READINGS IN

Human-Computer Interaction:

Toward the Year 2000

SECOND EDITION

READINGS IN

Human-Computer Interaction:

Toward the Year 2000

SECOND EDITION

WRITTEN AND EDITED BY

RONALD M. BAECKER, UNIVERSITY OF TORONTO

JONATHAN GRUDIN, UNIVERSITY OF CALIFORNIA, IRVINE

WILLIAM A. S. BUXTON, UNIVERSITY OF TORONTO

SAUL GREENBERG, UNIVERSITY OF CALGARY

MK

MORGAN KAUFMANN PUBLISHERS, INC.

SAN FRANCISCO, CALIFORNIA

Sponsoring Editor *Michael B. Morgan*
Production Manager *Yonie Overton*
Assistant Editor *Douglas Sery*
Editorial Coordinator *Marilyn Uffner Alan*
Production Editor *Cheri Palmer*
Cover Designer *Ross Carron, Carron Design*
Pasteup/Additional Composition *Susan M. Sheldrake*
Copyeditor *Ken DellaPenta*
Proofreaders *Patty Langstraat*
Printer *Courier Corporation*

Morgan Kaufmann Publishers, Inc.
Editorial and Sales Office
340 Pine Street, Sixth Floor
San Francisco, CA 94104-3205
USA

Telephone 415 / 392-2665
Facsimile 415 / 982-2665
Internet mkp@mkp.com

Printed in the United States of America

99 98 97 96 95 5 4 3 2 1

Library of Congress Cataloging-in-Publication Data

Readings in human-computer interaction : toward the year 2000 /
written and edited by Ronald M. Baecker ... [et al.]. -- 2nd ed.
p. cm.
Includes bibliographical references and index.
ISBN 1-55860-246-1
1. Human-computer interaction. 2. System design. I. Baecker, Ronald M.
QA76.9.H85R43 1995
004'.01'9--dc20 95-12073
CIP

Brief Contents

Detailed Contents

Preface

The man sitting next to me owned a transmission repair shop in Texas. He handed me his card and asked what I did. I told him. "Computers," he replied, "they're everywhere. When I hire a new guy, the first thing I do is send him to computer school for two weeks. The days when a kid learned to fix cars in the backyard under the apple tree are gone."

Computer systems are found throughout our society. Schoolchildren, scholars, secretaries, bank tellers, middle managers, executives, nurses, factory workers, animators, printers, architects, and planners are all discovering that computers are changing roles and expectations, enhancing some careers, trivializing or eliminating others.

Some computer systems run with little or no intervention, but most are interactive—they have human users who are engaged in computer-assisted tasks. The *human-computer interface*, also called the *user interface*, is often the single most important factor in the success or failure of an interactive system or application. Nielsen (1993) and Bias and Mayhew (1994) document numerous cases in which careful attention to the quality of the interface has yielded benefits such as cost savings, increases in system reliability, and decreases in user errors.

Narrowly defined, this interface comprises the input and output devices and the software that services them; broadly defined, the interface includes everything that shapes users' experiences with computers, including documentation, training, and human support.

The human-computer interface has become a very expensive part of software development. Sutton and Sprague (1978) gathered data on 22 interactive business applications in 10 large organizations from a variety of industries and found that the code required to support the human-computer interface averaged 59 percent of the total application code. Smith and Mosier (1984) surveyed 201 people concerned with information systems design, many involved in human factors engineering. The 83 who replied to the survey estimated that the interface took on average 30 to 35 percent of the software. Bobrow, Mittal, and Stefik (1986) report that the interface constitutes one-third to one-half of the code of typical expert or knowledge-based systems. A recent survey by Myers and Rosson (1992) drew 74 responses from developers, who estimated that 48% of application code and a comparable amount of development time is devoted to the interface.

Despite its importance, the human-computer interface is one of the most poorly understood aspects of most systems. The success or failure of an interface is determined by complex, subtly interrelated issues. For example, is it responsive or sluggish, forgiving or intolerant of human error, easy or difficult to learn, easy or difficult to use? Even whether or not it is attractive and fun to use can make a significant difference.

Diverse capabilities and disciplines are required to balance these and other factors. Interface design and development require software engineering and programming skills, of course, but can also benefit from the skills of graphic and industrial designers; human factors engineers and psychologists who understand human cognitive, perceptual, and motor skills; technical writers and training specialists; people knowledgeable in group and organizational dynamics; and those with expertise in input devices, display technologies, interaction techniques, dialogue design, and design methodologies. Individuals with an aptitude for elegance in system design play a crucial role. The growing use of sound, voice, video, animation, and three-dimensional display draw upon still other specialties. Computation now mostly supports activity in nonengineering domains, so those who have knowledge of such domains or who have the skills to acquire such knowledge become valuable contributors to the development process.

Effective interface development is thus a *multidisciplinary* process. A holistic view is required in approaching a design problem. More skills are required than any single individual is likely to possess.

Yet even if assembling a team of experts in all of these areas were possible, it would not guarantee success. Graphic design for computer displays, for example, is very different from the design taught in most art and design schools. The same is true of the other disciplines involved. What we need are new specialists, trained to understand and improve the ways in which humans interact with computers and broad enough in their outlook to work successfully on multidisciplinary teams.

THE PURPOSE OF THE BOOK

What materials are available to help one become a specialist at designing computers to interact with humans? Over a thousand papers relevant to the field are published annually. Most are written for experts—they cover relatively specialized topics and are located in journals or conference proceedings that are not widely available. A growing number of monographs and edited books on specific topics have been published. The excellent, although dated, *Handbook of Human-Computer Interaction* (Helander, 1988) contains 52 comprehensive and scholarly review papers. Useful elementary books (e.g., Rubinstein and Hersh, 1984; Norman, 1988; Perlman, 1989; Laurel, 1990; Heckel, 1991; Preece, 1993; Nielsen, 1993; Lewis and Rieman, 1993) and intermediate-level texts (e.g., Nickerson, 1986; Norman and Draper, 1986; Booth, 1989; Thimbleby, 1990; Shneiderman, 1992; Mayhew, 1992; Hix and Hartson, 1993; Dix et al., 1993; Eberts, 1994; Preece et al., 1994) summarize basic principles of human-computer interaction.

Yet these do not, in our view, sufficiently meet the needs of students, researchers, and practitioners interested in an overview of the significant concepts and results in the field and an introduction and comprehensive guide to the research literature. We want to provide both more breadth and more depth than do typical texts. We want to enable access to original sources rather than only to paraphrases and interpretations of the literature. That is the niche we seek to fill.

Why a Second Edition?

The first edition of this book (Baecker and Buxton, 1987) was published in 1987. In 1985, we had seen a need for appropriate teaching and learning materials that integrated, at an advanced level, relevant results from the research community, professional practice, and real applications. We therefore gathered, integrated, edited, and annotated with lengthy and scholarly introductions a source book of outstanding papers in ***human-computer interaction*** (HCI).

We feel that we succeeded. The book was well received and attracted high ratings from researchers, developers, and instructors. It continues to draw readers. However, eight years have passed. Eight years is a significant fraction of this young field's existence. The volume of work has grown rapidly. More has probably been published on human-computer interaction in the past five years than all that came before. Thus, a new edition was clearly needed.

As before, we have not merely collected and briefly introduced the reprinted papers. We have written comprehensive and integrative part, chapter, and case introductions that amount to over 20% of the pages of this volume and are actually a book within a book.

ORGANIZATION AND CONTENTS OF THE BOOK

Part I introduces human-computer interaction by presenting an illustrative case study of a real design problem, discussing user interface design in the context of the design of "everyday things," and describing the historical roots and intellectual development of the field.

In Part II we look at the process of developing interactive systems. We examine in depth the many varied approaches to design and evaluation. We also look at the social and organizational work contexts in which computers ultimately function, and consider their implications for the design process. We discuss how interface design is influenced by the nature of the systems development processes and the organizations encompassing it. Finally, we consider tools and techniques that facilitate implementation of interactive systems and their interfaces.

Part III focuses on the sensorimotor modalities through which users interact—visual, haptic (touch), and audio—and on the interaction styles and techniques that computers support, ranging from direct manipulation in graphical interfaces to the use of speech and natural language.

Part IV focuses on users and usage of interactive computer systems, on underlying cognitive processes, and on methods of modeling users and systems. Ways in which design can be responsive to human capabilities are examined, including error handling, documentation, training, workplace ergonomics, and interfaces for users with special needs.

Finally, Part V looks at research frontiers that are particularly significant as we approach the year 2000: computer-supported cooperative work and groupware; tailorable and adaptive systems; hypertext and multimedia; and cyberspace, which comprises three complementary visions of the future—global networking, virtual reality, and ubiquitous computing.

Each chapter and case study consists of an original introduction followed by key articles selected and reprinted from the literature. The introductions provide thorough reviews of each field, include comprehensive pointers to the literature, and explain why each paper was selected, what in it is of key importance, and how it relates to the other papers in the volume. Most articles are complete; a few important papers that could not be reprinted in their entirety are excerpted, either as short quotations in an introduction or as long passages included as readings.

ORGANIZATION AND CONTENTS OF THE BOOK

This volume is organized into five parts, consisting of fourteen chapters and three case studies analyzing specific systems and applications:

In choosing readings, we strove to include papers that

- maintain a balance between abstract and concrete, between universal and application-specific, between theory and practice. Theoretical papers appear alongside case studies of real systems and applications.
- describe both the possibilities and constraints of technology and the capabilities and limitations of humans.
- show the importance of the insights required for design and synthesis, as well as those needed for the very different processes of analysis and evaluation.
- deal with individual users of computer systems, and others that deal with communities of users. Some articles focus on a user's dialogue with the computer, others on the context surrounding human-computer dialogues.
- examine the past, the present, and the future of human-computer interaction. We describe approaches that are evolutionary as well as some that are revolutionary.

Despite the size of the volume, the large number of readings, and the additional excerpts, we do not claim to have included every desirable paper or to have made the *best* selection of papers in any absolute sense. We labored under constraints of space and time, the need to provide balance, and the ever-expanding volume of relevant literature. The more we read and study, the more we find there is to know. Yet we feel that this volume fills a gap in the literature and addresses the real needs cited above; later editions, or similar volumes by others, will carry this effort further and improve upon the result. We welcome suggestions for papers our readers feel should be included in the next edition. We also invite comments on experiences in using this edition. You may write to Ron Baecker at baecker@dgp.toronto.edu, Jonathan Grudin at grudin@ics.uci.edu, or the publisher via e-mail at mmorgan@mkp.com, or via snail mail to

Michael Morgan
Morgan Kaufmann Publishers
340 Pine Street, 6th Floor
San Francisco, CA 94104

Although the volume is intended as a sourcebook that brings together timely information, there is no central bibliography. We felt it best to list additional readings at the end of each chapter introduction, near the relevant material. Again, we had to be selective. To help readers initiate literature searches, we biased our choices towards recent papers. Our bibliography also includes references to over 200 available videotape demonstrations, since video is very effective at documenting, presenting, and explaining interactive systems. Excellent bibliographies are also included in many of the readings.

We hope that this volume serves both as a valuable free-standing collection and as a guide to the rich and rapidly evolving literature of human-computer interaction.

One Disclaimer

The field of human-computer interaction has in the past fifteen years focused on the needs of individual computer users, people who are often discretionary users working with personal computers, workstations, and minicomputer terminals. The field has been heavily influenced by cognitive psychologists and human factors engineers interested in problems arising in these contexts and by vendor companies that are developing for these markets. The overwhelming mood among those involved in the development and delivery of these technologies has been optimism, ranging from mild pleasure at tangible advance to euphoria and a belief in the liberating and enhancing effects of appropriate technology.

There is another field, with older roots in the mainframe computer era, that also focuses on the interaction of people and computers. Variously called data processing (DP), management information systems (MIS), and information technology (IT), this field has been heavily influenced by social and organizational psychologists, management theorists, and by large customer organizations, such as government agencies, banks, and hospitals. These researchers and practitioners (and others in computer science, sociology, philosophy, and law) are more evenly divided between optimism and pessimism. Questions they raise include: What is appropriate technology? How should it be applied? Of what use is it to enhance the human-computer interface if the purpose and the application are not ennobling and enriching?

The field of human-computer interaction has not usually dealt with the social implications of computing in any depth. The human-computer interaction focus is typically on development and refinement, not on the critique and analysis of fundamental change to which technology may contribute. The two fields are no longer entirely isolated. They have converged in forums such as the study of computer-supported cooperative work, but differences in emphasis remain.

Effects of computers on employment, personal privacy, safety from an accidental nuclear disaster, distribution of power and control in our society, and our self-image—to identify some of the serious issues raised by such scholars—are critical to the wise and humane use of computers and should be pondered and debated by all those active in the so-called "computer revolution."

Despite the importance of these issues, this volume is intended to represent, insofar as is possible in close to 950 pages, the major results and research contributions in the field of human-computer interaction as it is conventionally constituted today. Thus, only in Chapter 14 do we discuss the social impacts of computerization, and we do this so tersely that it does not do justice to the importance and complexity of the issues. Fortunately, we can recommend several excellent books devoted to this topic. Dunlop and Kling (1991) and its successor volume, Kling (1995), draw from diverse sources to provide valuable perspectives on many of these issues. Other good introductions are Forester and Morrison (1994), Erman, Williams, and Gutierrez (1990), Rosenberg (1992), and BBC (1992).

WHAT'S NEW IN THE SECOND EDITION?

What did we keep, what did we change? The simple answer is that this is really a new book as well as a second edition. Almost every reading is new; every part, chapter, and case introduction is new or mostly new with the exception of the historical Chapter 1 and Case B, and there are over 20% more pages than in the first edition. The first edition is thus still valuable as a companion volume. The overall structure of the book has been largely preserved, but significantly reordered.

Readers may be surprised, for example, to find design and evaluation covered in one (long) chapter. Pure cases of design exist, but the emphasis on prototyping and iterative development are eroding the barriers between design and evaluation. Good design practice often includes the evaluation of current practice, existing systems, and the use of prototypes. We did, however, include some papers that focus exclusively on either design or evaluation. (Note to instructors: Because Chapter 2 covers so much material, you may want to assign readings and teach it in two parts.)

Over the years, this book has often been used in courses that include a student project consisting of the design or evaluation of an interface. To assist students in carrying out such projects, we moved the chapters on development, design, and evaluation toward the front of the book. Material on the emerging psychology of human-computer interaction thus appears later, a change we made reluctantly.

A few other changes are noteworthy. Several burgeoning fields—groupware and computer-supported cooperative work; tailorable and adaptive systems; hypertext and multimedia; and cyberspace, including global networking, virtual reality, and ubiquitous computing—warrant significant attention and receive chapters of their own. We include more on the work environments, development organizations, and software engineering practices that surround most applications of human-computer interaction. On the other hand, we reduced the emphasis on studies of text editing and word processing, although there are still lessons to be learned from these mature application areas. Space limitations also forced us to drop the chapter on the psychology of computer programming, an important but very specialized topic.

RELATIONSHIP TO HCI CURRICULUM EFFORTS

In 1992 the ACM Special Interest Group on Human-Computer Interaction (SIGCHI) published a report of its Curriculum Development Group (CDG) entitled "ACM SIGCHI Curricula for Human-Computer Interaction" (Hewett et al., 1992). Section 2.3 (pages 13–28 of the report) is called "The Content of Human-Computer Interaction" and attempts to inventory "the current state of research results in the field of HCI." Instructors, students, and researchers wishing to review the field according to this inventory can find in this volume most of the topics described in the inventory, albeit organized in a different way (refer to box below).

The only CDG content area that is barely covered in our book is C4: Computer Graphics. This is almost always taught and studied as a separate subject. A comprehensive text is Foley et al. (1990). On the other hand, our Chapter 3, "Considering Work Contexts in Design," and Chapter 4; "Software Development Contexts," go significantly beyond the CDG proposal, and the topics of Part V; "Research Frontiers," are of greater significance today than when the CDG report was drafted.

More recently, another significantly larger committee considered the future of human-computer interaction education (Strong et al., 1994). Its differences with the CDG recommendations are modest yet extremely significant, and lie chiefly in suggesting the inclusion of material to aid in understanding the social and organizational contexts of technological change, and to help improve analysis, design, imple-

RELATIONSHIP TO HCI CURRICULUM EFFORTS

ACM SIGCHI CDG Inventory of HCI Topics		Location of Topics in This Book
N	*The Nature of HCI*	
	N1 (Meta-)Models of HCI	*Chapter 1*
U	*Use and Context of Computers*	
	U1 Human Social Organization and Work	*Chapters 3, 4, 11*
	U2 Application Areas	*Cases A–C, Chapters 11–14*
	U3 Human-Machine Fit and Adaptation	*Chapters 10, 12*
H	*Human Characteristics*	
	H1 Human Information Processing	*Chapters 9, 10*
	H2 Language, Communication, Interaction	*Chapters 6–8*
	H3 Ergonomics	*Chapter 10*
C	*Computer System and Interface Architecture*	
	C1 Input and Output Devices	*Chapters 6–8*
	C2 Dialogue Techniques	*Chapters 6–8*
	C3 Dialogue Genre	*Chapters 2, 6*
	C4 Computer Graphics	*Chapter 6*
	C5 Dialogue Architecture	*Chapters 5, 6*
D	*Development Process*	
	D1 Design Approaches	*Chapters 2, 6*
	D2 Implementation Techniques	*Chapters 2, 4, 5*
	D3 Evaluation Techniques	*Chapters 2, 3*
	D4 Example Systems and Case Studies	*Cases A–C, Chapters 11–14*
P	*Project Presentations and Examinations*	

mentation, and evaluation methodologies to be more sensitive to these contexts. Chapters 3 and 4 of this volume address these topics.

USING THIS BOOK IN TEACHING

The first edition of this book has been widely used in courses at the advanced undergraduate and graduate levels. For the second edition, we included material at beginner, intermediate, and advanced levels, as one explicit goal was to enable its use both for one-semester graduate courses and for one- or two-semester undergraduate courses. This has been successfully tested with draft manuscripts in the 1993–94 academic year. Another goal, as with the first edition, is to support independent study and project work in HCI.

The Curriculum Development Group report describes four prototypical courses, as follows (p. 30):

> *The proposed courses can be broadly characterized as either technology oriented (CS1: User Interface Design and Development and CS2: Phenomena and Theories of Human-Computer Interaction) or human-oriented (PSY1: Psychology of Human-Computer Interaction and MIS1: Human Aspects of Information Systems), and as moving from a general professional/practical orientation (CS1 and MIS1) to one that is more specialized and research oriented (CS2 and PSY1).*

The first term of a two-semester computer science HCI course (CS1) would draw most heavily from Part I, Chapters 2 and 5 in Part II, and selected topics from Part III and Part V, with one or two lectures dealing with material in Part IV. The second semester (CS2) would pick up additional topics from Parts II, III, and V, with significant emphasis on material in Part IV.

A one-semester course in psychology (PSY1) would begin with Part I, and choose in a balanced way material from Chapters 2 and 5, Parts III, and IV, using some material in Part V for motivation and illustration. The same is true for a one-semester course in management information systems (MIS1), except more emphasis would be given to material in Chapters 3 and 4, with a corresponding deemphasis on Part IV.

EXAMPLES ON VIDEO

Increasingly, developers of interactive systems and human-computer interfaces are documenting their work with videotaped demonstrations. Over 200 such video demonstrations are cited in chapter introductions and included in a special references section at the end of each chapter introduction. Most are from the *ACM SIGGRAPH Video Review* and can be ordered from

SIGGRAPH Video Review
c/o VI&A/First Priority
P.O. Box 576
Itasca, IL 60143-0576
Phone (within USA): . . .1-800-523-5503
Fax (within USA): 1-312-789-7185
Phone (outside USA): . . .+1-708-250-0807
Fax (outside USA): . . . . .+1-708-250-0038
e-mail: . . . . .svrorders@siggraph.org

ELECTRONIC DATA BASES AND RESOURCES

One happy new development is the creation of bibliographic data bases, central repositories of information relevant to the field that are available across the Internet or in other formats. The HILITES CD/ROM (Shackel, Alty, and Reid, 1992), last produced in 1993, is a commercial product containing information on about 32,000 items of HCI literature, including abstracts and full citations. Information can be obtained from K.E.Phillips@lut.ac.uk. The HCI Bibliography Project, organized by Gary Perlman (1991) at Ohio State University, provides free access via anonymous ftp, mail servers, and Macintosh and DOS floppy disks to a resource of over 11,000 entries, including keywords and abstracts. The bibliography has been developed through the efforts of over 100 volunteers from 13 nations. Information can be obtained from hcibib@cis.ohio-state.edu.

The World-Wide Web is increasingly proving to be a valuable resource for human-computer interaction. What was once known as the HCI Launching Pad is now the World-Wide Web Virtual Library on Human-Computer Interaction. Scanning the home page at http://www.cs.bgsu.ed/HCI/ gives you access to information on recent publications, bibliographies, and conferences and on HCI organizations, labs, educational standards, and practices. The WWW VL: HCI home page also incorporates a collection of pointers to personal Web pages where researchers are profiled and from which you can gain access to other sources of useful information (selected and posted by each researcher). Gary Perlman's home page at http://www.cis.ohio-state.edu/~perlman, for instance, directs you to resources, bibliographies, and other useful resources with which he is involved.

Current information about this book will be made available through the publishers World Wide Web Home Page, http://mkp.com. Readers will be able to find an electronic catalog of Morgan Kaufman books, which will contain information on this book including a complete table of contents. We will also, as time allows, include pointers to other sources of information useful for both teachers and students, such as online bibliographies, and links to researchers and to instructors.

ACKNOWLEDGMENTS

We have been privileged while working on both editions of this book to receive advice and assistance from many knowledgeable individuals, including Mark Ackerman, John Arnott, Barry Arons, Phil Barnard, Tom Carey, Jack Carroll, Lisa Covi, Susan Dumais, Tom Erickson, Julian Feldman, Roy Fielding, Jim Foley, Robert Glushko, John Gould, William Graves, Wayne Gray, Heinz Klein, John Leggett, Clayton Lewis, Gene Lynch, Rod Macintosh, Tom Malone, Marilyn Mantei, M. Lynne Markus, Tom Moran, Neville Moray, S. Joy Mountford, Dianne Murray, Ray Nickerson, Jakob Nielsen, Niels Christian Nielsen, Don Norman, Steven Poltrock, Jim Rhyne, Brian Shackel, Rod McIntosh Shand, Hank Strub, Berney Williams, and Patricia Wright. Students in two University of

California–Irvine classes provided useful comments on early drafts. We are especially indebted to Marc Davis, Rob Kling, Aaron Marcus, Joe McGrath, Brad Myers, and Gitta Salomon, who contributed original material or reworked existing material for this edition.

Students at the University of California–Irvine and the University of British Columbia assisted greatly by reading, evaluating, and commenting on the papers as part of the iterative design of this book. Nancy Silver of the University of Toronto also carried out a very useful review of the manuscript.

Despite this assistance, gratefully acknowledged and much appreciated, full responsibility for any errors and omissions lies with the author/editors. The architecture of the second edition is the work of Ron, Jonathan, and Bill. Ron took prime responsibility for the Preface; Chapters 1, 6, and 11; Case B; and (together with Jonathan) Chapters 2 and 13. Jonathan took prime responsibility for the Part Introductions; Cases A and C; Chapters 3, 4, 9, and 14; and (together with Ron or Saul) Chapters 2, 12, and 13. Bill took prime responsibility for Chapters 7 and 8. Saul took prime responsibility for Chapters 5 and 10, and (together with Jonathan) Chapter 12. The first major review pass was carried out by Ron and Saul; the very extensive final review pass was done by Ron and Jonathan.

Beki Grinter prepared the index with care and attention to detail. Laurie Harris, Ann-Barbara Graff, Diba Bot, Maria Casas, Kaia Kruus, Alex Mitchell, Ilona Posner, and Barbara Whitmer ably assisted the authors in many ways including bibliographic citations, library research, proofreading, and prepartion of figures. We are particularly indebted to Laurie and Ann-Barbara for their skill and resourcefulness.

We are grateful to Mike Morgan of Morgan Kaufmann Publishers for his support, advice, and forbearance through a lengthy series of missed deadlines and slipping schedules, and to members of his staff including Cheri Palmer, Yoni Overton, Doug Sery, and Marilyn Uffner Alan.

Lil and Aha brought much joy and enrichment to Ron's life during the last year and a half of work on this book, for which he is very grateful. Jonathan thanks those he loves for accepting his preoccupation during this difficult endeavor.

REFERENCES

Baecker, R., and Buxton, W. (Eds.) (1987). *Readings in Human-Computer Interaction: A Multidisciplinary Approach.* Morgan Kaufmann.

BBC (1992). *The Machine That Changed the World.* 5 hr. video series.

Bias, R., and Mayhew, D. (1994). *Cost-Justifying Usability.* Academic Press.

Bobrow, D., Mittal, S., and Stefik, M. (1986). Expert Systems: Perils and Promise. *Communications of the ACM* 29(9), 880–894.

Booth, P. (1989). *An Introduction to Human-Computer Interaction.* Lawrence Erlbaum Associates.

Dix, A., Finlay, J., Abowd, G., and Beale, R. (1993). *Human-Computer Interaction.* Prentice Hall.

Dunlop, C., and Kling, R. (Eds.) (1991). *Computerization and Controversy: Value Conflicts and Social Choices.* Academic Press.

Eberts, R. (1994). *User Interface Design.* Prentice Hall.

Erman, M., Williams, M., and Gutierrez, C. (Eds.) (1990). *Computers, Ethics, & Society.* Oxford University Press.

Foley, J., van Dam, A., Feiner, S., and Hughes, J. (1990). *Computer Graphics: Principles and Practice.* Second Edition. Addison-Wesley.

Forester, T., and Morrison, P. (1994). *Computer Ethics: Cautionary Tales and Ethical Dilemmas in Computing.* Second Edition. MIT Press.

Heckel, P. (1991). *The Elements of Friendly Software Design,* The New Edition. Sybex.

Helander, M. (Ed.) (1988). *Handbook of Human-Computer Interaction.* North-Holland.

Hewett, T., Baecker, R., Card, S., Carey, T., Gasen, J., Mantei, M., Perlman, G., Strong, G., and Verplank, W. (1992). ACM SIGCHI Curricula for Human-Computer Interaction, Report of the ACM SIGCHI Curriculum Development Group, ACM.

Hix, D., and Hartson, R. (1993). *Developing User Interfaces: Ensuring Usability Through Product & Process.* John Wiley & Sons.

Kling, R. (Ed.) (1995). *Computerization and Controversy: Value Conflicts and Social Choices.* Academic Press.

Laurel, B. (Ed.) (1990). *The Art of Human-Computer Interface Design.* Addison-Wesley.

Lewis, C., and Rieman, J. (1993). *Task-Centered User Interface Design.* Available on World-Wide Web URL ftp://fpt.cs.colorado.edu/pub/cs/distribs/clewis/HCI-Design-Book.

Mayhew, D. (1992). *Principles and Guidelines in Software User Interface Design.* PTR Prentice Hall.

Myers, B., and Rosson, M. (1992). Survey on User Interface Programming. *Proc. CHI '92,* ACM, 195–202.

Nickerson, R. (1986). *Using Computers: Human Factors in Information Systems.* MIT Press.

Nielsen, J. (1993). *Usability Engineering.* Academic Press.

Norman, D. (1988). *The Psychology of Everyday Things.* (*The Design of Everyday Things* in paperback.) Basic Books.

Norman, D., and Draper, S. (Eds.) (1986). *User Centred System Design: New Perspectives on Human-Computer Interaction.* Lawrence Erlbaum Associates.

Perlman, G. (1989). User Interface Development Curriculum Module. Software Engineering Institute, Carnegie-Mellon University, Pittsburgh, PA 15213.

Perlman, G. (1991). The HCI Bibliography Project. *SIGCHI Bulletin,* 23, 3, 15–20.

Preece, J. (1993). *A Guide to Usability: Human Factors in Computing.* Addison-Wesley.

Preece, J., Rogers, Y., Sharp, H., Benyon, D., Holland, H., and Carey, T. (1994). *Human-Computer Interaction.* Addison-Wesley.

Rosenberg, R. (1992). *The Social Impact of Computers.* Academic Press.

Rubinstein, R., and Hersh, H. (1984). *The Human Factor: Designing Computer Systems for People.* Digital Press.

Shackel, B., Alty, J., and Reid, P. (1992). HILITES—The Information Service for the World HCI Community. *SIGCHI Bulletin* 24, 3, 40–49.

Shneiderman, B. (1992). *Designing the User Interface: Strategies for Human-Computer Interaction.* Addison-Wesley.

Smith, S., and Mosier, J. (1984). The User Interface to Computer-Based Information Systems: A Survey of Current Software Design Practice. *Behaviour and Information Technology* 3(3), 195–203.

Strong, G., with contributions by Gasen, J., Hewett, T., Hix, D., Morris, J., Muller, M., Novick, D., and many others (1994). A Report: New Directions in Human-Computer Interaction Education, Research, and Practice. Available from the Interactive Systems Program, U.S. National Science Foundation, Washington, D.C. Available on World-Wide Web URL: http://www.sei.cmu.edu/arpa/hci/directions/TitlePage.html.

Sutton, J., and Sprague, R. (1978). A Study of Display Generation and Management in Interactive Business Applications. *IBM Research Report* RJ2392(31804). Yorktown Heights, NY.

Thimbleby, H. (1990). *User Interface Design.* ACM Press.

Acknowledgements

Norman, D.A. (1988). The Psychopathology of Everyday Things. Chapter 1 of D.A. Norman, *The Psychology of Everyday Things*, Basic Books, pp. 1–33. ©1988, Donald A. Norman. Reprinted by permission of Basic Books, a division of HarperCollins Publishers, Inc. Also available in paperback as *The Design of Everyday Things*.

Salomon, G.B. (1993). A Case Study in Interface Design: The CHI '89 Information Kiosk. Original paper.

Johnson, J., Roberts, T.L., Verplank, W., Smith, D.C., Irby, C.H., Beard, M., and Mackey, K. (1989). The Xerox Star: A Retrospective. (1989 IEEE. Reprinted, with permission, from *IEEE Computer* 22(9), pp. 11–29, September 1989.

Gould, J.D. (1988). How to Design Usable Systems (Excerpt). Revision of Chapter 35 of M. Helander (Ed.), *Handbook of Human-Computer Interaction*, pp. 757–779; 784–789. North-Holland. Reprinted by permission.

Lewis, C., and Rieman, J. (1993). Getting to Know Users and Their Tasks. Chapter 2 of *Task-Centered User Interface Design*. Self-published over the Internet, pp. 14–19.

Mountford, S.J., in *The Art of Human Computer-Interface Design* by Brenda Laurel. © 1990 by Apple Computer. Reprinted with permission of Addison-Wesley Publishing Company.

Vertelney, L. (1989). Using Video to Prototype User Interfaces. *ACM SIGCHI Bulletin* 21(2), pp. 57–61. © 1989, Association for Computing Machinery, Inc. Reprinted by permission.

Erickson, T.D., in *The Art of Human-Computer Interface Design* by Brenda Laurel. © 1990 by Apple Computer. Reprinted with permission of Addison-Wesley Publishing Company.

McGrath, J. (1994). Methodology Matters: Doing Research in the Behavioral and Social Sciences. Original paper.

Mack, R.L., and Nielsen, J. (1994). Usability Inspection Methods. Executive Summary of J. Nielsen and R.L. Mack (Eds.), *Usability Inspection Methods*, John Wiley & Sons, pp. 1–23. Reprinted by permission John Wiley & Sons, Inc.

Kennedy, S. (1989). Using Video in the BNR Usability Lab. *ACM SIGCHI Bulletin* 21(2), pp. 92–95. © 1989, Association for Computing Machinery, Inc. Reprinted by permission.

Orlikowski, W. (1992). Learning from Notes: Organizational Issues in Groupware Implementation. *Proc. CSCW '92*, ACM, pp. 362–369. © 1992, Association for Computing Machinery, Inc. Reprinted by permission.

Bannon, L. (1991). From Human Factors to Human Actors. In J. Greenbaum and M. Kyng (Eds.), *Design at Work: Cooperative Design of Computer Systems*, Lawrence Erlbaum Associates, pp. 25–44. © 1991 Lawrence Erlbaum Associates. Reprinted by permission.

Bødker, S., Grønbæk, K., and Kyng, M. (1993). Cooperative Design: Techniques and Experiences from the Scandinavian Scene. In D. Schuler and A. Namioka (Eds.), *Participatory Design: Principles and Practices*, Lawrence Erlbaum Associates, pp. 157–175. © 1993 Lawrence Erlbaum Associates. Reprinted by permission.

Good, M. (1992). Participatory Design of a Portable Torque-Feedback Device. *Proc. CHI '92*, ACM, pp. 439–446. © 1992, Association for Computing Machinery, Inc. Reprinted by permission.

Suchman, L.A., and Trigg, R.H. (1991). Understanding Practice: Video as a Medium for Reflection and Design (Excerpt). In J. Greenbaum and M. Kyng (Eds.), *Design at Work: Cooperative Design of Computer Systems*, Lawrence Erlbaum Associates, pp. 75–89. © 1991 Lawrence Erlbaum Associates. Reprinted by permission.

Holtzblatt, K., and Jones, S. (1993). Conducting and Analyzing a Contextual Interview (Excerpt). In D. Schuler and A. Namioka (Eds.), *Participatory Design: Principles and Practices*, Lawrence Erlbaum Associates, pp. 177, 181–88, 192–204, 207–210. © 1993 Lawrence Erlbaum Associates. Reprinted by permission.

Kling, R. (1995). Controversies about Computerization and the Organization of White Collar Work. Revised and updated version of a paper that appeared as R. Kling and C. Dunlop (1993). "Controversies About Computerization and the Character of White Collar Worklife" in *The Information Society* 9(1) (Jan–Feb, 1993): pp. 1–29.

Boehm, B.W. (1988). A Spiral Model of Software Development and Enhancement. © 1988 IEEE. Reprinted, with permission, from *IEEE Computer* 21(2), pp. 61–72, May 1988.

Grudin, J. (1991). Interactive Systems: Bridging the Gaps Between Developers and Users. © 1991 IEEE. Reprinted, with permission, from *IEEE Computer* 24(4), pp. 59–69, April 1991.

Kim, S., in *The Art of Human-Compute -Interface Design* by Brenda Laurel. © 1990 by Apple Computer. Reprinted with permission of Addison-Wesley Publishing Company.

Myers, B.A. (1993). State of the Art in User Interface Software Tools. In H.R. Hartson and D. Hix (Eds.), *Advances in Human-Computer Interaction*, Volume 4, Ablex, pp. 110–150. Reprinted by permission.

Pausch, R., Conway, M., and Deline, R. (1992). Lessons Learned from SUIT, the Simple User Interface Toolkit. *ACM Transactions on Information Systems* 10(4), pp. 320–344. © 1992, Association for Computing Machinery, Inc. Reprinted by permission.

Myers, B.A., Giuse, D.A., Dannenberg, R.B., Vander Zanden, B., Kosbie, D.S., Pervin, E., Mickish, A., and Marchal, P. (1990). Garnet: Comprehensive Support for Graphical, Highly Interactive User Interfaces. © 1990 IEEE. Reprinted, with permission, from *IEEE Computer* 23(11), pp. 71–85, November 1990.

Wiecha, C., Bennett, W., Boies, S., Gould, J., and Greene, S. (1990). ITS: A Tool for Rapidly Developing Interactive Applications. *ACM Transactions on Information Systems* 8(3), pp. 204–236. © 1990, Association for Computing Machinery, Inc. Reprinted by permission.

Roseman, M., and Greenberg, S. (1992). GroupKit: A Groupware Toolkit for Building Real-Time Conferencing Applications. *Proc. CSCW '92,* ACM, pp. 43–50. © 1992, Association for Computing Machinery, Inc. Reprinted by permission.

Schneiderman, B. (1991). A Taxonomy and Rule Base for the Selection of Interaction Styles. In B. Shackel and S.J. Richardson (Eds.), *Human Factors for Informatics Usability,* Cambridge University Press, pp. 325–342. Reprinted with the permission of Cambridge University Press.

Marcus, A. (1990) Principles of Effective Visual Communication for Graphical User Interface Design. *UNIX World,* August 1990, pp. 107–111, September 1990, pp. 121–124, and October 1990, pp. 135–138. Reprinted by permission.

Murch, G. (1985). Color Graphics—Blessing or Ballyhoo (Excerpt). *Computer Graphics Forum, 4,* North-Holland, pp. 133–135. Reprinted by permission.

Baecker, R., Small, I., and Mander, R. (1991). Bringing Icons to Life. *Proc. CHI '91,* ACM, pp. 1–6. © 1991, Association for Computing Machinery, Inc. Reprinted by permission.

Ahlberg, C., and Shneiderman, B. (1994). Visual Information Seeking: Tight Coupling of Dynamic Query Filters with Starfield Displays. *Proc.' CHI '94,* ACM, pp. 313–317; 479–480. © 1994, Association for Computing Machinery, Inc. Reprinted by permission.

Marcus, A. (1992). A Comparison of Graphical User Interfaces (Excerpt). In A. Marcus, *Graphic Design for Electronic Documents and Interfaces,* ACM Press, pp. 137–159; 187–188. © 1992, Association for Computing Machinery, Inc. Reprinted by permission.

MacKenzie, S. (1992). Movement Time Prediction in Human-Computer Interfaces. *Proc. Graphics Interface '92,* Morgan Kaufmann, pp. 140–150.

Buxton, W. (1986). Chunking and Phrasing and the Design of Human-Computer Dialogues. In H.-J. Kugler (Ed.), *Information Processing '86,* Proc. of the IFIP 10th World Computer Congress, North Holland, pp. 475–480. Reprinted by permission.

Goldberg, D., and Goodisman, A. (1991). Stylus User Interfaces for Manipulating Text. *Proc. Fourth ACM SIGGRAPH Symposium on User Interface Technology (UIST '91),* pp. 127–135. © 1991, Association for Computing Machinery, Inc. Reprinted by permission.

Pedersen, E., McCall, K., Moran, T., and Halasz, F. (1993). Tivoli: an Electronic Whiteboard for Informal Workgroup Meetings. *Proc. InterCHI '93,* ACM, pp. 391–398. © 1993, Association for Computing Machinery, Inc. Reprinted by permission.

Bier, E., Stone, M., Fishkin, K., Buxton, W., and Baudel, T. (1994). A Taxonomy of See-Through Tools. *Proc. CHI '94,* ACM, pp. 358–364. © 1994, Association for Computing Machinery, Inc. Reprinted by permission.

O'Malley, M. (1990). Text-to-Speech Conversion Technology. © 1990 IEEE. Reprinted, with permission, from *IEEE Computer* 23(8), pp. 17–23, August 1990.

Peacocke, R., and Graf, D. (1990). An Introduction to Speech and Speaker Recognition. © 1990 IEEE. Reprinted, with permission, from *IEEE Computer* 23(8), pp. 26–33, August 1990.

White, G. (1990). Natural Language Understanding and Speech Recognition. *Communications of the ACM* 33(8), pp. 72–82. © 1990, Association for Computing Machinery, Inc. Reprinted by permission.

Gaver, W., and Smith, R. (1990). Auditory Icons in Large-Scale Collaborative Environments. *Proceedings of Human-Computer Interaction—INTERACT '90,* Elsevier (North-Holland), pp. 735–740. Reprinted by permission.

Card, S.K., and Moran, T.P. (1986). User Technology: From Pointing to Pondering. *Proc. ACM Conference on History of Personal Workstations,* Palo Alto, pp. 183–198. © 1986, Association for Computing Machinery, Inc. Reprinted by permission.

Olson, J.R., and Olson, G.M. (1990). The Growth of Cognitive Modeling in Human-Computer Interaction Since GOMS. *Human-Computer Interaction* 5, pp. 221–265, Lawrence Erlbaum Associates. © 1990 Lawrence Erlbaum Associates. Reprinted by permission.

John, B.E. and Vera, A.H. (1992). A GOMS Analysis of a Graphic, Machine-Paced, Highly Interactive Task. *Proc. CHI '92,* ACM, pp. 251–258. © 1992, Association for Computing Machinery, Inc. Reprinted by permission.

Gray, W.D., John, B.E., Stuart, R., Lawrence, D., and Atwood, M.E. (1990). GOMS Meets the Phone Company: Analytic Modeling Applied to Real-World Problems. *Proc. Human-Computer Interaction—INTER-ACT '90,* Elsevier (North-Holland), pp. 29–34. Reprinted by permission.

Barnard, P. (1991). The Contributions of Applied Cognitive Psychology to the Study of Human-Computer Interaction. In B. Schackel and S.J. Richardson (Eds.), *Human Factors for Informatics Usability,* Cambridge University Press, pp. 151–182. Reprinted with the permission of Cambridge University Press.

Landauer, T.K. (1991). Let's Get Real: A Position Paper on the Role of Cognitive Psychology in the Design of Humanly Useful and Usable Systems. In J.M. Carroll (Ed.), *Designing Interaction,* Cambridge University Press, pp. 60–73. Reprinted with the permission of Cambridge University Press.

Norman, D.A. (1990). Human Error and the Design of Computer Systems. *Communications of the ACM* 33(1),pp. 4–5; 7. © 1990, Association for Computing Machinery, Inc. Reprinted by permission.

Denning, P.J. (1990). Human Error and the Search for Blame. *Communications of the ACM* 33(1), pp. 6–7. © 1990, Association for Computing Machinery, Inc. Reprinted by permission.

Lewis, C., and Norman, D.A. (1986). Designing for Error. In D.A. Norman and S.W. Draper (Eds.), *User Centered System Design,* Lawrence Erlbaum Associates, pp. 411–432. © 1986 Lawrence Erlbaum Associates. Reprinted by permission.

Carroll, J.M., and Mack, R.L. (1984). Learning to Use a Word Processor: By Doing, by Thinking, and by Knowing. In J. Thomas and M. Schneider (Eds.), *Human Factors in Computer Systems,* Ablex, pp. 13–51. Reprinted by permission.

Sellen, A., and Nicol, A., in *The Art of Human Computer Interface Design* by Brenda Laurel. © 1990 by Apple Computer. Reprinted with permission of Addison-Wesley Publishing Company.

Lazzaro, J.J. (1993). Computers for the Disabled, *BYTE,* pp. 59–64. Reprinted by permission.

Sauter, S.L., Chapman, L.J., and Knutson, S.J. (1985). Improving VDT Work: Causes and Control of Health Concerns in VDT Use (Excerpt). Madison, WI: University of Wisconsin, pp. 7, 9, 11–12, 27–32. Reprinted by permission.

Sproull, L., and Kiesler, S. (1991). Computers, Networks and Work. *Scientific American*, pp. 116–123. Reprinted with permission. © 1991 by Scientific American, Inc. All rights reserved.

Grudin, J. (1994). Groupware and Social Dynamics: Eight Challenges for Developers. *Communications of the ACM* 37(1), pp. 92–105. © 1994, Association for Computing Machinery, Inc. Reprinted by permission.

Baecker, R.M., Nastos, D., Posner, I.R., and Mawby, K.L. (1993). The User-Centered Iterative Design of Collaborative Writing Software. *Proc. InterCHI '93*, ACM, pp. 399–405, 541. © 1993, Association for Computing Machinery, Inc. Reprinted by permission.

Henderson, A., and Kyng, M. (1991). There's No Place Like Home: Continuing Design in Use. In J. Greenbaum and M. Kyng (Eds.), *Design at Work: Cooperative Design of Computer Systems*, Lawrence Erlbaum Associates, pp. 219–240. © 1991 Lawrence Erlbaum Associates. Reprinted by permission.

Cypher, A. (1991). Eager: Programming Repetitive Tasks by Example. *Proc. CHI '91*, ACM, pp. 33–39. © 1991, Association for Computing Machinery, Inc. Reprinted by permission.

Maes, P. (1994). Agents that Reduce Work and Information Overload. *Communications of the ACM* 37(7), pp. 31–40, 146, ACM. © 1994, Association for Computing Machinery, Inc. Reprinted by permission.

Fischer, G., and Reeves, B. (1992). Beyond Intelligent Interfaces: Exploring, Analyzing, and Creating Success Models of Cooperative Problem Solving (Excerpt). *Journal of Applied Intelligence*, Vol. 1, pp. 316–323, Kluwer. Reprinted by permission.

Egan, D.E., Remde, J.R., Landauer, T.K., Lochbaum, C.C., and Gomez, L.M. (1989). Behavioral Evaluation and Analysis of a Hypertext Browser. *Proc. CHI '89*, ACM, pp. 205–210. © 1989, Association for Computing Machinery, Inc. Reprinted by permission.

Glushko, R.J. (1992). Seven Ways to Make a Hypertext Project Fail. *Technical Communications* 2, MIT Press, pp. 226–230. Reprinted by permission.

Davis, M. (1993). Media Streams: An Iconic Visual Language for Video Representation. © 1993 IEEE. Reprinted, with permission, from *Proceedings of the 1993 Symposium on Visual Languages*, pp. 196–202.

Levine, S., and Ehrlich, S.F. (1991). The Freestyle System: A Design Perspective. In A. Klinger (Ed.), *Human-Machine Interactive Systems*, Plenum, pp. 3–21. Reprinted by permission.

Perkins, R., Blatt, L.A., Workman, D., and Ehrlich, S.F. (1989). Iterative Tutorial Design in the Product Development Cycle. *Proc. 33rd Annual Human Factors Society Meeting*, pp. 268–272. Reprinted with permission from *Proceedings of the Human Factors Society 33rd Annual Meeting*, 1989. © 1989 by the Human Factors Society, Inc. All rights reserved.

Francik, E., Rudman, S.E., Cooper, D., and Levine, S. (1991). Putting Innovation to Work: Adoption Strategies for Multimedia Communication Systems. *Communications of the ACM* 34 (12), pp. 53–63. © 1991, Association for Computing Machinery, Inc. Reprinted by permission.

Berners-Lee, T., Cailliau, R., Luotonen, A., Nielsen, H.F., and Secret, A. (1994). The World-Wide Web. *Communications of the ACM* 37(8), ACM, pp. 76–82. © 1994, Association for Computing Machinery, Inc. Reprinted by permission.

Ellis, S.R. (1991). Nature and Origins of Virtual Environments: A Bibliographical Essay (Excerpt). *Computing Systems in Engineering* 2(4), excerpts from pp. 321–347. Reprinted by permission.

Weiser, M. (1991). The Computer for the 21st Century. *Scientific American*, pp. 94–95, 98–102, 104, September 1991. Reprinted with permission. © 1991 by Scientific American, Inc. All rights reserved.

Part I

Introduction to Human-Computer Interaction

In Part I, we define human-computer interaction and relate it to our long history of designing artifacts for human use. A concrete example, the development of an information kiosk, introduces several issues in interactive system design and one approach to addressing them. We then review the history of human-computer interaction and the design of interactive computer systems. Part I concludes with a particularly important event in this history, the development of the Xerox Star, which led to what is now called the *graphical user interface.*

Human-computer interaction (HCI) can be defined in many possible ways. The Curriculum Development Group of the ACM Special Interest Group on Human-Computer Interaction (SIGCHI), for example, states (Hewett et al., 1992, p. 5):

> *Human-computer interaction is a discipline concerned with the design, evaluation and implementation of interactive computing systems for human use and with the study of major phenomena surrounding them.*

Dix et al. (1993, p. xiii) offer the following definition:

> *"Human-computer interaction" (or HCI) is, put simply, the study of people, computer technology and the ways these influence each other. We study HCI to determine how we can make this computer technology more usable by people.*

Finally, in a very recent book, Preece et al. (1994, p. 1) suggest:

> *Human-computer interaction (HCI) is about designing computer systems that support people so that they can carry out their activities productively and safely.*

The computer is a tool, a complex artifact that can extend our reach. The design discipline of human-computer interaction systematically applies knowledge about human purposes, human capabilities and limitations, and machine capabilities and limitations in order to enable us to do things that we could not do before. Another goal of HCI, as suggested in the definitions given above, is to enhance the quality of the interaction between people and computers. We strive, for example, to make technology easier for people to learn and easier for them to use.

Computers are our most complex creations. They have the potential for realizing an unlimited range of behaviors and interactions with their human users. Accordingly, the design of effective computer systems is very challenging. Happily, we do not approach this task in a vacuum: For centuries, people have designed and created artifacts, some simple, some complex. The design of the human interface to these artifacts has not always gone smoothly. We can learn a great deal from the problems encountered in "the design of everyday things," which is the title of a book by cognitive scientist and technology-watcher Donald A. Norman (1988).

Our first reading is the introductory chapter of Norman's book, originally titled *The Psychology of Everyday Things.* Norman examines the design of a multitude of common objects, such as doors, light switches, water faucets, stove controls, refrigerators, washer-dryers, slide projectors, telephones, VCRs, and watches. He finds examples of bad design almost everywhere, *even for objects far simpler than most human-computer interfaces.* Norman then introduces several concepts that he uses in his analyses of both good and bad design:

- *Affordances* are the perceived properties of an artifact that determine how it could possibly be used. For example, buttons are for pushing, menus are for choosing.
- *Constraints* are physical, semantic, cultural, and logical factors that encourage proper actions and prevent erroneous ones.
- *Conceptual models* are mental models of a system which allow users to understand the system, to predict the effects of their actions, and to interpret the results.
- *Mappings* describe the relationships between controls and their effects on a system. For example, moving a control to the left should move a corresponding display object left.
- *Visibility* in the design of a system makes apparent to users the conceptual model of the system and the actions they are allowed to take.
- *Feedback* from a system provides information about the effects of users' actions.

In the remainder of his important book, Norman introduces "The Seven Stages of Action" (a description of this theory appears in Chapters 2 and 9) to explain how people do things, why they make errors (see the paper by Lewis and Norman in Chapter 10), and how to apply the theory to do "user-centered design." He uses the six key concepts defined above in his prescriptions for user-centered design (p. 188):

- *Make it easy to determine what actions are possible at any moment (make use of constraints).*
- *Make things visible, including the conceptual model of the system, the alternative actions, and the results of actions.*
- *Make it easy to evaluate the current state of the system.*

- *Follow natural mappings between intentions and the required actions; between actions and the resulting effect; and between the information that is visible and the interpretation of the system state.*

  In other words, make sure that (1) the user can figure out what to do, and (2) the user can tell what is going on.

Norman tries to spur us to action in the conclusion of his book (pp. 216–217):

> *Now you are on your own. If you are a designer, help fight the battle for usability. If you are a user, then join your voice with those who cry for usable products. Write to manufacturers. Boycott unusable designs. Support good designs by purchasing them, even if it means going out of your way, even if it means spending a bit more. And voice your concerns to the stores that carry the products; manufacturers listen to their customers. . . .*
>
> *And enjoy yourself. Walk around the world examining the details of design. Take pride in the little things that help; think kindly of the person who so thoughtfully put them in. Realize that even details matter, that the designers may have had to fight to include something helpful. Give mental prizes to those who practice good design: send flowers. Jeer those who don't: send weeds.*

Further insights into human-computer interaction design are also provided by three other books authored or edited by Norman. Norman and Draper (1986) is a collection of thoughtful papers exploring why computer and other systems are so difficult to use, through an analysis of the "interface experience," which includes issues such as what users understand, how they use information, and what they do. Norman (1992) is a broad and somewhat lighthearted treatment of many of the issues raised in Norman (1988), including a new collection of "design follies" and some interesting examples dealing with reliability and safety in commercial aviation. Norman (1993) focuses more deeply on *cognitive artifacts*, "tools of thought . . . that complement abilities and strengthen mental powers," and on *abstraction* and *representation*, "the ability to represent perceptions, experiences, and thoughts in some medium other than that in which they have occurred, abstracted away from irrelevant details." The three books written by Norman have been issued as an interactive CD-ROM, which also includes exercises and video lectures (Norman, 1994).

Petroski (1985, 1993) also helps us place human-computer interaction in a broader perspective. He argues that analyses of failures have been crucial in advancing other engineering and design disciplines. This may be of particular interest in software development, where failures can disappear as quickly as a disk can be erased and reused, leaving only lingering traces in the minds of researchers and developers who are more interested in moving on to the next project than in dwelling on past difficulties. A nicely written review of Petroski by Updike (1993) focuses on the need to consider fashion, profitability, and novelty in understanding the history of design.

Computers may be by far the most complex machines we deal with, but they are also fortunately our most *flexible* machines, capable of continued adaptation and refinement. This happens through the creative process of design, with successive stages of concept formation; creative synthesis and execution; and subsequent observation and evaluation, analysis, and critique. Orchestrating these tasks is challenging, and is perhaps best learned using case studies and examples.

To illustrate key issues, Case A examines the design of an information kiosk intended for use by the participants at a conference. This project had both creative and evaluative elements. Some aspects of this project were unusual, although most are found in many projects. The developers describe their approach and what they learned from it. Of particular interest to us is the use of a visually oriented, iterative methodology with extensive reliance on behavioral analysis and empirical evaluation.

This and other design methodologies are presented in detail in Chapter 2. Yet it is helpful to gain some perspective before we proceed. The discipline of human-computer interaction is a rapidly moving target for anyone who sets out to master it. To anticipate where the field might be going, it is helpful—perhaps essential—to consider whence it has come. Chapter 1, "A Historical and Intellectual Perspective," provides an overview of the field's intellectual development, stressing the origin of key ideas whose subsequent realization in computer systems has sometimes come quickly, sometimes slowly, and in some cases not yet come. This chapter also serves to frame many of the results and contributions presented throughout this book.

Other papers in this volume that adopt historical perspectives are Grudin (Chapter 4), Card and Moran (Chapter 9), and Ellis (Chapter 14). It has been said that those who do not study the past are condemned to repeat it. Well, there is no chance that this field will return to its past, but we can better prepare for the future by comprehending the trajectory of change. Developers as well as users approach computers with beliefs and expectations about what computers are and what they can do. Our preconceptions are often based on our experiences. The experiences of today's users differ from past users. They will have different preconceptions, different needs. Insight into past change may enable us to anticipate and guide the changes that are coming.

Case B focuses on the early development of the modern *graphical user interface*, typically known as the GUI. It includes a detailed description of the Xerox Star, a pioneering system incorporating a GUI that was marketed in 1981. The Star leveraged much of the creative vision and laborious groundwork of the previous two decades. We also discuss the Apple Lisa and Macintosh, systems that followed and extended the work in the Xerox Star. These systems helped to inspire the rapid growth of human-computer interaction in the 1980s. Chapters 5 and 6 will bring the story of the graphical user interface up-to-date.

REFERENCES

Note: A ◈ before a reference indicates a reading.

Dix, A., Finlay, J., Abowd, G., and Beale, R. (1993). *Human-Computer Interaction.* Prentice-Hall.

Hewett, T., Baecker, R., Card, S., Carey, T., Gasen, J., Mantei, M., Perlman, G., Strong, G., and Verplank, W. (1992). ACM SIGCHI Curricula for Human-Computer Interaction, Report of the ACM SIGCHI Curriculum Development Group.

◈ Norman, D. (1988). The Psychopathology of Everyday Things. Chapter 1 in *The Psychology of Everyday Things.* (*The Design of Everyday Things* in paperback.) Basic Books, 1–33.

Norman, D. (1992). *Turn Signals Are the Facial Expressions of Automobiles.* Addison-Wesley.

Norman, D. (1993). *Things That Make Us Smart.* Addison-Wesley.

Norman, D. (1994). Defending Human Attributes in the Age of the Machine. CD-ROM. Voyager Books.

Norman, D., and Draper, S. (1986). *User Centered System Design: New Perspectives on Human-Computer Interaction.* Lawrence Erlbaum Associates.

Petroski, H. (1985). *To Engineer Is Human: The Role of Failure in Successful Design.* St. Martin's Press.

Petroski, H. (1993). *The Evolution of Useful Things.* Knopf.

Preece, J., Rogers, Y., Sharp, H., Benyon, D., Holland, H., and Carey, T. (1994). *Human-Computer Interaction.* Addison-Wesley.

Updike, J. (1993). Things, Things. *The New Yorker,* January 18, 104–106.

THE PSYCHOPATHOLOGY OF EVERYDAY THINGS

Donald A. Norman

"Kenneth Olsen, the engineer who founded and still runs Digital Equipment Corp., confessed at the annual meeting that he can't figure out how to heat a cup of coffee in the company's microwave oven."[1]

You Would Need an Engineering Degree to Figure This Out

"You would need an engineering degree from MIT to work this," someone once told me, shaking his head in puzzlement over his brand new digital watch. Well, I have an engineering degree from MIT. (Kenneth Olsen has two of them, and he can't figure out a microwave oven.) Give me a few hours and I can figure out the watch. But why should it take hours? I have talked with many people who can't use all the features of their washing machines or cameras, who can't figure out how to work a sewing machine or a video cassette recorder, who habitually turn on the wrong stove burner.

Why do we put up with the frustrations of everyday objects, with objects that we can't figure out how to use, with those neat plastic-wrapped packages that seem impossible to open, with doors that trap people, with washing machines and dryers that have become too confusing to use, with audio-stereo-television-video-cassette-recorders that claim in their advertisements to do everything, but that make it almost impossible to do anything?

1.1 Carelman's Coffeepot for Masochists. The French artist Jacques Carelman in his series of books *Catalogue d'objets introuvables (Catalog of unfindable objects)* provides delightful examples of everyday things that are deliberately unworkable, outrageous, or otherwise ill-formed. Jacques Carelman: "Coffeepot for Masochists." Copyright © 1969–76–80 by Jacques Carelman and A. D. A. G. P. Paris. From Jacques Carelman, *Catalog of Unfindable Objects,* Balland, éditeur, Paris-France. Used by permission of the artist.

The human mind is exquisitely tailored to make sense of the world. Give it the slightest clue and off it goes, providing explanation, rationalization, understanding. Consider the objects—books, radios, kitchen appliances, office machines, and light switches—that make up our everyday lives. Well-designed objects are easy to interpret and understand. They contain visible clues to their operation. Poorly designed objects can be difficult and frustrating to use. They provide no clues—or sometimes false clues. They trap the user and thwart the normal process of interpretation and understanding. Alas, poor design predominates. The result is a world filled with frustration, with objects that cannot be understood, with devices that lead to error. This book is an attempt to change things.

The Frustrations of Everyday Life

If I were placed in the cockpit of a modern jet airliner, my inability to perform gracefully and smoothly would neither surprise nor bother me. But I shouldn't have trouble with doors and switches, water faucets and stoves. "Doors?" I can hear the reader saying, "you have trouble opening doors?" Yes. I push doors that are meant to be pulled, pull doors that should be pushed, and walk into doors that should be slid. Moreover, I see others having the same troubles—unnecessary troubles. There are psychological principles that can be followed to make these things understandable and usable.

Consider the door. There is not much you can do to a door: you can open it or shut it. Suppose you are in an office building, walking down a corridor. You come to a door. In which direction does it open? Should you pull or push, on the left or the right? Maybe the door slides. If so, in which direction? I have seen doors that slide up into the ceiling. A door poses only two essential questions: In which direction does it move? On which side should one work it? The answers should be given by the design, without any need for words or symbols, certainly without any need for trial and error.

A friend told me of the time he got trapped in the doorway of a post office in a European city. The entrance was an imposing row of perhaps six glass swinging doors, followed immediately by a second, identical row. That's a standard design: it helps reduce the airflow and thus maintain the indoor temperature of the building.

My friend pushed on the side of one of the leftmost pair of outer doors. It swung inward, and he entered the building. Then, before he could get to the next row of doors, he was distracted and turned around for an instant. He didn't realize it at the time, but he had moved slightly to the right. So when he came to the next door and pushed it, nothing happened. "Hmm," he thought, "must be locked." So he pushed the side of the adjacent door. Nothing. Puzzled, my friend decided to go outside again. He turned around and pushed against the side of a door. Nothing. He pushed the adjacent door. Nothing. The door he had just entered no longer worked. He turned around once more and tried the inside doors again. Nothing. Concern, then mild panic. He was trapped! Just then, a group of people on the other side of the entranceway (to my friend's right) passed easily through both sets of doors. My friend hurried over to follow their path.

How could such a thing happen? A swinging door has two sides. One contains the supporting pillar and the hinge, the other is unsupported. To open the door, you must push on the unsupported edge. If you push on the hinge side, nothing happens. In this case, the designer aimed for beauty, not utility. No distracting lines, no visible pillars, no visible hinges. So how can the ordinary user know which side to push on? While distracted, my friend had moved toward the (invisible) supporting pillar, so he was pushing the doors on the hinged side. No wonder nothing happened. Pretty doors. Elegant. Probably won a design prize.

1.2 A Row of Swinging Glass Doors in a Boston Hotel. A similar problem to the doors from that European post office. On which side of the door should you push? When I asked people who had just used the doors, most couldn't say. Yet only a few of the people I watched had trouble with the doors. The designers had incorporated a subtle clue into the design. Note that the horizontal bars are not centered: they are a bit closer together on the sides you should push on. The design almost works—but not entirely, for not everyone used the doors right on the first try.

The door story illustrates one of the most important principles of design: *visibility.* The correct parts must be visible, and they must convey the correct message. With doors that push, the designer must provide signals that naturally indicate where to push. These need not destroy the aesthetics. Put a vertical plate on the side to be pushed, nothing on the other. Or make the supporting pillars visible. The vertical plate and supporting pillars are *natural* signals, *naturally* interpreted, without any need to be conscious of them. I call the use of natural signals *natural design* and elaborate on the approach throughout this book.

Visibility problems come in many forms. My friend, trapped between the glass doors, suffered from a lack of clues that would indicate what part of a door should be operated. Other problems concern the *mappings* between what you want to do and what appears to be possible, another topic that will be expanded upon throughout the book. Consider one type of slide projector. This projector has a single button to control whether the slide tray moves forward or backward. One button to do two things? What is the mapping? How can you figure out how to control the slides? You can't. Nothing is visible to give the slightest hint. Here is what happened to me in one of the many unfamiliar places I've lectured in during my travels as a professor:

The Leitz slide projector illustrated in figure 1.3 has shown up several times in my travels. The first time, it led to a rather dramatic incident. A conscientious student was in charge of showing my slides. I started my talk and showed the first slide. When I finished with the first slide and asked for the next, the student carefully pushed the control button and watched in dismay as the tray backed up, slid out of the projector and plopped off the table onto the floor, spilling its entire contents. We had to delay the lecture fifteen minutes while I struggled to reorganize the slides. It wasn't the student's fault. It was the fault of the elegant projector. With only one button to control the slide advance, how could one switch from forward to reverse? Neither of us could figure out how to make the control work.

All during the lecture the slides would sometimes go forward, sometimes backward. Afterward, we found the local technician, who explained it to us. A brief push of the button and the slide would go forward, a long push and it would reverse. (Pity the conscientious student who kept pushing it hard—and long—to make sure that the switch was making contact.) What an elegant design. Why, it managed to do two functions with only one button! But how was a first-time user of the projector to know this?

Taste (7) für Diawechsel am Gerät

Diawechsel vorwärts = kurz drücken,

Diawechsel rückwärtz = länger drücken.

Button (7) for changing the slides

Slide change forward = short press,

Slide change backward = longer press.

1.3 Leitz Pravodit Slide Projector. I finally tracked down the instruction manual for that projector. A photograph of the projector has its parts numbered. The button for changing slides is number 7. The button itself has no labels. Who could discover this operation without the aid of the manual? Here is the entire text related to the button, in the original German and in my English translation:

As another example, consider the beautiful Amphithéâtre Louis-Laird in the Paris Sorbonne, which is filled with magnificent paintings of great figures in French intellectual history. (The mural on the ceiling shows lots of naked women floating about a man who is valiantly trying to read a book. The painting is right side up only for the lecturer—it is upside down for all the people in the audience.) The room is a delight to lecture in, at least until you ask for the projection screen to be lowered. "Ah," says the professor in charge, who gestures to the technician, who runs out of the room, up a short flight of stairs, and out of sight behind a solid wall. The screen comes down and stops. "No, no," shouts the professor, "a little bit more." The screen comes down again, this time too much. "No, no, no!" the professor jumps up and down and gestures wildly. It's a lovely room, with lovely paintings. But why can't the person who is trying to lower or raise the screen see what he is doing?

New telephone systems have proven to be another excellent example of incomprehensible design. No matter where I travel, I can count upon finding a particularly bad example.

When I visited Basic Books, the publishers of this book, I noticed a new telephone system. I asked people how they liked it. The question unleashed a torrent of abuse. "It doesn't have a hold function," one woman complained bitterly—the same complaint people at my university made about their rather different system. In older days, business phones always had a button labeled "hold." You could push the button and hang up the phone without losing the call on your line. Then you could talk to a colleague, or pick up another telephone call, or even pick up the call at another phone with the same telephone number. A light on the hold button indicated when the function was in use. It was an invaluable tool for business. Why didn't the new phones at Basic Books or in my university have a hold function, if it is so essential? Well, they did, even the very instrument the woman was complaining about. But there was no easy way to discover the fact, nor to learn how to use it.

I was visiting the University of Michigan and I asked about the new

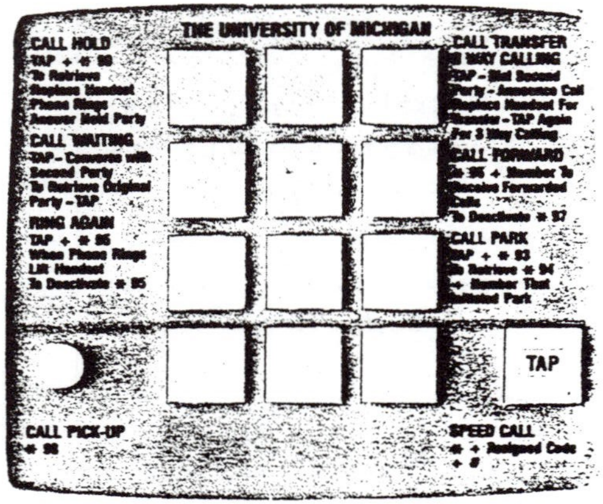

1.4 Plate Mounted Over the Dial of the Telephones at the University of Michigan. These inadequate instructions are all that most users see. (The button labeled "TAP" at the lower right is used to transfer or pick up calls—it is pressed whenever the instruction plate says "TAP." The light on the lower left comes on whenever the telephone rings.)

system there. "Yech!" was the response, "and it doesn't even have a hold function!" Here we go again. What is going on? The answer is simple: first, look at the instructions for hold. At the University of Michigan the phone company provided a little plate that fits over the keypad and reminds users of the functions and how to use them. I carefully unhooked one of the plates from the telephone and made a photocopy (figure 1.4). Can you understand how to use it? I can't. There is a "call hold" operation, but it doesn't make sense to me, not for the application that I just described.

The telephone hold situation illustrates a number of different problems. One of them is simply poor instructions, especially a failure to relate the new functions to the similarly named functions that people already know about. Second, and more serious, is the lack of visibility of the operation of the system. The new telephones, for all their added sophistication, lack both the hold button and the flashing light of the old ones. The hold is signified by an arbitrary action: dialing an arbitrary sequence of digits (*8, or *99, or what have you: it varies from one phone system to another). Third, there is no visible outcome of the operation.

Devices in the home have developed some related problems: functions and more functions, controls and more controls. I do not think that simple home appliances—stoves, washing machines, audio and television sets—should look like Hollywood's idea of a spaceship control room. They already do, much to the consternation of the consumer who, often as not, has lost (or cannot understand) the instruction manual, so—faced with the bewildering array of controls and displays—simply memorizes one or two fixed settings to approximate what is desired. The whole purpose of the design is lost.

In England I visited a home with a fancy new Italian washer-drier combination, with super-duper multi-symbol controls, all to do everything you ever wanted to do with the washing and drying of clothes. The husband (an engineering psychologist) said he refused to go near it. The wife (a physician) said she had simply memorized one setting and tried to ignore the rest.

Someone went to a lot of trouble to create that design. I read the instruction manual. That machine took into account everything about today's wide variety of synthetic and natural fabrics. The designers worked hard; they really cared. But obviously they had never thought of trying it out, or of watching anyone use it.

If the design was so bad, if the controls were so unusable, why did the couple purchase it? If people keep buying poorly designed products, manufacturers and designers will think they are doing the right thing and continue as usual.

The user needs help. Just the right things have to be visible: to indicate what parts operate and how, to indicate how the user is to interact with the device. Visibility indicates the mapping between intended actions and actual operations. Visibility indicates crucial distinctions—so that you can tell salt and pepper shakers apart, for example. And visibility of the effects of the operations tells you if the lights have turned on properly, if the projection screen has lowered to the correct height, or if the refrigerator temperature is adjusted correctly. It is lack of visibility that makes so many computer-controlled devices so difficult to operate. And it is an excess of visibility that makes the gadget-ridden, feature-laden modern audio set or video cassette recorder (VCR) so intimidating.

The Psychology of Everyday Things

This book is about the psychology of everyday things. POET emphasizes the understanding of everyday things, things with knobs and dials, controls and switches, lights and meters. The instances we have just examined demonstrate several principles, including the importance of visibility, appropriate clues, and feedback of one's actions. These principles constitute a form of psychology—the psychology of how people interact with things. A British designer once noted that the kinds of materials used in the construction of passenger shelters affected the way vandals responded. He suggested that there might be a psychology of materials.

AFFORDANCES

"In one case, the reinforced glass used to panel shelters (for railroad passengers) erected by British Rail was smashed by vandals as fast as it was renewed. When the reinforced glass was replaced by plywood boarding, however, little further damage occurred, although no extra force would have been required to produce it. Thus British Rail managed to elevate the desire for defacement to those who could write, albeit in somewhat limited terms. Nobody has, as yet, considered whether there is a kind of psychology of materials. But on the evidence, there could well be!"[2]

There already exists the start of a psychology of materials and of things, the study of affordances of objects. When used in this sense, the term *affordance* refers to the perceived and actual properties of the thing, primarily those fundamental properties that determine just how the thing could possibly be used (see figures 1.5 and 1.6). A chair affords ("is for") support and, therefore, affords sitting. A chair can also be carried. Glass is for seeing through, and for breaking. Wood is normally used for solidity, opacity, support, or carving. Flat, porous, smooth surfaces are for writing on. So wood is also for writing on. Hence the problem for British Rail: when the shelters had glass, vandals smashed it; when they had plywood, vandals wrote on and carved it. The planners were trapped by the affordances of their materials.[3]

Affordances provide strong clues to the operations of things. Plates are for pushing. Knobs are for turning. Slots are for inserting things into. Balls are for throwing or bouncing. When affordances are taken advantage of, the user knows what to do just by looking: no picture, label, or instruction is required. Complex things may require explanation, but simple things should not. When simple things need pictures, labels, or instructions, the design has failed.

A psychology of causality is also at work as we use everyday things.

1.5 Affordances of Doors. Door hardware can signal whether to push or pull without signs. The flat horizontal bar of *A* (above left) affords no operations except pushing: it is excellent hardware for a door that must be pushed to be opened. The door in *B* (above right) has a different kind of bar on each side, one relatively small and vertical to signify a pull, the other relatively large and horizontal to signify a push. Both bars support the affordance of grasping: size and position specify whether the grasp is used to push or pull—though ambiguously.

1.6 When Affordances Fail. I had to tie a string around my cabinet door to afford pulling.

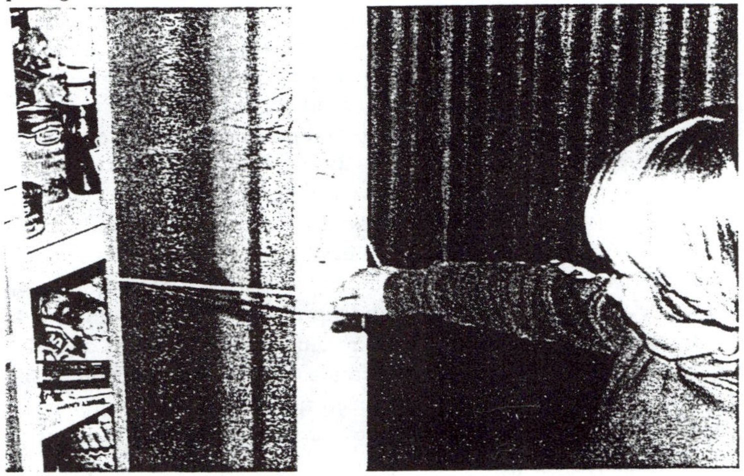

Something that happens right after an action appears to be caused by that action. Touch a computer terminal just when it fails, and you are apt to believe that you caused the failure, even though the failure and your action were related only by coincidence. Such false causality is the basis for much superstition. Many of the peculiar behaviors of people using computer systems or complex household appliances result from such false coincidences. When an action has no apparent result, you may conclude that the action was ineffective. So you repeat it. In earlier days, when computer word processors did not always show the results of their operations, people would sometimes attempt to change their manuscript, but the lack of visible effect from each action would make them think that their commands had not been executed, so they would repeat the commands, sometimes over and over, to their later astonishment and regret. It is a poor design that allows either kind of false causality to occur.

TWENTY THOUSAND EVERYDAY THINGS

There are an amazing number of everyday things, perhaps twenty thousand of them. Are there really that many? Start by looking about you. There are light fixtures, bulbs, and sockets; wall plates and screws; clocks, watches, and watchbands. There are writing devices (I count twelve in front of me, each different in function, color, or style). There are clothes, with different functions, openings, and flaps. Notice the variety of materials and pieces. Notice the variety of fasteners—buttons, zippers, snaps, laces. Look at all the furniture and food utensils: all those details, each serving some function for manufacturability, usage, or appearance. Consider the work area: paper clips, scissors, pads of paper, magazines, books, bookmarks. In the room I'm working in, I counted more than a hundred specialized objects before I tired. Each is simple, but each requires its own method of operation, each has to be learned, each does its own specialized task, and each has to be designed separately. Furthermore, many of the objects are made of many parts. A desk stapler has sixteen parts, a household iron fifteen, the simple bathtub-shower combination twenty-three. You can't believe these simple objects have so many parts? Here are the eleven basic parts to a sink: drain, flange (around the drain), pop-up stopper, basin, soap dish, overflow vent, spout, lift rod, fittings, hot-water handle, and cold-water handle. We can count even more if we start taking the faucets, fittings, and lift rods apart.

The book *What's What: A Visual Glossary of the Physical World* has more than fifteen hundred drawings and pictures and illustrates twenty-three thousand items or parts of items.[4] Irving Biederman, a psychologist who studies visual perception, estimates that there are probably "30,000 readily discriminable objects for the adult."[5] Whatever the exact number, it is clear that the difficulties of everyday life are amplified by the sheer profusion of items. Suppose that each everyday thing takes only one minute to learn; learning 20,000 of them occupies 20,000 minutes—333 hours or about 8 forty-hour work weeks. Furthermore, we often encounter new objects unexpectedly, when we are really concerned with something else. We are confused and distracted, and what ought to be a simple, effortless, everyday thing interferes with the important task of the moment.

How do people cope? Part of the answer lies in the way the mind works—in the psychology of human thought and cognition. Part lies in the information available from the appearance of the objects—the psychology of everyday things. And part comes from the ability of the designer to make the operation clear, to project a good image of the operation, and to take advantage of other things people might be expected to know. Here is where the designer's knowledge of the psychology of people coupled with knowledge of how things work becomes crucial.

CONCEPTUAL MODELS

Consider the rather strange bicycle illustrated in figure 1.7. You know it won't work because you form a *conceptual model* of the device and mentally simulate its operation. You can do the simulation because the parts are visible and the implications clear.

Other clues to how things work come from their visible structure—in particular from *affordances, constraints,* and *mappings.* Consider a pair of scissors: even if you have never seen or used them before, you can see that the number of possible actions is limited. The holes are clearly there to put something into, and the only logical things that will fit are fingers. The holes are affordances: they allow the the fingers to be inserted. The sizes of the holes provide *constraints* to limit the possible fingers: the big hole suggests several fingers, the small hole only one. The mapping between holes and fingers—the set of possible operations—is suggested and constrained by the holes. Moreover, the operation is not sensitive to finger placement: if you use the wrong fingers,

1.7 Carelman's Tandem "Convergent Bicycle (Model for Fiancés)." Jacques Carelman: "Convergent Bicycle" Copyright © 1969–76–80 by Jacques Carelman and A. D. A. G. P. Paris. From Jacques Carelman, *Catalog of Unfindable Objects,* Balland, éditeur, Paris-France. Used by permission of the artist.

the scissors still work. You can figure out the scissors because their operating parts are visible and the implications clear. The conceptual model is made obvious, and there is effective use of affordances and constraints.

As a counterexample, consider the digital watch, one with two to four push buttons on the front or side. What are those push buttons for? How would you set the time? There is no way to tell—no evident relationship between the operating controls and the functions, no constraints, no apparent mappings. With the scissors, moving the handle makes the blades move. The watch and the Leitz slide projector provide no visible relationship between the buttons and the possible actions, no discernible relationship between the actions and the end result.

Principles of Design for Understandability and Usability

We have now encountered the fundamental principles of designing for people: (1) provide a good conceptual model and (2) make things visible.

PROVIDE A GOOD CONCEPTUAL MODEL

A good conceptual model allows us to predict the effects of our actions. Without a good model we operate by rote, blindly; we do operations as we were told to do them; we can't fully appreciate why, what effects to expect, or what to do if things go wrong. As long as things work properly, we can manage. When things go wrong, however, or when we come upon a novel situation, then we need a deeper understanding, a good model.

For everyday things, conceptual models need not be very complex. After all, scissors, pens, and light switches are pretty simple devices. There is no need to understand the underlying physics or chemistry of each device we own, simply the relationship between the controls and the outcomes. When the model presented to us is inadequate or wrong (or, worse, nonexistent), we can have difficulties. Let me tell you about my refrigerator.

My house has an ordinary, two-compartment refrigerator—nothing very fancy about it. The problem is that I can't set the temperature properly. There are only two things to do: adjust the temperature of the freezer compartment and adjust the temperature of the fresh food compartment. And there are two controls, one labeled "freezer," the other "fresh food." What's the problem?

You try it. Figure 1.8 shows the instruction plate from inside the refrigerator. Now, suppose the freezer is too cold, the fresh food section just right. You want to make the freezer warmer, keeping the fresh food constant. Go on, read the instructions, figure them out.

1.8 My Refrigerator. Two compartments—fresh food and freezer—and two controls (in the fresh food unit). The illustration shows the controls and instructions. Your task: Suppose the freezer is too cold, the fresh food section just right. How would you adjust the controls so as to make the freezer warmer and keep the fresh food the same? (From Norman, 1986.)

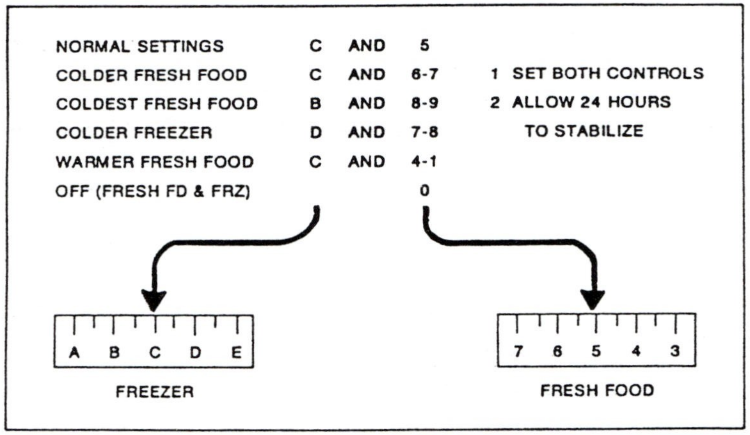

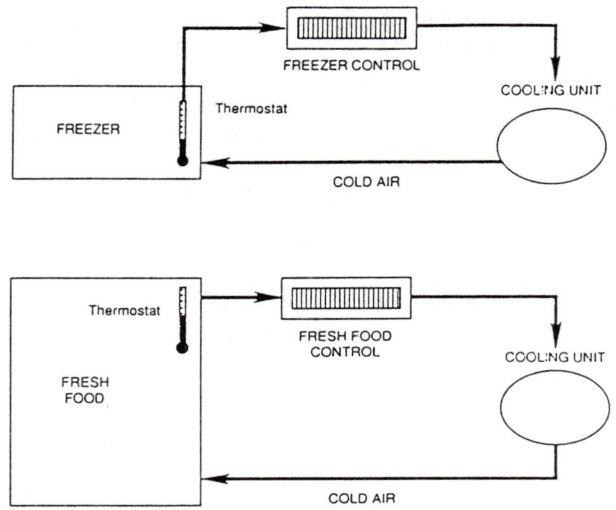

1.9 Two Conceptual Models for My Refrigerator. The model *A* (above) is provided by the system image of the refrigerator as gleaned from the controls and instructions; *B* (below) is the correct conceptual model. The problem is that it is impossible to tell in which compartment the thermostat is located and whether the two controls are in the freezer and fresh food compartment, or vice versa.

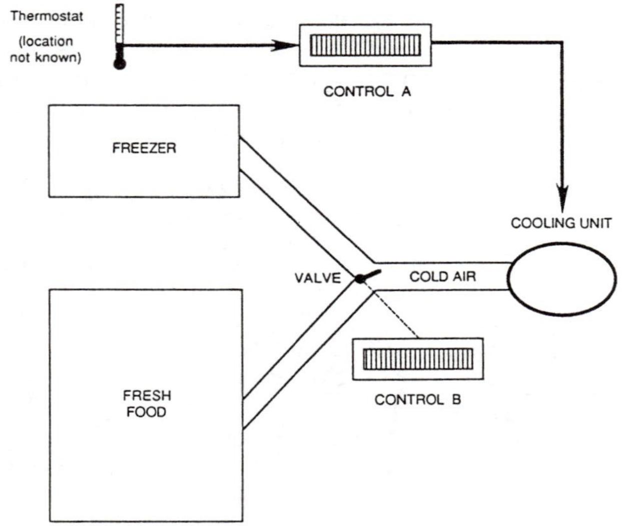

Oh, perhaps I'd better warn you. The two controls are not independent. The freezer control affects the fresh food temperature, and the fresh food control affects the freezer. And don't forget to wait twenty-four hours to check on whether you made the right adjustment, if you can remember what you did.

Control of the refrigerator is made difficult because the manufacturer provides a false conceptual model. There are two compartments and two controls. The setup clearly and unambiguously provides a simple model for the user: each control is responsible for the temperature of the compartment that carries its name. Wrong. In fact, there is only one thermostat and only one cooling mechanism. One control adjusts the thermostat setting, the other the relative proportion of cold air sent to each of the two compartments of the refrigerator. This is why the two controls interact. With the conceptual model provided by the manufacturer, adjusting the temperatures is almost impossible and always frustrating. Given the correct model, life would be much easier (figure 1.9).

Why did the manufacturer present the wrong conceptual model?

1.10 Conceptual Models. The *design model* is the designer's conceptual model. The *user's model* is the mental model developed through interaction with the system. The *system image* results from the physical structure that has been built (including documentation, instructions, and labels). The designer expects the user's model to be identical to the design model. But the designer doesn't talk directly with the user—all communication takes place through the system image. If the system image does not make the design model clear and consistent, then the user will end up with the wrong mental model. (From Norman, 1986.)

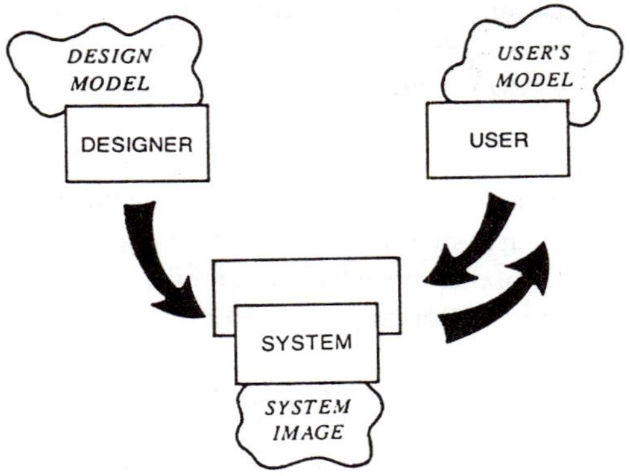

Perhaps the designers thought the correct model was too complex, that the model they were giving was easier to understand. But with the wrong conceptual model, it is impossible to set the controls. And even though I am convinced I now know the correct model, I still cannot accurately adjust the temperatures because the refrigerator design makes it impossible for me to discover which control is for the thermostat, which control is for the relative proportion of cold air, and in which compartment the thermostat is located. The lack of immediate feedback for the actions does not help: with a delay of twenty-four hours, who can remember what was tried?

The topic of conceptual models will reappear in the book. They are part of an important concept in design: *mental models,* the models people have of themselves, others, the environment, and the things with which they interact. People form mental models through experience, training, and instruction. The mental model of a device is formed largely by interpreting its perceived actions and its visible structure. I call the visible part of the device the *system image* (figure 1.10). When the system image is incoherent or inappropriate, as in the case of the refrigerator, then the user cannot easily use the device. If it is incomplete or contradictory, there will be trouble.

MAKE THINGS VISIBLE

The problems caused by inadequate attention to visibility are all neatly demonstrated with one simple appliance: the modern telephone.

I stand at the blackboard in my office, talking with a student, when my telephone rings. Once, twice it rings. I pause, trying to complete my sentence before answering. The ringing stops. "I'm sorry," says the student. "Not your fault," I say. "But it's no problem, the call now transfers to my secretary's phone. She'll answer it." As we listen we hear her phone start to ring. Once, twice. I look at my watch. Six o'clock: it's late, the office staff has left for the day. I rush out of my office to my secretary's phone, but as I get there, it stops ringing. "Ah," I think, "it's being transferred to another phone." Sure enough, the phone in the adjacent office now starts ringing. I rush to that office, but it is locked. Back to my office to get the key, out to the locked door, fumble with the lock, into the office, and to the now quiet phone. I hear a telephone down the hall start to ring. Could that still be my call, making its way mysteriously, with a predetermined lurching path, through the phones of the building? Or is it just another telephone call coincidentally arriving at this time?

In fact, I could have retrieved the call from my office, had I acted quickly enough. The manual states: "Within your pre-programmed pick-up group, dial 14 to connect to incoming call. Otherwise, to answer any ringing extension, dial ringing extension number, listen for busy tone. Dial 8 to connect to incoming call." Huh? What do those instructions mean? What is a "pre-programmed pick-up group," and why do I even want to know? What is the extension number of the ringing phone? Can I remember all those instructions when I need them? No.

Telephone chase is the new game in the modern office, as the automatic features of telephones go awry—features designed without proper thought, and certainly without testing them with their intended users. There are several other games, too. One game is announced by the plea, "How do I answer this call?" The question is properly whined in front of a ringing, flashing telephone, receiver in hand. Then there is the paradoxical game entitled "This telephone doesn't have a hold function." The accusation is directed at a telephone that actually *does* have a hold function. And, finally, there is "What do you mean I called you, you called me!"

Many of the modern telephone systems have a new feature that automatically keeps trying to dial a number for you. This feature resides under names such as automatic redialing or automatic callback. I am supposed to use this feature whenever I call someone who doesn't answer or whose line is busy. When the person next hangs up the phone, my phone will dial it again. Several automatic callbacks can be active at a time. Here's how it works. I place a phone call. There's no answer, so I activate the automatic callback feature. Several hours later my telephone rings. I pick it up and say "Hello," only to hear a ringing sound and then someone else saying "Hello."

"Hello," I answer, "who is this?"

"Who is this?" I hear in reply, "you called me."

"No," I say, "you called me, my phone just rang."

Slowly I realize that perhaps this is my delayed call. Now, let me see, who was I trying to call several hours ago? Did I have several callbacks in place? Why was I making the call?

The modern telephone did not happen by accident: it was carefully designed. Someone—more likely a team of people—invented a list of features thought desirable, invented what seemed to them to be plausible ways of controlling the features, and then put it all together. My university, focusing on cost and perhaps dazzled by the features, bought the system, spending millions of dollars on a telephone installation that has proved vastly unpopular and even unworkable. Why did the university buy the system? The purchase took several years of committee work and studies and presentations by competing telephone companies, and piles of documentation and specification. I myself took part, looking at the interaction between the telephone system and the computer networks, ensuring that the two would be compatible and reasonable in price. To my knowledge, nobody ever thought of trying out the telephones in advance. Nobody suggested installing them in a sample office to see whether users' needs would be met or whether users could understand how to operate the phone. The result: disaster. The main culprit—lack of visibility—was coupled with a secondary culprit—a poor conceptual model. Any money saved on the installation and purchase is quickly disappearing in training costs, missed calls, and frustration. Yet from what I have seen, the competing phone systems would not have been any better.

I recently spent six months at the Applied Psychology Unit in Cambridge, England. Just before I arrived the British Telecom Company had installed a new telephone system. It had lots and lots of features. The telephone instrument itself was unremarkable (figure 1.11). It was the standard twelve-button, push-button phone, except that it had an extra key labeled "R" off on the side. (I never did find out what that key did.)

The telephone system was a standing joke. Nobody could use all the features. One person even started a small research project to record people's confusions. Another person wrote a small "expert systems" computer program, one of the new toys of the field of artificial intelligence; the program can reason through complex situations. If you wanted to use the phone system, perhaps to make a conference call among three people, you asked the expert system and it would explain how to do it. So, you're on the line with someone and you need to add a third person to the call. First turn on your computer. Then load the expert system. After three or four minutes (needed for loading the program), type in what you want to accomplish. Eventually the computer will tell you what to do—if you can remember why you want to

1.11 British Telecom Telephone. This was in my office at the Applied Psychology Unit in Cambridge, England. It certainly looks simple, doesn't it?

1.12 Two Ways to Use Hold on Modern Telephones. Illustration *A* (below left) is the instruction manual page for British Telecom. The procedure seems especially complicated, with three 3-digit codes to be learned: 681, 682, and 683. Illustration *B* (below right) shows the equivalent instructions for the Ericsson Single Line Analog Telephone installed at the University of California, San Diego. I find the second set of instructions easier to understand, but one must still dial an arbitrary digit: 8 in this case.

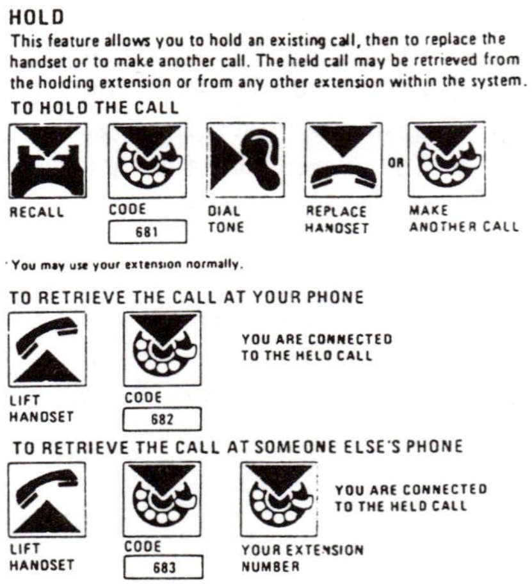

CALL HOLD/CALL PARK
With party on line
- Press R key
- Listen for recall dial tone (three beeps and dial tone)
- Hang up handset

TO RETRIEVE FROM SAME PHONE
- Lift handset; you are connected to the call

TO RETRIEVE FROM ANOTHER PHONE
- Lift handset
- Dial extension where call was parked; listen for busy tone
- Dial 8; you are connected to the call

NOTE: Call will remain parked for 3 minutes before re-ringing do it, and if the person on the other end of the line is still around. But, as it happens, using the expert system is a lot easier than reading and understanding the manual provided with the telephone (figure 1.12).

Why is that telephone system so hard to understand? Nothing in it is conceptually difficult. Each of the operations is actually quite simple. A few digits to dial, that's all. The telephone doesn't even look complicated. There are only fifteen controls: the usual twelve buttons—ten labeled 0 through 9, #, and *—plus the handset itself, the handset button, and the mysterious "R" button. All except the "R" are the everyday parts of a normal modern telephone. Why was the system so difficult?

A designer who works for a telephone company told me the following story:

"I was involved in designing the faceplate of some of those new multifunction phones, some of which have buttons labeled "R." *The* "R" *button is kind of a vestigial feature. It is very hard to remove features of a newly designed product that had existed in an earlier version. It's kind of like physical evolution. If a feature is in the genome, and if that feature is not associated with any negativity (i.e., no customers gripe about it), then the feature hangs on for generations.*

"It is interesting that things like the "R" *button are largely determined through examples. Somebody asks, 'What is the* "R" *button used for?' and the answer is to give an example: 'You can push* "R" *to access loudspeaker paging.' If nobody can think of an example, the feature is dropped. Designers are pretty bright people, however. They can come up with a plausible-sounding example for almost anything. Hence, you get features, many many features, and these features hang on for a long time. The end result is complex interfaces for essentially simple things."*[6]

As I pondered this problem, I decided it would make sense to compare the phone system with something that was of equal or greater complexity but easier to use. So let us temporarily leave the difficult telephone system and take a look at my automobile. I bought a car in Europe. When I picked up the new car at the factory, a man from the company sat in the car with me and went over each control, explaining its function. When he had gone through the controls once, I said fine, thanked him, and drove away. That was all the instruction it took. There are 112 controls inside the car. This isn't quite as bad as it sounds. Twenty-five of them are on the radio. Another 7 are the temperature control system, and 11 work the windows and sunroof. The trip computer has 14 buttons, each matched with a specific function. So four devices—the radio, temperature controls, windows, and trip computer—have together 57 controls, or just over 50 percent of the ones available.

Why is the automobile, with all its varied functions and numerous controls, so much easier to learn and to use than the telephone system, with its much smaller set of functions and controls? What is good about the design of the car? Things are visible. There are good mappings, natural relationships, between the controls and the things controlled. Single controls often have single functions. There is good feedback. The system is understandable. In general, the relationships among the user's intentions, the required actions, and the results are sensible, nonarbitrary, and meaningful.

What is bad about the design of the telephone? There is no visible structure. Mappings are arbitrary: there is no rhyme or reason to the relationship between the actions the user must perform and the results to be accomplished. The controls have multiple functions. There isn't good feedback, so the user is never sure whether the desired result has been obtained. The system, in general, is not understandable; its capabilities aren't apparent. In general, the relationships among the user's intentions, the required actions, and the results are completely arbitrary.

Whenever the number of possible actions exceeds the number of controls, there is apt to be difficulty. The telephone system has twenty-four functions, yet only fifteen controls—none of them labeled for specific action. In contrast, the trip computer for the car performs seventeen functions with fourteen controls. With minor exceptions, there is one control for each function. In fact, the controls with more than one function are indeed harder to remember and use. When the number of controls equals the number of functions, each control can be specialized, each can be labeled. The possible functions are visible, for each corresponds with a control. If the user forgets the functions, the controls serve as reminders. When, as on the telephone, there are more functions than controls, labeling becomes difficult or impossible. There is nothing to remind the user. Functions are invisible, hidden from sight. No wonder the operation becomes mysterious and difficult. The controls for the car are visible and, through their location and mode of operation, bear an intelligent relationship to their action. Visibility acts as a good reminder of what can be done and allows the control to specify how the action is to be performed. The good relationship between the placement of the control and what it does makes it easy to find the appropriate control for a task. As a result, there is little to remember.

THE PRINCIPLE OF MAPPING

Mapping is a technical term meaning the relationship between two things, in this case between the controls and their movements and the results in the world. Consider the mapping relationships involved in steering a car. To turn the car to the right, one turns the steering wheel clockwise (so that its top moves to the right). The user must identify two mappings here: one of the 112 controls affects the steering, and the steering wheel must be turned in one of two directions. Both are somewhat arbitrary. But the wheel and the clockwise direction are natural choices: visible, closely related to the desired outcome, and providing immediate feedback. The mapping is easily learned and always remembered.

Natural mapping, by which I mean taking advantage of physical analogies and cultural standards, leads to immediate understanding. For example, a designer can use spatial analogy: to move an object up, move the control up. To control an array of lights, arrange the controls in the same pattern as the lights. Some natural mappings are cultural or biological, as in the universal standard that a rising level represents more, a diminishing level, less. Similarly, a louder sound can mean a greater amount. Amount and loudness (and weight, line length, and brightness) are additive dimensions: add more to show incremental increases. Note that the logically plausible relationship between musical pitch and amount does not work: Would a higher pitch mean less or more of something? Pitch (and taste, color, and location) are substitutive dimensions: substitute one value for another to make a change. There is no natural concept of more or less in the comparison of different pitches, or hues, or taste qualities. Other natural mappings follow from the principles of perception and allow for the natural grouping or patterning of controls and feedback (see figure 1.13).

Mapping problems are abundant, one of the fundamental causes of difficulties. Consider the telephone. Suppose you wish to activate the callback on "no reply" function. To initiate this feature on one telephone system, press and release the "recall" button (the button on the handset), then dial 60, then dial the number you called.

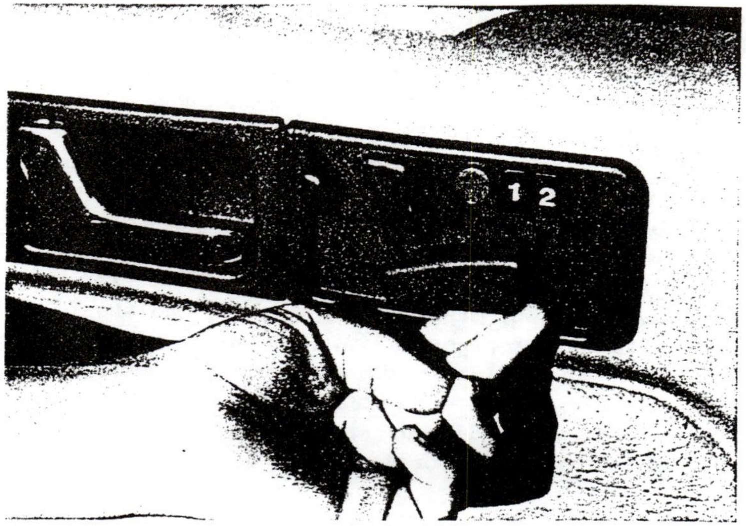

1.13 Seat Adjustment Control from a Mercedes-Benz Automobile. This is an excellent example of natural mapping. The control is in the shape of the seat itself: the mapping is straightforward. To move the front edge of the seat higher, lift up on the front part of the button. To make the seat back recline, move the button back. Mercedes-Benz automobiles are obviously not everyday things for most people, but the principle doesn't require great expense or wealth. The same principle could be applied to much more common objects.

There are several problems here. First, the description of the function is relatively complex—yet incomplete: What if two people set up callback at the same time? What if the person does not come back until a week later? What if you have meanwhile set up three or four other functions? What if you want to cancel it? Second, the action to be performed is arbitrary. (Dial 60. Why 60? Why not 73 or 27? How does one remember an arbitrary number?) Third, the sequence ends with what appears to be a redundant, unnecessary action: dialing the number of the person to be called. If the phone system is smart enough to do all these other things, why can't it remember the number that was just attempted; why must it be told all over again? And finally, consider the lack of feedback. How do I know I did the right action? Maybe I disconnected the phone. Maybe I set up some other special feature. There is no visible or audible way to know immediately.

A device is easy to use when there is visibility to the set of possible actions, where the controls and displays exploit natural mappings. The principles are simple but rarely incorporated into design. Good design takes care, planning, thought. It takes conscious attention to the needs of the user. And sometimes the designer gets it right:

Once, when I was at a conference at Gmunden, Austria, a group of us went off to see the sights. I sat directly behind the driver of the brand new, sleek, high-technology German tour bus. I gazed in wonder at the hundreds of controls scattered all over the front of the bus.

"How can you ever learn all those controls?" I asked the driver (with the aid of a German-speaking colleague). The driver was clearly puzzled by the question.

"What do you mean?" he replied. "Each control is just where it ought to be. There is no difficulty."

A good principle, that. Controls are where they ought to be. One function, one control. Harder to do, of course, than to say, but essentially this is the principle of natural mappings: the relationship between controls and actions should be apparent to the user. I return to this topic later in the book, for the problem of determining the "naturalness" of mappings is difficult, but crucial.

I've already described how my car's controls are generally easy to use. Actually, the car has lots of problems. The approach to usability used in the car seems to be to make sure that you can reach everything and see everything. That's good, but not nearly good enough.

Here is a simple example: the controls for the loudspeakers—a simple control that determines whether the sound comes out of the front speakers, the rear, or a combination (figure 1.14). Rotate the wheel from left to right or right to left. Simple, except how do you know which way to rotate the control? Which direction moves the sound to the rear, which to the front? If you want sound to come out of the front speaker, you should be able to move the control to the front. To get it out of the back, move the control to the back. Then the form of the motion would mimic the function and make a natural mapping. But the way the control is actually mounted in the car, forward and backward get translated into left and right. Which direction is which? There is no natural relationship. What's worse, the control isn't even labeled. Even the instruction manual does not say how to use it.

1.14 **The Front/Rear Speaker Selector of an Automobile Radio.** Rotating the knob with the pictures of the speaker at either side makes the sound come entirely out of the front speakers (when the knob is all the way over to one side), entirely out of the rear speakers (when the knob is all the way the other way), or equally out of both (when the knob is midway). Which way is front, which rear? You can't tell by looking. While you're at it, imagine trying to manipulate the radio controls while keeping your eyes on the road.

The control should be mounted so that it moves forward and backward. If that can't be done, rotate the control 90° on the panel so that it moves vertically. Moving something up to represent forward is not as natural as moving it forward, but at least it follows a standard convention.

In fact, we see that both the car and the telephone have easy functions and difficult ones. The car seems to have more of the easy ones, the telephone more of the difficult ones. Moreover, with the car, enough of the controls are easy that I can do almost everything I need to. Not so with the telephone: it is very difficult to use even a single one of the special features.

The easy things on both telephone and car have a lot in common, as do the difficult things. When things are visible, they tend to be easier than when they are not. In addition, there must be a close, *natural* relationship between the control and its function: a *natural mapping*.

THE PRINCIPLE OF FEEDBACK

Feedback—sending back to the user information about what action has actually been done, what result has been accomplished—is a well-known concept in the science of control and information theory. Imagine trying to talk to someone when you cannot even hear your own voice, or trying to draw a picture with a pencil that leaves no mark: there would be no feedback.

In the good old days of the telephone, before the American telephone system was divided among competing companies, before telephones were fancy and had so many features, telephones were designed with much more care and concern for the user. Designers at the Bell Telephone Laboratories worried a lot about feedback. The push buttons were designed to give an appropriate feel—tactile feedback. When a button was pushed, a tone was fed back into the earpiece so the user could tell that the button had been properly pushed. When the phone call was being connected, clicks, tones, and other noises gave the user feedback about the progress of the call. And the speaker's voice was always fed back to the earpiece in a carefully controlled amount, because the auditory feedback (called "sidetone") helped the person regulate how loudly to talk. All this has changed. We now have telephones that are much more powerful and often cheaper than those that existed just a few years ago—more function for less money. To be fair, these new designs are pushing hard on the paradox of technology: added functionality generally comes along at the price of added complexity. But that does not justify backward progress.

Why are the modern telephone systems so difficult to learn and to use? Basically, the problem is that the systems have more features and less feedback. Suppose all telephones had a small display screen, not unlike the ones on small, inexpensive calculators. The display could be used to present, upon the push of a button, a brief menu of all the features of the telephone, one by one. When the desired one was encountered, the user would push another button to indicate that it should be invoked. If further action was required, the display could tell the person what to do. The display could even be auditory, with speech instead of a visual display. Only two buttons need be added to the telephone: one to change the display, one to accept the option on display. Of course, the telephone would be slightly more expensive. The tradeoff is cost versus usability.[7]

Pity the Poor Designer

Designing well is not easy. The manufacturer wants something that can be produced economically. The store wants something that will be attractive to its customers. The purchaser has several demands. In the store, the purchaser focuses on price and appearance, and perhaps on prestige value. At home, the same person will pay more attention to functionality and usability. The repair service cares about maintainability: how easy is the device to take apart, diagnose, and service? The needs of those concerned are different and often conflict. Nonetheless, the designer may be able to satisfy everyone.

A simple example of good design is the $3\frac{1}{2}$-inch magnetic diskette for computers, a small circle of "floppy" magnetic material encased in hard plastic. Earlier types of floppy disks did not have this plastic case, which protects the magnetic material from abuse and damage. A sliding metal cover protects the delicate magnetic surface when the diskette is not in use and automatically opens when the diskette is inserted into the computer. The diskette has a square shape: there are apparently eight possible ways to insert it into the machine, only one of which is correct. What happens if I do it wrong? I try inserting the disk sideways. Ah, the designer thought of that. A little study shows that the case really isn't square: it's rectangular, so you can't insert a longer side. I try backward. The diskette goes in only part of the way. Small protrusions, indentations, and cutouts prevent the diskette from being inserted backward or upside down: of the eight ways one might try to insert the diskette, only one is correct, and only that one will fit. An excellent design.

Take another example of good design. My felt-tipped marking pen has ribs along only one of its sides; otherwise all sides look identical. Careful examination shows that the tip of the marker is angled and makes the best line if the marker is held with the ribbed side up, a natural result if the forefinger rests upon the ribs. No harm results if I hold the marker another way, but the marker writes less well. The ribs are a subtle design cue—functional, yet visibly and aesthetically unobtrusive.

The world is permeated with small examples of good design, with the amazing details that make important differences in our lives. Each detail was added by some person, a designer, carefully thinking through the uses of the device, the ways that people abuse things, the kinds of errors that can get made, and the functions that people wish to have performed.

Then why is it that so many good design ideas don't find their way into products in the marketplace? Or something good shows up for a short time, only to fall into oblivion? I once spoke with a designer about the frustrations of trying to get the best product out:

It usually takes five or six attempts to get a product right. This may be acceptable in an established product, but consider what it means in a new one. Suppose a company wants to make a product that will perhaps make a real difference. The problem is that if the product is truly revolutionary, it is unlikely that anyone will quite know how to design it right the first time; it will take several tries. But if a product is introduced into the marketplace and fails, well that is it. Perhaps it could be introduced a second time, or maybe even a third time, but after that it is dead: everyone believes it to be a failure.

I asked him to explain. "You mean," I said, "that it takes five or six tries to get an idea right?"

"Yes," he said, "at least that."

"But," I replied, "you also said that if a newly introduced product doesn't catch on in the first two or three times, then it is dead?"

"Yup," he said.

"Then new products are almost guaranteed to fail, no matter how good the idea."

"Now you understand," said the designer. "Consider the use of voice messages on complex devices such as cameras, soft-drink machines, and copiers. A failure. No longer even tried. Too bad. It really is a good idea, for it can be very useful when the hands or eyes are busy elsewhere. But those first few attempts were very badly done and the public scoffed—properly. Now, nobody dares try it again, even in those places where it is needed."

The Paradox of Technology

Technology offers the potential to make life easier and more enjoyable; each new technology provides increased benefits. At the same time, added complexities arise to increase our difficulty and frustration. The development of a technology tends to follow a U-shaped curve of complexity: starting high; dropping to a low, comfortable level; then climbing again. New kinds of devices are complex and difficult to use. As technicians become more competent and an industry matures, devices become simpler, more reliable, and more powerful. But then, after the industry has stabilized, newcomers figure out how to add increased power and capability, but always at the expense of added complexity and sometimes decreased reliability. We can see the curve of complexity in the history of the watch, radio, telephone, and television set. Take the radio. In the early days, radios were quite complex. To tune in a station required several adjustments, including one for the antenna, one for the radio frequency, one for intermediate frequencies, and controls for both sensitivity and loudness. Later radios were simpler and had controls only to turn it on, tune the station, and adjust the loudness. But the latest radios are again very complex, perhaps even more so than early ones. Now the radio is called a tuner, and it is littered with numerous controls, switches, slide bars, lights, displays, and meters. The modern sets are technologically superior, offering higher quality sound, better reception, and enhanced capability. But what good is the technology if it is too complex to use?

The design problem posed by technological advances is enormous. Consider the watch. A few decades ago, watches were simple. All you had to do was set the time and keep them wound. The standard control was the stem: a knob at the side of the watch. Turning the knob wound the spring that worked the watch. Pulling the knob out and turning it made the hands move. The operations were easy to learn and easy to do. There was a reasonable relation between the turning of the knob and the resulting turning of the hands. The design even took into account human error: the normal position of the stem was for winding the spring, so that an accidental turn would not reset the time.

In the modern digital watch the spring is gone, replaced by a motor run by long-lasting batteries. All that remains is the task of setting the watch. The stem is still a sensible solution, for you can go fast or slow, forward or backward, until the exact desired time is reached. But the stem is more complex (and therefore more expensive) than simple push-button switches. If the only change in the transition from the spring-wound analog watch to the battery-run digital watch were in how the time was set, there would be little difficulty. The problem is that new technology has allowed us to add more functions to the watch: the watch can give the day of the week, the month, and the year; it can act as a stop watch (which itself has several functions), a count-down timer, and an alarm clock (or two); it has the ability to show the time for different time zones; it can act as a counter and even as a calculator. But the added functions cause problems: How do you design a watch that has so many functions while trying to limit the size, cost, and complexity of the device? How many buttons does it take to make the watch workable and learnable, yet not too expensive? There are no easy answers. Whenever the number of functions and required operations exceeds the number of controls, the design becomes arbitrary, unnatural, and complicated. The same technology that simplifies life by providing more functions in each device also complicates life by making the device harder to learn, harder to use. This is the paradox of technology.

The paradox of technology should never be used as an excuse for poor design. It is true that as the number of options and capabilities of any device increases, so too must the number and complexity of the controls. But the principles of good design can make complexity manageable.

In one of my courses I gave as homework the assignment to design a multiple-function clock radio:

You have been employed by a manufacturing company to design their new product. The company is considering combining the following into one item:

- *AM-FM radio*
- *Cassette player*
- *CD player*
- *Telephone*
- *Telephone answering machine*
- *Clock*
- *Alarm clock (the alarm can turn on a tone, radio, cassette, or CD)*
- *Desk or bed lamp*

The company is trying to decide whether to include a small (two-inch screen) TV set and a switched electric outlet that can turn on a coffee maker or toaster.

Your job is (A) to recommend what to build, then (B) to design the control panel, and finally (C) to certify that it is actually both what customers want and easy to use.

State what you would do for the three parts of your job: A, B, and C. Explain how you would go about validating and justifying your recommendations.

Draw a rough sketch of a control panel for the items in the indented list, with a brief justification and analysis of the factors that went into the choice of design.

There are several things I looked for in the answer. (Figure 1.15 is an unacceptable solution.) First, how well did the answer address the

1.15 Possible Solution to My Homework Assignment. Completely unacceptable. (Thanks to Bill Gaver for devising and drawing this sample.)

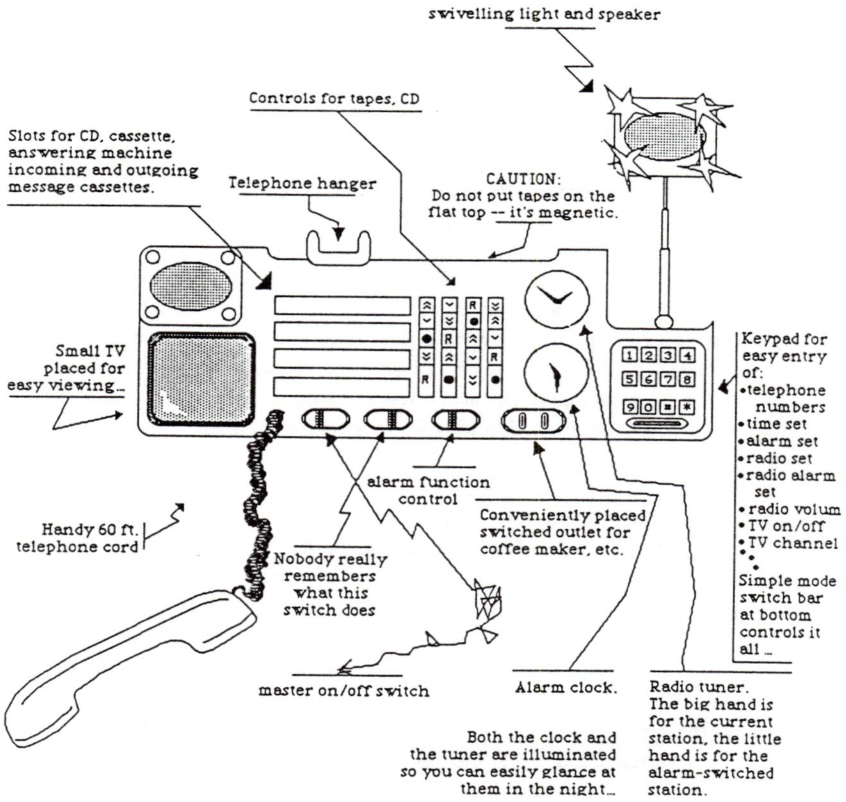

real needs of the user? I expected my students to visit the homes of potential users to see how their current devices were being used and to determine how the combined multipurpose device would be used. Next, I evaluated whether all the controls were usable and understandable, allowing all the desired functions to be operated with minimum confusion or error. Clock radios are often used in the dark, with the user in bed and reaching overhead to grope for the desired control. Therefore the unit had to be usable in the dark by feel only. It was not supposed to be possible to make a serious mistake by accidentally hitting the wrong control. (Alas, many existing clock radios do not tolerate serious errors—for example, the user may reset the time by hitting the wrong button accidentally.) Finally, the design was expected to take into account real issues in cost, manufacturability, and aesthetics. The finished design had to pass muster with users. The point of the exercise was for the student to realize the paradox of technology: added complexity and difficulty cannot be avoided when functions are added, but with clever design, they can be minimized.

Case A

Iterative Design of an Information Kiosk

Our first case study is the design of an interactive information kiosk that was used by people attending the CHI '89 conference in Austin, Texas (Salomon, 1990a, 1990b, 1993). Designed by the Human Interface Group at Apple Computer, it contained multimedia data about the city of Austin, the conference program, and the people attending the conference. This last point was an important element in its success: Participants created a "yearbook" by recording personal information and entering a digital photo of themselves. Users could browse and print out yearbook pages. The kiosk ran on 12 computers, was available around the clock, and was used over 5,000 times during the week of the conference.

Our reading focuses on the design of the kiosk, in particular the heavy use of a visually oriented, iterative methodology. Another interesting aspect of this project was the inclusion of a facility to collect usage data at the conference, providing further feedback to the developers (see also Salomon, 1990b).

Several aspects of the project were unusual. The information kiosk was not intended to be a product and was not used after the conference. The development team was relatively small. Yet the project resembled other design and development projects in several ways. It operated under a tight time schedule (six months, with no possibility for slippage). The system had to be robust. The project involved considerable risk: A company with a reputation for its human-computer interfaces was introducing a system at a conference attended by thousands of interface specialists!

Several additional points are significant:

- The system was tested with real users.
- The multimedia interface being developed, which included text, graphics, sound, and animation, required a multidisciplinary team of developers. Individuals with skills in graphic design, psychology, and programming were involved.
- The paper introduces a novel design concept. Communication of design specifications relied primarily on visual materials, not written specs. Many developers have commented on the weaknesses of text for specifying human-computer interfaces. For example, Gundry (1988) and Overmyer (1992) argue for broadening the concept of specifications based on their experiences with large systems. This project presents an alternative. Will it scale up? How far can it be pushed in developing real products? This paper cannot answer these questions, but challenges us to explore them.
- The importance of *iterative* design is highlighted. At each stage of development, there were imperfections in the then-current design, weaknesses that could not have been anticipated and solutions that emerged in the process of iterative testing and redesign.
- To make iterative design possible when facing budget or schedule constraints, a rapid prototyping approach is used to support mocking up and trying out interfaces and dialogues. The information kiosk developers used a variety of methods to obtain quick feedback on design proposals: paper sketches, HyperCard mock-ups, storytelling sequences, and functional prototyping.
- The author emphasizes the importance of behavioral analysis and empirical evaluation in the design process. Solutions and improvements were not merely postulated and assumed, they were tested. She cites Nielsen's (1989) "discount usability engineering." Usability engineering is a rigorous approach in which quantitative usability goals are established and the software is tested until they are met (Whiteside, Bennett, and Holtzblatt, 1988). Nielsen advocates a more constrained approach designed to capture obvious problems, consisting of testing small subsets of the system with relatively few users who think aloud as they work, and providing developers with a small number of guidelines or principles to use as a checklist.

Many of the methods described in Case A are revisited in later chapters. The multidisciplinary approach is discussed further by Kim in Chapter 4. Iterative design is emphasized by Gould in Chapter 2. Also in Chapter 2, Vertelney discusses storyboarding and other approaches to rapid prototyping (see also the Gould paper and the introduction to Chapter 5). Behavioral analysis and empirical evaluation are covered in detail in Chapter 2.

Case A also illustrates several common challenges:

- In spite of the use of iterative design and the overall success of the effort, the interface was not perfect. Seventy percent of users reported finding what they wanted, leaving room for improvement. Commendably, Salomon identifies specific problems found through analysis of the trace data from use at the conference. She also notes subtle methodological problems, such as premature debate over low-level design decisions.
- The developers relied on intuition in generating initial user requirements. Because they attend conferences, this seems plausible, but conference participants not from Apple could have different requirements. Someone from Montana might

wish to sort attendees by state, which may not be of great interest to a Californian. The example isn't important, but the principle is: It is dangerous for developers to rely only on their intuition about user needs. To their credit, the project team went outside their group and their company to find real users to test their designs.

In summary, the case study shows that a successful system can be built under a tight schedule, using iterative design with visual prototyping and extensive user involvement. The reader may also wish to compare and contrast the approach in the case study with some earlier Apple work on information kiosks (Kreitman, 1988 video) and with another successful example of kiosk design, the IBM Olympic Message System (Gould et al., 1987; IBM, 1985 video).

REFERENCES

Note: A ● before a reference indicates a reading.

Gould, J., Boies, S., Levy, S., Richards, J., and Schoonard, J. (1987). The 1984 Olympic Message System: A Test of Behavioral Principles of System Design. *Communications of the ACM* 30(9), 758–769.

Gundry, A. (1988). Humans, Computers, and Contracts. In Jones, D., and Winder, R. (Eds.), *People and Computers IV.* Cambridge University Press.

Nielsen, J. (1989). Usability Engineering at a Discount. In Salvendy, G., and Smith, M. (Eds.), *Designing and Using Human-Computer Interfaces and Knowledge-Based Systems.* Elsevier, 394–401.

Overmyer, S. (1992). Specifying Functional and HCI Requirements with Electronic Multimedia. *Proc. East-West International Conference on Human-Computer Interaction.* ICSTI, 429–436.

Salomon, G. (1990a). How the Look Affects the Feel: Visual Design and the Creation of an Information Kiosk. *Proc. Human Factors Society 34th Annual Meeting,* 277–281.

Salomon, G. (1990b). Designing Casual-Use Hypertext: The CHI '89 InfoBooth. *Proc. CHI '90,* ACM, 451–458.

● Salomon, G. (1993). A Case Study in Interface Design: The CHI '89 Information Kiosk. Original paper.

Whiteside, J., Bennett, J., and Holtzblatt, K. (1988). Usability Engineering: Our Experience and Evolution. In Helander, M. (Ed.), *Handbook of Human-Computer Interaction.* North-Holland, 237–255.

VIDEOS

IBM (1985). Olympic Message System. *ACM SIGGRAPH Video Review* 19.

Kreitman, K. (1988). MacWorld Information Kiosk: Visual Metaphors for Accessing Information. *ACM SIGGRAPH Video Review* 58.

A case study in interface design *The CHI '89 Information Kiosk*

Gitta Salomon

Introduction

Six months before the 1989 CHI (Human Factors in Computing Systems) Conference, a small team at Apple Computer undertook design of an interactive information kiosk for the conference. The team was interdisciplinary, composed of programmers, graphic designers and cognitive psychologists. The project goals were: to explore the interface design process; to make use of multimedia – in its infancy at the time; and, to expand the team's understanding of what constitutes a successful interface design, by observing a broad range of people using the system.

This chapter describes the system and the design process applied in its development. It provides a case study in user-centered, iterative design of a multimedia system. The material presented is primarily a synthesis of two previously published conference papers (see [9], [10]).

The system's content and functionality, as delivered, are described in the first section. The following section discusses how this final design evolved. It includes several examples illustrating the important role visual design played throughout development. In the final section, findings based on usage data collected at the conference are described.

An overview of the system

The final system consisted of two components: the *InfoBooth* and the *PhotoBooth*. The InfoBooth met the requirements of a *browsing system* hypertext [2]. It provided multimedia data about the conference program, the people in attendance, and the city of Austin, Texas, where the conference was held. It was intended for informal, short-term interactions. Consequently, the design was oriented towards ease of use, as opposed to providing a great deal of functionality. The PhotoBooth offered conference attendees a way to input information about themselves that was then included in the InfoBooth. Each of these components is described in greater detail below.

The InfoBooth

The InfoBooth was delivered on Apple Macintosh SE 30 computers, equipped with a mouse input device and no keyboard. The database, located on each machine's internal hard disk, approached 40 megabytes in size. Each InfoBooth computer was part of a station, containing 4 such computers and a laser printer. Three stations – 12 computers and 3 printers in all – were available throughout the conference.

The InfoBooth interface and database incorporated sound, graphics and text and were built in HyperCard® [1]. For those unfamiliar with HyperCard, its basic unit is a *card*, which is equivalent to a single *screen* (the terms screen and card will be used interchangeably here). Cards can contain *buttons* which, when pressed, take an action on the user's behalf, *fields* of text, and bit-mapped graphics. A group of cards residing in a single file are referred to as a *stack*.

Figure 1. The InfoBooth IntroScreen. Users selected one of four available information sections from this screen.

Content

Figure 1 depicts the IntroScreen, the starting point for interaction with the InfoBooth. This card used both animation and audio to describe the information available in the four main InfoBooth sections.

1 *Kiosk Information* This section provided information about how to use the kiosk and was intentionally kept small in size – it consisted of only one card. As in the design of the Olympic Message System [3,7], the team aimed for an easy to use interface, not requiring extensive on-line help.

2 *Presentation Information* This section primarily contained information about each conference presentation, appearing on individual *Presentation Cards* (see Figure 4f). Each card included the title, author(s), date and time of the presentation. In most cases, a brief multimedia animation about the presentation was also included, constructed from sound bites and graphics supplied by the presenter.

3 *Attendee Yearbook* This section contained information about the people attending the conference; each person was represented on a separate Yearbook Card (see Figure 8). While the content for the Presentation Information section was collected, designed and incorporated prior to the conference, the content for the Attendee Yearbook was obtained at the conference itself. Attendees created a digitized image of themselves, and entered information such as their name and title, by using the specially configured PhotoBooth stations described below.

4 *Austin Information* This section provided information about the city of Austin, Texas, including places of interest, and types and locations of restaurants. It was designed and developed by OZZ Research of Austin, Texas and will not be further discussed in this chapter.

Functionality

Since InfoBooth users were restricted to mouse-only interactions, all navigation through the four information sections was initiated by a mouse click on a graphical button. There were no text menus or type-in areas. In this way, all of the interaction possibilities were constantly visible to the user. This methodology, which strives to reduce cognitive load, has been applied to other HyperCard browsing interfaces [6, 11].

In brief, the InfoBooth supplied the following types of interactions:

- In the Kiosk Information section, the user could view a single card, describing use of the available functionality.
- In the Presentation Information section, users could locate specific Presentation Cards by using any of four sorting methods:
  A timetable;
  A listing of authors (i.e. anyone who appeared on the by-line of a presentation);
  A listing of presentation titles;
  A listing of topic areas.
  These sorting methods were offered to the user via the Sort Selection screen (see Figure 2) – the first screen a user saw upon entering the Presentation Information section. Upon selecting one of the four sorting method buttons, the user was taken to the appropriate sorting method card (Figures 3a–3d). The user could then navigate to a specific Presentation Card by clicking on the corresponding button. Individual Presentation Cards could be printed by using the "Print" button supplied.
- In the Attendee Yearbook, users could locate individual Yearbook Cards by using alphabetical indices or by sequentially moving, either backwards or forwards, through the cards. Users could choose to print any of the individual entries.

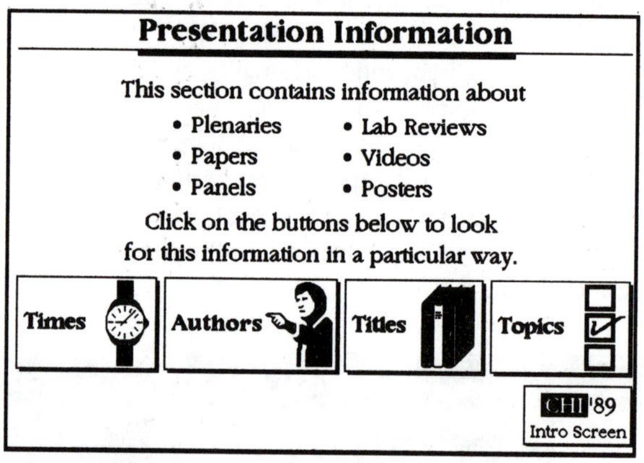

Figure 2. The Sort Selection Screen. Upon selecting Presentation Information from the IntroScreen, users were shown this screen. The desired sorting method was chosen by clicking on the appropriate button.

The PhotoBooth

Four PhotoBooths were available to conference attendees within the conference registration area. Each PhotoBooth was equipped with a standard Apple Macintosh SE 30, a keyboard and mouse, and third-party video digitizing hardware. During registration, each person was encouraged to use a PhotoBooth and enter data for later display as an InfoBooth Yearbook Card. The PhotoBooth's custom data collection program (created in HyperCard) assisted attendees in inputting data about themselves.

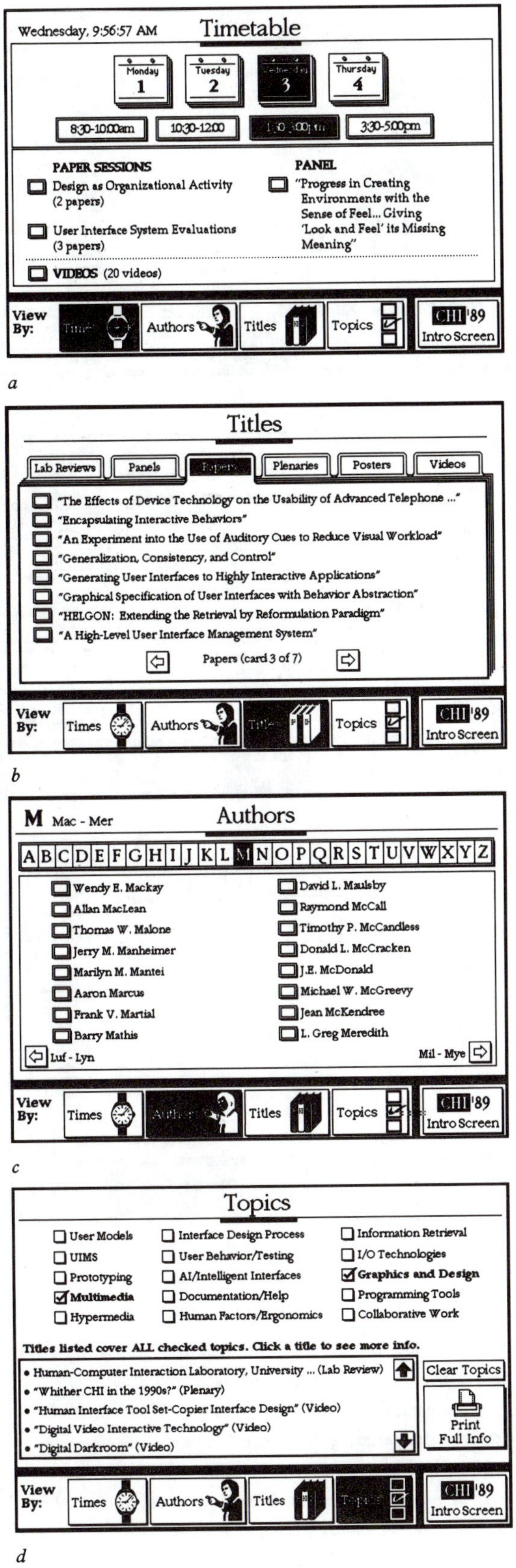

Design methodology and process

From the project's initiation, the team agreed to adopt an iterative design process, based on successively enhanced prototypes. This design process primarily followed the three principles of system design described in [3,4]. Because the design team was composed of typical CHI conference attendees, much of the early design sessions focused on what *we*, the designers, would want from the system.

Throughout the design process, the team concentrated on using visual materials to simulate the end user's experience, rather than on writing text specifications. Consequently, the final design was primarily the result of creating and improving visual prototypes. It was not based on carefully constructed flow charts or written design documents.

This iterative process progressed through three distinct phases: the *initial design specification* phase, the *storytelling prototype* phase and the *functional prototype* phase. Briefly, these phases can be described as follows. In the initial design specification phase, rough paper sketches and screen mock-ups were created. These designs allowed the team to examine and critique the system's basic functionality. In the next phase – the storytelling prototype phase – these designs were refined and used to 'tell stories' about the system's functionality to others. Feedback helped pinpoint areas where the interface design was potentially unclear or non-intuitive. In the third phase, the prototypes were made semi-functional. Informal user testing of these prototypes uncovered several problems which significantly effected usability. However, many of these problems were corrected by relatively small changes to the interface's visual appearance. Figure 4 depicts how the Presentation Card evolved through all three phases. In the following sections, each phase is examined in greater detail with specific examples from the Information Kiosk's development.

Figure 3. Example screens from the four Presentation Card sorting methods. They are: (a) the time-based sort, (b) the author's name sort, (c) the title sort, (d) the topic sort. Each method allowed users to find Presentation Cards in a different way. The bottom panel of buttons. a visually stable element in each of the designs, allowed users to switch to a different sorting method.

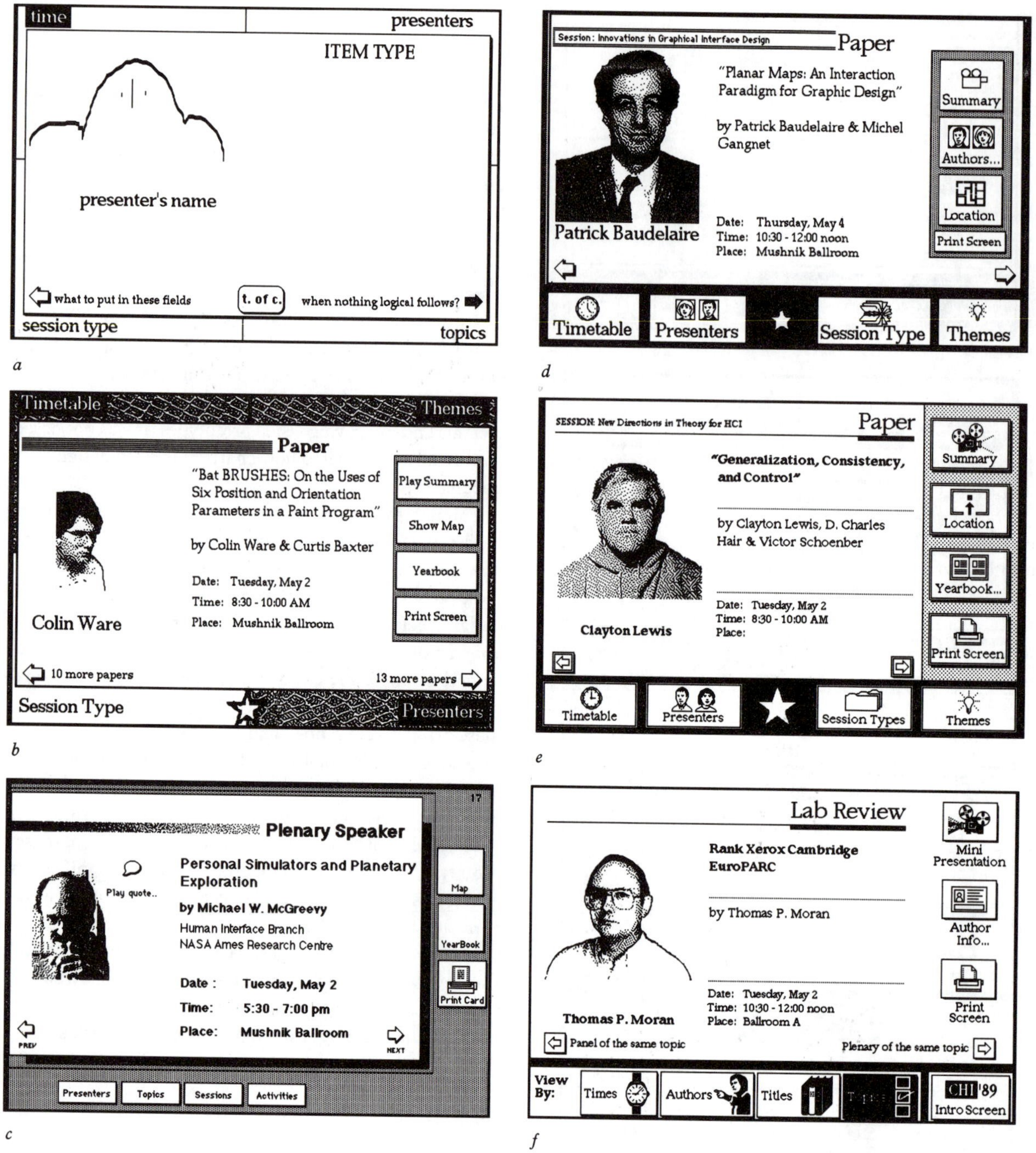

Figure 4. Evolution of a design: the Presentation Information Card. Figure (a) depicts an early design specification, applying "visual placeholders" to suggest possible functionality. An annotation describing a potential problem with the arrow labels was added during a design session. Figures (b) and (c) illustrate further development of the ideas in (a), as addressed by two different team members. Fake data was used where real information was not yet available. Both designs were used in storytelling prototypes and the feedback led to design (d). Functionality was then added to (d) and it was used in informal testing. Results led to design (e), in which all buttons were given a consistent appearance, icons were enhanced and the layout was refined. Figure (f) represents the final design, after several rounds of user testing. Several visual changes were made to correct misinterpretations. For example, the bottom row of buttons was grouped into a "view by" menu thereby emphasizing their interrelationship. Also, the right-hand column of buttons was made smaller and the bounding box was eliminated. Consequently, the buttons were visually tied to the actual presentation information on which they acted. Moreover, icon text labels were altered to better explain their functionality.

Initial design specification phase

After the team decided on the basic InfoBooth content (once again, this was assumed legitimate because the team members were typical system users), emphasis was placed on designing the interface functionality from a user's point of view. No written specifications were created. Early designs were communicated through paper sketches or HyperCard mock-ups.

These early designs were often very rough and made use of *visual placeholders* – simple text and/or items crudely drawn or borrowed from clip art – to demonstrate possible screen designs, functionality and sequencing. Team members without graphic design experience were encouraged to convey their ideas by placing simple graphics, buttons and text onto HyperCard cards. Even designs solely consisting of strategically placed text proved to be useful and important discussion aids.

The roughness of these designs often prompted team members to contribute ideas that might not have been elicited had the artwork appeared more final. By using a simple text label to indicate a button, the discussion centered around the functionality it implied, rather than on its graphical representation. Missing functionality was often uncovered through the use of these prototypes; it was typical for a team member to remark "I can see how the user would do this, but how would the user do that?" In fact, because of HyperCard's flexibility, design sessions were typically conducted around a computer. Often, a team member would take hold of the mouse and change the visual design to illustrate an alternative solution. In addition, comments about missing features or problematic areas were often typed directly onto the relevant screen (see Figure 4a). This technique supported easy recall of the outstanding issues.

Although the team was not concerned with appearance details during this phase, there was one visual issue that received some attention. Due to the limited screen size of a single HyperCard card at the time (approximately 4.5 by 6.75 inches), there was concern about the amount of information that could be shown at any one time. Through the use of on-screen designs, composed of visual placeholders, the team maintained awareness of potential visual clutter.

Storytelling prototype phase

Following this initial phase, team members elaborated on the prototype designs with the most potential. The seemingly strongest ideas were used to create sets of screens depicting a particular interaction sequence. Often, more than one design supporting the same functionality was pursued. These prototypes were primarily constructed in HyperCard, although they could have just as well been built using paper flipbooks, other software packages, or video[12].

These enhanced designs were then presented to colleagues and friends who were not intimately involved with the project. Because these prototypes were essentially 'slide shows' – screen designs with limited or no functionality – the presenter would tell a story describing how the user would arrive at each screen. Although the story line was completely predetermined, the storyteller could elicit useful feedback by asking users what they *thought* would happen if they pressed a depicted (although not functional) button. By taking individuals through typical usage stories, the team was able to note important oversights.

For example, an early storytelling prototype for the PhotoBooth program (the data collection program used to create Attendee Yearbook Cards) led the user through a five step sequence that requested the necessary information. Figure 5 shows two screens used in this prototype. The storytelling prototype viewers quickly became confused; their remarks indicated that they were unsure of

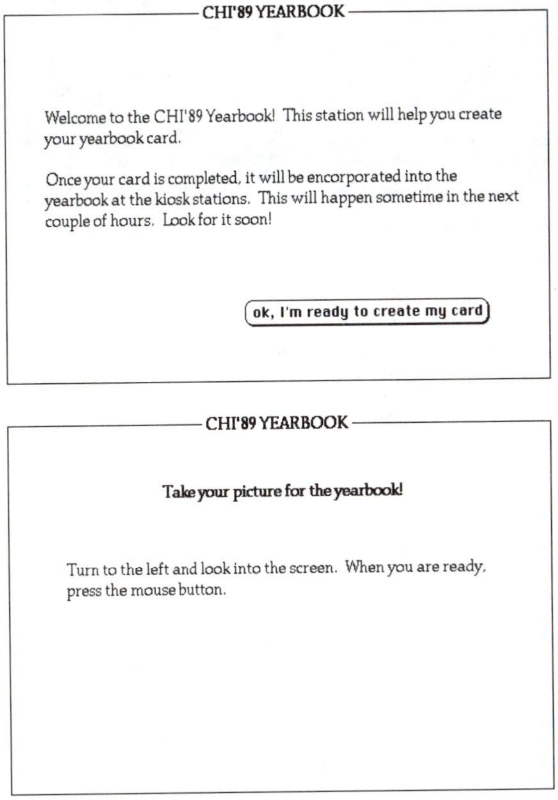

Figure 5. Example of a storytelling prototype. These two cards were used to simulate the functionality of the PhotoBooth program. Viewers of the 'slide show' constructed with these cards remarked that they were confused; they didn't understand what they were doing. Although the design team knew what a Yearbook Card was – and that there were five steps involved in creating it – this information was nowhere to be found in the interface.

Figure 6. Final design for the PhotoBooth program. The design problems noted in Figure 5 were addressed by this design. Users first viewed the top card. It explicitly stated that they would proceed through 5 steps. Users then viewed a voice-over animation that visually described the entire process and end result. This was followed by the lower card, which clearly marks the start of step one. Each subsequent step was carefully distinguished by a similar dividing screen, boldly stating the step number and title.

how many different things the program would require them to do, and what end result they were working towards. Basically, they did not recognize five distinct steps in the program.

If the program had been described to them verbally or in writing, rather than presented in rough visual form, this confusion might not have been detected. The team members realized that in giving a verbal description of the program, they always mentioned the five steps, even though this explanatory information was missing from the actual design. A written text specification would have certainly also masked this problem.

Figure 6 shows two screen designs used in the final implementation. The problems noted in the storytelling prototype were addressed in several ways. First, users were informed at the program's initiation that they would proceed through five steps. Distinctive dividing cards were added, clearly marking the beginning of each section. In addition, a voice-over animation was inserted between the two screens shown. It quickly and efficiently explained the entire process about to be undertaken, and presented the user with an example Yearbook Card.

Functional prototype phase

As the designs progressed, the team began including bits of underlying functionality. These semi-functional prototypes were informally tested with users and quickly reworked based on feedback. The goal was to improve the interface as much as possible through rapid redesign and retesting, before all of the functionality was put in place. Consequently, numerous iterations of these functional prototypes occurred.

The test subjects included some Apple Computer employees who planned to attend the conference. In addition, subjects were recruited from outside Apple to help uncover potential difficulties with HyperCard or the Macintosh that the team had not anticipated. Throughout the design, the team consciously tried to avoid using HyperCard interface conventions that might not be widely recognized; HyperCard or Macintosh familiarity could not be assumed in the target user group.

The style of testing resembled *discount usability testing* as described in [8]. Subjects were asked to perform specific tasks, as well as pursue items of interest. At the end of each session an interview was conducted to collect general impressions.

Many of the problems uncovered were related to misinterpreted functionality and surprisingly small changes to the visual representation corrected them. Three examples are now discussed. The third points out why any visual change needs retesting.

Representing functionality on presentation cards

Figure 4e was part of a functional prototype test of the Presentation Information section. The largest interface problem uncovered was related to the consistent button appearance the team had so carefully developed. By making all buttons visually similar, the team thought users would easily distinguish between active areas and passive information. However, because all buttons on a Presentation Card possessed this similar 'look,' users could not distinguish their differences in functionality. For example, users did not understand the difference between the global controls at the bottom of the card and the local controls (i.e., controls related to the specific presentation information shown) on the side of the card. The Texas star button – the one unique-looking button – only added to the confusion and users had trouble recalling its purpose.

These issues led to several redesign sessions. After literally dozens of attempts to graphically clarify and reinforce the functional differences of the buttons, the team arrived at the final design (see Figure 4f). Specifically,

- The buttons related to the presentation itself were slightly reduced in size and placed on the same white background as the other presentation-specific information.
- The sorting method buttons were grouped into a panel labelled "view by."
- The IntroScreen button replaced the Texas star button.

While all buttons maintained a common button look – a drop shadow – visual distinctions supporting their different uses were introduced. Retesting validated these changes; many of the problems had been eliminated.

Just before the conference, the "Location" button was eliminated. This allowed the other presentation-related buttons on the card's right side to be raised. The right arrow button could then be moved to the extreme right. This idea had surfaced in an earlier design (Figure 4d). Its reinstatement helped to solidify the top portion of the screen as a single entity. Testing showed this also helped users to locate and use the right arrow button.

The "Summary" button problem

During testing of the Presentation Information section, many of the button labels were not well understood by users. As a result, a number of wording changes were made as shown in Figure 4f. Most notably, few users clicked on the "Summary" button (see Figure 1e). This button activated a brief, screen-filling multimedia animation about the specific presentation. Some users indicated that "Summary" implied text and therefore the button wasn't interesting enough to click on. Even the use of a movie camera icon did not prevent this false interpretation.

The problem was addressed by a number of straightforward visual changes. The button's functionality was visually mimicked by animating the movie camera icon; the reels appeared to spin and a moving light stream emanated from the camera. The icon was also reoriented to face into the card, thereby indicating the area where activity would occur. In addition, the button was relabeled "Mini-Presentation" which more accurately described its function. Finally, a visual description of the button's purpose was included in the InfoBooth's *attract-mode* (an animation of the IntroScreen that played whenever the kiosk was not in use). In the same way that video games often provide a preview of their functionality when idle, the kiosk previewed the "Mini-Presentation" button's functionality. Retesting showed that users were more inclined to click on the button after these changes were made.

The Yearbook navigation problem

Although no yearbook entries existed prior to the conference, several typical entries were created for user testing in the functional prototype phase. Subjects had surprisingly few problems navigating within the yearbook given the design shown in Figure 7. The book metaphor was well understood; subjects used the letter tabs to move to certain parts of the book and the index tab to locate specific entries. However, users could not figure out how to leave the yearbook section altogether

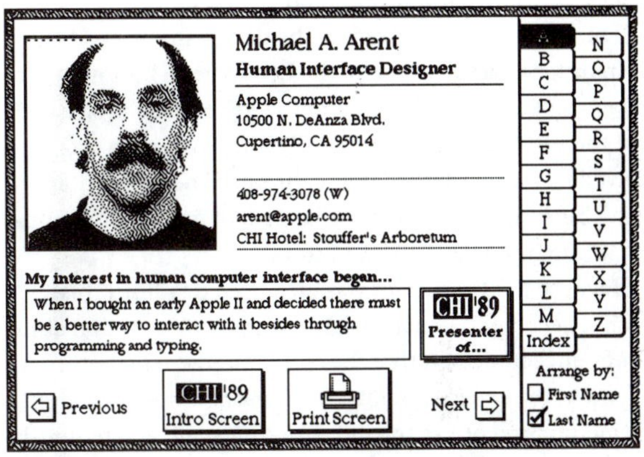

Figure 7. Early Yearbook Card design. In this design, a book metaphor is supported by the graphical letter and index tabs on the right. Testing showed that users did not experience difficulties in locating entries using this navigation device; they made use of both letter and index tabs. However, the location and visual appearance of the IntroScreen button made it difficult to find. Users felt themselves trapped in the yearbook; they couldn't find a button that allowed them to exit.

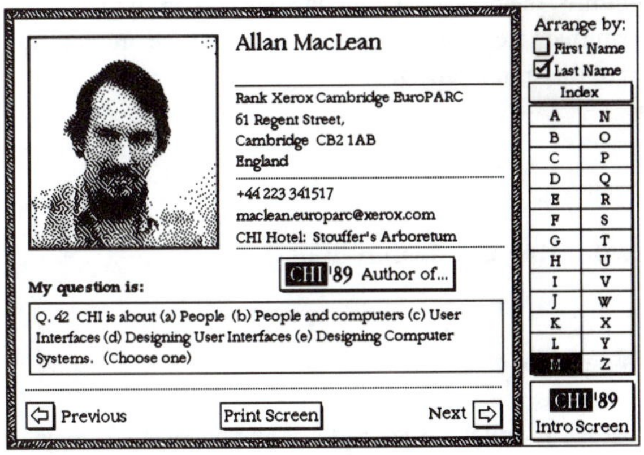

Figure 8. The final Yearbook Card design. In this design, the IntroScreen button was placed in the lower right corner where users expected to find it. It no longer presented a problem. However, due to space constraints, the graphical tabs were replaced with smaller buttons and the index button was moved to the top of the column. Consequently, many users completely failed to notice the index button and tediously used the arrow buttons to move to desired entries.

This problem was easily explained after it was noted. In the Presentation Information section, user testing had prompted a change in the take-me-to-the-first-screen button – it had been changed from the Texas star to the CHI '89 InfoBooth logo. This change was also made in the Yearbook section. Consequently, the logo was now being used twice on the Yearbook Card, in two buttons with similar shapes (i.e., it was also used on the "Presenter of..." button). As shown in Figure 7, this repetitive use created visual confusion. In addition, because the IntroScreen button was not located in the lower right corner, as on *every other* InfoBooth card, users couldn't find it.

This problem was solved by the design shown in Figure 8. In order to accommodate the IntroScreen button in the lower right corner, the letter tabs were reduced in size and lost their 'tab-like' appearance. The Index button was moved to the top of the letter columns. The "Presenter of..." button shape was also changed, to further differentiate it from the IntroScreen button.

Because the InfoBooth was on a fixed deadline, this design became the final design. Informal observation at the conference indicated that the earlier problem had been solved at the expense of introducing a new one. Few users seemed to find or use the index button at all, and tediously moved through screen after screen using the forward and backward arrows. Many people mentioned the need for an index in the conference questionnaire (L. Boorman, personal communication, May 21, 1989). Even though the index button had the visual appearance of a button – a drop shadow – its location caused it to be perceived as a column heading. By simply placing it at the bottom of the letter columns, the redesign might have succeeded. If time had permitted retesting might have uncovered the problem and led to this minor change.

Evaluating the design in use

Using trace data

In order to explore usage patterns and uncover where, in practice, the interface design was successful and where it was flawed, trace code was inserted into the InfoBooth program. This code unobtrusively and anonymously collected data about users' actions at the conference. After the conference, its analysis provided insight into widespread usage trends.

The data collected was recorded as ASCII text files; each user action was logged as a single line of text (see Figure 9). The recordings include mouse clicks, the time at which they occurred and information about the click location

```
1154082 openStack stack "opening"
1154084 openCard card "opening animation"
1206956 mouseUp card button "pres info"
1206985 openCard card "chi information"
1207442 mouseUp card button "Interest List"
1207489 openStack stack "sort themes"
1207495 openCard card "themes"
1207500 mouseUp bkgnd button "Clear Topics"
1207971 mouseUp card button "Theme 12"
1208529 mouseDown card button "down"
1208545 mouseDown card button "down"
1209120 mouseDown card button "up" button
```

Figure 9. An excerpt from a typical trace data file. Each line represents a user action. The initial number is a time stamp and is followed by a description of the specific action taken.

(i.e., a particular Hypercard field or button, or the card itself). In addition, the trace code tracked the opening of any card or stack (although transparent to the end user, the InfoBooth was composed of several stacks).

In an attempt to capture where one interaction session ended and another began, the trace code initiated a new trace file whenever the current session 'timed out.' That is, the current trace file was closed and a new one opened whenever the program automatically returned to the IntroScreen after being idle for a designated time period. However, because the program could not distinguish between the situation where one user left and was immediately replaced by another, from continuous, single user sessions, it cannot be assumed that a single file *necessarily* represents one session. The design team discussed this issue prior to the conference, but could not find a suitable way to require users to terminate their sessions given the casual interaction environment.

By the end of the conference over 5,600 files – slightly more than 23 megabytes of data – were recorded. While no rigorous evaluation of this data was undertaken, several informal analysis programs were written. These programs uncovered several interesting interface issues, some of which are described below.

Trace data insights: Presentation Information

In this section, three findings related to the Presentation Information section are discussed.

Design of selectable items

One of the first trace data analysis programs explored how users chose to view the Presentation Information cards. This program examined the sorting methods users selected from the Sort Selection screen (Figure 2). The findings were surprising. Out of 2,321 cases where a user arrived at the Sort Selection screen:

- 18% chose the timetable sort
- 21% chose the author sort
- 07% chose the title sort
- 17% chose the topic sort

However, 21% (499 users) clicked on the field containing the bulleted list, even though it was *not* an active hot spot. Upon inspection, the information in the bulleted list most closely resembles the information available within the title sort. Furthermore, the title sort was conspicuously the least selected sorting method. It seems plausible that users thought that clicking on the bullet points would take them to title sort information.

Only one other InfoBooth card displayed information as a bulleted list. User behavior on this card was somewhat similar: 189 users out of 1534 (12%) clicked on the bulleted list before clicking on anything else.

Throughout the InfoBooth's design the team aimed to establish an interface convention: all clickable items were either enclosed by drop shadow buttons or contained in fields specifically marked as clickable lists. Therefore, the bulleted list on the Sort Selection screen was solely intended as a means of clear visual representation; bullets are often used in print media to clearly represent list information. However, the usage pattern noted indicates that this graphical elements might carry expectations of interactivity in the computer domain. Its use, therefore, should be carefully considered. Furthermore, other print conventions might carry similar user expectations. Through more extensive testing prior to the conference, this particular representation issue may have been uncovered.

Built-in functionality and browsing strategies

Users could select a particular sorting method at each of the three different levels of hierarchy within the Presentation Information section. That is, they could:

1. Choose an initial sorting method from the Sort Selection screen (Figure 2).
2. Change a different sorting method while in another sorting method using the "view by" buttons (Figure 3a–3d).
3. Choose a sorting method from a Presentation Card using the same set of "view by" buttons (Figure 4f).

The InfoBooth could have provided fewer ways for a user to change sorting methods (e.g. just the first, or just the first and second). In fact, an evaluation of a similar system, the Glasgow Online, recommended requiring users to traverse extra levels of a database rather than providing this type of 'short-cut' functionality [5].

To better understand how people used the InfoBooth sorting methods, the trace data was processed to depict sorting method interactions as easily read patterns. Each user foray into the Presentation Information section was encoded as a string of letters. At a glance, it became obvious that many people used the available short-cuts. In some instances, the user returned to the sorting method currently in use, or even the initial Sort Selection screen, and *then* selected an alternative. But in most cases where a user took these actions, previous usage patterns showed a familiarity, as well, with the short-cut method. It appears it was beneficial to give users access to all three ways of selecting a sorting method.

The use of intelligent defaults

The time sort's design incorporated an assumption about usage: the system assumed that when the time sort was chosen, users would be most interested in what was occurring currently or in the near future. Therefore, whenever users entered the time sort, they were first shown the appropriate card for the current day and time (see Figure 3a).

It was difficult, if not impossible, to assess the value of this design decision prior to the conference. However, trace data analysis reinforced the decision: in more than half the cases, users made their selections from the screen they were shown first.

This finding suggests a potentially interesting interactive use for trace data. If the data is assessed *as* the system is used, it may be possible to provide users with responsive defaults – defaults that adjust themselves as user populations and needs change.

Trace data insights: the Yearbook section

Since the yearbook content was primarily created at the conference, trace data concerning it offered insights not obtainable during pre-conference user testing.

Lack of use of the index button

How bad was the "Index" button problem reported earlier? The trace data indicates that of the 4,677 times users arrived at the yearbook cover card, only 3% clicked on the index button first, while 74% selected a specific letter. Obviously, the index button was not found often. Possibly users expected to find an index for a letter – instead of the first entry under that letter – when they selected a specific letter button. The team considered this design at one point, but unfortunately discarded and forgot it before conducting any user tests. The other changes to the Yearbook Card may have made this design variant more desirable.

Improving trace data

In retrospect, there are a few ways the trace code might have been improved. For example, the code neglected to record the actual coordinates of a mouse click when it occurred on a card or within a field. This additional data would discern if the user selected specific graphics on a card, or assumed certain words or symbols within a field were 'hot.' For example, 10% of the users clicked on the yearbook cover when they first entered the yearbook section. Did they all select the same location? If so, the graphics at that location must have implied 'clickability.' Similarly, the largest number of stray clicks on individual Presentation Cards were on the card itself – which is surprising given that most of the card was covered by either buttons or fields that would have been specifically noted.

In conclusion

The design process described resulted in a successful information kiosk, suitable to a variety of users within a casual usage environment. Numerous people were observed using the system throughout the conference. In addition, 70% of the users who responded to the CHI conference questionnaire indicated that they were able to find desired information in the kiosk. The trace data further confirmed that much of the functionality provided was used.

The design process applied to constructing the kiosk was iterative and visually-based. It encouraged system development from the user's point of view. It stressed how it would actually *feel* to use the system.

The specific examples provided in this chapter illustrate how progressively more refined designs arose from initial rough ideas, and how early and frequent testing of prototypes uncovered problems that were not difficult to correct and were often related to the graphical representation.

The chapter also describes how analyses of usage data can uncover good and flawed aspects of an interface. Insights garnered from the trace data of one system can provide a basis for design decisions and/or influence where more extensive user testing should be applied in new systems.

As more system designers are confronted with these types of interface challenges, the need for examples increases. This case study provides readers with insight into the interface design process, and specific issues related to the design of interactive information systems.

Acknowledgements

Thanks are extended to the CHI '89 information kiosk team – Michael Arent, Penny Bauersfeld, Donna Cohen, Jonathan Cohen, Kate Gomoll, Mike Mills, Ian Small, and Laurie Vertelney – who made the experiences and system described here possible.

References

1. Apple Computer, Inc. *Macintosh® HyperCard® User's Guide.* 1987. Reading, MA: Addison Wesley.
2. Conklin, J. Hypertext: An Introduction and Survey. *IEEE Computer.* 20, 9 (Sept. 1987), 17-41.
3. Gould, J.D., Boies, S.J., Levy S., Richards, J.T. and Schoonard, J. The 1984 Olympic Message System: A Test of Behavioral Principles of System Design. *Comm. of the ACM.* 30, 9 (Sept. 1987), 758-769.
4. Gould, J.D. and Lewis, C. Designing for Usability: Key Principles and What Designers Think. *Comm. of the ACM.* 28, 3 (March 1985), 300-311.
5. Hardman, L. Evaluating the Usability of the Glasgow Online Hypertext. *Hypermedia.* 1, 1 (1989), 34-63.
6. Kreitman, K. MacWorld Information Kiosk: Visual Metaphors for Accessing Information. *Videotape* presented at CHI '88.
7. Ledgard, H.F. An Outstanding Example. *PC Tech Journal.* 5, 7 (July 1987), 193-194.
8. Nielsen, J. Usability Engineering at a Discount. In G. Salvendy and M.J. Smith (Eds.), *Designing and Using Human-Computer Interfaces and Knowledge Based Systems.* Amsterdam: Elsevier, (1989), 394-401.
9. Salomon, G. . Designing Casual-Use Hypertext: The CHI '89 InfoBooth. In *CHI '90 Conference Proceedings.* ACM Press, (Seattle, WA, 1990), 451-458.
10. Salomon, G. How the Look Affects the Feel: Visual Design and The Creation of an Information Kiosk. In *Human Factors Society 24th Annual Meeting Proceedings.* (Orlando, Florida, 1990), 277-281.
11. Salomon, G., Oren, T., and Kreitman, K. Using Guides to Explore Multimedia Databases in *Proc. of the Twenty-Second Annual Hawaii International Conference on System Science.* (Kailua-Kona, Hawaii, Jan. 3-6, 1989), IEEE Computer Society Press, vol. 4, 3-11.
12. Vertelney, L. (1989). Using Video to Prototype User Interfaces. *SIGCHI Bulletin,* 21 (2), 57-61.

Chapter 1

A Historical and Intellectual Perspective

When thinking about technology, we tend to anticipate the future and forget the past. Consider today's graphical user interfaces (GUIs). We know that they are typically patterned after the two innovative systems to be discussed in Case B: the Xerox Star, introduced in 1981, and the Apple Macintosh, introduced in 1984. Yet the groundwork for these systems was laid in the 1960s and 1970s.

In this chapter, we provide an historical perspective, introducing some seminal ideas, contributors, and systems. However, our objective is not a detailed, historically complete recitation of names, places, and dates. Our emphasis is intellectual, with a focus on the history of ideas. Today's new systems can be traced to the excitement generated by yesterday's imaginative speculations. Today's speculative ideas may be the seeds of tomorrow's systems.

THE MEMEX

Although the modern digital computer is grounded in ideas developed in the 18th and 19th centuries, important concepts and the technology required to implement the ideas only became available in the 1930s and the 1940s. The initial motivation was to speed the routine and laborious calculations required for ballistic (e.g., artillery) and atomic energy computations.

Perhaps the first person to see beyond these uses and conceive of the computer as a fundamental tool for transforming human thought and human creative activity was Vannevar Bush (1945). In his classic paper, "As We May Think," he described the increasing difficulty of managing and disseminating the results of research (pp. 101–102):

> *Professionally our methods of transmitting and reviewing the results of research are generations old and by now are totally inadequate for their purpose. If the aggregate time spent in writing scholarly works and in reading them could be evaluated, the ratio between these amounts of time might well be startling. Those who conscientiously attempt to keep abreast of current thought, even in restricted fields, by close and continuous reading might well shy away from an examination calculated to show how much of the previous month's efforts could be produced on call. Mendel's concept of the laws of genetics was lost to the world for a generation because his publication did not reach the few who were capable of grasping and extending it; and this sort of catastrophe is undoubtedly being repeated all about us, as truly significant attainments become lost in the mass of the inconsequential.*
>
> *The difficulty seems to be not so much that we publish unduly in view of the extent and variety of present-day interests but rather that publication has been extended far beyond our present ability to make real use of the record. The summation of human experience is being expanded at a prodigious rate, and the means we use for threading through the consequent maze to the momentarily important item is the same as was used in the days of square-rigged ships.*

To solve this problem, he sketched the outlines of a device he called the MEMEX (pp. 106–108):

> *Consider a future device for individual use which is a sort of mechanized private file and library. It needs a name, and, to coin one at random, "MEMEX" will do. A MEMEX is a device in which an individual stores all his books, records, and communications, and which is mechanized so that it may be consulted with exceeding speed and flexibility. It is an enlarged intimate supplement to his memory.*
>
> *It consists of a desk, and while it can presumably be operated from a distance, it is primarily the piece of furniture at which he works. On the top are slanting translucent screens, on which material can be projected for convenient reading. There is a keyboard and sets of buttons and levers. Otherwise it looks like an ordinary desk.*
>
> *In one end is the stored material. The matter of bulk is well taken care of by improved microfilm. Only a small part of the interior of the MEMEX is devoted to storage, the rest to mechanism. Yet if the user inserted 5,000 pages of material a day it would take him hundreds of years to fill the repository, so he can be profligate and enter material freely.*
>
> *Most of the MEMEX contents are purchased on microfilm ready for insertion. Books of all sorts, pictures, current periodicals, newspapers, are thus obtained and dropped into place. Business correspondence takes the same path. And there is provision for direct entry. On the top of the MEMEX is a transparent platen. On this are placed longhand notes, photographs, memoranda, all sorts of things. When one is in place, the depression of a lever causes it to be photographed onto the next blank space on a section of the MEMEX film, dry photography being employed.*
>
> *There is, of course, provision for consultation of the record by the usual scheme of indexing. If the user wishes to consult a certain book, he taps its code on the keyboard, and the title page of the book promptly appears before him, projected onto one of his viewing positions. Frequently used codes are mnemonic, so that he seldom consults his code book; but when he does, a single tap of a key projects it for his use. Moreover, he has supplemental levers. On deflecting one of these levers to the right he runs through the book before him, each page in turn being projected at a speed which just allows a recognizing glance at each. If he deflects*

it further to the right, he steps through the book ten pages at a time; still further at one hundred pages at a time. Deflection to the left gives him the same control backward.

A special button transfers him immediately to the first page of the index. Any given book of his library can thus be called up and consulted with far greater facility than if it were taken from a shelf. As he has several projection positions, he can leave one item in position while he calls up another. He can add marginal notes and comments, taking advantage of one possible type of dry photography, and it could even be arranged so that he can do this by a stylus scheme, such as is now employed in the telautograph seen in railroad waiting rooms, just as though he had the physical page before him.

All this is conventional, except for the projection forward of present day mechanisms and gadgetry. It affords an immediate step, however, to associative indexing, the basic idea of which is a provision whereby any item may be caused at will to select immediately and automatically another. This is the essential feature of the MEMEX. The process of tying two items together is the important thing.

When the user is building a trail, he names it, inserts the name in his code book, and taps it out on his keyboard. Before him are the two items to be joined, projected onto adjacent viewing positions. At the bottom of each there are a number of blank code spaces, and a pointer is set to indicate one of these on each item. The user taps a single key, and the items are permanently joined. In each code space appears the code word. Out of view, but also in the code space, is inserted a set of dots for photocell viewing; and on each item these dots by their positions designate the index number of the other item.

Thereafter, at any time when one of these items is in view, the other can be instantly recalled merely by tapping a button below the corresponding code space. Moreover, when numerous items have been thus joined together to form a trail, they can be reviewed in turn, rapidly or slowly, by deflecting a lever like that used for turning the pages of a book. It is exactly as though the physical items had been gathered together from widely separated sources and bound together to form a new book. It is more than this, for any item can be joined into numerous trails. . . .

Wholly new forms of encyclopedias will appear, ready made with a mesh of associative trails running through them, ready to be dropped in the MEMEX and there amplified. The lawyer has at his touch the associated opinions and decisions of his whole experience and of the experience of friends and authorities. The patent attorney has on call the millions of issued patents, with familiar trails to every point of his client's interest. The physician, puzzled by a patient's reactions, strikes the trail established in studying an earlier similar case and runs rapidly through analogous case histories, with side references to the classics for the pertinent anatomy and histology. The chemist, struggling with the synthesis of an organic compound, has all the chemical literature before him in his laboratory, with trails following the analogies of compounds and side trails to their physical and chemical behavior.

The historian, with a vast chronological account of a people, parallels it with a skip trail which stops only on the salient items, and can follow at any time contemporary trails which lead him all over civilization at a particular epoch. There is a new profession of trail blazers, those who find delight in the task of establishing useful trails through the enormous mass of the common record. The inheritance from the master becomes, not only his additions to the world's record, but for his disciples the entire scaffolding by which they were erected.

Bush's vision was remarkable. He foresaw the application of machines to information storage and retrieval, the value of associative indexing, and the multimedia nature of future computer use. He predicted the development of "a machine which types when talked to" and speculated on the possibility of someday establishing a path from the written word to the brain that is "more direct" than the senses—tactile, oral, and visual. With CD technology making a fully digital MEMEX possible and computer networks allowing us to build a distributed MEMEX, Bush's dream may become a reality.

MAN-COMPUTER SYMBIOSIS

In the 1950s, others began to see the computer's potential use as a facilitator of aspects of human creativity and problem solving. Between 1960 and 1965 there was an outpouring of ideas and prototype systems. Much of what has been achieved since then has been to implement and expand these ideas, to convert prototypes to products. What was special about the early 1960s? One factor was the arrival of transistor-based "second-generation" computers in 1958. The use of vacuum-tube computers had been sharply limited by their size, speed, and power requirements, and their maintenance cost. With transistors, the constraints on what could be imagined melted away, a process that accelerated in the mid-1960s as "third-generation" integrated circuit computers began to appear.

One of the most compelling new visions of the computer's potential was that of J.C.R. Licklider (1960), who conceived of a synergistic coupling of human and machine capabilities (p. 4):

The fig tree is pollinated only by the insect Blastophaga grossorum. *The larva of the insect lives in the ovary of the fig tree, and there it gets its food. The tree and the insect are thus heavily interdependent: The tree cannot reproduce without the insect; the insect cannot eat without the tree; together, they constitute not only a viable but a productive and thriving partnership. This cooperative "living together in intimate association, or even close union, of two dissimilar organisms" is called symbiosis.*

"Man-computer symbiosis" is a subclass of man-machine systems. There are many man-machine systems. At present, however, there are no man-computer symbioses. The purposes of this paper are to present the concept and, hopefully, to foster the development of man-computer symbiosis by analyzing some problems of interaction between men and computing machines, calling attention to applicable principles of man-machine engineering, and pointing out a few questions to which research answers are needed. The hope is that, in not too many years, human brains and computing machines will be coupled together very tightly and that the resulting partnership will think as no human brain has ever thought and

process data in a way not approached by the information-handling machines we know today.

Licklider asserted that the then-current generation of computers failed to facilitate this symbiosis (p. 5):

Present-day computers are designed primarily to solve preformulated problem. . . .

However, many problems that can be thought through in advance are very difficult to think through in advance. They would be easier to solve, and they would be solved faster, through an intuitively guided trial-and-error procedure in which the computer cooperates, turning up flaws in the reasoning or revealing unexpected turns in the solution. Other problems simply cannot be formulated without computing-machine aid. Poincare anticipated the frustration of an important group of would-be computer users when he said, "The question is not 'What is the answer?' The question is 'What is the question?'" One of the main aims of man-computer symbiosis is to bring the computing machine effectively into the formulative parts of technical problems.

The other main aim is closely related. It is to bring computing machines effectively into processes of thinking that must go on in "real time," time that moves too fast to permit using computers in conventional ways. Imagine trying, for example, to direct a battle with the aid of a computer on such a schedule as this. You formulate your problem today. Tomorrow you spend with a programmer. Next week the computer devotes 5 minutes to assembling your program and 47 seconds to calculating the answer to your problem. You get a sheet of paper 20 feet long, full of numbers that, instead of providing a final solution, only suggest a tactic that should be explored by simulation. Obviously, the battle would be over before the second step in its planning was begun. To think in interaction with a computer in the same way that you think with a colleague whose competence supplements your own will require much tighter coupling between man and machine than is suggested by the example and than is possible today.

Licklider suggested how computers could improve and facilitate thinking and problem solving (pp. 5–6):

In the spring and summer of 1957, therefore, I tried to keep track of what one moderately technical person actually did during the hours he regarded as devoted to work. Although I was aware of the inadequacy of the sampling, I served as my own subject.

It soon became apparent that the main thing I did was to keep records. . . .

About 85 per cent of my "thinking" time was spent getting into a position to think, to make a decision, to learn something I needed to know. Much more time went into finding or obtaining information than into digesting it. Hours went into the plotting of graphs and other hours into instructing an assistant how to plot. When the graphs were finished, the relations were obvious at once, but the plotting had to be done in order to make them so. At one point, it was necessary to compare six experimental determinations of a function relating speech intelligibility to speech-to-noise ratio. No two experimenters had used the same definition or measure of speech-to-noise ratio. Several hours of calculating were required to get the data into comparable form. When they were in comparable form, it took only a few seconds to determine what I needed to know.

Throughout the period I examined, in short, my "thinking" time was devoted mainly to activities that were essentially clerical or mechanical: searching, calculating, plotting, transforming, determining the logical or dynamic consequences of a set of assumptions or hypotheses, preparing the way for a decision or an insight. Moreover, my choices of what to attempt and what not to attempt were determined to an embarrassingly great extent by considerations of clerical feasibility, not intellectual capability.

The main suggestion conveyed by the findings just described is that the operations that fill most of the time allegedly devoted to technical thinking are operations that can be performed more effectively by machines than by men. Severe problems are posed by the fact that these operations have to be performed upon diverse variables and in unforeseen and continually changing sequences. If those problems can be solved in such a way as to create a symbiotic relation between a man and a fast information-retrieval and data-processing machine, however, it seems evident that the cooperative interaction would greatly improve the thinking process.

In a later paper, Licklider and Clark (1962) outline applications of human-computer communication to military command and control, mathematics, programming, war gaming and management gaming, planning and design, education, and scientific research. They report on some early experiments and prototype systems that demonstrate the potential of using computers in these applications. Then, showing remarkable foresight, they list ten problems whose solutions are prerequisites for true human-computer symbiosis. The first five they term "immediate," the next one "intermediate," and the last four "long-term":

- Time sharing of computers among many users
- An electronic input-output surface for the display and communication of correlated symbolic and pictorial information (the earlier paper cited this and computer-driven wall displays as essential)
- An interactive, real-time system for information processing and programming
- Systems for large-scale information storage and retrieval designed to make possible concurrent, cooperative problem solving in many disciplines
- The facilitation of human cooperation in the design and programming of large systems
- Combined speech recognition, hand-printed character recognition, and light-pen editing
- Natural language understanding, including syntactic, semantic, and pragmatic aspects
- Recognition of the speech of arbitrary computer users (the earlier paper stressed a need for automatic speech production, as well)
- The theory of algorithms—discovery, development, and simplification
- Heuristic programming

Time has proven Licklider and Clark to be remarkably accurate. Their immediate goals have been met. But despite some progress, their intermediate and long-term visions remain goals, thirty years later.

TIME SHARING AND NETWORKING

Even before Licklider's papers, John McCarthy and Christopher Strachey independently proposed the development of a system of time sharing, allowing the computer to work on several jobs simultaneously and to give each user the illusion of having a personal machine.

The realization of this idea was absolutely critical for interactive systems to succeed. Computers, which were very expensive, could run only one program at a time. It was too costly to allow such a computer to be idle waiting for a user to enter information, so "batch processing" was the rule: a program was read in, executed, and the result then printed out for the user to study. With time sharing, an "inactive" user does not hold up the system—it can work on other jobs while waiting.

The time-sharing concept was soon validated by experimental systems built in the early 1960s at Bolt Beranek and Newman, Inc., MIT, and System Development Corporation, among others (Davis, 1966; Fano and Corbato, 1966; Licklider, 1968). The viability and rapid development of time sharing advanced the art of human-computer interaction significantly:

- It dramatically increased the accessibility of computers and the size of user communities.
- Because a user could now afford to think at "the terminal" and not simply carry out preconceived actions, designers of interactive programs could pay more attention to users' behaviors at the terminal and to methods for making them maximally productive. One result was the development of new "interaction languages" such as JOSS (Shaw, 1964), which facilitated on-line control and programming of the machine (Davis, 1966; Licklider, 1968).
- New applications such as computerized text processing began to flourish, eventually resulting in full-screen editors and word processors (Meyrowitz and van Dam, 1982).
- Because each time-sharing computer had a community of users who could communicate directly with each other through messages, or indirectly through a shared file system, computer-mediated human-human interaction could also be enriched.

Starting in the mid-1960s, the latter achievement was greatly extended by the development of wide area computer networks, linking machines and users in geographically distant sites (Roberts, 1986). The availability of these networks ultimately led to the virtual communities we see today (Chapter 14).

The challenges to realizing time sharing and networking were primarily technical. Vision quickly became reality, providing the essential foundation for the development of interactive systems. Progress was slower, however, in implementing the concepts that facilitate fluid interaction between human and machine.

SKETCHPAD

Some computers of the early 1950s had displays, such as MIT's Whirlwind and the SAGE air-defense command and control system (Machover, 1978; Bell, 1986; Ross, 1986). Thus, by the middle 1950s it was obvious that the computer could be used to manipulate pictures as well as numbers and text. Researchers began exploring the potential for enhanced graphical communication between human and machine. The most successful was Ivan Sutherland (1963, 1963 video). His pioneering Sketchpad system, built at MIT Lincoln Laboratory, introduced powerful new ideas and concepts:

- *Hierarchic* internal structure of computer-represented pictures, defined in terms of subpictures
- A *master* picture with *instances* that are transformed versions of the master; this concept helped lay the foundation for modern object-oriented programming
- *Constraints* as a method of specifying details of the geometry of a picture; for example, a horizontal constraint applied to a line, or an equal distance constraint applied to pairs of points
- The ability to display and manipulate *iconic* representations of constraints
- The ability to copy as well as instance both pictures and constraints
- Elegant techniques for picture construction using a light pen as an input device
- Separation of the coordinate system in which a picture is defined from that in which it is displayed
- Recursive operations such as "move" and "delete" applied to hierarchically defined pictures

Sketchpad was tremendously influential, but it took years for many researchers or developers to get systems powerful enough to apply these ideas.

INTERACTIVE COMPUTER GRAPHICS

Others were actively exploring avenues for assisting design that were opened by the new interface technologies. Their excitement and intensity peaked at the same conference at which Sutherland unveiled Sketchpad, the 1963 Spring Joint Computer Conference. Work described there included a general outline of the requirements for a computer-aided design (CAD) system (Coons, 1963), a presentation of the requirements for CAD in terms of languages and data structures (Ross and Rodriguez, 1963), a description of hardware requirements for CAD (Stotz, 1963), and a method of generalizing Sketchpad to allow input and manipulation of three-dimensional line drawings (Johnson, 1963).

But further advances in hardware and software were needed to realize the tremendous potential of computer graphics suggested by Sutherland and the early CAD pioneers. Early graphics hardware was very expensive, requiring costly memory to store image representations and costly circuitry to eliminate flicker from cathode ray tube (CRT) displays. Invented in the 1950s, the direct view storage tube (Preiss, 1978) had by the early 1970s made low-cost graphics possible, providing a tremendous stimulus. Work was also underway on enhancing the expressive potential of the technology. This led to two areas of innovation: powerful display processors (Myer and Sutherland, 1968) capable of real-time manipulations of simple line drawings, and input technologies that accepted real-time input of sketches and gestures, such as data tablets (Davis and Ellis, 1964).

The software front saw progress in two major directions. Investigators at Lincoln Laboratory and other sites developed operating systems capable of supporting interactive graphics under time sharing, another step in making the technology more cost-effective (Sutherland, Forgie, and Morello, 1969). Languages were developed with embedded graphics support that facilitated the production of graphics applications (Rovner and Feldman, 1968).

These advances led to a flourishing of new applications of computation to mathematics, science, engineering, and art. Culler and Fried, for example, pioneered in the development of computer-aided mathematical laboratories (Culler, 1968). Typical of the new scientific applications was the use of 3D computer graphics in molecular modeling, begun by Levinthal (1966) and later refined by several groups (e.g., Brooks, 1977). In art, building on the pioneering work in computer-generated animation of Knowlton (1966) and others, Baecker (1969) provided a convincing example of how artists could specify and refine movies through an interactive language of sketches, direct actions, and real-time playback. Davis (1966), Licklider (1968), and a special issue of readings from *Scientific American* (1971) provide accounts of these early developments.

MEMEX REVISITED: TWO VISIONS OF AUGMENTING HUMAN INTELLECT

Also in the 1960s, two influential technological visionaries, Doug Engelbart (1963, 1982, 1986; Engelbart and English, 1968, 1968 video) and Ted Nelson (1965, 1973, 1981, 1987) elaborated Bush's concept of the MEMEX in imaginative ways. They envisioned computers building and manipulating richly structured complexes of interconnected, interlinked bodies of text, which Nelson termed *hypertext*. They realized, as Bush had not, that most information would be stored digitally rather than on microfilm.

The approaches of Engelbart and Nelson differed in substantive ways. Engelbart focused on defining an hierarchic structure for ordinary documents to enable computer support in their preparation; Nelson was more interested in lateral links and interconnections to create a text "space" unlike any that existed. Engelbart looked to support focused group creation and problem solving; Nelson was excited by individual exploration and extension of document structures that could combine contributions from people with no formal ties.

Engelbart conceived of his work as the "augmentation of man's intellect" (1963, pp. 1, 3–4):

> *By "augmenting man's intellect" we mean increasing the capability of a man to approach a complex problem situation, gain comprehension to suit his particular needs, and to derive solutions to problems. Increased capability in this respect is taken to mean a mixture of the following: the comprehension can be gained more quickly; that better comprehension can be gained; that a useful degree of comprehension can be gained where previously the situation was too complex; that solutions can be produced more quickly; that better solutions can be produced; that solutions can be found where previously the human could find none. And by "complex situations" we include the professional problems of diplomats, executives, social scientists, life scientists, physical scientists, attorneys, designers—whether the problem situation exists for twenty minutes or twenty years. We do not speak of isolated clever tricks that help in particular situations. We refer to a way of life in an integrated domain where hunches, cut-and-try, intangibles, and the human "feel for a situation" usefully coexist with powerful concepts, streamlined terminology and notation, sophisticated methods, and highly-powered electronic aids. . . .*
>
> *Our culture has evolved means for us to organize and utilize our basic capabilities so that we can comprehend truly complex situations and accomplish the processes of devising and implementing problem solutions. The ways in which human capabilities are thus extended are here called* augmentation means, *and we define four basic classes of them:*
>
> 1. ***Artifacts****—physical objects designed to provide for human comfort, the manipulation of things or materials, and the manipulation of symbols.*
> 2. ***Language****—the way in which the individual classifies the picture of his world into the concepts that his mind uses to model that world, and the symbols that he attaches to those concepts and uses in consciously manipulating the concepts ("thinking").*
> 3. ***Methodology****—the methods, procedures, and strategies with which an individual organizes his* goal-centered *(problem-solving) activity.*
> 4. ***Training****—the conditioning needed by the individual to bring his skills in using augmentation means 1, 2 and 3 to the point where they are operationally effective.*
>
> *The system we wish to improve can thus be visualized as comprising a trained human being together with his artifacts, language, and methodology. . . .*

Twenty years later, in reviewing his progress, Engelbart (1982) asserted that he had been successful in facilitating "almost all phases of any simple to complex document production process," and in providing a "dialogue support system" consisting of electronic mail and remote shared screen capabilities. Echoing Licklider, he stressed the importance of synergy (Engelbart, 1982, pp. 306–307):

> *It is extremely important to note the multiple levels of synergism at work here:*
>
> *(a) The synergistic effect of integrating many tools into one coherent workshop makes each tool considerably more valuable than if it were used alone—for instance, the value of teleconferencing is very much greater when the participants are already doing a large proportion of their everyday work on line, so that any of the working material is available for selective citing and accessing, and when the users are already at home with the basic techniques of preparing and studying on-line material and of organizing and finding related passages.*
>
> *(b) . . .the synergistic effect of integrating many augmented individuals into one coherent community makes each element of augmentation considerably more valuable than if it were applied just to support its one individual—this is derived from the collaborative communication capabilities as applied through extended organizational methods to integrate the augmented capabilities of individuals into augmented teams and communities.*
>
> *And finally, for any application of significant power—of which augmentation of an engineering project would be a good example—the adaptability and evolutionary flexibility*

of the computer-communication system is extremely important. The working methods of individuals will shift markedly as they settle into use of a comprehensive workshop, and with these new methods and skills will come payoff potential for changes and additions to their workshops—a cycle that will be significantly active for many years to come. A similar cycle will be even more dramatically evident at the organizational level.

Nelson (1965) contrasted his concept of hypertext to traditional text (p. 96):

> *Systems of paper have grave limitations for either organizing or presenting ideas. A book is never perfectly suited to the reader; one reader is bored, another confused by the same pages. No system of paper—book or programmed text—can adapt very far to the interests or needs of a particular reader or student.*
>
> *However, with the computer-driven display and mass memory, it has been possible to create a new, readable medium, for education and enjoyment, that will let the reader find his level, suit his taste, and find the parts that take on special meaning for him, as instruction or entertainment.*
>
> *Let me introduce the word* hypertext *to mean a body of written or pictorial material interconnected in such a complex way that it could not conveniently be presented or represented on paper. It may contain summaries, or maps of its contents and their interrelations; it may contain annotations, additions and footnotes from scholars who have examined it. Let me suggest that such an object and system, properly designed and administered, could have great potential for education, increasing the student's range of choices, his sense of freedom, his motivation, and his intellectual grasp. Such a system could grow indefinitely, gradually including more and more of the world's written knowledge. . . .*

Doug Engelbart was early in recognizing the need for experiments to test various approaches to the human-computer interface (English, Engelbart, and Berman, 1967). Nelson shares Engelbart's concerns about the quality of the interface, but takes a more passionate and less scientific approach. Typical of his style, for example, is his invention of the term "cybercrud," which he defines as "putting things over on people using computers," and the phrase "the psychic engineering of fantic fields," which anticipates what we now think of as the design of the conceptual models and metaphors through which users encounter and interpret interactive systems (1973, pp. 21, 23, 26):

> *The myth of technical determinism seems to hold captive both the public and the computer priesthood. Indeed, the myth is believed both by people who love, and by people who hate, computers. This myth, never questioned because never stated, holds that whatever is to come in the computer field is somehow preordained by technical necessity or some form of scientific correctness. This is cybercrud.*
>
> *Computers do what people want them to do,* at best. *Figuring out what we should want, in full contemplation of the outspread possibilities, is a task that needs us all, laymen no less. There is something right about the public backlash against computers: things don't have to be this way, with our bank balances unavailable from computers, the immense serial numbers of our drivers' licenses generated by computers, the unstaunchable rivers of junk mail sent to us by computers. And it is the duty of the computer-man to help demythologize, to help the intelligent layman understand the specifics of systems he must deal with, and to help the public explore the question,* what do we want?. . .
>
> *I can now state what I believe to be the central problem of screenworld design, and indeed of design of man-machine* anything—*that is, psychic architecture.*
>
> *By the psychic architecture of a system, I mean the mental conceptions and space structures among which the user moves: their arrangements and their qualities, especially clarity, integration and meshing, power, utility and lack of clutter.*
>
> *It should be noted that these notions are much like those by which we judge regular architecture, and indeed the relationship would seem very close. An architectural grand design—say, of a capitol building—embraces the fundamental concepts a user will have to know to get around: main places, corridor arrangement (visualization and symmetries), access structure. These concepts are the very same in a screenworld or other complex man-made virtual structure: main places, corridors or transition rules (and their visualization and symmetries), access structure. It is a virtual space much like a building (though not confined to three "normally" connected dimensions), and susceptible to the same modes of spatial understanding, kinds of possible movement within, and potential appreciation and criticism. . . .*
>
> *The psychic engineering of fantic fields—adult's hyperspaces of word and picture, child's gardens of verses—is our new frontier. We must look not to Asimovian robotics and the automated schoolmarm and librarian, but to the penny arcade and the bicycle, the clever diagram and the movie effect, to furnish this new realm.*

Bravo! Happily, Nelson has had a profound effect on many young people interested in computers through his lively and deeply humanistic vision of the creative potential of appropriate computer technology.

Interestingly, two subdisciplines of human-computer interaction recently emerged, each claiming one of these two men as an inspiration. Computer-supported cooperative work (CSCW) has applied Engelbart's insights into the importance of group and organizational activity (see Chapter 11). Hypertext has also become a booming field (see Chapter 13). These chapters include the recent history of the two topics.

HUMAN FACTORS, PSYCHOLOGY, AND THE DESIGN OF HUMAN-COMPUTER DIALOGUES

Recall Norman's suggestion that the design of human-computer interfaces be informed by the psychology and the design of everyday artifacts. The discipline that focuses on enhancing the quality of our use of artifacts is called *human factors* or *ergonomics* (McCormick and Sanders, 1982; Sanders and McCormick, 1987; Van Cott and Kinkade, 1972). This field originated in studies of work practices early in the century. Human factors drew particular attention during and after World War II, when it was applied to the evaluation of the complex new weaponry. Simple design flaws were found to have serious effects. For example, an escape hatch that was awkward for a fully equipped man to get through led to the unnecessary deaths of over 10,000 British bomber crew members (Dyson, 1979).

Human factors is therefore a branch of applied psychology devoted to guiding and enhancing the design of artifacts. Shackel's (1962) work on computer display design is an early example of empirically confirming design choices through quantitative validation of interface quality. Part IV discusses in greater depth the role of human factors and applied psychology in human-computer interaction. In the 1960s, psychological research began influencing the design of interactive computer systems and software in numerous ways, including

- comparisons of batch-processing and time-sharing computer use, off-line and on-line problem solving (Grant and Sackman, 1967; Lampson, 1967; Nickerson, Elkind, and Carbonell, 1968; Gold, 1969)
- the relationship between the efficacy of problem solving in a time-shared environment and system response time (Miller, 1968; Grossberg, Wiesen, and Yntema, 1976)
- human-computer cooperative problem solving (Yntema and Torgerson, 1961; Carbonell, Elkind, and Nickerson, 1968; Miller, 1969)

Yet, since most people who interacted directly with computers in the 1960s were programmers, human-computer interaction was at that time primarily programmer-computer interaction. This discipline is typically known as the *psychology of computer programming*.

Sackman (1970) published an important book applying psychological research methods to programming. After reviewing past research on problem solving in programming, he presented detailed results and analyses of a new set of experiments. Of particular interest is his attention to individual differences and his recommendations for a "scientific study of man-computer problem solving."

Even more influential than the Sackman book was one published by Weinberg (1971). It dealt broadly with programming as human performance, as an individual activity, and as a social activity. More than any other single work up to that time, the book focused attention on the human factors of programming and described the actual behavior and thought processes of programmers as they carried out their daily activities. By encouraging programmers to improve the interfaces to their own computerized tools, increasing their productivity and enhancing program reliability and maintainability, Weinberg led to a general recognition of the importance of anyone's interface to the machine.

A third significant book, Shneiderman (1980), reviews the psychology of programming through the 1970s. As programmers became a smaller and smaller fraction of computer users in the 1980s and 1990s, the psychology of programming became less central to human-computer interaction. Research continues, however, with particular emphasis on cognitive models of programming, object-oriented programming, and visual programming (Soloway and Iyengar, 1986; Olson, Sheppard, and Soloway, 1987; Koenemann-Belliveau, Moher, and Robertson, 1991). Two useful survey papers are Curtis et al. (1986), which is reprinted in Baecker and Buxton (1987)—the first edition of this book, and Curtis (1988).

By the 1970s, conditions had changed from the 1950s and 1960s, and more and more nonprogrammers were interacting directly with computers. Computer operators at terminals initiated batch-processing jobs and handled the output. In industries such as insurance, banking, and air transportation, data entry personnel used terminals. These users had little discretion over their work conditions. Although optimizing the interfaces on these systems was not usually a management priority, psychologists and human factors specialists increasingly stressed the need and the potential for improving human-computer interaction. Shackel (1969), Nickerson (1969), and Bennett (1972) wrote early influential proposals and reviews in this regard.

A landmark event in the consolidation and popularization of human-machine interface issues was the publication of *Design of Man-Computer Dialogues* by James Martin (1973), a widely published and influential data-processing consultant. The scope of his work includes the following:

- Categorization of terminal operators
- Alphanumeric dialogues, including natural language dialogues, programming dialogues, display techniques, and supporting hardware
- Dialogues using sound and graphics, including the role of pictorial representations, and the technology of voice answer-back systems
- Psychological considerations, including response time requirements, human channel and buffer capacity considerations, display encoding, and the role of creativity
- Training operators, including totally naive operators, computer-assisted instruction, information control rooms, and terminals for management
- Implementation considerations, including control of user errors, techniques for dealing with failures, "bullet proofing" systems, security and privacy, dialogue program generators, and simulation of human-machine interfaces

Three other influential works of that period were "User Engineering Principles for Interactive Systems" (Hansen, 1971), chapters on interactive graphical techniques and command languages in *Principles of Interactive Computer Graphics* (Newman and Sproull, 1973), and "The Art of Natural Graphic Man-Machine Conversation" (Foley and Wallace, 1974). Hansen's paper presented what is probably the first—and is certainly the shortest—enumeration of principles for the design of interactive systems:

- "Know the user."
- "Minimize memorization" by allowing selection of items rather than entry of data, using names instead of numbers, ensuring predictable behavior, and providing ready access to useful system information.
- "Optimize operations" by providing rapid execution of common operations, preserving display consistency, exploiting "muscle memory," and organizing and reorganizing commands based on observed system usage.
- "Engineer for errors" by providing good error messages, designing so common errors are not made, allowing

actions to be reversible, and guaranteeing system integrity in the face of hardware or software failure.

Martin's book acquainted the commercial data-processing world with the issues and importance of good interface design. The three works cited above raised the academic computer science community's awareness of human factors.

THE PERSONAL WORKSTATION

We now return to system and technology development, turning our attention to Xerox Palo Alto Research Center (PARC), formed in 1971. An incredible concentration of computer science talent converged on PARC just as the evolution of memory and processor technology offered new opportunities in computer design and implementation. This produced several major contributions by the mid-1970s, although most were not published until later (Pake, 1985; Perry and Wallich, 1985), and many were not exploited commercially by Xerox (Alexander and Smith, 1988).

- Xerox developed the Alto, a prototype of a new kind of computer called a "personal workstation" (Thacker et al., 1979; Thacker, 1986); intended for use by one individual, it had significant local processing power and memory, a high-resolution bit-mapped display, a keyboard, and a mouse, the latter being an innovation developed by Engelbart's group at Stanford Research Institute.
- Xerox pioneered the development of congenial graphical interfaces to systems and to the applications that ran on them, such as text editing, creation of illustrations, document creation, and electronic mail (Lampson, 1986). These interfaces incorporated windows, menus, scroll bars, mouse control and selection mechanisms, and views of abstract structures, all presented and integrated in a consistent manner. One important innovation was WYSIWYG, "what you see is what you get," in which a user sees and manipulates on the screen a representation of a document that looks identical to the eventual printed page.
- Xerox pioneered methods for the local area networking of workstations (Metcalfe and Boggs, 1976; Lampson, 1986). This provided users with the advantages of a personal machine along with access to shared resources, such as a central file server and high-speed printers.

Note that other, even earlier computers, such as the Whirlwind, the TX-0, the TX-2, the DEC PDP-1, and the Linc (Clark, 1986), were often used as "personal computers" (Bell, 1986). Yet only with the Alto and its successors did the concept of a computer intended for use by a single individual become technologically and economically realizable, first in highly capitalized, advanced research and development laboratories, and years later "for the rest of us."

THE DYNABOOK

Perhaps the most compelling vision amidst the excitement of the many new ideas and applications at Xerox was Alan Kay's concepts of the "Reactive Engine" (Kay, 1969) and the "Dynabook" (Kay and Goldberg, 1977; Kay, 1987 video). Kay and Goldberg (1977, pp. 31–32) wrote:

> *"Devices" which variously store, retrieve, or manipulate information in the form of messages embedded in a medium have been in existence for thousands of years. People use them to communicate ideas and feelings both to others and back to themselves. Although thinking goes on in one's head, external media serve to materialize thoughts and, through feedback, to augment the actual paths the thinking follows. Methods discovered in one medium provide metaphors which contribute new ways to think about notions in other media.*
>
> *For most of recorded history, the interactions of humans with their media have been primarily nonconversational and passive in the sense that marks on paper, paint on walls, even "motion" pictures and television, do not change in response to the viewer's wishes. A mathematical formulation—which may symbolize the essence of an entire universe—once put down on paper, remains static and requires the reader to expand its possibilities.*
>
> *Every message is, in one sense or another, a simulation of some idea. It may be representational or abstract. The essence of a medium is very much dependent on the way messages are embedded, changed, and viewed. Although digital computers were originally designed to do arithmetic computation, the ability to simulate the details of any descriptive model means that the computer, viewed as a medium itself, can be* all *other media if the embedding and viewing methods are sufficiently well provided. Moreover, this new "metamedium" is* active*—it can respond to queries and experiments—so that the messages may involve the learner in a two-way conversation. This property has never been available before except through the medium of an individual teacher. We think the implications are vast and compelling.*
>
> A dynamic medium for creative thought: *the* Dynabook. *Imagine having your own self-contained knowledge manipulator in a portable package the size and shape of an ordinary notebook. Suppose it had enough power to outrace your senses of sight and hearing, enough capacity to store for later retrieval thousands of page-equivalents of reference materials, poems, letters, recipes, records, drawings, animations, musical scores, waveforms, dynamic simulations, and anything else you would like to remember and change.*
>
> *We envision a device as small and portable as possible which could both take in and give out information in quantities approaching that of human sensory systems. Visual output should be, at the least, of higher quality than what can be obtained from newsprint. Audio output should adhere to similar high-fidelity standards.*
>
> *There should be no discernible pause between cause and effect. One of the metaphors we used when designing such a system was that of a musical instrument, such as a flute, which is owned by its user and responds instantly and consistently to its owner's wishes. Imagine the absurdity of a one-second delay between blowing a note and hearing it!*
>
> *These "civilized" desires for flexibility, resolution, and response lead to the conclusion that a user of a dynamic personal medium needs several hundred times as much power as the average adult now typically enjoys from timeshared computing. This means that we should either build a new resource several hundred times the capacity of current machines and share it (very difficult and expensive), or we should investigate the possibility of giving each person his own powerful machine. We chose the second approach.*

Hardware advances over the past two decades have enabled the realization of Kay's vision in terms of size and portability. Portable computers, then notebook computers, and most recently personal information managers have become significant segments of the computer marketplace. A challenge for the year 2000 is to develop software that will complete the realization of the vision.

THE PERSONAL COMPUTER

About the time that Kay was building and elaborating his Interim Dynabook, an article in *Popular Electronics* (Roberts and Yates, 1975) triggered a veritable revolution in the computing industry by describing the Altair, the first home computer. Personal computers increased the availability of computer power at an incredible rate and significantly broadened the usefulness of computers. No longer were they primarily the purview of a technical and mathematical priesthood at one end and tightly managed data entry clerks at the other. Instead, rapidly growing numbers of computer users were doctors and lawyers, teachers and librarians, business people and shopkeepers.

Whether professional users, amateurs, or hobbyists, most of the new computer users desired more congenial, forgiving, "user-friendly" interfaces than were available. The strength of this phenomenon resulted in the eventual successes of the Apple Macintosh, the first commercially successful implementation of the Xerox-style human interface, and the many graphical interfaces that followed it, as described in Case B.

The history of personal computer and workstation hardware and software is covered in Levy (1985), Goldberg (1988), and Ranade and Nash (1994).

THE ROLE OF ARTIFICIAL INTELLIGENCE

As Kay prototyped his Dynabook, Nicholas Negroponte (1970) in the Architecture Machine Group at MIT was developing a more radical view of the ultimate human-computer interaction (p. 1):

> *Computer-aided design cannot occur without machine intelligence—and would be dangerous without it. In our area, however, most people have serious misgivings about the feasibility and more importantly, the desirability of attributing the actions of a machine to intelligent behavior. These people generally distrust the concept of machines that approach (and thus why not pass?) our own human intelligence. In our culture an intelligent machine is immediately assumed to be a bad machine. As soon as intelligence is ascribed to the artificial, some people believe that the artifact will become evil and strip us of our humanistic values. Or, like the great gazelle and the water buffalo, we will be placed on reserves to be pampered by a ruling class of automata.*
>
> *Why ask a machine to learn, to understand, to associate courses with goals, to be self-improving, to be ethical—in short, to be intelligent?*
>
> *The answer is the underlying postulate of an architecture machine. A design machine must have an artificial intelligence because any design procedure, set of rules, or truism is tenuous, if not subversive, when used out of context or regardless of context. It follows that a mechanism must recognize and understand the context before carrying out an operation. Therefore, a machine must be able to discern changes in meaning brought about by changes in context, hence, be intelligent. And to do this, it must have a sophisticated set of sensors, effectors, and processors to view the real world directly and indirectly.*

Negroponte went on to describe the need for a rich language of interaction between human and machine, calling for dialogues specific to a particular person and particular machine that would evolve based on their shared history (pp. 9–13):

> *Each [a designer and a machine] should track the other's design maneuvers, evoking a rhetoric that cannot be anticipated. "What was mere noise and disorder or distraction before, becomes pattern and sense; information has been metabolized out of noise" (Brodey and Lindgren, 1967). The event is circular inasmuch as the designer-machine unity provokes a dialogue and the dialogue promotes a stronger designer-machine unity. This progressively intimate association of the two dissimilar species is the symbiosis. It evolves through mutual training, in this case, through the dialogue.*
>
> *Such man-machine dialogue has no historical precedent. The present antagonistic mismatch between man and machine, however, has generated a great deal of preoccupation for it. In less than a decade the term "man-machine communication" has passed from concept to cliché to platitude. Nevertheless, the theory is important and straightforward: in order to have a cooperative interaction between a designer of a certain expertise and a machine of some scholarship, the two must be congenial and must share the labor of establishing a common language. A designer, when addressing a machine, must not be forced to resort to machine-oriented codes. And in spite of computational efficiency, a paradigm for fruitful conversations must be machines that can speak and respond to a natural language.*
>
> *With direct, fluid, and natural man-machine discourse, two former barriers between architects and computing machines would be removed. First, the designers, using computer-aided design hardware, would not have to be specialists. With natural communication, the "this is what I want to do" and "can you do it" gap could be bridged. The design task would no longer be described to a "knobs and dials" person to be executed in his secret vernacular. Instead, with simple negotiations, the job would be formulated and executed in the designer's own idiom. As a result, a vibrant stream of ideas could be directly channeled from the designer to the machine and back.*
>
> *The second instruction overcome by such close communion is the potential for reevaluating the procedures themselves. In a direct dialogue the designer can exercise his proverbial capriciousness. At first a designer may have only a meager understanding of his specific problem and thus require machine tolerance and compatibility in his search for the consistency among criteria and form and method, between intent and purpose. The progression from visceral to intellectual can be articulated in subsequent provisional statements of detail and moment-to-moment reevaluations of the methods themselves.*
>
> *But, the tête-à-tête must be even more direct and fluid; it is gestures, smiles, and frowns that turn a conversation into a*

dialogue. "Most Americans are only dimly aware of this silent language even though they use it everyday. They are not conscious of the elaborate patterning of behavior which prescribes our handling of time, our spatial relationships, our attitudes towards work, play, and learning" (Hall, 1959). In an intimate human-to-human dialogue, hand-waving often carries as much meaning as text. Manner carries cultural information: the Arabs use their noses, the Japanese nod their heads. Customarily, in man-machine communication studies, such silent languages are ignored and frequently are referred to as "noise." But such silent languages are not noise; a dialogue is composed of "whole body involvement—with hands, eyes, mouth, facial expressions—using many channels simultaneously, but rhythmized into a harmoniously simple exchange" (Brodey and Lindgren, 1968).

Imagine a machine that can follow your design methodology and at the same time discern and assimilate your conversational idiosyncrasies. This same machine, after observing your behavior, could build a predictive model of your conversational performance. Such a machine could then reinforce the dialogue by using the predictive model to respond to you in a manner that is in rhythm with your personal behavior and conversational idiosyncrasies.

What this means is the dialogue we are proposing would be so personal that you would not be able to use someone else's machine, and he would not understand yours. In fact, neither machine would be able to talk directly to the other. The dialogue would be so intimate—even exclusive—that only mutual persuasion and compromise would bring about ideas, ideas unrealizable by either conversant alone. No doubt, in such a symbiosis it would not be solely the human designer who would decide when the machine is relevant.

An elaboration of this vision can be found in Negroponte (1975) and in a quarter century of work in the Architecture Machine Group, now the Media Laboratory, of MIT. Although inspirational, little of the promise of AI has yet been realized. Current progress is documented in our presentations of speech and natural language interaction in Chapter 8 and of work on tailorable and adaptive systems in Chapter 12. Each decade promises to be the one in which AI technologies will find widespread application. Will it happen by the year 2000? Negroponte and others think so ("Speech More Important," 1989; Straub and Wetherbe, 1989).

MODELING USERS AND INTERFACES

The 1960s saw relatively few scientific and behavioral studies of interfaces, other than those at Bolt Beranek and Newman, System Development Corporation, and MIT Lincoln Laboratory, cited earlier. The pace of effort picked up in the 1970s. An influential group was formed by John Gould at IBM Research around 1971. One early contribution was to study the interface to Zloof's (1975, 1976) concept of "Query by Example" before any code was written (Thomas and Gould, 1975).

Another influential group was the Applied Information Processing Psychology Project of Allen Newell, Stu Card, and Tom Moran, begun at Xerox PARC in 1974. Their approach drew from the field of "information processing psychology" (Lindsay and Norman, 1977). This field of psychology, described in Chapter 9, involves representing human information processing (perceiving, recognizing, learning, remembering, etc.) in formal terms, in some cases modeled by computer programs.

Newell, Card, and Moran developed a model of a human user of computer systems called the Model Human Information Processor (see Chapter 9) and a methodology for calibrating the model and applying it as predictive tool. Even though the resulting work, *The Psychology of Human-Computer Interaction* (Card, Moran, and Newell, 1983), raises more questions than it answers, it is a landmark contribution, the first major body of work that attempts to develop an underlying applied science of human-computer interaction.

EXPANDING RESEARCH FRONTIERS

Finally, on the applied side, the 1980s and 1990s saw a veritable explosion of research on new paradigms of human-computer interaction. Although here also the ideas had typically been introduced in the 1960s and 1970s, decades would need to elapse until technology had matured sufficiently to allow them to be explored. These paradigms include groupware and computer-supported cooperative work (Chapter 11); tailorable and adaptive systems (Chapter 12); hypertext and multimedia (Chapter 13); and cyberspace—virtual reality, ubiquitous computing, and global networks (virtual communities) (Chapter 14). The history of these areas appears in the chapters where they are discussed.

A DEVELOPING COMMUNITY OF SCHOLARS

In the late 1970s and early 1980s, many corporations joined IBM and Xerox in mounting major efforts to study and improve the human factors of computing systems. Some academic interest had arisen earlier. In England, Professor Brian Shackel of the University of Loughborough, who in the late 1950s pioneered work on the ergonomics of computers (Shackel, 1962), founded in 1970 an influential research group, Human Sciences and Advanced Technology (HUSAT). Other prominent scholars who helped expand the field in the late 1970s and early 1980s included Allen Newell at Carnegie-Mellon University; Don Norman at the University of California, San Diego; James Foley at George Washington University; Ben Shneiderman at the University of Maryland; and Phil Barnard, Nick Hammond, John Long, Patricia Wright, and Richard Young at the Medical Research Council Applied Psychology Unit in Cambridge, England.

This community grew rapidly in the United States and West Europe. The ACM Special Interest Group on Computer and Human Interaction (SIGCHI), formed in 1983, became the fastest-growing ACM special interest group. Local chapters of SIGCHI formed in several cities to schedule monthly technical presentations. The field has drawn increasing participation from Japan and other Asian countries, Australia, South America, and East Europe.

We end this account of the intellectual roots of the field of human-computer interaction in the mid-1980s. The researchers and developers whose work comprises this volume take up these threads and introduce many new ideas and discoveries from the subsequent decade. Before placing you in their hands, we list several forums of communication among members of the field. These have helped us and may assist you in further exploration:

- International Symposium on Man-Machine Systems, held in Cambridge, England, in 1969 (IEEE, 1969)
- *International Journal of Man-Machine Studies*, now called *The International Journal of Human-Computer Studies*, begun in 1969
- Software Psychology Society, based in Washington, D.C., which has met monthly since 1976 (Shneiderman, 1986)
- Human Factors Society Technical Group on Computer Systems, formed in 1971
- Conference on Easier and More Productive Use of Computing, held at the University of Michigan in 1981
- annual ACM SIGCHI CHI conferences, begun with an unexpectedly successful 1982 meeting in Gaithersburg, MD.; the proceedings are widely cited; the SIGGRAPH video series documents demonstrations shown at past conferences
- journal *Behaviour and Information Technology* (begun in 1982)
- IFIP INTERACT conferences (every three years since 1984)
- British Computer Society HCI conferences (annually since 1985)
- International Conference on Human-Computer Interaction (every two years since 1985)
- journal *Human-Computer Interaction* (since 1985)
- the *Handbook of Human-Computer Interaction* (Helander, 1988), a landmark 1,100-page compendium of 52 excellent original overview chapters
- journal *Interacting with Computers* (since 1989)
- journal *International Journal of Human-Computer Interaction* (since 1989)
- journal *ACM Transactions on Computer and Human Interaction* (since 1994)
- magazine *interactions* (ACM) (since 1994)

There are also specialized conferences dealing with user interface software technology, computer-supported cooperative work, hypertext, multimedia, intelligent interfaces, and virtual reality.

Human-computer interaction has also taken a place in general treatments of the history of computing (e.g., *ACM Annals of the History of Computing*; Friedman, 1989; BBC, 1992 video). Friedman does not focus exclusively on human-computer interaction or even on interactive systems—his focus is on systems in organizations, which includes a useful overview of the history of computer systems. In addition, more focused historical reviews have begun to appear (Gaines, 1985; Shackel, 1985; Grudin, 1990, 1991).

The study of human-computer interaction is underway. Is the field living up to its potential? You be the judge.

REFERENCES

Note: A ● before a reference indicates a reading.

Alexander, R., and Smith, D. (1988). *Fumbling the Future: The Story of Xerox & Personal Computing*. Morrow.

Baecker, R. (1969). Picture-Driven Animation. *AFIPS Conference Proceedings* 34, 273–288.

Baecker, R., and Buxton, W. (Eds.) (1987). *Readings in Human-Computer Interaction: A Multidisciplinary Approach*. Morgan Kaufmann.

Bell, G. (1986). Toward a History of Personal Workstations. *Proc. Conference on the History of Personal Workstations*, ACM, 1–17.

Bennett, J. (1972). The User Interface in Interactive Systems. *Annual Review of Information Science and Technology* 7, 159–196.

Brodey, W., and Lindgren, N. (1967). Human Enhancement through Evolutionary Technology. *IEEE Spectrum* 4(9), 87–97.

Brodey, W., and Lindgren, N. (1968). Human Enhancement: Beyond the Machine Age. *IEEE Spectrum* 5(2), 79–93.

Brooks, F. (1977). The Computer "Scientist" as Toolsmith—Studies in Interactive Computer Graphics. *IFIP Conference Proceedings*, 625–634.

Bush, V. (1945). As We May Think. *The Atlantic Monthly* 176, 101–108.

Carbonell, J., Elkind, J., and Nickerson, R. (1968). On the Psychological Importance of Time in a Time Sharing System. *Human Factors* 10(2), 135–142.

Card, S., Moran, T., and Newell, A. (1983). *The Psychology of Human-Computer Interaction*, Lawrence Erlbaum Associates.

Clark, W. (1986). The *LINC* was Early and Small. *Proc. Conference on the History of Personal Workstations*, ACM, 133–155.

Coons, S. (1963). An Outline of the Requirements for a Computer-Aided Design System. *AFIPS Conference Proceedings* 23, 299–304.

Culler, G. (1968). Mathematical Laboratories: A New Power for the Physical and Social Sciences. Reprinted in *Proceedings of the Conference on the History of Personal Workstations*. ACM, 1986, 59–72.

Curtis, W. (1988). Five Paradigms in the Psychology of Programming. In Helander, M. (Ed.) (1988), *Handbook of Human-Computer Interaction*, North-Holland, 87–105.

Curtis, W., Soloway, E., Brooks, R., Black, J., Ehrlich, K., and Ramsey, R. (1986). Software Psychology: The Need for an Interdisciplinary Program. *Proc. of the IEEE* 74(8), 1092–1106.

Davis, M., and Ellis, T. (1964). The Rand Tablet: A Man-Machine Graphical Communication Device. *AFIPS Conference Proceedings* 24, 325–331.

Davis, R. (1966). Man-Machine Communication. In Cuadra, C.A. (Ed.), *Annual Review of Information Science and Technology* 1, Interscience, 221–254.

Dyson, F. (1979). *Disturbing the Universe*. Harper & Row.

Engelbart, D. (1963). A Conceptual Framework for the Augmentation of Man's Intellect. In Howerton, P., and Weeks, D. (Eds.), *Vistas in Information Handling*, Vol. 1, Spartan Books, 1–29.

Engelbart, D. (1982). Integrated, Evolutionary, Office Automation Systems. In Landau, R., and Bair, J. (Eds.), *Emerging Office Systems*, Ablex.

Engelbart, D. (1986). The Augmented Knowledge Workshop. *Proc. Conference on the History of Personal Workstations*, ACM, 73–83.

Engelbart, D., and English, W. (1968). A Research Center for Augmenting Human Intellect. *AFIPS Conference Proceedings* 33, 395–410.

English, W., Engelbart, D., and Berman, M. (1967). Display-Selection Techniques for Text Manipulation. *IEEE Transactions on Human Factors in Electronics* HFE-8(1), 5–15.

Fano, R., and Corbato, F. (1966). Time sharing on Computers. *Scientific American* 214(9), 129–140.

Foley, J., and Wallace, V. (1974). The Art of Natural Graphic Man-Machine Conversation. *Proc. of the IEEE* 62(4), 462–470.

Friedman, A. (1989). *Computer Systems Development: History, Organization and Implementation.* Wiley.

Gaines, B. (1985). From Ergonomics to the Fifth Generation: 30 Years of Human-Computer Interaction Studies. *Proc. Interact '84* Elsevier (North-Holland), 3–7.

Gold, M. (1969). Time sharing and Batch-Processing: An Experimental Comparison of Their Values in a Problem-Solving Situation. *Communications of the ACM* 12(5), 249–259.

Goldberg, A. (Ed.) (1988). *History of Personal Computer Workstations.* Addison-Wesley. Material originally presented at an ACM conference by the same name held in 1986.

Grant, E., and Sackman, H. (1967). An Exploratory Investigation of Programmer Performance under On-Line and Off-Line Conditions. *IEEE Transactions on Human Factors in Electronics* 8(1), 33–48.

Grossberg, M., Wiesen, R., and Yntema, D. (1976). An Experiment on Problem Solving with Delayed Computer Responses. *IEEE Transactions on Systems, Man, and Cybernetics,* 219–222.

Grudin, J. (1990). The Computer Reaches Out: The Historical Continuity of Interface Design. *Proc. CHI '90,* ACM, 261–268.

Grudin, J. (1991). Interactive Systems: Bridging the Gaps between Developers and Users. *IEEE Computer* 24(4), 59–69. Reprinted in this volume.

Hall, E. (1959). *The Silent Language.* Doubleday.

Hansen, W. (1971). User Engineering Principles for Interactive Systems. *AFIPS Conference Proceedings* 39, Fall Joint Computer Conference. AFIPS Press, 523–532.

Helander, M. (Ed.) (1988). *Handbook of Human-Computer Interaction.* Elsevier.

IEEE (1969). *IEEE Transaction on Man-Machine Systems: Special Issue,* 10 Part II (4).

Johnson, T. (1963). Sketchpad III: Three Dimensional Graphical Communication with a Digital Computer. *AFIPS Conference Proceedings* 23, 347–353.

Kay, A. (1969). The Reactive Engine. Ph.D. Thesis, University of Utah.

Kay, A., and Goldberg, A. (1977). Personal Dynamic Media. *IEEE Computer* 10(3), 31–42.

Knowlton, K. (1966). Computer-Produced Movies. *Science* 150, November 1965, 1116–1120.

Koenemann-Belliveau, J., Moher, T., and Robertson, S. (Eds.) (1991). *Empirical Studies of Programmers: 4th Workshop.* Ablex.

Lampson, B. (1967). A Critique of "An Exploratory Investigation of Programmer Performance under On-Line and Off-Line Conditions." *IEEE Transaction on Human Factors in Electronics* 8(1), 48–51.

Lampson, B. (1986). Personal Distributed Computing: The Alto and Ethernet Software. *Proceedings of the Conference on the History of Personal Workstations,* ACM, 101–131.

Levinthal, C. (1966). Molecular Model-Building by Computer. *Scientific American* 214(6), 42–52.

Levy, S. (1985). *Hackers.* Anchor Press/Doubleday.

Licklider, J. (1960). Man-Computer Symbiosis. *IRE Transactions of Human Factors in Electronics* HFE-1(1), 4–11.

Licklider, J. (1968). Man-Computer Communication. *Annual Review of Information Science and Technology* 3, 201–240.

Licklider, J., and Clark, W. (1962). On-Line Man-Computer Communication. *AFIPS Conference Proceedings* 21, 113–128.

Lindsay, P., and Norman, D. (1977). *Human Information Processing: An Introduction to Psychology,* Second Edition. Academic Press.

Machover, C. (1978). A Brief, Personal History of Computer Graphics. *IEEE Computer* 11(11), 38–45.

Martin, J. (1973). *Design of Man-Computer Dialogues,* Prentice-Hall.

McCormick, E., and Sanders, M. (1982). *Human Factors in Engineering and Design,* Fifth Edition. McGraw-Hill.

Metcalfe, R., and Boggs, D. (1976). *ETHERNET:* Distributed Packet Switching for Local Computer Networks. *Communications of the ACM* 19(7), 395–404.

Meyrowitz, N., and Van Dam, A. (1982). Interactive Editing Systems: Part 1. *ACM Computing Surveys* 14(3), 321–352.

Miller, R. (1968). Response Time in Man-Computer Conversational Transactions. *AFIPS Conference Proceedings* 33, 267–277.

Miller, R. (1969). Archetypes in Man-Computer Problem Solving. *IEEE Transaction on Man-Machine Systems* 10 Part II (4), 219–241.

Myer, T., and Sutherland, I. (1968). On the Design of Display Processors. *Communications of the ACM* 11(6), 410–414.

Negroponte, N. (1970). *The Architecture Machine: Towards a More Humane Environment.* MIT.

Negroponte, N. (1975). *Soft Architecture Machines.* MIT.

Nelson, T. (1965). A File Structure for the Complex, the Changing, and the Indeterminate. *Proc. ACM National Conference,* 84–100.

Nelson, T. (1973). A Conceptual Framework for Man-Machine Everything. *Proc. National Computer Conference,* M21–M26.

Nelson, T. (1981). *Literary Machines,* Project Xanadu, 8400 Fredericksburg, #138, San Antonio, TX 78229.

Nelson, T. (1987). *Computer Lib* and *Dream Machines.* Revised Edition, Tempus Books.

Newman, W., and Sproull, R. (1979, 1973). *Principles of Interactive Computer Graphics.* McGraw-Hill.

Nickerson, R. (1969). Man-Computer Interaction: A Challenge for Human Factors Research. *Ergonomics* 12 (4), 501–517.

Nickerson, R., Elkind, J., and Carbonell, J. (1968). Human Factors and the Design of Time Sharing Computer Systems. *Human Factors* 10(2), 127–134.

Olson, G., Sheppard, S., and Soloway, E. (Eds.) (1987). *Empirical Studies of Programmers: 2nd Workshop.* Ablex.

Pake, G. (1985). Research at Xerox PARC: A Founder's Assessment. *IEEE Spectrum* 22(10), 54–61.

Perry, T., and Wallich, P. (1985). Inside the PARC: The "Information Architects." *IEEE Spectrum* 22(10), 62–75.

Preiss, R. (1978). Storage CRT Terminals: Evolution and Trends. *IEEE Computer* 11(11), 20–26.

Ranade, J., and Nash, A. (Eds.) (1994). *The Best of Byte: Two Decades on the Leading Edge.* McGraw-Hill.

Roberts, H., and Yates, W. (1975). ALTAIR 8800: The Most Powerful Minicomputer Project Ever Presented—Can Be Built for under $400. *Popular Electronics,* 33–38.

Roberts, L. (1986). The Arpanet and Computer Networks. *Proc. Conference on the History of Personal Workstations,* ACM, 51–58.

Ross, D. (1986). A Personal View of the Personal Work Station: Some Firsts in the Fifties. *Proc. Conference on the History of Personal Workstations,* ACM, 19–48.

Ross, D., and Rodriguez, J. (1963). Theoretical Foundations for the Computer-Aided Design System. *AFIPS Conference Proceedings* 23, 305–322.

Rovner, P., and Feldman, J. (1968). The LEAP Language and Data Structure. *IFIP Conference Proceedings,* 579–585.

Sackman, H. (1970). *Man-Computer Problem Solving: Experimental Evaluation of Time sharing and Batch Processing.* Auerbach.

Sanders, M., and McCormick, E. (1987). *Human Factors in Engineering and Design,* Sixth Edition. McGraw-Hill.

Scientific American (1971). *Readings from Scientific American: Computers and Computation.* W.H. Freeman & Co.

Shackel, B. (1962). Ergonomics in the Design of a Large Digital Computer Console. *Ergonomics* 5, 229–241.

Shackel, B. (1969). Man-Computer Interaction—The Contribution of the Human Sciences. *IEEE Transactions on Man-Machine Systems* 10 Part II (4), 149–163.

Shackel, B. (1985). Ergonomics in Information Technology in Europe—A Review. *Behaviour and Information Technology* 4(4), 263–287.

Shaw, J. (1964). JOSS: A Designer's View of an Experimental On-Line Computing System. *Proc. Fall Joint Computer Conference* 26, 455–464.

Shneiderman, B. (1980). *Software Psychology: Human Factors in Computer and Information Systems.* Winthrop Publishers.

Shneiderman, B. (1986). No Members, No Officers, No Dues: A Ten Year History of the Software Psychology Society. *SIGCHI Bulletin* 18(2), 14–16.

Soloway, E., and Iyengar, S. (Eds.) (1986). *Empirical Studies of Programmers.* Ablex.

Speech More Important Interface than Graphics, Media Lab's Negroponte Tells SIGGRAPH. (1989, November). *Byte,* p. 26.

Stotz, R. (1963). Man-Machine Console Facilities for Computer-Aided Design. *AFIPS Conference Proceedings* 23, 323–328.

Straub, D., and Wetherbe, J. (1989). Information Technologies for the 1990s: An Organizational Impact Perspective. *Communications of the ACM,* 32, 1328–1339.

Sutherland, I. (1963). Sketchpad: A Man-Machine Graphical Communication System. *AFIPS Conference Proceedings* 23, 329–346.

Sutherland, W., Forgie, J., and Morello, M. (1969). Graphics in Time sharing: A Summary of the TX-2 Experience. *AFIPS Conference Proceedings,* 34, 629–636.

Thacker, C. (1986). Personal Distributed Computing: The Alto and Ethernet Hardware. *Proc. Conference on the History of Personal Workstations,* ACM, 87–100.

Thacker, C., McCreight, E., Lampson, B., Sproull, R., and Boggs, D. (1979). Alto: A Personal Computer. In Siewiorek, D., Bell, G., and Newell A., *Computer Structures: Principles and Examples,* Second Edition, McGraw-Hill, 549–572.

Thomas, J., and Gould, J. (1975). A Psychological Study of Query by Example. *AFIPS Conference Proceedings* 44, 439–445.

Van Cott, H., and Kinkade, R. (Eds.) (1972). *Human Engineering Guide to Equipment Design,* Revised Edition. American Institutes for Research.

Weinberg, G. (1971). *The Psychology of Computer Programming.* Van Nostrand Reinhold.

Williams, G. (1984). The Apple Macintosh Computer. *Byte* 9(2), 30–54.

Yntema, D., and Torgerson, W. (1961). Man-Computer Cooperation in Decisions Requiring Common Sense. *IRE Transactions on Human Factors in Electronics,* 20–26.

Zloof, M. (1975). Query by Example. *AFIPS Conference Proceedings* 44, 431–437.

Zloof, M. (1976). Query by Example—Operations on Hierarchical Data Bases. *AFIPS Conference Proceedings* 45, 845–853.

VIDEOS

BBC (1992). *The Machine That Changed the World,* 5-hr. video series.

Engelbart, D., and English, W. (1968). A Research Center for Augmenting Human Intellect. *ACM SIGGRAPH Video Review* 106. Originally filmed in 1968, published in 1994.

Kay, A. (1987). Doing with Images Makes Symbols: Communicating with Computers. University Video Communications, P.O. Box 5129, Stanford CA 94309.

Sutherland, I. (1963). Sketchpad. *ACM SIGGRAPH Video Review* 13. Originally filmed in 1963, published in 1983.

Case B

The Emergence of Graphical User Interfaces

As described in Chapter 1, the Xerox Palo Alto Research Center (PARC) was an environment of enormous creativity in the 1970s (see also Pake, 1985; Perry and Wallich, 1985; Alexander and Smith, 1988). This included pioneering work in the design of personal computers, the invention of interactive techniques to exploit workstation capabilities and facilitate their use, and development of an applied cognitive psychology to help guide design. Late in the 1970s, in order to exploit these advances commercially, Xerox created a separate product development organization, the System Development Division.

THE XEROX STAR

These activities eventually resulted in the April 1981 announcement of the 8010 Star Information System, "a new personal computer designed for offices... intended for business professionals who handle information" (Smith et al., 1982; Smith and Irby, 1990 video). The Star was the first comprehensive direct manipulation system intended for business applications in an office environment.

The Star was greeted with much enthusiasm. The human-computer interface was an important area of innovation. It codified and made available many significant interface ideas developed at PARC and in other pioneering systems (see Chapter 1):

- The use of a *desktop metaphor*, yielding a familiar *user's conceptual model* with electronic documents on a simulated desktop
- *Direct manipulation*, with the ability to see and point to menus and icons rather than to remember and type written commands
- The use of *property* or *option* sheets to specify the appearance of objects
- *What you see is what you get* (WYSIWYG)
- *Universal* or *generic* commands such as Move, Copy, and Delete that are used throughout the system (Rosenberg and Moran, 1984)
- A relatively high degree of consistency
- Relatively few *modes*, states of the system where certain commands cannot be used (Tesler, 1981)

Our reading, Johnson et al. (1989), is a comprehensive retrospective look at the Star that includes more detail on these principles. Other important overview papers are Smith et al. (1982), reprinted in the first edition of this book—Baecker and Buxton (1987), and Miller and Johnson (1995), which is a recent retrospective look at the Star design process. Verplank (1988) reviews the design of the look-and-feel of the Star and some of the principles that emerged in that process. A more technical description of the interface components appears in Smith et al. (1982). Also relevant are Thacker et al. (1982), which describes the prototype Alto computer on which much of the earlier research had been done; Harslem and Nelson (1982), which describes the Star development environment and process; Lipkie et al. (1982), which describes the graphics implementation; and Purvy, Farrell, and Klose (1983), which describes the Star's record processing capability.

The high quality of the Star interface was only partly due to inspired design based on a decade of creative and relevant research and development. Another factor was the extensive prototyping of ideas, pencil-and-paper analyses, and human factors experiments with potential users. Some of these experiments are described in Bewley et al. (1983), reprinted in Baecker and Buxton (1987). Although not emphasized in our reading, this empirical work in iteratively refining the Star interface was an essential and successful part of the design process (Miller and Johnson, 1995).

For example, a set of 17 icons was needed. Four sets were designed and tested for the speed at which specific icons could be picked from a group and for the accuracy of identification when first encountered. One set was then selected and modified. Figure B.1 (page 50) describes some of the Star human factors tests.

The Star pioneered with its human-computer interface and with its orientation towards "knowledge workers" as intended users. Miller and Johnson (1995) assert that many aspects of the design process were done right:

- Commitment to design first, then code
- Use of objects-and-actions design methodology
- Attention to detail
- Participation of graphic designers

Yet Star was not a great commercial success. Often the technological trailblazer only paves the way for a second or third product to be successful. Perhaps Xerox was simply too early; the "knowledge worker" market did not exist in 1981. Other possible causes include the following:

- *Cost.* Each individual Star cost an amount approaching

FIGURE B.1

Partial listing of Star-1 functional tests (Bewley et al., 1983, p. 77)

Test Topic	Number of Subjects	Total Hours	Impact
Selection schemes	28	64	*Led to new design; validated new scheme*
Keyboard (6 layouts)	20	40	*Led to design of keyboard*
Display	20	10	*Specified display phosphor and refresh rate*
Tab-indent	16	16	*Caused redesign of tab and indent functionality*
Labels	12	6	*Caused change in property sheet and keyboard labels*
Property sheets	20	40	*Identified potential interface problems and redesigns*
Fonts	8	6	*Led to decision on screen-paper coordination*
Icons	20	30	*Led to design of icons*
Initial dialogue	12	36	*Led to design of training facility and materials*
HELP	2	6	*Validated HELP design ideas*
Graphics	10	65	*Led to redesign; validated new design*
Graphic idioms	4	16	*Contributed to redesigns*
J-Star labels	25	25	*Led to design of keyboard labels for Japanese-Star*

$15,000, including a proportional share of the network "file servers" and "print servers." 1981 also saw the introduction of IBM's much less expensive PC. In relationship to other available products, Star's benefits were not perceived to be worth the additional cost.

- The Star possessed *very limited functionality* (Hammer, 1984). Although aimed at a management and professional market, it did not include a spreadsheet, the application that propelled PC sales. Unproven benefits of the new interface could not compensate for missing functionality.
- The Star *lacked an open architecture*, technical and administrative mechanisms that encourage third-party software developers to create new software for the system. Its Customer Programming (CUSP) system (Purvy, Farrell, and Klose, 1983), a record processing language that was not initially a full programming language, was not suitable for application development. For a long time, Xerox would not license to third parties the tool they themselves used for programming, the Mesa development environment (Lauer and Satterthwaite, 1979; Johnsson and Wick, 1982).
- The Star was *perceived as slow.* Roberts and Moran's (1983) evaluation of nine text editors showed that despite the Star's long response time, its editor was the second fastest in carrying out a set of benchmark tasks. However, it is the *perception* of human users, and not any abstract reality, that ultimately determines user satisfaction. The authors of our reading attribute this problem to the failure to set clear usability criteria at the outset.
- The *direct manipulation interface*, employing a mouse to point at objects and select operations, is *not the best for every situation.* The authors note that slavish adherence to one metaphor is a problem if it prevents us from capitalizing on features outside the domain of the metaphor. Writing a few years later, Hutchins, Hollan, and Norman (1986) identify and analyze the features that led direct manipulation interfaces to succeed, but also note weaknesses: Repetitive actions are difficult to indicate directly. To use variables generally requires a symbolic description. High precision may be difficult to obtain directly. To access one item among thousands of similar items may be much easier if you can search by name than if you must find and point to it.

Despite these problems, the graphical user interface eventually prevailed in the marketplace (see Chapters 5 and 6). The Apple Macintosh, not the Star, reaped the benefits. Yet Apple, too, failed in its first attempt.

THE APPLE LISA

It is said that Steven Jobs, Apple's founder and chairman, visited Xerox PARC in 1979 and was incredibly impressed with the bit-mapped displays and the applications running on them (Perry and Wallich, 1985, p. 72). Early in 1983, Apple introduced the Lisa, a product with an interface similar to the Star (but see Marcus, 1984, for a discussion of some fine distinctions), but with some important differences:

- The Star was much more ambitious than the Lisa in networking and distributed computing.
- At roughly $10,000, the Lisa was somewhat less expensive than the Star.
- The Lisa was positioned between an office system and a personal productivity tool, to be used by individuals for such tasks as editing documents, building forecasting models with spreadsheets, and managing small data bases.

Williams (1983) and Apple (1983 video) describe the design and interface of Lisa. Morgan, Williams, and Lemmons (1983) discusses the design process. In contrast to most of the glowing accounts of Lisa's usability, Carroll and Mazur (1986) is an illuminating observational study of users learning the Lisa that shows that even a highly crafted interface can have significant weaknesses.

THE APPLE MACINTOSH

Because of its cost, its confused product positioning, and its inadequate application base, the Lisa was not successful and was withdrawn within three years. Then, in January of 1984, Apple introduced the Macintosh at a price of approximately $2,500. In about a year, its success was clear. Why, in contrast to the Star and the Lisa, did the Macintosh succeed?

- The Mac *did not need to trailblaze.* The Star and Lisa had prepared the ground in terms of the interface. IBM and other companies had created a market for professional personal computers.
- Since the Mac was in *a sense a second-generation Lisa,* Apple had the opportunity to learn from experience and eliminate many bugs (Tognazzini, 1986). The interface improved along the road from Star to Lisa to Mac.
- The product was *very aggressively priced.*
- Although product functionality was limited at first, a partially open architecture, a *powerful developer's toolkit* (Apple, 1985), and an aggressive program of third-party software development soon led to widespread availability of significant software applications. Apple worked hard to encourage developers to adhere to the overall interface concepts by providing them with guidelines, tools, and feedback when they strayed.
- Its excellent graphics and the availability of a reasonably priced 300 dot per inch laser printer (the Laserwriter) allowed the Macintosh to achieve early domination in the emerging market of *desktop publishing.* Again, Apple's timing was better than Xerox's. Xerox had done the pioneering work on the computer-controlled laser printer, but Apple was able to commercialize a high-quality implementation at a reasonable price.
- Apple was able to utilize successful *experience in the personal computer business.* Apple had marketing expertise, distribution channels, and experience in computer sales and support.

Williams (1984), Webster (1984), and Jennings (1984) describe the design and the interface of the Macintosh. Lemmons (1984), Markoff and Shapiro (1984), and Guterl (1984) discuss the design process.

CONCLUSION

The best interface design work in the world may be wasted if it is not coupled with a timely product that offers significant functionality at a reasonable price, skillfully marketed to appropriate customers.

REFERENCES

Note: A ● before a reference indicates a reading.

Alexander, R. C., and Smith, D. K. (1988). *Fumbling the Future: The Story of Xerox & Personal Computing.* Morrow.

Apple Computer Company (1985). *Inside Macintosh,* Volumes I, II, III. Addison-Wesley.

Baecker, R., and Buxton, W. (Eds.) (1987). *Readings in Human-Computer Interaction: A Multidisciplinary Approach.* Morgan Kaufmann.

Bewley, W., Roberts, T., Schroit, D., and Verplank, W. (1983). Human Factors Testing in the Design of Xerox's 8010 "Star" Office Workstation. *Proc. CHI '83,* 72–77.

Carroll, J., and Mazur, S. (1986). Lisa Learning. *IEEE Computer* 19(10), 35–49.

Guterl, F. (1984). Design Case History: Apple's Macintosh. *IEEE Spectrum,* December, 34–43.

Hammer, M. (1984). The OA Mirage. *Datamation,* February, 36–46.

Harslem, E., and Nelson, L.(1982). A Retrospective on the Development of Star. *Proc. 6th International Conference on Software Engineering,* IEEE Computer Society, 377–383.

Hutchins, E., Hollan, J., and Norman, D. (1986). Direct Manipulation Interfaces. In Norman, D., and Draper, S. (Eds.), *User Centered System Design,* Lawrence Erlbaum Associates, 118–123.

Jennings, M. (1984). Evaluating the Macintosh Finder. *Byte,* December, A94–A101.

● Johnson, J., Roberts, T, Verplank, W., Smith, D., Irby, C., Beard, M., and Mackey, K. (1989). The Xerox Star: A Retrospective. *IEEE Computer* 22(9), 11–29.

Johnsson, R., and Wick, J. (1982). An Overview of the Mesa Processor Architecture. *SIG Plan Notices,* 4, 17

Lauer, H., and Satterthwaite, E. (1979). The Impact of Mesa on System Design. *Proceedings of the 4th International Conference of Software Engineering.* IEEE Computer Society.

Lemmons, P. (1984). An Interview: The Macintosh Design Team. *Byte,* February, 58–80.

Lipkie, D., Evans, S., Newlin, J., and Weisman, R. (1982). Star Graphics: An Object-Oriented Implementation. *Computer Graphics* 16(3), 115–124.

Marcus, A. (1984). Corporate Identity for Iconic Interface Design: The Graphic Design Perspective. *IEEE Computer Graphics and Applications* 4(12), 24–32.

Markoff, J., and Shapiro, E. (1984). Macintosh's Other Designers. *Byte,* August, 347–356.

Miller, L., and Johnson, J. (1995). The Star User Interface: A Successful User Interface Design. In Rudisill, M., Lewis, C., Polson, P., and McKay, T. (Eds.) (1995), *Human-Computer Interface Design: Success Cases, Emerging Methods, and Real-World Context,* Morgan Kaufmann.

Morgan, C., Williams, G., and Lemmons, P. (1983). An Interview with Wayne Rosing, Bruce Daniels, and Larry Tesler: A Behind-the-Scenes Look at the Development of Apple's Lisa. *Byte,* February, 90–114.

Pake, G. (1985). Research at Xerox PARC: A Founder's Assessment. *IEEE Spectrum* 22(10), 54–61.

Perry, T., and Wallich, P. (1985). Inside the PARC: The Information Architects. *IEEE Spectrum* 22(10), 62–75.

Purvy, R., Farrell, J., and Klose, P. (1983). The Design of Star's Records Processing: Data Processing for the Noncomputer Professional. *ACM Transactions on Office Automation Systems* 1(1), 3–24.

Roberts, T., and Moran, T. (1983). The Evaluation of Computer Text Editors: Methodology and Experimental Results. *Communications of the ACM* 26(4), 265–283.

Rosenberg, J., and Moran, T. (1984). Generic Commands. *Proc. Interact '84.* Elsevier (North-Holland), 360–364.

Smith, D., Harslem, E., Irby, C., and Kimball, R. (1982). The Star User Interface: An Overview. *Proc. AFIPS 1982 National Computer Conference* 50, 515–528.

Smith, D., Irby, C., Kimball, R., Verplank, W., and Harslem, E. (1982). Designing the Star User Interface. *Byte* 7(4), April, 242–282.

Tesler, L. (1981). The Smalltalk Environment. *Byte*, August, 90–147.

Thacker, C., McCreight, E., Lampson, B., Sproull, R., and Boggs, D. (1982). Alto: A Personal Computer. In Siewiorek, D., Bell, D., and Newell, A. (Eds.), *Computer Structures: Principles and Examples*, McGraw-Hill.

Tognazzini, B. (1986). Usability Testing in the Real World. *Proc. CHI '86*, ACM, 212–215.

Verplank, W. (1988). Graphic Challenges in Designing Object-oriented User Interfaces. In Helander, M. (Ed.) (1988), *Handbook of Human-Computer Interaction*, North-Holland, 365–376.

Webster, B. (1984). The Macintosh: System Review. *Byte*, August, 238–251.

Williams, G. (1983). The Lisa Computer System. *Byte*, February, 33–50.

Williams, G. (1984). The Apple Macintosh Computer. *Byte*, February, 30–54.

VIDEOS

Apple Corp. (1983). Lisa. *ACM SIGGRAPH Video Review* 8.

Smith, D., and Irby, C. (1990). Xerox Star User Interface. *ACM SIGGRAPH Video Review* 56. Originally filmed in 1981, published in 1990.

The Xerox Star: A Retrospective

Jeff Johnson and Teresa L. Roberts, US West Advanced Technologies
William Verplank, IDTwo
David C. Smith, Cognition, Inc.
Charles H. Irby and Marian Beard, Metaphor Computer Systems
Kevin Mackey, Xerox

The Xerox Star has significantly affected the computer industry. In this retrospective, several of Star's designers describe its important features, antecedents, design and development, evolution, and some lessons learned.

Xerox introduced the 8010 "Star" Information System in April of 1981. That introduction was an important event in the history of personal computing because it changed notions of how interactive systems should be designed. Several of Star's designers, some of us responsible for the original design and others for recent improvements, describe in this article where Star came from, what is distinctive about it, and how the original design has changed. In doing so, we hope to correct some misconceptions about Star that we have seen in the trade press and to relate some of what we have learned from designing it.

For brevity, we use the name "Star" here to refer to both Star and its successor, ViewPoint. "ViewPoint" refers exclusively to the current product.

What Star is

Star was designed as an office automation system. The idea was that professionals in a business or organization would have workstations on their desks and would use them to produce, retrieve, distribute, and organize documentation, presentations, memos, and reports. All of the workstations in an organization would be connected via Ethernet and would share access to file servers, printers, etc.

Star's designers assumed that the target users were interested in getting their work done and not at all interested in computers. Therefore, an important design goal was to make the "computer" as invisible to users as possible. The applications included in the system were those that office professionals would supposedly need: documents, business graphics, tables, personal databases, and electronic mail. The set was fixed, always loaded, and automatically associated with data files, eliminating the need to obtain, install, and start the right application for a given task or data file. Users could focus on their work, oblivious to concepts like software, operating systems, applications, and programs.

Another important assumption was that Star's users would be casual, occasional users rather than people who spent most of their time at the machine. This assumption led to the goal of having Star be easy to learn and remember.

When Star was introduced in 1981, its bitmapped screen, windows, mouse-driven interface, and icons were readily apparent features that clearly distinguished it from other computers. Soon, however, others adopted these features. Today, windows, mice, and icons are more common. However, Star's clean, consistent user interface has much more to do with its details than with its gross features. We list here the features that we think make Star what it is, categorized according to their level in the system architecture: machine and network, window and file manager, user interface, and document editor.

0018-9162/89/0900-0011$01.00

Machine and network level. Important aspects of Star can be found in the lowest levels of its architecture: the machine and the network of which it is a part.

Distributed, personal computing. Though currently available in a stand-alone configuration, Star was designed primarily to operate in a distributed computing environment. This approach combines the advantages and avoids the disadvantages of the two other primary approaches to interactive computing: time-shared systems and stand-alone personal computers.

Time-shared systems, dominant through the sixties and seventies, allow sharing of expensive resources like printers and large data stores among many users and help assure the consistency of data that many must use. Timesharing has the disadvantages that all users depend upon the continued functioning of the central computer and that system response degrades as the number of users increases.

Personal computers, which have replaced timesharing as the primary mode of interactive computing, have the advantage, as one Xerox researcher put it, "of not being faster at night." Also, a collection of personal computers is more reliable than are terminals connected to a centralized computer: system problems are less apt to cause a total stoppage of work. The disadvantages of PCs, of course, are the converse of the advantages of timesharing. Companies that use stand-alone PCs usually see a proliferation of printers, inconsistent databases, and nonexchangeable data.

The solution, pioneered by researchers at Xerox (see "History of Star development" below) and embodied in Star, is to connect personal workstations with a local area network and to attach shared resources (file servers, database servers, printers) to that same network.

Mouse. An interactive computer system must provide a way for users to indicate which operations they want and what data they want those operations to be performed on. Users of early interactive systems specified operations and operands via commands and data descriptors (such as text line numbers). As video display terminals became common, it became clear that it was often better for users to specify operands — and sometimes operations — by pointing to them on the screen. It also became clear that graphic applications should not be controlled solely with a keyboard. In the sixties and seventies, people invented many different pointing devices: the light pen, the trackball, the joystick, cursor keys, the digitizing tablet, the touch screen, and the mouse.

Like other pointing devices, the mouse allows easy selection of objects and triggering of sensitive areas on the screen. The mouse differs from touch screens, light pens, and digitizing pads in that it is a relative pointing device: the movement of the pointer on the screen depends upon mouse movement rather than position. Unlike light pens, joysticks, and digitizing pads, the mouse (and the corresponding pointer on the screen) stays put when the user lets go of it.

To achieve satisfactory mouse-tracking performance, Star handles the mouse at a very low level. In some workstations, the window system handles mouse tracking, with the result that the mouse pointer often jerks around the screen and may even freeze for seconds at a time, depending upon what else the system is doing. The mouse is a hand-eye coordination device, so if the pointer lags, users just keep moving the mouse. When the system catches up, the mouse moves beyond the user's target. We at Xerox considered this unacceptable.

Star uses a two-button mouse, in contrast with the one-button mouse used by Apple and the three-button mouse used by most other vendors. Though predecessors of Star developed at Xerox Palo Alto Research Center (see "History of Star development" below) used a three-button mouse, Star's designers wanted to reduce the number of buttons to alleviate confusion over which button did what. Why stop at two buttons instead of reducing the number to one, as Apple did? Because studies of users editing text and other material showed that a one-button mouse eliminated button-confusion errors only at the cost of increasing selection errors to unacceptable levels.

Bitmapped display. Until recently, most video display terminals were character-mapped. Such displays enable vast savings in display memory, which, when memory was expensive, made terminals more affordable.

In the seventies, researchers at Xerox PARC decided that memory would get cheaper eventually and that a bitmapped screen was worth the cost anyway. They thus developed the Alto, which had a screen 8.5 inches wide and 10.5 inches tall and an instruction set specially designed for manipulating display memory.

Like the Alto, Star's display has a resolution of 72 pixels per inch. The number 72 was chosen for two reasons. First, there are 72 printer's points per inch, so 72 pixels per inch allows for a smooth interface with the world of typesetting and typography. Second, 72 pixels per inch is a high enough resolution for on-screen legibility of a wide range of graphics and character sizes (down to about eight points — see Figure 1), but not so high as to cause an onerous memory burden, which a screen that matched the 300 dots-per-inch printer resolution would have. Unlike many PC graphic displays, the pixel size and density are the same horizontally and vertically, which simplifies the display software and improves image quality.

Window and file manager level. Just above Star's operating system (not discussed here) are facilities upon which its distinctive user interface rests.

Windows. Systems now commonly allow several programs to display information simultaneously in separate areas of the screen, rather than each taking up the entire display. Star was the first commercial system to provide this capability.

Some windowing systems allow windows to overlap each other. Other systems don't; the system adjusts the size and position of windows as they are opened and closed. Star's windowing system could overlap windows and often did (for example, property sheets appeared in windows overlapping application windows). However, early testing revealed that users spent a lot of time adjusting windows, usually so they did not overlap. Because of this, and because Star's 17-inch screen reduced the need for overlapping windows, the designers decided to constrain application windows to not overlap. However, some situations benefit from overlapping application windows. This, added to a subsequent reduction in the standard screen size to 15 inches (with a 19-inch screen optional), resulted in optional constraints for ViewPoint, Star's successor, with the default setting allowing application windows to overlap one another.

Integrated applications. "Integrated" has become a buzzword used to describe many things. Here, it means that text, graphics, tables, and mathematical formulas are all edited inside documents. In many other systems, different types of content are edited in separate application

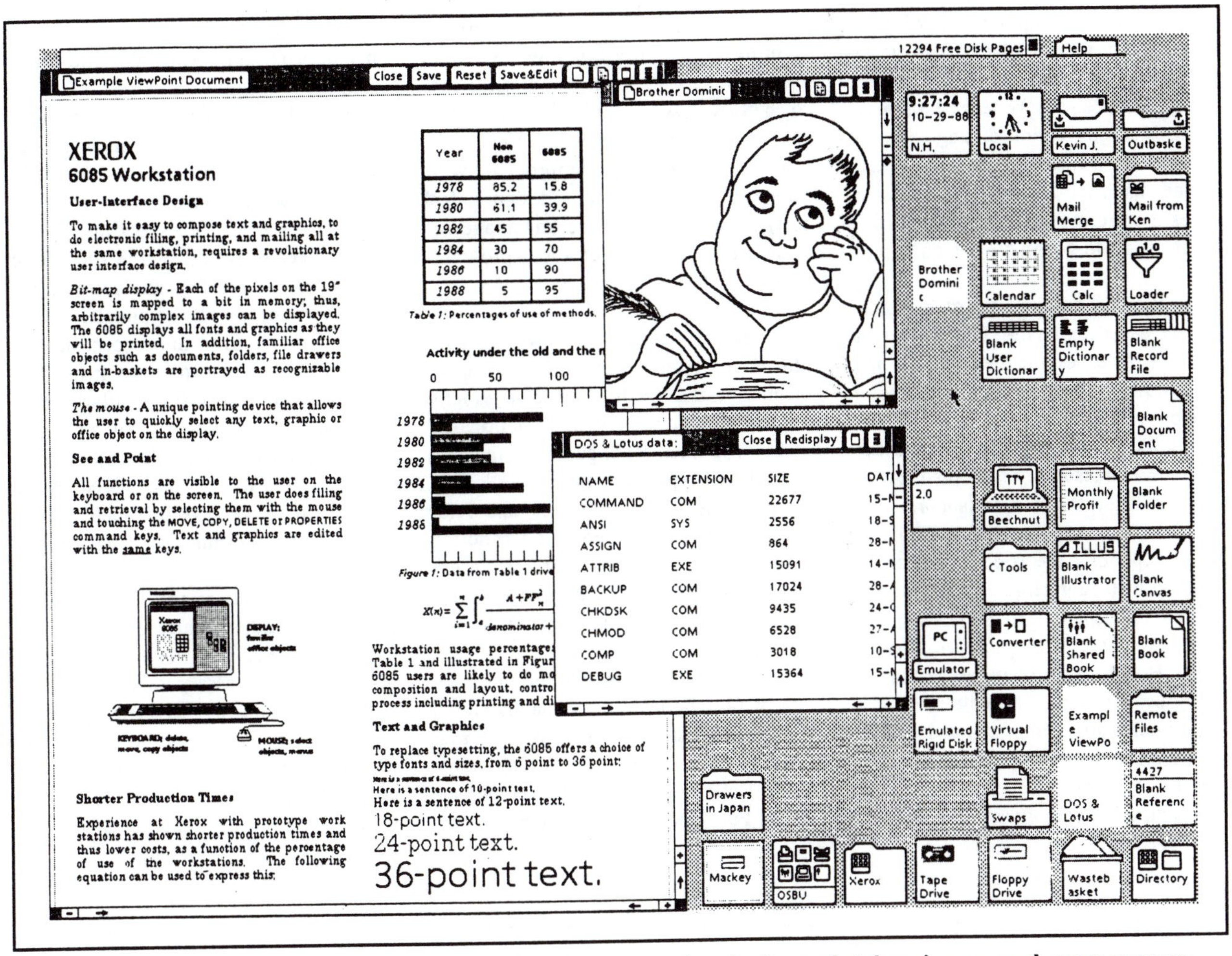

Figure 1. ViewPoint screen image. Star's bitmapped display, once unique in the marketplace, is now much more common. Such a display permits WYSIWYG editing, display of proportionally spaced fonts, integrated text and graphics, and graphical user interfaces.

windows and then cut and pasted together. For example, a MacDraw drawing put into a Microsoft Word or Aldus Pagemaker document can no longer be edited; rather, the original must be re-edited with MacDraw and then substituted for the old drawing in the document.

Not even Star is fully integrated in the sense used here. For example, though the original structured graphics editor, the new one (see "History of Star development" below), and the table and formula editors all operate inside text files, spreadsheets and freehand drawings are currently edited in separate application windows and transferred into documents, where they are no longer fully editable.

User-interface level. Star's user interface is its most outstanding feature. In this section we discuss important aspects of the interface in detail.

Desktop metaphor. Star, unlike all conventional systems and many window- and mouse-based ones, uses an analogy with real offices to make the system easy to learn. This analogy is called "the Desktop metaphor." To quote from an early article about Star:

> Every user's initial view of Star is the Desktop, which resembles the top of an office desk, together with surrounding furniture and equipment. It represents a working environment, where current projects and accessible resources reside. On the screen are displayed pictures of familiar office objects, such as documents, folders, file drawers, in-baskets, and out-baskets. These objects are displayed as small pictures, or icons.
>
> The Desktop is the principal Star technique for realizing the physical office metaphor. The icons on it are visible, concrete embodiments of the corresponding physical objects. Star users are encouraged to think of the objects on the Desktop in physical terms. You can move the icons around to arrange your Desktop as you wish. (Messy Desktops are certainly possible, just as in real life.) You can leave documents on your Desktop indefinitely, just as on a real desk, or you can file them away.[1]

Having windows and a mouse does not make a system an embodiment of the Desktop metaphor. In a Desktop metaphor system, users deal mainly with data files, oblivious to the existence of programs. They do not "invoke a text editor," they "open a document." The system knows the type of each file and notifies the relevant application program when one is opened.

Most systems, including windowed ones, use a Tools metaphor, in which users deal mainly with applications as tools. Users start one or more application programs (such as a word processor or spreadsheet), then specify one or more data files to edit with each. Such systems do not explicitly associate applications with data files. Users bear the burden of doing that— and of remembering not to try to edit a spreadsheet file with the text editor or vice versa. User convention distinguishes different kinds of files, usually with filename extensions (such as memo.txt). Star relieves users of the need to keep track of which data file goes with which application.

SunView is an example of a window system based upon the Tools metaphor rather than the Desktop metaphor. Its users see a collection of application program windows, each used to edit certain files. Smalltalk-80, Cedar, and various Lisp environments also use the Tools metaphor rather than the Desktop metaphor.

This is not to say that the Desktop metaphor is superior to the Tools metaphor. The Desktop metaphor targets office automation and publishing. It might not suit other applications (such as software development). However, we could argue that orienting users toward their data rather than toward application programs and employing analogies with the physical world are useful techniques in any domain.

The disadvantage of assigning data files to applications is that users sometimes want to operate on a file with a program other than its "assigned" application. Such cases must be handled in Star in an ad hoc way, whereas systems like Unix allow you to run almost any file through a wide variety of programs. Star's designers feel that, for its audience, the advantages of allowing users to forget about programs outweighs this disadvantage.

Generic commands. One way to simplify a computer system is to reduce the number of commands. Star achieves simplicity without sacrificing functionality by having a small set of generic commands apply to all types of data: Move, Copy, Open, Delete, Show Properties, and Same (Copy Properties). Dedicated function keys on Star's keyboard invoke these commands. Each type of data object interprets a generic command in a way appropriate for it.

Such an approach avoids the proliferation of object-specific commands and/or command modifiers found in most systems, such as Delete Character, Delete Word, Delete Line, Delete Paragraph, and Delete File. Command modifiers are necessary in systems in which selection is only approximate. Consider the many systems in which the object of a command is specified by a combination of the cursor location and the command modifier. For example, Delete Word means "delete the word that the cursor is on."

Modifiers are unnecessary in Star because exact selection of the objects of commands is easy. In many systems, the large number of object-specific commands is made even more confusing by using single-word synonyms instead of command modifiers for similar operations on different objects. For example, depending upon whether the object of the command is a file or text, the command used might be Remove or Delete, Duplicate or Copy, and Find or Search, respectively.

Careful choice of the generic commands can further reduce the number of commands required. For example, you might think it necessary to have a generic command Print for printing various things. Having Print apply to all data objects would avoid the trap that some systems fall into of having separate commands for printing documents, spread-

Direct manipulation

Jeff Johnson and Teresa L. Roberts

Star's Desktop metaphor is based upon the more general principle of "direct manipulation."[1,2] What, exactly, is direct manipulation? Consider the following passage from a description of Apple's Macintosh:

> Imagine driving a car that has no steering wheel, accelerator, brake pedal, turn signal lever, or gear selector. In place of all the familiar manual controls, you have only a typewriter keyboard.
>
> Anytime you want to turn a corner, change lanes, slow down, speed up, honk your horn, or back up, you have to type a command sequence on the keyboard. Unfortunately, the car can't understand English sentences. Instead, you must hold down a special key with one finger and type in some letters and numbers, such as "S20:TL:A35," which means, "Slow to 20, turn left, and accelerate to 35."
>
> No doubt you could learn to drive such a car if you had sufficient motivation and determination. But why bother, when so many cars use familiar controls? Most people wouldn't.[3]

Actually, it isn't familiarity that makes real cars easier to drive than the hypothetical "computer car" would be — cars are certainly not familiar to those who are just learning to drive them. What makes real cars easier to drive is the directness of their controls. Real cars have distinct interfaces to the speed control (the accelerator pedal), the direction control (the steering wheel), the gears (the gearshift handle), the radio (several knobs and buttons), etc. Each interface is specially designed for controlling its respective function. In contrast, the hypothetical "computer-car" has only one control: a keyboard.

Direct manipulation requires that distinct functions be invoked and controlled in spatially distinct locations, in ways that are specific and appropriate for the particular function being controlled. Data objects should be selected and operated on by simulated physical contact rather than by abstract verbal reference: "*That* one" rather than "The one in row 6." Continuous functions (such as screen brightness and color saturation) should be controlled via continuous controls such as sliders, knobs, and dials. Discrete functions (such as character font family) should be controlled via discrete means such as commands, multiposition switches, or menus. In effect, a direct manipulation system has a different input channel for every function the user can have it perform.

Conventional interfaces are indirect in that there is a single, general interface to all functionality (such as a keyboard and command language or a menu). In other words, there is only one input channel for all kinds of input; different kinds of input are distinguished linguistically, rather than spatially.

Having a different interface to each function may seem to contradict the goal of having a consistent interface, but in fact does not. Similar functions should indeed have similar user interfaces across contexts. Direct manipulation requires, however, that different functions should have distinct interfaces, just as a car has distinct interfaces to its various functions.

Directness versus indirectness is not a simple dichotomy: we can speak of degrees of directness. Consider a graphics editor for creating illustrations. In the following sequence of interfaces, each contains all of the indirection of the previous one and adds a new level:

sheets, illustrations, directories, etc., but it is nonetheless unnecessary. In Star, users simply Copy to a printer icon whatever they want to print. Similarly, the Move command is used to invoke Send Mail by moving a document to the out-basket.

Of course, not everything can be done via generic commands. Some operations are object-specific. For example, a word might use italics, but italics are meaningless for a triangle. In Star, object-specific operations are provided via selection-dependent "soft" function keys and via menus attached to application windows.

Direct manipulation and graphical user interface. Traditional computer systems require users to remember and type a great deal just to control the system. This impedes learning and retention, especially by casual users. Star's designers favored an approach emphasizing recognition over recall, seeing and pointing over remembering and typing. This suggested using menus rather than commands. However, the designers wanted to go beyond a conventional menu-based approach. They wanted users to feel that they are manipulating data directly, rather than issuing commands to the system to do it. Star's designers also wanted to exploit the tremendous communication possibilities of the display. They wanted to move away from strictly verbal communication. Therefore, they based the system heavily upon principles that are now known as direct manipulation and graphical control.

Star users control the system by manipulating graphical elements on the screen, elements that represent the state of the system and data created by users. The system does not distinguish between input and output. Anything displayed (output) by the system can be pointed to and acted upon by the user (input). When Star displays a directory, it (unlike MS-DOS and Unix) is not displaying a list of the names of the files in the directory, it is displaying the files themselves so that the user can manipulate them. Users of this type of system have the feeling that they are operating upon the data directly, rather than through an agent — like fetching a book from a library shelf yourself rather than asking someone to do it for you.

A related principle is that the state of the system always shows in the display. Nothing happens "behind the user's back." You needn't fiddle with the system to understand what's going on; you can understand by inspection.

One of Star's designers wrote

> When everything in a computer system is visible on the screen, the display becomes reality. Objects and actions can be understood purely in terms of their effects upon the display. This vastly simplifies understanding and reduces learning time.[2]

An example of this philosophy is the fact that, unlike many window-based computer systems (even some developed at Xerox), Star has no hidden menus — all available menus are marked with menu buttons.

For a more detailed explanation of direct manipulation, see the sidebar.

Icons and iconic file management. Computer users often have difficulty managing their files. Before Star existed, a secretary at Xerox complained that she couldn't keep track of the files on her disk. An inspection of her system revealed files named memo, memo1, memo071479, letter, etc. Naming things to keep track of

---

(1) The most direct interface for moving a circle would have the user point directly at the screen and pull the circle to its new location.

(2) Introducing a mouse, bitpad, or joystick adds one level of indirection: moving the mouse, bitpad stylus, or joystick on the desk moves the pointer on the screen. Some users have difficulty with this indirection.

(3) Arrow keys introduce another level — and another kind — of indirection: the keystroke movements required to move the screen pointer, and hence the circle, do not resemble the desired movement of the circle.

(4) Typing a command to move the circle is still more indirect. Though typing a command involves movements (keystrokes), we are inclined to think of the movements as incidental; they could just as well be speech. Thus, it is no longer a matter of movement — similar or not — in one place corresponding to movement in another place; rather, it is the syntax and semantics of the command that determine what happens.

Differences in directness can be very subtle. Contrast the following two methods of changing the size of a window on the display:

(1) Grabbing onto a corner of the window and stretching the window to the desired size.

(2) Clicking on the desired window, choosing Resize from a command pull-down menu, then pointing to where the window's new border is to be moved.

It is sometimes said that mouse-driven user interfaces are direct while keyboard user interfaces are indirect. Note, however, that both methods 1 and 2 above use a mouse, yet method 2 is less direct than method 1.

The above examples involve an illustration tool and a window manager. Such applications are actually in a special category with respect to direct manipulation, because the images on the screen are what the application is intended to manipulate. The purpose of many applications (such as databases, command and control, and file management) is to allow users to manipulate information that is only represented on the screen in some way (for example, pictorially or textually). Such applications therefore have one inherent level of indirection.

Systems having direct-manipulation user interfaces encourage users to think of them as tools rather than as assistants, agents, or coworkers. Natural-language user interfaces, which are inherently indirect, encourage the reverse. As direct-manipulation interfaces become more prevalent and as progress is made in natural-language understanding and generation, it will be interesting to see which way users prefer to think about their computers.

References

1. E. Hutchins, J. Hollan, and D.A. Norman, "Direct Manipulation Interfaces," in *User-Centered System Design*, D.A. Norman and S. Draper, eds., Erlbaum Associates, Hillsdale, New Jersey, 1986, pp. 87-124.

2. B. Shneiderman, "Direct Manipulation: A Step Beyond Programming Languages," *Computer*, Vol. 16, No. 8, Aug. 1983, pp. 57-68.

3. L. Poole, "A Tour of the Mac Desktop," *MacWorld*, Vol. 1, No. 1, 1984, pp. 16-21.

them is bothersome enough for programmers, but completely unnatural for most people.

Star alleviates this problem partly by representing data files with pictures of office objects called icons. Every application data file in the system has an icon representing it. Each type of file has a characteristic icon shape. If a user is looking for a spreadsheet, his or her eye can skip over mailboxes, printers, text documents, etc.

Furthermore, Star allows users to organize files spatially rather than by distinctive naming. Systems having hierarchical directories, such as Unix and MS-DOS, provide an abstract sort of "spatial" file organization, but Star's approach is concrete. Files can be kept together by putting them into a folder or simply by clumping them together on the Desktop, which models how people organize their physical worlds. Since data files are represented by icons, and files are distinguished by location and specified by selection rather than by name, users can use names like memo, memo1, letter, etc., without losing track of their files as easily as they would with most systems.

As bitmap-, window-, and mouse-based systems have become more common, the use of the term "icon" has widened to refer to any nontextual symbol on the display. In standard English, "icon" is a term for religious statues or pictures believed to contain some of the powers of the deities they represent. It would be more consistent with its normal meaning if "icon" were reserved for objects having behavioral and intrinsic properties. Most graphical symbols and labels on computer screens are therefore not icons. In Star, only representations of files on the Desktop and in folders, mailboxes, and file drawers are called icons.

Few modes. A system has modes if user actions differ in effects or availability in different situations. Tesler has argued that modes in interactive computer systems are undesirable because they restrict the functions available at any given point and force users to keep track of the system's state to know what effect their actions will have.[3] Though modes can be helpful in guiding users through unfamiliar procedures or for handling exceptional activities, they should be used sparingly and carefully.

Star avoids modes in several ways. One is the extensive use of generic commands (see above), which drastically reduces the number of commands needed. This, in turn, means that designers need not assign double-duty (that is, different meanings in different modes) to physical controls.

A second way is by allowing applications to operate simultaneously. When using one program (such as a document editor), users are not in a mode that prevents them from using the capabilities of other programs (such as the desktop manager).

A third way Star avoids modes is by using a noun-verb command syntax. Users select an operand (such as a file, a word, or a table), then invoke a command. In conventional systems, arguments follow commands, either on a command line or in response to prompts. Whether a system uses noun-verb or verb-noun syntax has a lot to do with how moded it is. In a noun-verb system such as Star, selecting an object prior to choosing a command does not put the system into a mode. Users can decide not to invoke the command without having to "escape out" of anything or can select a different object to operate on.

Though Star avoids modes, it is not completely modeless. For example, the Move and Copy commands require two arguments: the object to be moved and the final destination. Though less moded ways to design Move and Copy exist, these functions currently require the user to select the object, press the Move or Copy key, then indicate the destination using the mouse. While Star waits for the user to point to a destination, it is in Move or Copy mode, precluding other uses of the mouse. These modes are relatively harmless, however, because (1) the shape of the cursor clearly indicates the state of the system and (2) the user enters and exits them in the course of carrying out a single mental plan, making it unlikely that the system will be in the "wrong" mode when the user begins his or her next action.

Objects have properties. Properties allow objects of the same type to vary in appearance, layout, and behavior. For example, files have a Name property, characters have a Font family property, and paragraphs have a Justified property. Properties may have different types of values: the Name property of a file is a text string; the Size property of a character might be a number or a choice from a menu; the Justified property of a paragraph is either "on" or "off." In Star, properties are displayed and changed in graphical forms called property sheets.

Property-based systems are rare. Most computer systems, even today, allow users to set parameters for the duration of an interactive session or for the duration of a command, but not for particular data objects. For example, headings in Wordstar documents do not "remember" whether they are centered or not; whether a line is centered is determined by how the program was set when the line was typed. Similarly, directories in Unix do not "remember" whether files are to be listed in alphabetical or temporal order; users must respecify which display order they want every time they invoke the ls command.

Progressive disclosure. It has been said that "computers promise the fountains of utopia, but only deliver a flood of information."[4] Indeed, many computer systems overwhelm their users with choices, commands to remember, and poorly organized output, much of it irrelevant to what the user is trying to do. They make no presumptions about what the user wants. Thus, they are designed as if all possible user actions were equally likely and as if all information generated by the system were of equal interest to the user. Some systems diminish the problem somewhat by providing default settings of parameters to simplify tasks expected to be common.

Star goes further towards alleviating this problem by applying a principle called "progressive disclosure." Progressive disclosure dictates that detail be hidden from users until they ask or need to see it. Thus, Star not only provides default settings, it hides settings that users are unlikely to change until users indicate that they want to change them. Implicit in this design are assumptions about which properties will be less frequently altered.

One place progressive disclosure is used is in property sheets. Some objects have a large number of properties, many of which are relevant only when other properties have certain values (see Figure 2). For example, on the page layout property sheet, there is no reason to display all of the properties for specifying running header content and position unless the user actually specifies that the document will have running headers.

Another example of progressive disclosure is the fact that property displays in Star are temporary, displayed on demand. In some systems, the properties of the current selection are displayed at all times, through codes embedded in the text or in an area of the screen reserved for that purpose, even though the user usually doesn't care.

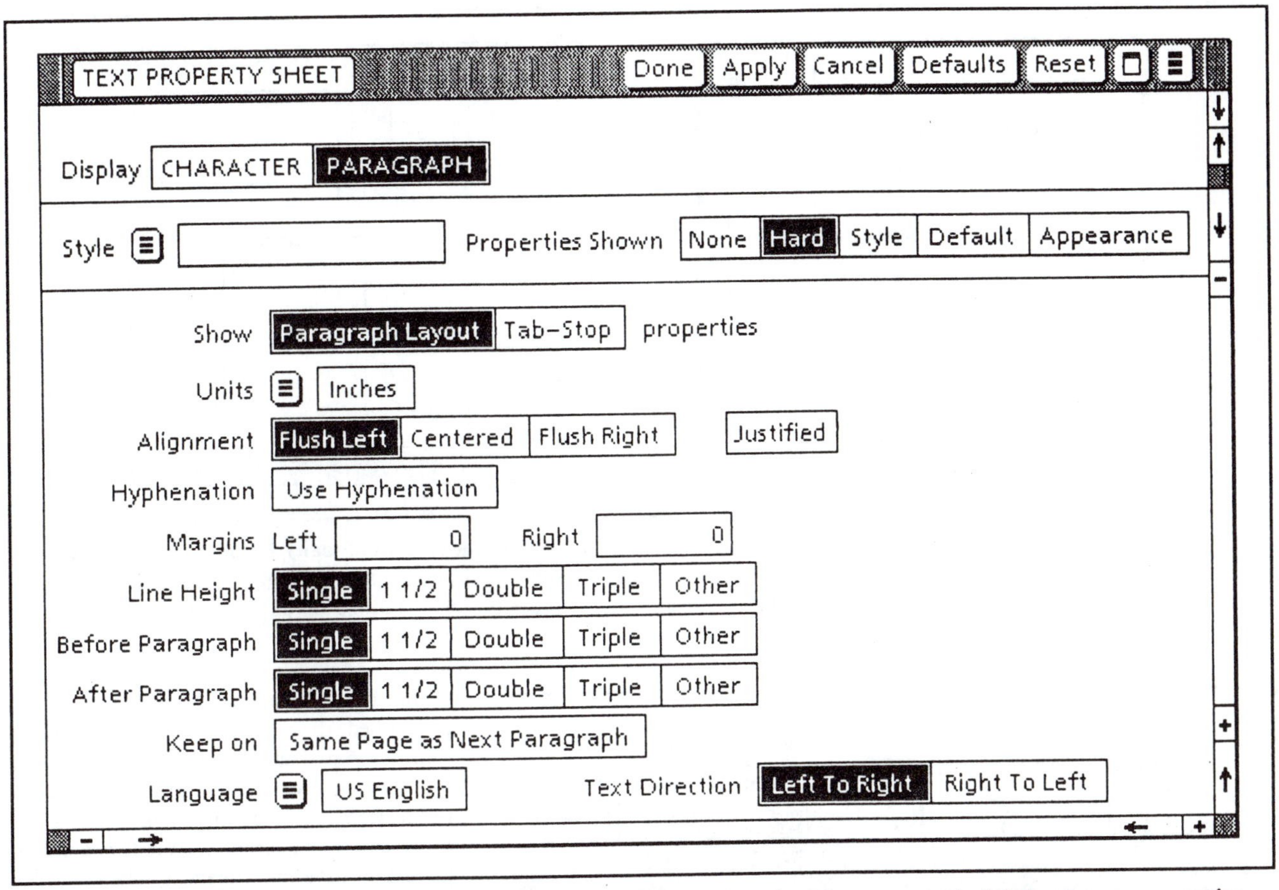

Figure 2. Progressive disclosure. Star's property sheets, like the rest of the interface, use a principle known as progressive disclosure to avoid overwhelming users with information. Usually, users don't need to see an object's properties: they only need to see and perhaps change its assigned style. Users see an object's properties only upon request. Also, even when a user sets a property sheet to show an object's properties, as shown here, some information remains hidden until the user asks to see it. For example, there is no need to clutter the property sheet here with boxes for entering numbers for "Other" values of Line Height, Spacing Before Paragraph, or Spacing After Paragraph until the user actually sets the property to "Other."

A highly refined manifestation of progressive disclosure recently added to ViewPoint is *styles*, which allows users to regard document content (such as a paragraph) as having a single style rule instead of a large number of properties. Thus, styles hide needless detail from users.

Consistency. Because Star and all of its applications were designed and developed in-house, its designers had more control over its user interface than is usually the case with computer systems. Because the designers paid close attention to detail, they achieved a very high degree of consistency. The left mouse button always selects; the right always extends the selection. Mouse-sensitive areas always give feedback when the left button goes down, but never take effect until the button comes up.

Emphasis on good graphic and screen design. Windows, icons, and property sheets are useless if users can't easily distinguish them from the background or each other, can't easily see which labels correspond to which objects, or can't cope with the visual clutter. To assure that Star presents information in a maximally perceivable and useful fashion, Xerox hired graphic designers to determine the appearance and placement of screen objects. These designers applied various written and unwritten principles to the design of the window headers and borders, the Desktop background, the command buttons, the pop-up menus, the property sheets, and the Desktop icons. The most important principles are

• The illusion of manipulable objects. One goal, fundamental to the notion of direct manipulation, is to create the illusion of manipulable objects. It should be clear that objects can be selected and how to select them. It should be obvious when they are selected and that the next action will apply to them. Whereas the usual task of graphic designers is to present information for passive viewing, Star's designers had to figure out how to present information for manipulation as well. This shows most clearly in the Desktop icons, with their clear figure/ground relationship: the icons stand by themselves, with self-contained labels. Windows reveal in their borders the "handles" for scrolling, paging, window-specific commands, and pop-up menus.

• Visual order and user focus. One of the most obvious contributions of good graphic design is appropriate visual order and focus on the screen. For example, in-

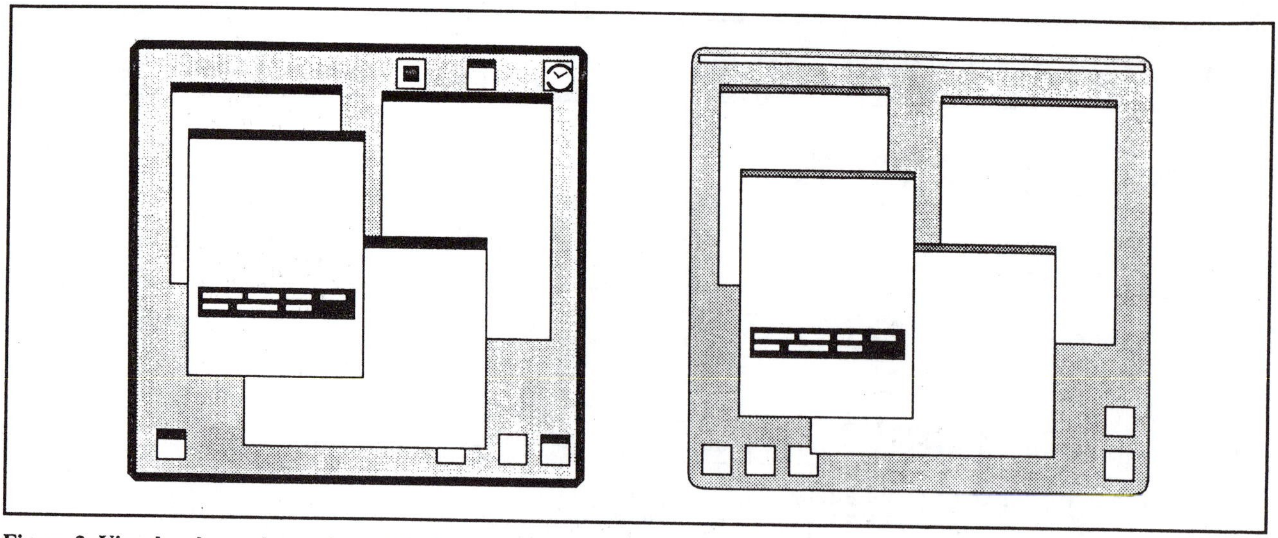

Figure 3. Visual order and user focus. The large amount of contrast present on the screens of many window systems (left screen) makes it difficult to focus on the relevant information. The selection should be the user's main focus: it is the object of the next operation. The right screen shows how Star/ViewPoint's screen design focuses attention on the selection.

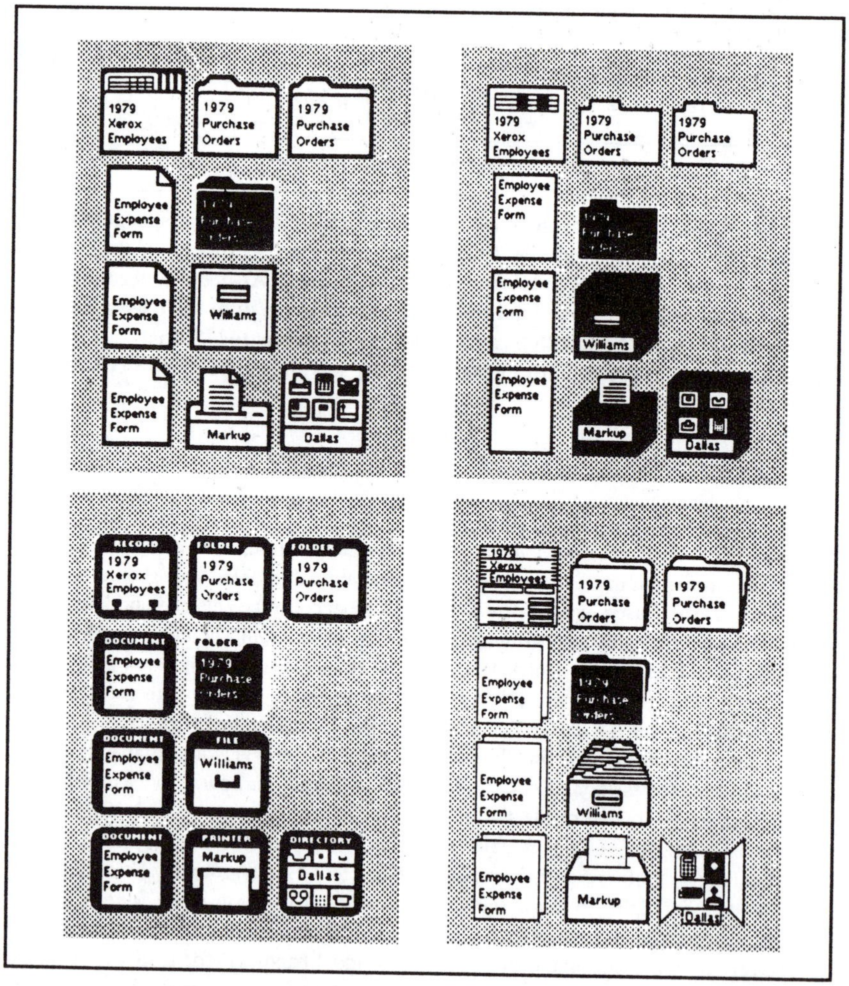

Figure 4. Visual order and user focus. Four candidate sets of icons were designed and tested for Star. A representative sample from each set is shown here. In Star, the icon selected by the user is indicated by inverting its image. Candidate icon sets in which the images are mostly white allow icons to stand out when selected. The set that best satisfies this criterion, the one on the upper left, was chosen.

tensity and contrast, when appropriately applied, draw the user's attention to the most important features of the display.

In some windowing systems, window interiors have the same (dark) color as the Desktop background. Window content should have high intensity relative to the Desktop, to draw attention to what is important on the screen. In Star, window content background is white, both for high contrast and to simulate paper.

Star keeps the amount of black on the screen to a minimum to make the selection stand out (see Figure 3). In most windowing systems, window headers and other areas of the screen are black, making the selection hard to find. This principle is so important that Star's designers made sure that the display hardware could fill the nonaddressable border of the screen with Desktop grey rather than leaving it black as in most systems. Star also uses icon images that turn from mostly white to mostly black when selected (see Figure 4) and allows at most one selection on the screen at a time.

• Revealed structure. Often, the more powerful the program used, the greater the distance between intention and effect. If only effect is displayed and not intention, the user's task of learning the connection is much more difficult. A good graphical interface can make apparent to the user these connections between intention and effect, that is, "revealed structure." For example, there are many ways to determine the position and length of a line of text on a page. It can be done with page margins, paragraph indentations, centering, tabs, blank lines, or spaces. The WYSIWYG, or "what you see is what you get," view of all these would be identical. That would be enough if all that mattered to the user was the final form on paper. But what will happen if characters are inserted? If the line is moved to another page, where will it land? WYSIWYG views are sometimes not enough.

Special views are one method of revealing structure. In Star, documents can show "Structure" and/or "Non-Printing Characters" if desired (see Figure 5). Another convenient means for revealing structure is to make it show up during selection. For example, when a rectangle is selected in a graphics frame, eight control points highlight it, any of which can attach to the cursor during Move or Copy and can land on grid points for precise alignment. The control point highlighting allows a user to distinguish a rectangle from four straight lines; both might produce the same printed effect but would respond differently to editing.

• Consistent and appropriate graphic vocabulary. Property sheets (see Figure 2) present a form-like display for the user to specify detailed property settings and arguments to commands. They were designed with a consistent graphic vocabulary. All of the user's targets are in boxes; unchangeable information such as a property name is not. Mutually exclusive values within choice parameters appear with boxes adjacent. Independent "on/off" or state parameters appear with boxes separated. The current settings are shown inverted. Some of the menus display graphic symbols rather than text. Finally, there are text parameters consisting of a box into which text or numbers can be typed, copied, or moved, and within which text editing functions are available.

• Match the medium. It is in this last principle that the sensitivities of a good graphic designer are most apparent. The goal is to create a consistent quality in the graphics that is appropriate to the product and makes the most of the given medium. Star has a large black and white display. The solutions the graphics designers devised might have been very different had the display had grey-scale or color pixels.

A common problem with raster displays is "jaggies": diagonal lines appearing as staircases. With careful design, jaggies can be avoided, for example, by using only vertical, horizontal, and 45-degree angles. Also important is controlling how the edges of the figures interact with the texture of the ground. Figure 6 shows how edges are carefully matched to the background texture so that they have a consistent quality appearance.

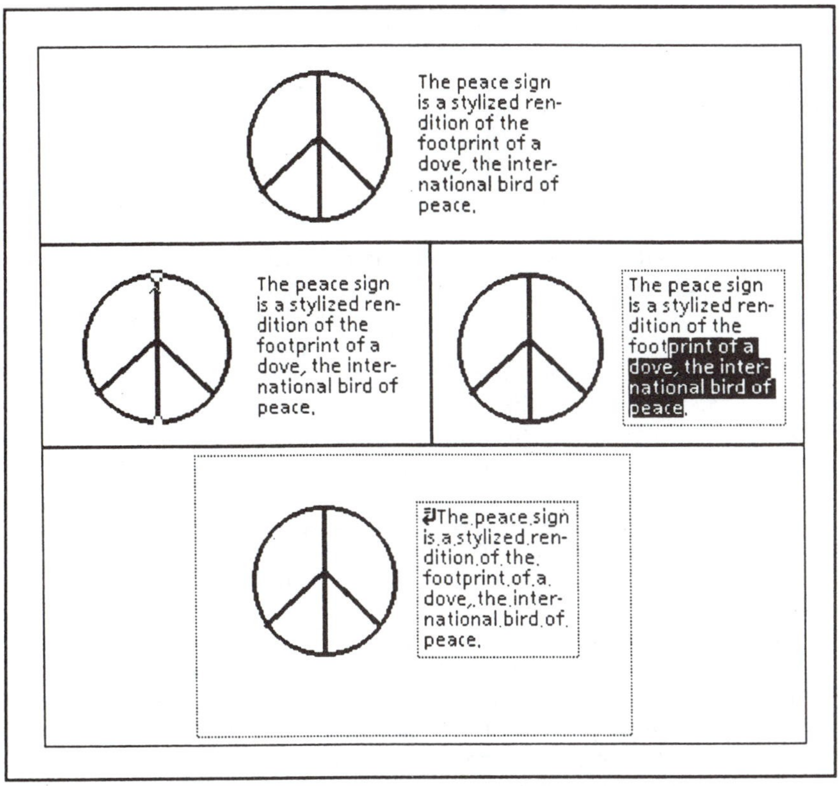

Figure 5. Revealed structure. At the top is the WYSIWYG view of mixed text and graphics. The middle two panels show that structure is revealed when an object is selected. When a line segment is selected, its control points are shown. When text is selected, the text string is revealed. The bottom panel shows the effect of the Show Structure and Show Non-Printing Characters commands, which is to reveal the location of embedded graphics and text frames (dotted lines) and "new paragraph" and Space characters.

Document editor level. At the top level of Star's architecture are its applications, the most prominent of which is the document editor.

WYSIWYG document editor. Within the limits of screen resolution, Star documents are displayed as they will print, including typographic features such as boldface, italics, proportional spacing, variable font families, and superscripts, and layout features such as embedded graphics, page numbers, headers, and footers. This is commonly referred to as "what you see is what you get," or WYSIWYG.

Star adheres to this principle even in domains where other WYSIWYG document editors do not. For example, mathematical formulas are created and edited in documents using a WYSIWYG editor that has knowledge built into it about the appearance and layout of mathematical symbols. A square root sign has a slot for an

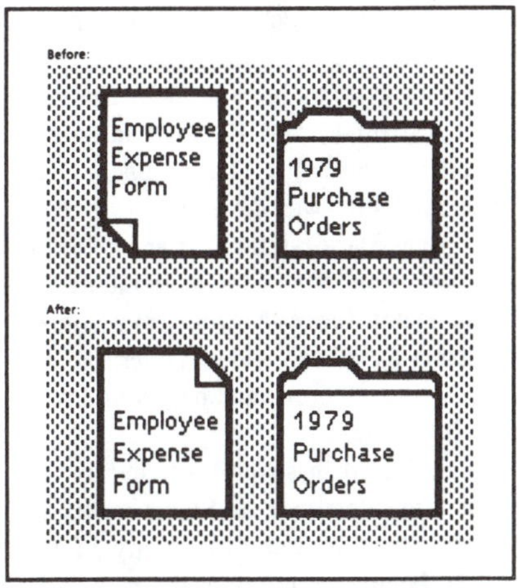

Figure 6. Match the medium. Many graphic refinements were made during the design process. For example, the turned corner of the document icon was moved to the top so that the three lines of label would line up with the labels of other icons. Also, icons were carefully sized and positioned against the gray background to create smoother lines.

expression and grows when the expression becomes large (see Figure 7). In most systems, mathematical formulas are created either by putting together special characters to make mathematical symbols or by using a special in-line notation (such as sqrt(sigma(1, n, (x*3)/2))) to represent the formula that will eventually be printed. Formulas created with such systems usually require several print-edit cycles to get right.

Extended character set for multilingual capability. Star uses 16-bit character codes, in contrast to most of the computer industry, which uses seven- or eight-bit character codes (for example, ASCII or EBCDIC). The Star character set is a superset of ASCII. The reason for a 16-bit code is a strong market requirement for enhanced multilingual capabilility coming from Xerox's subsidiaries in Europe and Japan. Most systems provide non-English characters through different fonts, so that the eight-bit "extended" ASCII codes might be rendered as math symbols in one font, Greek letters in another font, and Arabic in yet another. This has the effect that when any application loses track of font information while handling the text (which happens often in some systems), a paragraph of Arabic may turn into nonsensical Greek or math symbols or something else, and vice versa.

Star uses 16-bit character codes to permit the system to reliably handle European languages and Japanese, which uses many thousands of characters. All Star and ViewPoint systems have French, German, Italian, Spanish, and Russian language capabilities built in. The Japanese language capability was developed as part of the original Star design effort and released in Japan soon after Star's debut in the United States. Since that time, many more characters have been added, covering Chinese, Arabic, Hebrew, and nearly all European languages.

As explained in several articles by Joe Becker, the designer of Star's multilingual capabilities, handling many of the world's languages requires more than an expanded character set.[5] Clever typing schemes and sophisticated rendering algorithms are required to provide a multilingual capability that satisfies customers.

The document is the heart of the world and unifies it. Most personal computers and workstations give no special status to any particular application. Dozens of applications are available, most incompatible with each other in data format as well as user interface.

Star, in contrast, assumes that the primary use of the system is to create and maintain documents. The document editor is thus the primary application. All other applications exist mainly to provide or manipulate information whose ultimate destination is a document. Thus, most applications are integrated into the document editor (see "Integrated applications" above), operating within frames embedded in documents. Those applications that are not part of the document editor support transfer of their data to documents.

History of Star development

Having described Star and ViewPoint, we will describe where they came from and how they were developed. Figure 8 graphs this history, showing systems that influenced Star and those influenced by it.

Pre-Xerox. Although Star was conceived as a product in 1975 and was released in 1981, many of the ideas that went into it were born in projects dating back more than three decades.

Memex. The story starts in 1945, when Vannevar Bush, a designer of early calculators and one of President Franklin D. Roosevelt's science advisors, wrote an article describing his vision of the uses of electronics and information technology. At a time when computers were new, room-sized, and used only for military number-crunching, Bush envisioned a personal, desktop computer for non-numerical applications. He called it the Memex. Due to insufficient technology and insufficient imagination on the part of others, Bush's ideas languished for 15 years.

Sketchpad. In the sixties, people began to take interactive computing seriously. One such person was Ivan Sutherland. He built an interactive graphics system called Sketchpad that allowed a user to create graphical figures on a CRT display using a light pen. The geometric shapes users put on the screen were treated as objects: after being created, they could be moved, copied, shrunk, expanded, and rotated. They could also be joined together to make larger, more complex objects that could then be operated upon as units. Sketchpad influenced Star's user interface as a whole as well as its graphics applications.

NLS. Also in the sixties, Douglas Engelbart established a research program at Stanford Research Institute (now called SRI International) for exploring the use of computers "to augment the knowledge worker" and human intellect in general. He and his collegues experimented with different types of displays and input devices (inventing the mouse when other pointing devices proved inadequate) and developed a system commonly known as NLS.*

NLS was unique in several respects. It used CRT displays when most computers used teletypes. It was interactive (i.e., on-line) when almost all computing was batch. It was full-screen-oriented when the few systems that were interactive were line-oriented. It used a mouse when all other graphic interactive systems used cursor keys, light pens, joysticks, or digitizing tablets. Finally, it was the first system to organize textual and graphical information in trees and networks. Today, it would be called an "idea processor" or a "hypertext system."

The Reactive Engine. While Engelbart et al. were developing ideas, some of which eventually found their way into Star, Alan Kay, then a graduate student, was doing likewise. His dissertation, *The Reactive Engine*, contained the seeds of many ideas that he and others later brought to fruition in the Smalltalk language and programming environment, which, in turn, influenced Star. Like the designers of NLS, Kay realized that interactive applications do not have to treat the display as a "glass teletype" and can share the screen with other programs.

Xerox PARC. In 1970, Xerox established a research center in Palo Alto to explore technologies that would be important not only for the further development of Xerox's then-existing product line (copiers), but also for Xerox's planned expansion into the office systems business. The Palo Alto Research Center was organized into several laboratories, each devoted to basic and applied research in a field related to the above goals. The names and organi-

*The actual name of the system was On-Line System. A second system called Off-Line System was abbreviated FLS, hence NLS's strange abbreviation. NLS is now marketed by McDonnell Douglas under the name Augment.

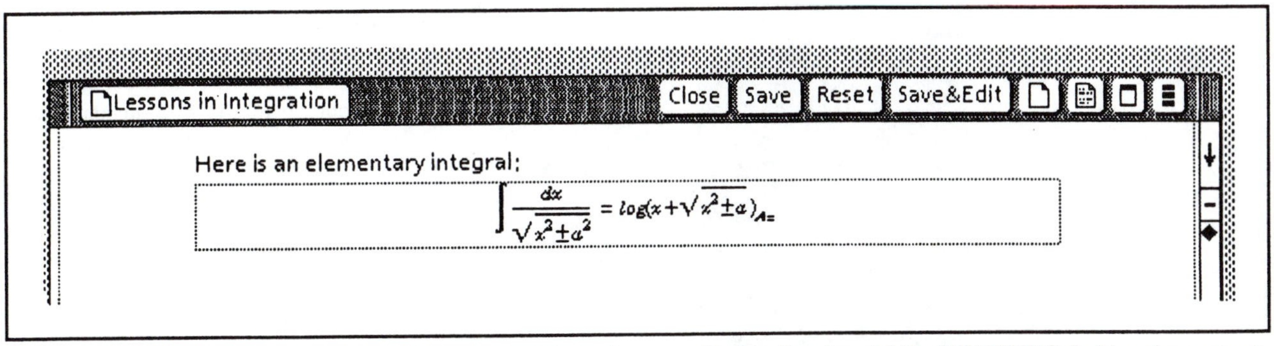

Figure 7. WYSIWYG formula editing. Mathematical formulas are edited in Star in a highly WYSIWYG fashion, in contrast to most systems, in which formulas are specified via in-line expressions or by constructing them from pieces in a special character font.

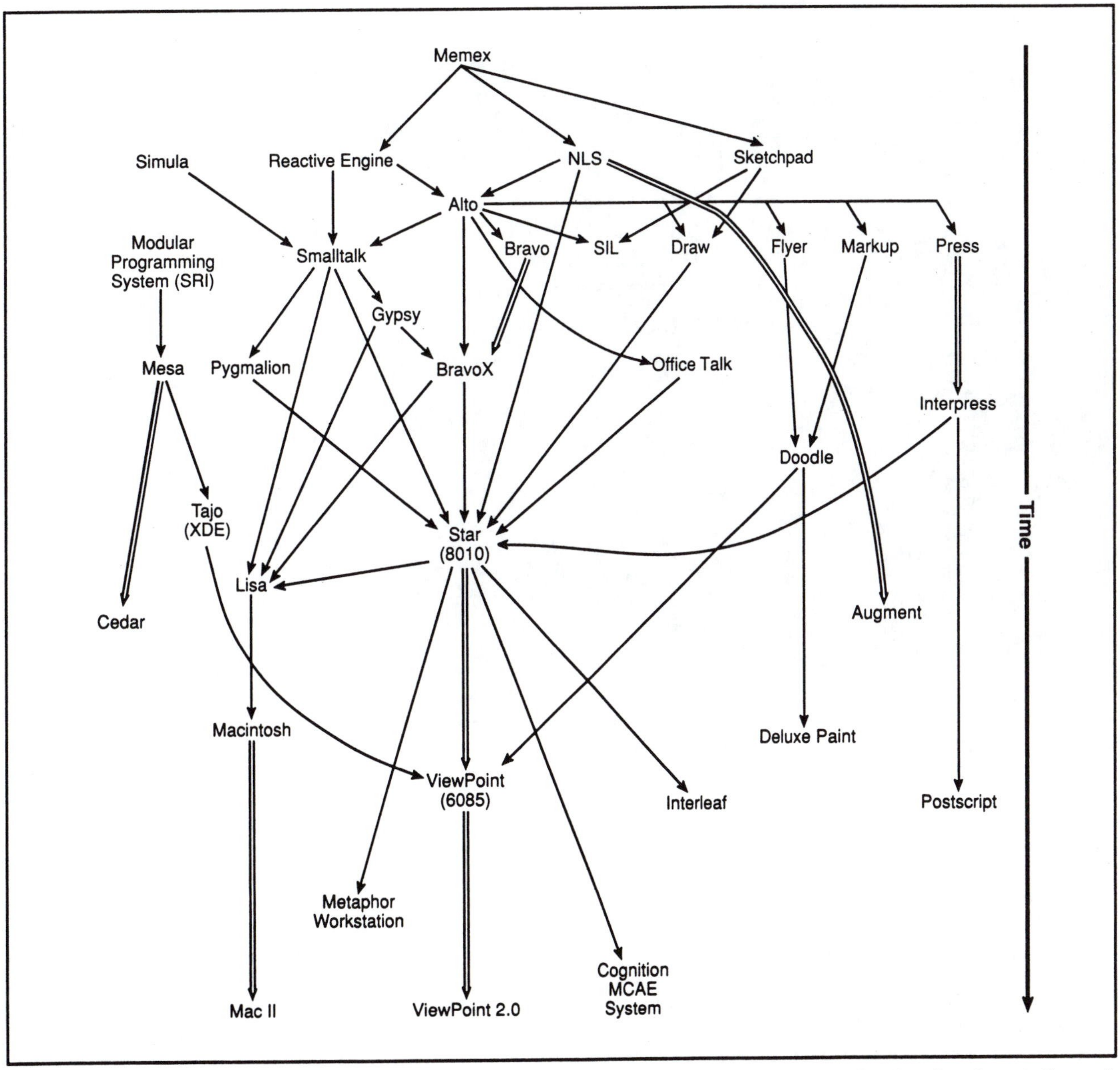

Figure 8. How systems influenced later systems. This graph summarizes how various systems related to Star have influenced one another over the years. Time progresses downwards. Double arrows indicate direct successors (i.e., follow-on versions). Many "influence arrows" are due to key designers changing jobs or applying concepts from their graduate research to products.

Figure 9. The Xerox Alto. The Alto, developed at Xerox PARC in the seventies, was a prototype for Star. Both its hardware design and the many programs written for it by PARC researchers strongly influenced Star's designers.

zation of the labs have changed over the years, but the research topics have stayed the same: materials science, laser physics, integrated circuitry, computer-aided design and manufacturing, user interfaces (not necessarily to computers), and computer science (including networking, databases, operating systems, languages and programming environments, graphics, document production systems, and artificial intelligence).

Alto. PARC researchers were fond of the slogan "The best way to predict the future is to invent it." After some initial experiments with time-shared systems, they began searching for a new approach to computing.

Among the founding members of PARC was Alan Kay. He and his colleagues were acquainted with NLS and liked its novel approach to human-computer interaction. Soon, PARC hired several people who had worked on NLS. In 1971, the center signed an agreement with SRI licensing Xerox to use the mouse. Kay and others were dedicated to a vision of personal computers in a distributed environment. In fact, they coined the term "personal computer" in 1973, long before microcomputers started what has been called the "personal computer revolution."

One result of the search for a new approach was the Alto (see Figure 9). The Alto was a minicomputer that had a removable, 2.5-megabyte hard disk pack (floppy disks did not exist at the time) and 128 to 256 kilobytes of memory. Unlike most machines of its day, the Alto also had a microprogrammable instruction set, a "full-page" (10½ × 8¼ inch, 600 × 800 pixel) bitmapped graphic display, about 50 kilobytes of high-speed display memory, and a mouse.

The first Alto became operational in 1972. At first, only a half-dozen or so Altos were built. After software that exploited the Alto's capabilities became available, demand for them grew tremendously, spreading beyond PARC into Xerox as a whole and even to external customers. Eventually, Xerox built more than a thousand Altos.

Ethernet. Another product of the new approach was the Ethernet. With its standardized, layered communications protocols, Ethernet provided a way of connecting computers much more flexibly than previously possible. Soon after the first Altos were built, they were networked together. Eventually, the network grew to thousands of workstations (Altos and Alto successors) within Xerox's worldwide organization.

Smalltalk. Alan Kay was one of the main advocates of the Alto. His Learning Research Group began using the Alto to build prototypes for a personal computing system "of the future" — a portable machine that would provide not canned applications but rather the building blocks necessary for users to build the tools and applications they needed to solve their own information processing problems. The technologies needed to build a lap computer with the power of the envisioned system (called the "DynaBook") were unavailable at the time and still are.

The prototypes developed by Kay's group evolved into the Smalltalk language and programming environment. Smalltalk further promoted the notion of personal computing; pioneered complete, interactive programming environments; and refined and solidified concepts of object-oriented programming that had been extant only in vestigial forms in previous systems. Most importantly for Star, Smalltalk demonstrated the power of graphical, bitmapped displays; mouse-driven input; windows; and simultaneous applications. This is the most visible link between Smalltalk and Star, and is perhaps why many people wrongly believe that Star was written in Smalltalk.

Pygmalion. The first large program to be written in Smalltalk was Pygmalion, the doctoral thesis project of David C. Smith. One goal of Pygmalion was to show that programming a computer does not have to be primarily a textual activity. It can be accomplished, given the appropriate system, by interacting with graphical elements on a screen. A second goal was to show that computers can be programmed in the language of the user interface, that is, by demonstrating what you want done and having the computer remember and reproduce it. The idea of using icons — images that allow users to manipulate them and in so doing act upon the data they represent — came mainly from Pygmalion. After completing Pygmalion, Smith worked briefly on the NLS project at SRI before joining the Star development team at Xerox.

Bravo, Gypsy, and BravoX. At the same time that the Learning Research Group was developing Smalltalk for the Alto, others at PARC, mainly Charles Simonyi and Butler Lampson, were writing an advanced document editing system for it called Bravo. Because it made heavy use of the Alto's bitmapped screen, Bravo was unquestionably the most WYSIWYG text editor of its day, with on-screen underlining, boldface, italics, variable font families and sizes, and variable-width characters. It allowed the screen to be split, so different documents or different parts of the same document could be edited at once, but did not operate in a windowed environment as we use the term today. Bravo was widely used at PARC and in Xerox as a whole.

From 1976 to 1978, Simonyi and others rewrote Bravo, incorporating many of the new user-interface ideas floating around PARC at the time. One such idea was modelessness, promoted by Larry Tesler[3] and exemplified in Tesler's prototype text editor, Gypsy. Simonyi et al. also added styles, enhancing users' ability to control the appearance of their documents. The new version was called BravoX.

Shortly thereafter, Simonyi joined Microsoft, where he led the development of Microsoft Word, a direct descendent of BravoX. Another member of the BravoX team, Tom Malloy, went to Apple and wrote LisaWrite.

Draw, Sil, Markup, Flyer, and Doodle. Star's graphics capability (its provisions for users to create graphical images for incorporation into documents, as opposed to its graphical user interface) owes a great deal to several graphics editors written for the Alto and later machines.

Draw, by Patrick Beaudelaire and Bob Sproull, and Sil (for Simple Illustrator) were intellectual successors of Sutherland's Sketchpad (see above): graphical object editors that allowed users to construct figures out of selectable, movable, stretchable geometric forms and text. In turn, Star's graphic frames capability is in large measure an intellectual successor of Draw and Sil.

Markup was a bitmap graphics editor (that is, a paint program) written by William Newman for the Alto. Flyer was another paint program, written in Smalltalk for the Alto by Bob Flegel and Bill Bowman. These programs inspired Doodle, a paint program written for a later machine by Dan Silva. Doodle eventually evolved into ViewPoint's Free-Hand Drawing application. Silva went on to write DeluxePaint, a paint program for PCs.

Laser printing. Fancy graphics capabilities in a workstation are of little use without hard-copy capability to match it. Laser printing, invented at PARC, provided the necessary base capability, but computers needed a uniform way to describe output to laser printers. For this purpose, Bob Sproull developed the Press page-description language. Press was heavily used at PARC, then further developed into Interpress, Xerox's commercial page-description language and the language in which Star encodes printer output. Some of the developers of Interpress later formed Adobe Systems and developed Postscript, a popular page description language.

Laurel and Hardy. A network of personal workstations suggests electronic mail. Though electronic mail was not invented at PARC, PARC researchers (mainly Doug Brotz) made it more accessible to nonengineers by creating Laurel, a display-oriented tool for sending, receiving, and organizing e-mail. The experience of using Laurel inspired others to write Hardy for an Alto successor machine. Laurel and Hardy were instrumental in getting nonengineers at Xerox to use e-mail. The use of e-mail spread further with the spread of Star and ViewPoint throughout Xerox.

OfficeTalk. One more Alto program that influenced Star was OfficeTalk, a prototype office automation system written by Clarence ("Skip") Ellis and Gary Nutt. OfficeTalk supported standard office automation tasks and tracked jobs as they went from person to person in an organization. Experience with OfficeTalk provided ideas for Star because of the two systems' similar target applications.

Summing up. The debt that Star owes to the Alto and its software is best summed up by quoting from the original designers, who wrote in 1982:

> Alto served as a valuable prototype for Star.... Alto users have had several thousand work-years of experience with them over a period of eight years, making Alto perhaps the largest prototyping effort in history. There were dozens of experimental programs written for the Alto by members of the Xerox Palo Alto Research Center. Without the creative ideas of the authors of these systems, Star in its present form would have been impossible.... In addition, we ourselves programmed various aspects of the Star design on the Alto...

Star. To develop Star and other office systems products, Xerox created the Systems Development Department. SDD was staffed by transferring people from other parts of Xerox, including PARC, as well as by hiring from outside. Thus, contrary to what has often been stated in the industry press, Star was not developed at PARC, but rather in a separate product-development organization.

When SDD was formed, a decision was made to use Mesa, an "industrial-strength" dialect of Pascal conceived at SRI and further developed at PARC, as the primary product programming language. SDD took over development and maintenance of Mesa from the Computer Science Laboratory at PARC, freeing CSL to develop Mesa's research successor, Cedar.

Star hardware. Star is often discussed as if it were a computer. In fact, Star is a body of software.* However, using the

*The official name for Star was the Xerox 8010 Information System. The machine was called the 8000 Series Network Systems Processor. Originally, "Star" was only an internal name.

name Star to refer to the machine is understandable since the machine was designed in conjunction with the software to meet the needs of the software design. This is in sharp contrast to the usual approach, in which software is designed for existing computers.

The 8000 Series workstation was based upon a microcoded processor designed within Xerox especially to run the object code produced by the Mesa compiler. Besides being microprogrammed to run Mesa, the processor provided low-level operations for facilitating display operations. For example, the bitblt operation for manipulating rectangular arrays of screen pixels is implemented as a single instruction. As sold, the machine was configured with at least 384 kilobytes of real memory (expandable to 1.5 megabytes), a local hard disk (10, 29, or 40 megabytes), a 17-inch display, a mechanical mouse, an eight-inch floppy disk drive, and an Ethernet connection. The price was initially $16,500 with software.

Even though the machine was designed to run Star, it also ran other software. In addition to selling it as the 8010 "Star" workstation, Xerox sold it as a server machine and as an Interlisp and a Smalltalk workstation.

Star software. Alhough Star incorporated ideas from a number of predecessors, it still required a mammoth design effort to pull all of those ideas — as well as new ideas — together to produce a coherent design. According to the original designers, ". . . it was a real challenge to bring some order to the different user interfaces on the Alto."[1] About 30 person-years went into the design of the user interface, functionality, and hardware.

To foster uniformity of specifications as well as thoughtful and uniform design, Star's designers developed a strict format for specifications. Applications and system features were to be described in terms of the *objects* that users would manipulate with the software and the *actions* that the software provided for manipulating objects. This "objects and actions" analysis was supposed to occur at a fairly high level, without regard to how the objects would actually be presented or how the actions would actually be invoked by users. A full specification was then written from the "objects and actions" version. This approach forced designers to think clearly about the purpose of each application or feature and fostered recognition of similar operations across specifications, allowing what might have seemed like new operations to be handled by existing commands.

When SDD was formed, it was split between two locations: Southern California (El Segundo) and Northern California (Palo Alto). Few people were willing to transfer one way or the other, leaving SDD with the choice of losing many competent engineers or being creative. SDD's management took the creative route: they put the Ethernet to work, attaching the development machines at both sites to a network, connecting the two sites with a 56-kilobit-per-second leased line, encouraging heavy use of electronic mail for work-related communication, and developing tools for facilitating distributed, multiparty development.

As might be expected from Star's origins, most of the design and prototyping work was done in Palo Alto, whereas most of the implementation was done in El Segundo. Though this split was handled creatively, some of Star's designers now believe it caused problems not overcome by extensive use of e-mail. For example, the implementors did not benefit from much of the prototyping done at PARC.

The development process has been recounted in detail elsewhere[6] and will not be repeated here. Suffice it to say that the Star development effort

- involved developing new network protocols and data-encoding schemes when those used in PARC's research environment proved inadequate;
- involved a great deal of prototyping and user testing;
- included a late redesign of the processor;
- included several software redesigns, rewrites, and late additions, some based on results from user testing, some based on marketing considerations, and some based on systems considerations (see below);
- included a level of attention to the requirements of international customers unmatched in the industry; and
- left much of what was in the Star Functional Specification unimplemented.

Tajo/XDE. Since the machine upon which Star ran was developed in parallel with the software, it was not available early-on for use as a software development platform. Early prototyping and development was done on Altos and successor research machines developed at PARC. Though the Mesa language ran on these machines, development aids for Mesa programmers were lacking.

When the 8000 Series workstation became available, the systems group within SDD began working on a suitable development environment. Known internally as Tajo and externally as Xerox Development Environment (XDE), the completed development environment and the numerous tools written to run in it were quickly adopted by programmers throughout SDD. Star's later improvements adopted many good ideas from Tajo.

ViewPoint. Though Star's introduction at NCC '81 was lauded in the industry press, initial sales were not what had been hoped. Almost immediately, efforts were launched to improve its performance, extensibility, maintainability, and cost.

ViewPoint software. Even before Star was released, the implementors realized that it had serious problems from their point of view. Its high degree of integration and user-interface consistency had been achieved by making it monolithic: the system "knew" about all applications, and all parts of the system "knew" about all other parts. It was difficult to correct problems, add new features, and increase performance. The monolithic architecture also did not lend itself to distributed, multiparty development.

This created pressure to rewrite Star. Bob Ayers, who had been heavily involved in the development of Star, rewrote the infrastructure of the system according to the more flexible Tajo model. He built, on top of the operating system and low-level window manager, a "toolkit" for building Star-like applications.

In the new infrastructure, transfer of data between different applications was handled through strict protocols involving the user's selection, thus making applications independent from one another. The object-oriented user interface, which requires that the system associate applications with data files, was preserved by having applications register themselves with the system when started, telling it which type of data file they correspond to and registering procedures for handling keyboard and mouse events and generic commands. User-interface consistency was fostered by building many of the standards into the application toolkit. The development organization completed the toolkit and then ported or rewrote the existing applications and utilities to run on top of it.

Other software changes included

- the addition of several applications and utilities, including a Free-Hand Drawing program and an IBM PC emulation application;
- optional window tiling constraints, so that users can have overlapping windows if desired;
- redesigned screen graphics (icons, windows, property sheets, command buttons, and menus) to accommodate a smaller screen and to meet the demands of a more sophisticated public; and
- improved performance.

To underscore the fact that the new system was a substantial improvement over the old, the name was changed from Star to ViewPoint. ViewPoint 1.0 was released in 1985.

ViewPoint hardware. In addition to revising the software, Xerox brought the hardware up to date by designing a completely new vehicle for ViewPoint: the 6085 workstation. The new machine was designed to take advantage of advances in integrated circuitry, reductions in memory costs, new disk technologies, and new standards in keyboard design, as well as to provide IBM PC compatibility. The 6085 workstation has a Mesa processor plus an optional IBM-PC-compatible processor, one megabyte of real memory (expandable to 4 megabytes), a hard disk (10 to 80 megabytes), a choice of a 15- or a 19-inch display, an optical mouse, a new keyboard, a 5¼-inch floppy disk drive, and, of course, an Ethernet connection. The base cost was initially $6,340 with the ViewPoint software. Like the 8010, the 6085 is sold as a vehicle for Interlisp and Smalltalk as well as for ViewPoint.

Recent ViewPoint changes. The recently released ViewPoint 2.0 adds many features relevant to desktop publishing. These include

- Xerox ProIllustrator, a new vector graphics editing application designed mainly for professional illustrators;
- Shared Books, support for groups of users working on multipart documents;
- a Redlining feature, for tracking deletions and insertions in documents;
- cursor keys, for moving the insertion point during keyboard-intensive work; and
- stylesheets, for facilitating control of document appearance.

Lessons from experience

So what have we learned from all this? We believe, the following:

Pay attention to industry trends. Partly out of excitement over what they were doing, PARC researchers and Star's designers didn't pay enough attention to the "other" personal computer revolution occurring outside of Xerox. By the late seventies, Xerox had its own powerful technical tradition (mouse-driven, networked workstations with large bitmapped screens and multiple, simultaneous applications), blinding Star's designers to the need to approach the market with cheap, stand-alone PCs. The result was a product that was highly unfamiliar to its intended customers: businesses. Nowadays, of course, such systems are no longer unusual.

Developing Star and ViewPoint involved developing several enabling technologies, for networking, communicating with servers, describing pages to laser printers, and developing software. At the time they were developed, these technologies were unique in the industry. Xerox elected to keep them proprietary for fear of losing its competitive advantage. With hindsight, we can say that it might have been better to release these technologies into the public domain or to market them early, so that they might have become industry standards. Instead, alternative approaches developed at other companies have become the industry standards. Xerox's current participation in the development of various industry standards indicates its desire to reverse this trend.

Pay attention to what customers want. The personal computer revolution has shown the futility of trying to anticipate all of the applications that customers will want. Star should have been designed from the start to be open and extensible by users, as the Alto was. In hindsight, extensibility was one of the keys to the Alto's popularity. The problem wasn't that Star lacked functionality, it was that it didn't have the functionality customers wanted. An example is the initial lack of a spreadsheet application. The designers failed to appreciate the significance of this application, which may have been more important even than word-processing in expanding the personal computer revolution beyond engineers and hobbyists into business. Eventually realizing that Star's closedness was a problem, Xerox replaced it with ViewPoint, a more "open" system that allows users to pick and choose applications that they need, including a spreadsheet and IBM PC software. Apple Computer learned the same lesson with its Lisa computer and similarly replaced it with a cheaper one having a more open software architecture: the Macintosh.

Know your competition. Star's initial per-workstation price was near that of time-shared minicomputers, dedicated word-processors, and other shared computing facilities. Star was, however, competing for desktop space with microcomputer-based PCs. ViewPoint has corrected that problem: The 6085 costs about the same as its competition.

Establish firm performance goals. Star's designers should have established performance goals, documented them in the functional specifications, and stuck to them as they developed Star. Where performance goals couldn't be met, the corresponding functionality should have been cut.

In lieu of speed, the designers should have made the user interface more responsive. Designing systems to handle user input more intelligently can make them more responsive without necessarily making them execute functions faster. They can operate asynchronously with respect to user input, making use of background processes, keeping up with important user actions, delaying unimportant tasks (such as refreshing irrelevant areas of the screen) until time permits, and skipping tasks called for by early user actions but rendered moot by later ones. ViewPoint now makes use of background processes to increase its responsiveness.

Avoid geographically split development organizations. Having a development organization split between Palo Alto and El Segundo was probably a mistake, less for reasons of distance per se than for lack of shared background in "PARC-style" computing. However, the adverse effect of sheer distance on communication was certainly a factor.

Don't be dogmatic about the Desktop metaphor and direct manipulation. Direct manipulation and the Desktop metaphor aren't the best way to do everything. Remembering and typing is sometimes better than seeing and pointing. For example, if users want to open a file that is one of several hundred in a directory (folder), the system should let users type its name rather than forcing them to scroll through the directory trying to spot it so they can select it.

Many aspects of Star were correct. Though certain aspects of Star perhaps should have been done differently, most of the aspects of Star's design described at the beginning of this article have withstood the test of time. These include

- Iconic, direct-manipulation, object-oriented user interface. The days of cryptic command languages and scores of commands for users to remember (a la Unix and MS-DOS) should have passed long ago.
- Generic commands and consistency in general. Even Macintosh could use some lessons in this regard: the Duplicate command copies files within a disk, but users must drag icons to copy them across disks and must use Copy-Paste to copy anything else.
- Pointing device. Although cursor keys have some advantages and certainly would have enhanced Star's market appeal (as they have ViewPoint's), Star's designers stand by the system's primary reliance on the mouse. This does not imply a commitment to the mouse per se, but rather to any pointing device that allows quick pointing and selection. As interfaces evolve in the future, high-resolution touch screens and other more exotic devices may replace mice as the pointing devices of choice.
- High-resolution display. Memory is now cheap, so the justification for character displays is gone.
- Good graphic design. Screen graphics designed by computer programmers will not satisfy customers. The Star designers recognized their limitations in this regard and hired the right people for the job. As color displays gain market presence, the participation of graphic designers will become even more crucial.
- 16-bit character set. An eight-bit character set (such as ASCII) cannot accommodate international languages adequately. Star and ViewPoint's use of a 16-bit character set and of special typing and rendering algorithms for foreign languages is the correct approach.
- Distributed, personal computing. Though the reorientation of the industry away from batch and time-shared computing toward personal computing had nothing to do with Xerox, PARC, or Star, it was an important part of the computing philosophy that led to Star.

Star has had an indisputable influence on the design of computer systems. For example, the Lisa and Macintosh might have been very different had Apple's designers not borrowed ideas from Star, as the following excerpt of a *Byte* magazine interview of Lisa's designers shows:

> Byte: Do you have a Xerox Star here that you work with?
> Tesler: No, we didn't have one here. We went to the NCC [National Computer Conference] when the Star was announced and looked at it. And in fact it did have an immediate impact. A few months after looking at it we made some changes to our user interface based on ideas that we got from it. For example, the desktop manager we had before was completely different; it didn't use icons at all, and we never liked it very much. We decided to change ours to the icon base. That was probably the only thing we got from Star, I think. Most of our Xerox inspiration was Smalltalk rather than Star.[7]

Elements of the Desktop metaphor approach also appear in many other systems.

The history presented here has shown, however, that Star's designers did not invent the system from nothingness. Just as it has influenced systems that came after it, Star was influenced by ideas and systems that came before it. It is difficult to inhibit the spread of good ideas once they are apparent to all, especially in this industry. Star was thus just one step in an evolutionary process that will continue both at Xerox and elsewhere. That is how it should be. □

Acknowledgments

When Star was announced, several articles on it appeared in trade magazines, journals, and at conferences. Many of these were reprinted in the Xerox publication *Office Systems Technology*.[8] Since then, several more articles have been published that are relevant to this retrospective. They include an article from MacWorld[9] that described the historical antecedents of Apple Computer's Lisa and Macintosh computers, which share much of Star's history. This retrospective owes a great deal to those previous writings. We also acknowledge the valuable contributions that Joe Becker, Bill Mallgren, Doug Carothers, Linda Bergsteinsson, and Randy Polen of Xerox, and Bob Ayers, Ralph Kimball, Dave Fylstra, and John Shoch made to this retrospective. Finally, we acknowledge the helpful suggestions made by the first and second authors' colleagues at US West Advanced Technologies and several anonymous reviewers to improve the quality of the article.

References

1. D.C. Smith et al., "The Star User Interface: An Overview," *Proc. AFIPS Nat'l Computer Conf.*, June 1982, pp. 515-528.
2. D.C. Smith, "Origins of the Desktop Metaphor: A Brief History," presented in a panel discussion, "The Desktop Metaphor as an Approach to User Interface Design," in *Proc. ACM Annual Conf.*, 1985, p. 548.
3. L. Tesler, "The Smalltalk Environment," *Byte*, Vol. 6, No. 8, Aug. 1981, pp. 90-147.
4. L. Winner, "Mythinformation," *Whole Earth Review*, No. 44, Jan. 1985.
5. J. Becker, "Multilingual Word Processing," *Scientific American*, Vol. 251, No. 1, July 1984, pp. 96-107. (See "Further reading" for other articles on Star's multilingual capability.)
6. E.F. Harslem and L.E. Nelson, "A Retrospective on the Development of Star," *Proc. Sixth Int'l Conf. on Software Engineering*, Sept. 1982, Tokyo, Japan. Reprinted in *Office Systems Technology*, OSD-R8203A, Xerox Corp., pp. 261-269.
7. G. Williams, "The Lisa Computer System," *Byte*, Vol. 8, No. 2, Feb. 1983, pp. 33-50.
8. *Office Systems Technology*, OSD-R8203A, Xerox Corp.
9. T. Nace, "The Macintosh Family Tree," *MacWorld*, Nov. 1984, pp. 134-141.

Further reading

For interested readers, we provide here a guide to further reading on Star and related topics. A more comprehensive and detailed version of this retrospective will appear in an upcoming Prentice-Hall book series. Also, the September issue of *IEEE Spectrum* includes an article, "Of Mice and Menus," on graphical user interfaces past and present. The authors of that article consulted several people who contributed to or are mentioned in this Star retrospective.

In the following bibliography, readings are categorized according to whether they pertain to work done prior to the establishment of Xerox PARC, to work done at PARC, to the original Star design done at Xerox SDD,[8] to enhancements to Star and ViewPoint, and to work on related topics.

Pre-Xerox

Bush, V., "As We May Think," *Atlantic Monthly*, Vol. 176, No. 1, July 1945, pp. 101-108.

Engelbart, D.C., and W.K. English, "A Research Center for Augmenting Human Intellect," *Proc. FJCC*, Vol. 33, AFIPS, 1968, pp. 395-410.

English, W.K., D.C. Engelbart, and M.L. Berman, "Display-Selection Techniques for Text Manipulation," *IEEE Trans. Human Factors in Electronics*, HFE-8, 1967, pp. 21-31.

Kay, A.C., *The Reactive Engine*, PhD thesis, University of Utah, Salt Lake City, 1969.

Sutherland, I.E., *Sketchpad: A Man-Machine Graphical Communications System*, PhD thesis, M.I.T., Cambridge, Mass., 1963.

Xerox pre-Star

Card, S., W.K. English, and B. Burr, "Evaluation of Mouse, Rate-Controlled Isometric Joystick, Step Keys, and Text Keys for Text Selection on a CRT," *Ergonomics*, Vol. 21, 1978, pp. 601-613.

Ellis, C., and G. Nutt, "Computer Science and Office Information Systems," Xerox PARC Tech. Report SSL-79-6, 1979.

Geschke, C.M., J.H. Morris, Jr., and E.H. Satterthwaite, "Early Experience with Mesa," *Comm. ACM*, Vol. 20, No. 8, 1977, pp. 540-553.

Ingalls, D.H., "The Smalltalk Graphics Kernel," *Byte*, Vol. 6, No. 8, Aug. 1981, pp. 168-194.

Kay, A.C., and A. Goldberg, "Personal Dynamic Media," *Computer*, Vol. 10, No. 3, March 1977, pp. 31-41.

Kay, A.C., "Microelectronics and the Personal Computer," *Scientific American*, Vol. 237, No. 3, Sept. 1977, pp. 230-244.

Smith, D.C., *Pygmalion: A Computer Program to Model and Simulate Creative Thought*, Birkhauser Verlag, Basel and Stuttgart, 1977.

Thacker, C.P., et al., "Alto: A Personal Computer," in *Computer Structures: Principles and Examples*, D. Siewioek, C.G. Bell, and A. Newell, eds., McGraw Hill, New York, 1982.

Star

Curry, G., et al., "Traits—An Approach to Multiple-Inheritance Subclassing," *Proc. ACM Conf. on Office Automation Systems (SIGOA)*, 1982.

Dalal, Y.K., "Use of Multiple Networks in the Xerox Network System," *Computer*, Vol. 15, No. 10, Oct. 1982, pp. 82-92.

Johnsson, R.K., and J.D. Wick, "An Overview of the Mesa Processor Architecture," *SIGPlan Notices*, Vol. 17, No. 4, 1982.

Lipkie, D.E., et al., "Star Graphics: An Object-Oriented Implementation," *Computer Graphics*, Vol. 16, No. 3, July 1982, pp. 115-124.

Shoch, J.F., et al., "Evolution of the Ethernet Local Computer Network," *Computer*, Vol. 15, No. 9, Aug. 1982, pp. 10-27.

Smith, D.C., et al., "Designing the Star User Interface," *Byte*, Vol. 7, No. 4, April 1982, pp. 242-282.

Sweet, R.E., and J.G. Sandman, Jr., "Empirical Analysis of the Mesa Instruction Set," *SIGPlan Notices*, Vol. 17, No. 4, 1982.

Star/ViewPoint enhancements

Becker, J., "Typing Chinese, Japanese, and Korean," *Computer*, Vol. 18, No. 1, Jan. 1985, pp. 27-34.

Becker, J., "Arabic Word Processing," *Comm. ACM*, Vol. 30, No. 7, July 1987, pp. 600-610.

Bewley, W.L., et al., "Human Factors Testing in the Design of Xerox's 8010 Star Office Workstation," *Proc. ACM Conf. on Human Factors in Computing Systems*, 1983, pp. 72-77.

Bushan, A., and M. Plass, "The Interpress Page and Document Description Language," *Computer*, Vol. 19, No. 6, June 1986, pp. 72-77.

Curry, G., and R. Ayers, "Experience with Traits in Star," *Programming Productivity: Issues for the Eighties*, IEEE Computer Society Press, Los Alamitos, Calif., 1986, Order #681.

Halbert, D., "Programming by Example," Xerox OSD Tech. Report OSD-T84-02, 1984.

Lewis, B., and J. Hodges, "Shared Books: Collaborative Publication Management for an Office Information System," *Proc. ACM Conf. on Office Information Systems*, 1988.

Miscellaneous

Bly, S., and J. Rosenberg, "A Comparison of Tiled and Overlapping Windows," *Proc. ACM Conf. on Computer-Human Interaction*, 1986, pp. 101-106.

Goldberg, A., *Smalltalk-80: The Interactive Programming Environment*, Addison-Wesley Publishing, Reading, Mass., 1984.

Goldberg, A., and D. Robson, *Smalltalk-80: The Language and its Implementation*, Addison-Wesley Publishing, Reading, Mass., 1984.

Halasz, F., and T. Moran, "Analogy Considered Harmful," *Proc. ACM Conf. on Human Factors in Computing Systems*, Gaithersburg, MD, 1982, pp. 383-386.

Houston, T., "The Allegory of Software: Beyond, Behind, and Beneath the Electronic Desk," *Byte*, Dec. 1983, pp. 210-214.

Johnson, J., "Calculator Functions on Bitmapped Computers," *SIGCHI Bulletin*, Vol. 17, No. 1, July 1985, pp. 23-28.

Johnson, J., "How Closely Should the Electronic Desktop Simulate the Real One?" *SIGCHI Bulletin*, Vol. 19, No. 2, Oct. 1987, pp. 21-25.

Johnson, J., "Modes in Non-Computer Devices," in press, *Int'l J. Man-Machine Studies*, 1989.

Johnson, J., and R. Beach, "Styles in Document Editing Systems," *Computer*, Vol. 21, No. 1, Jan. 1988, pp. 32-43.

Malone, T.W., "How Do People Organize Their Desks: Implications for the Design of Office Information Systems," *ACM Trans. on Office Information Systems*, Vol. 1, No. 1, 1983, pp. 99-112.

Rosenberg, J.K., and T.P. Moran, "Generic Commands," *Proc. First Int'l Conf. on Human-Computer Interaction (Interact-84)*, 1984, pp. 1,360-1,364.

Teitelman, W., "A Tour Through Cedar," *IEEE Software*, April 1984.

Whiteside, J., et al., "User Performance with Command, Menu, and Iconic Interfaces," *Proc. ACM SIGCHI '85*, 1985, pp. 185-191.

Jeff Johnson is a user-interface researcher at Hewlett-Packard Labs. While working on this article, he was a member of the Advanced User Interfaces Group of US West Advanced Technologies. Before that, he worked at Xerox designing and implementing enhancements to the Star/ViewPoint system, and at Cromemco as a software engineer and manager. He received BA and PhD degrees in cognitive psychology from Yale and Stanford universities, respectively.

Teresa L. Roberts is a user-interface researcher in the Advanced User Interfaces Group at US West Advanced Technologies. She spent 10 years at Xerox, designing and evaluating parts of the Star user interface. She received a PhD in computer science from Stanford University.

William Verplank is an interaction design consultant with IDTwo and a lecturer in human factors and design at Stanford University. He worked at Xerox from 1978 to 1986, doing user testing and user-interface design for Star and ViewPoint. He received a BS in mechanical engineering from Stanford University and MS and PhD degrees in man-machine systems from MIT.

David C. Smith received a PhD in Computer Science from Stanford University in 1975. He spent seven years at Xerox Office Systems Division as one of the principal designers of Star. After that, he was vice president of user communication at Cognition, Inc., an MCAE firm, and is now an advanced system designer at Apple Computer.

Charles H. Irby is vice president of Metaphor Computer Systems, Software Products Division. Previously, he managed the Advanced Development Group of Xerox Office Systems Division and in that capacity was one of the principal designers of Star. Prior to that, he worked with Douglas Engelbart at SRI developing the NLS system. He received a BA in physics and mathematics and an MS in computer science and electrical engineering from the University of California at Santa Barbara.

Marian Beard is director of release management at Metaphor Computer Systems. Before joining Metaphor, she managed user interface design for Xerox's 8000 and 6085 products, and was a member of the original Star design team. She received a BA in history from Stanford University and an MEd from the University of Missouri.

Kevin Mackey is a software engineer at Logitech. He worked at Xerox from 1982 to 1989, developing applications software for Star and ViewPoint, and in that capacity helped develop ViewPoint's PC-emulation facility. He received a BS in computer science from the University of California at Berkeley.

Readers may contact Jeff Johnson at Hewlett-Packard Labs, 1501 Page Mill Rd., 1AU, Palo Alto, CA 94303.

Part II

The Process of Developing Interactive Systems

Part I reviewed the historical development of human-computer interaction, emphasizing the emergence of graphical user interfaces. Parallels were drawn between the usability of interactive computer systems and everyday technologies and devices such as doors, showers, faucets, and stoves. We also presented two case studies of the interface design process.

In Part II we examine in detail the designing, building, and evaluating of interactive systems (also see Rudisill et al., 1995, a forthcoming collection of papers on interface design in the real world, and especially Card, 1995, which appears in this collection). In Chapter 2 we cover approaches to the design and evaluation of interactive systems. Chapter 3 broadens the focus of discussion to consider the work context in which systems are used and design approaches that focus on understanding the broad context of use. In addition to being *used* in organizations, interactive systems are designed and built by teams of people; software development contexts are the topic of Chapter 4. Chapter 5 focuses on tools and techniques that are used in such settings to construct graphical user interfaces.

Chapter 2 discusses design and evaluation together. Earlier HCI books have typically considered these topics separately. They parallel the approach of traditional software engineering, which emphasizes first getting the design right and then later evaluating its conformance to the requirements and functional specifications. A design-it-right-first approach was successful in building some kinds of noninteractive software. For most interactive systems, however, correct requirements and specifications are difficult to formulate in advance, for we rarely understand enough about the subtle effects of the design on users and their tasks. Therefore, evaluation of preexisting systems, new prototypes, and evolving products has become integral throughout the development process. This *user-centered, iterative design* approach was illustrated by the Apple Information Kiosk and Xerox Star case studies in Part I and will be a dominant theme throughout this book.

Chapter 2 presents some proven design methodologies and discusses the importance of studying users and their tasks at an early stage of the design process. We describe approaches to brainstorming and conceptualizing new interface ideas, to exploring them through processes of envisionment, and to prototyping them in a variety of ways. We emphasize methods that have proven themselves in real applications. The readings also introduce several evaluation methods and position them in the development process.

Most work in human-computer interaction has focused on the dialogue between individual users and a computer. In Chapter 3, "Considering Work Contexts in Design," we acknowledge that individuals work in a social context. The conditions under which people work should influence the design of the systems they use. What's more, as networks tie users together, the social aspects of computing become prominent.

It is easy for developers to lose track of the larger context in which users operate. Chapter 3 discusses a perspective that is crucial for interface designers—the nature of the organizational and work context in which computers and software are used. It also illustrates the potentially disastrous consequences, for users and developers alike, of losing track of the work context.

Interface design is usually carried out in the context of a systems development project of which it is one part. The context can vary dramatically depending upon whether development is done in-house, through custom contracts, or to create products. Most software engineering approaches do not adequately address the needs of interface development. The greatest challenge in developing a good system is often not in knowing what to do, but in finding the time, place, and resources to do it. Chapter 4, "Software Development Contexts," discusses these problems and identifies possible solutions.

When design turns to implementation, the tools available to build systems become important. In Chapter 5 we survey tools designed to assist the developers of interactive systems and interfaces, and we consider issues in tool design and implementation. Tools can, but often don't, support the evolution of a system from early interface mock-ups to working prototypes to final construction. A flexible toolkit enables early feedback on the strengths and weaknesses of an interface design and facilitates easy experimentation and rapid change. Tools to support development have become increasingly critical as the range of interface options increases and as interface software grows more complex.

REFERENCES

Card, S. (1995). Pioneers and Settlers: Methods Used in Successful User Interface Design. In Rudisill, Lewis, Polson, and McKay (1995), to appear.

Rudisill, M., Lewis, C., Polson, P., and McKay, T. (Eds.) (in press). *Human-Computer Interface Design: Success Cases, Emerging Methods, and Real-World Context.* Morgan Kaufmann.

Chapter 2

Design and Evaluation

"Getting it right the first time" plays a very different role in software design which does not involve user interfaces than it does in user interface design. This may explain, in part, the reluctance of designers to relinquish it as a fundamental aim. In the design of a compiler module, for example, the exact behavior of the code is or should be open to rational analysis. Even those factors which cannot be predicted exactly, such as frequencies of data with particular characteristics, may be amenable to statistical treatment. The choice of algorithms can and should be anchored securely in a reliable analysis of the data, the transformations to be carried out, and the performance characteristics of the system. Good design in this context is highly analytic, and emphasizes careful planning. Designers know this.

Adding a human interface to the system disrupts this picture fundamentally. A coprocessor of largely unpredictable behavior (i.e., a human user) has been added, and the systems algorithms have to mesh with it. There is no data sheet on this coprocessor, so one is forced to abandon the idea that one can design one's algorithms from first principles. An empirical approach is essential. The involvement of human users escalates the need for an empirical approach well above the usual requirements for testing to make sure a system works.

John Gould and Clayton Lewis (1985, p. 305)

Recognition of the need for an empirical approach came early. But effective methods for designing and evaluating interfaces have been slow in coming.

Unfortunately, no "silver bullet" appeared. And the design challenge increases as improved computer power, input and display hardware, and interaction techniques enable new applications and produce new challenges. Even advice that is easy to state, such as "know the user," is difficult to apply. No one approach covers all situations. Designing an entirely novel product is different from designing minor enhancements to an existing system. Sometimes functionality is the primary focus of interest; in other cases performance or aesthetics play the major role. Skillful developers learn to select appropriately from a broad range of techniques.

The fortunate news is that significant progress has been made. We have refined a broad range of methods. Formal development goals and rigorous quantitative testing fit well in the engineering context of early interface development. Over time, interfaces became more context-specific and less constrained by engineering considerations, and qualitative approaches became more prevalent. Recently we have also seen design methods anchored in theory. The readings in this chapter and discussions in the text review this wonderful and growing set of methods in a maturing and important field.

DESIGN AND EVALUATION CONSIDERED TOGETHER

Design, implementation, and evaluation were traditionally viewed as separate topics. It seems logical: Design something, build it, and evaluate what you've built. This chapter's readings emphasize, however, that interactive systems require *iterative* design. Rarely do we know enough about computer users and their work practices to design interactive systems and applications from basic principles. The most promising approach is to iterate design and evaluation until a satisfactory result is achieved. Evaluation pervades this process: evaluation of existing systems, evaluation of current work practices and organizational settings, evaluations of rapid prototypes and mock-ups, evaluations of alpha and beta versions. Figure 2.1 illustrates a possible iterative design cycle.

This chapter begins with approaches that have been developed and refined to address traditional human-computer interface design problems, typically involving single-user personal computer applications. We present a *multidisciplinary* perspective, drawing from engineering, programming, cognitive psychology, human factors, anthropology, and graphic design. Of these, typically only graphic designers have formal training in design; as a result, the literature is marked by collections of methods and principles with little in the way of systematic design theory. We present a relatively systematic approach to design in this chapter.

We then examine evaluation approaches—approaches for testing prototypes early in the design cycle or for evaluating software at any point in development. Evaluation approaches are categorized into those carried out by designers without the aid of users, and those that do involve users.

The themes of this chapter are continued in the next chapter, which covers recent approaches that bring in the essential contextual and social issues required for effective design of the integrated, multiuser systems needed today by groups and organizations.

THE DISCIPLINE OF HUMAN-COMPUTER INTERACTION DESIGN

As we shall see in Part III of this volume, modern interface designers have a great variety of interaction techniques and considerable interface knowledge at their disposal. As we shall see in Part IV, good design takes into account characteristics of the intended users and the work that they do. How can our knowledge of technological possibilities and user needs be duly considered and synthesized into an appropriate design? What process should be used? How can it be done most effectively?

Answers tend to be characterized as either principles or rules, guidelines or checklists, or methodologies. *Principles* are collections of statements that advise the designer on how to proceed (for example, "Know the user"). *Guidelines* are collections of tests that can be applied to an interface to determine if it is satisfactory; (e.g., provide an average response time of less than one second). Principles and guidelines are often confused, since the latter can be simple reformulations of the former—"design until *x* is achieved" replacing "achieve *x* in your design." In practice, guidelines are usually more specific and in some cases quantitative. *Methodologies* are more-or-less formalized procedures that are believed to guide and structure the process of effective design when followed in sequence.

We begin this section with a discussion of design principles. (Because design guidelines are used primarily in system and interface evaluation, their discussion is deferred to later in the chapter.) We then present several accessible and effective design methodologies. The section concludes with brief discussions of key issues that appear in most of the methodologies—getting to know users and their tasks, idea generation, envisionment and prototyping, metaphor, and multidisciplinary collaboration.

FIGURE 2.1

One possible iterative design process consisting of successive phases of a design-implement-evaluate loop.

Information collection
Questionnaires
...
Characterizations of users and tasks
Day in the life scenarios
Interviews with discipline specialists

↓

	Design →	**Implement** →	**Evaluate**
Concept design ↓	Initial design concept	Design mockups	Interviews with users; reactions to mockups
Functionality and interface design ↓	Design of system functionality & look-and-feel	Implementation of "smoke and mirrors" prototype	Usability test
Prototype implementation ↓	Design of "critical mass" of system	Implementation of partial working system	Heuristic evaluation
Deliverable system implementation ↓	Design and modification of deliverable system	Implementation and installation of this system	Usability tests
System enhancement and evolution	Design of monitoring and feedback system	Implementation of this system	Interviews and questionnaires, data collection and analysis

Design Principles

An early and insightful enumeration of principles for the design of interactive graphics systems is that of Hansen (1971):

- "Know the user."
- "Minimize memorization," by allowing selection of items rather than entry of data, by using names instead of numbers, by ensuring predictable behavior, and by providing ready access to useful system information.
- "Optimize operations," by providing rapid execution of common operations, by preserving display consistency, by exploiting "muscle memory," and by organizing and reorganizing commands based on observed system usage.
- "Engineer for errors," through the provision of good error messages, by designing so common errors are not made, by allowing actions to be reversible, and by guaranteeing system integrity in the face of hardware or software failure.

Subsequent lists of principles appeared in Foley and Wallace (1974), Norman (1983), and Gaines and Shaw (1984). Rubinstein and Hersh (1984) is a useful book that presents 93 design principles, including

1. *Designers make myths; users make conceptual models.*
2. *Separate design from implementation.*
3. *Describe before you leap.*
4. *Develop an explicit use model.*
5. *Maintain a consistent myth.*

. . .

9. *Make states visible and visibly distinguished.*
10. *Minimize conceptual load.*
11. *Respect the rules of human conversation.*
12. *Interrupt with care.*
13. *Respond with an appropriate amount of information.*
14. *Don't misrepresent capabilities.*
15. *Do not violate the rules of human conversation.*
16. *Be consistent in the use of language.*
17. *Teach by example, not by formalism.*
18. *Avoid arbitrary syntax.*
19. *Use application terminology.*
20. *Use standard language.*

. . .

30. *Treat learning aids as part of the system.*
31. *Write the user's guide first.*
32. *Support clear conceptual models for documentation.*
33. *Example, examples, examples.*

. . .

49. *Provide an easy way out.*
50. *No surprises.*

. . .

55. *Don't blame the user.*

. . .

62. *Make it easy to correct mistakes.*

. . .

87. *Articulate the evaluation goals.*
88. *Select subjects who are unfamiliar with the system.*
89. *Select subjects who are representative of the target population.*
90. *Use representative tasks.*

. . .

93. *Videotape real users.*

A readable book by Heckel (1991) is structured around thirty "design elements":

1. *Know your subject.*
2. *Know your audience.*
3. *Maintain the user's interest.*
4. *Communicate visually.*
5. *Lever the user's knowledge.*
6. *Speak the user's language.*
7. *Communicate with metaphors.*
8. *Focus the user's attention.*
9. *Anticipate problems in the user's perception.*
10. *If you can't communicate, don't do it.*
11. *Reduce the user's defensiveness.*
12. *Give the user control.*
13. *Support the problem-solving process.*
14. *Avoid frustrating the user.*
15. *Help the user cope.*
16. *Respond to the user's actions.*
17. *Don't let the user focus on mechanics.*
18. *Help the user to crystallize his thoughts.*
19. *Involve the user.*
20. *Communicate in specifics, not generalities.*
21. *Orient the user in the world.*
22. *Structure the user's interface.*
23. *Make your product reliable.*
24. *Serve both the novice and the experienced user.*
25. *Develop and maintain user rapport.*
26. *Consider the first impression.*
27. *Build a model in the user's mind.*
28. *Make your design simple. . .*
29. *But not too simple.*
30. *You need vision!!!*

Shneiderman (1992, pp. 72–73) formulates "eight golden rules of dialog design":

1. *Strive for consistency.*
2. *Enable frequent users to use shortcuts.*
3. *Offer informative feedback.*
4. *Design dialogues to yield closure.*
5. *Offer simple error handling.*
6. *Permit easy reversal of actions.*
7. *Support internal locus of control.*
8. *Reduce short-term memory load.*

Our final set of principles is an elegant formulation originally devised by Gould and Lewis (1985), later updated in Gould et al. (1987). It is presented in the first reading of Chapter 2, a slight revision of most of a landmark chapter that Gould (1988) published in the *Handbook of Human-Computer Interaction* (Helander, 1988). It is quite appropriately one of the longest readings in this volume.

The article pulls together a decade of work on design and evaluation techniques by many researchers. This work had produced a scattered assortment of strategies, practices, and tools that could be applied successfully in different situations (see Rudman and Engelbeck, 1995, and Olson and Moran, 1995, for recent attempts to structure and compare some of the many approaches to interface design). Gould did the field a great favor by collecting this work in one place, illustrating many of the techniques by referring to experiences in designing a messaging system for Olympic athletes (Gould et al., 1987; IBM, 1985 video). He structures the methods by placing them in a framework of four design principles he had developed with Clayton Lewis (Figure 2.2).

Design Methodologies

Although principles can assist as we design, they do not help to structure the process of design. The ideal design methodology might be a procedure that when followed in a more or less straightforward manner is likely to produce a good design. Although the ideal is unrealizable, we shall nonetheless review a number of insightful and useful formulations of design methodologies.

Gould's formulation of the design process can be viewed as an informal methodology. He describes work as occurring in four phases: "a gearing-up phase, an initial design phase, an iterative development phase, and a system installation phase." He notes that usability is determined by much more than the software controlling the interface and identifies a score of usability components, ranging from system performance to support groups. He then suggests a number of methods, classifying them under the most appropriate of the four design principles (Figure 2.3).

This is a splendid set of approaches, some of which will be elaborated by later readings in this chapter. Gould also gathers

FIGURE 2.2

Four user interface and system design principles (Gould, Boies, and Lewis, 1991, p. 75).

Early Focus on Users
Designers should have direct contact with intended or actual users—via interviews, observations, surveys, and participatory design. The aim is to understand users' cognitive, behavioral, attitudinal, anthropometric characteristics—and the characteristics of the jobs they will be doing.

Early—and Continual—User Testing
The only presently feasible approach to successful design is an empirical one, requiring observation and measurement of user behavior, careful evaluation of feedback, insightful solutions to existing problems, and strong motivation to make design changes.

Iterative Design
A system under development must be modified based upon the results of behavioral tests of functions, user interface, help system, documentation, training approach. This process of implementation, testing, feedback, evaluation, and change must be repeated to iteratively improve the system.

Integrated Design
All aspects of usability (e.g., user interface, help system, training plan, documentation) should evolve in parallel, rather than be defined sequentially, and should be under one management.

FIGURE 2.3

Methods for applying the design principles of Figure 2.2 (Gould, 1988).

Methods to Carry Out Early Focus on Users
Talk with users
Visit customer locations
Observe users working
Videotape users working
Learn about the work organization
Thinking aloud
Try it yourself
Participative design
Expert on design team
Task analysis
Surveys and questionnaires
Testable behavioral target goals

Methods to Carry Out Early—and Continual—User Testing
Printed or video scenarios
Early user manuals
Mock-ups
Simulations
Early prototyping
Early demonstrations
Thinking aloud
Make videotapes
Hallway and storefront methodology
Computer bulletin boards . . . and conferencing
Formal prototype test
Try-to-destroy-it contests
Field studies
Follow-up studies

Methods to Carry Out Iterative Design
Software tools
System development work organization

Methods to Carry Out Integrated Design
Consider all aspects of usability in the initial design
One person or group has responsibility for all aspects of usability

the methods into useful checklists that can be used in planning and carrying out a project. Some methods are particularly interesting because they are rarely seen in other discussions of development, such as "try-to-destroy-it contests" in which a system is turned over to a group who is challenged to find bugs, to crash the system, or to break into it.

Gould's article has been highly praised by readers with a variety of backgrounds. But, although it includes checklists that are useful in any situation, it is *not* a prescription to be applied in a cookbook fashion. As Gould notes, not all of the techniques are appropriate in every project. Which techniques to use, how heavily to rely on any one, how long to iterate, where to set criteria for success, and many other issues must be decided by designers or developers. Sometimes these approaches are also difficult to apply, due to conditions in development organizations that are explored in Chapter 4.

Another design methodology is the formulation of Rubinstein and Hersh (1984), who describe the process of system design as occurring in successive iterations of five stages—information collection, design, implementation, evaluation, and deployment:

- The gathering of information, including goals, market requirements, technical requirements, current state of the art, competing products, industry standards, government regulations, and the capabilities of the system builders. The key element is carrying out a *task analysis* of the activities done by users in their environment.
- System design, including specification of the *external myth* and *conceptual model* through which the users see and understand the system, the *use model* describing how the system is to be used, the documentation, and the methods for error handling and recovery.
- Implementation design and construction, first of a prototype, and then of the system itself.
- Testing and evaluation, both formal and informal, of the system.
- Delivery of the system, and evaluation of the reactions of the user and the marketplace to it.

Shneiderman (1992, pp. 498–499) presents a more elaborate, eight-stage "lifecycle for interactive systems development." Again, testing in every stage and iteration among the stages is required. He stresses the need for the involvement of and the nurturing of the user community and the careful planning for reliability, availability, security, integrity, standardization, portability, integration, timeliness, and affordability.

- Collect information, using interviews, questionnaires, and task analysis. Prepare a schedule and estimation of all costs. Design a testing strategy.
- Define requirements and semantics. Requirements include security, privacy, integrity, and adherence to standards. Semantics include task objects, actions, and sequencing. Obtain manager and customer agreement.
- Design syntax and support facilities, including response time, feedback for each action, error messages and error handling, on-line help and tutorials. Write user and reference manuals. Review all specifications. Carry out usability testing with mock-ups or prototypes.
- Specify physical devices, considering issues such as screen size, resolution, and color. Establish communication requirements. Consider ergonomic issues such as table space and lighting. Do more testing and design revisions.
- Develop software, using interface software development tools. Emphasize modifiability, maintainability, reliability, security, and adequate documentation. Enable monitoring of users and performance. Thoroughly test with realistic usage load.
- Integrate system and disseminate to users, via acceptance tests of both the software and the support facilities. Provide adequate training and consultation to users. Follow phased approach to dissemination, revising and fine tuning in response to user feedback.
- Nurture the user community, employing telephone and on-line consultants, newsletters and suggestion boxes, interviews and focus groups, electronic newsgroups and bulletin boards. Conduct both objective and subjective evaluations. Monitor usage frequencies and patterns, including occurrences of errors. Respond to user suggestions for improvements and to what is implied by the evaluations.
- Prepare evolutionary plan, including system design for easy repair and refinement, and availability of staff time. Use questionnaires and interviews for ongoing user feedback. Schedule regular revisions, informing users in advance.

Nielsen (1993, p. 72) stresses the need for "usability engineering" in the development of entire product families as they evolve over extended periods of time. He develops a "usability engineering lifecycle model" as a set of eleven stages with iterative design listed explicitly as one of the stages:

1. *Know the user*
   a. *Individual user characteristics*
   b. *The user's current and desired tasks*
   c. *Functional analysis*
   d. *The evolution of the user and the job*
2. *Competitive analysis*
3. *Setting usability goals*
   a. *Financial impact analysis*
4. *Parallel design*
5. *Participatory design*
6. *Coordinated design of the total interface*
7. *Apply guidelines and heuristic analysis*
8. *Prototyping*
9. *Empirical testing*
10. *Iterative design*
    a. *Capture design rationale*
11. *Collect feedback from field use*

We shall return below to a discussion of knowing the user and the user's tasks. Nielsen argues that competitive analysis can be a cost-effective way of studying and evaluating approaches to product functionality and interface design. He stresses the importance of setting quantitative usability goals, such as the number of user errors per hour, or the level of satisfaction expressed by users. These goals can then be translated into estimates of increased productivity, which in turn can be used to estimate the money to be saved for a customer or customer's organization.

Parallel design is useful in brainstorming, where it can increase the number of possible design approaches. Participatory design goes beyond "knowing" the user; instead, the user becomes one of the designers, as we shall see in more detail in Chapter 3.

Coordinating and increasing the consistency of the user interface is often achieved through corporate user interface standards and graphical user interface style guides (Marcus, 1992; see also the discussion in Chapter 6). Guidelines and heuristic evaluation, prototyping, and empirical testing will be discussed later in this chapter.

Lewis and Rieman (1993, p. 9) term their design methodology "the task-centered design process." Most of their shareware book is an elaboration of the following steps of their process:

- *figure out who's going to use the system to do what*
- *choose representation tasks for task-centered design*
- *plagiarize*
- *rough out a design*
- *think about it*
- *create a mock-up or a prototype*
- *test it with users*
- *iterate*
- *build it*
- *track it*
- *change it*

We shall return to Lewis and Rieman's methods of getting to know users and their tasks in the next subsection. Their tongue-in-cheek suggestion to "plagiarize" is perhaps too strong a way of expressing a solution to the problem that has been glossed over in the other design methodologies—inventing design ideas and creating an initial design. They suggest that designers work within existing interface frameworks, incorporate existing applications within their solutions, and copy interaction techniques from other systems (although this may have legal ramifications, as we shall see in Chapter 6). Design ideas can also be created through brainstorming, as we shall discuss below.

Getting to Know Users and Their Tasks

From Hansen's "know the user" to Lewis and Rieman's "task-centered design," the importance of understanding users and their tasks has never been in question. Yet there is no cookbook procedure for accomplishing this that works for all users and all tasks. Lewis and Rieman (1993) stress the importance of developing an understanding of users through close personal contact, and of choosing representative tasks that provide reasonably complete coverage of a system's intended functionality. The reading, which is Chapter 2 of their shareware book, gives a number of insightful examples of learning about users' tasks and codifying this knowledge as "concrete, detailed examples of tasks they perform or want to perform that your system should support." They suggest that *scenarios* then be produced for a set of key sample tasks that describe in detail "what a user would have to do and what he or she would see step-by-step in performing a task using a given system." Sometimes these are called "day in the life" scenarios. We shall return below to scenarios as a form of envisionment.

Understanding users and their tasks can be done at a number of levels. Often it is helpful to profile the characteristics of users. These include physical characteristics, such as age; knowledge and experience, such as education, computer and task literacy and experience, and reading and typing ability; and psychological characteristics, such as attitude and motivation. Jobs and tasks may also be categorized in terms of their structure and importance, the level of training and support provided, and the nature of system use, for example, regular or casual, mandatory or discretionary. These gross categorizations may sometimes be helpful in suggesting appropriate design approaches, such as the use of touch screens for an information kiosk to be used by one-time museum visitors who can have arbitrary degrees of computer literacy and experience.

Yet these general characteristics fail to capture the individual richness of user behavior in a specific work context. Lofland and Lofland (1984) is a very useful guide to qualitative observation and analysis of social settings. This often requires generic methods such as questionnaires and interviews. Payne (1951) and Sheatsley (1983) are accessible treatments of the art of asking questions. They stress how much the wording, ordering, and formatting of questions can influence the results of a survey. We shall also describe in Chapter 3 two approaches that involve interviews and observations in the workplace—contextual inquiry, and ethnography and interaction analysis.

It is also important to realize that human-computer interaction is not the first discipline to concern itself with understanding users and their tasks. The human-factors community has for many years worked on *task analysis*, which they characterize as follows (Kirwan and Ainsworth, 1992, p. 1; see also Phillips et al., 1988):

> *. . .a range of techniques used by ergonomists, designers, operators and assessors to describe, and in some cases evaluate, the human-machine and human-human interaction in systems. Task analysis can be defined as the study of what an operator (or team of operators) is required to do, in terms of actions and/or cognitive processes, to achieve a system goal. Task analysis methods can also document the information and control facilities used to carry out the task.*

Kirwan and Ainsworth (1992) describes a task analysis process; details 25 major techniques of task analysis for task data collection, task description, task simulation, task behavior assessment, and task requirement evaluation; and discusses a number of applications in the chemical, nuclear, offshore, military, and machine tooling industries.

Finally, human information processing psychology and approaches to cognitive modeling allow more precise formulations of task analysis that can then be used to guide design. We shall review this area in detail in Chapter 9.

Idea Generation

Yet ideas for innovative systems and excellent interfaces do not only come from understanding users and their tasks, but from the generation of new ideas and new approaches. Consider, for example, Dan Bricklin's invention of the spreadsheet in 1978, as described in Levy (1984) and Licklider (1989). The idea for the spreadsheet came to Bricklin as he was pondering how he might use his computer experience to facilitate the tedious calculations involved in projecting the financial implications of one company's acquisition of another. These calculations were typically done by accountants and analysts on large sheets of papers ruled with rectangular grids, usually known as "ledger sheets" or "spreadsheets." The financial modeling packages available on mainframes were not very accessible, and he conceived of the possibility of implementing an electronic spreadsheet on the tiny microcomputers that were then thought by many to be only toys. The rest, as they say, is history.

Both Bricklin's computer experience and his domain knowledge of financial modeling contributed to his electronic spreadsheet inspiration. The reading by Mountford (1990) suggests that ideas and inspiration for interface design can also be found in the fields of film, animation, theater, architecture, and the more closely related fields of industrial design and information display. She discusses interface metaphors and, not surprisingly, the importance of observing real-world tasks and environments. She concludes with a set of techniques for generating new ideas and enhancing creativity, primarily by different methods of "breaking set," forcing a different view of an object or situation. Other approaches to idea generation can be found in the popular literature on methods such as observation, listening, brainstorming, metaphor, sketching, scenario creation, free association, meditation, juxtaposition, searching for patterns, and "lateral thinking" (De Bono, 1970).

Envisionment and Prototyping

The creative aspect of designing for use has received remarkably little treatment in the human-computer interaction literature. The technical nature of development, the fact that most interfaces are developed by programmers, and the initially quite limited range of interface expression slowed the entry of graphic design and graphic art into the field. Yet these professionals are actually trained in designing for use, unlike programmers, human factors engineers, and others involved in interface construction. Today, the maturing of computer technology and the wider range of expression it now enables has led to growing recognition of the role for professional designers. One notable example is Aaron Marcus, whose work is sampled in Chapter 6. Another is William Verplank, one of the authors of our Case B retrospective look at the Xerox Star.

In an unpublished presentation, Verplank (1991) outlines ways in which sketching and metaphor can contribute to design. He notes that three metaphors have dominated human-computer interface design. First came the "computer as person," giving rise to command languages and dialogues. Next came the "computer as tool," with a focus on full representation and direct, continuous control. Now the "computer as medium" metaphor stresses the notion of reaching out to distant people and objects and information. Each of these metaphors brings with it many associations and constraints in thinking about the interface.

Verplank also discusses the use of "throw-away metaphors" to release creative associations and ideas, even if the metaphor never appears in the final interface. He described a project on insurance claims handling in which interviewing case workers led to a "detective metaphor." The designers thought in terms of looking for clues, following leads, gathering and organizing evidence, making deductions, and so forth. The notion of case workers "ruminating" over a case led to a playful series of digestive system metaphors, in which cases were seen as fodder to be processed in multiple stages. (Alimentary, my dear Watson?)

Envisionment of interfaces is therefore the formulation and exploration of system and interface ideas and metaphors at a very early stage of the design process. Verplank and the industrial designer Laurie Vertelney are two experts in the rapid sketching and graphic envisionment of interface ideas. Some methods of envisionment are presented in the next reading, Vertelney's (1989) paper "Using Video to Prototype User Interfaces." The title is a little misleading—video is required only as a medium for displaying simple mock-ups or prototypes produced to simulate and evaluate design ideas rapidly. These methods include stories, scenarios, storyboards, flipbooks, animated drawings, cutout animation, animation of real objects, computer animation, and computer-scripted interactive prototypes, such as those that can be produced with Claris HyperCard and MacroMedia Director. Rapid prototyping is further explored in Wilson and Rosenberg (1988).

Envisionment can also be done with "Wizard of Oz" techniques in which input to a simulated computer is fed to a human "behind the curtain" who types back responses designed to simulate a system that cannot now be built or has not yet been built (Thomas and Gould, 1975; Gould, Conti, and Hovanecz, 1983). These are further described as "simulations" in the reading by Gould (1988).

The Role of Metaphor

As we have seen, metaphor is a useful tool in both idea generation and in envisionment. Webster's Third New International Dictionary defines metaphor as "a figure of speech in which a word or phrase denoting one kind of object or action is used in place of another to suggest a likeness or analogy between them." Metaphors aid users in understanding a new *target domain* (e.g., a word processor) by allowing them to comprehend it (up to the point of "mismatch," to be discussed further below) in terms of a *source domain* they already understand (e.g., a typewriter). Metaphors aid designers because adoption of a metaphor allows them to structure aspects of the target system or interface in terms of familiar and commonly understood aspects of the source domain.

In our next reading, "Working with Interface Metaphors," Thomas Erickson (1990) builds his discussion around an interesting example—metaphors that were considered as part of a major development project. First he discusses uses of metaphor in everyday language, then uses of metaphor in interfaces. In describing the process of generating useful interface metaphors, he stresses the need to understand the two parties that the metaphor will connect: the users and the system. He also repeats advice introduced by Gould, such as the need for iterative design and a focus on users.

Erickson also notes that to get full value from a metaphor, designers should consider using as much of it as possible. If you choose a book metaphor, he says, don't forget to include a table of contents, page numbers, and an index!

Erickson's example is the interface to a system feature that automates the process of repeatedly making copies of an object that will frequently be changed. He explores different metaphors that might work, and leaves the reader in suspense by saying that further research as well as user testing are required to select the best approach. However, by exploring the Macintosh System 7, you can discover the choice that was made.

A more comprehensive review of metaphor appears in Carroll, Mack, and Kellogg (1988). The authors begin by enumerating metaphor source domains then in use in commercially available or prototype systems, including offices, desktops, documents, business forms, chalkboards, ledger sheets, and the physical world. After discussing three approaches to understanding metaphor—operational, structural, and pragmatic—they propose an approach to designing with metaphor that involves four steps (p. 77):

- *Identify candidate metaphors or composite metaphors.*
- *Detail metaphor/software matches with respect to representative user scenarios.*
- *Identify likely mismatches and their implications.*
- *Identify design strategies to help users manage mismatches.*

Mismatches need not be viewed as a liability. Smith (1987, p. 61; see also 1987 video), for example, in developing his "Alternate Reality Kit," suggests that we exploit our ability to create system features that are mismatches in terms of the interface metaphor, "magical features . . . that deliberately violate the metaphor in order to provide enhanced functionality."

The Role of Multidisciplinary Collaboration

As stressed in the introduction to this volume, and as highlighted by the discussion in this chapter, effective design involves a variety of skills—conceptual and technical, behavioral and aesthetic. Assembling a design team in which these skills are well represented requires drawing upon and effectively harnessing many backgrounds and disciplines, a subject that is explored beautifully in the paper by Kim in Chapter 4.

EVALUATING SYSTEMS AND THEIR USER INTERFACES

We now shift our focus from design to evaluation. As noted before, evaluation of existing practice often precedes design, and evaluation of prototypes and systems is used throughout the processes of design, implementation, and deployment.

Our next reading, "Methodology Matters: Doing Research in the Behavioral and Social Sciences" by Joseph McGrath (1994; see also McGrath, 1984), introduces an elegant and comprehensive framework for understanding methods of evaluation. In the social and behavioral sciences, McGrath states, "the phenomena of interest involve states and actions of human systems—of individuals, groups, organizations, and larger social entities—and the by-products of those actions." In studying human-computer interaction, we examine the states and actions of humans in their use of computers. For example, we may study the use of groupware (see Chapter 11) by a team of coworkers. We may do this in a laboratory setting or in a natural setting such as a workplace, and we may use a variety of techniques such as questionnaires, interviews, and observation. McGrath provides insight into the strengths and weaknesses of these methods, insights that apply to the study of human-computer interaction whether the interfaces are used by individuals, groups, or organizations.

McGrath introduces terminology that will appear in articles in this chapter and in subsequent chapters. He stresses that there are trade-offs among "*generalizability* of the evidence over populations of *actors*, *precision* of measurement of the *behaviors* that are being studied (and precision of control over extraneous factors that are not being studied), and *realism* of the situation or *context* within which the evidence is gathered, in relation to the contexts to which you want your evidence to apply." McGrath emphasizes that no single method can possess all three of these desirable attributes. He discusses *correlation* and *causality*, and the fact that we should not assume that a causal relationship exists between phenomena simply because their appearances are correlated. He introduces the technique of *randomization* and the concept of a *true experiment*, and explains the logic of *statistical inference*.

McGrath then explores the concept of *validity*. He suggests that there are four important and distinct notions—*internal validity*, *statistical conclusion validity*, *construct validity*, and *external validity*. A study lacking external validity, for example, may apply to the setting in which it is carried out, yet tell us nothing about the extent to which it applies in other settings. Finally, McGrath describes in detail six kinds of experimental measures, *self reports*, *trace measures*, *observations by a visible observer*, *observations by a hidden observer*, *public archival records*, and *private archival records*.

McGrath concludes with a summary of key points:

- *Results depend on methods. All methods have limitations. Hence, any set of results is limited.*
- *It is not possible to maximize all desirable features of method in any one study; tradeoffs and dilemmas are involved.*
- *Each study (each set of results) must be interpreted in relation to other evidence bearing on the same questions.*

An elegant part of McGrath's presentation is his taxonomy of research strategies (Figure 2.4).

This taxonomy provides a framework within which to organize and present human-computer interaction evaluation methods (Figure 2.5).

Experienced designers often report that unexpected factors in the workplace are a source of problems for systems they have developed. *Field strategies* allow us to study systems in use on real tasks in real work settings, and to observe the many important factors that cannot be explored in a laboratory, where we can control many details yet not reproduce the context of real technology use.

We distinguish between two kinds of field strategies, *field studies* and *field experiments*. Field study methods, such as *ethnography and interaction analysis* and *contextual inquiry*, techniques that we present and discuss in Chapter 3, observe process or technology in situ, disturbing the system we observe as little as possible. In *field experiments* we observe the impact of changing one aspect of the work environment, either over a short time frame as during the *beta testing* of a new product, or in a study of the medium- or long-term impact of technological change.

The second class of methods are called *experimental strategies*, typically carried out in a laboratory. The principle advantage is the degree of control it permits over the conditions of the study. Participants can be selected to meet specific criteria, the tasks can be chosen or constructed, the activity can be recorded, and the conditions can be repeated to allow quantitative measures of such metrics as performance, recurrence of errors, and subjective satisfaction.

We distinguish between two kinds of experimental strategies, *experimental simulations* and *laboratory experiments*. Laboratory experiments are controlled experiments in which we typically study the impact of some interface parameter such as screen size, design of icons, naming of menus, or choice of input device. We shall return to this topic later in this chapter. In experimental simulations we create in the laboratory a *real* system that is used *for*

FIGURE 2.4

Taxonomy of research strategies (McGrath, 1994).

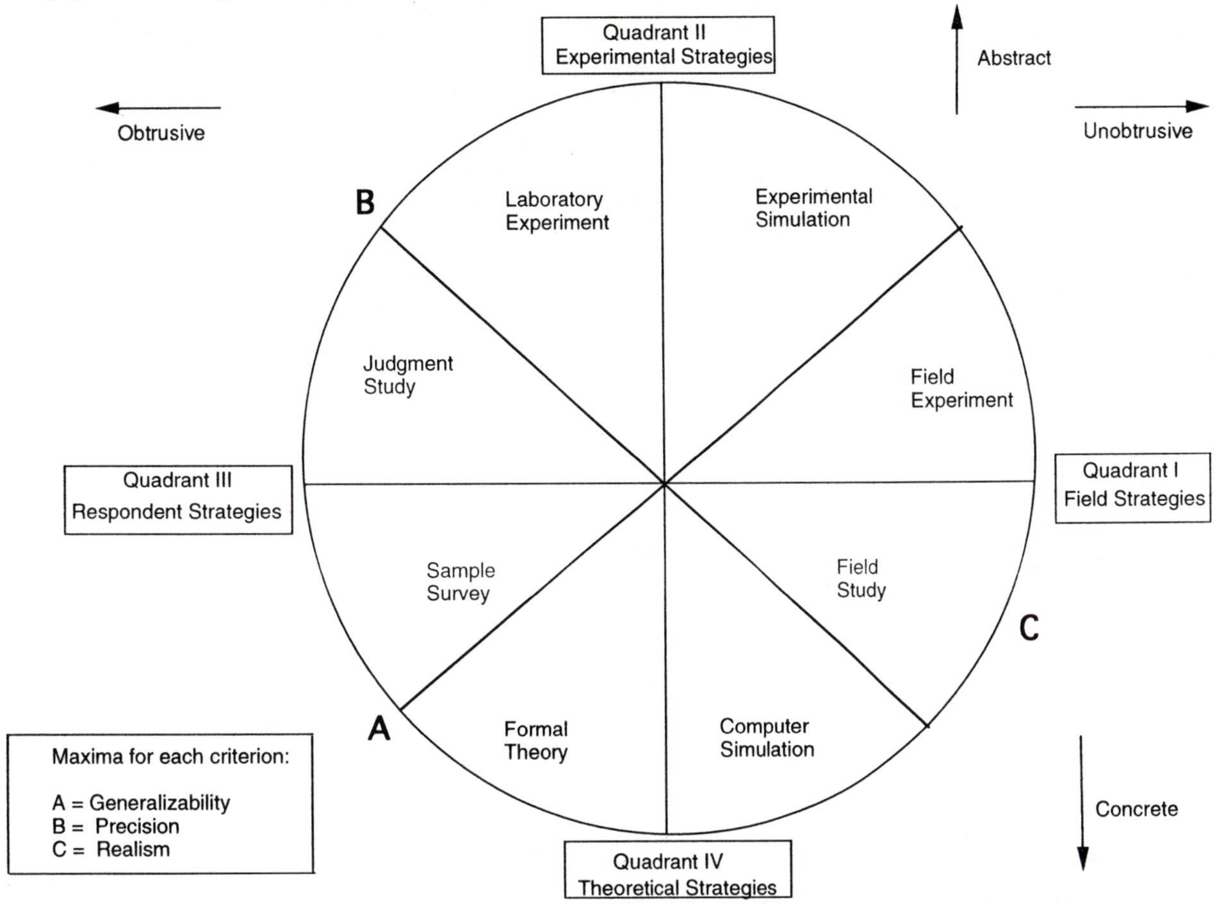

FIGURE 2.5

HCI research and evaluation strategies.

Field strategies
(Settings under conditions as natural as possible)

Field studies
- *Ethnography and interaction analysis*
- *Contextual inquiry*

Field experiments
- *Beta testing of products*
- *Studies of technological change*

Experimental strategies
(Settings concocted for research purposes)

Experimental simulations
- *Usability testing*
- *Usability engineering*

Laboratory experiments
- *Controlled experiments*

Respondent strategies
(Setting is muted or made moot)

Judgment studies
- *Usability inspection methods, e.g., heuristic evaluation*

Sample surveys
- *Questionnaires and interviews*

Theoretical strategies
(No observation of behavior required)

Formal theory
- *Design theory, e.g., Norman's 7 stages*
- *Behavioral theory, e.g., color vision*

Computer simulations
- *Human information processing theory*

experimental purposes by *real* potential users. We try to make the setting as much like an actual behavior setting as possible. Two such methods are called *usability testing* and *usability engineering*, topics to which we shall also return later in this chapter.

The third class of methods are called *respondent strategies*. These are in turn divided into *judgment studies*, in which we get responses from a relatively small set of "judges" about a carefully crafted set of stimuli, and *sample surveys*, in which we typically solicit more general kinds of information from a somewhat broader class of respondents. In judgment studies, responses are primarily designed to give information about the stimulus (e.g., an interface); in sample surveys, they are primarily designed to give information about the respondents. Sample surveys include questionnaires and interviews, which we have already discussed briefly in this chapter. Judgment studies include *usability inspection methods*, which we shall discuss later in this chapter.

The final set of methods are called *theoretical strategies*, which in turn are divided into *formal theory* and *computer simulations*. In both cases recommendations for the appropriateness of interfaces or interface approaches is based on evaluation with respect to a human-computer interaction theory. Although development of such theories is based on empirical evidence, their application typically does not involve any empirical observations, and in fact is often intended to obviate the need for empirical observations (see Chapter 9).

Formal theory is typically used qualitatively to provide insights into interface suitability. In computer simulations, however, models can be "run" on a computer to derive predictions of user performance as specific interface evaluations. In the ultimate case, one could evaluate a design without constructing it, as the design of an airplane wing can be tested with an aerodynamic model before any wind tunnel testing. The required models of interfaces, dialogues, and users are built from our understanding of human information processing. The best known of these techniques is GOMS; this and other human information processing approaches are introduced in Chapter 9.

Karat (1988) and Landauer (1988) are two other valuable treatments of research and evaluation methods in human-computer interaction.

In the remainder of this section, therefore, we shall discuss five approaches to system and interface evaluation:

- Heuristic evaluation with usability guidelines
- Cognitive walkthroughs
- Usability testing
- Usability engineering
- Controlled experiments

The last three approaches are experimental methods involving empirical work *with* users. The first two approaches are respondent strategies carried out by interface designers or usability specialists *without* the aid of users. They are the most prominent of a class of techniques known as *usability inspection methods*. This is the topic of our next reading, Mack and Nielsen (1994), which is the executive summary of a recent book reviewing work in this field. The reading describes inspection objectives, categorizes the methods, discusses methodological issues in carrying out inspections, positions inspections in the usability engineering lifecycle, and briefly introduces important research issues.

Heuristic Evaluation with Usability Guidelines

Usability guidelines are often indistinguishable from design principles, but they must be formulated in a way so as to be *testable*. Designers or evaluators can then examine an interface and determine whether or not it meets the guidelines. Smith and Mosier (1986), with 944 guidelines, Brown (1988), with 302 guidelines, and Mayhew (1992), with 288 guidelines, are particularly extensive sets of guidelines.

We need to be cautious in relying upon guidelines, because they are usually vague, are sometimes contradictory (Maguire, 1982), involving trade-offs between conflicting goals (Norman, 1983), and are often formulated at an inappropriate level of specificity (Smith, 1986). For example, opinions often differ as to what constitutes a good error message or how to prevent errors, and advice such as "be consistent" is not always helpful advice.

It is certainly true that unmotivated inconsistency is a common and annoying source of poor interface design. Yet we all recognize that it is possible to design a "foolish consistency." An interface that made us carry out every operation in one way with no shortcuts for frequently used paths might be consistent, but not optimal. In fact, Grudin (1989, 1992) demonstrates the complexity of the interface consistency issue and shows with some examples that good interfaces are not necessarily consistent.

It is also difficult to apply guidelines to real design problems (Mosier and Smith, 1986). Ideally, guidelines must specify the context in which they are to be applied. Yet it is impossible to describe fully the significant context for interface design. The significance of context in determining the appropriate design guideline is explored for the example of the naming of commands by Barnard and Grudin (1988).

Finally, it is very difficult to deal with huge sets of guidelines. Recently, Jakob Nielsen and his colleagues (Nielsen and Molich, 1990; Nielsen, 1992a, 1993, 1994a; 1994b) have developed a usability inspection method known as *heuristic evaluation*. A few usability specialists are asked to look for problems in an interface or interface design by judging its compliance with a small set of very general design guidelines or "heuristics." Evaluators are trusted to use their experience and intuition to identify whether a guideline makes sense or not in a particular context and how to apply it. Heuristics focus the evaluator's attention on aspects of an interface that are often sources of trouble, making the detection of problems more likely.

Nielsen and Landauer (1993) analyze usability problems described in 11 published projects and conclude that the maximum cost/benefit ratio for a medium-large software project would have been obtained through the use of four evaluators. Although this is a not a reliable magic number, it does indicate that heuristic evaluation satisfies Nielsen's goal of being a "discount usability engineering method" that can be successfully applied on a modest budget.

Nielsen (1992a) explores the finding of usability problems in a telephone-based voice response system as a function of evaluator expertise. Nor surprisingly, usability specialists performed better than nonspecialists, and "double experts" who also had expertise in the type of interface being evaluated performed even better. The reader may wish to see how many problems he or she can find in the interface, which is described in Figure 2.6.

Figure 2.7 lists ten design heuristics derived by Nielsen (1994a, 1994b) from a factor analysis that suggests which guidelines provide the best coverage of published usability problems. They are "common sense" guidelines that usability specialists are familiar with, but keeping them in mind while examining interfaces seems to help evaluators in identifying problems.

Yet even ten guidelines result in conflicts and trade-offs. It is always necessary to think about the context and how sensibly to apply any guidelines. Even more important is to carry out empirical testing of designs built with the aid of guidelines. Guidelines and heuristic evaluation should be used *together with* empirical

FIGURE 2.6

A sample problem in usability evaluation (Nielsen, 1992a).

Identify usability problems in the following telephone-based banking system dialogue. The dialogue was preceded by user identification and password entry, and the transaction failed because the user had not authorized the bank to accept transfers over the phone.

System: Enter '1' for account information, '3' for transfers between your accounts. . .

User: 3#

S: Enter account to transfer from

U: 1234567890# (savings account number)

S: Enter account to transfer to

U: # (an abbreviation for the checking account)

S: Enter amount in cents

U: 100000#

S: From account number twelve thirty-four fifty-six seventy-eight ninety to account number primary account, a transfer of one thousand dollars is to be made. Press one to confirm, zero to cancel.

U: 1#

S: You do not have access to use this function.

FIGURE 2.7

Ten usability guidelines derived from a factor analysis of 249 usability problems encountered in 11 projects (Nielsen, 1994a, p. 30; see also Nielsen, 1994b).

Visibility of system status
The system should always keep users informed about what is going on, through appropriate feedback within reasonable time.

Match between system and the real world
The system should speak the users' language, with words, phrases and concepts familiar to the user, rather than system-oriented terms. Follow real-world conventions, making information appear in a natural and logical order.

User control and freedom
Users often choose system functions by mistake and will need a clearly marked "emergency exit" to leave the unwanted state without having to go through an extended dialogue. Support undo and redo.

Consistency and standards
Users should not have to wonder whether different words, situations, or actions mean the same thing. Follow platform conventions.

Error prevention
Even better than good error messages is a careful design which prevents a problem from occurring in the first place.

Recognition rather than recall
Make objects, actions, and options visible. The user should not have to remember information from one part of the dialogue to another. Instructions for use of the system should be visible or easily retrievable whenever appropriate.

Flexibility and efficiency of use
Accelerators—unseen by the novice user—may often speed up the interaction for the expert user such that the system can cater to both inexperienced and experienced users. Allow users to tailor frequent actions.

Aesthetic and minimalist design
Dialogues should not contain information which is irrelevant or rarely needed. Every extra unit of information in a dialogue competes with the relevant units of information and diminishes their relative visibility.

Help users recognize, diagnose, and recover from errors
Error messages should be expressed in plain language (no codes), precisely indicate the problem, and constructively suggest a solution.

Help and documentation
Even though it is better if the system can be used without documentation, it may be necessary to provide help and documentation. Any such information should be easy to search, focused on the user's task, list concrete steps to be carried out, and not be too large.

user testing, not as a replacement for user testing (Smith and Mosier, 1986; Nielsen and Phillips, 1993).

Jeffries (1994) stresses the importance of building a good working relationship between usability inspectors and developers, cautions about the dangers of "false alarms," and makes recommendations for improving usability problem reports (p. 290):

1. *Describe the problem and the solution separately.*
2. *Provide justifications for the problem and the solution.*
3. *Include an assessment of the severity of the problem.*
4. *Explicitly consider possible trade-offs.*
5. *Evaluate carefully any solution that requires new functionality to be added to the application.*
6. *Be aware of biases that you, the evaluator, bring to the evaluation.*
7. *Try to look at each problem from multiple levels of abstraction.*
8. *Examine the problem reports as a collection, replacing local optimizations and trade-offs with general solutions that fit the application as a whole.*

Cognitive Walkthroughs

Cognitive walkthrough evaluation (Polson et al., 1992) is inspired by structured code walkthroughs, in which a group of software engineers examine code in a methodical search for problems. In cognitive walkthroughs of an interface design, a set of representative tasks is selected and stepped through, keystroke by keystroke, menu selection by menu selection. Whether based on a paper mock-up or a working prototype, the design must be fully specified, allowing the system response to any user action to be described.

As the developers consider each action, they fill out forms that require them to specify information about the users' goals, tasks and subtasks, knowledge, the visible state of the interface, and the relations and changes among these. The questions are based on a cognitive theory of the relationships between goals, actions, and the visible state of the interface, a theory based in part on the GOMS approach introduced in Chapter 9. Four questions are paramount (Wharton et al., 1994, p. 112):

- *Will the users try to achieve the right effect?*
- *Will the user notice that the correct action is available?*
- *Will the user associate the correct action with the effect trying to be achieved?*
- *If the correct action is performed, will the user see that progress is being made toward solution of the task?*

The theory underlying cognitive walkthroughs is based on the psychology of inexperienced users, and the approach is intended to evaluate a design for ease of learning, particularly by exploration. Use of the technique allows the detection of likely interface problems, such as when a label will not properly identify its function to a user. Cognitive walkthroughs suggest specific psychological explanations for problems, thereby pointing developers towards solutions.

When cognitive walkthrough evaluation was tried on complex systems in development settings (Wharton et al., 1992), it did detect some usability problems. Yet selecting appropriate tasks required knowledge that was not always available to the development team (a problem faced by all usability inspection methods). The low-level focus on keystrokes and mouse clicks often left high-level problems unrecognized. For example, one might examine a six-step sequence and find appropriate labels and system responses at each step, but fail to notice that the entire sequence could be eliminated by a higher-level change in the interface. Finally, the time demands of the process were not acceptable in the development organizations studied.

To address this last issue, the time demands, the developers of the method devised an automated tool for handling the forms (Rieman et al., 1991). Rowley and Rhoades (1992) also modified the technique to speed up the process, resulting in what they term the *cognitive jogthrough*. In doing this they encouraged more open discussion of observations by experts, thus adding elements of heuristic evaluation. This may have moved them further from the underlying cognitive theory, yet enabled the capture of higher-level problems and the immediate generation of design change suggestions. Further discussion of the evolution and current status of this technique appears in Wharton et al. (1994).

Two other interesting usability inspection methods are pluralistic walkthroughs (Bias, 1994) and inspection and design reviews (Wixon et al., 1994). *Pluralistic walkthroughs* are meetings in which actual users, product developers, and usability experts examine and discuss usability issues associated with the dialogue steps in a task scenario. *Inspection and design reviews* typically focus on consistency of an interface with respect to a product family and compliance of an interface to some interface standard.

Usability Testing

The above methods all rely on the good intuition of interface specialists. As stated above, we cannot rely only upon this, but need to augment these intuitions with evidence obtained from observing our artifacts being utilized by real users, which is known both as *usability testing* and *user testing*.

Most usability testing involves experimental tasks that reflect important or frequent uses of the system, which should be selected through contact with real users and work situations, not by intuition. Participants are recorded as they engage in the tasks; problems and "errors" are identified. Interface changes to make these problems and errors less likely can then be proposed. Features that take particularly long to identify or operate can be identified. Overall user satisfaction (or frustration) levels can be monitored, either informally or through questionnaires.

Generally, a number of people are asked to carry out the experimental task, in order to pick up a wider range of problems and to get some sense of the frequency and consequences of each. Nielsen and Landauer (1993) analyze usability problems described in 11 published projects and conclude that the maximum cost/benefit ratio for a medium-large software project would have been obtained through the use of three test users. Again, this is not a "magic number," but an indication that usability testing can be successfully carried out with only a modest budget.

In a formal scientific experiment, all subjects are asked to carry out precisely the same task. In usability testing, however, the evaluators may change the task or even the interface when a major error is first encountered, rather than spending additional

FIGURE 2.8

Guidelines for user testing with thinking aloud (based on Nielsen, 1992a).

Practical study design

- *Reflect on the participants' backgrounds and how they might affect the study.*
- *Be aware of problems that arise when experimenters know the users personally.*
- *Prepare for the study carefully (avoid last minute panic).*
- *Select the tasks carefully to be representative and to fit the allotted time.*
- *In general, start with an easier (but not frivolous) task.*
- *Write down features of the system that are not being tested as well as those that are!*
- *Define the start-up state for the study precisely.*
- *Define precise rules for when and how users can be helped during the study.*
- *Plan the timing and cut-off procedure (if subject gets stuck) for each part of the study.*
- *Include reasonable provisions for data collection (e.g., tape or video recorder, keystroke capture where appropriate).*
- *Plan data analysis techniques in advance.*
- *Carry out a pilot study (important but often overlooked).*

Written materials

- *Participant release form.*
- *Questionnaire covering prior experience, etc. (if relevant).*
- *Introduction to the study for users, including scenario of use.*
- *Checklist for experimenters.*
- *Evaluation survey (if relevant).*

Carrying out the study

- *Let users know that complete anonymity will be preserved.*
- *Let them know that they may quit at any time.*
- *Stress that the system is being tested, not the participant.*
- *Indicate that you are only interested in their thoughts relevant to the system.*
- *Demonstrate the thinking-aloud method by acting it out for a simple task, such as figuring out how to load a stapler.*
- *Hand out instructions for each part of the study individually, not all at once.*
- *Maintain a relaxed environment free of interruptions.*
- *Occasionally encourage users to talk if they grow silent.*
- *If users ask questions, try to get them to talk (e.g., "What do you think is going on?" and follow predefined rules on when to help or interrupt to help).*
- *Debrief each user after the experiment.*

Improving the study

- *The pilot study should "debug" the study. This minimizes changes during the study, allowing quantitative data analysis. But improvements may be warranted.*
- *Experimenters' role can be improved.*
- *Tasks given to participant can be improved.*
- *Written materials can be improved.*

effort documenting an obvious problem. The paper by Baecker, Small, and Mander in Chapter 6, for example, is an example of a *quasi-experiment* in which testing showing lack of comprehensibility of some static icons is followed by replacing them with animated icons, which are then shown to be comprehensible.

Often used in usability testing, the "thinking aloud" technique was first introduced to HCI by Clayton Lewis (1982; but see also Ericsson and Simon, 1980, 1984). A useful set of guidelines for using this procedure appears in Nielsen (1992b), and is adapted and extended in Figure 2.8. Many of these suggestions are good advice for *any* testing that involves users, such as stressing that it is the software that is being tested, not the participant, and that you know the software has problems ("After all, if you have no problems, this test is a waste of time!").

Our next reading, "Using Video in the BNR Usability Lab" by Kennedy (1989), is a nice example of usability testing that describes an alternative to the "thinking aloud" method. Called "co-discovery learning" by Kennedy and "constructive interaction" by others (Miyake, 1982; O'Malley, Draper, and Riley, 1984), the technique involves two people discussing a task as they carry it out. Although individual performance is typically the ultimate design goal, conversation while learning is often more natural than trying to think aloud while working alone. The two approaches are contrasted in a study by Hackman and Biers (1992).

Kennedy notes that seeing a videotape of people trying to use a system can motivate designers and management better than statistics do. The paper describes how she and her colleagues use a software tool called U-Test in order to manage and analyze video records and communicate the results to those concerned. Video is now an essential tool in most usability testing and in other behavioral methods used in human-computer interaction. This is further described in the reading by Suchman and Trigg in Chapter 3, and in papers by Harrison and Baecker (1992), Harrison, Owen, and Baecker (1994), Cuomo (1994), and Harrison (1995).

Brooks (1994), in the Nielsen and Mack (1994) book outlined in the previous reading, describes more recent approaches used at BNR. Many of the methods described by Kennedy are now standard elements in usability testing conducted at Microsoft, Apple, and other product development organizations. They are often used in conjunction with other approaches, such as contextual interviewing (described by Holtzblatt and Jones in Chapter 3).

Further general reading on usability testing may be found in

Maguire and Dillon (1993), Dumais and Redich (1993), and Rubin (1994). Nilesen (1994c) is a special issue of the journal *Behaviour and Information Technology* devoted to the increasingly important topic of corporate usability laboratories, which typically are equipped with special provisions such as multiple rooms, one-way mirrors, scan converters, and video recording equipment. Hoiem and Sullivan (1994) review the design and use of integrated data collection and analysis tools including both program event capture and video logging. Smilowitz, Darnell, and Benson (1994) present an evaluation of testing carried out in a usability laboratory and in actual work environments.

Palmitter et al. (1994) discuss how the usability lab can be brought "on the road" throughout the corporation and used in all phases of what they term "customer-centred design." They mention the use of many of the evaluation methods cited in Figure 2.5, including ones that we shall introduce in Chapter 3 as being responsive to the context in which users work.

Usability Engineering

Usability engineering (Nielsen, 1993) is user testing that is more formal in the sense that interface specialists or developers set explicit, quantitative performance goals known as *metrics*. For example, new users must be able to create and save forms in their first ten minutes with the system, or experienced telephone operators must on the average make fewer than 2% uncorrected errors while taking orders in no more than two minutes on the average.

There are two main arguments for explicit quantitative goals. Human factors engineers and other usability specialists are more likely to be taken seriously in engineering settings if they adopt the quantitative, objective approaches familiar to engineers. Developers who have explicit goals can chart their progress and recognize when they have succeeded.

Yet numbers will boost credibility only when they can be defended. Sometimes they can, as by measuring the time required for the same operation in a competing system. But often, especially with new or complex systems, numbers are arbitrary. Improving performance is desirable, but this involves more than adhering to strict numerical objectives, since users often respond most to the overall "feel" of a system.

Whiteside, Bennett, and Holtzblatt (1988) provide a good overview of usability engineering. In recounting their experiences, they also describe their evolution away from "development by numbers" and toward more qualitative approaches, such as contextual inquiry, which is discussed in Chapter 3.

Controlled Experiments

The McGrath reading discussed the purposes, advantages, and disadvantages of controlled experiments for studying groups (Ray and Ravizza, 1985; Hays, 1988). The advantage of the experimental method is considerably greater for studying individual behavior. Social, emotional, motivational, and communication variables that greatly complicate behavior in groups have less effect on individuals carrying out cognitive tasks such as reading or searching through a display, typing characters, or manipulating a mouse. Formal experiments can therefore help us understand the low-level perceptual, cognitive, and motor activities of individuals. As this individual behavior will ultimately occur in and be influenced by social settings, we must nevertheless remember that the use of an interface may be very different in a work setting from what it was in the laboratory.

One issue that arises in designing an experiment is whether to select a *within-subjects* design or a *between-subjects* design. A within-subjects design is one in which each subject or participant in the experiment experiences the different options being tested. If, for example, you are testing two mouse designs, each subject would try some tasks with one mouse, and then some with the other. In a between-subjects experiment, each subject tries just one of the alternatives being tested.

The advantage of the within-subjects approach is that it doesn't matter if some subjects happen to be particularly fast. This is *controlled for* or balanced out by the fact they use both designs, and you can see which they are faster with. On the other hand, these subjects in a between-subjects experiment may be using the slower mouse but could register a fast performance because they are speedier. A between-subjects experiment must therefore use more subjects to get the same level of confidence in the result. Yet often a between-subjects experiment is better because within-subjects participants can learn something from one condition that can affect their performance in the next condition. For example, using one mouse will improve their coordination and enable them to perform better on the second mouse, whichever one that may be. This can be addressed by techniques such as counterbalancing, that is, having half of the subjects try things in one order and half in the other order, but such techniques are not always effective due to asymmetries in practice effects.

In practice, one must carefully consider the trade-off between the economy of a within-subjects design versus the chance that learning effects can pollute the results.

One area that has seen considerable experimental work is that of menu design (Perlman, 1985; Paap and Roske-Hofstrand, 1988; Norman, 1991). Studies of menu design demonstrate both the possibilities and the perils of the experimental approach. On the one hand, they have provided reliable, reproducible answers to questions about whether to organize menus to be broad and shallow vs. narrow and deep. On the other hand, the experiments have ignored some important features of menus in the real world. For example, in experimental settings, the menu items that subjects are to select are generally chosen randomly, so each item is equally likely to be the target item. However, in real situations, we inevitably select some items much more frequently than other items. It is very likely that this would influence the breadth-vs-depth design decision, yet it is typically not studied. Results that ignore the impacts of frequency variations may therefore mislead as guides to design.

Nevertheless, for clearly defined questions, such as selecting the better of two mouse designs, formal interface experiments can be very useful in applied settings. We have already seen in Case B the effective use of such a study in the development of the Star. Chapter 13 presents an example of formal experimentation at its best in Egan et al.'s evaluation of Superbook, a hypertext-based browsing system. Shneiderman (1992) and his colleagues at the University of Maryland have also been active proponents and users of experimental methods.

Evaluating Evaluation

Recently, researchers have begun to carry out studies comparing and contrasting some of the evaluation methods we have discussed. We shall review four of these studies. The first attempts to characterize the pragmatics of user testing and heuristic evaluation. The other three seek to compare the effectiveness of user testing and usability inspection.

Nielsen and Landauer (1993) examines 11 user testing and heuristic evaluation exercises. In each of the studies, the experimenters felt they knew the complete set of problems in the interface, so it is possible to determine what percentage of the problems each evaluator found, and thus to determine the additional benefit from adding subjects. The authors use this to perform a cost-benefit analysis of these methods.

The authors estimate the optimal number is 9–21 heuristic evaluators or 7–20 user testing subjects, depending on project size. For medium-large projects, they suggest that the highest ratio of benefits to costs is achieved with 4 heuristic evaluators and 3 test users. A number of assumptions went into these calculations, which should therefore be regarded as speculative. Typical of laboratory studies, most of the interfaces that were examined were very small, and the evaluators did not work as they might in professional settings. (For example, in a study they might spend an hour evaluating an interface that would get days of attention in a work setting.) The figures are most plausible for small or very small projects. But the paper identifies an approach to tackling important issues in evaluation, and it should be followed by similar analyses of larger-scale projects in real work settings.

Jeffries et al. (1991) compared the interface to a single product using four evaluation techniques: cognitive walkthroughs, heuristic evaluation, usability testing, and reliance on interface guidelines. Heuristic evaluation and usability testing generally fared better than cognitive walkthroughs and the use of guidelines. Heuristic evaluation identified the greatest number of problems, including severe problems, but also uncovered many problems that were not severe. Usability testing was much more likely to focus in on severe problems and avoid problems that were not severe. Usability testing was more expensive, but heuristic evaluation required more expert evaluators.

Karat, Campbell, and Fiegel (1992) studied the relative effectiveness in identifying usability problems in two user interfaces of empirical usability testing and of walkthroughs carried out by individuals and pairs of evaluators. Usability testing identified the greatest number of problems, including a significant set of severe problems that were missed in the walkthroughs. Team walkthroughs typically fared better than individual walkthroughs. Empirical testing required the same or less time to identify the problems than did the walkthroughs. Only a third of the significant usability problems were identified in all three conditions, emphasizing the importance of using both experimental and respondent strategies.

Another comparison was reported in Nielsen and Phillips (1993). In this study, heuristic evaluation, usability testing, and the GOMS formal modeling approach (see Chapter 9) were used to estimate performance time for two interfaces. This is a very different task. Although all three methods were able to identify the better of the two interfaces, usability testing was the most accurate at identifying the relative advantage of the better interface, with GOMS next, and heuristic evaluation third. Since one interface was about 4 times as fast as the other, it was not remarkable that all methods identified it. This appears to indicate that heuristic evaluation is particularly good at detecting interface defects and not as good at identifying interface efficiency. GOMS is solely used to predict performance efficiency and does not identify design problems at all, so its superior performance in this task is understandable.

These studies are preliminary, and need to be viewed as the first of an ongoing series of attempts to compare methods systematically. At this point, the best approach appears to be a combination of heuristic evaluation and empirical usability testing. (Clearly, future methodological studies need to include this combination as one of the conditions to be evaluated.) Yet, even today, cognitive walkthroughs can lead to improved heuristics and better trained usability testers. The evolution and interplay of scientific theory and engineering practice is complex and unpredictable! The reader is referred to Nielsen (1993) and Nielsen and Mack (1994), which in late 1994 represented the best single sources on usability testing and usability inspection.

Positioning Evaluation in the Design Process

To conclude our discussion of evaluation methods, we return to the sample development process sketched in Figure 2.1 and suggest in Figure 2.9 where these methods could most appropriately be used. At any stage, there is a good selection of useful methods, many of which can be carried out at modest cost, so there is no longer any excuse for development carried out in splendid isolation from thoughtful critique by experts and effective participation and feedback by users.

THEORY-BASED DESIGN

So we can now see the crucial role that evaluation plays in the design process. Yet we are still left with an uncomfortable feeling. The design methodologies we have described are helpful, but not totally satisfactory. They must be tailored to different situations. It is not always obvious how to apply them. They provide advice, but neither exact prescriptions nor certainty. In response to these problems, some researchers have tried to put the craft of design on a more scientific footing by developing and applying theories of human-computer interaction to the process of design.

Don Norman (1986, 1988), for example, has formulated a theory, "The Seven Stages of Action," to explain how people do things. Versions of Norman's diagram appear both as Figure 9.4 and as Figure 1 of the Olson and Olson paper in Chapter 9. The theory postulates that there are seven stages of user activities involved in task performance. First is (1) deciding on a goal to be achieved.

To carry out the action requires three stages: (2) forming the intention, (3) specifying an action, and (4) executing this sequence. Finally, to assess the effect of the action requires three stages: (5) perceiving the state of the system, (6) interpreting that state as an outcome, and (7) evaluating that outcome in terms of the original goal.

FIGURE 2.9

Possible uses of evaluation methods in a sample development process.

Information collection
Interviews and questionnaires
Contextual inquiry
Interaction analysis

Concept design
Interviews
Heuristic evaluation
Usability testing
Controlled experiments

Functionality and interface design
Heuristic evaluation
Usability testing
Theory-based evaluations
Human information processing simulations

Prototype implementation
Usability testing
Heuristic evaluation

Deliverable system implementation
Usability testing
Quasi-experiments

System enhancement and evolution
Interaction analysis
Interviews and questionnaires
Field experiments

The problem with many artifacts, Norman argues, is that their design does not allow a user to move smoothly through these seven stages. In some cases, a system does not provide actions that correspond easily and directly to the intentions of the user. He terms this the "Gulf of Execution." For example, direct manipulation systems (Shneiderman, 1983; Hutchins, Hollan, and Norman, 1986) allow us to bridge this gulf because there is usually a straightforward correspondence between an intention and the action that needs be carried out to act on this intention. In other cases, a system does not provide a physical representation that can be easily perceived and interpreted in terms of the user's intentions and expectations. He calls this the "Gulf of Evaluation." Systems that provide meaningful and appropriate feedback in response to user actions allow us to bridge this gulf.

Norman suggests (1988, p. 53) that the seven-stage theory can be a valuable design aid, for it provides a checklist of questions to ensure that these gulfs can be bridged:

How easily can one:

1. *Determine the function of the device?*
2. *Tell what actions are possible?*
3. *Determine mapping from intention to physical movement?*
4. *Perform the action?*
5. *Tell if system is in desired state?*
6. *Determine mapping from system state to interpretation?*
7. *Tell what state the system is in?*

He also interprets this checklist in terms of concepts of good design already introduced in the Introduction to Part I (Norman, 1988, pp. 52–53):

- *Visibility. By looking, the user can tell the state of the device and the alternatives for action.*
- *A good conceptual model. The designer provides a good conceptual model for the user, with consistency in the presentation of operations and results and a coherent, consistent, system image.*
- *Good mappings. It is possible to determine the relationships between actions and results, between the controls and their effects, and between the system state and what is visible.*
- *Feedback. The user receives full and continuous feedback about the results of actions.*

Other theories that have been applied to guide the design process are the Syntactic-Semantic Model of User Knowledge (Shneiderman, 1992), the Task-Artifact Design Cycle (Carroll, Kellogg, and Rosson, 1991; Carroll and Rosson, 1992) and the Human Information Processor, GOMS, Keystroke-Level Model, and other human information processing models that are presented in Chapter 9.

PRESERVING DESIGN RATIONALE

Even these beginning steps towards developing a theory-based design science provide little encouragement for thinking that a good, widely useful interface design method will emerge from a purely logical analysis. Thoughtful, iterative design and evaluation enable the exploration of a potentially large design space. It is natural to want to preserve a record of what was tried, how it succeeded, and how it did not. Recording the design history or its rationale could serve several purposes. By focusing attention on the process of considering alternatives, it might lead to better design in the first place. A record of the decision making could also be very useful when modifications are being considered.

Many prominent HCI researchers have recently focused their attention on capturing and working with *design rationale*, exploring it as a theoretical approach to understanding and improving the design process. There has also been work on building tools to ease the time-consuming process of recording and manipulating the design rationale information. Carroll and Moran (1991, p. 198) summarize the approach as follows:

> *There are several motivations for constructing explicit design rationale: (a) to support reasoning processes in design, (b) to facilitate communication among the various players in the design process (designers, implementers, maintainers, users, etc.), and (c) to further the cumulation and development of design knowledge across design projects and products. Design rationale research addresses the issues involved in capturing, articulating, representing, and using explicit rationale for these various purposes. The goal of this research is to provide improved concepts, methods, and tools for design.*

This approach is immensely appealing from an intuitive perspective, but it has yet to prove convincingly that it can overcome several obstacles to fulfilling the promise. These obstacles include the distraction and labor that is required of designers to use the tools and methods; the fact that some decisions are made for reasons that are not entirely consciously understood (e.g., aesthetic) or that might be socially or politically too sensitive to record (e.g., this feature would be too difficult for the current staff to implement); and the possibility that descriptions cannot be easily understood at a time and place removed from that of the designer.

Despite these obstacles, the work on capturing design rationale has led to intellectually stimulating explorations of the design process, and greater benefits are likely to follow. Moran and Carroll (1995) is an edited collection that contains a significant fraction of recent work in this area. Rank Xerox EuroPARC (1993 video) and Carroll et al. (1994 video) document two approaches to design rationale.

REFERENCES

Note: A ● before a reference indicates a reading.

Baecker, R., and Buxton, W. (Eds.) (1987). *Readings in Human-Computer Interaction: A Multidisciplinary Approach.* Morgan Kaufmann.

Barnard, P., and Grudin, J. (1988). Command Names. In Helander (1988), 237–255.

Bias, R. (1994). The Pluralistic Usability Walkthrough: Coordinated Empathies. In Nielsen and Mack (1994), 63–76.

Brooks, P. (1994). Adding Value to Usability Testing. In Nielsen and Mack (1994), 255–271.

Brown, C. (1988). *Human-Computer Interface Design Guidelines.* Ablex.

Carroll, J., Kellogg, W., and Rosson, M. (1991). The Task-Artifact Cycle. In Carroll, J. (Ed.), *Designing Interaction: Psychology at the Human-Computer Interface,* Cambridge University Press, 74–102.

Carroll, J., Mack, R., and Kellogg, W. (1988). Interface Metaphors and User Interface Design. In Helander (1988), 67–85.

Carroll, J., and Moran, T. (1991). Introduction to This Special Issue on Design Rationale. *Human-Computer Interaction* 6(3–4).

Carroll, J., and Rosson, M. (1992). Getting Around the Task-Artifact Cycle: How to Make Claims and Design by Scenario. *ACM Transactions on Information Systems* 10(2), 181–212.

Cuomo, D. (1994). Understanding the Applicability of Sequential Data Analysis Techniques for Analyzing Usability Data. *Behaviour and Information Technology* 13(1–2), 171–182.

De Bono, E. (1970). *Lateral Thinking: Creativity Step by Step.* Harper & Row.

Dumais, J., and Redich, J. (1993). *A Practical Guide to Usability Testing.* Ablex.

Ericsson, K., and Simon, H. (1980). Verbal Reports as Data. *Psychological Review* 87, 215–251.

Ericsson, K., and Simon, H. (1984). *Protocol Analysis: Verbal Reports as Data.* MIT Press.

● Erickson, T. (1990). Working with Interface Metaphors. In Laurel, B. (Ed.), *The Art of Human-Computer Interface Design,* Addison-Wesley, 65–73.

Foley, J., and Wallace, V. (1974). The Art of Natural Graphic Man-Machine Conversation. *Proc. of the IEEE* 62(4), 462–471.

Gaines, B., and Shaw, M. (1984). *The Art of Computer Conversation.* Prentice Hall.

● Gould, J. (1988). How to Design Usable Systems. In Helander (1988), 757–789. (Revised, excerpt included 757–779, 784–789.)

Gould, J., Boies, S., Levy, S., Richards, J., and Schoonard, J. (1987). The 1984 Olympic Message System—A Test of Behavioural Principles of System Design. *Communications of the ACM* 30(9), 758–769.

Gould, J., Boies, S., and Lewis, C. (1991). Making Usable, Useful, Productivity-Enhancing Computer Applications. *Communications of the ACM* 34 (1), 74–85.

Gould, J., Conti, J., and Hovanecz, T. (1983). Composing Letters with a Simulated Typewriter. *Communications of the ACM* 26(4), 295–308.

Gould, J., and Lewis, C. (1985) Designing for Usability—Key Principles and What Designers Think. *Communications of the ACM* 28(3), 300–311.

Grudin, J. (1989). The Case against User Interface Consistency. *Communications of the ACM* 32(10), 1164–1173.

Grudin, J. (1992). Consistency, Standards, and Formal Approaches to Interface Development and Evaluation: A Note on Wiecha, Bennett, Boies, Gould, and Greene. *ACM Transactions on Information Systems* 10(1), 103–111.

Hackman, G., and Biers, D. (1992). Team Usability Testing: Are Two Heads Better than One? *Proc. 36th Annual Human Factors Society Meeting,* 1205–1209.

Hansen, W. (1971). User Engineering Principles for Interactive Systems. *AFIPS Conference Proceedings* 39, AFIPS Press, 523–532.

Harrison, B. (1995). Multimedia Tools for Social and Interactional Data Collection and Analysis. To appear in Thomas, P. (Ed.), *The Social and Interactional Dimensions of Human-Computer Interfaces.* Cambridge University Press.

Harrison, B., and Baecker, R. (1992). Designing Video Annotation and Analysis Systems. *Proc. Graphics Interface '92,* Morgan Kaufmann, 157–166.

Harrison, B., Owen, R., and Baecker, R. (1994). Timelines: An Interactive System for the Collection and Visualization of Temporal Data. *Proc. Graphics Interface '94,* Morgan Kaufmann, 171–178.

Hays, W. (1988). *Statistics,* Fourth Edition. Harcourt Brace.

Heckel, P. (1991). *The Elements of Friendly Software Design,* The New Edition. Sybex.

Helander, M. (Ed.) (1988). *Handbook of Human-Computer Interaction.* North-Holland.

Hoiem, D., and Sullivan, K. (1994). Designing and Using Integrated Data Collection and Analysis Tools: Challenges and Considerations. *Behaviour and Information Technology* 13(1–2), 160–170.

Hutchins, E., Hollan, J., and Norman, D. (1986). Direct Manipulation Interfaces. In Norman, D., and Draper, S. (Eds.) (1986), *User Centered System Design,* Lawrence Erlbaum Associates, 87–124.

Jeffries, R. (1994). Usability Problem Reports: Helping Evaluators Communicate Effectively with Developers. In Nielsen and Mack (1994), 273–294.

Jeffries, R., Miller, J., Wharton, C., and Uyeda, K. (1991). User Interface Evaluation in the Real World: A Comparison of Four Techniques. *Proc. CHI '91,* ACM, 119–124.

Karat, J. (1988). Software Evaluation Methodologies In Helander (1988), 891–903.

Karat, C., Campbell, R., and Fiegel, T. (1992). Comparison of Empirical Testing and Walkthrough Methods in User Interface Evaluation. *Proc. CHI '92,* ACM, 397–404.

● Kennedy, S. (1989). Using Video in the BNR Usability Lab. *SIGCHI Bulletin* 21(2), ACM, 92–95.

Kirwan, B., and Ainsworth, L. (1992). *A Guide to Task Analysis.* Taylor and Francis.

Landauer, T. (1988). Research Methods in Human-Computer Interaction. In Helander (1988), 905–928.

Levy, S. (1984). A Spreadsheet Way of Knowledge. *Harpers Magazine,* November 1984. Appears in Forester, T. (Ed.), *Computers in the Human Context: Information Technology, Productivity, and People,* MIT Press, 1989.

Lewis, C. (1982). Using the "Thinking-Aloud" Method in Cognitive Interface Design. *IBM Research Report RC 9265 (#40713).*

● Lewis, C., and Rieman, J. (1993). Getting to Know Users and Their Tasks. Chapter 2 of *Task-Centered User Interface Design,* self-published over the Internet, 14–19.

Licklider, T. (1989). Ten Years of Rows and Columns. *Byte,* December, 324–331.

Lofland, J., and Lofland, L. (1984). *Analyzing Social Settings,* Second Edition. Wadsworth.

● Mack, R., and Nielsen, J. (1994). Executive Summary. In Nielsen, J., and Mack, R. (Eds.), *Usability Inspection Methods,* John Wiley & Sons, 1–23.

Maguire, M. (1982). An Evaluation of Published Recommendations on the Design of Man-Computer Dialogues. *International Journal of Man-Machine Studies* 16(3), 237–261.

Maguire, M., and Dillon, A. (1993). Usability Measurement—Its Practical Value to the Computer Industry. *Proc. INTERCHI '93,* ACM, 145–148.

Marcus, A. (1992). *Graphic Design for Electronic Documents and User Interfaces.* Addison-Wesley.

Mayhew, D. (1992). *Principles and Guidelines in Software User Interface Design.* PTR Prentice Hall.

McGrath, J. (1984). Methods for the Study of Groups. Chapter 3 of McGrath, J. (Ed.), *Groups: Interaction and Performance.* Prentice Hall, 28–39.

● McGrath, J. (1994). Methodology Matters: Doing Research in the Behavioral and Social Sciences. Original paper.

Miyake, N. (1982). Constructive Interaction. *CHIP Report 113.* Center for Human Information Processing. University of California at San Diego.

Moran, T., and Carroll, J. (Eds.) (1995). *Design Rationale: Concepts, Techniques, and Use.* Lawrence Erlbaum Associates.

Mosier, J., and Smith, S. (1986). Applications of Guidelines for Designing User Interface Software. *Behaviour and Information Technology* 5(1), 39–46.

● Mountford, S. (1990). Tools and Techniques for Creative Design. In Laurel, B. (Ed.), *The Art of Human-Computer Interface Design.* Addison-Wesley, 17–30.

Nielsen, J. (1992a). Finding Usability Problems through Heuristic Evaluation. *Proc. CHI '92,* ACM, 373–380.

Nielsen, J. (1992b). Evaluating the Thinking Aloud Technique for Use by Computer Scientists. In Hartson, H., and Hix, D. (Eds.), *Advances in Human-Computer Interaction,* Volume 3, Ablex, 69–82.

Nielsen, J. (1993). *Usability Engineering.* Academic Press.

Nielsen, J. (1994a). Heuristic Evaluation. In Nielsen and Mack (1994), 25–62.

Nielsen, J. (1994b). Enhancing the Explanatory Power of Usability Heuristics. *Proc. CHI '94.* ACM, 152–158.

Nielsen, J. (Ed.) (1994c). Special Issue on Usability Laboratories. *Behaviour and Information Technology* 13(1–2).

Nielsen, J., and Landauer, T. (1993). A Mathematical Model of the Finding of Usability Problems. *Proc. INTERCHI '93,* ACM, 206–213.

Nielsen, J., and Mack, R. (Eds.) (1994). *Usability Inspection Methods.* John Wiley & Sons.

Nielsen, J., and Molich, R. (1990). Heuristic Evaluation of User Interfaces. *Proc. CHI '90,* ACM, 249–256.

Nielsen, J., and Phillips, V. (1993). Estimating the Relative Usability of Two Interfaces: Heuristic, Formal, and Empirical Methods Compared. *Proc. INTERCHI '93.* ACM, 214–221.

Norman, D. (1983). Design Principles for Human-Computer Interaction. *Proc. CHI '83,* ACM, 1–10.

Norman, D. (1986). Cognitive Engineering. Chapter 3 in Norman, D., and Draper, S. (Eds.) (1986), *User Centered System Design,* Lawrence Erlbaum Associates, 31–61.

Norman, D. (1988). *The Psychology of Everyday Things.* (*The Design of Everyday Things* in paperback.) Basic Books.

Norman, K. (1991). *The Psychology of Menu Selection: Designing Cognitive Control at the Human-Computer Interface.* Ablex.

Olson, J., and Moran, T. (1995). Mapping the Method Muddle: Guidance in Using Methods for User Interface Design. In Rudisill, Lewis, Polson, and McKay (1995).

O'Malley, C., Draper, S., and Riley, M. (1984). Constructive Interaction: A Method for Studying Human-Computer-Human Interaction. *Proc. INTERACT '84,* 269–274.

Paap, K., and Roske-Hofstrand, R. (1988). Design of Menus. In Helander (1988), 205–235.

Palmitter, S., Lynch, G., Lewis, S., and Stempski, M. (1994). Breaking Away from the Conventional "Usability Lab": The Customer-Centered Design Group at Tektronix, Inc. *Behaviour and Information Technology* 13(1–2), 128–131.

Payne, S. (1951). *The Art of Asking Questions.* Princeton University Press.

Perlman, G. (1985). Making the Right Choices with Menus. *Proc. Interact '84.* North-Holland, 317–321, reprinted in Baecker and Buxton (1987).

Phillips, M., Bashinski, H., Ammerman, H., and Fligg Jr., C. (1988). A Task Analytic Approach to Dialogue Design. In Helander (1988), 835–857.

Polson, P., Lewis, C., Rieman, J., and Wharton, C. (1992). Cognitive Walkthroughs: A Method for Theory-Based Evaluation of User Interfaces. *International Journal of Man-Machine Studies* 36, 741–773.

Ray, W., and Ravizza, R. (1985). *Methods Towards a Science of Behaviour and Experience*, 2nd Edition. Wadsworth.

Rieman, J., Davies, S., Hair, C., Esemplare, M., Polson, P., and Lewis, C. (1991). An Automated Cognitive Walkthrough. *Proc. CHI '91*, ACM, 427–428.

Rowley, D., and Rhoades, D. (1992). The Cognitive Jogthrough: A Fast-Paced User Interface Evaluation Procedure. *Proc. CHI '92*, ACM, 389–395.

Rubin, J. (1994). *Handbook of Usability Testing: How to Plan, Design, and Conduct Effective Tests*. John Wiley & Sons.

Rubinstein, R., and Hersh, H. (1984). *The Human Factor*. Digital Press.

Rudisill, M., Lewis, C., Polson, P., and McKay, T. (Eds.) (in press). *Human-Computer Interface Design: Success Cases, Emerging Methods, and Real-World Context*. Morgan Kaufmann.

Rudman, S., and Engelbeck, G. (1995). Lessons in Choosing Methods for Designing Complex Graphical User Interfaces. In Rudisill, Lewis, Polson, and McKay (1995).

Sheatsley, P. (1983). Questionnaire Construction and Item Writing. In Rossi, P., Wright, J., and Anderson, A. (Eds.), *Handbook of Survey Research*, Academic Press, 195–230.

Shneiderman, B. (1983). Direct Manipulation: A Step Beyond Programming Languages. *IEEE Computer* 16(8), 57–69.

Shneiderman, B. (1992). *Designing the User Interface: Strategies for Effective Human-Computer Interaction*, Second Edition. Addison-Wesley.

Smilowitz, E., Darnell, M., and Benson, A. (1994). Are We Overlooking Some Usability Testing Methods? A Comparison of Lab, Beta, and Forum Tests. *Behaviour and Information Technology* 13(1–2), 183–190.

Smith, R. (1987). Experiences with the Alternate Reality Kit: An Example of the Tension between Literalism and Magic. *Proc. CHI+GI '97*, ACM, 61–67.

Smith, S. (1986). Standards Versus Guidelines for Designing User Interface Software. *Behaviour and Information Technology* 5(1), 47–61.

Smith, S., and Mosier, J. (1986). *Guidelines for Designing User Interface Software*. Report No. 7 MTR-10090, ESD-TR-86-278. MITRE Corporation.

Thomas, J., and Gould, J. (1975). A Psychological Study of Query by Example. *Proc. 1975 National Computer Conference*, 439–445.

Verplank, W. (1991). Sketching Metaphors: Graphic Invention and User-Interface Design. Presented at *FRIEND21 Symposium*, November 1991.

Vertelney, L. (1989). Using Video to Prototype User Interfaces. *SIGCHI Bulletin* 21(2), ACM, 57–61.

Wharton, C., Bradford, J., Jeffries, R., and Franzke, M. (1992). Applying Cognitive Walkthroughs to More Complex User Interfaces: Experiences, Issues, and Recommendations. *Proc. CHI '92*, ACM, 381–388.

Wharton, C., Rieman, J., Lewis, C., and Polson, P. (1994). The Cognitive Walkthough Method: A Practitioner's Guide. In Nielsen and Mack (1994), 105–140.

Whiteside, J., Bennett, J., and Holtzblatt, K. (1988). Usability Engineering: Our Experience and Evolution. In Helander (1988), 791–817.

Wilson, J., and Rosenberg, D. (1988). Rapid Prototyping for User Interface Design. In Helander (1988), 859–875.

Wixon, D., Jones, S., Tse, L., and Casaday, G. (1994). Inspections and Design Reviews. In Nielsen and Mack (1994), 77–103.

VIDEOS

Carroll, J., Van Deusen, M., Wheeler, G., Alpert, S., Karat, J., and Rosson, M.B. (1994). Multimedia Folklore: Capturing Design History and Rationale with Raison d'Etre. *ACM SIGGRAPH Video Review (SGVR)* 106.

IBM (1985). Olympic Message System. *ACM SGVR* 19.

Rank Xerox EuroPARC (1993). QOC in Action: Using Deign Rationale to Support Design. *ACM SGVR* 88.

Smith, R. (1987). Alternate Reality Kit. *ACM SGVR* 27.

HOW TO DESIGN USABLE SYSTEMS
(EXCERPT)

John D. Gould
P. O. Box 704
IBM Research Center -- Hawthorne
Yorktown Heights, New York 10598

ABSTRACT

This paper describes a process of system design that, if you follow it, will help you design good computer systems for people -- systems that are easy to learn, easy to use, contain the right functions, and are liked. There are four key points in this usability design process: early focus on users; empirical measurement; iterative design; and integrated design, where all aspects of usability evolve together from the start. This paper focuses upon 20-30 informal methods to carry out these four points. Many of the methods can be used without extensive training in human factors. This is important because usability is so broad and so deep that there is not enough trained human factors people to work on it. Use of these methods is contrasted with other approaches frequently discussed today, including user interface standards, handbooks and guidelines, and formal models.

INTRODUCTION

The focus of this paper is on designing computer systems. It is aimed at system designers who want to know more about how to design useful, usable, desirable computer systems -- ones that people can easily learn, that contain the functions that allow people to do the things they want to do, and that are well liked. Throughout, "good computer systems" mean ones with these characteristics.

The intended audience, or users, of this paper are expected to be (1) human factors people involved, or getting involved, in system design; (2) experimental psychologists and other discipline-oriented people who may want to learn how to do behavioral system design work; and (3) system designers who are not trained in human factors but who are concerned about usability of systems. This latter group is particularly important since it is impractical for trained human factors people to work on all aspects of usability. There are not enough of them. Usability is too broad. And, besides, as a result of reading this paper, systems people can learn how usability people ought to work.

Reprinted, with some additions, from Martin Helander (Ed.), <u>Handbook of Human-Computer Interaction.</u> North-Holland: Elsevier, 1988, pp 757-789.

"There is no comprehensive and generally accepted manual on how to design good human factors into computer systems," wrote Shackel (1984). While not comprehensive, we hope this paper will at least be useful. It is intended to be tutorial, to identify and explain the main things you must do to design a good system. It provides indications of where to go for more information, and what you can expect to find when you get there. It is not a critical review of the literature, nor an examination of small technical differences. It brings together material from diverse sources that previously may have existed fairly independently of each other.

Overview

In this Introduction, we first note that usability consists of many pieces. Second, we briefly mention a process for system design which addresses all these pieces. We believe that the four key points ("principles") of this process are the required cornerstones for designing good systems. Third, as a means of showing where these principles fit into system design, we divide the design process into four rough phases. Next, in the main section we describe many methods to be used in carrying out this process of designing for usability. In sections at the end, we discuss tips on how to get started designing your system and various resources available to you; and we describe in more detail the status of user interface standards, guidelines, development manuals, and formal models.

TABLE 1. Components of usability.

System Performance
Reliability
Responsiveness
System Functions
User Interfaces
Organization
I/O Hardware
For end-users
For other groups
Reading Materials
End-user groups
Support groups
Language Translation
Reading materials
User interfaces
Outreach Program
End-user training
On-line help system
Hot-lines
Ability for customers to modify and extend
Installation
Packaging and unpacking
Installing
Field Maintenance and serviceability
Advertising
Motivating customers to buy
Motivating user to use
Support-group users
Marketing people
Trainers
Operators
Maintenance workers

Usability Has Many Aspects

There are many aspects to usability which must be taken into account if a system is to be good (Table 1). Generally designers focus on only one aspect of usability, e.g., knitting pre-given functions together into an user interface. This narrow focus almost guarantees missing the point that usability is made up of many important factors which are often mutually dependent (see Boies, Gould, Levy, Richards, and Schoonard, 1985 for a detailed example).

To illustrate the importance of the various aspects of usability, consider several of those shown in Table 1 that are perhaps least discussed in the literature.

System reliability and responsiveness are the sine qua non elements of usability. If the system is unavailable, it cannot be used. If the system is unreliable, users will avoid it regardless of how good it may be when it works. A survey of 4,448 computer users found that response time was the most important variable affecting their happiness (Rushinek and Rushinek, 1986). With increased system responsiveness user productivity goes up (Doherty and Kelisky, 1979; Doherty and Thadhani, 1982; but see Martin and Corl, 1986). Usability factors go deep, as well as being broad. System reliability and responsiveness go to the heart of system configuration.

It is often alleged that people buy systems for their functions, rather than for their user interface characteristics. (While this is probably historically true, the popularity of MacIntosh reflects the increased value users place on user interfaces.) In the Usability Design Process section below we address how to determine required functions.

Language translation is a serious and time-consuming process. Just the usability detail of putting all the messages in one file, rather than burying them in the code, eases the language translation process -- even makes it possible (see Boies et al., 1985 for a behavioral approach to language translation).

Unpacking and installing computer systems have been greatly improved and speeded up by work of human factors psychologists (Comstock, 1983; Granda, Personal Communication, 1980; Green, 1986).

What we call outreach programs, which include user training, reading materials, on-line help, and hot-lines,

TABLE 2. Usability Design Process -- The Four Principles.

EARLY -- CONTINUAL -- FOCUS ON USERS
Direct contact -- through interviews, observations, surveys, participative design -- to understand cognitive, behavioral, attitudinal, and anthropometric characteristics of users -- and their jobs.

EARLY -- AND CONTINUAL -- USER TESTING
Early on, intended users do real work with simulations and prototypes; their performance and reactions are measured qualitatively and quantitatively.

ITERATIVE DESIGN
System (functions, user interface, help system, reading material, training approach) is modified based upon results of user testing.
Testing cycle is repeated.

INTEGRATED DESIGN
All aspects of usability evolve in parallel;
All aspects of usability under one focus.

often do not reflect the general observation that people learn by doing and by observing others doing.

It is easy to overlook the fact that several other groups, besides the primary users, also need user interfaces, reading materials, and training. These include user trainers, system operators, maintenance workers, and salespeople. Ultimately, usability is seriously affected by the usability of what these people are taught and given. We have observed sales people who avoid giving demonstrations of even simple products (dictating equipment was one example) because of uncertainty about how the products work.

Usability Design Process -- The Four Principles

To design good systems, we believe that you must follow the four principles of system design shown in Table 2 in addressing each aspect of usability. These steps have been developed at IBM Research (Boies et al., 1985; Gould and Lewis, 1983; 1985). They will be discussed in the next main section.

Usability Design Phases

As a chronological framework for discussing what you must do to carry out the four steps in Table 2, we divide the work roughly into four phases: a gearing-up phase, an initial design phase, an iterative development phase, and a system installation phase.

Gearing-Up Phase. This is mainly an information gathering and conceptualization phase. Here you look for good STARTING POINTS, e.g., learn about related systems. You familiarize yourself with existing user interface STANDARDS, GUIDELINES, and any DEVELOPMENT PROCEDURES your organization may have. Each of these resources in capital letters is discussed in separate sections below.

Initial Design Phase. Here you need to make a preliminary specification of the user interface, drawing upon existing and leading systems, standards, and guidelines where appropriate; collect critical information about users and their work; develop testable behavioral goals; and organize the work to be done. Early focus on users takes center stage here. Integrated design, in which all aspects of usability are considered at the outset and evolve together, begins in this phase and is carried into the iterative development phase. All of this is elaborated on below.

Iterative Development Phase. With testable behavioral goals and ready access to user feedback established, continuous evaluation and modification of all aspects of usability can be achieved, as described below.

TABLE 3. Comments we have informally heard from system designers.

"We didn't anticipate THIS."

"But that's not how I thought it worked."

"What do users REALLY want"?

"I'm too pooped to change it now -- it took so long to get here."

"The manual and the user interface are different"!

"Even simple changes are hard."

"Why is user testing so late"?

"Why does user testing take so long"?

"Why don't we do user testing"?

"I would've tested, but...."

"We are surprised that..."

"It worked before..."

"The manual will take care of this..."

"The help system will take care of this..."

"A hot-line will take care of this..."

"We'll take care of it in the NEXT release."

"It's not broken; that's how it's supposed to work."

System Installation Phase. Here concentration centers on techniques for installing the system in customers' locations, introducing it to users, employing the training materials you developed earlier, ascertaining and assuring customer acceptance. (In the case of vendor products, this phase assumes successful marketing has occurred.) The work done on installation, customer support, and system maintenance now receives the ultimate test. For most systems, delivery to the customer should not signal the end of the road, since there are the inevitable follow-ons. Thus, it is just another iteration. If data logging programs to record user performance and acceptance have been incorporated, they will prove useful here. This phase is not discussed further in this paper.

USABILITY DESIGN PROCESS

Beyond Standards, Guidelines, Etc.

Table 3 contains revealing comments made by system designers. Behind them is the realization that relying on a blend of designers' own experiences and following standards, guidelines, or various rational and analytic design philosophies is not sufficient to arrive at good computer systems. Too many systems end up being hard to learn and use, have arbitrary inconsistencies with other systems, and lack the sparkle of insight into what users could really benefit from. From these experiences, several general points shown in Table 4 emerge.

TABLE 4. General observations about system design.

Nobody can get it right the first time.

Development is full of surprises.

Developing user-oriented systems requires living in a sea of changes.

Making contracts to ignore them does not eliminate the need for change.

Designers need good tools.

You can have behavioral design targets, just as you have other capacity and performance targets for other parts of the system, e.g., memory size, calculation time (Gould and Lewis, 1985).

Even if you have made the best system possible, users -- both novices and experienced -- will make mistakes using it.

TABLE 5. Generally required steps in designing good systems.

Define the problem the customer wants solved
Identify tasks users must perform
Learn user capabilities
Learn hardware/software constraints
Set specific usability targets (in behavioral terms)
Set specific usability targets (in behavioral
Sketch out user scenarios
Design and build prototype
Test prototype
Iteratively incorporate changes and test again until:
Behavioral targets are met
A critical deadline is reached
Install system at customer location
Measure customer reaction and acceptance

In response to these problems, several human factors people, apparently working independently, have in the last few years written relatively similar recommendations about how to do better (Bennett, 1984; Bury, 1984; Chapanis and students, e.g., Sullivan and Chapanis, 1983; Damodaran, Simpson, and Wilson, 1980; Meister, 1986; Reitman-Olson, 1985; Rubinstein and Hersh, 1984; Shackel (1984), the Usability Engineering group at DEC, e.g., Good, Spine, Whiteside, and George, 1986; Wixon and Whiteside, 1985; a group at IBM Research, Boies, et al., 1985; Gould and Lewis, 1985. Shackel (1985) has provided a historical summary. All this work represents a coming together of many earlier experiences. For example, the "application of empirical methods to computer-based system design" was the title of an experimental paper more than twenty years ago (Grace, 1966). These principles of system design have much in common with the characteristics of successful businesses, as observed in _In Search of Excellence_ and _A Passion for Excellence_ by Peters and colleagues. These books contain hundreds of examples describing the value of responding to the needs of customers (users).

There are many common procedural steps in the recommendations of all these people, summarized in Table 5, which should be used in carrying out the usability design process.

Principle 1. Early -- And Continual -- Focus On Users

Your Job. Your job is to design a system that has the right functions in it so people can do their work better and like it. You can't figure out what people want, need, can do, and will do without talking with them.

Decide Who the Users Will Be. A first step in designing a system is to decide (a) who the users will be and (b) what they will be doing with the system. This should be done either _before_ starting to design the system, or at a very early stage after obtaining some general ideas about it. Having done this, subsequent decisions, e.g., about system organization, required functions, user interface, must reflect these answers. The user population may ultimately be broader or more heterogeneous. If so, there is no a priori rule for aiming at the "lowest common denominator" or at the "average" user. Rather, your system will have to be tailored and tested for the other groups as well, and design tradeoffs may be required. But establishing one user set is much better than letting this decision continue to slip, as it forces design decisions that otherwise remain open too long. Open decisions about the intended users reflect slipperiness, not flexibility. We believe that the single best way to move advanced technology toward useful applications is by defining an intended user population and what they will do with it.

Designers Often Avoid This. We have observed two serious types of reluctance: one a reluctance to define the users, and the other a reluctance to take the definition seriously. First, as strange as it may seem, designers often avoid coming to grips with the question of who the users will be. This is due in part to the strong (and appropriate) effect the answer will have on subsequent design decisions. For example, designers cannot maintain that they are designing a toolkit system for non-programmers and make it so complicated ("powerful") that even their programming colleagues recognize the contradiction. Reviewers have suggested that this example is a paper tiger -- that no one would believe it. We did not make it up. The reluctance seems to be greatest in research environments, where people's goals are often mixed, e.g., advance the discipline of speech recognition versus build a listening typewriter, advance the discipline of expert systems versus build one to aid human operators or schedulers.

Second, even where designers define early who the users will be, the implications of this decision do not always drive subsequent design decisions in as powerful a way as they should. For example, setting out to design a picture editor for secretaries is laudable, but then building it so that only programmers can use it is inappropriate. We know of one advanced technology interface that is being developed for a specific list of executive users. Yet the designers have never talked with or visited the offices of these executives -- even though they work in the same building as they do. There is little relation between what the designers are building and what the intended users are likely to ever use.

<u>You Can't Rely Upon Descriptive Data.</u> Even if a description of the intended users were as complete as it possibly could be, it would not be an adequate basis for design. It would not substitute for direct interaction and testing.

Methods To Carry Out Early Focus On Users

Several methods for carrying out these principles apply to more than one principle. For convenience, however, we have grouped methods under the principle to which they are probably most relevant.

<u>Talk with Users.</u> Talk with the intended users. Ask them about their problems, difficulties, wishes, and what works well now. You may learn, for example, that morale is very low and that participative design, where some of the workers serve on the design team, is necessary for subsequent acceptance of your system. Tell them -- better, show them if you can -- what you have in mind and get their reactions. They may help you learn about other possible user groups. John Couch, a Ph.D. in Computer Science, worked each weekend incognito in a retail computer store while designing much of the software for the Lisa computer system. "I learned about the fears and frustrations of the average user and the more sophisticated ones firsthand. I believe it was the single most significant source of what we we came up." (Peters and Austin, 1985, p. 9).

You can't expect users to invent radically new ideas. Most users are not trained to think through a design -- but they can comment on your new ideas if you show the ideas in an appropriate form. Their reactions will be particularly helpful to the extent you can make these examples as concrete and relevant as possible. You may learn, for example, that they do not want menus -- they will only avoid them; or that English is a second language for a significant fraction of the intended users, which has serious implications for the design of the reading materials. You may learn how naive you have been about what handicapped people <u>really</u> want. Boies et al. (1985) provide further examples of this method, as well as of other methods mentioned below.

The intended users are the "experts," not, for example, their managers. To illustrate: reviewers of this chapter who were primarily system designers (a main intended user group) provided different recommendations on the topics to be covered, organization, and emphasis than did professional human factors people (more interested in the thoroughness and choice of references, for example) or the <u>Handbook's</u> editors.

Interviewing users focuses the design team's energy on people and not in other directions. You will encounter a dilemma: on the one hand, if you wait for a while to interview users you can ask them more pointed questions; on the other hand, you may be too far down the road to take advantage of other (perhaps more important) insights such interviews provide. The solution is to carry on these discussions throughout the development cycle. Schedule meetings in the users' areas. Put pictures of users, in their own work environments, in designers' offices. Where appropriate, move a designer's office to a user area.

Achieving <u>direct contact</u> with potential users is much better than exclusively relying upon intermediaries, such as marketing research people. Something is lost in the translation. Direct contact helps to reduce the often mentioned problem that designers and users do not speak the same language. Direct contact provides an "insider's view." One Levi executive spends one Saturday a month on the sales floor of a major retailer selling blue jeans. The executive reports that it provides a different view from the market research data. "It was quite an eye-opener for me to sell our own, to watch people buy other people's jeans." (Peters and Austin, 1985, p. 11). Many developers (ironically, rather than users) cannot seem to find time for this, however. We know of one group that was creating an "expert system" to aid computer operators, but members of the group were not planning to interview the operators or watch them work. Visiting directly with hungry or unemployed people has more impact on a person than reading about them. You may not have any idea about what you need to know about users and their environments until you see them. Imagine yourself designing a system to be used by inhabitants of the moon. Certainly you lack familiarity with these users, and need to learn much about them. You will not go wrong if you assume that you lack as much information about the potential users of your own system.

Visit Customer Locations. Visit potential locations for your system, particularly if these environments are new to you. More than a decade ago, Dick Granda (personal communication) visited IBM customer locations and watched them install very large computer systems (IBM 7090 systems). He observed, in the two weeks or so that it took to install such a system, all kinds of unnecessary but tolerated confusion and difficulties. His behavioral observations led IBM to make a number of changes, including color coding the cables, shipping the manuals in the cartons with the boxes they described, and reorganizing the packaging. These changes cut installation time to 1/5 of what it had been.

The Reverend Wyatt Tee Walker was Martin Luther King's trusted lieutenant in the American civil rights marches of the 1960's. "Before King demonstrated to desegregate public housing in Albany, Ga., in December 1961, Walker meticulously examined the area of the planned march, even sending a youngster, a middle-aged man and an elderly woman along the route days in advance to test whether it was manageable." And before the Birmingham, Alabama sit-ins of 1963, Walker "carefully planned the protest, learning as much as he could about the eateries by speaking to blacks in the area." (Waga, 1988.) The point here is that in designing a system to desegregate the South, Walker visited the customer's location and simulated what he intended to do.

Joseph Esherick, recipient of the the American Institute of Architects highest award -- the 1989 Gold Medal -- and famous for the design of San Francisco's Cannery and Monterey Bay Aquarium, says "If you want to design a restaurant talk to waiters, see if they'll let you get back in the kitchen. You'll learn how to ask questions and how to listen." "You ought to pay attention to how things work." (USA Weekend, 1989).

Customers' environments almost always contain surprises for designers. The president of Broadway Stores, a large up-scale retail chain, spends 40% of his time on the sales floor (as told to Stephen Boies, 1989). The 1984 Olympic Message System (OMS) was a voice message system used by Olympians from all countries (Boies, et al., 1985). In a field test of OMS conducted at the desert location of one of the events, it was learned that bugs (the living, multi-leg type) crawled into the computers at night to keep warm. Protection was required or damage could result. If you are designing self-service terminals, you may observe in public places that inexperienced customers are hesitant to insert their credit card for fear of losing it or getting unwanted bills. In factories you may learn that your system must be impervious to grease, dirt, vibration, and caustic materials. In schools you may learn how naive you are about today's learning problems and achievements. In offices you may learn about the sociology that affects the use of a system. A large insurance company that wanted its thousands of quasi-independent field agents to purchase and use terminals learned that the agents would use them only if they were quiet and did not generate much heat in their typically small offices.

Observe Users Working. Visit the workplaces of users. Most systems are follow-ons to existing ones. Learn what is hard about the existing work so you don't make the same mistakes. Observe potential users doing their jobs. You may feel self-conscious at first. Hang out. Blend in with the woodwork. Ask non-threatening questions as workers become less self-conscious. It will all go well. You may learn that operators avoid changing tapes and ribbons or adding paper to machines; that secretaries avoid transferring calls for fear of making an error. You may learn that space is very limited, or that workstations must be shared, or that no one comes to training sessions, or that no one reads manuals. You may learn what users do when they don't know something or get in trouble, which should help you in designing your outreach program. See what they have difficulty with and what they dislike. You may learn that construction workers don't wear their reading glasses and don't want to press small keys, particularly while wearing heavy gloves; that office workers will not use an electronic mail system that automatically recognizes their speech if they have to wait thirty seconds to activate it before each usage; that the operators expect that the new system will respond much faster than the present one (had you planned to make it that way?); that airline passengers lose their credit cards by inserting them in the wrong place (ticket dispenser); that management has no intention of buying any manuals. The implications of these findings must then be incorporated into the design of your system.

Videotape Users Working. Make a videotape of a few users working, and show it to other members of the design team or management. Brief (2 min.) videotapes of users having difficulty and illustrations of home-made remedies to solve design inadequacies carry more punch with people who count than do tables with lots of numbers. The tables, incidentally, can be obtained only with much more effort.

Learn about the Work Organization. Here the emphasis is upon understanding the organization of the work that your system is intended to help. This is particularly important where many different user groups are involved (see Mumford, 1981). A system with an user interface that was adequate and well liked, as reported in one case study of an IBM hospital care system (Fitter, Brownbridge, Garber, and Herzmark; 1985), was nevertheless under-utilized in its two installations because there was a mismatch between the system organization and the hospital organization.

Thinking Aloud. Have potential users think aloud as they are doing their actual work (see Lewis, 1982). Doing this while actually performing their job may yield different insights than having them reflect on their work later. There will be real time comments that may provide details important for all the little decisions you make everyday in designing your system. Like a politician who visits his constituency, you will learn what the real issues are. You may learn that the sales clerks don't want to fold clothes, check ids, have long lines at their check-out counters, or make change because of the implications of possible mistakes; that bank tellers don't want to share workstations or have it known that they can't work with fractions; that warehouse workers will probably avoid using a workstation if they have to walk a long way or wait for it to warm up each time they need to use it.

Try It Yourself. Sometimes it can be rewarding to try a worker's job yourself. You may learn, for example, that glare on the screen is really bothersome, a slow system leads to rude customers, your arms get tired, you can't handle all the interruptions. Of course, you must be careful not to confuse your expertise with that of the intended users. We have been told that Kentucky Fried Chicken executives are required to work for a period in retail outlets.

Participative Design. Make intended users part of the design team. This is particularly effective when designing an "in-house" system which you will be responsible for introducing once it is completed, e.g., a quality control system for your factory, a data entry system for your distribution center, an automated library for your division. Mumford (e.g., 1981) has written several papers on participative design. Participative design is not just a good thing to do politically. Experienced workers know a lot more about what they do than do drop-in designers. (Don't you know more about your work than, for example, a consultant to your manager's manager?) Glasson (1985) describes various roles users can play here. Eason (1982) describes some difficulties in accomplishing participative design.

Worker involvement in design allows workers to participate in decision-making about conditions that affect their work lives. Besides leading to better systems, this process leads to an increase in pride, self-esteem, and perhaps autonomy. Maybe productivity too. People want to be actively involved in their work, and in the decisions that affect their work lives. Sometimes people have to be helped here, though.

Expert on Design Team. Using an expert to consult on the design team of OMS, in that case a recent ex-Olympian, was valuable in designing that voice message system (Boies et al., 1985). This person was a consultant and not a full-fledged member of the design team. In some cases, for example having a physician as part of the team to design a patient monitoring system, might be more valuable if the person is committed to seeing the project to completion and not simply a consultant. Putting experts on the design team is simply another way to phrase "participative design." The term is sometimes used when the intended users are highly skilled individuals. Keep in mind, however, that people who do lower skill jobs are nevertheless the experts at their jobs.

Task Analysis. Probably the most formally worked out method of learning about users' jobs is task analysis. Task analysis is an analytical process used to determine the specific behaviors required of people in a man-machine system (Air Force definition). Formal task analysis is usually "operator-oriented," rather than "discretionary-user-oriented." This reflects the nature of most jobs in which it is used. Task analysis, says Drury (1983) in a tutorial, is a comparison between the demands the task places on the human operator and the capabilities of the operator to deal with them. It is the process of identifying and reporting the significant work activities, requirements, and technical and environmental conditions. It is usually carried out through observation, interviews, or questionnaires. A formal task or job description results.

Formal task analysis is regularly conducted by the Armed Services and government, and their contractors. This formality reflects the division of labor that often occurs in large system projects, e.g., a new, multi-person space system or a defensive missile system. Descriptions of pieces of a proposed system, e.g., the "personnel subsystem," are collected by one group and passed to another group, who passes them to yet another group. The literature on task analysis of government-funded systems (e.g., Kloster and Tischer, 1985; Meister, 1986) and the literature from the civilian computer industry (as illustrated, for example, in the CHI proceedings) have developed independently, it appears. There are many variations in task analysis. Mentemerlo and Eddowes (1978) reviewed many, and concluded that it is not possible to have a single cookbook approach that is universally applicable. While formal task analysis is valuable, the division of labor noted above can provide layers of insulation between the ultimate users and various designers along the way. It should not be carried out without having designers talk directly with users.

There are many informal, valuable informal task analysis approaches. At IBM Boca Raton, Happ and human factors colleagues (personal communication) have designers and users write each step that they believe is necessary to complete a task on a separate slip and put it on a wall. Happ reports that the design (with its flaws) comes to life, and that they discover multiple steps, confusions, left out operations, and exceptions. What results is an improved early conception of what will be required. In a different approach, not aimed at system design but aimed at identifying what executives do, Mintzberg (1976) followed each of several executives for two weeks, carefully observing and measuring their daily activities and talking with them about them.

Surveys and Questionnaires. The data obtained from surveys and questionnaires can be useful. Talking with a group of users first, and with other members of the design team, is necessary to know what questions to ask. Sometimes answers to questions can seem sterile, e.g., average years education, employee turnover. But the implications of these answers are powerful. If the users have relatively little education and high job turnover, then training must be brief and inexpensive.

Testable Behavioral Target Goals. Most new systems specify in advance physical performance and capacity targets, e.g., memory swap time, MIPS, mean time to failure estimates, instruction times. Explicit behavioral targets that new systems must meet can also be established (e.g., Bennett, 1984; Carroll and Rosson, 1984; Gould and Lewis, 1985; Shackel, 1985; Wixon and Whiteside, 1985). An example target goal is: business professionals with no experience using a new office services system must be able to retrieve and read three brief electronic messages from their system mailbox and reply to each within twelve minutes. They can ask the experimenter (a simulated "hot-line") for help no more than once. These explicit behavioral benchmarks go beyond general expectations, often implicit only, that a new system should not require more time or lead to more errors than the old (manual?) Table 6 provides additional partial examples of testable behavioral specifications.

Measurable behavioral targets, and where your developing system stands with respect to them, give management a metric to understand what progress has been made, and what is still required. This makes it possible to judge usability on the same basis as other system components.

Behavioral targets give phrases like "user friendly" or "easy to use" a technical basis. Wixon and Whiteside (1985) have worked out a methodology called "usability engineering" in which specific behavioral goals play a key role. The time requirements, the number of errors and help attempts, and the user acceptance ratings that form the behavioral targets are arrived at by discussions with users, discussions among the design team, and the characteristics of the existing systems that will be improved upon. Measurable usability targets stated in behavioral terms are required to determine whether the finished product fulfills its usability goals (Good, Spine, Whiteside, and George; 1986)

TABLE 6. Additional examples of testable behavioral specifications.

Example 1. Twenty experimental participants, familiar with the IBM PC but unfamiliar with query languages, will receive sixty minutes training using the new on-line query training system for novice users. They will then perform nine experimental tasks.

On Task 1, 85% of these tested users must complete it successfully in less than 15 minutes, with no help from the experimenter. They may use all reference and help materials, but no hot-lines. Task 1 consists of six steps:

1. Create a query on the displayed query panel using the table SCHOOL.COURSES.
2. Delete all column names except COURSE and TITLE.
3. Save the current query with the name CTITLE.
4. Run it once.
5. Get the current query panel displayed.
6. Clear the current query panel so that it contains nothing.

Example 2. For this integrated editor, any displayed messages encountered in the process of creating documents, tables, or drawings will be understood by secretaries with one or more years of word processing experience, as demonstrated by the ability of at least 90% of them to paraphrase correctly these messages. The system will provide error recovery mechanisms suitable for these users, as evidenced by the ability of at least 85% of them to execute successful recovery strategies in seven of the attached eight scenarios (adapted from Carroll and Rosson, 1984).

Example 3. Nine of ten participants, whose first language is not English, must be able to walk up and use this vending machine, get the target item within twenty seconds, and get the correct change. This must be done without watching anyone else use it and without asking the experimenter any questions.

Example 4. Test participants, a random sample from customers in retail computer stores who are willing to participate in this experiment, must be able to unpack this prototype home computer and connect the display, printer, mouse, keyboard, and special-effects card. They must initiate the system and then set the date and time on the computer. This work must be completed by at least 17 of the 20 participants in 60 minutes, using only the instructions contained in the manuals in the boxes.

A Checklist. Table 7 is a checklist to help you carry out early -- and continual -- focus on users.

TABLE 7. Checklist for achieving Early -- and Continual -- Focus on Users.

_____We defined a major group of potential users.

_____We talked with these users about the good and bad points of their present job (and system if appropriate).

_____Our preliminary system design discussions always kept in mind the characteristics of these users.

_____We watched these users doing their present jobs.

_____We asked them to think aloud as they worked.

_____We tried their jobs (where appropriate).

_____We did a formal task analysis.

_____We developed testable behavioral target goals for our proposed system.

Principle 2. Early -- And Continual -- User Testing

Your job is to design a system that works and has the right functions so that users can do the right things. You won't know whether it is working right until you start testing it.

From the very beginning of the development process, and throughout it, intended users should carry out real work using early versions of training materials and manuals, and simulations and prototypes of user interfaces, help systems, and so forth. The emphasis here is upon measurement, informal and formal. The basic premise is that you cannot get it right the first time, no matter how experienced or smart you are. This observation is not limited just to computer system designers. Heckel (1984), in writing about software design, asks "If Ernest Hemingway, James Michener, Neil Simon, Frank Lloyd Wright, and Pablo Picasso could not get it right the first time, what makes you think you will?" Heckel quotes others: "Plan to throw one away" (Fred Brooks). Rewrite and revise...it is no sign of weakness or defeat that your manuscript ends up in need of major surgery" (William Strunk and E. B. White). "The two most important tools an architect has are the eraser in the drawing room and the sledge hammer on the construction site" (Frank Lloyd Wright). If you measure and then make appropriate changes you can hill-climb toward an increasingly better system.

Methods To Carry Out Early -- And Continual -- User Testing

Printed or Video Scenarios. As a starting point, sketch out a few user scenarios on paper and show them to members of the design team. Provide exact details, e.g., the exact layout and wording on the screen, exactly what keys users must press, and the response of the system. These details will of course change -- but this presumptive exactness stimulates the right level of discussion. Members of the design team now must react to a proposal; removed is the misleading comfort of not realizing the design conflicts that lie hidden when these details are missing. These scenarios do not just lead to arguments about surface characteristics of an user interface. Since they inherently specify functions, it is our experience that they lead to discussions about required functions, and how they should be organized. This in turn will quickly identify deep systems organization issues.

Then carry the process one step further. Type up these scenarios, or perhaps make a brief video demonstration of them if you are designing a system where graphics, animation, or color is dominant. They are now in shape to be shown to prospective users for their reaction. In the meantime, other members of the design team have developed some shared realization of what the entire project is trying to create.

What you have done with this procedure is to identify and organize functions in a way that intended users can understand and react to. You are quickly getting informal data before even writing a line of code. You are designing the system from the users' point of view.

Early User Manuals. Begin writing the user manual before any code is written. Intended users can react to this helpfully, since the system is being described in the appropriate fashion. If you get inappropriate reactions, start re-writing the manual. When people ask questions, you have new items for the manual. The printed and graphic scenarios, prepared as suggested above, can be included as examples. This works. Designers at Digital Equipment Corporation wrote the user manual simultaneously with beginning to design an user interface for a workstation. They found, from informal evaluation of their user manual, that they were making their system too complicated, and modified it while there was still a chance to do so (Rubinstein and Hersh, 1984). Of particular significance, they also found that the user manual became their definitive design document -- in spite of the fact that all the traditional documents were also available. Cowlishaw (1984) first wrote and circulated for review the documentation for each major section of the the successful REXX language before he implemented that section. (REXX is an IBM interpretive language often used for command and macro programming, prototyping, education, and personal programming.) He reports that "The writing of documentation was found to be the most effective way of spotting inconsistencies, ambiguities, or incompleteness in a design. The majority of usability problems were discovered before they became embedded in the language." In making OMS, designers at IBM Research wrote the user guide first (Boies et al., 1985). Based upon people's reactions to it, they made changes to the planned system functions and organization. The designers put immediately into the user guide details that people suggested ought ultimately to be there.

With this approach,early manuals continually evolve, with their final version being very different from their first versions. In contrast, writing manuals today is usually done sometime after the system has been designed and implemented -- and by people in a different department. In just this situation, an IBM manual writer took the initiative to write part of a manual early. In explaining how to turn on the system, the writer made up a procedure, since the designers had not yet settled on one. A hardware designer read the manual, liked the "solution," and adopted it. The point: manuals can influence what other designers do. An experimental case study of re-writing an existing text editor manual provides several good leads on how to go about writing a user manual (Sullivan and Chapanis, 1983).

Mock-ups. Seminara (1985) discusses the advantages of mock-ups and models in developing systems, and draws on a power plant example. Boies et al., (1985) used a wooden mock-up to begin development of the kiosk that became an essential part of their outreach program for OMS. They put this mock-up in the main hallway of the Research Center. It led to innovative solutions to a difficult training situation they were facing. Rather than slow down the development process, it contributed to getting things done on time in a six month development schedule. The comments of passers-by were beneficial in designing all parts of the kiosk, e.g., physical locations of pamphlet holders, display, and telephone; messages; display color and scrolling techniques; security. It also led to the identification of issues that might not have been otherwise as easily envisioned, e.g., air conditioning requirements, required room inside for maintenance. As the life size mock-up evolved, it became the design model that was replicated by the fabricators.

Simulations. Much informal experimentation can be carried out by simulating important parts of the system. Sometimes this can be done with paper and pencil (Thomas and Gould, 1975). Sometimes successful simulations can be carried out with computer systems, separate from those that will ultimately be used in a product (Gould, Conti, and Hovanyecz, 1983; Kelley, 1984). Code iteratively developed in simulations need not be thrown away, but can be used in the actual product if planned properly (Richards et al., 1985). The OMS case history gives a detailed example of simulation (Boies et al., 1985).

More formal experimentation (i.e., carefully designed and controlled laboratory experiments with serious statistical analysis of the results) can be carried out with simulations also, if you have the expertise to do this. Erdmann and Neal (1971) simulated an airlines reservation system in an airport by having a hidden reservation agent actually respond to customers who were using it. Gould, Conti, Hovanyecz (1983) simulated a listening typewriter by having a hidden typist actually enter what users said (Figure 1). Kelley (1984) put himself in the human-computer loop to answer questions his natural language calendar system could not. Good, Whiteside, Wixon, and Jones (1984) intercepted inappropriate commands of novices using an electronic mail system, substituting the correct ones, but adding the inappropriate ones to a new extended command set. Some system tools allow the creation of relatively complete early collections of on-line user interface frames connected only to the few functions so far written. All these simulation techniques identified both how people used the systems and and how they felt about them.

Early Prototyping. Early prototyping can be made possible through the use of designer toolkits or user interface management systems (see section on Software Tools below). Try to develop pieces of your system to the point where potential users can carry out pre-defined problems (even if other pieces of the system are not yet working). You will learn things you have possibly missed through simulations, e.g., effects of multiple simultaneous users, side-effects of functions. Rapid prototyping changes work organization. It allows and stimulates discussions among workers. The discussions are much different than without it. People that could not previously make a contribution because of the form that the work existed in can now contribute usefully.

You can measure people's performance and feelings. In at least some cases how people feel about a new system better predicts actual discretionary use of it than does how effectively these people actually use it (Davis and Reitman-Olson, 1986). There are many testimonies to the value of early prototyping. For example, Woodmansee (1985) who, in writing about the experience of developing Visicorp's Visi On (R), suggests it could have been even better had early user interface prototyping been done. Alavi (1984) found that prototyping, in contrast to the traditional life-cycle approach to system development, facilitates communication between users and designers, but is harder to manage and control. Mitch Kapor, the inventor of Lotus 123, in reflecting on its development process, indicated that they continually prototyped their work. He served as the main experimental user, sometimes trying to get real work done, other times demonstrating the prototype to others and getting their comments, other times simply trying out a new version and providing feedback (talk given at the IBM Research Center, Hawthorne, 1989). See Case Study Evaluations below for examples of early prototyping.

Prototyping is expensive, but necessary. Our a priori understanding of users is imperfect at best. Guidelines and generic behavioral research (see Gruenenfelder and Whitten, 1985) provide at best only approximately good recommendations. And our systems contain bugs and inconsistencies.

Sometimes system programmers or management simply do not believe reports that users are having a difficult time learning, for example, a new prototype system. Videotapes of users having problems are often much more convincing than charts and oral reports. (Where possible, the effect can be even more powerful if you can get them to watch early testing themselves.)

Early Demonstrations. Demonstrate working pieces of your system to anyone who will take the time to watch. Simply going through the motions of using it, and honestly observing others' reactions will be instructive. Of course, it is even better to let them try it themselves on a brief task. Even a simple task can be revealing. For example, when the touchscreen does not work, you may be surprised to learn that users do not lift their finger and press again as your algorithm requires, but rather just press their finger even harder and wider. This problem would not show up in your demonstrations, but only when somebody else tries it. Successful demonstrations of pieces of your system and manuals give management and customers confidence that you are making progress.

Thinking Aloud. Performance measures, such as time and errors, do not give a clear indication of what is bothering users or what may be the source of an user error (Lewis, 1982). People simply do not make the mental transitions ("leaps") that system or manual designers expect of them. At Carnegie-Mellon University's Communications Design Center, students and faculty test out new user manuals by studying individuals talking out loud as they try to get things done. This results in both gross changes to the manual, e.g., identification of missing sections, and subtle modifications. Human factors people at DEC found that having two users think aloud, i.e., basically talk to each other, as they tried to install a small computer made it easier to obtain verbal n protocols from some users and led to additional insights (Comstock, 1983; see also Rubinstein and Hersh, 1984). Of course, requiring users to think aloud can affect the precision of time and error performance measures, and so when precise performance measurements are sought, then you may not want to collect verbal protocols.

Make Videotapes. Besides being useful for measuring time, errors, and user attitudes, brief videotapes of users attempting to use a new system have tremendous impact upon management, especially where users are having problems (see also Rubinstein and Hersh, 1984). Designers often find it impossible to believe that others cannot use their system. These vignettes can be mind-opening. These are often viewed over and over, and elicit vigorous reactions -- from colleagues and particularly from management.

Hallway and Storefront Methodology. Gould et al (1987) coined this term on the basis of their experience of putting parts of OMS during its development in the hallway of the IBM Research Center in Yorktown. By putting a mock-up, simulation, or an early prototype in an obvious public place (or restricted access "public" place in the case of a company confidential system), passers-by just naturally are attracted to use it. This provides a source of invaluable comments and surprises. Tognazzini in his talk at CHI86 described how Apple Computer started doing usability testing at local computer stores, "dragging along the programmers," as he put it, "and having a bunch of random people go through their latest software." "It was very effective," he said, "because not only did they quickly discover the pitfalls, but the programmers saw them too, avoiding all those arguments."

In hallway and storefront methodology, you must react quickly to all good suggestions, however, if you want to keep the flow of comments coming. This demands good tools for interface designers (see below under Iterative Design). Even trivial errors must be quickly corrected. For example, if a person notices a misspelling, correct it quickly. If it is there the next day, it will begin to affect the confidence of the passers-by that you are taking their comments seriously. Making changes quickly requires the project to be organized for integrated usability design (see above). What gets learned in storefront and hallway methodology is valuable for user guides, user interfaces, display sizes and colors, identification of required functions, help systems, and the design and looks of the workstation.

As an added benefit, hallway and storefront adds zest, gusto, fun to a project. It can give a project momentum that was not previously there. People notice what you are doing. Members of the project see better how their work fits in, and what other members are doing. Your project begins to emerge from a sea of other projects that may be going on around you.

Putting a mock-up or prototype in the hallway can help your cause with system colleagues whom you may be having trouble in getting to work on aspects of the system that contribute to usability. Passersby's reactions will quickly identify what is important, and may very quickly lead to a work re-organization. The whole project will benefit, for the right working relations will be identified.

Some people have expressed a concern that they cannot protect proprietary systems with hallway and storefront methodology. Maybe so in some cases, but there is still much that can be learned. At IBM Boca Raton lab where IBM PC plans are carefully guarded, the human factors people have placed displays in the library and cafeteria and obtained reactions from passers-by about color and screen layout. They were able to do this without associating these designs with any particular future product.

<u>Computer Bulletin Boards, Forums, Networks, and Conferencing.</u> Existing, extensive computer networks allow designers to send out a partial or an entire new user interface and obtain feedback from users all over the world -- most of whom would otherwise be unknown to the designer. Cowlishaw (1984) did this in a very serious way during the four years he was developing REXX, an interpretive language often used for command and macro programming, prototyping, education, and personal programming. "The most important factor in the development of REXX," he writes, "began to take effect when the first interpreter was distributed over the the IBM communications network known as VNET. (This network links over 1400 mainframe computers in forty countries.) From the beginning, many hundreds of people were using the language...from temporary staff to professional programmers. (They) provided immediate feedback to the designer on their preferences, needs, and suggestions for change. An informal language committee then appeared spontaneously and communicated among themselves and with the designer entirely electronically. The discussions...grew to hundreds of thousands of lines. Using the network, the designer could interactively explain and discuss the changes that were required." Cowlishaw concludes modestly that "Many if not most of the good ideas embodied in the language came directly from users. It is impossible to overestimate the value of the direct feedback from users." One factor that motivated users to provide feedback was the speed with which Cowlishaw responded to them.

Electronic bulletin boards allow you to "tack up" electronic requests for help, advice, comments. Like traditional bulletin boards, for example in universities or in super markets, people unknown to you will read your message. Computer conferencing facilities have enhanced the basic bulletin board notion by giving the reader many aiding functions. For example, the reader is provided with ways to look up all references on your topic, all messages you may have posted in the past on this subject, an easy way to reply to your request, and ways to run your program should you post a program on the bulletin board or forum (Flavin, Williford, and

Barzilai, 1986). Oftentimes forums develop on the basis of user comments about using an already-designed system, e.g., Lotus 1-2-3. These forums center on users sharing tricks in using the system of interest, and feedback to the designers for the next version. Clearly, however, on-going forums, either public or private, can be useful while design of a new system is on-going. People's comments are usually informal, but informed -- and come from ego-involved users.

Formal Prototype Test. Much of the emphasis so far has been upon informal experimental results, e.g., create a scenario, simulation, or prototype; measure the performance of some users doing real work; get their reactions; modify the user interface; then repeat the process. Informal empirical and experimental work are very valuable, and give an idea of where you stand vis a vis the behavioral targets you established earlier.

TABLE 8. The percentage of participants who successfully completed all three programming problems in each of four iterative tests of a system under development. Data adopted from Bury (1985).

Iteration 3 -- 75% tasks completed
Iteration 4 -- 33% tasks completed
Iteration 5 -- 65% tasks completed
Iteration 6 -- 92% tasks completed

NOTE: Data are based upon the three problems common to all iterations. Participants' performance improved during the first three iterations. The results "go up and down" because prior to Iteration 4 a new training approach was developed, and the deleterious effects of it were identified.

These activities can be carried out without some of the technical skills of trained human factors people, e.g., psychophysics, experimental design, or statistics. But we certainly encourage formal experimentation where possible. If skilled human factors people are available to develop the experimental and statistical designs, then an even more accurate and valuable assessment can be made. As shown in Table 8, Bury (1985) provides an example of how formal experimental iteration can improve a system. "Give me numbers like iterative design provides," said one corporate officer, "and you take user interfaces out of the realm of taste and preference only."

There are many formal behavioral methods for designing software systems (see, for example, a National Academy of Science/National Research Council recent report which summarizes many (Anderson and Olson; 1985)).

As your project nears its end, you are really busy and of necessity have become part salesperson to push it to completion. Thus, even though you have done much behavioral work already, it is better if you can have an outside group do the final evaluation. It is just too hard to be objective under the final pressures, even though you have been objective up to this point.

Try-to-Destroy-It Contests. The design team of OMS, near the end of development, turned over their system to a group of college students and let them try to find bugs, crash it, break into it, etc. (Gould, et al., 1987). College students require little extrinsic reward for doing this type of work! A sociology develops that may initially be humbling to you, but is ultimately of immense value. If there is a need to keep this test proprietary, it is still not hard to find cooperative, motivated people to carry it out.

Field Studies. Laboratory and hallway studies go only so far. Each methodology mentioned so far yields somewhat different information. Putting your system into the field for a test reminds you of problems that that you have put out of mind or identifies problems that other methodologies do not get at (see Boies et al. (1985) for a detailed example). While laboratory studies of computer installation are valuable, relates John Whiteside of DEC (personal communication, 1987), it took a field study to identify the customer problem of what to do with all the cartons and packing materials after installing a small system on the 32nd floor of a downtown building. Field test clearly suggest priorities about which problems to solve first. So-called "early customer shipment," vendor-customer agreements, and early site installations are mechanisms for doing field tests.

TABLE 9. Checklist for achieving Early User Testing.

_____We made informal, preliminary sketches of a few user scenarios -- specifying exactly what the user and system messages will be -- and showed them to a few prospective users.

_____We have begun writing the user manual, and it is guiding the development process.

_____We have used simulations to try out the functions and organization of the user interface.

_____We have used mock-ups to try out the functions and organization of the user interface.

_____We have done early demonstrations.

_____We invited as many people as possible to comment on on-going instantiations of all usability components.

_____We had prospective users think aloud as they used simulations, mock-ups, and prototypes.

_____We used hallway and storefront methods.

_____We used computer conferencing forums to get feedback on usability.

_____We did formal prototype user testing.

_____We compared our results to established behavioral target goals.

_____We met our behavioral benchmark targets.

_____We let motivated people try to find bugs in our systems.

_____We did field studies.

_____We included data logging programs in our system.

_____We did follow-up studies on people who are now using the system we made.

Follow-Up Studies. Once a system has been released, studying how actual customers use it has value for subsequent releases and related new products. This work serves as a validation of the earlier prototyping and iterative design efforts, and it is particularly important in assessing the usefulness of various functions and what new functions are required. These studies illustrate the need to provide automatic data collection tools in your system.

Studying hot-line calls or service center requests and complaints related to your system can be insightful in identifying problems users are having. For example, Sony Corporation's telephone-based "customer-information center" receives 1200 phone calls per day. A computer record summarizing the questions people asked is used to modify the company's user manuals (Schrage, 1986). At Apple, all senior executives learn of real user problems by listening to them on a toll-free 800 customer call-in line. Occasionally they try to answer the question (Peters and Austin, 1985).

A Checklist. Table 9 is a checklist to help you carry out early -- and continual -- user testing.

Principle 3. Iterative Design

The key requirements for iterative design are:

Identification of required changes.

An ability to make the changes.

A willingness to make changes.

The required or recommended changes can be identified with measurements made on intended users and the results compared against previously established behavioral goals. To make these changes, however, requires that designers have good tools, and that the work is organized in a way that enables them to be responsive.

When you find a problem, what to do about it may not be clear. There is no principled method to determine what the solution is. There are only empirical methods -- to be used after careful analysis, critical thinking, and innovation have been applied. The empirical methods can either be used during system development or they, in effect, will be used after the system is delivered -- which is usually an inopportune time. Sometimes you may make changes that will cause other problems. You will only know if you test them.

Methods To Carry Out Iterative Design

Software Tools. There has been recent widespread recognition of the importance of providing designers with good tools. In the past, particularly as deadlines approached, there has been great reluctance to make even simple changes to an user interface because these changes might introduce bugs into the application code. That is, code for an user interface and an application were mixed together. Experience with this problem has led to the development of toolkits (e.g, the MAC toolkit) and user interface management systems (UIMS).

You need good tools. First, tools are needed to make changes in an user interface possible and easy. Without this, there can be no iterative design, which is so necessary for the design of good systems. These tools can be the basis of rapid prototyping. Second, they bring an user interface within the control of human factors people and other non-programming specialists who understand the application. Third, good tools reduce cost by making individual programmers and designers more productive, and by speeding up schedules. This in turn further reduces cost by reducing disproportionately more the number of required people. Fourth, inherent in tools are "ways of doing things." These can automatically contribute to improved usability (or reduced usability if they enforce bad constraints). Fifth, good tools can facilitate user interface consistency and cross-system consistency.

The basic characteristic of UIMSs is that there is a separation between an user interface and the functions that it uses. That is, there is a well defined interface between that portion of the code that contains an user interface and that portion of the code that implements the functions of that user interface. The driving force for this separation is that it enables an user interface to co-evolve with an application. This separation reduces or eliminates the need to test application code each time a change is made in an user interface. That is, an user interface can be changed independently from the function code.

UIMSs are evolving from several orientations. Some UIMSs are created in the service of developing a specific system, e.g., as was the case in IBM's voice messaging systems (Richards, et al., 1985). These may have generality to other applications in the same domain. Some UIMSs are available only within the company that developed them, e.g., Xerox's Trillium (Henderson, 1986); tools from several aerospace companies (Overmyer, 1987). Some UIMSs provide a means of rapid prototyping, but once an user interface is settled on, then the system must be re-coded. Softright's DEMO is an example. The MAC toolkit, designed for application programmers, aims at reducing development costs and encouraging consistency in an user interface across applications. Some UIMSs are commercially available, e.g., Apollo Computer's ADM; Cosmic's (NASA software) TAE. The intent here is to handle a broad range of applications. Good general references to read on UIMSs are Bennett (1986); Buxton, Lamb, Sherman, and Smith (1983); Green (1985); Pfaff (1985).

Designers who have actually used UIMSs in the development of their own systems describe them in very positive terms (Richards, et al., 1985; Shulert, Rogers, and Hamilton, 1985; Hayes, Szekely, and Lerner, 1985)

Are UIMSs and toolkits easy for non-programmers to use? They are evolving, but ease of use does not seem to be the prime consideration. To be successful in using an UIMS, you must at present become a skilled user of it, even if not a skilled programmer.

System Development Work Organization. Required changes to various aspects of usability (Table 1) cannot be carried out in a coordinated way if the work is not organized to make change possible. Indeed, none of this will work at all if there is not a willingness to live in a sea of changes, and react to required changes quickly and appropriately. Busy white collar workers live in a sea of interruptions, and realize that unexpected changes are part of their job. It is part of the job of designing good systems to manage change, and not make contracts to ignore required change. You can't manage change by pretending it is not needed.

A Checklist. Table 10 is a checklist to help you carry out iterative design.

TABLE 10. Checklist for carrying out Iterative Design.

_____All aspects of usability could be easily changed, i.e., we had good tools.
_____We regularly changed our system, manuals, etc., based upon testing results with prospective users.

Principle 4. Integrated Design

As explained in Boies et al. (1985), we recommend that all aspects of usability evolve in parallel. At the outset, work should begin on sketching an user interface, user guides, other reading materials, the language translation approach, the help system, and so forth. In order for this to happen successfully, all aspects of usability should be under one focus or person. Of course, that person will probably have other usability people working for him/her. Usability cannot be coordinated otherwise. This one-focus recommendation presumes line-management responsibility, and is thus different from Usability Committees (Demers, 1984).

An example illustrates the need for integrated design. During a field test of OMS (Boies, et al., 1985) before the Olympics started it was learned that the word "Olympics" had to be changed to "Olympic." This would seem to be a trivial change. But alas. All user interface messages and all help messages with the word "Olympics" had to be changed. Since these messages were recorded in twelve languages, speakers for each of these languages had to be obtained. The user guides (and other printed material) had to be changed. These were in twelve languages also, some of which involved alphabets that most printers do not handle, e.g., Arabic, Russian. The lettering on signs had to be changed. Since one person was in charge of usability (and OMS was organized so that all messages were in one file), this clearly modest change was done in all appropriate places. Under the usual organization, however, this would have been much more difficult. For example, the required change might have been recommended by human factors people, who would have had to negotiate it with the several different managers (e.g., the project manager, user interface manager, help system manager, documentation manager, advertising manager). Even if they were all convinced, they would then have to negotiate it with their programmers or other relevant staff people. Then there would be the required inquiries to be sure all relevant people agreed to do it, and did it. This trivial change is typical of many, many trivial changes one discovers that need to be made during the last stages of development. He who has the stuff in his computer has the power. A more detailed example of the need for integrated design is in Boies, et al. (1985).

Methods To Carry Out Integrated Design

A project can be managed to only a few goals, e.g., low cost, processing speed, compatibility with the past, reliability, short development schedule, usability. With the methods described in this paper, you can measure usability, therefore control it, and therefore manage it. Integrated design is an essential approach if one of the goals of your project is usability.

The methods just outlined under early focus on users and those mentioned below to carry out user testing must be brought to bear on all aspects of usability. Technically, these methods are sufficient to guarantee an acceptable system. The main difficulty in carrying out integrated design will be organizational. Integrated design requires a departure from fractionated development practices where various aspects of usability are developed in different loosely-related departments, divisions, cities, companies.

Integrated design assumes a recognition at the very outset that usability is important, that it includes many factors (Table 1), and that work must begin on it from the start. Integrated design requires a sincere dedication to manage for usability.

Integrated design requires that one group, at the very beginning, be given sufficient resources (money, personnel, time, authority) to drive and control usability, and to invent what is needed to make usability good. This organization may have critical mass early enough to be an effective lobby for usability -- to assure that usability gets its share of the resources of the project. Integrated design requires that this group sign up to guarantee good usability. Their duties include carrying out the methods described under each of the other three principles, or see that others do.

Today development groups are not organized to facilitate integrated design. Development of the functions, user interface, manuals, help system, training materials, etc. are often each done in a separate department in large projects.

Because of these traditions integrated Design may be tough to carry out in many organizations. It requires that the usability people be outstanding, be given the responsibility (and accountability), and have good tools. It is not just a plug for more jobs for human factors people. The responsibility will be extremely demanding, especially on large systems. Very special people will be required. We have been told that no one person could possibly control all aspects of usability on large systems. This is simply not logical, since there is generally one person in charge of the whole system (of which usability is only a part).

A Checklist. Table 11 is a checklist to help you carry out integrated design.

TABLE 11. Checklist for achieving Integrated Design.

____We considered all aspects of usability in our initial design.

____One person (with an appropriate number of people) had responsibility for all aspects of usability.

____User manual

____Manuals for subsidiary groups, e.g., operators, trainers, etc.

____Identification of required functions

____User interface

____Assure adequate system reliability and responsiveness

____Outreach program, e.g., help system, training materials, hotlines, videotapes, etc.

____Installation

____Customization

____Field Maintenance

____Support-group users

Evaluation Of The Usability Design Process

In recent informal surveys we have made of system designers, we have been struck that most of their technical concerns would be addressed by using the methods just described.

A distinguishing feature of successful American companies e.g., fast food vendor, grocery store, computer manufacturer, and government units is their long term dedication to customer satisfaction (Peters and Waterman, 1982; Peters and Austin, 1985). Methodologically, people in these success stories stay close to their customers ("users"); they wander around. We have been told that several years ago a large corporation studied their twelve major business failures. They concluded that in each failure they did not know that particular "business" or "application" or "user set" for which they were creating a new product. IBM's market success has often been attributed to "knowing the customers' business better than they." The point here is that these examples illustrate the value of knowing and serving users.

We have talked about the process of design. As part of this process, it is possible to select as starting points good designs from an existing inventory, e.g., pull-down menus, pointing and selecting with a mouse, icons, Lotus "menu-bar," multiple windows on a screen. These designs have themselves stood the test of empirical usage. (see section on Starting Points below)

Comparison to Other Approaches. Gould and Lewis (1985) have compared usability design with other design approaches, e.g., getting it right the first time. You simply cannot fully specify a system in advance -- even when using a methodology that tries to do so (Swartout and Balzar, 1982). Further, Gould and Lewis (1985) explicitly raised, and then addressed, several reasons why the principles of usability design are often not used, e.g., belief that the development process will be lengthened, belief that iteration is just fine-tuning. Human factors is more than just frosting that can be spread on at the end. "What if the development schedule is so tight that you cannot afford the luxury of talking to users," we are sometimes asked. Talking to users is not a luxury; it is a necessity. The methods described here should help with achieving a schedule. They introduce reality into the schedule, since you must do all these things eventually anyway. "Can't talking to just a few people be misleading," we are sometimes asked. Yes, possibly -- but you will be far, far better off than if you talk to none. Talking to no one is a formula for failure.

Comparison to other "User Interface Principles". The process advocated here is procedurally or methodologically oriented. In contrast, sometimes designers use the term "design principles" to refer to certain features they believe are important to incorporate into their user interfaces, e.g., icons, desk-top metaphor, consistency. Case studies that illustrate this include Xerox's Star (R) system (Smith, Irby, Kimball, Verplank, and Harslen, 1982), Visicorp's Visi On (R) (Woodmansee, 1985), some IBM Research popular PC packages (Foulger, 1986).

Case Study Evaluations. Two common threads running through reports on the development of several recent computer systems are the need for using and the effectiveness of using the design methods described here: IBM's Audio Distribution System (ADS) (Gould and Boies, 1983); Tektronix's Graphic Input Workstation (Weiner, 1984); Boeing's banking terminal (Butler, 1985); Digital Equipment Corporation's VAX Text Processing Utility (Good, 1985); Xerox's Star system (Smith, Irby, Kimball, Verplank, and Harslen, 1982); Apple's Lisa (R) system (Williams, 1983); IBM Research Computer Systems Department systems (Foulger, 1986); IBM's QMF (Boyle, Ogden, Uhlir, and Wilson, 1985). See also Akscyn and McCracken (1985). When designers follow the process advocated here, they brag about it. Not so with most other design approaches. Indeed, we have heard presentations where designers claim to have done much of what is advocated here, but clearly have not.

The development process used in OMS (Boies et al., 1985) directly tested and demonstrated the value of this process for developing a significant system. So have other case studies (Good et al., 1986; Hewett and Meadow, 1986). Because of practical limitations, these have not been controlled experiments wherein another group of designers built the same system following a different design methodology. One study, in conjunction with a one-semester course, did use a controlled experimental paradigm to compare protyping and specifying design approaches (Boehm, Gray, and Seewaldt; 1984). They found that with prototyping these student designers wrote 40% less code, required 45% less time to complete their system, and created systems that were rated higher on ease of learning and use, compared with the systems created by the students in the specifying groups. Participants in the specifying groups, on the other hand, created systems that had more functions, were more robust, had more coherent designs, and their systems were more easily integrated.

Design is a series of on-going tradeoffs among hardware, software, usability, economic, and scheduling factors. The usability design process must be followed if usability is to receive its due.

Status. If all of this is so good, why doesn't everybody do it? We previously thought that the principles of the usability design process were almost trivially simple to follow -- they are so commonsensical, and they are not difficult technically to carry out. We were wrong. They are not commonsensical to many designers (Gould and Lewis, 1985). They are hard to carry out, mainly for organizational and motivational reasons. In addition, designers in the early stages of work on a new and innovative system (a relatively rare situation in most environments, since most systems are really follow-on systems) sometimes find it hard to map the principles and methods of usability design onto their work. Once a user group is defined this becomes easier, however.

Practicing usability design is especially difficult for managers. Being willing to live in a sea of changes, which the usability design process requires, on very large projects with hundreds of people presents a significant stumbling block. Groups that report practicing the usability design process typically have a strong, committed manager. These groups are often, but not always, relatively small.

Taking the opportunity to think about the process with which you will design something rather than the design of that something, can be difficult. Designers always seem to be in the middle of something -- and never at the beginning of something with time to think about global issues.

We have met designers who are certain that the development process will be lengthened and more expensive if they practice the usability design process. They would be adding on more work, they reason, and therefore more time and effort would be required. This view fails to recognize that you learn things with this approach which eliminate a lot of work that would otherwise go on (see Boies et al., 1985; Gould and Lewis, 1985). Imagine building a house without knowing pretty much what you wanted when you started. Without a plan, you would save some time getting started, but it would certainly cost you later.

Experimental psychologists sometimes see some of our recommended methods as requiring inordinate drudge work. "I don't want to sit and watch people for hours in the experiments." Observing, listening, and making notes provide valuable insights that can be gained no other way. "Why not just completely automate computer-controlled experiments"? This automation itself requires iteration; usually there is not enough time.

To some, user testing and iterative design may seem like a pessimistic design philosophy. Do I always have to start from scratch? When will we have a scientific, analytic approach that leads to getting a good user interface right the first time? User testing and iterative design will probably always be necessary to be sure you did get it right the first time. Even expert bridge players do not always make their bids.

Nevertheless, there appears to be an increase in the use of our recommended methods, and an increased desire on the part of individual designers to try them.

Recent Advances. Two recent conceptual advances are integrated design and usability engineering. First, integrated design was added to the process of Gould and Lewis (1985) based upon the OMS experience as a test case of the other three principles (Gould, et al., 1987) (see Table 2). It may prove, organizationally, to be the hardest to follow.

Second, usability engineering, formulated at DEC (Good, et al., 1984; 1985), is a methodical, quantitative way to improve usability. Typically, the design team, in cooperation with human factors people, develops behavioral goals about how much better they want their new system to be than a competitive or previous system. For example, they may want to reduce turn-around time of a process control report by 25% or reduce hot-line questions by 20%. Then in small formal experiments, participants are given benchmark tasks to carry out on the new system. They may also carry out very similar tasks on the comparison system if these results may have not been obtained previously. These comparative results, together with other usability observations, drive the next iteration on the new system. The team tries to identify components of the new system contributing the most to the comparative results (on the targeted goals of turn-around time and hot-line calls in the example) and then improve these components. John Whiteside (personal communication, 1987), the manager of this DEC human factors group, and his group have used this approach successfully on over twenty DEC development projects. As part of this, the group is increasingly spending up to fifty per cent of their time in the field (rather in their offices or labs) visiting and observing customers.

Necessary, But Not Sufficient. Using the methods advocated here does not guarantee a GREAT system. The methods are necessary but not sufficient, as pointed out in Boies et al. (1985), to achieve acceptable usability. As in all other professions, designers have a range of ability. By definition, most systems are designed by average designers. Practicing usability design greatly increases the probability that average designers will design systems with acceptable usability. Good starting points further help (see next Section). To go beyond this and design GREAT systems requires innovation and creativity, as in the invention of the electronic spreadsheet. Also required is an outstanding leader and very good, committed people, dedication, hard work, and lots of self-imposed pressure.

New Technologies. While the usability design process is certainly useful for development projects, it is less clear how they relate to the early stages of very new research technologies and ideas. When new ideas are just beginning, they are fragile; potentially good ones can often be rejected. Imagine some new technical ideas that hardly exist today, e.g., remote control technology (maybe eventually it might be used to control or monitor your lawn mowers, children, or as a mouse replacement); locator technology (that might eventually indicate within a few feet where a particular person or object is, no matter where in the world it is; would you ever lose anything again?); a new programming technology (with which people might eventually work very differently); a brain wave recognizer (which might eventually automatically drive a typewriter or word processor, or aid in world peace negotiations); storage technology a billion or trillion times larger than today's but with "immediate" response time. The key points with these examples are that the very tough early problems are (a) to demonstrate technical feasibility apart from any application, and (b) until then it is hard to study seriously or even envision many applications that may result from a new technology (but not impossible, see Gould, Conti, and Hovanyecz, 1983).

Since the original publication of this manual five years ago, we have learned a good deal about practicing usability design on very advanced new technologies, in this case a very advanced programming technology (Gould, Boies, and Lewis, 1991).

STARTING POINTS

Where should a designer start when designing a computer system? There are several beginning points, prior to talking with potential users.

Define The System

The most important starting point is to define at least in general terms what the system will be, e.g., who will use it, what should it do, and why the users and/or organization will benefit from it. Write these down, so everyone is getting the same message. Where appropriate, define in one simple sentence the problem this system will solve for the customer. While this may seem obvious and easy, it is our observation that it is often missing, largely because of mixed motives, organizational conflicts, and focus on other things. When this is done, especially at the outset, great progress has already been made on the design problem. These goals are at least as critical in the design space as are weight, cost, MIPS, disk size, etc. Try to develop a system that users and their organizations really want.

Follow-on Systems

Most computer systems are not new. They are new releases by a vendor of existing systems (e.g., Lotus 123 (R), version 2), or extensions of already existing in-house applications. In effect, the designer is not getting started, but is already started. On the one hand the existing release of a system helps define the new design problem, but on the other hand it puts compatibility constraints on what the designer may do. The constraints may involve a trade-off between establishing positive transfer for the existing users and greatly improving the system for new users. Of importance is that the architecture of an existing system allow for easy change although it often does not.

New Influential Systems

A frequently used source of ideas for all aspects of system usability is imitation of key advances made by designers of related user interfaces, manuals, maintenance strategies, training strategies, and system functions. In user interfaces, for example, it appears that many systems have adopted the use of a mouse, icons, windows, and desktop metaphor popularized in the Xerox Star system (see Smith, Irby, Kimball, and Verplank, 1982 for descriptions of these features), or the menu style popularized in Lotus 123.

New Technologies

New technologies are often the driving force to create new systems. Examples include very large-screen displays, speech recognition, handwriting recognition, touch screens. Such projects involve innovative research. The people involved attempt to solve very difficult technical challenges. As a consequence, the work is often technology-oriented, designed to demonstrate feasibility or to contribute to the scientific disciplines from which they emanate.

While inventors want to get their ideas into use, they are not always usability oriented. It is our view that the mid-stages of the development process of new technologies can be hastened if a usability approach as described in the section on Usability Design Process is taken.

User Circumstances

Sometimes a good starting point is to build on existing user knowledge, skills, and resources. What do users expect to happen in certain circumstances? Users of computers can often describe how they wish things could be. You could talk with users in their work environments or, if appropriate, attend meetings of large user groups. In the latter case, there are official user groups associated with most large computer companies, and a list of these groups has been recently published (Datamation, 1987). Discussing advanced research technology with relevant computer users, e.g., discussing a handmarking command language with secretaries, can identify useful directions to pursue. In some large organizations marketing groups sometimes use techniques like "focus groups" to elicit some of this information. Consistent with our recommendation of direct involvement of designers with users, we recommend that designers observe these sessions, and not get the data second-hand.

Journals, Proceedings, Demonstrations

Paging through journals and proceedings can be a source of starting ideas. Journals include Human Factors, Behaviour and Information Technology, Ergonomics, Human-Computer Interaction, International Journal of Man-Machine Studies, ACM journals, particularly Communications of the ACM. and SIGHCHI Bulletin. The Proceedings of the annual meeting of the Human Factors Society (e.g., 1986) and the Proceedings of Computer Human Interaction conferences (e.g., 1986) contain many relevant papers of the most recent work in the field. Such articles can be helpful, but they are usually not written in a tutorial or procedural way as are, for example, the handbooks described below. Demonstrations at national meetings, e.g., SIGCHI, and trade-shows can also be a source of ideas.

Other Designers And Consultants

Talk over your possible system with other designers. Let the attitudes of successful designers rub off on you. Benefit from lessons they have learned. These conversations can help you develop notions of good usability design and poor usability design. There are many analogies between designing good computer systems and designing other types of systems. Draw upon lessons you have learned, via successes and mistakes, in other domains. Think about how carefully you design something very important to yourself personally, e.g., a modification or addition to your house or living system. You probably have many conversations with your family (i.e., "the users") and with friends, architects, carpenters, electricians, plumbers, suppliers before going ahead with the project. Use this same sensitivity and care with the computer system you are designing.

You can obtain a list of possible consultants by looking in the Directory of the Human Factors Society. Associated with each member's name is a one-line description of their speciality and whether they are available as a consultant. You can find members living near you via the geographical area listing in it. University professors, and their students, are often interested in consulting and contract work. Try Psychology Departments and Computer Science Departments..

•
•
•

Sections on User Interface Standards, Handbooks and Guidelines, Development Procedures Books and Rules, and Formal Models for Design omitted because they duplicate material presented elsewhere in this book or because they too rapidly become out-of-date.

•
•
•

SUMMARY AND CONCLUSIONS

Usability is combination of many factors, each of which is often developed independently. User interface code is becoming an increasingly large percentage of the total system code. Standards are beginning to emerge for user interface design. Establishing standards for software aspects of user interfaces is probably premature. There are lots of guidelines for good system design. However, these are not enough for the design of good systems. You must at the very beginning and throughout development focus on prospective users and their work. We often hear that people buy computer systems for the functions in them. You are unlikely to figure out what the functions should be without talking with users. You must continuously measure each aspect of usability, and then iterate in a hill-climbing way toward a better system. All aspects of usability should begin evolving from the very beginning, and should be under one focus. Tests to date of this recommended approach lead to the conclusion that it is necessary for the design of a good system, but not sufficient. Innovation and creativity are still required to make a great system.

ACKNOWLEDGEMENTS

I thank Clayton Lewis for several influential early conversations about the organization of this paper; Stephen Boies for collaboration on the Software Tools section; Angie Fusca for gathering some source material and editorial help, particularly with the reference section; many human factors and system design people for careful reading of various iterations of this manuscript and for many helpful suggestions, including Amy Aaronson, Charles Collins, Don Davis, Gary Flatow, Liz Gould, Paul Green, Alan Happ, Rick Herder, Peter Kennedy, Tom Lanzetta, Susanne Maass, Bob Mack, Jim McGready, Ben Nathanson, Bucky Pope, Bob Riekert, Jim Schoonard, Linda Tetzlaff, Ann Marie Vosburgh. I also thank for their comments seven reviewers of this chapter for the Handbook of Human-Computer Interaction, including Warren Badger, C. J. Goddard, B. L. Nicholas, Stuart Parsons, Bob Remington. These interactions with intended users of this paper allowed me to use the usability design process recommended here to develop the manual.

This reprinted chapter contains a few examples not provided in the earlier version published in The Handbook of Human-Computer Interaction. It also contains some improvements suggested by Jonathan Grudin and his students, whom I thank for their encouragement.

In the five years since writing the original version, I and wonderful colleagues have collaborated on a software tools project (called ITS) aimed at technically facilitating iterative design of computer applications and at encouraging a new work organization under which the process of usability design can more easily and effectively be carried out (Boies, Bennett, Gould, Greene, S. L., and Wiecha, 1989; Gould, Boies, and Lewis, 1991). The results are encouraging (Wiecha, Bennett, Boies, Gould, and Greene, 1990; Boies, Ukelson, Gould, Anderson, Babecki, and Clifford, 1991; Gould, Sitnik, and Ukelson, 1991; Ukelson, Gould, Boies, and Wiecha, 1991).

TRADEMARKS

Star is a trademark of Xerox Corporation. Lotus 123 is a trademark of the Lotus Corportion. Lisa is a trademark of the Apple Corporation. Macintosh is a trademark of the Apple Corporation. Visi On is a trademark of Visicorp.

REFERENCES

Akscyn, R. M. and McCracken, D. L. (1985). ZOG and the USS CARL VINSON: Lessons in System Development. Proceedings of Interact'84 First IFIP Conference on Human-Computer teraction. Interaction. (pp. 303-308). Amsterdam: Elsevier Science Publishers.

ACM. (1986). Proceedings of the CHI'86 Human Factors in Computing Systems Conference. Available from ACM Order Department, P.O.Box 64145, Baltimore, Maryland 21264.

Aetna Life Insurance Company (1986). Software usability guidelines: Techniques for achieving "normal to use" systems. People/technology Issues and Programs. Hartford, Connecticut.

Alavi, M. (1984). An assessment of the prototyping approach to information systems development. Communications of the ACM, 27(6), 556-563.

Anderson, N. S. &amp. Reitman-Olson, J. (eds.). (1985). Methods for designing software to fit human needs and capabilities. Washington, D.C.: The National Academy of Sciences/National Research Council Committee on Human Factors.

Apple Human Interface Guidelines: The Apple Desktop Interface. Published by Apple Programjmer's and Developer's Association, 290 SW 43rd Street, Renton, Washington 98055, 1986.

Bell Telephone Laboratories. (1983). Video Display Terminals: Preliminary Guidelines for Selection, Installation, &amp. Use. New Jersey

Bennett, J. L. (1985). The concept of architecture applied to user interfaces in interactive computer systems. In Proceedings of Interact'84 First IFIP Conference on Human-Computer teraction. Interaction. (pp. 865-870). Amsterdam: Elsevier Science Publishers.

Bennett, J. L. (1986). Tools for building advanced user interfaces. IBM Systems Journal, 25, 354-368.

Bennett, J. L. (1984). Managing to meet usability requirements: establishing and meeting software development goals. In J. Bennett, D. Case, J. Sandelin, and M. Smith (Eds.) Usability issues and health concerns, (pp. 161-184). Englewood Cliffs, New Jersey: Prentice-Hall.

Boehm, B. W., Gray, T. E., Seewaldt, T. (1984). Prototyping versus specifying: A multiproject experiment. IEEE Transactions on Software Engineering, 10(3), 290-302.

Boies, S. J., Gould, J. D., Levy, S. E., Richards, J. T., Schoonard, J. W. (1985). The 1984 Olympic Message System -- A Case Study In System Design, IBM Research Report, RC-11138. Yorktown Heights, N.Y.: IBM.

Boies, S. J., Ukelson, J. U., Gould, J. D., Anderson, D., Babecki, M., and Clifford, J. (1991). Using ITS to Create an Insurance Industry Application -- A Joint Case Study. IBM Research Report, RC-16467.

Boyle, J., Ogden, W., Uhlir, S., Wilson, P. (1984). QMF usability: How it really happened. In Human Computer Interaction -- Interact '84, (pp. 877-882).

Boies, S. J., Bennett, W. E., Gould, J. D., Greene, S. L., and Wiecha, C. (1989). The Interactive Transaction System (ITS): Tools for Application Development. IBM Research Report RC-14694.

Bury, K. F. (1985). The iterative development of usable computer interfaces. In Human-Computer Interaction -- Interact '84, (pp. 343-348).

Butler, K. A., (1985). Connecting theory and practice: A case study of achieving usability goals. In Human Factors in Computing Systems Proceedings CHI'85, (pp. 93-98). New York: ACM.

Buxton, W., Lamb, M., Sherman, D., Smith, K. (1983). Towards a comprehensive user interface management system Computer Graphics, 17(3), 35-42.

Cakir, A., Hart, D. J., Stewart, T. F. M. (1979). The VDT Manual. Germany: Inca-Fiej Research Association.

Card, S. K., Moran, T. P., Newell, A. (1983). The Psychology of Human-Computer Interaction. Hillsdale, N.J.: Erlbaum Assoc.

Carroll, J. M., Rosson, M. B. (1984). Usability specifications as a tool in iterative development, IBM Research Report. Yorktown Heights, N.Y.: IBM.

Chaikin, G. (1984). The department of defense human factors standardization program. Applied Ergonomics, 15, 197-201.

Chaikin, G. (1976). Human engineering specifications and standards: Payoffs and pitfalls. Society of Automotive Engineers, 1-6.

Comstock, E. (1983). Customer installability of computer systems. In Proceedings of the Human Factors Society Annual Meeting, (pp. 501-504). Santa Monica, California: Human Factors Society.

Cowlishaw, M. F. (1984). The design of the REXX language. IBM Systems Journal, 23(4), 326-335.

Damodaran, L., Simpson, A., Wilson, P. (1980). Designing Systems for People. Manchester, England: NCC Publications.

Datamation. Datamation's Directory of User Groups. Datamation. December 15, 1987, 33 (24), 52-68,

Davis, F. D., Reitman-Olson, J. (1986). Integrating user motivation and task performance theories. Human Computer Interaction Lab -- VM Tech Report.

Davis, E. G., Swezey, R. W. (1983). Human factors guidelines in computer graphics: A case study. International Journal of Man-Machine Studies. 18, 113-133.

Demers, R. A. (1981). System design for usability Communications of the ACM, 24, 494-501.

Doherty, W. J., Kelisky, R. P. (1979). Managing VM/CMS system for user effectiveness IBM System Journal, 1, 143-163.

Doherty, W. J., Thadhani, A. J. (1982). The economic value of rapid response time. IBM Technical Report Publication #GE20-0752-0 (Available from author at IBM T. J. Watson Research Center.)

Drury,C. G. (1983). Task analysis methods in industry. Applied Ergonomics, 14(1), 19-28.

Eason, K. (1983). Methodological issues in the study of human factors in teleinformation systems. Behaviour and Information Technology, 2, 357-364.

Eason, K. D. (1982). The process of introducing information technology. Behaviour and Information Technology, 1, 197-213.

Eike, D. R., Fleger, S. A., Phillips, E. R. (1986). User interface design guidelines for expert troubleshooting systems. In Proceedings of the Human Factors Society -- 30th Annual Meeting, (pp. 1024-1028). Santa Monica, California: Human Factors Society.

Engel, S. E., Granda, R. E. (1975). Guidelines for man/display interfaces. IBM Technical Report, Poughkeepsie N.Y.: IBM.

Erdmann, R. L., Neal, A. S. (1971). Laboratory vs. field experimentation in human factors--An evaluation of an experimental self-service airline ticket vendor. Human Factors, 13, 521-531.

Fitter, M. J., Brownbridge, G., Garber, R., Herzmark, G. (1985). A human factors evaluation of the IBM Sheffield primary care system. Human-Computer Interaction -- Interact '84, (pp. 675-682).

Flavin, R. A., Williford, J. D., Barzilai, H. (1986). Computer conferencing data structures in the GRANDiose System. IEEE Transactions on professional communications, PC29(1), 34-44.

Foulger, D. (1986). Discovering the PC User Interface. Unpublished Manuscript. Available from the author at IBM T. J. Watson Research Center, Yorktown Heights, N.Y. 10598.

Gallaway, G. R. (1981). Response times to user activities in interactive man/machine computer systems. Human Factors Guidelines Series. NCR Technical Report HFP 81-25. Dayton, Ohio: NCR.

Gardner, A., Mayfield, T. F., Maguire, M. C. (1985). Human factors guidelines for the design of computer-based systems. In Human-Computer Interaction -- Interact '84, (pp. 649-654).

Glasson, B. C. (1985). Guidelines for user participation in the system development process. In Human-Computer Interaction -- Interact '84, (pp. 589-596).

Good, M. (1985). The iterative design of a new text editor. In Proceedings of the Human Factors Society -- 29th Annual Meeting, (pp. 571-574). Santa Monica, California: Human Factors Society.

Good, M., Spine, T. M., Whiteside, J., George, P. (1986). User-derived impact analysis as a tool for usability engineering. In Human Factors in Computing Systems CHI'86 Proceedings, (pp. 241-246). New York: ACM.

Good, M., Whiteside, J. A., Wixon, D. R., Jones, S. J. (1984). Building a user-derived interface. Communications of the ACM, 27, 1032-1043.

Goodwin, N. C. (1983). Designing a multipurpose menu driven user interface to computer based tools. In Proceedings of the Human Factors Society -- 27th Annual Meeting, (pp. 816-820). Santa Monica, California: Human Factors Society.

Gould, J. D., Boies, S. J., Levy, S., Richards, J. T., Schoonard, J. (1987). The 1984 Olympic Message System--A test of behavioral principles of system design. Communications of the ACM, (in press).

Gould, J. D., Conti, J., Hovanyecz, T. (1983). Composing letters with a simulated typewriter. Communications of the ACM, 26, 295-308.

Gould, J. D., Lewis, C. H.. (1983). Designing for usability--key principles and what designers think. In Proceedings of the 1983 Computer-Human Interaction Conference, (pp. 50-53).

Gould, J. D., Lewis, C. H.. (1985). Designing for usability - -key principles and what designers think. Communications of the ACM, 28, 300-311.

Gould, Sitnik, and Ukelson (1991). Case Study: Using ITS to Make a General Purpose Spreadsheet Program. Proceedings of Bould Conference on User Interface Design (in press).

Gould, J. D., Boies, S. J., and Lewis, C. (1991). Making Usable, Useful, Productivity-enhancing Computer Applications. Communications of the ACM. 34(1), 74-85.

Grace, G. L. (1966). Application of empirical methods to computer-based system design. Journal of Applied Psychology, 50, 442-450.

Granda, R. (1980). Personal Communication. IBM Corporation, Poughkeepsie, New York.

Green, M. (1985) The University of Alberta user interface management system. In Proceedings of SIGGRAPH'85: Computer Graphics, 19, (pp. 205-213).

Green, P. (1986). Customer setup of the NCR PC-8 personal computer: a case study. The University of Michigan Transportation Research Institute Report, UMTRI-86-25. Ann Arbor, Michigan.

Gruenenfelder, T. H. and Whitten, W. B., II. Augmenting Generic Research With Prototype Evaluation. Experience in Applying Generic Research To Specific Products. In Human-Computer Interaction -- Interact '84, (pp. 315-319).

Hamel, C. J. (1986). The CAI evaluation checklist: Guidelines for the design of computer-aided instruction. In Proceedings of the Human Factors Society -- 30th Annual Meeting, (pp. 136-138). Santa Monica, Ca.: Human Factors Society.

Hayes, P., Szekely, P., Lerner, R. (1985). Design alternatives for user interface managements systems based on experience with COUSIN. In Computer Human Interaction CHI'85 Conference Proceedings, (pp. 169-175).

Heckel, P. (1984). The Elements of Friendly Software Design. New York: Warner Books.

Henderson, D. A., Jr. (1986) The Trillium user interface design environment. In Proc. CHI'86 Human Factors in Computing Systems, (pp. 222-227). New York: ACM.

Hendricks, D., Kilduff, P., Brooks, P., Marshak, R., Doyle, B. (1986). Human Engineering Guidelines for Management Information Systems. U. S. Army Human Engineering Laboratory, Aberdeen Proving Ground, Maryland.

Hewett, T. T., Meadow, C. T. (1986). On designing for usability: An application of four key principles. In Human Factors in Computing Systems CHI'86 Proceedings, (pp. 247-252). New York: ACM.

Hirsch, R. S. (1982). National standards for the design of visual display terminals. In Proceedings of the Human Factors Society, (pp. 290-294). Santa Monica, CA: Human Factors Society.

Human Engineering Procedures Guide: Military Handbook. (1986). Department of Defense, Washington, D. C., MIL-HDBK-XXX, August.

Human Engineering Requirements for Military Systems. (1979). Equipment and Facilities. Military Specification, MIL-H-46855B, January.

Human Factors Society. Human-Computer Interaction Standards Committee. (1986). Draft Proposal, Version 1.0. Santa Monica, CA: Human Factors Society.

Human Factors Society. (1986). American National Standard for Human Factors Engineering of Visual Display Terminal Workstations. (HFS-100). Santa Monica, California: Human Factors Society.

Human Factors Society. Directory and Yearbook of Human Factors Society. (Available for $25 from The Human Factors Society, P.O.Box 1369, Santa Monica, California 90406.)

Human Factors Society. Proceedings of the Human Factors Society -- 30th Annual Meeting. (Available from The Human Factors Society, P.O.Box 1369, Santa Monica, California 90406.)

Human Factors of Workstations with Visual Displays. (1984) (Can be obtained from Human Factors Center, IBM, Publication #G320-6102-2, 5600 Cottle Road, San Jose, CA 95193)

Keister, R. S. (1981). Human factors guidelines for the content, layout, and format of CRT displays in interactive application systems: For the use of help screens and online documentation. Human Factors Guidelines Series, NCR Technical Report HFP 83-12. Dayton, Ohio.

Keiras, D., Polson, P. G. (1985). An approach to the formal analysis of user complexity. Intl. J. Man-Machine Studies, 22, 365-394.

Kelley, J. F. (1984). An iterative design methodology for user-friendly natural language office information applications. ACM Transactions on Office Information Systems, 2(1), 26-41.

Klein, G. A., Brezovic, C. P. (1986). Design engineers and the design process: Decision strategies and human factors literature. In Proceedings of the Human Factors Society -- 30th Annual Meeting, (pp. 771-775). Santa Monica, CA: Human Factors Society.

Kloster, G. V., Tischer, K. (1985). Man-machine interface design process. In Human-Computer Interaction -- Interact '84, (pp. 889-894).

Lewis, C. H. (1982). Using the "thinking aloud" method in cognitive interface design. IBM Research Report, RC-9265. Yorktown Heights, New York: IBM.

Lynch, G. (1985). American national standard for human factors engineering of visual display terminal workstations: A report to the Society. In Proceedings of the Human Factors Society -- 29th Annual, Meeting, (pp. 987-994). Santa Monica, CA: Human Factors Society.

Martin, G. L., Corl, K. G. (1976). System response time effects on user productivity Behaviour and Information Technology, 5(1).

McCormick, E. J. (1976). Human Factors in Engineering and Design. New York: McGraw Hill.

Meister, D. (1986). Human Factors Testing and Evaluation. Amsterdam, Netherlands: Elsavir.

Mentemerlo, M. D., Eddowes, E. (1978). The judgemental nature of tasks analysis. In Proceedings of the Human Factors Society, (pp. 247-250). Santa Monica, CA: Human Factors Society.

Mintzberg, H. (1976). The nature of managerial work. New York: Harper and Row.

Mosier, J. N., Smith, S. L. (1986). Application guidelines for designing user interface software. Behaviour and Information Technology, 5, 39-46.

Mumford, E. (1981). Participative system design: structure and method. Systems, Objectives, Solutions, 1, 5-19.

Olsen, R. A. (Ed.) (1981). Handbook for Design and Use of Visual Display Terminals. Report LMSC-D927602. Lockheed Missiles and Space Company, Sunnyvale, Calif.

Overmyer, S. P. (1987). Rapid prototyping in the design of large-scale interactive information systems. Human Factors Society Bulletin, 30, 3-4.

Peters, T., Waterman, R. H. (1982). In Search of Excellence.

Peters, T., Austin, N. (1985). A Passion for Excellence. New York: Random House.

Pfaff, G. R. (1985). User Interface Management Systems. Berlin: Springer Verlag.

Reed, P. (1986). Human factors standards for the software user interface: Genesis and evolution of the HFS human-computer interface. In Proceedings of the Human Factors Society -- 30th Annual Meeting, (pp. 1409-1411). Santa Monica, CA: Human Factors Society.

Reisner, P. (1981). Using a formal grammar in human factors design of an interactive graphics system. IEEE Transactions of Software Engineering, SE-7, 1409-1411.

Reitman-Olson, J. (1985). Expanded design procedures for learnable, usable interfaces. In Proceedings of the ACM-SIGCHI Human Factors in Computing Meeting, (pp. 1-3). New York: ACM.

Richards, J. T., Boies, S. J., Gould, J. D. (1985). Rapid prototyping and system development: Examination of an interface toolkit for voice and telephone applications. IBM Research Report, RC-11433. Yorktown Heights, NY: IBM.

Rose, C. (1985). Inside Macintosh. Apple Computer, Inc., 1, 27-70.

Rubinstein, R., Hersh, H. (1984). The Human Factor: Designing Computer Systems for People. Burlington, Massachusetts: Digital Press.

Rupp, B. A. (1981). Visual display standards: a review of issues. Proceedings of the SID, 22, 63-72.

Rushinek, A., Rushinek, S. F. (1986). What makes users happy? Communications of the ACM, 29, 594-598.

Schrage, M. (1986). It may be happened not to work. Minneapolis Star and Tribune, December 28, page 8D.

Seminara, J. L. (1985). Use of models and mock-ups in verifying man-machine interfaces. In IEEE Third Conference on Human Factors and Power Plants, (pp. 38-40).

Shackel, B. (1984). The concept of usability. In J. Bennett, D. Case, J. Sandelin, M. Smith (Eds.), Visual Display Terminals: Usability Issues and Health Concerns, (pp. 45-87). Englewood Cliffs, N.J.: Prentice-Hall.

Shackel, B. (1985). Human factors and usability -- Whence and whither? Software Ergonomics '85, 13-31.

Shackel, B. (1984). Information technology -- A challenge to ergonomics and design. Behaviour and Information Technology, 3, 263-275.

Shulert, A. J., Rogers, G. T., Hamilton, J. A. (1985). ADM - A Dialog Manager. In Human Factors in Computing Systems CHI'85 Proceedings, (pp. 177-183). New York: ACM.

Shurtleff, D. A. (1980). How to Make Displays Legible. La Mirada, CA: Human Interface Design.

Smith, D. C., Irby, C., Kimball, R., Verplank, B., Harslem, E. (1982). Designing the star user interface. Byte, 7(4), 242-282.

Smith, S. L. (1986). Standards versus guidelines for designing user interface software. Behaviour and Information Technology, 5, 47-61.

Smith, S. L., Aucella, A. F. (1983). Design guidelines for the user interface to computer-based information systems. U.S.A.F. Electronic Systems Division, Technical Report ESD-TR-83-122. Hanscom Air Force Base, Massachusetts (NTIS No. AD A127 345).

Smith, S. L., Mosier, J. N. (1984). Design guidelines for user-system interface software. Technical Report ESD-TR-84-190. U.S.A.F. Electronic Systems Division, Hanscom Air Force Base, Massachusetts (NTIS No. AD A154 907).

Smith, S. L., Mosier, J. N. (1986). Guidelines for designing user interface software. Technical Report ESD-TR-86-278, MTR 10090. Mitre Corporation, Bedford, Massachusettes.

Sullivan, M. C., Chapanis, A. (1983). Human factoring a text editor manual. Behavior and Information Technology, 2(2), 113-125.

Swartout, W., Balzer, R. (1982). On the inevitable intertwining of specification and implementation. Communications of the ACM, 25, 438-440.

Thomas, J. C., Gould, J. D. (1975). A psychological study of query by example. In Proceedings of the 1975 National Computer Conference, (pp. 439-445).

Tullis, T. S. (1983). The formatting of alphanumeric displays: A review and analysis. Human Factors, 25, 657-682.

Tullis, T. S. (1986). A system for evaluating screen formats. In Proceedings of the Human Factors Society -- 30th Annual Meeting, (pp. 1216-1220). Santa Monica, CA: Human Factors Society.

USA Weekend. (Anonymous Author) "Question of the Week." March 31-April 2, 1989, p 2.

VanCott, H. P., Kincade, R. G. (1972). Human Engineering Guide to Equipment Design. Washington, D.C.: U. S. Government Print Office.

VanNess, F. L. (1986) Space, colour and typography on visual display terminals. Behaviour and Information Technology, 5, 99-118.

Waga, P. "...and they help carry it on". The Reporter Dispatch. Gannett Westchester Newspapers, White Plains. Section 1, p. 10. Sunday, April 3, 1988.

Weiner, H. (1984). Human factors lessons from the design of a real product. TEK Technical Report, (Can be obtained from the author at Tektronix, Box 1000, Wilsonville, Oregon 97070).

Whiteside, J., Jones, S., Levy, P. S., Wixon, D. (1985). User performance with command, menu, and Iconic interfaces. In Human Factors in Computing Systems CHI'85, (pp. 185-191). New York: ACM.

Wiecha, C., Bennett, W., Boies, S., Gould, J., and Greene, S. (1990). ITS: A Tool for Rapidly Developing Interactive Applications. ACM Transactions on Office Information Systems 8, 204-236.

Williams, G. (1983). The Lisa computer system. Byte, 8(2), 33-50.

Wixon, D., Whiteside, J. (1985). Engineering for usability: Lessons from the user derived. In Human Factors in Computing Systems CHI'85, (pp. 144-147). New York: ACM.

Woodmansee, G. H. (1985). The Visi On experience--from concept to marketplace. In Human-Computer Interaction -- Interact '84, (pp. 871-876).

Woodson, W. E., Conover, D. W. (1964). Human Engineering Guide for Equipment Users. Los Angeles, CA: University of California Press.

Ukelson, J. P., Gould, J. D., Boies, S. J., and Wiecha, C. (1991). Case Study: Using ITS Style Tools to Implement IBM's CUA-2 User Interface Style. Computer Software and Practice (in press).

GETTING TO KNOW USERS AND THEIR TASKS

BY CLAYTON LEWIS AND JOHN RIEMAN

TO GET A GOOD INTERFACE you have to figure out who is going to use it to do what. You may think your idea for a new system is so wonderful that everyone will want it, though you can't think of a really specific example, and that it will be useful in some way to people, even though you can't say just how. But history suggests you will be wrong. Even systems that turned out to be useful in unexpected ways, like the spreadsheet, started out by being useful in some expected ways.

Example: The Illusory Customers

There was a startup here in Boulder a few years back that wanted to build a system to help people build intelligent tutoring systems. They raised a bundle of money, brought a lot of smart people in, and went to work. But they didn't stop to figure out EXACTLY WHO would use the system to do EXACTLY WHAT. The concept seemed too good, in those palmy days of AI madness, to require that kind of pedestrianism. The lack of specificity created some problems internally, since it was hard to make good decisions about what aspects of the new system were important. But the trouble became critical when the time came to line up test users, people who would try out the software and provide feedback to the developers. There were no takers! Not only were there no people waiting to fork out cash for the tool, there weren't even people who would take it for nothing. And this wasn't because the work wasn't quality. People just didn't want to do what the tool was supposed to help them do.

The company didn't just roll over; they searched around for something that people did want to do that they could do with something like the tool that had been built. Not surprisingly this didn't work out and the company folded its tents when the money ran out.

You may not have needed selling on this point. "Everybody" knows you have to do some kind of requirements analysis. Yes, but based on what, and in what form? Our advice is to insist that your requirements be grounded in information about real, individual people and real tasks that they really want to perform. Get soft about this and the illusions start to creep in and before you know it you've got another system that everybody wants except people you can actually find.

HyperTopic: Contracts and Requirements

"Fortunately I don't have to worry about this. I work on contract stuff and all the requirements have been spelled out for me before I start."

Not so fast! It's one thing to meet the requirements of a contract and another thing to build a good system. Are anybody's interests really served if you build a system that meets spec but is a failure? That's what is likely to happen if you work to requirements that have not been grounded in reality, even if it's not your fault. Being selfish, will you get repeat business, or will you get a good reputation from work like this?

Clayton did once talk with a contract developer who assured him that on his current job the success of the system was really not an issue under any conceivable future (no possibility of repeat business, etc.) He has also heard of third-world "development" projects in which the real game is to please the bureaucrat who turns the tap on the (U.S.- supplied) "development" money, rather than to make something work. But life is too valuable to spend on activities like these. Find something to do that matters.

2.1 GETTING IN TOUCH WITH USERS

So here's what to do. The first step is to find some real people who would be potential users of what you are going to build. If you can't find any you need to worry a lot. If you can't find them now, where will they come from when it's time to buy? When you have found some, get them to spend some time with you discussing what they do and how your system might fit in. Are they too busy to do this? Then they'll probably be too busy to care about your system after it exists. Do you think the idea is a real winner, and they will care if you explain it to them? Then buy their time in some way. Find people in your target group who are technology nuts and who'll talk with you because you can show them technology. Or go to a professional meeting and offer a unique T-shirt to people who'll talk with you (yes, there are people whose time is too expensive for you to buy for money who will work with you for a shirt or a coffee mug).

HyperTopic: Generic and Designer Users

"I don't have to bother about this stuff. My system will be a tool for any UNIX user, no matter what they are working on. There's no special user population I'm trying to support."

Unfortunately experience shows that many ideas that are supposed to be good for everybody aren't good for anybody. Why not check by finding somebody and making sure it's good at least for them?

"Well, I'm somebody and my tool is good for me."

Two points here. First, is it REALLY good for you? Do you actually USE it? Never work on something if you ought to be a user for it but you aren't. It's amazing how often this principle is violated. Second, there are lots of reasons why things often seem more useful to their designers than they do to other people. A big one is that the designer builds up his or her understanding of the thing over a long time and with a lot of thought. Usually the user wants to understand it right away, and often can't (Bruce Tognazzini makes this point very well in "Tog on Interface" Reading, MA: Addison Wesley, 1992, p. 8).

2.2 LEARNING ABOUT THE USERS' TASKS

Once you have some people to talk with, develop CONCRETE, DETAILED EXAMPLES of tasks they perform or want to perform that your system should support. Here's how this went for Clayton and colleagues in a recent project, disguised to avoid embarrassing anybody.

The aim was to develop a system for modelling traffic: street layout, traffic volumes, accidents and the like. The system was to provide a flexible, graphical interface that would make it easy to tweak the model and examine the results. We had good access to potential users, because the project was sponsored by an organization that included people who currently use an existing model that the new one was to replace.

But there was a delicate issue here, that you will often face. The particular people providing money for the project were not the users themselves, but a staff organization whose mission was to look after the needs of the users. Sounds OK? It's not: it meant that our direct contact was not with the people who really know firsthand what the problems are but people who are supposed to know the problems secondhand, a very different thing. Fortunately we knew what we wanted and were able to arrange a series of meetings with real users.

In these meetings we developed a list of twelve things the users would actually want to do with the system. They were specific, as for example:

> Change the speed limit on Canyon Boulevard eastbound between Arapahoe and 9th. Calculate projected traffic flows on Arapahoe west of 6th assuming Canyon speeds between 25 and 55 in increments of 5 mph.

Notice a few things about this example.

- It says what the user wants to do but does not say how the user would do it.

As stated, this task does not make any assumptions about the nature of the modelling tool or its interface. Therefore it can be used to compare different design alternatives for the system and interface in a fair way. If we said "change the speed limit by selecting a new value from a menu" we would have prejudged the right way for the user to perform this part of the task.

- It is very specific.

Not only does it say exactly what the user wants to do, it actually specifies particular streets. What's the point of this? It means that we can fill out this description of the task with any other details that may become relevant in evaluating designs. In fact, it forces us to do this. For example, if the model needs to divide streets into separate pieces for purposes of analysis, and the user then needs to select a number of pieces to do an analysis for a stretch of street, we can see in detail how this would work out for the real Canyon Boulevard. We can't avoid the problem as we could if we were thinking of any old generic street.

Dennis Wixon has an example that makes this point (In M. Rudissill, T. McKay, C. Lewis, and P.G. Polson (Eds.), "Human-Computer Interaction Design: Success Cases, Emerging Methods, and Real-World Context." Morgan Kaufman. In press.). Wixon and colleagues were developing an interface for a file management system. It passed lab tests with flying colors, but bombed as soon as customers got it. The problem was that it had a scrolling file list that was (say) twenty characters wide, but the file names customers used were very long, and in fact often identical for more than twenty characters (the names were made up by concatenating various qualifiers, and for many names the first several qualifiers would be the same.) Customers were not amused by needing to select from a scrolling list of umpty-ump identical entries that stood for different files. And this wasn't an oddball case, it was in fact typical. How had it been missed in the lab tests? Nobody thought it would matter what specific file names you used for the test, so of course they were all short.

- It describes a complete job.

Note that the task doesn't just say to fiddle the speed limit on Canyon, or just to calculate projections for Arapahoe. It says the user wants to do both. This means that in seeing how this task plays out for a particular design of the interface we are forced to consider how features of the interface work together, not just how reasonable they may look separately.

We once evaluated a phone-in bank service that had done well in lab tests. People had no trouble checking their balances, finding out if checks had cleared, and the like. But when we looked at what was involved in finding if a check had cleared AND THEN looking at a balance, we found big problems. The interface was supposed to support this kind of transition between functions, but the test tasks used in the lab had not required them.

Describing complete jobs is a key feature of our approach, and it's different from the usual way of doing things. Usually requirements lists are just that: lists of little things the system has to do. Meeting this kind of requirement does little to ensure that users can do a real job without going crazy: it just ensures that they can do all the PARTS of a real job.

An important angle on the complete job issue is seeing where inputs come from and where outputs go. In the example problem, where does the model the user is going to tweak come from? How does he or she obtain it? If there aren't good answers to these questions the system will be no good in practice, even if it does the tweaking and calculating parts very well.

Clayton worked on an early business graphics package whose sales were disappointing. Customer visits (done after ship, not before development when they should have been done) showed that the problem was that the package worked well when users had numbers to type in to make a graph, but badly when numbers were already in the system and needed to be extracted from a file. One user had temporarily hired typists to transcribe numbers from one screen, where a data file was displayed, onto another screen where the graph package was running. He was not eager to continue this arrangement. The majority of uses we saw were of this get-data-from-a-file kind, so the system was unsuited to requirements even though it did a good job on making the graph itself, the part of the whole job on which the designers concentrated.

So you want to choose tasks that represent complete jobs, and you want to be sure to scrutinize the edges of the tasks. Where does stuff come in from? Where does it go? What has to happen next?

• The tasks should say who the users are.

In the highway example we were dealing with a small, close- knit group of users, so we didn't specify in our example tasks WHO would be doing what: we took it as given. Probably we should have worried about this more, and probably you should. The success of a design can be influenced strongly by what users know, how the tasks supported by the system fit into other work they have to do, and the like. So you need to get a fix on these things early in design.

The design of Oncocin, a sophisticated cancer therapy advisor, illustrates what's at stake (Musen, M.A., Fagan, L.M., and Shortliffe, E.H. "Graphical specification of procedural knowledge for an expert system. In J.A. Hendler [Ed.], "Expert Systems: The User Interface." Norwood, NJ: Ablex, 1988, p. 15). Earlier experience with doctor users had shown that they are willing to invest very little time in becoming familiar with a new system. A system to be used directly by doctors therefore has to be different from one to be used by medical technicians, who can be told they HAVE to learn a new tool. The Oncocin designers needed to decide up front whether their users would be doctors or would be technicians working in support of doctors. They went for direct use by doctors. The interface they came up with is as much as possible a faithful copy of the paper forms for specifying therapy that doctors were already using.

So what should you say about users in specifying your tasks? If possible, name names. This allows you to get more information if it becomes relevant, just as saying it's Arapahoe Avenue allows you to bring in more detail about the task if you need to. Beyond that you should note characteristics of the users that you already know will be important, such as what their job is and what expertise they have.

In choosing the sample tasks for the traffic modelling system we were guided by two objectives. First, we wanted to be sure that we had examples that illustrated the kinds of support that we as designers thought the system should provide. That is, we had some general ideas about what the system was supposed to be good for, and we tried to find tasks that were examples of these. But second, we needed to reflect the interests of potential users in the examples. So we tried to find tasks that illustrated proposed functionality in the context of work users really wanted to do.

In the process some possible functions for the system dropped out. We had envisioned that the system might include some optimization functions that would manipulate the model to find the best of some range of alternatives with respect to some measure of quality. Users had no interest in this. They preferred to solve such problems by framing and evaluating alternatives themselves rather than having the system do this.

This is not an uncommon conflict, and one without a simple resolution. We thought, and still think, that users would eventually come to want optimization functions once more pressing modelling needs were met, so we didn't want to just take the users' word on this. But we put optimization on the back burner to be pushed again in the future.

This illustrates a key point about input from users: users are NOT always right. They cannot anticipate with complete accuracy how they will use new technology. As a designer your job is to build a system that users will want when it gets here, not to build the system users say they want as they see things today. You may well have insight into the future that users lack. But you need to be very careful about this. If you are like most designers, an outsider in the domain of work you are trying to support, you have to recognize that users know a whole lot more about what they are doing than you do. If you can't get users interested in your hot new idea, however hard you try to draw them into it, you're probably missing something.

HyperTopic: Participatory Design

In our discussion we have been assuming a split between the roles of designers and users that has been traditional in U.S. system design. Designers are not users; they gather information from users and reflect it in systems they build; they give these systems to users who use them or not. There is an alternative approach, pioneered by workers in Scandinavia, that rejects this structure. In participatory design, systems are designed by designers and users working together: a slogan is DESIGNING WITH rather than DESIGNING FOR. The power to make the system be one way rather than another is not reserved for the designers, as it is in most U.S. design practice, but rather is shared by designers and users working in collaboration.

The contrast between participatory design and standard U.S. practice reflects deep differences in political and philosophical outlook between Europe and the U.S.. Most European countries give workers very broad influence on working conditions, which are much more strictly regulated than in the U.S.. In many countries workers must have seats on the boards of directors of companies, and workers must be consulted on the introduction of new technology in the workplace. With this view of workers it is natural to think that workers should have a direct hand in shaping the systems they have to use. By contrast the prevailing view in the U.S. is that management should just decide what systems are good for productivity and then impose them on workers, whose views basically don't matter.

Many people in the U.S., if they think about these matters at all, assume that the U.S. way of doing things must be right. What is your reaction when you hear that in some European countries it is illegal to make someone work in a room without a window? Does that seem silly, or maybe wrongheaded, because of the restriction in places on freedom of enterprise? What do you think about it when you also learn that a number of countries in Europe have higher per capita productivity than the U.S., and that the U.S. is steadily losing export position, especially in advanced industries, and holding its own primarily in commodity exports like farm produce? For a fascinating, disturbing, and constructive look at these and related issues, read the book "The Competitive Advantage of Nations," by Michael Porter (New York: Free Press, 1990).

You can find a lengthy discussion of participatory design in the journal Human-Computer Interaction, (Floyd, C., Mehl, W.-M., Reisin, F.-M., Schmidt, G., and Wolf, G. "Out of Scandinavia: Alternative approaches to software design and system development." Human-Computer Interaction, 4 (1989), pp. 252-350), and a short and sweet discussion in an article by Jeanette Blomberg and Austin Henderson of Xerox in the CHI'90 proceedings (Blomberg, A.L. and Henderson, A. "Reflections on participatory design." In Proc. CHI'90 Conference on Human Factors in Computer Systems. New York: ACM, 1990, pp. 353-359). Blomberg and Henderson stress three defining attributes of participatory design: the goal of the activity is to improve the worklife of users (not, for example, to demonstrate how neat object-oriented technology is); the activity is collaborative, with all goals and decisions actively negotiated and not imposed; the activity is iterative, in that ideas are tested and adjusted by seeing how they play out in practice.

It's pretty easy to see how one could approach participatory design in in-house projects, though it would not be easy to get your organization actually to do it. For in-house projects it will be true at some level that designers and users share the same goals, though in the U.S. context these goals may not have much to do with the quality of worklife. But U.S. organizations usually have job demarcations which make it hard to get participatory design going. Usually, if my job is to be a user it is not to be a designer or to work on designs. That's the province of "experts" employed for the purpose, even though they have no idea what the real problems are that need to be solved.

For commercial projects there are further challenges. At bottom, your objective as a commercial developer may really not be to improve the quality of somebody else's work life, but rather to make money for yourself. So you don't have the right goal to begin with.

There are two ways to go from here. One is to forget about the defining goals of participatory design and go through the motions of it in service of your selfish goals. The idea is that you hope to produce a better design, and hence make more money, by engaging users in collaboration focussed on the user's goals. To draw users in to making the considerable investment of time they would have to make to work with you, you would offer them a piece of the action.

Developing new technology in close partnership with potential users like this is a good idea in many industries for lots of reasons not restricted to the peculiarities of user interfaces. As Michael Porter recounts, the modern printing press was developed by a new technology company that was supported by some of its potential users, big English newspapers. Such a relationship gets you the information you need to make your system really useful, and hence successful, as well as developing an early market.

Another response to the mismatch of your goal of making money and the participatory design goal of improving the quality of work life is to change your goal. Will money actually make you happy? Of course not. Will improving somebody's work life make you happy? Maybe so, if the work involved is itself something worthwhile, or if you just take satisfaction in doing something well. Even if you can't get this unselfish the logic of the situation is that you may do better all around, including monetarily, if you really care about the people who will use your system and what they do than if you only care about the money.

2.3 USING THE TASKS IN DESIGN

Back to the traffic modelling system and our sample tasks. What did we do with them after we got them? Taking a look at their fate may clarify what the tasks should be like, as well as helping to persuade you that it's worth defining them.

Our first step was to write up descriptions of all the tasks and circulate them to the users (remember, we're back in us-versus-them mode, with designers and users clearly different teams.) We included queries for more information where we felt the original discussion had left some details out. And we got corrections, clarifications, and suggestions back which were incorporated into the written descriptions.

We then roughed out an interface design and produced a SCENARIO for each of the sample tasks. A scenario spells out what a user would have to do and what he or she would see step-by-step in performing a task using a given system. The key distinction between a scenario and a task is that a scenario is design-specific, in that it shows how a task would be performed if you adopt a particular design, while the task itself is design-independent: it's something the user wants to do regardless of what design is chosen. Developing the scenarios forced us to get specific about our design, and it forced us to consider how the various features of the system would work together to accomplish real work. We could settle arguments about different ways of doing things in the interface by seeing how they played out for our example tasks.

Handling design arguments is a key issue, and having specific tasks to work with really helps. Interface design is full of issues that look as if they could be settled in the abstract but really can't. Unfortunately, designers, who often prefer to look at questions in the abstract, waste huge amounts of time on pointless arguments as a result.

For example, in our interface users select graphical objects from a palette and place them on the screen. They do this by clicking on an object in the palette and then clicking where they want to put it. Now, if they want to place another object of the same kind should they be made to click again on the palette or can they just click on a new location? You can't settle the matter by arguing about it on general grounds.

You can settle it by looking at the CONTEXT in which this operation actually occurs. If the user wants to adjust the position of an object after placing it, and you decide that clicking again somewhere places a new object, and if it's legal to pile objects up in the same place, then you have trouble. How will you select an object for purposes of adjustment if a click means "put another object down"? On the other hand, if your tasks don't require much adjustment, but do require repeated placement of the same kind of object, you're pushed the other way. Our tasks seemed to us to require adjustment more than repeated placement, so we went the first way.

This example brings up an important point about using the example tasks. It's important to remember that they are ONLY EXAMPLES. Often, as in this case, a decision requires you to look beyond the specific examples you have and make a judgement about what will be common and what will be uncommon. You can't do this just by taking an inventory of the specific examples you chose. You can't defend a crummy design by saying that it handles all the examples, any more than you can defend a crummy design by saying it meets any other kind of spec.

We represented our scenarios with STORYBOARDS, which are sequences of sketches showing what the screen would show, and what actions the user would take, at key points in each task. We then showed these to the users, stepping them through the tasks. Here we saw a big gain from the use of the sample tasks. They allowed us to tell the users what they really wanted to know about our proposed design, which was what it would be like to use it to do real work. A traditional design description, showing all the screens, menus, and so forth, out of the context of a real task, is pretty meaningless to users, and so they can't provide any useful reaction to it. Our scenarios let users see what the design would really give them.

"This sample task idea seems crazy. What if you leave something out? And won't your design be distorted by the examples you happen to choose? And how do you know the design will work for anything OTHER than your examples?" There is a risk with any spec technique that you will leave something out. In choosing your sample tasks you do whatever you would do in any other method to be sure the important requirements are reflected. As noted above, you treat the sample tasks as examples. Using them does not relieve you of the responsibility of thinking about how other tasks would be handled. But it's better to be sure that your design can do a good job on at least some real tasks, and that it has a good chance of working on other tasks, because you've tried to design for generality, than to trust exclusively in your ability to design for generality. It's the same as that point about users: if a system is supposed to be good for EVERYBODY you'd better be sure it's good for SOMEBODY.

HyperTopic: Integrating Task-Centered Design and Traditional Requirements Analysis

If you're working for a small company or developing small projects for a few internal users at a large firm, the task- centered design approach may be all you need. But for larger projects, you'll probably have to work within the structure of an established software engineering procedure. How to apply task-centered principles within that procedure will vary depending on the software engineering approach used at your company. But we can give some general guidelines that are especially useful in the early stages of development.

Most large software projects are developed using some version of the "waterfall method." The basic waterfall method assumes that a piece of software is produced through a clearly defined series of steps, or "phases":

- Requirements analysis
- Specification
- Planning
- Design
- Implementation
- Integration
- Maintenance.

In its strictest version, this method states that each phase must be completed before the next phase can begin, and that there's no chance (and no reason) to return to an earlier phase to redefine a system as its being developed.

Most software engineering specialists today realize that this approach is unrealistic. It was developed in the era of punch cards and mainframes, so it doesn't have a real place for considerations of interactive systems. Even in the mainframe era it was less than successful, because the definition of what's required inevitably changes as the system is developed.

Various modifications to the phases of the waterfall method and their interaction have been proposed. However, it's not unusual to find productive software development environments that still incorporate many steps of the method, partly for historical reasons and partly because the approach helps to define responsibilities and costs for various activities within a large software project. With some effort, the task- centered design approach can supplement the early stages of a waterfall environment.

Requirements Analysis

The waterfall method's initial "Requirements Analysis" phase describes the activity of defining the precise needs that the software must meet. These needs are defined in terms of the users and the their environment, with intentionally no reference to how the needs will actually be met by the proposed system.

This is exactly the same approach as we suggest for describing representative tasks: define what the user needs to do, not how it will be done. The difference is that the representative tasks in task-centered design are complete, real, detailed examples of things users actually need to do. The requirements produced by traditional software engineering, on the other hand, are abstract descriptions of parts of those representative tasks.

This is an important distinction, and we want to emphasize it most strongly:

> Task-centered design focuses on REAL, COMPLETE, REPRESENTATIVE tasks. Traditional requirements analysis looks at ABSTRACT, PARTIAL task elements.

Here's an example. For a document processing system, a representative task might be to produce this book. Not to produce "a book," but to produce "version 1 of Task-Centered Design, by Lewis and Rieman." That representative task supplements the detailed partial tasks collected in traditional requirements analysis, which might include things such as "key in text" and "check spelling" and "print the document."

So if you're doing a traditional requirements analysis, you need to supplement it by collecting some representative tasks. The two approaches complement each other nicely. The traditional approach helps to ensure that all important functions of the system are recognized, while the representative tasks in the task-centered approach provide an integrated picture of those functions working together.

Specification

In the traditional "Specifications" phase of software engineering, the requirements are used to produce a description of the system that includes the details needed by the software designers and implementers. The customers — the end users — can then sign off on this document, and the software team can begin to plan and design the actual system. This sounds like great stuff from a management point of view, but it practice it often falls apart. Users aren't experts at reading specifications documents, and they have trouble imagining how the system will actually perform. Various alternatives to written specifications have been proposed, including prototypes and a more iterative approach to design, both of which fit nicely into the task-centered design approach.

However, even if you're still doing written specifications, the representative tasks can be of value. Include those tasks, with some details about how they will be performed, in the specification document. The big win here is that the customers will be able to understand this part of the specifications. It will also force the specifications writer to consider a complete task, which may catch problems that could be missed when single functions are considered individually.

Notice that the description of the proposed software hasn't quite reached the stage where you could do a complete "scenario," as we have defined it. Many of the details, such as the names of menu items, the distribution of functionality among dialog boxes, etc., remain to be defined. But a high- level overview of the interactions can be described, and doing this well is a test of your understanding of the users' needs.

Planning, Design, and Beyond

From this point on, the strict waterfall method and the task- centered design approach take very different paths. Many of the principles we describe can be used in doing the first pass at system and interface design, but inherent in the task-centered approach is the need for iteration: it's very rare that the first design of an interface is a complete success. Several iterations of testing and redesign are required, and that may well involve jumping backward through the phases of the waterfall method, something that's traditionally not allowed. Fortunately, the strict forward- moving method is seldom adhered to today. Most development environments recognize the need for some iteration, and that should make it possible to accommodate the general spirit of the task-centered approach.

Tools and Techniques for Creative Design

S. Joy Mountford
Human Interface Group
Apple Computer, Inc.

"A WEEKDAY EDITION OF *THE NEW YORK TIMES* contains more information than the average person was likely to come across in a lifetime in seventeenth century England" [Wurman, 1989]. The world is rich with data, rapidly becoming more varied in media type—sounds, photos, FAX, computer-generated images, telephony, as well as text flood our lives. The challenge is how to best present and represent such data within the interface, to transform it into useful information.

For computer users, much so-called information is virtually inaccessible, not only because there is so much of it, but also because the many types of information formats and delivery systems are not integrated at the interface. Electronic mail, for instance, comes in a bewildering assortment of flavors: screen text, voice, or paper print-out; usenet, MCI, or interoffice e-mail; personal messages, electronic conferences, or bulletin boards. Telecommunications, service industries, entertainment companies, and educational institutions will use tomorrow's personal information environments to store and present enormous worlds of data. Several business areas do not yet provide extensive computer access to their workers; for example, theatrical production, fast-food chains, creative art and design companies, travel-related industries, bookings, and merchandise ordering in retail sales. Future interfaces need to incorporate new information types and to accommodate new types of users with additional customized real-world interface metaphors that make information easy to find and use.

With the onslaught of more varied information and application types, there is a great need for guidance in generating more creative, usable interface designs. We need techniques to help us do a better job of visualizing the look and feel of potential interfaces. Such interface prototyping tools as HyperCard have been a great step forward in enabling graphic designers to demonstrate their ideas, but we need even more powerful tools with which to emulate the "feel" of the interface in the hands of new users with new uses. A limited number of computer tools are available to assist in the design process (see the chapter by Wagner in this volume), but even fewer exist to help us decide which ideas are worthwhile.

The science and art of computer interface design is a relatively young discipline within a world of more mature design traditions. There are few success stories for interface designers to learn from, compared with traditional disciplines such as mathematics and biology. There are even fewer principles that can help us predict the behavior of our clients, the users. We have much to learn about interpersonal communication, group behavior, aesthetics, showmanship, and users' adaptability to change. Some of our new interface ideas will come from people who study thought, language, entertainment, and communication, as well as from people who study hardware, algorithms, data structures. We need to find better mechanisms for facilitating collaboration among designers from both artistic and scientific points of view, as articulated in "The Role of the Artist in the Laboratory" [Buxton, 1988].

This paper examines the emerging discipline of interface design in terms of established disciplines, the present state of the art, and techniques for generating new ideas. Looking to the past, we can identify mature design disciplines in other fields that can inform our own. The first section of this paper examines the areas of "traditional" animation, theater, architecture, industrial design, and information display for techniques and approaches that can be of use to human-computer interface designers. The second section looks at the more contemporary tools of metaphor and user observation. The final section of the paper surveys some techniques for designing the interfaces of the future through brainstorming and the creative juxtaposition of ideas.

New Wine from Old Vats

Film

Table 1 shows an insightful historical timeline indicating some of the changes that have occurred to various communication crafts as they moved from being inventions to being art forms (this table is taken from *The Elements of Friendly Software Design* [Heckel, 1984]). Heckel views "software as a newcomer to communication crafts." It is interesting to note that one of the most recent "arts" to change its form is filmmaking, which

Writing	Painting	Film	Drama	Photography	Architecture	Music	Computers
3300 BC Egyptian hieroglyphics	**20000 BC** Cave Paintings of Lascaux, France	**1884** Thomas Edison demonstrates kinetoscope	**600 BC** First Greek amphitheatre built for festival of Dionysos	**1839** Daguerre announces his photographic method	**2700 BC** Pyramids at Sakkara and Gizeh	**2000 BC** Invention of the Egyptian harp	**450 BC** First abacus
2300 BC Maxims of Ptohhotep	**3000 BC** Egyptian tomb paintings	**1903** Edwin Porter's *The Great Train Robbery*	**550 BC** Introduction of the chorus in Greek plays	**1861** Mathew Brady's civil war photographs	**400 BC** Parthenon Athens	**1306 AD** First pedal organ	**1864** Charles Babbage's analytic engine
1500 BC Development of phonetic alphabet	**1100 AD** Invention of oil paints	**1915** D.W. Griffith's *Birth of a Nation*	**442 BC** Sophocles' *Antigone*	**1882** Eastman develops Kodak camera	**1100 AD** Development of flying buttress	**1404** First clavichord	**1955** First commercial mainframe computer
800 BC Library of Assyria founded	**1497** Da Vinci's *Last Supper*	**1927** First Sound Movie: *The Jazz Singer*	**1580 AD** Establishment of the first repertory companies	**1902** Stieglitz's "Spring Showers"	**1400** Completion of Chartres Cathedral	**1520** First violin	**1958** Fortran: First high level language
1440 AD Gutenberg's invention of moveable type	**1654** Rembrandt's *Portrait of Jan Six*	**1941** Orson Welles' *Citizen Kane*	**1603** Shakespeare's *Hamlet*	**1947** Ansel Adams' Yosemite photographs	**1920** Invention of pre-stressed concrete	**1602** Monteverdi's first opera, *Orfeo*	**1975** First Personal Computer
1605 Cervantes' *Don Quixote*	**1937** Picasso's *Guernica*				**1936** Frank Lloyd Wright's "Falling Water"	**1720** J.S. Bach: *Well-Tempered Clavier*	**1978** VisiCalc
1719 First Modern Novel: Defoe's *Robinson Crusoe*						**1824** Beethoven's Ninth (Choral) Symphony	**1979** WordStar

Table 1: Most communications crafts started as inventions and evolved slowly in the direction of an art form. Software is a newcomer to the world of communications crafts. Figure from Heckel, Paul (1991). Elements of Friendly Software Design, *Sybex.*

likewise had its roots as an engineering discipline. Originally movies were viewed as having a fixed window within which some action occurred; they were often nothing more than continous slideshows of information. The roots of filmmaking changed with the production of *Birth of a Nation* by D. W. Griffith in 1914. Engineers who had controlled films actually lost out to those who saw the artistic possibilities for film. Griffith's success began the relatively recent tradition of films as an art form, communicating directly to an audience.

The next "new" communications medium is likely to be that of software design. Like film, software was originally dominated by those who knew how to program, but this has now expanded to include a much larger audience. The first most widely used successful piece of software was VisiCalc™, which was considered "friendly" and usable by a wide audience who had hitherto found financial packages rather cumbersome. Tools such as HyperCard™ have made the price of entry into so-called "programming," or rather scripting, much more accessible to a range of new, more artistic, skill sets. It would serve interface designers well to learn from the lessons of filmmaking, to facilitate the best growth directions for interface design. Our new interfaces will serve as future vehicles of communication to a large audience, the world's users.

Animation

Walt Disney Studios produced their most famous animation classics long before computer animation existed. Disney's goal was to create an animated form of communication that was as new in the 1920s as computers were in the 1960s. Both are powerful communicative forms that rely heavily on the use of graphics. We employ limited animation in the Macintosh interface today—the zooming effect for opening and closing of files, for instance. New uses for animation in human-computer interfaces are explored in the chapter by Baecker and Small in this volume. Tomorrow's personal computers have the potential to create animations rich enough to allow users to actually interact with dramatic dynamic events. The principles developed by the Disney animators, who worked without automated assistants, are likely to prove quite useful in interface design.

A set of twelve principles of animation is detailed in *Disney Animation: The Illusion of Life*, by Thomas and Johnston [1984]. Anticipation, for example, is a motion characteristic that can both provide information and produce powerful dramatic effects. Disney's animated characters exaggerate the way bodies prepare to move forward by pulling backwards slightly beforehand. Anticipation "telegraphs" the character's intent, adding visual continuity and a sense of realism that carries the audience forward with the character. Disney also used sound quite effectively to represent such aspects of events as position, direction, and speed of motion. Sound can be similarly applied to interface events to establish continuity and provide information for the user (see the chapter by Mountford and Gaver in this volume). Each of Disney's principles of animation contains valuable insights and techniques for interface designers.

Theater

The dramatic arts are full of promising ideas for interface design. Contemporary discussions of software agents with humanlike qualities brings one to consider exactly what makes characters effective and believable (see the chapter by Laurel in this volume). A recent research project at Apple called Guides demonstrated a way of searching a database with the help of different personal viewpoints. These personal guides gave users their individual viewpoints of a encyclopedic slice of Grolier's American history. Initial studies indicated that users found the guides engaging and informative (see the chapter by Oren et al. in this volume). Dramatic stories and characters are familiar and effective mechanisms for structuring thought and behavior. We have barely begun to scratch the surface in applying this body of knowledge to computer interface design.

Drama has the power to *engage* audience members both emotionally and cognitively. Interactive plays and novels are beginning to be studied to see what facets make them more or less effective with readers and viewers. By isolating the key factors contributing to audience involvement and participation, we can discover techniques for enhancing direct engagement through human-computer interfaces [Laurel, 1986].

ARCHITECTURE

Architecture and interface design have an important goal in common: to create livable, workable, attractive environments. The principle of "form follows function" maintains that the form of objects should follow their functional requirements. The architectural movement towards functionalism was initially contested in Victorian England, as the industrial age was trying to hide the impact of industrialization on people's everyday lives. Le Corbusier was initially viewed with skepticism when he proposed that a house was a *machine for living*, as opposed to the traditional idea that a house was a shelter. He likened a house to a ship or bridge in its function. Likewise, we are only just beginning to conceive of computers as extensions of our functional everyday lives.

The listing of all the requirements to be met on an architect's design project have become known as *programming*. The more precise these definitions can be made on a project, the less likely it is that variations will occur among the different contributors to any design project. In architecture, these requirements are often referred to as *constraints*, just as they are known to interface designers. In order to make the process of designing within constraints as systematic as possible for architects, Alexander [1964] devised a set of steps for listing all functional requirements for a given architectural design problem. As an example, he specifies 21 requirements for designing a tea kettle. He then studies the interactions between the requirements and groups them into related clusters that form a hierarchical order of relationships that will govern the final design.

Managing trade-offs becomes rather difficult when the architect cannot control all of the variables. For example, requirements for plenty of natural light and interior quiet may be in conflict. If the windows must face a noisy street for the best light, then a trade-off decision must be made. Such trade-off decisions can be made in isolation by even an inexperienced designer, but experienced designers can often generate better alternatives because they have a better feel for the relative importance of the various requirements. Experience can lead to more graceful solutions. As Pile observes:

> Satisfactory performance is invariably a matter of meeting a number of requirements—a vast number in the case of complex designs. The various requirements may be in conflict so that different satisfactory solutions can result from differing emphases on differing requirements. One most satisfactory solution only can emerge in the limited context of one particular evaluation of the relative importance of various desiderata. [Pile, 1979]

Alexander captures some of the wisdom of an experienced designer in his formal methodology. It can improve the performance of the inexperienced, and can help even an experienced designer make a more systematic analysis of the consequences of alternative solutions. This approach is controversial because it says little about beauty, harmony, or pleasure. Even so, it can be a spur to creativity in the fields of both architecture and interface designs.

Industrial Design

The experience of designing real-world objects for everyday use has a lot to teach us about how to design usable interfaces for software. Those designs which endure the test of time are mostly those that are reliable, offering straightforward ease of use and pleasurable user experiences. The chapter by Vertelney and Booker in this volume suggests principles and techniques of industrial design that can guide our interface work.

Information Display

In applications ranging from statistical graphics to scientific visualization, computers are used increasingly as tools for creating graphical displays of information. Often, however, the designers of such displays fail to take advantage of the techniques developed in "traditional" information display disciplines. The graphical prowess of today's computers has encouraged the production of a plethora of unreadable graphics, characterized by Tufte as "chartjunk" [see Verity, 1985]. Tufte goes on to observe that "people who don't see particularly well are designing interfaces to graphics machines. People have been doing books for 500 years and much wisdom has come from all that activity" [Tufte, 1983]. Not just interface designers, but American culture as a whole, seems to undervalue the established disciplines in this area—in Japan, for instance, there is an Annual Statistics Day contest and celebration! Experts in traditional fields like statistics and cartography can provide wisdom and techniques to the designer of graphical information displays (see figure 1).

The domain of classical mathematics employs a linear language of symbolic expression that is poorly suited to the representation of parallel events and processes, yet this is often the first "language" adopted by interface designers—the software for creating 3-D graphics on a leading graphics workstation, for instance, requires the user to define figures and specify

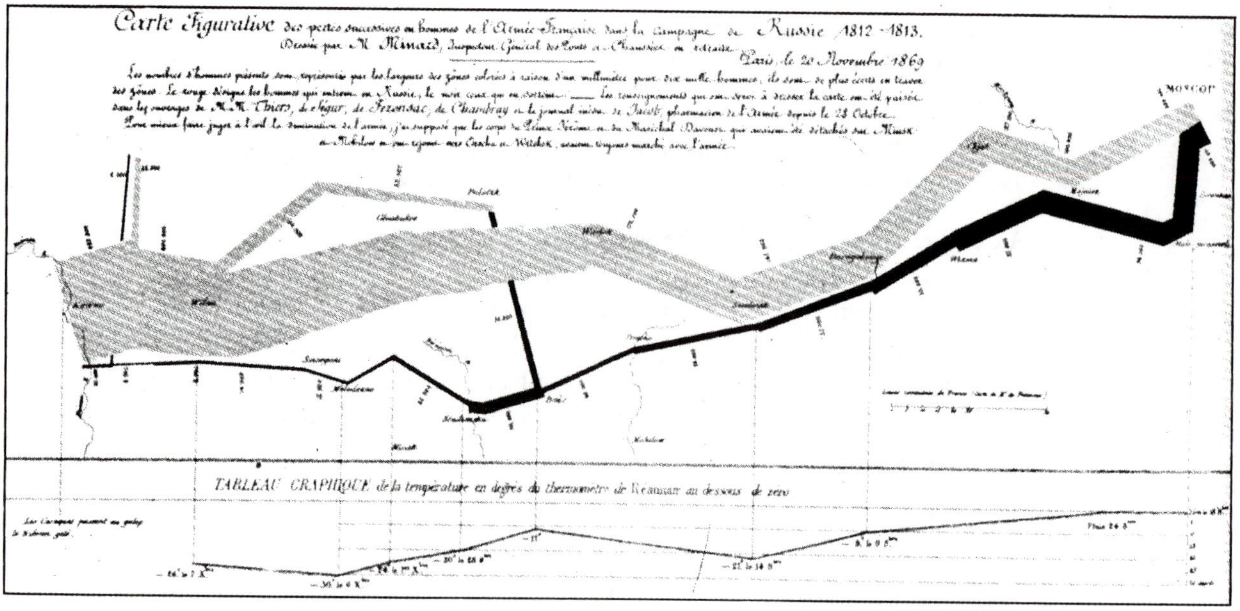

Figure 1: A map of the progress of Napoleon's invasion of Russia. Expert cartographers and statisticians can create graphical displays that are packed with accessible information. "Napoleon's March to Moscow: The War of 1812." Edward R. Tufte, The Visual Display of Quantitative Information. Cheshire, CT: Graphics Press, 1983.

their movements mathematically at the interface. A conversational metaphor provides a good alternative to the formal language of mathematics. Smalltalk, for example, exemplifies an object-oriented approach where "objects" are given "messages" specifying their desired behavior, placing the emphasis on "communication" among the elements of the program.

Within statistics, Deken [1985] takes the conversational motif a step further by proposing three types of agents to assist users in the analysis and evaluation of data. *Data-item agents* could capture data and verify its "fit" by applying expertise in handling approximations and noticing relationships among data. This data-item agent could likewise communicate with an *organizer agent* that could create an organizational structure for the data. A *reporter agent* could take care of providing a variety of useful representations of the data to the user, even to the point of suggesting relevant questions. Deken's model illustrates a dynamic and conversational approach to data transactions, borrowing from the dramatic arts in its use of the behavioral associations among actors/agents.

Most people have experienced the situation in which a good diagram can explain more than the prose one would use to describe it. Why and how a good diagram works, however, is poorly understood. A picture is not always worth a thousand words, and even great scientists could benefit from the support of artists in visually representing their work (see figure 2).

A general observation is that perceptual codes in diagrams convey less information than symbolic ones. Symbolic representations elicit conscious cognitive processing, whereas analogic, pictorial ones are perceived more

Figure 2: A sketch from Galileo's analysis of the strength of a beam. The sketch obscures its information content with a welter of irrelevant detail. Obtained from the Ann Ronan Picture Library, Somerset, England.

automatically. A map, for example, provides specific locational information using grid coordinates, which for some people is more useful than analogic spatial arrangement. Examples of frequently used perceptual codes are contour mapping, color coding of electrical systems, and auditory tone distinctions used in telephone systems. Venn diagrams are used to represent inclusion—a notion that is difficult to communicate through natural language, especially when more than two sets are involved. Flowcharts provide visual representations of connectedness and sequence. In musical notation, symbolic codes (the forms of notes themselves) give specific information about pitch (through the position of a note on the staff) and duration, and the perceptual effect of "blackness" on the staff provides general information about the speed of the music.

Such principles of information display as the effective use of perceptual and symbolic codes can be applied to a variety of problems in interface design. Successful graphic and layout techniques can even make computer programs easier to visualize. For example, Fitter and Green [1979] have found that understanding is enhanced when different programs are represented in ways that are as perceptually distinct as possible. Baecker and Marcus [1989] similarly have applied knowledge about information display to the task of visualizing programs written in C.

Contemporary Interface Design Tools: Metaphor and User Observation

In addition to the wealth of wisdom to be gained from the study of design in other traditional domains, the discipline of interface design has developed some methodologies of its own that are worth reviewing. Related to the notion of borrowing techniques from other domains is the idea of creating interface metaphors that can anchor users' understanding of the computer to something with which they are already familiar. Conversely, studying people as they perform familiar, well-understood tasks can provide valuable insights about possible ways to represent tasks on the computer.

Interface Metaphors

Interface design is a relatively new human endeavor and has benefitted much from the application of metaphor in helping interface designers who understand it mainly by virtue of being human:

> The metaphor is perhaps one of man's most fruitful potentialities. Its efficacy verges on magic, and it seems a tool for creation which God forgot inside one of His creatures when He made him. [y Gasset, 1925]

Metaphors are powerful verbal and semantic tools for conveying both superficial and deep similarities between familiar and novel situations. We are generally unaware of the extent to which metaphor is embedded in our thought and language (see Erickson's chapter on metaphor in this volume). As MacCormac describes them, "Metaphors not only communicate suggestive and expressive meanings but they also become iconic objects through their fusion of sense with sound" [MacCormac, 1985].

The Macintosh computer interface is a well-known example of the successful use of various metaphors to facilitate new users' understanding of the computer and its functions. During the development of the Lisa interface, Apple designers found that the "desktop metaphor" was preferred by users to a form-fill-in dialog box. Much of the ease of use of the Macintosh interface is attributable to the correspondence between the appearance, uses, and behaviors of such interface objects as documents and folders and their real-world counterparts; conversely, user difficulties are often attributable to differences between them.

Although some find the use of interface metaphors to be too constraining (see Nelson's chapter in this volume), designers can optimize the cognitive value of metaphors and minimize difficulties through careful selection and implementation. As Lakoff and Johnson [1980] observe, metaphors do not imply a complete mapping of every concrete detail of one object or situation onto another; rather they emphasize certain features and suppress others. Thorough examination of a candidate metaphor helps designers to discover its inherent selectivity and use it to their advantage.

Observing Real-world Tasks and Environments

Development of some worthy "new" ideas for introduction into the electronic world can come from careful examination of the "traditional" ways of performing tasks. As Don Norman exhorts elsewhere in this volume, designers must sit down in offices, factories, and schools and watch the problems people encounter and the tools they use to solve them in their everyday work and education.

Observation of a person at a traditional physical desk reveals typical and extended ways of working that are not supported by a computer system. For example, the person may start writing a small Post-it™ note to carry with them, then on another plain piece of paper draw a map sketch, and on another plain piece of paper paint in different colors. Today, trying to do the same thing using a computer is immensely more complicated. Typically, different applications have to be launched separately depending on the kinds of data to be created; writing, drawing, and painting are all separate applications and different data types. Individual elements must be pasted together, sometimes requiring that they be transformed into new data types, in order to create a finished document.

The observations above have led to the further refinement of a set of interface ideas often referred to as the *plain-paper metaphor*, likening the screen to a blank sheet of paper. Currently, users must break their work up into separate tasks and perform each within its associated environment—taking the tasks to the tools. The plain-paper metaphor would reverse this process by bringing the tools to the task. "Virtual" tools could be designed to correspond to "real-world" uses.

Metaphors have two distinct but related uses in interface design: as cognitive aids to users, and as aids to creativity for designers. Metaphors can help designers to use their own, often unconscious expectations to create new information links and mental structures. The creative use of metaphor and other techniques for formally facilitating creativity are reviewed in the next section.

Techniques for Generating New Ideas

No one really knows where good ideas come from or what actually makes them "good". Novelty is desirable, and so is a close fit between the idea and some real-world problem. Leverage and generality are also important. So where do these novel, useful, high-leverage, general ideas come from? What follows are some suggestions on how to stimulate thought by looking at the world in unusual and nontraditional ways.

Some people believe that new ideas are almost always the result of collisions—juxtaposition or recombinations of ideas [Koestler, 1964]. Consciously creating juxtapositions of normally unassociated referents may suggest new, previously unsuspected hypotheses about how to approach or solve a problem. Adams [1986] provides a series of brainstorming steps that can help designers expand existing metaphorical elements and generate new ideas. Designers can be encouraged more formally to think more broadly and openly about their interface designs by engaging in lateral thinking exercises. What follows is a series of interface design exercises based on Adams' axioms, many of which illustrate ideas that have been considered in the design of past interactive systems.

New Uses for the Object Consider the "desktop" interface. What else could a desktop be used for? People often use a real desk as a space for communication—laying out papers and showing intermediate stages of their work, marking them up together, putting them in a different order. The "desktop" could be used similarly as a space for shared work and as a communications area.

Adapt the Object To Be Like Something Else What if we adapt our "desktop" to be more like a kitchen? In kitchens, we find lots of basic and specialized tools that are used to create a myriad of different items (food). The same ingredient creates different foods when different tools are applied to it. For example, grating a carrot can produce fine-grained garnishes, but placing it in a blender produces juice. If we could identify or create some similar basic ingredients to serve as building blocks, they could serve as models for building better general-purpose tools. How would these ideas change the "contents" and organizational structure of an interface?

Modify the Object for a New Purpose What happens if we add the desire of providing information about the larger environment to our "desktop"? We might employ environmental sound, as in a real office, to provide information about adjacent activities. We might treat windows as periscopes or portholes through which we can observe or even travel to other parts of the environment (rather like Smalltalk project Views/Rooms from Xerox PARC).

Magnify—Add to the Object We could add various features to the "desktop" that are already present in a real desk; for example, a drawer with scissors, glue, tape, and other tools (PARC Cypress, 1977, and Apple II

Jane, 1983, are examples). We could add features like phones, calendars, diaries, FAX, newspaper service, or shopping lists. These items would enhance and extend its functionality.

Minimize—Subtract from the Object We might pare away the desk until all that is left is the "desktop" and a drawer with blank sheets of paper and a pencil in it. What could be accomplished with only these items? (This is usually described as the "plain paper metaphor," an idea that may actually predate the notion of separate applications.) This helps prevent the mind-set of always adding more and more isolated pieces of technology.

Substitute Something Similar A "desktop" may not be a useful metaphor for every user in every task domain. What about a delivery service? Instead of things like files and folders, the interface could be organized in terms of trucks, routes, and ordering systems. The trash can could become a dumpster. Another interesting metaphor is the idea of an interface with peel-off transparent layers.

Rearrange the Data What if we reorganized the basic layout of the "desktop" so that the scroll bars were at the top (as in Smalltalk) and the menu bar was at the bottom? Among other things, we may discover such biases as a layout for right-handed people. We might also use the same technique to generate ideas for designing an alternative interface for left-handed users.

Reverse or Transpose the Information Turning the metaphor inside out creates some interesting ideas. What would happen if windows were views from files to the desktop rather than the other way around? What if everything were circular rather than rectangular in form? What if we were to view the desktop from below rather than above? What if we saw it from very *far* above—what else would come into view? Ideas of different visual lenses come to mind; for example, fisheyes and magnifiers.

Combine the Data into an Ensemble What larger metaphor might the "desktop" be a part of? Beyond its area is perhaps a virtual office, a whole building-full of data-rooms, cities, or worlds of information. How might this larger metaphor be represented? How would the desktop fit into it?

ROLE PLAYING

In addition to Adams' exercises, thought provocation through role playing [von Oech, 1986] might help designers to create, evaluate, and develop ideas by assuming different points of view. Often it seems that the only point of view we have time for is the defense of our own existing positions, roles, and ideas. It is too easy to get blinded by our own myopic view.

Deliberately assuming different roles can be both creative and liberating. Von Oech describes four characters that are active in all of us to varying degrees and, depending on our job descriptions, that are allowed in different proportions to work on a problem:

The Explorer: This character gathers information on an issue, researching the problem before the solution set exists. Activities include reading, asking others about their views, and deciding which issues need additional work or definition.

The Artist: This character generates new ideas in the problem-solving phase. This phase is the most energetic and active. New problem definitions, potential solutions, and alternative next paths for action are produced.

The Judge: This character evaluates and filters the ideas that have been generated. At this stage some ideas must be discarded—a task that is less appealing to creative folks. New ideas won't emerge if the Judge is in charge at the beginning of the brainstorming process.

The Warrior: This character champions a particular idea and sets the course for the next round of problem-solving. This includes planning how the idea will be tested, evaluated, and developed.

Creative problem-solving can be enhanced by exercising mental agility—the ability to move easily between different roles. No one of these four types of characters can make an idea succeed without the other characters' participation. Knowing how and when to change character roles is crucial. A useful exercise is to take 30 minutes to brainstorm and to plan out a solution to any particular problem, alternating roles between the four described characters every 7 minutes. This approach can demonstrate how each of the different roles contributes to the overall decision. We have tried such exercises at Apple and have found that the transcripts of such role-playing sessions offer much food for thought even later.

Enhancing Creativity

Is creativity a talent, accessible only to a gifted few, or is it a skill that can be learned? This question has been debated and researched from a surprising variety of angles, from discussions by theorists such as Koestler [1964] and Harman and Rheingold [1984] to practical brainstorming and unblocking guidebooks from applied imagineers such as von Oech [1986], Adams [1986], and McKim [1972]. Current research into the cognitive underpinnings of human learning is making important contributions to the study of creativity. Books and exercises for enhancing creativity are worthwhile for interface designers, especially those connected with visual thinking [Hanks and Belliston, 1980] and right brain exercises [Edwards, 1986]. They all serve as platforms for individual and group exercises that can help us better understand our users' needs and propose some usable and creative solutions to their problems.

As software becomes a more powerful and pervasive tool for communicating and learning, the need will increase to find new ways to look at interfaces and their designs. Interface designers can learn from the past successes and failures of other design/communication disciplines. The idea of *visual thinking* as promoted by Arnheim [1969], McKim [1972], and others emphasizes the success designers can achieve by educating themselves in new perspectives. The development of new prototyping tools and hardware platforms with greater capabilities, as well as techniques for using traditional design knowledge with new creative methods and fresh perspectives, will facilitate the design of exciting new interfaces.

Interface designers must live in both the present and the future. While we are working on our present interface problems, we should be thinking about how to create tools to better build on our knowledge and make it reusable and available to others. The best contribution that we can make to the understanding of the communication interface is to create and build tools to be better able to do our own jobs. Right now we are just beginning to discover what these tools should be, creating specifications for their design, and experimenting with new methodologies. In the future, we will be challenged to make the most of this power to pass on our understanding both to other designers and to new users in the form of new, more powerful, more easily learnable, and more engaging ways to use computers.

Adams, J.L. (1986) *Conceptual Blockbusting*. 3rd Ed. Addison-Wesley.

Alexander, C. (1964) *Notes on the Synthesis of Form*. Harvard University Press.

Arnheim, R. (1969) *Visual Thinking*. University of California Press.

Baecker, R. and Marcus, A. (1990) *Human Factors and Typography for More Readable Programs*. Addison-Wesley.

Buxton, W. (1988) *The Role of the Artist in the Laboratory*. Meisterwerke der Computer Kunst. Ed. C. Schopf. TMS Verlag.

Decken, J. (1985) Machines and Metaphors. *Proc. of the 15th Symposium on Computer Science and Statistics*, March 80–83.

Edwards, B. (1986) *Drawing on the Artist Within*. Simon and Schuster.

Erickson, T. (1990) *Interface and Evolution of Pidgins. The Art of Human-Computer Interface Design*. Ed. B. Laurel. Addison-Wesley. 11–16. Further references to this text are abbreviated *AH-CID*.

Erickson, T. (1990) *Working with Interface Metaphors*. *AH-CID*: 65–74.

Fitter, M. and Green, T. (1979) When Do Diagrams Make Good Computer Languages? *Int. Jrnl of Man-Machine Studies*. (11) 235–261.

Hanks, K. and Belliston, L. (1980) *Rapid Viz*. Morgan-Kaufmann.

Harman, W. and Rheingold, H.L. (1984) *Higher Creativity*. Tarcher.

Heckel, P. (1984) *The Elements of Friendly Software Design*. 2nd Ed. Warner Software, Warner Books.

Koestler, A. (1964) *The Act of Creation*. Macmillan.

Lackoff, G. and Johnson, J. (1980) *Metaphors We Live By*. University of Chicago Press.

Laurel, B. (1986) *Interface as Mimesis. User-Centred System Design: New Perspectives on HCI*. Ed. Norman & Draper. Erlbaum Assoc.

MacCormac, E. (1985) *A Cognitive Theory of Metaphor*. MIT Press.

McKim, R. (1972) *Experiences in Visual Thinking*. PWS-Kent Publishers.

Mountford, S.J. and Gaver, W. (1990) *Talking and Listening to Computers*. *AH-CID*: 319–334.

Oren, T., Salomon, G., Kreitman, K., and Don, A. (1990) *Guides: Characterizing the Interface*. AH-CID: 367–382.

Papenek, V. (1985) *Design for the Real Work, Human Ecology and Social Change*. 2nd Ed. Academy Chicago Press.

Pile, J. (1979) *Design: Purpose, Form and Meaning*. University of Massachusetts Press.

Thomas, F. and Johnston, R. (1984) *Disney Animation: The Illusion of Life*. Abbeville Press.

Tufte, E. (1983) *Visual Display of Quantitative Information*. Graphics Press.

Verity, J. (1985) "Graphically Speaking with Dr. Edward R. Tufte." *Datamation* 7 (20) 88–90.

von Oech, R. (1986) *A Kick in the Seat of the Pants*. Harper Row.

Wurman, R.S. (1989) *Information Anxiety*. Doubleday.

y Gasset, J. O. (1925) *The Dehumanization of Art; and Other Essays on Art, Culture, and Literature*. Trans. A. McVitty, Jr. Princeton University Press, 1968.

USING VIDEO TO PROTOTYPE USER INTERFACES

LAURIE VERTELNEY

Abstract:

The Human Interface Group at Apple Computer uses video as a design tool to prototype and visualize ideas about how computers will be used in the future. This paper is for people who need to build visualizations of user interfaces that don't yet exist. It describes how to create effective interface simulations using animation and video techniques. The advantages and disadvantages of video as a user interface design and prototyping medium are also explored.

Deciding what interfaces to build:

Before you can build a prototype of a user interface you have to specify what tasks the interface will enable. This specification can take many forms: a user interface ERS (an engineering requirement specification that is used to describe how the user interface will work), a list of functions or commands or even a scenario or story which describes the interface in more detail. In any event, you will end up with a collection of tasks that will be automated by a technology. The next step will be to design how a user will interact with the technology in order to accomplish the task or use the functions you've listed in your specification. No matter how you specify your user interface you will probably need a way to illustrate your design ideas to others.

There are many techniques for simulating user interfaces. However, many of these techniques require the skills of a computer programmer and special purpose hardware or software. Until recently, user interface designers spent very little time actually *designing* user interfaces because there were no tools which enabled them to explore design alternatives. Designing often meant building.

How do you prototype your user interface ideas? You could set out to actually build them, but what if people don't like your design? How do you prototype a user interface to a product that does not yet exist? Visualization and animation techniques for prototyping or simulating user interfaces without actually building them will be addressed in this paper.

Developing storyboards and flipbooks:

You should have some ideas about how the eventual interface should look and 'respond' to the user. The next step is to create a storyboard or flipbook to help visualize the user interface interactions. Storyboards and flipbooks help designers work out timing and sequencing problems and quickly record design solutions. Storyboards are used in the film industry to describe the camera shots, action, and timing events for films. There are usually eight to twelve drawings on a page with supporting text in a window below the drawing. Flipbooks are used by animators. They have one drawing per page. Animators can 'fan' the pages of the book to get a rough approximation of the motion between drawings.

The following is an example of a storyboard that illustrates an interface for marking a shared calendar.

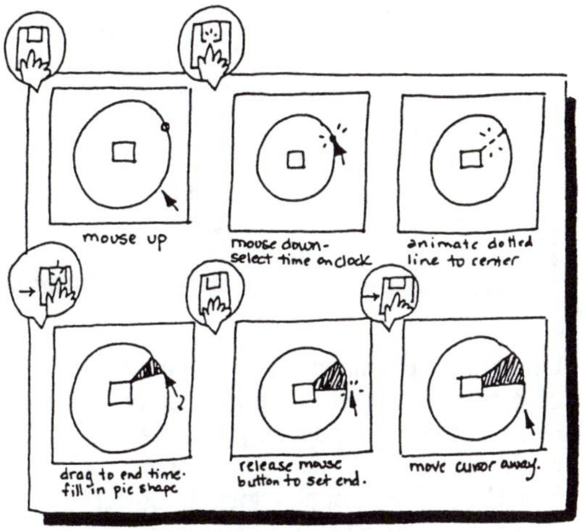

The storyboard was intended to describe:

- what the computer screen would look like
- how the user would manipulate the interface to accomplish a task
- the response the computer would make to the user's input.

Visualizing the interaction:

Storyboards and flipbooks are useful tools for interaction designers but they can be difficult for others to interpret as user interface specifications because they lack continuity and transition from one drawing to the next. Once the interface techniques are described on paper, they can be visualized in a more temporal medium, such as video, to illustrate the interactivity of the design.

There are several techniques that can be used to illustrate interaction concepts. They vary based on the degree to which the prototype must mimic the real product. I have used three types of prototypes: animated prototypes, computer scripted or interactive prototypes and prototypes which integrate video with other media.

Animating interaction techniques:

Animated Drawings:
The simplest animation effect is an animated drawing. To illustrate how to make an animated drawing let's imagine an interface for a shared calendar. To produce an animated drawing a simple sketch of the calendar interface is drawn on a piece of paper. The drawing is then reproduced on a copier so there are multiple copies of the original sketch. The interaction events, such as the steps required to make an appointment on the calendar, are then drawn on top of the copied drawing as in-between frames for the animation. These drawings can be filled in with color if desired. The drawings are placed, in sequential order, under a video camera and shot one drawing at a time for 10 to 20 seconds. A video editor is used to assemble the final animation so that each drawing is shown for the appropriate amount of time. The drawings, edited together in this fashion give the illusion of motion. (The ideal frame rate is 24 images per second, but the motion can be illustrated even at 1 frame per second.)

This method can produce many rough interface sketches in less than a day. The cost for materials, such as paper and pens, is minimal. And it is possible to create a crude but effective approximation of the interaction in the user interface even though the frame rate is course. However, if a close approximation of the finished interface is what you're trying to achieve, this method will not be appropriate.

Cutout animation:
A similar technique is cut out animation. Objects such as the calendar, can be cut out of paper or cardboard and placed on top of a background. The objects are then filmed as they are moved under the video camera. Smooth transitions such as moving or rotating an object are relatively simple. The object can be moved under the camera in real time; while the video camera is recording the action. But not all computer interactions are this simple to simulate. For example, to simulate the effect of scaling a window each frame of the animation must be recorded while the object is replaced sequentially with a smaller object. The video editor must be used later to remove the time between each frame.

Like the animated drawing technique, cutout animation can produce many rough interface sketches in less than a day at a minimal cost. It has the added advantage that objects can be used over and over without having to recreate them. However, it is difficult to choreograph the placement of the cutout objects so retakes of the shots are often required if mistakes are made while filming. Again, this method is not appropriate for close approximations of the finished user interface.

Animated objects:
I have recently discovered some techniques to accommodate prototyping user interfaces for three dimensional objects, such as interfaces for computer aided design. I built a foam core model of the objects, then used fishing line (which is transparent) to translate and rotate the objects in space. A small camera, suspended above the objects, can be moved through the space to give the illusion of walking through the model. Magnets, hidden from the camera's view, can be used to manipulate objects as if they are moving by themselves. I've also found magnets useful for moving cursors over flat planes.

One of the advantages of this method is that objects can be reused. Unfortunately, it is difficult to prototype manipulations that could not occur in real physical space such as scaling objects or changing an object's shape. But it can be faster and less expensive than creating and animating a computer generated model.

Computer animation:
Another prototyping technique is computer animation. Simple cell animation or flipcard animation can be accomplished with programs such as VideoWorks or HyperCard. Let's use our calendar interface as an example. The calendar can either be

drawn with a paint program or scanned into the computer from a sketch. Each frame of the animation must be drawn and placed as a cell on top of the background sketch. Reusable objects, such as the cursor, can be moved around on top of the calendar. Their positions are recorded for playback later.

This technique can produce results that closely resemble what the finished interface might look like. When our ideas become more concrete our paper sketches are converted to computer based prototypes. These computer animation tools are used most often to prototype interfaces for Macintosh. Computer generated animations are much easier to modify than the previous animation techniques. Unfortunately, not all computer animation programs are easy to use for prototyping user interfaces and special purpose hardware is required to get video out of the computer. Filming directly off of the computer screen produces poor quality scanning effects.

Computer scripting interactive prototypes:

An extension to computer animated prototypes are computer scripted prototypes. Animated prototypes simply play out a linear sequence of frames and are not interactive. Computer scripted prototypes are tightly confined to a series of interaction events. Some of the tools that we have used to make our prototypes somewhat interactive are VideoWorks Interactive, Prototyper and HyperCard.

The drawing below illustrates how HyperCard can be used to prototype an interface. I used the HyperCard paint tools to create a drawing of what the calendar would look like in it's normal rest state. Then I created a drawing of what the calendar would look like if the user had opened an appointment window. To simulate the effect of actually opening the appointment window, I connected or linked the two screens together with a button. When pressed, the button would flip from the illustration of the calendar in the rest state (figure A) to the illustration of the calendar with the appointment window opened (figure B). This gave the illusion that the calendar prototype actually worked, even through it was merely a user controlled animation.

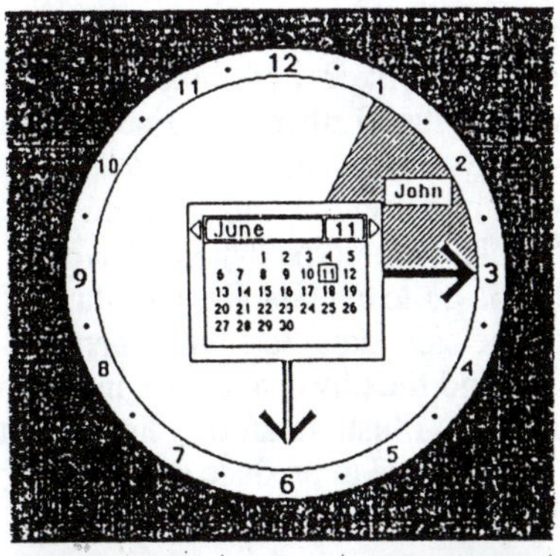

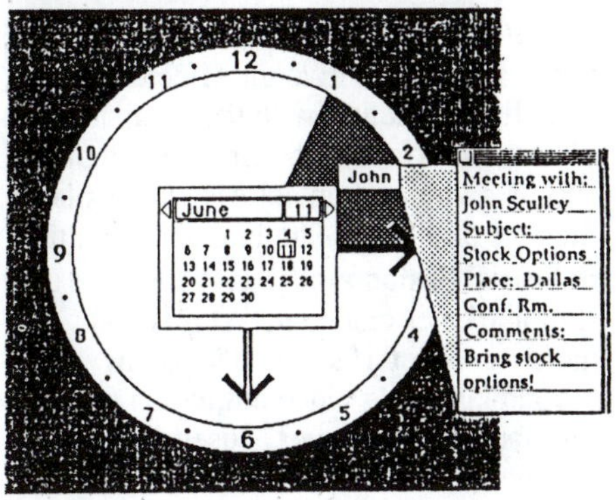

The biggest advantage to this technique is that it gives the illusion of being interactive. Tools such as these enable designers to produce quick prototypes in less than an hour or fully operational applications that require months to create. Again, there is some overhead required to learn how to use the application and to connect special adapters to convert high resolution screen images to recordable video.

Mixing media for more complex prototypes:

Emerging technologies include the capability to show video in a window, high resolution graphics, animation and more. Simulating user interfaces to these technologies require sophisticated prototyping techniques such as special purpose video production and computer graphic tools. It may be appropriate to work with a video production facility due to the equipment cost and professional expertise required to use this equipment. It is unlikely that you will need this level of production capability in-house. (An example of this kind of prototype, which was intended for marketing purposes, is Apple Computer's, "Knowledge Navigator".)

What would a prototype using these techniques look like? Let's take our calendar one step further. Imagine that you have written a script and constructed a storyboard of a user marking a shared calendar. The prototype that you have described is quite explicit about the task of marking the calendar, the environment the user is in, and the physical packaging of the computer. To illustrate all of your ideas it would be desirable to produce a video scenario.

The prototype will be constructed in layers and assembled to give the effect of a user actually interacting with the computer and it's user interface. The first layer that is shot is a video of an actress who is playing the part of a user. She interacts with the industrial design model as if she were using it to mark her calendar. At this point model has no user interface on it's display. The second layer is a video animation of the user interface. A computer is used to animate the sequence of events that show how the computer would look when marking a calendar. Finally, the video of the user interface is matted on top of the video of the industrial design model to give the illusion that the user is actually interacting with the physical device to mark her calendar.

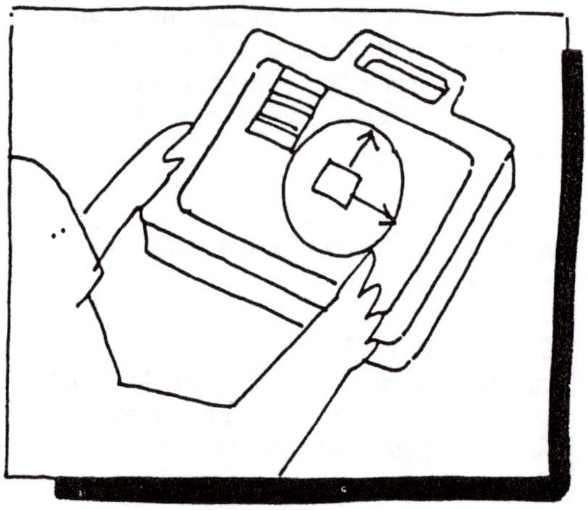

This technique produces an explicit representation of the user interface, both as a visual model and as an interaction model without the cost of actually implementing the user interface. Since this prototype is observed, the only thing lacking is interactivity. Unfortunately, the production costs can be very high, into the tens of thousands of dollars, and it can take months to produce.

Lessons learned:

Now that we've described several video prototyping techniques, let's take a look at what we have learned about video as a design tool.

Advantages:

- Video can provide an entire range of visual expression; from rough video sketches to highly refined and believable video productions.
- Video sketches enable designers, clients and end users to visualize interface ideas and get feedback early in the design process reducing the costs incurred by late design changes.
- Interface designers can produce many design alternatives in the same amount of time that it would take to implement just one design.
- Interface designers don't have to program computers to prototype user interfaces.
- Video is useful for specifying user interfaces for technologies which do not yet exist and can emulate the mechanics of real systems without actually having to build them.

Disadvantages:

- Video tools are expensive.
- Video is difficult to change or manipulate. Productions must be carefully planned ahead of time.
- It is difficult to simulate specific products with video. It is best to prototype in the target environment when possible. At Apple, HyperCard, VideoWorks and MacApp are used to prototype Macintosh user interfaces because they provide a better simulation of what the final design might look and feel like.
- Video can mislead people into believing that the prototype is the finished product. Since video can simulate reality, it is difficult to distinguish a prototype from a real working computer system.
- It is difficult to test video prototypes because they are not interactive.

Summary

Video is a useful design tool for prototyping user interfaces. It can provide immediate results in the form of video sketches or simulate final designs with finished video productions. Although it is not always the most appropriate design medium, video is especially useful when designing interfaces for technologies that do not yet exist.

Working with Interface Metaphors

Thomas D. Erickson
Advanced Technology Group
Apple Computer, Inc.

"METAPHOR," someone recently said to me, "seems to be the holy grail at Apple." It's true. Just about everyone at Apple knows the phrase "desktop metaphor" and fervently believes that a good metaphor is essential to an easy-to-use human interface. But just as the grail proved to be elusive, so is the knowledge of how metaphor really works.

The goal of this chapter is to provide designers with a deeper understanding of what metaphor is, and how to use it when designing an interface. First, we look at some of the characteristics of metaphor in language. These characteristics provide insights on how metaphor works in an interface. Next we look at an example of a poorly chosen interface metaphor and how it decreases the usability of the system. Finally, a design example is used to illustrate a method for coming up with interface metaphors and to present some rules of thumb for evaluating their value.

The Ubiquity and Invisibility of Metaphor

Many people think of metaphor as a flowery sort of language found chiefly in poetry and bad novels. This is not correct. Metaphor is an integral part of our language and thought. It appears not only in poetry and novels, but in our everyday speech about common matters. Mostly we don't notice; metaphor is such a constant part of our speech and thought that it is invisible.

The ubiquity of metaphor in language is convincingly demonstrated in the delightful book, *Metaphors We Live By* [Lakoff and Johnson, 1980]. The authors show that many of our basic concepts are based on metaphors. For example, without any intention of being poetic or fanciful, we speak of argument as though it is war. Arguments have *sides* that can be *defended* and *attacked*. Facts can be *marshaled* to support one's *position; strategies* can be employed. If a position is *indefensible*, one can *retreat* from it. Arguments can have *weak points*—they can even be *destroyed*; arguments can be *right on target*; arguments can be *shot down*. There is a whole web of concrete military language that we use to describe the rather abstract process of having an argument. It's also important to note that we don't just talk about argument as though it were war: being in an argument feels like a conflict; when we *lose* an argument, we feel bad.

The metaphorical way in which we talk and think about argument is the rule, not the exception. For example, the goal of this chapter is to provide a *deeper* understanding of metaphor. (Rather than just providing a *surface* treatment or *getting our feet wet*, I'd really like to *get into* the topic. Yet metaphor contains unexpected *depths*. Although we must avoid *getting in over our heads*; still, it would be nice to *plunge in* and *get to the bottom* of things.) In the next sentence, I say that we're going to *look at* metaphor as it's used in language. You *see*, we often speak of understanding an idea as seeing an object. Thus we may want to take a *closer look* at something, *shed some more light* on it, or *approach it from a different direction* so as to get a new *perspective* on it.

A word that is used in a metaphorical way is usually just the tip of the iceberg. A metaphor is an invisible web of terms and associations that underlies the way we speak and think about a concept. It is this extended structure that makes metaphor such a powerful and essential part of our thinking. Metaphors function as natural models, allowing us to take our knowledge of familiar, concrete objects and experiences and use it to give structure to more abstract concepts.

Metaphor in the Interface

The characteristics of metaphor in our language are the same ones that govern how metaphor works in an interface. Just as metaphors invisibly permeate our everyday speech, so do they occur throughout the interfaces we use and design. Just as we use military terms to make the rather abstract process of arguing more tangible, so we use object and container terms to make the Macintosh file system more concrete. And just as we experience arguments as real conflicts, most Macintosh users believe that when they move a document icon from one folder to another, they are really moving the document itself (what is "really" happening is that a pointer to the file is being moved—of course, *pointer* is a metaphor too . . .).

Because we use metaphors as models, an interface metaphor that suggests an incorrect model can cause difficulties for users. Consider the following scenario:

A visitor arrives. As previously agreed, she phones from the lobby to tell me she has arrived. However, I've stepped away from my desk for a moment, so the voice mail system answers:

"I'm not here now. But if you'll leave a message after the beep, I'll get right back to you."

She does so, and is quite properly annoyed when I show up in the lobby half an hour later and ask what kept her.

What neither of us knew was that there was a half hour delay between when she left the message in my mailbox and when it became available to me. Why the delay? The voice mail system resides on a machine in another building and, under conditions of heavy use, it can take as much as half an hour to notify me of a message.

It's easy to blame the system, but the real problem is that the system's metaphor has failed. The instruction manual and the on-line recordings inform users that they have *mailboxes* in which *messages* may be *left*. When the caller reaches the system, she hears a message in the callee's voice, saying "I'm not *here* now," followed by a beep—just as with an answering machine. A very clear model is presented: the caller has reached the callee's desk; the callee is not there; but the caller may leave a message in a *mailbox* that seems to act just like a conventional answering machine. Unfortunately, the model is incorrect. It provides no way for the users to understand that there might be a time lag between when a message is left in a mailbox and when the mailbox's owner can open it and find the message.

A more accurate metaphor would be an answering service metaphor. Messages would be left with an answering service, which would then forward the message to the appropriate person. Though this might not lead the user to expect a delay, it does provide grounds for appropriate suspicions when it becomes clear that something is wrong. The system need not even be redesigned for this metaphor to be used. Individual users could invoke the answering service metaphor just by having someone else record a message for them: "Tom's not at his desk. If you leave a message after the beep, I'll forward it to him." This is a small change, but it gives the user a different, more accurate model. No longer does the voice and language suggest that the message has reached its destination; instead, it's clear that an intermediary has the message and that it still must be forwarded.

The example of voice mail is a good one for several reasons. First, it clearly illustrates how an interface metaphor can provide the user with a model of the system, and how differences between the user's model and the real thing can cause problems. Second, it illustrates that a metaphor can make a difference even when there are no graphics or text associated with the interface. Too many people think that interface metaphors exist, or are important, only when icons and graphics are used. Finally, the example is good because it's so universal. Nearly everyone who uses this voice mail system has a message that presents the wrong model.

Why don't people use the more accurate metaphor? There are several possibilities. Many users don't understand how voice mail really works—they believe that the system's metaphor is real, that messages are really left in the boxy phones sitting on their desks. When incomprehensible delays occur, well, that's just the way high-tech stuff is sometimes. But that's not the full story, because even those who understand how the system really works continue to present the wrong model. Some of these users may not understand the purpose of an interface metaphor. They blame the hardware, and it doesn't occur to them that something as nebulous as a metaphor could in any way compensate for something as real as slow hardware. Finally, even users who understand that an interface metaphor should provide the user with a good model of the system may not know how to go about finding better metaphors.

Coming Up with Interface Metaphors

How do you come up with appropriate metaphors? This section describes the process of generating interface metaphors and applies it to a simple design problem. Although the design example is both hypothetical and oversimplified, it illustrates a useful approach to designing with metaphor.

Here's a brief overview of the process. Because the purpose of an interface metaphor is to provide users with a useful model of the system, the first step is to understand how the system really works. Second, because no metaphor can model all aspects of a system's functionality, the designer must identify what parts of it are most likely to give users difficulty. Finally, once the designer has identified the sort of model required, metaphors that support that model must be generated.

Functional Definition

To create a model of something, obviously you have to understand how the thing itself works. This includes not only what the system can do but when that functionality is available to the user and how quickly the system can perform various functions. Some of this information may not be available in the system specification; nevertheless, it is essential, and the interface designer must either experiment with the system or probe the appropriate technical people to obtain it.

Now let's take a look at our example. Because we're using a fictitious, over-simplified example, the functional definition process is easy: we just make up the specifications. To make the example somewhat more realistic, rather than starting from scratch, we will assume that we are going to add new functionality to the Macintosh.

In the Macintosh, data is shared between applications by copying and pasting. However, this can be cumbersome if the data in the source document is continually changing: every time it changes, you have to recopy it and then repaste it. Let's assume that our task is to automate this process. Users will be allowed to define links between parts of different documents, so that when a change is made to data in the source document, the change is copied automatically, sent over the link, and then pasted automatically into the receiving document. For the purposes of this example, we'll impose three constraints. First, links have directionality—that is, data can go only one way along a link: from source to recipient, or from beginning to end. Second, links can be one to many: one piece of data may be at the source end of many links, so that a change to it is sent to many different documents. Third, we'll assume that we can't guarantee that a change in data at the source end of a link can be transmitted instantly to the destination end of the link—there may be a time lag.

Identify Users' Problems

The second step is to figure out what users have problems with. What aspects of the functionality are new to them? What may look familiar, but will really be different? The best way to do this is to observe users (see Gomoll's chapter in this volume). Watch them using similar functionality and see what problems they have. Describe what you're doing and see if they understand. Show them prototypes of your system and watch them try to use it (see Wagner's chapter in this volume for a description of prototyping). Each of these methods has its drawbacks, but any is better than just guessing.

What do users understand and not understand about the functionality of links? For the purposes of this example, we'll just guess. Users may not understand that links have directionality—that data can flow one way along a link, but not the other. Or, users may not understand that links are one-to-many: data at the source end of a link may show up in many different documents. There are other likely problems that would most appropriately be identified by working with users, but these two will serve our purposes.

Metaphor Generation

The first step in generating metaphors is to note what metaphors are already implicit in the problem description. Because we use metaphors to talk about abstract concepts, it's almost certain that metaphors are lurking about in the description of the functionality. However, because the functionality is usually defined by technical people who aren't representative of end users, the metaphors are often inappropriate. Nevertheless, it is important to identify these metaphors if only because unrecognized metaphors, may limit the variety of metaphors you generate.

In the description of our example, we are using a metaphor. We speak of the functionality in terms of *links between* documents. We say that links have *sources* and *destinations* and that data is *sent along* the links. It is important to recognize that there are other possible metaphors. Perhaps data could be conceived of as flowing through pipes. Or one could imagine electronic connections—a link could be created by wiring it up. Or a link could be thought of as a path, and special porters could carry data along it. But note that these metaphors—"pipes," "wires," and "paths"—are all special cases of the "links" metaphor. Each is a special type of *connection* metaphor. It may be useful to look for metaphors that focus not on connections, but on the properties of the data at either end of the link.

Mountford's chapter in this volume describes various techniques that can be used to generate new metaphors. However, one particularly useful approach is to focus on the user problems you've identified and look for real-world events, objects, or institutions that embody some of the characteristics that users find difficult to understand. These make good candidates for new interface metaphors.

For example, what are some real-world things that exhibit directionality? Rivers flow in one direction; TV images are transmitted from a broadcaster to a receiver; newspapers are mailed from a publisher to subscribers; forces like gravity and magnetism have direction. Similarly, TV broadcasts and newspaper editions also originate from one point and end up in many places at once; rivers generally do the opposite; and gravity and magnetism don't work at all.

It should be possible to generate dozens of potentially useful metaphors. For the purpose of keeping this example brief, we'll look at only three: links (because with the advent of commercial hypertext this is an increasingly popular metaphor), TV broadcasting, and newspaper publishing.

Evaluating Interface Metaphors

Once several metaphors have been generated, it's time to evaluate and choose one through which to express the new functionality. For our purposes, we'll take our original metaphor—links—and the TV broadcasting and newspaper publishing metaphors described above. Here are five questions for evaluating the usefulness of an interface metaphor.

Amount of Structure

How much structure does the metaphor provide? A metaphor without much structure may not be very useful.

One problem with the links metaphor is that it doesn't have much structure. If you ask users what a "link" is, you'll get a lot of different answers—users don't have a clear notion of what a link is. Links can be one-way or two-way. Links may imply data flow, or they may just be physical connections. When users think of links, they may even think of chains, sausages, or golf. There's nothing in the links metaphor that suggests the directionality or one-to-manyness of the flow of data that the users need help in understanding.

In contrast, users know a lot about TV broadcasting and newspaper publishing. For example, newspapers have editions, subscribers, editors, delivery people, and delivery routes; they may be found at newsstands; and so on. TV broadcasting has networks, stations, channels, *TV Guide*, TV receivers, reruns, serials, shows, VCRs, and so on.

Applicability of Structure

How much of the metaphor is actually relevant to the problem? What is particularly important here is not what is irrelevant, but things that might lead the user in the wrong direction or raise false expectations.

For example, in comparing TV broadcasting and newspaper publishing, note that the broadcasting metaphor may lead the user astray because broadcasting implies instantaneous transmission of the data; in contrast, everyone knows that newspapers take a while to get delivered.

Representability

Is the interface metaphor easy to represent? Ideal interface metaphors have distinctive visual and auditory representations, as well as specific words associated with them.

This is another area where the link metaphor is weak. Even assuming that users understand that "link" means a "connection over which data can flow," what does a link look or sound like? In contrast, the broadcasting metaphor has many possibilities for representation; for example, a TV set for a receiver, a broadcasting tower for a transmitter, sounds for indicating transmission. The newspaper metaphor also has possibilities—one could imagine sounds and images of a printing press for the source end of the link and a newspaper as the receiving end. There are also rich vocabularies specifically associated with broadcasting (transmitting, receiving, tuning, reception range) and newspapers (publishing, issues, editions, circulation, delivery).

Suitability to Audience

Will your audience understand the metaphor? A metaphor may satisfy all the other criteria, but if your users don't grasp the metaphor, it's useless.

Suitability would, for example, probably rule out the use of pointers (in the computer science sense) as a metaphor for links, even though they do indicate directionality. In evaluating suitability, it is once again important for the designer to involve the user in the design process. It is exceedingly easy to become convinced of the suitability of a metaphor that, when tested on users, turns out to evoke completely inappropriate associations.

Extensibility

What else do the proposed metaphors buy you? A metaphor may have additional bits of structure that may be useful later on.

For example, it would be nice if links worked across networks. Because both broadcasting and newspaper publishing work across large distances, it's likely that they have structures that can provide a degree of support for data sharing across machines. For example, one might imagine each server on a network having a *newsstand*, which would be the recipient of *publications* from other machines.

It's also important to notice ways in which the metaphor may extend itself. For example, the broadcasting metaphor might encourage a use of the link functionality in a way that is very different from the data sharing that it was originally envisioned as supporting. It's easy to imagine users deciding to use the link functionality presented via the broadcasting metaphor to browse among the different *channels* available, just as they would switch from one TV channel to another. This sort of behavior seems much less likely to occur with the newspaper publishing metaphor.

What's Next?

Which metaphor should we choose for our example? It's not clear. To enable us to really address the question, the problem definition needs to be more detailed, more metaphors need to be generated and evaluated, and end users need to be consulted and observed throughout the design process.

Once a metaphor is settled on, it must be integrated into the interface. Although a discussion of this is beyond the scope of this chapter, one point should be made. Using the above criteria to select a good metaphor will be of little use unless the metaphor is used to its full extent. That is, having chosen a metaphor with a lot of structure, use as much of the structure as possible in the interface. Similarly, having chosen a representable metaphor, be sure to make full use of those representations.

Although the injunction to use and represent a metaphor fully may seem obvious, it's astonishingly easy to find examples where it has been ignored. For example, many HyperCard stacks start out using a book metaphor, usually by presenting a book-like background, but then fail to include such basic elements of books as page numbers, tables of contents, and indexes. Similarly, actions such as going to the next page are often represented by dissolving from one page to the next, rather than by using a visual effect to indicate that the page is being turned. These are all small details, but, as we saw in the voice mail interface, small details can make big differences.

Summary

Although metaphors are everywhere, they are often-difficult to notice. They are present whenever we speak or think about abstract concepts. Metaphors serve as natural models; they allow us to take our knowledge of familiar objects and events and use it to give structure to abstract, less well understood concepts.

Metaphors exhibit these same properties in interfaces. To the extent that an interface metaphor provides users with realistic expectations about what will happen, it enhances the utility of the system. To the extent it leads users astray, or simply leads them nowhere, it fails.

Designers need to do several things when working with metaphor. They need to notice what metaphors are already present in the system. They must understand the system's functionality. And, most important, they need to know which aspects of the functionality users may not understand. Armed with this knowledge, the designer can search for metaphors that best support the areas in that the user's understanding is the weakest.

References

Apple Computer, Inc. (1987) *Human Interface Guidelines: The Apple Desktop Interface*. Addison-Wesley.

Lakoff, G. and Johnson, M. (1980) *Metaphors We Live By*. University of Chicago Press.

METHODOLOGY MATTERS: DOING RESEARCH IN THE BEHAVIORAL and SOCIAL SCIENCES

JOSEPH E. MCGRATH

PSYCHOLOGY, UNIVERSITY OF ILLINOIS, URBANA

23 OCTOBER 1994

Material in this chapter draws on ideas from a number of my earlier publications, including: McGrath, J.E., 1984; McGrath and Brinberg, 1984; Brinberg and McGrath, 1985; Runkel and McGrath, 1972; McGrath, Martin, and Kulka, 1982.

"Doing research" simply means the systematic use of some set of theoretical and empirical tools to try to increase our understanding of some set of phenomena or events. In the social and behavioral sciences, the phenomena of interest involve states and actions of human systems — of individuals, groups, organizations, and larger social entities — and the by-products of those actions.

The meaning of research evidence, in any area of science, is inherently tied to the means or methods by which that evidence was obtained. Hence, to understand empirical evidence, its meaning, and its limitations, requires that you understand the concepts and techniques on which that evidence is based.

This chapter is about some of the tools with which researchers in the social and behavioral sciences go about "doing" research. It raises some issues about strategy, tactics and operations. Especially, it points out some of the inherent limits, as well as the potential strengths, of various features of the research process by which behavioral and social scientists do research.

SOME BASIC FEATURES OF THE RESEARCH PROCESS

Doing research, in the behavioral and social sciences, always involves bringing together three sets of things:

(a) some *content* that is of interest,
(b) some *ideas* that give meaning to that content, and
(c) some *techniques or procedures* by means of which those ideas and contents can be studied.

For example, the contents of a study might involve the behavior of a jury, conversations in a family about buying a new car, the voting behavior of members of a community, littering in a park, courtship patterns in a small town, and so forth. The ideas might include the concept of attitudes, the notion that education affects political preferences, the concept of conformity, the hypothesis that groups whose members like one another perform tasks better than groups whose members do not like each other, and so forth. The techniques might include a questionnaire to assess individual attitudes, toward a car or a candidate or group mates; a set of procedures for observing family discussions about cars and money; a means to gather election returns; a plan to evaluate the quality of group task products; and so forth.

I will refer to these three sets of things more formally, as three distinct, though interrelated, domains:

(a) The *Substantive* domain, from which we draw contents that seem worthy of our study and attention;
(b) The *Conceptual* domain, from which we draw ideas that seem likely to give meaning to our results; and
(c) The *Methodological* domain, from which we draw techniques that seem useful in conducting that research.

Furthermore, research always deals with several levels of phenomena: With *relations* between units or *elements* within a context or *embedding system*. The elements, relations, and embedding systems have different forms in each of the three domains [See Figure 1].

SUBSTANTIVE DOMAIN

In the substantive domain, I will call the units or elements Phenomena, and the relations among them Patterns of phenomena. These Phenomena, and Patterns of them, are the object of our study. For the behavioral and social sciences, the phenomena of interest involve the states and actions of some human systems —individuals, groups, organizations, communities, and the like — and the conditions and processes that give rise to and follow from those states and actions.

Another way to say this is to say that the behavioral and social sciences study "actors behaving toward objects in context". An example would be "an individual casting a vote in a county election". Another example would be "the number of units produced in the week of April 12th by group 32 of the production division of the Danville plant".

It must be understood that both "actors" and "context" here refer to human systems at any of a number of system levels —individual, group, community, organization, and so on. Different behavioral and social sciences specialize in the study of different human systems —that is, in the study of phenomena and patterns at different levels and of different kinds. The rest of this book presents material that illustrates many of the substantive phenomena and patterns that have been studied within the field of human-computer interaction.

CONCEPTUAL DOMAIN

For the social and behavioral sciences, the elements of interest in the conceptual domain are properties of the states and actions of those human systems that are the focus of study — properties of "actors behaving toward objects in context". These might include such familiar ideas as "attitude," "cohesiveness," "power," "social pressure," "status," as well as many others that are used in social and behavioral science research. *Relations* in the conceptual domain refer to any of a variety of possible ways in which two or more elements can be connected. Some of those ways are viewed as "causal" connections. Some are logical relations. Some simply are chronological relations. For example, two elements can be equal or unequal, they can be related linearly or non-linearly, one can be a necessary or sufficient cause of the other, one can include the other, the relation between them can be one way or reciprocal, and many more. Materials from the conceptual domain —properties, and relations among those properties — are the "ideas" that can give meaning to the phenomena and patterns that we study in the substantive domain.

METHODOLOGICAL DOMAIN

In the methodological domain, elements are methods. I will call the methods *Modes of Treatment* (of properties of phenomena). Modes of Treatment are different ways by which a researcher can deal with a particular feature of the human systems that are to be studied.

One set of such Modes of Treatment include various *techniques for measuring* some feature (that is, for assessing the state or magnitude of some property of some actors-behaving- in-context), so that the researcher can determine what value or level that feature has for each "case" to be studied. Measurement methods include such things as: a questionnaire, a rating scale, a personality test, instruments for observing and recording communications, techniques for assessing the quality of some products resulting from individual or group task performance, and the like. (More is said about kinds of measures near the end of this chapter.)

Modes of Treatment also include various *techniques for manipulating* some feature of a research situation (that is, some property of an actor-behavior-context). To carry out an experimental manipulation of a feature of the situation (sometimes referred to as "manipulating a variable") means making that feature have one particular predetermined value or level for certain "cases" to be studied and another specific preordained value or level for certain other "cases," so that the effect of differences in that property can be assessed by comparing those two sets of "cases." For example: You might want to study the effectiveness of a particular human-computer system by studying two sets of work groups, one set of groups working with that computer system and the other set doing the same tasks "manually". Social psychologists have tried to manipulate features of the systems they study by a number of techniques, such as:

(a) **giving instruction** to participants (e.g., trying to motivate them to try hard by telling them that there will be a valuable prize for the best product);
(b) **imposing constraints** on features of the environment (e.g., providing some participants with a particular software program that may help task performance, and providing other participants with a different or no program to carry out that function);
(c) **selecting materials** for use (e.g., trying to produce differences in task difficulty by giving some participants very difficult word problems to complete, and giving other participants easier problems of the same type);
(d) **giving feedback** about prior performances (e.g., trying to induce feelings of success or failure by telling some participants they did well, and telling others they did poorly, on a previous task);
(e) **using experimental confederates** (e.g., trying to establish different degrees of liking for fellow group members by having an experimental assistant who is pretending to be a normal participant work very hard in some groups and act indifferent in others).

(More is said about techniques for manipulating variables near the end of this chapter).

Modes of Treatment of variables also include a set of *techniques for controlling the impact of* various "extraneous" features of the situation — features that are important but that you are not going to measure or manipulate in a particular study. These include: techniques for *experimental control*, by which you make certain features take the same predetermined value for all cases in the study (e.g., study only 6-year-olds to control on age); techniques for *statistical control* by which you try to nullify the effects of variations in a given property within a study by "removing" those variations by statistical means; and techniques for *distributing the impact* of a number of features of the system and its context—without directly manipulating or controlling any one of them— so that such impact can be taken into account in interpretation of results. The most prominent means for distributing impact of a number of features is called *randomization*, and refers to procedures for the allocation of "cases" among various conditions within the study. These Modes for dealing with various features of the human systems to be studied — *measuring, manipulating, controlling* and *distributing impact* — are the basic sets of elements or "tools" by which social and behavioral scientists systematically gather empirical information.

Relations in the methodological domain have to do with the application of various *Comparison Techniques*. These are methods or techniques by means of which the researcher can assess relations among the values of two or more features of the human system under study. Such comparisons involve three sets of features of the systems under study: (a) the features that have been measured, and that are regarded as measures of the phenomena of interest (these are sometimes called "dependent variables"); (b) the features that have been measured or manipulated, and that are regarded as potential covariates of, or antecedents to, the phenomena of interest (these are sometimes called "independent variables"); and (c) all of the other features of the system that are relevant to the relations of interest (between dependent and independent variables), and that you have (or have failed to) control, or whose impact you have (or have failed to) distribute or otherwise take into account. Comparisons assess the covariation or association between the values of the first two sets (the dependent and independent variables), against the backdrop of the third set (i.e., other relevant features that were not studied directly but that nevertheless are a part of the meaning of results).

Most of the rest of this chapter will deal with features of the research process that emphasize the methodological domain, without much systematic consideration of either conceptual or substantive matters. The reader should keep in mind, though, that the research process, like a three-legged stool, always depends on materials from *all three* domains — content, ideas, and techniques.

DOMAINS

LEVELS	SUBSTANTIVE	CONCEPTUAL	METHOD-OLOGICAL
ELEMENTS	Phenomena	Properties	Modes of Treatment
RELATIONS	Patterns	Relations	Comparison Techniques
EMBEDDING SYSTEMS	Ongoing systems [e.g. human-computer systems	Conceptual Systems (e.g., field theory)	Research Strategies (e.g. laboratory experiment)

Figure 1: *Domains and levels of concepts in behavioral and social science research.*

RESEARCH METHODS AS OPPORTUNITIES AND LIMITATIONS

Methods are the tools —the instruments, techniques and procedures — by which a science gathers and analyzes information. Like tools in other domains, different methods can do different things. Each method should be regarded as offering potential opportunities not available by other means, but also as having inherent limitations. You cannot pound a nail if you don't have a hammer (or some functional equivalent). But if you do have a hammer, that hammer will not help you much if you need to cut a board in half. For that you need a saw (or the functional equivalent). And, of course, the saw would not have helped to drive the nail. So it is with the tools or methods of the social and behavioral sciences.

All research methods should be regarded as *bounded opportunities* to gain knowledge about some set of phenomena, some substantive domain. Knowledge in science is based on use of some combination of substance, concepts and methods. The meaning of that knowledge, and the confidence we can have in it, both are contingent on the methods by which it was obtained. All methods used to gather and to analyze evidence offer both opportunities not available with other methods, and limitations inherent in the use of those particular methods.

One good example of this dual nature of methods —both opportunities for gaining knowledge and limitations to that knowledge — is the widespread use of questionnaires and other forms of self-report in many areas of the social and behavioral sciences. On the one hand, self-report measures (questionnaires, interviews, rating scales, and the like) are a direct way, and sometimes the only apparent way, to get evidence about certain kinds of variables that are worthy of study: attitudes, feelings, memories, perceptions, anticipations, goals, values, and the like. On the other hand, such self-report measures have some serious flaws. For example: Respondents may try to appear competent, to be consistent, to answer in socially desirable ways, to please (or frustrate) the researcher. Sometimes respondents are reactive on such self-report measures without even being aware of it. These flaws limit, and potentially distort, the information that can be gained from such self-report measures. Other approaches to data collection, such as observation of visible behavior, may be difficult or impossible to use when studying particular kinds of variables. For example: How do you go about observing anxiety, or sadness, or some other emotion? In any case, while such methods may avoid some of the particular weaknesses of self-reports, those methods will have other different weaknesses.

Such is the dilemma of empirical science: All methods have inherent flaws, though each has certain potential advantages. You cannot avoid these flaws; but you can bring more than one approach, more than one method, to bear on each aspect of a problem. If you only use one method, there is no way to separate out the part that is the "true" measure of the concept in question from the part that reflects mainly the method itself. If you use multiple methods, carefully picked to have different strengths and weaknesses, the methods can add strength to one another by offsetting each other's weaknesses. Furthermore, if the outcomes of use of different methods are consistent, this way of proceding can add credibility to the resulting evidence. If the outcomes differ across different methods, then you can avoid misinterpretation of the resulting evidence by properly qualifying your conclusions.

This same general problem (that methods are inherently flawed, though each is flawed differently), and this same general prescription for dealing with it (by use of multiple methods), hold, as well, for research strategies, for comparison techniques and for research designs, all of which will be discussed subsequently in this chapter. For example, the research strategy called the laboratory experiment has some important strengths. It can permit precise measurement of effects resulting from deliberate manipulation of presumed causes, and therefore the drawing of strong inferences about cause-effect relations. But laboratory experiments also have some serious flaws. Researchers using laboratory experiments often greatly narrow the scope of the problem; they study it in artificial settings; and they are likely to use procedures and measures that make the situation seem even more artificial to the participants.

Several strategies that are alternatives to laboratory experiments are discussed later in this chapter. They include: field studies, sample surveys, and several others. Each of these other strategies offers different strengths, some of them offsetting the weakness-es of the laboratory; but each also has different inherent weaknesses, some of these being the very strengths of the laboratory strategy. No one strategy, used alone, is very useful; each of them is far too flawed. But again, the researcher needs to take advantage of multiple approaches. Usually, this cannot be done within a single study — often, the researcher must use a single strategy as a practical matter. But multiple strategies can be used over several studies of the same problem. The approaches need to be chosen so that the weaknesses of each strategy can be offset by the strengths of another. If we obtain consistent outcomes across studies using different strategies, we can be more confidant that those outcomes have to do with the phenomena we are studying, and not just with our methods.

To summarize:

(a) Methods enable but also limit evidence.
(b) All methods are valuable, but all have weaknesses or limitations.
(c) You can offset the different weaknesses of various methods by using multiple methods.
(d) You can choose such multiple methods so that they have patterned diversity; that is, so that strengths of some methods offset weaknesses of others.

Given these principles, it should be why it is not appropriate to ask whether any given study is flawless, and therefore to be believed (as in the query, "But is that study valid?"). Rather, we should ask whether the evidence from any given study is consistent with other evidence on the same problem, done by the same or other researchers using other strategies and other methods. If two sets of evidence based on different methods are consistent, both of those sets of evidence gain in credibility. If they are not consistent, that inconsistency raises doubts about the credibility of both sets. How much doubt we may have about the two sets of evidence depends on what else is known about the problem and the methods from still other studies. On the other hand, if all of the studies of a given problem have been based on the same methods, then that body of information is very much contingent on, and limited by, the flaws of those methods. Such a body of information must be regarded with some skepticism until you know whether it holds for a broader array of methods.

It should be noted here, though, that no one investigator is apt to be trained in the use of all methods, nor to have access to the resources needed for all of them. For example, some researchers have access to use of extensive and well designed laboratory facilities and are well trained in those methods but do not have ready access to the resources needed for a full scale sample survey, or for an elaborate field study. Other researchers may be in the reverse situation, with poor or no laboratory facilities but with excellent survey facilities and field study opportunities. What is crucial is not that a given researcher be able to use all methods on his or her research problem, but rather that the field as a whole make such use of diverse methods on each of its key problem areas. The fundamental principle, in behavioral and social science is that *credible empirical knowledge requires consistency or convergence of evidence across studies based on different methods.* These issues and their implications for behavioral and social science are discussed further in the parts of this chapter to follow, along with more detailed descriptions of strategies, comparison techniques, designs and methods.

RESEARCH STRATEGIES: CHOOSING A SETTING FOR A STUDY

Research evidence, in the social and behavioral sciences, always involves *somebody doing something, in some situation.* We can always ask about three facets: Who [which actors], what [which behaviors] and when and where [which contexts]. [The terms "actor", "behavior" and "context" are used here as technical terms with meanings somewhat different from ordinary usage. Actor refers to those human systems, at whatever level of aggregation (e.g., individuals, groups, organizations, communities) whose behavior is to be studied. Behavior refers to all aspects of the states and actions of those human systems that might be of interest for such study. Context refers to all the relevant temporal, locational and situational features of the "surround" within which those human systems are embedded.]

When you gather a batch of research evidence, you are always trying to maximize three desireable features or criteria:

A. **Generalizability** of the evidence over the populations of Actors.
B. **Precision** of measurement of the behaviors that are being studied (and precision of control over extraneous factors that are not being studied).
C. **Realism** of the situation or Context within which the evidence is gathered, in relation to the contexts to which you want your evidence to apply.

Although you always want to maximize all three of these criteria, A, B and C simultaneously, you cannot do so. This is one fundamental dilemma of the research process. The very things you can do to increase one of these three features reduces one or both

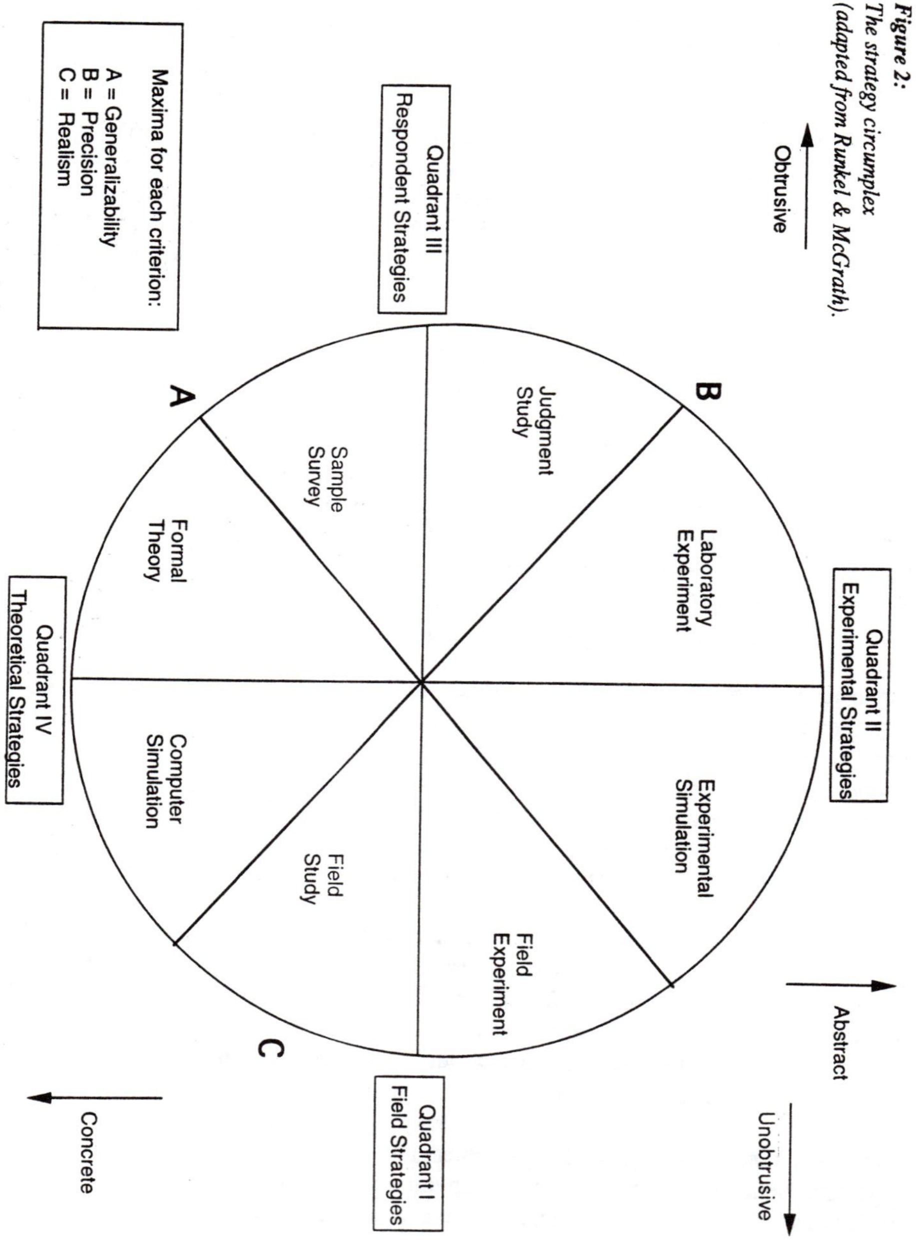

Figure 2:
The strategy circumplex
(adapted from Runkel & McGrath).

of the other two. For example: The things you can do to try to increase the precision with which you can measure behavior and control related variables (B) (for example, conducting a carefully conrolled laboratory experiment) will intrude upon the situation and reduce its "naturalness" or realism (that is, reduce C), and will also reduce the range of actors (A) to whom the findings can be generalized. Conversely, the things you can do to try to keep high realism of context (C) (for example, conducting a field study in a natural situation) will reduce both the range of populations to which your results can be applied (A) and the precision of the information you generate (B). As a third example, the things you can do to try to establish a high degree of generalizability over actors (A) (for example, conducting a well-designed sample survey) will reduce realism (C) by obtaining the measures out of context, and will reduce precision (B) both by having measures of only a limited number of behaviors, and by failing to control or otherwise take into account extraneous factors that may affect results.

You can appreciate this dilemma better by examining some of the major research strategies used in the behavioral and social sciences. Figure 2 shows a set of eight alternative research strategies, or settings for gathering research information. In that figure, the eight strategies are shown as lying in a circular arrangement in relation to two underlying dimensions: the degree to which the setting used in the strategy is universal or abstract vs. particular or concrete; and the degree to which the strategy involves procedures that are obtrusive, vs. procedures that are unobtrusive, with respect to the ongoing human systems (the actor-behavior-context units) that are to be the object of study. The four strategies on the right side of the circle involve fairly concrete or particularistic settings; the four on the left side use fairly universal or abstract settings. The procedures used in the four strategies in the lower half of the circle can be fairly unobtrusive. The four strategies in the top half of the circle necessarily use procedures that are fairly obtrusive, that is, they disturb the ongoing human systems (the actor-behavior-context units) that are being studied.

Figure 2 also shows where, among the strategies, each of the three desired features, or criteria is at its maximum. Criterion A, generalizability with respect to the population of Actors, is potentially maximized in the sample survey and in formal theory. Criterion B, precision with respect to measurement and control of behaviors, is potentially at its maximum in the laboratory experiment and in judgment studies. Criterion C, realism of context, is potentially at its maximum in the field study. The geometry of figure 2-1 emphasizes the dilemma just discussed, namely: strategies that maximize one of these are far from the maximum point for the other two. The very same changes in research procedures that would let you move toward the maximum of any one of these criteria —A, B, or C —at the same time would move you away from the maximum point of the other two. *It is not possible, in principle, to maximize all three criteria simultaneously.* Thus, any one research strategy is limited in what it can achieve. Research done by any single strategy is flawed, although the various strategies are flawed in different ways.

The eight strategies listed in Figure 2 are shown as four pairs, each occupying one quadrant of the circle. Quadrant I contains research strategies that involve observation of ongoing behavior systems under conditions as natural as possible. Quadrant II contains research strategies that are carried out in settings concocted for the purpose of the research. Quadrant III contains research strategies that involve gathering responses of participants under conditions in which the setting is muted or made moot. Quadrant IV contains research strategies that are theoretical, rather than empirical, in character. The two strategies in each of these quadrants will be described and illustrated briefly in the following paragraphs.

QUADRANT I: THE FIELD STRATEGIES

The two research strategies in quadrant I are the Field Study and the Field Experiment. In a field study, the researcher sets out to make direct observations of "natural", ongoing systems, while intruding on and disturbing those systems as little as possible. Much of the ethnographic work in cultural anthropology would exemplify this strategy, as would many field studies in sociology and many "case studies" of organizations.

A field experiment is a compromise strategy in which the researcher gives up some of the unobtrusiveness of the plain field study, in the interest of gaining more precision in the information resulting from the study. Typically, a field experiment also works within an ongoing natural system as unobtrusively as possible, except for intruding on that system by manipulating one major feature of that system. Field experiments use a manipulation of one important feature of the system in order to be able to assess the causal effects of the difference in that manipulated feature on other behaviors of the system. A number of studies in work organizations, such as the famous Western Electric or Hawthorne studies (Roesthlinger & Dickson, 1939), would exemplify the field experiment. Such studies introduce a major change in one feature of the organization (for example, a change in the formal communication structure), and study the changes that occur elsewhere in the organization subsequently. Sometimes such research also studies an unchanged but otherwise comparable organization, as a basis for comparison.

The essence of both of the strategies in quadrant I, the field study and the field experiment, is that the behavior system under study is "natural", in the sense that it would occur whether or not the researcher were there and whether or not it were being observed as part of a study. The two strategies of quadrant I differ in that the field study remains as unobtrusive as it can be (although no study is ever completely unobtrusive), at a cost in ability to make strong interpretations of resulting evidence; whereas the field experiment attempts to gain the ability to make stronger interpretations of some of the results (for example, that a behavior difference associated with the experimental manipulation may have been caused by the variables involved in that manipulation), but does so at a cost in obtrusiveness, hence in the naturalness or realism of the context.

QUADRANT II: THE EXPERIMENTAL STRATEGIES

The best known of the two strategies in quadrant II is the laboratory experiment. In that strategy, the investigator deliberately concocts a situation or behavior setting or context, defines the rules for its operation, and then induces some individuals or groups to enter the concocted system and engage in the behaviors called for by its rules and circumstances. In this way, the researcher is able to study the behaviors of interest with considerable precision (e.g., the investigator can be better prepared to measure certain behaviors because he or she can be confident about where and when those behaviors will occur), and to do so under conditions where many extraneous factors (that might be important but that are beyond the scope of the researcher's present interest) have been eliminated or brought under experimental control. The potential gain in precision in the measurement and control of behavior, which is the lure of the laboratory experiment, is paid for by increased obtrusiveness, hence reduced realism of context, and by a narrowing of the range of potential generalizability of results.

The other strategy of Quadrant II is the experimental simulation. In this strategy, the researcher attempts to achieve much of the precision and control of the laboratory experiment but to gain some of the realism (or apparent realism) of field studies. This is done by concocting a situation or behavior setting or context, as in the laboratory experiment, but making it as much like some class of actual behavior setting as possible.

One example would be research using ground-based flight simulators such as those used by both the U. S. Air Force and commercial airlines to train pilots for instrument flying. Another would be research that uses auto driving simulators like those sometimes used to train neophyte drivers. Still another would be research using military training exercises, or involving intra-squad practice games by an athletic team. Still another could be a monopoly game, or a stratgy game, or other similar board game, if they were used for research purposes and with some degree of control over "extraneous variables". Here, the key idea is that the researcher wants to create a system under his or her control, but at the same time have that system operate in a manner that simulates the operation of some particular class of naturally occurring system —the flight of airplanes, the steering of autos, the flow of "battle" in various sorts of two-sided combat or contests, or the operation of a "market" involving both strategic choices and chance factors.

The experimental simulation is a compromise strategy that attempts to retain the precision of the laboratory but at the same time to not give up so much realism of context. It risks introducing so much realism that precision of measurement and control are weakened, on the one hand, or retaining so much control that it becomes as "artificial" as the laboratory experiment on the other hand. An example of the former would be use of a military training exercise, in which the opposing "armies" are allowed to carry out any missions, anywhere and in any order, and thus make it impossible to observe and record the action for research purposes. An example of the latter would be to make such a "combat exercise" so stylized, and simplified in its flow — in the interest of good measurement and control — that all of the "realism" is nullified —that is, the system actually operating in the study does not function like the systems supposedly being simulated (that is, actual combat).

The two strategies in Quadrant II, in contrast to those of Quadrant I, involve concocted rather than natural settings. That is, the laboratory experiment and the experimental simulation are strategies that involve "actor-behavior-context" systems that would not exist at all were it not for the researcher's interest in doing the study. The distinction here is not between "real" and "unreal." The context of the laboratory experiment and the experimental simulation are certainly "real" for the participants once they are in the lab or simulation chamber; and the behaviors performed by the participants are certainly "real". Participants' behaviors are undoubtedly influenced by features of the experimental setting, but that is also the case in any other setting, natural or concocted. In fact, the exploration of such situational influences is, in large part, the point of behavioral and social science.

The distinction here, between the field research of Quadrant I and the experimental research of Quadrant II, has to do with whether the situation exists prior to and independent of the investigator, versus having been concocted by the researcher; and therefore whether the participants are taking part in it as an ongoing part of their lives or as part of a research endeavor. The issue is not one of reality, although much discussion of research strategies in the social sciences mistakenly treats it as such. Rather, the issue is one of motivation: Who has what stake in the behavior system under study.

Note that the difference between adjacent strategies are matters of degree. You can find "experimental simulations" (for example, varieties of strategy games) for which the task is so abstract that it becomes very close to a laboratory experiment. It also should be pointed out that few studies are "pure" examples of one strategy. These types of strategies represent a set of possibilities for carrying out research, rather than a description of concrete studies.

QUADRANT III: THE RESPONDENT STRATEGIES

In a sample survey, the investigator tries to obtain evidence that will permit him or her to estimate the distribution of some variables, and/or some relationships among them, within a specified population. This is done, typically, by careful sampling of actors from that population (thus potentially gaining a lot of generalizability, criterion A), and by systematically eliciting responses from those selected actors about the matters of interest. The many public opinion surveys on voting intentions, political preferences, buying intentions,and the like exemplify this strategy. While there is much emphasis on selection of sample, there is little opportunity for manipulation and/or control of variables and often little opportunity for much precision of measurement. Hence, this strategy is low on criterion B. And since the responses are gathered under conditions that make the behavior setting irrelevant, the question of realism of context is made moot (hence, this strategy is low on criterion C).

In a judgment study, the researcher concentrates on obtaining information about the properties of a certain set of stimulus materials, usually arranged so that they systematically reflect the properties of some broad stimulus domain. At the same time, such studies are usually done using "actors of convenience," so to speak. The focus of study is the set of properties of the stimulus materials, rather than some attributes of the respondents. Thus, studies using this strategy are often high on precision of measurement and control of both the stimulus materials and the responses (hence, high on criterion B). At the same time, they are often quite low on generalizability over population (hence, low on criterion A). Such studies are also usually done in a "neutral" behavior setting and with procedures that attempt to reduce or eliminate any properties of the behavior setting that might affect the judgments. Hence, they are low on criterion C. A good example of this strategy are studies in the area of psychology called psychophysics. These study the systematic relations between properties of the physical stimulus world and the psychological perception of those stimuli (e.g., the mapping of visible light and visual experience, of sound waves and auditory experience). Many "scaling" studies designed to explore the pattern of dimensions in some set of stimuli would also be examples of this strategy.

The two strategies of Quadrant III concentrate on the systematic gathering of responses of the participants to questions or stimuli formulated by the experimenter, in contrast to the observation of behaviors of the participants within an ongoing behavior system. Whereas the strategies of quadrant I focus on observation of behaviors within naturally occurring behavior settings, disturbed as little as possible by the research process, and the strategies of quadrant II focus on observation of behaviors within experimentally concocted behavior settings, the strategies of Quadrant III focus on observing behavior under conditions where the behavior setting is made irrelevant to the response. The sample survey does this by asking for responses that transcend the particular setting within which the responses are made. Questions such as how you intend to vote, whether you expect to buy a car next year, or how many children are living in your residence, are not related to the behavior setting within which a survey interview takes place (a doorstep, a living room, a shopping mall, an office). The judgment study makes the behavior setting irrelevant by attempting to neutralize or nullify the context of the behavior. To do this, the researcher attempts to mute, by "experimental controls," any of the features of the behavior setting that might "interfere with" the judgments being made. For example, psychophysical studies are usually done under "neutral" conditions of room temperature, lighting, chair comfort, and the like. The intent is to nullify any effects of the behavior setting or context on the judgments that are the topic of study.

The relation between the judgment study and the sample survey lies in their both emphasizing the behavior of some respondents in reaction to some stimulus materials, and deemphasizing the context within which those responses occur. The distinction between the judgment study and the sample survey has to do with two of their features: (a) whether the context is nullified by experimental controls or transcended by the nature of the responses elicited; and (b) whether the response of an individual to a stimulus is regarded as information about the stimulus (hence, a judgment study) or information about that respondent (hence, a sample survey).

QUADRANT IV: THE THEORETICAL STRATEGIES

Formal theory is a strategy that does not involve the gathering of any empirical observations (although it may be accompanied or preceded by much study of past empirical evidence). Rather, the researcher focuses on formulating general relations among a number of variables of interest. Generally, these relations —propositions, or hypotheses, or postulates —are intended to hold over some relatively broad range of populations. Hence this strategy is relatively high on the generalizability criterion A. At the same time, the formulation of theory in and of itself does not involve the operation of any concrete system (hence, it is relatively low on criterion C), nor does it involve the observation of any ongoing behavior (hence it is very low on criterion B). This strategy would be exemplified by any of the various general theories in behavioral and social sciences. Such theories are based on earlier empirical evidence (it is to be hoped), and they often lead to subsequent empirical studies. But the representation of the theory itself is not empirical — that is, it does not involve any "actors behaving in context".

The other non-empirical strategy in Quadrant IV is called Computer Simulation. It is like the experimental simulation strategy of quadrant II in that it is an attempt to model some particular kind of real-world system — a battle, a market, an aircraft in flight. But it is quite different from that strategy too. The computer simulation is a complete and closed system that models the operation of the concrete system without any behavior by any system participants. It does this because the researcher has designed a model that is complete and logically closed. All the important components of the system are specified by the investigator, and so are all of the relations among those components. Then, when the researcher starts a "run" of the system, all that ensues is the relatively predictable resultant of features built into the system. Such models are based on behavior in the sense that they must have all behavior parameters specified in advance, and this is often done on the basis of evidence from prior empirical research (at least for the parts about which the investigator has such past research available). But *no new behavior transpires during the run of the simulation.* And the "behavioral outcomes" that the simulation "shows" have the logical status of *predictions* from the theory that the researcher built into the model, rather than the status of behaviors occurring in nature independent of the control of the investigator. So this strategy is very low on criterion B. At the same time, it is potentially high on criterion C, in the sense that it is an attempt to model some concrete class of real world system (such as the geophysical processes going on in connection with the eruption of Mount St. Helens, or the prediction of the outcome of next year's Superbowl). But a computer simulation is designed to model some particular class of system; so the model is likely to have little generality over populations of actors or situations —or, more accurately, the question of generality over populations is moot. So this strategy is low on criterion A.

The two strategies of Quadrant IV are different in kind from the other six, but in a sense the pairs in each quadrant also differ in kind from those of the other quadrants. The inclusion of the two non-empirical strategies in this context is valuable for at least two reasons. First, the two theoretical strategies are related to the empirical strategies in several ways indicated in the diagram and in the preceding discussion. Second, the inclusion of these two strategies reminds us of the importance of the theoretical side of the research process. One major limitation of social psychology during much of its history (about 100 years) has been a reluctance to give full emphasis to the theoretical basis that is a necessary underpinning for any science. Inclusion of these two strategies also gives us the opportunity to note that one of the more powerful general strategies for research, and one that involves the use of multiple strategies on the same problem, is the simultaneous use of one of the theoretical strategies (say, the formulation of a general theory) and one of the empirical strategies (for example, a laboratory experiment).

SOME STRATEGIC ISSUES

Within the other chapters of this book, you will find studies done by all or most of the strategies discussed here. You should view that substantive material with two strategic issues in mind:

First, each strategy has certain inherent weaknesses, although each also has certain potential strengths. These weaknesses and strengths become part of the meaning of any evidence gathered with those strategies. So, an adequate interpretation of the available evidence on any given topic or problem should take those methodological strengths and weaknesses into account. The first strategy issue you are encouraged to address, in relation to material presented in the rest of this book, therefore is: Does the material, as presented, properly reckon with the strengths and weaknesses of the research strategies it encompasses?

Second, since all strategies are flawed, but flawed in different ways, to gain knowledge with confidence requires that more than one strategy —carefully selected so as to complement each other in their strengths and weaknesses— be used in relation to any given problem. While all of the research strategies discussed here are quite frequently used, there seems to be a tendency to use certain strategies for research on some problems or topics and other strategies for work on other problems or topics, but not to use multiple strategies on the same problem. The second strategic issue you are encouraged to address, with regard to the substantive material presented in the rest of this book, therefore is: To what extent is the research evidence on each problem or topic based on use of only a single research strategy, and therefore limited by the weaknesses of that strategy; and to what extent is that body of evidence based on use of multiple, complementary strategies, with agreement or convergence among the findings attained via the different strategies? The answers to those two issues are important indicators of how much the study of human-computer interaction has become a viable science with a cumulative body of credibly interpretable evidence.

STUDY DESIGN, COMPARISON TECHNIQUES, AND VALIDITY

In every empirical study, observations must be gathered, those observations must be aggregated and partitioned, and some comparisons must be made within that set of data. The comparisons to be made are the heart of the research. They reflect the relations that are the central focus of study. What comparisons are to be made in a given case depends on: (a) what has been included in the study at the element level from all three domains (what phenomena, what properties, what modes for treatment of variables have been used); (b) what systems are being worked from in all three domains (what substantive system is being studied, what conceptual paradigm is being used, what research strategy is being drawn upon); (c) what conceptual relations have been posited for the patterns of phenomena of interest (e.g., that a certain pair of properties, X and Y, are causally linked, with X causing Y); and, especially, (d) what comparison techniques are available, within the methodological domain, to ask such relational questions. This section will deal with some general features of the comparison techniques that are most commonly used within the current methodology of the social and behavioral sciences.

COMPARISON TECHNIQUES: ASSESSING ASSOCIATIONS AND DIFFERENCES

All research questions can be boiled down to variations of a few basic forms: baserates, correlations, and differences. The baserate question asks: How often (at what rate, or what proportion of the time) does Y occur? That is a purely descriptive question, but it is often a very crucial underpinning to the interpretation of other information. A second general form of comparison question, and one that has been given far more attention than the baserate question, is the relational question. Are X and Y related? Do they occur together? That relational question has two major forms, which together subsume most of the questions that are asked in behavioral and social science research: the correlational or covariation question, and the comparison or difference question.

Baserates. If I do not know how often Y occurs in the general case, then I really have no basis for deciding whether the rate of Y in some particular case is or is not "notably" high or low.

For example, some researchers recently found that there was a surprisingly high rate of birth defects among infants born to women who worked at jobs involving continual use of video display tubes. One set of people (Nine to Five, an organization concerned with the rights and well-being of working women) interpreted that data as indicating that video displays represented a health hazard, at least for pregnant women. Another set of people (agents of the organization whose women workers had shown such high rates of birth defects in their pregnancies) interpreted the same numbers as not being indicative of any hazard, arguing that we do not know the baserates of birth defects for the pregnancies of working women — of the same age, social class and so forth — who do not work with video display tubes. Incidentally, the policies advocated by the two groups, not surprisingly, were in similar sharp contrast to each other. Nine to Five urged some policies that would reduce the exposure of pregnant women to video displays and would protect their job rights at the same time. The management group urged "more research" — presumably in pursuit of the missing baserate information and perhaps in exploration of possible effects from the video displays — but no other changes in working conditions.

Such differences in interpretation of the same evidence are pervasive throughout the behavioral and social sciences. They are especially important in research dealing with various political, economic, and social issues. Those same kinds of disagreements also confront the physical and biological sciences: How much exposure to radiation is "acceptable"? What are tolerable levels of exposure to asbestos, dioxin, and many other environmental contaminants? Does smoking really "cause" cancer or heart disease, or is the evidence "merely correlational"?

Furthermore, the obvious influence of self-interest on those interpretations holds equally for the so-called "exact sciences" of physics, chemistry, physiology and the like, as it does for the admittedly less fully developed sciences that deal with human behavior. Researchers who are concerned with the spread of cancer, such as members of the American Cancer Society, are likely to see the evidence about cigarette smoking as damning; whereas researchers who are in some way reflecting the interests of the tobacco industry are more likely to dismiss that evidence as "mere correlations". Similarly, groups with environmental concerns see as hazardous the same levels of exposure to contaminants that representatives of chemical companies see as perfectly safe.

Such differences in interpretation are also frequent in the study of human-computer interaction. It often seems that the protagonists for particular systems find more virtues and fewer limitations in those systems than do other researchers.

While all of these differences in interpretation and policy recommendation would not be resolved by accurate baserate information, at least many of them would be put in more tractable form if scientists —physical and biological as well as behavioral and social — would give more attention to accumulating accurate baserate information, for complex sets of operating conditions, than has been the case for most topics in the past.

The correlational question. The relational question, in correlational form, asks whether there is systematic covariation in the values (or amounts or degrees or magnitudes) of two (or more) properties or features of some "system". In other words: Do the values of property X covary with the values of property Y? If X is high for some "case," is it likely that Y will also be high for that case as well? And if X is low for some case, is it likely that Y will also be low for that case? For example, does happiness vary with age?

A high positive correlation between X and Y means that when X occurs at a high value, Y is also likely to be at a high value; and that when X is at a low value, Y is also likely to be low. In the example noted above, this would mean that older people (that is people with high values of X, age) would by and large be happier (that is, have generally higher values of Y) than younger people? The correlation between X and Y could also be high and negative, if high values of X went with low values of Y and vice versa. If that were the case for the example, then younger people would be, by and large, happier.

When there is little or no correlation, positive or negative, between X and Y, then cases with high values of X will be just as likely to have low, medium, or high values of Y, and vice versa. In the example, that would mean that older and younger people both vary in happiness, with some of each having high levels of it and some of each having less of it. To say that there is a low or zero correlation or association between X and Y implies that knowing the value of X for any given case does not give us any clue at all about what value of Y that case is likely to have. Another way of saying that is to say that a zero correlation between X and Y implies that X has no predictive power with respect to Y. Still another way to put the matter is to say that a zero correlation means that X and Y do not covary.

Consider the example given above, of age and happiness. It might be the case that the highest level of happiness occurs at some age other than the very oldest or the very youngest. For example, happiness might tend to increase up to age 35, then remain roughly the same. That would indicate a *nonlinear* correlation. In such a case, the correlation or covariation could be just as strong, but more complicated in its form, than for the simple linear case. There are a number of statistical tools that allow the researcher to investigate nonlinear, as well as linear, correlations. Unfortunately, behavioral and social scientists far too often do not use such non-linear tools when the evidence to be examined might well require them. As the shape of the relation becomes more complicated —e.g., suppose on the average happiness decreased from young child to adolescent, then increased up to about age 45, then decreased again, but flattened out after 65 —our statistical tools become more cumbersome to use, and fewer of them are appropriate for the task of assessing such complex forms of relation.

Much research in the social and behavioral sciences makes use of correlations, linear and nonlinear, that involve two, three, or more variables. Such a correlational approach requires being able to measure the values of X, and of Y (and of the other variables, if more than two are involved), for a series of "cases" that vary on X and on Y (and on the other variables involved). ("Cases," here, mean "actors behaving in contexts," as discussed in the first section of this chapter.) In the example used above, that would mean getting a measure of age and of happiness for each of a series of individuals who make up the sample of a given study. The correlation between these two sets of values can tell you whether X and Y go together; but it cannot help you decide whether X is a cause of Y, or vice versa, or both, or neither. That is to say, the correlation comparison techniques can assess conceptual relations that imply covariation between two (or more) variables; but they cannot assess any conceptual relations that are causal in their implications.

The Difference Question. Another form of the relational question is the comparison or difference question. The difference question involves asking, essentially, whether Y is present (or at a high value) under conditions where X is present (or at a high value); and whether Y is absent (or at a low value) when X is absent (or low). For example, do groups perform assigned tasks better (Y) when members like each other (X) than when they do not.

You could approach the assessment of this question in either of two ways. One way would be to go around collecting measures of "liking" in groups until you had gathered a bunch that were high on liking and another bunch that were low on liking (and perhaps a bunch at intermediate levels), and then compare the average task performance scores for those batches of groups. That kind of study would be, in effect, a messy version of the correlational approach —one that gave up much of the power of correlations without gaining any advantage in making a stronger interpretation of causal direction in the results.

A more useful approach to the comparison question would be: To create some groups with members who do like each other, and some other groups with members who do not like each other; then, to give both sets of groups some common tasks to perform; and then, to see if the average task performance (Y) of the "high liking" groups (X) is higher than the average task performance of the "low liking" groups (not-X). For the comparison to be most useful, you would need to make sure that the two sets of groups were the same, or comparable, on all of the other factors that might affect task performance, such as: difficulty of the task, availability of task materials, quality of working conditions, task-related abilities of members, experience and training of members, and many more. You might render the groups comparable on some of those factors by controlling them, so that each factor occurred at a certain single constant value for all groups of both sets. For example, you probably would want to have all groups in both conditions do exactly the same tasks. For some other features of the situation, that you could not hold at a constant value for all "cases" — such as intelligence or task abilities of members — you might want to match the groups, on the average, between the two conditions, for those factors. You might even want to manipulate a second or third variable in addition to your manipulation of "group liking" — perhaps group size, for example —so that you could ask about task performance as a function of differences in that other factor, and of differences in the two factors at the same time. For example, you might want to assess whether group liking had more of an effect on task performance for small groups than for larger ones. (Questions about the joint effects of differences in two variables — say factor A and factor B — on the level of a third variable — say Y — are often referred to in the research literature as "interaction effects").

RANDOMIZATION AND "TRUE EXPERIMENTS"

You can only measure, match, control and manipulate a limited number of variables in any one study, and there are usually many more factors that are potentially important to the phenomena you are studying. You have to do *something else* about all of the rest of that rather large set of potentially relevant factors. The main "something else" that you can do is called Randomization, or random assignment of cases to conditions.

Randomization means using a random assignment procedure to allocate "cases" to "conditions." In the above example, that would mean using some random method for assigning individuals in your sample to groups that were to be high in liking and those that were to be low in liking (and to large and small groups of each kind). For an allocation procedure to be random, each case must be equally likely to end up in any given combination of conditions. Using the previous example, for instance, that would mean that any given individual is equally likely to be in a "high liking small size" condition, a "high liking large size" condition, a "low liking small size" condition, or a "low liking large size" condition. (You must take into account, of course, the difference in numbers of individuals that would be used in large and small groups).

Your study must include some procedure for random allocation of cases to conditions in order for your study to be what Campbell & Stanley (1966) call a "true experiment". (Their distinction between "pre-experiments," "true experiments" and various kinds of "quasi-experiments" are discussed in a later section of this chapter). If you do have such randomization, then you strengthen the credibility of your information about high X going with high Y (and low X with low Y). It is plausible that the difference you produced by manipulating X caused the observed difference in Y. It is not plausible that Y caused X (since you know that you caused X to be high in one set of groups and low in the other). And, since you assigned cases to high X and low X conditions by a random procedure, it is not likely (though it is possible) that the high X cases were all high on some extraneous factor that caused high Y, while the low X cases were all low on that same factor. For example, if you assigned individuals to "high liking" and "low liking" groups by a random procedure, as in the example given above, and then those groups differed later in their average task performance scores, it is unlikely (but not impossible) that they differed because all of the people who happened to end up in the "high" condition on a chance basis had more than average task ability, while all the people who, by chance, were assigned to the "low" groups happened to be below average in task ability.

Note that this line of argument involves likelihood or probability, not logical certainty. *A random allocation procedure does not guarantee an equal distribution of any, let alone all, of the potential extraneous factors* among the conditions being compared. Rather, a randomization procedure makes a highly unequal distribution on any one of them highly unlikely (but not impossible). So the reasoning from even a true experiment involves inductive rather than deductive logic, probability rather than certainty.

The effectiveness of randomization for actually rendering the sets of cases in different conditions "not different" from one another depends on the number of cases being allocated. Furthermore, you can never know for sure that some one particular factor did not end up —by the luck of the draw — quite mal-distributed across the conditions of your study. If such a factor is operating, and is also related to the phenomena you are studying, it will distort your results and you will have no way to know it. This is often called "confounding". Of course, if you had not used a random allocation procedure, such a mal-distribution across conditions would almost certainly have occurred, perhaps for many variables. You would also not know which ones or in what directions they were producing distortion in your data. And each of them would contribute to the confounding of your results. (Confounding in research evidence is like noise in a communication system. The more noise that is present, the more likely it is that the "signal" or "information" will be masked or distorted).

You can see that true experiments are potentially powerful techniques for learning about causal relations among variables. But, as in all aspects of research methodology, you buy this high power at a high price in two ways. First, you reduce the scope of your study, insofar as you hold variables constant, and insofar as you make your experimental variables (your X's) occur only at a few levels (e.g. high vs. low liking, or 3 person vs. 5 person vs. 8 person groups). The results of your study will thereby be limited in the range of conditions over which the findings can be generalized. Second, you reduce the realism of context of your study, inasmuch as your activities (rather than "nature") have created the groups, designed the tasks, and elicited behavior that served your — not the participants' — purposes.

SAMPLING, ALLOCATION AND STATISTICAL INFERENCE

The basis you use for choosing the cases that are to be included in your study, out of a larger population of potential cases, also has a substantial effect on the credibility of the evidence resulting from your study. Most of the ways that social scientists have to assess correlations and differences rely on statistical reasoning that requires that the cases in the study be a "random sample" of the population to which the results apply. So, your results really apply to that population of which your cases constitute a random sample. For example, suppose you chose cases by talking to all the people who left a dining hall by a certain door, starting at 12:30 Wednesday. Your results, strictly speaking, would apply to a population that does not include: people who do not eat at that dining hall, people who leave by another door, people who eat quickly, people who have a Wednesday class that goes through lunch hour, and, of course, people who refuse to talk to "interviewers" who stop them in public places. The question is not whether you "have a random sample." The question always is: given your procedures for selecting cases, what is the nature of the population of which you actually have a random sample? It is to that population, and only that one, that your results apply.

There is sometimes confusion in the use of the term random in discussing how one goes about choosing a sample of cases from a population, and in discussing how one allocates cases (already selected to be in the study) among the conditions of that study. Both selection and allocation of cases require that there be a random component in the procedure. In the sampling case, the procedure is designed to determine which cases, out of some larger population, will be included in a given study. In the allocation case, the procedure is designed to determine which conditions each given case —already selected as part of the study — will be assigned to. The two are alike in that, for both population sampling and allocation of cases to conditions, the term random refers to a procedure, not an outcome. You do not actually "select a random sample." You select a sample by using "a random procedure". There is no guarantee that the resulting sample will be a mirror of the population. That is, you have no guarantee that your random sample (the sample you select with a random procedure) will yield a representative sample (that is, a distribution of cases that mirrors the population from which you sampled). Similarly, you do not actually "allocate a random set of cases to each condition." You allocate cases among conditions by using "a random procedure". There is no guarantee that the sub-samples will in fact be comparable in any respect. But in both cases — sampling from a population and allocating cases to conditions within your study — using a random procedure is your best bet. That is, using a random procedure to sample from a population or to allocate cases gives you the best chance that the resulting population will be representative, and that the resulting allocation of cases to conditions will be unbiased.

The preceding discussion also suggests one reason why the size of samples used (the number of cases that are to be randomly allocated to conditions) is crucial to the credibility of experimental results. The larger the number of things to be allocated by some random procedure, the more the distribution of those cases will approach the "idealized" random distribution. For example, the probability that "heads" or "tails" will result from the flip of a coin is 50-50. But each actual flip is either heads or tails, and it would not be particularly surprising if the distribution of 10 flips was other than 5 to 5 — say, 6 to 4 or even 7 to 3. As the number of coin flips is increased (assuming, of course, an honest coin and an honest flip), the more the distribution of heads and tails is likely to approach 50-50. It will still not be surprising if, for 1000 flips, the results were close to but not exactly 500 each (say, if results were 513 heads to 487 tails). But a distribution of 700 heads to 300 tails for the flip of 1000 coins is much less likely than a distribution of 7 heads to 3 tails for the flip of ten coins.

This same kind of probabilistic reasoning is the basis for deciding whether a given difference, found within the comparisons of a research study, is or is not to be taken seri- ously. Suppose you have created conditions in which there are two sets of cases known to differ in a particular feature (i.e., having X and not having X, as in the preceding dis- cussion), known to be alike in many other respects (that is, to be alike on factors for which you exercised experimental control), and known to have been allocated to the two conditions by some random procedure (and therefore not likely to differ much on any particular other characteristic). Suppose, further, that the two sets do show a difference in their average values on a feature of interest, Y, that you had allowed to vary and mea- sured for each case. How do you know whether or not that difference in average Y val- ues (for the set of cases that had X versus the set that did not have X), is a "real" or "meaningful" difference, rather than being just a small difference that occurred by chance—like the case of the 1000 coin flips that ended up 513 heads and 487 tails?

The underlying logic of much statistical inference about differences (and correla- tions, too) can be illustrated by going back to the coin flip example. If we flipped a coin ten times, resulting in 6 heads and 4 tails, or 7 heads and 3 tails, we would not be espe- cially surprised. Nor would we suspect the coin or the flip to be biased, dishonest. With only ten flips, we might argue, such a distribution of results is likely to occur fairly often just by chance. But if we flipped the coin 1000 times, we would be quite surprised —and quite suspicious of the fairness of the coin or the underlying procedure — if the results were 600 heads and 400 tails, or 700 heads and 300 tails. Our surprise and sus- picion would arise because such an uneven distribution would not happen very often if only chance (that is, the effect of some random process) were operating. And from such a line of reasoning, we might arrive at the conclusion (suspicion) that *something other than chance* must be operating for the result to be such an unlikely distribution of out- comes. What we would expect that "something" to be would depend on what else we knew, or suspected, about the situation (for example, that the coin is uneven, that the flipper is cheating, or the like).

Returning now to the case of the obtained differences in Y values for sets of cases that did and did not have X: Suppose we assume that both the X and not-X cases are drawn from the same overall population of cases, and (for the moment) assume that the presence or absence of X really does not make any difference in the value of Y —that is, that the only reasons that the two samples have different average Y values are the operation of chance factors. Imagine that we could draw a series of pairs of samples of cases from that population, each sample being drawn in a truly random fashion and each sample being the size of the samples in our study. We can calculate the chances of drawing a pair of samples that differed in their average Y values by as much as our two samples do if only chance factors were affecting which cases from the larger popula- tion ended up in each of the samples. Just as we can estimate the probability of getting a distribution of coin flips that differs a certain amount from the idealized "random dis- tribution" of coin flips, given that we know the number of coin flips involved, so we can estimate the probability of getting an average difference of a certain size (on some measure, Y) between two groups of cases—if only chance factors were operating!. When such calculations indicate that a difference as big as the one we actually obtained in our study would only very rarely occur if chance alone had been operating, we are likely to draw the conclusion (as we would in the case of the 700 heads to 300 tails) that something other than chance is probably involved in the difference (in average Y values) between the group of cases that did have X, and the group that did not have X.

Since we can state the probability of the result (that is, the proportion of time it would have occurred) if only chance were operating, that *probability value* is a rela- tively precise and quantitative *estimate of how confident we can be that something other than chance was at work.* But that probability value in and of itself does not help us determine *what* that "something other than chance" might have been that was respon- sible for the disparate outcome. Even when we conclude that the difference in average Y values between cases with and without X is probably not a chance difference, it does not follow that the difference was caused, solely or even partly, by the presence or absence of X itself. As with the case of the mal-distribution of coin flips, what you con- clude or suspect about what caused the difference depends on what else you know (or suspect) about the situation: What other factors, not adequately taken into account by your measures, controls and randomization procedures, could have been operating dif- ferentially between the two groups? These suspicions are sometimes referred to as plausible rival hypotheses (rival, that is, to the hypothesis that the presence or absence of X is the main causal factor).

VALIDITY OF FINDINGS

The idea of validity is central to the research process, yet it is a diffuse concept. One quite comprehensive discussion of validity issues (Cook & Campbell, 1979) posits four different types of validity: internal validity, statistical conclusion validity, construct validity, and external validity. All four are discussed in this section, along with some other related considerations.

Internal validity has to do with the degree to which results of a study permit you to make strong inferences about causal relations. That is, how close can you come to asserting that the presence of X (or variations in level of X) caused the altered level of Y values? From the preceding discussion, it should be clear that the mere existence of a difference in average values of Y for sets of cases for which X was and was not pre- sent (or was high vs. low) is not a sufficient basis for the conclusion that X caused Y. For one thing, the difference might have arisen just by chance. Some of the considera- tions involved in determining the non-chance basis of a finding (e.g., sample sizes) were discussed in the previous section. It is those and related statistical considerations that are involved in a study's *statistical conclusion validity*, which has to do with whether a given result (such as a difference in Y associated with a difference in X) is to be regarded as not due to chance.

There are other reasons why a difference in Y associated with a difference in X does not necessarily imply a causal role for X. Some other variables might have been covarying with X, and they, rather than X, might have produced the change in Y. Any such factor, that was neither measured, manipulated, held constant, nor matched across groups in your study, is a candidate for the role of "other variable" that is a plausible alternative or rival hypothesis about the cause of the difference in Y. If your study included a random procedure by which cases were assigned to conditions, such randomization can help rule out many such plausible rival hypotheses about the cause of differences in Y. How many and which rival hypotheses can be ruled out in any given case depends on the procedures by which randomization, experimental controls, matching, and other features were carried out in your study design. The internal validity of your study's findings depends on how well you can rule out —by the logic of your procedures as well as through certain comparisons in your results—all of the plausible rival hypotheses.

Construct validity asks such questions as: How well defined are the theoretical ideas of your study? How clearly understood are the conceptual relations being explored? How clearly specified are the mappings of those concepts and relations to the substance and methods with which they are to be combined? This form of validity obviously is related to the "fit" of elements and relations from the conceptual domain with those from the other two domains. Just what problems arise in this context depend on which of several alternative study paths are followed in a given case.

External validity refers to how confident you can be that the findings of your study will hold up upon replication, and how confidently you can predict both the range over which your findings will hold and the limits beyond which they will not hold. Obviously, some features of a study have a direct bearing on whether that study's findings are likely to prove generalizable: the size, nature, and mode of selection of the sample of cases used in the study; the degree to which the study involved relatively artificial, versus relatively natural, settings and procedures; and the like. Nevertheless, determining the generalizability of any particular set of findings in any definitive sense requires conducting one or more follow-up studies. No one study "has" external validity, in and of itself. Later studies may shed some light on the generalizability of its findings; and it may have shed some light on the robustness of findings from prior studies.

Threats to validity. Campbell and his colleagues (see references) have developed an excellent list of more than thirty major classes of plausible rival hypotheses that are potential threats to these four forms of validity. Which of these different classes of threats to validity are most problematic depends on which type of study design is being used, and which type of research setting provides the strategic context for the study.

Campbell and associates also have developed a classification of some 21 major types of study designs that have been or can be used in the study of a variety of behavioral and social science topics, and indicated which sets of plausible rival hypotheses are and are not frequent problems for each type of design. Some of the design types are "true experiments" in the sense discussed in the preceding section. Some strong inferences about the X-Y relation potentially can be made from these, although even these true experiments do not by any means eliminate all plausible rival hypotheses. Some of the design types are what Campbell and colleagues call "pre-experimental" designs, meaning that they fail to cope with a very large number of potential rival hypotheses. Some of the design types are what Cook and Campbell call "quasi-experimental" designs. As the name implies, these have some but not all the virtues of the "true experiment." For example, they may have a non-random, but specifiable, basis for allocation of cases to conditions. Compared to true experiments, these designs can deal effectively with some, but not nearly so many, of the plausible rival hypotheses; they permit some, though weaker, inferences about the causal status of the X-Y relation.

Besides these issues in study design, and the issues related to research strategies that were discussed earlier, the researcher also needs to take into account the various techniques that are, or could be, available for measuring, manipulating, controlling or otherwise treating key properties of the human systems that are the focus of our behavioral and social science studies. Some features of these operational level techniques for the Modes of Treatment of variables are discussed in the next section of this chapter.

CLASSES OF MEASURES AND MANIPULATION TECHNIQUES

POTENTIAL CLASSES OF MEASURES IN SOCIAL PSYCHOLOGY

Social and behavioral scientists have used a wide variety of techniques to measure the presence or values of the specific features of the human systems that they wish to study. By far the most widely used type of measure involves questionnaires or other forms of self-report, some of whose main strengths and weaknesses were noted earlier in this chapter. But researchers have invented a number of other approaches, some of which offset the weaknesses of self-reports but, of course, do so at the cost of incurring other weaknesses. Campbell and colleagues have provided a useful taxonomy of measurement methods and indicated their major strengths and weaknesses (See Webb, Campbell, Schwartz & Sechrest, 1966). That schema has been extended and elaborated by McGrath and colleagues (See Runkel & McGrath, 1972; McGrath, 1984; McGrath, Martin & Kulka, 1982; Brinberg & McGrath, 1985). A brief and simplified form of those ideas will be presented here.

Whenever an investigator wants to obtain a measure of some feature of a system being studied, he or she must somehow arrange for a record of that feature to be made for each case that is to be in the study, and made in such a way that the investigator will have access to it later. The information contained in the record is always about the human system being studied (the actor- behaving- in- context, whether that is an individual, a group, or whatever). And it is always to be used by the investigator (that is, scored, aggregated with other records, used in comparisons, and so forth). But the record of it can be made by any one of three parties: by the actor, whose behavior is the focus of study (or some representative of the actor when that is a multi-person unit); by the investigator who is conducting the study (or some person or instrument serving as surrogate of the investigator); or by some external third party who is not involved in the research and who makes a record of the behavior for some other purpose (e.g., records of attendance made for administrative purposes).

When such a record of behavior is made —by any of the three recording agents, participant, investigator or external party — it is important to ask whether the actors whose behaviors are being recorded are aware that the recording process is taking place and that those records will or may later be used for research (or other quasi-public) purposes. When the actors are aware that their behaviors are or may be recorded and used for purposes other than their own (e. g., for research purposes or for certain other kinds of quasi-public purposes such as administrative assessments within an organization or political activities within a community), then the ensuing behavior cannot be regarded as altogether "natural." This constraint on "naturalness" is quite apart from any other aspects of the research methodology, such as use of field or experimental strategies, and quite different from the state of affairs in nonhuman sciences (e.g., physics, chemistry, biology). The investigator must take that potential "unnaturalness" of behavior, that has been induced by the measuring procedure, into account as he or she uses (that is, scores, aggregates, analyzes, interprets) that evidence. This problem is sometimes referred to as the reactivity of measures. It is one major way in which social and behavioral science research often loses realism (criterion C as discussed earlier in this chapter) even when that research is done in natural or field settings.

We can use the two distinctions discussed above — "who makes a record of the behavior?" and "is the participant aware that his or her behavior is being recorded and used for research purposes?" — to structure a classification of six major types of measures. Records that the participants knowingly make of their own behavior are called Self-Reports. Records that participants unwittingly make by their behavior are called Trace Measures. Records of behavior made by the investigator (or some agent or instrument working for the investigator) are called Observations — and they may be by an observor "visible" to, or hidden from, the participants. Records of behavior recorded by some third party, for non-research purposes, are called Archival Records — and they may be done either with the expectation that the information will be public knowledge or with the expectation that it will not be public. The material to follow examines those six classes of data collection methods — Self-Reports, Trace Measures, Observations by a Visible Observor, Observations by a Hidden Observor, Public Archival Records, and Private Archival Records.

Self-Reports. The first of these six classes are the self-reports of participants, always done under conditions in which the respondents know that their behavior is being recorded for research purposes. An example would be responses on a questionnaire that the participants were asked to complete.

Observations. A second way to get records of behavior is by means of observations. This term refers to records of behavior (such as a record of the sequence of speakers in a group), made directly by the investigator, or made by someone substituting for the investigator (e.g., an experimental assistant), or made by some physical instrument that is serving the investigator (e.g., an automatic electronic counter, or a stopwatch). Sometimes observations are made under conditions in which the participants know that they are being observed; but other times observations are made without the participants being aware of it. So it is important to distinguish two classes of observational measures: Observations by a Visible Observer and Observations by a Hidden Observer. The crux of that distinction is really between observations known to be taking place (whether the observer is literally in sight or not), versus observations that are not known (by the participants) to be taking place. Sometimes "visible observers" are actually out of sight (e.g., working behind one-way mirrors) but their presence is known to the participants. Sometimes "hidden observers" are not literally hidden, as when data are gathered by eavesdropping on conversations on a bus or in a restaurant.

Archival records. A third way to get records of behavior is to analyze material in existing archives. These are records and documents that have been gathered and/or preserved by some third party, external to the research activity, presumably for reasons not related to purposes of the researcher. Examples would be the information contained in newspaper morgues and the files of other communication media; or in public or organizational records of births, deaths, promotions, marriages, and the like; or in private documents such as diaries, letters and logs. None of these records were made for purposes of research. But some of those records may have been made under conditions where the actors were aware that the behavior was likely to be recorded and those records were likely to be used —not for research purposes but for administrative or political ones. For example, one would presume that the public speeches of politicians are made under the expectation that they would become part of the public record. And one would presume that some forms of official transactions within organizations—election or appointment to an office, attendance or absence from duty, levels of output and of expenditures —are such that the performers assume that others will know about the behavior or its consequences. So these kinds of archival records should be regarded as reactive in a way similar to but not exactly the same as the reactive effects on questionnaire responses and behavior in the presence of visible observers. Other forms of archival records, though — such as diaries, private letters and the like — we might presume to have been made without any expectation that they would be used later for research or other quasi-public purposes (unless the source was a public figure). Still other archival material —such as the number of births in a county, or the annual gross national product, or the number of highway fatalities on a certain weekend —are clearly not affected, consciously or unconsciously, by the participants' awareness that their behavior or its results will become a matter of record. So, we can identify two types of archival measures, called Records of Public Behavior (e.g., records of "State of the Union" speeches, or of promotions in an organization) and Records of Private Behavior (e.g., behavior contributing to the birth or accident rates, or to GDP).

Trace measures. One final type of measure has been called Trace Measures (see Webb, et. al, 1966). These are records of behavior that are laid down by the behavior itself, but without the actors being aware that they are making such a record. They include traces of the behavior that are accretions of some sort, and traces that are evidences of erosions. For example: Users of a museum inflict wear on the floor tiles. Other things being equal, there will be more wear in the paths leading to the more popular exhibits. So records of tile wear could be an unobtrusive measure of public preferences for the various exhibits. As another example: Smudges on pages of library books could be an unobtrusive index of their use. As still another example: The number and types of liquor bottles in the garbage of a particular household or community could be an indicator of drinking and other social habits of those actors. These are like self-reports, in that they are the result of "recording" done by the participants themselves. But they are unlike self-reports in that the participants are presumably not aware that there will be a record of their behavior that will be used for research purposes. Hence, trace measures are far less reactive than self-reports —although, of course, they are beset with a number of other weaknesses, some of which will be noted below.

STRENGTHS AND WEAKNESSES OF TYPES OF MEASURES

These six types of measures —self-reports and traces produced by the participants themselves, observations made by hidden or visible observers in the service of the investigator, and archival records of public and private behaviors gathered and preserved by third parties external to the research — subsume virtually all of the techniques by means of which social and behavioral scientists have obtained measures of the features of the "actors - behaving - in - context" that they have studied. Measures of each type have both important advantages and serious weaknesses for social and behavioral science researchers. As with other aspects of the research process, there is not one "right" or "best" way to measure; and exclusive use of any one type of measure can compromise the value of the resulting information.

Self-reports. Self-reports include questionnaire responses, interview protocols, rating scales, paper and pencil tests. They are by far the most frequently used type of measure in behavioral and social science, and there are some very good reasons for that popularity. Self-reports are versatile, both as to their potential contents and as to the population to which they can be applied. One can ask questions on a self-report measure that deal with virtually any idea that one can express in words. And one can adapt such questions for use with most humans except for very young children. Self-reports are relatively low in both initial setup costs and subsequent cost-per-case. They also have low "dross rates"; that is, little of the information that is gathered gets discarded (something that is not always true for observations, trace measures, and archival materials). They take relatively little time to construct and to apply. But self-reports have a serious Achilles' heel: They are potentially reactive, since the participants are aware that their behavior is being done for the researcher's, not the respondent's, purposes. Such knowledge may influence how they respond. Participants may try to make a good impression, to give socially desirable answers, to help the researcher get the results being sought (or, alternatively, to hinder that quest). Such influences may enter deliberately or unwittingly. All self-report evidence is thus potentially flawed, though self-reports are nevertheless a very useful form of evidence.

Observations. Observations by a visible observer share with self-reports the serious problem of reactivity. They also are vulnerable to observer errors that derive from the fact that both humans and physical instruments that might be used for the observation and recording of phenomena are fallible. Unlike self-reports, observations can be used only on overt behavior, not on thoughts or feelings or expectations. But within that limitation, they are relatively versatile in their contents and in the populations to which they can be applied. Relative to self-reports, observations are costly in both time and resources, and have a rather high dross rate (at least as viewed on a per-observer-hour basis). Use of a hidden observer may reduce the problem of reactivity considerably, but such observations are still vulnerable to observer errors, are still costly in time and money and high in dross rate, and are generally less versatile with regard to both content and population. Furthermore, use of hidden observers raises some rather serious ethical concerns.

Trace measures. Trace measures, physical evidences of behavior left behind as unintended residue or outcroppings of past behavior, offer a sharp contrast to self-reports in both strengths and weaknesses. Their greatest strength is that they are unobtrusive; they do not interfere with the ongoing flow of behavior and events, and they are not likely to be affected reactively by the participants' awareness of the role of the physical evidence in later research. On the other hand, trace measures are not nearly so versatile as to content or population as are self-reports or observations. They are simply not available for many concepts one might wish to study. Furthermore, they are often quite loosely linked to the concepts they are alleged to measure. For example, specific kinds of trash in a garbage can (such as liquor bottles) may indicate any or all of many features of the life style of the residents: social class, gregariousness, family size, the presence of a drinking problem, and so forth. Much wear on certain floor tiles may indicate differential popularity of a certain exhibit; but it also could mark a path to the rest rooms or the museum cafeteria, or simply denote the part of the floor that was least recently retiled. Trace measures are often very time consuming to gather and process; they sometimes are costly; and they sometimes have a very high dross rate. Yet, their relatively unique status as unobtrusive and nonreactive makes them a very valuable potential class of measures, though a class that has as yet seen relatively little use in social and behavioral science.

Archival records. Archival records refer to such things as census data, production records, court proceedings, diaries, material from newspaper, magazine, radio and TV "morgues," and official administrative records, documents and contracts. Some of them are records of public behavior (such as political speeches, votes in a legislature), and are created or recorded with an eye to their public use —for administrative or political purposes, rather than for research purposes. These are likely to be as reactive as a questionnaire or as behavior in the presence of a visible observer. Others are records of essentially private behavior (such as birth rates, records of consumer purchases, and the like), and would seem to be as free of reactive biases as are trace measures or data from hidden observers. Both kinds are like trace measures in some of their vulnerabilities:

relatively low versatility of content and population; relatively high dross rates; sometimes only a loose linkage between the record and the concept to be represented by it. They are often far less costly than trace measures, since someone else has already gathered them. But they are often the only records of whatever they contain. Therefore, in terms used by Webb, et al. (1966), when you use a set of archival records in research, they are "methodologically consumed" —meaning that there is no opportunity to "cross-validate" your findings by getting more data on another set of comparable cases, as there would be with self-reports or data from direct observations. Nevertheless, they sometimes offer "best evidence," perhaps the only reasonable evidence, for research problems dealing with times long past, or with extensive periods of time, or with features of very large social units (large organizations, nation states).

Concluding comment about types of measures. All types of measures, therefore, have both strengths and weaknesses. And, like research strategies, study designs and other aspects of the research process, the strengths of one type can compensate for and offset the weaknesses of another. But unlike strategies and designs, the investigator is not constrained to use them one at a time. On the contrary, it is both possible and crucial to get more than one type of measure for each key variable that is to be measured in your study.

TECHNIQUES FOR MANIPULATING VARIABLES

In social and behavioral sciences, the techniques for manipulating variables are not nearly as well specified as are techniques for measuring them. Some ideas on the topic are presented in Runkel & McGrath (1972); those are drawn upon and extended here. Recall that an experimental manipulation requires that the investigator somehow make sure that all of the cases of each condition will have a certain predetermined value of the independent variable that is to be manipulated, while that independent variable value will differ for different conditions of the study. There seem to be three general classes of techniques by means of which investigators can produce experimental manipulations of variables in their social psychological studies. The investigator can try to manipulate a variable by: (a) selecting cases with desired values and allocating them to appropriate conditions of the study; (b) intervening directly in the systems being studied to produce the desired values in the appropriate cases; or (c) inducing the desired values in the appropriate cases by indirect means. These three approaches differ, considerably, in their strengths and weaknesses as techniques for experimental manipulation of variables.

Selection. Selection is often the most convenient means to make sure that all cases of a given condition are alike on a certain variable —that all are 6-year-olds, or females, or juries-that-dealt-with-a-murder-case—and that all the cases of another comparison condition differ on that variable —being all 10-year-olds, or males, or juries-that-dealt-with-a-civil-suit. But that convenience costs dearly in the uncertainty associated with the nature of the variable that you thus "manipulate." Manipulation by selection does not make for a "true experiment" because you cannot assign cases at random to the conditions of your study. With selection, you assign cases so as to differ systematically on X, and they of course will also differ systematically on all of the other things that —unbeknownst to you —go along with X. When you get sets of cases that differ on a variable by means of selection, you have only a limited idea of just how those sets of cases differ from each other. What are all the ways in which 6-year-olds and 10-year-olds differ? Or males and females? Or the juries that end up assigned to criminal and civil cases? They probably differ in the ways you had in mind —e.g., the 10-year-olds are better at arithmetic than are the 6-year-olds, and the civil juries are less guilt-ridden if they deliver a guilty verdict. But they also probably differ in myriad other ways as well —such as the 10-year-olds' superior strength, size, emotional stability, knowledge of language, and so on, and the civil jury's expectations of a shorter trial and less publicity. So when you do a study comparing average Y values for a set of cases that had a particular value of X (say, 6-year-olds, or males, or civil juries) versus a set that had a different value of X (say, 10-year-olds, or females, or criminal juries), the X carried in your manipulation (selection) has a lot of surplus meaning in relation to the X you are likely to have in your conceptual formulations of the problem. Results of such a comparison are as equivocal in their meaning as is the "meaning" (that is, the scope and limits) of "X as manipulated."

Direct intervention. Manipulation by direct intervention in the structures and processes of the ongoing system that is being studied is the surest way of achieving a definite and specifiable manipulation, at least for those situations in which it can be done. If you want to compare 6-person juries versus 12-person juries, or groups working on difficult tasks versus groups working on easy tasks, you can do this directly by creating a number of cases of each. Furthermore, you can do this in a way that permits a random allocation of specific participants to the conditions of the study—- with any given participant having a proportionately equal chance of being in a 6 or 12 person jury, or in a group with hard or easy tasks. In that way, you have not only manipulated the specific variable you had in mind —jury size, or task difficulty—in a direct and relatively pure fashion. You have at the same time distributed the impact of "all those other variables" that you are not studying. Hence, it is unlikely (though not guaranteed) that any one of those "other variables" will confound your results by being distributed just like the X condition (that is, for example, by being high in all the randomly composed 6-person juries or all the groups with difficult tasks and being low in all the randomly allocated 12-person juries or all the groups with easy tasks). Direct interventions are not likely to be very costly or very time consuming, and they ordinarily have a very low dross rate —you get what you intended in each case, a difficult task or a 12-person jury, with relatively little slippage.

But direct intervention, too, has its limitations and its costs. For one thing, it is applicable only for relatively overt and tangible variables (see discussion of induction, below). So, while it will deliver specified values of X in relatively pure form, it will only work for relatively superficial X's. This is similar to the idea of low versatility in a type of measure. At the same time, in many cases such direct manipulations are apparent to the participants, so results may suffer from reactivity effects. For example, there is an extensive research literature on the presence of unintended "experimental demands" in many studies, and how to deal with them. Experimental demands are unintended cues in the situation facing an experimental participant, cues that may seem to tell him or her what the experimenter "really wants" the participants to do, and thus may influence the participant's behavior and thereby confound the results.

Inductions. Manipulations by less direct interventions are called experimental inductions. There are three main forms by which an investigator can attempt to manipulate a variable by indirect induction. One is by use of misleading instructions to the participants. For example, in one social psychological study, participants were told that they had been put into groups designed to be compatible (or not designed to be compatible) on the basis of personality assessments previously gathered from them. They in fact were randomly assigned to groups that got the high or low compatibility instructions —in accord with principles of good experimental design. These instructions were designed to induce one set of the groups to develop higher group cohesiveness than the other set, even though there was no real objective basis for such a difference. The study was concerned with the subsequent effects of high vs. low cohesiveness on communication, influence and performance in groups.

A second means for inducing a desired level of a variable is use of false feedback. For example, some participants might be told that they had been successful in their performance on an initial trial (and others told that they had not been successful), in order to study the effects of perceived success (or failure) on subsequent performance, or aspirations, or self-esteem. What is important from the experimenter's point of view is not that the feedback must be false, but rather that which person is to get which experimental condition is set by a (random) allocation procedure. Hence, the feedback is not contingent on the actual performance it is supposed to reflect.

A third means for indirectly inducing a desired level of a variable is the use of experimental confederates. Here, one or more persons pretend to be normal study participants, although they in fact are confederates of the investigator. During the course of the study, they carry out pre-planned activities (e.g., make false judgments, or start an argument, or deviate from the others in their opinions on the topic being discussed) designed to induce certain conditions in the naive study participants. In one classic study, for example, Asch (1954) had several confederates and only one naive participant making judgments about the relative length of lines displayed to them. On certain predetermined trials, the confederates all gave a certain incorrect answer. The study was designed to explore the effects of such social pressure on judgments by the naive participants, and on their feelings and beliefs as well.

Manipulation by indirect induction of the intended conditions is in some ways like use of a hidden observer. It involves deception, so it always raises some ethical issues. It also runs some risk of being detected by the participants, in which case it not only does not work as intended but also can backfire to the detriment of the overall research activity. At the same time, if it is carried out without raising the suspicions of the naive participants, then it potentially can produce the desired conditions for the appropriate cases, and do so without necessarily raising reactivity problems.

But what was said, above, about experimental demand certainly holds for these inductive conditions as well as for direct interventions. The situation may be teeming with "hints" as to what the experimenter really is up to, and what he or she wants the participants to do, or at least the naive participants may see the situation in that way. As with self-report measures, inductions are fairly versatile in the content of the variables to which they can be applied. They are ordinarily fairly low in cost and time —although they can be costly indeed if they backfire.

Manipulation by induction presents special problems for later analysis and interpretation. What should the investigator do if, after applying the inductions to sets of cases that were randomly allocated to treatment conditions, it turns out that the induction did not "take" for some of the cases? For example, what if some of the groups in the "low compatibility" condition turn out to be high in cohesiveness? Or what if some of the groups slated to receive high success feedback did so poorly that they can tell that they failed, regardless of what the experimenter tells them about their scores? Should the investigator eliminate the cases for which the induction did not work, thus testing the hypothesis about the relation of X and Y with a "purer" distinction on X —but also testing it on sets of groups for which the allocation to conditions no longer reflects a random procedure? Or should the investigator make the comparisons on all of the groups intended to be in the various conditions, thereby preserving the effectiveness of the random allocation procedure, even though it is known that some of the cases did not "have" X when they were supposed to, and some of them may have "had" X when they were not supposed to?

This problem points up, in a special case form, how two of the forms of validity that were talked about in the preceding section of this chapter are tied to one another in ways that do not permit them to be maximized simultaneously. The two ways to proceed in the above example pose a tradeoff between clarity of the concept in its manipulated form (that is, construct validity) and the integrity of the random allocation procedure (hence, internal validity). Needless to say, this and other forms of manipulation also have implications for the other two forms of validity —statistical conclusion validity and external validity—and these implications often arise in the form of tradeoffs, or dilemmas, within the research process.

CONCLUDING COMMENTS ABOUT THE RESEARCH PROCESS

There is much more to be said about all of these topics: About the nature of the research process and the main features of the research process; about strategies by which research can be carried out and some of the strategic issues that they imply; about study designs, comparison techniques, various forms of validity, and ways of dealing with various threats to them; and about types of measures and techniques for manipulating and controlling variables, and their various strengths and weaknesses. There is far more than can be said here. Some further reading on these questions is suggested in the list of books at the end of the chapter.

Here is a summary of some of the key points of this chapter:

(a) Results depend on methods. All methods have limitations. Hence, any set of results is limited.

(b) It is not possible to maximize all desirable features of method in any one study; tradeoffs and dilemmas are involved.

(c) Each study (each set of results) must be interpreted in relation to other evidence bearing on the same questions.

So, any body of evidence is to be interpreted in the light of the strengths and weaknesses of the methodological and conceptual choices that it encompasses: The strategies, the designs, and the techniques for measuring, manipulating and controlling variables and for analyzing relations among them. Evidence is always contingent on all of those methodological choices and constraints. It is only by accumulating evidence, over studies done so that they involve different —complementary — methodological strengths and weaknesses, that we can begin to consider the evidence as credible, as probably true, as a body of empirically-based knowledge.

On the other hand, these strategies, designs, and methods together constitute a powerful technology for gaining information about phenomena and relations among them. It is true that each piece of information gained through those techniques is not certain, but only probabilistic. It is also true that each piece of information is not totally general; each piece is contingent on the means by which and the conditions under which it was obtained. It is therefore true that each set of results, to be meaningful and credible, must be viewed in the context of the accumulated body of information on that same topic.

But this need for careful accumulation of evidence should not be viewed as a limitation of research, but rather as a challenge to the research community. It also can serve as a reminder that the research process is, at heart, a social enterprise resting on consensus.

REFERENCES

Asch, S. (1951). Effects of group pressure upon the modification and distortion of judgment. In H. Guetzkow (Ed.), Groups, leadership and men. Pittsburgh: Carnegie Press.

Brinberg, D. & McGrath, J. E. (1985). Validity and the Research Process. Beverly Hills, CA: SAGE Publications.

Campbell, D. T. & Stanley, J. C. (1966). Experimental and Quasi-Experimental Designs for Research. Chicago, Rand-McNally.

Cook, T. D. & Campbell, D. T. (1979). Design and analysis of quasi-experiments for field settings. Chicago, Rand- McNally.

McGrath, J. E., & Brinberg, D. (1984). Alternative paths for research: Another view of the basic vs. applied distinction. In S. Oskamp (Ed.). Applied social psychology annual (Vol.5). Beverly-Hills, Ca.: Sage Publications.

McGrath, J. E. , Martin, J., & Kulka, R. A. (1982) Judgment Calls in Research. Beverly Hills, CA: Sage Publications, Inc.

McGrath, J. E. (1984). Groups: Interaction and performance. Englewood Cliffs, N.J.: Prentice-Hall.

Runkel, P. J. & McGrath, J. E. (1972). Research on Human Behavior: A systematic guide to method. New Your: Holt, Rinehart & Winston.

Webb, E. J., Campbell, D. T., Schwartz, R. D., & Sechrest, L. (1966). Unobtrusive measures: Nonreactive research in the social sciences. Chicago, IL: Rand-McNally.

Usability Inspection Methods: Executive Summary

Robert L. Mack
IBM T. J. Watson Research Center

Jakob Nielsen
SunSoft

This chapter provides an overview of the main usability inspection methods, with reference to the chapters that treat individual issues in more depth.

1.1 *Definition of Usability Inspection*

Usability inspection is the generic name for a set of methods based on having evaluators inspect or examine usability-related aspects of a user interface. Usability inspectors can be usability specialists, but they can also be software development consultants with special expertise (e.g., knowledge of a particular interface style for graphical user interfaces), end users with content or task knowledge, or other types of professionals. The different inspection methods have slightly different goals (see Section 1.2), but normally, usability inspection is intended as a way of evaluating user interface designs. In usability inspection, the evaluation of the user interface is based on the considered judgment of the inspector(s). The individual inspection methods vary as to how this judgment is derived and on what evaluative criteria inspectors are expected to base their judgments. In general, the defining characteristic of usability inspection is the reliance on judgment as a source of evaluative feedback on specific elements of a user interface.

Mark, R.L., and Nielsen, J. (1994). Usability Inspection Methods. Executive Summary of J. Nielsen and R.L. Mack (eds.), *Usability Inspection Methods*, John Wiley & Sons, pp. 1–23. Reprinted by permission John Wiley & Sons, Inc.

We can contrast inspections to other kinds of evaluation methods. The four basic ways of evaluating user interfaces are: *automatically* (usability measures computed by running a user interface specification through evaluation software); *empirically* (usability assessed by testing the interface with real users); *formally* (using exact models and formulas to calculate usability measures); and *informally* (based on rules of thumb and the general skill, knowledge, and experience of the evaluators). Usability inspections correspond to the latter category of informal methods.

With the current state of the art, automatic methods do not work and formal methods are very difficult to apply and do not scale up well to complex, highly interactive user interfaces. Empirical methods are the main way of evaluating user interfaces, with user testing probably being the most commonly used method. Often, real users can be difficult or expensive to recruit in order to test all aspects of all the versions of an evolving design. In this respect, inspection methods are a way to "save users." Several studies of usability inspection methods have discovered that many usability problems are overlooked by user testing, but that user testing also finds problems that are overlooked by inspection. This suggests that the best results are achieved by combining empirical tests and inspections. The relationship between usability inspection and user testing is discussed in many chapters, and in particular, by Desurvire (Chapter 7), Karat (Chapter 8), and Brooks (Chapter 10).

We coined the term "usability inspection" in reference to function and code inspection methods that have long been used in software engineering for debugging and improving code (Ackerman et al. 1989; Fagan 1976, 1986; Freedman and Weinberg 1990; Russell 1991; Stevens 1989; Weller 1993). Admittedly, most usability inspection methods that began to appear in the published HCI literature around 1990 were developed without much explicit connection to the achievements in the program inspection field. The main exception to this historical fact is the formal usability inspection method described by Kahn and Prail (Chapter 6), which was explicitly intended to leverage off developers' program inspection methods.

1.2 *Inspection Objectives*

Typically, a usability inspection is aimed at finding usability problems in an existing user interface design, and then using these problems to make recommendations for fixing the problems and improving the usability of the design. This means that usability inspections are normally used at the stage in the usability engineering cycle when a user interface design has been generated and its usability (and utility) for users needs to be evaluated.

Identifying Usability Problems

Usability problems can be defined as aspects of a user interface that may cause the resulting system to have reduced usability for the end user. Usability is a fairly broad concept that basically refers to how easy it is for users to learn a system, how efficiently they can use it once they have learned it, and how pleasant it is to use. Also, the frequency and seriousness of user errors are normally considered to be constituent parts of usability. Thus, a user can find an interface element to be problematic for many reasons: It might make the system harder to learn; it might make it slower for users to perform their tasks; it may cause usage errors; or it may simply be ugly or otherwise unpleasing. Much of the work of usability inspection is concerned with classifying and counting the number of usability problems found in an inspection. Such analyses depend on the exact definition of what constitutes a usability problem and judgments as to how different phenomena might constitute manifestations of a single, underlying problem. It is difficult to make these distinctions, but often common sense is sufficient to determine what constitutes a usability problem. From the general definition of usability problem, one can say that any aspect of the design where a change would lead to improved system measures on one or more usability measures should be counted as a usability problem.

Usability Engineering Lifecycle

Identifying user interface problems, either in testing or through inspections is important, but it is only a part of a larger process. After the list of usability problems has been generated, a development team must redesign the user interface in order to fix as many of the problems as possible. To do so involves further types of information and analyses; these begin to point to a larger usability engineering context. We will discuss the role of inspections in the larger context of usability engineering in later sections, especially in Section 1.5. The following three points provide an overview of the use of inspection problem reports for influencing design.

- Fixes and other redesign suggestions must be generated. Usability inspection methods are generally better at finding problems than at driving the design of improved user interfaces, so additional considerations based on other usability methods may be needed for this stage. Typically, usability problem reports do contain suggestions for redesigns as noted by Jeffries (Chapter 11) and Desurvire (Chapter 7). In many cases it is also obvious just from knowing about a usability problem how it can be fixed. Furthermore, some inspection methods recommend including meetings of teams of developers and usability specialists (Wixon et al., Chapter 4; Kahn and Prail, Chapter 6) where redesign solutions can be hashed out.
- Effective use of a list of usability problems typically requires that these problems be prioritized with respect to the severity of each problem. As discussed in several chapters, most notably Brooks (Chapter 10), priorities are necessary to avoid expending disproportionate efforts on fixing usability problems that may not matter much to users anyway. Severity ratings are normally derived from an estimate of the expected user or market impact of each usability problem. In general, severity ratings are not a mainstream characteristic of usability inspection methods, but Nielsen (Chapter 2), Karat (Chapter 8), and Desurvire (Chapter 7) do give some examples of how to rate usability problems.
- Finally, it is necessary to get an estimate of the software cost associated with implementing the suggested redesigns. Several software engineering methods exist for estimating the programming cost. Although they may not be highly accurate, they can still provide useful information for the rough cost-benefit analysis that will be needed to make the final decision as to what usability problems can be fixed. Severe usability problems will normally be fixed no matter what their cost. It is often possible to fix many less severe problems that involve modest changes to the code. These trade-offs should not be considered part of the usability inspection method itself: It is preferable to have problem reports point out even those usability problems the inspector may judge to be too expensive to fix, because it is sometimes possible for design teams to develop alternative and much cheaper redesign suggestions.

Team Building and Education

Another objective of usability inspection methods can be the communication of information among the members in group inspection methods (Wixon et al., Chapter 4). As noted by Kahn and Prail (Chapter 6), there are considerable educational benefits to be gained as inspectors without usability expertise are made aware of the usability problems found by inspection. This exposure to additional usability concerns seems to be an effective way to increase developers' appreciation for the user-oriented perspectives in software development.

Usability inspection can also be used in traditional courses since the discussion of lists of usability problems is a good way to make usability issues and problems concrete for the students. Nielsen (Chapter 2) describes ways in which instructors can use usability inspection to provide rapid training of students in user interface design classes.

1.3 *Inspection Methods*

Usability inspection is the generic term for several methods, including at least the following eight:

- *Heuristic evaluation* (Chapter 2) is the most informal method and involves having usability specialists judge whether each dialogue element conforms to established usability principles. These principles are normally referred to as the heuristics (see Table 2.2 on page 30 for a sample list of heuristics) and give the method its name.
- *Guideline reviews* are inspections where an interface is checked for conformance with a comprehensive list of usability guidelines. However, since guideline documents contain on the order of 1,000 guidelines, guideline reviews require a high degree of expertise and are fairly rare in practice. This book does not contain a specific example of guideline reviews, but the method can be considered as somewhat of a cross between heuristic evaluation and standards inspection.
- *Pluralistic walkthroughs* (Chapter 3) are meetings where users, developers, and human factors people step through a scenario, discussing usability issues associated with dialogue elements involved in the scenario steps.
- *Consistency inspections* (Chapter 4) have designers representing multiple projects inspect an interface to see whether it does things in a way that is consistent with their own designs. Thus, consistency inspections are aimed at evaluating consistency across the family of products that has been evaluated by an inspection team.
- *Standards inspections* (Chapter 4) have an expert on some interface standard inspect the interface for compliance. Thus, standards are aimed at increasing the degree to which a given interface is in the range of other systems on the market that follow the same standards.
- *Cognitive walkthroughs* (Chapter 5) use a more explicitly detailed procedure to simulate a user's problem-solving process at each step in the human-computer dialogue, checking to see if the simulated user's goals and memory for actions can be assumed to lead to the next correct action.
- *Formal usability inspections* (Chapter 6) are intended to be very similar to the code inspection methods with which many software developers are already familiar. In this method, the various participants have well-defined responsibilities: A moderator is appointed to manage both individual and focused inspections, and the full team inspection meeting; a design owner is responsible for design and redesigns; the inspectors have the job of finding problems; and a scribe records all defects and issues identified during the meeting. Inspections are performed through a six-step process: planning, a kickoff meeting, a preparation phase where inspectors review the interface individually, the main inspection review when the inspectors' lists of usability problems are merged, and a follow-up phase where the effectiveness of the inspection process itself is assessed.
- *Feature inspections* focus on the function delivered in a software system; for example, whether the function as designed meets the needs of intended end users. Feature inspections can involve not only evaluation of a function, but can also involve the design of that function. Feature inspections are not discussed in any depth in this book, although several chapters refer to the need for inspections to focus on the usefulness of interface function, and not simply the usability of the interface, as an implementation of that function (e.g., Desurvire, Chapter 7). Another example referred to in this book is programming walkthroughs, discussed briefly by Wharton et al. (Chapter 5) as a variation of cognitive walkthroughs. The objective of the programming walkthrough is to design a programming language, starting from general attributes of the language, and elaborating the goals, subgoals, and actions required to accomplish a specific programming task. Programming walkthroughs are also discussed in depth in Bell (1992), and Bell et al. (1994).

1.4 *Inspection Methodology Issues*

Choosing a usability inspection method requires consideration of several methodology issues, beginning with the objectives of the inspection. Nearly all chapters discuss one or more of these issues. Moreover, inspection objectives are typically driven by development constraints, as much as by the appropriateness of a method for some usability-related objective. In this section we provide a brief summary of these methodology issues and pointers to chapters that focus discussion on them. We also recommend Chapter 4 by Wixon et al. for its suggested "lens of inspection" metaphor for making methodology decisions (see Figure 4.1 on page 80).

Objectives

We have already identified the high-level objectives of inspections: Identify potential usability problems and provide design-relevant information that can contribute to improving the usability of a product. In a software development context, however, these high-level objectives must be resolved into more specific objectives. Section 1.3 summarized several possible inspection methods, but selecting one of them requires a more specific objective. Objectives also often involve taking into account development constraints and trade-offs. Establishing clear objectives can only come with experience, informed by the experience of others as conveyed, for example, in case studies. All the chapters in this book discuss the importance of having clear objectives, but Chapter 10 by Brooks, Chapter 4 by Wixon et al., and Chapter 6 by Kahn and Prail, in particular, provide useful discussions and examples about the relation between the objectives of usability inspections and broader development contexts.

Inspection Framework

How does a usability inspection participant actually evaluate an interface? Each inspection method we summarized in Section 1.3 uses somewhat different guidelines. Heuristic inspections use heuristics that are derived from usability guidelines and principles. Examples are described in Chapter 2 by Nielsen, Chapter 8 by Karat, and Chapter 7 by Desurvire. Inspections based on evaluating conformity to an interface style, of course, adapt relevant guidelines in the form of checklists or heuristics. Examples are discussed in Chapter 4 by Wixon et al. These chapters also discuss variations in these heuristics which can reflect differences among users, the systems under evaluation, the user tasks involving those systems, and the objectives of the inspection in terms of what information the development team needs (again, see Chapter 10 by Brooks and Chapter 4 by Wixon et al.).

Cognitive walkthrough guidelines represent a clear contrast with interface guidelines and heuristics, at least on the surface. Cognitive walkthroughs are typically cast in the form of questions about the relationship between task goals attributed to users, and the interface actions needed to accomplish them (at least the actions the software designer intended). Chapter 13 by Wharton and Lewis and Chapter 6 by Kahn and Prail discuss the rationale and examples for such principles in depth; additional discussion can be found in Chapter 12 by Mack and Montaniz. These questions about goals and actions are generic, but are answered in the context of the specific task scenarios, appropriate for the users and task domain for which the interface is designed. Many variations in the specific form of cognitive walkthrough questions have been tried, and Chapter 6 by Kahn and Prail, Chapter 8 by Karat, Chapter 12 by Mack and Montaniz, and, of course, Chapter 5 by Wharton et al. provide or point to examples.

Deciding what guidelines to adopt is really deciding what usability inspection method to choose. This level of decision must be made by broader considerations, including the relative effectiveness of results provided by the method and how easy methods are to learn and use. These issues are further discussed later in the chapter.

Scenarios

Should inspectors evaluate an interface in terms of specific end-user tasks, or should they be encouraged to interact with the interface with more general and open-ended instructions? Most of the chapters that discuss applications of specific inspection methods make the case for asking inspectors to use specific task scenarios in their inspection. The rationale is that scenarios, properly chosen, represent how the system is intended to be used by end users. In this context, properly chosen means representative of end-user tasks or chosen explicitly to expose inspectors to particular aspects of the interface. Asking inspectors to evaluate the system in terms of task scenarios provides a task-oriented perspective on the interface. This perspective is essential for cognitive walkthroughs because task scenarios represent a structure and flow of goals and actions whose obviousness is precisely what inspectors are supposed to evaluate.

On the other hand, as Nielsen argues in Chapter 2, there are advantages to giving inspectors more open-ended instructions for evaluating a system. Real users will not necessarily be given explicit task scenarios. They will generate their own goals and combine exploration, inference, and training to map them into interface actions. Moreover, giving inspectors specific scenarios, while it controls their focus, also constrains what they might try doing with the system, and hence what they might discover. To the extent that inspectors create their own task-orientation, they will explore the interface through scenarios anyway.

The use of scenarios involves the obvious trade-off between ensuring that inspectors inspect an interface in terms of a specific focus and task flow that a usability specialist cares about, and allowing a potentially more open-ended and inspector-driven exploration and exposure to an interface. Scenarios ensure that certain interface features are evaluated. Controlled comparisons across users or other conditions are possible. When scenarios are not prescribed, there is potentially more opportunity for inspectors to explore more diverse aspects of the interface, although this depends on the instructions inspectors are given, and how complex the interface is. Inspectors who are not given specific scenarios typically explore the interface in terms of meaningful tasks of their own choice. As we suggested, the range of tasks that might be spontaneously carried out depends on how much inspectors are encouraged to explore and how task-oriented they are. Of course, in some cases, a system under inspection may have a limited set of tasks associated with it and scenario-driven inspection is constrained. Desurvire (Chapter 7) and Nielsen (Chapter 2) both discuss examples involving phone-based interface prototypes.

For the evaluation of very complex domain-specific systems, scenarios can be created from actual user task data to help the inspectors understand how users are expected to interpret and act on the interface. The scenario can thus supply the domain knowledge needed to operate the system that the inspectors may not have and allow them to perform their evaluation even when they are not domain specialists themselves (Bradford, Chapter 9; Nielsen, Chapter 2).

Inspector Experience

Who should carry out inspections? What experience and skills should inspectors have? Several chapters compare inspections carried out by groups with different types of expertise. Nielsen (Chapter 2), Desurvire (Chapter 7), and Karat (Chapter 8) discuss these questions for heuristic evaluation; and Kahn and Prail (Chapter 6), Mack and Montaniz (Chapter 12), and Wharton et al. (Chapter 5) discuss them for cognitive walkthroughs. Not surprisingly, experience with usability guidelines, user testing, and the design of user interfaces, leads to more effective usability inspection problem reporting. This is compared to inspectors who are software developers but lacking interface or usability expertise, or inspectors who are not experts in either software development or usability.

Who should do inspections could also depend on other objectives for inspection. One original objective, discussed by Wharton et al. (Chapter 5), was to allow usability specialists to conduct inspections themselves, as a way to leverage usability expertise and as an alternative for laboratory testing involving end users. Another objective, also discussed by Wharton et al., is to give software developers who might not have experience with usability issues or usability testing, experience with a user-centered perspective on interfaces. Yet another objective, exemplified in Nielsen's heuristic evaluation method, is to have nonexperts, perhaps even end users, carry out inspections, but to do so with much less control and formality; hence, less cost than would be entailed by formal user testing.

Clearly, there is considerable discretion in deciding who should do inspections, depending on the objectives of inspection. A mix of expertise and experience provides an opportunity to take advantage of fresh perspectives on the part of nonexperts and the more thoughtful evaluations likely to result from usability experts. The trade-offs here are obviously in time and effort at finding, training, and engaging inspectors from these different groups.

Individual or Group Inspection

Should individuals carry out inspections or should they be conducted by groups? Nielsen (Chapter 2), Wharton et al. (Chapter 5), and Desurvire (Chapter 7) make the case for individual inspections where the inspectors work independently of each other before their inspection reports are combined (though Wharton et al. also support the possibility of cognitive walkthroughs in group sessions). The rationale is to ensure that individuals have an opportunity to form their own intuitions about an interface and to feel free to make evaluations without being influenced by other opinions. Individual inspections can also be carried out by individuals at will, without the overhead of organizing group meetings.

On the other hand, there are advantages to having teams of more than one individual carry out inspections. Bias (Chapter 3), Desurvire (Chapter 7), Karat (Chapter 8), and Wixon et al. (Chapter 4) discuss these advantages in their chapters. People can reinforce each other, helping each other to notice problems that might not be seen individually. Conversely, there may be value to some level of critical evaluation of problems, if the problems that are "filtered out" are indeed implausible. Problem predictions that are not plausible end-user problems are potential false positives, and Jeffries (Chapter 11) discusses examples in more depth.

In fact, both individual and group inspections can be carried out in different phases of an inspection or as part of follow-on design activities. Nielsen (Chapter 2) discusses group debriefing of individual inspectors as one way of creating a group perspective on inspection problems, following a phase of individual inspections. Beyond the inspection (or end-user testing) process itself, the results of usability testing or inspection are typically presented to, and analyzed by, the larger design team. In this context it can be useful for the group as a whole to walk through interface screens in a scenario-driven way. Group design walkthroughs with a usability focus are an important type of design activity in a development project. Bias (Chapter 3), Kahn and Prail (Chapter 6), and Wixon et al. (Chapter 4), discuss group walkthroughs with this aim. (In Chapter 12, Mack and Montaniz also allude to examples of group design review and analysis, not otherwise discussed in this book: Karat and Bennett 1992a, b; Mack 1992.)

The trade-off in having both individual and group inspections is, of course, time. If time and inspectors are scarce, it may be necessary to make a decision about individual or group inspections. There are no clear-cut guidelines. It should be noted, however, that inspection results, like the results of user testing, must be analyzed beyond their raw form, in order to simplify them and derive implications for design. At some point, these follow-on analyses inevitably involve the larger development team.

Usability of Methods

Inspection methods need to be learned and applied efficiently. Existing inspection methods do differ in these two respects. One of the main motivations for heuristic evaluation is that it is relatively easy to learn and to apply. One of the main criticisms of cognitive walkthroughs is that the approach is not as easy to learn or to apply. This has led to several variations in the method; Chapter 5 by Wharton et al. discusses this evolution. Kahn and Prail (Chapter 6), and Mack and Montaniz (Chapter 12) also discuss potentially simpler variants.

The learnability and usability of an inspection technique is an important goal. With experience on the part of the HCI community, more efficient (and effective) methods will likely evolve. The cognitive jogthrough reported by Rowley and Rhoades (1992) may be an example (see also Wharton et al., Chapter 5). Of course, the effort to learn and to use a method could trade off with the effectiveness of the method in producing useful results. Currently, it is fair to say that the simpler technique, heuristic evaluation, is also the more effective in situations where the two techniques have been compared. However, it may be just as appropriate to view an inspection technique analogous to more traditional methods of usability testing and data analysis. A real mastery of empirical testing methods does require a degree of training and certainly experience with experimental design, data analysis, and so on. Analogously, cognitive walkthrough methods may require experience and only achieve their full potential over the long term. The cognitive walkthrough procedure takes time to learn, but once internalized, it can be applied efficiently (see Wharton et al., Chapter 5). For trained usability professionals, such an investment may be acceptable. For other professionals, such as software developers, this may not be the case. Finally, as Wharton et al. suggest there may be other objectives and results for which cognitive walkthroughs are better suited, such as generating design or interfaces.

1.5 *Usability Inspection and the Usability Engineering Lifecycle*

The preceding section discussed important methodological issues for choosing and adapting usability inspection methods, which motivated many of the discussions in the chapters of this book. Ultimately, however, we are interested in how usability inspection methods contribute to the larger context of usability engineering which certainly includes many other kinds of contributions by usability and software human factors specialists. This section continues to discuss methodology issues, but in the larger context. It is in this larger context that the objectives of usability inspection will be determined; hence, what specific method will be selected and where the results of inspections will be relevant. Consequently, the focus is on the validity of inspection data with respect to "real users'" experience, usefulness of data in influencing design, and the relationship between inspections, design and prototyping, and user testing.

Validity of Inspection Results

Ideally, we would want to answer many of the aforementioned methodology decisions by simply asking what set of decisions lead to the most effective results. Unfortunately, this turns out to be a difficult question to answer. The validity of inspection results can mean different things, but basically it is the answer to the question: How predictive are they of end-user problems? The answer to this question is important because ultimately we want to know how seriously to take problems identified by inspections, with respect to making recommendations for modifying software. Careful comparisons are hard to carry out and to interpret.

Jeffries (Chapter 11), Mack and Montaniz (Chapter 12), Nielsen (Chapter 2), Desurvire (Chapter 7) and Karat (Chapter 8) discuss in some depth the qualitative characteristics of concrete examples of usability problem reports and how well they predict (or fail to predict) end-user problems. We ask this question when inspection problem reports are obtained in place of user testing. We assume that problem reports predict problems that end users of the software are likely to actually have in laboratory testing. And the laboratory results are assumed, of course, to be representative of users' experience in the context of their work. The validity of inspection problem reports is analogous to the question of validity we have when we try to infer the usability of products in the marketplace from laboratory testing of usability involving representative end users.

In general, validity is defined relative to the criteria that are chosen to compare methods and results. The validity of results is related not to an absolute criteria, but to the goals and purpose of the work. This seems like a truism, but one often loses sight of it when discussing efficiency and validity which are sometimes treated as absolutes without mentioning a frame of reference.

The first comprehensive comparison of inspection techniques was done by Jeffries, Miller, Wharton, and Uyeda (1991). Their paper forms the background to several other comparisons reported in Chapter 7 by Desurvire, Chapter 8 by Karat (see also Karat et al. 1992), and Chapter 12 by Mack and Montaniz (see also Montaniz and Mack 1993). Jeffries et al. (1991) compared heuristic evaluation, cognitive walkthroughs, guideline-based inspection methods, and laboratory user testing. It is very difficult in any comparison to ensure that different inspection method and inspection group conditions are really comparable, but in general, the heuristic evaluation method resulted in problem reports that appeared to be better predictors of end-user problems (discovered in the laboratory testing) than cognitive walkthroughs or guideline-based inspections. Studies described by Desurvire and Karat in Chapters 7 and 8 report results consistent with the Jeffries et al. (1991) findings. In general, inspection problem reports typically do not predict end-user problems as well as we might wish, in order to confidently substitute inspection for end-user testing. Aggregated inspection problem predictions rarely do better than 30 to 50 percent of end-user problem types. Heuristic inspections appear to result in more overall predictions and better predictions of end-user problem types than cognitive walkthroughs. This is a broad generalization and the relative effectiveness of methods depends on many more specific factors, including the training and experience of inspectors, the type and severity of problem identified. The chapters by Desurvire (Chapter 7), Karat (Chapter 8), and Wharton et al. (Chapter 5) present in depth analyses of these interactions.

When considering the effectiveness of problem reports as problem predictions, not all problems are of equal interest. Identifying severe problems is especially important, and Jeffries (Chapter 11), Desurvire (Chapter 7), Karat (Chapter 8), Mack and Montaniz (Chapter 12), and Nielsen (Chapter 2) offer valuable suggestions on how to define severity, how to effectively classify the severity of problems, and how likely inspection techniques will identify severe problems. Severity is generally a derived measure based on how frequently a problem occurs and what impact it has on the user. Problems may be a nuisance, easily recoverable from, or may result in total task failure and extreme frustration for end users. These distinctions can be captured in severity ratings and, in some cases, in a qualitative analysis of problem content. There are no standards for analyzing severity, as Desurvire (Chapter 7) observes, but the chapters indicated above provide in-depth discussions of this important attribute of problem report content, as well as pointers to related literature.

Desurvire (Chapter 7), Jeffries (Chapter 11), and Mack and Montaniz (Chapter 12) discuss qualitative attributes of usability problems (predicted and observed in end-user testing) that may help explain misses or the failure of inspection problem reports to predict end-user problems. For example, in the case of inspections that are based on scenarios, it is possible that the problems end users have drive them into parts of an interface that create new tasks (and potential problems) which inspection participants do not experience in their more constrained situation. In effect, inspectors and end users are "evaluating" overlapping, but also partially incomparable sets of user task scenarios. Desurvire (Chapter 7), and Mack and Montaniz (Chapter 12) also distinguished different types of problems in terms of psychological function, noting that some types of problems may be easier for inspectors to infer and describe than others. For example, perceptual-motor problems involving the use of a mouse pointing device differ from seemingly more cognitive errors like choosing a wrong menu option. The former problems may not be obvious to inspectors unless they have experienced such problems themselves or observed them in others. Usability specialists with behavioral training or testing experience surely have an advantage here.

Nielsen (Chapter 2) offers a contrasting perspective on the predictability of inspection reports. Predicting end-user problems is highly desirable, of course, but if we grant that inspections are intended to substitute for testing, and that therefore we are not going to also collect end-user test data, we face a different problem in assessing the effectiveness of inspections. In this case we are interested in the relationship between number of inspections (and inspectors), and the number of problem types we can discover. This relationship has been the focus of Nielsen's work with heuristics evaluations, and is discussed in depth in his chapter. The good news for the "discount usability" perspective is that between four and five evaluators appear to be sufficient in most cases to identify 80 percent of the total usability problems we are likely to identify, in some asymptotic sense, with many more inspectors (and presumably would identify in end-user testing).

In addition to explaining the failure of inspection problem reports to predict end-user problems, we also need to account for problem predictions that do not correspond to end-user problems. These are false positives; Jeffries devotes much of Chapter 11 to discussing them. The issue for developers is whether and how to respond to predicted problems that do not occur for end users in a testing situation.

Finally, the validity of inspection problems, taken as end-user problems is the same question we must always ask with respect to more traditional end-user testing done in the laboratory. Inspections that do not use end users involve additional assumptions about how inspector intuitions (expressed in their problem reports) relate to "real" end-user problems. As Brooks (Chapter 10) quite effectively points out, however, usability problems are not the only thing a development team needs to worry about. She suggests that we assess the effectiveness of inspection methods and end-user testing against the insight they provide not only for usability, but also for the overall satisfaction customers ultimately come to have with the product in the workplace. Enhancing usability is important but not enough.

Effectiveness of Inspection Problem Information

Even more important than predicting end-user problems, is the effectiveness of inspection problem reports in improving the usability of an interface. This impact begins, of course, with a list of problem reports. Fixes and other redesign suggestions must be generated. Typically, usability problem reports do contain suggestions for redesigns as noted by Jeffries (Chapter 11) and Desurvire (Chapter 7); knowing about a usability problem is often sufficient to find an obvious way to fix it. However, usability inspection methods are generally better at finding problems than at driving the design of improved user interfaces, so additional considerations based on other usability methods may be needed for this stage. These considerations are also likely to require the involvement of the larger design team and additional methods that go beyond inspection procedures per se.

Several chapters, especially those of Desurvire (Chapter 7), Jeffries (Chapter 11), Kahn and Prail (Chapter 6), and Mack and Montaniz (Chapter 12), discuss qualitative characteristics of inspection report content and its relation to influencing interface design change. Inspectors often explicitly describe specific improvements or preferences in giving reports; these may be directly relevant to making potential design improvements. It can also be useful to encourage inspectors to describe potential problems in behavioral terms that describe possible underlying causes and consequences. These attributes of problem report content can provide useful clues for a design team about why problems occur and what to do about them. Similarly, it is useful when inspectors can make judgments about the potential severity of problems, whether in terms of quantitative ratings or in qualitative terms of describing the specific consequence of a user problem (e.g., losing data). Severity judgments can help to organize and prioritize problems. Jeffries' discussion in Chapter 11 of what makes an effective problem report is especially recommended.

Effective use of recommendations derived from usability problems typically requires that these problems be prioritized with respect to the severity of each problem and the cost estimated for implementing the suggested design change. As Brooks (Chapter 10) points out, priorities are necessary to avoid expending disproportionate efforts on fixing usability problems which may not matter much to users anyway. We discussed how problem severity can be analyzed in the preceding section. In general, severity ratings are not a mainstream characteristic of usability inspection methods. Severity ratings are normally derived from an estimate of the expected user or market impact of each usability problem; Nielsen (Chapter 2), Karat (Chapter 8), and Desurvire (Chapter 7) do give some examples of how to rate usability problems.

Another issue in problem analysis, discussed at length by Bradford (Chapter 9) and Jeffries (Chapter 11), is that software design problems are not always simple, but may involve larger design concepts that require more analysis and integration of results and implications across multiple interface features. A particular problem report may focus on a specific interface feature or issue, but on more careful examination, may point to larger issues or be correlated with other problem descriptions. In one example discussed at the workshop on which this book is based, an inspector predicted that some users might lose track of a newly created folder on a graphical windowing desktop. There was a visual discontinuity between the creation dialog and the desktop environment on which the newly created folder appeared, and the desktop was cluttered. This specific potential problem actually raised a more general question of how users find documents and folders on the desktop of this particular system. Inferring multiple views of a problem and synthesizing commonalities across superficially different problems requires the skills of a usability specialist.

Tackling these larger design issues also requires a good working relationship with the larger design and development team. These relationships are discussed by Brooks (Chapter 10), Kahn and Prail (Chapter 6), and Wixon et al. (Chapter 4). As Desurvire (Chapter 7) and Brooks (Chapter 10) point out, inspection data may not have the same surface credibility as user test data. For example, showing a video of a test user in a laboratory evaluation can be quite persuasive. It can be a challenge to establish the same kind of credibility for inspection data. Involving the design team in usability evaluations and inspections can be an effective way to increase the credibility of usability evaluations, as several contributors state, notably Bias (Chapter 3), Kahn and Prail (Chapter 6), and Wixon et al. (Chapter 4). Bias's "pluralistic walkthrough," involving end users, developers, and usability specialists in inspection teams is one promising possibility.

When to Use Inspection Methods

Given that usability inspections are part of a larger development process, it is also important to consider under what conditions inspections are appropriate or most effectively applied. With a few exceptions, such as feature inspection (discussed on page 6) inspection methods are not suited for use in the very early phases of the usability engineering lifecycle where no user interface design has been designed or implemented. During these early stages, methods like task analysis, competitive analysis, scenario writing, and envisioning can be used (Nielsen 1993a), but it is impossible to inspect and evaluate what does not yet exist. Similarly, inspection methods are poorly suited for usability engineering very late in the cycle, when the system has been released to the customers and the goal is to have them actually use it and get ideas for future versions. At this point, field studies, interaction logging, and the analysis of user-support calls are more appropriate than inspection methods.

In general, usability inspection methods require the existence of an interface design. They do not necessarily require this design to be *implemented*, however. Many inspection methods lend themselves to the evaluation of interface specifications because the methods do not require the inspector to actually *use* the system for anything. This means that inspections can be done relatively early in the design stage, especially compared to end-user usability testing (Bradford, Chapter 9).

Usability inspection methods are well suited as part of an iterative design process where they can be combined with other usability evaluation methods like user testing. A research result that has been replicated several times (Jeffries et al. 1991; Desurvire, Chapter 7; Karat, Chapter 8; Nielsen, Chapter 2) is that user testing and usability inspection have a large degree of nonoverlap in the usability problems they find. Consequently, it will pay off to use both methods in combination. A typical strategy is to apply a usability inspection method first to clean up the interface as much as possible, then to subject the revised design to user testing.

Cost-Benefit of Usability Inspection

Underlying decisions about what inspection method or method variant to use are trade-offs about time and resources. The cost and benefit of usability inspection, compared to end-user testing, or doing nothing, for that matter, is emerging as an important issue in the HCI community for planning and justifying the application of usability engineering methods in software development. Nielsen (Chapter 2) and Karat (Chapter 8) discuss the issue briefly in the context of usability inspections and provide pointers to more in-depth discussion (see Bias and Mayhew 1994).

Heuristic evaluation methods, for example, were originally motivated by Nielsen's "discount usability" perspective: Usability engineering activities are often difficult to justify and carry out in a timely way, but many activities can be done quickly and cheaply, and produce useful results. The methodology decisions we sketched in this section turn less on what is "correct" than on what can be done within development constraints. After all, with sufficient resources we would likely simply aim for rapid prototyping and end-user testing.

In contrast to the "discount usability engineering" perspective, cognitive walkthroughs appear more formal and "expensive." Learning the technique requires some exposure to psychological concepts and models of human problem solving and goal-oriented activity. The procedure itself involves a systematic question and answer protocol. With experience, the underlying concepts procedural formalities can be internalized and efficiently applied. The language of goals, actions, and task breakdown has considerable face validity in thinking about human-computer interaction, and the usability of user interfaces (see Wharton and Lewis, Chapter 13). The attractiveness of cognitive walkthrough for many practitioners likely lies in the fact that it bases itself on this perspective. The effectiveness of cognitive walkthroughs may be better judged in terms of long-term use and experience by specialists, and in the context of software design, in contrast to software evaluation.

The ultimate trade-off, as Nielsen notes in Chapter 2 (see also Nielsen 1994a), may be between doing *no* usability-related assessment of a developing product and doing *some* kind, however limited in scope or formality. We suspect that most methodology decisions, however unsatisfactory they might appear from some ideal perspective, will nonetheless result in an inspection process that will produce useful insights into the usability of an interface and contribute to improving that interface.

Virtually all usability inspection methods perform detailed evaluation of individual dialogue elements in a single user interface design. An exception is consistency inspection where the elements of two or more interface designs are compared in order to ensure that similar things are done the same way. Another exception is heuristic estimation (Nielsen and Phillips 1993; Polson et al. 1992b) where the overall usability characteristics of an user interface are assessed. A typical application of heuristic estimation is where some other usability method has found a usability problem with the interface design, but where the fix would be too expensive to implement without further justification. Heuristic estimation can then be used to estimate the time users would take to complete typical tasks with the interface and with the proposed revised design, resulting in task analysis that can serve as input to a cost-benefit analysis to determine whether the change should be implemented.

1.6 Research Directions

The methodological issues discussed in the preceding sections point to possibilities for direct methodological research. First, much work is needed to improve methods with respect to making more and better problem predictions and streamlining the inspection process (this is especially true of cognitive walkthroughs). One way to improve inspection methods would be to better understand the process of making inspections.

As suggested by Mack and Montaniz (Chapter 12), sensitivity to potential problems probably is driven largely by inspectors' own difficulties in using various interfaces, the likelihood of inspectors having similar problems, and inspectors' skill at reflecting on and generalizing these personal experiences. Similarly, in Chapter 2 Nielsen notes the similarity between usability inspection and having problems as a participant in an empirical end-user test. Research might be directed at finding ways to help inspectors become more aware of their own experience and generalizing it for purposes of making inspection judgments, as Desurvire suggests (Chapter 7). Can we provide tools or training that encourage problem report content that is informative with respect to describing concrete problems, problem severity, and possible design improvements? A better understanding of how users learn or accomplish goals with software tools may yet suggest more effective heuristics or evaluation frameworks. Analyzing the effectiveness of inspection guidelines may help. For example, Nielsen (Chapter 2) performed a factor analysis of a database of 249 usability problems to discover a set of heuristics that provided as broad explanations as possible of these problems. Cognitive theory may contribute here, as Wharton and Lewis argue in Chapter 13.

A second direction would directly tackle the question raised by several contributors, especially Brooks (Chapter 10), of how valid inspection data are with respect to the larger real-world context of software under inspection. What do inspections (or empirical data) really predict? Are schemes for characterizing problem severity valid in the marketplace? Answers to these questions bear on the cost-benefit justification for testing or inspections, on possibilities for improving inspection methods, or even for specifying what methods are best suited for what evaluation or design questions. A longitudinal study that focused on problems or feedback in terms specific enough to assess the relevance of earlier feedback during development, would be invaluable.

A third area of research would be to improve the way inspection data are analyzed and how results may be used more effectively in the larger development cycle. Design and evaluation should be, and typically are, tightly linked; this relationship needs to be understood and supported. Programming walkthroughs, mentioned earlier as an example of feature inspections (see Bell et al. 1994) suggest the possibility and value of closely integrating the evaluative and generative design capabilities of inspections. We suspect that many early design activities involve a close interleaving of generation and evaluation, sharing many of the attributes of cognitive and programming walkthroughs. Mack and Montaniz (Chapter 12) discuss examples of such design activities briefly, alluding to group design methods involving scenario-driven usability walkthroughs developed by Bennett (1984), and Karat and Bennett (1992a, 1992b). A recent example from our own (Mack's) laboratory involved taking seriously the often made recommendation to write a user manual for new software before a line of code is written. We wrote a quick reference guide for new users of a speech recognition interface for a graphical windowing environment (see J. Karat 1994), and used it to guide early interface design. We walked the design team through progressively more concrete versions of the design guide, comparing handwritten sketches of the designer's initial interface ideas against questions and tasks we thought were plausible for end users learning to use the system. We found this technique to be extremely useful in both evaluating design ideas and generating new ones. We did not use cognitive walkthroughs explicitly, but the language of goals and goal-action matches and mismatches was quite natural in this context.

Finally, we believe that there is a need to develop tools for cumulating, organizing, and helping to apply information based on inspections, not only within a single product development cycle but also across multiple products. Several chapters, especially Bradford (Chapter 9) and Jeffries (Chapter 11), suggested a need for methods of analyzing usability feedback, from inspections or from end-user testing, in more integrative ways for purposes analyzing broader design issues and trade-offs. We see promise in integrating design rationale schemes such as QOC (MacLean et al. 1991a, 1991b; see also MacLean and McKerlie 1994) with the analysis of design implications of inspection data. The QOC technique (an acronym for Question, Option and Criteria) lays out a space of design questions (or issues), and develops for each one a decision tree of design (or implementation) options associated with criteria that might be used for deciding among options. Important design issues and decision criteria can be raised by the results of empirical tests and inspections. The generation of design criteria for selecting among options might also be driven by inspection data. Issues can be compared and trade-offs made potentially more easily.

Blatt and Knutson (Chapter 14) discuss software tools under development at NCR that are intended to provide such criteria to give software developers access to usability and user interface design expertise and experience across multiple products. This online repository would include interface and usability guidelines, examples of usable design from previous products, and guidelines and support for conducting inspections and empirical testing.

1.7 Conclusions

The chapters in the book represent a wide range of applied experience with usability inspection methods and their role in the larger usability inspection context. Usability engineers who are considering adopting such methods, or who want to reflect on and refine similar methods already being used, should find these chapters very informative. Usability inspections are not yet a substitute for user testing, but appear to be quite effective for generating useful insight into the usability of a developing interface where end-user testing simply cannot be done quickly enough or with sufficient scope to answer all the usability questions that come up in a development process. Still, there is much room for improving these methods, and practitioners and HCI researchers are invited to take the opportunity to build on the solid work represented in this volume.

USING VIDEO IN THE BNR USABILITY LAB

SUE KENNEDY

Abstract: This paper describes the goals of the BNR Usability Lab and explains how we have achieved our goals by developing the "Co-Discovery Learning" testing methodology and designing "U-Test", a special interface for usability testing with video.

Bell-Northern Research (BNR) is the research and development arm of Northern Telecom. In the BNR Usability Lab, we videotape users as they "test-drive" Northern Telecom telephones and other communications products that are being developed by BNR. Our focus is on user interface testing, as other aspects of the product are tested by other groups in BNR. Quickly, we identify user interface problems, recommend improvements to the interface, and retest the modified interface. This iterative usability testing is done throughout the design process. Early in the design of a product we use computer simulations of the interface and prototypes, and in the later stages of development we test the working product.

Video is our main method of data collection, as well as the tool that we use to communicate the test results to our clients - the interface designers, documentation writers, product marketers, and management. These clients have responded enthusiastically to the use of video. They view usability testing as an essential part of the design process, which contributes considerably to the success and acceptability of Northern Telecom products in the marketplace. In the remainder of this paper, I will describe the goals of our usability lab and explain how we have achieved our goals by developing a new testing methodology, "Co-Discovery Learning" (Kennedy, Niergarth & Cuddy, 1985; Kennedy, 1986), and designing "U-Test", a special interface for usability testing with video.

Goals of the Usability Lab

The main goal of the usability lab is to identify all potential usability problems in the usability lab, rather than waiting until the product is released and customers start to complain. We want to improve the interface as early as possible because it becomes more difficult and costly to make changes as the development cycle progresses. It is also helpful to prioritize the changes that we recommend, so that developers can focus on implementing the most important changes first.

Once we have identified ways of improving the interface, we have to communicate the results of our usability tests to the interface designers, developers, and product managers. More important, we need to convince them to change the interface. This is the most challenging part of our job, since some of the improvements that we recommend may be costly and complicated and may delay product development considerably. Sometimes, the interface designers or developers try to convince us that the interface is great - but the documentation needs to be improved. It is tempting to try to improve usability by changing the user guide, but we realize that some users will never read the guide. Another common attitude is that , "Users will learn -- they just need a bit of practice." This is a dangerous assumption because users who get really frustrated and confused on their first attempt may never get any more practice. Although we try to be convincing, it is very important to express our recommendations about the interface objectively and diplomatically, in order to maintain an effective working relationship with the user interface designer and developers.

We have tried several ways of convincing developers to improve the product. Detailed descriptions of usability test results are not sufficient. Statistics do not convince them. In any case, it would be inappropriate to do a detailed statistical analysis of the effects of each proposed interface change because all of the changes interact together. We find that developers are most easily convinced if they actually see the users interact with the product. This is where video becomes an essential communication tool.

In our fast-paced product development environment, the turn-around time for usability tests must be extremely short. A team of two usability testers typically tests 10-20 users one week, and analyzes 35-40 hours of video data and presents the results and recommendations by the end of the next week. The presentation to the interface designers, managers, and product marketers often includes playing video segments to illustrate usability problems. The interface designers work with the usability testers to make changes to the user interface, and then the modified interface is retested. The testing team has another week to analyze the results and make final recommendations, and 1-2 weeks to prepare a video illustrating the results of the usability test.

How Video Helps Us Achieve our Goals

Over the past 5 years we have developed the "Co-Discovery Learning" testing method, which helps us identify and prioritize usability problems, communicate them convincingly, and recommend improvements to the interface. At the same time we designed "U-Test", a special interface for usability testing with video. With U-Test we can conduct the usability tests, collect and analyze data, and present the results easily, effectively and very quickly.

Co-Discovery Learning

Our usability testing method is called Co-Discovery Learning because we videotape two users as they cooperate or work together and discover how to use the product by trying it out. Usually, we do not provide a user guide or give any training. All we give the users is a list of standard tasks that we would like them to complete. Typical tasks for testing a telephone are, "Answer the next call and transfer it to Bob", and, "Program your phone so it will dial your home number automatically". Difficult tasks may be repeated again later in the list. Immediately after completing each task the users jointly rate the difficulty on a 7 point scale. Users require about 2 hours to complete all of the tasks on the list. Then, we interview both users together to find out what they like and dislike about the phone. We also evaluate their conceptual models of the phone by asking questions like, "What does the Rls button do?", or, "How can you tell if you have a call on hold?". The interview is also videotaped.

We find that two users working together experience the same problems as one user working alone. However, the conversation between the two users makes it much easier for us to understand their interaction with the product and pinpoint usability problems. Testing without a user guide or training has many advantages. Instead of reading the user guide and ignoring the phone, the users actually read the display and the names of buttons, look at flashing lights, and listen to tones. Because the users rely only on the interface, we know that the problems that they experience are interface problems, rather than problems with the training or user guide. This reduces the temptation to use the user guide to patch up interface problems. Instead, we adopt a minimalist approach to our documentation and include only the information that users cannot learn by discovery. The discovery learning approach also decreases our turn-around time because we can start testing before the user guide is written. Finally, testing without a user guide is quite realistic because many users are not willing to read one.

We used to test by having a single user "think aloud" while reading the user guide and completing tasks. The Co-Discovery Learning approach yields video that is much more interesting, informative, and convincing. When presenting our results, we describe how users completed each task and summarize the users' difficulty ratings. We play videotape segments to illustrate usability problems. We might also show two users deciding on a rating and discussing why they think a task was difficult, or show them experiencing the same problems that second time they attempt the task.

Similarly, replaying part of the interview may be used to illustrate that even after using the product for 2 hours the users did not develop an accurate conceptual model. If the interface has been changed and retested, we use video to illustrate usability improvements.

Although video segments are useful for communicating the results of usability tests, they do not satisfy some of our other important requirements. We need to prioritize usability problems, compare the usability of one product with another, decide when the product is usable enough, and convince designers to make changes. To address these issues, we need to do a detailed analysis of the videotapes in order to obtain quantitative measures of usability. Some of our measures include the time that users require to complete each task, the number of hints they require from the usability tester, and the number of times users refer to any online help or any form of documentation that is provided with the product. An especially important measure for telephones is the number of accidentally "dropped" calls.

The quantitative usability measures have an amazing impact on designers and management. For example, after testing an early simulation of one of our phones, we spent hours showing videotapes and trying to convince designers to change the procedures for transferring a call. Then we did a detailed analysis and told them that the average time for learning to transfer a call was 11 minutes. Immediately, they decided to modify the interface.

We use the quantitative measures to compare the usability of different phones, including those of our competitors. We establish quantitative usability goals for each phone and get the designers to agree to them before starting to usability test. For example, users should be able to transfer a call on their first attempt in less than 5 minutes, without reading a user guide, and without "dropping" the other caller. The goals are based on usability test results from our own and competitors' phones, and also on characteristics of the phone that we are testing, such as the size of the display and whether it has softkeys.

The quantitative usability meaures have also greatly improved the interface designers' attitudes about usability testing. Instead of viewing the usability test as a way to reveal negative aspects of the interface, designers now realize that it can show how well their interfaces compare to others, and help them concentrate on the parts of the interface can really be improved.

The main disadvantage of using quantitative usability measures and video segments to communicate interface problems is that considerable time is required to do a detailed analysis of the videotapes and pick out relevant segments. To speed up the process we designed U-Test, an interface to our video equipment which automates the analysis and enables us to do much of it in real time.

U-Test

To understand how U-Test works, pretend that you are a usability tester sitting in your experimenter's control room. Two users are sitting in the adjacent room with a plastic prototype of a telephone (driven by a computer simulation) and a list of tasks to complete. In front of you are two video monitors. One monitor shows a split screen image of the two users. On the left side of the screen you can see their facial expressions and notice that they are smiling and looking at the phone. On the right side of the screen is a close up view of the users pressing buttons and lifting up the handset. The second monitor shows what the users see as they use the phone. You can read the names of the keys and as the user touches buttons, you can see the indicator lights blink, softkeys appear, and words on the display change. This information helps you understand the users' comments as you listen and watch them trying to use the phone. Near the monitors are remote controls for the video cameras, an intercom for talking to the users, the computer that is running the simulation of the telephone, and the computer that runs U-Test. We originally designed U-Test to run on an IBM PC, but have recently switched to a Macintosh II which runs U-Test as a Hypercard application.

To start the usability test, you select the U-Test application from the screen and select "Start Experiment" from a pull-down menu. This turns on and synchronizes two VCR's which start recording the information on the two monitors. If for some reason they aren't recording, the computer will beep and remind you to check them. The first task on the users' list, "Call Joe's Plumbing at 479-1238", appears on your screen. The numbered list of procedures for completing the task are listed below it: "1. Lift handset, 2. Select external line, 3. Dial 479-1238". There is also a list of errors that you anticipate users might make while completing this task, based on pilot testing or testing of similar phones. For example, the first error on the list is "Get extension 47 on int line". This error occurs if the users lift the handset, which automatically selects an internal line, and start dialing 479-1238, which is an external number. They will end up calling the person at extension 47.

You use the intercom to tell the users to start the first task, and simultaneously press the function key labelled "Timer On". (All function keys also appear as buttons on the screen, so you can use the function key on the keyboard or use the mouse to click on the "Timer On" a button on the screen.) As you watch the users try to make the call, you can type in your observations and describe any problems that they are having. The users lift the handset and start dialing on an internal line. This is one of the errors that appears on your screen, so rather than typing it in you select it with the mouse. This is an excellent illustration of the problem, which would be very suitable for including in a usability testing video, so you also click on the "Video" button or press the function key. Then you continue typing in additional comments. When the users complete the phone call a computer- simulated voice answers "Joe's Plumbing". You press the "Timer Off " function key. You listen as the users rate the difficulty of the task and type in their rating and why they have rated it that way. As they start reading the second task on their list you select the "Next Task" button.

The next task, "Answer the call and transfer it to Bill at ext. 48." appears on top of your screen and the timer starts automatically. Another part of the screen reminds you to "Send external call", so that the users can answer it. You turn to the computer that runs the telephone simulation and select "Send external call" from a menu. The users' phone starts ringing and they answer it and attempt to transfer it. In the process, they accidently drop the call. You press the "Drop Call" function key and type in an explanation of how they dropped the call. You send the users another external call so they can start over again. You are not sure why they are having trouble and press the "Check" function key so you can replay the video and check it later on. Then, they almost succeed, but hang up before the transfer is completed. The timer on your screen indicates that they have been trying to transfer the call for 9 minutes and since they don't seem to be making any progress you decide to give them a hint. You select the "Hint" button and type in the hint that you gave them: " You have to press a key to complete the

Transfer before you hang up". Finally they transfer the call and you press the "Stop Timer" function key.

At the end of the test session you select "Print Data" from a pull-down menu. This prints out a data file which lists each usability task followed by your "comments" -- the information that you entered into the computer during the test. This includes typed comments, function key presses or button selections, and errors selected from the lists on your screen. Then, you click on the "Data Summary" icon and for each individual task, U-Test summarizes the completion times, number of hints, number of dropped calls, number of times each function key or button was pressed, and number of times the users made each of the errors that were listed on your screen. Using the U-Test data files and summaries, you can do much of the analysis of the usability test without replaying the videotapes.

When you do need to refer to the videotapes it is easy to locate the specific parts you want to play. U-Test uses time codes to synchronize the two videotapes of the usability test with the information in the data file. To playback a usability test, you put the videtapes in the VCR, start U-Test, and type in the name of the datafile. When you press the "Play", "Rewind", "Fast forward", and "Stop" function keys, both VCR's will operate together in synchrony, and the comments that you entered during the usability test will be displayed on the PC. You can also scroll through the comments until you find one that interests you, press the "Synch Tape to Comment" function key, and then play the corresponding parts of the videotapes. Or, you can "Search" the datafile to locate a particular comment. For example, you might want to search for and replay all the instances in which users dropped calls accidently, or received hints, or in which you pressed the "Check" function key.

U-Test's playback mode makes it very easy to select video segments of a particular usability task to show the designers. You check the data file and data summary for each subject pair and if they experienced the problem that you wish to illustrate and you entered a "Video" comment, then you replay it. After finding a good example, you can copy it on to a blank videotape, alternating images of the users with images of the product. Or, you can have the designers come into the usability lab to watch both videotapes synchronized together.

U-Test has increased the effectiveness of our usability tests considerably, while decreasing the analysis time by as much as 75%. The main disadvantage of U-Test is the cognitive load that it places on the usability tester during the test. The person who is operating U-Test spends at least two hours looking at two video screens and one computer screen, analyzing why users are having problems, typing in comments and pressing function keys. At the same time, the other usability tester communicates with the users via the intercom, operates the computer that is running the simulation of the product, and if necessary, adjusts the camera angles using the remote control equipment. After considerable practice, it is possible for one person to do this alone, but we find it more reliable and less stressful to have two usability testers work together. To facilitate this, when we changed U-Test to a Hypercard application, we duplicated the function keys on the screen. One usability tester can concentrate on using the keyboard to type in comments while the other uses the mouse to press the buttons on the screen. This improved the usability of U-Test considerably, but conducting the tests is still quite stressful. However, most usability testers would prefer the stress of doing the analysis in real time to the boredom of replaying hours of video and analyzing it afterwards. We wouldn't test without it!

Conclusions

The BNR Usability Lab has used the Co-Discovery Learning method and U-Test successfully on a variety of products including business and residential telephones, telephone installation equipment, attendant consoles, automated office systems, voice editors, and CAD/CAM tools. Quickly and effectively, we can identify, prioritize, and communicate usability problems, and work with developers to improve the user interface of Northern Telecom products. Our usability testing method leads to a successful product -- one that is easy to learn and well-accepted by users because it works the way they expect it to.

References:

Kennedy, S., Niergarth, J., and Cuddy, D. The behavioral evaluation of a visual voice editor testbed. *Proceedings of the 11th International Symposium on Human Factors in Telecommunications*, Rennes, 1985.

Kennedy, S. Usability Testing of the Meridian 3000 Touchphone. Video presented at *CHI'86 Conference on Human Factors in Computing Systems.*

Chapter 3

Considering Work Contexts in Design

This chapter focuses on the interplay between the design of computer systems and applications, and the social and organizational settings in which they are to be used. The context of work (or play) clearly affects "human-computer interaction" but seems to lie beyond the interface. Work contexts seem irrelevant when designing the appearance of menus and dialogue boxes or the functionality of generic "horizontal" applications such as word processors. Yet social and organizational considerations are critically important for design and grow more so with each passing year.

Consider a blind person, experienced at using a cane. Attention is focused at the tip of the cane—the surface struck by the tip is felt and in this manner the environment is understood. The tip of the cane is the *interface to the world.* The handle is the *interface to the tool.* The handle is carefully designed to convey accurately and comfortably useful information.

The human-computer interface is like the blind person's interface to a cane. Yet, like blind users of canes, computer users want to be primarily focused on their work in the world, not on their canes. Thus, just as designers of cane handles need consider the range of surfaces and collision angles and vibrations that will be encountered, interface designers benefit from learning about the environments in which their users will work. Brown and Duguid (1994, p. 6) put it this way:

> *Trying to define new practices without reference to users' past insights, common intuitions, shared understandings, and hard-won experience is actually far more difficult than grappling with context.*

When the first edition of this book was written, the typewriter was an endangered species, threatened by stand-alone PCs. Today, stand-alone PCs, which have been the basis of most of HCI research, are well down the road to extinction. Computers are now less likely to be used independently to produce information that will be exchanged in paper form, but are linked together in networks that carry the work of one computer user to others. Hence the design of applications must consider the organizational settings in which they are to be used.

When we worked on stand-alone machines and exchanged printed documents, for example, we could use any word processor. But now that we rely on exchanging documents electronically, word processor selection becomes a collective concern. Organizational factors create new design issues, such as interoperability.

Some applications are explicitly written to support group and organizational activity across networks. Readings in this chapter, Chapter 11 (Groupware and Computer-Supported Cooperative Work), and Case C (a groupware application) emphasize that the success of these systems is heavily governed by social, organizational, and environmental factors.

Not long ago, most direct users of computers were engineers and programmers. Developers' intuitions about their colleagues' preferences were often reliable. The range of interface options was limited. Today, computers enter environments for which developers have few intuitions. To learn about social organization and work outside their laboratories is not just a luxury for most developers, but a necessity. We hope that the readings in this chapter will make it clear why this is true and provide methods for accomplishing the learning efficiently and effectively.

Finally, much interface design has shifted from generic interfaces, such as the Macintosh or Windows, to *domain-specific* application interfaces. To excel at this, developers must combine interface design skills with knowledge of specific work domains—knowledge of the organizations, work culture, and work processes in which their systems will be used.

This chapter introduction starts with two case studies that illustrate why simple-minded notions of "usability" are not enough. In one, the reward system within an organization overrides usability issues in determining who uses an application and who doesn't. In the second, good usability methods are employed to produce a usable—but not useful—application. We then cover several design approaches that emphasize the understanding of work settings. Finally, we survey research and literature of the information systems field that is becoming of increasing relevance to human-computer interaction.

TWO CASE STUDIES

Our first reading, Orlikowski (1992), describes an office application introduced with 10,000 copies spread throughout "Alpha Corporation," a major consulting firm. It is an excellent demonstration that social and political concerns can be crucial for systems designers. Three categories of Alpha employees figure prominently in the story—consultants, partners, and technical support engineers.

Consultants, working under heavy pressure, do most of the daily work of the firm. After a period of time they are either promoted to more responsible positions or fired and replaced. After another interval elapses, they are reevaluated, and either become partners or leave the company.

Partners are responsible for overall management of the firm. Prior to the study, the partners observed that operations were highly redundant—one consultant would carry out a project without realizing that other consultants had done similar projects in the past. Experience was being wasted; people were continually reinventing the wheel. To address this, the partners acquired Lotus Notes for the consultants. Notes is a groupware product that combines features of electronic mail and shared data bases to promote rapid information sharing, to create an "organizational memory" for the corporation.

A team of *technical support engineers* was assigned the major undertaking of installing Notes at sites around the world.

Orlikowski focuses her analysis on the conflict between the goals of the partners, who wanted more cooperation, and the consultants, who needed to prove their individual worth in this intense "up or out" culture of promotion or firing. A consultant's value to the company lies in their experience and the information he or she controls; sharing this freely over the network is potentially threatening. The design of Notes, which allows information in a data base to be freely browsed by others on the network, seems to clash with the culture and reward system of this organizational context.

Thus, *the system would have problems regardless of how well the dialogues, response time, hardware, or documentation were designed and implemented.* The conflicting motivations of users were not taken into account.

Yet Orlikowski mentions that Notes was a great success among the technical support engineers. These employees were not part of the competitive culture of the consultants. They carried out similar tasks in different places and happily shared information and experiences. Thus, it was the reward structure, not the software, that guided the outcome. Notes's success in the engineering culture demonstrates that organizational context is a critical element in determining how employees will react to a system.

To be fair, the story of Alpha Corporation is not over. Later releases of Notes provided features that may enable it to succeed among the consultants, many of whom began using at least its basic e-mail capability. The partners, who remain committed to Notes, could also change the company's reward structure to create incentives for sharing information. Also, despite initial problems at Alpha Corporation, Notes has become, as of the mid-1990s, the most successful groupware application other than e-mail (Kirkpatrick, 1994).

Another case study, not included for reasons of space, provides a sharper warning (Keil, Beranek, and Konsynski, 1995; Markus and Keil, 1994). It covers the redesign of a system developed for a sales organization in a major computer company. Earlier, the company had documented costly errors made when sales representatives tried to specify appropriate system configurations to customers. To deal with this, the company built an expert system to configure products, a system of the kind made famous by Digital's XCON (Barker and O'Connor, 1989). The system was capable of accurately configuring products, but it was used for only a fraction of orders.

An inquiry uncovered complaints about the usability of the system. This led to the project reported in these studies, a redesign of the awkward interface. The redesign effort included many of the techniques recommended in Chapter 2 and throughout this book, notably iterative design with user feedback. Users from five pilot sites were trained on the new system. Despite this major investment, running into millions of dollars, the resulting system was used little more than the old one. Why?

A series of interviews showed that the system design had been based on the following model of the sales process: A customer identifies system requirements, then the sales force works out a configuration, and finally the price is calculated. This sounds rational, but in reality, most customers indicate how much they have to spend, and the sales force tries to identify an adequate system that can be obtained for that amount. The program did not support this "backwards" reasoning—it worked only in one direction, from configuration to price. Lacking this key functionality, the system did not help the sales force. The new interface made it *usable* but not *useful.*

In this case, *a major effort to increase system usability was futile.* Understanding why the result was not useful required discovering a "counterintuitive" work process in the organization.

This is an important lesson, but should be kept in perspective. Product developers often know that an application or a feature is useful from earlier versions or competing products. In a mature application area where functionality has settled down, usability and the human-computer interface become key concerns. However, when designing one-of-a-kind systems, novel applications, or new features, or when introducing a system into an organization for the first time, it is essential to understand the workplaces and tasks that are to be supported.

FROM HUMAN FACTORS TO HUMAN ACTORS

Our second reading, Bannon (1991), encourages an evolution to a broader perspective that we feel is important for many of us who have focused on interface design. Bannon encourages "understanding people as actors in situations, with a set of skills and shared practices based on work experience with others." After reviewing changes that encourage such a shift, he elaborates by suggesting a set of specific shifts in focus:

- *From product to process in research and design.* If we fix the design process, the product will take care of itself, Bannon argues, drawing on a Scandinavian tradition.
- *From individuals to groups.* The "PC islands" are disappearing. Thus, only by focusing on groups will we understand social and motivational factors.
- *From the laboratory to the workplace.* If we accept groups and organizations as important units, lab studies are less useful.
- *From novices to experts.* Studies of novice users are important, and easier to do, but as the field and users mature, more balance is needed.
- *From analysis to design.* Human factors training is primarily evaluative and neglects recognition of design skill. (We regard these as complementary, not competitive.)
- *From user-centered to user-involved design.* Again drawing on Scandinavian tradition, Bannon argues for involving users in design rather than testing designs on users.
- *From requirement specifications to prototyping and iterative design.*

Bannon's article ties together themes already introduced with those yet to be explored, and also provides a good transition to the readings that follow. Design as distinct from analysis was discussed in Chapter 2. The value of prototyping and iterative design is a major theme in this field, as is discussed in both Chapter 2 and in Chapter 4, "Software Development Contexts." The shift to group emphasis is taken up again in Chapter 11 and Case C. Finally, the ethnographic and participatory design approaches that Bannon cites are the subject of our next readings.

MAXIMIZING USER INVOLVEMENT: PARTICIPATORY APPROACHES TO DESIGN

In Chapter 2 we focused primarily on methods suitable for laboratory study. These studies can be invaluable once you know which factors can be safely controlled or ignored. Usability engineering requires the identification of important, meaningful targets. Usability testing, heuristic evaluation, and cognitive walkthroughs typically require "representative scenarios of use" for evaluation. What is representative? Laboratory methods require *domain knowledge* if they are to avoid being sterile exercises.

Knowledge of the application domain can be obtained in several ways. Relying on intuition is often used but very risky because developers usually do not work in environments like those of other users and because their knowledge of how software works gives them insights other users do not share. Many an atrocious interface is based on a good engineer's intuition.

Consulting an organization's standard practices or policies manual is a tempting but notoriously unreliable approach to understanding a workplace. Work practices rarely resemble their official description. The official description may be a goal or an idealized view. In reality, work is often marked by flexible exception handling and problem solving not represented in such manuals (Suchman, 1983, 1987).

Another common approach to obtaining domain knowledge is to hire a domain expert, a person with experience in the subject. This is very useful, but it relies on the experience and memory of one person whose knowledge may soon be out of date or who may be influenced by what they learn about system development (from you and others!).

How far can we take the notion of user involvement in system design? In Chapter 12 we discuss limitations of "end-user programming," providing users with tools to tailor or program their own environments. We see a trend toward greater user control, but users do not always have the knowledge or skill to design their own systems, which are rapidly increasing in complexity.

Thus we need creative design alliances between developers and users. Several approaches to achieve this have been developed in Europe, particularly in Scandinavia and England, under the names *sociotechnical system design*, *collaborative design*, and *participatory design*. These efforts drew wider attention in 1987 with the publication of *Computers and Democracy—A Scandinavian Challenge*, edited by Bjerknes, Ehn and Kyng. We shall now review a number of these participatory approaches, beginning with the work of the Scandinavian school.

Scandinavian Approaches to Collaborative Design

In our next reading, Bødker, Grønbæk and Kyng (1993), participatory design researchers from Aarhus University in Denmark, discuss the assumptions underlying their work, provide a brief history of their efforts, and describe several of the approaches that they have evolved and are currently extending.

Their focus as systems developers is to develop applications that enhance workplace skills through increased flexibility, in contrast to automating activity strictly to increase productivity at the risk of deskilling the work. They focus on the interplay between technology and the organization of work, recognizing that changes in technology will change the workplace and that organizational change can enable technological innovation.

Full cooperation of users and developers is not attained through good intentions alone. Developers must be immersed in the processes and culture of the workplace and users must be educated in technological possibilities. Since one cannot assume that either group will be fascinated by the other's message, much effort must go into experimenting with strategies to make the process interesting and engaging. As we have discussed to some extent in Chapter 2, a good method is to create *scenarios* of future system use, enabling users to draw on implicit knowledge of work practice that is not conveyed through written requirements. After presenting a case study, the authors describe in detail these *future workshops*, along with several other techniques they use: *organizational games*, *design mock-ups*, and *cooperative prototyping*.

Cooperative prototyping exemplifies a novel outcome yielded by their approach. Traditional prototyping involves these steps: A prototype is created, and it is tested by representative users. Then the prototype is modified, and the modification is tested. The Scandinavians' goal is to recreate a realistic work situation, so they strive to develop a prototyping system that can, to the greatest degree possible, be modified "on the fly" in the course of an interaction with a user. Each user may encounter a different prototype. Although quantitative analysis becomes impossible, this moves the process forward rapidly and minimizes time spent with prototypes that have already proved deficient.

The reader interested in these approaches now has many places to begin. For example, *Design at Work: Cooperative Design of Computer Systems* (Greenbaum and Kyng, 1991) is a set of essays by Europeans and Americans that centers on the Scandinavian approach to development. The Bannon reading in this chapter and the Henderson and Kyng reading on tailorable systems in Chapter 12 are from this book.

Participatory Design: Principles and Practices (Schuler and Namioka, 1993) is another set of original essays that includes the Bødker, Grønbæk, and Kyng and Holtzblatt and Jones readings. Many essays focus on adapting for more widespread use those European approaches to system design based on research into user and developer collaboration. Another chapter, Blomberg et al. (1993), explores the gulf between nonprescriptive ethnographic methods and the needs of design teams.

For the more adventurous, *Software Development and Reality Construction* (Floyd et al., 1992) is an eclectic set of essays, many with a strong philosophical element. A difficult but potentially rewarding chapter by Arne Raiethel (1992) presents the contributions to design of his extension of Activity Theory (discussed in Chapter 9).

Other literature presenting, critiquing, and exploring Scandinavian approaches includes Howard (1985); Docherty et al. (1987); Ehn (1989); Floyd et al. (1989); Bødker (1991); and Kyng (1994b). The Scandinavian approach is the subject of a lively debate between Morten Kyng of Aarhus University and two American researchers in the *Scandinavian Journal of Information Systems* (Kraft and Bansler, 1994a; 1994b; Kyng, 1994a).

Limitations of full participatory design include tripping over "boundary issues" or conflicting priorities among users (Ehn, 1989), and a conservative bias to perpetuate current practices rather than fully exploit the potential of new technologies (Clement and Van den Besselaar, 1993). Nevertheless, it is clearly a valuable inclusion in our array of design tools.

Importing Scandinavian Approaches

To what extent can these methods be applied elsewhere? Scandinavia is noteworthy for its cultural homogeneity, a welfare state inclined toward "empowering" rather than replacing workers, and "codetermination laws" that grant workers a voice in technological innovation in their workplaces. In addition, much of the Scandinavian work consisted of building unique systems within specific user organizations, whereas a lot of the North American interest is from developers of commercial products, a distinction that is explored in detail in Chapter 4.

Our next reading is a CHI conference presentation describing a high degree of user involvement in the design of an innovative product. Chemists participated with Michael Good (1992) in designing a novel interface to molecular modeling software. Although not all product design involves such significant innovation, the case study illustrates the benefits of participatory design in such situations.

Although this point is not emphasized by Good, as a result of feedback from the chemists, the design changed radically from the developers' original concept. The developers anticipated an opportunity for virtual reality technology, but were guided to a simpler force feedback device. Again, as with cooperative prototyping, participatory design allowed the designers to make major corrections.

Good is not alone in "importing" participatory design. Since 1990, participatory design conferences have been held every two years in the United States. Selected papers from the first two were published in Schuler and Namioka (1993) and Muller and Kuhn (1993). Muller has been an active early adopter (e.g., Muller, 1992).

Sociotechnical Design

The Scandinavians are not the only or even the first group to adopt a cultural rather than technical approach to the design of information systems. In the early 1970s, Enid Mumford developed sociotechnical design in Great Britain (Mumford, 1983,1993). Intended to give clerks and shop floor workers a greater voice in reorganizing work practices as part of the introduction of new systems and technology, sociotechnical design focuses on facilitated group meetings involving developers, managers, and future users.

Sociotechnical design has much in common with the Scandinavian approaches, which were influenced by it. A difference is that sociotechnical design is marked by greater acceptance of the business mission—increased efficiency—in contrast to the Scandinavians' primary focus on increasing the quality of working life.

Soft Systems Methodology

Soft systems methodology (Checkland and Scholes, 1990) is an approach to planning organizational change developed over the past twenty years. Although not restricted to information systems design, it has been used for this purpose, primarily in Europe. Its perspective draws on general systems theory and cybernetic traditions. This all-encompassing approach examines *all* aspects of a system, considering every element to have the properties of being a whole and of being a component of larger systems that have "emergent properties" not predictable from knowledge of the parts.

To obtain the necessary depth of understanding, soft systems methodology must be participatory at some level, but it has been criticized for requiring a single systems theoretician to pull the picture together. However, this systems approach has appealed to some as a structure for participatory design (e.g., Mathiassen and Neilsen, 1989).

Joint Application Design

A parallel approach to increasing user participation in in-house development projects, is joint application design (JAD) (e.g., Davidson, 1993). JAD is a more structured method intended to accelerate the development process. Carmel, Whitaker, and George (1993) contrast participatory design and joint application design, concluding that the former could benefit from additional structure and definition, and the latter could benefit from the creativity and attention to participant selection that mark participatory design.

ETHNOGRAPHY AND INTERACTION ANALYSIS

In our analysis of McGrath's Chapter 2 reading, we noted that field research can consist of ethnography (descriptive anthropology). Research ethnographers attempt to understand a workplace through immersion in and extended contact with it and through a subsequent analysis of this experience. Until recently it would have been considered very exotic to involve anthropologists in human-computer interface design, but they now carry out much of this field research. Notable examples are Lucy Suchman (1987), whose pioneering work we sample below, Constance Perin, with her study of e-mail use (Perin, 1991), Wanda Orlikowski (1992), whose case study of the adoption and impact of organizational memory technology we have already reviewed, and Bonnie Nardi, whose studies include spreadsheet use (Nardi and Miller, 1991) and end-user programming (Nardi, 1994).

Our next reading, "Ethnography and Interaction Analysis," is excerpted from an article by an anthropologist and a computer scientist (Suchman and Trigg, 1991). It describes two specific ethnographic approaches and a computer-based tool for supporting them. Video is also used, but in a slightly different way than in Chapter 2. These researchers do extremely detailed analyses of specific passages in order to obtain a deep understanding of behavior that they have observed. This approach is most useful very early in development, in order to build an understanding of existing work practices thorough enough to illuminate the possibilities for and implications of introducing technology.

If time and resources permit, ethnographic research can provide the most detailed understanding of a site of interest. Bowers (1994), for example, studied the use of a local area network and of commercial collaborative software in a government agency responsible for technology strategy. His methodology included two detailed interviews of up to three hours in duration with key personnel and *job shadowing* of these key personnel over an 18-month period. Although the users were relatively sophisticated and positive toward the technology, the study uncovered organizational problems that inhibited its use and almost doomed the network to failure. (This work also exemplifies the seminal role of research in Great Britain at the junction of technology and organizations, a thread present since the work of Mumford and Checkland in the 1970s.)

As we can see from the Bowers work, the principal cost of ethnographic study is the time required for collecting and analyzing data. However, it may cost far less than a failed development effort. The Francik et al. reading in Case C, to which ethnographer Constance Perin contributed, was undertaken when developers realized that innovative multiuser applications require detailed knowledge that cannot be obtained in other ways.

An important consideration is that ethnographers are not trained as designers. Quite the contrary, they are trained to "interfere" as little as possible with the community they observe. Ethnographic studies most often provide warnings—detailed descriptions of work practices that new technology might disrupt. Others may have to design ways to avoid the disruption or decide whether the benefits of change will outweigh the cost. But the first step is to anticipate the disruption.

A short, useful book for anyone considering field research is Lofland and Lofland's (1995) *Analyzing Social Settings: A Guide to Qualitative Observation and Analysis*. It is a useful compendium of advice and instruction for planning, executing, and analyzing field research, although it was not written specifically with the study of technology in mind.

In the past few years, developers and researchers have honed approaches that offer the possibility of designing technology for a better fit to the workplace, while taking into account the pressures imposed on real development. These include an energetic descendant of participatory design, contextual inquiry, to which we turn next.

CONTEXTUAL INQUIRY

A group working at Digital Equipment Corporation in the mid-1980s developed a design approach that falls squarely between observation and interview. (See Whiteside, Bennett, and Holtzblatt, 1988, for a review of the usability engineering background in which the method emerged, and Whiteside, 1995, for a design example in which the method was used.) Although the approach is very carefully crafted, at its heart is the idea of intensively interviewing people while they are working. At first glance this may seem to surrender benefits of either approach alone—and it does. By interrupting to ask questions, the interviewer inevitably disrupts the work to an unknown degree. Thus, the experiences is not quite "natural." Also, by letting the worker's activity control the direction of the interview, the interviewer gives up some control over the questions that get asked and the ground that is covered. However, this method can be used to obtain very useful information extremely efficiently. Contextual inquiry is a powerful tool that will reward a designer who masters it.

Michael Good drew on contextual inquiry as part of his iterative design of a portable torque-feedback system for use by chemists. Our next reading is a thorough description of the technique by two of its developers, Karen Holtzblatt and Sandra Jones (1993), who have trained over 400 members of engineering teams in its use (including one of the author-editors of this book).

Holtzblatt and Jones begin by outlining the goals of contextual inquiry, the challenges it set out to meet, and the underlying principles they developed.

The goals of contextual inquiry are familiar goals of system design: "to support, extend, and positively transform the work of individuals, teams, and businesses" through computer hardware, software, services, and support. The specific challenges that they faced were

- supporting people who do similar work in different business contexts and cultures, a challenge for developers of commercial products
- obtaining appropriate and helpful information about the work of these different users
- gathering the information quickly and efficiently

Holtzblatt and Jones succeeded in overcoming the obstacles that so often prevent product developers from involving users, obstacles discussed further in Chapter 4. Because usability requires a match between work practices and technology, contextual interviewers are steeped in the technology and focus the interviewing on understanding work practices. In addition, contextual inquiry emphasizes the difference between the work that people want to accomplish and the work required just to use the tool, the computer. If the people interviewed are not yet using a computer system, the interview will focus on the work they do and any noncomputer tools they employ. If the interviewees are already using a computer—perhaps an earlier version of the system being designed—then the interviewer considers both the existing computer use *and* the nature of the work.

Three principles guide the contextual inquiry process:

- Preserving the users' work *context* to obtain a more accurate and concrete understanding
- Creating a *partnership* with users to reach a shared understanding of the work processes being examined
- Attending carefully to the *focus* that the interviewer adopts (for example, it can be useful to consciously expand the focus, to ask questions that might otherwise go unasked, and to ask questions in areas of greater uncertainty)

The preparation, execution, and analysis of a contextual interview are described in depth in the long paper excerpts included in this volume. More detail about methods of analysis can be found in Holtzblatt and Beyer (1993). This involves the iterative construction and discussion, by the development team and users, of five kinds of work models:

- *Context models*: organizational culture, policies, procedures that affect work
- *Physical models*: the physical environment as it impacts work
- *Flow models*: the major roles and communication paths at work
- *Sequence models*: the temporal sequences of important activities in a setting
- *Abstract flow models*: composites used to discuss possible changes in work practice

THE INFORMATION SYSTEMS PERSPECTIVE

Another literature on computers and their impact on organizations and society emerged in the 1960s and 1970s, one that grew out of an analysis of the impact of the large mainframe and minicomputer systems that had long dominated the computer field. It has been labeled data processing (DP), information systems (IS), management information systems (MIS), and information technology (IT). The systems were originally primarily batch-processing systems, "number crunchers" with little in the way of direct human-computer interaction. The IS focus is on functionality, not interface issues. Much IS research is descriptive, not intended to influence design.

As interactive PCs and workstations emerged, designers faced very different issues. The IS and HCI research and development communities evolved independently, forming their own conferences, journals, literatures, and jargons. Both are about people and computers, but they have remained apart.

"Two countries divided by a common language." George Bernard Shaw observed that although the United States and Great Britain seem to speak the same language, we use words in very different ways. This is also true of the information systems and human-computer interaction literature. It is mostly written in English, but each group uses the same words in different ways, reflecting different priorities shaping each perspective.

A one-page essay adapted from Grudin (1993a) is included as an appendix to this chapter. It reviews the differences in meaning that surround common terms such as "user," "task," and "implementation." Before you read an article or book cited in this chapter—in fact, before you read the articles in this chapter—it is useful to think about which community the authors came from, what priorities they likely shared, and which use of terminology to expect from them. A traveler in an unfamiliar terrain profits from knowing a little of the local dialect!

Yet powerful forces are now bringing the information systems and human-computer interaction fields together. Networks and client-server architectures bridge large organizational systems and what have heretofore been PC "islands." Applications that run across networks affect and are affected by group and organizational activity, with profound consequences for their design.

Interface developers have always benefited from understanding the context of use of their systems, but now it is essential to consider social and organizational issues in design and development. Conferences that bring together people from the IS and HCI fields include computer-supported cooperative work, where the Orlikowski paper was first presented, as well as participatory design.

The final reading in Chapter 3, Kling (1995a), presents a lively and balanced overview of issues involving computerization and work that have emerged from information systems research. These issues are not traditional HCI fare, but some substantially influence our work, or will soon.

Kling starts with a brief historical overview of the interrelationships of work and computerization. Then he discusses two common modes of analysis: *utopian* (and anti-utopian) views of technology, and *social realism*, the empirical, "objective" approach that most of us probably endorse (with occasional fits of utopian fervor or anti-utopian gloom). The bulk of the article discusses the following issues and controversies arising from the analyses of social realists:

- *Control and coordination of work processes.* Topics include how work is managed, how communication takes place, how decisions are made, and the differential impacts on males and females. Electronic monitoring, work speedup, and telecommuting are prominent concerns.
- *Skill and support for computerization.* Does technology "deskill" or "routinize" work? Kling review the literature and show that these issues are more complex than we first thought.
- *The integration of computing into work.* Kling was among the first to stress the importance of attending to the broader infrastructure of computing. This section contains the most explicit discussion of design implications in the reading.
- *New forms of work organization.* Do computers "empower" or "informate" workers? The author reviews Zuboff's (1988) influential work.

Systems to support or interface to groups bring these social issues to the fore. They are not "just politics," outside the realm of engineering. They often have ethical implications. They have significant design implications however you look at them. Control and coordination in engineering environments is unlike that in many other work settings, so it is especially important for developers to avoid overgeneralizing from experience. Many of the issues are far from cut-and-dried. For example, workplace monitoring can make work excruciating, yet it also can save lives.

We close this section with a brief review of relevant literature from the information systems perspective.

Literature on organizational theory, management, and information systems. This literature is quite extensive. Pfeffer (1982) is a useful survey of organization theory. Crowston and Malone (1988) review the impact of technology on organizations from a number of perspectives. Mintzberg's (1989) functional decomposition and typology of organizations is an insightful perspective from which to think about how technology can fit within organizations, although the author does not emphasize this use of his work. Stinchcombe (1990) considers organizations as information-processing structures, completely independent of technology use (or nonuse). This perspective encourages reflection on the actual or potential roles of information-processing technology. Galegher, Kraut, and Egido (1990) is an excellent multidisciplinary collection of original essays discussing intellectual teamwork in the light of possible technological support.

Literature on information technology, organizations, and society. Some of this literature predates interactive systems or addresses systems in which functionality far outweighs the human-computer component in significance. Nevertheless, the reception of large systems by people in organizations can be illuminating to any developer whose interactive application must survive in group and organizational settings.

Friedman (1989) is a comprehensive, analytic review of the history of information systems. We strongly recommend this book for its history of the information systems field and the major issues. The bibliography is invaluable. Friedman considers three major historical phases: First, hardware constraints dominated the industry. Next, the principal constraints were in developing software. And now, he argues, responding to user needs is the dominant concern. From an organizational perspective, "user needs" applies first to the functions carried out by the computer, and only secondarily to the human-computer interface that is the primary focus of our book.

Our reading by Kling provides a comprehensive bibliography of over 100 relevant works. Two edited collections surveying this diverse literature are Kling (1995b) and Zerzan and Carnes (1991). Kraut (1986) is an older anthology of interesting and useful studies. Boland and Hirschheim (1987) is another good collection from the same series as Friedman's monograph. Ostberg and Chapman (1988) discuss myths that impede the successful introduction of new technologies.

LABORATORY STUDIES AND FIELD STUDIES

Do the laboratory usability methods of Chapter 2 conflict with the field contextual methods of this chapter? Can clear rules of thumb direct us to one or the other? Should the approaches be integrated into one methodology?

One consideration is the degree of novelty of the system or application for the people who will use it. Novelty is accompanied by risk and less well-formed intuitions, which call out for contextual, participatory work. Novelty also tends to bring a focus on functionality, which is closer to the actual work of participants. More mature products may attend more to the interface, which may be of equal significance for the success of that project, but which is further from the interests and knowledge of workers.

Consider the cooperative prototyping described by Bødker, Grønbæk, and Kyng (1993). It encourages quick, major course corrections, but it is less helpful for minor features to which each participant responds differently. Thus, we feel that any project can benefit from greater contextual knowledge, but it is particularly important to obtain it for novel projects when major changes are possible. Later in development, or for minor refinements of mature products, usability testing or usability engineering may be more beneficial.

Yet both perspectives are always useful. In the words of Brown and Duguid (1994, pp. 25–26):

> *Because social practice is extraordinarily rich and extremely complex . . . designers' chances of understanding it decrease almost exponentially with the distance between themselves and practitioners. In the gap—which human factors labs cannot bridge—ready-made prejudices and preconceptions and over-easy assumptions about "proper use" and "inherent functionality" substitute for insight and understanding. . . .*
>
> *Complete immersion is not, however, the antidote to the detachment of the lab. Problems of immersion actually mirror those of separation. Separation tends to view practice from across a no-man's land, thereby representing not so much what practice is like, as what it looks like from a distance, capturing the external relations, but missing the internal conditions. User-centered design (Norman, 1988; Norman and Draper, 1986) and work-oriented design (Ehn, 1989), by contrast, promote design around actual practice. These are a significant improvement on the human factors lab, but they nonetheless risk focusing on internal requirements at the expense of external ones. Both approaches, then, have complementary limitations. Design from across no-man's land expects practice to submit to external demands. Design in the trenches often proceeds as if only internal demands need to be considered.*
>
> *Designers need both to resist these traps and to position themselves to understand a practice both from within and from without—close enough to understand its internal requirements, but detached enough to observe external conditions and cross-boundary relations to other communities and to encompassing social structures....*

If these tensions and trade-offs between separation and immersion do not provide enough challenges to good design, we now turn in Chapter 4 to the impact of the organizational context in which design is carried out. As we shall see, for example, there are organizational factors in product organizations that can constrain working with users and can therefore impede the participatory design of products (Grudin, 1993b).

REFERENCES

Note: A ❁ before a reference indicates a reading.

❁ Bannon, L. (1991). From Human Factors to Human Actors. In Greenbaum and Kyng (1991), 25–44.

Barker, V., and O'Connor, D. (1989). Expert Systems for Configuration at Digital: XCON and Beyond. *Communications of the ACM* 32(3), 298–318.

Bjerknes, G., Ehn, P., and Kyng, M. (Eds.) (1987). *Computers and Democracy—A Scandinavian Challenge.* Gower.

Blomberg, J., Giacomi, J., Mosher, A., and Swenton-Wall, P. (1993). Ethnographic Field Methods and Their Relation to Design. In Schuler and Namioka (1993), 123–155.

Boland, R., and Hirschheim, R. (Eds.) (1987). *Critical Issues in Information Systems Research.* John Wiley & Sons.

Bowers, J. (1994). The Work to Make the Network Work: Studying CSCW in Action. *Proc. CSCW '94,* ACM, 287–298.

Brown, J., and Duguid, P. (1994). Borderline Issues: Social and Material Aspects of Design. *Human-Computer Interaction* 9(1), 3–36. See also commentaries on this paper in the same issue.

Bødker, S. (1991). *Through the Interface: A Human Activity Approach to User Interface Design.* Lawrence Erlbaum Associates.

● Bødker, S., Grønbæk, K., and Kyng, M. (1993). Cooperative Design: Techniques and Experiences from the Scandinavian Scene. In Schuler and Namioka (1993), 157–175.

Carmel, E., Whitaker, R., and George, J. (1993). PD and Joint Application Design: A Transatlantic Comparison. *Communications of the ACM* 36(6), 40–48.

Checkland, P., and Scholes, J. (1990). *Soft System Methodology in Action.* John Wiley & Sons.

Clement, A., and Van den Besselaar, P. (1993). A Retrospective Look at PD Projects. *Communications of the ACM* 36(6), 29–37.

Crowston, K., and Malone, T. (1988). Information Technology and Work Organization. In Helander (1988), 1051–1070.

Davidson, E. (1993). An Exploratory Study of Joint Application Design (JAD) in Information Systems Delivery. *Proc. 14th Int. Conf. on Information Systems,* 271–283.

Docherty, P., Fuchs-Kittowski, K., Kolm, P., and Mathiassen, L. (Eds.) (1987). *System Design for Human Development and Productivity: Participation and Beyond.* North-Holland.

Ehn, P. (1989). *Work Oriented Design of Computer Artifacts.* Lawrence Erlbaum Associates.

Floyd, C., Mehl, W.-M., Reisin, F.-M., Schmidt, G., and Wolf, G. (1989). Out of Scandinavia: Alternative Approaches to Software Design and System Development. *Human-Computer Interaction* 4(4), 253–349.

Floyd, C., Züllighoven, H., Budde, R., and Keil-Slawik, R. (Eds.) (1992). *Software Development and Reality Construction.* Springer-Verlag.

Friedman, A. (1989). *Computer Systems Development: History, Organization and Implementation.* John Wiley & Sons.

Galegher, J., Kraut, R., and Egido, C. (Eds.) (1990). *Intellectual Teamwork: Social and Technological Foundations of Computer-Supported Cooperative Work.* Lawrence Erlbaum Associates.

● Good, M. (1992). Participatory Design of a Portable Torque-Feedback Device. *Proc. CHI '92,* ACM, 439–446.

Greenbaum, J., and Kyng, M. (Eds.) (1991). *Design at Work.* Lawrence Erlbaum Associates.

Grudin, J. (1993a). Interface: An Evolving Concept. *Communications of the ACM* 36(4), 110–119.

Grudin, J. (1993b). Obstacles to Participatory Design in Large Product Development Organizations. In Schuler and Namioka (1993), 99–119.

Helander, M. (Ed.) (1988). *Handbook of Human-Computer Interaction.* North-Holland.

Holtzblatt, K., and Beyer, H. (1993). Making Customer-Centered Design Work for Teams. *Communications of the ACM* 36(9), 93–103.

● Holtzblatt, K., and Jones, S. (1993). Conducting and Analyzing a Contextual Interview. In Schuler and Namioka (1993), 177–210. (Excerpt included 177, 181–188, 192–204, 207–210.)

Howard, R. (1985). UTOPIA: Where Workers Craft New Technology. *Technology Review,* April, 43–49.

Keil, M., Beranek, P., and Konsynski, B. (1995). Usefulness and Ease of Use: Field Study Evidence Regarding Task Considerations. *Decision Support Systems,* 13, 75–91.

Kirkpatrick, D. (1994). Why Microsoft Can't Stop Lotus Notes. *Fortune,* 12 December, 141–157.

● Kling, R. (1995a). Controversies about Computerization and the Character of White Collar Worklife. Original.

Kling, R. (1995b). *Computerization and Controversy: Value Conflicts and Social Choices,* Second Edition. Academic Press.

Kraft, P., and Bansler, J. (1994a). The Collective Resource Approach: The Scandinavian Experience. *Scandinavian Journal of Information Systems* 6(1), 71–84.

Kraft, P., and Bansler, J. (1994b). Privilege and Invisibility in the New York Order: A Reply to Kyng. *Scandinavian Journal of Information Systems* 6(1), 97–106.

Kraut, R. (Ed.) (1986). *Technology and the Transformation of White-Collar Work.* Lawrence Erlbaum Associates.

Kyng, M. (1994a). Collective Resources Meets Puritanism. *Scandinavian Journal of Information Systems* 6(1), 85–96.

Kyng, M. (1994b). Scandinavian Design: Users in Product Development. *Proc. CHI '94,* ACM, 3–9.

Lofland, J., and Lofland, L. (1995). *Analyzing Social Settings: A Guide to Qualitative Observation and Analysis,* Third Edition. Wadsworth.

Markus, M. L., and Keil, M. (1994). If We Build It, They Will Come: Designing Information Systems That Users Want to Use. *Sloan Management Review,* Summer, 11–25.

Mathiassen, L., and Neilsen, P. (1989). Soft Systems and Hard Contradictions—Approaching the Reality of Information Systems in Organisations. *Journal of Applied Systems Analysis* 16, 75–88.

Mintzberg, H. (1989). *Mintzberg on Management: Inside Our Strange World of Organizations.* Free Press.

Muller, M. (1992). Retrospective on a Year of Participatory Design Using the PICTIVE Technique. *Proc. CHI '92,* ACM, 455–462.

Muller, M., and Kuhn, S. (Eds.) (1993). *Participatory Design. Communications of the ACM* 36(4).

Mumford, E. (1983). *Designing Human Systems.* Manchester Business School.

Mumford, E. (1993). The Participation of Users in Systems Design: An Account of the Origin, Evolution, and Use of the ETHICS Method. In Schuler and Namioka (1993), 257–270.

Nardi, B. (1994). *A Small Matter of Programming: Perspectives on End-User Computing.* MIT Press.

Nardi, B., and Miller, J. (1991). Twinkling Lights and Nested Loops: Distributed Problem Solving and Spreadsheet Development.

International Journal of Man-Machine Studies 34(2), 161–184.

Norman, D. (1988). *The Psychology of Everyday Things.* (*The Design of Everyday Things* in paperback.) Basic Books.

Norman, D., and Draper, S. (Eds.) (1986). *User Centered System Design.* Laurence Erlbaum Associates.

⊛ Orlikowski, W. (1992). Learning from Notes: Organizational Issues in Groupware. *Proc. CSCW '92,* ACM, 362–369.

Ostberg, O., and Chapman, L. (1988). Social Aspects of Computer Use. In Helander (1988), 1033–1049.

Perin, C. (1991). Electronic Social Fields in Bureaucracies. *Communications of the ACM* 34(12), 74–82.

Pfeffer, J. (1982). *Organizations and Organization Theory.* Pitman.

Raeithel, A. (1992). Activity Theory as a Foundation for Design. In Floyd, C., Züllighoven, H., Budde, R., and Keil-Slawik, R. (Eds.), *Software Development and Reality Construction,* Springer-Verlag, 391–415.

Schuler, D., and Namioka, A. (Eds.) (1993). *Participatory Design: Principles and Practices.* Lawrence Erlbaum Associates.

Stinchcombe, A. (1990). *Information and Organizations.* University of California Press.

Suchman, L. (1983). Office Procedures as Practical Action: Models of Work and System Design. *ACM Transactions on Office Information Systems* 1, 320–328.

Suchman, L. (1987). *Plans and Situated Action.* Cambridge University Press.

⊛ Suchman, L., and Trigg, R. (1991). Understanding Practice: Video as a Medium for Reflection and Design. In Greenbaum and Kyng (1991), 65–89. (Excerpt included 75–89.)

Whiteside, J. (1995). Applied Contextualism as a Design Methodology for a Computer-Supported Meeting System.

In Rudisill, M., Lewis, C., Polson, P., and McKay, T. (Eds.) (1995). *Human-Computer Interface Design: Success Cases, Emerging Methods, and Real-World Context.* Morgan Kaufmann.

Whiteside, J., Bennett, J., and Holtzblatt, K. (1988). Usability Engineering: Our Experience and Evolution. In Helander (1988), 791–817.

Zerzan, J., and Carnes, A. (Eds.) (1991). *Questioning Technology: Tool, Toy or Tyrant?* New Society Publishers.

Zuboff, S. (1988). *In the Age of the Smart Machine: The Future of Work and Power.* Basic Books.

POSTSCRIPT TO CHAPTER 3—TWO COMMUNITIES, TWO LANGUAGES

As the gap between system developers and system users grew, the systems development field fragmented, producing different communities with distinct priorities, approaches, conferences, journals, and languages. Important terms are used in different ways, often resulting in confusion when discussing a topic with or reading an article by someone from another context. Below, parallel descriptions of two communities highlight their conflicting uses of common terms.

Information Systems (IS)

This field arose in the late 1960s as mainframe systems proliferated and is also called data processing (DP), management information systems (MIS), and information technology (IT). These expensive systems were acquired to address major tasks within large organizations. They were operated by computer professionals, but organizations had to adjust in order to provide the data required by the system and to use the output. Management interest in understanding how best to use computers led to an academic focus divided between computer science and business or management schools, especially in the United States. Large "user organizations" are active in IS research and development. A key concern is system **implementation**, the process of introducing a system into an organization, which can—but need not—include the development of the system.

The **users** of these large systems are management or staff who use the output. Their contact with the computer is generally indirect: they read printed reports that it generates on topics they have defined; professional computer staff are responsible for the intervening steps. The **task** that the computer supports is a large organizational enterprise involving many employees, such as tracking inventory and orders. In developing a mainframe or minicomputer **application** for an organizational task, a **task analysis** is carried out to determine who in the organization is involved in the activity, what information they take in, how they act on it, and to whom they route it. The principal focus is on functionality. An **evaluation** of system use often occurs too late in development to be useful, so this job is often particularly unpopular.

The use of terminals spread, permitting direct data entry and creating a new category of computer user, called the **end user**. This supplanted the similar data preparation work of filling out forms, keypunching cards, and so forth. The people working at such tasks were affected by computerization. As a result, end-user concerns became a research focus, especially in Europe, where union influence on legislation, the high proportion of computers and research in the public sector, and philosophical or political disposition led many researchers to focus on the "end user" perspective. But in general, information systems research, as it appears in major journals such as *Management Science* and *MIS Quarterly,* has been dominated by the management perspective.

Human-Computer Interaction (HCI)

This field arose in the early 1980s as multitasking minicomputer and personal computer **systems** became widespread. These systems addressed the tasks of individuals. Users of these systems typically preprocess information, enter and work with it interactively, and process the output before making it available to their group or organization. Interest in personal information processing led to an academic focus divided between computer science and experimental (perceptual and cognitive) psychology. Early development and use of these systems was centered in the United States and to a lesser degree the United Kingdom. Large software development companies drive research in this area. One of their key concerns is **implementation**, which in this context means solely the development or coding of a system or application.

The **users** in this context are those who directly interact with the computer. They are more likely to be white collar or relatively autonomous blue collar workers, and thus in an organizational sense each is an IS "user" and "end user" rolled into one. In this community only the term "users" appears. From the perspective of interacting with the system, they more resemble the "end users" of the IS world. A computer-supported **task** is typically a small, individual activity, such as final document preparation. In developing an **application** such as a word processor for such a task, a **task analysis** determines the perceptual and cognitive activity within a user—how a person takes in, processes, and acts on information. The principal focus is on the human-computer interface. An **evaluation** of the use of an existing product can be a useful step in developing subsequent versions.

Off-the-shelf software product development is a smaller enterprise in Europe, so research on human-computer interaction has a somewhat different slant. Europeans show more interest in moving beyond the perceptual and cognitive focus to integrate this aspect of human-computer interaction into its social and organizational context. But in general, research in this area, as it appears in major journals such as *Human-Computer Interaction* and in the annual *Computer and Human Interaction (CHI) Conference Proceedings,* has been dominated by individual perceptual and cognitive processes.

LEARNING FROM NOTES: Organizational Issues in Groupware Implementation

Wanda J. Orlikowski

Sloan School of Management
Massachusetts Institute of Technology
50 Memorial Drive (E53-329)
Cambridge, MA 02139
(617) 253-0443 wanda@eagle.mit.edu

ABSTRACT
This paper explores the introduction of groupware into an organization to understand the changes in work practices and social interaction facilitated by the technology. The results suggest that people's mental models and organizations' structure and culture significantly influence how groupware is implemented and used. Specifically, in the absence of mental models that stressed its collaborative nature, groupware was intepreted in terms of familiar personal, stand-alone technologies such as spreadsheets. Further, the culture and structure provided few incentives or norms for cooperating or sharing expertise, hence the groupware on its own was unlikely to engender collaboration. Recognizing the central influence of these cognitive and organizational elements is critical to developers, researchers, and practitioners of groupware.

KEYWORDS
Groupware, Implementation, Lotus Notes, Organizational Factors, Technological Frames

INTRODUCTION
Computer-supported cooperative work, collaborative computing, and groupware have become common labels in our contemporary technological vocabulary. While some have discussed the potential for such technologies to enhance organizational effectiveness [3, 8, 9, 15], others have suggested that the implementation of such technologies is more difficult and yields more unintended consequences than is typically acknowledged [2, 10, 11, 12, 16]. Empirical studies of groupware usage in organizations are clearly needed to shed light on these diverse expectations. While there have been many field studies of electronic mail usage [1, 4, 5, 6, 13, 14, 17], groupware (that includes more collaborative features than electronic mail) has been studied less frequently.

In this paper I describe the findings of an exploratory field study which examined the implementation of the groupware product *Notes*® (from Lotus Development Corporation)[1] into one office of a large organization. My interest in studying the implementation and use of this product was to investigate whether and how the use of a collaborative tool changes the nature of work and the pattern of social interactions in the office, and with what intended and unintended consequences. The findings suggest that two organizational elements seem especially relevant in influencing the effective utilization of groupware: people's *cognitions* or mental models about technology and their work, and the *structural properties* of the organization such as policies, norms, and reward systems. The findings suggest that where people's mental models do not understand or appreciate the collaborative nature of groupware, such technologies will be intepreted and used as if they were more familiar technologies, such as personal, stand-alone software (e.g., a spreadsheet or word processing program). The findings further suggest, that where the premises underlying the groupware technology (shared effort, cooperation, collaboration) are counter-cultural to an organization's structural properties (competitive and individualistic culture, rigid hierarchy, etc.), the technology will be unlikely to facilitate collective use and value. That is, where there are few incentives or norms for cooperating or sharing expertise, goupware technology alone cannot engender these. Conversely, where the structural properties do support shared effort, cooperation, and collaboration, it is likely that the technology will be used collaboratively, that is, it will be another medium within which those values and norms are expressed. Recognizing the significant influence of these organizational elements appears critical to groupware developers, users, and researchers.

[1] Notes is an application development environment that can support communication, coordination, and collaboration within groups or organizations. While some features such as electronic mail are built-in, others need to be built by the adopting organization, e.g. discussion forums and customized views of shared databases. See Marshak (1990) for more details.

RESEARCH SITE AND METHODS

Field work was conducted within a large services firm, Alpha Corporation (a pseudonym), which provides consulting services to clients around the world. The career structure within Alpha is hierarchical with four primary milestones--staff consultant, senior consultant, manager, and principal. In contrast to the pyramidal career structure, the firm operates through a matrix form, with client work being executed and managed in a decentralized fashion out of local offices, while being coordinated through consulting practice management centralized in the headquarters office.

A few years ago, Alpha purchased and distributed Notes to all their consultants and support staff as part of a strategy, described by a senior principal as an attempt to "leverage the expertise of our firm." My research study examined the implementation of Notes in one large office of Alpha over a period of five months.[2] Detailed data collection was conducted through unstructured interviews, review of office documents, and observation of meetings, work sessions, and training classes. Over ninety interviews were conducted, each about an hour in length, with some participants being interviewed more than once over the period of study. In addition to the office where the study was conducted, I interviewed key players from Alpha's headquarters and technology group. Participants spanned various hierarchical levels and were either consultants in active practice, administrators supporting practice activities, or members of the centralized technology support function (see Table 1).

	Practice	Technology	Total
Principals	13	4	17
Managers	26	15	41
Seniors	12	13	25
Admin.	8	--	8
Total	59	32	91

Table 1: Number and Type of Interviews in Alpha

The research study was designed to examine how the groupware technology is adopted and used by individuals, and how work and social relations change as a consequence. The research study began in February 1991 before the Notes system was due to be installed within the office and continued through the implementation and early use of the Notes system (June 1991). The findings reflect participants' anticipations of as well as their early exposure to the Notes system.[3] These findings need to be interpreted cautiously as they only reflect the adoption and early use experiences of a sample of individuals within a specific office in what is a larger implementation process continuing over time in Alpha. While early, the findings to date are interesting as they reflect people's initial experiences and assessments of Notes in light of their current work practices and assumptions about technology. The initial period following the implementation of a technology is typically a brief and rare opportunity for users to examine and think about the technology as a discrete artifact, before it is assimilated into cognitive habits and work practices, and disappears from view [18]. It is possible that with time, greater use, and appropriate circumstances, these early experiences will change.

RESEARCH RESULTS

Background to the Notes Acquisition

In the late eighties, a few senior principals realized that Alpha, relative to its competitors and clients' expectations, was not utilizing information technology as effectively as they could. In response, they commissioned an internal study of the firm's technological capabilities, weaknesses, and requirements. On the basis of this study's recommendations, a new and powerful position--akin to that of a Chief Information Officer (CIO)--was created within Alpha with responsibility for the firm's internal use of information technology. One of the first tasks the new CIO took on was the creation of firm-wide standards for the personal computing environments utilized in Alpha offices. It was while reviewing communication software that the CIO was introduced to the Notes groupware system. As he remarked later, after a few days of "playing with Notes," he quickly realized that it was "a breakthrough technology," with the potential to create "a revolution" in how members of Alpha communicated and coordinated their activities. Shortly thereafter the CIO acquired a site license to install Notes throughout the firm, and announced that the product would be Alpha's communications standard.

The CIO began to market Notes energetically within various arenas of the firm. He gave numerous talks to principals and managers, both at national meetings and in local offices, during which he promoted his vision of how Notes "can help us manage our expertise and transform our practice." Through interest and persuasion, demand for Notes grew, and the physical deployment of the technology proceeded rapidly throughout the firm. The actual use of Notes within the office I studied, however, appeared to be advancing more slowly. While electronic mail usage had been adopted widely and enthusiastically, the use of Notes to share expertise, and the integration of Notes into work practices and policies had not yet been accomplished. The data I collected and analyzed during my field study of one office suggests that at least two organizational elements--cognitive and structural--influenced the participants' adoption, understanding, and early use of Notes.

2 henceforth referred to simply as "the office."

3 This research study represents the first of a series of studies that are being conducted within Alpha over time. Further analyses and observations are thus anticipated.

Cognitive Elements

Cognitive elements are the mental models or frames of references that individuals have about the world, their organization, work, technology, and so on. While these frames are held by individuals, many assumptions and values constituting the frames tend to be shared with others. Such sharing of cognitions is facilitated by common educational and professional backgrounds, work experiences, and regular interaction. In the context of groupware, those cognitive elements that have to do with information technology become particularly salient. Elsewhere, I have termed these *technological frames*, and described how they shape the way information technology is designed and used in organizations [7].

When confronted with a new technology, individuals try to understand it in terms of their existing technological frames, often augmenting these frames to accommodate special aspects of the technology. If the technology is sufficiently different, however, these existing frames may be inappropriate, and individuals will need to significantly modify their technological frames in order to understand or interact effectively with the new technology. How users change their technological frames in response to a new technology is influenced by (i) the kind and amount of product information communicated to them, and (ii) the nature and form of training they receive on the product.

(i) Communication about Notes

Employees in the office I studied received relatively little communication about Notes. Many of them first heard about the CIO's decision to standardize on Notes through the trade press. Others encountered it during Alpha's annual management seminars that form part of consultants' continuing education program. Most encountered it for the first time when it was installed on their computers. Without explicit information about what Notes is and why Alpha had purchased it, these individuals were left to make their own assumptions about the technology and why it was being distributed. This contributed to weakly developed technological frames around Notes in the office. Consider, for example, these remarks made by individuals a few weeks before Notes was to be installed on their computers:

> *I know absolutely nothing about Notes. I don't know what it is supposed to do.*
>
> *All I know is the firm bought it, but I don't know why.*
>
> *I first heard that the firm had bought Notes through the Wall Street Journal. Then your study was the next mention of it. That's all I know about it.*
>
> *I heard about Notes at the [management seminars] about eight months ago. I still don't know what it is.*
>
> *It has something to do with communications.*
>
> *It's big email.*
>
> *I've heard that it's hard copy of email ... but I am not very clear about what it is exactly.*
>
> *Is it a new version of 1-2-3?*
>
> *I believe Notes is putting word processing power into spreadsheets.*
>
> *It's a network... I don't know how the network works. Where does all this information go after I switch my machine off?*
>
> *It's a database housed somewhere in the center of the universe.*

Weakly developed technological frames of a new and different technology are a significant problem in technology transfer because people act towards technology on the basis of the meaning it has for them. If people have a poor or inappropriate understanding of the unique and different features of a new technology they may resist using it, or may not integrate it appropriately into their work practices. In the office, one consequence of such poor understanding was a skepticism towards Notes and its capabilities. For example, principals and managers in the office commented:

> *I first heard about Notes when I read in the Wall Street Journal that Alpha had purchased a revolutionary new piece of software. My first thought was -- how much is this costing me personally? ... [T]his kind of implementation affects all of our pocketbooks. ... I have [heard that] there is no value in information technology -- so you can imagine how I feel!*
>
> *When I first heard about it, I thought "Oh yeah? First hook me up to the network, and then I'll listen." Right now I still can't see the benefit.*
>
> *I don't believe that Notes will help our business that much, unless all of our business is information transfer. It's not. Business is based on relationships. Ideas are created in non-work situations, socially, over lunch, etc.*

Poor circulation of information about Notes was a consequence of the rapid installation of Notes that Alpha had pursued. The CIO had delegated responsibility for Notes deployment to the firm's technology group. Because demand for Notes was growing quickly, the technologists did not have an opportunity to plan the Notes rollout, and did not develop or pursue a formal implementation plan or information dissemination strategy. Two technology managers commented:

> *We tried to stay one step ahead of the firm's demand and [the CIO's] evangelism. We were swamped with requests. Every time [the CIO] gave a talk, we'd be deluged with requests for Notes. ... We had no time to do a formal plan or a grand strategy because [the CIO] had raised the level of enthusiasm in the firm, and there was no way we could say to the principals "wait while we get our act together."*
>
> *[The CIO] set the tone for the deployment strategy by generating interest in the product at the top. He was pushing a top-down approach, getting to all the principals first. So our deployment was driven by a lot of user pull and a little push from us. ... We were constantly struggling to keep up with demand.*

This rapid, demand-driven rollout was consistent with the CIO's assumption about how technologies such as Notes should be implemented. He commented that:

> *Our strategy was to blast Notes through our organization as quickly as possible, with no prototypes, no pilots, no lengthy technical evaluation. We want to transform the way we deliver service to clients.*

He believed that an "empowering" technology such as Notes should be put in the hands of as many people as possible, and that if the technology is compelling enough "they will drift into new ways of doing things." That is,

> *[I]f you believe that Notes is a competitive technology you have to deploy it quickly, and put it in the hands of the users as fast as possible. Critical mass is key.*

In particular, the CIO focused on convincing the key "opinion leaders" in the firm of the value of the technology, as he believed that these individuals would lead the charge in defining and spreading the uses of Notes throughout the firm.

(ii) Training on Notes

Training users on new technology is central to their understanding of its capabilities and appreciating how it differs from other technologies with which they are familiar. It also significantly influences the augmentation of existing technological frames or the development of new ones. Because the technologists were extremely busy deploying Notes and keeping it up and running, they did not have the resources to pay much attention to the education of users. Their first priority was to physically install hundreds of copies of Notes in multiple offices around the country and keep them operational. As one technology manager noted, it was a matter of priorities:

> *We made a conscious decision between whether we should throw it [Notes] to the users versus spending a lot of time training. We decided on the former.*

The under-emphasis on training was consistent with the CIO's general view that Notes does not require formal end-user training, and that it is through experimentation and use, not formal education programs that people begin to appreciate a technology's potential and learn to use it in different and interesting ways. This user-driven diffusion strategy, however, typically takes time, particularly in a busy services firm with considerable production pressures. Because this study did not detect any new user initiatives around the use of Notes in the office, it is possible that the timing of the research is simply too early in the implementation process. The following experiences thus represent the first encounters consultants had with Notes and how they initially appropriated it.

The training that was made available to users in the office I studied came in two forms, self-study and classroom training. The former provided users with a videotape and work-book, and covered Notes' basic functions and interfaces. The latter offered up to four hours of instruction and hands-on exercises by local computer support personnel. None of these training options emphasized its collaborative nature or possible business value. The training materials were relatively technical, individual-oriented, and non-specific in content. Trainees were exposed to the basic Notes functions such as electronic mail, editing, and database browsing. While facilitating the accessibility of the material to all individuals, from secretaries to principals, this "one size fits all" training strategy had the effect--at least initially--of not conveying the power of Notes to support specific consulting applications or group coordination.

This training on Notes resembled that of the training conducted on personal productivity tools. While useful for teaching the mechanics of Notes, it does not give users a new way of thinking differently about their work in terms of groupware. While Alpha was less concerned with collaborative or group work than with sharing expertise across the firm, the effect of the initial training was that participants in my study attempted to understand Notes through their existing frame of personal computing software. Such interpretations encouraged thinking about Notes as an individual productivity tool rather than as a collaborative technology or a forum for sharing ideas. For example, one manager noted:

> *I see Notes as a personal communication tool. That is, with a modem and fax applications I can do work at home or at a client site and use Notes to transfer work back and forth. In the office, instead of getting my secretary to make twenty copies of a memo she can just push a button.*

Further, the applications built for users by the technology group tended to automate existing information flows rather than creating new ones through the cooperative features of Notes. This reinforced the message that users received in their training, that Notes is an incremental rather than a transforming technology, and that new technological frames or new work practices around it are not required. Thus, in contrast to the technologists' vision of Notes as a technology that can "fundamentally change the way we do business," consultants in the office appeared to expect, at most, incremental improvements in operations. A manager noted:

> *The general perception of Notes is that it is an efficient tool, making what we do now better, but it is not viewed by the organization as a major change. Remember we're ... a management consulting firm and management consultants stick to management issues. We don't get into technology issues.*

Another said:

> *I think it will reduce the time of gathering information. I think it will cut down on frustration in transferring information. But it is not a radical change.*

As a result of the lack of resources that technologists had for communication and training, users of Notes in the office developed technological frames that either had weakly developed notions of Notes, or that interpreted Notes as a personal rather than a group or firm productivity tool. Because technological frames may change over time and with changing contexts, it is possible that the frames developed by the office participants will change over time. For example, if individuals are exposed to other applications of Notes developed elsewhere in the firm or in other firms, or if their increased use of Notes helps them understand how they can change the way they work, new understandings and uses of Notes may result. Our ongoing study of this implementation will monitor such possible developments.

Structural Elements

Structural properties of organizations encompass the reward systems, policies, work practices, and norms that shape and are shaped by the everyday action of organizational members. In the office, three such structural properties significantly influenced individuals' perceptions and early use of Notes.

(i) Reward Systems

Within Alpha there is an expectation--shared by many services firms--that all or most employee hours should be "billable," that is, charged to clients. This is a major evaluation criterion on which employees are assessed, and employees studiously avoid "non-billable hours." Because most of the participants did not initially perceive using Notes as a client-related activity (and hence as "not chargeable"), they were disinclined to spend time on it. Further, given their lack of understanding and skepticism of Notes, they were unwilling to give up personal time to learn or use it. Consider these comments from senior consultants and managers:

> *One of the problems is time. Given my billing rate, it makes no sense for me to take the time to learn the technology. In Alpha we put so much emphasis on chargeable hours and that puts a lot of pressure on managers. ... And now we've made an enormous commitment to Notes and Hardware, and LANs, but we haven't given people the time and opportunity to learn it. For them to do classes they have to work extra on weekends to meet deadlines.*
>
> *I think it is going to be a real issue to find time to use Notes. We don't have the time to read or enter information in Notes. What would I charge it to? We already complain that we can't charge our reading of our mail to anything. We end up having to charge it to ourselves [he reads his mail on the train going home].*
>
> *I don't think that Notes will ever be used in Alpha as effectively as it could be. We're not going to make sure everyone in the office has fifteen hours over the next year to spend time learning it. And if they expect us to take it out of our own time I'm not going to invest that time. I have another life too.*
>
> *The opportunity costs for me to take training in the office are very high. At my level, every week is a deadline, every week is a crisis. No accommodations are made in our schedules or workload to allow us to train on technology. So I won't learn it unless it's mandatory.*

Thus, one significant inhibitor of learning and using Notes was the office's reward system with its accompanying incentive schemes and evaluation criteria. Because the reward system had not changed since the implementation of Notes, consultants in the office perceived time spent on Notes as less legitimate than client work. While many used Notes for electronic mail or database browsing, these activities amounted to a few minutes a day, and hence were easily subsumed into client or personal time. However, any more extensive use of Notes was seen as potentially disrupting the balance between billable hours and personal time, and hence to be avoided. These concerns, however, varied by position in the office. Not surprisingly, principals were willing to take a longer-term and firm-wide perspective on Notes, being less preoccupied than were managers and senior consultants with time constraints, "billable hours," personal performance, and their own careers.

(ii) Policies and Procedures

Along with the few resources dedicated to Notes training and communication, the office--at the time of my study--had not formulated new work procedures or set new policies around data quality, confidentiality, and access control. Many participants indicated that their use of Notes was inhibited by their lack of knowledge about these issues, particularly concerns about liability (their own and Alpha's). Principals for example, worried about data security:

> *Security is a concern for me. ... We need to worry about who is seeing the data. ... Managers should not be able to access all the information even if it is useful, [such as] financial information to clients, because they leave and may go and work for competitors. So there should be prohibitions on information access.*
>
> *I am not sure how secure Notes is. Many times we have run into difficulties and things have got lost in never-never land.*
>
> *I have concerns about what goes into the databases and who has access to them and what access they have. ... But we haven't thought that through yet.*

Managers and senior consultants in the office were more anxious about personal liability or embarrassment:

> *I would be careful what I put out on Notes though. I like to retain personal control so that when people call me I can tell them not to use it for such and such. But there is no such control within Notes.*
>
> *My other concern is that information changes a lot. So if I put out a memo saying X today and then have a new memo two weeks later, the person accessing the information may not know about the second memo which had canceled the first. Also if you had a personal discussion you could explain the caveats and the interpretations and how they should and shouldn't use the information.*
>
> *I'd be more fearful that I'd put something out there and it was wrong and somebody would catch it.*

I would be concerned in using Notes that I would come to the wrong conclusion and others would see it. What would make me worry is that it was public information and people were using it and what if it was wrong? I would not want to be cited by someone who hasn't talked to me first. I'm worried that my information would be misconstrued and it would end up in Wichita, Kansas "as per J. Brown in New York" being used and relied on. You should be able to limit what access people have to what information, particularly if is your information. I would definitely want to know who was looking at it.

There is a hesitancy here because you don't want to put everything into public information as people may rely on that information and screw up, and it may reflect badly on you.

The lack of explicit procedures and policies around Notes highlights the difficulty of enforcing firm-wide policies in a decentralized firm. While the CIO has been able to institute standards around certain technology platforms--clearly a technical domain, instituting standard procedures and policies about data quality, control, and liability begins to encroach on the organizational domain--an arena where the CIO's authority is less established. As a result, the technologists have been careful about setting policies that would require organizational changes and that might invoke turf issues. Managers of local offices, however, had not devoted any attention to this issue, at least in the early adoption phase. As a result, there was some ambiguity about the locus and nature of responsibility and liability with respect to the intellectual content of Notes databases. This may have inhibited the application of Notes to a broader range of work practices in the early phase of implementation.

(iii) Firm Culture and Work Norms

Alpha shares with many other consulting firms a relatively competitive culture--at least at the levels below principal. The pyramidal structure and the hierarchical "up or out" career path promote and reinforce an individualistic culture among consultants, where those who have not yet attained principal status vie with each other to get the relatively few promotions handed out each year. In such a competitive culture, there are few norms around cooperating or sharing knowledge with peers. These comments by consultants in the office are illustrative:

This is definitely a competitive culture--it's an up or out atmosphere.

Usually managers work alone because of the competitiveness among the managers. There is a lot of one-upmanship against each other. Their life dream is to become a principal in Alpha, and they'll do anything to get there.

The atmosphere is competitive and cut-throat; all they want is to get ahead as individuals.

Interestingly, there was some evidence that there is much more collegiality at the highest levels of the firm, where principals--having attained tenure and the highest career rank--enact more of a "fraternal culture" than the competitive individualism evident at lower levels. This is also evident in service organizations with similar organizational structures, such as firms providing legal, accounting, or medical services. Below the principal level, however, managers and senior consultants in my study indicated that there was generally little precedent for sharing or cooperating with colleagues, and little incentive to do so as they needed to differentiate themselves from their peers. For example:

The corporate psychology makes the use of Notes difficult. Particularly the consultant career path which creates a back-stabbing and aggressive environment. People aren't backstabbing consciously, it's just that the environment makes people maximize opportunities for themselves.

I'm trying to develop an area of expertise that makes me stand out. If I shared that with you you'd get the credit not me.... It's really a cut-throat environment.

Power in this firm is your client base and technical ability. ... It is definitely a function of consulting firms. Now if you put all this information in a Notes database you lose power. There will be nothing that's privy to you, so you will lose power. It's important that I am selling something that no one else has. When I hear people talk about the importance of sharing expertise in the firm, I say "Reality is a nice construct."

The competitive individualism--which reinforces individual effort and ability, and does not support cooperation or sharing of expertise--is counter-cultural to the underlying premise of groupware technologies. It is thus not surprising that, at all but the highest career level, Notes is being used largely as an individual productivity tool in the office. Senior consultants and managers within this office feel little incentive to share their ideas for fear that they may lose status, power, and distinctive competence. Principals, on the other hand, do not share this fear and are more focused on the interests of the office and the firm than on their individual careers. An interesting contrast to this point, which further supports it, is that Notes is being used by Alpha technologists to exchange technical expertise. Not being subject to the competitive culture, individual-focused reward systems, "up-or-out" career pressures, and "chargeable hours" constraints of the consultants, the technologists appear to have been able to use the technology to conduct their work, that is, solving technical problems.

DISCUSSION

The results of this research suggest that the organizational introduction of groupware will interact with cognitive and structural elements, and that these elements will have significant implications for the adoption, understanding, and early use of the technology. Because people act towards technology on the basis of their understanding of it, people's technological frames often need to be changed to accommodate a new technology. Where people do not appreciate the premises and purposes of a technology they may use it in less effective ways. A major premise underlying groupware is the coordination of activities and people across time and space. For many users, such a premise may represent a radically different understanding of technology than they have experienced before. This suggests that a particularly central aspect of implementing groupware is ensuring that prospective users have an appropriate understanding of the technology, that is, that their technological frames reflect a perception of the technology as a collective rather than a personal tool.

At the time I conducted my study, many of the participants in the office did not have a good conception of what Notes was and how they could use it. Their technological frames around Notes were weakly developed and relied heavily on their knowledge and experience of other individually-used technologies. Given such cognitions, it is not surprising that in their early use of the technology, these participants had not generated new patterns of social interaction, nor had they developed fundamentally different work practices around Notes. Instead, they had either chosen not to use Notes, or had subsumed it within prior technological frames and were using it primarily to enhance personal productivity through electronic mail, file transfer, or accessing news services. As indicated above, however, these findings reflect an early phase of the participants' experiences with Notes. It is possible that these experiences will change over time as they get more accustomed to using Notes, and these are expected to change over time depending on their ongoing experiences with the technology.

Where a new technological frame is desirable because the technology is sufficiently unprecedented to require new assumptions and meanings, communication and education are central in fostering the development of new technological frames. Such communication and education should stress the required shift in technological frame, as well as provide technical and logistic information on use. A training approach that resembles that used for personal computing software is unlikely to help individuals develop an appreciation of groupware. For individuals used to personal computing environments and individual applications, shared technology use and cooperative applications are difficult to grasp. In these cases, concrete demonstrations of group applications can help to provide insight. Further, learning groupware collectively may foster joint understanding and expectations. Where individuals learn a shared technology in isolation, they may form their own assumptions, expectations, and procedures which may differ from those of the people they will interact with through the technology.

In situations where the premises underlying groupware are incongruent with those of the organization's culture, policies, and reward systems, it is unlikely that effective cooperative computing will result without a change in structural properties. Such changes are difficult to accomplish, and usually meet with resistance. Without such changes, however, the existing structural elements of the firm will likely serve as significant barriers to the desired use of the technology. For example, in the study described above, the existing norms, policies, and rewards appear to be in conflict with the premises of Notes. Because incentive schemes and evaluation criteria in the office had not been modified to encourage or accommodate cooperation and expertise sharing through Notes, members feared loss of power, control, prestige, and promotion opportunities if they shared their ideas, or if their lack of knowledge or misinterpretations were made visible. Thus, in a relatively competitive culture where members are evaluated and rewarded as individuals, there will be few norms for sharing and cooperating. If groupware is to be used cooperatively in such cultures, these norms need to be changed--either inculcated top-down through training, communication, leadership, and structural legitimation, or bottom-up through support for local opportunities and experimentation around cooperation. Without some such grounding in shared norms, groupware will likely be used primarily for advancing individual productivity.

In addition to norms, resources are a further important facilitator of shared technology use. Whether formally earmarked from some firm-wide R&D budget, or provided informally through local slack resources, occasions for experimenting with shared applications are needed to generate interest and use around cooperative computing. In the office, for example, there had been no change in the allocation of resources following the implementation of Notes, and members had not been given time to use and experiment with Notes. There was thus a tension between the structural requirement that all work be production-oriented, and the adoption of an infrastructure technology such as Notes which was perceived to be only indirectly related to production work. Where individuals are not given resources to learn and experiment with the new technology, or not given specific applications that help them accomplish their production work within the technology, the immediate pressures of daily production tasks and deadlines will tend to dominate their decisions around how they allocate their time.

This research study suggests that in the early adoption of a technology, cognitive and structural elements play an important role in influencing how people think about and assess the value of the technology. And these significantly influence how they choose to use the technology. When an organization deploys a new technology with an intent to make substantial changes in business processes, people's technological frames and the organization's work practices will likely require substantial change. An interesting issue raised by this requirement is how to anticipate the required structural and cognitive changes when the technology is brand new. That is, how do you devise a game plan if you have never played the game before? This is particularly likely in the case of an unprecedented technology such as groupware. One strategy would be to deploy the technology widely in the belief that through experimentation and use over time, creative ideas and innovations will flourish. Another strategy would prototype the technology in a representative group of the organization--on a pilot basis--and then deploy it to the rest of the organization once the technology's capabilities and implications are understood. This way the required structural and cognitive changes learned through the pilot can be transferred. Viewed in terms of these two strategies, aspects of Alpha's adoption activites now appear to resemble the former strategy. Our future studies should indicate how successful this strategy has been.

It is worth noting that while the early use of Notes in the office has proved more valuable for facilitating individual productivity than for collective productivity, the implementation of Notes has resulted in the installation of an advanced and standardized technology infrastructure. As one technology manager put it: "A side-benefit of Notes is that it got people into a more sophisticated environment of computing than we could have done otherwise." Most of the office members--from principals to senior consultants--now have ready and easy access to a network of personal computers and laser printers. Thus, while the initial experiences with Notes in the office may not have significantly changed work practices or policies, the office appears to be relatively well-positioned to use this platform to take advantage of any future technological or work-related initiatives.

In general, the findings presented here provide insight for future research into the structural and cognitive organizational elements that interact with and shape the adoption and early use of groupware in organizations. They also have practical implications, indicating how and where such organizational elements might be managed to more effectively implement groupware in various organizational circumstances.

ACKNOWLEDGMENTS

Support from MIT's Center for Coordination Science is gratefully acknowledged. Jolene Galegher, Bob Halperin, Tom Malone, and Judith Quillard provided helpful comments on an earlier version of the paper. Thanks are also due to the participants from Alpha Corporation.

REFERENCES

1. Bair, J.H. and Gale, S. An Investigation of the COORDINATOR as an Example of CSCW, *Proc. CSCW* (Portland, September 1988).

2. Bullen, C. and Bennett, J. Groupware in Practice: An Interpretation of Work Experience, *Proc. CSCW* (Los Angeles, October 1990), 291-302.

3. Dyson, Esther Why Groupware is gaining Ground, *Datamation* (March 1, 1990), 52-56.

4. Eveland, J.D. and Bikson, T.K. "Evolving Electronic Communication Networks: An Empirical Assessment," *Proc. CSCW* (Austin, August 1986), 91-101.

5. Feldman, M.S. Electronic Mail and Weak Ties in Organizations, *Office: Technology and People*, 3 (1987), 83-101.

6. Finholt, T. and Sproull, L.S. Electronic Groups at Work, *Organization Science*, 1:1 (1990), 41-64.

7. Gash, D.C. and Orlikowski, W.J. Changing Frames: Towards an Understanding of Information Technology and Organizational Change, *Academy of Management Best Papers Proc.*, 51st Annual Meeting (Miami Beach, August 1991), 189-193.

8. Govani, Stephen J. License to Kill, *Information Week* (January 6, 1992), 22-28.

9. Groupware: The Teamwork Approach, Supplement to *PC Week*, 8, 41 (October 14, 1991).

10. Grudin, J. Why CSCW applications fail: Problems in design and evaluation of Organization Interfaces, *Proc. CSCW* (Portland, September 1990), 85-93.

11. Kiesler, S. The Hidden Messages in Computer Networks, *Harvard Business Review* (January-February 1986), 46-59.

12. Kling, R. Cooperation, Coordination, and Control in Computer-Supported Work, *Comm. of the ACM*, 34, 2 (1991), 83-88.

13. Mackay, W.E. Diversity in the Use of Electronic Mail, *ACM Transactions on Office Information Systems*, 6:4 (1988), 380-397.

14. Markus, M. L.. Toward a 'Critical Mass' Theory of Interactive Media, *Communication Research*, 14:5 (October 1987), 491-511.

15. Marshak, David S. Lotus Notes: A Platform for Developing Workgroup Applications, *Patricia Seybold's Office Computing Report*, (July 1990).

16. Perin, C. Electronic Social Fields in Bureaucracies *Comm. of the ACM*, 34, 2 (1991), 75-82.

17. Sproull, L.S. and Kiesler, S. Reducing Social Context Cues: Electronic Mail in Organizational Communication, *Management Science*, 32, 11 (1986), 1492-1512.

18. Tyre, M.J. and Orlikowski, W.J. Windows of Opportunity: Creating Occasions for Technological Adaptation in Organizations, Sloan School of Management #3309, MIT (Cambridge, July 1992).

From Human Factors to Human Actors: The Role of Psychology and Human-Computer Interaction Studies in System Design

Liam J. Bannon

Man is one of the best general-purpose computers available and if one designs for man as a moron, one ends up with a system that requires a genius to maintain it. Thus we are not suggesting that we take man out of the system, but we are suggesting that he be properly employed in terms of both his abilities and limitations.

E. Llewellyn Thomas, 1965

I believe that there needs to be a better understanding among researchers, and among many system designers too, about the "users" of computer systems and the settings in which they work. Part of the problem resides in an implicit view of ordinary people which, if surfaced, would seem to treat people as, at worst, idiots who must be shielded from the machine, or as, at best, simply sets of elementary processes or "factors" that can be studied in isolation in the laboratory. Although psychology, particularly as represented by the field of human factors (HF) or ergonomics, has had a long tradition of contributing to computer systems design and implementation, it has often neglected vitally important issues such as the underlying values of the people involved and their motivation in the work setting.

Understanding people as "actors" in situations, with a set of skills and shared practices based on work experience with others, requires us to seek new ways of understanding the relationship between people, technology, work requirements, and organizational constraints in work settings. Studying such a multi-faceted and multi-layered issue requires that we go beyond more traditional controlled laboratory studies that are the hallmark of experimental human-computer interaction (HCI) studies. In this chapter I recount some experiences, give some background on the field of HCI, and point out some problems. I suggest some alternative perspectives and directions for more fruitful research on, or rather with, people in work settings that may assist in the design of more usable and useful computer systems.

A True Story

I once worked in the human factors group of a large organization and was asked to build an interface to a particular system. I was given the manuals from the previous system, some reports by investigators of problems noted with this system, and some specifications of the new hardware and software capabilities and the new functional specifications. Fine, as far as it went. My wish was to go out and talk with users of the current system, to get a better "feel" of the situation they were working in, and subsequently to interact with them in an iterative design process in order to make a usable interface. To my astonishment, I was informed that not only could I not proceed in this fashion, but—ultimate irony—I was not allowed, for political organizational reasons, to meet with even a single user throughout this process! I complained, but being in a very junior position, I was overruled, so I then spent some months on what seemed to me an insane task: developing a logically coherent, though naive, mapping of tasks onto a menu-based interface based solely on the paper specifications I had been given. A report was duly completed and forwarded to another level in the organization, and much of it was actually implemented, to my amazement. Given my deskbound, limited knowledge of the actual use situation, I am sure that many of my "logically" elegant design solutions turned out to be hopelessly complex and/or inappropriate in the real work situation.

I do not want to claim that such a situation is the norm, but I do claim that this true scenario is not nearly as far from normality as one would hope. Granted, the fault here does not lie solely at the feet of the HCI community. Within this organization, however, that group must take some of the blame for not stressing an iterative design process that insisted on *active* user participation. This is partly due to a rather limited perspective on what users can offer in the design process, compounded by organizational politics that sometimes makes contact between designers and users a more difficult process than one would suppose. Readers might keep this little story in mind as they read the rest of the text, as the link between it and some of the attitudes and practices of designers and researchers discussed here should emerge. In the next section I take a short tour of the landscape of human factors and user interface design, note a few pertinent examples of terminology which betray a certain limited view of the people that we aim to design for, and suggest some alternatives.

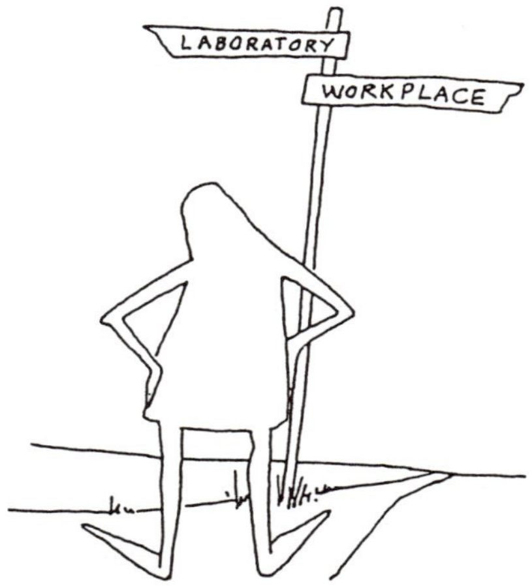

A Question of Perspective(s)

> Language does not simply symbolize a situation or object which is already there in advance—it makes possible the existence or appearance of that situation or object, for it is part of the mechanism whereby that situation or object is created. (Mead, 1934, p. 78)

Replacing Human Factors with Human Actors

The terms used in a discipline often give a clue as to how members "see" that field. Once certain distinctions are accepted and become part of the standard vocabulary, these terms can become a barrier to the reality that lies outside. For this reason, it is a useful exercise to periodically reexamine the language used to express our understanding of the world. I have chosen to use the terms human factors and human actors in the title of the chapter as I believe it highlights a difference in the perception of the person; the former connoting a passive, fragmented, depersonalized, unmotivated individual, the latter connoting an active, controlling one. I claim that traditional human factors work, although it undoubtedly has merit and has produced many improvements to existing technological systems, is often limited in scope with respect to its view of the person. Within the HF approach, the human is often reduced to being another system component with certain characteristics, such as limited attention span, faulty memory, etc., that need to be factored into the design equation for the overall human-machine system. This form of piece-meal analysis of the person as a set of components de-emphasizes important issues in work design. Individual motivation, membership in a community of workers, and the importance of the setting in determining human action are just a few of the issues that are neglected. People are more than a sum of parts; be they information-processing subsystems or physiological systems, they have a set of values, goals, and beliefs about life and work. This more encompassing interpretation of the human factors field is not signaled by the name, nor by the bulk of studies appearing under this topic in the journals so designated. By using the term *human actors* emphasis is placed on the person as an autonomous agent that has the capacity to regulate and coordinate his or her behavior, rather than being simply a passive element in a human-machine system. This change in terminology may help in adjusting one's perspective, emphasizing the holistic nature of the person acting in a setting, and contrasting with the view of the person as a set of information processing mechanisms which can be analyzed in the same manner as the information processing mechanisms of the technology.[1]

Re-thinking the Concept of "Users"

Another term ubiquitous in articles about the HCI field that deserves scrutiny is that of *users*. This general term refers to all people who use a particular computer system or application. It can be distinguished from the term "operators" in that the latter implies a greater involvement with the machine or system, presumably one where the person is more uniquely assigned to the device. The focus of the system design or HCI research group is biased towards the technology; the view of people is often simply as "users" of this piece of technology, and "naive users" at that. This can lead to problems. People may not know the technology, but they are not naive as to their work; rather it is the system designers who are "work naive." There is nothing inherently wrong in taking this stance—though in talking of naive users, I prefer the less judgmental terms "casual" or "discretionary users"—for periods when designing computer applications, but there is a danger in thinking of people as *nothing but* users. In fact, it is often still the case that computer users need to make some modifications to the system in various ways, tailoring the system before it is truly usable (see Chapter 11). So in a very real sense *users are designers* as well. Focusing on people simply as users can also blind us to the fact that

---

1 Similar concerns about the role of human factors, including reference to this issue of human actors, can be found in the work of Niels Bjørn-Andersen. See, for example, the paper "Are human factors human?" (Bjørn-Andersen, 1988).

the user's view of the technology we are developing may be very different from that of the designer's view. The user is often a worker who has a set of tasks to perform, and the use of the computer may be only one element necessary to the accomplishing of this work. We can become focused in design on one particular application and forget that the user has needs differing from that of simply performing the set of system operations. For example, Whiteside and Wixon (1987) note one case where a word processing clerk spent a lot of time manually counting the lines she had typed because she was paid by the line, but the particular system did not have a facility to do this (relatively straightforward) task. Often the user is involved in multi-tasking not just on the computer, but also with co-workers, perhaps with clients through the phone system, and sundry daily happenings. Neglecting this rich and complex set of "nonessential" but truly everyday work interactions can lead to unworkable or unwieldy systems (see Cypher, 1986). It is the ability to understand the user perspective, to be able to see a problem from other than the system viewpoint, to be able to empathize and work with the users of the intended system that marks the good design team.

Users are not Idiots

Although viewing computer users as naive is bad enough, viewing them as idiots is even worse. Apart from the values question that arises, there are clear design implications if this faulty view of users is implicitly adopted. Just because users do not understand how the machine works or have difficulty with the system designer's terminology, does not imply that they are stupid, as some developers apparently conclude, if we are to judge from the systems that are at times designed. The system design team should start out with the understanding that workers/users are competent practitioners, people with work tasks and relationships which need to be taken into account in the design of systems, and with whom they must collaborate in order to develop an appropriate computer system. The idea that we must design systems so that "any idiot can use them" bears close scrutiny. Taking this as a serious design goal can often result in systems that necessarily produce such stupid behavior (see Bannon, 1986a, for further comment). In addition, as noted in the opening quotation, a consequence of trying to make such a system is that an incredible amount of "intelligence" must go into its initial design and maintenance. Taken to the extreme, we have the prospect of artificially intelligent systems operated by morons—an absurd scenario. Fortunately, in recent years this particular problem seems to have diminished, probably as a result of designers and others finally developing a better understanding of the user's perspective. A slightly less obnoxious version of this can be seen in the overemphasis on "easy to learn" systems in HCI research. Certainly, there are some applications where a minimal interface that is easy to learn is desirable, but this is not usually the case when dealing with systems that will be used by people in their everyday long-term work. We need to pay attention to the capabilities of the system and allow users greater flexibility and expressiveness in their use of it.

Allow for Active Users

Whereas focusing attention on the user may be a positive step, users are not simply passive objects that others must study and design for, as some accounts would have it. People are, or can become, *active agents*. They often wish to accomplish tasks, to understand what is going on, and are willing to jump ahead and explore the computer system on their own if, for example, the tutorial material is unclear or pedantic. If the system does not give an explanation for its behavior, the user will often try to make one up in order to render the doings of the system comprehensible. People are always struggling to make sense of their world. Developing instruction sequences to be followed by rote, with inadequate explanation, fails to satisfy or even to work in most real situations. For example, in discussing LisaGuide, an on-line tutorial for the Lisa system, Carroll and Mazur (1986) note one user's reaction: "I'm getting impatient. I want to do something, not learn how to do everything." (p. 39). Understanding the needs of active users has been the subject of investigation by psychologists, with Carroll and his colleagues prominent among them (Carroll & Rosson, 1987). Here are the words of an office worker, a user whom I interviewed, which capture her wish to understand, and to learn what's going on.

> People have to know how to understand, they have to be able to rationalize things out, to work things out, in a logical sequence. If they don't understand something, or how it works, then they have to go back to either just learning it by rote, or by asking, or by just making the mistake, and going back, and asking, and then correcting. But if you understand the system a little bit then sometimes you can think it out ..... and if you can reason it out then it stays with you longer—it's easier to understand, to work with. But if you are just learning piecemeal, then you can't. If you are just learning by rote.... someone tells you, this is the way to do it, then you can memorize it, but you'll never fully understand it, and [never] be able to expand from there.

In summary, we can see on reflection that some of the concepts and terms common in the system design and HCI research fields contain at least an implicit, if not explicit, perspective on users of computer systems that I would claim is inaccurate and liable to lead to faulty design decisions. Likewise, within the theory and research areas of HCI, this perspective has led to a concentration on issues that can be studied in the laboratory at the expense of other concerns that might be more crucial in actual work settings. But exactly what is this HCI field, and how did it come about? In the next section, I give a brief account of the origins of the field, before proceeding to discuss the current status of HCI—some results, limitations, and possible future directions.

The Field of Human Factors and Human-Computer Interaction: Some Background

This section gives a short account of the changing relationship between people and the machines with which they work, and the contribution of human factors studies in these changes. It is evident that unless a process is totally automated there will still be a need for some human intervention. How to divide the work between the human and the machine becomes an important task. Traditionally, in human factors, this "allocation of functions" task proceeds according to sets of guidelines about general human and machine performance capacities. We also need to design an "interface" between the machine and the person—knobs, dials, displays, controls—so that they can interact at some level. In the early days of this century, the focus was on how to get a machine to perform to the required functionality. The human component was often reduced to yet another "cog" in the overall machine—one that was, at times, more expendable than the machine. The slow improvement in the conditions and nature of work for people operating with machines came about not simply for altruistic reasons, but partly also in the search for greater efficiency of operation. Poorly trained or motivated operators and poorly designed equipment could cause breakdowns in the smooth functioning of the industrial process. Better designed controls and tasks that reduced both mental and physical strain on the operator allowed for improved performance of the human-machine system. The attempt to fit the machine to the skills and limitations, both physical and mental, of the operator developed into a new field of applied study early this century. This new field was called *human factors engineering* in North America, and similar efforts in Europe became known as *ergonomics*, from the Greek words *ergon*, meaning work, and *nomos*, which can mean law or knowledge. People working in this field usually had a background in either behavioral science or industrial engineering. Physiologists and medical practitioners also contributed to the understanding of human capabilities and limitations in work settings—effects of stress, psycho-motor ability, perceptual acuity, mental processing workloads, etc. Out of this observational and occasionally experimental discipline arose a body of knowledge that could be useful in the design of complex human-machine systems (see Van Cott & Kinkade, 1972).

In the early days of this century the problem was to build machine systems to do something useful. The focus was on the machine performance, as I noted previously. Machines were not being substantially modified every year, so the *ease of learning* of the system was not a high priority. Training was a one-shot process. People could be trained to perform whatever operations were required and subsequently serve as operators of the machine. As computing developed, the separation between operating and programming developed. Focus was still on the functionality of the software rather than on its ease of use. Programmers spent years learning arcane languages to communicate with the system. The user community started to change from one that was focused either on studying the properties of the machines themselves (computer scientists) or on application programmers that mediated between user needs and the computer system. A growing number of people using computers could be classified as *discretionary* users, people who saw themselves as having a job or profession that was not primarily geared to the computing medium itself, but who used it directly as a tool in their everyday work. However, these people were frustrated by the difficulty of learning how to program computers for their work. With the advent of the personal computer over a decade ago it was obvious that their widespread acceptance would become more dependent on their ease of learning and use. Not everyone was willing to learn something akin to IBM's notorious Job Control Language (JCL) in order to operate a personal computer.[2]

The field of human-computer interaction (HCI) emerged in the early eighties partly as a response to these changing conditions. It was linked to, but somewhat distinct from, its human factors pro-

2 Paradoxically, this emphasis on making systems easy to learn and use has now resulted in an over-emphasis in research and design on this aspect of computer use, with a consequent decline in attention to how to allow for the growth of competence and skill on many computer systems. I elaborate on this point later in the chapter.

genitor in both its eclectic makeup and its more theoretical bias.[3] The older field, somewhat dismissively referred to as "knobs and dials" psychology, was seen as lacking in theoretical motivation by cognitive scientists. What was required was a better *cognitive coupling* between the human and the new universal machine, the computer, and not simply better designed surface characteristics of displays. Software engineers were also involved, as they were experimenting with the design of highly interactive interfaces and were concerned about how to conduct dialogues with users and present complex information effectively to them on graphic displays. Over the last decade the area of human-computer interaction has grown enormously, both within academic research environments and corporate research laboratories. This commercial concern was a major impetus for HCI studies, and "ease-of-use" and "user-friendliness" have become advertisements for particular computer systems.

Beyond Current Conceptions of HCI

Despite the legitimate advances that have been made in various arenas of human-computer interaction (see Shneiderman, 1987, for a collation of some of this material), there has been serious criticism of the field for its lack of relevance to practitioners in system design. Despite the widespread interest, no clear set of principles has emerged from this work. The experience of certain designers has been loosely codified, various long lists of design guide-lines are available, and a large number of evaluations of existing systems have been produced; but the attempt to place this applied science on a more rigorous footing has been difficult. Gray and Atwood (1988), in a review of a recent collection of papers (Carroll, 1987), noted the lack of any examples of developed systems in the papers and the general lack of contact of the work with "real world" design situations. They explicitly state that the skeptical designer will not be convinced of the relevance of the cognitive sciences to the design of better human-computer systems based on this work. Within this collection, a discussion section by Whiteside and Wixon (1987) makes a number of pointed observations about the limitations of cognitive theory in its application to everyday design situations.

If there is not too much in the way of theory that is directly relevant, can we utilize some of the sophisticated methods and techniques used in psychology to analyze user behavior, so that designers could find out how users perform on different versions of a system, or different prototypes, and not have to rely on intuition? Standard lab experimentation is too limited, costly, and time-consuming. What is needed are quick and dirty methods that can give rapid feedback to designers about the utility and usability of their products. This is happening in practice currently, in the work on *usability*. Design involves making many tradeoffs, and in many instances empirical data can assist in determining the appropriate choices. Such tasks as setting up small in workplace empirical studies, noting reactions, user preferences, taking verbal protocols from subjects to see how they view the application, etc., are all investigative methods familiar to psychologists which can be useful in an iterative design process.

Cognitive psychologists have also studied particular issues; for example, we now know a lot about how people learn to use word processors, about the kinds of errors they make on different systems, about the mental models they attempt to construct of systems; but the application of such findings to new situations is not always obvious. From the perspective of the designer, the work to date can highlight some pertinent issues, but we are still impoverished in our search for new ways of thinking about and developing systems. The hoped-for contribution of HCI to the design of completely novel interfaces has not yet materialized, though some believe that it may come, given a shift in priorities among psychology researchers (Carroll, 1989).

I believe that there are a number of limitations in much of the current work on HCI that needs to be remedied for the field to be more useful to designers in practical situations. In the following paragraphs I suggest some changes in direction within the field of HCI that might help bridge the gap between theory, experiment, system design, and the actual work setting.

From Product to Process in Research and Design

By this I mean that more attention needs to be paid to the *process* of design, that is, working with users in all stages of design, to see the iterative nature of design and the changing conception of what one is designing as a result of the process itself. This is in contrast to a view of design that proceeds from a set of fixed requirements without iteration and without involvement of the users. This change in orientation has been evident for some time in much of the system design work within the Scandinavian tradition (see Chapter 9). It is also evident in the work of Jones (1988) and Floyd (1987), from industrial design and software engineering backgrounds, respectively, and by Bannon and Bødker (1989) in the field of HCI.

3 Earlier human factors "man-machine communication" (sic) groups, were mainly working within military high-performance environments e.g. fighter aircraft cockpit displays. Another traditional area of concern for ergonomists was in general occupational heath and safety studies, e.g. determining noise safety levels in factory settings.

From Individuals to Groups

The majority of HCI studies to date take as their focus the individual user working on a computer system. This research focus totally neglects the importance of coordination and cooperation between work processes that is necessary in many work situations. Indeed, here again the applied field has been more astute than the theoretical. System designers have been aware of this coordinated aspect of work activity and have tried to support it from early on, albeit rather crudely. For example, much of the office automation work in the 1970s attempted to model work flows, but in too rigid a manner, thereby not allowing the human "components" in the overall system enough flexibility to make the system work. With a better understanding of how work gets accomplished coming from the research of Suchman and Wynn (1984), designers have a better "model" from which to build. The word "model" is in quotes here because such research shows that a strict model of human action in most work situations is not possible or appropriate; rather, human action is driven by the concrete situation that exists at any moment and is constantly changing. This implies that we should *support office workers in their activities*, rather than building *office automation systems*. Extending the focus of concern from the human-computer dyad to larger groups of people and machines engaged in collaborative tasks is an important area for research in the next period. The quick growth of this field, labelled Computer Support for Co-operative Work (CSCW), attests to its importance.[4]

From the Laboratory to the Workplace

Much of the early research done in the HCI field was confined to rather small, controlled experiments, with the presumption that the findings could be generalized to other settings. Examples of such studies were those done on command naming conventions (see Barnard & Grudin, 1988 for a review of this research). It has become increasingly apparent that such studies suffer from a variety of problems that limit their usefulness in any practical setting. First, by the time these studies are done the technology often makes the original concerns outdated. Witness the disappearance of line-oriented editors from commercial systems just as a "scientific" understanding of how people used them was being developed. Newell and Card (1985) refer to this problem as the race between the tortoise of cumulative science and the hare of intuitive design. Important contextual cues for the accomplishment of tasks were often omitted in this transfer from the real world to the laboratory, so the results of the lab studies became difficult to apply elsewhere. Increasingly, attention is shifting to in situ studies, in an effort to "hold in" the complexity of the real world situations, and a variety of observational techniques, especially video, are being employed to capture activities. We can see an increasing focus on the concept of "usability" among the research community—whether people can and do actually use the resulting systems designed for them.[5] From a design perspective, this means that we need a prototype or test system for users to experience in order to get information on the usability of the resulting system. There are many examples from recent large development projects that point out the importance of empirical methods for getting feedback on design decisions from users. For example, on the path-breaking Xerox Star system, both formal experiments (Bewley, Roberts, Schroit, & Verplank, 1983) and informal studies were used extensively. On the Apple Lisa, the designers note "Another thing we have done is user tests—taking our ideas and bringing in naive users and sitting them down and seeing what their impressions are. This has caused some changes, and I think that's all shown in the quality." (BYTE Interview, 1983, p. 100). Having psychologists on the design team can thus assist in the planning, conduct, and evaluation of such studies, whether or not detailed manipulations and data analyses are planned.

From Novices to Experts

The majority of experimental studies in HCI focus on first time learners of computer systems or applications. Typically, performance is monitored for the first hour or two on the system. Exceptionally, perhaps, use of an application is observed over a few days, but rarely for periods longer, such as weeks, never mind years. This has been due partly to the ease of obtaining naive subjects for experiments from subject-pools at universities and employment centers. While granting that there is some need for studying such users, the paucity of studies that are concerned with the process of development of expertise with a computer application is remarkable. The issue is not simply that expert performance needs further examination, but that we need to pay greater attention to how users become skilled in the use of the computer application.

4 See Greif, 1988, for a selection of papers in this area, and Bannon & Schmidt (1989) for an overview of the field.

5 For an excellent tutorial on designing for usability see the chapter by Gould in Helander (1988). The chapter by Whiteside, Bennett, and Holtzblatt on usability engineering in the same volume is also worth studying. What these articles note is how difficult it is to evaluate the usability of an artifact without investigating the situations of use of that artifact. See Bannon & Bødker (1989) for an extension of this argument.

What obstacles or incentives are there within the system to encourage the growth of competence? Additional issues relate to the difference in system learning and use between freshman university students and particular work groups with their own already-established set of work practices which may hinder or support learning and development of competence on the computer system.[6]

From Analysis to Design

Early human factors work tended to focus on evaluation of existing systems, and analysis of features that had been found in the use situation to be good or bad from the point of view of the user. However, the concern of people in HCI now is how to build better artifacts. We don't just want to know about systems after they have been built, we want to know how we should build them in the first place, and even what we should build.[7] HCI should be a design science: "Design is where the action is," to quote a memorable phrase of Allen Newell. The question is how can HCI contribute to the design of more usable and more useful artifacts? Newell and Card (1985) argue for the importance of giving designers approximate calculational models of the person performing a task for use in making design decisions about the human-computer interface. Many groups are currently active in such user modelling, looking at the structure, content, and dynamics of individual user cognition at the interface. Much work in the area continues the GOMS (Goals, Operators, Methods, and Selection rules) model tradition of Card, Moran, and Newell (1983), extending it in various ways. The practicality and utility of such low-level calculational models in actual design has been the subject of some debate (Carroll & Campbell, 1986). While some reject this approach as narrow and time-consuming, others have pursued even more generalized user models as design support aids. For example, the concept of Programmable User Models (PUMs) (Young, Green, & Simon, 1989) is based on a generalized architecture of human cognition. This approach to assisting system designers in understanding users' needs appears to be unduly narrow. Rather than moving designers closer to actual users, such a device, if it existed, would seem to support the view that actual contact with real users was unnecessary. The designer could just program the PUM in order to understand the constraints on usability, and potentially not have to observe actual users at all. The very vision of a PUM seems a rather abstract view of human activity in the world, and to imply a rather strange relationship, or lack of one, between designers and users. I would claim that both the GOMS work and that on PUMs support a human factor, rather than a human actor perspective discussed earlier. Such work can never replace prototyping and actual empirical user testing, although it might have a role at a certain stage in the design of a new system.

From User-Centered to User-Involved Design

As a first step towards focusing the attention of the designer on the needs of the user and away from a concentration on the hardware, there has been an increasing emphasis on taking a "user-centered" approach to design (Norman & Draper, 1986). Exactly what the term user-centered system design means, or how it can be achieved, is far from clear. In some cases it dissolves into platitudes such as "Know the User." Such kinds of general guidelines are of little use in practical situations of design due to their lack of specificity. Gould (1988) discusses how important it is to have an early and continuous focus on users, to develop iterative designs, and to have early and continuous user testing. This is a step in the right direction: Users are being given a larger role in the design process, but it is still a relatively passive role. Although actual participation by users on the design team is mentioned, it does not figure prominently in this user-centered approach. A more radical departure from current thinking within the mainstream HCI world is to look at users not simply as objects of study, but as active agents within the design process itself. This involvement of users in design is both a means for promoting democratization in the organizational change process and a way to ensure that the resulting computer system adequately meets the needs of the users. It is this approach that has been the hallmark of many of the Scandinavian studies mentioned in this book and evident in its chapters.

From User Requirements Specifications to Iterative Prototyping

Over the years, it has been acknowledged that the standard way of representing user requirements in the functional requirements specification document is often inadequate, and the question has begun to be asked whether this is because of some problems in the way of doing the studies locally, or whether there is a fundamental problem with the very assumption that we can map out in advance users' needs and requirements successfully through simple techniques of observation and interviewing. In Part II of this book, it is argued that users need to have the experience of being in the future use situation, or an approximation of it, in order to be able to comment on

---

6 For more on this issue of qualifications and computer use, see Bødker (1989).

7 Given how often new design emerges from old however, this distinction between analysis or evaluation of existing systems and design of new ones is perhaps too strict. In many cases, evaluation of current systems can provide important "feed-forward" into the next design as well, and usually does so in practice.

the advantages and disadvantages of the proposed system. Thus, some form of mock-up or prototype needs to be built in order to let users know what the future use situation might be. In the construction and evaluation of such prototypes, the skills of the psychologist can be useful. This particular issue is a part of the previously mentioned shift from a product to a process orientation in both research and development of systems.

Conclusion: HCI in System Design

Some distinctions can be drawn between different kinds of system development projects.[8] In the development of products the need to have a user-friendly interface is very high, as it can determine the success of the product in the marketplace. At the same time, the exact user group for the newly designed product is not clearly specified in advance. This can have implications for user-involvement in design, as discussed throughout this book. However, it does not invalidate the need to work with future users; it just means that we cannot be as sure about satisfying their needs as fully as we can on a system development project oriented towards a single application for a particular, specific group. We should be able to find representative users to at least allow us to iteratively prototype the design. Much of this book is dealing with another form of project, specific development projects, where the involvement of users is the least problematic because, at least in theory, we know who they are. In some projects, requirements specifications may be drawn up by third parties, other than the users and developers, and this can make it difficult though not impossible to utilize some of the user-involvement techniques outlined in Part II.

Understanding the needs and the tasks performed by the user is basic to the system development process. However, it is a mistake to think that simply having a human factors person on the design team is by itself sufficient to ensure that the human factor has been adequately taken into account, in the sense that is being discussed here. Even in companies where there exist groups specifically targeted to give human factors advice on projects, one often finds that they have little influence over the design process, and are often regarded as "add-ons" by the engineering staff. This state of affairs has sometimes been encouraged, unfortunately, by the human factors personnel themselves, who often seem unwilling to understand the complete project or product, but focus on the narrow aspects that are adjudged to require human factors input. Such an attitude can also be forced on human factors people as a result of the structure and functioning of the organization, with project support from the HF unit only allowed at certain periods, and the physical separation of the HF department from that of the software engineering group.

Human factors, or ergonomics considerations, are often incorporated into the design process simply as a set of specifications to which the delivered system must adhere. The actual work of the human factors personnel is seen as operator task analyses to be fed into these specifications, and perhaps some interface retouching near the end of the development cycle, when the system design has already been fixed. In general, the role of these people has been seen as ancillary to the main task of building the system. The role of HF or HCI in system design today should be more fluid and pragmatic. Input is vital in discussing the initial capabilities of the system and its required functionality, persisting in the development and evaluation of prototypes, and in final screen layout considerations.

What is being advocated here is an approach which, although acknowledging the contribution that different disciplines can make to the design process, ultimately depends upon the users themselves to articulate their requirements, along with the system design team composed of a variety of specialists acting in the capacity of consultants to the project. Design teams and users must be prepared to acknowledge each others' competencies and to realize that effort must be made by both parties to develop a mutually agreeable vocabulary of concepts that can be shared by the different groups comprising the project. It is no easy task for different disciplines and work activities to accomplish this; additional research would be valuable in this area.

Some of the efforts in Scandinavia on involving users in design (see, e.g., Bjerknes, Ehn, & Kyng, 1987) provide a promising start towards the alternative system design paradigm advocated here, at least for project system development. Within such an approach, the starting and end point of the design process is with the users themselves, from what they require, to how they evaluate the prototype, and the iterations that follow. Along the way, the services of a variety of disciplines may be required, not just those of the software engineer and the ergonomist, but also perhaps architects, sociologists, and anthropologists. These disciplines should come together in the overall design process as required, and not as dictated by some arbitrary flow model by which the system design gets handed around sequentially from one discipline to another. It is from the mutual interaction of these different perspectives, including that of the end users, focused on a particular design project, that good design may emanate.

---

8 These distinctions originate from remarks by Jonathan Grudin, and have been developed in subsequent discussions with Susanne Bødker, Kaj Grønbæk, and Jonathan Grudin.

Acknowledgments

Thanks to Niels Bjørn-Andersen, Susanne Bødker, Jonathan Grudin, Randy Trigg, and the Editors for helpful comments on earlier drafts.

References

Bannon, L. (1986a). Issues in design: Some notes. In D. A. Norman & S. W. Draper (Eds.), *User centered system design: New perspectives on human-computer interaction* (pp. 25-29). Hillsdale, NJ: Lawrence Erlbaum Associates.

Bannon, L. (1986b). Helping users help each other. In D. A. Norman & S. W. Draper (Eds.), *User centered system design: New perspectives on human-computer interaction* (pp. 399-410). Hillsdale, NJ: Lawrence Erlbaum Associates.

Bannon, L. & Bødker, S. (1989). Beyond the interface: Encountering artifacts in use. Aarhus, Denmark: Aarhus University, Computer Science Department. DAIMI PB-288. (To be published as a chapter in J. M. Carroll (Ed.), *Designing interaction: Psychological theory at the human-computer interface*).

Bannon, L. & Schmidt, K. (1989). CSCW: Four characters in search of a context. In *Proceedings of First European Conference on Computer Support for Cooperative Work* (pp. 358-372). Gatwick, UK.

Barnard, P. & Grudin, J. (1988). Command names. In M. Helander (Ed.), *Handbook of human-computer interaction* (pp. 237-255). Amsterdam: North-Holland.

Bewley, W., Roberts, T., Schroit, D., & Verplank, W. (1983). Human factors testing in the design of Xerox's 8010 "Star" office workstation. *Proceedings CHI'83 Conference on Human Factors in Computing Systems*. Boston, USA: ACM Press.

Bjerknes, G., Ehn, P., & Kyng, M. (1987). *Computers and democracy—a Scandinavian challenge*. Aldershot, UK: Avebury.

Bjørn-Andersen, N. (1988). Are "human factors" human? *The Computer Journal, 31* (5), 386-390.

Brown, J. S. (1986). From cognitive to social ergonomics and beyond. In D. A. Norman & S. W. Draper (Eds.), *User centered system design: New perspectives on human-computer interaction* (pp. 457-486). Hillsdale, NJ: Lawrence Erlbaum Associates.

Bødker, S. (1989). A human activity approach to user interfaces. *Human Computer Interaction, 4* (3), 171-195.

BYTE Interview (1983, February). An Interview with Wayne Rosing, Bruce Daniels, and Larry Tesler. *BYTE*, 90-114.

Card, S., Moran, T., & Newell, A. (1983). *The psychology of human-computer interaction*. Hillsdale, NJ: Lawrence Erlbaum Associates.

Carroll, J. M. (Ed.). (1987). *Interfacing thought: Cognitive aspects of human-computer interaction*. Cambridge, MA: Bradford/MIT Press.

Carroll, J. M. (1989). Evaluation, description and invention: Paradigms for human-computer interaction. In M. C. Yovits (Ed.), *Advances in Computers*, 29, 47-77. London: Academic Press.

Carroll, J. M. & Campbell, R. L. (1986). Softening up hard science: Reply to Newell and Card. *Human Computer Interaction*, 2, 227-249.

Carroll, J. M. & Mazur, S. A. (1986, November). LisaLearning. In *IEEE Computer, 19* (10), 35-49.

Carroll, J. M. & Rosson, M. B. (1987). The paradox of the active user. In J. M. Carroll (Ed.), *Interfacing Thought: Cognitive Aspects of Human-Computer Interaction*. Cambridge, MA: Bradford/ MIT Press.

Cypher, A. (1986). The structure of user's activities. In D. A. Norman & S. W. Draper (Eds.), *User centered system design New perspectives on human-computer interaction* (pp. 243-263). Hillsdale, NJ: Lawrence Erlbaum Associates.

Floyd, C. (1987). Outline of a paradigm change in software engineering. In G. Bjerknes, P. Ehn, & M. Kyng (Eds.), *Computers and democracy—a Scandinavian challenge* (pp. 191-212). Aldershot, UK: Avebury.

Giedion, S. (1969). *Mechanization takes command*. New York: W.W. Norton.

Gould, J. (1988). How to design usable systems. In M. Helander (Ed.), *Handbook of human-computer interaction* (pp. 757-790). Amsterdam: North-Holland.

Gray, W. D. & Atwood, M. E. (1988, October). Interfacing thought: Cognitive aspects of human-computer interaction [Review of *Interfacing thought: Cognitive aspects of human-computer interaction*.] *SIGCHI Bulletin*, 88-91.

Greif, I. (Ed.). (1988). *Computer-supported cooperative work: A book of readings*. San Mateo, CA: Morgan Kaufmann.

Helander, M. (Ed.). (1988). *Handbook of human-computer interaction*. Amsterdam: North-Holland.

Jones, J. C. (1988). Softecnica. In J. Thackara (Ed.), *Design after modernism* (pp. 216-226). London: Thames & Hudson.

Landauer, T. (1987). Relations between cognitive psychology and computer systems design. In J. M. Carroll (Ed.), *Interfacing thought: Cognitive aspects of human-computer interaction* (pp. 1-25). Cambridge, MA: Bradford/MIT Press.

Mead, G. H. (1934). *Mind, self and society*. Chicago: University of Chicago Press.

Newell, A. & Card, S. K. (1985). The prospects for psychological science in human-computer interaction. *Human Computer Interaction, 1*, 209-242.

Newell, A. & Card, S. K. (1986). Straightening out softening up: Response to Carroll and Campbell. *Human Computer Interaction*, 2, 251-267.

Norman, D. A. & Draper, S. W. (Eds.). (1986). *User centered system design: New perspectives on human-computer interaction*. Hillsdale, NJ: Lawrence Erlbaum Associates.

Reisner, P. (1987). Discussion: HCI—what it is and what research is needed. In Carroll, J. M. (Ed.), *Interfacing thought: Cognitive aspects of human-computer interaction*. Cambridge, MA: Bradford/MIT Press.

Shneiderman, B. (1987). *Designing the user interface: strategies for effective human-computer interaction*. Reading, MA: Addison-Wesley.

Suchman, L. & Wynn, E. (1984). Procedures and problems in the office. *Office: Technology and People*, *2* (2), 133-154.

Thomas, E. L. (1965). Human factors in design. In M. Krampen (Ed.), *Design and planning*. New York: Hastings House.

Thomas, J. & Kellogg, W. (1989, January). Minimizing Ecological Gaps in User Interface Design. *IEEE Software*, 78-86.

Van Cott, H. & Kinkade, R. (Eds.). (1972). Human engineering guide to equipment design. Washington: American Institute for Research. (Revised edition).

Whiteside, J. & Wixon, D. (1987). Discussion: Improving human-computer interaction—a quest for cognitive science. In J. M. Carroll (Ed.), *Interfacing thought: Cognitive aspects of human-computer interaction* (pp. 337-352). Cambridge, MA: Bradford/-MIT Press.

Young, R. M., Green, T., & Simon, T. (1989). Programmable user models for predictive evaluation of user interface designs. In *Proceedings of CHI'89 Conference on Human Factors in Computing Systems* (pp. 15-19). New York: ACM Press.

Cooperative Design: Techniques and Experiences From the Scandinavian Scene

Susanne Bødker
Kaj Grønbæk
Morten Kyng
Aarhus University, Denmark

This chapter is based on a vision, an ideal, of what system development should achieve and how it should take place. First of all, we see the ideal project as one that encourages the users-to-be in an organization, i.e., all the involved groups and individuals, to decide themselves how to develop their work by means of new computer support. This ideal is seldom realized, because organizations are characterized by conflicts, most significantly between management and labor, and because different groups have different power and resources in the organization. It is not only a matter of democracy, though. In our experience, most traditional systems development methods are too abstract and detached from the work and life of most people, even from management. Thus we need to develop and work with techniques that allow for more use of everyday experiences and professional skills in design.

At the Participatory Design Conference (PDC '90), Seattle, the authors of this chapter and their collaborators were invited to present their approaches to participatory design, together with other researchers and designers from Scandinavia. These approaches originate from a diversity of projects where researchers and designers have been cooperating closely with groups of workers, shop stewards, and other union representatives, and where the organizational framework provided by the local unions played an important role (Ehn & Kyng, 1987). Hence, one of the key questions discussed over the 2-day conference was whether the Scandinavian "Model" for system design, as summarized in our earlier vision could be applied in a North American setting—a setting where industrial democracy and strong union relationships cannot be assumed to be found in most organizations, as is the case in Scandinavia. We do not attempt here to answer this question. Rather, we do discuss a set of techniques to support our earlier vision. We also describe the underlying perspectives and leave it to the readers to judge whether the perspective and the techniques can be adopted in their particular settings. For detailed discussions of the techniques, and the rationale behind them, we refer to a recent book, *Design at Work: Cooperative Design of Computer Systems* (Greenbaum & Kyng, 1991).

To begin, we present our perspective on computer applications and design as a list of statements or assumptions:

Computer Applications

- When computer applications are brought into a workplace, they should enhance workplace skills rather than degrade them.
- Computer applications should be viewed as tools, and designed to be under the control of the people using them. They should support work activities, not make them more rigid.
- The introduction of computer applications changes the organization of work around them. The interplay between the computer application and work organizational issues should be a specific focus of the design and introduction of computer applications into organizations.
- Although computer applications are generally ordered to increase productivity, they also need to be looked at as a means to increase the quality of the results.

The Design Process

- The design process, as any process taking place in an organization, is a political one and leads to conflict. Managers who order an application see things differently from the workers who will use it. Different groups of users will need different things from the application, and system designers often pursue their own interests. Conflicts are inherent in the process. If they are ignored the solution may be less useful and continue to create problems.
- Computer applications that are created for the workplace need to be designed with full participation from the users—both from a democratic point-of-view and to insure that competencies central to the design are represented in the design group. Full participation, of course, requires training and active cooperation, not just token representation in meetings or on committees. We use the term *cooperative design* to designate such cooperation between users and designers. However, to users, designing a new computer application is a secondary activity whereas for designers it is their primary work. This means that the designers should know how to set up the process and need to make sure that everyone gets something out of the interaction.
- The design process highlights the issue of how computers are used in the context of work organization. We see this question of focusing on how computers are used, which we call the *use situation,* as a fundamental focus for the design process. We put our attention on how people work, and take the practice of the users as the starting point for the design process.
- Encouraging user participation and designing for skill means paying attention to things that are often left out of the formal specifications, like tacit knowledge or shared knowledge and communication. Computer applications are a lot more than the simple flow of information represented in the flowcharts that systems analysts present to their clients. When users participate in actual design activities it is necessary to use tools that are familiar to them. Traditional tools such as flowcharts, dataflow diagrams, and programming languages are insufficient (or even useless) as means for cooperating with users. In our experience, some of the techniques we discuss later do in fact encourage user participation and creativity.
- To enable users to contribute with their tacit knowledge in design, it is important to simulate future work situations, creating the illusion of actually working with the projected system. In this way changes in the use practice can, to some extent, be predicted and evaluated.

This perspective on computer applications and design processes has evolved over more than 15 years, strongly influenced by the experiences from several research projects of our own as well as those of other groups. An overview of this development follows.

HISTORICAL BACKGROUND

The research projects that we have been involved with since the early 1970s, have developed in interplay with the society around them. Employee influence through unions and cooperation with management has for a long time been an integral part of the industrial relations in the Scandinavian countries. The Scandinavian projects on worker influence on development and use of computers began in the early 1970s, when new legislation increased the possibilities for worker influence. The projects supplemented the earlier strategy, called codetermination, with a series of activities set up by central and local unions independent of employer organizations and management. In these "first generation" projects, workers aided by consultants and researchers struggled to develop a better, more coherent platform for worker influence on the use of new technology at the workplace. New work practices, focusing on group work and the development of local resources for action, were being shaped, tried out in practice, and reshaped in the projects. Some of the work groups produced criteria for better working environments and suggestions for applications to support groups of workers planning their own work. As a result of the first of these projects the existing legislation on worker influence was supplemented by Technology Agreements that gave workers a direct say in the development and use of technology in their workplaces. This also led to an extensive series of union education programs. The first of these projects was the NJMF project, set up by Kristen Nygaard and Olav-Terje Bergo together with the Norwegian Iron and Metal Workers' Union (Nygaard & Bergo, 1975). This was followed by the Swedish DEMOS project in which Pelle Ehn and Åke Sandberg played major parts, and the Danish DUE project organized by Morten Kyng, Lars Mathiassen, and Niels Erik Andersen together with the Trade Union Council (Ehn & Kyng, 1987).

In the 1970s these early projects introduced the notion of worker participation in decisions about technology, but, whereas workers had a legal say in workplace technology, the laws did little to shift the balance of power from a managerial perspective. And the rationalistic tradition embedded in computer system development did little to give workers a voice in putting forth their own ideas when trying to agree on the introduction of new technology. As in the United States, this was reflected in the tools of system development, which emphasized developing technical specifications rather than seeing the application from the perspective of the users.

By the early 1980s, a "second generation" of projects was initiated in Scandinavia. These projects focused on design of new kinds of computer support using skill and product quality to push computer system design more towards a users' perspective. They took the issue of dehumanization and put it on the table as a central problem in the design and use of computer systems. Thus, to put some muscle on the bones of the Technology Agreements, the issues of quality of work and product were put into the foreground of the new design-oriented projects. An example of this was the Utopia project, named both for its ideals and as an acronym for its use (Bødker, Ehn, Kammersgaard, Kyng, & Sundblad, 1987). In this project computer system developers and researchers worked with a group of typographers helping to formulate the ways that computer technology could be used to enhance their skills and better the typographic quality of newspapers. These researchers came from the Swedish Center for Working Life, the Technical University in Stockholm, and from Aarhus University.

From the first projects in the 1970s, developing strategies and techniques for worker influence on design and use of computer applications, through the focus on skill in the early 1980s, computer system development in Scandinavia developed the concept of user participation. In *Work Oriented Design of Computer Artifacts,* Pelle Ehn (1989) outlines the story of these changes and delves into some of the theoretical work that influenced the thinking of the earlier as well as later projects. Rethinking the actions and experiences in these projects he develops a theoretical understanding of design work based on phenomenology, marxism, and ordinary language understanding.

This theoretical understanding has been supplemented with inspiration from activity theory (Bødker, 1991; Christiansen, 1988), and the so-called work development research (Engeström, 1987; Bisgaard et al., 1989). Together with the insight developed during our writing of *Design at Work* (Greenbaum & Kyng, 1991) it has lead to a new round of empirical work, which we present in part next.

In retrospect, when looking at the strategies and techniques applied in the aforementioned projects, there has been continuous development and some major changes: In general, we have today a much better theoretical understanding of possibilities for and limitations to active user participation in design processes. This understanding comes from our interpretations of theories that can be grouped under the philosophical heading of social construction, seen in contrast with the rationalistic tradition of computer science. At the practical level this is reflected in our continued *revisions* of our set of development tools and techniques, where we try to modify those aspects of our techniques that are influenced by the older rationalistic perspective pervading system development theory and practice. One illustration of these revisions is our move from system descriptions to mock-ups and game-like design sessions (see the following). Also, where many of the techniques of the early projects followed the line of analyzing, followed by setting up goals, for example, for local unions, and then making action programs, today, many of our techniques use fantasy and imagined futures to move from problems in the present specific setting to reality and specific actions. This "substitution" of goals with positive visions/fantasy without the need for rationalistic arguments to support the visions is an important step in encouraging creative contributions from the users (Kyng, 1989).

CASE: THE AT PROJECT

The following case example is a project taking place at the National Labour inspection service (AT) office in Aarhus. The purpose of the project seen from the point-of-view of the managers and workers at AT is to design a number of computer applications for AT and to develop a long-term strategy for decentralized development and maintenance. Decentralization here is relative to the existing strategy in which all AT offices in Denmark subscribed to centralized computer applications run by a department in Copenhagen. This aspect, that the project is useful for the people in the participating organization, is central to our research. As with all the empirical projects that researchers from our tradition engage in, the project is one of action research, which in our understanding, means that the people we work with should get something out of the process as well. The purpose for the researchers is an improved understanding and further development of the techniques described in *Design at Work,* among others, and of the applied theoretical basis.

We use the case primarily for presenting our choice of techniques, based on experiences from previous cases. The AT project itself is still only in the first stages. Presenting the techniques by means of a concrete case also serves to illustrate the situated nature of our techniques. The way we combine and apply the techniques at AT is dependent on specific conditions at AT. So, for instance, the techniques are presented differently in *Design at Work*. And obviously, the way we planned the work at AT differs from what actually happened.

In the project, 8 researchers work together with the people at the AT office in Aarhus. This office is part of a country-wide labor Inspection service, under the auspices of the Danish State, mandated to take care of the workers' health inspection at all workplaces. Employed are inspectors, who are partly specialized in different areas, as well as administrative personnel, and a centrally located support staff of researchers. In the Aarhus office, the staff amounts to approximately 40 people.

The inspectors are trained in many different ways, as engineers, craftspeople, biologists, nurses, medical doctors, psychologists, and more. The contact between the inspectors and the companies takes place in three different ways: (a) an inspector selects, and visits, a randomly chosen company; (b) an accident is reported by a company, a doctor, or a shop steward, upon which the inspector may choose to pay a visit; (c) and through a so-called campaign. A campaign is a coordinated (often from the main office) effort to visit companies within a certain area, or where certain kinds of work hazards are very common. For example, all plastic-producing factories are paid visits to inform about cancer. The inspectors in general give information and advice, and they have the legal power to order changes in the production facilities when these are not in accordance with the law.

The administrative staff consists of office workers, who perform numerous support functions, maintain files of different kinds, and give immediate help to people calling on the phone.

For the researchers, this project is somewhat different from most previous projects in that we cooperate both with the local management and with the workers. Furthermore, the project from the outset includes all groups at the organization, with their different roles and skills.

Following are presentations of the techniques that the project works with as outlined in Fig. 8.1. We also discuss specific measures. The following activities were planned during the first part of the AT project:

- Researchers learning about the work at AT through workplace visits during which people from AT were interviewed and demonstrated their work practices.
- Compilation of an inventory of existing problems with and new ideas for

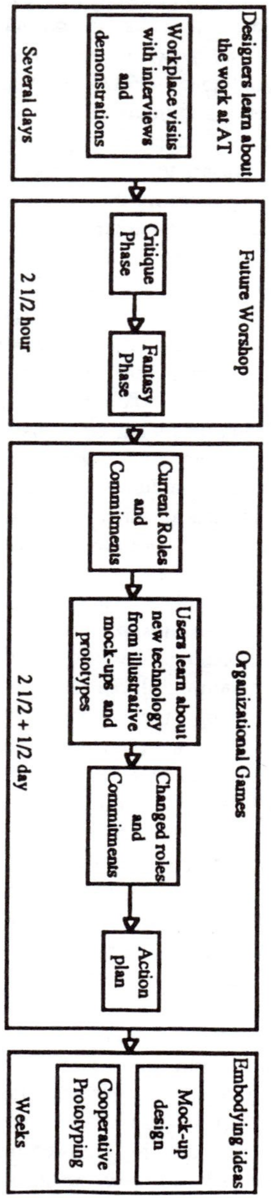

FIG. 8.1. Activities undertaken and planned for the AT project.

work organization and computer support through the critique and fantasy phases of a Future Workshop.

• An Organizational Game investigating current roles, new technological possibilities—illustrated by means of mock-ups and prototypes—and changed roles, and developing an action plan.

• Embodying ideas—continued cooperative design of selected computer applications using mock-up design and cooperative prototyping, and trying out new/modified work organizations.

At this point, a detailed plan for development of a strategy for decentralized system development or for the conclusion of the project has not been made.

The initial step of the first activity was for 4–5 researchers to visit the organization for a couple of days. We wanted to learn more about the work tasks of the inspectors and the administrative staff. Furthermore, we needed to focus on the materials and instruments that were applied in the different work tasks, and the cooperation between people in the work tasks. This involved following several of the inspectors on workplace inspections. In general the strategy was one of interviewing people in their offices or wherever they were working, asking them to demonstrate to us parts of their work tasks, the files that they keep, the instruments, in particular computer programs that they apply, etc. Inspired by Engeström (1987) and Bisgaard et al. (1989) focus was not only on the normal state of affairs, but also on exceptions and problems. The work of managers and workers was treated in the same way, and the outcome was improved knowledge of the organization as well as a number of ideas and problem areas to focus on in the process to come.

FUTURE WORKSHOPS

Following the workplace visits at AT, a Future Workshop was conducted to help focus more directly on the problems and ideas that the workers at AT had, or could bring forward collectively. In *Design at Work* (Greenbaum & Kyng, 1991) the use of the Future Workshop technique for system design is described in detail. (See Halskov Madsen & Kensing (1991) who have developed the Future Workshop technique for system development in combination with a technique denoted Metaphorical Design.)

Robert Jungk and Norbert Müllert (1987) originally developed the Future Workshop technique for citizen groups with limited resources who wanted a say in the decision-making processes of public planning authorities (town planning, environmental projection, energy crisis, etc.). The technique is meant to shed light on a common problematic situation, to generate visions about the future, and to discuss how these visions can be realized. Those participating should share the same problematic situation, they should share a desire to change the situation according to their visions, and they should share a set of means for that change. Usually, a Future Workshop is run by at least two facilitators, with no more than 20 participants. The facilitators attempt to ensure an equal distribution of speaking time and they should also ensure that all participants can follow the discussion, by letting the participants write their ideas as short statements on wall charts (a large sheet of paper taped to the wall). A Future Workshop is divided into three phases: the Critique, the Fantasy, and the Implementation phase. Essentially the Critique phase is designed to draw out specific issues about current work practice; the Fantasy phase allows participants the freedom to imagine "what if" the workplace could be different; and the Implementation phase focuses on resources needed to make realistic changes. These phases are surrounded by preparation and follow-up periods.

At the beginning of the Future Workshop the facilitators introduce the technique to the participants. Basically the Critique phase is like a structured brainstorming that focuses on current problems at work. Speaking time is allotted to all participants and is often restricted to 30 seconds to make it possible for everyone to speak. As a preparation for the next phase the statements are grouped under a number of critique-headings/themes. As the first part of the following Fantasy phase the critique themes are inverted to positive guiding themes. During the following brainstorming no statement about the future is considered too extreme—if somebody wants it, it's OK. As a preparation for the second part of the Fantasy phase the short statements are regrouped under a number of fantasy-headings/themes. Some of these are then selected for elaboration in the following group work, where they are elaborated into "utopian outlines." The Implementation phase may start by having each group present their version of a utopian outline. The general idea is to make plans for how to start acting in the immediate future of the workshop. In the AT project the Future Workshop idea was adapted as follows.

The researchers' understanding of the problems of the organization was mainly based on interviews with individuals at AT. After that, they encouraged workers to also formulate their own understanding of problems and changes, preferably as a collective. Not that they expected everybody to share needs and problems, but at least to create a mutual understanding of these.

Given previous experiences with Future Workshops where different groups were involved (see for example, *Design at Work,* Chapter 7), the researchers decided to ask management to stay away from the workshop and leave the scene to the workers. One of the problems experienced earlier in having a mixed group of managers and workers do a Future Workshop together is that the workers may be afraid of management retaliation if they express serious critique of current conditions in the organization. Also, in many organizations, the workers are less used to expressing themselves orally than management, resulting in a workshop where management interests set the agenda.

It is quite difficult to get everybody together in an organization like AT, where the inspectors are out a lot, and where many people work part-time. Thus, a 2½ hour slot in a regular monthly staff meeting was set aside for a meeting focusing on the Critique and Fantasy phases of a Future Workshop. In addition to this, a 2-day meeting for a smaller group was scheduled for later. For this meeting, the researchers decided to use the design-by-playing technique described shortly. In order to make the best possible use of the 2½ hours, the Implementation phase was seen as something going on after the meeting (in many ways, the rest of the project can be seen as implementation). To make use of the insight already collected two of the four researchers present in the meeting were to observe the statements in the Critique phase and try to come up with themes for the Fantasy phase. This also reflects an experience of ours saying that formulating themes is often hard and time consuming. The Fantasy phase was conducted in four groups, each of which had a different theme and had a researcher as facilitator. Some of the ideas that came up here were selected for further exploration in the Organizational Game. The themes arising out of the Future Workshop were used in setting up the playground of the Organizational Game, and the discussions as well as the earlier investigations were used in setting up the situations for the game.

ORGANIZATIONAL GAMES

The major problems in AT are centered around the organization of work and how this relates to the use of computer technology: For instance, much of the information that the inspectors report about their inspections is rewritten three times by the inspectors in slightly different forms. Following this, the information is filed by different secretaries into different files. It was suggested by the researchers, and accepted by AT, that the 2-day meeting should focus on such work organization problems. The Organizational Game technique, developed by Sjögren and Ehn (1991) seemed appropriate for this. It supports considering alternative work organizations by playing them out and confronting the different problems they create.

Organizational games build on the idea that:

- they make a difference for the participants
- implementation of the results is likely
- they are fun to participate in.

The first two points concern the political side of participation in design; the users must have a guarantee that their design efforts are taken seriously. The last point concerns the design process. No matter how much influence participation may give, it should transcend the boredom of traditional design meetings to really support design as meaningful and involved action. The design work is treated as a theatrical play. Furthermore the organizational games share with future workshops the idea that the overall structure of the game moves from the present situation, via an imagined future, back to reality. One of the early attempts to develop organizational games came from the UTOPIA project where an Organizational Kit was developed to enrich work with abstract system descriptions. The basic ideas behind the organizational design game in the UTOPIA project were that:

- It should be fast and easy for a group of people to work with;
- it should be cheap and flexible to use, allowing several alternatives to be tested during discussions; and
- it should be based on concepts relevant to the actual type of production and support design discussions of existing and future work and technology.

Based on experiences from UTOPIA and other projects, the technique has been developed and applied in several projects, by Sjögren and Ehn (1991). The main example of the use of the technique is the Desktop Publishing Game. It was developed for and played in a few public administration offices in Sweden, the main case being the Consumers Agency Konsumentverket. The technique borrows its way of thinking from theater. Its dramatic design context is based on six concepts:

The playground is a subjective and negotiated interpretation of the work organization in question. The professional roles are represented by both individual professional ambitions and organizational requirements. The situation cards introduce prototypical examples of breakdown situations. Commitments are made by individual role players as actions related to a situation card. Conditions for these commitments are negotiated, and an action plan for negotiations with the surrounding organization is formulated.

The game designed for AT was based on a group of 10–12 people from different parts of the organization, workers as well as management. The game started with a Prologue, where the rules of the game were introduced, and the roles and competences of the participants chosen. For Act 1, which followed the Prologue, the playground and situation cards were designed by the researchers to focus on the problems that had surfaced during the initial activities in the project, i.e., the workplace visits and the Future Workshop. In later parts of Act 1, the participants were to create and play their own situation cards. This was done to bring the game closer to the actual problematic situations of the organization, as perceived by the participants from AT. A lot of work was put into preparing Act 2, where some amount of not-yet-implemented or well-defined technology applications were to appear on the scene. The researchers decided to instantiate this technology by means of prototypes and mock-ups (see the following) letting participants get a chance to experience these as part of the game. Act 2 focused on possible new pieces of technology to be applied in the organization, and how they would affect the work in the organization. Act 3 focused on changes of roles and new commitments, with new technology. This act applied scenarios rather than situation cards. One scenario was the small autonomous group, and one was focused on process and product quality. Once again the roles and competences of the participants were negotiated. In the final part, a new playground was brought in, and the participants negotiated an action plan, based on the experiences from the game. This action plan focused both on what could be done here and now and by groups or individuals in AT, and on what needed external resources. All of this was scheduled to take place at a 2½-day seminar. However, we did not finish the action plan. This was done 10 days later at a half-day meeting.

The following two sections present some of the techniques we have developed to involve users actively and creatively in the design of computer applications. Their main value is that they allow users to experience future work-like situations where emerging new applications are tried out, evaluated, and changed or discarded—in cooperation between users and (system) designers. This use of the techniques is part of the action plan developed in the Organizational Game described earlier, but thus far the techniques have, in the AT project, only been used in a learning process, where the designers illustrated new technological possibilities by means of mock-ups and prototypes as part of the Organizational Game (cf. the second act described earlier). As Fig. 8.1 shows, mock-up design and cooperative prototyping activities are planned to embody a subset of the ideas that surfaced in the previous activities.

MOCK-UP DESIGN

The idea of mock-ups was developed in the UTOPIA project as a way to encourage active user involvement, as opposed to the use of traditional specification documents. In addition, they actually help users and designers transcend the borders of reality and imagine what is currently impossible, such as a screen of 100″ with 1000 pixels per inch. As opposed to descriptions, mock-ups remind the users of familiar work situations. And with mock-ups there are meaningful roles for them to play in the use of these design artifacts.

The idea of mock-ups is presented by Ehn and Kyng (1991). They ask why mock-ups work, despite having low functionality and being only a kind of simulacrum. Some of the answers, they suggest, are that mock-ups:

- encourage "hands-on experience," and thus support user involvement beyond the detached reflection that traditional system descriptions allow for;
- they are understandable, hence there is no confusion between the simulation and the "real thing," and everybody has the competence to modify them;
- they are inexpensive, hence many experiments can be conducted without big investments in equipment, commitments, time, and other resources; and last but not least,
- they are fun to work with.

Some of these characteristics are shared by mock-ups and prototypes, as described in the following section. However, some are not, and in the following we focus on these characteristics, that is, why at times it may be a good idea to design without computers. First, mock-ups are built with inexpensive materials. To buy expensive hardware and build advanced software early in a project may, in most situations, be directly counterproductive, especially given the possibilities of mock-ups. In other situations, however, the investments in hardware and software may not be a problem—PCs may already be massively used in the organization. Still, the use of mock-ups may pay off, because it can help generate new visions and new options for use. Second, the characteristics of these simple tools and materials are familiar to everybody in our culture. With this type of mock-ups nothing mysterious happens inside a 'black box.' If a picture taped to the blackboard drops to the floor everybody knows that this was due to difficulties of taping on a dusty chalkboard, and not part of the design. There is no confusion between the simulation and the 'real thing.' Third, such mock-ups lend themselves to cooperative modifications. The possible "operations" on the material using, for example, pens and scissors, are well known to all, and with simple paper-and cardboard mock-ups people often make modifications jointly or take quick turns changing the mock-up. The physical changes are visible, and, with proper display, visible to all the participants.

However, as with any tool or technique, simple mock-ups have their limitations, too. First, changes to a mock-up may be very time consuming. If, for example, a different way of presenting menus is chosen, changes may have to be done to dozens of drawings, or a whole new set of slides will have to be made. Second, it is hard to illustrate behavioral aspects of future applications as realistically as it can be done with prototypes. Third, although mock-ups allow a design group to experiment without the limitations of current technology, this freedom is only a partial blessing. In the end, good design results from a creative exploitation of the technological possibilities and limitations, not from ignoring them. Thus, as paradoxical as it may sound, the demands for computer knowledge in a design group using mock-ups are very high.

In the AT case, we plan to build mock-ups to explore more details of possible future technology, by managers, workers, and researchers in cooperation. Suggestions for where to use mock-ups and prototypes have arisen from the action program, as described next, but the specific areas in which to proceed remain to be chosen.

COOPERATIVE PROTOTYPING

The way we do prototyping—cooperative prototyping—is different from traditional prototyping in that traditional prototyping approaches mainly take the perspective of the developers: Analyst/Designers conduct investigations in the user organization and develop prototypes on their own. Such prototypes are tested by or demonstrated to users to give the developers feedback on their solution. It has a superficial resemblance to our use of prototypes for illustrating new technological possibilities, but whereas we see this use of prototypes as part of the users' learning, traditional approaches view it as part of the feedback to developers. Traditional approaches put little emphasis on active user involvement in the actual design process. Bødker and Grønbæk (1991) introduce a different approach called Cooperative Prototyping. The approach is an exploratory approach (Floyd, 1984) where prototyping is viewed as a cooperative activity between users and designers, rather than an activity of designers utilizing users' more or less articulated requirements. In cooperative prototyping the aim is to have users achieve a familiarity with the tools that comes close to what was achieved with mock-ups, although this may be infeasible in the immediate future.

The cooperative prototyping approach establishes a design process where both users and designers are participating actively and creatively with their different qualifications. A key point in facilitating such a process is to let the users experience prototypes in a fluent work-like situation. The users' current skills must be confronted with new technological possibilities. This can be done in a simulated future work situation or in a real use situation. When breakdowns occur in the simulated use situation, users and designers analyze the situation and discuss whether the breakdown occurred because of the need for training, a bad or incomplete design solution, or for some other reason. Breakdowns caused by bad or incomplete design solutions should rapidly be turned into improved designs, in order to reestablish the fluent work-like evaluation of the prototype. In many cases users can participate actively in improving the prototypes. Prototype modifications that can be made by direct manipulation are made immediately in the session, whereas modifications requiring a larger programming effort are postponed and made by designers after the session.

Setting up alternative prototypes is useful for users and designers to get their imagination going and thereby for the group to discuss different ways of organizing work. A Future Workshop often displays a diversity of alternative fantasies about how to improve work with computers or by changing work organization. Exploring some of these alternatives through prototyping is a fruitful way to move from fantasy into the actual development process and to focus on improving the users' work through computer support.

At present the prototypes for the AT case are seen primarily as learning vehicles for the workers and managers as part of the Organizational Game. This use of prototypes supports imagination and discussion about the future work with new technology. The Organizational Game becomes more concrete than if technology is just talked about. For instance, prior to the AT project, there had been a lot of talk about the inspectors carrying portable computers on their visits. But hardly any of the inspectors had seen one. Letting them experience the general capabilities of a portable computer in itself grounds the discussions. And of course experiencing prototypes of what the portable may be used for in their specific situation brings the discussion much further and also raises a number of questions related to work organization. For instance, if the inspectors directly enter into the computer the information that they now record on forms, what will happen to the work tasks of the secretaries who are now responsible for this data entry?

As with mock-ups these initial discussions help delimit areas in which to proceed with prototyping. And part of this is to let the users get more actively involved with the existing prototypes. To learn the best ways to set up these sessions, a diversity of questions are considered, such as: What is the purpose of the session? How stable should the prototype be in advance? To what extent should in-session modifications be done? What setting should be chosen? How should the outcome be documented/evaluated? In prototyping sessions, designers often like to demonstrate all the features they believe are wonderful. However, our claim is that demonstrations do not necessarily tell the users anything about how the prototype or the final application fulfills their needs. To fully experience the prototype, the users need to be in control of its use for some period of time, to try it out in work-like situations. If the prototypes are not sufficiently stable to let the users work on their own with it, the designer should be prepared to give first aid for breakdowns caused by the prototype. While designers are, initially, the ones who know how the process should be set up, it is important that the process be adjusted to the needs and wishes of the users.

The product of the prototyping process is not only a computer prototype. Prototyping is a learning process, and much of the new understanding must be spread to workers and managers who do not participate directly in the prototyping. One way is to use the different prototypes in a process in which all involved personnel are guided through a compacted version of the prototyping process (Bisgaard et al., 1989). In general, the prototypes are valuable means in the education of future users, because education can start while the final computer application is being implemented. Similarly, the participants from a prototyping process can often act as teachers. These ideas are being developed in the AT project.

GENERAL CONDITIONS

A design process in which a group of users and designers cooperate takes place in a complex context with different types of societal conditions and contractual relationships among the partners (see Chapter 5 by Grønbæk et al., this volume).

System designers in some settings will have to fight to involve users in the design process. For instance, the application to be developed may be specified in a product contract stating requirements and a fixed price. Or the application is a brand new product to be marketed. Thus it may be difficult to identify a suitable group of potential users.

One of the frequent obstacles to increased user involvement in design projects is resources, or rather, the lack of them. Throughout a design project resources must be secured for user participation if there is to be real cooperation. Users who get no reduction in their daily workload cannot be expected to engage themselves in a design project over long periods of time. But resources are not only time and money; they also include education and assistance from a variety of experts.

Another frequent obstacle to user involvement is the current structure and the traditions in the involved organizations. For instance, marketing groups within product development organizations may restrict user involvement in the development process even when the developers do find it important (see chapters by Grudin and by Grønbæk et al., in this volume). One such reason could be that the product development organization does not want to design a product that is tied too closely to a certain customer or customer type.

In most organizations, some groups have more power and resources than others. Those who have the most power and resources are usually management, not the end-users. To help users get a forum where they can take an active part in design means to set up situations where they can act according to their own interests and rules, and not simply according to those of their managers. The right to make decisions about how to spend resources is also a crucial aspect of the resource question mentioned before. Most projects have to follow the rules of the organization to which they belong. In some cases this implies that a project group consisting of designers and users collectively makes the decisions, as was the case with the UTOPIA project mentioned earlier. In most cases, however, standard managerial procedures will determine the way decisions are made. When a crisis or a conflict arises under these circumstances, decisions often run contrary to the wishes of users, and perhaps contrary to those of the designers as well. The result is usually that the users withdraw from the process, either totally by leaving the design group, or by becoming passive members, losing their initial belief in the possibilities of their influencing the design. To give users a better chance of continued participation, we recommend that from the outset the designers argue for a certain amount of resources to be allocated for user initiatives.

The weakest groups in particular need the strongest support in formulation of their demands and ideas for the future. There can be conflicting interests among the groups, but these conflicts may be turned into resources for the project, if the situations are set up in appropriate ways. This can mean that designers and users should not just establish one project group of all involved parties, but should work with different groups of people at different times (Ehn & Kyng, 1987; Ehn & Sandberg, 1979; Engeström, 1987). At the same time, the different groups need to be exposed to each other's demands and suggestions, which emphasizes the need for designers to be coordinators of the activities.

CONCLUDING REMARKS

One of the issues confronted when we tear down the barriers of traditional design is that the roles of the system developers shift from that of project managers to project facilitators. Cooperative design, which in our perspective means empowering users to fuller participation and cooperation, changes the rules of the game. Within traditional system development each step, from feasibility study through implementation, is supposed to be controlled by system developers and management through discrete procedures, and marked by clear-cut milestones and exit criteria. In our view, the traditional system approach makes it easier for designers to create the impression that things are under control. But often the supposedly last act, where a system is put into operation, shows that it does not fit the work of the users, and an almost unending epilogue of modifications begins. The cooperative design approach begins by creating an environment in which users and designers can actively consider the future use situation. It is a process where users and designers don't have to wait until the final act to know if the application will fit the practice of the users.

Finally, we recall the situated nature of cooperative design. Each application of the techniques described in this chapter will be different depending on the type of project in which they are applied. In *Design at Work* (Greenbaum & Kyng, 1991) the techniques have been presented using a variety of examples of their use; in this chapter we have done a somewhat similar thing using a single project as our example. A reader who examines both sources will see that the techniques have been applied differently. The point is that the next application of the techniques will again be different. This is why we think example driven presentations, like the one here, are more appropriate than stating general guidelines and methods. Trying to apply techniques that have been described by example will force the reader to consider similarities and differences between the described example and the current situation. This exercise will move the attention towards how to fit the technique to the current setting, rather than just sticking to a guideline that most likely doesn't fit the situation.

ACKNOWLEDGMENTS

Many people have been involved in the work on which this chapter is based. Pelle Ehn, Joan Greenbaum, Kim Halskov Madsen, Finn Kensing, and Dan Sjögren were principal "methodology developers" and fellow writers on the

Design at Work book (Greenbaum & Kyng, 1991). Pelle, Joan, Kim, and Merete Bartholdy were members of the group who did the workshops at the Participatory Design Conference held in Seattle, March/April 1990. The researchers in the project that we use as our case include Ellen Christiansen, Pelle Ehn, Randi Markussen, Preben Mogensen, and Randy Trigg, as well as the authors of this chapter. Ellen, Randi, Preben, and Susanne have done many of the initial investigations in the project, and together with Pelle and Randy they have planned and coordinated the workshop activities we discuss. The chapter would not have been possible without the contributions of the many collaborators in the different empirical cases that constitute our frame of reference, including those of the people at AT-Aarhus. Pelle Ehn commented helpfully on an earlier draft.

REFERENCES

Bisgaard, O., Morgensen, P., Nørby, M., & Thomsen, M. (1989). *Systemudvikling som lærevirksomhed, konflikter som basis for organsationel udvikling* [Systems development as a learning activity, conflicts as the origin of organizational development]. (DAIMI IR-88). Aarhus: Aarhus University.

Bødker, S. (1991). *Through the interface: A human activity approach to user interface design*. Hillsdale, NJ: Lawrence Erlbaum Associates.

Bødker, S., Ehn, P., Kammersgaard, J., Kyng, M., & Sundblad, Y. (1987). A Utopian experience. In G. Bjerknes, P. Ehn, & M. Kyng (Eds.), *Computers and democracy: A Scandinavian challenge* (pp. 251–278). Aldershot, UK: Avebury.

Bødker, S., & Grønbæk, K. (1991). Design in action: From prototyping by demonstration to cooperative prototyping. In J. Greenbaum & M. Kyng (Eds.), *Design at work: Cooperative design of computer systems* (pp. 197–218). Hillsdale, NJ: Lawrence Erlbaum Associates.

Christiansen, E. (1988). *Den realistiske vision: et humanistisk-datalogisk perspektiv på systemudvikling* [The realistic vision]. Unpublished doctoral dissertation, Aalborg: Aalborg University.

Ehn, P. (1989). *Work-oriented design of computer artifacts*. Stockholm: Arbetlivscentrum.

Ehn, P., & Kyng, M. (1987). The collective resource approach to systems design. In G. Bjerknes, P. Ehn, & M. Kyng (Eds.), *Computers and democracy: A Scandinavian challenge* (pp. 251–278). Aldershot, UK: Avebury.

Ehn, P., & Kyng, M. (1991). In J. Greenbaum & M. Kyng (Eds.), *Design at work: Comparative design of computer systems*. Hillsdale, NJ: Lawrence Erlbaum Associates.

Ehn, P., & Sandberg, A. (1979). *Företagsstyrning och löntagarmakt*. Stockholm: Prisma.

Engeström, Y. (1987). *Learning by expanding*. Helsinki: Orienta-Konsultit.

Floyd, C. (1984). A systematic look at prototyping. In R. Budde, K. Kuhlenkamp, L. Mathiassen, & H. Zullighover (Eds.), *Approaches to prototyping* (pp. 1–18). Berlin/Heidelberg: Springer-Verlag.

Greenbaum, J., & Kyng, M. (Eds.). (1991). *Design at work: Cooperative design of computer systems*. Hillsdale, NJ: Lawrence Erlbaum Associates.

Halskov Madsen, K., & Kensing, F. (1991). Generating visions: Future workshops and metaphorical design. In J. Greenbaum & M. Kyng (Eds.), *Design at work: Cooperative design of computer systems* (pp. 155–168). Hillsdale, NJ: Lawrence Erlbaum Associates.

Jungk, R., & Mullert, N. (1987). *Future workshops: How to create desirable futures*. London: Institute for Social Inventions.

Kyng, M. (1989). Designing for a dollar a day. *Office, Technology, and People, 4*(2), 157–170.

Nygaard, K., & Bergo, O. T. (1975). Trade unions: New users of research. *Personnel Review 4*(2).

Sjögren, D., & Ehn, P. (1991). From system description to scripts for action. In J. Greenbaum & M. Kyng (Eds.), *Design at work: Cooperative design of computer systems* (pp. 269–280). Hillsdale, NJ: Lawrence Erlbaum Associates.

PARTICIPATORY DESIGN OF A PORTABLE TORQUE-FEEDBACK DEVICE

Michael Good

Digital Equipment Corporation
110 Spit Brook Road (ZKO2-1/N42)
Nashua, NH 03062-2698 USA
1-603-881-2296, good@baviki.enet.dec.com

ABSTRACT

Customer-driven design processes such as participatory design can be used to develop new presence, or virtual reality, technology. Chemists worked together with computer company engineers to develop scenarios for how presence technology could be used to support future molecular modeling work in drug design. These scenarios led to the development of a portable torque-feedback device which can be used with either workstation or virtual reality technology. This paper discusses both the experience with the participatory design process and the novel features of the portable torque-feedback device.

KEYWORDS: Presence, virtual reality, participatory design, force feedback, molecular modeling, chemistry.

INTRODUCTION

Whether it is called virtual reality, artificial reality, cyberspace, or presence, the technology that enables participants to see, hear, feel, and walk around a computer-generated world has captured the public imagination. Accompanying this enthusiasm are serious questions about the usefulness of presence technology. One belief is that "Artificial reality will just be a gadget for rich countries," affecting only military and Nintendo game applications [3].

How might we take presence technology beyond gadgetry and make it useful for diverse people doing different types of work? My approach has been to apply the techniques of participatory design [1, 9] to the development of presence technology. In Digital's Presence project, chemists collaborated with computer engineers to develop new prototypes of presence technology. As Laurel [11] suggests, our starting point is to design the experience that we want people to have when using computers in their work.

In this paper, I will first set the context by briefly describing the portion of the chemists' drug design work on which we focused, and then describing the technological background in presence that the computer engineers brought to the project. I will then discuss our experience with the participatory design process, and how it led to the development of a new force-feedback device, the portable torque-feedback device (patent pending).

CONTEXT

Participatory design is a collaborative process. Computer users are the experts in their work, while computer designers are the experts in computer technology. Participatory design brings these two backgrounds together to create new systems with the goal of improving the quality of work life, as shown in Figure 1.

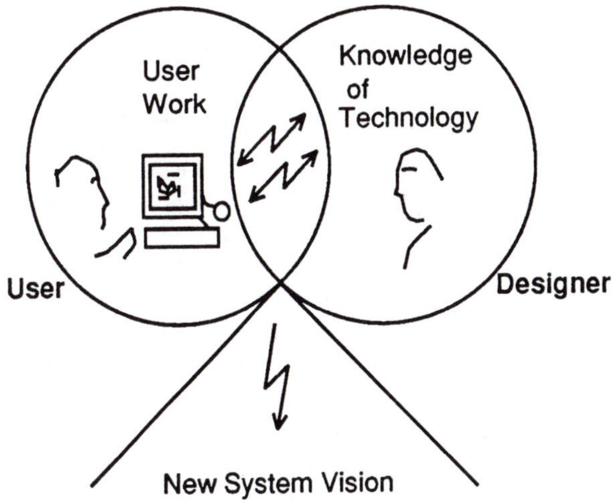

Figure 1: Dynamic Interaction Between Technology and Work

Blomberg and Henderson [1] describe three basic aspects of participatory design: the goal of improving the quality of work life, a collaborative orientation, and an iterative process. An important part of participatory design is what

Ehn [4] calls the balance between tradition and transcendence. In participatory design, new technology explicitly incorporates the history of how work has been done in the past while simultaneously improving how work can be done in the future.

Molecular Modeling

Our customers were members of a molecular modeling group at a pharmaceutical company, working in the drug discovery process. The discovery and development of new drugs is a long, complex process. We focused on one piece of the discovery process for one category of drugs called enzyme inhibitors.

Enzyme inhibitors are small molecules that can dock, or bond, with larger enzyme molecules at an active site. By docking at the active site, the small molecules inhibit or stop an undesired chemical reaction produced by the enzyme. Stopping the chemical reaction can serve to relieve undesired symptoms. The inhibitor might be made up of about sixty atoms while the enzyme itself is made up of thousands of atoms.

One of the many problems in enzyme docking is that neither the enzyme inhibitor nor the enzyme is rigid. Both can twist into many different layouts, called conformations. Exploring these different layouts is called exploring the conformational space of the molecules. One common goal is to look for conformations with low energy for both the enzyme inhibitor and the enzyme, since this tends to make docking easier.

Exploring conformational space is one of many applications of molecular modeling. Chemists have many molecular modeling tools available. Perhaps the most popular tools are physical models, such as Dreiding stick models. These physical models are similar to the ball-and-stick models used in chemistry classes, but adapted for professional use. Many computerized molecular modeling systems are also available [e.g. 13].

While the computerized systems are becoming more frequently used, they are resisted by many chemists. Cost is a major issue, but there are usability issues as well. Even a system that appears well-designed and based on established graphical user interface principles can distance a chemist from a physical understanding of the nature of the enzyme and the candidate enzyme inhibitor molecules.

The chemists' goal for the project was to find new technologies that could be used as the basis for new molecular modeling tools for enzyme docking. These tools would combine the benefits and usability of existing physical and computerized modeling tools.

Presence

The computer engineers brought a particular technical focus to participatory design. This technical focus was to increase the quality of presence for computer users.

Presence has several characteristics. Presence is related to a feeling of computer transparency, where the interface to a computer fades into the background [7]. As presence or transparency increases, so does the experience of working on a task as opposed to working on a computer. This has long been a goal in developing usable systems.

From a design perspective, presence expresses the qualities of a product that can be perceived by one or more of our senses [5]. Research in multisensory human-computer interaction currently focuses on making greater use of the senses of vision, touch, and hearing.

From a perspective in rhetoric and argumentation, presence is the quality which makes certain elements important and pertinent to an audience [15]. One historical method to increase presence is to use concrete rather than abstract objects.

Our use of the term "presence" refers to the quality of human-computer interaction that makes systems more transparent to the user, makes greater use of the senses, and makes the abstract concrete. Presence is not a distinct category of computer technology like menu systems, direct manipulation, or virtual reality [18]. Many different technologies can be used to achieve greater presence through computers, depending on the nature of the work and on individual and group preferences.

Our technological focus started with virtual reality technology [16]. Our participatory design experience expanded that focus to include workstation technology enhanced with multisensory I/O devices. Artificial reality [10] is another technology for achieving presence in some contexts. We did not include it in our technological focus due in part to the lack of tools for developing working prototypes.

The computer engineers' goal for the project was to develop new presence technology that could improve work life for our customers in the future by providing more transparent, sensory, and concrete systems. Molecular modeling has already been a driving problem behind the multisensory research at the University of North Carolina [2]. We expected that working with chemists would be especially useful for developing new ways to support the sense of touch in the use of computers.

PARTICIPATORY DESIGN EXPERIENCE

Participatory design offers rich methodological possibilities for building powerful computer application systems. This project applied participatory design methodology to a somewhat different area: the development of presence technology. The computer engineers worked in the context of product development organizations that have traditionally built general-purpose systems for diverse customers.

My initial conception of the participatory design process was to view it in five steps:

1. Building relationships. We would spend enough time to ensure a good fit between customer-participants and the Presence project. This included familiarizing our customers with presence technology.

2. Contextual inquiry. Contextual inquiry emphasizes interview methods conducted in the context of the participant's work and building an understanding of work in context [19]. The computer engineers needed to build an understanding of the customer's work before we could collaborate as co-designers.

3. Brainstorming. Brainstorming sessions, where all ideas are recorded and criticism of ideas is forbidden, would generate many ideas for how presence technology could improve work life.

4. Storyboarding. Customers and computer engineers would develop some of the most promising brainstorming ideas into illustrated scripts of a "day in the life" of a customer using presence technology in the future [14].

5. Iterative design. Using the storyboards as specifications, the computer engineers would build prototypes that would be tested by the customer-participants on a regular basis. All the previous steps would continue in an iterative fashion.

Our participatory design work with chemists was one of three simultaneous participatory design projects for developing presence technology. In the other projects, where the computer users were toy designers and computer industrial designers, we followed this 5-step process. After spending several months in building relationships, the initial design visits lasted 2 days. The first day was spent in contextual inquiry, and the second day was divided between brainstorming and storyboarding. Subsequent iterative design sessions lasted 1 day.

With the chemists, however, the initial design session was less structured. Contextual inquiry and storyboarding activities flowed together, and brainstorming activity was generally absent. Storyboarding did not produce a full illustrated script, but rather a scenario for use of new technology. We adapted the design techniques on the fly in response to the work context. Participatory design is a collaborative approach to design, not a rigid set of design methods.

In the rest of this section I will describe our experience in working with the chemists in building relationships, contextual inquiry, and storyboarding. The next section will then describe our progress in moving from the scenario to the prototype tested in our first iterative design session.

Building Relationships

Conducting participatory design in a large product development organization presents many challenges. Grudin [6] identifies many of these challenges and their various sources in the nature of product development, in the division of labor within product development organizations, and in the use of standard software development procedures and techniques. Two of these challenges took months for us to overcome: identifying appropriate customer participants, and then obtaining access to the participants.

I tried several approaches in order to find appropriate customer participants for this project. One approach that did not work was simply to call or send electronic mail to the sales representative in charge of a promising account. A much more successful technique was to discuss this project in Digital's VAX Notes conferences, which serve as electronic bulletin boards for a variety of technical and employee interests. Interested sales representatives then contacted me in response to these notes. These contacts could take days or months to develop. Two months elapsed from the time I placed a note in the pharmaceutical industry conference before a sales representative contacted me about the project.

Initial contacts enabled the customers and me to build a working relationship before beginning the actual design sessions. The pharmaceutical customers had already planned a visit to Digital to hear about future technologies in other areas, so my presentation was included in that visit. This meeting took place 2 months after the initial contact with the Digital sales representative. Two months later we arranged the first design meeting.

Overall, 5 months elapsed between the first contact with the sales representative for the pharmaceutical company and the first on-site participatory design visit. It took only half that time to then develop the torque-feedback device and presence software prototypes for molecular modeling and have them ready for the first iterative design session.

Part of the reason that the process took so long is systemic, as Grudin discusses, but part is particular to the nature of this project. We needed to find customer groups who were already familiar with state-of-the-art computer systems for their applications and whose mission included looking for new technology which could help solve their difficult problems. These groups also needed to include intended users of the new technology: chemists who were familiar with computers, not just computer people who were familiar with chemistry. Research and development groups made the best candidates for this work.

Contextual Inquiry

We use contextual inquiry to understand the nature of the user's work, how computers are involved in that work, and how the use of computers supports and disrupts the work process. Interviewing customers as they use a computer system is particularly effective for understanding the ongoing usage of a computer system, rather than the summary experience that customers recollect after the fact. Such interviews are often hit-or-miss regarding job content, though, and are not usually sufficient by themselves to get an overall understanding of the work process.

One technique we use to provide more context is to have customers give us an overview of their entire work process, using artifacts of that process wherever possible. An overview of the entire drug design process would have been too complex for the computer designers to follow. Instead, our customers focused on the portion of drug design that they viewed as most relevant: the creation of drugs from enzyme inhibitors. After reviewing the basic chemistry, the molecular modelers demonstrated some current modeling techniques with both physical models and computer models. All the computer engineers had extensive collegiate math and science backgrounds, which helped in understanding the chemists' work.

One chemist's work was particularly inspiring for future designs. He had found the current computerized representation of the enzyme active site too limiting, even with the use of stereoscopic displays and fast 3-D rendering systems. He constructed an elaborate foam-core physical model of the enzyme active site, with the cavity of the model representing the conformation of the enzyme that was of the greatest interest. After constructing this model he was very excited, so he rushed to get his Dreiding model of the enzyme inhibitor and physically experiment with moving the Dreiding model of the enzyme inhibitor around the foam core model of the enzyme active site. But this did not work either: the problem was simply too complex for either the physical model or the computer model to be fully understandable on their own. The chemist wound up going back and forth between the physical model and the computer model to figure out the proper conformation of the enzyme inhibitor which would lead to a good dock.

This and similar sessions led to the idea of combining the advantages of computer models and physical models. Physical models in many ways provide greater presence for the chemists and are closer to the traditional work practice. Computerized models offer many ways to transcend the current work practice, including the ability to get quantitative results. Why not combine the two into an electronic Dreiding model, where the computer model can be manipulated physically, like existing Dreiding models?

A key element of contextual inquiry involved having the computer engineers tour the work facilities. Most of our participatory design work at the pharmaceutical company took place in conference rooms, but we did tour the molecular modeling laboratory and individual offices, as well as getting a walking tour of the entire complex. Absorbing the physical feeling of the workplace helped the computer engineers better understand the context of the customers' work.

After doing some storyboarding around the electronic Dreiding model ideas, we returned for further contextual inquiry sessions. Another chemist demonstrated the use of the group's existing molecular modeling software package in more detail. This demonstration then fed into further storyboarding work.

Storyboarding

"Day in the life" scenarios and storyboards both can serve as specifications for prototypes. Both techniques emphasize narrative, rather than theory, as the primary source for design [17]. Scenarios describe situations where customers would use new technology in the future. Storyboarding goes to an additional level of detail by creating an illustrated script for this scenario. Storyboarding thus can provide a more detailed specification for prototype software. In this case, our scenario was simple enough that the lack of an illustrated storyboard did not hamper our later prototyping work.

The molecular modelers developed a scenario based on an electronic version of the mechanical stick models that chemists already use. The electronic model could be physically manipulated like the mechanical models while supporting several new capabilities, such as ease of filing and providing quantitative energy calculations. Physical manipulation keeps the kinesthetic presence that is missing in current molecular modeling software. Quantitative results such as energy calculation and minimization provide important and pertinent information that is not present for chemists when using the mechanical models.

This scenario illustrates the balance between traditional work practice and the new possibilities offered by presence technology. It based on the existing work practice of the Dreiding models, but adds numerous capabilities that are not provided by those models. The visual representation of the electronic Dreiding model would follow the practice of the chemists' existing molecular modeling software.

FROM SCENARIO TO PROTOTYPE

Developing Prototype Hardware

These participatory design sessions confirmed our initial impression that force-feedback devices to support the sense of touch would be particularly useful in molecular modeling.

General-purpose force-feedback devices are not currently commercially available, so we had to design and build our own. Our initial force-feedback prototype, developed prior to our participatory design work, was based on Minsky's 2-D force-feedback joystick [12]. We were also influenced by the 6-D robotic arm used by Brooks et al. for enzyme docking [2], and by the force-feedback steering wheel used in Atari's Hard Drivin' arcade game [16]. Since the work started we have become aware of other related devices, including Iwata's 9-D manipulator [8] and the force-feedback versions of instrumented gloves [16].

Our participatory design sessions suggested a smaller and simpler force-feedback device that would be more useful in molecular modeling applications than the 2-D joystick. This hand-held device would have one torque motor to provide torque feedback: as the participant twisted the shaft, the device could twist back as appropriate. This was directly suggested by the idea for an electronic Dreiding model for molecular modelers, where the modelers could deal with a computer model of a molecule in the same physical ways that they currently deal with physical Dreiding models of molecules.

Our portable torque-feedback device uses the same basic electronics as our version of the 2-D joystick, but much simpler mechanics. The 2-D joystick converts the output of torque motors into position offsets in the X and Y directions, whereas the torque-feedback device has no need for such conversion.

Figure 2, drawn to scale, shows the relative size and shape of our initial 2-D joystick versus the later 1-D device. The 2-D force-feedback joystick was about 28 inches tall and 20 inches square. The portable torque-feedback device was about 7½ inches tall and 2½ inches in diameter.

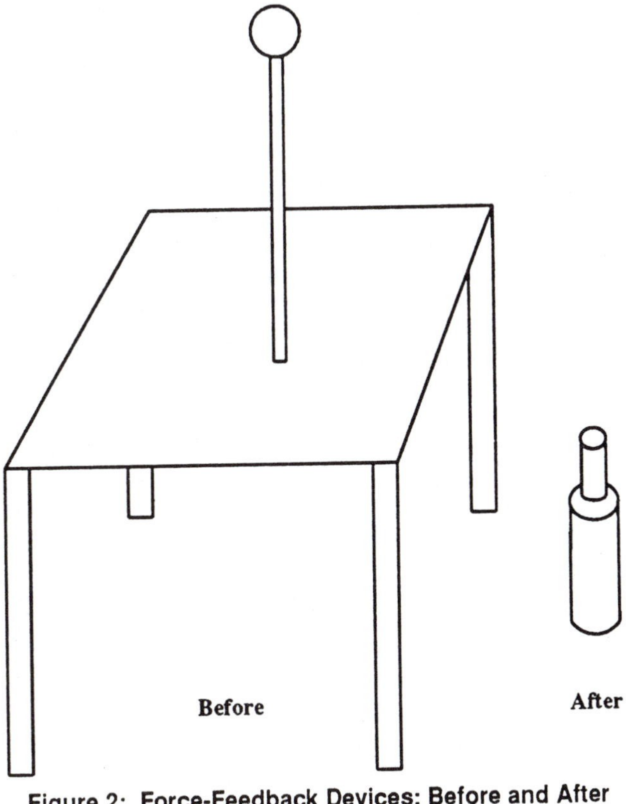

Figure 2: Force-Feedback Devices: Before and After Participatory Design with Chemists

Developing Prototype Software

The scenario of electronic Dreiding models led to the development of our initial software prototype which the chemists tested a few months later in a visit to one of our laboratories. In this prototype, the participant selects the molecule to be studied, and data is read in from a text file in standard PDB (Protein Data Bank) format. The chemists provided PDB data for several small 30-60 atom molecules. The molecule was displayed in a window on the screen in a color-coded format similar to that used in the customer's existing molecular modeling software.

After reading in the molecular data, there were several modes available: twisting the entire molecule using a 6-D magnetic sensor, moving the entire molecule using the sensor, and selecting a bond that the participant would like to rotate. All this mode selection, including the specification of the bond, was done via the keyboard. We focused our time developing the presence features within each mode, rather than on improving the usability of the control structures of the protoype.

Selecting a bond to rotate started the mode that used the torque-feedback device. As the participant rotated the molecule around the bond, the device provided feedback based on an estimate of molecular forces. This energy curve was also displayed on the screen along with the graphical display of the molecule. The torque on the device was proportional to the gradient of the energy curve, based on the rotation of the shaft of the torque-feedback device. The graphical display of the energy curve also indicated the current position on the curve. In this first prototype, the energy curves were randomly selected from three precomputed functions, so any relationship to actual molecular forces was coincidental.

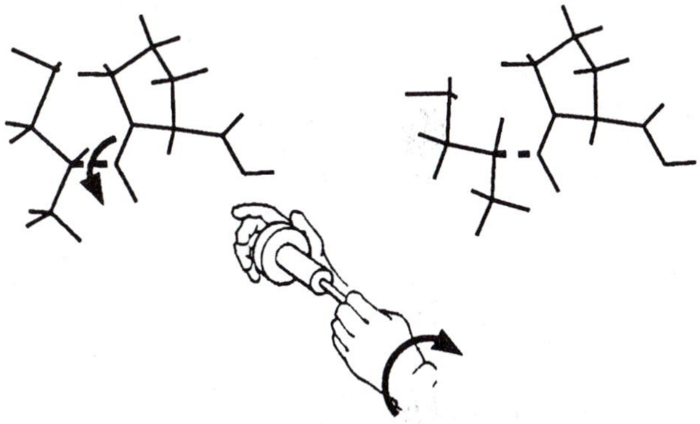

Figure 3: Rotating an Enzyme Inhibitor Around a Selected Bond

Figure 3 shows a black-and-white representation of the color display of a sample enzyme inhibitor. Moving from the conformation on the left-hand side of the figure to the conformation on the right involves two steps. First, the chemist selects the bond (indicated in Figure 3 with the thick dotted line) so that the left-hand side of the molecule would be rotated. The chemist then rotates the shaft of the torque-feedback device about 60 degrees towards him- or herself, and the left-hand side of the molecule also rotates about 60 degrees towards the chemist.

As the shaft is rotated, the chemist feels resistance to the rotation based on the gradient of a molecular energy curve. In this first prototype, this energy curve was based on random data. In a more advanced prototype, the energy gradient would be based on the varying differences in distance between the atoms in the molecule. In the example in Figure 3, this would lead to a decrease of energy at first, as the top-most atoms move further apart. At the local energy minimum, no torque output is produced. The energy would increase again towards the end of the rotation as the bottom-most atoms move closer together, leading to greater resistance or torque output.

Iterative Design Results

Despite the limitation of the arbitrary energy curves, the prototype was compelling for the chemists. The most experienced chemist noted that the prototype was "Very nice... I'm already playing... Feels great to me... This is really neat."

Torque feedback played a different role in exploring the molecular model than the chemists had expected. The senior chemist noted that instead of using torque feedback to find good conformations (how the molecule should be twisted around different bonds), he was using the graphical display for that purpose. The torque feedback aided him in developing a physical understanding of the molecule. The combination of the graphical and force display seemed to provide a "very rapid way to examine the conformational space."

We had told the chemists before the demonstrations began that the energy curves displayed on screen and via the torque-feedback device were randomly generated. Nevertheless, the chemists felt as if they were dealing with an approximation of the actual energy curves for the molecule. This demonstrated the power of the combined video and force display for conveying a sense of presence. It also showed that high presence can amplify the "garbage in garbage out" problems that can plague computer-based systems.

This iterative design session also uncovered two limitations with the prototype torque-feedback device itself. The first limitation was the inability to turn the torque feedback off. In one scenario, the chemist may want to choose a bond, rotate it to the desired position, then keep choosing other bonds and rotating as desired. In this scenario it is important to have a mode where the torque feedback is off, because the chemist may want to leave a bond in a relatively high-energy conformation. That could not be done if the torque feedback is pushing the chemist away from that position towards a local energy minimum. A button on the device is useful for this and other control functions.

The second limitation was the quantization of the device. In this prototype, the torque feedback was quantized in 5-degree increments of the 360 degrees of rotation. The junior chemist believed this reduced the feel of the torque-feedback unit as a high-resolution device, even though this level of quantization was the highest he had seen for computing molecular forces in existing molecular modeling computer software. We speculate that adding some interpolation, or doing unequal sampling where the energy is sampled most at the lowest levels of change (the lowest values of the first derivative) would add more presence. Despite this limitation, the chemist felt the prototype gave "a feel for the degree of fineness of the rotational space around bonds."

Participatory design involves being prepared to discard technological ideas if new paths better meet customer needs. Customer participation includes making decisions, not simply being asked for advice. During our first iterative design session, the molecular modeling customers spent about 1 hour with prototypes involving the force-feedback devices and about 2 minutes with another prototype which used the head-mounted display. Their experience confirmed their initial hunch that force feedback met their needs while the head-mounted display did not. A revised scenario focused on supporting the senses of touch and hearing to complement screen-oriented displays.

Our participatory design sessions have not yet resulted in a finished product. Further work needs to be done to make this invention into a practical product for molecular modeling use. Iterative participatory design work has been hampered by financial cutbacks at both the pharmaceutical and computer companies. This seems a particular hazard when conducting participatory design of new technology during an economic recession.

CONCLUSIONS

When we started our participatory design work, we expected to learn new ways to apply presence technology to make it useful in different work contexts. We did not expect to invent a new presence technology device as we did here. In this case, participatory design led to the invention of a simpler device that was cheaper and easier to build than our initial prototype, while also being more useful in some work contexts.

The portable torque-feedback device adds to the repertoire of presence devices, especially those that support the sense of touch in human-computer interaction. Its portability makes it suitable for use in combination with current head-mounted display systems as well as with workstations. Because the torque feedback is presented to the hand by a grasped device rather than to the fingers via computerized clothing, a wider range of forces can be applied safely than is the case with force-feedback gloves.

Applications of the portable torque-feedback device are not limited to molecular modeling. The device can be used for other applications where torque feedback is useful. These applications could include the industrial design of the feel of knobs and dials as well as general purpose information visualization. Usability for these different applications could be enhanced by a set of "Swiss Army" style attachments to the shaft of the device, such as knobs, dials, and steering wheels.

Participatory design is an approach that responds to its context, rather than a fixed set of procedures used in all situations. Our design sessions with the chemists succeeded, even though they did not take place in the five discrete steps I had initially anticipated. Specific design activities proceeded as needed in the context of a collaborative relationship.

Our difficulties with participatory design came in initiating and sustaining the process, not in applying the process in design sessions at customer and computer company sites. Finding and enrolling appropriate customer participants for the participatory design process remains a challenge for engineers in large product development organizations. Our use of the company's internal electronic network to find participants eventually worked, but it was slow. Sustaining a commitment to participatory design work for new technology also was a problem for us.

Developing useful, enjoyable, and appropriate technology that enhances presence for computer users is an ongoing challenge. Participatory design has steered computer engineers and chemists in some new design directions. This experience indicates that participatory design can be used to develop new computer technology as well as new computer-based application systems.

ACKNOWLEDGMENTS

Tom Stockebrand dubbed our collaboration the Presence project and moved this project from mockups to working prototypes, among many other contributions. James Munson was co-inventor of the portable torque-feedback device. The prototypes were developed by James Munson, RuthAnn Abruzzi, John Gilstrap, Robert Clemens, Pete Pittman, and Pin Fong Ng. Figure 1 was provided by Karen Holtzblatt and Sandy Jones. Eliot Tarlin and Minette Beabes provided the design and rhetoric perspectives on presence, respectively.

DISCLAIMER

The views expressed in this paper are those of the author and do not necessarily reflect the views of Digital Equipment Corporation.

REFERENCES

1. Blomberg, J. L. and Henderson, A. Reflections on participatory design: Lessons from the Trillium experience. In *Proc. CHI '90 Human Factors in Computing Systems* (Seattle, WA, April 1–5, 1990), ACM, New York, 353–359.

2. Brooks, F. P., Jr., Ouh-Young, M., Batter, J. J. and Kilpatrick, P. J. Project GROPE — Haptic displays for scientific visualization. *Computer Graphics, 24*, 4 (August 1990), 177–185. Proc. SIGGRAPH '90 (Dallas, TX, August 6–10, 1990).

3. Ditlea, S. Another world: Inside artificial reality. *PC/Computing, 2*, 11 (November 1989), 90–102.

4. Ehn, P. *Work-Oriented Design of Computer Artifacts*. Arbetslivscentrum, Stockholm, 1988. Available from Lawrence Erlbaum Associates, Hillsdale, NJ.

5. Gilles, W. The presence of products: A question of perspective. *Innovation, 4*, 3 (1985), 5–8.

6. Grudin, J. Systematic sources of suboptimal interface design in large product development organizations. *Human-Computer Interaction, 6*, 2 (1991), 147–196.

7. Holtzblatt, K. A., Jones, S. and Good, M. Articulating the experience of transparency: An example of field research techniques. *SIGCHI Bulletin, 20*, 2 (October 1988), 45–47.

8. Iwata, H. Artificial reality with force-feedback: Development of desktop virtual space with compact master manipulator. *Computer Graphics, 24*, 4 (August 1990), 165–170. Proc. SIGGRAPH '90 (Dallas, TX, August 6–10, 1990).

9. Johnson, J., Ehn, P., Grudin, J., Nardi, B., Thoresen, K. and Suchman, L. Participatory design of computer systems (panel). In *Proc. CHI '90 Human Factors in Computing Systems* (Seattle, WA, April 1–5, 1990), ACM, New York, 141–144.

10. Krueger, M. W. *Artificial Reality II*. Addison-Wesley, Reading, MA, 1991.

11. Laurel, B. *Computers as Theatre*. Addison-Wesley, Reading, MA, 1991.

12. Minsky, M., Ouh-Young, M., Steele, O., Brooks, F. P., Jr. and Behensky, M. Feeling and seeing: Issues in force display. *Computer Graphics, 24*, 2 (March 1990), 235–243. Proc. 1990 Symposium on Interactive 3D Graphics (Snowbird, UT, March 25–28, 1990).

13. Mohamadi, F., Richards, N. G. J., Guida, W. C., Liskamp, R., Lipton, M., Caufield, C., Chang, G., Hendrickson, T. and Still, W. C. MacroModel — An integrated software system for modeling organic and bioorganic molecules using molecular mechanics. *Journal of Computational Chemistry, 11*, 4 (April 1990), 440–467.

14. Mountford, S. J., Buxton, B., Krueger, M., Laurel, B. and Vertelney, L. Drama and personality in user interface design (panel). In *Proc. CHI '89 Human Factors in Computing Systems* (Austin, TX, April 30–May 4, 1989), ACM, New York, 105–108.

15. Perelman, Ch. and Olbrechts-Tyteca, L. *The New Rhetoric: A Treatise on Argumentation.* Trans. J. Wilkinson and P. Weaver. University of Notre Dame Press, Notre Dame, IN, 1969. Original French version published in 1958.

16. Rheingold, H. *Virtual Reality.* Summit Books, New York, 1991.

17. Rorty, R. *Essays on Heidegger and Others: Philosophical Papers Volume 2.* Cambridge University Press, Cambridge, 1991.

18. Wixon, D. and Good, M. Interface style and eclecticism: Moving beyond categorical approaches. In *Proc. Human Factors Society 31st Annual Meeting* (New York, October 19–23, 1987), Human Factors Society, Santa Monica, CA, Vol. 1, 571–575.

19. Wixon, D., Holtzblatt, K. and Knox, S. Contextual design: An emergent view of system design. In *Proc. CHI '90 Human Factors in Computing Systems* (Seattle, WA, April 1–5, 1990), ACM, New York, 329–336.

Understanding Practice: Video as a Medium for Reflection and Design (Excerpt)

Lucy A. Suchman and Randall H. Trigg

• • •

Ethnography and Interaction Analysis

Informed by these perspectives, our work makes use of two related methods for research: ethnography and interaction analysis. Ethnography, the traditional method of social and cultural anthropology, involves the careful study of activities and relations between them in a complex social setting. Such studies require extended participant observation of the internal life of a setting, in order to understand what participants themselves take to be relevant aspects of their activity. Importantly, this may include things that are so familiar to them as to be unremarkable (and therefore missing from their accounts of how they work), although being evident in what they can actually be seen to do.

Interaction analysis is concerned with detailed investigation of the interaction of people with each other and with the material environment.[3] Our use of interaction analysis is inspired by prior work in anthropology and sociology, particularly ethnomethodology and conversation analysis (see for example Atkinson & Heritage, 1984; Garfinkel, 1986; Goodwin, 1981; Goodwin & Heritage, 1990; Heritage, 1984; Sacks, Schegloff, & Jefferson, 1974). In work settings, where our studies have been centered, our analyses focus on the joint definition and accomplishment of the work at hand, through the organization of interaction and the use of supporting technologies and artifacts.

Situations of Use

Our goal in doing studies of work is to identify routine practices, problems, and possibilities for development within a given activity or setting. In the case of the airport operations room, we learned about the difficulties of propagating changes to complex sheets by recording an instance of everyday trouble, as well as by hearing Ops Room members' stories about misdirected baggage. The ideal site for investigations of technology in use, in our view, are these "naturally occurring" occasions of work activity, in the settings in which such activities ordinarily take place. That is, in settings designed by the participants themselves, over time, rather than contrived by the researcher for purposes of the analysis. The first task for such studies is to come to understand peoples' current work practices, using the technologies that are available to them.

A variation on this approach is to investigate the organization of work practice and the use of technologies in situations that we, as researchers, construct. Within those situations, we invite the participants to use whatever tools they choose, and to organize their work in whatever ways they choose. So, for example, we might be interested in understanding how people use shared drawing spaces such as whiteboards or poster paper to do joint design work (Tang, 1989). We ask people who use whiteboards in the course of their everyday practice to come and do some of their own work, but at a time and place that we propose, and with video cameras set up to record their interaction. A further variation occurs when we have an early prototype of a new tool, and invite people to come in to use the prototype, again to do their work but in a time and place that we propose (see for example, Minneman & Bly, 1990).

A situation constructed for purposes of investigation, in contrast to a study carried out wherever the activities of interest are under way, is itself a kind of prototyping. That is, rather than experimental "control," we are really after a way of prototyping either our methods for looking at the details of work practice, or a tool, ideally based on prior study in actual work settings, that we are not quite ready to put out into the world. Like all prototyping, such studies should be done as rapidly as possible, with as strong a feedback mechanism as we can design. And as soon as we can, we should get ourselves out into the world again.

What We Record

In recording within actual work settings, our strategy is to find multiple solutions to the problem of capturing the complex activities that work involves.

Setting-oriented records are made using a stationary camera, positioned to cover as much as possible of the activity in a given physical space. The use of the complex sheet described earlier was recorded with camera and microphone positioned to include all four seated operations room workers in the field of view, and to pick up as much of their talk as possible.

Person-oriented records, in contrast, attempt to understand the work from a particular person's point of view. Depending on the nature of their work, this may require recording equipment that travels with the person being recorded. For example, in order to

3 For more details on both interaction analysis and its application to design see Jordan, Henderson, and Tatar (in prep.).

understand the use of the complex sheet by ramp crew members in more detail, we would need to accompany them as they move around the planes and in the terminal.

An object-oriented record would track a particular technology or artifact. We might trace a complex sheet from the time it is first generated (as an empty matrix) through its markup and highlighting by operations room members, to its filing and possible eventual recovery by auditors. Instrumenting the computers used by operations room personnel to provide machine audit trails yields a different sort of object-oriented record.

Finally, task-oriented records may require multiple recordings of distributed individuals working toward a common goal. A prime example of a task-oriented record would be if during the aircraft swap described above we could have had access not only to activity inside the operations room itself, but also at the two relevant gates and out on the ramp.

How We Work as Researchers

The first analysis we undertake after recording an extended sequence of activity is a rough content log of the entire videotape. Such a log describes observed events and indexes them chronologically by clock time. This rough summary of what happened can expedite the process of searching for particular remembered instances. In addition, the log identifies issues raised in the course of viewing the tape again. Such issue-based logging might include, for example, marking an event as being of inherent interest and possibly representative of a new theme or category (e.g., extending a complex sheet across two complexes); labelling an event as being representative of a given theme or category (e.g., modifiability of artifacts); or generating proposals for further fieldwork (e.g., studying the use of the complex sheet on the ramp).

Frequently, a sequence of recorded activity is picked out as being of particular interest and deserving of more systematic analysis. A first step toward such analysis is a careful transcription (see Jefferson, 1984). Though transcribing talk is almost always central to any interactional study, detailed sequential analyses can also focus on non-vocal dimensions of interaction such as the participants' gaze, gestures, and body positions (see Goodwin, 1981; Heath, 1986; Kendon, 1985). Furthermore, in our work, we have found it valuable to analyze activity in terms of peoples' interactions with various artifacts or technologies. This requires detailed transcriptions of the actions of people using machines, concatenated with machine records to show the interactional organization between person and machine, and the interrelation of that human-machine interaction with the talk and activity of other people (see, for example, Suchman, 1987, chap. 6).

The task of interaction analysis is to uncover the regularity and efficacy of peoples' relations with each other and their use of the resources that their environment affords. To see this regularity requires a productive interaction between an emerging theory and a rich body of specific instances. As we accumulate studies of interaction in specific settings we begin to develop a set of both general observations (e.g., the interorganization of talk and nonvocal activity) and specific analyses (e.g., the specialized concerns and practices of people in this particular domain and/or this particular setting). As an analysis begins to develop over a body of videotapes, it becomes necessary to construct "collections"; that is, instances of interaction that one wants to see as a class. In setting such instances side by side, the commonalities and distinctive features among them are made more visible:

> For example, on one videotape of an American hospital birth it was noted that at the beginning of a particular uterine contraction the eyes of all those present—nurse, husband, medical student—went to the electronic fetal monitor by the woman's bedside. A behavioral pattern was proposed that when a monitor is present, birth attendants' eyes will move to that equipment when a contraction begins. The pattern was checked against other contractions in this particular labor, on tapes of other American hospital births where monitors were present, as well as against monitored contractions in European hospitals. It was found that the pattern held overwhelmingly. In the few cases where it did not, evidence for some competing local activity was available to explain the discrepancy, e.g., the woman was very distraught or the doctor was just at that time doing an examination and therefore had his or her eyes on her. When examining videotapes of births where monitors were not used, it was found that crossculturally in the absence of monitoring equipment, the focus of attention almost always shifts to the woman when a contraction begins. A generalization was then proposed which states that in the presence of high-technology equipment the attentional focus of medical personnel as well as of non-staff attendants shifts from the patient to the machinery. (Jordan, Henderson, & Tatar, in prep.)

Having a videotape in hand in no way eliminates the need for thoughtful interpretation of the meaning of the events it records. However, video-based interaction analysis affords a powerful corrective to our tendency to see in a scene what we expect to see:

> For example, in certain circumstances we expect a couple who are in close physical proximity and who are smiling at each other to

> also touch each other. Observers frequently report that they have seen such touches even though on replay it is clear that none occurred. Errors of this sort are invisible on a paper-and-pencil record, but a tape segment can be played over and over again, and questions of what is on the tape versus what observers think they saw can be resolved by recourse to the tape as the final authority. This jolting experience of periodically having one's confidence in what one (thinks one) saw shaken, instils a healthy skepticism about the validity of observations that were made without the possibility to check the record more than once. (Jordan, Henderson, & Tatar, in prep.)

The work of interaction analysis is time consuming and labor intensive for the researcher. It requires the painstaking work of viewing, transcribing and searching videotapes for sequences relevant to a developing analysis. However, a compelling case for the value of this labor is made in Jordan, Henderson, & Tatar (in prep.):

> Even for a trained observer, it is simply impossible to note the overlapping activities of several persons with any accuracy or any hope of catching adequate detail. Consider an excerpt from fieldnotes, a paper-and-pencil snapshot of a birth: "midwife bathing baby; mother in hammock; father out to dispose of placenta; grandmother rummaging in cardboard box" (Jordan, 1983). The videotape provides an incomparably richer record. The kind of talk (or silence) going on at the time, the procedural details of the bath, the mother's eyes on the infant, the grandmother's rummaging for oil and baby wraps, the looks, the body orientations, all of that is lost and probably not recoverable from memory. It is also not recoverable from the memory of participants by interviewing after the fact. Similarly, the details of manipulative procedures such as the arranging of flight-status strips on the work panel of air traffic controllers (Anderson, forthcoming) or the details of moving a cursor while text editing, are impossible to capture in words, both because of the density of behavioral details and because we lack a ready descriptive vocabulary for bodily behavior which could be captured in notes.

This work is not easily delegated. Particularly where conceptual categories are under construction, it is difficult to instruct another as to where to look. More importantly, it is precisely in the repeated, careful working through of the primary materials that theoretical insights arise. In this way, analysis is something like iterative design. Articulations of themes and categories arise from familiarity with the materials and are constantly reevaluated against those materials. This in turn renews and extends one's familiarity. Furthermore, the identification of new themes and categories can lead one to return to the field or workplace to gather new materials.

Tools for Activity Analysis

As we have seen, the work of video-based interaction analysis involves a continual interweaving of multiple activities: viewing and re-viewing video records both individually and in groups, generating activity or "content" logs for each record, conducting detailed sequential analyses of selected portions of the records, integrating multiple records (often in different media) of the same activity, identifying conceptual categories and gathering "collections" of instances, and finally, juxtaposing multiple analytic perspectives on the same activity.

Assume for a moment that we have obtained a set of video records of activity in a workplace, including practitioners' work with a particular technology of interest. What tools, in particular what computer-based resources, are available to help manage and manipulate them? The sort of video analysis discussed here suggests possibilities for computer support: the need to generate useful abstractions while retaining their relation to unique instances and the need to capture multiple perspectives on the same piece of recorded activity.

Figure 3 shows part of an ongoing analysis of the operations room activity discussed earlier. The image is taken from the screen of a computer-based "activity representation" tool that we are in the process of developing.[4] Our tool is an example of a hypermedia system in that it represents information in linked, browsable networks.[5] Nodes in the network could include verbal transcripts, records of participants' gaze or other non-vocal activity captured in some graphical notation, brief comments or annotations, or indeed, a videotape itself.

Three "windows" appear in Figure 3: a text window displaying a portion of the verbal transcript, a graphics window depicting our understanding of the three-way aircraft switch, and a three-paned "worksheet" window used to control and annotate the video record. The worksheet's "Content log" pane serves as a canvas on which bits of text and graphics are positioned, ordered chronologically according to the time of the events they depict.

---

4 The tool described here was designed and prototyped in collaboration with Jeremy Roschelle and Roy Pea of the Institute for Research on Learning, with support from Apple Computer.

5 For an introduction to hypermedia and a survey of the major systems, see Conklin (1987).

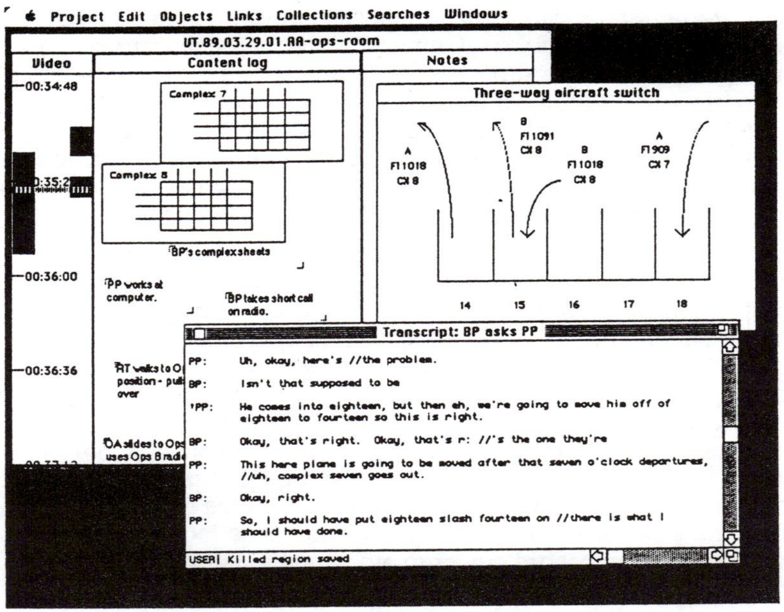

Figure 3. A computer-based environment for video analysis.

The "Video" pane includes ruler-like markings indicating relative time from the start of the tape. The small scroll bar appearing just under "00:35:24" indicates the current position of the videotape. When the videotape is playing this scroll bar moves down the pane. The three filled rectangles in the video pane mark the locations of *active links*. As the scroll bar moves past these link markers, the linked materials are automatically displayed in separate windows. The larger rectangle is linked to the graphics displayed in the "Three-way aircraft switch" window while the two smaller rectangles link to positions within the transcript.

The tool enables us to maintain and interrelate multiple perspectives on a work activity. Perspectives can differ on the basis of the dimension of activity picked out (e.g., talk, gaze, gesture, use of technology), or the viewer (e.g., different researchers, designers, and practitioners). In doing cooperative design we need to share materials: If video provides the catalyst for multidisciplinary collaborative work, then tools with which to study, represent, and discuss video records provide the ongoing support.

Who Participates

Most video-based analysis of activity makes use of a preconceived coding scheme, carried along largely unchanged from one study to the next. Our approach, in contrast, is to craft and refine our conceptual framework through the ongoing work of analysis. A basic strategy is to use multiple perspectives, drawing on designers, people informed about interaction analysis, and those able to unravel the intricacies of practice in a given domain. Although our use of these methods to date has been primarily in the context of traditional research, we believe they can be developed in the service of cooperative design. In our current working group, researchers bring tapes and transcripts from their respective projects to a weekly two-hour meeting.[6] The group offers a forum in which researchers can identify the possibilities that a particular tape affords. The entire working session is audiotaped, so that with those proposals and insights in hand, individual researchers or project groups can direct their more intensive work outside the lab to a particular line of analysis. Lines of analysis developed outside the lab in turn can be brought back to the larger group for reactions and new insights.

In a typical session, someone provides a brief introduction to the setting of the recorded activity and the project's interests in coming to understand that activity better. The group then works from a running videotape that is stopped whenever anyone observes something of interest. Group members propose interpretations for what is going on, attempting to provide some grounding or evidence in the materials at hand. Such proposals usually require repeated reviewings of the tape, until alternative formulations are laid out or the group agrees on one interpretation. Often an observation leads to further questions to be asked out in the field, at which point the questions are noted and viewing continues.

As well as being the focus of discussion for researchers and designers, video records can afford a basis for conversation with work practitioners. In a process developed most extensively by Frankel (1983) in working with student physicians, participants in a recorded interaction review the tape along with researchers. They are invited to stop the tape at any point and offer comments on what they see. Their comments are audiotaped, and then flagged at the place on the videotape that occasioned them.

This gives some idea of how participants structure the event, i.e. where they see significant segments as beginning and ending; it

6 We do this regularly through the Interaction Analysis Laboratory, a joint activity of Xerox PARC and the Institute for Research on Learning in Palo Alto, and through the Design Interaction Analysis Laboratory at Xerox PARC.

> also gives information on troubles that may be invisible to the analyst, on resources and methods used by participants to solve their problems, and on many other issues of importance to participants. Frankel, for example, asked patients and physicians who had been videotaped during medical consultations to stop the tape when they saw something of interest. There was a substantial overlap in *where* they stopped the tape, but the explanations they gave for *why* they stopped the tape were widely divergent between patients and physicians, indicating substantially different views of what their interactions were about. Elicitation based on video tapes has the advantage of staying much closer to the actual events than if one were to ask questions in a situation removed from the activity of interest to the researcher. (Jordan, Henderson, & Tatar, in prep.)

With these experiences as background, we hope to engage practitioners themselves in the process of analysis in order to collaborate on both work and system development.

Applying Video Analysis to System Design

Together with colleagues at Xerox Palo Alto Research Center (PARC), we have been exploring the technological as well as the social-interactional resources of collaborative work practice, focusing on the use of available artifacts. In particular, this has involved extensive studies of the use of shared drawing surfaces (see, for example, Tang, 1989; Tang & Minneman, 1990). To illustrate the power of video-based study for design, we trace the experience of two of our colleagues building a prototype shared drawing tool.

The objective of these studies is to understand how the use of the shared workspace both supports and is organized by the emergent structure of the ongoing activity. The conventional view of a shared writing/drawing space as a medium for the communication and recording of individual ideas is displaced by a detailed analysis of the use of such a shared workspace. By looking closely at each instance where participants in a working session put pen to paper, we begin to understand the complex sequential relationship between writing and talk in the joint accomplishment of the work at hand.

Scott Minneman and Sara Bly are currently engaged in a process of design that incorporates these observations. In what follows we briefly summarize their experience; the interested reader should consult Minneman and Bly (1990) for a full discussion.

Prior to designing Commune, their multi-user drawing tool, Minneman and Bly were involved in studies of collaborative drawing activity using traditional media. In particular, Bly conducted studies of a pair of user interface designers working in three communicative environments: face-to-face, in offices joined by a slow-scan video link, and over the telephone. This research revealed the work required to maintain coordination and co-presence as interactional and representational resources became less accessible and more difficult to share. In the Office Design Project (Weber & Minneman, 1987; Stults, 1988), three architects collaborated for two days on the design of an office space, communicating only via audio and video links. As Minneman and Bly (1990) put it:

> The results of these examples of using Media Spaces for everyday drawing activities indicated that better tools were needed to support individuals and groups collaborating remotely. It was also believed that such tools might easily generalize to support collaborative design work in other environments. The need for finding a solution to shared drawing support was apparent: the next step was to understand how and why drawing surfaces were already being used. (p. 2)

One resource for gaining such understandings is a workgroup at PARC consisting of anthropologists, computer scientists and designers called the Designer Interaction Analysis Lab (DIAL) (described in Tatar, 1989). This group meets regularly to apply the methods of interaction analysis to concrete problems in system design. The group views videotapes of people working with traditional as well as prototype technologies, noting the subtleties of established work practices with familiar artifacts, as well as the problems and adaptations encountered by practitioners using new technologies.

> One major finding from [DIAL-related] studies has been the importance of the *process* of the collaboration in contrast to the actual artifacts or markings on the shared work surface. Process includes the use of gestures, the ability to interact in the same space, the use of references, the lack of distraction caused by the drawing action, and the feeling of close interaction. Observing the use of drawing surfaces has pointed out the potential value of providing not only shared marks in a tool for distributed use but also support for the interactive process. (Minneman & Bly, 1990, p. 3)

The studies left several questions unanswered, however, suggesting "that the capabilities of a shared drawing tool might best be *evolved* through use, rather than through analysis and design alone" (p. 3). This led to a minimalist design for the Commune shared drawing tool, modeling the user interface after a single shared sheet of paper with marking pens. The first prototype could thus be developed in short order and made available to casual "walk-up" users almost immediately thereafter. Videotapes were made of these encounters as well as of one extended working session by two user interface designers. Initial study of this data indicates the "ease with which almost all users began using the system..." (p. 5).

As Minneman and Bly (1990) point out, such careful use-based prototyping isn't always the most natural path for designers:

> Despite the initial success of our development cycle for Commune, there is considerable temptation to revert to design evolution based solely on intuitions and the technological possibilities offered by the prototyping platform. (p. 6)

Our purpose in applying video analysis to design is to resist such temptation by developing methods that encourage the move from analysis to development to further analysis. The goal is to tie both intuitions and technological possibilities to detailed understandings of real work practice.

Reflection and Design

During meetings in the course of assembling this book, Pelle Ehn provided what we found to be a helpful formulation of the relations among the book's authors. Some of us are reflective practitioners, he said, referring to the book by Donald Schön (1983). And others of us are practicing reflectors. What we share is the goal of bringing the two together. Theorizing or reflecting and engaging in some form of practice are essential to every kind of human endeavor, be it research, design, or any other form of work practice. To develop simultaneously our ways of working together and our technological systems will require a joint enterprise that recognizes, encourages, and develops both the quality of our work practice and our powers of reflection, with respect for both and without privilege to either.

In Figure 4, this joint enterprise is depicted in the form of a triangle linking three perspectives: research, design, and practice. We deliberately have not said researchers, designers, and practitioners, because our goal is to view these not only as a division of labor between participants in the system development process, but as places from which to look. Depending on where one stands, at which corner of the triangle, one adopts a different perspective.

As a consequence of personal preference, experience, and training, we are likely to distribute ourselves differently across these perspectives. We believe that the most satisfactory organization may take the form of collaborations wherein some of us take on primary responsibility for one of these perspectives, and others of us for other perspectives. However, we want to think of these, not as absolute, fixed positions but as relative to each other. And we want all to have facility at moving between perspectives.

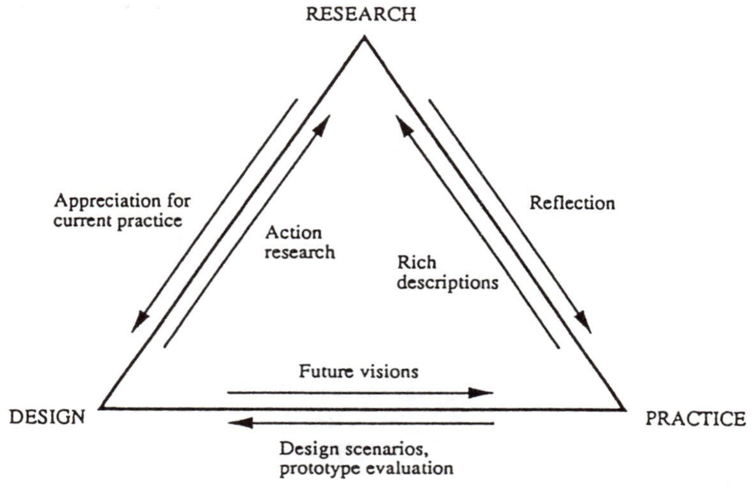

Figure 4. Video as a medium for conversation and learning.

In Figure 4, the arrows appearing along the edges of the triangle indicate the kind of contributions that one perspective can make to another:

- Using the perspective of research, practitioners reflect on their current practice;
- Using the perspective of design, practitioners envision future work practices and new technologies;
- Using the perspective of practice, researchers gain the insights that only confrontations with reality can provide;
- Using the perspective of design, researchers bring an action-oriented involvement to their traditional analytic work practice;
- Using the perspective of practice, designers working with users better understand the implications of prototypes and scenarios for new designs;
- Using the perspective of research, designers gain new insights from observing current practice so as to respect the present when designing for the future.

Examples of such pairwise collaborations can be found throughout research and industry wherever people concern themselves with work practice and technology. What we now hope to foster are collaborations among all three perspectives simultaneously, that is, activity occurring in the center of the triangle. Consider the case of the videotaped working session excerpted at the start of this paper. In a joint session of practitioners, researchers and designers looking at the recording, the various groups might have overlapping but not identical goals. All might share the goal of understanding better what happened in the interaction, though the participants might be reflecting on their work together, the researchers investigating the interactional organization of the work, and the designers searching for ideas for new prototypes. We hope that such cross-perspectival cooperations become the norm in the future, particularly in cases that today involve only one of the parties. We believe that the video medium can catalyze such collaborations to the greater understanding and imagination of all concerned.

Acknowledgments

We are grateful to Liam Bannon, Susanne Bødker, Bengt Brattgård, Bo Dahlbom, Pelle Ehn, Joan Greenbaum, Austin Henderson, Berit Holmqvist, Jana Kana-Essig, Morten Kyng, Jens Kaasbøl, and Jesper Strandgaard Pedersen, for comments on earlier drafts of this paper.

References

Akrich, M. (1987). How can technical objects be described? Paper presented at the Second Workshop on Social and Historical Studies of Technology, Twente University, The Netherlands.

Anderson, R. J., Hughes, J. A., Schapiro, D. Z., & Sharrock, W. W. with Harper, R. & Gibbons, S. (forthcoming). Flying planes can be dangerous: A framework for analysing the work of air traffic control. Submitted to *Human-Computer Interaction.* Hillsdale, NJ: Lawrence Erlbaum Associates.

Atkinson, J. M. & Heritage, J. C. (1984). *Structures of social action: Studies in conversation analysis*. Cambridge, UK: Cambridge University Press.

Blomberg, J. & Henderson, A. (1990). Reflections on participatory design: Lessons from the Trillium experience. *Proceedings CHI'90 Human Factors in Computing Systems* (Seattle, April 1-5). ACM, New York, 353-360.

Conklin, J. (1987). Hypertext: A survey and introduction. *IEEE Computer, 20* (9), 17-41.

Frankel, R. (1983). The laying on of hands: Aspects of the organization of gaze, touch and talk in a medical encounter. In S. Fisher & A. Todd (Eds.), *The social organization of doctor-patient communication* (pp. 10-33). Washington, DC: Center for Applied Linguistics.

Garfinkel, H. (Ed.). (1986). *Ethnomethodological studies of work.* London: Routledge & Kegan Paul.

Goodwin, C. (1981). *Conversational organization: Interaction between speakers and hearers.* New York: Academic Press.

Goodwin, C. & Heritage, J. (1990). Conversation Analysis. Prepared for *Annual Review of Anthropology*, 1990.

Heath, C. (1986). *Body movement and speech in medical interaction.* Cambridge, UK: Cambridge University Press.

Hellman, R. (1989). Emancipation of and by computer-supported cooperative work. In *Scandinavian Journal of Information Systems, 1*, 143-161.

Heritage, J. C. (1984). *Garfinkel and ethnomethodology*. Cambridge, UK: Polity Press.

Jefferson, G. (1984). Caricature versus detail: On capturing the particulars of pronunciation in transcripts of conversational data. *Tilburg Papers on Language and Literature No. 31*, University of Tilburg, Netherlands.

Jordan, B. (1983). *Birth in four cultures* (3rd ed.). Montreal: Eden Press.

Jordan, B. (1987). High Technology: The Case of Obstetrics. *World Health Forum 8*(3), 312-319. Geneva: World Health Organization.

Jordan, B., Henderson, A., & Tatar, D. (In preparation). *Interaction analysis: Foundations and practice.* Palo Alto: Xerox Palo Alto Research Center.

Kendon, A. (1985). Behavioural foundations for the process of frame attunement in face-to-face interaction. In G. Ginsburt, M. Brenner, & M. von Cranach (Eds.), *Discovery Strategies in the Psychology of Action.* London, UK: Academic Press, 229-253.

Latour, B. (1986). *How to write* The Prince *for machines as well as for machinations*. Working paper, Seminar on Technology and Social Change, Edinburgh.

Minneman, S. & Bly, S. (1990). Experiences in the development of a multi-user drawing tool. *Proceedings of the Third Guelph Symposium on Computer-mediated Communication*. Ontario: University of Guelph.

Sacks, H., Schegloff, E. A., & Jefferson, G. (1974). A simplest systematics for the organization of turn-taking for conversation. *Language*, *50*, 696-735.

Schön, D. (1983). *The reflective practitioner*. New York: Basic Books.

Stults, R. (1988). Experimental uses of video to support design. Palo Alto, CA: Xerox Palo Alto Research Center.

Suchman, L. (1987). *Plans and situated actions*. Cambridge, UK: Cambridge University Press.

Suchman, L. & Jordan, B. (1989). Computerization and women's knowledge. In K. Tijdens, M. Jennings, I. Wagner, & M. Weggelaar (Eds.), *Women, work and computerization: Forming new alliances* (pp. 153-160). Amsterdam: North-Holland.

Tang, J. C. (1989). *Listing, drawing and gesturing in design: A study of the use of shared workspaces by design teams*. Technical report SSL-89-3 (Ph.D. Dissertation, Stanford University). Palo Alto, CA: Xerox Palo Alto Research Center.

Tang, J. C. & Minneman, S. (1990). VideoDraw: A video interface for collaborative drawing. *Proceedings CHI'90 Human Factors in Computing Systems*, *Seattle, April 1-5* (pp. 313-320). New York: ACM.

Tatar, D. (1989). A preliminary report on using video to shape the design of a new technology. *SIGCHI Bulletin*, *21*, 2, 108-111.

Weber, K. & Minneman, S. (1987). *The office design video project* [Videotape]. Palo Alto, CA: Xerox Palo Alto Research Center.

Winner, L. (1980). Do artifacts have politics? *Daedalus*, *109*, 121-136.

Conducting and Analyzing a Contextual Interview

(Excerpt)

Karen Holtzblatt
InContext Enterprises, Inc. Sudbury, MA

Sandra Jones
Digital Equipment Corporation, Nashua, NH

Our goal in system design is to support, extend, and positively transform the work of individuals, teams and businesses through computer systems. We use the term *system* to refer to a complete system that includes hardware, software, services, and support. Contextual inquiry was developed to help achieve this goal and to meet three challenges.

1. We needed to identify a process for designing systems that support people who engage in similar work in many different business contexts and cultures. As Grudin (1990) pointed out, large computing systems are in the business of delivering general purpose computing systems. At Digital Equipment Corporation, engineering does not produce systems for a specific user with whom we can work continuously and to whom we are delivering a system tailored to a specific work process and culture.

2. We needed to identify an expedient process for gathering user information in the time available. Time and resource constraints within engineering and on the part of our customers limit the amount of time we can spend working with users.

3. We needed to identify a means of gaining appropriate and helpful information about users' work. Traditional information collection practices do not seem to provide a context in which users can articulate their requirements in a form that helps engineering design a system that meets our goal.

Contextual inquiry grew out of these organizational challenges. It supports the production of general purpose systems and provides us with a way to work for short periods of time with users at multiple customer sites that are geographically dispersed. It helps people crystallize and articulate their work experience. It also fosters team work and the development of a shared, consistent system vision among team members. (Team members include hardware and software engineers, people and product managers, writers, marketing personnel, and customer support personnel.)

Contextual inquiry is a technique that fosters participatory design. It provides a way for users to participate in the design of general purpose systems. It is a technique for working with users to help them articulate their current work practices, system practices, and associated experiences. The technique contributes to initial design concepts by providing an understanding of the nature of user's work through inquiry with users. We represent this understanding through models of current work practice and descriptions of fundamental work concepts that were developed through interviews with users. This understanding is then used to design a system model that supports user's work.

•

•

•

PRINCIPLES OF THE CONTEXTUAL INQUIRY PROCESS

Contextual inquiry does not provide a set of steps to follow for collecting and interpreting user information. Rather, it provides a set of concepts that guide the design and implementation of information collection and analysis sessions. Three principles guide the contextual inquiry process: context, partnership, and focus.

Context

We have claimed that the definition of a system that supports and positively transforms users' work is derived from an understanding of users' work. Understanding users' work is, therefore, critical to system design.

The best way to understand the work is to talk to people in their actual work environment. Design information is present in its richest form when we speak with people during ongoing work or using work artifacts. Work artifacts are the results of work. For instance, the artifacts that an application developer generates usually include functional specifications and code modules.

People Speak About Their Work in Abstractions. Typical data collection techniques, like surveys, structured interviews, or focus groups, collect information about what people do or what they want in a new system.

The notion of collecting system requirements suggests that people have the information that we need to design a system. If we ask people what they *want* they will be able to tell us. And, if we collect all this information we can then design a system to meet users' wants. This assumes that people are aware of what they are doing, and know what they need to improve the system.

We claim that people do not usually think about their work process and the impact of computer tools on their work as they work. People are engaged in doing work; they are not simultaneously reflecting upon their experience of doing work. Our focus of attention throughout the day depends on our particular concerns. For example, people who are building aircraft do not simultaneously think about the design of the computer tools they are using. The perspective from which computer designers observe users' work differs from the users' perspective.

We have found that when we talk to people about their work in an informal way or in traditional interviews, they tend to speak in abstractions and summaries about what they do and how they work. People have typical tasks that they can talk about. If we ask them to describe these tasks, they speak in abstractions about typical meetings, what usually happens, a philosophy of work, and other musings about their roles. This alone is not information that we can use to design a system.

On a visit to one of Digital's customers, we asked a user to describe the process for application development. The user started to describe the roles of various people and then showed us volumes of documentation that describe their processes. He said, "This is the way we work." We then asked about his current project. We asked whether he used the processes described in the volumes for his current project. "Well, no. There were extenuating circumstances and resource issues. Parallel development was needed." When we asked about his previous project, we got the same answer.

We find that process descriptions are idealized models of what should be or could be a way of working, but they rarely describe the actual work flow of people trying to accomplish a task. Similarly, descriptions of personal work processes are abstractions of general and common features of work derived from many instances of work, each with its own particular character.

The farther away we are from actual work, the more abstract the descriptions of work become. If we design a system based on these abstractions, we will likely fail because we do not know the actual ways that people get things done.

Through contextual inquiry, which focuses people on articulating their work experience as they work, we can help people to be concrete. Through dialogue with users, we develop an understanding of their everyday work flow by focusing them on particular instances of work. We can then create a system work model that supports users' work.

The Difference Between Summary Information and Ongoing Experience. When asked about a computer system, people provide a summary statement, or their opinion of the system. This summary statement is an abstraction derived from everyday experience. For example, when a writer was asked what she liked about the text editor she used, she said:

> I like it because it was really easy to learn. It uses this keypad with the labeled keys so I don't have to remember what key to press. I also like the multiple buffers.

She liked the multiple buffers feature in the editor. Frequently, people are not aware of what they like about a system, because it works well and does not call attention to itself. Or, they might tell us what features they like, but not sufficient detail about the feature and how it supports their work flow.

If we are present when the person is actually using the system, we can capture the detail of ongoing experience. For instance, during the contextual interview when the writer was editing a document, she began using multiple buffers, saying:

> This is a really usable feature. I position myself in one buffer, get the buffer I want to select from, return to the first and just pop it in—the cursor holds my place. I love it! It's a great productivity gain.

The ability to cut and paste between buffers easily was central to the usability of multiple buffers. Editing between buffers is usable because the editor maintains the last cursor location in each buffer. Multiple buffers without cursor placeholding would not be as usable. Similarly, when asked what she disliked about the editor, she said:

> Well I can't think of anything. There are little things that get in the way on a daily basis, but right now I don't know what they are.

Such summary information does not provide us with insights about what is "in the way." However, during the contextual interview she pointed out a problem with the way the editor failed to handle text formatting. The editor did not automatically wrap text as text was being edited. This prevented her from reading all of the sentence as she edited. She spoke of the disruption this caused:

> This is a biggy. I wish they would fix this.

Outside of the context of actually doing work with the editor, she was unable to recall this problem. It was the experience of encountering the problem that brought it to memory. In fact, she mentioned the problem before it actually occurred on the screen. As an experienced user of the editor, she had developed a workaround to the problem, a way of avoiding the situation. As she was about to use the workaround, she remembered the problem and discussed it. Even though the problem did not occur, the disruption to her work did occur.

Only by being present when work is happening can we see and discuss the details of what supports or what hinders work. When people are not in the context of actual work, they are not aware of the details. If something is very disruptive and causes work problems, it stands out in their memory. Little things build up over time. People might not know what the problems are; they only know that they do not like the system. On rating scales they rate the system low, on open-ended questions they list major problem areas to improve, and at interviews they discuss *bug* lists and *wish* lists (their design solutions) saying: "Support me; fix the system."

If we ask people to tell us what they do, what works for them, what problems they have with a system and how they work with others, we get summary experience. It is likely that we will, at best, collect attitudes about the system, abstract descriptions of work and lists of very disruptive problems. None of this *information* tells us what to design to support the work. Moreover, people do not naturally conceptualize their work, the work process, or the elements of design that support or disrupt that work. These are not users' major concerns; their major concern is doing the work. However, these are the computer designer's major concerns, which can be discovered by talking with users about their work while they work.

Accessing Ongoing Experience. Being present in the work context leads to more information than other kinds of information gathering. The workplace is filled with *touchstones* that help people recall their work experience: books and documentation that are open or unwrapped, crib sheets taped to the walls or computer monitors, documents used in meetings, files stored in a structure that supports the work, the coworker down the hall who is the source of problem solving, office mates, the broken door on the workstation from frustrated rebooting, the calendar with appointments, and the artifacts that people produce.

Walking with people through their work place and focusing them on their concrete experiences produces concrete information. People see something that reminds them of what worked and what did not work, and of stories about how things happened on the last project. The things in the environment provide the designer with opportunities to ask how objects are used now or how artifacts were produced. The people in the environment become the source of conversation about teamwork and organizational culture. The set-up of the environment, office layout, dress and degrees of neatness, lead to conversations about structure in the organization, interpersonal work, and expectations.

Contextual inquiry focuses people on their work and tool experience in the context of actual, ongoing work. Being present while the person works with a tool or with others allows the designer to witness the person's work and system experience as it occurs. Through the use of paper prototyping in actual work contexts users can imagine the effect of a potential system design on their work. Through dialogue with users in their work context, we can design a usable system work model and user interface.

Partnership

To design effective systems, we need to understand users' *experience* of work and systems. This information is invisible; we cannot access it by standing on the outside of a process, watching people's behavior and writing down what happens. We need to talk with users to understand their experience. To have an effective dialogue, we form partnerships with our users.

The principle of partnership recognizes that only through dialogue can designers become aware of users' experience of work and tool use. Together designers and users create a shared understanding of work practice that reveals technological opportunities and problems that occur in work processes and in system use. From this shared understanding designers create usable systems.

The User is the Expert. We recognize that in the area of personal experience and work, users are the experts. As such, users must act as informants in their relationship with designers. Designers do not know the users' experience; users must speak their experiences.

Acknowledging users as the experts and the source of understanding has two important results:

First, when we say that users know and the designer does not know, it becomes acceptable for the designer to ask questions. The designer's role is not to solve problems or give answers. Rather, the designer's role is to understand users' work and experience in order to imagine technological solutions. Since users know, and we do not, we can free ourselves from the expectation that we should already know and let ourselves inquire about what is going on.

Second, acknowledging that users know, protects us from misinterpretation. Interpreting another's behavior into our own experience is a normal occurrence. We do not look at a behavior like a smile and say only that Joe is smiling. We usually assume something about Joe's inner experience. We say that Joe is happy. We also look at the context and assume something about the cause. Joe is happy because Mary smiled at him. We only witnessed behaviors. Yet, we derived meaning from these observations. However, our interpretation may be incorrect.

We interpret users' behavior based on our experience and previous knowledge of the work context and tools. When we observe behavior, we impose our interpretation on the person's intention and experience. When we make assumptions about "what is going on," we can be wrong. Through dialogue we let users shape our assumptions and the meaning that we derive from a situation.

For example, during an interview we thought it annoyed the person to have to press several keys to correct a typographical error. When we asked the person about our interpretation of her behavior, she said that correcting the error was "like one keystroke." The layout of the function keys allowed her to correct common errors quickly with little disruption to her work. Acknowledging that users are the experts frees us to ask questions, to let go of the need to provide answers to technical problems, and ensures that we shape our interpretations by the users' experience.

Sharing Control During the Inquiry. In a traditional interview or survey, the "asker" generally has the power. The asker arrives with a list of questions. In this setting, users understand that their role is to answer the questions. The asker controls the pace and content of the conversation. Generally, one of the unspoken rules is that users do not question the questions. Users answer the questions.

But we have said that users have all the information, including what is important for us to know about. We could form a list of questions that comprise our best guess about what is important, but we might be wrong. We are not users, and we do not understand their work context. The purpose of going to the user is to find out what is important. If we come in with a question asking format, it implies that we have already decided what is important even if we later ask: "What have I left out?" Because we are the designers, users might conclude that we already know what we need to find out.

To create equal dialogue in which both people create and direct the conversation, the designer must deliberately let go of control and create a situation that allows users to share control. Partnership means that we empower users to direct the conversation along with the designer.

We give up control by giving up the role of expert, by using open-ended questions that invite users to talk, and by letting users lead the conversation. Rather than entering with a list of questions, we enter with a few areas of concern (the focus) which we share with users. This communicates the scope of the conversation. Alternatively, the conversation can begin with a request to: "Tell me about your work and your current project." The dialogue that takes place while users are working and involves probing what is going on. "What are you doing now?" "Is that what you expected to happen?" When we are talking about artifacts, we ask how, why, and when the artifact was created and used. In most cases, the central question brought to the inquiry is "What is going on here?"

The flow and pace of the conversation tell us whether we have formed a partnership of shared control. If the conversation is jerky (stop and go), if the person waits for us to ask a question, we have probably generated an "I ask; you answer" situation. When we are in dialogue together, the inquiry flows, ideas arise, and the interaction is conversational.

Often we enter the interview with a concern about covering all the issues with every person. Since each person's experience is unique, each dialogue is unique. Users cover the issues that are important to their work. We need not cover every issue with every person. There are additional users from whom we can get information. During the interview, the inquiry evolves. No two people are ever treated alike because we intend to articulate their unique experience.

Creating Shared Meaning. It is often the case that we do not actively listen and build on what others say. Consider a typical meeting: Person A makes a point. Person B thinks of a response. Person C gets his point in first while Person B develops his idea. Person D makes his point. Person B looks for an opening. Finding a pause in the conversation, Person B makes his point. However, the point does not follow from what C or D said, and B barely knows what they said because he was busy preparing his comment. The result is not shared meaning, but individuals getting in their points.

In this case, person B was self-listening—paying attention to his own thoughts rather than listening to others. When we self-listen, we develop our own interpretations rather than a shared interpretation with another.

Tape recorders are useful for capturing words, but they do not necessarily capture shared meaning. What will these words mean later on? If we have not actively created meaning during the interview, we have to impose an interpretation on the words after the interview. Each time we stop listening to users we fall out of partnership and fail to create meaning together.

To maintain the partnership, the designer must stop or change the conversation when either person seems unengaged. Self-listening naturally happens. We get design ideas. When we design in our head while users are talking, we are no longer letting the user shape our understanding. But if we simply share our design ideas as they occur, we both remain in partnership and we can codesign with users. In this way, users' experience of work can be directly translated into system possibilities. By sharing design ideas and interpretations as they occur, ideas get quickly shaped and validated, and the user partnership is maintained.

Reflection and Engagement. The key to partnership is to maintain a conversation that allows users and the designer to reflect on, question, and create shared meaning about the work experience. This process is one of oscillation between engagement and reflection. Engagement occurs when we actively listen and speak with users about their ongoing experience of work. Active engagement has the sense of a stream of consciousness discussion. Reflection occurs when we stop to consider and integrate information into our evolving understanding. Together we step back to make sense of the ongoing experience. Then, we return to the stream of conversation while users continue working.

We maintain an equal partnership by allowing both people to steer the conversation. Together we create an understanding of work and design ideas that can support the work. Maintaining our relationship to users and balanced control is key to the principle of partnership. Partnership creates the opening for participatory design.

•
•
•

CONDUCTING A CONTEXTUAL INTERVIEW

A contextual interview is a manifestation of the principles of contextual inquiry. In this section, we describe the setup that is required and the structure of an interview. We include practical hints based on our experience conducting interviews.

Identifying Customers

We begin the interview process by asking: Who is the customer? We think of the customer in two ways: as the business or industry that we expect to buy our product and as the individuals interacting with or getting value from the system. We work with marketing and sales representatives to determine the market for the product. From this discussion, we generate a list of key industries. Because we would like to return to users throughout the development cycle, we try to establish customer partnerships with key customers. Key customers include industries that are critical to our business success that engage in the kind of work the system will support. These may not be the only customers we work with, but they are a core group that represents a good cross section of the marketplace. Once we determine a set of potential customer partners, we work through business channels to contact user representatives.

Arranging the Visit

Before contacting the customer, we develop a framework for our visit that includes our purpose, a structure for the day of the visit, specific requests regarding the roles of users we want to interview and the amount of time the interview will require. The framework helps us to talk with user representatives about what we would like to do. We vary it according to specific situations. We also discuss our intended use of audio or video recording and send a copy of the form that we use to procure written permission before the visit.

A typical day at a customer site might look like the following:

- 9:00–9:30
  Interviewers meet group of customers to describe the product area and the process and to pair off. This group may include management and other contact people.
- 9:30–12:00
  Contextual interviews in offices or work place.
- 12:00–1:00 Lunch as a group.
- 1:00–3:30
  Second round of contextual interviews with a second set of users.
- 3:30–4:00
  Team consolidation and quick review of interviews if possible.
- 4:00–4:30
  Discussion with hosts about the results including a summary of major understandings.

We send thank-you notes after the visit.

Selecting Initial Users

Once we have determined what users we want to work with, our focus determines the particular individuals we want to interview. In determining who to interview, we consider the following roles:

- People who use the system directly (users),
- People who manage the users,
- People who receive products from the system (recipients),
- People who test the system and provide purchasing recommendations to management,
- People who make the purchasing decision, and
- People who use competitive products.

In a large work domain, our users have many different kinds of work. For example, the work domain of system management leads us to talk with operators, system managers, managers of the group, network managers, PC network managers, hotline operators, and the decision-makers. The team needs to identify the kinds of work that will be done with the planned system and who will be using the system. They can then identify people in key roles to be interviewed at a single site. When each interviewer works with a person doing a different type of work, the team will gather a sense of the business, culture, team interaction, and particular work when the information is combined.

We have found that it is best to schedule one visit at a time. This allows time between visits to analyze the information and refocus for the next set of interviews. We want to be in a position where we can make decisions about who to interview next based on our evolving focus rather than on an a priori decision.

Selecting Subsequent Users. Focus directs the interview; focus also directs the decision of who to talk with next. We use the time between visits to synthesize the information and frame our unanswered questions and concerns. This understanding guides us in selecting users for the next interviews.

Through the interview process, we are seeking to expand our focus and make it consistent with the users' experience. As such, we look for mismatches with what we already know; we are not trying to replicate experience. We select users who we think will challenge and develop our understanding. We are less concerned about replication than about whether our current understanding remains valid as we move from person to person, industry to industry, team to team, and across different kinds of work. To create a generic system we are looking for relationships between fundamental elements of the work domain. In addition, we attend to site-specific information that will tell us how to design customization and preference options in the system.

We are often asked how many people we need to talk with before beginning design. We accept that within engineering we are always designing from partial understanding. When we have no user design information, we are designing from an n of 1, where 1 is the designer. We recognize that we can never talk to *enough* people to ensure completeness for a generic population. As we continuously expand the base of users we work with, our understanding expands to respond to a larger segment of the targeted market.

Using Multiple Interviewers

Multiple interviewers contribute to expanding the team's focus and the understanding of users' work issues. There are several reasons for using multiple interviewers:

1. If a team collects information from several users within a project at a site, the information collected will reveal how people work together and the flow of work in the organization. This is a way of seeing a cross-section of a customer's business.
2. Interviewers with different functions, such as documentation, engineering, product management, training, and support, have different perspectives. Although the interviewers are working from the same focus, each person sees things from the perspective of their expertise. This difference is a strength. Through team analysis, the different perspectives are incorporated into a system vision. Interviewers with different functions can also incorporate each other's perspective in future interviews.
3. Interviewers with the same function, such as engineers, also have different perspectives. Each person sees things differently. Through team analysis, each member comes to understand and incorporate other perspectives into the system vision.

We deliberately develop cross-functional teams to conduct interviews. We bring small teams of three to five people to a customer site. Usually, each person conducts two interviews with different users within one day.

We have also conducted interviews in pairs or small teams. The advantage of this approach is that the team develops a shared understanding during the interview. The disadvantage is that it reduces the number of people we can interview during a visit.

Setting the Focus Before the Interviews

Before going to the interview site, the team of interviewers meets to articulate their focus for this visit. If the team will be talking to people who do different types of work, the group discusses what aspects of that work will be probed. The team deliberately articulates its entering assumptions and focus, making notes on key areas identified from previous information, and clarifying its purpose. The interviewer discusses these notes with the user to focus the conversation. These notes can be referred to during the interview to regain focus if the conversation becomes undirected.

Structure of a Contextual Interview

A typical contextual interview has three parts described in this section:

- Introduction: Establishing a relationship
- Ongoing work inquiry
- The wrap-up

During the interview we take notes. In our notes, we write down:

- What users do
- What users say
- Our interpretations
- Disruptions that occur to the users' work including workarounds
- Aspects of tool use that support the users' work

Our focus directs what we discuss. During the interview, we integrate information continuously into an understanding of users' work, and share the understanding with users. We do not try to structure or categorize the information during the interview.

It is more important to maintain the inquiry with the user than to take notes. However, when we are in the middle of capturing a thought and users move to the next point, we ask them to wait until we are finished recording. If we are unable to use recording equipment, we might work in pairs and have a colleague take notes to supplement our notes.

Introduction: Establishing a Relationship. A contextual interview begins by establishing a relationship. We introduce ourselves to users, tell them why we are there, assure them that all they say is confidential, and ask for their permission to record the interview. (We might use written consent forms when using recording equipment.) We tell them that we are interested in learning about their work process and how they experience their work and the tools they use. We enlist them as partners in the inquiry by telling them that we are there to learn about their work and use of computer tools.

We tell people how long we intend to be there, and that they can take a break or end the interview at any time. We ask them to give us an overview of their work and to discuss what specific work they will be doing during our visit. We ask for their opinions of the tools they use.

People always have things they want to tell us, such as software *bugs* or *wish* list items. Sometimes they want to demonstrate software. We listen to what they say. This conversation gives us hints about what to look for during the ongoing work part of the interview. Until they tell us what they need to tell us, they cannot focus on doing their ongoing work.

Ongoing Work Inquiry. As we move into the ongoing work part of the interview, we ask questions and share ideas as users work. We tell users that we will be interrupting, and ask them to tell us if we interrupt them at an inconvenient time. When we do interrupt at an inconvenient time, we make a note of our thought or question and ask it later.

As users work, we do not talk all the time; we also watch in silence. In fact, there are often long periods of quiet. The objective is to build a shared understanding of users' work. To do this requires discussion, but we do not sit there generating questions. We are engaged in an inquiry with the user. Our work is to maintain that partnership. We do this by sharing our interpretations and design ideas.

After we have been assimilating information continuously we may reach an overload point and need to go away and put our ideas together. We either suggest a break or that we end the session. (It is often the case that the interviewer tires before the users.) If we are tired, we say so and end the conversation.

We need to ensure that users are equally involved in the partnership. The role expectations often cause users to avoid requesting the session stop. Therefore we attend to any nonverbal and subtle cues (looking at watches, mentioning hunger) that suggest that users need a break or want to end, and suggest this.

Our goal is to articulate a coherent understanding of the user's work process, uncover the needs for the work, and uncover what supports or hinders the work. We let users lead the discussion by keeping the questions open-ended. We need to be careful not to narrow our focus too quickly, and try to keep specific questions until the wrap-up. We probe behind solutions and follow-up comments that contradict our entering assumptions. By so doing, we expand our focus and co-interpret the work with users. If users go off on a track that is not useful, we redirect the conversation.

We stay concrete and keep people concrete by attending to the ongoing work and work artifacts. For example, if they say, "People here do this," we ask: "What do you do?" If they refer to a "DFD," we ask them to explain the acronym and to show us one. We speak from concrete artifacts, ongoing work, or recently finished projects. When they refer to something, we ask to see examples.

When people are using computer tools for their work, we ask to see them use these tools. Some questions that we ask to keep the conversation going are:

What are you doing?
Why are you doing that?
Is that what you expected?

We ask them to tell us about workarounds that they have developed to avoid problems. Probing workarounds reveals how people think about and structure their work.

We bring out assumptions that we have (our focus) when people refer to that area to see if what we thought matches what they think. This is an opportunity to validate or invalidate our assumptions. Similarly, we share our interpretations and design ideas for validation:

I'm hearing you say such and such. Am I on track?
What you're saying leads me to conclude . . .
What if the application did . . . ?

The Wrap-Up. To conclude the interview, we summarize what we learned by referring to our notes. This is a good time to clarify any uncertainties. If particular questions or concerns were not raised during the interview, we discuss them at this time. We need to be careful about interpreting users' response; just to be polite they might say that they like an idea. This is an important time to validate or invalidate our assumptions. Finally, if users are using a product with which we have experience, we give them tips that help them be more efficient.

We ask if we can call later if we have additional questions, and invite them to contact us if they think of something after we leave. We close by thanking them for their time.

Variations in the Use of Contextual Inquiry

The principles of contextual inquiry direct us to collect information about work and system use from people as they work. Within Digital, it is not practical to spend days, weeks, or months with users. Therefore, we seek to maximize our information by spending several hours watching and talking with people as they work. Typically we spend two to three hours and we may make return visits. However, not all work can be seen in a day or less, and not all work can be interrupted. We use the principles of context (closeness in time, concrete instances, and accessing ongoing experience) to design alternative information collection schemes.

For example, application software development takes place over months and years. To get the flavor of this work within 2 hours, we take a team of three to five people to the customer site to interview different people performing different kinds of work on the same project. This gives us a sense of the way work overlaps and is coordinated. We also have people speak from their current project in the context of the artifacts that they produce and tools that they use. This allows us to talk with users about work process in a concrete way within a limited period of time.

For work that is difficult to interrupt, we might videotape a work session and immediately review the tape with the person in order to interpret what happened. The videotape is used to evoke the experience that the person had in the moment. In this and other ways, the principles of contextual inquiry can guide the design of information collection sessions.

ANALYZING CONTEXTUAL INQUIRY INFORMATION

Analyzing contextual inquiry information is interpretive and results in a shared understanding of users' work and system use that informs design. Throughout the process we are building an understanding of user and organizational work practices, a system vision, and specific design ideas. We are also generating questions for technology and future users. Analysis takes place both during and after the interviews.

During the interview, we engage in simultaneous information gathering and analysis. We share design ideas that are pertinent to the work being discussed and we engage users in design conversations. Together with users, we cointerpret their experience of work and usability. At the end of each interview, we have an understanding of their work and system usage.

The process of postinterview analysis is similar to the interview process. However, rather than having a dialogue with the person we dialogue with the text by reading the transcript and asking questions from a particular focus. Our interpretation continues as we analyze the text. To date we have not had users present during postinterview analysis. However, we have generated questions for clarification and followed-up with previous users.

The team performs additional analysis after the interview. We recommend team analysis over individual analysis and will describe a process that uses Affinity diagramming to support team analysis. Affinity diagramming is a technique for building a structure of ideas from a set of unstructured ideas. It is an inductive way to conceptually group information (Cohen, 1988).

Analysis by a team has many benefits. It integrates multiple perspectives and creates a shared vision of the system and a shared focus for subsequent interviews. It builds team spirit and saves time in the long run. We have found that individual analysis used by others results in the individual compiling documents that are neither read nor convincing. The individual ends up explaining conclusions and team time is used to redo what was done alone. Although the logistics of working as a team can be difficult, in the long run working as a team saves time. Team analysis also contributes to group ownership and builds a clear understanding of the whole system vision.

The following description of analysis focuses on a team process. Readers can abstract principles and apply them to individual analysis situations.

Transcribing the Interview

It is important to transcribe notes and tapes while the interview is still fresh in memory. Reviewing the interview helps us refocus for the next set of interviews. As we create the transcript we may include comments, insights, or questions that arise, using notation that differentiates our comments from the interview content.

Transcription can be time consuming (we estimate a 2–1 or 3–1 ratio for audiotape transcription). We have had secretaries and a transcription service transcribe the tapes so as to minimize the time team members spend on this activity. It is much easier for the team to work from a transcript or typed notes than from the original tapes or handwritten notes. At the beginning of the transcript, we include an orientation to the user's work and any other relevant demographic information.

Fixing and Evolving the Focus of Analysis

It is important to clarify our focus before beginning analysis. When we are doing analysis with a team, the team clarifies their focus together. We ask: What is our purpose or design concern? Without a clear focus, we can get lost in the information. Our focus directs what we include and what we exclude.

If we were developing a tool for debugging software programs, for example, our focus could be: "What is the work of debugging?" "How do the tools that users have support or disrupt the work of debugging?" As we read the transcript, we look for responses to these questions. After reading a section of text, we ask: "What is going on here?" "What does this tell us about the work of debugging?" We exclude information that is not about debugging. If we changed our focus, we would include different information.

Interpretation results from this dialogue between our questions and the transcript. We read and reuse the person's language, moving back and forth between specific instances and the entire session. As we interpret the text, questions may arise. In fact, the postinterview analysis may generate an interpretation that needs to be validated either with the person who was interviewed or with a new person. These questions, together with our current understanding of the users' work, form our entering focus for subsequent interviews. Before the next visit the team reviews these questions as part of setting their entering focus.

Analysis of the transcripts has the same effect as analysis during the interview: Our understanding of users' work changes and our focus expands and is grounded, inductively derived from the user information.

Interpreting the Information

The focus that we bring to the information guides our interpretation. As we change our focus, different aspects are revealed in the information. The deliberate shifting of focus provides a rich understanding. As a result, the same information can be analyzed with different foci revealing different things.

The transcript is used as a catalyst to direct team discussions about the user's work and the system. We interpret the text by alternating between reading the text silently and then sharing design ideas, questions, and work observations, and identifying technical issues. If more than one person has conducted interviews, information from one interview reminds us of information from another. This related information is shared to build an understanding of how people work together and the relationship between different types of work.

As we interpret the information, we do not critique ideas. We include ideas that seem technologically impossible or impractical. We keep the same attitude that we brought to the interview; we imagine the impossible. We do not want to constrain our creative ideas. There is no commitment to action at this point; commitment comes later.

We use and reuse the user's language, listening to the user's language carefully. What are users saying? We quote users verbally and in writing to discern the meaning which might have gone unattended during the interview. We consciously resist the temptation to rephrase their words in a way that supports our agenda items. As we move back and forth between the specific instance being examined and the whole session, we develop an integrated understanding of user work. As we understand the work, design ideas naturally emerge. We record design ideas, system work models, and user interface ideas.

The understanding that we develop is specific to the particular context within which we gathered the information. However, the knowledge is also reusable; it is carried across interviews. The knowledge that we develop from analysis becomes our entering focus for subsequent interviews. In addition, some of the knowledge extends beyond the specific context. Knowledge about work structure, work concepts, and usability concepts apply in other contexts. In this way, the understanding that we develop acts as a theory of work and theory of usability that transcends a particular domain. The concept of disruption is an example of a reusable concept that was articulated through analysis of contextual inquiry information. Holtzblatt et al. (1988) found instances of the system disrupting the work, such as when the writer had a problem with text not wrapping in the editor. We now consciously look for and discuss disruption by the system with users in a variety of work domains.

This reusable knowledge provides us with a framework or "hooks" that we use whenever we do interviews. These hooks include attending to:

- Work structure or work flow
- Problems accomplishing the work
- Problems in system use
- Disruptions caused by the system
- Workarounds that are used to avoid disruption from the system

- Transparency of the system
- Aspects of work process and system use that support work

Recording Understandings

As we interpret the text, we record our understandings. This can be done in the transcript by using a coding scheme to distinguish between the text of the interview and the postinterview interpretations. Another way of recording understanding is by using note cards or Post-its.[3] When working alone or in a team we have found Post-its an effective medium as they allow us to group and regroup information easily with the Affinity diagramming process.

When working in a team, everyone has a copy of the interview transcript. The person who conducted the interview begins by giving an overview of the interview and talking about the user's work and background. The team reviews the transcript together and one person acts as scribe by writing the understandings onto Post-its. Another person takes online notes to elaborate the words on the Post-its. The compiled notes represent meeting minutes. The team review is done by reading aloud and stopping when we want to record something, or by reading a section silently and then discussing and recording the understandings.

We do not recommend streamlining the process until the first transcript is walked through in this way. This could take 4 to 8 hours for a 3-hour interview. By this time members of the team learn each other's focus and the team's focus has broadened enough to challenge their entering understandings of the system and users' work. Analyzing the first transcript is slow because it draws in related information from other transcripts and because the team is learning to work together. To streamline the process, people can identify key aspects of the transcripts before the meeting and then share and discuss them, screening redundancies. Also, individuals can each take one transcript (not their own), identify key aspects, and guide the walk-through of the transcript.

We record:

- A description of users' work
- The flow or structure of the work
- A description of problems in their work
- A description of problems with the computer tools
- Design ideas that emerge from our understanding of their work
- Questions for subsequent interviews

[3]Post-it is a registered trademark of 3M.

Questions naturally fall out of the inquiry process. Sometimes the questions direct us to specific users to interview. They can also indicate things that we need to find out from a particular person, or questions about technological possibilities.

A key to successful recording is to avoid structuring the information during interpretation. If we make duplicate points, they will be handled in the structuring process that follows. We also avoid judging the value of ideas. Decision making is separate from information analysis.

Structuring the Understanding

Some analyses have generated hundreds of Post-its. To work effectively with such a large amount of information requires some structuring.

Structuring contextual inquiry information is inductive not deductive: It is a bottom-up process. We use Affinity diagramming, a technique that supports inductive thinking. It is a way to synthesize qualitative information into conceptual groupings.

To begin, we divide the Post-its among the team members. The objective is to systematically group Post-its that are conceptually related while avoiding the use of predetermined categories. We want the groupings to emerge from the information.

Developing an Affinity Diagram is a team process that requires facilitation by one of the team members. We begin by selecting an arbitrary piece of information, placing it on a white board and asking: "What relates to this piece of information?" Someone else puts a related piece of information on the board and the discussion begins. As information is put on the board, people talk about the relationships they see or do not see between the information.

As the groupings emerge, individual items move between groups. This process continues until the groups seem fairly stable. When the groups stabilize, the team systematically reviews each group and assigns the group a name. The name might come from an individual item in that group. The group names are intended to crystallize our understanding of the specific items in the group. It is through the conversations about the items that a shared meaning is developed within the team. The meaning of the information guides the design and development effort.

When the groupings are stable, the team reviews and labels each group. We suggest limiting the individual items in each grouping to five. This forces new concepts to emerge so that the detail and complexity of the information is revealed. The first level groupings can then be further grouped into a second and third level grouping to form a hierarchy. Figure 9.2 shows the hierarchical structure of an Affinity diagram.

When complete, the headings represent domains of work and design areas for the system. The individual items represent design ideas and the details of users'

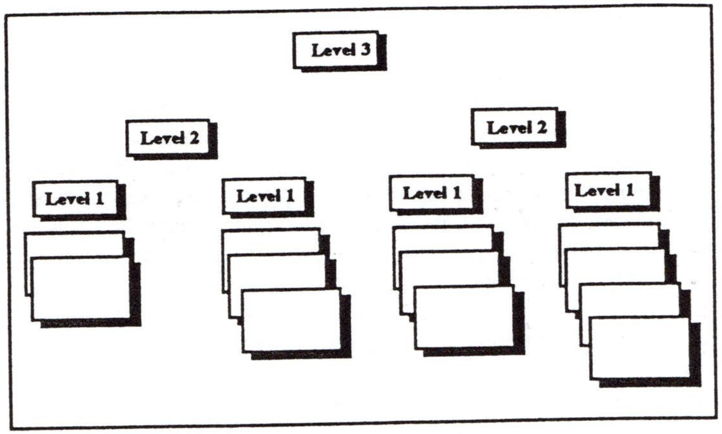

FIG. 9.2. Affinity diagram.

work. The team then reviews the "wall" to determine what is missing in the items. These missing items are recorded and direct the next focus.

We recommend working with no more than 300 Post-its at a time. Multiple Affinity diagrams can be completed as more information is collected. We do not recommend deliberately trying to integrate later Post-its into the first affinity headings. Rather a new structure should be created. When these structures are placed side by side, they represent a full picture of the information. Overlapping headings can be integrated later.

We have found it effective to use large pieces of paper as a background for the Affinity diagram. Flipchart paper works well. We tape the paper vertically so that it can be rolled up like a scroll, removed from the room, and reused as necessary. It is also effective to use white boards as the Post-its surface, and then place the groupings in a notebook for portability.

When the Affinity diagram is recorded, it represents an effective means of communicating the emerging system vision. This information can be used in requirements documents, decision-making processes, and to focus design meetings.

•
•
•

USING CONTEXTUAL INQUIRY THROUGHOUT THE SYSTEM DEVELOPMENT CYCLE

Each phase of development has key questions and tasks to which engineering teams must respond. Although our design practices are generally iterative and involve simultaneous requirements definition and design, we use a water-fall model of development to show where and how contextual inquiry can be used throughout the development cycle.

The question during the first phase of development is: "What should we build?" The key tasks are to determine a product strategy and product requirements.

We have used contextual inquiry to gather system requirements for a variety of products and systems. We use contextual inquiry with users of our systems and competitive systems. The focus for these inquiries is:

- What is the user's work?
- What tools are currently used?
- What works well and why?
- What are the problems that we can address with our technology?

Inquiry with users results in an understanding of system requirements that becomes the first cut at a product requirements document. Information at this stage is also used with planning tools, such as Quality Function Deployment (QFD). We use QFD to map user's needs to system requirements (Cohen, 1988). It provides a systematic process that is sensitive to customers' business needs, engineering resources, and marketing needs. QFD is one way that we separate design from decision making.

The requirements gathering phase is an opportune time to establish partnerships with strategic customers that we can work with intermittently throughout the development life cycle.

The second phase of development is focused on project planning and preliminary design. We have used contextual inquiry at this stage with paper prototyping to define the system work model. This is also the time that we use Metaphor Workshops, scenario building, and user participation in design meetings.

Design and coding of the implementation are the key tasks of the third phase of development. We have used contextual inquiry to codesign the system work model and user interface with users. Initially, the designs are represented as paper prototypes and later as software prototypes or early versions of the software system. When software is available for restricted use, we conduct *test drives*. Test drives provide users with an opportunity to explore the system while engaging in dialogue with designers about work flow, work concepts, and interface mechanisms. Although some test drives do not take place at the user's work site, designers use the principles of contextual inquiry in their interaction with users.

External field test of the system occurs during the fourth phase of development. During field test and after the product ships, we conduct contextual inquiry sessions with users in their environment while they are using the system for their work. Initially, we focus on ease of learning and later on experienced usage of the system.

Throughout the development cycle, user collaboration and system design are part of an ongoing, iterative process. The results of the inquiries are incorporated into the design of the system. After the product ships, results of inquiries can be incorporated into subsequent versions of the product or into a new product. The system development cycle in Fig. 9.4 illustrates how contextual inquiry can be used throughout the development cycle.

The type and extent of impact that contextual inquiry has on a system depends on when it is used. At the beginning of the product cycle, there is greater opportunity to define the product. This is the time to determine fundamental issues related to product functions and system structure that supports user's work flow and work concepts. Later in the development cycle, the design focus narrows to issues specific to the user interface, such as interface terminology and sequence of steps. The design of a system work model that supports user work and the design of the user interface is equally important. Working with users throughout the development cycle ensures that we consider both of these areas, not simply user interface issues.

Contextual inquiry is used as a method for collaborating with users throughout the system development cycle. As such, it provides a way for users to participate in the design process. This participation can be limited to a contextual inquiry session that focuses on user's work and tool use, or it can be expanded to include codesign of the system through the use of prototypes and participation in design meetings. In Digital, we are combining contextual inquiry with other participatory design practices and quality decision-making processes. When used together we have been able to powerfully impact the direction of products and the ways that design teams work.

We invite you to try contextual inquiry. Take from us what we have learned, try it in your organization, and tell us how you have improved upon our ways of bringing the users' voice into the design and development process.

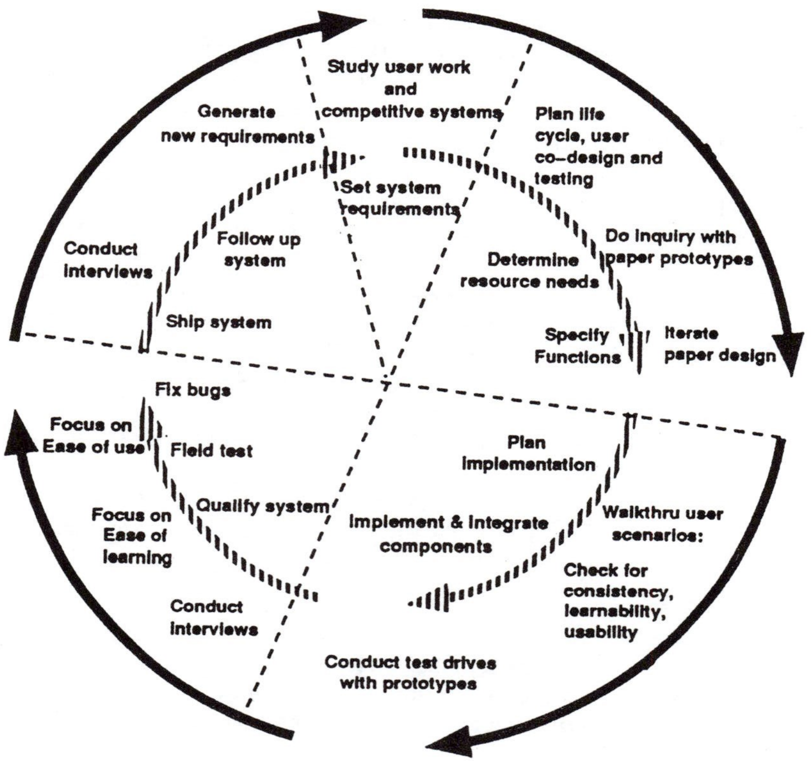

FIG. 9.4. System development cycle.

ACKNOWLEDGMENTS

The efforts of several people contributed to this chapter. We especially thank Melinda Thomas for her careful reviews of this chapter. We also thank Hugh Beyer, Michael Catano, Julie Dingee, Anne Duncan, Michael Good, Glen Lupton, Claudia Marcus, and Dennis Wixon for their comments. We thank John Bennett, Steve Knox, and Dennis Wixon for their help in developing the contextual inquiry course on which this chapter is based.

REFERENCES

Bennett, J., Holtzblatt, K., Jones, S., & Wixon, D. (1990, April). *Usability engineering: Using contextual inquiry.* Tutorial presented at CHI '90: Conference on Human Factors in Computer Systems, Seattle, WA.

Blomberg, J., & Henderson, A. (1990). Reflections on participatory design: Lessons from the Trillium experience. In *Proceedings of CHI'90: Conference on Human Factors in Computing Systems* (pp. 353–359). Seattle, WA. New York: Association for Computing Machinery.

Cohen, L. (1988). Quality function deployment: An application perspective from digital equipment corporation. *National Productivity Review, 7*(3), 197–208.

Darroch, V., & Silvers, R. (Eds.). (1982). *Interpretive human studies: An introduction to phenomenological research.* Washington, DC: University Press of America.

Ehn, P. (1988). *Work-oriented design of computer artifacts.* Stockholm: Arbetlivscentrum.

Ehn, P., & Kyng, M. (1991). Cardboard computers: Mocking-it-up or hands on the future. In J. Greenbaum & M. Kyng (Eds.), *Design at work: Cooperative design of computer systems* (pp. 169–196). Hillsdale, NJ: Lawrence Erlbaum Associates.

Gentner, D., & Grudin, J. (1990). Why good engineers (sometimes) create bad interfaces. In *Proceedings of CHI'90: Conference on Human Factors in Computing Systems* (pp. 277–282). Seattle, WA. New York: Association for Computing Machinery.

Glaser, B., & Strauss, A. (1967). *The discovery of grounded theory: Strategies for qualitative research.* Chicago: Aldine.

Good, M. (1989). Seven experiences with contextual field research. *SIG-CHI Bulletin, 20*(4), 25–33.

Gould, J. D., Boies, S. J., & Lewis, C. (1991). Making usable, useful and productivity enhancing computer applications. *Communications of the Association for Computing Machinery.*

Grudin, J. (1990). Obstacles to participatory design in large product development organizations. In *Proceedings of PDC'90: Participatory Design Conference* (pp. 14–21). Seattle, WA. Palo Alto: Computer Professionals for Social Responsibility.

Heidegger, M. (1962). *Being and time,* (J. Macquarrie & E. Robinson, Trans.) New York: Harper & Row.

Holtzblatt, K., Jones, S., & Good, M. (1988). Articulating the experience of transparency: An example of field research techniques. *SIGCHI Bulletin, 20*(2), 45–47.

Jones, S. (1989). *Learning DECwrite in the workplace: Using contextual inquiry to articulate learning* (Digital Equipment Corp. Tech. Rep., DEC-TR 677). Nashua, NH: Digital Equipment Corp.

Kensing, F., & Madsen, K. (1991). Generating visions: Future workshops and metaphorical design. In J. Greenbaum & M. Kyng (Eds.), *Design at work: Cooperative design of computer systems.* Hillsdale, NJ: Lawrence Erlbaum Associates.

Kuhn, T. S. (1962). *The structure of scientific revolutions.* Chicago: University of Chicago Press.

Kyng, M. (1988). Designing for a dollar a day. In *Proceedings of CSCW'88: Conference of Computer-Supported Cooperative Work* (pp. 178–188). Portland, OR. New York: Association for Computing Machinery.

Nygaard, K. (1990). Program development as a social activity. In *Proceedings of PDC'90: Participatory Design Conference* (pp. 4–13). Seattle, WA. Palo Alto: Computer Professionals for Social Responsibility.

Packer, M. J. (1985). Hermeneutic inquiry in the study of human conduct. *American Psychologist,* pp. 1081–1093.

Whiteside, J., Bennett, J., & Holtzblatt, K. (1988). Usability engineering: Our experience and evolution. In M. Helander (Ed.), *Handbook of human-computer interaction* (pp. 791–817). New York: North-Holland.

Winograd, T., & Flores, F. (1986). *Understanding computers and cognition.* Norwood, NJ: Ablex.

Wixon, D., Holtzblatt, K., & Knox, S. (1990). Contextual design: An emergent view of system design. In *Proceedings of CHI'90: Conference on Human Factors in Computing Systems* (pp. 329–336). Seattle, WA. New York: Association for Computing Machinery.

Controversies About Computerization and the Organization of White Collar Work

Rob Kling

*Department of Information & Computer Science
and
Center for Research on Information Technology and Organizations

University of California at Irvine,
Irvine, CA 92717, USA
kling@ics.uci.edu

February 1995

ABSTRACT

The way that computerization changes white collar work is the subject of significant controversies in the research and professional communities. This paper examines some of the key controversies about the way that computerization influences patterns of coordination and control in workplaces, including monitoring. It examines debates about upskilling and deskilling, and the role of organizational infrastructure in making computerized systems more usable. It also examines the ways that computerization might foster new forms of work organization.

Keywords: Computerization, worklife, workplace control, gender, telecommuting, technological utopianism, organizational change.

Acknowledgements: The paper gained considerably from discussions with Jonathan P. Allen, Robert Anderson, Joey George, Suzanne Iacono, Kate Kaiser, John Leslie King, Hannes P. Lubich, Wanda Orlikowski, Karen Ruhleder, Sang-Min Whang and Mary Zmuidzinas. Jonathan Grudin's enthusiasm was helpful throughout, and our discussions about technological change influence several parts of the paper. Production of this paper was partially funded by a UC-Irvine Faculty Fellowship and NSF grant SRB-9321375 for research about ethical issues and value conflicts in the design of computerized systems.

THE IMPORTANCE OF WORK

This article examines some key controversies about how work with computer-based systems is organized to affect the quality of working life for clerical workers, administrative staff, professionals, and managers. These controversies are sometimes self evident in the literature, as when one author explicitly criticizes a specific study or theoretical position. However, many of the key debates are implicit in the body of research and professional literature, even though researchers and professionals sometimes debate them verbally with colleagues. If you read a broad sample of books or articles about computerization and changing work, you will find that groups of authors seem to be writing about completely different universes. Some focus on older technologies while others focus on the latest technologies. A few writers will focus on those professionals who have significant influence over the organization of their activities and the technologies they use, while others focus on workers who have little discretion in the types and performance of their work. Analysts may examine managerial practices exclusively, or write as if technology itself

Revised and updated version of a paper that appeared as "Controversies About Computerization and the Character of White Collar Worklife." in The Information Society. 9(1) (Jan-Feb, 1993):1-29.

creates new forms of work. Some writers examine gender differences, while most ignore issues of gender when discussing computers and worklife. In short, there exists a plethora of conflicting interpretations regarding computerization and work. This paper will help sort some of the key areas of conflict. Since a full treatment could easily be book-length, I do not pretend this article is a complete or systematic analysis of all the major controversies.

While this article focuses upon areas of controversy, there are tacit agreements among the scholars and professionals who write about computerization and changes in work. Perhaps the most important point of agreement is that some computer technologies have important potentials in changing key assumptions about work and fundamental work practices. Writers differ in their opinions as to which technologies are most likely to catalyze major changes. Some hold that special technologies, such as PCs, networking, groupware, or notebook computers with cellular modems will create more flexible and interesting work. Others emphasize special forms of interfaces, such as windows, pens or voice recognition. It is also argued that a wide variety of computer systems can be used to restructure work to either improve or degrade its quality.

A second tacit agreement is that the quality of working life is an important aspect of social life. The relevance of work quality as a major topic in the information systems field is itself controversial. Many writers focus on the economic effects of computerization and ignore the quality of working life(e.g., Cash, McFarland, McKenney, and Applegate, 1992). I do not share this economic view. Following are some key reasons why I believe that the quality of worklife should be a central topic in discussions of computerization

First, wage earning is a major component of many people's lives. Wage income is the primary way that most people between the ages of 22 and 65 obtain money for food, housing, clothing, transportation, etc. The United States' population is about 260 million and well over 110 million men and women work for a living. Major changes in the nature of work — the number of types of jobs, job content, career opportunities, social relations and working conditions of various kinds — can affect a significant segment of society.

Second, in the United States, most wage earners work 30 - 60 hours per week — a large fraction of their waking lives. People's work experiences shape other aspects of their lives as well. Work pressures or pleasures can be carried home to families. Better jobs give people room to grow when they seek more responsible, or complex positions, while stifled careers often breed boredom and resentment in comparably motivated people. Although people vary considerably in the kinds of experiences and opportunities they want from a job, few people would be satisfied with a well paid, but monotonous and socially isolated job.

Third, many of the arguments advanced for the economic value of new forms of computer technologies make tacit assumptions about how people will work with them. Understanding the relationship between computer use and organizational productivity is paramount. It is crucial to know what people's work practices and (dis)satisfactions actually are. In the late 1980s, an array of PC-based applications commonly referred to as "productivity tools" were introduced. Most of the evidence regarding the use and value of the applications tends to be anecdotal (e.g., Baily, 1991; Salerno, 1991). No extensive studies are available which assess how these applications increased the productivity of the men and women who use them. It is known that productivity among North American office workers during a period of intense computerization in the 1980's resulted in a period of slow growth (Kling, 1995b; Strassman, 1990). There are interesting analyses that focus on how people actually work with computerized systems (Attewell, 1995). While some computer applications improve productivity by decreasing the number of jobs, most computer systems are used by only a few to support the majority of workers.

Fourth, computerization has had a visible direct effect on more people in their workplaces than in any other setting; home, school, church, etc. Workplaces are good places to examine how the dreams and dilemmas of computerization work out for tens of millions of people under a variety of social and technical conditions.

In the next section, I sketch some ways that work and technology have changed in the last 150 years. I will then examine some common approaches to the analysis of technology and changing work — technological utopianism and anti-utopianism. These two discussions begin our examination of some key controversies about computerization and the quality of worklife.

THE RELEVANCE OF HISTORICAL PERSPECTIVES: A SECOND INDUSTRIAL REVOLUTION?

"The design of the factory of the past will shape the office of the future" (cf. Garson, 1988). Our understanding of the past is never complete, and is periodically reconstructed. Our images of previous periods shape our evaluations of the present and our perceptions of future possibilities. When specialists discuss computerization and work, they often appeal to strong images relevant to the transformations of work in the last one hundred years, and the role that technologies have played in these changes. Stories about the industrial revolution and the nature of factories play an important role in understanding computerization and worklife. In 19th-century North America, there was a major shift from farms to factories as the primary workplaces. Those shifts — associated with the industrial revolution — continued well into the early 20th century. Industrial technologies such as the steam engine played a vital role in the rise of industrialism. Methods of organizing work altered significantly. The assembly line with high-volume, low-cost production and standardized, fragmented jobs was a critical advance in the history of industrialization.

During the last 100 years, farms became increasingly mechanized, replacing horse-drawn plows and hand-held tools with motorized tractors, harvesters and other powerful equipment. Farming itself has reorganized drastically. Family farms run by small groups have rapidly declined, and been bought (or replaced by) huge corporate farms with battalions of managers, accountants, and hired hands.

The economy of the United States during the late 20th-century is characterized by the rise of service businesses such as banking, insurance, travel, education, and health. Many of the earliest commercial computer systems were bought by large service organizations such as banks and insurance companies. (It has been estimated that during the 1980's, finance industries bought approximately 30% of the computer hardware in the US.) Although large firms are still the dominant investors in computer-based systems, in the last three decades computer use has spread to virtually every type of workplace. Since offices are the predominant site of computerization, I will focus on the role that these computer systems play in altering office work.

It is now commonplace for farm and factory management to implement computer systems support in their offices. Approximately 50% of the staff of high tech manufacturing firms are white collar workers who use such systems — engineers, accountants, marketing specialists, etc. Computerization in factory production lines is increasing dramatically, via the introduction of numerically controlled machine tools and industrial robots. Issues such as worklife quality and managerial control are as vital on the shop floor as in white collar areas (see Shaiken, 1986; Zuboff, 1988). While this paper examines white collar work, I invite the reader to consider the parallels between the computerization of blue collar work and white collar work. Many studies on the computerization of blue collar work focus on factories (e.g., Noble, 1984; Shaiken, 1986; Zuboff, 1988). Although factories employ a significant fraction of blue collar workers, they do not comprise a majority. Major blue collar occupations which are not factory jobs include: bus and truck drivers, heavy equipment operators, construction workers, appliance repair personnel, automobile and airplane mechanics, gas station attendants, dockworkers, gardeners and janitors. Factories are often the site of major computerization projects, as in the use of robots for welding and painting, or the use of numerically controlled machinery in production scheduling and inventory systems. Ironically, factories are growing areas of white collar employment, especially for specialists who organize or use such applications.

THE TRANSFORMATION OF OFFICE WORK

Office work has always involved keeping records. There are not many detailed accounts of early offices — pre-Middle Age. Prior to the 20th century, the majority of offices were small and often the workplace of a single businessman or professional who kept informal records (Delgado, 1979). Today, offices with dozens of clerical workers carrying out similar tasks are commonplace. The character of offices — the way work is organized, the role of women in their operation, the career lines, and office technologies — has been radically transformed in the last 100 years.

Novelists like Charles Dickens have written vivid descriptions of 19th- century English clerks. Clerks were often viewed as a dull bunch of sickly men with safe, but tedious jobs. In the 19th century, information was recorded by clerks using pen and ink. All copying was done by hand. No powerful technologies for assisting one's hand in writing, copying, or calculating existed. Filing systems were makeshift, and there were no standardized sizes of forms such as 3 x 5" cards or letter-size paper. Clerical work was a man's job. It was a common venue for evolving from clerk to businessman and/or owner.

JoAnn Yates (1989) documents how the technology and organization of office work underwent substantial change after the mid-19th century. Railroads and large manufacturing firms with complicated inventories and thousands of workers were the leading adopters of office innovations. The earliest innovations focused on standardizing the sizes of file boxes and forms. The vertical file for storing masses of correspondence was devised in the 1890s (Yates, 1989:56-63). By the early twentieth century, firms were using telephones and typewriters. Both evolved during the latter part of the 19th century. By the 1930s and 1940s, manufacturers were devising electromechanical machines to manipulate, sort and tally specialized paper records automatically. Expensive pieces of equipment, such as specialized card-accounting machines, were more affordable and justifiable in organizations that centralized their key office activities.

While managers often adopted new equipment to enhance the efficiency of their offices, its uses were tied to widespread changes in the shape of organizations: the shifts in control to central administrators, and an increase in the number of clerical jobs that were being filled by women. Women began to work in offices as typewriter operators and clerks. They were usually viewed as being short-term job-holders; young women in their twenties, after graduation and before marriage. As larger firms hired professional managers, many aspiring professionals turned to graduate schools rather than apprenticeships to learn their craft. Increasingly, specialized colleges rather than on-the-job training became the key entry point for professional and managerial careers. As these careers became predominantly male, the majority of clerical workers became female. Women were often discouraged from seeking jobs in the upper cadres of the professions or management.

This sketch indicates some of the key themes that permeate discussions of computerization and the quality or worklife: how efficient and flexible work will be, who controls the work that is done and how it is organized, how work is divided by gender, and who shares in the benefits of technological and organizational change.

CHANGES IN COMPUTER TECHNOLOGY

Businesses such as insurance companies and banks, along with public agencies, adopted computer-based information systems on a large scale in the 1960s. Many of the early digital computer systems replaced electromechanical paper-card systems. The earliest systems were designed for batch operation. Clerks filled in paper forms with information about a firm's clients, and the forms were periodically sent to a group of keypunchers to be translated onto cardboard cards. These "Hollerith cards" each stored one line of data of up to 80 characters. They were punched with a series of holes for each character or number. Keypunch machines were clanky devices with a typewriter-style keyboard, a bin for storing blank cards, and a holder for the card being punched. There was no simple way for a keypunch operator to correct an error. Cards containing errors (e.g., a letter "s" instead of an "a") had to be completely repunched. The punched cards were then taken to a data-processing department for a weekly or monthly "run," during which records were updated and reports produced. Errors often took a few cycles — sometimes weeks or months — to identify and correct. Using these early computerized systems required immense precision and care, since inaccuracies were detected and corrected very slowly. In addition, the data from one information system were usually formatted in a way that did not make them accessible to other systems. Professionals and managers often waited months for a new kind of report. Reports that required merging data from several separate systems were often viewed as prohibitively complex, time-consuming, and expensive to create. The earliest computer systems were speedier than the hand in processing large volumes of highly specialized transactions, but they were also rigid and cumbersome to use.

Furthermore, the transaction-processing and report-generating programs were usually written by programmers who were organized into specialized data-processing departments. Often, large computer systems, their operators and programmers were all located in basement offices — isolating them from organizational life. During the last 20 years, most organizations have reorganized their computer-based information systems to be more responsive and flexible, and to support a richer array of organizational activities. Terminals connected to shared data-bases or microcomputers are commonplace today. Many computer scientists, management scholars, and journalists advocate whole new families of computing technologies, such as groupware or voice recognition. Have jobs improved in a way that is commensurate with the recent technical improvements in computer systems? What roles are new technologies likely to play in altering worklife?

COMMON MODES OF ANALYSIS: UTOPIAN AND SOCIAL REALIST

Technological Utopianism and Anti-Utopianism

Every year thousands of articles and dozens of books comment on the meaning of new computer technologies for people, organizations, and society. A large fraction of literature about computing describes emerging technologies and ways in which they can expand the limits of human possibility. Faster, tinier computers can make it easier for people to access information in a wider variety of places. Larger memories can make more data accessible. Richer display devices can help people communicate more readily with computerized systems through pictures and text. High speed networks, such as Usenet and Internet, link thousands of computer systems and people in ways which were only dreamed of in 1970. The rapid evolution of computer capabilities in a relatively short span of time continues to amaze both the creators and beneficiaries of modern technology.

Accounts of the powerful information processing capabilities of computer systems are central to countless stories of computerization and social change. Authors write about changes in technology and social life with a range of analytical and rhetorical strategies. They bombard us with their glowing vision of technical wonders able to rapidly manipulate large amounts of information with little effort — to enhance control, to create insight, to search for information, and facilitate cooperative work between people. Others concentrate on a darker social vision in which computerization only serves to amplify human misery — people dependent on complex technologies which they do not understand, or doomed to routine work, because computers have usurped the interesting intellectual tasks. Both views reflect utopian and anti-utopian themes — genres of social analysis that are about 500 years old, and predate the social sciences by about 350 years.

Technological utopianism portrays specific technologies, (i.e. computers, nuclear energy, or other low-energy low-impact technologies,) as being the key enabling elements of an ideal world (Dunlop and Kling, 1991 Section I; Kling, 1994). It does not refer to exotic technologies, such as portable pocket laser printers or voice recognition on wrist-size computers. It refers to a kind of narrative that makes technologies, even simple ones, the key elements to a lifestyle that is admired as being fundamentally good and eminently desirable.

An interesting example of technological utopianism is found in "The Mechanization of Office Work" by Vincent Giuliano (1991). Giuliano examines the shift of office technologies from pen and paper through typewriters, mechanical devices, and finally, the interactive computer-based systems available on every desk. He argues that the social organization of office work is evolving through three stages: (a) an informal "preindustrial" office; (b) a highly regimented "industrial" office; and (c) a flexible "information-age" office in which operations are more integrated than in the industrial office. There are major technological differences in Giuliano's illustrations of these archetypal offices. His preindustrial office relies on telephones, paper, and organized files. The industrial office relies on batch-run computerized information systems, as well as paper and telephones. An information-age office relies on desktop computing linked to interactive data-bases on every desk. Giuliano characterizes the information-age office as

> one which exploits new technology to preserve the best aspects of the preindustrial office and avoid their failings. Ideally, it combines terminal-based work stations, a continuously updated data base, and communications to attain high efficiency. This is achieved

> with a return to people-centered rather than machine-centered work. Machines are paced to the needs and abilities of the people who run them. . . . The mechanization of office work is an essential element in the transformation of American society to one in which information work is the chief economic activity.

Giuliano portrays information-age office work in utopian terms — flexible, efficient, cooperative and interesting. His argument illustrates technological utopianism because it assumes that better technologies necessarily create better jobs. This does not mean Giuliano is completely "wrong", but it can lead the critical reader to ask whether advanced computer systems might not also be compatible with the informal pre-industrial office or formalized and regimented industrial office organizations. Giuliano's article illustrates the typical confusion between (a) information-oriented work and (b) the use of specific technologies. All of his illustrations refer to offices that are exclusively devoted to information-handling in some form. There is no substantive rationale for labeling any of these office forms as "information-age" offices. The label glamorizes the kind of office technology that Giuliano would like to see widespread — interactive computer systems linked to integrated data bases. Giuliano overlooks the fact that there was a substantial information work force in the United States by 1900, and it approached 30% of the work force by 1950 — long before electronic computer systems of any kind were routine fixtures of white collar work (see Kling 1990).

Other analysts who examine computerization and work articulate visions whose bleakness contrasts strongly with Giuliano's technological utopianism. Technological anti-utopianism is almost a mirror image of technological utopianism. In a technologically anti-utopian narrative, technologies are a key cause of human suffering. For example, Langdon Winner portrays newer forms of office automation in these vivid terms:

> To enter the digital city one must first be granted access. Having "logged on," one's quality of participation is determined by the architecture of the network and its map of rules, roles and relationships. Technical professionals are usually greeted by a computerized version of the social matrix, an organizational form in which there is at least superficial equality and ready access to information and one's coworkers. They experience computer networks as spheres of democratic or even anarchic activity. Especially for those ill at ease in the physical presence of others (a feeling not uncommon among male engineers), the phenomenon of disembodied space seems to offer comfort and fulfillment. Here are new opportunities for self-expression, creativity, and a sense of mastery! Some begin to feel they are most alive, most free when wandering through the networks; they often "disappear" into them for days on end.
>
> Ordinary workers, on the other hand, typically face a radically different set of possibilities. They become the objects of top-down managerial control, required to take orders, complete finite tasks, and perform according to a set of standard productivity measures. The working structure is one which incorporates the authoritarianism of the industrial workplace and augments its power in ingenious ways. No longer are the Taylorite time-and-motion measurements limited by an awkward stopwatch carried from place to place by a wandering manager. Now workers' motions can be ubiquitously monitored in units calculable to the nearest microsecond. For telephone operators handing calls, insurance clerks processing claims, and keypunch operators doing data entry, rates of performance are recorded by a centralized computer and continuously compared to established norms. Failure to meet one's quota of phone calls, insurance claims, or keystrokes is grounds for managerial reprimand or eventual dismissal. For those who manage the systems of computerized work, the structures and processes offer a wonderfully effective means of control. A report issued by the Office of Technology Assessment revealed that by the late 1980's, four to six million American office workers are already subject to such forms of computer-based surveillance. Such systems do not, as utopian dreams of automation prophesied, "eliminate toil and liberate people for higher forms of work." (Winner 1992, pp: 57-58).

Technological utopian and anti-utopian analysts suggest that the changes they foresee are certain to happen if certain technologies are developed and disseminated. Their arguments gain rhetorical force through linear logics and the absence of important contingencies. This causal simplification is, in my view, a fatal flaw of utopian and anti-utopian speculations. They explore the character of possible social changes as if they were the only likely social changes.

Clear and fairly coherent stories do not always match important patterns of computerization. For example, the information-age office is the only office type that Giuliano describes as having computer terminals which are located on almost every desk. It is also the only office that his diagram depicts as having plants! There is a photograph of a computerized office in Giuliano's article. It is an insurance claims office which combines an industrial work organization of a matrix of desks in an open area with the information-age elements of a terminal on every desk . . . and plants! Oddly, Giuliano does not comment on the way that this glimpse of the world undermines his clean topology of three ideal types.

Utopian and anti-utopian analysts share important common conventions. Their narratives are usually future oriented, universalizing experiences with technologies, homogenizing experiences into one or two groups, and portraying technologies as totalizing elements that dominate important social interactions. They take extreme, but different, value positions. They portray computerization with monochromatic brushes: white or black. The technological anti-utopians' characterizations of the tragic possibilities of computerization provide an essential counterbalance to the giddy-headed optimism of the technological utopian accounts. The romances and tragedies are not all identical. While some anti-utopian writings examine the possibilities of computerized systems for coercion, others emphasize alienation.

Although utopian and anti-utopian analyses often purport to offer visions of where computerization is taking us, it is worth noting that this literature is not merely descriptive. Rather, they seek to stimulate or inhibit their respective future scenarios (Kling and Iacono, 1991). Attractive alternatives to utopian analysis should be more credible in their characterization of conflict in a social order, or the distribution of knowledge. A more pragmatic approach to problems created by these new technologies should rest upon less deterministic logics of social change. They should also identify the social contingencies that make technologies (un)workable and social changes benign or harmful for various social groups.

Social Realism

One approach which incorporates these features is social realism. Social realism uses empirical data to examine computerization as it is actually practiced and experienced. Social realists are careful to note in their articles and books that they have: "carefully observed computerization in some key social settings and . . . will tell you how it really is." The most common methods are the journalistic and the social science approaches involving critical inquiries and ethnography. Social realism gains its force through gritty observations about the social worlds in which computer systems will be used.

Social realists do not all agree on the basic categories for conceptualizing technology and work: they differ in some key theoretical assumptions, such as the role of conflict in workplaces (Kling, 1980). In "Reading 'All About' Computerization" (1994), Kling examines the strengths and weaknesses of social realism as an approach. In the following sections, I will emphasize controversies which are anchored in social realist accounts of computerization and changing work.

CONTROL AND COORDINATION ISSUES

Gender and the Organization of Work

The majority of books and articles about computerization and changing work tend to ignore gender differences. Analysts who are most interested in gender issues write and focus on female-dominated occupations. The controversies about gender differences involving computerization and work focus on the extent to which men benefit more than women by computerization. The debates about gender differences focus on two kinds of issues: (1) occupational structures in which a majority of women's jobs are routinized and men have disproportionate opportunities to be offered the best jobs; (2) gender differences in cognitive and social style which lead men and women to prefer different software designs. I will focus on the first issue.

Discussions of women and computing often focus on clerical work because about one-third of the women in the work force are clerks. Conversely, about 80% of the 20 million clerks in the United States in 1993 were women. Women work in every occupation from janitors to Ambassadors for the Federal government, but they are not equally represented in the higher status and better paid professions. Less than 30% of the nation's 1.3 million programmers and systems analysts were women in 1993. But the nation's 16.1 million female clerks vastly outnumbered the nation's 412,000 female programmers and systems analysts in 1993. Female computer users today are more likely to be clerks who processes transactions, such as payroll, inventory, airline reservations, than to be information and computer professionals.

Iacono and Kling (1987) examine how the dramatic improvements in office technologies over the past 100 years have diversified clerical jobs, creating a higher level of interest, flexibility and skill enrichment. It is also observed that these changes, especially those involving increased skill requirements, have not initiated commensurate improvements in career opportunities, influence, or salaries. They examine the evolution of clerical work in the last 100 years, from the introduction of the first typewriters through whole generations of office equipment — mechanical accounting machines, telephones, and photocopiers. Each generation of equipment has made certain tasks easier. Clerical work also shifted from a predominantly male occupation, which provided an entry route to higher levels of management, to a predominantly female occupation with little provision for upward mobility. Iacono and Kling criticize Giuliano's technological utopianism by arguing that a new generation of integrated computer-based office systems will not automatically alter the pay, status, and careers of clerical workers without specific considerations.

These observations become more meaningful because the vast majority of working women are still concentrated in a few occupations, despite the growing numbers of women who have entered the professions and management in the last two decades (Reskin and Padavic, 1994). About 80% clerical workers in the U.S. in 1993 were women. In contrast, about 42% the executives and managers and 53% of the professionals were women. However, women professionals were clustered in nursing, social work, library jobs, and school teaching. For example, 75% of school teachers were women while less than 20% of architects were women. In 1988 only 30% of employed computer scientists and 10% of employed doctoral-level computer scientists were women (Pearl, et. al., 1990) and the percentages have not changed substantially since then (see also Klawe and Leveson, 1995).

In the last 25 years increasing numbers of women have chosen technical fields. Approximately 0.4% of the B.S. engineering degrees in 1966, were awarded to women compared to almost 14% in 1987. Slightly more than one third of the B.S. degrees in computer and information science in 1987 were earned by women. Bear in mind, however, that the clerical work force is about seven times as large as the segment of the work force devoted to professional engineering and computer work. Consequently, the way in which clerical work is computerized affects a huge percentage of working women.

Control and Coordination of Work Processes

An important aspect of worklife that recurs in social realist studies is the issue of who controls how work is organized, how workers are encouraged to coordinate and communicate at their various skill levels. Part of the controversy is between analysts who emphasize control and those who ignore (or pay little attention to) control issues. Analysts frequently assume that technologies labelled as "computer support for cooperative work" will usually be used in cooperative workgroups and that the elegant groupware will readily improve a work group's performance. In the 1988 Computer Supported Cooperative Work Conference, Pelle Ehn argued that all group work required cooperation and that cooperation is a *dominant* element in work groups. Kling (1991B) criticized this position and wrote:

> Most workplaces are much less coercive than chain gangs. But the primary alternatives are not simply limitless cooperation, as if these are all-or-nothing characteristics of group relations. As Grudin points out in the case of group calendars, most professionals are not so eager to cater to their managers' preferences that they will continually inconvenience themselves and lower their productivity in order to help their manager's secretary schedule meetings. They are somewhat cooperative, but also somewhat autonomous and self-oriented. Further, some kinds of conflict in groups is critical for identifying alternative lines of action and avoiding groupthink, as long as conflicts are resolved constructively and with dignity. In practice, many working relationships can be multivalent, mix elements of cooperation, conflict, conviviality, competition, collaboration, commitment, caution, control, coercion, coordination and combat (just to stay with some "c-words"). They also involve attention to substantive tasks, managing the organization of work, genuine sociability, and even play.

In the 1980s, many professionals became enamored with microcomputers. They were the new electronic typewriters for all. Engineers set aside their slide rules and electronic calculators for software which mechanized their calculations and produced graphical data displays. Accountants helped drive the demand for micros with their passion for computerized spreadsheets. And so on. They became hooked on the relative ease and speed of their computer tools, and dreaded any return to manual work. They adopted and adapted computers to their work in ways that enhanced individual control. Work remained labor intensive, since the working week did not diminish in length (Schor, 1991). Work sometimes became more fun, or at least less tedious. However, there is major controversy about the extent to which the romance between professionals and computing may be short lived.

First, the individualism which allows the individual to select software and configure systems to personal preferences often increases coordination costs when people work together. Standards, even if local, are a constraint which undermines the utopian ideal of enhanced freedom in electronic work.

There are issues of managerial control as well. In Giuliano's account, managers organized "industrial age" offices for efficiency. They organized "information-age" offices in ways that enhanced the quality of jobs as well. Observers argue that managers are incapable of relinquishing substantial control to their subordinates. Andrew Clement, for example, argues that the close monitoring of employee behavior represents the logical extension of a dominant management paradigm — pursuit of control over all aspects of the business enterprise. Indeed some believe that to manage is to control. ". . . [M]anagement may be called 'the profession of control'" (Clement, 1984:10).

Some analysts argue that the industrialization of clerical work sets the stage for the industrialization of professional work as well. In "The Social Dimensions of Office Automation" (1986), Abbe Mowshowitz summarizes his vision in these concise terms:

> Our principal point is that the lessons of the factory are the guiding principles of office automation. In large offices, clerical work has already been transformed into factory-like production systems. The latest technology — office automation — is simply being used to consolidate and further a well-established trend. For most clerical workers, this spells an intensification of factory discipline. For many professionals and managers, it signals a gradual loss of autonomy, task fragmentation and closer supervision — courtesy of computerized monitoring. Communication and interaction will increasingly be mediated by computer. Work will become more abstract . . . and opportunities for direct social interaction will diminish.

Andrew Clement (1988) expands Mowshowitz's theme in "Office Automation and the Technical Control of Information Workers". He examines IBM's attempt to require mainframes as intermediaries for PC-to-PC communication via its Systems Network Architecture (SNA). He notes:

> ....the prospect is that personal computing will be steadily absorbed into a subordinate role within the central hierarchy of corporate computing systems. . . . If this comes about, then the current wave of PCs can be seen as Trojan horses. Introduced under the guise of tools offering autonomy to users, they will be turned into extensions of the central computing systems and as the means of extending managerial control. (Clement, 1988, p. 241).

In these studies, Clement, Giuliano, and Mowshowitz make powerful arguments which gain some of their force identifying systematic conflicts between managers and their subordinates. But they treat organizations as if they share similar strategies of managerial control. They gain intellectual force by using the rhetorical strategies of technological anti-utopianism, suggesting that only one "social logic" can be dominant (Kling, 1994). Clement is correct in noting that central systems offer more possibilities for tightened technical standards and control over work. The controversial question is whether they require it. Electronic mail is a premier example of a computer-system that can open new possibilities for flexible communication because it requires a shared communication system. The extent to which new information technologies necessarily tighten managerial control, even when they offer workers more autonomy has set off a massive controversy. One argument against stand-alone workstations is that they do not support electronic communication, by person-to-person mail or group bulletin boards. It was hoped that new computer-communication technologies, such as electronic mail, would enable workers to bypass rigid bureaucratic procedures (e.g., Hiltz and Turoff, 1978:142). I will discuss this issue below.

Neo-Marxists divide the work world into two broad categories: owners and their managerial representatives on the one hand, and workers of various kinds on the other. They assume that these groups are usually in conflict. Owners and managers seek to maximize their profits by reducing the costs of producing goods and services by many means, including lowering labor costs. An influential analyst, Harry Braverman (1974), argued that the logic of capitalism requires owners and managers to relentlessly enhance their control over workers to reduce labor costs. Braverman's theory has been influential in shaping critical studies of technology in worklife. In the images of Mowshowitz, Clement, and Perrolle (which follow Braverman's argument), managers computerize so as to tighten control at every turn.

During the last decade, Braverman's labor process theory has been subject to significant criticism (Attewell, 1987; Kuhn, 1989; Wood, 1989:10-11). Critics of Braverman's labor processes theory fault him for treating workers as purely passive agents. Further, Braverman's theory ignores the variety of managerial approaches for improving productivity, such as those which increase responsibility, pay and morale, rather than tightening control and de-skilling (Jewett and Kling, 1990). Braverman's labor process theory ignores the way that workers are able to undermine managerial control systems. There is a rich tradition of industrial sociology which examines the methodology workers employ in undermining managerial incentive and monitoring systems (e.g., Whyte, Dalton, Roy, Sayles and Associates, 1955 Part I).

Electronic Workplace Monitoring and Speedup

Analysts who fear that managers will use computer systems to tighten control over workers have focussed on the issue of electronic monitoring (see the quotes from Winner and Mowshowitz, above). Defenders of electronic monitoring argue that managers have a right to know how effectively their subordinates are working, and whether they are slacking off. When computerized work is relatively private and reflected in shifting screens rather than lines of people or stacks of paper, managers need new ways to learn how their subordinates are working. Critics of electronic monitoring argue that it is oppressive, unobtrusive and pervasive. The manager who walks around to see how her staff are working can talk with them about the nature of the work, the organization, and their personal lives. They can build solidarity in their work groups, although much depends upon their abilities to develop rapport and communicate. In contrast, the supervisor who stays at a distance from her subordinates and has frequent measures of activities such as keystrokes, transactions or phone calls can create a pervasive judgmental presence. They have fewer occasions to build workgroup solidarity and motivate through commitment rather than fear.

In "Big Brother and the Sweatshop" (1991), Paul Attewell examines five theoretical approaches to help understand the typical uses of computerized workplace monitoring. He notes variations in the way that business firms and public agencies organize work and technology. Attewell examines the differing predictions which one would make by using five different theoretical approaches: corporate culture, neo-Marxism, product lifecycle, contingency theory, and industrial sociology. He argues that managers have tremendous incentives in principle to learn about and control the work of their subordinates. But he observes that many practical conditions weigh against their using computer systems as instruments of surveillance in the vast majority of workplaces. Attewell's article is specially important because of the care with which he examines a variety of supervisory strategies and how managers work with and without computerized monitoring systems. He notes that managers are concerned with controlling many resources, not just labor. For example, it's likely that the manager of a work group that manages multi-million dollar investments will pay more attention to the quality of decisions being made rather than a few thousand dollars in salary costs. In contrast, the manager of a work group where labor is the most costly resource and where judgmental errors are unlikely to be catastrophic may be very anxious to shave a few thousand dollars off of the payroll by having people work to their maximum. Attewell (1991:252) develops an alternative model that integrates elements of the organizations' environment, culture, business strategy, work organization and labor market conditions.

While Attewell asks about the conditions under which organizations will monitor the activities of their staffs, Grant and Higgens (1991) ask about the effectiveness and repercussions of monitoring service workers, such as those who audit insurance claims. They developed a rich, multi-dimensional concept of monitoring which includes features such as the granularity of data, the range of data collected, and the variety of people who routinely see data about a person's work. They found that many people did not object to computerized monitoring. But they also fond that monitoring does not always improve performance and the quality of service. In fact, service seemed to degrade most when many aspects of performance were monitored and made available to supervisors. Grant and Higgens view monitoring as a legitimate but subtle form of managerial intervention which can often backfire when system designers and managers do not pay close attention to people's indirect responses to monitoring.

Kling and Iacono (1984) take a very different approach to workplace monitoring and the control of work. Their empirical study examines the ways in which computerization alters social control and coordination in workplaces. Most analysts who examine the use of computer-based systems to tighten social control employ a model of managerial authority, even those who criticize Braverman's labor process theory. Their study introduces a new ("institutional") model of social control in which information can flow in any direction (up, down, and laterally) and in which people in different organizational units can try to enforce organizational norms for people in other units. Kling and Iacono observe complex patterns of negotiation and control that go beyond the traditional hierarchy. They rigorously examine the explanatory power of the institutional model compared with two other models: managerial authority and lateral negotiations. The institutional model is an important model of social control because it indicates that social behavior can be controlled through information flows and people that extend beyond the immediate behavior setting in which workers use computer-based information systems. Kling and Iacono focussed their study on complex inventory control systems in manufacturing firms. But their points pertain to groupware or any other computerized system where peers can see each other's work performance through the system.

Control Over the Location of Work

Managers often computerize work with several competing logics. They may be concerned with maintaining some control over their subordinates' time and pay, but also with allowing sufficient flexibility and self-direction to insure quality work and retain good employees. Certain organizations will pay less and offer attractive working conditions. One of the interesting possibilities of computerized work would allow full time workers to work at home part of the work week. This is relatively rare because of the problems created with workplace control. Many self-employed people work at home. Futurists like Alvin Toffler have been enamored with the possibility that people who commute to a collective office could elect to work at home. In *The Third Wave*, Toffler (1980) portrayed homes with computer and communications equipment for work as "electronic cottages". This concept, with labels like "telecommuting" and "telework," have been the subject of numerous studies. The pros and cons of firms giving their employees computer equipment to use at home while communicating with their shared offices via electronic mail opens up endless possibilities (Kraemer & King, 1982; Olson, 1983; Olson, 1989a; Huws, Korte, and Robinson, 1990). Working at home has the advantages of decreasing urban congestion during commuting hours, gives parents more opportunity for contact with young children, and allows people to spend more time in their neighborhoods. However, people who work a substantial fraction of the time at home may be unavailable for meetings, less visible to their peers and (therefore) passed over for promotions, and would be difficult to supervise unless they worked on a piece-rate system. Still other employees may lack sufficient self-discipline for work at home.

Popular accounts are wont to emphasize that home may be a less distracting place to work than the collective office. I do a significant fraction of my work, especially reading and writing, at home. Experience has taught me that home is a different kind of place to work — with its own privacies and distractions. Homeworkers report a different set of attractions and distractions at home: sociable neighbors may expect to be able to drop in any time; children returning from school demand attention in the middle of the afternoon, the refrigerator may beckon others too frequently, and so on. Some parents choose to work at home because they can spend time with their babies and pre-school children, but they often accomplish less than at their collective offices. Olson's (1989a) study of full-time work at home by computer professionals exemplifies some of the empirical studies. She found reduced job satisfaction, reduced organizational commitment and higher role conflict in her sample. She also wonders whether work-at-home practices can exacerbate workaholism.

Forester (1989B) recently critiqued the visions of full-time work at home via telecommuting as a romantic preference. After coming to appreciate the social isolation reported by several people who worked at home full time, he speculates that many of the most ardent advocates of full-time work at home with computing have never done it themselves. Whether organizations will allow substantial fractions of their workforce to work at home with computing part time (1-3 days a week), for reasons of personal flexibility or to reduce commuting remains an open question. Few homes are designed for significant home offices, and there are many important questions about the pros and cons of part time work at home with computing (and fax) for those who prefer this option.

A few organizations have conducted limited pilot tests of telecommuting. But these organizations and others keep the majority of their desk-bound work force keystroking in the office rather than at home. Workers may be given computer equipment to use for unpaid overtime work. To date, however, no large firms have dispersed a large fraction of their full-time work force to their homes or even satellite work centers to work with computer systems. Members of a few professions, such as journalists, professors, salesmen, and accountants take notebook computers on the road when they travel.

The desire to maintain control underlies many managers' fears of having their employees work full-time at home (Kling and Jewett, 1994). It is much easier for managers to be sure that people are putting in a fair day's work in an office from nine to five, than to work out elaborate contracts about the work to be done each week or month. Further, officeworkers often find it easier to coordinate with people who are often wanted for meetings if they are in their collective offices. Work at home increases tensions about control over work. This is most evident when high technology firms whose marketers promote the visions of bountiful technology for all refuse to let a significant fraction of their professionals work at home part time as an alternative to the daily grind of urban commuting.

It has been speculated that richer multimedia information systems, such as those supported by Integrated Services Digital Network (ISDN), may lead to more telecommuting because they would support more effective video and voice conferencing. The controversy here argues that better conferencing systems may facilitate conferencing but the control issues are not resolved by the technology, against technological utopian dreams that minimize the perennial importance of managerial control issues.

A few firms, such as IBM and Chiat/Day, have conducted pilot tests of the telecommuting and "virtual offices." And the members of a few occupations, such as journalists, professors, salesmen, and accountants often take notebook computers on the road when they travel. But the vast majority of firms keep their office-bound work force keystroking in the office rather than at home. Some workers are given computer equipment to use for unpaid overtime work. To date, however, no large firms have dispersed a large fraction of their full-time work force to their homes to work with computer systems.

It seems that the desire to maintain control underlies many managers' fears of having their employees work full-time at home. It is much easier for managers to be sure that their subordinates are putting in a fair day's work in an office from nine to five (sometimes called "face work"), than to develop and monitor subtle contracts about the amount of work ("deliverables") to be produced each week or month. See Kling and Jewett (1994) and Kling (1995c) for more extended discussions of the debates about telecommuting and virtual offices.

SKILL AND SUPPORT FOR COMPUTERIZATION

The Skilling Debates

There has been substantial debate about the extent to which organizations will design or adopt new computer technologies that lead to a less skilled, less professional workforce, with commensurate reductions in the interest of their work, autonomy and pay. As with many other debates about computerization and social life, the technological utopian analyses set some of the background. In this debate, they portray computerization as leading to a workplace of contented workers, whether the use of computing simplifies or complicates work. The main counterposition is informed by neo-Marxism.

In "Intellectual Assembly Lines" (1991), Judith Perrolle examines how managers can use expert systems and other advanced computer technologies to reduce the skill levels of professional jobs. As an analyst of class politics, Perrolle examines the work world in terms of structural conflicts between owners and their managerial representatives on the one hand, and workers of various kinds on the other. In this analysis owners and managers seek to maximize their profits by reducing the costs of producing goods and services by many means, including reducing the costs of labor.

Perrolle draws on Harry Braverman's (1974) argument that owners and managers relentlessly try to enhance their control over workers to reduce labor costs. One major managerial strategy is reducing the skills required for most jobs, thus enabling them to hire less expensive workers. Perrolle illustrates this theme through the example of computerized "application generators". Some of these facilities simplify the production of computer programs so they can be written by clerical workers paid $20,000 per year. A firm that delegates a large proportion of programming to clerical workers rather than to university-trained programmers paid $40,000 per year might reduce labor costs substantially. But Perrolle argues that expert systems may also be applied toward reducing the skill levels required for professional jobs. As skill levels of jobs are reduced, so is their pay, autonomy, status, and perhaps their intrinsic interest. Perrolle also argues that as intellectual skills lose their status, the criterion for being human will shift from an emphasis on intellect to an emphasis on feeling. (She cites research from Sherry Turkle that indicates that this shift has begun.)

The debates about up-skilling and de-skilling are complex and subtle, because a de-skilled job may be up-skilling for a person with lower skill levels (Attewell 1987). For example, a law firm might tailor routine document production for secretaries rather than lawyers. That set of tasks — put into a full-time job — might bore a skilled lawyer. But the same tasks may prove fascinating for someone who normally types correspondence and is eager to enter a paralegal line of work.

Workers often have no systematic voice in the direction of large computerization projects. Sometimes jobs appear to be upskilled when managers do not pay direct attention to skill issues (Danziger and Kraemer, 1986). A few firms have attempted to involve workers in redesigning their own jobs as part of computerization projects (Levering, 1988; Jewett and Kling, 1990; Clement and Van den Besselaar, 1993). However, most organizations remain authoritarian or paternalistic. Unions are the primary means workers have used to counter the preferences of self-interested managements. Yet, white collar workers seldom unionize and professionals, the subject of Perrolle's article, remain hostile toward unions.

Similarly, Perrolle ignores fundamental aspects when examining the computerization of professional jobs in the U.S. Spreadsheets, like Lotus 1-2-3 and Microsoft's Excel, are the primary software types that fueled the market for PCs in businesses in the mid-1980s. While it is possible to regiment and de-skill jobs with spreadsheets, the majority of applications are geared towards professionals and/or their clerical assistants. It is likely that professionals and managers, rather than clerical workers, will be the major users of any new information systems, absorbing these innovations at a higher rate than local programmers can devise them. Organizations and work groups frequently standardize their software; word processors, databases, and spreadsheets. This does not automatically regiment the overall character of work, by no means.

In a rich and provocative field study, Wanda Orlikowski (1991) examines how a large international computer-consulting firm used Computer Assisted Software Engineering (CASE) tools to reorganize work. The firm hires college graduates and MBAs with no significant professional computing experience and trains them with their own methods. It reviews the newer consultants with tough "up or out" hurdles every two years. Orlikowski's account of this firm's use of customized CASE tools has some important parallels with Perrolle's (1991) characterization of intellectual assembly lines. The CASE tools were designed to enforce a specific sequence of design activities, for example by requiring that data tables be fully defined before they are used in a program. The firm spent less effort in training newer recruits than they spent on similar cohorts of previous years. She reports that the younger consultants did not realize that their jobs required less skill for them than for consultants who had worked without the CASE tools. In fact, they liked the windowed CASE tools with nifty menus and the ability to easily edit changes without rewriting whole documents. Some of the intermediate level consultants had found key ways to work around some of the CASE tools' restrictions when they were working in a time crunch, but their own managers frowned on these workarounds. In addition, managers reported that the CASE system allowed them to bill the work of its users at higher multiples than the work of previous cohorts who used system paper-based design methods.

THE INTEGRATION OF COMPUTING INTO WORK

The vast majority of articles and books about computerization and work are written as if computer systems are highly reliable and graceful instruments. There are relatively few published studies of the ways that people actually use software systems in their work — which features do they use, how do they meet and resolve problems caused by systems or gaps in their own skills and how does the use of computerized systems alter the coherence and complexity of work?

There are no easy answers to these questions. Organizations may computerize jobs to simplify them. An extreme example are fast food chains with their computerized cash registers. Clerical workers input the menu items by selecting the appropriate register buttons, rather than the price of a cheeseburger or malts. This tactic enables them to hire clerical workers with limited math skills. Kraut, Dumais, and Koch (1989) report a case study of customer service representatives in which simplifying work was a major consequence of computerization.

In "The Integration of Computing and Routine Work" (1986), Les Gasser studied anomalies common in the daily use of computing systems. Anomalies are discrepancies between a person's expectation of behavior and the actuality. Anomalies include system bugs, but they go much further. For example, in 1990 the State of Massachusetts billed the city of Princeton, MA one cent in interest after it paid a bill for a ten cent underpayment of taxes. Each of these transactions cost a postage stamp, as well as several dollars in staff time and computing resources. The Wall Street Journal reporter viewed the situation as anomalous because one would not expect organizations to routinely invest many dollars in attempting to collect a few cents. However, the computer program was probably working as it was designed — to compute interest on all underpayments and produce accurate bills for interest due to the State of Massachusetts.

Gasser views computer use as a social act rather than as an individual act. He discusses computerized information systems that are developed, used, maintained, and repaired, by teams of people — people who relay their beliefs about system values, uses, limits, and problems to their co-workers. In addition, the individuals in Gasser's study depend upon other groups in their organization for key resources such as data, training, and equipment fixes. Anomalies occur due to the interactions between these groups, which are not organized like firemen to race to each other's aid at a moment's notice.

Gasser argues that discrepancies are widespread. The anomalies of computing may be reduced by improved equipment, but they cannot be eliminated. Gasser's argument sheds some light on the question of why computerization may not enhance productivity as readily as many analysts expect. It gives us insight as to why certain jobs become more complex with computerization — since men and women who use computers sometimes need to account for these differences and work around them.

Infrastructure

Workable computing arrangements depend upon a set of supporting physical, technological or social resources. Physical resources include space for equipment. Technological resources can require electricity and communication lines. Social resources may comprise of people skilled in the use and repair of equipment as well as the practices for allocating resources. These collective resources are termed the computing infrastructure by Kling and his colleagues (Kling and Scacchi, 1982; Kling, 1987B; Lepore, Kling, Iacono and George, 1989; Kling, 1992). Their conception differs from that of Shulman, Penman and Sless (1990) who rigidly distinguish between the "technical infrastructure" in organization and the "human infrastructure" and neglect interdependencies.

Computing infrastructure is a key element in facilitating any computerization effort (Kling and Scacchi, 1982; Gasser, 1986; King and Kraemer, 1986; Kling, 1987B; Kling, 1992; Clement, 1990; Jewett and Kling, 1990; George, Iacono, and Kling, 1991; Jewett and Kling, 1991; Bullen and Bennett, 1995). People report having better quality worklives in workgroups where the computing infrastructure for supporting training and consulting is best developed (Lepore, Kling, Iacono, and George, 1989). Further, financially poorer organizations, like many public schools, sometimes have trouble effectively using gifts of advanced computer systems because of weakness in their computing infrastructure. Training is one aspect of computing infrastructure that receives some attention. But computing infrastructure refers to a much richer array of resources and practices.

It is common for images of simplification to dominate talk about computerization, regardless of the complexity of systems. Clement (1990) reports a case of computerization for secretaries in which managers characterized new systems as "super typewriters" that did not require special training. They were very much mistaken. Many of the popular "full featured" PC software packages for text processing, spreadsheets, and databases include hundreds of features. Narratives that focus on the capabilities of systems usually suggest that people can readily have all the advantages that the features offer. Actual behavior often differs from these expectations. The majority of people who use these powerful programs learn only a small fraction of the available capabilities — enough to do their most immediate work. Moreover, it is increasingly common for many workers to use multiple computer systems, often with conflicting conventions, further complicating people's ability to "use computer systems to their fullest advantage." This dilemma can be partially resolved through the adoption of comparatively uncomplicated systems. Providing staff training and having available consultants can increase the practicality of the system. Still, cost efficiency is a factor. Managers often decide that supporting computer use with training and consulting is too expensive. Training is not cheap; an organization may pay $500 in labor time for a professional to learn to use a package that costs $150 to purchase. One of the authors vividly remembers a research administrator of a major food processing firm who was using a popular and powerful spreadsheet for budget projects. He wanted to print out reports in different fonts, such as printing budget categories in larger bolder print. But he did not know how to do this. He believed that "it could be done easily" because he saw such a report in an advertisement. And, most important, he treated his ignorance as a personal failing. However, he would have had to learn his spreadsheet's macro facility to print in varied fonts. His manual provided no clues about the techniques for changing fonts within a report. In some organizations he might have turned to an information center with skilled consultants. In this company, the PC consultants were overworked installing new PCs and had no time to train the men or women who use them or consult with them on software use. This was not a critical problem for the manager. But it is indicative of how many organizations expect white collar workers to learn to effectively use computer systems on their own, with little support besides limited manuals and advice from co-workers. Windowing systems are another complex family of environments whose actual use has many nuances. They are sold as easy to use. The reality is that they can daunt non-specialists who try to configure them without expert help. Computer systems do not work perfectly, further adding to the skills people need to develop and complicating their work (see Kling and Scacchi, 1982; Gasser, 1986; Clement 1990; Jewett and Kling, 1990).

Christine Bullen and John Bennett (1995) concentrated on how people actually integrate computer systems to support collaborative work in groups (groupware) into their work. They report how several work groups attempted to use some of today's best commercially available groupware systems with mixed results. Their informants found the value of the electronic mail features of these systems to be significant, despite the fact that a number of the electronic mail features were not used to full advantage. Others found many of the offered features hard to use, or not worth the effort (also see Grudin, 1989).

Notably, Bullen and Bennett discovered that many groups eventually reorganized their work to take the best advantage of their groupware. For example, the usage of electronic calendars to schedule meetings requires that all participants keep detailed calendars up to date on the computer system, even if they spend much of their time out of the office. Many managers and professionals hope that they can computerize effectively by installing appropriate equipment, rather than by reorganizing work when they (re)computerize. Bullen and Bennett make a provocative attempt to characterize high performing groups and found that they are not always the most computerized. They argue that group members and their managers have worked hard to create work environments that have "clear elevating goals," and which support and reward commitment. These groups have developed effective social systems with coherent goals and related rewards as well as adopting technologies that might help improve their performance.

There is considerable unpublished controversy about this kind of analysis, since many technologists and computer vendors try to convince computer using organizations that appropriate new technologies alone will improve working styles and organizational effectiveness. During the 1990s interesting technologies such as expert systems, groupware and graphical interfaces will be written about by technologists and journalists as if they can significantly improve the ways that people work without requiring important changes in the way groups organize their work. Careful studies of work with new computing technologies, like Bullen and Bennett's study, suggest that new technologies alone are unlikely to be magic potions that can automatically improve work just by appearing in a workplace (also see Jewett and Kling, 1990).

Social Design of Computerized Systems and Work Settings

One of the most exciting recent developments has been the efforts by a variety of computer scientists and social scientists to draw on the social sciences in designing computer systems and the social environments in which they are used (see Kling and Jewett, in press). The controversies appear in print in a rather one-sided manner. Some analysts explicitly examine the social design of computerized systems, while others ignore these possibilities entirely.

In "Understanding the Nature of the Office for the Design of Third Wave Office Systems" (1991), Jan Mouritsen and Niels Bjorn-Anderson reflect on the manner in which highly rationalistic conceptions of office work have undermined the ability of technologists to design "successful" office systems. There are many criteria for assessing the "success" of a computerized office (Kling, 1984), e.g., whether or not the systems are used routinely, how much they reduce costs, the kinds of new services they provide, and the extent to which they improve work by making the content more interesting or the process more flexible. No computerized system is likely to foster substantial improvements in all of these aspects of organizations simultaneously. The choice of criteria to emphasize depends upon whose values should be held preeminent in an organization, as well as the range of technical possibilities. Mouritsen and Bjorn-Anderson identify eight themes that could enrich the range of system designs, and are likely to produce systems that are attractive to those whose work is most affected by them. Their first point is to replace the concept of human factors with a concept of the men and women who use systems as conscious and reflective people who may or may not work in accord with designers' expectations. (For example, people may stick Post-its on their terminals in addition to using a flexible but sluggish text database.) Their remaining points amplify this idea to help designers understand the organizational conditions under which people work, the significance of informal organization, the legitimacy of world-view clashes and organizational politics, etc.

Their article is part of a larger literature about strategies for designing computerized systems to improve the work-lives of those who work with them (for example, Kling, 1984; Kling, 1987A; Hirschheim, 1985; Ehn, 1989; Winograd, 1988; Bikson, Eveland and Gutek, 1989; Ehn, 1991; Wagner, 1993; Clement, 1994). Ehn (1991) suggests a curriculum for computer systems designers who want to work from a social perspective. He argues that mathematics is appropriate for examining the efficiency of algorithms, but it is an inappropriate foundation for the design of "end-user" computer systems. Ehn's curriculum rests on Herbert Simon's behavioral approach to design and uses architecture as a reference point. In contrast, Kling (1985) argues that urban planning is a more appropriate reference point since urban planners study complex social ecologies with many artifacts and diverse lifestyles. But Kling, Ehn and others who develop this stream of analysis agree that the traditional focus of systems design on mathematical foundations is an intellectually limited approach (Kling, 1993). Analysts who limit themselves to mathematical formulations naively pursue the mirage of "rigorous methods" while being unable to characterize important human relationships in workplaces.

Many of the social analysts argue that the effective design of computer systems must go hand in hand with redesigning the way that work is organized. They also argue that organizations will not reap important economic benefits from new computer systems without parallel changes in the structure of work responsibilities, relationships, and rewards. Jewett and Kling (1990) report the case of a pharmaceutical firm in which sales managers radically restructured the responsibilities of sales clerks from passive order-takers to be more proactive sales representatives. The department held extensive meetings to reconceptualize their roles, and the staff rewrote all of the job descriptions. The department's managers also commissioned the development of a new computerized information system to provide richer searching capabilities to support the restructured jobs. In this case, the configuration of the information systems was part of a larger social design which included the explicit reconceptualization of key jobs (see Kling and Jewett in press and Chapter 4 of Levering, 1988.)

These strategies usually require that systems analysts and designers understand many of the work practices, schedules, resource constraints, and other contingencies of the people who will use the new computerized systems. They also require that people who use systems have a substantial role in specifying their designs as well as altered work practices. One reason that stand-alone microcomputers may have been so attractive for many people is that they offered more control over the form of computerization and changes in work than systems which ran on shared computer systems. In addition, microcomputer users' work methods made them less dependent upon having access to busy full time computer professionals to design and modify systems. This made their arrangements more adaptable. Many organizations implemented PC systems with a tacit social design that gave their workers more autonomy.

The main alternative approaches rely on more formal conceptions of information flows and work (Ellis and Naffah, 1987; Mills, Linger and Hevner, 1986). Mouritsen and Bjorn-Anderson (1991) criticize office and information systems designed from formal models that don't take the social nature of work and organizations as an intellectual foundation, (see also Bansler and Bodker 1993 for an empirical study of the limits of formal design methods in practice).

One way to insure that systems are designed effectively for people who will use them is to include user representatives on design teams (Kling, 1984; Clement, 1994). This kind of participation by people who use systems is particularly effective in the design of customized information systems. While most computer systems professionals are likely to label themselves as "user oriented," only a fraction of organizations in the United States effectively integrate the men and women who use these systems into design projects. In Norway, participation has been institutionalized through laws requiring unionized workers be informed of computerized systems early on in their planning and design, and be given positions on design committees. This approach gives workers more voice than they often have in systems designs. There are however, problems of integrating people with weak technical skills into design teams dominated by managers and technologists. It is easiest to effectively involve people in the design of information systems when the number of participants is small, perhaps less than 50, than when it is large. Large scale, important computer systems, e.g., airline reservations, police data, and social service payments systems, etc. are used by thousands of people. In these cases, some participation is better than none, but it is not a panacea. There are no perfect systems or systems design strategies. Interesting design work aims to develop computerized systems which are organizationally effective, yet allows the men and women who use them to have a significant voice in shaping their destinies. Design or implementation strategies that exclude the people who use the systems from influencing their design, selection, or integration into work seem paternalistic at best, oppressive at worst. Even so, practitioners who design or implement large systems have learned that strategies which effectively involve a representative and adequately motivated set of men and women in their designs demand care and an intuitive understanding of their preferences for working effectively, (see especially Clement and Van den Besselaar, 1993 and also Kling 1995c for further discussion).

NEW FORMS OF WORK ORGANIZATION

I began this article with the controversies surrounding computerization and how it changes the organization of work. This debate used traditional forms of regimented assembly lines as a major reference point. Another related controversy is the extent to which new computing technologies, especially those which support communications open up new forms of work. Does electronic mail eliminate organizational hierarchies and facilitate the formation of flexible (virtual?) work groups? Do new forms of computerization create novel possibilities for organizational learning (Zuboff, 1991)?

There are few empirical studies which support these speculations, and the existing evidence is mixed. In one intriguing study, Tom Finholt and Lee Sproull found that electronic mail can give groups more ability to develop their own culture (Finholt and Sproull, 1990). Others argue that electronic mail reduces the barriers to communication between people at different levels of hierarchy in an organization (Sproull and Kiesler, 1991).

Zuboff (1988) reports on an exceptional case which may dim these unbridled enthusiasms and lead us to wonder about the conditions most likely to generate these transformations. In a large drug company she studied, managers claimed that their electronic communications were being treated as policy statements, even when they wanted to make an informal observation or ad-hoc decisions. Further, when a group of about 130 professional women formed a private conference that threatened male managers, participation was discouraged by upper managers and many participants dropped out (Zuboff, 1988:382-383). I suspect that electronic communications systems can encourage the forming of groups that upper managers deem to be safe, except in those special organizations — like universities and R&D labs — where there are strong norms against censorship. The controversy between technological utopians who see technologies as improving human and organizational behavior and those who see social systems as changing slowly in response to other kinds of social and economic forces will not be resolved by one or two case studies. But the cases are instructive to help focus the debate about what is possible and the conditions under which computer systems of specific kinds alter social life (see Kling, 1995d).

One of the most intriguing and popular conceptualizations is Zuboff's distinction between automating work and informating work (Zuboff, 1988; Zuboff 1991).

> To 'automate' is to replace human activity with a machine (computer) which is faster, more reliable, more subject to control, etc. The typical goals of automation "have typically been those of cost reduction, efficiency, and roductivity....Automation...means applying technology in ways that increase the self acting and self regulating capacities of machine systems, thus minimizing human intervention."
>
> "Intelligent technology can be used to automate, but even as this occurs, the technology has the capacity to translate those automated activities into data and to display those data. Information technology symbolically renders processes, objects, behaviors and events so that they become visible, knowable and sharable in a new way." ... The word I have coined to describe this second function is 'informate.' 'To informate' means to translate and make visible; 'informating' occurs as processes, objects, behaviors and events are translated and made visible as explicit information.... As the informating process unfolds, the organization is increasingly imbued with an electronic text that implicitly represents many forms of data which were once implicit, private or minimally codified. Thus the work environment becomes increasingly 'textualized.'
>
> By textualization' I mean that an increasing proportion of the information in the work environment is presented through the medium of the electronic text.
>
> Under these conditions, 'to work' becomes more abstract, since it depends upon an understanding of, responsiveness to, and ability to manage and create value from information. In an informated environment, skills are refined." ... "It requires the construction of a new kind of knowledge, one that is more analytical, abstract, and conceptual....It is in terms of this second informating function that information technology represents a radical discontinuity in the history of work and the evolution of industrial technology." (Zuboff, 1991:3-5).

Zuboff reports an intriguing case of informating in her study of an Expense Tracking System (ETS) in a paper plant (Bronsema and Zuboff, 1984; Walton 1989:142-149;Zuboff, 1988: 255-267). Operators in the paper plant acquired information about the costs of making paper from a computerized system that had been added to their existing papermaking equipment. By experimenting with their equipment controls they were able to significantly reduce the costs of producing paper. The costs of chemicals and other ingredients in paper-making were previously unavailable to operators in real-time. The ETS is a great illustration of informating.

The worm in the ETS case was the implementation process. While upper managers in the firm originally viewed the ETS as a risky project, they were pleased with the cost reductions and praised the staff involved. The managers who initiated the ETS bypassed some middle managers and worked directly with the machine operators to help give them a sense of ownership over the ETS (Bronsema and Zuboff, 1984). When the operators' results from using the ETS proved valuable to managers in corporate headquarters, these middle managers felt left out and worried about the security of their jobs. They tried to share in the glory of ETS' use by adding their names to key reports. Later they initiated policies to limit and impede operators' abilities to experiment with it. Informating the machine operators empowered them in ways that threatened their immediate managers, who in turn, acted to protect their jobs and status. However the concept of informating focusses upon the closed system of a job, information recorded about some work processes, and feedback to workers' about their performance. As Zuboff shows in the ETS case, managers who are located outside of this segment of a work system can play a major role in facilitating or impeding an informating strategy.

Zuboff's distinction between informating and automating has become the center of significant attention and unpublished controversy. Her catchy and vivid imagery has stimulated some scholars to rethink their approaches to computerization (e.g., Walton, 1989; Morton, 1991). I have found that some of our students and colleagues like the resonance of the term "informate" because it suggests a positive and upbeat approach to computerization. I have also been intrigued by the way that some of these same students and faculty have a hard time articulating what an informated workplace would be like, and how much their conceptions often diverge from Zuboff's formulation.

Part of Zuboff's contribution is to squarely place the analysis of computerization and work in a moral framework which values the possible innovations from all workers, including clerks and production workers. And Zuboff's case studies provide vivid testimony to the ways that many managers are frightened of tapping the creative potential of their workers, and thus also risking a loss of their own authority and power. Informating is a great buzzword. Unfortunately, it is hard to identify how many kinds of work could be effectively informated based on Zuboff's particular definition. For example, how would one informate the job of a person who is word processing legal contracts? Zuboff's conceptualization of informating seems to have been inspired by "closed loop" process control systems where blue collar workers can become more analytical when they obtain data (and training) to help them monitor and analyze their own work.

The moral force of informating derives from the use of new technologies and reconceptualized work to empower and ennoble workers. Her conception of informating focusses on people and their work in isolation, even though empowerment tacitly refers to social relationships which extend outside of a particular workgroup. The informating concept isn't rich enough to help us understand when organizations will experiment with new forms of work — or when these experiments will be successfully sustained over a period of time (and when they will be quickly abandoned). Unfortunately, the body of writing about informating seems to be driven more by zeal to inspire managers with a new vision than by an interest in exploring the value, boundaries and problematics of the concepts.

The controversy about the possibility of computerization fostering new forms of work organization is very engaging. Enthusiasts of the position that computerization can lead to new forms of work have the advantage of offering exciting possibilities. However, they rarely face the issues of control and support systems which I have examined in this paper. When they ignore recurrent themes from previous eras of computerization, they risk being blindsided by perennial issues in new guises.

CONCLUSIONS

During the 1990s organizations will continue to computerize work — automating new activities and replacing earlier systems with newer technologies. The controversies about how to change work with computer systems will continue to have immense practical repercussions. The relevant research is multi-disciplinary and scattered in the books and journals of several disciplines. This article identified some of the key controversies that pervade this diffuse literature — those that pertain to gender equity, control, support systems, social design and new ways of organizing work. I have noted that many of the controversies are implicit, since authors often take positions without carefully discussing the alternative positions and debates.

I have not tried to resolve these key controversies here, even though our own beliefs shape our selection of topics and illustrations. But there are some useful conclusions that we can draw from the existing research. Further systematic research can help resolve some controversies, such as the possibilities of effective social design, the conditions which engender new forms of work organization, and the extent to which they create higher quality workplaces. However, these controversies also pertain to the concrete behavior of organizations, and questions about what they do and will do, not just what they should do.

Organizations and workplaces differ and consequently, their appropriate work organization technologies differ. The research shows that no single logic has been applied towards changing work with computerization. So key controversies cannot be automatically resolved by a new kind of computer technology, such as pen-based systems, or voice recognition. New technologies create new opportunities, but do not always require that the opportunities will be exploited, for better or worse. For example, the research shows that few organizations utilize fine grained computer monitoring systems as intensively as critics of automated monitoring suggest. On the other hand, relatively few organizations systemically and broadly exploit the possibilities of more flexible work schedules that telecommuting can provide. And it is common for organizations to underinvest in the support for helping people effectively integrate computerized systems into their work.

The choices of how to computerize involve practical judgments about what makes workers more productive, but it also engages managers' preferences for control, innovation. Controversies over control pervade the literature about computers and worklife. They also pervade numerous workplaces. They entail controversies that have no inherent resolutions.

But good research can at least help men and women at work in understanding the issues and some of their most significant repercussions. After all, on a large scale, the resulting choices will affect the lives of tens of millions of people.

The practical situation is worsened when advocates of some new family of technologies write as if all that has been learned from the last 30 years of computerization is totally irrelevant to help us understand how their systems can be integrated into work or serve as a catalyst for reorganizing work. In this article, I have criticized technological utopianism and anti-utopianism as key genres which informs many normative accounts about how organizations should or should not computerize work. I have seen a reliance on these genres in a large body of professional writing about new families of computing which are technologically discontinuous with past devices. Expert systems, personal computing, groupware, and networking have often been the subject of analyses which are anchored in technological utopian premises. I expect to see a similar body of misleading literature develop to characterize new worlds of work with other exciting technologies, such as "personal digital assistants."

A more realistic body of scholarly and professional analyses can develop in two ways. First, if analysts are willing to learn from the past, such as the nature of control issues in work and the importance of infrastructure and social design, in their relentless search for a better future (see Kling and Jewett, 1994). And, second, if the technological community is willing to devote some resources to sponsor serious empirical inquiry into the opportunities, limitations, problems of specific families of new technologies.

The modest band of systematic empirical researchers can only study a small fraction of the diverse array of workplace technologies, occupations, industries, and organizational conditions. But I have found key themes that relate to new technologies, and diverse occupations and industries. Despite the limitations of the current body of research, certain perennial themes recur. While there are many important and open research questions, there is a body of good research to help inform better choices now.

REFERENCES

Attewell, Paul. 1987. "The Deskilling Controversy." *Work and Occupations*. 14(3):323-346.

Attewell, Paul. 1991. "Big Brother and the Sweatshop: Computer Surveillance in the Automated Office." in Dunlop and Kling.

Attewell, Paul. 1995. "Information Technology and the Productivity Challenge." in Kling (1995a).

Baily, Martin Neal. 1991. "Great Expectations: PCs and Productivity" in Dunlop and Kling.

Bansler, Jorgen and Keld Bodker. (1993). A Reappraisal of Structured Analysis: Design in an Organizational Context. ACM TOIS 11(2)(April):145-193.

Bikson, Tora & J.D. Eveland & Barbara A. Gutek. 1989. "Flexible Interactive Technologies for Multi-Person Tasks: Current Problems and Future Prospects." in Olson 1989b, Pp. 89-112.

Bikson, Tora K. 1987. "Understanding the Implementation of Office Technology." in Kraut 1987B, Chapter 9, Pp. 155-176.

Blomberg, Jeanette. 1988. "The Variable Impact of Computer Technologies on the Organization of Work," Chapter 28 in Greif.

Braverman, Harry. 1974. *Labor and Monopoly Capital*. New York: Monthly Review Press.

Bronsema, Gloria and Zuboff, Shoshana. 1984. "Expense Tracking at Tiger Creek" Harvard Business School Case 9-485-057).

Bullen, Christine and John Bennett. 1995. Groupware in Practice: An Interpretation of Work Experience" in Kling.

Cabins, Lucius. 1990. The Making of a Bad Attitude. in Carlsson and Leger, Pp. 94-102.

Carlsson, Chris with Mark Leger. eds. 1990. *Bad Attitude: The Processed World Anthology*. New York: Verso.

Cash, James, W. McFarland, James McKenney and Linda Applegate. 1992. *Corporate Information Systems Management* 3rd Ed.

Clement, Andrew and C.C. Gotlieb. 1987. "Evolution of an Organizational Interface: The New Business Department at a Large Insurance Firm." *ACM Transactions on Office Information Systems*.5(4):328-339.

Clement, Andrew. 1990. "Computer Support for Cooperative Work: A Social Perspective on Empowering End Users." *Proceedings of the Conference on Computer Supported Cooperative Work*.Los Angeles Ca.

Clement, Andrew. 1984. "Electronic Management: New Technology of Workplace Surveillance." *Proceedings, Canadian Information Processing Society Session 84*, Calgary, Alberta. May 9-11:259-266.

Clement, Andrew. 1988. "Office Automation and the Technical Control of Information Workers." Chapter 11 in *The Political Economy of Information*. edited by Vincent Mosko and Janet Wasko. Madison, Wisconsin: University of Wisconsin Press.

Clement, Andrew. 1994. Computing at Work: Empowering Action by 'Low-level Users'. *Communications of the ACM*(37)1 (Jan):52-65. Reprinted in Kling (1995a).

Clement, Andrew and Pater Van den Besselaar. 1993. A Retrospective Look at Participatory Design Projects. *Communications of the ACM*36(4) (June):29-37.

Cockburn, Cynthia. 1988.*Machinery of Dominance: Women, Work and Technical Knowhow*.Boston, MA: Northeastern University Press.

Danziger, James and Kenneth Kraemer. 1986.*Computers and People: The Impacts of Computing on End Users in Organizations*. New York: Columbia University Press.

Delgado, Alan. 1979. *The Enormous File: A Social History of the Office*. London: John Murray.

Dunlop, Charles and Rob Kling. eds. 1991. *Computerization and Controversy: Value Conflicts and Social Choices*. San Diego: Academic Press.

Ehn, Pelle. 1989. *Work-Oriented Design of Computer Artifacts*. Stockholm: Arbetslivcentrum 1988. US Edition: Hillsdale, New Jersey: Lawrence Erlbaum.

Ehn, Pelle. 1991. "The Art and Science of Designing Computer Artifacts." in Dunlop and Kling.

Ellis, Clarence Arthur and N. Naffah. 1987. *Design of Office Information Systems*. New York: Springer-Verlag.

Finholt, Tom and Lee Sproull. 1990. "Electronic Groups at Work." *Organization Science*.1(1):41-64.

Forester, Tom. 1989A. *Computers in the Human Context: Information Technology, Productivity, and People*, edited by Tom Forester. Cambridge, Ma: The MIT Press.

Forester, Tom. 1989B. "The Myth of the Electronic Cottage." in Forester 1989A.

Galegher, Jolene, Robert Kraut and Carmen Egido, eds. 1990. *Intellectual Teamwork: Social and Technological Foundations of Cooperative Work*.Hillsdale, New Jersey: Lawrence Erlbaum Associates.

Garson, Barbara. 1988. *Electronic Sweatshop: How Computers are Transforming the Office of the Future into the Factory of the Past*.New York: Simon and Schuster.

Gasser, Les. 1986. "The Integration of Computing and Routine Work." *ACM Transactions on Office Information Systems*.4(3):205-225.

George, Joey, Rob Kling and Suzanne Iacono. 1990. "The Role of Training and Support in Desktop Computing" in *Desktop Information Technology: Organizational Worklife in the 1990s*,edited by Kate M. Kaiser and Hans J. Oppeland. Amsterdam: Elesevier/North Holland.

Gerson, Elihu M., and Susan Leigh Star. 1986. "Analyzing Due Process in the Workplace". *ACM Transactions on Office Information Systems*. 4(3):257-270

Giuliano, Vincent E. 1991. "The Mechanization of Work" in Dunlop and Kling.

Glenn, Evelyn, & Feldberg, Rosalyn. 1979. "Proletarianizing Clerical Work: Technology and Organizational Control in the Office." in *Case Studies in the Labor Process,*. edited by A. Zimbalist. New York: Monthly Review Press.

Grant, Rebecca and Chris Higgins. 1991. "The Impact of Computerized Performance Monitoring on Service Work: Testing a Causal Model." *Information Systems Research*. 2(2):116-141.

Greif, Irene. ed. 1988. *Computer Supported Cooperative Work: A Book of Readings*. San Mateo, Ca: Morgan Kaufman.

Grudin, Jonathan. 1989. "Why Groupware Applications Fail: Problems in Design and Evaluation." *Office: Technology and People*. 4(3):245-264.

Gutek, B., & Bikson, T. 1985. "Differential Experience of Men and Women in Computerized Offices." *Sex Roles*.13:123-136.

Hiltz, Starr Roxanne and Murray Turoff. 1978. *The Network Nation: Human Communication via Computer*. Reading, Massachusetts: Addison-Wesley Publishing Company, Inc.

Hirschheim, Rudi. 1985. *Office Automation: A Social and Organizational Perspective*. New York: John Wiley.

Huws, Ursula, Werner Korte, and Simon Robinson. 1990. *Telework: Towards the Elusive Office*. New York: John Wiley.

Iacono, Suzanne and Rob Kling. 1987. "Changing Office Technologies and the Transformation of Clerical Jobs." Chapter 4 in Kraut, 1987B.

Jewett, Tom and Rob Kling. 1990. "The Work Group Manager's Role in Developing Computing Infrastructure." *Proceedings of the ACM Conference on Office Information Systems*. Boston, Ma.

Jewett, Tom and Rob Kling. 1991. "The Dynamics of Computerization Social Science Research Team: A Case Study of Infrastructure, Strategies, and Skills." *Social Science Computer Review*. 9(2)(Summer):246-275.

Klawe, Maria and Nancy Leveson, 1995. "Women in Computing: Where are we Now?" *Communications of the ACM*. 38 (1)(January):29-35.

Kleiner, Art, ed. "The Health Hazards of Computers: A Guide to Worrying Intelligently." *Whole Earth Review*. (48):80-93.

Kling, Rob. 1980. "Social Analyses of Computing: Theoretical Perspectives in Recent Empirical Research." *Computing Surveys*. 12(1):61-110.

Kling, Rob. 1984. "Assimilating Social Values in Computer-based Technologies." *Telecommunications Policy*. (June):127-147.

Kling, Rob. 1987A. "Computerization as an Ongoing Social and Political Process." in *Computers and Democracy : A Scandinavian Challenge*,edited by Gro Bjerknes, Pelle Ehn, Morten Kyng. Brookfield, Vermont: Gower Pub.Co.

Kling, Rob. 1987B. "Defining the Boundaries of Computing Across Complex Organizations." *Critical Issues in Information Systems*. edited by Richard Boland and Rudy Hirschheim. London: John Wiley.

Kling, Rob. 1990. "More Information, Better Jobs?: Occupational Stratification and Labor Market Segmentation in the United States' Information Labor Force." *The Information Society*7(2):77-107.

Kling, Rob. 1991A. "Computerization and Social Transformations." *Science, Technology and Human Values*. 16(3):342-367.

Kling, Rob. 1991B. "Cooperation, Coordination and Control in Computer-Supported Work. *Communications of the ACM*.34(12):83-88.

Kling, Rob. 1992. "Behind the Terminal: The Critical Role of Computing Infrastructure In Effective Information Systems' Development and Use." Chapter 10 in *Challenges and Strategies for Research in Systems Development*. edited by William Cotterman and James Senn. Pp. 153-201. New York: John Wiley.

Kling, Rob. 1993. "Organizational Analysis in Computer Science." *The Information Society*. 9(2) (Mar-May, 1993):71-87

Kling, Rob. 1994. "Reading 'All About' Computerization: How Genre Conventions Shape Social Analyses" *The Information Society*10:147-172.

Kling, Rob. 1995a. *Computerization and Controversity: Value Conflicts and Social Choices*.2nd ed. San Diego: Academic Press.

Kling, Rob. 1995b. "The Centrality of Organizations in the Computerization of Society" in Kling (1995a).

Kling, Rob. 1995c. "Computerization at Work" in Kling (1995a).

Kling, Rob. 1995d. "Social Relations in Electronic Forums: Hangouts, Salons, Workplaces and Communities" in Kling (1995a).

Kling, Rob and Suzanne Iacono. 1984. "Computing as an Occasion for Social Control." *Journal of Social Issues*. 40(3): 77-96.

Kling, Rob and Suzanne Iacono. 1989. "Desktop Computerization and the Organization of Work." in Forester, 1989A.

Kling, Rob and Suzanne Iacono. 1991. "Making the Computer Revolution" in Dunlop and Kling.

Kling, Rob and Tom Jewett. 1994. "The Social Design of Worklife With Computers and Networks: A Natural Systems Perspective." in Marshall Yovits (ed.) *Advances in Computers. vol 39* . Orlando Fl: Academic Press

Kling, Rob and Walt Scacchi. 1982. "The Web of Computing: Computer Technology as Social Organization." *Advances in Computers*. vol. 21. New York: Academic Press.

Kraemer, Kenneth L., and John L. King. 1982. "Telecommunications-Transportation Substitution and Energy Productivity." *Telecommunications Policy*.Part I, 6(1):39-59, Part II, 6(2):87-99.

Kraemer, Kenneth, L., and James Danziger. 1990. "Social Impacts: The Impact of Computer Technology on the Worklife of Information Workers. *Social Science Computer Review*. 8(4):592-613.

Kraemer, Kenneth L., and Allain Pinnsoneault. 1990. "Technology and Groups: Assessments of Empirical Research." Chapter 14 in Galegher, Kraut, and Egido.

Kraut, Robert E. 1987A. "Predicting the Use of Technology: The Case of Telework," in Kraut 1987B. Pp. 113-133.

Kraut, Robert E. (ed.). 1987B. *Technology and the Transformation of White Collar Work*, Hillsdale, New Jersey: Lawrence Erlbaum and Associates.

Kraut, Robert, Susan Dumais, and Susan Koch. 1990. "Computerization, Productivity and Quality of Worklife." *Communications of the ACM*. 32(2):220-238.

Kuhn, Sarah. 1989. "The Limits to Industrialization: Computer Software Development in a Large Commercial Bank." in Wood.

Kyng, Morton and Joan Greenbaum. 1991. *Design at Work: Cooperative Work of Computer Systems*. Hillsdale, NJ.: Lawrence Erlbaum.

Lepore, Stephen, Rob Kling, Suzanne Iacono, and Joey George. 1989. "Implementing Desktop Computing, Infrastructure, and Quality of Worklife." *Proceedings of the 10th Annual Conference on Information Systems*. Boston, MA: December.

Levering, Robert. 1988. *A Great Place to Work: What Makes Some Employers So Good (and Most So Bad)*.New York: Random House.

Mills, Harlan D., Richard C. Linger, and Alan R. Hevner. 1986. *Principles of Information Systems Analysis and Design*. Orlando: Academic Press.

Morton, M. S. (Ed). 1991. *The Corporation of the 1990s: Information Technology and Organizational Transformation*.New York, Oxford University Press.

Mouritsen, Jan and Niels Bjorn-Anderson. 1991. "Understanding Third Wave Information Systems," in Dunlop and Kling.

Mowshowitz, A. (1986). The Social Dimension of Office Automation. In Marshall Yovits, (Ed.) Advances in Computers. New York: Academic Press.

Noble, David F. 1984. *Forces of Production: A Social History of Industrial Automation*. New York: Knopf.

Olson, Margrethe H. 1983. "Remote Office Work: Changing Work Patterns in Space and Time." *Communications of the ACM*.26(3):182-187.

Olson, Margrethe H. 1989a. "Work at Home for Computer Professionals: Current Attitudes and Future Prospects." *ACM Transaction on Information Systems*7(4):317-338.

Olson, Margrethe H., ed. 1989b. *Technological Support For Work Group Collaboration*. Hillsdale, NJ: Lawrence Erlbaum Associates, Inc.

Orlikowski, Wanda. 1991. "Integrated Information Environment or Matrix of Control? The Contradictory Implications of Information Technology." *Accounting, Management and Information Technology*1(1):9-42.

Pearl, Amy; Martha E. Pollack, Eve Riskin, Becky Thomas, Elizabeth Wolf, and Alice Wu. 1990. "Becoming a Computer Scientist: A Report by the ACM Committee on The Status of Women in Computing Science." *Communications of the ACM*. 33(11)(November):47-58.

Perrolle, Judith. 1986. "Intellectual Assembly Lines: The Rationalization of Managerial, Professional and Technical Work." *Computers and the Social Sciences*. 2(3):111-122. Reprinted in Dunlop and Kling (1991).

Reskin, Barbara and Irene Padavic. 1994. *Women and Men at Work.*Thousand Oaks, CA: Pine Forge Press.

Salerno, Lynne. 1991. "What Happened to the Computer Revolution?" in Dunlop and Kling.

Schneider, Leslie & Claudio Ciborra. 1983. "Technology Bargaining in Norway." in *Systems Design For, With, and by the Users : Proceedings of the IFIP WG 9.1 Working Conferenceon Systems Design For, With, and by the Users, Riva del Sol, Italy, 20-24 September 1982.* edited by U. Briefs, C. Ciborra, L. Schneider New York: North-Holland Pub. Co.

Schor, Juliet. 1991. *The Overworked American : The Unexpected Decline of Leisure.* New York, N.Y.: Basic Books.

Shaiken, Harley. 1986. *Work Transformed: Automation and Labor in the Computer Age.*Lexington, Massachusetts: Lexington Books.

Shulman, Arthur D. Robyn Penman, and David Sless. 1990. "Putting Information Technology in its Place: Organizational Communication and the Human Infrastructure." Pp. 155-192, in *Applied Social Psychology in Organizational Settings,* edited by John S. Caroll. Hillsdale, N.J.: Lawrence Erlbaum.

Sproull, Lee and Sara Kiesler. 1991. *Connections: New Ways of Working in the Networked Organization.* Cambridge, Mass.: MIT Press.

Sprousse, Martin (Ed.) 1992. *Sabotage in the American Workplace: Anecdotes of Dissatisfaction, Mischief, and Revenge.* San Francisco, Ca: Pressure Drop Press.

Starbuck, William H., and Jane Webster. 1991. "When is Play Productive." *Accounting, Management and Information Technology*1(1):71-90.

Toffler, Alvin. *The Third Wave.* New York, Bantam Books, 1980.

Turoff, Murray and Roxanne Hiltz. 1983. "Working at Home or Living in the Office." Pp. 719-725. *Information Processing, 1983: Proceedings of the IFIP 9th World Congress, Paris France. September 1983.*New York: North Holland.

Wagner, Ina. 1993. "A Web of Fuzzy Problems: Confronting the Ethical Issues." *Communications of the ACM*36(4) (June):94-101. RE[rinted in Kling (1995).

Walton, Richard. E. 1989. *Up and Running: Integrating Information Technology and the Organization.* Boston, MA. Harvard Business School Press.

Whyte, William F., Melville Dalton, Donald Roy, Leonard Sayles, and Associates. 1955. *Money and Motivation: An Analysis of Incentives in Industry.*New York: Harper and Rowe.

Winner, Langdon. 1992. "Silicon Valley Mystery House" in *Variations on a Theme Park: The New American City and the End of Public Space.*edited by Michael Sorkin. New York: Noonday Press.

Winograd, Terry. 1988. "A Language/action Perspective on the Design of Cooperative Work." *Human-Computer Interaction*3:1 (1987—88), 3-30. Reprinted in Irene Greif, ed. *Computer-Supported Cooperative Work: A Book of Readings,* San Mateo, California: Morgan-Kaufmann. 1988:623-653.

Wood, Stephen. 1989. "The Transformation of Work, in *The Transformation of Work: Skill, Flexibility and the Labour Process.*edited by Stephen Wood. London: Unwin Hyman.

Yates, JoAnne. 1989. *Control through Communication: The Rise of System in American Management.*Baltimore: Johns Hopkins University Press.

Zuboff, Shoshana. 1988. *In the Age of the Smart Machine: The Future of Work and Power.* New York: Basic Books.

Zuboff, Shoshana. 1991. "Informate the Enterprise." *National Forum.*Summer:3-7.

Chapter 4

Software Development Contexts

In Chapter 2 we covered approaches to designing and evaluating interactive systems and their human-computer interfaces. Chapter 3 enlarged the scope of this discussion to consider the social, organizational, and work context in which systems are to be used. Chapter 5 will survey tools that support interface development, but before doing so we must step back to examine the software engineering process of which interface development is a part. We shall begin by considering the different organizational contexts or environments in which development occurs. This will be followed by an exploration of relationships between human-computer interaction and software engineering. We shall end the chapter with some additional reflections on the multidisciplinary and multifaceted nature of system and interface design.

THREE DEVELOPMENT CONTEXTS

Why is the larger context important? The answer is that methods that are appropriate in one situation may not work in another. For example, you work in a clinic developing software to support nine nurses. A participatory design effort that involves the nurses makes sense. But if your next job is for a huge software company developing a new off-the-shelf product, you will not know who the (hopefully millions of) users will be or how to get their participation. And what about that last job, developing software under government contract—here contact with the eventual users was sharply restricted by distance, security, and legal considerations! One size will not fit all.

In our first selection, Grudin (1991a) focuses on three principal contexts in which interactive software is developed and various conditions that affect the development process. The contexts are those mentioned above: internal or *in-house development* of a system for a specific set of users, commercial *product development* of "shrink-wrap" software intended for a large market of users, and competitively bid *contract development*. The different circumstances of each case greatly affect the approaches and tools that are likely to be used.

To appreciate the differences, consider when the development team and the software users can be identified in each context. In contract development, the users are known first, when the system is being specified; the developers are not identified until after the contract is awarded. Product development is the reverse: The development team is known early, but the users are not really known until the product sells—often the users are not those predicted by the developers. With in-house development, both groups are identifiable from the outset. Do these differences affect the prospects for user and developer interaction in design? Of course they do!

The human-computer interaction field has been dominated by research and development with a focus on products, primarily single-user applications. In-house development and contract development are rarely mentioned. But these different development contexts are becoming increasingly intertwined as individual users are networked into larger groups and as commercial software products become important components of large organizational systems.

Other important factors in establishing the development context are the size of the development organization, the novelty of the software being developed, the nature of the competition (if any), and so on. For example, if a feature has been included because a competitor has obtained a marketing advantage by advertising it, you will have difficulty arguing for eliminating it based on field testing that shows it is not useful.

Additional reading is available on each of these development contexts. Gundry (1988) and Overmyer (1990) describe interface development in contract projects, describing the obstacles resulting from the tyranny of the contract and approaches to improving the situation and to work within the structure of existing government regulations. A report by Buie and Winkler (1994) describes "HCI Challenges in Government Contracting," a special interest group meeting at CHI '94.

Friedman (1989) provides a wonderful look at internal development. As we mentioned in Part I, Friedman's book is organized historically, but as it proceeds it covers many aspects of developing systems within user organizations. Friedman argues that in-house development has gone through three eras, in which first hardware, then software, and now user needs (including functionality) were development bottlenecks. Among the approaches to user involvement considered by Friedman are the Scandinavian approach described by Bødker, Grønbæk, and Kyng in Chapter 3 and end-user programming, covered in Chapter 12.

Grudin and Poltrock (1989) surveyed over 200 interface developers in several large product development companies. They describe patterns of communication and coordination among the contributing software engineers, human factors engineers, technical writers, industrial design engineers, training developers, and marketing specialists. Grudin (1991b) provides a detailed account of the forces at work within these companies. Obstacles to direct contact between developers and users include challenges in motivating the developers, identifying appropriate users, obtaining access to users, motivating the users, and in benefiting from user contact when established. Grudin proceeds to analyze what goes wrong when users are not involved, describing many subtle forces at work in development organizations that have unfortunate influences on the interface.

For example, an important goal is to communicate the interface design, usually as a written specification. It might seem logical that the design most easily communicated will be the best for users, but this is not the case: A written specification is a static, physically dispersed object; human-computer interaction is dynamic and focused. A set of menus that can be scanned easily when laid out on paper may be full of minefields for a confused user wandering through them one at a time.

Another example is noted in an elegant essay by Conway (1968). He presents a surprising semiformal argument that the designs produced by an organization will, under certain conditions, reflect the structure of the organization. This can be applied to the interface, the software architecture—any design contributed to by individuals distributed across an organization. Naturally there is no reason to think that an interface structured to match the development organization will be ideal for users.

Grudin (1991b) suggests ways for product developers to proceed: He notes supportive features of such environments, process changes that could involve users, and technology to facilitate communication. He suggests greater use of mediators to communicate between developers and users, and changes in the nature and purpose of the development organizations themselves.

Participant observer studies of interface development by Poltrock and Grudin (1994) identify why some product developers have difficulty following Gould's principles (Chapter 2): early focus on users, early and continual user testing, iterative design, and integrated design. The visibility of the software interface creates problems for iterative design, since interface changes lead to fears of a lack of progress and create problems for those writing documentation and training materials. Integrating all aspects of usability under one management is difficult because of, in part, the historic dispersal of these activities throughout a company.

THE INFLUENCE OF SOFTWARE ENGINEERING

Large government contracts propelled the computer industry throughout the 1950s and led to the first model of software development—the waterfall model. The waterfall model is a development method geared toward contract development of large batch (noninteractive) systems. Development is broken down into a progression of steps or phases: feasibility study, requirements analysis, preliminary design, detailed design, coding, integration, installation, and maintenance. Minor variations have been proposed, but these "stage models" consist of sequential development steps with little iteration or prototyping.

The stage models were developed in government settings in the 1950s and 1960s, and reached full expression in the waterfall model proposed at TRW (Royce, 1970). Subsequently, IBM encouraged their mainframe customers to use this development method, although most were developing information systems for internal use, not government contracts. When commercial software became a significant force in the late 1970s and early 1980s, the larger product development companies also tried to adopt the best-known approach to development, the waterfall model. Thus, this model has been very influential, as depicted in Figure 4.1.

However, the waterfall model was created for one development context, contract development. Two important factors in that context at the time were the following:

- The developers and users were separated by spatial, temporal, and organizational barriers.
- The systems being developed were not interactive—programs were started and ran to completion with no interruptions by users.

Under these conditions, it was often necessary and even appropriate to adopt the "design it first" waterfall approach. But some internal developers realized that the first condition did not apply to them: They worked for the same organization as their users, so it made sense for them to consult more closely with the users throughout development. This reaction to the waterfall model was first represented in the European sociotechnical and participatory design approaches discussed in Chapter 3. Later, product developers realized that the second condition no longer applied and that interactive systems could rarely be designed right the first time, leading to the iterative, prototyping approaches discussed in Chapter 2. Still later, these two new approaches came into contact through a mutual interest in computer-supported cooperative work (CSCW).

In the software engineering community, the waterfall model was refined, in particular by Barry Boehm, author of the classic book *Software Engineering Economics* (1981). In our second reading, Boehm (1988) observes the inadequacies of the waterfall model *particularly for systems with a human-computer interface.* He proposes a spiral model of development specifically designed to incorporate prototyping and iteration. The spiral model also includes periodic risk assessment, providing points at which a futile project can be abandoned.

Boehm describes the use of the spiral model in an internal development project. He notes that iteration and prototyping present particular challenges for contract development and suggests methods to address the challenges.

Boehm also includes a useful prioritized list of problems affecting software projects. The first five are the following:

- Personnel shortfalls
- Unrealistic schedules and budgets
- Developing the wrong software functions
- Developing the wrong user interface
- Gold plating

Boehm's list reminds us of the importance of software functionality. This is sometimes underemphasized in writings on human-computer interaction. Our focus is generally on design that comes after functionality is established. Yet one must reflect on the larger context in which we work. Only by fully understanding our situation can we prioritize, anticipate challenges, plan strategically, and recognize which aspects of the environment can be changed, and which cannot.

INTEGRATING HCI AND SOFTWARE ENGINEERING

The past fifteen years have seen other refinements of traditional software engineering approaches. Although slowly expanding their coverage of the human-computer interface, these methods focused on software functionality and relegated the interface to a very subordinate role. Structured analysis and design initially limited interface design to one subphase of development (De Marco, 1978). "Jackson System Development," also widely embraced, "excludes the whole area of human engineering in dialogue design [and] excludes procedures for system acceptance" (Jackson, 1983). Because these software development methods are widely promoted, some human-computer interaction researchers have made efforts to integrate them with modern interface design approaches.

A structured human factors methodology has been developed by Lim, Long, and Silcock (1991), who extend the Jackson System Development method by grafting human factors methods onto the structured analysis and redesign of a recreational facility booking system. Although the authors note the desirability of iterative design, their human factors stream consists of four phases, each a series of proceduralized stages, that proceed in a traditional sequence from preliminary to detailed design and onto implementation and evaluation. As a redesign effort there is an existing system to test, but no provision for prototyping and testing improvements is described. Lim and Long (1992) position most interface design methods that have been proposed in the context of a larger task analysis and development effort.

More detailed examples of task analysis and system development incorporating HCI approaches with structured system development and Jackson System Development are described in Sutcliffe and McDermott (1991) and Sutcliffe and Wang (1991). Unfortunately, the constraints of their formalism were not flexible enough to handle the unpredictable order in which users desire to carry out tasks. Their approach did not anticipate a

FIGURE 4.1

The influence of stage models (solid lines) and responses to them in different development contexts.

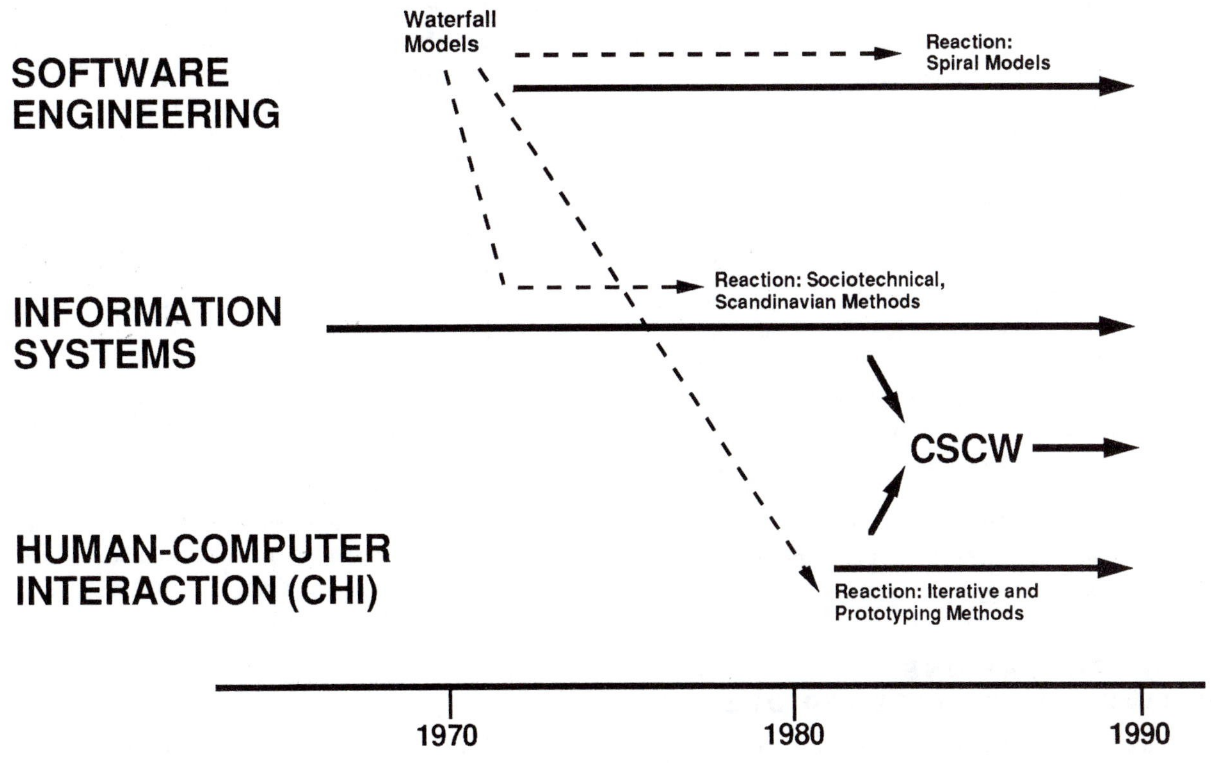

mismatch between the users' models of an application's functional hierarchy and the conceptual model created by a structural analysis that was shaped by automated procedures of no interest to users. Some aspects of their method are rudimentary—for example, the proposed complexity metrics lack mathematical rigor.

These efforts to integrate usability engineering and software engineering are not yet practical, but they are praiseworthy first steps toward bringing together two largely noncommunicating fields, steps down a path many are likely to follow. A 1995 book, *Software Engineering and Human-Computer Interaction* (Taylor and Coutaz, 1995) emerged from a workshop designed to bring these communities together.

INTEGRATING HCI AND SOFTWARE DEVELOPMENT

In practice, software development is often carried out without relying on a formal process. Faced with this lack of structure, practitioners wrestle with the organizational and temporal placement of human factors expertise and techniques.

At the CHI '85 conference, Marilyn Mantei presented a tutorial titled "Techniques for Incorporating Human Factors in the Software Design Process," and Robert Mack chaired a panel on human factors in computer interface design. Grudin, Ehrlich, and Shriner (1987) stepped back from the typical perspective of an individual project to look at human factors deployment in environments in which successive versions of a product are built and in which middle- and upper-level managers oversee entire product lines.

Panelists at CHI '88 debated five approaches to integrating human factors and software development:

- Create a central human factors laboratory
- Disperse human factors personnel among development groups
- Place human factors engineers in charge of development projects
- Hire human factors consultants
- Use human factors personnel to educate software engineers in interface design and development (Grudin et al., 1988)

Persuasive arguments can be marshaled for each position. Concentrating human factors engineers in a laboratory permits economies of scale and helps assure qualified management, but can lead to a "human factors ghetto" ignored by development teams that might accept a permanently assigned human factors engineer. Consultants are often granted more respect but have more limited involvement. Efforts at educating the software engineers who typically design the interfaces are worthwhile in principle, but the most influential developers have the least time to spare. No one approach is appropriate in all contexts, and a mix can provide the greatest benefit.

COST JUSTIFICATIONS FOR ITERATIVE, USER-CENTERED DESIGN

"It will cost too much and take too long." This argument is often used to oppose iterative design and other methods for building more useful, usable systems. In Chapter 2, John Gould denied the truth of this claim but provided no quantitative details.

There is no question that the computer and software industries now accept the importance of usability. Nielsen (1993, p. 9) notes:

> *The trade magazine InfoWorld assigns explicit weights in its software reviews: Ease of learning is weighed at 4–10%, ease of use at 8–13%, and quality of documentation at 5–8%, with the exact weights determined by the type of application being reviewed. These three review criteria account for between 18% (spreadsheets) and 30% (word processors) of the final review scores. Error handling is assigned a further 5–8% of the review weight as a combined category including both user errors (a usability issue), software bugs, and recovery from hardware crashes. Notice, by the way, how favorably these percentages compare with the allocation of 6–10% of a development project's budget to usability . . . usability is a comparatively cheap way to improve product quality.*

Thus early testing and iterative design would seem easy to justify. It is clearly cheaper to correct design errors if they are caught early. Yet one argument against testing is that flawed interfaces are acceptable because people can adapt to anything, although Chapter 10 suggests that there are serious limitations to this crass position. Other factors also may prevent the application of human factors methods. A project racing against the clock or competing with a parallel project may face premature termination if it does not produce something tangible in a set period of time. A manager may postpone diverting resources to the interface until after a critical milestone is passed, even if more resources will be required later and the interface will suffer. Such economic considerations vary in different development contexts (Grudin, 1994).

A stronger argument is that testing is too costly. To counter this feeling, several researchers have attempted to establish a sound business case for usability testing by estimating the costs of using the methods and the benefits that result. Mantei and Teorey (1988) estimated the costs in time and money for 13 human factors activities variously carried out at the scoping, functional specification, design, implementation, and testing stages. They assumed software development based on Boehm's (1981) constructive cost model (COCOMO), modified to incorporate the human factors methods. They also estimated the savings to the users and suggested that, for medium and large projects, these outweigh the costs.

Nonetheless, their cost estimate for a medium-scale software project (roughly 32,000 lines of code) was nearly $130,000. Subsequently, several other researchers have extended and refined this work, many of them reaching significantly more favorable cost projections for the adoption of these techniques (e.g., Rosenberg, 1989; Tognazzini, 1990). Nielsen (1994, pp. 247–49) suggests that the figure could be halved by the use of his "discount usability engineering" method, and reminds us of Voltaire's dictim "*le mieux est l'ennemi du bien*" (the best is the enemy of the good).

Several useful papers on the cost-benefit and business case analysis of usability testing and usability engineering are Bias (1994), Mayhew and Mantei (1994), Karat (1994), Ehrlich and Rohn (1994), Dray and Karat (1994), Mauro (1994), Mayhew (1994), and Aykin (1994), all of which appear in a book that establishes an economic case for applying human factors methods in a variety of contexts (Bias and Mayhew, 1994). The usability engineering literature covered in Chapter 2 also includes discussions of cost justification. These economic analyses typically compute savings accruing from a variety of factors:

- Increased user productivity
- Decreased errors
- Decreased training costs
- Decreased employee turnover
- Decreased workplace injuries and lost time
- Decreased implementation costs due to late design changes
- Increased sales
- Decreased maintenance and support costs

A number of estimates of cost savings in specific cases may be found in Chapter 1 of Nielsen (1993) and in many chapters of Bias and Mayhew (1994). Given this research coupled with the increasing acceptance of the importance of usability, we expect to see growing recognition that usability flaws are software bugs that must be discovered and corrected in every development project. Nevertheless, we are all too often reminded of Conway's (1968) lament, "There's never enough time to do something right, but there's always enough time to do it over."

THE MULTIDISCIPLINARY AND MULTIFACETED NATURE OF DESIGN

Our chapter concludes with an inspirational essay by software designer and graphic artist Scott Kim (1990). He urges every developer to be an "interdisciplinary ambassador"—to be nosy, playful, a tour guide, patriot, traveler, pen pal, raconteur, and world citizen! Interface design is multidisciplinary, but few people are. Therefore, we must build and use bridges between the many relevant disciplines and perspectives.

Multimedia was the province of research laboratories in the 1980s. By the end of the 1990s, it is safe to say that it will be pervasive. Color graphics, high-quality audio, animation, and video will be standard features. This presents extraordinary possibilities for interface development, but requires development teams who have expertise in graphic design, sound design, cinematography, and animation in addition to software and interface design. Applications are also becoming more specialized, meaning that the best design will be based on extensive knowledge of specific task domains. Increasing competition rewards greater attention to marketing considerations.

Internationalization of markets brings issues of cross-cultural understanding into sharp focus. The *SIGCHI Bulletin* initiated an "International Perspectives" column in 1991. Workshops on cross-cultural perspectives were held at CHI '92 (Kellogg and Thomas, 1993) and INTERCHI '93 (Nakakoji, 1993). Internationalization affects interface text, of course, but also has subtle effects on icon interpretation (Horton, 1994). Nakakoji (1994) reviews some of the issues affecting cross-cultural influences on interface design.

We can view the extraordinary increase in complexity as an opportunity to be exploited or a challenge to be coped with. But how do we proceed? We can borrow liberally from other designs. We can seek out the tools that generally emerge to help us confront such challenges. And of course we can recruit as many skills as possible into our team, build bridges to others in our organization, hire consultants, and so forth.

Yet managers have long been aware that an effective team is more than a set of skills. It is also an appropriate combination of personalities, each making a contribution. Consider a favorite "team" in an adventure novel or movie. Very likely one member will be cerebral; a second, physical; and a third, aesthetically oriented. Different personality types are important in facing unknown challenges.

Greenbaum (1990) critiques systems development environments and methods from this perspective, arguing that they emphasize logic, rationality, and analytic approaches. These approaches are good for programming and for dealing with technological issues, but she observes that different skills, centering on empathy and emotion, are necessary for understanding users and their motivations.

Greenbaum's argument has two parts. She lays out a dichotomy of attributes or orientations (Figure 4.2).

FIGURE 4.2

Attributes present (left) and often missing (right) in development environments (Greenbaum, 1990).

Objective	**Subjective**
Reason	**Feeling**
Impersonal	**Personal**
Rational	**Emotional**
Power	**Love**
Things	**People**

In systems development, as in many engineering disciplines, the first set of attributes is typically valued and the second is not. This may work out well when the critical problems faced in work deal with designing efficient circuitry. However, Greenbaum argues, these values are skewed for the development of interactive systems that will be used in workplaces by individuals with a broad range of preferences, motivations, and experiences. The development team must obtain insight into the needs of users in these environments. To do this, the team must be capable of understanding and working with the subjective, emotional, motivational, and social characteristics of people. In Chapters 2 and 3 we stressed the importance of user involvement; working with users and benefiting from their contributions requires its own skill set. Greenbaum argues that these "softer" skills are not valued in systems development contexts and that people who value these skills are often made to feel out of place. This is an obstacle to the development of interactive systems.

Women can, of course, be analytic and rational, and men can be empathic and tuned to emotions, but as Greenbaum notes, our culture tends to produce men who value the first set of attributes and women who value the second. Thus, engineering environments that overemphasize the rational and analytic are more likely to discourage women, many of whom have skills that are crucial for developing good interactive systems.

This observation is extended in a more recent article that is included in a book on the topic of gender and information technology design (Bødker and Greenbaum, 1993). The authors note that the stress on technology and objectivity is reflected in a linguistic bias (favoring "systems" over "applications"). They extend the participatory design framework described by Bødker et al. in Chapter 3 to include both rational and empathic orientations in building office systems and applications.

Many of us feel a little uneasy contemplating interface designers as goodwill ambassadors with one or another set of gender attributes. Approaches must be adapted to the development context at hand, and an interdisciplinary gadfly who serves a tremendously useful role in a young, expanding organization can look expendable in a contracting organization. But Kim is right, the field is in constant flux and evolution, and the contributions of individuals who stand still will diminish over time.

REFERENCES

Note: A ● before a reference indicates a reading.

Aykin, N. (1994). Reuse: A Case Study on Cost-Benefit of Adopting a Common Software Development Tool. In Bias and Mayhew (1994), 177–202.

Bias, R. (1994) Wherefore Cost Justification of Usability: Pay Me Now or Pay Me Later—But How Much? In Bias and Mayhew (1994), 3–8.

Bias, R., and Mayhew, D. (Eds.) (1994). *Cost-Justifying Usability.* Academic Press.

Boehm, B. (1981). *Software Engineering Economics.* Prentice-Hall.

● Boehm, B. (1988). A Spiral Model of Software Development and Enhancement. *IEEE Computer* 21(2), 61–72.

Buie, E., and Winkler, I. (1994). HCI Challenges in Government Contracting. *SIGCHI Bulletin* 26(4), ACM, 49–50.

Bødker, S., and Greenbaum, J. (1993). Design of Information Systems: Things Versus People. In Green, E., Owen, J., and Pain, D. (Eds.), *Gendered by Design, Information Technology and Office Systems,* Taylor & Francis.

Conway, M. (1968). How Do Committees Invent? *Datamation,* April, 28–31.

De Marco, T. (1978). *Structured Analysis and System Specification.* Yourdon Press.

Dray, S., and Karat, C.-M. (1994). Human Factors Cost Justification of an Internal Development Project. In Bias and Mayhew (1994), 111–122.

Ehrlich, K., and Rohn, J. (1994). Cost Justification of Usability Engineering: A Vendor's Perspective. In Bias and Mayhew (1994), 73–110.

Friedman, A. (1989). *Computer Systems Development: History, Organization and Implementation.* Wiley.

Greenbaum, J. (1990). The Head and the Heart: Using Gender Analysis to Study the Social Construction of Computer Systems. *SIGCAS Bulletin* 20 (2), ACM, 9–17.

● Grudin, J. (1991a). Interactive Systems: Bridging the Gaps between Developers and Users. *IEEE Computer* 24(4), 59–69.

Grudin, J. (1991b). Systematic Sources of Suboptimal Interface Design in Large Product Development Organizations. *Human-Computer Interaction* 6(2), 147–196.

Grudin, J. (1994). Evaluating Opportunities for Design Capture. In Moran, T., and Carroll, J. (Eds.), *Design Rationale: Concepts, Techniques, and Use.* Lawrence Erlbaum Associates.

Grudin, J., Carroll, J., Ehrlich, S., Grisham, M., Hersh, H., and Seybold, P. (1988). Integrating Human Factors and Software Development. *Proc. CHI '88,* ACM, 157–159.

Grudin, J., Ehrlich, S., and Shriner, R. (1987). Positioning Human Factors in the User Interface Development Chain. *Proc. CHI+GI '87,* ACM, 125–131.

Grudin, J., and Poltrock, S. (1989). User Interface Design in Large Corporations: Coordination and Communication across Disciplines. *Proc. CHI '89,* ACM, 197–203.

Gundry, A. (1988). Humans, Computers, and Contracts. In Jones, D., and Winder, R. (Eds.) *People and Computers IV.* Cambridge University Press.

Horton, W. (1994). *The Icon Book: Visual Symbols for Computer Systems and Documentation.* John Wiley & Sons.

Jackson, M. (1983). *System Development.* Prentice-Hall.

Karat, C.-M. (1994). A Business Case Approach to Usability. In Bias and Mayhew (1994), 45–70.

Kellogg, W. A., and Thomas, J. C. (1993). Cross-Cultural Perspectives on Human-Computer Interaction: A Report on the CHI '92 Workshop. *SIGCHI Bulletin* 25(2), ACM, 40–45.

● Kim, S. (1990). Interdisciplinary Cooperation. In Laurel, B. (Ed.), *The Art of Human-Computer Interface Design,* Addison-Wesley, 31–44.

Lim, K., Long, J., and Silcock, N. (1991). Integrating Human Factors with the Jackson System Development Method: An Illustrated Overview. *Ergonomics* 35 (10), 1135–1161.

Lim, K., and Long, J. (1992). A Method for (Recruiting) Methods: Facilitating Human Factors Input to Systems Design. *Proc. CHI '92,* ACM, 549–556.

Mack, R., Moran, T., Olson, J., Wixon, D., and Whiteside, J. (1985). Computer Human Factors in Computer Interface Design. *Proc. CHI '85,* ACM, 137–147.

Mantei, M., (1985). Techniques for Incorporating Human Factors in the Software Design Process. Tutorial Notes. ACM.

Mantei, M. and Teorey, T. (1988). Cost/Benefit Analysis for Incorporating Human Factors in the Software Lifecycle. *Communications of the ACM* 31(4), 428–439.

Mauro, C. (1994). Cost-Justifying Usability in a Contractor Company. In Bias and Mayhew (1994), 123–142.

Mayhew, D. (1994). Cost-Benefit Analysis of Upgrading Computer Hardware. In Bias and Mayhew (1994), 159–175.

Mayhew, D., and Mantei, M. (1994). A Basic Framework for Cost-Justifying Usability. In Bias and Mayhew (1994), 9–43.

Nakakoji, K. (1993). Cross-Cultural Considerations in Designing Human-Computer Interaction. *American Programmer* 6(10), 18–24.

Nakakoji, K. (1994). Crossing the Cultural Boundary. *BYTE* 19(6), 107–109.

Nielsen, J. (1993). *Usability Engineering.* Academic Press.

Nielsen, J. (1994). Guerrilla HCI: Using Discount Usability Engineering to Penetrate the Intimidation Barrior. In Bias and Mayhew (1994), 245–272.

Overmyer, S. (1990). The Impact of DoD-Std-2167A on Iterative Design Methodologies: Help or Hinder? *ACM SIGSOFT Software Engineering Notes* 15(5), 50–59.

Poltrock, S., and Grudin, J. (1994). Organizational Obstacles to Interface Design and Development: Two Participant Observer Studies. *ACM Transactions on Computer-Human Interaction* 1(1), 52–80.

Rosenberg, D. (1989). A Cost Benefit Analysis for Corporate User Interface Standards: What Price to Pay for a Consistent Look and Feel? In Nielsen, J. (Ed.), *Coordinating User Interfaces for Consistency,* Academic Press.

Royce, W. W. (1970). Managing the Development of Large Software Systems: Concepts and Techniques. *Proc. Westcon*. Also available in *Proc. ICSE 9*, Computer Society Press, 1987.

Sutcliffe, A., and McDermott, M. (1991). Integrating Methods of Human-Computer Interface Design with Structured Systems Development. *International Journal of Man-Machine Studies* 34, 631–655.

Sutcliffe, A., and Wang, I. (1991). Integrating Human-Computer Interaction with Jackson System Development. *The Computer Journal* 34(2), 132–142.

Taylor, R., and Coutaz, J. (Eds.) (1995). *Software Engineering and Human-Computer Interaction*. Springer Verlag, Lecture Notes in Computer Science.

Tognazzini, B. (1990). Usability Testing on the Cheap. Chapter 14 of *Tog on Interface*. Addison-Wesley.

A Spiral Model of Software Development and Enhancement

Barry W. Boehm, TRW Defense Systems Group

"Stop the life cycle—I want to get off!"
"Life-cycle Concept Considered Harmful."
"The waterfall model is dead."
"No, it isn't, but it should be."

These statements exemplify the current debate about software life-cycle process models. The topic has recently received a great deal of attention.

The Defense Science Board Task Force Report on Military Software[1] issued in 1987 highlighted the concern that traditional software process models were discouraging more effective approaches to software development such as prototyping and software reuse. The Computer Society has sponsored tutorials and workshops on software process models that have helped clarify many of the issues and stimulated advances in the field (see "Further reading").

The spiral model presented in this article is one candidate for improving the software process model situation. The major distinguishing feature of the spiral model is that it creates a *risk-driven* approach to the software process rather than a primarily *document-driven* or *code-driven* process. It incorporates many of the strengths of other models and resolves many of their difficulties.

This evolving risk-driven approach provides a new framework for guiding the software process.

This article opens with a short description of software process models and the issues they address. Subsequent sections outline the process steps involved in the spiral model; illustrate the application of the spiral model to a software project, using the TRW Software Productivity Project as an example; summarize the primary advantages and implications involved in using the spiral model and the primary difficulties in using it at its current incomplete level of elaboration; and present resulting conclusions.

Background on software process models

The primary functions of a software process model are to determine the *order of the stages* involved in software development and evolution and to establish the *transition criteria* for progressing from one stage to the next. These include completion criteria for the current stage plus choice criteria and entrance criteria for the next stage. Thus, a process model addresses the following software project questions:

(1) What shall we do next?
(2) How long shall we continue to do it?

Consequently, a process model differs from a software method (often called a methodology) in that a method's primary focus is on how to navigate through each phase (determining data, control, or "uses" hierarchies; partitioning functions; allocating requirements) and how to represent phase products (structure charts; stimulus-response threads; state transition diagrams).

Why are software process models important? Primarily because they provide guidance on the order (phases, increments, prototypes, validation tasks, etc.) in which a project should carry out its major tasks. Many software projects, as the next section shows, have come to grief because they pursued their various development and evolution phases in the wrong order.

Evolution of process models. Before concentrating in depth on the spiral model, we should take a look at a number of others: the code-and-fix model, the stagewise model and the waterfall model, the evolutionary development model, and the transform model.

The code-and-fix model. The basic model used in the earliest days of software

0018-9162/88/0500-0061$01.00©1988 IEEE

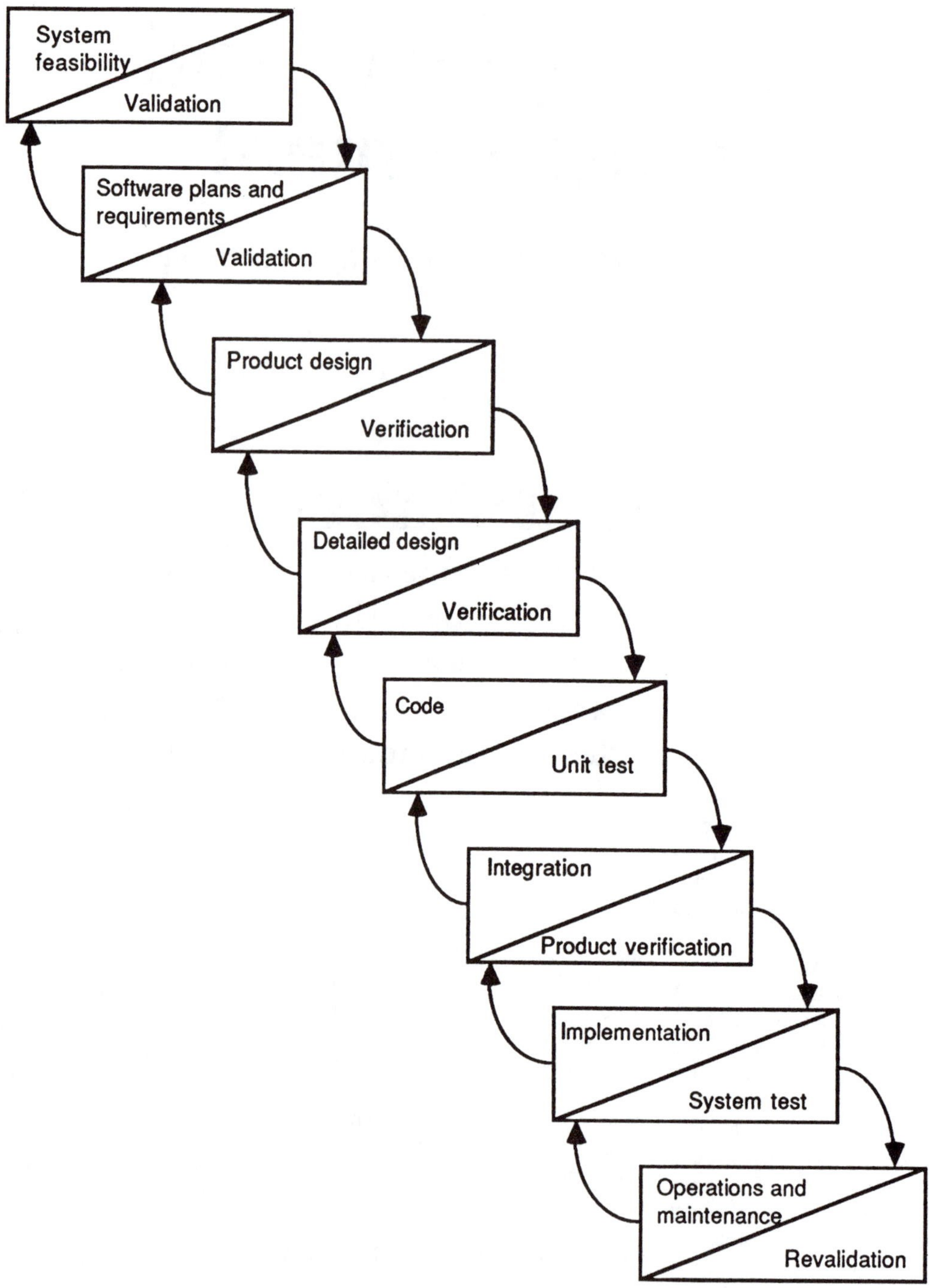

Figure 1. The waterfall model of the software life cycle.

development contained two steps:

(1) Write some code.

(2) Fix the problems in the code.

Thus, the order of the steps was to do some coding first and to think about the requirements, design, test, and maintenance later. This model has three primary difficulties:

(a) After a number of fixes, the code became so poorly structured that subsequent fixes were very expensive. This underscored the need for a design phase prior to coding.

(b) Frequently, even well-designed software was such a poor match to users' needs that it was either rejected outright or expensively redeveloped. This made the need for a requirements phase prior to design evident.

(c) Code was expensive to fix because of poor preparation for testing and modification. This made it clear that explicit recognition of these phases, as well as test-and-evolution planning and preparation tasks in the early phases, were needed.

The stagewise and waterfall models. As early as 1956, experience on large software systems such as the Semi-Automated Ground Environment (SAGE) had led to the recognition of these problems and to the development of a stagewise model[2] to address them. This model stipulated that software be developed in successive stages (operational plan, operational specifications, coding specifications, coding, parameter testing, assembly testing, shakedown, system evaluation).

The waterfall model,[3] illustrated in Figure 1, was a highly influential 1970 refinement of the stagewise model. It provided two primary enhancements to the stagewise model:

(1) Recognition of the feedback loops between stages, and a guideline to confine the feedback loops to successive stages to minimize the expensive rework involved in feedback across many stages.

(2) An initial incorporation of prototyping in the software life cycle, via a "build it twice" step running in parallel with requirements analysis and design.

The waterfall model's approach helped eliminate many difficulties previously encountered on software projects. The waterfall model has become the basis for most software acquisition standards in government and industry. Some of its initial difficulties have been addressed by adding extensions to cover incremental development, parallel developments, program families, accommodation of evolutionary changes, formal software development and verification, and stagewise validation and risk analysis.

However, even with extensive revisions and refinements, the waterfall model's basic scheme has encountered some more fundamental difficulties, and these have led to the formulation of alternative process models.

A primary source of difficulty with the waterfall model has been its emphasis on fully elaborated documents as completion criteria for early requirements and design phases. For some classes of software, such as compilers or secure operating systems, this is the most effective way to proceed. However, it does not work well for many classes of software, particularly interactive

The waterfall model has become the basis for most software acquisition standards.

end-user applications. Document-driven standards have pushed many projects to write elaborate specifications of poorly understood user interfaces and decision-support functions, followed by the design and development of large quantities of unusable code.

These projects are examples of how waterfall-model projects have come to grief by pursuing stages in the wrong order. Furthermore, in areas supported by fourth-generation languages (spreadsheet or small business applications), it is clearly unnecessary to write elaborate specifications for one's application before implementing it.

The evolutionary development model. The above concerns led to the formulation of the *evolutionary development* model,[4] whose stages consist of expanding increments of an operational software product, with the directions of evolution being determined by operational experience.

The evolutionary development model is ideally matched to a fourth-generation language application and well matched to situations in which users say, "I can't tell you what I want, but I'll know it when I see it." It gives users a rapid initial operational capability and provides a realistic operational basis for determining subsequent product improvements.

Nonetheless, evolutionary development also has its difficulties. It is generally difficult to distinguish it from the old code-and-fix model, whose spaghetti code and lack of planning were the initial motivation for the waterfall model. It is also based on the often-unrealistic assumption that the user's operational system will be flexible enough to accommodate unplanned evolution paths. This assumption is unjustified in three primary circumstances:

(1) Circumstances in which several independently evolved applications must subsequently be closely integrated.

(2) "Information-sclerosis" cases, in which temporary work-arounds for software deficiencies increasingly solidify into unchangeable constraints on evolution. The following comment is a typical example: "It's nice that you could change those equipment codes to make them more intelligible for us, but the Codes Committee just met and established the current codes as company standards."

(3) Bridging situations, in which the new software is incrementally replacing a large existing system. If the existing system is poorly modularized, it is difficult to provide a good sequence of "bridges" between the old software and the expanding increments of new software.

Under such conditions, evolutionary development projects have come to grief by pursuing stages in the wrong order: evolving a lot of hard-to-change code before addressing long-range architectural and usage considerations.

The transform model. The "spaghetti code" difficulties of the evolutionary development and code-and-fix models can also become a difficulty in various classes of waterfall-model applications, in which code is optimized for performance and becomes increasingly hard to modify. The transform model[5] has been proposed as a solution to this dilemma.

The transform model assumes the existence of a capability to automatically convert a formal specification of a software product into a program satisfying the specification. The steps then prescribed by the transform model are

- a formal specification of the best initial understanding of the desired product;
- automatic transformation of the specification into code;
- an iterative loop, if necessary, to improve the performance of the resulting code by giving optimization guidance to the transformation system;
- exercise of the resulting product; and
- an outer iterative loop to adjust the specification based on the resulting operational experience, and to rederive, reoptimize, and exercise the adjusted software product.

The transform model thus bypasses the difficulty of having to modify code that has become poorly structured through repeated reoptimizations, since the modifications are made to the specification. It also avoids the extra time and expense involved in the intermediate design, code, and test activities.

Still, the transform model has various

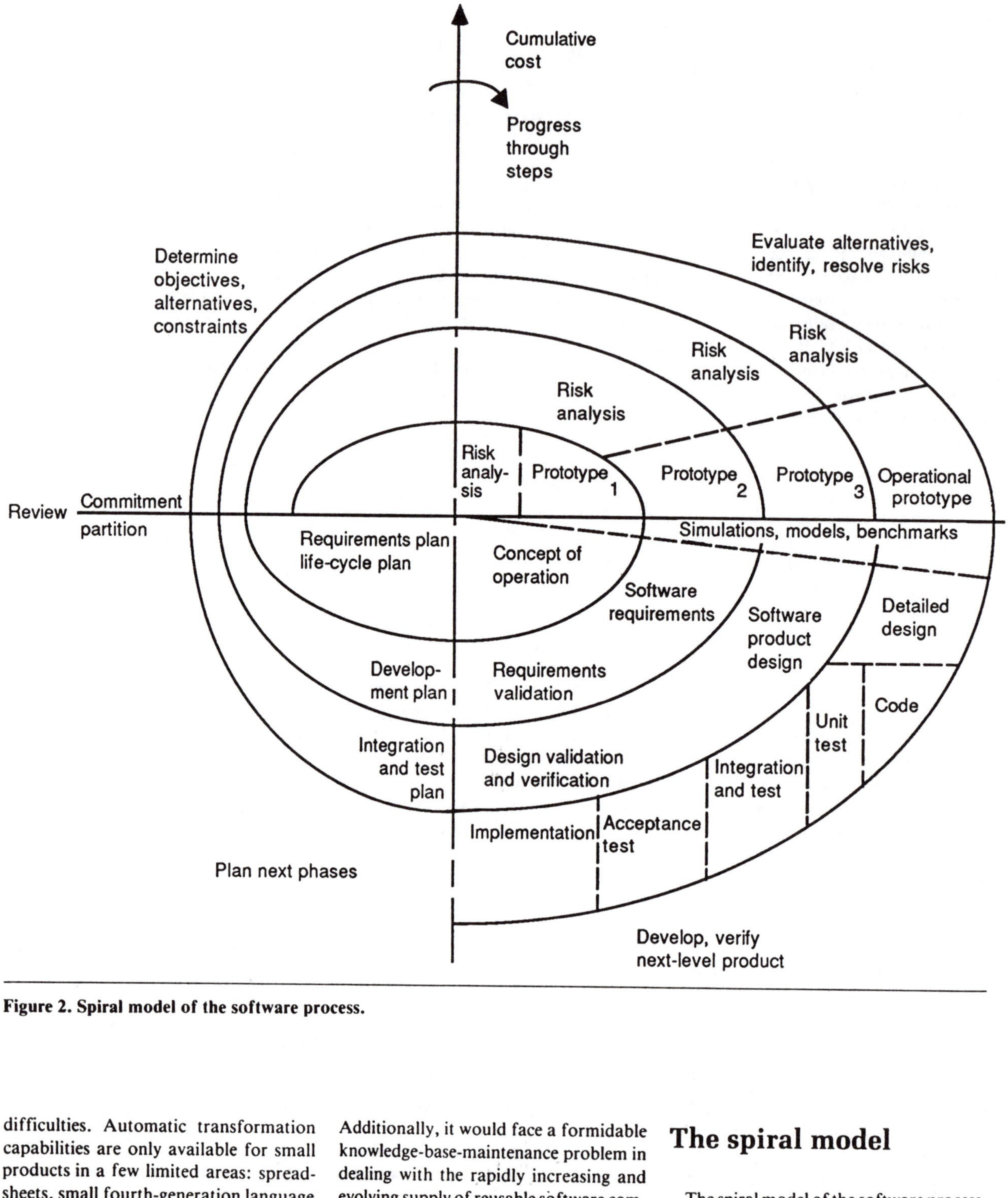

Figure 2. Spiral model of the software process.

difficulties. Automatic transformation capabilities are only available for small products in a few limited areas: spreadsheets, small fourth-generation language applications, and limited computer-science domains. The transform model also shares some of the difficulties of the evolutionary development model, such as the assumption that users' operational systems will always be flexible enough to support unplanned evolution paths. Additionally, it would face a formidable knowledge-base-maintenance problem in dealing with the rapidly increasing and evolving supply of reusable software components and commercial software products. (Simply consider the problem of tracking the costs, performance, and features of all commercial database management systems, and automatically choosing the best one to implement each new or changed specification.)

The spiral model

The spiral model of the software process (see Figure 2) has been evolving for several years, based on experience with various refinements of the waterfall model as applied to large government software projects. As will be discussed, the spiral model can accommodate most previous models as special cases and further provides guidance as to which combination of previous models best fits a given software situation. Development of the TRW Software Productivity System (TRW-SPS), described in the next section, is its most complete application to date.

The radial dimension in Figure 2 represents the cumulative cost incurred in accomplishing the steps to date; the angular dimension represents the progress made in completing each cycle of the spiral. (The model reflects the underlying concept that each cycle involves a progression that addresses the same sequence of steps, for each portion of the product and for each of its levels of elaboration, from an overall concept of operation document down to the coding of each individual program.) Note that some artistic license has been taken with the increasing cumulative cost dimension to enhance legibility of the steps in Figure 2.

A typical cycle of the spiral. Each cycle of the spiral begins with the identification of

- the objectives of the portion of the product being elaborated (performance, functionality, ability to accommodate change, etc.);
- the alternative means of implementing this portion of the product (design A, design B, reuse, buy, etc.); and
- the constraints imposed on the application of the alternatives (cost, schedule, interface, etc.).

The next step is to evaluate the alternatives relative to the objectives and constraints. Frequently, this process will identify areas of uncertainty that are significant sources of project risk. If so, the next step should involve the formulation of a cost-effective strategy for resolving the sources of risk. This may involve prototyping, simulation, benchmarking, reference checking, administering user questionnaires, analytic modeling, or combinations of these and other risk-resolution techniques.

Once the risks are evaluated, the next step is determined by the relative remaining risks. If performance or user-interface risks strongly dominate program development or internal interface-control risks, the next step may be an evolutionary development one: a minimal effort to specify the overall nature of the product, a plan for the next level of prototyping, and the development of a more detailed prototype to continue to resolve the major risk issues.

If this prototype is operationally useful and robust enough to serve as a low-risk base for future product evolution, the subsequent risk-driven steps would be the evolving series of evolutionary prototypes going toward the right in Figure 2. In this case, the option of writing specifications would be addressed but not exercised. Thus, risk considerations can lead to a project implementing only a subset of all the potential steps in the model.

On the other hand, if previous prototyping efforts have already resolved all of the performance or user-interface risks, and program development or interface-control risks dominate, the next step follows the basic waterfall approach (concept of operation, software requirements, preliminary design, etc. in Figure 2), modified as appropriate to incorporate incremental development. Each level of software specification in the figure is then followed by a validation step and the preparation of plans for the succeeding cycle. In this case, the options to prototype, simulate, model, etc. are addressed but not exercised, leading to the use of a different subset of steps.

This risk-driven subsetting of the spiral model steps allows the model to accommodate any appropriate mixture of a specification-oriented, prototype-oriented, simulation-oriented, automatic transformation-oriented, or other approach to software development. In such cases, the appropriate mixed strategy is chosen by considering the relative magnitude of the program risks and the relative effectiveness of the various techniques in resolving the risks. In a similar way, risk-management considerations can determine the amount of time and effort that should be devoted to such other project activities as planning, configuration management, quality assurance, formal verification, and testing. In particular, risk-driven specifications (as discussed in the next section) can have varying degrees of completeness, formality, and granularity, depending on the relative risks of doing too little or too much specification.

An important feature of the spiral model, as with most other models, is that each cycle is completed by a review involving the primary people or organizations concerned with the product. This review covers all products developed during the previous cycle, including the plans for the next cycle and the resources required to carry them out. The review's major objective is to ensure that all concerned parties are mutually committed to the approach for the next phase.

The plans for succeeding phases may also include a partition of the product into increments for successive development or components to be developed by individual organizations or persons. For the latter case, visualize a series of parallel spiral cycles, one for each component, adding a third dimension to the concept presented in Figure 2. For example, separate spirals can be evolving for separate software components or increments. Thus, the review-and-commitment step may range from an individual walk-through of the design of a single programmer's component to a major requirements review involving developer, customer, user, and maintenance organizations.

Initiating and terminating the spiral. Four fundamental questions arise in considering this presentation of the spiral model:

(1) How does the spiral ever get started?
(2) How do you get off the spiral when it is appropriate to terminate a project early?
(3) Why does the spiral end so abruptly?
(4) What happens to software enhancement (or maintenance)?

The answer to these questions involves an observation that the spiral model applies equally well to development or enhancement efforts. In either case, the spiral gets started by a hypothesis that a particular operational mission (or set of missions) could be improved by a software effort. The spiral process then involves a test of this hypothesis: at any time, if the hypothesis fails the test (for example, if delays cause a software product to miss its market window, or if a superior commercial product becomes available), the spiral is terminated. Otherwise, it terminates with the installation of new or modified software, and the hypothesis is tested by observing the effect on the operational mission. Usually, experience with the operational mission leads to further hypotheses about software improvements, and a new maintenance spiral is initiated to test the hypothesis. Initiation, termination, and iteration of the tasks and products of previous cycles are thus implicitly defined in the spiral model (although they're not included in Figure 2 to simplify its presentation).

Using the spiral model

The various rounds and activities involved in the spiral model are best understood through use of an example. The spiral model was used in the definition and development of the TRW Software Productivity System (TRW-SPS), an integrated software engineering environment.[6] The initial mission opportunity coincided with a corporate initiative to improve productivity in all appropriate corporate operations and an initial hypothesis that software engineering was an attractive area to investigate. This led to a small, extra "Round 0" circuit of the spiral to determine the feasibility of increasing software productivity at a reasonable corporate cost. (Very large or complex software projects will frequently precede the "concept of operation" round of the spiral with one or more smaller rounds to establish feasibility and to reduce the range of alternative solutions quickly and inexpensively.)

Tables 1, 2, and 3 summarize the application of the spiral model to the first three rounds of defining the SPS. The major features of each round are subsequently discussed and are followed by some examples from later rounds, such as preliminary and detailed design.

Round 0: Feasibility study. This study involved five part-time participants over a two- to three-month period. As indicated in Table 1, the objectives and constraints were expressed at a very high level and in qualitative terms like "significantly increase," "at reasonable cost," etc.

Some of the alternatives considered, primarily those in the "technology" area, could lead to development of a software product, but the possible attractiveness of a number of non-software alternatives in the management, personnel, and facilities areas could have led to a conclusion not to embark on a software development activity.

The primary risk areas involved possible situations in which the company would invest a good deal only to find that

- resulting productivity gains were not significant, or
- potentially high-leverage improvements were not compatible with some aspects of the "TRW culture."

The risk-resolution activities undertaken in Round 0 were primarily surveys and analyses, including structured interviews of software developers and managers, an initial analysis of productivity leverage factors identified by the constructive cost model (Cocomo)[7]; and an analysis of previous projects at TRW exhibiting high levels of productivity.

The risk analysis results indicated that significant productivity gains could be achieved at a reasonable cost by pursuing an integrated set of initiatives in the four major areas. However, some candidate solutions, such as a software support environment based on a single, corporate, maxicomputer-based time-sharing system, were found to be in conflict with TRW constraints requiring support of different levels of security-classified projects. Thus, even at a very high level of generality of objectives and constraints, Round 0 was able to answer basic feasibility questions and eliminate significant classes of candidate solutions.

The plan for Round 1 involved commitment of 12 man-months compared to the two man-months invested in Round 0 (during these rounds, all participants were part-time). Round 1 here corresponded fairly well to the initial round of the spiral model shown in Figure 2, in that its intent was to produce a concept of operation and a basic life-cycle plan for implementing whatever preferred alternative emerged.

Table 1. Spiral model usage: TRW Software Productivity System, Round 0.

Objectives	Significantly increase software productivity
Constraints	At reasonable cost Within context of TRW culture • Government contracts, high tech., people oriented, security
Alternatives	Management: Project organization, policies, planning, control Personnel: Staffing, incentives, training Technology: Tools, workstations, methods, reuse Facilities: Offices, communications
Risks	May be no high-leverage improvements Improvements may violate constraints
Risk resolution	Internal surveys Analyze cost model Analyze exceptional projects Literature search
Risk resolution results	Some alternatives infeasible • Single time-sharing system: Security Mix of alternatives can produce significant gains • Factor of two in five years Need further study to determine best mix
Plan for next phase	Six-person task force for six months More extensive surveys and analysis • Internal, external, economic Develop concept of operation, economic rationale
Commitment	Fund next phase

Round 1: Concept of operations. Table 2 summarizes Round 1 of the spiral along the lines given in Table 1 for Round 0. The features of Round 1 compare to those of Round 0 as follows:

- The level of investment was greater (12 versus 2 man-months).
- The objectives and constraints were more specific ("double software productivity in five years at a cost of $10,000 a person" versus "significantly increase productivity at a reasonable cost").
- Additional constraints surfaced, such as the preference for TRW products (particularly, a TRW-developed local area network (LAN) system).
- The alternatives were more detailed ("SREM, PSL/PSA or SADT, as requirements tools etc." versus "tools"; "private/shared" terminals, "smart/dumb" terminals versus "workstations").
- The risk areas identified were more specific ("TRW LAN price-performance

within a $10,000-per-person investment constraint'' versus ''improvements may violate reasonable-cost constraint'').

• The risk-resolution activities were more extensive (including the benchmarking and analysis of a prototype TRW LAN being developed for another project).

• The result was a fairly specific operational concept document, involving private offices tailored to software work patterns and personal terminals connected to VAX superminis via the TRW LAN. Some choices were specifically deferred to the next round, such as the choice of operating system and specific tools.

• The life-cycle plan and the plan for the next phase involved a partitioning into separate activities to address management improvements, facilities development, and development of the first increment of a software development environment.

• The commitment step involved more than just an agreement with the plan. It committed to apply the environment to an upcoming 100-person testbed software project and to develop an environment focusing on the testbed project's needs. It also specified forming a representative steering group to ensure that the separate activities were well-coordinated and that the environment would not be overly optimized around the testbed project.

Although the plan recommended developing a prototype environment, it also recommended that the project employ requirements specifications and design specifications in a risk-driven way. Thus, the development of the environment followed the succeeding rounds of the spiral model.

Round 2: Top-level requirements specification. Table 3 shows the corresponding steps involved during Round 2 defining the software productivity system. Round 2 decisions and their rationale were covered in earlier work[6]; here, we will summarize the considerations dealing with risk management and the use of the spiral model:

• The initial risk-identification activities during Round 2 showed that several system requirements hinged on the decision between a host-target system or a fully portable tool set and the decision between VMS and Unix as the host operating system. These requirements included the functions needed to provide a user-friendly front-end, the operating system to be used by the workstations, and the functions necessary to support a host-target operation. To keep these requirements in synchronization with the others, a special minispiral was initiated to address and resolve these issues. The resulting review led to a commitment to a host-target operation using Unix on the host system, at a point early enough to work the OS-dependent requirements in a timely fashion.

• Addressing the risks of mismatches to the user-project's needs and priorities resulted in substantial participation of the user-project personnel in the requirements definition activity. This led to several significant redirections of the requirements, particularly toward supporting the early phases of the software life-cycle into which the user project was embarking, such as an adaptation of the software requirements engineering methodology (SREM) tools for requirements specification and analysis.

It is also interesting to note that the form of Tables 1, 2, and 3 was originally developed for presentation purposes, but subsequently became a standard ''spiral model template'' used on later projects. These templates are useful not only for organizing project activities, but also as a residual design-rationale record. Design rationale information is of paramount importance in assessing the potential reusability of software components on future projects. Another important point to note is that the use of the template was indeed uniform across the three cycles, showing that the spiral steps can be and were uniformly followed at successively detailed levels of product definition.

Table 2. Spiral model usage: TRW Software Productivity System, Round 1.

Objectives	Double software productivity in five years
Constraints	$10,000 per person investment Within context of TRW culture • Government contracts, high tech., people oriented, security Preference for TRW products
Alternatives	Office: Private/modular/. . . Communication: LAN/star/concentrators/. . . Terminals: Private/shared; smart/dumb Tools: SREM/PSL-PSA/. . .; PDL/SADT/. . . CPU: IBM/DEC/CDC/. . .
Risks	May miss high-leverage options TRW LAN price/performance Workstation cost
Risk resolution	Extensive external surveys, visits TRW LAN benchmarking Workstation price projections
Risk resolution results	Operations concept: Private offices, TRW LAN, personal terminals, VAX Begin with primarily dumb terminals; experiment with smart workstations Defer operating system, tools selection
Plan for next phase	Partition effort into software development environment (SDE), facilities, management Develop first-cut, prototype SDE • Design-to-cost: 15-person team for one year Plan for external usage
Commitment	Develop prototype SDE Commit an upcoming project to use SDE Commit the SDE to support the project Form representative steering group

Succeeding rounds. It will be useful to illustrate some examples of how the spiral model is used to handle situations arising in the preliminary design and detailed design of components of the SPS: the preliminary design specification for the requirements traceability tool (RTT), and a detailed design rework or go-back on the unit development folder (UDF) tool.

The RTT preliminary design specification. The RTT establishes the traceability between itemized software requirements specifications, design elements, code elements, and test cases. It also supports various associated query, analysis, and report generation capabilities. The preliminary design specification for the RTT (and most of the other SPS tools) looks different from the usual preliminary design specification, which tends to show a uniform level of elaboration of all components of the design. Instead, the level of detail of the RTT specification is risk-driven.

In areas involving a high risk if the design turned out to be wrong, the design was carried down to the detailed design level, usually with the aid of rapid prototyping. These areas included working out the implications of "undo" options and dealing with the effects of control keys used to escape from various program levels.

In areas involving a moderate risk if the design was wrong, the design was carried down to a preliminary-design level. These areas included the basic command options for the tool and the schemata for the requirements traceability database. Here again, the ease of rapid prototyping with Unix shell scripts supported a good deal of user-interface prototyping.

In areas involving a low risk if the design was wrong, very little design elaboration was done. These areas included details of all the help message options and all the report-generation options, once the nature of these options was established in some example instances.

A detailed design go-back. The UDF tool collects into an electronic "folder" all artifacts involved in the development of a single-programmer software unit (typically 500 to 1,000 instructions): unit requirements, design, code, test cases, test results, and documentation. It also includes a management template for tracking the programmer's scheduled and actual completion of each artifact.

An alternative considered during detailed design of the UDF tool was reuse of portions of the RTT to provide pointers to the requirements and preliminary design specifications of the unit being developed. This turned out to be an extremely attractive alternative, not only for avoiding duplicate software development but also for bringing to the surface several issues involving many-to-many mappings between requirements, design, and code that had not been considered in designing the UDF tool. These led to a rethinking of the UDF tool requirements and preliminary design, which avoided a great deal of code rework that would have been necessary if the detailed design of the UDF tool had proceeded in a purely deductive, top-down fashion from the original UDF requirements specification. The resulting go-back led to a significantly different, less costly, and more capable UDF tool, incorporating the RTT in its "uses-hierarchy."

Spiral model features. These two examples illustrate several features of the spiral approach.

- It fosters the development of specifications that are not necessarily uniform, exhaustive, or formal, in that they defer detailed elaboration of low-risk software elements and avoid unnecessary breakage in their design until the high-risk elements of the design are stabilized.
- It incorporates prototyping as a risk-reduction option at any stage of development. In fact, prototyping and reuse risk analyses were often used in the process of going from detailed design into code.
- It accommodates reworks or go-backs to earlier stages as more attractive alternatives are identified or as new risk issues need resolution.

Overall, risk-driven documents, particularly specifications and plans, are important features of the spiral model. Great amounts of detail are not necessary unless the absence of such detail jeopardizes the

Table 3. Spiral model usage: TRW Software Productivity System, Round 2.

Objectives	User-friendly system Integrated software, office-automation tools Support all project personnel Support all life-cycle phases
Constraints	Customer-deliverable SDE ⇒ Portability Stable, reliable service
Alternatives	OS: VMS/AT&T Unix/Berkeley Unix/ISC Host-target/fully portable tool set Workstations: Zenith/LSI-11/. . .
Risks	Mismatch to user-project needs, priorities User-unfriendly system • 12-language syndrome; experts-only Unix performance, support Workstation/mainframe compatibility
Risk resolution	User-project surveys, requirements participation Survey of Unix-using organizations Workstation study
Risk resolution results	Top-level requirements specification Host-target with Unix host Unix-based workstations Build user-friendly front end for Unix Initial focus on tools to support early phases
Plan for next phase	Overall development plan • for tools: SREM, RTT, PDL, office automation tools • for front end: Support tools • for LAN: Equipment, facilities
Commitment	Proceed with plans

project. In some cases, such as with a product whose functionality may be determined by a choice among commercial products, a set of weighted evaluation criteria for the products may be preferable to a detailed pre-statement of functional requirements.

All of the projects fully using the system have increased their productivity at least 50 percent.

Results. The Software Productivity System developed and supported using the spiral model avoided the identified risks and achieved most of the system's objectives. The SPS has grown to include over 300 tools and over 1,300,000 instructions; 93 percent of the instructions were reused from previous project-developed, TRW-developed, or external-software packages. Over 25 projects have used all or portions of the system. All of the projects fully using the system have increased their productivity at least 50 percent; indeed, most have doubled their productivity (when compared with cost-estimation model predictions of their productivity using traditional methods).

However, one risk area—that projects with non-Unix target systems would not accept a Unix-based host system—was underestimated. Some projects accepted the host-target approach, but for various reasons (such as customer constraints and zero-cost target machines) a good many did not. As a result, the system was less widely used on TRW projects than expected. This and other lessons learned have been incorporated into the spiral model approach to developing TRW's next-generation software development environment.

Evaluation

Advantages. The primary advantage of the spiral model is that its range of options accommodates the good features of existing software process models, while its risk-driven approach avoids many of their difficulties. In appropriate situations, the spiral model becomes equivalent to one of the existing process models. In other situations, it provides guidance on the best mix of existing approaches to a given project; for example, its application to the TRW-SPS provided a risk-driven mix of specifying, prototyping, and evolutionary development.

The primary conditions under which the spiral model becomes equivalent to other main process models are summarized as follows:

- If a project has a low risk in such areas as getting the wrong user interface or not meeting stringent performance requirements, and if it has a high risk in budget and schedule predictability and control, then these risk considerations drive the spiral model into an equivalence to the waterfall model.
- If a software product's requirements are very stable (implying a low risk of expensive design and code breakage due to requirements changes during development), and if the presence of errors in the software product constitutes a high risk to the mission it serves, then these risk considerations drive the spiral model to resemble the two-leg model of precise specification and formal deductive program development.
- If a project has a low risk in such areas as losing budget and schedule predictability and control, encountering large-system integration problems, or coping with information sclerosis, and if it has a high risk in such areas as getting the wrong user interface or user decision support requirements, then these risk considerations drive the spiral model into an equivalence to the evolutionary development model.
- If automated software generation capabilities are available, then the spiral model accommodates them either as options for rapid prototyping or for application of the transform model, depending on the risk considerations involved.
- If the high-risk elements of a project involve a mix of the risk items listed above, then the spiral approach will reflect an appropriate mix of the process models above (as exemplified in the TRW-SPS application). In doing so, its risk-avoidance features will generally avoid the difficulties of the other models.

The spiral model has a number of additional advantages, summarized as follows:

It focuses early attention on options involving the reuse of existing software. The steps involving the identification and evaluation of alternatives encourage these options.

It accommodates preparation for life-cycle evolution, growth, and changes of the software product. The major sources of product change are included in the product's objectives, and information-hiding approaches are attractive architectural design alternatives in that they reduce the risk of not being able to accommodate the product-charge objectives.

It provides a mechanism for incorporating software quality objectives into software product development. This mechanism derives from the emphasis on identifying all types of objectives and constraints during each round of the spiral. For example, Table 3 shows user-friendliness, portability, and reliability as specific objectives and constraints to be addressed by the SPS. In Table 1, security constraints were identified as a key risk item for the SPS.

It focuses on eliminating errors and unattractive alternatives early. The risk-analysis, validation, and commitment steps cover these considerations.

For each of the sources of project activity and resource expenditure, it answers the key question, "How much is enough?" Stated another way, "How much of requirements analysis, planning, configuration management, quality assurance, testing, formal verification, etc. should a project do?" Using the risk-driven approach, one can see that the answer is not the same for all projects and that the appropriate level of effort is determined by the level of risk incurred by not doing enough.

It does not involve separate approaches for software development and software enhancement (or maintenance). This aspect helps avoid the "second-class citizen" status frequently associated with software maintenance. It also helps avoid many of the problems that currently ensue when high-risk enhancement efforts are approached in the same way as routine maintenance efforts.

It provides a viable framework for integrated hardware-software system development. The focus on risk-management and on eliminating unattractive alternatives early and inexpensively is equally applicable to hardware and software.

Difficulties. The full spiral model can be successfully applied in many situations, but some difficulties must be addressed before it can be called a mature, universally applicable model. The three primary challenges involve matching to contract software, relying on risk-assessment expertise, and the need for further elaboration of spiral model steps.

Matching to contract software. The spiral model currently works well on internal software developments like the TRW-SPS, but it needs further work to match it to the world of contract software acquisition.

Internal software developments have a great deal of flexibility and freedom to accommodate stage-by-stage commitments, to defer commitments to specific options, to establish minispirals to resolve critical-path items, to adjust levels of effort, or to accommodate such practices as prototyping, evolutionary development, or design-to-cost. The world of contract software acquisition has a harder time achieving these degrees of flexibility and freedom without losing accountability and control, and a harder time defining contracts whose deliverables are not well specified in advance.

Recently, a good deal of progress has been made in establishing more flexible contract mechanisms, such as the use of competitive front-end contracts for concept definition or prototype fly-offs, the use of level-of-effort and award-fee contracts for evolutionary development, and the use of design-to-cost contracts. Although these have been generally successful, the procedures for using them still need to be worked out to the point that acquisition managers feel fully comfortable using them.

Table 4. A prioritized top-ten list of software risk items.

Risk item	Risk management techniques
1. Personnel shortfalls	Staffing with top talent, job matching; teambuilding; morale building; cross-training; pre-scheduling key people
2. Unrealistic schedules and budgets	Detailed, multisource cost and schedule estimation; design to cost; incremental development; software reuse; requirements scrubbing
3. Developing the wrong software functions	Organization analysis; mission analysis; ops-concept formulation; user surveys; prototyping; early users' manuals
4. Developing the wrong user interface	Task analysis; prototyping; scenarios; user characterization (functionality, style, workload)
5. Gold plating	Requirements scrubbing; prototyping; cost-benefit analysis; design to cost
6. Continuing stream of requirement changes	High change threshold; information hiding; incremental development (defer changes to later increments)
7. Shortfalls in externally furnished components	Benchmarking; inspections; reference checking; compatibility analysis
8. Shortfalls in externally performed tasks	Reference checking; pre-award audits; award-fee contracts; competitive design or prototyping; teambuilding
9. Real-time performance shortfalls	Simulation; benchmarking; modeling; prototyping; instrumentation; tuning
10. Straining computer-science capabilities	Technical analysis; cost-benefit analysis; prototyping; reference checking

Table 5. Software Risk Management Plan.

1.	Identify the project's top 10 risk items.
2.	Present a plan for resolving each risk item.
3.	Update list of top risk items, plan, and results monthly.
4.	Highlight risk-item status in monthly project reviews. • Compare with previous month's rankings, status.
5.	Initiate appropriate corrective actions.

Relying on risk-assessment expertise. The spiral model places a great deal of reliance on the ability of software developers to identify and manage sources of project risk.

A good example of this is the spiral model's risk-driven specification, which carries high-risk elements down to a great deal of detail and leaves low-risk elements to be elaborated in later stages; by this time, there is less risk of breakage.

However, a team of inexperienced or low-balling developers may also produce a specification with a different pattern of variation in levels of detail: a great elaboration of detail for the well-understood, low-risk elements, and little elaboration of the poorly understood, high-risk elements. Unless there is an insightful review of such a specification by experienced development or acquisition personnel, this type of project will give an illusion of progress during a period in which it is actually heading for disaster.

Another concern is that a risk-driven specification will also be people-dependent. For example, a design produced by an expert may be implemented by non-experts. In this case, the expert, who does not need a great deal of detailed documentation, must produce enough additional documentation to keep the non-experts from going astray. Reviewers of the specification must also be sensitive to these concerns.

With a conventional, document-driven approach, the requirement to carry all aspects of the specification to a uniform level of detail eliminates some potential problems and permits adequate review of some aspects by inexperienced reviewers. But it also creates a large drain on the time of the scarce experts, who must dig for the critical issues within a large mass of non-critical detail. Furthermore, if the high-risk elements have been glossed over by impressive-sounding references to poorly understood capabilities (such as a new synchronization concept or a commercial DBMS), there is an even greater risk that the conventional approach will give the illusion of progress in situations that are actually heading for disaster.

Need for further elaboration of spiral model steps. In general, the spiral model process steps need further elaboration to ensure that all software development participants are operating in a consistent context.

Some examples of this are the need for more detailed definitions of the nature of spiral model specifications and milestones, the nature and objectives of spiral model reviews, techniques for estimating and synchronizing schedules, and the nature of spiral model status indicators and cost-versus-progress tracking procedures. Another need is for guidelines and checklists to identify the most likely sources of project risk and the most effective risk-resolution techniques for each source of risk.

Highly experienced people can successfully use the spiral approach without these elaborations. However, for large-scale use in situations where people bring widely differing experience bases to the project, added levels of elaboration—such as have been accumulated over the years for document-driven approaches—are important in ensuring consistent interpretation and use of the spiral approach across the project.

Efforts to apply and refine the spiral model have focused on creating a discipline of software risk management, including techniques for risk identification, risk analysis, risk prioritization, risk-management planning, and risk-element tracking. The prioritized top-ten list of software risk items given in Table 4 is one result of this activity. Another example is the risk management plan discussed in the next section.

Implications: The Risk Management Plan. Even if an organization is not ready to adopt the entire spiral approach, one characteristic technique that can easily be adapted to any life-cycle model provides many of the benefits of the spiral approach. This is the Risk Management Plan summarized in Table 5. This plan basically ensures that each project makes an early identification of its top risk items (the number 10 is not an absolute requirement), develops a strategy for resolving the risk items, identifies and sets down an agenda to resolve new risk items as they surface, and highlights progress versus plans in monthly reviews.

The Risk Management Plan has been used successfully at TRW and other organizations. Its use has ensured appropriate focus on early prototyping, simulation, benchmarking, key-person staffing measures, and other early risk-resolution techniques that have helped avoid many potential project "show-stoppers." The recent US Department of Defense standard on software management, DoD-Std-2167, requires that developers produce and use risk management plans, as does its counterpart US Air Force regulation, AFR 800-14.

Overall, the Risk Management Plan and the maturing set of techniques for software risk management provide a foundation for tailoring spiral model concepts into the more established software acquisition and development procedures.

We can draw four conclusions from the data presented:

(1) The risk-driven nature of the spiral model is more adaptable to the full range of software project situations than are the primarily document-driven approaches such as the waterfall model or the primarily code-driven approaches such as evolutionary development. It is particularly applicable to very large, complex, ambitious software systems.

(2) The spiral model has been quite successful in its largest application to date: the development and enhancement of the TRW-SPS. Overall, it achieved a high level of software support environment capability in a very short time and provided the flexibility necessary to accommodate a high dynamic range of technical alternatives and user objectives.

(3) The spiral model is not yet as fully elaborated as the more established models. Therefore, the spiral model can be applied by experienced personnel, but it needs further elaboration in such areas as contracting, specifications, milestones, reviews, scheduling, status monitoring, and risk-area identification to be fully usable in all situations.

(4) Partial implementations of the spiral model, such as the Risk Management Plan, are compatible with most current process models and are very helpful in overcoming major sources of project risk.□

Acknowledgments

I would like to thank Frank Belz, Lolo Penedo, George Spadaro, Bob Williams, Bob Balzer, Gillian Frewin, Peter Hamer, Manny Lehman, Lee Osterweil, Dave Parnas, Bill Riddle, Steve Squires, and Dick Thayer, along with the *Computer* reviewers of this article, for their stimulating and insightful comments and discussions of earlier versions of the article, and Nancy Donato for producing its several versions.

References

1. F.P. Brooks et al., *Defense Science Board Task Force Report on Military Software*, Office of the Under Secretary of Defense for Acquisition, Washington, DC 20301, Sept. 1987.
2. H.D. Benington, "Production of Large Computer Programs," *Proc. ONR Symp. Advanced Programming Methods for Digital Computers*, June 1956, pp. 15-27. Also available in *Annals of the History of Computing*, Oct. 1983, pp. 350-361, and *Proc. Ninth Int'l Conf. Software Engineering*, Computer Society Press, 1987.
3. W.W. Royce, "Managing the Development of Large Software Systems: Concepts and Techniques," *Proc. Wescon*, Aug. 1970. Also available in *Proc. ICSE 9*, Computer Society Press, 1987.
4. D.D. McCracken and M.A. Jackson, "Life-Cycle Concept Considered Harmful," *ACM Software Engineering Notes*, Apr. 1982, pp. 29-32.
5. R. Balzer, T.E. Cheatham, and C. Green, "Software Technology in the 1990s: Using a New Paradigm," *Computer*, Nov. 1983, pp. 39-45.
6. B.W. Boehm et al., "A Software Development Environment for Improving Productivity," *Computer*, June 1984, pp. 30-44.
7. B.W. Boehm, *Software Engineering Economics*, Prentice-Hall, 1981, Chap. 33.

Further reading

The software process model field has an interesting history, and a great deal of stimulating work has been produced recently in this specialized area. Besides the references that appear at the end of the accompanying article, here are some additional good sources of insight:

Overall process model issues and results

Agresti's tutorial volume provides a good overview and set of key articles. The three recent *Software Process Workshop Proceedings* provide access to much of the recent work in the area.

Agresti, W.W., *New Paradigms for Software Development*, IEEE Catalog No. EH0245-1, 1986.

Dowson, M., ed., *Proc. Third Int'l Software Process Workshop*, IEEE Catalog No. TH0184-2, Nov. 1986.

Potts, C., ed., *Proc. Software Process Workshop*, IEEE Catalog No. 84CH2044-6, Feb. 1984.

Wileden, J.C., and M. Dowson, eds., Proc. Int'l Workshop Software Process and Software Environments, *ACM Software Engineering Notes*, Aug. 1986.

Alternative process models

More detailed information on waterfall-type approaches is given in:

Evans, M.W., P. Piazza, and J.P. Dolkas, *Principles of Productive Software Management*, John Wiley & Sons, 1983.

Hice, G.F., W.J. Turner, and L.F. Cashwell, *System Development Methodology*, North Holland, 1974 (2nd ed., 1981).

More detailed information on evolutionary development is provided in:

Gilb, T., *Principles of Software Engineering Management*, Addison Wesley, 1988 (currently in publication).

Some additional process model approaches with useful features and insights may be found in:

Lehman, M.M., and L.A. Belady, *Program Evolution: Processes of Software Change*, Academic Press, 1985.

Osterweil, L., "Software Processes are Software, Too," *Proc. ICSE 9*, IEEE Catalog No. 87CH2432-3, Mar. 1987, pp. 2-13.

Radice, R.A., et al., "A Programming Process Architecture," *IBM Systems J.*, Vol. 24, No.2, 1985, pp. 79-90.

Spiral and spiral-type models

Some further treatments of spiral model issues and practices are:

Belz, F.C., "Applying the Spiral Model: Observations on Developing System Software in Ada," *Proc. 1986 Annual Conf. on Ada Technology*, Atlanta, 1986, pp. 57-66.

Boehm, B.W., and F.C. Belz, "Applying Process Programming to the Spiral Model," *Proc. Fourth Software Process Workshop*, IEEE, May 1988.

Iivari, J., "A Hierarchical Spiral Model for the Software Process," *ACM Software Engineering Notes*, Jan. 1987, pp. 35-37.

Some similar cyclic spiral-type process models from other fields are described in:

Carlsson, B., P. Keane, and J.B. Martin, "R&D Organizations as Learning Systems," *Sloan Management Review*, Spring 1976, pp. 1-15.

Fisher, R., and W. Ury, *Getting to Yes*, Houghton Mifflin, 1981; Penguin Books, 1983, pp. 68-71.

Kolb, D.A., "On Management and the Learning Process," MIT Sloan School Working Article 652-73, Cambridge, Mass., 1973.

Software risk management

The discipline of software risk management provides a bridge between spiral model concepts and currently established software acquisition and development procedures.

Boehm, B.W., "Software Risk Management Tutorial," Computer Society, Apr. 1988.

Risk Assessment Techniques, Defense Systems Management College, Ft. Belvoir, Va. 22060, July 1983.

Barry W. Boehm is the chief scientist of the TRW Defense Systems Group. Since 1973, he has been responsible for developing TRW's software technology base. His current primary responsibilities are in the areas of software environments, process models, management methods, Ada, and cost estimation. He is also an adjunct professor at UCLA.

Boehm received his BA degree in mathematics from Harvard in 1957 and his MA and PhD from UCLA in 1961 and 1964, respectively.

Readers may write to Boehm at TRW Defense Systems Group, One Space Park, R2/2086, Redondo Beach, CA 90278.

Interactive Systems:

Bridging the Gaps Between Developers and Users

Jonathan Grudin, Aarhus University

Today, user needs are recognized to be important in designing interactive computer systems, but as recently as 1980, they received little emphasis. In most major systems development companies, the basic organizational structures and development processes were defined in an earlier era, when the dialogue between computer systems and computer users did not have to be considered.

This point is of more than historical interest; it raises some basic questions: Can these companies develop effective interactive systems? What changes would bring greater knowledge of users and their work environments into systems development? How long will it take to translate this new understanding into reliable, effective practice?

Until 15 years ago, most computer system users were engineers and programmers. Developers were designing systems for their own use or for other technically proficient users. They felt no need to seek user participation in design. Now, however, computer use has spread to workplaces that are very unlike engineering laboratories. Contact with system users is required, but determining how direct or extensive this contact need be and actually achieving it have been surprisingly difficult.

Three development contexts provide a framework for understanding interactive software development projects: competitively bid, commercial product, and in-house/custom development.

Toward a user focus. Early proponents of greater user involvement included both human factors specialists and systems developers. An IBM usability research group stressed "an early focus on users" in the 1970s, and an influential 1983 paper recommended that "typical users (e.g. bank tellers, as opposed to a 'group of expert' supervisors, industrial engineers, programmers) ... become part of the design team from the very outset when their perspectives can have the most influence, rather than using them to 'review,' 'sign off on,' 'agree' to the design before it is coded."[1] Perhaps coincidentally, this paper appeared when popular books such as *In Search of Excellence* were urging industry to cater to the customer. A user focus was further emphasized in *User Centered System Design*,[2] an influential 1986 collection of research papers. Also in the 1970s and 1980s, Europeans experimented with greater user involvement in systems design. In particular, the Scandinavian "participatory design" approach, in which users collaborate as full development team members, attracted attention (see Suchman's review, "Designing with the User").[3]

The challenge of designing better interactive systems has not gone unnoticed in software engineering. Boehm observes that the dominant waterfall development model "does not work well for many classes of software, particularly interactive end user applications."[4] His proposal, a "spiral model" of software development, incorporates user involvement, prototyping, and iterative design. Yourdon recently wrote, "The first, and by far the most important, player in the systems game is someone known to systems analysts as a user."[5]

The spiral model is not yet widely used, and as Boehm notes, it may be difficult to apply in some contexts. Similarly, Yourdon's observation has not been fully translated into practice. The software methods that are employed widely today were developed before interactive end user applications became important. They do not provide for an early and continual focus on users — quite the contrary. Traditional structured analysis relegates the task of establishing a "man-machine interface" to one subphase of system development.[6] Jackson System Development "excludes

0018-9162/91/0400-0059$01.00 © 1991 IEEE

the whole area of human engineering in such matters as dialog design .... It excludes procedures for system acceptance, installation, and cutover."[7] Because such methods do not specify user involvement in design, project plans do not anticipate it, and development organizations are not structured to facilitate it. In fact, organizational structures and processes often work against user participation.

Many development projects do not include direct user involvement. Such projects indirectly acquire knowledge about system users, finding ways to bridge the gap between developers and users. These indirect methods sometimes work, but they may not meet the rising expectations of computer buyers and users.

Terminology. The authors above employ the term "user" when referring to the people directly engaged with the system, sometimes called "end users." I follow their lead in equating "user" with "end user." Terms such as "customer" and "buyer" refer to other people involved in system acquisition and use. Similarly, "developers" refers to active members of a development project, a relatively narrow definition that excludes those in management and support roles, whose contributions are described separately. Of course, developers are also users of the tools and the development system.

The term "functionality" describes the high-level system or application functions or operations that relate to the work the software supports, while "interface" or "user interface" describes the lower level operations and features that define the way users interact with the system. From the users' perspective, the functionality and the interface are intertwined aspects of usability and utility, but in a given project, the terms can be defined at different times by different people.

Identifying developers and users

Figure 1 presents three paradigms for software project development based on when users and developers are identified. The left edge of each horizontal bar represents the point when many of the project's developers or eventual users are known. Of course, not every project matches one of these time courses precisely. Also, it can be difficult to pin down events to one moment in time.

This framework best applies to projects that begin with a decision to build, modify, or replace a system or application and include a planned completion or delivery date. The three development paradigms describe a large set of projects that have significantly influenced interactive systems development.

In contract development or software acquisition, the user organization is known from the outset, but the development organization is identified after a contract is awarded. The clearest cases involve competitive bidding; for example, a government agency prepares a design specification for a new computer system and awards the contract to the developer with the most responsive bid. Actual practice can involve ambiguity or complications. The user organization may have some idea of who will get the contract; the user population may change before the system is completed, perhaps due to system personnel requirements; and contracts may be awarded in stages. But the essence of contract development is that the users are identified before the developers.

In product development, also called commercial off-the-shelf or shrink-wrap software development, the developers are known from the outset, but the users often remain unknown until the product is marketed. Of course, all product development begins with some idea of the intended customers, whether existing or new. But uncertainty about the eventual user population is an important facet of product development, as the unexpected fates of many products, positive as well as negative, remind us. The IBM PC and the Apple Macintosh are successful systems whose markets were not initially foreseen, whereas the designers of countless failed products anticipated user populations that did not materialize.

Finally, in in-house development, also called internal or information systems development, both the users and the developers are known at the project outset. (For example, a bank's computer services division develops a system for the bank's platform managers.) The user population may evolve or be too large or too dispersed to deal with individually, but the degree of initial identification is very high. This also occurs in custom development, where a specific external developer is engaged from the start to produce a system for a specific customer.

Projects may not be pure expressions of one paradigm. When a contract is negotiated without bidding, the developer has greater early involvement and encounters fewer restrictions on user access, a situation that lies somewhere between competitively bid contract development and in-house/custom development. Another paradigm merge occurs when a development company acquires a contract for a single system with the idea of subsequently developing it into a product. Similarly, an in-house project acquires some characteristics of product development when the organization features a large, diverse, and geographically dispersed user population (for example, when a bank's data processing department develops a system for branches that vary in size and operation).

It is not surprising that conditions for user participation vary across these development contexts. The timing gap between user and developer involvement in a prod-

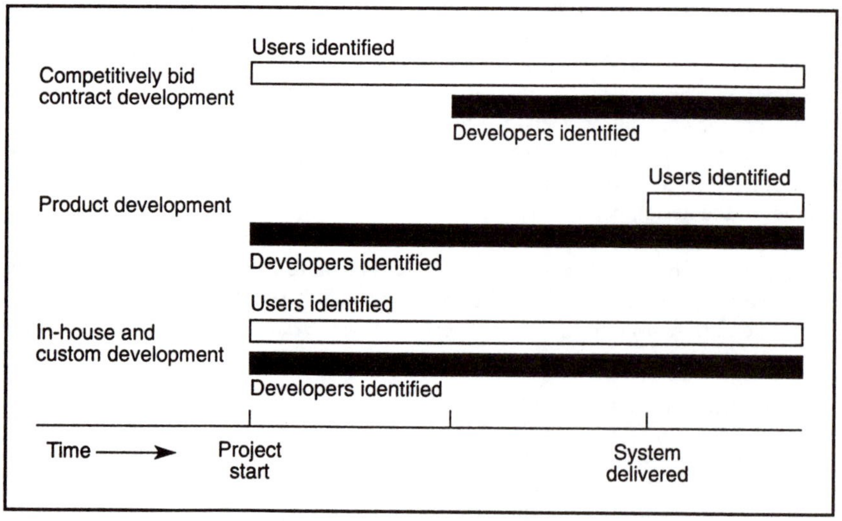

Figure 1. Project time lines with points of user and developer identification.

uct or competitively bid contract development project is an obstacle to collaboration. Many aspects of development practice have evolved to "communicate across time" — to bridge the gaps shown in Figure 1 — as well as to bridge the physical distances that often separate developers and users. These "bridges" or mediators include consultants, independent or third-party software developers and vendors, domain experts hired by development companies, internal market research or development groups, users and standards organizations, and flexible or multistage contracts.

Such mediation works better in some cases than in others. Keep in mind the chorus of recommendations that interactive systems developers establish and maintain continual contact with users, and the widening gulf between development and user environments. Intuition has become a less reliable guide to development, and the effectiveness of replacing it with indirect contact between developers and users must be continually reexamined.

The reliance on specifications documents imposes a "wall" between users and developers.

Three development contexts

Each of the paradigms or contexts in Figure 1 has contributed to contemporary practices of developing interactive systems while maintaining its own history, literature, and even language. Contract development has been central to the evolution of software project management methods; product development has focused attention on computer interfaces to individual users; and in-house development has explored social and organizational aspects of system use. Many people work exclusively in one paradigm or another. Understanding the different perspectives can eliminate some of the resulting confusion and allow us to evaluate approaches that are based on unfamiliar research and development experiences.

Contract development and a focus on software methods. From the beginning of commercial computer development, government contracts have been a powerful force in the industry. The United States government has been and remains the largest computer user.[8] Government-initiated large-scale projects focused attention on software development methods.

Major contributions to the stage model of systems development were first described at a 1956 Office of Naval Research Symposium and a 1966 Air Force Exhibit.[4] The waterfall model of the software life cycle became the basis for most government software-acquisition standards. This model describes an unvarying sequence of phases in which feasibility is established, requirements are specified, and preliminary and detailed designs are drawn up prior to coding. Then, these phases are followed by testing, integration, implementation (or installation), operation, and maintenance. This provides minimal opportunity for prototype testing and iterative design, which form the basis of ongoing user involvement.

The waterfall model restricts prototyping to "build-it-twice" development and restricts further iteration to feedback from adjacent phases. These limitations were recognized early by some software development managers and have been a source of criticism that has gathered force with the spread of interactive systems. But, the waterfall model is a natural fit to competitive contract development, where the user organization determines feasibility, prepares a requirements specification, and then issues one or more contracts for design, development, administration, and maintenance.

The waterfall model and its refinements were suited in other ways to the large, often government-contracted systems that dominated early systems development. The heavy emphasis on early design is more successful for relatively predictable, noninteractive systems, which have less uncertainty about requirements than systems that support substantial user interaction. In addition, the documentation and the distinct phases facilitate creation of an audit trail.

Strongly promoted by IBM, the waterfall model became the foundation for many structures and procedures found in most systems development. However, for today's interactive systems developer, the reliance on specifications documents imposes a "wall" between users and developers. This wall may not be impenetrable, but it clearly impedes user-based iterative design. The other development contexts are slowly freeing themselves from the problematic organizational structures and development practices that originated in contract development.

Product development and a focus on the user interface. As hardware costs fell and the market for computer systems broadened during the 1960s and 1970s, off-the-shelf product development grew in importance, especially in the United States. The discretionary nature of product acquisition means that systems must appeal to people, rather than meet written requirements specifications. However, product developers are buffered from end users by two intermediaries: the market and the customer.

With a large number of possible users, a product can do very well if only a fraction of the market finds it acceptable. In addition, especially in less mature markets, the product generally has to appeal to the customer — the person who makes the purchasing decision, often a manager or information systems specialist — not the end user. These customers share with the product development company the job of assuring system acceptance. The customer can hire systems administrators, provide training, establish internal development groups to tailor the product, supplement the product with third-party software, or even mandate use. Thus, just as the specification requirement in contract development is a wall between developers and users, the market and the customer in product development represent a thick hedge. Information about users' needs gets through, but it takes time and is muffled. Individual voices are not heard.

The delay in responding to users' needs allowed product development companies to focus on functionality, even if they met the usability needs of only a fraction of the potential users. Product development organizations could postpone attending to the human-computer dialogue while slowly finding indirect methods (consultants, market research, user groups, shows, trade press, etc.) to learn about major user needs. Now, as usability expectations increase in more mature software markets, product development companies are entering the phase in which users' needs replace software constraints as the dominant influence on development. We will see that the indirect, mediating organizational structures and processes that product developers formed to bridge the gap to users often inhibit direct user-developer contact.

Muffling individual users' voices meant that in the 1980s, as computer use spread and usability became an issue, product developers focused on the generic aspects of the human-computer dialogue that are shared by almost all users. Motor control, perception, and lower cognitive processes — the "look and feel" of software — were explored by researchers and developers in the field of human-computer interaction. Since the hardware, the software environment, and product functionality are typically specified before a product development team is formed, only these aspects of the user interface design remain to be defined.

A community focused on interface issues coalesced in 1983 with the formation of the ACM Special Interest Group on Computer and Human Interaction (SIGCHI). Industry representation at the annual CHI conferences and in the related journals (such as *Human-Computer Interaction*, established in 1985) has come predominantly from product development companies.

Developers could safely ignore social or organizational concerns when the spread of multitasking systems and personal computing made single-user systems and applications very profitable. The design and use of word-processor or spreadsheet programs, for example, are relatively independent of the social context in which they are used. The profits enabled American product development companies to form research groups, recruit heavily from leading universities, and influence the direction of academic research.

This field, human-computer interaction, has had less involvement from those working in contract development, where usability is taking even longer to come into focus. In-house development also remains relatively uninvolved, due in large part to differing interests: Internal development must focus on the individual and group differences and social dynamics that product developers can ignore; these are central to the acceptance of a specific in-house or custom-built system. In addition, the narrow "user interface" focus is less useful to in-house developers, who are more likely to consider functionality and its interface together.

In-house and custom development and a focus on user participation. In-house or internal development, in which the developers and users work under the same corporate roof, was the original development context. The early developers were also the users of their own systems. In the United States today, the other contexts have achieved greater visibility through their concentration of resources and association with the major computer manufacturers. But in-house development is a major generator of software (and in much of Europe, it is the most visible). This paradigm affords an obvious potential advantage to user participation in design: The developers and the eventual users are known when the project is initiated.

There is growing competitive pressure for usability in the marketplace and greater focus on the human-computer dialogue in contracts.

Potential obstacles to success do exist. Projects for multiuser systems are more challenging than single-user applications. Also, along with any benefits received by adopting the specifications-based waterfall model, internal developers created the documentation "wall" between themselves and users. This wall has less purpose in this environment, and it comes down immediately when the system is completed.

Many system design challenges for end users were first experienced in in-house development, where success required that a predefined set of users accept the system. Successful contract development requires conformance to a written specification; successful product development does not depend on appealing to a specific individual or group. But an internal development project must be accepted by a set group of users.

By the late 1970s or early 1980s, user needs replaced software constraints as the dominant concern within internal systems development.[8] It is not surprising that this occurred as soon as interactive systems began replacing batch processing. (A similar transition is under way, a decade later, in product development. Its arrival has been delayed by the market and the customer, which stand between off-the-shelf product developers and their users.) Design approaches based on active user involvement gathered strength, notably in British and Scandinavian projects. Many were collaborations between researcher-developers and specific user organizations; they shared the in-house development characteristic of identifying developers and prospective users at the outset.

Cultural and political factors, including a strong trade union movement, are often credited for the Scandinavian interest in collaborative design. While these factors surely contribute, the dominance of the in-house and custom development paradigm in these countries presented precisely the right motivation and conditions for such experiments. Unlike the situation in the United States, research and development resources were not absorbed by large competitively bid government contracts or by product development, contexts in which user needs have been slower to come into focus and in which conditions for engaging users in development are less favorable.

Today, usability is becoming more important to product and contract development organizations. These organizations are still to some extent buffered from the end users by the size of the product market and by the reliance on contract documents. However, resistance to unfriendly systems is growing. There is growing competitive pressure for usability in the marketplace, particularly in mature application domains, and greater focus on the human-computer dialogue in contracts. The success of the Macintosh in the mid-to-late 1980s was a turning point — a good interface drove hardware and software sales.

Product and contract developers who foresaw the importance of usability encountered obstacles to involving users. Few successful cases of user participation in development have been reported. For this reason, some researchers and developers are turning to Europeans who have a track record in such collaborations. For example, at the 1988 ACM-sponsored Conference on Computer Supported Cooperative Work held in Portland, Oregon, six of the 30 presentations were based on the Scandinavian approach. (Recent books and articles on this approach are listed in "Further reading.") Thus, just as contract and product development have influenced interactive systems development, work originating in in-house development contributes techniques and approaches.

Product and contract developers can gain

insight from the European approaches, but must bear in mind that in-house development is a different context. Today, product development projects in particular have acquired the same motivation to involve users that in-house development projects had 10 years ago. However, they experience different conditions within which to engage users. Roadblocks to a strong focus on users include the timing of involvement shown in Figure 1, as well as the organizational structures and processes that were established before the importance of the interaction dialogue. Adapting to the new situation may ultimately require substantial organizational change. We can guide that change, and work effectively in the meantime, by identifying each paradigm's unique advantages and disadvantages for realizing successful user participation in design and by understanding the alternatives to direct user involvement and their limitations.

Product development projects in particular have acquired the same motivation to involve users that in-house development projects had 10 years ago.

Factors influencing interactive systems development

Before exploring the opportunities and obstacles that each paradigm offers, let's consider several constraints on development projects that influence the conditions for user contact. One constraint, the time for involving development partners, was used to identify the three development paradigms: a single user organization for which there are many potential developers (contract development), a single development group with many potential users (product development), and a single development group with a single user organization (in-house development). Other factors include the size, charter, and structure of the development organization; the nature of the user population; the degree of design uncertainty; the presence or absence of other partners or contributors to the project; the nature of the commitments and agreements among the parties involved; societal conditions that the partners may be unable to control; and changes encountered over the life of the project.

The size of the development company or organization. This article generally focuses on projects in large organizations. A start-up or a small product development company may have fewer resources, less division of labor, fewer installed customer base concerns, and may succeed with far fewer sales than a larger company. These factors permit greater flexibility, more latitude for (inexpensive) innovation, and, particularly significant for user involvement, the possibility of focusing on a few potential customers (perhaps even finding a customer willing to cosponsor development). In these ways, a small product development company takes on some characteristics of in-house or custom development.

At the other end of the size continuum, very large companies also present mixed appearances. A large telecommunications company, for example, blends substantial internal development with opportunities for product development provided by its large, identifiable market. Similarly, in a highly divisionalized company, one division may "sell" its product to another or even bid for an internal contract to deliver a system.

The charter of the company or organization. Organizational charters vary, and a company may work in more than one paradigm. For example, large product-development companies pursue government contracts for systems that can be built on or around their products. A separate Federal Systems Division may manage these projects, but influences often cross divisional boundaries. Paradigms also blur when a product development company that considers entry into a new market experiments by custom building a system for one customer to obtain domain expertise. The Scandinavian UTOPIA project (an acronym in the Scandinavian languages for "training, technology, and products from the quality of work perspective") did the reverse experiment: Methods from the in-house/custom development paradigm were adapted to a product development effort.[9] An organizational charter shifts gradually when a company develops a system under contract to one user organization, then decides to market it more broadly. Finally, several influential Scandinavian projects have involved development teams drawn from university research laboratories, small groups with a mixed agenda of research and development interests.

Organizational structures and procedures. Companies that do similar work do not necessarily divide responsibilities and meet obligations in the same way. While certain job descriptions and work procedures are widespread in the industry, companies of similar size and charter organize, distribute authority, and approach system development differently. Marketing divisons drive some companies, while engineering drives others. Some are hierarchical bureaucracies, others are strongly divisionalized into semiautonomous subunits, and some have experimented with almost ad hoc approaches. An in-house project in a large, divisionalized company may be managed through a contract competed for by internal development groups. Even where high-level approaches to organizational structure and process are similar, small variations in structure and process can greatly affect individual development projects. Within a single company, such variation results from internal reorganizations.

The nature of the system user population. The generic term "user" masks a tremendous diversity of computer users and contexts of use. This diversity will continue to increase — even if progress in hardware development stopped today, current technology would take decades to realize its potential. The number and heterogeneity of users is often a particular concern to in-house development. More generally, some users are captive audiences, who use systems acquired for them by others, while others are discretionary users. At the extreme end of discretionary use, those who pay for their own systems become involved through their personal economic stake. An Apple developer told me, "We don't have to ask our users for advice; they volunteer it."

The physical separation of developers from some or all users is often critical, as are barriers of class, culture, or language. The sensitivity of the users' work is another factor: A group designing a system for the CIA may have to accept a limit to their ability to "know the users."

The degree of design novelty or uncertainty. The uncertainty that arises in designing for a new market or in utilizing a new medium not only affects the motivation for working with users but also affects the conditions for doing so. Experienced users are more easily found in a mature application area, and mediators — consultants, trade publications, empirical research — are more reliable sources of information about users or technical alternatives.

Mediators: additional partners in the development project. Although I have primarily considered users and developers, projects generally involve other parties. These parties include other groups within the development and user organizations, as well as external consultants, subcontractors, value-added resellers, independent software vendors, third-party developers, product user organizations, trade unions, and standards organizations. Inanimate mediators include published guidelines, trade publications, and trade shows.

The roles of such mediators are sometimes central, sometimes incidental; they include informing developers of users' needs and informing users of technological opportunities. A critical uncertainty in interactive systems development is the adequacy of these channels for indirect collaboration in development.

Commitments and agreements among the groups involved. Commitments vary in formality and scope, ranging from informal understandings between individuals within one organization to binding contracts among companies. They also vary in content, focus, and flexibility. The content can be restricted to technical aspects of the system or can include such commitments to the users as organizational impact statements, installation, or training. Similarly, an agreement can be restricted to the system to be developed or can specify aspects of the development process, including techniques to facilitate user involvement, such as prototyping or scheduled reviews. Contracts vary in flexibility — even a formal contract might include a level-of-effort provision or specify times at which its terms can be reconsidered, permitting design changes based on user involvement.[4,10]

Societal conditions and change over time. Projects encounter dynamic influences that the development partners cannot directly control.[10] These influences include aspects of the labor market, economic considerations of supply and competition, available technology, formal standards, and legal restrictions on technology use or safeguard requirements. Finally, the factors described in this section are subject to change within the life of a project; it is a rare project that enjoys static conditions from start to finish.

Focusing on users: Opportunities, obstacles, and mediators

Each project has particular advantages and disadvantages for involving users and specific strategies to cope with the gaps between developers and prospective users. These are explored here at the more general level of the three development paradigms.

Contract development. User involvement faces the most formidable obstacles in this context, especially with fixed-cost competitively bid contracts.

Opportunities. Starting with a well-defined user population is an advantage in obtaining user involvement. Of course, the users themselves do not write the specifications, but the opportunity exists to enlist their cooperation. (However, when specifications address only system function, such user involvement stops short of contributing to the user interface.) Also, contract development projects are often relatively large and slow moving (in contrast with an application upgrade, for example), which could provide substantial resources and time for iterative development with user involvement. High-level management is committed to the success of the project, which is an important factor in system acceptance. Finally, within constraints described below, the user organization has the power of authoring the contract and thus can obtain greater user involvement either directly or indirectly (that is, contract provisions may require prototyping or periodic review; interface features, usability targets, training requirements, or an organizational impact statement may be specified).

Obstacles. Consider a composite case described by Gundry[11]: The user organization, a large government agency, prepares a requirements specification. This is followed by a request for proposals (RFP) to develop the system design. A contract is awarded. This work results in a design specification that is the basis for an RFP for system development, which leads to the development contract award.

In the initial requirements specification executed within the large bureaucracy, user involvement is not assured. If a task analysis is done at all, it may rely on a few interviews of users or supervisors. Although interaction can occur before the RFP is issued, communication between designers in the bidding organizations and anyone in the user organization is then sharply curtailed and monitored to prevent a bidder from acquiring an unfair advantage.

When the contract for design is awarded, the designers work to the specification; by avoiding contact with the user organization, they avoid influencing the subsequent bidding on the more lucrative development contract. Since the follow-on development contract can be awarded to another company, the designers do not necessarily know who the developers will be. And, when the same company does obtain both the design and development contracts, as often happens, the development team is usually distinct from the design team, which has moved on to other design proposals. In addition, companies minimize risk by preparing joint bids, which spreads development across two or more organizations.

Contact with users continues to be controlled during development. This is for security or geographic separation reasons or to avoid influencing later bidding (on system administration, for example, or on system maintenance, which is often the most lucrative contract of all).

The designers and developers have another reason to avoid contact with users. Contract compliance is based on conformance to the written specifications. Any deviation from the specification is to be avoided: Programmers have been known to code nonfunctioning procedures described in miswritten specifications to avoid jeopardizing compliance. The development organization might prefer to commit to a relatively comprehensible and static document rather than try to satisfy unpredictable users. Usability requirements in contracts for interactive systems can be as vague as "the system shall present information succinctly" or "the system shall be easy to operate efficiently."[11]

Some contracts require that prototypes be demonstrated to users yet preclude or discourage changes based on feedback from the demonstrations. This only serves to alert users to the inadequacies of the system they will receive. When changes are possible, the developers may not learn much beyond "the system is unusable."

Mediators. Figure 2 shows several groups that serve as intermediaries, educating system users about contract developers and vice versa. Within a user organization, system analysts or engineers specify requirements, and contract specialists or monitors handle negotiations. Similar professionals in the development organizations write proposals and negotiate contracts, with developers not assigned to a project until contract award.

External consultants help the user organization by playing a surrogate developer role during requirements definition, providing the contracting organization with insight into feasible technologies. Although consultants are more likely to deal with managers or specialists, they may actively participate with users. Contractors working on one phase of the project are in a sense consulting on subsequent phases; for example, those who write the design specification provide guidance to the as-yet-unidentified developers. Similarly, developers who are barred from direct access to real users employ consultants familiar with the target environment to serve as surrogate users or hire domain experts away from a large customer to help staff the project.

User organizations address eventual shortcomings in the system through modifications by in-house or third-party developers. More broadly, contractors communicate their needs by working collectively with vendors to develop formal standards, adherence to which may be mandated in subsequent contracts. (A large enough customer organization, such as the United States Department of Defense, can by itself promote standards development and compliance.) Gundry[11] proposes that the contracting organization supplement the requirements specification with a "concepts of use" document: an extended description of the users, their work practices, and their working organization. That this static view of the users' environment is perceived by Gundry as a major step forward is a dramatic statement of how little contact between developers and users currently exists.

Government contracts impose further challenges to developing more usable systems. Cost-plus contracts reduce the incentive to reuse successful components; in fact, using a similar interface can suggest that the government is being charged twice for the same work. In addition, contractors who are also engaged in product development may be reluctant to place their best work in the public domain by including it in a government-owned system.

On the positive side, concurrent engineering and computer-aided acquisition and logistic support are new approaches that reduce development time by using centralized databases and multidisciplinary teams to reduce the emphasis on phased development. While designed for other purposes, the increased communication and coordination could promote continuous customer and user participation. Also, as noted above, the contract itself may be used to open up communication. Contractors may be required to describe planned human factors activities. Where legal barriers do not intervene, user involvement can be specified. Even a formal contract may address the uncertainties of dialogue design by providing points for renegotiation of contract terms based on prototype testing.[10] Experiments have been tried with design-to-cost contracts, reward-for-effort contracts, and "buy-downs" or "fly-offs": multistage contracts with a "competitive conceptual development phase" in which several developers build and test prototypes before the final development contract competition.

Product development. This context provides a strong incentive to increase usability, but user involvement is a challenge when the potential users are numerous yet faceless.

Opportunities. Because development costs are amortized over many sales, product development organizations typically have considerable resources and many potential users that could be drawn upon to improve usability. Competition in the marketplace provides a motive for doing so — the attention given to "look and feel" reflects the growing awareness of the importance of usability. Product development companies are major employers of human factors engineers, technical writers, and other user interface specialists. Continual

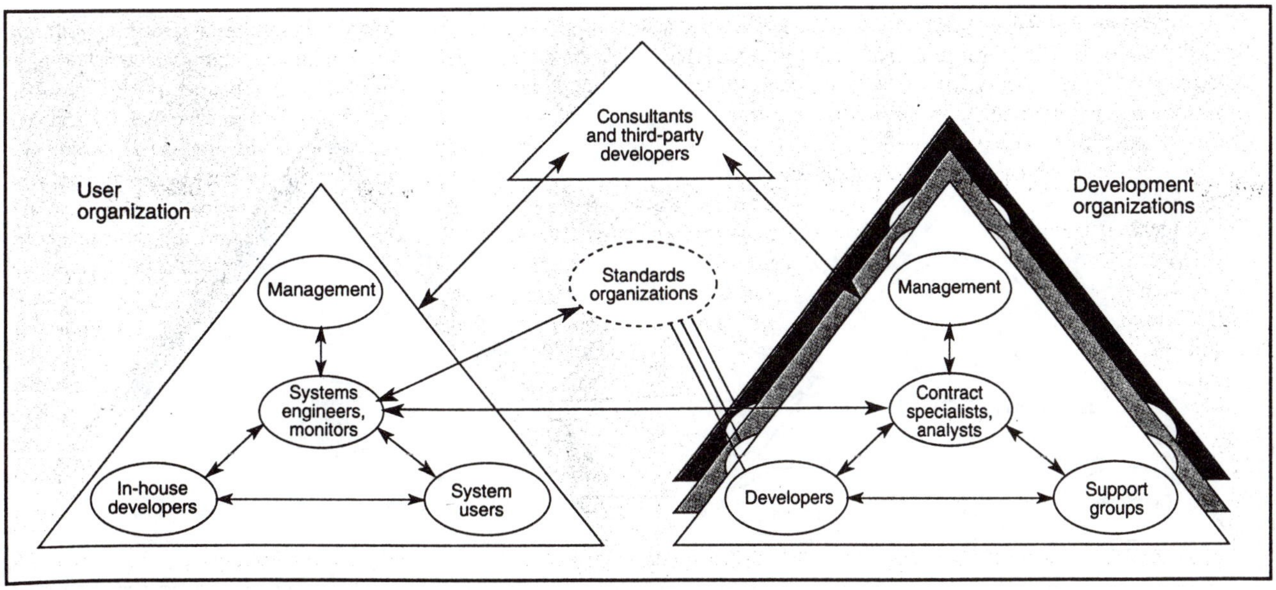

Figure 2. Contract development: Only the users are specified fully at the outset.

product upgrades or new releases free some developers from "single-cycle" development. They evaluate existing practice and feed it into the next version's design, and they may save good ideas that arrive too late for one project for use on another one. Finally, while these companies can succumb to inertia or conservative forces, they were founded on change and at some level recognize that survival requires openness to new ideas and approaches.

Obstacles. First, the development team members must commit to involving users. Developers who are isolated in large engineering laboratories may not empathize or sympathize with users who are inexperienced, nontechnical, or have different values and work styles. Even identifying the development team is difficult: Functionality is defined by management or marketing before the project team is formed, project membership changes over time, and the developers of different user interface components — such as software dialogue, documentation, and training — often communicate very little. In many companies, placing all aspects of a product's usability under the same management would conflict with deeply rooted aspects of organizational structure and process.

Also, the difficulty of identifying future users is a major obstacle to involving them. Strategic marketing decisions are carefully guarded by upper management to prevent the competition from using the information. Development teams often do not know which applications will be marketed as packages. In addition, before reaching an end user, many products are extensively modified or tailored by third-party developers or by the customer's in-house developers. These developers are users of the product, too.

Another obstacle is accessing potential users once they are identified. They work in different organizations, perhaps even different countries. Also, product development companies tend to shield developers from the time-consuming task of responding to individual user requests.

Figure 3 identifies several groups charged with knowing the needs of users: product management, marketing, and customer support in the development organization, and information systems specialists in the user organization. These go-betweens or mediators often discourage direct developer-user contact, either overtly or by partly alleviating the need for it.

These mediators are often ineffective conduits for usability information because the task is difficult and the usability concerns are new. It is particularly difficult in this context to obtain adequate time from potential users, who have little at stake. When contact does occur, product developers risk overgeneralizing from a few contacts, and they must contend with conflicting views of different users. (Careful selection of test sites happens primarily for major products and relatively late in development.) Finally, information that is obtained must be worked into the development process, which is fraught with competing interests and trade-offs. The process was designed to maximize the predictability and reliability of developing noninteractive systems; it does not work as well for developing the less predictable interactive systems.

Another obstacle is the pressure to produce new releases of existing products — the relatively short development cycle favors small enhancements over substantial innovation and does not provide enough time for users and developers to educate one another. Caution is also encouraged by the new fear of incurring an interface copyright infringement suit. Emphasis on rapid development engenders attempts to routinize the process through the early approval of specifications and schedules, which limits flexibility.

One approach that product developers pioneered to overcome their separation from users is providing customized or tailored systems, which is a useful step but not a panacea. Another approach has been to rely on mediators.

Mediators. As shown in Figure 3 and described above, sales and marketing departments, management, customer support, and other groups within large product-development companies mediate between users and developers. Other developers form part of a corporate memory that for usability issues can operate more effectively than formal records. External consultants serve as surrogate users, providing developers with detailed product critiques and information on market direction. Consulting, market research, and competitive

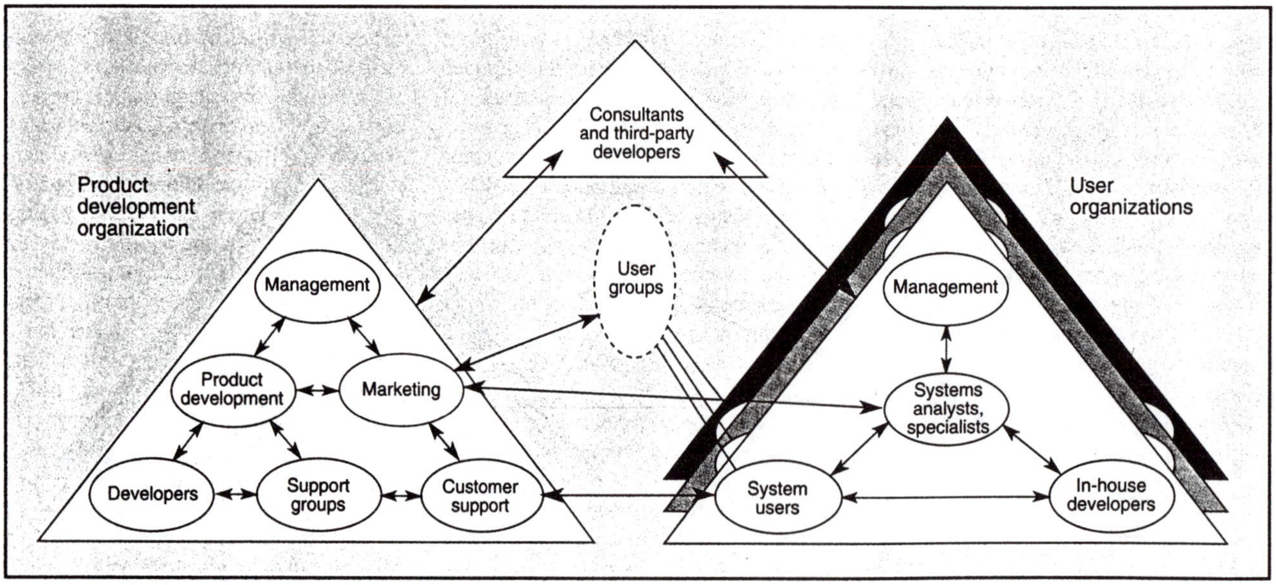

Figure 3. Product development: Only the development group is fully specified at the outset.

analysis, although undertaken to support the marketing of existing products, can also guide developers. Value-added resellers, third-party developers and independent software vendors, who adapt or match products to specific markets, stand between development and user organizations. Customer organizations engage consultants as surrogate developers to advise them about purchasing or installation. Buyers also rely on in-house developers to supplement or tailor products.

Most customers exert little direct influence on product development companies individually, but user groups representing many customers have more influence. However, this communication channel is less effective when meetings are attended by customers or buyers rather than users and by marketers rather than developers.

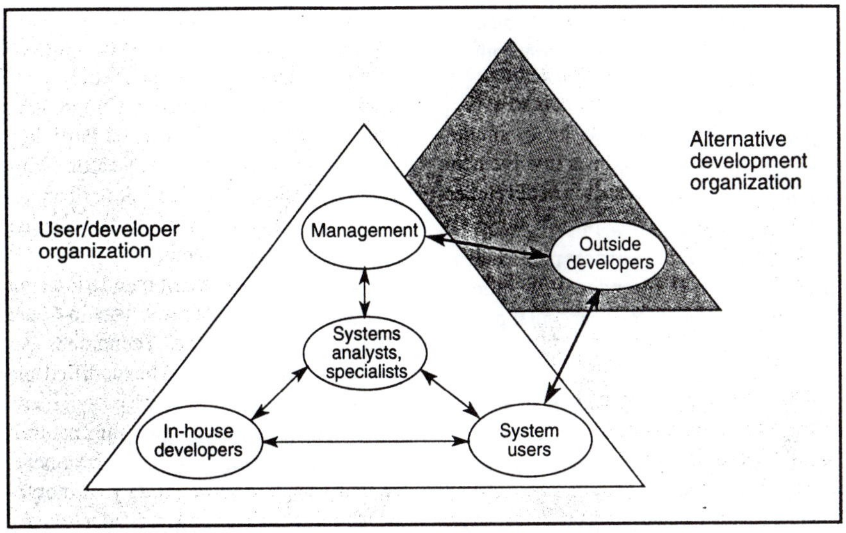

Figure 4. In-house and custom development: Developer and user populations are known at the outset.

In-house development. This development context appears to offer good prospects for collaboration among users and developers, but the challenges are substantial. One challenge is that internal development is often modeled on contract development, adopting methods that work against user involvement.

Opportunities. Collaboration is logically easier when users and developers are known from the beginning (see Figure 4). An early relationship can lead to parallel work on the functionality and the interface and is needed for prototyping and iterative design. User involvement can also help with system acceptance because participating users acquire an interest in the outcome; they may accept system features that they otherwise would have resisted.[8] In in-house development, communication between developers and users can be enhanced by the shared corporate culture (but see below). Also, the transitions across development phases are smoother; in particular, the developers are accessible during product introduction and use. A further advantage is that these projects have strong management support, an important element in obtaining system acceptance. Finally, they often enjoy a less pressured, more flexible development schedule — shifting focus from the product to the development process occurs most naturally in this environment.

Obstacles. In-house projects are generally systems or major applications designed to support organizations, which are more difficult than the single-user applications that dominate software product development. In addition, identifying future users is easier than ensuring collaboration. Large companies may impose geographic as well as organizational separations. Conflicts of interest exist within organizations: Management or information systems staff themselves may be the principal beneficiary of a project; if their interests conflict with the end users', user alienation is more likely than cooperation. Conflicts also occur among different worker groups — Ehn[9] describes jurisdictional disputes among typesetters, journalists, and administrative workers in one project. Friction between developers and users can result from differing codes of values, conduct, and dress, as well as disparities in age and salary.[8]

Selecting representative users is a challenge. Not all potential users have the time or inclination to participate fully, management may wish to participate or to control participant selection, and workers with greater knowledge of technology may be more interested but less representative. Potential participants' political roles in the organization must be balanced against their roles as system users. In addition, some techniques must be used very carefully in internal development — rapid prototyping can unduly raise users' expectations of the system's capabilities or state of completion. (This problem also appears as the rapid-prototyping technique is introduced in contract development; in product development, where disappointing one potential user is not as serious, the risk is that development management will be misled.)

Fewer resources may be available to in-house development projects than to contract or product-development projects. Building a single system to be used for many years provides less opportunity for evaluation, feedback, and catching missed opportunities the next time around than is found in product development. Prototyping and iterative design are not infinitely flexible, so the in-house development team must plan very carefully, considering, for example, the likely organizational impact. Such planning is beneficial, but given the inherent uncertainty of interactive systems development, the need to anticipate correctly is not an advantage.

Mediators. The spread of interactive systems in the early 1980s immediately confronted in-house developers with the needs of end users. The mediators who enabled the other developers to adjust slowly while delaying their entry into this phase are less available to in-house developers. Only upper management or human resources departments typically intervene between internal developers and users.

Friedman[8] explores five possible approaches to bridging the gap between users and developers in internal development: direct user participation in development based on traditional methods, end user computing (effectively, trying to eliminate developers by providing systems that can be tailored or customized by users), decentralizing the information center (to bring developers into closer contact with users), changing the systems development approach (through a process focus, notably an emphasis on prototyping and iterative design), and relying more heavily on information systems specialists with both domain expertise and development skills. These are not mutually exclusive: The Scandinavian experiments have simultaneously employed direct user involvement, prototyping, and the education of developers about the domain area. In fact, these approaches are all forms of user participation, if participation is extended to include the education that precedes a particular project.

Several convergent forces push interactive systems development toward greater concern for users' needs. First, reaching untapped markets requires learning more about them. Computer versatility enhances the likelihood of finding a way to support a group of people whose concerns are properly understood. Second, users who can choose their tools will be influenced by usability in exercising this discretion. The focus on "look and feel," while reflecting aesthetic as well as utility judgments, arises from the availability of functionally equivalent product alternatives in mature markets. Third, understanding user needs is more central to software support of groups.

Until recently, mainframe systems focused on supporting organizations while most micro- and minicomputer applications focused on supporting individuals. Now, networking and multitasking systems make group-level support feasible. "Groupware" product developers face issues that were previously encountered mainly in in-house development as the focus of application development shifts from individual similarities (with the goal of appealing to a large group of similar people) to individual differences and social dynamics (to attract all members of groups, independent of background, role, or preferences). Here, application developers are at a disadvantage relative to system developers, since there is less corporate commitment to ensuring the acceptance of a groupware product than a large system. Finally, the cost of computation was a major obstacle to providing more usable systems. As processing time, memory, and maintenance costs continue to fall, more computational power is devoted to handling user interaction. Today, the price to obtain a better interface is not much more than the cost of building or buying one.

In summary, computer vendors' interests, computer users' interests, and economic factors work in concert to encourage the development of more usable software. Further progress will result from sharing experiences across the three development contexts. Conferences such as the 1988 Computer Supported Cooperative Work Conference and the 1990 Participatory Design Conference in Seattle bring together Scandinavian and American researchers and developers from in-house and product development.

Boehm[4] outlines recommendations for contract development drawn from in-house development experience. Techniques developed in one context can be modified and applied in others. The process focus and low-cost techniques that developed naturally in in-house development environments are being applied more broadly. Prototyping techniques first used in product development are being adapted to in-house projects. Further contact occurs as in-house projects come to rely more heavily on off-the-shelf software product components and as contracts specify more standard platform products.

The prevalence of specific development contexts may shift with societal changes. For example, the current integration of the European community will promote competitively bid contract development to ensure equal access to large projects. Europeans may profit from American experience and find ways to introduce approaches that achieve higher levels of user involvement.

Such communication requires effort. Many interests are not shared; there are specialized terminologies, journals, trade publications, conferences, and shows. Even word meanings vary across development contexts; for example, "implementation" is a synonym for "development" or "coding" to product developers, while it means "installation" or "adoption" elsewhere. "End user" or "operator" to an in-house developer is just "user" in a product environment.

Procedures take on different appearances: To a contract or in-house developer, a "task analysis" generally addresses repetitive activity carried out in an organizational context by an "operator" hired to perform it, whereas to a product developer, a "task analysis" is more often a cognitive analysis of individual behavior in a less structured, discretionary use situation.

Techniques are viewed differently: Internal developers (and many in the research community) link software "evaluation" to testing that occurs late in development, when only minor design changes are possible; in contrast, product design is more likely to begin with the evaluation of existing products or versions, so "evaluation" has a less negative ring to product developers.

Finally, confusion may result from failing to differentiate among the contexts, as illustrated by the debate over the routinization of software development. In large product development organizations, strong competition and the pressure for frequent releases create a strong desire to control the development process and to render it immune to the loss of any individual — conditions leading to "deskilling," where individual developers are given less responsibility and become more expendable. However, a tendency toward deskilling is not reported in internal development, where competitive pressures are lower and developers increase their value to their organization by acquiring domain knowledge.[8]

References to "the computer industry" disguise the multiplicity of computer industries that have evolved. They share a need to examine current practices and search for new ones to meet the challenge of developing usable, useful interactive software. Only by recognizing the range of existing conditions and their effects can we adapt the hard-earned lessons of one development context and apply them in others. The potential benefits are new techniques, processes, and organizational structures for development. ■

Acknowledgments

Morten Kyng and the Systemarbejde Group at Aarhus University provided the time and inspiration for developing this paper. Kaj Grønbæk, Susanne Bødker, and Liam Bannon participated in its iterative design. Andrew Friedman's book was further inspiration and an excellent resource on internal development. Bob Glushko, Henry Lahore, Jane Mosier, Scott Overmyer, Steve Poltrock, and Craig Will contributed to my understanding of contract development, although their full understanding is not reflected. Elizabeth Dykstra and Tom Erickson provided useful suggestions. Students at Aarhus University commented helpfully on earlier drafts. Also, anonymous *Computer* reviews were invaluable.

References

1. J.D. Gould and C.H. Lewis, "Designing for Usability — Key Principles and What Designers Think," *Proc. CHI83 Human Factors Computing Systems*, 1983, pp. 50-53.

2. D.A. Norman and S.W. Draper, *User Centered System Design: New Perspectives in Human-Computer Interaction*, Lawrence Erlbaum Associates, Hillsdale, N.J., 1986.

3. L. Suchman, "Designing with the User," ACM *Trans. Office Information Systems*, Vol. 6, 1988, pp. 173-183.

4. B. Boehm, "A Spiral Model of Software Development and Enhancement," *Computer*, Vol. 21, No. 5, May 1988, pp. 61-72.

5. E. Yourdon, *Modern Structured Analysis*, Yourdon Press, New York, 1989.

6. T. De Marco, *Structured Analysis and System Specification*, Yourdon Press, New York, 1978.

7. M. Jackson, *System Development*, Prentice Hall, Englewood Cliffs, N.J., 1983.

8. A.L. Friedman, *Computer Systems Development: History, Organization and Implementation*, John Wiley & Sons, Chichester, UK, 1989.

9. P. Ehn, *Work-Oriented Design of Computer Artifacts*, Arbetslivcentrum, Stockholm, 1988.

10. K. Grønbæk et al., "Cooperative System Design: Shifting from Product to Process Focus," to be published in *Participatory Design*, D. Schuler and A. Namioka, eds., Lawrence Erlbaum Associates, Hillsdale, N.J., 1991.

11. A.J. Gundry, "Humans, Computers, and Contracts," *People and Computers IV*, D.M. Jones and R. Winder, eds., Cambridge University Press, Cambridge, United Kingdom, 1988.

Further reading

In-house development: the new interest in Scandinavian approaches. As noted in the text and described in the cited work of Friedman and Suchman, interest is growing in the Scandinavian participatory design approach based on the in-house and custom development paradigm. Examples of recent or forthcoming publications:

Bjerknes, G., P. Ehn, and M. Kyng, eds., *Computers and Democracy — A Scandinavian Challenge*, Gower, Aldershot, United Kingdom, 1987.

Bødker, S., *Through the Interface: A Human Activity Approach to User Interface Design*, Lawrence Erlbaum Associates, Hillsdale, N.J., 1991.

Docherty, P., et al., eds., *System Design for Human Development and Productivity: Participation and Beyond*, North-Holland, Amsterdam, 1987.

Ehn, P., *Work-Oriented Design of Computer Artifacts*, Lawrence Erlbaum Associates, Hillsdale, N.J., 1989.

Floyd, C., et al., "Out of Scandinavia: Alternative Approaches to Software Design and System Development," *Human-Computer Interaction*, Vol. 4, No. 4, 1989, pp. 253-349.

Greenbaum, J. and M. Kyng, eds., *Design at Work: Cooperative Design of Computer Systems*, Lawrence Erlbaum Associates, Hillsdale, N.J., 1991.

Howard, R., "Utopia: Where Workers Craft New Technology," *Technology Review*, April 1985, pp. 43-49.

Schuler, D. and A. Namioka, eds., *Participatory Design*, Lawrence Erlbaum Associates, Hillsdale, N.J., to be published in 1991.

Product development: the focus on usability in the late 1980s. Among the many works published, articles explicitly considering the product development environment include:

Gould, J.D., "How to Design Usable Systems," M. Helander, ed., *Handbook of Human-Computer Interaction*, North-Holland, Amsterdam, 1988.

Grudin, J., "Systematic Sources of Suboptimal Interface Design in Large Product Development Organizations," to be published in *Human-Computer Interaction*, Vol. 6, No. 2, 1991.

Grudin, J., and S. Poltrock, "User Interface Design in Large Corporations: Coordination and Communication Across Disciplines," *Proc. CHI89 Human Factors Computing Systems*, Apr. 1989.

Poltrock, S.E., "Innovation in User Interface Development: Obstacles and Opportunities," *Proc. CHI89 Human Factors Computing Systems*, Apr. 1989.

Contract development: starting to address usability concerns. In addition to the Gundry paper cited in the text there are the following sources:

Overmyer, S.P., "The Impact of DoD-Std-2167A on Iterative Design Methodologies: Help or Hinder?" *ACM SIGSoft Software Engineering Notes*, Vol. 15, No. 5, pp. 50-59, 1990.

Smith, S.L., "User-System Interface Design in System Acquisition," Tech. Report ESD-TR-84-158 Air Force Electronic Systems Division, Hanscom Air Force Base, Mass., 1984.

Jonathan Grudin is a visiting associate professor of computer science at Aarhus University, Denmark. His interests include systems development in large organizations and the effects of systems on organizations.

He received a BA in mathematics/physics from Reed College, an MS in mathematics from Purdue University, and a PhD in psychology from University of California at San Diego.

After spending several years as a systems developer at Wang Laboratories, he worked in the MCC Human Interface Laboratory, studying the development process at MCC shareholder companies. Past publications range from *Byte* to the *Communications of the ACM*.

The author can be reached at Aarhus University, Computer Science Department, Ny Munkegade, Building 540, 8000 Aarhus C, Denmark; e-mail jgrudin@daimi.aau.dk.

Interdisciplinary Cooperation

Scott Kim
Look Twice, Inc.

#$(*&% @ to You, Too!

IN THE EARLY DAYS, computers and software were designed by engineers for engineers. Nowadays they are designed by teams that include psychologists, artists, and writers, as well as engineers and programmers. Because many of these alliances are new, misunderstandings naturally arise. Here is a typical exchange between a graphic designer and a programmer.

Designer: *I'm interested in computers. Can you help?*

Programmer: *Gladly! What would you like to know?*

Designer: *What can I do with this computer?*

Programmer: *Anything you want.*

Designer: *Marvelous! Show me a page of text.*

Programmer: *Okay.*

Designer: *But that looks ugly.*

Programmer: *That's the font that's built into the machine.*

Designer: *I guess that's the way computers look.*

Programmer: *No, you could change the font, too.*

Designer: *Okay, let's redesign it.*

Programmer: *But it would take a lot of work. And besides, I don't see anything wrong with this one.*

Designer: *Can't you see what's in front of you?*

Programmer: *Can't you tell me the rules?*

Both people walk away frustrated. The programmer feels annoyed that the artist doesn't appreciate the work involved; the designer feels outraged that the programmer cannot see the obvious. Yet both people started with good intentions. What is going on? How can such situations be improved?

This article is about interdisciplinary cooperation and how to make it work better. The ideas are based on my recent studies at Stanford University as an interdisciplinary graduate student in computers and graphic design. I conclude that disciplines are like cultures: for disciplines to work well together they must learn to appreciate one another's language, traditions, and values. I raise these issues here because human-computer interface design is a particularly interdisciplinary field. For interface design to thrive, many disciplines must cooperate.

Different Disciplines Have Different Priorities

Different disciplines have different priorities, different thinking styles, different values. When people from different disciplines get together, their values collide. What one person finds valuable others do not even notice. And they do not notice that they do not notice.

I first understood this effect some years ago when I started as a graduate student at Stanford. Computer science professor Donald Knuth had just developed a programming language for typeface design called Metafont. I liked Metafont's mix of artistic and technical considerations.

Metafont allows a designer to design a typeface by writing a program, rather than by drawing shapes on paper. Programming a typeface allows a designer to make systematic variations—like changing the thickness of all strokes—without having to redraw each letter individually. Knuth's dream was to enable designers to express the structural ideas of their typefaces in a precise notation akin to music notation.

As the resident programmer/artist I had the pleasure of demonstrating Metafont to many outstanding typeface designers. Over and over I heard the same demand: make it more visual. Designers said they would prefer to work directly with images on the screen, rather than type programs to produce images.

The obvious solution was a more graphic version of Metafont, similar to computer-aided design or painting programs that are common today. But I felt there was a deeper issue. I decided to keep probing.

The key question seemed to be "What is the difference between the thinking styles of a computer scientist and a graphic designer?" (Here I am lumping the concerns of typeface designers with the concerns of visual communicators in general.) The computer science department proved a hostile environment for thinking about this question. The art department was no better. Each found the other way of thinking incomprehensible.

The explanation was simple: computer scientists and graphic designers have different priorities. Computer scientists value the program and how it works; graphic designers value the picture and how it looks. This difference is the primary source of misunderstanding between computer scientists and graphic designers.

In computer science, the life or death struggle is getting the program to run. The entire programming environment supports this single task. Other things matter also—a computer will not run without electricity—but those jobs can be delegated. Until the program works, a programmer feels obsessed. It is hard for a programmer to say "Oh, my program crashed, no problem. I'll just go home and come back tomorrow." If you want to talk to a programmer, it is important to know that you will not be trusted unless you have written a program. The program can be simple; all that matters is that you have experienced the basic drama of programming.

In graphic design, the life or death struggle is getting the picture to look right. The entire studio environment supports this single task. Other things matter also—a painting will not survive without proper paint chemistry—but those jobs can be delegated. Until the picture works, an artist feels obsessed. It is hard for an artist to say "Oh, my composition doesn't balance, no problem. I'll just go home and come back tomorrow." If you want to talk to an artist, it is important to know that you have not gotten down to the real business until you start looking at pictures. It does not matter what you say; the proof is in the portfolio.

Programs and pictures—each of these priorities is so obvious to someone within the discipline that it goes without saying, but so foreign to someone outside the discipline that it is almost unthinkable. As a result, outsiders not already attuned to the priorities of a discipline have difficulty breaking in.

Any self-respecting programmer will probably be outraged that I have reduced programming to mere coding. Isn't solving the user's problem the true priority of programming? Likewise, designers will be outraged that I have reduced design to mere production. Isn't clear communication the true priority of design? In both cases I emphasize the bottom-line survival priorities of a field rather than the conceptual goal-oriented priorities, because it is the survival priorities of a field that shape its culture.

Once I had isolated the issue of priorities, I was free to wonder what would happen if priorities were rearranged. Metafont is a computer scientist's approach to a graphic design task. The reverse of computer-aided design is design-aided computation. What would be a graphic designer's approach to a computer science task? This led me to my dissertation, which asks how computers might be different if they were designed for use by visual artists.

Flexible Humans and Rigid Disciplines

Here is a theory of disciplines that explains why miscommunication between disciplines occurs.

Disciplines Develop When Flexible Humans Meet Recurring Situations

When a human encounters a new situation, the human must invent a new response. If the situation occurs repeatedly, the human may find it more economical to develop a single habitual response than to invent a new response each time.

If the repeated situation affects many people, society may find it worthwhile to teach the habit as a practice. If the practice is worth improving, society may find it worthwhile to create a field of study around the practice. The field of study is a discipline.

Disciplines, like all human tools, are by nature rigid. A hammer must be hard, or it does not work. A theory must be precise, or it cannot be tested. A discipline must have traditions, or it cannot be passed on. Rigid tools give humans leverage.

Every Discipline Has a Hierarchy of Priorities Derived from the Survival Needs of the Original Situation

The same holds for habits or practices. In life itself, priorities include eating, sleeping, and breathing. In driving, priorities include staying on the road, having enough gas, and not colliding with other cars. In computer science, priorities include getting programs to run, not losing data, and keeping programs maintainable. In graphic design, priorities include anticipating the appearance of a printed piece before it is printed, communicating instructions accurately to printers, and visual consistency.

Priorities pervade every aspect of a discipline, including social organization, physical artifacts, training procedures, and specialized language. Priorities are not necessarily easy to meet; but because they are a matter of survival, enormous effort goes into their maintenance.

Everyone must eat, so society is organized to deliver food. Cars need roads, so an enormous network of roads webs the nation. Programs must be maintainable, so programmers organize programs according to conventions of structured programming. Colors must be printed accurately, so printers use special language for naming colors.

When a Discipline Becomes a Way of Life, Priorities Become Invisible

The nature of habit is to be unconscious. If you had to think about every footstep, walking would be mentally exhausting.

When you are surrounded by people who share the same habit, the habit becomes accepted as part of the natural order of things. It is hard to hear your own speech as having an accent, unless you have learned more than one way of speaking. Likewise, it is hard for programmers to remember that not everyone thinks in sequential logical terms, and for graphic designers to remember that not everyone looks for visual patterns.

Current society links personal identity to job category. You are not a person who drives buses; you are a bus driv*er*. You are not a person interested in philosophy; you are a philosopher. Because jobs are linked to physical survival in the form of money, disciplinary priorities become personal priorities.

The invisibility of disciplinary priorities is both good and bad. On the one hand, they allow people within the same discipline to communicate more efficiently. On the other hand, they prevent people from noticing that their responses may no longer be appropriate.

When Priorities Are Threatened, Survival Feels Threatened

When people from different disciplines get together, their priorities are bound to misalign. The mismatches lead to the upsetting feeling that what one person considers important is being ignored by the other person.

This would not be a problem except for two points: because people identify with their disciplines, the insult is taken personally, and because priorities are invisible, the matter is not available for discussion. Each person feels personally attacked, and cannot figure out why.

I want to emphasize that interdisciplinary miscommunication is a direct result of the rigid nature of disciplines. It is not anybody's fault. It is not to be taken personally. And it is not insurmountable.

Why You Should Stick Your Nose into Other People's Business

Interdisciplinary cooperation sounds good in principle. In practice, there are many doubts.

It's Not My Job

Certainly your first responsibility in a work situation is your job. But part of your job is to know what is not your job. Unless you understand where your job ends and someone else's begins, you will try to do work that is beyond your ability. And you will miss opportunities for creative synergy.

For instance, programmers who do not understand the contribution of artists to visual interface design often try to design screen layouts themselves and resist suggestions for improvement. Graphic designers who do not understand the capabilities of computers often design for the screen as if it were paper and miss the visual continuity problems of a dynamic medium. Together, a programmer and a graphic designer can create something much stronger than what either could create alone.

Yes, But It Really Is Someone Else's Job

You may be right. But sometimes circumstances force us to do jobs outside our area of expertise, especially in small companies or innovative projects.

Yes, But My Job Really Is Self-contained

It is true that some jobs require less cooperation than others. If you are working by yourself on a job with tightly defined goals, you may have little need to talk with others. Talking with others can still help by giving you new ways of thinking about your discipline.

I Already Know What I Need to Know

No job in the computer industry stays the same for long. Job definitions keep changing as computers themselves change. For instance, technical writers need to keep learning more about graphic design as publishing software unifies text and illustration.

I Can't Afford the Time

Of course you cannot spend all your time learning about other disciplines. Decide for yourself how much time you can afford, then think about how to use it efficiently. If you never take time to explore, you will never find out what you are missing.

I Can't Go Back and Get Another Degree

Social pressures make it seem like you have to study for years before you are qualified to ask questions. The truth is that beginners often ask the most profound questions. And you do not have to be an expert to make good use of expert advice. You need to learn only as much as you find useful. No matter where you are, you can always make the best use of what you know.

I Tried, But I Couldn't Make Sense of the Jargon

People within a discipline often have trouble communicating what they know to outsiders. This is frustrating to everyone. Your best guide is probably someone from your own discipline who has already learned the new jargon.

I'm Scared of Looking Stupid

To take the pressure off yourself, imagine you are a reporter assigned to do a story on this other discipline. Ask intelligent questions readers might be interested in. Insist the answers be in terms that you, as a representative of your readers, can understand. If that is still too scary, take along a bodyguard. Treat your subject as you would like to be treated if the roles were reversed. If someone came to you and cheerfully mentioned that they would love to learn about a subject you know well, how would you respond?

I Can't Think That Way

You may feel like you cannot think about some other discipline, but such feelings are probably due to early discouragements ("math isn't lady-like," "art is for sissies"). Given enough support, there is no reason you cannot learn anything you want. Imagine you are an actor playing the role of an expert in another discipline. Rise to the occasion despite feelings of insecurity.

When I Need to Know, I'll Hire a Specialist

That is fine, as long as you know enough about the specialty to bring the specialist in early enough. A good solution is to talk to the specialist at the very beginning of a project, to figure out when the expertise will be most helpful. The specialist must also know about your area; otherwise, communication will be difficult.

How Do I Know It Will Be Relevant?

You don't. It is a risk. But not risking can be risky too. So you might as well give it a try. No one can judge relevance but you. And you cannot make judgments until you have collected all the facts impartially. Collect now, judge later.

This Is How We've Always Done It

Consider changing. Human-computer interface design is certainly improving, but without better interdisciplinary cooperation the field will continue to suffer large holes. For instance, most psychologists studying computers assume text dialog or window/menu interfaces. But these are only two possible interface styles among thousands. Unless psychologists talk to designers who are free to imagine alternate interface styles, their studies have no basis for drawing general conclusions.

It's Too Hard

It was once. But it does not have to be. That is what this paper is about.

How To Be an Interdisciplinary Ambassador

Disciplines are like cultures. For disciplines to work well together they must transcend national boundaries and learn to appreciate one anothers' cultures. Here are six steps you can take to improve interdisciplinary understanding.

1. **Patriot.** Start by being proud of your own discipline. If your discipline is systematically undervalued, you may find this exercise difficult. But before you can appreciate others you must be able to appreciate yourself.

   Think of a patriot. Appreciate the struggles and triumphs of your people. Recall what first interested you about your discipline. List persuasive reasons why your discipline has tremendous value. Value your discipline without devaluing other disciplines.
2. **Tour guide.** The first step towards interdisciplinary understanding is to welcome visitors from other disciplines, just because they are who they are, whether or not you understand anything about their culture. Interdisciplinary communication can happen only where there is unconditional respect.

   Think of a tour guide. Your job is to make your guests feel comfortable, learn a bit about them, and share aspects of your land they will find interesting. Your job is not to criticize your visitors for being from the wrong place, to convince them that your way is right, or to protect your secrets.
3. **Traveler.** The next step is to learn about other disciplines. Interdisciplinary understanding can happen only when both disciplines have experienced the other's culture.

   Think of a world traveler. Make plans to visit another discipline. Read about the discipline's history, learn a bit of the language, talk to travelers who have been there before. Live as a native. Be open to new experiences. Do not only eat hamburgers. Replace fear of the unknown with curiosity and a spirit of adventure. Once you start traveling, you will find yourself in the company of other travelers.
4. **Pen pal.** Interdisciplinary relationships are based on personal relationships. Start building your worldwide community one person at a time.

   "I'm interested in hearing about what you do, and telling you about what I do. I realize we come from different backgrounds, but there's no reason we can't be friends. Your way of thinking is just as valid as my way, I can learn to appreciate its value, and it will be valuable for me to understand it. Ask me anything you want to know about my discipline and I will do my best to answer."
5. **Ambassador.** The next step is to establish diplomatic relations between pairs of disciplines.

   Think of an ambassador. Learn to speak both languages. Learn to live in both cultures. Work with people in both disciplines toward common goals. Be committed to overcoming inevitable disagreements. Diplomacy is a slow process of building trust. Building trust requires active testing of faith. Do not accept simple answers. Question everything and do what it takes to find out the truth.

   Diplomatic relations are difficult if the two disciplines are fighting over the same turf, so do not wait until a crisis before you step in. To maintain neutrality, an ambassador should not be in a power relationship with either discipline.

   When explaining one discipline to people in another discipline, your first responsibility is to explain persuasively why they need to know about this other discipline, not to turn them into instant experts. Start from where they are. Use examples they care about. Show the effects of the other discipline on their discipline. Demonstrate the bad consequences of ignoring this other discipline. Outline the general principles of the other discipline; avoid details. Standard introductory courses probably will not work, because they are often addressed to people who are already in the same frame of mind as the discipline.
6. **World citizen.** Think of the world as your home. Take pleasure in the diversity of cultures. Borrow freely from all disciplines. Get help when

> you need it. Where one discipline is weak, look for another that is strong. See to it that all disciplines benefit. Assemble interdisciplinary teams that work together as equals from the beginning. Agree on goals early.
>
> When disciplines merge, the results can be outstanding. The painting program MacPaint, which gave thousands of people their first positive experience of computers and of art, came from a tight collaboration between software artist Bill Atkinson and visual artist Susan Kare.

Yes, this is an ambitious charter. My purpose here is to give you all the options. You do not have to do it all. Any piece is fine. And you do not have to do it alone. We are all in this together.

How to See the Nose on Your Face

As you reach out to other disciplines, it is important to keep noticing the assumptions in your own discipline that might limit your view of the world. Seeing your own assumptions is like seeing your own nose. It is such a constant part of your visual field that you have to do something special to become aware of it, like close one eye, cross your eyes, or focus unusually closely. Here are games to bring your assumptions into focus.

Be Playful

Nothing locks in assumptions like seriousness. Put aside practicality for a moment and take an irreverent attitude toward your discipline. Tell someone about your discipline as if it were astonishing news: "You'd never believe it!" Describe everyday practices as if they were strange alien rituals. Chuckle at the little absurdities of your discipline. Spout technical jargon. Apply the full weight of your discipline to a simple everyday activity, making it hopelessly complex.

Tell the Story of Your Life

How did you get to be where you are now? Telling the story of your life helps remind you (and others) of the choices you made along the way to your current occupation, and of your identity as a human being apart from your work. Recall early delights that got you interested in your current field. Take turns with other people telling life stories and listening. You will be fascinated by the curious similarities and differences.

Tell the Story of Your Discipline

Disciplines spend so much time defending their boundaries that we forget that the boundaries are arbitrary and can be changed. Research the history of your discipline. How did it start? What was the original question? Whose big idea was it anyway? How have its boundaries changed over time? Why did it evolve the way it did? Imagine how it could have evolved differently had circumstances been different. Imagine how it might change. When historians five hundred years from now look back at our times, how might they tell the story of your discipline?

Draw a Map

The quickest way to sound like an expert in a field is to know how it is organized. Draw a map showing your discipline and how it is divided into different factions. Draw neighboring disciplines. Label mountains, rivers, cities, and wilderness.

Write a Tour Guide

Pretend your discipline is a foreign country. Write a tour guide for visitors. Design a poster that will attract interest. Rave about scenic wonders. Draw a state flag. Include a short dictionary of useful phrases. Give tips on local customs. Offer package tours. Make up tacky souvenirs.

Write an Emergency Guide

It takes years of training to become a doctor, but everyone needs to know first aid. Write a one-page guide to your discipline in the style of the first aid guides that appear at the beginning of some phone books. It does not have to be serious. Give short, clear instructions on what to do in crisis situations. Include diagrams.

Argue Persuasively That Another Discipline Is Far More Important Than Yours

In this book you will find arguments for the importance of many different approaches to user interface design, including industrial design, writing, computer games, sound, gesture, psychology, drama, help systems, and education. Choose an approach that you find boring. Enthusiastically list reasons why that approach is the most interesting and important of all, while the approach of your discipline hardly matters. Enjoy demolishing any pompous self-importance your field may have developed.

Imagine How People in Other Disciplines Would Solve a Problem in Your Discipline

Changing your point of view is a basic technique of generating new ideas. Use the friction between different disciplines to spark new ideas. By systematically trying out other points of view, you can overcome limitations in your own point of view. For further ideas on creative brainstorming, see Mountford's and Erickson's chapters in this volume.

Interdisciplinary People . . .

. . . carry messages between castles.

. . . fall in the cracks.

. . . build bridges so others may cross.

. . . sit on the fence.

. . . wear many hats.

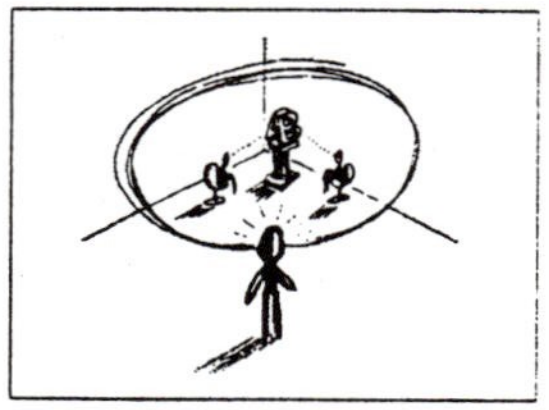

. . . see more than one point of view.

List All the Roles You Play Throughout the Day

You are already interdisciplinary, by virtue of the many roles you play through the day: friend, spouse, parent, child, driver, pedestrian, student, teacher. Even the simplest job usually requires several distinct skills. How do you juggle all these roles? What do you do when they overlap? What are the priorities in each situation? Interview yourself as if you were the world's leading expert on juggling roles.

List the Priorities of Your Discipline

What are the most important priorities to teach beginners in your field? Order priorities by importance. For each priority, recall a story that explains its importance. Compare how the same priorities look to beginners and experts.

Remarks

The assumptions of different disciplines are usually compared only in jokes about different people's stereotypical responses to the same situation ("A doctor, a lawyer, and a politician were walking down the street . . ."). Such jokes perpetuate the belief that people cannot change. The purpose of these exercises is to replace stale cynicism with fresh imagination.

The Center for Explanation and Other Fantasies

Here are some other interesting opportunities I see for future interdisciplinary work.

Providing Inspiring Examples

Traditional schools and businesses discourage interaction between disciplines. To raise our hopes of what is possible, we need inspiring examples of good interdisciplinary work. Search out and document existing interdisciplinary work. Compare how people in different disciplines approach the same problem, as Arent, Vertelney, and Lieberman do in their chapter in this volume. Set uncompromisingly pure goals, even if the scope of the project has to be narrow. Teams work best if they are small, allow everyone to participate equally from the beginning, and can agree early on common goals.

Raising the Lowest Common Denominator

Interdisciplinary work often flounders for lack of adequate tools. For instance, a graphic designer cannot participate in graphic user interface design without adequate graphic prototyping tools. To raise our expectations of what is practical, we need better everyday standards. Research the minimal requirements of each discipline. Build the minimum requirements into everyday tools and procedures. Set standards that are universally accepted, even if the details have to be compromised. Standards work best if they are expressed precisely, presented in language that users understand, and adapt well to particular cases.

Changing Organizational Priorities

Large-scale change requires clear commitment from those in charge. An organization's structure must reflect its priorities or it will not be effective. When Alan Kay set up the group that created Smalltalk and the much of desktop metaphor at the Xerox Palo Alto Research Center in the early 70s, he built the importance of the user interface into every aspect of the group. The group opened the door to a constant stream of young users, hired people with backgrounds in music and philosophy, designed a dedicated personal computer with a large bitmapped screen, and pioneered a simpler type of software environment. In contrast, most computer research centers are closed to outside users, hire only engineers, use existing machines, and build on layers of complex software designed for sophisticated programmers. In such an environment it is hard for user interface design to be a priority.

Interdisciplinary Disciplines

Several existing disciplines study relations between different social groups. Anthropologists and sociologists document cultural behavior. Organizational development people assemble teams in business. Educators and psychologists analyze different thinking styles. Journalists and writers present specialized topics to general audiences. All of these fields can contribute to better interdisciplinary cooperation.

The Center for Explanation

I see a new profession emerging: interdisciplinary connectors who are skilled at explaining any discipline to any another. Such connectors would help members of an interdisciplinary team communicate with each other.

This brings me to the Center for Explanation. Writers, illustrators, and filmmakers all learn to tailor explanations of ideas to particular audiences. Usually the explanations follow rigid explanatory conventions. For instance, popular science is usually presented in a slightly detached authoritative voice that says "isn't science wonderful," whereas academic science is usually presented in a dry formal voice that says "I'm so objective." Only parodists break the conventions.

Nowhere is there a place to explore explanatory styles themselves freely. Occasionally a new explanatory style will sweep a field, as happened with graphical techniques and statistics. But these are isolated instances. The Center for Explanation would systematically explore all possible ways of explaining an idea, both after the fact for a general audience, and during the process for a specialized audience.

Rethinking *Interdisciplinary*

I have always been proud to be interdisciplinary. But the word makes me feel scattered. To find out why, I listed all meanings of *interdisciplinary*. They are cartooned on the previous pages.

I concluded that the word is backwards. *Interdisciplinary* means you cut up the world into disciplines, then try to glue it back together. The word maintains a fragmented view of the world, even though it advocates unity. The opposite approach might be to call an interdisciplinary field a *generality*, and to characterize anyone who specializes in only one aspect of a generality as being *subgeneral*.

There is only one world. Disciplines are ways for people to subdivide the world. If you treat disciplines as primary divisions you can build bridges between particular disciplines. But if the disciplines move, the bridges no longer connect anything. It is better in the long run to let disciplines play a secondary role, and to build bridges between people on the basis of mutual understanding and respect.

References

Kim, S. (1988) *Viewpoint: Toward a Computer for Visual Thinkers*. Ph.D. diss. Computer Science Department, Stanford University.

Koberg, D., and Bagnall, J. (1973) *The Universal Traveler*. William Kaufmann.

Chapter 5

Development Tools

Human-computer interaction is concerned with the design, evaluation and implementation of interactive computer systems for human use (Hewett et al., 1992). This book thus far has concentrated on design (interpreted broadly) and evaluation (especially Chapter 2), claiming correctly that good interfaces can only arise by taking a user perspective.

Yet design based on human considerations is not enough, for design can rarely be detached from implementation. Today's computers, unfortunately, are not particularly malleable. They lend themselves to particular interface paradigms. Designs that deviate from these paradigms even slightly may be prohibitively expensive or impossible to build. Just as an architect must design human-usable structures around the properties of building materials and the capabilities of tradespeople, so must the interface designer understand the affordances of *interface development tools*, and what an application programmer can reasonably do with them.

This section discusses development tools, concentrating mostly on GUIs (graphical user interfaces, see Case B and Chapter 6). This introduction will first describe what development tools are, and then present a brief overview of the conventional and novel tools now available. The readings delve into greater detail. The first paper by Myers (1993a) provides an excellent taxonomy and survey of the state of the art. The remaining readings describe four development tools, SUIT, Garnet, ITS, and GroupKit, each with distinct perspectives and philosophies.

SUIT provides excellent examples of the offerings now found in most interface toolkits; it has the added advantage that it is freely available, is easy to learn, and has been tested as a teaching tool in classroom settings (Pausch, Conway, and Deline, 1992). The Garnet toolkit illustrates several novel approaches to interface development, such as constraints and programming by demonstration, and is perhaps one of the most comprehensive development tools now available (also for free) for advanced students and researchers (Myers et al., 1990; Myers, 1994a). The Interactive Transaction System (ITS) considers interface development as part of the software engineering life-cycle, and layers its capabilities to correspond to the work roles of development team members (Wiecha et al., 1990). Finally, GroupKit considers the different requirements that a groupware toolkit must satisfy from both a programmer and an end-user perspective (Roseman and Greenberg, 1992).

Although this chapter will restrict itself to tools for GUI construction, development tools go far beyond that. Because toolkits provide visible interface components, we must be concerned with their graphical design (Chapter 6) and how people can interact with them (Chapters 7 and 8). Domains other than conventional GUIs also require development support. These include 2D and 3D graphics and animation systems (see, e.g., the paper by Baecker, Small, and Mander reprinted in Chapter 6), end-user programming (the paper by Cypher in Chapter 12), hypertext (Chapter 13), multimedia (the paper by Gaver and Smith in Chapter 8, and also Case C and Chapter 13), and virtual environments (the paper by Ellis in Chapter 14).

WHAT ARE DEVELOPMENT TOOLS?

What do we mean when we talk about interface development tools? One definition, provided by Dix et al. (1993) is, "tools that provide programming support for implementing interactive systems." Yet this does not tell the whole story.

First, a development tool should minimize the effort it takes to translate the semantics of the interface design into the semantics of the toolkit offerings. At one extreme, any graphical interface could be implemented—at ridiculous cost in time and effort—as long as the procedures "set pixel" and "get input event" were available. At the other extreme, the tool components would exactly match the design components. For example, a file selection tool would satisfy the design semantics that require a user to select a file. Existing tools are somewhere between these two ends. While most provide low-level matches between interface building blocks and design semantics—buttons for triggering actions, menus for selecting from a list, fields for entering text—a design specification requiring anything out of the ordinary is usually difficult to implement.

Second, a tool should be integrated into the interface development process. There are several approaches to this. Abstract interface specification could be automatically translated into an implementation. Design layout and storyboarding could occur within a single interface tool, minimizing the distinctions between the design, prototyping, and implementation stages (Nielsen, 1993). The tool itself could be an active participant in the testing and verification process, perhaps by checking for consistency and correctness. At the very least, the system should be malleable enough to encourage iterative modification, conceivably by the end user.

Taking these points into consideration, we now extend the goal and definition of development tools to

> tools that help a developer convert interface specifications into an interactive system, and that support all phases of system refinement including prototyping, implementation, testing, maintenance, and system enhancement.

There are a wide variety of GUI development methods and tools in existence, and while many address some of the goals listed above, none address all of them. In order to get a feel for the offerings, a survey of contemporary approaches to development tools is useful. The first reading by Myers (1993a) supplies this through an in-depth discussion of the state of the art in interface software tools. Myers explains why interfaces are difficult to build (see also Myers, 1993c and 1994b), lists the advantages of using development tools, and sets the goals the tools should strive to achieve. He then describes a thorough taxonomy of both conventional and novel user interface software approaches, accompanied by many examples of commercial and experimental systems.

The rest of this chapter introduction will set the stage for the readings by presenting popular approaches to interface software tools. This section will look at several important approaches to conventional development tools: windowing systems, toolkits, interface builders, user interface management systems, and tools specialized to specific application domains. Novel approaches to interface development are discussed afterwards: capabilities of the next generation of GUI tools, how tools can support more of the development cycle, and how tools must adapt to new interface paradigms such as groupware.

CONVENTIONAL DEVELOPMENT TOOLS

Windowing systems constrain each application or application component to a particular frame on the screen (a window). They provide an *input model*, where user interactions within a particular window are passed to the application as events that can be interpreted further. They also provide a *graphics model*. The application specifies the output graphics, and the windowing system guarantees that graphics are drawn only in that window. Some degree of *window management* is also provided to the user and programmer, where windows can be opened, closed, resized, moved, iconified, and so on. Finally, they usually enforce some kind of *presentation style*, which determines their overall look and feel. Popular examples of windowing systems are X for Unix (Scheifler and Gettys, 1986), the Apple Macintosh Toolbox (Apple Computer, 1985), Microsoft Windows (Microsoft, 1993b), and the Presentation Manager for IBMs.

The X Window system deserves special mention, for it is snetwork-based and uses a client-server architecture (Scheifler and Gettys, 1986). Its power is akin to the way terminal emulators handle local and remote programs, except that X handles all aspects of a GUI as well. Any X application, called a *client*, can run on any machine in the network. A *server* process, which resides on the user's workstation, mediates all user input and display output. The server translates a person's input into X events and sends it to the appropriate client. The client interprets these events, and sends graphics directives to the server on how to update the display. A special kind of client is the *window manager*, which is responsible for the overall look and feel of the window frames. That is, the window manager decorates and arranges windows on the screen, and provides the mechanism by which a user controls the windows and the input to them. The beauty of X is that all this is transparent to the developer of clients; machine independence is acquired "for free."

Figure 5.1 below illustrates an example of the way the X process architecture is typically used. A Unix workstation, a file server, and an X terminal are shown. Since both the workstation and the X terminal have a display running X Windows, they must run their own X server. The window manager processes are also shown residing on their local machine, although they could be (but rarely are) located on different machines. Client processes are shown spread over the network. The workstation is running two client applications locally (I and J) with the third (K)—perhaps a compute-intensive application—executing on the file server. Regardless of their location, all clients receive input and display output from and to the workstation. The X terminal, an X display device that cannot execute client programs, runs all its client applications (M and N) on the file server.

FIGURE 5.1

An example of the X Windows process architecture.

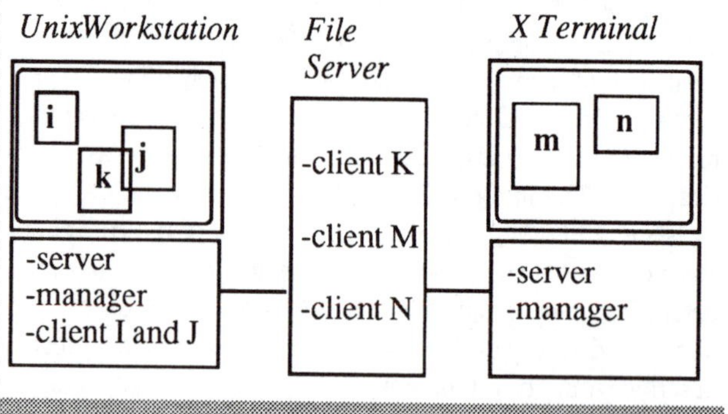

Further descriptions of windowing systems can be found in the first reading by Myers, and also in Marcus (1992, excerpted in Chapter 6). Pike (1983 video), Myers (1985b video), Cohen (1987 video), and Carnegie Mellon University (1989 video) document important early research windowing systems.

In spite of these offerings, windowing systems provide too low-level an abstraction for building applications (Myers, 1993c). More suitable layers, such as toolkits, interface builders, and user interface management systems, are usually implemented on top of window systems. These are described below.

Toolkits collect a variety of interface building blocks (called *widgets*) and a language for putting them together. Although good toolkits are extremely hard to develop, the effort is justified by the decrease in complexity and increase in quality of applications developed on top of them. Toolkits are most useful when the widget set closely matches the components in the interface design.

Example toolkits are Motif (Open Software Foundation, 1989; Heller, 1992), the XView implementation of Open Look (Heller, 1990; Sun Microsystems, 1990b), InterViews (Linton, Vlissides, and Calder, 1989), SUIT (the second reading, Pausch, Conway, and Deline, 1992), MacApp (Apple Computer, 1987), and TCL/TK (Ousterhout, 1994).

Typical widgets found in toolkits are buttons, menus, sliders for specifying numbers, scrollbars, text editors, canvases for drawing graphics, terminal windows, and so on. Examples of widgets can be found in all readings in this chapter, as well as in Marcus (1992, excerpted in Chapter 6 of this book).

There are also many videos on widgets. Myers (1990 video) is a comprehensive collection of the ways various vendors have implemented the look and feel of a number of widgets, including scroll bars, menus, palettes, various buttons, text editors, dialog boxes, desktops, and window managers. Myers (1985a video) discusses the design of percent-done progress indicator widgets. Plaisant and Wallace (1992 video) shows how even a simple touchscreen toggle widget requires iterative design. Particularly innovative recent widgets are the Toolglass and Magic Lenses (Bier et al., 1994 video; see also the discussion and paper in Chapter 7).

Interfaces that are built using toolkits are constructed by programming. The developer encodes a widget's placement in the window, its attributes, and what "callback" procedures should be executed when a user activates the widget. For example, Figure 5.2 contains the complete TCL/TK code to create the button shown in the window in that figure. We first instruct the window manager to set the window's title to "Demo". We then create the button containing the text "Press Me", and the attached callback will print "Hello world" when the button is pressed. Finally, we position the button at the top of the window with some padding (white space) around it.

FIGURE 5.2

A button in a window, and the TCL/TK code that created it.

```
wm title . Demo
button .mybutton
        -text "Press Me"
        -command "puts "Hello world"
pack .mybutton -side top
        -padx 10 -pady 10.
```

Some toolkits even support multiple styles of widget look and feel, so the same program can present itself as, say, a Motif or an OpenLook system (e.g., InterViews; Linton, Vlissides, and Calder, 1989).

While toolkits are popular for building interfaces, they do have limitations. First, widget sets are small, and restrict the interaction techniques a developer can include in the interface. Second, toolkits—while good at creating "control panels"—provide poor support for what would actually occur in the application window (Myers, 1993c). As a result, programmers often revert to low-level graphics and text-editing constructs. Third, programming in an abstract language is an inefficient way of putting widgets together, and many compile cycles are required before a widget's appearance and placement on the screen are correct. Interface builders remedy this last fault.

Interface builders provide a direct manipulation graphical interface to toolkits. Some are integrated into the toolkit environment, while others are separate add-ons. Examples are the NeXT Interface Builder (NeXT, 1991), Visual Basic (Microsoft, 1993a), SUIT's integrated interface builder (Pausch, Conway, and Deline, 1992, included as a reading), the XF builder for TCL/TK (Delmas, 1993), and Garnet's Lapidary (Myers, Vander Zanden, and Dannenberg, 1989). The implementor selects a widget from a palate, places it onto a screen, and sets its attributes through form-filling or direct manipulation. Links are made to callbacks, which are still written as procedures. Some builders can even attach multimedia events to widgets, e.g., a "sound stream" can be dropped onto a button, which is then played whenever the button is pressed (NeXT, 1991).

Interface builders allow developers to test interfaces as they are being constructed—each widget will behave with the expected look and feel. Sophisticated builders will also link widgets to their callbacks during testing, allowing the developer to try out the evolving application at any time (e.g., XF; Delmas, 1993). As with toolkits, some builders support multiple styles of widget look and feel (e.g., DevGuide; Sun Microsystems, 1990a). Unfortunately, if nonstandard interface and widget behavior is required, the developer will usually have to dip back to coding the toolkit or even the window layer.

Finally, we should make special mention of two systems: MacroMedia Director and HyperCard (Goodman, 1987). Because they facilitate the building of interface prototypes of even unusual interfaces, both are excellent for design exploration. Yet since they have relatively weak underlying languages, the interface and application behaviour is more a simulation than the real thing, and they are poor choices for building complex deliverable systems.

User interface management systems (UIMSs) would more appropriately be termed "user interface development environments." They typically separate an application into three modules: the *presentation graphics* (what a person sees), the *dialog control* (how a person's inputs are managed and passed to the application), and an *application interface* (how the interface hooks into the actual application code, and how the two communicate input/output events to each other) (Olsen, 1992). A run-time component typically manages the interaction between the three. The advantage is that the interface and application are separated; ideally the interface can be altered without changing the application code at all. The disadvantage is that it is hard for the designer to separate the two in practice, since interfaces (especially direct manipulation ones) are often tightly intertwined with the application.

Example UIMSs include the User Interface Language for Motif (Open Software Foundation, 1989), Chiron (Taylor and Johnson, 1993), and the UofA* UIMS (Singh and Green, 1991). Chapter 12 of the first edition of this book, Baecker and Buxton (1987), contains an extensive review of early work on UIMSs. Early videos on UIMSs and other advanced programming environments are the University of Toronto UIMS (Buxton, 1983 video), the Flair rapid prototyping system (Wong, 1983 video), the Tiger UIMS (Kasik, 1983 video), the Cousin UIMS (Hayes, 1985 video), and Sassafras (Hill, 1987 video).

There are a wide variety of *application-specific tools* that are designed around particular application styles. For example, most modern PC-based data bases include facilities for specifying not only the data bases, but the interfaces for graphical query and report generation as well (e.g., Claris' Filemaker-Pro, ACI's 4D). Similarly, some hypertext systems (discussed in Chapter 13) provide tools for building particular types of browsers, links, nodes, and node behaviors (e.g., HyperCard; Goodman, 1987). Other tools are available to build particular types of applications, such as graphical editors (e.g., Unidraw; Vlissides and Linton, 1990).

An Example

Many conventional development tools have a large learning curve, because they assume an audience of highly proficient GUI developers who are willing to invest time in return for toolkit power. The Suit Simple User Interface Toolkit, described by Pausch. Conway, and Deline (1992) and included as a reading in this chapter, is an excellent example of a tool designed for novice GUI developers, such as computer science majors. It was deliberately simplified to make it learnable in a few hours, versus four to six weeks for Xtk (McCormack and Asente, 1988), Andrew (Palay et al., 1988; Carnegie Mellon University, 1989 video), InterViews (Linton, Vlissides, and Calder, 1989), and Motif (Heller, 1992). While not as powerful as the others, it makes an excellent teaching tool. Its highlights are the following:

- Portability across platforms
- Standard widget set
- Running application plus application builder
- Capability for authoring custom widgets

SUIT is portable over the Macintosh, IBM, and Unix/X platforms. This is achieved by employing a standard language (C), and by having minimal operating system dependencies. Common high-level graphics are built on top of platform-specific low-level graphics packages.

SUIT contains a reasonable set of standard widgets, such as buttons, scrollable lists, menus, and geometry managers (for determining the layout of widgets in a window). Widgets are manipulated by changing their properties, rather than by hard-coding. Widgets can also be abstract data types. For example, an abstract widget that tracks a minimum, current, and maximum value of a range can appear as a pie chart, a valuator, a gauge, or a scroll bar.

A SUIT program is both a running application and an interface builder. Users can rapidly switch from the application mode into a builder mode by a simple keypress, and alter the interface as desired. The minimal distinction between a test and a build mode greatly reduces the time bottleneck typical with edit-compile-test cycles.

SUIT developers can author custom widgets. While this is still difficult for the uninitiated, it satisfies Pausch's philosophy that hard things should be possible.

Because SUIT is freely available, it a reasonable and accessible platform that students and practitioners alike can use to learn about GUI toolkit fundamentals. Another easy to learn toolkit is TCL/TK (Ousterhout, 1994), also available for free. On the commercial side, Visual Basic (Microsoft, 1993a) is a reasonably priced and popular interface builder for the IBM PC environment, one that is growing in importance since it became the language for user extensions of Microsoft applications running under Windows. Neuron Data's Open Interface and Visiz's Galaxy are other state-of-the-art examples of powerful commercial toolkits.

NOVEL APPROACHES TO DEVELOPMENT TOOLS

While the tools described above reduce the effort of building GUIs, they still have a long way to go. Several new approaches to tool design may ease the development burden even further. These include techniques for incorporating constraints, separating object look and feel, and programming by demonstration (as illustrated by Garnet); for supporting the software development process (as illustrated by ITS); and for implementing groupware (as illustrated by GroupKit). These approaches will be explained within the context of the remaining readings in this chapter.

Comprehensive Advanced GUI Tools

The Garnet project is described in the third reading and its addendum; the original Garnet description is presented first (Myers et al., 1990), followed by an update of new work (Myers, 1994a). Garnet incorporates both traditional and contemporary development tools to make a comprehensive GUI toolkit. Garnet, which is both a system and a set of tools, combines four novel features:

- Easy manipulation of graphical objects and their behavior
- Constraints
- Interactors
- Programming by demonstration

Garnet enables easy manipulation of graphical objects and their behavior. Unlike most toolkits and interface builders, Garnet developers can create and edit application-specific graphical objects as well as predefined widgets. All objects are defined within the Opal graphical object tool, which is in turn implemented on top of KR, a prototype-instance object-oriented system. If the developer directly edits the prototype (such as a menu object), all its instances automatically reflect the changes.

Garnet supports *constraints* (see also the discussion of this topic in Chapter 6). Interactive systems often incorporate massive dependencies among interface, data, and program components. Changes to one component usually affect many others. An example is a flow chart—if one box is moved, it should remain connected to other boxes by repositioning the arrows that join them. Constraint-based tools let the developer specify relationships between components. The run-time system would enforce these constraints by making sure that changes in one object are reflected on others.

The idea of constraints in graphical interfaces was first seen in SketchPad (Sutherland, 1963), and later in ThingLab (Borning, 1979). More recently, Garnet embeds constraints into both Opal and KR, and maintains them at run-time (see also Myers, 1993b). Garnet also provides the C32 spreadsheet, a tool that lets designers specify, monitor, and debug constraints while the interface is running. Constraints have also been applied to maintain consistency across multiuser applications in the Rendezvous toolkit (Patterson, 1991; Hill et al., 1993).

Garnet includes constructs known as *interactors* for input handling. Most toolkits hardwire the "feel" of an object (i.e., its input handling) directly into each widget. Garnet separates the look from the feel by encapsulating behaviors of input devices in "interactors" (Myers, 1990). For example, a menu interactor allows a user to select one or more items from a set, regardless of how the set is actually displayed on the screen. This allows many different types of menus to be constructed on top of the same interactor mechanism. This approach is similar to Smalltalk's model-view-controller paradigm (Krashner and Pope, 1988). The model is the prototype-instance object specification, the view is the graphical object system, and the controller is the interactor. A constraint system connects the three.

Garnet supports *programming by demonstration (PBD)*. PBD allows developers to demonstrate, instead of program, examples of what they want to the computer. The system then automatically generates a program from those examples, perhaps generalizing where necessary. The Marquise tool and Lapidary interface builder in Garnet illustrates how demonstration techniques can extend existing tools supplied by the toolkit (see also Myers, 1993b).

Garnet's approach was derived from Myer's earlier work on the Peridot interface development system (Myers, 1988; Myers and Buxton, 1986). A recent book (Cypher et al., 1993) gives a thorough perspective on PBD and is a rich collection of historical and contemporary PBD systems. Some noteworthy PBD systems that are applied to domains other than interface construction are Metamouse (Maulsby et al., 1992), Eager (Cypher, 1991), Triggers (Potter, 1993) and Tourmaline (Myers, 1991). Cypher (1991, reprinted in Chapter 12) describes how PBD can be applied to customizing end-user applications.

A video snapshot of the Garnet system is Myers et al. (1994 video). Its Lapidary interface builder is shown by Vander Zanden and Myers (1991 video). On the programming by demonstration scene, Peridot (Myers, 1988 video) illustrates how GUI widgets can be created by example; Metamouse (Maulsby, 1990 video) illustrates how a system can infer a procedure for carrying out a graphical editing task. Kurlander (1993 video) shows Chimera, a system built to explore new demonstrational techniques in the domains of graphical editing and interface building. For something completely different, Triggers (Potter, 1993 video) lets people program GUI interactions by giving it examples of screen changes at the pixel level.

Tools for the Entire Development Cycle

Implementation is only one aspect of interface design. Toolkits should support interface specification, implementation, and testing (Perlman, 1988). Interface builders already help with rapid prototyping, for the designer and user can work together on the interface appearance. Because UIMSs separate application and interface code, the jobs of interface design, prototyping, and implementation can also be separated.

A different way of supporting the development life cycle is to move away from the strictly "artifact centered" approach of existing tools, and towards a semantically driven user interface design. The idea is that a semantic model of the interface is developed as a declarative description, and that the model becomes a plan that is used to let the developer manipulate the interface in a way that is appropriate to its stage in the life cycle. For example, the developer would apply tools to the model for design exploration, automatic design, design assistance, design criticisms, and so on (Puerta and Szekely, 1994). While no such system yet exists for the entire life cycle, several are moving towards this direction, including Humanoid (Szekely, Luo, and Neches, 1993; Luo, Szekely, and Neches, 1993), the User Interface Design Environment (UIDE) (Kim and Foley, 1990; Sukaviriya, Foley, and Griffith, 1993; Byrne et al., 1994), Mechano (Puerta et al., 1994), and the Interactive Transaction System (ITS) (summarized below).

IBM's Interactive Transaction System (ITS) is a model-based system that contains four major components (Wiecha et al., 1990, included as a reading in this chapter; also see Gould, Boies, and Lewis, 1991; Gould, Ukelson, and Boies, 1993, 1995):

- An *action layer* implements the semantics of application functions independent of the interface.
- A *dialog layer* treats the interface as a set of logical frames containing objects, and defines the flow of control between the frames and the actions associated with them.
- *Style rules* define the presentation and behavior of interaction widgets; the rules codify user interface standards usually found in the style guides of interface vendors.
- *Style programs* implement the actual widgets.

One of the main points of the ITS layers is that each corresponds to the work roles of the development team members. Application programmers work with the action layer, application experts compose dialog rules, graphic designers compose style rules, and style programmers build style programs. ITS also promotes reuse. Because it is heavily modularized, new interfaces to existing actions can be created quickly, styles substituted, and dialogues altered.

Does ITS work in practice? Gould, Ukelson, and Boies (1993, 1995) claim it does. They examine several case studies of ITS being used to develop quite different interfaces and applications. All show a several-fold decrease in the person-months required to produce them. Some of the implementations are production quality, the most notable being the Expo '92 Visitor Information System that was used by an estimated 40 million visitors to Spain's World Fair.

ITS also reveals a potential danger of automating system construction from rules. For example, Wiecha et al. (1990) claim in the reading that rules are an excellent way of capturing design decisions, with the added benefit that they are embodied into the interface in a consistent, rather than ad hoc, manner. Grudin (1992) notes that the paper has altered the example taken from Grudin (1989) and argues that ITS's claim that rules produce consistency is problematic, since almost anything, including English spelling, can be generated by a large enough rule set. He also suggests that a rigidly enforced consistency may not be desirable. It is all too easy for a designer to blindly apply rules that, while reasonable for the general case, may cause problems at particular points in the interface. As Wiecha states (1992, p. 114):

> *The important issues are . . . related to the appropriateness and quality of style rules in addition to the level of conformance to them found in an interface.*

Groupware Toolkits

A recent paradigm shift in user interfaces is the realization that work is often collaborative. Groupware, described further in Chapter 11, is software that supports and augments group work (Greenberg, 1991; Baecker, 1993). Conventional toolkits are inadequate for building groupware, for they do not support many of the requirements of groupware. The GroupKit project, covered in Roseman and Greenberg (1992, included as a reading in this chapter), describes capabilities that a groupware toolkit for real-time distributed work must afford over traditional GUI builders. These cluster into two categories:

- Programmer-centered design requirements
- Human-centered design requirements

The toolkit must handle technical problems associated with groupware and its management of multiple and distributed processes. The goal is to remove a programmer's tedium when specifying how a conference's processes and communication channels are initiated, maintained, and torn down. Minimal capabilities include robust interprocess communication, concurrency control, graceful conference maintenance, a persistent object store, and an appropriate multiuser graphics model (see also Olson et al., 1993).

Groupware toolkits should also support fundamental human factors requirements identified for effective group work. Even the conceptually simple idea of multiple cursors on a display and annotation of artifacts (used for promoting gesturing, awareness, and note taking over a visual work surface) is incredibly difficult to do well with conventional toolkits (Hayne, Pendergast, and Greenberg, 1993/94). Another requirement is direct support for meeting processes. This includes handling the various ways people join conferences, updating latecomers, and providing mechanisms for turntaking.

The GroupKit toolkit described in the reading illustrates how these requirements can be implemented. Other groupware toolkits for real-time distributed meetings include Rendezvous (Patterson, 1991; Hill et al., 1993), Suite (Shen and Dewan, 1992), and MMConf (Crowley et al., 1990). Another approach to groupware development is to support the asynchronous conversational structure between people, e.g., Oval (Malone, Lai, and Fry, 1992), the Conversation Builder (Kaplan et al., 1992), and Strudel (Shepherd, Mayer, and Kuchinsky, 1990). Given the prevalent nature of group work, we believe that interface toolkits should all be developed with multiuser extensions in mind.

Video examples of multiuser widgets can be found in Baecker et al. (1994 video); Greenberg et al. (1992 video); Bier, Freeman, and Pier (1992 video); and Dewan (1992 video).

Other Novel Approaches

There are many other innovative approaches to building interface development tools. For example, a new frontier in human-computer interaction is three-dimensional virtual environments. These typically include a head-mounted display for stereoscopic vision, motion detectors that allow people to "move" through 3-space, a data glove or suit for manipulating objects, and directional sound (see Ellis 1991, reprinted in Chapter 14 of this book). A completely new style of toolkit is required to address these types of interface, for they must maintain the integrity of the underlying graphics data base and views, as well as managing the difficult problem of three-dimensional multimodal input (Jacob et al., 1993; see also discussions in Chapters 6 and 7).

FormsVBT (Avrahami, Brooks, and Brown, 1990 video) is a toolkit that provides three tightly linked views onto a project: the interface builder, an editor onto the code, and a test mode. The developer can work on the project in whatever view is appropriate to them, and changes in one view are immediately propagated to the others. Gray et al. (1992 video) illustrates how semantic models can be used to drive interface design.

OTHER SOURCES

You can keep up-to-date with new advances in development tools by following the ACM Symposium on User Interface Software and Technology (UIST) conference, the main forum for researchers in this area. Proceedings are available from ACM Press. You can also find a research agenda for development tools in Olsen et al. (1993).

You can also try out toolkits. Several of the systems described in this introduction and the readings are available "for free" via anonymous ftp. All include documentation. They are suitable for teaching students about toolkit use, or as a tool for constructing interfaces. Installation, if done by a systems person, is usually straightforward. The Internet address and directory/file paths of the distributions are listed below, however availability and details may change over time:

SUIT

```
cs.virginia.edu
pub/suit/*
```

runs on Unix/X, DOS, Windows, Macintosh

Garnet

```
a.gp.cs.cmu.edu
/usr/garnet/garnet/*
```

runs on Unix/X, requires LISP

TCL/TK

```
sprite.berkeley.edu
tcl/tcl7.3.tar.Z
tcl/tk3.6.tar.Z
```

runs on Unix/X

GroupKit 2.2b

```
ftp.cpsc.ucalgary.ca
pub/projects/grouplab/software/groupkit-*.tar.Z
```

runs on Unix/X, requires TCL/TK and TCL-DP

REFERENCES

Note: A ● before a reference indicates a reading.

Apple Computer (1985). *Inside Macintosh.* Addison-Wesley.

Apple Computer (1987). *MacApp: The Expandable Macintosh Application.* Apple Programmer's and Developer's Association.

Baecker, R. (1993). *Readings in Groupware and Computer-Supported Cooperative Work: Assisting Human-Human Collaboration.* Morgan Kaufmann.

Baecker, R., and Buxton, W. (Eds.) (1987). *Readings in Human-Computer Interaction: A Multidisciplinary Approach.* Morgan Kaufmann.

Borning, A. (1979). Thinglab—A Constraint-Oriented Simulation Laboratory. Technical Report SSL-79-3, Xerox Palo Alto Research Center.

Byrne, M., Sukaviriya, P., Wood, S.D., Foley, J., and Kieras, D. (1994). Automating Interface Evaluation. *Proc.CHI '94,* ACM, 232–237.

Crowley, T., Baker, E., Forsdick, H., Milazzo, P., and Tomlinson, R. (1990). MMConf: An Infrastructure for Building Shared Applications. *Proc. CSCW '90,* ACM, 329–342.

Cypher, A. (1991). EAGER: Programming Repetitive Tasks by Example. *Proc. CHI '91,* ACM, 33–39. Reprinted in Chapter 12 of this volume.

Cypher, A., Halbert, D., Kurlander, D., Lieberman, H., Maulsby, D., Myers, B., and Turransky, A. (Eds.) (1993). *Watch What I Do: Programming by Demonstration.* MIT Press.

Delmas, S. (1993). XF: Design and Implementation of a Programming Environment for Interactive Construction of Graphical User Interfaces. Technische Universitat Berlin.

Dix, A., Finlay, J., Abowd, G., and Beale, R. (1993). *Human-Computer Interaction.* Prentice Hall International.

Goodman, D. (1987). *The Complete HyperCard Handbook.* Bantam Books.

Gould, J., Boies, S., and Lewis, C. (1991). Making Useful, Usable, Productivity-Enhancing Computer Applications. *Communications of the ACM* 34(1), 79–85.

Gould, J., Ukelson, J., and Boies, S. (1993). Improving Application Development Productivity by Using ITS. *International Journal of Man-Machine Studies* 39(1), 113–146.

Gould, J., Ukelson, J. and Boies, S. (1995). Improving User Interfaces and Application Productivity by Using the ITS Application Development Environment. In Rudisill, M., Lewis, C., Polson, P., and McKay, T. (Eds.) (1995), *Human-Computer Interface Design: Success Cases, Emerging Methods, and Real-World Context,* Morgan Kaufmann.

Greenberg, S. (Ed.) (1991). *Computer Supported Cooperative Work and Groupware.* Academic Press.

Grudin, J. (1989). The Case against User Interface Consistency. *Communications of the ACM* 32(10), 1164–1173.

Grudin, J. (1992). Consistency, Standards, and Formal Approaches to Interface Development and Evaluation: A Note on Wiecha, Bennett, Boies, Gould, and Greene. *ACM Transactions on Information Systems* 10(1),103–111.

Hayne, S., Pendergast, M., and Greenberg, S. (1993/94). Implementing Gesturing with Cursors in Group Support Systems. *Journal of Management Information Systems,* Fall/Winter.

Heller, D. (1990). *XView Programming Manual.* The Definitive Guides to the X Window System, 7. O'Reilly & Associates.

Heller, D. (1992). *Motif Programming Manual.* The Definitive Guides to the X Window System, 6. O'Reilly & Associates.

Hewett, T., Baecker, R.M., Card, S., Carey, T., Gasen, J., Mantei, M., Perlman, G., Strong, G., and Verplank, W. (1992). ACM SIGCHI Curricula for Human-Computer Interaction, Report of the ACM SIGCHI Curriculum Development Group.

Hill, R., Brinck, T., Patterson, J., Rohall, S., and Wilner, W. (1993). The Rendezvous Language and Architecture. *Communications of the ACM* 36(1), 62–67.

Jacob, R., Leggett, J., Myers, B., and Pausch, R. (1993). Interaction Styles and Input/Output Devices. *Behaviour and Information Technology* 12(2), 69–79.

Kaplan, S., Tolone, W., Bogia, D., and Bignoli, C. (1992). Flexible, Active Support for Collaborative Work with ConversationBuilder. *Proc. CSCW '92,* ACM, 378–385.

Kim, W., and Foley, J. (1990). DON: User Interface Presentation Design Assistant. *Proc. UIST '90,* ACM, 10–20.

Krashner, G., and Pope, S. (1988). A Description of the Model-View-Controller Paradigm in the Smaltalk-80 System. *Journal of Object-Oriented Programming* 1(3), 26–49.

Linton, M., Vlissides, J., and Calder, P. (1989). Composing User Interfaces with InterViews. *IEEE Computer* 22(2), 8–22.

Luo, P., Szekely, P., and Neches, R. (1993). Management of Interface Design in HUMANOID. *Proc. INTERCHI '93,* ACM, 107–114.

Malone, T., Lai, K., and Fry, C. (1992). Experiments With Oval: A Radically Tailorable Tool for Cooperative Work. *Proc. CSCW '92,* ACM, 289–297.

Marcus, A. (1992). *Graphic Design for Electronic Documents and User Interfaces.* ACM Press.

Maulsby, D., Witten, I., Kittlitz, K., and Franceschin, V. (1992). Inferring Graphical Procedures: The Compleat Metamouse. *Human-Computer Interaction* 7(1), 47–89.

McCormack, J., and Asente, P. (1988). An Overview of the X Toolkit. *Proc. UIST '88,* ACM, 46–55.

Microsoft (1993a). Microsoft Visual Basic, Version 3.0.

Microsoft (1993b). Microsoft Windows, Version 3.1.

Myers, B. (1988). *Creating User Interfaces by Demonstration.* Academic Press.

Myers, B. (1990). A New Model for Handling Input. *ACM Transactions on Information Systems* 8(3), 289–320.

Myers, B. (1991). Text Formatting by Demonstration. *Proc.CHI '91,* ACM, 251–256.

● Myers, B. (1993a). State of the Art in User Interface Software Tools. In Hartson, H., and Hix, D. (Eds.), *Advances in Human-Computer Interaction* 4, Ablex, 110–150.

Myers, B. (1993b). Garnet: Uses of Demonstrational Techniques. In Cypher, Halbert, Kurlander, Lieberman, Maulsby, Myers, and Turransky (1993), 219–236.

Myers, B. (1993c). Why Are Human-Computer Interfaces Difficult to Design and Implement? Research Report CMU-CS-93-183. Computer Science Department. Carnegie Mellon.

⊛ Myers, B. (1994a). Addendum: Changes to Garnet Since November, 1990. Original paper.

Myers, B. (1994b). Challenges of HCI Design and Implementation. *Interactions* 1(1), 73–83.

Myers, B., and Buxton, W. (1986). Creating Highly-Interactive and Graphical User Interfaces by Demonstration. *Computer Graphics* 20(3), 249–258. Reprinted in Baecker and Buxton (1987).

⊛ Myers, B., Giuse, D., Dannenberg, R., Zanden, B., Kosbie, D., Pervin, E., Mickish, A., and Marchal, P. (1990). GARNET: Comprehensive Support for Graphical, Highly-Interactive User Interfaces. *IEEE Computer* 23(11), 71–85 (see Myers, 1994a).

Myers, B., Vander Zanden, B., and Dannenberg, R. (1989). Creating Graphical Objects by Demonstration. *Proc. UIST '89*, ACM, 95–104.

NeXT (1991). *NeXTStep and the NeXT Interface Builder.* 900 Chesapeake Drive, Redwood City, CA 94063.

Nielsen, J. (1993). *Usability Engineering.* Academic Press.

Olsen Jr, D. (1992). *User Interface Management Systems: Models and Algorithms.* Morgan Kaufmann.

Olsen Jr., D., Foley, J., Hudson, S., Miller, J., and Myers, B. (1993). Research Directions for User Interface Software Tools. *Behaviour and Information Technology* 12(2), 80–97.

Olson, J., Card, S., Landauer, T., Olson, G., Malone, T., and Leggett, J. (1993). Computer-Supported Co-Operative Work: Research Issues for the 90s. *Behaviour and Information Technology* 12(2), 115–129.

Open Software Foundation (1989). *OSF/Motif, Programmer's Reference Manual.* Open Software Foundation.

Ousterhout, J. (1994). *An Introduction to Tcl and Tk.* Addison-Wesley.

Palay, A., Hansen, W., Kazar, M., Sherman, M., Wadlow, M., Neuendorffer, T., Stern, Z., Badler, M., and Peters, T. (1988). The Andrew Toolkit: An Overview. *Usenix Technical Conference Proceedings*, 9–21.

Patterson, J. (1991). Comparing the Programming Demands of Single-User and Multi-User Applications. *Proc. UIST '91*, ACM, 87–91.

⊛ Pausch, R., Conway, M., and Deline, R. (1992). Lessons Learned from SUIT, the Simple User Interface Toolkit. *ACM Transactions on Office Information Systems* 10(4), 320–344.

Perlman, G. (1988). Software Tools for User Interface Development. In Helander, M. (Ed.) (1988), *Handbook of Human-Computer Interaction*, North-Holland, 819–833.

Potter, R. (1993). Guiding Automation with Pixels: A Technique for Programming in the User Interface. *Proc. INTERCHI '93*, ACM, 530.

Puerta, A., Eriksson, G., and Musen, M. (1994). Toward Ontology-based Frameworks for Knowledge-Acquisition tools. *Proceedings of the Eighth Knowledge-Acquisition Workshop for Knowledge-Based Systems.*

Puerta, A., and Szekely, P. (1994). Model-based Interface Developement. Tutorial Notes #20 at ACM CHI '94 Conference.

⊛ Roseman, M., and Greenberg, S. (1992). GroupKit: A Groupware Toolkit for Building Real-Time Conferencing Applications. *Proc. CSCW '92*, ACM, 43–50.

Scheifler, R., and Gettys, J. (1986). The X Window System. *ACM Transactions on Graphics* 5(2), 79–109.

Shen, H., and Dewan, P. (1992). Access Control for Collaborative Environments. *Proc. CSCW '92*, ACM, 51–58.

Shepherd, A., Mayer, N., and Kuchinsky, A. (1990). Strudel—An Extensible Electronic Conversation Toolkit. *Proc. CSCW '90*, ACM, 93–104.

Singh, G., and Green, M. (1991). Automating the Lexical and Syntactic Design of Graphical User Interfaces: The UofA* UIMS. *ACM Transaction on Graphics* 10(3), 213–254.

Sukaviriya, P., Foley, J., and Griffith, T. (1993). A Second Generation User Interface Design Environment: The Model and the Runtime Architecture. *Proc. INTERCHI '93*, ACM, 375–382.

Sun Microsystems (1990a). *The DevGuide User's Manual.*

Sun Microsystems (1990b). *DeskSet Environment Reference Guide.*

Sutherland, I. (1963). Sketchpad: A Man-Machine Graphical Communication System. *Proceedings of the National Computer Conference.* AFIPS, 329–346.

Szekely, P., Luo, P., and Neches, R. (1993). Beyond Interface Builders: Model-Based Interface Tools. *Proc. INTERCHI'93*, ACM, 383–390.

Taylor, R., and Johnson, G. (1993). Separations of Concerns in the Chiron-1 User Interface Development and Management System. *Proc. INTERCHI '93*, ACM, 367–374.

Vlissides, J., and Linton, M. (1990). Unidraw: A Framework for Building Domain-Specific Graphical Editors. *ACM Transactions on Information Systems* 8(3), 237–268.

Wiecha, C. (1992). ITS and User Interface Consistency: A Response to Grudin. *ACM Transactions on Information Systems* 10(1), 112–114.

⊛ Wiecha, C., Bennett, W., Boies, S., Gould, J., and Greene, S. (1990). ITS: A Tool for Rapidly Developing Interactive Applications. *ACM Transactions on Information Systems* 8(3), 204–236.

VIDEOS

Avrahami, G., Brooks, K., and Brown, M. (1990). FormsVBT: A Two-View Approach to Constructing User Interfaces. *ACM SIGGRAPH Video Review (SGVR)* 56.

Baecker, R., Glass, G., Mitchell, A., and Posner, I. (1994). SASSE: The Collaborative Editor. *ACM SGVR* 97.

Bier, E., Freeman, S., and Pier, K. (1992). MMM: The Multi-Device Multi-User Multi-Editor. *ACM SGVR* 76.

Bier, E., Stone, M., Pier, K., Fishkin, K., Baudel, T., Conway, M., Buxton, W., and DeRose, T. (1994). Toolglasses and Magic Lenses: The See-Through Interface. *ACM SGVR* 97.

Buxton, W. (1983). Towards a Comprehensive UIMS. *ACM SGVR* 11.

Carnegie Mellon University (1989). An Overview of the Andrew System. *ACM SGVR* 46.

Cohen, E. (1987). Siemens RTL Tiled Window System. *ACM SGVR* 33.

Dewan, P. (1992). Coupling the User Interface of a Multi-User Program. *ACM SGVR* 87.

Gray, M., deBaar, D., Foley, J., and Mullet, K. (1992). Coupling Application Design and User Interface Design. *ACM SGVR* 76.

Greenberg, S., Roseman, M., Webster, D., and Bohnet, R. (1992). GroupSketch. *ACM SGVR* 87.

Hayes, P. (1985). The Cousin User Interface Management System. *ACM SGVR* 18.

Hill, R. (1987). Sassafras Demo. *ACM SGVR* 34.

Kasik, D. (1983). Tiger System Demonstration. *ACM SGVR* 12.

Kurlander, D. (1993). Graphical Editing by Example. *ACM SGVR* 89.

Maulsby, D. (1990). Metamouse: End-User Programming by Demonstration. *ACM SGVR* 56.

Myers, B. (1985a). Percent Done Indicator. *ACM SGVR* 19.

Myers, B. (1985b). The User Interface for Sapphire. *ACM SGVR* 19.

Myers, B. (1988). Creating User Interfaces by Demonstration: The Peridot User Interface Management System. *ACM SGVR* 59.

Myers, B. (1990). All the Widgets. *ACM SGVR* 57.

Myers, B., Giuse, D., Mickish, A., Vander Zanden, B., Kosbie, D., McDaniel, R., Landay, J., Goldberg, M., and Pathasarathy, R. (1994). The Garnet User Interface Development Environment. *ACM SGVR* 97.

Pike, R. (1983). Blit. *ACM SGVR* 13.

Potter, R. (1993). Guiding Automation with Pixels: A Technique for Programming in the User Interface. *ACM SGVR* 89.

Plaisant, C., and Wallace, D. (1992). Touchscreen Toggle Design. *ACM SGVR* 77.

Vander Zanden, B., and Myers, B. (1991). The Lapidary Graphical User Interface Design Tool. *ACM SGVR* 63.

Wong. (1983). Rapid Prototyping Using FLAIR. *ACM SGVR* 12.

State of the Art in User Interface Software Tools*

Brad A. Myers

School of Computer Science
Carnegie Mellon University

INTRODUCTION

The *user interface* of a computer program is the part that handles the output to the display and the input from the person using the program. The rest of the program is called the *application* or the *application semantics*. Experience and studies have shown that creating the software for user interfaces is a very expensive and difficult task. The easy-to-use "Direct Manipulation" interfaces popular with most modern systems are among the most difficult to implement. In these interfaces, the objects of interest are visible on the screen, and the user can operate on them by direct reference and rapid, reversible, incremental actions (Shneiderman, 1983). Examples include most programs running on systems with *windowing systems* (that divide the screen into separate rectangular areas) such as Macintosh, Microsoft Windows, Presentation Manager, SunView, X, etc.

This chapter discusses why user interface software is so difficult to create, and what kinds of tools have been created to help with this process. There have been many previous surveys on this topic (Myers, 1989a; Hartson & Hix, 1989), but since this is a fast-changing field, a new one seemed in order. In addition, this chapter takes a broader approach and includes more components of user interface software, including windowing systems. However, it is now impossible to discuss *all* user interface tools, since there are so many. For example, there are over 100 commercial graphical user interface builders, and many new research tools are reported every year at conferences like the annual ACM User Interface Software and Technology Symposium (UIST) and the ACM SIGCHI conference. There are also probably at least three Ph.D. theses on user interface tools every year. Therefore, this chapter tries to provide an overview of the most popular approaches, rather than an exhaustive survey.

User interface tools have been called various names over the years, with the most popular being *user interface management systems (UIMS)*. However, many people feel that the term UIMS should be used only for tools that handle the sequencing of operations (what happens after each event from the user), so other terms like *toolkits*, *user interface development environments*, *interface builders*, and *application frameworks* have been used. This chapter will try to define these terms more specifically, and use the general term *user interface tool* for all software aimed to help create user interfaces. Note that the word *tool* is being used to include what are called *toolkits*, as well as higher level tools, such as interface builders, that are *not* toolkits.

Four different classes of people are involved with user interface software, and it is important to have different names for them to avoid confusion. The first is the person using the resulting program, who is called the *end user* or just *user*. The next person creates the user interface of the program, and is called the *user interface designer* or just *designer*. Working with the user interface designer will be the person who writes the software for the rest of the application. This person is called the *application programmer*. The designer may use special user interface tools specifically created to help create user interfaces. These tools are created by the *tool creator*. Note that the designer will be a user of the software created by the tool creator, but we still do not use the term *user* here, to avoid confusion with the end user. Although this classification discusses each role as a different person, in fact, there may be many people in each role, or one person may perform multiple roles. The general term *programmer* is used for anyone who writes code and may be a designer, application programmer, or tool creator.

WHY USER INTERFACES ARE HARD TO BUILD

It is the conventional wisdom that user interface software is difficult and expensive to create. Many surveys have shown that the user inter-

* For help with this chapter, I would like to thank Jim Foley, Brad Vander Zanden, John Turner, Robert Seacord, Bernita Myers, and the referees.

This research was sponsored by the Avionics Lab, Wright Research and Development Center, Aeronautical Systems Division (AFSC), U. S. Air Force, Wright-Patterson AFB, OH 45433-6543 under Contract F33615-90-C-1465, Arpa Order No. 7597. The views and conclusions contained in this chapter are those of the authors and should not be interpreted as representing the official policies, either expressed or implied, of the U.S. Government.

face portion of the software accounts for over half of the code and development time. For example, a new survey reports that, over a wide class of program types, machine types, and tools used, the percentage of the design time, the implementation time, the maintenance time, and the code size devoted to the user interface was about 50% (Myers & Rosson, 1992). In fact, there are a number of important reasons that user interface software will *inherently* be among the most difficult kinds of software to create, as described below.

Iterative Design

It is notoriously difficult to *design* a user interface that will be easy to use, and there are no design strategies that will guarantee that the resulting user interface will be learnable, easy to use, and "user friendly." Consequently, the only reliable method for generating quality user interfaces is to test prototypes with actual end users and modify the design based on the users' comments and performance (Gould & Lewis, 1985; Swartout & Balzer, 1982). As reported by Sheil (1983, p. 136) "complex interactive interfaces usually require extensive empirical testing to determine whether they are really effective and considerable redesign to make them so." This methodology is called *iterative design* and has been used in the creation of some of the best user interfaces: the Xerox Star (Bewley, Roberts, Schroir, & Verplank 1983), the Apple Lisa and Macintosh (Morgan, Williams, & Lemmons, 1983), and the Olympic Messaging system (Boies, Gould, Levy, Richards, & Schoonard, 1985). A recent survey reported that 87% of the development projects used iterative design in some form (Myers & Rosson, 1992).

The need for iterative design means that the conventional software engineering approach to software design (Yourdon, 1989) is inadequate. It is impossible to fully specify the user interface of a system, then implement it, and later test it. Instead, the specification, the implementation, and the testing must be intertwined (Swartout & Balzer, 1982). Furthermore, it can be very difficult to schedule and manage user interface development when it is not clear how many iterations of reimplementation will be necessary.

Multiprocessing

As discussed below, almost all windowing systems queue "event" records to deliver the keyboard and mouse inputs from the user to the user interface software. Users expect to be able to abort and undo actions (for example, by typing control-C or Command-dot) and to freeze the output of the program if it is scrolling by too fast (for example, using control-S). Also, if a window's picture needs to be redrawn by the application, the window system notifies the application by adding a special event to the queue. Therefore, the user interface software must be structured so that it can accept input events at all times, even while executing commands. Consequently, any operations that may take a long time (such as printing, searching, global replace, repaginating a document, or even repainting the screen) should be executed in a separate process.[1] Therefore, most programmers creating user interface software will encounter the well-known problems of multiple processes (synchronization, maintaining consistency among multiple threads, deadlocks, etc.).

Real-time Programming

Most graphical, direct manipulation interfaces will have objects that are animated or move around with the mouse. In order for this to be attractive to users, the objects must be redisplayed between 30 and 60 times per second without uneven pauses. Therefore, the programmer must insure that any necessary processing to calculate the feedback can be guaranteed to finish in about 16 milleseconds. Many of the problems of real-time programming therefore also appear in user interface programming.

Robustness

When the user provides erroneous input to a program, the program should respond with a helpful error message, and allow the user to repair the error and continue. This means that programs should *never* crash or go into a debugger. Whereas a programmer might define the interface to an internal procedure to only work when passed a certain type of value, the user interface must always accept any possible input and continue to operate. As a result, there is a tremendous requirement for robustness in user interface software.

To make the task even more difficult, user interfaces should allow the user to abort and undo any operation. Therefore, the programmer must implement all actions in a way that will allow them to be aborted while executing and undone after completion.

Testability

A related problem is the difficulty of testing user interface software for correctness. Since systems may have hundreds of commands, and they

[1] Alternatively, the long jobs could poll for input events in their inner loop, and then check to see how to handle the input, but this is essentially a way to simulate multiple processing.

may interact in many ways, it is difficult to exercise all possible paths through the program. Automated testing tools are rarely useful for direct manipulation systems, since they have difficulty pretending to be users. Techniques such as making a transcript of the mouse movements and button presses do not work if elements of the user interface are moved around or change type, since then the transcript will no longer work. Also, how would the testing program compare the output with the expect values, since the output is usually directed at the screen?

Modularization

One of the most important ways to make software easier to create in general is to appropriately modularize the different parts. The standard admonition in textbooks is that the user interface portion should be separated from the rest of the software, in part so that the user interface can be easily changed (for iterative design). Unfortunately, programmers find in practice that it is difficult or impossible to separate the user interface and application parts (Rosson, Maass, & Kellogg, 1987), and changes to the user interface usually require reprogramming parts of the application also.

Complexity of the Tools

The existing tools for creating user interface software are notoriously difficult to use. Manuals for the tools often run to many volumes and contain hundreds of procedures (for example, the Macintosh ToolBox manuals, Apple, 1985, now fill six books, and the X documentation is similar). In spite of this, many of the provided functions may not be flexible enough to achieve the desired effect. For example, in the Macintosh and Motif toolkits, it is easy to have a keyboard accelerator that will perform the same operation as a menu item, but very difficult to have a keyboard command do the same thing as an on-screen button. Some tools even require the programmer to learn an entirely new special-purpose programming language to create the user interface.

Using the underlying graphics packages is also quite difficult. Since the human eye is quite sensitive to small differences, the graphic displays must essentially be perfect: a single pixel error in alignment will be visible. Most existing graphics packages provide no help with making the displays attractive.

Language Support

Most computer programming languages do not contain primitives for graphical input and output. Many, however, have input–output primitives that will read and write strings. For example, Pascal uses readln and writeln. Unfortunately, using these produces a very bad user interface, where the user is required to answer questions in a highly modal style, and there are no facilities for undo or help. Therefore, the built-in input/output facilities must be ignored and special libraries must be used.

Many user interface tools have found other important language features lacking. For example, many people agree that user interface software should be "object-oriented," but most languages do not have an appropriate object system (see "Toolkit Intrinsics" below). The creators of the Xtk toolkit (McCormack & Asente, 1988) (in which Motif and OpenLook are implemented), and the Andrew toolkit (Palay et al., 1988), decided that existing object systems (such as C++ and Objective-C) were unacceptable, and decided to implement their own special object-oriented facilities to C. Similarly, Apple added an object system to Pascal for MacApp (Wilson, 1990), and Garnet (Myers et al., 1990) added a special object system to Lisp.

OVERVIEW OF USER INTERFACE SOFTWARE TOOLS

Since user interface software is so difficult to create, it is not surprising that people have been working for a long time to create tools to help with the process. Today, many of these tools have progressed from research into commercial systems, and their effectiveness has been amply demonstrated. For example, the MacApp system from Apple has been reported to reduce development time by a factor of four or five (Schmucker, 1986). Research systems also continue to evolve quickly, and the systems that were popular 5 years ago have been made obsolete by more effective tools and new styles of user interfaces.

Advantages of Using Tools

Naturally, the user interface tools attempt to overcome the problems in creating user interface software listed above. In particular, the claimed advantages of using tools include:

- **The quality of the interfaces should be higher.** This is because:
  - Designs can be rapidly prototyped and implemented, possibly even before the application code is written.
  - It is easier to incorporate changes discovered through user testing.
  - There can be multiple user interfaces for the same application.
  - More effort can be expended on the tool than may be practical on

  any single user interface, since the tool will be used with many different applications.
  - Different applications are likely to have more consistent user interfaces if they are created using the same user interface tool.
  - Conversely, some user interface tools make it easier to investigate different styles for a user interface, and thereby provide a unique "look and feel" for a program.
  - A UI tool should make it easier for a variety of specialists to be involved in designing the user interface, rather than having the user interface created entirely by programmers. Graphic artists, cognitive psychologists, and human factors specialists may all be involved. In particular, professional user interface designers, who may not be programmers, can be in charge of the overall design.
  - It will be easier to customize the interfaces to fit the needs of the users.
  - The ability to rapidly modify interfaces should allow system designers and salesmen to try different interfaces on products in front of customers and end users, and immediately incorporate their suggestions.
- **The user interface code will be easier and more economical to create and maintain.** This is because:
  - Interface specifications can be represented, validated, and evaluated more easily.
  - There will be less code to write, because much is supplied in standard libraries.
  - There will be better modularization due to the separation of the user interface component from the application. This should allow the user interface to change without affecting the application, and a large class of changes to the application (such as changing the internal algorithms) should be possible without affecting the user interface.
  - Training and learning costs for the user interface designers and implementers should be less, since the tools are easier to use than the underlying system.
  - The level of expertise of the interface designers and implementers can be lower, because the tools hide many of the complexities of the underlying system.
  - The reliability of the user interface should be higher, since the code for the user interface is created automatically from a higher level specification.
  - It should be easier to port an application to different hardware and software environments since the device dependencies are isolated in the user interface tool.

Goals for User Interface Software Tools

This section discusses some of the things that you might want a user interface tool to help with. The list can be used to evaluate the various tools to see how much they cover. Naturally, no tool will help with everything, and different user interface designers may put different emphasis on the different goals.

In general, the tools might:

- help *design* the interface given a specification of the end users' tasks,
- help *implement* the interface given a specification of the design,
- create easy-to-use interfaces,
- allow the designer to rapidly investigate different designs,
- allow nonprogrammers to design and implement user interfaces,
- automatically evaluate the interface and propose improvements, or at least provide information to allow the designer to evaluate the interface,
- allow the end user to customize the interface,
- provide portability, and
- be easy to use themselves.

This might be achieved by having the tools:

- automatically choose which user interface styles, input devices, widgets, etc., should be used,
- help with screen layout and graphic design,
- validate user inputs,
- handle user errors,
- handle user-specified aborting and undoing of operations,
- provide appropriate feedback to show that inputs have been received,
- provide help and prompts,
- update the screen display when application data changes,
- notify the application when the user updates application data,
- deal with field scrolling and editing,
- help with the sequencing of operations, and
- insulate the application from all device dependencies and the underlying software and hardware systems.

Components of User Interface Software

As shown in Figure 1, user interface software may be divided into various components. Some systems layer the components differently, but most have a part that fills each of the roles shown.

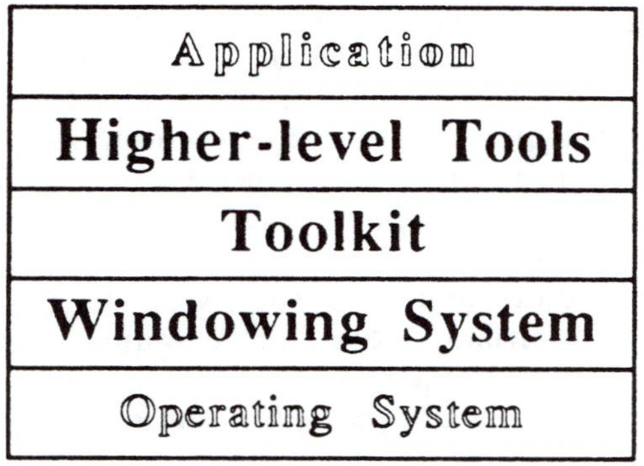

Figure 1. The components of user interface software discussed in this paper.

The *windowing system* supports the separation of the screen into different (usually rectangular) regions, called *windows*. Some modern windowing systems divide the functionality into a *window system*, which provides the functional or programming interface, and a *window manager* which provides the user interface. This terminology comes from the X system (Scheifler & Gettys, 1986). However, many people and systems use the name *window manager* to refer to both the base layer and the user interface layer. This chapter will use the X terminology, and use the term *windowing system* when referring to both layers.

The *window system* part provides procedures that allow the application to draw pictures on the screen and get input from the user. The *window manager* allows the end user to move windows around, and is responsible for displaying the title lines, borders, and icons around the windows. On top of the windowing system is the *toolkit*, which contains many commonly used *widgets* such as menus, buttons, scroll bars, and text input fields. On top of the toolkit might be higher level tools, which help the designer use the toolkit widgets. The following sections discuss each of these components in more detail.

WINDOWING SYSTEMS

A *windowing system* is a software package that helps the user monitor and control different contexts by separating them physically onto different parts of one or more display screens. A survey of various windowing systems appears in Myers (1988a).

The first windowing systems were implemented as part of a single program or system. For example, the EMACs text editor (Stallman, 1979), and the Smalltalk (Tesler, 1981) and DLISP (Teitelman, 1979) programming environments, had their own windowing systems. Later systems implemented the windowing system as an integral part of the operating system, such as Sapphire for PERQs (Myers, 1984), SunView for Suns, and the Macintosh and NeXT windowing systems. In order to allow different windowing systems to operate on the same operating system, some windowing systems, such as X and Sun's NeWS, operate as a separate process, and use the operating systems interprocess communication mechanism to connect to applications.

Structure of Windowing Systems

A windowing system can be logically divided into two layers, each of which has two parts (see Figure 2). The *window system*, or *base layer*, implements the basic functionality of the windowing system. The two parts of this layer handle the display of graphics in windows (the *output model*) and the access to the various input devices (the *input model*), which usually includes a keyboard and a pointing device such as a "mouse." The primary interface of the base layer is procedural, and is called the windowing system's *application* or *program interface*.

The other layer of a windowing system is the *window manager* or *user interface*. This includes all aspects that are visible to the user. The two parts of the user interface layer are the *presentation*, which is comprised of the pictures that the window manager displays, and the *commands*, which are how the user manipulates the windows and their contents. Figure 3 shows windows that demonstrate different aspects of the presentation, including patterns or pictures for the area where there are no windows, title lines and borders for windows, icons, etc. Examples of the operations that may be provided for windows include moving them around on the screen and specifying their size.

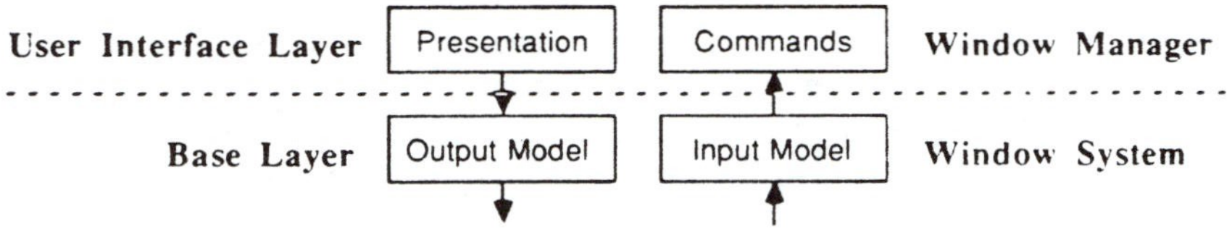

Figure 2. The windowing system can be divided into two layers, called the *base* or *window system* layer, and the *user interface* or *window manager* layer. Each of these can be divided into parts that handle output and input.

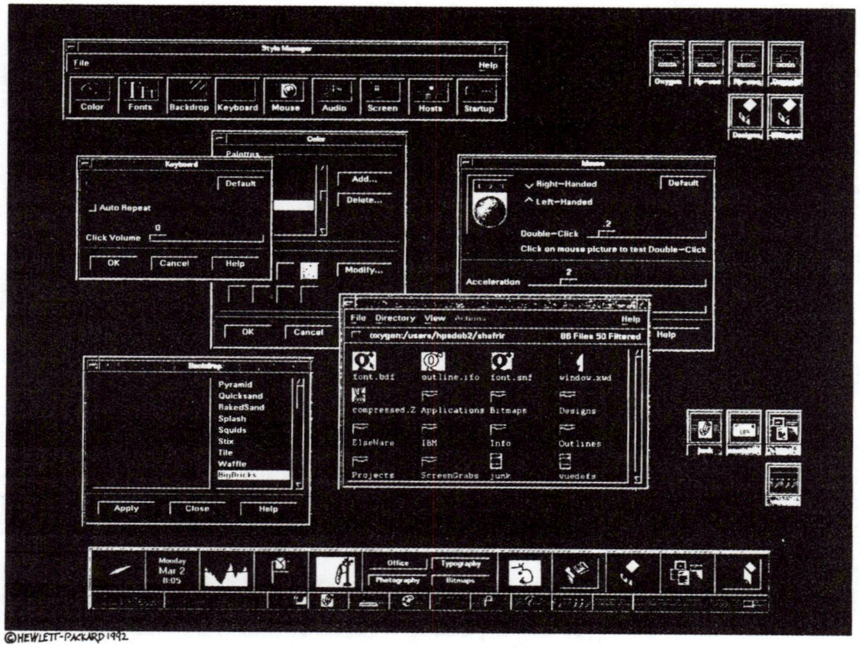

Figure 3. An example screen running a covered window system. This is a Hewlett-Packard HP VUE screen, which is using Motif under X/11. (Courtesy of the User Interaction Design Group, Hewlett-Packard, copyright 1991, used by permission.)

Base Layer

The *base layer* is the procedural interface to the windowing system. In the 1970s and early 1980s, there were a large number of different windowing systems, each with a different procedural interface (at least one for each hardware platform). People writing software found this to be unacceptable because they wanted to be able to run their software on different platforms, but they would have to rewrite significant amounts of code to convert from one window system to another. The X windowing system (Scheifler, 1986) was created to solve this problem by providing a hardware-independent interface to windows. X has been quite successful at this, and has driven virtually all other windowing systems out of the workstation hardware market (the notable exception is the NeXT system; and, of course, some older windowing systems, such as SunView, continue to be supported). In the small computer market, the Macintosh runs its own window system, or X, and IBM PC-class machines primarily run Microsoft Windows or IBM's Presentation Manager.

Output model. The output model is the set of procedures that an application can use to draw pictures on the screen. It is important that all output be directed through the window system so that the graphics primitives can be clipped to the window's borders. For example, if a program draws a line that would extend out of a window's borders, it must be clipped so that the contents of other, independent, windows are not overwritten. Most windowing systems provide special escapes that allow programs to draw directly to the screen, without using the window system's clipping. These operations can be much quicker but are very dangerous and therefore should seldom be used. Most modern computers provide graphics operations that are specially optimized to work efficiently with the window system.

In early windowing systems, such as Smalltalk (Tesler, 1981), Blit (Pike, 1983), and Sapphire (Myers, 1986), the primary output operation was *BitBlt* (also called *RasterOp*). This takes a rectangle of pixels from one part of the screen and copies them to another part. Various boolean operations can be specified for combining the pixel values of the source and destination rectangles. For example, the source rectangle can simply replace the destination, or it might be XORed with the destination. BitBlt can be used to fill a rectangle with a particular color, display text, scroll windows, and perform many other effects (Ingalls, 1981).

Later windowing systems, such as the Macintosh and X, added a full set of drawing operations, such as filled and unfilled polygons, text, lines, arcs, etc. A few windowing systems, such as NeWS, NeXT, and the latest versions of DECWindows, allow the full Postscript imaging system (Adobe, 1985) to be used to create images on the screen. Postscript provides device-independent coordinate systems and arbitrary rotations and scaling for all objects, including text. Another advantage of using Postscript for the screen is that the same language can be used to print the windows on paper (since many printers accept Postscript).

As shown in Figure 4, the earlier windowing systems assumed that a graphics package would be implemented using the windowing system. For example, the CORE graphics package was implemented on top of the SunView windowing system. As mentioned above, most newer systems, including the Macintosh, X, NeWS, and NeXT, have implemented the graphics system as *part* of the windowing system.

Input model. It is somewhat surprising that, although there has been substantial progress in handling of the output in windowing systems, input is still handled in essentially the same way that the original windowing systems handled it: as a stream of event records sent to the

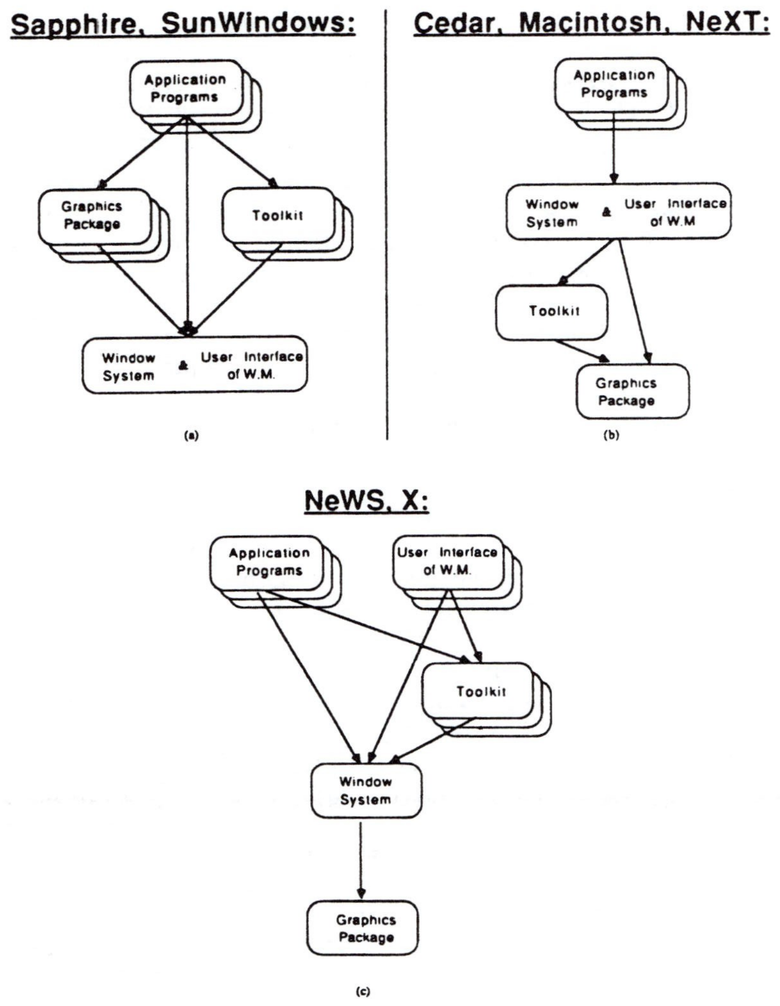

Figure 4. Various organizations that have been used by windowing systems. Boxes with extra borders represent systems that can be replaced by users. Early systems (a) tightly coupled the window manager and the window system, and assumed that sophisticated graphics and toolkits would be built on top. The next step in designs (b) was to incorporate into the windowing system the graphics and toolkits, so that the window manager itself could have a more sophisticated look and feel, and so applications would be more consistent. Most recently, (c) windowing systems have allowed different window managers and different toolkits, while still embedding sophisticated graphics packages.

window. Each event record typically contains the type and value of the event (e.g., which key was pressed), the window that the event was directed to, a timestamp, and the x and y position of the mouse. The windowing system queues keyboard events, mouse button events, and mouse movement events together (along with other special events) and programs must dequeue the events and process them.

The problems with this model are that:

- There is no provision for special abort or stop-output events (control-C, command-dot), so these will be queued with the other input events.
- The same event mechanism is used for special messages from the windowing system. When a window gets larger or becomes uncovered, the program must usually be notified so it can adjust or redraw the picture in the window. Most window systems communicate this by enqueuing special events into the event stream, which the program must handle.
- The application must always be willing to accept events in order to process aborts and redrawing requests, as discussed above in "Multiprocessing."
- The model is device dependent, since the event record has fixed fields for the expected incoming events. If a 3-D pointing device or one with more than the standard number of buttons was used instead of a mouse, then the event mechanism could not handle it.
- Because the events are handled asynchronously, there are many race conditions that can cause programs to get out of synchronization with the window system. For example, in the X windowing system, if you press inside a window and release outside, under certain conditions the program will think that the mouse button is still depressed. Another example is that refresh requests from the windowing system specify a rectangle of the window that needs to be redrawn, but if the program is changing the contents of the window, the wrong area may be redrawn by the time the event is processed. This problem can occur when the window is scrolled.

Although these problems have been known for a long time, there has been little research on new input models (an exception is the Garnet Interactors model—Myers, 1990a).

User Interface Layer

The user interface of the windowing system allows the user to control the windows. In X, the user can easily switch user interfaces by killing one window manager and starting another. Popular window managers under X include *uwm* (which has no title lines and borders), *twm*, *mwm* (the Motif window manager), and *olwm* (the OpenLook window manager). There is a standard protocol through which programs and the base layer communicate to the window manager, so that all programs continue to run without change when the window manager is switched. It is possible, for example, to run applications that use Motif widgets inside the windows controlled by the OpenLook window manager.

For a complete discussion of the options for the user interfaces of window managers, see Myers (1988a). Also, the video *All the Widgets* (Myers, 1990b) has a 30-minute segment showing many different forms of window manager user interfaces.

The user interface of a windowing system, which is sometimes called its *look and feel*, can apparently be copyrighted and patented. This is the source of a number of the look-and-feel lawsuits (Samuelson, 1989).

Presentation. The *presentation* of the windows defines how the screen looks. One very important aspect of the presentation of windows is whether they can *overlap* or not. Overlapping windows, sometimes called *covered* windows, allow one window to be partially or totally on top of another window, as shown in Figure 3. This is also sometimes called the *desktop metaphor*, since windows can cover each other like pieces of paper can cover each other on a desk.[2] The other alternative is called *tiled* windows, which means that windows are not allowed to cover each other. Figure 5 shows an example of tiled windows. Obviously, a window manager that supports covered windows can also allow them to be side-by-side, but not vice-versa. Therefore, a window manager is classified as *covered* if it allows windows to overlap. Although the tiled style was popular for awhile, it is now rarely seen, because users generally prefer overlapping.

Another important aspect of the presentation of windows is the use of *icons*. These are small pictures that represent windows (or sometimes files). They are used because there would otherwise be too many windows to conveniently fit on the screen and manage. When a window is not in use, it can be removed and replaced with its icon, and later conveniently retrieved when needed. Figure 6 shows examples of icons from various window managers. Some window managers allow

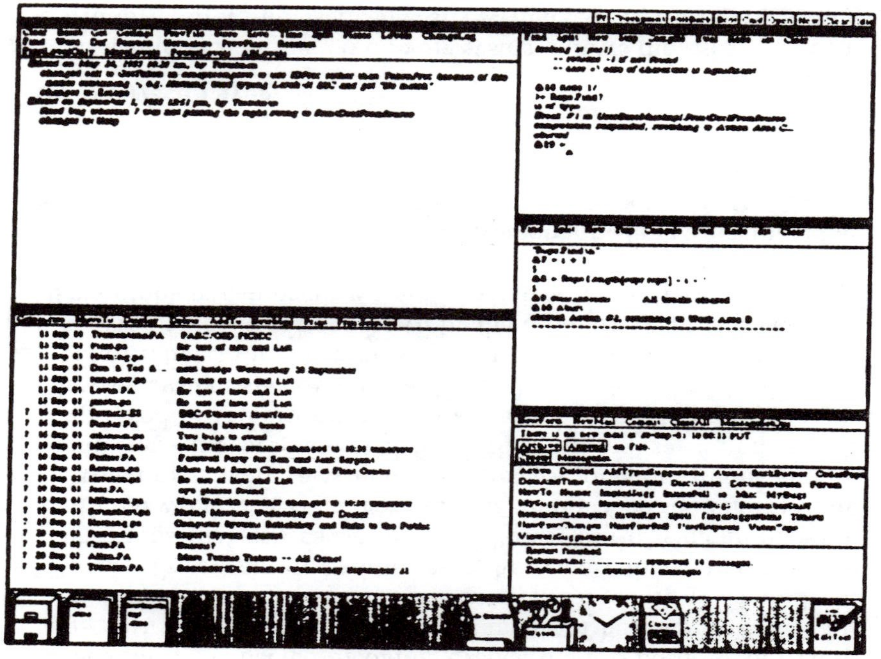

Figure 5. A screen from the Cedar [Swinehart, Zellweger, Beach, & Hagmann, 1986] windowing system. Windows are "tiled" into two columns. There is a row of icons along the bottom. Each window has a fixed menu of commands below the title line.

applications to control parts of the icons for their own user interfaces. For example, Sapphire allows the icon to be a bitmap picture and to contain progress bars, and Motif allows the icon to contain arbitrary graphics, that might even be animated.

Other aspects of the presentation include whether the window has a title line or not, what the background (where there are no windows) looks like, and whether the title and borders have control areas for performing window operations.

Commands. Since computers typically have multiple windows and only one mouse and keyboard, there must be a way for the user to control which window is getting keyboard input. This window is called the *input* (or *keyboard*) *focus*. Another term is the *listener*, since it is listening to the user's typing. Older systems called the focus the *active window* or *current window*, but these are poor terms, since in a multiprocessing system many windows can be actively outputting in-

[2] There are usually other aspects to the desktop metaphor, however, such as presenting file operations in a way that mimics office operations, as in the Star office workstation (Smith, Irby, Kimball, Verplank, & Harslem, 1982).

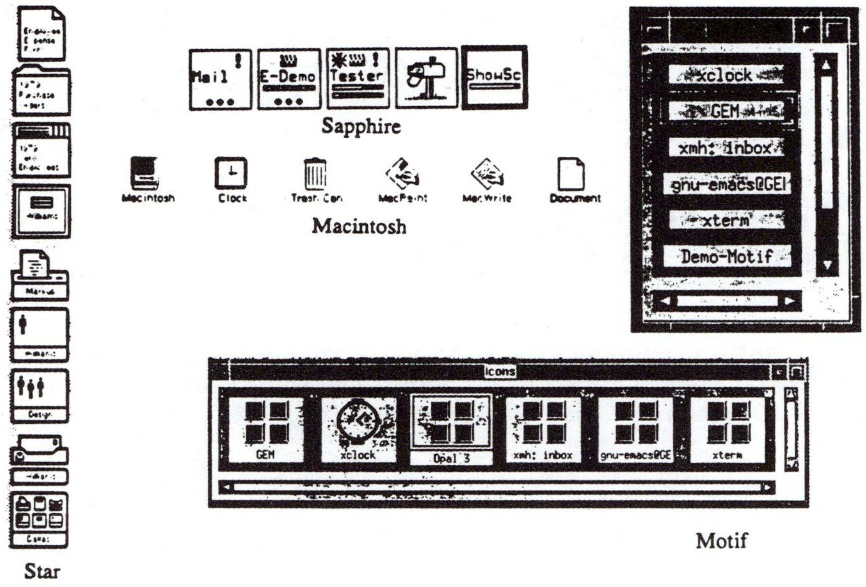

Figure 6. Examples of icons from different systems: Sapphire [Myers, 1984], Macintosh, Star [Smith et al., 1982] and two styles of icons for the Motif Window Manager for X.

formation at the same time. Window managers provide various ways to specify and show which window is the listener. The most important options are:

- *click-to-type*, which means that the user must click the mouse button in a window before typing to it. This is used by the Macintosh.
- *move-to-type*, which means that the mouse only has to move over a window to allow typing to it. This is usually faster for the user but may cause input to go to the wrong window if the user accidentally knocks the mouse.

Most X window managers (including the Motif and OpenLook window managers) allow the user to choose which method is desired.

All covered window systems allow the user to change which window is on top (not covered by other windows), and usually to send a window to the bottom (covered by all other windows). Other commands allow windows to be changed size, moved, created, and destroyed.

TOOLKITS

A *toolkit* is a library of interaction techniques that can be called by application programs. An *interaction technique* is a way of using a physical input device to input a certain type of value. Interaction techniques are also often called *widgets* or *gadgets*. Typically, widgets in toolkits include menus, buttons, scroll bars, dialog boxes, etc. Figure 7 shows some examples of widgets. Toolkits can only be used by programmers, since they only have procedural interfaces.

Using a toolkit has the advantage that the final UI will look and act similarly to other UIs created using the same toolkit, and each application does not have to rewrite the standard functions, such as menus. A problem with toolkits is that the styles of interaction are limited to

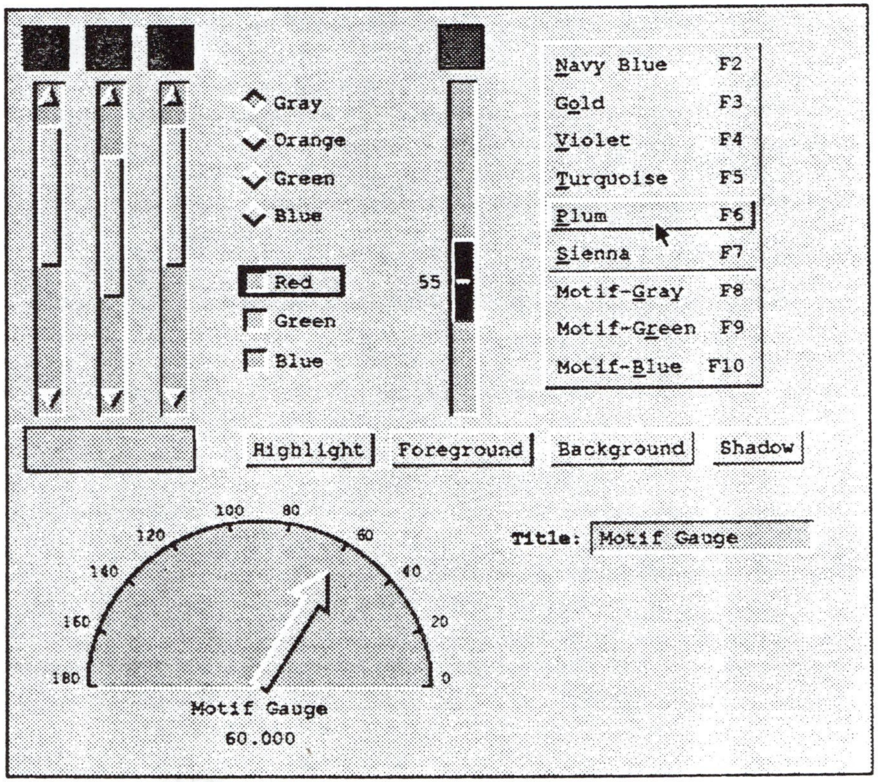

Figure 7. Some of the widgets with a Motif look-and-feel provided by the Garnet toolkit.

those provided. In addition, the toolkits themselves are often expensive to create: "The primitives never seem complex in principle, but the programs that implement them are surprisingly intricate" (Cardelli & Pike, 1985, p. 199). Another problem with toolkits is that they are often difficult to use, since they may contain hundreds of procedures, and it is often not clear how to use the procedures to create a desired interface.

As with the graphics package, the toolkit can be implemented either using or being used by the windowing system (see Figure 4). In the Macintosh, the toolkit is at a low level, and the window manager user interface is built using it. The advantage of this is that the window manager can then use the same toolkit routines for its user interface. In other systems, such as X, the toolkit is on top of the windowing system. Here, is it easier to switch toolkits (for example, the Xtk—McCormack & Asente, 1988), InterViews (Linton, Vlissides, & Calder, 1989), or Garnet (Myers et al., 1990) toolkits can be used on top of X), but the window manager must usually implement its user interface from scratch.

In the terminology of the Xtk toolkit (McCormack & Asente, 1988) for the X Window System, a toolkit may be divided into two layers. The *widget set* is the collection of widgets, and the *intrinsics* layer is how the widgets are implemented. The intrinsics provide the common services, such as techniques for object-oriented programming, etc. Multiple widget sets with different looks and feels can be implemented on top of the same intrinsics layer (Figure 8a), or else the same look-and-feel can be implemented on top of different intrinsics (Figure 8b).

Toolkit Intrinsics

Toolkits come in two basic varieties. The most conventional is simply a collection of procedures that can be called by application programs. Examples of this style include the SunTools toolkit for the Sun View

(a) (b)

Figure 8. (a) At least three different widget sets that have different looks and feels have been implemented on top of the Xtk intrinsics. (b) The Motif look and feel has been implemented on at least three different intrinsics.

windowing system, and the Macintosh Toolbox (Apple, 1985). The other variety uses an object-oriented programming style that makes it easier for the designer to customize the interaction techniques. Examples include Smalltalk (Tesler, 1981), Andrew (Palay et al., 1988) and the Xtk toolkit (McCormack & Asente, 1988) for the X Window System.

The advantages of using object-oriented intrinsics are that it is a natural way to think about widgets (the menus and buttons on the screen *seem* like objects), the widget objects can handle some of the chores that otherwise would be left to the programmer (such as refresh), and it is easier to create custom widgets (by subclassing an existing widget). The advantage of the older, procedural style is that it is easier to implement, no special object-oriented system is needed, and it is easier to interface to multiple programming languages.

To implement the objects, the toolkit might invent its own object system, as was done with Xtk, Andrew, and Garnet, or it might use an existing object system, as was done in InterViews (Linton et al., 1989), which uses C++, and NeXTStep (NeXT, 1991), which used Objective-C.

The usual way that object-oriented toolkits interface with application programs is through the use of *call-back procedures*. These are procedures defined by the application programmer that are called when a widget is operated by the end user. For example, the programmer might supply a procedure to be called when the user selects a menu item. Experience has shown that real interfaces often contain hundreds of call-backs, which makes the code harder to modify and maintain (Myers & Rosson, 1992). In addition, different toolkits, even when implemented on the same intrinsics like Motif and OpenLook, have different call-back protocols. This means that code for one toolkit is difficult to port to a different toolkit. Therefore, research is being directed at reducing the number of call-backs in user interface software (Myers, 1991a).

Some research toolkits have added novel things to the toolkit intrinsics. For example, GROW (Barth, 1986) and the Garnet toolkit (Myers, 1990a) allow the objects to be connected using *constraints*, which are relationships that are declared once and then maintained automatically by the system. For example, the designer can specify that the color of a rectangle is constrained to be the value of a slider, and then the system will update the rectangle if the user moves the slider.

Widget Set

Typically, the intrinsics layer is look-and-feel independent, which means that the widgets built on top of it can have any desired appearance and behavior. However, a particular widget set must pick a look and feel. The video *All the Widgets* shows many examples of widgets that have been designed over the years (Myers, 1990b). For example, it shows 35 different kinds of menus. Like window manager user interfaces, the widgets' look and feel can be copyrighted and patented.

As was mentioned above, different widget sets (with different looks and feels) can be implemented on top of the same intrinsics. In addition, the same look and feel can be implemented on top of different intrinsics. For example, there are Motif look-and-feel widgets on top of the xtk, InterViews, and Garnet intrinsics (Figure 8b). Although they all look and operate the same (so would be indistinguishable to the end user), they are implemented quite differently and have completely different procedural interfaces for the programmer.

VIRTUAL TOOLKITS

Although there are many small differences among the various toolkits, much remains the same. For example, all have some type of menu, button, scroll bar, text input field, etc. Although there are fewer windowing systems and toolkits than there were 5 years ago, people are still finding that they must do a lot of work to convert their software from Motif to OpenLook to the Macintosh and to Microsoft Windows.

Therefore, a number of systems are being developed that try to hide the differences among the various toolkits, by providing *virtual* widgets which can be mapped into the widgets of each toolkit. The code can then be linked to different actual toolkits, and will run without change. An example is the XVT system (XVT, 1991), which provides a C or C++ interface that hides the differences of the Motif, OpenLook, Macintosh, MS-Windows, and OS 2-PM toolkits (and also character terminals).[3]

The interface to the virtual toolkit is still procedural, however, so the designer must be an experienced programmer. Typically, the virtual toolkits take a "least common denominator" approach and only provide functions that appear in all toolkits. Therefore, a designer may not be able to achieve the desired result. In addition, the resulting interface may not be completely compliant with the look and feel of the target system, due to features of the target toolkit that do not appear in other toolkits.

[3] This can be distinguished from a toolkit that supports multiple looks and feels. For example, both the InterViews and Garnet toolkits provide a set of widgets with the Motif look and feel, and another set of widgets with a custom look and feel. To be called a *virtual toolkit*, a system must link to the native implementations of the underlying toolkits, rather than replacing them.

HIGHER LEVEL TOOLS

Since toolkits are hard to use, there is a tremendous interest in higher level tools that will make the user interface software production process easier.

Phases

Many higher level tools have components that operate at different times. The *design time component* helps the user interface designer design the user interface. For example, this might be a graphical editor which can lay out the interface, or a compiler to process a user interface specification language. The next phase is when the end user is using the program. Here, the *run-time component* of the tool is used. This usually includes a toolkit, but may also include additional software specifically for the tool. Since the run-time component is "managing" the user interface, the term *user interface management system* seems appropriate for tools with a significant run-time component. There may also be an *after-run-time component* that helps with the evaluation and debugging of the user interface. Unfortunately, very few user interface tools have an after-run-time component. This is partially because tools that have tried, such as MIKE (Olsen & Halversen, 1988), discovered that there are very few metrics that can be applied by computers.

Specification Styles

High-level user interface tools come in a large variety of forms. One important way that they can be classified is by how the designer specifies what the interface should be. As shown in Figure 9, some tools require the programmer to program in a special-purpose language, some provide an application framework to guide the programming, some automatically generate the interface from a high-level specification, and others allow the interface to be specified graphically. Each of these types is discussed below. Of course, some tools use different techniques for specifying different parts of the user interface. These are classified by their predominant or most interesting feature.

Language based. With most of the older user interface tools, the designer specified the user interface using a special-purpose language. This language can take many forms, including context-free grammars, state transition diagrams, declarative languages, event languages, etc. The language is usually used to specify the syntax of the user interface, i.e., the legal sequences of input and output actions. This is sometimes called the *dialog*. Green (1986) provides an extensive comparison of grammars, state transition diagrams, and event languages.

Specification Format	Examples
Language Based	
State Transition Networks	[Newman, 1968], [Jacob, 1986]
Context-Free Grammars	YACC, LEX, Syngraph [Olsen & Dempsey, 1983]
Event Languages	ALGAE [Flecchia & Bergeron, 1987], Sassafras [Hill, 1986], HyperTalk
Declarative Languages	Cousin [Hayes et al., 1985], Open Dialog [Schulert et al., 1985], Motif UIL
Constraint Languages	Thinglab [Borning, 1981], C32 [Myers, 1991b]
Application Frameworks	MacApp [Wilson, 1990], Unidraw [Vlissides & Linton, 1990]
Automatic Generation	MIKE [Olsen, 1986], UIDE [Foley et al., 1989], ITS [Wiecha et al., 1990]
Direct Graphical Specification	
Prototypers	Bricklin's Demo [Sage, 1990], Director [MacroMind, 1990], HyperCard
Cards	Menulay [Buxton et al., 1983], HyperCard
Interface Builders	DialogEditor [Cardelli, 1988], NeXT Interface Builder [NeXT, 1991], Prototyper [SmethersBarnes, 1990], UIMX [VisualEdge, 1990]
Graphical Editors	Peridot [Myers, 1988b], Lapidary [Myers et al., 1989]

Figure 9. Ways to specify the user interface, and some tools that use that technique.

State transition networks. Since many parts of user interfaces involve handling a sequence of input events, it is natural to think of using a state transition network to code the interface. A *transition network* consists of a set of states, with arcs out of each state labeled with the input tokens that will cause a transition to the state at the other end of the arc. In addition to input tokens, calls to application procedures and the output to display can also be put on the arcs in some systems. In 1968, Newman implemented a simple tool using finite state machines that handled textual input. This was apparently the first user interface tool. Many of the assumptions and techniques used in modern systems were present in Newman's: different languages for defining the user interface and the semantics (the semantic routines were coded in a normal programming language), a table-driven syntax analyzer, and device independence (Newman, 1968).

State diagram tools are most useful for creating user interfaces where a large amount of syntactic parsing is necessary or when the user interface has a large number of modes (each state is really a mode). For example, state diagrams are useful for describing the operation of low-level widgets (e.g., how a menu or scroll bar works), or the overall global flow of an application (e.g., this command will pop-up a dialog box, from which you can get to these two dialog boxes, and then to this other window, etc.). However, most highly interactive systems attempt to be mostly *mode free*, which means that, at each point, the user has a wide variety of choices of what to do. This requires a large number of arcs out of each state, so state diagram tools have not been successful for these interfaces. In addition, state diagrams cannot handle interfaces where the user can operate on multiple objects at the same time. Another problem is that they can be very confusing for large interfaces, since they get to be a "maze of wires," and off-page (or off-screen) arcs can be hard to follow.

Recognizing these problems, but still trying to retain the perspicuousness of state transition diagrams, Jacob (1986) has invented a new formalism, which is a combination of state diagrams with a form of event languages (described below). There can be multiple diagrams active at the same time, and flow of control transfers from one to another in a co-routine fashion. The system can create various forms of direct manipulation interfaces.

Context-free grammars. Many grammar-based systems are based on parser generators used in compiler development. For example, the designer might specify the user interface syntax using some form of BNF. Examples of grammar-based systems are parsers built with YACC and LEX in Unix, and Syngraph (Olsen & Dempsey, 1983).

Grammar-based tools, like state diagram tools, are not appropriate for specifying highly interactive interfaces, since they are oriented to batch processing of strings with a complete syntactic structure. These systems are best for textual command languages.

Event languages. With event languages, the input tokens are considered to be "events" that are sent to individual event handlers. Each handler will have a condition clause that determines what types of events it will handle, and when it is active. The body of the handler can cause output events, change the internal state of the system (which might enable other event handlers), or call application routines.

The ALGAE system (Flecchia & Bergeron, 1987) uses an event language that is an extension of Pascal. The user interface is programmed as a set of small event handlers, which ALGAE compiles into conventional code. Sassafras (Hill, 1986) uses a similar idea, but with an entirely different syntax. This system also adds local variables called "flags" to help specify the flow of control. As described below the HyperTalk language that is part of HyperCard for the Apple Macintosh can also be considered an event language.

Most of the tools in this category are explicitly designed to handle multiple processes, which can be important in user interfaces. For example, research has shown that people can be more effective when operating multiple input devices at the same time (Buxton & Myers, 1986). Also, it is often easier to program multiple interactions that are available at the same time (so the user can pick which one to use) using multiple processes. The disadvantage of these event languages is that it can be very difficult to create correct code, since the flow of control is not localized and small changes in one part can affect many different pieces of the program. It is also typically difficult for the designer to understand the code once it reaches a nontrivial size.

Declarative languages. Another approach is to try to define a language that is declarative (stating what should happen) rather than procedural (how to make it happen). Cousin (Hayes et al., 1985) and HP/Apollo's Open-Dialogue (Schulert et al., 1985) both allow the designer to specify user interfaces in this manner. The user interfaces supported are basically forms, where fields can be text typed by the user, or options selected using menus or buttons. There are also graphic output areas that the application can use in whatever manner desired. The application program is connected to the user interface through "variables," which can be set and accessed by both.

Another type of declarative language is the layout description languages that come with many toolkits. For example, Motif's UIL allows the layout of widgets to be defined. Since the UIL is interpreted when an application starts, users can (in theory) edit the UIL code to customize the interface. UIL is not a complete language, however, in the sense that the designer must still write C code for many parts of the interface, including any areas containing dynamic graphics.

The advantage of using declarative languages is that the user interface designer does not have to worry about the time sequence of events and can concentrate on the information that needs to be passed back and forth. The disadvantage is that only certain types of interfaces can be provided this way, and the rest must be programmed by hand in the "graphic areas" provided to application programs. The kinds of interactions available are preprogrammed and fixed. In particular, these systems provide no support for such things as dragging graphical objects, rubber-band lines, or drawing new graphical objects.

Constraint languages. A number of user interface tools allow the programmer to use constraints to define the user interface (Borning & Duisberg, 1986). Early constraint systems include Sketchpad (Sutherland, 1963), which pioneered the use of graphical constraints in a drawing editor; and Thinglab (Borning, 1981), which used constraints for graphical simulation. Subsequently, Thinglab has been extended to aid in the generation of user interfaces (Borning & Duisberg, 1986).

The use of constraints as part of the intrinsics of a toolkit was mentioned above. A number of research toolkits now supply constraints as an integral part of the object system (e.g., Garnet; Myers et al., 1990). In addition, some systems have provided higher-level interfaces to constraints. Graphical Thinglab (Borning, 1986) allows the designer to create constraints by wiring icons together, and NoPump (Wilde & Lewis, 1990) and C32 (Myers, 1991b) allow constraints to be defined using a spreadsheet-like interface.

The advantage of constraints is that they are a natural way to express many kinds of relationships that arise frequently in user interfaces. For example, that lines should stay attached to boxes, that labels should stay centered within boxes, etc. However, a disadvantage with constraints is that they require a sophisticated run-time system to solve them efficiently. Another problem is that they can be hard to debug when in error, since it is difficult to trace the causes and consequences of values changing. However, a growing number of research systems are using constraints, and it appears that modern constraint solvers and debugging techniques may solve these problems, so they have a great potential to simplify the programming task.

Summary. In summary, there have been many different types of languages that have been designed for specifying user interfaces. One problem with all of these is that they can only be used by professional programmers. Some programmers have objected to the requirement for learning a new language for programming just the user interface portion (Olsen, 1987). Furthermore, it seems more natural to define the graphical part of a user interface using a graphical editor. However, it is clear that for the forseeable future, much of the user interface will still need to be created by writing programs, so it is appropriate to continue investigations into the best language to use for this. Indeed, a new book is entirely devoted to investigating the languages for programming user interfaces (Myers, 1992).

Application frameworks. After the Macintosh Toolbox had been available for a little while, Apple discovered that programmers had a difficult time figuring out how to call the various toolkit functions, and how to insure that the resulting interface met the Apple guidelines. They therefore created a software system that provides an overall *application framework* to guide programmers. This is called MacApp (Wilson, 1990) and uses the object-oriented language Object Pascal. Classes are provided for the important parts of an application, such as the main windows, the commands, etc., and the programmer specializes these classes to provide the application-specific details, such as what is actually drawn in the windows and which commands are provided. MacApp has been very successful at simplifying the writing of Macintosh applications.

Unidraw (Vlissides & Linton, 1990) uses a similar approach, but it is more specialized for graphical editors. This means that it can provide even more support. Unidraw uses the C++ object-oriented language and is part of the InterViews system. Unidraw has been used to create various draw and CAD programs, and a user interface editor (Vlissides & Tang, 1991). Even more specialized are various graph programs, such as Edge (Newbery, 1988) and TGE (Karrer & Scacchi, 1990). These provide a framework in which the designer can create programs that display their data as trees or graphs. The programmer typically specializes the node and arc classes, and specifies some of the commands, but the framework handles layout and the overall control.

All of these frameworks require the designer to write code, typically by creating application-specific subclasses of the standard classes provided as part of the framework. Another class of systems that might be considered "frameworks" help create user interfaces that are composed of a series of cards, such as HyperCard from Apple. These systems are discussed below because their primary interface to the designer is graphical.

Automatic generation. A problem with all of the language-based tools is that the designer must specify a great deal about the placement, format, and design of the user interfaces. To solve this problem, some tools use *automatic generation* so that the tool makes many of these choices from a much higher level specification. Many of these tools, including Mickey (Olsen, 1989), Jade (Vander Zanden & Myers, 1990), and Chisel (Singh & Green, 1989), have concentrated on creating menus and dialog boxes. Chisel and Jade allow the designer to use a graphical editor to edit the generated interface if it is not good enough.

Another approach is to try to create a user interface based on a list of the application procedures. MIKE (Olsen, 1986) creates an initial interface that is menu-oriented and rather verbose, but the designer can change the menu structure, use icons for some commands, and even make some commands operate by direct manipulation. The designer uses a graphical editor, like those described in the next section, to specify these changes.

UIDE (the user-interface design environment) (Foley et al., 1989) requires that the semantics of the application be defined in a special-purpose, Pascal-like language, and therefore might be included with the language-based tools. It is placed here instead because the language is used to describe the functions that the application supports and not the desired interface. The description includes pre- and postconditions of the operations, and the system uses these to reason about the operations, and to automatically generate an interface. One interesting part of this system is that the user interface designer can apply "transformations" to the interface. These change the interface in various ways. For example, one transformation changes the interface to have a currently selected object instead of requiring an object to be selected for each operation. Another transformation provides functions specialized for various types ("delete-square" and "delete-triangle"), rather than general-purpose functions ("delete"). UIDE applies the transformations and insures that the resulting interface remains consistent. Another feature of UIDE is that the pre- and postconditions are used to automatically generate help (Sukaviriya & Foley, 1990).

Another rule-based system is ITS (Wiecha et al., 1990), which is being used to create the visitor information system for EXPO 1992 in Seville. Unlike the other systems described above, the designer in EXPO is expected to write some of the rules used to generate the interface, rather than just writing a specification that the rules work on. In particular, the design philosophy of ITS is that all design decisions should be codified as rules so that they can be used by subsequent designers, which will hopefully mean that interface designs will get easier and better as more rules are entered. As a result, the designer should never use graphical editing to improve the design, since then the system cannot capture the reason that the generated design was not sufficient.

While the idea of having the user interface generated automatically is appealing, this approach is still at the research level, because the user interfaces that are generated are generally not good enough. A further problem is that the designer must often use special-purpose specification languages, which can be difficult to learn and use properly. The most promise currently seems to be for the generation of dialog-box and menu-based interfaces.

Direct graphical specification. The tools described next all allow the user interface to be defined, at least partially, by placing objects on the screen using a pointing device. This is motivated by the observation that the visual presentation of the user interface is of primary importance in graphical user interfaces, and a graphical tool seems to be the most appropriate way to specify the graphical appearance. Another advantage of this technique is that it is usually much easier for the designer to use. Many of these systems can be used by nonprogrammers. Therefore, psychologists, graphic designers, and user interface specialists can more easily be involved in the user interface design process when these tools are used.

The tools that support graphical specifications can be classified into four categories: prototyping tools, those that support a sequence of cards, interface builders, and editors for application-specific graphics.

Prototyping tools. The goal of *prototyping tools* is to allow the designer to quickly create some examples of what the screens in the program will look like. Often, these tools cannot be used to create the real user interface of the program; they just show how some aspects will look. This is the chief factor that distinguishes them from other high-level tools. Many parts of the interface may not be operable, and some of the things that look like widgets may just be static pictures. In many prototypers, no real toolkit widgets are used, which means that the designer has to draw simulations that look like the widgets that will appear in the interface. The normal use is that the designer would spend a few days or weeks trying out different designs with the tool, and then completely reimplement the final design in a separate system. Most prototyping tools can be used without programming, so they can, for example, be used by graphic designers.

Note that this use of the term *prototyping* is different from the general phrase *rapid prototyping*, which has become a marketing buzz-word. Advertisements for just about all user interface tools claim that they support "rapid prototyping," by which they mean that the tool helps create the user interface software quicker. The term *prototyping* is being used here in a much more specific manner.

Probably the first prototyping tool was Dan Bricklin's Demo (Sage, 1990). This is a program for an IBM PC that allows the designer to create sample screens composed of characters and "character graphics" (where the fixed-size character cells can contain a graphic like a horizontal, vertical, or diagonal line). The designer can easily create the various screens for the application. It is also relatively easy to specify the actions (mouse or keyboard) that cause transitions from one screen to another. However, it is difficult to define other behaviors. In general, there may be some support for type-in fields and menus in prototyping tools, but there is little ability to process or test the results.

For graphical user interfaces, designers often use tools like MacroMind Director (MacroMind, 1990) for the Macintosh, which is actually an animation tool. The designer can draw example screens, and then specify that when the mouse is pressed in a particular place, an animation should start or a different screen should be displayed. Components of the picture can be reused in different screens, but again the ability to show behavior is limited. HyperCard for the Macintosh is also often used as a prototyping tool.

The primary disadvantage of these prototyping tools is that they cannot create the actual code for the user interface. Therefore, the interfaces must be recoded after prototyping. There is also the risk that the programmers who implement the real user interface will ignore the prototype.

Cards. Many graphical programs are limited to user interfaces that can be presented as a sequence of mostly static pages, sometimes called *frames* or *cards*. Each page contains a set of widgets, some of which cause transfer to other pages. There is usually a fixed set of widgets to choose from, which were coded by hand.

An early example of this is Menulay (Buxton et al., 1983), which allows the designer to place text, graphical potentiometers, iconic pictures, and light buttons on the screen and see exactly what the end user will see when the application is run. The designer does not need to be a programmer to use Menulay. Trillium (Henderson, 1986), which is aimed at designing the user interface panels for photocopiers, is very similar to Menulay. One strong advantage that Trillium has over Menulay is that the cards can be executed immediately, as they are designed, since the specification is interpreted rather than compiled. Trillium also separates the behavior of interactions from the graphic presentation and allows the designer to change the graphics (while keeping the same behavior) without programming. One weakness is that it has little support for frame-to-frame transitions, since this rarely is necessary for photocopiers.

Probably the most famous example of a card-based system is HyperCard from Apple. There are now many similar programs, such as GUIDE (OWL, 1991), Spinnaker Plus (Spinnaker, 1991), and Tool Book (Asymetrix, 1990). In all of these, the designer can easily create cards containing text fields, buttons, etc., along with various graphic decorations. The buttons can transfer to other cards. HyperCard provides a scripting language, called HyperTalk, to provide more functionality for buttons. As mentioned above, HyperTalk is really an event language, since the programmer writes short pieces of code that are executed when input events occur.

Interface builders. A related kind of tool allows the designer to create dialog boxes that are to be part of a larger user interface. These are often called *Interface Builders*. They allow the designer to select from a predefined library of widgets, and place them on the screen using a mouse. Other properties of the widgets can be set using dialog boxes. Usually, there is also some support for sequencing, such as bringing up subdialogs when a particular button is hit. Examples of research interface builders are DialogEditor (Cardelli, 1988), vu (Singh & Green, 1988) and Gilt (Myers, 1991a). There are literally hundreds of commercial interface builders. Just a few examples are the NeXT Interface Builders (NeXT, 1991), Prototyper for the Macintosh (Smethers-Barnes, 1990), WindowsMAKER for Microsoft Windows on the PC (Blue Sky, 1991), and UIMX for X Windows and Motif (Visual Edge, 1990).

Although Interface Builders make laying out the dialog boxes and menus easier, this is only part of the user interface design problem. For any kind of program that has a graphics area (such as drawing programs, CAD, visual language editors, etc.), Interface Builders do not help with the contents of the graphics pane.

Editors for application-specific graphics. When an application has custom graphics, it would be useful if the designer could draw pictures of what the graphics should look like rather than having to write code for this. The problem is that the graphic objects usually need to change at run time, based on the actual data and end user's actions. Therefore, the designer must draw an *example* of the desired display, which will be modified at run-time. This distinguishes these programs from the graphical tools of the previous three sections, where the full picture can be specified at design time. As a result of the *generalization* task of converting the example objects into parameterized prototypes that can change at run-time, all of these systems are research prototypes. However, some of the ideas are beginning to appear in commercial systems.

Peridot (Myers, 1988b) allows new, custom widgets to be created. The primitives that the designer manipulates with the mouse are rectangles, circles, text, and lines. The system generalizes from the designer's actions to create parameterized, object-oriented procedures like those that might be found in toolkits. Peridot can also be used by non-programmers. Lapidary (Myers et al., 1989) extends the ideas of Peridot to allow general application objects to be drawn. For example, the designer can draw the nodes and arcs for a graph program. The DEMO system (Wolber & Fisher, 1991) allows some dynamic, run-time properties of the objects to be demonstrated, such as when objects should be created.

Specialized Tools

For some application domains, there are customized tools that provide significant high-level support. These tend to be quite expensive, however. For example, in the aeronautics and real-time control areas, there are a number of high-level tools, including AutoCode (Integrated Systems, 1991) and InterMAPhics (Prior, 1991).

EVALUATING USER INTERFACE TOOLS

There are clearly a large number of approaches to how tools work, and there are research and commercial tools that use each of the techniques. When faced with a particular programming task, the designer might ask which tool is the most appropriate. Different approaches are appropriate for different kinds of tasks, and orthogonally, there are some dimensions that are useful for evaluating all tools. An important point is that in today's market, there is probably a higher level tool appropriate for most tasks, so if you are programming directly at the window manager or even toolkit layer, there may be a tool that will save you much work.

Approaches

Using the commercial tools, if you are designing a command-line style interface, then a parser-generator like YACC and Lex is appropriate. If you are creating a graphical application, then you should definitely be using a toolkit appropriate to your platform. If there is an application framework available for your platform, it will probably be very helpful. For creating the dialog boxes and menus, an Interface Builder is very useful, and generally easier to use than declarative languages like UIL. If your application is entirely (or mostly) pages of information, possibly with some fields for the user to fill in, then the card tools might be appropriate.

Among the approaches that are still in the research phase, constraints seem quite appropriate for specifying graphical relationships, automatic generation may be useful for dialog boxes and menus, and graphical editors will allow the graphical elements of the user interface to be drawn.

Dimensions

There are many dimensions along which you might evaluate user interface tools. The importance given to these different factors will depend on the type of application to be created, and the needs of the designers.

- **Depth.** How much of the user interface does the tool cover? For example, interface builders help with dialog boxes, but do not help with creating interactive graphics. Does the tool help with the evaluation of the interfaces?
- **Breadth.** How many different user interface styles are supported, or is the resulting user interface limited to just one style, such as a sequence of cards? Can new interaction techniques be added?
- **Portability.** Will the resulting user interface run on multiple platforms, such as X, Macintosh and Windows?
- **Ease of use of tools.** How difficult are the tools to use? For toolkits and most language-based higher level tools, highly trained professional programmers are needed. For some graphical tools, even inexperienced end users can generate user interfaces. Also, since the designers are themselves users of the tools, the conventional user-interface principles can be used to evaluate the quality of the tools' own user interface. Typically, the tools with the best ease of learning are also the least functional, in terms of depth and breadth.
- **Efficiency for designers.** How fast can designers create user interfaces with the tool? This is often related to the quality of the user interface of the tool.
- **Quality of resulting interfaces.** Does the tool generate high-quality user interfaces? Does the tool help the designer evaluate and improve the quality? Many tools allow the designer to produce any interface desired, so they provide no specific help in improving the quality of the user interfaces.
- **Speed of resulting interface.** How fast does the resulting user interface operate? Some tools interpret the specifications at run-time, or provide many layers of software, which may make the resulting user interface too slow on some target machines.
- **Price.** Some tools are provided free by research organizations, such as the Xtk toolkit from MIT and Garnet from CMU. Most personal computers and workstations today come with a free toolkit. Commercial higher level tools can range from $200 to $50,000, depending on their functionality.
- **Robustness and Support.** The free research tools are likely to have less support than commercial ones.

Naturally, there are tradeoffs among these criteria. Generally, tools that have the most power (depth and breadth) are more difficult to use. The tools that are easiest to use might be most efficient for the designer, but not if they cannot create the desired interfaces.

As tools become more widespread, reviews and evaluations of them are beginning to appear in magazines. Also, there are a few formal studies of tools (Hix, 1989).

RESEARCH ISSUES

Although there are many user interface tools, there are plenty of areas in which further research is needed. A report prepared for an NSF study discusses future research ideas for user interface tools at length (Marchionini & Siebert, 1991). Here, a few of the important ones are summarized.

Increased Depth

Many researchers are trying to create tools that will cover more of the user interface, such as application-specific graphics and behaviors. The challenge here is to allow flexibility to application developers while still providing a high level of support. Tools should also be able to support Help, Undo, and Aborting of operations.

Today's user interface tools mostly help with the *generation* of the code of the interface, and assume that the fundamental user interface *design* is complete. What are also needed are tools to help with the generation, specification, and analysis of the design of the interface. For example, an important first step in user interface design is task analysis, where the designer identifies the particular tasks that the end user will need to perform. Research should be directed at creating tools to support these methods and techniques. These might eventually be integrated with the code generation tools, so that the information generated during early design can be fed into automatic generation tools, possibly to produce an interface directly from the early analyses. The information might also be used to automatically generate documentation and run-time help.

Another approach is to allow the designer to specify the design in an appropriate notation, and then provide tools to convert that notation into interfaces. For example, the UAN (Hartson, Siochi, & Hix, 1990) is a notation for expressing the end user's actions and the system's responses.

Finally, much work is needed in ways for tools to help evaluate interface designs. Initial attempts, such as in MIKE (Olsen & Halversen, 1988), have highlighted the need for better models and metrics against which to evaluate the user interfaces. Research in this area is continuing by cognitive psychologists and other user interface researchers.

Increased Breadth

We can expect the user interfaces of tomorrow to be different from the conventional window-and-mouse interfaces of today, and tools will have to change to support the new styles. For example, most tools today only deal with two-dimensional objects, but there is already a demand to provide 3-D visualizations and animations. New input devices and techniques will probably replace the conventional mouse and menu styles. For example, gesture recognition is already appearing in commercial products, such as the notepad computers designed by GO (GO, 1991). "Virtual reality" systems, where the computer creates an artificial world and allows the user to explore it (often using a DataGlove—Foley, 1987), cannot be handled by any of today's tools.

A more immediate concern is supporting interfaces that can be moved from one natural language to another (like English to French). This is not simply a matter of translating the labels, however, since the labels will be different sizes, so interfaces must be redesigned. Can the tools do this automatically? Also, some languages are entered from right to left or top to bottom (or a combination of these), and the input mechanisms should deal with this.

End-User Programming and Customization

One of the most successful computer programs of all time is the spreadsheet. The primary reason for its success is that end users can program (by writing formulas and macros). However, *end-user programming* is rare in other applications. More effective mechanisms for users to customize existing applications and create new ones are needed. However, these should not be built into individual applications as is done today, since this means that the user must learn a different programming technique for each application. Instead, the facilities should be provided at the system level, and therefore should be part of the underlying toolkit. Naturally, since this is aimed at end users, it will not be like programming in C, but rather at some higher level.

New models

It is well recognized that the tools in use today have some fundamental problems. For example, the input model used by windowing systems and toolkits is device dependent and causes synchronization problems. Another problem is that the object-oriented model of toolkits does not make it easy enough to customize widgets. Fundamentally different models might be useful for future user interface tools.

Application and UI Separation

One of the fundamental goals of user interface tools is to allow the better modularization and separation of user interface code from application code. However, a recent survey reported that modern toolkits actually make this separate more difficult, due to the large number of call-back procedures required (Myers & Rosson, 1992). Therefore, further research is needed into ways to better modularize the code, and how tools can support this.

Tools for the Tools

It is very difficult to create the tools described in this chapter. Each one takes an enormous effort. Therefore, work is needed in ways to make the tools themselves easier to create. For example, the Garnet toolkit is exploring mechanisms specifically designed to make high-level graphical tools easier to create (Myers & Vander Zanden, 1991). The Unidraw framework has also proven useful for creating interface builders (Vlissides & Tang, 1991). However, more work is needed.

CONCLUSIONS

User interface software is inherently difficult to create, because it combines some of the most difficult aspects of programming, including multiprocessing, real-time programming, the need for absolute robustness and frequent, iterative changes to the specification. As a consequence of this, the area of user interface tools is expanding rapidly. Five years ago, you would have been hard pressed to find any successful commercial higher level tools, but now there are over 100, and chances are that today, whatever your project is, there is a tool that will help. Tools coming out of research labs are covering increasingly more of the user interface task, and are creating better user interfaces. As more companies and researchers are attracted to this area, we can expect the pace of innovation to continue to accelerate. There will be many exciting and useful new tools available in the near future.

REFERENCES

Adobe Systems, Inc. (1985). *Postscript Language Reference Manual*. Reading, MA: Addison-Wesley.

Apple Computer, Inc. (1985). *Inside Macintosh*. Reading, MA: Addison-Wesley.

Asymetrix Corporation. (1990). *Toolbook*. Bellevue, WA: Author.

Integrated Systems. (1991). *Autocode*. Santa Clara, CA: Author.

Barth, P. (1986, April). An object-oriented approach to graphical interfaces. *ACM Transactions on Graphics*, 5(2), 142–172.

Bewley, W. L., Roberts, T. L., Schroit, D., & Verplank, W. L. (1983, December). Human factors testing in the design of Xerox's 8010 'Star' Office Workstation. Human Factors in Computing Systems. *Proceedings SIGCHI'83*, pp. 72–77. Boston, MA.

Blue Sky Software Corporation. (1991). *WindowsMAKER*. Las Vegas: Author.

Boies, S. J., Gould, J. D., Levy, S., Richards, J. T., & Schoonard, J. W. (1985). The 1984 Olympic Message System—A Case Study in System Design. *IBM Research Report*, Vol. RC-11138.

Borning, A. (1981, October). The programming language aspects of Thinglab; a constraint-oriented simulation laboratory. *ACM Transactions on Programming Languages and Systems*, 3(4), 353–387.

Borning, A. (1986, April). Defining constraints graphically. Human factors in computing systems. *Proceedings SIGCHI'86*, pp. 137–143. Boston, MA.

Borning, A. & Duisberg, R. (1986, October). Constraint-based tools for building user interfaces. *ACM Transactions on Graphics*, 5(4), 345–374.

Buxton, W., Lamb, M. R., Sherman, D., & Smith, K. C. (1983, July). Towards a comprehensive user interface management system. *Computer Graphics*, *17*(3). (Also in *Proceedings SIGGRAPH'83*, pp. 35–42. Detroit, MI.)

Buxton, W., & Myers, B. (1986, April). A study in two-handed input. Human factors in computing systems. *Proceedings SIGCHI'86*, pp. 321–326. Boston, MA.

Cardelli, L. & Pike, R. (1985, July). Squeak: A language for communicating with mice. Computer graphics. *Proceedings SIGGRAPH'85*, pp. 199–204. San Francisco, CA.

Cardelli, L. (1988, October). Building user interfaces by direct manipulation. ACM SIGGRAPH Symposium on User Interface Software and Technology. *Proceedings UIST'88*, pp. 152–166. Banff, Alberta, Canada.

Flecchia, M. A., & Bergeron, R. D. (1987, April). Specifying complex dialogs in ALGAE. Human factors in computing systems (pp. 229–234). Toronto, Canada: CHI+GI'87.

Foley, J. D. (1987, October). Interfaces for advanced computing. *Scientific American*, pp. 127–135.

Foley, J., Kim, W. C., Kovacevic, S., & Murray, K. (1989, January). Defining interfaces at a high level of abstraction. *IEEE Software*, *6*(1), 25–32.

GO Corporation. (1991). *PenPoint*. Foster City, CA: Author.

Gould, J. D., & Lewis, C. H. (1985, March). Designing for usability—Key principles and what designers think. *Communications of the ACM*, *28*(3), 300–311.

Green, M. (1986, July). A survey of three dialog models. *ACM Transactions on Graphics*, 5(3), 244–275.

Hartson, H. R., & Hix, D. (1989, March). Human-computer interface development: Concepts and systems for its management. *Computing Surveys*, *21*(1), 5–92.

Hartson, H. R., Siochi, A. C., & Hix, D. (1990, July). The UAN: A user-oriented representation for direct manipulation interface designs. *ACM Transactions on Information Systems*, *8*(3), 181–203.

Hayes, P. H., Szekely, P. A., & Lerner, R. A. (1985, April). Design alternatives for user interface management systems based on experience with COUSIN. Human factors in computing systems. *Proceedings SIGCHI'85*, pp. 169–175. San Francisco, CA.

Henderson, D. A., Jr. (1986, April). The Trillium user interface design environment. Human factors in computing systems. *Proceedings SIGCHI'86*, pp. 221–227. Boston, MA.

Hill, R. D. (1986, July). Supporting concurrency, communication and synchronization in human-computer interaction—The Sassafras UIMS. *ACM Transactions on Graphics*, 5(3), 179–210.

Hix, D. (1989, November). A procedure for evaluating human-computer interface development tools. ACM SIGGRAPH Symposium on User Interface Software and Technology. *Proceedings UIST'89*, pp. 53–61. Williamsburg, VA.

Ingalls, D. H. H., (1981, August). The Smalltalk graphics kernel. *Byte Magazine*, *6*(8), 168–194.

Jacob, R. J. K. (1986, October). A specification language for direct manipulation interfaces. *ACM Transactions on Graphics*, 5(4), 283–317.

Karrer, A., & Scacchi, W. (1990, October). Requirements for an extensible object-oriented tree/graph editor. ACM SIGGRAPH Symposium on User Interface Software and Technology. *Proceedings UIST'90*, pp. 84–91. Snowbird, UT.

Linton, M. A., Vlissides, J. M., & Calder, P. R. (1989, February). Composing user interfaces with InterViews. *IEEE Computer*, *22*(2), 8–22.

MacroMind. (1990). *Director*. San Francisco, CA: Author.

Marchionini, G., & Sibert, J. (Ed.). (1991, October). An agendy for human-computer interaction: Science and engineering serving human needs. *SIGCHI Bulletin*, *23*(4), 17–32.

McCormack, J., & Asente, P. (1988, October). An overview of the X Toolkit. ACM SIGGRAPH Symposium on User Interface Software and Technology. *Proceedings UIST'88*, pp. 46–55. Banff, Alberta, Canada.

Morgan, C., Williams, G., & Lemmons, P. (1983, February). An interview with Wayne Rosing, Bruce Daniels, and Larry Tesler. *Byte*, *8*(2), 90–114.

Myers, B. A. (1984, December). The user interface for Sapphire. *IEEE Computer Graphics and Applications*, *4*(12), 13–23.

Myers, B. A. (1986, September). A complete and efficient implementation of covered windows. *IEEE Computer*, *19*(9), 57–67.

Myers, B. A. (1988a, September). A taxonomy of user interfaces for window managers. *IEEE Computer Graphics and Applications*, *8*(5), 65–84.

Myers, B.A. (1988b). *Creating user interfaces by demonstration*. Boston: Academic Press.

Myers, B. A. (1989, January). User interface tools: Introduction and survey. *IEEE Software*, *6*(1), 15–23.

Myers, B. A., Vander Zanden, B., & Dannenberg, R. B. (1989, November). Creating graphical interactive application objects by demonstration. ACM SIGGRAPH Symposium on User Interface Software and Technology. *Proceedings UIST'89*, pp. 95–104. Williamsburg, VA.

Myers, B. A., Guise, D. A., Dannenberg, R. G., Vander Zanden, B., Kosbie, D. S., Pervin, E., Mickish, A., & Marchal, P. (1990, November). Garnet: Comprehensive support for graphical, highly-interactive user interfaces. *IEEE Computer*, *23*(11), 71–85.

Myers, B. A. (1990a, July). A new model for handling input. *ACM Transactions on Information Systems*, *8*(3), 289–320.

Myers, B. A. (1990b). All the Widgets. *SIGGRAPH Video Review*, *57*.

Myers, B. A. (1991a, November). Separating application code from toolkits: Eliminating the spaghetti of call-backs. ACM SIGGRAPH Symposium on User Interface Software and Technology. *Proceedings UIST'91*, pp. 211–220. Hilton Head, SC.

Myers, B. A. (1991b, April). Graphical techniques in a spreadsheet for specifying user interfaces. Human factors in computing systems. *Proceedings SIGCHI'91*, pp. 243–249. New Orleans, LA.

Myers, B. A., & Rosson, M. B. (1992, May). Survey on user interface programming. Human factors in computing systems. *Proceedings SIGCHI'92*. Monterey, CA.

Myers, B. A. (Ed.). (1992). *Languages for developing user interfaces*. Boston, MA: Jones and Bartlett.

Myers, B. A. & Vander Zanden, B. (1992, February). Environment for rapid creation of interactive design tools. The Visual Computer. *International Journal of Computer Graphics*, 2, 94–116.

Newbery, F. J. (1988, October). An interface description language for graph editors. 1988 IEEE Workshop on Visual Languages (pp. 144–149). Pittsburgh, PA: IEEE Computer Society Order Number 876.

Newman, W. M. (1968). A system for interactive graphical programming. *AFIPS Spring Joint Computer Conference*, *28*, 47–54.

NeXT, Inc. (1991). *NeXTStep and the NeXT Interface Builder*. Redwood City, CA: Author.

Olsen, D. R., Jr., & Dempsey, E. P. (1983, July). Syngraph: A graphical user interface generator. Computer graphics. *Proceedings SIGGRAPH'83*, pp. 43–50. Detroit, MI.

Olsen, D. R., Jr. (1986, October). Mike: The menu interaction kontrol environment. *ACM Transactions on Graphics*, *5*(4), 318–344.

Olsen, D. R., Jr. (1987, April). Larger issues in user interface management. *Computer Graphics*, *21*(2), 134–137.

Olsen, D. R., Jr., & Halversen, B. W. (1988, October). Interface usage measurements in a user interface management system. ACM SIGGRAPH Symposium on User Interface Software and Technology. *Proceedings UIST'88*, pp. 102–108. Banff, Alberta, Canada.

Olsen, D. R., Jr. (1989, April). A programming language basis for user interface management. Human factors in computing systems. *Proceedings SIGCHI'89*, pp. 171–176. Austin, TX.

Owl International, Inc. (1991). *Guide*. Bellevue, WA: Author.

Palay, A. J., et al. (1988, February). The Andrew toolkit—An overview. *Proceedings Winter Usenix Technical Conference*, pp. 9–21. Dallas, TX.

Pike, R. (1983, April). Graphics in overlapping bitmap layers. *ACM Transactions on Graphics*, *2*(2), 135–160. (Also appears in *Computer Graphics: SIGGRAPH'83 Conference Proceedings*, *17*(3), *3*, *July 25–29*, 1983, pp. 331–355.)

Prior Data Sciences. (1991). *InterMAPhics*. Kanata, Ontario Canada: Author.

Rosson, M. B., Maass, S., & Kellogg, W. A. (1987, April). Designing for designers: An analysis of design practices in the real world. *Human Factors in Computing Systems* (pp. 137–142). Toronto, Canada: CHI+GI'87.

Sage Software, Inc. (1990). *Dan Bricklin's Demo II, Version 3.0*. Beaverton, OR: Author.

Samuelson, P. (1989, May). Why the look and feel of software user interfaces should not be protected by copyright law. *Communications of the ACM*, *32*(5), 563–572.

Scheifler, R. W., & Gettys, J. (1986, April). The X Window System. *ACM Transactions on Graphics*, *5*(2), 79–109.

Schmucker, K. J. (1986, August). MacApp: An Application Framework. *Byte*, *11*(8), 189–193.

Schulert, A. J., Rogers, G. T., & Hamilton, J. A. (1985, April). ADM-A Dialogue Manager. Human factors in computing systems. *Proceedings SIGCHI'85*, pp. 177–183. San Francisco, CA.

Sheil, B. (1983, February). Power tools for programmers. *Datamation*, *29*(2), 131–144.

Shneiderman, B. (1983, August). Direct manipulation: A step beyond programming languages. *IEEE Computer*, *16*(8), 57–69.

Singh, G., & Green, M. (1988, October). Designing the interface designer's interface. ACM SIGGRAPH Symposium on User Interface Software and Technology. *Proceedings UIST'88*, pp. 109–116. Banff, Alberta, Canada.

Singh, G., & Green, M. (1989, November). Chisel: A system for creating highly interactive screen layouts. ACM SIGGRAPH Symposium on User Interface Software and Technology. *Proceedings UIST'89*, pp. 86–94. Williamsburg, VA.

SmethersBarnes. (1990). *Prototyper 3.0*. Portland, OR: Author.

Smith, D. C., Irby, C., Kimball, R., Verplank, B., & Harslem, E. (1982, April). Designing the Star User Interface. *Byte, 7*(4), 242–282.

Spinnaker Software. (1991). *Spinnaker PLUS*. Cambridge, MA: Author.

Stallman, R. M. (1979, August). *Emacs: The extensible, customizable, self-documenting display editor* (Tech. Rep. 519). Cambridge, MA: MIT Artificial Intelligence Lab.

Sukaviriya, P., & Foley, J. D. (1990, October). Coupling a UI framework with automatic generation of context-sensitive animated help. ACM SIGGRAPH Symposium on User Interface Software and Technology. *Proceedings UIST'90*, pp. 152–166. Snowbird, UT.

Sutherland, I. E. (1963). SketchPad: A man-machine graphical communication system. *AFIPS Spring Joint Computer Conference, 23*, 329–346.

Swartout, W., & Balzer, R. (1982, July). The inevitable intertwining of specification and implementation. *Communications of the ACM, 25*(7), 438–440.

Swinehart, D., Zellweger, P., Beach, R., & Hagmann, R. (1986, October). A structural view of the Cedar programming environment. *ACM Transactions on Programming Languages and Systems, 8*(4), 419–490.

Teitelman, W. (1979). A display oriented programmer's assistant. *International Journal of Man-Machine Studies, 1*, 157–187. (Also Xerox PARC Technical Report CSL-77-3, Palo Alto, CA, March 8, 1977.)

Tesler, L. (1981, August). The Smalltalk environment. *Byte Magazine, 6*(8), 90–147.

Vander Zanden, B., & Myers, B. A. (1990, April). Automatic, look-and-feel independent dialog creation for graphical user interfaces. Human factors in computing systems. *Proceedings SIGCHI'90*, pp. 27–34. Seattle, WA.

Visual Edge Software Ltd. (1990). *UIMX*. Montreal: Author.

Vlissides, J. M., & Linton, M. A. (1990, July). Unidraw: A framework for building domain-specific graphical editors. *ACM Transactions on Information Systems, 8*(3), 204–236.

Vlissides, J. M., & Tang, S. (1991, November). A Unidraw-based user interface builder. ACM SIGGRAPH Symposium on User Interface Software and Technology. *Proceedings UIST'91*, pp. 201–210. Hilton Head, SC.

Wiecha, C., Bennett, W., Boies, S., Gould, J., & Greene, S. (1990, July). ITS: A tool for rapidly developing interactive applications. *ACM Transactions on Information Systems, 8*(3), 204–236.

Wilde, N., & Lewis, C. (1990, April). Spreadsheet-based interactive graphics: From prototype to tool. Human factors in computing systems. *Proceedings SIGCHI'90*, pp. 153–159. Seattle, WA.

Wilson, D. (1990). *Programming with MacApp*. Reading, MA: Addison-Wesley.

Wolber, D., & Fisher, G. (1991, November). A demonstrational technique for developing interfaces with dynamically created objects. ACM SIGGRAPH Symposium on User Interface Software and Technology. *Proceedings UIST'91*, pp. 221–230. Hilton Head, SC.

XVT Software, Inc. (1991). *XVT*. Boulder, CO: Author.

Yourdon, E. (1989). *Modern structured analysis*. Englewood Cliffs, NJ: Prentice-Hall.

Lessons Learned from SUIT, the Simple User Interface Toolkit

RANDY PAUSCH, MATTHEW CONWAY, and ROBERT DELINE
University of Virginia

In recent years, the computer science community has realized the advantages of GUIs (Graphical User Interfaces). Because high-quality GUIs are difficult to build, support tools such as UIMSs, UI Toolkits, and Interface Builders have been developed. Although these tools are powerful, they typically make two assumptions: first, that the programmer has some familiarity with the GUI model, and second, that he is willing to invest several weeks becoming proficient with the tool. These tools typically operate only on specific platforms, such as DOS, the Macintosh, or UNIX/X-windows.

The existing tools are beyond the reach of most undergraduate computer science majors, or professional programmers who wish to quickly build GUIs without investing the time to become specialists in GUI design. For this class of users, we developed *SUIT*, the *S*imple *U*ser *I*nterface *T*oolkit. SUIT is an attempt to distill the fundamental components of an interface builder and GUI toolkit, and to explain those concepts with the tool itself, all in a short period of time. We have measured that college juniors with no previous GUI programming experience can use SUIT productively after less than three hours. SUIT is a C subroutine library which provides an external control UIMS, an interactive layout editor, and a set of standard "widgets," such as sliders, buttons, and check boxes. SUIT-based applications run transparently across the Macintosh, DOS, and UNIX/X platforms. SUIT has been exported to hundreds of external sites on the internet. This paper describes SUIT's architecture, the design decisions we made during its development, and the lessons we learned from extensive observations of over 120 users.

Categories and Subject Descriptors: D.2.2 [**Software Engineering**]: Tools and Techniques—*software libraries, user interfaces*; D.2.6 [**Software Engineering**]: Programming Environments—*interactive*; D.2.m [**Software Engineering**]: Miscellaneous—*rapid prototyping, reusable software*; I.3.4 [**Computer Graphics**]: Graphics Utilities—*application packages, graphics packages, software support*; I.3.6 [**Computer Graphics**]: Methodology and Techniques—*device independence, interaction techniques*; K.3.2 [**Computers and Education**]: Computer and Information Science Education—*computer science education*

General Terms: Experimentation, Design, Human Factors

Additional Key Words and Phrases: Export, graphical user interface, GUI, learnability, pedagogy, portability, rapid prototyping, software tools, UIMS, user interface toolkit.

INTRODUCTION

This is a practice and experience paper that describes our experience with SUIT, the Simple User Interface Toolkit. In recent years, support tools for building GUIs, called UIMSs, UI toolkits, and interface builders have gained popularity, but they have been heavily skewed toward programmers who are willing to invest a large amount of time in mastering them. While these tools are appropriate for many professionals in the field, their extended learning curves make them prohibitive for undergraduate students or other programmers who wish to build GUIs, but who do not wish to invest weeks in mastering the tool base. GUI building tools can be very deceptive: providing an interactive builder that provides mouse-based interface editing can obscure the fact that if the programmer is not familiar with the callback model for GUIs, attempting to attach functionality to the screen components will be extremely confusing.

In academia, we should be exposing our students to good GUI-building tools, not as a speciality item in a graduate level graphics course, but in mainstream courses, such as undergraduate software engineering or "projects" courses. Unfortunately, these courses cannot sacrifice several weeks in order to teach the concepts hidden inside the GUI model, nor can they afford the luxury of allowing the students several weeks to master complicated GUI tools. Outside of academia, a similar situation exists, where many professional programmers who do not specialize in GUI design often have need to quickly build "graphical front ends" for various application software, but can never take the time to master complex GUI development tools.

In SUIT, the Simple User Interface Toolkit, we have attempted to distill the essential components of good GUI building tools and provided those essentials in a form that can be used by programmers who come prepared with nothing but competency in the C programming language. Our goal is not to provide new capabilities in the GUI-building realm, but to combine existing techniques in a clean design that can be learned quickly. In this respect, we hope SUIT can provide the same contribution to the interface builder community that Pascal did for the programming language community. We certainly have heard many (older) GUI programmers comment that the current state of the art in GUI tools is similar to programming languages in the 1960s and 1970s. The Motif Widget Set, for example, exhibits many of the same "interference of features" problems as did PL/I.

SUIT succeeds not by providing a new "silver bullet" idea, but by making dozens of independent design decisions which, when taken in combination, produce a system which is easy for novice GUI programmers to learn. The design methodology was relatively straightforward: be willing to rewrite the implementation many times, perform stringent user testing to every phase in an iterative fashion, and be willing to sacrifice "well-known" design principles for ease of use in the face of evidence from user observation. We have performed direct observations of over 120 separate users within a two-year time span during SUIT's development. The end result is a ten-page tutorial which requires new users to spend between 1.5 and 3 hours learning to use SUIT, at which time they can begin using SUIT for programs of their own choice. This is a vast improvement over a four to six week learning curve we observed for our students with systems like **Xtk** [10], the Andrew Tool Kit [13], Interviews [4], and the Motif Widget Set. SUIT also provides a 160-page reference manual, much of which is also available via on-line help.

Authors' address: Computer Science Department, Thornton Hall, University of Virginia, Charlottesville, VA 22903; email: pausch@virginia.edu

DESIGN APPROACH

Throughout SUIT's development, we applied the following principles:

—exploit knowledge and skills the user already has,
—make the easy things easy and the hard things possible, and
—perform end-user testing early and often.

Current UI toolkits and UIMSs tend to violate the first point by forcing their users to learn a new programming language. For example, the NeXT Interface Builder [9] requires learning objective-C, and Interviews requires learning C++. While these languages are required to support the model each system provides, users who are focused on their task at hand often fail to use advanced tools because the learning threshold of these languages is too high.

Our design strategy was to leverage off the only existing skill we could assume our users would have: the ability to program in C. Therefore, anything that could not be specified with SUIT's interactive tools would have to be done by having the user write C code. Also, we acknowledged early on that any new concepts we needed our users to understand, such as inheritance of information in a class-based object-oriented model, SUIT would have to teach to them via its interactive tools. As our final design goal, we looked to the production of a ten-page written tutorial which would walk the new user through the system. We explicitly chose a written, rather than on-screen tutorial format for two reasons: First, our most limited resource was screen real-estate, and putting the tutorial on paper reduced demand for screen space. The second reason was that we wanted to avoid confusion between "tutorial areas" and "real areas" on the screen. By using a paper-based tutorial, we could use the SUIT screen layouts without problem. While we do not argue that on-screen tutorials are appropriate in many applications, we felt that for SUIT's target audience, a paper-based tutorial would be superior. The last design constraint was in the type of users we targeted during our testing of the software. Working with the very best students, or even average students who were interested in GUIs, would have been a mistake. We wanted to target users for whom creating GUIs was a means to an end, not an end in itself. Therefore, we used a captive audience: students in undergraduate software engineering courses who had been assigned projects that required GUIs, but who would be graded on the overall result of their effort, of which the GUI was a small fraction.

By constantly observing new users, we were able to maintain perspective on the difficulties they face when trying to understand the SUIT model. This sort of user testing is well understood in some corporate cultures, most notably at Apple Computer. This technique was also used with great success in the development of Trillium [3].

ARCHITECTURE

This section gives a high-level description of SUIT's internal architecture and describes SUIT's basic data model. We begin by discussing platform portability, then cover several popular UI builder models, SUIT's definition of an object, its interactive tool set, and how it composes and links objects together.

Portability

A user interface toolkit requires three basic forms of support: an implementation language, operating system support, and a graphics package. Our implementation language had to be either C or Pascal, since they are the only languages widely known by undergraduates. Although Pascal is more widely used and is simpler than C, implementing SUIT in Pascal was not technologically feasible. Pascal exists on all three platforms, but it varies widely [19]. Also, standard Pascal is not powerful enough to support the external control model: it lacks the ability to store function addresses as variables. Therefore, we chose ANSI-C. Our operating system dependency was very small: we only needed to be able to read and write an ASCII text file, and the standard C I/O libraries always support this.

For graphics, we needed a common, low-level graphics package that supported operations such as DrawLine and DrawFilledCircle on each of the platforms. We were surprised to find few graphics packages implemented for all three platforms. Most researchers we contacted said that they had always ported between platforms by implementing small compatibility libraries for the specific graphics commands they used in their applications. This made porting their systems unnecessarily time consuming, so we determined that we would use a well-defined common graphics layer from the beginning of the project.

We chose to use SRGP, the Simple Raster Graphics Package, which was being distributed by the Addison-Wesley Publishing Company with the second edition of *Fundamentals of Interactive Computer Graphics*, by Foley et al. [7]. SRGP was already implemented for the Macintosh and X windows; we ported it to Turbo C on DOS, on top of Borland's BGI graphics driver. Our DOS version of SRGP is now distributed with the textbook. Figure 1 shows the software layering that makes SUIT portable.

SRGP has several drawbacks. To overcome them and to provide a wider range of functionality, we layered a thin graphic package called GP (Graphics Package) on top of SRGP. GP allows widget authors to avoid screen coordinates by providing arbitrary floating point coordinate systems and performing standard window-to-viewport mapping. In addition, GP converts the mixed sample/event input model of SRGP into a strict event model (mouse motion is treated as a discrete event). GP also provides a color-and-font naming layer so that color-and-font table values can be properly set across different platforms. Because GP was already providing support for fonts, we augmented its drawText primitive to implement a small, extensible language for special characters and effects, including:

@i(text)	*Example Text*
@b(text)	**Example Text**
@u(text)	Example Text
@+(text)	Example Text
@−(text)	Example Text

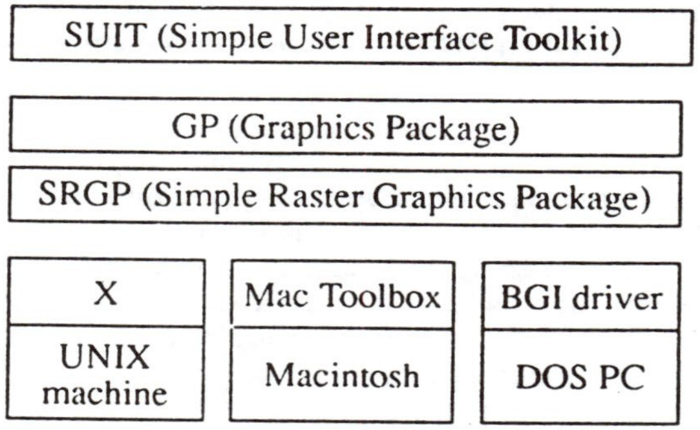

Fig. 1. Layered software for portability.

As long as SUIT-based applications are restrained in their choice of fonts and the number of colors they use, the applications will port across Macintosh, DOS, and UNIX/X-windows platforms with identical look-and-feel. The only remaining point of potential inconsistency is the number of buttons on the mouse: SUIT's interactive tools assume a one-button mouse, and we recommend that applications do the same, although we provide access to whatever mouse buttons are provided by the current hardware.

Another feature of GP is its handling of colors. In most graphics packages, if an application is developed for a color display, when it is ported to a monochrome display, various artifacts appear. Consider Figure 2, where a red arrow is drawn on a green background. In most systems, when drawn on a monochrome display, both (nonwhite) colors would map to black. GP's solution is to define the color of each primitive as a pair [color, monochrome appearance], as in ["purple", "black"]. When SUIT's interactive tools are used to set an object's color, a set of color chips appears when on a color screen, but a toggle button appears on a monochrome screen.

A very different approach to portability is taken by XVT [14, 18], which provides a virtual toolkit on top of the native toolkit layer on each platform. The advantage of the XVT approach is that on each platform the application has the same look and feel as other applications built locally on that platform. There are two major drawbacks to this approach. First, XVT is forced to provide only those function common to all platforms—the lowest common denominator solution. Second, the user must use different support tools (e.g., layout editors) on each platform.

SUIT's Data Model

Most user interface toolkits for compiled languages use a "code dumping" model. The user runs a builder application and interactively lays out what the screen interface should look like. When the user exits this builder program, it "dumps" the skeleton of a program and the user then edits the interior of the "callback" routines, which are called when user interface actions, such as a button press, occur. The motivation for code dumping programs is that the vast majority of the code to interact with screen widgets is ugly and can be mechanically generated. The drawback to dumping code is that if the user ever wishes to go back and change, say, the location or color of a button, the builder program must be able to "parse back" the code that it had dumped. Of course, this requires preventing the user from editing the dumped code, although that can usually be done by dumping the callback skeletons in separate files from other code regarding things like object creation.

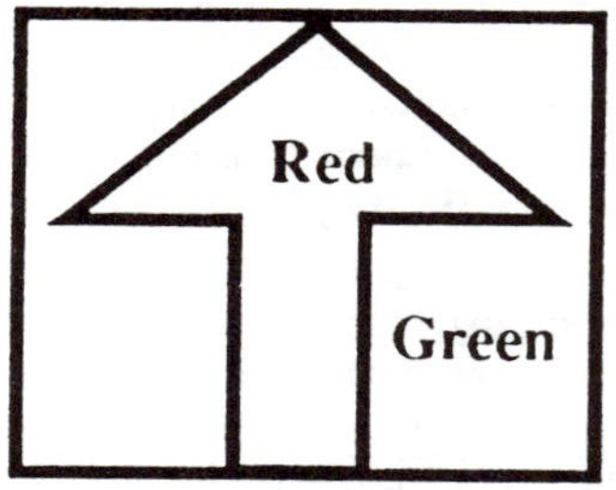

Fig. 2. Colors on monochrome.

The code dumping model is also awkward: to make a change to the interface, the programmer must fire up a separate builder application, drag a button to a new location, dump new code, and then recompile, relink, and rerun the application.

SUIT uses a different model. In fact, it is fair to say that SUIT is best understood if thought of as a subroutine library that provides a front end to a database. The SERPENT system uses a similar approach [1]. The database maintains information about all screen objects, such as their location and color. When an application exits, SUIT writes the database to permanent storage, and when the application is next invoked, SUIT queries the database to see where objects should go and what color to make them. If we had not been interested in platform portability, we would have used the .Xresources file as our permanent storage, instead we write a separate file, called foo.sui, for an application named foo.

Applications programmers create objects by making calls such as

```
void Hi(SUIT_object obj)
{
    printf("hello, world \ n");
}
SUIT_createButton("hello", Hi);
```

which creates a screen button and attaches a callback function that is called when the button is pressed. The first time this program runs, the button has no screen location, so it appears at some random location on the screen. While the application is running, we provide the ability to interactively lay out widgets on the screen (more on that later). If the user moves the button, SUIT records the location in the database and upon exit, the database is written to disk. The next time this program runs, the SUIT_createButton call will create the button, examine the database, and find the screen location that was stored during the previous execution. Thus, interfaces can be modified at any time that a program is running.

SUIT provides a collection of screen objects, where each object is described by

—its state, contained in a property list,
—a C procedure that examines the object's state and displays it on the screen, and
—a C procedure that handles user input to the object and updates the object's state.

The property list containing an object's state is a set of [name, type, value] triples, as in the following.

```
["label",            "text",            "pizza"]
["diameter",         "floating point",  10.5]
["number of slices", "integer",         6]
["has anchovies",    "boolean",         FALSE]
```

Once users understand that a SUIT-based application is a collection of objects, we introduce external control by explaining that SUIT maintains a table of all on-screen objects (this is the database SUIT maintains), and that SUIT multiplexes keyboard and mouse input based on the location of the cursor. Users quickly understand that three different slider objects share code for their input handling and display procedures, but have a distinct property lists in the state table. The contents of this table are written to human-readable ASCII text file between executions of the program.

After users understand that SUIT maintains a table of objects, we explain that SUIT's interactive tools are provided by accepting some of the user's input as commands to SUIT, rather than to a particular screen object. When user input occurs, SUIT queries the state of the CONTROL and SHIFT keys: if they are both down when mouse buttons are pressed, SUIT interprets the input as a command to move or resize a screen object and updates the object table accordingly. This use of keyboard modifiers allows us to avoid the "run versus build" mode used by other interface buiders, such as the NeXT Interface Builder. Avoiding this mode switch is important for new users, and we have experienced almost no cases of users being confused about when they are giving input to SUIT and when they are giving input to the application. The combination of SHIFT and CONTROL was chosen for very pragmatic reasons: very few window managers "grab" this combination by default, and they are two keys that most users can easily locate on the keyboard.

The "main loop" of a SUIT-based application then looks like

```
forever do
{
  wait for an input event
  IF(SHIFT & CONTROL) are down
      THEN handle as a SUIT-command
      ELSE
      {
      figure out widget we're over
      call its input handler
      }
  paint any objects who've changed
}
```

SUIT maintains a "needs to be repainted" bit next to each object: if any properties of an object change, then SUIT sets this bit. At the bottom of the loop, all "needs to be repainted" objects are repainted and their bits are reset. This provides two important sources of repaint optimization: first, if an object will change several times in on pass of the loop, it will be painted only once; second, we can avoid some repainting altogether by not repainting an object if its properties have not changed.

Having grasped how external control works, many users find it mildly unsettling, because they have become accustomed to using the flow of control in programs to sequence actions. Users do not, however, find external control to be nearly as difficult as their first introduction to either pointer variables or recursion. Once users understand the basic mechanism that drives SUIT, we explain that a standard set of screen objects has already been implemented and stored in a library. This motivates the question of how screen objects can be made to invoke application procedures, or "callbacks." In the example of a slider, users understand how the input handler and painting procedure will cause the slider to behave properly, but are not sure how an application routine can be informed that a value contained in that slider has changed. We then explain that a callback function can be added to the slider object's property list. If such a property exists, the input handler calls the function after changing the state of the slider object. This attachment of user-level callbacks is the most difficult intellectual leap for most users.

As a final comment on external control, we had originally implemented SUIT as strictly external control: each application's main procedure looked something like

```
{
createObject{ . . . }; createObject{ . . . };
. . .
letSuitRun();
}
```

Of course, one of the objects was usually a Done button that would call an exit function to terminate the program. We added support for "internal control" applications by adding a routine that would check to see if any mouse or keyboard input had occurred:

```
{
createObject(...);
createObject(...);
...
while (⟨application's test⟩)
   {
⟨whatever the application wanted⟩
SUIT_checkAndProcessAnyInput();
}
```

This was extremely important for some applications, expecially those needed to poll real-time I/O devices, but it underscores the fact that internal versus external control is not necessarily a large difference.

Objects as Abstract Data Types

Many students tend to confuse the notion of an object's state and the mechanisms that affect that state. We have had good success combatting this by treating objects as abstract data types that have multiple mechanisms for displaying state. For example, SUIT supports a bounded value object with the following properties:

```
["minimum value",    "floating point", 0.0]
["current value",    "floating point", 0.7]
["maximum value",    "floating point", 1.0]
```

which can appear as any of the following display styles [6, 16], shown in Figure 3. A keystroke command (again, with keyboard modifiers down) cycles between the various display styles, and this has been very effective in establishing the difference between an object's state and the mechanism for displaying and altering that state. For many students, it is the most visceral experience they have had in understanding the general concept of an abstract data type.

User Defined Property Types

Users may define their own types for use in property lists by registering subroutines with SUIT that initialize, copy, destroy, convert the type to ASCII, and convert from ASCII to the type. The ASCII conversion allows SUIT to write the interface file that is saved between executions, and to convert one arbitrary type to another by going through an ASCII representation. Users may also register a custom widget that interactively edits that type.

The Class Mechanism

Subclassing and inheritance are complex ideas. When we first show students SUIT, we explain that SUIT provides a collection of screen objects, each of which belongs to one class, and can inherit some portion of their state from that class. When motivating the class and inheritance mechanisms, we find it necessary to briefly lie to our students; they are not ready to appreciate the real reasons, which are of course based on issues such as modularity and abstraction, upon which weaker undergraduates have a tenuous grip. Students understand concrete explanations much better than abstract ones, and once they understand the concept, one can revisit the motivation for it. Therefore, we explain that having each object store values for each possible property is wasteful, expecially when many widgets often have the value for a property. Although the storage savings are not really of concern to us, they provide a motivation that students readily accept. When a program requires the value of a property, SUIT looks first in the property list containing that object's state. If SUIT does not find the requested property, it then looks in a property list stored with the object's class. If the property is not found at that level, SUIT looks in a global property list. If the property is not found in the global property list, SUIT creates it using the type's initialization routine to establish a default value.

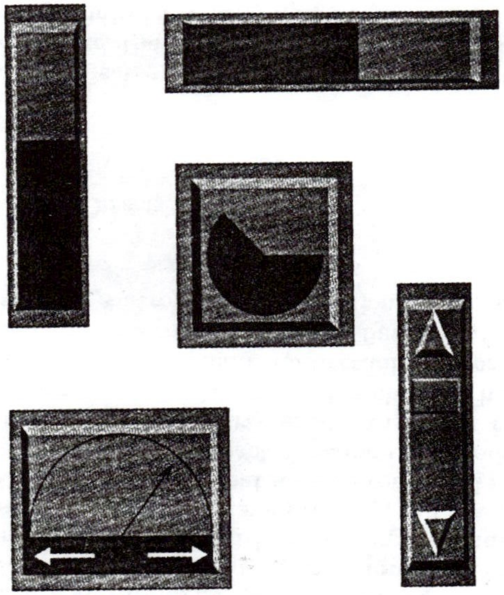

Fig. 3. Bounded value display styles.

The Property Editor

Students do best with concrete, visible items. Screen objects are good for explaining object-oriented programming, as shown by the early success in Smalltalk [8]. The problem with class and global property lists is that they are no longer implicitly visible. The prototype-instance architecture [11] does not really solve this problem, because prototype objects are typically not visible on-screen. We provide a direct manipulation [15] property editor that allows users to interactively examine and alter the state of objects. The SUIT property editor, which is shown in Figure 4, always displays the object, class, and global property lists when allowing the user to edit the state of an object.

Users alter a property's value by clicking on that property with the mouse; boolean properties toggle when clicked, and other properties either bring up a type-in box or a type-specific dialog box, such as the dialog box for type font shown in Figure 5. If an object is currently inheriting a value from its class, the user can take that property value and drag it from the class level to the object level, thereby copying it. If a property is currently specified at the object level and the user wishes to have that property default to the class's specification, the user drags the property from the object level to the trash can, deleting the object level property. In the same way, properties can be manipulated at the global level. An exrcise in the SUIT tutorial asks the reader to make all labels in an application blue, and then have one particular label override that default and be red.

Property sheets date back to (at least) the Xerox Star [2]. Other systems use a spreadsheet model for accessing attributes of objects [12, 20]. Our contribution is to always expose the fixed three levels on every invocation. This produces some screen clutter, but also avoids having the student learn the mechanisms for accessing inherited state. The property editor has been tremendously successful; it allows our students to understand and use state inheritance in less than five minutes. We believe this is due to the combination of limiting the class hierarchy to a single level—exposing information at all three levels—and using direct manipulation.

Other systems, such as Sun's DevGuide, use custom panels for each widget class, rather than a scrollable list of properties as in the SUIT property editor. The drawback to using a custom panel per widget class is that it either requires the authors of new classes to create those panels by hand, or requires the system to provide an automatic layout tool for an arbitrary set of properties, a task beyond most current systems. With SUIT, if a user defines a new widget class, the property editor will work automatically with that class.

Linking Objects to Other Objects

By default, SUIT provides a very simple linkage mechanism. Application-level callbacks can be registered with objects, and those callbacks are invoked by the input handlers for the screen objects. A more complicated problem is how to provide a general linkage mechanism between screen components and arbitrary user routines. The NeXT Interface Builder solves the problem by allowing the user to draw a connection between two screen objects and then prompting the user to specify details about the linkage via a sequence of dialog boxes. SUIT provides a simpler but more limited form of linkage that handles a large number of common cases and avoids the novice's usual confusion about whether the first object is linked to the second, or the second is linked to the first.

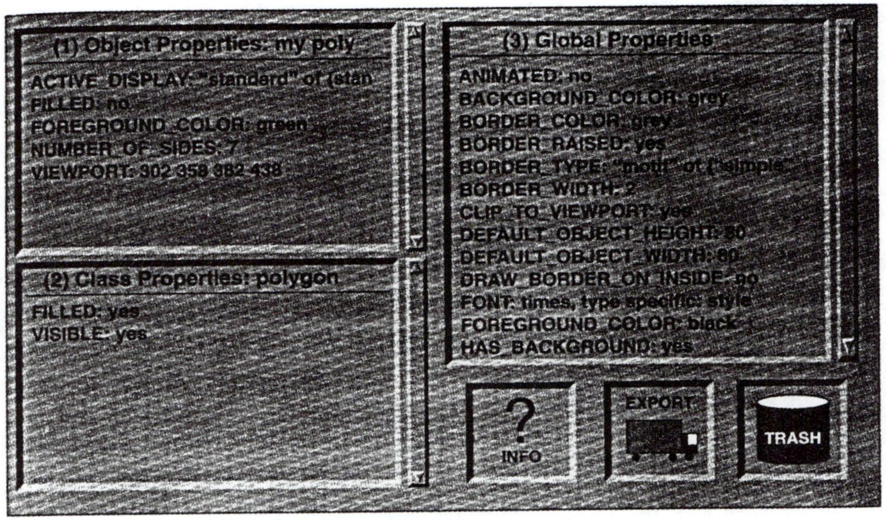

Fig. 4. Property editor.

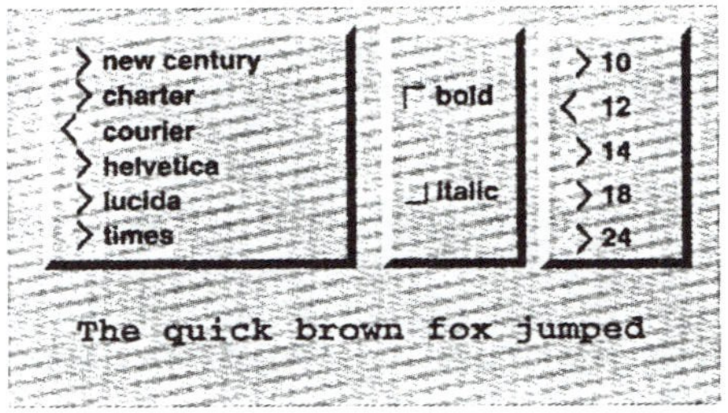

Fig. 5. Font panel.

Many linkages between on-screen objects merely allow one object to control a particular aspect, or property, of another. For example, in the polygon drawing program in Figure 6, the slider controls the number of sides in the polygon. Rather than attempting to link two existing objects, a SUIT user would start with only the polygon object and then invoke the property editor. The user would then drag the "number of sides" property to the "EXPORT" icon (a picture of a moving van), which causes SUIT to create a new object that controls that property. This also has the side effect of locking the property, which is shown with a small "lock" icon in the property editor. This avoids the ambiguous situation of the user modifying the polygon's "number of sides" in the property editor after exporting it.

In fact, the program shown in Figure 6 can be created with no programming, starting with a blank screen. The user creates a "polygon object" via

Fig. 6. Polygon application.

the menu of standard objects and then exports that polygon object's "number of sides" and "filled" properties.

In a similar fashion to the EXPORT icon, the INFO icon can be used to gain information about a property. Users can drag a property to this icon and get on-line help describing the data type of the property and a textual description of what the property is used for.

Hierarchy

With most interface toolkits, novices confuse the logical tree of subclasses with the geometric tree that visually nests objects. We avoid this problem in SUIT by limiting classes to one level and by hiding the geometric hierarchy from novice users. As an aside, the motivation for providing rich subclasses of objects is somewhat weak; it may help the implementor of the toolkit, but most users of the toolkit do not want to have to know that class "button" has been derived from class "label" in order to use it properly. In theory, this should make it easier to create custom widgets by subclassing existing ones, but our discussions with Motif users revealed that most find the process more frustrating than helpful.

Although some basic SUIT objects are actually hierarchical collections of other objects, we provide procedural and interactive operations that treat these objects atomically. By providing interactive tools that allow users to move and resize multiple objects at one time, we sidestep the only motivation most novices have for wanting to compose basic objects into a hierarchy.

Once users are comfortable with the basic system, we introduce them to interactive manipulation of hierarchy. SUIT allows users to create a composite object which geometrically contains other objects. One type of composite object, the bulletin board, does no rearrangement of its children. Another, the stacker, has vertical and horizontal tiling display styles (vboxes in Interviews/TeX terminology). A third, the pull down menu, hides its children until it is pressed. Screen objects can be nested within a composite object by dragging them inside it. Any object can be nested into any of the composite objects, and new users are often delighted when they discover they can place clocks and sliders in pulldown menus.

When objects are inside a composite object, there is ambiguity as to which object should receive input. For regular input, this is simple: the input handler for the outer object merely passes the input down to the appropriate child. Input directed toward SUIT's interactive tools, such as an attempt to move an object, is more problematic. This is resolved by allowing the user to *open* a composite widget. When an object is open, SUIT draws a special border around it to indicate that its children, and not the outer object, will receive SUIT commands. If a child is moved outside the boundaries of its geometric parent, it becomes autonomous, moving up to be a sibling of its parent in the geometry tree.

Geometric hierarchy adds semantic complexity in several ways. First, property lookup is affected: if a button is inside a pulldown menu and does not specify its color, should it be the color of its class (all buttons), or of its geometric parent (the pulldown menu)? There is no one, correct answer. One could implement a flag per property in each object indicating "not specified, but look at parent, not class," which provides all possible options at the cost of implementation and intellectual complexity. Instead, SUIT uses a simple rule: if an object does not specify a property, we look first at its class's property list, and if we still do not find the property, we walk up the parent chain until an answer is found. The class property lists of the ancestors are not consulted; we concede this is an arbitrary decision, but so are all other solutions.

Employees

In SUIT, each object represents an abstract data type, which can have multiple representations called display styles. Each of these display styles may be simple or may be composed of other SUIT objects. If a display style consists of other objects, these objects are known as the employees of that display style. Figure 7 shows the display styles for a bounded value object. The speedometer and thermometer display styles are simple because they have no employees, while the scrollbar display style has three employees: two arrow buttons and an elevator.

The employees of a display style appear only while the object is in that display style. When one "cycles" a bounded value object from the scrollbar to the thermometer, the scrollbar's three employees are no longer needed. In SUIT this is implemented through visibility. Invisible objects in SUIT are neither painted nor sent input. When one cycles an object from one display style to another, the employees of the old display are made invisible and those of the new display are made visible. We chose to change the employees' visibility rather than create and destroy them as necessary, so that the employees' properties would be retained when the user cycles away from the display style and back to it again.

In terms of geometrical composition, employees are very similar to children. Both children and employees move and resize with their parents and may inherit their parent's properties. The only difference between them is that a child exists for each of the parent's display styles while an employee exists for only one. To make this distinction clear, consider a possible implementation of an object that allows the user to scroll through a picture. One display style might use scrollbars along each axis to represent the

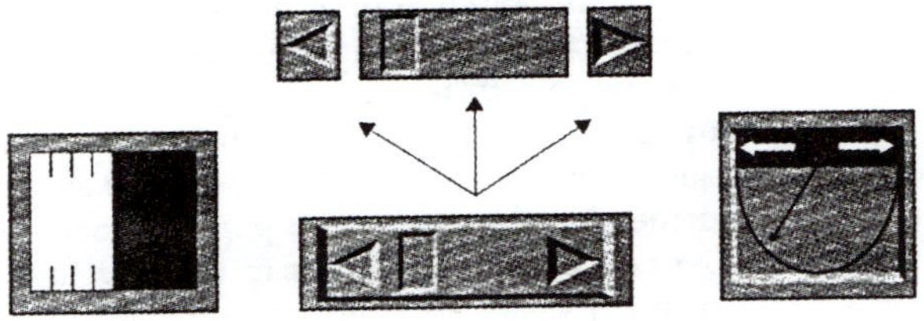

Fig. 7. Employees in display styles.

portion of the picture currently being viewed. Another might use a panner object (a rectangle within another rectangle) to represent the same information. In the implementation, the picture object would be a child, since it would necessarily be in every display style. The scrollbars would be the employees of the first display style, and the panner would be the employee of the second.

In practice, employees are rarely used. The only object in SUIT's standard library that uses them is the scrollbar mentioned above. There are two main reasons for this. The first is that, if an abstraction is sufficiently complicated to merit breaking it down into several component objects, then there is often only one good way to represent this abstraction; thus the object would have only one display style. An object with only one display style has no need for employees. The second reason is that those who use SUIT to build applications usually have a particular interface in mind, and therefore only design one display style for each of their objects. Again, having one display style makes employees unnecessary.

The last portion of the architecture supports semantic linking of state: many systems, such as Garnet, support a *constraint* model where the programmer specifies a relationship that should remain true, and the system ensures that it does. For example, the programmer can make one object state "above" another on the screen by establishing a constraint between their viewports.

SUIT's model is similar: we allow the programmer to register an *interest* in an object by specifying a procedure to call each time any property of that object changes. The procedure is called with parameters indicating the object that is in question, the name of the property that changed, and the old and new values. This interest routine will then set any properties for that (or any other) object. This is, in fact, how SUIT makes sure that buttons are the same size as their text. It registers an interest in each button, and if the "label" property of a button changes, SUIT recomputes a new "viewport" property based on the size of the text. While this behavior could have been implemented in a specialized constraint language, we believe that simply writing a subroutine in C is the most straightforward way to establish the relationship we wish to maintain between the string in the button and the button's viewport.

OUR EXPERIENCE WITH USERS

The next two sections are our most important contribution, both of which are based on our experience with our users and the changes in the system that they motivated. These two sections are delineated by whether the change was to the programmer interface and the data model or to the set of interactive tools that we provided in the interface builder. We begin with the lesson we learned from the programmer's interface.

Our most important observation is that we were defeated on only one front: the general idea of callback-based programming was something we were never able to have the tool teach as part of the process. We were able to write a four-page addition, to be read before the tutorial, which makes it possible for most students to understand external control. In hindsight, we should not have been surprised that external control was the single most difficult concept for college juniors. Introductory programming courses stress writing programs whose execution paths closely follow the order that the statements are read in the source code. Callback functions are typically not covered, nor are subroutines that take functions as parameters. In fact, in ANSI-Standard Pascal, external control is not even possible, because function pointers cannot be stored into variables.

All but the very best undergraduates are accustomed to encoding state in the flow of their programs, and they have great difficulty adjusting to the model in which they write small fragments that can be called in any order, at any time. In fact, a common "coping strategy" we saw was for a single button's callback procedure to encapsulate a huge chunk of program functionality. Students also tended toward moded interfaces, where they attempted to force the user dialog at each step, trying to mimic a command-line prompt interface within a GUI.

Custom Widget Authoring

Another major observation is that, although creating new widgets is relatively painless in SUIT, and early versions of the tutorial had students do so, we found that students went to great extremes to avoid writing their own custom widgets. The end result of this is very positive. Whether motivated by fear, laziness, or by good software engineering principles, students reused existing code wherever possible.

When students did write custom widgets, we saw two major recurring problems. The first common problem was in using coordinate systems. The abstract floating point "world" coordinate system is much easier and more flexible, but is not what students expected. Concrete things are almost always easier to grasp than abstract ones, and students uniformly expressed the desire to draw in screen pixels. However, after students had written several custom widgets, they usually began to appreciate the abstract coordinate system.

The second major problem with custom widget authors was a general lack of understanding of the SUIT "database model," in which input procedures change properties in the database and paint procedures may only examine the database. This division caused major problems: almost every student attempted to paint within the input procedure. We considered mechanically disabling the graphics library routines before calling a user's input handler and then reenabling them after the call, so that any painting inside a hit procedure would trigger a run-time error. We abandoned this because it probably would not have helped a student understand what they were doing wrong.

Students were able to write most programs without creating their own custom widgets. When they attempted to create custom widgets, they often had difficulty. Based on these two facts, we removed the section of the tutorial on creating custom widgets. Students who needed to create custom widgets were eventually provided with an example program that created a simple widget. Students were more successful in modifying this program to meet their needs than they had been working from a clean slate.

Make Easy Things Easy

In several places, we were able to apply design principle of "make easy things easy, and hard things possible." The first was with moded interaction techniques: dialog boxes that grabbed the input focus and required an answer from the user before other screen objects would again accept input. We identified the most commonly requested cases and provided simple functions for them:

```
SUIT_inform (char *message);
SUIT_askYesNo(char *question);
SUIT_askOKCancel(char *question);
SUIT_askYesNoCancel(char *question);
SUIT_ask(char *question, char *answer1, char *answer2);
```

In addition to these, we provided one general-purpose moded dialog box. When passed an arbitrary SUIT object as a parameter, it nests in it an OK/Cancel dialog box and allows the user to interact with the widget until the user presses either the OK or Cancel button. These routines seemed to meet all of our user needs for moded dialog boxes.

Another common case was the need by users for dynamic interaction techniques, such as rubber-banding lines or dragging objects around the screen. We provided a simple routine that XOR'd a rectangle at the current mouse position as long as the button stayed down. The final screen coordinate would then be functionally returned. This, combined with a utility function SUIT_ObjectAt(x, y), made it easy for users to implement simple drag-and-drop techniques, such as dragging objects to a trash can. In addition to the rectangle drag, we provided a text string drag routine and a general-purpose drag routine that called an application callback each time the mouse moved.

Most of the time, the rule of thumb is that anything one sees on the screen is part of the SUIT interface, is stored in the database, and is restored "as is" the next time the application is run. In some instances, this is not desirable; for example, in some applications it makes more sense for scrollable lists to return to the top of the list than retain their old location. To support this, we added calls to make particular properties temporary. In a similar fashion, an entire object could be declared temporary—meaning none of its state would be saved between application invocations.

Name Space Issues

Like other dynamic systems, we rapidly developed a problem due to the lack of static checking on our name spaces. For example, property names in SUIT are just character strings, searched at runtime using string compares. Since users need not declare a property before using it, a common user error is to misspell a property's name, thus generating a new property with a default value. A classic story involves one poor student who was trying to remove the border of an object and spent several hours trying to figure out why the following line of code:

```
SUIT_setBoolean(myObject, "has boarder", FALSE);
```

had no effect. By mispelling the "has border" property, the student created a new Boolean property, never again examined. This is a common problem in most LISP-based systems, such as Garnet, where accidental *slot* creation is a problem.

Users often need to create new properties. We kept this flexibility, but avoided spelling problems for the SUIT-provided properties by using the C preprocessor and including a line such as

```
#define HAS_BORDER "has border"
```

in the suit.h include file for each SUIT-provided property name in the standard set. This, combined with the decision to make all string compares in SUIT be case-insensitive, effectively solved our dynamic name space problems.

Other Programmer Issues

Under certain conditions, it became necessary to prohibit users from altering a property via the property editor. For example, users tended to randomly play with various global-level properties, which often caused problems. Therefore, we *locked* some properties, so that the user could no longer change them with the interactive property editor. The remaining semantic question was whether this would also prohibit the application programmer from setting the property. (We rejected the idea of having two different lock bits per property to specify both cases.) Because the programmer also had the ability to query whether properties were locked, and to lock and unlock them, we decided to make the lock prohibit the interactive user only from changing the property, and this has worked well in practice.

From the beginning, we felt it was important to support animation in the toolkit. In our demonstration programs, we provide bouncing balls that move at a constant twenty pixels per second, regardless of the speed of the underlying hardware. (If the hardware is slow, the balls will appear at a lower number of intermediate positions, and their motion will be choppier; if the hardware is fast, their motion will appear smoother). In order to support this, we needed to provide a device-independent SUIT_getCurrentTime function, which we added to GP because it was the most convenient layer. We also found it useful to support a boolean *animated* property for all widgets; if this property is true, SUIT automatically calls the object's paint procedure, whether or not any of the object's properties have changed.

INTERACTIVE TOOL OBSERVATIONS

We present here a variety of insights that we gained from watching people use SUIT's interactive tools.

Gathering Feedback

Gathering feedback from experts was relatively easy. We encouraged all our users to send electronic mail to the SUIT account if they had questions or comments. From the mail we received, we were able to deduce which parts of SUIT were causing programmers the most trouble, and therefore, which parts needed fixing, better documentation, or both.

By comparison, gathering feedback from novices was much harder. The only real way to find out which parts of SUIT were hardest for novices to learn was to give the SUIT tutorial to novices and watch them as they worked through it. Our standard observation protocol was to seat pairs of students at UNIX workstations with an observer from the SUIT team sitting behind them, silently taking notes on the session.

Pairing the students off was a vital part of the observation. When two people are told to work together they talk to each other, often saying what is going on in their minds as they work through the tutorial. This forces into the open a dialog that, with one person, would be entirely internal. By eavesdropping on a pair of collaborating students, we can learn about which parts of SUIT (and the tutorial itself) that new users find easy and which cause confusion. SUIT's design was changed innumerable times because of difficulties we saw from these silent observation sessions.

Keeping the observers quiet during the observation sessions was crucial. One reason user testing is hard is that the observer can often influence the observed—a problem quite familiar to anyone who designs surveys. This is especially true here, because it was often the SUIT implementors themselves who did the observing. We maintained a strict policy of "sitting on our hands" during the observations; under no circumstance were the observers allowed to get up from their chairs and help the users get out of a bind that SUIT or its tutorial had put them into. If they did, we required the observers to deliver a standard apology: "I'm sorry I wrote such bad software. Here, let me help you with that." Needless to say, the observers remained seated.

We tested SUIT and its tutorial as often as possible and with as many people as we could. This often meant living off the kindness of the professors in the department teaching software engineering. This gave us a pool of approximately 45 students per semester from this one class alone. Other classes gave us more opportunities to test the software on novices. Because of the large number of people that went through the user testing process, video taping was never a practical alternative to real, live observation.

We would like to note that everyone benefits from a massive user testing experience. The observers benefit from the experience of learning how to take notes and to be observant; the observed from a kind of "cultural" lesson, i.e., that computer scientists really field test as part of their craft; and the programmers from relearning what parts of the software will confuse new users.

The user testing and the electronic mail from our more advanced users yielded a great deal of practical knowledge, which we can summarize under three categories: SUIT's basic feedback techniques. SUIT's different interaction techniques, and SUIT's methods of creating and composing widgets.

Feedback Techniques

XOR is dangerous. As useful a technique as this is for moving graphics interactively, we found that XOR was not nearly as portable as one might imagine. Some platforms define the bit representation of "black" to be all zeros, which has no effect in XOR mode! The solution here is to always use a representation that is all ones as the color to XOR with, not the "black" that is provided by the native graphics environment.

On platforms with color displays, the XOR problem is even worse because the result of an XOR operation is ill-defined in color. XORing two colors results in a third color, the value of which depends on the values loaded into the color table, which cannot be predicted. Often, we found that we got "lucky," but of course, anything can change the color table—so sometimes SUIT XOR's a faint blue line onto a light grey background.

Take care when drawing handles. SUIT uses the standard feedback technique of drawing "handles" on objects that are "selected" for the purposes of some direct manipulation operations (e.g., resize). As is the convention, we drew these handles as small black squares in the corners and on the edges of whatever objects were selected. Users complained that we sometimes drew these squares on parts of widgets that were already black, meaning that the handles were essentially invisible black on black.

Choosing some other color was clearly not the solution; doing so merely transferred the problem of someday drawing red on red, or blue on blue. Eventually, we solved this problem by outlining each of the black handles with a 1-pixel-wide white border, producing a handle that is visible under all circumstances. We learned that sometimes the best answer to an interface problem isn't with engineering, but with graphic design.

Animation draws attention and raises expectations. We use animation in SUIT as a way of drawing the user's attention to a particular part of the screen, especially when there is an abrupt change to the interface. Animation has the effect of saying, "Look here! This just changed!" For example, when the user creates a new widget interactively, SUIT animates a rectangle that collapses from the edges of the window down toward the center of the screen, where the new widget appears, much the same way as the Macintosh animates a rectangle when a new folder is opened. SUIT's export icon also animates when a property is exported—a truck drives off the icon as feedback that the property was exported. This charmed most users who saw it, but other users were disappointed because other icons and buttons didn't animate. Whether the whimsical charm of the moving truck is different enough to warrant its removal is a matter of debate.

Interaction Techniques

Muscles as modes. SUIT is unlike some other interface builders that have separate "run" and "build" modes. SUIT's interactive tools are present with the program as it runs, blurring the difference between running and building. To distinguish between events that are meant for the application and those meant for SUIT, we use a keyboard modifier. If the SHIFT and CONTROL keys are held down when the mouse is clicked, we sent the event to SUIT, otherwise the event is passed on to the application. Unlike a moded interface, the chance of confusing run and build mode are zero; the user holds down the SHIFT and CONTROL keys, so there is a constant reminder of "who you're talking to."

Direct manipulation beats menus. We originally used a "cut and paste" menu-driven model in the design of SUIT's property editor, with dreadful results. Changing a property entailed clicking on a property, then accessing a menu to choose the desired operation: move a property up a level, move down a level, delete, and so on. The temptation to drag the property itself in order to move, copy, or delete it was overwhelming. The menus always seemed to put the properties "at arm's length" from the user. We eventually abandoned the menus in favor of a "direct-manipulation" style of editing.

With direct manipulation, users could now simply click on the property to produce a widget that allowed them to edit that property's value. For example, clicking on a color property produced a selection of colors to choose from and clicking on a font produced a listing of available faces, sizes, and styles. Text properties are the only ones that break this "click, get a dialog box, press OK to accept the change" model of interaction. Clicking on a text property wraps a type in a field around the currently displayed characters for the value of that property. This is clearly an irregularity, but one that is a benign exception to the rule—rather than strict adherence to consistency, we opted for keeping the user's attention focused on the string he is already looking at, rather than producing a dialog box in some other part of the screen.

Moving a property from the class level to an object level was done by the familiar "drag and drop" action. Users clearly liked this style better than the old menu "move up a level" command. Users also showed in testing that they had no trouble understanding that dropping a property on the "info" widget produced a dialog box with information about the property or that dropping it on the trash can deleted it.

As it turns out, the presence of the trash can implied power that SUIT did not (at first) possess. We observed that users extended the "drag and drop" metaphor in their own minds to apply to the whole *widgets* as well as properties; in many tutorial observation trials, users dragged widgets to the trash can and were startled to discover that nothing happened. It seems that our users understood the concept of "regularity" before we did.

We always saw the property editor as a place where properties, not widgets, were being dragged from place to place, but so many people tried to delete widgets with the property trash can that we added the feature and made our users happy. By extending this principle further, we also provided help strings for widgets dropped on the info widget. Dropping a widget on the "export" button still does nothing, as the semantics for this are not well defined.

By providing this harmless but useful level functionality, we obeyed the "law of least astonishment" at the expense of the "purity" of the model.

Widget Creation and Composition

Users liked "export." If a user drops a property onto the property editor's "export" widget, SUIT creates a widget corresponding to the type of the property. Color properties produce color chips, text properties produce text entry widgets, and so on. The widget then controls the value of the property that was "exported," providing a short cut to the full-blown property editor by giving the user a single widget in the application interface that controls the value of a property. This was seen by many of our users as a way of avoiding a fair bit of uninteresting code in their applications.

Interactive widget creation is only for demos and decoration. While always impressive in a demo, the ability to create new buttons and sliders on the fly is really not very useful. Items that act merely as decoration, such as labels, can be added nicely, but most items have attached functionality that must be specified. Because SUIT is based on C, runtime binding would be much harder than in a LISP-based system like Garnet; SUIT would need to compile and link code on the fly—something that a LISP-based system need not worry about. If the user creates a button interactively, how does he or she attach a callback function to it? Attaching the callback is usually done with the creation call, but here the button has already been created!

At present, the only way to do this is by hand: the programmer opens up the C source code file and makes a function call that attaches a function pointer to the button, referring to the button by its unique string name provided when the widget was created interactively. Spelling the name incorrectly results in a fatal runtime error.

As a practical matter, SUIT's interactive creation of widgets is really only of use for widgets with no functionality—labels and "place mats" (rectangles that exist purely for show).

Composition of Widgets

In the begining, we saw the need for a *composition* widget–a widget whose only purpose is to contain other widgets. In a fit of whimsy, we dubbed this new widget type *tupperware*. Tupperware was seen as a general-purpose container class that could be used for horizontal and vertical stacking geometry managers, pulldown menus, dialog boxes, and any other type of widget that might contain other widgets. To us, the only distinction between these different screen objects was in the way they displayed their subordinates (or "children" in SUIT parlance). We therefore implemented a tupperware class with display styles bulletin board,menu,vertical stacker, and horizontal stacker.

Our users saw things differently. To them, a menu and a bulletin board (dialog box) were two different things, and pretending that they were the same only served to confuse them. As it turned out, we had difficulty in maintaining the code for this behemoth widget, and so reimplemented it as several different widgets. This removed bugs and cleared the way considerably for our users. Again, cleanliness of the model was sacrificed for the learning curve of our user base.

CONCLUSIONS

By using a reduced model for subclassing, hiding geometric hierarchy, and providing direct manipulation tools for property setting and linkage, we were able to radically reduce the learning time and complexity for a user interface toolkit. By keeping the toolkit's implementation lightweight and building it on top of an easily ported graphics package, we have been able to implement SUIT on a wide variety of platforms.

College juniors who were not familiar with external control, and had never seen another UI toolkit, were able to use SUIT productively after roughly two and a half hours. Our undergraduate software engineering class projects have been able to expand their scope significantly by using SUIT, and the students were highly motivated by being able to easily produce professional-looking interfaces for their projects.

The best validation of a tool like SUIT is when it is used by external sites, which must rely only on our printed documentation and limited correspondence via electronic mail. At the time of this writing, SUIT has been FTP'd to over 100 external internet machines, and is being adopted for use in undergraduate courses at a number of universities. Professional research laboratories are also finding SUIT attractive; as is often the case, a powerful tool that is easy for novices to use is often attractive to experts as well.

Our original desire was merely to produce a tool that would introduce students to relatively difficult concepts, specifically external control and inheritance. We had presumed that after spending a few weeks with SUIT they would outgrow it and move on to other more mature and complex systems such as UIMX [17], based on Motif Widget set, or Interviews. Instead, we have observed the phenomenon that also occurred with Pascal: unless students discovered a specific need to move to a more advanced platform, they continued to use SUIT for their own research projects.

Our major regret is that we implemented geometrically hierarchical widgets. This more than doubled the complexity of the system, and we estimate its end value to most users at less than five percent.

In this paper, we have presented the final incarnation of SUIT; it is important to remember that SUIT's development was a continuous, iterative process, with dozens of versions released and tested for feedback with real students.

Getting SUIT

SUIT is provided without charge to academic and nonprofit organizations. Readers with access to the internet can type finger suit@uvacs.cs.virginia.edu for directions on how to get and run the software.

ACKNOWLEDGMENTS

We would like to thank Roderic Collins, Jim Defay, Pramod Dwivedi, Brandon Furlich, Rich Gossweiler, Drew Kessler, James Leatherby, Chris Long, William McClennan, Kim Passarella, Anne Shackelford, Hans-Martin Werner, and Nathaniel Young, all of whom contributed to SUIT's development. We also thank all of our users, especially Anita Jones and Marc Brown, who allowed us to use their students as guinea pigs for early versions of SUIT. We acknowledge the help of the anonymous referees, whose comments led to substantial improvements in the paper.

SUIT should not be confused with SUITE [5], a project at Purdue with a similar name.

REFERENCES

1. Bass, L. J., Clapper, B. M., Hardy, E. J., Kazman, R. N., and Seacord, R. C. Serpent: A user interface environment. In *Proceedings, Winter* 1990 *USENIX Technical Conference*, (Washington, D.C., Jan. 1990), pp. 245–258.
2. Bewley, W., Roberts, T., Schroit, D., and Verplank, W. Human factors testing in the design of Xerox's 8010 'Star' Office Workstation. In *Proceedings of ACM CHI'83 Conference on Human Factors in Computing Systems* (Boston, Dec. 12–15, 1983), pp. 72–77.
3. Blomberg, J., and Henderson, A. Reflections on participatory design: Lessons from the Trillium Experience. In *Proceedings of ACM CHI'90 Conference on Human Factors in Computing Systems*, (Seattle, Wash., Apr. 1–5, 1990), pp. 353–359.
4. Calder, P., Linton, M., and Vlissides, J. Composing user interfaces with interviews. *IEEE Computer 22*, (Feb., 1989), 8–22.
5. Dewan, P. *A Guide to Suite*. Software Engineering Research Center, Purdue Univ. SERC-TR-60-P, Feb. 1990.
6. Foley, J. D., and McMath, C. F. Dynamic process visualization. *Comput. Grah. Appl. 6*, 3 (Mar. 1986), 16–25.
7. Foley, J., Van Dam, A., Feiner, S., and Hughes, J. *Computer Graphics: Principles and Practice (2nd Edition)*. Addison-Wesley Publishing Co., Reading, MA, ISBN 0-201-12110-7; T385.C587, 1990.
8. Goldberg, A., and Robson, D. *Smalltalk—80: The Language*. Addison-Wesley, Reading, Mass., 1989.
9. Mahoney, M. Interface Builder and Object-Oriented Design in the NeXTstep Environment. In *Tutorial Notes from the ACM SIGCHI Human Factors in Computer Systems Conference*, (New Orleans, LA, 1991). Available from NeXT, Inc., 900 Chesapeake Drive, Redwood City, CA 94063 415-424-0200.
10. McCormack, J., and Asente, P. An overview of the X toolkit. In *Proceedings of the ACM SIGGRAPH Symposium on User Interface Software* (Banff, Alberta, Canada, Oct. 1988), pp. 46–55.

11. Myers, B., Giuse, D., and Dannenberg, B. Garnet: Comprehensive support for graphical, highly interactive user interfaces. *IEEE Comput. 23*, 11 (Nov. 1990).
12. Myers, B. Graphical Techniques in a spreadsheet for specifying user interfaces. In *Proceedings of ACM CHI'91 Conference on Human Factors in Computing Systems* (New Orleans, LA, Apr. 27–May 2, 1991), pp. 243–250.
13. Palay, A. J., Hansen, W. J., Kazar, M. L., Sherman, M. S., Wadlow, M. G., Neuendorffer, T. P., Stern, Z., Badler, M., and Peters, T. The Andrew toolkit—An overview. In *USENIX Technical Conference Proceedings* (Dallas, TX, Feb. 1988), pp. 9–21.
14. Rochkind, M. J. Technical overview of the extensible virtual toolkit. Advanced Programming Institute, Ltd., January 16, 1989, API Ltd., Box 17665, Boulder, CO 80308 (303) 443-4223.
15. Schneiderman, B. Direct manipulation: A step beyond programming languages. *IEEE Comput. 16*, 8 (Aug. 1983), 57–69.
16. Sibert, J., Hurley, W., and Bleser, T. An object-oriented user interface management system. *Comput. Graph. 20*, 4 (Aug. 1986). Also in *Proceedings of SIGGRAPH* '86.
17. User Interface Management Toolkit for X. Visual Edge Software Ltd, 101 First St., Suite 443, Los Altos, CA 94022 (415) 948-0753.
18. Valdes, R. A virtual toolkit for windows and the Mac. *BYTE 14*, (Mar. 1989), 209–210.
19. Welsh, J. Ambiguities and Insecurities in Pascal. *Softw. Prac. Expe. 7*, (1977), 685–696.
20. Wilde, N., and Lewis, C. Spreadsheet-based interactive graphics: from prototype to tool. In *Proceedings of ACM CHI'90 Conference on Human Factors in Computing Systems* (Seattle, Wash., Apr. 1–5, 1990), pp. 153–159.

Garnet

Comprehensive Support for Graphical, Highly Interactive User Interfaces

Brad A. Myers, Dario A. Giuse, Roger B. Dannenberg, Brad Vander Zanden, David S. Kosbie, Edward Pervin, Andrew Mickish, and Philippe Marchal
Carnegie Mellon University

User interface software is difficult and expensive to implement.[1] Highly interactive interfaces are among the hardest to create, since they must handle at least two asynchronous input devices (such as a mouse and keyboard), real-time feedback, multiple windows, and elaborate, dynamic graphics.

The Garnet research project is creating a set of tools to aid the design and implementation of highly interactive, graphical, direct manipulation user interfaces. Garnet also helps designers rapidly prototype different interfaces and explore various user interface metaphors during early product design.

Most graphical interfaces are created using toolkits, collections of interaction techniques (sometimes called "widgets" or "gadgets") such as menus, scroll bars, and buttons. Examples include the Macintosh Toolbox and Xtk for the X Window System. Unfortunately, these toolkits are often difficult to use, since they contain literally hundreds of procedures. Also, many toolkits do not help the programmer create the most important part of the application — the graphics that appear in the main application window. In particular, the application must handle all input events (expressed at a low level as "the left mouse button went down," "the mouse is at (30,345)," etc.), deciding which operation to perform on objects and drawing objects with the underlying graphics package (which usually supplies operations such as "draw-line" and "draw-circle"). Furthermore, modifying or creating toolkit items is usually difficult or impossible.

Garnet helps create highly interactive user interfaces by emphasizing easy specification of object behavior, often by demonstration and without programming.

Higher level tools such as interface builders and user interface management systems[1] have not adequately addressed these problems. A conventional interface builder lets a designer graphically place user interface components in a window, thereby creating menus, palettes, and dialogue boxes. Examples include Next's Interface Builder, Smethers Barnes' Prototyper for the Macintosh, and UIMX for X Windows. These programs let a designer place only preprogrammed interaction techniques in windows, and they usually allow only a few parameters to be set. Often, a designer will type the name of a procedure to be called when the interaction technique is executed. Designers cannot modify or design the interaction techniques themselves, and the interface builders do not address application-specific graphics at all.

A user interface management system helps a designer handle the dialogue, or sequencing, aspects of the user interface — that is, what happens after each user action. Such systems have generally not addressed the creation of toolkit components (menus, scroll bars, etc.) or the specification or management of application-specific graphical objects (the contents of application windows).

A number of features differentiate Garnet from other user interface tools, including an emphasis on handling objects' runtime behavior (how they change when the user operates on them) and on handling all visual aspects of a program's user interface, including its graphics and the contents of all application-specific windows.

For example, when creating an application that lets the user manipulate boxes connected by arrows (such as a graph edi-

0018-9162/90/1100-0071$01.00 © 1990 IEEE

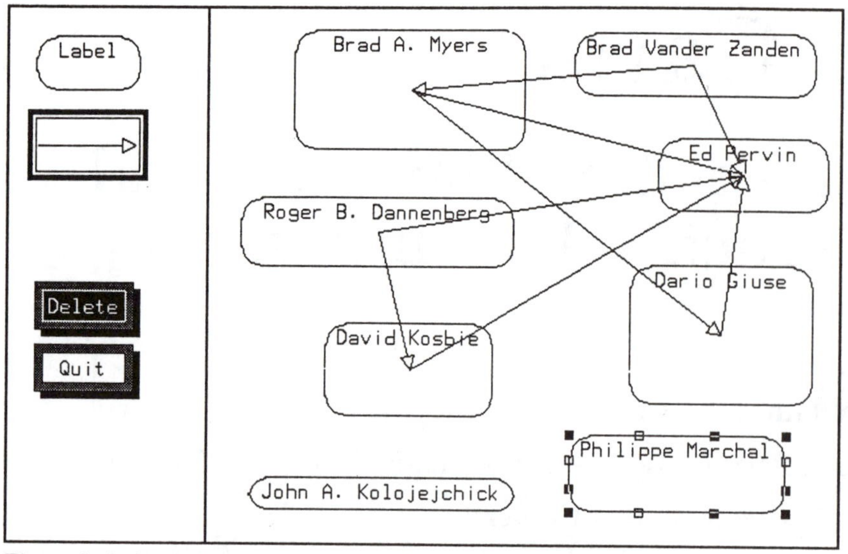

Figure 1. A simple boxes-and-arrows editor created with Garnet. An arbitrary number of new boxes and arrows can be added, and their initial position is specified using the mouse. Any existing box or arrow can also be selected, changed in position or size, and deleted. This entire editor was implemented in about three hours using the Garnet Toolkit.

tor or project-planning chart — see Figure 1), Garnet's user interface builder lets the designer draw the boxes and arrows and demonstrate how they should respond to the mouse. Menus, palettes, and dialogue boxes can be generated automatically or added graphically. Toolkits and interface builders in other systems might help build the menus and palettes, but they don't let the designer implement and manage the boxes and arrows themselves. Designers using those programs must code these elements directly using the underlying graphics package and input device handlers. Typically, coding application-specific graphics requires 10-100 times more effort than dealing with menus and buttons, so Garnet should save programmers significant time.

This article provides an overview of all parts of Garnet, which stands for "generating an amalgam of real-time novel editors and toolkits." Previous articles[2-5] have concentrated on individual aspects of the system. (There is also a complete reference manual for the Garnet Toolkit.[6])

Garnet is entirely "look-and-feel independent," which means the designer can either create user interfaces with an original graphical appearance and behavior or choose from a set of predefined appearances and behaviors.

The system contains both low-level and high-level tools. The low-level tools, called the Garnet Toolkit, use a number of mechanisms to help implement user interfaces, including a prototype-instance object system, a constraint system (which allows relationships among objects to be declared once and then maintained by the system), automatic graphical object updating (so that the system refreshes the display when objects change), and separate specification of input handling from graphics.

Garnet's high-level tools include the Lapidary interface builder; the Jade dialogue box creation system, which automatically creates menus and dialogue boxes from a list of their contents; and the C32 spreadsheet for specifying complex constraints. Garnet is implemented in Common Lisp and uses the X Window System through the standard CLX interface from Common Lisp to X Windows. A version for the Macintosh is also being developed. Garnet is therefore portable and runs (so far) on CMU, Lucid, Allegro, Harlequin, and TI Common Lisps and on many hardware platforms. Garnet does not use the Common Lisp Object System (CLOS) or any Lisp or X Windows toolkit (such as Interviews,[7] CLUE, CLIM, or Xtk).

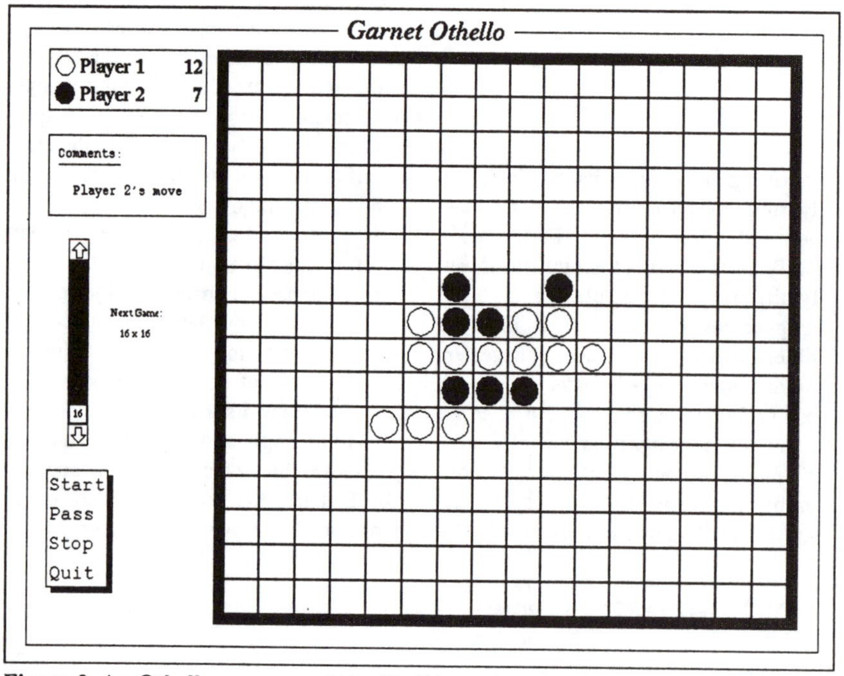

Figure 2. An Othello game created with Garnet.

Coverage

Garnet is designed to handle user interfaces that let users operate on graphic objects with the mouse and keyboard. Since the objects often represent application data, and since changes made on the screen to the graphics are translated into changes to the data, the user has the feeling he or she is directly manipulating the data. Similarly, the screen reflects changes the application makes to the data, possibly in response to external events.

Garnet is suitable for

- box and arrow diagram editors (see Figure 1), like MacProject;
- conventional drawing programs, such as MacDraw;
- icon manipulation programs, like the Macintosh Finder;
- graphical programming languages in which computer programs are constructed using icons and other pictures, such as a flowchart;
- tree and graph editing programs, including semantic networks, neural networks, and state transition diagrams;
- board games, such as chess or Othello (see Figure 2);
- simulation and process monitoring programs, in which the user interface shows the status of the monitored simulation or process and lets the user manipulate it;
- user interface construction tools (we implemented Garnet using itself); and
- some forms of CAD/CAM programs.

Garnet does not have a significant text editing component, but it does provide small editable strings that might be used as labels or fields in a table or dialogue box.

Garnet's primary influence is Peridot,[8] a construction tool that lets users create toolkit items without programming. Peridot lets nonprogrammers create many types of interaction techniques, including most kinds of menus, property sheets, buttons, scroll bars, percent-done progress indicators, sliders, and iconic and title line window controls. Like Garnet, Peridot uses constraints. However, Peridot lacks a programming interface and offers no way to use existing toolkit items or create application-specific graphic objects. (Many systems, including Thinglab[9] and Apogee,[10] have used constraints; see the sidebar.)

Garnet's Jade dialogue editor, which automatically constructs dialogue boxes from high-level specifications, was influenced by the Interactive Transaction System.[11]

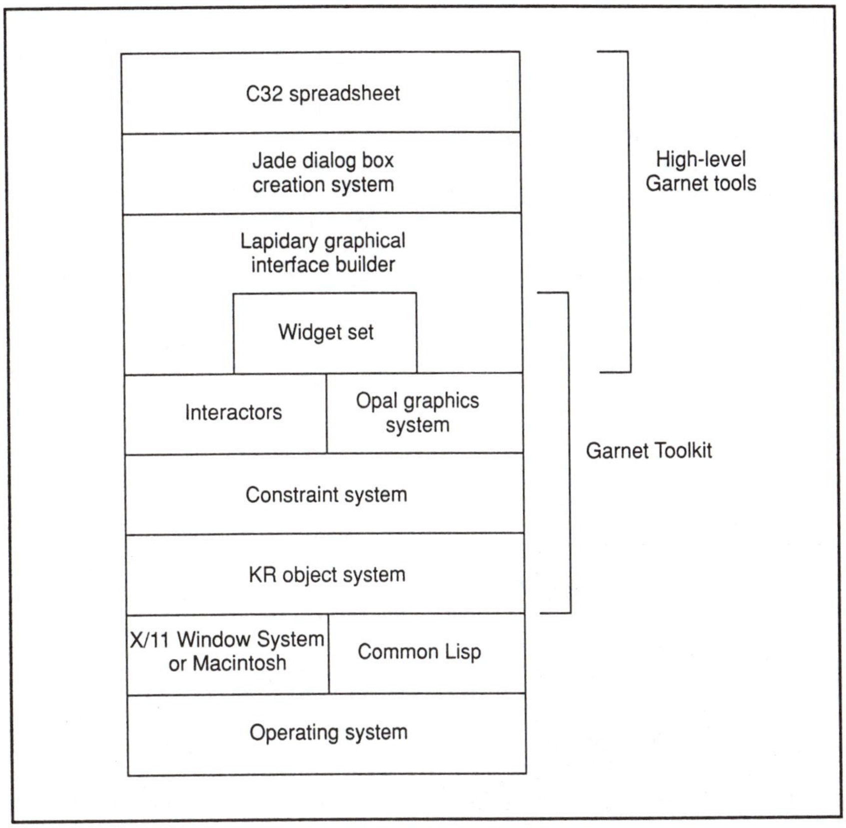

Figure 3. The structure of the Garnet system.

The Garnet Toolkit

Garnet contains a number of different components grouped into two layers. The Garnet Toolkit (the lower layer) supplies the object-oriented graphics system and constraints, a set of techniques for specifying the objects' interactive behavior in response to the input devices, and a collection of interaction techniques. Designers using this layer must write procedures. The higher layer contains tools that let designers draw pictures to show how the interface should look and behave and to define parts of the interface at a high level. These tools automatically create code based on the user's specifications.

The toolkit itself is divided into several components (see Figure 3):

- an object-oriented programming system,
- a constraint system,
- a graphical object system,
- a system for handling input, and
- a collection of gadgets or widgets.

Using the X toolkit's terminology, the first four parts of the Garnet Toolkit are intrinsics (the mechanisms supporting the implementation) and the fifth is the widget set (a collection of menus, scroll bars, etc., with a prespecified look and feel).

Object-oriented programming system. Garnet's object-oriented programming system, called KR (for "knowledge representation"), supports a prototype-instance model for objects rather than the conventional class-instance model used by Smalltalk and C++. A prototype-instance model does not distinguish between instances and classes; any instance can be a "prototype" for other instances. All data and methods are stored in "slots" (sometimes called fields or instance variables). Slots that are not overridden by a particular instance inherit their values from their prototypes. Actually, KR does not distinguish between data and method slots. Any slot can hold any type of value, and in Common Lisp a function is just a type of value. Slot names start with colons and can contain any number of printing characters (for example, :left, :interim-selected, :obj-over).

An instance can also add any number of new slots. Unlike conventional class-instance models, this means that the number of slots in each object is highly variable — each object can have a different number of local slots, depending on which properties it wants to accept as defaults and which it wants to override. In fact, the number of slots can change dynamically. Slots can be explicitly removed from objects at any time. If a program sets the value of a slot that does not exist, then the slot is created automatically. The advantage of this feature is that it is easy to create slots to hold local data. For example, if a rectangle's color represents an application temperature, the application can create an instance of a rectangle and a slot in it called :temperature. A disadvantage of this flexibility is that compile-time or even runtime checking of slot accessing and setting is impossible, since all slot names are legal. Also, since slots can hold any type of value, there is no type checking at the KR level.

As an example of inheritance, assume that a top-level rectangle prototype has slots containing values for the rectangle's left, top, width, height, and color (see Figure 4). An instance using that rectangle as a prototype will typically — but not necessarily — override some of the values. A programmer could create an instance with a particular color and size, and then create more instances of that instance (see Figure 4). If a prototype's slot value changes, all instances of that prototype that do not override that slot immediately inherit the new value. Similarly, if an instance's slot is removed, the corresponding slot of its prototype will be used instead, if it exists. All objects (prototypes and instances) can be displayed on the screen.

The methods that implement messages sent to the objects can also change dynamically, which is not possible in conventional object systems like Smalltalk. In Garnet, the designer need only assign a new procedure to the appropriate slot; the new method will be used subsequently.

The prototype-instance model is more dynamic and flexible than the familiar class-instance model. A high-level tool such as

A constraints primer

Brad Vander Zanden and Brad A. Myers

Any large, complex application contains thousands of interdependent relationships. For example, a graphical application must deal with the relationships arising from laying out objects, displaying feedback for input operations, and keeping views consistent with the underlying data they represent. These relationships might include keeping text labels centered in boxes, making feedback objects follow the cursor during a move operation, and setting the color of an airplane icon according to whether a flight is early, on time, or delayed.

Constraints provide a convenient way to specify relationships and have them automatically maintained at runtime by a constraint solver. In contrast, a conventional programming language requires the application to both specify the relationships and do all the bookkeeping to maintain them. For example, suppose that an arrow must stay connected to the center of a box and that a label on the arrow must stay centered on the arrow. In constraint programming, whenever the application changes the box's position or size, the constraint solver automatically repositions the arrow and its label. In contrast, a conventional language forces the designer to write code to reposition the arrow and the label. This might not seem too onerous a task, but when an application contains thousands of such relationships, the bookkeeping needed to maintain them increases so rapidly that adding new functionality to the application becomes difficult, and the time required to debug the changes also increases substantially.

In addition to simplifying the creation of an application and increasing its robustness, constraints lend themselves to incremental recomputation. When a user changes one or more parameters in an application, or adds or deletes a number of constraints, most of the existing constraints remain satisfied and only a small number must be reevaluated. An incremental constraint-solving algorithm can automatically identify which constraints must be reevaluated and limit its solving to these constraints. Such an algorithm can be used with any application written for that constraint system. In contrast, a conventional language requires the designer to create a new incremental algorithm for each application. Of course, a conventional language also lets the designer take advantage of any special characteristics of the application, so that he or she can write a custom algorithm that might be faster than a general-purpose constraint solver.

Types of constraints

Constraints can be either one-way or multiway. One-way constraints let the constraint solver change only one object in the constraint to satisfy it; multiway constraints allow any object to change. For example, the arrow in Figure 5 (in the main text) is connected to the circle and the box by one-way constraints. If either the box or the circle moves, the arrow also moves to resatisfy the constraints. However, if the arrow moves, neither the box nor the circle moves — the constraints that tie the arrow to the box or circle are violated or removed. If these constraints were multiway, then the constraint solver would move the box or circle when the arrow moved, thus satisfying the constraints.

Multiway constraints are obviously more powerful than one-way constraints, but this increased expressiveness comes at a price. One-way constraint solving algorithms only have to evaluate constraints, making them simpler to implement and more efficient than multiway constraint solvers that must also choose which variable in a constraint should be modified.

Multiway constraints can also introduce ambiguity at the design level. For example, suppose we have the constraint $A - B - C = 0$. If A changes, the constraint solver must choose whether to change B, C, or both. In this case, we should adhere to the principle of least astonishment — a user's editing operation should change the result in a way consistent with the user's expectations.[1,2] One approach to eliminate this ambiguity — constraint hierarchies[2] — divides constraints into hierarchies or priority levels. The constraint solver then tries to satisfy as many constraints as possible, solving the highest priority constraints first, then the next highest, and so on. One issue that constraint hierarchies do not address is how to specify that multiple values should change (for example, when both B and C should change when A changes).

Constraint solving

Constraints can be solved in either a lazy or eager fashion. Lazy evaluation evaluates a constraint only if it affects a result the Garnet interface builder can display a prototype on the screen and let the user edit it. All instances of that prototype automatically reflect these edits. For example, if a designer changes the standard look and feel of a menu prototype, all menus in the system immediately change accordingly. In most class-instance systems, changing the class structure when instances exist is either very expensive or makes the instances invalid.

A potential disadvantage of the prototype-instance model is that getting a slot's value could require a search up the entire inheritance hierarchy, since slots must be inherited from the prototypes if they are not present in an object. Garnet alleviates this problem by keeping local caches of inherited values. Another efficiency problem is that, since new slots can be added at any time, a fixed storage scheme like a structure or record cannot be used. Rather, a dynamic list of slot names and slot values must be kept. Garnet addresses this problem by keeping the most commonly accessed slots in a Lisp record structure so they can be accessed quickly, and by keeping any new slots in a list.

The efficiency of Garnet's object system is actually better than other Lisp object systems, such as CLOS. For example, on a Sun 3/60 workstation running Allegro Common Lisp, the simplest slot accessing function takes 49.8 microseconds in Portable Common Loops (an implementation of CLOS), but only 27.3 microseconds in KR. Creating an instance in CLOS (16,160 microseconds) takes about 15 times longer than in Garnet (1,117 microseconds).

that the user requests; eager evaluation evaluates a constraint immediately when values change. Thus, a lazy-evaluation system can contain variables whose values are out of date. Lazy evaluation avoids unnecessary work if relatively few values are needed to compute the result the user requests. For example, if portions of a drawing are off screen, they might not have to be recalculated. However, lazy evaluation also introduces extra bookkeeping, since the constraint solver must keep track of out-of-date variables. In addition, lazy evaluation can result in potential delays when the values of out-of-date variables are demanded. Lazy evaluation is most effective in applications where the user wants to view only a limited portion of the application's data and where changes are occurring to all parts of the application's data. Otherwise, eager evaluation is preferable, since it is conceptually cleaner than lazy evaluation (everything is always up to date).

Constraint systems

Examples of graphical systems that use constraint technology abound.[3] Sketchpad[4] pioneered the use of graphical constraints in a drawing editor in the early 1960s. Thinglab[1] took constraints a step further and introduced them into the realm of graphical simulation. More recently, Thinglab has been refined to aid in the generation of user interfaces.[2] Both Sketchpad and Thinglab provide multiway constraints. However, most user interface development systems use one-way constraints because of their simplicity and efficiency; Grow,[5] Peridot,[6] and Apogee[7] are three examples. Grow was the first comprehensive user interface development system to use constraints. Peridot was the first to try to infer constraints. Apogee was the first to employ lazy evaluation. Constraint[8] provided a user interface development environment that used multiway constraints and introduced a new constraint-solving algorithm that made multiway constraints efficient enough to be solved in real time.

The Garnet way

Garnet currently provides one-way constraints and uses lazy evaluation. Whenever a user changes a variable, all constraints that directly or indirectly depend on that variable are marked as out of date. When a user requests the value of an out-of-date variable, the constraint solver demands the values of all variables that this constraint depends on. If these variables are out of date, their constraints will in turn be evaluated, and so on. Eventually, the constraint solver reaches variables whose values are either atomic (that is, not computed by a constraint) or up to date, at which point the constraint solver can work its way back to the originally requested variable.

Future versions of Garnet will probably provide a limited form of multiway constraints and eager evaluation. We have found that almost all constraints in interfaces created with Garnet have to be reevaluated when the display is updated; thus lazy evaluation does not avoid the evaluation of enough constraints to justify the increased bookkeeping it requires. Also, the preliminary design for the new multiway algorithm seems to be very efficient.

References

1. A. Borning, "The Programming Language Aspects of Thinglab: A Constraint-Oriented Simulation Laboratory," *ACM Trans. Programming Languages and Systems*, Vol. 3, No. 4, Oct. 1981, pp. 353-387.
2. B.N. Freeman-Benson, J. Maloney, and A. Borning, "An Incremental Constraint Solver," *Comm. ACM*, Vol. 33, No. 1, Jan. 1990, pp. 54-63.
3. A. Borning and R. Duisberg, "Constraint-Based Tools for Building User Interfaces," *ACM Trans. Graphics*, Vol. 5, No. 4, Oct. 1986, pp. 345-374.
4. I.E. Sutherland, "Sketchpad: A Man-Machine Graphical Communication System," *AFIPS Spring Joint Computer Conf.*, 1963, pp. 329-346.
5. P. Barth, "An Object-Oriented Approach to Graphical Interfaces," *ACM Trans. Graphics*, Vol. 5, No. 2, Apr. 1986, pp. 142-172.
6. B.A. Myers, *Creating User Interfaces by Demonstration*, Academic Press, Boston, 1988.
7. T.R. Henry and S.E. Hudson, "Using Active Data in a UIMS," *Proc. ACM SIGGraph Symp. User Interface Software*, Oct. 1988, pp. 167-178.
8. B. Vander Zanden, "Constraint Grammars — A New Model for Specifying Graphical Applications," *Proc. Conf. Human Factors in Computing Systems (SIGCHI 89)*, Apr. 1989, pp. 325-330.

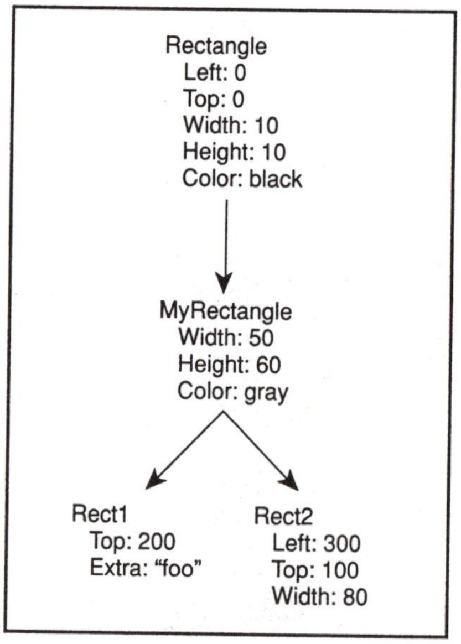

Figure 4. Inheritance in a prototype-instance model. Rect1 and Rect2 are instances of MyRectangle, which is an instance of Rectangle. MyRectangle inherits the left and top of Rectangle. Rect1 inherits all the values of MyRectangle except top, which it overrides. It also adds a new slot. If the left of Rectangle changes, then the lefts of MyRectangle and Rect1 immediately change also. Even though they may be prototypes for other objects, all of these are "real" objects in that they can be displayed on the screen.

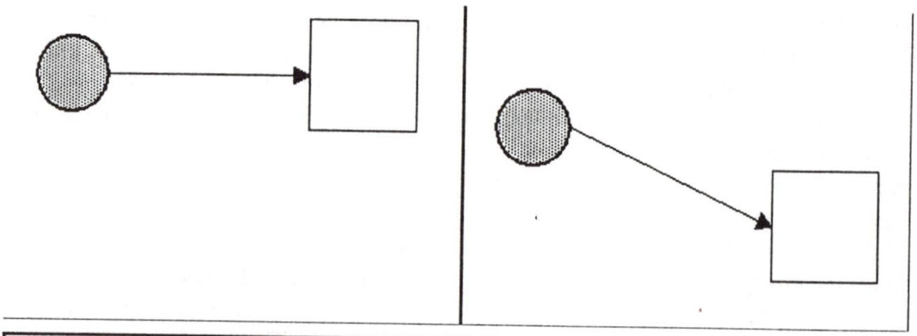

```
(create-instance 'myline arrow-line
   (:x1 (formula (gv circle1 :right)))
   (:y1 (formula (gv circle1 :center-y)))
   (:x2 (formula (gv box1 :left)))
   (:y2 (formula (gv box1 :center-y))))
```

Figure 5. The line stays attached to the box and circle even when they move. Below the graphic is the code to define the constraints on the line.

Constraint system. A constraint is a relationship among objects that is maintained when any of the objects changes. Constraints are a natural way to express common relationships in graphical user interfaces. For example, in an editor that supports boxes attached by arrows, the designer could specify a constraint that the arrows must stay attached to the boxes. Then, when the boxes are moved by a program or the mouse, the system automatically moves the arrows as well. (The sidebar discusses constraints and their implementation in more detail.)

Coral[2] was an early version of Garnet's constraints, but it was abandoned because it wasn't fast or flexible enough. Constraints are now integrated with the KR object system.

Constraints in Garnet are arbitrary Common Lisp expressions, stored in object slots. When a program accesses a slot, it cannot tell whether the slot contains a simple value (like a number) or a constraint that calculates the value. Within constraints, references to other objects' slots use the form "(gv other-object slot-name)," where "gv" stands for "get value." Whenever the value of the referenced slot changes, the formula is reevaluated. For example, the code in Figure 5 could be used to keep an arrow attached to two objects.

These formulas are one-way constraints; if the other object changes, the object with the formula is reevaluated, but not vice versa. For example, when the circle or box in Figure 5 moves, the line also moves; however, if the line moves, the circle and box do not move. This type of constraint is also used in Peridot,[8] Apogee,[10] and many other constraint-based user interface systems. As a special case, Garnet can handle cycles in the constraint dependencies (so object *A* can depend on *B*, and *B* can depend on *A*), in which case Garnet goes around the loop exactly once.

Other systems have used more powerful multiway constraints, which we might add to Garnet later. The primary advantage of the current scheme, however, is that constraint evaluation is very efficient. Garnet can reevaluate more than 3,500 constraints per second on the IBM RT PC implementation, which means that many objects with dozens of constraints can be updated in real time as objects are dragged with the mouse. Of course, Garnet ensures that formulas whose values do not change are not reevaluated, so user interfaces can contain many thousands of constraints.

An interesting and novel feature of Garnet's constraints is that the object referenced in the constraint can be accessed indirectly through a variable. For example, a feedback object in a menu might be constrained to be the same size as whatever object it is on top of. A slot would hold the object that the feedback should appear over. Whenever this slot changes, Garnet automatically reevaluates the formulas that depend on the slot, thus moving the feedback object. To make indirection easy, the gv function can be passed a list of slots to use as indirect references. For example, (gv :SELF :other-obj :left) means: "Look in this object's :other-obj slot. The contents of the slot will be another object. Go to that object and get its left." Since this form is common, (gv-indirect . . .) can be used instead of (gv :SELF . . .).

As an example of indirection, the reverse video rectangle in Figure 6 moves whenever the value of the :obj-over slot changes. This mechanism lets designers keep the input-handling specification independent of the graphics. For example, the interactor object that handles menu behavior (described in the "Input handling" section) simply sets the :obj-over slot to the object that the mouse is over, and the constraints ensure that the graphics that handle feedback change appropriately. The interactor does not need to know anything about the appearance of the graphics.

Because any slot of any object can contain constraints, the use of constraints in Garnet is not limited to the position and size of graphical objects. Constraints are used throughout the system to control many kinds of behaviors. For example, a constraint can be used to set the mode to determine whether an object will change size or grow based on which mouse button is pressed:

```
(:grow-the-object
  (formula (eq (gv-indirect :which-button)
               :rightdown)))
  ; grow if right button is pressed,
  ; otherwise move
```

Constraints can also be used to connect graphical objects to application-specific objects. For example, the value of a gauge displayed on the screen could be constrained to a temperature data value in the application.

Graphical object system. Opal, Garnet's graphical object system, is designed to make creating and editing graphical objects easy. Opal provides default values for all object properties, so simple objects can be drawn by specifying only the necessary parameters. For example, to create a rectangle at (10,20) with size 30 by 40, a designer need only write:

```
(create-instance 'myrect rectangle
   (:left 10) (:top 20) (:width 30)
   (:height 40))
```

The object system is integrated with the constraint system, so that any object property can be specified with formulas instead of numbers, as shown in the code in Figure 5.

Opal also automatically handles object drawing and erasing. If any object property changes, Opal automatically refreshes the screen and redraws that object. If that object overlaps others on the screen, Opal ensures they are also redrawn correctly (see Figure 7). In addition, if the modifications change other objects due to constraints, these other objects are also redrawn automatically.

Rather than simply redrawing all the objects, Opal tries to minimize the number of objects that are erased and redrawn. This is very important for complex scenes. For example, moving one object through a window containing 200 other objects takes 25.6 milliseconds per move (39 moves per second) rather than the 568 milliseconds (1.76 moves per second) it would take if Opal redrew all the objects.

Because Opal knows where all objects are, it can also handle window refresh (when the window is uncovered). Opal's clients never have to worry about the window system's refresh events. In fact, Opal and the interactors completely hide all window system functions.

To make an object appear in Opal, the designer only has to add it to an Opal window. Removing the object from the window makes the object disappear. To change an object's color or size, the designer sets the appropriate slots. Therefore, the programmer never calls the draw or erase methods on objects directly; these methods are only called from internal Opal routines. In this respect, Opal departs significantly from other graphical object systems.

An important aspect of Opal is its ability to group graphical objects into collections called *aggregates*. When an aggregate is used as a prototype, its instances contain copies of the entire collection of objects. Thus, there is an instance for each component of the aggregate as well as for the aggregate itself (see Figure 8). Changes to the aggregate are immediately reflected in

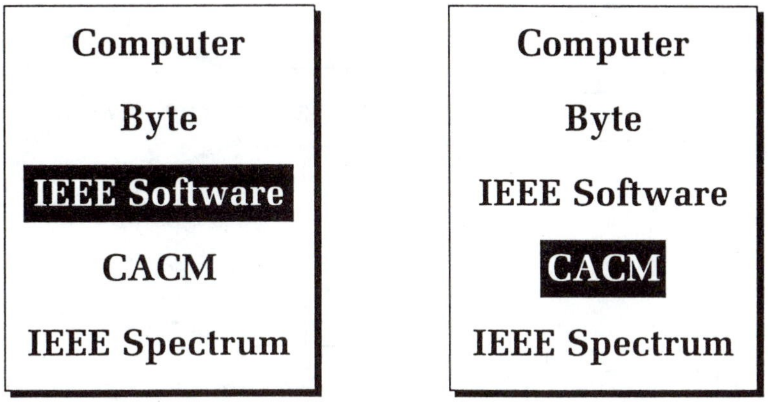


```
(create-instance 'feedback-box Rectangle
   (:obj-over NIL)                            ; The object that should be
                                              ; highlighted
   (:visible (formula (gv-indirect :obj-over)))  ; I am visible if there is an object
                                              ; in :obj-over
   (:left (formula (gv-indirect :obj-over :left)))  ; The size and position is the same
                                              ; as whatever I am over
   (:top (formula (gv-indirect :obj-over :top)))
   (:width (formula (gv-indirect :obj-over :width)))
   (:height (formula (gv-indirect :obj-over :height)))
   (:draw-function :xor))                     ; XOR this rectangle
```

Figure 6. Setting the :obj-over slot of the feedback-box rectangle makes it appear over that object because of the constraints on the size and position.

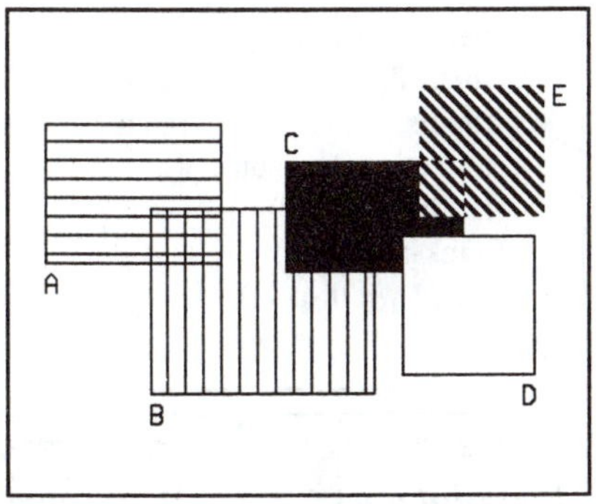

Figure 7. Opal lets graphics overlap opaquely and automatically refreshes damaged parts. If C is erased, B, D, and E will need to be redrawn. Opal uses a clipping region so that only the parts of B, E, and D that overlap C are affected, and so that A does not have to be redrawn. B is drawn with the OR drawing function, E is drawn with XOR, and the others are drawn with Copy.

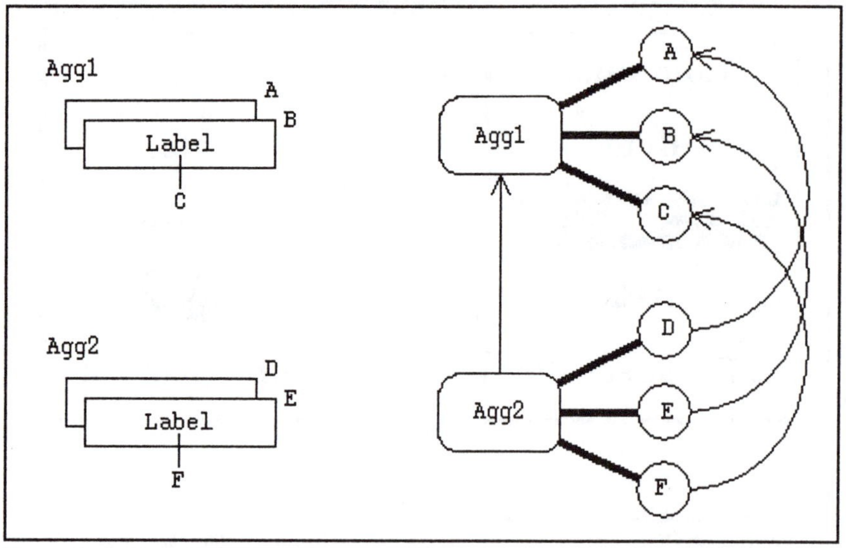

Figure 8. A, B, and C are components of the aggregate Agg1. Making an instance of Agg1 automatically makes instances of each of its components. The dark lines are component links, and the arrow lines are instance links. If Agg1 or any of its components change, Agg2 and its components would change automatically.

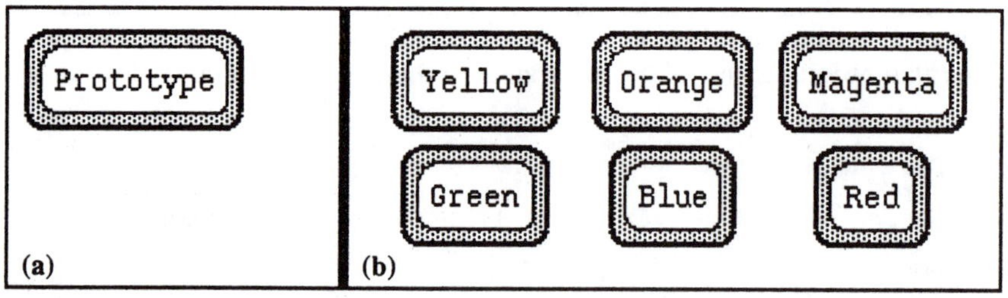


```
(create-instance 'colorlist AggreList
   (:left 150)(:top 10)
   (:Item-Prototype My-Roundtangle-Prototype)
   (:Items '("Yellow" "Orange" "Magenta" "Green" "Blue" "Red"))
   (:direction :horizontal)
   (:h-align :center)          ; Center the objects in the field
   (:rank-margin 3)            ; Go to next line after 3rd object
   (:fixed-width-p T))         ; All fields have same width
```

(c)

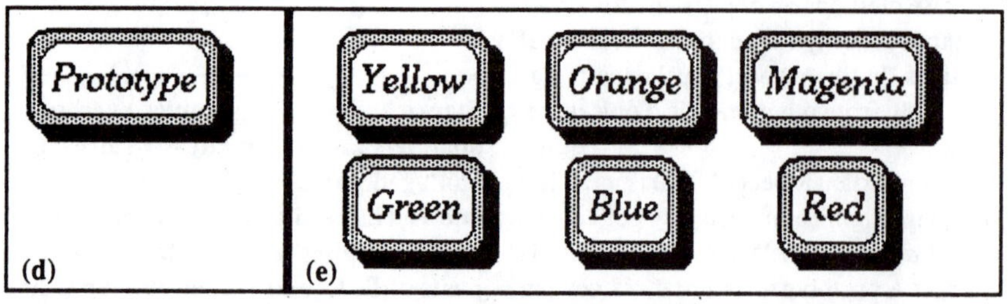

Figure 9. A prototype for the menu items (a) and a two-dimensional aggrelist using instances of that prototype for each element (b). The actual code to display the menu is shown in (c). If the prototype is subsequently edited to add a drop shadow and change the font (d), all instances immediately inherit the new values and structure (e).

all instances, including when components are added or deleted from the prototype, in which case the corresponding components are immediately added or deleted from all instances. Previous implementations of the prototype-instance model have not supported such structural changes to instances.

As an example, consider a graphical tool that lets the user design menus. The user might draw a prototype button (Figure 9a) and then create many instances of that button in the interface (Figure 9b). If the prototype is subsequently edited—perhaps to add a drop shadow and change the text font (Figure 9d) — Opal insures that all instances immediately inherit the changes (Figure 9e). This requires that Opal add a new object for the shadow to each instance.

Of course, each instance can override any of the slots, making it easier to build prototypes for complex, composite objects like menus and scroll bars. The prototype contains example values for slots (like the text strings in the menu), and the instances override these values.

A special form of aggregate is an *aggrelist*, which is used to lay out a list or table of elements. An aggrelist contains a single prototype for all the elements, and each element uses a different value for some value of that prototype. For example, menus are usually implemented as an aggrelist with a single prototype for the items but with a different string value displayed in each item. The prototype in Figure 9a is an aggregate containing the two rounded rectangles (one grey and one white) and the example string "Prototype." Aggrelists allow the items to be displayed horizontally, vertically, and in multiple rows, or the programmer can specify a layout (as for the gauge labels shown later in Figure 12f). We are also working on the implementation of aggregraphs and aggretrees to lay out graphs and trees.

Input handling. One of the most difficult tasks when creating highly interactive user interfaces is handling the mouse, keyboard, and other input devices. Window managers and user interface toolkits typically provide only a stream of device-dependent mouse positions and keyboard events, and they require that the programmers handle all interactions themselves. Garnet provides significantly more help through the use of interactors, which are encapsulations of input device behaviors.[3]

There are few distinct behaviors in user interfaces. For example, although graphics can vary significantly and the specific mouse buttons can change, all menus operate in essentially the same manner. Another example is the way objects move when being dragged with the mouse. The interactors capture these common behaviors in a central place while still allowing a high degree of customizing by application programs.

Other advantages of the interactors are:

• They are entirely look independent; any graphics can be attached to a particular feel (see Figures 10 and 11).

• They let designers separate the details of object behavior from the application and the graphics (long a goal of user interface software design).

• They support multiple input devices operating in parallel.

• They let users operate on any of a number of different applications running in separate windows in the same Lisp process and same address space, thereby supporting a form of multiprocessing.

• Opal and the interactors hide the complexities of X Windows graphics and event handling, making Garnet easier to use than X Windows and allowing Garnet to be ported to other graphics packages, such as Macintosh Quick Draw or Display Postscript, without changing Garnet applications.

There are only six types of interactors in Garnet, and these cover all the kinds of interactions used in graphical user interfaces:

• *Menu-Interactor*. For choosing one or more items from a set, or for a single stand-alone button.

• *Move-Grow-Interactor*. For moving or changing the size of an object or one of a set of objects using the mouse. This interactor can be used for one- or two-dimensional scroll bars and horizontal and vertical gauges, and for moving or growing application objects in a graphics editor.

• *New-Point-Interactor*. For entering one, two, or an arbitrary number of new points using the mouse; for example, for creating new lines or rectangles in an editor.

• *Angle-Interactor*. For calculating the angle at which the mouse moves around some point. It can be used for circular gauges or for rotating objects.

• *Trace-Interactor*. For capturing all the points the mouse goes through between start and end events, as needed for free-hand drawing.

• *Text-String-Interactor*. For inputting a small (optionally multiline) string of text.

Each interactor is parameterized in various ways, so the programmer can control the mouse or keyboard events that make it start and stop and the optional application procedures to be called on completion. The most significant parameters, however, are the objects where the interactor operates and the (optional) objects to handle feedback. Each type of interactor controls the graphics with a well-defined protocol. For example, the menu interactor sets the :obj-over slot of the feedback object. Therefore, to turn the list of items in Figure 9b into a menu using the feedback object from Figure 6, we need only the following code:

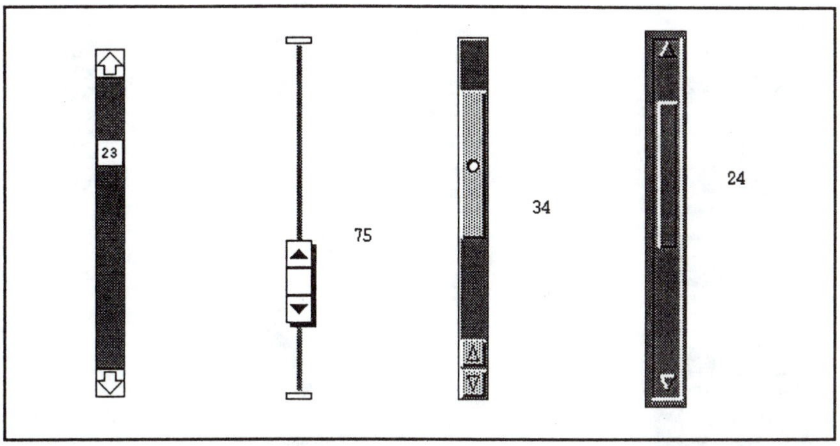

Figure 10. The same type of interactor can handle different graphic looks. Here, move-grow-interactors for the indicators and menu-interactors for the arrow buttons handle scroll bars that look like those in the Macintosh, Open Look, Next, and OSF/Motif environments.

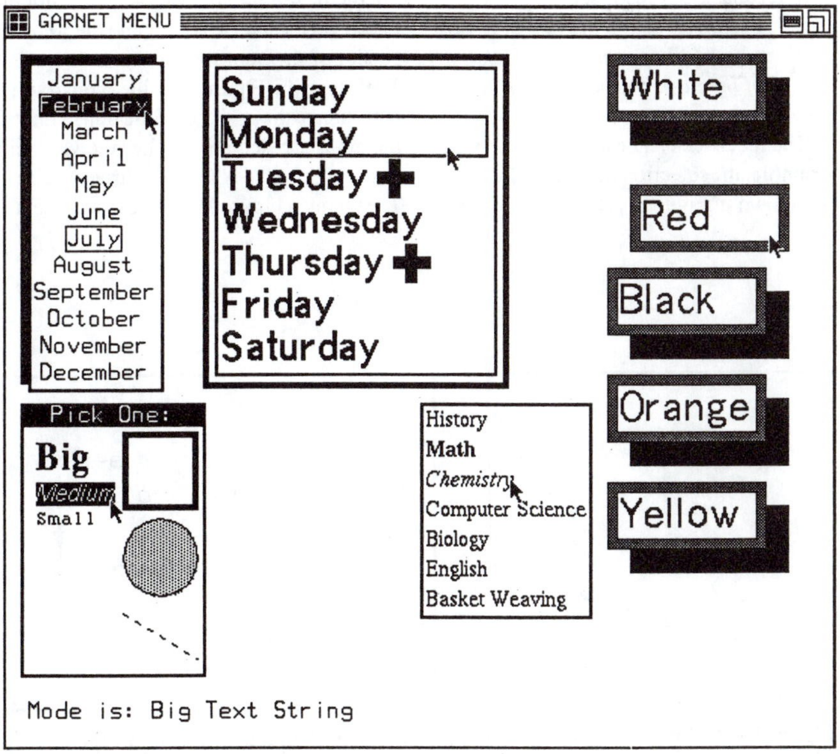

Figure 11. The menu-interactor can handle menus with many different looks and feels. The items in (c) simulate floating by moving when the mouse is over them. The items in (e) change to italic when the mouse is over them; the final selection is bold.

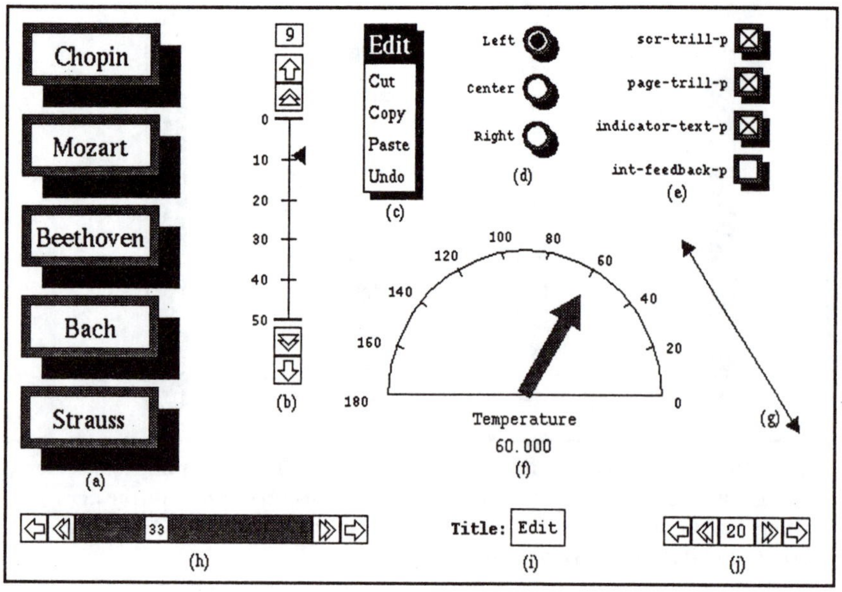

Figure 12. Some of Garnet's gadgets: (a) floating buttons, (b) a number slider, (c) a menu, (d) floating radio buttons, (e) floating check boxes, (f) a semicircular gauge, (g) an arrow-line, (h) a scroll bar, (i) a labeled text entry field, and (j) a number entry field.

```
(create-instance 'color-selector
                 menu-interactor
  (:start-where '(:element-of colorlist))
    ; Colorlist is defined in Figure 9c
  (:feedback-obj feedback-box))
    ; Feedback-box is defined in Figure
    ; 6 and will appear over whichever
    ; of the items the mouse is over
```

The feedback can be a set of objects, for example, the selection handles in Figure 1. As shown in Figure 11, the feedback does not even have to be a separate object. Instead, some property of the object itself can change in response to the mouse. If the :feedback-obj is not supplied, the menu interactor sets the :interim-selected slot of the object the mouse is over and the :selected slot of the item the mouse ends up on. The menu in Figure 11c has constraints that change the position of the object under the mouse, based on whether the value of :interim-selected is T or NIL (true or false). The menu in Figure 11e decides whether to use a Roman, bold, italic, or bold-italic font based on the values of both :interim-selected and :selected.

An important feature of interactors is that a single interactor can handle a set of objects. For example, there is a single interactor for each menu, rather than one for each menu item. Similarly, a single move-grow interactor can be used for an entire set of objects that can be moved with the mouse (as in Figure 1). The interactor will choose which object to move based on where the mouse button is pressed.

The interactors are based on Smalltalk's Model-View-Controller.[12] In Garnet, the application objects correspond to the model, the Opal graphical objects correspond to the view, and the interactors correspond to the controller. In Smalltalk, however, if a programmer wants a new style of object, he or she usually has to write code for all three parts. In Garnet, programmers almost never need to create new forms of interactors, even for application-specific objects; it is sufficient to create an instance of one of the supplied types of interactors and then supply appropriate parameters to achieve the desired behavior. New types of interactors would be needed in Garnet only for radically different types of behaviors, such as gesture recognition or new kinds of physical input devices (such as a 3D joystick). Constraints in Garnet connect the models, views, and controllers.

Gadgets. On top of Opal and the interactors is a collection of interaction techniques — called gadgets — that provide a starting point for applications. There are gadgets for menus, scroll bars, buttons, gauges, etc. Figure 12 shows some of the gadgets supplied with Garnet (more are being created). These can be used by designers who do not want their applications to have a custom look and feel. Most of the gadgets have a number of parameters to let designers vary many aspects of the appearance and behavior.

In some toolkits, such as Xtk and Interviews, each gadget is a window. This significantly limits what gadgets can do. In Garnet, however, gadgets are not windows, so there is a gadget, for example, that is a line with an attached arrowhead (Figure 12g). An even more sophisticated gadget in Garnet handles object selection (see Figure 13). It displays selection handles around the selected object and lets the user move or grow the object by pressing on the handles. Therefore, to support graphical object selection, a designer using Garnet need only create an instance of an object-selec-

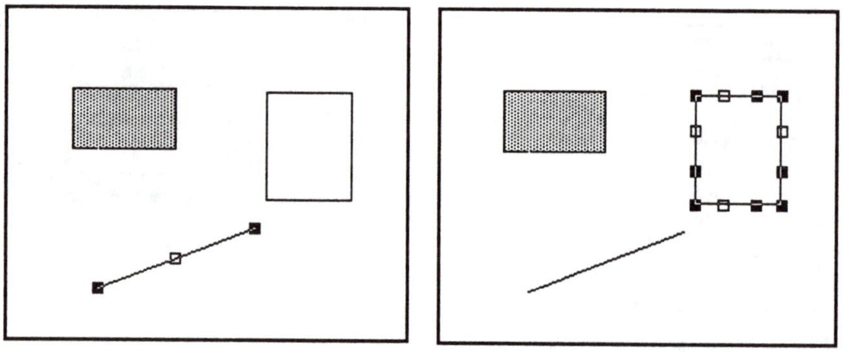

Figure 13. The graphics selection gadget shows control handles around the selected object. Pressing on a white handle moves the object, and pressing on a black one changes the object's size. When a line is selected, only three control points are shown: the black ones change the end points and the white one moves the line, keeping the same length and slope.

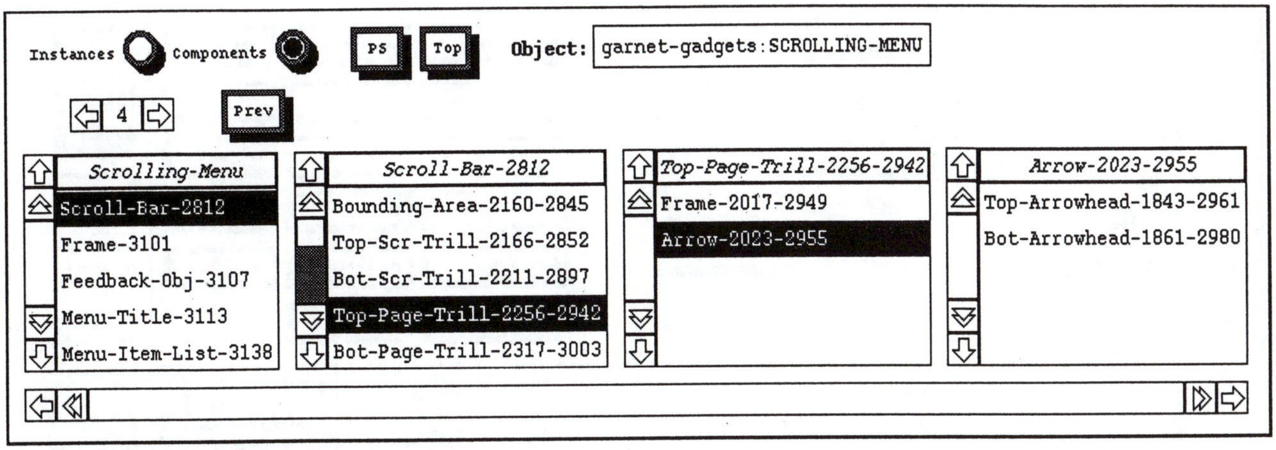

Figure 14. A browser that will show either the components of an aggregate or the instances of a prototype. We created this with the Garnet Toolkit, and it can be used to debug Garnet code.

tion gadget (assuming he or she finds the Garnet look and feel acceptable).

Since creating new gadgets with Garnet is easy, we expect many designers to create their own gadgets rather than use the supplied ones. By using Lapidary (detailed in the next section) or by programming using Opal and interactors, programmers can create new styles of menus and buttons in minutes.

Debugging tools. Defining user interfaces with constraints and interactors is natural and effective, but it can be difficult to find bugs in the code. Since with constraints, a bad value in one place can cause many different objects to have bad values, the effects of a bug are not local.

Garnet provides a large and growing number of debugging tools to help with program implementation. These tools provide tracing mechanisms to show how a slot got its current value, where objects are on the screen or why they are not visible, and what happens when the mouse or keyboard is used. The tools also provide extensive checking for legal values of graphics slots and convenient ways to inspect objects, including browsers (see Figure 14).

The interface builder

Lapidary. On top of the Garnet Toolkit layer are a number of tools to make creating user interfaces easier. The most important is the Lapidary interface builder.[4] Lapidary provides a graphical front end to most of the underlying toolkit features, so that a program's graphical aspects can be specified pictorially. In addition, the behavior of these objects at runtime can be specified using dialogue boxes and by demonstration.

In particular, Lapidary lets the designer, who does not have to be a programmer, draw pictures of application-specific graphical objects that the application will create and maintain at runtime. These objects include the graphical entities the end user will manipulate (such as the components of the picture), the feedback showing which objects are selected (such as small squares that serve as handles on the sides and corners of an object), and the dynamic feedback objects (such as hairline boxes to show where an object is being dragged). The designer creates prototypes of the objects in Lapidary, and the application program then creates instances of the prototypes as needed.

In addition, Lapidary supports the construction and use of gadgets, such as menus, scroll bars, buttons and icons. Lapidary therefore supports both the use of a predefined library of gadgets and the definition of new gadgets with a unique look and feel. Both types can even be combined in the same application. The designer can specify the runtime behavior of these objects in a straightforward way using constraints and abstract descriptions of their interactive response to the input devices. Lapidary generalizes from the specific example pictures to let the designer specify the graphics and behaviors by demonstration.

The designer can specify the behavior of objects in various ways. Graphical constraints can be attached to objects using iconic menus (see Figure 15). If an object should move with the mouse, it can be selected and declared a feedback object. Lapidary will automatically generalize the constraints on the feedback object so that they refer to whatever graphical object the mouse is over. For example, in Figure 15b the check mark is constrained to the Stop button, but Lapidary generalizes this constraint to use a variable (like the :obj-over slot of Figure 6) so that the check mark can appear next to any of the buttons.

Also, if an object should change based on some user action, the designer can specify this by demonstration. The designer draws one state, then another, and Lapidary automatically constructs the constraints to change the object between the two states. The menus of Figures 11c and 11e can be defined in this way.

Consider how a designer might create the boxes and arrows for a graph editor. First, the designer draws a picture of the boxes, say, using rounded rectangles (Figure 16a). Then, he or she creates an example text label and uses the iconic constraint menus to center it at the top (Figure 16b). This will serve as the prototype for the boxes the application will create, so the designer selects the entire group and saves it as a named prototype. Lapidary asks the designer for the object parameters, so the designer specifies the position and size of the box and the string for the label. Lapidary then writes this prototype to a file and defines it in memory (in case the application is running concurrently with Lapidary).

Next, the designer creates a copy of the

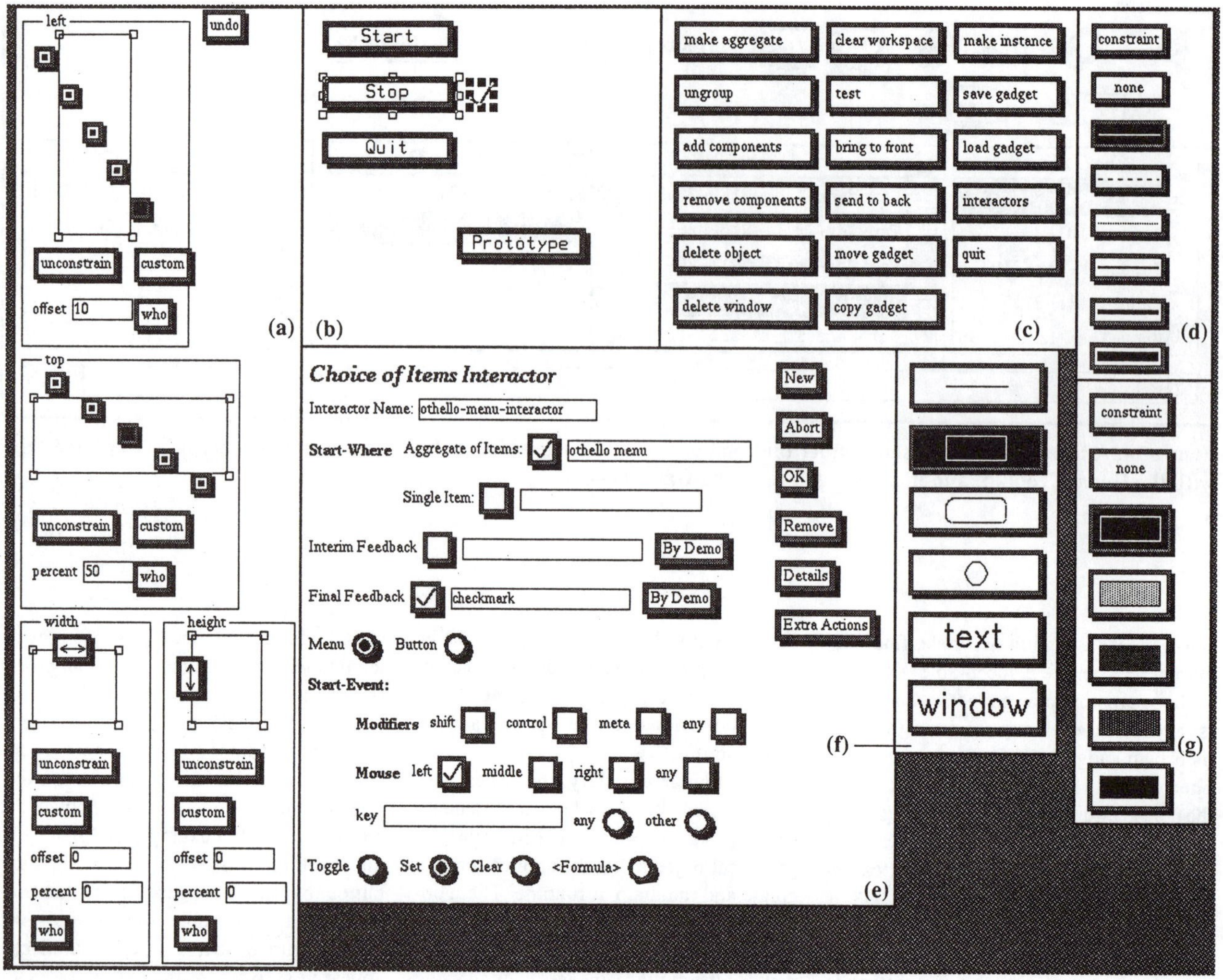

Figure 15. Lapidary in action. The work window (b) contains a prototype and three buttons made from it. The check mark icon is the primary selection (indicated by black squares) and the center button is the secondary selection (indicated by white squares). The iconic constraint menu (a) shows that the primary selection is constrained to be 10 pixels to the right of the secondary selection and centered by it vertically. Window (c) contains the main Lapidary commands. The menus on the right determine the type of the next object to be created (f), the line style (d), and the fill style (g). The large window in the center (e) is a dialogue box for specifying the behavior of the menu being created; it shows that the check mark icon will be the final feedback to show which item is selected when the left mouse button is pressed. This dialogue box was created using Jade.

box, draws an arrow-line (Figure 16c), and uses the line constraint menu to specify that the ends of the line should be centered in the boxes (Figure 16d). Then the designer selects only the line and saves it as a prototype. Lapidary notes that the prototype has constraints to objects that are not being saved, so it asks the designer if the objects are to be parameters of the line prototype. The designer specifies that the parameters should be called from-obj and to-obj. Now the application can create instances of the lines, supplying the objects for the from-obj and to-obj slots, and new lines will appear in the application window. The application knows nothing about the graphics used for the lines, and the designer did not have to write any graphics code. This entire design session takes about four minutes.

Jade. It is sometimes easier to list the contents of a dialogue box or menu than to meticulously draw it. The Jade dialogue box creation system automatically creates a dialogue box or menu from a specification of its contents.[5] In addition to being simple to work with, the specification passed to Jade has the additional advantage of being independent of any particular look and feel. The textual specification has a Lisp-like syntax and lists only the string labels to appear in the dialogue box, the type of input required (such as the choice of one item of a set, or of a number in a range). When Jade is given a particular look and feel (Macintosh, Motif, Garnet standard, etc.), it can choose the correct interaction techniques, which themselves can be designed using Lapidary. The heuristic rules that determine the placement of various parts of the interface are specific to a particular look and feel. For example, the set of buttons that make a dialogue box go away ("OK," "Cancel," etc.) will be at the

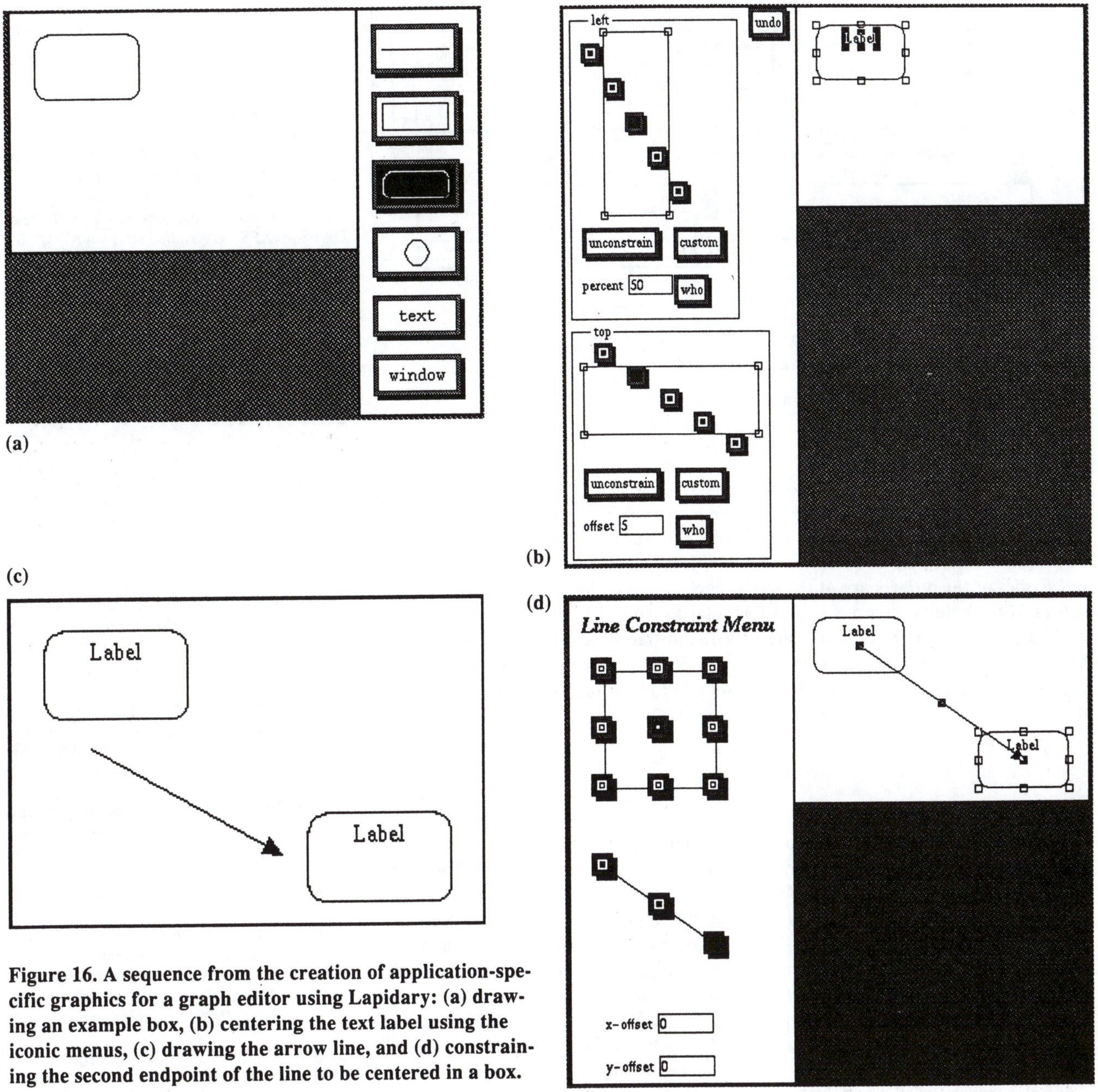

Figure 16. A sequence from the creation of application-specific graphics for a graph editor using Lapidary: (a) drawing an example box, (b) centering the text label using the iconic menus, (c) drawing the arrow line, and (d) constraining the second endpoint of the line to be centered in a box.

right for a Macintosh-like dialogue box and at the top for a Xerox Star-like one. Jade created the dialogue box in Figure 15e automatically.

The heuristics for placing objects in dialogue boxes attempt to create an attractive display based on graphic arts principles. If the designer is not happy with the dialogue box, however, he or she can edit it in Lapidary, adding decorations (such as extra rectangles and lines) and moving parts around. These changes are saved in an exceptions file so they can be reapplied even if the original textual specification is edited and the dialogue box regenerated.

C32 spreadsheet. Although many desired constraints can be specified using Lapidary's iconic menus, designers occasionally need more powerful constraints. The C32 spreadsheet program in Garnet lets designers enter arbitrary Lisp constraint expressions. It provides many of the advantages for graphics that financial spreadsheets provide for business. In particular, C32 lets the designer monitor and debug interfaces by watching spreadsheet values while the user interface is running. It also provides extensible command menus, automatic generation of appropriate object references from mouse clicks in graphics windows, and automatic generalizations of example constraints so they can be used in multiple formulas. Figure 17 shows a typical C32 session.

The Garnet Toolkit is operational and has many local and external users. More than 80 companies and universities are licensed to use Garnet. (Garnet is available free from Carnegie Mellon University. Designers interested in using Garnet should contact Myers at the CMU address listed after the biographies.) We are working to increase the toolkit's

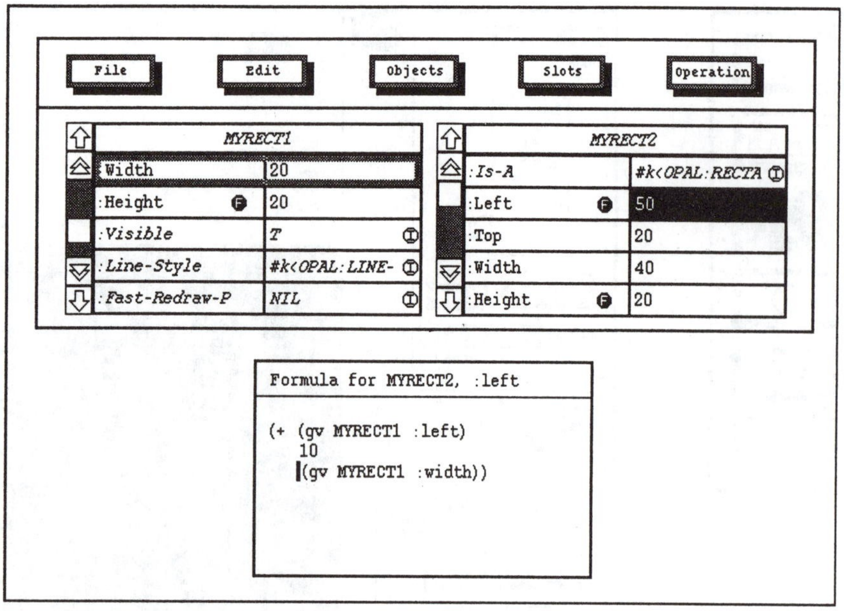

Figure 17. Viewing two objects in the Garnet C32 spreadsheet. At the top of the window is a set of pull-down menus. Each object has its own set of columns. The slot names of the objects are at the left of each column, along with the current values. If the value is computed by a formula, an icon with an "F" is shown. Inherited values are in italics and marked with a different icon. At the bottom is a formula display window for the selected slot. When the user clicks on a slot or an object in a graphics window, a reference to that object is inserted into the formula.

functionality and performance and to find new ways to support the design and implementation of application user interfaces. We hope the toolkit will be widely distributed and used in the Common Lisp community. Lapidary is working but is not yet releasable. Jade is partially working and has been used to generate the Lapidary dialogue boxes. The C32 system is just now being implemented.

We plan to work on allowing more of the interface to be specified by demonstration rather than through dialogue boxes and coding. For example, Lapidary could infer graphical constraints and mouse dependencies from the user's drawing, in a manner similar to Peridot.[8] We also hope to extend Garnet to handle other input and output technologies, such as physical dials and switches, speech input and output, and gesture recognition.

Finally, we plan to provide a high-level graphical editor framework that provides many of the operations common in systems that let the user create and manipulate graphical objects. These might include support for a palette of object types; selecting objects; changing object size, position, and other properties; deleting objects; automatically laying out objects as a list, table, graph, or tree; saving and restoring objects to a file; printing; and undoing. For many programs, this subsystem will provide most of the standard functionality, and designers will need to specify only the application-specific parts.

Garnet has only been working for a short time, but it has already demonstrated that it makes the creation of graphical, highly interactive user interfaces easier. For example, in an informal experiment, creating a simple graphical editor like that in Figure 1 took various people two to four hours with the Garnet Toolkit but 10-20 hours with other toolkits such as Apple's MacApp and Sun's Open Look. When Lapidary and the other high-level tools are released, we expect programmer productivity to increase even more. ■

Acknowledgments

In addition to the authors, others who have helped design and implement Garnet include Pedro Szekely, Pavan Reddy, Jake Kolojejchick, and Lynn Baumeister. Amy Moormann Zaremski and Pedro Szekely were brave early users of the Garnet Toolkit and helped us debug it. Bernita Myers, Amy Moormann Zaremski and the referees provided helpful comments on this article.

This research was sponsored in part by the Defense Advanced Research Projects Agency, under contract F33615-87-C-1499, ARPA Order No. 4976, Amendment 20, monitored by the Avionics Laboratory, Air Force Wright Aeronautical Laboratories, Aeronautical Systems Division (AFSC), Wright-Patterson AFB, Ohio 45433-6543.

References

1. B.A. Myers, "User Interface Tools: Introduction and Survey," *IEEE Software*, Vol. 6, No. 1, Jan. 1989, pp. 15-23.

2. P.A. Szekely and B.A. Myers, "A User Interface Toolkit Based on Graphical Objects and Constraints," *Proc. ACM Conf. Object-Oriented Programming, Systems Languages, and Applications* in *SIGPlan Notices*, Vol. 23, No. 11, Nov. 1988, pp. 36-45.

3. B.A. Myers, "Encapsulating Interactive Behaviors," *Proc. Conf. Human Factors in Computing Systems (SIGCHI 89)*, Apr. 1989, pp. 319-324.

4. B.A. Myers, B. Vander Zanden, and R.B. Dannenberg, "Creating Graphical Objects by Demonstration," *Proc. ACM SIGGraph Symp. User Interface Software and Technology*, Nov. 1989, pp. 95-104.

5. B. Vander Zanden and B.A. Myers, "Automatic, Look-and-Feel-Independent Dialogue Creation for Graphical User Interfaces," *Proc. Conf. Human Factors in Computing Systems (SIGCHI 90)*, Apr. 1990, pp. 27-34.

6. B.A. Myers et al., "The Garnet Toolkit Reference Manuals: Support for Highly Interactive, Graphical User Interfaces in Lisp," Tech. Report CMU-CS-90-117, Carnegie Mellon University, Computer Science Department, Mar. 1990.

7. M.A. Linton, J.M. Vlissides, and P.R. Calder, "Composing User Interfaces with Interviews," *Computer*, Vol. 22, No. 2, Feb. 1989, pp. 8-22.

8. B.A. Myers, *Creating User Interfaces by Demonstration*, Academic Press, Boston, 1988.

9. A. Borning, "Thinglab — A Constraint-Oriented Simulation Laboratory," Tech. Report SSL-79-3, Xerox Palo Alto Research Center, July 1979.

10. T.R. Henry and S.E. Hudson, "Using Active Data in a UIMS," *Proc. ACM SIGGraph Symp. User Interface Software*, Oct. 1988, pp. 167-178.

11. C. Wiecha et al., "Generating User Interfaces to Highly Interactive Applications," *Proc. Conf. Human Factors in Computing Systems (SIGCHI 89)*, Apr. 1989, pp. 277-282.

12. G.E. Krasner and S.T. Pope, "A Description of the Model-View-Controller User Interface Paradigm in the Smalltalk-80 System," *J. Object-Oriented Programming*, Vol. 1, No. 3, Aug. 1988, pp. 26-49.

Roger B. Dannenberg is a research computer scientist at Carnegie Mellon University. His research interests include programming language design and implementation and the application of computer science techniques to the generation, control, and composition of computer music.

Dannenberg received a BA from Rice University in 1977, an MS from Case Western Reserve University in 1979, and a PhD from Carnegie Mellon in 1982. He is a member of Phi Beta Kappa, Sigma Xi, Tau Beta Pi, Phi Mu Alpha, the ACM, SIGCHI, and the Computer Music Association.

Edward Pervin is a research programmer at Carnegie Mellon University, where he is working on Garnet. Pervin received his MS and BSc degrees in mathematics from Carnegie Mellon.

Brad A. Myers is a research computer scientist at Carnegie Mellon University, where he is the principal investigator for Garnet. His research interests include user interface development systems, user interfaces, programming by example, visual programming, interaction techniques, window management, programming environments, debugging, and graphics.

Myers received the MS and BSc degrees from the Massachusetts Institute of Technology, and he received a PhD in computer science at the University of Toronto, where he developed the Peridot user interface management system. He is a member of the IEEE, the Computer Society, the ACM, SIGGraph, and SIGCHI.

Brad Myers can be reached at the School of Computer Science, Carnegie Mellon University, Pittsburgh, PA 15213-3890. Electronic mail can be sent to garnet@cs.cmu.edu.

Brad Vander Zanden is an assistant professor at the University of Tennessee and an active participant in the Garnet project. He was a postdoctoral fellow at Carnegie Mellon University for two years. His interests include user interface development systems, user interfaces, constraint systems, incremental constraint satisfaction, programming environments, and graphics.

Vander Zanden received his BS degree from Ohio State University, and his MS and PhD degrees from Cornell University. He is a member of the IEEE, the Computer Society, the ACM, SIGGraph, and SIGPlan.

Andrew Mickish received a BS degree from Carnegie Mellon University, where he worked on the Garnet project as an undergraduate. He plans to enter graduate school to pursue interests in user interfaces and artificial intelligence.

Dario A. Giuse is a senior computer scientist at Carnegie Mellon University. His research interests include user interface development environments, constraint satisfaction, graphics, knowledge representation systems, tutoring systems for foreign languages, medical informatics, and interactive knowledge acquisition systems.

Giuse received the Dr.Ing. degree (summa cum laude) in computer science from the Politecnico di Milano, Italy, in 1979. He is a member of the IEEE Computer Society, the ACM, the AAAI, and the Mathematical Association of America.

David S. Kosbie is a graduate student at Carnegie Mellon University, where he is a member of the Garnet project. His research interests include user interface development systems, user interfaces, and methods for simplifying graphical programming. Kosbie received the BA degree from Harvard University in 1987. He is a member of the IEEE and the Computer Society.

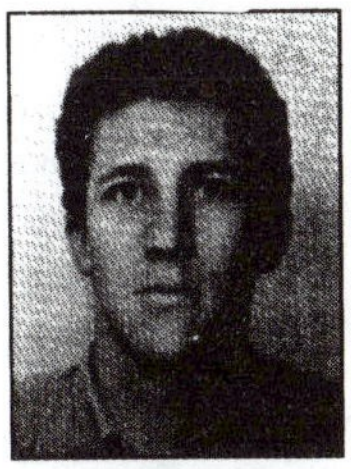

Philippe Marchal is a member of the Human-Computer Interaction group of the European Computer-Industry Research Center in Munich. He is a former visiting scientist at Carnegie Mellon University, where he was a researcher in the Garnet project. His research interests include user interfaces, user interface management systems, interaction techniques, human factors, graphics, and object-oriented programming. Marchal graduated from the University of Grenoble, France.

Addendum: Changes to Garnet Since November, 1990

Brad A. Myers
Human Computer Interaction Institute
Carnegie Mellon University
http://www.cs.cmu.edu:8001/Web/Groups/garnet/garnet-home.html

Introduction

There have been significant improvements to Garnet in the five years since the accompanying article was written, and we have started a new system in C++ called Amulet based on the Garnet ideas. This addendum highlights some of the more important changes.

The Garnet Toolkit

There have been a number of improvements to the constraint system. In particular, we discovered that an important problem was the space overhead of constraints, but that up to 95% of the constraints were evaluated only once at object creation time. Therefore, we added a unique mechanism that eliminates the constraints that only depend on constant values.

The Opal object system has been enhanced with objects to support multiple-font, multiple-line text editing, including embedding arbitrary graphical objects in the string, and a special mode to support Lisp code editing. This new object removes the restriction that Garnet not be used for applications with significant text components. To make Garnet practical for use for maps and visualizations with thousands of graphical objects, we added a special feature to eliminate most of the per-object overhead when there are lots of similar objects.

Gesture recognition has been added to the Garnet input model so that designers can investigate advanced user interfaces. The desired gestures can be specified by simply giving examples.

The widget set in Garnet has been significantly expanded, including a complete set of widgets with the Motif look-and-feel which have been implemented entirely using the Garnet low-level tools. The debugging tools have also been substantially expanded. A new ''Inspector'' tool views and edits the properties of objects. Other views show the object hierarchies and the dependencies of constraints.

Garnet provides several editing functions in a manner that should be usable by most graphical editors *without change*, unlike other application frameworks where programmers must subclass these operations. These include cut, copy, paste, delete, duplicate, group, ungroup, refresh, to-top, to-bottom, save, open, etc. Garnet will also create a postscript file for any window, so printing is easy.

Higher Level Tools

There are two entirely new tools in Garnet. The first is the Gilt interface builder, which allows users to select widgets from a palette and place them into a window. Gilt provides access to the full set of widgets, including pop-up widgets like menubars and option buttons. When complete, the interface design can be tested and saved to a file. There are two important innovations in Gilt: dependencies among widgets and filtering of values can be demonstrated [2], and graphical styles can be defined so that widgets will look consistent across multiple dialog boxes and applications [1].

The Marquise tool [3] allows the overall interactive behaviors of an application to be described by demonstration. Other Garnet tools allow pieces of an application to be created, but a tool to put it all together had been missing. With Marquise, the user can demonstrate the overall design of application windows and how the various widgets control the behaviors. Innovative features in Marquise include: the ability to demonstrate graphical palettes that control what kinds of objects are created and the properties of objects (color, font, etc.); control over where the user must click for a behavior to start, and special icons to show where the events occurred.

Distribution

Garnet is now in the public domain, and it is available by anonymous FTP. It runs on both X/11 and the Macintosh. To get Garnet, FTP to `a.gp.cs.cmu.edu`. Change to `/usr/garnet/garnet/` and retrieve `README` for instructions, or you can send electronic mail to `garnet@cs.cmu.edu`. The distribution includes the entire toolkit, plus Gilt, C32 and Lapidary. We make sure that Garnet works in any Common Lisp environment, including Allegro, Lucid, CMU, Harlequin, AKCL, CLISP, and Macintosh Common Lisps on Sun, DEC, HP, Apollo, IBM 6000, SGI, Macintosh, and many other machines. As a result, there are now over 80 projects all over the world using Garnet to create a wide variety of applications.

Amulet

Amulet is a new C++ environment that incorporates the best ideas of Garnet along with many new innovations including toolkit-level support and interactive tools to for gesture recognition, speech recognition, animated 2-D and 3-D objects, visualizations including maps and large data sets, World-Wide-Web browsing and editing, and multiple people interacting with the system at the same time. Amulet will run on Unix, Microsoft Windows, and the Macintosh. For more information on Amulet, send mail to `amulet@cs.cmu.edu` or see http://www.cs.cmu.edu:8001/Web/Groups/amulet/amulet-home.html.

Acknowledgements

Additional members of the Garnet project since 1990 include: James Landay, Rich McDaniel, Matt Goldberg, Rajan Parthasarathy, and Don Hopkins.

References

1. O. Hashimoto and B.A. Myers. Graphical Styles for Building User Interfaces By Demonstration. Proceedings UIST'92, Nov., 1992, pp. 117-124.

2. B.A. Myers. Separating Application Code from Toolkits: Eliminating the Spaghetti of Call-Backs. Proceedings UIST'91, Nov., 1991, pp. 211-220.

3. B.A. Myers, R.G. McDaniel, and D.S. Kosbie. Marquise: Creating Complete User Interfaces by Demonstration. Proceedings INTERCHI'93, April, 1993, pp. 293-300.

ITS: A Tool for Rapidly Developing Interactive Applications

CHARLES WIECHA, WILLIAM BENNETT, STEPHEN BOIES, JOHN GOULD, and SHARON GREENE
IBM T.J. Watson Research Center

The ITS architecture separates applications into four layers. The action layer implements back-end application functions. The dialog layer defines the content of the user interface, independent of its style. Content specifies the objects included in each frame of the interface, the flow of control among frames, and what actions are associated with each object. The style rule layer defines the presentation and behavior of a family of interaction techniques. Finally, the style program layer implements primitive toolkit objects that are composed by the rule layer into complete interaction techniques. This paper describes the architecture in detail, compares it with previous User Interface Management Systems and toolkits, and describes how ITS is being used to implement the visitor information system for EXPO '92.

Categories and Subject Descriptors. D.2.2 [**Software Engineering**]: Tools and Techniques—*software libraries, user interfaces*; H.1.2 [**Models and Principles**]: User/Machine Systems—*human factors*; H.4 [**Information Systems Applications**]: General; I.3.6 [**Computer Graphics**]: Methodology and Techniques—*device independence, ergonomics, interaction techniques, languages*; K.6.1 [**Management of Computing and Information Systems**]: Project and People Management—*systems analysis and design, systems development*; K.6.3 [**Management of Computing and Information Systems**]: Software Management—*software development, software maintenance.*

General Terms: Design, Human Factors, Languages, Management, Standardization

Additional Key Words and Phrases: Management systems, user interface

1. INTRODUCTION

Application developers today face a problem of great complexity. Because of the diversity of users and of their equipment, applications must run in many different configurations. They must support displays of varying size, resolution, and color depth. Different types of input devices are required, from keyboards to touch screens. Applications must run in different countries and be able to reformat messages in varying lengths in each language. Messages should be available in large font sizes for vision-impaired users. Interface style should be consistent with other applications running on similar hardware. Style should at the same time conform to guidelines being developed by many organizations for presentation and interaction behaviors.

Historically, two types of layered architectures have been developed in attempts to provide the required flexibility in applications: User Interface Management Systems (UIMS) and toolkits. UIMS separate the application from its interface. Back-end computations are separated from dialog control and style. Style, however, is often treated in a single interface layer. Toolkits separate style from the application. Dialog control remains in the back end while the implementation of interaction techniques is hidden in a code library.

ITS is a four-layer architecture with separate tools for back-end computation, dialog control, definition of interface style, and implementation of graphic primitives used in the style. We begin by reviewing previous work done in UIMS and toolkits. Then we show how the layers of the ITS architecture combine the benefits of both UIMS and toolkits. After describing each layer of the architecture we show how ITS is being used to implement the visitor information system for EXPO '92 in Seville.

2. RELATED WORK

2.1 User Interface Management Systems

User Interface Management Systems, by analogy to Data Base Management Systems, divide applications into two layers. An application layer implements the underlying computations, while an interface layer implements the details of interface presentation and interaction. According to the traditional Seeheim [18] architecture, the interface layer defines the connection to the application, dialog flow of control, and presentation style. The application layer is structured as a set of callback routines executed in response to user actions or external interrupts.

The goals of separating the application from its interface are well documented [9, 10], and include reusing a given application in multiple interfaces, consistency among a family of applications that run using a common interface, and independent tools for application and interface developers. We believe previous UIMS have had limited success in meeting these goals because of two problems: They have not sufficiently decomposed the interface layer, and they have provided inadequate tools for interface designers.

The Seeheim model calls for separate dialog control and presentation components in the interface layer. Much of the previous work on UIMS has focused on the dialog component. Less attention has been paid to presentation. Previous systems sometimes represented presentation and dialog in a single layer. Serpent [20], for example, allows for control over style by composing primitive graphic objects into compound interaction techniques. However, this composition is specified together with dialog control flow.

In other systems, work has only recently begun to refine the presentation layer. One example is UIDE [6]. UIDE refines dialog into several layers for application data objects, commands, and control. Recent work focuses on new layers for intelligent control over presentation style [7]. The UofA* UIMS [22] separates dialog control from interface style. Interface style is generated automatically.

Portions of this paper have previously appeared in the proceedings of the 1989 and 1990 ACM Symposia on User Interface Software and Technology.
Authors' address: IBM T.J. Watson Research Center, P.O. Box 704, Yorktown Heights, NY 10598. email: wiecha@ibm.com

The rules that control style, however, are not exposed in a layer of their own. Rather, the interface designer tunes the interface once it has been automatically generated.

For those systems that do allow designer control over style, two approaches have been taken: manual editing with WYSIWYG or constraint-based editors, and automatic generation using executable style rules. An early example of the editing approach is the WYSIWYG form editor in Cousin [10]. Using such a tool, a designer may position command buttons or menu items and link them to application actions by direct manipulation.

Early editors supported only static screen designs. They specified *what* objects should appear and unconditionally *where* they should be located. These editors are inadequate for developing applications that must meet criteria of portability across hardware, end-user language, and type of user. An application that runs even in just two languages such as English and Spanish has different layouts driven by the translation of its messages. If it must run on displays of different resolutions or under a window system with resizable windows, its layout must change even more dramatically.

Work on interface workbenches has begun to respond to these challenges. More recent systems [3, 11] are based on layout constraints. Constraints describe *how* to reflow objects when window size or other variables change. However, constraints still do not capture *when* and *why* objects should appear, that is, the specifications in a style guide or the designer's knowledge that led to the given layout. Such knowledge is required if each screen is not to be designed individually or if the design is to be altered automatically under changing conditions.

Examples of systems that automatically generate interfaces include APEX [5], APT [15], Jade [25], and ITS [2, 26]. These systems all have the goal of encoding interface style in a set of executable rules. One dimension that helps distinguish among them is the intended role of their rules relative to an interface designer using the system. We can distinguish between design formulation and execution. Formulation involves making decisions such as what gridding to use in screen layout or what color values are appropriate for representing concepts such as errors, values, or prompts. Execution involves being able to apply these decisions automatically by executing style rules. APEX, for example, stresses the formulations of style. It consists of metarules for constructing style. In contrast, a graphic artist or human factors engineer formulates the design in ITS. Style rules are the language for representing and executing that design. The usability of the style language for designers is therefore of much greater concern in ITS than in previous work.

2.2 Toolkits

Toolkits differ from UIMS in the architectural separation that they make between application and interface. Toolkits are code libraries of common interface components such as standard windows, dialog boxes, menus, and dials. Applications developed using toolkits do not separate code for user interaction from the rest of the application. As in conventional applications, toolkit applications control internally the selection of interaction techniques and the sequencing of the user's dialog with them. To use a menu rather than a text entry field, for example, the programmer must change application code. To allow the user to interact nonmodally with a set of menus rather than step sequentially through them also requires changes to application code. In most UIMS both the selection and control of interaction techniques are external to the application.

Tookits do remove the composition and implementation of interaction techniques from applications. Thus a window may be composed of a hierarchy of objects including title bar, resize icon, and scrollbar. To the application programmer the window is created and manipulated as a single object. The implementation of each of these objects is also hidden in code reused from the toolkit. Thus the useful abstraction that toolkits offer application programmers is in the implementation of interaction techniques, not in their selection or design.

Historically, toolkits evolved out of the window system community in a variety of environments. The best known examples are MacApp [19] and the several X toolkits, Xtk [27], Atk [17], and Interviews [14]. Some of these toolkits gained quick commercial success because of their reduction of the complexity of programming interfaces.

The second factor driving their success is the growing interest in interface consistency and standards. By hiding the composition of interaction techniques from application programmers, toolkits control the implementation of interface style. An application that requests a window will by default get the toolkit standard definition of that window automatically.

Toolkits have two major problems in supporting the growing interest in consistency and standards. First, new interaction techniques can usually be composed only by programming. To create an analog clock object, for example, one must write a new toolkit object that instantiates, sizes, and positions a set of more primitive objects for clock hands and numbers. Nonprogramming graphic artists and human factors engineers therefore still lack appropriate tools to create styles themselves.

Toolkits are also poor tools for supporting consistency since they do not capture the rules governing when to use each interaction technique. These rules, an essential part of style, are contained only in hardcopy style guides. Such guides have now been published for a variety of styles, including the MacIntosh [1], Open Look [23], OSF/Motif [16], and Common User Access [12].

Hardcopy style guidelines are specifications for the presentation and interaction behavior of user interfaces. They may include general design philosophy, such as "adopt an object-action style" or "keep the user in control of the application at all times." Guidelines may also include more specific rules for implementing the interface, such as "the first item in a pull-down bar must appear below and one character to the right of the action bar item that leads to it." Based on informal observations of experience at IBM and elsewhere, guidelines are difficult to interpret by programmers and omit important details necessary for the complete definition of a style.

3. THE ITS ARCHITECTURE

3.1 Overview

The ITS architecture has four layers as shown in Figure 1. Actions read and write data values without concern for dialog control (when or in what sequence they will be called). They do not change depending on whether, or how many,

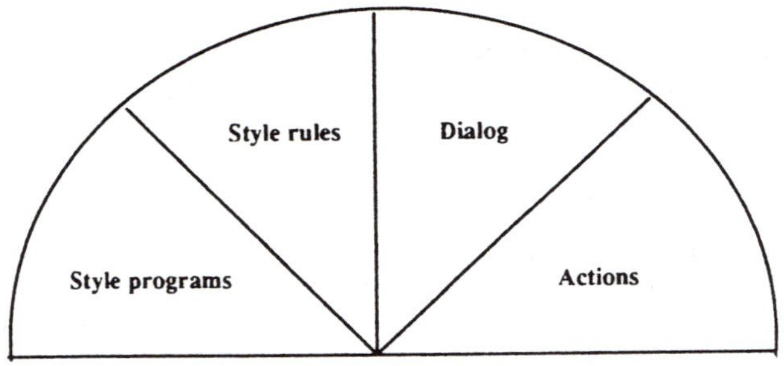

Fig. 1. Architecture of ITS applications.

views are attached to the data values they compute. The style of those views may change independently as well, for example, from tables to graphs. Actions are written in C.

Dialog is specified in the next layer of the system. Dialog includes the content of logical *frames* and the control flow among them. Separating dialog from actions allows actions to be reused in different applications. An airline reservation system intended for public access, for example, might not include some functions that are available to reservations agents. The dialog written for the reservations agent would have *frames* for those additional functions and the control flow necessary to access them. Two versions of the application can be created by writing different dialogs without having to change the actions themselves.

So far the application is not committed to a style, screen layout, language, or window system. The rule layer composes style programs into interaction techniques for each object in the dialog. An example of one type of style decision is whether to represent a *choice* the user must make as a radio button menu or action bar. These decisions are made automatically by a set of executable style rules. Style rules are written, and are open to modification, by interface designers. Style can be changed at any time by the appropriate selection of the rule base to be used in a given application.

Style rules are executed at compile time. Run-time changes in the dialog are managed by the style program layer. Example style programs include routines for text formatting, tree layout, row and column table layout, circular menus, raster images, scalable border decorations, and selectable hot spots on maps or images. Style programs can be added to the toolkit as required.

Style programs commit the application to screen layout, including the size and line wrapping of individual items. Layout is initially decided as each frame is drawn at run-time. Layout can later change when, for example, the user resizes a window.

3.2 Combining UIMS and Toolkit Layering

The split between actions and dialog in Figure 1 corresponds to the familiar separation between the application and its interface in previous UIMS. The remaining three layers further divide the interface into style-independent dialog control, definition of style, and implementation of the toolkit objects used in creating styles. To understand the benefits of this layering consider a simple example, which might appear in an airlines reservation kiosk. Figure 2 shows the opening *frame* of dialog for the kiosk. The *frame* appears in one style as shown in Figure 3. *Choice* and *choice item* (*ci*) statements are keywords in the dialog language. *Messages* provide descriptive text that can be used variously as titles, prompts, or defaults under control of style rules. The dialog branches to the *frame* named by the *activate* attribute when the user *executes* an item.

```
:frame id=main
  :choice purpose=overview, message="Select an item to"
    :ci message="View flights for today", activate=check_today
    :ci message="View future flights", activate=check_by_date
    :ci message="Make a reservation", activate=reserve
  :echoice
:eframe
```

Fig. 2. Dialog for opening frame of example airline reservations kiosk.

Fig. 3. Opening frame of the airlines reservation example shown in one possible style.

To appear as shown in Figure 3, one or more style rules must fire and transform the *choice* into the tree shown in Figure 4. The rules introduce additional nodes for components of the menu not coded in the dialog. The style rules add a *title* and an object that arranges children horizontally (in this case the choice items). Style rules also decorate each node with attributes controlling presentation (such as color, font, margins, horizontal and vertical layout) and interaction behavior.

Splitting the interface into separate layers for style-independent dialog, rule base, and toolkit has three benefits. First, the dialog remains independent of style. Dialog can be mapped into any style simply by firing the appropriate rule. Second, interface designers now control style rather than application programmers. Application designers build dialogs only from style-independent objects such as *choice*. The rule layer represents the selection criteria for all interaction techniques. As we have seen, this knowledge is not captured in executable form in toolkit applications, only in hardcopy style guides.

The third consequence of the ITS architecture is that new interaction techniques can be composed by style rules from existing toolkit objects. In conventional toolkits, new interaction techniques are also composed from existing objects, but usually by programming. The example menu here was constructed

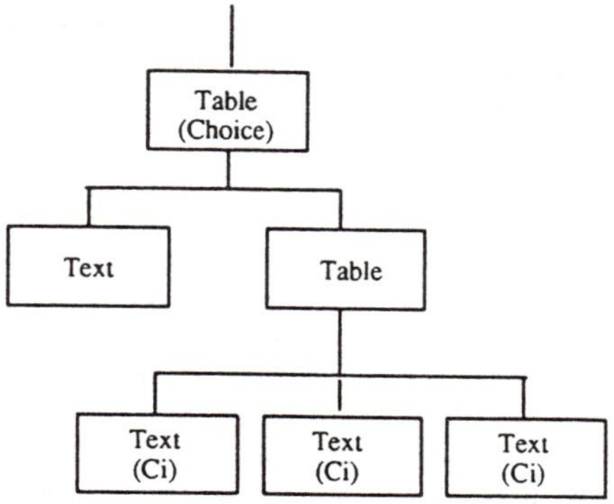

Fig. 4. Tree of units for an action bar menu. Types of nodes originally coded in the dialog are given in parentheses.

from only three toolkit objects: text, raster icons, and tabular layout. The style decisions on how to compose them into the final menu are made entirely by rules.

Since the menu is created by rules, a "menu" object is never added to the toolkit. The menu exists only as the coordinated behavior of the primitive objects. Since the toolkit need contain only primitive objects, programmers themselves have less need to implement new objects as style changes. As a result, interface designers enjoy control over style independent both of application and of toolkit programmers.

New objects are added to the toolkit whenever an interaction technique cannot be built simply by composing existing objects. Of course, these new objects are then available for reuse in composing other interaction techniques that may wish to build upon them.

3.3 Usability of Design Tools by Nonprogrammers

If application and style designers are to be truely independent from programmers, their dialog and rule languages must be highly usable. A financial analyst should be able to create a tax application, or an airline route planner a crew-scheduling application, with minimal application or style programming support. We want to give application and style experts executable tools to engage them as first class participants in application design. Currently their role is often restricted to providing input to systems analysts or programmers implementing widgets in a toolkit. Without appropriate software tools, admonitions toward user-driven design will remain only that.

Each layer in the ITS architecture corresponds to one of four roles in application development: application programmer, application expert, style expert, and style programmer. Of course, these roles may be played by one or several people as appropriate to the particular application.

An application expert is familiar with some problem domain, such as the airline industry, and wants to implement an application in that domain. The application expert typically is neither trained in programming, nor part of an information systems department. Traditionally the application expert interacts with a systems analyst to produce a design specification. Later, the specification is implemented by application programmers. Application designs produced by the analyst are not executable, but usually are represented as natural language or pseudocode algorithms. These incomplete specifications create opportunities for costly design errors. In ITS the application expert is the dialog author.

The style expert has had perhaps the poorest tool support in traditional application development. A style expert may be a graphic artist or human factors engineer. Style experts in the past have worked by drafting design guidelines or evaluating prototypes. They have had no separable work product, such as an executable style definition. Since they have had to influence designs indirectly through software developers, they have had difficulty having significant impacts. Rules give them direct control over style in ITS.

4. THE ACTION LAYER

A dialog depends on actions to implement the semantics of application functions. Actions are separated from dialog to create a library of reusable functions, to reduce the complexity of the dialog itself, and to allow changes in back-end computations independent of the interface. To communicate, the dialog and actions must share both data and control.

4.1 Data Sharing between Actions and Interface

Actions read values from data tables and return results to the same or other fields in tables. All communication between the application and interface occurs by passing values stored in data tables (see Figure 5). The collection of all data tables active in an application is called the data pool.

A particular instance of a data table is stored only once in the data pool. As in the Andrew Toolkit or Smalltalk Model-View-Controllers [13], any number of dialog objects may refer to a data table. Thus the same data may be shown in both tabular and graphical form if it is viewed simultaneously by two dialog objects. Whenever a value is changed by an action or by the user, all dialog objects representing it will be notified automatically. Each object then updates the display in whatever way is appropriate. The actions themselves have no knowledge of the number or type of dialog objects viewing the tables they manipulate in the data pool.

The update mechanism that sends style program messages about changed values is a hybrid of program-initiated and automatic notification [24]. Actions take the initiative in setting a bit in the data pool to indicate they have changed a field. This change flag is then propagated to style programs automatically by the dialog manager. Further, only those views of the changed field that are currently visible on the screen receive update notices. Others redraw only when they become visible.

4.2 Calling Actions

Control lies with the dialog manager until a user event triggers a call to an action. These events include *frame initialization* and *termination, selection, keyboard entry*, and *execution*. When called, the action is passed the event type and current dialog object. The events and parameters define the ITS architecture for actions. An action must be able to respond to one or more events. Otherwise actions are

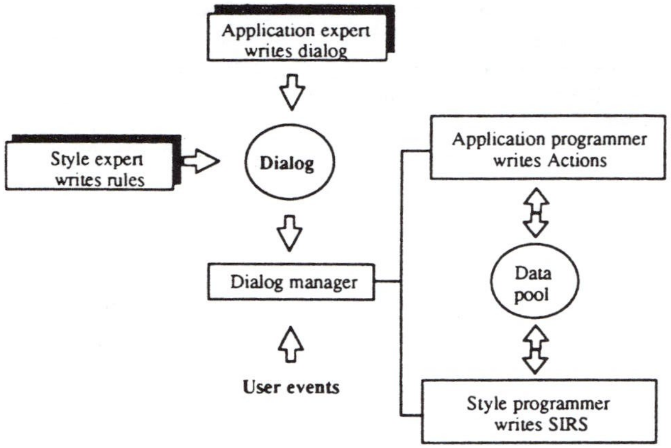

Fig. 5. The dialog manager calls actions in response to user events. Actions read and write values in the data pool. Change flags in the data pool trigger update notices to all style programs currently displaying the changed values.

conventional C library functions. In the OS/2 version of ITS they are typically stored in dynamically linked libraries and demand loaded.

This "external" model of control [10] can be interrupted asynchronously by an action that independently notices an error or other condition requiring user action. The action causes an interrupt by marking an arbitrary field in the data pool as changed. The resulting update notices may cause the dialog manager to branch to an error frame or to call other actions to correct the error.

5. THE DIALOG LAYER

The application expert in ITS is responsible for defining the *content* of the interface in the dialog layer. *Content* consists of two parts: tables that describe the data to be stored in the data pool and frames that define the application dialog itself.

5.1 Data Tables

Application actions receive input from the data pool and write output back to the data pool. ITS organizes these values using two data structures: *forms* and *lists*. A single set of *fields* is called a *form*; a set of *forms* is called a *list*. Both structures can be drawn, of course, in any number of styles not necessarily similar to physical forms and lists.

The application expert defines the structure of the data pool by writing table definitions. Tables are templates for the *fields* in each *list* and *form*. One or more instances of a table can be created in the pool under dialog control. Each instance is called a *generation* of the data object. Multiple *generations* are particularly useful when *frames* are called recursively and need private data spaces.

```
:form table=flight_info
  :fi field=destination, rangename=cities, size=20
  :fi field=departure_time, size=10
  :fi field=departure_date, size=20
  :fi field=airline, rangename=airlines, size=20
  :fi field=number_stops, size=5
:eform

:list listname=flights, numrecords=10
  :li field=destination, rangename=cities, size=20
  :li field=departure_time, size=10
  :li field=departure_date, size=20
  :li field=airline, rangename=airlines, size=20
  :li field=number_stops, size=5
:elist
```

Fig. 6. Data definition file. A form is a named collection of fields. A list is an array of forms with "numrecords" elements.

Tables for the airlines reservation example are shown in Figure 6. Each *field* has a name and an optional set of descriptive attributes. The *datatype* may be used by style rules in selecting appropriate interaction techniques for the *field*. The *size* attribute can be used in estimating the screen space required for the *field*. A *message* can be used as a title or prompt if no *message* is given in the dialog file.

Tables describe the data in a family of applications. Attributes given in the tables are inherited by a dialog when it refers to each *field*. Thus a family of dialogs may be built using the same table definitions and reuse attributes coded only once in the table.

5.2 Dialog

The dialog layer defines the content of a set of *frames* and the flow of control among them. Traditionally, application programs have fully controlled the sequencing of user dialog. Input and output statements were intermixed with those performing application computations. The application decided when and in what order interaction would take place. Nearly all UIMS remove control of dialog sequencing from the application and place it instead either in a central dialog manager [10] or in a distributed set of interaction objects that jointly regulate user interactions [21].

As we saw in Figure 2, control branches to the frame named by the *activate* attribute when the user executes a dialog statement. *Activated* frames are put on a run-time stack and popped from the stack as the user returns from them. Since the user can follow multiple dialog paths simultaneously, perhaps by interacting in different windows in parallel, the stack is really a tree of *frame* activations.

The *attachto* attribute controls where a *frame* is added to the execution stack. According to its intended lifetime in the dialog a *frame* may be attached near the root or near the leaves of the tree. For example, *frames* that are attached at the root of the stack exist until the user explicitly terminates them or leaves the application. *Frames* that are attached to lower branches of the stack terminate when any *frame* above them terminates. Since generations of *forms* and *lists* in the data pool are also linked to nodes in the stack, a *frame* may be bound to different data depending on where it appears in the stack.

Name	Description
Session	Indicates the start of a tag file or complete tag set.
Frame	Indicates the start of a group of conceptually related dialog blocks.
List	Indicates the start of a set of related items, e.g., a set of employees in an organization.
Li	List item. Specifies a field that should be included in a list built by an enclosing list tag.
Form	The start of a form, e.g., a related collection of fields.
Fi	Form item. Names a field to be included in a form built by an enclosing form tag.
Choice	Indicates the start of a set of alternatives to be chosen by the user.
Ci	Choice item. Specifies one of the choice items in the list enclosed by a Choice tag.
Info	Information block. A static panel of help information.
Ii	Information item. An item in a help panel.

Fig. 7. Objects used to specify dialog content.

Name	Values	Definition
Action	⟨action name⟩	Name of the action to call on frame entry, item selection, or execution.
Activate	⟨frame id⟩	Transfers control to frame "id" when an item is selected.
Purpose	Elaboration	Specifies the intention of the application expert in creating the frame. Can be used by style to set colors, titles, or controls appropriately.
	Example	
	Feedback	
	Group	
	Help	
	Instructional	
	Overview	
	Useraction	
	Warning	
Structure	Continuum	Description of the underlying nature of the data contained in the field. Used to choose appropriate interaction techniques.
	Scale	
	Order	
	Set	
	Points	
	Label	
	Disjoint	
UserCan	Delete	Specifies the actions the user can perform on the specified field.
	Filter	
	Hide	
	Modify	
	Search	
	Select	
	Show	
	Sort	

Fig. 8. Selected dialog attributes.

Next, the application expert defines the content of each *frame* in the dialog. To simplify the application expert's job, we chose a small fixed set of dialog objects. These objects are listed in Figure 7. Each statement may include a number of attributes, some of which are listed in Figure 8. Attributes are used to specify the *actions* executed, *values* set, and *messages* displayed by each dialog object.

```
:frame id=check_today, action=getlist,
        listname=flights, value=flights.dta
  :list listname=flights, number=5
    :li field=destination, message="To"
    :li field=departure_time, message="Departure"
    :li field=airline, message="Carrier"
    :li field=number_stops, message="Stops"
  :elist
  :frame message="To search for selected flights"
    form table=flight_info
      :fi field=destination, message="Enter destination city"
    :eform
    :choice purpose=useraction
      :ci message="Ok", action=select_flights,
          table=flight_info, listname=flights
    :echoice
  :eframe
:eframe
```

Fig. 9. Frame for viewing and selecting flights in example airline reservation kiosk.

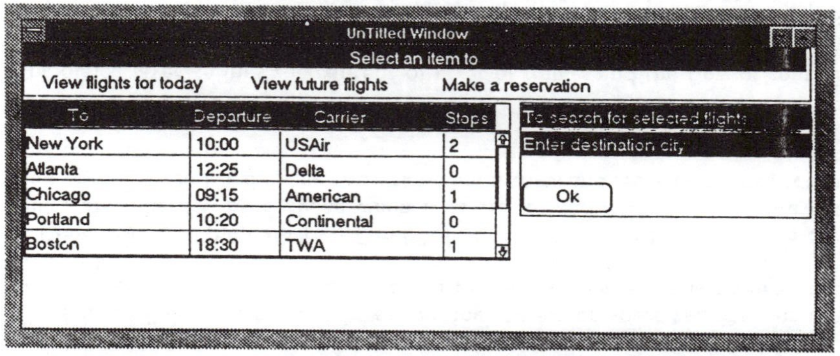

Fig. 10. Flight list and controls for selecting particular flights in the example airline reservation kiosk.

Figure 9 shows how these objects have been used to display a list of flights in the airline reservation example. The *frame* is shown in one possible style in Figure 10.

The *frame* contains a *list* showing four of the five *fields* defined for "flights" in the data definition file. Each *field* is coded on a list item (*li*) statement. The list items define the *fields* displayed in each *record* of the list. Five *records* will be presented to the user at a time. *Lists* and *forms* defined in the dialog file are views onto data values themselves, which are stored in the data pool. All views of "flights" will be synchronized by update messages from the dialog manager whenever any of them modify the data pool.

The *subframe* in Figure 9 groups a *form* and *choice* into a control for selecting particular flights. "Select_flights" will be called when the user *executes* "Ok." The action uses all nonnull fields of the table "flight_info" as search keys into the "flights" list. It replaces "flights" with the set of *records* satisfying the search. Dialog manager update messages then cause all views of the list to be redrawn.

6. THE RULE LAYER

What is style? One definition of style is a coordinated set of decisions on the appearance and behavior of the interaction techniques used in a family of applications. Three dimensions of this definition are important: (1) it refers to both the output and the input characteristics of interaction techniques, (2) it considers both style in the small (individual techniques) and in the large (a coordinated set of decisions), and (3) it applies to more than one application.

For a family of applications, both consistency and identity of style are important. Consistency means that similar functions in an interface, such as choosing a single item from a list of mutually exclusive options, are represented and interact with the user similarly wherever found in an interface. Consistency does not mean that such a function is identical throughout the interface, just that where appropriate the technique is similar and where differences exist, those differences have meaning.

Consider Grudin's example of a potentially destructive menu operation [8]. In his example, when a menu appears it defaults to the last item executed by the user. This helps the user repeat nondestructive operations such as copy or select. If, however, the last item executed was delete, then the menu defaults to another item. Grudin argues that this is an example of desirable, though inconsistent, behavior. We believe, rather, that this is consistent behavior. Consistency can mean a hierarchy of default rules and subrules for special cases. In our view, users will in fact perceive the consistency in behavior of dangerous operations even if that behavior differs from the default rule.

ITS represents the range of general to special cases as such a hierarchy of rules. In ITS, the different types of *choices* are represented with one or more rules that describe how they are similar, together with subrules that give the particular characteristics of each one of them.

What we call identity is perhaps as important as consistency. Identity is the customer's requirement of being able to create styles that users associate with their applications. Interface style is now an area of competitive advantage in itself. The identity of excellent styles is becoming strategically important to the success of our customers.

ITS style rules support each of these requirements. They control both presentation and interaction in style. They support style in the large by representing not just individual interaction techniques but the *conditions* under which each of them should be used. And they are an open architecture that allows customers to modify standard styles and create entirely new styles of their own.

6.1 The Rule Mechanism

Each rule has a *conditions* part and a *results* part. The *conditions* determine when a rule will be executed. *Conditions* may test the type of dialog statement (e.g., *choice*, *list*, *form*). Any dialog attribute can also be tested so that, for example, a rule will fire only for those *choices* that have *kind* = *1_and_only_1*. Other *conditions* may test for particular numbers or kinds of children. Thus a rule for

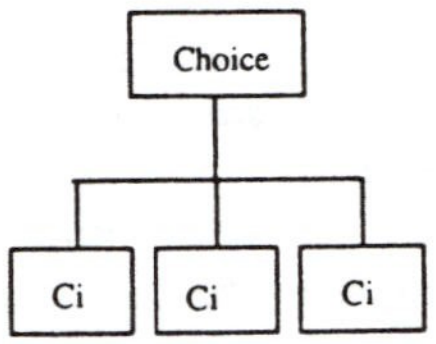

Fig. 11. The choice before style matching.

forms may fire only when a *form* has fewer than ten *fields*. Another rule that uses less screen space might fire when there are more than ten *fields*.

All of these *conditions* can be applied to a dialog object's children. A rule for *frames* that contain images can test for the presence of an image and can refer to the child that matches that test in the *results* part of the rule. That child might be positioned specially, or it might be assigned attributes to draw or interact with it differently than the other children.

All of a rule's tests must succeed for the rule to be considered for execution. Thus the current rule language supports only conjunctive *conditions*. Our experience to date does not suggest the need for more sophisticated conditionality including both conjunctive and disjunctive *conditions* within a single rule. Cases where the same *results* should occur for two different *conditions* can be handled by two rules with similar *results*. The language does support a null *condition* to catch all cases not otherwise coded. Thus if the rule base handles only the *1_and_only_1 kind* of *choice*, all others can be matched by a single rule with null *conditions*.

Five types of *result* statements can be nested with a rule:

—*Units*: to create and modify the dialog structure,
—*Set or Conditions*: to control the execution of nested rules,
—*Kids*: to collect or match on characteristics of the children of the dialog block being matched,
—*Attributes*: to set default values for style attributes, and
—*Content*: to generate dialog under style control.

6.2 Creating and Modifying Dialog Structure

Let us begin with structure. We have seen that the application expert codes a *choice* as shown in Figure 2. The set of allowed *choice items* are coded on separate *ci* statements. Before it has been matched by a rule, only the abstract *choice* exists as shown in Figure 11. The job of the style rule is now to refine this structure into one such as shown in Figure 12 by giving a template to control how each dialog node will be represented.

As style experts, assume we want all *choices* to be menus (rather than, say, entry fields). Structurally, a menu is simply a set of *choice items* arranged vertically or horizontally, perhaps under a *title*. Additional nodes are required beyond those shown in Figure 11 for the *title* and to group the *choice items* together.

Figure 13 shows a rule for creating simple menus. The *conditions* statement matches only on the type of dialog object, in this case all *choices*. The nested set

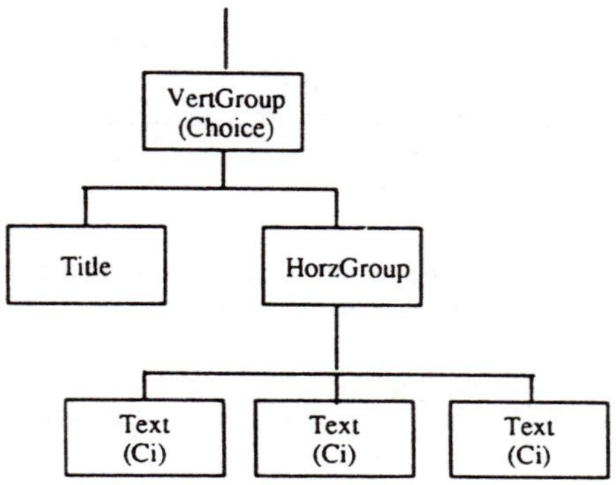

Fig. 12. Tree of units describing a simple menu in ITS. Title and HorzGroup units are added automatically by the style rule.

```
:conditions source=choice
    fire for all choices
  :unit type=VertGroup
    the block arranges the title vertically
    above the set of items
    :unit type=Title
    :eunit
    :unit type=HorzGroup
    the item is replicated for all children of
    the choice, i.e. all ci statements
      :unit type=Message, replicate=all
      :eunit
    :eunit
  :eunit

:econditions
```

Fig. 13. Style rule creating a simple menu with title.

of *units* describes the structure of the *choice* for this style. Thus the menu has a parent node that controls the layout of the *title* relative to the *choice items*. The child *unit* is *replicated* for all of the *ci* statements in Figure 11.

Unit structure is created by taking the rule as a template. Several *units* in the rule may derive from a given dialog object. For example, the single *choice* node in Figure 2 is redefined into a *vertgroup*, *title*, and *horzgroup unit* in Figure 13. Dialog attributes from the *choice* are assigned to all three *units* that derive from it. In this way style programs have ready access to all dialog attributes.

This is very helpful when the dialog node is bound to an object in the data pool. Then all *units* derived from it are bound to the same object. They are simply multiple views of the same data. Each *unit* will get update messages about changes to the data, but can decide to respond to them in very different ways.

Each parent *unit* handles the layout of its immediate children. Thus the *vertgroup unit* aligns the *title* above the set of *choice items*, and the nested *horzgroup* aligns the individual *items* horizontally. Vertical and horizontal directions themselves are defined by the *fillorder* attribute. *Fillorder* equals *colsfirst* in a *vertgroup* type and *rowsfirst* in a *horzgroup* type.

```
:conditions source=choice
    still match on all choices
  :unit type=VertGroup
    :unit type=Title
    :eunit
    pick the best one of the following subrules
    :set apply=best
    when only one choice item can be selected at a time
    (1_and_only_1), refine each item into separate dingbat
    icon and text for the radio buttons
    :conditions kind=1_and_only_1
      :unit type=VertGroup
        :unit type=HorzGroup, replicate=all
          :unit type=Dingbat
          :eunit
          :unit type=Message
          :eunit
        :eunit
      :eunit
    :econditions
    in the default case, each choice item is simply a text label
    as before
    :conditions
      :unit type=HorzGroup
        :unit type=Message, replicate=all
        :eunit
      :eunit
    :econditions
    :eset
  :eunit

:econditions
```

Fig. 14. Style rule creating a radio button menu or a simple menu, according to the kind attribute.

Now override this default rule to draw single-option choices as radio buttons. These *choices* should still have *titles*, but we now want the *items* to be stacked vertically. Each *choice item* should now include an *icon* for the button (called a *dingbat* by typesetters) and a *message*. Figure 14 shows the revised rule. The outer *conditions* statement still matches on all *choices*. The top *vertgroup* and *title units* are the same for both types of menu. *Choices* coded with *kind* equal to *1_and_only_1* are refined with separate *units* for the *icon* and *message*. Separate *units* are required since they will be decorated with different attributes. The *message* string, unlike the *icon*, redraws itself in reverse video when the user tracks into an *item*.

6.3 Matching on Characteristics of Children

In mapping from dialog to style, rules can change the order of children. The style expert may want to group all *items* together that *activate* other *frames*. Say, for instance, all *items* that transfer control to another *frame* should come first and have an urgent *background* color. The revised rule to do this is shown in Figure 15.

```
:conditions source=choice

    Name the set of kids that transfer control "go_kids".
    These are just the ci statements that have activate attrib-
    utes

  :kids name=go_kids, present=activate
  :unit type=VertGroup
    :unit type=Title
    :eunit
    :unit type=VertGroup

    each ci with an activate attribute is drawn as a text label
    with arrow icon to its right

      :unit type=HorzGroup, replicate=go_kids
        :unit type=Message
        :eunit
        :unit type=icon, shape=down_arrow
        :eunit
      :eunit

    other ci's are simply drawn as text items

      :unit type=Message, replicate=rest
      :eunit
    :eunit
  :eunit

:econditions
```

Fig. 15. Style rule reordering kids so that choice items that transfer control (i.e., have activate attributes) appear before others. In addition, they are drawn with an icon emphasizing that they are branches.

The *kids* statement collects groups of children that meet its *conditions.* In Figure 15 the rule again matches all *choices.* Any *choice items* that have *activate* attributes (*present=activate*) are included in the "go_kids" group. The name is simply an internal label used to refer to the set later in the rule.

Replicate names a set of children that should be refined using a given subtree of *units.* So, in Figure 15, the rule first *replicates* over the members of the "go_kids" group and then over the remaining children. *Rest* is a keyword that means all children not named in any group of *kids.* The *items* that transfer control are refined into three *units*: a *message,* an *icon* reminding the user that the *item* transfers control, and a parent horizontal group. Other *items* are drawn simply as *messages.*

6.4 Setting Default Values for Style Attributes

Style attributes control the appearance and behavior of *units.* Some of the attributes supported in the current system are listed in Table I. They control space and layout negotiations between parent and child *units,* presentation including font and colors, and interaction including the mapping between *physical* and *logical* events. Attributes are parameters to the style programs that render *units* on the screen. The style programs themselves are named on each *unit* by its *techid* attribute.

Table I. Selected Style Attributes Currently Supported in ITS

Name	Values	Definition
AnswerWidth	Children SelfCalc SelfFixed PopAdjust	Compute the width (depth) of this unit by summing the requests of the child units, by a nonstandard method, by using fixed estimates, or by combining the child requests and then adjusting them.
Layout	Count Space	How units should be fit into available space. By Count fits a given number of units, e.g., 3 × 4, into the space. By Space flows as many units as will fit into the available space, then wraps to the next vertical or horizontal free space.
TopMargin	⟨integer⟩	Number of screen units in top (bottom, left, or right) margin.
TechId	⟨program⟩	Name of the Style Program (P) that will draw this unit.
NomWidth	⟨integer⟩	Estimate of the Width (Depth) of this unit in screen units.

Attributes are assigned to *units* by labeling the *unit* with a *type.* Some of the style *types* we have used so far include *title, dingbat, message, horzgroup,* and *vertgroup.* Each *type* defines a set of attribute *values.* The set of attributes is the same for all *types*; only their *values* change among the *types.* Thus *prompt* and *title* may have a different font, horizontal justification, and color values. The *icon type* may be drawn with a raster style program, rather than the text formatter used by *prompt* and *title.* Justification and color attributes, however, can still be coded.

Style experts can create default attribute *values* and then override them later in subrules. The parent/child hierarchy of *units* defines the scope over which a *type's values* are defined. Most *types* are defined at the root of the dialog and are global. Those that are overridden at lower levels are changed only within the subtree where they are overridden.

Assume that several rules have refined the flight reservation frame in Figure 9 into the *unit* tree shown in Figure 16. Figure 17 shows how the *session* rule assigns defaults at the root node. Another rule has overridden the *font* for *title* below the *choice.* Note that the override occurs just for that individual *choice.* Other *choices* that may not have triggered the rule making this override will draw their *titles* as given in the root definition.

Two features of this design are significant. First, attributes inherit within each *type* independently of whether any *units* are actually assigned the *type.* Thus a style expert can write rules that define and override *title* attributes without concern for which interaction techniques may or may not actually use *title.* Attributes and *units* are defined separately.

Second, the *unit* hierarchy allows each parent to control *types* for its subtree. This can be done no matter how many levels exist between the *unit* that defines the *type* and the *unit* that uses it. For example, we may want the color of *titles* in a dialog box to be different from other *titles* on the screen. Pop-up dialog boxes, new windows, or areas of an existing window are all ways of representing *frames.* One of a set of alternative *frame* rules will be selected as the best match

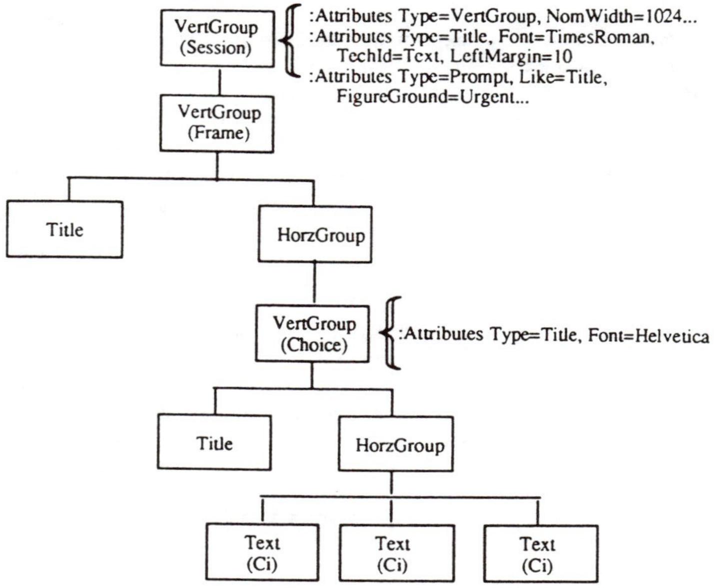

Fig. 16. The dialog tree after frame, nested subframe, and choice rules have fired. The font of titles has been overridden in this subframe.

```
:conditions source=session
    Start by defining default attributes for types used in this style. These
    defaults will be attached to the unit at the session, i.e. root, level.
    They will then inherit to lower units according to the type of each
    unit.
  :Attributes type=VertGroup, NomWidth=1024...
  :Attributes type=Title, Font=TimesRoman, TechId=text, LeftMargin=10, ...
  :Attributes type=Prompt, Like=Title, FigureGround=Urgent, ...
    Then define the unit structure for the session. We don't want titles
    here, so just create a single unit.
  :unit type=VertGroup
  :eunit
:econditions
```

Fig. 17. Any rule may assign default attributes. Those defaults are saved at the node that matches the rule. Defaults at the session level, as here, are global to the style.

for each *frame* statement in the dialog. This winning rule can override *title* colors set at higher levels of the dialog tree. The new color then is inherited by *titles* within the *frame*. Therefore, *titles* created by the same *choice* rule within different *frames* can take on different colors.

```
:conditions source=frame
  :unit type=VertGroup
    frames have titles above the set of frame contents
    :unit type=Title
    :eunit
    :unit type=HorzGroup
    Frame contents are arranged horizontally. The type isn't
    assigned here, but in other rules that match later on the spe-
    cific frame contents.
      :unit replicate=all
      :eunit
    :eunit
    each frame has Help and Quit buttons added automatically
    by the rule. The choice will be matched itself later as any
    other block.
    :content
      :choice purpose=useraction
        :ci message=Help, activate=AppHelp
        :ci message=Quit, action=shutdown
      :echoice
    :econtent
  :eunit
:econditions
```

Fig. 18. This rule creates Help and Quit buttons automatically in each frame.

6.5 Generating Dialog within Style

Finally, style rules can themselves generate dialog and delay committment to its style. A rule, for example, can add standard command buttons to each *frame* automatically. The rule in Figure 18 codes the same *choice* statements that could be used by an application expert to create Help and Quit buttons. Thus the *frame* rule does not have to say how they should appear, just that they should appear in each *frame*. The appropriate *choice* rule will fire later to create the button style. This technique has been used to generate "Yes" and "No" *choice items* for fields with Boolean data types. Rules have also automatically generated pull down menus for text entry *fields* where a fixed set of values is allowed for the *field*.

7. THE STYLE PROGRAM LAYER

7.1 Space Negotiations

Style programs, like actions, must respond to a standard set of messages from the dialog manager. The most important messages are sent to request screen space estimates, to paint to the screen, and to inform the style program when the user indicates *activation, selection,* or *execution*. The style expert can set attributes that control whether style programs receive each message or take the default response.

The problem in space negotiation is to request and then allocate screen space for each *unit* based on its requirements and the requirements of its children.

Space negotiation is a three-step process that balances performance with the need for high-quality layout. The first step is to determine the space requirements of each *unit*. The second, and optional, step is for the parent to adjust the space required for children. The third step assigns a specific location to each object that will be displayed.

Space requirements are determined by a depth first, left-to-right traversal of a *frame*. The first step occurs when moving downward. During this phase each *unit* is asked to respond with its own space requirements. Many *units* defer this question until their children have responded to it first. The second step of space allocation occurs during the upward search (looking for the next right-hand sibling) of each subtree. During this step each *unit* is asked to integrate and possibly adjust the space requirements of its children. An example would be a *unit* asking for enough space to give each of its children the same depth as that of the deepest child.

Space assignment is done by a second tree traversal. During this phase each *unit* receives its screen assignment, both location and size. This process is top down. From its allocation, each *unit* reserves what it requires and allocates the remaining space to its children. Each *unit* can, of course, have a different policy for allocating space.

7.2 Other Operations

Each of the above processes place their results only in documented attributes on the *unit* tree. This means that these results are publicly visible and hence are easily available for reuse. One such use is to be queried by children needing to make their own space or drawing decisions. For example, a text object that wants to set its font size relative to a parent can respond to a repaint message by setting its size as some increment on the size attributes in the parent block.

Mouse tracking or touch-paint location also benefits from standardized attribute definitions. The run-time manager can provide a default tree traversal for correlating mouse position with a displayed object. In ITS this default mapping is determined by the smallest display rectangle surrounding the mouse position. As such, mouse event mapping is similar to that in the X toolkit. However, alternative mappings are often required, as when a parent wants to redirect a mouse event to a child different than the one directly under the mouse (as in the Andrew toolkit). An attribute on each *unit* determines whether the *unit* wants to assume responsibility for pointer correlation within its borders. ITS thus combines a strong default method and the flexibility to override this method with alternative ones.

8. THE EXPO 92 VISITOR INFORMATION SYSTEM

To test the ITS application development tools, we are using them to build a visitor information system for the 1992 EXPO in Seville, Spain. ITS allows us to build this system iteratively as a series of progressively more complete prototypes. These prototypes are functioning applications and test each layer of ITS: actions, dialog, style rules, and style programs.

8.1 What Is the EXPO Visitor Information System?

The EXPO visitor information system will offer information and services to an estimated 20 million visitors from April through October, 1992. Information to be provided includes maps and directions for navigating around the two square kilometer site, up-to-the-minute schedules of events, and background information on countries and organizations participating in EXPO. In addition, the system will provide visitors with services beyond those traditionally found in information kiosks. These include person-to-person and group electronic messaging, automated restaurant reservations, public opinion polling, and locators for lost family members. Since we also believe the kiosk should be fun to use, it will provide a variety of standalone and networked games for use during offpeak hours.

8.2 What Are the Requirements for the EXPO Visitor Information System?

Developing a style for EXPO is a good test for ITS since both the application and the developers pose difficult challenges. The application must support several languages, including several dialects of Spanish, as well as English, French, and German. Most visitors will be extremely inexperienced computer users. Since we expect them to spend only a very few minutes at the information system, it must be operable with little or no training. To be visually attractive it must be of world-class graphic design quality and operate with multiple types of media: high-quality text, graphics, and images.

The developers, too, pose challenges the ITS tools must help meet. Our development team is distributed between two locations in Seville and New York. ITS must help integrate application functions developed in both locations. In addition, we maintain working prototypes in other locations for demonstration, including Madrid and visitor centers on the EXPO construction site. These prototypes must be attractive enough even in early versions to promote the desired image of a quality product in the works.

8.3 Dialog and Actions

The starting *frame* of the application is shown in Figure 19. Its appearance in the EXPO style is shown in Figure 20. The user can take an electronic walk through EXPO by selecting hotspots in maps and images at the left of the screen, take an opinion poll, draw a picture using a finger-painting program (Figure 21), send or receive electronic mail (Figure 22), or make a restaurant reservation.

In Figure 19, the "startexpo" and "stuff_caption" actions are called when the *frame* initially appears on the screen. "Startexpo" reads several data files to initialize the image network and opinion poll. "Stuff_caption," when called with the *frame initialize* message, sets up the caption of the current image in the image title area. Later, when "stuff_caption" is called with *select* messages, it replaces the caption with short titles describing each hotspot as they are selected on the image. Since no actions are coded on the messaging or opinion poll choice items, when *executed* they simply transfer control to the *frames* given by their *activate* attributes.

The image network panel is built from a *form* and two *lists* grouped together as a *subframe*. *Version = fit* is recognized by style rules to fit the *subframe* into

```
:frame id=basic_frame, level=a, action=startexpo, listname=nav_list,
        table=eachframe
  :choice message="Explore picture or", purpose=navigation, version=icon
    :ci message=Poll, value="opinion.bmp", activate=opinion_poll
    :ci message=Paint, value="paint.bmp", activate=finger_painting
    :ci message=Meals, value="meals.bmp", activate=reservations
    :ci message=Read,  value="read.bmp", activate=read_message
    :ci message=Send, value="send.bmp", activate=send_message
    :ci message=Vote, value="vote.bmp", activate=voting
  :echoice

  :frame version=fit, purpose=group
    :form version=almost
      :fi table=eachframe, field=ndx_title, purpose=overview
      :fi table=imagetext, field=label, purpose=feedback
    :eform

    :list listname=hotlist, datatype=image, number=11, table=eachframe,
      field=pic_file, message=the picture, action=stuff_caption
      :li field=index, action=newimage
    :elist

    :list listname=piclist,number=5, datatype=set_of_image
      :li field=small_pic_file,action=poptoimage
    :elist
  :eframe

  :frame purpose=navigation
    :choice structure=disjoint, purpose=useraction
      :ci message='Empezar en espanol', action=lang_and_size,value=spn
      :ci message="Let's Start in English", action=lang_and_size,value=eng
    :echoice
  :eframe
:eframe
```

Fig. 19. Dialog statements of the beginning EXPO frame as coded by the application expert. A choice block allows the user to select an EXPO service. Value attributes on choice items name the icon to be displayed with each choice. A form gives title and caption information for the image and its list of hotspots. A second list displays the route the user has traversed through the tree of images about EXPO.

the left-hand two-thirds of the screen and to be sure it appears there regardless of the order in which it is coded in the dialog statements. *Purpose = group* indicates to this style that all contents of the *subframe* are related, and hence they are drawn together on a gray background with no separating gaps or lines. *Structure = disjoint* is coded, in contrast, on the *choice* between Spanish and English. The EXPO style therefore separates these *choice items* visually on the screen.

Within the image *subframe*, the *form* contains two *form items* for the image title and caption. *Version* and *purpose* attributes are used here to guide style in choosing appropriate fonts, margins, and separating lines between the title and caption. The *list* with *datatype* = image contains the image and its set of hotspots. The image file name is found in the *field* "pic_file" in the *table* "eachframe." An image's hotspots are stored as *records* of the *list*. Each *record* contains *fields* for

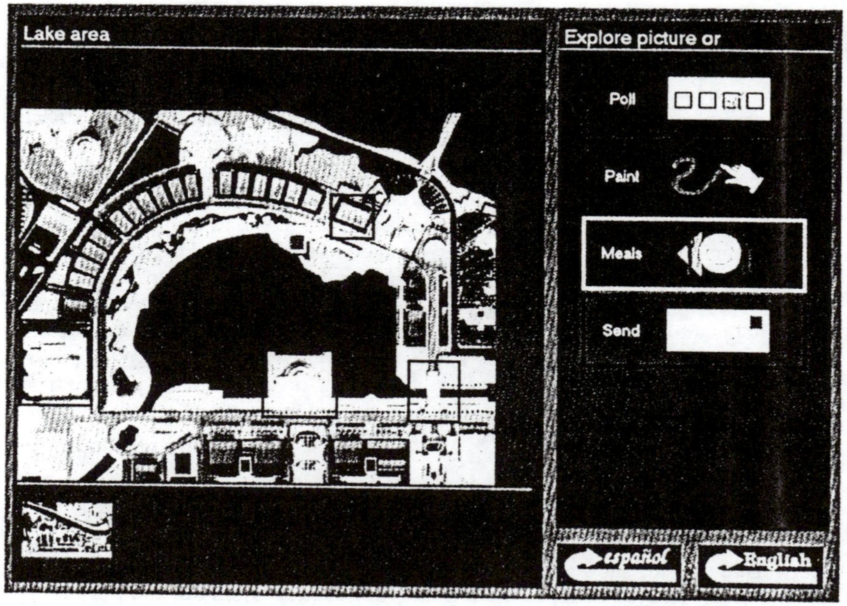

Fig. 20. Maps and images with selectable hotspots provide an electronic walk through EXPO.

the position and size of the hotspot. These *fields* are used by a style program to size and position the hotspot on the image.

To help users navigate, miniature pictures show the path of images taken from the root of the network. In Figure 19, the *list* with *datatype* = set_of_image stores this breadcrumb trail. This *list* is simply a view of the internal picture stack maintained by the "newimage" action. Each time "newimage" is called by *executing* a hotspot, it pushes a small picture file name onto the stack. "PopToImage," the action coded on *items* in the breadcrumb *list*, pops the stack to return directly to any image on the path to the root.

Note that all navigation through the image network is coded within a single *frame* in the dialog. No *activate* attributes transfer control outside that *frame* when users pick hotspots or pop the image stack. Rather, actions simply modify the contents of the data pool to point to new images and hotspots. Update messages propagated by the dialog manager to style programs cause repaints of only those parts of the screen that need to change to show the new image. All of the borders, title bars, and menu controls remain unchanged by these repaints. The effect minimizes disruption for the user.

8.4 Style Programs Needed to Implement EXPO

Eight different style programs are needed to control the screen in Figure 20. A text formatter draws titles, menus, command buttons, and explanatory text.

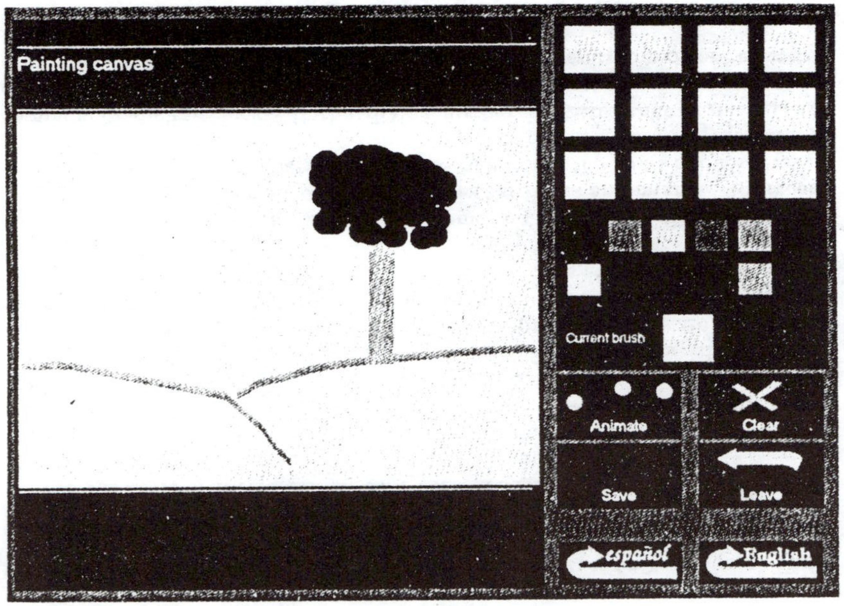

Fig. 21. Finger painting using a touch screen.

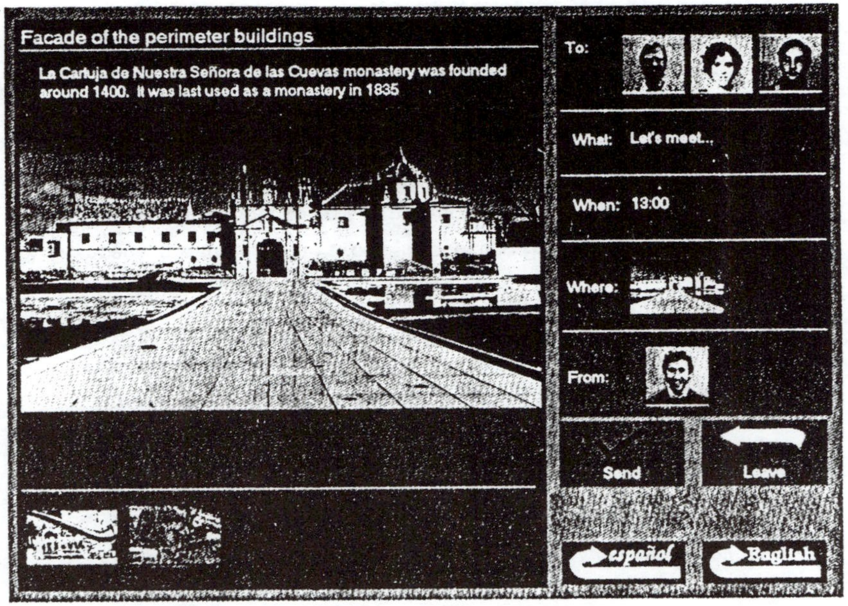

Fig. 22. Sending a message to family members. The "where" field of the message at right tracks the currently displayed image. "When" and "what" fields are set by graphical dialogs appearing in the image area.

Pictures are displayed from true color images mapped offline to a 256-entry color table. Drop shadows and other decorative borders are computed from scalable bitmap definitions so they can wrap around units of any size. Selectable hotspots are computed from position data and superimposed over images. The same style program that highlights each hotspot is wrapped around the small images below the picture and around each selectable menu item. To cause all items to highlight when the user touches anywhere on the screen, a style program at the root of the screen's *unit* tree propagates finger down and up events to all interested *units* below it. Finally, rectangular layout is controlled by a style program using a gridded design [4]. In gridding, style experts specify the number of columns in a *frame*. *Units* within that *frame* are sized as multiples of the column width. A gridded *frame*, by having only a small number of *unit* sizes, typically looks more balanced than one with arbitrary sizes.

The text, gridded frame layout, picture, and drop shadow programs were reused from the toolkit. The programs for positioning hotspots, drawing their borders, and propagating touch events were added during the implementation of EXPO.

8.5 EXPO 92 Rules

The structure of the map *frame* is shown schematically in Figure 23. *Units* shown in bold correspond to the original content coded by the application expert in Figure 19. Other *units* are added automatically by style to control layout, to refine original content nodes into more elaborate structure, and to create content not originally coded by the application expert.

Unit 1 in Figure 24 is the *frame* coded by the application expert. This root *unit* controls the entire group of hotspots contained within the *frame*. Hotspots are controlled from the root of the *frame* so they are all drawn and erased together wherever the touch occurs.

Units 2, 3, and 4 are created automatically by the rule in Figure 24 to control the placement of the image and language buttons within the *frame*. *Unit* 2 creates a horizontal group across the entire screen. *Unit* 3 at the left contains the image *subframe* (*unit* 5) and its three children, *units* 6 through 8. *Unit* 4 is a vertical group of the remaining *frame* contents. The buttons for changing languages are forced to the bottom of this right-hand column. Each of these objects are further refined by the firing of appropriate rules elsewhere in the style.

9. DISCUSSION

9.1 Layering not Separation

User Interface Management Systems traditionally have been used to build generic interface controls such as menus, buttons, and scroll bars. Large "client areas" have been left as terra incognita, into which the application has been allowed to

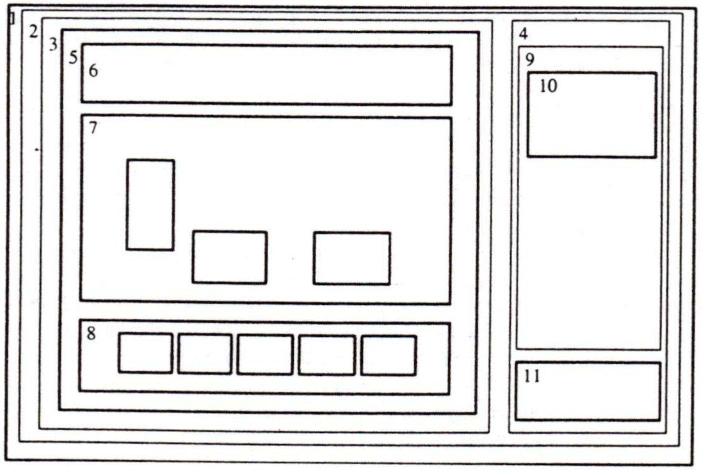

Fig. 23. Structure of map frame. The rule moves the image to the left of the screen as unit 7. Selectable hotspots are positioned by unit 7 according to locations provided by the application. Other frame contents are arranged vertically as children of unit 9. Only units in bold are coded by the application expert; others are added automatically by style rules to control layout and behavior.

write at will to handle more application-specific interaction techniques. Thus, the modularity gained by defining an interface externally from the application is lost for large segments of the interface. This is true because the application defines the style of interaction within the client area. Changes to the style of that part of the interface require changes to the application.

The alternative is to generate all of the interface within the UIMS and to eliminate the client area. This leads to the view that information about the application, in particular about its data types, is not hidden from style rules. Rather than separating application from style, ITS applications delay commitment to style. Delayed commitment means that application layers are not allowed to talk about style. Once we have committed to a particular style, however, application information is freely available to style rules and programs.

As an example, in the EXPO visitor information system users can select the time of day for a restaurant reservation. Time is a data type defined within the EXPO application as a pair of integer ranges for hours and minutes. By recognizing the use of the time data type, a style rule draws the hours and minutes in the correct sequence and automatically inserts a colon between them as is common in digital clocks. If the dialog further indicates that a given usage of time is for display only (by coding *usercan = show*), the rule reduces the separation between the *fields*, since space is no longer required for selectable hotspots around them.

```
:conditions source=frame
    Start by naming the contents of the frame that we want to handle specially, these include the buttons to change languages (purpose=navigation)...
:kids name=bottom, source=frame, purpose=navigation
    ...and the image panel that should fit into the left side of the screen.
:kids name=fits, version=fit
    Then define the unit tree for the frame.
  :unit type=Group
    Type=Group creates a unit to control the group of all hotspots on the
    screen. Draw messages are sent to each one from here, at the root of the
    frame, so they all appear and disappear together.
    :unit type=HorzGroup
    The horizontal group arranges an image panel at the left of the screen...
      :unit type=VertGroup
        :unit replicate=fits
        :eunit
      :eunit
      :unit type=VertGroup
    ...then rest of the frame contents are stacked vertically at the right side of
    the screen.
        :unit type=vertgroup, extradepth=accept
    This extra vertical group accepts extra depth, while the language buttons
    below reject it. That forces them to the bottom of the screen.
          :unit replicate=rest
          :eunit
        :eunit
    Buttons for changing languages come at the bottom of the right hand column.
        :unit replicate=bottom, extradepth=reject
        :eunit
      :eunit
  :eunit
:econditions
```

Fig. 24. Style rule for location finder frame in EXPO. Other rules will fire for the individual contents of the frame, including the list for hotspots and the choices for personal services and languages.

9.2 Comparison with General-Purpose Production Systems

Style rules are not simple to write and understand in ITS. They are, however, much simpler to write and understand than general-purpose expert system languages such as OPS-5. ITS rules are specialized for generating interfaces in their syntax for the structure of interaction techniques, in the simple depth-first traversal used to match blocks in an application, and in the strategies supported for resolving conflicts among multiple rules that may match a given block.

The nonprocedural syntax is the most notable feature of how rules specify *units* in an interaction technique. Rules do not say how to transform dialog into specific styles. Instead, rules require the style expert to say only what the final structure should look like. The job of the ITS system is to transform the application expert's abstract tree into that style.

To be usable, the process of executing rules must also be simple. General-purpose expert systems execute rules until no new elements are added to working memory and all rules that match working memory elements have been fired. To simplify the process ITS considers each *unit* only once during a depth-first traversal of the dialog. The rule cycle consists of three steps: (1) select the next *unit* in the depth-first traversal, (2) fire one or more rules that match the selected *unit* according to a conflict resolution strategy described below, and (3) replace the *unit* with the refined subtree created by the rules just fired. Since each *unit* is replaced in the tree with a subtree refined according to the current style, rules often add new *units* that are visited for matching themselves later on. In this way rules control children but not siblings or parents of a selected node.

A typical style file contains different rules for each type of dialog statement. In addition, each statement (such as a *choice*) typically has several variant styles depending on the attributes coded on it by the application expert. *Choices*, for example, may appear differently depending on their *kind*, *purpose*, or *emphasis* attributes. How are conflicts resolved and the appropriate rule selected?

Two kinds of conflict resolution have been implemented in ITS: Execute the best rule that matches the *unit* under consideration, and execute all rules that match it in the order from most general to most specific. These two possibilities allow both for selection among competing alternatives (execute the best rule) and execution of a series of rules that progressively override defaults or make independent decisions (execute all matching rules in sequence).

The scope over which conflict resolution takes place is also more constrained in ITS than in general expert systems. ITS rules are organized into a hierarchy of sets. A set of alternative rules for *choices* might be nested inside a single set. This set itself would be contained in a set of sets for other attributes that rules might match on such as the *emphasis* or *state* of a data value. The organization of the two sets is shown graphically in Figure 25. Consider how a dialog *choice* will be processed by these rules. *Apply = each* tells the top-level set to fire each the two sets nested beneath it. As many rules in the left-hand set as match should be executed, since they make decisions on orthogonal attributes. Only one of the rules in the right-hand set should fire, since each applies to a different type of object.

9.3 Other Application Experience

In addition to EXPO '92 we have focused our application work on workbenches for the application expert. Two dialog workbenches are currently being built. One presents the dialog as a spreadsheet whose rows are dialog statements and columns contain attributes. The dialog is edited by typing into cells of the matrix or by selecting from ranges of values automatically maintained about the dialog being built.

The second workbench is based on two abstractions of the dialog: the control graph of *activations* among *frames* and the dialog tree within each *frame*. A *frame* can be selected from the control graph and its tree drawn in another window.

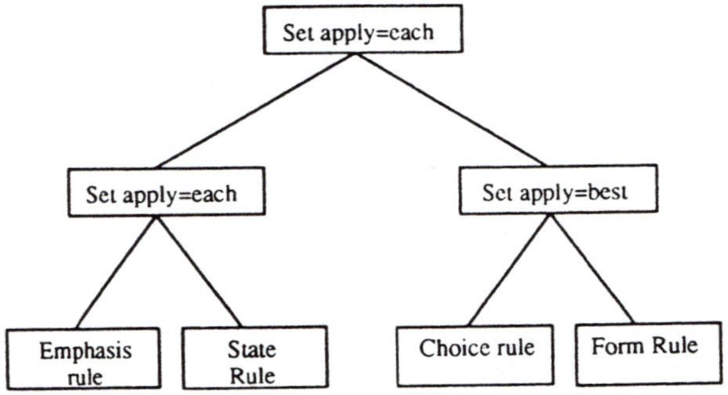

Fig. 25. Tree of sets of style rules.

Details of each object in the *frame* are shown in attached panels as the mouse tracks into nodes in the tree.

The two workbenches are complementary in that the first is a good tool for editing "in-the-small;" the second helps to view the overall structure of the dialog "in-the-large." We hope to combine them soon into an integrated tool.

9.4 Feedback into Improved Rules

We have described the benefits of generating interfaces automatically. Executable style rules greatly reduce the time required to build an interface. Given an excellent style, they also can improve the quality of an interface over that produced by untrained designers. But it is often argued that automatic style will not beat the quality of interfaces individually handcrafted by excellent designers. Is it not a good idea to allow designers to hand-tune automatically generated designs to bring them up to snuff?

While it is tempting to do so, it is a bad idea for two reasons. First, styles need to be tuned when they are missing knowledge that could have caused them to generate a better design in the first place. By manually tuning the output of the rule-base we would miss an opportunity to add the missing knowledge. No one else would benefit from our work.

Second, we ourselves would benefit from our hand-tuning only temporarily. The next time we modified the application, and regenerated its interface, we would have the opportunity to hand-tune the style again. Since maintenance is a fact of life, we need instead to write the new rules that let us use the improved style as often as needed.

Nonetheless, style workbenches do have a role in aiding interface design. Understanding and modifying the behavior of styles can be complex problems. A workbench could help by searching for rules whose behavior might be altered by style changes. The workbench could also provide visual examples of the results produced by firing rules. Direct manipulation changes to these displays, for example, to change the font of a title could be used together with prompts for entering the appropriate conditions of the changed rule.

9.5 Using Applications in Different Styles

We used to talk about writing styles that were truly separate from applications. These generic styles would work with all applications. We now believe that, while possible, this is not always desirable. This shift of view is captured by the shift from speaking about a separation between application and style in favor of a delayed commitment to style.

Styles with rules that match only on the fixed set of dialog statements and attributes (Figure 7 and Figure 8) work equally well when used with any application. These statements and attributes are standard components of all applications and so styles can be secure in matching on them.

Styles with rules that match also on application data types will not work equally well when used with any application. They have specialized knowledge about how to interact with particular types of data. On the other hand, they need not work any less well with other applications than do the generic styles. For an application with data types not matched by the style with application-specific rules, the generic rules will still fire. Rules that select for particular types of application data only improve a style.

9.6 Behavioral Experience

To understand the usability of our tools outside of our immediate group we have concentrated on two activities: teaching classes on interface design using ITS and transferring ITS to external customers. This experience has focused so far on the action and dialog layers, rather than the rule and style program layers. To date, we have taught ITS to roughly 25 people from within and outside IBM and from widely varying backgrounds. These classes are week-long, hands-on working sessions where students arrive with their own design problems and leave with working interfaces.

ITS has also been transferred to one customer external to IBM. A major insurance company has sent several of its programmers and style experts to our course. Subsequently, these programmers, working independently, successfully coded all of the actions and dialog for several prototype applications at their home locations.

CONCLUSIONS

We have described the four layers of the ITS architecture. The action layer implements back-end application functions. The dialog layer defines the content of the user interface, independent of its style. Content specifies the objects included in each frame of the interface, the flow of control among frames, and what actions are associated with each object. The style rule layer defines the presentation and behavior of a family of interaction techniques. Finally, the style program layer implements an extensible toolkit of objects that are composed by the rule layer into complete interaction techniques. Example style programs include routines to format text, render raster images, and arrange units in gridded rectangular layouts.

Our experience has shown that ITS is capable of implementing highly interactive applications. Highly interactive applications respond intimately to user actions based on the current application state. They require a tighter coupling between the application and interface than was provided by early UIMS. ITS provides this coupling by allowing actions to update the data pool on any user event and by reflecting these updates to all views of the changed data automatically.

Our experience has also suggested a number of extensions to both the dialog and rule layers. Many of the rules in the EXPO style, for example, match on the type of *list* or *form* being rendered. Examples include the time data type discussed above, as well as "labeled images" (an image together with descriptive text), "messages" (fields in an email message), and restaurant reservations.

The dialog layer will be extended with a more powerful type language. A type hierarchy will allow new types to be created as extensions of existing ones. The message type, for example, might be defined as a specialization of a flat collection of fields. Structured types will also be supported to help group fields in complex data such as messages and reservations.

The style rule layer will be extended at the same time to support the new type mechanism. The matching algorithm currently recognizes a type only by exact match. To avoid a proliferation of rules specific to single data types, the algorithm will be extended to recognize generalizations of a type if no rules are otherwise found. An instance of the message type, for example, might be matched by a more general rule for a flat collection of fields if no rule is given specifically for messages.

ACKNOWLEDGMENTS

The ITS System has been developed by the combined efforts of our entire group, including Chris Cesar, Tom Cofino, Lauretta Jones, Joe Kesselman, Rich Mushlin, Susan Spraragen, and Jacob Ukelson.

The EXPO '92 visitor information system is being developed jointly with Paco Curbera, Angel Llopis, Javier Martinez, Juan Rojas, and Luis Sopena of IBM's Madrid Scientific Center.

REFERENCES

1. Apple Computer, Inc. *Human Interface Guidelines: The Apple Desktop Interface*. Appie Programmers and Developer's Association. Renton, Wash, 1986.
2. Bennett, W., Boies, S., Gould, J., Greene, S., and Wiecha, C. Transformations on a dialog tree: Rule-based mapping of content to style. In *Proceedings of the ACM SIGGRAPH Symposium on User Interface Software and Technology* (Williamsburg, Va., Nov. 13–15). ACM, New York, 1989, pp. 67–75.
3. Cardelli, L. Building user interfaces by direct manipulation. In *Proceedings of the ACM SIGGRAPH Symposium on User Interface Software* (Banff, Alberta, Canada, Oct. 17–19). ACM. New York, 1988, pp. 152–166.
4. Feiner, S. A grid-based approach to automating display layout. In *Proceedings of Graphics Interface '88* (Edmonton, Canada, June). Morgan Kaufmann, Palo Alto, Calif., 1988, pp. 192–197.
5. Feiner, S. An experiment in the automated creation of pictorial explanations. *IEEE Comput. Graph. Appl. 5*, 11 (1985). 29–37.
6. Foley, J., Gibbs, C., Kim, W., Kovacevic, S. A knowledge-based user interface management system. In *Proceedings of CHI 1988* (Washington, D.C., May 15–19). ACM, New York, 1988, pp. 67–72.
7. Foley, J. Personal communication, 1989.

8. Grudin, J. The case against user interface consistency. *Commun. ACM 32*, 10 (Oct. 1989), 1164–1173.
9. Hartson, H. R., and Hix, D. Human-computer interface development: Concepts and systems for its management. *ACM Comput. Surv. 21*, 1 (1989), 5–92.
10. Hayes, P., Szekely, P., and Lerner, R. Design alternatives for user interface management systems based on experience with COUSIN. In *Proceedings of CHI '85* (San Francisco, April 14–18). ACM, New York, 1985, pp. 169–175.
11. Hudšon, S. Graphical specification of flexible user interface displays. In *Proceedings of the ACM SIGGRAPH Symposium on User Interface Software and Technology* (Williamsburg, Va., Nov. 13–15). ACM, New York, 1989, pp. 105–114.
12. IBM Corp. *Systems Application Architecture, Common User Access Panel Design and User Interaction.* SC26-4351-0. Dec. 1987.
13. Krasner, G., and Pope. S. A cookbook for using the model-view-controller user interface paradigm in Smalltalk-80. *J. Object Oriented Program.* (Aug./Sept. 1988).
14. Linton, M., Vlissides, J., and Calder, P. Composing user interfaces with interviews. *IEEE Comput. 22*, 2 (1989), 8–22.
15. Mackinlay, J. Applying a theory of graphical presentation to the graphic design of user interfaces. In *Proceedings of the ACM SIGGRAPH Symposium on User Interface Software* (Banff, Alberta, Canada. Oct. 17–19). ACM, New York, 1988, pp. 179–189.
16. Open Software Foundation. *OSF/Motif Style Guide, Revision 1.0.* Open Software Foundation, Cambridge, Mass.
17. Palay, A., Hansen, W., Kazar, M., Sherman, M., Wadlow, M., Neuendorffer, T., Stern, Z., Bader, M., and Peters. T. The Andrew toolkit: An overview. Tech. Rep. Carnegie Mellon Univ. Information Technology Center.
18. Pfaff, G., Ed. *User Interface Management Systems.* Springer-Verlag, Berlin, 1985.
19. Schumucker, K. *Object-Oriented Programming for the Macintosh.* Hayden Books, Hasbrouck Heights, N.J., 1986.
20. SEI. Serpent, a user interface management system overview, version 1. Tech. Rep. 89-UG-2. Carnegie Mellon Univ./Software Engineering Institute, Feb. 1989.
21. Sibert, J., Hurley, W., and Bleser, T. An object-oriented user interface management system. In *Proceedings of SIGGRAPH '86* (Dallas, Tex., Aug. 19–22). ACM, New York, 1986, pp. 259–268.
22. Singh, G., and Green, M. Chisel: A system for creating highly interactive screen layouts. In *Proceedings of the ACM SIGGRAPH Symposium on User Interface Software and Technology* (Williamsburg, Va., Nov. 13–15). ACM, New York, 1989, pp. 86–94.
23. Sun Microsystems and ATT. *Open Look, Graphical User Interface Application Style Guidelines.* Addison-Wesley, Reading, Mass.,
24. Szekely, P. Separating the user interface from the functionality of application programs. Ph.D. thesis, Dept. of Computer Science, Carnegie-Mellon Univ., 1988.
25. Vander Zanden, B., and Myers, B. Automatic, look-and-feel independent dialog creation for graphical user interfaces. In *Proceedings of CHI '90* (Seattle, Wash., April 1–5). ACM, New York, 1990, pp. 27–34.
26. Wiecha, C., and Boies, S. Generating user interfaces: Principles and use of ITS style rules. In *Proceedings of the ACM SIGGRAPH Symposium on User Interface Software and Technology* (Snowbird, Utah, October 3–5). ACM, New York, 1990, pp. 21–30.
27. *X Toolkit Intrinsics Programming Manual, The X Window System Series*, vol. 4. O'Reilly and Associates, Sebastobol, Calif., 1989.

GROUPKIT
A Groupware Toolkit for Building Real-Time Conferencing Applications

Mark Roseman
Saul Greenberg

Department of Computer Science
University of Calgary
Calgary, Alberta, Canada T2N 1N4
(403) 220-6015 roseman@cpsc.ucalgary.ca

ABSTRACT
This paper presents our approach to the design of groupware toolkits for real-time work, and how the design is instantiated in our toolkit, GROUPKIT. The design is based on both the technical underpinnings necessary for real-time groupware, and on user-centered features identified by existing CSCW human factors work. We also present three strategies for building GROUPKIT's components. First, an extendible, object-oriented *run-time architecture* supports managing distributed processes and the communication between them. Second, *transparent overlays* offer a convenient method for adding general components to various groupware applications, for example supporting gestures via multiple cursors and annotation via sketching. Third, *open protocols* allow the groupware designer to create a wide range of interface and interaction policies, accommodating group differences in areas such as conference registration and floor control.

KEYWORDS
real-time groupware, toolkit, development tools

INTRODUCTION
Real-time computer conferencing applications have been a major focus of groupware development efforts. Often motivated by CSCW research, we have recently seen the creation of numerous systems, such as shared text editors [23], freehand sketching systems [13,22], structured drawing programs [15], and group support systems [24]. Yet construction of these applications is fraught with difficulties. Besides all the normal problems of building single-user applications, the groupware developer must be concerned with technical issues such as synchronization, concurrency, communications, registration and more. The developer must also understand and incorporate the fundamental CSCW human factors issues identified for effective group work. *Groupware toolkits* are now emerging that address some of these issues. By providing the key components for common groupware needs, the toolkits can reduce development effort, enable rapid prototyping, and increase product quality of multi-user applications.

Of course, there are many potential groupware applications, and no one toolkit could cover all possibilities. In our case, we are concerned with toolkits that assist in constructing real-time *work surfaces* — shared visual environments where one user's actions are made immediately visible to other users [11]. These work surfaces are useful in both face to face and geographically distributed meetings. At its simplest, a work surface is a "What You See Is What I See" (WYSIWIS) space [27] that conference participants use for creating, importing, displaying, and interacting with their artifacts — usually text and graphics of some sort. Thus work surfaces include generic applications such as shared windows, whiteboards, structured drawing systems, and shared editors. But work surfaces can be far more powerful and specialized than that. For example, WYSIWIS could be relaxed so that people could view the work surface from different perspectives; an example would be a competitive card game [26]. Specialized applications could expand the notion of work surface to include tools for voting, brainstorming, organizing ideas, and so on.

This paper discusses our toolkit design philosophy, as embodied in GROUPKIT. We begin by listing a preliminary set of requirements for groupware toolkits, derived from both human factors work and technical innovations in CSCW. The following section presents an overview of GROUPKIT, with a detailed description of its technical architecture. Examples of three strategies for designing toolkit component are then given.

TOOLKIT DESIGN REQUIREMENTS

In this section we propose and defend some of the underlying design requirements we feel are important for a real-time conferencing toolkit. We do not believe this list is complete, nor will every item be necessary for every groupware application. However, we do feel the requirements listed will apply to a wide range of real time conferencing applications, and that they provide a reasonable starting point for discussion. Requirements listed in the first section are human-centered, and those in the second are programmer-centered.

Human-centered design requirements

Supporting multi-user actions over a visual work surface.
We believe there are several general but critical activities that people do over a shared work surface, regardless of its contents. Two of these, gesturing and annotation, are described below.

a) Provide support for gesturing. Researchers at Xerox PARC studied the use of conventional drawing surfaces by small groups [28]. A critical finding was that participants frequently gesture over the drawing surface: to enact ideas, to signal turn-taking, to focus the attention of the group, and to reference objects on the surface. Several recent computer systems emulating group drawing surfaces support gesturing with multiple cursors appearing on all displays [13,2,15], and their usability studies confirm the ubiquity of gesturing. We believe that gesturing can enhance communication in many diverse types of conferences, and should be supported at the toolkit level.

b) Provide support for graphical annotation. The Xerox studies also noticed many instances of annotations made to existing drawings, serving both as gestures (eg underlining text while saying "this one here") and as meta-level notes. Several systems now incorporate graphical annotations of their objects. FREESTYLE users, for example, can verbally and graphically annotate bitmap snapshots; the results can be mailed to others who can then play back the transcript [9]. Both PROOF-MARKS in *vmacs* [18], and the commercial MARKUP application allow comments and markup symbols to be added to written documents. As with gesturing, we believe that real-time group graphical annotation over a work surface is useful in many situations and should be supported by the toolkit.

Structuring group processes during a meeting
Some researchers believe that groupware should impose a social model of interaction on the group. This is an explicit attempt, based on management theory, to provide methods for keeping the group on task, enforcing roles and commitments, and making the group more efficient and productive. There is certainly controversy between those who believe that social protocol should be determined only by the group members (eg [7]), by the software (eg [24]), and somewhere in between (eg [16,14]). We believe that some group process primitives should be provided by the toolkit, accommodating groupware that wishes to control meeting structure. The list below discusses only a few group process requirements.

c) Provide various floor control policies. Floor control or turn-taking mechanisms provide a way to mediate access to shared work items. Lauwers [19] and Greenberg [14] recommend that systems should "support a broad range of [floor control] policies" to suit the users' needs. Systems such as SHAREDX [10] and ASPECTS (from Group Technologies) support a few different policies, while SHARE [14] strives to provide complete flexibility. Floor control can be important in many situations, such as shared screens allowing only serial interaction, or systems following strict interaction models, such as a teacher controlling which students can access the work surface.

d) Support different registration methods. Another part of group process controls who is allowed to join the meeting. For some meetings, anyone may be allowed to join. For others only a select group can participate, or perhaps new users must be "sponsored" by an existing user. Sometimes more spontaneous creation of conferences is desired [17] while other situations require a central facilitator to handle registration [24]. Toolkits should provide the flexibility to support any reasonable registration process.

e) Support latecomers to the conference. A consequence of spontaneous conferences is that all users will not join the conference at the start. Provisions should exist allowing newcomers to join at any time, as well as allowing existing members to leave. Strategies must also be supported to assist the newcomers in "getting up to speed." This may involve simply sending the current conference state to the new user [15] or providing summary information on how the conference has progressed over its lifetime.

Integration with conventional ways of doing work.
Groupware should not impose a barrier between "individual" and "group" ways of working. For example, the system should provide group members with ready access to their individual work, and allow them to import it to a conference. Additionally, all normal communication channels (eg telephone, email) should be readily available.

f) Integrate other forms of communication. Voice communication is an important factor in most conferences [4], and given the ubiquity of telephones, we should assume that a voice channel is available. While many real-time conferencing systems assume a voice channel is present, they do not explicitly support creating voice links. Ideally, there should be a mechanism in the conferencing system to establish voice conferencing — perhaps automatically when a data conference is started. Similar arguments hold for other channels that may be available such as video links.

g) Allow use of single-user applications. Soon, most computer applications may be designed to support multiple users. Unfortunately, most of today's applications support single users only. There are several reasons why single-user programs should be available in multi-user conference settings. Groupware counterparts to single-user programs may not exist; a person's work may be accessible only through a particular application; people are skilled on particular applications. Conference users should be able to view and interact with single-user systems through shared screen or shared windows eg SHARE [12] and SHAREDX [10]. The toolkit should provide shared windows or the means to incorporate other shared window systems.

Programmer-centered design requirements

Technical support of multiple and distributed processes. Most groupware, especially for geographically distributed conferences, will require an architecture where multiple (perhaps distributed) processes can communicate with each other. While most operating systems provide process control and inter-process communication, the programmer's job of initiating, maintaining and tearing down processes and their communication channels is a tedious one. As well, state information about sessions may need to survive beyond the lifetime of a single process or meeting.

h) Provide processes for basic conference management. Groupware applications must oversee all conference management, which include activities such as participant registration, initiation and teardown of meeting processes, communications, and so on. Groupware toolkits have placed much emphasis in providing capabilities for conference management eg LIZA [11], CONFERENCE TOOLKIT [3], and MMCONF [5]. We too believe that the basic run-time infrastructure for conference management must be supplied by the toolkit.

i) Provide a robust communications infrastructure. Any groupware toolkit must provide the communications facilities on which to build conferencing components. At the very least, it must be possible for any process to send messages to specific processes owned by conference users, and it is preferable if a multi-cast facility is available to broadcast a single message to all. Of course, the communications demands will depend heavily on the way the process architecture is determined. The trade-offs between centralized and replicated architectures are well-documented [20], with centralized architectures simplifying concurrency control and replicated architectures being more efficient and robust to machine failure.

j) Provide support for persistent sessions. Often computer conferences will span more than a single session, for example decision support meetings [24]. It is desirable to maintain session state information over the full duration of the conference. There should exist a general mechanism whereby conference objects can be made persistent.

Technical support of a graphics model. A visual work surface will require graphical and textual primitives. Yet shared graphics require several capabilities that are not present in single user systems.

k) Provide primitives to a shared graphics library. Many groupware applications require graphical library primitives for creating multi-user objects such as shared lines, rectangles, circles and text. Greenberg, Roseman et al's discussion of GROUPDRAW [15] describes technical issues of a shared object-oriented drawing package, and provides their design of an abstract drawing object that can be sub-classed into concrete objects such as shared lines [15]. Similarly, the fine-grained editing of simple graphics and text objects in Bier and Freeman's MMM system gives insight into how shared objects should behave [1]. Similar extendible graphics libraries should be provided by toolkits, so that programmers can easily create shared interactive graphical objects on the display.

l) Provide object concurrency control. Many groupware conferencing systems support access to some type of shared object, be it structured graphics or a text buffer. Concurrency control is often needed to mediate access to the object, for example, two people trying to manipulate the same point on a line. In fact several concurrency schemes have already been implemented in groupware toolkits [25,26,11]. Concurrency can be achieved through simple locking, transaction mechanisms, or numerous other schemes [8]. In addition, the degree of concurrency and access to shared objects can be specified through the notion of flexible coupling [6].

m) Separate the view of an object from its underlying representation. Many single-user graphical systems separate the properties of an object from its view on the screen. Patterson argues that this separation is critical in groupware [25,26], and that abstractions should be used to create an interface-independent representation of data. As a consequence, users can have multiple perspectives on the same data.

GROUPKIT

GROUPKIT is a toolkit a programmer can use to develop real-time computer conferencing applications for geographically distributed or face to face meetings. It provides not only support for basic connectivity, but also support for higher-level human factors concerns. As it is still being developed, we have not yet incorporated all our design principles. However components are provided for flexible policy conference registration, communications support, flexible floor control, and gestural and annotative communication.

GROUPKIT is written in C++, on top of the INTERVIEWS toolkit [21]. Applications built using GROUPKIT will run on any machine supporting INTERVIEWS, that is, Unix workstations running X-Windows. GROUPKIT relies on the INTERVIEWS glyph mechanism for its user interface constructs. Glyphs are lightweight objects (similar to widgets in other toolkits) that are composed to make interfaces. The INTERVIEWS Dispatch library — a front end to normal Unix sockets — is used for communications.

Process and Communications Run-Time Support
GROUPKIT's technical infrastructure is based upon a replicated architecture and communications support, as illustrated in Figure 1. The infrastructure supports conference registration and the subsequent communication between processes owned by conference participants. This is comparable to the communications support in RENDEZVOUS [25] and the CONFERENCE TOOLKIT [3]. The remainder of this section describes the infrastructure components by walking through an example scenario.

Registration. Suppose a user wants to create a shared drawing surface, perhaps to discuss a design problem with a remotely located colleague. On initiating the GROUPKIT-based program, the user must first create a conference. This is done through the *Registrar Client*, which provides an interface to the central *Registrar*.

The Registrar allows the user to create, join or leave one or more conferences. The Registrar Client is responsible for implementing particular registration policies, eg deciding who enters the conference, how they do so, and what the interface looks like. While GROUPKIT allows new Clients to be programmed, it also provides a library of predefined Registrar Clients implementing particular registration policies and user interfaces. One novel aspect of this scheme is that it allows group members to use different Registrar Clients to enter a single conference.

The Registrar is an independent process (invisible to the user) that maintains a list of all conferences and their users. One central Registrar would exist at each installation. The Registrar itself is *policy-free*, and leaves it to the Registrar Clients to implement a particular registration policy and to present a reasonable interface to the user. This allows different policies and interfaces to be implemented in order to accommodate group differences.

Conference Initiation. In our scenario, the user has just requested a new conference through the Registrar Client, which in turn passes the request on to the Registrar. Next, the Registrar Client asks the *Coordinator* to create a new *Conference* object. The Coordinator acts as an intermediary between the Registrar Client and application Conferences, permitting multiple conferences (eg sketching and editing applications) to share a common registration mechanism. Its main duties are to create Conferences at the request of the Registrar Client, and to direct requests from the Client to the appropriate Conference.

The Coordinator then spawns a new process which instantiates a Conference object. It is the Conference object that actually runs the specific groupware application. GROUPKIT provides a generic Conference object, which the developer may subclass to provide extra functionality required by the application. In this case, the generic

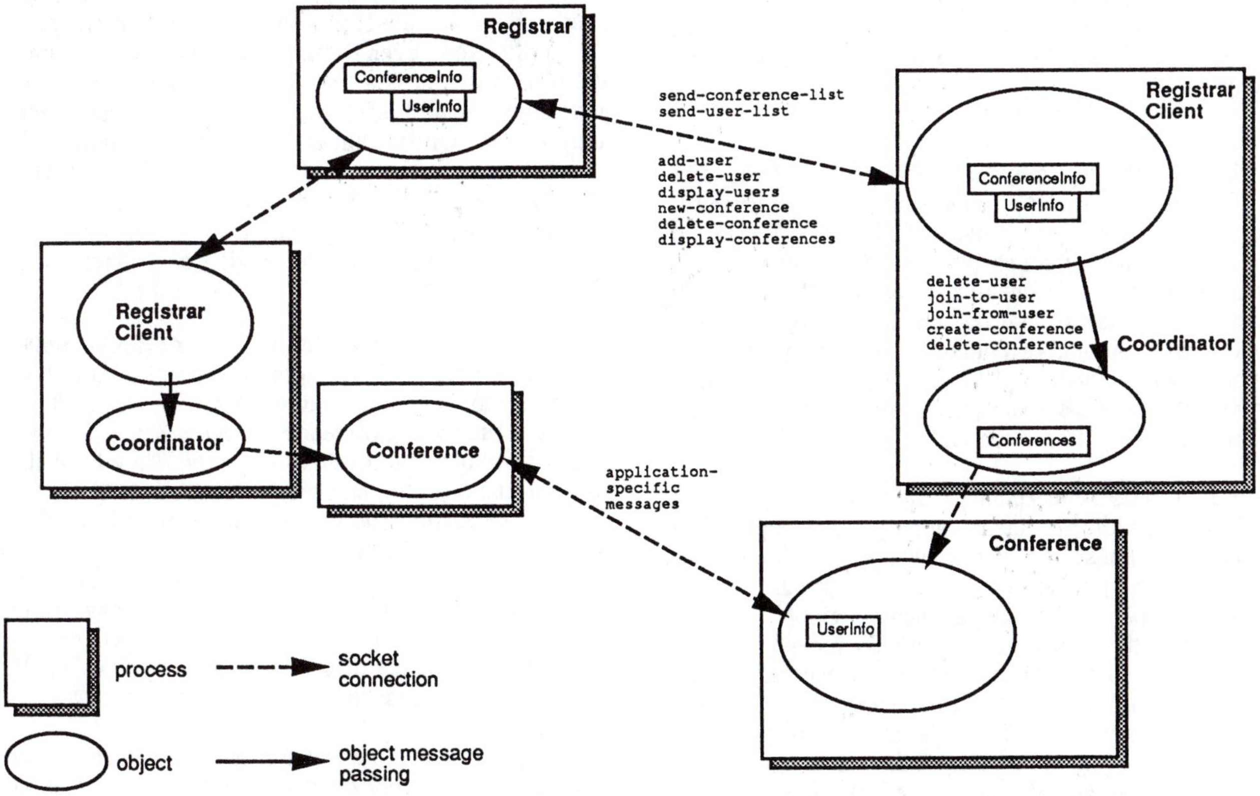

Figure 1. Communications infrastructure of GROUPKIT, showing message passing between objects. Here, objects owned by one user (rightmost Registrar Client, Coordinator, and Conference) interact with objects owned by another user, as well as the central Registrar. Small font text indicates the message passing protocol.

Conference object is used, along with a programmer-defined glyph (graphical interface) supporting a shared drawing surface.

Conference Maintenance. Other users can also create Conference objects. As each Conference locates the meeting participants via the Registrar, communications channels will be opened between all Conference objects. Facilities in the generic Conference are provided for exchanging messages with other user processes.

Communications between distributed processes are maintained by *messaging objects*. The two types of messaging objects ("Writer" and "Reader") provide a convenient method of communicating with processes owned by remote conference participants. These objects, derived from the INTERVIEWS Dispatch library, provide a primitive Remote Procedure Call (RPC) facility. Writer objects specify messages they can send, while Reader objects provide functions to be called when messages are received.

Conference Leaving and Termination. As with initiation, conference leaving and termination is handled through the Registrar Client. If a user wishes to leave the conference without terminating it, their Registrar Client sends the `delete-user` message (Figure 1) to the Registrar. Some Clients may permit explicit conference termination, allowing any user to terminate the conference, while more typically the Registrar Client for the last user to leave will terminate the conference. This is done by sending a `delete-conference` message to the Registrar, which will be rebroadcast to any remaining users' Registrar Clients.

Overlays

GROUPKIT provides components that may be included in any Conference object through an *overlay* strategy. Overlays are transparent "windows" placed on top of the main application graphics shown by the Conference object. Currently, overlay components have been implemented for gestural communication (via multiple cursors over a surface) and annotative communication (via freehand drawing over a surface). The motivation is that such components could be useful for a variety of groupware applications, as mentioned earlier.

Figure 2 provides a conceptual picture of adding an overlay for displaying multiple cursors on an existing application graphic. The transparent cursor overlay is written as an INTERVIEWS glyph that overlays any other glyph. Neither the cursor glyph nor the main application glyph need any knowledge of the other. Input events are received by the cursor glyph, which updates cursors as necessary. The event (eg cursor motion) is then passed to the application glyph, to use as needed. The application glyph need not even know the event went through the cursor glyph. As with single-cursor window systems, event-driven drawing operations are performed normally by the application glyph, based on these events, with the cursor glyph sketching the cursors on top of the normal graphics.

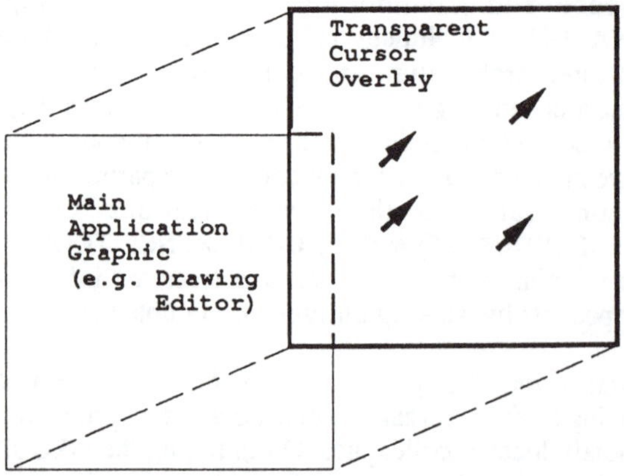

Figure 2. Adding a multiple cursor overlay.

To incorporate the multiple cursor overlay into an application, the programmer instantiates a CursorOverlay which surrounds the application's graphic. Code in the overlay's constructor allows the CursorOverlay to communicate with remote conference objects and inquire about new conference users.

This technique, also used to implement the freehand sketching overlay, seems very promising. Through the composition mechanism, adding overlay components to applications is extremely straightforward. As well, the overlays are kept separate — conceptually and in the code — from the underlying applications. Its strength is that the overlay does not interfere with the underlying graphics of the application, even if those graphics are changing. Because of this, it is a trivial matter to add, for example, annotation capabilities on top of a "live" shared terminal application. Unlike other systems that only allow annotation of screen snapshots (eg MMCONF [5]), the underlying application can be fully active. It is expected that further research will suggest other components that could be transparently added to a variety of conferences.

Open Protocols

One design requirement for GROUPKIT is to provide flexible policies where appropriate, allowing group processes to be structured during a meeting, and to accommodate group differences. *Open protocols* provide a means of implementing this flexibility. They have three components: a controlled object, a controller object, and a protocol describing how the two communicate. The controlled object's behavior does not incorporate any policy determining how its state can be manipulated. Instead, a protocol is defined, and the object will obey any external requests made to it to change its state. The controller is just an external object that implements a particular policy by the requests it sends to the controlled object.

Currently, two components have been implemented using open protocols, a floor control module and a registration module. We concentrate here on the registration module. Figure 3 shows the message protocol (beside the arrows) between the Registrar (the controlled object) and its Clients (the controllers). Here, the Registrar responds to *any* request from its clients, allowing any client to ask the Registrar to create a new conference, or conceivably even to delete any user out of any conference. While this does make it possible to create a "super-user" version of the Client, it also provides the flexibility to create any number of other Clients interfacing to the Registrar, without making any changes to the Registrar itself. As examples of this, the implementations of both a *free* and a *restricted* registration policy are now described. Under a free registration policy, new users may join any existing conference. The implementation here is straightforward. The Registrar Client sends an `add-user` message to the Registrar, which is broadcast to the other Registrar Clients in the selected conference. The Registrar Client also requests the Coordinator to create a new application Conference. The Conference makes connections with the other users, and the interaction proceeds normally.

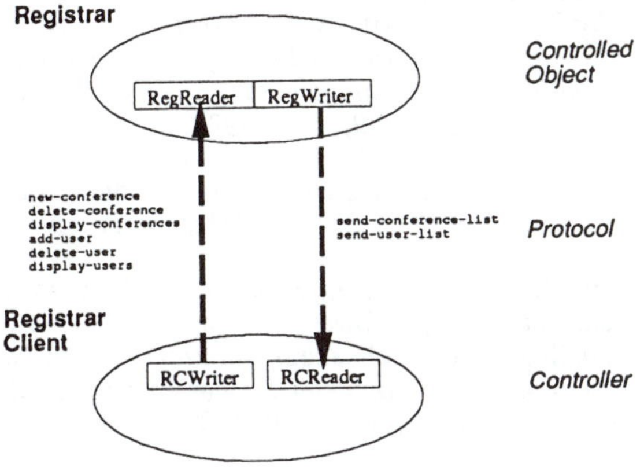

Figure 3. Registration Protocol.

In contrast, a restricted registration policy does not permit new users to join an existing conference unless "sponsored" by an existing conference participant. Here, the Registrar Client again sends an `add-user` message, which is rebroadcast to the other users. At this point, the local Registrar Client does *not* ask the Coordinator to create a new conference. The remote users are asked by their Registrar Clients if the new user should be accepted. A remote user can accept the new user, and sends them a message, prompting the new user to create the conference as before. If rejected (either explicitly or by timeout), the `delete-user` message is sent to the Registrar.

Floor control policies are handled similarly [14]. Each user has a flag, specifying if their actions should affect the conference or not. Any user can examine or change any other user's flag. A preemptive floor control scheme for serial interaction, where a user can immediately seize control from the current floor holder, can be implemented by setting the local flag to `write` and setting all others to `no-write`. The end result is that the local user gains control of the floor until preempted by another user. A ring-passing policy, where the floor may be seized only if it is free (ie the previous floor holder has released it), is implemented by setting the local flag to `write` only if all others are currently set to `no-write`. MMCONF [5] uses a similar strategy for floor control, but manipulates only a single token, thus allowing less flexibility in protocols.

Again, this strategy seems useful in general. By providing a simple protocol to change states, building new policies becomes a simple matter of expressing the policy's semantics in the language of the protocol.

BUILDING AN EXAMPLE APPLICATION

This section describes the steps necessary to build applications using GROUPKIT. The steps include specifying the application-specific graphical presentation and interaction, initializing objects to send and receive application messages, selecting an application Conference object, and initializing a Coordinator object.

As an illustration, we describe the construction of a simple multi-user freehand sketching program using the multiple cursor overlay. The interface is similar to GROUPSKETCH [13]: multiple cursors are always visible, any user can draw at any time, and fine-grained actions are immediately visible on all displays. Note that although GROUPKIT provides a sketching overlay, for illustration we will not use it.

Graphical presentation

The application needs one or more INTERVIEWS glyphs to manage the graphical presentation and user interaction aspects of the interface, as well as any internal data structures. For a freehand sketching application, this involves creating a glyph holding a bitmap, and providing tools (pencil and eraser) that respond to mouse events for changing the bitmap. To incorporate the cursor overlay, the bitmap glyph is "composed within" the cursor glyph.

Designing this part of the sketching application is comparable to designing a single user version of the group application. There are some general conventions that are helpful to follow, such as separating event handling (cause) and the result of events (effect) into different routines. This facilitates use of common routines for local and remote invocations [15].,

Messaging objects

Writer and Reader objects are used to send and receive application-specific messages. The routines in Writer objects are invoked as a result of local actions, for example, transmitting coordinates of a drawn line segment to the other replicated applications. Callbacks in the Reader objects interpret these messages, usually calling routines in the graphical presentation object to handle requests. In the example, the Reader instructs the sketchpad glyph to draw the line specified in the message. The standard objects must be initialized to include the required callbacks.

Coordinator

The Coordinator connects the registration mechanism (via the Registrar Client) to the application Conference objects running as separate processes. Available conference types must be specified to the Coordinator, using the standard X resource mechanisms (ie .XDefaults).

Application Conference

The application Conference maintains communications channels with other distributed applications. In our example, the generic GroupKit conference has sufficient functionality. The main program instantiates this object, and "attaches" to it the bitmap glyph described earlier, so that the glyph can send and receive messages.

The Conference is notified when users join or leave. Routines in the base Conference class manage the low-level socket connections between users. However, other classes may be notified when new users join or leave, to manipulate application data structures maintained for each conference user. For example, the cursor overlay uses this information to add or remove cursors as users join or leave.

FUTURE WORK

The work presented here should be seen as an initial attempt to formalize the design and implementation of general groupware conferencing toolkits. The design requirements emphasize the important abstractions needed in real-time CSCW applications, and provide a basis for generalizing existing application or toolkit features. The three strategies presented — a run-time process and communication architecture, overlays and flexible policies — should be seen as general strategies that can be used to implement certain design features. It is expected that further design principles and strategies will evolve.

GROUPKIT has proven to be a flexible platform for testing our ideas. We have already built prototype drawing programs and shared terminals, and we will be constructing more elaborate and robust applications shortly. Currently, several of the design principles have not yet been embodied in the toolkit. Our immediate plans are to address the concurrency control issues, building a layer of support for generic shared graphical objects, that follow ideas presented in [15]. Ideally, a framework for building domain-specific group graphical editors could be created, drawn from the ideas in Unidraw [29].

Some other work has focussed on blurring the distinction between synchronous and asynchronous groupware, by providing a system that determines the appropriate means of conferencing (synchronous or asynchronous) and makes available various communication channels (text, voice, video). The choices offered the user depend on environmental information (ie who is currently around, what communication channels are available). The registration mechanisms in GROUPKIT provide the flexibility to implement such a scheme.

Groupware toolkits still have a long way to go to catch up to their single-user counterparts. We look forward to the day when all toolkits will incorporate multi-user features, and its interface components (such as control panels and editing widgets) have multi-user capabilities built into them. When that day comes, the artificial distinction between single and multi-user systems will disappear.

Note: GROUPKIT will be available for anonymous ftp by conference time, from the Department of Computer Science, University of Calgary (`cpsc.ucalgary.ca`).

REFERENCES

1. Bier, E.A. and Freeman, S. MMM: A User Interface Architecture for Shared Editors on a Single Screen. In *User Interface Software and Technology (UIST '91)*, Nov. 11–13 1991, pp. 79-86.

2. Bly, S.A. and Minneman, S.L. Commune: A shared drawing surface. In *Proceedings of the Conference on Office Information Systems (COIS '90)*, Apr. 25–27 1990, pp. 184-192.

3. Bonfiglio, A., Malatesa, G., and Tisato, F. Conference Toolkit: A framework for real-time conferencing. In *Proceedings of the 1st European Conference on Computer Supported Cooperative Work (EC-CSCW '89)*, Sept. 1989.

4. Chapanis, A. Interactive human communication. *Scientific American 232*, 3 (1975), 36-42.

5. Crowley, T., Baker, E., Forsdick, H., Milazzo, P., and Tomlinson, R. MMConf: An infrastructure for building shared applications. In *Proceedings of the Conference on Computer-Supported Cooperative Work (CSCW '90)*, Oct. 7–10 1990.

6. Dewan, P. Flexible user interface coupling in collaborative systems. In *Proceedings of the ACM CHI'91 Conference on Human Factors in Computing Systems*, Apr. 27–May 2, 1991, pp. 41-48.

7. Dykstra, E.A. and Carasik, R.P. Structure and support in cooperative environments: The Amsterdam Conversation Environment. *IJMMS 34*, 3 (Mar. 1991), pp. 419–434.

8. Ellis, C.A., Gibbs, S.J., and Rein, G.L. Groupware: Some issues and experiences. *Comm. ACM 34*, 1 (1991).

9. Francik, E., Rudman, S.E., Cooper, D., and Levine, S. Putting innovation to work: Adoption strategies for multimedia communication systems. *Comm. ACM 34*, 12 (Dec. 1991), pp. 37–63.

10. Garfinkel, D., Gust, P., Lemon, M., and Lowder, S., "The SharedX multi-user interface user's guide, version 2.0," , HP Research report, no. STL-TM-89-07, Palo Alto, California, 1989.

11. Gibbs, S.J. LIZA: An Extensible Groupware Toolkit. In *Proceedings of the ACM CHI'89 Conference on Human Factors in Computing Systems*, Apr. 30–May 4 1989, pp. 29-35.

12. Greenberg, S. Sharing views and interactions with single-user applications. In *Proceedings of the Conference on Office Information Systems (COIS '90)*, Apr. 25–27 1990, pp. 227–237.

13. Greenberg, S. and Bohnet, R. GroupSketch: A multi-user sketchpad for geographically-distributed small groups. In *Proc. Graphics Interface (1991).*

14. Greenberg, S. Personalizable groupware: Accomodating individual roles and group differences. In *Proceedings of the 2nd European Conference on Computer Supported Cooperative Work (EC-CSCW '91)*, Sept. 1991.

15. Greenberg, S., Roseman, M., Webster, D., and Bohnet, R. Human and technical factors of distributed group drawing tools. In *Interacting with Computers (Special Edition on CSCW, in press).*

16. Johnson-Lenz, P. and Johnson-Lenz, T. Post-mechanistic groupware primitives: rhythms, boundaries and containers. *IJMMS 34*, 3 (Mar. 1991), pp. 385–418.

17. Kraut, R.E., Egido, C., and Galegher, J. Patterns of contact and communication in scientific research collaborations. In *Intellectual Teamwork: Social Foundations of Cooperative Work.* Lawrence Erlbaum Associates, pp. 149–172, 1990.

18. Lakin, F. Visual languages for cooperation: A performing medium approach to systems for cooperative work. In *Intellectual Teamwork: Social Foundations of Cooperative Work.* Lawrence Erlbaum Associates, pp. 453–488, 1990.

19. Lauwers, J.C. *Collaboration transparency in desktop teleconferencing environments*, Ph.D. dissertation, Technical Report CSL-TR-990-435, Stanford University, Computer Systems Lab, CA, 1990.

20. Lauwers, J.C., Joseph, T.A., Lantz, K.A., and Romanow, A.L. Replicated architectures for shared window systems: A critique. In *Proceedings of the Conference on Office Information Systems (COIS '90)*, Apr. 25–27 1990, pp. 249-260.

21. Linton, M.A., Calder, P.R., Interrante, J.A., Tang, S., and Vlissides, J.M., *InterViews Reference Manual*, Stanford University, Sept. 1991.

22. Minneman, S.L. and Bly, S.A. Managing a trois: A study of a multi-user drawing tool in distributed design work. In *Proceedings of the ACM CHI'91 Conference on Human Factors in Computing Systems*, Apr. 27–May 2 1991, pp. 217-224.

23. Neuwirth, C.M., Kaufer, D.S., Chandhok, R., and Morris, J.H. Issues in the Design of Computer Support for Co-Authoring and Commenting. In *Proc. of the Conference on Computer-Supported Cooperative Work (CSCW '90)*, Oct. 7–10 1990.

24. Nunamaker, J.F., Dennis, A.R., Valacich, J.S., Vogel, D.R., and George, J.F. Electronic meeting systems to support group work. *Communications of the ACM 34*, 7 (July 1991), pp. 40-61.

25. Patterson, J.F., Hill, R.D., Rohall, S.L., and Meeks, W.S. Rendezvous: An architecture for synchronous multi-user applications. In *Proce. of the Conference on Computer-Supported Cooperative Work (CSCW '90)*, Oct. 7–10 1990.

26. Patterson, J.F. Comparing the programming demands of single-user and multi-user applications. In *Proc. User Interface Software and Technology (UIST '91)*, Nov. 11–13 1991, pp. 87-91.

27. Stefik, M., Bobrow, D.G., Foster, G., Lanning, S., and Tatar, D. WYSIWIS revised: Early experiences with multiuser interfaces. *ACM Trans. on Office Information Systems 5*, 2 (1987), pp. 147–167.

28. Tang, J.C. Findings from observational studies of collaborative work. *IJMMS 34*, 2 (1991), pp. 143–160.

29. Vlissides, J.M. and Linton, M.A. Unidraw: A Framework for Building Domain-Specific Graphical Editors. In *Proc. of User Interface Software and Technology*, Oct. 1989.

PART III

Interacting with Computers

In Part I we established the importance of the context in which computer systems are used and looked at examples of the process of system and interface design. Part II examined the design process in detail, stressed the need to ground design in terms of real users and their tasks and work practices, and presented effective methods for doing this and for evaluating the results. We shall now examine in detail individual computer use, which has been a primary focus of research in human-computer interaction.

Here is a puzzle for the reader: Why have we relied overwhelmingly on one sensory modality, the visual modality, for communicating from the computer to users, and a different modality, manual operation, for communicating in the other direction? Could it have been the other way around? Could one modality have sufficed? Why hasn't more use been made of auditory or other sensory modalities?

Since punch cards and paper tape went the way of the dinosaurs, we have used visual display units (VDUs, also called VDTs for visual display terminals, and CRTs for cathode ray tubes, the central element in many of them) to display information produced by the computer, paper for longer-term access to results, and keyboards and mice as input devices of choice. If we set aside taste and smell, we have the three senses of sight, touch, and sound, giving us the potential for three modalities from computer to human and three modalities from human to computer. We've typically only used one each direction. Can we do better than that?!

Computer vision is an active and challenging area within artificial intelligence (AI). In theory, computers could have an eye, or two, or even three! Yet our inability to automate effective general real-time object recognition has relegated computer vision to very specialized applications. On the other hand, video cameras are increasingly used to input and retransmit information that enriches computer use without the need for intelligent intervening processing.

Robotics is another active, challenging AI topic. Will computers reach out and touch us? Controlling in a trustworthy manner mechanical moving parts is difficult, so current uses are primarily manufacturing and applications for users with special needs.

What about the auditory modality? We use it so heavily in human-human communication that its neglect in human-computer interaction is surprising. Once again, part of the reason is that it is hard. Speech recognition, the most desirable exploitation of audition, is another difficult AI frontier. There has been some progress, but adoption of the technology has been slow. There are fewer technical problems in achieving computer-generated speech and sound, but aesthetic challenges remain. Synthetic speech is generally understandable but doesn't sound great. Nonspeech audio of high quality is possible but needs to find significant uses and overcome concerns about noise pollution (we can close our eyes but not our ears).

In Part III we examine these three modalities of sight, touch, and sound. We begin, however, with a review of interaction *styles*, approaches or techniques that may favor one modality or may appear in different modalities. For example, *menu systems* typically appear on displays, yet voice answering systems also make use of auditory menus. *Command languages* have been a common manual interaction style, and also are suitable for speech recognition systems.

Part III therefore begins with an overview reading. Shneiderman (1991) provides a taxonomy of conventional interaction styles and rules governing their use. The interaction styles examined are *menu selection*, *form fill-in*, *command languages*, *natural language interfaces*, and *direct manipulation* or *graphical interfaces*. Shneiderman describes the relative advantages and disadvantages of each. Then, examining each in turn, he provides examples and a checklist of considerations for developers planning to use the style. He concludes by discussing blends of interaction styles. A more comprehensive treatment of this material appears in Shneiderman (1992).

Chapter 6 explores the visual modality, paying particular attention to the use of graphic design, information display, color, three-dimensional display, and animation. Chapter 7 explores ongoing research and development into the manual or haptic channel, emphasizing the role of touch (as in touchscreens), gesture (as a rich vehicle for communication), and marking (as in the recent emergence of pen-based computing). Chapter 8 explores the auditory modality, including nonspeech audio, as well as recent developments in speech recognition and its perennial sidekick, natural language understanding: For speech recognition to go beyond simple commands or dictation, the computer must be able to process what is being said, yet another HCI challenge to AI.

Each chapter looks at the modality from three points of view. We examine the human perceptual or motor system that uses the channel, specifically, visual perception, manual motor skills, and auditory perception. We also look at the kinds of devices available for mediating human-computer dialogues that ideally should exploit the properties and characteristics of these human sensorimotor systems. In the case of the visual system, we additionally review some of the insights that the field of graphic design offers to the structuring of effective human-computer communication. And finally, we examine interaction styles particularly appropriate for each modality.

One other trend is worth mentioning, and that is the coordinated use of multiple sensory modalities in systems that transact in what is commonly known as *multimedia*. A *multimedia* computer system is one that transacts or interacts in more than one medium, i.e., carriers of information such as text, audio, still graphics, animation, and video. It is important to distinguish this concept from that of a ***multimodal*** system, one that supports multiple styles of interaction using different sensory modalities, for example, voice and gesture. The two typically occur together, and we use one term or the other depending upon whether our focus is on the means by which information is conveyed or on the style of interaction.

Multimedia is hot. Both ACM and IEEE have recently begun journals and conferences on the topic. New and established companies are rushing to lay claim to territory they only vaguely understand. We shall return to multimedia in Chapter 13 and with the Freestyle system in Case C. Several papers in Chapters 6, 7, and 8 hint at the possibilities. An early classic multimodal interactive system is Put That There (Bolt, 1980, 1984; Schmandt and Hulteen, 1982; Schmandt, 1984 video). Part II of Blattner and Dannenberg (1992) and Cohen (1992) are good introductions to multimodal interaction, a topic we shall discuss in Chapters 7 and 8.

REFERENCES

Note: A ● before a reference indicates a reading.

Blattner, M., and Dannenberg, R. (Eds.) (1992). *Multimedia Interface Design.* ACM.

Bolt, R. (1980). "Put-That-There": Voice and Gesture at the Graphics Interface. *Computer Graphics* 14(3), 262–270.

Bolt, R. (1984). *The Human Interface: Where People and Computers Meet.* Lifetime Learning Publications.

Cohen, P. (1992). The Role of Natural Language in a Multimodal Interface. *Proc. UIST '92,* ACM, 143–149.

Schmandt, C., and Hulteen, E. (1982). The Intelligent Voice Interactive Interface. *Proc. Conference on Human Factors in Computer Systems,* ACM, 363–366.

● Shneiderman, B. (1991). Taxonomy and Rule Base for the Selection of Interaction Styles. In Shackel, B., and Richardson, S. (Eds.), *Human Factors for Informatics Usability,* Cambridge University Press, 325–342.

Shneiderman, B. (1992). *Designing the User Interface: Strategies for Effective Human-Computer Interaction.* Second Edition. Addison-Wesley.

VIDEO

Schmandt, C. (1984). Put That There. *ACM SIGGRAPH Video Review* 13.

A TAXONOMY AND RULE BASE FOR THE SELECTION OF INTERACTION STYLES

BEN SHNEIDERMAN

1. Introduction

Recent empirical research has shed much light on the design of interactive systems. As researchers, we now understand more precisely the strengths and weaknesses of system variants. As system developers we now have substantially improved evaluation techniques. Academic and industrial researchers have begun to develop predictive and descriptive theories, while thoughtful professionals have compiled useful guidelines documents for practitioners. In spite of all this progress, designers who confront a new application are often reduced to mimicking familiar examples or extrapolating intuitively from experience.

This attempt at a set of design guidelines is intended to aid designers in choosing among the primary interaction styles and in refining their design to suit specific user communities performing specific tasks. The first step is an understanding of the five primary interaction styles: menu selection, form fill-in, command language, natural language, and direct manipulation. Variants and combinations are possible, but these basic styles are a useful taxonomy (Shneiderman, 1987). The second step is an understanding of the factors that guide designers in choosing among the five primary interaction styles. A formal decision procedure would be attractive, but for the moment we must rely on informal rules which although they often stem from extrapolations of experiments need to be validated and refined.

2. Taxonomy of interaction styles

There are many ways of interacting with a computer. The variations result from differences in tasks, computer concepts, and interface devices. The five primary interaction styles described in this paper could each accomplish the full range of interactions, although some would be awkward in certain situations (see Table 1 for an overview). The remainder of this section reviews each style, shows an example, and offers guidelines for improving the design.

Menu selection
- Advantages: shortens training, reduces keystrokes, structures decision-making, permits use of dialog management tools, easy to support error handling
- Disadvantages: danger of many menus, may slow frequent users, requires screen space, requires rapid display rate

Form fill-in
- Advantages: simplifies data entry, requires modest training, assistance is convenient, shows context for activity, permits use of form management tools
- Disadvantages: consumes screen space, requires typing skills

Command language
- Advantages: flexibility, supports user initiative, appeals to 'power' users, potentially rapid for complex tasks, supports macro capability
- Disadvantages: requires substantial training and memorisation, difficult to retain, poor error handling

Natural language
- Advantages: relieves burden of learning syntax
- Disadvantages: requires clarification dialog, may require more keystrokes, may not show context, unpredictable

Direct manipulation
- Advantages: visually presents task, easy to learn, easy to retain, errors can be avoided, encourages exploration, high subjective satisfaction
- Disadvantages: may require graphics display/pointing devices, more programming effort until tools improve, may be hard to record history or write macros

Table 1: Overview of interaction styles with their advantages and disadvantages.

2.1 *Menu selection*

In menu selection systems the computer displays a list of items from which the user selects. If the items are meaningful to the user then menu selection can be a rapid, accurate, and satisfactory approach. If the items are hard to understand or appear similar to each other, users can become confused and make errors. Menu selection is advantageous because it decomposes a complex interaction into a series of smaller steps and because it provides structure for decision-making. On the other hand this same decomposition process can be too rigid for some users and it may slow down the knowledgeable frequent user.

For many situations menu selection can substantially reduce the number of keystrokes necessary and thereby reduce error rates and performance times. Menu selection mechanisms can be the familiar numbered menus, lettered menus, mnemonic lettered menus, or unlabelled menus. Unlabelled menus operate by movement of a highlight bar over the items, under the control of arrow keys, a mouse, a joystick, a graphics tablet, etc. Table 2 provides a brief set of guidelines while Smith and Mosier (1987) offer extensive guidelines for menu selection systems. Shneiderman (1987) reviews empirical studies and suggests practical design rules.

- Use task semantics to organise menus (single, linear sequence, tree structure, acyclic and cyclic networks)
- Prefer broad/shallow trees
- Show position by graphics, numbers, or titles
- Items become titles for trees
- Meaningful groupings of items
- Meaningful sequencing of items
- Brief items, begin with keyword
- Consistent grammar, layout, terminology
- Type-ahead, jump-ahead, or other short-cuts
- Jumps to previous and main menu
- Consider: online help, novel selection mechanisms, response time, display rate, screen size

Table 2: Menu selection guidelines.

Figure 1 is.an example of menu selection as applied to airline reservation systems when the users are air travellers making reservations from a hotel or airport lobby. This hypothetical example for Boswash Airlines will be used to illustrate all five interaction styles. Each version is merely a sketch for a system, meant to encourage discussion and to emphasize differences. A full system might have more instructional material, online help, a mixture of interaction styles for different parts of the task, special hardware, greater provision for reversibility of action, more informative feedback, etc.

In Figure 1 the user is confronted with a rigid sequence of menus that force the user to make decisions in a system-defined order. Users who would be willing to change their departure time or date to find a cheaper flight would become frustrated with this design. The numbered menus do help structure the users' work, but more knowledgeable users might be annoyed that items such as the date were broken into

```
          BOSWASH AIRLINES RESERVATIONS MENU SYSTEM

What month do you want to take your trip?

1  January      4  April      7  July        10  October
2  February     5  May        8  August      11  November
3  March        6  June       9  September   12  December

Type the number of your choice and press RETURN: __
```

---------- New screen ----------

```
Type the date in the month you want to take your trip: __
```

---------- New screen ----------

```
What is your departure city?

1  Albany, NY                  5  Philadelphia, PA
2  Boston, MA                  6  Washington, DC
3  Hartford, CT                7  White Plains, NY
4  New York, La Guardia

Type the number of your choice and press RETURN: __
```

---------- New screen ----------

```
What is your arrival city?

1  Albany, NY                  5  Philadelphia, PA
2  Boston, MA                  6  Washington, DC
3  Hartford, CT                7  White Plains, NY
4  New York, La Guardia

Type the number of your choice and press RETURN: __
```

---------- New screen ----------

```
What time of day do you wish to take your trip?

1      7:00 AM  to  10:30 AM
2     10:01 AM  to   3:00 PM
3      3:01 PM  to   6:00 PM
4      6:01 PM  to  10:00 PM

Type the number of your choice and press RETURN: __
```

Figure 1: Menu selection approach, with occasional form fill-in for fields such as names, phone numbers or charge numbers.

two separate items. They might prefer a form fill-in approach. Also the layout, wording of items, instructions, and error handling might all be improved. On the other hand, some form of menu selection system is likely to be the most successful in a public waiting room environment where computer and typing skills are not uniformly high.

2.2 *Form fill-in*
In a form fill-in interaction the users' main task is to provide data in labelled fields clustered on one or more screens. Sometimes the data items are merely binary choices (Yes/No or Male/Female) or selections from short lists (days of the week or a set of colours), but they can also be taken from large domains (personal names or chemical formulae) or may be essentially unbounded (explanatory paragraphs or meteorological data). Of course, it is possible to replace form fill-in with a series of menu choices, but this strategy can become extremely tedious. Keyboards or other input devices are effective ways of inputting lengthy data fields. The keyboard may be seen as a continuously displayed menu that permits rapid selection using a well-learned skill. Increasingly data entry is handled more automatically as is done in reading magnetic stripes on charge cards to get names and account numbers or grocery packages with bar codes.

Form fill-in requires that users learn to use the keyboard with tab, cursor control, and backspace keys. If the users are competent keyboard operators and field labels are meaningful then form fill-in is an effective approach that produces a quite rapid rate of data entry, a moderate level of errors, and good user satisfaction. There has been very little research in the design of form fill-in systems but there are several sources of design guidelines (Galitz, 1980, 1981; Smith and Mosier, 1987) (see also Table 3 for a brief list).

The Boswash Airlines example as a form fill-in (Figure 2) demonstrates the increased density of information that can be supplied on a single screen when compared with menu selection. Presumably the user can press arrow or tab keys to move around the form and perform error correction. The keyboard usage might reduce the number of potential users when compared to menu selection, but might increase the willingness of more knowledgeable and frequent users to work with the system.

Research issues include very basic questions of appropriate layout, justification, spacing, grouping, sequencing, handling of optional fields, and online help. A combination of form fill-in with menu selection might help the novice user. For example, the list of departure cities might be made available when the cursor is moved to that field; then the user could select a city instead of typing it and it would be displayed in the field. A useful conjecture, that needs validation, is that as user experience increases, the density of fields on a single screen can be increased while the field labels can be shortened.

- Meaningful title
- Comprehensible instructions
- Logical grouping and sequencing of fields
- Visually appealing layout of the form
- Familiar field labels
- Consistent terminology and abbreviations
- Visible space and boundaries for data entry fields
- Convenient cursor movement
- Error correction for individual characters and entire fields
- Error messages for unacceptable values
- Optional fields should be marked
- Explanatory messages for fields

Table 3: Form fill-in guidelines

```
                 BOSWASH AIRLINES RESERVATIONS FORM

 Type the information required and press RETURN:

 Departure date: __/__/__  (09/08/87 indicates September 8, 1987)
 Departure city: ____________
   Arrival city: ____________
 Departure time: __:__ _    (8:30 P indicates 8:30 in the evening)
Number of seats: _
      Last Name: ____________         First Name: ____________
   Phone Number: (___) ___-____
    Charge Card: __  (MC=MasterCard, AE=American Express, or VI=Visa)
  Charge Number: ____ ____ ____ __
```

Figure 2: Form fill-in provides guidance, but requires knowledge of field labels, permissible values, and typing.

2.3 *Command language*
Knowledgeable frequent users do not want to be distracted by having to locate an item in a list, nor do they want to have to view and move a cursor over a form. They can manipulate the possibilities in their mind and want concise notations for issuing commands with modest informative feedback. These 'power' users want to be able to put several commands on a single line and even create new commands that encapsulate the work of several frequently used command sequences. The learning time may be

days or weeks, but since usage is frequent the benefits of concision are great.

Often command languages emerge from familiar notations such as mathematics, boolean logic, or music, but many command languages have been created to deal with novel task domains such as text and string manipulation, hotel reservations, or information retrieval. There has been much research in command language design for text editors and other applications. Consistency in structure, meaningfulness, orderly abbreviations, small number of commands, and congruent pairs of commands have been shown to be important determinants of rapid learning, rapid use, low error rates, high satisfaction, and easy retention over time (see Table 4 for a brief set of guidelines).

- Create explicit model of objects and actions
- Choose meaningful, specific, distinctive names
- Try for hierarchical structure
- Provide consistent structure
  (hierarchy, argument order, action-object)
- Support consistent abbreviation rules
  (prefer truncation to one letter)
- Offer frequent users the capability to create macros
- Consider command menus on high-speed displays
- Limit number of commands and ways of accomplishing a task

Table 4: Command language guidelines.

Airlines reservations systems used by travel agents and airlines employees use a very concise and cryptic command language strategy. The Boswash Airlines command language (Figure 3) is modelled after the American Airlines SABRE system that has been in use for approximately 25 years. The information is packed in a coded form without delimiters and the feedback is also quite dense, but these are advantages to the frequent user.

```
BOSWASH AIRLINES RESERVATIONS COMMAND SYSTEM

READY FOR COMMANDS:  A08SEPDCALGA0830

  Command code:    Date:             Departure/      Time:
  A=Availability   Two digit date    Arrival:        Four digits
  C=Confirm        Three letter      Three letter
  D=Delete         month             airport codes
  U=Update

  Computer Response:

DCA  LGA  08  SEP
BA   412    0800   0859     FY   0  727
NY   854    0830   0952     K    0  DC9
BA   414    0900   1000     FY   0  727
QF   018    0900   1044     Y    1  737

  User's command to indicate Need for 2 seats on flight BA 414:

N2BA414

  Computer response:

BA   414    0900   1000     FY   0  727

  User's command to indicate name, phone number, and charge card:

SHNEIDERMAN,BEN/202-555-8767/MC524298785656
```

Figure 3: Command language style requires special knowledge of fields and permissible field values. Command language style requires few keystrokes but potentially substantial training.

2.4 *Natural language*

Many computer scientists and computer users propose that the "ultimately desirable" way of using a computer is through natural language interaction. They argue that people already know their own natural language and therefore learning to use the computer would be simplified if the computer accepted natural language input. This vision has propelled many researchers over the years as they tried to make natural language interaction systems for programming, database retrieval, or expert systems usage. There are commercial products such as INTELLECT (Artificial Intelligence Corporation) or Q & A (Symantec) but the success could only be considered to be modest. Relieving the user of the burdens of syntax is only a small part of the problem in using a computer and is of benefit only to novice and intermittent users. The much more complex part is understanding the computer concepts and the task domain. Relief from syntactic details does not ensure that the users will know that files must be saved before quitting or that stock market purchases must be in blocks of 100 shares.

Furthermore, natural language interaction systems constantly confront the user with the problem of uncertainty about whether a particular input will be acceptable to the machine. This inhibits planning ahead since users must always be ready to engage in clarification dialogue. Improved designs will mitigate this problem and speech input might reduce the penalty of typing, but the users will still be struggling to discover the syntactic and semantic scope of the system. Therefore, this author is sceptical that natural language interaction will become widely used. The reader should be cautioned that there are still many people who hold a more optimistic view. Natural language generation and natural language parsing of textual databases are likely to be more successful applications of the technology of computational linguistics. Finally, the special case of interactive fiction and adventure games should be cited as a highly successful application of natural language interaction. The success stems from the fact that in this situation part of the challenge and fun is to discover the syntactic and semantic bounds of the program. Table 5 summarizes some of the issues concerning natural language interaction.

- Reducing syntactic load is not enough
- Computer and task semantics should be represented
  predicate calculus, boolean algebra, set theory, normalisation theory, database entities and values, permissible operations and constraints
- Make syntactic and semantic scopes visible
- Therefore, NLI might work best for:
  - Users who are knowledgeable about task domain
  - Intermittent users who cannot retain syntax
  - Users with moderate computer skills
  - Good typists (until speech I/O improves)

Table 5: Natural language interaction guidelines.

The scenario for Boswash Airlines (Figure 4) is meant to be positive and attractive. It is not clear that such a system could be built or that it would be sufficiently successful to be commercially viable. It might be improved by more instructional information and some display of the previously made decisions.

2.5 *Direct manipulation*

The first four interaction styles emerged from a 'teletype mentality' or at best a text-oriented view of the task. However, many designers are breaking away from the constraints of teletype and keyboard designs and employing screen-oriented, form-oriented, visual and graphic approaches with pointing devices such as arrow keys, a

BOSWASH AIRLINES RESERVATIONS SERVICE

WHAT DAY DO YOU WANT TO TRAVEL?

September 8, 1987.

WHERE DO YOU WANT TO FLY FROM?

I want to fly from New York.

ASSUMING YOU MEAN LAGUARDIA AIRPORT IN NEW YORK CITY.
IS THIS CORRECT?

Yes.

WHERE DO YOU WANT TO FLY TO?

Boston.

WHAT TIME DO YOU WANT TO TRAVEL?

Around nine in the morning.

ASSUMING YOU MEAN 9:00 AM THEN THERE IS A FLIGHT:
BOSWASH AIRLINES 414,
DEPARTS LAGUARDIA AT 9:00 AM AND ARRIVES BOSTON AT 10:00 AM.
HOW MANY SEATS DO YOU WANT?

One seat, no smoking, on the aisle.

RESERVATION CONFIRMED.

Figure 4: Natural language style could work well in this example because the users are familiar with airline terminology and concepts. However, it requires substantial user input, clarification of possibly ambiguous phrases, and may cause difficulty in situations when unfamiliar terms are used. Also, the users may be uncertain as to what the scope of the semantics and syntax are.

mouse, touchscreens, or a graphics tablet. These new designs often depend on bit-mapped high resolution displays, but the concepts of direct manipulation can be applied with simple text screens and a simple pointing device.

The key to direct manipulation design is to create a visual representation of the 'world of action' that includes selectable displays of the objects and actions of interest. Then with pointing, zooming, and panning the user can rapidly perform operations, see the results immediately and reverse operations if necessary. These ideas have been applied in the Xerox STAR, Apple Macintosh, videogames, many word processors, and other applications (Shneiderman, 1983, 1987). The benefits include relatively rapid learning with high retention over time and high user satisfaction. Errors can often be prevented because the representation shows the users the impossibility of performing a task and because typographic errors are eliminated when the user selects from a set of displayed objects. Exploration is often encouraged in direct manipulation environments, especially when reversibility of actions is ensured. There are disadvantages in current direct manipulation designs. It is often difficult to create programs and recording the history of a session can be troublesome.

Developing direct manipulation systems is difficult with current software tools, but improvements are expected. There is some concern also for visually impaired users. For some tasks, frequent users may prefer command language approaches (unseen manipulation) because they prefer not to be distracted by having to locate objects and actions on the screen and then select them. The definition of direct manipulation with some of the benefits and concerns is in Table 6.

- Create visual representation of the 'world of action'
  - Objects and Actions are shown
  - Tap analogical reasoning
- Rapid, incremental, and reversible actions
- Replace typing with pointing/selecting
- Make results of actions immediately visible

Benefits

Control/display compatibility
Less syntax reduces error rates
Faster learning and higher retention
Encourages exploration

Concerns

Increased system resources, possibly
Some actions may be cumbersome
Macro techniques are often weak
History/tracing may be difficult
Visually impaired have more difficulty

Table 6: Direct manipulation guidelines with benefits and concerns.

The Boswash Airlines example (Figures 5a–e) shows a form that provides the context for the decision process. Users can touch a field to begin the flight selection process. Then with the form still on the screen, they might be presented with a map showing departure cities. After selecting the departure city the screen would show a map with arrival cities accessible from the selected departure city. Then to choose the date, the calendar provides familiar context, avoids the questions of data entry format, and can be very rapid. Finally, the results of each selection are displayed on the form allowing continuous visibility of status and an opportunity to make changes.

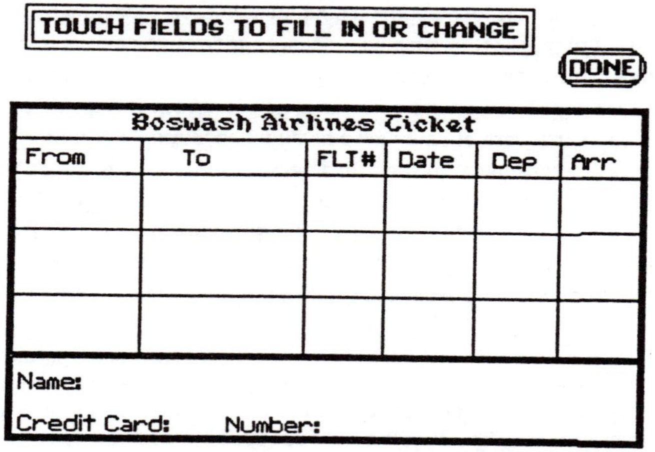

Figure 5a: Form to be filled. The user has some flexibility in order.

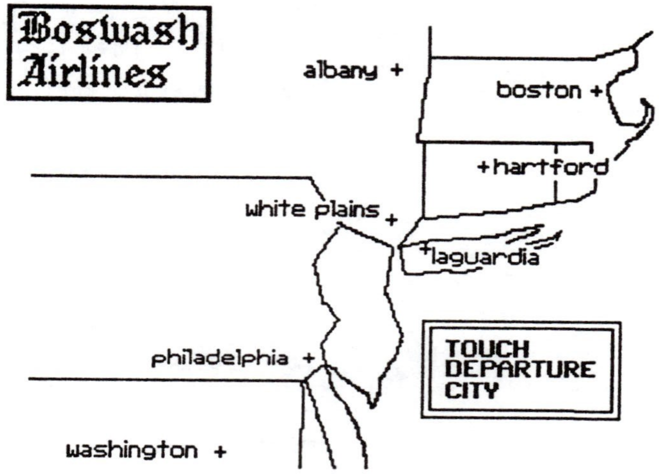

Figure 5b: Map to select departure city shows geographic relationships.

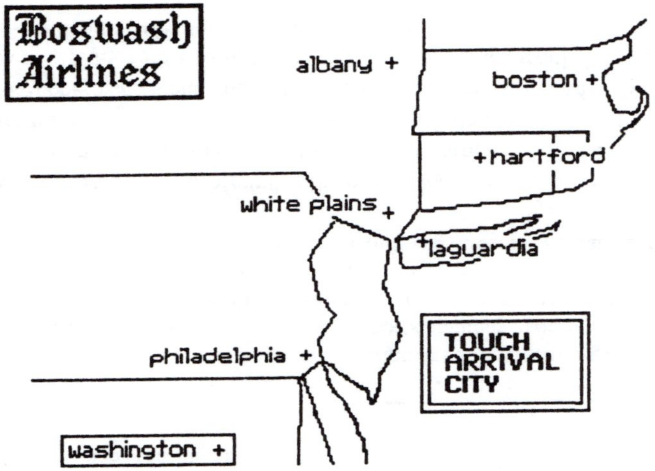

Figure 5c: Map to select arrival city.

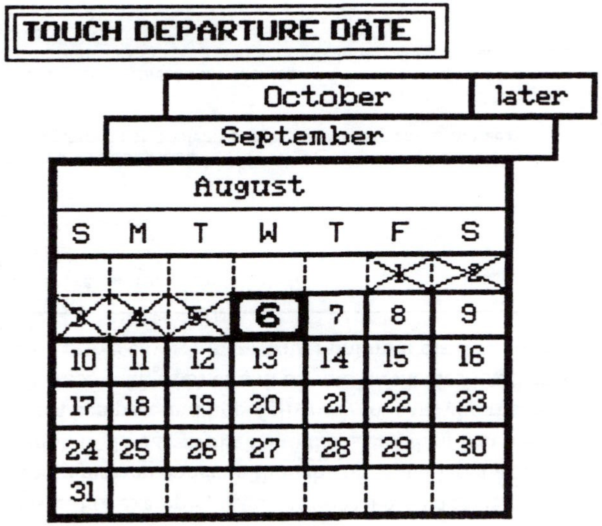

Figure 5d: Calendar to select date with indications of past (crossed out), current (boxed in and made bold), and future dates.

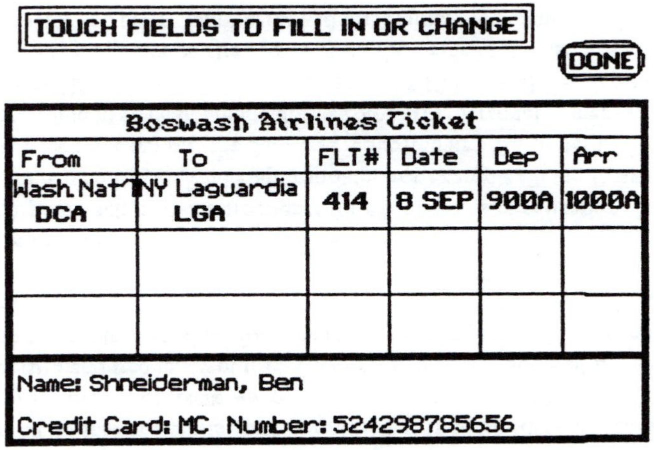

Figure 5e: Form as it looks filled in with cities, times, and date. Name and credit card number are supplied by simply 'dipping' card in reader.

3. Choosing an interaction style

Like good cooking, good user interface design is a blend of measurable aspects (calorie counts, fat percentages, vitamin levels) with subjective issues (smell, texture, colour, taste) and stylistic variations (Szechuan, French, Northern Italian) plus contemporary fashion (nouvelle cuisine, par-boiled vegetables, rare meat). Designers absorb each problem situation thoroughly, then apply reason and intuition combined with experience to produce a solution. Some designers favour menu selection or command language for all situations because they are familiar with the strategies for design and implementation. In other cases the availability of form management software may sway designers to depend heavily on this approach.

As a design field, human-computer interaction is moving beyond depending only on the intuition of designers; empirical evidence is accumulating to guide designers. Still interface design is a new field and much work remains to be done before reliable designs for multiple situations are available.

3.1 *Factors influencing choices*

What follows is the author's attempt to suggest rules for designers to follow in selecting appropriate interaction styles. The rules are presented in an informal rule-based notation that is similar to what is used in expert systems. Much work remains to refine these rules. Undoubtedly there are exceptions, missing criteria, or simply poor decisions. However, this first attempt is meant to be compact, be narrowly focused, and therefore to provide a basis for discussion and improvement.

Table 7 lists some of the aspects of the task domain that influence the selection of interaction style. For example, if the task has a high degree of data entry, then form fill-in is strongly recommended, although command language can be used. If a familiar notation is already available to the users, then that notation should be converted into a compact and hopefully easy to learn command language. If exploration is important, as in circuit or automobile design, then direct manipulation can provide a flexible environment with minimum distraction from the task.

```
IF high degree of data entry
==> ff | cl

IF paper form exists
==> ff

IF familiar notation exists
   (e.g., arithmetic or boolean expressions, chemical formulae)
==> cl

IF natural visual representation exists
| modest number of objects and actions can represent the task domain
==> dm

IF multiple decisions are required
| selection from a large unfamiliar state space
==> ms | dm | cl

IF poor keyboard skills
==> ms | dm | (nl with speech input)

IF exploration and intuition are important goals
==> dm
```

Table 7: Task factors are an important determinant of interaction styles. This informal rule based representation expresses the author's opinions in design situations; there will undoubtedly be exceptions and refinements. The notation uses ==> to mean *then*, & for *and*, and | for *or*. The interaction styles are menu selection (ms), form fill-in (ff), command language (cl), natural language (nl), and direct manipulation (dm).

User skill level has a profound influence on the selection of an interaction style (Table 8). With novices, menu selection or some form of direct manipulation present familiar words or visual representations of the task domain. These styles require limited keyboard skills and computer knowledge. More knowledgeable users can work more rapidly with a form fill-in approach. Knowledgeable intermittent users can work with any style. As frequency of use and proficiency increases, users will

```
IF novice
==> ms | dm

IF modest knowledge of task domain with some computer skills
==> ms | dm | ff

IF intermittent knowledgeable
==> ms | dm | ff
 | (cl with online help or pocket guide)
 | nl

IF frequent user
==> (cl with macros)
 | (ms with type-ahead)
 | (dm with adequate shortcuts)
 | (ff with dense display)
```

Table 8: User skill levels are a key determinant of interaction style. These informal rules capture some of the possible combinations. Undoubtedly there are exceptions or a more thoughtful way of forming the rules.

seek more rapid and productive styles with less to look at on the screen. Expert users expect short response time and macro facilities to encapsulate frequent sequences of actions into a single command.

In addition to the interaction style, there are a host of variables that have to be adjusted as a function of the users' knowledge and frequency of use (Table 9). For example, novices need meaningful labels, while knowledgeable intermittent users prefer abbreviations so that more information can be shown in a single display. Expert frequent users may prefer to eliminate some labels and use concise codes, thereby speeding up screen scanning and permitting still denser displays. Similarly, the desire for informative feedback when actions are taken generally decreases with increased expertise and frequency of use. These rules describe some of the design features that vary with the users' profile. There are certainly other features and exceptions to these rules.

3.2 *Blending interaction styles*

The five primary interaction styles are meant for exposition and education. In real systems, designers blend styles where appropriate. For example, in the Boswash Airlines menu selection example, the date was requested as a fill-in item, because menu selection would have been preposterous. Similarly, personal names are usually handled as a form fill-in item. For a short list, say 2 to 12 items, if the display rate is reasonably fast, a menu selection strategy is often the best. As the list gets longer the designer must weigh the users' familiarity with the items, the potential and

IF novice ==> high density of meaningful labels
& high density of informative feedback
& slower pace
& introductory tutorial/demo
& limited subset of actions and functionality

IF knowledgeable intermittent ==> modest use of labels
& modest use of informative feedback
& moderate pace
& online help to explain objects and actions
& chance to move up to more powerful actions, but protection danger

IF frequent user (knowledgeable about task/computer/syntax) ==> short, sparse, or no labels
& short, sparse, or no informative feedback
& faster pace
& online reference with elaborate search mechanisms
& abbreviations, shortcuts, user-defined macros, with access to system internals

Table 9: User skill levels are a key factor in determining a variety of aspects of the interaction design. These rules are an informal representation of the author's opinions that will undoubtedly have exceptions and will need to be refined. It is meant as a first attempt to provoke discussion.

seriousness of an error, the speed of interaction required, and the length of the items. All but the final criteria are difficult to assess quantitatively, leaving the designer with the responsibility for making a tough judgment.

A few versions might be built and subjected to empirical testing. Sometimes a blend of interaction styles can help resolve the problem. For example, maybe the user is presented with a form fill-in for the departure and arrival cities. Those who wish to can type in the city name or the short three letter airport code if they know it. Alternatively, the placement of the cursor in the field may generate a pop-up window with a menu of cities that can be selected by pointing (mouse or arrow keys). Then the selected city name is automatically displayed in the form. Form fill-in can be nicely supplemented by pop-up menus for less knowledgeable users.

Similarly, command language systems can be supplemented by a form fill-in or menu selection strategy for less knowledgeable users. For example, many text editors (e.g., Wordstar or Finalword) start with a command language approach that has a hierarchical structure. After pressing the first key for the first part of the command, the user can immediately type more characters to complete the command, but if they are less familiar with the commands a menu will appear automatically after 4 – 6 seconds.

Some users prefer to make the menus visible all the time, others prevent them from ever appearing. A quite similar approach, that might be called command menus, has been implemented in LOTUS 1-2-3. The top line of the screen shows a menu with items that are selected by arrow keys or typing the first letter. Then another one-line menu appears, or arguments are typed in, going down as many as five levels in the tree structure. Novice users walk slowly through the menus while experts type ahead rapidly enough that the menus appear on the screen for only a fraction of a second.

Another blending approach is to offer a form fill-in and allow the knowledgeable user to type a long sequence of commands in the field. Direct manipulation systems often revert to menu selections approaches when a visual representation cannot be found. Some direct manipulation systems offer a menu of visual items, such as a colour or texture palette. Tennant, Ross and Thompson (1983) offer an imaginative blend of natural language and menu selection. The users select from a menu of syntactically and semantically acceptable sentence fragments. As each choice is made, the permissible sentence fragments change. With a rapid display and pointing device, the user can quickly assemble a syntactically and semantically correct query for a database. These are but a few of the possibilities. Identifying useful and appropriate blends for different users in different situations is an important goal for researchers and system designers.

4. Conclusions

Designers of interactive systems have had to work from their own experience and intuition, validating their designs by costly and time consuming iterative testing. There is some hope that we can more precisely understand when to apply a particular interaction style and how to refine it so that it produces rapid user performance, low error rates, high satisfaction, ease in learning, and ease in retention over time. Blends of interaction styles can be very effective in serving a range of users and in dealing with certain interaction tasks. A massive program of empirical research will be necessary to guide this research, but the payoff in more reliable and effective designs can be enormous. Finally, a useful psychological theory, tied to the interaction styles would be a tremendous benefit.

Galitz, W.O. (1980) *Human Factors in Office Automation*. Atlanta, GA: Life Office Management Association.

Galitz, W.O. (1981) *Handbook of Screen Format Design*. Wellesley, MA: Information Sciences.

Shneiderman, B. (1983) Direct Manipulation: a step beyond programming languages. *Computer*, 16(8), 57–69.

Shneiderman, B. (1987) *Designing the User Interface: Strategies for Effective Human-Computer Interaction*. Reading, MA: Addison-Wesley.

Smith, S.L., and Mosier, J.N. (1987) *Design Guidelines for User-System Interface Software*. Bedford, MA: The MITRE Corporation.

Tennant, H.R., Ross, K.M., and Thompson, C.W. (1983) Usable natural language interfaces through menu-based natural language understanding. *Proceedings of CHI '83 Conference on Human Factors in Computer Systems*, available from ACM Order Dept., P.O. Box 64145, Baltimore, MD.

Chapter 6

Vision, Graphic Design, and Visual Display

There is much talk today about information highways, the information economy, and the information revolution. Yet what modern technology has achieved thus far is better described as a data explosion. Data does not become information until it informs, that is, until it can be used as the basis for problem solving and decision making. One primary goal of interactive computer systems must therefore be to help us extract data that is required for a task from the mass of data available, and to suppress that which is superfluous or irrelevant.

But simply providing a selective "filter" is not enough. In every transaction with a computer, the user is making decisions. We need to provide the relevant information for the task at hand, and to provide it in the most articulate, succinct, and appropriate manner possible. In doing so we exploit the human capacity for perceiving structure and organization—in short, for understanding.

The main vehicle today for delivery of information from a computer to a human being is the visual channel. This chapter deals with the visual representation, presentation, perception, and comprehension of information. It also deals with the discipline of graphic design, which has as its mission the design of effective visual presentations. Finally, it deals with methods and technologies for producing effective visual presentations and delivering them to users.

FROM SENSATION TO PERCEPTION

Effective human-computer interaction requires the presentation of information so that the eye and brain can see what the presenter intended to be seen. This is not always a trivial problem because the viewer does not perceive an image that conforms exactly to the physical image displayed on a computer screen. The visual sensations reaching the eye are translated into perceptual experience by the brain through processes such as pattern recognition. We therefore need to acquaint ourselves with how we experience and perceive such phenomena as brightness, contrast, flicker, motion, and color.

We can only hint at the relevant material in this volume and provide pointers to generally accessible literature. Different sources provide complementary insights—the literatures of psychophysics and the psychology of perception, human factors, and graphic design and visual presentation. In this section we review principles of psychophysics and visual perception.

Although the chapter deals with vision, certain characteristics of the human sensorimotor system apply regardless of the modality. One of these is the difference between the magnitude of a physical stimulus and the magnitude of the psychological sensation of that stimulus. We must distinguish between visual intensity and brightness, between wavelength and hue, between aural intensity and loudness, and between frequency and pitch. Research in *psychophysics* has concluded that psychological magnitude is related to physical stimulus by a power law that applies across a wide variety of sensory phenomena, with exponents ranging from 0.33 for visual brightness to 3.5 for the subjective strength of electric current applied to the finger (Stevens, 1961). Thus we cannot rely blindly upon the physical properties of a visual or auditory display, but must instead consider carefully how particular colors or sounds will be received by a human observer.

The science of psychophysics also contributes a number of other useful concepts (Van Cott and Kinkade, 1972), including

- sensitivity range along a stimulus scale from minimum perceivable to maximum tolerable for a human observer
- relative discrimination sensitivity, measuring an observer's ability to distinguish between two stimuli or to detect a change in one stimulus, also known as the "just noticeable difference" (JND)
- ability to make absolute judgments of stimuli or of their magnitude along some scale, expressed as a number of distinguishable values (Miller, 1956)

Absolute judgments are typically much more difficult than relative judgements. Thus, although we can distinguish several hundred different intensities of light or sound on a relative basis, we can only reliably identify on the order of a half dozen or a dozen different absolute stimuli arrayed along a single psychophysical dimension, such as brightness, hue, saturation, or value. Figure 6.1 reproduces a summary of visual coding methods, and provides some guidelines regarding our ability to discriminate displays that are coded using various individual stimulus dimensions. Multiple stimulus dimensions can often be combined to give us more discriminable stimuli.

FIGURE 6.1

Visual coding methods. The approximate number of levels that can be discriminated on an absolute basis under optimum conditions (Sanders and McCormick, 1993, p. 126)

Alphanumeric, single numerals	10
Alphanumeric, single letters	26
Color (hue of surfaces)	9
Color (hue, saturation, and brightness combinations)	24
preferable limit	9
Color (hue of lights)	10
preferable limit	3
Geometric shapes	15
preferable limit	5
Size of forms (such as squares)	5
preferable limit	3
Brightness of lights	3
preferable limit	2

The process of organizing sensations into perception also shares common elements independent of sensory modality (Lindsay and Norman, 1977, Chapter 1). Perhaps the most important of these is the brain's attempt to organize sensory messages into meaningful *patterns* and *structures*. It does this by applying rules that summarize its model of the way the world is organized and the way it should appear in various contexts. This allows us to integrate often incomplete and sometimes inconsistent sensations into a plausible perception of the structure of the source of the sensations.

Perception is an *active process*. What is seen is not merely a passive response to visual input, but the result of hypothesis formation and testing conditioned by our expectations. Lindsay and Norman (1977) describe this as the combination of "data driven" and "conceptually driven" processing, what computer scientists might call "bottom up" and "top down" computation.

What kinds of hypotheses are generated? Haber and Wilkinson (1982, p. 25) suggest how we attempt to perceive *structure* in the images we see:

> *The human visual system is designed to produce organized perception. Information consisting of a variety of such spatial features as size, shape, distance, relative position, and texture is structured by the mind to represent visual scenes. These spatial features are perceived as properties of things, objects in the scene, and not merely as abstract lines or surfaces. We do not perceive lines or unattached extents; we perceive objects. All parts of each object are perceived together in one construction—not as separate, independent, and free-floating elements. And all the objects are perceived as related to each other—near, far, behind, adjoining, and so forth. . . .*

Examples of perceived structure include the "perceptual constancies" that result in buildings appearing to stand still, people remaining the same size and shape, and snow remaining white, despite the fact that the retinal images may have radically different positions, shapes, and brightnesses depending upon the viewing conditions. Another central concept that emerges is that of *context*, how what is seen in one part of an image is affected by what appears in adjoining parts in space (within the current scene) and in time (in the immediate recent past). More generally, what is seen is very often not what is presented—*optical illusions* are perhaps the most dramatic example of this. Illusions are often the result of multiple possible structures and competing interpretations, as in the familiar figure-ground phenomena or the Neckar cube illusion (Figure 6.2). Thus, in structuring our screens, we must not automatically assume that our intentions can be easily translated into effective presentation and communication—we must work to achieve the desired results.

FIGURE 6.2

The Neckar cube—an optical illusion. Notice how one stimulus causing one optical sensation can result in two dramatically different perceptions of the figure.

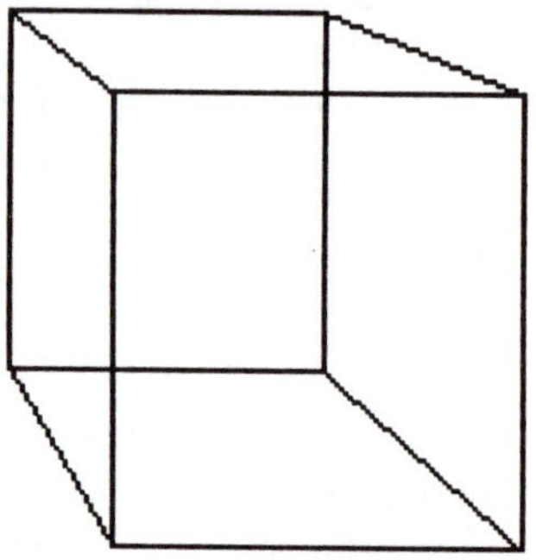

Given this framework, the interested student can access the literature to fill in other needed background—the basic anatomical and physiological properties of the eye and of the neural pathway to the brain, the dimensions of vision and the perception of brightness, contrast, flicker, motion, and color. Particularly useful is a superb publication that presents an encyclopedic survey of perception and human performance (Boff, Kaufman, and Thomas, 1986). Other useful sources in the psychology literature are Thompson (1985), Chapters 2 and 3 of Lindsay and Norman (1977), and the book by Gregory (1966).

The human factors literature is complementary, focusing on the optimum characteristics of specialized kinds of displays. Typical treatments are Chapter 3 of Van Cott and Kinkade (1972), Chapter 7 of Kantowitz and Sorkin (1983), and Chapters 4 and 5 of Sanders and McCormick (1993). These consider, among other topics, the appropriate design of alphanumeric displays, visual codes and symbols, quantitative and qualitative displays of data, status indicators, signal and warning lights, and representational displays.

GRAPHIC DESIGN FOR EFFECTIVE VISUAL COMMUNICATION

The literature of psychology, psychophysics, and human factors typically describes and quantifies the possibilities and limits of human visual performance. The results tell us what cannot be done, what cannot possibly work. *Graphic design* is the art of the possible, the discipline of effective visual communication. Its application is essential to the design of effective displays and usable interfaces. We cannot here provide a course on graphic design, but can introduce key concepts and provide reliable pointers to the literature.

Bowman (1968) provides a brilliant and systematic introduction to the visual language of effective graphic communication. He describes a vocabulary of *form* elements—point, line, shape, value, and texture; a grammar of *spatial organization*—plane, multiplane, and continuous; an idiom of *volumetric perspective*—parallel, angular, and oblique; and a syntax for *phrasing the image*—relationship, differentiation, and emphasis. Then he discusses the visualization process in terms of the three basic steps of concept, design, and production. He concludes with an extensive design library of examples illustrating how to show

- *what*—natural appearance, physical structure, and organization of parts in relation to the whole
- *how*—physical movement, system of flow in relation to component parts, and process as a succession of related events
- *how much*—physical size, numerical quantity, trend of increase or decrease, and division of its parts in terms of the whole
- *where*—natural area, environmental location, and position with respect to other individual elements

Dondis (1973) stresses that the process of *composition* is the most crucial step in visual problem solving. She illustrates with examples combining what she defines as the basic elements of visual communication—the dot, the line, shape, direction, tone, color, texture, scale, dimension, and movement. The compositional technique she views as most important is that of *contrast*, and she devotes some effort to its explication. She also presents a variety of purposely polarized techniques for visual communication, for example, balance and instability, symmetry and asymmetry, regularity and irregularity, simplicity and complexity, and unity and fragmentation.

A third source of design ideas is Hofmann (1965), a catalog of challenging visual design examples organized around the themes of the dot, the line, confrontation, and letters and signs.

These volumes may seem far removed from human-computer interaction, but their insights can and must be applied to the design of effective displays and usable interfaces. No designer has within the past fifteen years argued this more forcefully and more articulately than Aaron Marcus (1983, included as a reading in Baecker and Buxton, 1987). Good introductions to the discipline of graphic design and its application to interface design are Marcus (1990), included here as a reading, and a recent book, Marcus (1992). He presents examples that demonstrate the importance of careful selection and arrangement in using typography, signs and symbols, charts and diagrams, color, and spatial and temporal arrangement. Echoing insights from psychology, he suggests the use of consistent layout and formatting conventions applied with reference to an appropriate grid. The resulting visual structure serves to guide the eye as the brain attempts to parse and interpret an image, and helps the user to navigate through the succession of displays and images presented by a system in the course of its use.

Marcus develops his recommendations for effective visual communication in terms of three basic principles—*organize*, *economize*, and *communicate*. He stresses that the application of design principles to the medium of computer displays and interactive systems is not a trivial process. The medium typically has numerous special features and restrictions such as limited spatial extent and resolution. Thus there is a compelling need to enlist the participation of skilled graphic designers in the design of screens and human-computer interfaces.

A comprehensive review of research results that inform effective screen design is Tullis (1988). Videos that deal with graphic design for effective visual communication include Easel Corp. (1992 video) and Henry Dreyfuss Associates (1992 video).

Typography at the Interface

The most basic element of graphic design, as it affects each and every user interface, is *typography*. The craft of typography begins with the design of attractive and legible *letterforms* in a variety of *typefaces* or *fonts*, that may be either *serif* or *sans serif*, and that are arranged in families encompassing variations in *weight*, such as *regular* and *bold*, and variations in slant, such as *roman* and *italic*. Typography includes the careful arrangement of sequences of letterforms on the page with the goal of enhancing readability. This is done by controlling parameters of individual characters, such as *point size* and *letterspacing*, of words, such as *word spacing*, and of lines, such as *line length*, *leading*, and *justification*. Finally, typography encompasses the augmentation of raw text with simple graphic elements such as *rules*, *leader lines*, and *logotypes*. These typographic parameters and possibilities are illustrated in Figure 6.3.

FIGURE 6.3

Some typographic variations. These are only a few of the many possibilities.

A line of 10 point type, Times Roman serif font.

A line of 10 point type, Helvetica sans serif font.

A line of 10 point type, Helvetica bold.

A line of 10 point type, Helvetica italic.

`A line of fixed-width type.`

Type with normal letter spacing.

Type with condensed letter spacing.

A n d   w i t h   e x p a n d e d   l e t t e r   s p a c i n g .

Two lines with a
shorter line length.

Two lines of type

with increased leading.

A line of type flush left.

A line of type flush right.

A line of type centered.

The discipline of typography was always relevant to screen design, even in the days of single font fixed-width 24 x 80 character displays (Marcus, 1982a). Bit-mapped displays on personal computers and workstations allow for richer possibilities, yet restraint is required. The computer scientist's undisciplined delight in typography sometimes leads to "fontitis," the inclusion of so many fonts and point sizes in a single display that the result is visual chaos. As the eminent graphic designer Chuck Bigelow cautioned at CHI+GI '87, "What good is all this power if you lay waste to the literate landscape?"

Rosen (1963) presents a catalog of classic typefaces whose grace and expressiveness put to shame the typical appearance of our screens and printouts. Ruder (1967) presents a rich body of evocative examples showing some of the uses and appearances of typography within design.

Bigelow and Day (1983, included as a reading in Baecker and Buxton, 1987), introduces some of the issues of digital typography including letterform design, representation of digital letterforms, letterform quality, legibility and readability of digital text at different resolutions, and the problem of *aliasing*, in which high spatial frequencies in an original image are reproduced as local spatial frequencies, leading to the characteristic *jaggies* that are still often seen in low-resolution digital images. Morris (1989) reviews the history and key research issues of digital typography. More comprehensive treatments may be found in Seybold (1984), which presents digital typesetting in the context of the entire typesetting and printing process, and Rubinstein (1988), which pays particular attention to the technology of composition and layout.

Within the literature of computer science, Witten (1985) presents the fundamentals of computer typography and some solutions to the difficult problems of line breaks, hyphenation, justification, and page makeup. Brown (1989) reviews and critiques two international standards for the representation and exchange of structured documents, the Office Document Architecture (ODA) and the Standard Generalized Markup Language (SGML). Naiman (1991) is a comprehensive treatment of technical and perceptual issues in the use of grayscale for improved character presentation. Bibliographies and research results on digital typography may be found in van Vliet (1986, 1988), Andre and Hersch (1989), and Naiman (1991).

There is also much to be learned from the literature on the legibility and readability of typography. Tinker (1963, 1965) and Huey (1968) present some classic research on the legibility of type and on the psychology of reading. Hartley (1978, 1980); Kolers, Wrolstad, and Bouma (1979, 1980); Felker (1980); and Felker et al. (1981) are more modern collections of articles on the readability of documents and structured text.

Generally, text on screens has been found to be less legible than text on paper. Gould et al. (1987) surveys much of the relevant literature and presents the results of some experiments that fail to explain why this is so, but demonstrate some of the contributing factors. Gould et al. (1986) and Gould et al. (1987) show that reading speeds equivalent to that on paper may be obtained through the use of high-quality antialiased fonts displayed with dark characters on a light background on a high-resolution screen.

Videos dealing with typography include Xerox (1985a video, 1985b video), Russell (1987 video), Giannitrapani (1987 video), and Small, Ishizaki, and Cooper (1994 video).

Color in Interfaces

Color is another key component of graphic design for effective human-computer interaction. The appropriate use of color is difficult. Our reactions to color result from a complex set of physiological, perceptual, and cognitive phenomena, which are translated into principles and guidelines for the effective use of color in the third part of the reading by Marcus (1990), and also in the reading consisting of a short excerpt from a paper by Murch (1985), which in turn summarizes a longer treatment (Murch, 1984). Murch (1985) is reprinted in its entirety in Baecker and Buxton (1987). Two other readable introductions to the use of color in computer displays and interfaces are Marcus (1982b) and Salomon (1990).

Both Murch and Marcus stress the need for restraint in the use of color, avoiding the "fruit salad" appearance resulting from the undisciplined use of color. The serious student of color will need to review considerable material from the art and design literature, for example, Itten (1961), Albers (1963), Chevreul (1967), Yule (1967), Birren (1969a, 1969b), Hunt (1975), and Wong (1987). Wyszecki and Stiles (1982) is a comprehensive treatment of color science, including colorimetry, photometry, and color vision.

The computer science literature has tended to focus on issues of choosing the appropriate color space and of automating the mapping from one space to another (Joblove and Greenberg, 1978; Meyer and Greenberg, 1980; Smith, 1978). Robertson and O'Callaghan (1986) deals with the use of color to display quantitative information. In 1986, the journal *Color Research and Application* contained the proceedings of a meeting covering a broad range of issues in both softcopy and hardcopy computer-generated color. Stone, Cowan, and Beatty (1988; see also Stone, 1987 video; Beretta and Stone, 1990 video) discusses the problem of mapping gamuts of display monitor colors to gamuts of printer colors in order to enable the faithful reproduction of screen images on paper.

Two recent books are particularly valuable. Travis (1991) reviews color display hardware, color vision, methods of color specification, and the appropriate use of color. Durrett (1987) discusses many of the same issues, and then examines the use of color in applications ranging from process control to cartography to education.

Pictures, Symbols, Signs, and Icons

Human-computer interfaces increasingly incorporate images as well as text. Arnheim (1969) states that images can function as *pictures, symbols,* and *signs.*

> *An image serves merely as a* sign *to the extent to which it stands for a particular content without reflecting its characteristics visually. . . . Images are* pictures *to the extent to which they portray things located at a lower level of abstractness than they are themselves. They do their work by grasping and rendering some relevant qualities—shape, color, movement—of the objects or activities they depict. . . . An image acts as a* symbol *to the extent to which it portrays things which are at a higher level of abstractness than is the symbol itself. . . .*

One trend in user interfaces, arising from advances in computer graphics, is the incorporation of increasingly realistic three-dimensional portrayals (Greenberg, 1982). Mills (1982, 1985) suggests that this by itself is not sufficient to make optimal use of the medium of computer graphics and argues that we need also pay attention to the insights into pictorial representation and communication that arise out of art, art history, design, and the psychology of visual perception (Arnheim, 1954; Gombrich, 1961). Mills shows how man's background, history, and knowledge are embodied in his "cognitive schemata" and his capacity for metaphorical thinking, and how the choice of pictorial representation can facilitate his understanding of images and his problem-solving ability. The imaginative and appropriate choice of visual representation is thus a key determinant of the success of a user interface.

Another trend is that of incorporating in the interface *icons*, images representing system commands, objects, states, or results. Many icons function as pictures. For example, a schematic pen may be used to indicate that the user may now paint, or a short thick line can indicate that lines about to be input will be drawn with a thick stroke. Some icons function as symbols, as for example, in the use of an hourglass, clock, spinning globe, or "smiling Buddha" to indicate that the system is working and the user should be patient. A discussion of the development and testing of icons for use in the Xerox Star appears in the introduction to Case B.

The design of icons is a demanding craft. Dreyfuss (1972) has catalogued the incredible variety of icons in his guide to some of the 20,000 known international graphic symbols. The American Institute of Graphic Arts (AIGA) has analyzed the strengths and weaknesses of passenger/pedestrian-oriented symbols in three distinct dimensions: *semantic, syntactic*, and *pragmatic* (1981, p. 20):

> *The* semantic *dimension refers to the relationship of a visual image to a meaning. How well does this symbol represent the message? Do people fail to understand the message that the symbol denotes? Do people from various cultures misunderstand this symbol? Do people of various ages fail to understand this symbol? Is it difficult to learn this symbol? Has this symbol already been widely accepted? Does this symbol contain elements that are unrelated to the message?*
>
> *The* syntactic *dimension refers to the relationship of one visual image to another. How does this symbol look? How well do the parts of this symbol relate to each other? How well does this symbol relate to other symbols? Is the construction of this symbol consistent in its use of figure/ground, solid/outline, overlapping, transparency, orientation, format, scale, color, and texture? Does this symbol use a hierarchy of recognition? Are the most important elements recognized first? Does this symbol seriously contradict existing standards or conventions? Is this symbol, and its elements, capable of systematic application for a variety of interrelated concepts?*
>
> *The* pragmatic *dimension refers to the relationship of a visual image to a user. Can a person see the sign? Is this symbol seriously affected by poor lighting conditions, oblique viewing angles, and other visual "noise"? Does this symbol remain visible throughout the range of typical viewing distances? Is this symbol especially vulnerable to vandalism? Is this symbol difficult to reproduce? Can this symbol be enlarged and reduced successfully?*

Every aspect of this discussion applies equally well to the design of icons for computer systems. The difficulty of the task is illustrated in a reading included in Baecker and Buxton (1987) that provides excerpts from AIGA (1981) showing possible designs for icons representing "information," "arriving flights," and "exit."

Horton (1994) is an excellent recent comprehensive guide to the roles, design, construction, and testing of icons for computer systems and documentation. He stresses that the perceived meaning of an icon depends upon the context in which it appears and the background, knowledge, and interests of the viewer. Thus, icons are not automatically universal and do not necessarily work in all cultures, but must be carefully designed and tailored for international use. Horton presents a process for developing icons that reflects the principles of task-centered, iterative design we have presented throughout this book.

Is the use of icons in interfaces a fundamental breakthrough enabling new levels of ease of learning or ease of use, or a fad, eventually to disappear and be replaced with traditional textual representations? Arguments on both sides of this debate are presented in the reading by Baecker, Small, and Mander (1991). Both sides would likely agree that the meaning of an icon should be obvious to experienced users of a system, and be evocative and self-evident to new users. Some icons fail to meet the former criterion; many fail to meet the latter criterion. The reading suggests that the use of animation could be a solution to the problem of icon comprehensibility and provides some evidence for this hypothesis through a quasi-experiment comparing static to dynamic, animated icons. We shall return below to a further discussion of the possible roles of animation at the interface.

PRINCIPLES FOR EFFECTIVE VISUALIZATION

A special class of images used increasingly in computer-generated displays are those portraying quantitative data, geographic data, and complex symbolic relationships. This is done by encoding and interpreting the data and relationships in a chart, graph, map, or diagram. The formulation and generation of intelligent varieties of these images can contribute significantly to the communicative and expressive power of computer displays.

No individual has presented this case more eloquently than Edward R. Tufte (1983). His goal is *graphical excellence*, which he defines (p. 13) as "the efficient communication of complex quantitative ideas":

> *Excellence in statistical graphics consists of complex ideas communicated with clarity, precision, and efficiency. Graphical displays should:*
>
> - *show the data*
> - *induce the viewer to think about the substance rather than about methodology, graphic design, the technology of graphic production, or something else*
> - *avoid distorting what the data have to say*
> - *present many numbers in a small space*
> - *make large data sets coherent*
> - *encourage the eye to compare different pieces of data*
> - *reveal the data at several levels of detail, from a broad overview to the fine structure*
> - *serve a reasonably clear purpose: description, exploration, tabulation, or decoration*
> - *be closely integrated with the statistical and verbal description of a data set.*

"Graphics *reveal* data," says Tufte. He then presents in his beautiful book "a language for describing graphics and a practical theory of data graphics." He concludes with humility and a healthy skepticism (p. 191):

> *Design is choice. The theory of the visual display of quantitative information consists of principles that generate design options and that guide choices among options. The principles should not be applied rigidly or in a peevish spirit; they are not logically or mathematically certain; and it is better to violate any principle than to place graceless or inelegant marks on paper. Most principles of design should be greeted with some skepticism, for word authority can dominate our vision, and we may come to see only through the lenses of word authority rather than with our own eyes.*
>
> *What is to be sought in designs for the display of information is the clear portrayal of complexity. Not the complication of the simple; rather the task of the designer is to give visual access to the subtle and the difficult—that is, the* revelation of the complex.

Those wishing to learn about the art of "the revelation of the complex" will need to supplement the Tufte book with additional readings. His more recent work, Tufte (1990), is another beautiful and insightful compendium of heuristics and examples of effective information visualization.

Another useful source to consult is Cleveland (1985), which presents principles of graphical construction, a catalog of appropriate graphical methods, and a paradigm for graphical perception. The use of a theory of visual perception and experimental results on visual perception to guide the design of displays is a welcome addition to the literature.

Three valuable books with a nice "how-to" flavor are Spear (1969), Schmid and Schmid (1979), and Schmid (1983). These three books, as well as the classic by Huff (1954) and the more recent Monmonier (1991), include illustrations of what not to do, that is, how to lie with graphic presentation. Far more insidious, however, is the well-intentioned but ill-conceived *chartjunk* (Tufte's term) intended to enliven and entertain, but actually conceals or even distorts the data. Herdeg (1981), a classic catalog of lively diagrams now in its fourth edition, presents numerous examples of imaginative and appropriate work interspersed with chartjunk. Holmes (1984) is even more replete with chartjunk. The student should look at these various books and think about what makes a visual presentation honest, communicative, and effective.

The advanced student can eventually progress to the monumental works of Tukey and Bertin. Tukey (1977) focuses on the exploratory analysis of data, and the use of novel forms of graphic presentation to assist in the task. Bertin (1983) begins from a cartographic perspective, but enlarges this to a comprehensive exploration of methods of applying graphic presentation to the construction of complex yet communicative diagrams, networks, and maps.

INFORMATION VISUALIZATION SOFTWARE

Charts, graphs, maps, and diagrams are examples of vehicles for what is now known more generally as *information visualization* (McCormick, DeFanti, and Brown, 1987; Gershon et al., 1994; Visualization Software, 1991 video; see also the proceedings of the new ACM and IEEE conferences on scientific visualization). As computers are used to manage larger and larger sets of more and more complex data, better means of manipulating, analyzing, and visualizing data are needed (Goldstein and Roth, 1994). Traditional methods of portraying data such as charts and graphs are being augmented by new computer-based techniques for information visualization.

The reading by Ahlberg and Shneiderman (1994; 1994 video), for example, describes the use of dynamic query filters and starfield displays to facilitate the process of visual information seeking. Dynamic query filters allow the rapid updating of search results as query parameters are adjusted with sliders and buttons. Starfield displays are two-dimensional scatterplots of sets of results (for an early example of such a display, see the last scene of Baecker, 1981 video). Zooming and panning over the displays, and recomputing them rapidly as queries are reformulated, powerfully support human capabilities for intelligent browsing and pattern recognition.

Part VI of Shneiderman (1993) reviews other work on information visualization carried out in Shneiderman's lab, including earlier papers on dynamic queries (Ahlberg, Williamson, and Shneiderman, 1992; Shneiderman, Williamson, and Ahlberg, 1992 video; Plaisant and Jain, 1994 video) and their application to searching a real-estate data base (Williamson and Shneiderman, 1992). Another technique is that of tree maps (Johnson and Shneiderman, 1991; Turo, 1994 video), which displays large tree structures by partitioning a rectangular display space into a collection of hierarchically nested rectangular bounding boxes.

Viewers of large information visualizations need to perceive both local detail and global context (see Spence, 1983 video, for an early demonstration of this). Traditional computer graphic systems allow users to pan and zoom over information spaces. Unfortunately, when one is zoomed in to see detail, the context is not visible, and when one is zoomed out for purposes of orientation, the detail cannot be seen. A solution to this problem is to provide overview and detail displays in multiple windows with independent pan and zoom capabilities, yet this can lead to divided visual focus, as well as screen clutter or window overlap.

Furnas (1986) proposed *generalized fisheye views* as another solution to the problem of providing both context and detail in a single information display. The key idea is to show "local" detail in full while displaying successively less detail for "global" information at the periphery. This can be done in three ways, by graphically distorting the view, thereby shrinking the peripheral information; by filtering the view, so that less detail appears at the periphery; or by replacing details at the periphery with smaller representations, abstractions, and clusters. Examples of such approaches are Sarkar and Brown (1992; Brown, 1993 video), which proposes fisheye displays of graphs; Rao and Card (1994), which investigates fisheye displays of tables; and Noik (1993) and Schaffer et al. (1995), which study the fisheye display of hierarchically clustered networks and graphs. The latter paper also includes a recent review of this literature and an experiment comparing the efficacy of fisheye and full-zoom methods in a process control application.

Another area of recent research is work on intelligent automatic information visualization. A pioneeering work in this area is Mackinlay's Ph.D. thesis (1986a, 1986b) exploring the automated design of graphical presentations of relational information. This is accomplished using AI techniques, graphic design expressiveness and effectiveness criteria, and a composition algebra that composes a small set of primitive graphical languages. More recent work in this area includes Roth et al. (1994), which uses automated design knowledge to assist both in the process of creating new designs and in the process of finding and customizing relevant existing designs, and Myers, Goldstein, and Goldberg (1994), which shows how to create charts by demonstration.

Videos documenting work in information visualization include Hill and Hollan (1992 video) and Tweedie et al. (1994 video).

Finally, one kind of information visualization that deserves special mention is *software visualization*, the use of interactive computer graphics and the disciplines of graphic design, typography, animation, and cinematography to portray the function, structure, and behavior of algorithms and computer programs. Pioneering work in this area is represented by *Sorting Out Sorting*, a 30-minute computer-animated portrayal of sorting algorithms (Baecker, 1981 video); Balsa, an elegant system for the interactive construction and display of such visualizations (Brown, 1988); and Baecker and Marcus (1988), which applies graphic design principles to improve the presentation of computer program source code. Recently, Eick and his colleagues have developed lovely applications of high-resolution color data visualization to aid in the comprehension of large computer programs, networks, relational data bases, and other complex systems (Eick, Steffen, and Sumner, 1992; Eick, Nelson, and Schmidt, 1994; AT&T Bell Laboratories, 1994; AT&T Bell Laboratories, 1993 video).

A comprehensive recent overview of work in this field is Price, Baecker, and Small (1993). Other videos presenting work in software visualization as well as programming environments with superior visualization capabilities include CCA (1983 video), Abelson (1985 video), Lieberman (1985 video), Xerox (1985c video), Tektronix (1985 video), Eisenstadt and Brayshaw (1988 video), ParcPlace Systems (1989 video), Carnegie Mellon University (1991 video), and Brown (1992 video).

DISPLAY METHODS AND TECHNOLOGIES

Our final topic in this chapter examines a number of methods for defining and creating user interfaces and visual presentations—three-dimensional displays, animation, structured editors, and graphical user interfaces (GUIs)—as well as the technology whereby such displays are produced and presented to users.

Three-Dimensional Display

Most interactive applications to date have used the computer to display two-dimensional worlds. The dominant conceptual model is that of the "desktop metaphor," originally pioneered with the Star personal workstation which we analyzed in Case B. Yet the field of three-dimensional computer graphics (Foley et al., 1990) has vividly demonstrated the power of three-dimensional modeling, rendering, display, and interaction through compelling applications to fields such as computer animation and computer-aided mechanical, industrial, and architectural design.

Why limit ourselves to two-dimensional metaphors in human-computer interaction? An early attempt to use three-dimensional representations for information visualization of complex semantic networks was the MCC SemNet project (Fairchild, Poltrock, and Furnas, 1988; Fairchild and Poltrock, 1987 video).

More recently, Card, Robertson, and Mackinlay (1991), Robertson, Mackinlay, and Card (1991 video), and Robertson, Card, and Mackinlay (1993) apply human information-processing principles (see Chapter 9) to suggest that information workspaces be mediated and accessed through three-dimensional representations. A prototype information visualizer suggesting how to facilitate information retrieval is presented in these papers, and in more detail in two companion papers, Mackinlay, Robertson, and Card (1991), which proposes 3D, fisheye-like views of linear information; and Robertson, Mackinlay, and Card (1991), which explores cone trees, animated 3D visualizations of hierarchical information.

Gomez et al. (1994) is a recent review of issues in facilitating 3D interaction. Brookshire Connor et al. (1992) explore the design of three-dimensional widgets. One interesting example is the "interactive shadow" widget, which provides valuable perceptual cues about the spatial relationship between objects and also a direct manipulation interface to constrained transformation techniques (Herndon et al., 1992) More recently, Zeleznik et al. (1993) discuss the design of a toolkit for constructing 3D widgets. Further discussion of 3D interaction appears in Chapter 7.

The most comprehensive vision of the potential of three-dimensional display and interaction is that of immersing users in an environment that is rendered and portrayed so vividly that it appears to be real. We shall return to this concept of *virtual reality* in Chapter 14.

Animation

Interactive computer systems should portray phenomena using dynamic displays as well as static images, so we require, in addition to the skills of the graphic designer, the skills of the cinematographer and animator. We can look to the language of cinema for models of how our interfaces should behave. They should enable us to include, as *global* changes to the entire screen, the *cut*, the *fade in* (*fade out*), the *dissolve*, the *wipe*, the *overlay* (superimposition), and the *multiple exposure* (image combination). *Locally*, within a region of the screen, interfaces should allow the *pop on* (*pop off*), the *pull down* (*pull up*), the *flip*, and the *spin*. Finally, they should allow, as either global or local phenomena, *reverse video*, *color changes*, *scrolling*, *panning*, *zooming in* (*zooming out*), the *close up*, and *full motion*, possibly through simulations of three-dimensional worlds and environments. With such effects, an interface can more easily be made memorable and vivid, captivating and enjoyable to use.

We have already presented one reading that illustrates this very well. Baecker, Small, and Mander (1991) employ animation to make icons livelier and more comprehensible. The addition of movement enabled viewers who were confused by several static icons to identify their roles quickly and accurately.

Baecker and Small (1991) is a systematic analysis of possible roles of animation at the interface. Card, Robertson, and Mackinlay (1991), Robertson, Mackinlay, and Card (1991 video), and Robertson, Card, and Mackinlay (1993) employ animation to facilitate exploration and perception of large information spaces. Sukiviriya and Foley (1990) demonstrate the automatic generation of context-sensitive animated help.

The Structure and Editing of Graphic Representations

The pioneering work of Ivan Sutherland (1963, 1963 video) demonstrated that the underlying structure of displays is even more important than what appears on the screen. A number of videos present recent advances in exploring this concept. Pier (1989 video) deals with the processing of digital images. Bier (1989 video) considers "graphical search and replace" in synthetic pictures. Furnas (1990 video) demonstrates a prototype system capable of reasoning about graphical interfaces. Pier and Bier (1991 video) presents a prototype system in which documents act as user interfaces in the sense that any document element can behave as a "button." Gleicher (1992 video) demonstrates the use of constraints in a direct manipulation graphical editor, and Karsenty (1993 video) explores ways in which the computer can assist the user in dealing with constraints. Finally, so that users need not think about two representations, what is on the screen and what underlies it, Kim (1988 video) treats the pixel on the screen as the sole representation, *the* state of the system.

The Technology of Visual Displays

As interface designers, we need to understand the kinds of images that facilitate human-computer interaction, and also be aware of the technology capable of generating and displaying these images. The process occurs in four steps: (1) understanding the fundamental characteristics of images as represented on computer displays; (2) understanding the kinds of changes to images that must be supported by the technology to enable interactive applications to be effective; (3) understanding the basic technology and architecture of display systems; and (4) understanding how to apply this technology to the generation of appropriate imagery and the dynamic changes to the imagery that are required.

The technology is advancing at breakneck speed (compare, for example, Sproull, 1986, to Baecker, 1979). Sproull (1986), which is included as a reading in Baecker and Buxton (1987), is an overview of the technology and architecture of current visual displays. It focuses on how technological parameters and architectural design of display update processors, frame buffer memories, and video generators can either facilitate or hinder the production of the displays, picture changes, and interactive techniques that interface designers require. These techniques include the incorporation of color and antialiasing, smooth scrolling and dragging, rapid pop-up menus and color table animation. Chapter 4, "Graphics Hardware", and Chapter 18, "Advanced Raster Graphics Architecture" of Foley et al. (1990) are more recent treatments of computer graphics hardware, with an emphasis in the latter chapter on the use of pipelined and parallel architectures for computing in hardware relatively realistic renderings of three-dimensional scenes.

Of equal or often greater importance to the interface designer are the physical and pragmatic characteristics of the resulting workstation and terminal. The last two decades have seen increasing interest in the use of *flat panel displays* to overcome the fundamental problems of too much size, weight, and power consumption that characterize cathode ray tube (CRT) terminals. Work has concentrated on three technologies:

- *Liquid crystal displays* (LCDs), in which a voltage reorients molecules within a layer of liquid crystals sandwiched between glass plates so that light is reflected or absorbed
- *Electroluminescent displays*, in which a thin film deposited in layers on a glass plate glows when a voltage is applied
- *Plasma displays*, in which neon gas sandwiched between glass plates is ionized and thereby emits light

A number of books and survey papers (Refioglu, 1983; Aldersey-Williams and Graff, 1985; Perry et al., 1985; Tannas, 1986; Castellano, 1992; Werner, 1993) report that flat panel technologies are capturing an increasing percentage of the market for computer displays. Yet the only technology with significant success has been LCDs, both passive and active matrix, because of their use in laptop computers. Meanwhile, the CRT has continued its many decades of improvement in brightness, luminous efficiency, color, resolution, and cost. The interested reader may want to begin with Tannas (1985) and Castellano (1992), which present comprehensive overviews of the technologies of visual displays, and with the monthly *Information Display Magazine* (published by the Society for Information Display). Snyder (1988) reviews both vision science and display hardware determinants of image quality.

One important realization of the past two decades has been of the significance of *scale*, that is, physical size of devices, in enabling new kinds of computer use. First came *personal computers*, which are now daily tools of hundreds of millions of individuals around the world. Next came *laptop computers*, which allow machines to be used free of the desk and the office. This was followed by *palmtop computers*, sometimes known as *personal digital assistants* (PDAs), which reduce the size and weight and increase the mobility of computational devices even further. Even more recently, researchers have begun to work on what has become known as *ubiquitous computing* (see Chapter 14 and especially the reading by Weiser), in which highly portable tiny badges and tabs as well as large wall-size displays, all of which contain compute engines, are interconnected and communicating in order to enable new kinds of applications.

Putting It All Together: GUIs

Ultimately, typography and layout, symbolism and color, dimensionality and animation, must be brought together in an interface style for a particular program, system, or environment. The term *graphical user interface*, or GUI, is variously used to refer to the "look and feel" of an interface style, the common functionality available to a user, and the underlying software that implements and supports user interactions. Employing the terminology introduced in Chapter 5, we can state that the look and feel of a GUI is typically implemented by a user interface toolkit sitting on top of a windowing system.

Recall our discussion of consistency in Chapter 2. Users would find it very difficult if every application and every computer system presented a different look and feel. The software industry is trying to respond to this problem. Apple Computer (1992), for example, is a published set of human interface guidelines intended to encourage those developing software for the Macintosh to provide consistent interfaces. Corresponding documents from other dominant look-and-feels are IBM (1991), Microsoft (1992), Open Software Foundation (1992), and Sun Microsystems (1990).

Marcus (1992) defines a "common user interface" as "a set of rules used across a group of products that formally specifies the visual presentation of data and functions, the user's interaction, and the logical organization and behavior of information," and suggests defining and documenting the common user interface in a "user interface standards manual." Smith (1988) compares the use of standards versus guidelines in designing user interface software.

Despite the generally shared goal of interface consistency, there are many different GUIs in use today. The reading by Marcus (1992) describes six that in 1992 had established a strong market presence or had been important to the development of the field. After introducing these six—the Macintosh, NextStep, Open Look, Windows, Presentation Manager, and Motif—he presents an overview of key windowing system concepts, and then describes how windows and menus are realized in the six annoyingly different, yet tantalizingly similar systems. More recently, Marcus, Smilonich, and Thompson (1995) is a detailed comparison of the technology, appearance, interaction, and common actions of six GUIs (those listed above with Open Look replaced by Windows NT), thereby providing a framework for developers to design and implement cross-platform applications that nonetheless have a consistent look-and-feel.

Users would likely benefit if all look-and-feels were identical, as they would be able to learn new systems with greater ease. Yet this goal is unlikely to be realized. Premature standardization could damage the industry more than inconsistent interfaces. Furthermore, GUI and other software developers produce unique interfaces and look-and-feels because they believe they can do it better than others have before them, and they desire to establish a distinctive appearance for their products. They then seek to protect their developments and prevent others from copying and using their work. This has led to look-and-feel copyright infringement lawsuits, an area of intense legal activity whose outcome is as of the writing of this book still in question (Shneiderman, 1991; Samuelson, 1992, 1993).

CONCLUDING REMARKS

We have reviewed some of the disciplines involved in enhancing interactive computing through the use of the human visual channel. In isolation, individual factors such as typography and color are already complicated. The issues become even more subtle, however, in the combined and interacting effects of typography, symbolism, graphics, layout, and color. Because the contributing factors are numerous and difficult to control, and the effects of task and context profound, it is difficult to see how to generalize the few concrete results we have from the human factors literature. See, for example, such studies as Tullis (1981, 1983), Dickson, DeSanctis, and McBride (1986), and Bensabat, Dexter, and Todd (1986).

Good progress may therefore best be achieved through the multidisciplinary collaboration of the technologist telling us what is possible, the psychologist telling us what not to do, and the designer suggesting what to do.

REFERENCES

Note: A ● before a reference indicates a reading.

● Ahlberg, C., and Shneiderman, B. (1994). Visual Information Seeking: Tight Coupling of Dynamic Query Filters with Starfield Displays. *Proceedings of CHI '94*, ACM, 313–317, 479–480.

Ahlberg, C., Williamson, C., and Shneiderman, B. (1992). Dynamic Queries for Information Exploration: An Implementation and Evaluation. *Proc. CHI '92*, ACM, 619–626.

Albers, J. (1963, 1975). *Interaction of Color.* Yale University Press.

Aldersey-Williams, H., and Graff, G. (1985). The Flat Panel Challenge. *High Technology*, 39–45.

American Institute of Graphic Arts (1981). *Symbols Signs: The System of Passenger/Pedestrian Oriented Symbols Developed for the U.S. Department of Transportation.* Hasting House.

Andre, J., and Hersch, R. (Eds.) (1989). *Raster Imaging and Digital Typography.* Cambridge University Press.

Apple Computer (1992). *Macintosh Human Interface Guidelines.* Addison-Wesley.

Arnheim, R. (1954). *Art and Visual Perception: A Psychology of the Creative Eye.* University of California Press.

Arnheim, R. (1969). *Visual Thinking.* University of California Press.

AT&T Bell Laboratories (1994). Data Visualization at AT&T Bell Laboratories. Unpublished report. For further information contact Brian Johnson at bsj@research.att.com.

Baecker, R. (1979). Digital Video Display Systems and Dynamic Graphics. *Computer Graphics* 13(2), 48–56.

Baecker, R., and Buxton, W. (1987). *Readings in Human-Computer Interaction: A Multidisciplinary Approach.* Morgan Kaufmann.

Baecker, R., and Marcus, A. (1988). *Human Factors and Typography for More Readable Programs.* ACM Press.

Baecker, R., and Small, I. (1991). Animation at the Interface. In Laurel, B. (Ed.), *The Art of Human-Computer Interface Design.* Addison-Wesley, 261–267.

● Baecker, R., Small, I., and Mander, R. (1991). Bringing Icons to Life. *Proceedings of CHI '91*, ACM, 1–6.

Bensabat, I., Dexter, A., and Todd, P. (1986). An Experimental Program Investigating Color-Enhanced and Graphical Information Presentation: An Integration of the Findings. *Communications of the ACM* 29(11), 1094–1105.

Bertin, J. (1983). *Semiology of Graphics: Diagrams, Networks, Maps.* University of Wisconsin Press.

Bigelow, C., and Day, D. (1983). Digital Typography. *Scientific American* 249(2), 106–119.

Birren, F. (Ed.) (1969a). *Principles of Color.* Van Nostrand Reinhold Company.

Birren, F. (Ed.) (1969b). *A Grammar of Color: A Basic Treatise on the Color System of Albert H. Munsell.* Van Nostrand Reinhold.

Boff, K., Kaufman, L., and Thomas, J. (1986). *Handbook of Perception and Human Performance.* 2 volumes. John Wiley & Sons. See esp. Chapters 4–10, 28–29, and 33–38.

Bowman, W. (1968). *Graphic Communication.* John Wiley & Sons.

Brookshire Connor, D., Snibbe, S., Herndon, K., Robbins, D., Zeleznik, R., and van Dam, A. (1992). Three-Dimensional Widgets. *Computer Graphics* 25(2), 183–188.

Brown, H. (1989). Standards for Structured Documents. *The Computer Journal* 32(6), 505–514.

Brown, M. (1988). *Algorithm Animation.* ACM Distinguished Dissertation. MIT Press.

Card, S., Robertson, G., and Mackinlay, J. (1991). The Information Visualizer, An Information Workspace. *Proceedings of CHI '91*, ACM, 181–188.

Castellano, J. (1992). *Handbook of Display Technology.* Academic Press.

Chevreul, M. (1967). *The Principles of Harmony and Contrast of Colors and Their Application to the Arts.* Van Nostrand Reinhold.

Cleveland, W. (1985). *The Elements of Graphing Data.* Wadsworth Advanced Books. Color Research and Application (1986). Supplement to Volume 11. John Wiley & Sons.

Dickson, G., DeSanctis, G., and McBride, D. (1986). Understanding the Effectiveness of Compter Graphics for Decision Support: A Cumulative Experimental Approach. *Communications of the ACM* 29(1), 40–47.

Dondis, D. (1973). *A Primer of Visual Literacy.* MIT Press.

Dreyfuss, H. (1972). *Symbol Sourcebook: An Authoritative Guide to International Graphic Symbols.* Van Nostrand Reinhold.

Durrett, J. (Ed.) (1987). *Color and the Computer.* Academic Press.

Eick, S., Nelson, M., and Schmidt, J. (1994). Graphical Analysis of Computer Log Files. *Communications of the ACM* 37(12), 50–56.

Eick, S., Steffen, J., and Sumner, E. (1992). Seesoft (TM)—A Tool for Visualizing Line Oriented Software Statistics. *IEEE Transactions on Software Engineering* 18(11), 957–968.

Fairchild, K., Poltrock, S., and Furnas, G. (1988). SemNet: Three-Dimensional Graphic Representations of Large Knowledge Bases. In R. Guindon (Ed.), *Cognitive Science and Its Applications to Human-Computer Interaction.* Lawrence Erlbaum Associates.

Felker, D. (Ed.) (1980). *Document Design: A Review of the Relevant Research.* American Institutes for Research.

Felker, D., Pickering, F., Charrow, V., Holland, V., and Redish, J. (1981). *Guidelines for Document Designers.* American Institutes for Research.

Foley, J., van Dam, A., Feiner, S., and Hughes, J. (1990). *Computer Graphics: Principles and Practice.* Second Edition. Addison-Wesley.

Furnas, G. (1986). Generalized Fisheye Views. *Proceedings of CHI '86,* ACM, 16–23.

Gershon, N., Bushell, C., Mackinlay, J., Ruh, W., Spoerri, A., and Tesler, J. (1994). Information Visualization: The Next Frontier. *Proc. SIGGRAPH '94,* ACM, 485–486.

Goldstein, J., and Roth, S. (1994). Using Aggregation and Dynamic Queries for Exploring Large Data Sets. *Proc. CHI '94,* ACM, 23–29.

Gombrich, E. (1961). *Art and Illusion: A Study in the Psychology of Pictorial Representation,* Second Edition. Pantheon Books.

Gomez, J., Carey, R., Fields, T., van Dam, A., and Venolia, D. (1994). Why Is 3-D Interaction So Hard and What Can We Really Do about It? *Proc. SIGGRAPH '94,* ACM, 492–493.

Gould, J., Alfaro, L., Barnes, V., Finn, R., Grischkowsky, N., and Minuto, A. (1987). Why Reading Is Slower from CRT Displays than from Paper: Attempts to Isolate a Single Variable Explanation. *Human Factors* 29(3), 269–299.

Gould, J., Alfaro, L., Finn, R., Haupt, B., and Minuto, A. (1986). Reading from CRT Displays Can Be as Fast as Reading from Paper. *IBM Research Report* RC-12083.

Gould, J., Alfaro, L., Finn, R., Haupt, B., Minuto, A., and Salaun, J. (1987). Why Reading Was Slower from CRT Displays than from Paper. *Proc. CHI+GI '87,* ACM, 7–11.

Greenberg, D. (1982). An Overview of Computer Graphics. In Greenberg, D., Marcus, A., Schmidt, A., and Gorter, V. (Eds.), *The Computer Image: Applications of Computer Graphics,* Addison-Wesley, 7–75.

Gregory, R. (1966). *Eye and Brain: The Psychology of Seeing.* World University Library.

Haber, R., and Wilkinson, L. (1982). Perceptual Components of Computer Displays. *IEEE Computer Graphics and Applications* 2(3), 23–35.

Hartley, J. (1978). *Designing Instructional Text.* Kogan Page Limited.

Hartley, J. (Ed.) (1980). *The Psychology of Written Communication.* Kogan Page Limited.

Helander, M. (Ed.) (1988) *Handbook of Human-Computer Interaction.* North-Holland.

Herdeg, W. (1981). *Diagrams: The Graphic Visualization of Abstract Data,* Fourth Expanded Edition. Graphics Press Corp.

Herndon, K., Zeleznik, R., Robbins, D., Brookshire Connor, D., Snibbe, S., and van Dam, A. (1992). Interactive Shadows. *Proc. UIST '92,* ACM, 1–6.

Hofmann, A. (1965). *Graphic Design Manual.* Van Nostrand Reinhold.

Holmes, N. (1984). *A Designer's Guide to Creating Charts and Diagrams.* Watson-Guptill Publishing Company.

Horton, W. (1994). *The Icon Book: Visual Symbols for Computer Systems and Documentation.* John Wiley & Sons.

Huey, E. (1968). *The Psychology and Pedagogy of Reading.* MIT Press.

Huff, D. (1954). *How to Lie with Statistics.* W.W. Norton.

Hunt, R. (1975). *The Reproduction of Color,* Third Edition. John Wiley & Sons.

IBM (1991). *IBM Systems Application Architecture: Common User Access: Advanced Interface Design.*

Itten, J. (1961). *The Art of Color.* Van Nostrand Reinhold.

Joblove, G., and Greenberg, D. (1978). Color Spaces for Computer Graphics. *Computer Graphics* 12(3), 20–25.

Johnson, B., and Shneiderman, B. (1991). Treemaps: A Space-Filling Approach to the Visualization of Hierarchical Information Structures. *Proc. 2nd International IEEE Visualization Conference,* 284–291.

Kantowitz, B., and Sorkin, R. (1983). *Human Factors: Understanding People-System Relationships.* John Wiley & Sons.

Kolers, P., Wrolstad, M., and Bouma, H. (1979). *Processing of Visible Language,* Vol. 1. Plenum Press.

Kolers, P., Wrolstad, M., and Bouma, H. (1980). *Processing of Visible Language,* Vol. 2. Plenum Press.

Lindsay, P., and Norman, D. (1977). *Human Information Processing: An Introduction to Psychology,* Second Edition. Academic Press.

Mackinlay, J. (1986a). Automated Design of Graphical Presentations. Stanford University Department of Computer Sciences Report No. STAN-CS-86-1138.

Mackinlay, J. (1986b). Automating the Design of Graphical Presentations of Relational Information. *ACM Transactions on Graphics* 5(2), April 1986, 110–141.

Mackinlay, J., Robertson, G., and Card, S. (1991). The Perspective Wall: Detail and Context Smoothly Integrated. *Proc. CHI '91*, 173–179.

Marcus, A. (1982a). Designing the Face of an Interface. *IEEE Computer Graphics and Applications* 2(1), 23–29.

Marcus, A. (1982b). Color: A Tool for Computer Graphics Communication. In Greenberg, D., Marcus, A., Schmidt, A., and Gorter, V., (Eds.)*The Computer Image: Applications of Computer Graphics*, Addison-Wesley, 76–90.

Marcus, A. (1983). Graphic Design for Computer Graphics. *IEEE Computer Graphics and Applications* 3(4), 63–70.

Marcus, A. (1990). Principles of Effective Visual Communication for Graphical User Interface Design. *UnixWorld*, August 1990, 107–111; September 1990, 121–124; and October 1990, 135–138 (revised and reformatted).

Marcus, A. (1992). A Comparison of Graphical User Interfaces. In Marcus, A. *Graphic Design for Electronic Documents and User Interfaces*, ACM Press (Excerpt included 137–159, 187–188).

Marcus, A., Smilonich, N., and Thompson, L. (1995). *The Cross-GUI Handbook for Multiplatform User Interface Design*. Addison-Wesley.

McCormick, B., DeFanti, T., and Brown, M. (1987). Special Issue on Visualization in Scientific Computing. *Computer Graphics* 21(6).

Meyer, G., and Greenberg, D. (1980). Perceptual Color Spaces for Computer Graphics. *Computer Graphics* 14(3), 254–261.

Microsoft (1992). *The Windows Interface: An Application Design Guide*. Microsoft Press.

Miller, G. (1956). The Magical Number Seven, Plus or Minus Two: Some Limits on Our Capacity for Processing Information. *Psychological Review* 63, 81–97.

Mills, M. (1982). Cognitive Schema and the Design of Graphics Displays. *Proc. Graphics Interface '82*, 3–12.

Mills, M. (1985). Image Synthesis: Optical Identity or Pictorial Communication? *Proc. Graphics Interface '85*, 303–308.

Monmonier, M. (1991). *How to Lie with Maps*. The University of Chicago Press.

Morris, R. (1989). Rendering Digital Type: A Historical and Economic View of Technology. *The Computer Journal* 32(6), 524–532.

Murch, G. (1984). The Effective Use of Color, Part 1: Physiological Principles. *Tekniques* 7(4), 13–16; Part 2: Perceptual Principles. *Tekniques* 8(1), 4–9; Part 3: Cognitive Principles. *Tekniques* 8(2), 25–31. Tektronix Corporation.

Murch, G. (1985). Color Graphics—Blessing or Ballyhoo? *Computer Graphics Forum* 4, North-Holland, 127–135. (Excerpt included 133–135.)

Myers, B., Goldstein, J., and Goldberg, M. (1994). Creating Charts by Demonstration. *Proc. CHI '94*, ACM, 106–111, 475.

Naiman, A. (1991). The Use of Grayscale for Improved Character Presentation. Ph.D. Thesis, Department of Computer Science, University of Toronto, March.

Noik, E. (1993). Exploring Large Hyperdocuments: Fisheye Views of Nested Networks. *Proc. ACM Conference on Hypertext and Hypermedia*, 192–195.

Open Software Foundation (1992). *OSF/Motif Style Guide*. Prentice Hall.

Perry, T., Wallich, P., Apt, C., and Baldauf, D. (1985). Computer Display: New Choices, New Tradeoffs. *IEEE Spectrum*, July, 52–73.

Price, B., Baecker, R., and Small, I. (1993). A Principled Taxonomy of Software Visualization. *Journal of Visual Languages and Computing* 4(3), 211–266.

Rao, R., and Card, S. (1994). The Table Lens: Merging Graphical and Symbolic Representations in an Interactive Focus+Context Visualization for Tabular Information. *Proc. CHI '94*, ACM, 318–322, 481–482.

Refioglu, H. (Ed.) (1983). *Electronic Displays*. IEEE Press.

Robertson, G., Card, S., and Mackinlay, J. (1993). Information Visualization Using 3D Interactive Animation. *Communications of the ACM* 36(4), 57–71.

Robertson, G., Mackinlay, J., and Card, S. (1991). Cone Trees: Animated 3D Visualizations of Hierarchical Information. *Proc. CHI '91*, ACM, 189–194.

Robertson, P., and O'Callaghan, J. (1986). The Generation of Color Sequences for Univariate and Bivariate Mapping. *IEEE Computer Graphics and Applications* 6(2), 24–32.

Rosen, B. (1963). *Type and Typography: The Designer's Type Book*. Van Nostrand Reinhold.

Roth, S., Kolojejchick, J., Mattis, J., and Goldstein, J. (1994). Interactive Graphic Design Using Automatic Presentation Knowledge. *Proc. CHI '94*, ACM, 112–117, 476.

Rubinstein, R. (1988). *Digital Typography: An Introduction to Type and Composition for Computer System Design*. Addison-Wesley.

Ruder, E. (1967). *Typography: A Manual of Design*. Hastings House Press.

Salomon, G. (1990). New Uses for Color. In Laurel, B. (Ed.) (1990), *The Art of Human-Computer Interface Design*, Addison-Wesley, 269–278.

Samuleson, P. (1992). Updating the Copyright Look and Feel Lawsuits. *Communications of the ACM* 35(9), 25–31.

Samuleson, P. (1993). The Ups and Downs of Look and Feel. *Communications of the ACM* 36(4), 29–35.

Sanders, M., and McCormick, E. (1993). *Human Factors in Engineering and Design*, Seventh Edition. McGraw-Hill.

Sarkar, M., and Brown, M. (1992). Graphical Fisheye Views of Graphs. *Proc. CHI '92*, ACM, 83–91.

Schaffer, D., Zuo, Z., Greenberg, S., Bartram, L., Dill, J., Dubs, S., and Roseman, M. (forthcoming). Navigating Hierarchically Clustered Networks through Fisheye and Full-Zoom Methods. *ACM Transactions on Information Systems*.

Schmid, C. (1983). *Statistical Graphics: Design Principles and Practice*. John Wiley & Sons.

Schmid, C., and Schmid, S. (1979). *Handbook of Graphic Presentation*, Second Edition. John Wiley & Sons.

Seybold, J. (1984). *The World of Digital Typesetting*. Seybold Publications, Inc.

Shneiderman, B. (1991). Protecting Rights in User Interface Designs. *ACM SIGCHI Bulletin* 22(2), 18–19.

Shneiderman, B. (Ed.) (1993). *Sparks of Innovation in Human-Computer Interaction.* Ablex.

Smith, A. (1978). Color Gamut Transform Pairs. *Computer Graphics* 12(3), 12–19.

Smith, S. (1988). Standards Versus Guidelines for Designing User Interface Software. In Helander (1988), 877–889.

Snyder, H. (1988). Image Quality. In Helander (1988), 437–474.

Spear, M. (1969). *Practical Charting Techniques.* McGraw-Hill.

Sproull, R. (1986). Frame-Buffer Display Architectures. In *Annual Review of Computer Science*, Annual Reviews, 19–46.

Stevens, S. (1961). The Psychophysics of Sensory Function. In Rosenblith, W. (Ed.), *Sensory Communication*, MIT, 1–34.

Stone, M., Cowan, W., and Beatty, J. (1988). Color Gamut Mapping and the Printing of Digital Color Images. *ACM Transactions on Graphics* 7(4), 249–292.

Sukiviriya, P., and Foley, J. (1990). Coupling a UI Framework with Automatic Generation of Context-Sensitive Animated Help. *Proc. UIS '90*, ACM, 152–166.

Sun Microsystems (1990). *Open Look Graphical User Interface Application Style Guidelines.* Addison-Wesley.

Sutherland, I. (1963). Sketchpad: A Man-Machine Graphical Communication System. *AFIPS Conference Proceedings* 23, 329–346.

Tannas, L. (1985). *Flat-Panel Displays and CRTs.* Van Nostrand Reinhold.

Tannas, L. (1986). Electroluminescence Catches the Public Eye. *IEEE Spectrum* 23(10), 37–42.

Thompson, P. (1985). Visual Perception: An Intelligent System with Limited Bandwidth. In A. Monk, (Ed.), *Fundamentals of Human-Computer Interaction*, Academic Press.

Tinker, M. (1963). *Legibility of Print.* Iowa State University Press.

Tinker, M. (1965). *Bases for Effective Reading.* University of Minnesota Press.

Travis, D. (1991). *Effective Color Displays: Theory and Practice.* Academic Press.

Tufte, E. (1983). *The Visual Display of Quantitative Information.* Graphics Press.

Tufte, E. (1990). *Envisioning Information.* Graphics Press.

Tukey, J. (1977). *Exploratory Data Analysis.* Addison-Wesley.

Tullis, T. (1981). An Evaluation of Alphanumeric, Graphics, and Color Information Displays. *Human Factors* 23(5), 541–550.

Tullis, T. (1983). The Formatting of Alphanumeric Displays: A Review and Analysis. *Human Factors* 25(6), 657–682.

Tullis, T. (1988). Screen Design. In Helander (1988), 377–411.

Van Cott, H., and Kinkade, R. (Eds.) (1972). *Human Engineering Guide to Equipment Design*, Revised Edition. American Institutes for Research.

Van Vliet, J. (Ed.) (1986). *Text Processing and Document Manipulation.* Cambridge University Press.

Van Vliet, J. (Ed.) (1988). *Document Manipulation and Typography.* Cambridge University Press.

Werner, K. (1993). The Flat Panel's Future. *IEEE Spectrum* 30(11), 18–26.

Williamson, C., and Shneiderman, B. (1992). The Dynamic Home Finder: Evaluating Dynamic Queries in a Real-Estate Information Exploration System. *Proc. SIGIR '92*, ACM, 338–346.

Witten, I. (1985). Elements of Computer Typography. *International Journal of Man-Machine Studies* 23, 623–687.

Wong, W. (1987). *Principles of Color Design.* Van Nostrand Reinhold.

Wyszecki, G., and Stiles, W. (1982). *Color Science: Concepts and Methods, Quantitative Data and Formulae*, Second Edition. John Wiley & Sons.

Yule, J. (1967). *Principles of Color Reproduction.* John Wiley & Sons.

Zeleznik, R., Herndon, K., Robbins, D., Huang, N., Meyer, T., Parker, N., and Hughes, J. (1993). An Interactive 3D Toolkit for Constructing 3D Widgets. *Computer Graphics* 27(3), 81–84.

VIDEOS

Abelson, H. (1985). Boxer: Applications of a Personal Computing Environment. *ACM SIGGRAPH Video Review (SGVR)* 18.

Ahlberg, C., and Shneiderman, B. (1994). Visual Information Seeking Using the FilmFinder. *ACM SGVR* 97.

AT&T Bell Laboratories (1993). High Interaction Data Visualization—Using Seesoft to Visualize Program Change History. *ACM SGVR* 88.

Baecker, R. (1981). *Sorting Out Sorting.* 30-minute computer-animated teaching film. Distributed by Morgan Kaufmann Publishers. Excerpted in *ACM SGVR* 1.

Beretta, G., and Stone, M. (1990). Color Selection. *ACM SGVR* 55.

Bier, E. (1989). MatchTool: Interactive Graphical Search and Substitute. *ACM SGVR* 48.

Brown, M. (1992). An Introduction to ZEUS. *ACM SGVR* 77.

Brown, M. (1993). Browsing Graphs Using a Fisheye View. *ACM SGVR* 88.

Carnegie Mellon University (1991). GENIE: Developing and Assessing State-of-the-Art Integrated Programming Environments. *ACM SGVR* 65.

CCA (1983). Program Visualization. *ACM SGVR* 13.

Easel Corp. (1992). Graphic Design of an Executive Information System. *ACM SGVR* 78.

Eisenstadt, M., and Brayshaw, M. (1988). Visualizing the Execution of Prolog Programs. *ACM SGVR* 58.

Fairchild, K., and Poltrock, S. (1987). SemNet 2.1. *ACM SGVR* 27.

Furnas, G. (1990). Graphical Reasoning for Graphical Interfaces. *ACM SGVR* 56.

Giannitrapani, L. (1987). Three Dimensional Font Design. *ACM SGVR* 34.

Gleicher, M. (1992). Briar—A Constraint-based Drawing Program. *ACM SGVR* 77.

Henry Dreyfuss Associates (1992). Computer Interface Design 1992. *ACM SGVR* 78.

Hill, W., and Hollan, J. (1992). Pointing and Visualization. *ACM SGVR* 77.

Karsenty, S. (1993). Inferring Graphical Constraints with Rockit. *ACM SGVR* 89.

Kim, S. (1988). Viewpoint: Toward a Computer for Visual Thinkers. *ACM SGVR* 58.

Lieberman, H. (1985). ZStep: A Stepper for LISP-based Visual Inspection. *ACM SGVR* 19.

ParcPlace Systems (1989). A Navigator for UNIX. *ACM SGVR* 46.

Pier, K. (1989). Digital Darkroom. *ACM SGVR* 48.

Pier, K., and Bier, E. (1991). Documents as User Interfaces. *ACM SGVR* 63.

Plaisant, C., and Jain, V. (1994). Dynamaps: Dynamic Queries on a Health Statistics Atlas. *ACM SGVR* 97.

Robertson, G., Mackinlay, J., and Card, S. (1991). Information Visualization Using 3D Interactive Animation. *ACM SGVR* 63.

Russell, A. (1987). MIT Visible Language Workshop. *ACM SGVR* 33.

Shneiderman, B., Williamson, C., and Ahlberg, C. (1992). Dynamic Queries: Database Searching by Direct Manipulation. *ACM SGVR* 77.

Small, D., Ishizaki, S., and Cooper, M. (1994). Typographic Space. *ACM SGVR* 97.

Spence, R. (1983). Office of the Professional. *ACM SGVR* 13.

Stone, M. (1987). Color Selection Tool. *ACM SGVR* 33.

Sutherland, I. (1963). Sketchpad. *ACM SGVR* 13. Originally filmed in 1963, published in 1983.

Tektronix (1985). Magpie. *ACM SGVR* 19.

Turo, D. (1994). Hierarchical Visualization with Treemaps: Making Sense of Pro Basketball Data. *ACM SGVR* 97.

Tweedie, L., Spence, R., Williams, D., and Bhogal, R. (1994). The Attribute Explorer. *ACM SGVR* 97.

Visualization Software (1991). Special Issue on Visualization Software. *ACM SGVR* 70.

Xerox (1985a). Human Interface Aspects of Typefounder. *ACM SGVR* 18.

Xerox (1985b). Multilingual Typing. *ACM SGVR* 18.

Xerox (1985c). Cedar Programming Environment. *ACM SGVR* 19.

Principles of Effective Visual Communication for Graphical User Interface Design

Aaron Marcus, President, Aaron Marcus and Associates, Inc.
1144 65th Street, Suite F, Emeryville, California 94608-1109 USA
Tel: 510-601-0994, Fax: 510-547-6125, Internet Email: marcus.1@applelink.apple.com

Abstract

Researchers and developers should develop a high-quality, integrated approach to the graphical presentation of all elements of human-computer (user) interface (HCI) design. Principles from information-oriented, systematic design can assist in providing guidance for simple, clear, consistent solutions to the design of menus, windows, icons, dialogue boxes, and control panels that are not explicitly specified by current graphical user interface (GUI) paradigms.

Introduction

Some researchers and developers think their user interface design problems are solved because industry conventions for window managers have emerged. However, programmers have discovered that graphical user interface (GUI) paradigms such as Microsoft Windows™, Motif™, Apple Macintosh™, or NextStep™ do not solve the essential task of visually communicating a product's data and functions.

In this tutorial article, you will learn how information-oriented, systematic graphic design can benefit graphical user interface design in conveying information about data and functions. Some basic principles of visual communication can go a long way towards achieving better graphical user interface design.

In the article, I introduce the terminology of visible language and discuss how to achieve effective visual communication in graphical user interfaces, electronic publishing, and presentations. I emphasized three basic principles: organize, economize, and communicate. I show how to apply those principles to the essential elements of typography, symbolism, and layout inherent in all menus, control panels, icons, and dialogue boxes whose visual attributes are not sufficiently specified by current GUI. In the concluding part of my tutorial, I cover the subject of color. This complex and interesting topic requires some detailed examination.

GUIs and Graphic Design

A GUI design must account for the following:

- A comprehensible mental image (metaphor)
- Appropriate organization of data, functions, tasks, and roles (cognitive model)
- Efficient navigation schema among these data and functions, tasks, and roles
- Quality appearance characteristics (the look)
- Effective interaction sequencing (the feel)

Graphic design can help GUIs achieve their potential to communicate. Information-oriented, systematic graphic design is the use of typography, symbols, color, and other static and dynamic graphics to convey facts, concepts, and emotions. Graphic design is found in almost every facet of life, from the design of books, films, magazines, and videos, to the design of exhibits, highway signage, and maps.

Information-oriented, systematic graphic design helps people understand complex information. So, why shouldn't graphic design help users find *their* way through data and functions, and make the trip more pleasant as well?

Information-oriented, systematic graphic design can help in almost every phase of product development providing effective communication for every kind of user, application, platform, and GUI

How is this possible? Because successful visual communication through information-oriented, systematic graphic design relies on some fundamental graphic design principles. Once you are aware of these principles, you will be able to appreciate why some displays are better than others, and, after a little practice, you'll find your own decision making and accomplishments are improving. You can apply these principles to the design of all typical GUI components: screens, windows, menus, dialogue boxes, control panels, icons, and pointers/cursors.

Design Considerations for Successful GUIs

When designing successful GUIs, development, usability, and acceptance factors are of critical importance.

Development factors include the following: platform constraints, tool kits and component libraries, support for rapid prototyping, and customizability. In all of these areas, graphic design can help by improving visual communication.

Usability factors typically include the following: human abilities, product identity, clear conceptual model, and multiple representations. Again, graphic design principles can assist by taking into account human factors and expressing a strong visual identity.

Finally, acceptance factors include these: installed base, corporate politics, international markets, and documentation and training.

All of these factors benefit from improved visual communication in the user interface. A conceptually distinct organization, a visually consistent presentation, and an effective use of visible language contribute to improved visual communication.

Visible Language

The term "visible language" may not be familiar to you. The concept of visible language refers to all the graphical techniques used to communicate the message or content. The term includes the following:

- Layout: formats, proportions, and grids; two-dimensional and three-dimensional organization.
- Typography: selection of typefaces and typesetting, including variable-width sans-serif and serif fonts as well as fixed-width fonts found on most computer displays.
- Color and texture: color, texture and light that convey complex information and pictoral reality.
- Imagery: signs, icons, and symbols, from the photographically real to the abstract.
- Animation: a dynamic or kinetic display that is especially important for video-related imagery.
- Sequencing: the overall approach to visual storytelling.
- Sound: abstract, vocal, concrete, or musical cues. These have been called "earcons", a pun on icons.
- Visual identity: the additional, unique rules that lend overall consistency to a user interface.

All information-oriented, systematic graphic design relies on these visual signs to convey meaning to a viewer. Notice that two strange items appear in the list. Obviously, sound is not visual, but acoustic cues increasingly will be part of the repertoire of the information designer of GUIs. The last item, visual identity, refers to overall decisions about how the corporation or the product line expresses itself in visible language.

The basic technique in achieving effective visual communication involves establishing explicit rules, specifications, and guidelines for visible language that affect the user interface.

Principles of User Interface Design

The manipulation of visible language is a basic task of user interface design. This set of principles can be a useful guide to professional practice, research, and development.

- **Organize:** Provide the user with a clear and consistent conceptual structure.
- **Economize:** Maximize the effectiveness of a minimal set of cues.
- **Communicate:** Match the presentation to the capabilities of the user.

Let's look at each of these principles in detail.

Principle 1: Organize

The first principle is to get organized (see Figure 1). The Bauhaus artist and designer Josef Albers (*Despite Straight Lines*, Yale University Press) expressed it this way:

To design is to plan and organize,
to order, to relate, and to control.

In short, it embraces all means
opposing disorder and accident.

Therefore, it signifies a human
need and qualifies man's thinking
and doing.

There are several important concepts within the major principle of organization: consistency, screen layout, relationships, and navigability

Consistency

There are four important aspects of consistency: internal consistency, external consistency, real world consistency, and when *not* to be consistent, i.e., when to deviate from the norm.

The principle of internal consistency says: observe the *same* conventions and rules for *all* elements of the GUI. Figure 2 provides an example.

Casual differences should be avoided. Without a strong motivating reason, these casual differences cause the viewer to work harder to understand the essential message of the display.

The second point is external consistency: follow existing platform and cultural conventions across user interfaces. Figure 3 provides an example.

The lack of external consistency can cause confusion for users moving across applications. Imagine the chaos on the interstate highway network if the Stop sign changed visually from state to state! What we need for GUIs is the same kind of consistency for *conceptual* landscapes. Remember: designing a GUI is like designing a city full of exciting and useful people, places, and activities.

The third point is real world consistency: make the conventions consistent with real world experience. Figure 4 provides an example.

The fourth and last point is innovation: deviate from existing conventions only when doing so provides a clear benefit to the user. In other words, have a good reason for being inconsistent! In an article on the topic of consistency, Jonathan Grudin, a GUI researcher (see Bibliography), showed that sometimes it is impossible to avoid some kinds of inconsistency, and that inconsistency even can be beneficial. However, as a general rule, strive for consistency, without being slavish about it.

Screen Layout

The second major way to organize visual displays is to design their spatial layout or composition. There are three primary ways of achieving organization of screen layout: use a grid structure, standardize the screen layout, and group related elements.

Grids of horizontal and vertical lines can help locate items in menus, major window components, and other two-dimensional compositions such as dialogue boxes or control panels. The exact measurements must be worked out very carefully to take into account the content to be displayed, spaces between text groups, the screen resolution, and the viewing conditions. Generally, the maximum number of major divisions in the horizontal or vertical direction follows what human factors specialists call Miller's magic number, namely, 7 ± 2. This recommendation derives from the maximum number of coding items we can easily remember in short-term memory.

The same idea can be applied to a control panel, menu, dialogue box, or even the small area of icons, in which case a small grid helps to locate individual pieces of these pictograms and ideograms. Figure 5 shows some examples.

Relationships

Another technique helpful in achieving visual organization is to establish clear relationships by linking related elements and disassociating unrelated elements. This simple precept may be complex to carry out in practice. Figure 6 presents an example.

Navigability

The final means of organizing visual elements is navigability. Important techniques include these: provide an initial focus for the viewer's attention, direct attention to important, secondary, or peripheral items, and assist in navigation throughout the material. Figure 7 provides an example.

Principle 2: Economize! (or Make Do with What You Have)

In this first part of the tutorial we have introduced the subject of information-oriented, systematic graphic design for GUIs and the idea of visual language. We have looked at one important principal for achieving effective visual communication: organization. In this next section, we shall investigate how to use the best techniques to reach the user with the message of functions or data that the user interface must communicate.

The second major principle is to economize (doing the most with the least). Don Norman, a cognitive scientist, comments on economy, in his book *The Psychology of Everyday Things* (Basic Books, New York, 1969). Here are some excerpts:

- *How many controls does a device need?*
- *The fewer the controls, the easier it looks to use and the easier it is to find the relevant controls...*
- *To make something look easy, minimize the number of controls.*

The concept of economy can be broken down into four major subtopics: simplicity, clarity, distinctiveness, and emphasis.

Simplicity suggests that we include only those elements that are essential for communication. In addition, we should be as unobtrusive as possible.

As they say in the business world, use the KISS method: Keep it *Supremely Simple*. Do *not* assume that your audience is stupid; we all have natural limits to the rate at which we can take in informational-rich content. If you exceed natural limits, you will induce indifference, boredom, or anxiety.

No matter to whom you're communicating, simplicity is a virtue, unless your objective is to confuse, entertain, or beautify, in which cases, overindulgence *may* be justified. In general, the GUI components should be modest and *not* overly attract the viewer's attention. Users should be almost unconscious of the GUI working to convey meaning. Figure 8 provides an example.

Keep It Crystal Clear

The second technique for being economical is clarity: design all components so that their meaning is not ambiguous. Figure 9 provides an example.

The third technique for achieving economy is distinctiveness: distinguish important properties of essential elements. Figure 10 illustrates this technique.

The final technique of economizing is emphasis. In general, make the most important elements *salient*, i.e., easily perceived. De-emphasize non-critical elements and minimize clutter so that critical information is not hidden. Figure 11 makes this point.

Principle 3: Communicate!

The previous comments explored the principles of organization and economy. The third main principle is, communicate! The visual communication researcher Sol Worth puts it this way in his book, *Studying Visual Communication* (University of Pennsylvania Press, Philadelphia)

Communication...is...a social process, within a specified context, in which signs are produced and transmitted, perceived, and treated as messages from which meaning can be inferred.

To communicate successfully, a GUI must keep in balance these factors: legibility, readability, typography, symbolism, multiple views, and color/texture.

The first factor is legibility: design individual characters, symbols, and graphic elements to be easily noticeable and distinguishable. Figure 12 shows some examples.

Typefonts, desktop icons, control panel symbols, etc. all need to be designed so that their parts show up well. You must select visualization techniques that are appropriate to the output display technology (*e.g.*, the spatial resolution, color, and animation characteristics). Keep in mind that many viewers over 40 years of age often need help with glasses or contact lenses just to see the screen well.

Another factor to remember is that dark screen backgrounds in brightly lighted rooms may cause distracting reflections that can diminish screen legibility. In contrast, brightly lighted screens in dark rooms may be too glaring and hard to see.

Closely related to legibility is readability. The term readability means that the display is comprehensible, i.e., easy to identify and interpret, as well as inviting and attractive. Figure 13 presents an example.

One of the key contributors to legibility and readability is the use of typography in the user interface. We still rely on text, tables, lists, and annotation, even if we are showing charts, diagrams, or other graphical displays. Typography includes the characteristics of individual elements (typefaces and typestyles) and their groupings (typesetting techniques).

Use a small number of typefaces of suitable legibility, clarity, and distinctiveness to distinguish between different classes of information. Within each typeface, select a set of enhanced letterforms, punctuation marks, and symbols. Figure 14 provides some examples. Usually, one to three typefaces are sufficient for most situations, even the very complex code displays that Ron Baecker and I recommend for code visualization in our book *Human Factors and Typography For More Readable Programs* (see Bibliography).

The third and final typographic recommendation concerns typesetting: Within menus, dialogue boxes, control panels, forms, and other window components, adjust the point size, word spacing, paragraph indentation, and line spacing to enhance the readability and to emphasize critical information.

The following are some basic recommendations:

- Generally, you should use a maximum of three typefaces in a maximum of three sizes, no matter what the application.
- Lines of text should have from 40 to 60 characters maximum, and words should be spaced correctly, usually the width of a lower case "r" or "i" for a variable-width text.
- Text should be set in appropriate formats, that is, set text flush left, set numbers flush right, avoid centered text in lists, and avoid short justified lines

of text.

- For fixed-width fonts, justified lines of text can slow reading speed by 12 percent.

Use upper and lower case characters whenever possible, i.e., avoid all capital lines of text, which can also slow reading speed by 12 percent.

Of course, one can always find exceptions to these guidelines, but the basic recommendations should serve for most typographic settings.

Making Sense of Symbolism

Typographic characters are not the only visible language elements that must be designed so that they communicate their content efficiently. Icons, symbols, charts, maps, diagrams, and photographic imagery used in the displays also must be carefully selected and refined to communicate the desired contents.

The specific principles for designing charts, maps, diagrams, pictograms and ideograms are more numerous than space permits at this time. The Bibliography provides references to some outstanding sources of guidelines and case studies, such as the work of Tufte, Bertin, and Ota.

Multiple Views

One important technique for improving communication in the user interface is to provide multiple perspectives on the display of complex structures and processes. An important principle of good design, then, is making use of these multiple views:

- Multiple forms of representation
- Multiple levels of abstraction
- Simultaneous alternative views
- Links and cross references
- Metadata, metatext, metagraphics

Figure 15 shows two examples.

Color/Texture

Our final topic, color, is a very complex subject and will be treated specially to conclude this tutorial. Color can be a powerful tool for communication if used correctly. The basic recommendation is this: use appropriate highlighting and deemphasis techniques to convey meaningful semantic distinctions.

A human factors researcher, Dr. Gerald Murch, comments on color in his paper "The Effective Use of Color in Visual Displays: Text and Graphics Applications" this way: "Color can be a powerful tool to improve the usefulness of an information display in a wide variety of areas if color is used properly. Conversely, the inappropriate use of color canseriously reduce the functionality of a display system."

Color Terms and Concepts

Color discussions can be confusing because scientists, artists, designers, programmers, and marketing professionals describe color phenomena in different ways. Let's first discuss the color terms using one useful set of dimensions: hue, value, and chroma. These color terms are derived from the Munsell system of color used by artists, designers, and manufacturers. The dimensions differ from the red, green, and blue basis of the "RGB" color system familiar to users of CRT display devices. The approach also differs from another color system, the International Commission on Illumination (CIE), which uses specific spectral measurements to unambiguously specify color.

Hue is the spectral wavelength composition of a color that produces perceptions of being blue, orange, green, etc. Value is the relative amount of lightness or darkness of the color in a range of black to white (also called intensity). Chroma is the purity of the color in a scale from gray to the most vivid variant of the perceived color (also called saturation). Figure 16 shows the interrelations of all of these dimensions. Brightness, a fourth key term, refers to the amount of light energy creating the color. Different amounts levels of brightness affect the shape and size of the hue-value-lightness solid.

The circle of hues, the vertical range of values, and the range of chromas going out from the central vertical axis provide a basic specification of the color. Note that one further dimension, brightness, is required, which refers to the amount of energy in the light. In effect, there is a color solid for each brightness level, and the detailed, shape of the color solid change somewhat, based on the human eye's performance characteristics.

One important point to bear in mind is that color combinations can take place in different media in several ways. Figure 17 shows three typical means of combining color. At the left, primary colors of illuminated light like red, blue, and green, additively combine in pairs to produce magenta, cyan, and yellow, and together produce white light.

In the center, primary colors of pigment like red, blue, and yellow subtractively combine to produce a dark brown-black. CRT screens typically combine light additively, while most hardcopy color is obtained through subtractive mixtures of pigments, dyes, or tints.

At the right is an example of optical mixture in which small lines blend into a single color. Typical four-color process printing of images on paper uses closely spaced small dots of cyan, yellow, and magenta, plus black (the graphic arts industry's CYMK specification of color) to achieve an optical mixing of colors due to the eye's inability to resolve the individual color elements in "full-color" graphic arts printing.

A typical need for screen design is to combine colors so they make visual sense. Artists and designers have proposed several basic approaches to harmonious combinations, which are illustrated in Figure 18.

Beyond the basic technology of color for screen display, it is important to understand how color can help communication. Here are some basic advantages:

- Emphasize important information
- Identify subsystems or structures
- Portray natural objects realistically
- Portray time and progress
- Reduce errors of interpretation
- Add coding dimensions
- Increase comprehensibility
- Increase believability and appeal

With respect to learning and comprehension, color is superior to black-and-white in terms of the viewer's processing time and emotional reactions, and there is a difference in a viewer's ability to interpret information. People often can learn more from a color display if color is used correctly. Another crucial factor is that color is more enjoyable. With respect to memory performance, memory for color information appears to be superior to black-and-white.

These benefits indicate that color can work for you in communicating facts, concepts, and emotions; but color is definitely a complex tool. At the same time, color has these potential drawbacks:

- Color requires more expensive and complicated display equipment.

- Color displays may not accommodate color deficient vision, which occurs in about 8 percent of Caucasian males.

- Some colors may cause visual discomfort and afterimages.

- Color may contribute to visual confusion or may catalyze negative associations through cross-disciplinary and cross-cultural connotations.

Because color can be misused easily, there is a clear need for guidelines. Establishing complete rules or specifications for color use is difficult. The International Standards Organization (ISO) has begun by publishing draft standards for some aspects of basic color legibility. Their report and some general guidelines on color are referred to in the Bibliography.

Color Design Principles

To keep recommendations simple, we can refer to the original three basic principles, but this time apply them to color. We'll examine selected guidelines under each principle: color organization, color economy, and color communication.

Color Organization

The first set of recommendations about color concerns consistency of organization. Use color to group related items, and use a consistent color code for screen displays, documentation, and training materials. Figure 19 presents an example.

In general, similar colors should imply a relation among objects. A viewer can sense the relatedness by color over space and over time in sequences of images. Be complete and consistent in your color groupings. For example, command and control colors in menus should be avoided for information coding within a work area, unless a specific connection is intended. Another recommendation is to use similar background colors for related areas. This color coding can subtly orient the viewer to the conceptual link among these areas.

Once color coding is established, the same colors should be used throughout the GUI and all related publications. This color continuity may require designing colors to appear in different media. Remember: CRT screens use additive color mixtures, while most hardcopy devices use subtractive color mixtures. The color gamuts (that is, available color ranges) of these two media usually are not identical.

Color Economy

The next recommendations concern economical use of color:

The principle of color simplicity suggests using a maximum of 5 ± 2 colors where the meaning must be remembered. Note that this maximum is even less than the so called Miller's magic number from human factors, 7 ± 2. If appropriate, use redundant coding based on shape as well as color.

The basic idea is to use color to enhance black-and-white information, that is, design the display to work well first in black-and-white.

For documentation tasks, for example, using color to portray an object, the maximum number of colors needed is dependent on the application. For aesthetic purposes such as design style, emotional expression, or realism, many more colors may be required. Figure 20 shows some examples of using minimal color.

In figure 20 at the left, 5±2 colors may use a set of a few grays and some strongly different hues, or the set may use only different values for a given hue.

In the center, the rainbow is a reminder to use spectral order in color coding. To code a large set of colors, use the spectral sequence: red, orange, yellow, green, blue, and violet. Francine Frome, a human factors researcher (see Bibliography), has shown that viewers see a spectral order as a natural one and would select red, green, and blue as intuitive choices for the front, middle, and back layers, respectively, when viewing a multi-layer display.

Note, however, that brightness can change a viewer's perception of depth. If the colors are balanced, then red seems to come forward.

At the right, the images are a reminder to use redundant coding of shape as well as color, which aids those with color deficient vision and makes the display more resilient to color distortions caused by ambient light changes or by medium-to-medium conversion. Ambient light can cause changes in perceived hue, value, and chroma. Conversion from one medium to another can cause unforeseen and sometimes uncontrollable changes. Remember that among Caucasian viewers, 8% of males have some form of color-deficient viewing.

Color Emphasis

Among the remaining principles, color emphasis suggests using strong contrast in value and chroma to focus the user's attention on critical information.

The use of bright colors for danger signals, attention getters, reminders, and cursors is entirely appropriate. High chroma red-alerts seem to aid faster response than yellow or yellow-orange if brightness is equal, but of course this also depends upon the background colors. When too many figures or background fields compete for the viewer's attention, confusion arises, as can happen in the Las Vegas approach to color design. The hierarchy of highlighted, neutral, and lowlighted states for all areas of the visual display must be carefully designed to maximize simplicity and clarity. Here again we find the basic maxim: simplicity, clarity, and consistency are especially important for color design.

Use saturated or high-chroma colors for older viewers, or for those who have viewed displays for very long periods of time. Bear in mind that frequent, but short term viewing can benefit from low-chroma displays, and that very bright displays of letters, symbols or lines tend to bloom, that is, the light spreads out against the background.

Color Communication

In color communication, recommendations for legibility include the following: use colors appropriately for the central and peripheral areas of the visual field. Use color combinations whose discriminability is influenced least by the relative area of each color. Do not use colors that are simultaneously high in chroma and spectrally extreme. Figure 21 presents some examples.

The outer edges of the retina are not particularly sensitive to colors in general. Thus, red or green should be used in the center of the visual field, not in the periphery, as in the example at the left. If they are used at the periphery, some signal to the viewer must be given to capture attention, e.g., size change or blinking. Use blue, black, white, and yellow near the periphery of the visual field. The retina remains sensitive to these colors near the periphery.

With regard to the example in the center of Figure 21, use blue for large areas, not for text type, thin lines, or small shapes. Blue-sensitive color receptors are the least numerous in the retina (approximately 5%), and are especially infrequent in the eye's central focusing area, the fovea. Blue is good for screen backgrounds.

If the colors change in size in the imagery, you should bear in mind the following: As color areas decrease in size they appear to change their value and chroma. You also may be able to see this in the center example.

At the right of Figure 21, you see colors that have a strong contrast. Use colors that differ both in chroma and value (lightness). Do not use adjacent colors that differ only in the amount of pure blue, because the edge between the two colors will appear to be fuzzy. To avoid this you might use a dark blue and a light blue.

Regarding use of simultaneously high-chroma, spectrally extreme colors, you can see that strong contrasts of red/green, blue/yellow, green/blue, and red/blue can create vibrations, illusions of shadows, and after-images. Unless you need to create a special visual effect, avoid these combinations.

In general, use light text, thin lines, and small shapes (white, yellow, or red) on medium to dark backgrounds (blue, green, or dark gray) for dark viewing situations. Typical low ambient-light viewing situations are those for slidepresentations, workstations, and video. Video displays produce colors that are lower chroma.

Use dark (blue or black) text, thin lines, and small shapes on light (light yellow, magenta, blue, or white) backgrounds for light viewing situations. Typical viewing situations are those for overhead transparencies and paper. Reserve the highest contrast in figure-field relationships for text type.

Color Interactions

The interaction of color is a very complex subject that cannot be presented in this limited space. The basic text on the subject is Albers' book, *The Interaction of Color* (see Bibliography). Designers of user interfaces need to become familiar with there phenomena, which students of art and design often study. Figure 22 shows two examples of color interaction phenomena.

Color Symbolism

Finally, we recall the importance of symbolism in communication: use color codes that respect existing cultural and professional usage. Figure 23 shows typical examples.

Use color connotations with great care. Connotations vary strongly among different kinds of viewers, especially from different cultures. The correct use of color requires careful analysis of the experience and expectations of the viewers.

For example, mailboxes are blue in the USA, bright red in England, and bright yellow in Greece. If color is used in an electronic mail icon on the screen, this suggests that color sets might be changed for different countries to allow for differences in international markets.

Conclusion

The many recommendations of this tutorial are based on three basic principles: organize! economize! and communicate! These principles may not solve all of the precise GUI design challenges that researchers, developers, and other professionals face when using available GUI paradigms, but these principles can point you in the right direction and get you started.

The next task is to incorporate these principles into your own individual design efforts so that your GUI prototypes and products are better because they communicate their message more effectively. A next stage is to incorporate the principles into your own styleguides, templates, and clip-art so that others may adapt and apply these principles of effective communication.

Developing better visual communication in GUIs will make it possible for everyone to benefit from the capability of high performance computer graphics systems to communicate more efficiently and effectively through high performance graphic design.

Acknowledgments

This article is a slightly edited version of three articles that appeared in *UnixWorld*, 1990, cited in the Bibliography and are reprinted with the permission of *UnixWorld* and McGraw-Hill. The article is based on principles identified in Baecker and Marcus, *Human Factors and Typography for More Readable Programs* (see Bibliography). The current formulation was developed for *MacWeek*'s first national user's conference on user interface design for the Macintosh, MacWeek ID 89, October 1989, and are presented in a videotape available from Aaron Marcus and Associates, Inc. The author would like to thank the following past and current members of his staff for their assistance in preparing this article in its original form: David Collier, N. Gregory Galle, Grant Letz, Sherry Markwart, Adam Miramon, Kevin Mullet, and Sandra Ragan.

Bibliography

Albers, Josef, *Interaction of Color*, Yale University Press, New Haven, 1975.

Baecker, Ronald, and Marcus, Aaron, *Human Factors and Typography for More Readable Programs*, Addison-Wesley, Reading, Mass., 1990.

Bertin, Jacques, *Semiology of Graphics,* University of Wisconsin Press, 1083.

Durrett, H. John, ed., *Color and the Computer*, Academic Press,Orlando, Florida, 1987.

Durrett, John and Judi Trezona, "How to Use Color Displays Effectively," *Byte,* Vol. 7, No. 4, April 1982, pp. 50-53.

Frome, Francine, "Incorporating the Human Factor in Color CAD Systems," *IEEE Proceedings of the 20th Design Automation Conference,* 1983, pp. 189-195.

Grudin, Jonathan, "The Case Against User Interface Consistency," *Communications of the ACM,* Vol. 32, No. 10, October 1989, pp. 1164-1173.

International Standards Organization (ISO)

"Computer Display Color," Draft Standard, Doc. 9241-8, ISO, Zurich, 1989.

Jones, Gerald E., "Color Use, Abuse in Presentations," *Computer Graphics World*, Vol. 9, No. 5, May 1986, pp. 119-120ff.

Marcus, Aaron, "Color: A Tool for Computer Graphics Communication," in Greenberg, Donald, *et al.*, *The Computer Image*, Addison-Wesley, Reading, 1982, pp. 76-90.

Marcus, Aaron, "Users Must Establish Own Rules for Color, " *Computer Graphics Today*, Vol. 2, No. 9, September 1985, pp. 7ff.

Marcus, Aaron, "The Ten Commandments of Color," *Computer Graphics Today,* official publication of the National Computer Graphics Association, Media Horizons, Inc., New York, November 1986, pp. 7ff, reprinted in part in *Color News*, Vol. 2, No. 2, Pantone Color Institute Newsletter, Pantone, Inc.,1987.

Marcus, Aaron, "The User Interface Standards Manual: A Tool for Effective Management," *Proceedings*, National Computer Graphics Association National Conference, Philadelphia, 22-26 March 1987, Vol. 3, Technical Sessions, pp. 461-470.

Marcus Aaron, "Computer Iconographics: Readings on Signs," *Computer Graphics Today*, official publication of the National Computer Graphics Association, Media Horizons, Inc., New York, Vol. 4, No. 7, July 1987, pp. 19-20.

Marcus, Aaron, "Design Tips for Winning Forms," *Computer Graphics Today*, Vol. 5, No. 11, November 1988, pp. 27ff., and in excerpted form in Marcus, Aaron, "Design Tips for Developing Good Form," *Publish!*, Vol. 3, No. 6, PCW Communications, San Francisco, June 1988, p. 68.

Marcus, Aaron, "Visual Arts: Tips for Icon Design," *Computer Graphics Today,* official publication of the National Computer Graphics Association, Media Horizons, Inc., New York, Vol. 6, No. 1, January 1989, pp. 24.

Marcus, Aaron, "Designing Graphical User Interfaces," three-part article, *UnixWorld*, Vol. 7, No. 8, August 1990, pp. 107-116; No. 9, September 1990, pp. 121-127; No. 10, October 1990, pp. 135-138.

Murch, Gerald M., "Effective Use of Color: Cognitive Principles,"*Tekniques*, Vol. 8, No. 2, Summer 1984, pp. 25-31.

Murch, Gerald M., "Physiological Principles for the Effective Use of Color," *IEEE Computer Graphics and Applications*, Vol. 4, No. 11, November 1984, pp. 49-54.

Ota, Yuko, *Pictogram Design*, Kawashi Shobo Publishers, Tokyo, Japan, 1987

Rehe, Rolf F., *Typography: How to Make it Legible,* Design Research International, Carmel, Indiana, 1974.

Taylor, Joann M. and Gerald M. Murch, "The Effective Use of Color in Visual Displays: Text and Graphics Applications," *Color Research and Application,* Vol. 11, Supplement 1986, pp. S3-S10.

Thorrell, L. G. and W. J. Smith, *Using Computer Color Effectively: An Illustrated Reference*, Prentice Hall, Englewood Cliffs, NJ. 1990.

Tufte, Edward R., *The Visual Display of Quantative Information Maters,* Graphics Press, Chelshive, Connecticuit, 1983.

Author's Biography

Aaron Marcus received a BA in physics from Princeton University (1965) and a BFA and MFA in graphic design from Yale University Art School (1968). He is an internationally recognized authority on the design of human-computer interfaces and electronic publishing documents, including chart, form, document, icon, and screen design. He has given tutorials at SIGGRAPH, NCGA, and SIGCHI conferences in addition to seminars at businesses and academic institutions in the USA, Canada, Australia, Israel, Finland, Singapore, and Japan.

As president of Aaron Marcus and Associates, Inc., he and his staff design user interfaces, electronic publishing documents, multimedia, and information displays, such as the visualization of complex structures and processes, executive presentations, and libraries of clip art and templates for computer graphic systems for such clients as Apple, Canon Information Systems, Digital Equipment, Dupont, Eastman Kodak, Hewlett-Packard, IBM, MCC, McDonnell-Douglas, Motorola, NCR, Prime-Computervision, Reuters, Ricoh, and 3M, among others.

Figures

Figure 1: Chaotic Screen, Ordered Screen. This figure summarizes the ideas of being consistent, using an organized screen layout, making relationships clear, and assisting the user's navigation. This example is *not* intended to imply that tiled screen layouts are always the *correct* solution.

Figure 2: Internal Consistency: Dialogue Boxes. In general, you should maximize the similarity of the major components of a user interface, i.e., maximize the regularity of the location and appearance of all items. In the two examples of dialogue boxes, notice that the same kinds of elements are shown in the same place, and those with different kinds of behavior each have their own special appearance.

Figure 3: External Consistency for Text Tool Icons. These text tool icons come from different applications but generally have the same meaning in desktop publishing. The obvious lack of consistency has a negative impact on users using new or similar products.

Figure 4: Real World Consistency: Highway Signage for Screen Display Icons. It is possible to take advantage of objects, processes, or events that are already familiar to the user and build upon this knowledge. This principle is the basis of the success of the desktop metaphor.

Figure 5: Screen, Control Panel and Icon Grids. Screen, control panel and icon grids show how a set of horizontal and vertical lines control size, location, and extent of visual elements.

Figure 6: Relationships. In the example at the left, shape, location, and color can all create strong visual relationships that may be completely inappropriate. Ask yourself if all the bold items are related. Probably not. In the improved example on the right, the relationships are clear, consistent, appropriate, and strong. These monochrome examples are not intended to suggest that monochrome displays are superior, only that the out-of control visual relationships in the example at the left have been brought into greater control.

Figure 7: Navigation. In this example of poor design and improved design, notice how very simple techniques of spatial layout and color (in this case gray values) can help focus the viewer's attention to the most important titlebar areas of the display. Then, the bulleted items guide the viewer through the secondary contents.

Figure 8: Complicated and Simpler Designs. In the example on the left, the design is overdone, with useless differentiation. At the right, the presentation is simpler, with fewer extraneous changes of direction, typefaces, and capitalization. Once you have reduced the display to its utmost simplicity, you can *then* begin to add more as soon as you can justify the additions.

Figure 9: Ambiguous and Clear Icons. In these examples of icons, notice how the ones on the left can be confusing, while the ones on the right are more understandable. Note that the same symbol appears in two situations.

Figure 10: Too Little and Too Much Distinctiveness. The first example shows a typical screen design in which everything is too bland, too much the same. The second example shows a typical Las Vegas approach in which *every* component is trying to be too distinctive. A happy medium is the correct solution.

Figure 11: Too Much and Improved Emphasis. The busy figure that you have seen before emphasizes too many things at once, making a clutter. The second example establishes a clear hierarchy. Remember that this approach can be used in achromatic (black, gray, white) as well as polychrome displays.

Figure 12: Illegible and Legible Texts. The top left example is a classic case of an illegible font. The example below it shows differences in size that are too minimal.

Figure 13: Unreadable and Readable Texts. The top example shows a more unreadable text in which it is difficult to detect the presence of a subtitle. The second example shows a more readable arrangement of the same contents.

Figure 14: Typefaces and Typestyles. Small caps, and special characters that are routinely available for CRT display, as for laser printers, and other hard copy devices.

Figure 15: Verbal and Visual Multiple Views. With multiple views, you can provide the user with the ability to view simultaneously a major "focus" plus additional information on a single screen. You can also provide links and cross references among these views to facilitate navigation through the contents.

Figure 16: Color Dimensions. The image presents color interrelationships in a simplification of a hue, value, and chroma space based on the TekHVC color model. Detailed descriptions of this color space and others appear in the Appendix on color specification systems.

Figure 17: Color Mixtures Showing Additive, Subtractive, and Optical Mixtures. Typical display media use different means of achieving color mixtures. CRT displays use additive mixtures while hardcopy devices use subtractive. Both can use optical mixtures.

Figure 18: Color Harmonies. The approaches show (beginning at the top left) adjacent hues, varying values of a single hue, varying chromas of a single hue, opposing hues (complementary hues), nearly opposing hues (split complements), and equidistant hues (triads).

Figure 19: Color Consistency. On the left, multiple elements unrelatead but with similar colors, can cause confusion about which elements should be understood as a group. On the right, color is used together with location to reinforce grouping. Keep in mind that different values of the same color or different shapes of the same hue can be used to group related elements.

Figure 20: Color Simplicity. Limiting the number of colors, in color codes using a spectral order, and/or using redundant coding of shape increase the simplicity of a color display.

Figure 21: Color Legibility. Correct use of colors that account for the retina's physiological characteristics can improve the legibility of color displays.

Figure 22: Color Interactions. Color interactions with the background color fields can create illusions like that shown in the first example: one color appears like two and two different colors appear like one. This illusion often occurs in area maps or complex diagrams. Colors must be chosen to avoid these illusions. The second example shows Mach banding, in which flat areas of color give a fluted effect, like the sides of a column.

Figure 23: Color Symbolism. Commonly used codes are the traffic light at the left (often used in executive displays for exception reporting); the colors of writing: (black on white with red highlighting, used in financial accounting) and the typical colors of water, earth, and vegetation used in maps.

Figure 1: Chaotic Screen, Ordered Screen

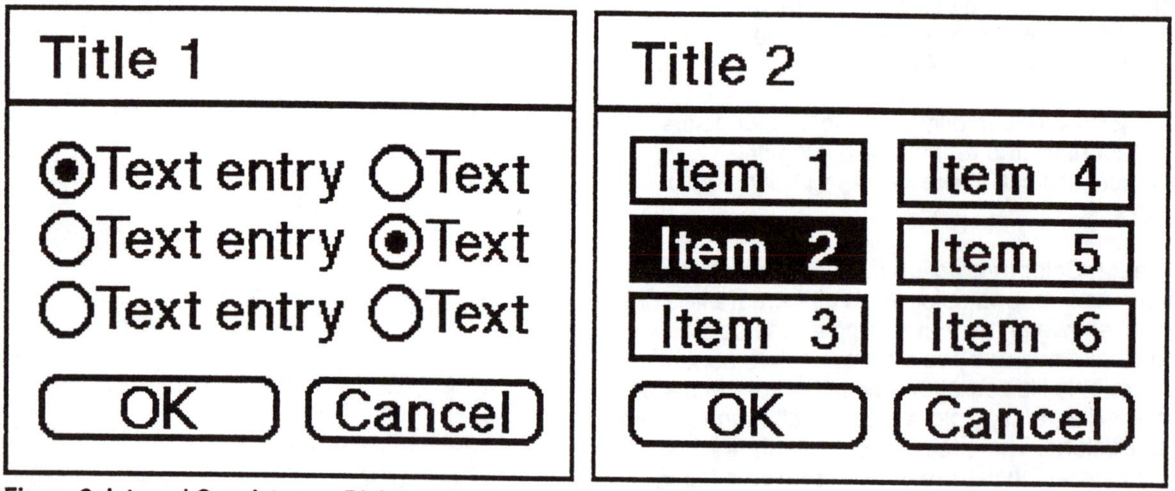

Figure 2: Internal Consistency: Dialogue Boxes

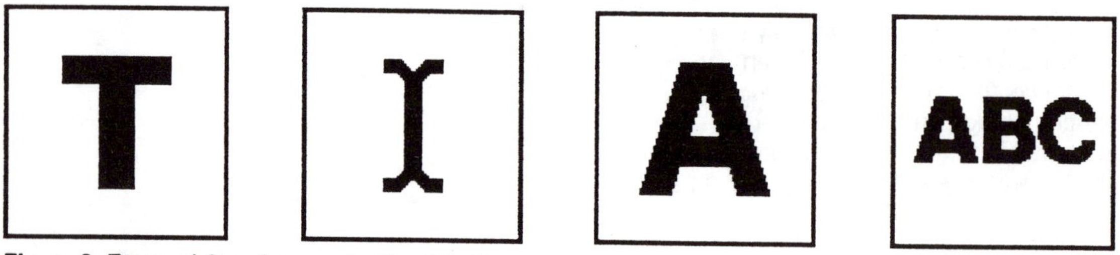

Figure 3: External Consistency for Text Tool Icons

Figure 4: Real World Consistency: Highway Signage for Screen Display Icons

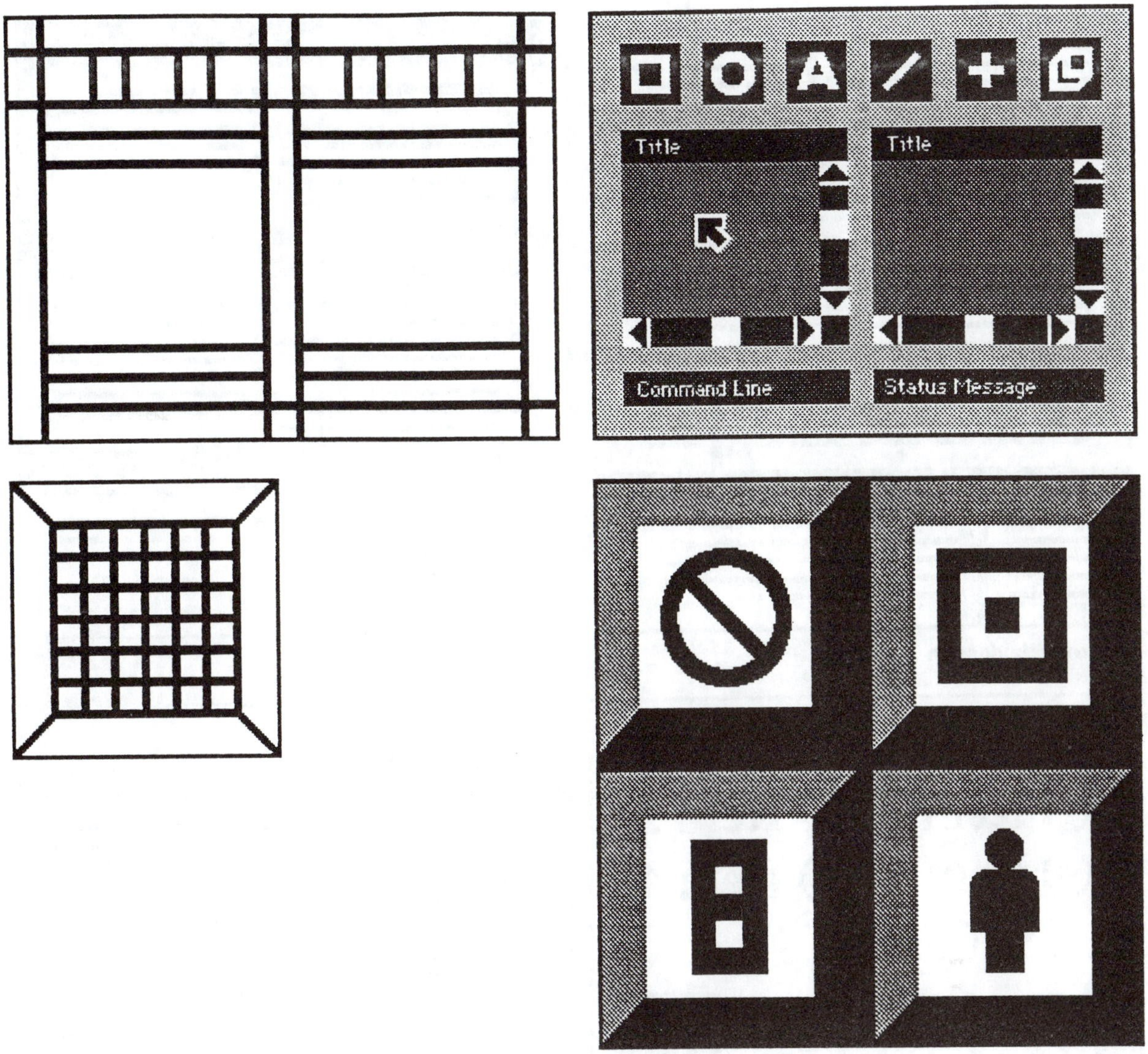

Figure 5: Screen, Control Panel and Icon Grids

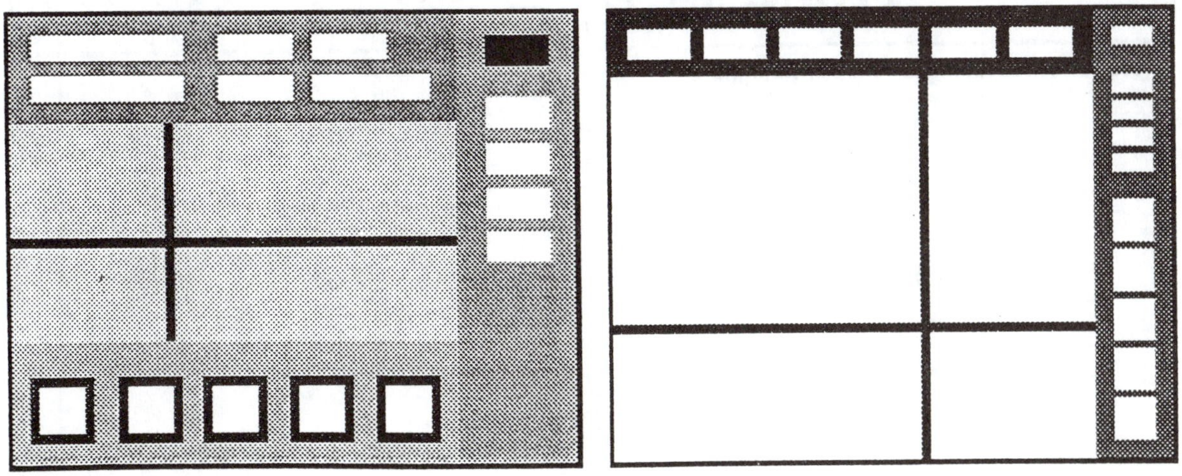

Figure 6: Relationships

Figure 7: Navigation

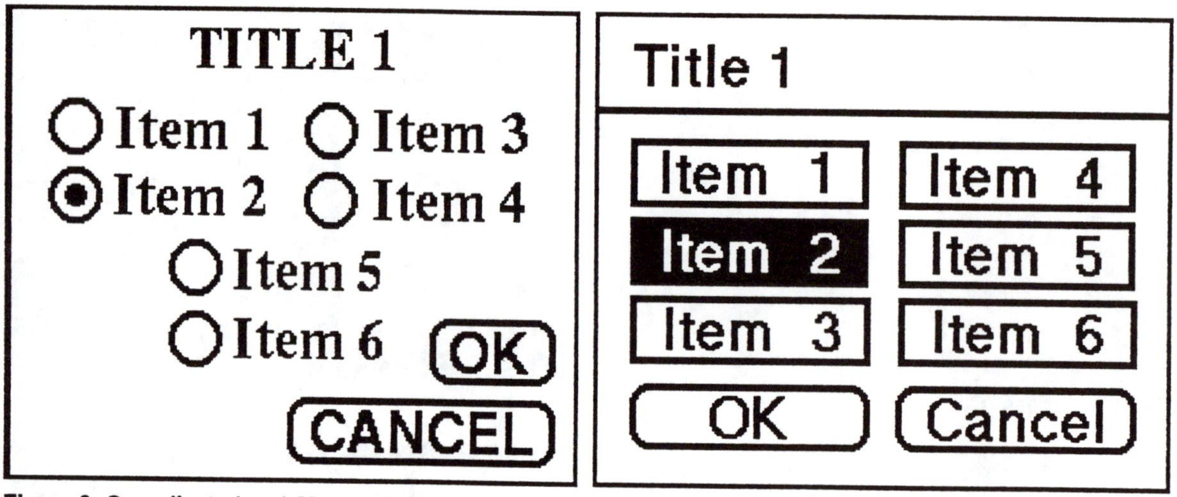

Figure 8: Complicated and Simpler Designs

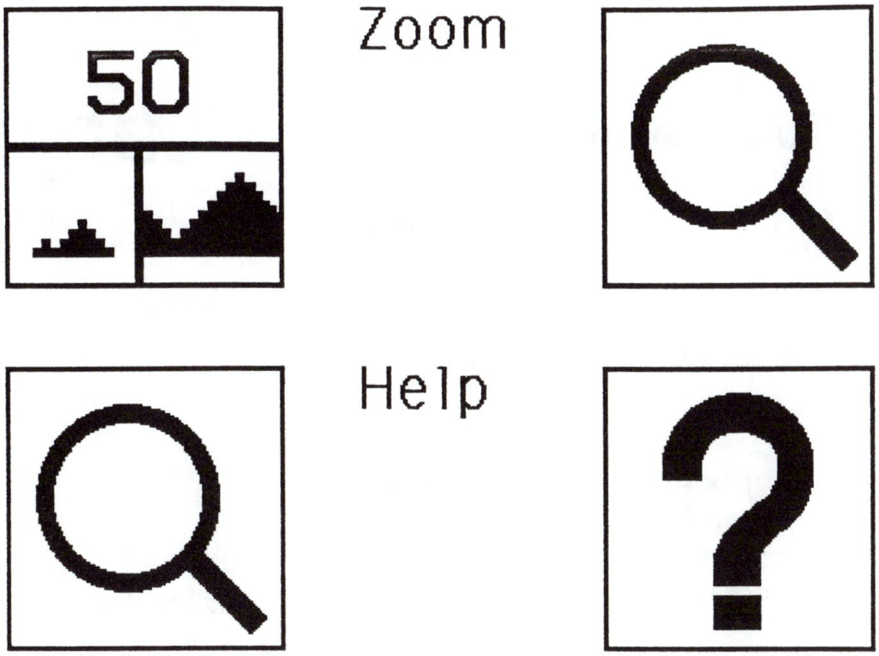

Figure 9: Ambiguous and Clear Icons

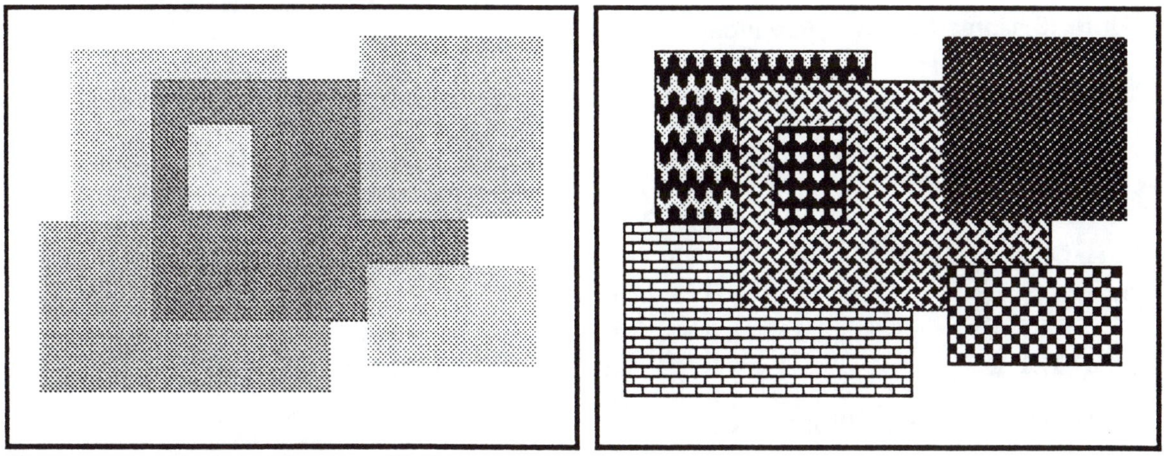

Figure 10: Too Much and Too Little Distinctiveness

Figure 11: Too Much and Improved Emphasis

Illegible	Legible	Illegible	Legible
Text set in Old English	Text set in Univers	Large Medium Small	Large Medium Small

Figure 12: Illegible and Legible Texts Based on Fonts and Relative Sizes

Unreadable: Design components to be easy to interpret and understand. Design components to be inviting and attractive

Readable

Design components to be easy to interpret and understand.

Design components to be inviting and attractive

Figure 13: Unreadable and Readable Texts

Univers
Helvetica
Times Roman
Palatino
Courier

ABCDEfghijkl
ABCDEfghijkl
AAaBBbCCcDDd

Uchbφ=>IQm∃

Figure 14:Typefaces and Typestyles

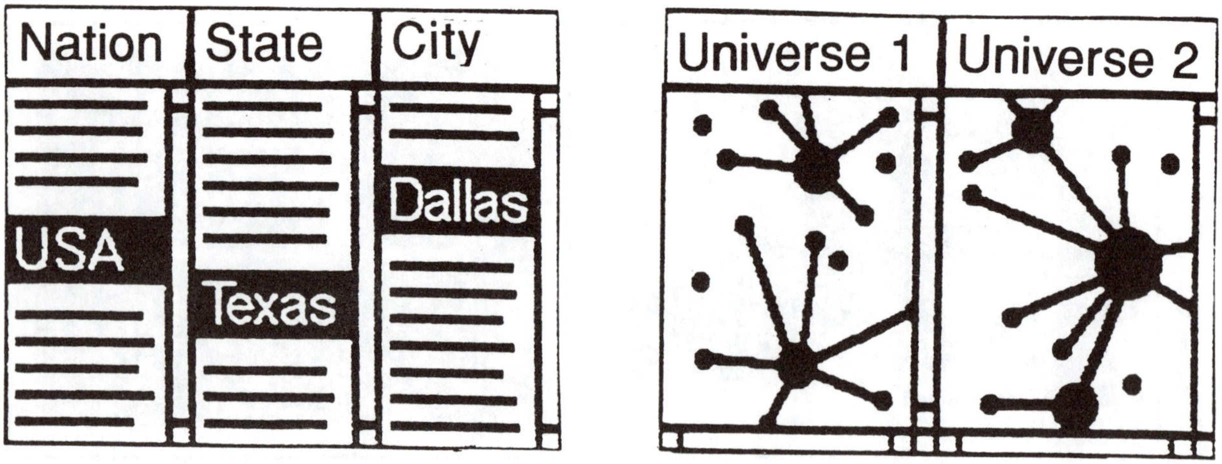

Figure 15: Verbal and Visual Multiple Views

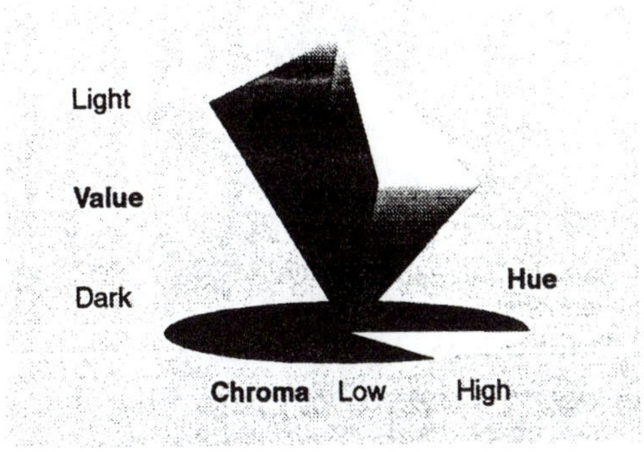

Figure 16: Color Dimensions

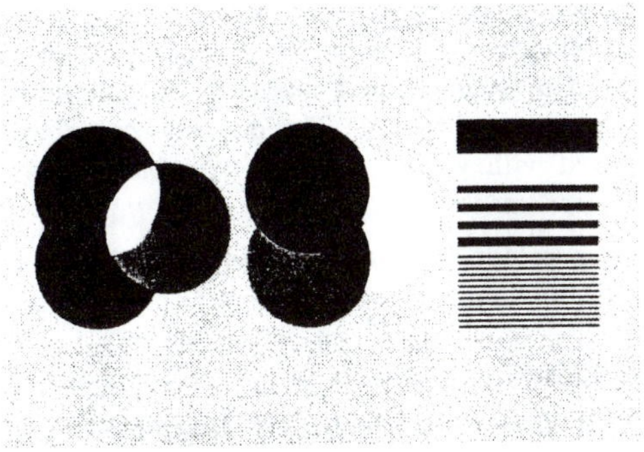

Figure 17: Color Mixtures

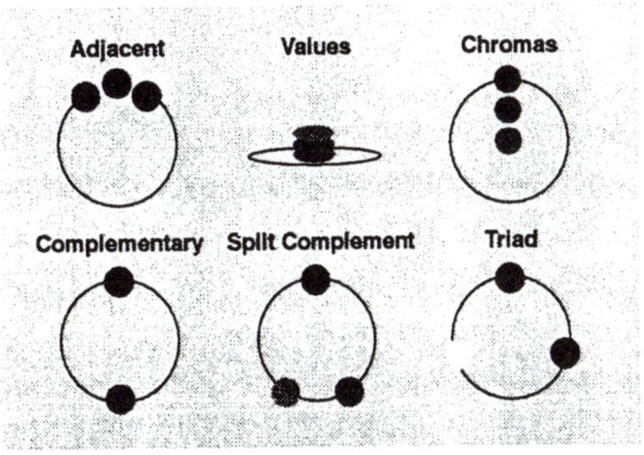

Figure 18: Color Harmonies

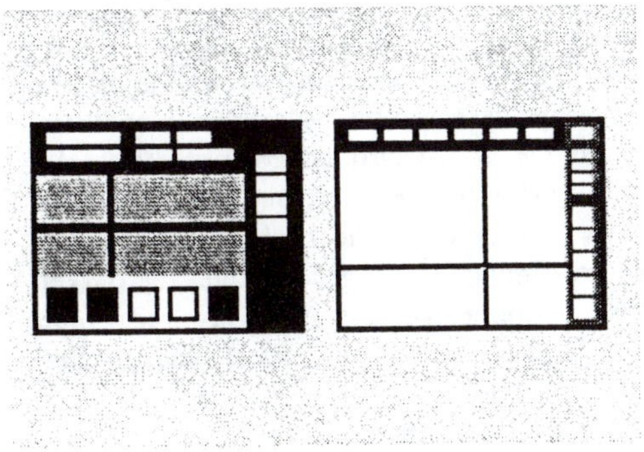

Figure 19: Color Consistency

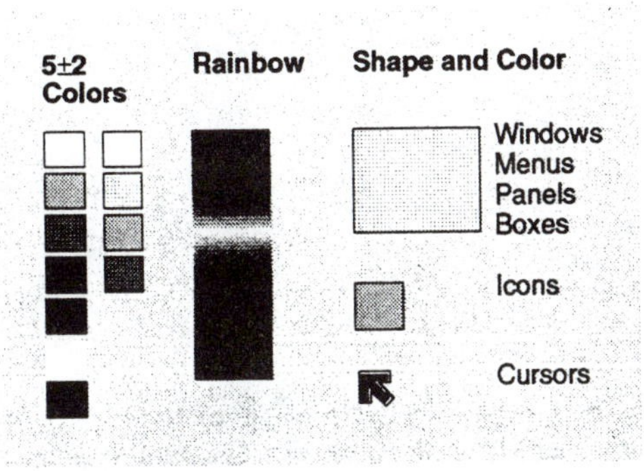

Figure 20: Color Simplicity

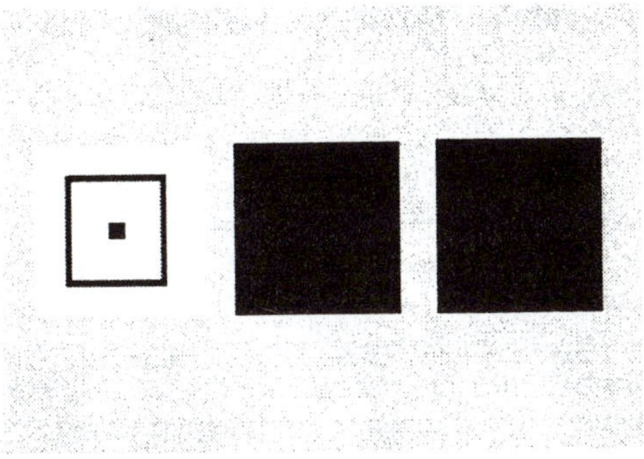

Figure 21: Color Legibility

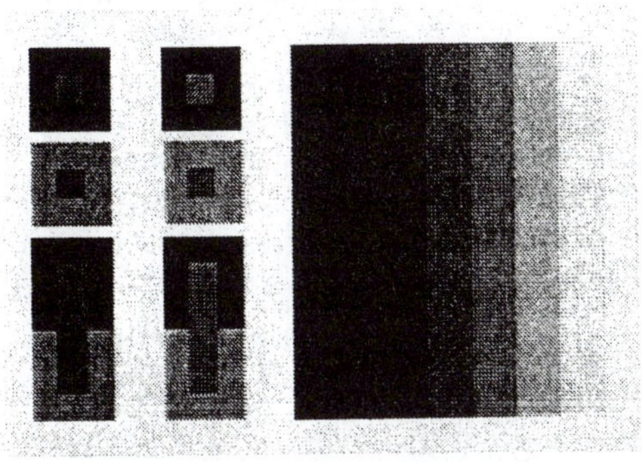

Figure 22: Color Interactions

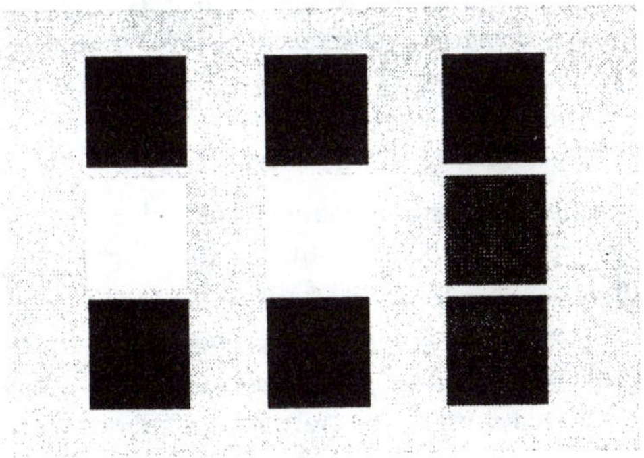

Figure 23: Color Symbolism

Please see the inside front cover for color images C1 through C8 which correspond to Figures 16 through 23.

Color Graphics—Blessing or Ballyhoo

(Excerpt)

G. Murch

• • •

5. Guidelines for Effective Colour Usage

Based on the preceding discussion, some general guidelines for colour usage can be stated. They are listed here according to the area of their derivation — physiological, perceptual, or cognitive.

5.1. Physiological guidelines

Avoid the simultaneous display of highly saturated, spectrally extreme colours. Reds, oranges, yellows, and greens can be viewed together without refocusing, but cyan and blues cannot be easily viewed simultaneously with red. To avoid frequent refocusing and visual fatigue, extreme colour pairs such as red and blue or yellow and purple should be avoided. However, desaturating spectrally extreme colours will reduce the need for refocusing.

Avoid pure blue for text, thin lines, and small shapes. Our visual system is just not set up for detailed, sharp, short-wavelength stimuli. However, blue does make a good background colour and is perceived clearly out into the periphery of our visual field.

Avoid adjacent colours differencing only in the amount of blue. Edges that differ only in the amount of blue will appear indistinct.

Older viewers need higher brightness levels to distinguish colours.

Colours change appearance as ambient light level changes. Displays change colour under different kinds of ambient light — fluorescent, incandescent, or daylight. Appearance also changes as the light level is increased or decreased.

On the one hand, a change occurs due to increased or decreased contrast, and on the other, due to the shift in the sensitivity of the eye.

The magnitude of a detectable change in colour varies across the spectrum. Small changes in extreme reds and purples are more difficult to detect than small changes in other colours such as yellow and blue-green. Also, our visual system does not readily perceive changes in green.

Difficulty in focusing results from edges created by colour alone. Our visual system depends on a brightness difference at an edge to effect clear focusing. Multi-coloured images, then, should be differentiated on the basis of brightness as well as of colour.

Avoid red and green in the periphery of large-scale displays. Due to the insensitivity of the retinal periphery to red and green, these colours in saturated form should be avoided, especially for small symbols and shapes. Yellow and blue are good peripheral colours.

Opponent colours go well together. Red and green or yellow and blue are good combinations for simple displays. The opposite combinations - red with yellow or green with blue - produce poorer images.

For colour-deficient observers, avoid single colour distinctions.

6. Perceptual Guidelines

Not all colours are equally dicernible. Perceptually, we need a large change in wavelength to perceive a colour difference in some portions of the spectrum and a small one in other portions.

Luminance does not equal brightness. Two equal-luminance but different hue colours will probably appear to have different brightness. The deviations are most extreme for colours towards the ends of the spectrum (red, magenta, blue).

Different hues have inherently different saturation levels. Yellow in particular always appears to be less saturated than other hues.

Lightness and brightness are distinguishable on a printed hard copy, but not on a colour display. The nature of a colour display does not allow lightness and brightness to be varied independently.

Not all colours are equally readable or legible. Extreme care should be exercised with text colour relative to background colours. Besides a loss in hue with reduced size, inadequate contrast frequently results when the background and text colours are similar. As a general rule, the darker, spectrally extreme colours such as red, blue, magenta, brown, etc. make good backgrounds while the brighter, spectrum-centered, and desaturated hues produce more legible text.

Hues change with intensity and background colour. When grouping elements on the basis of colour, be sure that backgrounds or nearby colours do not change the hue of an element in the group. Limiting the number of colours and making sure they are widely separated in the spectrum will reduce confusion.

Avoid the need for colour discrimination in small areas. Hue information is lost for small areas. In general, two adjacent lines of a single-pixel width will merge to produce a mixture of the two. Also, the human visual system produces sharper images with achromatic colours. Thus for the fine detail, it is best to use black, white, and grey while reserving chromatic colours for larger panels or for attracting attention.

6.1. Cognitive guidelines

Do not overuse colour. Perhaps the best rule is to use colour sparingly. The benefits of colour as an attention getter, information grouper, and value assigner are lost if too many colours are used. Cognitive scientists have shown that the human mind experiences great difficulty in maintaining more than five to seven elements simultaneously; so it is best to limit displays to about six clearly discriminable colours.

Be aware of the nonlinear colour manipulation in video and hard copy. At this point, algorithms do not exist for translating the physical colours of an imaging device into a perceptually structured colour set. Video or hard-copy systems cannot match human perception and expectations on all fronts.

Group related elements by using a common background colour. Cognitive science has advanced the notion of set and preattentive processing. In this context, you can prepare or set the user for related events by using a common colour code. A successive set of images can be shown to be related by using the same background colour.

Similar colours connote similar meanings. Elements related in some way can convey the message through the degree in similarity of hue. The colour range from blue to green is experienced as more similar than the gamut from red to green. Along these lines, saturation level can also be used to connote the strength of relationships.

Brightness and saturation draw attention. The brightest and most highly saturated area of colour display immediately draws the viewer's attention.

Link the degree of colour change to event magnitude. As an alternative to bar charts or tic marks on amplitude scales, displays can portray magnitude changes with progressive steps of changing colour. A desaturated cyan can be increased in saturation as the graphed elements increase in value. Progressively switching from one hue to another can be used to indicate passing critical levels.

Order colours by their spectral position. To increase the number of colours on a display requires imposing a meaningful order on the colours. The most obvious order is that provided by the spectrum with the mnemonic ROY G. BIV (red, orange, yellow, green, blue, indigo, violet).

Warm and cold colours should indicate action levels. Traditionally, the warm (long wavelength) colours are used to signify action or the requirement of a response. Cool colours, on the other hand, indicate status or background information. Most people also experience warm colours advancing toward them — hence forcing attention — and cool colours receding or drawing away.

While these guidelines offer some suggestions, they certainly should not be taken as binding under all circumstances. There are too many variables in colour display, colour copying, human perception, and human interpretation to make any hard and fast rules. So, by all means, experiment.

• • •

BRINGING ICONS TO LIFE

Ronald Baecker,[1] Ian Small,[1,2] and Richard Mander [2,3]

1. Dynamic Graphics Project
Computer Systems Research Institute and Department of Computer Science, University of Toronto

2. Human Interface Group, Apple Computer, Inc.

3. Department of Educational Psychology, Stanford University

This research completely conducted at the Human Interface Group, Apple Computer, Inc.

ABSTRACT

Icons are used increasingly in interfaces because they are compact "universal" pictographic representations of computer functionality and processing. *Animated icons* can bring to life symbols representing complete applications or functions within an application, thereby clarifying their meaning, demonstrating their capabilities, and even explaining their method of use. To test this hypothesis, we carried out an iterative design of a set of animated painting icons that appear in the HyperCard tool palette. The design discipline restricted the animations to 10 to 20 second sequences of 22x20 pixel bit maps. User testing was carried out on two interfaces — one with the static icons, one with the animated icons. The results showed significant benefit from the animations in clarifying the purpose and functionality of the icons.

KEYWORDS

Icons, interaction techniques, dialogue methods, iterative design, empirical studies, HyperCard.

INTRODUCTION

WIMP (Windows, Icons, Menus, and Pointers) interfaces of the 80's have empowered millions of new computer users. Nonetheless, as systems become more sophisticated, and as functionality continues to expand, interfaces become more complex, sometimes arcane and even bizarre. They are often neither easy to learn nor easy to use.

New developments in interface technology can help deal with the problem of interface comprehensibility. One such development is non-speech audio (Buxton, 1989; Gaver, 1986, 1989). This paper deals with an example of another such development: the *animated interface* (Baecker and Small, 1990).

Why do we believe that animation could help make interfaces more understandable? The reason is that animation is an effective means of portraying complex processes evolving over time. This paper describes ten specific ways in which animation could assist a user. It then focuses on one specific kind of animation: the *animated icon*.

We define animated icons and discuss how animation might solve some of the problems associated with icons while preserving their traditional strengths. We then discuss the design of animated icons and describe our first attempt at a set of animations for the HyperCard tool icons. Weaknesses discovered through user testing led to a redesign which is also described. The second set of animated icons was then user tested in comparison with traditional static icons. The results of these tests are reported and interpreted.

USES OF ANIMATION AT THE INTERFACE

Ten basic ways in which animation could assist a user may be described in terms of questions about a system or interface that animation can help answer (Baecker and Small, 1990, 257-266):

- **Identification:** What is this?
- **Transition:** Where have I come from and gone to?
- **Orientation:** Where am I?
- **Choice:** What can I do now?
- **Demonstration:** What can I do with this?
- **Explanation:** How do I do this?
- **Feedback:** What is happening?
- **History:** What have I done?
- **Interpretation:** Why did that happen?
- **Guidance:** What should I do now?

For example, many home computer games display animated identifications while the system is loading. The outline zoom (an animated transition) which accompanies the opening (and closing) of an icon on many desktops orients the user to the location of the new window which appears on the desktop. The "Guided Tours" which are distributed with some Apple products are animated explanations. Two well-known examples of animated feedback are the animated icons in the Sapphire windowing environment (Myers, 1984) and the now common *percent-done progress indicators* (Myers, 1985).

MOTIVATION

Myers used animated icons to provide feedback about the status of system-level functions and processes. We have begun to explore another kind of animated icon, one that brings to life the symbols representing applications (such as writing, painting, and drawing programs) and the functions within an application (such as the painting tools within HyperCard). Why might one want to do this? What are some of the strengths and weaknesses of icons?

Easterby (1970) stresses the advantages for international use of symbolic displays over those that are language-based. Lodding (1983) asserts that, because people find images "natural," because the human mind has powerful image memory and processing capabilities, because icons can be easily learned and recognized, and because images "can possess more universality than text," iconic interfaces can "reduce the learning curve in both time and effort, and facilitate user performance while reducing errors." Gittens (1986) notes the ease with which graphical attributes of icons such as style and colour can be used to represent common properties of a collection of objects.

Manes (1985), on the other hand, asserts that icons may be confusing, wasteful of space, and totally ineffective in dealing with large numbers of similar commands, files, or concepts. Gittens (1986) notes the difficulty of finding "obvious pictographic equivalents" of computer system concepts, and of using icons to deal with the specification of large numbers of command parameters. Kolers (1969) notes that the claims for the "immediacy" and "directness" of the understanding of pictograms are exaggerated, and that recognizing even realistic icons requires "a great deal of perceptual learning, abstracting ability, and intelligence."

Despite this debate, there is little experimental evidence documenting the advantages and disadvantages of icons and specifying how they can be used appropriately and optimally (Baecker and Buxton, 1987). In terms of the questions presented above, icons typically serve as *identifications* of applications and functions, answering the "what is this?" question. Ideally, the meaning of an icon should be obvious to experienced users of a system, and also be evocative and self-evident to new users. Many icons fail to meet the former criterion; most fail to meet the latter criterion.

Our hypothesis was that animating icons would reduce this problem: animated icons should be easier to recall for experienced users, and more obvious in their meaning to new users. The work to be described tests this latter conjecture. It also tests the conjecture that animating icons can allow icons to provide a *demonstration* function as well, answering the "what can I do with this?" question.

ITERATIVE DESIGN

We chose the HyperCard tool palette as a suitable domain for testing our conjecture. Each of the 18 icons is a 22 pixel x 20 pixel bit map. The appearance, name, and location of each icon is shown in Figure 1.

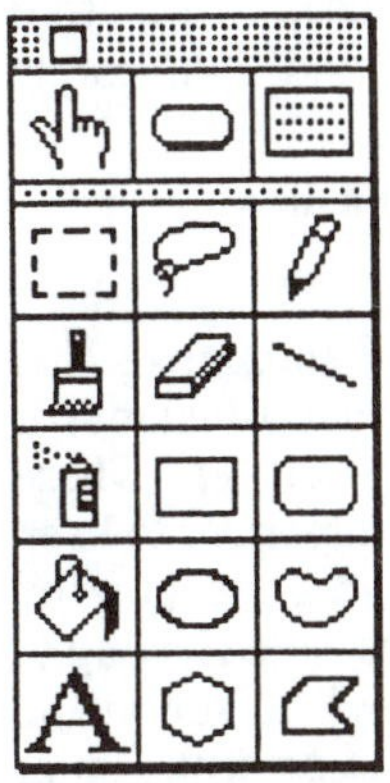

Browse	Button	Field
Selection	Lasso	Pencil
Paint Brush	Eraser	Line
Spray Can	Rectangle	Rounded Rectangle
Paint Bucket	Oval	Curve
Text	Regular Polygon	Irregular Polygon

Figure 1: The HyperCard tool palette

Animation describing an icon could occupy an arbitrary portion of the screen. To keep the animation from occluding other icons or obscuring the user's context, we adopted a severe design discipline requiring that each icon should animate in place, within its 22x20 area.

An experienced animator, familiar with the Macintosh and its animation capabilities, was hired to create the prototype animations. The task was extremely laborious: we lacked tools suitable for designing, editing, and playing miniature animated bit maps. Yet the initial results were encouraging, suggesting that miniature animations could be effective. Some key frames from several prototype animations appear in Figure 2.

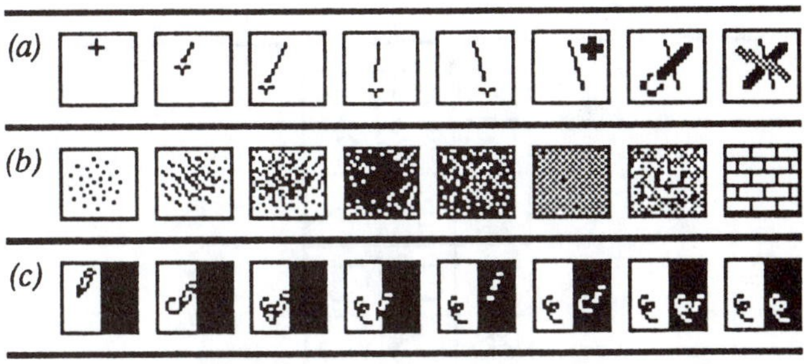

Figure 2: Keyframes from prototype animations (shown actual size). While it is difficult to get a sense of the animation from a static representation, imagine the animation flowing smoothly through the images shown.
(a) the Line tool
(b) the Spray Can tool
(c) the Pencil tool

We conducted a preliminary test by observing the reactions to the animated icons of five experienced HyperCard users from varying backgrounds. We also submitted the animations to detailed scrutiny, looking for cases in which the animations were:

- Wrong, showing something that was incorrect.
- Misleading, easy to misinterpret.
- Confusing, capable of multiple reasonable interpretations.
- Inconsistent, with respect to the other animations.

- Structured poorly, not presenting uses of a tool progressing from the most important and simplest to those less important and more complex.
- Incomplete, omitting something fundamental.
- Too long, trying to show too much.

Our scrutiny revealed several instances of animations that were misleading, either because of visual illusions or because the animator was trying to be too clever. These problems demonstrated that it was clearly important to keep the animations simple, both visually and conceptually. There were also a number of inconsistencies, some having to do with accurate renditions of a simulated cursor in the animations, and some relating to the order of presentation of a tool's capabilities.

Aside from identifying many of these problems, the five subjects were also concerned about the level of detail conveyed by the animations. Some expected complete *explanations*, believing the scope of the animations to be larger than it was. It was clear that this was not possible, as the goals of each animation were constrained by spatial and temporal considerations. In fact, the initial animations of the Browse, Button, and Field tools were clearly not successful in conveying the complex abstract concepts they represent.

We then planned a more detailed study. In order to simplify the subject requirements, and because of the difficulties in animating the Browse, Button, and Field tools in so little time and space, we opted to eliminate these tools from the palette (see Figure 3).

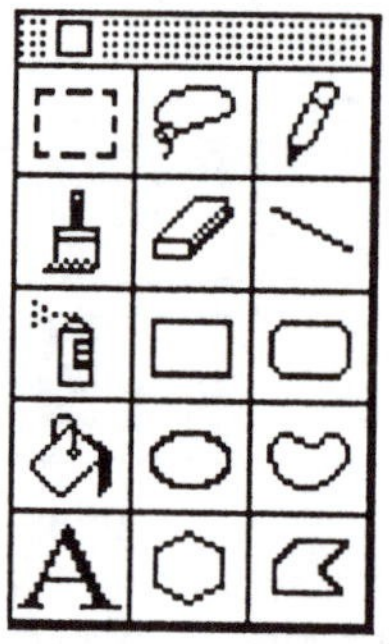

Figure 3: The test palette

Based on the feedback summarized above, we modified or completely redesigned eight paint tool animations (see Figure 4, which shows four of the original animations and their redesigns). The changes ranged from simple ones, such as adding a miniature cursor to the Rectangle tool animation, through more complex modifications, such as reordering the Oval tool animation to depict the simplest case first, to complete conceptual redesign, such as creating new Lasso and Selection tool animations in an attempt to emphasize the similarities and differences between the two.

We left untouched two animations, the Spray Can tool and the Regular Polygon tool, which probably could have been improved. Five painting animations were deemed satisfactory in their original form.

EMPIRICAL EVALUATION

The animated icons used in this study were designed to represent the functionality of HyperCard's painting tools. Our goal was to determine whether or not animations could help users understand this functionality.

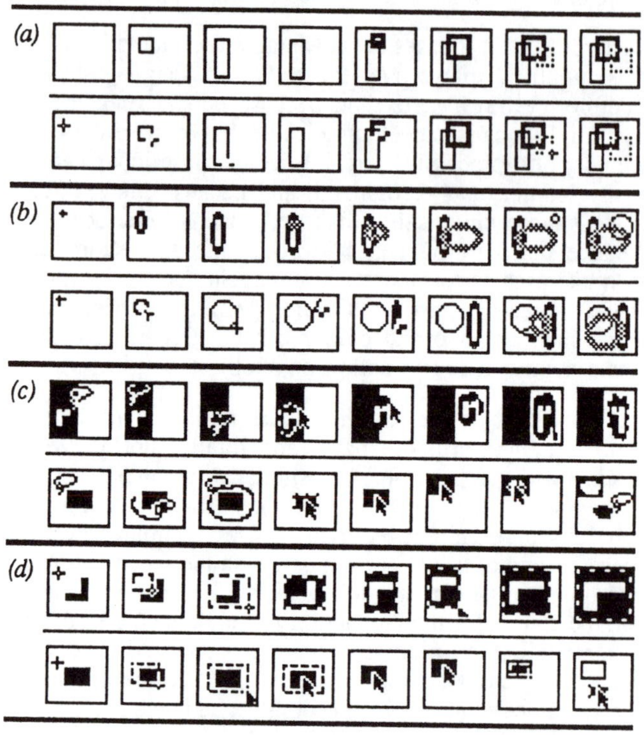

Figure 4: Four of the animations and their redesigns
(a) the Rectangle tool
(b) the Oval tool
(c) the Lasso tool
(d) the Selection tool

Since the animations were designed for novice painters, we created a simple set of painting tasks in a HyperCard stack. This stack consisted of 11 cards, each showing a picture on the left and a partially completed copy on the right, as demonstrated in Figure 5. The artwork was put in the background layer of the card so that the user could paint on the card and erase errors without affecting the preliminary material. The tasks were designed to be progressive, beginning with one that required the Pencil tool, then moving to more complex painting tools, and finally to the Lasso and Selection tools. However, the tasks were also designed to provide more than one way to complete the painting. Thus it would not be obvious to users which tool to use.

Nine subjects, four having no experience with Macintosh paint programs, four having some familiarity, and one having considerable experience with drawing programs, were selected for the study. The results from one novice were not included in the data because the animations were different, but the results were comparable to the others. All subjects completed the entire task set. Test sessions were monitored by two observers, and were audio and videotaped for later analysis.

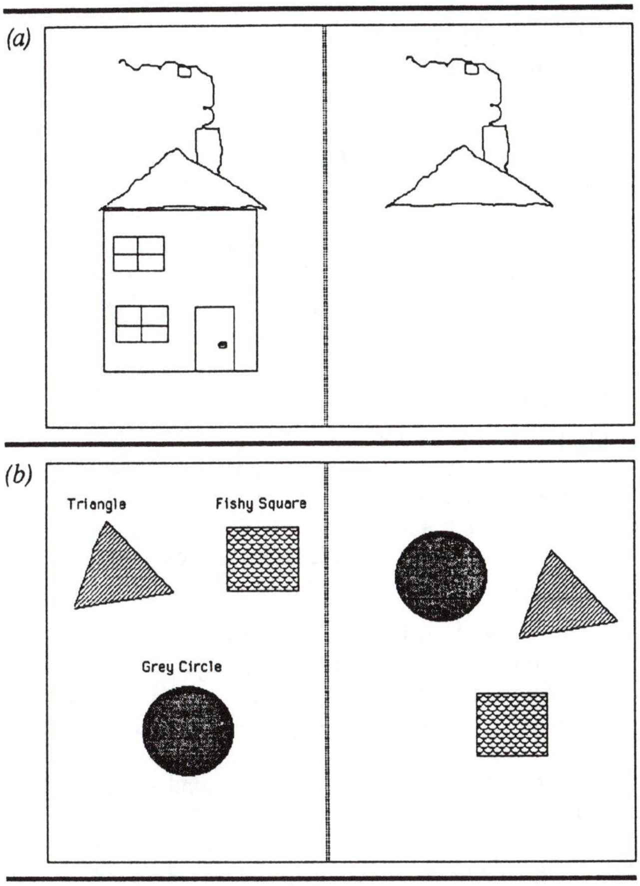

Figure 5: Two of the painting tasks in the user study

We structured the study to provide data describing user comprehension of tool functionality after viewing the static icons, after viewing the animated icons, and finally after using the tools. Before starting the painting tasks, each user was shown the static tool palette and asked to describe what each tool might do. We relied on intrusive questioning to provide this information during the test, questioning subjects after they had viewed a tool's animation but before they had used the tool itself. A final interview provided the required data after users had gained experience with the tools. This test procedure bears some similarity to the first part of the "Naming Test" of the "Icon Shape Test" described in Bewley et al. (1983).

Static Icons

Users' reactions to the Lasso, Pencil, Paint Brush, Eraser, Line, Spray Can, Rectangle, Rounded Rectangle, Oval, and Text tool icons indicate that these static images convey the functionality of the tools they represent. Novice users often found the remaining five tool icons confusing (see Table 1).

While most users thought that the Lasso and Selection tools were for selecting objects, the exact differences between their functionalities were not clear. Users not identifying the Selection tool correctly thought that it drew rectangles with broken lines. The Paint Bucket tool was not recognized as such by any of the novice users. They dubbed it the graduation cap; one user continued to refer to it as a graduation cap that tipped paint even after determining its functionality.

None of the subjects was able to identify the Curve tool properly, although two subjects thought it drew kidney beans. The Regular Polygon tool was often thought to make hexagons and the Irregular Polygon tool to make objects with parallel sides.

Animated Icons

All subjects liked the animations, reporting that they found them very useful. Novice users noticed the animations early in the testing session, typically during the first painting task, and would then look at the animations to find out what the tools did and to confirm their expectations of a tool's functionality. Table 1 demonstrates that in every case the users understood the purpose of each icon after viewing the animations.

One user commented that the animations made selecting an icon less like a memory game in which you had to remember the icon's purpose, since you could view its animation any time as a reminder.

User experiences demonstrated that every detail of an animation needed to be clear and not subject to misinterpretation, which could arise from the strangest of coincidences. Searching for an appropriate tool for adding a chimney to a house, one subject noticed that the Paint Bucket tool's animation featured a chimney-like shape (see Figure 6). Selecting and using the chimney tool resulted in a completely black painting and a very disgruntled user, rather than the elegant chimney desired. Experiences such as this demonstrate the difficulties of creating effective animation which is sufficiently generic and abstract to avoid confusion.

Figure 6: How unexpected confusion can occur
(a) the chimney task
(b) the Paint Bucket tool animation

	Novice (3)		Familiar (4)		Expert (1)	
	Static	Anim.	Static	Anim.	Static	Anim.
	1	All	All	All	All	All
	All	All	All	All	All	All
	All	All	All	All	All	All
	All	All	All	All	All	All
	All	All	3	All	All	All
	2	All	All	All	All	All
	All	All	All	All	All	All
	2	All	All	All	All	All
	2	All	All	All	All	All
	0	All	1	All	All	All
	2	All	All	All	All	All
	0	All	1	All	0	All
	All	All	All	All	All	All
	0	All	0	All	All	All
	1	All	1	All	All	All

Table 1: User comprehension of static and animated icons. The number of users who understood the static icons, and their animated counterparts, is indicated. For example, only 1 novice user understood the static Selection tool, but all 3 understood the animated version.

User context and expectation also affect interpretation of the animations, and must be taken into account during the design process. The Spray Can tool animation depicts several different patterns being sprayed, culminating in the brick pattern. Some users interpreted this to mean that the tool could spray on walls, rather than being able to spray a wall-like pattern.

Similarly, some users interpreted the Selection and Lasso tool animations as meaning that the tools selected objects, rather than regions. While the animations were designed to emphasize the subtle differences between the two tools, users tended to miss details, such as the shrinking nature of Lasso selection, which conflicted with their expectations.

Animated Icons With Sound

A number of the animations, such as the Rectangle tool, conveyed usage as well as functionality. Others, such as the Irregular Polygon tool, were less successful. We believe that this extension to animated explanation would be greatly assisted by the addition of sound effects such as mouse clicks. Multiple media such as animation and sound can be combined to produce compelling help and assistance systems. For example, in the case of the Irregular Polygon tool animation, novice users did not understand how to end a polygon. Adding the sound of mouse clicks to the animation, including the double click required to end the polygon, should clarify this. While we have experimented with prototype implementations that make use of sound, we have not yet subjected them to testing.

INTERFACE ISSUES

While our goal for this study was to address the macro-interface issue of whether animated tool icons provided assistance to novice users, the session recordings enabled us to identify some micro-interface issues as well. Although we had predicted some of the micro-interface behaviour that we observed, other aspects were surprising to us.

We considered allowing all animations to play simultaneously, but rejected this technique as "too busy." After experimenting with a number of methods for accessing the animations, we provided our subjects with a palette that was configured to trigger the animations whenever the mouse cursor passed into a new icon's bounding box. Upon triggering an animation, most users would try to move the mouse out of the way in order to get a clear view of the animation, only to have the animation stop when the mouse was moved outside the icon's bounding box. After a few false starts, users became adept at keeping their mouse just on the edge of the bounding box to maximize their view of the animation. This training process occurred much more rapidly than anticipated.

Two of the more experienced users selected tools so quickly that they completed the painting tasks without ever seeing the animations. This was possible because of a short delay between entering an icon and the noticeable start of its animation. These users liked this feature because of the control it gave them. Unfortunately, some novice users initially found the dissolve associated with this delay to be confusing because it made them think that the tool was unavailable for their particular task.

Users were frequently confused between selecting a tool and animating it. This confusion manifested itself in user behaviour which involved watching the animation of a tool which was not the currently selected tool, and then immediately attempting to use that tool without first selecting it.

Animations which depicted sequences of different tool modes sometimes confused users by making them think that they could select the different modes by carefully timing their selection click with respect to the evolving animation. While this may be a valuable interface technique, animations which caused such user reactions were clearly in need of redesign.

SUMMARY AND CONCLUSIONS

The users found animated icons useful and helpful. In every case in which static icons were not understood, the dynamic icons were successful in conveying the purpose of the tool. In some cases, changes or simplifications to the animations are required to depict tool functionality more accurately.

While the results of this study are positive, there are many issues which are still outstanding. From an authoring standpoint, there are few clear rules regarding length, content, ordering, and visual representation which will guarantee effective animations, particularly for tools with more abstract functionality. Even iterative design can fail to achieve success, as shown by some of our results. Furthermore, the lack of tools for designing miniature bit mapped animations makes prototyping more laborious than it should be.

From an interface standpoint, we have not yet accomplished a completely satisfactory accessing scheme. Neither have we determined how animated icons relate and fit into the context of a much larger and extensive help system. Both these issues are extremely important.

Finally, we need to determine whether we can provide animated icons which can be helpful with more complex functionality and to all levels of users. A different style of animation may be needed to demonstrate effectively complex abstract concepts such as those represented by the Browse, Button, and Field icons. Also, by providing different animations for novice, familiar and expert users, we may be able to extend this help technique to a more general application.

APPENDIX: A NOTE ON THE IMPLEMENTATION

We conducted preliminary evaluations using a prototype implementation which displayed the animations in isolation from the surrounding HyperCard environment. While sufficient for obtaining initial feedback, this implementation lacked the functionality required for supporting novice users attempting real tasks.

A more complete implementation was prepared for the second round of user testing. We replaced the standard HyperCard tool palette with our own abbreviated animated tool palette, thereby allowing users to conduct all their interaction through the new experimental interface. The animations were displayed using a low-level animation playback system developed earlier during our research. The low-level engine ensured that animations played at a constant speed despite system load, by dropping frames from the display list as required. Sound was supported either as a single continuous sound track attached to the animation, or as sound events attached to individual frames within the animation.

ACKNOWLEDGEMENTS

This work was conducted in the Human Interface Group of the Advanced Technology Group of Apple Computer, Inc. We are indebted to Eric Martin, who created the initial animation prototypes; Ruth Ritter, who helped to redesign animations based on user feedback; and to Anne Nicol, Kate Gomoll, Shifteh Karimi, and S. Joy Mountford, for assistance including user testing, animation redesign, research support, and comments on this paper.

REFERENCES

Baecker, R. and Buxton, W. (1987). *Readings in Human-Computer Interaction: A Multidisciplinary Approach.* Morgan Kaufmann.

Baecker, R. and Small, I. (1990). Animation at the Interface. In Laurel, B. (Ed.), *The Art of Human-Computer Interface Design*, Addison-Wesley, 251-267.

Bewley, W., Roberts, T., Schroit, D., and Verplank, W. (1983). Human Factors Testing in the Design of Xerox's 8010 'Star' Office Workstation, *Proceedings of CHI '83*, 72-77.

Buxton, W. (1989). Introduction to this Special Issue on Non-Speech Audio. *Human-Computer Interaction* 4(1).

Easterby, R. (1970). The Perception of Symbols for Machine Displays. *Ergonomics* 13(1), 149-158.

Gaver, W. (1986). Auditory Icons: Using Sound in Computer Interfaces. *Human-Computer Interaction* 2(2), 167-177.

Gaver, W. (1989). The Sonic Finder: An Interface that Uses Auditory Icons. *Human-Computer Interaction* 4(1).

Gittens, D. (1986). Icon-Based Human-Computer Interaction. *International Journal of Man-Machine Studies* 24, 519-543.

Kolers, P. (1969). Some Formal Characteristics of Pictograms. *American Scientist* 57(3), 348-363.

Lodding, K. (1983). Iconic Interfacing. *IEEE Computer Graphics and Applications* 3(2), March/April 1983, 11-20.

Manes, S. (1985). Pushing Picture-Perfect Programs: Smash That Icon! *PC Magazine,* June 1985, 64.

Myers, B. (1984). The User Interface for Sapphire. *IEEE Computer Graphics and Applications* 4(12), 13-23.

Myers, B. (1985). The Importance of Percent-Done Progress Indicators for Computer-Human Interfaces. *Proceedings of CHI '85*, 11-17.

Visual Information Seeking: Tight Coupling of Dynamic Query Filters with Starfield Displays

Christopher Ahlberg and Ben Shneiderman*
Department of Computer Science,
Human-Computer Interaction Laboratory & Institute for Systems Research
University of Maryland, College Park, MD 20742
email: ahlberg@cs.chalmers.se, ben @cs.umd.edu

ABSTRACT

This paper offers new principles for visual information seeking (VIS). A key concept is to support browsing, which is distinguished from familiar query composition and information retrieval because of its emphasis on rapid filtering to reduce result sets, progressive refinement of search parameters, continuous reformulation of goals, and visual scanning to identify results. VIS principles developed include: dynamic query filters (query parameters are rapidly adjusted with sliders, buttons, maps, etc.), starfield displays (two-dimensional scatterplots to structure result sets and zooming to reduce clutter), and tight coupling (interrelating query components to preserve display invariants and support progressive refinement combined with an emphasis on using search output to foster search input). A FilmFinder prototype using a movie database demonstrates these principles in a VIS environment.

KEYWORDS: database query, dynamic queries, information seeking, tight coupling, starfield displays

INTRODUCTION

In studying visual information seeking (VIS) systems for expert and first time users, we have found several user interface design principles that consistently lead to high levels of satisfaction. This paper defines these principles and presents a novel VIS system, the FilmFinder.

The exploration of large information spaces has remained a challenging task even as parallel hardware architectures, high-bandwidth network connections, large high-speed disks, and modern database management systems have proliferated. Indeed, these advances have left many users with the feeling that they are falling further behind and cannot cope with the flood of information [3, 18]. Now, the user interface design principles for VIS have the potential to reduce our anxiety about the flood, find needles in haystacks, support exploratory browsing to develop intuition, find patterns and exceptions, and even make browsing fun.

The key to these principles is understanding the enormous capacity for human visual information processing. By presenting information visually and allowing dynamic user control through direct manipulation principles, it is possible to traverse large information spaces and facilitate comprehension with reduced anxiety [14,16]. In a few tenths of a second, humans can recognize features in mega-pixel displays, recall related images, and identify anomalies. Current displays of textual and numeric information can be extended to incorporate spatial displays in which related information is clustered in 2-dimensional or higher spaces. This use of proximity coding, plus color coding, size coding, animated presentations, and user-controlled selections enable users to explore large information spaces rapidly and reliably.

KEY CONCEPTS

The principles of direct manipulation were a good starting point for design of visual information seeking applications [16]:

- visual representation of the world of action including both the objects and actions
- rapid, incremental and reversible actions
- selection by pointing (not typing)
- immediate and continuous display of results

However, when designing systems especially for information seeking tasks [11], additional principles are needed. A key VIS principle is to support browsing, which is distinguished from familiar concepts of query composition and information retrieval because of its emphasis on rapid filtering to reduce result sets, progressive refinement of search parameters, continuous reformulation of goals, and visual scanning to identify results. These goals are supported by the VIS designs developed in this paper:

dynamic query filters: query parameters are rapidly adjusted with sliders, buttons, etc.

---

* Current address: Dept. of Computer Science, Chalmers University of Technology, S-412 96 Göteborg, Sweden

CHI94-4/94 Boston, Massachusetts USA

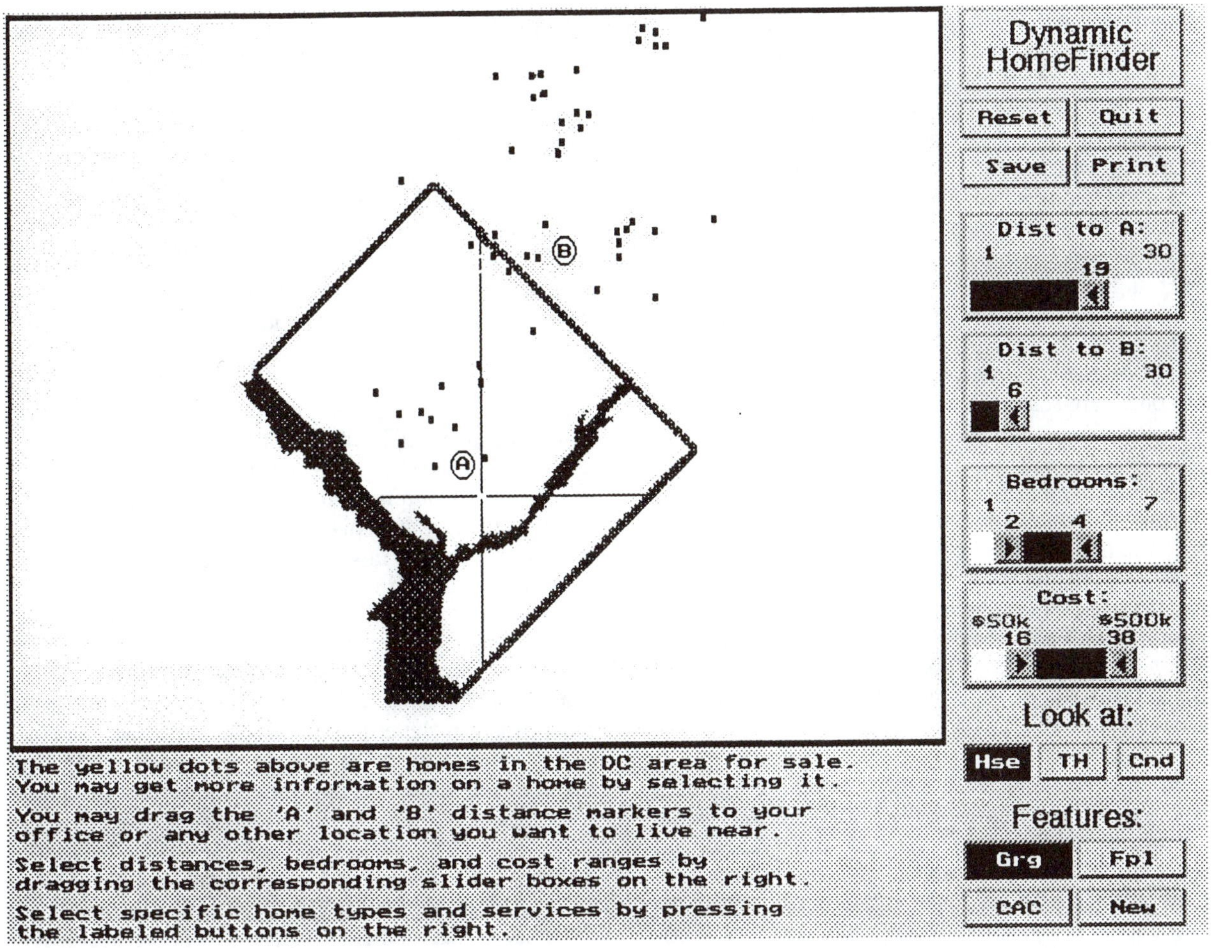

Figure 1: In the Dynamic HomeFinder query system each point satisfies the query described by the sliders for location, cost, number of bedrooms, home type (house, townhouse, or condominium), and buttons (Garage, Fireplace, Central Air Conditioning, or New construction). The points of light can be selected to generate a detailed description.

- starfield display: result sets are continuously available and support viewing of hundreds or thousands of items
- tight coupling: query components are interrelated in ways that preserve display invariants and support progressive refinement. Specifically, outputs of queries can be easily used as input to produce other queries.

Dynamic Query Filters

Our early work on dynamic queries [2, 6, 20] demonstrated dramatic performance improvements and high levels of user satisfaction. By allowing rapid, incremental and reversible changes to query parameters, often simply by dragging a slider, users were able to explore and gain feedback from displays in a few tenths of a second. For example, the Dynamic HomeFinder enabled users to adjust upper and lower bounds on home prices and see points of light on a map indicating available properties (Figure 1). This allowed users to immediately identify high or low cost communities, or find low cost homes in high-priced communities. Users could similarly adjust a slider to indicate number of bedrooms, and select toggles to indicate desire for garage, central air-conditioning, fireplace, etc.

Each of these query components (sliders, buttons, etc.) acted as a filter, reducing the number of items left in the result set. The effects were combined with simple AND logic, accounting for most naturally occurring queries. In situations where OR logic was required, users were usually quite satisfied, or actually preferred, generating a sequence of queries. This approach allowed users to see the size of the ORed components rather than merely the union of the result sets.

The work reported in this paper advances dynamic queries by demonstrating the efficacy of selection of items in alphanumeric lists with the Alphaslider [1, 12]. This query component allows users to select one item from a list of 10,000 or more, with a simple selection tool that takes little screen space, avoids use of the keyboard, and prevents typing errors.

Starfield Display

In our early work on dynamic queries the output was based on a naturally occurring spatial display. For example, the chemical table of elements was used with color highlighting of chemical names to indicate inclusion in the result set. In the Dynamic HomeFinder, points of light on a map of Washington, DC indicated properties that matched the query components. One step in the direction of generality was to build a version of the HomeFinder that had textual output as might be found in the tuples of a relational database display. As the query components were adjusted, the display remained stable, but when the user let go of the mouse button, the screen was refreshed with the correct result set.

To further support the widespread application of dynamic queries it seemed necessary to find other approaches to visual information display [4, 5, 7, 17]. Points of light are convenient because they are small yet highly visible, could be color coded, are selectable objects, and can be displayed rapidly. But if a natural map did not exist for an application, such as a set of documents, photos, songs, etc., could we create one that would be suitable? While we need to try further examples, our initial answer is affirmative. For many situations we have been able to create meaningful two-dimensional displays by selecting ordinal attributes of the items and use them as the axes. This starfield approach is a scatterplot with additional features to support selection and zooming. Our intuitions about what choices are most effective is still rough, but there is hope that we can formalize our decisions.

For example, in a database of documents, the year the document was written might be the horizontal axis while length in words might be the vertical axis. Large old documents might be at the upper left while short new documents might be at the lower right. Other attributes such as an author assigned importance value, number of co-authors, or number of references could also be used. In a database of people, the axes might be the age, number of years of education, salary, number of children, or other demographic variables.

Tight Coupling

The principle of tight coupling of interface components began to emerge in some direct manipulation graphic user interfaces. For example, if a user saves a document, the SAVE menu item becomes grayed out until a change is made. Tight coupling helps reveal the software state, and often constrains the user from making erroneous or useless actions.

A more complex example of tight coupling is the interrelationship between the text in a word processor, the position of the thumb in the scroll bar, and the page number displayed on the window border. Moving the thumb causes the text to scroll and the page number to be updated. We could write a logical proposition describing the relationship among these three display components. Such a statement would begin by indicating that when the top of the document is displayed, the thumb is at the top of the scroll bar and the page indicator is set at 1. Good program design would ensure the preservation of the display invariants. However, some word processors may fail to preserve this invariant when sections of the document are deleted or when the document is reformatted with a larger font. To compensate, some word processors may include a repaginate command, or update the thumb position only when it is moved. These errors violate the principle of tight coupling.

Tight coupling also applies to components of a query facility. In a well-designed facility, users should be able to see the impact of each selection while forming a query. For example, if a user specifies that they want films before 1935, then only certain actors or directors are selectable. This is to prevent users' from specifying null sets, e.g. films made before 1935 and directed by Francis Ford Coppola.

Another aspect of tight coupling is the linkage of *output-is-input* to support efficient use of screen space by eliminating the distinction between commands/queries/input and results/tables/output. In short, every output is also a candidate for input. This principle first emerged in our 1983 hypertext work [9] in which the notion of embedded menus replaced the earlier designs that had a paragraph of output followed by a menu to select further information. It seemed more logical to have highlighted words in the text and simply allow users to select those words with arrow keys, a mouse, or a touchscreen. The outputs-are-inputs principle reduced screen clutter by eliminating redundancy, and focused users' attention to a single location for gathering information and for applying an action to get more information.

This principle was applied in the chemical table of elements in which each element could be selected causing the sliders to be set to that element's values [2], in our health statistic map in which a state could be selected to retrieve its detailed data [13], and in the HomeFinder in which a point of light could be selected to retrieve detailed information or a photo, if it were available.

That database output can be used as input can be compared to functionality in spreadsheets where there is no such thing as input cells or output cells, or the Query by Example system [21] where input can be treated as output and vice versa. It has been referred to as a notion of Equal Opportunity [15]. In information retrieval systems this is useful as users can easily explore branches of a search and follow their associations as they come along -- associative database searching.

Tight coupling has several aspects:

- comprehensible and consistent affordances to guide users (highlighted words or areas, explicit handles, scrollbars, etc.).
- rapid, incremental, and reversible interactions among components.
- constraints on permissible operations to preserve *display invariants* (logical propositions relating the components, e.g. that the scroll bar thumb position constantly reflects the position in the document) and prevent errors.
- *continuous display* to always show the users some portion of the information space that they are

exploring. They begin by seeing a typical result set or item, which helps to orient them to what is possible in this information seeking environment. This seems more effective than starting with a blank screen or a form to fill in.

- *progressive refinement*, in which users can alter the parameters to get other results [18]. If the users see that there are too many items in the result set, they can reformulate their goal and seek a more restrictive value for one of the attributes.
- allow users to select *details on demand* [9]. This is the heart of hypermedia, but it applies to most designs. Instead of older query facilities which required alternation between query composition and result interpretation, our designs show results and invite further selections if details are needed. In the Dynamic HomeFinder, homes were shown as simple points of light until the user selected one of the points to get the details. This principle reduces clutter while the query is being shaped and allows users to get further information when they need it.

FILMFINDER DESIGN

To test these principles of visual information, we created a tool for exploring a film database, the FilmFinder. Watching a film is often a social activity so this tool was designed to encourage discussions and make the decision process easier for groups of viewers. Existing tools for learning about films include encyclopedias, such as *Leonard Maltin's Movie and Video Guide* [10]. They typically provide an alphabetic organization, with additional indexes, but these are difficult to use. Recently, computer-based encyclopedias such as Microsoft's Cinemania have appeared on the market. Although some of them employ novel approaches such as hypertext links they still do not provide users with an overview of the data. They employ a traditional approach to database queries with commands or form fill-in, and then provide a textual response in the form of scrolling lists. If the users are unhappy with the result, they compose a new query and wait for the new result. Progressive refinement can take dozens of steps and many minutes.

Before designing the tool, informal interviews were conducted with video store clerks and film aficionados. The FilmFinder [Color plate 1] tries to overcome search problems by applying dynamic queries, a starfield display, and tight coupling among components. Dynamic queries were applied by having a double box range selector to specify film length in minutes, by having buttons for ratings (G, PG, PG-13, R), large color coded buttons for film categories (drama, action, comedy, etc.), and our novel Alphasliders for film titles, actors, actresses, and directors.

The query result in the FilmFinder is continuously represented in a starfield display [Color plate 1]. The X-axis represents time and the Y-axis a measure of popularity. The FilmFinder allows users to zoom into a particular part of the time-popularity space [Color plate 2]. As users zoom in the colored spots representing films grow larger, giving the impression of flying in closer to the films. The labels on the axes are also automatically updated as zooming occurs. When fewer than 25 films are visible, their titles are automatically displayed.

To obtain more information about a particular element of the query results, users click on that element, getting desired details-on-demand [Color plate 3]. An information card which provides more information about attributes such as actors, actresses, director and language, is displayed. In a traditional retrieval system users would obtain more information by starting a new query. In the FilmFinder users can select highlighted attributes on the information card and thereby set the value of the corresponding Alphaslider to the value of that attribute. This forms the starting point for the next query and allows graceful and rapid exploration with no fear of error messages.

Tight coupling is strongly supported in the FilmFinder. When users select categories of movies using the category toggles, the starfield display and the query ranges of the Alphasliders are immediately updated [Color plate 2]. This effectively eliminates empty and invalid query results. The same is possible when users zoom into a particular part in the search space -- only those films that appear during that range of years and are in the particular popularity range will be part of the Alphaslider query range. The Alphasliders can even affect each other, selecting Ingmar Bergman on the Director slider would set the Actor slider to only operate over those actors who appear in Ingmar Bergman's movies. This interaction between the query widgets, and the possibility to use query results as input, creates a tightly coupled environment where information can be explored in a rapid, safe, and comprehensible manner.

FILMFINDER SCENARIO

Tools like the FilmFinder might be found in video stores, libraries, and homes - they might even come as a part of standard television sets. Imagine the Johnson family sitting down at their TV Saturday night to watch a movie that they all like. They turn on the TV and are presented with a FilmFinder's starfield visualization and a number of controls [Color plate 1]. All controls are operable by a wireless mouse and no keyboard is needed.

The family members don't have a specific film in mind, but they know that they want to see something popular and recent. After some discussion they agree on the categories for a search: drama, mystery, comedy, or an action film. To cut down the number of films further they select an actor that they all like, in this case Sean Connery. Observe in [Color plate 2] how the category toggles have been manipulated - and the Alphaslider indexes updated to contain appropriate values, the visualization has zoomed into the correct part of the information space, and Sean Connery has been selected with the Actor slider.

Now the number of films in the starfield has been cut down from about 2000 to 25 and the Johnsons decide to look further at *The Murder on the Orient Express*. They select it with their remote control and are presented with an information card [Color plate 3]. The description and image remind the Johnsons that they have already seen this film, so the information card can now become the tool to further refine their search.

Mr. Johnson sees Anthony Perkins' name and decides he wants to see a movie starring Anthony Perkins, while Mrs. Johnson wants to see a movie with Ingrid Bergman. To resolve the disagreement they select both actors in the information card, and the selection is reflected in the Alphaslider settings. When the information card is closed, the query result is updated and the Johnsons are presented with one movie with both Anthony Perkins and Ingrid Bergman which they decide to watch [Color plate 4].

FUTURE WORK

The dynamic queries approach has much to recommend it, but it must be extended to deal with larger databases, more varied kinds of information, and a greater range of query types. Current dynamic queries do not satisfy the demands of relational completeness, but they offer other features that depend on spatial output that are not available in existing relational databases. It appears productive to combine the strengths of both approaches.

When searching films - as well as for other information - it would be desirable to incorporate fuzzy searching to find similar films. To include such functionality in the FilmFinder would probably be desirable - but first algorithms must be devised and more importantly, the issue of to what extent the mechanisms should be user controlled must be examined.

When browsing the information space by zooming, it is important that this is done smoothly so users get a feeling of flying through the data. New algorithms and data structures are necessary to support the smooth flying through the data. A natural extension would be to add a third dimension so that some films would appear closer than others.

The tight coupling among query components in the FilmFinder was helpful - but there may be cases when such interrelationships not are desirable. Formal specification of the logical propositions for display invariants is a useful direction, because it could lead to proofs of correctness and advanced tools to build such interfaces rapidly.

REFERENCES

1. Ahlberg, C. and Shneiderman, B., 1993. The Alphaslider: A rapid and compact selector, *Proc. ACM CHI'94 Conference.*
2. Ahlberg, C., Williamson, C., and Shneiderman, B., 1992. Dynamic queries for information exploration: An implementation and evaluation, *Proc. ACM CHI'92 Conference*, 619-626.
3. Borgman, C. L., 1986. Why are online catalogs hard to use? Lessons learned from information-retrieval studies, *Journal of the American Society for Information Science 37*, 6, 387-400.
4. Buja, A., McDonald, J. A., Michalak, J., Stuetzle, W., 1991. Interactive data visualization using focusing and linking, *Proc. IEEE Visualization '91*, 156-163.
5. Egenhofer, M., 1990. Manipulating the graphical representation of query results in Geographic Information Systems, *1990 IEEE Workshop on Visual Languages*, IEEE Computer Society Press, Los Alamitos, CA, 119-124.
6. Eick, Steven, 1993. Data visualization sliders, AT&T Bell Laboratories Report, Napervillie, IL.
7. Feiner, S. and Beshers, C., 1990. Worlds within worlds: Metaphors for exploring n-dimensional virtual worlds, *Proc. User Interface Software and Technology '90*, ACM, New York, NY, 76-83.
8. Koved, L. and Shneiderman, B. 1986. Embedded menus: Selecting items in context, *Comm. of the ACM 29*, 4 (April 1986), 312-318.
9. Kreitzberg, Charles B., Details on Demand: Hypertext models for coping with information overload, in Dillon, Martin (Editor), *Interfaces for Information Retrieval and Online Systems*, Greenwood Press, New York, 1991, 169-176.
10. Maltin, L., 1993. *Leonard Maltin's Movie and Video Guide*, Penguin Books, New York.
11. Marchionini, G., 1993. *Information Seeking*, Cambridge Univ. Press, Cambridge, UK.
12. Osada, M., Liao, H., Shneiderman, B., Alphaslider: searching textual lists with sliders, *Proc. of the Ninth Annual Japanese Conf. on Human Interface*, Oct. 1993.
13. Plaisant, C., 1993. Dynamic queries on a health statistics atlas, Forthcoming Technical Report, Human-Computer Interaction Laboratory, University of Maryland, College Park, MD.
14. Robertson, G. G., Card, S. K., and Mackinlay, J. D., 1993. Information visualization using 3-D interactive animation, *Comm. of the ACM 36*, 4, 56-71.
15. Runciman, C. and Thimbleby, H., 1986. Equal opportunity interactive systems, *Int'l Journal of Man-Machine Studies 25* (4), 439-51.
16. Shneiderman, B., *Designing the User Interface: Strategies for Effective Human-Computer Interaction: Second Edition*, Addison-Wesley Publ. Co., Reading, MA (1992), 573 pages.
17. Singers, R., Endres, L., 1993, Metaphoric abstraction, the starfield and complex systems, in preparation, Johnson Controls, Milwaukee, WI.17. Welty, C., 1985. Correcting user errors in SQL, *Int'l Journal of Man-Machine Studies 22*, 463-477.
18. Welty, C., 1985. Correcting user errors in SQL, *Int' Journal of Man-Machine Studies 22*, 463-477.
19. Williams, M., 1984. What make RABBIT run? *Int'l Journal of Man-Machine Studies 21*, 333-352.
20. Williamson, C. and Shneiderman, B., 1992. The Dynamic HomeFinder: Evaluating dynamic queries in a real-estate information exploration system, *Proc. ACM SIGIR Conference*, 339-346.
21. Zloof M. Query-by-Example, *National Computer Conference*, AFIPS Press (1975), 431-437.

Please see the inside back cover for color image C9 which corresponds to Ahlberg and Shneiderman, Color Plate 1.

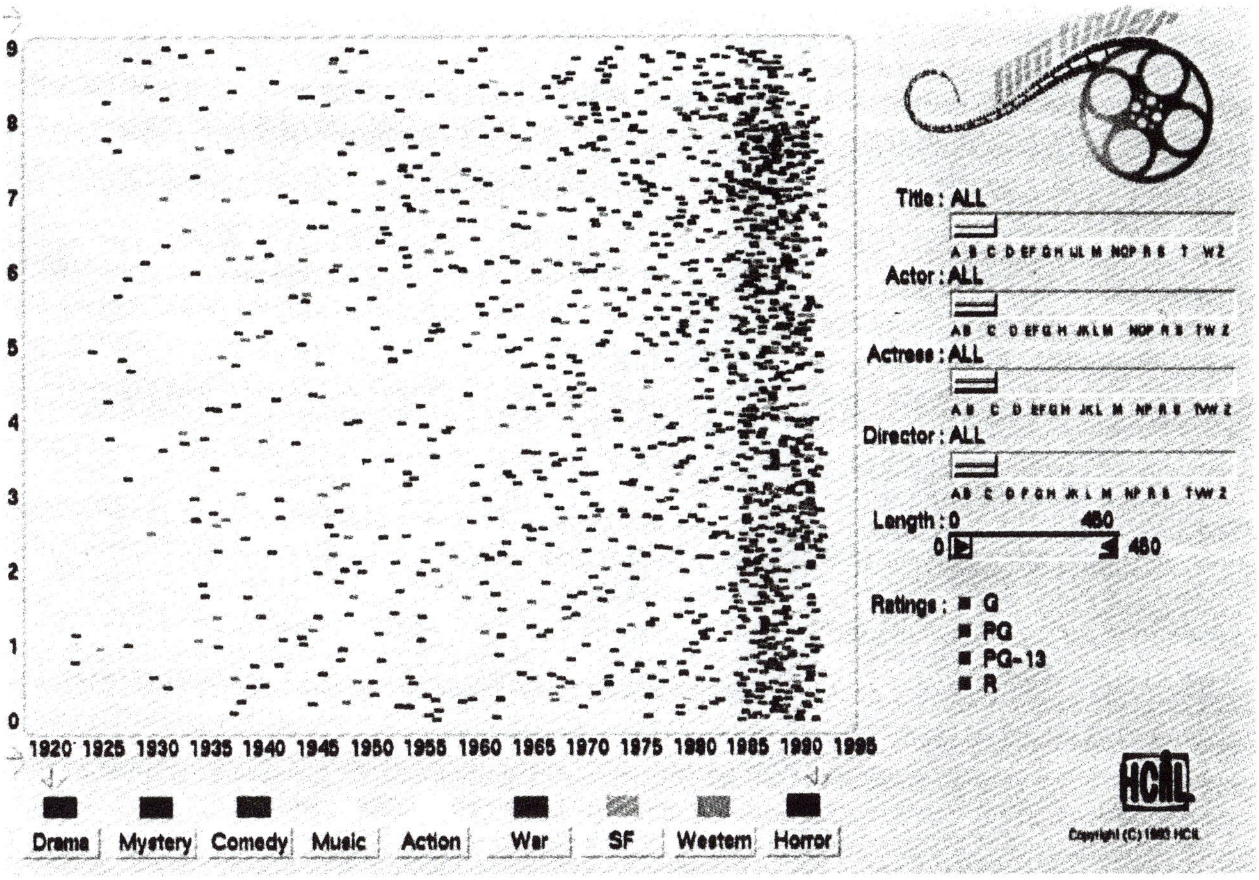

Ahlberg & Shneiderman, Color plate 1. The FilmFinder.

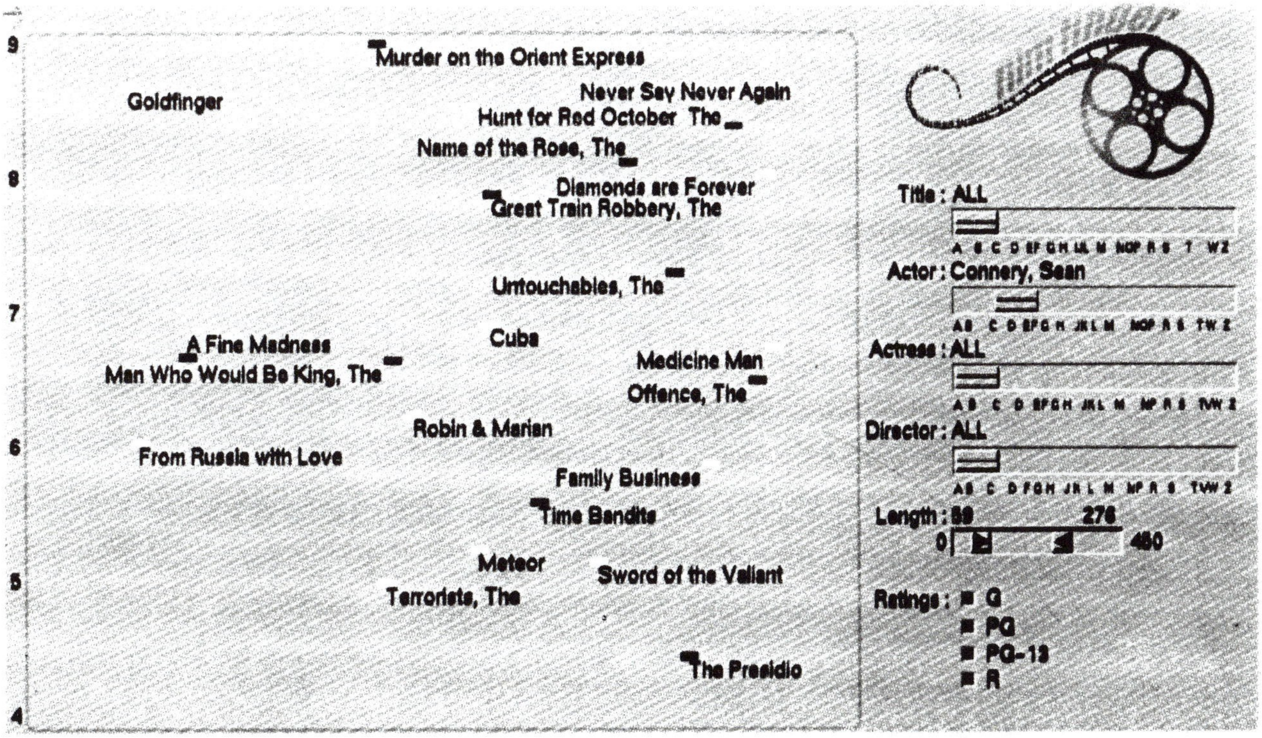

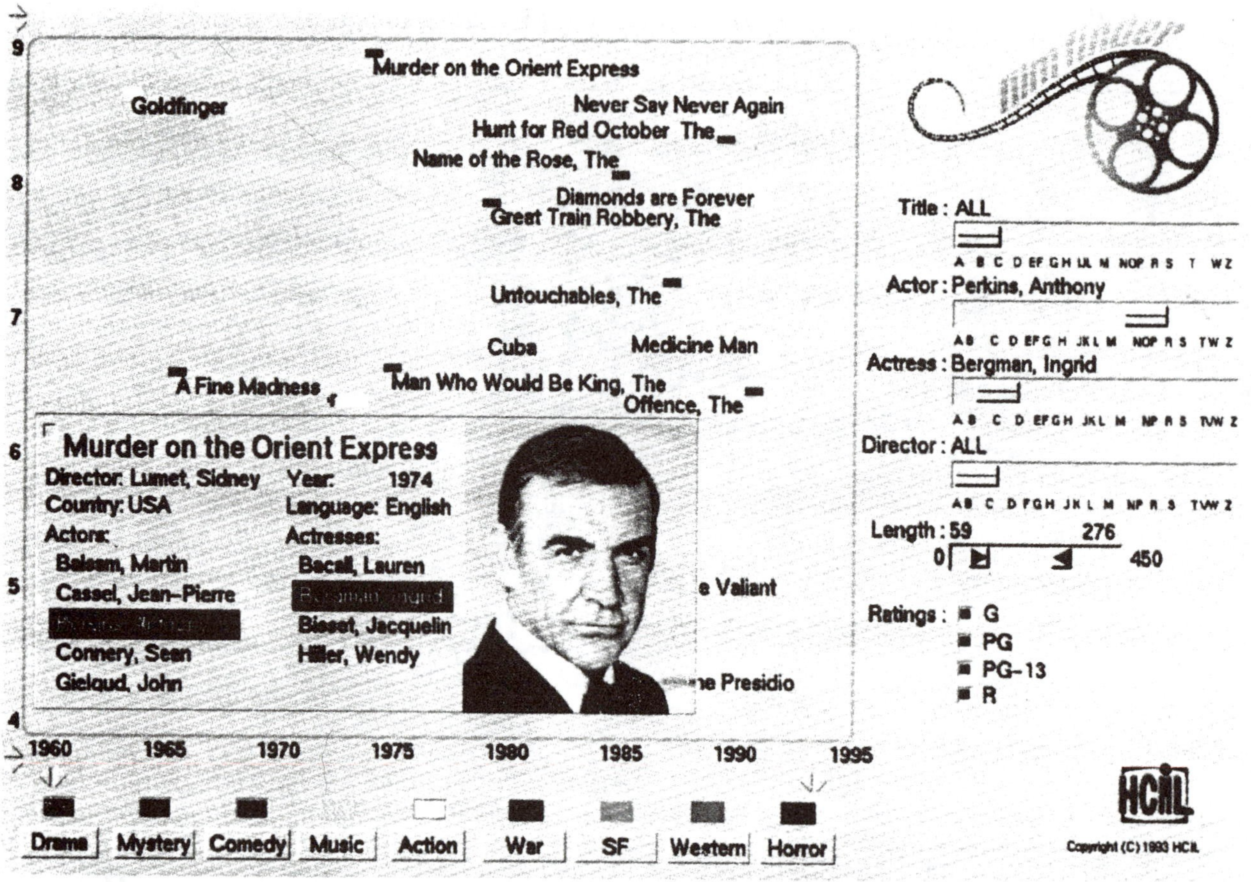

Ahlberg & Shneiderman, Color plate 3. Anthony Perkins and Ingrid Bergman has been selected in the information card - which is reflected in the Alphasliders.

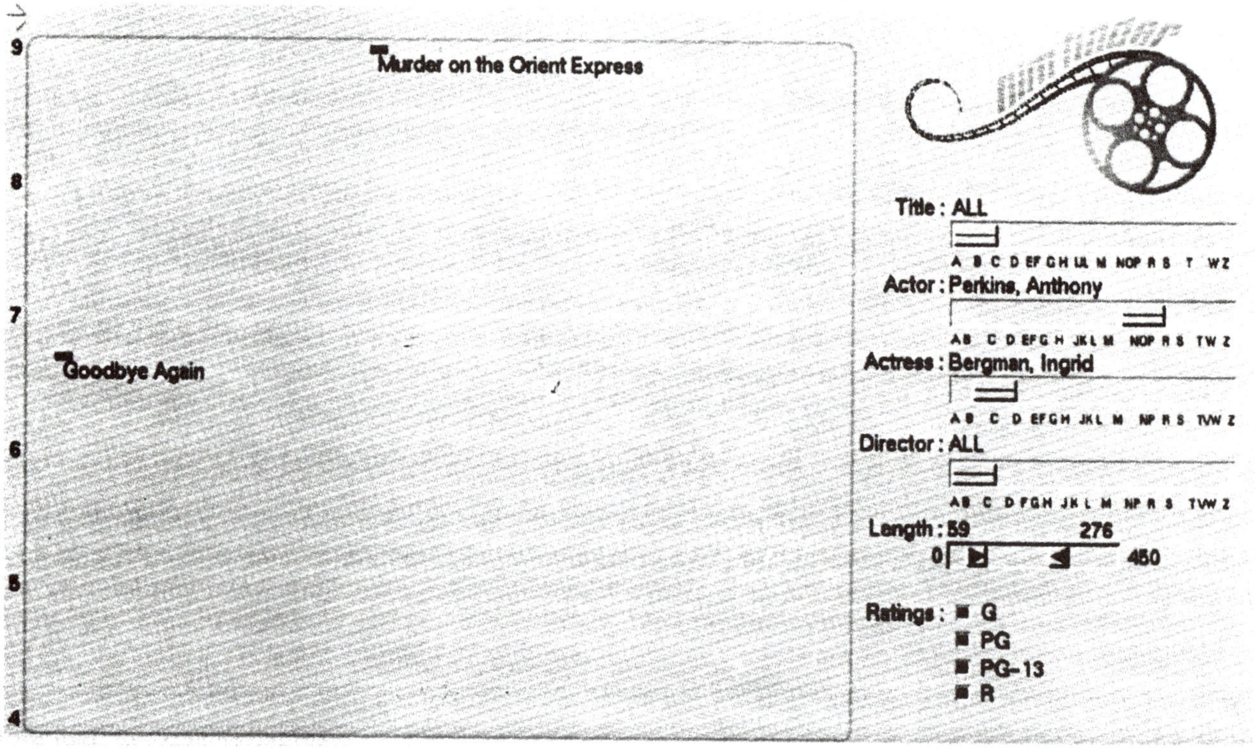

A Comparison of Graphical User Interfaces (Excerpt)

Aaron Marcus

To assist designers of graphical user interfaces, this section details similarities and differences among six major graphical user-interface (GUI) products. This chapter addresses the functional capabilities and usability characteristics of the following windowing systems:

Apple Macintosh OS
NextStep
OPEN LOOK GUI
Microsoft Windows
OS/2 Presentation Manager
OSF/Motif Window Manager and Toolkit

The windowing system is similar to an operating system. Instead of file systems or CPU cycles, however, the windowing system manages resources such as screen space and input devices. In GUIs, the windowing system acts as a front end to the operating system by shielding the end-user from the abstract and often confusing syntax and vocabulary of a keyboard-oriented command language.

The following chapter is divided into four parts. Section 7.1 offers explanations of the selected windowing systems. Sections 7.2-7.7 describe the basic components of six windowing systems. These sections also provide comparative data in figures containing tables and screen images. Section 7.8 examines a number of frequently performed tasks in terms of the steps users must take to accomplish them in each of the six windowing systems. Section 7.9 reviews the performance, configurability, and standardization of the windowing systems and closes with a brief summary that highlights the most important differences among the six products reviewed.

Additional detailed information describing the components of each system is presented in Appendixes A and B. The order in which the systems are described is the same for each section of the chapter so that information for a particular product can be located quickly. To facilitate cross-product comparisons while maintaining a consistent order of presentation, similar products such as Windows, Presentation Manager, and Motif are placed in adjacent positions in the sequence.

The Macintosh appears first because it is the oldest and most established of the windowing systems. For a large segment of the user population, the Macintosh defined the standard against which newer products must compete. NextStep is considered next because of its similarity to the Macintosh from the standpoint of its target user population and the level of complexity of the conceptual model presented by the GUI.

The OPEN LOOK GUI is similar to both NextStep and Motif. It appears third and is followed by Motif, which is grouped with Windows and Presentation Manager. This arrangement allows the two simple user model systems (Macintosh and NextStep), the three workstation class machines (NeXT, OPEN LOOK, Motif), and the three IBM-standard systems (Motif, Windows, Presentation Manager) to be grouped simultaneously. The same order of presentation used in the text is maintained in the column organization of the figures.

This chapter employs a single set of generic terminology to describe the components of the products being compared. Note that product references refer to the state of the products in early 1990.

7.1 Windowing Systems

Introduction

Each of the windowing systems discussed in this chapter has a unique place in the history of GUIs. Each system also has unique features, which are reviewed briefly in this section.

Macintosh

The Apple Macintosh was introduced in 1984 as the first mass-market computer featuring a high-resolution, bit-mapped graphic display and a direct manipulation interaction style. Its windowing system is built on top of a proprietary library of operating-system and user-interface toolkit routines in the Macintosh ROM.

The classic Macintosh is a single-tasking system with a high level of responsiveness and a very simple user model. Apple has succeeded in creating widespread acceptance among third-party software developers for their standard human-interface components. As a result, knowledge about familiar Macintosh applications can ease the task of learning new applications.

The Macintosh was the first computer system with a GUI to gain widespread market acceptance and experience significant commercial success. Its popularity, particularly in nontechnical market segments traditionally unreceptive toward computing, can be attributed in large part to Apple's commitment to the creation of a consistent and user-supportive human interface.

Because of its historical precedence and market penetration, the Macintosh has established the standard of interaction by which GUIs are judged. The degree of responsiveness to the actions of the user demonstrates the quality of interaction that is possible when the windowing system is integrated tightly with a particular hardware and software environment.

NextStep

The NextStep user interface provides a windowing system and graphical desktop environment for the NeXT Computer, which began shipping in 1988. The four component modules of the NextStep user interface are the Window Server, the Workspace Manager, the Application Kit, and the Interface Builder.

NextStep was the first in a series of products to adopt a simulated three-dimensional appearance for its standard components. The Window Server uses Display PostScript to create high-quality grayscale screen displays providing graphics that can be output on any PostScript printer.

The Application Kit provides a standard set of object-oriented components that can be customized by application developers. The Interface Builder is an end-user oriented tool that allows users to link these objects to system- and application-level functions with no additional programming. With this tool, standard OPEN LOOK human-interface components can be used to automate the user's tasks.

Like the Macintosh human interface, NextStep is oriented toward the needs of the nontechnical user. A straightforward conceptual model, a simple set of controls, and a well-developed collection of software tools shields the user from the complexity of the operating system and increases the suitability of the system for the initially targeted users (students and scholars) in higher education. Although the sophisticated UNIX-based operating system makes some degree of complexity inevitable, the design of the NextStep human interface makes the system accessible even for completely UNIX-naive users.

OPEN LOOK

The OPEN LOOK GUI was developed jointly by Sun Microsystems and AT&T as the standard operating environment for UNIX System V.4. The GUI exists as a layer on top of a base windowing system that provides the imaging-model and network-communication services. Versions of OPEN LOOK have been implemented on top of both the X Window System and Sun's Network-extensible Window System (NeWS).

Guidance for OPEN LOOK developers is provided by an exemplary functional specification and style guide. An explicit goal of the OPEN LOOK designers was to avoid potential legal challenges by creating innovative appearance and behavior characteristics. As a result, many of the conventions adopted deviate significantly from the industry norm.

A contrasting approach is adopted by OPEN LOOK. Its orientation toward maximum functionality is evident in the numerous context-sensitive and mode-specific operations it provides. While it, too, should make the UNIX world relatively accessible even for inexperienced users, the extended functionality of OPEN LOOK itself introduces an additional layer of complexity that is not seen in NextStep or the Macintosh human interface.

OSF/Motif

OSF/Motif is a window-manager and user-interface toolkit developed by DEC and Hewlett-Packard for the Open Software Foundation (OSF). Motif provides an alternative to OPEN LOOK that is linked to the OSF version of standard UNIX.

Like OPEN LOOK, the Motif Window Manager exists as a software layer atop the network-oriented X Window System. Appearance can be modified independently of the functional characteristics of the resulting system, and individual vendors are encouraged to customize the functional shell with their own proprietary widget sets.

The standard appearance and behavior of the Motif Window Manager are based on the OS/2 Presentation Manager. PC users familiar with that system or with Microsoft Windows will have little difficulty adapting to Motif on a workstation-level machine. Like NextStep, the Standard Motif widget set provides a simulated three-dimensional appearance.

OSF/Motif provides a GUI for a high-end, network-based computing environment whose appearance and behavior is consistent with that of Microsoft Windows and the OS/2 Presentation Manager. Because of their de facto standardization on IBM and compatible platforms, these operating environments are expected to predominate in the movement toward GUIs for PC-based systems. OSF anticipates that knowledge of Windows and the Presentation Manager will transfer easily to Motif, making it the windowing system of choice when PC users upgrade to workstation platforms.

The implementation of Motif on top of the network-transparent X Window System allows Motif to leverage an emerging standard in the workstation environment as well. Motif provides a windowing system that can serve as a bridge between the PC and workstation environments. Its potential for easing this transition will increase the attractiveness of Motif for organizations integrating high-performance workstations with existing PC networks.

Microsoft Windows and OS/2 Presentation Manager

Microsoft Windows was created in 1985 as a multitasking, graphics-oriented alternative to the character-based environment provided by MS-DOS on PC-compatible systems. The bit-mapped displays and mouse-driven menus provided by Windows first opened the door to graphics-oriented software on the PC.

Initially, Windows was limited by many of the design characteristics (640K address space, low-quality display, etc.) of the DOS environment on which it was built. Recent enhancements, however, have increased the responsiveness and graphical quality of Windows, particularly on 80386-based machines.

The OS/2 Presentation Manager was developed jointly by Microsoft and IBM in 1987 as the standard graphics-based end-user environment for the operating system replacing MS-DOS. Presentation Manager will become the standard operating environment for IBM and compatible microcomputers in the 1990s. The appearance and behavior of Presentation Manager are derived primarily from Windows, which will eventually provide an identical user model for users in the MS-DOS environment.

Microsoft Windows and the OS/2 Presentation Manager must satisfy a very different market consisting largely of existing MS-DOS users in business and technical environments. The extensive support for keyboard-based control provided by these products reflects the heritage of the character-based DOS interface, which has historically relied heavily on keystroke combinations for selecting from menus and dialogue boxes.

7.2 Windowing-System Overview

Introduction

Windowing systems divide the display screen into multiple functional areas that provide a means of monitoring and controlling multiple application programs or manipulating multiple data objects in a graphical environment. The windows in which documents and applications are presented provide a set of well-defined visual and functional contexts that allow multiple processes to time-share a single set of input devices (mouse, keyboard, etc.) and a limited amount of physical display space. The windowing code (software architecture, the method of window management, and the base window system's imaging model) can have noticeable effects on the quality of the displays and the level of interaction experienced by the user. These factors are described in this section.

Software Architecture

The location and organization of the code that implements the windowing system can influence the responsiveness, device dependence, and resource requirements of the resulting system. Kernel-based architectures, for example, provide high levels of interactivity but are dependent on the architecture and available resources of a single machine. Client-server architectures allow a single instance of the windowing system code to be shared across entire networks of heterogeneous machines, but response times may be limited by the communication bandwidth of the network.

Kernel-Based Architecture

In kernel-based systems, windowing services are provided by some portion of the operating system itself, or by a standard add-on module that resides along with the operating system in RAM- or ROM-based libraries. Kernel-based windowing codes and operating systems share the same physical memory space and are accessed in essentially the same way.

Client-Server Architecture

Client-server architectures provide a means for sharing windowing-system resources among multiple processes and machines. A server is a computer running software that provides a particular capability to an entire network of interconnected machines. A client is a piece of software on the same network that requests and uses the capabilities provided by the server.

Even the best client-server implementations incur significant communication overhead that can lead to noticeable performance degradation compared to kernel-based windowing systems. Kernel-based systems achieve higher performance at the cost of device dependence and the need to redundantly execute the same code on each machine.

Window Management

Window-management facilities allow the system to maintain spatial relationships between windows as they are moved, resized, and depth-arranged. Several options are available in window control menus that feature automatic arrangement of windows. Of particular importance are tiled, overlapping, and cascading windows. While the historical controversy over the relative merits of tiled and overlapping windows appears to have been resolved in favor of overlapping window management, tiled windows may still be useful in large or high-resolution displays.

Tiled Windows

Tiled windows are arranged automatically by the windowing system to completely fill the available display space (which may be either the entire display screen or an entire content area of a window). Windows are prevented from overlapping. When any window is resized, other windows must be sized in the opposing direction to compensate.

Overlapping Windows

Overlapping windows have an associated depth value that represents their distance from the viewer. At each pixel, only the contents of the nearest window covering that portion of the display are presented. The window with the lowest depth value thus obscures the contents of any other windows occupying the same display space, creating an illusion of physical overlapping. The resulting window stack is comparable to a pile of papers on the user's desk and allows users to take advantage of existing spatial-management skills.

Cascading Windows

Cascading windows are a special case of overlapping window management in which the windows are arranged automatically in a regular progression that prevents any window from being completely obscured. The origins (that is the upper-left corner) of each successive window is offset slightly in both the horizontal and vertical directions to conserve display space while simplifying the task of bringing any window to the front of the stack.

Imaging Model

The imaging model is embodied in the set of functions used by the window manager to translate mathematical descriptions of graphical elements into pixel images in the physical buffers of the display device. The two major classes of imaging model are based on raster images (bitmaps) that correspond directly to the resolution of the output device or on vector-based drawing languages such as PostScript, which maps abstract procedural image descriptions to the physical coordinates of the output device.

Because the image is defined procedurally and must be decoded by the windowing-system software, the rendering time for a vector-based language such as Display PostScript is dependent on the complexity of the image involved. Raster-based models, in contrast, provide rendering speed that is independent of image complexity.

The coordinate system, color capabilities, and image transfer mode defined by the imaging model can significantly affect the performance of the windowing system and the quality of the displays it can support. Device-dependent imaging models produce optimum performance, but may constrain the quality of printed output and produce displays that must be recoded whenever the platform changes. Sophisticated, device-independent imaging models can be scaled to match the resolution of any output devices, but the transformations may noticeably reduce rendering speed.

X Window System

The X Window System, developed jointly by MIT and DEC, is becoming rapidly the de facto standard for GUIs in workstation- and network-computing environments. X, V. 11 (X11) provides a high-throughput, network-transparent mechanism permitting communication between client programs and window servers.

Either the client, the server, or both may reside on the local machine. The X Window System provides a substrate for network communications and imaging across a wide variety of displays that is totally independent of the appearance and behavior of the GUI layer. Both Motif and OPEN LOOK leverage this capability by providing variations in appearance and behavior on top of the basic X11 functionality.

Windowing-System Components

The appearance and behavior of the windowing system as experienced by the user is determined by a small group of standard components. The systems make use of essentially the same set of human-interface objects, but the names by which these components are identified vary significantly among vendors (see Fig. A.1, Appendix A). The following set of terms will streamline cross-product comparisons by identifying standard components consistently and unambiguously.

Windows

From the viewpoint of the window manager, a window is any discrete area of the visual display that can be moved, sized, and rendered independently on the display screen. Even though most of the components are actually implemented and managed as windows by the system, we consider windows from the user's point of view. The definition we employ will therefore include only those display objects that allow the user to change the view of their contents using techniques such as sizing, scrolling, or editing.

Menus

Menus provide users with a means of command retrieval that enables them to see and point instead of remembering and typing. The menu system allows problems caused by the limitations of human memory to be greatly reduced at the expense of slightly reduced motor performance. The benefits are substantial, particularly when the number and complexity of commonly used applications limits the user's expertise with individual command sets.

Controls

Any visually represented window component that can be manipulated directly with the mouse or keyboard is a control. Each of the windowing systems defines standard sets of controls that can be incorporated by applications to provide consistent interaction protocols across products.

Dialogue Boxes

Dialogue boxes provide a visual and functional context for presenting options from which the user can select. Any interactive exchange of information between the user and the system that takes place in a limited spatial context considered a dialogue.

Although three distinct classes of dialogue box are described (control panels, query boxes, and message boxes), there may be considerable overlap between classes. Any dialogue box can be characterized by a clearly defined scope that determines the effect on the state of the system and the subsequent operations permitted.

Modeless Dialogues

Modeless dialogue boxes are limited in scope and do not restrict the subsequent operations of the user. Modeless dialogues may incorporate some basic window functions such as sizing and positioning. Users can continue to work without responding, if necessary, and may be allowed to keep the modeless dialogue on display even after a response has been made.

Modal Dialogues

Modal dialogue boxes require the user to respond before any other action can be taken. Application modal dialogues prevent the user from invoking any application functions until the dialogue has been satisfied, while system modal dialogues prevent the user from performing any operations anywhere in the system.

Control Panels

Control panels appear at the implicit or explicit request of the user and provide information reflecting the current state of a number of related system parameters, any of which can be changed interactively while the panel remains on display. Changes to the system state do not take effect until the user explicitly accepts the new settings.

Query Boxes

Query boxes appear in response to user actions, but are not requested explicitly by the user. Query boxes prompt the user for a single piece of information, such as a yes-or-no answer to a single question, and provide a context in which the necessary information can be provided. Like control panels, query boxes allow the user to cancel the action that led to the query.

Message Boxes

Providing critical information to the user is the primary function of message boxes, which are not requested by the user and typically appear only when the system has entered, or is about to enter, an unrecoverable and potentially dangerous state. The user's response options are typically limited to a simple yes-or-no decision, or in irreversible system states, simple acknowledgment of the message.

Mouse/Keyboard Interface

The systems use a mouse and keyboard as the primary interaction devices. Each device is well-suited to certain types of interaction tasks. The mouse provides an efficient means of accomplishing tasks that require spatial manipulation, such as menu navigation and window sizing and positioning. The keyboard is more efficient for sequential tasks, such as text entry and window shuffling.

Conclusion

Having discussed briefly the differences of implementation, I shall discuss the various typical components of window systems in the following sections.

7.3 Windows

Introduction

The windowing systems discussed in this chapter all provide a standard window structure within which application programs and documents are displayed for and controlled by the user. Most of these systems define a number of standard window types that can be customized by applications as necessary. For the purpose of comparison, this section describes standard windows that implement the basic features provided by the windowing system.

Application and Document Windows

An application window is the first object that appears in the workspace when a program is launched. The application window may contain data itself or it may provide a top-level context for one or more "child" windows (that is, dependent windows created by the independent, or "parent," window) that actually contain the data being processed. Child windows containing data that can be freely modified by the user are usually described as document windows, because they are typically associated with a single data object such as a text file or drawing.

The structure of document windows is similar or identical to that of application windows. Document windows provide a context within which to store and display the data for a single object as it is being created. Most applications support multiple document windows that allow users to work with more than one file at a time. The parent window's application menu affects only the document window that is currently receiving user input.

Window Icons

Window icons conserve display space by reducing the size of windows during periods in which no input from the user is required. Window icons help the user to maintain a global context by providing a visual reminder of the currently active applications and documents. These icons also allow previous local contexts to be immediately restored through direct interaction with visible objects.

Overall Appearance

A recent trend in GUIs is the creation of windows and window components that appear to be three-dimensional, resembling real-world controls on familiar devices such as automotive dashboards or hi-fi equipment. The stylistic treatment has useful functional implications as well, because raised three-dimensional

Macintosh

NextStep

OPEN LOOK

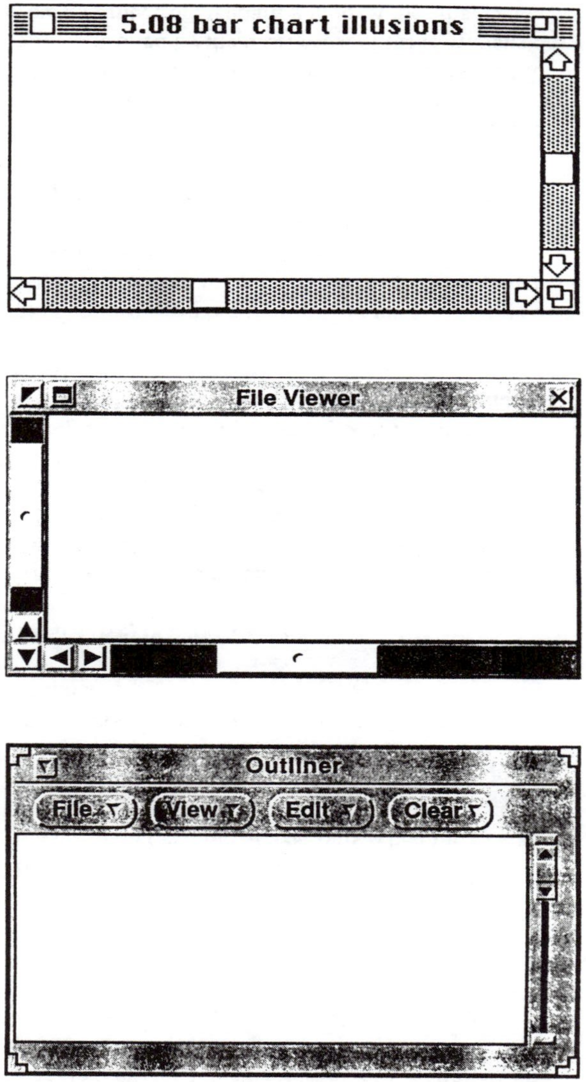

Figure 7.1Window Systems Gallery 1

OSF/Motif

Microsoft Windows 3.0

OS/2 Presentation Manager

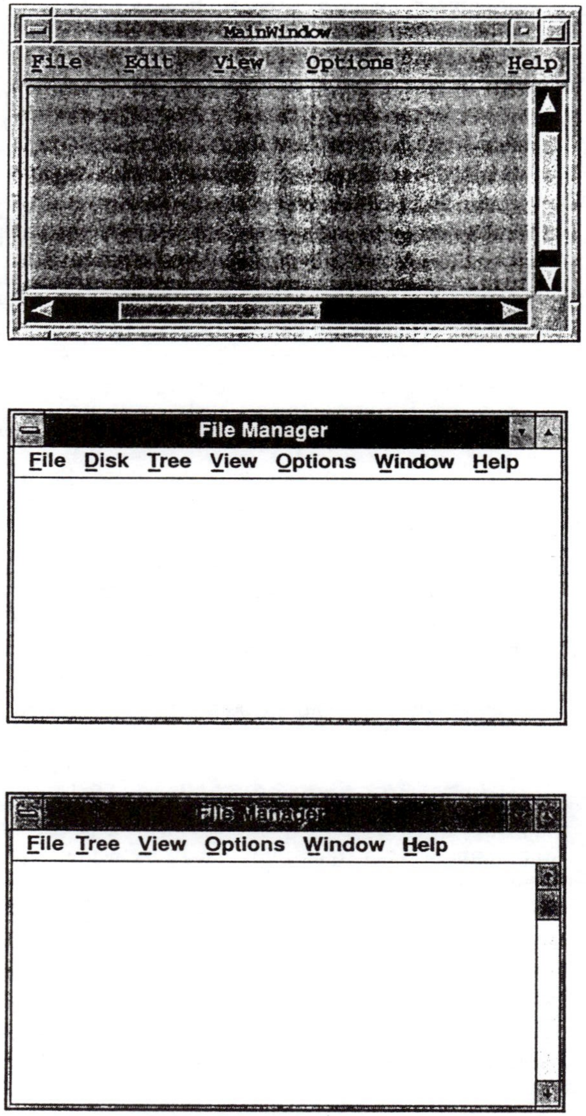

Figure 7.2 Window Systems Gallery 2

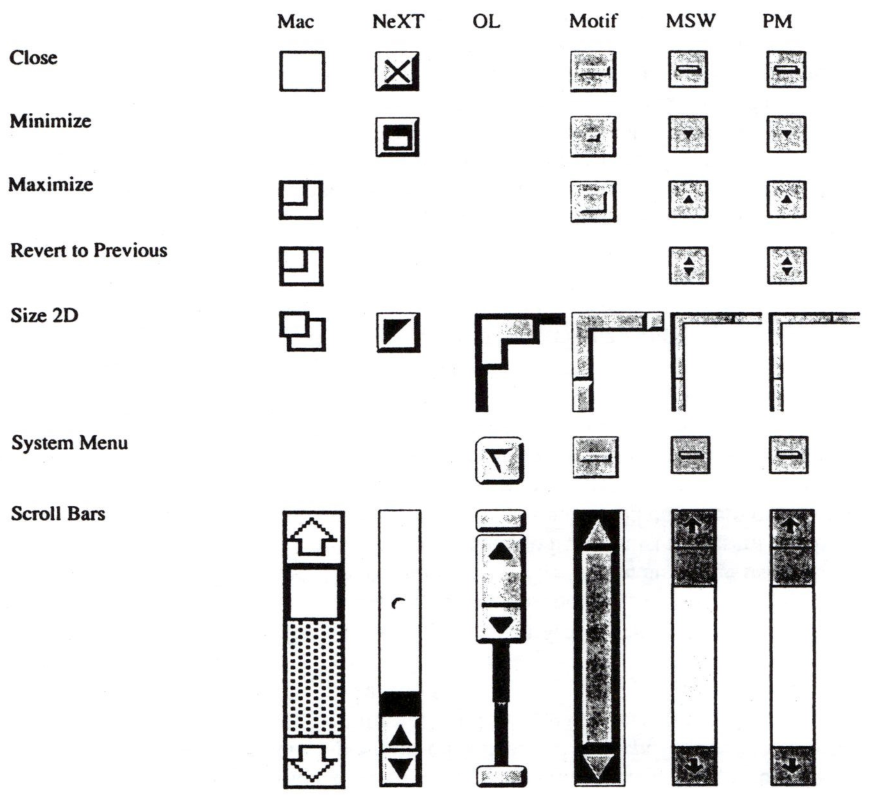

Figure 7.3 Standard Window Controls

areas can be easily differentiated from their surroundings and identified as graspable or pushable objects.

Window Structure

The structure of application and document windows varies considerably across systems. Most windows have a border region controlled by the windowing system and a content region that the application can freely modify. The Windowing System Galleries pictured in Figs. 7.1 and 7.2 provide a visual catalogue of the overall structure and major components of a full-featured basic window in each of the six systems. See Figs. B.1 and B.2 for an annotated version identifying components using system-specific terminology.

Standard Window Controls

As the technology of windowing systems has matured, the set of standard user controls for window management and manipulation has become relatively stable (see Fig. 7.3). The system-specific details of each of these fundamental window-management operations are described more extensively in Section 7.8.

Conclusion

Windows provide the means of displaying application-related data. To modify the data, menus are required to provide the relevant functions. The various kinds of menus are discussed in the following section.

7.4 Menus

Introduction

Menus provide a means for the user to issue commands without having to remember the name and syntax of the particular command required. Each of the window systems being compared uses the select-then-operate command paradigm. The user first selects the object or objects to which the operation is to apply, then chooses the appropriate command from the menu.

The six windowing systems each provide a menu interface for the majority of their capabilities. At the most general level, the systems all display menus as vertical lists of commands. Beyond this, however, the appearance and behavior of menus varies substantially across systems. Figures 7.4 and 7.5 display a representative sample of the standard menus provided by each system. The following discussion describes the major differences in menu appearance, behavior, and standardization across applications. This section will define a limited number of menu classes based on these fundamental menu characteristics. Some further distinctions bear mentioning: representation, duration, and navigation.

Representation: Implicit pop-up menus appear whenever the mouse menu button is depressed within a particular region of the display. The region may be the entire screen or some well-defined area such as a window or window border, but no feedback is provided to remind the user of the presence of a menu. In explicit pop-up menus, areas from which menus can be accessed are designated by a specific symbol or visual treatment applied to a standard control. A special case is the pull-down menu, in which the menu is attached to a menu bar at the top of the window or the display screen.

Duration: The presentation of a menu may be either static, with the menu displayed continuously in a particular location, or dynamic, with the menu displayed only until the user makes a selection. Stay-up menus provide a combination of these behaviors. These menus are positioned in a convenient location and remain on display even after a selection has been made, allowing the user to select repeatedly from the options presented.

Navigation: Menu hierarchies are traversed by using the mouse menu button with either apress-drag-release or a click-position-click protocol. Except for the Macintosh, each of the six windowing systems supports both methods of selection.

Menu Appearance

The visible language characteristics of the menu can strengthen the conceptual model of the GUI presented by the windowing system. The visible language used to reflect the state of the menu items must represent (1) the currently selected state of any multistate item or group of items, (2) the eligibility of an item for selection, (3) the presence of attached submenus or dialogue boxes, and (4) the keyboard shortcut that can be used to access a particular item. Appropriate visual feedback must also be provided to identify the menu item currently selected by the mouse pointer or key-board cursor as the user navigates through the menu system.

In each of the windowing systems, items that cannot be selected are emphasized less than valid selections. Attached submenus are represented by arrows or triangles, while dialogue boxes are represented by the ellipsis character (see Fig. 7.4). OPEN LOOK is the only system that does not provide explicit representation of keyboard menu shortcuts. The other systems all place the name of the "accelerator," or "hot," key and its qualifiers at the right edge of the associated menu item.

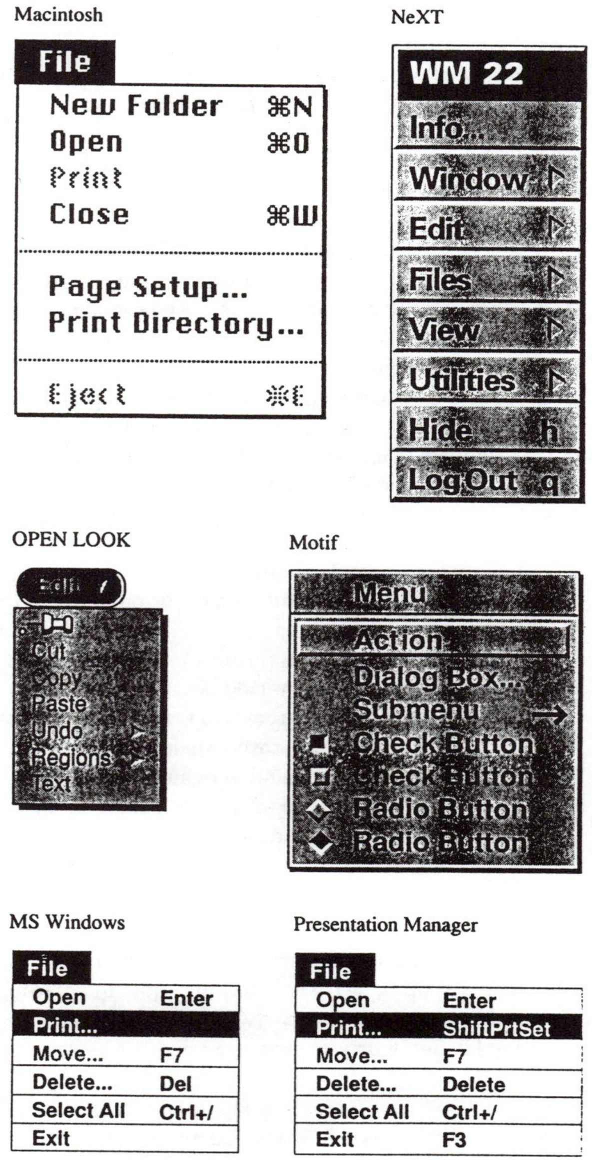

Figure 7.4 Menu Gallery

	Mac	NeXT	OL	Motif	MSW	PM
Pull-Down Menus	●		●	●	●	●
Implicit Pop-Up Menus		●	●	●	●	●
Explicit Pop-Up Menus	●	●	●			
Stay-up Menus	●	●	●			

Figure 7.5 Menu Presentation Techniques

Mac	NeXT	OL	Motif	MSW	PM
	Info	File	System	Control	System
File	Window	View		File	File
Edit	Edit	Edit		Edit	Edit
		Props		View	View
				Window	Window
				Help	Help

Figure 7.6 Standard Menu Commands

Menu Behavior

The behavioral aspects of menus constrain the ways in which they can be manipulated by the user and the manner in which they respond to user interaction. Individual classes of menus can be described by their representation, duration, and navigation characteristics. Except for NextStep, the systems all support pulldown menus attached to the individual application or document windows or (on the Macintosh) to the top of the display screen. Each system also provides pop-up menus represented either implicitly or explicitly (see Fig. 7.5).

Standard Menus and Menu Items

The standard menus items defined by each windowing system are listed in Fig. 7.6 Menus containing windowing-system commands are generally provided by the system itself. Other menus are defined by the application and may differ from the system menus in presentation or behavior. Both types of menu rely on standardization to help users locate the desired command.

Window-Control Menus

Task- and window-management functions allow multiple windows to share display space. The Macintosh and NextStep provide only a few of these system-level functions in the same set of menus used by application programs. Users of these systems must rely on the controls provided in the window borders for most of their window-management tasks. The remaining systems place window-control functions in menus that are physically or conceptually distinguished from the menus used by application programs.

Component Menus

OPEN LOOK provides implicit pop-up menus for various structural regions of the window as well as for certain controls such as textfields, scrollbars, and scrolling lists. These component menus, which are required for conforming to OPEN LOOK implementations, are described in greater detail in Appendix B.

Application Menus

Applications normally require their own set of menus, which may be presented separately or integrated with the system menus in both application and document windows. Some application functions are universal and appear in the menus of virtually every program. If the names and locations in the menu structure of these common functions vary significantly across applications, the system may be unnecessarily difficult to learn and use. Most windowing systems therefore provide recommendations or standards to produce a menu configuration that is consistent across applications (see Fig. 7.7).

Conclusion

Additional adjustments of application windows that cannot be accomplished with the menus directly require further adjustment of data. The data parameters and their annotation are provided by controls, which are discussed in the following section.

	Macintosh	NextStep	OPEN LOOK	OSF/Motif	MS Windows	OS/2-PM
Window Types						
Window with Keyboard Focus	Active Window	Key Window	Input Area	Active Window	Active Window	Active Window
Child Window	Document Window	Standard Window	Base Window	Secondary Window	Document Window	Document Window
Modeless Dialog Box	Dialog Box	Panel	Pop-up Window	Modeless Dialog Widget	Modeless Dialog Box	Modeless Dialog Box
Modal Dialog Box	Modal Dialog Box	Attention Panel	Notice	Modal Dialog Widget	Modal Dialog Box	Modal Dialog Box
Query Box	Dialog Box	Panel	Command Window	Secondary Window	Dialog Box	Dialog Box
Message Box	Alert			Message Box	Message Box	Message Box
Window Structure						
Title Bar	Title Bar	Title Bar	Header	Title Area	Title Bar	Title Bar
Window Menu Bar			Control Area	Menu Bar	Menu Bar	Menu Bar
Message Area			Footer		Message Line	Message Line
Window Controls						
Close Control	Close Box	Close Button		System Menu Button	Control Menu Box	System Menu Box
Size Control	Size Box	Resize Button	Resize Corner	Border Resize Handle	Window Frame	Window Frame
Minimize Control		Miniaturizing Button		Minimize Button	Minimize Box	Minimize Box
Maximize Control	Zoom Box			Maximize Button	Maximize Box	Maximize Box
Restore Control	Zoom Box				Restore Box	Restore Box
Scrollbar	Scrollbar	Scroller	Scrollbar	Scrollbar	Scrollbar	Scrollbar
Scrollbar Handle	Scroll Box	Scroll Knob	Drag Area	Slider	Scroll Box	Scroll Box
Scrollbar Arrow	Scroll Arrow	Scroll Button	Arrow	Arrow	Scroll Arrow	Scroll Arrow
Menu Types						
Pull-Down Menus	Menu		Button Menu	Pull-down Menu	Drop-down Menu	Drop-down Menu
Implicit Pop-Up Menu		Menu	Pop-up Menu	Pop-up Menu	Contextual Menu	Contextual Menu
Explicit Pop-Up Menu	Pop-up Menu	Pop-up List	Button Menu			
Stay-Up Menu	Tear-off Menu	Detached Menu	Pinned Menu			

Figure A.1 Windowing-System Component Terminology

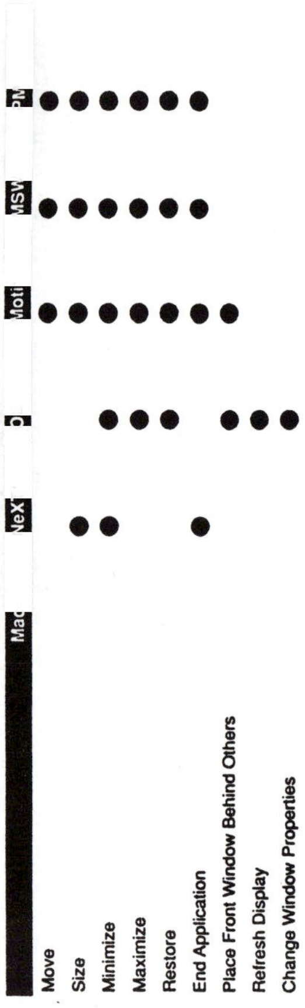

Figure 7.7 Window Control Menu Commands

Appendix A

Windowing-System Component Terminology

Figure A.1 outlines some of the product-specific terminology used to describe standard components that appear in nearly all windowing systems. Cells for components with no direct equivalent in a particular system are left blank in the resulting terminology matrix.

Chapter 7

Touch, Gesture, and Marking

This chapter investigates input to computer systems. Although there has been much progress since the pioneering Sketchpad system of the early 1960s (Sutherland, 1983 video), this is still an area of human-computer interaction in which there is great potential for further improvement.

Our discussion will focus on what we call *haptic* input. This term haptic comes from a Greek word having to do with *contact.* Hence, haptic input is input that involves physical contact between the computer and the user. This contact may be via the hands using a mouse, feet using a pedal, or even the tongue using a special joystick.

There are also nonhaptic means of input. The main one, speech, is covered separately in Chapter 8. Eye-tracking is another possibility. Since it is still more of a future technology than something that can be used today in mainstream applications, we shall merely refer the reader to Hutchinson et al. (1989), Jacob (1991), Koons, Sparrell, and Thorisson (1993), and Thorisson, Koons, and Bolt (1992 video).

We can't discuss haptic input without at least also mentioning output. *Every* haptic input device also provides output through the tactile or kinesthetic feedback it gives to users. The quality and appropriateness of this "feel" may be very important in determining a device's effectiveness and acceptance. Some devices, such as certain joysticks, actually provide force feedback (Iwata, 1990). Others, such as devices producing output in Braille, even use the haptic channel solely for output.

What we are *not* going to do in this chapter is provide a complete catalogue of input devices and how they work. This information is available in sources such as Chapanis and Kinkade (1972), Seibel (1972), Sherr (1988), Greenstein and Arnaut (1988), and Potasnak (1988). A condensed presentation can be found in Chapter 8 of Foley et al. (1990). The focus of our discussion will be on the human use rather than on the mechanics of the technology. We shall begin by looking at sample tasks by which devices can be compared. We shall also present a taxonomy of input that helps differentiate devices along dimensions meaningful to the designer.

RELATING TASK AND TECHNOLOGY

Each input device has its own strengths and weaknesses, just as each application has its own unique demands (Gaver, 1991). With the wide range of available input devices, a problem confronting the designer is to obtain a match between application and input technology. The designer must recognize the relevant dimensions along which an application's demands can be characterized, and must know how each technology being considered performs along those dimensions. These topics are addressed below and in Buxton (1986a).

One way to try and understand these issues is to experiment with a diverse set of representative tasks. Each task has its own idiosyncratic demands. We can determine which properties are relevant to a particular application, and then test the effectiveness of various technologies in their performance. This allows us to match technology to the application. Furthermore, the set of representative tasks provides a reminder of what dimensions should be considered in the selection process.

We shall now describe a basic set of generic tasks. Like any such list, this one is not complete. It was chosen to reflect the types of 2D tasks typically found in graphical user interfaces, such as those illustrated in the excellent collection of widgets compiled in Myers (1990 video). Text entry and 3D input are not emphasized. We leave it as an exercise for the reader to expand the list.

Pursuit Tracking

In this test, a target (a fly) moves over the screen under computer control (Figure 7.1). The operator uses the control device to track the fly's motion. Feedback about the operator's performance is given by a tracking symbol in the form of a fly swatter. The idea is to see how many times the fly can be killed by positioning the swatter over the fly and pushing a button device.

The main statistic in this test is how many times the fly can be swatted in a given time interval. A number of parameters should be variable in order to develop an understanding of their influence on task performance. One of these is the speed that the target moves. Another is the *control:display (C:D) ratio.* The C:D ratio is the ratio between the distance the controller must be moved in order to cause the tracker to move a given distance on the display. For example, if the C:D ratio is 2:1, two centimeters of motion by the controller result in only one centimeter of motion by the tracker.

FIGURE 7.1

Pursuit tracking. A moving target (a fly) moves over the screen. The tracking symbol is a fly swatter. When the swatter is over the fly, the user pushes a button device to swat the fly.

A high C:D ratio is useful for fine cursor positioning, and for users who do not have well developed motor coordination (such as the aged or physically disabled). A low C:D ratio permits one to traverse the display with relatively little motion of the controller.

Notice that with devices that use the same surface for both control and display, such as touch screens and light pens, the C:D ratio is almost always 1:1. Such devices therefore have a directness not shared by most other technologies (Nelson, 1983 video; Minsky, 1985; Pickering, 1986; Potter, Shneiderman, and Weldon, 1988; Potter, Berman, and Shneiderman, 1989; Plaisant and Shneiderman, 1991 video; Sears and Shneiderman, 1991; Shneiderman, 1991; Plaisant and Wallace, 1992 video), which makes them particularly appropriate for systems to be used by anyone who walks up to them, such as information and museum kiosks.

With appropriate technology, the C:D ratio may be changed. Sometimes this is done by the user, and in other cases it is changed automatically. The C:D ratio also need not be linear. On the Macintosh computer, for example, the C:D ratio varies, based on the speed that the controller (the mouse) is moved. In effect, the C:D ratio is governed by an "automatic transmission."

One other parameter to consider in this test is the button push that is required to swat the fly. For example, can this be activated with the same hand that is providing the spatial control? This may be difficult if a trackball or a touch tablet (Buxton, Hill, and Rowley, 1985) is used.

Target Acquisition

In this task, the user must select each of a number of rectangles displayed on the screen (Figure 7.2). A rectangle is selected by positioning the tracking symbol over it and signaling the system with a button event. Rectangles should be selected left to right, top to bottom.

FIGURE 7.2

Target acquisition. Select each rectangle in turn, left to right, top to bottom. Notice how selection time is related to target size.

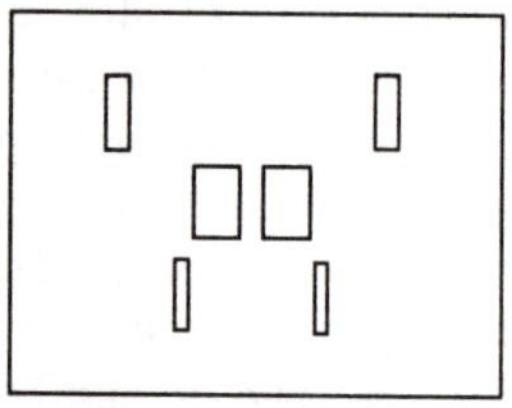

The most interesting statistic is how long it takes to select the full set of targets. One should also examine how target size affects the speed of target acquisition. The smaller the target, the longer it will take to acquire, because of the fine motor control required. This is generalized as *Fitts' Law* (Fitts and Peterson, 1964), and was first used to study HCI in Card, English, and Burr (1978) (see also English, Engelbart, and Berman, 1967).

Fitts's Law states that the movement time, *MT*, to acquire a target with a continuous linear controller is a function of the distance over the target size. More precisely, the time *MT* to move the hand to a target of width *W*, which lies at distance *D* away is

$$MT = a + b \log_2 (D/W + 1)$$

where *a* is a constant, and (according to Card, Moran, and Newell, 1983, p. 241) $b = 100[70\sim120]$ msec/bit.

The most current and thorough discussion of Fitts' Law is MacKenzie (1992a). The reading by MacKenzie (1992b) summarizes important points for the practitioner and presents examples of how this law can be applied.

As in the pursuit-tracking task, issues such as C:D ratio and what button device is used will affect performance. There are a number of variations on this basic task. Each brings to light important aspects of the input technology:

- *Homing time:* If an application involves frequently moving between a text entry device (usually a QWERTY keyboard) and a pointing device, this movement affects user performance. This is the homing time discussed in the keystroke model (Card, Moran, and Newell, 1980). To get a feeling for the effect of homing time, have the user push a key on the keyboard (the spacebar, for example), after each square is selected. Also, using the same tablet, what is the difference in performing this task between using a puck and a stylus?
- *Number of dimensions:* Fitts' Law deals with movement in one dimension. Some studies have used it to predict and analyze performance in higher dimensional tasks. The two main questions are, (a) What is the effective target width in two or more dimensions? and (b) What is the effect of approach angle? The former question can be understood by considering selecting a word, which is graphically short in the vertical dimension but wide horizontally. Should the width or height be used? The second question has to do with whether or not we can move more effectively horizontally or vertically. These are points discussed in MacKenzie (1992b), and more fully in MacKenzie and Buxton (1992).
- *Dragging and rubber-band lines:* In this variation, an object is dragged (or a rubber-band line is stretched) from square to square. As shown by MacKenzie, Sellen, and Buxton (1991), dragging between targets is also a Fitts' Law task, and the act of maintaining the dragging state (by holding down a button on the mouse, for example) can negatively affect the acquisition of the target. In particular, different devices are affected to different degrees by state maintenance. Hence, if dragging is an important part of the interaction style, devices should also be evaluated in this mode.
- *Left hand vs right hand:* It is interesting to see how devices perform in Fitts' Law tasks when carried out using the left or the right hand. Kabbash, MacKenzie, and Buxton (1993)

found that the degradation in moving from the dominant to nondominant hand varied across devices. The lesson is to be sure that devices are evaluated in the context in which they are to be used.

Free-Hand Inking

Attempting to input a facsimile of your handwritten signature places yet another set of demands on the input technology. To get a feeling for the degree to which various devices lend themselves to this type of task, present the user with a screen ruled with lines of decreasing spacing. Have users sign their names once in each space (Figure 7.3). Use a simple subjective evaluation of the quality of signatures as a means of comparing devices.

FIGURE 7.3

Free-hand inking. A device's ability to capture a good facsimile of your signature is a good measure of its effectiveness for inking and drawing tasks. Comparisons should be made for different sizes.

The attributes of this handwriting exercise are relevant to several other common tasks, such as those seen in drawing programs, marking interfaces, and systems that utilize character recognition.

Tracing and Digitizing

In applications such as cartography, computer-aided design, and the graphic arts, it is important to be able to trace material previously drawn on paper, or digitize points from a map. *Relative* devices such as mice and trackballs are almost useless in this regard. *Absolute* devices such as tablets vary widely in how well they can perform such a task. Demands on resolution and linearity vary greatly across applications. In cartography, for example, the accuracy of digitization required is often far beyond what is needed to digitize a sketch.

Constrained Motion

In some applications it is important to be able to move the tracker rapidly along a straight-line path. One example is in using the scrollbar mechanism of some systems. Another is where you want to use the motion of a mouse in one dimension, say Y, to control one parameter, without changing the value of another parameter being controlled by motion in the X dimension. Different devices vary in the ease with which this can be done. X/Y thumbwheels, for example, would outperform a mouse in this task if the motion were along the primary axes.

In the example task of Figure 7.4, the tracking symbol is a ball that is dragged along a linear path defined by two parallel lines. The object is to move along the path without crossing the parallel lines. How is speed affected by the input device used and the path width? Are similar results obtained if the path is vertical or diagonal?

A variation of the previous example is to see how well the user can specify a circular motion within a constrained region (Figure 7.5). This type of control is useful in manipulating 3D objects, for example, and is described in Evans, Tanner, and Wein (1981). As in the previous example, different results will be obtained from different devices. Results will also vary according to C:D ratio and the width of the path.

FIGURE 7.4

Constrained linear motion. How quickly can the ball be moved along the straight path without crossing the lines?

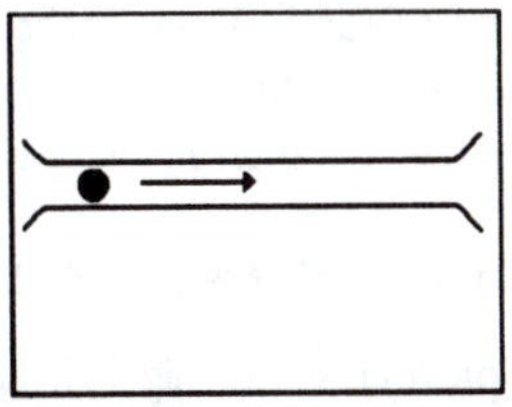

FIGURE 7.5

Constrained circular motion. How fast can the tracking symbol be moved around the circular shaded path without crossing the borders?

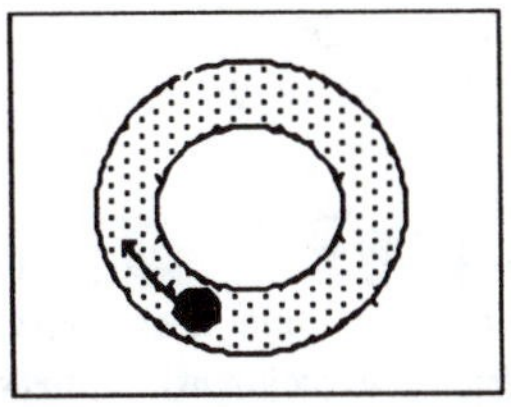

Three-Dimensional Input and Interaction

All of the tasks discussed thus far involve 2D control. As the power of graphics displays increases, 3D interfaces are becoming increasingly important to the user interface designer. Issues that used to concern only computer graphics specialists are now relevant to designers of general applications.

One consequence of this is that designers need to devise the 3D equivalents of the representative 2D tasks discussed in the previous section (see, for example, Myers and Zeller, 1990 video). Another is that the designer must decide what devices to use in supporting applications of higher dimensionality. At one extreme, does one need special devices such as those described in Brooks et al. (1983 video) and Brooks et al. (1990), or the instrumented gloves of virtual reality systems (Zimmerman et al., 1987; Zacharey, 1987 video; Weiner and Ganapathy, 1990 video)? Or can one support 3D interaction using the same, relatively nonintrusive devices found in conventional 2D interfaces?

A number of important studies show that the latter is often possible. One of the more compelling examples is the Information Visualizer described in Mackinlay, Card, and Robertson (1990), Mackinlay, Robertson, and Card (1990), and Mackinlay, Card, and Robertson (1990 video) and discussed more fully in Chapter 6.

Chen, Mountford, and Sellen (1988) is a good introduction to the problem of controlling 3D worlds with 2D devices. It introduces a novel new technique, the *virtual 3D trackball.* It also contains an excellent comparative evaluation of a number of techniques, many of them deriving from earlier work by Evans, Tanner, and Wein (1981; see also Evans, Tanner, and Wein, 1981 video; and Shoemake, 1992, for a variation of the virtual 3D trackball.)

Other publications dealing with novel 3D input devices, interaction techniques, and experimental studies include Schmandt (1983), Ware and Jessome (1988), Ware and Osborne (1990), Hill and Hollan (1992 video), MacKenzie and Ware (1993), and Zhai, Buxton, and Milgram (1994).

Finally, the reader should compare two different approaches to a 3D drawing package. Gargoyle 3D (Bier and Pier, 1987 video; Bier, 1989 video; Bier, 1990) and 3-Draw (Sachs, Stoop, and Roberts, 1989, 1990 video) are similar in that they use *constraints* and "snapping" techniques, but they differ greatly in how input is handled.

A TAXONOMY OF INPUT DEVICES

The examples of the previous section highlight how different devices lend themselves to different tasks. In this section, we develop a categorization of input devices that is based on the properties that cause these differences. Our approach is shown in Figure 7.6.

The table uses a hierarchy of criteria to organize the devices. It is limited, considering only continuous, manually operated devices. Hence, the first two (implicit) organizational criteria are

- continuous versus discrete
- agent of control (hand, foot, voice, etc.)

The table is divided into a matrix whose primary partitioning into rows and columns delimit

- what is being sensed (position, motion, or pressure)
- the number of dimensions being sensed (1, 2, or 3)

These primary partitions are delimited by solid lines. For example, both the rotary and sliding potentiometers fall into the box associated with one-dimensional position-sensitive devices (top left-hand corner). These primary rows and columns are then further subdivided by dotted lines into secondary regions that group

- devices that are operated using similar motor skills (subcolumns)
- devices that are operated by touch versus those that require a mechanical intermediary between the hand and the sensing mechanism (subrows)

Grouping by motor action can be seen in examining the two-dimensional devices. Since they are in the same subcolumn, Figure 7.6 implies that tablets and mice utilize similar types of hand control and that this motor action is different from that used by joysticks and trackballs, which appear in a different subcolumn.

The use of different subrows to differentiate between devices that are and are not touch-activated can be seen in comparing the light pen and the touch screen. While each utilizes similar motor control, the light pen requires the use of a stylus.

FIGURE 7.6

Taxonomy of input devices. Continuous manual input devices are categorized. The first-order categorization is property sensed (rows) and number of dimensions (columns). Subrows distinguish between devices that have a mechanical intermediary (such as a stylus) between the hand and the sensing mechanism (indicated by "M"), and those which are touch sensitive (indicated by "T"). Subcolumns distinguish devices that use comparable motor control for their operation (Buxton, 1983).

Property Sensed	Number of Dimensions: 1	1	2	2	2	2	3	
Position	Rotary Pot	Sliding Pot	Tablet & Puck	Tablet & Stylus	Light Pen	Isotonic Joystick	3D Joystick	M
Position				Touch Tablet	Touch Screen			T
Motion	Continuous Rotary Pot	Treadmill	Mouse			Sprung Joystick Trackball	3D Trackball	M
Motion		Ferinstat				X/Y Pad		T
Pressure	Torque Sensor					Isometric Joystick		T
	rotary	linear	puck	stylus finger horiz.	stylus finger vertical	small fixed location	small fixed with twist	

Thus we see that the table models the structure that exists in the domain of input devices. It helps in finding appropriate equivalencies, which is useful in dealing with issues of device independence (to be discussed below). It also helps us relate devices to one another. For example, a tablet is to a mouse what a joystick is to a trackball.

Furthermore, if the taxonomy can suggest new transducers in a manner analogous to the way the periodic table of Mendelev has predicted new elements, then we can have even more confidence in it. We make this claim and cite the "torque sensing" one-dimensional pressure-sensitive transducer as an example. To our knowledge, no such device exists commercially. Nevertheless it is a potentially useful device, an approximation of which has been demonstrated by Herot and Weinzapfel (1978).

Three novel input devices demonstrated on video are the bicycle as workstation (Roberts, 1989 video), the pointing stick (Rutledge and Selker, 1990 video), and the cue ball (Theil, 1991 video).

Generality and Extensibility

Choosing the input technologies to be used with a workstation often involves a trade-off between two conflicting demands. Every task has specialized needs that can be best addressed by a specialized technology, yet each workstation is used for multiple tasks. Supplying the optimum device for each task is generally impossible, so a trade-off must be made.

Devices must be chosen to give the best coverage of the demands of the range of tasks. An important criterion in comparing devices, therefore, is how broad their coverage is. Stated differently, how many squares in Figure 7.6 can a particular device be used to fill? For example, graphics tablets can emulate many other transducers (Evans, Tanner, and Wein, 1981). The tablet is what could be called an *extensible* device. This property of extensibility is an important but seldom considered criterion that should be used in device selection.

Relative versus Absolute Controllers

Another important characteristic of input devices is whether they sense absolute or relative values. This has a very strong effect on the nature of the dialogues that the system can support with any degree of fluency. As we have seen, a mouse cannot be used to digitize map coordinates or trace a drawing because it does not sense absolute position. An example taken from process control, the *nulling problem*, occurs when absolute transducers are used in designs where one controller must be used for different tasks at different times (Buxton, 1986a).

What Our Taxonomy Doesn't Show

Perhaps the main weakness of the taxonomy presented above is that it considers only the continuous aspect of devices. As the sample tasks discussed earlier in this chapter illustrated, other factors, such as the integration of button devices with continuous controllers, has a strong impact on a device's performance. An example is the case of trying to "pick up" and drag an object with a mouse (where the button is integrated) compared to performing the same transaction using a trackball (where it is difficult to hold down the button, which is not integrated, with the same hand that is controlling the dragging motion).

An approach to capturing this aspect of devices is found in Buxton (1990a). A three-state model is developed that can be used to characterize both input *devices* and *tasks*. By providing a common vocabulary to describe both, a means of arriving at an appropriate match between the two is provided.

The reader is also referred to Foley, Wallace, and Chan (1984), an important early approach to characterizing input; Card, Mackinlay, and Robertson (1990, 1991), an excellent taxonomy of input devices that extends the model developed above; and Lipscomb and Pique (1993), a complementary means of categorizing input devices.

CHUNKING AND PHRASING

Much of the rest of this chapter deals with alternative ways of articulating commands to the computer. The reading by Buxton (1986b) is intended to lay a theoretical foundation for this. The main thesis of the paper is that human-machine dialogues can benefit by appropriate phrasing similar to that used in written and spoken language, and in music.

Phrasing not only groups together things that are associated in meaning or purpose, but also makes clear points of *closure*, that is, points at which one can be interrupted, or take a break. Most human-machine dialogues are *compound*, for example, selecting and positioning, positioning and scaling, navigating and selecting (Buxton, 1982; Buxton, 1984 video). The structure that emerges from appropriate phrasing can accelerate the process whereby novice computer users "chunk" together concepts, thereby building cognitive skill. Relevant to this issue is Mantei (1990 video), a delightful and thought-provoking collection of short clips documenting a variety of mouse use behaviors.

The reading discusses the nature of skill acquisition and the use of phrasing in its acquisition. In so doing, it lays the foundation for how some of the literature on cognitive modeling can be extended to apply to the *pragmatic* and *device* levels of the interface. Finally, it prepares the reader for the sections that follow—those that deal with marking, gesture, and two-handed input.

Modes and Mode Errors

As originally defined by Norman (1981), a *mode error* is the misclassification of a situation resulting in actions that are inappropriate for the true situation. Whenever a particular action has different consequences depending upon the state of the system, mode errors may occur. The classic example of this is in text editors with command-line interfaces. Here, for example, typing the word "add" may be interpreted as a *command*, indicating that you are about to add text, or as just another word that you want to enter into the document.

Reducing mode errors is one of the main attractions of direct manipulation interfaces (Tesler, 1981). Yet mode errors still occur. The best way to prevent them is to provide continuous and meaningful feedback to the user. For example, pressure and movement feedback has been shown to be effective in reducing mode errors (Sellen, Kurtenbach, and Buxton, 1992).

MARKING

There is increasing interest in a style of interaction that has been variously called "paperlike," "pencentric," "pen based," "character recognition," or "gesture driven." Yet many of these are not like paper, and many do not use a pen. What all have in common is that the user's input is in the form of a stream of *x,y* coordinates that could be called *digital ink*. Hence, we will refer to these as *marking* interfaces, applications, or systems.

One of the main claims made for such systems is that they are more natural and easier to use. In many ways, we agree. Our discussion on chunking and phrasing emphasizes their potential. However, it is important to realize that *knowing how to use a pen is no more a ticket to mastering marking systems than knowing how to type is a ticket to mastering Unix or MS-DOS*. Most marking systems are extremely difficult to learn and are very prone to *mode errors*. This is true even of the best of the currently available systems, such as Carr (1991) and Carr and Shafer (1991). A good discussion of problems with marking interfaces is Briggs et al. (1993).

Who Does the Recognition?

Recognition lies at the heart of marking systems, whether they deal with block characters, cursive script, proofreader's symbols, or other annotations. Computer recognition is far from perfect, even when user's have training and are careful. This is not likely to change in the near future. In many ways, computer recognition is a "black hole" that has diverted energy and attention away from other aspects of marking-based systems that in the long run may be far more important than recognition.

This is because there are many benefits of electronic documents that do not require the computer to recognize their contents—particularly when marking-based systems are used in computer-mediated human-human interaction (see Chapter 11), rather than just in human-computer interaction.

We should therefore pay more attention to applications where recognition of the marks is done by a human rather than by a computer. As with notebook applications, this may be where the "recognizer" is also the author, or annotation systems, where the marked-up document is read by someone else. The markings might be recognized as they are written, as with electronic whiteboards (Elrod et al., 1992), or at a later time, as in fax or e-mail type applications.

The Freestyle system discussed in Case C (Levine and Ehrlich, 1991, included as a reading; Wang Laboratories, 1989 video) is a good example of how computer recognition can be sidestepped. Electronic mail and voice mail are integrated with markings to provide a creative system for annotating electronic documents.

While both Hardock, Kurtenbach, and Buxton (1993) and the reading by Goldberg and Goodisman (1991) show how Freestyle-like systems can be augmented with recognition, we want to emphasize that the application does not depend on it.

What Is Recognized?

If the computer does do mark recognition, this typically means character or script recognition. An early system is shown in Ward (1985 video). Good discussions of this topic can be found in Pittman (1991), Plamondon, Suen, and Simner (1989), and Suen (1990). The reading by Goldberg and Goodisman (1991) gives a brief introduction to character recognition, and a detailed analysis of how to handle recognition errors.

Recognizing characters and script is typically expensive both in terms of computational effort and the user's investment in training the system. Powerful applications can result when the recognition focuses on higher-level marks such as proofreader symbols. Such marks are frequently easier to recognize and can be user-independent. This is illustrated in the Tivoli electronic whiteboard application presented in the reading by Pedersen et al. (1993). Apte, Vo, and Kimura (1993) show how recognition can be applied to geometric shapes.

User-definable graphical marks have also been demonstrated by some researchers (Rubine, 1991; Wolf, Rhyne and Ellozy, 1989, 1989 video).

Self-Revelation and Marking Menus

A "paperlike" interface has the potential to be almost indistinguishable from Unix or MS-DOS. Just consider the similarity between a blank piece of paper and a screen that is blank other than for a "%" or "A>" prompt.

Without some help, the user has no means of knowing what state the system is in, or what options are available. So marking-based systems often assume a *form-filling* style (see the introduction to Part III), or a style similar to classical GUIs. Yet such interface styles may not be appropriate. Consider, for example, applications for very small displays, such as personal digital assistants (PDAs), where screen real estate is not available.

Recently, another design option has been developed, that of *marking menus* (Kurtenbach and Buxton, 1991a, 1991b, 1993, 1994). Marking menus are an extension of "pie menus" (Callahan et al., 1988). The novice user presses down on a stylus and waits for a short interval of time (approximately 1/2 second). A pie menu of the available commands then appears directly under the cursor (Figure 7.7a). The user may then select a command from the pie menu by keeping the stylus tip depressed and making a stroke through the desired sector or slice of the pie. The slice is highlighted and the selection is confirmed when the pressure on the stylus is released.

The other option is to "mark ahead" by making the mark without waiting for the pie menu to pop up (Figure 7.7b). The physical movement involved in selecting a command is identical to the physical movement required to make the mark corresponding to that command. For example, a command that requires movement up and to the right for pie menu selection requires marking up and to the right in order to invoke that command. The concept is similar to that of accelerator keys in many of today's applications. A user is reminded of the keystrokes associated with particular menu items every time a menu is displayed since the name of the corresponding keys may appear next to the commands. With marking menus, the user is not only reminded, but actually rehearses the physical movement involved in making the mark every time a selection from the menu is made. We believe that this further enhances the association between mark and command.

FIGURE 7.7

Marking menus. The transition from novice to expert reflected in two ways of invoking commands (Kurtenbach and Buxton, 1991b).

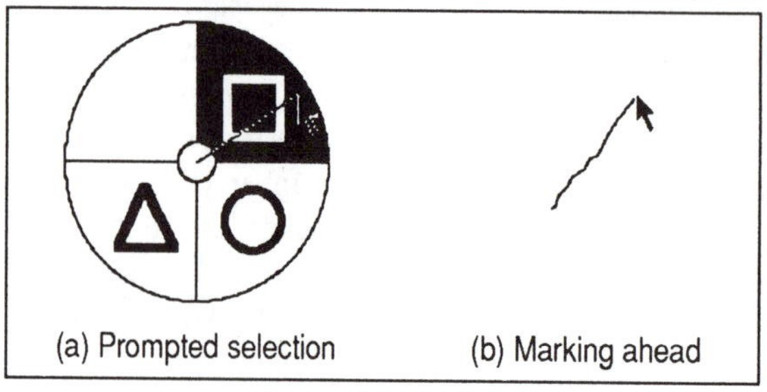

Supporting markings with pie menus in this way helps users make a smooth transition from novice to expert. Novices in effect perform menu selection. Users almost always wait for the pop-up menu and then select the desired sector when they first encounter a new menu. Yet waiting for the menu takes time. Thus, as users begin to memorize the layout (as they become expert), they begin to mark ahead to invoke the commands. We have also observed an intermediate stage where users may begin to make a mark, and then wait for the menu to pop-up in order to verify their choice of action.

Why not just use pie menus rather than marks? Marks are faster after one has memorized the layout of the menu. Even if a user did not have to pause to signal for the menu to be popped up, one would still have to wait for the menu to be displayed before making a selection. In many systems, displaying the menu can be annoyingly slow and visually disturbing. There is anecdotal evidence that expert users avoid these problems by "mousing ahead" in pie menu systems (Hopkins, 1991).

One disadvantage of this technique is that "reselection" is not possible using marks, in other words, one lacks the ability to change the item being selected before actually executing an item. For example, one can pop-up the menu and highlight a series of items before releasing the mouse button while on the desired item. Typically this behavior is exhibited by novices who are unfamiliar with the menu items. However, once familiar with a menu, users rarely use reselection. Hence an expert using marks has little need for reselection.

Working Within the Marking Idiom

In music, composers choose instruments that best match their musical ideas, and then write in the appropriate *idiom*. Problems with current marking interfaces are sometimes caused by designers not adequately conceptualizing the idiom of marking systems.

Let us assume, for example, that character and cursive script recognition were 100% accurate. The systems might still not be successful. Even cursive writing is much slower than three-fingered typing. Why then write? Reasons include the ability to do free-form layout, include sketches, and incorporate graphical aspects of text layout. For example, it is faster to write "$2^2 \neq 22$" than to type it on a keyboard: Yet virtually none of the properties of these benefits are captured by current recognizers, which force the user to write rectilinear text, more often than not in little bounding boxes.

If one merely needs to enter linear text and a keyboard is not available, it is faster to enter text with a stylus on a graphical keyboard than it is to print it or to write it cursively. The text thus entered will be more accurate and more legible than that which is written. (For example, there will be no more confusion between the letter *O* and the digit *0*.)

A graphical keyboard may not be appropriate or desirable. On a palmtop computer, for example, it would not fit unless the "keys" were inordinately small. If one is to enter text using marks, yet is concerned with speed, then an alternative is to use *shorthand*. While recognizing traditional shorthand has been investigated (Leedham et al., 1984), it is technically problematic. There are relatively few people who have the skill, and the skill is not easy to acquire. In some applications, however, the designer can invent an effective shorthand notation that does not have these disadvantages. The music shorthand illustrated in Buxton (1986b) is one such example. A more generally applicable example is the Unistrokes shorthand developed by Goldberg and Richardson (1993, 1993 video).

The Unistrokes alphabet is shown in Figure 7.8. In keeping with the name, each character is represented by a single stroke mark. The alphabet must be learned, but this only takes about an hour, aided by the use of mnemonics (Figure 7.9).

FIGURE 7.8

The Unistrokes alphabet.

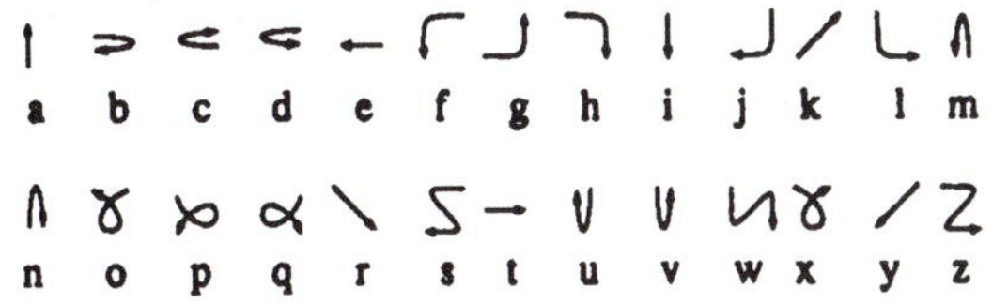

FIGURE 7.9

Unistroke mnemonics.

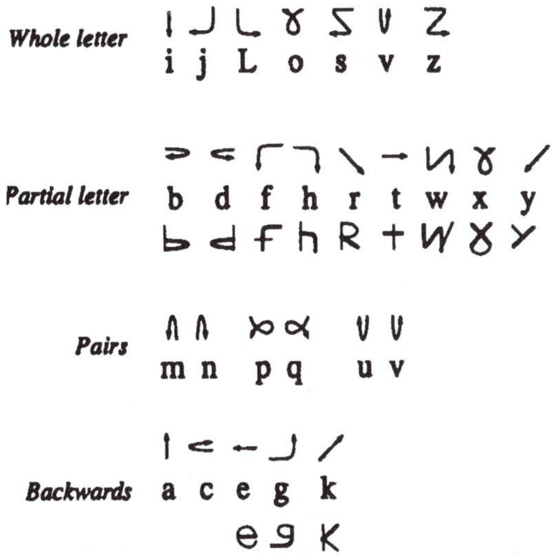

Unistrokes are interesting for at least two reasons beyond the potential for faster input. Since each character is fully specified by a single stroke, there is no *segmentation problem*. That is, the system need not invest any energy trying to figure out which stroke belongs to which character. Hence there is no need to print characters within the confines of bounding boxes. Characters can even be recognized when the Unistrokes are written one on top of the other. This would be useful in entering data into a wristwatch computer by writing on a touch-sensitive watch face, which may be superior to using the microkeyboards now on some wristwatches.

Second, because of the lack of segmentation problems, one need not look at the "page," or display, when writing Unistrokes, so "heads up" writing is possible. Unlike paper and pen technologies, one can visually attend to the whiteboard in a lecture, or a document which one is transcribing, and still take legible notes. So we obtain one of the key benefits of touchtyping in a marking interface.

Another aspect of the idiom is that, unlike direct manipulation GUIs, it is natural for marking systems *to leave an explicit audit trail of the user's actions*, as shown in Hardock, Kurtenbach, and Buxton (1993). In their MATE system, users mark annotations on electronic documents and then return them to the author. The author sees two views of the document: one with the annotated original text, the other with the modified, or edited text (Figure 7.10).

FIGURE 7.10

MATE in incorporation mode. In incorporation mode, a user can view the annotated document and select which annotations to incorporate. Annotations (seen in the left window) that have been "executed" appear as thin lines (e.g., "ed"). Annotations that have not been executed appear as thick lines. Annotations are color coded based on who made them. Annotations that represent commands can be executed by selecting them with the stylus. Annotations that have been executed can be "undone" by reselecting them. The document's current state appears in the right window. The user can navigate (scroll) independently or concurrently in each window (Hardock, Kurtenbach, and Buxton, 1993).

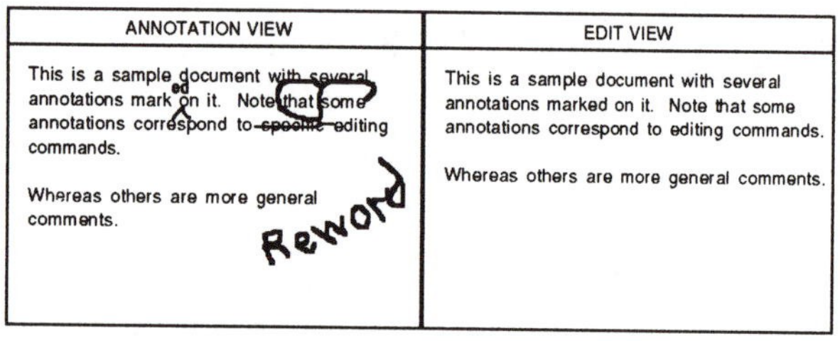

Unlike Freestyle, the annotations can be invoked by the author to effect the indicated change. This is done by a point/select operation on the annotation. When invoked, the annotation remains visible, but "grayed out" so as to be distinguished from annotations that have not yet been acted upon. These grayed out marks represent the audit trail of actions taken. The benefit comes when one wants to *undo* an action. This is effected simply by reselecting a grayed-out mark. This differs from conventional direct manipulation systems in that it largely doesn't matter when the undone command was originally invoked. Since all past operations are visible (as grayed-out marks), one has an effective undo capability without needing to be too concerned about the order in which things were done.

Finally, one of the most important aspects of the marking idiom is the *figure/ground* relationship that exists between computer-printed vs. human-printed text. Even from a distance, it is absolutely clear which marks were made from the computer and which by hand. This property makes marking very powerful in annotation applications.

Situated Design

Even if character and cursive script recognition were perfect, this would not solve the problems of marking systems. No matter how good the recognition, it is still usually faster to find an address in your address book than in your personal digital assistant (PDA). The same is true for checking appointments in a calendar, looking up a word in the dictionary, or starting to take notes in a meeting.

When we specify systems, performance of the display, bus, and disk drive are rigorously defined. It is strange that we do not do the same in specifying applications. As an exercise, take any of the transactions described above (and others for which PDAs are used) and time them with a stopwatch. The times obtained from the status quo paper and pen condition should set the *minimum* specification for the electronic version, or there had better be a very good reason why not. It is not enough to have the "best" calendar program on the market. It must also be there when I need it and where I need it, and be superior to existing technologies.

Designers must, therefore, pay more attention to the context in which tools are to be used and the constraints these contexts imply.

Summary

Marking interfaces have great potential. For this potential to be realized, we have to abandon the preoccupation with character and script recognition, and also pay attention to other important issues.

The weaknesses of current systems is largely due to a lack of user-centered design. We have already shown examples where use and context should help define performance specifications. Too much design is still carried out without real user involvement and user testing (see Chapter 2). A notable exception is the work by Wolf and her colleagues (Wolf, 1986, 1988, 1992; Wolf and Morrel-Samuels, 1987).

A good way to monitor recent developments in mark-based computing is to subscribe to the bimonthly newsletter *Pen-Based Computing* (1995).

GESTURES

Many people use the term "gesture" to refer to marking interfaces. While every mark is based on a gesture, it is the resulting mark and not the gesture that is used as input to the system. There is a distinct class of system in that it is truly the gesture itself which is recognized. Typically, such systems leave no marks and produce more dimensions of input than the *x,y* point stream of marking input.

One common way to capture manual gestures, particularly in virtual reality applications (Chapter 14), is using the instrumented glove mentioned above. Fels and Hinton (1990) describe a novel alternative, a prototype neural network system called Glovetalk, which recognizes manual sign language as input and produces continuous speech as output.

One of the pioneers in gesture-based input is Myron Krueger (1991, 1985 video, 1988 video). What is novel about his work is that it does not require any intrusive technology such as gloves. The input is acquired by the system via a video camera. By coupling the video signal with real-time image processing, the computer is able to "see" and recognize the manual gestures.

Gesture is even more powerful when combined with other modalities, such as direct manipulation (Rubine, 1992 video), and especially voice (Bolt, 1984; Schmandt et al., 1984 video; Thorisson, Koons, and Bolt, 1992 video; Koons, Sparrell, and Thorisson, 1993; Koons and Sparrell, 1994 video). This is a topic that we explore further in Chapter 9.

Gestures in Collaborative Work

Computer-supported collaborative work (Chapter 11) is an area that puts special demands on input. Effective meetings require rapid and fluid interaction (Wolf et al., 1991; Elrod et al., 1992).

In meetings where people are at different sites, however, the remote awareness problem arises. Consider distributed audio/graphic conferencing using shared view software such as the

Tivoli system discussed in the reading by Pedersen et al. (1993). If the people at the remote site want to point or indicate something, their only means is via a remote cursor, or telepointer. What this does is reduce their gestural vocabulary to little more than that of a fruit fly. Although a great improvement over no pointing and gesturing, it falls short of what one can do in face-to-face meetings.

What is missing is the superimposition of the hands' and arms gestures over the work surface. This shortcoming has been addressed in innovative papers by Tang and Minneman (1991a, 1991b). What they do is capture the image of the hands over the work surface and transmit it to the remote site, where it appears as a shadow. Hence far richer gestural interaction is possible. Further advances in enriching machine-mediated gestural communications may be seen in the elegant work of Hiroshi Ishii described in Chapter 11 (see Ishii, Kobayashi, and Arita, 1994; Ishii, Arita, and Kobayashi, 1992 video). What remains is to add Krueger's recognition capabilities to these approaches.

TWO-HANDED INPUT

Consider how people use their hands in performing tasks in the everyday world, such as painting, threading a needle, taking notes, opening a book, and driving a car. Each is an example of people's ability to coordinate the action of their two hands. Each contrasts with how the two hands are typically used today in interacting with computers.

Both hands are certainly used in typing, but this is a single task made up of discrete events. We also see two-handed usage in activating function and/or accelerator keys with one hand, while pointing with a mouse with the other. In this case, the button pushes are discrete and the pointing continuous. The class of interaction rarely seen in interacting with computers, and illustrated by the real-world examples given above, has both hands performing continuous tasks in concert. Incorporating such *asymmetrical bimanual action* can greatly improve the quality of direct manipulation interaction.

Guiard (1987) claims that bimanual asymmetric actions in the everyday world can be characterized by three properties:

- *The nondominant hand determines the frame of action of the dominant hand.* Two examples are holding a nail that is to be hammered, and holding a needle that is to be threaded.
- *The sequence of action is nondominant hand, then dominant.* This is seen in the nail and the needle examples, as well as that of a painter moving his or her palette to a convenient location, then dipping his or her brush into the desired paint pot.
- *The action of the nondominant is coarse relative to the fine action of the dominant hand.* This is seen in the example of the painter's palette. The positioning of the palette is not as demanding as the accuracy required in dipping the brush into the appropriate paint pot.

If we are to design our user interfaces to exploit everyday skills, then these three characteristics suggest how the two hands can be used. Buxton (1990b) works through a MacPaint example, where one is "painting" and wants to continue to paint on a part of the "page" that is not visible in the window. It contrasts the complexity of scrolling the page and resuming painting using two techniques: the standard "hand" dragging tool, versus using a trackball in the nondominant hand. The former takes eight steps, the latter, one. The former interrupts the flow of action (painting). In the latter, as in the physical world, one does not have to lay the "paint brush" down in order to reposition the paper.

The ideas underlying the previous example were tested formally in an experiment by Buxton and Myers (1986). People spontaneously used two hands in performing compound tasks when there was a good match between task and action. This study refutes the often heard complaint about two-handed action—"It is difficult to rub your stomach while tapping your head." Although there are cases where two-handed action is very difficult and requires a high degree of skill, there are many bimanual tasks in which users are already skilled. Buxton and Myers demonstrated that these skills could be applied in performing *compound tasks*, such as *positioning and scaling*, and *navigation and selection*.

More recently, Bier et al. (1993) have developed a new two-handed paradigm of interaction that is consistent with Guiard. The paradigm is called the *see-through interface*, and it uses two new classes of widgets called *tool glass* and *magic lenses*. It is best thought of as a 2 ½ D interface that functions on three planes:

- The *desktop* on which icons sit. This is consistent with conventional GUIs.
- The *cursor* that floats above the desktop and its icons. This is typically manipulated by the dominant hand, with a device such as a mouse. This is consistent with conventional GUIs.
- The *magic lens* and *toolglass sheets*, which lie between the cursor and the desktop. These sheets are much like the plastic protractors and rulers that one gets with drafting sets: you can see the tool and the markings on it, but also see what is on the "paper" below them. The magic lens and toolglass sheets are repositioned using the nondominant hand, using a trackball or small touch tablet, for example.

The relationship among these three levels is illustrated in Figure 7.11. The example shows a toolglass sheet with three *click-through buttons* on it. Each represents a different texture that might be assigned to the icon on the desktop. A particular texture is assigned by aligning the cursor and the desired toolglass button over the icon (as represented by the vertical broken line in the figure) and clicking the mouse button.

Magic lenses are also manipulated using the nondominant hand. They are visualization widgets that can be thought of as analogous to magnifying glasses with a diverse range of optical properties. For example, they enable one to highlight vertices, provide X-ray views of scenes, or filter out all objects except those of a particular color.

Bier et al. (1993), Stone, Fishkin, and Bier (1994), Bier et al. (1994), which is included as a reading, and Bier et al. (1994 video) provide an expanded view of the design space. Kabbash, Buxton, and Sellen (1994) presents an experiment that illustrates the usability and utility of toolglass widgets.

FIGURE 7.11

Click-through buttons. Three click-through buttons are shown on a sheet of toolglass. Each button represents a different texture with which icons can be coloured. The button with the desired texture is aligned with the cursor over the icon. Clicking "through" the button over the icon causes it to acquire that button's texture.

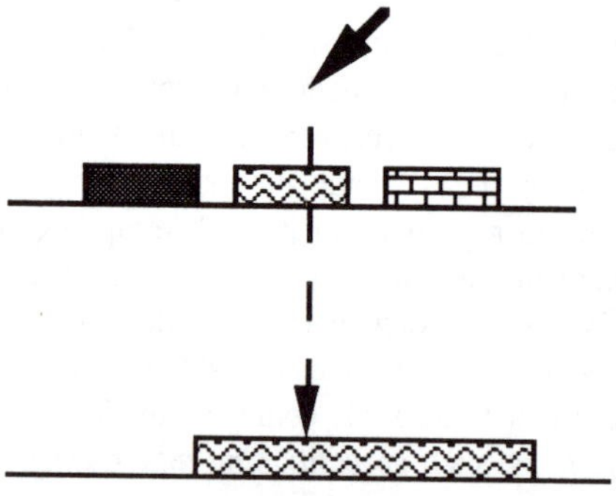

Asymmetric bimanual input will be supported by future GUIs. It is perhaps the best way to improve both the "directness" and the "manipulation" of so-called *direct manipulation* interfaces. However, two hands is *not* always better than one. Opportunites for bad design are everywhere, and this includes two-handed interfaces. Using two cursors, one for each hand, for example, should be avoided, as is shown in Kabbash, Buxton, and Sellen (1994) and in Dillon, Edey, and Tombaugh (1990). As with any interaction technique, we need appropriate human-centered design.

REALIZING INPUT'S FULL POTENTIAL

Unfortunately, we are hard-pressed to use the haptic channel to its full potential. We need more experience before this situation can be altered. In many cases this experience is hard to obtain. If, for example, we want to compare two devices systematically, we will very often find that they are incompatible physically, electronically, or logically. Hence, what should be a simple comparison turns into a logistical nightmare.

Yet things are starting to improve, because of the introduction of the *Apple Desktop Bus (ADB).* This is a standard bus for connecting input devices that was introduced by Apple (but available on some other computers, such as from Silicon Graphics). Because of its design, one can easily switch from one input device to another, thereby enabling one to study their respective properties.

The ease with which devices can be exchanged in an interface should be a prime consideration when choosing a platform for studying HCI.

Transparent Access and the Physically Disabled

For most users, the problems of connecting different input devices to a system, as outlined in the previous section, are an annoyance. However, for users with physical disabilities, these problems can determine whether or not they are able to use a computer at all, and thus can have a major impact on their quality of life. To put it in extreme terms, our discussion of two-handed input assumes that users have the use of two hands. Clearly, designs have to accommodate the special needs of those who do not.

For most common input devices there exist special-purpose transducers that permit people with different physical disabilities to supply comparable signals. A mouse may be replaced by a tongue-activated joystick, or a button replaced by a blow-suck tube. It is reasonable to expect disabled persons to acquire such special-purpose devices. However, it is economically unreasonable and socially unacceptable to expect them to be dependent upon custom applications in order to interact with their systems.

What is required is *transparent access* to standard applications. That is, existing applications should be able to be used by simply plugging in the specialized replacement transducer. The difficulties in providing transparent access are exactly the same difficulties that we encountered above where we wanted to replace one input device with another for comparative purposes. In recognizing that this is a problem "handicapping" all of us, perhaps the achievement of generalized transparent access will become a greater priority than it has been up to now. These and related issues are raised in more detail in Chapter 10.

Device Independence and Virtual Devices

Recently there have been some efforts to overcome some of the problems that stand in the way of transparent access through development of the concept of device-independent graphics.

Just as machine-independent compilers facilitated porting code from one computer to another, device-independent programming constructs have been developed for input-output. With input, the principle idea is that all devices more or less reduce to a small number of generic *virtual devices.* For example, an application can be written in a device-independent way such that it need not know if the source of text input is via a keyboard or a speech-recognition system. All the application need know is that text is being inputted. Similarly, the application need not know what specific device is providing location information (in pointing, for example). All that it need know is what the current location is.

This idea of device independence has been discussed by Foley and Wallace (1974), Wallace (1976), Newman (1968), and Rosenthal et al. (1982). It was refined and integrated into the standardized graphics systems (GSPC, 1977, 1979; ISO, 1983).

Within the Graphical Kernel System (GKS) standard (ISO, 1983), the virtual devices are defined in terms of the values that they return to the application program. The virtual devices for input in GKS are

- locator: a pair of real values giving the coordinate of a point in world coordinates
- stroke: a sequence of x/y coordinates in world coordinates
- valuator: a single real number
- pick: the name of a segment
- string: a string of characters
- choice: an integer defining one of a set of alternatives

For the designer of user interfaces, the main advantage of device-independent graphics has been that one can experiment with different devices without usually having to modify the applications code. All that needs to be changed (from the software perspective) is the actual device driver. The application doesn't care what driver is being used for a particular device because the standard is defined in terms of the calling protocol and the number and type of parameters returned.

Device-independent graphics has aided us in rapidly prototyping user interfaces (Chapter 2), yet it has also led to problems because some practitioners have confused technical interchangeability with functional interchangeability. Just because I can substitute a trackball for a mouse does not mean that the resulting user interface will still be satisfactory. As we have seen, devices have idiosyncratic properties that make them well suited for some tasks, and not for others (to consider this issue in terms of text input, for example, see Seibel, 1962; Conrad and Longman, 1965; Devoe, 1967; Klemmer, 1971; Kroemer, 1972; Owen, 1978; Rochester, Bequaert, and Sharp, 1978; Montgomery, 1982; Norman and Fisher, 1982; Noyes, 1983; Darragh, Witten, and James, 1990; and Matias, MacKenzie, and Buxton, 1993). Further discussion of problems with the concept of device independence appears in Baecker (1980).

CONCLUSION

Although the difficulties of physically and logically interfacing input devices to applications have impeded development, these logistical problems are diminishing. Perhaps more significant is that many people think about input only at the device level, as a means of obtaining improved time-motion efficiency through use of the sensorimotor system. The reading (Buxton, 1986b) makes clear that this is a big mistake. Effectively structuring the pragmatics of input can also have a significant impact on the cognitive level of the interface. This chapter has been directed towards exploiting that potential.

REFERENCES

Note: A ◉ before a reference indicates a reading.

Apte, A., Vo, V., and Kimura, T. (1993). Recognizing Multistroke Geometric Shapes: An Experimental Evaluation. *Proc. UIST '93*, ACM, 121–128.

Baecker, R. (1980). Towards an Effective Characterization of Graphical Interaction. In Guedj, R., ten Hagen, P., Hopgood, F., Tucker, H., and Duce, D. (Eds.), *Methodology of Interaction*, North Holland, 127–148. Reprinted in Baecker and Buxton (1987).

Baecker, R., and Buxton, W. (1987). *Readings in Human-Computer Interaction: A Multidisciplinary Approach*. Morgan Kaufmann.

Bier, E. (1990). Snap-Dragging in Three Dimensions. *Computer Graphics* 24(2), ACM, 249–262.

◉ Bier, E., Stone, M., Fishkin, K., Buxton, W., and Baudel, T. (1994). A Taxonomy of See-Through Tools. *Proc. CHI '94*, ACM, 358–364.

Bier, E., Stone, M., Pier, K., Buxton, W., and DeRose, T. (1993). Toolglasses and Magic Lenses: The See-Through Interface. *Computer Graphics* 27(3), ACM, 73–80.

Bolt, R. (1984). *The Human Interface: Where People and Computers Meet*. Lifetime Learning Publications.

Briggs, R., Dennis, A., Beck, B., and Nunamaker, J. (1993). Whither the Pen-Based Interface. *Journal of Management Information Systems* 9(3), 71–90.

Brooks, F., Ouh-Young, M., Batter, J., and Kilpatrick, P. (1990). Project GROPE—Haptic Displays for Scientific Visualization. *Computer Graphics* 24(3), ACM, 177–185.

Buxton, W. (1982). An Informal Study of Selection-Positioning Tasks. *Proc. Graphics Interface '82*, 323–328.

Buxton, W. (1983). Lexical and Pragmatic Considerations of Input Structures. *Computer Graphics* 17(1), ACM, 31–37.

Buxton, W. (1986a). There's More to Interaction Than Meets the Eye: Some Issues in Manual Input. In Norman, D., and Draper, S. (Eds.), *User Centered System Design*, Lawrence Erlbaum Associates, 319–337.

◉ Buxton, W. (1986b). Chunking and Phrasing and the Design of Human-Computer Dialogues. In Kugler, H. J. (Ed.), *Information Processing '86*, Proc. IFIP 10th World Computer Congress, North Holland, 475–480.

Buxton, W. (1990a). A Three State Model of Graphical Input. In *Proc. INTERACT '90*, Elsevier Science (North-Holland), 449–456.

Buxton, W. (1990b). The Natural Language of Interaction: A Perspective on Non-Verbal Dialogues. In Laurel, B. (Ed.), *The Art of Human-Computer Interface Design*, Addison-Wesley, 405–416.

Buxton, W., Hill, R., and Rowley, P. (1985). Issues and Techniques in Touch-Sensitive Tablet Input. *Computer Graphics* 19(3), ACM, 215–224.

Buxton, W., and Myers, B. (1986). A Study in Two-Handed Input. *Proc.CHI '86*, ACM, 321–326.

Callahan, J., Hopkins, D., Weiser, M., and Shneiderman, B. (1988). An Empirical Comparison of Pie vs. Linear Menus. *Proc. CHI '88*, ACM, 95–100.

Card, S., English, W., and Burr, B. (1978). Evaluation of Mouse, Rate Controlled Isometric Joystick, Step Keys and Text Keys for Text Selection on a CRT. *Ergonomics* 21(8), 601–613.

Card, S., Mackinlay, J., and Robertson, G. (1990). The Design Space of Input Devices. *Proc. CHI '90*, ACM, 117–124.

Card, S., Mackinlay, J., and Robertson, G. (1991). A Morphological Analysis of the Design Space of Input Devices. *ACM Transactions on Information Systems* 9(2), 99–122.

Card, S., Moran, T., and Newell, A. (1980). The Keystroke Level Model for User Performance Time with Interactive Systems. *Communications of the ACM* 23(7), 396–410.

Card, S., Moran, T., and Newell, A. (1983). *The Psychology of Human-Computer Interaction*. Lawrence Erlbaum Associates.

Carr, R. (1991). The Point of the Pen. *Byte* 16(2), 211–221.

Carr, R., and Shafer, D. (1991). *The Power of PenPoint*. Addison-Wesley.

Chapanis, A., and Kinkade, R. (1972). Design of Controls. In Van Cott, H., and Kinkade, R. (Eds.), *Human Engineering Guide to Equipment Design*, Revised Edition, U.S. Government Printing Office, 345–379.

Chen, M., Mountford, J., and Sellen, A. (1988). A Study in Interactive 3-D Rotation Using 2-D Control Devices. *Computer Graphics* 22(4), ACM, 121–129.

Conrad, R., and Longman, D. (1965). Standard Typewriter Versus Chord Keyboard: An Experimental Comparison. *Ergonomics* 8, 77–88.

Darragh, J., Witten, I., and James, M. (1990). The Reactive Keyboard: A Predictive Typing Aid. *IEEE Computer* 23(11), November, 41–49.

Devoe, D. B. (1967). Alternatives to Handprinting in the Manual Entry of Data. *IEEE Transactions on Human Factors in Electronics* 8(1), 21–32.

Dillon, R., Edey, J., and Tombaugh, J. (1990). Measuring the True Cost of Command Selection: Techniques and Results. *Proc. CHI '90,* ACM, 19–25.

Elrod, S., Bruce, R., Goldberg, D., Halasz, F., Janssen, W., Lee, D., McCall, K., Pedersen, E., Pier, K., Tang, J., and Welch, B. (1992). Liveboard: A Large Interactive Display Supporting Group Meetings, Presentations and Remote Collaborations. *Proc. CHI '92,* ACM, 599–607.

English, W., Engelbart, D., and Berman, M. (1967). Display Selection Techniques for Text Manipulation. *IEEE Transactions on Human-Factors in Electronics* 8(1), 5–15.

Evans, K., Tanner, P., and Wein, M. (1981). Tablet-Based Valuators That Provide One, Two, or Three Degrees of Freedom. *Computer Graphics* 15(3), ACM, 91–97.

Fels, S., and Hinton, G. (1990). Building Adaptive Interfaces with Neural Networks: The Glove-Talk Pilot Study. In *Proc. INTERACT '90,* Elsevier (North-Holland), 683–688.

Fitts, P., and Peterson, J. (1964). Information Capacity of Discrete Motor Responses. *Journal of Experimental Psychology* 67, 103–112.

Foley, J., and Wallace, V. (1974). The Art of Graphic Man-Machine Conversation. *Proceedings of IEEE* 62(4), 462–470.

Foley, J., Wallace, V., and Chan, P. (1984). The Human Factors of Computer Graphics Interaction Techniques. *IEEE Computer Graphics and Applications* 4(11), 13–48.

Foley, J., van Dam, A., Feiner, S., and Hughes, J. (1990). *Computer Graphics: Principles and Practice.* Addison-Wesley.

Gaver, W. (1991). Technology Affordances. *Proc. CHI '91,* ACM, 79–84.

● Goldberg, D., and Goodisman, A. (1991). Stylus User Interfaces for Manipulating Text. *Proc. UIST '91, ACM,* 127–135.

Goldberg, D., and Richardson, C. (1993). Touch-Typing with a Stylus. *Proc. InterCHI '93,* ACM, 80–87.

Greenstein, J., and Arnaut, L. (1988). Input Devices. In Helander (1988), 495–520.

GSPC (1977). Status Report of the Graphics Standards Planning Committee. *Computer Graphics* 11(3), ACM.

GSPC (1979). Status Report of the Graphics Standards Planning Committee. *Computer Graphics* 13(3), ACM.

Guiard, Y. (1987). Asymmetric Division of Labor in Human Skilled Bimanual Action: The Kinematic Chain as Model. *Journal of Motor Behavior* 19(4), 486–517.

Hardock, G., Kurtenbach, G., and Buxton, W. (1993). A Marking Based Interface for Collaborative Writing. *Proc. UIST '93,* ACM, 259–266.

Helander, M. (Ed.) (1988). *Handbook of Human-Computer Interaction.* North-Holland.

Herot, C., and Weinzapfel, G. (1978). One-Point Touch Input of Vector Information from Computer Displays. *Computer Graphics* 12(3), 210–216.

Hopkins, D. (1991) The Design and Implementation of Pie Menus. *Dr. Dobb's Journal,* December 1991, 16–26.

Hutchinson, T., White, K., Martin, W., Reichert, K., and Frey, L. (1989). Human-Computer Interaction Using Eye-Gaze Input. *IEEE Transactions on Systems, Man, and Cybernetics* 19(6), 1527–1534.

Ighii, H., Kobayoshi, M., and Arita, K. (1994). Interactive Designof Seamless Collaboration Media: from Team Work Station to Clear Board. *Communications of the ACM* 37 (8), 83–97.

ISO (1983). *Information Processing-Graphical Kernel System (GKS) Functional Description.* International Standards Organization, ISO/DP 7942.

Iwata, H. (1990). Artificial Reality with Force-Feedback: Development of Desktop Virtual Space with Compact Master Manipulator. *Computer Graphics* 24(3), ACM, 165–170.

Jacob, R. (1991). The Use of Eye Movements in Human-Computer Interaction Techniques: What You Look At Is What You Get. *ACM Transactions on Information Systems* 9(3), 152–169.

Kabbash, P., Buxton, W., and Sellen, A. (1994). Two-Handed Input in a Compound Task. *Proc. CHI '94,* ACM, 417–423.

Kabbash, P., MacKenzie, I. S., and Buxton, W. (1993). Human Performance Using Computer Input Devices in the Preferred and Non-Preferred Hands. *Proc. InterCHI '93,* ACM, 474–481.

Klemmer, E. T. (1971). Keyboard Entry. *Applied Ergonomics* 2(1), 2–6.

Koons, D., Sparrell, C., and Thorlsson, K. (1993). Integrating Simultaneous Input from Speech, Gaze, and Hand Gestures. In Maybury, M. (Ed.), *Intelligent Multimedia Interfaces,* AAAI Press / MIT Press, 257–276.

Krueger, M. (1991). *Artificial Reality II.* Addison-Wesley.

Kroemer, K. H. (1972). Human Engineering the Keyboard. *Human Factors* 14(1), 51–63.

Kurtenbach, G., and Buxton, W. (1991a). GEdit: A Testbed for Editing by Contiguous Gesture. *SIGCHI Bulletin* 23(2), ACM, 22–26.

Kurtenbach, G., and Buxton, W. (1991b). Integrating Mark-Up and Direct Manipulation Techniques. *Proc. UIST '91,* ACM, 137–144.

Kurtenbach, G., and Buxton, W. (1993). The Limits of Expert Performance Using Hierarchic Marking Menus. *Proc. InterCHI '93,* ACM, 482–487.

Kurtenbach, G., and Buxton, W. (1994). User Learning and Performance with Marking Menus. *Proc. CHI '94,* ACM, 258–264.

Leedham, C., Downton, A., Brooks, C., and Newell, A. (1984). On-Line Acquisition of Pitman's Handwritten Shorthand as a Means of Rapid Data Entry. *Proc. Interact '84,* Vol. 2, Elsevier (North-Holland), 86–91.

Levine, S., and Ehrlich, S. (1991). The Freestyle System: A Design Perspective. In Klinger, A. (Ed.), *Human-Machine Interactive Systems,* Plenum Press, 3-21. Appears in Case C of this volume.

Lipscomb, J., and Pique, M. (1993). Analog Input Device Physical Characteristics. *SIGCHI Bulletin* 25(3), 40–45.

MacKenzie, I. S. (1992a). Fitts' Law as a Research and Design Tool in Human-Computer Interaction. *Human Computer Interaction* 7(1), 91–139.

● MacKenzie, I. S. (1992b). Movement Time Prediction in Human-Computer Interfaces. *Proc. Graphics Interface '92,* Morgan Kaufmann, 140–150.

MacKenzie, I. S., and Buxton, W. (1992). Extending Fitts' Law to Two-Dimensional Tasks. *Proc. CHI '92*, ACM, 219–226.

MacKenzie, I. S., Sellen, A. and Buxton, W. (1991). A Comparison of Input Devices in Elemental Pointing and Dragging Tasks. *Proc. CHI '91*, ACM, 161–166.

MacKenzie, I. S., and Ware, C. (1993). Lag as a Determinant of Human Performance in Interactive Systems. *Proc. InterCHI '93*, ACM, 488–493.

Mackinlay, J., Card, S., and Robertson, G. (1990). Rapid Controlled Movement through a Virtual 3D Workspace. *Computer Graphics 24(3)*, ACM, 171–176.

Mackinlay, J., Robertson, G., and Card, S. (1990). Rapid Controlled Movement through Virtual 3D Workspaces. *Proc. CHI '91*, ACM, 455–456.

Matias, E., MacKenzie, I. S., and Buxton, W. (1993). Half-QWERTY: A One-Handed Keyboard Facilitating Skill Transfer from QWERTY. *Proc. InterCHI '93*, ACM, 88–94.

Minsky, M. (1985). Manipulating Simulated Objects with Real-World Gestures Using a Force and Position Sensitive Screen. *Computer Graphics* 18(3), ACM, 195–203.

Montgomery, E. (1982). Bringing Manual Input into the 20th Century. *IEEE Computer* 15(3), 11–18. See also follow-up letters in the May, June, and October 1982 issues.

Newman, W. M. (1968). A Graphical Technique for Numerical Input. *Computing Journal* 11, 63–64.

Norman, D., (1981). Categorization of Action Slips. *Psychology Review* 88 (1), 1–15.

Norman, D. and Fisher, D. (1982). Why Alphabetic Keyboards Are Not Easy to Use: Keyboard Layout Doesn't Much Matter. *Human Factors* 24(5), 509–519.

Noyes, J. (1983). The QWERTY Keyboard: A Review. *International Journal of Man-Machine Studies* 18, 265–281.

Owen, S. (1978). QWERTY Is Obsolete. *Interface Age*, January 1978, 56–59.

● Pedersen, E., McCall, K., Moran, T., and Halasz, F. (1993). Tivoli: An Electronic Whiteboard for Informal Workgroup Meetings. *Proc. InterCHI '93*, ACM, 391–398.

Pen-Based Computing: The Journal of Stylus Systems (1995). Stylus Publishing, P.O. Box 876, Sandpoint, Idaho 83864-0876. Tel: (208) 265-5286. e-mail: nickbarab@bix.com.

Pickering, J. (1986). Touch-Sensitive Screens: The Technologies and Their Applications. *International Journal of Man-Machine Studies* 25(3), 249–269.

Pittman, J. A. (1991). Recognizing Handwritten Text. *Proc. CHI '91*, ACM, 271–275.

Plamondon, R., Suen, C. Y., and Simner, M. (Eds.) (1989). *Computer Recognition and Human Production of Handwriting*. World Scientific Publishing.

Potasnak, K. (1988). Keys and Keyboards. In Helander (1988), 475–494.

Potter, R., Berman, M., and Shneiderman, B. (1989). An Experimental Evaluation of Three Touch Screen Strategies within a Hypertext Database. *International Journal of Human-Computer Interaction* 1(1), 41–52.

Potter, R., Shneiderman, B., and Weldon, L. (1988). Improving the Accuracy of Touch Screens: An Experimental Evaluation of Three Strategies. *Proc. CHI '88*, ACM, 27–32.

Rochester, N., Bequaert, F., and Sharp, E. (1978). The Chord Keyboard. *IEEE Computer* 11(12), 57–63.

Rosenthal, D. S., Michener, J. C., Pfaff, G., Kessener, R., and Sabin, M. (1982). Detailed Semantics of Graphical Input Devices. *Computer Graphics* 16(3), ACM, 33–43.

Rubine, D. (1991). Specifying Gestures by Example. *Computer Graphics* 25(4), ACM, 327–337.

Sachs, E., Stoop, D. and Roberts, A. (1989). 3-Draw: A Three Dimensional Computer Aided Design Tool. *Proceedings of the 1989 IEEE International Conference on Systems, Man and Cybernetics*, Cambridge, MA, 1194–1196.

Schmandt, C. (1983). Spatial Input/Display Correspondence in a Stereoscopic Computer Graphic Work Station. *Computer Graphics* 17(3), ACM, 253–261.

Sears, A., and Shneiderman, B. (1991). High Precision Touchscreens: Design Strategies and Comparisons with a Mouse. *International Journal of Man-Machine Studies* 34, 593–613.

Seibel, R. (1962). A Feasibility Demonstration of the Rapid Type Data Entry Station. *Research Report No. RC 845*, IBM T. J. Watson Research Center.

Seibel, R. (1972). Data Entry Devices and Procedures. In Van Cott, H., and Kinkade, R. (Eds.), *Human Engineering Guide to Equipment Design*, Revised Edition, Washington: U.S. Govt. Printing Office, 311–344.

Sellen, A., Kurtenbach, G., and Buxton, W. (1992). The Prevention of Mode Errors through Sensory Feedback. *Human Computer Interaction* 7(2), 141–164.

Sherr, S. (Ed.) (1988). *Input Devices*. Academic Press.

Shneiderman, B. (1991). Touch Screens Now Offer Compelling Uses. *IEEE Software* 8(2), 93–107.

Shoemake, K. (1992). ARCBALL: A User Interface for Specifying Three-Dimensional Orientation Using a Mouse. *Proc. Graphics Interface '92*, Morgan Kaufmann, 151–156.

Stone, M., Fishkin, K., and Bier, E. (1994). The Movable Filter as a User Interface Tool. *Proc. CHI '94*, ACM, 306–312.

Suen, C. (Ed.) (1990). *Frontiers in Handwriting Recognition: Proceedings of the International Workshop on Frontiers in Handwriting Recognition*. Centre for Pattern Recognition and Machine Intelligence, Concordia University, Montreal, Quebec, Canada H3G 1M8.

Tang, J., and Minneman, S. (1991a). VideoDraw: A Video Interface for Collaborative Drawing. *ACM Transactions on Information Systems* 9(3), 170–184.

Tang, J., and Minneman, S. (1991b). Videowhiteboard: Video Shadows to Support Remote Collaboration. *Proc. CHI '91*, ACM, 315–322.

Tesler, L. (1981). The Smalltalk Environment. *Byte*, August, 90–147.

Wallace, V. (1976). The Semantics of Graphical Input Devices. *Proceedings of the Siggraph/Sigplan Symposium on Graphical Languages*, 61–65.

Ware, C., and Jessome, D. (1988). Using the Bat: A Six-Dimensional Mouse for Object Placement. *IEEE Computer Graphics and Applications* 8(6), 65–70.

Ware, C., and Osborne, S. (1990). Exploration and Virtual Camera Control in Virtual Three Dimensional Environments. *Computer Graphics* 24(2), ACM, 175–183.

Wolf, C. (1986). Can People Use Gesture Commands? *SIGCHI Bulletin* 18(2), ACM, 73–74.

Wolf, C. (1988). A Comparative Study of Gestural and Keyboard Interfacess. *Proc. 32nd Annual Meeting of the Human Factors Society*, 273–277.

Wolf, C. (1992). A Comparative Study of Gestural, Keyboard and Mouse Interfaces. *Behaviour and Information Technology* 11(1), 13–23.

Wolf, C., and Morrel-Samuels, P. (1987). The Use of Hand-Drawn Gestures for Text-Editing. *International Journal of Man-Machine Studies* 27, 91–102.

Wolf, C., Rhyne, J., and Ellozy, H. (1989). The Paper-Like Interface. In Salvendy, G., and Smith, M. J. (Eds.), *Designing and Using Human-Computer Interfaces and Knowledge-Based Systems*, Elsevier (North-Holland), 494–501.

Wolf, C., Rhyne, J., Zorman, L., and Ossher, H. (1991). WE-MET (Window Environment-Meeting Enhancement Tools). *Proc. of CHI '91*, ACM, 441–442.

Zhai, S., Buxton, W., and Milgram, P. (1994). The "Silk Cursor": Investigating Transparency for 3D Target Acquisition. *Proc. CHI '94*, ACM, 459–464.

Zimmerman, T., Lanier, J., Blanchard, C., Bryson, S., and Harvill, Y. (1987). A Hand Gesture Interface Device, *Proc. CHI+GI '87*, ACM, 189–192.

VIDEOS

Bier, E. (1989). Gargoyle 3D: Snap-Dragging in 3D. *ACM SIGGRAPH Video Review (SGVR)* 47.

Bier, E., and Pier, K. (1987). Snap-Dragging and the Gargoyle Illustration System. *ACM SGVR* 33.

Bier, E., Stone, M., Pier, K., Fishkin, K., Baudel, T., Conway, M., Buxton, W., and DeRose, T. (1994). Toolglasses and Magic Lenses: The See-Through Interface. *ACM SGVR* 97.

Brooks, F., et al. (1981). The Grip-75 Man-Machine Interface. *ACM SGVR* 4.

Buxton, W. (1984). Selection-Positioning Task Study. *ACM SGVR* 12.

Evans, K., Tanner, P., and Wein, M. (1981). Graphics Interaction at NRC. *ACM SGVR* 4.

Goldberg, D., and Richardson, C. (1993). Touch Typing With a Stylus. *ACM SGVR* 88.

Hill, W., and Hollan, J. (1992). Pointing and Visualization. *ACM SGVR* 77.

Ishii, H., Arita, K., and Kobayashi, M. (1992). Toward Seamless Collaboration Media: From Team Work Station to Clear Board. *ACM SGVR 87*.

Koons, D., and Sparrell, C. (1994). Iconic: Speech and Depictive Gestures at the Human-Machine Interface. *ACM SGVR* 97.

Krueger, M. (1985). Videoplace Sampler, *ACM SGVR* 20.

Krueger, M. (1988). Videoplace '88, *ACM SGVR* 40.

Mackinlay, J., Card, S., and Robertson, G. (1991). Rapid Controlled Movement through a Virtual 3D Workspace. *ACM SGVR* 65.

Mantei, M. (1990). The Strauss Mouse. *ACM SGVR* 56.

Myers, B. (Ed.) (1990). All the Widgets. *ACM SGVR* 57.

Myers, R., and Zeller, B. (1990). Silicon Graphics Workspace. *ACM SGVR* 56.

Nelson, D. (1987). Magnetic Fusion Experiment Control Center. *ACM SGVR* 13.

Plaisant, C., and Shneiderman, B. (1991). Scheduling Home Control Devices. *ACM SGVR* 63.

Plaisant, C., and Wallace, D. (1992). Touchscreen Toggle Design. *ACM SGVR* 77.

Roberts, S. (1989). 16,000 Miles on a Bicycle. *ACM SGVR* 47.

Rubine, D. (1992). Combining Gestures and Direct Manipulation. *ACM SGVR* 77.

Rutledge, J., and Selker, T. (1990). In-Keyboard Analog Pointing Stick: A Case for the Pointing Stick. *ACM SGVR* 55.

Sachs, E., Stoop, D. and Roberts, A. (1990). 3-Draw: A Tool for the Conceptual Design of 3D Shape. *ACM SGVR* 55.

Schmandt, C., et al. (1984). Put That There. *ACM SGVR* 13.

Sutherland, I. (1983). Sketchpad. *ACM SGVR* 13. Film originally produced in 1961.

Theil, D. (1991). The Cue Ball as Part of a Gestural Interface. *ACM SGVR* 63.

Thorisson, K., Koons, D., and Bolt, R. (1992). Multi-Modal Natural Dialogue. *ACM SGVR* 76.

Wang Laboratories (1989). Wang Freestyle. *ACM SGVR* 45.

Ward, G. (1985). Software Control at the Stroke of a Pen. ACM *SGVR* 18.

Weiner, D., and Ganapathy, S. (1990). Three-Dimensional Interfaces in Shared Environments. ACM *SGVR* 55.

Wolf, C., Rhyne, J. and Ellozy, H. (1989). The Paper-Like Interface. *ACM SGVR* 47.

Zacharey, G. (1987). The Dataglove. *ACM SGVR* 27.

Movement Time Prediction in Human-Computer Interfaces

I. Scott MacKenzie
Department of Computing and Information Science
University of Guelph
Guelph, Ontario, Canada N1G 2W1
519-824-4120, mac@snowhite.cis.uoguelph.ca

Abstract

The prediction of movement time in human-computer interfaces as undertaken using Fitts' law is reviewed. Techniques for model building are summarized and three refinements to improve the theoretical and empirical accuracy of the law are presented. Refinements include (1) the Shannon formulation for the index of task difficulty, (2) new interpretations of "target width" for two- and three-dimensional tasks, and (3) a technique for normalizing error rates across experimental factors. Finally, a detailed application example is developed showing the potential of Fitts' law to predict and compare the performance of user interfaces before designs are finalized.

Keywords: human performance modeling, Fitts' law, input devices, input tasks

Introduction

Movement is ubiquitous in human-computer interaction. Our arms, wrists, and fingers busy themselves on the keyboard and desktop; our head, neck, and eyes move about attending to graphic details recording our progress. Matching the movement limits and capabilities of humans with interaction techniques on computing systems, therefore, can benefit from research in this important dimension of human behaviour.

One focus in HCI research is in predicting and modelling the time for humans to execute tasks. Although encompassing a vast territory to be sure, one dimension is the time invested in movement. In fact, movement is an integral, seemingly innocuous component of many research questions in HCI: Are popup menus superior to menu bars? Which input device affords the quickest and most accurate interaction? Should a scroll bar in a text editor be on the left or right side of the CRT display? Can gestures replace commands in text editing?

In this review paper, we will explore Fitts' law, a powerful model for the prediction of movement time in human-computer interaction. We are motivated by (a) apparent problems in previous work, (b) the difficulty in interpreting and comparing published results, and (c) the need to guide future research using Fitts' law.

We begin with a brief tour of Fitts' law, and follow by describing some refinements to correct flaws or to improve its prediction power. Finally, derived models are used in an application example to illustrate the potential of Fitts' law in assessing and comparing interface scenarios before they are finalized in products.

A Brief Tour of Fitts' Law

The application of information theory to human performance modeling dates to the 1950s when experimental psychologists (e.g., Miller, 1953) embraced the work of Shannon, Wiener, and other information theorists as a framework for understanding human perceptual, cognitive, and motor processes. Models, or "laws", that persist today include the Hick-Hyman law for choice reaction time (Hick, 1952; Hyman, 1953) and Fitts' law for movement time (Fitts, 1954; Fitts & Peterson, 1964).

According to Fitts, a movement tasks' difficulty (*ID*, the "index of difficulty") can be quantified using information theory by the metric "bits". Specifically,

$$ID = \log_2(2A / W) \qquad (1)$$

where A is the distance or amplitude to move and W is the width or tolerance of the region within which the move terminates. Because A and W are both measures of distance, the term within the parentheses in Equation

1 is without units. The unit "bits" emerges from the somewhat arbitrary choice of base 2 for the logarithm. From Equation 1, the time to complete a movement task is predicted using a simple linear equation, where movement time (*MT*) is a linear function of *ID*.

Figure 1 shows the serial tapping task used by Fitts (1954). In this experiment, subjects alternately tapped as quickly and accurately as possible between two targets of width *W* at a distance *A*. Obviously, as targets get farther away or as they get smaller, the tasks get more difficult and more time is required to complete the task. In Fitts' experiment *A* and *W* each varied over four levels. The easiest task had $A = 1$ inch and $W = 1$ inch for $ID = \log_2(2A/W) = \log_2(2) = 1$ bit. The hardest task had $A = 16$ inches and $W = 0.25$ inches for $ID = \log_2(128) = 7$ bits.

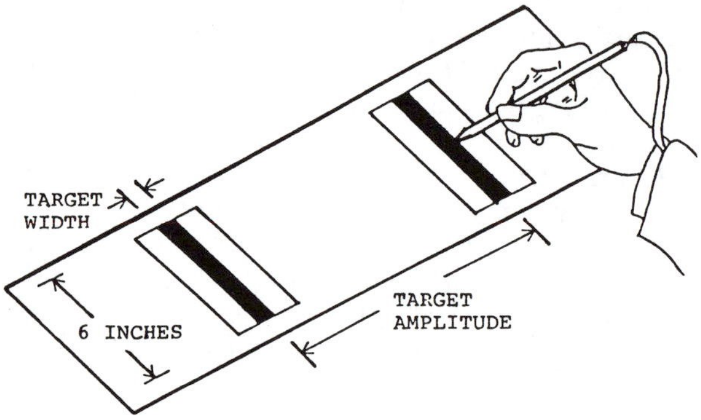

Figure 1. The serial tapping task used by Fitts (1954).

The task in Figure 1 can be implemented on interactive graphics systems using targets displayed on a CRT and a cursor manipulated by an input device. A common variation is the discrete task — a single movement toward a target from a home position (see Figure 2). Target selection is usually accomplished by a button push when the cursor is over the target.

The first use of Fitts' law in HCI research was the work of Card, English, and Burr (1978) who applied the model on data collected in a text selection task using a joystick and a mouse. Subjects were required to move the cursor from a home position to a target — a word — and select it by pushing a button. Numerous other HCI researchers have subsequently used Fitts' law. Examples include Boritz, Booth, and Cowan (1991); Gillan, Holden, Adam, Rudisill, and Magee (1990); Card, Mackinlay, and Robertson (1990); Epps (1986); MacKenzie, Sellen, and Buxton (1991); Walker and Smelcer (1990); and Ware and Mikaelian (1987).

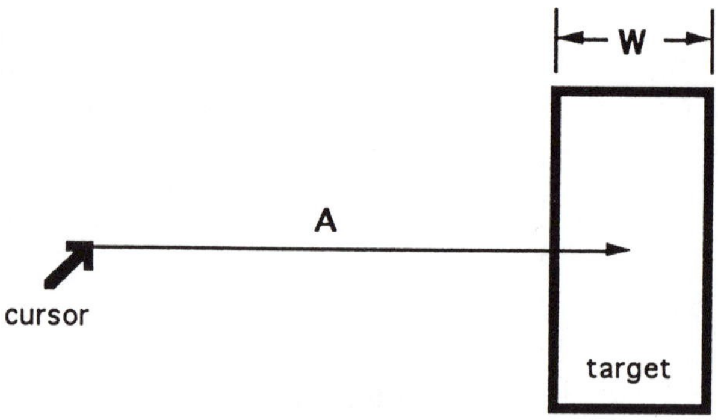

Figure 2. A discrete task using a cursor and a target displayed on a CRT.

A movement model based on Fitts' law is an equation predicting movement time (*MT*) from a task's index of difficulty (*ID*). Figure 3 shows the general idea.

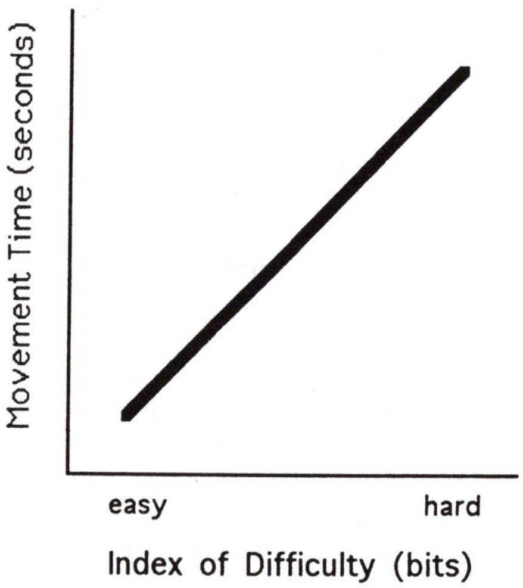

Figure 3. Movement time prediction.

As expected, movement time for hard tasks is longer than for easy tasks. The prediction equation for the line in Figure 3 is of the form

$$MT = b\,ID \qquad (2)$$

or

$$MT = a + b\,ID \qquad (3)$$

depending on whether or not the line goes through the origin. In both cases, b is the slope of the line.

Since task difficulty is analogous to information, the rate of task execution can be interpreted as the human rate of information processing. For example, if a task rated at, say, $ID = 4$ bits is executed in 2 seconds, then the human rate of information processing is $4/2 = 2$ bits/s. This is also evident by examining Figure 3. Since the vertical and horizontal axes carry the units "seconds" and "bits" respectively, the slope of the line is in "seconds/bit". The reciprocal of the slope is in "bits/s". The latter measure Fitts called the index of performance (*IP*). Since *IP* is in bits/s, the term "bandwidth" is also used.

Intuitively, the higher the bandwidth the higher the rate of human performance since more information is being articulated per unit time. One of the strengths in Fitts' law is that measures for *IP*, or bandwidth, can motivate performance comparisons across factors such as device, limb, or task. It follows that performance in a human-computer interface can be optimized by selecting and combining those conditions yielding high bandwidths.

Equation 2 is ideal since the prediction line goes through the origin. This is important for the intuitive reason that a movement task rated at $ID = 0$ bits is predicted by Equation 2 to take zero seconds, as desired. By Equation 3, however, a non-zero intercept implies that a task rated at $ID = 0$ bits will take "a" seconds to execute. (This point will surface again later.)

Building a Fitts' Law Model

In building a Fitts' law model, the slope and intercept coefficients in the prediction equation are determined through empirical tests. The tests are undertaken in a controlled experiment using a group of subjects and one or more input devices and task conditions. On interactive computing systems, this could range from manipulating a cursor with a mouse and selecting icons to manipulating a virtual hand with an input glove and grabbing objects in a 3D virtual space.

The design of experiments for Fitts' law studies is simple. Tasks are devised to cover a range of difficulties by varying A and W. For each task condition, multiple trials are conducted and the time to execute each is recorded and stored electronically for statistical analysis. Errors are also recorded (and analysed as discussed later). Generally, measurements are aggregated across subjects resulting in one data point for each task condition. A typical data set is shown in Table 1 for a stylus in a serial point-select task mimicking Fitts' serial tapping task (MacKenzie, 1991).

Table 1
Data From an Experiment Using a Stylus in a Point-Select Task

A[a]	W[a]	*ID* (bits)	*MT* (ms)	Errors (%)	*IP* (bits/s)
8	8	1	254	0.0	4.3
8	4	2	353	1.9	6.1
16	8	2	344	0.8	6.4
8	2	3	481	1.7	6.4
16	4	3	472	2.1	6.6
32	8	3	501	0.6	6.2
8	1	4	649	8.8	6.3
16	2	4	603	2.1	6.8
32	4	4	605	2.7	6.7
64	8	4	694	2.5	5.9
16	1	5	778	7.0	6.6
32	2	5	763	3.4	6.6
64	4	5	804	2.3	6.3
32	1	6	921	8.5	6.6
64	2	6	963	3.3	6.3
64	1	7	1137	9.9	6.3
		Mean	645	3.6	6.3
		SD	243	3.1	0.6

[a]experimental units; 1 unit = 8 pixels

The first three columns contain the independent variables target amplitude (A), target width (W), and the associated index of difficulty (*ID*) calculated using Equation 1. A and W each varied over four levels, yielding *ID*s of 1 to 7 bits. In the last three columns are the dependent variables movement time (*MT*), error rate, and the index of performance ($IP = ID/MT$). Each row entry is the mean of about 470 trials. The grand means were 645 ms for movement time, 3.6% for error rate, and 6.3 bits/s for the index of performance, as shown in the second last row.

The next step in model building is to enter the 16 *MT*-*ID* points in tests of correlation and linear regression. The data in Table 1 yield a regression line with movement time (ms) predicted as

$$MT = 53 + 148\, ID \tag{4}$$

with a correlation of $r = .992$. Correlations above .900 are considered very high for any experiment involving measurements on human subjects. A high r suggests that the model provides a good description of observed behaviour.

The prediction equation has an intercept of 53 ms and a slope of 148 ms/bit. Converting the slope to its reciprocal yields an index of performance, or bandwidth, of 6.8 bits/s. Often the data points and regression line are shown together in a scatter plot (see Figure 4).

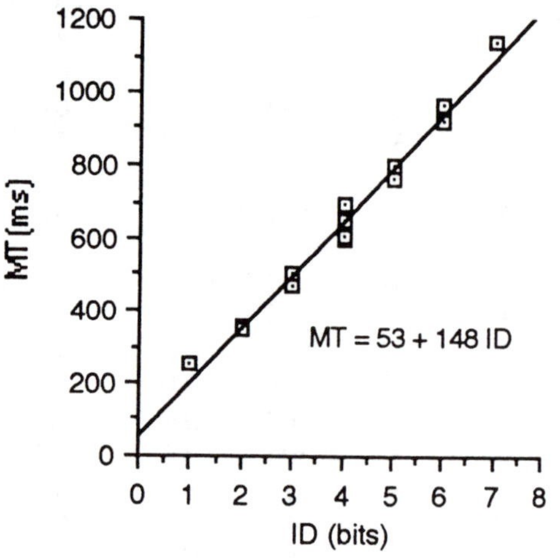

Figure 4. Scatter plot and regression line for the data in Table 1.

As just shown, the index of performance can be calculated using a direct division of mean scores ($IP = ID/MT$) or through linear regression ($IP = 1/b$, from $MT = a + b\,ID$). The two methods yielded slightly different results: 6.3 bits/s using the direct method vs. 6.8 bits/s using the slope reciprocal. Although the disparity seems small, the correct method of calculation is in doubt. Fitts used the direct method in his 1954 paper and linear regression in a subsequent study (Fitts & Peterson, 1964). Most (but not all) current researchers use linear regression. Notably, the disparity is systematic: If the line in Figure 4 is rotated counter-clockwise forcing it through the origin, the slope increases and the slope reciprocal decreases, thus reducing the disparity.

If the regression line intercept is small the difference between the two bandwidth measures will be slight. If the intercept is large, the difference may be appreciable. In the latter case, a consistent, additive component of the task (such as a button push) may be the source of the intercept.

An example is the model built by Card et al. (1978) for the mouse in a text selection task:

$$MT = 1030 + 96\,ID \tag{5}$$

Although the fit was again very good ($r = .91$), this equation has one of the largest intercepts in published Fitts' law research. The implication, of course, is that a movement task rated at $ID = 0$ bits will take 1.03 seconds.

The large intercept also casts doubt on the validity of the slope reciprocal as a measure for bandwidth. The slope of 96 ms/bit translates into a bandwidth of 10.4 bits/s. The Card et al. (1978) experiment used 20 task conditions with a mean *ID* of 2.63 bits/s. The mean movement time was reported as 1.29 s; so, the bandwidth calculated using a direct division of means is 2.63/1.29 or 2.0 bits/s. This differs from the slope reciprocal bandwidth by a factor of five! This is a concern if one wishes to generalize findings in terms of the human rate of information processing. Is the rate in this case 10.4 bits/s or 2.0 bits/s? As evident in Table 2, the regression line equations (and resulting bandwidths) vary tremendously in previous Fitts' law research using the mouse in point-select tasks.

A third possibility for calculating the prediction model is regression-through-the-origin. Although it has never been employed, the method will produce the best-fitting line passing through the origin.

Since linear regression produces the prediction line with the best fit, it is the preferred choice for model building. However, the proviso is added that the intercept must be small. "Small" in this context is on the order of a few hundred milliseconds — a value which can reasonably be attributed to random variation in measurements.

Table 2
Prediction Equations and Bandwidths From Fitts' Law Studies Using a Mouse in Point-Select Tasks

Study	Prediction equation (ms)	Bandwidth (bits/s)
Boritz et al., 1991	$MT = 1320 + 430\,ID$	2.3
Epps, 1986	$MT = 108 + 392\,ID$	2.6
MacKenzie et al., 1991	$MT = -107 + 223\,ID$	4.5
Han et al., 1990	$MT = 389 + 175\,ID$	5.7
Card et al., 1978	$MT = 1030 + 96\,ID$	10.4
Gillan et al., 1990	$MT = 795 + 83\,ID$	12.0

Refinements to Fitts' Law

Despite an extremely good fit in empirical tests, Fitts' law is a frequent target for critical reviews (e.g., Meyer, Smith, Kornblum, Abrams, & Wright, 1990; MacKenzie, in press; Welford, 1968). Numerous problems surface under close examination or when findings are compared across studies. These have motivated corrections or refinements to the model. In this section we review these and offer suggestions to guide researchers in applying the law.

Formulation for Index of Difficulty

Early examinations of the law noted a consistent departure of data points above the regression line for "easy" tasks ($ID < 3$ bits). A new formulation for ID was proposed by Welford (1960) to correct this:

$$ID = \log_2(A/W + 0.5). \quad (6)$$

Many researchers, including Fitts, noted an improved fit using Equation 6. The Welford formulation was used by Card et al. (1978), whose findings were subsequently elaborated in the *Psychology of human-computer interaction* (Card, Moran, & Newell, 1983). Not surprisingly, many HCI researchers citing Card and colleagues adopt the Welford formulation (e.g., Boritz et al., 1991; Gillan et al., 1990).

It has also been argued that Fitts, in formulating his model, deviated unnecessarily from Shannon's original work in information theory (MacKenzie, 1989; Shannon & Weaver, 1949), and that a more theoretically sound formulation for the index of task difficulty is

$$ID = \log_2(A/W + 1). \quad (7)$$

In terms of MT, the prediction model becomes

$$MT = a + b \log_2(A/W + 1). \quad (8)$$

Equation 8, known as the Shannon formulation, is preferred because it

- provides a slightly better fit with observations,
- exactly mimics the information theorem underlying Fitts' law, and
- always gives a positive rating for the index of task difficulty.

The last point above is understood by examining the three formulations for ID. Using the Fitts or Welford formulation (Equations 1 & 6), the index is negative if the amplitude is less than half the target width; that is, $A < W/2$. At the very least, a negative rating for task difficulty is a nuisance. From Equation 7, as A approaches zero (for any W), ID approaches 0 bits, but never becomes negative. Obviously, the latter effect has strong intuitive appeal. Although for the one-dimensional paradigm an amplitude less than $W/2$ only occurs when the starting position is inside the target (see Figure 2), very small $A{:}W$ ratios are fully possible when the law is applied in two dimensional tasks. This is demonstrated in the next section.

Extension to Two Dimensions

It is important to remember that the experiments undertaken by Fitts and most other experimental psychologists tested one dimensional movements. This is evident in Figures 1 and 2. Since both target amplitude and target width are measured along the same axis, it follows that the model is inherently one dimensional.

HCI researchers employing Fitts' law invariably use target selection tasks realized on a two-dimensional CRT display. The shape of the target and the angle of approach, therefore, must be considered carefully in applying the model. If the targets are circles (or perhaps squares), then the one-dimensional constraint remains largely intact. (The "width" of a circle is the same, regardless of the angle of measurement!) However, if targets are rectangles (e.g., "words"), the situation is confounded. We can still view the amplitude as the distance to the centre of the target; but the definition of target width is unclear. This is illustrated in Figure 5.

In applying the model in 2D tasks, a critical question arises: What is target width? The default strategy is to consistently use the horizontal extent of the target. We call this the "STATUS QUO" model for target width. Unfortunately, a STATUS QUO model yields unrealistically low (sometimes negative!) estimates for task difficulty when, for example, a short and wide target, such as a word or series of words, is approached from above or below at close range. At least two examples of this exist in the literature. Gillan et al. (1990) used Fitts' law in a target selection task using strings of characters as targets while varying the approach angle and approach distance. One extreme condition saw a 26-character (6 cm) target approached diagonally from a distance of 2 cm. Welford's formulation was used, so the index of task difficulty was $ID = \log_2(A/W + 0.5) = \log_2(2/6 + 0.5) = -2.6$ bits. The negative rating is troublesome. (A similar example is found in Card et al., 1978).

One result of task difficulty extending to the left of $ID = 0$ bits is that it becomes certain that a positive (probably large) intercept emerges under linear regression. This is because conditions with $ID = 0$ bits or less correspond to conditions that *actually occurred* in the experiment.

No doubt, such tasks will take a non-trivial (positive) amount of time.

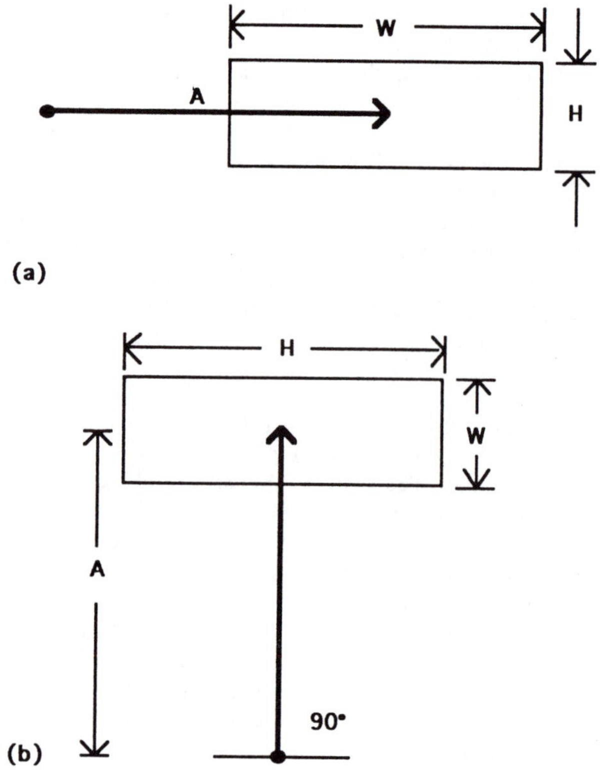

Figure 5. Fitts' law in two dimensions. The roles of width and height reverse as the approach angle changes from 0° to 90°.

We suggest two ways to correct this problem. The first is to use the Shannon formulation for *ID*, which for the example above would increase the rating to $\log_2(2/6 + 1) = +0.42$ bits.

A second and additional strategy is to substitute for *W* a measure more consistent with the 2D nature of the task. Consider Figure 6. The inherent 1D constraint in the model is maintained by measuring *W* along the approach axis. This is shown as *W'* (read "W prime") in the figure. Notwithstanding the assertion that subjects may "cut corners" to minimize distances, the *W'* model is appealing because it allows a 1D interpretation of a 2D task.

Another possible substitution for target width is "the smaller of W or H". This pragmatic approach has intuitive appeal in that the smaller of the two dimensions seems more indicative of the accuracy demands of the task. We call this the "SMALLER-OF" model. This model is computationally simple since it can be applied only knowing *A*, *W*, and *H*. The *W'* model, on the other hand, requires *A*, *W*, *H*, and θ_A, and a geometric calculation to determine the correct substitution for *W*. The SMALLER-OF model is limited to rectangular targets, however.

An experiment was conducted to test the different models for target width on a standard target selection task using a mouse. The design employed a balanced range of short-and-wide and tall-and-narrow targets approached from various angles. The results indicate that both the SMALLER-OF and *W'* models are empirically superior to the STATUS QUO model and that the difference between the SMALLER-OF and *W'* models is insignificant (MacKenzie & Buxton, in press).

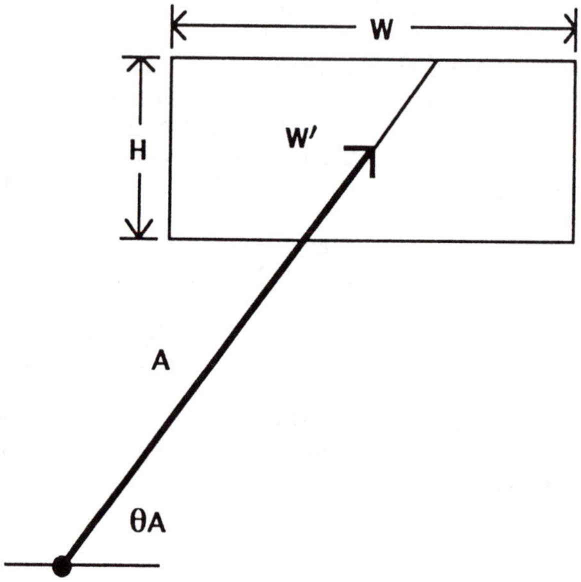

Figure 6. What is target width? Possibilities include *W'* (the width of the target along an approach vector) or the smaller of *W* or *H*.

In summary, the SMALLER-OF or *W'* model is recommended in applying Fitts' law to two dimensional tasks. We should note that extensions to three dimensional tasks easily follow from the arguments above; although Fitts' law has yet to be tested in 3-space. Finally, note that the *W'* model reduces to the STATUS QUO model for one dimensional tasks.

Normalization and the Speed-Accuracy Tradeoff

The reciprocity between the speed of actions and the subsequent accuracy of responses has been well documented in experimental psychology and human factors engineering (e.g., Hancock & Newell, 1985;

Pew, 1969). Despite this, researchers all too often base performance analyses solely or largely on task completion time measurements while paying little regard to the errors that accompanied — and equally contributed to — performance. Comparative evaluations based on movement time criteria are difficult when faced with disparities in error rates. That is, if condition A was faster than condition B, but had more errors, it is uncertain which condition is better.

The most important refinement to Fitts' law, perhaps, is the technique for accommodating spatial variability or errors in responses. The techniques calls for target width to be adjusted based on the distribution of "hits" (selection coordinates) about each target. Thus, at the model building stage, W is a dependent variable rather than an independent variable. The claim is that the technique increases the power of Fitts' law since normalized models inherit a known and consistent error rate. In particular, comparisons within and between studies are strengthened by a "level playing field".

The output or "effective" target width (W_e) is derived from the observed distribution of "hits", as described by Crossman and Welford (Welford, 1968, p. 147). This adjustment lies at the very heart of the information-theoretic metaphor — that movement amplitudes are analogous to "signals" and that end-point variability (viz., target width) is analogous to "noise".

The technique is illustrated in Figure 7. When a nominal error rate of 4% occurs (Figure 7a), no adjustment is required ($W_e = W$). When a different error rate occurs, target width is adjusted by multiplying it by a ratio of z scores obtained from statistical tables for the unit-normal curve. For example, if 2% errors were recorded on a block of trials when selecting a 5 cm wide target, then $W_e = 2.066/2.326 \times 5 = 4.45$ cm (Figure 7b).[1] The analyses proceed as before except using "effective *IDs*", calculated using W_e instead of W.

Applying this technique is essential if comparisons within or across studies are attempted. Rephrasing and earlier point, if performance on condition A was 6 bits/s and performance on condition B was 5 bits/s, we'd like to conclude that condition A was superior; however, in the absence of identical or normalized error rates, such a conclusion is weak and perhaps wrong. Fitts' law models have appeared in published research accompanied by error rates from 0% to 25% (see MacKenzie, in press); yet the technique is rarely applied. It is strongly recommended that future research adopt the method.

[1] The technique is described elsewhere in full detail with examples (MacKenzie, in press).

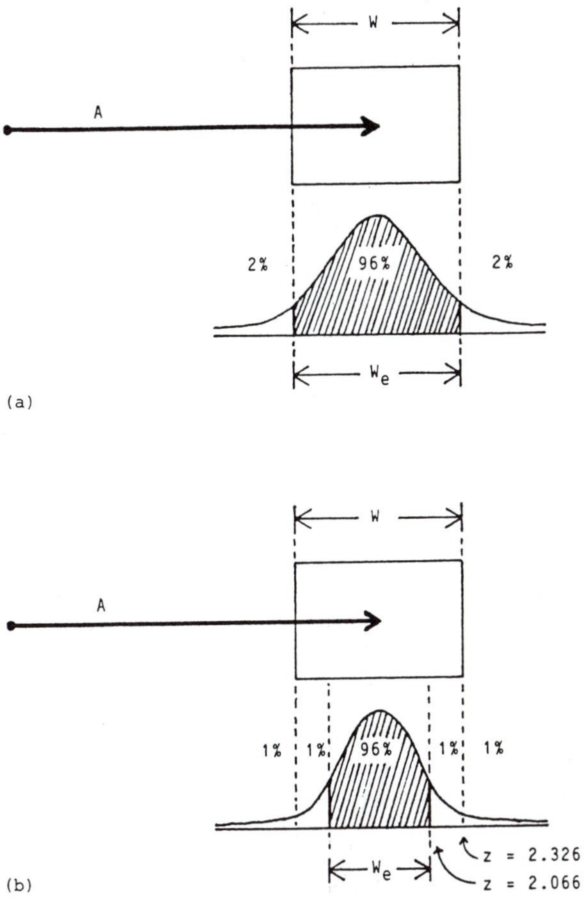

Figure 7. The method for normalizing responses. In (a) the error rate is 4% so no adjustment is needed. In (b) the rate is 2% so an adjustment is made.

Applying Fitts' Law: An Example

One challenge in research is relating the findings to real-world problems confronting practitioners in the field. Despite its recognition as one of the more robust models for human movement, Fitts' law has rarely migrated from the research lab.

An instance of Fitts' law actually being used in a product is a computer-aided design tool called *Jack*, developed at the University of Pennsylvania (Badler, Webber, & Kalita, 1991). In *Jack* three dimensional human figures (simulated on a CRT display) are programmed to execute motions such a picking up objects or making adjustments on a simulated control panel. Since the researchers did not know how fast to program movements in *Jack*, they called upon Fitts' law. A derived Fitts' law model was embedded in *Jack* to provide the duration for movements, based on the distance to move and the size of the terminating region for the move. The visual result is quite natural.

In this section, further applications for Fitts' law models are explored and a specific example is developed.

First, we must recognize when *not* to use Fitts' law. The law is a prediction model for rapid, aimed movement. A variety of user input activities do not fit this description, including drawing, inking, writing cursive script, and other temporarily constrained tasks. Furthermore, some devices are inadequately modeled by Fitts' law. Isometric joysticks are force sensing and undergo negligible motion. As a model for human movement, it seems odd to apply Fitts' law where no limb movement takes place. Card et al. (1978) found that performance data for an isometric joystick were poorly described by Fitts' law. After the data were decomposed by amplitude, however, the model fit well, yielding a series of parallel lines across amplitude conditions. Other devices, such as those for velocity control, may also display characteristics inappropriate for a Fitts' law model.

For the more common pointing devices (such as the mouse, trackball, or stylus), and for common point-select or drag-select tasks, however, Fitts' law has the potential to assist in the design and evaluation of graphical user interfaces. Questions of the form "How long will this task take?" can be answered using Fitts' law prediction equations if certain conditions exist. If the tasks are rapidly executed with negligible or known mental preparation time, system response time, device homing time, etc., then there is a good chance Fitts' law can assist in evaluating alternative methods.

Consider the case of deleting a file (icon) on the Apple *Macintosh* computer. Three possible methods are listed below.

DRAG-SELECT: Drag the icon to the trash-can. (This is the traditional *Macintosh* method.)

POINT-SELECT: Select the file icon with a point-select operation, then select the trash-can icon with a second point-select operation.

STROKE-THROUGH: Stroke through the icon. This method uses a button-down action beside the file icon followed by dragging (stroking) through the icon and a button-up action on the opposite side.

The STROKE-THROUGH method is an example of input which mimics a natural gesture in manuscript editing (Hardock, 1991; Kurtenbach & Buxton, 1991). A reasonable assumption for the stroking gesture is that the button-down action occurs on the left of the icon in the centre of a region the same size as the icon, and that the button-up action occurs similarly in a region on the right of the icon.

A possible screen layout is shown in Figure 8. The trashcan icon is located at the bottom right of the screen. The file icon is placed in the middle of the screen at a distance of 14 cm from the trashcan. Both icons are 2 cm square. The button-down and button-up regions for the stroking gesture are shown in dotted lines.

The calculations proceed using derived pointing and dragging models for the mouse (MacKenzie et al., 1991):

Pointing model:

$$MT = 230 + 166\ ID \quad (IP = 6.0 \text{ bits/s}) \tag{9}$$

Dragging model:

$$MT = 135 + 249\ ID \quad (IP = 4.0 \text{ bits/s}) \tag{10}$$

The pointing model applies to the POINT-SELECT method, while the dragging model applies to the DRAG-SELECT and STROKE-THROUGH methods. Note also that for the STROKE-THROUGH method the amplitude is 4 cm, rather than 14 cm.

Once the initial move to the icon is complete, the time to delete the file icon using each method is calculated as follows:

DRAG-SELECT:

$$\begin{aligned} MT &= 135 + 249 \log_2(14/2 + 1) \\ &= 135 + 249 \times 3 \\ &= 882 \text{ ms} \end{aligned} \tag{11}$$

POINT-SELECT:

$$\begin{aligned} MT &= 230 + 166 \log_2(14/2 + 1) \\ &= 230 + 166 \times 3 \\ &= 728 \text{ ms} \end{aligned} \tag{12}$$

STROKE-THROUGH:

$$\begin{aligned} MT &= 135 + 249 \log_2(4/2 + 1) \\ &= 135 + 249 \times 1.58 \\ &= 528 \text{ ms} \end{aligned} \tag{13}$$

This result suggests, using Fitts' law analyses, that the traditional method of deleting a file on the *Macintosh* is slower than two alternate methods. (The STROKE-THROUGH method is 40% faster.) The example is simplistic, however. Other issues such as methods for deleting multiple files or for un-deleting files must be considered too.

Even though the rate of information processing is lower during dragging than during pointing, the STROKE-THROUGH method, which is a dragging operation, is faster than the POINT-SELECT method. This is due to the combined effect of the intercepts in the prediction equations and the different movement amplitudes. Using the stroke-through method, the predicted *MT* is independent of the distance (A) between the file icon and the trashcan icon since the movement amplitude is nominally set at twice the file icon's width. However, the predicted *MT* decreases with A for the POINT-SELECT method. This suggests there may be a cross-over point below which the POINT-SELECT method is faster. Knowledge of this may play a critical role in selecting an appropriate method. In the current example, the cross-over point is calculated by equating the POINT-SELECT and STROKE-THROUGH predictions as follows:

$$230 + 166 \log_2(A/2 + 1) = 135 + 249 \log_2(A/2 + 1) \quad (14)$$

Solving Equation 14 yields $A = 2.72$ cm. So, the point-select method is faster than the STROKE-THROUGH method only for amplitudes less than 2.72 cm. Certainly, this is a minority of cases. Other possibilities could be explored too, such as increasing the size of the trashcan icon relative to file icons.

Future Possibilities

In the hard science-soft science debate, Newell and Card (1985) hold that "striving to develop a theory that does task analysis by calculation is the key to hardening the science" (p. 237). Indeed, future applications of Fitts' law may include "embedded models" as an

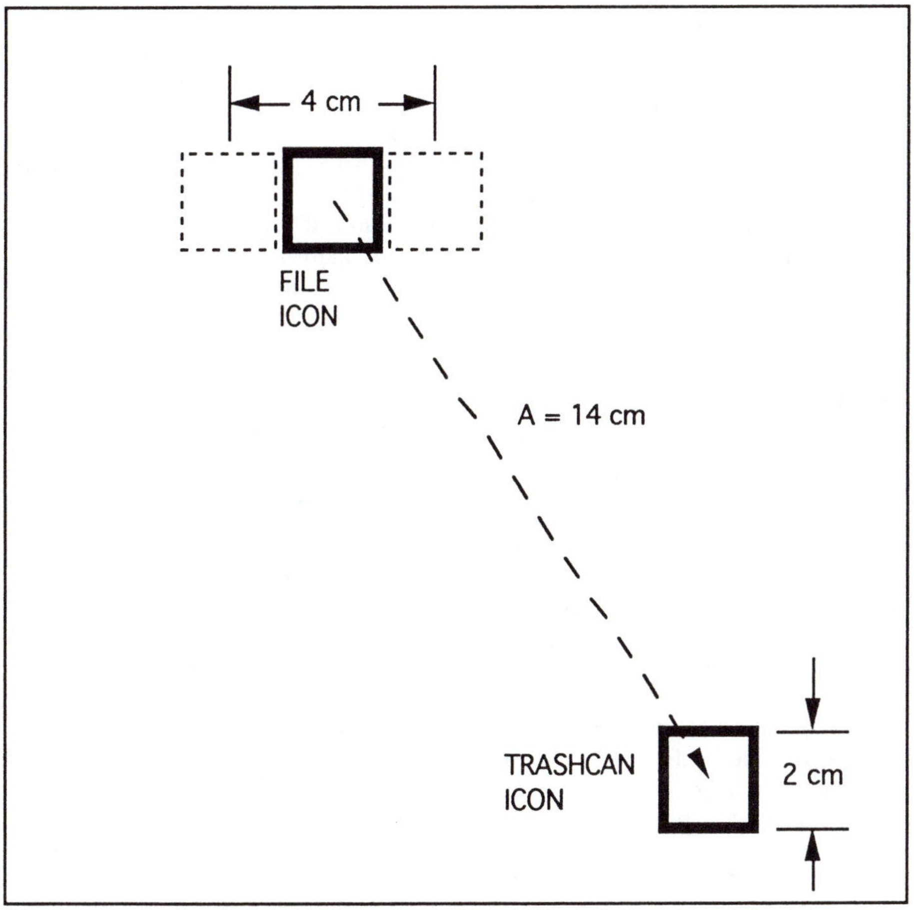

Figure 8. Screen layout for Fitts' law example.

integral part of user interface design and management systems. The scenario envisioned goes something like this: A user interface is patched together in story-board fashion with a series of screens (with their associated soft buttons, pull-down menus, icons, etc.) and interconnecting links. The designer puts the embedded model into "analyse mode" and "works" the interface — positioning, drawing, selecting, and "doing" a series of typical operations. When finished, the embedded model furnishes a predicted minimum performance time for the tasks (coincident with a nominal or programmable error rate). The designer moves, changes, or scales objects and screens and requests a reanalysis of the same task.

This is a rough first approximation. At a higher level, an embedded model is an "agent" in beta testing, monitoring activities and profiling performance. The profile catalogs a variety of facets of the interface. For example, a "locus of control" could identify frequently used screens or high-use regions on a display. In a word processing system, for example, depending on the implementation for scrolling, a user may work mostly at the bottom of the screen. Knowledge of this may imply that a menu bar could be placed at the bottom of the display rather than at the top.

A more powerful embedded model performs sequence analysis. How long does it take to get from point A to point B through a series of intermediate steps? Or, of alternate ways, which is the fastest? Hypermedia environments with embedded links facilitate such analyses, since an explicit and external state-transition description may not be needed. The agent acts on the screen definitions and links (as they exist in the application) in evaluating alternative or optimal paths.

An embedded model is more than a software routine incorporating Fitts' law. System and user performance constants are needed, similar to those in the Keystroke-Level Model (Card, Moran, & Newell, 1980). A parametric analysis could identify bottlenecks or optimal combinations. For example, decreasing pointing time by 10% vs. decreasing user keystroke time by 10% may have vastly different effects on overall task completion time. If a task can be accomplished two ways (e.g., 4 point-select operations vs. 20 keystrokes), which is the fastest? A parametric analysis could identify cross-over points across settings (as shown earlier). The designer could establish ranges and weights for parameters, and an agent, armed with embedded models, would take it from there.

Fitts' law may also participate in user-adaptive systems — systems with a human interface which changes to accommodate a user's capabilities and limitations (Rouse, 1988). Control systems for air traffic, ground traffic, power generation or industrial processes are potential instances. One can imagine several human operators interacting with a complex system by manipulating iconic controls in response to system events. As system dynamics change, the demands on operators change. Models such as Fitts' law (and/or the Hick-Hyman law) could measure the load on operators (in bits/s) or predict their performance. In safety-critical settings, it may be possible to systematically allocate tasks to workers to maintain set-points of sub-maximal performance.

Human-computer interaction has advanced by leaps and bounds in recent years. We can attribute this primarily to the improved interfaces advanced through the technologies of mouse input and bit-mapped graphic output. There is an ongoing and valuable need for the prediction and modelling of user activities within such environments. As human-machine dialogues evolve and become more "direct", the processes and limitations underlying our ability to execute rapid, precise movements emerge as performance determinants in interactive systems. Powerful models such as Fitts' law can provide vital insight into strategies for optimizing performance in a diverse design space.

Acknowledgement

This paper is based on research conducted at the Computer Systems Research Institute in the University of Toronto. The financial support of the Natural Sciences and Engineering Research Council of Canada, Xerox Palo Alto Research Center, and Digital Equipment Corp. is gratefully acknowledged.

References

Badler, N. I., Webber, B. L., & Kalita, J. (1991). Animation from instructions. In N. I. Badler, B. A. Barsky, & D. Zeltzer (Eds.), *Making them move: Mechanics, control, and animation of articulated figures* (pp. 51-93). San Mateo, CA: Morgan Kaufmann

Boritz, J., Booth, K. S., & Cowan, W. B. (1991). Fitts's law studies of directional mouse movement. *Proceedings of Graphics Interface '91* (pp. 216-223). Toronto: CIPS.

Card, S. K., English, W. K., & Burr, B. J. (1978). Evaluation of mouse, rate-controlled isometric joystick, step keys, and text keys for text selection on a CRT. *Ergonomics*, *21*, 601-613.

Card, S. K., Mackinlay, J. D., & Robertson, G. G. (1990). The design space of input devices. *Proceedings of the CHI '90 Conference on Human Factors in Computing Systems* (pp. 117-124). New York: ACM.

Card, S. K., Moran, T. P., & Newell, A. (1980). *Psychology of human-computer interaction.* Hillsdale, NJ: Erlbaum.

Epps, B. W. (1986). Comparison of six cursor control devices based on Fitts' law models. *Proceedings of the 30th Annual Meeting of the Human Factors Society* (pp. 327-331). Santa Monica, CA: Human Factors Society.

Fitts, P. M. (1954). The information capacity of the human motor system in controlling the amplitude of movement. *Journal of Experimental Psychology, 47*, 381-391.

Fitts, P. M., & Peterson, J. R. (1964). Information capacity of discrete motor responses. *Journal of Experimental Psychology, 67*, 103-112.

Gillan, D. J., Holden, K., Adam, S., Rudisill, M., & Magee, L. (1990). How does Fitts' law fit pointing and dragging? *Proceedings of the CHI '90 Conference on Human Factors in Computing Systems* (pp. 227-234). New York: ACM.

Han, S. H., Jorna, G. C., Miller, R. H., & Tan, K. C. (1990). A comparison of four input devices for the Macintosh interface. *Proceedings of the 34th Annual Meeting of the Human Factors Society* (pp. 267-271). Santa Monica, CA: Human Factors Society.

Hancock, P. A., & Newell, K. M. (1985). The movement speed-accuracy relationship in space-time. In H. Heuer, U. Kleinbeck, & K.-H. Schmidt (Eds.), *Motor behavior: Programming, control, and acquisition* (pp. 153-188). New York: Springer-Verlag.

Hardock, G. (1991). Design issues for line-driven text editing/annotation systems. *Proceedings of Graphics Interface '91* (pp. 77-84). Toronto: CIPS.

Hick, W. E. (1952). On the rate of gain of information. *Quarterly Journal of Experimental Psychology, 4*, 11-26.

Hyman, R. (1953). Stimulus information as a determinant of reaction time. *Journal of Experimental Psychology, 45*, 188-196.

Kurtenbach, G., & Buxton, W. (1991). GEdit: A testbed for editing by contiguous gesture. *SIGCHI Bulletin, 32*(2), 22-26.

MacKenzie, I. S. (1989). A note on the information-theoretic basis for Fitts' law. *Journal of Motor Behavior, 21*, 323-330.

MacKenzie, I. S. (1991). *Fitts' law as a performance model for human-computer interaction.* Doctoral dissertation. University of Toronto.

MacKenzie, I. S. (in press). Fitts' law as a research and design tool in human-computer interaction. *Human-Computer Interaction.*

MacKenzie, I. S., & Buxton, W. (in press). Extending Fitts' law to two dimensional tasks. *Proceedings of the CHI '92 Conference on Human Factors in Computing Systems.* New York: ACM.

MacKenzie, I. S., Sellen, A., & Buxton, W. (1991). A comparison of input devices in elemental pointing and dragging tasks. *Proceedings of the CHI '91 Conference on Human Factors in Computing Systems* (pp. 161-166). New York: ACM.

Meyer, D. E., Smith, J. E. K., Kornblum, S., Abrams, R. A., & Wright, C. E. (1990). Speed-accuracy tradeoffs in aimed movements: Toward a theory of rapid voluntary action. In M. Jeannerod (Ed.), *Attention and performance XIII* (pp. 173-226). Hillsdale, NJ: Erlbaum.

Miller, G. A. (1953). What is information measurement? *American Psychologist, 8*, 3-11.

Newell, A., & Card, S. K. (1985). The prospects for psychological science in human-computer interaction. *Human-Computer Interaction, 1*, 209-242.

Pew, R. W. (1969). The speed-accuracy operating characteristic. *Acta Psychologica, 30*, 16-26.

Rouse, W. B. (1988). Adaptive aiding for human/computer control. *Human Factors, 30*, 431-443.

Shannon, C. E., & Weaver, W. (1949). *The mathematical theory of communication.* Urbana, IL: University of Illinois Press.

Walker, N., & Smelcer, J. B. (1990). A comparison of selection times from walking and pull-down menus. *Proceedings of the CHI '90 Conference on Human Factors in Computing Systems* (pp. 221-225). New York: ACM.

Ware, C., & Mikaelian, H. H. (1989). A evaluation of an eye tracker as a device for computer input. *Proceedings of the CHI+GI '87 Conference on Human Factors in Computing Systems and Graphics Interface* (pp. 183-188). New York: ACM.

Welford, A. T. (1960). The measurement of sensory-motor performance: Survey and reappraisal of twelve years' progress. *Ergonomics, 3*, 189-230.

Welford, A. T. (1968). *Fundamentals of skill.* London: Methuen.

CHUNKING AND PHRASING AND THE DESIGN OF HUMAN-COMPUTER DIALOGUES

INFORMATION PROCESSING 86, H.-J. Kugler (ed.)
Elsevier Science Publishers B.V. (North-Holland)

William BUXTON
Computer Systems Research Institute, University of Toronto
Toronto, Ontario, Canada, M5S 1A4

Invited Paper

ABSTRACT

The use of physical gestures to reinforce cognitive chunking is discussed. The thesis presented is that muscular tension and motion can be used to phrase human-computer dialogues. These phrases can be used to reinforce the chunking of low-level tasks that correspond to the higher-level primitives of the mental model that we are trying to establish. The relationship of such gestures to the issue of compatibility is also discussed. Finally, we suggest how to improve the use of grammar-based models in analysing and designing interaction languages.

1. INTRODUCTION

It is no secret that the user interface of most computer systems could be improved. Systems are often intimidating, prone to error, and require a high investment in effort before productive work can be undertaken. A desire to make systems easier to use is a good starting point, but we can't get very far without some theory.

"Easier to use" is easy to say, but it suggests little about *how* to reduce errors and frustration and promote faster learning. In order to make some headway, we might best reformulate the problem as "How can we accelerate the process whereby novices begin to perform like experts?". Underlying this formulation is an assumption that there is a qualitative difference between how experts and novices achieve particular goals. This assumption is supported by much of the recent literature in problem solving and the acquisition of cognitive skills [1].

Experts and novices differ in the coarseness of granularity with which they view the elements of a particular problem or task. Novices are attentive to low-level details. For example, operational details such as finding a particular character on the keyboard or remembering the name of a command involve the novice conciously in problem solving. The result is that valuable cognitive resources are diverted from the central problem at hand.

With experts, these low-level details can be performed automatically. Hence, the size of the chunks of the problem to which they are attentive are much larger. The skills that permit these tasks to be performed automatically, however, must be highly learned, usually through repetition [19]. The acquisition of skills, therefore, can be characterized by developing an ability to perform ever-larger chunks of a problem automatically.

We can now return to our reformulation of the problem at hand, "How can we accelerate the process whereby novices begin to perform like experts?". Our premise is that there should be as close a match as possible between the structure of how we think about problems and the language or representation that we use in solving them.

The term *pragmatics* has been used to describe the device and kinesthetic components of the user interface [6]. Pragmatics, therefore, concern the human gestures of a dialogue and the transducers that capture them. They are the primary representation through which the user directly articulates concepts to the system. This representation should, therefore, be engineered to match how the expert thinks about the problem domain and reinforce the mental model that we are trying to develop for the novice. Another way of stating this is that the dialogue structure, especially the pragmatics, should be engineered so as to maximize compatibility [12][17] between concept and action.

2. SYNTAX: TWO APPROACHES

The design of the syntax has a major effect on the quality of the user interface of an interactive system. It affects learnability, the frequency and nature of user errors, the retention of skills (as with non-regular users) and the speed of task performance. A major problem for users is the cognitive load imposed by remembering the tokens of a command and their order (see, for example, [4]).

There are many approaches that designers have taken to avoid such problems. One is to limit the number of arguments to a command. This is the approach taken in the *MacWrite* program of the Apple Macintosh computer [3]. (We use the Macintosh as the basis of our example because many readers will be familiar with it, and also because it has a good user interface. It provides, therefore, an excellent foil for discussing new concepts of design.)

MacWrite limits operators to one explicit argument. This causes problems, however, for operations such as *move* which require both a direct and indirect object. To get around this, *MacWrite* replaces the single command *move* with two lower-level commands *cut* and *paste*. While the new primitives have a simpler syntax, the user's mental model must be restructured to map the concept move onto them. Rather than simplifying the user interface, therefore, it is possible that the single-operand-per-verb strategy simply redistributes the cognitive loading.

An alternative design strategy exists. If *move*, for example, is the primitive that most closely corresponds to the user's model, then the design problem is to use it while minimizing the burden of remembering the arguments and their ordering. One approach to doing so can be seen in how files are moved to the garbage can using the Macintosh's *finder*. Another approach is offered by proof-reader's symbols. An example is shown in fig. 1.

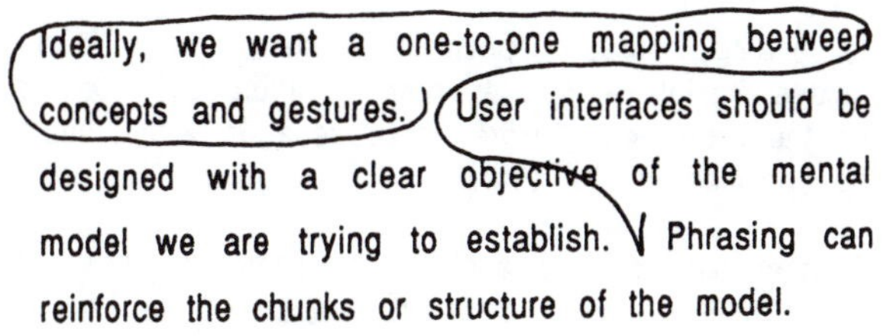

Fig. 1: Proof-Reader's Symbol Specifying "Move."Contrast the directness of this example, or moving files to the Macintosh's garbage can with the "cut-and-paste" strategy used by *MacWrite* [3].

There are at least three points worth noting about these examples, especially in contrast with the "cut-and-paste" strategy for specifying *move* :

- the entire transaction, verb, direct object, and indirect object are all specified in a single gesture;
- there will never be an error in syntax since the ordering is implicit in the gesture;
- the operation is specified using existing skills and does not require restructuring of existing mental models.

3. PHRASING AND GESTURE

We can think about the components of the move command in the previous example as being woven together by a thread of continuity similar to that which binds together a musical phrase. The "statement" is initiated in a state of neutrality, is articulated by a continuous gesture, and upon closure, returns to a neutral state where another phrase can be introduced by either party. As in music, the phrase is characterized by tension (in this case muscular) and the neutral state by relaxation.

One of our main arguments is that we can use tension and closure to develop a phrase structure to our human-computer dialogues which reinforces the chunking of the mental model that we are trying to establish.

Human input to the majority of today's systems is *haptic*. That is, it involves physical contact with transducers such as mice, keyboards and pedals. In the "body-language" of haptic input, kinesthetics and muscular tension are the raw materials of establishing a phrase structure. There is evidence that such periods of tension (or *arousal*) are accompanied by a heightened state of attentiveness and improved performance [21]. This is illustrated in fig. 2. Hence, we have maximum attention during task performance. On closure, transactions are followed by periods of relaxation which indicate that it permissible to be interrupted, or move on to the next step.

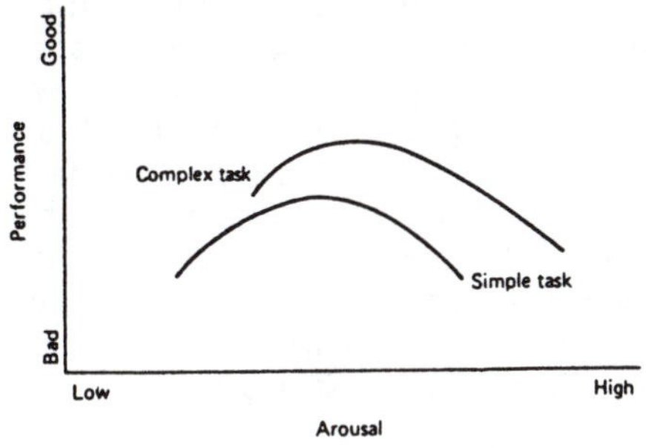

Fig. 2: Yerkes-Dodson law (From [18] p. 606). Within limits, attention and performance increase with arousal, or tension.

4. COMPOUND TASKS

Problems that we saw previously in the syntax of a single command also appear at another level of the human-computer dialogue. In actual applications, many of the transactions which we perform consist of *compound tasks*. Selecting an electrical component and positioning it in a circuit board layout would be an example of a *selection/positioning* task [6]. Similarly, identifying a word by finding it in a document and then selecting it would be an example of a *navigation/selection* task [9]. In many such cases, we would argue that users model a compound task as a single entity. In such cases, having to address the sub-tasks independently may result in an additional burden comparable to using *cut* and *paste* instead of *move*. We claim that the use of phrasing through kinesthetic gesture can be used to overcome this problem.

Pop-up menus provide a good example to illustrate our point. In general, one would consider making a selection from a pop-up menu as a single task.

However, on closer examination, it is seen to consist of three sub-tasks:

- *invoke the menu* : by depressing the mouse button;
- *navigate to selection* : by moving mouse while button is depressed;
- *make selection and return* : by releasing the mouse button.

In this case, the "glue" that ties the sub-tasks together is the tension of holding the mouse button down throughout the transaction. By designing the dialogue in this way, errors of syntax and mode errors are virtually impossible to make since the concluding action (articulated by releasing the mouse button) is the unique and natural consequence to the initial action (depressing the mouse button). Furthermore, the tension of the finger holding down the button gives constant feedback that we are in a temporary state, or mode. (There is a slight irony to this, since it is precisely in so-called "modeless" interfaces that pop-up menus are most commonly found.)

5. PHRASING AND COGNITIVE SKILLS

In their 1983 study [11], Card, Moran and Newell discussed how experts collapsed low-level text editing tasks into cognitive "subroutines" that they termed "routine cognitive skills". Anderson [2] describes the acquisition of such skills as being based upon the compilation and proceduralization of knowledge about the underlying sub-tasks. We believe that phrasing can be used to organize these sub-tasks to accelerate this process.

6. PRAGMATICS AND THE COMPONENTS OF INPUT

If Card, Moran and Newell's routine cognitive skills are compilations of lower-level primitives, one could try to determine the basic building blocks. One possible answer comes from Foley, Wallace and Chan [13]. They tried to characterize human input to computer systems from the user's perspective. In so doing, they came up with six basic primitives:

- *Select* an item in 1, 2, or 3D;
- *Position* an item in 1, 2, or 3D;
- *Orient* (rotate) an item in 1, 2, or 3D;
- *Path* : specify a path, such as in inking in a paint program;
- *Quantify* : specify a numerical value;
- *Text* : enter text, as in word processing

On closer examination, however, we see that these primitives are not necessarily all at the same level. Let us use the *position* primitive as an example.

If we use a mouse or a tablet, positioning an object in 2D can be viewed as a single task. However, the moment that we change transducers and use a QWERTY keyboard, specifying the same coordinates involves two primitives, namely *quantifyX* and *quantifyY*.

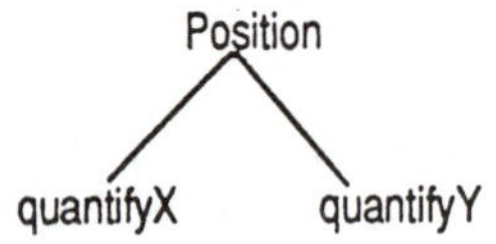

Fig. 3. Position as an Aggregate of 2 Quantify Tasks

We see from this example that even Foley, Wallace and Chan's six primitives have a deep structure. Whether the sub-tasks are consciously perceived, however, is very much influenced by the gesture (and capturing transducer) used. When appropriate, a single gesture (pointing) can be used to articulate a single concept (position).

We can build upon this positioning example. Let us look at an example from music where we want to enter notes into a score. Using the QWERTY keyboard we could enter a command line to specify each note. The line:

C#4 1/4 6/4

for example, could specify a C sharp in the fourth octave having a quarter note duration and starting on the sixth beat. Here, three separate values must be specified by the user.

Another technique to achieve the same result would be to use a mouse to select a quarter note from a menu and then drag it to the desired position in pitch and time on the staff. This technnique is commonly used, and can be seen in the popular *Deluxe Music Construction Set* for the Apple Macintosh [5]. Using this technique the specification of entry point and pitch collapse into a single positioning task, so adding a note reduces to a compound selection/positioning task.

We can further integrate the underlying tasks using a technique developed by Buxton, Sniderman, Reeves, Patel and Baecker [10]. Here, a simple short-hand notation is used to enter notes in a single gesture. Using a stylus and digitizing tablet, the user points at where a note is to appear and enters one of the shorthand symbols shown in fig. 4.

The use of this system to enter a 16th note is shown in fig. 5.

Of the three techniques discussed, the third is the fastest and the one that most directly corresponds to what a musician is trained to do using pencil and paper. While the technique requires the user to memorize the short-hand symbols, their design makes this easy to do and the benefits in increased speed of transcription make the investment worthwhile.

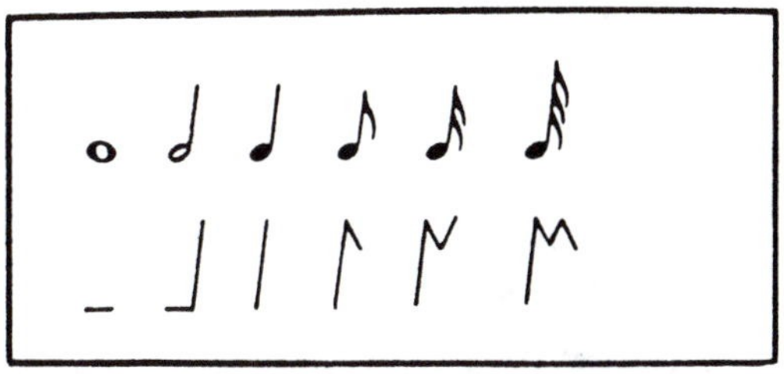

Fig. 4. Short-Hand Symbols for Transcribing Musical Notation [10]. The short-hand symbols are shown under the note durations that they represent. Note the correspondence between number of flags and number of changes of direction in the stems of the short-hand symbols.

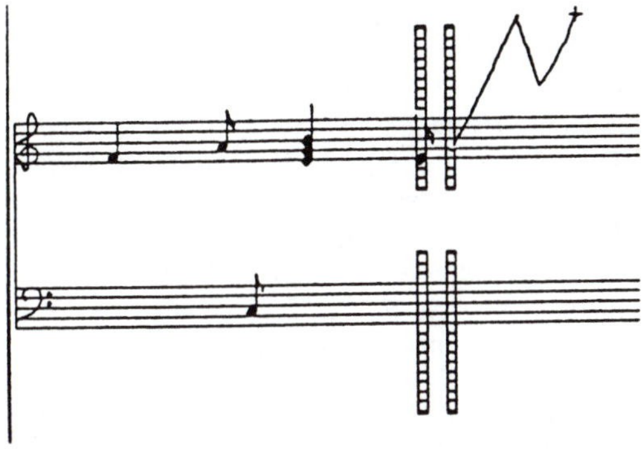

Fig. 5. Entering a 16th Note Using a Single Gesture. Note duration is determined by symbol drawn. The entry point and pitch of the note is determined by where the the short-hand symbol is drawn.

7. GRAMMARS, PRAGMATICS AND COMPLEXITY

The *add note* transaction of the previous examples can be represented as a grammar. This is shown in tree form in fig. 6. Here we see the sub-tasks that make up the complete transaction. However, the number of *distinct* actions that the user was required to make in order to specify these sub-tasks was seen to depend on the interaction technique used.

Having the sub-tasks of a transaction form aggregates as in this example can be viewed as a form of chunking imposed by the pragmatics of the dialogue. The effect of such chunking has important implications for grammar-based modeling of interaction languages, such as that pioneered by Reisner [20], and further developed by Green and Payne [14] and Green, Payne, Gilmore and Mepham [15].

In her original work, Reisner developed a set of heuristics which she used to analyze the grammar of the interaction language of a particular system. From this analysis she would derive a value which gave a measure of the system's learnability and proneness to error. The heuristics that she used were based upon:

- Number of productions
- Number of terminals
- Length of productions

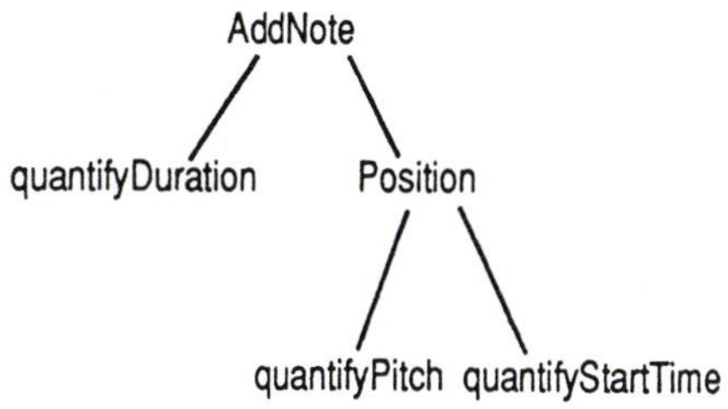

Fig. 6. Task Hierarchy in AddNote Task Adding a note can be seen to involve specifying a duration, pitch and entry point. The specification of pitch and entry point can collapse into a single 2D positioning task. The entire transcation can collapes into a single aggregate and be expressed by a single gesture using the short-hand transcription technique illustrated in fig. 5.

A simplified version of such an analysis can be applied to the grammar of our AddNote primitive. The grammar itself is shown below in production form. Non-terminals start with upper casė characters and terminals start with lower case characters.

AddNote := quantifyDuration PositionPitchTime
PositionPitchTime := quantifyPitch quantifyStartTime

Let the weight of each production and each terminal equal one unit. Since we have two productions and three terminals, the total weight is therefore five. Let us assume that this is an accurate measure of the complexity of the transaction using the command-line technique described.

This being the case, we would argue that the heuristics must be adjusted when using the selection/positioning technique. Namely, the entire *PositionPitchTime* sub-task should be treated as a single terminal. This is based on the aggregation of the *quantifyPitch* and *quantifyStartTime* sub-tasks due to the interaction pragmatics. Consequently, the weight of the transaction using this technique would be three units (one production and two terminals).

Finally, using the short-hand character recognition technique, we would argue that the weight of the *entire transaction* is about equivalent to that of a single terminal, namely one unit.

Having implemented and informally tested each of the techniques described [16][10], we believe these weight estimates to be about accurate when considering speed of learning and speed of task performance. There are important implications of these observations on grammar-based analyses of interaction languages. In particular, such analyses should accomodate the pragmatics of the language so as to establish where sub-trees collapse into a single unit. The non-terminals at the root of such collapsed sub-trees should be treated as virtual terminals.

In our opinion, making such considerations explicit will focus attention on the effect of pragmatics on the complexity of a dialogue. Furthermore, when such models are used prescriptively, such considerations have the potential to aid in designing interaction languages that better exploit such chunking mechanisms to reinforce desired mental models.

9. GESTURES AND TRANSDUCERS

The importance of pragmatics and physical gesture is central to virtually all of the examples discussed. However, gestures are meaningless if there is no transducer that can capture them. Unfortunately, the range of options open to designers today is very limited. The available transducers are limited, and even those that are available are poorly understood [8]. The lack of pressure sensitive devices (such as mouse buttons to control line thickness) and foot controls are two obvious examples of the shortcomings of current resources. The paucity of techniques that effectively use both hands is another [9].

10. CONCLUSIONS

We have argued that user interface pragmatics can be designed to accelerate the acquisition of expert operational skills. The key is gesture-based phrasing to chunk the dialogue into units meaningful to the application. Concepts or transactions that can be described in a single word or phrase can often be articulated using a single gesture. This desired one-to-one correspondence between concept and gesture leads towards interfaces which are more *compatible* with the user's model.

The work described is based on practice and experience rather than formal experimentation. It is preliminary, and a great deal of research remains to be done. However, the examples discussed are sufficiently persuasive to warrant an examination of current design practice.

ACKNOWLEDGEMENT

I would like to acknowledge the contribution of many of my colleagues and students in the preparation of this paper. Brad Myers, Ron Baecker, Ralph Hill, Peter Rowley, Wendy Walker and Allison Lee have all helped improve the presentation. I would also like to acknowledge the support of Tony Waserman who provided the catalyst that brought this paper about.

Finally, I would like to acknowledge the Natural Sciences and Engineering Research Council of Canada who's continued financial support has made this research possible.

REFERENCES

[1] Anderson, J.R. (Ed.) (1980). *Cognitive Skills and their Acquisition*, Hillsdale, N.J.: Lawrence Erlbaum & Associates.

[2] Anderson, J.R. (1982). Acquisition of Cognitive Skill, *Psychological Review*, **89(4),** 369-406.

[3] Apple (1984), *MacWrite User's Manual*, Apple Computer Inc., Cupertino, CA.

[4] Barnard, P.J., Hammond, N.V., Mortan, J., Long, J.B. & Clark, I.A. (1981). Consistency and Compatibility in Human-Computer Dialogue, *IJMMS*, **15(1),** 87-134.

[5] Brown, G. (1985). *Deluxe Music Construction Set*, San Mateo, CA: Electronic Arts.

[6] Buxton, W. (1982). An Informal Study of Selection-Positioning Tasks, *Proceedings of Graphics Interface '82*, 323-328.

[7] Buxton, W. (1983), Lexical and Pragmatic Considerations of Input Structure, *Computer Graphics*, **17(1)**, 31-37.

[8] Buxton, W. (1986). There's More to Interaction Than Meets the Eye, in Norman, D. & Draper, S. (Eds.) (1986) *User Centered System Design: New Perspectives on Human-Computer Interaction*, Hillsdale, N.J.: 319-337.

[9] Buxton, W. & Myers, B. (1986). A Study in Two-Handed Input, *Proceedings of CHI '86*, to appear.

[10] Buxton, W., Sniderman, R., Reeves, W., Patel, S. & Baecker, R. (1979). The Evolution of the SSSP Score Editing Tools. *Computer Music Journal*, **3(4),** 14-25.

[11] Card, S., Moran, T. & Newell, A. (1983), *The Psychology of Human-Computer Interaction*, Hillsdale, N.J.: Lawrence Erlbaum Associates.

[12] Fitts, P.M. & Seeger, C.M. (1953), S-R compatibility: Spatial characteristics of stimulus and response codes. *Journal of Experimental Psychology,* **46,** 199-210.

[13] Foley, J., Wallace, V.L. & Chan, P.(1984), The Human Factors of Computer Graphics Interaction Techniques, *IEEE CG&A*, **4(11),** 13-48.

[14] Green, T.R.G. & Payne, S.J. (1984). Organization and Learnability in Computer Languages, *IJMMS*, **21(1)**, 7-18.

[15] Green, T.R.G., Payne, S.J., Gilmore, D.J. & Mepham, M. (1984). Predicting Expert Slips, *Proceedings of Interact '84*, Vol. 1, 92-98.

[16] Hogg, J. & Sniderman, R. (1979). Score Input Tools Project Report, Unpublished manuscript, C.S.R.I., University of Toronto.

[17] John,B.E., Rosenbloom, P.S. & Newell, A. (1985). A Theory of Stimulus-Response Compatibility Applied to Human-Computer Interaction, *Proceedings of CHI'85*, 213-220.

[18] Kantowitz, B.H. & Sorkin, R.D. (1983). *Human Factors: Understanding People-System Relationships*, New York: John Wiley & Sons.

[19] Newell, A. & Rosenbloom, P.S. (1980). Mechanisms of Skill Acquisition and the Law of Practice, in Anderson, J.R. (1980). *op cit.*

[20] Reisner, P. (1981). Formal Grammar and Human Factors Design of an Interactive Graphics System, *IEEE Transactions on Software Engineering,* **7 (2)**, 229-240.

[21] Yerkes, R.M. & Dodson, J.D. (1908). The Relative Strength of Stimulus to Rapidity of Habit-Formation, *Journal of Comparative and Neurological Psychology,* **18**, 459-482.

Stylus User Interfaces for Manipulating Text

David Goldberg and Aaron Goodisman *
Xerox Palo Alto Research Center
3333 Coyote Hill Road, Palo Alto, CA 94304
goldberg@parc.xerox.com

Abstract

This paper is concerned with pen-based (also called stylus-based) computers. Two of the key questions for such computers are how to interface to handwriting recognition algorithms, and whether there are interfaces that can effectively exploit the differences between a stylus and a keyboard/mouse.

We describe prototypes that explore each of these questions. Our text entry tool is designed around the idea that handwriting recognition algorithms will always be error prone, and has a different flavor from existing systems. Our prototype editor goes beyond the usual gesture editors used with styli and is based on the idea of leaving the markups visible.

1 Introduction

Common experience with keyboards and pens suggest that keyboards are optimized for text entry, and pens for drawing. With the appearance of small, portable pen-based computers such as the GridPad, whose primary input device is a stylus (i.e. an electronic pen) used directly on a display, we are faced with the problem of how to use a stylus to manipulate text. This paper studies two aspects of this problem.

First, what is a good user interface to a handwriting recognizer? There have been many papers on handwriting recognition (see [11] for a survey), but very few on user interfaces to recognizers (the most completely described interface is PenPoint [3]). Our system is based on the philosophy that recognizers will always make errors, and that the interface must be designed from the beginning to accomodate that fact. This results in a substantially different interface from PenPoint (and was developed before the publication of [3]).

The second problem is this: can we find an interface that exploits the differences between a stylus and a mouse/keyboard? If we cannot, then there is a real question as to whether pen-based computers are viable, since text entry is slower and more error prone with a stylus than with a keyboard, and since it is feasible to build a notebook sized pen-based computer with a keyboard and thumb operated trackball with similar functionality to a mouse (such as the portable Macintosh).

Two of the primary differences between a stylus and a mouse are (1) styli have much finer control than mice (try writing your signature with a mouse), and (2) while it is easy to manipulate three buttons on a mouse, it is difficult to use the same hand to both hold a stylus and press one of three buttons. Most previous work with styli has focused on using gestures as editing commands ([2], [3], [4], [8], [14] are examples). This works well because it doesn't require buttons, and it is easier to draw gestures with a stylus than a mouse. However, all these editors simply provide a different way to do the same tasks that can be performed with mice and keyboards. We propose that a markup editing

*also with Dept. of Computer Science, Massachussetts Institute of Technology, Cambridge, MA 02139

interface (which extends gesture based editors by leaving the gestures visible) is more appropriate for pen computers, because it can perform some common tasks that are very awkward with traditional keyboard/mouse systems.

There is a continuum of evaluation techniques for studying user interfaces, ranging from formal user studies to informal testing by a few users. Since the space of stylus-based user interfaces is just beginning to be explored, we felt that informal observation of users was the appropriate way to evaluate our prototypes. Once the informal exploration has identified a few promising UI techniques, then formal studies will become more important.

This paper has four parts. First, we describe the hardware used in our studies. Next, we classify the different types of recognition systems and explain the choices we made for our system. In the third part, we describe our text entry program, which uses a number of techniques to compensate for the error-prone analogue nature of handwriting recognition. Finally, we describe our markup editor, and single out what we feel is a key design principle for such editors. More details on the programs can be found in [6].

2 The Hardware

We did all our studies with a *scratchpad*, which is a PARC-built peripheral to a Sun Microsystems SPARCstation. A scratchpad consists of an 1120 by 780 LCD display, on top of which is a transparent tablet made by Scriptel Corporation. The display is driven by a custom SBus card. To SPARCstation software, the scratchpad looks like a second display, and our programs wrote directly onto the display using Sun's pixrect library.

The Scriptel stylus we used for these studies is tethered to the tablet, and has a microswitch in the tip to detect when the stylus is in contact with the tablet, but has no buttons on the side of the barrel (the newest styli from Scriptel do have a side button). The stylus plugs into an RS-232 port at the back of the SPARCstation, and reports the location of the pen at a rate of 200 locations/second, with a resolution of about 400 dots/inch, which is roughly four times the resolution of the display. The stylus can accurately report its position even when it is above the display, that is, when the tip of the stylus is not in contact with the tablet. Each location report contains a bit telling whether or not the tip switch is depressed.

Because the Scriptel tablet lies between the pen and the display surface, there is a fair amount of parallax between the tip of the pen and the display. Although we tried to compensate for this by displaying a cursor, most users had some difficulty pointing the stylus because of the parallax.

3 Parameters of Text Entry Systems

There are five major parameters that characterize handwriting recognition systems.

Printing/Cursive Script Electronic styli can detect when the pen is in contact with the tablet. This gives a way to mark the beginning and ending of strokes, namely by when the pen is lifted off the tablet. In printing the pen is lifted between each character (and also perhaps between strokes within a character). In cursive script writing, the pen will not always lift between two characters.

Upper/Mixed Case Does the system recognize only upper case letters, or does it accept mixed case?

Boxed/Unboxed The key issue is who decides how to group strokes into letters. In a boxed system, each letter is in a separate box, so the user groups strokes into letters by writing different letters in different boxes. In an unboxed system, the system provides only a line to write on rather than a row of boxes, and the system itself must compute how to group strokes into letters.

Recognition Feedback Does the system provide feedback after each letter, immediately displaying the result of the recognition? Or does the user signal the system after entering a unit of text, at which point the system recognizes that whole block of text at once.

Writer Dependent/Independent Is the system writer independent, or does it require each user to first train the system to learn his handwriting.

3.1 Discussion

Here are the choices we made for our text entry tool. Our system recognizes printed text. Cursive script recognition was not chosen because there are no script systems known to the authors that have consistently high recognition rates.

Our system recognizes mixed case. Although some commercial systems (Pencept, GridPad) recognize upper case only, we feel that mixed case systems are necessary for the acceptance of stylus text input.

Even though our recognizer can perform in an unboxed mode (that is, it can do the segmentation itself), we chose to do all our UI studies in boxed mode. There were several reasons for this. First, recognition in boxed mode is more accurate, because there are no segmentation errors. Second, correction and editing are greatly simplified when each letter is in a box.[1] Based on our informal studies, we identified a third advantage to boxed input, which may be most important of all: when users are given only lines to write on, some writers frequently slip into a script mode where they join pairs of letters. For recognizers that can recognize only discrete characters, this obviously results in poor recognition rates. Boxes greatly reduce the chance that a writer will join pairs of letters.

Our system recognizes one letter at a time. We did not study tradeoffs of recognition by blocks versus by character, however we can make the following observation. In our system, you can correct at any time (and we provide two correction gestures: one to delete a letter and one to open up space). Systems that recognize a block at a time essentially require a mode for correction, since you can't correct until you see that the recognizer has made an error, and thus you can't correct without first instructing the system to perform the recognition. However, block recognition does provide more context to help in performing the recognition.

[1]PenPoint finesses this point by allowing unboxed input, but then after recognition, redisplaying using boxes.

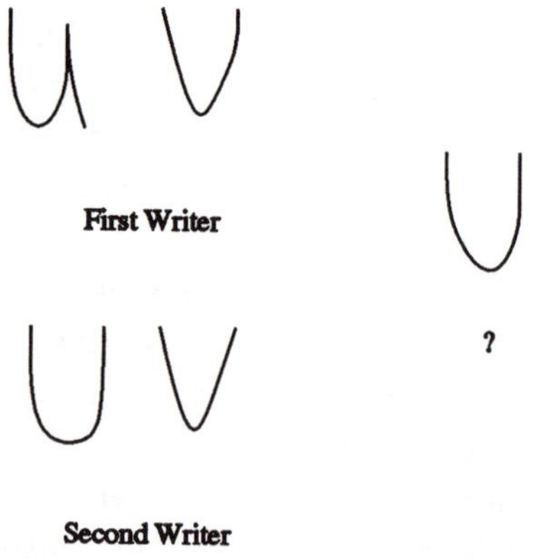

Figure 1: Lower case u, v for two different writers

3.2 Writer Independence

The last item on our list is the most interesting tradeoff. If writer independent systems had the same accuracy of writer dependent ones, then writer independent systems would be the obvious choice. However, writer dependent systems are more accurate. This is only partly due to imperfect recognition technology. Consider the pair of letters *u* and *v*, written by two different writers, and the unidentified letter shown in Figure 1.

If the unidentified character was printed by the first writer, it is obviously a *v*, whereas for the second writer it is a *u*. This illustrates that even for human recognition of letters, knowledge about the writer is important. The importance of writer-dependent information is even more crucial for mixed case systems than for upper-case only, for the simple reason that there are more easily confused pairs like *u* and *v*.

Our system is writer dependent and requires training. This is partly because we wanted to focus on user interfaces and minimize the effort on building a recognizer. A trained recognizer is easier to write because it doesn't require collecting a large database of user writing styles. But we also feel that trained systems (or hybrid systems that modify their behavior with training) are necessary for achieving high accuracy.

There are two disadvantages to trained systems:

first, they must be trained, and second, before using them, you must identify yourself to the system so that it can locate your training database. For pen-based computers that will be used for several hours a day, the overhead of a training session is small. Hybrid systems have the advantage that they can be used immediately, but we believe that virtually all users will eventually want to go through a training session to improve accuracy.

The potentially larger problem with trainable systems is that you must identify yourself to the system before you begin writing. Similar issues arise in speech recognition ([5]), but the inconvenience of identification with stylus systems is much less than with speech systems. First, there is often no overhead to begin using a speech system: you simply begin speaking. Thus the relative overhead of an extra identification step can be significant. Imagine an elevator where you speak the floor number. Having to first identify yourself would take longer than performing the actual task of speaking a floor number! For stylus applications, there is built-in overhead, because you have to pick up the pen and place it on the writing surface. Thus the relative cost of identifying yourself is less. Second, with speech there is a problem when several people alternate speaking (say at a meeting). Identifying the speaker after each speaker change is a significant problem. With multiple writers, the common case will be for each writer to have a separate pen, and thus once a mapping between people and pens has been established, there is no further overhead to identification.

Once you've decided to use a trained system, there is the question of how to do the training. Perhaps the best method is to do it automatically, so that each time the user draws a letter, that is used as training data. The disadvantage of this technique is that a letter may be misrecognized, and if the user doesn't bother to correct it then incorrect training data will be used. Our system requires explicit training instead. With explicit training, we believe that it is important to make training as simple as possible. Thus we do not require the user to invoke a special program to train. Instead, whenever the user is entering text, he can get a display which enables him to examine and modify his training samples via a single tap. Details are in section 4.2. Experience with our prototype shows that users often write somewhat differently in a formal training session than when performing real-life tasks. Thus the accuracy of the training data improves if it is based on input during actual tasks, and that in turn is more likely if there if very low overhead to modifying training samples.

4 The Text Entry Program

The primary difference between keyboard and styli are that keyboards are discrete. When you hit the *A* key, you will always get the character *A*. On the other hand, when you write the letter *A*, because recognizers are heuristic, sometimes you won't get *A*, but rather *H* or some other incorrect letter. Even the best recognizers will occasionally misinterpret a letter that seems unambiguous to the writer. Thus a successful user interface to a character recognizer must have a strategy for overcoming the analogue nature of handprinted input. Our text entry prototype uses two major techniques to improve accuracy.

4.1 Segmenting Cursor

First, it uses boxed entry, which eliminates segmentation errors and discourages run-on pairs of letters. Some users, however, find it awkward to write in an input area filled with boxes. So we developed a technique we call the segmenting cursor[2] to gain the segmenting advantages that boxes give, without having to fill the input area with boxes.

The basic idea is simple. The user is presented with a single box. This is like the cursor in computer keyboard systems, except that this box is the outline of a box, rather than a solid box. The user writes the first letter inside the cursor/box. When all the strokes of the first letter are completed, the user begins the first stroke of the next letter outside and to the right of the box. At this point, the

[2]This was based on a suggestion by David Gifford of MIT, although we later discovered a similar idea in the patent literature [12].

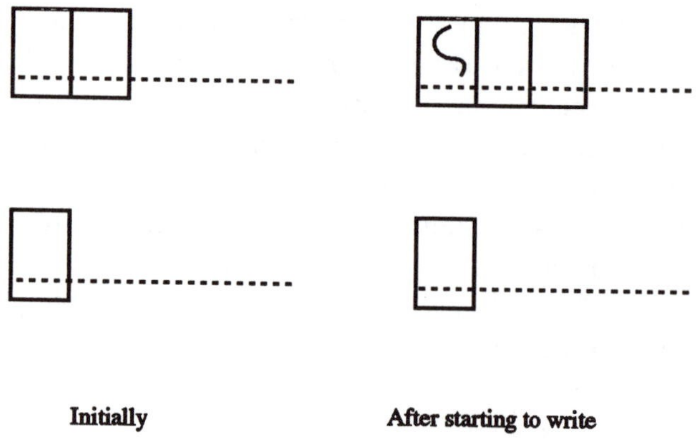

Figure 2: Segmenting Cursor

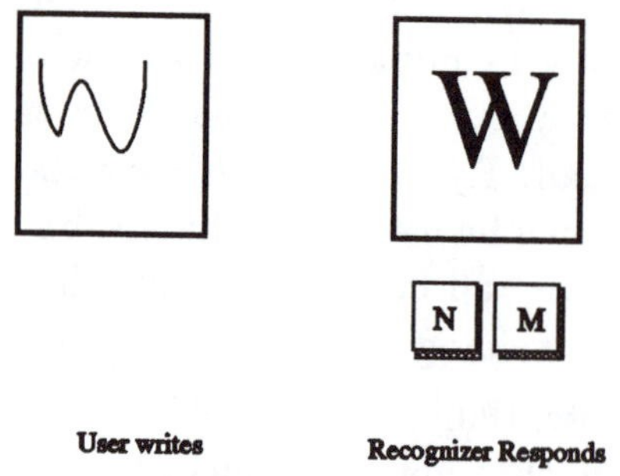

Figure 3: Initial attempt at correction

box/cursor moves to surround the letter now being written.

In practice, we have discovered that a few refinements to this basic idea are necessary. First of all, if the user is allowed to write on more than one line, there should be a box at the beginning of the line following the line being written on. That way, when the user wants to skip to the next line, he knows where to write the first character af that line.

Second, we found that it helps if the cursor is actually a pair of boxes. The user writes the first letter in the left-most box. As soon as he sets the stylus into the second box, the first box disappears and a new box appears to the right of the second box. The reason this helps users is that at the moment the user lifts the pen from the last stroke of a letter, he would like to see the following box. But the system cannot know to create the next box until the pen touches down outside the current box. Thus having a pair of boxes ensures that when a user wants to write a new letter, the box for it will be there in time to aim the beginning of the first stroke of that new letter.

Finally, if the writer wants to leave a space to begin a new word, it helps to have a visible box where the new word will appear. Thus, the initial cursor has two boxes, but after the user begins to write, we put up a third box. See figure 2.

Some users find that erasing of old boxes and drawing of new boxes distracting. Having the "buffer" of boxes as just described helps minimize this problem, because the drawing of the new cursor/box does not appear directly under where the pen is writing. Although many users find the segmenting cursor a pleasant entry interface, even with this buffering some still find the moving cursor distracting. Thus a system that uses the segmenting cursor will probably want to provide a mode where the writing area is filled with traditional boxes.

4.2 Tap-Correction

One obvious way to deal with the fact that recognizers make errors, is to leverage off the fact that when the recognizer is wrong, its second guess is usually right. Our first attempt to exploit this idea was as follows: after printing a letter, the user would be presented with the first guess by having his drawn letter replaced by the recognizer's best guess. We also presented two smaller boxes containing the second and third choices (see Figure 3). If the first guess was correct, the user would go on and print the next letter. If the first guess was not correct, then the user could either redraw the letter, or touch one of the buttons with alternate choices. Our expectation was that most of the time, the correct choice would be in one of the smaller boxes, and that the user save effort by clicking on the appropriate small box, rather than having to reprint the letter.

However, our informal experiments showed that users rarely clicked on the small correction boxes. It seems that the effort of reading what was in the boxes and deciding if they were correct required too much cognitive overhead, and so users prefered to simply rewrite the letter.

With that failure behind us, we tried a new idea. The simplest gesture to make with a stylus is to tap, and so in our next system if a letter was misrecognized, the user could tap on it and the system would display the recognizer's second choice. This was much more successful. When the recognizer was wrong, but the second choice was correct, users tended to perceive this as not really being an error. We call this system "tap-correction".

This technique does have a downside, which is illustrated by the letter *i*. Normally, the system echos pen motion, spreading "ink" to mark the path of the stylus, just as a real pen would. When the system recognizes a letter, it replaces the ink with a nicely drawn version of the recognized letter either when the user begins the next letter, or when one second has elapsed with no input. So if a user writes a lower case *i* by first drawing the vertical stroke and then a dot, the recognition will not occur until he moves on to the next letter (or pauses). However, if a user writes slowly, and one second elapses between the time of the vertical stroke and the dot, the dot will be intepreted to mean "choose the second choice", rather than as dotting the *i*. Our experience suggests that this is not a major problem, and can be minimized by allowing users to change the one second time-out.

The next issue is what meaning to assign to a second tap. There are three possible actions: display the third best recognition, clear the writing area so the user can rewrite the letter, or just escape into a system that displays a keyboard so the user can select the key with his letter. We chose to have the second tap clear the display, allowing the user to rewrite the character. At the same time, a small box appears. Tapping on this box jumps to a display that not only contains a keyboard, but also displays the reference characters and buttons to modify them. This provides the easy access to reference characters that was mentioned earlier.

We also found that after the second tap, when the user was going to rewrite the letter, it was useful to redisplay the original ink. This has two advantages. First, sometimes a user would forget what letter he was writing. This usually happened when the user wrote a stretch of letters, and then went back to correct the errors. Seeing the redisplayed original letter was often a faster way to recall the original letter than rederiving it from context. Second, redisplaying the ink gives the user useful feedback on why the recognizer failed. After the recognizer has replaced the users ink with an incorrect guess, there is no longer any hint as to why the recognizer failed. When the ink is redisplayed, it is often obvious what the problem was. The input letter may have been poorly formed, or perhaps the user drew a letter that is ambiguous (e.g. *u*, *v*). Redisplaying the original ink helps remove an air of mystery from the whole system.

One important aspect of tap-correction is that if you make an error, you cannot immediately rewrite the letter: you must tap twice before you can rewrite. However, in practice a double tap is a sufficiently simple gesture, so that this is not an obstacle to directly proceeding to a rewrite. The advantage of this approach is that users are "trained" to use the built-in fast correction: you must go thru the "tap for second choice" step before you can rewrite a letter.

5 The Editing Program

Most tasks performed on a computer involve some text creation. Although there are some people who have a strong aversion to keyboards and prefer handwriting recognition to typing, for most users the fact that handwriting recognition is slower and more error prone than typing is a major drawback to stylus systems. Thus if the stylus is to become widely used as an input device, we must identify common tasks for which a stylus is superior to a keyboard (and/or mouse). Our candidate for such a t¡ask is a markup editor, others are discussed in [16].

A typical scenario that can benefit from markup editing is when two people collaborate (possibly at remote sites) on a document. Author one produces a draft and gives it to author two. With current tools, author two has two choices. He can print the draft and mark it up with a pen, sending the marked up paper back to author one, or he can receive the draft online, edit it, and then resend it to author one. In the first case, author one can clearly see the changes, but must key in the edits by hand. In the second case the changes are already keyed in, but there is no easy way to see the changes.[3] A markup editor combines the best features of both approaches. The edits are made using marks such as strikeout to erase a word. The editor does **not** perform the edit and erase the word. Instead, it recognizes the edit (or gesture), and signifies its recognition by replacing the strikeout ink with a nicely drawn strikeout, in complete analogy with a character recognizer that replaces the ink of a hand drawn letter with one from a nicely tuned font. Because the gesture was recognized, the edit that it stands for can later be carried out automatically. Markup editors combine the ideas of gesture editing with two-view editors ([1] is a recent example) in that there are two views of the document: one with the edits as gesture marks, and the other with the edits applied.

In most previous work on gesture-based text editors, the gesture commands have either been carried out immediately ([2], [3], [4], [8], [14]), or the marks have been left unintepreted ([13]). The work of Suenaga and Nagura ([9]) is closest to ours. They mark up a printed (possibly handwritten) document with gestures, and then read the document and marks with a FAX receiver. The marks are interpreted, and a revised document is then printed on a FAX transmitter. [4]

Experience with our prototype suggests that markup editors have two significant advantages that might make markup editors desirable even for ordinary editing tasks. First of all, undo operations become much more flexible. Traditionally, editors let you undo operations in reverse order, but you since can't see what those edits were, you can only infer them from watching the undo. A few editors (such as Tioga [10]) will display a list of your recent edits, but only as textual descriptions which are not the same as the mouse/keyboard actions that created the edits. With our editor, when a user undoes an edit, he makes a rubout gesture on top of the edit mark, so there is no ambiguity about what is being undone. Furthermore, the edits can be undone in any order: there is no longer a constraint that the edits be undone in the reverse order to which they were made. Of course, there is the complication of two different edit operations that interact,[5] but no matter what solution is provided to this problem, we feel that "random access" undo is a significant advantage to this type of editor.

The second advantage of markup editors is that they tie in very nicely with version control. At a certain point, the document will be filled with marks, and the user will wish to see what the document looks like when the edits are applied. This provides a natural checkpoint at which to make a new version of the document.

5.1 Analogies with Paper

One popular approach to stylus-based editors is to mimic what people do with pencil and paper ([15]). Although this is a valuable approach, we want to emphasize the opposite. After all, if a stylus-based system can do only what paper and pencil does, then why not just use paper? We propose that an important design principal for stylus editors (and stylus interfaces in general) is to try to go beyond what can be done with paper and pencil.

An example of an interface that uses a stylus like a pencil is Wang FreeStyle ([13]). In this system, to erase you turn the pen over and rub, just as you would with a pencil. Although this technique is easy to remember, it is not the best approach for stylus editors for the following reasons.

FreeStyle allows you to make only uninterpreted marks on paper, so the only operation (besides marking) is erasing. With a stylus text editor, however, you should also be able to move, copy and perform other editing actions. It doesn't make sense to single out one editing action (erasing) to

[3] Of course it is possible to develop a program that takes two input files and tries to show the changes by marking up the original, but this seems inferior because (1) edits can be made in more than one way, and the precise edit is lost and (2) marginal notes or "comments" (that is ink that is meant for the reader but performs no editing function) are lost.

[4] After completing this paper, we received a copy of [7], which describes the use of markup in a collaborative editor.

[5] For example, if you move a block of text, and then edit that text, what happens when you undo the move operation? Will that replace the original copy or the edited copy?

be performed in a special way. Furthermore, the potential advantage of erasing with the other end of a stylus is that it is easy to remember; however, this advantage is minimal because remembering that action doesn't carry over to the other editing actions (eg. copy, move) that a stylus can perform.

Erasing by rubbing perpetuates an action which is clumsy and awkward to perform with a pencil. In one of our prototypes, we used the action of clicking a side button on a pen to indicate erase. Users loved it, because a simple click is much simpler and faster than having to turn a pencil (or stylus) around in your hand. This isn't to say that the best use of a side button is for erasing, but simply to indicate that a stylus affords much simpler methods of erasing than the use of more metaphorical techniques.

Here are two examples that arise in editing, which illustrate the principle that editor interfaces should go beyond simply mimicking paper and pencil practice.

First, consider moving text. The common practice with paper is to circle the source, then draw an arrow to the destination. A markup editor could use this as the gesture that it leaves on the screen. But it is possible to go beyond this and do something that can't be done easily with paper: the editor can also insert a copy of the source at the destination (preferably in a different font). This is especially useful when the source and destination are separated by many lines. Placing a copy of the inserted text at the insertion point is a simple idea, but one that is easy to overlook when merely imitating paper practice.

A second example is selection. With paper, selection tends to be done by circling, and this has been adopted by some systems (for example [4]). But as other have observed (e.g. [14]), it is awkward for selections that span multiple lines. A better idea is inspired by mouse-based systems: simply indicate the beginning and end of the selection, and let the computer highlight the rest.

6 Summary

We draw two main conclusions from our work.

First, it is possible to design a text entry interface that compensates for the imperfections of handwriting recognition algorithms. Unlike PenPoint, our prototype allows users to correct errors without having to rewrite a misrecognized letter; in our system, a single tap corrects. We also observed that writer-dependent, boxed-text entry was more accurate than unboxed text entry, and we devised techniques (e.g. the segmenting cursor and the ability to modify the reference characters at any time) for making this type of input work more smoothly than the obvious implementation.

Second, we believe we have identified a type of stylus usage (markup editing) that can accomplish many editing tasks more easily than can be done with paper or with a keyboard/mouse system. An important principle in designing stylus-based user interfaces is to focus not on imitating paper, but rather on performing tasks that are difficult to do with paper. The two-view nature of our markup editor is an example of something that cannot be done with a paper-only system.

7 Acknowledgements

We would like to thank Jim Gasbarro who designed the scratchpad hardware, Russell Brown who implemented the character recognizer, Bill Buxton for many enlightening conversations, and Dan Swinehart for a careful reading of the manuscript.

References

[1] Avrahami, G., Kenneth Brooks, M. H. Brown. "A Two-view approach to constructing user interfaces," *Computer Graphics* 23(3), 1989, pp. 137-146.

[2] E.R. Broklehurst. "The NPL electronic paper project," *Int. J. Man-Machine Studies* 34(1), 1991, pp. 69-95.

[3] Robert Carr and Dan Shafer. *The Power of PenPoint*, Addison-Wesley, 1991.

[4] Michael L. Coleman. "Text Editing on a Graphic Display Device Using Hand-drawn Proofreader's symbols," *Pertinent Concepts*

In Computer Graphics, Proceedings of the Second Univeristy of Illinios Conference on Computer Graphics, 1969, pp. 282-290.

[5] Gearge R. Doddington and Thomas B. Schalk. "Speech recognition: turning theory to practice," *IEEE Spectrum*, 18(9), September, 1981, pp. 26-32.

[6] Aaron Goodisman. *A Stylus-Based User Interface for Text: Entry and Editing*, MIT Masters Thesis, 1991.

[7] Gary Hardock. "Design Issues for Line-Driven Text Editing / Annotation Systems," *Proceedings of Graphics Interface '91*, Calgary, Alberta, June 3-7 1991, Morgan Kaufmann, pp 77-84.

[8] Arto Kankaanpaa. "FIDS – A Flat-Panel Interactive Display System," *IEEE Computer Graphics and Applications*, 8(2), March 1988, pp. 71-82.

[9] Yasuhito Suenaga and Masakazu Nagura. "A facsimile based manuscript layout and editing system by auxiliary mark recognition," *Proceedings 5th International Conference on Pattern Recognition*, Miami Beach, Florida, December 1980, pp. 856 - 858.

[10] Daniel C. Swinehart, Polle T. Zellweger, Richard J. Beach, and Robert B. Hagmann. "A Structural View of the Cedar Programming Environment," *ACM Transactions on Programming Languages and Systems*, 8(4), October 1986, pp. 419-490.

[11] C.C. Tappert, C.Y. Suen, and T. Wakahara. "On-Line Handwriting Recognition — A Survey," *Ninth International Conference on Pattern Recognition*, 1989, pp. 1123-1132.

[12] Fumio Togawa and Hitoshi Hirose. "Handwritten Character-Recognizing Apparatus for Automatically Generating and Displaying Character Frames," *United States Patent 4,953,225*, August 28, 1990.

[13] Wang FreeStyle *SigGraph Video Review* 45(3), 1989.

[14] L.K. Welbourn, R.J. Whitrow. "A Gesture Based Text Editor," *Proc. of the Fourth Conference of the British Computer Society of Human Computer Interaction*, 1988, pp. 363-371.

[15] Catherine G. Wolf and Palmer Morrel-Samuels. "The Use of Hand-drawn Gestures for Text-Editing," *International Journal of Man-Machine Studies*, 27(11), 1987, pp. 91 - 102.

[16] Catherine G. Wolf, James R. Rhyne and Hamed A. Ellozy. "The Paper-Like Interface," in *Designing and Using Human-Computer Interfaces and Knowledge Based Systems*, Edited by G. Salvendy and M. J. Smith, Elsevier Science Publishers, 1989, pp. 494 - 501.

Tivoli: An Electronic Whiteboard for Informal Workgroup Meetings

Elin Rønby Pedersen, Kim McCall, Thomas P. Moran, Frank G. Halasz*
Xerox Palo Alto Research Center
3333 Coyote Hill Road
Palo Alto, CA 94304, U.S.A.
Email: elin@dat.ruc.dk, {mccall,moran,halasz}@parc.xerox.com

ABSTRACT

This paper describes Tivoli, an electronic whiteboard application designed to support informal workgroup meetings and targeted to run on the Xerox Liveboard, a large screen, pen-based interactive display. Tivoli strives to provide its users with the simplicity, facile use, and easily understood functionality of conventional whiteboards, while at the same time taking advantage of the computational power of the Liveboard to support and augment its users' informal meeting practices. The paper presents the motivations for the design of Tivoli and briefly describes the current version in operation. It then reflects on several issues encountered in designing Tivoli, including the need to reconsider the basic assumptions behind the standard desktop GUI, the use of strokes as the fundamental object in the system, the generalized wipe interface technique, and the use of meta-strokes as gestural commands.

INTRODUCTION

Most of the early attempts to build computer support for meeting rooms, such as the Colab project [11], included whiteboard-sized displays to provide a shared focus of attention for the meeting participants. However, these displays were controlled at a distance by keyboard and mouse (just like a workstation). Meeting participants did not interact directly with the display surfaces as they would with ordinary whiteboards. Empirical studies of collaborative work at shared drawing surfaces [2,12] show that the physical actions around the surface itself are as important as the actual marks made on the surface to support the collaboration. Thus, the *Liveboard* system [7] was created at PARC to provide a "directly interactive, stylus-based, large-area display."[1] The Tivoli project was started to develop software for the Liveboard technology addressing two goals: (1) to discover and explore the user interface techniques appropriate to this new kind of technology and (2) to discover and implement the functionality needed to actually support small working meetings at the Liveboard.

Nature of the User Interface

The basic direction was influenced by our early Liveboard experiences. After a dozen Liveboards had been deployed throughout PARC in meeting rooms and common areas, the most widely-used application was *Whiteboard* [7], a simple multipage pen-based image editor. It simulated a whiteboard by allowing freehand drawing and erasing. This system provided for the kind of unselfconscious, freeform scribbling that is prevalent in small group interactions, and it confronted us with the issues of the appropriate interaction techniques for and the basic nature of this genre of user interface.

The basic function of the board is to support interaction between people (and in this we agree with [4] that it is a "conversation board"). As such, the most important criteria for the user interaction with the board are to be *unselfconscious* — so as not to draw the attention of the participants from their interaction with each other — and to be *fluid* — to allow unhindered expression of ideas. While it is true that the user's "text-graphic performance" [9] involves the creation of various kinds of text-graphic objects, it does not follow that users should be required to declare these as they would be by a structured drawing program like MacDraw. In this sense we disagree with [4]. Further, we deliberately do not provide for handwriting recognition, for it would be disruptive in this context.

The Liveboard, as one component of a vision of ubiquitous computing [13], "blends into the woodwork" and appears to be just a familiar whiteboard. To follow through on this, the board should also behave as a simple whiteboard, at least initially. This not only allows first-time users immediate use of the board, but also allows users to build from their current work practices involving whiteboards.

Pen-based computing is still in its infancy. Operating system support, such as PenPoint [6] and Microsoft Windows for Pen

1. Other large-surface displays are also becoming available, such as the Smart Technologies 2000 and the WACOM Meeting Staff.

*Elin R. Pedersen's current address is: Department of Computer Science, Roskilde University, DK-4000 Roskilde, Denmark.

Figure 1: Photograph of Tivoli running on a Xerox Liveboard being used in an informal meeting.

Computing, is just now being provided. We want to discover appropriate ways to utilize the pen as an input device. The motions that are natural for a pen are quite different from those for a mouse. Because we are operating on a large surface, we want to keep as much facility "at hand" as possible. Gesturing (i.e. creating marks to be interpreted as commands) is an obvious extension beyond drawing and erasing. Other pen-based systems are oriented to using marks as annotations and gestures as commands over structured material, such as form-filling applications. Our situation is somewhat different in that all our material consists of informal handmade marks, and we want to preserve this look and feel. This raises new user interface issues that we are beginning to address.

Functionality for Small Working Meetings

Tivoli is targeted at supporting small working meetings, because this kind of meeting activity is prevalent at PARC and is well suited to the Liveboard. By "working" meetings (as opposed to, say, presentations) we mean meetings where the participants work closely together on a problem or an idea. For these a scribbling surface is useful for generating, communicating, and clarifying ideas and for keeping track of information. Such a working group usually needs to be small: up to about 8 people (also, the physical size of the Liveboard image, 46" x 32", precludes more people being able to gather around it effectively). Because meetings are small and informal, there is no official facilitator or scribe; all participants can have access to the board.

Our goal with Tivoli was to extend the functionality of a simple whiteboard program while preserving its basic features, spirit, and style. The early ideas for new functionality were numerous and diverse — much more than we could possibly implement. As a design strategy to sort these out, we developed a series of 14 scenarios of various kinds of meetings — varied both in content (design, review, brainstorming, administrative meetings) and in style (small to medium, informal to structured, co-located and distributed meetings). Each scenario was a 2-9 page narrative description of a meeting and its use of available wall displays, including whiteboards, flipcharts, copyboards, and Liveboards. Half the scenarios were *documentaries* of actual meetings, and half were *envisionments* of possible meetings. Writing these scenarios served to

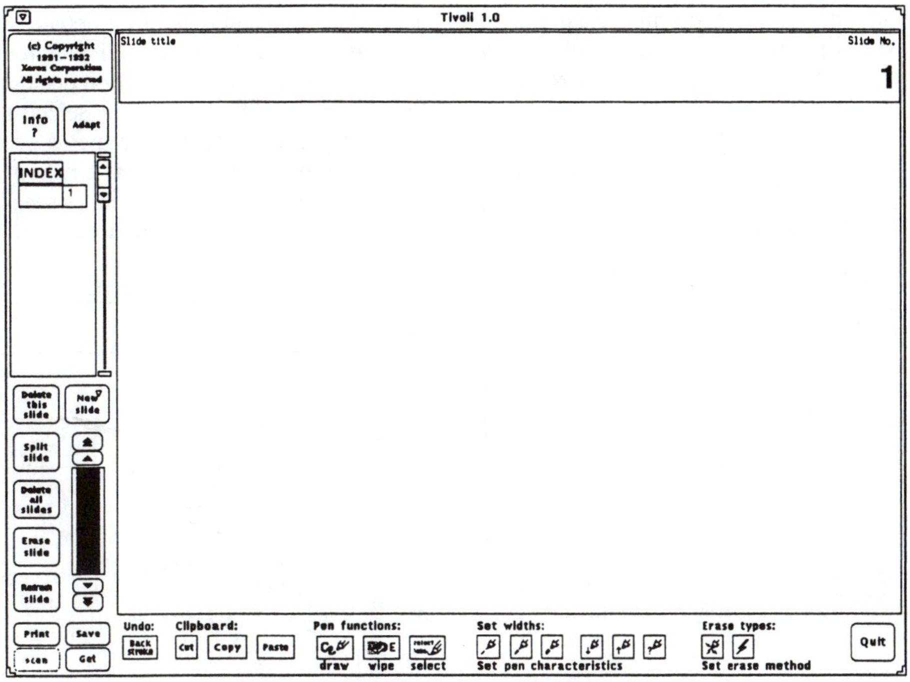

Figure 2: Tivoli window with blank slide.

integrate and concretize inputs from a variety of people, including both designers and potential users.

Analysis of these scenarios resulted in the identification of a coherent *core* of functionality needed across all meeting types and the classification of the remaining functionality into different research *thrusts*. The core functionality included simple pen and gesture scribbling and editing, multiple pages, saving and retrieving, printing, and importing images. The thrusts involved remote collaboration (shared drawing), meeting management tools, and integration with other "ubiquitous" devices. Tivoli was designed to implement the core functionality on an architecture that anticipated the explorations into the extended functionality. In this paper, we describe and discuss Tivoli 1.0, the first release that implements the core functionality.

A SCENARIO OF TIVOLI USE

The following scenario illustrates the main features of Tivoli 1.0 and motivates many of the design issues discussed in the next section. Elin, Kim, Tom, and Frank are starting a design meeting in which they intend to discuss the Tivoli object hierarchy and the possibility of implementing the "decorations" that appear on the Tivoli drawing surface as objects within that hierarchy. Elin goes to the Liveboard, which is displaying the Tivoli window shown in Figure 2. The window at this point consists of a blank *slide* for drawing in and control panels along the bottom and left edges.

In a long box at the top of the slide Elin writes "Objects in the Tivoli World." She does this as naturally and directly as if she were writing with a marker on a whiteboard. Then she lists the main classes of user-generated objects, "Stroke," "Character," and "Image." Kim points out that "Images" are now called "Pictures," so Elin taps the **wipe** button at the bottom of the window. The pen's cursor turns into an eraser. As she sweeps the pen over the word "Images," each stroke she'd drawn is erased as a unit as soon as she touches it. She taps the **draw** button, sees her usual drawing cursor again, and writes "Picture."

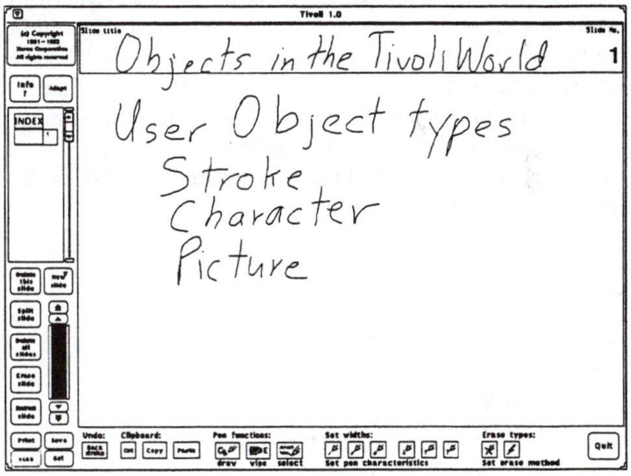

Figure 3

Elin wants a heading for these terms, but needs to create room above them to write it. She taps on the **select** button and draws a circle around the three terms, which then become selected. Then, she draws a line to show how far she wants to have the selected objects moved, which they do when she lifts up the pen. Above them she writes "User Object types." The result is shown in Figure 3.

Tom complains that Elin has been writing with too fine a pen. So she circles her list again and taps on the button for a thicker pen width. All the selected strokes get thicker as can be seen in Figure 4. But she failed to completely include the first 'U', which she deals with separately. But she has still left out the title at the top. She again taps the **wipe** button. But rather than just sweeping across the title (which would erase it), she first "dips" the pen into the button representing the preferred pen width. Now as she wipes it across the title strokes, they are all repainted at the new width. A tap of the **draw** button gives her back her regular pen.

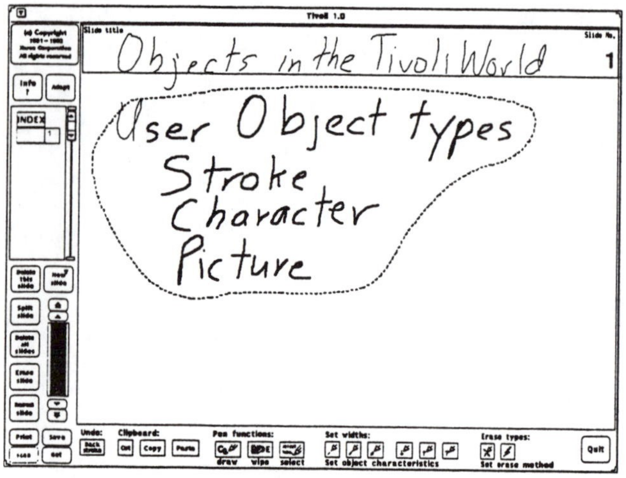

Figure 4

Elin starts a list of system-generated objects or slide "decorations." The list reaches the bottom of the slide, but Frank mentions a couple of items that were left out and really belong near the top of the list. Elin draws a horizontal line across the slide (what we call a "tear" gesture) where she wants more room and quickly taps the pen twice. Everything below the line gets selected, and she moves it down. Then she writes the desired items in the space just opened up. Some of the list is no longer visible, so she taps a small arrow button to scroll the slide. A scroll indicator near the arrow reflects where the current viewport is on the entire slide. The scrolled slide is show in Figure 5.

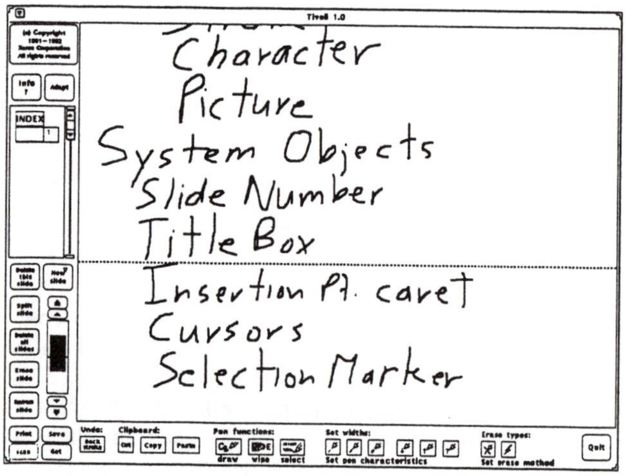

Figure 5

Now it's time to list issues concerning the objects, and Elin decides to start listing them on a separate slide; so she taps the **New Slide** button and gets a blank slide. At the top she writes "Issues" and then lists several issues as people mention them. A *slide list* to the left of the slide area contains a numbered list of all of the slides she has created. She taps on the numbers to switch between the two slides.

The group gets embroiled in a debate on the virtues of special-case representations and display routines. Elin is taking notes on the arguments, but soon decides this discussion belongs on a separate slide; so she selects it all and cuts it with a pigtail gesture. She then creates a new slide and taps the **Paste** button. The strokes that had been cut show up on the new slide. They remain selected, as seen in Figure 6, inviting her to move them, which she does.

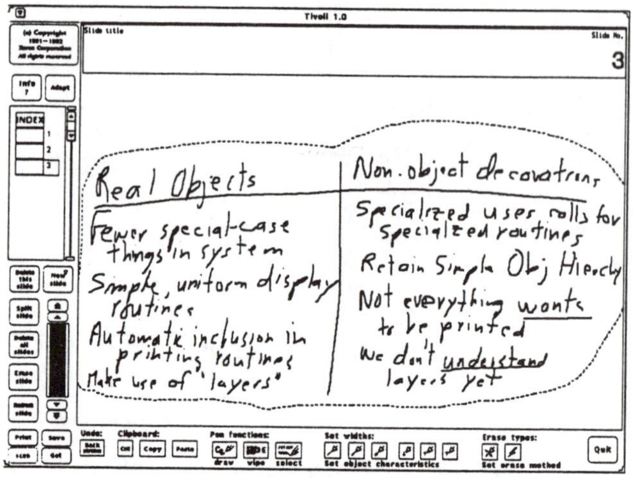

Figure 6

As the discussion starts to get very technical, Frank begins to worry about its implications for the display and object management aspects of the implementation. Kim remembers that he once prepared a slide for a formal talk illustrating the implementation modules. He goes to the Liveboard, taps the **Get** button, and selects from a dialog window the file containing his slides for that talk. Those slides are all added into the current folder of slides, which now number eight.

Unsure of which of the five new slides was the desired one, Kim taps the **INDEX** entry at the top of the slide list. This produces a system-created slide which consists of the title areas from the other slides, as shown in Figure 7. He sees that the desired Architecture slide is number seven. He thinks about just going to that slide, but decides instead to clean things up by deleting the unwanted slides. He uses the slide index to go to each slide in turn and delete it by tapping the **Delete this slide** button.

Then he goes to the Architecture slide and starts annotating it with circles and arrows. The resulting slide is shown in Figure 8. Occasionally he erases some of these, toggling back and forth between drawing and erasing by a rapid tap-tap of the pen. Because the illustration is in the *background* it is indelible. Only the annotations get erased. At one point he erases too much, deleting one arrow too many. He taps on the **Back stroke** button until he has recovered the lost arrow.

Elin wants to propose a new twist, but Kim is monopolizing the group's attention, so Elin draws a picture on a piece of paper before the idea escapes her. When the opportunity presents itself she sticks the paper into the Liveboard's attached scanner, taps the **Scan** button, and waits a minute. Then she

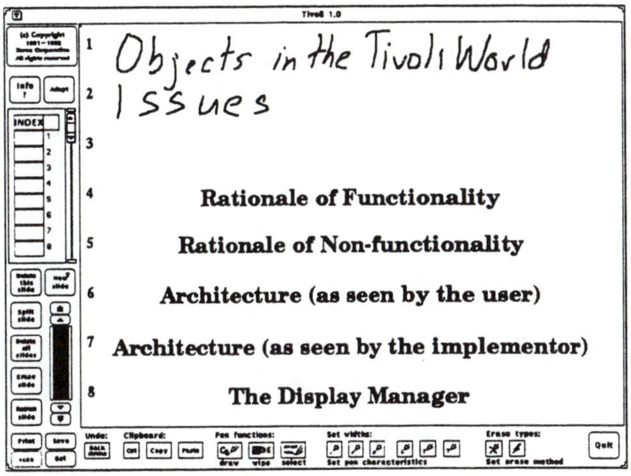

Figure 7

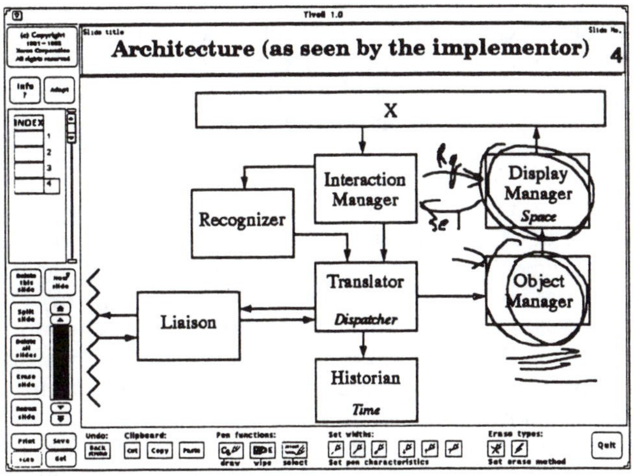

Figure 8

presses a button that imports the scanned image as the background of the current slide. Then she explains it and further annotates it.

Before anything is decided, the meeting's time has expired. Frank wants a hardcopy of the slides, so he taps the **Print** button, selects the **4 slides per page** option so that they'll all show up on one sheet, and sends it off to the printer. Tom is nominated to see whether he can condense the discussion to anything actionable. Frank finally taps the **Save** button. A dialog window comes up that suggests a default file name under which to save it. But Frank thinks up a better one, and *for the first time in the entire meeting* he uses the Liveboard's attached keyboard to specify the desired file name.

A few hours later, Tom runs Tivoli on his office workstation and reads in the folder in order to review the meeting. Imagining that this folder will form the basis for the next meeting, he decides to create another slide summarizing outstanding issues. But since his workstation has no stylus for drawing, he decides to do most of his writing with the keyboard.

The group's next meeting starts by reading in and reviewing Tom's revised version of the folder.

DESIGN FEATURES AND ISSUES

We now discuss some of the more interesting design features of Tivoli and the user interface design issues that they raise.

Assumptions Reconsidered

User interface design has converged onto a broad set of principles defining the generic graphical user interface (GUI). However, the GUI is tied to a set of assumptions about the technology (such as the mouse and the keyboard) and the usage situation (a single user at a workstation on a desk). Both our technology and our usage situation are different for Tivoli, and we found ourselves reconsidering many tacit assumptions. We give three examples:

Pen vs. mouse

A mouse is designed for pointing, whereas a pen is also for writing and drawing. Thus gestural techniques are much more natural for a pen than a mouse. A mouse is indirect in the sense that computation mediates the relationship of the physical movement of the mouse to the movement of the cursor on the display. On the other hand, the Liveboard pen is pointed directly at the surface of the display. There does not necessarily need to be a cursor; it should be where the pen is pointing (within the limits imposed by calibration error). This directness provides for a more direct interaction with objects on the display. However, the system needs to respect this physical directness. For example, we use an OpenLook scroll bar to implement the slide list. When the user points to a scroll arrow, the scroll arrows ride up and down the scrollbar like an elevator. With the mouse this is fine, because the cursor is adjusted to ride the elevator. But with the pen the elevator slides out from underneath the stationary pen, throwing the user off the scroll arrow.

Very Large Interactive Surface

Even with a large workstation display, the user can have a reasonable overview of the display from the normal viewing distance. A user standing at a Liveboard, however, is too close to have such an overview. Thus, we have had to adjust the size and placement of pop-up messages to make sure the user will always notice them. Also, tools such as buttons and menus can be physically out of the user's reach on the Liveboard. (This becomes apparent when running off-the-shelf workstation software on the Liveboard.) This implies some obvious design constraints, such as not requiring users to reach the top of the display to press a button. More generally, it places greater emphasis on keeping user control at the pen, especially for frequent actions and for actions that occur within the flow of scribbling. This is another motivation for utilizing gestural commands, which are issued from the pen *at* the place of application. The problem with gestures is that novice users may not remember them, and so we provide redundant screen buttons where possible. For example, the user can toggle between drawing and erasing either by a double tap of the pen or by reaching down and tapping the **draw** and **erase** buttons at the bottom of the display.

Multiple Users and Pens

A Liveboard is large enough to have more than one person working at it at a time — a natural working situation [11, 12]. The Liveboard is designed to have three pens to accommodate multiple users, and Tivoli was designed to operate with multiple pens. One consequence is that tools on the display are shared. For example, we cannot highlight an icon to show the current pen line thickness, since it can be different for different pens. This is yet another argument for gestural actions, which are localized to specific pens and do not have to rely on shared on-screen tools. In general, in our implementation we have had to distinguish *pen state* from *system state* (see also [3]). This distinction is not always clear-cut. For example, we consider a selection of objects to be part of a pen's state, and thus a second user cannot operate on the first user's selection (without taking the first pen). Another example is that we mark all actions with the ID of the pen that produced them, and we restrict the undoing of actions to be by the same pen (i.e, pen_2 cannot undo the relocation of strokes performed by pen_1, although pen_2 can erase those strokes).

Atomic Objects

Tivoli has an informal look and feel that is much like that of paint programs. But a major feature of the Tivoli design that distinguishes it from paint programs is that drawings are represented as *stroke objects*, not as pixel map images. A stroke is simply a series of line segments describing the path of the pen from the time it touches down on the display surface until it is lifted. A stroke is created over time, and the system cannot wait until it is completed before displaying it (as it does with keystrokes). Therefore, we provide an "inner loop" of feedback that instantly inks the display surface as the pen is moved over it. Only after the pen is lifted does the system create a stroke object.

The stroke-level granularity of this representation manifests itself when operating on the drawing. For example, erasing is done by wiping over the surface with the pen in erase mode. As the eraser goes over each stroke, that whole stroke disappears (i.e., the stroke object is deleted from the representation). This has proved to give a very nice "power boost" when erasing small to medium size strokes, such as handwriting (sweeping across a word gets rid of it without having to fuss with every little pixel). But this sometimes causes surprises when a long stroke (e.g., a large box or a long arrow) disappears when only a small portion of it has been touched by the eraser. The general issue is that objects are not homogeneous, and operations need to be designed to have a desirable effect. This issue needs much further exploration.

Another advantage of strokes as atomic units is that they provide objects for holding properties (e.g., color and thickness). Stroke properties can be changed, e.g., the color of a whole stroke can be changed, no matter how entangled it is with other strokes. And because they are geometrically defined, strokes are transformable.

Generalized Wiping

Tivoli expands the notion of object-based erasing to generalized *wiping*. Wiping is a user's back-and-forth motion across the display surface with a pen, which in wipe mode is called a *wiper*. The wiping motion *dynamically* selects objects as the wiper passes over them. A wiper has an associated operator, which it applies to objects as it selects them. Erasing is accomplished when the wipe operator is DELETE. When the user enters wipe mode, the default operator is DELETE; and thus a novice user can simply think of this as an eraser. But the wipe operator can be changed just by tapping any on-screen button with the wiper. For example, tapping the red button changes the wipe operator to MAKE-RED, after which wiping makes all selected objects red. This has proved to be a natural and powerful technique for dynamically selecting and applying operations to objects.

Gestures (Meta-Strokes)

We have noted several motivations for the use of gestural techniques with the pen. By the term "gesture" we mean a *meta-stroke*, i.e., a stroke that is not just taken to be an element of the drawing, but is to be *interpreted as a command.* A gesture is drawn as a regular stroke and then interpreted. This has the beneficial effect in a group situation that the non-drawing participants can see the gesture before the action takes place and thus not be surprised by unexpected behavior. The most common gesture is the selection gesture, which is drawn as a closed loop of arbitrary shape around a set of objects, defining them as the *selection*. Subsequent gestures then operate on the selection: a pigtail gesture deletes the selected objects; a stroke that starts inside the selection loop moves the selection to the other end of the stroke (the encircled objects remain selected so that they can be operated on again).

One of the main design issues is how to indicate that a stroke is a gesture. There are several classes of techniques, involving devices (e.g., a gesture pen vs. a drawing pen), modes (e.g., gesture mode vs. drawing mode), "tense modes" [5] (e.g., holding down button on the pen to indicate a gesture), and so on. We attempted to avoid modes in the first version of Tivoli, and so we explored a different technique: the *postfix indicator*, which converts the preceding stroke into a gesture. For example, to select and delete a word, first draw a loop around the word, then give the indicator (which repaints the loop in the distinguished gesture color), then draw a pigtail.[2] The postfix technique allows gestures to be embedded in the drawing process. For example, a loop can be drawn (which at this point is just a regular stroke) and, if it isn't correct, erased and redrawn before indicating that it is to be interpreted as a gesture.

We explored a *double tap* of the pen as the postfix indicator (by analogy to a double-click on a mouse button). There is an inherent ambiguity with a double tap during drawing: how to distinguish it from two intentionally small drawing strokes, such as a colon or a quote mark. Thus a user writing "To:" might find that the system attempts to interpret the "o" as a gesture (unsuccessfully because the "o" is an empty loop) and all that is left is a "T".[3]

Faced with this difficulty in distinguishing double taps, especially for users with a "choppy" style of handwriting, we have moved to using a pen button as the gesture indicator in the more recent versions of Tivoli.

2. The pigtail does not require an indicator since it is indicated implicitly by context: When a selection is made, the system expects the user to next operate on it; and thus any stroke starting within the selection loop is taken to be a gesture.

STATUS AND FUTURE DIRECTIONS

Tivoli was first released in December 1991 and since then has been installed as the primary application on the Liveboards at PARC. It runs on Sun Sparcstations and utilizes the X Window System. It is implemented in C++ and currently uses the XView toolkit to implement control panels and buttons.

Tivoli 1.0 is only the first step in our attempt to build a collaborative meeting tool for the Liveboards. Among the many improvements and extensions we hope to eventually explore, we are currently focusing our effort on three issues: (1) a multi-site, shared version of Tivoli; (2) making the interface more accessible, or perspicuous, for casual users; and (3) exploring how Tivoli can be used to support specific meeting practices.

Multi-Site Tivoli

Our vision is to make Tivoli a true collaborative tool, supporting both multiple users standing shoulder-to-shoulder around a single Liveboard and multiple users utilizing two or more geographically-separated Liveboards (This draws inspiration from other work on shared drawing systems. such as [2, 8]. The version of Tivoli described in this paper is implemented to support only the single Liveboard case. We have implemented a multi-site version of Tivoli (Tivoli 2.0) that preserves all of the functionality in the current version [10].

Although the current version supports multiple users around a single Liveboard, the majority of our experience to date has been with situations where only a single user operates Tivoli at any given time. It remains an open question whether our current design will provide appropriate support for the multiple user (single Liveboard) case. In particular, the current Tivoli includes little mechanism for coordinating the actions among multiple users (e.g., preventing one user from changing slides while another is drawing), with the idea that such coordination can be accomplished using social rather than technological means. As we gain experience with the multiple user situation, we will be able to assess if this is in fact the case.

Another usage scenario for Tivoli involves a single meeting room containing a single Liveboard communicating with a (pen-based) laptop for each meeting participant. We hope to explore how the principles we are using to design a multi-site Tivoli will apply this co-located, multi-host case.

The Casual User

The design of Tivoli represents a deliberate balance between two often conflicting goals: interface simplicity and functionality. On the one hand, our goal was to design a Liveboard interface that maintains the natural, facile, immediately obvious feel of a conventional whiteboard. In particular, we were interested in maintaining the whiteboard's ease-of-use to casual (or never-before) users. Liveboards were designed to be placed into public meeting spaces. We wanted to make it easy for a person who has never used a Liveboard to walk up and figure out how to accomplish what they could on an ordinary whiteboard (draw in multiple colors, erase) plus a few obvious extensions (change slides, print) with little or no training. Meeting this requirement tended to push the Tivoli user interface towards simplicity, with the control panel displaying only a few straightforward buttons.

On the other hand, the Liveboard is a computational device. Another of our goals in designing Tivoli was to use this computational power to the user's advantage in supporting and augmenting the capture and organization of ideas in meetings. Accomplishing this goal tended to introduce sophisticated features and functionality into Tivoli (e.g., the generalized wipe operations) whose interface was either complex or non-intuitive or both. Moreover, the more such features we added to the program, the more widgets and buttons needed to be added to the interface.

It's clear from the feedback we've received from our user community that our current user interface design has erred in favor of increased functionality over intuitiveness, or perhaps 'interface perspicuity'. The never-before user who walks up to a Liveboard tends to find the interface so complex that she has some difficulty figuring out how to do the basics. We consider this a major problem and are exploring a revised user interface design which improves the walk-up-ability of Tivoli without decreasing the level of functionality.

Support for Specific Meeting Practices

A very explicit goal of the Tivoli project is to develop research prototypes with sufficient functionality and robustness that they can be put into widespread use in real meeting situations. Tivoli 1.0 is the first step in achieving this goal. Tivoli is currently in use on the 10 Liveboards throughout PARC, and we are beginning to accumulate feedback from users engaged in a variety of tasks and meeting types. At minimum, this feedback will guide us in making incremental improvements to Tivoli. More importantly, we are interested in examining in some detail how Tivoli is utilized for specific meeting practices. Our goal is to better understand what functionality could be added to Tivoli in order to support or augment these meeting practices. For example, Tivoli is frequently used to support brainstorming meetings. We are currently exploring how Tivoli could be expanded to support typical brainstorming activities such as list-making, categorization, and voting without altering its fundamental whiteboard-like nature.

In some sense, our search to expand Tivoli to provide support for more specific meeting practices reflects the other side of the tension between a simple, facile, whiteboard-like interface and an application that takes maximum advantage of the computational power behind the Liveboard to support its users' work practices. Clearly, the design challenge for this kind of system is to satisfy both of these goals.

3. Actually, the situation was much worse. The double tap was also loaded with a second function: to indicate a switch between drawing and wiping mode. A double tap would first cause the previous stroke to be interpreted as a gesture; if the gesture recognizer did not recognize it, then it caused a mode jump. Thus, an inadvertent double tap usually threw the user into wipe mode without warning, a dangerous move to say the least! This mode toggling functionality was removed from double tap in subsequent versions.

REFERENCES

1 Sara A. Bly. A Use of Drawing Surfaces in Different Collaborative Settings. *Proceedings of CSCW 88 Conference on Computer Supported Cooperative Work*. Portland, 1988, pp. 250-256.

2 Sara A. Bly and Scott L. Minneman. Commune: A Shared Drawing Surface. In *SIGOIS Bulletin*, Massachusetts, 1990, pp. 184-192.

3 Eric A. Bier, Steve Freeman. MMM: A User Interface Architecture for Shared Editors on a Single Screen. *Proceedings of the ACM Symposium on User Interface Software and Technology*, UIST'91, 1991.

4 Tom Brinck, Louis M. Gomez. A Collaborative Medium for the Support of Conversational Props. To appear in *Proceedings of CSCW 92 Conference on Computer Supported Cooperative Work*. Toronto, 1992.

5 William Buxton. Chunking and phrasing and the design of human-computer dialogues, *Proceedings of the IFIP World Computer Congress*, Dublin, Ireland, 1986, pp. 475-480.

6 Robert Carr, Dan Shafer. *The Power of the PenPoint*. Addison-Wesley, 1991.

7 Scott Elrod, Richard Bruce, David Goldberg, Frank Halasz, William Janssen, David Lee, Kim McCall, Elin R. Pedersen, Ken Pier, John Tang and Brent Welch. Liveboard: A large interactive display supporting group meetings, presentations and remote collaboration. *Proceedings of CHI '92 Conference on Human Factors in Computing Systems*, Monterey, CA, 1992.

8 Hiroshi Ishii, Minoru Kobayashi, Jonathan Grudin. Integration of Inter-personal space and shared workspace: ClearBoard design and experiments. *Proceedings of CSCW 92 Conference on Computer-Supported Cooperative Work*, Toronto, 1992, pp. 33-42

9 Fred Lakin, John Wambaugh, Larry Leifer, Dave Cannon, Cecelia Sivard. The Electronic Design Notebook: Performing Medium and Processing Medium. *Visual Computer: International Journal of Computer Graphics*, 214-226, August 1989.

10 Kim McCall, Thomas Moran, Bill van Melle, Elin Pedersen, Frank Halasz. Design principles for sharing in Tivoli, a whiteboard meeting-support tool. *Position paper for the Workshop on Real Time Group Drawing and Writing Tools, CSCW 92 Conference on Computer-Supported Cooperative Work*, Toronto, 1992.

11 Mark Stefik, Greg Foster, Danny Bobrow, Ken Kahn, Stan Lanning, Lucy Suchman. Beyond the Chalkboard: Computer support for collaboration and problem solving in meetings. *Communications of the ACM, 30(1)*, 1987. Also in Irene Greif, editor, *Computer Supported Work: A Book of Readings*, Morgan Kaufmann Publishers, 1988, pp. 335-366.

12 John Tang. *Listing, Drawing, and Gesturing in Design: A Study of the Use of Shared Workspaces by Design Teams*. Ph.D. Thesis. Stanford University, Department of Mechanical Engineering, 1989.

13 Mark Weiser. The Computer for the 21st Century. *Scientific American, Sept. 1991*.

A Taxonomy of See-Through Tools

Eric A. Bier, Maureen C. Stone, Ken Fishkin, William Buxton†, Thomas Baudel‡
Xerox PARC, 3333 Coyote Hill Rd., Palo Alto, CA 94304
†University of Toronto, CSRI, Toronto, ON, Canada, M5S 1A4
‡Université de Paris-Sud, LRI, 91 405 Orsay Cedex, France
E-mail: {bier, stone, fishkin} @parc.xerox.com, willy@dgp.toronto.edu, thomas@lri.fr

ABSTRACT

In current interfaces, users select objects, apply operations, and change viewing parameters in distinct steps that require switching attention among several screen areas. Our See-Through Interface™ software reduces steps by locating tools on a transparent sheet that can be moved over applications with one hand using a trackball, while the other hand controls a mouse cursor. The user clicks *through* a tool onto application objects, simultaneously selecting an operation and an operand. Tools may include graphical filters that display a customized view of application objects. Compared to traditional interactors, these tools save steps, require no permanent screen space, reduce temporal modes, apply to multiple applications, and facilitate customization. This paper presents a taxonomy of see-through tools that considers variations in each of the steps they perform. As examples, we describe particular see-through tools that perform graphical editing and text editing operations.

CR Categories and Subject Descriptors: I.3.6 [**Computer Graphics**]: Methodology and Techniques—interaction techniques; H.5.2 [**Information Interfaces and Presentation**]: User Interfaces—interaction styles; I.3.3 [**Computer Graphics**]: Picture/Image Generation—viewing algorithms; I.3.4 [**Computer Graphics**]: Graphics Utilities—graphics editors

Key Words: user interface, control panel, transparent, multi-hand, viewing filter, button, lens, menu, macro

INTRODUCTION

With software applications becoming more complex, it is difficult to organize user interfaces so that application functionality is easy to find, easy to learn, and quick to use. Limited screen space encourages the use of tools such as pop-up menus and hierarchical menus, which take time and attention to activate, and temporal modes, which cause confusion. Users must often select objects, apply operations, and change viewing parameters in distinct steps that require switching attention among several screen areas. In addition, the non-dominant hand is often relegated to trivial activities, such as holding down a modifier key, that do not make full use of its capabilities. A new user interface paradigm, the See-Through Interface™ system, addresses these issues.

Our interface allows users to interact with applications through a set of movable semi-transparent tools, called *see-through tools* or *click-through tools*. These tools are organized onto a sheet, called a Toolglass™ sheet. Tools may include graphical filters, called Magic Lens™ filters, that present a modified view of the shapes underneath them. The toolglass sheet can be positioned with the non-dominant hand and triggered with the dominant hand. For example, a right-handed user may translate and resize the sheet using a trackball and thumbwheel with the left hand and apply the tools by positioning a cursor using a mouse in the right hand. Together, the cursor, toolglass sheet, and applications create a three-layer interface as shown in figure 1. Tools are grouped into units called *tiles*. A toolglass sheet displays one tile at a time, just as a HyperCard stack [10] displays one card at a time.

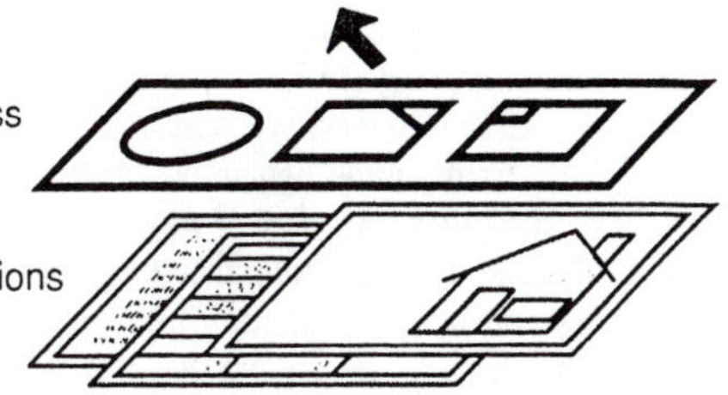

Figure 1. The three layers of our interface.

Click-through tools are used in two, possibly simultaneous, steps. First, the user positions the tool over an application object. Second, the user clicks on that object, through the tool, with a cursor. For example, in figure 2, the user has placed a color-changing tool (shown in thick lines) over a circle and a triangle (shown in thin lines). The triangle in the upper left corner of the tool shows the color that it applies. The user applies the color to the circle by clicking a mouse button while the cursor arrow is over both the tool and the circle.

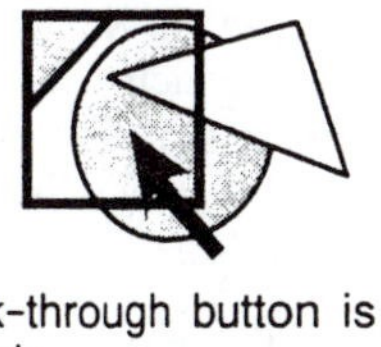

Figure 2. A click-through button is used to change the area color of a circle.

Click-through tools can save steps relative to traditional interactors. For example, the tool in figure 2 selects both an operation to apply (change color) and an object to apply it to (the circle) in a single two-handed gesture. This can save time and reduce cognitive load, because the user can combine more steps into a single mental "chunk" [6]. Initial user studies show performance improvements and user preference for click-through tools [13].

Toolglass sheets can be moved from application to application, providing a common interface to several applications. For example, the same button can be used to change the color of a shape in a graphical editor or a word in a text editor. In addition, our interface alters the traditional relationship of application programs and data; instead of loading a document into an application program and then working within the limitations of that program, the user can bring applications, in the form of

CHI94-4/94 Boston, Massachusetts USA
© 1994 ACM 0-89791-650-6/94/0358...$3.50

see-through tools, to the document.

See-through tools make good use of the coarse-positioning skills of the non-dominant hand, which have been described by Guiard [11]. However, unlike interfaces that require holding down modifier keys, this interface can be used, with reduced speed, when only one hand is available; the user can drag a tool into place with the mouse cursor and then apply it.

These tools have many other potential advantages. Toolglass sheets take up no permanent screen space. See-through tools replace temporal modes, which can be difficult to get into and out of, with spatial modes, which are entered and exited by moving the sheet. They allow the user's gaze and the mouse cursor to remain in the work area. They can be rearranged by copying or dragging. They can be composed by overlapping, providing users with a visual way to create their own macros. They can be added incrementally to a user interface based on traditional interactors. Finally, when a tool includes a magic lens filter, it provides the user with a modified view of the application objects that helps in the use of that tool.

The discovery of many examples of useful see-through tools has made it clear that they define a large new design space for user interfaces. In this paper, we describe some tools that we have found interesting and instructive. We also describe a taxonomy of see-through tools, which provides both an overview of the see-through interface system for those interested in understanding its potential, and an understanding of the ways that these tools may vary that will aid implementors of such tools. We structure this material as a taxonomy because our own exploration of the see-through interface paradigm proceeded by discovering particular tools and then categorizing them. A previous paper on this interface describes its implementation and its uses for graphical editing and visualization [4].

See-through tools have been implemented on several platforms. Most of the tools described here are implemented in the Multi-Device Multi-User Multi-Editor (MMM) framework [3] in the Cedar programming environment [22], which runs on SunOS. Tools for visualizing maps and editing graphics are implemented in C++ in the X Window system. An implementation on the Apple Macintosh is in use for human factors studies [13]. The tools of figures 5, 6, 11, 14 and 15 are envisionments of tools that will be implemented in the future; the rest are existing tools.

The rest of this paper is organized as follows. We describe related work. Then we describe five basic steps in the operation of a see-through tool. The next five sections describe a set of see-through tools that illustrate variations in each of these five basic steps. In addition, each of these sections describes one or more types of variation of a given basic step and expresses each type of variation as an axis of our taxonomy. The remaining sections summarize the taxonomy and present conclusions and plans for future work.

RELATED WORK

Our work on see-through tools builds on a large body of previous work in a number of disciplines, including two-handed interfaces, movable tools, transparent tools, and visual filters. In addition, the taxonomy presented here relates to previously published taxonomies of user interface components.

Two-handed interfaces. As in VIDEOPLACE, our interface allows the use of two hands simultaneously [14]. However, our tools make an asymmetric use of the hands, with the non-dominant hand defining a coarse frame in which the dominant hand works. As noted by Guiard, such asymmetric bimanual activity is both natural for people and very common in everyday activities [11]. Buxton and Myers showed in a scrolling and text selection activity that users tend to overlap the use of both hands [7]. Our interface takes advantage of this insight to support a general-purpose user interface paradigm.

Movable tools. Previous systems allow the user to position commands over the application work area. For example, Macintosh tear-off menus [16] can be dragged by their borders and positioned for later use. Our tools differ in that the tool and cursor can move independently.

Transparent tools. Many CAD tools display partly-transparent stationary menus on top of the application work area. The Markup graphics editor displayed a semi-transparent pop-up menu of modes [17]. Recent work allows menus to be made transparent in X windows [1]. One author has proposed the use of transparent windows [20]. Our tools are unique in that they are both two-handed and use the position of the cursor over a tool and over the underlying application to determine the result of an interaction.

Visual filters. Many window systems include a movable pixel magnifier to enlarge a region of the screen. Recent image processing systems support a wide variety of filter operations including composition of overlapping filters [19]. *A portal* in the Pad system can present a modified view of the part of the workspace seen through it [18]. Related work on visual filters has been described in more detail [4]. Previous systems did not allow the filter to be moved with the non-dominant hand nor to be combined with click-through tools.

Taxonomies. In their classic paper, Foley and Wallace describe the value of virtual devices and identify *pick*, *button*, *locator*, and *valuator* as categories of tools [9]. See-through tools blur some of these categories. A click-through *button* can also be a *pick* because the user can click on a button and an application object at the same time. Likewise, a *button* can also be a *locator* because the user can click on a button and specify an application position at the same time. While their taxonomy is concerned almost exclusively with function, ours includes issues of triggering, appearance, motion, and instantiation.

OPERATION OF SEE-THROUGH TOOLS

The toolglass sheet is a layer between the cursor and the application, as shown in figure 3. A tool on the sheet intercepts input from the user and delivers modified input to the application. Likewise, it intercepts display requests from the application and produces a modified image on the screen. The tool can be moved relative to both the application and the cursor.

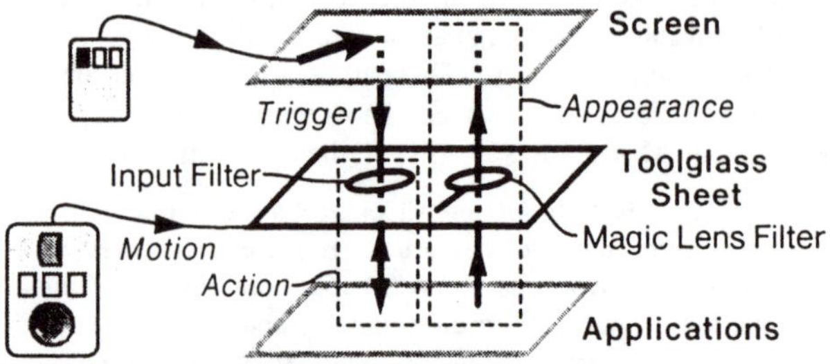

Figure 3. Information flow in a see-through tool.

The italic labels in figure 3 show four steps in the operation of a see-through tool: receiving a triggering event from the user (*Trigger*), computing an action based on that event and having an application perform that action (*Action*), computing the appearance of the tool and the application as seen through it (*Appearance*), and moving over application objects (*Motion*). A fifth step, instantiation on a toolglass sheet (*Instantiation*), is not shown. This section defines and describes these five steps.

Trigger. As with traditional tools, the user can trigger a see-through tool with a variety of actions including mouse clicks or pen gestures. Any trigger may come to a tool via another see-through tool that overlaps it.

Action. In response to a triggering event, a see-through tool produces a command to be executed. This command may be executed by the tool itself or passed to the application underneath it. The action may cause data to flow from the tool to the application and/or from the application to the tool, as indicated by the bidirectional arrows in figure 3. While many actions consist of a short message, actions may contain a large quantity of data, such as an entire disk file. The action produced may be applicable to only a single application, or may be expressed in an application-independent format. Application-independent commands implemented in our system include selection, creation, deletion, and modification of graphical properties, such as font and color. When several see-through tools are composed by overlapping them, the action may include contributions from each of these tools.

Appearance. Like traditional tools, a see-through tool may draw a picture that identifies its boundary and function. However, because it overlaps underlying applications, a tool's picture often contains elements that are transparent, translucent, or small in order to avoid obscuring the application underneath. In addition, a tool may modify the appearance of the application underneath using a magic lens filter [4][5][21]. For example, a tool that selects text characters may display visible symbols to distinguish SPACEs from TABs. A related paper describes many uses of movable filters in user interfaces [21]. Thus, we discuss filters only briefly in this paper.

Motion. In general, a toolglass sheet and all of its tools translate as a unit under the control of a 2D valuator such as a trackball and resize as a unit under the control of a 1D valuator such as a thumbwheel. However, some tools may change their relationship to the sheet (and to other tools), e.g., by translating, rotation, or resizing. This relative motion may be triggered either by an explicit request or in response to the presence of particular applications or application objects below the tool.

Instantiation. Before it can be used, a see-through tool must be instantiated on a toolglass sheet. The tool may appear whenever this sheet is used, only when this sheet is in a particular temporary mode, or only when this sheet is in a particular position relative to the application. The tool may be customized to a greater or lesser degree by the user. A tool may be built from any number of see-through components; a simple tool will have only one component, a complex tool may have dozens or more.

Each of the next five sections considers one of the five steps, presenting examples that illustrate variations in that step's behavior. Where several types of variation are present for a single step, each type is discussed in its own subsection. Each type of variation is an axis of our taxonomy.

TRIGGER

This section describes one axis of our taxonomy: trigger type.

The user can trigger a tool in a variety of ways, including clicking with a mouse, dragging (pressing a mouse button, moving the mouse while the button is held down and then releasing at a new position), or gesturing (e.g., drawing a stroke, character or symbol on the tool). In addition, tools can receive input from other see-through tools that are layered above them.

While the triggering events are familiar, doing them over see-through tools instead of over editors or traditional interactors allows more information to be extracted from each event; the tool and the application are both under the cursor position, so each token of the input can operate on the tool, the application or both. For example, one click on the button of figure 1 chooses a command and an operand simultaneously.

Dragging events may begin inside a click-through button and end outside of it. When applied to a shape creation palette this results in a "drop-and-drag" (not drag-and-drop) operation, as shown in figure 4. Here, each dashed shape is a click-through button. When the mouse button goes down over a shape, a copy of that shape is added to the scene, made opaque, and attached to the cursor. The object then moves with the cursor until the mouse button goes up, allowing fine positioning of the new shape.

Figure 4. Drop-and-drag from a shape palette.

Dragging may also begin outside of a tool and end inside it. For example, a shape may be dragged in a traditional way to a printer icon located on the toolglass sheet, causing the document to be printed. This is drag-and-drop with the target of the drop on the sheet.

A stroke gesture may begin in one part of a tool and end in another. Figure 5 shows a tool that combines single stroke gestures (like those used in Kurtenbach's Marking Menus [15]) with pie menus [12]. In figure 5(a), the user strokes from a graphical shape (a triangle) positioned under the circular center button of the menu to a button labelled "Fill Color", to apply the fill color of the triangle to the rectangular prototype object that is part of the tool. Conversely, in figure 5(b), the user strokes from the "Dashes" button to the circular center button to apply the dash pattern of the prototype to the triangle. Figure 5(c) shows the result.

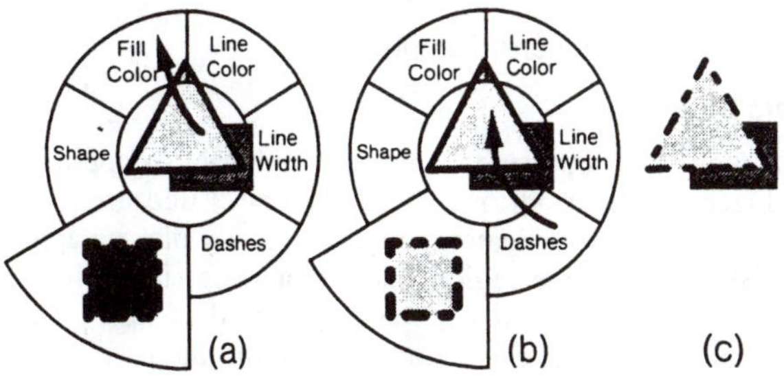

Figure 5. Property Sampler/Applicator. (a) Sampling fill color. (b) Applying dashes. (c) The result.

A common problem with gesture interfaces is that it is hard for the system to distinguish input that is intended as a gesture from input intended as writing or drawing. Our solution is to use a see-through tool as the gesture interpreter. In figure 6, the user moves a gesture-interpreting tool (solid black lines) over a drawing and deletes a triangle with a gesture. Note that the same gestures can be used in multiple applications because the gesture interpreter can be moved from one application to another.

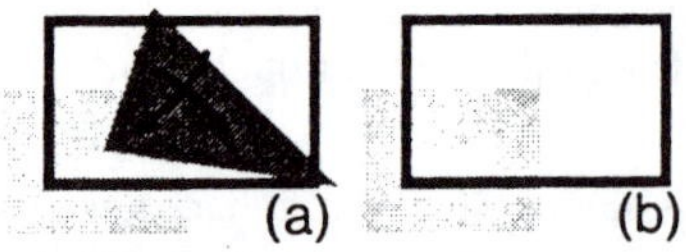

Figure 6. A gesture tool. (a) A deletion gesture, 'X', is made. (b) The triangle is deleted.

ACTION

This section describes seven axes of our taxonomy that are related to the action step of a tool: input transparency, data direction, data magnitude, application independence, application, operation class, and composition.

Input Transparency

In addition to *click-through* tools, which pass commands and cursor coordinates to the application beneath them, toolglass sheets include traditional, *click-on*, tools, whose function does not depend on the relative position of the cursor and the application. Our click-on tools include simple buttons, radio buttons, cycling-value buttons, on-off buttons, sliders and dials. Several of these buttons are used in the Lens Sampler tool shown in figure 7. This tool uses radio buttons to select a lens shape and filter type. The slider modifies a lens parameter. "Settings" is an on-off button that makes the radio buttons appear or disappear. The navigation buttons are simple buttons that cause a different tile (set of tools), to be displayed. Finally, the "Trackball Button" is a simple button that connects the trackball and thumbwheel to this sheet, allowing them to move and resize it. This connection is needed because several sheets may be on-screen at once.

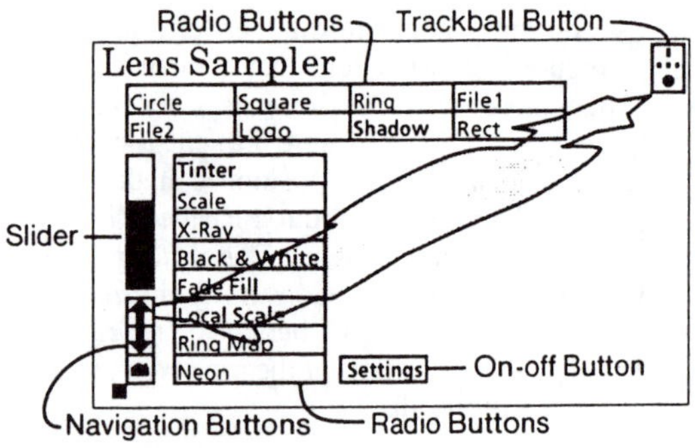

Figure 7. The Lens Sampler tile.

Data Direction

Our tools can both send commands and data to applications and receive commands and data from them. Because it is positioned over the application, a tool can easily pick up application shapes from the region under it or drop shapes into this region. For example, the graphics clipboard of figure 8 picks up a shape when the clipboard is empty and the user clicks on a shape, as shown in figure 8(a). As the clipboard moves, it displays a fragment of the copied shape (figure 8(b)). The entire shape can be pasted somewhere else (figure 8(c)). Moving the clipboard leaves the new copy behind while the fragment continues to move with the tool (figure 8(d)). Clicking the square in the upper left corner clears the tool for reuse.

Some tools mostly *send* information to the application, such as the shape creation palette of figure 4. Others mostly *receive* information. For example, the Print Tool of figure 9(a) picks up application shapes, clips them to a rectangle, positions them on a page of specified size and creates a file that prints as shown in figure 9(b).

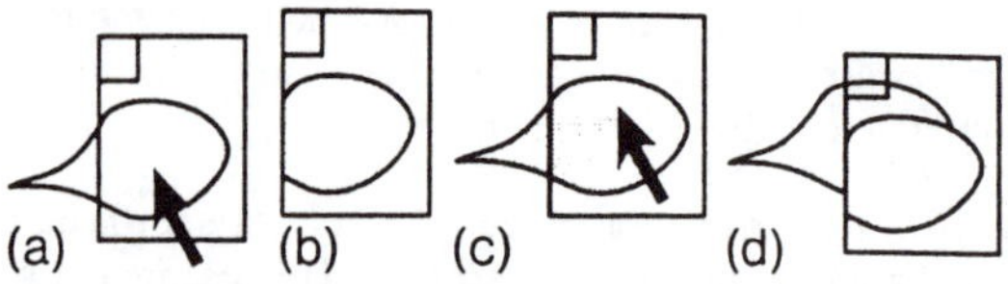

Figure 8. Graphics Clipboard.

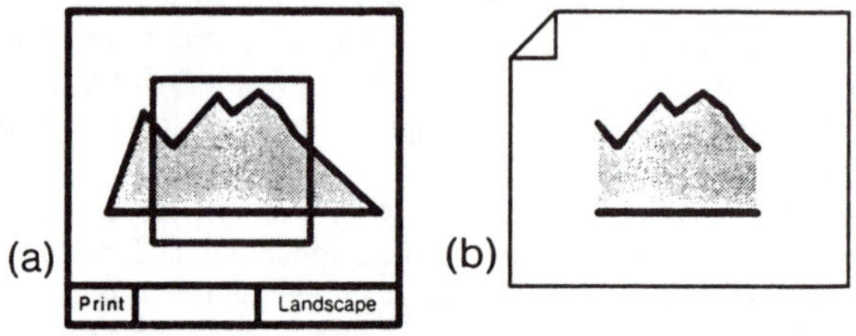

Figure 9. The Print Tool (a) Specifying the print parameters. (b) The resulting printed page.

Data Magnitude

Some tools send only a small amount of information to the application. The color-changing button of figure 2, for example, sends two short commands, one to select the shape at the mouse coordinates and another to change the color of that shape. Other tools may send large amounts of information. For example, the Clip Art tool, shown in figure 10, can transfer an entire illustration in a single click. The bottom part of this tool is a hierarchical file browser, showing the sub-directories and files in the current directory. Pressing the UP button causes the tool to display the parent directory of the current one. Clicking on a file icon with the left mouse button drops the contents of the file into the application below. Clicking with the middle mouse button causes the contents of that file to be shown in the upper part of the tool; the tile of figure 10 shows the picture "/ClipArt/Arrows/TriangleArrows". These shapes can then be drop-and-dragged into the application.

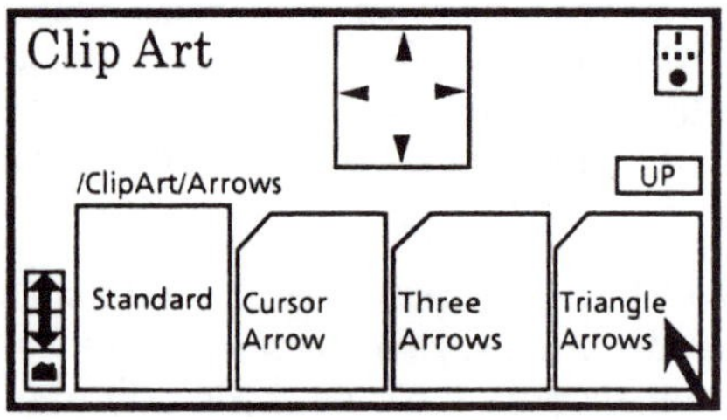

Figure 10. The Clip Art tool.

Application Independence

Tools can be designed either to work over a single application or to work over multiple applications. In the first case, the tool and application can exchange commands and data in formats specific to that application. In the second case, the tool must either express commands and data in a standard format, or must contain software to handle the data and commands of each application over which it is used.

Application-independent tools are more valuable because the

investment in learning to use them pays off in many different contexts. This is in contrast to current tools that are bound to an application, requiring, as Bruce Tognazzini put it, "having to slide your entire house inside a hammer before you can hang a picture on the wall" [8].

Application

See-though tools can be used over virtually any screen-based application, including illustrators, text editors, 3D modelers, spreadsheets, and CAD packages. Another interesting possibility is to use see-through tools over traditional tools. For example, figure 11 shows a tool that creates a graphical macro by picking up click-on buttons from a traditional control panel. Figure 11(a) shows part of the control panel of a graphics editor. These traditional iconic buttons set dash patterns and determine whether lines will have round or square ends. Figure 11(b) shows the macro tool. The upper part of this tool is a clipboard that copies buttons. The user has picked up a dash pattern button and a round-line-ends button by clicking on them through this region (recall figure 8). The resulting tool is placed over an oval shape (which originally had a solid border) and applied. The resulting oval has a dash pattern with round dots as shown.

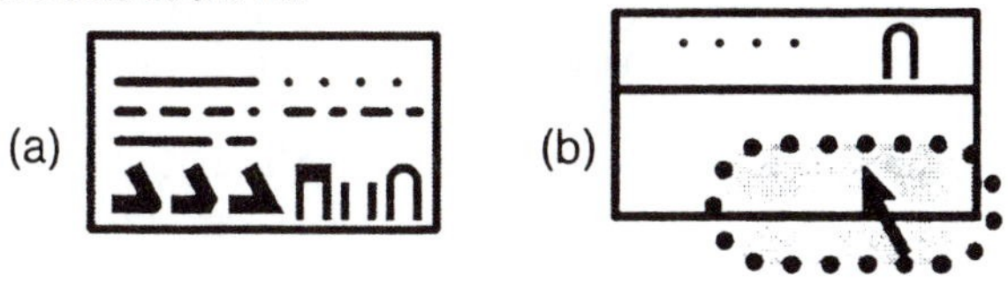

Figure 11. Making a macro. (a) A traditional control panel. (b) Applying a macro to an oval.

Operation Class

See-through tools can perform any operation that traditional buttons can perform, plus other operations normally associated with modes. In a graphics editor for example, these tools can select, create, delete, and modify shapes. Examples of these operations are shown throughout this paper. Here we describe some unusual tools for deletion and modification.

Deletion tools can be built with magic lens filters that make it easy to find the object to be deleted and make it easy to undo a mistake. For example, a filter in the tool can show the objects that were most recently deleted. Clicking on a "ghost" object causes its deletion to be undone.

Of the many modification tools, see-through tools that modify shape, position, size, or orientation are particularly interesting because they can incorporate visual guidelines, such as the alignment lines and circles of snap-dragging [2]. Figure 14, which will be described below, is an example.

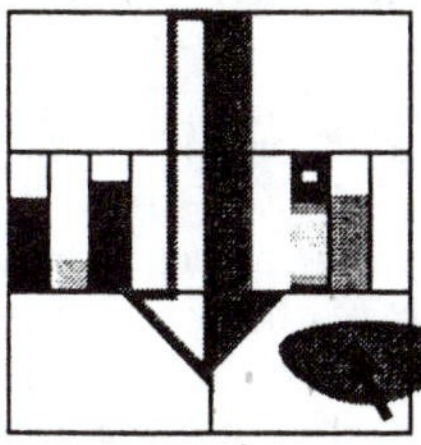

Figure 12. Color editor for fill and line colors.

See-through tools can also integrate the process of getting a current value, modifying it, and applying it. The color editor of figure 12 has four click-through buttons and six sliders. The upper-left and upper-right rectangles pick up a line color and fill color respectively. The red-green-blue sliders on the left or the hue-saturation-value sliders on the right can modify the color. The arrow in the middle shows the resulting color. The lower-left and lower-right rectangles apply this color to lines or filled regions, respectively. The shape in figure 12 is receiving a new fill color.

Composition

Some see-through tools compose with other tools when the tools are overlapped to form a stack. For example, we can combine a fill-color setting tool with a line-color setting tool to form a tool that sets both fill and line color.

To support composition, a tool must be willing to accept a command that has come from another tool and emit a modified command that blends its function into the received command. This blending may be done in several ways: A tool may append its command to end of the incoming one, prepend its command to the beginning, or modify the incoming command in a more general way. For example, a tool that protects illustrations from being edited would remove, from any command it receives, all requests to edit the objects below.

APPEARANCE

This section describes two axes related to appearance: output transparency and lens presence.

Output Transparency

Well-designed see-through tools must be visible enough to see, but simple enough so as not to clutter the user's view of the applications below. For some tools, an acceptable appearance may require using stippled, translucent, or transparent regions. Some of our translucent tools use a color-tinting magic lens filter [4] to draw their interiors.

Lens Presence

Adding a magic lens filter to a click-through tool can improve the usability of the tool by revealing information appropriate to the tool's operation. Conversely, adding input handling to a filter increases its utility, by making it possible to act on the information revealed by the filter. Figure 13(a) shows a click-through tool being used to select the hidden upper left corner of a square. Figure 13(b) shows a filter that produces a wireframe view of objects seen through it. Figure 13(c) is a tool that combines the click-through tool and the filter to create a tool that aids selection of hidden corners.

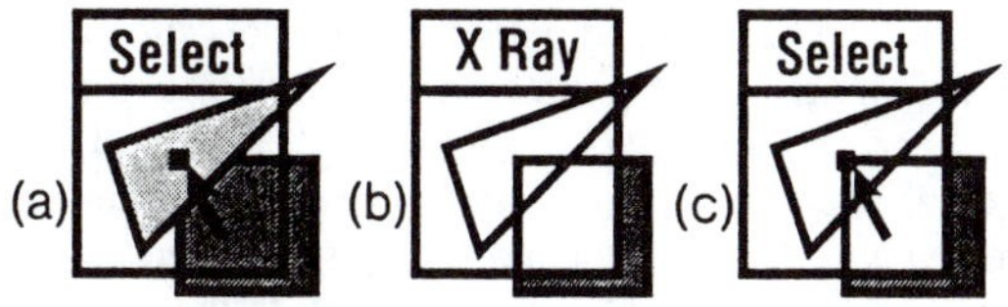

Figure 13. Three tools. (a) Vertex selector. (b) X-ray filter. (c) Vertex selector with x-ray filter.

MOTION

This section describes one axis related to motion: moves with.

The toolglass sheet moves relative to objects on other layers, including the cursor, the screen, and applications. Each of these other objects provides a reference frame that a see-through tool may move with. Most of our tools move and resize as a unit with the sheet. However, our grid tools draw their grids relative to the coordinate system of the screen (to allow inter-application alignment) or relative to a particular application.

Some tools are a hybrid, moving with the sheet some of the time and with scene objects at other times. So long as the object doesn't move into the space of other tools, these motions cause little confusion. For example, figure 14(a) shows a tool whose parts translate relative to scene objects. This alignment tool consists of two circles. When the center of the tool is positioned near a scene vertex, the circles move to snap their centers to that vertex using snap-dragging gravity [2] as shown in figure 14(b). The user can then use the circles to add a new line of known length as shown in figure 14(c). This tool is like a template that is held in the non-dominant hand while the user draws with the dominant hand.

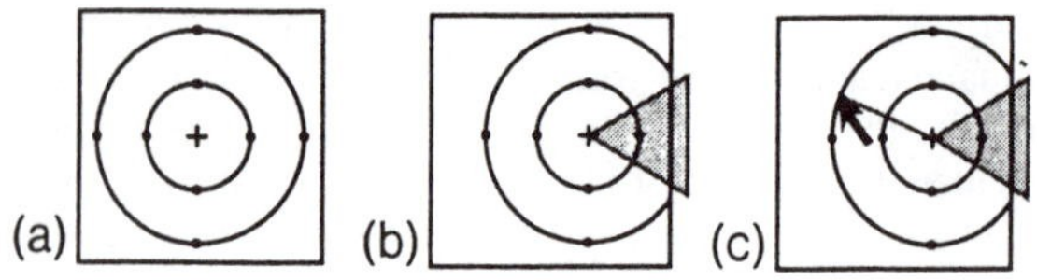

Figure 14. An alignment circles tool.

Tools may even move with specific application objects. For example, the large rectangle in Figure 15(b) is a magic lens filter that creates a small control panel next to the left edge of *each* text object. The control panel displays the current font size of the text and includes arrows that increase or decrease the font size when pressed. This tool replaces traditional tools that select text, query its current size, and change that size.

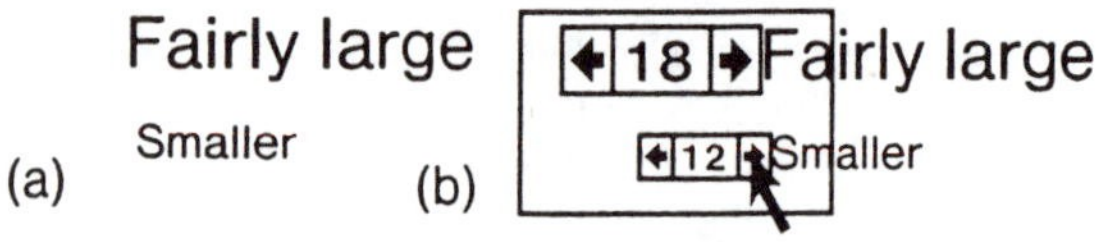

Figure 15. A font-size tool. (a) Some text. (b) The filter reveals font size controls. The user makes some text larger.

Tools may move in a variety of ways including translating, rotating, or scaling. For example, we envision a text creation tool that can be rotated relative to the sheet. By rotating this tool, the user indicates the orientation that new text will have.

INSTANTIATION

This section describes our final three axes, which relate to instantiation: customization, persistence, and complexity.

Customization

See-through tools can be customized in a variety of ways. Parameters can be changed with click-on tools such as sliders, dials, and multi-valued buttons. In addition, a tool can be moved or copied within a tile by clicking on a small button in one corner of the tool with different mouse buttons. Alternatively, when two toolglass sheets are overlapped, tools can be "punched through" from one sheet to the other. If one tool is copied on top of another tool, the tools are composed, if possible, to form a macro. Customized tiles can be saved to disk and retrieved for later use.

Persistence

Some see-through tools always appear in the same place on a particular tile, or on all tiles (e.g., like the background card in HyperCard). For example, the Navigation and Trackball buttons in figure 7 appear on all tiles of our Cedar implementation.

On the other hand, to reduce screen clutter, other tools appear only when needed. For example, the radio buttons in figure 7 appear when the button named "Settings" is on and disappear when it is off. Likewise, the font-size changing buttons of figure 15 appear only when text strings are present.

Complexity

While many of the tools described here have only a small number of components, powerful tools can be built having many. For example, the color editor of figure 12 has two color lifting buttons, two color applying buttons and six sliders. Useful tools may be much more complicated than this, perhaps combining all of the functionality of existing control panels or property sheets into a single see-through tool.

SUMMARY OF THE TAXONOMY

Table 1 summarizes the axes of variation discussed in this paper. This taxonomy is not complete. There are other kinds of variation for each of the operational steps that have been discussed and other operational steps to consider. However, this taxonomy does provide an initial map of the design space for see-through tools.

While a few of these 14 axes depend on each other, they are largely orthogonal. Thus, any value on one axis can be combined with almost any value on any other axis, resulting in a large design space. The Composition and Input Transparency axes are related, in that composition rules on input make sense only if some overlapped tools are click-through. Persistence and Moves With are related in that tools that appear in response to data will most likely move with that data rather than with something else.

Trigger Type:	Click, Drag-out, Drag-in, Drag-out-and-in, Gesture, Overlapped tool
Input Transparency:	Click-through, Click-on
Data Direction:	Down, Up, Both
Data Magnitude:	Simple command, ..., Database
Application Indep.:	No, Yes
Application:	Graphics, Text, Other click-throughs, Traditional tools, ...
Operation Class:	Select, Create, Delete, Modify, ...
Composition:	Append, Prepend, Modify
Output Transparency:	Opaque, Stippled, Translucent, Transparent
Moves With:	Sheet, Application, Both, Object, Cursor
Lens Presence:	No, Yes
Customization:	None, Parameters, Editable
Persistence:	Always, Temporal mode, Appears in context
Complexity:	Single part, ..., Many parts

Table 1. 14 Taxonomy Axes and Typical Values.

As the examples in this paper indicate, interesting tools can be found throughout the space determined by these axes.

CONCLUSIONS

We have constructed a taxonomy of see-through tools by looking for variability in the ways they respond to five basic events: triggering, generating an action, drawing, moving, and instantiating. For each of these categories of response, we found one or more types of variability, producing 14 axes in our taxonomy. At the same time, we have presented over a dozen examples of novel see-through tools that motivate the different kinds of variability.

This paper does not present the only possible taxonomy of see-through tools, and none of our example tools is likely to be the best see-through tool for performing a given function. However, our examples and taxonomy do show that, far from being just a new way to present transparent menus, the see-through interface system is a vast new design space for user interface tools. Furthermore, effective tools can be found throughout the space, making it well worth exploring.

This paper should help to stimulate the imaginations of those interested in creating see-through tools. In addition it should be of value to those building toolkits for see-through tools. Each of our axes suggests a kind of tool variability that the toolkit may need to support.

FUTURE WORK

Work continues to explore and extend our taxonomy of tools, and to build and test these tools on a variety of platforms. Tools are being designed for use over new applications, including text editors, map visualizers, multi-media and spreadsheets. We are developing alternative ways to position, size, and navigate through these tools, including use with one hand. Finally, we are designing additional human factors studies to extend our understanding of how see-through tools are used in practice.

ACKNOWLEDGMENTS

We thank John Tukey for stimulating conversations and for coining "Toolglass" as one word. We thank Randy Pausch for ideas and encouragement, Tony DeRose for co-inventing the magic lens filter concept, and Matt Conway for implementations of see-through tools on a new platform (X windows) and in new domains. We thank Jock Mackinlay, Polle Zellweger, Ken Pier and our anonymous reviewers for substantive comments that lead to an improved taxonomy and paper. Finally, we thank Xerox for its support.

REFERENCES

1. Joel F. Bartlett. Transparent controls for interactive graphics. WRL Technical Note TN-30, Digital Equipment Corporation, Palo Alto, CA, July 1992.
2. Eric A. Bier and Maureen Stone. Snap-dragging. Proceedings of Siggraph '86 (Dallas, August), *Computer Graphics*, Vol. 20, No. 4, ACM, 1986, pp. 233-240.
3. Eric A. Bier and Steve Freeman. MMM: a user interface architecture for shared editors on a single screen. *Proceedings of the ACM SIGGRAPH Symposium on User Interface Software and Technology* (South Carolina, November), ACM, 1991, pp. 79-86.
4. Eric A. Bier, Maureen C. Stone, Ken Pier, William Buxton, and Tony D. DeRose. Toolglass and Magic Lenses: The See-Through Interface. Proceedings of Siggraph '93 (Anaheim, August), *Computer Graphics* Annual Conference Series, ACM, 1993, pp. 73-80.
5. Eric A. Bier, Maureen C. Stone, Ken Pier, Ken Fishkin, Thomas Baudel, Matt Conway, William Buxton and Tony DeRose. Toolglass and Magic Lenses: The See-Through Interface (videotape, 10 minutes). In the formal video program of this conference.
6. William Buxton. Chunking and phrasing and the design of human-computer dialogues. *Proceedings of the IFIP World Computer Congress* (Dublin, Ireland), 1986, pp. 475-480.
7. William Buxton and Brad A. Myers. A study in two-handed input. *Proceedings of CHI '86 Human Factors in Computing Systems* (Boston, April), ACM, 1986, pp. 321-326.
8. A. Brady Farrand, Marc Rochkind, Jean-Marie Chauvet, Bruce Tognazzini, David C. Smith. Common elements in today's graphical user interfaces: the good, the bad, and the ugly. *Proceedings of Interchi '93, Human Factors in Computing Systems* (Amsterdam, April), ACM, 1993, pp. 470-473.
9. J. D. Foley and V. L Wallace. The art of natural graphic man machine conversation. *Proceedings of the IEEE*, Vol. 62, No. 4, April 1974. Reprinted in IEEE Tutorial on Computer Graphics (2nd ed.), pp. 315-324.
10. Danny Goodman. *The Complete HyperCard Handbook*. Bantam Books, 1987.
11. Yves Guiard. Asymmetric division of labor in human skilled bimanual action: the kinematic chain as a model. *The Journal of Motor Behavior*, Vol. 19, No. 4, 1987, pp. 486-517.
12. Don Hopkins. The design and implementation of pie menus. *Dr. Dobb's Journal*, Vol. 16, No. 12, December 1991, pp. 16-26.
13. Paul Kabbash, Abigail Sellen, and William Buxton. A comparison of two-handed click-through tools to traditional menu input. Included in these proceedings.
14. Myron W. Krueger, Thomas Gionfriddo, and Katrin Hinrichsen. VIDEOPLACE—An artificial reality. *Proceedings of CHI '85, Human Factors in Computer Systems* (San Francisco, April), ACM, 1985, pp. 35-40.
15. Gordon Kurtenbach and William Buxton. Issues in combining marking and direct manipulation techniques. *Proceedings of the ACM Symposium on User Interface Software and Technology* (UIST '91, S. Carolina, November), ACM, 1991, pp. 137-144.
16. *MacDraw Manual*. Apple Computer Inc. Cupertino, CA 95014, 1984.
17. William M. Newman. Markup. *Alto User's Handbook*, Xerox Palo Alto Research Center, 3333 Coyote Hill Rd., Palo Alto, CA 94304, 1979.
18. Ken Perlin and David Fox. Pad: an alternative approach to the computer interface. *Proceedings of Siggraph '93* (Anaheim, August), *Computer Graphics* Annual Conference Series, ACM, 1993, pp. 57-64.
19. *ImageVision*, Silicon Graphics Inc., Mtn. View, CA.
20. Loretta Staples. Representation in virtual space: visual convention in the graphical user interface, figure 14. *Proceedings of Interchi '93, Human Factors in Computing Systems* (Amsterdam, April), ACM, 1993, pp. 348-354.
21. Maureen C. Stone, Ken Fishkin, Eric A. Bier. The movable filter as a user interface tool. Included in these proceedings.
22. Daniel C. Swinehart, Polle T. Zellweger, Richard J. Beach, and Robert B. Hagmann. A structural view of the Cedar programming environment. *ACM Transactions on Programming Languages and Systems*, Vol. 8, No. 4, ACM, 1986, pp. 419-490.

Chapter 8

Speech, Language, and Audition

Natural language and the audio channel are the primary means of human-to-human communication, but they are little used between human and machine. Yet times are changing, and in this chapter we investigate user interface issues associated with speech, nonspeech audio, and natural language.

When one considers communicating with sound, speech generally comes to mind first. Envisionments of future systems often involve people conversing with their computers as with a friend. Two good examples are the interactions with the computer Hal in the film *2001: A Space Odyssey* and the Knowledge Navigator system envisionment video (Apple, 1992).

Conversing so freely with our computer in the near future is not too likely. Nor is it necessarily desirable. But there are real benefits in using speech, even with limited recognition or no recognition at all. Speech can also be used effectively with other modes of interaction, such as pointing and gesturing.

The audio channel is not restricted to speech. It is suited to a wide variety of other audio-based interaction. We see examples of this in everyday activities, such as responding to a ringing telephone or whistling for a taxi. Similarly, nonspeech audio can play an important role in computer-mediated interactions, for example in factory process control or in aircraft flight management systems.

If audio is such a powerful mode of communication, why is it not more often used in human-computer interaction? Sometimes it is because audio is simply inappropriate in the given context. For example, we can only be attentive to one stream of spoken instructions at a time. Consequently, in cases where we need to control more than one process simultaneously, speech (alone) is generally not an effective mode of communication. Like all other modes of interaction, audio has strengths and weaknesses that need to be understood for it to be used effectively. Finally, technical and economic difficulties have often discouraged the use of audio input and output.

These obstacles to using audio, and to some degree speech, have recently been reduced, so they are now feasible design alternatives generating increased interest. A recent workshop on "The Future of Speech and Audio in the Interface" contains a bibliography of recent work (Arons and Mynatt, 1994) to supplement the articles cited below.

We have five main objectives in this chapter:

- To relate work in natural language to that in speech
- To put speech input/output in realistic perspective
- To show that there is more to the audio channel than speech
- To emphasize that speech- and audio-based communication with computers is now technologically and financially feasible
- To help bring audio into the mainstream of user interface design

SPEECH AND NATURAL LANGUAGE INTERFACES

One of the main hopes for speech and natural language technologies is to make interaction with machines more resemble interaction with people. Yet this may not result in the panacea that many expect. We shall see that the ability to converse with your computer as with a friend or colleague is neither technologically feasible nor always desirable. Yet speech and natural language technologies are practical and very useful in some applications. Often, recognition and understanding are not even required, as in voice mail or in voice annotation.

One theme of this chapter (see also Chapter 7) is that speech is often far more effective when coupled with other modalities of interaction, especially gestures such as pointing and marking. Just as face-to-face conversation is much richer due to the ability to see the accompanying body language, so is it the case when interacting with computers.

Speech has a number of properties that need to be taken into account by the designer. For example, while it is faster to speak than to write, it is faster to read than to listen. This is good for input, bad for retrieval. Speech is effective in communicating many concepts, but spatial and temporal relationships are often far better articulated with gestures or markings. Speech, and audio in general, is ubiquitous; the visual channel is localized—you have to be looking at something to see it—but the ringing of a telephone can be heard anywhere. If the call is for me, this is an advantage. If not, it is an intrusion.

In the orchestra, there is no single "right" instrument. Composers choose the instruments that will give voice to their ideas depending on their suitability to express that particular idea. Every instrument is best for something and worst for something else. So is it with speech and natural language technologies. They can be immensely powerful when effectively used, and a disaster when not. Sometimes they are best used "solo," other times in counterpoint or harmony with other interaction techniques. This chapter provides the background that should enable better orchestration of such human-computer dialogues.

Stored Speech

One of the most powerful uses of speech is when it is applied to computer-mediated *human-human* communication, rather than *human-computer* interaction. Here there is typically no need for computer recognition, since the message is intended for a human and not a machine. Speech is stored in computer memory, and later retrieved for playback or processing. This is a very common computer application, including many telephone answering machines and all voice mail.

Few people think of the audio cassette of their answering machine as a "file system," or their answering machine as an e-mail server, but that is what they are. These systems are physically, logically, and conceptually remote from our conventional workstations, yet this need not be so.

Likewise, dictating machines can form the model for a new generation of small mobile speech capture and filing devices. An excellent example is the innovative VoiceNotes system of Stifelman et al. (1993).

Integrating voice *store-and-forward* capability into our systems can take many other forms. Gould and Boies (1983, 1984), for example, describe the human factors of developing an early telephone-based messaging system that used the keypad for control and handset for speech input/output. This system was the subject of the first case study in Baecker and Buxton (1987). The system supported editing, filing, retrieval, and distribution of voice messages. The design challenge was to support this functionality using limited I/O resources. While such systems are now common, the user-centered iterative methodology employed by the authors is still an outstanding example for designers.

A second excellent example, showing yet another "packaging" of a voice store-and-forward system is the Olympic Messaging System shown in Gould (1985 video) and mentioned in Case A of this volume. Here the user interface had to work for users who had no training, came from many different cultures, and spoke a number of different languages.

While going beyond simple answering machines, these systems were still telephone-centric. They were forerunners to the voice-messaging systems that are commonplace today. Xerox PARC's Etherphone system (Zellweger et al., 1988 video; Vin et al., 1991) illustrates how basic telephone voice-messaging functionality can be integrated into a workstation environment and lays a foundation for the workstation as voice server.

One of the main benefits of voice store-and-forward comes in integrating voice messaging with other document types, such as written text. In so doing, one can move from voice mail to voice annotation. This capability is now starting to find its way into popular PC word processors.

Chalfonte, Fish, and Kraut (1991) compared the relative effectiveness of written and voice annotations of written documents. In their study, written annotations appeared on the paper document itself and voice annotations were spoken onto an audio cassette. The main finding was that there was a significant difference in the kinds of annotations for which voice was used compared to writing. Voice was used mainly for global, high-level comments; written annotations lent themselves to local, low-level comments.

One conclusion that could be drawn is that both kinds of annotations should be supported. Yet the lack of any way of easily anchoring voice annotations to specific locations in the document may have prejudiced against using voice for more localized comments. This weakness is an artifact of the technology used in the study. It would be interesting to repeat this study using a system that would let you "attach" voice annotations to specific locations on the document, as well as write them on the manuscript. This, and more, is enabled by our next example, Wang's Freestyle.

Freestyle (Levine and Ehrlich, 1991; Wang Laboratories, 1989 video; see also Case C of this volume) enabled users to annotate electronic documents by writing using an electronic stylus or by voice. Most significantly, one could point, mark, and speak *simultaneously,* and have the result captured for later review. The resulting document, with the dynamics of voice and gesture intact, could then be returned or distributed using electronic mail. The elegance of this system is its minimalist design: there is *no* use of speech or character recognition. Its effectiveness comes through matching the media to the task. In addition to static marks and conventional voice messaging, it recognized the importance of synchronized voice and gesture in annotation.

A problem encountered with speech files is in searching and retrieving information. One can visually skim written documents and search them by content. How to skim spoken messages is less clear. Yet Arons (1992, 1993, 1993 video) has laid the groundwork for systems to have this capability. Thus there is hope for being able to perform content-based search and retrieval from within speech files, without full speech recognition. Lie, Dybvik, and Rygh (1994 video) shows a visual environment for navigating the data space of voice messages.

Current research in *word spotting* (Wilcox, Smith, and Bush, 1992; Wilcox, Smith, and Bush, 1992 video) may well permit users to speak a "key" and have the file searched for an occurrence. There is some kind of recognition going on with such systems, but it is not speech recognition as discussed later in this chapter. Current systems still have limitations. They are not speaker-independent, for example (that is, the key must be uttered by the same speaker who uttered the file being searched).

Speech Synthesis

Speech synthesis, the speech technology most available to designers and users, is now standard on a many personal computers. This technology typically takes ASCII text (such as a document from a word processor) as its input and gives speech as its output. It usually does this by following a set of production rules, without dictionary look-up for context checking. (Therefore, it cannot determine if "wind" should be pronounced as "I will wind my watch," or "The wind is blowing.")

This synthetic *text-to-speech* technology is efficient and more general than the computer playback of a recorded human voice. It can be done in software or hardware relatively economically. In other cases, however, such as the directory assistance systems used by most North American telephone companies, recordings of a real human voice are use. Here the digits are spoken, stored, and then recalled for playback. The difficulty is in achieving smooth speech by splicing together numbers recorded in isolation. This is achieved by recording several versions of each digit, and then choosing the one that will result in the most natural transition with the digits preceding and following it. The justification of such specialized systems must be based on the need for high-quality natural sounding speech, not cost, since they are generally expensive and difficult to implement. The reading by O'Malley (1990) gives a good overview of the current state of the art of text-to-speech technologies.

Text-to-speech has been used in a number of applications. Schmandt (1984), for example, developed a system called ***mailtalk***, which enabled users to retrieve their e-mail by having it "read" to them over the phone, rather than logging in to a system via computer.

Text-to-speech can also be used to deliver stored system messages and on-line help rather than using stored voice messages. However, since a sentence written in ASCII is much more compact than a recorded sentence (even with modern compression), the text-to-speech solution is far more economical. Even more significantly, if the messages are synthesized, they can be composed on the fly. The system can therefore be more flexible and adaptable than one made up of fixed prerecorded messages.

The quality of synthetic speech is variable. At the low end, speech output typically sounds like a prototypical robot, speaking in a near monotone. Moody, Joost, and Rodman (1987) discuss the effects of various types of speech output on speaker recognition. Pisoni, Nusbaum, and Greene (1985) show that the demands on voice quality vary with the application. Human factors of voice quality in text-to-speech systems are discussed in Thomas and Rosson (1984). That the actual voice quality plays an important factor in how systems are accepted by users is shown in Rosson and Cecala (1986).

Michaelis and Wiggins (1982), Kaplan and Lerner (1985), Klatt (1987), and Streeter (1988) are good reviews of speech synthesis systems, technologies, and applications. Davis (1989 video) demonstrates the use of synthetic speech to give spoken directions to drivers.

Speech Recognition

Speech recognition systems recognize spoken words. This is often confused with natural language understanding. A speech recognition system has no idea what the words mean. It only knows that they are words and what words they are. To be of any use, these words must be passed on to higher-level software for syntactic and semantic analysis. If the spoken words happen to be in the form of natural language (for example, English), then they may be passed on to a natural language understanding system (although, as we will see later, this is generally not the case).

It is important to understand that the "words" that make up the recognition vocabulary need not be words in the normal sense. Rather, such systems typically work by matching the acoustic pattern of an acoustic signal with the features of a stored template. Within the confines of the system's resolution, these signals could be words, short phrases, whistles, or any other discernible acoustic signal or utterance. (Of course, since they are intended for speech, the pattern-matching heuristics are optimized to work on the characteristic features of speech signals.)

Speech recognition systems are not yet in general use, although they are used extensively in specialized applications such as in telephony. Workstations and personal computers are now being delivered with built-in recognizers. Such systems are very relevant to users who are physically disabled, such as quadriplegics, or in cases where the eyes or hands are unavailable, as when one is occupied in performing a task such as driving a vehicle or is wearing special clothes. Good examples would be a surgeon who cannot touch a keyboard for fear of contamination, or a mechanic whose hands are too greasy to use a keyboard effectively.

Speech recognition is significantly more difficult than speech synthesis. Systems vary along a number of dimensions:

- *Speaker-dependent or -independent:* Does the system have to be trained separately for each different user? Most large vocabulary systems are speaker-dependent and require training. This is usually not true for systems with very limited vocabularies.
- *Size of vocabulary:* How many words can the system recognize? Low-end systems recognize tens of words, while state-of-the-art high-end systems can recognize on the order of 50,000. Increasing the vocabulary can expand the utility of a system. However, it also raises the capital cost and the cost that need be invested in training the system. With some systems, the cost of this training increases with vocabulary size. With others, however, training time is a constant, independent of vocabulary size. The system developed for IBM by Jelinik (1985) is an example.
- *Isolated word or continuous speech recognition:* One of the hardest problems in speech recognition is determining when one word ends and the next one begins. In order to sidestep the problem, most systems force the user to issue commands a single word at a time. Typically, words must be separated by a gap of on the order of 300 milliseconds. Since this is unnatural, speech recognition systems that require multiword commands may require special training for users. One perspective on this is presented in Biermann et al. (1985).

The overview of the panel session on voice-based communication which took place at CHI+GI '87 (Aucella et al., 1987) presents a fairly broad perspective on the topic in a relatively small amount of space. Robin Kinkead, for example, discusses issues that must be taken into account when designing such systems:

> *Continuous versus discrete speech is a non-issue, and yet it is the most hotly debated, claimed and counter-claimed and misunderstood variable in speech recognition. Before the advent of functional large vocabulary systems, it was frequently cited as the single largest barrier to the acceptance of speech recognition by the public. The real issues of accuracy,*

repeatability of performance, vocabulary size, cost, flexibility, amount of training needed, ease of modification, location of microphone, complete voice control over the system, and performance in variable conditions were frequently dismissed in favor of debate over what has been shown (in studies, in use, and in demonstrations) to be a minor point, whether one must speak with pauses between words or not. (Kinkead, in Aucella et al., 1987, p. 42)

The reading by Peacocke and Graf (1990) provides a good introduction to the field (see also Levinson and Liberman, 1981, and Das and Nadas, 1992). One of the best single sources for an overview of speech recognition is the book of readings by Waibel and Lee (1990). Good articles on speech recognition appear in special issues of *IEEE Computer* (Kamel, 1990) and of the *Proceedings of the IEEE* of November,1985. In the latter issue, Jelinik (1985) describes a IBM recognition system with a 5,000-word vocabulary, Levinson (1985) addresses structural issues affecting speech recognition, and Zue (1985) discusses knowledge-based techniques. Helander, Moody, and Joost (1988) is a good review paper on the field. Rudnicky (1990 video) demonstrates an excellent speech recognition system.

While we are waiting for speech recognition to improve, there is still debate about its utility. There are a number of empirical studies of speech recognition systems. Karl, Pettey, and Shneiderman (1993) did a comparison of speech versus mouse specification of commands to a word processor. Subjects reacted favorably to the speech interface. Overall, it was 18% faster at task performance than the mouse. However, users had real concerns with problems of accuracy, response time, and the inadequacy of the feedback to their actions. (This is a theme repeated in a number of other studies.)

Perhaps the most interesting result of the Karl et al. study was one that was unexpected by the authors, that the use of speech to issue commands interfered with short-term memory tasks that constituted part of the experiment. Subjects had to build a table of symbols. For each, they would select and copy a symbol from a list, memorize its description, page down to the table, paste in the symbol, and then type its description from memory. Using voice for the cut-and-paste commands interfered with the task of remembering the description.

In retrospect, this result should not be a surprise, since it is consistent with earlier findings in the human factors literature. Wickens, Mountford, and Schreiner (1981) showed how different modalities of interaction were appropriate for different classes of messages. The likely reason that speech interfered with the memory task, while using the mouse did not, is that speech and linguistic memory compete for the same cognitive resources. The mouse-issued commands use a different, noncompetitive channel.

The lesson for user interface designers is that one has to pay careful attention to the full range of tasks to be performed, and what resources (motor, sensory, and cognitive) each consumes. A key rationale for multimodal interfaces is to enable tasks to be distributed over noncompetitive channels. This was not the case in the experiment by Karl et. al.

Other studies of potential interest are those by Rudnicky, Sakamoto and Polifroni (1990), who studied voice interaction in a spreadsheet task, Martin (1989), Franzke et al. (1993), and Allen (1983).

Finally, there are a number of important earlier studies by Gould and his associates: Gould (1982), Gould and Alfaro (1984), and Gould, Conti, and Hovanyecz (1983). The last study investigates the potential of composing letters with a listening typewriter, and suggests that large-vocabulary isolated-word recognition may provide the basis for a useful listening typewriter.

Perhaps as interesting to the student of human-computer interaction is the "Wizard of Oz" methodology this study used. Since a practical listening typewriter was not available, the authors simulated one by having a human transcribe the subjects' speech and echo it back on a CRT. This illustrates the use of limited resources to test the validity of an idea before making a heavy investment in its development. Newell et al. (1991) present an improved environment for performing such studies. Hauptmann (1989) uses a similar technique to investigate voice in combination with gesture in working with 3D graphical objects. Maulsby, Greenberg, and Mander (1993) use a Wizard of Oz approach in a voice- and gesture-based programming-by-demonstration system.

Speaker Recognition

While not in the mainstream of speech recognition, the identification of individuals from their speech is an active research area relevant to human-computer interaction. There are two topics of interest:

- *Speaker verification:* test against a single template, verify that it is X
- *Speaker recognition/identification:* test against a set of *n* possibilities (including "no match") to identify a speaker

The former has relevance in applications such as security. An example would be using a spoken utterance as one's password ("passvoice") to log on to a system or enter a secured area.

Speaker recognition also has several other potential applications, such as to keep track of who is speaking at any given time during a videotaped meeting. This would support queries such as "Show me the segment when Jane started to speak after John, about 5 minutes into the meeting." Such techniques can be used in studying collaborative work (Kurtenbach and Buxton, 1994) and do not require the content of the speech to be recognized.

The reading by Peacocke and Graf (1990) contains some discussion of speaker recognition and verification techniques. Doddington (1985) surveys the field and has a good bibliography.

Natural Language Recognition

Natural language understanding and generation would appear to be primarily an HCI issue. Yet the literature mostly describes applications where the main concern is typically not on the human-machine dialogue, such as automatic translation, data base query, and information retrieval.

What the literature often misses is that natural language human-human dialogues do not generally consist of grammatically correct complete sentences. They make use of interruption, misunderstanding detection, and conversational repair mechanisms. These concerns seem peripheral to the above applications, yet should be a major part of any natural language interface to interactive applications. We must look to artificial intelligence for treatments of these issues. Peria and Grosz (1993) is a summary of recent work on natural language processing, published as a special volume of the journal *Artificial Intelligence.* Ogden (1988) and Scha (1988) are reviews of the design and use of natural language interfaces. Stock (1993 video) demonstrates a natural language interface for a multimedia system.

Natural language systems are distinct from speech-based systems in that the input and output is ASCII text rather than speech. Readers might naturally assume that speech recognition and synthesis systems have a natural language system underneath them. However, as the reading by White (1990) points out, this is not normally the case. Speech-understanding systems more typically operate by phrase or pattern matching, rather than by any deep underlying model of natural language. White discusses how speech and natural language technologies might be combined in order to improve the performance of future systems. Central to his approach is a technique known as Hidden Markov Models (HMM), an important topic also discussed in the reading by Peacocke and Graf (1990).

White emphasizes that knowledge from various sources contributes to the meaning of an utterance;

- *Syntactic:* having to do with grammar, or structure
- *Prosodic:* having to do with inflection, stress, pitch, timing, and other aspects of articulation
- *Pragmatic:* having to do with the situated context within which utterance takes place—issues such as location, time, cultural practices, speakers, hearers, and surroundings
- *Semantic:* having to do with meaning of words

Natural language understanding systems must have uniform methods for representing and communicating knowledge from each of these sources.

Pragmatics is currently the hardest for systems to collect from the environment automatically. This is an area where the technologies of *ubiquitous computing* (discussed in the reading by Weiser in Chapter 14) may help in the future.

How "natural" are current natural language systems? Ogden and Sorknes (1987), for example, investigated the performance of a commercially available natural language interface for data base queries, used by individuals with no formal query training. In their study, only 28% of their first questions resulted in a correct response. Perhaps even more significant, 16% of the problems were thought to have been answered correctly, but were not. The authors make the point that to operate any system, users must learn two things:

- What the system is capable of doing
- The language with which one invokes these capabilities

They note that with conventional interfaces, one learns the capabilities as one learns the language. This is less true with a natural language understanding system, since the language is already "known." Nonetheless, one still has to learn the system's capabilities and limitations, so training must be provided.

As mentioned earlier, information retrieval is one application of natural language technology. The proceedings of a series of DARPA sponsored conferences on "message understanding" (MUC, 1991, 1992) report on work directed at a very specific task: to read a large body of English wire-service-like electronic messages, identify those that deal with a specific topic (Latin American terrorism), and provide a standard form summarizing key information for each. While not dealing with foreground interaction, per se, this aspect of natural language technology will have increasing relevance to users as distributed on-line information systems become more widely available.

Natural Language Generation

Messages from computers sometimes come in the form of "natural language" phrases or sentences describing status, errors, or options. Such messages are mostly precomposed and stored, either as speech or text. While the language used is "natural," these do not count as "natural language" systems in the sense that the term is usually intended. There is no natural language system underlying the messages. There is no way that new messages can be composed automatically to accommodate new circumstances. If all situations have not been anticipated, and the message is not in the original repertoire, it cannot be uttered.

The generation of messages on the fly is the heart of natural language generation in interactive systems. This is especially true when the output goes beyond the provision of system messages, and begins to include more "conversational" interfaces. Imagine, for example, a calendar management program that uses natural language input and output.

Consider generating responses to queries such as, "What am I doing next Thursday?" or "When can I meet James for an hour next week?" Notice that these are not questions for which there are stock answers that can be prerecorded, or which follow simple templates. As with natural language understanding, generating appropriate responses requires access to deeper knowledge sources about the domain and context.

The literature on natural language generation and understanding largely overlap. As with recognition, it is mainly rooted in artificial intelligence. In addition to the references already cited, see Rich (1984) for an older but still relevant overview, and Fedder (1990), which presents a brief coverage of the importance of the mappings between domain and language concepts in natural language generation.

Speech, Gesture, and Multimodal Interaction

So-called "natural language" systems are not always the most natural way to interact (Buxton, 1990; Lee and Zeevat, 1990). Gestures can often convey the intent of an utterance much more naturally than speech or written language. Pointing and selecting one object from among many similar ones is often easier than trying to identify it by describing it verbally. On the other hand, it may be easier to say "All red triangles" than to point and select every red triangle from among many objects. Both demonstrative and descriptive techniques are valuable, and the "natural" language for each is different. Perhaps the greatest benefit comes when speech and gesture can be used together. Cohen (1992) outlines strengths and weaknesses of direct manipulation and language, concluding that they are complementary rather than competing approaches.

Wang Freestyle, discussed earlier (and in Case C), is a wonderful example of the power of combining speech and gesture, even when there is no recognition of either by the machine.

The pioneering example of the use of speech and gesture, and still one of the most compelling examples, is Put That There (Schmandt and Hulteen, 1982; Bolt, 1984; Schmandt, 1984 video).

Put That There enabled users to interact with objects on a wall-sized map using voice input combined with pointing. The system also provided feedback graphically (on the map) and by speech, using text-to-speech technology. Some of the benefits of the system can be understood from the name. For example, the pronoun "that" and adverb "there" can only be understood (in the absence of additional context) when accompanied by gesture. Without the gesture, the vocabulary of the speech recognizer would have to include the proper nouns for all selectable objects, and the simple adverb "there" would have to be replaced by a much more complicated clause. The multimodal approach allows the dialogue to be more succinct for the user and less complicated for the system.

Others have used voice and pointing, following the path laid by Put That There. Salisbury et al. (1990), for example, describe an interface for a military radar defense system (AWACS) that uses speech recognition and speech output in combination with a mouse to point at targets. MCC (1989 video) demonstrates a tool set for constructing multimodal interfaces.

Hauptmann (1989) ran a Wizard of Oz study of people performing seven different operations on a wireframe cube seen on a display. Three different modalities were tested: voice alone, gesture alone, and voice and gesture together. More than twice as many subjects preferred to use voice and gesture together than preferred voice alone or gesture alone. Subjects used a rather limited vocabulary, indicating that within restricted domains, small vocabulary recognition systems may be sufficient. Rudnicky and Hauptmann (1992) presents a further discussion of this multimodal use of speech.

Weimer and Ganapathy (1989, 1990 video) describe a prototype system that starts to integrate ideas discussed by Hauptmann into a working system. Users interact with a 3D world seen through stereoglasses by using speech and hand gesture as input. In this virtual reality system, hand gesturing implements a virtual control panel.

Thorisson, Koons, and Bolt (1992, 1992 video), Koons, Sparrell, and Thorisson (1993), and Koons and Sparrell (1994 video) present a prototype system for interacting with a map data base using speech, hand gesture, and eye tracking. They present an excellent discussion of methods and issues that arise in interpreting simultaneous multimodal inputs. A key challenge is to build a single meaning from the input from various sources.

Using a taxonomy of gestures presented by Rimé and Schiaratura (1991), they discuss how systems could interpret the following:

- *Symbolic gestures:* These are gestures that, within the culture, have come to have a single meaning. The "OK" gesture is one such example. However, recognizing American Sign Language would also fall into this category.
- *Deictic gestures:* These are the types of gestures most generally seen in HCI. These are the gestures of pointing, or otherwise directing the listener's attention to specific events or objects in the environment.
- *Iconic Gestures:* As the name suggests, these gestures are used to convey information about the size, shape, or orientation of the object of discourse.
- *Pantomimic gestures:* These are gestures typically used in showing the use of movement of some invisible tool or object in the speaker's hand.

A key observation made by the authors is that only the first class, symbolic gestures, can be interpreted without further context. Either this context has to be provided sequentially by another gesture or action (as is the case in direct manipulation systems), or by another channel, such as voice, working in concert with the gesture. The former is typical of current methods of HCI. The latter is more like communication in the everyday world.

Applications

There are a number of papers addressing the issue of integrating speech-based interaction into more conventional GUIs and window managers. Some of this work, such as Mynatt and Edwards (1992), uses both speech and nonspeech audio. Their main concern is providing access to users who have various disabilities. Schmandt et al. (1990) and Schmandt, Ackerman, and Hindus (1990) discuss extending the X windowing environment to support voice interaction. Kamel, Emami, and Eckert (1990) discuss an architecture that would enable a workstation to support a range of applications such as a telephone manager, screen telephone, answering machine, calendar program, and voice editor. Their concern is with the toolkits that bind the applications with the various hardware components required.

Most work on voice-based interfaces and applications (e.g., Schmandt and McKenna, 1988; Schmandt and Arons, 1987 video) has centered around telephony. While the telephone has traditionally been perceived as distinct from the computer, today the distinction is becoming blurred. Voice is now being used to access services over the phone (Lennig, 1990). Nakatsu (1990) presents a system for presenting banking services delivered via the telephone. This system uses both speech synthesis and recognition. Wattenbarger et al. (1993) provide a good discussion of the human factors issues involved in telephone-based speech systems.

Lawrence and Stuart (1990) and Sola and Shepard (1990) discuss telephone attendant support and dialing services, respectively. Brennan et al. (1991) is a summary of a panel of a number of people involved in telephony applications discussing their experience with voice-based applications.

The applications that will have the most impact may not be ones that are centered around "familiar" technologies such as the workstation or the telephone. With emerging miniaturization and wireless technologies, a new range of information/communication devices are emerging. In the coming world of "ubiquitous computing" (see the reading by Weiser in Chapter 14), we will likely see the emergence of small "intimate" computing devices that have a strong speech component. The VoiceNotes handheld voice notetaker (Stifelman, et al., 1993) is a good example of this class of technology. Schmandt (1993) is an excellent discussion of the transition from desktop to mobile use of voice in computing.

Other Sources

The August 1990 issue of IEEE Computer was devoted to the voice in computing (Kamel, 1990). Simpson et al. (1985) is an older (but still relevant) human factors perspective on speech-based interaction. Cowley (1990 video) and Cowley and Jones (1993 video) provide human factors guides to the use of speech. Strathmeyer (1990) and Rudnicky, Hauptmann, and Lee (1994) are good up-to-date overviews of speech technology. Roe and Wilpon (1993) and Rabiner and Juang (1993) present good up-to-date discussions of speech recognition. Schmandt (1985) is an excellent overview, while Schmandt (1994) is a book giving a detailed practical guide to the use of speech synthesis and speech recognition.

The *Encyclopedia of Artificial Intelligence* (Shapiro, 1992) has entries for a number of topics covered above, including natural language generation, natural language understanding, discourse understanding, and speech understanding. These are written mainly from an AI rather than HCI perspective, but are useful to anyone trying to obtain a deeper understanding of the issues involved.

The proceedings of the annual *DARPA Workshop on Speech and Natural Language* (DARPA, 1989, 1990, 1991, and 1992) present a rich package of papers dealing with theory, technology, and applications. The proceedings of the annual IEEE International Conference on Acoustics, Speech, and Signal Processing (ICASSP) is another rich concentrated source.

NONSPEECH AUDIO

Unless we are hearing impaired, we have used nonspeech audio cues on a daily basis all of our lives. Crossing the street, answering the phone, diagnosing problems with our car engine, and whistling for our dog are common examples. Despite the widespread use of this rich mode of interaction in our lives, it has had little impact on how we interact with computers. This need not be so. There are significant potential benefits to be reaped by developing such capabilities.

The audio messages in such systems generally fall into one of three categories:

- Alarms and warning systems
- Status and monitoring indicators
- Encoded messages and data

Although alarms and warning systems dominate, video games illustrate the potential of nonspeech audio to effectively communicate higher-level messages. Just compare an expert player's score when the audio is turned on with the score when the audio is turned off. The likely significant drop in score indicates that the audio conveys strategically critical information, and is more than just an acoustic "lollipop."

For nonspeech audio to be effective, the meaning of each signal must be known to the intended listener. Just like any other language, this is a learned vocabulary. We are not born knowing the meaning of a fog horn, fire alarm, or police siren. If audio cues are to be used in interactive systems, then their design is of utmost importance. As graphic design is to effective icons, so is acoustic design to effective auditory signs, or *earcons*.

Learning and Remembering

One way to assist users in remembering the meaning of nonspeech audio signals is by metaphor—have the meaning associated with a sound correspond to the meaning of similar sounds in the everyday world. Yet the extent to which existing acoustic signs can be exploited remains to be seen. Although the application of fog horn and fire alarm sounds to computer applications is limited, Gaver (1986, 1989) presents compelling examples that make effective use of existing world knowledge of the acoustic environment. One such example makes use of our association of reverberation with empty space. He proposes that if there were a reverberant clunk when we saved a file, then the amount of reverberation would provide a good cue as to how much free space was left on the disk. Similarly, on the Apple Macintosh, placing a file into the "trash can" could be accompanied by an appropriate "tinny crash."

On first impression, such use of the audio channel to provide feedback may seem frivolous or unnecessary. However, most actions in the physical world are accompanied by acoustic feedback that is important to performing the associated task. This is seen in something as common as starting a car. When we are next to a jackhammer that masks the sound of the engine, most of us have tried to start an already running car, with the consequent grinding of gears of the starting motor. Such feedback can benefit the performance of computer-based tasks as well. This is especially true for the visually impaired and those working in critical applications where audio feedback can reduce the risk of error.

Musical and Everyday Listening

Gaver identifies two approaches to nonspeech audio:

- Musical listening
- Everyday listening

In musical listening, the "message" is derived from the relationships among the acoustical components of the sound, such as its pitch, timing, and timbre. In everyday listening, what one hears is not perceived in such an analytical way. What one hears is the *source* of the sound, not its acoustic attributes. For example, if one hears a door slam, one pays attention to the fact that it was a door, perhaps how big it was, what material it was made of (wood or metal?), and how hard it was slammed. The musical listening analysis of the same thing would deal with issues like whether it was a long or short sound, low or high pitched, and loud or soft. The *auditory icons* described in the reading by Gaver and Smith (1990) are an excellent example of auditory design targeting at everyday listening.

The raw materials of auditory design based on musical listening are as follows. These are the musical equivalent to typography, layout, and colour in graphic design:

- *Pitch:* the primary basis for traditional melody
- *Rhythm:* relative changes in the timing of the attacks of successive events
- *Tempo:* the speed of events
- *Dynamics:* the relative loudness of events (static or varying)
- *Timbre:* the difference of spectral content and energy over time, which is what differentiates a saxophone from a flute
- *Location:* where the sound is coming from

Consider the use of *leitmotiv* in Wagner's operas, or Prokofiev's use of musical themes to identify the characters of Peter and the Wolf. First, they show that humans can learn and make effective use of cues based on these musical parameters. Without trying to trivialize Wagner, we have seen the same type of audio cue effectively applied in the video game Pacman. On the other hand, the example of Wagner's operas also serves to show that if you are not intimately familiar with the themes, all of the references will be lost on you. Some researchers, such as Blattner, Sumikawa, and Greenberg (1989) have proposed using just such motivic encoding for messages in user interfaces. While the ideas warrant exploring, it must also be pointed out that there is little experimental evidence validating this approach (a notable exception being the study by Brewster, Wright, and Edwards, 1993, which showed some benefit of messages employing melodic encoding).

Testing and Validation

Testing and validation are important. While missing a few references in an opera may not be life threatening, the opposite is true in piloting an aircraft or monitoring a nuclear power plant. In the Three Mile Island power plant crisis, for example, over 60 different auditory warning systems were activated (Sanders and McCormick, 1987, p. 155).

Momtahan, Hétu, and Tansley (1993), for example, performed a study on the audibility and identification of auditory alarms in the operating room (OR) and intensive care unit (ICU) of a hospital. Staff were able to identify only a mean of 10 to 15 of the 26 alarms found in the OR. Only a mean of 9 to 14 of the 23 alarms found in the ICU were identified correctly by nurses who worked there. Only in the OR was the ability to identify alarms positively correlated with their importance.

The biggest problem leading to the results of this study is that there were simply too many alarms in these critical areas, and those that were there were poorly designed. Not only are they hard to distinguish on their own, but some were "masked" (that is, inaudible) due to the noise of machinery (such as a surgical drill) used in the space in normal practice. Because of the design, some alarms actually masked other, simultaneously occurring, alarms. Although sound can be a valuable channel of communication, this study shows the risk of bad design and implementation.

Nielsen and Schaefer (1993) studied the effect of nonspeech audio in a computer paint program on users who were between 70 and 75 years old. In the program studied, they found that the sound contributed nothing positive, and served to confuse some of the users. Clearly, the use of sound is no panacea. If audio cues are to be employed, they must be clear and easily differentiable. Careful design and testing is required for them to be effective.

Human Factors

There is ample human factors literature from which the designer can obtain useful guidelines about the use of nonspeech audio cues. Three excellent sources are Deatherage (1972), Kantowitz and Sorkin (1983), and Sanders and McCormick (1987). Each uses the term "audio display" to describe this use of the audio channel. Figure 8.1 summarizes Deatherage's view as to when to use audio displays rather than visual ones.

Perhaps the prime attribute of computer-generated audio output is that messages can be conveyed without making use of the visual channel. Visual messages must be seen to be understood. Audio messages are received regardless of where one is looking. This is of particular importance in cases where the visual channel is focused elsewhere, or where the task does not require constant visual monitoring. When the amount of information to be conveyed is high and pushes the visual channel to the limits, the audio channel can also be used to carry some of the information, thereby reducing the overall load. Conversely, one person's auditory icon is another person's noise. The ergonomics of noise is one of the topics covered in Chapter 10.

Pragmatics of Using Sound on Computers

In the past, one of the biggest problems in exploring the use of audio signals was a logistical one. In her research, for example, Bly had to build special hardware and interface it to her computer (Bly et al., 1985). Some important recent developments have changed this situation dramatically. The change is a technological one that has resulted from the music industry adopting a standard protocol for interfacing electronic sound synthesis and processing equipment to computers. This standard is known as MIDI, the Musical Instrument Digital Interface. Because of MIDI, there is a wide range of equipment and interfaces readily available to the researcher who wants to study this area. In addition to the specification (IMA, 1983), an excellent general introduction to MIDI can be found in Loy (1985).

As personal computers become ever more powerful, and memory cheaper, one needs to rely less on peripherals to produce sounds. Digital recordings of sounds can be stored in memory and played back on demand in the same way as stored speech messages. This is especially appropriate for "everyday" auditory icons, such as used by Gaver.

Complex sounds can also be synthesized "on the fly" in real time from some compact representation. Gaver (1993) discusses

FIGURE 8.1

When to use audio or visual displays. Guidelines for determining whether to use the audio or visual channel in displaying information (Deatherage, 1972, p. 124).

Use auditory presentation if:

1. *The message is simple.*
2. *The message is short.*
3. *The message will not be referred to later.*
4. *The message deals with events in time.*
5. *The message calls for immediate action.*
6. *The visual system of the person is overburdened.*
7. *The receiving location is too bright or dark—adaptation integrity is necessary.*
8. *The person's job requires him to move about continually.*

Use visual presentation if:

1. *The message is complex.*
2. *The message is long.*
3. *The message will be referred to later.*
4. *The message deals with location in space.*
5. *The message does not call for immediate action.*
6. *The auditory system of the person is overburdened.*
7. *The receiving location is too noisy.*
8. *The person's job allows him to remain in one position.*

new and potent techniques for doing so. The approach is analogous to the use of text-to-speech techniques. Ludwig, Pincever, and Cohen (1990) describe a novel approach to using spatial cues in sound in a manner analogous to the use of windows in displays.

Finally, Wenzel et al. (1993) summarizes a panel discussion that tries to relate hardware requirements to perceptual performance, and brings together useful perspectives for the designer of nonspeech audio systems.

Perception and Psychoacoustics

We have discussed the importance of good design of acoustic stimuli to communicate information. This can be aided by using the rich literature on psychoacoustics and the psychology of music. Psychoacoustics tells us a great deal about the relationship between perception and the physical properties of acoustic signals. Music and the psychology of music tell us much about the human's ability to compose and understand higher-level sonic structures. The literature is quite extensive in addressing issues such as the perception of pitch, duration, and loudness of acoustic signals. It also helps provide an understanding of masking—the phenomenon of one sound (for example, noise) obscuring another one (such as an alarm or a voice). Elementary information is available in any first-year psychology text book. More advanced information is in Tobias (1970), Evans and Wilson (1977), Carterette and Friedman (1978), Scharf and Buus (1986), Scharf and Houtsma (1986), Hawkins and Presson (1986), and Moore (1989).

One aspect of perception that is not covered in the above references is the topic of signal detection theory, which has been an important part of the classical human factors approach to audio signals. References that address this at an introductory level are Deatherage (1972), Kantowitz and Sorkin (1983), and Sanders and McCormick (1987). A good summary of speech perception can be found in Jusczyk (1986).

Under a different name, *acoustic design* has had a thriving life as *music*. While music perception is not a part of mainstream human factors, it does have something to contribute. In particular, classic psychoacoustics has dealt primarily with simple stimuli. Music, on the other hand, is concerned with larger structures. Hence, melodic recognition and the perception and understanding of simultaneously sounding auditory streams (as in counterpoint) is of great relevance to audio's use in the human-computer interface. As a reference to this aspect of auditory perception, therefore, we recommend Roederer (1975) and Deutsch (1982, 1986).

Applications

Some of the earliest work using nonspeech audio was in data display, or "auralization." This can be considered the acoustic equivalent of scientific visualization. Typically, multidimensional data was presented acoustically by having each dimension of a datum map onto one of the dimensions of a sound. For example, this technique was used to perform analysis of variance and to present "sound graphs."

Some of the early work is summarized by Bly et al. (1985) and expanded in Frysinger (1990). Lunney and Morrison (1990) describes their system for presenting the infrared spectra of various chemical compounds using such techniques. (Like many other researchers in the field, their work was motivated by making scientific data accessible to those with visual impairments.)

In the Lunney and Morrison work, the computer presented sounds and the user then performed recognition. Smith, Bergeron, and Grinstein (1990) and Grinstein and Smith (1990) describe an interactive system that uses graphical and acoustical "textures" to represent data sets. One moves the cursor over a surface and hears a texture, not isolated sound events. The effect is very different, and does not employ musical listening.

Audio interfaces clearly have strong relevance for those with impaired vision (Edwards, 1989). Yet note that we *all* are visually impaired to some degree when working with computers. This is especially true in collaborative work at a distance, where one cannot always visually monitor the activities of one's collaborators. This is one of the areas where sound has the most potential. The reading by Gaver and Smith (1990; see also Gaver, Smith, and O'Shea, 1991) is an excellent exploration of some of this design space.

Finally, a recent exploration of the use of sound in interfaces for programmers is DiGiano and Baecker (1992).

Other Sources

Readers interested in nonspeech audio should consult a special issue of the journal *Human Computer Interaction* devoted to the topic (Buxton, 1989), the proceedings of a special SPIE conference (Farrell, 1990), and the proceedings of the first International Conference on Auditory Design, ICAD (Kramer, 1994).

CONCLUSION

The audio channel is an underutilized resource in human-computer interaction. One need only consider the position of visually impaired users to realize that the need is compelling. It becomes even more so when we come to the realization that in some (often critical) situations, all of us are visually impaired, perhaps because of the visual system being saturated, loss of light, or age. This is therefore an area that deserves and must receive more attention. With MIDI and the widespread availability of personal computers, there is now no excuse for not doing so.

REFERENCES

Note: A ● before a reference indicates a reading.

Allen, R.B. (1983). Composition and Editing of Spoken Letters. *International Journal of Man-Machine Studies* 19(2), 181–193.

Arons, B. (1992). Techniques, Perception, and Applications of Time-Compressed Speech. *Proceedings of the American Voice I/O Society Conference, AVIOS '92,* 169–177.

Arons, B. (1993). SpeechSkimmer: Interactively Skimming Recorded Speech. *Proc. UIS '93,* ACM, 187–196.

Arons, B., and Mynatt, E. (1994). The Future of Speech and Audio in the Interface. *SIGCHI Bulletin 26*(4), 44–48.

Aucella, A., Kinkead, R., Schmandt, C., and Wichansky, A. (1987). Voice: Technology Searching for Communication Needs. Panel Summary, *Proc. CHI + GI '87,* ACM, 41–44.

Baecker, R. and Buxton, W. (1987). *Readings in Human Computer Interaction: A Multidisciplinary Approach.* Morgan Kaufmann.

Biermann, A., Rodman, R., Rubin, D., and Heidlage, J. (1985). Natural Language with Discrete Speech as a Mode for Human-to-Machine Communication. *Communications of the ACM* 28(6), 628–636.

Blattner, M., Sumikawa, D., and Greenberg, R. (1989). Earcons and Icons: Their Structure and Common Design Principles. *Human-Computer Interaction* 4(1), Spring 1989.

Bly, S.. Frysinger, S., Lunney, D., Mansur, D., Mezrich, J., and Morrison, R. (1985). Communicating with Sound. *Proc. CH '85,* ACM, 115–119.

Bolt, R. (1984). *The Human Interface: Where People and Computers Meet.* London: Lifetime Learning Publications.

Brennan, P., Deffner, G., Lawrence, D., Marics, M., Schwab, E., and Franzke, M. (1991). Should We or Shouldn't We Use Spoken Commands in Voice Interfaces? *Proc. CHI '91,* ACM, 369–372.

Brewster, S., Wright, P., and Edwards, A. (1993). An Evaluation of Earcons for Use in Auditory Human-Computer Interfaces. *Proc. InterCHI '93,* ACM, 222–227.

Buxton, W. (1989). Introduction to this Special Issue on Non-Speech Audio. *Human-Computer Interaction* 4(1), 1–9.

Buxton, W. (1990). The Natural Language of Interaction: A Perspective on Non-Verbal Dialogues. In Laurel, B. (Ed.), *The Art of Human-Computer Interface Design,* Addison-Wesley, 405–416.

Carterette, E., and Friedman, M. (Eds.) (1978). *Hearing, Handbook of Perception, Volume IV.* Academic Press.

Chalfonte, B., Fish, R., and Kraut, R. (1991). Expressive Richness: A Comparison of Speech and Text as Media for Revision. *Proc. CHI '91,* ACM, 21–26.

Cohen, P. (1992). The Role of Natural Language in a Multimodal Interface. *Proc. UIST '92,* ACM, 143–149.

DARPA (1989). Proceedings of the 1989 DARPA Workshop on Speech and Natural Language. Morgan Kaufmann.

DARPA (1990). Proceedings of the 1990 DARPA Workshop on Speech and Natural Language. Morgan Kaufmann.

DARPA (1991). Proceedings of the 1991 DARPA Workshop on Speech and Natural Language. Morgan Kaufmann.

DARPA (1992). Proceedings of the 1992 DARPA Workshop on Speech and Natural Language. Morgan Kaufmann.

Das, S., and Nadas, A. (1992). The Power of Speech. *Byte* 17(4), 151–160.

Deatherage, B. H. (1972). Auditory and Other Sensory Forms of Information Presentation. In Van Cott, H., and Kinkade, R. (Eds), *Human Engineering Guide to Equipment Design,* Revised Edition, U.S. Government Printing Office.

Deutsch, D. (Ed.) (1982). *The Psychology of Music.* Academic Press.

Deutsch, D. (1986). Auditory Pattern Recognition. In Boff, K., Kaufman, L., and Thomas, J. (Eds.), *Handbook of Perception and Human Performance, Volume II,* John Wiley & Sons, 32.1–32.49.

DiGiano, C., and Baecker, R. (1992). Program Auralization: Sound Enhancements to the Programming Environment. *Proc. Graphics Interface '92,* Morgan Kaufmann, 44–52.

Doddington, G.R. (1985). Speaker Recognition Identifying People by Their Voices. *Proceedings of the IEEE* 73(11), 1651–1664.

Edwards, A. (1989). Soundtrack: An Auditory Interface for Blind Users. *Human-Computer Interaction* 4(1), 45–66.

Evans, E., and Wilson, J. (Eds.) (1977). *Psychophysics and Physiology of Hearing.* Academic Press.

Farrell, E. (Ed.) (1990). *Extracting Meaning from Complex Data: Processing, Display, Interaction.* Proceedings of the SPIE, Vol. 1259.

Fedder, L. (1990). Recent Approaches to Natural Language Generation. *Proc. INTERACT '90,* Elsevier (North-Holland), 801–805.

Franzke, M., Marx, A., Roberts, T., and Engelbeck, G. (1993). Is Speech Recognition Usable? An Exploration of the Usability of a Speech-Based Voice Mail Interface. *SIGCHI Bulletin* 25(3), ACM, 49–51.

Frysinger, S.P. (1990). Applied Research in Auditory Data Representation. In Farrell, E. (Ed.), *Extracting Meaning from Complex Data: Processing, Dsplay, Interaction.* Proceedings of the SPIE, Vol. 1259, 130–139.

Gaver, W. (1986). Auditory Icons: Using Sound in Computer Interfaces. *Human Computer Interaction* 2(2), 167–177.

Gaver, W. (1989). The SonicFinder: An Interface That Uses Auditory Icons. *Human-Computer Interaction* 4(1), 67–94.

Gaver, W. (1993). Synthesizing Auditory Icons. *Proc. InterCHI '93,* ACM, 228–235.

Gaver, W., and Smith, R. (1990). Auditory Icons in Large-Scale Collaborative Environments. *Proc. INTERACT '90,* Elsevier (North-Holland), 735–740.

Gaver, W., Smith, R., and O'Shea, T. (1991). Effective Sounds in Complex Systems: The ARKola Simulation. *Proc. CHI '91,* ACM, 85–90.

Gould, J. (1982). Writing and Speaking Letters and Messages. *International Journal of Man-Machine Studies* 16(2), 147–171.

Gould, J., and Alfaro, L. (1984). Revising Documents with Text Editors, Handwriting Recognition Systems, and Speech-Recognition Systems. *Human Factors* 26(4), 391–406.

Gould, J., and Boies, S. (1983). Human Factors Challenges in Creating a Principal Support Office System—The Speech Filing Approach. *ACM Transactions on Office Information Systems* 1(4), 273–298. Reprinted in Baecker and Buxton (1987).

Gould, J., and Boies, S. (1984). Speech Filing an Office System for Principals. *IBM Systems Journal* 23(1), 65–81. Reprinted in Baecker and Buxton (1987).

Gould, J., Conti, J., and Hovanyecz, T. (1983). Composing Letters with a Simulated Listening Typewriter. *Communications of the ACM* 26(4), 295–308.

Grinstein, G., and Smith, S. (1990). The Perceptualization of Scientific Data. In Farrell, E. (Ed.), *Extracting Meaning from Complex Data: Processing, Display, Interaction.* Proceedings of the SPIE, Vol. 1259, 190–199.

Hawkins, H., and Presson, J. (1986). Auditory Information Processing. In Boff, K., Kaufman, L., and Thomas, J. (Eds.), *Handbook of Perception and Human Performance, Volume II,* John Wiley & Sons, 26.1–26.64.

Hauptmann, A. (1989). Speech and Gestures for Graphic Image Manipulation. *Proc. CHI '89,* ACM, 241–245.

Helander, M. (Ed.) (1988). *Handbook of Human-Computer Interaction.* North-Holland.

Helander, M., Moody, T., and Joost, M. (1988). Systems Design for Automated Speech Recognition. In Helander (1988), 301–319.

IMA (1983). MIDI Musical Instrument Digital Interface Specification 1.0. IMA, 11857 Hartsook St., North Hollywood, CA 91607.

Jelinek, F. (1985). The Development of an Experimental Discrete Dictation Recognizer. *Proceedings of the IEEE* 73(11), 1616–1624.

Jusczyk, P.W. (1986). Speech Perception. In Boff, K., Kaufman, L., and Thomas, J. (Eds.), *Handbook of Perception and Human Performance, Volume II,* John Wiley & Sons, 27.1–27.57.

Kamel, R. (Ed.) (1990). Voice in Computing. Special issue of *IEEE Computer* 23(8), August 1990.

Kamel, R., Emami, K., and Eckert, R. (1990). PX: Supporting Voice in Workstations. *IEEE Computer* 23(8), 73–80.

Kantowitz, B., and Sorkin, R. (1983). *Human Factors: Understanding People-System Relationships.* John Wiley & Sons.

Kaplan, G., and Lerner, E. (1985). Realism in Synthetic Speech. *IEEE Spectrum* 22(4), 32–37.

Karl, L., Pettey, M., and Shneiderman, B. (1993). Speech versus Mouse Commands for Word Processing: An Empirical Evaluation. *International Journal of Man-Machine Studies* 39(4), 667–687.

Klatt, D.H. (1987). Review of Text-to-Speech Conversion for English. *Journal of the Acoustical Society of America* 82, 737–783.

Koons, D., Sparrell, C., and Thorisson, K. (1993). Integrating Simultaneous Input from Speech, Gaze and Hand Gestures. In Maybury, M. (Ed.), *Intelligent Multimedia Interfaces,* AAAI Press/MIT Press, 257–276.

Kramer, G. (Ed.) (1994). *Auditory Display.* Addison-Wesley.

Kurtenbach, G., and Buxton, W. (1994). User Learning and Performance with Marking Menus. *Proc. CHI '94,* ACM, 258–264.

Lawrence, D., and Stuart, R. (1990). Case Study of Development of a User Inerface for a Voice Activated Dialing Service. *Proc. I NTERACT '90,* Elsevier (North-Holland), 773–777.

Lee, J., and Zeevat, H. (1990). Integrating Natural Language and Graphics in Dialogue. *Proc. INTERACT '90,* Elsevier (North-Holland), 479–484.

Lennig, M. (1990). Putting Speech Recognition to Work in the Telephone Network. *IEEE Computer* 23(8), 35–41.

Levine, S., and Ehrlich, S. (1991). The Freestyle System: A Design Perspective. In Klinger, A. (Ed.), *Human-Machine Interactive Systems,* Plenum Press, 3–21.

Levinson, S. (1985). Structural Methods in Automatic Speech Recognition. *Proceedings of the IEEE* 73(11), 1625–1650.

Levinson, S., and Liberman, M. (1981). Speech Recognition by Computer. *Scientific American* 244(4), 64–76.

Loy, G. (1985). Musicians Make a Standard: The MIDI Phenomenon. *Computer Music Journal* 9(4), 8–26.

Ludwig, L., Pincever, N., and Cohen, M. (1990). Extending the Notion of a Window System to Audio. *IEEE Computer* 23(8), 66–72.

Lunney, D., and Morrison, R. (1990). Auditory Presentation of Experimental Data. In Farrell, E. (Ed.), *Extracting Meaning from Complex Data: Processing, Display, Interaction.* Proceedings of the SPIE, Vol. 1259, 140–146.

Martin, G. (1989). The Utility of Speech in Human-Computer Interfaces. *International Journal of Man-Machine Studies* 30(4), 355–375.

Maulsby, D., Greenberg, S., and Mander, R. (1993). Prototyping an Intelligent Agent through Wizard of Oz. *Proc. InterCHI '93,* ACM, 277–284.

Michaelis, P., and Wiggins, R. (1982). A Human Factors Engineer's Introduction to Speech Synthesizers. In Badre, A., and Shneiderman, B. (Eds.), *Directions in Human/Computer Interaction,* Ablex, 149–178.

Momtahan, K., Hétu, R., and Tansley, B. (1993). Audibility and Identification of Auditory Alarms in the Operating Room and Intensive Care Unit. *Ergonomics* 36(10), 1159–1176.

Moody, T., Joost, M., and Rodman, R. (1987). The Effects of Various Types of Speech Output on Listener Comprehension Rates. *Proc. INTERACT '87,* Elsevier (North Holland), 573–578.

Moore, B. (1989). *An Introduction to the Psychology of Hearing.* Academic Press.

MUC (1991). *Proceedings of the Third Message Understanding Conference (MUC-3).* Morgan Kaufmann.

MUC (1992). *Proceedings of the Fourth Message Understanding Conference (MUC-4).* Morgan Kaufmann.

Mynatt, E., and Edwards, K. (1992). Mapping GUIs to Auditory Interfaces. *Proc. UIST '92,* ACM, 61–70.

Nakatsu, R. (1990). Anser: An Application of Speech Technology to the Japanese Banking Industry. *IEEE Computer* 23(8), 43–48.

Newell, A., Arnott, J., Dye, R., and Cairns, A. (1991). A Full-Speed Listening Typewriter Simulation. *International Journal of Man-Machine Studies* 35(2), 119–131.

Nielsen, J., and Schaefer, L. (1993). Sound Effects as an Interface Element for Older Users. *Behaviour and Information Technology* 12(4), 208–215.

Ogden, W. (1988). Using Natural Language Interfaces. In Helander (1988), 281–319.

Ogden, W., and Sorknes, A. (1987). What Do Users Say to Their Natural Language Interface? *Proc. INTERACT '87,* Elsevier (North-Holland), 561–566.

◈ O'Malley, M. (1990). Text-to-Speech Conversion Technology. *IEEE Computer* 23(8), 17–23.

◈ Peacocke, R., and Graf, D. (1990). An Introduction to Speech and Speaker Recognition. *IEEE Computer* 23(8), 26–33.

Peria, F., and Grosz, B. (Eds.) (1993). Special Volume on Natural Language Processing. *Artificial Intelligence* 63(1–2).

Pisoni, D., Nusbaum, H., and Greene, B. (1985). Perception of Synthetic Speech Generated by Rule. *Proceedings of the IEEE* 73(11), 1665–1671.

Rabiner, L., and Juang, B. (1993). *Fundamentals of Speech Recognition.* Prentice Hall.

Rich, E. (1984). Natural-Language Interfaces. *IEEE Computer,* 39–47.

Rimé, B., and Schiaratura, L. (1991). Gesture and Speech. In Feldman, R., and Rim, B. (Eds.), *Fundamentals of Nonverbal Behaviour.* Press Syndicate of the University of Cambridge, 239–281.

Roe, D., and Wilpon, J. (1993). Whither Speech Recognition: The Next 25 Years. *IEEE Communicatons* 31(11), 54–62.

Roederer, J. (1975). *Introduction to the Physics and Psychophysics of Sound,* Second Edition. Springer-Verlag.

Rosson, M. B., and Cecala, A. (1986). Designing a Quality Voice: An Analysis of Listeners' Reactions to Synthetic Voices. *Proc. CHI '86,* ACM, 192–197.

Rudnicky, A., and Hauptmann, A. (1992). Multimodal Interaction in Speech Systems. In Blattner, M., and Dannenberg, R. (Eds.), *Multimedia Interface Design*, Addison-Wesley, 147–171.

Rudnicky, A., Hauptmann, A., and Lee, K. (1994). Survey of Current Speech Technology. *Communications of the ACM* 37(3), 52–57.

Rudnicky, A., Sakamoto, M., and Polifroni, J. (1990). Spoken Language Interaction in a Spreadsheet Task. *Proc. INTERACT '90*, Elsevier (North-Holland), 767–772.

Salisbury, M., Hendrickson, J., Lammers, T., Fu, C., and Moody, S. (1990) Talk and Draw: Bundling Speech and Graphics. *IEEE Computer* 23(8), 59–65.

Sanders, M., and McCormick, E. (1987). *Human Factors in Engineering and Design* (6th Edition). McGraw-Hill.

Scha, R. (1988). Natural Language Interface Systems. In Helander (1988), 941–956.

Scharf, B., and Buus, S. (1986). Audition I: Stimulus, Physiology, Thresholds. In Boff, K., Kaufman, L., and Thomas, J. (Eds.), *Handbook of Perception and Human Performance*, Volume I, John Wiley & Sons, 14.1–14.71.

Scharf, B., and Houtsma, A. (1986). Audition II: Loudness, Pitch, Localization, Aural Distortion, Pathology. In Boff, K., Kaufman, L., and Thomas, J. (Eds.), *Handbook of Perception and Human Performance*, Volume I, John Wiley & Sons, 15.1–15.60.

Schmandt, C. (1984). Speech Synthesis Gives Voiced Access to an Electronic Mail System. *Speech Technology*, August–September, 66–88.

Schmandt, C. (1985). Voice Communication with Computers. In Hartson, H. (Ed.), *Advances in Human-Computer Interaction*, Volume I, Ablex Publishing, 133–160.

Schmandt, C. (1993). From Desktop Audio to Mobile Access: Opportunities for Voice in Computing. In Hartson, H., and Hix, D. (Eds.), *Advances in Human-Computer Interaction*, Volume 4, Ablex Publishing, 251–283.

Schmandt, C. (1994). *Voice Communicaton with Computers*. Van Nostrand Reinhold.

Schmandt, C., Ackerman, M., and Hindus, D. (1990). Augmenting a Window System with Speech Input. *IEEE Computer* 23(8), 50–56.

Schmandt, C., Hindus, D., Ackerman, M., and Manandhar, S. (1990). Observations on Using Speech Input for Window Navigation. *Proc. INTERACT '90*, Elsevier (North-Holland), 787–793.

Schmandt, C., and Hulteen, E. (1982). The Intelligent Voice Interactive Interface. *Proc. Conference on Human Factors in Computer Systems*, ACM, 363–366.

Schmandt, C., and McKenna, M. (1988). An Audio and Telephone Server for Multi-Media Workstations. *Proceedings of the 2nd IEEE Conference on Computer Workstations*, 150–159.

Shapiro. S. (Ed.) (1992). *Encyclopedia of Artificial Intelligence (2nd Edition)*, Vol. 1 and 2. John Wiley & Sons.

Simpson, C., McCauley, M., Roland, E., Ruth, J., and Willeges, B. (1985). System Design for Speech Recognition and Generation. *Human Factors* 27(2), 115–141.

Smith, S., Bergeron, R., and Grinstein, G. (1990). Stereoscopic and Surface Sound Generation for Exploratory Data Analysis. *Proc. CHI '90*, ACM, 125–132.

Sola, I., and Shepard, D. (1990). A Voice Recognition Interface for a Telecommunications Basic Business Group Attendant Console. *Proc. INTERACT '90*, Elsevier (North-Holland), 779–785.

Stifelman, L., Arons, B., Schmandt, C., and Hulteen, E. (1993). VoiceNotes: A Speech Interface for a Hand-Held Notetaker. *Proc. InterCHI '93*, ACM, 179–186.

Strathmeyer, C. (1990). Voice in Computing: An Overview of Available Technologies. *IEEE Computer* 23(8), 10–15.

Streeter, L. (1988). Applying Speech Synthesis to User Interfaces. In Helander (1988), 321–343.

Thomas, J., and Rosson, M. B. (1984). Human Factors and Synthetic Speech. *Proceedings of the Human Factors Society*, Volume 2, 763–767.

Thorisson, K., Koons, D., and Bolt, R. (1992). Multi-Modal Natural Dialogue. *Proc. CHI '92*, ACM, 653–654.

Tobias, J. (Ed.) (1970). *Foundations of Modern Auditory Theory*, Vol. I and II, Academic Press.

Vin, H., Zellweger, P., Swinehart, D., and Rangan, V. (1991). Multimedia Conferencing in the Etherphone Environment. *IEEE Computer* 24(10), 69–79.

Waibel, A., and Lee, K. (Eds.) (1990). *Readings in Speech Recognition*. Morgan Kaufmann.

Wattenbarger, B., Garberg, R., Halpern, E., and Lively, B. (1993). Serving Customers with Automatic Speech Recognition—Human-Factors Issues. *AT&T Technical Journal* 72(3), 28–41.

Weimer, D., and Ganapathy, S. (1989). A Synthetic Visual Environment with Hand Gesturing and Voice Input. *Proc. CHI '89*, ACM, 235–240.

Wenzel, E., Gaver, W., Foster, S., Levkowitz, H., and Powell, R. (1993). Perceptual vs. Hardware Performance in Advanced Acoustic Interface Design. *Proc. InterCHI '93*, ACM, 363–366.

White, G. (1990). Natural Language Understanding and Speech Recognition. *Communications of the ACM* 33(8), 72–82.

Wickens, C., Mountford, S.J., and Schreiner, W. (1981). Multiple Resources, Task-Hemispheric Integrity, and Individual Differences in Time Sharing. *Human Factors* 23, 211–230.

Wilcox, L., Smith, I., and Bush, M. (1992). Wordspotting for Voice Editing and Audio Indexing. *Proc. CHI '92*, ACM, 655–656.

Zellweger, P., Terry, D., and Swinehart, D. (1988). An Overview of the Etherphone System and Its Applications. *Proc. 2nd IEEE Conference on Computer Workstations*, 160–168.

Zue, V. (1985). The Use of Speech Knowledge in Automatic Speech Recognition. *Proceedings of the IEEE* 73(11), 1602–1615.

VIDEOS

Apple Computer (1992). The Knowledge Navigator. *ACM SIGGRAPH Video Review (SGVR)* 79.

Arons, B. (1993). Hyperspeech, *ACM SGVR* 88.

Cowley, C. (1990). A Human Factors Guide to Computer Speech. *ACM SGVR* 65.

Cowley, C., and Jones, D. (1993). Talking to Machines. *ACM SGVR* 88.

Davis, J. (1989). Direction Assistance. *ACM SGVR* 48.

Gould, J. (1985). Olympic Messaging System. *ACM SGVR* 19.

Koons, D., and Sparrell, C. (1994). Iconic: Speech and Depictive Gestures at the Human-Machine Interface. *ACM SGVR* 97.

Lie, H., Dybvik, P., and Rygh, J. (1994). SCREAM: Screen-based Navigation in Voice Messages. *ACM SGVR* 97.

MCC (1989). Human Interface Tool Set—Copier Interface Design. *ACM SGVR* 47.

Rudnicky, A. (1990). Spoken Language Interfaces: The OM System. *ACM SGVR* 64.

Schmandt, C. (1984). Put That There. *ACM SGVR* 13.

Schmandt, C., and Arons, B. (1987). Conversational Desktop. *ACM SGVR* 27.

Stock, O. (1993). The Alfresco Interactive System. *ACM SGVR* 88.

Thorisson, K., Koons, D., and Bolt, R. (1992). Multi-Modal Natural Dialogue. *ACM SGVR* 76.

Wang Laboratories (1989). Wang Freestyle. *ACM SGVR* 45.

Weiner, D., and Ganapathy, S. (1990). Three-Dimensional Interfaces in Shared Environments. ACM *SGVR* 55.

Wilcox, L., Smith, I., and Bush, M. (1992). Wordspotting for Voice Editing and Audio Indexing. *ACM SGVR* 76.

Zellweger, P., Swinehart, D., Terry, D., and Pier, K. (1990). More Voice Applications in Cedar. *ACM SGVR* 59.

Text-To-Speech Conversion Technology

Michael H. O'Malley
Berkeley Speech Technologies

Text-to-speech (TTS) conversion transforms linguistic information stored as data or text into speech. It is widely used in audio reading devices for blind people. In the last few years, however, use of text-to-speech conversion technology has grown far beyond the disabled community to become a major adjunct to the rapidly growing use of digital voice storage for voice mail and voice response systems, which provide telephone information access. For example, text-to-speech technology can convert electronic mail to voice mail for audio access by phone. It can also permit field personnel to access large text databases, like parts inventories, by telephone.

The rapid expansion of text-to-speech technology comes in part from the advances in delivery methods and speech quality over the past 30 years. This article discusses the historical and theoretical bases of contemporary high-performance TTS systems and their current design. Because of space limitations, I have drawn examples mainly from Berkeley Speech Technologies' proprietary text-to-speech system, T-T-S.

Reading an English text out loud is currently the most successful simulation by a computer of a complex human mental function. This article shows how it can be done.

What is TTS?

Any text-to-speech system consists of two major elements. Starting with the output, we need some type of sound-generating mechanism whose function is analogous to that of the human vocal tract. A mouth by itself cannot talk, so we also need a module whose input is the text or other linguistic information to be spoken and whose output drives the sound-generating mechanism. In modern technology, both of these components are software. We can implement them in such a way that they can run on many kinds of hardware platforms.

A schematic of the human vocal tract appears in Figure 1. Air pressure developed in the lungs flows through the trachea and the vocal folds in the larynx. This opening between the vocal folds is called the glottis, and the air flow as a function of time is called the glottal waveform.

For voiced sounds, the correct combination of air pressure and muscle tension causes the vocal folds to vibrate, generating a series of pulses of air. For aspirate sounds such as /h/, the vocal folds adjust to generate turbulent air flow. For many sounds, we also generate noise in a higher part of the vocal tract.

Some of the noise in fricative sounds (/s/, /z/, /f/, etc.) actually results from turbulent air flowing through a constriction between the tongue and the roof of the mouth. On the other hand, the main source of noise in plosive sounds (/b/, /d/, /k/, etc.) is a burst from the sudden release of air pressure built up behind a closure of the vocal tract, followed by a short period of frication. In English and certain other languages, "voiceless" stops such as /k/ are also followed by a period of aspiration noise when they occur in particular linguistic environments.

The noise generated at the glottis or elsewhere in the vocal tract is modified as it passes through the oral and nasal cavities and radiates from the head as a speech waveform. As it progresses along the vocal tract, some of the flow reflects backwards. In fact, some energy even reflects back through the glottis toward the lungs. These reflections induce resonances (frequencies at which the sound is reinforced) and antiresonances (frequencies at which the sound is absorbed).

The frequency of the glottal pulses is one of the important parameters characterizing voiced sounds, corresponding to the fundamental frequency or pitch of the voice. However, finer details of the vocal

0018-9162/90/0800-0017$01.00 © 1990 IEEE

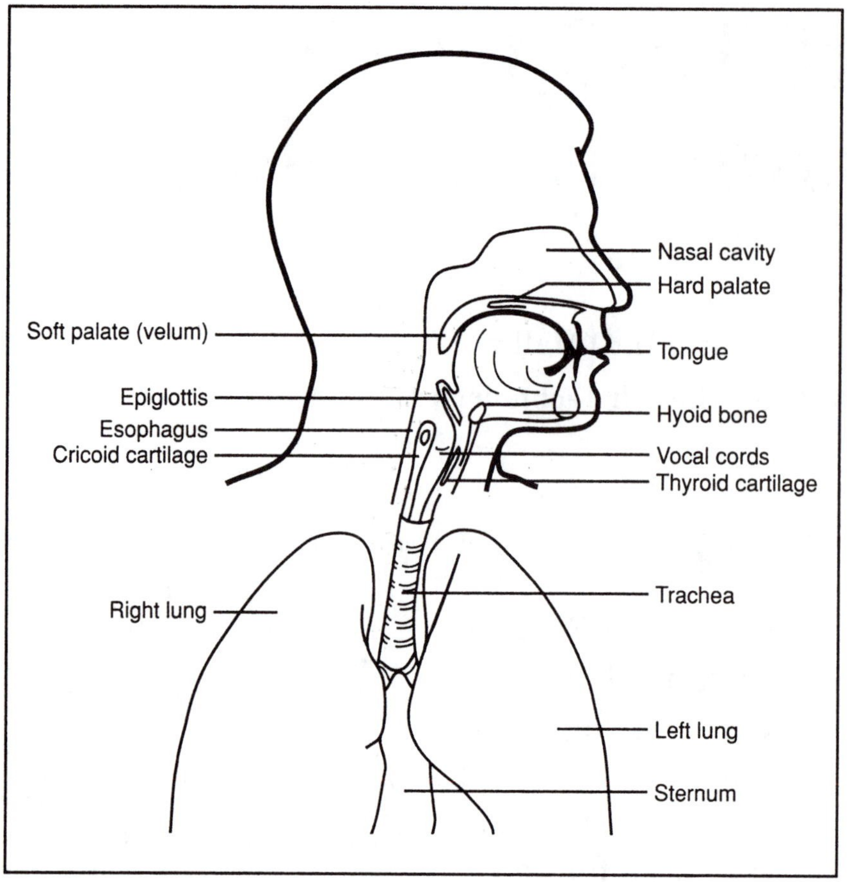

Figure 1. Schematic diagram of the human vocal mechanism.

fold vibrations as well as other elements of the sublaryngeal system also affect the overall sound quality.

Above the larynx, the shape of the tongue and lips and the size of the velar opening to the nasal cavity are major factors in determining the resonances of the vocal tract and thus the sound of the radiated speech waveform. Here again, even an obscure factor, such as the compressibility of the cheeks, can have some effect on the perceived sound.

The major features of the vocal tract and how they influence our perception of speech have been understood, at least in a general way, for years.[1,2] Because of the tremendous complexity of the vocal tract, however, the attempt to understand and model the human speech production mechanism remains an active research topic in current acoustic and physiological phonetics research.[3]

Our current understanding does permit the synthesis of intelligible speech, but our models, especially in their dynamic behavior, are not yet adequate to make synthetic speech that is indistinguishable from human speech.

Vocal tract models based on the physical shape and the physiology of the sound production mechanism provide many scientific insights but are rather difficult to use. The complex relationship between these physical parameters and the resulting speech waveform involves nonlinear equations. A small change in one of the model's parameters often makes a major change in the resulting sound.

Speech can also be modeled in strictly acoustic terms as a continuously changing spectrum (see Figure 2). The most common parameterization in this domain is in terms of the resonances and antiresonances (poles and zeros), familiar from traditional engineering models of linear systems. In this model, the speech production process consists of an excitation source, presumably representing the glottal waveform, which drives a "filter," presumably representing the oral and nasal cavities.

The most important acoustic parameters for speech synthesis are the fundamental frequency of the glottal waveform and the frequencies of the first three narrow bandwidth resonances, or formants. For a typical male voice, the fundamental varies over about an octave centered around 120 Hz, while the first three formants vary around 500 Hz, 1,500 Hz, and 2,500 Hz, respectively. The fundamental frequency for a female voice typically falls closer to 200 Hz, while the formant frequencies, which are inversely proportional to head size, measure about 10 percent higher.

This source/filter model of speech production is the most widely used model for acoustic phonetic research as well as for the most sophisticated applications of speech technology. However, it is only one of many possible parameterizations of the speech production mechanism.

For example, another model with wide applicability approximates the vocal tract by a cascade of short cylinders, each of a different diameter. This model is mathematically related to the widely used linear predictive coding (LPC) technique used in speech transmission systems and for recording human speech in compressed form on chips.

This multitube model has the advantage that it is easy to fit human speech to the model automatically, so we only need to transmit the model parameters rather than the full speech waveform. However, it is very difficult to relate the parameters of this multitube model to the usual scientific descriptions of speech. Therefore, this model has had limited applicability in the most sophisticated speech synthesis and recognition systems.

In my work at the University of Michigan in the 1960s, the real-time parametric voice module was actually a hardware analog filter. The hardware consisted of three voltage-controlled filters, a noise generator, and a pulse generator connected to an IBM 1800 computer with a total of only 8 kilowords of memory.

The filters modeled the resonances of the vocal tract and the pulse generator modeled the glottal waveform. We entered speech parameters by hand into the computer, which then sent them in real time to the hardware. By varying the parameters, we could study the effect of changing the voice model. The system helped in studying human speech production and perception, but was not sufficiently powerful to support the automatic conversion of text into speech in real time.

One major factor in the progress toward this goal has been the development of digital simulation of the kind of hardware used in the early systems. In general, an analog resonator can be simulated digitally by a very simple program consisting of addition, multiplication, and some storage

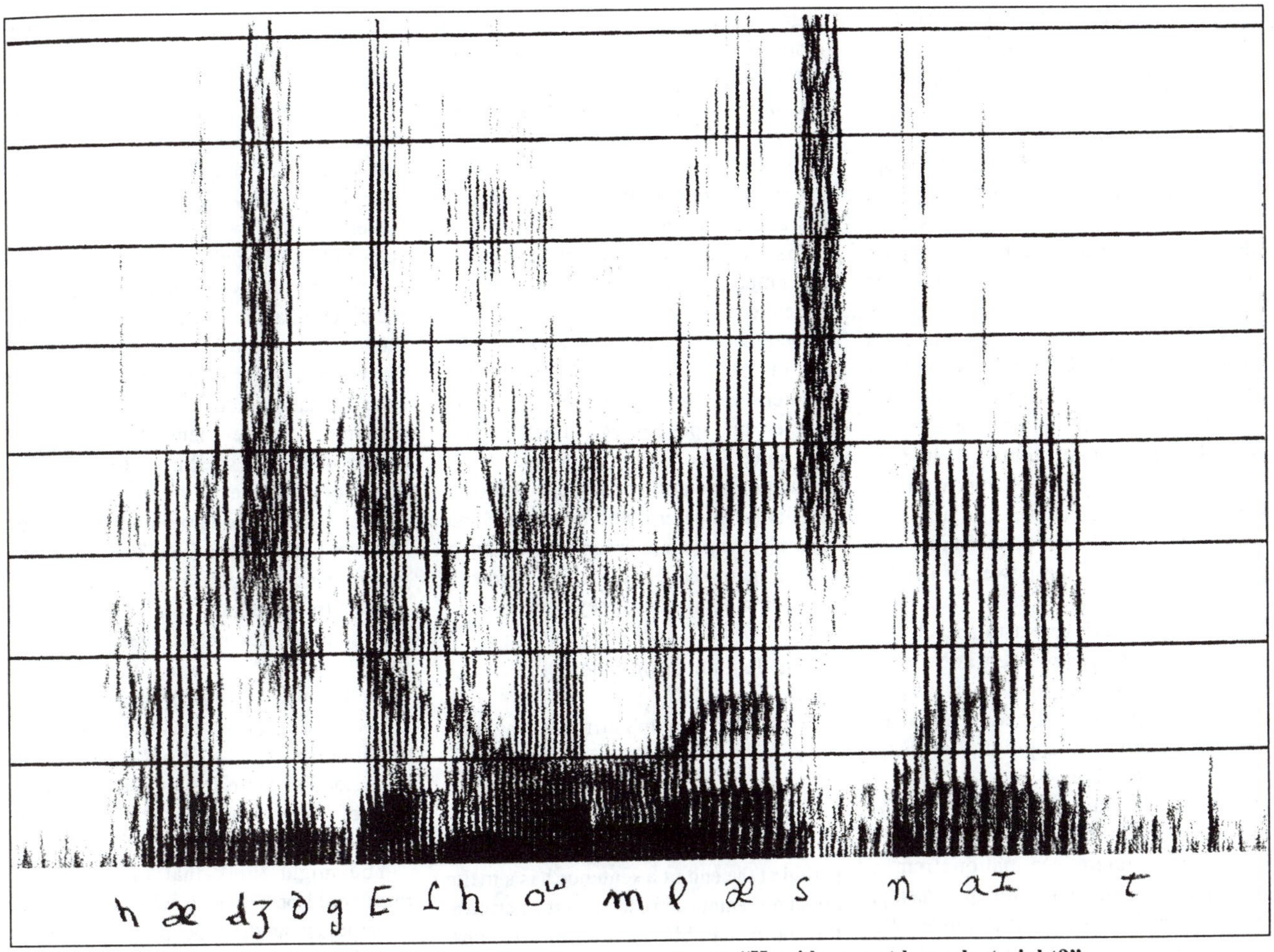

Figure 2. Speech modeled in acoustic terms as a continuous spectrum: "How'd you get home last night?"

locations. Approximately 20 multiplications are required in order to generate a single speech sample for a typical vocal tract model.

"Telephone quality" speech requires 8,000 samples per second, although most speech researchers prefer a somewhat higher bandwidth — 10,000 to 20,000 samples per second. With the computing power available by the 1970s, researchers could replace analog human sound production models by digital synthesizers in almost all research applications. Even when they lacked the computing power necessary for real-time synthesis, developing a more powerful, all-digital model and running it in batch mode was preferable to trying to make do with an inadequate hardware analog of the vocal tract. Thus, for more than 10 years most speech synthesizers have been software.

In 1978 Texas Instruments developed the "Speak & Spell" LPC chip. This chip can perform an integer multiply/add in less than 5 microseconds and therefore can implement a 10-pole lattice filter digitally. Unfortunately, this chip implements the multitube vocal tract model, with the consequent difficulty in generating synthetic parameters. However, because we can easily extract these filter coefficients from natural human speech, these chips found widespread use delivering speech in a number of products such as toys and talking cars. Of course, human voice stored and compressed by algorithm is not truly "synthetic" in the ordinary sense of "artificial" or "not of natural origin," but is more properly considered a low-bit-rate recording. True synthesis implies a model of a speaker, not an actual speaker.

During the 1980s, easily programmable digital signal processing chips became available. These chips, such as the Texas Instruments TMS320, could perform a multiply/add cycle in less that one microsecond. This meant that, at least for audio frequencies, even the most complex research voice models could be programmed to run in real time in a relatively inexpensive system. After this, practical hardware or computational limitations on the implementation of a synthesis voice model no longer existed.

However, the voice model constitutes a very small part of the text-to-speech synthesis problem. A voice model requires from a few hundred to at most a few thousand computer instructions. In contrast, the text-to-parameter model for a high-quality synthesizer requires from 100 to 1,000 times as much memory as the voice model to capture the extensive linguistic knowledge required for true synthesis.

It is interesting to compare the relative computational complexity in current speech recognition and speech synthesis systems. A speech recognition system must have some kind of speech analysis module, which functions as an "inverse" of the voice model of a speech synthesis system. However, this analysis task is more difficult than the corresponding synthesis because the signal is "real" rather than the result of a simplifying model. The better speech recognition models are related to the synthesis voice model, but they normally occupy a larger fraction of the available computer resources.

A speech recognition system must also have a "language model" to guide the mapping from the analysis parameters to the recognized text. In some sense, this module is the inverse of the text-to-parameter conversion module in a speech synthesis system.

In actuality, the language module for a speech recognition system is often rather simple and "algorithmic" rather than knowledge intensive. In fact, some recognition language models contain no linguistic information at all. They work with any language or even with nonlanguage sounds. However, even these simple language modules tax the power of current computer systems.

Generally speaking, text-to-speech systems are limited by our current knowledge of linguistics. Speech recognition systems are more limited by computing resources and by our ability to apply the linguistic knowledge available.

The text-to-parameter conversion module takes as input an English text (or, more usually, structured information from a database) and generates the parameters that can then drive a vocal tract model. We can think of this module as a model of how we convert linguistic information into parameters that drive the speech production mechanism. In other words, how do we read aloud from a printed text?

Of course, we know much less about how we process language than we know about how the human vocal tract works. However, we know a great deal about the structure of language. Linguistics is an old science and, especially over the past 30 years, researchers have developed a number of models for various parts of language. The text-to-parameter module might not really provide a good model of how we generate speech, but it does incorporate a great deal of knowledge about the English language.

The process of converting text into speech parameters breaks down into a number of stages, as shown in Figure 3. The following sections summarize these various subprocesses.

Text normalization

Actual texts have a great deal of symbolic material such as numbers, abbreviations, acronyms, and information signaled by graphic layout. The first step in a text-to-speech conversion system converts such information into a standard text format. The complex conversion process involves various types of local parsing. While the details lie beyond the scope of this article, some examples can illustrate the various difficulties.

First, consider the different ways we can read numbers. For example, we can read the sequence "415" in three different ways depending on whether it is an area code, part of an address, or a dollar amount. Furthermore, the rules for converting numbers into spoken English will differ in the United States and in England.

The pronunciation of various abbreviations is often determined by context. For example, the pronunciation of letter/punctuation mark sequences differs markedly depending upon where they occur:

- Dr. Jones lives on Jones Dr.
- St. James St.
- Jan. 22 is my wife's birthday; her name is Jan.

The effect of punctuation marks is also often context determined. For example, a period at the end of a sentence has a major effect on sentence prosody. But a period at the end of an abbreviation, in a decimal number, or after a middle initial in a name has a very different significance and must not be misinterpreted as a sentence termination in pronunciation. Columnar lists of items, pronounced as if they ended with a period, often do not have any punctuation at all. In this case, the text-to-speech system must recognize the two-dimensional shape of the text to pronounce it correctly.

All of the above phenomena can be handled reasonably successfully, but they require an extensive, nonalgorithmic computer program. Such a program captures facts about normal American English written text that almost every literate person knows implicitly. It probably does not provide a good model of our mental processing, but it does model human knowledge in the same sense that a good chess program models a chess master's knowledge of chess.

Word pronunciation

How we pronounce English words today depends on 2,000 years of history, dozens of wars, and many population migrations. Because of this, English has by far the most complex relationship between spelling and word pronunciation of any alphabetic language.

We all learned the rule that a final "e" makes the preceding vowel tense — the rule that turns "dud" into "dude." However, a reasonably accurate text-to-speech system requires several thousand such rules to handle English.

Any language with an alphabetic writing system has rules that convert spelling into sound. However, words borrowed from another language tend to reflect the rules of that language, modified to fit the patterns of the new language. The complexity of English spelling derives from its diversity of sources.

For example, the large number of English words borrowed from Romance languages tend to be stressed on the third syllable from the end ("intelligent"). However, some affixes move the stress location ("intelligibility"), while others do not ("intelligently"). English speakers often stress names and other words of recent non-English origin, such as "Dukakis," on the second syllable from the end, regardless of their stress in their original language.

You might think that pronunciation rules could be replaced with a large dictionary: just put the exact pronunciation of each English word in a table and then look it up. In fact, a text-to-speech system must use a dictionary to pronounce certain exceptional words. However, the ordinary English speaker encounters a large number of words and an even larger number of names. For example, it has been estimated that the average American high school student might encounter any one of 500,000 different words.[4] In the United States, the 1970 census listed more than 2 million different last names, any one of which might occur in a typical computer database. Furthermore, our culture adds new words and new names every day, which means that a dictionary would always be out of date. A large dictionary, by itself, cannot provide a solution.

The word pronunciation module for a high-performance text-to-speech system must combine a dictionary with sophisticated pronunciation rules. The dictionary handles words with a syntactic or context-dependent effect, as well as words not regular enough to justify a rule. The rules then handle the rest of the words, including new words and names. Of the several million words and names possible, the majority will thus be pronounced correctly by an efficient system.

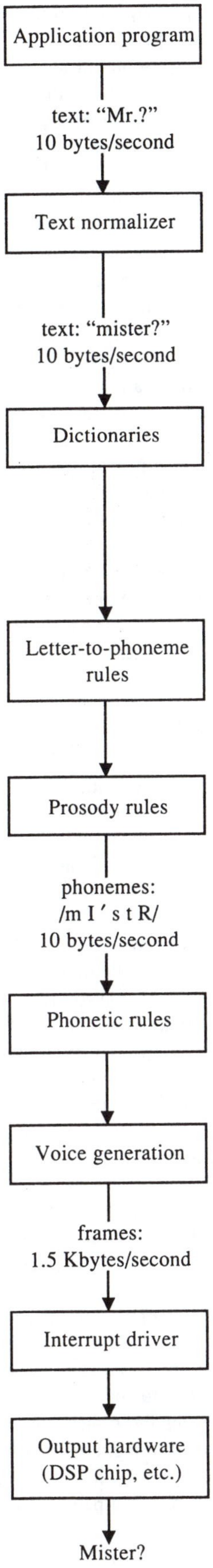

Text data made up of English words and numbers is the output of many kinds of application programs: word processors, electronic mail systems, databases, optical character readers, etc. This forms the initial input for BST T-T-S. We always need some kind of application program to create the text T-T-S reads.

The text normalizer converts everything in the text stream to letters. For example, "1990" becomes "nineteen ninety" and "Dr." becomes either "doctor" or "drive," as appropriate. The current normalizer is quite large and complex. We could use a much simpler one, but a normalizer is always needed. Custom normalizers help optimize performance in vertical market applications, which often have their own standard abbreviations.

Some words in English are not pronounced in accordance with the basic rules for English pronunciation. The word "of," for example, is the only case where a final "f" is pronounced "v." To say these words correctly, the system stores a phonemic transcription of their exact pronunciation in an exception dictionary. The dictionary is also needed to store grammatical information about particular words for use by other modules in the system.

The letter-to-phoneme rules convert English spelling into phoneme transcriptions, which are a more exact representation of pronunciation. For example, the word "cat" is represented as "k æ t." Grammatically significant endings such as "-ness," "-ly," and "-ing" are also identified.

The prosody rules create the intonation pattern, or rhythm, of sentences in the text. All text-to-speech systems have somewhat robotic prosodies because the computer, unlike human speakers, follows rigid rules. However, end users can insert prosodic "diacritics" into a text to get special intonation patterns.

The "fine tuning" of pronunciation takes place in the phonetic rules. For example, the phoneme "t" is pronounced differently in "tom," "atom," and "cat." Users can enter phonemes directly into the T-T-S system at this point, bypassing the text-to-phoneme modules, for complete control of pronunciation.

The voice generation module turns phonemes into more than 5,000 smaller speech units, which are then converted to voice parameters. T-T-S allows the creation of an unlimited number of different voices. Three default "head models" can be extensively modified, using text instructions alone, to produce many different character voices.

The interrupt driver takes frames and sends them to the output hardware at regular intervals of from 5 to 25 milliseconds.

Various kinds of output hardware can be used for the final stages of T-T-S. T-T-S can drive the general-purpose digital signal processing chips, such as the Texas Instruments TMS320, found in standard voice processing systems. However, it also produces excellent results with inexpensive consumer electronics speech chips and can even run without any special speech chips.

Figure 3. The process of converting text into speech parameters in Berkeley Speech Technologies T-T-S system.

Prosodies

The prosodic component of speech involves such phenomena as rhythm, intonation, and the emphasis or de-emphasis of particular words. For any given text, a human speaker might produce thousands of possible prosodic interpretations, but an even larger number would not be considered natural under reasonable circumstances.

As you listen to speech, certain words will seem more prominent than others. Often, these words carry the information focus of the message. On the other hand, such word stress patterns might simply signal that the word is part of a multiword compound: "Jones Street"; "history teacher."

Speech usually divides into a number of shorter phrases. Some of the division points will be accompanied by actual silence, while some will be marked only by an apparent slowing. However, each phrase will contain at least one of the emphasized words.

In addition to emphasized words and division into phrases, speech has an intonation contour. For example, some of the phrases typically end either with a falling pitch or with a fall followed by a low rise — a "period" or a "comma" intonation.

If part of a conversation, speech will exhibit quite elaborate prosodic phenomena that might carry a significant portion of the message's meaning. But speech as read from a text, especially by a person neither interested in nor knowledgeable about the text, will provide much more regular prosodic information.

Prosodies have been studied extensively in linguistics. However, they seem to be one of the most complex parts of language, and the information needed to generate them correctly from a text is not always available from current computational linguistic technology.

For example, prosodies depend in part upon syntactic structure. Usually, a prosodic break occurs between a long subject and the predicate in an English sentence. Because no current natural language parser is robust enough for use with general written English texts, we cannot always find this break reliably.

Prosodies generally prove the most difficult part of language for a text-to-speech conversion system. A very good prosodic component would probably require that the computer actually "understand" the text. However, an adequate if rather monotonic or dull reading is possible using the most neutral or general case of current prosodic models. For example, textual punctuation marks usually indicate prosodic boundaries, and the last word in a phrase normally gets the primary emphasis. Articles and prepositions are de-emphasized and associated with minor phrase boundaries.

The resulting speech sounds somewhat boring, but most attempts to make it more lively result in some sentences having a foolish-sounding prosody. Most people might also, when presented with a text and asked to read it aloud, use something closer to the prosody produced by a text-to-speech system than they would use in speaking naturally.

Phonetic rules

After we have applied the text normalizer, word pronunciation rules, and prosody rules, the utterance consists of a string of phonemes. Phonemes are the symbols used by some dictionaries to represent pronunciation. Although a long way from actual speech sounds, they represent the finest distinctions that most people not trained in phonetics normally notice. The concept of "the phoneme" covers a range of recognizable expressions, not a point. The distribution pattern for various phoneme realizations is part of what defines dialects. Ordinary, casual speech represents phonemes in about the same way that messy human handwriting represents the abstract ideal graphic letters of the alphabet.

The phonetic rule module takes phonemes as input to produce a detailed description of the sounds of the utterance. The rules in this module do things such as assign a duration to each phoneme according to context, for example, lengthening the final vowel in a phrase by up to 50 percent. Other rules remove parts of phonemes, for example, deleting the aspiration of a stop such as /k/ in a number of different contexts.

Phonetic rules play the major role of describing the co-articulation between phonemes. Each phoneme strongly influences the parameters in the adjacent phoneme. In some cases, this influence might extend over several adjacent phonemes.

A great many phonetic rules must be programmed in a text-to-speech conversion system. Without these rules, the speech output might be somewhat recognizable, but it would sound very unnatural. In American English, for example, the phoneme /t/ should sound quite different in the words "Tom," "cat," and "butter."

In rapid human speech, the application of phonetic rules is sometimes quite extreme. Consider, for example, the classic case of the phrase "Did you eat yet?" This phrase can reduce to something closer to "Chee chet?"

People can make such reductions because they understand and get feedback from their communication environment. Thus, they can judge the degree to which reduction is appropriate. If it is not appropriate, they can always speak more formally.

While we could certainly program such "fast speech" rules for a text-to-speech conversion system, it is probably more appropriate to maintain a more formal style of speech. For example, "want to" or "thank you" often reduce to "wanna" or "thank ya" when spoken. However, an electronic mail system that read its messages aloud over the telephone in such an informal style would seem odd and out of place in a business context.

Voice tables

The phonetic rules provide a detailed phonetic description for an utterance. The voice table module converts this description into numeric targets for use by the voice model. The phonetic rules in conjunction with the voice tables are the primary determinants of voice intelligibility.

Intelligibility is the likelihood that a human listener will be able to identify a particular word spoken. In one standard test,[5] a modern, high-quality text-to-speech system typically scores approximately 95 percent. In contrast, low-end systems score from 60 to 75 percent. Careful human speakers typically produce about half the listener error rate of the best text-to-speech systems, although some communication channels carrying human speech elicit scores as low as 85 percent on this test.

One major function of the voice tables is to handle differences in bandwidth. Speech researchers have usually assumed a minimum speech bandwidth of 5 or 6 kHz. Unfortunately, telephone system designers have traditionally employed a bandwidth of 3.5 kHz, and even the newest digital telephones have perpetuated that bandwidth.

Important features of fricatives and stops occur in the frequency range of 4 to 6 kHz. Human speech is so redundant that generally we don't miss this frequency range. However, text-to-speech systems can easily suffer losses unless we account for this difference in frequency range.

Our solution is to have different sets of voice tables for different frequency ranges. For applications involving telephones, some of the frequency components above 4 kHz can be mapped to a lower frequency, potentially contributing to overall speech quality and intelligibility.

Hardware implementation

In the work that we at Berkeley Speech Technologies have done on our own text-to-speech system, a major goal has been to develop a highly portable version of text-to-speech conversion software. We want to be able to deliver the same high quality of speech on any hardware platform that meets certain minimum requirements.

In terms of computational complexity, our text-to-parameter conversion process requires from 250 to 350 kilobytes of memory and a processing power of about 0.2 million instructions per second. Since this module is not very computationally demanding, we coded it entirely in the C language.

The voice model, on the other hand, requires less than 1 Kbyte of code but on the order of 1 MIPS. Since this module is small and usually time critical, we almost always encode it in assembly language.

The design of our software, coupled with recent advances in available hardware, has allowed us to successfully implement text-to-speech capability on a wide variety of hardware platforms. These include

- A pocket-sized talking dictionary with an 83,000-word vocabulary. It contains no digital signal processing chip, but synthesizes words in real time in an 8-MHz NEC V20 microprocessor.
- A telephone voice-response board that simultaneously generates 16 channels of speech from text in real time, then converts the speech waveforms into 32 kilobit-per-second ADPCM (adaptive delta pulse code modulation) coded speech.
- A stand-alone text-to-speech conversion unit with a built-in speaker and a 12-volt power supply, designed for speaking text messages sent to trucks by satellite.
- A personal speech-output device for blind people. Using CMOS hardware makes possible portability and battery-powered use with laptops. It speaks up to 700 words a minute.

Other approaches

The principal high-end commercial text-to-speech systems for American English are Digital Equipment's DECtalk, Centigram's Speech Plus, and our own BST T-T-S. Both DECtalk and Speech Plus are based on the work of Dennis Klatt at the Masschusetts Institute of Technology.[6]

Broadly speaking, Klatt's approach resembles the approach described in this article, based on an elaborate, fully synthetic, formant-based model of voice production. While the systems differ in many ways, the overall effect is roughly similar.

At the other end of the spectrum, a number of "toy" quality synthesizers have appeared on the market for use with low-end personal computers. Generally, they have relied either on recorded waveforms or on one of the "speech synthesis" chips.[7]

The main problem with this approach is that these chips are programmed to take phonemes as input and to generate between 64 and 128 presynthesized segments. However, these chips have not implemented the large number of phonetic rules that map phonemes into speech sounds, so have been fairly unintelligible.

Another approach, under the names "demi-syllable," "diphone," or "dyad" synthesis, involves recording several thousand segments of human speech using some form of LPC encoding.[8] These segments represent all of the theoretically possible transitions between adjacent phonemes or sequences of phonemes. Such an approach eliminates the need for some of the co-articulation rules but in return makes some of the other phonetic rules more difficult to apply. Some good research implementations have used this approach but, I believe, it does not solve any significant problems. Moreover, it has not been adopted in the highest quality commercial text-to-speech systems.

Unrealistic expectations for dramatic future improvement in text-to-speech technology sometimes arise from an unsophisticated view of the complex linguistic information involved. Improvement will continue at the same slow, steady pace that has produced incremental progress in accuracy, intelligibilty, and naturalness over the past three decades. However, we can expect faster progress in methods of delivering the technology. ■

References

1. G. Fant, *Acoustic Theory of Speech Production*, Mouton and Co., 's-Gravenhage, Netherlands, 1960.
2. J.L. Flanagan, *Speech Analysis Synthesis and Perception*, 2nd ed., Springer-Verlag, New York, 1972.
3. D.H. Klatt and L.C. Klatt, "Analysis, Synthesis, and Perception of Voice Quality Variations Among Female and Male Talkers," *J. Acoustical Society of America*, Vol. 87, Feb. 1990, pp. 820-857.
4. J.B. Carrol et al., *Word Frequency Book*, American Heritage, New York, 1971.
5. J.S. Logen, B. G. Greene, and D.B. Pisoni, "Segmental Intelligibility of Synthetic Speech Produced by Rule," *J. Acoustical Society of America*, Vol. 86, No. 2, Aug. 1989, pp. 566-581.
6. D.H. Klatt, "Review of Text-to-Speech Conversion for English," *J. Acoustical Society of America*, Vol. 82, No. 3, Sept. 1987, pp. 737-793.
7. I.H. Witten, *Principles of Computer Speech*, Academic Press, New York, 1982.
8. J.P. Olive, "Rule Synthesis of Speech from Diadic Units," *Proc. 1977 IEEE Int'l Conf. Acoustics, Speech, and Signal Processing*, Vol. ICASSP-77, pp. 568-570.

Michael H. O'Malley founded Berkeley Speech Technologies (initially called Berkeley Systems Works) in 1979. As president and chief scientist at BST, he has been engaged in the development of advanced text-to-speech systems since 1980. He has engaged in speech research since 1961, when he worked for IBM Research on a text-to-speech project while still a student at the California Institute of Technology. He did his PhD work in the University of Michigan Program in Communications Sciences, where he studied computer science, electrical engineering, linguistics, and biological systems.

From 1968 through 1973 O'Malley directed the Phonetics Laboratory at the University of Michigan as a member of the faculty. He was a principal investigator in the ARPA Speech Recognition Project, which he began at Michigan and continued at the University of California at Berkeley as a member of the UC Computer Science Department.

Readers can contact the author at Berkeley Speech Technologies, 2409 Telegraph Ave., Berkeley, CA 94705.

An Introduction to Speech and Speaker Recognition

Richard D. Peacocke and Daryl H. Graf
Bell-Northern Research

Speech recognition, the ability to identify spoken words, and speaker recognition, the ability to identify who is saying them, are becoming commonplace applications of speech processing technology.

Being able to speak to your personal computer, and have it recognize and understand what you say, would provide a comfortable and natural form of communication. It would reduce the amount of typing you have to do, leave your hands free, and allow you to move away from the terminal or screen. You would not even have to be in the line of sight of the terminal. It would also help in some cases if the computer could tell *who* was speaking.

If you want to use voice as a new medium on a computer workstation, it is natural to explore how speech recognition can contribute to such an environment. Here, we will review the state of speech and speaker recognition, focusing on current technology applied to personal workstations.

Limited forms of speech recognition are available on personal workstations. Currently there is much interest in speech recognition, and performance is improving. Speech recognition has already proven useful for certain applications, such as telephone voice-response systems for selecting services or information, digit recognition for cellular phones, and data entry while walking around a railway yard or clambering over a jet engine during an inspection.

Nonetheless, comfortable and natural communication in a general setting (no constraints on what you can say and how you say it) is beyond us for now, posing a problem too difficult to solve. Fortunately, we can simplify the problem to allow the creation of applications like the examples just mentioned. Some of these simplifying constraints are discussed in the next section.

Speaker recognition is related to work on speech recognition. Instead of determining what was said, you determine who said it. Deciding whether or not a particular speaker produced the utterance is called *verification*, and choosing a person's identity from a set of known speakers is called *identification*. The most general form of speaker recognition (text-independent) is still not very accurate for large speaker populations, but if you constrain the words spoken by the user (text-dependent) and do not allow the speech quality to vary too wildly, then it too can be done on a workstation.

See the sidebar "Applications" for a description of typical speech and speaker recognition applications.

Factors affecting speech recognition

Modern speech recognition research began in the late 1950s with the advent of the digital computer. Combined with tools to capture and analyze speech, such as analog-to-digital converters and sound spectrograms, the computer allowed researchers to search for ways to extract features from speech that allow discrimination between different words. The 1960s saw advances in the automatic segmentation of speech into units of linguistic relevance (such as phonemes, syllables, and words) and on new pattern-matching and

0018-9162/90/0800-0026$01.00 © 1990 IEEE

Applications

Although the performance of speech and speaker recognition systems is far from perfect, these systems have already proven their usefulness for certain applications.

Speech recognition. Currently, speech recognition is most often applied in manufacturing for companies needing voice entry of data or commands while the operator's hands are otherwise occupied. Related applications occur in product inspection, inventory control, command/control, and material handling. Speech recognition also finds frequent application in medicine, where voice input can significantly accelerate the writing of routine reports.

Speech recognition over the telephone network, although less used, has the greatest potential for growth. Automating the telephone operator's job can greatly reduce operating costs for telephone companies. Furthermore, speech recognition can help users control the personal workstation or interact with other applications remotely when touch-tone keypads are not available. (Telephone network applications are described in articles by Matthew Lennig and Ryohei Nakatsu elsewhere in this issue.)

Finally, speech recognition offers greater freedom to the physically handicapped.

Typical real-world applications:

- Delco electronics employs IBM PC/AT-Cherry Electronics and Intel RMX86 recognition systems to collect circuit board inspection data while the operator repairs and marks the boards.
- Southern Pacific Railway inspectors now routinely use a PC-based Votan recognition system to enter car inspection information from the field by walkie-talkie.
- Michigan Bell has installed a Northern Telecom recognition system to automate collect and third-number billed calls. AT&T has also put in field trial systems to automate call-type selection in its Reno, Nevada, and Hayward, California, offices.

Speaker recognition. Speaker recognition has been applied most often as a security device to control access to buildings or information. One of the best known examples is the Texas Instruments corporate computer center security system. Security Pacific has employed speaker verification as a security mechanism on telephone-initiated transfers of large sums of money. In addition to adding security, verification is advantageous because it reduces the turnaround time on these banking transactions. Bellcore uses speaker verification to limit remote access of training information to authorized field personnel. Speaker recognition also provides a mechanism to limit the remote access of a personal workstation to its owner or a set of registered users.

In addition to its use as a security device, speaker recognition could be used to trigger specialized services based on a user's identity. For example, you could configure an answering machine to deliver personalized messages to a small set of frequent callers.

classification algorithms. By the 1970s, a number of important techniques essential to today's state-of-the-art speech recognition systems had emerged, spurred on in part by the Defense Advanced Research Projects Agency speech recognition project. These techniques have now been refined to the point where very high recognition rates are possible, and commercial systems are available at reasonable prices.

Five factors can be used to control and simplify the speech recognition task[1]:

(1) *Isolated words.* Speech consisting of isolated words (short silences between the words) is much easier to recognize than continuous speech because word boundaries are difficult to find in continuous speech. Also, coarticulation effects in continuous speech cause the pronunciation of a word to change depending on its position relative to other words in a sentence. For example, "did you?" is not the same as "did" + short silence + "you?" Other effects depend on the rate of speaking as well, such as our tendency to drop the "t" in want when saying "want to" casually and quickly.

Error rates can definitely be reduced by requiring the user to pause between each word. For example, in a study by Bahl et al.,[2] error rates of 9 percent for continuous recognition decreased to 3 percent for isolated-word recognition. However, this type of restriction places a burden on the user and reduces the speed with which information can be input to the system (from a range of about 150-250 words per minute down to about 20-100 words per minute).

(2) *Single speaker.* Speech from a single speaker is also easier to recognize than speech from a variety of speakers because most parametric representations of speech are sensitive to the characteristics of the particular speaker. This makes a set of pattern-matching templates for one speaker perform poorly for another speaker. Therefore, many systems are speaker dependent — trained for use with each different operator. Relatively few speech recognition systems can be used by the general public. A rule of thumb used by many researchers is that, for the same task, speaker-dependent systems will have error rates roughly three to five times smaller than speaker-independent ones.

One way to make a system speaker independent is simply to mix training templates from a wide variety of speakers. A more sophisticated approach will attempt to look for phonetic features that are relatively invariant between speakers.

(3) *Vocabulary size.* The size of the vocabulary of words to be recognized also strongly influences recognition accuracy. Large vocabularies are more likely to contain ambiguous words than small vocabularies. Ambiguous words are those whose pattern-matching templates appear similar to the classification algorithm used by the recognizer. They are therefore harder to distinguish from each other. Of course, small vocabularies composed of many ambiguous words can be particularly difficult to recognize. A famous example is the E-set, which consists of a subset of the English alphabet and digits: "B," "C,"

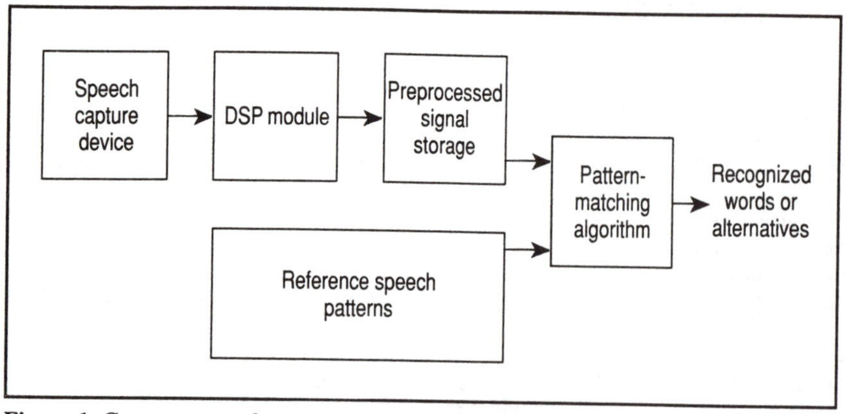

Figure 1. Components of a typical speech recognition system.

"D," "E," "G," "P," "T," "V," "Z," and "three."

The amount of time it takes to search the speech model database also relates to vocabulary size. Systems containing many pattern templates typically require pruning techniques to cut down the computational load of the pattern-matching algorithm. By ignoring potentially useful search paths, pruning heuristics can also introduce recognition errors.

(4) *Grammar*. The grammar of the recognition domain defines the allowable sequences of words. A tightly constrained grammar is one in which the number of words that can legally follow any given word is small. The amount of constraint on word choice is referred to as the *perplexity* of the grammar. Systems with low perplexity are potentially more accurate than those that give the user more freedom because the system can limit the effective vocabulary (and search space) to those words that can occur in the current input context. For example, a system described in Kimbal et al.[3] had an error rate of 1.6 percent with perplexity 19 (tightly constrained), while the error rate hit about 4.5 percent with perplexity 58 (more loosely constrained).

(5) *Environment*. Background noise, changes in microphone characteristics, and loudness can all dramatically affect recognition accuracy. Many recognition systems are capable of very low error rates as long as the environmental conditions remain quiet and controlled. However, performance degrades when noise is introduced or when conditions differ from the training session used to build the reference templates. To compensate, the user must almost always wear a head-mounted, noise-limiting microphone with the same response characteristics as the microphone used during training.

Components of a speech recognition system

Most computer systems for speech recognition include the following five components (see Figure 1):

(1) A *speech capture device*. This usually consists of a microphone and associated analog-to-digital converter, which digitally encodes the raw speech waveform.

(2) A *digital signal processing module*. The DSP module performs endpoint (word boundary) detection to separate speech from nonspeech, converts the raw waveform into a frequency domain representation, and performs further windowing, scaling, filtering, and data compression.[4] The goal is to enhance and retain only those components of the spectral representation that are useful for recognition purposes, thereby reducing the amount of information that the pattern-matching algorithm must contend with. A set of these speech parameters for one interval of time (usually 10-30 milliseconds) is called a *speech frame*.

(3) *Preprocessed signal storage*. Here, the preprocessed speech is buffered for the recognition algorithm.

(4) *Reference speech patterns*. Stored reference patterns can be matched against the user's speech sample once it has been preprocessed by the DSP module. This information is stored as a set of speech templates or as generative speech models.

(5) A *pattern matching algorithm*. The algorithm must compute a measure of goodness-of-fit between the preprocessed signal from the user's speech and all the stored templates or speech models. A selection process chooses the template or model (possibly more than one) with the best match.

Two major types of pattern matching in use are template matching by dynamic time warping and hidden Markov models. Artificial neural networks applied to speech recognition have also had some success, but this work is still in the early stages of research.[5] Moreover, linguistic knowledge incorporated into the pattern-recognition algorithm can enhance performance. However, such sophisticated techniques lie outside of the scope of this article (see, for example, O'Shaughnessy[4] and Mariani[6]).

Template matching by dynamic time warping became very popular in the 1970s. Template matching is conceptually simple. You want to compare the preprocessed speech waveform directly against a reference template by summing the distances between respective speech frames. However, biological limitations tend to produce nonlinear variations in timing from utterance to utterance. Consequently, the various frames of a word may be out of alignment with the corresponding frames of the given template. Since the order of speech events is fairly constant, you correct the misalignment by stretching the template in some places and compressing it in others to find an optimum match. Dynamic programming helps compute the optimum match. The sidebar "Dynamic time warping" illustrates the resulting time warp process.

Hidden Markov models are used in most current research systems because this technique produces better results for continuous speech with moderate-size vocabularies. HMMs are stochastic state machines that associate probabilities of producing sounds with transitions from state to state. An ideal HMM models speech with the same variations that occur in human speech due to coarticulation and other effects. Speech generated by a human being is matched against an HMM by computing the probability that the HMM would have generated the same utterance or by finding the state sequence through the HMM that has the highest probability of producing the utterance. The fact that HMMs generate poor-quality speech explains why recognition based on HMMs is still not perfect.

The sidebar "Hidden Markov models" further details the use of HMMs. Markov chains, although known about for almost a century, have only been successfully used in the context of speech recognition for the past 15 years or so. Until recently, no method existed for optimizing the model

Dynamic time warping

Frame distances between the processed speech frames and those of the reference templates are summed to provide an overall distance measure of similarity. But, instead of taking frames that correspond exactly in time, you would do a time "warp" on the utterance (and scale its length) so that similar frames in the utterance line up better against the reference frames. A dynamic programming procedure finds a warp that minimizes the sum of frame distances in the template comparison. The distance produced by this warp is chosen as the similarity measure.

In the illustration here, the speech frames that make up the test and reference templates are shown as scalar amplitude values plotted on a graph with time as the *x* axis. In practice, they are multidimensional vectors, and the distance between them is usually taken as the Euclidean distance. The graphs show how warping one of the templates improves the match between them. (For further information, see chapter 10 of O'Shaughnessy.[4])

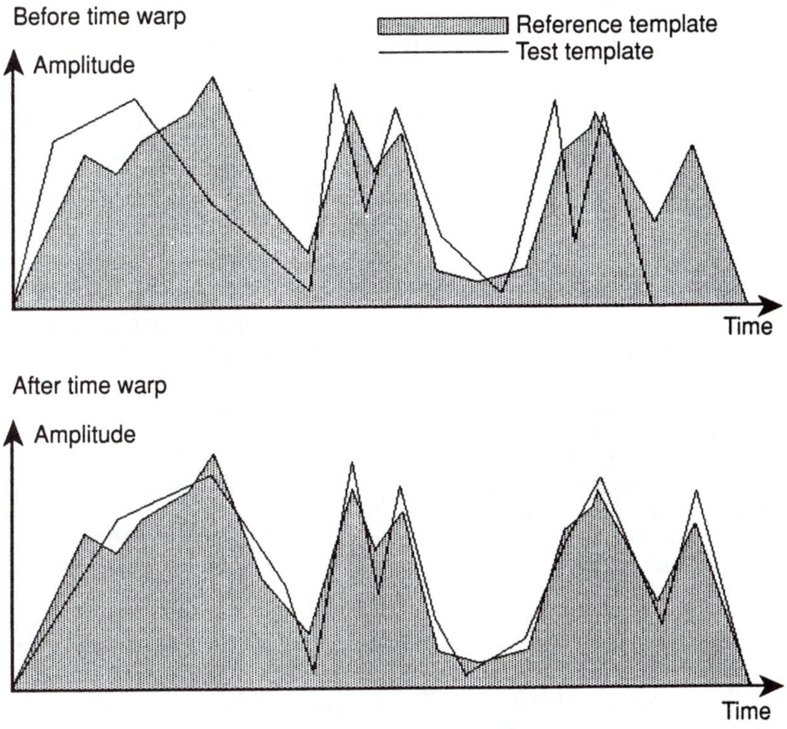

parameters to generate observed speech patterns. (The US Department of Defense actually suppressed publication of the advances in HMM algorithms for a while in the mid-1970s, probably because of their use in cryptanalysis.) As well as representing low-level speech segments and transitions, hidden Markov models provide a framework on which you can model higher level structures in continuous speech signals and incorporate other knowledge about the communication.

Current speech recognition systems

Current speech recognition systems can be categorized according to the types of constraint they place on the speech. At one end of the spectrum fall speaker-independent, continuous, unconstrained-grammar, large-vocabulary systems. These systems are still very much in the research stage.

Several systems among those representing the state of the art were trained and tested on the same speech data — the DARPA resource management database — and are easily compared. The DARPA resource management task involves queries and commands to a database of warships. The associated database consists of a 997-word vocabulary and grammars with various complexities. Sphinx, a recognizer developed at Carnegie Mellon University, has a maximum word-recognition accuracy of 93.7 percent for a grammar of perplexity 60 and 70.6 percent for a grammar of perplexity 997.[1] BBN's Byblos[7] and a system developed at Lincoln Labs[8] have word accuracies of 88.7 percent and 87.4 percent, respectively, for the perplexity 60 grammar (BBN's system requires about two minutes of speech to adapt to a particular speaker before reaching this level of performance). Texas Instruments* and Stanford Research Institute[9] have reported systems with 44.3 percent and 40.4 percent accuracy on the perplexity 997 grammar. These systems have considerably lower *sentence* accuracies.

Representative of the state of the art in speaker-dependent, isolated-word, large-vocabulary recognizers are systems like IBM's Tangora recognizer, which is capable of 97 percent accuracy for a 20,000-word vocabulary[10] and NEC's 97.5 percent accurate, 1,800-word system.[11]

A variety of other systems trade off constraints on the input speech for higher recognition accuracies. Among these are the AT&T Bell Labs telephone-grade, speaker-independent, connected-digit recognizer (98.5 percent accurate when the number of digits is known[12]) and a speaker-dependent version of BBN's Byblos, which measured 94.8 percent accurate on the perplexity 60 DARPA resource management task.

At the highly constrained speech end of the spectrum fall speaker-dependent, single-word, small-vocabulary recognition systems. A variety of such systems developed can achieve accuracies above 99 percent.

Various commercial systems have appeared for Sun workstations and IBM-compatible PCs over the past few years. Table 1 summarizes the capabilities, costs, and manufacturers' claimed accuracies of a sample of these commercial products. Although several companies advertise speaker-independent, continuous, large-

* See Kai-fu Lee,[1] p. 133.

Hidden Markov models

A hidden Markov model (HMM) is a doubly stochastic process for producing a sequence of observed symbols. An underlying stochastic finite state machine (FSM) drives a set of stochastic processes, which produce the symbols. When a state is entered after a state transition in the FSM, a symbol from that state's set of symbols is selected probabilistically for output. The term "hidden" is appropriate because the actual state of the FSM cannot be observed directly, only through the symbols emitted. In the example here, the sequence of symbols AAaaB could have been produced by any of three different state transition sequences.

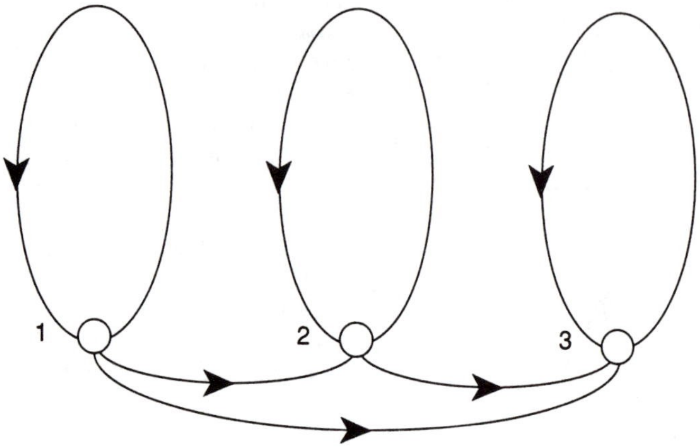

State	Possible Outputs
1	A,a
2	a
3	B

AAaaB could be produced by the following state sequences:

→ 1 → 1 → 1 → 1 → 3
or → 1 → 1 → 1 → 2 → 3
or → 1 → 1 → 2 → 2 → 3

Although not shown in the example, probabilities are attached to the finite state transitions, and discrete probability distributions control the symbol output for each state (continuous density HMMs also exist). In the case of isolated word recognition, each word in the vocabulary has a corresponding HMM. These HMMs might actually consist of HMMs that model subword units such as phonemes connected to form a single word-model HMM. In the case of continuous word recognition, a single HMM corresponds to the domain grammar. This grammar model is constructed from word-model HMMs. The observable symbols correspond to (quantized) speech frame measurements.

An algorithm known as the forward/backward (or Baum-Welch) algorithm finds a set of state transition probabilities and symbol output distributions for each HMM. This gradient descent algorithm uses training data to iteratively refine an initial (possibly random) set of model parameters such that the HMM is more likely to generate patterns from the training set.

After this initial training stage, a word or sentence to be recognized is spoken, and speech measurements are made that reduce the utterance to a sequence of symbols. In the case of isolated word recognition, the forward algorithm computes the probability that each word model produced the observed sequence of symbols — the model with the highest probability represents the recognized word. In the case of continuous recognition, the Viterbi algorithm finds the state transition path, through the grammar model, with the maximum likelihood of generating the set of measurements. The sequence of word models on this path corresponds to the recognized sentence. (For further information see "Introduction to Hidden Markov Models" by L.R. Rabiner and B.H. Juang, published in *IEEE Trans. Acoustics, Speech, and Signal Processing*, Jan. 1986, pp. 4-16.)

vocabulary speech recognition, they carefully avoid making strong claims about the accuracy of their products. With commercial systems, you typically get what you pay for. Products available for less than $1,000 US are isolated-word, small-vocabulary recognizers. Speaker-dependent, isolated-word, large-vocabulary recognizers for automated dictation are available for a few thousand dollars. You'll see an order of magnitude leap in price when you move to large-vocabulary, speaker-independent, continuous-speech recognizers.

Speaker recognition — the voice, not just the words

Speaker recognition is related to speech recognition. When the task involves identifying the person talking rather than what is said, the speech signal must be processed to extract measures of speaker variability instead of being analyzed by segments corresponding to phonemes or pieces of text one after the other. For speaker recognition, only one classification is made, based on part or all of an input test utterance. Although various studies have shown that certain acoustical features work better than others in predicting speaker identity, few recognizers examine specific sounds because of difficulties in phone segmentation and identification.

Both automatic speaker verification and speaker identification use a stored database of reference patterns (templates) for *N* known speakers. Both involve similar analysis and decision techniques. Verification is simpler because it only requires comparing the test pattern against one reference pattern and it involves a binary decision: Is there a good enough match against the template of the claimed speaker? The error rate for speaker identification can be much greater because it requires choosing which of the *N* voices known to the system best matches the test voice or "no match" if the test voice differs sufficiently from all the reference templates.

Comparing test and reference utterances for speaker identity is much simpler for identical underlying texts, as in text-dependent speaker recognition. With cooperative speakers you can apply speaker recognition straightforwardly by using the same words to train the system and then test it. This usually happens in verification, but speaker identification often requires

Table 1. A sample of commercially available speech recognition systems (for IBM PCs unless otherwise indicated).

Recognizer	Constraints (Speaker/Speech/Vocabulary)	Price (US $)	Percent Word Accuracy (per the manufacturer)
Dragon Voice-Scribe 400	Speaker dependent Isolated-word recognition 400 words	$995	>95
Dragon Dictate	Speaker adaptive Isolated-word recognition 30,000 words	$9,000	>90
ITT VRS 1280/PC	Speaker dependent Continous-speech recognition 2,000 words	$9,000	>98
Phonetic Engine* (Speech Systems Inc.)	Speaker independent Continous-speech recognition 10,000-40,000 words	$10,500-$47,100	95
Telerec (Voice Control Systems)**	Speaker independent Connected-word recognition 50 words	$3,000	>98
Verbex series 5000, 6000, 7000	Speaker dependent Continuous-speech recognition 80-10,000 words	$5,600-$9,600	>99.5
Voice Card (Votan)	Speaker dependent or independent Continuous-speech recognition 300 words	$3,500	>99 (speaker dependent), 95 (speaker independent)
Voice Comm Unit (Fujitsu)	Speaker dependent Connected-word recognition 4,000 words	Only in Japan	99.9
Voice Master Key (Covox)	Speaker dependent Isolated-word recognition 64 words	$150	95-96
Voice Navigator† (Articulate Systems)	Speaker dependent Isolated-word recognition 1,000 words	$1,300	95
Voice Pro (Voice Processing Corp.)	Speaker independent Continuous-speech recognition 13 words	$5,000	97-99
Voice Report (Kurzweil AI)	Speaker dependent Isolated-word recognition 20,000 words	$18,900	98

* Available for Sun workstations   ** VCS technology is used in Dialogic products   † Available for Macintosh (based on Dragon Systems technology)

text-independent methods. Higher error rates for text-independent methods means you will need much more speech data both for training and testing.

Automatic speaker recognition by computer has been an active research area since the early 1960s. A 1962 paper introduced the spectrogram as a means of personal identification, and this stimulated a good deal of further research. The term "voiceprint" also appeared in that paper. Unfortunately, the analogy with fingerprint reading is incorrect. As pointed out by Doddington,[13] the spectrogram is a function of the speech signal, not of the physical anatomy of the speaker. The speech signal depends far more on the speaker's actions, themselves a complex function of many factors, than on the shape of the speaker's vocal tract. The term "voiceprint" is misleading.

Speaker recognition systems

Speaker recognition by computer has only had limited success to date in applications using free text (text independent). Nonetheless, text-independent recognition of speakers has become an increasingly popular area of research, particularly for applications such as forensic, intelligence gathering, and passive surveillance of voice circuits. Free-text recognition usually lacks control over conditions that influence system performance, including variability in the speech signal and distortions and noise in the communications channel. The recognition task faces multiple problems: unconstrained input speech, uncooperative speakers, and uncontrolled environmental parameters. This has made it necessary to focus on features and characteristics of speech unique to the individual.

Performance of text-independent systems has lagged behind that of text-dependent systems, as you might expect. However, Markel and Davis[14] achieved excellent results with a linguistically unconstrained database of unrehearsed speech. Using voice pitch and linear predictive coding (LPC) reflection coefficients in their model, they reached 2 percent identification error and 4 percent verification error rates for 40-second segments of input speech. Results were not nearly as good with shorter input speech segments, even though the system avoided operational problems of microphone degradation, acoustic noise, and channel distortion. In text-independent recognition of nine male speakers over a radio channel at Bolt Beranek and Newman, the best performance was a 30 percent error rate for input speech segments of about two seconds.[15]

Text-independent recognition seems mainly slated for unobtrusive surveillance of individuals. As mentioned earlier, text-independent speaker identification poses a difficult problem. The accuracy of state-of-the-art text-independent identification is low, and it requires continuous use of computing power. Text-dependent speaker verification has the greatest potential for practical application at the moment. A number of organizations have research and development programs in speaker verification, and Texas Instruments and AT&T Bell Labs have both made major efforts in this research area.

AT&T Bell Labs has concentrated on speaker recognition over telephone lines, which faces difficult problems of microphone and channel distortion. Speaker recognition over telephone lines opens up an enormous set of possible uses, such as identification for various kinds of transaction processing in banking, shopping, and database access.

AT&T Bell Labs started its automatic speaker verification system in 1970. Researchers there chose measurements that are largely insensitive to the phase and spectral amplitude distortions likely over telephone lines. In an early five-month operational simulation, the system showed a user rejection rate and impostor acceptance rate of about 10 percent initially for new users, dropping to about 5 percent for experienced users and fully adapted templates. A more recent system used over telephone lines has achieved error rates (rejection of true speakers and acceptance of impostors) of approximately 2 percent.[16]

Texas Instruments has applied speaker verification to control access to its corporate computer center.[13] The gross rejection rate of the operational system measured 0.9 percent, with a casual impostor acceptance rate of 0.7 percent. The system has been operational 24 hours a day for more than a decade. The verification step uses a comparison of dynamic features, and time alignment is established using a simplified form of dynamic time warping. Verification utterances are constructed randomly using a four-word fixed phrase structure, for example, "Proud Ben served hard." As well as indicating what the user should say, the voice prompt helps stabilize pronunciation because the user tends to say it in the same way as prompted. Because a single utterance cannot provide the high level of verification performance desired, the system employs a sequential decision using multiple phrases when necessary. In operation, the actual number of phrases used averages 1.6.

Several companies offer speaker verification products, and voiceprints have emerged again. The claim of a voiceprint technique comes from Ecco Industries of Danvers, Mass. Ecco hopes to market a $300 voice-recognition security device for consumers this year. The intention is to create a digital picture of an individual's vocal tract so that bad colds or mimics will not trip up the device. US Sprint is testing a phone card that can be used to recognize the caller's voice. Card holders initiate calls in the usual way by dialing an 800 number, then dialing a personal identification number. A voice prompt asks callers to speak their password. The system is intended to reduce credit card fraud, including elimination of card-swapping. Bellcore has developed a similar credit card, which stores the template of a spoken word as 6,400 bits. According to Bellcore, the system recognizes the speaker 99 percent of the time, but the error rate can double to 2 percent if the speaker has a cold.

Speech recognition technology has migrated from mini- and mainframe computers to workstations and personal computers, and applications are already running on them. As embedded digital signal processors become more prevalent on workstations (such as the Next computer), we expect to see much wider use of speech and speaker recognition.

Current applications depend on the use of various simplifying constraints that make speech recognition feasible, as discussed above. The dependence on them means that, although useful practical applications of speech recognition exist, we have not yet achieved comfortable and natural communication with computers through voice. Text-dependent speaker recognition exists in the form of operational systems, but accurate text-independent speaker recognition remains a target.

Improvements in the speech and speaker recognition techniques discussed here will no doubt advance the performance of recognition systems, but it seems likely that we will also need natural language understanding before we can achieve comfortable and natural communication with computers through voice. ■

Acknowledgments

We are grateful for suggestions from the anonymous referees, which have improved the article, and to Jérôme Chiabaut and Taro Shibahara for help with an earlier version.

References

1. K. Lee, *Automatic Speech Recognition: the development of the Sphinx System*, Kluwer Academic Publishers, Norwell, Mass., 1989.

2. L. R. Bahl et al., "Speech Recognition of a Natural Text Read as Isolated Words," *Proc. IEEE Int'l Conf. Acoustics, Speech, and Signal Processing*, April 1981, pp. 1,168-1,171.

3. D.O. Kimbal et al., "Recognition Performance and Grammatical Constraints," *Proc. DARPA Speech Recognition Workshop*, Feb. 1986, pp. 53-59.

4. D. O'Shaughnessy, *Speech Communication: Human and Machine*, Addison-Wesley, Reading, Mass., 1987.

5. M.A. Franzini, M.J. Witbrock, and K.-F. Lee, "Speaker-Independent Recognition of Connected Utterances Using Recurrent and Nonrecurrent Neural Networks," *Proc. Int'l Joint Conf. Neural Networks*, Vol.2, Washington, DC, June 1989, pp.II-1 to II-6.

6. J. Mariani, "Recent Advances in Speech Processing," *Proc. IEEE Int'l Conf. Acoustics, Speech, and Signal Processing*, Glasgow, Scotland, May 1989, pp. 429-440.

7. M.-W. Fung et al., "Improved Speaker Adaptation Using Text-Dependent Spectral Mappings," *Proc. IEEE Int'l Conf. Acoustics, Speech, and Signal Processing*, New York City, 1988, pp. 131-134.

8. D.B. Paul, "The Lincoln Robust Continuous Speech Recognizer," *Proc. IEEE Int'l Conf. Acoustics, Speech, and Signal Processing*, Glasgow, Scotland, 1989, pp. 449-452.

9. H. Murveit and M. Weintraub, "1,000-Word Speaker-Independent Continuous-Speech Recognition Using Hidden Markov Models," *Proc. IEEE Int'l Conf. Acoustics, Speech, and Signal Processing*, New York City, 1988, pp. 115-118.

10. W. Wylegala, "A 20,000-Word Recognizer Based on Statistical Evaluation Methods," *Speech Technology Magazine*, Apr./May 1989, pp. 16-18.

11. K. Yoshida, T. Watanabe, and S. Koga, "Large Vocabulary Word Recognition Based on a Demi-Syllable Hidden Markov Model Using a Small Amount of Training Data," *Proc. IEEE Int'l Conf. Acoustics, Speech, and Signal Processing*, Glasgow, Scotland, 1989, pp. 1-4.

12. L.R. Rabiner, J.G. Wilpon, and F.K. Soong, "High-Performance Connected-Digit Recognition, Using Hidden Markov Models," *Proc. IEEE Int'l Conf. Acoustics, Speech, and Signal Processing*, New York City, 1988, pp. 119-122.

13. G. R. Doddington, "Speaker Recognition — Identifying People by their Voices," *Proc. IEEE*, Vol. 73, No. 11, Nov. 1985, pp. 1,651 1,664.

14. J.D. Markel and B. Davis, "Text-Independent Speaker Recognition from a Large Linguistically Unconstrained Time-Spaced Database," *IEEE Trans. Acoustics, Speech, and Signal Processing*, Vol. ASSP-27, No. 1, 1979, pp. 74-82.

15. M. Krasner et al., "Investigation of Text-Independent Speaker Identification Techniques Under Conditions of Variable Data," *Proc. IEEE Int'l Conf. Acoustics, Speech, and Signal Processing*, 1984, Paper 18B.5.

16. M.R. Birnbaum, L.A. Cohen, and F.X. Welsh, "A Voice Password System for Access Security," *AT&T Tech. J.*, Vol. 65, No. 5, Sept./Oct. 1986, pp. 68-74.

Richard D. Peacocke is a member of the Computing Research Laboratory at Bell-Northern Research in Ottawa. At BNR he has worked on office communications and software engineering and has led groups working in software quality assurance and artificial intelligence. He has published a number of technical papers, including several on expert systems and telecommunications. His current research interests include AI, knowledge-based software, and speech technology.

Peacocke is president of the Canadian Society for Computational Studies of Intelligence and a member of the IEEE Computer Society, AAAI, and ACM. He is also an adjunct professor in the Department of Systems and Computer Engineering at Carleton University, Ottawa.

Peacocke has a PhD in computer science from the University of Toronto, Canada. He received a BA in mathematics from Cambridge University and an MS in computing science from the University of Alberta, Canada.

Daryl H. Graf is a member of the Computing Research Laboratory at Bell-Northern Research in Ottawa, Canada. Since joining BNR in 1979, he has acquired extensive experience in the telecommunications field. As a former manager of BNR's international operator services design group, he is interested in the application of speech processing technology to the operator services area. His current research interests include adaptive systems for pattern classification, and he has published technical papers on the use of neural networks for robot control.

Graf received the BS with honors in computer science from the University of Calgary in 1979 and the MCS with distinction from Carleton University, Ottawa, in 1988. He is a member of the IEEE, CSCSI, INNS, and AAAI.

Readers may contact the authors at the Computing Research Laboratory, Bell-Northern Research, PO Box 3511 Station C, Ottawa, Ontario, Canada K1Y 4H7, Bitnet: richard@bnr.ca or dgraf@bnr.ca.

NATURAL LANGUAGE UNDERSTANDING AND SPEECH RECOGNITION

George M. White

Natural language understanding must be an integral part of any automatic speech recognition system that attempts to deal with interactive problem solving. The methods for representing and integrating knowledge from different sources may be valuable for the understanding process as well as speech recognition.

Natural language understanding (NLU) refers to computer understanding of *human* language, which includes spoken as well as typed communication. Most of the techniques developed for NLU over the last 25 years are largely concerned with syntax analysis of grammatically correct *typed* sentences. These techniques may not be useful in dealing with the nongrammatical nature of normal speech. This article focuses on speech understanding and the marriage of NLU techniques with speech recognition techniques needed to achieve *speech understanding.*

Automatic speech recognition (ASR) as a field of research has proceeded on a parallel but separate track from NLU for more than 20 years. For most of this time, ASR research has been preoccupied with translating acoustic information into computer commands or text without involving formal NLU techniques. (We use the term "recognition" as distinct from "understanding" when *no* linguistic or semantic analysis is involved.) It might appear reasonable for speech *understanding* to be achieved by acoustic phonetic analysis followed by NLU analysis. However, the subtleties of normal speech render it impractical to create a simple feed-forward interface between an acoustic analysis stage and current NLU techniques that expect reliable word-sized units as input.

For normal spontaneous speech, acoustic-phonetic analysis techniques by themselves will never be able to produce an unambiguous stream of text equivalent to the typed input expected for NLU systems. Thus, at the very least, an NLU stage would have to be modified to handle errorful input. In addition, a feedback mechanism should be provided between the NLU and acoustic phonetic stages. Otherwise, the acoustic-phonetic stage must increase the data processed by an order of magnitude in order to produce a sufficient set of alternatives to be passed on the NLU stage. In other words, *both* NLU and acoustic analysis stages must be modified to achieve a computationally efficient system.

Historically, NLU research has focused on grammatically correct typed queries of databases and automatic language translation of textbook documents, (e.g. technical journals, legal briefs, financial statements). The most successful commercial examples of NLU systems are computerized information retrieval systems from typed queries (e.g. Symantec's Q&A [9]). There are only a few language translation systems and they work with restricted sources of text [16]. There are no commercially successful NLU systems built specifically to work with speech input. (There are dozens of firms offering ASR, most are for personal computers, and none contain NLU technology to assist in the recognition of utterances.)

It is widely believed that NLU techniques must be used in conjunction with acoustic analysis techniques to achieve recognition of continuous speech. This is because continuous speech is normally filled with acoustic ambiguity which can only be resolved through the use of higher sources of knowledge, principally semantic and pragmatic sources. The Defense Advanced Projects Research Agency (DARDA), which provides the major funding for nonproprietary ASR research as well as natural language understanding, is sponsoring interdisciplinary projects explicitly to combine NLU and ASR disciplines. The VOYAGER system, developed at the Laboratory for Computer Science at MIT, is an example of this type of interdisciplinary project. VOYAGER is a speaker-independent, continuous speech-understanding system that employs a natural language component to understand and answer queries concerning the locations of public buildings in the Harvard/MIT area. The system is able to handle about 66 percent of the spontaneous questions asked of it in spoken English within its task domain.

Even though DARPA first began sponsoring speech-understanding research (SUR) in 1970, DARPA contractors are just beginning to successfully merge NLU and ASR research disciplines. Earlier SUR work produced systems that had semantic and prosodic components that theoretically were integrated with acoustic phonetic analysis components. However, these integrated systems were not successfully demnstrated because of inadequate computing power. Most ASR research has not focused on NLU but rather on the recognition of isolated utternces, or continuous utterances from highly constrained vocabularies (such as the digits); or speaker-dependent input instead of speaker-independent input; or carefully articulated continuous speech in narrow task domains with artificial language syntax constraints.

Meanwhile, the need for integrating NLU and ASR techniques has continually increased as the opportunity for spoken language communication with personal computers has increased, fueled by the increasing computational power of personal computers (and "workstations") for interactive problem solving.

Natural language understanding plays two roles in translating speech queries or statements into useful computer commands. The first role is imputing the correct meaning of the speech so the computer gets the right message...is of little concern here. The second, more subtle role (and main focus of this article) is reducing acoustic phonetic ambiguity in normal speech based on "understanding" of meanings.

Without NLU techniques, ASR systems using a purely acoustic-phonetic analysis perform well only on slowly pronounced isolated words. This is not the way we usually talk to one another, and pronouncing words in isolation is slow and tedious compared to continuous speech. However, it is useful and is the basis of a 30,000 word recognition system, DragonDictate [2] from Dragon Systems. This is the largest vocabulary system commercially available in the world. The automatic recognition of continuous speech for thousands of words is much more difficult because continuous speech is filled with acoustic-phonetic shorthand.

The extent of acoustic-phonetic shorthand can be understood from research performed by Dennis Klatt [11]. After recording normal continuous speech, Klatt would splice out individual words and play them back to listeners in random order. Typically, listeners could only understand about 70 percent of the words. Yet listeners got 100 percent of the words right when the words were played in the correct order. The conclusion of this experiment is that it is the grammatical rules, prosodics, and semantic content of a message that allow humans to overcome acoustic ambiguity in at least 30 percent of the words in normal conversation.

ASR system builders have long been aware that semantic and syntactic knowledge must be integrated with acoustic phonetic sources to deal with most forms of continuous speech. Integrating diverse knowledge sources has been at the heart of DARPA-sponsored ASR research for nearly 20 years. An early solution was put forth in the blackboard model of HEARSAY [7] developed at CMU (circa 1974) which simply states that all knowledge sources (KSs) should work in parallel. In addition, KSs should exchange results via a common memory scheme or *blackboard*. This solution, while general enough to cover all situations of interest, does not actually guide the integration of KSs. The HEARSAY model was eclipsed by a system based on Hidden Markov Models (HMMs) that implicitly addressed the issue of combining scores from different KSs.

The technique used with HMM systems for integrating KSs was to represent knowledge as finite state networks with transition probabilities between states, with integration being achieved by allowing different KSs to influence the transition probabilities. The HMM technique was *not* conceived as a technique for integrating KSs, but rather as a technique for applying sound stochastic modeling techniques to the problem of decoding strings of elemental sound symbols. However, HMM techniques did succeed at integrating information from at least three KSs. The KSs were

1. phone temporal duration,
2. phone level elemental sound similarity, measurements and,
3. word pair statistics.

The most notable and recent of these HMM systems was Sphinx [12] (circa 1988)—the world's first speaker-independent, continuous speech recognition system operating on a large vocabulary (1,000 words or more). Today, the HMM approach is the most widely used pattern-matching technique in ASR systems worldwide.

Despite the widespread use of the HMM approach, it has not had much impact on NLU or integration of NLU techniques into ASR systems. In fact the potential of HMM methodology to guide integration of diverse KSs is not at all obvious. It was first mentioned by Jim Baker in his doctoral thesis [3] which was also the first published explanation of HMM applied to ASR. Unfortunately, the Baker thesis only suggested that the HMM approach might apply to NLU.

In fact, it appears that it is not the hidden Markov process itself that is relevant; rather it is the state machine representation, and the methodology of processing the time evolution of the state machine that are relevant.

The Nature of Understanding

Computerized *understanding* of any subject raises philosophical issues. We operationally avoid these issues by defining understanding as the ability to respond appropriately to directives or queries in normal human language based solely on information we already possess.

NLU by machines is the decoding of messages encoded with the symbols and conventions that humans use among themselves. Extensive use of *context* is required since human communication is so extensively conditioned by the world models of the sender and receivers of messages. If the communication is written, the symbols are restricted to text and a few punctuation and highlighting symbols. Speech, on the other hand, contains more symbol carriers, namely pitch, volume and segment duration which together are said to supply prosodic information. To understand the conventions for imparting meaning to sequences of utterances, we need to understand the roles of syntax, pragmatics, and semantics. These are cornerstone issues in human communication.

Communication is the exchange of messages that describe the state of a model or a change in state of a model. These models are typically mental models but they can be computer models equally well. The messages are serial encodings that serve to *compress information and distribute it over ordered sets of symbols*. Serial encoding, and the possibilities for contextual information thus created are powerful information compression methodologies. They are fundamental not only to efficient communication, but probably to intelligence itself.

Contextual information is the local environment provided by nearby symbols that literally redefine a symbol. The fact that any given symbol can take different meanings depending on context means that communication can proceed with fewer symbols than would otherwise be needed.

To appreciate the extraordinary power of contextual information to build meaning into simple sequences, consider two extreme forms, providing the most powerful compression known: information encoding in chromosomes and fractals.

Chromosomes in the germ cells in

no way specify directly how many cells of any sort should appear in an adult being. Rather, they specify how each cell should react to differing *contexts* provided by other cells through chemical and electrical interchanges as the body matures. The collective behavior is striking as new cell characteristics are created according to the *sequences* of cell development. The full message encoded in a chromosome cannot be read directly, but must be allowed to create all the intermediate contexts in order to give expression to the final form.

Fractals [8] encode information in much the same way. As pointed out in *Scientific American* [13], fractals provide the most powerful techniques for picture data compression invented to date. They work by creating irregular geometric shapes that reproduce themselves on smaller and smaller scales, using the "context" of their previous larger structures to guide the smaller ones.

These are examples of extreme data compression using recursive contextual information encoding, in which context begets new context, which begets new context, etc. While not directly applicable to natural language understanding, such examples serve to focus attention on the data compression aspect of contextual information processing and the extraordinary power of context to reveal information to decoders with sufficient memory to utilize it.

If spreading information over sequences makes an efficient coding scheme, we could argue on principles of least effort that it would be used widely in human communication. And we see empirically that context is everywhere in human discourse.

Returning to the core issues of syntax, pragmatics, and semantics, it would appear that they address different levels of contextual information encoding provided by strings of words.

From among these three KSs, the shortest strings and most local context is the realm of language syntax. Syntax rules are typically concerned only with phrases and sentences rather than information spread over paragraphs or books.

Pragmatic and semantic models deal with larger contexts than encoded in isolated sentences. They generally cover encodings that span several sentences.

Pragmatic models reflect the intermediate states of mind that might be put in place by the progress of discourse or exposition.

Semantic models impart meaning to messages. Semantic models are the objects that messages describe the state of or the changes in. They are also called world models and are the ultimate repository of intelligence in a system. This is the true frontier of NLU and artificial intelligence in general, which will properly be the focus of research for years to come.

The underlying notion behind NLU semantic models is that meaning can be derived from models of the domain of discourse rather than

FIGURE 1 Knowledge Sources (KSs) shown in hierarchy according to the span of discourse covered

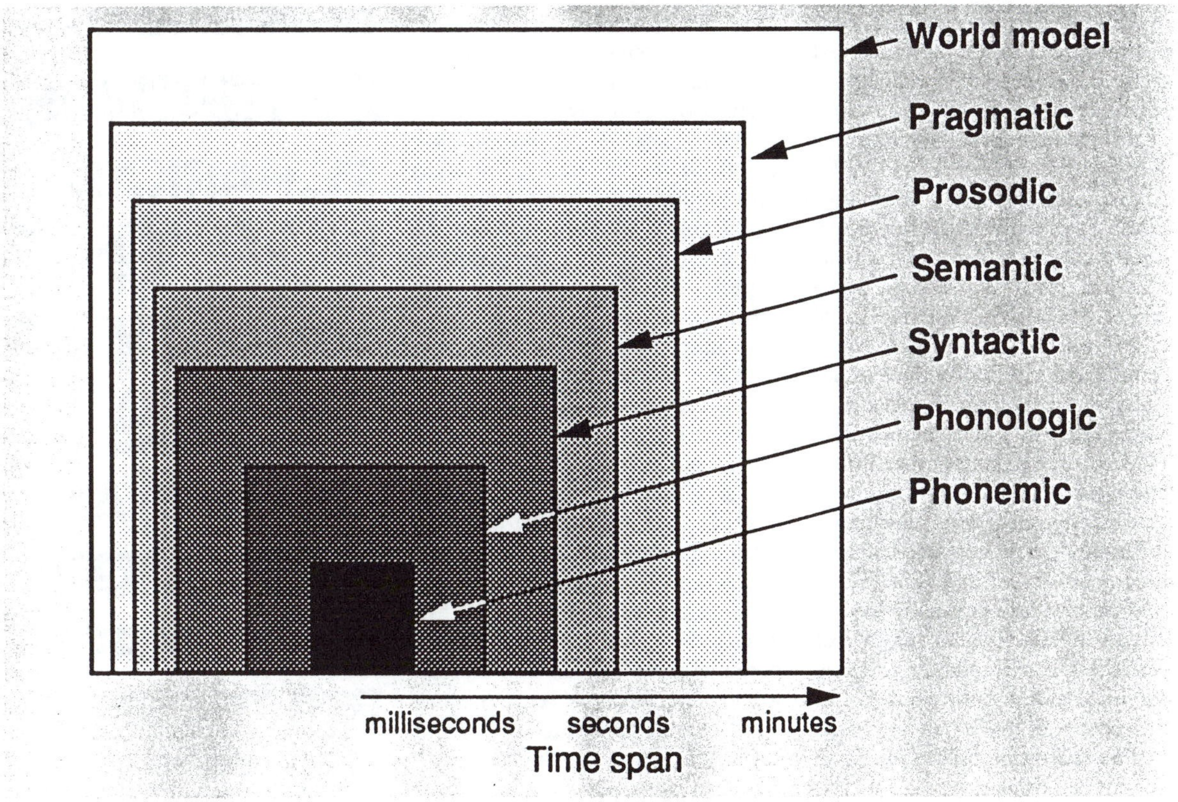

exhaustive enumeration of word sequences.

This reduces the problem of recognizing word strings, from a possibly infinite number of variations, to a problem of paraphrasing or transforming a finite number of manipulations that can be performed on finite world models.

In other words, there may be an infinite number of ways of saying the same thing; and the way to handle this situation is to encode the basic information once and use procedures to generate the different ways of saying it. Furthermore, in many domains of discourse, the basic underlying information may be small and represented well in a semantic model with a relatively small number of facts and properties. In this case, the problem of modeling human discourse is largely an issue of finding the right semantic models and combining them with the right linguistic transformation rules.

Roger Schank's [13] suggestion that the world of normal everyday discourse might be reduced to a few hundred generic situational models with 30 or so underlying actions that might be performed on the models, is another example. Sentences that could be parsed were interpreted as a paraphrase of these basic actions and the paraphrase was to be guided by conceptual dependency networks.

Noam Chomsky's [6] famous transformational grammars which transform a finite set of basic sentence structures, (deep structures), into an infinite number of ways of actually composing sentences (surface structures) provide another example. Semantics are encoded at the deep structure level. Transformational grammars play the role of conceptual dependency networks by translating underlying information embodied in the deep structures into the expressive forms actually found in normal human communication.

In summary, it is not the goal of NLU to prerecord all reasonable statements that might be made about any nontrivial subject and attach intended meanings. The goal is to create semantic models from which meanings may be generated and then to develop pragmatic and syntactic encoder/decoders (and prosodic encoder/decoders for speech) to spread the meaning over a serial stream of words.

The Nature of Speech

Speech is remarkable for the variety of rules it follows and even more remarkable for the rules it violates. Written sentences may be expected to obey most grammatical rules most of the time. However, spontaneous speech has at least some grammatical probabilistic errors most of the time; [4] it contains false starts, dangling phrases, mixed cases, mixed tenses, etc. I have a foreign friend who simply leaves out verbs and nouns at random: "Children making kites. All day running in the park. Hot. Tired. Sweaty. We going home now." Makes perfect sense, doesn't it? But it certainly is not grammatically correct.

In his scholarly book, "On Human Communication" Colin Cherry [5] points out that we can strip off all grammatical clues and still communicate (p122): "woman, street, crowd, traffic, noise, thief, bag, loss, scream, police... ."

While spontaneous speech may not be as "nongrammatical" as this, it still violates many of the rules on which typical NLU systems are based. On the other hand, most users of computerized NLU systems, whose goal is presumably to help the dumb machine understand, could be expected to obey most of the rules most of the time. Since most talkers obey many more grammatical rules than they disobey, syntactic information is certainly present. When the speakers fail to be perfect, however, it must not stop the NLU processes, just slow them down.

NLU systems need to extract meaning from partially completed parses (i.e. when the parse has gone as far as it can and it is not yet finished); they must shed light on the potential completions and what each would mean if completed. At the very least, this will require a change from deterministic to a probabilistic parsing strategy. In fact, probabilistic parsing is essential and one of the more important messages of this article.

NLU systems use many grammars for parsing (e.g. transformational, ATN, chart, bottom up, top down, semantic, conceptual dependency) and most may be gracefully applied to imperfections of real speech, *...but only if parsing is modified to be probabilistic.* In other words, decisions to follow particular branches in a parse tree must be treated as tentative rather than final (i.e. the decision to pursue any particular branch must be handled as a probabilistic decision); and provisions must be incorporated to retrace steps to follow alternative branches if the probability of the processed branch grows too low. Pioneering work in this area has been done by Seneff [15]. Such search strategies are well developed in the world of information-coding theory and automatic speech recognition. An appropriate approach for NLU is probably *stack decoding* [10].

While it might be universally agreed that probabilistic parsing is a

SPEECH IS REMARKABLE FOR THE VARIETY OF RULES IT FOLLOWS AND EVEN MORE REMARKABLE FOR THE RULES IT VIOLATES.

great goal and that ASR systems would be more accurate if they incorporated syntactic, prosodic, pragmatic, and semantic knowledge sources, there is little agreement on how to encode this knowledge and how to apply it. However, it is clear that a uniform method for representing and communicating between syntactic, prosodic, pragmatic, and semantic knowledge sources would help to promote information sharing between these different levels.

A proposal was put forth by Jim Baker [3] to provide a uniform representation in the form of "finite state machines." The idea was to represent all knowledge sources (semantic, prosodic, pragmatic, syntactic, phonemic and phonologic) as networks (or finite state machine equivalents) and then to determine what states are most probable using the mathematics of the HMM approach. The approach has been applied with great success to the lower sources of knowledge, namely phonologic, phonemic, and word order syntax based on simple word pair statistics.

Figures 2 thru 7 show popular finite state machine models associated with the HMM approach. Figure 2 shows how finite state machines might be used in an operational ASR system. This description is applied to the current leading ASR systems worldwide and is similar to the one described in Kai Fu Lee's paper on Sphinx [12].

It is important to note that figures 2 through 7 do not directly address the use of NLU techniques. They do not address semantic, prosodic, or pragmatic knowledge sources. Instead, they only show one way to integrate the *lower* sources of knowledge (phone to phoneme, phoneme to word, and word to word syntax). This integration has been implemented by embedding the lower sources explicitly within higher ones (see Figure 2).

Unfortunately Baker's thesis did not actually combine *higher* sources of knowledge (semantic, pragmatic and prosodic) nor did it explain how to do it beyond suggesting that finite state

2

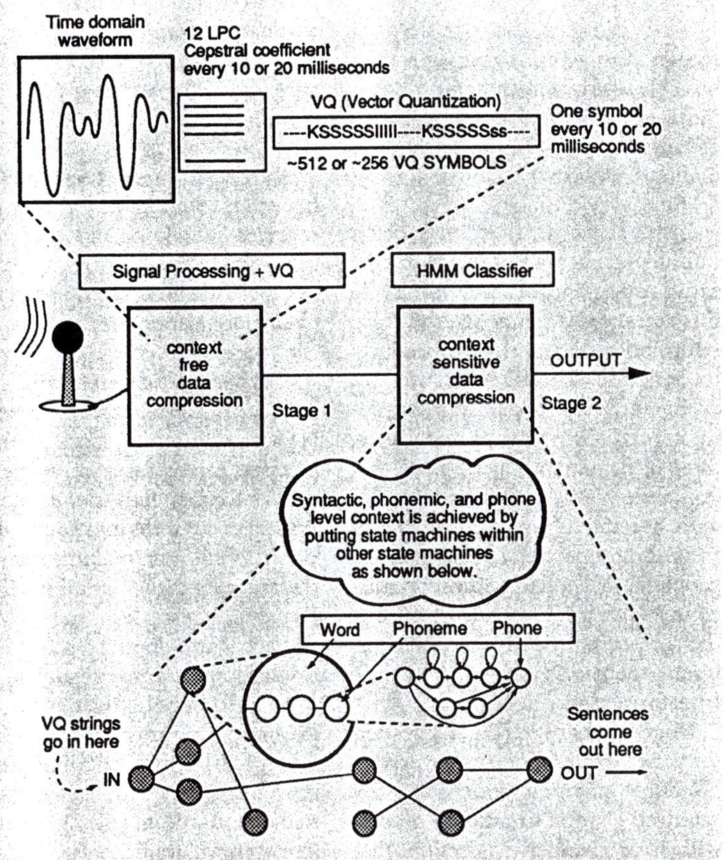

3

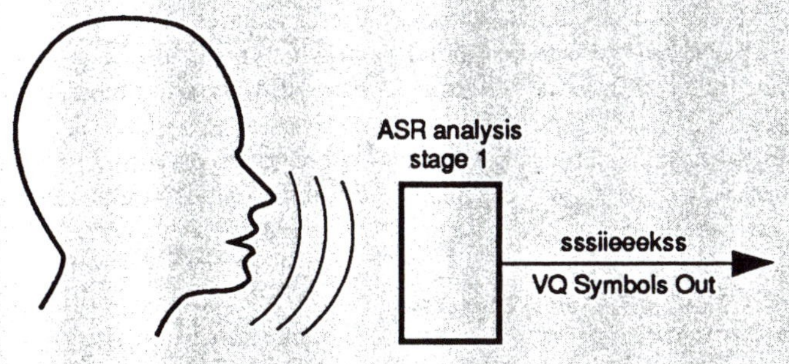

4

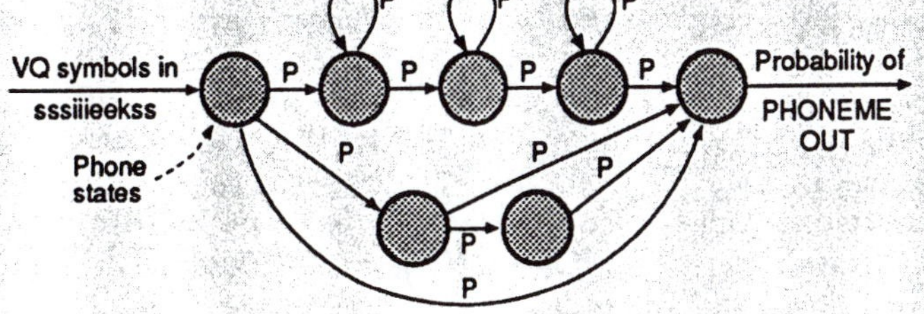

5

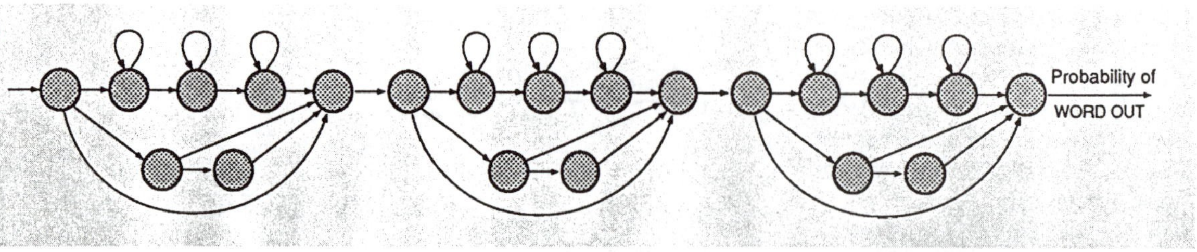

6

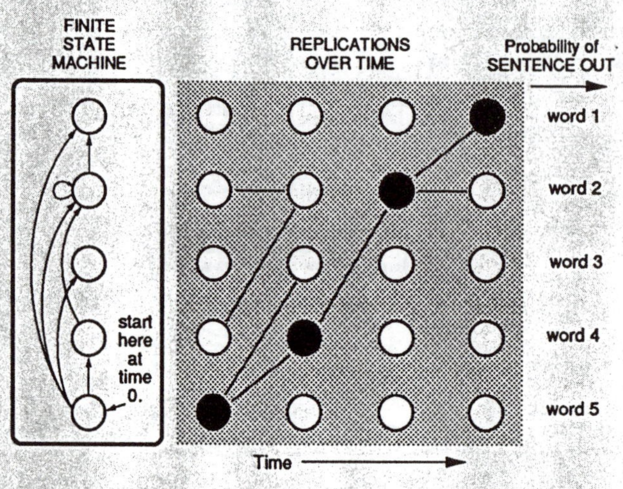

7

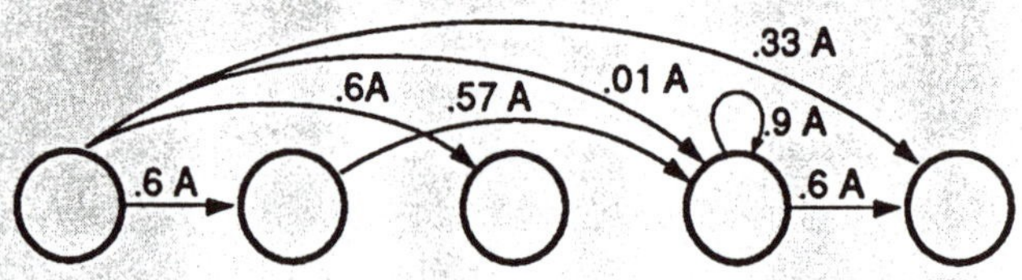

8

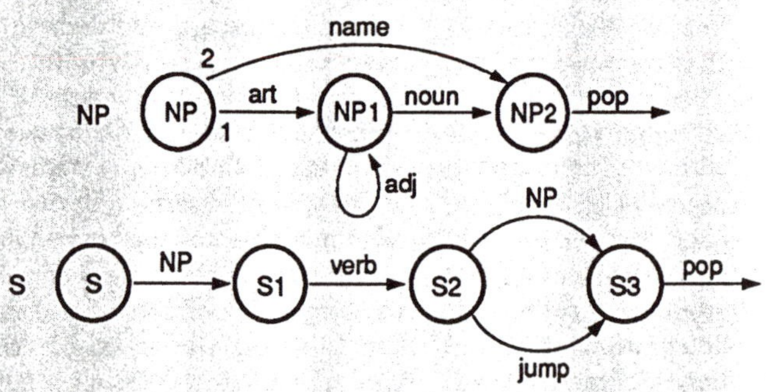

9

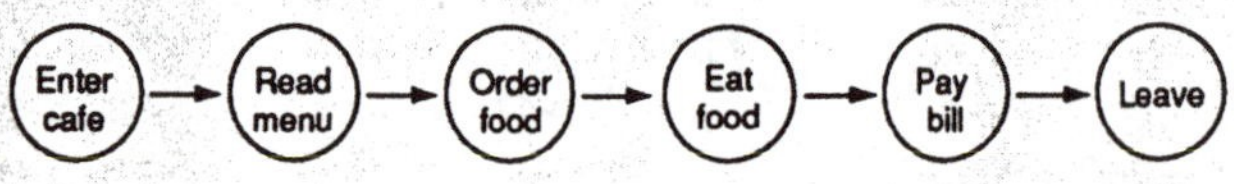

FIGURE 2 A typical ASR System combining KSs from phone, phonemic, and word levels showing production of VQ symbols followed by HMM state machine network

FIGURE 3 Initial stage of a typical ASR system, such as Sphinx, showing the reduction of speech input into a series of phone labels called VQ (vector quantization) symbols

FIGURE 4 Phones to Phonemes. Phones (VQ symbols) are processed by state machines for "phonemes." These phoneme models are described by [12]. The phoneme provides the context for the phone states within.

FIGURE 5 Phonemes to words. Three phonemes are shown concatenated to form a word. The transition probabilities inside the phonemes can be trained using the local context, namely the identity of the word. Context can alternately be provided by the two adjacent phonemes. This context was dubbed "triphones" by Lee [12].

FIGURE 6 Words to sentences. Sentences are created by replicating the states in a finite state machine over time. Each state represents a word. Links between those words with high probabilities are shown by lines in the word matrix. Words that form the sentence are shown in black.

FIGURE 7 Generic finite state machine showing compound probabilities associated with transitons, e.g. ".9A" = .9*A. When the nodes represent the words, the first probability is the language model. The second probability, "A," can be determined by acoustic measurements alone. However, it can also contain information from language syntax, prosodics, pragmatics, etc. as shown in Figure 11.

FIGURE 8 Syntactic knowledge encoded as ATN, (Augmented Transition Network) [16].

FIGURE 9 Roger Schank's restaurant script as example of state machine encoding of task domain knowledge. The key idea here is that the act of eating at a restaurant includes well-defined stages. The stages are small in number. Each stage provides scripts of probable dialogues.

10

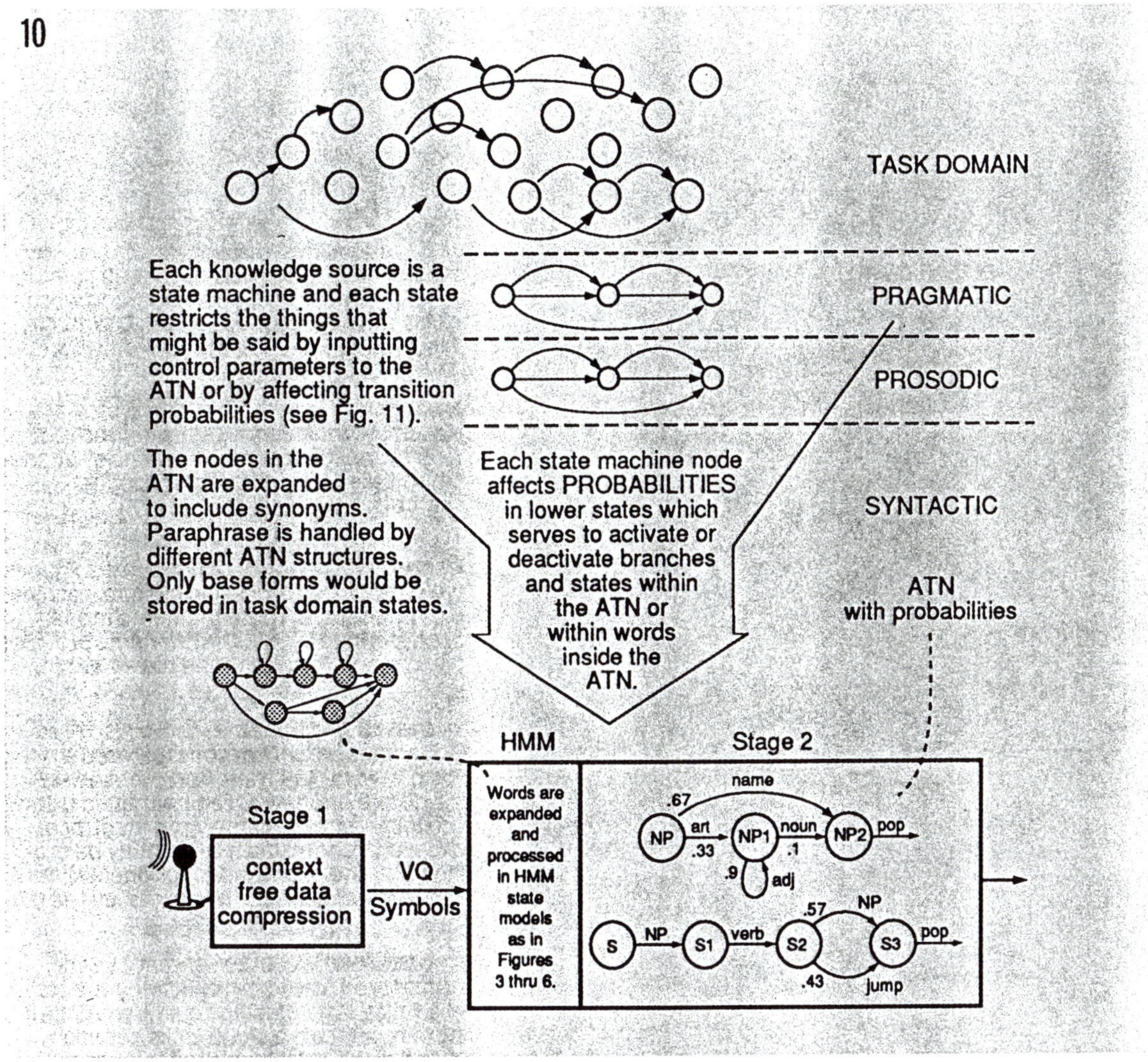

FIGURE 10 State Machine Networks for task domain, pragmatic, prosodic, and syntactic knowledge sources. Base forms for phrases and sentences originate in the task domain and are modified—expanded or encoded—by the pragmatic and prosodic domains before taking effect ATN. The ATN expands into a graph or network that can be searched to yield a parse of speech input. Higher knowledge sources in the form of state machines control the operation of another state machine, an ATN (or other grammar) by influencing transition probabilities.

FIGURE 11 Integration of indifferent KSs achieved by using conditional probabilities to link transitions in any given context to larger context provided by more global KSs

machines and the HMM formalism should be helpful. It is only now, 15 years later, that we have enough experience with state machines to appreciate why they might be useful for integrating higher sources of knowledge.

The main purpose of this article is to explore the elements of current HMM ASR methodology and show how they might be extended to encompass the integration of NLU with ASR. These techniques have not been put forth to solve this problem before but they are nonetheless well known techniques.

The main thesis of this article is, then, that NLU knowledge sources can and should be integrated with ASR sources by: first, developing probabilistic state machine networks for semantic, pragmatic and prosodic types of knowledge; and then developing a scheme for interconnecting different knowledge domains.

Once this is done, the time evolution of the probabilities of states can be treated in the same way that the lower model states are treated. We can see from Figure 2, that one way is to simply embed some finite state models within the states of other finite state models. We seek a more general answer here.

The state machines shown in Figure 11 are symbolic structures used simply to illustrate how conditional probabilities increase as contextual scope changes. The bottom state machine with generic transition prob-

11

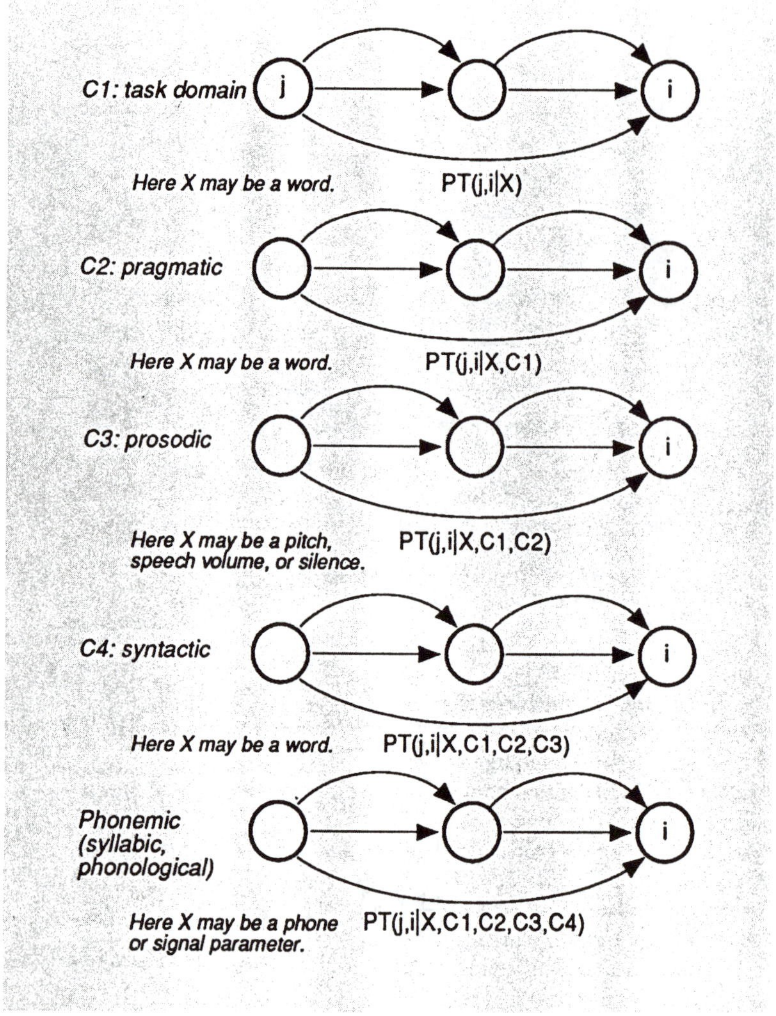

ability $PT(j,i|X,C1,C2,C3,C4)$ says that the probability of transition between elemental sound units is conditioned by (dependent on) the states occupied at the syntactic (C4), prosodic (C3), pragmatic (C2), and semantic (C1) levels. In practice, the different domains may be treated as independent. For example: $PT(j,i|X,C1,C2,C3,C4) = PT(i,j|X,C4)*P(C4|C3)*P(C3|C2)*P(C2|C1)$ where $P(Ci|Cj)$ is the probability of being in state, Ci, in the ith level given that the state Cj is occupied in the jth level.

Operationally, the conditional probabilities may be interpreted to mean that lower level models should be trained on data labeled by higher level states, and the same set of transition probabilities so gathered should be used during the recognition phase when the specified higher level states are active.

Recall Figure 1 and the hierarchy of contexts provided by task domain, pragmatic, prosodic, syntactic, phonemic, and phonological domains. The lower their position in the hierarchy, the more conditional are the probablities. More precisely, the longer the time span, the more global the context; and domains of lesser extent should be conditioned by the context of more global ones.

Figures 8, 9, and 10 show higher level knowledge sources represented as state machines. Figure 11 summarizes the method for integrating the NLU and ASR knowledge sources discussed in this article.

I believe the correct way to combine NLU and ASR is to specify task domain states first and then proceed to specify the lower states. In other words, first determine the different system states that might occur for each application. Next, determine the questions the user might ask and the commands the user might give for each state. This information would be encoded in grammars that are customized for particular situations. Grammars are preferred to simple lists of statements, even with paraphrase and morphological rules to achieve data compression, because grammars take up less memory.

The challenge is to assign probabilities to the various statements, and to pass these probabilities along to the lower domains of knowledge. The single most fruitful area is likely to be probability assignments to task domain states and to the sentences that would issue from these states. Initially, the key statistic may be $PT4(i,j|X,C1)*P(C4|C1)$ (in place of the current probabilities that are used by ASR systems that would correspond to $PT\,4(i,j|X)$). Later, it will be possible to add prosodic and pragmatic knowledge sources when they are better understood.

Conclusion

I have noted that NLU as a research discipline has not given great consideration to the needs of speech recognition per se. However, it is widely believed that NLU techniques will someday significantly improve performance of ASR systems. An obstacle to fruitful collaboration between ASR and NLU research areas has been the lack of a good theory combining information from different knowledge sources, a fundamental question in artificial intelligence research. I have a tentative answer to this question.

The solution I propose requires that knowledge be represented as networks of states. Communication as the time evolution of a network of states is envisioned. The time evolution is treated as a first order Markov process in a state machine, (i.e., the

SUMMARY

To Integrate Different Knowledge Sources:

1. Encode each knowledge source as a finite state network of relationships.
2. Treat the act of communicating as movement in the network driven by the encoding and decoding of messages.
3. Model the time evolution of the network as a message decoded as a stochastic process in a state machine, (i.e. assign transition probabilities to all legal transitions between states and update all probabilities after each time increment]. Let the probability of being be a state i at time t, P[i,t], be the sum of all path probabilities that come to state i where each path probability is the product of a precursor state probability, P[j,t-1], and its transition probability, PT[j,i|X]. Then P[i,t] = P[j,t-1]*PT[j,i|X] where X is the observation variable. It is the input that drives communication. It can be a phone, a word, or an acoustic measurement.
4. Cause one KS to affect another by treating the transition probabilities as conditional upon the context in which they occur. For instance PT[j,i|X,C1,C2,...] is the probability of going from state j to i given the context specified by X, C1, and C2...

states are linked together with transition probabilities with new state probabilities being computed from old state probabilities multiplied times the transition probabilities ...with summation over all products that connect old states to new ones). A significant element in the proposal is that the transition probabilities be conditioned both by the states (context) of more global state machines and also by the new acoustic information driving the communication.

This is not a simple extension of the HMM approach. There is no need to treat a hidden process in the model proposed here. On the other hand, most of the background work that has a direct bearing on this approach comes from the literature on HMM. It is expected that readers will want to refer to the HMM literature to see specific examples of the use of probability to combine knowledge sources.

It should be noted that knowledge sources at different levels may be processed asynchronously, in parallel, instead of serially. This has important consequences for improving the computational underpinnings for machine intelligence in general since parallel processing avoids the Von Neumann bottleneck by promoting the use of multiple hardware processors to increase the power of computing hardware.

I believe the approach described in this article will be immediately applicable to natural language understanding for well defined domains of discourse with limited vocabularies, and a manageable set of semantic alternatives that are characteristic of the task domains within text editors, page layout programs, spreadsheets, telecommunications systems, and databases. These are the areas of practical interest to personal computer manufacturers and significant progress can be expected in these areas. The time has come in the evolution of our society for us to start talking to our computers. The NLU community can play a key role in ushering in this new modality, possibly by using the techniques suggested.

Acknowledgments.
I would like to thank Victor Zue, Gary Hendrix, and Bill Luciw for reviewing the paper and contributing constructive criticism. ◼

References

1. Allen, J. *Natural Language Understanding.* The Benjamin Cummings Publishing Company, Inc., 1988.
2. Jim Baker. Dragon Dictate. *Speech Tech. J.*, Media Dimensions, New York, N.Y., (Spring 1989), 20-25.
3. Baker, J., Stochastic modeling for speech recognition. Doctoral thesis, Dept. of Computer Science Carnegie Mellon University, Pittsburgh, PA 1976.
4. Bodmer, F. *The Loom of Language.* W.W. Norton & Company, New York, 1944.
5. Cherry C. *On Human Communication.* MIT Press, Cambridge, Mass. April 1975.
6. Chomsky, N., *Aspects of the Theory of Syntax.* MIT Press, Cambridge, Mass., 1965.
7. Erman, L.D., Lesser, V.R. *Trends in Speech Recognition.* W. Lea, Ed. Prentice Hall, Englewood Cliffs, NJ, 1980, pp. 361-381.
8. Feder, J. *Fractals.* Plenum Press, New York and London, 1988.
9. Harvey, Hendrix, G. *Mastering Q&A.* Sybex, 1988.
10. Jelinek, F. Design of a Linguistic Statistical Decoder for the Recognition of Continuous Speech, *Automatic Speech and Speaker Recognition*, Dixon and Martin, IEEE Press, 1979, 231-237.
11. Klatt, D. personal communication.
12. Lee, K.F., Reddy, R., Hsiao-Wuen Hon. An overview of the SPHINX speech recognition system. *IEEE Trans. Acous. Speech, and Sig. Process. 38,* 1, (January 1990), 34-45.
13. Schank, Roger
14. Not just a pretty face; compressing pictures with fractals. *Sci Am.* (March, 1990), 77-78.
15. Seneff, S. TINA: A probabilistic syntactic parser for speech understanding systems. Tech. Rep. LCS Laboratory for Computer Science, MIT, Cambridge, MA, 1989.
16. Slocum, J. *Mach. Transl. Syst.* Cambridge Union Press, 1988.
17. Zue, V. et. al. The voyager speech understanding system: Preliminary development and evaluation. In *Proceedings of ICASSP* 90.

About the Author:
GEORGE M. WHITE began research in Automatic Speech Recognition (ASR) as the Stanford Artificial Intelligence Project in 1969. Today, he is manager of speech recognition research at Apple Computer. Author's Present Address: Apple Computer, 20525 Mariani Ave., Cupertino, CA 95014.

Human–Computer Interaction – INTERACT '90
D. Diaper et al. (Editors)
Elsevier Science Publishers B.V. (North-Holland)

AUDITORY ICONS IN LARGE-SCALE COLLABORATIVE ENVIRONMENTS

William W. Gaver
Rank Xerox EuroPARC
61 Regent Street
Cambridge, UK

Randall B. Smith
Xerox Palo Alto Research Center
3333 Coyote Hill Road
Palo Alto, CA, USA

We discuss the potential for auditory icons to address several common problems in large-scale, multiprocessing, and collaborative systems. These problems include those of confirming user-initiated actions, providing information about ongoing processes or system states, providing adequate navigational information, and signalling the existence and activity of other users who may be working in a part of the system that is not visible. We provide several examples of useful auditory icons drawn from a large, shared, multitasking environment called SharedARK, and discuss their implications for other systems.

1. INTRODUCTION

Auditory icons are everyday sounds meant to convey useful information to computer users by analogy with the sounds produced by everyday events (Gaver, 1986, 1989). The strategy of using everyday sounds is based on the observation that, in general, we listen to the world, not just to sounds. That is, when hearing a sound while walking down a street we are, hopefully, more likely to be aware that it is made by a large car accelerating in our direction than to notice to its pitch, loudness and timbre. Pitch, loudness, and timbre are perceptual attributes of the sound itself; their experience is one of *musical listening*. Size, force, and bearing are perceptual attributes of a sound's source; their experience is one of *everyday listening* (Gaver, 1988).

In this paper, we suggest ways that auditory icons can be used to enhance the usability of systems which employ multiprocessing and modes, extended or layered displays, and collaborative workspaces. Our suggestions are illustrated by examples drawn from our work in adding auditory icons to a large, shared virtual environment called SharedARK (Smith, 1988). SharedARK is a collaborative version of the Alternative Reality Kit (ARK; Smith, 1987). The system serves as a virtual physics laboratory for distance education, allowing one or a number of users to interact simultaneously with objects in an environment that extends far beyond the view offered by their screens. Users manipulate the mouse to control hands that may pick up, carry or even throw objects in the world. This interface has been shown to be relatively easy for novices to learn and use (Smith, et. al., 1989), but several problems remain. These problems include those of confirming user-initiated actions, providing information about ongoing processes or system states, providing adequate navigational information, and signalling the existence and activity of other users who may be working in a part of the system that is not visible. Of course, these problems are not unique to this system, but shared by most (if not all) systems that rely on direct manipulation, multiprocessing, extended or layered views, and/or collaboration.

We believe that auditory icons can address many of these problems. In SharedARK, for example, we have added auditory cues that are meant to help users interact with the system and each other. The auditory icons we use in the SharedARK interface are, for the most part, recorded environmental sounds. We avoid using synthesized or musical instrument tones in accordance with the philosophy that things in the virtual world of the computer should sound like things in the everyday world to which we are accustomed. However, several "sound effects" are also used to indicate events that have no counterparts in the real world (though even these were developed by modifying naturally-occurring sounds).

In what follows, we describe three groups of auditory icons, based on their functions for a single user. First are those that provide confirmatory feedback to users which is largely redundant with visual displays. Second are those that provide information about ongoing processes and system states. Third, we discuss the use of auditory icons to aid navigation in complex systems. Finally, we address how these sounds might aid collaboration by providing users information about the existence, location and actions of others. For each group, we provide several examples drawn from SharedARK, and discuss their implications for other systems.

2. CONFIRMATORY SOUNDS

In our everyday lives, we often rely on auditory feedback as confirmation of our actions. As I type this, for instance, I rely as much on the sounds of the keys as I do on watching the letters appear (and sometimes more). Yet computer interfaces rely almost entirely on visual cues to provide confirmation that user actions have been accepted. This presents problems in many direct-manipulation systems. For instance, a common mistake in such interfaces occurs when objects are dragged to some target. Often one either misses hitting the target, or accidently hits the wrong one. The results of such errors are usually annoying, and sometimes catastrophic. Visual highlighting, perhaps the most common visual cue added to indicate target acquisition, is not entirely effective in helping users avoid these problems.

Auditory icons can be used to provide the kind of auditory confirmations that we rely on in the everyday world. A simple strategy for designing such sounds is to use simple everyday sounds (like taps, clicks and scrapes) to supplement or replace visual highlighting. For instance, in SharedARK, many of the actions users may perform are accompanied by the sorts of sounds such actions might make in the everyday world.

An example of an interaction which involves many confirmatory sounds is shown in Figure 1. In this example, the user creates a Xerox button, and uses it to copy a ball for teleportation to a user in another part of the system (so, for instance, the other user can use it to experiment with gravity). In SharedARK, commands are embodied as labeled buttons (like the Xerox button showed in Figure 1, which copies other objects). Commands are issued by placing buttons on the relevant object and then activating the button.

In A, the user selects the Xerox button on a menu; the choice is confirmed by a clicking sound like that of a key being pressed. In B, the Xerox button makes a popping sound (which depends on what size it is) as it appears from nowhere. The user then carries the Xerox button to the ball and drops it on (C). The wooden clanking sound reflects a successful button attachment to the object. When the user activates the Xerox button (D), it makes a sound like a machine going through one cycle of activity to indicate that it is processing a command. Another popping sound accompanies the appearance of the new ball. In E, the user sets a teleporter on the ball, and again a clank indicates a successful attachment. When the teleporter is activated, the ball is instantly moved to a linked teleporter, and a science-fiction-like zapping sound indicates that the move is successful. This sound is an example of a sound effect, a non-arbitrary extension of everyday sounds to those meant to provide information about wholly synthetic events (see Gaver, 1989).

The auditory icons used to represent events in these examples are almost completely redundant with visual feedback already present in the system. Menu selection is usally indicated by the appearance of a new object. Appearance itself is of course visually indicated, as is contact between a button

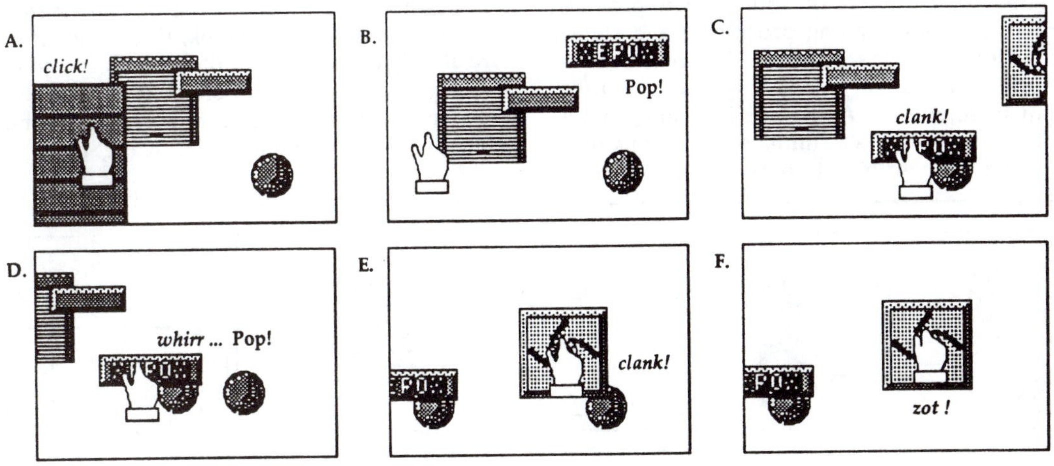

Figure 1. An example of an interaction which involves many confirmatory sounds.

and an object. Yet these sounds seem to provide feedback about actions in a way that is immediate, intuitive, and engrossing.

3. PROCESS AND STATE INFORMATION

Just as we listen to the world to tell the moment when our actions have successfully been performed, so we listen to ongoing events and processes to find out about their state. Experienced drivers seldom look at their tachometers in judging when to change gears, but instead listen to their engines. Hang-glider pilots often listen to the rush of wind around their heads to judge their speed, as watching the ground can be seriously misleading. Finally, computer users listen to the sounds their disk-drives, modems, and printers make to know what their machines are doing.

There are several reasons that sound is a particularly effective medium for displaying process and state information from computer systems. Sounds can serve to remind users about continuous states or ongoing processing without depending on windows that are likely to be occluded or to use unnecessary space. In addition, hearing auditory feedback about some change in the system does not rely on visual attention to that change. This property is important for any system, and crucial for those like SharedARK, in which events are not necessarily visible on the screen. Finally, changes in processes or state are usually most important to users, and sounds tend to be most noticeable when they change. Thus continuous sounds can be designed that fade into the perceptual background when they are unchanging, but which are quickly noticed when they change (Buxton, 1989).

A number of examples of sounds that provide information about ongoing processing and states may be found in SharedARK. Figure 2 shows several instances of processes that produce continuous sounds. In A, the user is turning on the law of motion, which is a simulated "law of nature" controlling whether objects move (a mode of the system). When this law is on, it makes a quiet, low pitched humming noise reminiscent of an electrical appliance. This sort of sound tends to fade into the perceptual background after a short time, so that it does not annoy or distract users. However, it can be heard if one wants to ascertain its status, and when motion is turned off the change to silence is immediately noticeable.

When the law of motion is turned on, two balls begin bouncing around a nearby room (B). With each collision comes a tapping sound that depends on the object's size. In C, the user has moved to a raincloud in a different area of the system and turned it on. As the raindrops fall, they make a dripping sound. The drips' repetition rate depends on the density of the rain and how fast it is falling.

Sounds that reflect the state of the system (such as the activation of a law of nature) and the activity of ongoing processes are quite helpful when the associated visual indicators are not visible or when the screen is crowded. Without the sound, one must look at the law of motion object to determine whether it is on, or throw an object to see if it moves. Such tests, simple as they might be, are often inconvenient and time-consuming, and in fact sometimes misleading. Hearing the state of the system and its processing is often more efficient than relying on graphical displays or tests of its performance.

Most systems to not include bouncing balls or falling rain, but they often do make use of multiple continuous processes and changing system states or modes. In such systems, sounds can be used as they are in this example to remind users of the state of their system and the activation of processes. Simple sounds have been shown to be effective in reminding users of the state of their system and avoiding mode errors (Monk, 1986). Similarly, other relatively continuous auditory icons can be used to represent the activity of ongoing processes such as background printing, copying, and formatting. There is great potential for using these sort of

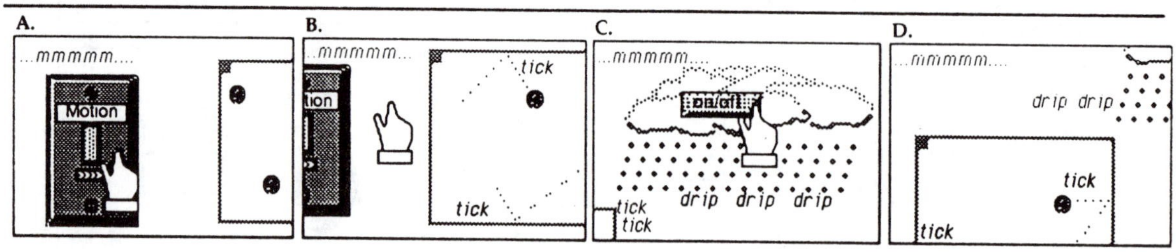

Figure 2. States and processes in SharedARK make sounds; their relative volumes depend on their distance.

auditory cues in any system which involves multitasking.

4. SOUNDS IN VERY LARGE ENVIRONMENTS

As the user moves to the raincloud in Figure 2, the balls continue to bounce around the room, but the sounds they make are quieter because the user has moved away from them. The dripping sounds, on the other hand, are relatively loud, indicating the user's proximity to them.

In general, the amplitudes of all sounds in SharedARK are changed and they are low-pass filtered to indicate the distance of their virtual sources from the user (low-pass filtering provides the attenuation of high frequency energy typical of distant sounds). In D, for instance, as the user moves back towards the bouncing balls the sounds they make become louder, while those made by the rain drops become softer. The humming noise made by law of motion remains constant, because it is a property of the entire system and is not associated with a particular location.

Auditory icons which depend on the distance between their sources and the user's virtual location have the potential to help users navigate. Such sounds produce auditory neighbourhoods, so that one can move away from one sound source and towards another without seeing either. Visually-disabled people commonly make use of continuously present sounds in their environment such as those of ventilator ducts or traffic crossings for orientation (Jenkins, 1985); we believe sounds can play a similar role in computer systems.

We have created objects we call *soundholders*, to explore the utility of such auditory landmarks. Soundholders continuously emit sounds whose volume decreases as the user moves away from them. The sounds they produce are randomly varied, with users having control over their average frequency and amplitude, as well as the frequency and amplitude ranges and the average repetition rate. By choosing different sounds and setting these parameters, a wide range of auditory environments can be created. As soundholders are associated with working areas, they make easier the task of moving around a space larger than can be seen at any given time. This seems true not only for systems with extended displays like SharedARK, but for layered systems as well.

Figure 3 shows how soundholders may be used as auditory landmarks. In A, the user has put a soundholder near one area of the system and started its sound (in this case, a series of bird calls). In B, the user has associated a different soundholder with another working space. This soundholder makes sounds like a burbling stream. As the user moves over the otherwise unmarked plane between the two regions, the rise and fall of their associated sounds provides information about the relative distance to each part of the system.

In any interface that uses sound, annoyance is an important issue. We have found that environmental sounds such as bird chirps, waves, and crickets seem to work well as continuously present auditory landmarks. They have the disadvantage that they are not meaningfully related to the areas with which they are associated; nonetheless, listening to a virtual aviary, for instance, seems much more pleasant than hearing a room full of machinery or typing. It is interesting to note in this context that there is a semantic component to sounds that make acoustically-based predictions of annoyance somewhat unreliable (Swift, et al., 1989). For instance, though birdsong is a highly abrupt and complex sound (and thus might be expected to be aversive) it is much less annoying than other more continuous sounds such as passing traffic.

Just as using auditory cues about the state of the system and processes frees users from relying solely on visual input, so do auditory landmarks enable users to navigate with reference to parts of the

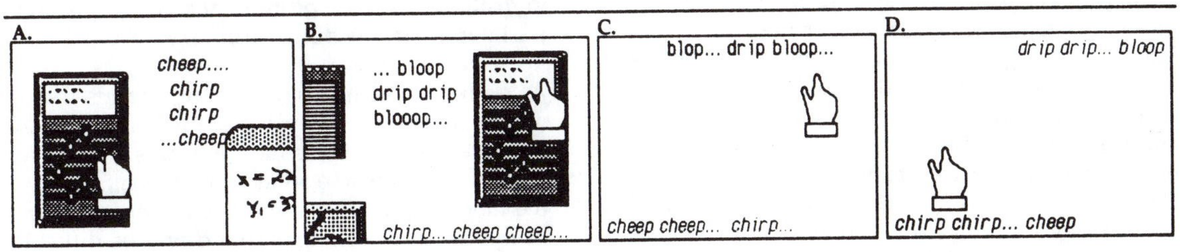

Figure 3. The user associates two sound holders with different regions of the SharedARK space. Navigation between the two auditory neighbourhoods thus created is aided by their sounds.

system they might not be able to see. Providing information about the distance between the user and important landmarks could be a useful tool in creating interfaces for the visually disabled. But as Buxton (1989) points out, we are all visually disabled to some degree when working with computers, especially those in which not all items of interest are necessarily visible. Auditory landmarks are useful for interfaces such as SharedARK, in which objects may be offscreen. Similarly, they have the potential to aid navigation in layered systems in which parts of the interface may be occluded or simply not shown. For instance, many CAD systems rely on invisible layers to simplify displays. Associating auditory landmarks with key layers to indicate proximity could help users find their way in such systems. Similarly, sounds could be used to indicate the nature and importance of linked areas in hypertext systems, helping users find paths in complex mazes of information.

5. LISTENING TO OTHER USERS

The functions outlined above are all relevant to individual users of large-scale multiprocessing environments. These auditory icons may play an equally important role in shared systems, in which more than one user may be working in the environment at a given time. For instance, all the auditory icons we incorporated into the SharedARK system are heard by all users of the system. The sounds thus perform the dual role of providing feedback to an acting user as well as new information to others. The addition of sound seems to add to the feeling of presence of other users, and to aid in coordinating activities. This is particularly true when users are working in spatially separated areas of the system.

Sounds that provide confirmatory feedback to one user might well be the only indication to another that certain actions are being performed. In the situation described in Figure 1, for instance, the sounds made in the process of copying and teleporting the ball – the pops, clanks, and whirring noises – assure the waiting user that his or her request is being carried out, and the sound of the teleporter tells him or her that the ball has arrived. Similarly, the sounds made by continuous processes and states are helpful in knowing what others are doing and the expected results of various actions ("Oh, you turned on the law of motion – I guess I'd better make sure none of my things are moving."). Finally, auditory landmarks are useful in helping to locate and guide other users ("Are you near the aviary? You should go over to the stream to find that button.").

Sound opens up a new dimension of meaningful reference points in this system which can help collaborative users overcome the limitations of the visual display. We have observed users collaborating on a spatially-distributed task in this system, both with and without sound. In general, it seems that users working with sound are much more likely to comment on each other's actions even when working in separate parts of the system That is, users working without sounds must ask one another about activities they cannot see, while those with auditory feedback can comment directly on the things they hear. In general, auditory icons can help users collaborate effectively even when they do not share the same view, as for instance when working on different portions of a document using a group editing tool.

6. CONCLUSIONS

The use of varied sounds in computer interfaces is new, but we feel it has much potential for increasing the usability of complex systems. With multiprocessing, the limitations of screen-size for representing objects and events becomes more apparent. Such limitations are inherent to complex interfaces that rely on spatial encoding. Strategies to overcome them such as layering and extending the virtual world outside the screen are potentially quite powerful, but many objects may be invisible at a given time. The same is true for many collaborative systems, in which users may work together on different aspects of a task. As more items are placed outside of view in such systems, being able to hear the status of the system could become more important.

There are a number of issues to address in designing effective auditory icons. The first involves the sort of mapping used between sounds and the information they are to convey. We believe that using environmental sounds chosen to have some semantic relation to their referents is often the best method for maintaining identifiability. It is difficult to relate synthesized or musical sounds to events in the interface in any but an arbitrary way.

A second problem is in designing sounds that will not be confused. Choosing sounds with different temporal patterns is the most effective way to create a set of discriminable sounds (Patterson, 1989). But the more sounds that are played at once, the more likely that any particular sound will be difficult to distinguish. Care must be taken to design a set of sounds that work well together, forming a well-balanced acoustic ecology.

Finally, sounds in the interface can be annoying. What seems cute and clever at first may grow tiresome after a few exposures. Sounds should be concise and unobtrusive, and should reflect a number of data dimensions at once to avoid repetition (for instance, varying sounds to reflect the size of associated objects is informative and adds variety). In general, the aim should be to use sounds that fit in with the environment in which the system will be used. In addition, users should have control over the sounds they hear, at least to the extent of being able to turn off individual sounds.

Although these issues can be difficult to resolve, auditory icons have much potential in providing feedback from complex systems. The addition of sound to SharedARK helps to demonstrate the wide range of functions that auditory icons can perform. By designing sounds that accompany user actions in the system, salient confirmatory feedback is provided to users in a way that seems more noticeable than visual cues. Sounds which reflect the status of the system and ongoing processes can be useful in allowing users to know about events without having to be in the same area of the system. Using amplitude and filtering to reflect the distance of virtual sound sources can aid navigation, and in combination with auditory landmarks helps to divide the otherwise homogeneous surface of the virtual world into distinct neighbourhoods. Finally, using these sounds in a collaborative context adds new information about other users and their activities, and provides new points of reference to all users.

ACKNOWLEDGEMENTS

We thank Allan Maclean and Judy Olson for their comments on this paper.

REFERENCES

Buxton, W. (1989). Introduction to this special issue on nonspeech audio. *Human-Computer Interaction*. 4 (1).

Gaver, W. W. (1986). Auditory icons: Using sound in computer interfaces. *Human-Computer Interaction*. 2, 167 - 177.

Gaver, W. W. (1988). Everyday listening and auditory icons. Doctoral Dissertation, University of California, San Diego.

Gaver, W. W. (1989). The SonicFinder: An interface that uses auditory icons. *Human-Computer Interaction*. 4 (1).

Jenkins, James J. (1985). Acoustic information for objects, places, and events. in Warren, W. H., & Shaw, R. E., *Persistence and change: Proceedings of the first international conference on event perception*. Hillsdale, NJ: Lawrence Erlbaum Associates.

Monk, A. F. (1986). Mode errors: A user-centered analysis and some preventative measures using keying-contingent sound. *International Journal of Man-Machine Studies*. 24, 313 - 327.

Patterson, R. D. (1989). Guidelines of the design of auditory warning sounds. *Proceedings of the Institute of Acoustics 1989 Spring Conference*. *11* (5), 17 - 24.

Smith, R. B. (1989). A prototype futuristic technology for distance education. *Proceedings of the NATO Advanced Workshop on New Directions in Educational Technology*. Nov. 10 - 13, 1988, Cranfield, U.K..

Smith, R. B. (1988). The Alternate Reality Kit: an example of the tension between literalism and magic. *Proceedings of CHI + GI 1987*. April 5 - 9, Toronto, 61 - 67.

Smith, R. B., O'Shea, T., O'Malley, C., Scanlon, E., & Taylor, J., (1989). Preliminary experiments with a distributed, multi-media, problem solving environment. *Proceedings of the European Conference on Computer Supported Cooperative Work*.

Swift, C. G., Flindell, I. H., & Rice, C. G. (1989). Annoyance and impulsivity judgments of environmental noises. *Proceedings of the Institute of Acoustics 1989 Spring Conference*. *11* (5), 551 - 555.

Part IV

Psychology and Human Factors

The disciplines of human-computer interaction and human factors are closely related. Human factors or ergonomics is a branch of applied psychology that has been characterized by Sanders and McCormick (1987, p. 5) as follows:

> *Human factors discovers and applies information about human behavior, abilities, limitations, and other characteristics to the design of tools, machines, systems, tasks, jobs, and environments for productive, safe, comfortable, and effective human use.*

Psychological issues, such as users' capabilities and preferences and the degree to which interfaces support their activities, are a central concern in HCI. Psychologists address these issues with empirical investigation, theory, and modeling.

Formal experiments can identify and quantify differences in performance, usability, and learnability among interfaces, input-output devices, and interaction techniques. As discussed in Chapter 2, the advantage of good formal experiments is the high degree of confidence we can have in the internal validity of the results. Nice examples of the role of experiments in design appear in Case B and in the Egan et al. study of a hypertext system in Chapter 13. In this section we focus on the use of experimentation to uncover general properties of human behavior. Knowledge of human behavior could then guide decisions without the need for further experimentation.

The difficulties of carrying out meaningful experiments and of achieving external validity so that we can generalize from them were described in Chapter 2 and by Liam Bannon in Chapter 3. For almost any aspect of design, we can compare some alternatives, but we cannot test every approach that clever designers may propose. Furthermore, we often cannot do our testing in the appropriate context of use.

Consider menu search, for example. How people scan visual displays is a well-researched topic in cognitive psychology. Many HCI experiments have examined people searching menus (see, for example, Perlman, 1985; Paap and Roske-Hofstrand, 1988; Norman, 1991). Guidelines have been written that try to specify an optimal organization. They deal with issues such as how many items should be in each menu, how many levels deep menu trees should go, and what is the optimum trade-off between breadth and depth in the design of menus. Unfortunately, all experiments have assumed that each menu item is chosen equally often. In real use, people generally use some menu items frequently and others rarely or never. Such patterns of use will influence the optimal depth, breadth, and organization of a menu, so we cannot use the guidelines with confidence. Innovations such as pie menus or voice selection menus have also typically not been considered in the experiments done to date.

An alternative to relying on empirical results is to develop analytic models that make quantitative predictions about a user's performance before an interface is built. Such models can minimize the need to build multiple versions and carry out lengthy experiments. Although limited by our lack of precise knowledge of human psychology, modeling approaches are being refined and applied. Serious students of HCI should be familiar with this work.

Chapter 9, "Human Information Processing," therefore, presents the development of over two decades of work on models of the human users of interactive computer systems and of their perceptual, cognitive, and motor behavior. It surveys attempts to develop a comprehensive psychological "science" of human-computer interaction that seeks to model and predict in advance, at least in some respects, how systems and interfaces will be used. The chapter also includes essays in which leading researchers examine and debate the role and contributions of psychology to the field of human-computer interaction.

Chapter 10, "Designing to Fit Human Capabilities," steps back to examine the broader view of the human-computer experience that was emphasized in Chapter 2. We explore human error, crucial to understanding how to improve users' experience. On-line help, documentation, and training are discussed. Building systems that conform or adapt to individual differences is always an issue, and interfaces for the disabled present a special case of designing for human capabilities. Computers are capable of greatly assisting those with special needs—if applications are designed with such needs in mind. Finally, we consider the physical environment and health concerns that arise with intense use of computer keyboards and displays. Problems with vision, hearing, posture-related back problems, and carpal tunnel or repetitive stress syndrome, to cite prominent examples, seem to be on the rise as users increase in number and age; dealing with such problems is essential if we are to foster the productive and humane use of computer technology.

REFERENCES

Norman, K. (1991). *The Psychology of Menu Selection: Designing Cognitive Control at the Human-Computer Interface.* Ablex.

Paap, K., and Roske-Hofstrand, R. (1988). Design of Menus. In Helander, M. (Ed.) (1988), *Handbook of Human-Computer Interaction,* North-Holland, 205–235.

Perlman, G. (1985). Making the Right Choices with Menus. *Human-Computer Interaction—Proc. Interact '84,* North-Holland, 317–321. Reprinted in Baecker, R., and Buxton, W. (Eds.) (1987), *Readings in Human-Computer Interaction: A Multidisciplinary Approach,* Morgan Kaufmann.

Sanders, M. S., and McCormick, E. J. (1987). *Human Factors in Engineering and Design,* Sixth Edition. Wiley.

Chapter 9

Human Information Processing

Of the many disciplines contributing to human-computer interaction, psychology and computer science are obvious candidates for foundation sciences. Courses on human-computer interaction are most often found in a computer science curriculum, but many leading researchers into interface design and evaluation began by studying human information processing in departments of cognitive psychology. Cognitive science (Gardner, 1985), which emerged more recently, draws on cognitive psychology, linguistics, artificial intelligence, and other disciplines, and may contribute even more to our understanding of human-computer interaction.

Many empirical studies of interactive computer use have no theoretical orientation. Data is collected, but no underlying model or theory of the process exists to be confirmed or refuted. Such a theory would be very useful because with many design decisions there are too many alternative proposals to test by trial and error. A strong theory or performance model could reduce the set of plausible alternatives to a manageable number for testing.

The readings in this chapter describe efforts to apply theory and models from cognitive psychology to the design of human-computer interfaces and dialogues. We also include two papers in which prominent researchers reflect on their experience and discuss the relationship between psychological research and human-computer interaction.

This chapter introduction presents key cognitive issues and terms. It is not a short course, but may serve as a catalyst and guide the reader to pursue the issues more deeply in the books and articles cited.

THE HUMAN INFORMATION PROCESSOR

Today, computer scientists can draw on psychology for guidance in design. Not long ago, the reverse was true: Psychology borrowed from computer science to construct a model of human information processing.

Radical behaviorism, then the dominant school of psychology, avoided using abstract mental concepts or mechanisms to explain behavior. After all, they reasoned, earlier explanations for behavior relied on demons and spells. Shouldn't scientists therefore restrict themselves to what can be observed, recorded, and reproduced? The advent of computers suggested that this logic needed to be challenged. Concepts such as input and output, memory, processing, and resource limitations are very useful in explaining a computer's observable behavior. Why not also try to apply these concepts to human behavior?

Using a computer metaphor for human information processing does *not* imply that the brain's functioning is analogous to a computer's functioning or that we are all walking around with Von Neumann machines in our heads. What we are saying instead is that the concepts and vocabulary of information processing can help in formulating theories of human cognition and in explaining aspects of human behavior.

Another important influence in legitimizing the study of humans as information processors came from "human factors" work that began with efforts to improve workplace efficiency early in the 20th century. This work assumed great importance in World War II with the need to improve the design and use of complex military technology, including complex visual displays. Experimentation on monitoring and extracting information from displays led to mathematical modeling of human behavior and new applications of statistical analysis.

A third source of support for thinking about mental phenomena in terms of information processing was an earlier tradition of psychology based on unobservable mental constructs. This included early empirical work by Fechner, Wund, and Helmholtz; introspective analyses such as those of William James, and psychodynamic contributions by Freud and his colleagues. (For example, concepts such as the id, ego, and superego can be viewed as concurrent processes.)

Ulric Neisser's *Cognitive Psychology* (1967) defined this new field. Subsequently, Lindsay and Norman published a widely used introduction, *Human Information Processing* (1977). A computer metaphor for mental processing was firmly established.

Thus psychology borrowed computer concepts and applied them to mental processing. Now the debt is being repaid as computer developers seek psychological knowledge to guide design. Most early computers had no visual displays, but human factors studies could help organize controls for loading registers and displaying the internal system status. Also, as described in Chapter 1, studies of "software psychology" emerged, including problem solving in programming, debugging strategies, and the effects of visual format on comprehension of programs.

The need to design the displays and keyboards for interactive computer systems led to a great influx of perceptual and cognitive psychologists. The study of human information processing is often categorized into studies of sensation, perception, cognition, and motor control, all of which are relevant to system design.

Sensation and Perception

Part III covered applications of sensation and perception in the visual and auditory systems. Sensation refers to the first nervous system responses to activity of the sensory organs of sight, sound, touch, olfaction, and taste—the latter two as yet playing little role in human-computer interaction! Sensation is relatively easy to study because the sense organs are located outside the skull and are similar to those of more easily studied animals.

Perceptual psychologists study the way people perceive sensory stimuli, particularly conscious perception. The Chapter 6 introduction illustrated the difference between sensation and perception with the Neckar cube illusion—a single sensory stimulus that can be perceived in different ways. Whether viewing an image, listening to music, or touching an object, what we perceive depends on our present context and past experience. Thus, there is no neat boundary between perception and cognition. Good overviews of sensation and perception include Cornsweet (1970), Kaufman (1974), Gregory (1978), and DeValois and DeValois (1988) on vision, and Green (1976), Yost and Nielsen (1977), and Pickles (1988) on hearing.

THE STUDY OF COGNITION TODAY

Research into cognition is highly interdisciplinary. This is reflected in the backgrounds of researchers who have published good general books on cognition. Anderson (1983, 1989) is a cognitive psychologist who focuses on experimental studies and models of the cognitive processes involved in memory and learning. Fodor (1983) is a philosopher who has collaborated with psychologists in developing psychological theory. Minsky's (1986) approach to the study of the mind is tied to his work in artificial intelligence. Linguistics (e.g., Pinker, 1990) has also been central to the evolution of cognitive science and contributes to the study of human-computer interaction. Excellent multiauthored collections have been edited by Osherson (1990), a developmental psychologist, and Posner (1989), a cognitive psychologist.

Cognition is often subdivided into topics. These include *attention* (Parasuraman and Davies, 1984), *categorization* (Neisser, 1987), *learning and expertise* (Osherson and Weinstein, 1984; Chi, Glaser, and Farr, 1988), *reasoning and problem solving* (Holyoak and Spellman, 1993; Kahneman, Slovic, and Tversky, 1982; VanLehn, 1989), and *performance* (Goodale, 1990; Jeannerod, 1990).

Also included is *memory*, often subdivided into *working memory* or *short-term memory*—for example, keeping a telephone number in mind for the short time needed to dial it (Baddeley, 1986); *episodic memory*, the recollection of specific events (Rubin, 1986); *semantic memory*, our general knowledge of the world and how things interrelate (Johnson-Laird, Hermann, and Chaffin, 1984; Shallice, 1988); and *implicit memory*, memories that guide our behavior without our being consciously aware of the details, including the memory involved in carrying out motor tasks such as riding a bicycle (or operating a trackball) (Jacoby, Lindsay, and Toth, 1992; Squire, 1987).

Another aspect of cognition is *mental representation*, which includes *spatial representation and imagery* (Anderson, 1978; Landau and Jackendoff, 1993) and *connectionist models* (Rumelhart, McClelland, and the PDP Research Group, 1986). *Mental models* (Gentner and Stevens, 1983) are an aspect of mental representation that has been heavily applied in human-computer interaction.

Cognitive neuroscience is a new frontier in the study of cognition. New technologies permit real-time measurement of neuronal activity in specific areas of the cerebral cortex of the brain as people are engaged in tasks. This basic research promises to contribute to a better understanding of human information processing.

For now, however, the most direct influences from cognitive sciences come from its parent disciplines of artificial intelligence, linguistics, philosophy, and psychology. General readings in cognitive science that may be particularly useful include Johnson-Laird (1986), Simon (1981), and Winston (1984).

RESOURCES IN HUMAN INFORMATION PROCESSING

We shall now explore concepts from information processing that suggest how psychology can be applied to human-computer interaction. The discussion begins with the basic concept of *resources*. These have analogs in the computer domain: memory, processing cycles, and bandwidth. Human resources have some similar properties and some dissimilarities.

We start with two important kinds of resources:

- Critical resources
- Limited resources

Critical resources are those required to perform a particular task or to execute a particular process. *Limited resources* are resources that may be in short supply relative to their need. In cognition, as in operating systems, problems arise when critical resources are limited and supply cannot meet the demand.

Perhaps the best-known human resource limitation is "the magic number seven" discussed by George Miller (1956). We can generally hold around seven "chunks" of information at a time in our short-term or working memory, such as a seven-digit phone number. This fact can be used in designing systems, but can be misused as well: Some claim that menu displays should contain seven items, but items visible on a display need not be held in short-term memory!

Various tasks and cognitive activities can be discussed in terms of the type and quantity of resources that they consume. Norman and Bobrow (1975) characterized processes as being limited by either

- the processing resources available, or
- the quality of data available.

The availability of processing *resources* depends on memory, processing "cycles," and internal communications channels. If additional resources would improve performance, a task is said to be *resource limited.*

Data quality is determined by what is being processed, rather than what is doing the processing. When adding processing resources will not improve performance, the process is said to be *data limited.* That is, no improvement in performance can be achieved without improving the quality of the data available for processing.

Data-limited processes can be subdivided into those having either

- signal data limits, or
- memory data limits.

Signal data limits depend on input quality. For example, we might describe an auditory case as having a poor "signal-to-noise" ratio. If you try to hold a conversation beside a running jackhammer, you will never get beyond a certain level of communication, regardless of how closely you listen. Similarly, if text is presented in a terrible typeface and with very poor background contrast, your reading speed will be limited despite your best efforts.

Memory data limits are less straightforward, but equally important. They do not describe the amount of memory (a resource limit), but instead the nature or quality of memory. Consider again the example of trying to read poorly presented text. You may use "world knowledge," your knowledge about what letters are likely to follow each other, for example. Your ability to use your experience affects your reading effectiveness. Someone reading a font for the first time will probably read more slowly than someone who has experience with it. This illustrates the idea that our past experiences make a difference. The nature of the stored information influences the processing of new information. The quality of stored information is an example of a memory data limit.

The relationship between resource and data limitations in performance is shown in Figure 9.1. Beyond a necessary minimum resource allocation (point R_{min}), performance improves as resources are added, up to the point R_{dl}. To this point, the task is resource limited. Beyond R_{dl}, the task is data limited. Unless the data improves, performance beyond this point will not improve even if additional resources are allocated.

In the sample task, the quality of data is constant and the allocated resources are increased. If the quality of the data was improved instead, the same performance would likely be achieved using fewer resources (or better performance achieved with the same resources). There is a trade-off between resources and data quality. A primary design objective should be to ***minimize resource consumption by improving data quality.*** Improved display quality and graphic design are techniques for pushing back signal data limits. Training and the use of appropriate mental models can push back memory data limits.

FIGURE 9.1

Data and resource limitations in performing a simple task. Increase in performance is shown on the vertical axis. Increase in resources is shown along horizontal axis. Certain minimal resources (R_{min}) are required to initiate the task. Performance levels off at a certain point (R_{dl}), when the task becomes data limited (Norman and Bobrow, 1975, p. 48).

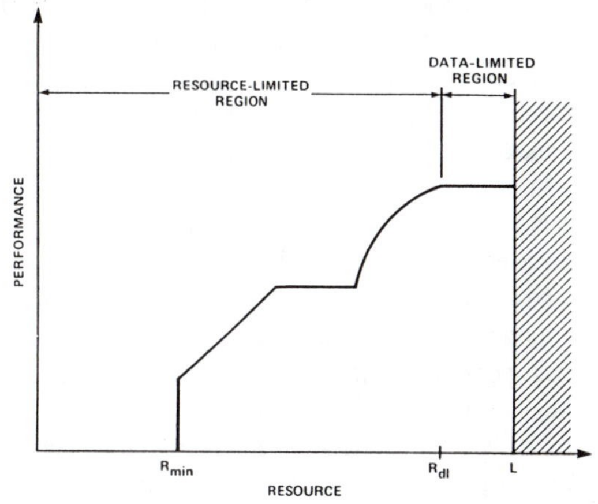

Why do we need to minimize the cognitive resources required to perform a task or complete a given amount of work? Cognitive resources are in short supply and there is a high demand. Hence, there is a cost associated with their use. A good measure of the complexity or difficulty of a task is its demand on resources. This measure is known as *cognitive load.* Cognitive load correlates directly with factors such as

- learning time
- fatigue
- stress
- proneness to error
- inability to "time-share"

Cognitive load is an important consideration in the design of isolated tasks as well as large systems, but the calculation is not always simple. For example, consider the different loads imposed in making a selection with a one-, two-, or three-button mouse. This was studied experimentally in designing the two-button mouse for the Xerox Star (Bewley et al., 1983, reprinted in the first edition of this book). Testing individual cases may indicate that the one-button mouse has the lowest load, since there is no overhead in determining which button to select. However, in the larger context, there may be a penalty "down the road" with a one-button mouse: for example, in learning when to double-click or when to use other methods to carry out commands. Rather than reducing the overall load of the system, we may only have shifted the load to another place or time.

This issue was debated at length by Apple Macintosh developers, who chose a one-button mouse. No clear resolution has appeared. Suffice it to say that the example illustrates how complexity and design must always be considered in context, since almost every decision has side effects.

Sometimes a critical resource is limited and cannot be allocated to a task. This may occur when performing a task with a particularly high cognitive load or when two tasks make simultaneous demands on the same resource. Consider the experience of a parent listening to two children who are talking at once.

In other situations, we can do more than one thing at a time; there are enough resources to go around—listening to a radio program while driving, for example. But if the car goes into a skid, the driver is very likely to stop listening to the radio and concentrate on getting the vehicle back under control. Full attention is focused on the driving task and no surplus resources are available to concentrate on the radio, no matter how interesting the program may be.

Degradation in the performance of one task because of competition with another task for critical resources is known as *interference*. Sometimes, processes mutually interfere and the performance of each degrades. More often, as in the driving example, a priority mechanism determines which of the competing tasks is more important and allocates resources accordingly. The performance of the higher-priority task is maintained at the expense of the other.

Many tasks performed using a computer have a high cognitive load, so they are susceptible to interference. One design goal is to reduce the likelihood of interference. Two approaches are reducing the load associated with task performance, and, as discussed earlier, improving the quality of data available to users.

Yet another way to reduce interference is to minimize the likelihood of competition. For example, different sensory modalities utilize different resources. While tracking a moving target on a display (using a mouse, for example), you are more likely to be able to perform a simultaneous verbal task than another visual or manual one. As emphasized in Chapters 7 and 8, we have underutilized sensory modalities that can supplement, rather than compete with, the visual.

The human factors community has considered these and other issues discussed later in this chapter in the context of process control and what they term "supervisory control." They term their approach *cognitive engineering*. Excellent reviews of this field are Woods and Roth (1988), Sheridan (1988), and Rasmussen and Goodstein (1988).

SKILLED PERFORMANCE

We all know people who perform tasks effortlessly that we find very difficult. For us, if the task can be done at all, it involves attentive, problem-solving behavior. Playing a piano, sailing a boat, writing computer programs, and solving math problems are possible examples. Experts in such activities are performing the same complex tasks, but their behavior is very different from our own. They are *skilled* in that particular activity. Skill is a continuum, of course, as seen in the ratings, handicaps, and belts used to grade performance in competitive activities such as chess, golf, and the martial arts.

Unlike the demands on our attention when we are learning, many aspects of skilled task performance are *automatic*, consuming negligible cognitive resources. Consequently, skilled performance is less susceptible to interference. The resources thus released can sometimes be allocated to another task performed synchronously with the skilled task. One visible clue that a subject is skilled is the execution of two or more complex tasks in parallel. (Of course, the extent to which this is possible also depends on the tasks.)

Many properties of skilled and unskilled behaviors can be observed watching people in a Chinese restaurant. Have a meal with someone who has never used chopsticks, someone who has used chopsticks since childhood, and someone whose skill level lies in between. Eating occupies a novice's full attention. The slightest distraction results in spilled food. Diners who are slightly beyond the novice level may seem to eat effortlessly, but if you ask a difficult enough question (i.e., one that generates enough interference), they too will drop food. With experts, no task affects their eating if it doesn't interfere with their use of hand or mouth. Expert chopsticks-users can talk, read, or recite poetry while eating. They are skilled.

To gain insight into the nature of skill, Card and Moran (1986) observed expert text editors in the work described in our first reading. They report that experts have built up a repertoire of techniques, or *methods*, for dealing with standard document-editing situations. One can think of these methods as the cognitive equivalent of macros or subroutines. The individual steps, or *operators*, required to perform a particular learned task are bound together. In text editing, the expert need only recognize the problem, *select* the most appropriate method for dealing with it, and invoke it.

However, identifying all of the methods used in a task may not be easy. For example, despite intense study of chess expertise, it is not yet clear precisely what steps are involved. Thus, skilled humans currently outperform the best computers even though the computers can consider many millions of moves more than the experts appear to consider in the time allowed.

Skill Acquisition and Skill Transfer

Achieving a skilled level of proficiency in most tasks is difficult. Many cognitive skills, like sensorimotor skills, are learned through repetition. With complex tasks, repetition is a necessary but not sufficient aspect of skill acquisition. Not all skills have the same difficulty of acquisition. Most of us can master riding a bicycle. Fewer of us can learn to fly a helicopter or become a virtuoso on the violin. The *learning curve* for a number of diverse skills is shown in Figure 9.2.

Crossman (1959) is an important early paper on skill acquisition. It emphasized methods and their selection and laid the groundwork for the modeling covered in the first readings in this chapter.

Training is a part of the human-computer interface that is becoming more important. The number of features in mature applications increases, the number of applications available on a system increases, networks vastly expand what is available, more people become users—all of these build the demand for learning and training, discussed in more detail in Chapter 10.

We now encounter a dilemma. Skilled performance has the desirable property of minimizing the cognitive load during task execution. However, acquiring skill takes time and effort. How do we know whether we are just transferring effort from execution time to learning time? How do we know when there is a net improvement?

FIGURE 9.2

Learning curves for several diverse tasks. (1) Reading inverted text (minutes/text); average 6 subjects. (2) Text processing with Wordstar editor (minutes/core editing tasks); benchmark test with 50 core editing tasks (9 subjects). (3) Typing alphanumeric material (seconds/keystroke); average of 18 employees each group. (4) Mail sorting (seconds/letter); average of 30 employees. (5) Cigar making (minutes/cigar); average of several employees (Bösser and Melchior, 1985, p. 344).

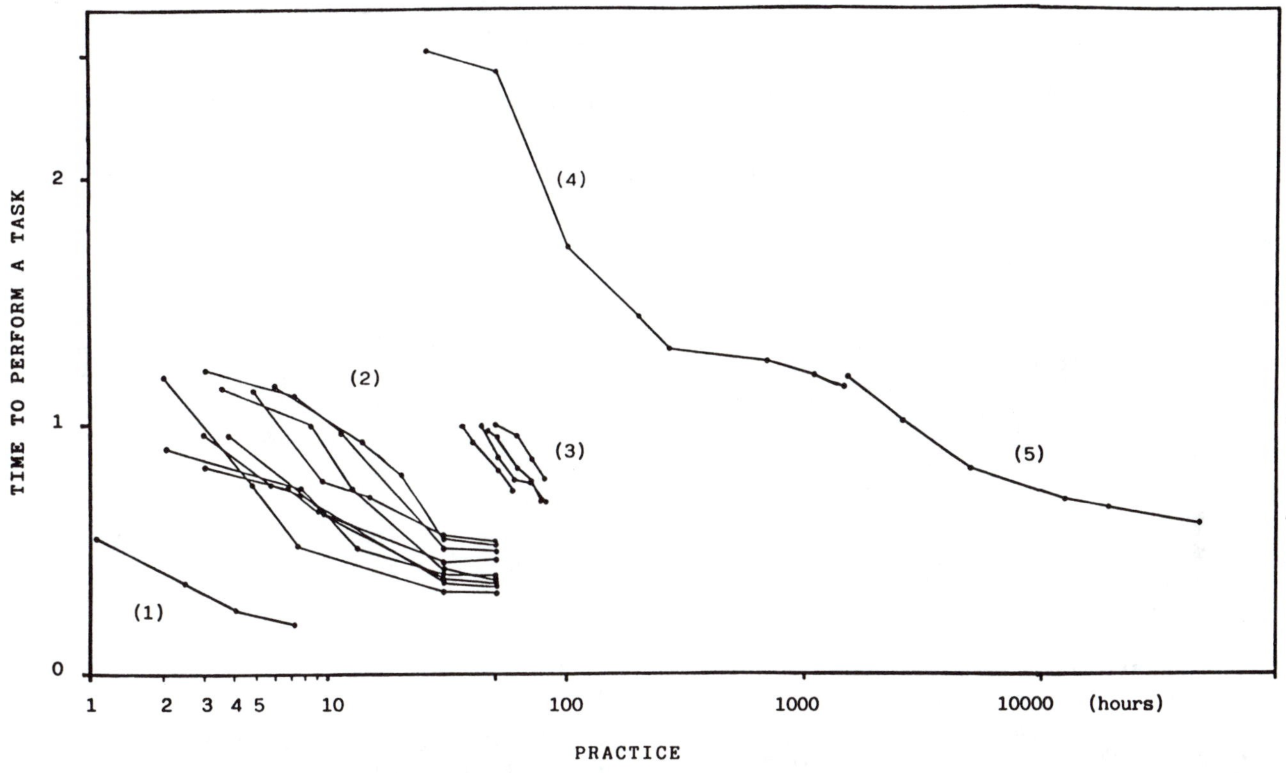

Sometimes the answer is clear, but often a trade-off exists, with no one right answer. Training is not a good investment if a skill will rarely be exercised. But for most cases we can side-step some of these questions by being clear about what we want to accomplish. Vague concepts like "ease of use" and "user friendly" don't help. A clearer formulation of our goal is that we want to *accelerate the process whereby novices begin to perform like experts*.

Even when skill is difficult to acquire, new users don't come to a system completely unskilled. Life equips us with a large repertoire of highly developed skills. The skills required to operate an application need not be learned from scratch.

Generally, the more specialized the application, the easier it is to design around existing skills. For example, any accountant can already touch-type on numerical keypads and draftsmen can already work a drafting machine with one hand while using a pencil in the other. These skills can form the basis for a powerful and *appropriate* design. Analyzing the target population for exploitable skills gives a whole new direction and bite to the platitude, "know the user."

When a new skill is required, we may get a head start in training by using an existing skill as a point of departure. The use of metaphor, discussed in Chapter 2, is one aspect of this. The use of existing skills as the basis for performing new tasks is known as *skill transfer*. Four guidelines for successfully designing an interface to maximize this transfer are the following:

- Build upon the users' existing set of skills.
- Keep the skills required by the system to a minimum.
- Use the same skill wherever possible in similar circumstances.
- Use feedback to identify similar contexts and distinguish ones that are dissimilar.

By keeping the repertoire of skills small, the skills are used more often. This practice, in turn, helps a novice attain a skilled level of proficiency.

Beyond the issue of practice, an underlying cognitive principle is that if interfaces require the same skills in similar contexts, the exploitation of existing skills is maximized. That is, in a well-designed system, when a user confronts a new situation, all of the feedback mechanisms shout "this is like this other task that you have done before," and the user can transfer what has already been learned to the new situation. This was discussed in Chapter 7 in Buxton's reading, "Chunking and Phrasing in the Design of Human-Computer Dialogues."

As computer use becomes more widespread, the problematic side of transfer of training is increasingly important (and frustrating) to developers. Users familiar with one interface pay a penalty if they have to retrain on a new interface, even if it is better. The reluctance to retrain, and its cost, has led to greater emphasis on "backwards compatibility." The fact that the QWERTY keyboard layout is universal as we enter the 21st century, despite scientific evidence since the 1930s that there exist better designs, is ample evidence of the power of "the installed base of users." Empirical evidence that switching will pay off in the long run can help the argument, but often only a substantially improved design will motivate change.

APPLIED COGNITIVE PSYCHOLOGY AS A FOUNDATION FOR HCI

Published in 1983, *The Psychology of Human-Computer Interaction* (Card, Moran, and Newell, 1983) has served as the foundation for the single most sustained effort to create a science base "for an applied psychology concerned with the human users of interactive computer systems" (p. vii). This psychology, they insist, should be "theory-based, in the sense of articulating a mechanism underlying the observed phenomena" (p. 13). Their pragmatic goal, to develop an applied psychology that is relevant to design, is illustrated with the following scenario (p. 9):

> *A system designer, the head of a small team writing the specifications for a desktop calendar-scheduling system, is choosing between having users type a key for each command and having them point to a menu with a lightpen. On his whiteboard, he lists some representative tasks users of his system must perform. In two columns, he writes the steps needed by the "key-command" and "menu" options. From a handbook, he culls the times for each step, adding the step times to get total task times. The key-command system takes less time, but only slightly. But, applying the analysis from another section of the handbook, he calculates that the menu system will be faster to learn; in fact, it will be learnable in half the time. He has estimated previously that an effective menu system will require a more expensive processor: 20% more memory, 100% more microcode memory, and a more expensive display. Is the extra expenditure worthwhile? A few more minutes of calculation and he realizes the startling fact that, for the manufacturing quantities anticipated, training costs for the key-command system will exceed unit manufacturing costs! The increase in hardware costs would be much more than balanced by the decrease in training costs, even before considering the increase in market that can be expected for a more easily learned system. Are there advantages to the key-command system in other areas, which need to be balanced? He proceeds with other analyses, considering the load on the user's memory, the potential for user errors, and the likelihood of fatigue. In the next room, the Pascal compiler hums idly, unused, awaiting his decision.*

Newell and Card (1985) elaborate on their approach. They argue that "hard science" always drives out "soft science," relegating the latter to second-class status and low influence. How do we prevent computer science from driving out contributions from psychological science? Their solution: "Transform the psychology of the interface into a hard science. By that we mean producing engineering theories of the user—task analysis, calculation and approximation." Task analysis is required because human users "attempt to adapt to the task environment to attain their goals." Calculation is needed because "the ability to do calculations is the heart of useful, engineering-oriented applied science." Approximation is needed because "if calculations are going to be made rapidly, they are necessarily going to be oversimplified" (Card, Moran, and Newell, 1983, pp. 10–11).

The first four readings in this chapter describe the applied psychology of human-computer interaction to which they contributed, and some applications of the theory. In the first paper, Card and Moran (1986) review their work from its inception at Xerox PARC in 1974 as a project in "understanding the nature of the human user" based on the newly emerging "psychology of cognitive behavior." They studied the use of different input devices, for example, not only to determine which were most effective, but to understand why, and to model their performance.

The Model Human Processor

Card, Moran, and Newell began by reviewing and codifying the existing scientific base that was relevant to their applied psychology. The central idea is the *Model Human Processor*, an idealized information-processing model of the human perceptual, motor, and cognitive systems that is shown on the fourth page of the Card and Moran reading (see also Card, 1984, excerpted in Baecker and Buxton, 1987). The Model Human Processor is a "simplified architecture of the user, described in terms of three processors, four memories, 19 parameters of these, and 10 principles of operation." The purpose of the model is not to build a robot, it is to aid designers by providing predictions of human performance, thus saving the effort of building and testing inferior designs: "The Model Human Processor can be used to compute predictions about human performance: how fast people can read, how fast they can scribble. . . ."

GOMS and the Analysis of Routine Cognitive Skills

Viewing people as information-processing systems leads naturally to trying to formalize the procedures involved in carrying out tasks interactively with a computer. Card, Moran, and Newell found that even crude models could provide predictive power. They studied text editing, describing it as a *routine cognitive skill* (see Roberts and Moran, 1983, reprinted in Baecker and Buxton, 1987; Roberts, 1988). Text editing and word processing were very successful computer applications in the 1970s, used first by programmers and then by a wider population. The authors also contributed to the design of the Xerox Star, for which text editing was an important application (see Case B).

The model they develop, *GOMS*, represents a user's cognitive structure in terms of

- *goals*
- *operators* (actions belonging to a user's repertoire of skills)
- *methods* (sequences of subgoals and operators often carried out in an automatic fashion to achieve goals)
- *selection rules* (for choosing among different possible methods for reaching a particular goal)

Their model predicts the methods that a skilled person will employ to carry out editing tasks and the time that they will take. Within the model, text editing is described at several levels of detail, starting at a gross level and progressing to finer representations. They refer to the levels as the *unit-task* level, the *functional* level, the *argument* level, and the *keystroke* level. For further detail, see Card, Moran, and Newell (1980a), reprinted in Baecker and Buxton (1987).

The Keystroke-Level Model

The level studied in the greatest detail could be called the *lexical* level: the individual keystrokes, mouse movements, and other motor activities on which a dialogue depends. The first reading describes the Keystroke-Level Model, a simplification of GOMS that predicts aspects of expert, error-free performance for command language interfaces (see also Card, Moran, and Newell, 1980b, reprinted in Baecker and Buxton, 1987). The input to the model is

- a description of a task
- a system's command language
- estimates of a user's motor skill parameters
- response time parameters of the system
- methods to be used for the task

The model then predicts the time it will take an expert user to perform the task using the specified methods on the specified system.

This approach exemplifies the theory-based cognitive engineering tools sought by the authors, tools that allow predictions of performance time, definition of system performance benchmarks, and the carrying out of a parametric analysis. A prediction is a function of particular task variables, allowing a sensitivity analysis to derive the effects of changes in task or model parameters. They also investigated how successively better approximations would affect the predictive power of the model.

In our reading, Card and Moran then describe empirical investigations into the nature of users' mental models, which is discussed further below. Collecting reports from people as they solved problems, they discovered that people who are given a conceptual model of their task do not automatically use this model in problem solving; it is just one "tool" that they may rely upon. Thus, providing users with a conceptual model may be less useful than was hoped.

Finally, Card and Moran complete their historical retrospective by describing the hypertext-based Notecards system developed as an idea organizer; we will return to Notecards in Chapter 13.

The Limitations of GOMS Models

In 1986, an interesting debate broke out in the pages of the journal *Human-Computer Interaction.* We already have cited Newell and Card's 1985 article calling for hardening up the soft psychological science of HCI. Carroll and Campbell (1986) responded to this article, and Newell and Card (1986) replied. Carroll and Campbell defend the advances made by the "soft science" of human factors, citing successes of the prototyping and iterative development methods laid out in Chapter 2. They claim that computer science is not "hard" in the sense of delivering predictive models of performance, and thus won't displace psychological contributions to design. They then explore four faults with the GOMS work that Newell and Card themselves raised: the work is too low level, too limited in scope, arriving too late to influence design, and too difficult to apply.

Figure 9.3 (Newell and Card, 1985) illustrates the charge that the model is too low level. Actions covered by the Keystroke-Level Model and GOMS models are in the band labeled "psychological," particularly in the lower two-thirds of it. Many activities of interest to computer users and developers take place in the band labeled "bounded rationality." In Chapters 3 and 11, we note that events in the upper band are also important for developers. How useful is a model that does not represent these actions?

FIGURE 9.3

The time scales of human action. Time durations in powers of 10 seconds and approximate equivalent units; characteristic actions and associated memory units (LTM = long term memory; STM = short term memory); classes of theories that engage actions at each level (Newell and Card, 1985, p. 226).

Time (sec)	Time (common units)	Action	Memory	Theory
10^9	*(decades)*	*Technology*	*Culture*	
10^8	*(years)*	*System*	*Development*	*Social and*
10^7	*(months)*	*Design*	*Education*	*Organizational*
10^6	*(weeks)*	*Task*	*Education*	
10^5	*(days)*	*Task*	*Skill*	
10^4	*(hours)*	*Task*	*Skill*	*Bounded*
10^3	*(ten mins)*	*Task*	*LTM*	*Rationality*
10^2	*(minutes)*	*Task*	*LTM*	
10	*(ten secs)*	*Unit task*	*LTM*	
1	*(secs)*	*Operator*	*STM*	*Psychological*
10^{-1}	*(tenths)*	*Cycle time*	*Buffers*	
10^{-2}	*(centisecs)*	*Signal*	*Integration*	*Neural and*
10^{-3}	*(millisecs)*	*Pulse*	*Summation*	*Biochemical*

Newell and Card (1986) replied to Carroll and Campbell, but unfortunately the exchange increasingly broke down into clarifications of misunderstandings. Newell and Card in essence argued for addressing the four faults by extending the model. Our next reading addresses the subsequent history of work that set out to do just that. In the meantime, one claim of Newell and Card bears scrutiny. They argue that the field is not advancing too rapidly for modeling to keep pace: "About every 5 years a new canonical interface comes to dominate the scene," perhaps 10 years after it first appears. They list TTY (teletype), typewriter, Glass TTY, semigraphic CRT, and bit-mapped CRT. (The latter was not yet dominant when they wrote in 1985.) Multimedia interfaces are a candidate for the next canonical interface (see Chapter 13). However, this progression overlooks the fact that each successive interface has not added equally to the possible design space. Quite the contrary, the last few advances have widened the range of design possibilities tremendously, raising doubts that we can keep pace in generating predictive models for all plausible interface designs.

BEYOND GOMS: COGNITIVE MODELING FACES ITS EARLY LIMITATIONS

In our next reading, Judy and Gary Olson (1990) briefly review the GOMS and Keystroke-Level Model work before covering the five years of progress in cognitive modeling that followed. This excellent overview also contains a large bibliography.

After noting where early GOMS models perform well, Olson and Olson list several shortcomings, first identified by Card, Moran, and Newell themselves. In particular, the models

- apply only to highly skilled users, omitting novice or intermediate users and the learning process
- account only for error-free performance, which is a serious flaw, since common slips can easily wipe out gains in error-free performance
- fail to consider individual differences
- focus on low-level sensorimotor performance and touch on cognition, but ignore the broader work context and its role in constraining design
- assume serial performance of task components, whereas many tasks permit parallel execution
- do not address mental workload
- do not address system functionality, but only usability
- do not address fatigue
- address performance but not user preference

Olson and Olson discuss extensions of GOMS that have been undertaken to address some of these limitations. One is to model users' "grammatical rules" for carrying out actions—to identify patterns in the sequences of operations that make up methods, analogous to the patterns in spoken language that make up the grammar learned by every speaker. Variations of this approach had been explored by Reisner (1981, 1984) and Payne and Green (1986). Green built on an early, influential paper by Moran (1981) in which the interface is described in terms of six levels:

- Task level: the set of tasks the system is intended to accomplish
- Semantic level: the conceptual objects and actions of the system
- Syntactic level: the command language with which users communicate with the system
- Interaction level: the physical actions associated with each element of the syntactic level, which corresponds to the "lexical level" in language
- Spatial layout level: the arrangement of input and output devices and the graphics display
- Device level: all the remaining physical features

Not surprisingly for 1981, the article was oriented toward command language interfaces and very low-level tasks. A typical example would be the following:

- Task level: copying text from one location to another
- Semantic level: conceptual objects include "segments of text," "copy," and "delete"
- Syntactic level: a command syntax might be (i) select text; (ii) issue copy command; (iii) move cursor to new location; (iv) issue paste command
- Interaction level: specifies exactly what happens when each of these actions is taken, for example, "paste" leaves copied text in a buffer
- Spatial layout level: determines where command names are placed on the display (if at all)
- Device level: for example, the pixel pattern used to place a character on a particular display

Moran noted that a design must address each of these levels.

Cognitive modeling was also influenced by the work of Donald Norman, notably an essay (Norman, 1986) in a book he co-edited (Norman and Draper, 1986). He presents a model of task performance in terms of seven stages of user activities, shown in Figure 9.4.

FIGURE 9.4

Seven stages of user activities involved in the performance of a task. The primary, central stage is the establishment of the goal. Then, to carry out an action requires three stages: forming an intention, specifying an action sequence, and executing the action. To assess the effect of the action also requires three stages, each in some sense complementary to the three stages of carrying out the action: perceiving the system state, interpreting the state, and evaluating the system state with respect to the original goals and intentions (Norman, 1986, p. 42).

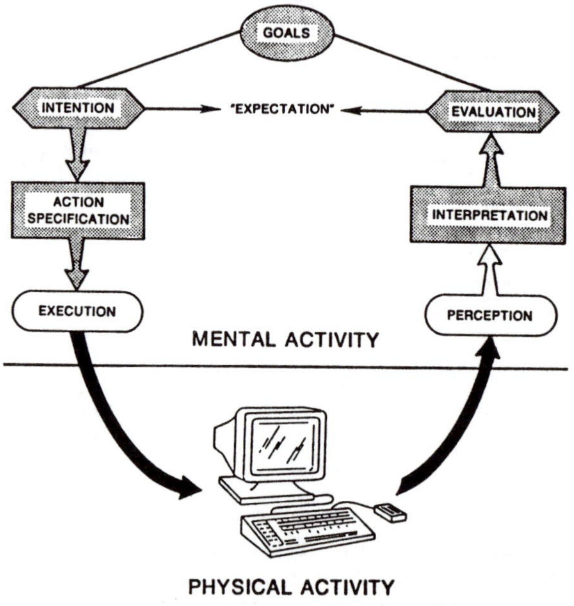

Although not quantitative, Norman's model provides insights that guided subsequent model development. As we have seen in the longer discussion of this approach that appears in Chapter 2, these insights are also useful in the process of interface design.

GOMS models have also been implemented in executable production systems that enable completeness and accuracy to be determined (Kieras, 1988; Bovair, Kieras, and Polson, 1990). Production systems are a modeling approach borrowed from artificial intelligence. Productions each consist of "triggering conditions" and an action. When the triggering conditions are met, the action is executed, changing the system in some way. All productions then check to see if the new state satisfies their triggering conditions, and the first one for which this is true "fires," carrying out its action. Constructs such as working memory are included. The goal is to build a model of human processing that can be used to test designs. The model can be checked by contrasting its output with actual human performance.

Olson and Olson describe "cognitive complexity theory" (Kieras and Polson, 1985), an extension of GOMS that incorporates learning and transfer of training. This approach is further extended in Polson and Lewis (1990) to incorporate a predictive model for a "walk-up-and-use" interface that requires no training, such as those for bank teller machines or airport kiosks. Olson and Olson also discuss "critical path analysis," a tool borrowed from operations research, where it is widely used to model industrial processes. In our context it is used to model human behavior that can go on in parallel: reading while typing, for example.

A direct descendant of GOMS discussed by Olson and Olson is the SOAR work at Carnegie Mellon University, an ambitious effort to develop a "unified theory of cognition" (Laird, Newell, and Rosenbloom, 1987). An imaginative use of SOAR in conjunction with task-action grammars is the "programmer user models" of Howes and Young (1991). A programmable user model is an architecture that represents a simulation of a user. A designer develops an interface, then simulates it by programming a simulated user. The authors claim that if the developer has difficulty programming the simulated user to use the interface, then a real user will have difficulty using the interface. Whether simulated users will be effective surrogates for real users in design remains to be seen.

Another cognitive modeling approach, "interacting cognitive subsystems," is discussed in the reading by Barnard described below.

Cognitive Modeling in the Present

The Olsons conclude by outlining serious limitations to modeling approaches as they have been developed to date. Only a limited class of errors has been modeled because our theoretical understanding of the cause of errors is weak. The models do not yet incorporate individual differences that we know are important, or fatigue, which affects people differently. Higher-level cognitive processes have thus far resisted modeling. As the adoption of standard platforms such as the Macintosh and Windows "resolves" many low-level interface design issues, developers now focus on higher-level issues such as training, planning, and complex problem solving. Functionality is still not addressed by the models, which may help catch relatively minor low-level interface problems while missing serious higher-level design flaws.

Nevertheless, cognitive modeling has achieved some notable successes. We include two short reports of useful applications of GOMS. John and Vera (1992) conducted a GOMS analysis of a video game. This graphic task proves that the method is not limited to a text display. The example suggests some limits of the approach: It describes a Super Mario Brothers expert as he traverses World 1, Level 1. Although such a player navigates this familiar ground automatically, the model cannot cover an expert's problem-solving activity upon reaching a new level of the game with new challenges.

Gray et al. (1990) use analytic modeling to solve a mystery: Why was a new keyboard, universally preferred by the operators who used it, slower than the keyboard it replaced? The analysis revealed that a new procedure adopted with the keyboard shifted an operation that was formerly carried out in parallel with others into the critical path, slowing down the task. This article was written as the results were coming in and captures the experimental method very nicely. The results confirmed the initial findings and can be found in more detail in Gray, John, and Atwood (1992, 1993) and Atwood, Gray, and John (1995).

The task explored by Gray et al. was especially well adapted for modeling: highly expert operators carrying out routine tasks involving primarily sensorimotor activity. Performance speed was clearly the critical measure. The fact that the slower keyboard was preferred—that performance and preference can diverge—can be important in other circumstances (Grudin and MacLean, 1984; Nielsen, 1993, pp. 33–37). Of the numerous usability goals of systems design, such as speed of performance, ease of learning, minimization of error, retention of memory over time, and personal preference, modeling has thus far focused mainly on performance speed, with some attention to ease of learning.

MENTAL MODELS

It is generally assumed that users apply *mental models* in trying to understand and predict system behavior, and that their success in using a system depends on how well their mental model corresponds to a model represented in the system design. Carroll and Olson (1988) describe the confusion that has reigned over the use of the term "mental model," but conclude that the most common use is "a representation (in the head) of a physical system or software being run on a computer, with some plausible cascade of causal associations connecting the input to the output."

Norman (1983) published an influential discussion in a book on mental models edited by Gentner and Stevens (1983). Norman's essay is included in the first edition of this book. He notes that our mental models fall short of the rigor of scientific or engineering models: They are incomplete, unstable, and often superstitious. Their boundaries are not clear, we make an effort to merge or simplify them, and our ability to "run" our mental models is limited.

Norman considers the use of mental models in design, observing that it is not easy to discover a user's mental model, given the imprecision of these models. He concludes (p. 14):

> *The moral of this story is that it is important for us to distinguish among several different kinds of models and conceptualizations. Our conceptualization of a target system should not be confused with the mental model that a user creates of that system. The designer's conceptualization may also differ from the image that the system itself presents to the user. In the ideal world, the system image will be consistent with the designer's conceptualization, and the user's mental model will thereby be consistent with both.*

As noted above, the Card and Moran reading discusses the concept of mental models and describes empirical findings that people only use mental models intermittently when confronting problems.

The role of mental models in design was actively discussed in the 1980s. Moran, (1981), Card, Moran and Newell (1983), Newell and Card (1985), Norman (1986), and Carroll and Olson (1988), all mentioned previously, discuss the topic, as do Young (1983), Carroll (1984), Streitz (1988), and Nielsen (1990). Several of these authors propose formalisms for distinguishing the multiplicity of roles and models involved.

Discussion of the "mental model" concept has fallen off. The maturing of our field may have diminished its usefulness. The design task is increasingly distributed: Some of the design is dictated by the platform, other features are added by various developers. "Users" can include people involved with marketing, installing, enhancing, and using an application. Rarely does one person have an overall conception of the system and its use (Grudin, 1993).

Whether or not the term "mental models" is revived, our need for a deep understanding of the contexts of use is growing, as discussed in Chapters 3 and 11 and Case C. In the past, much of the focus was on users' views of computer systems in general; now, with experienced computer users, our focus is on their mental representations of specific and often complex application domains.

ACTIVITY THEORY

The human information-processing model is not the only school of psychology relevant to human-computer interaction. Recently, a number of researchers have been impressed with *activity theory*, an approach that spans cognitive, developmental, and cultural psychology. The linking of cognitive and cultural approaches fits nicely with the efforts to design for individual activity in work contexts, discussed in Chapter 3. Indeed, the Bannon and the Bødker et al. readings in Chapter 3 are influenced by activity theory. Raeithel (1992) and Kuutti (1992) are a theoretical analysis and a case study, respectively, of activity theory applied to system design.

Activity theory focuses on actions (physical, verbal, mental) and how our interactions in the world affect individual, social, and cultural development. For our purposes, its principal advantage over other approaches is that it sees people such as computer users not as static information processors, but as individuals who are continually being shaped by our ongoing pattern of activity. This perspective brings into focus issues that are pushed into the background by other approaches, including individual differences, cross-cultural differences, and differences based on experience or occupation. For example, an activity theorist would anticipate that interfaces designed for today's users may have to be replaced for a generation that has the different experience of growing up with computers.

Whether or not you completely embrace activity theory, becoming acquainted with it should be useful. Nardi (in press) is a set of essays on activity theory and human-computer interaction, many of which originated in the second annual East-West HCI Conference held in St. Petersburg, Russia, in 1992 (reviewed by Grudin, MacLean, and Overmyer, 1993).

LINGUISTICS AND PSYCHOLINGUISTICS

Linguistics contributes to human-computer interaction design in several ways. The obvious hope, noted in Chapter 8, is that computational linguistics will eventually provide natural language understanding (NLU) systems. Applied to text, this is the basis of language translation programs that make a "first pass" to help human translators. Applied to voice, NLU will be essential if speech recognition is ever to achieve wide use. Chapter 8 also covered multimodal interfaces that combine, for example, language and gesture. Computational linguistics is finding other roles as well—for example, in automatic generation of multimedia document layouts (Weitzman and Wittenburg, 1994).

In addition to these specialized applications, linguistics can contribute to our understanding of most human-computer interaction. Any extended interaction of a person and a system is a dialogue. "Languages" have always been involved, as can be seen in the following examples: Engineers interact with computers through machine *language*. Early programmers worked with assembly *language*. Later, programmers interacted with computers using higher-level *languages*. The first interactive use of computers relied on command *languages*, in which users issue commands and the system responds. Data base query *languages* are also widely employed (Reisner, 1988).

We don't think of a mouse-driven graphical user interface as a language, yet a dialogue takes place. Grudin and Norman (1991, p. 611) write:

> *Consider, for example, this sequence of events in discarding a document on a Macintosh. As you move the mouse, the arrow or pointer moves across the display. When the pointer is above the icon that represents the document, you press and hold down the button on the mouse. The icon switches to "reverse video" (interchanging black and white), signaling that you have succeeded in selecting it. You move the mouse and an outline image of the icon moves, indicating your position and telling you that you remain in control of the document. When the pointer and the outline image reach the vicinity of an icon in the shape of a trash can, that image spontaneously switches to reverse video, signaling that when you release the mouse button, the document icon will disappear and effectively be discarded. You do so, and the sides of the trash can bulge slightly, indicating that the document is inside. . . . This entire sequence can be considered to be a dialogue, although no words are used. The system and you monitor one another; you communicate by mouse movements and button presses, the system communicates by moving objects, switching them to reverse video, making them appear and disappear, and changing their shape.*

The potential for applying linguistic knowledge to human-computer dialogue design has not been fully exploited, although some useful work has been done.

Nickerson (1977), reprinted in the first edition of this book, proposes ways in which person-computer conversations should and should not resemble person-person conversations. Reichman (1985) examines the structure of discourse and its implications for human-computer interaction. For example, two people, interrupted in mid-sentence, will not pick up precisely where they left off if they resume their conversation 10 minutes later. They will reestablish the context. A person who leaves a computer application in mid-operation and returns some time later may also have forgotten the context, but the computer will carry on as though no time had passed, often confusing the person. Reichman's examples use an understanding of human dialogues to stimulate design ideas.

Wittenburg (1990) and Cohen (1992) present rationales for drawing on linguistic understanding to extend direct manipulation interfaces. Considering dialogue design very broadly, Grudin and Norman (1991) examine forces that historical linguistics holds responsible for language evolution:

- Language should be clear and consistent.
- Language should be quick and easy to use.
- Language should allow a broad range of expression.
- Language should be humanly processible in real time.

These forces trade off against each other, forcing compromises. For example, languages are not completely consistent, because of the pressures to abbreviate and to allow economic expression of many different meanings. The authors find parallels in human-computer dialogues, trade-offs that are reflected in interface design. For example, interface consistency is usually good, but usability testing might determine that it is appropriate to violate consistency to speed up a frequent operation or slow down a dangerous one.

DISTRIBUTED COGNITION AND ARTIFACT ANALYSIS

In recent years, several leading theorists have used psychological theory to contribute to human-computer interaction in a different fashion. Instead of searching for general design guidelines and design principles, they focus on an examination of successful artifacts—software systems and other useful objects. By examining the use of such objects, we can discover which features of the objects contribute to their success and, in doing so, how the features interact with people and task environments.

Norman (1991) discusses "cognitive artifacts," devices that "maintain, display, or operate upon information in order to serve a representational function and that affect human cognitive performance" (p. 17). He notes that artifacts can be viewed from the personal perspective of those interacting with them, but that they can also be viewed from the perspective of the "system" consisting of the person and their context.

The concept of "distributed cognition" is explored in more depth in books by Norman (1993) and Hutchins (1994). Again, the focus is on the way information in the environment interacts in subtle ways and is relied upon by people engaged in many activities. Although partially descriptive and theoretical, this work has considerable implications for design.

Carroll, Kellogg, and Rosson (1991) and Carroll and Rosson (1995) focus more specifically on software systems and applications in undertaking "artifact analysis," carefully studying the ways that artifacts are used and understanding what features are responsible for their success, and why. They argue that in this way we can accelerate the "task-artifact cycle," the iterative process of designing new artifacts for tasks, which then change in response to the innovations, which then require modified artifacts, and so on.

THE ROLE OF PSYCHOLOGY IN INTERFACE DESIGN: A SUMMING UP

Several recent edited collections have surveyed and reflected on the contributions of psychologists to human-computer interaction (Carroll, 1987; Long and Whitefield, 1989; Shackel and Richardson, 1991; Carroll, 1991). In our final two readings of this chapter, drawn from this corpus, two eminent cognitive psychologists who have worked on issues in human-computer interaction for close to two decades summarize their experiences and their conclusions.

Phil Barnard (1991) provides a systematic overview of the contributions of applied cognitive psychology to our field. His organizing schema, similar to aspects of that presented by McGrath (Chapter 2), identifies three sets of research methods: exploratory field studies of user behavior and developer practice, formal models such as those discussed at length above, and controlled laboratory studies of systems or tasks. He sees these interacting with hypotheses about human information processing, ultimately leading to tools for system developers.

Barnard discusses achievements in each area. Exploratory studies contribute to reformulating design issues and cognitive issues. For example, when research showed that users differ widely in their view of the appropriate names for commands and other objects, designers could stop seeking the (nonexistent) perfect label and focus on ways to support variation (see Barnard and Grudin, 1988, for a review of the literature on command naming).

After outlining his interacting cognitive subsystems modeling approach, Barnard critiques the results of formal experimentation. Formal models based on experimental results have produced mixed results, especially when the models are used by people other than their developers. Experimenters hope to produce design principles, but Barnard notes the riskiness of generalizing from the experiments. How much of a result was due to factors other than those being directly tested? The contradictions among experimental results show that uncontrolled factors play a big role.

Barnard concludes with mixed optimism and caution toward applying psychology to design. He notes that research lags design, but suggests that a set of agreed-upon "benchmark" scenarios could help by providing a basis for collecting considerable empirical data for a range of models.

In our final reading, Tom Landauer (1991) takes a combative stance. He argues that useful theory is impossible, but that in the hands of psychologists, empirical models, iterative evaluation, and some rules of thumb will lead to innovation. He notes the limitations of the Keystroke Model and argues that because of the complexity of human cognition and behavior, theory is *not* the avenue to progress.

Landauer recommends that we start by empirically examining a task, through observation or controlled experiments. Design ideas that result must be tested iteratively, again drawing on methods developed by psychologists. Landauer illustrates his points with the Bellcore experience developing SuperBook, a hypertext-based document browser discussed by Egan et al. in Chapter 13. (You might wish to read this paper in conjunction with the Landauer paper.)

The interrelationships among science, engineering, and development are complex and subject to strong views. Barnard and Landauer represent two perspectives. For other interesting views, see the books mentioned at the beginning of this section, as well as Thimbleby (1990) and Rudisill et al. (in press).

REFERENCES

Note: A ❁ before a reference indicates a reading.

Anderson, J. (1978). Arguments Concerning Representations for Mental Imagery. *Psychological Review* 85, 249–277.

Anderson, J. (1983). *Architecture of Cognition.* Harvard University Press.

Anderson, J. (1989). *Cognitive Psychology and Its Implications,* 3rd Edition. W. H. Freeman.

Atwood, M., Gray, W., and John, B. (1995). Project Ernestine: Analytic and Empirical Methods Applied to a Real-World CHI Problem. In Rudisill, Lewis, Polson, and McKay (Eds.) (in press).

Baddeley, A. (1986). *Working Memory.* Oxford University Press.

Baecker, R., and Buxton, W. (Eds.) (1987). *Readings in Human-Computer Interaction: A Multidisciplinary Approach.* Morgan Kaufmann.

❁ Barnard, P. (1991). The Contributions of Applied Cognitive Psychology to the Study of Human-Computer Interaction. In Shackel, B., and Richardson, S. (Eds.), *Human Factors for Informatics Usability,* Cambridge University Press, 151–182.

Barnard, P., and Grudin, J. (1988). Command Names. In Helander (1988), 237–255.

Bewley, W., Roberts, T., Schroit, D. and Verplank, W. (1983). Human Factors Testing in the Design of Xerox's 8010 "Star" Office Workstation. *Proc. CHI '83,* ACM, 72–77.

Bovair, S., Kieras, D., and Polson, P. (1990). The Acquisition and Performance of Text-Editing Skill: A Cognitive Complexity Analysis. *Human-Computer Interaction* 5, 1–23.

Bösser, T., and Melchior, E. (1985). Learning to Control Complex Technical Systems. In Willumeit, H. (Ed.), *Human Decision Making and Manual Control,* North-Holland.

Card, S. (1984). Human Limits and the VDT Computer Interface. In Bennett, J., Case, D., Sandelin, J., and Smith, M. (Eds.), *Visual Display Terminals: Usability Issues and Health Concerns,* Prentice-Hall, 117–155. Excerpted in Baecker and Buxton (1987).

❁ Card, S., and Moran, T. (1986). User Technology: From Pointing to Pondering. *Proc. ACM Conference on History of Personal Workstations,* 183–198.

Card, S., Moran, T., and Newell, A. (1980a). Computer Text-Editing: An Information-Processing Analysis of a Routine Cognitive Skill. *Cognitive Psychology* 12, 32–74. Reprinted in Baecker and Buxton (1987).

Card, S., Moran, T., and Newell, A. (1980b). The Keystroke-Level Model for User Performance Time with Interactive Systems. *Communications of the ACM* 23(7), 396–410. Reprinted in Baecker and Buxton (1987).

Card, S., Moran, T., and Newell, A. (1983). *The Psychology of Human-Computer Interaction.* Lawrence Erlbaum Associates.

Carroll, J. (1984). Mental Models and Software Human Factors. *IBM Research Report RC 10616.* Yorktown Heights, NY: IBM.

Carroll, J. (Ed.) (1987). *Interfacing Thought: Cognitive Aspects of Human-Computer Interaction.* MIT Press.

Carroll, J. (Ed.) (1991). *Designing Interaction: Psychology at the Human-Computer Interface.* Cambridge University Press.

Carroll, J., and Campbell, R. (1986). Softening Up Hard Science: Response to Newell and Card. *Human-Computer Interaction* 2(3), 227–249.

Carroll, J., Kellogg, W., and Rosson, M.B. (1991). The Task-Artifact Cycle. In Carroll, J.M. (Ed.), *Designing Interaction,* Cambridge University Press.

Carroll, J., and Olson, J. (1988). Mental Models in Human-Computer Interaction. In Helander (1988), 45–65.

Carroll, J., and Rosson, M.B. (1995). Getting Around the Task-Artifact Cycle: How to Make Claims and Design by Scenario. In Rudisill, Lewis, Polson, and McKay (Eds.) (in press).

Chi, M., Glaser, R., and Farr, M. (Eds.) (1988). *The Nature of Expertise.* Lawrence Erlbaum Associates.

Cohen, P. (1992). The Role of Natural Language in a Multimodal Interface. *Proc. UIST '92,* 143–149.

Cornsweet, T. (1970). *Visual Perception.* Academic Press.

Crossman, E. (1959). A Theory of the Acquisition of Speed-Skill. *Ergonomics* 2(2), 153–166.

DeValois, R., and DeValois, K. (1988). *Spatial Vision.* Oxford University Press.

Fodor, J. (1983). *Modularity of Mind.* MIT Press.

Gardner, H. (1985). *The Mind's New Science: A History of the Cognitive Revolution.* Basic Books.

Gentner, D., and Stevens, A. (Eds.) (1983). *Mental Models.* Lawrence Erlbaum Associates.

Goodale, M. (Ed.) (1990). *Vision and Action.* Ablex.

Gray, W. , John, B., and Atwood, M. (1992). The Precis of Project Ernestine or An Overview of a Validation of GOMS. *Proc. CHI '92,* ACM, 307–312.

Gray, W. , John, B., and Atwood, M. (1993). Project Ernestine: A Validation of GOMS for Prediction and Explanation of Real-World Task Performance. *Human-Computer Interaction* 8(3), 237–309.

❁ Gray, W., John, B., Stuart, R., Lawrence, D., and Atwood, M. (1990). GOMS Meets the Phone Company: Analytic Modeling Applied to Real-World Problems. *Proc. INTERACT '90.* Elsevier (North-Holland), 29–34.

Green, D. (1976). *An Introduction to Hearing.* Lawrence Erlbaum Associates.

Gregory, A. (1978). *Eye and Brain,* 3rd Edition. McGraw-Hill.

Grudin, J. (1993). Interface: An Evolving Concept. *Communications of the ACM* 36(4), 110–119.

Grudin, J., and MacLean, A. (1984.) Adapting a Psychophysical Method to Measure Performance and Preference Tradeoffs in Human-Computer Interaction. *Proc. INTERACT '84,* North-Holland, 338–342.

Grudin, J., MacLean, A., and Overmyer, S. (1993). Report on the 1992 East-West International Conference on Human-Computer Interaction. *SIGCHI Bulletin* 25(2), 36–39.

Grudin, J., and Norman, D. (1991). Language Evolution and Human-Computer Interaction. *Proc. 13th Annual Conference of the Cognitive Science Society.* Lawrence Erlbaum Associates, 611–616 .

Helander, M. (Ed.) (1988). *Handbook of Human-Computer Interaction.* North-Holland.

Holyoak, K., and Spellman, B. (1993). Thinking. *Annual Review of Psychology,* 44, 265–315.

Howes, A., and Young, R. (1991). Predicting the Learnability of Task-Action Mappings, *Proc. CHI '91,* ACM, 113–118.

Hutchins, E. (1994). *Cognition in the Wild.* MIT Press.

Jacoby, L., Lindsay, D., and Toth, J. (1992). Unconscious Influences Revealed: Attention, Awareness, and Control. *American Psychologist* 47, 802–809.

Jeannerod, M. (Ed.) (1990). Motor Control & Representation. In *Attention & Performance XIII.* Lawrence Erlbaum Associates.

❁ John, B., and Vera, A. (1992). A GOMS Analysis of a Graphic, Machine-Paced, Highly Interactive Task. *Proc. CHI '92,* ACM, 251–258.

Johnson-Laird, P. (1986). *The Computer and the Mind: An Introduction to Cognitive Science.* Harvard University Press.

Johnson-Laird, P., Hermann, D., and Chaffin, R. (1984). Only Connections: A Critique of Semantic Networks. *Psychological Bulletin* 96, 292–315.

Kahneman, D., Slovic, P., and Tversky, A. (Eds.) (1982). *Judgment under Uncertainty: Heuristics and Biases.* Cambridge University Press.

Kaufman, L. (1974). *Sight and Mind.* Oxford University Press.

Kieras, D. (1988). Towards a Practical GOMS Model Methodology for User Interface Design. In Helander (1988), 135–157.

Kieras, D., and Polson, P. (1985). An Approach to the Formal Analysis of User Complexity. *International Journal of Man-Machine Studies 22,* 365–394.

Kuutti, K. (1992). Identifying Potential CSCW Applications by Means of Activity Thoery Concepts: A Case Example. *Proc. CSCW '92,* ACM, 233–240.

Laird, J., Newell, A., and Rosenbloom, P. (1987). Soar: An Architecture for General Intelligence. *Artificial Intelligence* 33, 1–64.

Landau, B., and Jackendoff, R. (1993). "What" and "Where" in Spatial Language and Spatial Cognition. *Behavioral and Brain Sciences* 16, 217–238.

● Landauer, T. (1991). Let's Get Real: A Position Paper on the Role of Cognitive Psychology in the Design of Humanly Useful and Usable Systems. In Carroll, J. (Ed.) *Designing Interaction.* Cambridge University Press, 60–73.

Lindsay, P., and Norman, D. (1977). *Human Information Processing: An Introduction to Psychology,* 2nd Edition. Academic Press.

Long, J., and Whitefield, A. (Eds.) (1989). *Cognitive Ergonomics and Human-Computer Interaction.* Cambridge University Press.

Miller, G. (1956). The Magic Number Seven, Plus or Minus Two: Some Limits on Our Capacity for Processing Information. *Psychological Review* 63, 81–97.

Minsky, M. (1986). *Society of Mind.* Simon and Schuster.

Moran, T. (1981). The Command Language Grammar: A Representation of the User Interface of Interactive Computer Systems. *International Journal of Man-Machine Studies* 15, 3–50.

Nardi, B. (Ed.) (in press). *Context and Consciousness: Activity Theory and Human Computer Interaction.* MIT Press.

Neisser, U. (1967). *Cognitive Psychology.* Appleton-Century-Croft.

Neisser, U. (Ed.) (1987). *Concepts and Conceptual Development: Ecological and Intellectual Factors in Categorization.* Cambridge University Press.

Newell, A., and Card, S. (1985). The Prospects for Psychological Science in Human-Computer Interaction. *Human-Computer Interaction* 1(3), 209–242.

Newell, A., and Card, S. (1986). Straightening Out Softening Up: Response to Carroll and Campbell. *Human-Computer Interaction* 2(3), 251–267.

Nickerson, R. (1977). On Conversational Interaction with Computers. *User-Oriented Design of Interactive Graphics Systems,* ACM, 101–113. Reprinted in Baecker and Buxton (1987).

Nielsen, J. (1990). A Meta-Model for Interacting with Computers. *Interacting with Computers* 2(2), 147–160.

Nielsen, J. (1993). *Usability Engineering.* Academic Press.

Norman, D. (1983). Some Observations on Mental Models. In Gentner and Stevens (1983), 7–14. Reprinted in Baecker and Buxton (1987).

Norman, D. (1986). Cognitive Engineering. In Norman, D., and Draper, S. (1986), 31–61.

Norman, D. (1991). Cognitive Artifacts. In J. Carroll (Ed.), *Designing Interaction: Psychology at the Human-Computer Interface.* Cambridge University Press.

Norman, D. (1993). *Things That Make Us Smart.* Addison-Wesley.

Norman, D., and Bobrow, D. (1975). On Data-Limited and Resource-Limited Processes. *Cognitive Psychology* 7, 44–64.

Norman, D., and Draper, S. (Eds.) (1986). *User Centered System Design.* Lawrence Erlbaum Associates.

● Olson, J., and Olson, G. (1990). The Growth of Cognitive Modeling in Human-Computer Interaction Since GOMS. *Human-Computer Interaction* 5, 221–265.

Osherson, D. (Ed.) (1990). *Invitation to Cognitive Science,* Vols. I–III. MIT Press.

Osherson, D., and Weinstein, S. (1984). Formal Learning Theory. In Gazzaniga, M. (Ed.), *Handbook of Cognitive Neuroscience,* Plenum Press, 275–292.

Parasuraman, R., and Davies, D. (Eds.) (1984). *Varieties of Attention.* Academic Press.

Payne, S., and Green, T. (1986). Task-Action Grammars: A Model of the Mental Representation of Task Languages. *Human-Computer Interaction* 2, 93–133.

Pickles, J. (1988). *An Introduction to the Physiology of Hearing.* Academic Press.

Pinker, S. (1990). Language Acquisiting. In Osherson, D. (Ed.), *Invitation to Cognitive Science,* Vol. 1, MIT Press.

Polson, P., and Lewis, C. (1990). Theory-Based Design for Easily Learned Interfaces. *Human-Computer Interaction* 5(2–3), 191–220.

Posner, M. (Ed.) (1989). *Foundations of Cognitive Science.* MIT Press.

Raeithel, A. (1992). Activity Theory as a Foundation for Design. In Floyd, C., Züllighoven, H., Budde, R., and Keil-Slawik, R. (Eds.), *Software Development and Reality Construction,* Springer-Verlag, 391–415.

Rasmussen, J., and Goodstein, L. (1988). Information Technology and Work. In Helander (1988), 175–201.

Reichman, R. (1985). *Getting Computers to Talk Like You and Me: Discourse Context, Focus, and Semantics.* MIT Press.

Reisner, P. (1981). Formal Grammar and Human Factors Design of an Interactive Graphics System. *IEEE Transactions on Software Engineering* SE-7(2), 229–240.

Reisner, P. (1984). Formal Grammar as a Tool for Analyzing Ease of Use: Some Fundamental Concepts. In Thomas, J., and Shneider, M. (Eds.), *Human Factors in Computer Systems,* Ablex.

Reisner, P. (1988). Query Languages. In Helander (1988), 257–280.

Roberts, T. (1988). Text Editors. In Helander (1988), 655–672.

Roberts, T., and Moran, T. (1983). The Evaluation of Computer Text Editors: Methodology and Empirical Results. *Communications of the ACM* 26(4), 265–283. Reprinted in Baecker and Buxton (1987).

Rubin, D. (Ed.) (1986). *Autobiographical Memory*. Cambridge University Press.

Rudisill, M., Lewis, C., Polson, P., and McKay, T. (Eds.) (in press). *Human-Computer Interface Design: Success Cases, Emerging Methods, and Real-World Context*. Morgan Kaufmann.

Rumelhart, D., McClelland, J., and the PDP Research Group (1986). *Parallel Distributed Processing: Explorations in the Microstructure of Cognition*. MIT Press.

Shackel, B., and Richardson, S. (Eds.) (1991). *Human Factors for Informatics Usability*. Cambridge University Press.

Shallice, T. (1988). *From Neuropsychology to Mental Structure*. Cambridge University Press. (Especially Chapter 12.)

Sheridan, T. (1988). Task Allocation and Supervisory Control. In Helander (1988), 159–173.

Simon, H. (1981). *Sciences of the Artificial*, Second Edition. MIT Press.

Squire, L. (1987). *Memory and Brain*. Oxford University Press. (Especially pp. 152–174.)

Streitz, N. A. (1988). Mental Models and Metaphors: Implications for the Design of Adaptive User-System Interfaces. In Mandl, H., and Lesgold, A. (Eds.), *Learning Issues for Intelligent Tutoring Systems*, Springer-Verlag.

Thimbleby, H. (1990). *User Interface Design*. ACM Press.

VanLehn, K. (1989). Problem Solving and Cognitive Skill Acquisition. In Posner, M. (Ed.), *Foundations of Cognitive Science*, MIT Press.

Winston, P. (1984). *Artificial Intelligence*, Third Edition. Addison-Wesley.

Weitzman, L., and Wittenburg, K. (1994). Automatic Presentation of Multimedia Documents Using Relational Grammars. *Proc. ACM Multimedia '94*, 443–451.

Wittenburg, K. (1990). The Position for NL. *Proc. CHI '90*, ACM, 54–55.

Woods, D., and Roth, E. (1988). Cognitive Systems Engineering. In Helander (1988), 3–43.

Yost, W., and Nielsen, D. (1977). *Fundamentals of Hearing*. Holt, Rinehart and Winston.

Young, R. (1983). Surrogates and Mappings: Two Kinds of Conceptual Models for Interactive Devices. In Gentner and Stevens (1983).

User Technology: From Pointing to Pondering

Stuart K. Card and Thomas P. Moran
Xerox Palo Alto Research Center

From its beginning, the technology of personal workstations has been driven by visions of a future in which people would work in intimate partnership with computer systems on significant intellectual tasks. These visions have been expressed in various forms: Memex (Bush, 1945), Man-Machine Symbiosis (Licklider, 1960), NLS (Engelbart, 1963), Dynabook (Kay, 1977), and others.

The tight coupling between human and computer required by these visions necessitated advances in the ways humans and computers interact. These advances have slowly begun to accumulate into what might be called a *user technology*. This user technology includes hardware and software techniques for building effective user interfaces: bitmapped displays, menus, pointing devices, "modeless" command languages, animation, and interface metaphors. But it must include a technical understanding of the user himself and of the nature of human-computer interaction. This latter part, the scientific base of user technology, is necessary in order to understand why interaction techniques are (or are not) successful, to help us invent new techniques, and to pave the way for machines that aid humans in performing significant intellectual tasks.

In this paper, we trace some of the history of our understanding of users and their interaction with workstations—the personal part of personal workstations. In keeping with the spirit of other papers at this conference, we have centered this review around our own experiences, perspectives, and work and have not attempted a complete history of the field. In concentrating on our own work, we do not wish to mimimize the importance of others' work; we simply want to tell our own story. Our focus is on what we have learned about users in our years of studying them and how we see our findings relating to the original visions of the personal workstation.

1. The Vision of an Applied User Psychology

The opportunity to tackle a science of the user brought us to PARC in 1974 (collaborating with Allen Newell, as consultant). As other PARC researchers were beginning to pursue the vision of highly graphic, interactive, network-based personal workstations, we were following a vision of our own. The idea was to draw concepts from cognitive psychology and artificial intelligence to create an applied cognitive science of the user. We called our project the Applied Information-processing Psychology Project (AIP). A 1971 memo by Allen Newell proposing this project to PARC stated the basic argument this way:

> (1) There is emerging a psychology of cognitive behavior that will permit calculation of behavior in new situations and with new humans. . . .
>
> (2) Several of the tasks that are central to the activities of computing—programming, debugging, etc.—are tasks that appear to be within the early scope of this emerging theory.
>
> (3) Computer science in general is extremely one-sided (for understandable reasons) in the treatment of its phenomena: almost no effort goes into understanding the nature of the human user. . . .
>
> (4) There is a substantial payoff (in dollars) to be had by really designing systems with detailed understanding of the way the human must process the information attendant thereto.

In 1974, we were in the position of having to create a new field. Psychological theories and methodologies held the promise of being able to represent and manage complex cognitive tasks, but the only body of research pertaining to human-computer interaction was in the field of human factors, where studies were largely empirical and evaluative, concentrating mostly on sensory-motor questions like the best shape for a switch. Human-computer interaction, involving two active agents each capable of initiating an exchange of information, inherently involves human cognitive processing. Our vision was to create a science of the user rooted in cognitive theory. But we also wanted the science to be practical, providing the system designer with the conceptual tools to think about the key characteristics of the user and the calculational tools to take account of the user's behavior.

To simplify a rather complex history for the purposes of this paper, we will narrate just a few strands of what unfolded. Each strand is organized around a particular aspect of the interface between the user, the system, and the task. The strands are organized into a sequence of ever-broader interfaces, from the physical interaction of the user with devices and displays to the symbiotic interaction of the user with the system while grappling with complex intellectual tasks—that is, from pointing to pondering:

> *The physical interface:* The user interacts with a system by means of physical input devices, such as a keyboard and a mouse, and output devices, such as a high-quality graphical display.
>
> *The cognitive interface:* The user has certain characteristics as an information processor, such as a limited working memory, that together with the goals he is trying to achieve determine his behavior.
>
> *The conceptual interface:* The computer system is also a complex information processing mechanism, and the the user needs to have some kind of mental model of it in order to effectively interact with it.
>
> *The task interface:* Systems are designed to help their users do tasks, not only small, routine tasks, but also larger, difficult intellectual tasks that are the object of the grand visions of personal workstations.

The story within each strand of our work is chronological; but the first three strands, representing our previous work, overlap in time. The last strand represents our current work.

2. The Physical Interface: Pointing

Bill English, who had among other thing engineered and built the mouse for Doug Engelbart (English, Engelbart, and Berman, 1967), was one of the people who migrated to PARC when it was founded. We worked for English when we first came to PARC. Engelbart and English had always considered the mouse to be an interim device, and English wanted to see if it was possible to invent other devices that would improve on its speed. In particular, he was interested in whether one could put a key on the keyboard that would sense force and direction without requiring the user to remove his hands from the keyboard. He had a number of devices built, and we helped design an experiment to test them. The results (Figure 1) showed that none of the devices tested improved on the mouse either for speed or for error rate (Card, English, & Burr, 1978).

This was a typical human factors experiment: we compared a set of systems to determine which one performed best. But this direct empirical comparison between devices was just the sort of methodology of human factors testing that we wanted to improve: we wanted to understand the reasons why the results came out the way they did. We therefore made mathematical models of each device and tested them against the data until we found models that fit. The model for the mouse was particularly instructive. The mouse was best modeled by a version of Fitts's Law:

$$Movement\ Time = Constant + .1 \log_2(D/S + .05) \text{ sec},$$

Device	Trials	Movement Time for Non-Error Trials						Error Rate	
		Homing Time		Positioning Time		Total Time			
	N	*M* (sec)	*SD* (sec)	*M* (sec)	*SD* (sec)	*M* (sec)	*SD* (sec)	*M*	*SD*
Mouse	1973	.36	.13	1.29	.42	1.66	.48	5%	22%
Joystick	1869	.26	.11	1.57	.54	1.83	.57	11%	31%
Step Keys	1813	.21	.30	2.31	1.52	2.51	1.64	13%	33%
Text Keys	1877	.32	.61	1.95	1.30	2.26	1.70	9%	28%

Figure 1. Overall pointing times for all devices. Homing Time is the time to move the hand from the keyboard to the device, Positioning Time is the time to move the cursor to the target. Times are based on a standardized set of distances and target widths. Averages are computed on the basis of four users x 600 trials/users. *Reprinted from Card, Moran, & Newell (1983, Fig. 7.4) with the permission of Lawrence Erlbaum Associates, Inc.*

where D is the distance the hand moves to the target and S is the target width (see Figure 2). The significance of this result is that this is the same law that describes movement time for the hand alone, with about the same constant of proportionality. The limiting factor in moving the mouse, therefore, is not in the mouse, but in the eye-hand coordinate system itself. That, in turn, means the mouse is nearly optimal, at least with respect to the set of muscles used. Therefore, designing a device that is faster than the mouse would be difficult.

Here was a prototypical example of the kind of theory we wanted to build—a model precise enough to enable designers to perform back-of-the-envelope calculations, a model that identified key constraints in the design space for pointing devices. With this model we could be sure that the data giving comparisons among devices would probably generalize to new situations, because we knew the main factors that governed the results. Furthermore, the model provided guidance for interface designers: make distant buttons large, for example. These studies were heavily used in the debate within Xerox that led to the decision to depart from tradition by including a mouse with the new Star product.

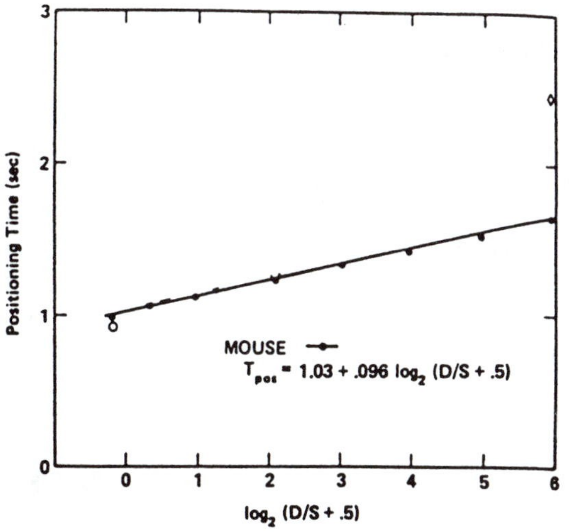

Figure 2. Positioning time for the mouse as a function of Fitts's Index of Difficulty. The fit of positioning time data to the straight line in the figure shows that time for the mouse is governed by Fitts's Law (is proportional to Fitts's Index of Difficulty). The constant of proportionality, .096 sec/bit (= 10.4 bits/sec), is approximately the same value as for pointing with the hand alone. *Reprinted from Card, Moran, & Newell (1983, Fig. 7.8) with the permission of Lawrence Erlbaum Associates, Inc.*

3. The Cognitive Interface: Cognitive Skill

The Model Human Processor

An interesting result of the mouse study was the way an evaluation of pointing devices led to a consideration of human information processing characteristics. This experience pointed to the need for an engineering model of users that would summarize such characteristics. We knew of many phenomena scattered in the literature of psychology, such as Fitts's law, that would be helpful for system design.

To someone who is not a specialist, such as a designer, this literature appears disorganized and contradictory. Psychologists love to split hairs and find small contradictions in published models. The robust but approximate generalizations that might be made to work for engineering tend to get trampled in the debates. Although we had the notion of such a model from about 1974, it wasn't until 1982, when we were nearing the completion of our book, that we were able to formulate it. The model, called the *Model Human Processor,* was inspired by the processors, memories, and switches (PMS) notation of Bell and Newell (1971) for describing the architecture of computing systems. It was a simplified architecture of the user, described in terms of three processors, four memories, 19 parameters of these, and 10 principles of operation (Figure 3).

As an example of the sort of calculation that can be done with the Model Human Processor, consider the case where a programmer is programming a video game version of billiards. He needs to know how long he has after the collision of two balls to compute the balls new trajectory before the illusion of causality breaks down. The Model Human Processor tells us that every event that occurs within 100 msec will be perceived as a single event, so a rough estimate is 100 msec. But it also recognizes that second-order phenomena can change this number, so it also supplies a range of uncertainty for this number (in this instance, 50 to 200 msec).

In this case, we can say that if the programmer can make the balls move within the 50 msec lower bound for this parameter, then it is pretty certain that users will perceive the collision as the cause of the balls change in direction, regardless of secondary effects such as brightness or contrast ratio of the screen.

The Model Human Processor can be used to compute predictions about human performance: how fast people can read, how fast they can scribble, the effect of different abbreviation schemes on memory error, and so on. Derivations based on the Model Human Processor were used to set the maximum velocity of the mouse on the workstation for the Xerox Star.

Text Editing and Cognitive Skill

The Model Human Processor also contains, as one of its principles of operation, Herbert Simon's bounded rationality principle. Our version of this principle may be stated:

> *A person acts so as to attain his goals through rational action, given the structure of the task, his*

> *inputs of information, and bounded by limitations upon his knowledge and processing ability.* (Card, Moran, & Newell, 1983).

That is, in order to predict a person's behavior, one needs to analyze the task he is trying to do, because the person will simply do what is rational to accomplish the task, constrained by limitations in his knowledge and ability to process information. Studies of how people solve problems had shown (Newell & Simon, 1972) that their behavior could be modeled as a search through a space of states of the problem, a *problem space.* We expected that in studies of human-computer interaction we would find users searching through problem spaces to accomplish goals, trying various solutions, backing off and taking other tacks when they ran into trouble.

Two early decisions we made led us to results which were contrary to our expectations. Although we had come to PARC initially with the intention of studying computer programming, we decided once we arrived that there were strategic advantages to studying text editing. A second, tactical, decision was to work with expert subjects rather than novices, in order to have more stable behavior to analyze. Further, to make sure that all our subjects had the

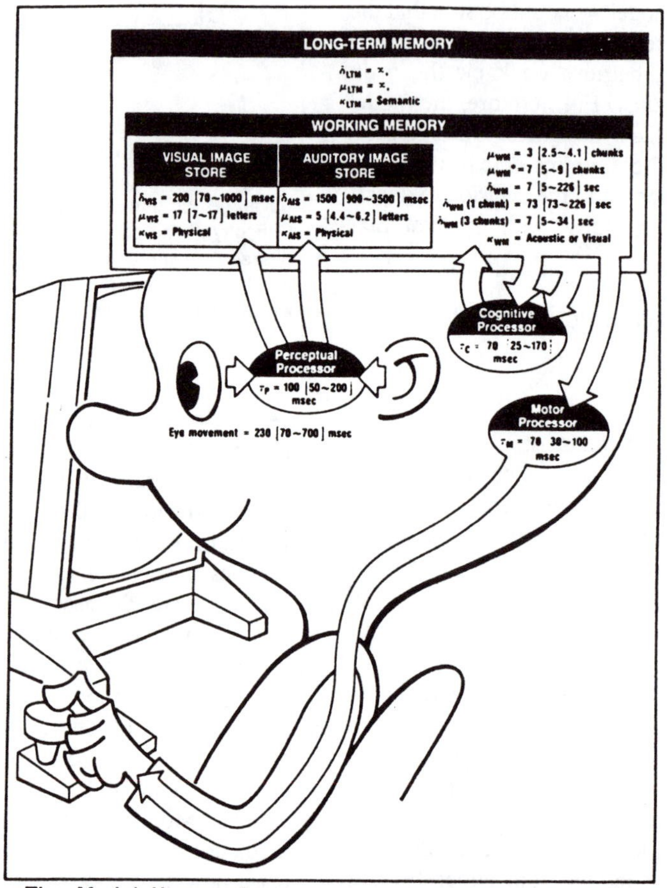

Figure 3. The Model Human Processor memories and processors. Depicted schematically in the figure are the memories, processors, and constants used for making simple computations. The basic architecture of the model can be summarized thus: Sensory information flows into Working Memory through the Perceptual Processor. Working Memory consists of activated chunks in Long-Term Memory. The basic principle of operation of the Model Human Processor is the Recognize-Act Cycle of the Cognitive Processor: On each cycle of the Cognitive Processor, the contents of Working Memory initiate actions associatively linked to them in Long-Term Memory; these actions in turn modify the contents of Working Memory. The Motor Processor is set in motion through activiation of chunks in Working Memory.

Predictions are made using time constants from the figure and a set of associated Principles of Operation: (P0) The Recognize-Act cycle of the Cognitive Processor; (P1) The Variable Perceptual Processor Rate Principle; (P2) The Encoding Specificity Principle; (P3) The Discrimination-Principle; (P4) The Variable Cognitive Processor Rate Principle; (P5) Fitts's Law; (P6) The Power Law of Practice; (P7) The Psychological Uncertainty Prinicple; (P8) The Rationality Principle; and (P9) The Problem Space Principle. *Reprinted from Card, Moran, & Newell (1983, Fig. 2.1.) with the permission of Lawrence Erlbaum Associates, Inc.*

same goals in mind, we presented them with a fairly explicit task—the "manuscript editing task"—which required them to work from a marked-up manuscript, making the changes explicitly indicated.

When we analyzed videotaped protocols of our subjects doing this task, we were surprised to find little of the search behavior of problem solving that we had expected. Subjects simply looked at the tasks and did them. The tasks were not problematic. The subjects had done similar tasks many times before, and had built up a large repertoire of methods that could be applied to the tasks. This wasn't problem solving; we came to call it *cognitive skill* and set out to build models to characterize and predict this mode of behavior.

We applied our theories of human information processing to the kind of specific skills necessary for the text-editing task. The result was a class of models in which the user's cognitive structure consists of four components: (1) a set of familiar Goals that the user would recognize when faced with a specific task; (2) a set of primitive Operators (actions) that the user was skilled at performing and could deploy whenever necessary; (3) a set of Methods, consisting of "compiled" sequences of subgoals and operators, that the user could use to attain his goals; and (4) a set of Selection rules that enable the user to choose among competing methods for goals. We call a model specified by these components a *GOMS model* (Figure 4 shows an example of one). Together, these components constitute the user's cognitive skills for performing tasks. If a user has enough knowledge of this kind, it isn't necessary to use problem-solving strategies. All that is needed is to examine the task, characterize it in terms of a specific goal, select the appropriate method, and then execute it.

In order to test our GOMS models, we ran a set of experiments to determine whether we could explicitly specify this kind of GOMS knowledge and thus predict what users would actually do. We also wanted to learn how the degree of resolution—the grain of specified detail of such a model—affects the degree of accuracy of predictions based on the model. We expected fine-grained models to yield increased accuracy. Knowing that it takes a lot more work to develop a fine-grained model, a practical question related to the applicability of our models was whether the additional work of constructing a fine-grained model was worth the effort.

To find out, we built a family of models in the GOMS framework that characterized the behavior of users of a specific computer text-editing system and ran experiments to test our predictions from these models. We were surprised to discover that fine-grained models did not yield a worthwhile or even a significant increase in prediction accuracy (Card, Moran, & Newell, 1976, 1980a). More felicitous, practically speaking, was our discovery that even the crude models seemed to capture and predict behavior fairly well. These properties suggested that the GOMS model could be turned into the kind of engineering tool that a designer could use to model and predict skilled user behavior in computer-mediated tasks. That was what we proceeded to try next.

```
                          KEYSTROKE LEVEL
Model K2:
 GOAL: EDIT-MANUSCRIPT
 .  GOAL: EDIT-UNIT-TASK                         . repeat until no more unit tasks
 .  .  GOAL: ACQUIRE-UNIT-TASK                   . . if task not remembered
 .  .  .  GOAL: TURN-PAGE* (see below)           . . . if at end of manuscript page
 .  .  .  GOAL: GET-FROM-MANUSCRIPT*
 .  .  GOAL: EXECUTE-UNIT-TASK                   . . if an edit task was found
 .  .  .  GOAL: LOCATE-LINE                      . . . if task not on current line
 .  .  .  .  CHOOSE-COMMAND
 .  .  .  .  [select GOAL: USE-QS-METHOD
 .  .  .  .             .  GOAL: SPECIFY-COMMAND*
 .  .  .  .             .  GOAL: SPECIFY-ARG*
 .  .  .  .          GOAL: USE-LF-METHOD
 .  .  .  .             .  GOAL: SPECIFY-COMMAND*]   . . . . . repeat until at line
 .  .  .  .  GOAL: VERIFY-LOC*
 .  .  .  GOAL: MODIFY-TEXT
 .  .  .  .  CHOOSE-COMMAND
 .  .  .  .  [select GOAL: USE-S-COMMAND
 .  .  .  .             .  GOAL: SPECIFY-COMMAND*
 .  .  .  .             .  GOAL: SPECIFY-ARG*
 .  .  .  .             .  GOAL: SPECIFY-ARG*
 .  .  .  .          GOAL: USE-M-COMMAND
 .  .  .  .             .  GOAL: SPECIFY-COMMAND*
 .  .  .  .             .  GOAL: SPECIFY-COMMAND*    . . . . . repeat until at text
 .  .  .  .             .  GOAL: SPECIFY-ARG*
 .  .  .  .             .  GOAL: SPECIFY-COMMAND*]
 .  .  .  .  GOAL: VERIFY-EDIT*

* Expansion of goals appearing several times:

          GOAL: TURN-PAGE
          . LOOK-AT-MANUSCRIPT                   . repeat twice
          . ACTION
          . MOVE-HAND                            . repeat twice
          . TURN-PAGE
          GOAL: GET-FROM-MANUSCRIPT
          . LOOK-AT-MANUSCRIPT
          . SEARCH-FOR
          . LOOK-AT-DISPLAY                      . optional
          GOAL: SPECIFY-COMMAND
          . GOAL: GET-FROM-MANUSCRIPT*           . if not already selected
          . CHOOSE-COMMAND                       . if not already selected
          . GOAL: TYPE-STRING*
          GOAL: SPECIFY-ARG
          . GOAL: GET-FROM-MANUSCRIPT*           . optional
          . CHOOSE-ARG
          . GOAL: TYPE-STRING*
          GOAL: VERIFY
          . LOOK-AT-DISPLAY
          . GOAL: GET-FROM-MANUSCRIPT*           . optional
          . COMPARE
          GOAL: TYPE-STRING
          . HOME                                 . optional
          . LOOK-AT-KEYBOARD                     . optional
          . LOOK-AT-DISPLAY                      . optional
          . TYPE-STRING
```

Figure 4. GOMS Model K2 for the text editor PØET. This model has a grain of about 0.5 sec/operator. The user is using a line-oriented editor to make changes to a computer file previously marked on a paper manuscript. *Reprinted from Card, Moran, & Newell (1983, Fig. 5.12) with the permission of Lawrence Erlbaum Associates, publishers.*

The Keystroke-Level Model

In simplifying the GOMS models into an engineering model that we could hand to a designer, we constructed an idealized prediction problem:

> *Given a task (possibly involving several subtasks), the command language of a system, the motor skill parameters of the user, the response time parameters of the system, and the method used for the task, predict how long an expert user will take to execute the task using the system, providing he uses the method without error.* (Card, Moran, & Newell, 1980b)

The Keystroke-Level Model enables a system designer to make such predictions with a "back-of-the-envelope" style of calculation.

To do the calculation, the designer codes the method a user employs to do a task in terms of a set of operations derived from one of the fine grain GOMS models (Figure 5). In this simplified model, all keystrokes are assumed to take a constant amount of time; and pointing with the mouse is also assumed to take a constant amount of time. Mental activity by the user is reduced to a single generic mental preparation operation, and rules governing when it will occur are provided.

A typical use of the model to analyze a method is given in Figure 6. This method is one way in which a hypothetical text-editor could be used to replace a word recently typed by the user. Each action of the method is described in terms of the operators of the model, then a time for the method is computed. In this case, the method is expected to take the same amount of time regardless of how many words back the word to be replaced is located. Figure 7 shows the expected time for performing this methods and two other methods available in the editor as a function of the number of words back the to-be-changed word is located. It can be seen that the time profiles of the three methods are quite different and that each is fastest at different times.

Even though our GOMS study suggested that simple models could be effective, and even though the Keystroke-Level Model was a careful simplification of one of the GOMS models, we felt that it was necessary to rigorously text the explicit performance assumptions of the model. To validate the Keystroke-Level Model, we ran a large set of experiments in which people performed tasks with text editors, graphics editors, and executive

Operator	Description and Remarks	Time (sec)
K	PRESS KEY OR BUTTON. Pressing the SHIFT or CONTROL key counts as a separate K operation. Time varies with the typing skill of the user; the following shows the range of typical values:	
	Best typist (135 wpm)	.08
	Good typist (90 wpm)	.12
	Average skilled typist (55 wpm)	.20
	Average non-secretary typist (40 wpm)	.28
	Typing random letters	.50
	Typing complex codes	.75
	Worst typist (unfamiliar with keyboard)	1.20
P	POINT WITH MOUSE TO TARGET ON A DISPLAY. The time to point varies with distance and target size according to Fitts's Law, ranging from .8 to 1.5 sec, with 1.1 being an average. This operator does *not* include the (.2 sec) button press that often follows. Mouse pointing time is also a good estimate for other efficient analogue pointing devices, such as joysticks (see Chapter 7).	1.10
H	HOME HAND(S) ON KEYBOARD OR OTHER DEVICE.	.40
$D(n_D, l_D)$	DRAW n_D STRAIGHT-LINE SEGMENTS OF TOTAL LENGTH l_D CM. This is a very restricted operator; it assumes that drawing is done with the mouse on a system that constrains all lines to fall on a square .56 cm grid. Users vary in their drawing skill; the time given is an average value.	$.9n_D + .16l_D$
M	MENTALLY PREPARE.	1.35
$R(t)$	RESPONSE BY SYSTEM. Different commands require different response times. The response time is counted only if it causes the user to wait.	t

Figure 5. The operators of the Keystroke-Level Model. The figure lists the operators needed to analyze user interface methods and to make calculations of user performance with these methods. *Reprinted from Card, Moran, & Newell (1983, Fig. 8.1) with the permission of Lawrence Erlbaum Associates, Inc.*

Method R (Replace):

Terminate type-in mode	MK[ESC]
Point to target word and select it	H[mouse] P[word] K[YELLOW]
Call Replace command	H[keyboard] MK[R]
Type new word	4.5K[word]
Terminate Replace command	MK[ESC]
Point to last input word and select it	H[mouse] P[word] K[YELLOW]
Re-enter type-in mode	H[keyboard] MK[I]

$$T_{execute} = 4t_M + 10.5t_K + 4t_H + 2t_P$$
$$= 12.1 \text{ sec.}$$

Figure 6. Encoding of Method R. Use of the Keystroke-Level Model to describe one possible method in a mouse-based display editor for replacing a word previously mistyped. It is assumed the word is still visible on the screen. *Reprinted from Card, Moran, & Newell (1983, p. 289) with the permission of Lawrence Erlbaum Associates, Inc.*

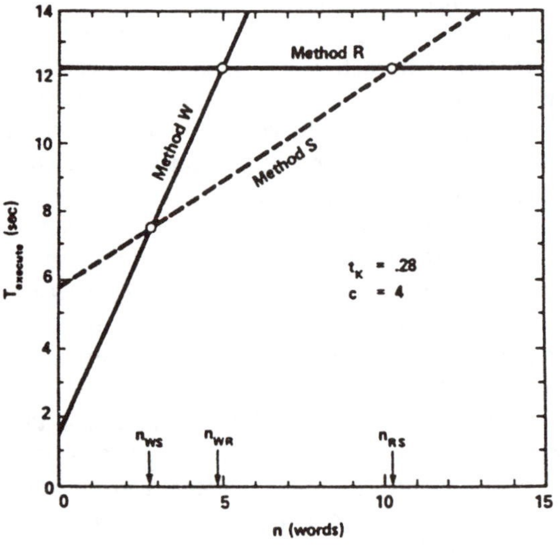

Figure 7. Execution time of three methods for the misspelled-word task as a function of *n*. This figure shows the use of the Keystroke-Level Model for the parametric comparison of three different methods for accomplishing the same goal. In this case each method appears to be superior in a certain range of *n*. *Reprinted from Card, Moran, & Newell (1983, Fig. 8.12a) with the permission of Lawrence Erlbaum Associates, Inc.*

subsystems. The results (Figure 8) showed a good fit between predictions derived from the model and observed times required for the tasks. Therefore, our simple approximative model would be of some use in making practical time estimates.

The Keystroke-Level Model has actually proved useful in real system design. One application was the determination of the number of buttons on the mouse for the Xerox Star product. Several schemes for selecting text in the Star text editor were proposed. These schemes required different numbers of buttons. The goal was to make a mouse with the smallest number of buttons possible, so that it was easy to learn to operate. Experiments to test the schemes were reasonably easy to run with novice subjects. Everyone is a novice subject on a new system, and being a novice doesn't require training. But understanding how well the schemes would work for expert users (which most users would be for most of their time on the system) was expensive, because a long time would have to be spent training the users. The solution was to run experiments for novices and to use the Keystroke-Level Model for predicting expert performance.

The Keystroke-Level Model allowed us to carry through, at least in regard to a very specific kind of behavior, part of our original vision of packaging psychological knowledge into a model that designers can use to calculate user performance with a variety of interactive computer systems.

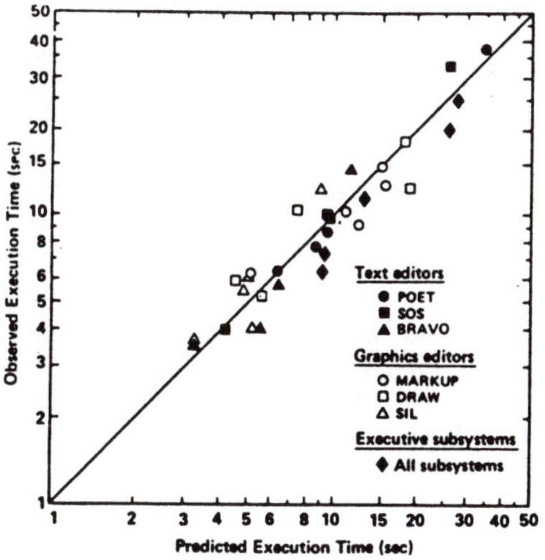

Figure 8. Predicted vs. observed execution times in tests of the Keystroke-Level Model. Predicted execution times were calculated from the Keystroke-Level Model. Observed execution times come from empirical observation. *Reprinted from Card, Moran, & Newell (1983, Fig. 8.6) with the permission of Lawrence Erlbaum Associates, Inc.*

The Unit Task

Not all skill characteristics can be reduced to simple counting, however. In studying text editing, we observed a characteristic of cognitive skill that is fundamentally cognitive, namely the organization of user behavior into short, quasi-independent tasks, which we call *unit-tasks.* Figure 9 shows a typical timeline of user behavior, in this case from a protocol of an electrical engineer using a graphic CAD system to design a VLSI circuit. The figure shows that the behavior is divided into chunks, each consisting of a a few seconds of pause (to formulate a task to do) followed by a few seconds of activity (to execute the task). Each think-execute chunk of behavior is a unit task.

The unit task structure of cognitive skill is interesting because the performance limitations of the user show through the purely rational organization of his behavior. The most significant reason why the unit task breakdown of behavior arises is because of limitations in the user's working memory. If the user can manage input and output streams in his working memory, then the user's behavior will have a continuous structure, as in touch typing from a manuscript. But, when conditions on the inputs and outputs do not allow this, then behavior must be structured into a series of unit tasks.

```
Clock |         10        20        30        40        50        60 sec
 Time |....:....|....:....|....:....|....:....|....:....|....:....|

Transcription Phase

 0:18 |-------DDDD=DDD=DDDDDDDDD=DDDD=DDDDDD
 0:55 |------D=D=D
 1:06 |-----D===DDDDDDDDDD
 1:25 |-----DD==DD
 1:36 |-------------------------AAAAAAAAAAAAAAAA
 2:17 |----------DDDDDD===DDDD=DDDDDDDDD
 2:50 |--------DDD=DDDDDDDDDD==DDD=D==DDDDD
 3:30 |----DDDD==DDDDD
 3:41 |--------D---------DD
 4:01 |-------------AAAAAAAA
 4:22 |------A=A
 4:31 |-------DDDDDD=DDD==DD
 4:52 |---------------------------D=DD
 5:23 |-----DD
 5:30 |-----A=A
 5:38 |-------DD====DDDDD=DDD
 6:00 |---------------D==DD
 6:20 |-----DDDD=DDDDDDDDDD
 6:44 |---D-D------D==DD
 6:57 |------------DDDDDDDDD=DDDD
 7:23 |------------D---DD----D
 7:46 |----------AAAAAAAA==AAAAA
 8:11 |-------A=A=AAA=AAAAAAA
 8:33 |---------D===DDDD=DDDD==DDDD
 9:01 |---------D=DD
 9:14 |-----------DDDD==DDD=DDD==DDDDD
 9:45 |--------------D==D=DD=DDDDDDDDDDD
10:18 |-----DDDD==DDD===DDD
10:38 |--------DD=DDDDD
10:54 |-----------D==D=DD===DDD
11:18 |-----D=DD==DDDD==DDDDD
11:44 |----MM
11:46 |----------D-DDDD----DDDD==DDDDDDD
12:21 |C----------------------------------------------
13:05 |A=AA
13:09 |-----------DDDDD=DDDDD=DDDDDDD====DDDD
13:47 |-------DDDDD=DDDDDDD
14:07 |-------------------
```

Symbol Code:

- `-` Task acquisition
- `D` Draw task execution
- `A` Alter task execution
- `M` Dimension task execution
- `C` Check task execution
- `=` Intra-execution pause
- `+` Pause within Move command

Figure 9. Time line representing the user's behavior sequence in a VLSI design session. Each single-character symbol represents one second of behavior. The symbol sequence begins on a new line at the beginning of each unit task, and the clock time is the time at the beginning of the unit task. *Reprinted from Card, Moran, & Newell (1983, Fig. 10.7) with the permission of Lawrence Erlbaum Associates, Inc.*

Figure 10 portrays a trace of the working memory load of the user, based on logical considerations of when information must be available in memory in order to do a task. As we can see, memory requirements build from a low point at the start of a unit task to a high within the unit task, where information for the task has been assembled, and back to a low point at the end of the unit task, where the information is no longer needed. If the information in working memory should reach a level higher than the working memory capacity, then user performance will suffer, usually manifested by the user committing errors. To avoid these errors, the user must break down the overall task into smaller (unit) units, each of which can be managed in the available working memory.

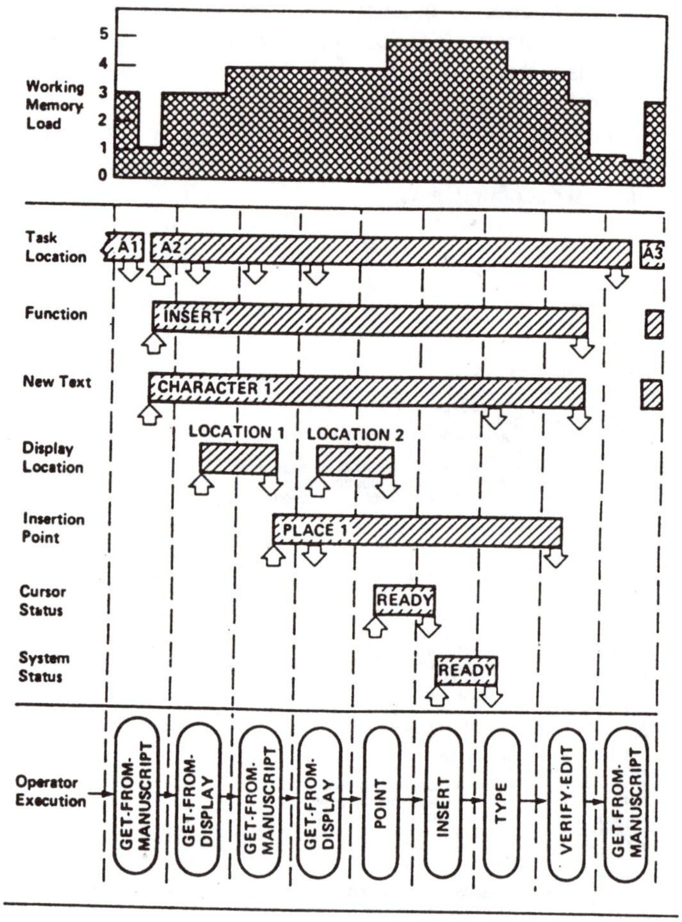

Figure 10. Data in Working Memory during a unit task. This figure is an hypothetical trace of the performance of one unit task. Time runs to the right on the horizontal axis. The bars indicate the time during which each piece of information about the task is needed. The arrows indicate the initial time data is available and the subsequent times it is needed. The histogram on the top plots the total Working Memory load over time, showing how the load peaks within a unit task and dips between unit tasks. *Reprinted from Card, Moran, & Newell (1983, Fig. 11.12) with the permission of Lawrence Erlbaum Associates, Inc.*

Unit-task behavior is at present a theoretical notion based on empirical observation (see Card, Moran, Newell, 1983, for further discussion). But it represents an important feature of user behavior—a sort of "cognitive rhythm"—that should be taken into account in designing user-computer interfaces that are sensitively tuned to the user's capabilities.

The Psychology of Human-Computer Interaction

In 1978, one of us had completed a doctoral thesis (Card, 1978) that consolidated much of the work we had been doing. The thesis helped convince us that the time was appropriate for writing a book presenting our vision of an applied science of the user. Work on the book gave us the opportunity to focus on the larger vision instead of just the pieces, and we became aware of some missing unifying theoretical work that we felt we had to do.

Although we had several calculational models (Fitts's law for the mouse, GOMS models, the Keystroke-Level Model, plus other minor models), there were questions of relating these to the classical literature in cognitive psychology and human factors. We had long sought a unifying framework for tying together the relevant psychological knowledge about users (one of our 1974 working papers called this conception the "Handbook of Cognitive Man"), but had made little progress. In preparing the book we revived this goal and came to a much more satisfying conception, the Model Human Processor, which captured the relevant psychological literature in the terms of a unified, approximative model. This model also provided a foundation for our other models.

The other big missing piece for us was to understand the relationship between the cognitive skill we had discovered and the classical notion of problem solving in cognitive psychology. Here we built a theory of the behavioral continuum between problem solving and cognitive skill and showed how practice on a task would gradually change problem solving behavior into skilled behavior. This is an active area of research in cognitive psychology today (e.g., Anderson, 1981).

The result of these efforts was the book, *The Psychology of Human Computer Interaction* (Card, Moran, & Newell, 1983). However, the book represented only the main line of our research efforts that fit together into a tightly knit view. There were many other areas of our work that we decided not to put into the book, such as the issues of learning and of users' mental models.

4. The Conceptual Interface: Mental Models

The early effort of the AIP Project was focused on understanding expert user performance. As we explained in the previous section, skilled performance is characterized by methods that users know and quickly execute to accomplish tasks. That is, we were focused on what is typically called procedural knowledge ("how-to-do-it" knowledge). However, from the beginning, we were aware that methods are not sequences of meaningless actions, but that expert users also have an understanding of what the procedures cause the machine to do. That is, the expert users have some sort of *mental model* of what is happening inside the computer ("how-it-works" knowledge).

The first AIP memo in 1974 proposed the notion of the "user's model," which refers to the conceptual model that the user can have of the system. A user's conceptual model is distinct from (but related to) the designer's implementation model. It is an abstraction of the system's architecture and software structures—the conceptual entities that the architecture and software implements—that is simple enough for non-technical users to grasp. (For example, a user might not know how the mechanism of the delete buffer of a text-editor works, but would simply know that the deleted text goes into a "clipboard.") A user's model would typically include knowledge of where information is stored (core memory, local disk files, remote file servers). It is important for the user to have an understanding of these kinds of features, for they are often not visible to the user.

The user's model provides an integrated package of knowledge that allows the user to predict what the system will do if certain commands are executed, to predict the state of the system after the commands have been executed, to plan methods for novel tasks, and to deal with odd error situations (by characterizing the system's state according to the model, then choosing operations necessary to leave that state).

Early Encounters with Conceptual Models

Early in our research we tried to write down rudimentary descriptions of the elements of conceptual models, which included the conceptual objects, their properties, how they related to each other (the characters in a text editor, for example, including the notion of a blank space as a character), and the conceptual operations that could be performed on those objects (inserting, moving, or deleting characters, including blank spaces).

Given the obvious importance of this kind of knowledge for the user, we were surprised to find that almost no system documentation ever clearly laid out a conceptual model of the system for the user. We were also surprised to discover what a difficult inductive task it is to specify such a model, even for a seemingly simple text editor. It was a detective game in which we were forced to hypothesize and test elements of possible models in order to find a succinct conceptual characterization of how the system worked. It was a game that took us days (not minutes) to do, hence not a game in which busy users were likely to engage.

It is clear that users attempt to make sense—by building mental models—of the behavior of a system as they use it. If a simple model is not explicitly or implicitly provided, users formulate their own myths about how the system works. These user-invented models may be inaccurate or misleading outside the very limited situation from which they emerged. Therefore, we believed that if the user is to understand the system, the system has to be designed with an *explicit* conceptual model that is easy enough for the user to learn. We call this the *intended user's model,* because it is the model the designer intends the user to learn. Just what mental model the user actually forms is another issue, which depends on how clearly the intended user's model is designed, how well it is implemented, and how well it is documented.

Although we were very concerned about the mental model issue, we didn't pursue explicit studies for several reasons: we didn't have a satisfactory methodology for studying it, we didn't have satisfactory representations of it, and we were busy pursuing the performance issues we have discussed. Still, we felt that the intended user's model was an important consideration in the user-interface design process.

User Interface Design Methodology

The practical application of our concerns came when Xerox began arranging the technology transfer between PARC and the Systems Development Division (SDD), which was created to develop office system products based on the research at PARC. In the Spring of 1976, a joint PARC/SDD committee (which included one of us) was formed to advise SDD on the design of the user interface of the office systems.

The committee decided not to try to design an actual interface, but to propose a methodology for SDD designers to follow in designing their interfaces. The methodology (Irby et al., 1977) included four parts: (1) analyze what tasks the user will want to do and the steps they go through to accomplish the tasks; (2) design an intended user's model in terms of which the tasks may be cast; (3) design a command language to make that model work; and (4) design an information display to reflect the operations of the system in terms of the conceptual model.

Thus, we recommended that the designer should lay out an intended user's model before designing the command language and the information display. The whole design effort should be oriented toward keeping this model "under control," i.e., keeping it simple, consistent, and clear enough for users to grasp.

The original designers of the Xerox Star interface, the workstation product SDD built, used this methodology. The conceptual model was clearly laid out in the system's functional specifications, and the designers worked hard to keep the model consistent. Although this model was represented informally, the fact that the designers focused on it contributed heavily to the widely recognized success of Star's user interface. The conceptual model is an under-appreciated aspect of Star's interface, but Star's more widely-touted icons and desktop metaphor only make sense with respect to its underlying conceptual model.

William Newman, another member of the committee, presented this methodology in the second edition of his book with Bob Sproull (Newman & Sproull, 1979).

Empirical Studies

By 1979, we were ready to tackle some empirical studies in order to understand the role of the user's model. The first study was an attempt to elicit the knowledge that real users of real systems have about the systems they use every day. The system we chose to study was the Alto Executive, a system which was in wide use at PARC for several years by nontechnical support people as well as programmers.

We wanted to find out what Alto users knew about the Executive. The goal was to see whether we could find some kind of mental models buried in the user's knowledge. The methodology we used was to transcribe interviews with several users into logical propositions and then classify them into categories.

The surprising result was that many nontechnical expert users (e.g., secretaries who used the system effectively every day) gave no evidence of having anything but very shallow models of how the system worked. (Perhaps we shouldn't have been surprised, because no conceptual model was documented and training was informal.) This led us to consider more carefully the role of the user's model.

In order to characterize the role a user's mental model would play in the use of a system, we performed experiments with the simplest kind of system we could devise, a simple stack-based calculator (Halasz & Moran, 1983; Halasz, 1984). We thought that a model of a stack might well be useful to help rationalize what for many users is a nonintuitive postfix command language. The formal experiment compared one group of users who were taught an explicit conceptual model of the stack, and a group of users who were carefully shielded from the stack model. The model group was trained in relation to a specific model and were told how that model related to the methods for solving arithmetic problems. The no-model group was only taught specific methods for performing the same tasks. Then we gave the two groups sets of problems that were categorized as simple routine tasks, slightly more complex tasks, and very difficult "invention tasks" (which required the user to invent new methods to solve).

The results (see Figure 11) revealed no difference between the two groups in both the routine and complex problems, but the model group performed much better on the invention tasks. The most surprising result was that even some of the no-model group were able to perform some of the invention tasks. We wanted to account for these results according to the cognitive theories we understood, so we analyzed the protocols gathered from the users as they performed the tasks.

Problem Type	No-Model Users	Model Users
Routine	98	95
Complex	87	88
Invention	25	67

Figure 11. Percentage of problems correctly done in the calculator experiments. There were two groups of users; one was taught an explicit conceptual model of the calculator's stack and the other group was prevented from having such a model. There were three types of problems, each of a different difficulty relative to what the users were taught.

Problem Type	No-Model Users				Model Users			
	Skilled Method Execution	Problem Solving			Skilled Method Execution	Problem Solving		
		Model Space	Methods Space	Task Space		Model Space	Methods Space	Task Space
Routine	90	0	8	2	89	11	0	0
Complex	94	0	6	0	91	7	0	2
Invention	2	0	84	14	7	71	19	3

Figure 12. Partitioning of the users' behavior in the calculator experiments. The users' behavior was devided into four behavioral modes: skilled method execution plus three problem solving modes, which are distinguished according to which problem space they were working in. The partitioning is based on an analysis of verbal protocol records; each line of protocol was categorized into the mode it manifested. The numbers in the table are the percentages of lines of protocol in each behavior mode. We believe that this measure underestimates the amount of work in the task space.

We divided the users' behavior into skilled method execution, as we had modeled in our earlier studies, and problem-solving. We found (see Figure 12) that in the routine and complex problems, the behavior was almost all skilled method execution: the subjects had been taught what to do, and they did it; even for the complex problems it wasn't difficult to knit together the methods they had learned for solving the problems.

Our hypothesis going into the study was that the conceptual model we taught the model group of users would provide them with a problem space through which they could search in order to find solutions. According to this theory, the user would characterize a difficult "invention" task in terms of this problem space: the state of the system when they started, the state of the system they would like to achieve, and a set of operations to move them through that space; they would solve the problem using generic problem-solving strategies.

However, when we analyzed the users protocols, we found two other kinds of problem spaces in which the users worked when they were problem solving. One was a *task space* within which they manipulated the given arithmetic task in various ways, such as dividing it into subtasks that could be solved by known methods. Another space in which they worked was a *methods space*, where they took known solution methods as strings of steps, manipulated those steps in various ways to produce new methods, and tried them to see how they worked.

We found that the most critical (although not very time consuming) problem solving was in the task space, where the user analyzed the given task into subtasks and delegated them to the model space or the methods space. The main difference between the users who had a model and those who didn't was that they had different problem spaces in which to work (see Figure 12). The model space was an effective problem space, within which the solution to the invention problems could be found; the method space was not particularly effective, but it was sufficient to allow some non-model users to stumble onto solutions to some of the invention problems (often, much to their surprise).

We concluded that mental models can be useful for novel task situations, but we found that users only use their models in specific subtasks; there was a lot of switching between the task space and other problem spaces. Users were cautious about going into a mode of behavior that involved thinking through a mental model. Model-based problem solving appears to be very mentally intensive, so users avoid it if they can apply cognitive skills. But, if users don't have appropriate methods available, they will retreat to some kind of problem solving. In these cases, a good conceptual model provides an effective problem space in which to work.

Thus, system designers should think of a conceptual model of a system as not just a simple view of a complex system, but as a problem space through which users can search for solutions to a variety of novel problems. The conceptual entities and operators in the intended user's model should be closely related to the kinds of tasks the users are likely to do, and the users should be provided with heuristics for moving through the model space.

Theoretical Studies: Task Mapping

We also worked on a theoretical analysis of conceptual models to show where they fit into the overall structure of the user interface. The Command Language Grammar formalism (Moran, 1978, 1981) shows how models relate to the task domain, the command language, and the detailed user-computer interactions. According to this theory, the conceptual model provides the user with a link between his task domain and the syntax of the interactive dialogue. That is, on the one hand the conceptual model serves as the semantics of the dialogue actions, while on the other hand it serves as a base into which the task can be mapped into the system.

Richard Young called this kind of mechanistic conceptual model a *surrogate model* (Young, 1983). Interactions on these issues with Young, who was exploring the domain of simple calculators, led to the discovery of a new kind of mental model—*task-action mappings* (Young, 1981). The properties of radically different calculator designs, such as algebraic versus stack calculators, could be best understood by an analysis of how well calculation tasks could be directly mapped into the actions available on the calculators. Surrogate models were completely bypassed in this analysis, which helps explain why people sometimes seem to get along with systems without having surrogate models of them.

In further work along this line, we have proposed a calculus, called *ETIT analysis*, for task mapping (Moran, 1983). The "fit" of a system to a task domain can be assessed by enumerating rules for reformulating system-independent task descriptions ("external tasks") into system-specific task descriptions ("internal tasks"). Rule-based system description techniques, such as this or Payne's (1984) *task-action grammar*, are beginning to provide a way to help us formalize the fuzzy notion of the *consistency* of a system (both internal consistency and consistency with respect to a task domain). Such techniques look promising as a way provide system designers with calculational techniques for predicting the learnability and "guessability" of systems.

5. The Task Interface: Pondering Ideas

Let us now turn to the role of a science of the user in the future development of the personal workstation. For us, the real challenges for user technology are now at the larger task level in which users are grappling with complex intellectual tasks. This is, of course, a return to working directly on a modern version of the original vision of augmentation workstations.

We now have workstations powerful enough to give each user a personal system equivalent to one that only a decade ago would have been shared with a hundred other users, and we are on the verge of major upgrades to even greater computing and communication power. We now have a much more developed base for user technology—not only techniques for designing user interfaces, but also models for understanding users. Thus, we are now in a better position than ever before to explore systems that can really augment human intellectual endeavors.

The challenge is to create systems that, through intimate cognitive interaction with users, aid them in structuring and manipulating their ideas. With such systems to help them, people will then be able to cope with more and more complex intellectual tasks of all sorts—authoring books and multi-media presentations, designing products and programs, composing music, analyzing experiments, the arguing points of law and policy, reasoning about scientific and social issues, and on and on.

The key to building such systems is to find ways by which a user can act on his ideas as objects, just as current text editors allow him to act on words as objects. This is difficult, since ideas are often tacit and ill-formed. A means is needed to *externalize* the ideas, to get them out of the user's head and into a form that can be organized and shaped. Two problems require solution:

(1) The user needs new ways to *represent* his ideas—to get the user's mind around the ideas, as it were. For this we can exploit advances in artificial intelligence and cognitive science.

(2) The user needs new ways to *manipulate* his ideas—to get the user's hands on the ideas. For this we can exploit advances in interactive computer graphics.

These problems are part of our current research agenda. In this endeavor we must not only build on our current base of understanding of the user, but also advance that understanding. For one thing, we have to launch studies into the nature of the complex intellectual tasks we wish to augment. This calls for a shift in our research strategy from studying users of existing systems to studying users of new systems that we ourselves build, which enables us to understand the nature of the tasks and the limits of users and systems for dealing with them. We give illustrations of this strategy from some of our own current projects.

Representation: Idea Structuring

Word processors and text editors, even powerful ones, are tailored for the final stages of writing a paper—crafting the text and graphics of the final product. Outline processors help with the previous stage of outlining. Although the latter are sometimes called "idea processors," it is clear that idea processing begins well before the stage of outlining. A genuine idea processor should allow the user to deal with ideas that are vague and ill-structured and help him gradually add structure as it is discovered.

We use the term *authoring* to refer to the larger intellectual task of gathering information, extracting and discovering ideas, structuring them, and finally composing them into a readable product. Authoring in this sense is a highly general task composed of generic subtasks, as illustrated in Figure 13. One begins by collecting sources of information; from these a set of notes (idea-sized units) are created to represent potentially relevant facts and ideas. As notes accumulate, they need to be filed in a structure suitable for retrieval, such as a topic hierarchy. But these notes also need structures that organize the ideas into meaningful, coherent themes. Such structures must be discovered, elaborated, supported by evidence in the notes and other sources. One then communicates these ideas by composing them into an interpretable product—a document, a slide presentation, or a browsable network of ideas.

The key research issue here is to help the users develop explicit mental models of idea structures, so they can see them, play with them, and evaluate them. This requires the invention of representations for *externalizing* ideas and idea structures. Cognitively, these representations serve the

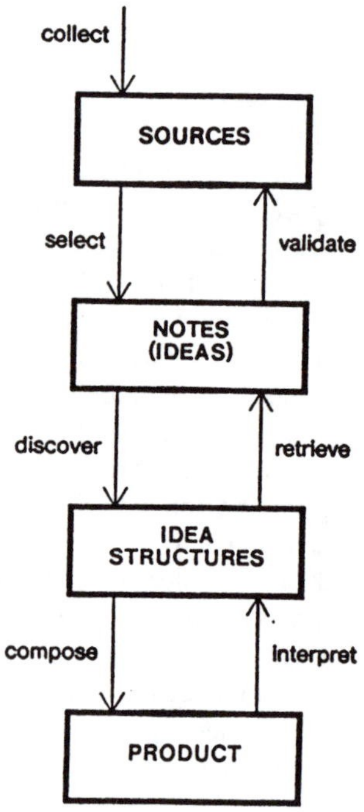

Figure 13. Schematic diagram of the generic authoring task. The boxes are the types of information to be managed in the authoring process, and the arrows are some of the processes for generating and transforming the information.

users as problem spaces; and new representations can fundamentally alter the way they are able to deal with ideas. Some representations should be "weak" in the sense that they can easily capture a large variety of even vague ideas; other representations should be "strong" in the sense that they can precisely capture and process particular classes of idea structures; and facilities must be provided to help users transform weak representations into strong ones.

We are developing a system, called *NoteCards*, to explore the broad nature of the authoring task. NoteCards supports the orienting metaphor of the notecard as a medium for capturing an idea. Notecards can be stored in fileboxes and linked into complex structures, which can then be viewed in graphic representations (such as the one shown in Figure 14). NoteCards is designed to be an open, flexible environment, so that we can use it as a "laboratory" to explore new representations and tools to support authoring tasks. Because it is an open system, NoteCards users are faced with the problem of devising appropriate ways to use the system, that is, mapping their particular tasks onto the basic elements of the system. This leads to a further interface issue of making the environment tailorable by users themselves to the wide variety of situations that we encourage them to bring to NoteCards (paper and documentation writing, scientific and legal argumentation, instruction authoring, design analysis). Thus, in contrast to our earlier methodology of observing a controlled, skilled user population, we are now observing a population of idiosyncratic, exploratory users.

Manipulation: Idea Browsing

The representations in an idea-structuring environment must be assimilated and manipulated with facility and speed. Idea-processing tasks are difficult for users, because they involve the retrieval, tracking, and manipulation of a large number of ideas (as is being attempted in Figure 14). Authoring a paper, for example, may require hundreds of notes and scores of references; programming may require hundreds of routines. But, as the Model Human Processor

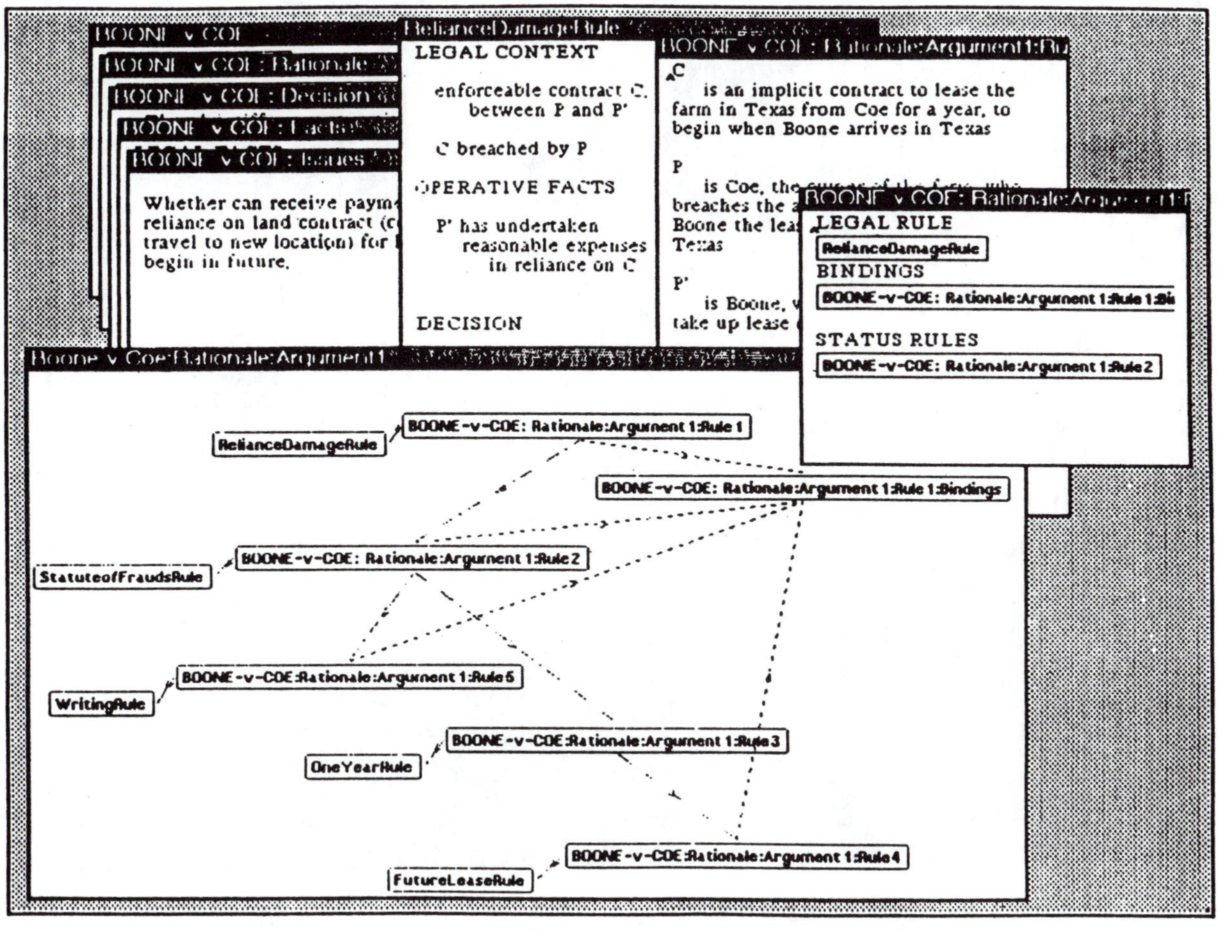

Figure 14. A screen image of the NoteCards system. The application shown is the analysis of a legal argument. A variety of legal rules must be brought to bear in arguing a particular case. The graph shows how the rules are related by applicability conditions and by bindings to the particulars of the case.

shows, only limited amounts of information can be handled in the user's working memory. These limitations lead the user to structure his behavior into unit-task bursts.

These considerations lead us to ask how a computer system can compensate for human cognitive limitations. The display can be used as an external memory to augment the user's internal working memory. This partly explains what has made the "desk-top" metaphor successful: users can use windows and icons to keep track of more documents, notes, and messages from other users than with the previous style of command language interfaces. By having these things visible as reminders, the user's effective working memory is increased, enabling him to do more complex tasks.

But the problem is that these techniques, which work well with with a few dozen objects, do not scale well up to the several hundred or even thousands of objects necessary for the idea-processing tasks we wish to do. Here, it helps to begin with a better understanding of the nature of the problem. Again, our method for gaining that understanding is through approximative models of user behavior. In this case, we have sketched a model called the Window Working Set Model (Card, Pavel, & Farrell, 1984) that analyzes access to screen objects in a manner analogous to the analysis of virtual memory operating systems. Informally, this model suggests that screen space itself is the key constraint and that at some point as the number of, say, overlapped windows required increases, user performance will decrease in a sudden and non-linear way, sending the user into the window version of thrashing.

Thus there are limitations on the uses of current graphical interface techniques for browsing large sets of ideas. Advanced graphics systems, however, open up a new set of possibilities. Figure 15 shows a fragment of an

Figure 15. Experimental Dandelris browser for organization charts. The photograph shows a view of a fragment of an organization chart as seen by a user flying around this chart. The chart is laid out on a simulated 2-dimensional whiteboard. The user can change his location in simulated 3-dimensional space, his direction of gaze, and by pointing with the mouse to indicate focus, the relative sizes of different organization chart boxes. (The experimental program was written by S. Card, A. Henderson, L. Lovstrand, and B. Verner.)

organization chart from an experimental browsing system we are implementing (the DandeIris, combining a Xerox DandeTiger Lisp machine and a Silicon Graphics Iris graphics processor). The node that is the user's focus is largest and is readable in the most detail. Nodes become smaller with distance from the focus. The user can fly around this chart to see it from different points of view and change his direction of gaze; if he points at a node, indicating a new focus of attention, it grows larger. The transitions are all animated in real-time, color, three-dimensional representations to help the user keep track of the transformed identities of various objects.

Such a display is designed to help the user navigate among a large number of objects; only a few of these objects would be visible in detail at any time, but many more would be visible as orienting cues and retrieval keys. The visual movement techniques is coupled with other retrieval techniques for allowing the user to focus on a limited number of items at a time (as required by our understanding of user's processing capacity) while retaining rapid access to a large number of items (as required by our understanding of the requirements of complex intellectual tasks). By coupling experimental programming with the analysis of user behavior, we hope to find theory-based techniques to aid the user in keeping track of and maintaining effective browsing and retrieval capability for large information structures.

6. Conclusions

What has been learned about users and how does this relate to the original visions of personal workstations? The short answer is that, unlike the early 1970's when little was known scientifically about computer users, we now have a vision of the form of an applied science of the user and a few areas of knowledge where that vision has been realized. In this paper we have narrated some of our efforts at building this applied science:

At the physical interface level, we have discovered that user performance with pointing devices is constrained by the information-processing capacity of the user. We have learned the quantitative law describing this constraint and have determined that certain devices, such as the mouse, are at the performance limits allowed by this law.

At the cognitive level, we have learned that routine human-computer interaction, such as text-editing, does not involve problem solving, but rather cognitive skills based on the execution of known methods. We can see the information-processing constraints of the user show through this skilled performance in the unit task of users. We have characterized cognitive skill to the extent of developing an engineering model for use by user-interface designers.

At the conceptual level, we have learned that users often have mental models of the systems they use, and that such models enable performance of novel tasks. System conceptual models provide the basis for users to acquire mental models, and thus are an important basis for system design. But mental models are cognitively intensive, and users will avoid them by attempting to map directly from their tasks to the actions required in a system. Theories of task mapping are just beginning to emerge.

At each of the above levels, it has been possible to base an applied science on a theory of the cognitive mechanisms underlying user behavior. At each level, the applied science was shown to be practical, in particular by being influential in the design of the Xerox Star.

The challenge for us today is to use our understanding of users to discover new ways to augment users in complex intellectual endeavors. Thus, we are concentrating our efforts in those areas where users' cognitive limitations need to be overcome and where users' cognitive abilities can be aided with computer-based tools. We believe that the most interesting problems are at the task level: understanding the nature of complex intellectual tasks and finding ways to build idea-structuring tools, both representation tools for structuring ideas and display tools for browsing ideas.

Whereas we once studied users empirically using existing systems in order to understand the nature of human-computer interaction, we now use what we have learned about users to help drive the creation of new experimental systems.

REFERENCES

Anderson, J. R. (1981). *Cognitive skills and their acquisition.* Hillsdale, NJ: Lawrence Erlbaum Associates.

Bell, C. G., & Newell, A. (1971). *Computer structures: readings and examples.* New York: McGraw-Hill.

Bush, V. (1945). As we may think. *The Atlantic Monthly,* August.

Card, S. K. (1978). Studies in the psychology of computer text editing systems. Unpublished doctoral dissertation, Carnegie-Mellon University, Department of Psychology.

Card, S. K., English, W. K., & Burr, B. J. (1978). Evaluation of mouse, rate-controlled isometric joystick, step keys, and text keys for text selection on a CRT. *Ergonomics, 21,* 601-613.

Card, S. K., Moran, T. P., & Newell, A. (1976). *The manuscript editing task: A routine cognitive skill* (Technical Report SSL-76-8). Palo Alto, CA: Xerox Palo Alto Research Center.

Card, S. K., Moran, T. P., & Newell, A. (1980a). Computer text-editing: an information-processing analysis of a routine cognitive skill. *Cognitive Psychology, 12,* 32-74.

Card, S. K., Moran, T. P., & Newell, A. (1980b). The keystroke-level model for user performance time with interactive systems. *Communications of the ACM 23,* 396-410.

Card, S. K., Moran, T. P., & Newell, A. (1983). *The psychology of human-computer Interaction.* Hillsdale, NJ: Lawrence Erlbaum Associates.

Card, S. K., Pavel, M., & Farrell, J. E. (1984). Window-based computer dialogues. *Proceedings of IFIP Interact '84,* 355-359. London: IFIP.

Engelbart, D. (1963). A conceptual framework for the augmentation of man's intellect. In P. W. Howerton and D. C. Weeks (Eds.), *Vistas in Information Handling,* Vol. 1. Washington, D.C.: Spartan Books.

English, W. K., Engelbart, D. C., & Berman, M. A. (1967). Display-selection techniques for text manipulation. *IEEE Transactions on Human Factors in Electronics, HFE-8,* 5-15.

Halasz, F. G. (1984). *Mental models and problem solving in using a calculator.* Unpublished Ph.D. Dissertation. Stanford, CA: Stanford University.

Halasz, F. G., & Moran, T. P. (1983). Mental models and problem solving in using a calculator. *Proceedings of the CHI '83 Conference on Human Factors in Computing Systems.* New York: ACM.

Irby, C., Bergsteinsson, L., Moran, T. P., Newman, W., & Tesler, L. (1977). *A methodology for user interface design.* Palo Alto, CA: Xerox Palo Alto Research Center.

Kay, A. (1977). Microelectronics and the personal computer. *Scientific American,* September, 230-244.

Licklider, J. C. R. (1960). Man-computer symbiosis. *IRE Transactions on Human Factors in Electronics, HFE-1* (March), 4-11.

Moran, T. P. (1978). *Introduction to the Command Language Grammar* (Technical Report SSL-78-3). Palo Alto, CA: Xerox Palo Alto Research Center.

Moran, T. P. (1981). The command language grammar: A representation for the user interface of interactive computer systems. *International Journal of Man-Machine Studies, 15,* 3-50.

Moran, T. P. (1983). Getting into a system: external-internal task mapping analysis. *Proceedings of the CHI '83 Conference on Human Factors in Computing Systems.* New York: ACM.

Newell, A., & Simon, H. A. (1972). *Human problem solving.* Englewood Cliffs, NJ: Prentice-Hall.

Newman, W., & Sproull, R. (1979). *Principles of interactive computer graphics,* 2nd ed. New York: McGraw-Hill.

Payne, S. J. (1984). Task-action grammars. *Proceedings of Interact '84: First IFIP Conference on Human-Computer Interaction,* London. Amsterdam: Elsevier.

Young, R. M. (1981). The machine inside the machine: users' models of pocket calculators. *International Journal of Man-Machine Studies, 15,* 51-86.

Young, R. M. (1983). Surrogates and mappings: two kinds of conceptual models for interactive devices. In D. Gentner & A. L. Stevens (Eds.), *Mental models.* Hillsdale, NJ: Lawrence Erlbaum Associates.

HUMAN-COMPUTER INTERACTION, 1990, Volume 5, pp. 221-265

The Growth of Cognitive Modeling in Human-Computer Interaction Since GOMS

Judith Reitman Olson and **Gary M. Olson**
The University of Michigan

ABSTRACT

The purpose of this article is to review where we stand with regard to modeling the kind of cognition involved in human-computer interaction. Card, Moran, and Newell's pioneering work on cognitive engineering models and explicit analyses of the knowledge people need to perform a procedure was a significant advance from the kind of modeling cognitive psychology offered at the time. Since then, coordinated bodies of research have both confirmed the basic set of parameters and advanced the number of parameters that account for the time of certain component activities. Formal modeling in grammars and production systems has provided an account for error production in some cases, as well as a basis for calculating how long a system will take to learn and how much savings there is from previous learning. Recently, we were given a new tool for modeling nonsequential component processes, adapting the "critical path analysis" from engineering to the specification of interacting processes and their consequent durations.

Though these advances have helped, there are still significant gaps in our understanding of the whole process of interacting with computers. The cumulative nature of this empirical body and its associated modeling framework has further highlighted important issues central to research in cognitive psychology: how people move smoothly between skilled performance and problem solving, how people learn, how to design for consistent user interfaces, how people produce and manage errors, how we interpret visual displays for meaning, and what processes run concurrently and which depend on the completion of prior processes.

In the bigger picture, cognitive modeling is a method that is useful in both initial design (it can narrow the design space and provide early analyses of design alternatives), evaluation, and training. But it does not extend to broader aspects of the context in which people use computers, partly because

Authors' present address: Judith Reitman Olson and Gary M. Olson, Cognitive Science and Machine Intelligence Laboratory, The University of Michigan, 701 Tappan, Ann Arbor, MI 48109-1234.

CONTENTS

there are significant gaps in contemporary cognitive theory to inform the modeling and partly because it is the wrong form of model for certain kinds of more global questions in human–computer interaction. Notably, it fails to capture the user's fatigue, individual differences, or mental workload. And it is not the type of model that will aid the designer in designating the set of functions the software ought to contain, to assess the user's judgment of the acceptability of the software, or the change that could be expected in work life and the organization in which this work and person fits. Clearly, these kinds of considerations require modeling and tools of a different granularity and form.

---

1. GOMS AS COGNITIVE MODELING

The ability to predict how users will interact with proposed designs is a useful tool for the system designer. Being able to make such predictions is one of the principal goals of a class of cognitive models that has emerged following on the work of Card, Moran, and Newell (1980a, 1980b, 1983). In this article, we examine the strengths and weaknesses of such models, focusing in particular on confirmations and extensions that have emerged since the original proposals. New work has addressed some of the well-known weaknesses of the original approach, but it is still important to understand exactly the limits of these kinds of models.

In very few design fields does the process of design proceed from first principles. Rather, new designs most often arise from old designs, from analogies, or from other sources of creative thought. First principles are then used to screen these candidate designs. This is exactly the role for which cognitive models are best suited (Newell & Card, 1985, 1986). To be concrete, cognitive models are useful in:

1. Initially constraining the design space, so that one does not build an interface, for example, that requires more items to be kept in memory than will fit in working memory (WM).
2. Answering specific design decisions, so that one can decide, for example, between a dialogue that requires few keystrokes but difficult retrieval from memory or one that involves more keystrokes but is easier to remember.
3. Estimating the total time for task performance with sufficient accuracy to make decisions about how many people are needed to staff the performance of a repetitive operational task on a computer.
4. Providing the base from which both to calculate training time and to guide training documentation to help the user determine in which situations which method is most efficient.
5. Knowing which stages of activity take the longest time or produce the most errors, in directing research toward the aspects of human-computer interaction that will have strong future performance implications.

Card et al. (1980a, 1980b, 1983) proposed a framework for building such analytic models of human performance with computers. This framework represented a significant advance from modeling in cognitive psychology in that many of the processes contributing to the full cycle of perception to action were modeled together and the knowledge that is considered necessary to perform a task was described in enough detail to generate predictions about human behavior in real, naturalistic tasks.

The framework has two key components. The first is a general characterization of the human information-processing system, in terms of both a system architecture and quantitative parameters of component performance. This they called the *Model Human Processor* (MHP), and it summarized a large body of research from cognitive psychology. The second key component is a way of describing what the user needs to know in order to perform computer-based tasks, a model called *GOMS*. The GOMS model—actually a family of models—describes the knowledge necessary and the four cognitive components of skilled performance in tasks: goals, operators, methods, and selection rules.

The GOMS framework provided Card et al. with the basis for predicting the methods and operators users would follow in carrying out a particular well-known task (the goal) and, given a method, how long that task would take. Figure 1 shows the steps a user proceeds through in using a piece of software (adapted from Norman, 1986). The user perceives activity on the screen, evaluates whether it is what is expected given the goals the user is trying to accomplish, sets up an intention of the next step, retrieves the way to enact this intent on this system, and executes the appropriate motor movements. This produces new activity on the screen, and the user cycles through the process again. The original GOMS framework focused on explaining the selection from memory of methods appropriate to the situation (the goal and intention phases of Figure 1) and the time to specify and to execute the action.

The strength of this approach is its ability to predict the time it takes a skilled user to execute a task based on the composite of actions of retrieving plans from long-term memory, choosing among alternative available methods depending on features of the task at hand, keeping track of what has been done and what needs to be done, and executing the motor movements necessary for the keyboard and mouse. To make useful predictions, GOMS assumes that routine cognitive skills can be described as a serial sequence of cognitive operations and motor activities. Each of these actions has a time parameter that is independent of the particular context within a task and is

Figure 1. **The seven steps of user activities involved in the performance of a computer-based task (based on Norman, 1986).**

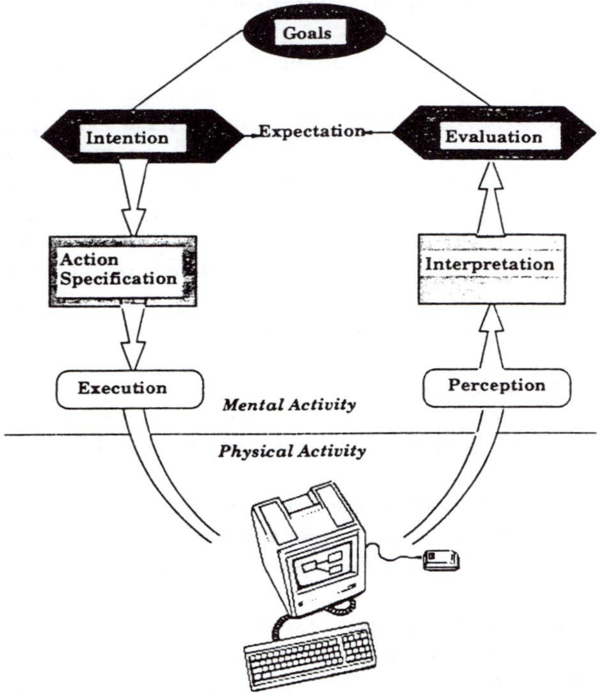

constant across tasks. Card et al. (1983) proposed such a theory, more constrained than general cognitive theories, in order to make engineering calculations.

Time parameters for external actions (and one internal action, that of retrieving the next unit of a plan) were estimated from empirical data derived from people using text editors, graphics systems, and some functions from the operating system of a variety of software. These numbers were generally obtained from a regression model, in which each unit task was assumed to consist of a set of keystrokes, hand movements, mental retrievals, and the like. Over a wide set of unit tasks from a variety of systems, values were obtained for these component processes. In later work, times for new parameters were derived in a similar manner except by Olson and Nilsen (1988). In their work, they recorded the time for every external act in a "keystroke capture" program, not just the total time for a task. Their regression analyses, therefore, included many more data points, each of smaller size, with each data point being a composite of a set of parameters relevant to that individual moment, not a sum over many different acts.

Card et al. (1983) found parameters that were very consistent across tasks. Of note were:

1. A keystroke, called **k,** for a midskilled typist is **280 msec.**
2. A single mental operator, called **M,** often interpreted as the time to retrieve the next chunk of information from long-term memory into WM is **1.35 s.**
3. Pointing, called **P,** to a target on a small display with a mouse takes on average **1.1 sec** (though the time is variable according to Fitts's law).
4. Moving the hands, called **H,** from the keyboard to the mouse takes **400 msec.**

An analyst or designer using these parameters to predict how long a particular task would take was given heuristics about where in the task retrieval of the next unit theoretically took place (where to put the **M**s) and when to insert the amount of time the system takes to respond. For example, retrieval (**M**) occurs at each unit boundary (a word, a single symbol or function key, a string of movements with a step key). Accordingly, if a subject were going to enter a formula in a spreadsheet by pointing with cursor-step keys to the cells that contain the desired values, a formula for adding the contents of cells from B22 to B29 would include:

```
@   s  u m  (   ^ ^ ^ ^ ^ ^ ^ ^ ^ ^ ^ ^  ·   ^  ^ ^ ^ ^ ^  )<ret>
MK  Mk k k  Mk  Mk k k k k k k k k k k  Mk  Mk k k k k k  Mk Mk
```

which adds up to:

8 **M**s and 26 **k**s
$8(1.35) + 26(.280) = 18.08$ s.

Using the small set of parameters with associated times derived from a large set of tasks, they were able to account for 90% of the variance in predicting unit task times such as the foregoing (Card et al., 1983, p. 294).

1.1. Limitations of the GOMS Approach

From the outset, it was clear that the GOMS approach to user modeling had well-defined strengths and weaknesses. Various GOMS models, particularly the keystroke-level model, provided good quantitative fits to the performance times of skilled users during errorless performance. Indeed, the parameters were stable enough so that performance in appropriate new situations could be predicted without the need to estimate parameters from the data. This ability to derive parameter-free estimates is part of what makes the GOMS approach useful in design, because it allows comparisons of different design alternatives. This is the key feature of the engineering approach that the GOMS models reflect.

One potential limitation of the GOMS model is that the initial work reported by Card et al. was carried out in a limited range of domains. There is always the question of whether the framework holds up when it is taken into new domains.

But there are more serious questions about the value of GOMS. Although there are many critiques of GOMS (e.g., Carroll & Campbell, 1986; Karat, 1988; Wilson, Barnard, Green, & MacLean, 1988), the most explicitly detailed list came from Card et al. (1980) themselves in their original framing of the model. A compilation of these shortcomings includes:

1. The model applied to skilled users, not to beginners or intermediates. Such *nonskilled users* spend considerable time engaged in problem-solving activities, rather than simply retrieving and executing plans, and move smoothly between problem solving and skilled behavior.
2. The model gave an account of skilled performance at asymptote but no account of either *learning* of the system or its *recall* after a period of disuse, nor how to design an easily learned consistent interface.
3. The model focused on errorless performance and, thus, gave no account of the *errors* that frequently occur even in skilled performance.
4. The model was most explicit about elementary perceptual and motor components of skilled behavior but tended to treat the *cognitive processes* in skilled behavior in a less differentiated fashion.
5. The model was developed exclusively for tasks in which the principal components that were being modeled could reasonably be assumed to be serial in nature. However, tasks have a substantial number of component processes that, at some level, must occur in *parallel*.
6. The model does not address *mental workload*—how much must be held in mind while using the system.
7. The model addresses only the usability of a task on a system and does not address *functionality*, that is, what tasks should be performed by the computer.
8. The model does not address the amount and kind of *fatigue* users experience using a system.
9. The model does not account for *individual differences* among users.
10. The model does not provide guidance in predicting whether users will judge the system to be either useful or satisfying, or whether the system will be globally *acceptable*.
11. The model stops short of addressing any aspects of how computer-supported work fits or misfits office or organizational life.

It is useful to ask which of these objectives have been addressed in subsequent work, which remain possible but unexplored, and which seem entirely beyond the scope of even an extended GOMS model.

1.2. Plan of This Article

The purpose of this article is to review these advances in cognitive modeling and to outline the significant problems that remain for both the designer in search of guidance and the cognitive psychologist interested in how cognitive processes interact to produce behavior of the sort exhibited in human-computer interaction. We do this by addressing the three main points.

First, we review the extent to which the quantitative estimates of task components described by Card et al. (1983) have held up in further research. Subsequent studies of skilled performance in several different domains have provided strong confirmation for the original work.

Second, a number of investigators have taken the Card et al. (1983) framework in new directions. We examine three in particular: the study of learning and transfer, the study of errors, and the analysis of parallel processes. In each case, the basic Card et al. framework is preserved, but additional value is added.

Third, a number of limitations remain, either because cognitive science currently provides no guidance to this aspect of human-computer interaction or because the questions require a wholly different modeling approach. We close with an examination of the place of cognitive modeling in the broader context of research on human-computer interaction.

2. ADVANCES IN MODELING SPECIFIC SERIAL COMPONENTS

A number of researchers have followed the spirit of GOMS and the MHP in empirical explorations. These investigations are direct tests of both the assumption of serial processing and the assumption that time parameters are constant across a wide range of tasks.

We have gathered the different parameters that various researchers have found; displayed them in Figures 3, 5, and 6; and summarized them in Figure 7. Each figure displays parameters as found in Card et al.'s (1983) empirical work and in their review of the relevant cognitive psychology literature as summarized in the MHP. Added to these parameters are values found in studies with a similar spirit: studies of entering editor commands with keystroke codes, entering formulas in spreadsheets, and so on. The new parameters are listed in italics in these three figures.

Figure 2. The seven steps of user activities involved in the performance of a computer-based task, annotated with known cognitive processes.

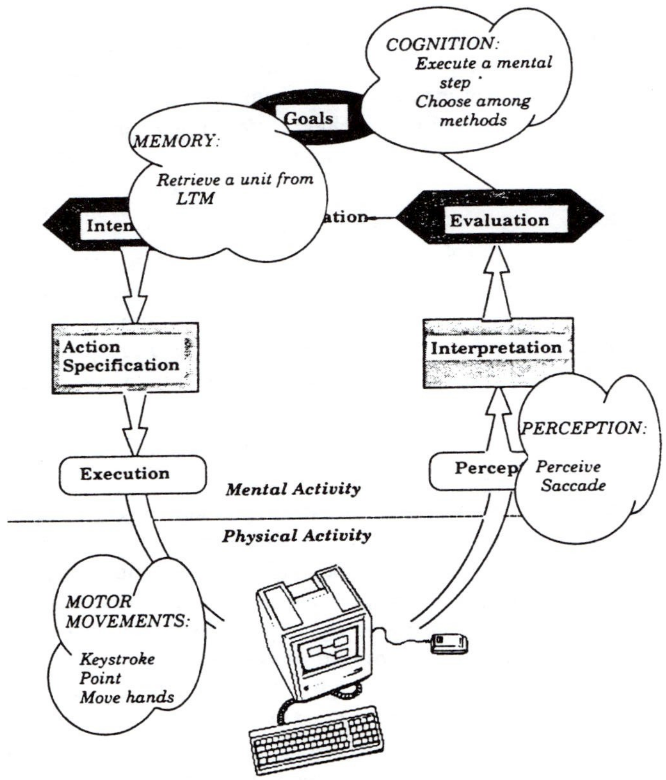

The parameters cluster into three general classes: motor movement, perception, and memory and cognition. These general classes of behavior map onto the seven steps of user activity as shown in Figure 2.

2.1. Motor Movements

Figure 3 summarizes the values found in various studies relevant to keyboard entry, using a mouse, and moving hands back and forth from keyboard to pointing devices.

Keying

A set of parameters accounts for the time to enter a keystroke in a normal typing task, the actual value depending on the skill level of the typist, the

Figure 3. **Parameters describing component processes in motor movement.**

Enter a keystroke		
Average non-secty typist	280 msec	CMN
Best typist (120 wpm)	80 msec	CMN
Good typist	120 msec	CMN
Average skilled typist (60 wpm)	200 msec	CMN
Typing random letters	500 msec	CMN
Typing complex codes	750 msec	CMN
Worst typist	1200 msec	CMN
Entering spreadsheet formulas		
Lotus	*330 msec*	*O&N*
Multiplan	*220 msec*	*O&N*
Entering column/width commands		
Lotus	*280 msec*	*O&N*
Multiplan	*230 msec*	*O&N*
Enter command abbreviations	*230 msec*	*J&N*
Expert typing cross-hand digraphs	*170 msec*	*J&N*
Expert typing same-hand digraphs	*220 msec*	*J&N*
Point with a mouse		
Average value, small screen, menu shaped target	1100 msec	CMN
Varies with distance and size of target	$1.0 + .10 \log_2(D/S+.5)$sec	CMN
Average value, small distance, menu target	*1900 msec*	*WSN*
Varies with distance and size of target	$.80 + .23 \log_2(D/S+.5)$*sec*	*WSN*
Move hands from keyboard to pointing device or back		
To mouse	360 msec	CMN
To joystick	260 msec	CMN
To cursor(arrow) keys	210 msec	CMN
To function keys	320 msec	CMN

CMN = Card, Moran, and Newell, 1983
O&N = Olson and Nilsen, 1988
J&N = John and Newell, 1989
WSN = Walker, Smelcer, and Nilsen, 1988

frequency with which the particular key is used, and the predictability and continuity of the text to be typed. That is, regular transcription typing is faster than entering formulas, for example, because numerals are less frequently typed and often the placement of the number and symbol keys requires perceptual search in addition to simple hand motor movements. Card et al. (1983) reported parameters ranging from 80 msec per keystroke for a typist of 135 words per minute (wpm) to 1200 msec per key for a user unfamiliar with the keyboard. An average typist is reported to take 280 msec per keystroke.

Two other researchers confirmed the basic keystroke parameters. Olson and Nilsen (1988) found two separate keystroke times from their examination of the moment by moment activity in entering and changing spreadsheets. They found a keystroke time of 330 and 220 msec for entering formulas in Lotus and Multiplan, respectively, and 280 and 230 msec for entering keystrokes in a task that changes the widths of columns in Lotus and Multiplan, respectively.

In their investigations of users entering command abbreviations, John and her colleagues (John & Newell, 1987, 1989, in press; John, Rosenbloom, & Newell, 1985) found keystrokes to be 230 msec in one, and 269 msec in the other. A more recent investigation (John & Newell, 1989) found that in tasks involving transcription typing, each keystroke was heavily dependent on skill level and task, with values ranging from 70 msec to 220 msec per key. These times correspond to the 200 msec for an average typist (60 wpm) from Card et al. (1983) if we assume a 50–50 distribution of crosshand, same-hand pairs:

$$(170 + 220)/2 = 195 \text{ msec.}$$

All these values are very close to the middle of the range of values designated by Card et al. (1983) and slightly smaller than the value designated in their work to represent typing random letters. These tasks, however, are much more predictable than typing random letters and are often performed by more skilled users.

Moving a Mouse

Pointing with a mouse at objects whose distances and target sizes covered a variety of screens requires an average 1100 msec per selection, according to Card et al. (1983). Although this value is appropriate for standard interfaces, such as choosing a ⅜-in. sized menu item on an 8½-in. diagonal screen (as in a Macintosh SE), it is known to vary with the distance of the movement and the size of the target, following Fitts's law (Fitts & Peterson, 1964). Because screens now regularly exceed the standard 8½ in., and the user more often needs to point to scroll bars, window sizers, graphic-object "handles," and icons that are both small and widely scattered on big screens, more detail is needed to assess this movement time accurately.

Card et al. (1983) explored the relationship between target size and distance travelled in mouse movements, empirically determining the constants in Fitts's law:

$$T = 1.03 + .096\log_2(D/S + .5).$$

The form of this relationship is interesting. There is a large constant time of 1 s to begin moving, no matter what the distance. Adjustments to this base time are in increments of 100 msec each time the distance traveled is 1½ times as long as the size of the target. That is, this formula suggests that it takes about 300 msec to reach the top of the screen from the middle[1] and 100 msec to travel about ½ in. (to the second menu item) on the Macintosh to hit the ⅜-in. menu item, about 1400 msec total.

Walker, Smelcer, and Nilsen (1989) explored the variations in this relationship to predict the time to choose items from nested menus, menus that present a second array of choices after the user chooses from a first menu, usually in side-by-side strips. Their empirical evaluation determined that the time to move to a target on the menu did indeed follow Fitts's law:

$$T = .81 + .23\log_2(D/S + .5).$$

Although the initial movement time of 810 msec is close to the 1030 msec of Card et al. (1983), the increment of 230 msec per unit distance and target size is twice that found earlier. This difference is likely accounted for by the fact the distance in the nested menus they used included a composite of the user selecting the first item with a single downward motion, a turn to the right in the item's slot, and a move to the edge, where the second set of items is displayed. Thus, the distances used in the Walker et al. (1989) study include the turns, as well as horizontal and vertical distance segments. The time is slower because it includes other, more subtle component processes.

An Example of the Application of GOMS and MHP to Design Generation

Walker et al. (1989) went a step further, using these facts to drive a design process, by demonstrating how GOMS can constrain a designer's search in such a way as to lead to large improvements in performance.

With the goal of shortening this total menu-selection time, Walker et al. made three adjustments to the design of menus. One redesign shortened the total distance the user had to travel to select an item by making the menu "pop

[1] But see the discussion of borders, later in this section.

Figure 4. **Fittsized menus: Menus whose target areas grow with the distance the user has to travel to get to them. In these particular menus, the cursor begins in the middle-left of the menu. On the right panel is the menu with "borders" on the top, right, and bottom edge, boundaries beyond which the cursor cannot move.**

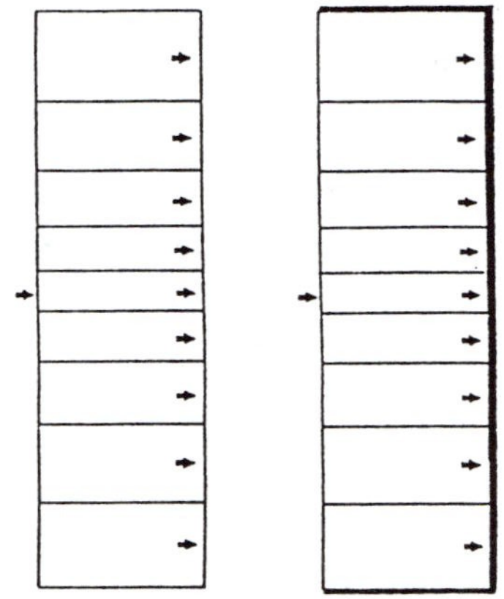

up" to the right of the cursor instead of below it. Though the average travel distance in this design would be halved, there was question whether the user might experience additional delays due to the uncertainty about which direction the movement had to be launched. The results showed that the time to select an item was far shorter when the menu popped up to the right of the cursor than when the menu appeared below it. The time to travel to the target was a much larger determinant of the total time than the small increment of time to decide whether to begin to move up or down.

Two new menu types followed, both intended to reduce the selection time by making the target bigger. Menus can be constructed so that the target size grows as the distance from the cursor's starting position increases. These are called "Fittsized menus" displayed on the left of Figure 4. In this menu, the further the user has to travel, the bigger the target. The mean reduction in this study, however, was only 80 msec, a small effect. Fitts's law, however, tells us to expect this small effect. It is a complicated arrangement, because as the targets grow, so does the overall distance to be traveled. But, in general, we would have to increase the size of the furthest target by a factor of nearly 3 to reduce the travel time over 100 msec, for example, making the fourth target item 1 in. tall if the first target item is the standard Macintosh ⅜ in.

In the third design on the quest for shorter selection times, Walker et al. (1989) made the target size effectively much bigger by putting a virtual border on the top, right, and bottom edges of the pop-up menu, a border beyond which the cursor could not move even though the mouse moved. This is similar to the border that the Macintosh interface has at the top of the screen. The cursor will not move off the screen, even though the user has moved the mouse to a place that would translate beyond the screen edge if it were unconstrained. In this situation, shown on the right-hand side of Figure 4, the target size is effectively very large and much easier to hit. This kind of menu reduced the selection time by a large amount. The average selection time over all menu positions in the original design was 1.9 s. Adding the borders reduced the average time by 450 msec, a reduction of nearly 25%.

Hand Movements

Hand movement time is the time needed to move from the space bar of the keyboard until the pointing control begins to move the cursor. This is a large-muscle movement also well characterized by Fitts's law; the time to reach a target (in this case, the mouse or joystick) is a function of the distance to the target and its size. This time was calculated from behavioral data to be approximately 360 msec, a relatively small, fixed amount of time because the mouse is typically in about the same position each time, and the target itself is large (see Card et al., 1983, Figure 7.4). This is a much smaller time than pointing with the mouse to a specific intercharacter location on the screen because of the large effect of size of the target on the overall time.

Card et al. (1983) found empirical variation among parameters for different pointing devices, presumably because they were at various distances from the home position on the keyboard and because the targets are of different sizes. The user took 360 msec to find a mouse and start to move, 260 msec to find the joystick (because it is bigger), 210 msec to find the cursor or arrow keys (both nearer and smaller), and 320 msec to find the function keys (presumably because they are a few inches away but relatively small).

2.2. Perception

Summary values for the known aspects of seeing items on the screen are summarized in Figure 5. These values are primarily from the summary of the literature included in Card et al.'s (1983) MHP, although John and Newell (1989, in press) add some recent empirical support for these values.

Clearly, by recognizing features of the current task and assessing some of the parameters necessary to do a task (e.g., the letters to be edited or components of the formula to be entered), perception and scanning are involved. The perceptual processor is clocked at **100 msec** in the summary of the MHP in Card et al. (1983, Figure 2.1) and a saccade (the time to move and take in information in each jump) at **230 msec.** Although neither perception nor scanning parameters are included in the empirical work of Card et al. (1983), John and Newell (in press) used the 100 msec for the perception of lights and simple symbols in a stimulus-response compatibility

Figure 5. **Parameters describing component processes in perception.**

Recognize or perceive

Time to respond to brief light	100 msec	MHP
It varies with intensity, brighter is faster	50 -- 200 msec	MHP
Recognize a 6-letter word	*340 msec*	*J&N*
	314 msec	*J&N*

Make a saccade

Time for the eye to jump to next location	230 msec	MHP

MHP = Model Human Processor from Card, Moran, and Newell, 1983
J&N = John and Newell, in press and 1989

task. When they combined it with a cognitive operator (discussed later) and standard information theory to calculate how many bits of information had to be processed by the cognitive processor, they obtained very good predictions. This is not a direct derivation of the perceptual parameter, but indirect support for its value.

Similar in style, John and Newell (1989, in press) determined that perceiving a six-letter word took **314 msec** in a stimulus–response compatibility task that involved entering abbreviations for command names. Because perception of words includes recognition, some verbal encoding, or retrieval of meaning in addition to simple perception, it is not surprising to find this value a bit higher than the others.

Let us consider an example of application of the theory. A related "scanning" parameter was identified in the Olson and Nilsen (1988) study of experts using spreadsheet software. The Olson and Nilsen scanning parameter was identified in situations in which the user was scanning a screen for additional information, the row and column coordinates on the spreadsheet border, in known locations. This scanning took an additional 2300 msec. Why is this so much longer than the perception values discussed earlier? Obviously, from the discrepancy in not just the value but the order of magnitude of these parameters, something more than simple perception is likely to be operating.

In the Olson and Nilsen task, the user must look for the cell addresses by following the row or column guide lines to the border where the row or cell indicators are displayed (e.g., *B,* on the column indicator and *22* on the row indicator) and then retrieve them for execution as keystrokes. The total time for this composite of scanning, storing, and retrieving was measurred at **2300 msec.** If we use the available parameters for a saccade and memory retrieval (in Figure 3), then we can calculate a reasonable storage time (one for the *B,* one for the *22*) to be 130 msec, close to the parametric value to perceive something. In more detail, if the 2300 msec is a composite of:

A saccade to the row line	230 msec
A storage of the row label	*130 msec*
A saccade to the column head	230 msec
A storage of the column label	*130 msec*
A saccade to the cell in which typing is to start	230 msec
Retrieval of the row and column labels	1350 msec
Total	2300 msec

where the 130 msec for storing a row label in working memory is the *derived* value from this calculation.

These parameter estimates, of course, warrant further empirical verification. But it is intriguing that this task can so nicely be decomposed into reasonable processes with time parameters from cognitive engineering.

This example illustrates the use of GOMS and MHP in understanding a design issue. The parameter Olson and Nilsen (1988) found was an order of magnitude too large; GOMS identifies this as an issue of grain size of task. It encourages closer examination of a linear sequence of more microscopic operations identified in previous research. Here, the result was that the 2.3 s time was not simple perception, but rather a series including search, storage, and recall, the last of which is known to have an associated long time. This might lead the designer from a solution that makes scanning per se shorter to one that eliminates the need for users to store and recall coordinate values.

2.3. Memory and Cognitive Processes

Figure 6 summarizes the values found in various studies relevant to memory retrieval, executing steps in a mental procedure, and choosing among methods.

Memory Retrieval

At the heart of the Card et al. (1983) model is *M,* called "mental," often interpreted as the time to retrieve the next unit of information. It is assumed from the listed heuristics about when this special operation occurs that this is

Figure 6. **Parameters describing component processes in memory and cognition.**

Retrieve a unit from LTM to WM		
Retrieve a command name or delimiter	1350 msec	CMN
Retreive a random command abbreviation	*1200 msec*	*J&N*
	1209 msec	*J&N*
	1200 msec	*J&N*
Retrieve the next part of a formula		
Multiplan (cursor method)	*1100 msec*	*O&N*
Lotus (cursor method)	*990 msec*	*O&N*
Lotus (typing method)	*1350 msec*	*O&N*
Retrieve command part in column width task		
Multiplan	*1160 msec*	*O&N*
Lotus	*1080 msec*	*O&N*
Repeated retrieval of same command		
Lotus	*660 msec*	*O&N*
Execute a mental step		
Cognitive Processor (the contents of WM initiate associatively-linked actions in LTM)	70 msec	MHP
Execute next rule in a formal model of skilled performance	*100 msec*	*BKP*
Execute next step in decoding abbreviations	*66 msec*	*J&N*
	60 msec	*J&N*
	50 msec	*J&N*
Choose among methods		
"Mental" operator, choose, retrieve	620 msec	CMN
Choose whether to type or point to cells in entering a spreadsheet formula	*1760 msec*	*O&N*

MHP = Model Human Processor from Card, Moran, and Newell, 1983
CMN = Card, Moran, and Newell, 1983
BKP = Bovair, Kieras and Polson, 1985
J&N = John and Newell, 1985, 1989,1989, in press.
O&N = Olson and Nilsen, 1988

retrieval of well-known units from long-term memory (LTM) for placement in WM, ready then to be either executed by a motor processor or further decomposed by subsequent retrieval from LTM. This value is empirically determined to be **1350 msec**.

John and Newell (1987, 1989, in press) and John et al. (1985) empirically determined a parameter for retrieval from LTM to be **1200 msec**. This is described as being retrieval of a completely arbitrary association between a stimulus word and its required letter-combination response. Olson and Nilsen (1988), in their study of spreadsheet software use, found a parametric value for retrieval of syntax parts in entering a formula as **1100 msec** in Multiplan and **1350 msec** in Lotus 1-2-3. Retrieving the command parts (e.g., the keyboard equivalent for a command from a menu) in a column-width task was **1160 msec** in Multiplan and **1080 msec** in Lotus.

Olson and Nilsen found another interesting result in their study of Lotus 1-2-3. In their study, the user entered the column width command four times in a row. Lotus 1-2-3 has no feature that allows you to set the column width for a range of columns. One can set either the whole spreadsheet's default column width or one column at a time. Thus, the only way to set a range (which we asked them to do) is to repeat the same action once for each of the columns desired. Again the times for memory retrieval were calculated. The first time the user set the column width, the retrieval time was **1100 msec**. On the second, third, and fourth trials (repeated rapidly in succession), the retrieval times dropped and remained flat, calculated to be **660 msec**, half that of the first retrieval. This is not a simple practice effect; the repeated act speeded up only the memory access, not the keying times. The times for the keystrokes were calculated individually for each trial and found to be constant at 280 msec.

Executing Steps in a Task

GOMS provides an explicit representation of the mental steps involved in executing a task. It catalogues the retrieval of a goal and its subgoals, the decision to select a method to fit the particulars of the current situation, the retrieval of the motor movements necessary to execute the command, and the execution of each of those command components. Card et al. (1983) estimated from the psychological literature that the execution of each procedural step should take about **70 msec**.

Kieras and Polson (Kieras, 1988; Kieras & Bovair, 1986; Kieras & Polson, 1985; Polson & Kieras, 1985; Polson, Muncher, & Engelbeck, 1986) made the GOMS representation much more explicit by programming the procedures in production system formalism, discussed in more detail later in this article. This formalism allowed a number of predictions of behavior far wider than those covered in Card et al. (1983), many of which are mentioned in later sections. Of note here is that from empirical studies of people carrying out a wide variety of procedures, they estimate that each production requires about **100 msec** to execute.

Similarly, John et al. (1985), John (1988), and John and Newell (1987, 1989, in press) determined from their studies of people entering command abbreviations that each mental step that translates the command word into an abbreviation takes **between 50 and 70 msec**. Even though these mental steps include a variety of processing acts, for example, storing notes in WM, calculating, and deciding, as well as very different specification languages that defined the cognitive steps, the finding across studies is remarkably consistent.

Choosing Among Methods

In the MHP, Card et al. (1983) assumed that the more choices for a response, the longer the expected response time. This is based on the work of Hick (1952) on choice reaction time tasks. Card et al. (1983) estimated that mental operators for choosing among appropriate methods is **620 msec**. Very little additional empirical validation followed this initial determination.

Olson and Nilsen (1988) found a much higher value for a similarly described process. When a system presents the user with a choice of methods, the user requires additional time to make the choice. In Lotus 1-2-3, the user has choices for indicating the elements of a formula—by typing in the cell coordinates (e.g., B22) or by pointing to the appropriate cell with the cursor, moved by step keys. In Multiplan, the contrasted piece of software in the study, there is only one way—pointing to the appropriate cell with the cursor using the step keys. Although the time to enter the formulas with the same method took exactly the same amount of time across the two packages, users of Lotus took an additional **1760 msec** before entering to decide which method to use. The time to start the formula in Lotus (which offered two methods) was 4.63 s, whereas in Multiplan (which offered only one method) it took only 2.87 s. In contrast, in another task, setting column widths, in which both Lotus and Multiplan offered only one method, the start times were identical.

Although the overall direction of this choice relationship and Hick's law are the same, the effects are a different order of magnitude. Hick's law predicts a set of simple, noncognitive reaction times in the range of 200 msec, similar in size to the MHP cognitive step. The time to choose among methods in Card et al. (1983) is 600 msec; in the study of spreadsheets, the time is on the order of 2 s. This difference suggests that a choice between methods in human-computer interaction is a more complex cognitive task, requiring several to many cognitive steps to be executed. These steps would differ from task to task. Also, some of the conditions on which methods are chosen require an estimate (e.g., of how far away certain values are), some perception of values on the screen, or a quick examination of how immediately memorable some parameters are, all of which would add complex component times to this overall effect.

Figure 7. **Summary of cognitive engineering parameters derived as the median of values obtained in Figures 3, 5, and 6.**

Enter a keystroke	230 msec
Point with a mouse	1500 msec
Move hands to mouse	360 msec
Perceive	100 msec
Make a saccade	230 msec
Retrieve from memory	1200 msec
Execute a mental step	70 msec
Choose among methods	1250 msec

2.4. Predicting Composite Performance From These Parameters

The data from Figures 3, 5, and 6 are summarized in brief engineering form in Figure 7. For each of the components, we have taken as the single value the median of the values obtained in similar circumstances. For example, for the time to retrieve from memory, we take the median of the nine values in the top of Figure 6, resulting in a value of 1200 msec. The one exception to this is the value for moving hands is listed for the movement to a mouse, the most common motion in the applications we have analyzed.

Let us consider an example of using these parameters in a wholly new task. We use these times to analyze a very different task studied in a different laboratory to illustrate the generality of the parameters and the component processes involved in GOMS and MHP.

Young and MacLean (1988) measured the times of people entering a block of values in a spreadsheet two different ways. The user could either enter each value separately, pointing to the next cell with the mouse (called the *Mouse* method), or set up a procedure by which each Enter key would advance the cursor automatically into the cell to the right of the last one. In this second method (called the *Menu* method), the user then had to use the mouse only when the next line was started. They found that the Mouse method took 4.19 s for each cell to be entered; the Menu method took 2.81 s to start each line and 2.46 to type each cell's two-digit number with the Enter key advancing the location to the right.

Using parameters from Figure 7, we calculate that the Mouse method consists of:

Moving the hand to the mouse	360 msec
Clicking the mouse (same as a keystroke)	230 msec
Moving the hand to the keyboard	360 msec
Retrieving two digits	1200 msec
Typing two digits @230 each	460 msec
Retrieving the end action	1200 msec
Typing the <ret> key	230 msec
Total	4040 msec

This result compares well with the **4.19 s** obtained in the study, a 3% error.

We further assume that task of starting each new line in the Menu method involves:

Moving hand to mouse	360 msec
Pointing to a new line with mouse	1500 msec
Clicking the mouse	230 msec
Moving hand to keyboard	360 msec
Total	2450 msec

This result compares with the **2.81 s** found, with a 13% error.

And the task of typing each number into the cell in the Menu method involves:

Retrieving (or looking for) two digits	1200 msec
Typing two digits @230 msec each	460 msec
Retrieving the end action	1200 msec
Typing the <ret>	230 msec
Total	3090 msec

This result compares with **2.46 s** found in the empirical study, a 26% error.

These calculations could be challenged in a number of ways, each challenge focusing on the inclusion or exclusion of an operation, especially the unobservable mental ones. These challenges would be important if we were interested in the details of skilled performance in these specific tasks, and the challenges should be pursued when we are doing research on the discovery of new parameters. What is more important for cognitive engineering and its use in design, however, is that these calculated values are within an average of 14% error of the observed values, accurate enough at this level of analysis to be useful in the calculation of overall task times. They are certainly in the right order of magnitude, even within the 20% error criterion often acceptable in early design stages. These numbers are accurate enough, for example, for us to determine in a large task how many task units could be performed each day by a dedicated clerk and, thus, how many clerks would have to be on staff to perform a work load of a target size.

In summary, although there are potential problems with the basic assumptions of GOMS and the MHP that the component processes are serial (discussed later in the Parallel Processes section) and that performance times in any one task are independent of context, these assumptions have served well in a variety of basic computer-based tasks. These tasks include remembering and entering different kinds of keyboard commands, using a text editor, manipulating files in an operating system, using graphics programs, and entering formulas and changing column widths in spreadsheet programs. All in all, within the limits imposed by the initial formulation, the model has done quite well in subsequent evaluations.

3. EXTENSIONS OF THE BASIC FRAMEWORK

Many critics have argued that the original ground rules set up for such models are overly restrictive and, thus, limit the usefulness of this approach for human-computer interaction applications. In this spirit, a number of investigators have tried to take this cognitive engineering approach beyond the scope of the original GOMS formulation. We now turn to these extensions, focusing on three areas: the analysis of learning and transfer, the analysis of errors, and the treatment of parallel processes.

The first two classes of extensions have been made possible by the explicit modeling of the user's knowledge of grammatical rules and of both knowledge and performance in terms of production systems.

Grammars. Reisner (1981, 1984) and Payne and Green (1986) used grammars to make explicit the knowledge a user must have in order to translate from goals to actions in a particular system. Grammatical rules are similar in spirit (though not form) to the goal decomposition and methods in GOMS. They are more a model of knowledge content (competence) than of a full system that can "run" to produce user performance (Green, Schiele, & Payne, 1988). In the spirit of cognitive engineering, however, these representations do provide a countable entity: the number of rules. And, in Payne and Green's (1986) Task-Action Grammar (TAG), there is an explicit aspect of the content that predicts learning: the relationship between the features encoded in the rules and the natural world associations of the user.

To illustrate what the elements of a grammar look like, we use the TAG notation for a small segment of a full grammar. TAG consists of commands, features of the goal (e.g., the direction of movement in which you want to move a cursor in text, like forward or backward), a "dictionary of tasks" (which shows the full set of actions covered and helps analysts count the coverage of each rule), and rules that translate goals into actions. Figure 8

Figure 8. **A portion of a task-action grammar for EMACS, for moving a cursor around text (adapted from Green, Schiele, & Payne, 1988).**

Commands:

Goal	Action
Move cursor one character forward	cntl-C
Move cursor one character backward	meta-C
Move cursor one word forward	cntl-W
Move cursor one word backward	meta-W

Features, possible values:

Direction	forward, backward
Unit	character, word

Rules

Task[Direction,Unit]	→ Symbol[Direction] + Letter[unit]
Symbol[forward]	→ "cntl"
Symbol[backward]	→ "meta"
Letter[word]	→ "W"
Letter[character]	→ "C"

illustrates the commands, the features, and the rules that map a small set of goals of moving a cursor around text to the word processor EMACS. The small set of rules here says that if the task is to move in a direction a particular unit of jump, you should type a symbol for direction, where forward is <cntl> and backward is <meta>, and follow it with a typed letter for the unit, where a unit the size of a word is *W* and the size of a character is *C*. This illustrates the form of the rules, their size, and an example of a good real-world mapping in that the letter used for units the size of a character and word are their own first letters.

Production Systems. Kieras and Polson (Bovair, Kieras, & Polson, 1990; Kieras, 1988; Kieras & Bovair, 1986; Kieras & Polson, 1985; Polson & Kieras, 1985; Polson et al., 1986) have used production systems to represent the GOMS structure of task knowledge and significant aspects of the MHP (significantly, the goal stack and a WM for storing parameters). This substantially improves the original GOMS theory, because it, like the grammars, makes the underlying knowledge much more explicit. Further, although the production system may be difficult to write (Kieras, 1988), once it is specified, one can run the program to check it for completeness and accuracy. And, once programmed, one can quantify a number of features of the knowledge and processing to predict both errors and learning time behavior.

To illustrate what a production system formalism of GOMS looks like, Figure 9 presents a section of the production system for writing a database

Figure 9. **Five rules written in production system formalism. These rules help guide the behavior of a user in deciding to write a crucial join statement in a database query in the popular language, SQL.**

```
Rule 1:    (StartUp.SeeIfJoinNeeded
  IF       ((GOAL SeeIfJoinNeeded)
           (NOT(NOTE SeeingIfJoinNeeded TRUE))
  THEN     ((Add NOTE SeeingIfJoinNeeded TRUE)
           (Add STEP CountTables)))
Rule 2:    (CountTables
  IF       ((GOAL SeeIfJoinNeeded)
           (STEP CountTables))
  THEN     ((DoTask Count NumberOfTables *NumberOfTables)
           (Add NOTE Number OfTables *NumberOfTables)
           (Delete STEP CountTables)
           (Add STEP AddJoinNote)))
Rule 3:    (IfNumberOfTables=2ThenAddNOTEJoinAndCleanup
  IF       ((GOAL SeeIfJoinNeeded)
           (STEP AddJoinNote)
           (NOTE NumberOfTables 2))
  THEN     ((Add NOTE JoinNeeded TRUE)
           (Delete STEP AddJoinNote)
           (Delete NOTE NumberOfTables ?NumberOfTables)
           (Add STEP CleanUp)))
Rule 4:    (IfNumberOfTablesNot=2, ThenCleanup
  IF       ((GOAL SeeIfJoinNeeded)
           (STEP AddJoinNote)
           (NOTE NumberOfTables 1))
  THEN     ((Delete STEP AddJoinNote)
           (Delete NOTE NumberOfTables ?NumberOfTables)
           (Add STEP Cleanup)))
Rule 5:    (CleanUp.SeeIfJoinNeeded
  IF       ((GOAL SeeIfJoinNeeded)
           (STEP CleanUp))
  THEN     ((Delete NOTE SeeingIfJoinNeeded TRUE)
           (Delete STEP CleanUp)
           (Add NOTE SawIfJoinNeeded TRUE)))
```

query in SQL, a popular language that has become the de facto standard in the industry (Smelcer, 1989). In this illustration are five IF–THEN rules that guide a user in deciding if in an SQL query a closing special statement (called a "join statement") is needed. It is needed if the user has asked for data that reside in two or more tables. The join statement tells the system how to link the data elements in the two tables. In Figure 9, the first rule sets up the goal, leaving a NOTE and a STEP in WM. The second rule performs the act of counting the number of tables used, stores that value in WM, deletes the goal of counting tables, and adds the STEP to add a note to the WM about needing the join statement. Each IF part of each rule checks for a match to the current goal (e.g., "GOAL SeeIfJoinNeeded" in the first rule) and the current notes in WM (e.g., "NOTE NumberOfTables 2" in the third rule). If there is a match, it executes other processes and adds and deletes notes and steps. This example illustrates the form and size of the productions and the putting and taking things off WM, both used in the discussions of learning and errors.

3.1. Learning and Transfer

Time to Learn

A significant shortcoming of the original GOMS framework was its restriction to skilled performance. A significant advance on this front is the work of Kieras and Polson focusing on both the time to learn new procedures and the transfer of training between procedures having various relationships to each other. For them, the explicit modeling of GOMS through production systems is the key. Kieras and Polson developed an extension of GOMS they called *Cognitive Complexity Theory* (see Polson, 1987, 1988). This theory provides a basis for making quantitative predictions about the time to learn each new piece of a task and the amount of transfer that could be expected in learning one new system or task after another.

Kieras and Polson first determined the number of steps in a procedure by counting the steps as encoded in a specialized language called NGOMSL. NGOMSL is the higher level programming language developed by Kieras (1988) to make the job of programming production system representations much easier. They then assessed the time it takes a person to learn the procedures. They studied learning under highly restrictive and controlled conditions, necessary in order to make the variance in learning times of a magnitude where one had some confidence in the quantitative estimates. They found that the time to learn each step took **30 s**, assuming a start-up or learning context time of 30 to 60 min.

This is much longer than the time estimated by Newell and Simon (1972), who calculated that learning each "chunk" of information took 5 to 10 s. The learning they referred to, however, is equivalent to learning a nonsense syllable, whereas for Kieras and Polson the learning was of steps in procedural knowledge, both the conditions under which it is appropriate and the actions associated with it. Ziegler, Vossen, and Hoppe (1986) report a **17 s** per production system step when the learning situation has some explanation associated with each piece to be learned. And Card (personal communication, January, 1989) reported **20 s** per production learning time.

These estimates vary. The authors themselves, however, claim that the variation has to do with the conditions under which the user is learning—for example, whether there is explanation associated with the steps being learned or whether opportunities for transfer are pointed out. And, of course, learners do not acquire knowledge about new systems under the carefully controlled, artificial circumstances of Kieras and Polson's research. Thus, it is much harder to know how to quantify learning times in more naturalistic situations.

What we find more promising, however, is that the values are the same order of magnitude over widely different situations and laboratories. Though nuances of training time per production will be interesting and research on this topic is to be encouraged, for our purposes here, the current "best guess" parameter is about **25 s** per production.

TAG (Payne & Green, 1986), because they also represent concrete aspects of the knowledge users must have to perform a task, similarly provides a basis from which to predict learning. Early rationales for using grammar representations were based on the argument that the number of rules determined the ease of learning, in that the more often a rule can be used, the more consistent a system is. Payne and Green (1989) argued that the number of rules is less critical than whether the features of those rules follow real-world features encoded in the user's memory already. Their empirical work demonstrated just this. A system described by 28 rules that had features described by well-known categories, one feature into one action, was learned nearly three times faster than one with 12 rules, but with complicated descriptions of the features of the situation to be attended. Although Payne and Green could have quantified learning time per rule, they did not because their argument made the content of the rules, not their number, the critical determinant of learning.

Transfer of Training From One System to the Other

Another, perhaps more generalizable aspect of Kieras and Polson's research has been the analysis of transfer between systems or components of systems. Their production system models make explicit exactly what it is that a person has to learn in acquiring knowledge of a new system. If productions are the units of learning, then a reasonable hypothesis is that the number of productions the two systems share provides a good metric for predictions of the amount of transfer. In other words, this analysis allows one to specify the exact effects of design consistency across systems.

In a series of studies, Kieras and Polson (Bovair et al., 1990; Kieras, 1988; Kieras & Bovair, 1986; Kieras & Polson, 1985; Polson & Kieras, 1985; Polson et al., 1986) have shown the predictive power of this approach. In a typical study, subjects learned to do various specific procedures on a computer system, and the time to master a new procedure was predicted to be a function of the number of new productions that would need to be learned. Because the procedures shared varying numbers of productions, there ought to be varying amounts of transfer or savings in learning as subjects learned a series of procedures. Figure 10 shows the results from a typical study. Here, subjects

Figure 10. **The fit of predictions of learning time to the number of new rules that have to be learned (from Polson, 1988).**

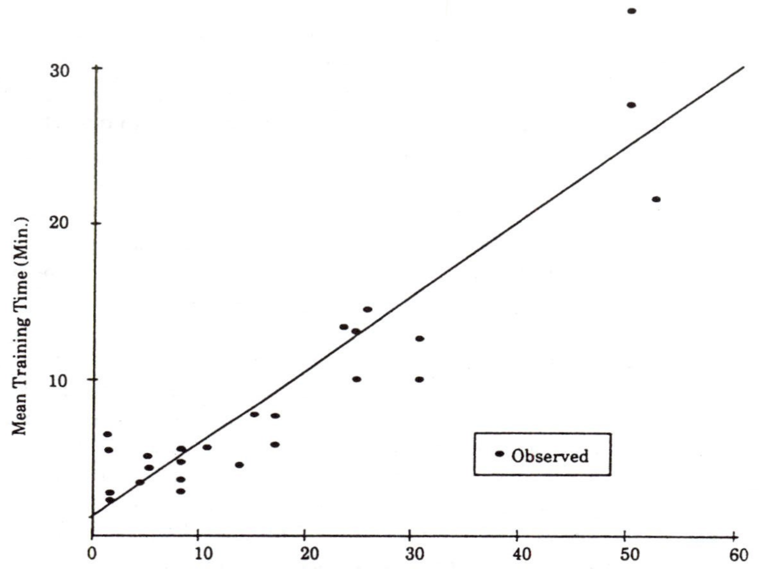

learned simple utility procedures for a floppy-disk-based microcomputer system, such as duplicating a diskette or printing a document stored on a diskette. Predicted values were based on the number of new productions to be learned, and observed values were based on learning the procedure to a criterion of learning under strict control.

These results are typical of a wide range of studies that have reviewed the learning of simple procedures. For example, Singley and Anderson (1988) found strong support for what is called the "identical elements model of transfer based on a production system representation of cognitive skill" (p. 223) in their study of transfer of text editors, both similar and dissimilar. This body of data shows the predictive power of the production system implementation of the GOMS model for characterizing transfer between procedures. In particular, it makes explicit and quantifiable the advantages of consistency in design.

Although these transfer results were obtained under the same kind of learning conditions as in the studies of learning time, there is less concern for their artificiality here. First, because there was a great deal of transfer, people were performing well; they did not often experience the somewhat harsh error-correction method. Second, in using these methods for doing comparative analyses of different systems, what one most cares about is the relative transfer among system components. Because production system models can be built for systems still under design, it is possible to assess the relative costs of differing degrees of consistency among procedures.

Like production systems, TAG has the potential of aiding the design process by assessing the amount of transfer expected from one system to another, aiding, for example, the consistency in a "family of products." Although the metric of counting the number of rules the two systems have in common is possible (and mentioned in Green et al., 1988), there has been no empirical verification to date.

3.2. The Analysis of Errors: Forgetting From Working Memory

Card et al. (1983) recognized that one of the causes of errors could be overload of WM or the goal stack. They tracked (see Card et al., 1983, Figure 11.12) the contents of WM during the performance of a task. As mentioned earlier, Kieras and Polson's formalism allows one to keep track explicitly of both the contents and the resident duration of each piece of information in WM. They stated that they expect errors to increase as soon as more than five items are held in WM (Kieras, 1988). However, neither they nor Card et al. empirically tested the prediction that the more items in WM, the greater the likelihood of errors.

Two researchers, however, recently tested these predictions in laboratory studies. The first of these, Lerch (Lerch, 1988; Lerch, Mantei, & Olson, 1989), developed a GOMS representation of skilled users writing out formulas in Lotus 1-2-3 (e.g., D23–D38), and in Interactive Financial Planning System (IFPS; e.g., PROFIT = REVENUES - COSTS). These two pieces of software differ in whether the user has to find and remember the coordinates of the cells in the formula (e.g., D23) or can refer to them by name, with adjectives such as *previous* to indicate relative location.

These two systems require various levels of WM load for different types of standard formulas commonly entered on the job. For example, any formula that requires temporary storage of values from different rows and columns puts a much greater load on WM in the Lotus representation than it does on IFPS representation. Figure 11 shows the WM load for the two systems in successive units of time, determined from the GOMS notation.

The results show that WM load for the two different interface styles and different kinds of formulas (those that are simple, single-column formulas and those that require cells from different columns and different rows) predict the occurrence of errors well. The higher the WM load, the more errors. For example, for formulas with cells in different rows and columns (the most complicated), the number of items that passed through WM for Lotus was 19[2] and for IFPS was 14. People writing in Lotus made errors on 14% of the formulas of this type, whereas people writing in IFPS made errors on only 6% of the formulas. Extrapolation of this relation suggests that when there are fewer than eight items in WM, errors would be eliminated.

Similarly, Smelcer (1989) examined the errors that users make while querying databases using SQL. In making queries, many people forget to put in an additional, necessary statement when information from two or more separate tables is used. This omission turns out to be a serious error, because unlike syntax errors that are caught by the system and corrected by the user, these “join errors” are syntactically correct and often return information that may be misleading. The difficult aspect of writing such a query is that the join statement is to be written last. The user has to remember to write it. Often there are steps in between that also require use of WM, making the likelihood of forgetting the crucial last step higher.

Smelcer calculated the WM load for different kinds of queries, those that have several steps in the middle of the query and those that have none. For example, a query that asks only for the names of all the employees of a company and their departments uses information from two tables and requires a join statement, but has no intervening “restriction” statements. On the other hand, a query that asks for the names of the employees who live in New Jersey and make over $40,000 a year has two statements between the initial part of the query and the final join statement.

Smelcer found a direct relationship between the number of intervening restriction statements (each of which requires many items to be stored in WM if calculated from the production system model) and the likelihood of people forgetting the last, crucial join statement. With no restrictions, people made 1.7% errors (20 out of 1200 opportunities); with two restrictions intervening before the join statement, they made 4.2% errors (50 out of 1200). The greater the WM load, the greater the number of omission errors.

In neither of these analyses do we know if the critical variable is the peak load in WM (in which we assume things are “bumped out”) or the length of stay of each of the items (where we assume that information decays with time). Calculating exactly how heavy the load in WM has to be before items are forgotten is difficult to assess. It is likely that people adopt strategies in which they do not attempt to hold too much in WM, using clues from the external environment to remind them of things needed in the task instead.

There are, of course, many causes of errors other than WM overload. The analyses just described only open the door on the treatment of errors within

[2] This value is derived from the number of items in WM (notes and steps, not goals), summed over the number of time steps that items were held in WM.

Figure 11. **Working memory load during the specification of various formulas that refer to cells in the same row or column or different rows and columns in two different languages: a language that requires the user to specify cells by coordinate values (e.g., B22) and one that refers to cells by name, with location specified relative to the current cell (e.g., Previous Sales).**

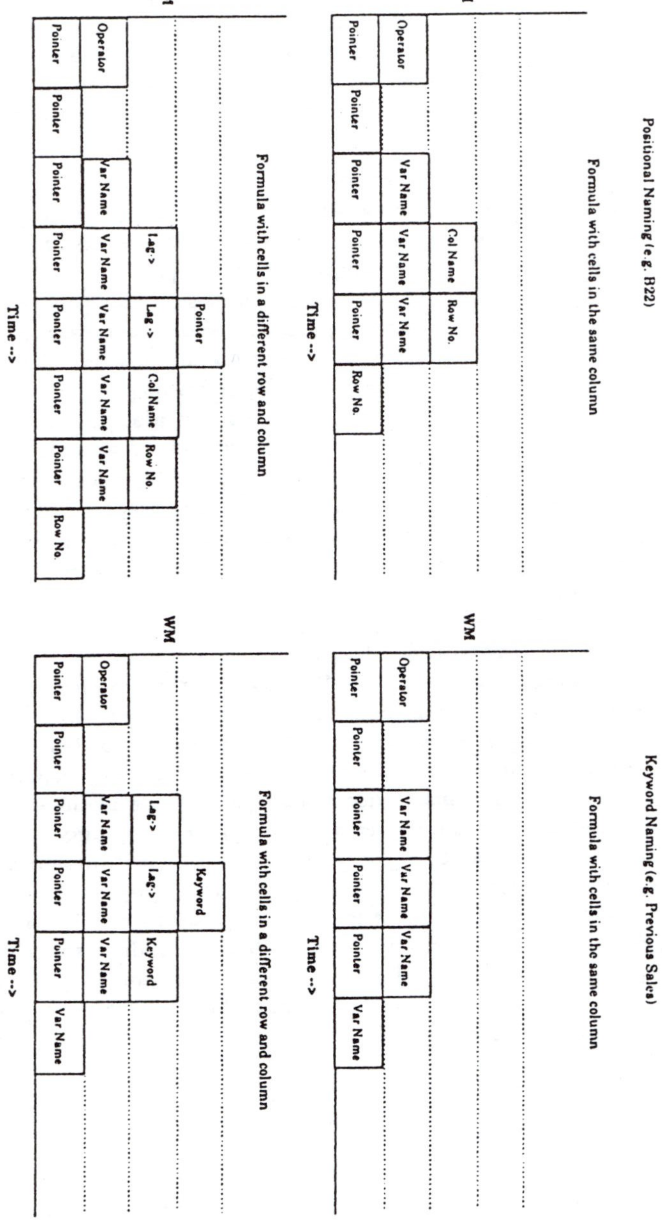

the GOMS framework, but the work described offers a significant beginning toward addressing one of the major shortcomings of the GOMS models.

3.3. Parallel Processes

Although the MHP assumes that processes can go on in parallel, for simplicity in engineering calculations, most work carried out in the GOMS framework assumes that the elementary processes captured in the models are serial. This simplifies the quantitative modeling, because total task time is assumed to be the sum of the times of a number of subcomponents. Further, it is consistent with a long tradition of cognitive modeling that assumes that much cognitive activity, at any rate, is fundamentally serial in nature (e.g., Newell & Simon, 1972). However, even Card et al. (1983) acknowledged that there are important cases where key components of performance may operate in parallel. Certainly tasks where perceptual or motor activities dominate, such as expert transcription typing, are likely to be best characterized by processes operating in parallel. The expert typist is reading input, translating it into motor output, and executing actions that type characters, all at a speed that demands an account in terms of parallel cognitive activities.

Card et al. (1983, Figure 5.10) illustrated the family character of GOMS by presenting a number of specific models of text editing that vary in grain of analysis. At the coarsest level, the model characterizes performance in terms of unit tasks; at their finest, the model accounts for individual keystrokes as a user interacts with the system via the keyboard. Such factors as the specific task, the level of expertise of the user, and the details of system operation could introduce parallelism at any level in such a hierarchy of models. The analyst might adopt the strategy of choosing the largest grain size at which there is no parallelism, if it were deemed important to keep the analytic advantages of working with serial models. Alternatively, methods such as those we are about to describe could be used to model performance at a grain size that includes substantial parallelism. Whether the behavior should be modeled by a serial or by a parallel model, however, is in large part determined by the grain size of the behavior selected by the analyst.

An analysis of a typical situation involving a user and a computer reveals numerous opportunities for parallel or cascading processes.

1. The user is bombarded with a set of external signals that sometimes occur in parallel. For example, keypresses are "echoed" on the screen while beeps alert the user of inappropriate action.
2. Mental events perhaps occur in parallel, sending cascaded information from one to the next. For example, plans of action might be retrieved for the next task while instructions about the immediately preceding task are executed.
3. External actions are elicited in parallel. For example, keys are pressed while eyes seek confirmation or new information to guide the next actions.

Rapid typing clearly requires a parallel model. For instance, those keystrokes that occur after one on the opposite hand are faster than if the same finger hits the key twice. This is probably because motions cascade; that is, one can be executing while another is begun. It is clear that the models have to incorporate notions of parallel processes.

This phenomenon appears in more than just use of a keyboard. Practical experience tells us that, at certain levels of analysis, skilled human–computer interaction is made up primarily of cascading internal processes. For example, in certain routine computer-supported tasks, such as imprinting bank checks with the amount (which is handwritten on the check) so that the whole check can be machine processed, the clerk is simply reading the handwritten amount from the check and keying in that same amount. How fast can the clerk key?

The keystroke model seriously overestimates the times:

> A saccade takes 230 msec; recognition takes 314 msec.
>
> Each numeral keystroke takes a minimum of 80 msec (for key entry times approaching 135 wpm), and typically there are four to five of them, plus an Enter key, which advances the display to the next check to be read, at an estimate of 1.35 s for retrieval (or less) and a 280 msec for entry.

This adds up to over 2 s per item. Real clerks are reported to complete them at less than .5 s each (J. O. Kerns, personal communication, February, 1989). Clearly, some of the processes are overlapping. Interestingly, the keying system just described allows the clerk to set a value that automatically displays the next item after a fixed number of keystrokes of the current item have been entered. Some of the best clerks are so fast that they set the system to display the next item while they are keying in the third numeral (out of five or six) of the previous item. They finish the keying of the last two numerals while they are looking at the next handwritten amount on the screen.

Furthermore, in this same situation, clerks accurately recognize that they have made a keying error after entering the whole next item. That is, the process that recognizes the miskeying finishes after the whole next item has been entered. Clerks have been known to correct check entries two checks back, never reaccessing the one just entered. Clearly, cascading of processes is occurring.

In our own experience, we recognize this same phenomenon when trying to apply the cognitive engineering model to menu design. Our observations show that when people know the menu item's name and location, visual search (for confirmation and guidance) and motor movement take place simultaneously. When users know the word they are looking for in a menu but not its location, the search is slower, and the motor movement seems to glide along with the visual scan. When the user knows neither the precise name nor the location, the time to find the item is fully dependent on reading time. The movement traces the eyes' reading time; as soon as the item is recognized, the cursor is at the right location.

For the expert user, then, the limiting or predicting time is fully dependent on the motor movement speed; for the novice, it is dependent on the reading speed. Predicting the actual performance time requires knowledge about what processes are occurring in parallel (or cascading or altered as they work in concert), which processes depend on each other (which must complete their processing before the next can begin), and which of them has a speed that is the limiting factor in the task at hand.

3.4. Critical Path Analysis: An Approach to Parallel Processing

Schweikert (1978, 1980) first proposed an analysis of nonserial processes in timed cognitive tasks using critical path analysis. He offered a very general set of procedures for constructing the graph of task components from the patterns of reaction times across experimental conditions. Recently, John (1988) also used concepts from critical path analysis to analyze tasks in the domain of human–computer interaction. Critical path analysis is a tool from operations engineering that provides a useful framework for the modeling of cascading mental and external processes.

John (1988) focused on the task of continuous typing. She wrote:

> The parallel operation and sequential dependencies of the three processors make the processes of typing difficult to analyze and talk about. Fortunately, there is an analysis technique, borrowed from engineering project management that allows easy analysis of parallel resources (the three processors [perceptual, cognitive and motor]) working with sequential dependencies (outlined by the typing-specific assumptions). The technique is called *critical path analysis*. (italics added, p. 49)

Critical path analysis allows analysts to specify the component processes, their duration, and the dependencies among them. A program for this analysis will calculate the path through this network that determines how long the total process can take. The program recognizes that some processes that occur simultaneously with others and take less time never enter into the calculation of the total duration of the task.

John's example analyses show how typing times can be calculated across situations in which the typist types words or random letters, with various numbers of letters displayed on the screen. Figure 12 depicts two examples of the processes involved. The top row of activity represents the perceptual processor (which is looking ahead at letters to type), the middle row is of the cognitive process (which is retrieving the individual letters of words read), and the bottom row is of the motor processor (which is enacting keypresses from either the same or different hands). The lines that connect the individual acts show the processes that theoretically must be completed before the next can start. For example, the motor processor cannot type a letter until it is retrieved, and keys on the same hand cannot be initiated until the cognitive processor intervenes.

In Figure 12, we compare the critical path for world-class and regular typists (who have motor times of 30 msec and 200 msec, respectively) in the top and bottom halves of the picture. After specifying the parameters for perceptual and cognitive processing (which are the same for both levels of skill) and calculating the critical path through the network, we find that the world-class typist is limited by the speed of the cognitive processor, whereas the regular typist is limited by the motor speed.

Critical path analysis is the kind of modeling tool that will help us in predicting times that seem to have parallel components. For example, it could help us predict the total time it takes a user to select an item from a menu if the user variously does or does not know the name of the item or where it is located. Figure 13 shows what this analysis looks like with the expert at the top, the person who knows the name but not the location in the middle, and the person who knows neither name nor location on the bottom. Simple serial GOMS modeling will not do. For these fast, simple tasks, some representation of the explicit dependencies of parallel processes as well as their component times is necessary.

In the past, we have been able to verify from observation the moment-by-moment fit of the components and their associated times. With critical path analysis, it is much harder to identify which aspects of one's assumptions about times and dependencies are right and which are wrong. Although Schweikert (1978, 1980) made some of the problem of discovery of processes and their interaction tractable, the modeling and confirmation process is still difficult. We will have to be very clever in our comparisons of performance across task demands or users' knowledge to make the inferences necessary to confirm or disconfirm the model and its parameters. However, doing the engineering predictions (of total time for the task) may have sufficient

Figure 13. **Critical path analysis for people who know the name and/or the location of items on the menu.**

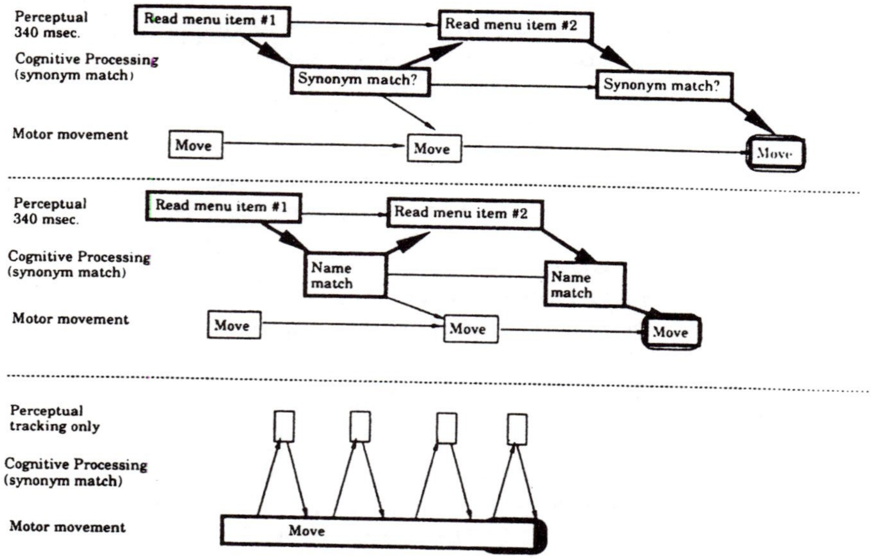

accuracy for design questions; what is difficult is the test of the underlying psychological model.

4. THE PLACE OF COGNITIVE MODELING IN HUMAN-COMPUTER INTERACTION

We have looked at examples of how cognitive modeling has been extended to cover learning and transfer, errors, and parallelism. In this section, we examine two issues: (a) the other kinds of useful extensions that could be made to give the framework even more scope; and (b) where, in the larger scheme of things pertaining to the study of human-computer interaction, even an extended and confirmed cognitive modeling framework would stand. These comments separate into those areas in which the framework might stand, but the kinds of information we need from cognitive theory does not yet exist to inform this extension. And there are questions about human-computer interaction that appear to require a wholly different kind of modeling. These assessments are categorized in Figure 14 and discussed next.

4.1. Additional Plausible and Useful Extensions

In this section, we follow the list of shortcomings reviewed in Section 1 of this article. The first category includes the areas that we feel could be

Figure 12. **Critical path analysis for two typists. The top one represents the typing speed of a world-class typist (30 msec/keystroke); the bottom one represents that of an average skilled typist (170 msec/keystroke).**

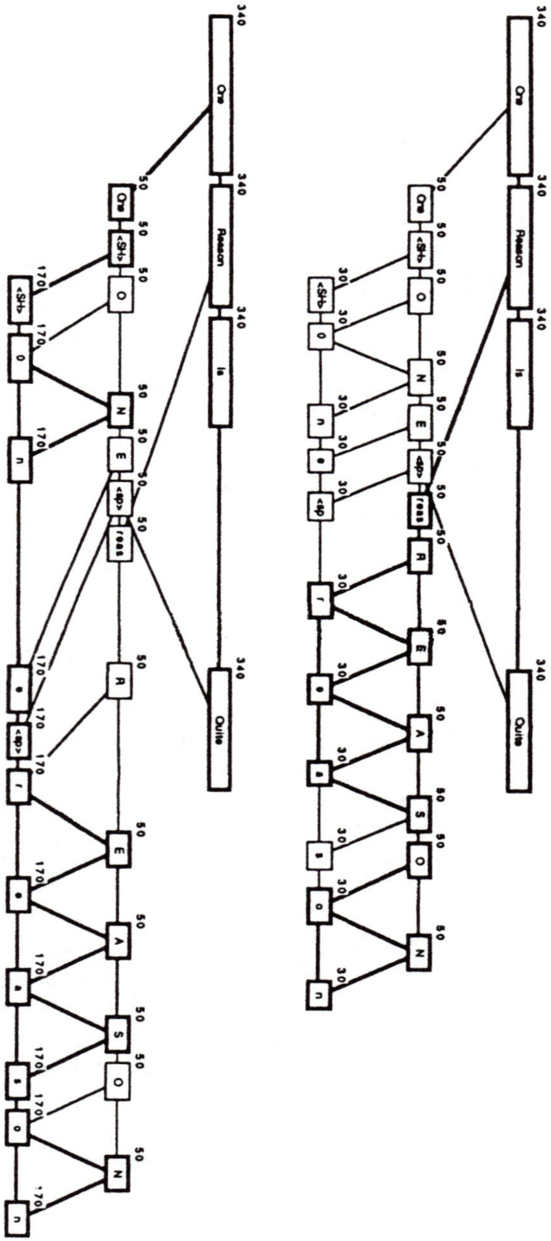

addressed within the original framework and its extensions but that have not yet been fully explored.

Nonskilled or Casual Users

Engineering models apply best to those situations that have skilled users of a particular system. Many such situations exist in industry, where clerks enter and change entries all day long. And not all of this work is simple data entry; with more advanced capabilities of systems at a price that makes them more widely available, people who do routine problem solving (e.g., debugging or error rectification) need systems with easy to use interfaces for rapid processing.

But many others of us are not skilled users of any particular system; we use a variety of systems to do our work, and we know some parts of each system better than others. Thus, some of the time in our interactions we are not simply retrieving and acting out plans. We retrieve the command appropriate to another system or inferred from its style; we often make errors of commission and figure out what must be done next given where we are now. We move smoothly from cognitive skill to problem solving and back. How people do this is of immense theoretical interest to cognitive psychologists. The article by Polson and Lewis (1990) is a step in this direction.

A second active research program that is relevant to this topic of casual user performance is the SOAR project (Laird, Newell, & Rosenbloom, 1987). SOAR is a running, growing model of the architecture of cognition. In style similar to that of cognitive engineering, SOAR could provide the detail necessary to answer the questions about how long it takes to recognize an impasse in skill, how long it takes to set up a new goal, how quickly similar productions are retrieved and analyzed, and how many steps are executed before a solution is found. All these parameters could likely be predicted in the SOAR framework (provided with a good task analysis) for situations in which a user is faced with learning a new system after knowing one that shares some relevant features.

Learning

One of the biggest, longest lasting issues in psychology is learning. People generate explanations of how a system works by watching the system respond to their inputs. We learn by asking and learn by watching. We need to know how that works; how productions grow and are integrated into methods; and what the psychological realities of methods, as opposed to chunked sequences, are.

Although we know that consistency in a system may make that system easier to learn (fewer productions to learn) and easier to operate (well-known productions can be used over and over again), we do not know much more than that. We know from the work of Kieras and Polson that a system that

Figure 14. **Summary of those issues addressed by new work on GOMS, those addressed by extensions to models in the GOMS tradition, and those judged not easily accommodated in GOMS because either there is not enough known in cognitive theory to inform the effort, or the level of analysis represented in GOMS is inappropriate for such questions.**

	Some Work Has Addressed This Topic	Straightforward Extension Seems Possible	Cognitive Science Does Not Inform Us	Requires Another Kind of Modeling
Nonskilled users	–	X	–	–
Learning	X	X	–	–
Errors	X	X	–	–
Cognitive processes	X	X	X	–
Parallel processes	X	X	X	–
Mental workload	–	X	–	–
Functionality	–	–	–	X
Fatigue	–	–	X	–
Individual differences	X	–	–	–
Acceptance	–	–	–	X
Fit to organizational life	–	–	–	X

shares productions with a system already known will be easier, but we do not know exactly how to design to that prescription. We do not know which system to base a new one on. Suppose the first system is internally inconsistent. We do not know if we would benefit more from reusing the old, inconsistent, confusable productions or from spending the time and effort to learn the new, consistent productions. Some phenomena from verbal learning literature seem applicable here, but as several researchers have found, not all phenomena from paired-associate learning apply (e.g., Singley & Anderson, 1988).

Errors and Mental Workload

Even in skilled performance with computers, we still make errors. As discussed earlier, some of these errors arise from an interface design that requires too much to be held in a limited-capacity WM. Users come to learn that such errors can be caught. They monitor their performance more closely by both checking concurrently for errors and breaking at the end of a task to assess whether errors have been committed. They also change their methods to include such things as writing down the address of a critical cell in a spreadsheet or printing out a document so that it can be scanned quickly for a target word in the area in which they want to work next. Understanding how people monitor their own behavior for errors and how they adapt their methods is critical to the full understanding of performance on the kinds of tasks for which analytic modeling was designed. And, as we have seen, analytic models can provide an explicit account of aspects of mental workload during tasks in terms of activity through the WM. Additional aspects of workload having to do with the use of the cognitive processor and the work involved in retrieval of procedures and facts could follow.

Cognitive Processes

Of those aspects of skilled performance in human–computer interaction that are underspecified in the models to date, interpretation of visual displays may be the most important. We know that Gestalt principles will drive some of the user's interpretation of what is on the screen, but we do not know much about how meaning is imparted on the whole display. We need to know this not only to determine how to display information for the slow, deliberate problem-solving processes involved in high-level decision making, but also for the fast, repetitive operational tasks such as those in keying handwritten characters in checks. Recent work by Tullis (1983, 1988) and Mackinlay (1986) made significant inroads in this area, but more work is called for, both in the application of what we know and in the discovery of basic facts about how people interpret what they see.

Parallel Processes

Concurrent or cascading processes seem to occur in rapid, skilled performance. We noted that clerks imprinting checks with machine-readable numerals could detect that they had made an error two checks past. This phenomenon indicates not only the existence of concurrent perception and motor movement but also that there may be some process that actively checks the accuracy of the behavior soon after that behavior has occurred. This is a natural case of simultaneous tasks. We need to know how this works and how many processes such as this background monitoring exist.

John's (1988) adoption of the critical path method of modeling concurrent, dependent processes requires us to characterize in great detail our assumptions of processes involved and their dependencies in these kinds of tasks. The literature in cognitive psychology provides even less guidance on these dependencies than it does in finding appropriate parameters. To illustrate the detail needed, John's modeling of the continuous typing task makes strong assumptions about which kinds of processes depend on the completion of other processes. For example, she stated that:

> The perceptual processor cannot perceive the next piece of information unless there is room in working memory for that information. . . . A character on the same hand cannot be initiated with a cognitive operator until the motor processor execution of the previous character is complete. (p. 47)

Though such simplifying assumptions may achieve success in some domains and at some levels of analysis, it is important to recognize that the existing psychological literature does not support such strong assumptions. Finding the kinds of links that do exist among processes is critical to this kind of modeling success.

Individual Differences

Card et al.'s (1983) original clocking of different motor operators of people with different skill levels and John's (1988) work on various levels of skill in typing exemplify how we might explore the implications of individual differences in human–computer interaction. Though these differences in motor operators clearly have an effect on predicting the total time that a task will take, there are likely large differences in perceptual and cognitive operations that similarly have large effects. People clearly differ in rate of learning, speed of retrieval, and reasoning or strategy formation. Egan (1988) reviewed a variety of ways in which individuals differ in their use of computers. This work and the more detailed parametric work in Gomez, Egan, Wheeler, Sharma, and Gruchacz (1983) and Gomez, Egan, and

Bowers (1986) could guide the further exploration of the effect of differences in the rate and form of cognitive processing on predictions of time and errors in the spirit of GOMS modeling.

4.2. Cognitive Modeling in Human-Computer Interaction

In the broader picture of providing tools for designers of human-computer interfaces, several important aspects of human-computer interaction do not seem to lend themselves to the approach described here. First, this approach does not capture the impact of fatigue on the times and errors associated with performance. Our models never tire; people do. Some extensions from research on the effect of time and mental workload may be relevant here, but the interplay of stress from the task itself from the physical environment (e.g., chairs and lighting) and the higher level aspects of one's job (e.g., work supervision, control over pacing, incentive and rewards, etc.) are beyond the scope of cognitive engineering as we see it. Some of this arises because of the little we know about the causes of fatigue on mental processing, and some arises from the possibility that when we do know, the GOMS-like modeling framework includes the wrong set of constructs.

Second, we do not see a possible extension of these models that would include assessment of people's perception of the acceptability of an interface. People's judgments of ease of use are not always in concordance with their actual productivity (e.g., Davis, Bagozzi, & Warshaw, 1989). Perceptions of whether the software's functionality is actually what the user needs and the ease with which the system can be learned all contribute to the acceptance of a piece of software and its eventual regular use. These do not appear to fit the style of analytic modeling, because they refer to an entirely different level of granularity of behavior and a different set of relevant features.

Perhaps the most important step in building a successful piece of software may be the analysis of the functions it will perform, in what order it will allow the user to do them, and how they fit into the larger picture of work and organizational roles. This point is made strongly under the rubric of "situated cognition," the understanding of work, its task and setting, and the eventual design of computers to support it (see Suchman, 1987). The topic of discovering useful functions has been explored in the management literature (e.g., Sasso, Olson, & Merten, 1987) and in the literature on traditional human factors (e.g., Sheridan, 1988), based on a broad analysis of what people do best and what computers do best. These approaches, however, do not yet converge at a level specific enough to be useful to a system designer. And the assessment of how computers change work and organizational life is as yet still at the descriptive, not theoretical, level (e.g., Markus, 1984). A kind of modeling different from that provided by the analytic models described in this article appears to be required to answer these kinds of important questions.

Despite these limitations, large classes of applications can be characterized in just the way that GOMS and its successors require. Every day thousands of people carry out computer-based interactions that are highly repetitive and stylized. Airline reservations, telephone directory assistance, troubleshooting of discrepancies in forms such as bank deposits all are examples of tasks in which cognitive modeling can play an important role in the design of learnable and usable systems. In these kinds of tasks, the approach is very powerful. Because we now have reasonably useful quantitative estimates of a number of task components, predictions about performance can be made for designs without our having to build prototype systems and run extensive, time-consuming user tests. User tests can, of course, reveal other things such as errors, problem solving, and initial learning and representation difficulties; however, cognitive models can screen out certain classes of poor designs for these kinds of tasks.

Acknowledgments. This article benefited greatly from very careful readings and thoughtful suggestions from Peter Polson, John Karat, Clayton Lewis, Thomas Green, Richard Young, and Bonnie John. We remain responsible for any faults in the clarity, accuracy, and opinions of the result but are grateful for the help these people gave us.

Support. This work was partially funded by the Army Research Institute, MDA903-89-K-0025.

REFERENCES

Bovair, S., Kieras, D. E., & Polson, P. G. (1990). The acquisition and performance of text-editing skill: A cognitive complexity analysis. *Human-Computer Interaction, 5,* 1-48.

Card, S. K., Moran, T. P., & Newell, A. (1980a). Computer text-editing: An information-processing analysis of a routine cognitive skill. *Cognitive Psychology, 12,* 32-74.

Card, S. K., Moran, T. P., & Newell, A. (1980b). The keystroke-level model for user performance time with interactive systems. *Communications of the ACM, 23,* 396-410.

Card, S. K., Moran, T. P., & Newell, A. (1983). *The psychology of human-computer interaction.* Hillsdale, NJ: Lawrence Erlbaum Associates, Inc.

Carroll, J. M., & Campbell, R. L. (1986). Softening up hard science: Reply to Newell and Card. *Human-Computer Interaction, 2,* 227-250.

Davis, F. D., Bagozzi, R. P., & Warshaw, P. R. (1989). User acceptance of computer technology: A comparison of two theoretical models. *Management Science, 35,* 982-1003.

Egan, D. E. (1988). Individual differences in human-computer interaction. In M. Helander (Ed.), *Handbook of human-computer interaction* (pp. 543-568). Amsterdam: North-Holland.

Fitts, P. M., & Peterson, J. R. (1964). Information capacity of discrete motor responses. *Journal of Experimental Psychology, 67,* 103–112.

Gomez, L. M., Egan, D. E., & Bowers, C. (1986). Learning to use a text editor: Some learner characteristics that predict success. *Human–Computer Interaction, 2,* 1–23.

Gomez, L. M., Egan, D. E., Wheeler, E. A., Sharma, D. K., & Gruchacz, A. M. (1983). How interface design determines who has difficulty learning to use a text editor. *Proceedings of the CHI '83 Conference on Human Factors in Computing Systems,* 176–181. New York: ACM.

Green, T. R. G., Schiele, F., & Payne, S. J. (1988). Formalisable models of user knowledge in human-computer interaction. In G. C. Van der Veer, T. R. G. Green, J.-M. Hoc, & D. M. Murray (Eds.), *Working with computers: Theory vs. outcome* (pp. 47–88). New York: Academic.

Hick, W. E. (1952). On the rate of gain of information. *Quarterly Journal of Experimental Psychology, 4,* 11–16.

John, B. E. (1988). *Contributions to engineering models of human–computer interaction.* Unpublished doctoral dissertation, Carnegie Mellon University, Pittsburgh.

John, B. E., & Newell, A. (1987). Predicting the time to recall computer command abbreviations. *Proceedings of the CHI '87 Conference on Human Factors in Computing Systems,* 33–40. New York: ACM.

John, B. E., & Newell, A. (1989). Cumulating the science of HCI: From S-R compatibility to transcription typing. *Proceedings of the CHI '89 Conference on Human Factors in Computing Systems,* 109–114. New York: ACM.

John, B. E., & Newell, A. (in press). Toward an engineering model of stimulus-response compatibility. In R. W. Gilmore & T. G. Reeve (Eds.), *Stimulus–response compatibility: An integrated approach.* Amsterdam: North-Holland.

John, B. E., Rosenbloom, P. S., & Newell, A. (1985). A theory of stimulus–response compatibility applied to human-computer interaction. *Proceedings of the CHI '85 Conference on Human Factors in Computing Systems,* 213–219. New York: ACM.

Karat, J. (1988). Software evaluation methodologies. In M. Helander (Ed.), *Handbook of human–computer interaction* (pp. 891–904). Amsterdam: North-Holland.

Kieras, D. E. (1988). Towards a practical GOMS model methodology for user interface design. In M. Helander (Ed.), *The handbook of human–computer interaction.* (pp. 135–158). Amsterdam: North-Holland.

Kieras, D. E., & Bovair, S. (1986). The acquisition of procedures from text: A production-system analysis of transfer of training. *Journal of Memory and Language, 25,* 507–524.

Kieras, D. E., & Polson, P. G. (1985). An approach to the formal analysis of user complexity. *International Journal of Man–Machine Studies, 22,* 365–394.

Laird, J. E., Newell, A., & Rosenbloom, P. S. (1987). Soar: An architecture for general intelligence. *Artificial Intelligence, 33,* 1–64.

Lerch, F. J. (1988). *Computerized financial planning: Discovering cognitive difficulties in model building.* Unpublished doctoral dissertation, University of Michigan, Ann Arbor.

Lerch, F. J., Mantei, M. M., & Olson, J. R. (1989). Translating ideas into action: Cognitive analysis of errors in spreadsheet formulas. *Proceedings of the CHI '89 Conference on Human Factors in Computing Systems,* 121–126. New York: ACM.

Mackinlay, J. D. (1986). *Automatic design of graphical presentations.* Unpublished doctoral dissertation, Stanford University, Department of Computer Science, Stanford, CA.

Markus, L. (1984). *Systems in organizations: Bugs and features.* New York: Plenum.

Newell, A., & Card, S. K. (1985). The prospects for psychological science in human-computer interaction. *Human–Computer Interaction, 1,* 209–242.

Newell, A., & Card, S. K. (1986). Straightening out softening up: Response to Carroll and Campbell. *Human–Computer Interaction, 2,* 251–267.

Newell, A., & Simon, H. A. (1972). *Human problem solving.* Englewood Cliffs, NJ: Prentice-Hall.

Norman, D. A. (1986). Cognitive engineering. In D. A. Norman & S. W. Draper (Eds.), *User centered systems design: New perspectives on human–computer interaction* (pp. 31–61). Hillsdale, NJ: Lawrence Erlbaum Associates, Inc.

Olson, J. R., & Nilsen, E. (1988). Analysis of the cognition involved in spreadsheet software interaction. *Human–Computer Interaction, 3,* 309–350.

Payne, S. J., & Green, T. R. G. (1986). Task-action grammars: A model of the mental representation of task languages. *Human–Computer Interaction, 2,* 93–133.

Payne, S. J., & Green, T. R. G. (1989). The structure of command languages: An experiment on task-action grammar. *International Journal of Man–Machine Studies, 30,* 213–234.

Polson, P. G. (1987). A quantitative theory of human-computer interaction. In J. M. Carroll (Ed.), *Interfacing thought: Cognitive aspects of human–computer interaction* (pp. 184–235). Cambridge, MA: MIT Press.

Polson, P. G. (1988). The consequences of consistent and inconsistent interfaces. In R. Guindon (Ed.), *Cognitive science and its applications for human–computer interaction* (pp. 59–108). Hillsdale, NJ: Lawrence Erlbaum Associates, Inc.

Polson, P. G., & Kieras, D. E. (1985). A quantitative model of the learning and performance of text editing knowledge. *Proceedings of the CHI '85 Conference on Human Factors in Computing Systems,* 207–212. New York: ACM.

Polson, P. G., & Lewis, C. H. (1990). Theory-based design for easily learned interfaces. *Human–Computer Interaction, 5,* 191–220.

Polson, P. G., Muncher, E., & Engelbeck, G. (1986). A test of a common elements theory of transfer. *Proceedings of the CHI '86 Conference on Human Factors in Computing Systems,* 78–83. New York: ACM.

Reisner, P. (1981). Formal grammar and human factors design of an interactive graphics system. *IEEE Transactions on Software Engineering,* SE-7, 229–240.

Reisner, P. (1984). Formal grammar as a tool for analyzing ease of use: Some fundamental concepts. In J. Thomas & M. Schneider (Eds.), *Human factors in computer systems.* Norwood, NJ: Ablex.

Sasso, W. G., Olson, J. R., & Merten, A. (1987). The practice of office analysis: Objectives, obstacles, and opportunities. *Office Knowledge Engineering, 2,* 11–24.

Schweickert, R. (1978). A critical path generalization of the additive factor method: Analysis of a Stroop task. *Journal of Mathematical Psychology, 18,* 105–139.

Schweickert, R. (1980). Critical path scheduling of mental processes in a dual task. *Science, 209,* 704–706.

Sheridan, T. (1988). Task allocation and supervisory control. In M. Helander (Ed.), *Handbook of human–computer interaction* (pp. 159–174). Amsterdam: North-Holland.

Singley, M. K., & Anderson, J. R. (1988). A keystroke analysis of learning and transfer in text editing. *Human–Computer Interaction, 3,* 223–274.

Smelcer, J. B. (1989). *Understanding user errors in database query.* Unpublished doctoral dissertation, University of Michigan, Ann Arbor.

Suchman, L. A. (1987). *Plans and situated actions: The problem of human-machine communication.* Cambridge, England: Cambridge University Press.

Tullis, T. S. (1983). The formatting of alphanumeric displays: A review and analysis. *Human Factors, 25,* 657-682.

Tullis, T. S. (1988). Screen design. In M. Helander (Ed.), *Handbook of human-computer interaction* (pp. 377-411). Amsterdam: North-Holland.

Walker, J. N., Smelcer, J. B., & Nilsen, E. (1989). *Fitts' Law and its design implications: Attempting to optimize speed and accuracy of menu selection.* Unpublished manuscript, University of Michigan, Human Computer Interaction Laboratory, Ann Arbor.

Wilson, M. D., Barnard, P. J., Green, T. R. G., & MacLean, A. (1988). Knowledge-based task analysis for human-computer systems. In G. C. Van der Veer, T. R. G. Green, J.-M. Hoc, & D. M. Murray (Eds.), *Working with computers: Theory vs. outcome* (pp. 3-46). New York: Academic.

Young, R. M., & MacLean, A. (1988). Choosing between methods: Analysing the user's decision space in terms of schemas and linear models. *Proceedings of the CHI '88 Conference on Human Factors in Computing Systems,* 139-143. New York: ACM.

Ziegler, S. E., Vossen, P., & Hoppe, H. U. (1986). *On using production systems for cognitive task analysis and prediction of transfer of cognitive skill.* Paper presented at the Third European Conference on Cognitive Ergonomics, Paris.

HCI Editorial Record. First manuscript received April 13, 1989. Revision received June 20, 1989. Final manuscript received October 4, 1989. Accepted by Peter Polson. —*Editor*

A GOMS Analysis of a Graphic, Machine-Paced, Highly Interactive Task.

Bonnie E John
School of Computer Science
& Department of Psychology

Alonso H. Vera
Department of Psychology

Carnegie Mellon University
Pittsburgh, PA 15213
(412) 268-7182
bej@cs.cmu.edu

ABSTRACT
A GOMS analysis was used to predict the behavior of an expert in a graphic, machine-paced, highly interactive task. The analysis was implemented in a computational model using the Soar cognitive architecture. Using only the information available in an instruction booklet and some simple heuristics for selecting between operators, the functional-level behavior of the expert proved to be virtually dictated by the objects visible on the display. At the keystroke-level, the analysis predicted about 60% of the behavior, in keeping with similar results in previous GOMS research. We conclude that GOMS is capable of predicting expert behavior in a broader range of tasks than previously demonstrated.

KEYWORDS: user models, cognitive models, GOMS, Soar, video games.

GOMS AND HIGHLY INTERACTIVE TASKS

GOMS analyses have been used to model many tasks in a diversity of domains [13]. Early analyses were of tasks with a static visual display. Editing tasks used red marks on a paper copy, choice reaction time stimuli were presented at a single position on a CRT screen, spreadsheet formulae and database queries were described on hard-copy, and typing tasks primarily involved transcription from hard-copy or from a single position on a CRT screen. Also, in many of the tasks, the user was free to work at his or her own pace; the user did not have to wait for critical information to appear, and critical information did not disappear. Subtasks were not thrust upon the user by a changing environment. Thus, these early studies did not demonstrate the appropriateness of the GOMS method for interactive tasks.

Recently, we extended the scope of GOMS analyses with an analysis of telephone operator call handling ([6], [3]). This task involved fleeting auditory and visual input, that could occur before or after the information was needed in the task. It also included speech input and output. Although the input was in real-time and the rate of task completion primarily driven by the task environment rather than the operator's skill, the knowledge of the goals, operators, methods, and selection rules associated with the task was sufficient to predict behavior. Additionally, we have also discovered GOMS-like behavior in an information retrieval task with an interactive computer browser [14].

The goal of the present work is to apply GOMS to even more highly interactive tasks. We believe video games are extreme examples of such tasks. The interaction in many video games seems largely driven by the game rather than by the player. Goals seem to be interrupted, suspended and returned to. Yet, similar to other domains successfully modelled by GOMS, an expert's behavior looks to be highly knowledge intensive and eventually becomes routine.

Some researchers have suggested that GOMS-style analyses cannot model behavior in real-time, dynamic, interactive tasks [1]. They argue that such tasks can only be modeled with completely reactive systems involving no planning at all. The question is therefore whether real-time constraints prevent the application of expert knowledge in such tasks or whether an expert's knowledge of a highly interactive, perceptually-driven motor task can be applied under these time constraints to yield routine plan-like behavior. If the latter is true, then this behavior should be captured by GOMS's goals, operators, methods, and selection rules. In this paper we argue that planning-based methods successfully describe behavior in such highly interactive domains and that this is a significant extension of these tools.

THE TASK

In response to a professional challenge (a panel at the Human Factors Society Meeting 1990), we did a GOMS analysis of Nintendo's Super Mario Bros. 3®.[1] This is a typical adventure game with treasures to collect, enemies to avoid or kill, and super powers to acquire and use. The

[1] Super Mario Bros. 3, Nintendo, and the games and characters discussed in this paper are trademarks of Nintendo of America Inc.

player manipulates the character Mario through the world by pressing buttons on a hand held controller. Four buttons on the controller are pressed with the left thumb to move Mario left, right, up or down; two buttons are pressed with the right thumb to make Mario jump, pick up objects, or increase speed.

The task used in this analysis is to traverse part of World 1, Level 1, collecting as many points as possible. A videotape of a nine-year-old expert, KP, performing the task provided observed behavior against which to measure the predictions of the GOMS analyses.

TWO GOMS ANALYSES IMPLEMENTED IN SOAR

GOMS suggests that the goals, operators, and methods can be defined from an objective analysis of the task. We conducted the GOMS analyses with as little reference to the expert's behavior as possible, opting instead, for taking the knowledge explicit in the instruction booklet and reasoning about the task itself.

The analyses were carried out at two levels: the *functional-level*, where operators are at the level of searching a block that or killing an enemy, and the *keystroke-level*, where operators are at the level of individual finger movements on the game's control panel. Each level is considered a separate GOMS analysis, as in Chapter 5 of Card, Moran, & Newell [2]. The two analyses will be described in parallel, beginning with the goals, operators, methods and selection rules for each, then describing the process of applying this information to the task of playing the game.

Goals, Operators, Methods, and Selection Rules

The instruction booklet [12] provides the overall *goals* of the game: to finish each level, to increase your standing (e.g. with points, or coins), and to avoid danger. These goals can be accomplished by performing *functional-level operators*. Functional-level operators appear in the instruction manual as direct commands or warnings. For instance, the command "Hit blocks...A useful item might pop out!" is implemented as a functional-level operator called `search-in-block`, and the warning "BEWARE! THE FOLLOWING ARE DEADLY" is implemented as a functional-level operator called `avoid-danger`.

Functional-level operators are accomplished through *keystroke-level operators* [2], which correspond to pressing the buttons on the controller described above. The instruction booklet also provides *methods*, or sequences of motor operators, for accomplishing some of the functional-level operators. For instance, the booklet shows the keystrokes necessary to pick up a shell, run with it, throw it at a block on the ground, and thereby break the block to find the treasure within.

Occasionally, there is more than one method available for accomplishing a functional-level operator, e.g. an enemy can be attacked either by jumping on its back or hitting it with Mario's tail (a desirable appendage acquired when a series of treasures are collected). Although the instruction booklet describes the alternative methods, it does not provide the selection rules necessary to decide between them. These are presumably acquired by the user as he or she experiments with the different methods in the course of playing the game. We produced selection rules for our analysis by preferring the method that gave the most points. For instance, in one case, the jump-on method described above gives 200 more points than the hit-with-tail method. Where there were no point differences, we produced a selection rule favoring an old technique familiar from previous versions of the game over a new technique peculiar to this version. For this segment of the game, these two considerations were sufficient to explain all of the expert's method selections.

The Soar Implementation of the GOMS Analysis

These goals, functional-level operators, keystroke-level operators, methods, and selection rules, were built into a computational model using the Soar architecture. Soar is a unified theory of cognition embodied in a production system architecture that has been used by researchers to model users performing several HCI tasks, including using automatic teller machines [15], browsing through a help system [14], and learning task-action mappings for an interface [4]. We chose to create a Soar implementation for several reasons. First, a Soar model can be run dynamically, like a computer program, making it easier to assess interactive behavior than typical hand-simulation of GOMS models. Furthermore, as will be discussed later, Soar allows us to back-up from the expert GOMS model and use Soar's inherent learning mechanisms to investigate how methods and selection rules might be acquired through experience.

HI-Soar (for Highly-Interactive-Soar) was constructed as a direct implementation of the GOMS analysis. Functional-level operators are proposed in response to objects appearing on the display, and accomplished through methods comprised of individual keystroke-level operators. HI-Soar interacts with a Lisp system which simulates the content of the display after each keystroke-level operator is applied. This simulation is not real-time, nor is it a full simulation of the game, rather, it gives HI-Soar an encoded representation of the objects on the display that would result from the particular keystroke at that particular point in the game.

Since many relevant objects appear on any one display, more than one functional-level operator is applicable at any one time. An analogous situation occurred in early GOMS

---

2 The terms *goals*, *functional-level operators* and *keystroke-level operators* are used to distinguish between three different levels in the typical GOMS goal hierarchy. This distinction is drawn to fascilitate exposition, and does not reflect a theoretical distinction between goals and operators. As Kieras [9] observes for GOMS analyses in general, "this distinction is intuitively-based, and it is also relative; it depends on the level of analysis."

analyses of text-editing [2] because the stimulus manuscript had between 3 and 11 editorial marks per page; the user had to select which edit to perform next and comprehend the editing marks to set the goal of the unit task. Card, Moran and Newell incorporated these selection processes into the GET-NEXT-TASK operator. Because text manipulation is highly regular in a left-to-right, top-to-bottom sequence, these selection processes were not discussed at length in early GOMS work. However, in a videogame, the selection of what to do next has much more importance to the outcome of the game and is more subject to individual differences. For our analysis, we developed preferences to select between functional-level operators based on common-sense reasoning about the game. For instance, when many blocks are available, `search-in-block` is proposed for each of them. We posited a preference for searching in the block closest to Mario. A description of the full set of preferences is beyond the scope of this paper; we refer the reader to John, Vera and Newell [8] for a more detailed account.

As an example of operator proposal and preferences, at the start-up display of the game there are four Question Boxes (QB1 through QB4, where QB1 is closest to Mario and QB4 is the furthest away) and one enemy (a "Goomba") visible on the display. This causes the functional-level operators `search-in-block(QB1)`, `search-in-block(QB2)`, `search-in-block(QB3)`, `search-in-block(QB4)`, and `attack-enemy(Goomba)` to be proposed. The preferences dictate that `search-in-block(QB1)` be chosen because it is closest to Mario and the Goomba is not an immediate threat.

Once a particular functional-level operator is selected HI-Soar must determine what method to use to accomplish the functional-level operator. The selection of the method is contingent on many aspects of the situation: powers possessed by Mario, tools available, etc. HI-Soar then selects and applies the appropriate keystroke-level operators to perform the method. When a keystroke-level operator is applied, it sends a message to the external Lisp system which provides information about the contents of the new display back to the perceptual level of HI-Soar.

After each keystroke-level operator is performed, the state of display changes and must be re-evaluated. New functional-level operators have an opportunity to take precedence over the current functional-level operator. Continuing the example, in service of `search-in-block(QB1)`, Mario moves to the right under the control of the `press-right-button` keystroke-level operator. Simultaneously, the Goomba moves left, closer to Mario. At the point where the Goomba becomes an immediate threat, the preference for `attack-enemy(Goomba)` overrides that for `search-in-block(QB1)` and the current functional-level operator changes to `attack-enemy(Goomba)`. This invokes the `jump-on` method and, in turn, the `press-A-button` keystroke-level operator. After the Goomba is killed, the preference for `search-in-block(QB1)` again takes precedence and Mario is moved right until he is under QB1; `press-A-button` is again invoked causing him to jump to complete the `search-in-block` operator.

Thus, given the changes visible on the game screen as input, HI-Soar model predicts the sequence of functional-level operators, methods, and keystroke-level operators that the expert will perform.

RESULTS OF THE GOMS ANALYSES

We compared the operators predicted by HI-Soar to the operators observed in the videotape for the first 30 seconds of the expert's game. Figure 1 shows the comparison at the functional-level and Figure 2 shows the comparison at the keystroke-level. In both figures, the operator names are listed along the vertical axis. The horizontal axis is labelled with a display number that indicates the opportunity for new functional-level operators to be selected. This designation corresponds roughly to time, where each display represents about a second's worth of activity.

In the figures, a black dot marks the inferred function of the expert's observed behavior at each display and a gray dot marks the operator HI-Soar performed at that display. The sense of these figures is that when the black and gray lines track each other, the model is making good predictions of observed behavior. Where the black and gray lines do not track, the model is not predicting the observed behavior.

Occasionally, the expert's behavior cannot be unambiguously inferred. For example, moving to the right could be in service of searching in a block located to the right, attacking an enemy located to the right, or just moving toward the end of the world. In these cases, no black dot appears in the display column and all the HI-Soar operators consistant with that behavior are shown as thin black circles. Where there is a haze of thin black circles above or below the gray dots, the behavior is consistent with many possible functions and it is likely that any prediction will track behavior; where black circles are few, the observed behavior is consistent with only a few functions and the model must be accurate to track behavior.

Figure 2 uses the same graphic conventions as Figure 1 for the keystroke-level operators. For the operators and predictions, each horizontal unit, delineated by dotted lines, corresponds to the functional-level operator implemented by the keystroke-level operators shown in that unit and also to the display that caused the selection of that functional-level operator. Therefore, each horizontal unit is labelled at the top with its corresponding display number and at the bottom with its associated functional-level operator.

Figure 1, the comparison of the observed behavior to the predicted functional-level operators, shows some interesting features of the analysis. Most striking is the excellent agreement between the predicted functional-level operators and the observed behavior. Only once in 31 opportunities is a functional-level operator selected that is inconsistent with observed behavior (Display.21). This instance is at a point

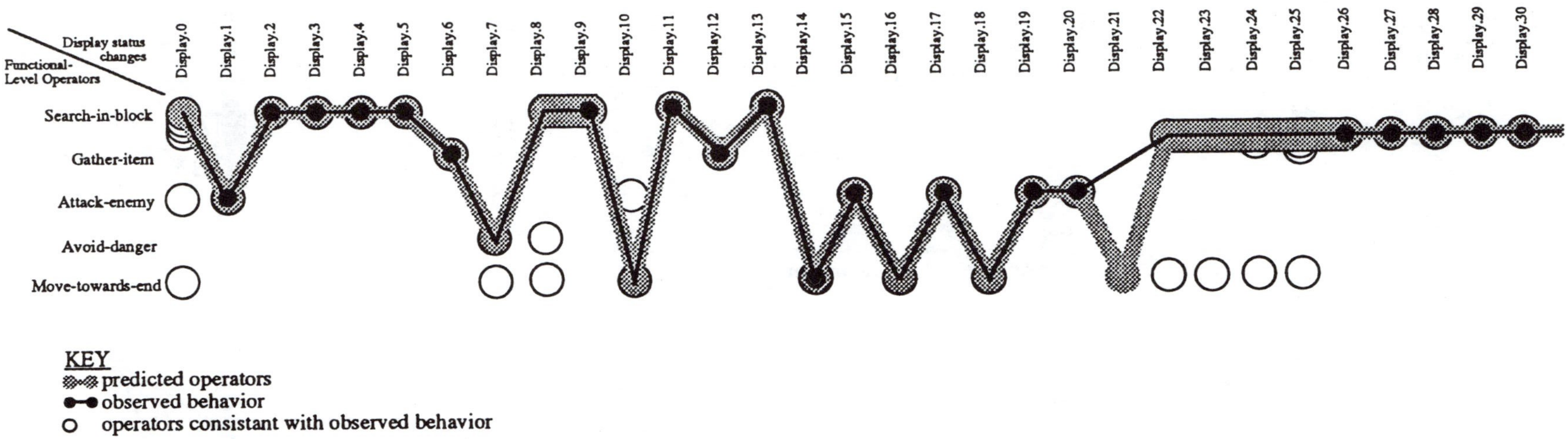

Figure 1. Comparison of the function-level model predictions with the observed behavior.

Black dots indicate functions inferred from the observed behavior. For instance, when Mario hits a block, we inferred that the intended function was to search in that block. Gray dots indicate the predicted functional-level operators. When an functional-level operator is predicted but a corresonding function cannot be unambiguously inferred from the observed behavior, a gray dot appears, but no black dot is drawn in the same Display column. In that case, all the functional-level operators consistent with the observed behavior are indicated with thin black circles. Gray lines connect the predicted functional-level operators and black lines connect the inferred functions. When no function can be unambiguously inferred, the black line passes through the predicted functional-level operator if that operator is consistent with the behavior, and does not pass through the predicted functional-level operator if that operator is contradictory to the observed behavior. Elongated gray circles represent consecutive displays in which the same functional-level operator, with the same argument, is selected. Elongated black circle indicate that the behavior observed throughout those displays is inferred to be in the service of the same function.

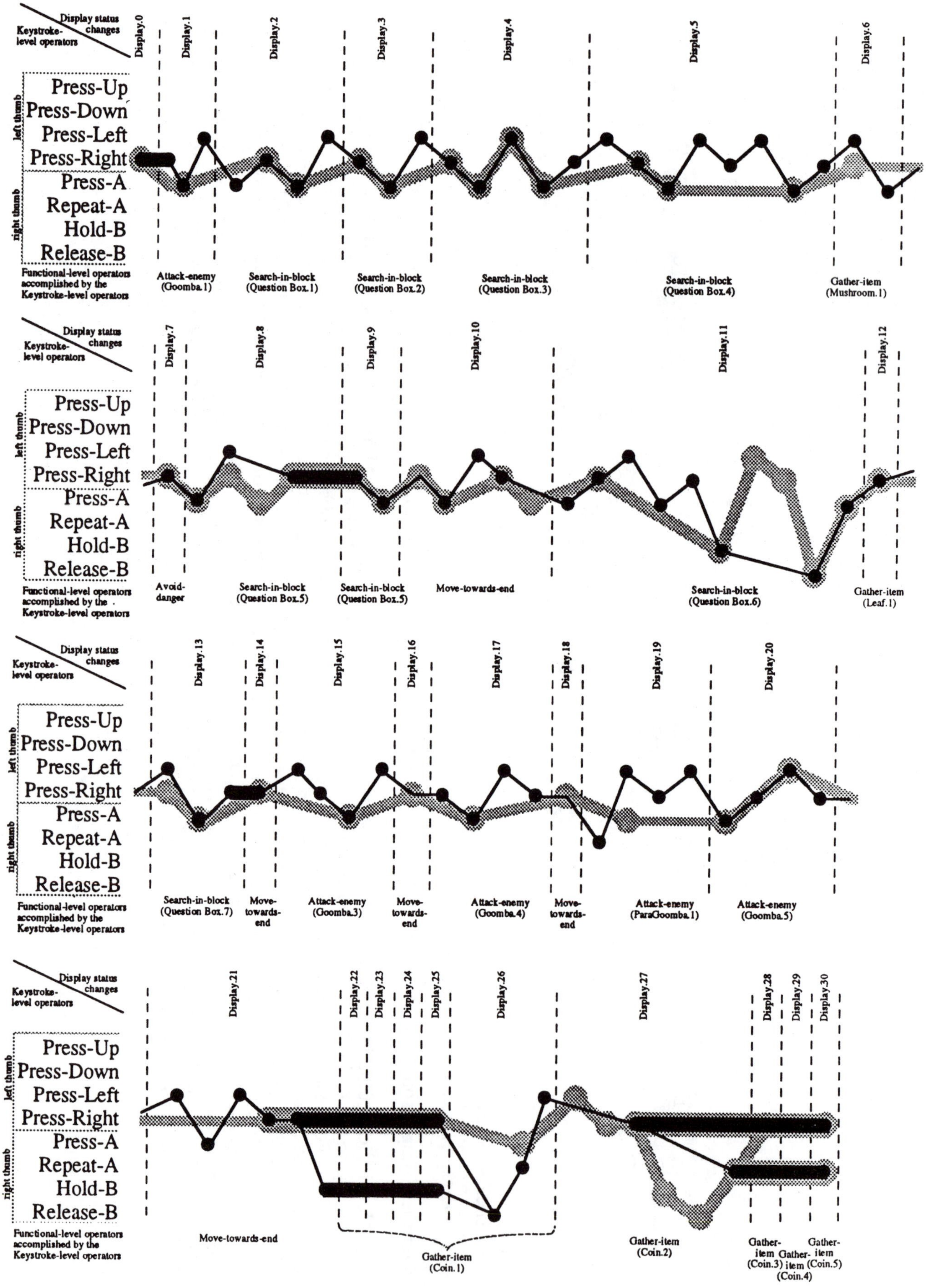

Figure 2. Comparison of keystroke-level predictions to observed behavior
(description same as that of Figure 1.)

in the game where the expert seems to anticipate gathering some coins that are not yet visible on the screen and for which he must attain flying speed. He moves left to get a running start for take-off. The model does not have the prior knowledge that coins will eventually appear to the right, and moves towards the end of the level (to the right) until it sees the coins, and then gathers them. Thus, the expert moves to the left in anticipation of flying, while the model moves to the right until it sees something to gather. As soon as the model sees the coins, the model and the expert have the same knowledge and they come back into synch.

The comparison of keystrokes inferred from the observed behavior and the motor operators predicted by the keystroke-level model, (Figure 2), also has several interesting features. The most striking is the dramatic difference in predictive power between the functional-level and keystroke levels; the functional-level predictions are almost perfect while the keystroke-level model predicts only about half of the observed behavior (46 of the 96 observed keystrokes). This is the same pattern of results obtained in Card, Moran, and Newell's analyses of text editing (1983), with functional-level operators predicting close to 100% of text-editing behavior and motor operators predicting about 60%.

Such a large drop in predictive power indicates that the keystroke-level models, both for the text-editing task and the game-playing task, may be missing important features that correspond to the unexplained behavior. For the text-editing task, Card, Moran, and Newell state that much of the unexplained behavior involved hand movements outside the model, e.g. the user licked her fingers before turning each page, an act not included in their model. In this analysis, there seems to be a similar type of unexplained behavior, twisting while jumping.

Twenty-four of the 37 observed keystrokes not predicted involve turning Mario left or right while jumping or floating. Experts tell us that this twisting motion slows Mario's horizontal motion while in the air. This indicates that the motor model used in this analysis is too simple to capture the interaction of forces in Mario's world (e.g. the equivalents of gravity and friction).

DISCUSSION OF THE GOMS ANALYSES

The results of this analysis indicate that GOMS can capture the knowledge necessary to predict the course of this highly interactive behavior. The functional-level operators in this segment of behavior are literally dictated by some simple heuristics derived from the overriding goals of the game, the operators and methods described in the instruction booklet, and the elements visible on the display.

Pengi, a video-game playing system built by Agre and Chapman [1], has been used to argue that planning-oriented frameworks such as GOMS cannot adequately predict behavior in highly-interactive, externally-driven environments. We believe that the results presented here demonstrate that this is not the case. Clearly, the sequence of expert behavior at the functional level is predicted very well.

We have not yet produced predictions of the timing of keystroke-level operators from our analyses, as we have in other GOMS analyses (e.g., [7], [3]). However, preliminary analyses indicate that this model will behave reactively enough to simulate the time-course of the game. In the expert's performance, the average time between the onset of keystrokes is about 300 msec, with the range for same-hand keystrokes of 50 msec to over 2 seconds, and the range for alternate-hand keystrokes of 0 msec (simultaneous use of both hands) to over 1 second. The time for a cognitive operator in Soar has been estimated to be on the order of 100 msec [11]. At this level of expertise, Soar predicts that the elements in the environment will trigger the selection of an appropriate keystroke with only one or two cognitive operators. These operators could be buffered to produce the simultaneous use of both hands and the delay between same-hand keystrokes equal to a single cognitive operator (similar to the typing model in [5]). Thus, we believe that a GOMS model can perform in this fast-paced situation using plans (methods) to produce behavior that is sufficiently reactive.

As well as demonstrating that GOMS could produce such interactive behavior, this work provides evidence that a system like Pengi could not mimic human behavior without plan-like information. For instance, at one point in the game, the expert begins to search in a block that is the closest one to Mario. However, on the way to searching in the target block, Mario must go beyond it and pass closer to another block. The expert ignores the closer block and continues to the original target. HI-Soar also continues to the original target block because it has a preference for continuing to implement an incomplete method for the current `search-in-block` functional-level operator rather than switching to a new `search-in-block` functional-level operator. A system like Pengi, on the other hand, would almost certainly switch to the second block when it became the closest to Mario.[3] We would argue that some level of planning, similar to the methods in GOMS models at least, is necessary to produce human-like behavior in this domain.

BEYOND GOMS

The HI-Soar model allows us to go beyond traditional GOMS models to investigate how users can acquire the methods and selection rules through experience with the computer system. Previous studies of the acquisition of routine cognitive skill have typically involved directly providing subjects with a set of methods that, if properly applied, will lead to successful completion of the task (e.g., [10]). Such studies have not examined what happens when the appropriate method is not given or when no selection

3 However, Pengi may have plan-like information encoded in its deictic representation. For example, "the-block-I-am-going-to-search-in", as distinct from "the-block-closest-to me", would allow it to prevent interruption of the goal.

rules are supplied. How do people acquire methods or selection rules through experience? The Soar unified theory of cognition provides an inherent learning mechanism, *chunking*, with which to address these questions. By examining the content of the HI-Soar model, we can identify knowledge that the expert exhibits but is not in the instruction booklet, remove that knowledge from the model, and show how the HI-Soar can learn that knowledge though playing the game.

For example, we described the first display of the game, where four Question Blocks and an enemy could be acted upon. The expert version of HI-Soar has a preference for searching in the closest block, hence, `search-in-block(QB1)` is selected. We eliminated the selection rules from a second version of HI-Soar and, instead, gave it an evaluation function based on how many points would be gotten from each of the proposed functional-level operators. This version of the model successfully chooses the same functional-level operator for the start-up display as the model with the explicit selection rules.

In another case, we looked at how the method of jumping onto a scaffold to search an otherwise unreachable block might be learned. The expert HI-Soar model has hand-coded knowledge that when searching in a block that is out of reach, Mario should jump on the scaffold under it. In a less expert version of HI-Soar, the model can recognize that a block is out of reach and use means-ends analysis to figure out that jumping on a scaffold would allow Mario to reach the block. Chunking integrates the solution as a new method and HI-Soar then transfers that knowledge to all subsequent blocks that are out of reach.

These investigations into how HI-Soar can learn methods and selection rules provide predictions about how people can learn from experience. We are continuing these explorations into learning by manipulating the knowledge in HI-Soar, the situations presented to it, and by comparing its predictions to the behavior of humans as they learn to play the game.

CONCLUSIONS

In summary, this work indicates that a GOMS model can predict functional-level behavior in the highly interactive domain of video games. To a lesser extent, GOMS can predict keystroke-level behavior as well, although a more detailed model of perceptual-motor behavior and the dynamics of the game world would probably lead to more accurate predictions. This work, therefore, represents an extension of the GOMS methodology to much more interactive, machine-paced, and graphic-based applications than has been previously demonstrated. However, given the limited nature of this demonstration, with a single user for less than a minute of behavior, continued investigation is necessary to establish the veracity of these conclusions. In addition, the implementation of these GOMS analyses in a Soar model allows us to investigate how GOMS methods and selection rules might be learned through experience.

ACKNOWLEDGEMENTS

This research was done in preparation for a panel at the Human Factors Society Meeting in Orlando, Oct. 5-12, 1990, organized by Wayne Gray and Mike Atwood of the Intelligent Interfaces Group at the NYNEX Science and Technology Center and we thank them for the professional challenge. This work was supported by the Office of Naval Research, Cognitive Science Program, Contract Number N00014-89-J-1975N158. The views and conclusions contained in this document are those of the authors and should not be interpreted as representing the official policies, either expressed or implied, of the Office of Naval Research or the U. S. Government. We would also like to thank Kyle Gray, Jay Anderson, and Billy Esch for their expert advice about playing Super Mario Bros. 3®.

REFERENCES

1. Agre, P. E. and Chapman, D. Pengi: An implementation of a theory of activity. In *Proceedings of the Sixth National Conference on Artificial Intelligence*, 268-272. Menlo park, Calif: American Association for Artificial Intelligence, 1987.

2. Card, S. K., Moran, T. P., & Newell, A. *The psychology of human-computer interaction.* Lawrence Erlbaum, Associates, Hillsdale, NJ, 1983.

3. Gray, W. D., John, B. E., & Atwood,, M. E. (submitted to Human-Computer Interaction) Project Ernestine: Validating GOMS for predicting and explaining real-world task performance.

4. Howes, A. and Young, R.M., Predicting the Learnability of Task-Action Mappings, In proceedings of *CHI 1991* (New Orleans, April 30-May 4, 1989) ACM, New York, 1991.

5. John, B. E. *Contributions to engineering models of human-computer interaction.* Doctoral dissertation, Carnegie Mellon University, 1988.

6. John, B. E. Extensions of GOMS analyses to expert performance requiring perception of dynamic visual and auditory information. In proceedings of *CHI 1990* (Seattle, Washington, April 30 - May 4, 1990) ACM, New York, 1990, 107-115.

7. John, B. E. & Newell, A., Toward an engineering model of stimulus response compatibilty. In *Stimulus Response Compatibillity: an Integrated Perspective.* R. W. Procter & T. G. Reeve (eds.) North-Holland: New York, NY, 1990.

8. John, B. E., Vera, A. H., and Newell, A.. *Towards real-time GOMS.* Carnegie Mellon University, School of Computer Science Technical Report CMU-SCS-90-195, 1990.

9. Kieras, D. E. Towards a practical GOMS model methodology for user interface design in M. Helander

(ed.) *Handbook of Human-Computer Interaction..* North-Holland: Elsevier Science Publishers B. V., 1988.

10. Kieras, D. E. and Bovair, S. The acquisition of procedures from text: A production system analysis of transfer of training. *Journal of Memory and Learning*, **25**, 507-524, 1986.

11. Newell, A. *Unified theories of cognition.* Cambridge, Mass: Harvard University Press, 1990.

12. Nintendo of America, *Super Mario Bros. 3 Instruction Booklet.*

13. Olson, J. R. & Olson, G. M. The growth of cognitive modeling in human computer interaction since GOMS. *Human Computer Interaction.*, 1989.

14. Peck, V. A., & John, B. E. (Submitted) "Browser-Soar: A computational model of a highly interactive task" School of Computer Science, Carnegie Mellon University.

15. Wharton, C. (In Preparation) Implications of the Differences Between Cognitive Architectures for Human-Computer Interaction. Ph.D. Dissertation Thesis, University of Colorado, Boulder.

Human–Computer Interaction – INTERACT '90
D. Diaper et al. (Editors)
Elsevier Science Publishers B.V. (North-Holland)

GOMS Meets the Phone Company: Analytic Modeling Applied to Real-World Problems

Wayne D. Gray[1], Bonnie E. John[2], Rory Stuart[1], Deborah Lawrence[1], & Michael E. Atwood[1]

[1]NYNEX Science & Technology Center, 500 Westchester Avenue, White Plains, NY 10604, USA.
[2]School of Computer Science, Carnegie Mellon University, Pittsburgh, PA 15113, USA.

GOMS analyses were used to interpret some perplexing data from a field evaluation of two telephone operator workstations. The new workstation is ergonomically superior to the old and is preferred by all who have used it. Despite these advantages telephone operators who use the new workstation are not faster than those who use the old but are, in fact, significantly slower. This bewildering result makes sense when seen with the aid of GOMS. With GOMS we can see that very few of the eliminated keystrokes or ergonomic advantages affect tasks that determine the operator's work time. Indeed, GOMS shows that some presumed procedural improvements have the contrary effect of increasing the time an operator spends handling a phone call. We conclude that if GOMS had been done early on, then the task, not the workstation, would have been redesigned.

1. INTRODUCTION

In the world of the phone companies, small differences in time per call can result in large savings of dollars. For example, NYNEX estimates that each second reduction per call in work time for its Toll & Assistance Operators (TAO) saves three million US dollars per year. With such an economy of scale, a newly introduced workstation that promised up to 2.5 seconds reduction in average operator work time (AWT) (or $7.5 million US per year) appeared very attractive[1]. However, the potential savings in yearly operating costs must be balanced against a capital cost of $10 to $15 thousand (US) per workstation. Since NYNEX has approximately 1,000 TAO workstations the initial investment in new technology is large and the cost of making a bad buying decision is great.

To evaluate the actual AWT saved by the new workstation with realistic call traffic, our group at the NYNEX Science & Technology Center helped to conduct a six-month field trial. Unfortunately, empirical trials are often long, expensive, and hard to control under real-world conditions. Analytic models, such as GOMS (Card, Moran, & Newell, 1983), have the potential to replace empirical trials but have not been validated with large-scale, complex systems. Therefore, in addition to the empirical component of this project, we have built GOMS models and are testing their predictions against the empirical results.

With its ergonomic enhancements, the new workstation was expected to improve (decrease) AWT. The new workstation had a 1200-baud, graphic display while the old workstation was a line and character-oriented 300-baud display. The new workstation eliminated many keystrokes and those that remained took place on a keyboard specifically designed for the TAO task. In contrast, the old keyboard had evolved through years of functional changes, adding new keys wherever space allowed.

As we framed it, the job was clear cut. We would collect data showing how much better the new workstation was than the old. Of special interest to the phone companies would be data showing for which call-types the new workstation had the greatest advantage and for which it had the least advantage. For the GOMS part we would compare the empirical data with GOMS models for accuracy, reliability, and cost (Gray, et al, 1989).

The empirical data surprised us. No matter how we looked at it, it showed that operators who used the old workstation to be faster than those who used the new workstation. To understand this unexpected result we turned to the GOMS analyses. These analyses show why the old workstation is faster than the new, and, most importantly, they indicate that it would be very difficult for any new workstation to be faster than the current one.

In this paper we provide an overview of the methodology of the study, the ***WHAT*** of the empirical data, and the ***WHY*** provided by GOMS. This is our first published report, more detailed reports will follow.

2. METHODOLOGY

2.1. Design

2.1.1. Task

The task of the TAO is to assist the customer in completing calls and recording the correct billing. Among others, TAOs handle person-to-person calls, collect calls, credit-card calls, and calls billed to a third number.

2.1.2. Office

The phone company office used in the study employs over 100 TAOs and handles traffic in the Boston, Massachusetts area. For purposes of the study, 12 existing workstations were removed and 12 new workstations installed.

2.1.3. Participants

All participants were NET employees who had worked as TAOs for a minimum of two years. Twenty-four participants were selected for the new workstations (the ***NEW*** condition) from a list of approximately 60 volunteers. Each new participant was paired with an ***OLD***, control participant matching for shift worked (that is, time of day), and AWT on the old workstation. The NEW condition was assigned a full-time manager from the management staff of the office.

2.1.4. Training

All NEW participants went through three days of training on the new workstation. The course was conducted on-site, by regular NET trainers. The course taught the techniques and procedures advocated by the manufacturer. The course itself was for ***conversion*** training, not new training; that is, it was intended for TAOs familiar with call handling and billing, who were simply being taught a new workstation. As such, it was very similar to other commonly taught conversion training courses .

2.1.5. Duration

The trial began in April 1989 and was originally scheduled to continue for six months. It was interrupted during the fifth month by a work stoppage (AKA strike) that affected all 60,000 NYNEX employees who belonged to a union. NEW and OLD participants worked their normal shifts during the trial. From the perspective of the NEW participants their tasks and duties as a TAO was identical to their pretrial job in all respects but one; namely, a new workstation was used. For the OLD participants nothing had changed.

2.2. Empirical Data Collection

In GOMS terminology, TAO performance is tracked at the level of the ***unit-task***, where a unit-task is one completed phone call (one completed customer request). For billing purposes, a database is maintained of every completed customer request handled by every operator in each office. Reports generated for each office randomly sample one out of every ten calls that pass through that office. We used this office database to extract data on the calls handled by our 24 NEW and 24 OLD participants.

In the database each completed call is classified as one out of over 250 call-types. Pretrial analysis showed that 19 call-types accounted for over 90% of all completed calls. Both the empirical and GOMS parts of this study included just these 19 most frequent call-types.

2.3. Data for GOMS

The GOMS analyses are based on previous human performance research and task specific information (John, 1990). The task specific information includes commonly used TAO training materials, observations of TAOs handling actual calls with the old workstation, pretrial AWT statistics, and videotapes of TAO handling staged calls with the old workstation. Staged calls, placed by a TAO supervisor and identified for the TAO, are a standard phone company practice used to debug new equipment or software; for this study, they were videotaped. Using these sources we can estimate the knowledge and procedures used by experienced TAOs, and produce estimates of system response times and customer conversation time. GOMS analyses for the new workstation are based only on manufacturer-supplied training materials and performance estimates from the old workstation. No observations or AWT data for the new workstations were used because our goal in using GOMS was to predict performance on the new workstation without empirical evidence.

3. WHAT: EMPIRICAL DATA

3.1. Pretrial

Pretrial matching of participants was based upon data collected by TAO managers at the phone company office. After the trial began we were able to use database information to check whether our two groups showed pretrial equivalence on this measure. The average difference between groups was small, 0.06 seconds, and insignificant, $F(1, 46) < 1$[2,3]. From this we conclude that our two groups, NEW and OLD, were equivalent on pretrial performance on the old workstation.

3.2. Trial

3.2.1. By Month

For the analysis by month we collapsed over call-type and chose the median time for each participant for each month. The data show that median work time (MWT) for the NEW group is 104% that of the OLD[4]; that is, the new workstation requires 4% more time on an average call than does the old workstation. This difference is significant. A two (group) by four (months) ANOVA (with months as a within subject variable) yields $F\ (1, 44) = 4.17$. The main effect of month is also significant, $F\ (3, 132) = 12.11$. This main effect reflects seasonal fluctuations in call-mix that affect MWT for both groups of TAOs.

More interesting, as shown by a non-significant interaction ($F\ (3, 132) = 1.39$, $p > 0.10$), between group differences in work time do not converge over the four month period. (From April through July work times for the NEW group are, respectively, 6%, 3%, 5%, and 4% higher than for the OLD.) This lack of an interaction suggests that the NEW participants master the new workstations very fast and reach asymptotic performance during the first month of the trial.

3.2.2. By Call-Type

For the analysis by call-type we collapsed over months and chose the median time for each participant on each of 18 call-types[5]. The two (group) by 18 (call-type) ANOVA (with call-type as a within subject variable) yielded a significant effect of group, $F\ (1, 46) = 5.92$, again indicating that the new workstation was slower than the old.

The main effect of call-type was also significant, $F\ (17, 782) = 101.27$, indicating that different call-types required different amounts of time to process. To our surprise, call-type did not interact with group, $F\ (17, 782) < 1$.

3.3. Summary of Empirical Results

Not only was the new workstation NOT faster than the old, but it was significantly slower. The approximate 4% difference translates to about a one second loss in MWT. Using the heuristic of $3 million (US) dollars per second per year, the 1 second difference would cost NYNEX $3 million per year.

Clearly something is wrong. How could an ergonomically engineered, modern workstation be slower than ergonomically indifferent, 5 year old technology?

The obvious answers seem to be wrong. First, the NEW participants were very motivated and very interested in "beating" their old work times. Managers reported that the NEW participants enjoyed the new workstations and actively tried to lower their work times. Second, although the study lasted for four rather than six months, all the data we have examined indicates that the NEW group had already reached asymptote and would not have improved their MWT with more practice. Indeed, preliminary analyses suggests that asymptotic performance was reached in the first week of the study.

4. WHY: GOMS

TAO's do several things in parallel when processing a customer's request: they listen to the customer, they perceive information on the CRT screen, they move their hands to appropriate keys and strike them. We represented this parallelism in a PERT chart, displaying all perceptual, cognitive, and motor operators (as boxes) and the dependencies between them (as lines connecting the boxes) according to goal decomposition and operator-placement heuristics (Card, et. al, 1983; John, 1990).

Figures 1 and 2 show the first and last segments of a GOMS analysis for one 15 second phone call. For each figure, the top chart represents the call using the new workstation while the bottom shows the GOMS analysis for the same call using the old workstation. For this report we make a virtue of necessity. A readable version of the full GOMS analysis would require more pages than this proceedings permits; also, a readable form would tend to draw the reader's attention to details which, while interesting in their own right, are tangential to this paper. The reduced version allows us to avoid such details while drawing attention to the overall pattern.

An important concept in analyzing the total task time for complex parallel tasks is "critical path". In project management, the critical path is "the sequence of tasks that determines the soonest the project can finish" (p. 6, CLARIS Corp, 1987); in GOMS analyses, it is the perceptual, cognitive, and motor operators that determine the total time for the task. For example, consider three partially overlapping activities: the TAO saying "New England Telephone, may I help you?", the TAO moving his/her right hand towards specific function keys, and the customer's saying "Operator, bill this to . . ." The TAO must perceive the customer's request before s/he can either press the appropriate key or make the appropriate verbal response, however, experienced TAOs can prepare for the most likely request in advance. In this case, the TAO moves towards likely function keys while still saying the greeting. Since saying the greeting takes longer than moving to the function keys, and customers typically wait for the operator to finish the greeting before they state their request, the movement toward the function keys is said to have "slack time" and is not on the critical path. This slack time is observed in the videotapes as the TAO hovering over some function keys waiting for the customer to give information that will dictate which key is to be pressed. In Figures 1 and 2, the critical path is shown as bold lines and boxes.

Figure 1 has two striking features. First, the analysis for the new (top) workstation has 10 fewer boxes than the analysis for the old (bottom) workstation, representing two fewer keystrokes. Second, none of the deleted boxes were on the critical path so the total task time for this portion of

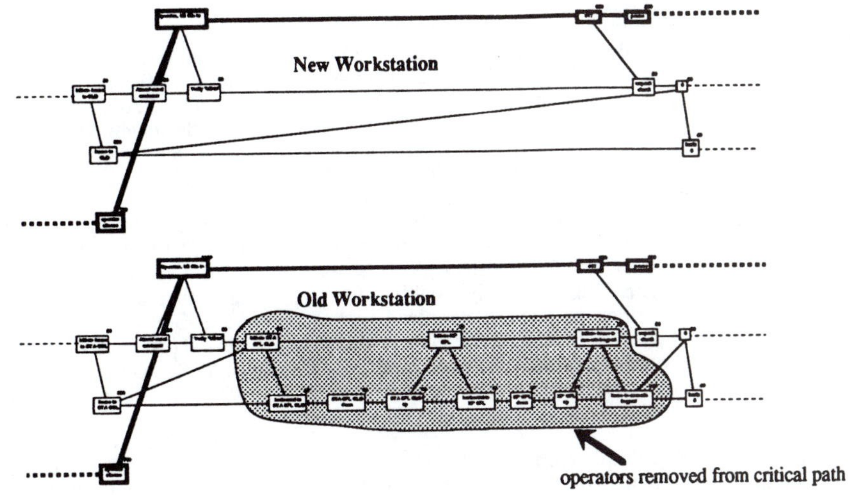

Figure 1. Section of GOMS analysis from near the beginning of the call. Notice that the new workstation (top) has removed two keystrokes (which had required 7 motor and 3 cognitive operators) from this part of the call. However, none of the ten operators removed were along the critical path (shown in bold). (Note: the print in the boxes is intentionally illegible.)

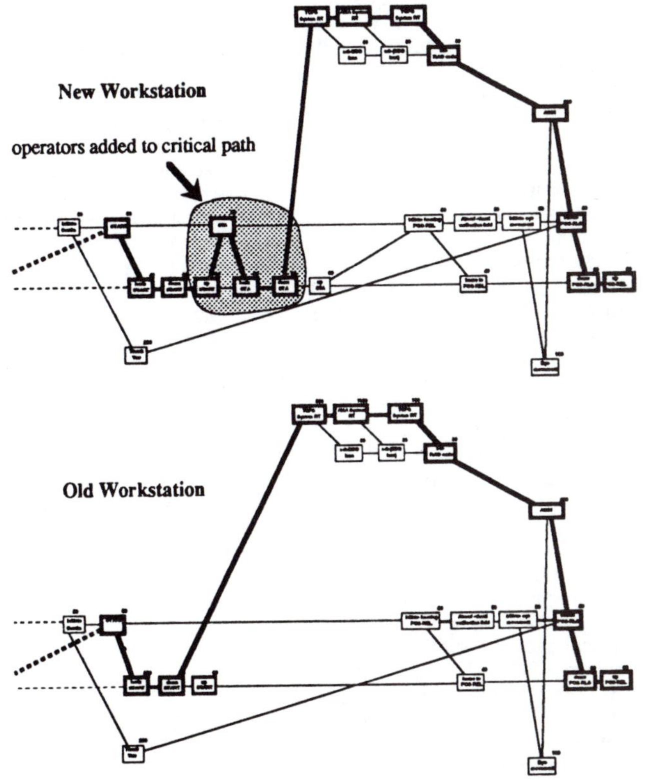

Figure 2. Section of GOMS analysis from the end of the call. Notice that the new workstation (top) has added one keystroke to this part of the call which results in four operators (three motor and one cognitive) being added to the critical path (shown in bold). (Note: the print in the boxes is intentionally illegible.)

the task would not change between workstations. At this point in the task the critical path is determined by the TAO greeting and getting information from the customer. Removing keystrokes here does nothing to affect the TAO's work time; that is, work time is controlled by the conversation, not by the keystrokes and not by the ergonomics of the keyboard.

The missing middle of the analysis (the activities between those shown in Figures 1 and 2) is identical for both workstations and essentially shows the critical path being driven by how fast the customer says the ten-digit number to which the call should be billed. TAOs are taught to "key along" with the customer. While a rapidly speaking customer could force the critical path to be determined by the TAO's keying speed, given that both workstations use the standard numeric keypad, the critical path (and resulting speed of keying in numbers) would be the same for both workstations.

If the new workstation simply eliminated the two keystrokes required by the old workstation in the beginning of the call, then GOMS would predict equivalent performance. However, for the new workstation, the procedure has been changed so that one of the keystrokes eliminated at the beginning of the call (Figure 1) now occurs later in the call (Figure 2). In this analysis, the keystroke moves from a position off of the critical path to one that is on the critical path. Hence, the cognitive and motor time required for this keystroke now adds to the time required to process this call. Thus, GOMS predicts that the AWT for this call would be slower for the new workstation than it would be for the old workstation. Indeed, the empirical data show that this call is 5% slower on the NEW than OLD workstation (a marginally significant difference, $F(1,46) = 3.14$, $p < 0.10$).

This analysis also speaks to the unexpectedly fast learning curve found in the empirical data. On the old workstation, the critical paths for many call-types are dominated by TAO and customer conversation time, and system response time, with individual keystrokes having as much as several seconds of slack time. Previous research with expert typists suggests that at most, the duration of keystrokes would increase from approximately 100 msec to approximately 1000 msec for the least experienced, hunt-and-peck keying on an unfamiliar keyboard (John & Newell, 1989, Card, et. al., 1983). Thus, it is unlikely that initial difficulty with the new workstation would change the critical path to being dominated by keystrokes. Therefore, most of the learning would be off the critical path and thus unobservable in the MWT.

To date, we have performed GOMS analyses for five call-types. The above example is representative of what we are finding. Generally the new workstation removes keystrokes that are off the critical path. Most of these are eliminated while some are placed onto the critical path. Current analyses are very specific to protocols obtained from individual TAOs. It is our intention to generalize the analysis for each call-type to all TAOs and to then assess the goodness of fit against the empirical data.

5. CONCLUSION & SUMMARY

The new workstation is ergonomically superior to the old and is preferred by all who have used it. Despite these advantages TAOs who use the new workstation are not faster than those who use the old. Indeed, statistical analyses show that the NEW TAOs are significantly slower than the OLD.

This bewildering result makes sense when seen with the aid of GOMS. With GOMS we can see that very few of the eliminated keystrokes or ergonomic advantages affect tasks that are on the critical path of the example call. Indeed, GOMS shows that some of the procedural changes moved previously non-critical keystrokes onto the critical path. Such changes add to the predicted work time even when the net result is fewer keystrokes.

Although the GOMS analyses is ongoing, the emerging conclusion is that there is very little that could be done to a workstation itself that would decrease work time for TAOs. The factors most limiting performance are neither the display nor entry of information, but system response time (other than workstation time) and customer conversation time. Clearly, if GOMS had been done early on, then the task, not the workstation, would have been redesigned.

For the TAO job, GOMS can be used in one of two ways. First, based upon GOMS, we can redesign TAO procedures to reduce the number of bottlenecks along the critical path. Second, and longer term, we can use GOMS to redesign the task itself. With GOMS we can ask whether it is worth while to speed up a component of the system. For example, when calling cards are used, a database is accessed to verify the number. What affect would a 50% decrease in time for database access have on operator work time? (If waiting for verification is not on the critical path then a faster access time would not reduce work time.) As another example, we can ask whether some parts of the customer interaction might best be automated.

Our main conclusion concerns GOMS itself. GOMS is an important and valuable tool that can be applied to tasks other than text-editing or spreadsheets. While it will continue to be useful to academic researchers, the time is ripe to apply GOMS to complex, real-world tasks.

ACKNOWLEDGEMENTS

Thanks are due to Karen O'Brien for her sponsorship, support, and assistance throughout all stages of the trial. Thanks also to Sandy Esch.

FOOTNOTES

[1] Reductions in AWT is just one of the many features of the new workstation. Its other features are such as to make it attractive to NYNEX even if AWT remained constant.

[2]Note that all all comparisons, ANOVAs, and figures are based upon median work time (MWT).

[3]The level of significance chosen for this report is $p < .05$.

[4]Note that the absolute magnitude of work time of NYNEX TAOs is considered proprietary information. Therefore, here and in several other places in this report, we have made an attempt to accurately depict the relative results without compromising corporate information

[5]One of our call-types was chosen not because of its frequency but because of interest in the procedure required to process it. Because many of our participants had such low numbers of recorded calls of this type (< 16) we excluded it from the current analysis.

REFERENCES

Card, S. K., Moran, T. P., & Newell, A. (1983). ***The psychology of human-computer interaction.*** Hillsdale, NJ: Erlbaum.

CLARIS Corporation (1987). ***MacProject II Manual.*** Mountain View, CA: CLARIS Corporation.

Gray, W. D., John, B. E., Lawrence, D., Stuart, R., & Atwood, M. E. (1989). ***GOMS meets the phone company, or, can 8,400,000 unit-tasks be wrong?*** Poster presented at CHI '89 (Austin, Texas, April 30-May 4).

John, B. E. (1990). Extensions of GOMS analyses to expert performance requiring perception of dynamic visual and auditory information. In the ***Proceedings of CHI, 1990*** (Seattle, WA, April 1-5). New York, ACM.

John, B. E., & Newell, A. (1989). Cumulating the science of HCI: From S-R compatibility to transcription typing. In ***Proceedings of CHI, 1989*** (Austin, Texas, April 30-May 4 1989). New York: ACM, pp. 109-114.

THE CONTRIBUTIONS OF APPLIED COGNITIVE PSYCHOLOGY TO THE STUDY OF HUMAN-COMPUTER INTERACTION

PHIL BARNARD

1. Introduction

1.1 *Human-computer interaction: the research context*

When a user is interacting with a computer system, two highly complex information processors are effectively conducting a dialogue. One of these, the user, will be engaged in some purposeful activity which is directed towards achieving a task objective in the home or workplace. The other, the computer system, is the tool that mediates the achievement of those objectives. Both parties to the dialogue are manipulating and acting upon information that represents concepts or entities in a particular task domain, for example, business accounts; the component reactions in a chemical plant; spaceships in a game; documents; or even computer programs themselves.

In order to achieve their particular objectives, individual users cannot typically rely on their knowledge of the task domain alone (cf. Morton *et al.*, 1979). They must also learn something about the way in which the tool behaves. They need such knowledge to interpret the state of information in the system; to assess how that state relates to their immediate goals; and to communicate to the system what action to take in order further to pursue those goals. These activities of interpretation, assessment and pursuing a course of action all occur in a specific context.

Obviously, that context is very much shaped by the particular style or form of human-computer interface that the system offers. As processors of information, any given generation of system is subject to the constraints of design practices within current hardware and software capabilities. Equally, the user shapes the context of a particular interaction. As processors of information, users are subject to different constraints — those of natural human cognition, their experience, their specific needs for using a computer tool and their broader motivations for doing so. The context is also determined by representations of the specific entities in the task domain that are being thought about by the user and manipulated by the system. In the course of a particular dialogue sequence these have a history. That history is likely to constrain both the user's interpretation of the system state and the system actions that can be carried out.

The study of human-computer interaction seeks to understand what it is about the factors within this total context that lead to productive and efficient use of computer tools. Once gained, that understanding should enable us to design new and better tools to support human endeavour and even to extend its horizons.

It has often been emphasised that this is essentially a multidisciplinary enterprise (e.g., Gaines, 1984; Norman and Draper, 1986; Carroll, 1987; Hammond, Christie and Marshall, 1987). In the process of development, software specialists, industrial designers and human factors engineers have all contributed to the evolution and enhancement of user interfaces. In the process of research many different disciplines have brought their concepts and methodologies to bear on the problems of usability. Computer science and its associated disciplines have led to enhancements in both hardware and software capabilities. The behavioural and cognitive sciences have also had very real influences. Some of these, such as psychology, ergonomics and sociology have assisted in the definition and analysis of the phenomena of actual tool use. Others such as linguistics and artificial intelligence have yielded important insights into the representation of knowledge and its manipulation.

In practical terms, cross-disciplinary understanding and cooperation are clearly of great importance for the productive advancement of both research and development projects. It is equally important for the effective transfer of new ideas from the research to the development communities. In more theoretical terms cross-disciplinary understanding is becoming essential. Although individual disciplines have their own objectives, methodologies and concepts, there is substantial cross-fertilisation. Both computers and users are representing and processing information and knowledge. Hence, concepts and techniques originating in one discipline are frequently of value in another.

For example, in order to analyse and explore the properties of the human information processor, psychologists may draw upon architectural concepts (e.g., transient and permanent storage) or functional concepts (e.g., executive processes) whose origins lie in computer science. Likewise, in order to analyse and explore how people represent and manipulate knowledge, psychologists may draw upon linguistics and artificial intelligence. Such intensive cross-fertilisation inevitably leads to a blurring of the boundaries between disciplines.

1.2 *Applied cognitive psychology*

Since its rapid evolution in the 1960s (e.g., see Neisser, 1967) cognitive psychology has sought to improve our scientific understanding of the fundamental properties of the human information processing mechanism. Its primary emphases have been upon developing and testing theories concerning the ways in which that mechanism constructs, manipulates and acts upon mental representations. Individual theories cover perception, language understanding and production, memory, problem solving, consciousness, intention and the control of action and many more. These areas of concern are all potentially relevant to the ways in which users will behave in the course of interacting with a computer.

Applying cognitive psychology directly to the problems of human-computer interaction is far from straightforward. Typically, individual theories are tested and evolve in the context of rather abstract laboratory tasks. These seek to isolate the influences upon behaviour of the component processes and mental representations which underlie cognition. Although substantial progress has been made towards defining and characterising important cognitive phenomena, there is little consensus concerning the theoretical concepts and principles that best explain them.

Typically, laboratory experiments focus upon repeated measurement of relatively "local" episodes of behaviour — as when subjects respond to discretely presented stimulus material. The basic phenomena obtained in these settings and the theories developed to account for them do not readily generalise beyond the confines of particular experimental paradigms. Also, it is often far from clear how the phenomena and theories relate to the settings of human-computer interaction where the component processes of cognition are coordinated to control extended and purposeful sequences of behaviour (e.g., see Barnard, 1987).

Applied cognitive psychology attempts to bridge the gap between the properties of cognition as studied in the more abstract laboratory tasks and those phenomena that are characteristic of cognition in the tasks of everyday life. There is considerable conceptual and methodological overlap between the core discipline of cognitive psychology and its applied counterpart. There are also differences. In the laboratory, hotly debated theoretical issues may focus upon predictions concerning relatively small differences in behaviour whose detection requires carefully controlled experimental conditions. The variables that give rise to those effects may be contributing relatively little to the overall ease or difficulty of carrying out the tasks of everyday life. As Landauer (1987) has remarked: "the point of applied research is to understand what matters in realistic contexts."

Knowing what is likely to matter in advance can be extremely difficult. There are many different ways in which an interface design may prove problematic. It might, for example, have an elegant and consistent command language. Users may nevertheless err when the command structures are incompatible with the organisation of information on the VDU (e.g., see Barnard *et al.*, 1981). Alternatively, a command language may prove problematic because it requires frequent use of shift key combinations on the keyboard (e.g., see Hammond *et al.*, 1980). Empirical evaluation may of course identify such problems. They nevertheless invite theoretical and practical analysis.

From a theoretical perspective this may require taking an integrated approach to the analysis of perception, cognition and action. This in turn may mean that our basic theoretical approaches need rethinking. Their scope may need to be substantially increased and this may require the development of concepts and techniques that enable us to generate approximate, but applicable, characterisations of cognition (e.g., see Card, Moran and Newell, 1983; Norman, 1986; Young and Barnard, 1987). From a more practical perspective, an integrated analysis of contributory factors may focus upon the various trade-offs that need to be taken into account in the actual process of system design (e.g., see Norman, 1983; 1986). Enhancing one attribute of an interface (e.g., displaying more helpful information) may have associated costs (it takes time to present and occupies VDU space). Viewed in this way there may be no clear resolution of a design problem, only trade-offs among alternative options.

Given the diversity of methods and theoretical concepts, as well as the broad range of practical issues associated with human-computer interaction, there are many different ways of pursuing research in applied cognitive psychology. The potential pay-offs are substantial. Sophisticated empirical methods, principled knowledge of the characteristics of user-system interactions and applicable models of user cognition could do much to enhance system designs and streamline their development. In moving towards these practical objectives, significant insights may also emerge concerning more fundamental theoretical issues, thereby also enhancing the core discipline of cognitive psychology itself.

1.3 *Key questions for this chapter*

The present chapter is set against the background of an interdisciplinary research context and the challenges of establishing systematic behavioural principles that encompass practical concerns. Its primary purpose will be to assess the contributions that can and are being made by applied cognitive psychology to the study of human-computer interaction. The blurring of boundaries between disciplines and between theoretical and practical issues means that the assessment will inevitably encompass a range of concepts and techniques. There is also a vast amount of research activity.

Hence, the assessment must be restricted to illustrations of the various types of contribution.

Many of the issues associated with design concepts and the application of behavioural methodologies within the development process are covered in Anderson and Olson (1985) and by other chapters in this book (e.g., Shneiderman; Shackel). Here the assessment will focus upon the use of interactive systems by those who are not specialists in a computer discipline. It will also concentrate upon two core questions: What progress is being made within applied cognitive psychology towards contributing a principled understanding of the phenomena or system use? What are the prospects for the systematic application of that principled understanding?

2. The visions

2.1 *Alternative objectives*

Cognitive psychologists actually turned their attention to the problems of human-computer interaction almost as soon as the technology became available to them. Over and above the immediate objectives of a particular study, most of the researchers had some broader vision concerning the potential of their concepts and methods.

Some concentrated upon the traditional goals of human factors. The measurement of performance with an appropriately sampled population of users could help choose among alternative interfaces with considerably better reliability than a designer's intuitions (e.g., see Ledgard *et al.*, 1980). Others were concerned with using behavioural evidence to formulate guidelines and principles which could be more generally applied early in the design process (e.g., see Black and Sebrechts, 1981). Systematic analysis also offered the prospect of potentially powerful alternatives to traditional emphases on empiricism and guidelines.

Such alternatives included the possibility of using formal methods to represent alternative interface designs in a way that would reveal their overall complexity or the presence of internal inconsistencies (e.g., Reisner, 1982). Others advocated using specifically psychological assumptions to model and predict key attributes of user behaviour — such as the time it would take users to learn a system or to perform specific tasks (e.g., Card *et al.*, 1983). For many of these approaches to apply, system and task specifications had to be predefined. For these, the visions remained essentially evaluative in nature. For others the vision included a more creative component. If cognitive concepts and methods were applied to furnish a deep understanding of the problems experienced by users, then that understanding could be used much more directly — to "invent" new types of interfaces that resolve the problems (e.g., see Landauer, 1985). A representative sample of these approaches will be examined in subsequent sections.

2.2 *An organising schema*

Before considering research achievements, it is helpful to have some kind of organising schema that can encompass key points of the different visions. In very general terms applied cognitive psychology can be viewed as bringing an empirical and conceptual "toolkit" to bear on the problems of human-computer interaction. Like any toolkit, its constituent elements fulfil different functions. One way of organising these elements into a broader research strategy is illustrated in Figure 1 (from Hammond and Barnard, 1984).

Some of the empirical methods focus upon observation and the acquisition of problem-defining data (cf. the "field" studies of Figure 1). They enable key phenomena of system use or user cognition to be charted. The problems associated with existing systems are, for example, frequently studied by obtaining session protocols of users attempting a realistic sample of tasks. Such information may be supplemented by measures of user perceived difficulties as assessed from their verbal comments or via assessment of their preferences. Such techniques are equally well suited to the exploration of the problems faced by designers as well as those faced by users. Alternatively, issues may initially be explored by studying users' basic conceptualisations within a task domain.

Explorational data of this type can fulfil both practical and research functions. They can, of course, be used to provide feedback to designers concerning usability. They can also provide a rich hunting ground for ideas and insight concerning the more basic causes of difficulties. Gradual accumulation of patterns of difficulties provide important signposts as to "what really matters" in human-computer interaction. This in turn helps to formulate hypotheses and to frame the requirements that our analytic and conceptual methods must meet (the "formal" tools of Figure 1).

Many of the more formal analytic methods can also have an exploratory character. Such is the case, for example, with many forms of task analysis. However, once such analyses are initially framed, or preliminary hypotheses formed on the basis of observational evidence, their ramifications can be tested in the laboratory using more classic experimental procedures and designs. Such tests may involve truly interactive systems or simulations of them. Alternatively, they may take key variables and study their consequences in tasks that are closely allied to those that might be accomplished with a computer system. If closely modelled upon a particular application, such studies can furnish a direct input to the design process. However, where variables are systematically manipulated they primarily serve to help define

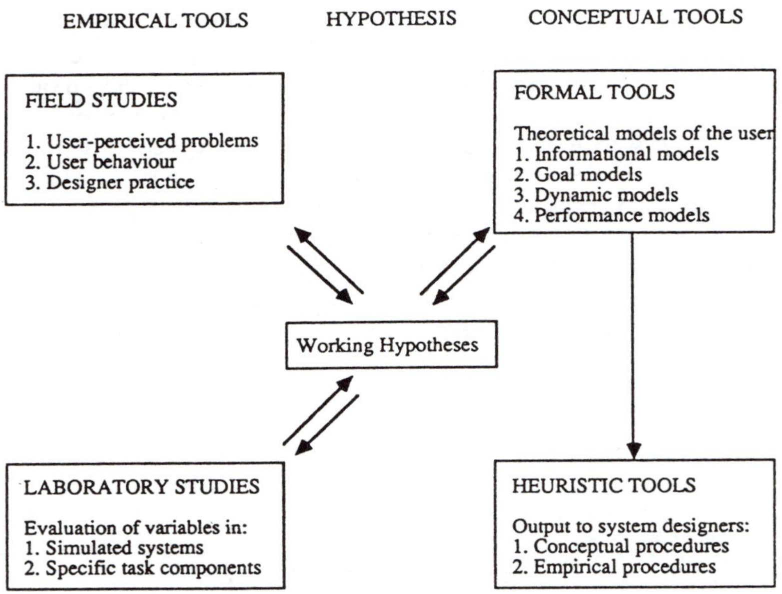

Figure 1. The toolkit organised into a research strategy (from Hammond and Barnard, 1984).

and delineate relationships between attributes of users, tasks and systems and attributes of performance. In short, such studies help us to understand the phenomena of system use.

Equally, those studies provide a basis for evaluating whether or not our more conceptual and analytic methods are accurately capturing and predicting what users are likely to do. Once such relationships are validated, the wider enterprise can really talk about heuristic engineering tools: conceptual and empirical procedures that can actually be used in system design and development. Naturally, the schema shown in Figure 1 does not accurately capture all the different research visions. The elements of the "toolkit" can be structured and used in a variety of ways. Research achievements can nevertheless be considered in terms of how our working hypotheses have been shaped (1) by exploratory studies; (2) by more conceptual analyses; (3) by experimental investigations of potential principles; and in terms of (4) the prospects for translating the products of such research into truly applicable tools.

In the following sections, each of these points will be considered in turn. The achievements will be presented in terms of the progress being made by the different kinds of activities. Since they all represent developing rather than mature research topics, there are many possible criticisms of the various studies and ideas. These will not be pursued in great detail in the context of outlining the achievements. A subsequent section (Section 4) will consider some of the general criticisms that apply to the field as a whole.

3. The achievements

3.1 *Achievements of exploratory empiricism*

In the context of longer term research programmes, exploratory studies have served to shape working hypotheses in a number of specific ways. For example, those hypotheses may be shaped towards the reformulation of a design issue, towards further scientific clarification of cognitive issues, or towards the more methodological concern of clarifying the properties of particular methods and measures.

3.1.1 Re-formulations of design issues

Work carried out by a group currently at Bell Communications Research (e.g., see Furnas *et al.*, 1982; 1983; Gomez and Lochbaum, 1984; Landauer, 1987) provides an excellent example of the reformulation of a design issue. One problem on which this group focused involved the way in which people name and categorise things: a problem of central importance to the design of information retrieval systems and command languages. The problem of naming and categorising was explored using a range of empirical methods such as name/descriptor generation, category assignment and sorting tasks. These techniques were applied across such diverse domains as text-editing, the contents of "yellow page" directories, cooking, and goods "wanted/for sale".

The common theme to emerge across studies, users and domains concerned the inherent variability in the way in which people name things. People can and do use a variety of different names or descriptions when referring to the same concept. The empirical data obtained in these studies added more than the simple identification of the problem. First, the variability could be quantified. The likelihood of any two people using the same name to refer spontaneously to the same concept ranged from a paltry 0.07 to a meagre 0.18. This reveals the likely extent of the problems for standard keyword retrieval systems which rely on the user generating one or only a few names that are the same as those chosen by the original designer of the system. Second, statistical simulations based upon the data were used to explore the probable success of alternative accessing schemes. Where target information could only be referred to by a single name, the probability of first try success was low (10–20%). However, the simulated probability of retrieval success could be dramatically improved (e.g., to 75-85%) by multiple "aliasing" — where the system accepts many, not necessarily unique, names for target information (Furnas *et al.*, 1983).

The same research group then went on to examine experimentally the issue of whether or not such enriched search vocabularies would actually enhance performance without an unacceptable cost in terms of the system retrieving many non-target items. Gomez and Lochbaum (1984) report one such study in which they systematically manipulated the richness of the search vocabulary with a database of 188 recipes drawn from cookbooks. As the size of the vocabulary was increased, so successful retrieval increased from some 12% to some 73%. Furthermore, the enriched vocabularies required fewer entries on average to reach the target than did the leaner vocabularies.

Another example of exploratory research with similar properties is provided by an IBM research group. Here the general problems of learning to use word processing systems were the focus of concern (e.g., see Mack, Lewis and Carroll, 1983; Carroll, 1984). In this case an initial study was conducted to identify the kinds of problems that "first time" users encountered. A small sample of users were asked to learn basic text entry and revision tasks by following a self-study training manual. While carrying out the tasks, users were asked to "think aloud" — to verbalise what they were trying to do and what they thought was going on. Records were preserved of both the explicit user-system exchanges and the users verbal commentary.

On the basis of these qualitative data, the investigators provide a rough taxonomy of the problems. Many of the difficulties could be attributed to a lack of very basic knowledge and the consequential difficulties of interpreting what the concepts and jargon mean. They report one user thinking that she might be "the printer". Similarly, users often did not appear to know what was relevant; they made *ad hoc* interpretations and inferences on the basis of very limited information; they generalised knowledge from their experience of typewriting; they assumed consistency of similar operations; they had trouble following directions and in gaining benefit from the help system and so on. Further examples of the individual categories need not be pursued here — they are well illustrated in Mack *et al.* (1983). Carroll (1984) concludes: "Learning in this situation appears to be very frustrating. System interfaces are inscrutable to the novice and the accompanying training materials provide little help in penetrating these mysteries."

The more general picture concerning user cognition during learning is evident from the taxonomic descriptions themselves. These make frequent reference to interpretation, assumptions, inference, and generalisation. Users were not slavishly following instructions, they were highly active participants in the learning process. Neither the training manual nor the interface provided appropriate support for active learners. In consequence, the researchers went on to explore ways of achieving more effective support.

In one series of studies, they examined alternatives to conventional documentation. The alternatives included "guided exploration cards" and "minimal manuals" (see Carroll, 1984). For example, the minimal manual drastically cut the amount of information presented; oriented the instructional material towards real tasks (rather than exercising facilities or functions); provided for more learner initiative (e.g., learners are left to explore deletions and insertions in a letter "on their own"); and provided greater error recovery information. Empirical verification of this approach showed that such manuals could be considerably more effective than their more conventional counterparts both in terms of acquiring basic skills and in terms of transfer to more advanced skills.

In a related series of studies, this same research group also examined a possibility for reducing initial learning difficulties. One way of protecting an active, exploratory user from making errors and getting into difficulties is to reduce the number of ways in which they can go wrong. This was achieved in a "training wheels" word processing system by initially disabling a whole range of functions required to carry out the more sophisticated tasks. In this system, the "first time" user only has access to very basic functionality. The more complex functions remained in the interface itself — as menu items in their appropriate contexts. However, if selected, the user was advised that that function was not available. Experimental studies were conducted in which basic tasks were learned on the training wheels system or on the complete commercial system. As with the minimal manual, the data suggested that the training wheels approach saved time and facilitated learning (again, see Carroll, 1984).

The achievements of this general approach are very real, whether applied to enriched keyword vocabularies, training manuals, or systems tailored for first time users. In each case, a mismatch between current design practice and users' natural predispositions has been identified and represented in terms of a general property of user cognition — variability in naming, or the active nature of human learning. In each case, the design problem is reformulated from the perspective of user cognition and the potential advantages of a possible solution are supported by empirical evidence. The "solutions" actually evaluated are not, of course, commercial products. They nevertheless stand in marked contrast to design "intuition" and constitute a clear demonstration of the potential benefits that could accrue were such solutions to be actively pursued in development projects.

3.1.2 Clarification of cognitive issues

Exploratory research has also helped to shape hypotheses primarily concerned with the further clarification of specific cognitive issues. For example, Hammond *et al.* (1980) studied users of an early relational database system which relied upon a highly notational command language. As with the Mack *et al.* (1983) study, the initial methodology involved obtaining session logs and "thinking aloud" protocols while users tried to solve a series of pre-set problems. Again, the investigators developed a taxonomy of errors and difficulties. Users frequently had problems with the form and content of the command language. One specific exchange was:

user types:	*t <- avg(age,people)
system responds:	age is an unset block

In this case, the command language required the arguments to be specified in a particular order — the block of data referred to had to be specified before the attribute over which the averaging was to be done. This kind of error could potentially have been due to users simply converting a natural language representation of the problem (I want the average age of the people) into a command string. However, such errors occur in the context of a set of command argument structures and in the context of other representations relevant to the particular instance of command entry (e.g., information on the VDU).

Having identified possible factors that could contribute to this class of error, Barnard *et al.* (1981) went on to explore experimentally their respective contributions to learning and performance in general. Several schemes for sequencing arguments were compared. In two schemes a pivotal argument always occurred in a constant position. In two other schemes the position of that pivotal argument varied. In these schemes the arguments were ordered in such a way as to be compatible or incompatible with users' natural language biases.

Three of these schemes led to roughly equivalent overall performance across initial learning. One scheme enhanced performance. That scheme involved placing the pivotal argument in a particular position (the first element) within the argument string. Positional consistency did not demonstrably enhance performance with the pivotal argument elsewhere in the string (i.e., the second element). Incompatibilities with natural language biases did not appear to retard learning and only contributed to argument reversal errors when the position of the pivotal argument varied from command to command.

Irrespective of the particular scheme for ordering arguments, performance was adversely affected when an information field presented argument identities on the VDU in an order that was incompatible with their ordering in command entry. A subsequent experimental study (Hammond, Barnard *et al.*, 1987) went on to show that the learning of argument structures was also influenced by the explicit prompting of command operations and by properties of the names used to refer to those operations.

The achievements and potential benefits of exploratory research of this kind are more indirect than those of the two preceding illustrations. These more factorial studies provide indications of the conditions under which particular variables can influence performance. They also provide some clues as to the relative magnitude of influences on user behaviour. However, the link to full blown designs with much greater functionality and richer tasks is often unclear. With larger command sets or different detailed constraints for argument ordering users may well behave differently.

What such studies achieve is twofold. First, knowing about the boundary conditions under which particular phenomena occur provides constraints for our working hypotheses concerning user cognition. As such constraints emerge over a series of studies they help us refine and reformulate our ideas as to what really contributes to error or ease of learning. Second, the nature of the phenomena enable us to pinpoint and illustrate how and why very general principles, such as maintaining consistency or natural language compatibility, may not necessarily be expected to provide the kinds of benefit often assumed by designers.

3.1.3 Methods and measures

The broader value of exploratory research clearly depends upon the properties of the methods used and upon the way in which qualitative and quantitative data are interpreted. The collection of "thinking aloud" protocols in conjunction with session logs, which played a part in two of the illustrations given above, is now a popular exploratory method. Its use, however, is not unproblematic. As a technique, it is highly laborious. In consequence, data are usually only collected for a relatively small number of tasks and users. This raises issues about the representativeness of such qualitative data. In addition, when users are reporting their thoughts verbally, they may not be performing the tasks in the same way as they would without concurrent verbalisation (e.g., Ericsson and Simon, 1980).

Such methodological concerns have led investigators to refine the techniques either to reduce the overall amount of effort involved (e.g., Hammond *et al.*, 1984), or to acquire other forms of verbal protocols. For example, O'Malley, Draper and Riley (1984) asked pairs of users openly to discuss problems during interactive sessions. This kind of technique provides enriched qualitative data concerning users' current concepts, rationales and explanations of system functioning. In contrast, Barnard, Wilson and MacLean (1986) discouraged verbalisation during actual interactive performance. What users could verbalise about the system was separately and quantitatively assessed using a different technique in which users described and explained pictures of system states to an experimenter.

In the Barnard *et al.* (1986) study, all users were queried on the same system states at two stages of experience. The contents of the protocols were quantified using techniques from the text memory literature in cognitive psychology. In this way the development of users' articulatable knowledge could be assessed and related to performance. As learning progressed the measures indicated that users' descriptions contained an increasing number of true statements about the system. Furthermore, this correlated with performance. Those users who performed well also verbalised a greater number of true statements about system operation. In marked contrast, the number of false statements about system operation did not decrease over the course of learning studied. Although apparently unrelated to overall improvements in performance, the pattern of false statements did appear related to the errors made during interactive performance. This led the authors to conjecture different relations between user knowledge and performance measures.

Other relationships among different "measures" have also been the subject of exploratory research. One major problem in relating design issues to research information is that alternative behavioural measures can tell different stories. This is often the case with measures of performance and measures of preference.

In one recent example, user preference and performance was explored in the context of different methods for entering data into a spreadsheet (MacLean, Barnard and Wilson, 1985). One method for entering data relied entirely upon the use of a mouse to point to each successive cell into which data had to be entered. An alternative method enabled the cursor to move automatically from cell to cell in a row or column. This method required a number of menu selections to determine the mode of cursor movement. This latter method required time and effort to set up but then saved on the number of mouse movements required during row or column entry. On this basis it would be efficient for entering large tables of data. However, for small tables the time cost of the additional menu selections should not be worthwhile.

MacLean *et al.* asked a sample of users to practise each method and then allowed them to make their own choice. This was done across tables of increasing size. To accrue maximum benefit from the alternative methods available, users should switch from the mouse method to the menu method when it becomes temporally efficient to do so. However, when the trade-off function was plotted, it was found that users tended to choose the menu method for the smaller sizes of table in spite of the fact that they were actually faster with the mouse method.

As with factorial studies aimed at clarifying cognitive issues, the potential benefits of exploratory studies of methods and measures are indirect. They are nevertheless of crucial importance: they help us to understand the nature of evidence and how it may relate to design issues. As with the uncovering of different relations among articulatable knowledge, overall performance and error (Barnard *et al.*, 1986), novel methodological techniques can provide a new perspective on an otherwise unclear problem. Likewise, understanding the relationship between performance and preference can help assess the validity of particular assumptions concerning, for example, user modelling. The MacLean *et al.* data queries the safeness of the assumption (Card *et al.*, 1983) that users will choose temporally efficient methods.

3.2 *The achievements of analytic approaches*

Empirical explorations of user performance help to define "what matters" in human computer interactions; to delineate phenomena; and to strengthen methodologies. However, the systematisation of our empirical knowledge requires conceptual analyses of the properties of systems, tasks and users. Many "conceptual frameworks" are currently under development (e.g., see Olson, 1987). Here, a distinction will be made between those frameworks that focus on the knowledge requirement of tasks, and those that focus on the cognitive processes that occur during the execution of tasks. In a richly interdisciplinary context, broad distinctions obviously oversimplify the true state of affairs. Individual frameworks typically differ in their detailed objectives and in the precise way in which concepts are used. The distinction between knowledge- and process-based approaches nevertheless enables some of the major contrasts and similarities to be drawn out.

3.2.1 Knowledge based analyses

Since early systems more often than not made use of artificial command languages, several investigators made use of linguistic techniques to describe the ideal knowledge that a user would require to operate a system without error. Among the pioneers in this area were Reisner (1981; 1982), Moran (1981), and Payne and Green (1983).

The actual notations proposed by these investigators have very different properties. Reisner (1982), for example, proposed a kind of "psychological" BNF (Backus-Naur Form[1]). This distinguished overt actions that a user must perform ("input" actions) and mental operations ("cognitive" actions) associated with their execution. Key characteristics of user performance were assumed to be related to the number of terminal symbols in the "sentences" of the grammar and the overall number of grammatical rules required to describe dialogues.

Similar assumptions were made by Payne and Green (1983) in the development of their task action grammar (TAG). They argued that the kind of BNF form adopted by Reisner failed to capture high level regularities in command languages that users

---

[1] Backus-Naur Form is a notation for representing the syntax of a programming language.

were likely to abstract. They therefore proposed a two-level grammatical model which distinguished sets and rules. The sets represented entities with common properties in the relevant domain; while the rules determined how sets of elements could legally be combined into sequences. The authors argued that this was not only more realistic from a cognitive viewpoint but also that it was technically more economic. Systems could generally be described with fewer rules than would be required in a BNF grammar.

Moran's (1981) command language grammar (CLG) was developed to enable designers to separate different levels of system knowledge and their relationships. It distinguishes three components. The first is a conceptual component which represents task and semantic levels of description. A communications component distinguishes a syntactic level and an interaction level; while a physical component distinguishes low level considerations such as spatial layout and device requirements. The grammar specifies how symbols at one level of description are mapped onto lower level symbols. In this framework it is not assumed that users necessarily require all these levels to operate a system — they could rely on knowledge at an interaction level. However, without an elaborated conceptual component users would get into difficulties when something goes wrong.

Other notational techniques with similar characteristics have been developed to analyse the properties of tasks. Moran (1983) has himself proposed another form of analysis (ETIT — mapping from the External Task to the Internal Task) in which notations are used to represent an external task space (e.g., in terms of entities in documents such as paragraphs and words) and an internal task space (in system internal terms such as lines and character strings). The complexity of the mapping from one form of representation to the other is presumed to be related to ease of learning or of transfer from one system to another. In a different vein, Johnson and his colleagues (Johnson, Diaper and Long, 1984; Johnson, 1985) have utilised a form of action-object grammar to describe what people need to know about computer related tasks.

Perhaps the most influential form of task notation for human-computer interaction is the GOMS (Goals, Operators, Methods and Selection rules) approach proposed by Card *et al.* (1983). In this approach, high level goals, such as "edit manuscript", are decomposed into lower level goals, such as "delete word". Operators are elementary perceptual, motor or cognitive acts which change the task environment or a user's mental state. Methods are the procedures which must be followed to achieve individual goals. Selection rules are heuristics for resolving conflicts where more than one method is available. Explicit specification of these elements can be used to model how long it will take an expert to perform the tasks. As with the hierarchy of rules in CLG, GOMS models can be constructed at several levels of detail.

This general approach has recently been developed into production system simulations of the knowledge users need to acquire to support error free expert performance (e.g., Kieras and Polson, 1985; Polson, 1987). As with other approaches, properties of the set of production rules required to simulate a user's how-to-do-it knowledge are utilised to predict learning and transfer effects (e.g., see Polson, Muncher and Engelbeck, 1986). Ease of learning is viewed in terms of the "cognitive complexity" of the production rule representations that need to be "acquired"; while ease of transfer can be assessed in terms of the number of common elements shared by pre- and post-transfer knowledge.

Several of the formal approaches outlined above are given a much more detailed treatment in this book by Ziegler and Bullinger. They also consider their relative strengths and limitations. Their most obvious strength is that the notations make explicit otherwise informal constructs like the consistency or complexity of an interface design. Since specification forms a potential basis for assessing such designs, showing how this can be done is itself a considerable achievement.

As representations designed to predict key aspects of usability, their main limitation is their tendency to assume relatively simple relations between "knowledge" and user "behaviour". They also tend to focus upon rather idealised, error free, expert knowledge. Typically, the analyses make little reference to the kinds of mental activities that are involved in task execution — such as interpretation or problem solving. Likewise, very real constraints on human cognition, such as memory retrieval and the limited capacity of mental processing, tend to play only a minor part in the derivation of predictions. These aspects are the focus of attention for process based approaches.

3.2.2 Process based approaches

As a part of their general effort to provide a scientific basis for the study of human-computer interaction, Card *et al.* (1983), adopted a particular perspective on the constraints on human information processing. This they encapsulated in their "model human information processor". The model distinguished different processors and memory systems (see Figure 2). Each was assigned relevant quantitative parameters such as cycle times or capacities. These parameters were abstracted from the relevant psychological literature.

The model provided a general background against which their calculational methods could be developed. Indeed, these investigators gave a number of simple illustrations of the ways in which such parameter estimates could be used to work through fragmentary components of user behaviour. It is not difficult to see how a framework of this sort can be used to guide the construction of performance models concerning the temporal attributes of expert skills. However, it is difficult to relate it

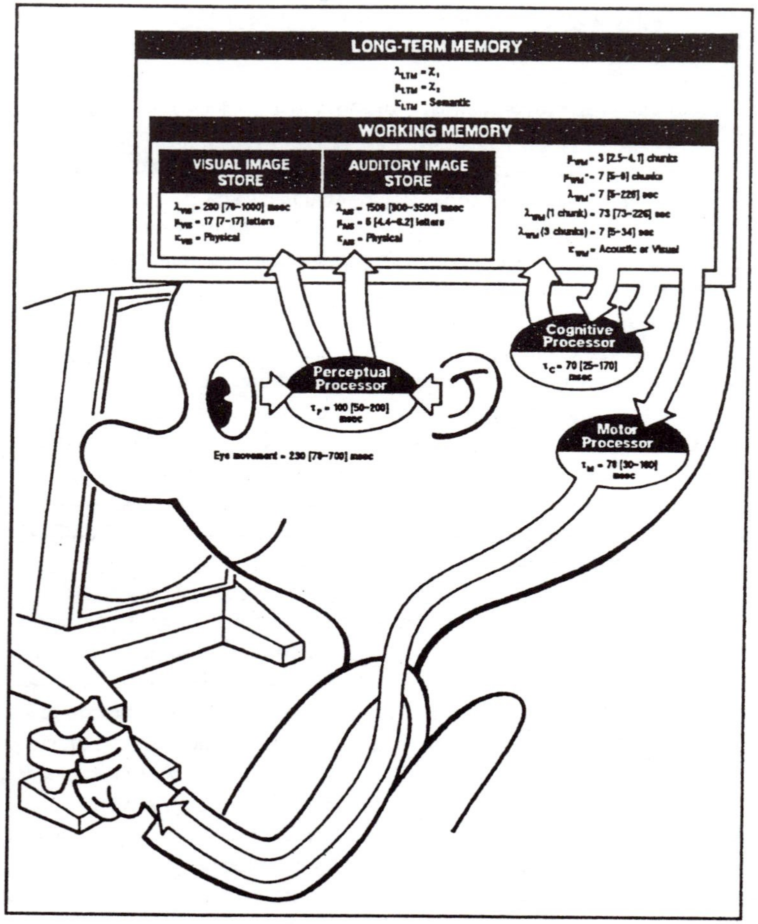

Figure 2: The model human information processor (from Card *et al.*, 1983).

directly to more qualitative aspects of cognition — such as how users manipulate their representations of knowledge. In fact, subsequent developments of the GOMS approach have tended to carry over only the more general assumptions concerning limited capacity working memory (e.g., Polson and Kieras, 1984) or the kinds of parameters required in memory access (e.g., John and Newell, 1987).

A rather different perspective is advocated by Norman (1986). His analysis focuses on the kinds of mental activities that occur in the control of action at an interface. Seven stages of activity are currently distinguished. In common with most other approaches, goals serve a pivotal rôle. Once a goal is formed, three further stages are involved in generating an action: forming an intention to act; specifying the action sequence; and executing it. The effect of that action is again assessed through three stages: perceiving the system state, interpreting that state; and evaluating that interpretation in relation to the original goal. These stages are viewed as approximations and need not be strictly seriated.

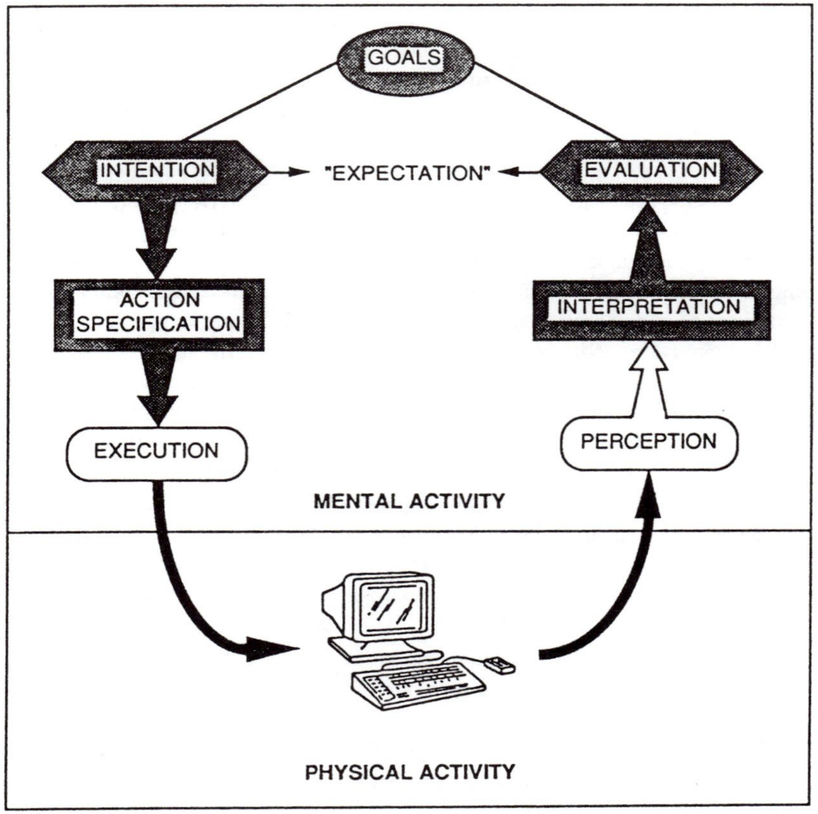

Figure 3: Seven stages of user activity (from Norman, 1986).

Norman's framework is not quantitatively predictive. Rather, it provides a basis for representing and understanding the cognitive consequences of particular designs. Menus, for example, can be thought of as devices that assist intention formation and action specification. Requirements for successive menu selections may nevertheless slow down execution in comparison to direct command entry. Likewise, it provides a clear conceptualisation of the potential benefits of direct manipulation interfaces. The use of iconic representations and pointing devices serve to reduce "the gulfs" between the system and the user. Users are directly acting upon representations of concepts in the task domain without requirements in action specification for command names or indirect menu selections. Similarly, where the consequences of an action are directly visible interpretation and evaluation are facilitated.

A framework that combines basic features of the two process based approaches outlined above has recently been proposed by Barnard (1987). This approach assumes a distributed architecture for human cognition with substantial capabilities for parallel processing of information (Figure 4). On this view different subsystems of cognition contain explicit processes that map from one kind of mental code to another (e.g., from a raw visual representation to an object based code). These processes embody the procedural knowledge required to execute the mapping. They also have access to declarative representations of information stored in "image records" (episodic memory structures) associated with each subsystem. On this view, there is no general purpose working memory. Cognition is viewed as being dynamically controlled via representations passed among subsystems.

The explicit decomposition of the memory and processing resources of cognition enabled Barnard to define a form of cognitive task analysis. It was assumed that key attributes of user behaviour could be inferred from a description of the way in which cognitive resources would function during task execution. The description incorporates components that refer both to knowledge and to information processing constraints:

User Behaviour <— Fn(Process Configuration and Procedural Knowledge and Record Contents and Dynamic Control)

In addition, different phases of cognitive activity, such as command entry or the interpretation of system states, are viewed as drawing upon different process configurations and memory resources. As with other approaches, this implies a family of models. In this case, members of the family describe the phases of activity that occur during task execution in a manner not dissimilar from Norman's overall view.

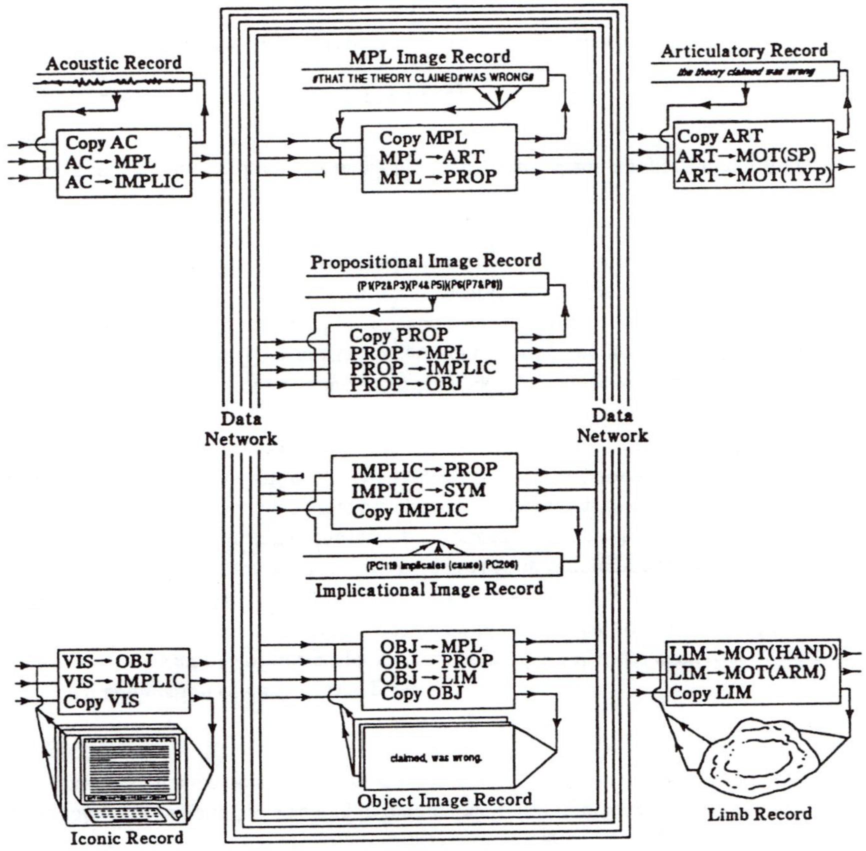

Figure 4. The interacting cognitive subsystems framework (from Barnard, 1987).

This approach is also intended to be predictive. Common patterns of mental activity are assumed to give rise to similar patterns of user behaviour. Such prediction requires principled relationships to be defined among the elements of the analysis and Barnard (1987) has proposed a number of such principles on the basis of experimental research on interactive dialogues. An illustrative example of the derivation of such principles will be given in the next section.

The process-based approaches illustrated here all attempt to capture, in an approximate manner, one or more aspects of what is going on in the user's head. In this respect, they complement the knowledge-based approaches described earlier. The key assumptions concerning user behaviour tend to be concentrated upon processes and their temporal or substantive properties. The assumptions concerning knowledge representation tend to be captured in a far more approximate way than is the case with grammars or production system representations. In effect, the individual analytic techniques are committed to different trade-offs in the depth and breadth of their coverage.

The advantages and disadvantages of the various different trade-offs is, of course, a matter for debate. However, user cognition is undoubtedly complex and it has often been pointed out that no single analytic technique will be sufficiently rich to capture all relevant features of user cognition (cf. Morton *et al.*, 1979). Against this background, the systematic development of a whole range of principled approaches can be regarded as a healthy state of affairs (cf. Norman and Draper, 1986). In contrast to the more classic style of theory typical of cognitive psychology, these approaches are making very real progress towards finding ways of specifying approximate models of systems, tasks and users.

3.3 *The achievements of experimental investigations of principles*

The experimental literature in human-computer interaction is now substantial. A significant proportion of this work has been directed at evaluating general issues associated with design alternatives. One example of an empirical "issue" is whether a few menus with many items are more effective than many menus each involving a few items (e.g., see Miller, 1981; Snowberry, Parkinson and Sisson, 1983). An earlier section (3.1) outlined other examples where experimental techniques were used to evaluate potential design alternatives (Gomez and Lochbaum, 1984; Carroll, 1984); as well as one example of experimental techniques being used to explore more cognitively oriented issues (Barnard *et al.*, 1981).

If our understanding of user behaviour is to advance in a systematic manner, then experimental research must go beyond the empirical facts to explicit statements of principles that can be generalised to new settings. For this to occur prototype principles and models need to be tested. Since the emphasis of the previous section was on the general properties of the different frameworks, experimental assessments of their predictions were not discussed. Indeed, as yet, the empirical ramifications of only some of those frameworks have been explored. The largest concentration of these concern various derivatives of the GOMS family of models (e.g., see Card *et al.*, 1983; Polson, 1987; John and Newell, 1987). There is also some data for the more grammatical formulations (e.g., see Payne and Green, 1983; Payne, 1984).

Where such assessments have been carried out, it is generally reported that the data fit the predictions of the model with reasonable accuracy. However, it is important to note that most of this type of empirical work is carried out by the originators of the model under test — and they get to choose the "testing ground". Where models have been evaluated by third parties, the fits can be less than impressive. Such was the case with an independent assessment (Allen and Scerbo, 1983) of the "keystroke level model" of Card *et al.* (1983).

As the various models evolve, it can be expected that many debates will focus upon concerns with the predictive accuracy and scope of the various modelling approaches. Rather than pursuing such detailed issues here, the present section will simply provide two illustrations in which experimental research is focused on an issue of principle. In the first illustration, classic principles from experimental psychology are applied to a setting in human-computer interaction. In the second illustration, evidence obtained in human-computer interaction is itself used to derive a principle.

3.3.1 An application of classic principles

In the opening sections of this chapter, it was pointed out that links between classic laboratory psychology and complex applied problems can be difficult to establish. Although they are relatively rare, there are clear cases where known principles of behaviour have been found to have utility in analysing problems in human-computer interaction. One such instance concerns principles that govern human choice and movement time. Indeed, such principles played a substantial rôle in the kinds of analyses advocated by Card *et al.* (1983). The present illustration concerns the application of principles to the depth/breadth issue in menu searches (Landauer and Nachbar, 1985).

In selecting items from a menu, users are making a choice among a specific number of alternatives. They must also carry out a movement to execute that choice. Hick's law governs the relationship between choice time and the number of alternatives; while Fitts' Law governs movement time as a function of target size and movement distance. Both of these laws have a logarithmic form:

Hick's law (choice reaction time) $T = c + k\log_2 b$

where b is the number of equally likely alternatives and c and k represent constants, and:

Fitts' Law (movement time) $T = c' + k'\log_2 d/w$

where d represents the distance, w the width of the target and c' and k' are again constants.

Landauer and Nachbar examined the applicability of these laws for menu choice where the user made a selection by pointing at a touch sensitive screen. This is an ingenious setting because the application of Fitts' law can be directly related to the number of menu options. The distance from the screen (d) is a constant under these circumstances and as the number of menu options available on the screen increases so the space available for each response sensitive area will reduce. Thus, both movement time and decision time could be expected to be a logarithmic function of the number of alternatives — or more conventionally, the branching factor in menu search.

Landauer and Nachbar report two experiments in which the depth and breadth menu searches were examined for a database of 4096 items. In the experiments, each menu contained 2, 4, 8 or 16 choices. In one case the targets were integer numbers; in the other they were alphabetically organised words. Pre-terminal choices were made by touching a sensitive band on the screen in which either an integer or alphabetic range was specified. In both cases the mean touch time per screen proved to be a linear function of the log of the number of alternatives in each panel. Their data are reproduced in Figure 5.

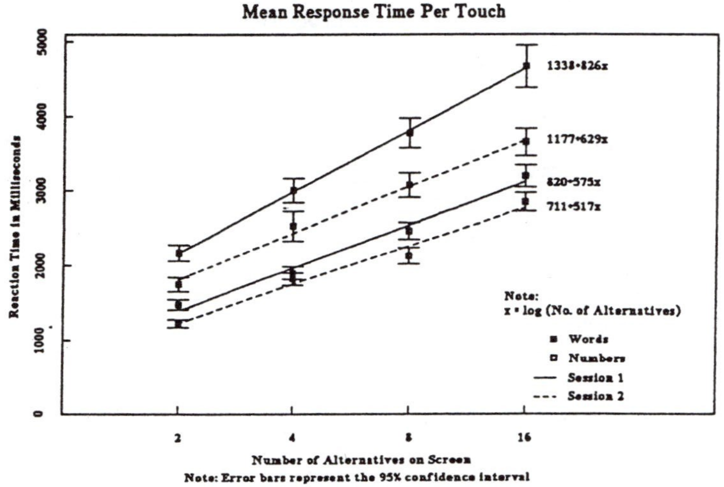

Figure 5. The logarithmic fit obtained by Landauer and Nachbar (1985).

Thus, in this setting, both laws applied. There must have been no substantial contribution from other processes, such as perceptual scanning, that was other than a constant or a log function of the number of alternatives. In terms of both mean and total search times the depth/breadth trade-off could be resolved in favour of breadth. Of course, in this instance there could be no ambiguity in the assignment of a target digit or word to a particular range. With fuzzier categories of information (such as those characteristic of viewdata systems) other decisional processes may come into play. The generality of such results therefore requires further empirical examination.

3.3.2 From experimental evidence to principles

Demonstrations of the application of known principles seem unlikely to form a basis for resolving many of the issues in human-computer interaction. Novel approximate principles need to be sought. In developing an approach to cognitive task analysis (see section 3.2.2), Barnard (1987) attempted to define principled relationships between cognitive activity and overt performance on the basis of experimental evidence. Some of the principles were motivated on the basis of a particular experiment concerned with the learning of command namesets.

The experiment (Grudin and Barnard, 1984) examined the learning of five different namesets for text editing tasks. The namesets involved semantically specific names (e.g., delete); abbreviations of those names (dlt); known words whose meaning was unrelated to their function in the text editing context (e.g., parole); novel "pseudowords" (e.g., ragole); and random consonant strings (e.g., FNM). Over the course of initial learning, the specific names were learned relatively efficiently. The abbreviations and unrelated words incurred some performance costs; while the pseudowords and consonant strings incurred even greater costs. Representative learning data are reproduced in Figure 6.

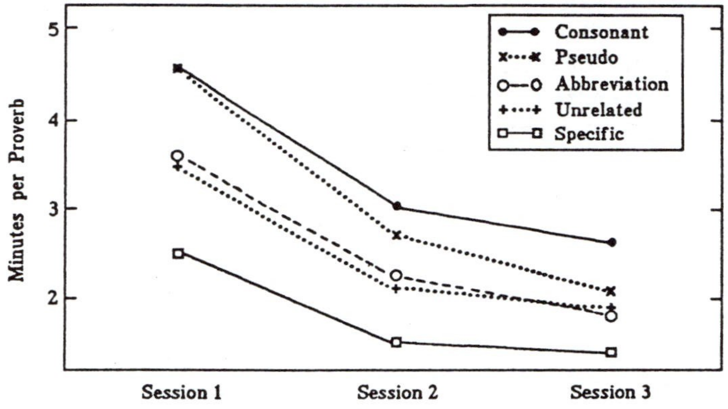

Figure 6. The mean editing times for learning the five command name sets (from Grudin and Barnard, 1984).

Barnard (1987) considered these data in relation to the demands placed upon the individual mental processes incorporated within his theoretical framework (see Figure 4). In order to issue a command name, separate processes must be recruited to map a semantic representation of the command operation onto its surface structure form (i.e., the name to be entered) and that surface structure form must be mapped onto motor actions for the control of keystroking. It was assumed that if individual processes do not embody appropriate procedural knowledge for effecting these mappings, then the dynamic control of action requires access to memory representations or inferential processing. These require additional information processing transactions among the subsystems of cognition. These extra transactions take time and increase the cognitive workload.

The Grudin and Barnard data suggested that the extra load could be approximated by assuming a principled relationship between the number of processes for which new procedural knowledge needed to be acquired and the complexity of dynamic control required within the human information processing mechanism. For the specific command names, it could reasonably be assumed that users would possess appropriate procedural knowledge both for the mapping from meaning to form and for the mapping from form to the required keystroke sequence.

With the abbreviations and unrelated words procedural knowledge would be absent for one processing component. In the case of abbreviations, procedural knowledge would be in place for mapping from meaning to the form of the full command word, but not for the precise sequence of characters to be keystroked. In contrast, with the unrelated words, the mapping from meaning to form would not be proceduralised. However, since the actual lexical items were known, the mapping from form to keystroke sequence would be proceduralised. With the pseudowords and consonant strings neither form of mental mapping would be known.

The resulting principles were specified in terms of general relationships between process configurations, procedural knowledge, record contents and the dynamic control of human processing activity (see section 3.2.2). Namely, if all elements in a configuration of processes required to support a phase of cognitive activity are fully proceduralised, then output can be controlled relatively automatically from the contents of a single image record. Where one process within a required configuration does not embody appropriate procedural knowledge then output cannot be controlled automatically and extra information processing transactions are required to control action. Where two (or more) processes are unproceduralised then many extra information processing transactions will be required.

These principles essentially account for the differences in initial performance depicted in Figure 6. However, performance with the pseudoword vocabulary improves faster than that for the consonant strings. In order to account for this pattern it is necessary to call upon another principle through which memory retrieval is enhanced by structural descriptions of possible lexical forms. The kinds of command names actually studied by Grudin and Barnard can be regarded as somewhat archaic when compared to more recent text editing systems. However, the important point is that the principles proposed are not restricted to that form of dialogue. They are stated in a very general form that can equally well be applied to the analysis of iconic interfaces or as yet undeveloped forms of dialogue style.

3.4 *Theory as a means to pragmatic tools*

In moving towards an applicable cognitive science, the various research projects described in this chapter have utilised very different tactics for calling upon principles and psychological theory. Some tactics have called for only the weakest form of synthesis. In problem-based solutions derived from exploratory research (section 3.1), such as the use of multiple aliasing or minimal manuals, theories were not systematically used. Rather, a psychological description of a usability issue is used to motivate a form of design. In these instances a general purpose application tool is not proposed. The gap between research and application is bridged by practical demonstration. This directly displays the plausibility of the idea to its target audience — system designers.

In other cases cognitive theory plays a direct rôle. In some instances, the application of the theory is best viewed in terms of a tool for thought rather than a tool for prediction. Such is the case with Norman's (1986) stages of mental activity. The kinds of subdivision proposed by Norman do not require a great deal of psychological expertise to understand. Accordingly, the distinctions themselves can have direct utility when supported by a few examples of how they relate to particular designs. They can help human factors practitioners, or even software designers, to conceptualise the nature of a design issue from the perspective of user cognition. Indeed, such conceptualisations are often felt to convey what is important about cognitive issues in a more relevant and digestible form than highly focused and technically presented models (e.g., see Whiteside and Wixon, 1987).

Much of the analytic emphasis in the study of human-computer interaction has been directed at stronger forms of synthesis. In strong synthesis, models based upon psychological principles are used to predict aspects of user behaviour in learning and performance. The intention here is generally to create tools that can be used to supplement empirical assessments. There are powerful arguments (e.g., see Reisner, 1987, Whiteside and Wixon, 1987) against any proposal to abandon empirical evaluations of designs and simply replace them with user modelling.

The encouraging feature of modelling activities in human-computer interaction research is the emphasis upon a rapid transition from theoretical discussion to the exploration of possible pragmatic tools. What research programmes have often strived to achieve is a practical demonstration of the utility of a tool and a methodology for its use. Representing a system dialogue in a formal grammar is, for example, a methodology in its own right. Although early examples tended to have an illustrative form, the potential utility of such techniques is now being demonstrated with significant coverage of the features of commercial products (e.g., see Green, Schiele and Payne, 1988).

The work of Card *et al.* (1983) also demonstrated a rapid transition from a theoretical representation (the model human information processor), to approximate engineering tools with very different methodological characteristics from grammars. In their case, the tools demonstrated were akin to mathematical methods employed in engineering disciplines. Task analysis and empirical estimates of relevant parameters could be used in mathematical modelling to predict key aspects of user performance. such as task execution times. These authors illustrate how such modelling could assist in design decisions concerning, for example, the range of different methods to incorporate into a system or the relative efficiency of different forms of input devices.

Although initially based upon the GOMS framework of Card *et al.* (1983), the work of Kieras and Polson has involved the demonstration of a different type of tool for use in an evaluative methodology (e.g., see Polson, 1987). In this case, a theory of cognitive complexity is explicitly realised in a working production system. This production system formalism is carried out with a real or envisaged system. Likewise, the way in which that system actually works is represented in a generalised transition network (GTN). The explicit representation of how-to-do-it and how-it-works knowledge enables both the user and the system to be simulated. Such simulations can then be applied iteratively both to explore properties of designs and to provide quantitative predictions concerning ease of learning and use.

The actual simulation of user knowledge means that some of the effort of a design team must be devoted to representing user knowledge. In order to do this, it is clear that someone on that team must have specialist how-to-do-it knowledge of cognitive complexity theory and how to implement it. Approaches that seek to avoid a requirement for specialist knowledge of cognitive theory are also under development. One possibility is to simulate theoretical constraints on human cognition, such as a programmable model of the user (Young and Green, 1986; Runciman and Hammond, 1986).

Operating within such a cognitively constrained architecture, designers would "program" user tasks that they have in mind for their envisaged system. If the designer finds it difficult to program the task, then by implication, users are also likely to find the task difficult. This kind of methodology involves designers using their own specialist skills to identify potential usability issues. By uncovering and exploring the nature of the problem for themselves, they should gain insight into how to create an alternative design that would avoid the problem.

A rather different kind of tool has been developed from Barnard's (1987) cognitive task analysis. In this analysis, a theoretical decomposition of cognitive resources (see Section 3.2.2 and Figure 4), is used as a language to describe mental processing. Principles governing cognitive activity were then inferred from empirical studies and represented in this resource based language (e.g., see Section 3.3.2). These were then supplemented by explicit rules for mapping from the principles to specific types of software application and to specific properties of user behaviour. These principles and mapping rules were then represented in the knowledge base of an expert system. A demonstrator system has been implemented for a restricted range of issues associated with command names, command sequences and menu sequencing (e.g., see Barnard, Wilson and MacLean, 1987).

This expert system builds approximate models of the way in which the human information processing mechanism will cope with the demands of a particular interface. On the basis of these models, the system draws principled inferences about both quantitative and qualitative aspects of user behaviour. Use of this tool does not require detailed specialist knowledge of the modelling process. The tool is aimed at human factors practitioners or designers with some knowledge of cognitive science. In addition, it does not require extensive formal specification of the interface. An analyst can approach the expert system with a specific design issue in mind. The system will elicit just that information it needs in order to build an appropriate "cognitive task model". Once that model is built, the system issues a textual report on the likely properties of user behaviour. If need be, the analyst can use the "what if" capability of the expert system to explore the consequences of modifying design features.

4. The realities of achievement

In the introduction to this chapter two key questions were posed. These concerned the extent to which applied cognitive psychology was contributing a principled understanding of the phenomena of system use and the prospects of that understanding being applied. There is a great deal of research activity, many empirical methods, a plethora of conceptual frameworks, a lot of evidence, and some prototype tools based upon theory. The ultimate value of research achievements in applied science must rest on the use of that science in design.

Obviously, much remains to be done by way of developing the various visions (Section 2) into a mature discipline that is routinely incorporated into system development. For such visions to be fully realised it is important to have a firm grasp of practical realities and to be in a position to respond in a positive way to more critical appraisals of the progress being made. From a purely scientific perspective, it is clear that there are many difficulties with our ideas, methodologies and evidence.

Exploratory methodologies have been used to great advantage and are being improved (Section 3.1). However, as Landauer (1987) has pointed out, the core discipline of experimental psychology has not been particularly productive in evolving the kinds of sophisticated exploratory paradigms that are really needed. It is also necessary to learn more about how to gain maximum benefit from those paradigms. In the case of exploratory studies using protocol methodologies, it is easy enough to collect the data. Then, much depends upon the skill and insight of a particular researcher in abstracting interesting or salient issues. Doing this successfully, particularly in relation to applicable theory, is often a matter of experience and judgement. Indeed, applied psychologists who are good at doing it may not be able to articulate how they do it.

Similarly, the different conceptual frameworks (Section 3.2) can all be regarded as capturing something important about cognition. However, they do make different trade-offs in modelling and in relation to the issues they address. The contrast between knowledge-based approaches (3.2.1) and process-based approaches (3.2.2) illustrated the kinds of trade-offs made. Most of the approaches remain partial and as yet have only been worked through for very restricted sets of circumstances. In this context, relatively little theoretical progress has been made towards dealing with all the different facets of interface use in an integrated way.

There are also problems with the kinds of assumptions made by the individual conceptual approaches. Predictions are usually based, not on a single simple assumption, but on a combination of assumptions. Under such circumstances a great deal has to be taken on trust. Sometimes constituent assumptions are open to debate. Most process-based approaches outlined earlier assume that human cognition is constrained by a central working memory of limited capacity. At least one makes a fundamentally different assumption. Barnard (1987) assumes that the restricted capability of the human cognitive mechanism to handle information in the short term is related to the coordination and control of distributed processes.

On other occasions, assumptions are implicit or only informally stated. This can make it difficult for people to agree on the content of a particular form of analysis. Such considerations can have profound consequences. To take just one example, the production system notation advocated by Polson (1987) enforces explicitness in the representation of user knowledge. However, the complete predictive mechanism assumes that productions are written in a particular "style". Variation in the style of writing individual production rules could in principle alter the outcome of the simulation (e.g., see Green *et al.*, 1988).

Uncovering and validating principles on the basis of experimental evidence (Section 3.3) can also be a difficult and lengthy process. The accuracy and generality of particular findings are a constant cause for concern. Furthermore, in some instances different pieces of evidence relating to a common topic can show markedly different patterns. Such has been the case with two of the topics considered earlier. Different experiments on the "naturalness" of command names for text editing have yielded superficially different results, sometimes coming down in favour of natural terminology (e.g., Ledgard *et al.*, 1980); sometimes in favour of computer-oriented terminology (Scapin, 1981); and sometimes showing that choice of terminology makes relatively little difference to performance (Landauer, Galotti and Hartwell, 1983).

Likewise, some studies of the breadth/depth issue in menu search have come out in favour of breadth (e.g., Landauer and Nachbar, 1985), while others have come down in favour of intermediate branching factors (Kiger, 1984; Miller, 1981). To the non-expert user of behavioural evidence these differences can be perplexing. However, it is frequently the case that factors other than the central topic of concern, such as the technique of assessment or the materials employed, are also varying from study to study. The real problem for the derivation of principles is to establish how all the relevant factors interact to determine the phenomena of system use. Such principles are unlikely to emerge from isolated or fragmentary pieces of evidence on any given topic.

In many respects applied research occupies the uncomfortable position of being squarely placed between the deep blue sea of science and the devil of practical application. There are equally powerful general criticisms from the perspective of those concerned with the practicalities of design and development. Many of the salient points have been recently discussed by Newell and Card (1985). They reinforce the general point that the theoretical contribution of applied science is too limited in scope. They also point out that there tends to be not enough knowledge to answer real design issues of current concern; and that when the researchers have obtained appropriate knowledge, its input is too late to be of real value. Thus, by the time scientific data for line editors is understood and accurately modelled, designers are building display editors; and by the time behaviour with these is understood, design attention is focused upon iconic interfaces, and so on.

There are also plenty of more detailed questions concerning the kinds of design tools that are under development (Section 3.4). One issue is the extent to which they are actually capturing the things that really matter in interface design. There is an argument, for example, that models of error free performance times for expert users are deficient in this respect. A substantial proportion of the variance in real performance times may be caused by a very small number of highly costly errors

(Landauer, 1987). Similarly, these models do not capture the real context in which users are likely to interact with a system. Whiteside and Wixon (1987) point out that modelling the complexity of the procedure for inserting a diskette is unlikely to predict very relevant problems in the context of system use. They report a user who physically inserted a diskette into a seam on the machine's plastic case rather than into the actual drive.

Another issue is the extent to which the kinds of tools being proposed actually mesh with the politics, schedules and practicalities of development teamwork (again, see Whiteside and Wixon, 1987). Theoretically motivated modelling may be all very well in principle, but it may call upon too many resources for too little gain in the context of a hard pressed development team. The kinds of theoretical models being developed are also primarily evaluative. With the possible exception of the idea of programmable user models (Young and Green, 1986), they do little to support creative design.

5. The future

Many of the critical points raised in the previous section can be answered sensibly. User cognition is complex. Although our scientific knowledge of the principles that govern these complexities is insufficient, enough is known to be of immediate conceptual and empirical value. The intuitions of system designers often display quite erroneous beliefs about user cognition (e.g., see Hammond *et al.*, 1983). In addition, the various criticisms and weaknesses are grounds, not for ignoring the progress that is being made towards an applied science of human-computer interaction, but for improving the discipline.

Thus, much can be done to address the problems of complexity, restricted scope, and the tendency for research to lag behind design (e.g., see Newell and Card, 1985). Issues associated with the complexity of cognition and the scope of our theories can be tackled by developing new forms of approximate cognitive modelling that have generalisable and cumulative properties. It may also be possible to speed up that process by making use of new methodologies for assessing the scope of models. For example, Young and Barnard (1987) have recently proposed a technique that involves a preliminary assessment of a model's scope by exploring how it copes with a range of scenarios describing different types of user-system interactions. This kind of assessment is itself approximate and could reduce our dependence upon lengthy experimental tests.

The particular issues raised by considering research achievements and their limitations also have implications for where future effort needs to be concentrated. In the present chapter the coverage has necessarily been selective. No reference has been made to popular concepts such as mental models (e.g., see Young, 1981; Halasz and Moran, 1983) or to the use of design "metaphors" (e.g., see Carroll and Thomas, 1982). On the basis of the issues that have served as illustrations here, three topics would seem to merit considerable future attention.

In order to deal with the many different things that can go wrong with an interface design, models are needed that integrate over the various perceptual, cognitive and motor resources of human cognition (e.g., see Barnard, 1987). In order to deal with the inherent variability of user behaviour, concepts are required to deal with the properties of individual differences and strategic variations in cognition (e.g., see Egan and Gomez, 1985). In order to develop our prospective design tools, it is necessary to improve our understanding of the ways in which designers make decisions and to find out what tools they really need (e.g., see Rosson, Maass and Kellogg, 1987).

6. Further reading

Many of the issues raised in this chapter are covered more extensively in the various chapters in J.M. Carroll (ed.) (1987) *Interfacing Thought: Cognitive Aspects of Human-Computer Interaction.* Cambridge, MA: MIT Press. Particular attention is drawn to the editor's introduction; to the chapter by Landauer; and that by Whiteside and Wixon. The rôle of cognitive psychology in system design is also the topic of a chapter by Hammond, Gardiner, Christie and Marshall in M. Gardiner and B. Christie (eds.) (1987) *Applying Cognitive Psychology to User-Interface Design.* Chichester: Wiley. Another critical appraisal of progress is provided by Newell and Card (1985) The prospects for psychological science in human-computer interaction. *Human-Computer Interaction*, **1**, 209-242.

Allen, R.B., and Scerbo, M.W. (1983) Details of command-language keystrokes. *ACM Transactions on Professional Communication*, PC–24, 30–37.

Anderson, N.S., and Olson, J.R. (1985) *Methods for Designing Software to Fit Human Needs and Capabilities*. Washington, DC: National Academy Press.

Barnard. P.J., Hammond, N.V. Morton, J., Long, J., and Clark, I.A. (1981) Consistency and compatibility in human-computer dialogue. *International Journal of Man-Machine Studies*, 15, 87–134.

Barnard, P.J., Wilson, M.W., and MacLean, A. (1986) The elicitation of system knowledge by picture probes. *Proceedings of CHI '86: Human Factors in Computer Systems*. New York: ACM. 235–240.

Barnard, P.J., Wilson, M.W., and MacLean, A. (1987) Approximate modelling of cognitive activity toward an expert system design aid. *Proceedings of CHI + GI '87: Human Factors in Computing Systems*. New York: ACM. 21–26.

Barnard, P.J. (1987) Cognitive resources and the learning of human-computer dialogs. In J.M. Carroll (ed.) *Interfacing Thought: Cognitive Aspects of Human-Computer Interaction*. Cambridge, MA: MIT Press. Ch. 6, 112–158.

Black, J., and Sebrechts, M. (1981) Facilitating human-computer communication. *Applied Psycholinguistics*, 2 146–177.

Card, S.K., Moran, T.P., and Newell, A. (1983) *The Psychology of Human-Computer Interaction*. Hillsdale, NJ: Lawrence Erlbaum Associates.

Carroll, J.M. (1984) Minimalist design for active users. In B. Shackel (ed). *Human-Computer Interaction—Interact '84*. Amsterdam: North-Holland, 39–44.

Carroll, J.M. (1987) Preface to J.M. Carroll (ed.) *Interacting Thought: Cognitive Aspects of Human-Computer Interaction*. Cambridge, MA: MIT Press. ix–xv.

Carroll, J.M. and Thomas, J.C. (1982) Metaphor and cognitive representation of computing systems. *IEEE Transactions on Systems, Man and Cybernetics*, SMC–12(2). 107–116.

Egan, D.E., and Gomez, L.M. (1985) Assaying, isolating and accommodating individual differences in learning a complex skill. In R.F. Dillon (ed.) *Individual Differences in Cognition, Volume 2*. London: Academic Press. 174–217.

Ericsson, K., and Simon, H. (1980) Verbal reports as data. *Psychological Review*, 87, 215–251.

Furnas, G.W., Gomez, L.M., Landauer, T.K., and Dumais, S.M. (1982) Statistical semantics: how can a computer use what people name things to guess what things people mean when they name things? *Proceedings of Human Factors in Computer Systems*. New York: ACM. 251–253.

Furnas, G.W., Gomez, L.M., Landauer, T.K., and Dumais, S.M. (1983) Statistical semantics: analysis of the potential performance of key-word information systems, *The Bell System Technical Journal*, 1753–1806.

Gaines, B.R. (1984) Perspectives on fifth generation computing. *Oxford Surveys in Information Technology*, 1, 1–53.

Gomez, L.M. and Lockbaum, C.C. (1984) People can retrieve more objects with enriched keyword vocabularies. But is there a performance cost? In B. Shackel (ed). *Human-Computer Interaction—Interact '84*. Amsterdam: North-Holland, 257–261.

Green, T.R.G., Schiele, F., and Payne, S.J. (1988) Formalisable models of user knowledge in human-computer interaction. In G. van der Veer, T.R.G. Green, J.-M. Hoc and D. Murray (eds). *Working with Computers: Theory versus Outcome*. London: Academic Press, 3–41.

Grudin, J.T. and Barnard, P.J. (1984) The cognitive demands of learning command names for text editing. *Human Factors*, 26, 407–422.

Halasz, F.G., and Moran, T.P. (1983) Mental models and problem solving in using a calculator. *Proceedings of CHI '83: Human Factors in Computer Systems*. New York. ACM. 212–216.

Hammond, N.V., and Barnard, P.J. (1984) Dialogue design: characteristics of user knowledge. In A. Monk (ed.) *Fundamentals of Human-Computer Interaction*. London: Academic Press, Ch. 9, 127–164.

Hammond, N.V., Long, J.B., Clark, I.A., Barnard, P.J., and Morton, J. (1980) Documenting human-computer mismatch in interactive systems. *Proceedings of the Ninth International Symposium on Human Factors in Telecommunications*, Red Bank, NJ, 17–24.

Hammond, N.V., Barnard, P.J., Morton, J., Long, J.B., and Clark, I.A. (1987) Characterising user performance in command rive dialogue. *Behaviour and Information Technology*, 6, 159–205.

Hammond, N.V., Christie, B., and Marshall, C. (1987) The role of cognitive psychology in user-interface design. In B. Christie and M. Gardiner (eds.) *Applying Cognitive Psychology to User Interface Design*. Chichester: Wiley. Ch. 2, 13–53.

John, B.E. and Newell, A. (1987) Predicting the time to recall computer command abbreviations. *Proceedings of CHI + GI '87: Human Factors in Computing Systems*. New York: ACM. 33–39.

Johnson, P. (1985) Towards a task model of messaging. In P. Johnson and S. Cook (eds.) *People and Computers: Designing the Interface*. Cambridge: Cambridge University Press, 46–62.

Johnson, P., Diaper, P., and Long, J. (1984) Tasks, skills and knowledge: task analysis for knowledge description. In B. Shackel (ed). *Human-Computer Interaction—Interact '84*. Amsterdam: North-Holland, 499–503.

Kieras, D.E., and Polson, P. (1985) An Approach to the formal analysis of user complexity. *International Journal of Man-Machine Studies*, 22, 365–394.

Kiger, J.I. (1984) The depth/breadth trade-off in the design of menu driven user interfaces. *International Journal of Man-Machine Studies*, 20, 201–213.

Landauer, T.K. (1985) Psychological research as a mother of invention. *Proceedings of CHI '85: Human Factors in Computer Systems*. New York: ACM. 44.

Landauer, T.K. (1987) Relations between cognitive psychology and computer systems design. In J.M. Carroll (ed.) *Interacting Thought: Cognitive Aspects of Human-Computer Interaction.* Cambridge, MA: MIT Press. Ch. 1, 1–25.

Landauer, T.K., and Nachbar, D.W. (1985) Selection from alphabetic and numeric menu trees using a touch screen: depth, breath and width. *Proceedings of CHI '85: Human Factors in Computer Systems*. New York: ACM. 73–77.

Landauer, T.K., Galotti, K.M., and Hartwell, S. (1983) Natural command names and initial learning: a study of text editing terms. *Communications of the ACM*, 26, 495–503.

Ledgard, H., Whiteside, J. Singer, A., and Seymour, W. (1980) The natural language of interactive systems. *Communications of the ACM*, 23, 556–563.

Mack, R.L., Lewis, C.H., and Carroll, J.M. (1983) Learning to use word processors: problems and prospects. *ACM Transactions on Office Information Systems*, 1, 254–271.

MacLean, A., Barnard, P.J., and Wilson, M.W. (1985) Evaluating the human interface of a data entry system: user choice and performance measures yield different trade-off functions. In P. Johnson and S. Cook (eds.) *People and Computers: Designing the Interface*. Cambridge: Cambridge University Press, 172–185.

Miller, D.P. (1981) The depth/breath trade-off in hierarchical computer menus. *Proceedings of the Human Factors Society*, 296–300.

Moran, T.P. (1981) The Command Language Grammar: a representation for the user interface of interactive computer systems. *International Journal of Man-Machine Studies*, 15, 3–50.

Moran, T.P. (1983) Getting into a system: external-internal task mapping analysis. *Proceedings of CHI '83: Human Factors in Computing Systems*. New York: ACM, 45–49.

Morton, J., Barnard, P.J., Hammond, N.V., and Long, J. (1979) Interacting with the computer: a framework. In E.J. Boutmy and A. Danthine (eds.) *Teleinformatics '79*. Amsterdam: North-Holland. 201–208.

Neisser, U. (1967) *Cognitive Psychology*. New York: Appleton-Century-Crofts.

Norman, D.A. (1983) Design principles for human-computer interaction. *Proceedings of CHI '83: Human Factors in Computing Systems*. New York: ACM, 1–10.

Norman, D.A. (1986) Cognitive engineering: In D.A. Norman and S.W. Draper (eds.) *User Centred System Design*. Hillsdale, NJ: Lawrence Erlbaum Associates. 31–62.

Norman, D.A., and Draper, S.W. (1986) *User Centred System Design*. Hillsdale, NJ: Lawrence Erlbaum Associates.

O'Malley, C., Draper, S.W., and Riley, M.S. (1984) Constructive interaction: a method for studying human-computer interaction. In B. Shackel (ed). *Human-Computer Interaction—Interact '84*. Amsterdam: North-Holland, 269–274.

Olson, J.R. (1987) Cognitive analysis of people's use of software. In J.M. Carroll (ed.) *Interacting Thought: Cognitive Aspects of Human-Computer Interaction.* Cambridge, MA: MIT Press. Ch. 10, 260–293.

Payne, S.J. and Green, T.R.G. (1983) The user's perception of the interaction language: a two-level model. *Proceedings of CHI '83: Human Factors in Computing Systems*. New York: ACM, 202–206.

Polson, P.G. (1987) A quantitative theory of human-computer interaction. In J.M. Carroll (ed.) *Interacting Thought: Cognitive Aspects of Human-Computer Interaction.* Cambridge, MA: MIT Press. Ch. 8, 184–235.

Polson, P.G., and Kieras, D.E. (1984) A formal description of users' knowledge of how to operate a device and user complexity. *Behaviour Research Methods, Instruments and Computers*, 16, 249–255.

Reisner, P. (1981) Formal grammar and human factors design of an interactive graphics system. *IEEE Transactions on Software Engineering*, SE–7, 229–240.

Reisner, P. (1982) Further developments towards using formal grammar as a design tool. *Proceedings of Human Factors in Computer Systems*. New York: ACM. 304–308.

Rosson, M.B., Maass, S., and Kellogg, W. (1987) Designing for designers: an analysis of design practice in the real work. *CHI + GI '87: Human Factors in Computing Systems*. New York: ACM.

Runciman, C., and Hammond, N.V. (1986) User programs: a way to match computer systems and human cognition. In M.D. Harrison and A.F. Monk (eds.) *People and Computers: Designing for Usability*. Cambridge: Cambridge University Press. 464–481.

Scapin, D.L. (1981) Computer commands in restricted natural language: some aspects of memory of experience. *Human Factors*, 23, 365–375.

Shackel, B. (1991) Usability–Context, Framework, Definition, Design and Evaluation. In B. Shackel and S. Richardson (ed.) *Human Factors for Informatics Usability*. Cambridge: Cambridge University Press. 21–37.

Shneiderman, B. (1991) A Taxonomy and Rule Base for the Selection of Interaction Styles. In B. Shackel and S. Richardson (ed.) *Human Factors for Informatics Usability*. Cambridge: Cambridge University Press. 325–342.

Snowberry, K., Parkinson, S.R., and Sisson, N. (1983) Computer display menus. *Ergonomics*, 26, 699–712.

Whiteside, J. and Wixon, D. (1987) Improving human-computer interaction: a question for cognitive science. In J.M. Carroll (ed.) *Interacting Thought: Cognitive Aspects of Human-Computer Interaction.* Cambridge, MA: MIT Press. 353–365.

Young, R.M. (1981) The machine inside the machine: users' models of pocket calculators. *International Journal of Man-Machine Studies*, 15, 51–85.

Young, R.M., and Barnard, P.J. (1987) The use of scenarios in human-computer interaction research: turbocharging the tortoise of cumulative science. *Proceedings of CHI + GI '87: Human Factors in Computing Systems.* New York: ACM. 291–296.

Young, R.M., and Green, T.R.G. (1986) Toward programmable user models. *Alvey Programme Annual Report 1986 Poster Supplement*. London: Alvey Directorate. Project MMI/112, p. 319.

Let's Get Real: A Position Paper on the Role of Cognitive Psychology in the Design of Humanly Useful and Usable Systems

Thomas K. Landauer

For the most part, useful theory is impossible, because the behavior of human–computer systems is chaotic or worse, highly complex, dependent on many unpredictable variables, or just too hard to understand. Where it is possible, the use of theory will be constrained and modest, because theories will be imprecise, will cover only limited aspects of behavior, will be applicable only to some parts of some systems, and will not necessarily generalize; as a result, they will yield little advantage over empirical methods.

Some useful theory will be of familiar homely kinds and have minor impact; examples include Fitts's Law, Hick's Law, the "Power" Law of practice, and laws of visual and auditory perception. More useful "theories" will be of new but mundane kinds. Example here include data-based simulations; qualitative understanding of task performance factors; rules of thumb for the use of color or optimal soft-key shapes; and empirical generalizations about user needs and characteristics.

But direct empirical models, rules of thumb, and formative evaluation together are a more-than-adequate base for important inventions and advances.

To explain and support somewhat this skeleton of dismal assertions and discordantly hopeful moral, I will add a little argument and some case examples.

Mostly, Useful Theory Is Impossible

I claimed that theory is impossible because the behavior of HC systems is chaotic or worse, highly complex, or dependent on many unpredictable variables. Let me be a little clearer about what I mean by "theory" here. In the first place, I mean a theory that is good enough to dictate system design characteristics that support much better human–computer interactive performance than are now produced by art and emulation alone. The problems of such design now involve primarily cognitive issues – how the mind of the user functions in interaction with the information processing and display dynamics of the computer.

A theory to guide such design would have to be both very broad in its coverage of human and machine information-processing phenomena and very accurate in capturing the effects of all the details that can have important effects. I do not mean to imply that theory will be of no help at all; I plan later to give examples of how even presently available theory can sometimes help to improve certain aspects of a given design. But the general theme of this collection of papers suggests to me that people somewhere are expecting much more: broad, detailed, and accurate theories that will replace empirical cut-and-try as the foundation of design. My contention is simply that the theory of human cognition is now and may forever be too weak to be the main engine driving HCI. Nor will it even serve an infrequent (see Carroll, this volume) but crucial role as it has in some other technologies – for example, nuclear energy and semiconductors.

This said, let me continue the case against theory. Human cognition and behavior are manifestly highly complex and exceedingly difficult to model to any useful degree. They are based on a physical processing system with O (10^{11}) heterogeneous nonsimple elements operating largely in parallel-cooperative statistical fashions, using a huge amount of genetic (10^{10} bits?), remembered (10^9 bits?), and currently received (10^9 bits/sec ?) data that are only partially the same for any two people and manifest behaviors that are well beyond current understanding or simulation – speech, language, and vision, to mention just a few. There has been a great deal of hopeful talk about the possibility that human behavior will be discovered to manifest important regularities at some "emergent level" of organization at which useful broad theories can be built. However, even though the imminent arrival of such theories has been frequently announced from the beginnings of modern psychology almost 100 years ago up to the present (Newell, 1989), nothing remotely resembling what one would hope for as a basis for HCI, nothing with substantial generality, power, and detail at the required level of cognition has ever materialized.

The excuse that the field is young will no longer do; many other sciences have made dozens of stunning advances in the time that psychology has existed. Nor will small numbers or lack of talent explain away the failure. From the mid-sixties to the early eighties scientific psychology was immensely popular at universities, and well-funded graduate programs attracted students with higher average aptitude scores than any other field. This talented group has now had time and grant support enough to test well the opportunities for theoretical advance.

But perhaps we should not expect progress in cognitive science from psychology, but instead from computer science, where the smart money has been going for the last decade. But even the most optimistic protagonists of artificial intelligence talk of 200 person-years of work to encode an adequate approximation to the consensually available part of the conscious portion of the minimum amount of linguistically expressible knowledge required as a base for the acquisition by reading and experience of the rest of the knowledge needed for ordinary human cognition (Lenat & Guha, 1989). Modeling by computer simulation the phenomena of "low-level" perceptual processes (like speech-sound comprehension or visual pattern recognition) seems at least as complex, and the influence of emotional and physiological factors add still more complication, as do social processes.

Now consider that present computer programs and systems have sufficient complexity that most programs cannot be proved, and that irreducible bugs are the norm, and it is apparent that the other side of the interface is also severely limited in its theoretical tractability. When we then put humans and computers together into a jointly functioning interactive whole, we are almost certain to have a situation in which all of the prediction-defying pathologies of highly complex nonlinear dynamical systems will abound. True, it is conceivable that simply understood "emergent properties" may yet appear from the interaction of these two very complex systems. But for the time being, it seems foolish to pin our hopes on such an expectation. It will, I think, be much more realistic, and fruitful as well, to expect that the phenomena of HCI will (a) sometimes manifest extreme sensitivity to starting variable value differences, as happens in weather systems for example, and may occur in HCI as a function of context, memory content, or individual performance trajectories; (b) simply be too computationally complex to calculate in real time to sufficient accuracy, as is the case for fluid flow over surfaces for example, and may occur in HCI as a function of the unlimited content-addressability of human memory, the flood of current contextual influences on individual and group behavior, or the mere combinatorial complexity of the joint states available to two Turing machines; and (c) be subject to too many important variables that are impossible to know in advance in any practical way (which users at company X will have looked up the syntax for rare query type Y?); or (d) be subject to extreme random variation (who will make a typographical error that invokes a rare program bug that causes a crash that takes the administrator three days to fix because backups are done only by a rival department?).

Where Possible, the Use of Theory Will Be Constrained and Modest

I proposed that theories will be imprecise, will cover only limited aspects of behavior, will be applicable only to some parts of some systems, and will not necessarily generalize, and thus will yield little advantage over empirical methods.

As a first example here, let us take the "keystroke model" of Card, Moran, and Newell (1983). It is certainly among the most successful attempts to provide theory for HCI, yet (a) at best its time predictions are good within only about 20–50%; (b) it does not predict or model the consequences of errors, which probably account for the majority of time, individual differences, and dissatisfactions in most computerized tasks; (c) it applies only to the skilled psychomotor performance aspects of tasks, not to visual pattern recognition, knowledge-based activities, or complex decision processes, and it is mute on motivational, learning, and social issues. If a different task were the target, let us say drawing or doing financial analysis, instead of the typing-centered tasks for which it was developed, it does not seem likely that the keystroke model would describe much of the interesting action at all. My guess is that these sorts of limitations are inherent and unavoidable, that the keystroke model is *not* an early poor example, soon to be superseded by grand general theories of cognition (it certainly hasn't happened yet). Rather, the keystroke model is a particularly successful example – because it deals with aspects of behavior that are relatively simple and well understood (because most understandable). Nonetheless, I would guess that the descriptive precision, and certainly the amount of insight into process, offered by the keystroke model could be easily exceeded in any real design problem by the empirical evidence of a crude prototype test with a handful of users or examination by a small panel of experts (Nielsen 1989; Nielsen & Molich, 1990). For a second example, to which I will refer several more times, take the Bellcore group's work on keyword query and hierarchical information display methods. Quite successful modeling of the benefits of full-text indexing has

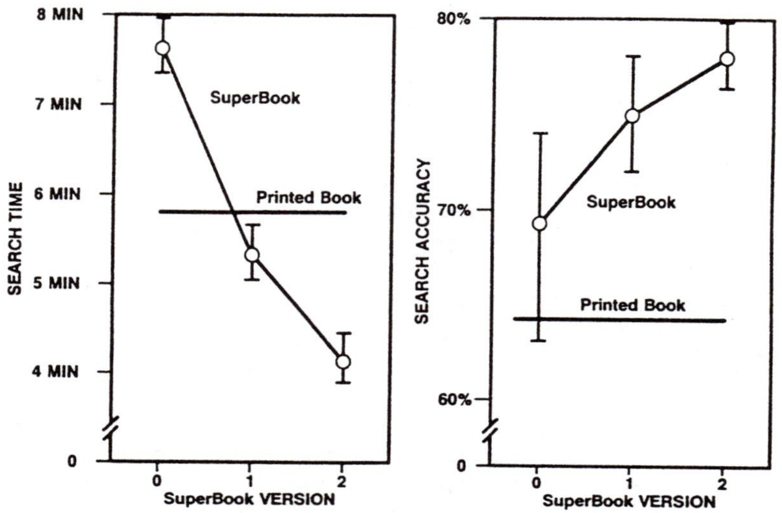

Figure 5.1. Information retrieval performance with successive versions of SuperBook. Version 0 was based on several previously formulated principles and incorporated successfully demonstrated features. Data are from an experiment in which students found answers to a variety of questions in a statistics book in its original print form or online with SuperBook. Versions 1 and 2 reflect the results of formative evaluation and redesign. About half of the time difference between versions 0 and 1 is attributable to faster code, the result to improved user–system interaction protocol.

been achieved (Furnas, Landauer, Gomez, & Dumais, 1987; Gomez, Lochbaum, & Landauer 1990), and a nice formal model of the value of fisheye views has been stated and verified (Furnas, 1986). When this "theoretical" understanding was applied to the design of the SuperBook™[1] text browser, the zero-order version (before testing and redesign) was probably better, from a usability perspective, than previous "seat-of-pants" designs, but not by very much. On the other hand, three short, empirical, formative design-evaluation cycles reduced average information retrieval times by over 50% and increased success rates by about 25%. This progression is shown graphically in Figure 5.1.

One kind of important design information discovered by empirical testing is exemplified by an observation made in the first evaluation of an attempt to add on-screen graphics to the browser. When pictures came up automatically, they sometimes covered the table of contents, making it impossible to continue search by the most effective method, posting keyword hits against the outline. This flaw illustrates the problem of complexity; so many things can happen in the interaction of a human with a machine that it is impossible to anticipate everything that can go wrong. It is hard to imagine any "theory" that would help.

1. SuperBook is a trademark of Bell Communications Research, Inc.

What does one do in such a situation? Well, one approach is to use human empathy and intuition to model the phenomenon; humans can perform immensely complex, nonlinear, fuzzy, satisficing cognition, so maybe they can put themselves in the place of other humans, and in the place of theories, and generate, perhaps unconsciously, the understanding needed for design. Some such process seems to be required in the use of scenario techniques as described by Carroll in this volume, the heuristic evaluation methods demonstrated by Nielsen and Molich (1990), or even the "theory-based walkthrough" method proposed by Lewis, Polson, Wharton, and Rieman (1990). It would appear to be the only basis for hope in the hermeneutic and contextual research positions (Wixon, Holtzblatt, & Knox, 1990) where not only theory but systematic data collection and analysis as well are rejected.

Another approach is to rely primarily on empirical methods. "But," the interlocutor will respond, "there is no such thing as a purely empirical method. An interface never steps into the same river twice, so in using the results of an evaluation study you necessarily generalize; thus use some implicit theory to tell what situation and design variations are unimportant." "Got me!" admits the philosopher, "and I must be using the same 'intuitive theory' approach I have lately ridiculed, *but,*" he hastens to add, "I am minimizing the risk by reducing the scope of theory." (It's just about what situations are very similar, and other kinds of theory would have to do that as well as the fancier things they attempt.)

Let me add an example of more constructive design guidance resulting from empirical testing. In one of Dennis Egan's "formative evaluation" studies of the SuperBook browser, college-student subjects wrote "open book" essay exams (Egan et al., 1990). Half the students were using a normal printed paper textbook on a statistics topic. The others were using the automatically generated SuperBook on-line version of the same book. The SuperBook students averaged scores 1.5 standard deviations higher than those using the original print text, roughly the difference between an A– and a C grade.

Closer analysis of the data revealed that the SuperBook students had all found a particular section of the text that had much of the information needed for a good answer. At first we jumped to the conclusion that the superior search facilities of the on-line version were responsible for its advantage. But Egan is too careful an empiricist to let the matter rest so easily. He ran a control study with users of the paper book watched by video, and discovered that they just as often found the relevant page as did the SuperBook users! Moreover they got to the relevant page just as quickly, and spent the same amount of time examining it. It appears that the reformatting – rearrangement and highlighting – of the page, or perhaps the search context in which it was found, caused one group of users to notice and absorb the information where the others passed it over. In SuperBook the section containing user search terms is promoted to the top of the "page," the relevant context is conveyed by the dynamically updated hierarchical heading structure displayed just above the text, and the typographical emphasis created by the author for linear reading is largely suppressed. We now call this "dynamic page recomposition," and list it as a feature.

This single empirical data point suggests some very interesting directions for future design experiments. One intriguing aspect of the situation is that many designers and critics have supposed that it would be optimal to reproduce print composition as exactly as possible in electronic browsers, the rationale being that we have no supportable basis for improving on the well-evolved art and conventions of print design. I leave it to the reader to judge whether the apparently counterintuitive lead of Egan's finding is likely to generalize, and to what extent similar leads have come or are likely to come from "cognitive theory" as usually imagined. Wright (1987) remarked that psycholinguistics had offered almost no guidance to text design. I would add that, up to now at least, theoretical work on discourse analysis, natural-language processing, or information retrieval has not either.

Some Useful Theory Will Be of Familiar Homely Kinds, and Have Minor Impact

The examples I mentioned included Fitts's Law, Hick's Law, the "Power" Law of practice, and various laws of visual and auditory perception. I do not want to push the radical pessimist view too far. To be sure, some important phenomena of behavior have been captured by tidy theories that hold widely, and we should certainly apply them where we can and pray for more. My favorite example is Fitts's Law. In designing the browser we used mouse-actuated "soft buttons" for several functions, and we think we improved the speed of operation in a late version by moving buttons closer to the point from which they would usually be operated and making their active target area larger. We probably saved tens of milliseconds per 5-minute browse. This really is not bad, as such things go; it's often not done in commercial systems, and is economically worthwhile in our expected applications, which have large multipliers. I think saving small fractions of a second by optimal button placement is probably a good illustration of the real but limited impact that traditional psychological theory can have if diligently applied.

And I believe that there could be many more profitable applications of known psychological principles. Let me give just a few more examples to communicate the flavor. Color psychophysics prescribes uses of color coding for graphic data presentation that are quite at variance with common practice. Hue is a metathetic as opposed to a prothetic continuum (Stevens & Galanter, 1957), meaning that hue differences will not map onto a one-dimensional monotonic scale of subjective quantity, and thus should not be used to indicate degree, as in temperature or altitude, as they often are.

Another example from our laboratory is the derivation from Hick's Law for decision time that hierarchical menus should be made as flat as possible, a prediction confirmed by our own and others' empirical tests (Landauer & Nachbar, 1985; Tullis, 1985.). Barnard, in this volume, describes some additional documented success stories in which theory from laboratory-based psychology has driven design and invention.

However, let us be realistic. Even the best examples of theory applications have produced only small quantitative and/or local gains in usability. Moreover, it seems likely that the design improvements they suggest would often have also been suggested by observations of trial users. Where such tests were not done, it is hard to prove that they would have substituted for theory. But if one watched users trying to hit small, distant keys, interpret red as "low," or work their way through deep menu hierarchies, it would not be surprising if one reached the same conclusions dictated by the relevant theories. And because usability evaluation studies will always be needed to catch the infinite variety of flaws and interaction effects (Landauer, 1987; Landauer & Galotti, 1984) not foreseeable by theory, it may be more efficient to skip the theory stage entirely.

More Useful "Theories" Will Be of New but Mundane Kinds

Examples here are data-based simulations, qualitative understanding of task performance factors, or empirical generalizations about user needs and characteristics. For discussion, let us take the information retrieval research as an example again. Early on, a set of empirical studies was done to measure the variation in terminology applied by different people in forming "keyword"-style indexing terms, category labels, and command names for several different domains (Furnas, Landauer, Gomez, & Dumais, 1983, 1987). The statistical characterization of these data was translated directly into a numerical simulation model that could be used to predict the empirical probability distributions of correct and erroneous hits when representative users pose queries against data bases in which the objects are named by various schemes. For example simulations showed that rich indexing – by collecting keywords from large numbers of potential users instead of single indexers, or by full-text indexing – expectedly improves recall (the proportion of wanted things found) by factors of two to five without much of a decrease in precision (the proportion of found things wanted). Several completely separate empirical studies at Bellcore (Gomez et al., 1990), and elsewhere (e.g., Good, Whiteside, Wixon, & Jones, 1984) have produced remarkably similar results for success rates of prototype command or information retrieval interfaces as a function of "pointer" vocabulary size. Although quantitative model predictions have not been made, experimentally observed search success for SuperBook is about 25% better than for comparable paper books with good but much smaller indexes. And a prototype "adaptive index" in which user words are monitored and added semiautomatically quickly produced very large gains in access success for users of an on-line directory (Furnas, 1985).

This sort of "theory" is different from what has usually been dignified by that title in psychology or computer science, and from what proponents of theory in HCI like Newell and Card (1985) seem to have in mind. But my belief is that it can be widely very useful. The central characteristic of such theory is that it is empirically based modeling of user behavior in a task for which a computer tool may be designed. Such models answer the question: Given a particular performance goal and general method, how often will representative users do what? In the example, the task was finding information by offering query words to match index words. If the task were spelling correctly, one might collect data on how often typical users in typical situations of composition or copy typing omit, substitute, or transpose particular letters or position-specific *n*-grams, or, in more detail, how often each misspelled word in a large sample was a mutation of what other words. Then simulations could reveal how well various schemes for spelling correction would work. Astonishingly, to my knowledge no such empirical modeling approach has ever been used to construct spelling correctors (cf. Kernighan, Church, & Gale, 1990), designers having depended instead on ad hoc "metrics" of the differences between strings – for example, the distances between letters on keyboards, or crude point scores for omissions, deletions, and transpositions.

Empirical models also both offer opportunity for qualitative understanding of important aspects of HCI – for example, that information retrieval fails very frequently because of vocabulary differences – and can generate useful descriptions of user characteristics and needs, such as how many spelling errors at what time cost do most people make, which can point the way to needed design features and functions.

But Direct Empirical Modeling and Formative Evaluation Are Enough

Distributional data on task behavior, simulations accomplished by simple calculations on them, naturalistic observations of current task performance and prototype use seem most inelegant and unexciting sources for technological progress. But they are, if not all, at least much of what is now needed as the basis of a vast range of new and wonderful artifacts. Computers and communications hardware and software are already extremely powerful and flexible. The reason they have been of so little utility – witness the fact that U.S. productivity has not improved during the information revolution, either globally or in most of the industries that have adopted it (Dertouzos, 1990) – is that they have not done much that is actually of significant net help to the user. For the most, past computer systems have been designed either (a) to mimic on a computer (but often less well) what we can already do some other way – for example, desktops and text on tiny screens for business tasks; (b) to do something you cannot do without a computer merely because you can (or because it's a challenge) – for example incomprehensible icons instead of words, or spaghetti tangles of links instead of searchable verbal descriptors (see Lenat & Guha, 1989, chap. 9, for a sad case history); or (c) on the basis of one or more programmer's unimproved hunch (the "wouldn't it be neat if . . ." design method) – for example, mouse-operated virtual calculators on the screen, or joint scheduling calendars (see Grudin, 1988, for a critique). Moreover, most actual system design is done by software engineers and programmers whose attention and creative energies are rightly focused on the mechanism, on how to write the program efficiently and elegantly, how to maximize performance and maintainability – not on usefulness or usability.

Thus what we really stand in need of is a usefulness-and-usability–oriented design discipline. The few successful computer and HCI inventions, such as spreadsheets, to date have come from lucky hunches, discovered useful essentially by market-selection factors, not from product ideas obviously good from the start but hard to achieve. Contrast the new functions provided by computers with those that motivated the development of better light sources, faster vehicles, or long-distance communication. But just intending to do right and paying attention to usefulness and usability will not suffice. What is badly needed or dramatically desirable in information-using human activities is not as obvious as it has been in these other fields.

Similarly, evaluating whether an invention or new design is superior, or even acceptable, is not as easy in HCI as it is in most engineering disciplines. The inventor can tell whether a steam engine works better than the last model by personal observation. Personal observation of one's own system is one of the worst ways to assess usability. We need a reliable and valid feedback signal, an "objective function," with which to measure success and guide evolution. Here modern psychological science can serve us well. Psychologists know how to observe, record, and analyze behavioral data, how to get behavioral data to yield valid conclusions. They know what to do and not do with single-case, single-observer impressions, and how to overcome biased intuition and the persuasive force of anecdote and social compliance. There is no reason in this age of science to rely solely on the noisy and inefficient informal evaluations that have shaped much of the technical advance of the past (Carroll, this volume) in all fields, but most especially the creation of cognitive tools.

The fact that disciplined investigation can easily disclose what people cannot do well and suggest ways in which a computer could help them is not widely appreciated. But the mundane empirical methods and models I have discussed can do this very effectively. The step from the level of understanding provided by such empirical studies to the creation of new cognitive tools can sometimes be a short one. Rich indexing is just one example of something a computer could easily do for people once it was known that is was needed. There are many more opportunities for similar innovations that will not be identified by deep or elegant general theory of the kind I believe to be impossible, but by simple empirical analysis of what is wrong with the way things are.

Another necessary component of success in HCI will be a way to deal with the complexity of the HCI system, with the certainty that there will be many things wrong with any initial design. Even if a new design includes genuinely valuable innovations, the "nuggets" of gold may be entirely hidden in the dirt. Fortunately, there is a straightforward methodology that works extremely well to separate the good aspects from the bad – iteratively test, analyze, and revise. This is a familiar and powerful expedient in almost all fields of engineering and design (and certainly HCI is either engineering or design). Wings and cars are tested in wind tunnels, beams in stress tests, ships in model tanks, building designs in balsa models and renderings, computer programs by compilation and exercise. That there has been so much resistance to the test-cycle approach to computer usability defies understanding.

Possibly to belabor the obvious, the point is that if human–machine behavior is too complex to design or predict from theory, as I claim, then initial designs will always have unexpected properties. By the usual statistics of evolutionary processes, almost all of these unexpected properties are likely to be undesirable, and only a few will be improvements over past designs. Insofar as the defects and novel advantages of the new design are large, they will be noticeable on the basis of a moderate amount of observation. So far, practical experience, as well as some experimental evidence, suggests that tests with 2 to 10 users usually reveal most glaring flaws, and sometimes offer strong guidance for positive improvements (Egan et al., 1990; Good et al., 1984; Nielsen, 1989; Tesler, 1983). Thus hope for major progress without the aid of strong theory is quite justified.

Let me bring this brief case for empiricism to a close by reviewing the history of one case of reasonably successful HCI invention and design. I take my text from the design of SuperBook on the grounds that it has eventuated in the deployment of a system that is demonstrably better than the preexisting noncomputerized technology. This is a surprisingly rare accomplishment in HCI (and in computer applications generally). In the domain of textual information access and use there is a clear baseline, ordinary paper and print books. Insofar as computer-based text systems have been evaluated against comparable book technology, they have either lost badly or barely tied, both in formal studies (Egan et al., 1990; review in Shneiderman, 1987; Weyer, 1982) and in commercial experience. Interestingly, this negative comparison is at least as true of existing hypertext systems (McKnight, Dillon, & Richardson, 1989). SuperBook, in the version currently being deployed by telephone companies, by contrast, results in much more efficient use of textual information than is obtained by experienced users with the familiar high-quality paper documents from which the on-line SuperBook version is automatically generated.

How did SuperBook get this good? Figure 5.2 depicts the history of the information retrieval and display research work in Bellcore's Cognitive Science group. Theoretical work is indicated by underlining, empirical data or analysis by plain type, principles and methods by straight bold, prototypes and systems by italics. The empirical contributions include true experiments, systematic observations, empirical modeling of indexing schemes, tests against standard data bases of queries and targets, formative evaluations of prototypes, and acceptance testing of a product. For this line of work, we still lack data on how resulting products are actually used in large-scale office environments. As previously shown in Figure 5.1, the prior "fundamental" research on which the first version of SuperBook was based led to a design that was somewhat (not reliably) better for accuracy but reliably slower than print. That was actually good compared to previous on-line text systems, especially since part of the slowness was the fault of the development language. But in the most important sense it was a complete failure. It is not our job to produce clever computer applications that reduce productivity However, analysis of the good and bad properties of that initial version, and two more design revision cycles based on similar observations produced a very large improvement.

I hardly want to claim that this experience will be repeated everywhere. But at least in this one case, I believe it was clear that the two essential ingredients for success were (1) a good analysis of what people needed to achieve their goals that prior technology did not provide well enough (rich indexing with good disambiguation, good contextual and organization support for orientation and navigation), and (2) iterative formative evaluation of designs to remove the flaws and

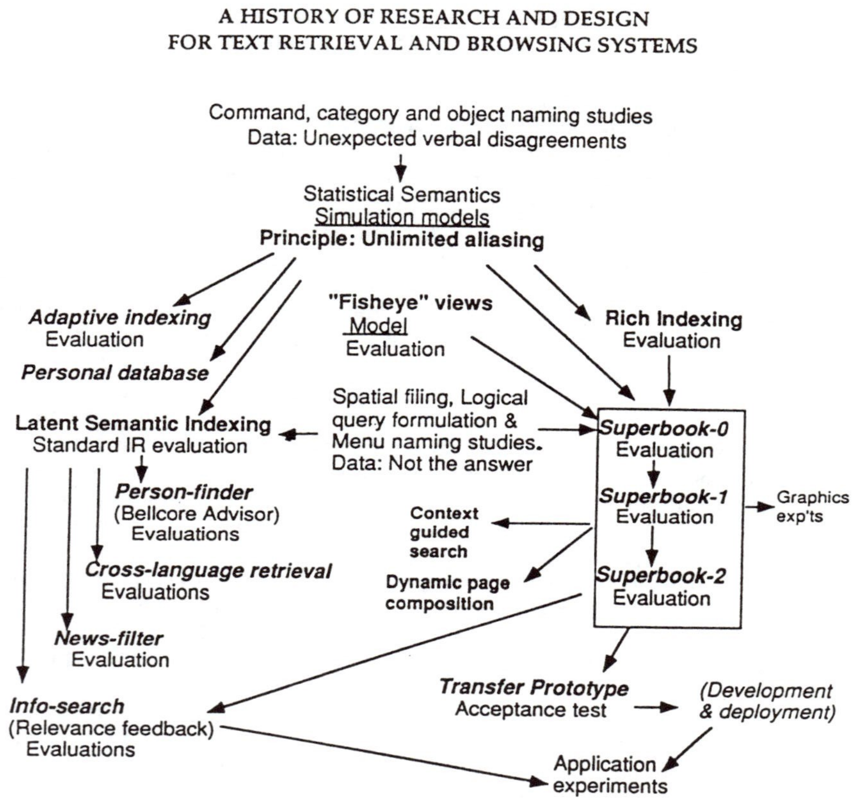

Figure 5.2. Schematic history of work on textual information in Bellcore's Cognitive Science group. Plain text indicates empirical data collection and analysis, boldface indicates principles and methods, italics prototypes and products. Theories and models are indicated by underlined text.

improve the flows (better interaction protocol, controls, dialog, screen design, code.)

Received cognitive theory found only a very minor role. Furnas's "degree-of-interest" function (1986) provided a theoretical rationale for the dynamic table of contents, although similar hierarchical TOCs have been invented without its help. Similarly Fitts's Law was in our minds when we positioned and sized the soft buttons and scroll bars, but did not make a major contribution. Our empirical work on "statistical semantics" leading to the principle of "unlimited aliasing" caused us to choose full-text indexing where it has often been eschewed (especially in other hypertext systems). We have not yet incorporated a true adaptive index because we have not yet learned how to implement it well in the text-browser environment. (Version 2 SuperBook does have a synonym creation facility, but that's quite different, and inferior; it makes two terms equivalent rather than adding a pointer from a term to a single object.)

There were some other lines of work that also contributed useful insights. One was research on the use of traditional data base query expressions (Greene, Devlin, Cannata, & Gomez, 1990; Greene, Gomez, & Devlin, 1986). It showed that most people have enormous difficulty composing logical information descriptors even though they have no trouble choosing appropriate data from a table. This suggested using a method other than boolean queries for disambiguating the results of full-text search. The invention of "context-guided search" – posting hits against the expandable table of contents – was an expression of this insight. There was also considerable research done on the creation and labeling of menu graphs for ad hoc information collections, to the conclusion that menus alone are not a general solution (Dumais & Landauer, 1984), and on spatial cues for filing and retrieval, to the conclusion that screen location is almost worthless for more than a handful of items (Dumais & Wright, 1986). In addition, of course, the literature on HCI and information retrieval contains many reports of empirical observations and experience on which we drew. This is not the place for a review of this literature, but relevant work is cited in the papers that are referenced here, and much of it is reviewed in Dumais (1988).

Another cognitive-tool invention that arose from the same starting observations and "statistical semantics" analyses was Latent Semantic Indexing (LSI). Latent Semantic Indexing uses a powerful statistical method for noise reduction that has been widely applied in signal processing to reduce significantly the "synonym" problem in word-based search. We also have not yet found a completely satisfactory way to combine LSI with a browser, although explorations continue. To reach the prototype system stage, LSI went through a separate series of formative design evaluations and improvements. In this case, early evaluations were based on standard query and relevance judgment data bases; more recent ones involve laboratory studies. While we made use of previous empirical comparisons of various accessory techniques for automatic indexing (e.g., how best to preweight terms), the extensive *theoretical* literature of information retrieval, linguistics, cognitive psychology of language, and computational natural language processing has been virtually no help at all. If anything, I expect the theory–applications relation to supply a benefit in the other direction. Latent semantic indexing seems to capture important aspects of human relevance judgments (see Deerwester, Dumais, Furnas, Landauer, & Harshman, 1990). It does so by using statistical methods to acquire an abstract "deep structure" representation of word meanings from the analysis of large amounts of representative text. Who knows, perhaps this model will lead the way to a new theory of human meaning representation and acquisition.

Perhaps the most important new technique in SuperBook is the posting of term-search hits against the table of contents. We're not entirely sure where this idea came from, although knowledge of the value of full text indexing along with the awareness that it would carry with it the need for disambiguation, was certainly important. And our and others' research showing that logical query expression is very difficult to learn and use, plus results from our statistical semantics work (Gomez et al., 1990) indicating that it will not give good results anyway, discouraged the use of boolean queries. However, this feature, which we now call *context-guided search,* was first introduced as an empirical design experiment. It was formative evaluation that led to the realization of its power and to refining it and making it a central interactive tool.

For me, the lesson of our work on information access is clear. Not coincidentally, it reflects my view of HCI in general. That is, the empirical methods of task and performance analysis and simulation coupled with formative design evaluation are sufficient and strong guides; theory is a weak adjunct. The field, if it is to succeed, should put its effort into the former.

References

Card, S. K., Moran, T. P., & Newell, A. (1983). *The psychology of human–computer interaction.* Hillsdale, NJ: Lawrence Erlbaum Associates.

Deerwester, S., Dumais, S. T., Furnas, G. W., Landauer, T. K., & Harshman, R. (1990). Indexing by latent semantic analysis. *Journal of The American Society for Information Science 41, 391–407.*

Dertouzos, M. (1990). Redefining tomorrow's interface. In J. C. Chew & J. Whiteside (Eds.), *Proceedings of CHI '90: Human Factors in Computing Systems* (p. 1). New York: ACM.

Dumais, S. T. (1988). Textual information retrieval. In M. Helander (Ed.), *Handbook of human–computer interaction.* Amsterdam: Elsevier Science Publishers.

Dumais, S. T., & Landauer, T. K. (1984). Describing categories of objects for menu retrieval systems. *Behavior Research Methods, Instruments and Computers, 16,* 242–248.

Dumais, S. T., & Wright, A. L. (1986). Reference by name vs. location in a computer filing system. *Proceedings of the Human Factors Society 30th Annual Meeting* (pp. 824–828).

Egan, D. E., Remde, J. R., Gomez, L. M., Landauer, T. K., Eberhardt, J., & Lochbaum, C. D. (1990). Formative design-evaluation of SuperBook. *ACM Transactions on Information Systems, 7,* 30–57.

Furnas, G. W. (1985). Experience with an adaptive indexing scheme. In L. Borman & B. Curtis (Eds.), *Proceedings of CHI '85: Human Factors in Computing Systems* (pp. 185–191). New York: ACM.

Furnas, G. W. (1986). Generalized fisheye views. In M. Mantei & P. Orbeton (Eds.), *Proceedings of CHI '86: Human Factors in Computing Systems* (pp. 16–23). New York: ACM.

Furnas, G. W., Landauer, T. K., Gomez, L. M., & Dumais, S. T. (1983). Statistical semantics: Analysis of the potential performance of keyword information systems. *Bell System Technical Journal, 62,* 1753–1806.

Furnas, G. W., Landauer, T. K., Gomez, L. M., & Dumais, S. T. (1987). The vocabulary problem in human–system communications. *Communications of the ACM, 30,* 964–971.

Gomez, L. M., Lochbaum, C. C., & Landauer, T. K. (1990). All the right words: Finding what you want as a function of richness of indexing vocabulary. *Journal of the American Association for Information Science 41, 547–559.*

Good, M. D., Whiteside, J. A., Wixon, D. R., & Jones, S. J. (1984). Building a user-derived interface. *Communications of the ACM, 27,* 1032–1043.

Greene, S., Gomez, L. M., & Devlin, S. J. (1986). A cognitive analysis of database query production. *Proceedings of the Human Factors Society 30th Annual Meeting* (pp. 9–13).

Greene, S. L., Devlin, S. J., Cannata, P. E., & Gomez, L. M. (1990). No IFs, ANDs, or ORs: A study of database querying. *International Journal of Man–Machine Studies, 32,* 303–326.

Grudin, J. (1988). Why CSCW applications fail: Problems in the design and evaluation of organizational interfaces. *Proceedings of 'CSCW '88 Conference on Computer-Supported Cooperative Work* (p. 85–93). New York: ACM.

Kernighan, M., Church, K., & Gale, W. (1990). *A spelling correction program based on a noisy channel model.* Helsinki, Finland: COLING.

Landauer, T. K. (1987). Relations between cognitive psychology and computer system design. In J. M. Carroll (Ed.), *Interfacing thought: Cognitive aspects of human–computer interaction* (pp. 1–25). Cambridge, MA: MIT Press.

Landauer, T. K., & Galotti, K. M. (1984). What makes a difference when? Comments on Grudin and Barnard. *Human Factors, 26,* 423–429.

Landauer, T. K., & Nachbar, D. W. (1985). Selecting from alphabetic and numeric menu trees using a touch screen: Breadth, depth and width. In L. Borman & B. Curtis (Eds.), *Proceedings of CHI '85: Human Factors in Computing Systems* (pp. 73–78). New York: ACM.

Lenat, D. B., & Guha, R. V. (1989). *Building large knowledge-based systems.* Reading, MA: Addison-Wesley.

Lewis, C., Polson, P., Wharton, C., & Rieman, J. (1990). Testing a walkthrough methodology for theory-based design of walk-up-and-use interfaces. In J. C. Chew & J. Whiteside (Eds.), *Proceedings of CHI '90: Human Factors in Computing Systems* (pp. 235–242). New York: ACM.

McKnight, C., Dillon, A., & Richardson, J. (1989). A comparison of linear and hypertext formats in information retrieval. Paper presented at Hypertext II Conference, York, England.

Newell, A. (1989). *Unified theories of cognition: The 1987 William James lectures.* Cambridge, MA: Harvard University Press.

Newell, A., & Card, S. K. (1985). The prospects for psychological science in human–computer interaction. *Human–Computer Interaction, 1,* 209–242.

Nielson, J. (1989). Usability engineering at a discount. In G. Salvendy & M. J. Smith (Eds.), *Designing and using human–computer interfaces and knowledge based systems* (pp. 394–401). Amsterdam: Elsevier Science Publishers.

Nielsen, J., & Molich, R. (1990). Heuristic evaluation of user interfaces. In J. C. Chew & J. Whiteside (Eds.), *Proceedings of CHI '90: Human Factors in Computing Systems* (pp. 249–256). New York: ACM.

Shneiderman, B. (1987). *Designing the user interface: Strategies for effective human–computer interaction.* Reading, MA: Addison-Wesley.

Tullis, T. S. (1985). Designing a menu-based interface to an operating system. In L. Borman & B. Curtis (Eds.), *Proceedings of CHI '85: Human Factors in Computing Systems* (pp. 79–84). New York: ACM.

Weyer, S. A. (1982). The design of a dynamic book for information search. Doctoral dissertation, Stanford University, Palo Alto, CA.

Wixon, D., Holtzblatt, K., & Knox, S. (1990). Contextual design: An emergent view of system design. In J. C. Chew & J. Whiteside (Eds.), *Proceedings of CHI '90: Human Factors in Computing Systems* (pp. 329–336). New York: ACM.

Chapter 10

Designing to Fit Human Capabilities

People and computers have quite different—often diametrically opposite—capabilities, as illustrated in Figure 10.1. With a "good" interface, human and computer should augment each other to produce a system that is greater than the sum of its parts. Computer and human share responsibilities, each performing the parts of the task that best fit its capabilities. The computer enhances our cognitive and perceptual strengths, and counteracts our weaknesses. People are responsible for the things the machine cannot or should not do. (See also Nickerson, 1977, reprinted in the first edition of this book, for an insightful exploration of this theme.)

Designing simultaneously for both human and computer capabilities requires trade-offs and compromises. Unfortunately, concessions in system design are often made at the expense of the person because of the last two rows of Figure 10.1: people are excellent at adapting to suboptimal situations, whereas computers are inflexible and their performance does not degrade gracefully.

"Creativity, adaptability, and flexibility are [human] strengths," says Don Norman (1990, p. 4) in the first reading in this chapter. Indeed, it is remarkable how people can accommodate to—and even enjoy—the very worst interfaces, albeit at the expense of training time, inefficiencies, and errors. Just consider how many people still use—and how many programmers swear by—the abysmal Unix interface (Norman, 1981)! Although even our best interfaces require people to adapt to some extent to the computer, designers have to recognize critical areas where the computer has to support human capabilities and augment our weaknesses. When people do have to adapt to the computer, the computer should assist that process. This brings us to the theme of this chapter—designing interfaces that best take advantage of human capabilities.

FIGURE 10.1

Capabilities of computers and people. Adapted from lecture notes, D. Hill, University of Calgary.

Capability	Computer	Human
Precision and repeatability	√	
Fast and accurate calculations	√	
Reliable memory	√	
Tirelessness	√	
Objectivity	√	
Patience	√	
Physical robustness	√	
Holistic pattern matching		√
Creativity		√
Initiative and exception handling		√
Ability to learn from experience		√
Ability to handle ill-defined problems		√
Good motor skills		√
Judgment		√
Sense of ethics and responsibility		√
Ability to apply social context to task		√
Ability to fail gracefully		√
Flexibility and adaptability		√

Some aspects of a system interface *must* be designed to accommodate particular human characteristics, for neglecting to do so would seriously compromise the effectiveness of the human-computer system:

- *Designing for human error.* Failing to account for the certainty of human error in a human-computer system is a recipe for disaster; interfaces should be constructed to minimize the number and the effects of errors.
- *Helping people learn systems and tasks through training and help.* Human knowledge is incomplete, difficult to acquire, and hard to remember. Since all systems require learning, we should support this process with high-quality training programs, documentation, active exploration, and on-line interactive help.
- *Devising interfaces for users with special needs.* A surprising number of people have some kind of physical or mental disability. An interface can block such individuals from using a computer—or it can minimize and even overcome the effect of these disabilities.
- *Accommodating us physically.* The design of workstation, furniture, and rooms that ignores our physical frailties leads to inefficiency, discomfort, and even injury. The field of "workstation ergonomics" studies and designs physical environments to fit people.

Although this chapter concentrates on these points, the topic is intimately tied to all aspects of design covered in this book. In particular, Parts I ("Introduction to HCI") and II ("The Process of Developing Interactive Systems") recommend design as an essential way to match people, human capabilities, machines, organizational requirements, and social context. Indeed, the philosophies of user-centered and task-centered design aim to fit applications to people and to their tasks, respectively (Norman and Draper, 1986; Lewis and Rieman, 1993). Chapter 2 also proposes "evaluation" as a way of detecting mismatches, ultimately leading to iterative changes to the system. Part III ("Interacting with Computers") considers how human and computer fit at the interaction level. Its chapters illustrate how machine output is assimilated easily by people if it is displayed appropriately (Chapters 6 and 8), and how people can converse with machines through natural mechanisms (Chapters 7 and 8).

The point to remember is that a "good" interaction technique maximizes human strengths, while a "poor" one exposes their limitations. Chapter 12 takes this one step further and suggests that because people vary greatly in their needs and requirements, and because individuals change over time, no design is perfect. It proposes that a way to fine-tune design (and consequently adapt to human capabilities) is to build flexibility and adaptability into the system.

DESIGNING FOR HUMAN ERROR

Even highly motivated and skilled users are guaranteed to make errors. Consider these scenarios:

- A regular user of an automated teller accidentally leaves her card in the machine (reported on Internet's comp.human-factors).
- When finished using a popular word processor, a person forgets to save the changes and loses a full day's work (personal experience).
- A controller omits a letter in a series of commands to the Phobos 1 Mars satellite, sending it into a tumble from which it never recovers (Waldrop, 1989, see also the Norman reading).
- In 1976, the police, operating a computerized highway sign system, fail to change speed limits on a major highway when fog descended.—34 vehicles crashed, 3 people were killed, and 11 were injured (D. Hill, personal communication).

The consequences of human error range from minor annoyance and frustration to loss of productivity, loss of profits, and loss of life. In our search for blame, we fault ourselves for our own errors, we laugh when we see others make petty mistakes, and we indict people for serious errors.

But who is really at fault? In the first reading, Norman argues that our propensity to err is a fact of life and that good system design should predict, accommodate, and minimize the effects of errors. He considers "human error" a misnomer, an artifact arising from system design that does not account for natural human behavior. Both Norman and Denning (in the next reading) suggest that we should not search for blame when so-called human error occurs. Instead we should regard failure as a breakdown in design that should be identified and remedied.

Norman and Denning argue that computer professionals should have mechanisms for reporting and publishing accounts of breakdowns, and for creating standards that minimize human errors. Interface professionals should honor standards, alter them when recurrent breakdown is observed, and admit and learn from our mistakes. This is beginning to happen at the Internet grass roots level, where people post and discuss usability problems (e.g., in the newsgroup comp.human-factors).

Many other fields consider the reporting and analysis of accidents and failures caused by human error a valuable resource for improving design, especially when safety is involved. We should learn from those industries and report—not cover up—errors. Perhaps the best model is in avionics, where pilots and air traffic controllers voluntarily report critical incidents to NASA's Aviation Safety Reporting System (Chappell and Tarrel, 1992; also see Stager, Hameluck, and Jubis, 1989). The NASA data base holds more than 100,000 entries, largely because the report process safeguards contributors from punishment. Critical incident investigation is standard practice in the nuclear industry (e.g., Armstrong, 1989; Hallbert et al., 1992; Malone, 1990), and we would be quite concerned if it were not! Many medical specializations attempt to minimize causes of human error, for example, intensive care units (Gopher et al., 1989). Other areas include mining (Shaw and Sanders, 1989), engineering (Petroski, 1985), and land/sea transportation (Lauber, 1987; Sanquist, 1992; Wagenaar and Groeneweg, 1987).

To design error-resistant systems, we must first understand what causes errors. Lewis and Norman (1986), in our next reading, divide errors into two broad categories: *mistakes* and *slips* (initially proposed in Norman, 1983). A *mistake* occurs when we have an incorrect mental model of what will happen when we do something. We consciously believe our action will meet our intention, but the result is not what we expected. With a *slip*, we intend to do the correct action, but somehow our performance gets misdirected and a different action is substituted. Slips usually occur in skilled behavior when we are not paying attention; we often notice the error too late. Lewis and Norman further categorize these errors and proceed to suggest methods for minimizing the possibility of errors or misunderstandings, methods for detecting errors, and methods for correcting errors.

There are other good sources for reading about error in human-computer systems. Norman (1988, Chapter 5) develops and applies the ideas in the Norman and Lewis reading to enhance the design of everyday things. Two of the ten essential usability heuristics (see Figure 2.7) proposed by Nielsen (1994) deal with errors, namely:

- Error prevention. Make it impossible or very unlikely for the user to make mistakes.
- Help users recognize, diagnose, and recover from errors. Provide good error messages. Let the user know what the problem is and how to correct it.

Before we can prevent errors, we have to understand their cause. Rouse and Rouse (1983) provide a theoretical classification of errors within a framework similar to Norman's stages of user activity. Woods and Roth (1988) review proposed error categorizations and consider error management within a cognitive engineering approach that seeks a better match between a person and a machine. A classification proposed by Booth (1990) enabled designers in one field to successfully classify 98.5% of the user-system errors.

While preventing human error is optimal, Rasmussen and Vicente (1989) argue, with Norman and Denning, that it is impossible to eliminate errors. The focus should thus be on controlling their effects. One method is to produce understandable error messages, and Shneiderman (1982a, 1982b) counsels us on the importance of a message's wording. Dean (1982) continues this theme with an insightful analysis for constructing error messages under the banner of how computers should talk to people; his recommendations were summarized on page 608 of the first edition of this book.

Additional general readings on human error include Wiener's presidential address to the Human Factors Society (Wiener, 1989), Miller and Swain's (1987) introduction to human error and reliability, and Reason's (1990) book on human error.

TRAINING, DOCUMENTATION, AND HELP

Can we expect less need for training, documentation, and help as interfaces improve? Can any application become a "walk up and use" system, if only the interface is good enough? In this section, we argue instead that training and help are more critical now than ever before. Computer functionality is increasing, hence people must know what is possible and how to achieve it. Computers are integrated into more aspects of work, hence people must learn new tasks and new roles in an organization. Because computer interfaces cannot be "perfectly" designed and systems cannot always evolve in lockstep with changing task requirements, people must learn how to adapt to system imperfections. After elaborating on this position, we shall discuss several methods for supplying training, documentation, and help.

Why Training and Help Are Important

Computer users need training and help in order to

- understand their evolving role in an organization and the changing context in which they work
- understand task domain concepts
- understand computer domain concepts
- be aware of the computer syntax required to complete the interaction

The last three are derived from the syntactic-semantic model of human-computer interaction (Shneiderman, 1994).

Because software can change the way we work, people must be trained to understand new work contexts and their changing roles within an organization. Organizations introduce software to change the work process to a hopefully better and more efficient one. In many cases, however, people are so immersed in the old work context that they may see little benefit of changing to a new one. Training is important here, both to ease the transition from the old to the new, and to promote "buy in" by making people aware of how they can benefit from the software. For example, the success or failure of the Coordinator, a structured e-mail system, depended heavily on whether people were trained on its underlying theory and the potential benefits (Bair and Gale, 1988; see also discussion in Chapter 11). However, training can be a double-edged sword, for people begrudge the time spent learning when they feel the functionality gained is not worth the learning effort (Carasik and Grantham, 1988).

Users of software may not have a complete understanding of the task domain. Areas that were once the domain of expert practitioners are now embodied in computer applications for the masses. If in the 1980s greater "ease of use" was brought to simple task domains, then the 1990s should see complex domains made accessible to end users.

However, accomplishing this presents challenges. The integration of typography and word processing has created desktop publishing, providing end users with control over aspects of typography such as font, leading, and layout, previously the responsibility of typographers. Merging technical art into drawing packages gives engineers computer-aided design (CAD) and the responsibilities once held by professional draftspeople. Spreadsheets give people the power of accounting ledgers, but not the knowledge of accountants. We have the decision-making capability of typographers, draftspeople, and accountants, but not their knowledge or training. On-line training and assistance to teach the rudiments of these fields is critical. If users are to take advantage of the capabilities, they must learn how to use the applications to accomplish particular tasks and solve particular problems.

Users of software may not have a complete understanding of the relevant computer semantics. Even when people know the task domain, they must translate their task goals into terms or actions the computer can recognize (Shneiderman, 1994; Norman, 1988). For example, a professional printer who is using a GUI-based typesetting system for the first time will have to learn about computer concepts such as windows, menus, and files. Good design can minimize the distinctions between the task and computer semantics, but some compromise is often necessary. Training and documentation can help people understand and bridge the unavoidable gulfs between computer and task semantics.

Users require constant reminders of computer syntax. Shneiderman (1994) reminds us that computer users must remember a wide variety of interface and device-dependent details. Command-based systems were notorious for this; people had to remember particular commands and their parameters. GUIs have lessened, but not eliminated, the need to know computer syntax. Windows still have to be adjusted, menus traversed, icons understood, and shortcuts remembered. Quick-reference guides or cheat sheets are common aids, reminding people of the system offerings as well as the correct incantations to invoke actions.

Within this framework of four reasons people require training and help, we can enumerate the types of questions that people ask. Sellen and Nicol (1990), included as a reading, emphasize a user-centered approach to help. They argue that the information delivered to the user and the way in which it is presented should depend upon the kind of question the user is asking. Figure 10.2 lists question types drawn in part from Sellen and Nicol and from Baecker, Small, and Mander's (1991) reading in Chapter 6.

FIGURE 10.2

Questions that computer users have.

Question Types	Example Questions
• *Informational*	*What kinds of things can I do with this program?*
• *Descriptive*	*What is this? What does this do?*
• *Procedural*	*How do I do this?*
• *Interpretive*	*What is happening now? Why did that happen? What does this mean?*
• *Navigational*	*Where am I? Where have I come from and gone to?*
• *Choice*	*What can I do now?*
• *Guidance*	*What should I do now?*
• *History*	*What have I done?*
• *Motivational*	*Why should I use this program? How will it benefit me?*
• *Investigative*	*What else should I know? Did I miss anything?*

Wright (1991) articulates the process that people follow to solve problems with documentation. Before reading any help text, people must formulate the problem as a question and find the text section that may hold the answer. When reading the text, they have to understand it, and as a result, decide what action they should take. Finally, they execute the action and evaluate the outcome to see if the answer was correct.

Training, documentation, and help must also match the way people actually learn computer applications in the real world. Carroll and Mack (1984), our next reading, studies human learning of complex materials in a realistic setting. Although the system learned by their subjects is an old text-based word processor, their observations on how people learn are still applicable to today's interfaces. In essence, people are active learners, and they teach themselves by

- trying things rather than only reading about them
- developing and testing hypotheses about why the system operates the way it does
- applying their knowledge of their tasks and prior experiences to interpret their experiences

Carroll and Mack believe that people learn *by doing, by thinking,* and *by knowing.* Their observations explain the success of active exploration through good tutorials and through simplified, forgiving interfaces (for learning by doing); interface and training systems that promote good conceptual models (for learning by thinking); and appropriate reference documentation that helps people answer specific questions (for learning by knowing).

Documentation and Training

Documentation and training are an essential part of the human-computer interface. In Chapter 2, Gould recommended that all aspects of usability design be integrated under one management. This principle, as well as those of user-centered and iterative design, apply equally well to documentation, on-line help, and training. Wright (1991) details how documentation—whether paper or on-line—must fit users' needs. It must match the conceptual model of readers, the wording and organizational structure must help them find answers to questions and make the contents understandable, and iterative development is required to tune the "usability" of the document. Perkins et al. (1989), included as a reading in Case C, is a good case study of iterative tutorial design.

Manuals are still the most popular type of help material, whether embodied as paper documents, on-line information systems, or hypertext. Manuals may consist of hundreds or thousands of pages of detailed information. A vast quantity of information can make a manual unusable—since a person's goal is to get on with his or her work, it is no wonder that people rarely or only superficially read these manuals! To get around the information glut problem, many modern applications now encourage an exploratory approach to learning, based on the theory presented in the Carroll and Mack reading that people learn best through "active learning" and "guided exploration," setting their own goals and solving problems at their own initiative and in their own way (see also Carroll, 1985, 1990).

This idea has been developed in two lines of research, *training wheels* interfaces and the *minimal manual.*

The training wheels approach is named for the two stabilizing wheels added to a child's bicycle during initial practice, also called starter wheels. They allow a child to practice basic operations—pedaling, braking, turning, and some balancing—without getting into trouble. Jack Carroll and his colleagues at IBM assumed that most learners of a new system only require a handful of functions from a system's rich offerings to get started. Rather than learn everything at once, training wheels make only simple, essential, and safeguarded functions available to learners. Users are given an exploratory environment for active learning. A number of principles are proposed:

- *Learn simple things first.* Nonessential parts of the system are prohibited, either by hiding them from the user or indicating that they are not available.

- *Positive transfer of learning.* All items learned in the stripped down version of the system are available in the full version and accessed in an identical fashion.
- *Common error states are unreachable.* Because learners are encouraged to explore, they must be protected somewhat from serious errors. This is achieved by limiting access to only the safe parts of the system, or by altering system behavior to reduce or eliminate consequences of erroneous actions.

The approach was tested in two experimental studies, Carroll and Carrithers (1984a, 1984b) and Catrambone and Carroll (1987).

Carroll and Carrithers compared the learning of novice users of a commercial system with novice users of a modified version of the system in which only basic functions were enabled. Other menu choices were visible but not active. They found that novices learned the basic functions more quickly. Users of the full system wandered through the menu structure and did not learn the key operations as soon. This left an important question unanswered: What happens when the "training wheels" are removed and users move on to the full system? Will the unnecessary "wandering" of the users who did not use training wheels now pay off? Catrambone and Carroll found that the learning advantage of the training wheels continued after they were removed, when the full system was encountered. Apparently the time spent wandering around the menu structure by unblocked users simply confused them. Unfortunately, this elegant and important work, which was not at all obvious, has not been followed up sufficiently in the years since it was published.

Another approach to training, the minimal manual (also called "minimalist design"), has met with mixed results. Main points drawn from Carroll (1985), which appeared in the first edition of this book, Carroll (1990), and Carroll et al. (1987–1988) are the following:

- *There is less to read.* Only basic topics are included, and material not related to a task is eliminated or reduced. Candidates for elimination include all repetition, summaries, reviews, practice exercises, indexes, troubleshooting guides, detailed descriptions of interface components, and welcome messages.
- *Learner initiative is encouraged.* The user is cast into an active role by modules that explain procedures as abbreviated steps, leaving a learner to infer or discover the missing steps. The manual encourages users to attend to the display by performing an action and observing the results.
- *Topics are modularized into very small chunks of 1 to 5 pages.* Modules reflect real user tasks. Their titles are task-oriented and become an index into the document. Realistic open-ended exercises foster the connection between training and use.
- *There is more error recovery information.* The manual assumes that learners will make mistakes. Modules list typical errors and recovery procedures.
- *Manuals may be used as references after training.* Because modules are task-centered, people can use the manual as a reference to remind them how to do particular task-related functions.

The final three points are relatively uncontroversial, but the first two may not be appropriate for all learners and situations. For a critique and literature review, see Williams and Farkas (1992).

Lewis and Rieman (1993) review learning theory and propose principles for designing a training program consistent with the training wheels approach:

- People learn facts best if they work with them—that is, through discovery, application, and recall.
- Skills improve with practice, and spaced practice (by interspersing a repetitive lesson with other tasks) is more effective.
- To be effective, practice requires feedback to let people know whether or not what they have done is right.
- People are best at learning a few things at a time—avoid unnecessary lesson complexity.
- People need to learn basic skills before undertaking advanced training.

Training wheels and minimal manuals don't solve all learning and help needs. For example, they don't respond to all the user-centered questions listed in Figure 10.2. Help designers may have difficulty identifying the essential user tasks and system functions; users of complex applications often use unique subsets of available functions (Greenberg, 1993; Draper, 1984). Also, people have different learning styles. For such reasons, most vendors supply multiple training approaches and document types to help new users, including "getting started" primers, multimedia tours through system basics, and training tutorials that include sample documents that people can work on. Figure 10.3 lists the offerings that come with a popular word processor of great functionality and complexity. Despite the number of these offerings, users still experience significant difficulties in mastering this complexity.

Experienced users also need help and training. Mayer (1988) describes differences between novice and expert computer users. Although he only mentions training in passing, his list indicates what novices need to learn before becoming experts, and that experts require quite a different kind of help.

On-Line Help

Documentation is moving on-line. Shneiderman (1994, in particular Chapter 12) lists a variety of standard on-line help approaches, each addressing particular types of questions.

- *On-line manuals* typically make paper manuals available electronically. More capabilities are available, such as string searching, multiple views into the document, and electronic bookmarking. Hypertext is an especially powerful way to search and navigate on-line manuals, facilitating rapid cross-referencing and browsing (discussed further in Chapter 13 of this book).
- *Keyword and keystroke* lists are quick-reference guides that inform or remind a user as to what is available and how to invoke an action.
- *Context-sensitive help* tunes the help message to the current context of a user. For example, the Apple Macintosh balloon help explains the meaning of the screen item being pointed to (see Figure 4 in the Sellen and Nicol reading).
- *Tutorials, demonstrations, and animations* introduce novice users to a system by presenting essential concepts and letting them try tutorial exercises. Animation is especially appealing when done within the existing interface. For example, static screen icons are "brought to life" by animating them, thereby

FIGURE 10.3

Training and documentation materials supplied with Microsoft Word 5.1, Macintosh version.

Learning to Use Word

- *A "Getting Started" book includes both basic and advanced tutorial instruction. The tutorial is based upon active learning—it expects people to work with sample documents included with the software. Other sections describe what the application is for and how to install it.*
- *For expert users, a "What's New" booklet lists the major differences between the new and old versions, and how to use the new capabilities.*
- *A "Jumpstart" reference guide provides "at a glance" training for experts who just want to get on with things. Its four pages summarize system installation, the meaning of major visible components and when they should be used, common errors, and answers to frequently asked questions.*
- *Separate "User Guide" booklets are included for training in the use of embedded applications such as drawing and equation tools. They are written as a combination of minimal manual and tutorial.*

Reference Materials and On-line Help

- *A very detailed hard-copy reference manual is included.*
- *An on-line manual, organized by topics, is included. Although not as detailed as the hard-copy manual, it summarizes salient information and indicates where to find further details in the hardcopy.*
- *Context-sensitive help is provided in two ways. Pressing the help key and pointing to a screen object brings up the relevant manual section. Also, Macintosh balloon help gives brief descriptions explaining menus and screen items when the mouse pointer is passed over them.*
- *Two quick reference guides are available. The hard-copy "Jumpstart," mentioned before, acts as a visual reminder of basic functionality. On-line, a scrollable "Commands" dialog lists all available commands, where they can be found in the hierarchical menus and dialogs, and what shortcuts are associated with them, if any.*

clarifying their meaning, demonstrating their capabilities, and explaining the procedure of use (Baecker, Small, and Mander, 1991, reprinted in Chapter 6).

- *Guides* are interface agents that actively guide people through a task, perhaps by "hand holding" or by taking a particular point of view toward the material (Oren et al., 1990).
- *Intelligent help* tries to infer what the user knows and doesn't know and offers help, lessons, and advice within that framework. Microsoft's "Intellisense" feature on some applications is an early commercial example.

Guides and intelligent help are discussed again in Chapter 12. In this area, reasoning and knowledge-based systems from artificial intelligence can aid HCI. The research of Gerhard Fischer and his colleagues, represented in the Fischer and Reeves excerpt in Chapter 12, foreshadows how such approaches can aid the creation of training and help systems for complex domain-specific applications.

Many of the techniques listed above are available today in the better applications. The reader should explore such systems to get a feel for their offerings. Microsoft Word is one popular example that can be used as a case study to illustrate how vendors are paying serious attention to training, documentation, and on-line help (Figure 10.3).

On-line help does have its detractors. Lewis and Rieman (1993) bemoan the effectiveness of on-line help, noting that few products have been shown to successfully deliver large volumes of on-line information better than traditional manuals. (Notable exceptions are Superbook—see Egan et al., 1989, in Chapter 13, and the Document Examiner—Walker, 1987, 1985 video, discussed in Chapter 13.) Reasons for mediocre performance include unwieldy search and browsing mechanisms, reading problems due to visual display quality, the difficulty of marking useful pages and sections, and the lack of skills required to use on-line help systems (see Wright, 1991). Lewis and Rieman encourage developers to use on-line help only for brief descriptions and facts.

We have a more optimistic view. Many early studies were based on old interfaces and screen technologies; we now find more positive results (see Perkins, et al. 1989, in Case C, and Egan et al., 1989, in Chapter 13). On-line help has traditionally received few resources, and when it does, effort may go into building a clever help system at the expense of producing good documentation. Good help interfaces are important, but studies by Borenstein (1985), summarized in Chapter 13 of the first edition of this book, indicate that the most important determinant of help system quality is the quality of the text!

Another pragmatic reason for putting manuals on-line, even if they are no better than paper versions, is that electronic help is always available, whereas paper manuals can be locked in cabinets, stored in other locations (as when working with a portable computer), or just inconvenient to obtain. On-line help has its benefits, and its effectiveness will improve as interface limitations are addressed.

Asking Others for Help

One of the most efficient ways to obtain help is to ask a knowledgeable person. Systems can mediate between users and experts. This is the tack taken by the Andrew Advisor, built on a multimedia mail and bulletin board system (Borenstein and Thyberg, 1991). The Advisor routes a question to human advisors. If they know the answer, they answer it immediately; otherwise, they post it to a bulletin board for others to answer. The bulletin board system contains a rich structure of groups based on patterns of questions and advisor expertise. Another approach is embodied in Ackerman and Malone's (1990) Answer Garden, a system that creates and grows a tree structure containing answers to commonly asked questions. If a questioner works through the tree structure and does not find an answer, the question can be sent to an expert, who can reply and, if the question is likely to occur again, insert the answer into the branching network. A similar system is proposed in Kurisaki (1990). Computer-mediated help "in real time" is provided by screen and window-sharing programs, and desktop- and videoconferencing systems, described in Chapter 11.

Other Sources

Several books deal specifically with help systems. Kearsley (1988) includes detailed chapters on design alternatives, system examples, discussions of research, implementation issues, and guidelines for building help systems. Horton (1990) considers the design and writing of on-line help for both file-based and hypertext-based systems.

Several authors have concentrated on how help systems should be designed. Elkerton (1988) categorizes design principles for online advice based on a GOMS model analysis (see Chapter 9): help is directed toward determining goals, clarifying operators, detailing steps in procedures, and selecting particular rules. Egan (1988) argues that a system can cater to individual differences of users through appropriate training and help. He recommends training environments (such as training wheels), making systems intelligent enough to coach people on individual problems, and implementing full-scale training curricula where people master steps in sequence. Wright (1988) identifies issues in the design of manuals that center on questions of manual content and presentation.

Some researchers have investigated how people use help and what questions they ask. Campagnoni and Ehrlich (1989) report that people using a hypertext-based help system eschewed indexes, preferring to page through topics or browse tables of contents. Guindon (1991) describes the language people use to form help requests and considers the requirements of a restricted natural language interface that might understand these requests.

Computer-aided instruction (CAI) and intelligent tutoring systems (ITS) are distinct, relevant fields of research, reviewed by Wenger (1987) and Eberts and Brock (1988). CAI systems provide on-line teaching programs for learners; ITS seek to take a more active role in determining what a student knows and how a lesson should proceed. Chapter 13 covers relevant hypermedia systems. You may also find it worthwhile to explore the proceedings of the System Documentation Conferences (ACM Press).

Innovative approaches to documentation and help are demonstrated in Walker (1985 video), Kirston et al. (1988 video), Shea (1989 video), and Sukaviriya (1989 video).

Conclusions

Documentation and support materials must be rich enough to reflect the diversity of learning styles and help situations. More research into the phenomena of active learning would be welcome.

USERS WITH SPECIAL NEEDS

"Empowerment" is a heavily used word, projecting a pleasant image of computers that enhance and extend human capabilities. Nowhere is this more true than in interfaces for users with special needs, such as the blind, the deaf, and the motor-disabled. Two kinds of contributions are possible:

- By designing interfaces for use by those with special needs, we can provide them with equivalent access to information and computer tools enjoyed by other computer users.
- We can design interfaces to be a prosthetic that lessens or overcomes a person's disability, providing an individual with some or all of the physical, mental, and social capabilities that others take for granted.

Making interfaces accessible to users with special needs is not only an altruistic exercise, but it is also a large and growing market. In an introduction to an issue of *Communications of the ACM* devoted to "Computers and People with Disabilities," Glinert and York (1992) note that 500,000 Americans are legally blind (NSF, 1990), 700,000 suffer from cerebral palsy (Pausch and Williams, 1992), three million are speech- or language-impaired (Kukich, 1992), and one million are hearing-impaired (Kukich, 1992). In a recent survey of ACM members, 5% reported a disability (Davies and Dipner, 1992)! Many of our aging population may eventually join their ranks, since improvements in medicine enable people to live longer despite any dysfunctions (Newell, 1994). Czaja (1988) reviews issues related to enabling the productive use of microcomputers by the elderly.

Our reading by Lazzaro (1993; see also Lazzaro, 1990, and Brown, 1992) outlines contemporary computer technology that opens doors for the disabled. It is encouraging that most of the systems listed by Lazzaro run on standard computers and are reasonably affordable. To supplement Lazzaro's article, this section provides a sample of current research and technology to show its richness and diversity. The approaches and inventions below are loosely categorized into the impairments they address: seeing, speaking, hearing, moving, and thinking. It is a rough categorization, since people have different levels of impairment, and multiple disabilities often occur together.

Helping the Blind and Visually Impaired See

How can people who have limited vision or none at all "see" computer displays? A sad irony is that the obvious answer of converting text to audio has been made more difficult and less useful by the development of graphical and multimedia interfaces that enhance the experience of unimpaired users. Happily, Lazzaro (1994a) reports on recent progress in adapting GUI software for the blind. Approaches to helping the impaired see include the following:

- *Text to speech:* Blind people can access books through equipment that uses optical character recognition (OCR) to scan text, which in turn drives a speech synthesizer (but see Blenkhorn, 1994, for caveats). Screen readers can be extended to verbalize not only text, but icons, menus, dialog boxes, and other graphical components (Edwards, 1989a, 1989b; Mynatt and Edwards, 1992).
- *Text to Braille:* Although a declining proportion of the blind can read Braille, there are Braille keyboards, Braille screens, and even Braille printers. Weber (1994) describes advanced interaction methods for Braille displays.
- *Spatial control of text-to-speech synthesis:* Innovative graphics tablets help the blind maximize their spatial abilities. The Touch 'n Talk workstation (Hill and Gries, 1988) presents users with a textured tablet as a spatial representation of a visual display. Users control the audio output of a screen display by touching different parts of the tablet.

- *Magnification:* People with limited visual ability can magnify portions of their screen to improve legibility. This is almost standard with modern computers, which let users adjust font size.
- *First-class auditory interfaces:* Mynatt and Edwards (1994) and Edwards (1988) argue that we can build auditory interfaces to replace or augment visual ones. Several inventions support their case. Soundtrack is a word processor for the blind that includes an auditory interface. Visual widgets, such as scroll bars, can be enhanced by an auditory interface (Brewster, Wright, and Edwards, 1994).

Helping the Speaking-Impaired Speak

Another beneficial use of a computer as prosthesis is to help people who are otherwise speaking impaired talk to other people. Talking typewriters can help in some cases, as suggested by the first example below. However, people whose speaking problems arise from severe motor impairments must resort to other schemes since they cannot type quickly; these are covered by the other examples.

- *Text to intelligible speech:* Kukich (1992) describes how speech-impaired people can use the telephone network without human intermediaries by using a speech synthesis system driven by typed text. One problem is that misspellings in typed messages often translate into unintelligible speech. Kukich describes a spelling correction approach that minimizes this problem.
- *Conversational moves:* Alm, Arnott, and Newell (1992) describe CHAT, a system that helps people who are both physically and speaking impaired to communicate with others by simulating natural dialog. They employ a conversational model that allows people to select conversational moves, with the system predicting moves and generating phrases (or choices) appropriate to the occasion. Newell et al. (1994) presents other systems developed by this group.
- *Gesture to speech:* Pausch and Williams (1992, 1994) are developing an articulator-based speech synthesizer for nonverbal children with cerebral palsy. Gesture and motion recognition is mapped to a speech synthesizer. The goal is to allow children to use natural mouth movement and other motions to generate speech.
- *Evaluating a speech prosthesis:* Strong (1994) evaluated the long-term use of a popular speech prosthesis system by a cerebral palsy victim (his daughter). This usability study found that although the existing system does work, specific improvements could make it far more usable and beneficial to disabled users.

Helping the Hearing-Impaired Hear

Conventional approaches to helping the deaf "hear" rely on shifting from speech to text. For example, telephones are used by the deaf through special telecommunications devices for the deaf (TDDs), boxes that let people type to each other over the phone system. Of course, TDDs can be replaced by computers, giving the deaf access to a full computer communication network as well. Some other methods are the following:

- *Speech transcription systems* that provide a written version of speech for a deaf person need not provide a perfect rendition of speech. The output must only be readable and be provided at close to verbatim speed (Brooks and Newell, 1985).
- *Sign language interfaces* allow the deaf to store, retrieve, and manipulate computer information through the deaf sign language. A panel on this topic at INTERCHI '93 described several systems (Frishberg et al., 1993).

Helping the Motor-Disabled Interact with Computers and Other Devices

Severely motor-disabled people have access to equipment designed for particular disabilities and tasks. Computers can provide tailored input mechanisms to help people control these devices. Examples include voice recognition, a head-controlled mouse, and special keyboards. There are even eye-wink interfaces for controlling word processors and wheelchairs (Shaw, Loomis, and Crisman, 1994)!

- Demasco and McCoy (1992) investigate methods that allow people with severe motor impairments to generate text. First, they look at predictive strategies that make it easy for people to select likely letters or words. Next, they explore "sentence compansion" that translates abbreviated sentences (such as "apple eat john") into well-formed ones ("the apple is eaten by John").
- Darragh and Witten (1992) describe in detail the "reactive keyboard," a text entry system for the physically disabled that greatly speeds typing by predicting a user's next response. Because predictions are based on previous input, they adapt to whatever text is being entered.
- More generally, Greenberg et al. (1994) survey "predictive interfaces" that help people for whom any manual input represents a challenge. In addition to text prediction, approaches and systems that are discussed include adaptive menus, reuse mechanisms, and programming by demonstration.
- Matias, MacKenzie and Buxton (1993) developed software for a one-handed keyboard that allows people to transfer two-handed touch-typing skills to touch-typing with one hand on a standard keyboard.

Helping the Mentally Challenged Think

Mental disability has received much less attention in computer interface design, perhaps because of the extreme variability of mental handicaps, which could require highly customized software. Still, interfaces can be modified to address particular disabilities. For example, Elkind and Shrager (1994) applied GOMS modeling to understand the writing bottlenecks suffered by people with dyslexia, which led to recommendations for speech recognition systems that would better support writing.

Other Sources

One excellent collection of articles on using computers to help people overcome disabilities is the special issue of *Communication of the ACM* mentioned above (Glinert and York, 1992). Another is the book *Extra-Ordinary Human-Computer Interaction* (Edwards, 1995), a collection of essays and papers from HCI specialists who work on interfaces for the disabled. Lazzaro (1994b) is a recent 250-page illustrated guide describing how to adapt personal computers for individuals with vision, hearing, motor, and speech impairments. The book contains practical, how-to-do-it sections as well as descriptions of more than

120 specific adaptive products. A demonstration of an interactive system facilitating communication with aphasic individuals is VA Medical Center (1989 video).

Conclusions

Designing for users with special needs is important. By seeing ideas and systems profoundly benefit people's lives, a designer earns a strong feeling of accomplishment. Because many people are disabled, there may be a substantial potential for financial returns. Since we and our friends and families all suffer accidents and grow old, we are investing in our own personal future.

THE PHYSICAL ENVIRONMENT AND WORKSTATION ERGONOMICS

The physical environment strongly influences the quality of human-computer interaction through

- workstation ergonomics (including the design of screens and keyboards)
- lighting
- temperature and noise
- health and safety

A bad physical environment can render the most technologically advanced system useless. Conversely, and often ignored by management and technologists alike, this is an area in which we can often get the greatest improvement in human performance and satisfaction for the lowest cost!

Many interface designers consider the physical environment, however important, to be beyond their control. After all, they usually produce software and have no power to control the furniture, keyboards, work habits, lighting, and noise levels of the workers' offices. However, it is part of an interface designer's role to consider the complete environment.

Low-cost solutions exist for surprisingly many problems. For example, light glare on a visual display unit (VDU) can be minimized by repositioning the screen, installing curtains over windows, or changing the internal room lighting. Noise discomfort can be reduced by ear plugs or a headset. Physical discomfort associated with long hours at a workstation can be diminished by adjusting furniture and exercising periodically. At the very least, interface designers should list potential environment problems and provide a customer or user with recommendations of how to avoid them or mitigate their effects.

Workstation Ergonomics

In this section we use the term "workstation" to designate the computer and furniture employed by an operator. The design problem is to match physical devices to the operator's body dimensions and capabilities. The introduction of ergonomically designed furniture can result in significant improvements in the workplace (Dainoff, Fraser, and Taylor, 1982; Shute and Starr, 1984; Smith, 1984).

Kroemer (1988) provides an excellent overview of computer workstation design. He notes that many complaints associated with workstation design are related to posture (caused by poorly designed and ill-placed furniture and equipment) and viewing (VDUs and documents that are outside people's "visual zone of comfort"). Kroemer provides tables of standard anthropometric measurements of the human body and recommendations for furniture design and equipment placement. However, he warns that measurements are important and useful only when *appropriately applied.* Many recommendations assume an average person sitting upright with elbows, hips, and knees at right angles—ignoring actual body sizes, working postures, and expected human variations (also see Grandjean, 1984). Other problems with measurements include the following:

- Some measures taken decades ago assume average heights that are quite different today.
- Some measures were based on atypical groups such as males in the military.
- Measurements can have an unwarranted air of rigor or authority.
- Measurements can be susceptible to misinterpretation by nonspecialists.

Since each of us is different, one might argue that furniture should be designed to be adjusted to individual needs. This philosophy has resulted in the much-touted "ergonomic furniture" that allows adjustments such as the height of the seat cushion and the tilt angle of the back. Yet adjustability can cause problems. People rarely understand the reasons behind adjustable features and often leave furniture as they receive it, or adjust it improperly.

Povlotksy and Dubrovsky (1988) observed that when people make serious efforts to adjust their furniture, almost all positions are very close to those recommended in standards. If any benefit is to be obtained by choosing adjustable furniture instead of well-designed nonadjustable furniture, there must also be an investment in educating users on its proper adjustment (Oman et al., 1989). Wallach (1994) lists commercial ergonomic products, indicating what the furniture does, its cost, and the address of the manufacturer or distributor.

In many cases, a simpler solution is possible. An operator needs a chair and desk that fit. If furniture is not shared, then inexpensive solutions can achieve the desired fit—tables can be lowered, chairs exchanged, and monitors elevated. Simple alterations can often address minor problems (a hacksaw does wonders!). If you understand the *cause* of a problem, then you are better equipped to tailor an individual solution. If your feet do not reach the floor, an angled support (such as a three-ring binder) can solve the problem very nicely.

Keyboard use demands particular attention. Typing injury due to repetitive motion is becoming a widespread and potentially devastating disability. Our reading on this topic (Sauter, Chapman, and Knutson, 1985) first summarizes typical problems in VDU work and organizational approaches to solving these problems. It then gives a physiological introduction to the musculoskeletal system and how strain is induced. Problems range from fatigue to tendon and nerve damage, such as carpal tunnel syndrome, a serious disability. People can guard against typing injury by following fairly simple rules:

- Provide periodic support for the arms and hands.
- Position work materials in a way that avoids unusual hand and arm postures; wrists should not be bent while typing.
- Make sure arms do not contact hard edges of tables and keyboards.

- Vary motion patterns, take breaks, and intersperse other activities and highly repetitive tasks.

Sauter, Chapman, and Knutson identify specific problems and solutions in keyboard placement and design, arm and hand support, and highly repetitive tasks. Because the designs of many keyboards and mice often force people into unnatural postures, vendors now sell "ergonomic" keyboards and mice. One example is Apple's adjustable keyboard, actually two keyboards (one for each hand) connected by a hinge that allows them to be spread apart. The "spreading" design stops people from turning their hands outwards when typing (see figures 9-7 and 9-9 in Sauter, Chapman, and Knutson). There is also software that detects highly repetitive activity, suggests breaks, and recommends exercises (Wallach, 1994). Introductions and overviews to workstation ergonomics are found in Grandjean (1987), Van Cott and Kinkade (1972), Kantowitz and Sorkin (1983), Frome (1984), and Sanders and McCormick (1987). Snyder (1988) provides detailed aspects of image quality on computer displays. Bosman and White (1990) reports specifically on character visibility in VDUs. More specific information can be found in other sources, such as Cakir, Hart, and Stewart (1980), Eastman Kodak (1983), and Smith (1984).

A continuously updated source of "frequently asked questions and answers" on typing injuries and related software and ergonomic products is available through the Internet (Wallach, 1994). In turn, Wallach recommends a pamphlet produced by New Zealand's Occupational Safety and Health Service (Wigley et al., 1992). Our reading by Sauter, Chapman, and Knutson (1985) is an excerpt from an excellent, clearly written booklet on VDU use that should be read by anyone interested in these issues.

This literature clarifies issues such as reach, zone of visual comfort, and desk height, but one must be careful to apply the metrics with care and discretion. Effective workstation design must incorporate a healthy balance between theory and field work.

Lighting

The most common environmental problem affecting workstations is glare on the surface of the screen caused by poorly controlled lighting. One way to address this is with an antiglare filter: optical coating (generally the best), etched or polarized glass, or mesh mounted over the screen surface. Comparative studies of filter techniques are found in Beaton and Snyder (1984) and Morse (1985).

Although such filters reduce glare, they also diffuse the light emitted from the CRT and can blur the display. These problems are minimal with the best filters and are less serious than glare. But even when using excellent filters, the problem should also be attacked at its source—lighting.

Comprehensive lighting design is complex, requiring consideration of color, drapes, furniture layout, and structural design, but simple, direct steps can also be taken. Sauter, Chapman, and Knutson (1985) suggest baffles on fluorescent lights, alignment of desks with lights and windows, and use of vertical venetian blinds (the section on lighting is excerpted in the first edition of this book). Comparative studies have shown that office workers prefer indirect to direct lighting (Hedge, 1991) and prefer particular levels of glare, ambient light, and document luminance (Konz and Bennett, 1987).

Temperature and Noise

Also requiring consideration are the noise and heat (e.g., Bauer, 1991) generated by workstations.

Heat is important because even moderate changes in temperature can affect performance. Added heat can lead to drowsiness and reduced concentration. A room with a workstation generates far more heat than a nonequipped equivalent next door, so local control over air temperature and circulation is required to adjust the ormer without adversely affecting other regions of the workplace.

Similarly, noise can influence concentration, stress level, and other aspects of performance. Even noises we don't notice can cause stress. For example, sometimes only when an air conditioner is switched off do people, surprised at how quiet it is, realize how loud the air conditioning was. The prevalence of modern open-concept offices exacerbates noise because computer and peripheral noise (fans, disk drives, beeping sounds, and keyboard clatter), as well as human conversation and movement, are merged into a single space. Mital, McGlothlin, and Faard (1990) note that the noise people find annoying in an open office is attributed to these sounds rather than to building machinery.

Acoustic design can minimize these effects through, for example, knowledgeable room furnishing. Rooms with soft furniture, carpets, and acoustic ceiling tiles are far quieter than those with hard floors and concrete ceilings. An irony in acoustic design is that a common strategy for controlling noise is to introduce more noise (Eastman Kodak, 1983)! By distributing relatively low-level broadband noise (something like the sound of the ocean), other potentially distracting sounds will be *masked*, i.e., hidden or muffled. The dilemma is that steady-state noise is subliminal and fatiguing, but a quiet workplace can be interrupted by intermittent sounds.

In extreme cases, a person can control the acoustic environment by wearing ear protectors. Quality ear plugs, for example, are reasonably comfortable, reduce noise by about 20 dB, and cost a dollar or two, yet still permit normal conversation in person or on the telephone. Sophisticated, technical approaches to hearing protection that do not compromise auditory and speech detection are discussed by Casali (1992).

Air temperature and sound issues can often be addressed at their source. Heat and noise radiation should be one of the parameters seriously considered before equipment is acquired. Although air conditioning can be added to reduce heat, it may increase the noise level. Isolating noisy and heat-producing machines (such as printers and disk drives) in closets can also be effective.

The bibliography lists readings on noise and the acoustic environment. Jones and Broadbent (1987) provide an overview of noise, including topics such as interference with speech by noise, the effects of noise on well-being and health, and general recommendations. Kryter (1970) presents a detailed account of the effects of noise on people. Koelega and Brinkman (1986) nicely summarize the literature on the effects of noise on vigilance tasks. Propst and Wodka (1975) is a comprehensible, practical handbook for dealing with acoustic problems in open-plan offices. As noted in Chapter 8; "Speech, Language, and Audition," sound is now more often being incorporated into interfaces, adding complexity and urgency to the problem of controlling noise in the workplace.

Achieving Health and Safety in the Workplace

With the introduction of any technology into the workplace or home, the effects on health and safety should be considered. This is an important issue in collective bargaining and in legislating standards.

Considerable attention has recently been focused on health issues stemming from computer use, primarily because of the widespread appearance of repetitive strain injuries, including carpal tunnel syndrome. Three recent overviews are Stigliani (1995), Pascarelli and Quilter (1994), and Pinsky (1993). Putz-Anderson (1988) is an older collection focusing on upper limb problems. Hedge (1987) provides an annotated bibliography covering the literature on technology-related health issues in office systems at that time. For a treatment of one topic in the medical literature, see Rempel, Harrison, and Barnhart (1992).

The Internet is a good place to seek information on health topics. The active newsgroup sci.med.occupational every month posts an extensive set of "frequently asked questions" (FAQ) messages. These FAQ files provide further pointers to WWW addresses and ftp sites for different subtopics. There is an *RSI Electronic Network Newsletter*, which also has pointers to WWW and ftp sites. To subscribe, send e-mail to majordomo@world.std.com with a body consisting of the two words "subscribe rsi" (the subject line doesn't matter).

Largely because of health and safety issues, several national and international organizations are working on standards for workplace ergonomics (Amick, 1987; Bevan, 1991). Examples are "ANSI/HFS 100-1988 Human Factors Engineering of Visual Display Workstations" and ISO 9241, "Ergonomics of Visual Display Terminals." These standards are still evolving. Updates on their status appear in the "Standards Factor" column of the *ACM SIGCHI Bulletin*. Standards are only useful when they are based on good scientific knowledge, applied in the context and conditions for which they are intended, and kept current with changes in technology. Yet politics, such as the desire to protect markets from imports, have sometimes influenced standards legislation. Therefore, do not assume that equipment that "meets the *X* standard" is automatically the best solution (Springer, 1985).

REFERENCES

Note: A ● before a reference indicates a reading.

Ackerman, M., and Malone, T. (1990). Answer Garden: A Tool for Growing Organizational Memory. *Conf. Office Information Systems*, ACM, 31–39.

Alm, N., Arnott, J., and Newell, A. (1992). Prediction and Conversational Movement in an Augmentative Communication System. *Communications of the ACM* 35(5), 46–57.

Amick, B. (1987). The Politics of the Quality of Worklife in Automated Offices in the USA. *Behaviour and Information Technology* 6 (4), 467–482.

Armstrong, M. (1989). Human Factors in Incident Investigation. *Proc. Human Factors Society 33rd Annual Meeting*, 1024–1028.

Baecker, R., and Buxton, W. (1987). *Readings in Human-Computer Interaction: A Multidisciplinary Approach*. Morgan Kaufmann.

Baecker, R., Small, I., and Mander, R. (1991). Bringing Icons to Life. In *Proc. CHI '91*, ACM, 1–6. Reprinted in Chapter 6.

Bair, J., and Gale, S. (1988). An Investigation of the Coordinator as an Example of Computer Supported Cooperative Work. Hewlett Packard Laboratories.

Bauer, W. (1991). Climate Problems in Areas with High VDU Density: Results of Traders Desks. *Proc. 4th Int'l. Conf. Human-Computer Interaction* 1, 162–166.

Beaton, R., and Snyder, H. (1984). The Display Quality of Glare Filters for CRT Terminals. *SID 84 Digest*, Society for Information Display, 298–301.

Bevan, N. (1991). Standards Relevant to European Directives for Display Terminals. *Proc. 4th Int'l. Conf. Human-Computer Interaction* 1, 533–537.

Blenkhorn, P. (1994). Producing a Text-to-Speech Synthesizer for Use by Blind People. In Edwards (1995), 285–292.

Booth, P. (1990). Identifying and Interpreting Design Errors. *International Journal of Human-Computer Interaction* 2(4), 307–332.

Borenstein, N. (1985). The Design and Evaluation of On-Line Help Systems. PhD Thesis, Carnegie-Mellon University.

Borenstein, N., and Thyberg, C. (1991). Power, Ease of Use and Cooperative Work in a Practical Multimedia Message System. *International Journal of Man-Machine Studies* 34(2), 229–259. Reprinted in Greenberg, S. (Ed.) (1991), *Computer Supported Cooperative Work and Groupware*, Academic Press.

Bosman, D., and White, T. (1990). On the Visibility of Character Features on a VDU. *Proc. INTERACT '90*. North-Holland, 729–734.

Brewster, S., Wright, P., and Edwards, A. (1994). The Design and Evaluation of an Auditory-Enhanced ScrollBar. *Proc. CHI '94*, ACM, 173–179.

Brooks, C., and Newell, A. (1985). Computer Transcription of Handwritten Shorthand as an Aid for the Deaf—A Feasibility Study. *International Journal of Man-Machine Studies* 23(1), 45–60.

Brown, C. (1992). Assistive Technology Computers and Persons with Disabilities. *Communications of the ACM* 35(5), 36–44.

Cakir, A., Hart, D., and Stewart, T. (1980). *Visual Display Terminals: A Manual Covering Ergonomics, Workplace Design, Health and Safety, Task Organization*. John Wiley & Sons.

Campagnoni, F., and Ehrlich, K. (1989). Information Retrieval Using a Hypertext-Based Help System. *Transactions on Information Systems* 7(3), ACM, 271–291.

Carasik, R., and Grantham, C. (1988). A Case Study of CSCW in a Dispersed Organization. *Proc. CHI '88*, ACM, 61–66.

Carroll, J. (1985). Minimalist Design for Active Users. In Shackel, B. (Ed.), *Proc. Interact '84*, North-Holland, 39–44. Reprinted in Baecker and Buxton (1987).

Carroll, J. (1990). *The Nurnberg Funnel: Designing Minimalist Instruction for Practical Computer Skill*. MIT Press.

Carroll, J., and Carrithers, C. (1984a). Training Wheels in a User Interface. *Communications of the ACM* 27(8), 800–806.

Carroll, J., and Carrithers, C. (1984b). Blocking Learner Error States in a Training-Wheels System. *Human Factors* 26(4), 377–389.

● Carroll, J., and Mack, R. (1984). Learning to Use a Word Processor: By Doing, by Thinking, and by Knowing. In Thomas, J., and Schneider, M. (Eds.), *Human Factors in Computer Systems*, Ablex, 13–51.

Carroll, J., Smith-Kerker, P., Ford, J., and Mazur-Rimetz, S. (1987–1988). The Minimal Manual. *Human-Computer Interaction* 3, 123–153.

Casali, J. (1992). Technology Advancements in Hearing Protection: Active Noise Reduction, Frequency/Amplitude-Sensitivity, and Uniform Attenuation. *Proc. Human Factors Society 36th Annual Meeting* 1, 258–262.

Catrambone, R., and Carroll, J. (1987). Learning a Word Processing System with Training Wheels and Guided Exploration. *Proc. CHI+GI '87,* ACM, 169–174.

Chappell, S., and Tarrel, R. (1992). Incident Retrieval from NASA's Aviation Safety Reporting System. *Proc. Human Factors Society 36th Annual Meeting* (2), 1048.

Czaja, S. (1988). Microcomputers and the Elderly. In Helander (1988), 581–598.

Dainoff, M., Fraser, L., and Taylor, B. (1982). Visual, Musculoskeletal and Performance Differences between Good and Poor VDT Workstations: Preliminary Findings. *Proc. Human Factors Society 26th Annual Meeting.*

❁ Denning, P. (1990). Human Error and the Search for Blame. *Communications of the ACM* 33(1), 6–7.

Darragh, J., and Witten, I. (1992). *The Reactive Keyboard.* Cambridge University Press.

Davies, D., and Dipner, R. (1992). ACM Membership Survey of Disability and Disability Issues. *Communications of the ACM* 35(5), 91–93.

Dean, M. (1982). How a Computer Should Talk to People. *IBM Systems Journal* 21(4), 424–453.

Demasco, P., and McCoy, K. (1992). Generating Text from Compressed Input: An Intelligent Interface for People with Severe Motor Impairments. *Communications of the ACM* 35(5), 68–78.

Draper, S. (1984). The Nature of Expertise in UNIX. *Proc. INTERACT '84,* North-Holland, 465–471.

Eastman Kodak (1983). *Ergonomic Design for People at Work.* Lifetime Learning Publications.

Eberts, R., and Brock, J. (1988). Computer-Based Instruction. In Helander (1988), 599–627.

Edwards, A. (1988). The Design of Auditory Interfaces for Visually Disabled Users. *Proc. CHI '88,* ACM, 83–88.

Edwards, A. (1989a). Soundtrack: An Auditory Interface for Blind Users. *Human-Computer Interaction* 4(1), 45–66.

Edwards, A. (1989b). Modelling Blind Users' Interactions with an Auditory Computer Interface. *International Journal of Man-Machine Studies* 30(5), 575–589.

Edwards, A. (Ed.) (1995). *Extra-Ordinary Human Computer Interaction: Interfaces for Users with Disabilities.* Cambridge University Press.

Egan, D. (1988). Individual Differences in Human-Computer Interaction. In Helander (1988), 543–568.

Egan, D., Remde, J., Landauer, T., Lochbaum, C., and Gomez, L. (1989). Behavioural Evaluation and Analysis of a Hypertext Browser. *Proc. CHI '89,* ACM, 205–210.

Elkerton, J. (1988). On-line Aiding for Human-Computer Interfaces. In Helander (1988), 345–364.

Elkind, J., and Shrager, J. (1994). Modelling and Analysis of Dyslexic Writing Using Speech and Other Modalities. In Edwards (1995), 133–155.

Frishberg, N., Corazza, S., Day, L., Wilcox, S., and Schulmeister, R. (1993). Sign Language Interfaces. *Proc. INTERCHI '93,* ACM, 194–197.

Frome, F. (1984). Improving Color CAD Systems for Users: Some Suggestions from Human Factors Studies. *IEEE Design and Test* 1(1), 18–27.

Glinert, E., and York, B. (1992). Computers and People with Disabilities. *Communications of the ACM* 35(5), 32–35.

Gopher, D., Olin, M., Badihi, Y., Cohen, G., Donchin, Y., Bieski, M., and Cotev, S. (1989). The Nature and Causes of Human Errors in a Medical Intensive Care Unit. *Proc. Human Factors Society 33rd Annual Meeting* (2), 956–960.

Grandjean, E. (1984). Postures and the Design of VDT Workstations. *Behaviour and Information Technology* 3(4), 301–311.

Grandjean, E. (1987). Design of VDT Workstations. In Salvendy, G. (Ed.), *Handbook of Human Factors,* John Wiley & Sons, 1359–1397.

Greenberg, S. (1993). The Computer User as Toolsmith: The Use, Reuse, and Organization of Computer-based Tools. *Cambridge Series on Human-Computer Interaction.* Cambridge University Press.

Greenberg, S., Darragh, J., Maulsby, D., and Witten, I. (1994). Predictive Interfaces: What Will They Think of Next? In Edwards (1995), 93–128.

Guindon, R. (1991). Users Request Help from Advisory Systems with Simple and Restricted Language: Effects of Real-Time Constraints and Limited Shared Context. *Human-Computer Interaction* 6(1), 47–75.

Hallbert, B., Rodriguez, M., Harbour, J., Caccamise, D., and Keller, J. (1992). Development of Job Performance Aids to Increase Human Performance Reliability: A Case Study in the Evaluation of Human Factors Principles. *Proc. Human Factors Society 36th Annual Meeting* (2), 1138–1142.

Hedge, A. (1987). Office Health Hazards: An Annotated Bibliography. *Ergonomics* 30(5), 733–773.

Hedge, A. (1991). The Effects of Direct and Indirect Office Lighting on VDT Workers. *Proc. Human Factors Society 35th Annual Meeting* 1, 536–540.

Helander, M. (Ed.) (1988). *Handbook of Human-Computer Interaction.* North-Holland.

Hill, R., and Gries, C. (1988). Substitution for a Restricted Visual Channel in Multimodal Computer-Human Dialogue. *IEEE Transactions on Systems, Man and Cybernetics* 18(2), 285–303.

Horton, W. (1990). *Designing and Writing On-line Documentation: Help Files to Hypertext.* John Wiley & Sons.

Jones, D., and Broadbent, D. (1987). Noise. In Salvendy, G. (Ed.), *Handbook of Human Factors,* John Wiley & Sons, 623–649.

Kantowitz, B., and Sorkin, R. (1983). *Human Factors: Understanding People-System Relationships.* John Wiley & Sons.

Kearsley, G. (1988). *On-line Help Systems: Design and Implementation.* Ablex.

Koelega, H. and Brinkman, J. (1986). Noise and Vigilance: An Evaluative Review. *Human Factors* 28(4), 465–481.

Konz, S., and Bennett, C. (1987). An Evaluation of Some VDT Lighting Variables. *Proc. Human Factors Society 31st Annual Meeting,* 1109–1112.

Kroemer, K. (1988). VDT Workstation Design. In Helander (1988), 521–539.

Kryter, K. (1970). *The Effects of Noise on Man.* Academic Press.

Kukich, K. (1992). Spelling Correction for the Telecommunications Network for the Deaf. *Communications of the ACM* 35(5), 80–90.

Kurisaki, M. (1990). Help Systems: An Information-Sharing Approach. *Proc. INTERACT '90,* North-Holland, 529–534.

Lauber, J. (1987). New Technology, Human Performance and Transportation System Safety. *Proc. Human Factors Society 31st Annual Meeting,* 15–20.

Lazzaro, J. (1990). Opening Doors for the Disabled. *BYTE,* August, 258–268.

Lazzaro, J. (1993). Computers for the Disabled. *BYTE,* June, 59–64. The author can be contacted on BIX at lazzaro@bix.com or on the Internet at lazzaro@world.std.com

Lazzaro, J. (1994a). Adapting GUI Software for the Blind Is No Easy Task. *BYTE,* May, 33.

Lazzaro, J. (1994b). *Adaptive Technologies for Learning and Work Environments.* American Library Association, 50 East Huron Street, Chicago IL 60611, 1-800-545-2433.

Lewis, C., and Norman, D. (1986). Designing for Error. In Norman, D., and Draper, S. (Eds.), *User Centered System Design,* Lawrence Erlbaum Associates, 411–432.

Lewis, C., and Rieman, J. (1993). *Task-Centered User Interface Design.* A shareware book available via anonymous ftp from ftp.cs.colorado.edu.

Malone, T. (1990). Human Factors and Human Error. *Proc. Human Factors Society 34th Annual Meeting* (1), 651–654.

Matias, E., MacKenzie, I., and Buxton, W. (1993). Half-QWERTY: A One-Handed Keyboard Facilitating Skill Transfer from QWERTY. *Proc. INTERCHI '93,* ACM, 88–94.

Mayer, R. (1988). From Novice to Expert. In Helander (1988), 569–580.

Miller, D., and Swain, A. (1987). Human Error and Human Reliability. In Salvendy, G. (Ed.), *Handbook of Human Factors,* John Wiley & Sons, 219–250.

Mital, A., McGlothlin, J., and Faard, H. (1990). Noise in Open-Plan Computer Rooms. *Proc. Human Factors Society 34th Annual Meeting* 1, 729–733.

Morse, R. (1985). Glare Filter Preference: Influence of Subjective and Objective Indices of Glare, Sharpness, Brightness, Contrast and Color. *Proc. Human Factors Society 29th Annual Meeting,* 782–786.

Mynatt, E., and Edwards, W. (1992). Mapping GUIs to Auditory Interfaces. *Proc. UIST '92,* ACM, 61–70.

Mynatt, E., and Edwards, W. (1994). Metaphors for Non-Visual Computing. In Edwards (1995), 187–206.

Newell, A. (1994). Extraordinary Human Computer Interaction. Intelligent Systems for Speech and Language Impaired People: A portfolio of Research. In Edwards (1995), 83–103.

Newell, A., Arnott, J., Cairns, A., Ricketts, I., and Gregor, P. (1995). In Edwards (1995), 78–92.

Nickerson, R. (1977). On Conversational Interaction with Computers. In *User-Oriented Design of Interactive Graphics Systems,* ACM, 101–113. Reprinted in Baecker and Buxton (1987).

Nielsen, J. (1994). Enhancing the Explanatory Power of Usability Heuristics. *Proc. CHI '94,* ACM, 152–158.

Norman, D. (1981). The Trouble with UNIX: The User Interface Is Horrid. *Datamation,* November, 139–150.

Norman, D. (1983). Design Rules Based on Analyses of Human Error. *Communications of the ACM* 26(4), 254–258.

Norman, D. (1988). *The Design of Everyday Things.* Doubleday.

Norman, D. (1990). Human Error and the Design of Computer Systems. *Communications of the ACM* 33(1), 4–5, 7.

Norman, D., and Draper, S. (Eds.) (1986). *User Centered System Design: New Perspectives on Human-Computer Interaction.* Lawrence Erlbaum Associates, 526.

NSF (1990). Report of the NSF Task Force on Persons with Disabilities. *CISE Directorate's Office of Cross-Disciplinary Activities.* October. Cited in Glinert and York (1990).

Oman, P., Gomes, C., Rains, K., and Morandi, M. (1989). Posture and VDU Operator Satisfaction. *SIGCHI Bulletin* 20(3), ACM, 52–57.

Oren, T., Salomon, G., Kreitman, K., and Don, A. (1990). Guides: Characterizing the Interface. In Laurel, B. (Ed.), *The Art of Human-Computer Interface Design,* Addison-Wesley, 367–381.

Pascarelli, E., and Quilter, D. (1994). *Repetitive Strain Injury: A Computer User's Guide.* John Wiley & Sons.

Pausch, R., and Williams, R. (1992). Giving CANDY to Children: Gesture Input Driving an Articulator-based Speech Synthesizer. *Communications of the ACM* 35(5), 58–66.

Pausch, R., and Williams, R. (1994). Giving Candy to Children: User-tailored Gesture Input Driving an Articulator-based Speech Synthesizer. In Edwards (1995), 156–168.

Perkins, R., Blatt, L., Workman, D., and Ehrlich, S. (1989). Iterative Tutorial Design in the Product Development Cycle. *Proc. Human Factors Society 33rd Annual Meeting* 1, 268–272. Reprinted in Case C.

Petroski, H. (1985). *To Engineer Is Human: The Role of Failure in Successful Design.* St. Martin's Press.

Pinsky, M. (1993). *The Carpal Tunnel Syndrome Book: Preventing and Treating CTS.* Warner.

Povlotksy, B., and Dubrovsky, V. (1988). "Recommended" versus "Preferred" in Design and Use of Computer Workstations. *Proc. Human Factors Society 32nd Annual Meeting* 1, 501–505.

Propst, R., and Wodka, M. (1975). *The Action Office Acoustic Handbook: A Guide for the Open Plan Facility Manager, Planner, and Designer.* Herman Miller Research Corp., 3970 Varsity Drive, Ann Arbor, Michigan 48104.

Putz-Anderson, V. (1988). *Cumulative Trauma Disorders: A Manual for Musculoskeletal Diseases of the Upper Limbs.* Taylor and Francis.

Rasmussen, J., and Vicente, K. (1989). Coping with Human Errors through System Design: Implications for Ecological Interface Design. *International Journal of Man-Machine Studies* 31(5), 517–534.

Reason, J. (1990). *Human Error.* Cambridge University Press.

Rempel, D., Harrison, R., and Barnhart, S. (1992). Work-Related Cumulative Trauma Disorders of the Upper Extremity. *Journal of the AMA* 267(6), 838–842.

Rouse, W., and Rouse, S. (1983). Analysis and Classification of Human Error. *IEEE Transactions on Systems, Man, and Cybernetics* 13(4), 539–549.

Sanders, M., and McCormick, E. (1987). *Human Factors in Engineering and Design (6th Edition).* McGraw-Hill.

Sanquist, T. (1992). Human Factors in Maritime Applications: A New Opportunity for Multi-Modal Transportation Research. *Proc. Human Factors Society 36th Annual Meeting* 2, 1123–1127.

● Sauter, S., Chapman, L., and Knutson, S. (1985). *Improving VDT Work: Causes and Control of Health Concerns in VDT Use,* University of Wisconsin (Excerpt included 7, 9, 11–12, 27–32). Excerpts on "Preventing Back Strain" (13–19) and "Lighting Control" (58–61) were reprinted in Baecker and Buxton (1987).

● Sellen, A., and Nicol, A. (1990). Building User-Centered On-line Help. In Laurel, B. (Ed.), *The Art of Human-Computer Interface Design,* Addison-Wesley, 143–153.

Shaw, B., and Sanders, M. (1989). Research to Determine the Frequency and Cause of Injury Accidents in Underground Mining. *Proc. Human Factors Society 33rd Annual Meeting* 2, 1004–1008.

Shaw, R., Loomis, A., and Crisman, E. (1994). Input and Integration: Enabling Technologies for Disabled Users. In Edwards (1995), 243–258.

Shneiderman, B. (1982a). Designing Computer System Messages. *Communications of the ACM* 25(9), 610–611.

Shneiderman, B. (1982b). System Message Design: Guidelines and Experimental Results. In Badre, A., and Shneiderman, B. (Eds.), *Directions in Human/Computer Interaction.* Ablex, 55–78.

Shneiderman, B. (1994). *Designing the User Interface.* 2nd Edition. Addison-Wesley.

Shute, S., and Starr, S. (1984). Effects of Adjustable Furniture on VDT Users. *Human Factors* 26(2), 157–170.

Smith, M. (1984). Human Factors Issues in VDT Use: Environmental and Workstation Design Considerations. *IEEE Computer Graphics and Applications* 4(11), 56–63. Reprinted in Baecker and Buxton (1987).

Snyder, H. (1988). Image Quality. In Helander (1988), 437–474.

Springer, T. (1985). The Statutes and Standards Movement. *Office Ergonomics Review* 2(2), 14–15.

Stager, P., Hameluck, D., and Jubis, R. (1989). Underlying Factors in Air Traffic Control Incidents. *Proc. Human Factors Society 33rd Annua! Meeting* 1, 43–46.

Stigliani, J. (1995). *High-Tech Health: The Computer User's Survival Guide.* O'Reilly and Associates.

Strong, G. (1994). An Evaluation of the PRC TouchTalker with Minspeak: Some Lessons for Speech Prosthesis Design. In Edwards (1995), 45–55.

Van Cott, V., and Kinkade, R. (Eds.) (1972). *Human Engineering Guide to Equipment Design.* Supt. of Documents, U.S. Government Printing Office, Washington, D.C., 20402.

Wagenaar, W., and Groeneweg, J. (1987). Accidents at Sea: Multiple Causes and Impossible Consequences. *International Journal of Man-Machine Studies,* 27 (5, 6), 587–598.

Waldrop, M. (1989). Phobos at Mars: A Dramatic View—and Then Failure. *Science* 245, 1044–1045.

Walker, J. (1987). Document Examiner: Delivery Interface for Hypertext Documents. *Proc. Hypertext '87,* ACM, 307–323.

Wallach, D. (1994). Typing Injury FAQ (frequently asked questions). Available in the Internet comp.human-factors newsgroup, or via anonymous ftp rtfm.mit.edu: directory pub/usenet/news.answers/typing-injury-faq.

Weber, G. (1994). Reading and Pointing—New Interaction Methods for Braille Displays. In Edwards (1995), 169-186.

Wenger, E. (1987). *Artificial Intelligence and Tutoring Systems: Computational and Cognitive Approaches to the Communication of Knowledge.* Morgan Kaufmann.

Wiener, E. (1989). Reflections on Human Error: Matters of Life and Death. *Proc. Human Factors Society 33rd Annual Meeting* 1, 1–7.

Wigley, Turner, Blake, Darby, McInnes, and Harding (1992). *Occupational Overuse Syndrome. Treatment and Rehabilitation: A Practitioner's Guide.* Occupational Safety and Health Service, Department of Labour, Wellington, New Zealand.

Williams, T., and Farkas, D. (1992). Minimalism Reconsidered: Should We Design Documentation for Exploratory Learning? *SIGCHI Bulletin* 24(2), ACM, 41–50.

Woods, D., and Roth, E. (1988). Cognitive Systems Engineering. In Helander (1988), 3–43.

Wright, P. (1988). Issues of Content and Presentation in Document Design. In Helander (1988), 629–652.

Wright, P. (1991). Designing and Evaluating Documentation for I.T. Users. In Shackel, B., and Richardson, S. (Eds.), *Human Factors for Informatics Usability,* Cambridge University Press, 343–358.

VIDEOS

Kirston, D., Carroll, J., Eckhoff, R., Kelley, J., and Canetti, S. (1988). Specialist Help Using Multiple Media. *ACM SIGGRAPH Video Review (SGVR)* 58.

Shea, T. (1989). Sun 386i On Line Help. *ACM SGVR* 46.

Sukaviriya, P. (1989). Context-Sensitive Animated Help. *ACM SGVR* 46.

VA Medical Center (1989). Cooking with VIC. *ACM SGVR* 45.

Walker, J. (1985). Document Examiner. *ACM SGVR* 19.

viewpoint

by Donald A. Norman

COMMENTARY: HUMAN ERROR AND THE DESIGN OF COMPUTER SYSTEMS

In 1988, the Soviet Union's Phobos 1 satellite was lost on its way to Mars. Why? According to *Science* magazine, "not long after the launch, a ground controller omitted a single letter in a series of digital commands sent to the spacecraft. And by malignant bad luck, that omission caused the code to be mistranslated in such a way as to trigger the test sequence" (the test sequence was stored in ROM, but was intended to be used only during checkout of the spacecraft while on the ground) [7]. Phobos went into a tumble from which it never recovered.

What a strange report. "Malignant bad luck?" Why bad luck: why not bad design? Was not the problem the design of the command language that allowed such a simple deviant event to have such serious consequences.

The effects of electrical noise on signal detectability, identification, and reliability are well-known. Designers are expected to use error-detecting and correcting codes. Suppose interference from known sources of electromagnetic noise had corrupted the signal to Phobos 1. We would not blame the ground controllers; we would say that the system designers did not follow standard engineering practice, and we would reconsider the design of the system so as to protect against this problem in the future.

People err. That is a fact of life. People are not precision machinery designed for accuracy. In fact, we humans are a different kind of device entirely. Creativity, adaptability, and flexibility are our strengths. Continual alertness and precision in action or memory are our weaknesses. We are amazingly error tolerant, even when physically damaged. We are extremely flexible, robust, creative, and superb at finding explanations and meanings from partial and noisy evidence. The same properties that lead to such robustness and creativity also produce errors. The natural tendency to interpret partial information—although often our prime virtue—can cause operators to misinterpret system behavior in such a plausible way that the misinterpretation can be difficult to discover.

Quite a lot is known about human performance and the way it applies to system interaction [1]. Several classes of human error have been identified and studied, and conditions that increase the likelihood of error can be specified in advance [3–5]. Communication systems can be designed to be error-tolerant and error-detecting or correcting. In a similar way, we could devise a science of error-tolerant detection or minimization interactions with human operators [2].

Many advances have been made in our understanding of the hardware and software of information processing systems, but one major gap remains: the inclusion of the human operator into the system analysis. The behavior of an information processing system is not a product of the design specifications; it is a product of the interaction between the human and the system. The designer must consider the properties of all the system components—including the humans—as well as their interactions. The various technical publications of the field attest to a concern with software and hardware, but emphasis on human functionality and capability is lacking. Many failures of information systems are attributed to human error rather than to the design. We are going to suffer continued failures until we learn to change our approach.

One of the first things needed is a change in attitude. The behavior we call human error is just as predictable as system noise, perhaps more so. Therefore, instead of blaming the human who happens to be involved, it would be better to try to identify the system characteristics that led to the incident and then to modify the design either by elimination of the situation or at least minimization of the impact for future events. One major step would be to remove the term "human error" from our vocabulary and to re-evaluate the need to blame individuals. A second major step would be to develop design specifications that consider the functionality of the human with the same degree of care that has been given to the rest of the system.

In the case of the Soviet Mars probe, *Science* wrote its report as if the incompetence of the human controller had caused the problem. Roald Kremnev, director of the Soviet Union's spacecraft manufacturing plant, was interviewed. Here is how *Science* reported the discussion:

> . . . what happened to the controller who made the error? Well, Kremnev told *Science* with a dour expression, he did not go to jail or to Siberia. In fact, it was he who eventually tracked down the error in the code. Nonetheless, said Kremnev, "he was not able to participate in the later opera-

tion of Phobos" [7].

Both the reporter's question and the answer presuppose the notion of blame. Even though the operator tracked down the error, he was still punished (but at least not exiled). But what about the designers of the language and software or the methods they use? Not mentioned. The problem with this attitude is that it prevents us from learning from the incident and allows the error-prone situation to remain.

Stories of related failures of computer systems due to "human error" are easy to find in every industry: nuclear power, aviation, business, the stock market, and of course, the computer industry itself. In the August 1989 issue of *Communications of the ACM*, the following item appeared in the section News Track:

> A computer operator at Exxon's Houston headquarters has been fired for inadvertently destroying computer copies of thousands of documents with potentially important information relating to the Alaskan oil spill . . . The ex-employee, however, says he is being used as a scapegoat and that none of the tapes he erased were labeled "Do Not Destroy."

The information provided about this incident is too sparse to form a conclusion, but if the system had been designed with the characteristics of human operators in mind, the preservation of tapes would not depend upon the existence of a simple (human-generated?) label: "Do Not Destroy." Thus, either the incident would not have happened, or the excuse would not have been plausible.

Perhaps it is time for ACM to take the lead in this matter for the design of computational systems. There is considerable expertise among its members, including the Committee on Computers and Public Policy and one special interest group devoted to related issues (SIGCHI, the Special Interest Group on Computer-Human Interaction).

There is also a convenient place to start. On the electronic computer networks, Peter Neumann moderates the valuable forum on risks to the public in computers and related systems, labeled as an activity of the ACM Committee on Computers and Public Policy. This RISKS forum collects, reports, and comments on incidents that include human error and design, but these are not sufficiently precise or authoritative to be used for professional advancement of the field. The sources of the information are often reports in the media that are incomplete, usually written before all relevant information is gathered, and subject to other sources of inaccuracies and biases. (The items from *Science* and *Communications*' News Track that I cited exhibit all these sources of unreliability.) There is a lot of potential benefit to be gained through the careful study of design failures. Namely, other disciplines have learned to benefit through such careful review and analysis [6]. In reviewing the cases presented in the RISKS forum, why not use them as guides to better design?

There are several existing systems used in other industries that could provide a model. One major source of valuable advice in the aviation community is a collection of incidents known as ASRS, the Aviation Safety Reporting System, run by NASA-Ames with a computer-readable database administered by Battelle. Here, people in the aviation community who witness or commit errors or other related problems write a description of the incident and their interpretation and mail them to ASRS. The ASRS investigators may call back to check accuracy or get more information, but once the information has been confirmed and clarified, the part of the form that contains the submitter's identification is returned to that individual. ASRS also removes all identifying information to make it impossible for the particular submitter or incident to be determined. This anonymity is critical to the accuracy and completeness of the database. Because NASA has no regulatory power and has a good record for keeping the sources confidential, this database has become trusted by the aviation community. People are now willing to describe their own actions if they believe the report will be useful for the improvement of aviation safety. A variable number of improvements in cockpit and other parts of aircraft x design have been made by designers who have studied the variable patterns of errors that can be seen in this database.

Instead of blaming the human who happens to be involved, it would be better to try to identify the system characteristics that led to the incident and then to modify the design either by elimination of the situation or at least minimization of the impact for future events.

A critical aspect of the ASRS system is that the reports are not seen by any supervisors of the submitters. Similar attempts in other industries have failed because their reports were submitted through a chain of authority that included the person's supervisor or plant management personnel—people who have biases to sanitize the report or to form negative judgements of the reporter. Thus, the incident reporting system for the nuclear industry is not an impartial guide to actual operating practices. Anonymity and self-reporting have worked well, along with a system of verification and clarification such as is performed by the NASA/ASRS team (mostly composed of retired aviation professionals).

In similar fashion, the United States National Transportation Safety Board (NTSB) performs a detailed analysis of transportation accidents (aviation, highway, ma-

(*continued on p. 7*)

Viewpoint (*continued from p. 5*)

rine, railroad, and pipeline). These reports are extremely valuable and are a major force in the improvement of safety in the relevant industries. (The NTSB reports are, by statute, not allowed to be used in legal proceedings to determine culpability for an event. This kind of protection is essential in today's litigious society to allow the investigation to proceed without fear that the results will be misinterpreted or misused.)

Should ACM sponsor similar initiatives? I do not know, for its issues are different from those faced by other industries. But I propose that ACM investigate the possible ways of improving this part of the profession. ACM could take the lead in establishing some positive and constructive actions to elevate the human side of computing to a level of concern and respectability equal to that of the physical and symbolic side.

REFERENCES

1. Helander, M., Ed. *Handbook of Human–Computer Interaction*. North-Holland, New York, 1988.
2. Leveson, N.G. Software safety: Why, what, and how. *ACM Comput. Surv. 18*, 2 (June 1986), 125–163.
3. Norman, D.A. *The Psychology of Everyday Things*. Basic Books, New York, 1988.
4. Norman, D.A. Design rules based on analyses of human error. *Commun. ACM 26*, 4 (April 1983), 254–258.
5. Perrow, C. *Normal Accidents*. Basic Books, New York, 1984.
6. Petroski, H. *To Engineer is Human: The Role of Failure in Successful Design*. St. Martin's Press, New York, 1985.
7. Waldrop, M.M. Phobos at Mars: A dramatic view—and then failure. *Sci.*, 245 (1989), 1044–45.

Donald A. Norman is professor and chair of the Department of Cognitive Science at the University of California, San Diego.

by Peter J. Denning, editor-in-chief

editorial

HUMAN ERROR AND THE SEARCH FOR BLAME

The ACM RISKS Forum, moderated by Peter Neumann of SRI International, is an electronic dialog among a community of network users concerned about risks to the public in computer systems. A frequent topic is the role of human error in mishaps involving computers. These discussions have raised interesting questions for me. What is the phenomenon we call human error? Why does it keep coming up so often in discussions about risks of using computers?

Most of us associate errors with mistakes. When I say I made a mistake, I usually mean one of two things. I may mean that I misjudged the consequences of an action I took and the consequences had an unwarranted or unreasonable cost that must now be compensated. Or I may mean that I had no way of foreseeing the unintended consequence, and now I regret having taken the action.

In the first case I had a choice but took action in the face of the risk, while in the second case I was blind to the consequences and had no real choice at all.

But these notions about mistakes are rational. In the background of our thinking about mistakes is an automatic, irrational reaction that they are wrong. Our emotions have not been conditioned to regard mistakes as basic constituents of the human condition or as opportunities to learn; instead our emotions have us think that mistakes should not have happened and that their occurrences are problems in need of correction. I will return to this point shortly. Let me continue with the rational side.

When certain actions recurrently have unwanted consequences, we usually establish standards that tell us what action is desired or what action is to be avoided. Such standards evolve in a community over time. When we are about to take an action we can evaluate it against the standard; we do not have to wait until some time later when the unwanted consequence appears.

The domain of engineering practice illustrates this. The designer of a communication device is expected to use accepted error-correcting codes to resist transmission noise. That designer commits a design error by omitting the codes; we say he may be held liable if a user of the equipment encounters a mishap because an erroneous signal was accepted by the device. The important point here is that there are accepted practices and that the engineer in question did not follow them.

But what about the case where there are no standards or accepted practices? The designer has no standard against which to assess the design. The community has no way to assess whether a design is risky—it is a new case. Software engineering is like this. Having noted the recurrent difficulties of constructing dependable software systems, some observers of the field of software engineering have begun to suspect that the current practices of the field (including methodologies and theories) are incapable of producing dependable software—something unseen is missing. A designer operating within these currently accepted practices is therefore likely to produce systems that produce breakdowns that he could not foresee. In what sense is he responsible for the error?

How we answer this depends on how we understand responsibility. Our ordinary everyday understanding associates responsibility with fault, blame, guilt, and liability. We have been trained by our legal system to think in terms of evidence to prove who is at fault and of compensation to the injured parties. The search for blame digs deeply. We live our lives under the supposition that somewhere, there is someone or some organization that is ultimately responsible for everything. Our litigiousness keeps us constantly looking for something to blame and someone to hold liable. We persist in this search despite the evidence of everyday observation that many human practices "just evolved" without anyone's planning them or anticipating them.

Look at how this way of thinking inclines us to interpret breakdowns produced by software systems. It is always easy, with 20/20 hindsight, to say that the design that has produced a breakdown was weak or flawed. We are automatically drawn into a search for blame. Our first target is the designer. Are we justified in saying that the designer, who operated without the benefit of the hindsight, can be held liable for the flaw? Some of us say that it is unfair to blame the designer who operated in good faith within the standards of the field; we look elsewhere for the blame. Our next target may be the organization that employs the designer. If we continue the search long enough we will be led to saying that the designers of the standard practices are to blame. This can bring us to the curious position that the authors of software engineering textbooks, or the officers of the professional societies that recommended practices and curricula, are to blame for flaws detected in systems designed with these methodologies. This sounds almost preposterous—except that I have read accounts of exactly such proposals!

Let us consider another interpretation of responsibility, as it is used in phrases such as "professional responsibility." Here responsibility is a declaration that a person or organization has influence on the outcome or on people's interpretation of the outcome, and is prepared to take action consistent with that declaration. This understanding of responsibility would have us act as follows:

(1) We would honor the standards the community has established in the domain in which we take responsibility;
(2) Having observed recurrent breakdowns, we would work to alter the standards and practices of the domain to anticipate the breakdowns in the future;
(3) We would be prepared to admit and learn from our mistakes and to extend the same privilege to others; and
(4) As a community, we would be open to being shown systematic blindnesses in our standard practices and to taking actions to improve them.

Within this interpretation, a responsible software designer would make it a point to know and abide by the standards and practices of software engineering; and the designer would forever be a student of the breakdowns of software systems and would where necessary work to alter the standards of the field. New practices such as rapid prototyping, design, teams including users, participatory design and anonymous databases of design flaws and mishaps can all contribute to overcoming our blind spots and to supporting us in these responsibilities.

The background supposition that there is always someone to blame is an illusion which blinds us to effective action within the domain of engineering. The search for blame prevents us from seeing the limitations of current engineering methodology and distracts us from improving our discourse of design. Indeed, the fear of being singled out for blame may well disincline us from trying courses of action whose consequences cannot be foreseen—the fear of our own blindness perpetuates our blindness.

Designing for Error

CLAYTON LEWIS and DONALD A. NORMAN

longjmp botch: core dumped
Fatal error in pass zero
awk: syntax error near line 1
awk: bailing out near line 1
cp: asd: No such file or directory

The above messages illustrate the surface of the difficult problem of dealing with error. The messages all result from the fact that the user has done something that the system cannot respond to. The result is for the system to produce an error message, much like the five examples shown above.

The difficulty with error messages is well known. Shneiderman (1980) and du Boulay and Matthew (1984), among others, have pointed out that the format and tone of these messages are often offensive, especially for beginners, leading them to believe that they, personally, have performed some serious misdeed due to their own incompetence. Moreover, even if a user tries to correct the fault that is being signaled, the information provided them is not always sufficient to allow them to find the problem. Indeed, the messages are often presented in such a way as to encourage the sorts of false explanations described by Lewis in Chapter 8.

> *The examples that opened this chapter were are all real. The "longjmp botch" message comes courtesy of the "more" program in 4.2BSD UNIX, discovered (repeatedly) by D. Norman (see Draper & Norman, 1984). Note that the error message does not even say which program has had the difficulty, so that if many procedures are being used at the same time (as is often the case), the user does not even have any idea of which routine has caused the problem, how to recover, or how to avoid the difficulty in the future. The "Fatal error in pass zero" message comes from a compiler heavily used by students. It is discussed in du Boulay and Matthew (1984). The "awk" errors are two of the more famous exit lines of the UNIX program "awk" when it finds the situation hopeless. You might think that "awk" was being helpful by identifying itself and then indicating roughly where in the file the difficulty occurred. You would be wrong. The two errors both resulted from specifying a nonexistent file (the command used was* "**awk asd**." *"Awk" is perfectly capable of determining that its difficulty came from the fact that the file "asd" did not exist. Instead, it gives the erroneous and misleading error messages appropriate had the file existed with a non-intelligible first line. Other UNIX programs, such as "cp" (the copy command) do better: The command sequence* "**cp asd**" *yields the last error message in the list: meaningful and useful. Even it could have done better, however, by aiding the user to make the correction rather than simply quitting, forcing the user to retype the sometimes lengthy command line for what might have been an error in a single character.*

Why are these situations called "errors"? In fact, what is really meant is that the system can't interpret the information given to it. By convention, this is called an error, a fault generated by the user. This is a rather arrogant point of view coming from a system designed to serve its users. A more appropriate point of view should really be that of apology:

> *I am very sorry, but I seem to have gotten confused. Could you help me out?*

After all, if User Centered Design is to be taken seriously, then the interaction with a system is to be thought of as a cooperative endeavor: The task is not to find fault and to assess blame but rather to get the task done. Failures to understand are commonplace and normal. Conversation is riddled with speech errors, from incomplete sentences to erroneous choice of words. But certainly we do not expect the people with whom we talk to respond to our speech errors with:

> *Your sentence was not grammatical. Say it again. (But do it right this time. Please.)*

In conversation, minor speech errors get repaired so automatically that the speaker often does not even realize they were made. And when the utterance cannot be understood, the listener can ask for correction of only the single word or phrase that caused the trouble:

> *I'm sorry—where should I put the glass?*

In the normal conversational situation, both participants assume equal responsibility in understanding. If there is a failure to understand, both take responsibility for repairing the difficulty. The analogous statement in a computer system would be something like this—the response that we classify later in this chapter as "Let's talk about it":

> *I can't find the filename you mention:*
> *   /csl/norman/HCIbook/LewisNorman/designingForError*
> *Do you mean:*
> *   1: DesigningForError*
> *   2: design-notes*
> *Please type which number or specify a new name:*

Consider the last three error messages in the opening example of the chapter. Those responses would have the user retype that entire, lengthy file specification (49 characters long!) simply for failure to capitalize the "d" in the last term of the expression. If the system took some of the responsibility, talking about the difficulty rather than assigning blame, the result would be a much more cooperative endeavor.

Although we do not believe it possible to design systems in which people do not make errors, we do believe that much can be done to minimize the incidence of error, to maximize the discovery of the error, and to make it easier to recover from the error. The focal theme of this chapter is to examine ways of treating a person's error in such a way that discovery and recovery are simple, natural, and even pleasant. The ideal situation would be one in which the error recovery was so graceful that it was not noticed

DEALING WITH ERROR

We would prefer not even to use the term "error." Misunderstandings, problems, confusions, ambiguities: Any other term would be preferable. The very term "error" assigns blame, yet as we just pointed out, the system is just as much to blame for its failure to understand as is the user for a failure to be perfectly, unambiguously, precise. Nonetheless, the term and the concept is with us. So for the while we should learn to deal with "error" as gracefully as possible.

We can do several things with error. One is to try to devise systems that eliminate or minimize errors. Another is to try to make it easier to deal with error when it exists, first by providing clear indication of the problem and its possible causes and remedies, second by providing tools that make correction easier. Finally, because many errors—sometimes serious ones—go undetected for surprisingly long times (because the actions being performed are legal and even sensible under other circumstances), the system should provide the kind of information that helps the user understand the implications of the actions being followed. For all of these procedures it is useful first to start with an understanding of error.

Understanding Error

Several theoretical analyses of errors exist (Norman, 1981a, 1983b; Reason & Mycielska, 1982). These analyses have been useful, but for current purposes we simply need to note the major categories of errors and the major difficulties that are associated with them. We divide errors into two major categories: *mistakes* and *slips*. The division occurs at the level of the intention: A person establishes an intention to act. If the intention is not appropriate, this is a *mistake*. If the action is not what was intended, this is a *slip*. It is of course possible to perform both a mistake and slip simultaneously; form an erroneous intention, and then carry it out improperly.

Slips can be analyzed and categorized into their causes. Interestingly enough, many forms of slips do not occur with beginners: The highly practiced, automated behavior of the expert leads to the lack of focused attention that increases the likelihood of some forms of slips. Slips are usually not as serious a problem as mistakes, and within mistakes, the greatest problems seem to result from misinterpretation or misdiagnosis of the situation. There are several consequences that follow from misdiagnosis, perhaps the most obvious being that the behavior that follows is then likely to be inappropriate for the situation. Worse, misinterpretation hampers detection of the effort, and even serious errors may go undetected for hours (and in the case of program bugs, sometimes for years). Detection of misdiagnosis is hampered by several factors, including the prevalence of the explanations discussed by Lewis in Chapter 8. We return to these later when we consider how people detect error.

MINIMIZING ERROR

Although we do not believe that it is possible to design systems that eliminate error, much can be done to minimize it. One factor is simply good system design, including the physical layout of the components and displays of the interface, intelligent choice of command names, and so on. These topics are well covered in standard human factors procedures and numerous studies of command names: We will not pursue them further. Another factor comes from providing good explanatory tools, a good conceptual model, a system image that matches that model. (This topic is of central concern for most of the chapters within this section of the book.) In similar fashion, the more effort that the person must exert to bridge the Gulfs of Execution and Evaluation (Chapters 3 and 5), the more room for errors of understanding and of interpretation. Some errors can be reduced through careful choice of representation: Thus, some task representations rule out whole classes of errors present with other representations.

Avoiding Error Through Appropriate Representation

Consider the problem of specifying a nonexistent file, the problem that led to the last three error messages in the opening illustration of the chapter. Why might a nonexistent file be specified? Here are reasons: The intended file perhaps didn't really exist; it might exist, but its name might be misremembered or misspelled; the file name might be correct, but the user might be working in the wrong directory. We could imagine many ways of providing better information about which files existed and what their names were. We could imagine spelling correctors or intelligent search procedures that would correct for some errors and for some instances of improper directories. And we could imagine improved error messages and error correcting techniques.

But note that the class of errors results from the representational format chosen by the system: Files are represented by typed strings of characters, thus requiring exact specification of the character string. If a different representational format for files were used, the entire class of errors would no longer exist. Thus, if files were indicated by icons on the screen and specification were done by pointing at an icon, it would not be possible to point at a nonexistent file. Directory errors would be noted by the physical absence of the desired icon and by the surrounding context, and spelling errors would no longer be a factor. The representational system has the *intrinsic* property of foreclosing a whole class of errors found with other forms of representation. (File selection by pointing at icons is really a form of menu selection, and the same comments therefore apply to any system in which files are specified through menu options.)

Note that we are not attempting to advocate file specification through the use of menus or icons over other forms of specification. We are simply pointing out that every choice of representation provides a set of intrinsic properties, sometimes eliminating whole classes of errors that are troublesome with other representations. But every design decision is a tradeoff, and this form of representation makes difficult some desirable operations, such as specifying a file from within a program (without user intervention) or specifying a class of files, such as "all files whose names start with 'test.doc'." Moreover, some old problems remain, although in slightly different form. Thus, although one cannot specify a nonexistent file or misspell a file name when files are specified by pointing, it is still quite possible to point at the wrong file.

Avoiding False Understandings

Some difficulties arise through false understanding of the system's properties. As a result, this class of errors can be minimized by giving more information. Some false understandings arise because people can generalize more from a single experience than is really appropriate. The positive side of this is to increase the efficiency of learning. The negative side is to make false inferences.

> *We can illustrate this point through an example given to us by a student during a class discussion of an early draft of this book. Student* S *commented that he often learned system commands in the "indirect" manner discussed by Owen in Chapters 9 and 17. Thus, when he first moved to a UNIX system, he could not figure out how to "delete" a file. But one day he watched someone "rm" a file, and decided that in UNIX, "delete file" was referred to as "remove file, with "remove" abbreviated as "rm." This is a positive example of*

learning indirectly: One observation resulted in a general rule. In class it was pointed out that this was a false generalization: There might actually be many different ways of deleting files, and "rm" might only be one special way. There isn't, but on one exposure, **S** *really was taking a risk by making such a generalization.*

S *agreed, and gave this second example of just that problem. He learned the UNIX mail system by watching someone else use it. The person read his mail and left the mail system with the command "x" (for "exit").* **S** *thereafter read his mail in the same way. However, he noticed that although he would "delete" many of the messages as he read his mail, on each new use those "deleted" messages were still present. Eventually, he sent a message to the system administrator, explaining that there was an error in his mail program. The administrator, obviously skilled with the mail program, suggested that* **S** *was using the wrong command to terminate the mail session: He should have been using the command "q" for "quit." The command "x" is the abnormal exit, one that aborts without updating records. The normal way to terminate the mail program is with "q": it updates all the mail files.*

Note that **S** *made the same form of inference in both the "rm" and the mail system examples. In one case it was correct, but in the other case erroneous. In neither case did* **S** *entertain the notion that there might be several versions of the command.*

These are examples of learning by induction, a procedure that is both powerful and problematic. When learning is accomplished in this manner, its success depends critically upon getting the right sequence of examples (see especially the work of VanLehn & Brown, 1980, and Winston, 1975). This implies that the problems faced by the learners won't be solved by such things as improvements in the system image. Rather, we need to contrive ways to get users to try some alternatives—and just the right alternatives at that.

Minimizing Errors That Result From Slips

Analysis of slips can yield suggestions for the design of systems that minimize the incidence of this class of errors. One such analysis was done by Norman (1983b): We summarize here the major findings of that study. There are several categories of slips, but the most relevant for system design are mode errors, capture errors, and description errors. Let us examine each briefly.

Mode errors suggest the need for better feedback. A large class of errors are classified as mode errors: doing the operation appropriate for one mode when in fact you are in another. Modes will be with us as long as we wish to be able to do more operations than it is sensible to have special keys for. Most complex devices end up having them, be they digital watches, aircraft automatic pilots, or text editors. Even "modeless systems" have modes, but disguised. *Smalltalk*, the text editor *Emacs*, the *Macintosh* operating systems: all have numerous states where the first operation performed changes the interpretation of subsequent keypresses or mouse clicks. Avoiding modes entirely is not practical, but one can minimize modes. Feedback is essential so that the user can tell in what mode the system is in: Make sure that the modes are distinctively marked.

Description errors suggest the need for better consistency. A description error occurs when there is insufficient specification of the action, and the resultant ambiguity leads to an erroneous act being performed. The name emphasizes the fact that the description of the action was correct, but insufficiently specified, so the act that got done in error matched many characteristics of the correct one. One class of description errors occurs when a person attempts to rederive an action sequence and does so improperly, forming a sequence appropriate for an action different from the one intended. This occurs primarily through a lack of consistency in command structure, so that the appropriate structure for one command is not the same for another, even though the commands appear to be related and share a common description of purpose, action, and even part of the command format. The basic concept involved here is that when people lack knowledge about the proper operation of some aspect of a machine, they are apt to derive the operation by analogy with other, similar aspects of the device. The "derivation" may be unconscious, and it can influence behavior without the person realizing that it is happening.

Capture errors suggest the need for better feedback. A capture error occurs when there is overlap in the sequence required for the performance of an infrequent and a frequently performed action, and in the course of attempting the infrequent one, the more common act gets done instead. One possible way of avoiding this class of error is to minimize overlapping sequences, but this may not be possible, especially when the infrequent action sequence is simply a modification of the frequent one. A second way of avoiding the error is to try to catch it where it occurs. The error occurs at the critical place where the sequences deviate, so it is here that the problem must be faced. If the system knows what the intention of the user is (perhaps by requiring the user to indicate the overall intention), it could be designed so that at the critical choice point the proper path was flagged or in some other way brought to the attention of the operator. In addition, sufficient feedback about the state of the system should be provided to offer reminders as to the deviation from the intention. A major issue here is simply to know the critical place at which the errors occur so that remedial action can be built into the system at that critical point.

DETECTING ERROR

Detecting an error is the first step toward recovery. Early detection of error is extremely important. Delayed detection obviously wastes time and effort as the user works through steps that will not be effective because of an earlier error. As steps pile up, the diagnosis of the error becomes harder: The more that has happened, the more places there are to look for something wrong. This is especially a problem for the new user, who cannot partition what has been done into the surely right and the possibly wrong—the "bootstrapping" problem discussed in the Introduction to this section of the book. And in most systems the repair aids, "undo"s or inverse operations, often can only be applied right after the error, or within a small number of steps of it. Making errors show up clearly and quickly is a key design goal.

Slips are easier to detect than mistakes. In a slip, the action that was performed differs from the action intended: Detection occurs by comparing the outcome with the intention. In a mistake, it is the intention that is wrong, so if the person compares the outcome with the intention, it matches, so the person is apt to say, "yup, things are going just fine." As a result, it can be remarkably difficult to discover an error. Slips, mind you, are not always easy to discover. A major problem in the discovery of slips is the problem of levels: The level at which actions take place in the world differ from the level at which the intention is formed. Detection of misdiagnosis is hampered by a *cognitive hysteresis*—the tendency to stick with a decision even after the evidence shows it to be wrong.[1] As we argue later, this cognitive hysteresis appears to result from a bias to search only for confirming evidence, the danger of partial explanations, and the similarity between the actual and the perceived event. Developing a system that can provide sufficient information to help in effective diagnosis and in getting out of the cognitive hysteresis should be a major design consideration.

How Should the System Respond?

Now let us get to the heart of the matter: How should the system respond when it can not interpret the information given to it by the user? There are two goals here: one is to figure out what is intended so that the system can proceed with its operations; the other is to warn when something inappropriate has taken place (or is about to take place). Let us first examine this latter goal, that of providing a signal to the user thus signifying that something has gone wrong.

One basic response that helps signal the occurrence of difficulty is to construct the system in such a way that difficulties prevent continued operation. We call this property a *forcing function*: something that prevents the behavior from continuing until the problem has been corrected. This guarantees self-detection. Suppose you get into your automobile and start to drive away, but without ever starting the engine (the error does actually occur). This error cannot go undetected—the car simply will not move: This is a forcing function and the error is self-correcting. The fact that something is wrong is brought forcefully to attention. Forcing functions are sometimes carefully constructed by the designer, but can often fall out of the system operation naturally—as in the example of the automobile keys.

Note that the forcing function is not to be thought of as an error message. Rather, the sequence of operation is so designed that one simply cannot proceed, but the observation occurs naturally, in the normal course of events. No error bells or messages need occur in the automobile example. Starting the engine is a natural prerequisite to driving the automobile: The lack of movement serves as the indication that something has gone wrong. It is not always possible to develop such natural sequences. Thus, removing the ignition keys from the

[1] We use the term *cognitive hysteresis* because it takes less information to reach a particular interpretation of the situation than it does to give up that interpretation. Indeed, it sometimes appears that people can form judgments of a situation rapidly, but that it takes an enormous amount of information, time, and energy to cause them to discard that initial judgment. The psychological terms "set" and "functional fixation" refer to related concepts.

automobile at the end of the trip is not on a natural sequence of prerequisite events. As a result it is not uncommon to leave the keys in the car. (Requiring the use of the keys to lock the auto doors may seem inconvenient to some, but it does provide a natural forcing function, making it impossible to lock one's only set of keys in the car: an event that happens with some frequency in cars that can be locked without the use of keys.)

Forcing functions guarantee detection of a problem, but not proper identification of it. Failure to load the proper floppy diskette into a computer has a forcing function: The program will not work properly. However, the user may be only aware of the fact that something wrong has happened, but unaware of the cause. Determining the cause requires more feedback from the system.

> *In the early days of the UNIX text editor* Ed *it was possible to spend hours on the terminal editing a file, then quit—failing to save the work in permanent storage (the computer disk). As a result, all the work would be lost. (The event happened more frequently than might be expected.) The solution was to add a forcing function: An attempt to quit without first saving the text will fail. In the UNIX* vi *text editor (a grandchild of* Ed*) the failure is accompanied by the message:* No write since last change (:quit! overrides). *This response is both a forcing function and an explanation, describing why the command has not been executed, and stating how the command can be done, if that is really what is desired. On many small business and personal computers, it is still possible to stop editing without saving the work by removing the diskette. The Macintosh computer attempts to prevent this with a forcing function: The diskette cannot normally be removed unless the application has been terminated properly. This still does not prevent the user from simply turning off the power, however.*

A forcing function is simply one of many responses the system can make when it senses difficulties. In fact, we identify six possible responses: *Gag, Warn, Do Nothing, Self Correct, Teach Me,* and *Let's Talk About It.* In the next sections we discuss these six kinds of responses.

Gag. The automobile that will not move unless the key is in the ignition provides a good illustration of the technique we call *gag.* "Gag" is a forcing function, one that deals with errors by preventing the user from continuing, thus preventing the user from expressing impossible intentions. Some systems deal with error by locking the keyboard, preventing further typing until the user has "reset" the terminal. This is an effective gag, but one that at times appears to use brute strength when a friendly reminding would do: If the goal is to antagonize the user, this method works well.

A more successful illustration of "gag" comes from a tutorial language system called FLOW, developed by Raskin (1974). In this system, commands are typed in and processed one character at a time. If the user attempts to key a character that does not have a continuation into a legal command, the character is not accepted. You just can't type anything that isn't a legal command in the given context.

> *FLOW was an elementary programming language, designed by Raskin for beginning computer users from the fine arts, students who normally cringed at the thought of mathematics or computers. Raskin used to demonstrate this system by closing his eyes and pounding upon the keyboard, gleefully pointing out that not only did no system error messages appear, but that at the end, there would be a legal, syntactically correct program. (Of course the program was meaningless.) The result, explained Raskin, was that his students were not afraid to experiment. The lack of error message associated with syntax and text entering increased their confidence. (An excellent tracing program that stepped through the program line-by-line, showing which statement was being executed and what result would occur, helped the understanding of the semantics of the language.)*

"Gag" transfers the users' concern from trying to do things to trying to say them: The front-line problem is typing something the system will accept. Rather than letting the user try out various intentions, which may not work, the system intervenes to block the expression of the intention, perhaps before it is fully formulated. This may interfere with learning, especially learning through experimentation. But, as in Raskin's FLOW system, it can also relieve the frustrations associated with low-level typing errors, allowing the user to concentrate upon the major themes to be learned.

Warn. Several types of warnings are possible. In many automobiles, a buzzer warns when the seatbelts are not fastened, but the auto can be operated even if the warning is ignored. In some computer systems, similar warnings tell of files that are not write-protected, or other conditions that are not set up in normal fashion. Here, the philosophy is to note the occurrence of a potentially dangerous situation, to tell the user, but then to let the user decide how to respond. "Gag" forces itself on the user: "Warn" is less officious.

The Macintosh interface uses a related approach. Here, the menus show all possible actions, including ones that are not legal at the current state. The user is warned of the illegal actions: The commands not available at the moment are signaled by being shaded in gray as a warning that they cannot be selected at the moment. The user is not forced: The user can still attempt to select the command. In some sense, "warn" is presenting the error message before the fact, and as such might also be considered as an error-preventing procedure rather than as an error message.

Do nothing. Some direct manipulation interfaces use the *do nothing* approach. If you attempt an illegal action it just doesn't work. Nothing special happens, and you are left to infer that you tried something forbidden. The lack of movement after the attempt to drive an automobile without starting the engine is an example of a "do nothing" response. In the *Pinball Construction Set* (Budge, 1983), if you try to change the color of an object whose color can not be changed, you can go through all the motions, but nothing happens. "The paint won't stick" is how one user characterizes it. Note that the users of neither the automobile nor the construction set consider the "do nothing" response to be an error message. It is simply the way the system works: In the real world, some operations don't work on some objects. The pinball world is similar: Not all operations have effects. One could argue the merits of the "do nothing" strategy, but in this particular type of situation it seems to be very effective, both in conveying the error and in avoiding any disruption or ill feeling on the part of the user.

The "do nothing" method relies on visibility of the effects of its operations to convey the gap between intentions and outcomes. "Do nothing" is mostly seen in direct manipulation systems. But it isn't linked to the direct manipulation concept in any fundamental way, except that if it is to be effective, the lack of action must be readily apparent: In the terms used in earlier chapters of this book, the Gulf of Evaluation must be small or nonexistent.

> *Not all system designers seem aware of the requirement that "do nothing" can be used only where there is good feedback. Thus, in the Berkeley 4.2BSD UNIX system, the "remote copy" command, "rcp," copies files between computers. It requires a minimum of two arguments. If only one argument is given, the command fails, but with no indication. If two arguments are given, but neither refers to a legal file, the command still appears to work. "rcp" follows the "do nothing" philosophy of error message, much to the frustration of the user. UNIX does not provide automatic display of the state of its file system, so in this case the "do nothing" philosophy is inappropriate. (The normal copy command, "cp," does not misbehave in this way: It responds to a non-existent file with a message, as shown by the last example at the start of the chapter.)*

"Do nothing" is the simplest error technique and, when used properly, seems to have some important advantages. The user stays focused on the domain of actions and their effects, rather than being drawn out to process error messages. The user may have to do some experimenting to discover why what was tried didn't work, but this has its good side: The user is kept in a mode in which trying things out seems reasonable.

"Do nothing" also seems superior to "warn" in situations as complex as the *Pinball Construction Set.* Thus, even though when the user invokes the paint brush, the system knows that the intention is to color some objects, but when the display is complex with a large number of objects, an attempt to "warn" which objects were colorable and which not might result in a display that was visually more confusing than revealing.

Self correct. Another approach is for the system to try to guess some legal action that might be what the user would like to do. Simple spelling correction is an example of this approach. The ultimate in such systems is probably *DWIM: Do What I Mean,* the corrector available on the InterLisp system (Teitelman & Masinter, 1981). Note that automatic correction facilities, such as DWIM are only acceptable when there is a good "undo" facility, so if DWIM does something inappropriate, it is easy to "undo" it. As the designer of the system (Teitelman) once put it: "If you have made an error, you are going to have to correct it anyway. So I might as well have DWIM try to correct it. In the best case, it gets it right. In the worst case it gets it wrong and you have to undo it: but you would have had to make a correction anyway, so DWIM can't make it worse."

DWIM becomes a way of life, a fundamental part of InterLisp that changes the way people think of the system. DWIM is powerful enough that it is used deliberately. Because DWIM remembers corrections given it, one can deliberately introduce a new term that will cause the system to call upon DWIM, then tell DWIM that it means whatever it is that was really wanted, and forever after type a simple term instead of a more complex one, letting DWIM "correct" the term, simplifying the typing. DWIM has even been used to introduce Algol-like notation to Lisp: When the user typed in Algol expressions, DWIM "corrected" it to Lisp syntax. DWIM also can be annoying, for it can sometimes get carried away, correcting things that ought not to be corrected. Some users swear by DWIM, some swear at it. As an error correcting facility, DWIM seems superb. Its negative features result from the overgeneralization of its facilities. Although DWIM can be asked to query the user before making changes (and it can be turned off entirely), the problem is that the user wants some of the features, but not all, and this is not easy to arrange.

> *DWIM—and presumably other "intelligent" error correction systems, can sometimes be too smart, frustrating the user. Here is one user's description of the problem:*
>
> *One especially annoying thing that DWIM can do is this: You are composing Lisp code and in true Lisp tradition, you want understandable variable and function names. Suppose you define and call a function "(get-next)." DWIM sees the expression and helpfully decides that you have made a typing error: You clearly mean to subtract "next" from "get" but forgot both the spaces and also the proper Lisp notation that requires the action to be listed first. So, DWIM politely, elegantly transforms your name "(get-next)" into the Lisp code "(minus get next)." When you try to run the program, you get an error message: "get" was discovered to be an unbound variable, found while Lisp was executing IDIFF, the routine for taking differences between integers. The problem, of course, is the hyphen in the function name. Using hyphenated names is common practice in other Lisp environments, but is to be avoided in InterLisp. There the convention is to capitalize initial letters, so the function would be called "GetNext" instead of "get-next." One learns these conventions after being burned a few times, but the first few times it happens, it can be very difficult to debug. Remember you never thought you mentioned a variable "get" and perhaps you didn't do any subtraction. Worse yet, maybe you did do some subtraction, and so you waste much time trying to fix the place in your program where you were subtracting. Argghhhh!*

Simpler instances of "self correct" can be found. Some operations are insensitive to the order of arguments, yet the command insists upon a particular ordering. This requirement could be weakened, or at the least, the system could try all orders and ask the user if it was OK. Calling the text editor upon a nonexistent file is usually treated through a "self correct" philosophy. Most editors interpret this as wanting that file to exist—a guess that is often correct, and when not, not costly to repair. "Self correct" can probably be used a lot more than it is. There are numerous simple cases where not much intelligence is required to determine what the user might really have meant, if only the designer would have thought to try.

Let's talk about it. Some systems respond to problems by initiating a dialog with the user: We call this strategy "Let's talk about it," and we consider it a major step forward toward true interaction. A good example is the way that many Lisp systems respond when they get into trouble: a message describing the problem to the best of the system's ability, but then, automatic entry into the "Lisp Debugger" allows the user to interact with the system and explore the various candidates for trouble. For the class of experienced users for whom such systems are designed, there is a high likelihood that the user can simply fix the problem and proceed. Here we have shared responsibility between user and system to explore the problem and come up with a solution.

Teach me. And finally, there is the response we call "Teach me," the system that queries the user to find out just what a particular phrase or command might have meant. In the best of these systems, for example, *Clout* (a natural language inquiry system for the *Microrim* relational database system), when the system finds a word it does not understand, it asks the user for a definition. Any words in the definition that are not understood are then themselves asked about. This continues until all the terms have been defined. The new terms are then retained by the system so that the same phrases can be used in the future.

The Problem of Level

One major problem associated with error messages is to convey just where the problem is. It is often the case that the system detects an error, the user recognizes that an error has been made, but there is still considerable difficulty in determining just what the error is. A major factor is the existence of numerous levels of intentions. The situation that led to the "longjmp botch" error with which we opened this chapter illustrates the problem. It was first found while formatting files on the terminal, using a program that internally invoked "more," the screen-display program. "More" got into trouble and collapsed most ungracefully, displaying the message *longjmp botch: core dumped.* What is a "longjmp botch?" Why is the user being told this? Of what use is this information?

One problem with this message is that it is presented at the lowest level of program execution whereas the user is thinking at a fairly high level of intention: The user is formatting a file, unaware that "more" is even involved. But the error message does not give any hint as to what level the trouble is at: The user assumed it was a problem either with the text file or with the formatter.

Suppose a task is performed, but the end result is not satisfactory. Why not? The reason could lie at any level. There are many places for error, many places where intentions could fail to be satisfied. If the operation were carried out manually, one step at a time, then it might be relatively easy to detect the place where the problem lies. But in many situations this is not possible: All we know is that the intention has not been satisfied. Many of us have experienced this problem, spending hours "fixing" the wrong part of a program or task because we did not have the information required to judge the level at which the problem had occurred. The question, however, for the system designer is: What information is most useful for the user?

The question is very difficult to answer. For the system programmer who is trying to debug the basic routines, the statement *longjmp botch* might be very useful—just the information that was needed. The problem is not that the error message is inappropriate; the problem is that sometimes it is appropriate, other times not.

One approach to the levels problem is to know the intention. If the program knew it was being used by a person who was intending to format a file, it could make one set of responses. If it knew it was being used by someone trying to track down a problem, it could make another set. However, although knowing user intentions and levels often helps, it does not guarantee success. In studies of human errors there are found numerous cases where knowledge of the intention would not help. Consider the following example:

> *X leaves work and goes to his car in the parking lot. X inserts the key in the door, but the door will not open. X tries the key a second time: It still doesn't work. Puzzled, X reverses the key, then examines all the keys on the key ring to see if the correct key is being used. X then tries once more, walks around to the other door of the car to try yet again. In walking around, X notes that this is the incorrect car. X then goes to his own car and unlocks the door without difficulty.*

It is easy to generate a large collection of examples like this, some involving cars, others apartments, offices, and homes. The common theme is that even though people may know their own intentions, they seem to tackle the problem at the lowest level, and then slowly, almost reluctantly, they pop up to higher levels of action and intention. If the door will not unlock, perhaps the key is not inserted properly. If it still won't work, perhaps it is the wrong key, and then, perhaps the door or the lock is stuck or broken. Determining that the attempt is being made at the wrong door seems difficult. Now perhaps the problem is the error messages are inappropriate: The door simply refuses to open. It would be better if the door could examine the key and respond "This key is for a different car." Can programs overcome this problem? (See Chapter 16 by Draper for one possible direction—a solution based on the notion of "responsibility.")

> *The "Let's Talk About It" strategy provides a possible solution to the problem of levels. Suppose the message indicating difficulty was always presented at the highest level, indicating that there has been a problem and its seriousness. Then, let the user be given tools to explore the problem to whatever depth is desired. Let the user be able to trace down the levels, to see where the original mismatch occurred, how that level was reached, and the state of the system at each level. The programmer can explore in detail: The experienced user can explore until the basic problem is clear, and the uninterested can remain uninterested. Such exploratory tools will require some skills to be constructed, but the multiwindow, run-time support for Lisp Machines (and even Macintosh Pascal and Basic) offer suggestions of how to proceed. But this kind of constructive interaction with the system has the possibility of solving the levels problem along with the error message problem.*

The Failure to Detect Problems

Often actions will accomplish a legal effect, and so cannot be detected as errors by the system, but are still problems in that they neither advance the user towards the goal nor do what the user intended. As we saw in the chapter by Lewis (Chapter 8), the users' ability to detect such states is unreliable. Word-processor learners can explain away even disastrous errors: They adjust their idea of what should be happening to fit what appears to be happening. Our studies of error bring out the same phenomenon: Serious failures may not be detected even though the available evidence appears (in hindsight) to be fully adequate. Norman (1984b, 1986) proposes three hypotheses that may account for these difficulties in detecting errors: relevance bias, partial explanation, and overlap between model and world.

Relevance bias. People seem to have an apparent bias toward seeking confirmatory evidence when evaluating a hypotheses, though looking for disconfirming evidence is often more useful (Johnson-Laird, 1983). This bias may be forced by the need to select evidence to consider from a large pool, too large to permit full examination. In selecting evidence one has to make judgments of relevance: One cannot afford to waste time processing irrelevant evidence. But judgments of what is relevant must be based on what one thinks is happening: in short, based on one's hypotheses. If confirming evidence is more likely to look relevant to a hypothesis than disconfirming evidence, the bias toward confirmation can be reinterpreted as a bias toward relevant-seeming evidence.

An example discussed by Lewis (Chapter 8) seems to fit Norman's analysis. When the learner searched for a page number and found a line number instead, the learner was satisfied, even though the label on the number made no sense in this context. The message looked relevant because it contained a number. And because it looked relevant, its very presence lent support to the hypothesis that it was what was wanted.

Partial explanation. The second conjecture is that errors are not detected because people accept crude agreement between what they expect and what they see. The example just discussed shows this mechanism at work as well. The learner interpreted the number in a way that accounted for the number, but not for the rest of the message. As noted, the rest of the display message indicated that the number was a line number, not a page number, but the learner did not require a complete interpretation. Like relevance bias, acceptance of partial explanations can be seen as a necessary response to limitations in processing capacity. One simply could not function if everything in the environment had to be fully interpreted.

Overlap of model and world. The final suggestion is that error detection is impeded by the fact that one's model of the world is likely to agree to a great extent with the way the world really is, even if the model is wrong in part. If one's model were too far off it would have to be adjusted. As a result of this rough agreement, finding points of disagreement is hard. Most things that one does will produce the results predicted by one's model, which is thus supported.

CORRECTING ERROR

If an error is detected the user needs to recover from it. Some existing systems provide general (or intended to be general) "undo" facilities, so that one can back up to an earlier state after making an error. Other systems aim to structure their operations so that they have natural inverses: Erasing a line is the inverse of drawing, and vice versa. It seems clear that, at the very least, *undo* is a desirable element of a system. It allows users to experiment more freely, it reduces anxiety and tension, and it permits ready recovery of many simple errors. Implementation of *undo* is nontrivial, however. An "undo" command that recovers from the last command is relatively easy, but many operations that the user thinks of as a single event can launch several different actions, only the last of which will be recoverable from with a single-step undo. But as soon as we go beyond recovery of the last operation, numerous technical and conceptual issues arise that have not yet been solved. Even single-step undo routines can be expensive of resources if one wishes to be able to recover from any command, including writing and reading from files and accidental or erroneous exits from the program.

Nievergelt has argued strongly for the essential kind of information a user must have in order to recover from error (Nievergelt & Weydert, 1980). Essentially, the user needs to know what the current state of the system is (*sites*), where one came from (*trails*) and what the possible alternatives are (*modes*). He bases the design of his experimental system around these three concepts: sites, modes, and trails.

The "Let's Talk About It," Teach Me," and the "Self Correct" strategy of dealing with problems seem like important directions to pursue. Certainly human-to-human communication makes very heavy use of these techniques.

CONCLUSION

In this chapter we have examined some of the ways that a system designer can deal with error. We think that error is the natural result of a person attempting to do a task. An error results for several reasons, including accidental mishaps, slips of action, and sincere mistakes. In many cases, the erroneous action represents the person's best attempt at the desired action. It is this case that most interests us, for here is where the spirit should be one of genuine cooperation. The user tried, and got it wrong. Think of the input not as an error, but as the user's first iteration toward the goal. The system should do its best to help. If it can figure out what was intended, so much the better. If not, it should explain gracefully where its problem is, perhaps making suggestions. It should not require retyping a long sequence or redoing a long set of operations when only one detail was in error. Human conversation does not require such correction.

Sometimes the responses of the person are not easily detected as being in error. That is, they are legal operations, but not appropriate for the situation. This is a more difficult case, for only the most intelligent of systems can detect this situation, and probably not even then. The solution here is to provide sufficient feedback and exploratory aids that the person is aware of the actions and of the system state. It should be easy for the user to examine the system, to find the consequences of actions, and to modify those actions. Undo facilities are desirable, but undo with the extra information that allows for intelligent use of the facility, including knowledge of how the operation got to its current state and what alternatives exist.

At times the best strategy is for the system simply to provide warnings, or not to respond at all. Sometimes it is possible to correct the error without further input from the person, although because the system too can make errors, this should only be done with consultation and permission. More important, it is often possible to avoid whole classes of error simply by reformulating the problem, eliminating aspects that would otherwise have caused trouble. This chapter does not attempt to be comprehensive in its treatment. The chapter is meant to provide the spirit of the enterprise: that error should be considered a normal part of operation, not an exception.

There already exists a system that accepts erroneous statements gracefully, usually managing to interpret actions correctly in spite of error, other times providing elegant correction procedures. The system?—human speech. Normal speech contains many errors and corrections, yet people have evolved such skillful procedures for correction that the listener seldom notices either the errors or the corrections. In a conversation, we do not complain of "syntax errors," even though there are many. Even simple errors of meaning can be tolerated if it is clear what was meant. When a speaker detects an error, the erroneous part of the utterance can be corrected while leaving the surrounding material unchanged, reducing effort and trauma by all concerned parties. When we fail to understand what a person has said we ask for correction. But we act as a cooperative team and minimize the effort required to deal with the error. Basically, we assume the person is trying to tell us something, so that even errors or local incoherence are still informative attempts. We treat understanding as a cooperative endeavor, requiring effort from both speaker and listener.

If we think of interaction with a computer as a cooperative endeavor we see that each side has certain talents. The person is good at setting goals and constructing intentions. The computer is great on the details. Let the two work together, with the person in charge. And let the computer go out of its way to make things easy for the user, to make corrections easy, to go that extra step toward understanding that makes conversation with an intelligent colleague so fruitful.

Budge, B. (1983) *Pinball construction set* (computer program). San Mateo, CA: Electronic Arts.

Draper, S. and Norman, D.A. (1984) Software Engineering for User Interfaces. In *Proceedings of the 7th International Conference on Software Engineering*. Silver Spring, MD: IEEE, 214–220.

du Boulay, B. and Matthew, I. (1984) Fatal error in pass zero: How not to confuse novices. *Behaviour and Information Technology*, 3, 109–118.

Johnson-Laird, P.N. (1983) *Mental Modes*. Cambridge, MA: Harvard University Press,

Nievergelt, J., and Weydert, J. (1980) Sites, modes and trails: Telling the user of an interactive system where he is, what he can do, and how to get places. In R. A. Guedji, P. ten Hagen, F.R. Hopgood, H. Tucker and D.A. Duce (eds.) *Methodology of interaction*. Amsterdam: North-Holland. 327–338.

Norman, D.A. (1981a) Categorization of action slips. *Psychological Review*, 88, 1–15.

Norman, D.A. (1983b) Design rules based on analyses of human error. *Communications of the ACM*, 4, 254–258.

Norman, D.A. (1984b) *Working papers on errors and error detection*. Unpublished manuscript, University of California, San Diego, Institute for Cognitive Science, La Jolla, CA.

Norman, D.A. (1986) New views of information processing: Implications for intelligent decision support systems. In E. Hollnagel, G. Mancini and D. Woods (eds.) *Intelligent decision aids in process environments*. New York: Springer-Verlag.

Raskin, A.J. (1974) The flow-language for computer programming. *Computers and the Humanities*, 8, 231–237.

Reason, J., and Mycielska, K. (1982) *Absent Minded? The psychology of mental lapses and everyday errors*. Englewood Cliffs, NJ: Prentice-Hall.

Shneiderman, B. (1980) *Software Psychology: Human factors in computer and information systems*. Cambridge, MA: Winthrop.

Teitelman, W., and Masinter, L. (1981, April) The Interlisp programming environment. *Computer*. 25–33.

VanLehn, K., and Brown, J.S. (1980) Planning nets: A representation for formalizing analogies and semantic models of procedural skills. In R.E. Snow, P.A. Federico, and W.E. Montague (eds.) *Aptitude, learning, and instruction: Volume 2. Cognitive process analyses of learning and problem solving*. Hillsdale, NJ: Lawrence Erlbaum Associates, 95–137.

Winston, P.H. (1975) Learning structural descriptions from examples. In P. H. Winston (ed.) *The psychology of computer vision*. New York: McGraw-Hill. 157–209.

Learning to Use a Word Processor: By Doing, by Thinking, and by Knowing

JOHN M. CARROLL
ROBERT L. MACK

Learning to use a word processor provides a study of real complex human learning that is fundamentally "active," driven by the initiatives of the learner—which are, in turn, based on extensive domain-specific knowledge and skill, and on reasoning processes which are systematic yet highly creative. State-of-the-art application systems and their training materials presuppose "passive" learners and are—to that extent—unusable. Some general design implications of active learning were discussed.

Suppose that people learned "passively." That is, suppose that designers of systems and of their training materials could place new users in a carefully programmed learning environment with confidence that through this experience new users would become skilled experts. These passive learners would presumably read descriptions and explanations of the system's functional capabilities; they would carefully follow exercises to drill and develop their skill and understanding; and gradually these experiences would converge on a mature stereotype of skill and understanding.

In point of fact, the above is pretty much what designers of state-of-the-art application systems and training material have supposed. Were this supposition correct, the human factors of computer systems would be in good shape today: the technology for "passive" learning of systems is well developed. But unfortunately, the supposition is almost totally wrong. As we will argue here, people learn *actively* not passively. The problems new users have with existent systems and training are testimony to this contention. That people do learn to use such systems via such training programs is testimony to the adaptability and intellectual tenacity of people. This point will also be amply illustrated in our discussion.

In order to be more usable, future application systems and their training support will need to accommodate the real (= "active") learner, rather than what might have been—from the perspective of the system designer and manual writer—the ideal (= "passive") learner. Toward the end of this chapter we will sketch some general design proposals along these lines and attempt to theoretically bring our work to bear on the analysis of human behavior and experience in realistic situations that is developing in current Cognitive Science (Norman, 1981).

METHOD AND OVERVIEW

The research discussed consists of studies of office personnel learning to use word processing equipment. In this chapter, we are not concerned with issues regarding particular systems (see Mack, Lewis, & Carroll, 1983). Our principal focus will be on the learning strategies (actually the classes of learning strategies) we have identified in the course of this work. The three classes of strategies we address are learning by doing, learning by thinking, and learning by knowing.

Our view is that these are natural—albeit complex—strategies for people to adopt when confronted by a learning task of nontrivial complexity. The learners we have studied are almost entirely "innocent" with respect to computer technology. In the context of learner innocence, we argue, these "natural" strategies entail severe and wide ranging learning problems. Analysis of these problems, in turn, suggests research directions for the analysis of real human learning within contemporary cognitive science and practical directions in which computer systems, and the educational technologies that support their training and use might evolve.

The Learners and Their Task

In this research project, ten office temporaries spent four half-days learning to use one of two possible word processing systems in our laboratory. Four were given a subset of the word processing operations for a general purpose, command-based system. The other six were asked to learn basic functions of a commercially available word processor which was menu-based.

These people were highly experienced in routine office work, but quite naive with respect to computers in general and word processing systems in particular. We asked them to imagine a scenario in which a word processing system had recently been introduced to their office, and they had been asked to be the first to learn it (to then pass this knowledge on to colleagues). The point was that they were to learn to use the system using the training materials that accompany it as their only resource. The manual we used was designed to be used as the nucleus of a "self-study" training method, although, in fact, such material is rarely used in complete isolation from other methods such as tutorial assistance (which is not surprising in light of our results, see below).

The materials we asked our learners to study addressed basic letter entry and revision skills (including formatting, printing, document retrieval, and document merging), and, in the case of the commercially available system, the use of command menus, the interpretation of messages, and the use of the on-line Help facility.

Learners spent varying amounts of time with this task, but we stopped them in any case after about 12 hours in order to ask them to try a simple "transfer task," involving typing in, revising, formatting, and then printing out a one-page letter. This transfer task was not part of the self-study manual; it served as a sort of benchmark achievement test. Finally, we asked learners about their prior work background, about specific queries that occurred to us during the course of the learning sessions, and about their overall impressions of the system and the experience.

Our concern here is not to detail the results of the project; they can be found in Mack et al. (1983). Suffice it to say that a great many problems cropped up during the sessions and that even after the 12 hours or so of self-study learning not a single learner was able to complete the transfer task without some kind of serious difficulty in editing subtasks such as document creation, retrieval or printing, or in actually entering and revising text.

Two very general points should be stressed about this project. First, the domain in which we studied learning is drawn from the real world of actual learning that real people must cope with: we studied real word processing systems, real training books, and users drawn from the population to whom the system and the books were targeted. We take this project to constitute an "ecologically valid" investigation of human learning. Second, the systems and the manuals which were our materials for this work are state-of-the-art. Thus, our findings—especially those pertaining to learner problems—are not abstract effects of "materials," but rather have immediate and specific practical implications for the design of technology in the word processing domain (see Mack et al., 1983).

Thinking Aloud

Our method involved prompting learners to "think aloud" as they worked through the training materials. They were to report questions that were raised in their minds, plans and strategies they felt they might be considering or following out, and inferences and knowledge that might have been brought to awareness by ongoing experiences. We remained with the learners to keep them talking and to intervene, if at any time it appeared that a problem was so grave that a learner might leave the experiment if we did not help out. Our prompting remained nondirective, and indeed once learners got going we needed to prompt very infrequently at all. We had to actually intervene rarely.

Throughout the learning sessions, video and sound recordings were made (in what we hoped was an unobtrusive manner). Our analysis consisted first of an enumeration of "critical incidents" which were cataloged and classified in various ways. This was constrained by the consensus of the three experimenters (the authors and Clayton Lewis). The chief goal of this was to form a picture of the typical experience of a learner, and it is this induced "prototype" learning experience to which we will refer in what follows (for details, see Mack et al., 1983). Our method of reporting will be to cite induced generalizations and to illustrate these by concrete examples transcribed from our audio recordings.

We are aware that the thinking aloud technique has been of great methodological interest recently, but this topic lies outside the scope of the present study (see Ericsson & Simon, 1980; Nisbett & Wilson, 1977).

How People Learn

Perhaps the most apt description of the world of the new user of a word processor is that often quoted phrase of William James: "a bloomin' buzzin' confusion." People in this situation see many things going on, but they do not know which of these is relevant to their current concerns. Indeed, they do not know if their current concerns are the appropriate concerns for them to have. The learner reads something in the manual; sees something on the display; and must try to connect the two, to integrate, to interpret. It would be unsurprising to find that people in such a situation suffer conceptual—or even physical—paralysis. They have so little basis on which to act.

And yet people do act. Indeed, perhaps the most pervasive tendency we have observed is that people simply strike out into the unknown. If the rich and diverse sources of available information cannot be interpreted, then some of these will be ignored. If something *can* be interpreted (no matter how specious the basis for this interpretation), then it will be interpreted. Ad hoc theories are hastily assembled out these odds and ends of partially relevant and partially extraneous generalization. And these "theories" are used for further prediction. Whatever initial confusions get into such a process, it is easy to see that they are at the mercy of an at least partially negative feedback loop: things quite often get worse before they get better.

Designers of word processors and training technology probably would have liked things to have been different. The easiest way to teach someone something is, after all, to tell them. However, what we see in the learning-to-use-a-word-processor situation is that people are so busy trying things out, thinking things through, and trying to relate what they already know (or believe they know) to what is going on that they often do not notice the small voice of structured instruction crying out to them from behind the manual and the system interface.

What's wrong? We would argue that the learning practices people adopt here are typical, and in many situations adaptive. The problem in this particular learning situation is that new learners of word processors are *innocent* in the extreme. Each feature of a word processing system may indeed have a sensible design rationale from the viewpoint of the systems' engineer, but this rationale is frequently far beyond the grasp of the new user. "Word processor," so far as we know, is not a natural concept. People who do not know about word processors have little, possibly nothing, to refer to in trying to actively learn to use such things. Innocence turns reasonable learning strategies into learning problems. This is what this study is about.

LEARNING BY DOING

Our learners relentlessly wanted to learn by trying things out rather than by reading about how to do them. In part this was impatience: they were reluctant to read a lot of explanation or get bogged down following meticulous directions. But it also devolved from mismatched goals: Learners wanted to discover how to do specific things at particular times, and this did not always accord with the sequence in which topics were treated in the manual.

Jumping the Gun

Half of our learners impatiently tried to sign on to the system before reading how to do so. Table 1 presents highlights of one such learner. The learner had reached a point in the manual which showed the sign on display. This was intended as orientation and included no instruction about how to sign on.

The learner immediately incurs a number of errors which prevent her from signing on easily, and she is forced to try out various actions on her own initiative in order to deal with these ancillary problems. Indeed, it is only after considerable exploration of keys and commands that she is able to sign on. The specific character of her errors, and the exploration she engages in reveal a profound lack of knowledge about computers.

TABLE 1
Signing on the Word Processing System

(1) *Learner has been trying to type the letter string "abc" on display in order to observe cursor movement and practice backspacing. She is typing this string on the operator name field for the sign-on menu. Due to a number of errors which include prematurely trying to sign-on with "abc" as the incorrect—and inadvertent—operator name, the learner decides to simply start over.*

L: So now let's see. Could I turn it off and start all over? That's what I would do. Will it hurt anything?
E: You're in control.
L: Let's see what happens. If I were all alone that's what I would do.
E: Yup! You're all alone!

Powers off, and immediately back on. A new sign-on menu display appears.

(2) *Correctly types operator name "learner6" in the sign-on menu field labeled "operator name."*

L: Uh, the six [*i.e., of "learner6"*] was right next to it [*i.e., no space*] and it entered without typing anything. Do I have to make it, press "enter" to make it stay? No. Didn't say anything about that so we will forget about that.

Reference unclear, but she does not "enter" the filled-in sign-on menu. Instead, she continues with the next exercise, involving typing the letters "abc" and backspacing. This is intended to be done on the sign-on menu to illustrate how one can correct mistakes made while filling in menu parameters.

(3) L: Okay now we are off. [*Reads aloud*] "If you have worked with this type "abc" and watch the cursor move."

Now she types "abc" right after the operator name which causes an error signalled several ways: audio message, a message about exceeding the length of the menu field, an indicator light signaling the need to take corrective action (labeled "reset/help"), and a locked keyboard which can only be unlocked by pressing a reset key.

L: Whoops!
E: What do you think happened then?
L: A bell rang. A buzzer or something.

(4) L: *Reads instructions on Sign-on menu display.* "Enter to finish" Okay let's see what happens. [*Presses the enter key*]

E: You pressed enter?
L: I pressed enter and nothing happened. [*The keyboard is locked*]

Reads more fragments of manual, stops at: "Ask your training administrator for help." How do I get the menu? Request the menu again. All right. Press request, cancel.

Presses keys labeled request and cancel, to no effect because of the locked keyboard. Reference to "the menu" is not clear but may reflect her current understanding that she has not signed on yet or that she needs some other kind of display to proceed.

Okay. I didn't get the original menu to press anything.

Learner believes she needs a different menu, one which lists the tasks or commands available (e.g., create or retrieve or print a document). It appears after one completes sign-on.

Oh "enter" it. Nothing.

TABLE 1—*Continued*

Presses enter, which would have the effect of bringing up another display, but to no effect because of locked keyboard.

Now presses request key which is not relevant to anything here.

E: You pressed request?
L: Request and enter, trying to find that menu page because this page is not; I don't know how to get off this page. *Not clear what she is referring to here, but clearly she believes that she must have a different display to work on.*

All right. Come on. *Reads more fragments of manual referring to functions which advance and return the function from one menu parameter field to another.*

Okay. Pressed that.
E: Variable advance?
L: Right. "Watch the cursor . . ." Nothing. [*Keyboard is still locked.*] Great!
E: Okay what are you pressing there?
L: Variable Advance. [*then*] "Enter" to see if anything different might happen. Okay. Let's try it once more. Nothing!

(5) Still nothing. Okay. If I wanted to go back I would use the . . . ". . . look on the front . . .". Where is the "code" key? Now I'm trying the variable advance key and the code key to see if anything happens. Nothing happens! For all the punching I'm doing nothing at all is happening.

E: Do you have any idea why that might be?
L: Ah, I can't understand why it isn't entering, even entering the mistakes if I'm making mistakes. It's coming up with nothing. They did not tell me to get off this page.

New Audio Tape—some interaction may have been lost.

Now I'm touching the backspace key and it is not erasing anything. [*because keyboard remains locked*] So I have made some kind of error that has locked everything in here.

E: Nothing seems to be working?

(6) L: Right. Reset/Help? [*Presses the reset key, which is the correct remedy*]
E: Pressing reset?
L: I pressed reset/help to see what would happen there.
E: What do you think happened?
L: Nothing, really. [*In fact, the reset/help indicator light went off, signaling the unlocking of keyboard.*]
E: Why did you press that?
L: I'm trying to get back to a beginning. To start over.

All right. What would happen if I put it on "test"? *Referring to a button on the display unit which is labelled "test status." It is used to diagnose problems with the unit. It is totally irrelevant here.*

Turns test status "on" and a diagnostic pattern overlays screen.

Beautiful!

E: What happened?

(*continued*)

TABLE 1—*Continued*

L: I decided to put it on test. Status is "test" rather than normal. Now let's see what happens if you backspace.

Backspace works and she does so, deleting the incorrect string "learner6abc."

Oh, my gosh, are you sure this isn't hurting everything. Oh, hey, hurrah! Good! Very good! Now we are in business.

Now if we backspace, it takes it off. Okay. Fine. Now where did it tell me that I should have started at "test"?

(7) [*Sometime later the learner is reading the manual.*]
E: Can you summarize what you were just doing there?

L: Well I was looking at this [*page*] 1–8. I was looking at this diagram and it says "The reset/help indicator is on." So then I figured out that these are indicators. I didn't know that before this. *Summarizes what other indicator lights mean.*

Now I pressed the correct key and nothing happened, which is exactly what they tell you in the directions will happen. "When you are in a reset [*condition*] you cannot move the cursor or type anything." Now this was my probem before. But I wasn't up to page 1–9 so I didn't know that if the reset/help key, uh indicator is on the machine is going to do nothing. So you need to press . . .

E: Was that your problem before?
L: Yes.
E: Huh?
L: I didn't realize that it would not act as long as that was on, that I have to do something to get it back to acting again.
Okay. To be able to continue you need to press the reset key. So I press that. Now the . . . did they call it a code? An indicator. The indicator went off. The reset/help indicator went off. So evidentally we are back in business.

(8) Well, um. Do you want . . . maybe I should go back and put it on normal and see if I could do the same thing?

E: Well, you're in control.

Puts test status button on "normal" setting. Now it's on "normal." Let's do everything we did and see if it will work on this because we may still have been on the reset/help button over there. I don't know.

We'll type the "abc" [*types "abc" in the operator name sign-on menu field*] and see what happens. Then we'll try to backspace [*does so, deleting the "abc" she has just typed*] Does that alright. We'll go backwards and do the things they told us to do.

Tries function to advance the cursor to a new menu field. Which moves the cursor. Now they want us to move back. We'll code it in and we're back. [*i.e., when user uses cursor advance function in conjunction with a code key, the cursor returns or moves up to the next menu field*]

Okay. I'm running back through the instructions and it is working with it set on "normal." [*Reads fragments of manual—repeats exercise on making "invalid key" errors and pressing reset*] Okay I could have done the exercise on "normal."

E: Is that what you conclude?
L: That's what I concluded. Evidentally when I heard the bell before and I didn't

TABLE 1—*Continued*

know that the reset/help indicator was on or didn't realize what was happening in that column. In other words I got into trouble before I got to [*page*] 1–8! So now we know why nothing was registering because I hadn't read on page 1–9 that I had to press the reset key.

Okay. Now I am going on to exercise two. We're going to find out how to sign on.

At this point begins following directions to sign-on.

For example, in segment 2 the learner has typed her operator identification but she does not immediately realize that she must press the "enter" key to execute the sign on task. When she later tries the enter key (segment 4) she has in the meantime incurred an additional error that has locked the keyboard (segment 3). Hence, enter has no effect after all. In segment 5 she begins to appreciate that there is a problem after trying out a number of other function keys to no avail (e.g., a backspace to delete the erroneous typed parameter entry). Finally, in segment 6 the learner manages to solve the locked keyboard problem, but she confuses that action with an immediately following—and perhaps some salient—operation (involving a "Test Status" key) and so misinterprets the solution to her problem.

Jumping the gun is not always traceable to "mere" impatience. Often learners strike out on their own because their specific goals do not match those implied by the manual designers. As the first few segments of Table 2 reveal, the learner is not certain of the point of the exercise. She wants very much to learn how to correct typing errors but this topic is not covered until later. The current practice exercise is about a prerequisite cursor movement skill.

The learner's uncertainty about the exercise and her own specific concerns encourage her to try correcting a typing error on her own (beginning of segment 2). However, her attempt fails because she has not yet learned how to correct typing errors (it involves positioning the cursor and using backspace or delete keys), and is not able to work out how to do so from what she already has learned or can guess. Indeed, the learner ultimately inserts blank lines into her text (segment 6) and botches the exercise. These errors arise because she incorrectly tries to move the cursor using the space and return keys (segments 5 and 6, respectively) which are not appropriate on the word processing system (i.e., these keys actually change what one has typed because the system is always in insert mode, that is, spaces and line breaks are inserted into the text line wherever the cursor happens to be).

TABLE 2
Correcting a Typing Mistake Prematurely

(1) E: What are you thinking?
L: I'm trying to figure out what exercise is supposed to be for [*pause*] line advance? Supposed to be an exercise on errors, but am I supposed to be trying to make errors and then move back?

Types first three lines of file. At end of third line, types comma instead of a period. Realizes her mistake after she has already carrier returned. Wants to know how to move the cursor back to make the correction.

(2) Oh, I see, so now . . .
E: What are you thinking?
L: I made a mistake up here, now if I want to go back I guess I would. . . . *Looks in the manual for information.*
E: What are you looking at, page 3–4? [*Pause*] What is that telling you?
L: Well, I'm trying to figure out how I can go back to correct that mistake. Am I supposed to correct my mistake yet, or am I supposed to just not worry about the mistakes or . . . I'm going to try to go back.

(3) *Backspaces with the cursor at the beginning of current line in order to move cursor back to immediately preceding line. This is not allowed and incurs a beep error message.*
Oh! It didn't like that.

(4) *Presses line return, which moves the cursor to the beginning of the previous sentence with the comma which she wants to correct.*
E: OK, what did you hit?
L: I pressed line return.

A function that moves the cursor up one line

E: On page 3–4 again, what's that telling you?
L: I'm still trying to figure out . . . press and hold down line return until the cursor moves to the first line . . . that's a step but. . . . *Trying to adapt the manual instructions to her situation.*

(5) *Hits the space bar to move the cursor to the right through the line, which puts a space at the beginning of the line. Then immediately backspaces, which deletes it.*

E: You hit a space then a backspace?

Pressing backspace deletes the unintended spaces at the beginning of the line.

L: Yes. I'm just going to leave that mistake and press return.

(6) *The cursor is at the beginning of the third line, so when she presses return she inserts a blank line above it.*

Whoa!
E: OK, what are you thinking?
L: I didn't know it was going to do that. Wonder how I can bring it back.

(7) *Hits code key.*

E: What did you hit?
L: I pressed code . . .

TABLE 2—*Continued*

	E: What are you thinking?
	L: I'm going to try to bring it back to where it was.
	E: Bring what back?
	L: Bring back the line, although I'm not really sure if it matters . . . space in between there. [*points to blank line*] I press return . . .
(8)	*Presses required return and inserts yet another empty line.* Don't go any further! I'm having difficulty because I'm trying to bring it back up.
	Uses line advance to move cursor down to the line that needs to be "moved back up."
	I'm trying to remember how to bring it back. I don't even know if it matters if it has a space in between. I can just continue typing.

Instruction Sequences Are Fragile

Learning by trying things out according to a personal agenda of needs and goals is not merely a preference. Learners who try to follow out manual instructions are often unable to do so. The instruction sequences are fragile in the sense that it is easy to get sidetracked and there is no provision in them for recovery. One example is a learner who inadvertently paginated (reformatted) a document at the beginning of an exercise on revising documents. This not only rearranged the lines in the file to make right margins even, it also stored the document away. The learner had not yet learned how to retrieve documents and the manual itself provided no recovery information for this type of error. Accordingly, she was forced to try to discover how to retrieve the document on her own. She was ultimately unable to do so and we had to intervene.

Once we restored the document to her display, she was faced with an equally staggering problem: the pagination operation had rearranged the lines of her file so that the revising instructions did not refer to the same document. An experienced user who understood reformatting could have reinterpreted the instructions and adapted them to this rearranged text. But this learner had no idea what she had done, and thus was hopelessly puzzled by the fact that the instructions seemed to be wrong.

The fragility of instruction sequences, coupled with the propensity of learners to try to recover by initiating exploratory forays, can result in problem tangles: Learners, who may not even fully understand the individual operations, have little basis for appreciating the subtle interdependence of clusters of word processor operations. They may be unable to diagnose or even recognize the problems they encounter.

Passive Learning

When learners do not, or cannot, follow directions the problems that arise can result in their losing track of what they are trying to do. It is likely, of course, that this loss of task orientation contributes to the overall failure of learning—as indicated by the trouble all learners had applying their learning experiences to the routine typing "transfer task" after training.

What is more surprising perhaps is that even when learners were able to successfully follow instruction sequences out, they still seemed to experience a loss of task orientation, as evidenced by comments like: "What did we do?" "I know I did something, but I don't know what it is!" or "I'm getting confused because I'm not actually doing anything except following these directions." For these subjects, the overall orientation toward accomplishing meaningful tasks (e.g., type a letter, print something out) has been subverted by a narrower orientation toward following out a sequence of instructions.

This is ironic, since self-study educational technology is predicated upon learning-by-doing mix of exposition and practice. The materials we used provided expository information about how to do things with the word processing system along side of step-by-step practice with those procedures. The problem seems to be that "learning by doing" means different things to manual designers and new users: following programmed exercises is "active" from the viewpoint of the designers but "passive" from the viewpoint of the learners. Unfortunately for the learners, their innocence about computers prevents them from actively learning by doing on their own with much success—at least given state-of-the-art system/training constellations.

LEARNING BY THINKING

Just as learners take the initiative to try things on their own, so also are they active in trying to make sense of their experience with the system. Learning passively by rote assimilation of information is atypical. Rather, learners actively try to develop hypotheses about why it operates the way it does. These quests after meaning can be triggered by new and salient facts. They can be forced by discrepancies between what is expected and what actually happens. They can be structured by the learner's personal agenda of goals and queries, referred to as new problems arise. And they can be resolved by analysis into elementary procedures in the context of some word processing goal. In each case, learners' lack of knowledge about word processing makes it difficult for them to reason out coherent solutions that accurately represent the objective operation of the word processor.

Constructing Interpretations

Because learners have no basis for recognizing and ruling out irrelevant connections, their interpretations of word processing systems are often influenced by spurious connections between what they think they need and what they perceive. The protocol example in Table 3 provides an example.

A learner is trying to find some way of using a "create document" command to retrieve a document (beginning of segment 2). The command is initiated by filling in parameters of a create document task menu. However, "create document" won't retrieve a document that already exists. Hence, when she fills in the name of the stored document (toward the end of segment 2), she incurs an error. Because the learner does not know what is relevant to getting a document back, she grasps for other possibilities (segments 6–8). The word "number" in a menu parameter called "document charge number" suggests to her that typing in page numbers will retrieve those pages for her. The word "originator" in the parameter called "document originator" suggests that typing in her operator name might somehow tell the system she wants *her* document. Neither parameter has anything to do with document retrieval, and both merely evoke further errors.

Learners are often faced with situations where they perceive a need to interpret some fact or observation in order to make sense of it. Often these interpretations are not necessary for understanding how to do something, but simply reflect their desire to *make sense of their experience.* For example, more than one learner was troubled by an inconsistency in the functions which are used to move the cursor around the screen. One set of functions is used to move the cursor within a menu display, while another set is used to move it around a typing display. The learner reconciled herself to the distinction by reasoning that a cursor movement function which moved the cursor from one line of a document file to another would not work in a menu display, because there could be more than one field on a line of a menu and she decided the function would not be able to move from one field to another *within* a line of a menu. In both cases, the learners could have simply accepted the way things were accomplished. Instead, they tried to construct rationales for why things were done the way they were.

In other cases, learners are faced with the need to *interpret discrepancies* between what happens to them, and what they think should happen. Because they lack knowledge about how the system operates, these ex-

TABLE 3
Not Knowing What Is Relevant to Retrieving a Document

(1) L: Did that make any sense to you? It didn't to me. I don't know why we had to do that, that was ridiculous. Now, let's see how do we get the pages back, that's going to be fun.

(2) *In a selection menu listing things users can do, learner presses enter to bring up a menu which when filled in and entered will create a new document file.*

You know what it's probably going to do now, it's going to tell me that there is a memo in there already. [*She is correct: i.e., she has already created a document named "Memo"; she wants to retrieve, not create this*]

Looks in manual for help.

E: What are you thinking?

L: Well, they were supposed to tell me anyway how to get these pages that I just lost.

In the create document menu she types the name of the document that she wants to get back. A message, "document name already exists," appears.

Document name already exists, I knew that was going to happen because I just typed it in.

(3) *Presses some other keys.*

I don't know how to do this.

E: What did you just press there?
L: Reset.
E: And before that?
L: This again, cancel [*which has no effect when the selection menu for tasks like create or revise is on the display, because there is nothing to cancel*].

Request. *Presses request, cursor in now on "request line."*

I'm just going to type "memo1" and press page return to see if it comes up [*"memo1" is the name of the document*]

Presses request. Looks in manual for help.

E: What are you looking up?

(4) L: I might have to look it up in one of these documents [*refering to tasks listed on the menu. The task or command she needs is listed there*]

I don't remember which one it was. [*Because she has not learned it yet*] Create a document . . . I can't use that.

(5) E: Why don't you think about it a little bit more, and if you still can't figure it out we'll help.

Reads the manual. Presses an invalid key.

L: Invalid key . . .
E: What were you looking for there?
L: Some solution to this problem. . . . We're at a stand still here. . . .

(6) E: You pressed reset a couple of times there?

Without answering presses request, types "cre," and the create document menu appears.

TABLE 3—*Continued*

(7) E: What are you thinking?
L: Would this be, "document charge number," would that be the page number? [*It has nothing to do with page number—she is still in effect trying to create a document*]
Maybe I have to look it up by the page number.
E: What are you thinking?
L: Last time I wrote the document name in there it didn't take it the way I wanted it to take it.

Advances cursor to the "document charge number" parameter.

E: What did you conclude from that, what you just read there?
L: No, No, I didn't read this. [*i.e., she had not noticed the "document charge number" parameter before in the menu for creating a new document*]

Deletes the "001" charge number and types in "0002" page number but overflows the menu field limits and gets an error message to this effect.

Doesn't fit. [*Presses reset to acknowledge error*]

E: Press reset there?

Deletes the "0002."

(8) L: [*Reads*] "document originator," would that be me?

Advances cursor to yet another menu parameter, this one called "document originator." This is where one indicates whose document one is typing, e.g., in an office, one's boss.

She types "learner1", presses enter to enter the create document menu; but because she has not specified a name for this "new" document, she incurs an error "Parameter omitted or not valid." The actions are irrelevant to retrieving a document anyway.

(9) E: What are you thinking?

Learner realizes that she has "paginated" document prematurely rather than after she has completed the exercise she was about to begin. That they should explain that it was going to be done later on. [*i.e., paginate or cause the rearranging of lines of text to right justify*] Cause they said before you do all of this you have to paginate. You will also, oh, no before printing it. So, in other words I assumed that I was supposed to do it right at the beginning, but where as I like wiped myself out. [*In fact, she has not deleted anything—she simply does not know how to retrieve the document file*] But it was done much later on, down here.

planations often are not accurate representations of what is really happening. In one case, a learner tried to decide if a "file" command has stored a document file away. It was not stored because the command was entered in a text input mode where all typed strings are interpreted as text, and not executed as commands. But she assumed that the file had been stored, and adduced evidence to confirm this premise. Not knowing what is really relevant, the learner found two features of the screen that were superficially similar to what one might hypothesize if the file command had been successful, and the learner concluded the document had been stored. For example, at one point she notices a status message "input mode 1 file" which indicates that she is in the text input mode. However, the word "file" matched her file command, and this was enough to suggest some kind of feedback that her "file" (as in store document) command had worked.

Table 4 illustrates a slightly different kind of reasoning in which a learner copes with a number of problems as she tried to sign on to a command-based word processing system we studied. For example, in segment 1 she is trying to decide where to enter the password. The correct point is the command line on the bottom of the display (where other commands have been entered). However, the explanation of signing on that she is following is not explicit about this, and the learner fills in by trying to type the password at the top of the display next to the "password:" prompt (perhaps she thought of this as a blank line of a form that one might fill out). This area of the display is a protected area and her attempt to type locks the keyboard and cursor. But in segment 3 she hypothesizes that inability to move the cursor at that point means the cursor is already in the right location to type! Finally, in segment 4 the learner seems to conclude that the lack of response to her password is the result of heavy load on the system!

How can we characterize these reasoning processes? In some cases, reasoning appears to consist in *adducing* factual support to a premise the learner would like to hold as true. Table 4 shows that the learner began with the hypothesis that she had stored the document file away, and sought evidence to confirm that this was the case. Her adduction here was incorrect because she did not know which facts were relevant to verifying the premise. She was persuaded that the superficially relevant word "file" in the status message signaled successful storing of the file.

In other cases, reasoning appears to consist in *abducing* (Peirce, 1958) a hypothesis when it, together with other assumptions the learner may already hold, is consistent with some fact or observation. An example in Table 4 (segment 1) is the learner's hypothesis the password is entered like an item in a form, that is, after the password prompt with the colon (rather than on the command line like other entries into the system). Other examples of abduction and a fuller discussion can be found in Lewis and Mack (1982).

Abductions and adductions are often incomplete and partial: people do not test them against all potentially relevant data. In particular, people tend to reason only from confirming evidence—and to overlook potentially disconfirming evidence (see Nisbett & Ross, 1980). As a consequence, learners are able to construct and verify ad hoc interpretations of what happens which may misrepresent the situation they are actually in.

Nevertheless, adductive and abductive reasoning processes are important in that they afford net growth in knowledge without requiring extensive prerequisite knowledge. In contrast, both classical methods of reasoning—deductive and induction—impose this requirement. Deduction requires an extensive knowledge base of principles from which univocal predictions can be derived. Induction requires an extensive and systematic empirical data base—and in any case cannot guarantee the validity of its conclusions. Neither of these two methods would be appropriate for our learners. This is because the information they have available about the system is typically too impoverished to allow them to build up representations by systematic induction and deduction, even assuming that people are sophisticated and motivated enough to do this. Abduction and adduction provide means of generating and supporting hypotheses from limited information.

Setting Goals and Solving Problems

Beyond merely trying to interpret experiences, learners often set goals which they actively pursue by trying to solve problems. They are hampered in this by not knowing the appropriate problem space, or domain of possible actions and interpretations relevant to accomplishing goals and addressing queries. Accordingly, their strategies are often local and fragmentary; they have difficulty integrating information or other experiences, and in formulating their concerns in ways that map transparently onto system functions. Learners appear to construct a personal agenda of goals and queries as they go along. As situations arise, this agenda is referred to opportunistically: fragmentary aspects of the local situation are assimilated to some standing goal or query.

Table 3 provides an example of the local and fragmentary character of setting goals and solving problems. Recall that the learner in this example is trying to retrieve a document she has inadvertently stored, but does not yet know how to do this. Segments 2 and 4 suggest that the learner has a relatively accurate general idea of what her problem is and what goal she should pursue: retrieve a document. In segment 4 she even tumbles to a relatively good strategy for solving the problem, namely, look for a command listed on the selection menu which could retrieve her document. Unfortunately, the correct command, while listed there in fact, evidently does not have a suggestive name and the learner drops that strategy without trying anything out.

Instead, beginning in segment 6, the learner tries to exploit a create document task with which she is already quite familiar. While the learner again reveals partial insight into her the adequacy of her strategy by suggesting (correctly) the she will incur an error using the create task (users cannot "recreate" existing files), she nevertheless incurs an error when she tries to retrieve her document using this command.

TABLE 4
Abductive Inferences in Signing On to the Text-Processing System

(1) L: OK, let's try it again. [*i.e., type password*] I'm on the wrong keys. Password, now type in your password. Now I can only type by going up correct? It's not telling me that. I'm assuming I can take the cursor up there.

I.e., learner does not know where to put cursor. In fact, it is already on the command line where the password should be entered. But the learner decides to move the cursor up the display right after the password prompt at the top of the screen.

(2) *After moving the cursor up the screen, she tries to type password, but this is a protected area of display which causes the keyboard to lock until a reset key is pressed. An "input inhibited" light also comes on.*

I expected it to come out. I expected to see the word. [*i.e., password*] but it's . . .

E: What happened?
L: It probably fed it and I made, umm, contact without showing it here, because it is a password and not everybody knows it generally. So it's sort of a secret between me and the computer.

Rereads description of password.

"The password will not print what you typed. If you are correct the display will blink and in a moment a few lines of greeting messages . . ." and evidently it's not right.

E: OK, what makes you think it's not right?
L: Cause it's not blinking. OK, do I? Ok, let's see the display will, at this point the display will . . . the word will appear, um.

The keyboard is locked, the cursor is in a protected area to the right of the password prompt.

(3) I assume maybe I should space one [*after the password*] Would that maybe [*work*]?

Tries moving cursor one space to the right of colon using space bar, cursor movement blocked because of locked keyboard condition.

Well it doesn't even space so I'm in my right position.

Tries typing password again

E: Ok, you just typed it again.
L: Shouldn't I hit enter?

(4) *Notices the input inhibited light on the display.* What do you think that means?

E: What were you pointing at?
L: The input inhibited [*light on the display*]. Is that possibly why that's not accepting that at the moment?

[*After brief digression*] I've seen that all too often. *She had had some experience using terminals for data entry.*

E: Well, what do you think that means?
L: So it's being held up temporarily. I don't think there's anything you can do at the moment until the light goes off. Oh it might be accepting my, it could be accepting my . . . what I put in and it will go off as soon as it's um . . . When you put information on there now maybe it . . . the input, the fact that you're putting in . . .
The learner is unable to develop any hypothesis as to why the system will not respond or accept input. The experimenters later were forced to intervene.

In light of these experiences, segments 7 and 8 are especially interesting. Despite her interpretation of the inappropriateness of the "create document" task for retrieving the document (segments 2 and 4), the learner returns to this menu and hypothesizes that other parameters of the task might be relevant to getting her document back. As we discussed in the preceding subsection, the learner does not know what is relevant to her goal, and so can entertain even specious hypotheses about what might be relevant based on very superficial resemblances. For example, the learner fills in the page number in a menu field labeled "document charge number" because the word "number" suggests page numbering.

Table 2 describes another example of how difficult it is for learners to formulate goals, and find information relevant to solving them. In segment 8 the learner tried to delete a blank line she had inadvertently inserted between two sentences. However, she did not describe her problem in this way, but thought of it as one of bringing the bottom sentence back under the first one (segment 6). The relevance problem arises during her search for some way to "bring the sentence back": the label "Required Return" on a carrier return key seemed to be relevant to this problem. In fact, the connection is specious. The Required Return function is just another version of the return key and resulted in the learner inserting yet another blank line.

When learners cannot solve a problem or resolve some query immediately, it may be saved away on a task agenda—with the hope that an answer will be found later. The goals and queries on this task agenda are typically addressed opportunistically rather than through systematic problem solving. (See Hayes-Roth and Hayes-Roth, 1979, for related views of planning behavior.) An example is the learner who initially misinterpreted why the word processing system did not let her sign on (i.e., in segment 6 of Table 1, the learner thinks she must be in a "Test Mode" to work on the system). Later (segment 7), when she dealt with a similar problem situation it occurred to her that her current (correct) interpretation was probably applicable to her earlier difficulty. Not only did this learner reconsider her earlier erroneous interpretation, she actually tried (segment 8) to recreate the original problem situation.

The learner in Table 2 who tried to correct a typing error before she had learned how to do so had been anxious for some time to discover how to correct typos. In another case (not shown in tables), a learner had unintentionally accumulated a number of special characters ahead of the cursor. The system is always in insert state so this material was pushed along as she typed. Of course, she wanted to eliminate this unsightly mess but did not know how (the delete key would have worked). It was only much later while she was learning how to delete another kind of special character that she realized the same operation might solve her earlier problem: indeed, when she next had the opportunity, she performed the appropriate deletion.

Consolidating Procedures

The word processing domain is highly procedural. Learners must analyze basic procedures in the context of various word processing goals. This is not a matter of rote learning and passive assimilation; even the simplest procedures like word deletion or replacing a letter reveals the difficult task of identifying relevant elements of these procedures and trying to integrate them into a smooth operation. Learners' understanding of procedures works by successive approximations. Learners form general schemata or rules for those elements relevant to a procedure. These general schemata are then filled out in the course of interacting with the word processing system.

Table 5 shows an example of a learner who is trying to delete the underscoring for the three words, ". . . will not change." The underscoring itself looks normal but it is marked by a special underscore character which is a block of reversed video superimposed on the space immediately following the word. To delete it, the user must position the cursor "under" the character in such a way that a message "word underscore" appears on an information line at the top of the display. (It is not enough that the cursor is spatially under the reversed video block.)

The learner's attempts to coordinate her initial understanding of this delete operation demonstrate the *revelatory nature* of trying actions out: a sequence of actions and events is consolidated into a procedural concept. The learner has the correct general idea of positioning the cursor under a character and then using a delete function to delete it (evidenced in segments 1 and 2), but does not incorporate the critical feedback from the information line at the top of the screen. The procedure has been incompletely instantiated. Even though the learner has read all this, and as the example shows will read about it all again (e.g., segment 5), its significance only becomes apparent through careful and detailed attempts (segment 6) to actually integrate and exercise the procedure.

One obstacle to integrating the elements of procedures, again, is the learner's innocence. In Table 5 (segments 7 through 11), the learner tries to replace a small "t" with a capital "T" in the word "the." The learner deletes the "t" correctly, but then formulates her goal of replacing it with a "T" to be one of replacing the space at the front of the string "_he" rather than simply inserting the "T" at the beginning of the string. Of course, the "T" is in effect inserted in the existing string which now includes a space, producing the string "T_he." In segments 9 through 11 she struggles to understand this procedure by tying the

TABLE 5
Deleting a Word Underscore and Replacing a Letter

(1) *The learner is trying to delete the underscore from the second of three words "will not change." She is not locating the cursor in a way that identifies the special underscore character*

L: What happened? The line [*underscore line*] didn't disappear, now what did I do? Was I over too many spaces? I could have been.

(2) Let me try again. I can replace the other one anyway. *Presses character delete, deleting the "c" of the third word "change." Not clear why she did this.*

What's happening?

Positions cursor immediately after the third word and "under" the underscore instruction, so that the character delete operation correctly deletes the underscore from that word.

It worked on that one, I don't understand. *Here is the problem: Underscore is represented by a special character symbol. To delete, the cursor must be positioned "under" this symbol and then deleted as any other character. The learner did not enter underscore instruction at the correct location for the second word but did so for the third. Therefore her action of locating cursor "under" the underscore character works as per instructions for the third, but not the second word. The learner does not understand what the instructions really mean or she would be able to recognize the discrepancy, and modify the instructions for the second word.*

(3) *Presses word delete key, and deletes the third and fourth words.*

E: What did you just press there?
L: I just pressed word delete.

Moves cursor to the next word and deletes it.

Oh, wait a minute, that keeps moving all of them. [*i.e., the line adjusts after material has been deleted*]

Looks in manual for information Checking out something here under [*the topic of*] word delete.

E: What is it that you're looking for?
L: I'm just trying to see . . .

(4) *"Not" is still underlined and every word in the line after "not" has been deleted.*

I got a little paranoid when I saw everything moving backward. I thought "wait a minute." Now, I realized I wanted to erase the whole thing anyway and retype it and then. . . . Because I lost a space in there and I couldn't get rid of the line under "not."

E: What were you looking for when you looked under [*the topic of*] word delete?
L: Yes, for some reason I was afraid. I saw this moving over and I saw this moving over and I was afraid that I was going to erase. I don't know I'd . . . I'd forgotten that everything was going to move over anyway as you erase, as you delete. So, I didn't want to go on to the next word, although actually I may have to erase that also. OK, I'll see, I'll see if I can type this, retype this line . . .

Types in the rest of the sentence, after underscored "not."

Oh, that's OK, alright.

(5) *Moves the cursor back to the space before the underscored word "not."*

(*continued*)

TABLE 5—*Continued*

E: What are you looking for now?
L: OK, I'm just looking to see what it says here again. [*I want to*] start again with the underscore . . . deleting the underscore. . . . Yes, no I'm just going over what I did before.

Still trying to delete the underscore line under "not," places the cursor under the space after the "t" and deletes a space.

Oh, what did I do?

(6) *Moves the cursor under the "t" in "not," then moves the cursor to the space after the "t."* I see, OK, I didn't realize that before. I didn't realize it [*the cursor*] has to pass through . . . the underscore. It has to pass through the underscore from what I understand.

E: How did you find that?
L: Um, under the, under the delete underscore instructions.

When she moves the cursor under the "t," the message "word under" appears on the screen.

I did that automatically before. It was supposed to be under the last letter of the underscore. *Presses a delete function with the cursor "under" the underscore symbol; the underscore is deleted.*

(7) *Learner moves on to another instruction for revising, this one involving replacing of a "t" with a "T" in the word "the" which is the first word of a newly revised sentence.*

(8) *She deletes the "t" in "the" to produce the string "he" with the cursor positioned under the "h." But before she tries to type the "T" she moves the cursor to the left, back under the space before the "he." Thus when she types "T" she actually inserts it in front of the space to produce "T he"; i.e., with a gap.*

E: What are you thinking?
L: OK, um, when I deleted the "t" and typed the capital "T," I created a space. Why is it doing this?

(9) *Looks in manual for help.*
E: Where are you reading now?
L: OK, I'm reading under character delete, I'm just . . . I'm trying to find out why when I retyped another character in place of the one I just deleted . . . um, I'm just wondering, there's another space after that now separating "T" and "h."

(10) *Places the cursor in the space between "T" and "h" and inserts another "T." Perhaps she is convincing herself that this really happened. Then she turns back to the manual section on deleting material.*

It says they move together.

E: Was that a particular thing you just said?
L: OK, it says, the instructions say that when you delete something the letters will move together to fill it in. OK, now that. . . . I don't understand why there's a space there as soon as I type the other one.

(11) [*Sometime later learner speculates*] When you delete, you take out. Do you add when you put in?

"addition" of text to her earlier experience deleting it. As she puts it in segment 11: "When you delete, you take out. Do you add when you put in?" Her real problem though is not recognizing that an important element of this procedure is the fact that the word processing system is always in insert mode.

A second problem, we have also seen before, that confronts this process of integrating basic procedures is that of problem tangling. In Table 5, for example, the learner had incorrectly underscored the second word of the triple (i.e., in the triple "will not change," the underscore character for "not" was originally entered at the last letter of the word, not under the interword spacing). Thus, while the learner was able to delete the underscoring for the third word "change" (segment 2), the same procedure mysteriously does not seem to work for the second word "not." The problem could be solved either by recognizing the earlier error, or by recognizing the correct feedback for locating the underscore character. Since the learner cannot untangle these problems, she cannot properly execute the procedure, which remains mysterious to her.

These examples suggest that even the simplest operations present learners with serious challenges. They must translate expository descriptions of operations into actions. They must coordinate multiple sources of information (on display, in manual, and from memory). And it is clear that the significance of the various elements of procedures (what they accomplish, what prerequisites are needed, what are relevant outcomes, etc.) only become tangible to learners in the context of their actually interacting with the system.

LEARNING BY KNOWING

Learning by reasoning and problem solving presupposes a well-defined "problem space": knowledge of what is relevant to particular goals, of how to constrain interpretations and goal-related actions, etc. Our learners understood the problem space of the conventional office, but not that of the "electronic office"—in particular, they did not understand the problem space of word processing. Nevertheless, they spontaneously referred to substantive prior knowledge from the former domain in order to understand the latter. We will refer to this as "learning by knowing"; it has often been called "metaphor" (Bott, 1979; Carroll & Thomas, 1982; Rumelhart & Ortony, 1977).

To this point, we have argued that a new user of a word processor relies without instruction on active exploration and ad hoc reasoning as learning strategies. However, not all possibilities are explored and not all hypotheses that could be reached are reached. What constrains these strategies is a sense of what could be appropriate—and this devolves from prior knowledge on the part of the learner: knowledge about devices "like" word processors (e.g., typewriters), knowledge about office routine and work in general, even knowledge culled from interacting with the word processor up to that point in time.

The Typewriter Metaphor

Office personnel learning to use a word processor typically have an extensive and fairly coherent body of knowledge regarding typewriters to which they can refer. Indeed, our learners were not able to resist referring to their prior knowledge about typewriters as a basis for interpreting and predicting experience with word processors.

One of our learners came to a halt as she read an instruction in the manual which said "Backspace to erase." It seemed that she could not interpret this instruction for, as she pointed out, backspace does not erase anything. She had irresistibly availed herself of her knowledge of how backspacing works on a typewriter, unable to even consider that this knowledge might be inappropriate for the present case. The incident had a sad ending, too. In wrestling with this problem, she accidentally incurred a "reset" condition, repositioning the cursor at the beginning of the word. Hence, when she finally elected to plunge ahead and "backspace to erase," it in fact did not work.

For a second example, recall the learner in Table 2 who was trying to move the cursor through a line of text to correct a typing mistake. Without any hesitation, she presses the space bar. She is surprised to see that this inserts a space into her text. Now, just as automatically, she presses the backspace key. This deletes the space. What is interesting in this example is first, that the space bar is expected to advance the cursor without inserting spaces, as it would do on a typewriter. Second, it is notable that when it fails to behave as anticipated, backspace is employed as an inverse operation—again just as it is on the typewriter. Neither of the expectations is thought out, rather both are immediately available in virtue of the learner's prior knowledge of typewriters. Fortunately, although the first expectation is thwarted, the second obtains: the space bar fails to provide a vehicle for cursor movement through text, but backspace succeeds in inverting the operation (including the undesired side effect).

To continue with this example (segment 5), the learner decides to abandon the goal of correcting her typing error (possibly because she cannot manage to get the cursor to the site of the error). She now wishes to advance the cursor and continue entering text. Again, with no deliberation, she keypresses the carriage return (segment 6): a blank line is inserted into the text. "Whoa!" The learner is surprised by this. Like the side effect of the space bar, it is discrepant with her expectations based on typewriters (where carriage return advances the typing point but does not insert lines)—and worse, there is no obvious predictable inverse operation available to her.

Expectations about Work

Our learners were experienced with conventional office work: typing letters, filing, etc. Their knowledge about how these routine tasks are organized in the office creates expectations in them about how analogous tasks ought to be performed in the "office of the future" (as represented by the word processor in our laboratory). Thus, one response to revising a letter task is to retype. This is striking since it is the capability of the word processor to store and retrieve documents—for revision, among other things—that is its fundamental advance over previous office technologies.

Another example of mismatched expectations is the correspondence between the typing page on the word processor and what learners expect a typing page to be from typewriting. The system ostensibly frees users from worrying about margins and formatting by doing these things automatically during printing, and having default settings. But new users can be troubled by these labor-saving features: the differences between a familiar piece of paper in a typewriter and the typing display raise many questions that are not easily answered early in learning. Learners wonder where the top and bottom, left and right margins are located on the display. They wonder how the length of the typing display corresponds to the length of a printed page (this is a relationship automatically controlled by the pagination feature). And they wonder whether error and status messages which appeared on the typing display would be part of their final product.

The learner's expectations about work transcend knowledge of how office procedures are carried out. They include motivational expectations about work-related learning and sociological expectations about power and control in work-related settings. These expectations can differ remarkably, as evidenced by comparing our learners to a college teacher learning to use a programmable calculator (Carroll & Lasher, 1981). This person was in fact, suffering many of the problems we have described above. In one particular incident, she was unable to make sense of several passages in the training manual.

Now in analogous situations our typist-learners typically concluded that the fault was their own, that they were too stupid to understand properly. However, our Ph.D. learner came to an entirely different conclusion: she decided that the manual contained misprints or other errors and could not, therefore, be used. She discarded it at that point—*never* considering the possibility that she was too stupid to understand in general, or even that the specific trouble was in part due to her own miscoordination of information. We believe that this manifest difference in attitudes is partly because the typist subjects identify with social powerlessness and hence expect to be victimized in work-related undertakings. However, we are basing this on a single comparison subject, and our interpretation must be weighed accordingly.

A final point we will simply make now and then return to later is that our learners seemed to expect a dichotomy between work-related learning and play. Of course work and play *are* different classes of activities for most people, but in learning it can be useful to adopt some aspects of a play orientation. Just as a causal observation, it seems that the capacity to shift gears a little and to treat work as play is characteristic of successful adult learners and problem solvers. The reluctance of our learners to do this (which was something the manual encouraged) may constitute a fairly abstract orientational learning obstacle.

Integrating Bits and Pieces

As a learning experience progresses, the learner is acquiring and organizing new bits of knowledge. The ultimate goal—and the final measure of success in the learning situation—is that of assembling these pieces into a coherent fabric, an understanding of the word processor. Along the way, any prior bit of knowledge is available for use as a basis for expectations concerning successive interactions with the system. Learners expect functional consistency from operations with similar names. One system we studied contained inconsistencies of this sort. Thus, to delete a word, one positions the cursor under the word's initial character and keypresses a word delete. However, to underscore a word, one positions the cursor under the final character of a word and keypresses the word underscore command.

This inconsistency caused one learner to misexecute one and then the other of these two operations in a dismal cycle of negative transfer as illustrated in Table 6. In two earlier episodes (not described in the table) the learner had followed explicit instructions for underscoring and deleting, and understood both. The episodes shown in segments 1–7 reveal that the learner eventually formed correct rules to cover both cases. For example, after learning how to underscore and delete on the first

TABLE 6
Learning Where to Position the Cursor for Deleting, Underscoring, and Backspacing

(1) *On Day 3 learner is about to underscore the word "solutions" but has positioned the cursor under the first letter, rather than at the correct position at the end of the word*

E: What are you doing?
L: I'm trying to code word underline [*i.e., To underline a user must press a word underline function in conjunction with a code function*]

Today I remembered which key it is [*she had trouble finding the word underscore key the day before*] but evidentally I didn't hit it in the right sequence.

Not clear what reference is, but in her first experience with the function the day before, she had pressed the code key after the word underscore key, which is the wrong sequence for underscoring—but her current problem derives from having a wrong cursor position.

Why didn't it underline? Oh, I should have . . .

E: Can you talk aloud about what you are thinking?

(2) L: Yes. Ah. I'm thinking, I'm looking at the word "solutions" on page 3–19. I wanted to underline it. I brought the cursor back under the "s" [*first "s" of the word*] before I hit the code underline. And I think that the code underline should have been hit at the end of the word. [*She is correct: i.e., the cursor should have been at end of word, not beginning.*]
E: Why do you think that?
L: Because it only underlined one thing [*the first "s" of "solutions"*]. I think.

She is correct. She then moves the cursor to the end of word and correctly underscores

(3) *On Day 2, learner is trying to reconstruct the correct position of the cursor in order to delete a word. She had learned the day before that the correct position is at the beginning of the word*

L: They have a code word delete. [*i.e., reference to the necessity of holding a code key while pressing a key labeled "word delete"*]
E: They what?
L: Code word delete. Now what I'm trying to figure out . . . in these instructions they didn't tell me where the cursor should be when I do the deletion. I think probably right after the last character of the word. So we'll go see.

We're going to get the cursor down to the word we want to work on. So we are going to line advance twice. [*i.e., press function to advance the cursor down a line*] And the word we want to work on is "have." So we are going to word advance to that [*i.e., use a function which advances the cursor to the next word within a line*]

Cursor positioned at beginning of "have." Now I think probably that I want to be at the end of it to eliminate it. *Uses character advance key to position cursor at end of "have."*

Okay as though I had just typed it and now they have a two down [*numbered manual instruction*] they want me to code word delete. So. Find "word." I want to be sure I'm watching [*the display*] so that I can see what happens.

(4) *Pressed code plus word delete and deletes space between "have" and next word so they are concatenated*

Oh no!
E: What happened?

(*continued*)

TABLE 6—*Continued*

L: I lost the space. So I have to put the space back in.
Presses backspace which deletes the "e"
Oh no! Now I lost the "e"!
E: What . . .?
L: Terrible!
E: What did you press to [*try to*] put the space back in?
L: I pressed the backspace [*which deletes*].

(5) Okay, now let's see. I tell you what I'm going to do. I going to press the "e" which I lost. [*Inserts "e" to restore "have"*] It moves it over [*i.e., inserts*]. Then I'll press a space which I lost *Presses space bar to insert space between "have" and next word.*

I'm going to take the cursor and character return it to the "e" [*i.e., uses function to return cursor one position left; in this case under "e" of "have"*] and then I'm going to code word delete again and see what happens there.

Ah, my whole problem here is. . . . *Positions cursor under "e" and presses code followed by word delete which again deletes the "e." Repeats to now delete the interword space.*

No, that wasn't the answer either.

E: What did you do?
L: I pressed code word delete and all I lost was a letter [*i.e., "e"*].
E: That's not what you expected?
L: No. I expected to lose [*delete*] the whole word "have."
E: What makes you think that?
L: Well, I thought it would take the whole word out.

(6) Now maybe I coded word delete in the wrong place. So let's put the "have" back in, the "have" and the space. Um. Is the space in? I'm going to go all the way back to the beginning of "have" with the cursor.

Repositions cursor under "h" of "have." And at the beginning of "have" I'm going to put code word delete and see if it takes the whole word "have" out.

Presses code and word delete which deletes "have". Yeah. That was the proper way. So when you use that you have to be at the beginning of the word you want to delete.

(7) E: Can you think of any particular reason why you thought that? That it had to be at the end of a word rather than at the beginning?

L: Because you can't delete it unless its already there. And if you were typing on you might decide you wanted to delete something right after you typed it.
E: I see.
L: And you would do it at the end. But I see that wouldn't work. You would have to get the cursor back to the beginning of the word if you wanted to delete the whole word.
E: Does that make sense to you now?
L: Yes. It's all right. If that's the way it works, that's fine. I still don't know why I was told to code line delete at the other one instead of coding word delete. And I'm very grateful but I don't know why I didn't lose one of those lines.

(8) *On Day 4, learner is reconstructing how to underscore a word. She tries to position the cursor at the beginning of the word, rather than correctly at the end as she learned on at least two previous occasions.*

TABLE 6—*Continued*

L: Just sitting in the office I would just take a chance that that would underline.

Pressing word underscore with the cursor under the first letter of the word underscores that letter only, and superimposes a block of reversed video to mark the underscore character.

If it didn't I would have to go to the book and find out.

(9) E: Well, this is just a question. I think we are beginning to wrap up. In the past when you used the word underline did it actually put underlining on the screen?
L: I can't remember today [*in fact, it had underlined completely*]
E: You can't remember whether it does or doesn't?
L: Whether it did or did not. But I'm not particularly worried, because the rectangle means there is an instruction at that point and the only instruction I put in was word underline.
E: Right
L: And I think I put it in at the right place. I think to give an instruction you have to be at the first character of that word. Like in other words to delete the word I found out you don't delete it at the end. You can't type delete just after you typed the word.

You have to get the cursor under the first character of the word and then type word delete to take out the word.

(10) E: Can I ask you a question about that? For awhile we noted that when you wanted to delete a word or a line you put the cursor at the end of that respective unit, whether word or line
L: Yeah, I didn't know how to do it.
E: Why did you do that?
L: Because I figured that it was the last thing entered and that it might just erase the last thing entered. Not a very . . . oh, also I think on a line delete I did that, too. I don't remember what happened whether it took out the next line or it didn't because the carriage return was in there. I really don't know what happened.

She is referring to an earlier experience in which she tried to delete the last part of a line with the cursor incorrectly located at the end of that line. It didn't work but was sufficiently ambiguous that this may not have impressed her.

day, segments 1 and 2 reveal that on the third day the learner erroneously tried to underscore with cursor at the *beginning* of the word ("solutions"). Why did she assume this after learning the correct procedure earlier? The protocols are not clear in this segment, but the same problem arose on the fourth day and in this case the learner's explanation suggests a generalization based on deleting words.

This second instance of trying to underscore with the cursor at the beginning (rather than at the end) of a word is shown in segments 8–10. When we finally asked her why she did this, she suggested: "I think to give an instruction you have to be at the first character of that word. Like, in other words, to delete the word I found out you don't delete it at the end [i.e., with cursor at the end of the word] . . . You have to get the cursor under the first character of the word and then type word delete, i.e., press the word delete function, to take out the word". This generalization about deleting, was hard-won in its own right as segments 3–7 reveal. The learner spent considerable time working out the fact that she must put the cursor at the beginning of the word she wants to delete, rather than at the end.

A similar inconsistency in this system involved cursor movement. In a menu, the cursor is advanced from one line to the next by pressing a variable advance key. However, in text the cursor is properly advanced from one line to the next by means of a *line* advance key. Learners tended not to acknowledge this distinction and to flop back and forth depending on whether they had more recently been on a menu or a typing display. Of course, this reliance on immediately prior experience led to numerous errors.

The problem of prior knowledge is not a simple one. On the one hand, we might say that learners will rely on their prior knowledge, and that developers of new technologies ought to take this fact of human cognitive learning into account in designing systems and in designing the educational technologies that accompany and introduce them. However, this is paradoxical: can we reasonably expect that new technologies can be constrained by old ones in this way?

More specifically, should long-term innovations in word processors be constrained by nonoptimal properties that typewriters merely happen to have as an accident of their history? Can we even find suitable metaphors for presenting new technologies to learners? Again, to be specific, should a radical innovation in word processing be eschewed merely because there is no apparent way to couch it as an extended super-typewriter?

DESIGNING FOR EASE OF LEARNING

Learning, as we have tried to suggest, is an active process. It is inescapably directed by the learner. This fact is not altered when educational technologies—like self-instruction manuals (and the systems to which they refer)—are designed to place the learner in a relatively passive role. Rather, the learning experience becomes chaotic, frustrating, and inefficient.

Cognitive science, by focusing attention on ecologically valid learning situations of nontrivial complexity, can address the theoretical and practical issues underlying the current misfit of state-of-the-art learning technology to human learners. We close this discussion by sketching three projects this might encompass.

Conceptual Framework

Learners do not "absorb" knowledge: they create, explore, and integrate knowledge. New word processor technologies, and the educational technologies that support them, must take this picture of learning seriously. Prior knowledge, for example knowledge of typewriters and routine office tasks, seems to be almost accidentally relevant—sometimes transfer is positive and sometimes negative. And this is not to presume that the issues are simple; it is merely to observe that they have not been addressed seriously to date.

We should stress that we are not urging that metaphors be explicitly and discursively presented to new users (cf. Halasz & Moran, 1982). If a metaphor must be explicitly taught to a new user, it is contributing to the amount of material that must be learned instead of relieving this burden. The best metaphor is obviously one that is implicitly and automatically suggested to the user merely by the appearance and behavior of a system. Such a metaphor maximizes the potential savings in learning effort. The well-known Query-By-Example system (Zloof, 1977) did just this by suggesting the metaphor of paper tables to users of a data base query system. The Smalltalk programming language also attempted to make use of familiar metaphors (Ingalls, 1981).

Of course, not all aspects of all systems can be as easily and elegantly fitted to metaphors. Indeed, our experience in studying the learning process in this area, inclines us to stress how easy it is to *underestimate* the subtlety, the novelty, and the complexity of the design features of computer systems. What metaphor might cover the "data stream" concept. that is the fact that the system's internal representation of objects like the "typing page" are actually linear strings of symbols? Failure to appreciate the data stream concept may indeed underlie many of the "quirks" our learners struggled with regarding insert mode, line return characters, and the like (e.g., a "blank line" on the "typing page" is represented internally as a single character). Suggesting a misleading or inconsistent metaphor through a feature of a user interface may create more learning problems than it mitigates.

Must new technology be burdened with "metaphoric compatibility" constraints? In designing the word processors of the future, will we always have to try to pretend that they are typewriters for the sake of our innocent new users? It seems to us that this is not the way to put things. For example, one can imagine the following possibility: a new office system is created—it is indeed not merely just another super typewriter (we leave open what it might be). How can it presented to new users to reap the benefits of prior knowledge and avoid the pitfalls?

A programmatic solution would be to envision a series of user interfaces; the first very much like a typewriter (in effect concealing from the user much of the innovative function that the system has to offer). The second user interface, is richer—less strictly tied to typewriter concepts—and for users who have progressed to mastery of the initial interface. The program should be clear. No one today thinks of a typewriter as a super pencil, and no one would seriously argue that technology should stop with typewriters. However, this does not mean that the cognitive–social transition from typewriters to super word processors must necessarily be as uncoordinated as was that from pencils to typewriters (but cf. Schrodt, 1982).

Indeed, the approach we have just sketched can be elaborated somewhat. It may be too strict a constraint to expect that a single metaphor or a patently obvious metaphor (like the typewriter metaphor) will always be immediately available (or even imaginable) in new areas of technological innovation. So far, we have limited our consideration to monolithic metaphors spontaneously generated by learners as they begin to interact with a system. The possibility is open—and intriguing—that aspects of prior knowledge could be brought to consciousness and assembled into composite metaphors.

The kind of educational technology we are imagining here has simply not been developed. Accordingly, there is little more we can offer at this time. Even if one eschews an active orientation toward the construction of learning metaphors, it seems crucial to guide learners at least to the extent that they should be warned about the limits to which a metaphor can be employed. The implicit typewriter metaphor we identified in our learner's conceptualizations often caused problems for them when it was inappropriate: such cases should be ferreted out and identified for new users.

Exploratory Environments

If the picture of learning we have given here is anything close to correct, it suggests that an optimal learning environment for new users will differ from that provided by current systems. Indeed, the disparity between what exists currently and what would seem to constitute a reasonable learning environment is so great that we are only able to capture the grossest properties of what we imagine would be an optimal learning environment. By definition we will refer to this as an "exploratory environment"; our reason for choosing this term will become clearer presently.

One property of an exploratory environment is that it provides learners with *an appropriate orientation toward the task:* learners approach the task of learning to use a word processor with highly discrepant expectations about what it will be like and how difficult it will be. They—and their bosses—may understand from popular misconception that word processors are easy to learn to use and that using them will result in immediate and substantial productivity increases. This might even be true if the means of instruction is personal tutoring. However, if the means of instruction is contemporary self-study, this is far from the truth—as our studies demonstrate. Realistic expectations about the difficulty of learning to use word processing equipment would at the very least discourage attributions of self-blame on the part of learners. And this, in turn, would at the very least make learning to use these systems more pleasant.

Another aspect of realistic task orientation involves learner responsibility and control. Manuals and system interfaces implicitly attempt to place the learner in a passive role, but as we have seen learners take charge regardless. Nevertheless, the conflict between a manual/system ensemble that directs rote exercises on, say, cursor movement, and an active learner who decides in spite of this to explore techniques of typo correction is problematic: the learner will "fail" in some sense no matter what the outcome. An exploratory environment establishes and reinforces a role of responsibility and control for the learner *via* the system interface and training materials. (Some of our current research work is addressed to this and we return to it briefly in the final section of this study.)

A second property of an exploratory environment is *system simplicity:* learner problems will tangle to the extent that systems afford problem tangling. Systems should, therefore, be designed to minimize potential for tangling. However, this does not at al mean that "function" must be traded for simplicity vis-à-vis the user interface. Earlier we suggested a "staged" sequence for user interfaces. The initial user interface, on this proposal, would indeed trade function for simplicity, but it would do this by shielding the new user from potentially tangling function. In any case, new users are not the ones who complain about limitations of function. Successive interfaces would increase the amount of revealed function—and therefore the potential for problem tangling—but staged in a way that would minimize the risks to learning at any given point in the process.

An alternative approach to achieving this sort of simplicity has been called "progressive disclosure" (Smith, Irby, Kimball, Verplank, & Harslem, 1982). An interface organized this way stages each function separately and places the staging sequence under the user's control. This is a more flexible approach than that of staging the entire interface as a whole and *shielding* the user from control, even awareness, of this. On the other hand, progressive disclosure, although it quite literally makes the learner "ask" for trouble, does allow such requests to be fulfilled.

Simplicitly connects directly to several other properties of exploratory environments, in particular to *clarity* and *safety*. Systems are often unclear in the sense that they do not inform the user of what state they are currently in, what they are currently doing, or even what they must have just done. In one system we studied, even the command to sign-off occasioned no confirmation message at all: the system merely put up the sign-on menu (presumably for the next user). New users do not recognize that "hello" *means* "good-bye" in systems. They frequently signed on again and then asked us how they were ever going to get off of the system!

In the same system, the command to print a document elicited a confirmation message that was routed to a "message reservoir." Here the message waited for the user to request it to be displayed. The trouble is that a user might not realize what has happened and/or might not know how to display a message. This could result in the message being displayed at a time much later than that at which it was sent. Thus when one least expected it, one could learn that file such-and-such had been printed. These problems of the amount and the timing of feedback are rather easily dealt with, at least in principle: why not have more feedback and present it in a more timely fashion? (The relevant design trade off here is that the presentation of feedback might interrupt a succeeding task and thereby distract the user—but this rationale doesn't make printing any less inscrutable for the learner.)

But a further, and far less trivial, feedback problem is that the content of messages is not typically "problem-oriented." Learners do not want to read messages like "parameter omitted or not valid." They want to find out what they did wrong *in that case* with regard to their own current goals—and they would like to know what to try next to achieve those goals. This kind of situation is devastating for current Help systems. We have many times seen subjects examine a Help screen which, in fact, contained the information they needed, but which presented that information in a problem-neutral manner. Since the learners were construing their needs in a problem-oriented "vocabulary," they simply failed to see the relevance of the Help.

Addressing this problem at all would require a task-analysis-driven approach to interface design that regards *learning* as a key user task. Addressing it comprehensively would require building in some sort of "intelligence" to the system interface. Nevertheless, an exploratory environment is "clear" in the sense that it provides abundant, timely, and problem-oriented feedback to the learner.

Safety is the capacity of the system to protect the learner from demoralizing penalty. The issue arises because, as we have seen, the learning strategies people adopt lead them into trouble with current word processors. A system that was safe to learn by doing would be one whose function was organized modularly with respect to real tasks. An error committed while correcting a typo in a menu field would not tangle with reset to alter the applicability of procedures for correcting the typo (recall Table 1). Training materials also should be organized modularly with respect to real tasks: learning by doing does not mean following out a cursor movement exercise by rote; it means typing in a letter (and "incidentally" learning to move the cursor about).

In such a system, recovering from an error might be more than a hopeless jump into an endless morass of problem tangles. Indeed, we view error recovery as a paradigmatic learning situation: the learner is highly task-oriented, primed to take action, and engaged in the system's responses. In current unsafe systems, all this is for naught since the learner is quite likely to end up lost. In a safe system, all this very constructive motivation might be effectively channeled into learning by discovery. Learners must be safe in taking action.

If the strategy of learning by thinking is to operate safely, the inferences, deductions, and abductions that people are prone to make must be correct. In some cases, this point can be codified simply: operations that have apparent natural inverses (space and backspace, line advance and line return) should indeed *be* inverses; they should mutually undo each other's effects; they should have predictably inverted names (Carroll, 1982a). In many other cases, designing systems that can be learned by being reasoned out is not nearly so straightforward. We simply do not understand human reasoning in these complex task environments well enough to derive from principles appropriate design strategies.

And of course, if the strategy of learning by knowing is to be safely employed then care must be taken to present a system interface which is consistent with prior knowledge: if word processors are thought of as super typewriters then, at least the initial interface should contain either nothing inconsistent with this, or if it does contain inconsistent features these should be well-marked for the new user (Carroll & Thomas, 1982). An exploratory environment is safe with respect to the strategies of learning by doing, thinking, and knowing. System operations and training materials are modular with respect to real tasks; natural inferences, deductions, and abductions entail correct expectations about the system's behavior; and prior knowledge which people regard as relevant *is* relevant.

These properties straightforwardly suggest the hypothesis that learning, as we have described it here, is facilitated in an exploratory environment. However, in closing this section, we want to observe that this facilitation may not merely be "cognitive." Exploratory environments may enhance task oriented motivation as well. Computer games manifest many of the properties of exploratory environments, and have been argued to increase task-oriented motivation (Malone, 1980, 1981). The argument is murky, however, since the games differ from word processors in a great many irrelevant ways as well.

The game of Adventure may be an important case with respect to this both because it is so widely popular and because its "maze learning" problem scenario is analogous in many ways to learning the conceptual maze codified in a structure of interconnected menus in a word processor (Carroll, 1982b). Indeed, the similarities between Adventure and current word processing systems can be pushed quite far—which raises the question of why the game is so attractive to people. Part of the answer might be that the types of properties we have clustered into the concept of an exploratory environment—properties like feedback, safety, modularity, learner control—nurture a motivational orientation in game learners that is precluded for learners of current word processors.

Clearly, these are empirical questions that can be addressed only by developing systems that comprise exploratory environments and by studying how people manage to learn to use them. This is the direction of our own current work.

Active Learning

In the early days of cognitive psychology, it was often necessary to rail against "stimulus–response" analyses of learning that went like this: items in the world come around and get paired with responses (or dispositions to respond) in the organism (generally because the pairing led to a good effect of some sort). This is a somewhat barren analysis of human learning to be sure, and cognitive psychology succeeded in doing away with it. The solution offered by cognitive psychology then, and now, was to turn the question of "learning" into the question of "memory." This was probably a good idea; after all, successful learning ought to lead to memory and stimulus–response psychology had nothing to say about how even simple aspects of memory organization could be explained.

In turning the question around like this, however, cognitive psychology overlooked another striking problem with the stimulus–response analysis of learning: learning—in that view—is a mechanically *passive* matter of pairing and then incrementing the strength of pairing. The active initiatives of the learner do not figure in at all. In turning the learning question into the memory question, cognitive psychology effectively finessed this problem: memory structures, after all, *ought* to be stable, relatively static, and so on. Reducing the analysis of memory to a set (albeit an increasingly large set) of mechanisms was viewed as an entirely proper way to scientifically approach the matter (but cf. Jenkins, 1974).

In sum, *both* stimulus–response psychology and cognitive psychology—in their approaches to the problems of analyzing learning and memory, respectively—share a basic orientation: the processes involved are "passive" with respect to the initiative of the learner–memorizer. They in fact share one other basic orientation. Neither school of psychology focused its principal empirical concern on the analysis of full-scale problems of human behavior and experience. This is as true of the classic Sperling and Sternberg brand of memory research as it is of the classic Skinnerian studies of pigeon pecking. While it may be true that in highly constrained situations or in infrahuman species active self-initiative is muted, this may not bear at all on the nature of real and complex human learning.

The treatment of learning in both stimulus–response psychology and subsequently in cognitive psychology share a picture of learning that approaches it as passive with respect to the initiative of the learner, and a methodological orientation that focuses analysis on highly constrained laboratory situations. Our examination of a more full-scale learning situation questions these premises (as has other recent work in cognitive science; Norman, 1981). Learning to use a word processor provides a study of real complex human learning that is fundamentally "active," driven by the initiatives of the learner—which are, in turn, based on extensive domain-specific knowledge and skill, and on reasoning processes which are systematic and yet highly creative.

Where do we go from here? Our examinations of current word processing systems have led us to a conception of learning, and in particular of learning to use a word processor. In the prior two sections we have summarized and projected in very general terms what we think we have learned. However, recognizing that current word processing systems might be improved from the learner's perspective by providing a conceptual framework and ensuring an exploratory environment is far short of *understanding what learning would be like in such a situation.* If the problems that learners experienced were less debilitating, we might be able to analyze learning at a finer grain and expose cognitive mechanisms that are simply lost in the confusion when people try to learn current systems. At the least, we could contrast learning in the two situations.

To address this, we are attempting to codify our suggestions for training and system design into concrete experimental prototypes. A rude approximation of this involves merely altering the training materials learners receive. The system they interact with is one we have studied previously, and one which has very little in common with exploratory environments. Nevertheless, by providing modular, problem-oriented training and training materials which make explicit the basic elements of procedures (e.g., what the goal is, what actions are required, including prerequisites, and what are the outcomes), we have been able to reduce training time without impairing learning performance (as measured by our transfer task).

These are preliminary results (our analysis is in progress) but they are encouraging. The next step for us is to exert direct control over the system interface itself. Only in this way can we seriously assess what learning may be like in an exploratory environment.

The nature of active learning remains for the most part an open question in current cognitive science. Since theory in this area is not very developed or abstract, the most promising strategy seems to be one of representatively examining a variety of accessible and realistic learning domains. Each domain must of course be probed as deeply as possible on its own terms, since we have no way of knowing antecedently which generalizations we identify will turn out to be domain-independent and which will turn out to be properties specific to particular domains or sets of domains. The current study can be placed into this programmatic framework: its chief results are its indications of what needs to be done next.

ACKNOWLEDGMENTS

We are greatly indebted to Clayton Lewis who was a full collaborator in this research and an originator of many of the ideas presented here. He was unable to participate in writing this chapter. We are also grateful to Karen Greer who helped to transcribe from tape-recordings the material presented in tables. Some of this material appeared in a slightly different form in Carroll and Mack (1983).

REFERENCES

Bott, R. *A study of complex learning: theory and methodology.* CHIP Report 82. University of California at San Diego, La Jolla, CA, 1979.

Carroll, J. Learning, using, and designing command paradigms. *Human Learning: Journal of Practical Research and Application. 1,* 31–62, 1982. (a).

Carroll, J. M. The adventure of getting to know a computer. *Computer, 15(11)*, 49–58, 1982. (b)

Carroll, J. & Lasher, M. Getting to know a small computer. Manuscript, IBM Watson Research Center, 1981.

Carroll, J. M., & Mack, R. Actively learning to use a word processor. In W. Cooper (Ed.) *Cognitive aspects of skilled typewriting*. New York: Springer-Verlag, 1983. Pp. 259–281.

Carroll, J., & Thomas, J. Metaphor and the cognitive representation of computing systems. *IEEE Transactions on Systems, Man and Cybernetics, 12*, 107–116, 1982.

Ericsson, K., & Simon, H. Verbal reports as data. *Psychological Review, 87*, 215–251, 1980.

Halasz, F., & Moran, T. Analogy considered harmful. *Proceedings of the Conference on Human Factors in Computer Systems*. National Bureau of Standards, Gaithersburg, MD, 1982.

Hayes-Roth, B., & Hayes-Roth, F. A cognitive model of planning. *Cognitive Science, 3*, 275–310. 1979.

Ingalls, D. Design principles behind Smalltalk. *Byte*, 286–298, August 1981.

Jenkins, J. J. Remember that old theory of memory? Well, forget it! *American Psychologist, 29*, 785–795, 1974.

Kinneavy, J. *A theory of discourse*. Englewood Cliffs, NJ: Prentice-Hall, 1971.

Lewis, C. *Using thinking aloud protocols to study the "cognitive interface"*. Research Report RC 9265, IBM Thomas J. Watson Research Center, Yorktown Heights, NY, 1982.

Lewis, C. & Mack, R. The role of abduction in learning to use text-processing systems. Paper presented at the annual meeting of the American Educational Research Association, New York, March 19–24, 1982.

Mack, R., Lewis, C., & Carroll, J. Learning to use office systems: Problems and prospects. *ACM Transactions on Office Information Systems, 1*, 10–30, July 1983.

Malone, T. *What makes things fun to learn? A study of intrinsically motivating computer games*. Cognitive and Instructional Sciences Series CIS-7 (SSL-80-11). Xerox Palo Alto Research Center, August, 1980.

Malone, T. What makes computer games fun? *Byte*, 258–277, December 1981.

Nisbett, R., & Wilson, T. Telling more than we can know: Verbal reports on mental processes. *Psychological Review, 84*, 231–259, 1977.

Nisbett, R., & Ross, L. *Human inference: Strategies and shortcomings of social judgment*. Englewood Cliffs, NJ: Prentice-Hall, 1980.

Norman, D. A. (Ed.). *Perspectives on cognitive science*. Norwood, NJ: Ablex, 1981.

Peirce, C. S. The logic of drawing history from ancient documents. In A. Burks (Ed.), *Collected papers of Charles Sanders Peirce*. Cambridge, MA: Harvard University Press, 1958.

Rumelhart, D., & Ortony, A. The representation of knowledge in memory. In R. C. Anderson, R. Spiro, & W. Montague (Eds.), *Schooling and the acquisition of knowledge*. Hillsdale, NJ; Erlbaum, 1977.

Schrodt, P. The generic word processor: A word-processing system for all your needs. *Byte*. 32–36, April 1982.

Smith, D., Irby, C., Kimball, R., Verplank, B., & Harslem, E. Designing the STAR user interface. *Byte*, 242–282, April 1982.

Zloof, M. Query-by-example: A data base language. *IBM Systems Journal, 16*, 324–343, 1977.

Building User-centered On-line Help

Abigail Sellen
University of California at San Diego
Summer Intern, Apple Computer, Inc.

Anne Nicol
Advanced Technology Group
Apple Computer, Inc.

INTERACTING DAILY with a computer usually presents us with no complicated problems or unpleasant surprises. We use certain applications with functions we understand for a small, familiar set of tasks. But ask us to try to accomplish an unfamiliar task (like make an index for a document), or ask us to use a different word processor, or even to write the document on a different kind of computer, and the experience is quite different. Now our goals are less clear, we probably have a poorer understanding of the interface, and we have difficulty interpreting the response of the system to our actions.

We need help. But, even if there is on-line help available, the unfortunate fact is that most help systems tend to exacerbate users' problems. Finding the simplest piece of information can turn into a complicated exercise. Forget about looking up something quickly, the information will probably be buried deep in the recesses of the help database. If and when we find what we need, it will probably take a long time to get back to the task we were working on, if we can even remember what it was. The process is time-consuming and effortful, and is apt to leave us feeling ineffective and frustrated.

As a consequence, some people do not even try to use the help provided: in our laboratory, we notice that even when help is available, subjects frequently do not use it. People prefer to flounder around in their work environment, or better yet turn to an in-house expert, rather than use the on-line help provided by the system.

Why Do Users Avoid Using Help?

Researchers have addressed this question by studying use of various on-line help systems [See Borenstein, 1985, and Hysell, 1986, for example]. It turns out that users have several common complaints:

- Difficulty in finding information
- Failure to deliver relevant information
- Difficulty of switching between help and the working context
- The complexity of the help interface
- The quality and layout of help information

In this chapter, we discuss major issues that arise in the design of help systems to address user needs and complaints; we describe the research approach we took, some results of that research, and some of our prototype solutions and guidelines. Finally, we speculate on future directions for on-line help. Although our discussion and examples are based on a specific project (described below), we have found that the issues and guidelines apply generally to interface design decisions for on-line help.

How Can We Design Help That's Useful and Easy to Use?

This question is the focus for an ongoing research and development effort at Apple. For the past two years, engineers, writers, and researchers from several departments have collaborated in the design of interfaces to on-line help that will meet users' needs across a variety of applications. The project is "user-centered" in that users are involved throughout the design process. The process begins by observing the way that users naturally do something (such as asking for help). Users provide feedback on the interface at each stage in its evolution. (See the chapters by Norman and Gomoll in this volume for expansion on both of these points.) The aim of the project is not only to produce prototypes of on-line help interfaces, but also to explore and extend the range of possibilities for help and to construct guidelines for the design of help.

What Makes Many Help Systems Difficult to Use?

An analysis of common users' complaints (above) and of our own experiences sheds some light on this issue. For example, consider the problem I (Abi) had in trying to find out how to put a box around text in Microsoft Word 3.02 (although we use Microsoft Word Help as a negative example here, the system in fact has many excellent features and has been mentioned by numerous developers as a model help system).

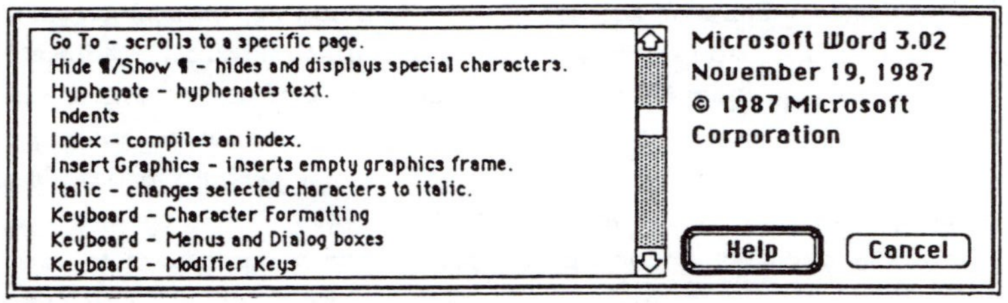

Figure 1

Although I had a specific task in mind, nothing in the list of topics in the on-line help seemed to be remotely related to what I wanted to do. By pure chance, and after much frustration, I found the information I needed under the heading *Paragraph-changes paragraph formatting.* Why did I have so much difficulty in finding it? There are at least two reasons:

- Not having had much experience with the program, I lacked the necessary knowledge to relate my problem, one of drawing a box around text, to a problem of paragraph formatting.

  Lesson: The conception of the problem that the user has may be very different from the conception of the expert, and people who design on-line help tend to be experts.
- My question was a question in terms of a task. Very few help topics laid out in Microsoft Word Help are organized in terms of tasks (see figure 1). In fact, there seems to be no consistent criterion used to designate how the help entries are presented. They are a combination of task-oriented topics (for example, Keyboard and Character Formatting), menu commands that often list the commands just as they appear in the menus (for example, Insert Graphics), and general definitions (for example, Indents).

  Lesson: Search time could have been greatly reduced if the form of the help topic corresponded to the kind of question I was asking.

This second point is also related to the problem of help not delivering the relevant information. It is not surprising that a user who wants to be presented with procedures will have difficulty when presented with definitions and descriptions. Similarly, a database that is task-oriented will tend to deliver information that is inappropriate for a user who wants a short description. In my example, the fact that I was asking a question in terms of a task meant that I needed a procedure. *The point is that the kind of question asked often determines the type of information required.*

Following the initiative of O'Malley [1986], we argue that one way of building an effective on-line help system is to start by noting the kinds of questions users ask when they need help. Each kind of question has important implications for the design of help in the interface.

Question Type	Canonical Form of the Question
1. **Goal-oriented**	What kinds of things can I do with this program?
2. **Descriptive**	What is this? What does this do?
3. **Procedural**	How do I do this?
4. **Interpretive**	Why did that happen? What does this mean?
5. **Navigational**	Where am I?

Figure 2

Different Help for Different Questions

As a first step in designing the interface, a series of studies was conducted in order to discover what questions users ask. Pairs of users were given a set of tasks to complete using unfamiliar Macintosh software with no on-line help provided. Instead, the users were encouraged to ask questions when they needed help, either of one another or of the experimenters. We then recorded and classified the questions, resulting in the five categories presented in figure 2.

Design Implications

The first implication for on-line help design is that *the kind of information delivered should be different depending on the question asked.* If the information is separated according to the kind of question, the amount of search time needed can be significantly reduced while the relevance of the information delivered is increased.

The second implication is that *the way in which information is accessed and presented should depend on the question asked.* A beginner faced with the Macintosh desktop for the first time might point to the trash can and ask, "What is this thing?" Descriptive questions are nicely served by a help system in which pointing accesses information. Contrast this with the novice who wants to know, "How do I remove a file?" The ability to point to something on the screen is not an integral part of the question-asking. The interface for procedural help should therefore look and function quite differently from the interface for descriptive help.

Different Interfaces for Different Kinds of Help

Here is a more specific look at how help for each kind of question might be approached:

Goal-oriented Questions: "What Can I Do with This Program?" In order to interpret the interface of an application, the user must first have some idea of the different kinds of tasks it supports. Further, the user must have in mind a goal appropriate to the software before successfully embarking on a task. Most people are familiar with the purpose of the software they

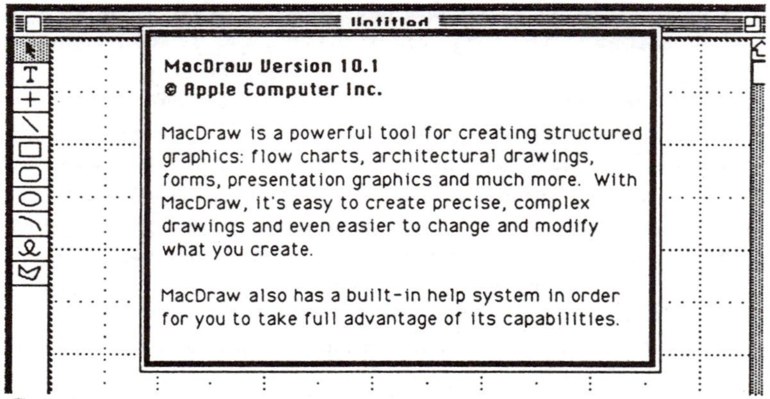

Figure 3

use, but occasionally users we observed asked that it be stated explicitly. Other times, users were not aware of the full range of functionality of a program. Two characteristics define this kind of help: 1) people who need it are unfamiliar with the interface; and 2) the information needs to be delivered only once or twice at most.

What are the implications for design?

- Introduce the information such that it will be easily accessible and highly visible to the novice user, without worrying whether it can be accessed quickly.
- Provide information that informs the user about the range of capabilities of a program, especially pointing out uses and functionality that users would not normally discover.

An example of how this kind of information might look for MacDraw is shown in figure 3.

Descriptive Questions: "What Is This? What Is It for?" Descriptive questions arose in a number of different situations, from trying to discover the name of an icon to finding out about the functional details of a menu item. There were essentially two behavioral modes in which users wanted definitions and descriptions of parts of the interface. The first was an exploratory mode in which users wanted to be able to point to objects on the screen or to menu items and ask for a description. The second was a task-specific mode in which the course of carrying out a task, some object or term needed to be defined.

The implications are that users should be able to ask for a definition both by pointing to items (especially important in graphical interfaces) and by asking in terms of a verbal label. Figure 4 shows how short descriptions might be delivered by pointing. In this case, the user might be new to the

Figure 4

Macintosh and exploring the Finder. The interface should support browsing as well as quick access to definitions for particular terms relevant to the task being performed. With regard to browsing, it seems important to support exploration of the current working context in addition to providing a glossary for terms and concepts that users otherwise may not know exist. A keyword search would be one solution to serving task-specific descriptive questions.

Procedural Questions: "How Do I Do This?" In our observations, procedural questions outnumbered any other kind of question. The form ranged from the very abstract in terms of high-level goals ("How do I start?") to the very specific in terms of executing particular actions ("How do I make this button disappear?"). The problem the user faces is that of translating intentions into the "language" of the interface. One possible solution is to provide access to procedural help through a menu so that users can recognize their questions rather than being forced to generate them. Further, recognition of the kind of question they want to ask can be facilitated by exploiting users' language rather than designers' language. That is, the vocabulary and formulation of tasks generated by users can be used to determine the structure of the procedural help menu.

Procedural questions are usually framed in terms of tasks users want to do. The options should therefore be articulated in task-oriented language. Further, research by O'Malley et al. [1983] shows that people looking for task-specific help tend to try to discover it through functionally related groups of commands. We found that the information was best presented in list form, with heavy use of graphics.

Finally, it is critical that this kind of help information be presented without obscuring or deactivating the working context, because procedures may be long and may need to be referred to while working. Figure 5 shows how information on how to change the size of a window might be presented in the Finder.

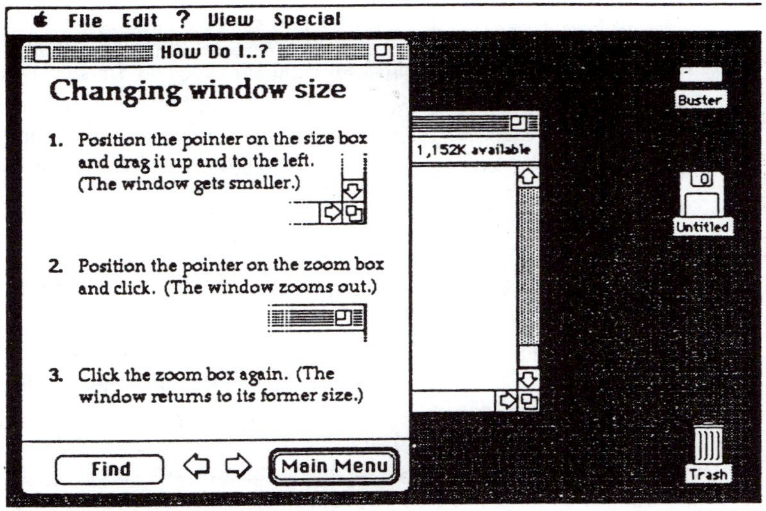

Figure 5

Interpretive Questions: "Why Did That Happen?" Interpretive questions arise when the system responds in an unexpected way. An error message is one obvious time at which a user may be faced with an unexpected situation. But there are many situations in which the user might not understand the system response, whether or not an error message is displayed. The Macintosh environment, for example, is one in which very few actions are actually "illegal."

From the designer's point of view, it is an easier task to offer an explanation of what went wrong at the same time that an error message is presented rather than forcing the user to inquire. Consider the problem, though, of telling the user why the system responded as it did when no obvious error was committed. The computer must either infer what the user's true intention was (infer what task the user was trying to accomplish) or provide a way for the user to diagnose the problem by providing the necessary tools.

Inferring the user's intention is a difficult problem, and in part depends on the "intelligence" and tracking capabilities of the computer. Even if the computer is able to track a user's activities and store templates of procedures for typical tasks, many tasks can be performed in a number of different ways and thus may look nothing like the stored prescriptions. Another complication is that users may carry out multiple activities that overlap [see Miyata and Norman, 1986]. Further, users may have a completely different intention in mind than their actions would suggest as a result of incomplete or faulty knowledge about the interface. Users may not be aware of their own intentions. Thus the task of inferring intention is complex and bound to be error-prone.

One approach might be for the computer to offer an interpretation of the user's task that the user can then critique, perhaps by referring to a menu of alternative interpretations. Once the user agrees with the computer's interpretation, help could be provided in the form of a diagnosis of the problem. This kind of help could also be supplemented by providing tools with which users could carry out their own diagnoses. One example would be providing users with a way of viewing a history of their past actions. This would be useful in cases where the user committed a minor, undetected error (unintentionally selecting the wrong menu item, for example). Another useful diagnostic tool might be a list of common errors committed during the task at hand.

Navigational Questions: "Where Am I?" The number of questions concerning navigation is very much application-dependent. Typically they arise most frequently with applications that are structurally complex and that contain a large amount of information. Hypertext-based software is one obvious example; hierarchically structured systems are another. Users tend to make heavy use of spatial metaphors: they report feeling "lost," speak of going "up" and "down" between levels or going "in" and "out" of situations.

Users often spontaneously construct spatial mental models or mental "maps" in order to move easily from one context to another. This has obvious implications for design. Reducing the memory load on the user is one benefit of making these mental "maps" explicit. Users can refer to the map instead of trying to retrieve information from memory to tell them "where they are." Another benefit is that a map can form the basis of a mental model on which the user relies to infer how to get from point A to point B without having to keep in mind a set of procedures for navigation. Thus, by exploiting spatial metaphors and allowing the user to make the inference, designers can help users avoid having to ask the question, "How do I get from point A to point B?"

Conceptual maps of this sort could take many different forms. These can be modeled after road maps, for example, or "You are here" maps like those found in department stores and subways. For a hierarchically based system (such as UNIX), a picture of the hierarchy that is updated automatically as the user creates and removes directories is another example of a solution to "navigating" around files. Obviously, the nature of the map will depend on the structure of the application.

Answers Instead of Questions?

We have focused so far on users' questions as the basis for providing help. But sometimes, users don't know what questions would give them useful information. David Owen [1986] constructed a help facility for UNIX called "Did You Know?" to help users execute commands more quickly and efficiently and to use the full range of capabilities of the system. In response to the user's typing "DYK," the system provides useful pieces of information and suggestions that are characteristic of the kind of information that experts or "power users" tend to possess. For example, it might offer information of the form "Did you know that there is an easier way to clear the clipboard?" or "Did you know you could have four windows open at once?" We see this approach as a complementary, perhaps even a necessary, part of a complete help system along with the kind of question-asking facility suggested here.

Help Design as a Function of Its Medium

Just as it is critical for a help system to be tailored to user needs, it must also be designed for the medium that conveys it. Many on-line help systems are really electronic manuals, obeying the conventions and constraints of physical manuals. One point in favor of this approach is that the new user knows what to expect: the documentation will have book conventions like a table of contents and an index. But electronic manuals lack other desirable features of physical manuals: the ease of browsing or thumbing through the information; the immediate sense of knowing where one is in the book; the ability easily to shift one's attention back and forth between the physical manual and the screen; and the added confidence that, because the manual is a separate object, referring to help can't possibly have unexpected or irrevocable effects on the electronic working context.

What are the advantages of help delivered on-line? On-line help is not subject to the physical constraints of a book: it can be interactive and action-dependent. It can be dependent on the user's working context or on the history of a user's actions, and can take account of a user's skill level. On-line help can also be dynamic. Instead of having users read pages of printed text, help information can be presented using animation, even with voice overlay. Other features that can be incorporated into on-line help, impossible to deliver from a manual, are the ability to do keyword searches, and the ability to cut information directly out of the help text and paste it into the working environment. Finally, on-line help is more portable—an important consideration in light of the recent trend toward lap-top computers.

Implicit versus Explicit Help

The distinction between on-line help and the user interface is not necessarily clear-cut. In a sense, any actions that the interface either affords or constrains constitute help for the user. What menus are available and what options are on those menus inform the user (theoretically at least) of the range of possibilities for performing a task. Any sort of feedback that may be given to the user, whether as a prompt to the next action in a series of actions or in the form of an error message, could also be considered on-line help. This kind of help is *implicit* help provided by the interface. Usually, however, we use the term "on-line help" to refer to supplemental aid provided on-line once the design of the interface has been established. This is *explicit* help.

One understandable concern is that good explicit help may become an excuse for a bad interface. Help systems might be viewed as a way to "patch up" poor interface design. The other side of the same coin is that a well-designed interface should not need a help system. The aim should be to provide simple, self-explanatory interfaces. Although the ideal is commendable, reaching it seems unrealistic at the moment, especially considering the imbalance between the power and flexibility that much contemporary software affords and the state of the art in intelligent interfaces.

Future Directions

As interfaces become more adaptive and supportive, the need for explicit, self-contained help systems will diminish. The more truly context-sensitive we are able to make help, the less obtrusive it will be for users. But this will require more than a superficial understanding of context. For example, there will be times when the help you want is either unrelated to your current context or should *not* be related to your current context. For example, you may be between tasks and need help initiating a new one. It then becomes tedious to have to make sure to return to a different context in order to get the help you need. Alternatively, you may be in your current context in error. Any restriction on the help options available or any context-dependent information is likely to confuse you further. A human tutor would know when to ignore the context, or when to point out an error that caused you to be in the wrong context. Context-dependent help must either incorporate such inferential capabilities or provide a means for the user to carry on a dialogue with the computer.

Suggesting that future help will be more fully integrated into the interface implies that help may be more active. Now people usually have to ask for help, but more intelligent systems could anticipate user needs. This would be particularly useful for situations in which users may recognize the need for help but not know how to ask for it. Truly intelligent, active help would reinterpret the actions according to users' intentions. At the very least, help could complete commands, or prompt for the next action. More advanced systems would not only tell you how to carry out a task but actually perform it for you.

Active help systems may present their own special problems and obstacles, however. First, as discussed previously, there is the difficulty of designing a system that can interpret users' intentions. In the absence of this capability, the system is prone to develop wrong interpretations, leading to diagnoses and advice that may be entirely inappropriate, further confusing the user. Another pitfall discussed by Norman [1986] is that of the computer taking too much control from the user, leaving the user feeling like a bystander. The user is put in the position of being a passive observer rather than an active participant. Computer-initiated help in the form of unsolicited advice is potentially intrusive and irritating, just as a person looking over your shoulder offering advice can be.

Do we need to wait for advanced inference capabilities to provide more adaptive and supportive help? We don't think so. Using both the interactivity of the situation and users' intelligence, we can design help that "nudges" users towards making appropriate decisions and choices. And we can use advances in other arenas to make help more accessible. Different modes of access for help should be considered, for example. Voice activation is one obvious possibility; gesture is another (see Hulteen and Kurtenbach's chapter in this volume).

With regard to the method of presentation of information, animation deserves further exploration. In their chapter in this volume, Baecker and Small discuss ways in which motion can effectively add a whole new dimension to the way information is conveyed. Many of these ideas can be applied to the domain of helpful interfaces. The use of animation to present a history of a user's past actions is one example. Animation is already used in "guided tour" tutorials for the computer. This idea could be extended to become more interactive and integrated into the interface.

One of our objectives in the project at Apple has been to provide guidelines for developers based on our research and discussions. This will be a continuing effort as the work progresses, and the guidelines will become increasingly specific as we build an interface model. But the general philosophy for the design will remain the same. It is expressed in the following five principles:[1]

- On-line help should never be a substitute for good interface design.
- Help should be context-sensitive; it should not take the user away from the task at hand.
- Help systems should assist users in framing their questions and provide different help for different questions.
- Help systems should be dynamic and responsive.
- Users shouldn't need help to get help.

[1] These principles are listed in a document titled, "Guidelines for the Design of On-line Help," published by the Human Interface Group, Apple Computer, Inc., 1988.

Figure Captions:

Figure 1: Part of the list of help topics for Microsoft Word 3.02.

Figure 2: Five kinds of questions users ask.

Figure 3: Answering the question, "What can I do with this program?" Users find it helpful to know the range of capabilities of a program, as well as its special features.

Figure 4: Answering the question: "What is . . . ?" Pointing and clicking gives the user a short description of graphical objects in the Finder. More detailed information could be accessed through a glossary.

Figure 5: Answering the question, "How do I change the size of a window?" in the Finder.

References:

Borenstein, N.S. (1985) *The Design and Evaluation of On-line Help Systems*. Ph.D. diss. Carnegie Mellon University.

Erlandsen, J., and Holm, J. (1987) Intelligent Help Systems. *Information and Software Technology*. 3 (29) 115–21.

Hysell, D. (1986) Planning Considerations for Online Documentation. *Proc. of the IEEE Professional Communication Society*. 61–66.

Miyata, Y., and Norman, D.A. (1986) Psychological Issues in Support of Multiple Activities. *User Centred System Design: New Perspectives on HCI*. Ed. Norman & Draper. Erlbaum Assoc. 265–84.

Norman, D.A. (1986) Cognitive Engineering. *User Centred System Design*. 31–61.

O'Malley, C.E. (1986) Helping Users Help Themselves. *User Centred System Design*. 377–98.

O'Malley, C.E., Smolensky, P., Bannon, L., Conway, E., Graham, J., Sokolov, J., and Monty, M.L. (1983) A Proposal for User Centred System Documentation. *Proc. of the CHI '83 Conference*. 282–85.

Owen, D. (1986) Answers First, Then Questions. *User Centred System Design*. 361–75.

Computers for the Disabled

JOSEPH J. LAZZARO

Adapting desktop computers to meet the needs of disabled workers is easier than you might think

Sal has all the makings of a good telemarketer: He's bright, outgoing, and persistent. He is also blind. Phyllis wants to hire him, but she has some concerns. How will he be able to use the company's database if he can't see the monitor? How will he read office correspondence? And more important, what will it cost the company to adapt the workplace to accommodate him?

Phyllis *must* accommodate him, since her company is in the U.S., and therefore subject to the Americans with Disabilities Act, or ADA (see the box "For More Information"). But she needn't worry. The latest adaptive technology for personal computers provides a cost-effective way to allow Sal and workers with other disabilities to do their jobs with independence.

Getting Access

Personal computers are directly compatible with many adaptive hardware and software products. You simply install them as you would any other add-in board or application. The majority of adaptive products are developed for the platforms that are commonly used in business environments: MS-DOS, Windows, and the Macintosh. Fewer products are available for Unix, but development work is under way due to the influence of the ADA.

When adapting a personal computer, you should pay special attention to hardware requirements (see the box "Adaptation Needs"). Both PCs and Macs require at least 25 MHz of processing power to run many adaptive applications, such as OCR or speech-synthesis programs, in conjunction with mainstream programs, such as spreadsheets.

Memory is another major consideration. For adaptation, many systems require a minimum of 1 MB of RAM—4 MB if you're running Windows or if you're attached to a network. The number of expansion slots is also vital. For instance, if you have a machine with five slots, you can install a speech synthesizer and an optical scanner alongside your video and drive controllers and still have one slot free.

Another important issue is how many serial and parallel ports your computer has. Many adaptive devices interface to the computer through serial ports, using standard nine- or 25-pin connectors.

Analyze, Then Adapt

The first task in adding adaptive technology to a computer is to determine the specific needs of the disabled worker in question. "It's very important to analyze the job thoroughly," says John Robichaud, a rehabilitation engineer with the Occupational Rehabilitation Group (Cambridge, MA), "and this goes way beyond just the PC." Robichaud's company looks at each job in terms of its component tasks and all the systems at the site used to perform those tasks.

continued

Adaptation Needs

HARDWARE: Both PCs and Macs require at least 25 MHz of processing power to run many adaptive applications, such as speech-synthesis programs, in conjunction with mainstream programs, such as spreadsheets.

MEMORY: Many systems require a minimum of 1 MB of RAM—4 MB if you're running Windows or if you're attached to a network.

EXPANSION SLOTS: With five slots, you can install a speech synthesizer and an optical scanner alongside your video and drive controllers and still have one slot free.

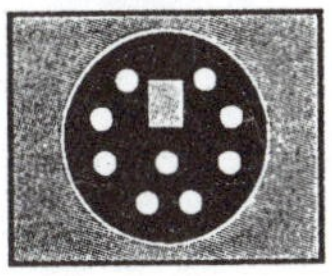

PORTS: Many adaptive devices interface to the computer through serial ports, using standard nine- or 25-pin connectors.

ROBERT BURGER © 1993

The next step is to focus on the employee's abilities. If he or she has no vision, then a speech or braille output package is recommended. For someone with limited but usable vision, a software magnification package may be appropriate. For a hearing-impaired worker, a Baudot/ASCII modem is a logical investment. For a motor-disabled user, an adapted keyboard or a Morse-code entry system is feasible.

To assist with adaptive technology, mainstream companies are providing consulting services and adaptive equipment to comply with the ADA. The SNAP (Special Needs Access Program) is a joint project of AT&T and NCR. It offers engineering consulting services and adaptive hardware and software for fees ranging from $75 to $125 per hour.

Cortez Martin, civil rights manager for the FAA Technical Center at the Atlantic City International Airport, used the SNAP to help accommodate a visually impaired worker. "We gave the consultants a real thumbs-up for their efforts and the approximately 20 hours of training they provided," he says. "The software and hardware they suggested made [our] employee more productive and more efficient."

DEC is using its DECtalk speech-synthesis system to help blind people to read and nonverbal people to speak. DEC has also created an Assistive Technology Group. In addition, Apple Computer and IBM have produced and sponsored assistive technology for their respective computer platforms. Their developments include everything from graphics-based speech-synthesis systems to sticky-key software (i.e., programs that electronically lock and hold the Shift, Ctrl, and Alt keys).

Adapting to a Specific Need

To work effectively, most vision-impaired users need to have their computers adapted with technologies such as speech synthesis, magnification, braille, and OCR. Speech-synthesis systems interface to a computer through 8- or 16-bit slots or through standard RS-232 serial ports. They rely on TSR packages, known as screen readers, to drive them.

A PC for a blind user, *equipped with an Oscar optical scanner and a braille printer, both by TeleSensory. The optical scanner converts text into ASCII code or into proprietary word processing format. Files saved on disk can then be translated into braille and sent to the printer. Visually impaired users can also enlarge the text on the screen by loading a TSR software magnification program.*

One example of a speech-synthesis system is VertPro from TeleSensory (Mountain View, CA). This $1795 product can read MS-DOS-based word processors, databases, spreadsheets, and other text-based software. Window Bridge from Syntha-Voice (Hamilton, Ontario, Canada) is a $695 Windows-based screen reader. This product can verbalize both MS-DOS- and Windows-based applications, and it will drive most speech synthesizers.

Magnification software can enlarge text appearing on the screen by up to 16 times. ZoomText Plus ($595) from AI Squared (Burlington Center, VT) and Magic Deluxe ($295) from MicroSystems Software (Framingham, MA) can both enlarge text on MS-DOS and Windows applications. Berkeley Systems (Berkeley, CA) markets inLarge, a $195 Mac-based software package that magnifies most commercial applications.

For braille output, the Juliet printer

DRAWINGS: TOM CENTOLA © 1993

This deaf user's PC *is connected to a telephone via an Ultratec Intele-Modem Baudot/ASCII modem. The user is sending and receiving messages to and from someone at a remote site who is using a telecommunications device for deaf people (right).*

($3995) from Enabling Technologies (Stuart, FL) interfaces to any standard RS-232 serial or parallel port. Juliet can emboss braille on both sides of a page at a speed of 40 characters per second. The Reading Edge OCR ($5495) from Xerox Imaging Systems (Peabody, MA) and the Arkenstone Open Book Unbound ($2190) from Arkenstone (Sunnyvale, CA) can read printed material to blind people and send the text to a PC.

TOM CENTOLA © 1993

This motor-disabled person *is communicating with a PC using a Pointer Systems optical head pointer to access all keyboard functions on a virtual keyboard shown on the PC's display. The user can "strike" a key in one of two ways. He can focus on the desired key for a user-definable time period (which causes the key to be highlighted), or he can click an adapted switch when he chooses the desired key.*

For users with hearing impairments, there's a long list of available adaptive hardware and software that you can add onto PCs. For example, SeeBeep ($20) from MicroSystems Software translates IBM speaker output into visual signals. Computers that are equipped with Baudot/ASCII modems can act as telecommunications devices for deaf people and also communicate with other PCs. Examples of this type of modem are the $329 Intele-Modem by Ultratec (Madison, WI) and the $349 CM-4 from Phone-TTY (Hackensack, NJ).

To adapt equipment for motor-impaired workers unable to type on a standard keyboard, you can employ adapted keyboards, sticky-key software, head pointers, and Morse-code systems that bypass the keyboard and enter data through the RS-232 serial port. In tandem with these add-ons, you can install software to display a picture of the keyboard on the screen. These products use a head-mounted pointing device. Examples include HeadMaster ($1195) from Prentke Romich (Wooster, OH) and the FreeWheel ($1395) from Pointer Systems (Burlington, VT).

With these systems, a motor-impaired person can bypass the physical keyboard with an external adaptive switch to select menu choices or virtual keys from an onscreen keyboard. Adaptive switches come in a variety of forms that can be activated by eye movements, breath control, or any other reliable muscle movement.

Another way of controlling computers is via a Morse-code system. Such a system consists of adaptive switches and software for people who can't type on a full keyboard but have the ability to physically push at least one key. HandiCode ($495) from MicroSystems Software is such a program. Voice-recognition systems permit people to issue verbal commands to a computer to perform data entry. Among the available voice systems are two from Dragon Systems (Newton, MA): DragonDictate-30K ($50) and VoiceType ($1995 plus board).

What's in the Works?

Adaptive technology must struggle to keep pace with the mainstream computer industry. For instance, numerous DOS-based screen readers exist, but few GUI screen readers are available. The use of multimedia could prevent blind users from accessing the information servers of the future unless a method can be found to translate animation into either speech output or braille. Pen-based computers could prevent the use of adaptive equipment for two reasons: They lack expansion slots for specialized hardware, and the heavily visual operating system isn't friendly to blind users.

Another problem is the long stretches of time between the appearance of mainstream products, such as spreadsheets and word processors, and those products' ability to interact with adaptive equipment. Ideally, this lag time will decrease as companies consider adaptive access early on in the design stage.

On July 26, 1994, companies with as few as 15 employees will be mandated to comply with the ADA. This criterion will make the ADA applicable to many more businesses. Because of the implementation of this new law, and the ever-increas-

For More Information

- **By calling the toll-free hot line at The National Institute on Disability Rehabilitation and Research (NIDRR) in Washington, D.C., at (800) 949-4232, you will be directly connected to your nearest ADA technical assistance center.**
- **You can obtain a free handbook (in either hard-copy or electronic form) about how to add adaptive technology to personal computers from the Clearinghouse on Computer Accommodation (COCA) of the Information Resources Management Service, General Services Administration. Write to: Susan A. Brummel, Director, COCA, c/o GSA, Room 2022, KGDO, 18th and F Sts. NW, Washington, DC 20405.**
- **State rehabilitation agencies, which are usually located in your state capital and listed in the phone directory, are a source of free information on ways to comply with the ADA.**
- **DOS-Abledata is a CD-ROM database from the Trace Center in Madison, Wisconsin. You can purchase this CD-ROM directly from the Trace Center for $25. You can also access its contents via the Massachusetts Commission for the Blind's BBS at (617) 451-5327 or via Project Enable (a disability-oriented BBS) at (304) 766-7842.**
- **The Internet has at least two newsgroups covering disability-related issues. These groups are called misc.handicap and alt.education.disabled. On-line services such as GEnie, BIX, CompuServe, and Delphi also have forums dedicated to adaptive technology.**
- **The Department of Justice runs a BBS dedicated to providing information on the ADA. To access it by modem, call (202) 514-6193.**

ing pervasion and decreasing costs of PCs, the future of adaptive technology is on a rising curve.

The payoff of the availability of adaptive equipment benefits everyone. "Building access for disabled people is the same as building better interfaces for all users," says Janina Sajka, project manager of the World Institute on Disability Network (Oakland, CA). "By studying the needs of disabled workers, we have the opportunity to build better access for everyone." ■

Joseph J. Lazzaro is director of the Adaptive Technology Program at the Massachusetts Commission for the Blind in Boston. He is the author of Adaptive Technologies for Learning and Work Environments *(American Library Association, forthcoming). You can contact him on BIX as "lazzaro@bix.com" or on the Internet at lazzaro@world.std.com.*

Improving VDT Work: Causes and Control of Health Concerns in VDT Use (Excerpt)

S.L. Sauter, L.J. Chapman, and S.J. Knutson

• • •

Nature and Seriousness of Stress Problems in VDT Work

The available research allows several general conclusions regarding the nature of strains experienced by VDT users. They are enumerated below. It is important to recognize that these conclusions are *generalizations.* We are sometimes misled by popular accounts to believe that all VDT users naturally experience all the problems specified. This is not so. Many experience none of these problems, and some experience all plus many more.

The types of strain most often associated with VDT use are eyestrain and musculoskeletal strain and, to a lesser extent, emotional or psychological strain.

Eyestrain in VDT work is usually characterized by sensations of irritation to the eye (burning or painful eyes) or eye fatigue (heavy or tired eyes). Eyestrain seems to be the most common complaint among VDT users and, generally speaking, may be the type of strain most likely to occur in excess in VDT users in comparison to more conventional office workers. Contrary to some popular beliefs, reports by VDT users of loss of ability to see clearly (blurred vision) or distorted perceptions of colors are quite rare.

With the exception of certain types of musculoskeletal strain such as backache or neckache, musculoskeletal aches and pains are generally less commonly reported than eyestrain.

The category of psychological strain contains several different types of disturbances which are grouped together because they all involve changes in emotional or motivational status. Of these disturbances, fatigue is probably the most common. Not infrequently, tension and anxiety are also reported. Where VDT users are asked simply whether or not they are satisfied with their jobs in general, the responses are usually quite positive. Yet, VDT users often express dissatisfaction with particular aspects of their jobs. In particular, complaints of dull routine and heavy workload demands are not uncommon.

How important or serious are these strains? Although eye, musculoskeletal, and certain psychological strains may be relatively abundant among VDT users, there is at present little evidence to link VDT use with actual physical or psychological injury or disease. A panel of scientific experts from across the country recently concluded that VDTs pose no threat of eye damage, although the issue is not so clear with respect to musculoskeletal disorders. Scientific evidence from around the world also indicates that, at worst, the strain of VDT use may be only slightly more intense or abundant than in more traditional clerical office work.

If this is the case, why all the fuss? Does this mean the problems are not threatening or can be ignored? The only thoughtful response to this question is an emphatic NO!

Although strain with VDT use may be only slightly elevated in comparison to traditional office work, it must be recognized that the actual levels of specific types of strain among office workers can be quite high. A research study of State of Wisconsin employees (Sauter, et al., 1983) found that about 20 to 30 percent of the clerical level office workers surveyed reported frequent eyestrain and backache or neckache at work. The incidence rates were a few percentage points higher for VDT users. While these discomforts have yet to be linked to physical disease or damage, they certainly are not trivial in terms of one's personal sense of well-being as anyone who has experienced chronic eyestrain or backache can attest to. Importantly, workplace conditions that cause eye and musculoskeletal strain have been linked with impaired office work performance, as demonstrated in recent research by the National Institute for Occupational Safety and Health (Dainoff et al., 1983).

These threats become particularly worrisome considering the rapidly expanding use of VDT's in the labor force. It has been projected that by 1990, 40 to 50 percent of all American workers will be making daily use of electronic terminal equipment (Guiliano, 1982).

Implementing Solutions: Guidelines and Precautionary Notes

Should It Be Fixed If It Doesn't Appear Broken?

It is not unusual to find VDT operations in which complaints over health disturbances or working conditions are rare. This should not be automatically interpreted as a sign that stress is absent and that preventive or corrective measures are unnecessary. As described further on, some ailments may require years to progress to the point where they are bothersome enough to cause VDT users to complain. By this stage, harm may already be done. Alternately, VDT users are sometimes reluctant to report discomforts for fear of job consequences, or because they may accept these problems as unavoidable aspects of the job.

Begin with VDT Users Most at Risk

Research suggests that job and health complaints are most common in basic clerical jobs characterized by heavy VDT use, repetitive and short cycle tasks, low skill requirements, heavy attentional or workload demands, and little personal control over the work process. An example is data entry. Priority in preventive or corrective efforts should be given to these types of VDT jobs.

Analyze the Job First

Efforts to upgrade the design of VDT jobs and workplaces to prevent stress should begin with a careful look at the requirements and demands of the job. The usefulness and appropriateness of various control measures depend upon the specific characteristics of the job. For example, a high quality video display or glare control is less essential in a task involving only modest VDT viewing in comparison to tasks with heavy dependence upon video display; pneumatic controls for easy adjustment of chair height are most important where the chair is used by different operators; additional rest pauses may be most beneficial in tasks with little variety. Together with job analysis, a preliminary survey of discomforts or the needs VDT users perceive can help pin down problems and prioritize control measures.

Encourage Innovation

Innovation can lead to improved and inexpensive methods of resolving job and workplace design problems in VDT use, and ways of coping with problems for which ready "off-the-shelf" solutions don't exist. Importantly, solutions don't always have to look nice to be effective. A low technology solution such as elevating a video display to an appropriate desk top height with blocks of wood may be as effective in some situations as a commercial product designed for this purpose.

Involve End Users in Decision Making

Participation of VDT users in planning of ways to control stress improves satisfaction by providing them with a degree of control over their fate. Don't forget, too, that the individual knows best where the shoe pinches. VDT end users have first hand knowledge of their particular job needs and the circumstances which interfere with their comfort and job performance. Thus, they can be a valuable source of information for identifying and correcting problems.

Proceed Slowly

Actions to prevent or correct job and health problems should proceed slowly and systematically so that their impact can be evaluated and "bugs" can be worked out before costly and potentially irreversible commitments are made. Changes in the organization of tasks or physical aspects of the workplace including equipment and furnishings should be evaluated on a trial or model basis before sweeping changes are made.

Ongoing Surveillance

Even carefully conceived and tested solutions are liable to result in unanticipated problems. Ongoing reporting or survey procedures should be established in VDT workplaces so that evolving problems can be detected and corrected before they mushroom into major disturbances.

Solutions Should Be Flexible

Excessive standardization in workplace design can create problems. While equipment or furnishings need to be adjustable to accommodate individual and task differences, it is unlikely that any single product or workstation configuration will be satisfactory for everyone. The chair is a good example. Regardless of the adjustability of a particular chair, it will not be comfortable for all individuals. To the extent possible, VDT workplace designs should be flexible in terms of allowing varied configurations or adjustment of equipment, as well as varied product designs.

Don't Overlook Training

Even the best designed workplace will be ineffective in controlling job and health problems in VDT use if operators are unfamiliar with methods of adjustment or operation of equipment and facilities. Training should focus not only on the *mechanisms* of operation, but also *principles*—for example, adjustment of chair height to prevent undue pressure beneath the thighs and why this is important. Understanding of underlying principles of adjustment or operation allows VDT users to adapt as situations change and to seek innovative solutions.

Training should be realistic—for example, "on the job" so that it can be readily applied. But it should also be formal so that correct and complete information is obtained.

Introduction to Musculoskeletal Strain

The Musculoskeletal System

Musculoskeletal strain refers to disorders and discomfort associated with stress to one or more of the components of the musculoskeletal system. The main components of the musculoskeletal system consist of (figure 6–1):

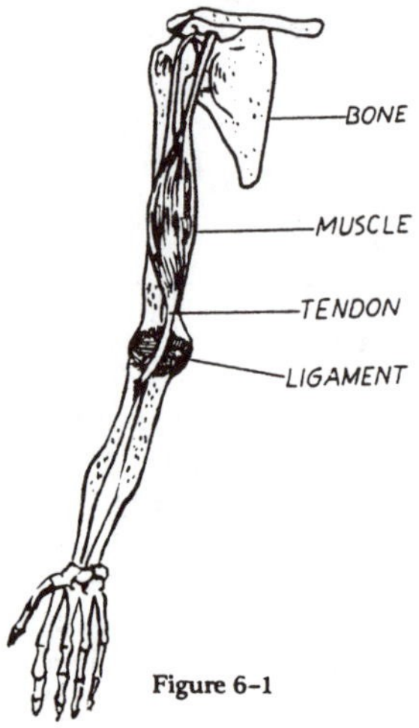

Figure 6–1

- The *bones* which provide the framework for the body.
- The *muscles* which exert forces to create movement and hold the body in various postures.
- *Ligaments* which connect bones to one another.
- *Tendons* which attach the muscles to the bones.

Also important are the *nerves* which transmit control signals out from the brain to the muscles, and carry sensory information back to the brain.

Symptoms

The most common type of musculoskeletal discomfort in VDT work is soreness or aching, usually in the back and neck. Aching and abnormal sensations such as numbness or tingling in the extremities are also reported by VDT operators, but less frequently than soreness in the torso.

Causes and Significance

The musculoskeletal system is both a living biological and a mechanical system. Like all mechanical systems, it is subject to wear and breakdown. Mechanical wear and tear to the components of the musculoskeletal system identified above is one source of discomfort in VDT work. Another source of discomfort involves problems meeting the biological requirements of the musculoskeletal system. When muscles are not adequately supplied with nourishment, or waste products are not adequately removed, muscle fatigue and discomfort quickly develop. This is probably the most common source of musculoskeletal discomfort in VDT work.

At first thought, it may not be readily apparent how VDT work can produce mechanical wear or fatigue of the musculoskeletal system. On the surface, this type of work seems to involve little of the dangerous activities such as lifting heavy loads or strenuous exercise which are frequently associated with musculoskeletal disorders. Yet close inspection of VDT work reveals several job characteristics which place workers at risk for musculoskeletal strain.

Static Muscular Efforts and Muscle Fatigue

One characteristic is the *stationary nature of VDT work*. VDT workers commonly remain seated for long periods in fixed postures. Computers have taken over responsibility for activities which require movement such as filing, sorting, delivering, and retrieving documents. However, just because VDT work is quite stationary does not necessarily mean that work is not being performed by the muscles and that fatigue is unlikely.

It is the rhythmic contraction and relaxation of the muscles which is responsible for the circulation of blood through the muscles, supplying them with nourishment and removing waste products. During contraction, blood vessels in the interior of the muscle are compressed by the tension created by the contracting muscle. This causes blood containing waste products to be squeezed or pumped out of the muscle. During relaxation the tension on vessels subsides and blood carrying nutrients can pass into the muscle. As work activities become more stationary, rhythmic muscle action is reduced and circulation through muscles is diminished. Now, of course, this is no problem if the muscles are truly at rest and their metabolic needs are therefore low. However, this is usually not the case in VDT work.

When maintaining fixed postures (for example, sitting erect or leaning forward at a desk, holding the arms outstretched to manipulate a keyboard), muscles of the back, shoulders, and arms are in a nearly constant state of contraction. This type of muscular effort is referred to as *static* effort. During static effort, metabolic needs are great, but circulation through muscles is impaired. Muscle fatigue and pain then quickly develop as muscles become laden with waste products and devoid of ingredients needed to produce energy. Hold your arms outstretched horizontally. Within just a few seconds you will begin to experience discomfort in the upper arm and shoulder caused by the steady contraction of muscles in this region. It is the buildup of one waste product—called "lactic acid"—which causes the pain.

Although static muscular effort can be extremely uncomfortable, it will not cause damage to the muscles.

Wear From Biomechanical Forces

Poorly designed VDT jobs and workstations can produce biomechanical forces that accelerate wear and tear of the musculoskeletal system. A case in point is wear to the spine. When the spine is misaligned in leaning or twisting toward poorly arranged work materials, or in slouching in response to fatigue from long periods of sitting, abnormal forces are placed upon the structures of the spine. This may advance the gradual degenerative changes in the spine that occur as a normal part of aging.

We don't want to create the impression that excessive musculoskeletal wear is certain to occur in VDT work. In fact, at present there is no data showing this type of damage among VDT users. On the other hand, it must be remembered that wear may require years, if not decades, to accumulate to the point where it becomes noticeable. Fortunately, enough is known about good workstation and job design so that these problems should be almost completely avoidable.

Wear from Repetitive Motion

The repetitive motion characteristics of some VDT jobs also hold the potential for musculoskeletal disorders. As mentioned, with the industrial revolution has come a tendency to reduce the scope of tasks performed by workers so that each individual performs one fairly narrow type of task as quickly as possible. This is what happens on assembly-lines, and what is sometimes observed in VDT work. For example, some VDT jobs consist of little more than simply operating a number pad throughout the course of the day.

One concern with this type of work is that continuous high speed performance of the same movement pattern can overwhelm the natural insulation and restorative processes that protect against friction and wear to the bones and other tissues of the musculoskeletal system. Irritation, inflammation and pain then results. An example of a site of particular concern is the wrist. Several tendons controlling the fingers share a narrow passageway through the bones of the wrist with a major nerve to the hand. Tendon and nerve irritation or damage may occur in this area when the hands and fingers are over-used.

Again, there is presently little evidence of repetitive motion disorders among VDT users. But still there is some cause for concern. Repetitive motion disorders have been observed in jobs with activities somewhat similar to VDT tasks (telegraph operators, typists, cashiers).

Emotional Factors and Musculoskeletal Strain

Finally, although the physical demands of the job are likely the chief sources of musculoskeletal strain in VDT work, emotional or psychological stress as caused by any number of job or personal factors may also have a contributing role. The reason is that psychological stress is often associated with an increase in muscle tension. Can you recall how you clench your jaw during stress, or the experience of pressing down so hard on a pencil that the lead breaks when you are under pressure? Thus, fatiguing or wearing muscular forces may be unnecessarily intense when psychological stress is present in VDT work.

Preventing Problems in the Arms and Hands

Disorders in the upper extremities are frequently seen in people whose jobs require high speed repeated performance of the same motion patterns. Assembly-line work and meat cutting are examples of occupations where arm and hand problems are quite common. And they are occasionally seen among typists as well. To date, arm, wrist, or hand discomfort among VDT users has been far less frequently reported than back or neck discomfort. But when these problems do occur, they can be serious and require medical attention. Discomfort in these areas sometimes signals wear or potential damage, as opposed to simple muscle fatigue. In order to help understand why these problems occur and how the control measures we suggest might prevent these problems, it is helpful to take a look at the design of the arms and hands.

Workings of the Arms and Hands

Moving and holding the arms outstretched over the desk top and keyboard are accomplished by muscles of the shoulder and upper arm.

The motion of the upper arm is controlled by shoulder muscles, and the muscles of the upper arm control the forearm. The muscle shown in figure 9-1 is the "biceps". It is the prominent muscle you can feel when you "make a muscle". It helps to hold your forearms as you suspend them over the keyboard.

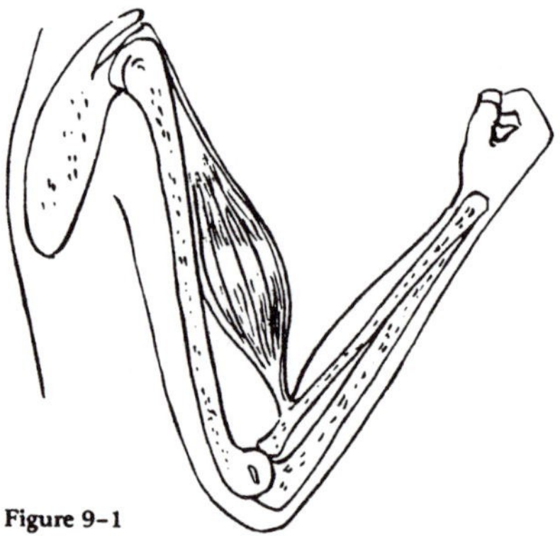

Figure 9-1

As illustrated in figure 9-1, the arm muscles attach to the bones they control at a position close to the joint. This arrangement results in greater muscular effort in holding the arms in any position than if the muscles were to be attached further out. It is like using a fishing pole. The fish feels heavier and greater effort is required to lift it out of the water at the end of a pole than if it is lifted straight up by the line.

What this means is that simply holding the arms, without support, over a keyboard requires quite a bit of static effort that quickly gives way to fatigue. Try simply holding your hands outstretched in front of you. It will take about 10-15 seconds at the most before you begin to develop a burning aching sensation in your shoulders and upper arms that is caused by muscle fatigue.

As suggested above, in VDT work problems of wear to the structures of the arms and hands are of greater concern than muscle fatigue. The structures susceptible to wear are mainly the nerves and tendons, particularly the tendons from the muscles controlling the hands and fingers.

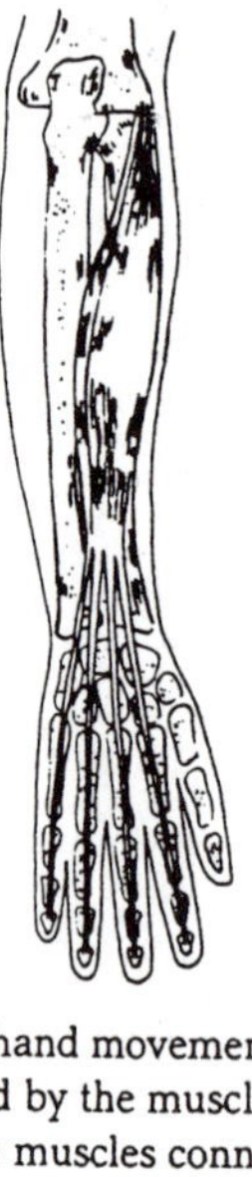

Figure 9-2

Finger and hand movement (as in typing) is governed by the muscles of the forearm. These muscles connect via tendons near the elbow on one end, and on the other end connect to tendons which travel through the wrist and connect to the hands and fingers (figure 9-2). The muscles and tendons shown in figure 9-2 are those on the back of the arm and hand. When these muscles contract, they pull the fingers and hand back (called extension), as shown in figure 9-3 (top). There exists a similar set of muscles and tendons on the bottom side of the arm which cause the fingers and hands to curl under, as when striking a key (figure 9-3, bottom).

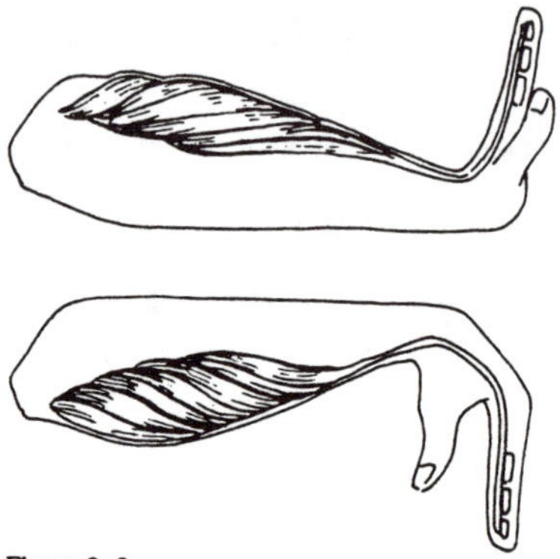

Figure 9-3

Signals from the brain stimulating the arm muscles to action are carried by nerves which originate from the spinal cord in the neck area. They travel out from between the neck vertebrae, around and between the muscles and bones of the shoulder, and down through and to the muscles of the arms and hands. These nerves also carry sensory information back to the brain.

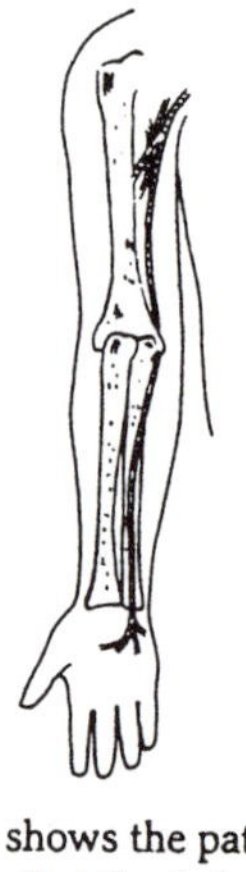

Figure 9-4

Figure 9-4 shows the path of one of these nerves called the "ulnar" nerve. Its territory includes the little finger and part of the next finger.

A second nerve of concern is the "median" nerve. On its way to the hand, the median nerve passes through a narrow tunnel formed on the top side of the wrist by the wrist bones, and on the bottom by a ligament (figure 9-5). As also seen in figure 9-5, this space is shared too by the tendons from the forearm muscles responsible for curling or closing of the hand and fingers. This narrow channel is called the "carpal tunnel". Blood vessels to the hand also pass through it. This structure is of special concern because it is a major site where nerve and tendon problems can originate.

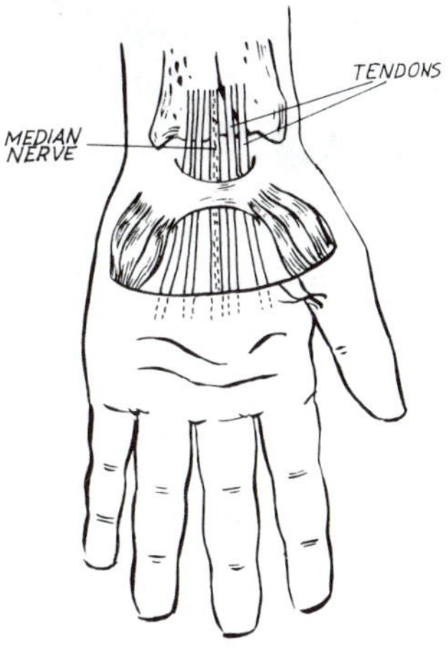

Figure 9-5

Things That Can Go Wrong with the Arms and Hands in VDT Work

Adjusting to New Activities

Any time we begin a new activity which involves the strenuous use of the arms and hands, we can expect some aching, soreness, or stiffness. The cause is often related to the fact that the muscles involved simply have not been used this way before. After a few days, the muscles should strengthen and recover, and the discomfort disappear.

Fatigue

Another type of reversible discomfort of the arms comes from muscle fatigue. As indicated above, holding the arms and hands outstretched over the keyboard requires static efforts of the muscles of the upper arms and shoulder-chest region. Again, discomfort can result from muscle fatigue due to steady contraction of these muscles. This problem is readily corrected by occasionally resting the arms or hands, and by keeping reach distances to work materials such as the keyboard to a minimum.

Wear and Tear

Poor arm-hand postures and highly repetitive actions, especially together, may cause physical damage to tendons and nerves. While rare, these types of problems are serious because once they develop, they may require medical treatment to correct them.

Nerve Irritation

Wear and tear to nerves and tendons is most likely at two sites—the elbow and wrist.

When the elbow is bent, as in the typing posture, tension is placed upon the ulnar nerve as it wraps around the elbow (figure 9-4). There is also little to protect the nerve from external forces such as a hard armrest at this site. This area is sometimes called the "funny bone" since irritation of the ulnar nerve at this point produces an unusual tingling sensation in the little finger.

When the arms are twisted inwards, as when laying the palms flat on a keyboard, the muscles responsible for this action may have a tendency to compress the median nerve just below the elbow.

Median nerve problems may also arise as the hands are bent backwards and outwards during keying. Remember the narrow tunnel (carpal tunnel) through which the median nerve, tendons, and blood vessels to the fingers pass? Bending of the wrists constricts this passageway. Compression of the contents of the carpal tunnel may damage the median nerve at this site and lead to a disorder known as "carpal tunnel syndrome". Of all arm-hand problems that might occur in VDT use, this is one of the most serious. But fortunately, it is also rare.

Symptoms of carpal tunnel syndrome include numbness, tingling, or prickling sensations in the hands, mainly the first three fingers, usually in the evening or early morning hours. Sometimes these sensations will extend up the arm as well. Weakness or frequent dropping of objects may also occur. VDT operators with recurrent symptoms like this should seek medical attention. Such symptoms may also signal nerve problems further up the line towards the neck.

CHECK OUT YOUR WRISTS FOR A POTENTIAL CARPAL TUNNEL PROBLEM:

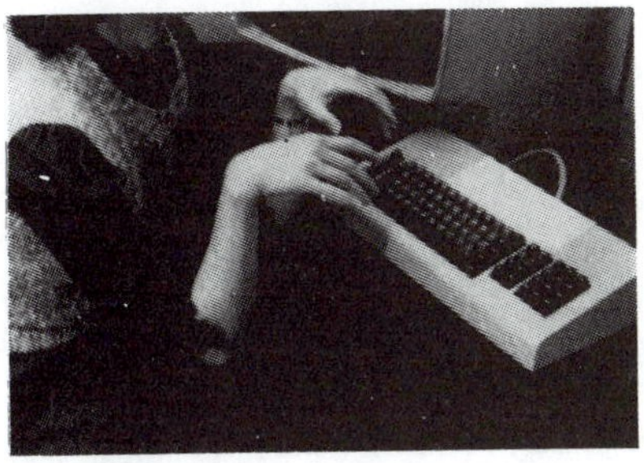

Figure 9-6

Sustained and extreme bending of the wrist may bring a potential carpal tunnel problem to light before the disorder progresses too far. One test you can perform on yourself is known as the "Phalens wrist flexion test."

Sit, resting your elbows on a table with your forearms in the air. Allow your hands to hang loose as shown in figure 9-6 for about one minute. If you develop pain, numbness, or *obvious* "pins and needles" sensations in your hands, have your doctor check you out. Another sign is "tingling" which radiates to your finger tips when you tap the underside of the wrist gently.

Tendon Irritation

It is not uncommon for typists and VDT operators to make many thousand key strokes per hour. Each stroke requires the contraction of a muscle and movement of a tendon in the forearm. With high movement rates, the possibility exists for irritation of tendons as they slide against one another or other structures in the arms or wrist. Tendons may also develop small tears at points near their connection to bones. Elbow pain may be related to such damage to the tendons holding the muscles of the forearm in place at the elbow. As with nerve injury, tendon problems become more likely when the arms and hands are used in awkward positions. Also like nerve injuries, tendons are not likely to recover well from injury without rest or a change in work routine. While tendon disorders can be quite debilitating, they seem to be fairly remote among office workers—probably no more likely than nerve problems.

Superficial Irritation

Finally, the arms and hands may become irritated from friction or repeated contact with hard or sharp surfaces of the worktable or chair. The elbow is one site. More common is irritation at the wrists. Sometimes a blister, callus, or inflammation will occur. While irritating, these disorders are usually not serious and can be readily corrected by use of a cushion, and good furniture and equipment design.

Workplace Causes and Control of Arm-Hand Disorders

To summarize, upper-extremity problems in VDT jobs may be caused by fatiguing postures, poor arm-hand positioning, highly repetitive tasks, and external forces to the arms and hands. To control these problems, it is important that:

- Opportunity for periodic support or rest of the arms and hands be provided.
- Work materials be positioned so as to avoid highly deviant arm and hand postures.
- Chair, table, and keyboard surfaces which contact the arms and hands be free of hard or cutting edges.
- Tasks be varied in terms of motion patterns; or rest breaks or relief activities be provided when tasks involve the high-speed performance of similar motion patterns.

Common examples of problems in these areas, as well as control procedures are given below.

Keyboard Placement and Design

Problems

Even the "normal" typing posture involves an outward deviation of the hands at the wrist (figure 9-7).

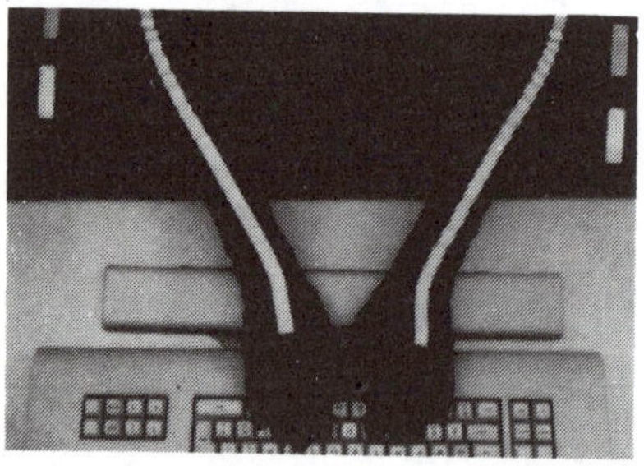

Figure 9-7

Several factors can lead to greater wrist deviation and thus increased pressure in the carpal tunnel.

One factor is simply poor positioning of the keyboard (figure 9-8). Attempts to

Figure 9-8

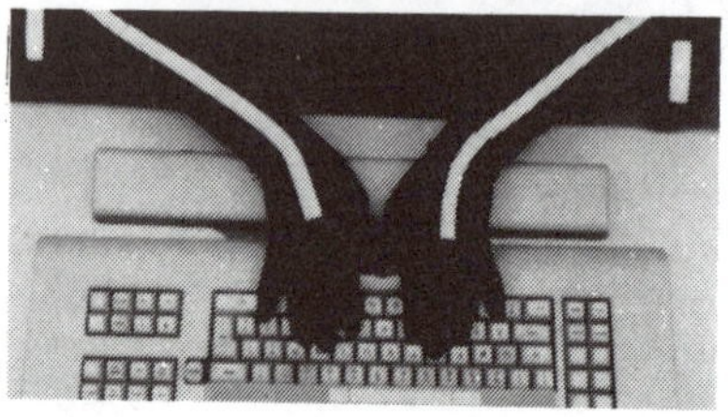

Figure 9-9

use the chair armrests while typing also leads to poor hand posture (figure 9-9).

Another problem is extension of the hand. When the hands are bent back sharply as shown in figure 9-10, there is a three-fold increase in the pressure in the carpal tunnel (in comparison to a straight alignment of the hands). Hand posture like this is common with a tall keyboard and no way to support the palms or wrists other than on the table top (figure 9-11). Operators are frequently seen to rest their hands in this fashion during brief pauses from keying.

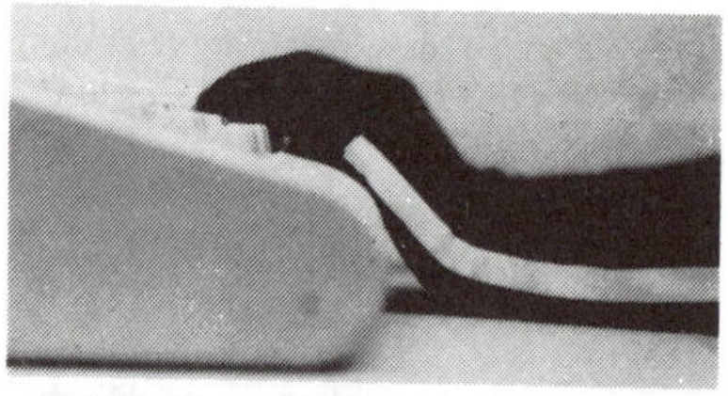

Figure 9-10

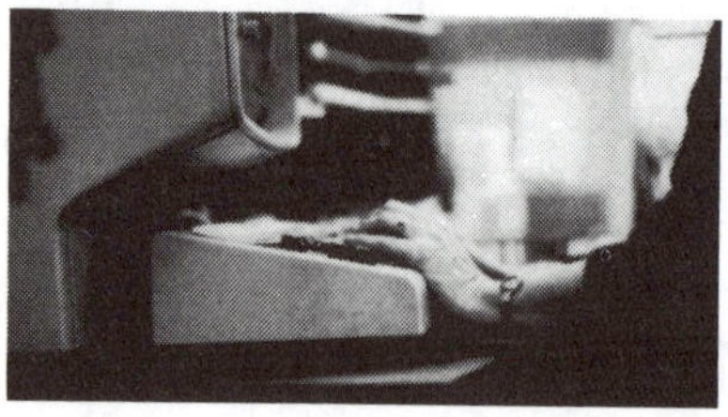

Figure 9-11

Solutions

Keyboard Alignment. The objective is to keep the arm-hand alignment as straight as possible. For conventional typing, this means that the keyboard should be placed squarely in front of the operator. However, in cases of only single-handed keying (as in data entry via number pad), a better position is for the keyboard to be placed off to either side of the operator so that the wrist need not be bent at all (figure 9-12).

Figure 9-12

Keyboard Thickness/Wristrests. A thin keyboard or use of a wristrest can help to minimize extension (backward bending) of the hand when resting the hand against or before the keyboard (figure 9-13). Sometimes the front edge of the keyboard will be broad enough for supporting the palms and wrists (figure 9-14).

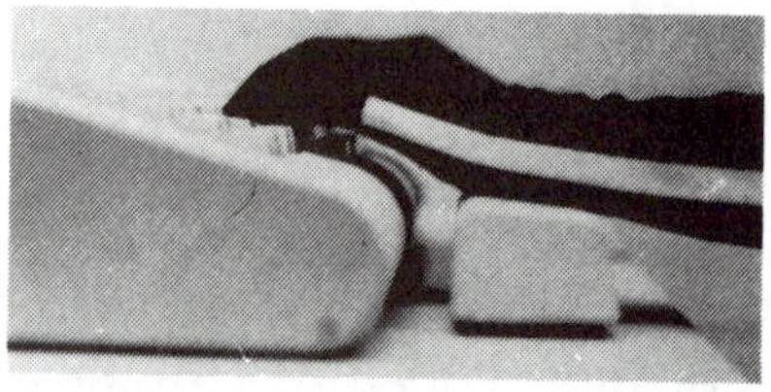

Figure 9-13

Figure 9-14

Wristrests specially designed for use with VDT keyboards are commercially available. Good design features for a wristrest are described below in the discussion of arm-hand rest systems. Importantly, if the wristrest is not well designed, it may be worse than no rest at all. When the wrist or palm is rested on a hard or sharp object, the pressure exerted may increase the opportunity for internal or external trauma to the wrist or palm.

Keyboard Height/Angle. Some keyboards are equipped with "legs" which allow height-angle adjustment (figure 9-15). Some multi-surface VDT tables enable height and angle adjustment of the keyboard support (figure 9-16). These features provide the opportunity to make adjustments to improve arm-hand postures and comfort.

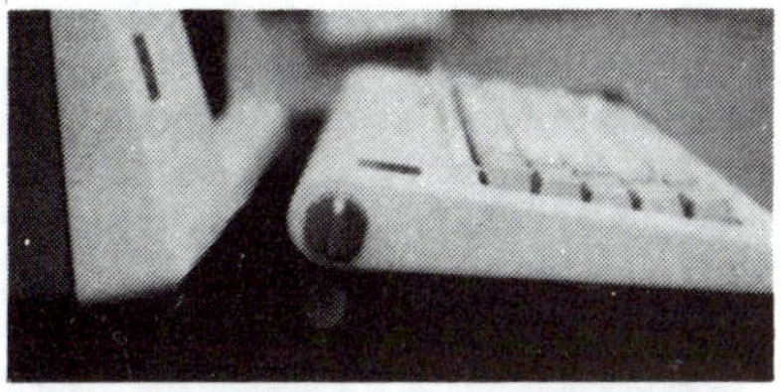

Figure 9-15

Figure 9-16

Arm-Hand Support

Problems

Worktable design sometimes makes it difficult to periodically rest the hands. Commonly, the table is too narrow, leaving no room for a wristrest or for resting the forearms or hands on the table (figure 9-17).

Figure 9-17

Wrists, palms or forearms are sometimes supported against a sharp edge of the desk or VDT chassis (figure 9-18).

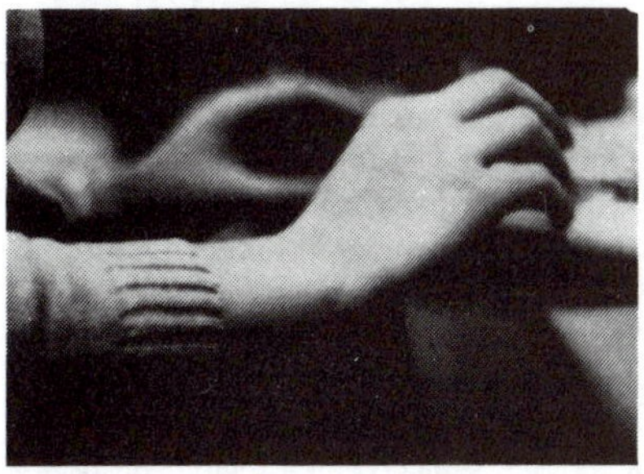

Figure 9-18

Pressures at this point can be substantial since a small area absorbs the full weight of the limb. Even resting the palms or wrists against the hard exterior of a keyboard or wristrest may result in problems if contact is continuously made at the same point.

Narrow, cutting, or unpadded armrests may create irritation at the elbow (figure 9-19). The usefulness of armrests is reduced to the extent that muscular efforts are required to hold the arm in place on the rest. This can happen with narrow, slippery armrests.

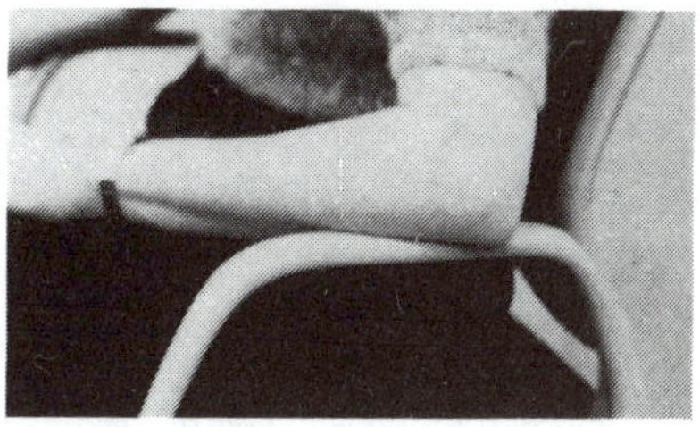

Figure 9-19

Solutions

Elbow-Armrest Design. Careful attention needs to be given to the design of chair supports for the arms or elbows in terms of length, height, separation, width, and padding. Poorly designed supports may create more problems than they resolve. Design specifications for these features are provided in the preceeding chapter on preventing neck and shoulder strain, and in Appendix A (Chair Checklist and Evaluation).

Wristrests. First of all, to use a separate wristrest or to support the hands upon the table top, the table will usually need to be deeper than the conventional typing table or "return" of a conventional office desk. Comfortable VDT positioning, leaving room for hand support, may require 30-36 inches of depth. A temporary solution for a narrow table (such as a desk return) is to overlay the table with a surface of a larger area (figure 9-20).

Figure 9-20

Figure 9-21

A good wristrest should have a fairly broad surface (a couple inches would seem appropriate) with a rounded front edge to prevent cutting pressures (figure 9-21). Padding further reduces the opportunity for compression and irritation. Height adjustability is important so the wristrest can be set to a preferred level. While wristrests are available commercially, they can also be readily fabricated. A firm piece of foam rubber is inexpensive and can be readily shaped and covered with fabric for aesthetic purposes, if desired (figure 9-22). Some operators will tape the rest to the front of the keyboard.

Figure 9-22

Any edges, such as the front of the keyboard or front of the desk which contact the palm, wrist, or forearm should be rounded. Padding may help if they are not (figure 9-23). Some operators find it comfortable to lightly pad the top front surface of the keyboard when using it as a palm support (figure 9-24).

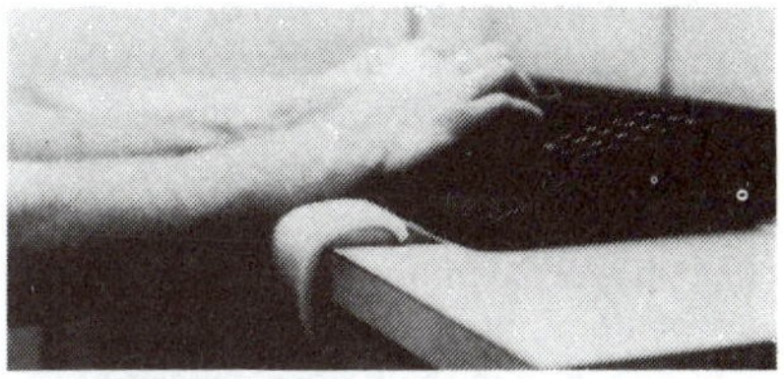

Figure 9-23

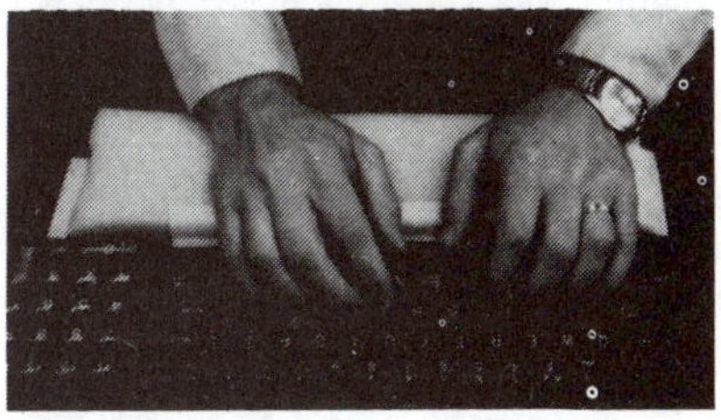

Figure 9-24

Highly Repetitive Tasks

Some VDT jobs (for example, key-to-disc data entry) have very little built-in variety. Nearly identical motion patterns are continuously repeated at a high rate of speed. In such cases the potential for irritation or wear to the structures of the arms and hands becomes a concern.

The ultimate solution to this problem is to redesign the job to eliminate highly repetitive tasks. But the first step is to correct poor postures of the arms and hands. Remember, the opportunity for injury is greater when repeated motions are combined with poor arm-hand posture.

If posture correction does not succeed in eliminating discomfort associated with repetitive tasks, then some degree of redesign of the job routine will be necessary.

Options include:

- Expanding (enlarging) the job of each operator beyond the scope of the repetitive task.
- Rotation of operators among different jobs or tasks.
- Introducing additional rest pauses.
- Redesign of the repetitive task.

The first two solutions are the best. Broadening the variety of tasks performed means that each person spends less total time at the repetitive task. The alternate tasks can provide relief as well as productive activity. Unfortunately, the variety of activities in many VDT facilities is too limited to make these options feasible. In this case, the solution is a more limited work spell or additional breaks.

One further option is redesign of the repetitive task. If one looks closely enough, it is possible to find some opportunity for variety in all VDT jobs. Begin by carefully itemizing all the different subtasks performed and their schedule. Long periods during which a single task such as data or text entry are performed can be broken up by rescheduling. Instead of keying for 20 minutes before proofing, key for 10 minutes. Place only one document at a time in the holder instead of three or four. Build new activities into your job. Move your phone to a position you have to walk to, or the printer across the room. The forced change in routine may appear inefficient, but you might be surprised. The variation in activity can help prevent or relieve fatigue, and this may actually boost performance. At the same time, sore hands and arms are getting a needed rest.

We cannot specify exactly how the work pattern should be reorganized. It depends upon the nature of the particular job. However, the starting point is to list all of the activities performed, however small, so you know just exactly what you have to work with.

Emotional Stress

Emotional stress shows up in increased muscle tension in the arm and hands, just as in the back and neck. For example, most of us have had the experience of pressing down so hard on a pencil that the lead breaks when writing while angry or under pressure. In VDT operators, a common reaction to stress is to strike the keys much harder than necessary. The result is increased wearing shock to the joints and tendons of the arms and hands. Of course, steady tension in the muscles also promotes muscle fatigue.

The best solution is to control the circumstances that cause stress to begin with. Additionally, it is possible to bring emotion related muscle tensing reactions under control as described in Appendix D. Be alert to how hard you and other operators around you strike the keyboard. Then consciously practice using only enough force to be certain that the key depresses sufficiently. You will find that it won't affect your performance at all, and loosening up may also take the edge off the stress you feel.

Sometimes keys are struck hard because they don't provide any auditory feedback or "feel" indicating that the key is sufficiently depressed. Some VDTs prevent this problem with a speaker that provides a click or beep when the key is depressed. This option is a definite plus.

Personal Factors Contributing to Arm-Hand Disorders

Poor Arm-Hand Posture

A number of personal characteristics and habits of operators can contribute to arm-hand disorders. VDT operators need to pay attention to their personal postural habits at the job and away from the job. How many times have you seen someone resting their head on their hand as shown in figure 9-25? Notice the backward bend of the hand at the wrist. The same posture is sometimes seen in grasping bicycle handlebars (figure 9-26). Even sleeping is sometimes associated with poor arm-hand postures. The head is often supported on the bent arm, or the hands and fingers curled. Doctors will sometimes prescribe splinting of the wrists at night to prevent poor wrist posture while sleeping.

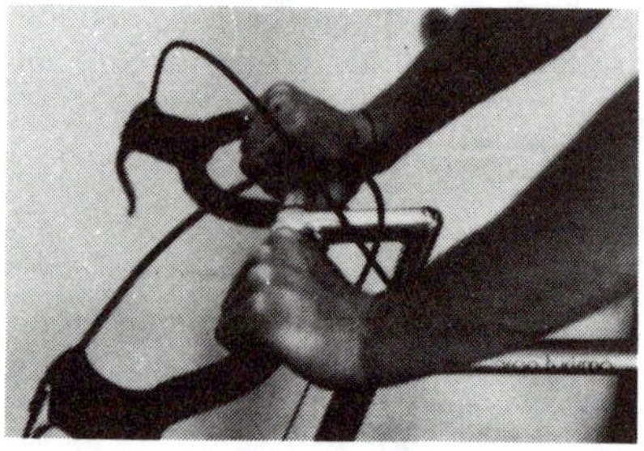

Highly Repetitive Activities

Certain leisure activities such as needlepoint or crocheting involve highly repetitive motions which operators may find add to the discomfort they experience from repetitious tasks at work.

Diet

Diet may have an influence on the development of arm-hand disorders. The B vitamins, obtained in protein such as meat or eggs, are necessary for the repair and protection of nerve cells. B vitamins are not stored well in the body so they need to be replaced on a regular basis.

Consider too the influence of coffee or other stimulants. While improving mental alertness, they also contribute to increased muscle tension which is bad for the arms and hands as well as the back and neck.

Other Factors

Individual operators can do something about all of the preceding factors. There are other provocative factors that the individual has little control over. Aging, gender, and a number of diseases such as diabetes are associated with increased nerve problems in the arms and hands. Women seem to have a greater incidence of carpal tunnel syndrome than men. The incidence increases in older women. Pregnancy is also associated with an increase in carpal tunnel problems, possibly due to increased swelling in the wrists.

This means that we have to be especially alert for arm-hand problems among individuals who are particularly at risk, and pay greater attention to the design of their jobs and workstations.

• • •

Part V

Research Frontiers in Human-Computer Interaction

When a new land is being explored, the frontier is everywhere. Almost every topic covered in this book remains an active area of research. Although frustrating to developers, because we have relatively few definitive answers, it makes the territory very exciting for those embarking on research.

We need to know much more about work, social organization, and impacts of technology. Design and evaluation present new challenges (and we haven't yet solved all the old ones!) as systems grow more and more complex. With greater emphasis on portability and interoperability, and on managing software complexity, development methods and tools remain an active area of research. Sound, animation, video, pen-based computing—only the first steps have been taken. Human psychology changes much more slowly, but our theories are still rudimentary. Designing for human capabilities is challenged by the rapid changes in environments that require mutual fit and adaptation of humans and computers.

The preceding chapters have covered the mainstream of human-computer interaction. In the remaining four chapters, we examine newer areas that have come from relative obscurity to prominence in the last few years. In each case, there is now vigorous activity on both the research and commercial fronts.

Chapter 11 covers computer-supported work and groupware. Human-computer interaction has to date largely focused on individual users working with devices such as keyboard and mouse. Despite adding novel input and output devices, the focus has typically remained on individual work. As networks link more and more users, however, this perspective is inadequate. We are compelled to develop software to support groups of people and entire organizations. Yet application developers accustomed to thinking in terms of individual users may not be sensitive to the issues surrounding cooperative work and may therefore be ill-prepared for the new challenges presented by groupware. Personal computers stood as small islands in the 1980s, each supporting one person. As the islands connect, software must become "group aware" or risk extinction.

Chapter 12 covers tailorable and adaptive systems, seen as a way to get developers "out of the loop." As everyone becomes a user and desires software tailored to their personal (and group) needs, there are not enough developers to go around. When the telephone company had insufficient operators to service its growing community of users, it solved the problem by using technology to turn each user into an operator. We now enter information that operators once looked up or handled for us. Likewise, many envision "end-user programming" as the solution to application development. With the proper tools, this argument goes, users can create their preferred environments without having to learn formal programming languages. Others feel that the remaining developers will be put out of business by introducing artificial intelligence into interfaces (at last?!), interface agents that will adapt to our needs and do our bidding.

Chapter 13 covers hypertext, multimedia, and hypermedia. Hypertext allows us to enrich documents by adding structure that facilitates organization, browsing, and retrieval of information. The decades-old visions of Bush, Engelbart, and Nelson continue to inspire research and development, but we are now able to support large-scale explorations and applications of the systems they imagined. Advances in algorithms and in processor and memory design have also allowed us to enrich the textual data in these documents to include graphics, voice, sound, animation, and video. Interfaces become livelier and more appealing, and we as researchers have an exciting set of new problems to solve.

Before moving on to the final chapter, we digress with one more case study, a look at the pioneering Freestyle system developed by Wang Laboratories in the 1980s. Freestyle brings together many of the themes developed in earlier chapters, especially pen-based computing, gestural interfaces, computer-supported collaborative work, and multimedia. It is also a good example of iterative design that attempted with mixed success to be responsive both to individual needs for training and support and to the organizational conext in which the technology was introduced. Yet this pioneering system failed commercially; our presentation will explore some of the reasons.

Finally, in Chapter 14, we explore cyberspace, a term which means different things to people. We shall define it to include three utopian visions: global networking, virtual reality, and ubiquitous computing.

The grass roots phenomenon of global networking has received a tremendous boost and incredible attention from the growth of the Internet and the appearance of Mosaic and the World-Wide Web. Although the technologies underlying virtual communities are fairly simple, their effects are profound. Text-based bulletin boards and computer-mediated communication systems are now active places for information exchange, argument, and discussion for millions of Internet users. Gopher, Mosaic, and the World-Wide Web provide mechanisms for retrieving and self-publishing information in a global hypertext system. The virtual communities now forming around these technologies are growing very rapidly, and may be a harbinger of the much hyped "information highway."

Virtual reality has seized the imagination of much of the public like no computer technology other than the Internet. The goal of immersing users in rich sensory artificial worlds limited only by our imagination has also inspired computer scientists to do the slow, hard work of solving the technical and human adaptation problems that stand in the way of realizing this vision.

Finally, ubiquitous computing represents a profound shift in perspective. Computers are no longer boxes with displays and keyboards, but specialized and often invisible computational elements populating many niches in our environment and acting synergistically with one another.

As we move toward the year 2000, the ideas and technologies presented in this book will progress from research ideas to working prototypes to products. Some will develop in ways that our authors predict, others in radically different and perhaps barely recognized forms. The only certainty is that our society will change as the new technologies are adopted. Virtual communities, virtual reality, and ubiquitous computing, in particular, bring with them bright utopian and dark antiutopian visions. To behave ethically, we must thoughtfully anticipate and consider implications of the use of these technologies. Hopefully we will then be able to influence their development and use for the benefit of all humanity.

Chapter 11

Groupware and Computer-Supported Cooperative Work

Computer-supported cooperative work or CSCW (Greif, 1988; Baecker, 1993) is computer-assisted coordinated activity carried out by groups of collaborating individuals. Examples of such activities include communication, problem solving, and coauthoring a document. CSCW seeks to become a scientific discipline guiding the thoughtful and appropriate design and development of *groupware*, the multiuser software that supports such activities. Groupware has been defined by Malone (cited in Coleman and Shapiro, 1992) as "information technology used to help people work together more effectively."

There is controversy over the definition of groupware. Some investigators include network file servers, some include data base software, some include electronic mail, and some include none of these. One view is that of Lynch, Snyder, and Vogel (1990, p. 160), who write:

> *Groupware is distinguished from normal software by the basic assumption it makes: groupware makes the user aware that he is part of a group, while most other software seeks to hide and protect users from each other. . . . Groupware . . . is software that accentuates the multiple user environment, coordinating and orchestrating things so that users can "see" each other, yet do not conflict with each other.*

The term *groupware* was coined by Peter and Trudy Johnson-Lenz (1982, p. 47), who defined it to be "intentional GROUP processes and procedures to achieve specific purposes" plus "softWARE tools designed to support and facilitate the group's work." Their early and insightful paper included discussions of structured communication forms such as messaging, conferencing, filtered exchanges, relational structures, voting, and decision support tools.

Today, groupware is a distinct product category and market, yet by the year 2000 many or most software tools will probably be "group aware," supporting coordinated group activity in addition to the use by individuals that is more conventional now.

The phrase "computer-supported cooperative work" was coined by Irene Greif and Paul Cashman in 1984 in the call for an invitation-only workshop on CSCW held in Cambridge, Massachusetts. The much-heralded "office automation" efforts of the 1970s and early 1980s were falling far short of expectations, and this was part of a recognition that it would be useful to bring together people from diverse disciplines—technical, social, economic—who shared an interest in issues of communication and coordination.

Thoughtful introductions to CSCW are found in Ellis, Gibbs, and Rein (1991), Bannon and Schmidt (1991), Robinson (1991), and Grudin (1994a). These papers debate the definition and nature of CSCW. They examine hardware and software technologies; design issues; lessons from experience; system descriptions; the nature of group work; core concepts and issues; differences in focus in Europe, America, and Asia; and analyses of the backgrounds and priorities of the diverse people who work in CSCW.

Greenberg (1991) notes that the term *computer-supported cooperative work* may be misleading: we study technologies *other than the computer*, the technology can *disrupt* activities of individuals while assisting the group overall, they support *competition* as well as cooperation, and they can assist *casual and social interactions* as well as those more typically thought of as work. Independent of what CSCW is or should be, we adopt in this chapter the pragmatism of Bannon, Bjorn-Andersen, and Due-Thomsen (1988):

> *We believe that for the moment the name CSCW simply serves as a useful forum for a variety of researchers with different backgrounds and techniques to discuss their work, and allows for the cross-fertilization of ideas, for the fostering of multi-disciplinary perspectives on the field that is essential if we are to produce applications that really are useful.*

"Forum" is indeed a nice metaphor: People come from different places with different priorities to examine the work of others with an eye to what might be useful, then return home. There is no expectation of a common goal or even a common language, and with participants from HCI, management information systems, software engineering, social science, and computer science backgrounds, to name a few, much diversity and some confusion are unavoidable.

A PARADIGM SHIFT FOR COMPUTING

Groupware and CSCW represent a paradigm shift in computer use. *Human-human* interaction rather than *human-machine* interaction is the primary focus; the computer facilitates human communication rather than acting as a purely computational device.

This paradigm shift results from several converging phenomena:

- Pervasive networking that enables widespread computer-based interpersonal and data communications
- The extension of personal computing technology to support small group productivity, sometimes known as *work-group* computing
- The maturing of technology developed by information systems researchers to support executive and managerial group decision making
- The merging of telecommunications and computing, as telecommunications companies seek new applications such as videoconferencing that exploit bandwidth
- The growing interest in telecommuting and work at a distance
- The introduction of new technologies and standards, such as ISDN (the Integrated Standard Digital Network)

Hence groupware use is now widespread and growing rapidly.

Electronic mail (e-mail), the most successful CSCW technology, is the topic of this chapter's first reading (Sproull and Kiesler, 1991a). Structured electronic mail, in which messages are often organized by topic and discussions sometimes mediated by a convenor, is called *computer conferencing* (Hiltz and Turoff, 1993). (Netnews, newsgroups, and electronic bulletin boards are other terms used for these increasingly popular forms of communication.) With the convergence of telecommunications and computation, CSCW can incorporate *teleconferencing*, the use of audio and video links while conferring at a distance.

The computer can also facilitate joint problem solving rather than communication per se, as, for example, in systems for *collaborative writing or drawing* (Sharples, 1993; Greenberg, Haynes, and Rada, 1995). Departments of management information systems (MIS) in schools of management or business study problem solving directed at issue organization and decision support, using the term *group decision support system* (GDSS). A key element in GDSSs is the *electronic meeting room.*

Thus, CSCW systems can integrate *shared interpersonal communication spaces* with *shared task workspaces* (Buxton, 1992) and support work that occurs both synchronously and asynchronously. Groupware technology expands the concepts of meeting and of collaborative work, allowing participants to transcend the requirements of being in the same place and working together at the same time.

Much groupware is designed for relatively small groups. Yet technologies such as electronic mail and conferencing systems can facilitate the synergistic functioning of large numbers of individuals. We shall consider systems and applications both for *groups* and for *organizations*, although we will emphasize the former.

A CSCW TAXONOMY

De Sanctis and Gallupe (1987) presented a broad typology of group support systems, subsequently refined by Johansen (1988) into the widely used 2-by-2 matrix shown in Figure 11.1. This typology differentiates groupware technologies in terms of their abilities to bridge time and to bridge space. Group members may work together at the same time, or work whenever they please. They may meet in a single room, or be on different floors, buildings, cities, or continents. Sample applications are included in each quadrant of Figure 11.1. The different activities create different technical challenges for the people who build tools to support them. Use of the tools also gives rise to different social and behavioral challenges.

FIGURE 11.1

Time and space-based views of CSCW technologies.

	One meeting site (same places)	**Multiple meeting sites (different place)**
Synchronous communications (same time)	**Face to Face Interactions** • *Public computer displays* • *Electronic meeting rooms* • *Group decision support systems*	**Remote Interactions** • *Shared view desktop conferencing systems* • *Desktop conferencing with collaborative editors* • *Video conferencing* • *Media spaces*
Asynchronous communications (different times)	**Ongoing Tasks** • *Team rooms* • *Group displays* • *Shift work groupware* • *Project management*	**Communication and Coordination** • *Vanilla e-mail* • *Asynchronous conferencing, bulletin boards* • *Structured messaging systems* • *Workflow management* • *Version control* • *Meeting schedulers* • *Cooperative hypertext, organizational memory*

Extensions of this widely used taxonomy have been proposed. De Sanctis and Gallupe (1987) placed a greater emphasis on differences in group size. Nunamaker et al. (1991) also differentiated between multiple individual sites and multiple group sites. Grudin (1994a) refined both time and place dimensions to include *same, different but predictable,* and *different and unpredictable,* reasoning that supporting an activity that is restricted to a few sites or a limited period of time creates different constraints than more open-ended activity.

These taxonomies can be useful, but most real work involves activities centered in more than one cell. The activity in a meeting is linked to earlier activities that may have been physically dispersed. A system that does not provide capabilities from several quadrants can create problems—participants in a meeting may expect a computer system there to be networked to the computers in their office to retrieve material worked on at a different time, for example. Thus, systems are moving toward "any time, any place" support. Nevertheless, this taxonomy is useful as a way to present and remember the different activities and applications in the world of groupware. We shall use it in this chapter, considering first asynchronous and then synchronous groupware.

ASYNCHRONOUS GROUPWARE

Asynchronous groupware supports communication and problem solving among groups of individuals who contribute at different times, and typically also are geographically dispersed. We consider three categories of approaches:

- Electronic mail and computer conferencing systems
- Structured messaging systems that use rules or knowledge to process mail, perhaps helping to manage and coordinate the flow of work within an organization
- Cooperative hypertext and hypermedia systems for constructing data bases and knowledge repositories that serve as *organizational memories*

Electronic Mail and Computer Conferencing

Electronic mail is arguably the most successful form of groupware developed and deployed to date. It is asynchronous, fast, can be addressed to multiple receivers, and has a built-in external memory that can be processed by computer (Sproull, 1991). Although e-mail has typically consisted only of text, increasingly it is multimedia, incorporating static images, voice, and even video (Borenstein, 1993).

The original intent of electronic mail was to facilitate point-to-point communication, very much like conventional surface mail (also called "snail mail"), but with greater speed and efficiency. Because e-mail can be addressed to multiple receivers, the identical base technology can facilitate discussion by groups or networks of individuals. This technology, variously known as *computer conferencing systems* or *electronic bulletin boards (bboards),* organizes user access and message transmission by topic or time rather than by the names of individual recipients (Kerr and Hiltz, 1982; Hiltz, 1984; Hiltz and Turoff, 1993; Hiltz, 1994). Bulletin board messages are usually organized by *time*; the emphasis is on the broadcasting of information to a community of interest. Conferencing system messages are usually organized by *topic*; the emphasis is on the dialogue that is facilitated among members of a community. Sometimes *distribution lists* are used to route messages to individual electronic mailboxes; at other times, users must access a central repository.

Many organizations have internal e-mail facilities. A rapidly increasing number, though, permit access to the global Internet, which distributes individual e-mail as well as thousands of topically arranged *newsgroups.* Thousands of local community bboards exist, often operated out of a person's home. Major private providers of e-mail and bulletin board facilities, such as Compuserve, Prodigy, and America OnLine, serve millions of people. All of these now have "gateways" to the Internet, allowing messages to flow back and forth to a potential community of tens of millions of individuals (see Chapter 14).

Thus, e-mail enables not only faster and efficient communications, but connections and linkages that were not heretofore possible and that "change the conventional patterns of who talks to whom and who knows what" (Sproull and Kiesler, 1991a, p. 116). The reading by Sproull and Kiesler sketches how computer networks can significantly change the structure of organizations and the conduct of work. They report recent results from laboratory experiments and field studies.

One series of laboratory studies investigated how electronic messaging affects group work (Sproull and Kiesler, 1991b; Kiesler and Sproull, 1992). In these experiments, computer-mediated small group decision making typically involves longer decision times, more equal participation, more difficult consensus-building processes, and more willingness to choose risky options than do face-to-face meetings. In interpreting this result, keep in mind that the richness of face-to-face interactions is lost in the limited interaction possible in text-based computer conferencing.

A significant role of electronic communications (described in detail in Chapter 5 of Sproull and Kiesler, 1991b) is in increasing the informational and emotional connections of employees, particularly those who are "peripheral," geographically or hierarchically distant from the center of activity. A field study summarized by Sproull and Kiesler and described in more detail in Eveland and Bikson (1988) illustrates this phenomena. Matched groups of active workers and retirees spent a year planning a company's retirement policy. One group had the option of using electronic communication; the second task force did not. The electronically supported group developed a structure that achieved greater breadth of access and a greater opportunity to lead or participate. They also maintained a higher degree of contact than the other group, felt more involved in the work of the group, and reported less communication isolation.

A broader treatment of the use and impacts of electronic mail and computer conferencing is the book *Connections* by Sproull and Kiesler (1991b). The book covers issues such as the coordinating effects of computer-mediated communications (CMC), "electronic etiquette" in CMC, changes in group dynamics between face-to-face meetings and electronic meetings, the role of CMC in allowing employees at an organization's periphery to feel connected, and the problems of authority, control, and influence that arise through the use of CMC.

Problems of authority and control are also highlighted in a paper by Perin (1991), who shows how CMC can create *electronic social fields* that challenge and stress conventional bureaucratic structures within organizations. A classic case of this documented by Zuboff (1988, Chapter 10) is that of "DrugCorp," where enthusiastic use of CMC for "access to information, thoughtful dialogue, and social banter" seriously threatened management when the content of supposedly closed conferences became public knowledge. The eventual result was the demise of the system's vitality. Clearly, e-mail can be a powerful technology for challenging and possibly transforming the patterns of communication and methods of control in an organization.

Structured Messages, Agents, and Workflow

The dramatic success of e-mail has also led to a number of problems such as an overabundance of e-mail, the receipt of large quantities of unwanted electronic "junk mail," and the inability to find needed information in huge data bases of conference messages. Structured messaging systems represent an attempt to provide users with better methods of organizing, classifying, filtering, and managing messages. One goal is the creation of "intelligent" messaging systems in which useful tasks are delegated to computer processes typically known as agents (see Chapter 12). In some cases the role of messages is to define, embody, and manage workflow in a corporation.

Malone and his coworkers (Malone et al., 1987a, 1987b, 1989; Malone, 1987 video) developed the Information Lens as an environment for intelligent e-mail management using *semistructured messages*, and methods for mail management via the specification of rules for processing messages. They later generalized the Information Lens to allow the description of cooperative work procedures other than electronic mail. Object Lens (Lai, Malone, and Yu, 1988) and Oval (Malone, Lai, and Fry, 1992) enable unsophisticated computer users to create their own cooperative work applications using simple, powerful building blocks. These include the representation of things in the world as semistructured *objects* with template-based interfaces, the summarizing of collections of objects in customizable *views*, and the development of rule-based agents for performing active tasks for people without requiring their attention or direct intervention.

Two other generalizations of the message concept have recently gained popularity. *Multimedia mail* (see also Chapter 13) allows data other than text, such as images, audio (see IBM, 1985 video), and video, to be sent over a network. Freestyle (see Wang Labs, 1989 video), discussed in Case C, was an early pioneer in this area. A popular modern standard is MIME (Multipurpose Internet Mail Extensions) that uses the standard Internet mail carrier (Borenstein, 1993). *Computational mail* is "the embedding of programs within electronic mail messages" (Borenstein, 1992). The resulting *active messages* can carry out particular interactions with recipients in addition to transmitting information (Borenstein and Thyberg, 1991; Goldberg, Safran, and Shapiro, 1992).

One way in which interdependencies among coworkers are managed and mediated and coordination is achieved is through language. A *language/action perspective* on the design of cooperative work has been presented by Winograd (1987–1988). Winograd defines *conversation* "to indicate a coordinated sequence of acts that can be interpreted as having linguistic meaning." A request, for example, can be followed by accepting that request, or by declining, or by making a counteroffer. Each of these conversation steps is followed by other steps in a "conversation for action." Flores et al. (1988) explain the language/action perspective—their theory of "language as social action" and show how it was made the basis for an early commercial groupware product (The Coordinator).

The language/action perspective was very influential, and work on such systems continues (De Michelis and Grasso, 1994). It has, however, touched on a key controversy in CSCW, and in HCI more generally. Information must be formally represented in a system if the system is to act on it intelligently, yet it is unclear how much of our tacit understanding of the world can usefully be represented formally. When is a formal representation a simplification, and when is a simplification more of a hindrance than a help? Perhaps no other groupware application has been as controversial in this regard as The Coordinator (e.g., Bowers and Churcher, 1988; Bannon and Schmidt, 1991; Robinson, 1991). See Suchman (1994) and Winograd (1994) for a debate on this topic, which is to be commented upon by others in the journal *CSCW* in 1995. The larger issue of the limits to the usefulness of formally representing knowledge also influences the discussion of workflow systems and organizational memories noted below, and is central to the discussion of critics, agents, and other intelligent interface support in Chapter 12.

Recently, more comprehensive systems for workflow management within organizations have been proposed and built (Medina-Mora et al., 1992). Because speech act structures must be tailored to different group needs and organizational flavors, toolkits have been developed that allow particular conversational structures to be specified, e.g., Strudel (Shepherd, Mayer, and Kuchinsky, 1990), Oval (Malone, Lai, and Fry, 1992), and the Conversation Builder (Kaplan et al., 1992). Workflow systems are apparently succeeding in application domains marked by fairly routinized activity, but are only beginning to be discussed in the CSCW research literature (e.g., Abbott and Sarin, 1994).

Cooperative Hypertext and Organizational Memory

In e-mail, the focus is on the process of messaging; in workflow processing, the focus is on messages that define process. Yet some applications focus instead on the corpus of messages or other computer documents and their interrelationships. They may then best be described as *cooperative hypertext systems*, in which a web of complex information is recorded and structured into a hypertext (see Chapter 13). Applications of such systems include collaborative knowledge building, asynchronous collaborative writing, and creating an *organizational memory*.

For example, Schatz (1991, 1991–1992) considers how to enhance the process of cooperative knowledge building in carrying out scientific research. The goal of the Community Systems project is to build an electronic scientific community by collecting "all" of a community's scientific knowledge into a digital library and then making it transparently available and manipulable over nationwide networks. The Telesophy system is being used by a community of 500 researchers studying the nematode worm *C. elegans*, a model organism in molecular biology.

Conklin (1992) proposes stronger criteria for organizational memory, arguing that organizations must shift from a document-

and artifact-oriented paradigm to one that embraces *process* as well. He suggests that this can be done with software that integrates three technologies—hypertext, groupware, and a *rhetorical method*, such as the *Issue-Based Information System (IBIS)*. The rhetorical method can improve the quality of the dialogue process within an organization by providing a structure for the discussion of complex problems, and it can provide an improved "conversational record" in which conversations are structured according to issues instead of chronology. IBIS development and use is described in Conklin and Begeman (1988), Burgess Yakemovic and Conklin (1990), and Conklin and Burgess Yakemovic (1992). Of course, organizational memory can be applied by HCI professionals to the interface design process; the notion of preserving the design rationale of what was tried, what succeeded, and what did not was discussed in Chapter 2 of this book (see also Carroll et al., 1994 video).

IBIS systems are another example of structuring information to facilitate its processing. A lively debate over the utility of organizational memory was held at the CSCW '94 Conference. The positions are briefly summarized on pp. 445–446 of the proceedings.

Lotus Notes is, in the mid-1990s, the most successful organizational memory product, and arguably one of the most successful groupware products developed to date (Kirkpatrick, 1994). Notes is "an integrated communications and data base network application, designed to gather, organize and distribute information among work groups, regardless of individual members' physical locations" (Connor, 1992). It is also "a platform for developing workgroup applications" (Marshak, 1990). Notes can be used for message routing, report distribution, idea discussion, and for the tracking and management of projects, sales leads, and customer support information. Notes achieves this through the use of a replicated data base algorithm designed for an environment in which servers are "rarely connected" (Kawell et al., 1988). How long information is retained in a Notes application will vary; it can thus be used for ephemeral discussions and is also a reasonable long-term repository in many environments.

The most substantial and longest-term use of Notes other than at Lotus itself has been at Price-Waterhouse (PW). Laube (1992), the PW chief information officer, states that three major business issues confronting their corporation motivated the purchase of tens of thousands of Notes licenses:

- Nobody knew who had the knowledge needed to solve a particular problem.
- Price Waterhouse professionals were constantly reinventing the wheel, solving, on a worldwide scale, the same problems over and over again.
- There was a need for better communications throughout the corporation.

Unlike many technology adoptions, Notes at Price Waterhouse was introduced from the top down rather than from the bottom up, resulting in virtually 100% penetration among the roughly 1,000 partners. The following impacts were predicted by Laube (1992):

- Retention of knowledge, a "filing cabinet in the sky"
- Support for global collaboration and global discussions
- Enhanced communication

The reading by Orlikowski (1992) included in Chapter 3 presents a less enthusiastic view. She analyzes the adoption of Notes by "Alpha Corporation" in terms of the mental models of Notes users and the incentive structure and workplace norms found in the organization. Her study took place in the initial months of the introduction of Notes into Alpha, and therefore may not characterize long-term sustained use in that setting, but it points to the importance of cognitive and motivational factors in groupware use and adoption.

SYNCHRONOUS GROUPWARE

Our second major collaboration technology category is *synchronous* groupware, software that assists a group of individuals in working together *at the same time* to carry out a task such as making a decision, planning a new initiative, structuring a proposal, writing a paper, or sketching a design. The goal of achieving a *shared digital workspace*, allowing collaborators at different workstations to examine and edit a shared view of a document, typically leads to a style of interface and to a set of implementation problems that distinguish synchronous systems from asynchronous ones.

Synchronous groupware can be subdivided into four classes:

- Desktop conferencing systems, which are workstation-based applications for collaborative work at a number of desktops, for example, outlining, writing, sketching, drawing, or building a spreadsheet
- System infrastructure for supporting and implementing desktop conferencing across workstations, for example, via shared screens or shared windows
- Electronic meeting and decision rooms such as group decision support systems
- Media spaces that include computer-controlled audio-visual networks and virtual meeting environments

Desktop Conferencing Systems

One of the earliest demonstrations of a desktop conferencing system was the NLS shared-screen conferencing system (Engelbart and English, 1968, 1994 video). Originally intended for augmenting face-to-face interactions, it was later expanded to support distance conferencing. The idea was simple: all participants saw the same things on their screen (a "shared view"), and each could take turns interacting with the system.

The next milestone in desktop conferencing was Xerox PARC's Colab project, which contained a variety of synchronous multiuser interfaces (Stefik et al., 1987; Xerox PARC, 1988 video; Stefik et al., 1987; Tatar, Foster, and Bobrow, 1991). Tools for collaborative brainstorming, argument development, and freestyle sketching were used by small groups of two to six individuals working in the Collaboration Laboratory meeting room. Each individual had a workstation that was linked to all other workstations, and to a large touch-sensitive screen at the front of the room.

While Colab was designed for face-to-face meetings, many of its ideas are highly relevant to distributed desktop conferencing. For example, a central theme is *WYSIWIS (What You See Is What I See)*, an idealization of multiuser interfaces in which everyone sees exactly the same image of the shared meeting workspace and can see where everyone else is pointing. WYSIWIS is axiomatic to screen-sharing approaches, but more general multi-user interfaces often relax the abstraction consciously to allow for private workspaces and individual activities that need not be in lockstep with the group.

Since then, there has been an explosion of work on desktop conferencing systems. All CSCW collections contain readings and system descriptions relevant to desktop conferencing. Greenberg, Haynes, and Rada (1995) is a specialized collection focusing on groupware systems for real-time drawing. (See also Bier, Freeman, and Pier, 1992 video; Greenberg et al., 1992 video.)

A detailed example of one desktop conferencing tool is offered by Baecker et al. (1993), included as a reading in this chapter. It documents the design of a collaborative writing tool that supports both synchronous and asynchronous work over local and wide area networks, and that allows both WYSIWIS and decoupled views of a document. Design of their system, called SASSE, is an excellent example of following the user-centered, iterative process described in Chapter 2. It was informed by interviews with writers who had worked together collaboratively (Posner and Baecker, 1992) and by a laboratory study of writers working on a specific task using a variety of tools and communications media. It consisted of repeated cycles of design, implementation, and user testing. (See also Baecker et al., 1994 video, and Egido et al., 1987 video.)

System Infrastructure for Desktop Conferencing

There are two general approaches to building groupware. *Collaboration transparency* describes a single-user application wrapped by special system software to make it usable by a group (Lauwers and Lantz, 1990). A *collaboration-aware* system requires an application to be significantly modified or rewritten from scratch. Both approaches raise serious design and implementation issues. Implementing synchronous groupware across a network forces one to deal with difficult problems in distributed processing such as keeping replicated information consistent, creating and maintaining real-time consistent views of a shared digital workspace, and dealing with subtle issues of synchronization and concurrency control (Greenberg and Marwood, 1994).

The most straightforward way of enabling the synchronous collaborative use of interactive software is to provide a collaboration-transparent mechanism that distributes the display of a conventional single-user application program to multiple workstations and that accepts input from any one of the workstations as the program's input. This requires running the program on each of the workstations under control of a *screen sharing* system (Greenberg, 1990; Crowley, 1992).

An alternative to screen sharing is *window sharing*, which has the advantage that users can continue to work in their private workspaces while collaborating within a window that represents the public workspace. Useful papers discussing this approach are Ahuja, Ensor, and Lucco (1990; see also AT&T Bell Labs, 1989 video); Crowley et al. (1990), Lauwers et al. (1990), and Lauwers and Lantz (1990). Many of these authors discuss the advantages and disadvantages of a *replicated architecture* versus a *centralized architecture* for building desktop conferencing systems.

Shared-view systems, whether screen or window sharing, leverage existing software into groupware: off-the-shelf products can thereby be used for desktop conferencing. This major benefit comes with two serious limitations. First, because the shared software application is collaboration-transparent (i.e., thinks only one person is using it), the system offers limited "group" capabilities. This often forces the group to work around the system. For example, participants cannot work simultaneously, and must take turns interacting with the display. The second problem is technical. To make applications shareable, builders must "work around" the limitations of the operating system and application infrastructure. As a result, many collaboration-transparent systems are designed to meet technical rather than user needs, tend to have performance limitations, are buggy, or are missing essential usability features.

Increasingly, researchers are moving beyond the investigation of operating system issues for supporting groupware to the design and construction of environments, toolkits, and languages for building groupware. The GroupKit system (Roseman and Greenberg, 1992; Greenberg and Roseman, 1994 video), which directly supports the implementation of real-time groupware, is discussed and reprinted in Chapter 5 of this book.

A second toolkit for this domain is Rendezvous (Patterson et al., 1990; Patterson, 1991; Hill, 1992; Hill et al., 1993; Rohall, Patterson, and Hill, 1992 video; Brinck, 1992 video). A third approach to the design of a language and system for programming both collaboration-transparent and collaboration-aware multiuser programs is described in Dewan and Choudhary (1991a). The kind and degree of sharing or *coupling* among various views displaying a shared workspace is treated in some depth in Dewan and Choudhary (1991b) and Dewan (1992 video). Dourish (1995) examines requirements for systems to facilitate customization and application evolution.

Electronic Meeting and Decision Rooms

Synchronous groupware differs as to where the collaborators are located. Decision support systems usually involve individuals working in an *electronic meeting room*, where the activity may be carried out independently "in parallel" or may involve a common focus of attention and discussion. (But see Zachary, 1988, for a view of decision support that stresses the role of computation rather than interpersonal communication to aid human decision making.)

Meeting support systems are an unusual category of groupware in that the pioneering early work was done not in computer science departments or product development companies but in schools of management and business schools (Kraemer and King, 1988). This community has long referred to meeting support software (often in conjunction with other groupware) as *group decision support systems* (GDSS). The name derived from the fact that decision making was seen as the main activity of the principal customers of this work, executives and upper corporate or governmental management. More recently, these systems have been generalized and are often called group support systems and electronic meeting rooms.

GDSS systems have tools to facilitate idea generation (brainstorming), idea organization, prioritizing, and voting (Bostrom, Watson, and Kinney, 1992; Jessup and Valacich, 1993). Often participants contribute ideas and vote anonymously, a technique that encourages participation from those who might otherwise be too shy or too intimidated to speak up. Dennis et al. (1988), Valacich, Dennis, and Nunamaker (1991), and Nunamaker et al. (1991) describe these systems and studies of their impacts.

Architectural and ergonomic design was applied to electronic meeting rooms in the Capture Lab (Mantei, 1989; Elwart-Keys et al., 1990; Austin, Liker, and McLeod, 1990) and in the Hohenheim CATeam Room (Ferwagner et al., 1989; Lewe and Krcmar, 1990). Aspects of room layout, the placement of people in the meeting room, and the method of user participation in the meeting can affect the effectiveness and usability of the entire system. The interior design and colors of the room, the shape of the table, the position of the workstations with respect to the table, and the nature of the participants' chairs have a substantial effect on participant interactions.

Electronic blackboards or whiteboards (e.g., Begeman et al., 1986) have gone from being simply public displays to allowing interactive sketching, gesturing, and slide presentation (Elrod et al., 1992). Software that uses such a display is described by Pederson et al. (1993), a reading in Chapter 7.

Although use of these systems long lagged behind expectations for them (Kraemer and King, 1988), several companies began marketing products in 1989. Causing this turnaround, along with improved software and lower hardware costs, was a greater realization of the importance of stressing the process of use, as noted in our reading by Grudin.

Proponents of these systems have used them for a wide range of meeting types, but the ability to work in parallel and generate large lists has favored brainstorming applications. The more tedious task of idea organization has been attacked by using semantic analysis programs to make a first pass at clustering items. Although imperfect, it has been found that people enjoy this stage more when the software has made a first pass (Nunamaker and Briggs, 1994).

Media Spaces

In contrast to computer-supported meeting rooms are efforts to support synchronous problem solving by people in different locations. A *media space* is a computer-controlled teleconferencing system in which audio and video communication and shared digital workspaces are used to overcome the barriers of physical separation (Stults, 1986, 1988; Bly, Harrison, and Irwin, 1993). Media spaces support what Buxton (1992) calls a shared *interpersonal space* as well as a shared *task space*. They not only support an application in use, but give its users an awareness of who is around and how they can be reached (see also Cockburn and Greenberg, 1993).

Media spaces were investigated at Xerox PARC as a tool to support design, beginning in the mid-1980s (Stults, 1986, 1988; Xerox PARC, 1989 video; Harrison and Minneman, 1990; Bly, Harrison, and Irwin, 1993). Researchers concluded that video can reduce physical barriers (through transmission over a network) and temporal barriers (through recording and playback). Designers can learn quickly to make effective use of video as an alternative to face-to-face interaction and as a means of sharing a workspace.

The first geographically distributed media space designed for cooperative work applications was created by Xerox PARC when it established a remote laboratory in Portland, Oregon, in the mid-1980s and linked the two sites with audio and video communication over a 56-kilobit-per-second leased line (Abel, 1990; Olson and Bly, 1991). The central feature of the connection was a *video window* between the commons areas at the two sites. This was later supplemented with a computer-controllable video network that connected most locations in both sites. Although somewhat crude, the media space produced enough cohesion for the two labs to function and feel like one group and to convey a sense of "presence" of remote individuals. On the other hand, certain verbal and nonverbal cues were not transmitted as well as they would be in a face-to-face situation. This resulted in the need to alter social protocols, to supplement video meetings with occasional face-to-face meetings, and to be sensitive to issues of privacy.

The recent media space work of Hiroshi Ishii has been particularly significant because of its innovation, its immediate appeal to audiences, and its attention to the finer issues of collaborative interaction. The evolution of this work is documented in Ishii (1990); Ishii and Miyake (1991); Ishii and Kobayashi (1992); Ishii, Arita, and Kobayashi (1992 video); Ishii, Kobayashi, and Grudin (1993); Ishii, Kobayashi, and Arita (1994); Ishii (1994 video).

Ishii's early work on TeamWorkStation demonstrates the potential for special-purpose hardware to visually combine the displays of shared digital workspaces with the displays of drawing surfaces and desktop materials. Following Stefik's suggestion (Xerox PARC, 1988 video) of the importance of *seamlessness* between individual and group work, Ishii suggests that it is of equal importance to eliminate the seam between a computer application and work without a computer, using paper, pens, and pencils on a desktop. TeamWorkStation achieves this by overlaying translucent workspace images—live video analog images of computer screens and physical desktop surfaces. The computer screen, which is also overlaid, is itself a shared screen, combining windows from individual collaborators.

TeamWorkStation creates a shared interpersonal space using small windows displaying a live video image of one's collaborator, but there is a "seam" between the video window and the task windows. With his ClearBoard system, Ishii removes that seam, achieving "a smooth transition between face-to-face conversations and shared drawing activities." The ClearBoard metaphor is "talking *through* and drawing *on* a *transparent glass window*." By using half-silvered mirrors and polarizing filters, the collaborator's image appears as though behind the display, permitting direct eye contact and an awareness of the direction of the partner's gaze at the objects on the display that appears to be between the two people.

A team at Keio University has adopted another approach to achieving direct eye contact and awareness of gaze direction using a technique that permits more than two collaborators. An arced screen behind each user's desk has a surface that reflects images of remote participants projected from above and behind the user, while allowing cameras behind the screen to record the user and project images to remote participants (Okada et al., 1994). The net effect is remarkably like sitting across one's desk from two or more collaborators.

Other notable media space work has been carried out in the University of Toronto CAVECAT project (Mantei et al., 1991; Mantei and Louie, 1994 video; Sellen, Buxton and Arnott, 1992 video); at Xerox EuroPARC (Gaver et al., 1992); at Bellcore (Bellcore, 1989 video; Cool et al., 1992; Fish et al., 1993; Bellcore

Information Networking Research Laboratory, 1993); and at SunSoft (Isaacs, Morris, and Rodriguez, 1994; Tang, Isaacs, and Rua, 1994; Tang and Rua, 1994 video). (See also Koved, 1992 video; Ropa and Ahlström, 1992 video; University of Maryland, 1993 video; Dybvik and Lie, 1994 video; Pankoke-Babatz, 1994 video; Tani et al, 1994 video.)

Much of this work has involved exploring different interface metaphors to handle these new forms of communication. Unfortunately, often it has involved colleagues whose offices were close, removing the need to make heavy use of the systems. Cruder technologies such as the Internet's MBONE (see Chapter 14) may achieve more use because they address the more severe connectivity needs of those who are geographically remote. When real-time connectivity cannot be established, applications such as video mail can be used instead (Magee, and Cox, 1992 video; Hopper, 1992 video). At Olivetti, media spaces have also been abetted with the use of active badges worn by participants, enabling the system and other users to locate an individual or automatically see who is in a room outside a camera's range (Hopper, 1993 video; Richardson et al., 1994 video; see also Chapter 14). In conclusion, media spaces in the year 2000 may be very different from those of today's research prototypes.

THE ADOPTION, DEPLOYMENT, AND USE OF GROUPWARE

It all sounds like wonderful technology, but will it be used? We have seen that success or failure of conventional single-user computer systems usually depends upon how accurately designers have satisfied the true needs of users and upon the skill and sensitivity with which the technology is deployed. This is proving to be even more true of groupware.

An influential paper by Grudin (1988) focused on three challenges in developing, deploying, and using groupware:

- Most groupware requires that all group members use the application, but not everyone benefits, thereby diminishing its prospects for success.
- Intuition is a less reliable guide in developing and selecting groupware than single-user applications.
- Evaluating groupware is more difficult than evaluating single-user applications because it must be studied in the field over a period of time (an attempt to extend traditional lab methods to groupware evaluation is found in van der Velden, 1992 video).

Our next reading, Grudin (1994b), extends these points to address five additional challenges:

- The need to reach a critical mass of users and avoid "prisoner's dilemma" problems (see also Markus, 1990)
- The difficulty of supporting existing social conventions and not disrupting social processes or threatening political structures
- The high degree of exception handling and improvisation that characterizes much group activity
- The challenge in designing features to be unobtrusive yet accessible when needed
- The requirement that groupware designers and developers think much more carefully about the processes of adoption and use than they have in the past

The eight challenges are illustrated with examples. For each of them, a contrast is made between the experiences of single-user application developers and those of large (mainframe) application developers. Approaches to meeting the challenges are outlined. The last challenge is further explored in Case C, which reviews the design and deployment of an innovative but ultimately unsuccessful groupware application.

Groupware is not the only information technology whose introduction depends critically upon the social and political context in which it is to be used and which in turn modifies the work environment after it is in use, as the discussion in Chapter 3 indicates. However, issues of group setting that made little difference to word processor designers, for example, may become crucial to those developing a coauthorship system.

The goal is to meet these challenges and provide support for *all* members of many groups and organizations, to overcome limitations of separation in space and in time. Yet the results will not necessarily be beneficial to all. Workflow management systems and ubiquitous video in the workplace raise serious issues of privacy and allow new kinds of workplace monitoring and control (e.g., Robinson, 1991, and Clement, 1994). There is perhaps inevitably a tension between using technology to augment individual capabilities and using it to reduce the workforce. Our lack of knowledge about existing work practices and the likely effects of new technology on these practices can stand in the way of success.

For these reasons, one important thread in CSCW has been studies of workplace activity—in some cases, workplaces into which new technology has been introduced, but in other cases, workplaces for which technology support is simply a possibility. Examples of such work, carried out by ethnographers, sociologists, and psychologists, include Bowers (1994); Rogers (1994); Blomberg, Suchman, and Trigg (1994); Bentley et al. (1992); and Xerox PARC (1989 video). Translating the findings of such studies into design is never easy (e.g., Blomberg et al., 1993). Yet we optimistically think that by becoming acquainted with a range of such studies, CSCW researchers and developers can better define the constraints acting on groupware design and create better infrastructures for supporting groups. Dourish (1995) is an interesting effort in this direction.

GUIDE TO FURTHER READING

CSCW conferences have been held in North America every two years since the first in Austin, Texas, in 1986 (Greif, 1986). The proceedings of all except the first—Suchman (1988), Halasz (1990), Turner and Kraut (1992), and Furuta and Neuwirth (1994)—are available from ACM Press. European conferences have been held on odd-numbered years since 1989. Selected papers from the first were published in Bowers and Benford (1991). Subsequent European CSCW conference proceedings are Bannon, Robinson, and Schmidt (1991) and De Michelis, Simone, and Schmidt (1993). Papers from three other relevant conferences are found in Olson (1989), Gibbs and Verrijn-Stuart (1990), and Hendriks (1991). The ACM-sponsored Conferences on Office Information Systems and Organizational Computing Systems also include many relevant papers. The annual ACM SIGCHI Conference invariably has sessions devoted to CSCW and groupware. There are also proceedings from trade-oriented groupware conferences (Coleman, 1992, 1993), which provide more detail on some topics than is available in the research literature, notably workflow management systems.

Greif (1988) was the first of several edited collections of major papers. As with so many aspects of modern computing, Doug Engelbart had one of the earliest visions of CSCW, and Greif reprints four of his papers. In the mid-1960s Engelbart demonstrated hypertext and hierarchically structured documents that could be accessed in shared workspaces and discussed over audio and video links. Greif includes influential papers mentioned in Chapter 1 of this book by Bush and Licklider, and then surveys work through the 1970s and mid-1980s, including reprints of eight papers from the out-of-print CSCW '86 Conference proceedings.

Subsequent edited collections include Galegher, Kraut, and Egido (1990); Greenberg (1991); Bostrom, Watson, and Kinney (1992); Marca and Bock (1992); and Baecker (1993). As of this writing, Baecker (1993) is the most recent collection of classic CSCW papers and book chapters. It includes over 70 selections. Included are reviews of all topics discussed in this chapter, as well as three additional topics: the behavioral foundations for CSCW (the psychology of groups, the sociology of organizations, the psychology of media, interaction analysis, and conversational analysis); case studies of cooperative work practice; and enabling technologies for groupware—networks, multimedia technology, windowing environments, hypertext, coordination theory, and distributed systems and concurrency control.

Other resources include an annotated bibliography of papers published through early 1991, included in Greenberg (1991). In addition, the conference proceedings are part of the on-line HCI bibliography described in the introduction to this book (hcibib@cis.ohio-state.edu). The "unOfficial Yellow Pages of CSCW," a description of over 400 experimental and commercial groupware systems, can be obtained by ftp from gorgon.tft.tele.no in pub/groupware or via Word Wide Web at URL http://www.tft.tele.no/cscw/.

The most relevant journals are *Computer Supported Cooperative Work* (Kluwer, first published in 1992); *Collaborative Computing* (Chapman and Hall, since 1994); and *Journal of Organizational Computing* (Ablex, since 1991). Special issues of *Communications of the ACM* devoted to CSCW are December 1991, January 1993, and January 1994, as is the June 1994 issue of *IEEE Computer*.

Reviews focused on specific groupware topics may have begun with Licklider and Vezza (1978), included in Greif (1988), a comprehensive and insightful review of the technical characteristics and political, social, and economic impacts of information networks. Turoff (1991) reviews the early history and significant developments in computer conferencing. Kraemer and King (1988) survey two decades of work on group decision-making support.

Myron Krueger (1991) reviews 25 years of his own pioneering work on media spaces. His Videoplace system, for example, linked the body movements of one individual with the hand movements of another in a collaborative video screen dance, thereby demonstrating compelling possibilities for computer-supported cooperative *play*.

Videos of CSCW systems can be found in several editions of the *ACM SIGGRAPH Video Review*, especially issues 87 and 106, which contain the video proceedings of the ACM CSCW '92 and '94 conferences, respectively.

REFERENCES

Note: A ● before a reference indicates a reading.

Abel, M. (1990). Experiences in an Exploratory Distributed Organization. In Galegher, Kraut, and Egido (1990), 489–510. Reprinted in Baecker (1993), 792–802.

Abbott, K., and Sarin, S. (1994). Experiences with Workflow Management: Issues for the Next Generation. *Proc. CSCW '94*, 113–120.

Ahuja, S., Ensor, J., and Lucco, S. (1990). A Comparison of Application Sharing Mechanisms in Real-Time Desktop Conferencing Systems. *Proc. Conf. on Office Information Systems*, ACM, 238–248.

Austin, L., Liker, J., and McLeod, P. (1990). Determinants and Patterns of Control over Technology in a Computerized Meeting Room. *Proc. CSCW '90*, ACM, 39–51.

Baecker, R. (1993). *Readings in Groupware and Computer-Supported Cooperative Work: Assisting Human-Human Collaboration.* Morgan Kaufmann.

● Baecker, R., Nastos, D., Posner, I., and Mawby, K. (1993). The User-Centred Iterative Design of Collaborative Writing Software. *Proc. InterCH '93*, 399–405.

Bannon, L., Bjorn-Andersen, N., and Due-Thomsen, B. (1988). Computer Support for Cooperative Work: An Appraisal and Critique. In Bullinger, H. (Ed.), *Eurinfo '88. Information Systems for Organizational Effectiveness*, North-Holland.

Bannon, L., Robinson, M., and Schmidt, K. (Eds.) (1991). *Proceedings of ECSCW '91, the Second European Conference on Computer Supported Cooperative Work.* Kluwer.

Bannon, L., and Schmidt, K. (1991). CSCW: Four Characters in Search of a Context. *Proc. ECSCW'89*, 3–16. Reprinted in Baecker (1993), 50–56.

Begeman, M., Cook, P., Ellis, C., Graf, M., Rein, G., and Smith, T. (1986). Project Nick: Meetings Augmentation and Analysis. *Proc. CSCW '86*, ACM, 1–6. Extended version published in *ACM Transactions on Office Information Systems*, 5(2), 1987.

Bellcore Information Networking Research Laboratory. (1993). The Touring Machine System. *Communications of the ACM* 36(1), 68–77.

Bentley, R., Rodden, T., Sawyer, P., Sommerville, I., Hughes, J., Randall, D., and Shapiro, D. (1992). Ethnographically-Informed Systems Design for Air Traffic Control. *Proc. CSCW '92*, ACM, 123–129.

Blomberg, J., Giacomi, J., Mosher, A., and Swenton-Wall, P. (1993). Ethnographic Field Methods and Their Relation to Design. In Schuler, D., and Namioka, A. (Eds.), *Participatory Design: Principles and Practices*, Lawrence Erlbaum Associates, 123–155.

Blomberg, J., Suchman, L., and Trigg, R. (1994). Reflections on a Work-oriented Design Project. *Proc. PDC '94 Conference on Participatory Design*, CPSR, 99–109.

Bly, S., Harrison, S., and Irwin, S. (1993). Media Spaces: Bringing People Together in a Video, Audio, and Computing Environment. *Communications of the ACM* 36(1), 28–47.

Borenstein, N. (1992). Computational Mail as Network Infrastructure for Computer-Supported Cooperative Work. *Proc. CSCW '92*, ACM, 67–74.

Borenstein, N. (1993). MIME: A Portable and Robust Multimedia Format for Internet Mail. *Multimedia Systems* 1, 29–36.

Borenstein, N., and Thyberg, C. (1991). Power, Ease of Use and Cooperative Work in a Practical Multimedia Message System. *International Journal of Man-Machine Studies* 34(2), 229–259. Also appears in Greenberg (1991), 99–129, and in Baecker (1993), 485–500.

Bostrom, R., Watson, R., and Kinney, S. (Eds.) (1992). *Computer Augmented Teamwork: A Guided Tour.* Van Nostrand Reinhold.

Bowers, J. (1994). The Work to Make a Network Work: Studying CSCW in Action. *Proc. CSCW '94,* ACM, 287–298.

Bowers, J., and Benford, S. (Eds.) (1991). *Studies in Computer Supported Cooperative Work: Theory, Practice, and Design.* Proc. First European Conference on Computer Supported Cooperative Work. Held in 1989. North-Holland.

Bowers, J., and Churcher, J. (1988). Local and Global Structuring of Computer Mediated Communication: Developing Linguistic Perspectives on CSCW in Cosmos. *Proc. CSCW '88,* ACM, 125–139.

Burgess Yakemovic, K., and Conklin, J. (1990). Report on a Development Project Use of an Issue-Based Information System. *Proc. CSCW '90,* ACM, 105–118. Reprinted in Baecker (1993), 566–579.

Buxton, W. (1992). Telepresence: Integrating Shared Task and Person Spaces. *Proc. Graphics Interface '92,* Morgan Kaufmann, 123–129. Reprinted in Baecker (1993), 816–822.

Clement, A. (1994). Considering Privacy in the Development of Multimedia Communications Systems. *Computer Supported Cooperative Work* 2(1–2), 67–88.

Cockburn, A., and Greenberg, S. (1993). Making Contact: Getting the Group Communicating with Groupware. *ACM Conference on Organizational Computing Systems,* 31–41.

Coleman, D. (1992). *Proc. Groupware '92.* Morgan Kaufmann.

Coleman, D. (1993). *Proc. Groupware '93.* Morgan Kaufmann.

Coleman, D., and Shapiro, R. (1992). Defining Groupware. Special Advertising Section to *Network World,* June 22, 1992.

Conklin, J. (1992). Capturing Organizational Memory. In Coleman (1992), 133–137.

Conklin, J., and Begeman, M. (1988). gIBIS: A Hypertext Tool for Exploratory Policy Discussion. *ACM Transactions on Office Information Systems* 6(4), 303–331.

Conklin, J., and Burgess Yakemovic, K. (1992). A Process-Oriented Approach to Design Rationale. *Human-Computer Interaction* 6(3–4), 357–391.

Connor, D. (1992). Making the Most of Information. In Coleman (1992), 63–68.

Cool, C., Fish, R., Kraut, R., and Lowery, C. (1992). Iterative Design of Video Communication Systems. *Proc. CSCW '92,* ACM, 25–32.

Crowley, T. (1992). Commercial Multimedia Groupware. In Coleman (1992), 421–422.

Crowley, T., Milazzo, P., Baker, E., Forsdick, H., and Tomlinson, R. (1990). MMConf: An Infrastructure for Building Shared Multimedia Applications. *Proc. CSCW '90,* ACM, 329–342. Reprinted in Baecker (1993), 637–650.

De Michelis, G., and Grasso, M. (1994). Situating Conversations within the Language-Action Perspective: The Milan Conversation Model. *Proc. CSCW '94,* ACM, 89–100.

De Michelis, G., Simone, C., and Schmidt, K. (1993). *ECSCW '93.* Proc. Third European Conference on Computer Supported Cooperative Work. Kluwer.

Dennis, A., George, J., Jessup, L., Nunamaker, J., and Vogel, D. (1988). Information Technology to Support Electronic Meetings. *MIS Quarterly* 12(4), 591–624.

DeSanctis, G., and Gallupe, B. (1987). A Foundation for the Study of Group Decision Support Systems. *Management Science* 33(5), 589–609.

Dewan, P., and Choudhary, R. (1991a). Primitives for Programming Multiuser Interfaces. *Proc. UIST '91,* ACM, 41–48. Reprinted in Baecker (1993), 681–690.

Dewan, P., and Choudhary, R. (1991b). Flexible User Interface Coupling in a Collaborative System. *Proc. CHI '91,* ACM, 41–48.

Dourish, P. (in press). Developing a Reflective Model for Collaborative Systems. *ACM Transactions on Computer-Human Interaction.*

Ellis, C., Gibbs, S., and Rein, G. (1991). Groupware: Some Issues and Experiences. *Communications of the ACM* 34(1), 39–58. Reprinted in Baecker (1993), 9–28.

Elrod, S., Bruce, R., Gold, R., Goldberg, D., Halasz, F., Janssen, W., Lee, D., McCall, K., Pederson, E., Pier, K., Tang, J., and Welch, B. (1992). Liveboard: A Large Interactive Display Supporting Group Meetings, Presentations and Remote Collaboration. *Proc. CHI '92,* ACM, 599–607. Reprinted in Baecker (1993), 709–717.

Elwart-Keys, M., Halonen, D., Horton, M., Kass, R., and Scott, P. (1990). User Interface Requirements for Face to Face Groupware. *Proc. CHI '90,* ACM, 295–301.

Engelbart, D., and English, W. (1968). A Research Center for Augmenting Human Intellect. *Proc. Fall Joint Computer Conference* 33(1), 395–410. Reprinted in Greif (1986).

Eveland, J., and Bikson, T. (1988). Work Group Structures and Computer Support: A Field Experiment. *ACM Transactions on Office Information Systems* 6(4), 344–379. Reprinted in Baecker (1993), 443–445.

Ferwanger, T., Wang, Y., Lewe, H., and Krcmar, H. (1989). Experiences in Designing the Hohenheim CATeam Room. In Bowers and Benford (1991), 251–265.

Fish, R., Kraut, R., Root, R., and Rice, R. (1993). Video as a Technology for Informal Communication. *Communications of the ACM* 36(1), 48–61.

Flores, F., Graves, M., Hartfield, B., and Winograd, T. (1988). Computer Systems and the Design of Organizational Interaction. *ACM Transactions on Office Information Systems* 6(2), 153–172. Reprinted in Baecker (1993), 504–513.

Furuta, R., and Neuwirth, C. (Eds.) (1994). *CSCW '94: Proc. Conference on Computer Supported Cooperative Work.* Chapel Hill, NC, Oct. 22–26, 1994. ACM.

Galegher, J., Kraut, R., and Egido, C. (Eds.) (1990). *Intellectual Teamwork: Social and Technological Foundations of Cooperative Work.* Lawrence Erlbaum Associates.

Gaver, W., Moran, T., MacLean, A., Lövstrand, L., Dourish, P., Carter, K., and Buxton, W. (1992). Realizing a Video Environment: EuroPARC's RAVE System. *Proc. CHI '92*, ACM, 27–35.

Gibbs, S., and Verrijn-Stuart, A. (Eds.) (1990). *Multiuser Interfaces and Applications.* North-Holland.

Goldberg, V., Safran, M., and Shapiro, E. (1992). Active Mail: A Framework for Implementing Groupware. *Proc. CSCW '92*, ACM, 75–83.

Greenberg, S. (1990). Sharing Views and Interactions with Single-User Applications. *Proc. Conference on Office Information Systems*, ACM, 227–237.

Greenberg, S. (Ed.) (1991). *Computer-Supported Cooperative Work and Groupware.* Academic Press.

Greenberg, S., Haynes, S., and Rada, R. (in press). *Designing Groupware for Real Time Drawing.* McGraw-Hill.

Greenberg, S., and Marwood, D. (1994). Real Time Groupware as a Distributed System: Concurrency Control and its Effect on the Interface. *Proc.. CSCW '94*, ACM, 207–217.

Greif, I. (Ed.) (1986). *CSCW '86: Proc. Conference on Computer-Supported Cooperative Work.* Austin, Texas, Dec. 3–5, 1986. Microelectronics Computer Corporation.

Greif, I. (Ed.) (1988). *Computer-Supported Cooperative Work: A Book of Readings.* Morgan Kaufmann.

Grudin, J. (1988). Why CSCW Applications Fail: Problems in Design and Evaluation. *Proc. CSCW '88*, ACM, 85–93. Minor revision published as Why Groupware Applications Fail: Problems in Design and Evaluation. *Office: Technology and People* 4(3), 245–264.

Grudin, J. (1994a). Computer-Supported Cooperative Work: History and Focus. *IEEE Computer* 27(5), 19–26.

▩ Grudin, J. (1994b). Groupware and Social Dynamics: Eight Challenges for Developers. *Communications of the ACM* 37(1), 92–105.

Halasz, F. (Ed.) (1990). *CSCW '90: Proc. Conference on Computer-Supported Cooperative Work.* Los Angeles, Oct. 7–10, 1990. ACM.

Harrison, S., and Minneman, S. (1990). The Media Space: A Research Project into the Use of Video as a Design Medium. *Proc. Conference on Participatory Design*, Computer Professionals for Social Responsibility, Seattle, WA, March 31–April 1, 1990, 43–58. Excerpted in Baecker (1993), 785–791.

Hendriks, P. (Ed.) (1991). *Groupware 1991: The Potential of Team and Organisational Computing.* Software Engineering Research Centre (SERC), P.O. Box 424, 3500 AK Utrecht, The Netherlands.

Hill, R. (1992). Languages for the Construction of Multiuser Multimedia Synchronous (MUMMS) Applications. In Myers, B. (Ed.) (1992), *Languages for Developing User Interfaces*, Jones and Bartlett, 125–143. Reprinted in Baecker (1993), 672–680.

Hill, R., Brinck, T., Patterson, J., Rohall, S., and Wilner, W. (1993). The Rendezvous Language and Architecture. *Communications of the ACM* 36(1), 62–67.

Hiltz, S. (1984). *Online Communities: A Case Study of the Office of the Future.* Ablex.

Hiltz, S. (1994). *The Virtual Classroom: Learning without Limits via Computer Networks.* Revised Edition. Ablex.

Hiltz, S., and Turoff, M. (1993). *The Network Nation: Human Communication via Computer.* Revised Edition. The MIT Press.

Isaacs, E., Morris, T., and Rodriguez, T. (1994). A Forum for Supporting Interactive Presentations to Distributed Audiences. *Proc. CSCW '94*, ACM, 405–416.

Ishii, H. (1990). TeamWorkStation: Towards a Seamless Shared Workspace. *Proc. CSCW '90*, ACM, 13–26.

Ishii, H., and Kobayashi, M. (1992). ClearBoard: A Seamless Medium for Shared Drawing and Conversation with Eye Contact. *Proc. CHI '92*, ACM, 525–532. Reprinted in Baecker (1993), 829–836.

Ishii, H., Kobayashi, M., and Arita, K. (1994). Iterative Design of Seamless Collaboration Media: From TeamWorkStation to ClearBoard. *Communications of the ACM* 37(8), 83–97.

Ishii, H., Kobayashi, M., and Grudin, J. (1993). Integration of Inter-Personal Space and Shared Workspace: ClearBoard Design and Experiments. *ACM Transactions on Information Systems* 11(4), 349–375.

Ishii, H., and Miyake, N. (1991). Toward an Open Shared Workspace: Computer and Video Fusion Approach of TeamWorkStation. *Communications of the ACM* 34(12), 37–50.

Jessup, L., and Valacich, J. (Eds.) (1993). *Group Support Systems: A New Perspective.* Macmillan.

Johansen, R. (1988), *Groupware: Computer Support for Business Teams.* The Free Press.

Johnson-Lenz, P., and T. (1982). Groupware: The Process and Impacts of Design Choices. In Kerr and Hiltz (1982), 45–55.

Kaplan, S., Tolone, W., Bogia, D., and Bignoli, C. (1992). Flexible, Active Support for Collaborative Work With ConversationBuilder. *Proc. CSCW '92*, ACM, 378–385.

Kawell, L., Beckhardt, S., Halvorsen, T., Ozzie, R., and Greif, I. (1988). Replicated Document Management in a Group Communication System. Presented at CSCW '88. In Marca and Bock (1992), 226–235.

Kerr, E., and Hiltz, S. (1982). *Computer-Mediated Communication Systems: Status and Evaluation.* Academic Press.

Kiesler, S., and Sproull, L. (1992). Group Decision Making and Communication Technology. *Organization Behaviour and Human Decision Processes* 52(1), 96–123.

Kirkpatrick, D. (1994). Why Microsoft Can't Stop Lotus Notes. *Fortune*, 12 December 1994, 141–157.

Kraemer, K., and King, J. (1988). Computer-based Systems for Cooperative Work and Group Decision Making. *ACM Computing Surveys* 20(2), 115–146.

Krueger, M. (1991). *Artificial Reality II.* Addison-Wesley.

Lai, K.-Y., Malone, T., and Yu, K.-C. (1988). Object Lens: A "Spreadsheet" for Cooperative Work. *ACM Transactions on Office Information Systems* 6(4), 332–353. Reprinted in Baecker (1993), 474–484.

Laube, S. (1992). Talk at Groupware '92 Conference, San Jose, 3 August 1992.

Lauwers, J., Joseph, T., Lantz, K., and Romanow, A. (1990). Replicated Architectures for Shared Window Systems: A Critique. *Proc. Conference on Office Information Systems*, ACM, 249–260. Reprinted in Baecker (1993), 651–662.

Lauwers, J., and Lantz, K. (1990). Collaboration Awareness in Support of Collaboration Transparency: Requirements for the Next Generation of Shared Window Systems. *Proc. CHI '90*, ACM, 303–311. Reprinted in Baecker (1993), 663–671.

Lewe, H., and Krcmar, H. (1990). The CATeam Meeting Room Environment as a Human-Computer Interface. In Gibbs and Verrijn-Stuart (1990), 143–158.

Licklider, J., and Vezza, A. (1978). Applications of Information Networks. *Proceedings of the IEEE* 66(11), 1330–1346. Reprinted in Greif (1988), 143–183.

Lynch, K., Snyder, J., and Vogel, D. (1990). The Arizona Analyst Information System: Supporting Collaborative Research on International Technology Trends. In Gibbs and Verrijn-Stuart (1990), 159–174.

Malone, T., Grant, K., Lai, K.-Y., Rao, R., and Rosenblitt, D. (1987a). Semistructured Messages Are Surprisingly Useful for Computer-Supported Coordination. *ACM Transactions on Office Information Systems* 5(2), 115–131.

Malone, T., Grant, K., Lai, K.-Y., Rao, R., and Rosenblitt, D. (1989). The Information Lens: An Intelligent System for Information Sharing and Coordination. In Olson (1989), 65–88. Reprinted in Baecker (1993), 461–473.

Malone, T., Grant, K., Turbak, F., Brobst, S., and Cohen, M. (1987b). Intelligent Information Sharing Systems. *Communications of the ACM* 30(5), 390–402.

Malone, T., Lai, K.-Y., and Fry, C. (1992). Experiments with Oval: A Radically Tailorable Tool for Cooperative Work. *Proc. CSCW '92*, ACM, 289–297.

Mantei, M. (1989). Observation of Executives Using a Computerized Supported Meeting Environment. *International Journal of Decision Support Systems* 5, June 1989, 153–166. Reprinted in Baecker (1993), 695–708.

Mantei, M., Baecker, R., Sellen, A.. Buxton, W., Milligan, T., and Wellman, B. (1991). Experiences in the Use of a Media Space. *Proc. CHI '91*, ACM, 203–208. Reprinted in Baecker (1993), 803–808.

Marca, D., and Bock, G. (Eds.) (1992). *Groupware: Software for Computer-Supported Cooperative Work*. IEEE Computer Society Press.

Markus, M. (1990). Towards a "Critical Mass" Theory of Interactive Media. In Fulk, J., and Steinfield, C. (Eds.), *Organizations and Communication Technology*, Sage Publications, 194–218.

Marshak, D. (1990). Lotus Notes: A Platform for Developing Workgroup Applications. *Patricia Seybold's Office Computing Report* 13(7), July 1990.

Medina-Mora, R., Winograd, T., Flores, R., and Flores, F. (1992). The Action Workflow Approach to Workflow Management Technology. *Proc. CSCW '92*, ACM, 281–288.

Nunamaker, J., and Briggs, R. (1994). CMI and Ventana Corporation. *CHI '94 Conference Companion*, ACM, 169–170.

Nunamaker, J., Dennis, A., Valacich, J., Vogel, D., and George, J. (1991). Electronic Meeting Systems to Support Group Work. *Communications of the ACM* 34(7), 40–61. Reprinted in Baecker (1993), 718–739.

Okada, K., Maeda, F., Ichikawaa, Y., and Matsushita, Y. (1994). Multiparty Videoconferencing in Virtual Social Distance: MAJIC Design. *Proc. CSCW '94*, ACM, 385–393.

Olson, M. (Ed.) (1989). *Technological Support for Work Group Collaboration*. Lawrence Erlbaum Associates.

Olson, M., and Bly, S. (1991). The Portland Experience: A Report on a Distributed Research Group. *International Journal of Man-Machine Studies* 34(2), 211–228. Also appears in Greenberg (1991), 81–98.

Orlikowski, W. (1992). Learning from Notes: Organizational Issues in Groupware Implementation. *Proc. CSCW '92*, ACM, 362–369. Reprinted in Chapter 3 of this volume.

Patterson, J. (1991). Comparing the Programming Demands of Single-User and Multiuser Applications. *Proc. UIST '91*, ACM, 87–94.

Patterson, J., Hill, R., Rohall, S., and Meeks, W. (1990). Rendezvous: An Architecture for Synchronous Multiuser Applications. *Proc. CSCW '90*, ACM, 317–328.

Pederson, E., McCall, K., Moran, T., and Halasz, F. (1993). Tivoli: An Electronic Whiteboard for Informal Workgroup Meetings. *Proc. InterCHI '93*, ACM, 391–398. Reprinted in Chapter 7 of this volume.

Perin, C. (1991). Electronic Social Fields in Bureaucracies. *Communications of the ACM* 34(12), 75–82.

Posner, I., and Baecker, R. (1992). How People Write Together. *Proc. 25th Annual Hawaii International Conference on the System Sciences*, Vol. IV, 127–138. Reprinted with slight revisions in Baecker (1993), 239–250.

Robinson, M. (1991). Computer Supported Cooperative Work: Cases and Concepts. In Hendriks (1991), 59–75. Reprinted in Baecker (1993), 29–49.

Rogers, Y. (1994). Exploring Obstacles: Integrating CSCW in Evolving Organisations. *Proc. CSCW '94*, ACM, 67–77.

Roseman, M., and Greenberg, S. (1992). GroupKit: A Groupware Toolkit for Building Real-Time Conferencing Applications. *Proc. CSCW '92*, ACM, 43–50. Reprinted in Chapter 5 of this volume.

Schatz, B. (1991). Building an Electronic Scientific Community. *Proc. the 24th Annual Hawaii International Conference on the System Sciences*, 739–748.

Schatz, B. (1991–1992). Building an Electronic Community System. *Journal of Management Information Systems* 8(3), Winter 1991–92, 87–107. Reprinted in Baecker (1993), 550–560.

Sharples, M. (Ed.) (1993). *Computer-Supported Collaborative Writing*. Springer-Verlag.

Shepherd, A., Mayer, N., and Kuchinsky, A. (1990) Strudel—An Extensible Electronic Conversation Toolkit. *Proc. CSCW '90*, ACM, 93–104.

Sproull, L., and Kiesler, S. (1991a). Computers, Networks, and Work. *Scientific American* 265(3), September 1991, 116–123.

Sproull, L., and Kiesler, S. (1991b). *Connections: New Ways of Working in the Networked Organization*. MIT Press.

Sproull, R. (1991). A Lesson in Electronic Mail. In Sproull and Kiesler (1991b), 177–184. Reprinted in Baecker (1993), 403–406.

Stefik, M., Bobrow, D., Foster, G., Lanning, S., and Tatar, D. (1987). WYSIWIS Revised: Early Experiences with Multiuser Interfaces. *ACM Transactions on Office Information Systems* 5(2), 147–167. Reprinted in Baecker (1993), 585–595.

Stefik, M., Foster, G., Bobrow, D., Kahn, K., Lanning, S., and Suchman, L. (1987). Beyond the Chalkboard: Computer Support for Collaboration and Problem Solving in Meetings. *Communications of the ACM* 30(1), 32–47. Also appears in Greif (1988), 335–366.

Stults, R. (1986). Media Space. Xerox Palo Alto Research Center Technical Report.

Stults, R. (1988). Experimental Uses of Video to Support Design Activities. Xerox Palo Alto Research Center Technical Report SSL–89–19.

Suchman, L. (Ed.) (1988). *CSCW '88: Proc. Conference on Computer-Supported Cooperative Work*. Portland, Oregon, Sept. 26–29, 1988, ACM.

Suchman, L. (1994). Do Categories Have Politics? The Language/Action Perspective Reconsidered. *CSCW: An International Journal* 2(3), 177–190.

Tang, J., Isaacs, E., and Rua, M. (1994). Supporting Distributed Groups with a Montage of Lightweight Interactions. *Proc. CSCW '94*, ACM, 23–34.

Tatar, D., Foster, G., and Bobrow, D. (1991). Design for Conversation: Lessons from Cognoter. *International Journal of Man-Machine Studies* 34(2), 185–209. Also appears in Greenberg (1991), 55–79. Reprinted in Baecker (1993), 403–406.

Turner, J., and Kraut, R. (Eds.) (1992). *CSCW '92: Proc. Conference on Computer-Supported Cooperative Work*, Toronto, Canada, Oct. 31–Nov. 4, 1992, ACM.

Turoff, M. (1991). Computer-Mediated Communication Requirements for Group Support. *Journal of Organizational Computing* 1, 85–113. Excerpted in Baecker (1993), 407–417.

Valacich, J., Dennis, A., and Nunamaker, J. (1991). Electronic Meeting Support: The GroupSystems Concept. *International Journal of Man-Machine Studies* 34(2), 262–282. Also appears in Greenberg (1991), 133–154.

Winograd, T. (1987–1988). A Language/Action Perspective on the Design of Cooperative Work. *Human-Computer Interaction* 3(1), 3–30. Also appears in Greif (1988), 623–653.

Winograd, T. (1994). Categories, Disciplines, and Social Coordination. *CSCW: An International Journal,* 2(3), 191–197.

Zachary, W. (1988). Decision Support Systems: Designing to Extend the Cognitive Limits. In Helander, M. (Ed.) (1988), *Handbook of Human-Computer Interaction,* North-Holland, 997–1030

Zuboff, S. (1988). *In the Age of the Smart Machine: The Future of Work and Power.* Basic Books.

VIDEOS

AT&T Bell Labs (1989). Rapport. *ACM SIGGRAPH Video Review (SGVR)* 45.

Baecker, R., Glass, G., Mitchell, A., and Posner, I. (1994). SASSE: The Collaborative Editor. *ACM SGVR* 97.

Bellcore (1989). Cruiser. *ACM SGVR* 45.

Bier, E., Freeman, S., and Pier, K. (1992). MMM: The Multi-Device Multiuser Multi-Editor. *ACM SGVR* 76.

Brinck, T. (1992). The Conversation Board. *ACM SGVR* 87.

Carroll, J., van Deusen, M., Wheeler, G., Alpert, S., Karat, J., and Rosson, M. (1994). Multimedia Folklore: Capturing Design History and Rationale with Raison d'Etre. *ACM SGVR* 106.

Dewan, P. (1992). Coupling the User Interfaces of a Multiuser Program. *ACM SGVR* 87.

Dybvik, P., and Lie, H. (1994). Combining Realtime Multimedia Conferencing with Hypertext Archives in Distance Education. *ACM SGVR* 106.

Egido, C., et al. (1987). Multimedia Technology for Collaborative Writing. *ACM SGVR* 27.

Engelbart, D., and English, W. (1994). A Research Center for Augmenting Human Intellect. *ACM SGVR* 106. Originally filmed in 1968.

Greenberg, S., and Roseman, M. (1994). GroupKit: A Groupware Toolkit. *ACM SGVR* 106.

Greenberg, S., Roseman, M., Webster, D., and Bohnet, R. (1992). GroupSketch. *ACM SGVR* 87.

Hopper, A. (1992). The Pandora Multimedia System. *ACM SGVR* 87.

Hopper, A. (1993). The Active Badge System. *ACM SGVR* 89.

IBM. (1985). Olympic Message System. *ACM SGVR* 19.

Ishii, H. (1994). Seamless Media Design. *ACM SGVR* 106.

Ishii, H., Arita, K., and Kobayashi, M. (1992). Toward Seamless Collaboration Media: From TeamWorkStation to ClearBoard. *ACM SGVR* 87.

Koved, L. (1992). Rubber Rocks. *ACM SGVR* 87.

Magee, B., and Cox, G. (1992). Enhanced Factory Communications. *ACM SGVR* 87.

Malone, T. (1987). The Information Lens. *ACM SGVR* 34.

Mantei, M., and Louie, G. (1994). CAVECAT: Computer Audio Video Enhanced Collaboration at Toronto. *ACM SGVR* 106.

Pankoke-Babatz, U. (1994). CSCW for Government Work: POLIKOM-Video. *ACM SGVR* 106.

Richardson, T., Bennett, F., Mapp, G., Harter, A., and Hopper, A. (1994). Teleporting—Making Applications Mobile. *ACM SGVR* 106.

Rohall, S., Patterson, J., and Hill, R. (1992). Go Fish! A Multiuser Game in the Rendezvous System. *ACM SGVR* 76.

Ropa, A., and Ahlström, B. (1992). A Case Study of a Multimedia Co-Working Task. *ACM SGVR* 76.

Sellen, A., Buxton, B., and Arnott, J. (1992). Using Spatial Cues to Improve Desktop Videoconferencing. *ACM SGVR* 76.

Tang, J., and Rua, M. (1994). Montage: Multimedia Glances for Distributed Groups. *ACM SGVR* 106.

Tani, M., Horita, M., Yamaashi, K., Tanikoshi, K., and Futakawa, M. (1994). Courtyard: Integrating a Shared Large Screen and Individual Screens. *ACM SGVR* 106.

University of Maryland (1993). Exploring Remote Images: A Telepathological Workstation. *ACM SGVR* 88.

van der Velden, J. (1992). Delft-WITLab: Research Issues and Methods for Behavioral Analysis. *ACM SGVR* 87.

Wang Labs (1989). Freestyle. *ACM SGVR* 45.

Xerox PARC (1988). Experiments in Computer Support for Teamwork. *ACM SGVR* 58.

Xerox PARC (1989). The Office Design Project. *ACM SGVR* 45.

Computers, Networks and Work

Electronic interactions differ significantly from face-to-face exchanges. As a result, computer networks will profoundly affect the structure of organizations and the conduct of work

by Lee Sproull and Sara Kiesler

Although the world may be evolving into a global village, most people still lead local lives at work. They spend the majority of their time in one physical location and talk predominantly to their immediate co-workers, clients and customers. They participate in only a few workplace groups: their primary work group, perhaps a committee or task force and possibly an informal social group.

Some people, however, already experience a far more cosmopolitan future because they work in organizations that have extensive computer networks. Such individuals can communicate with people around the world as easily as they talk with someone in the next office. They can hold involved group discussions about company policy, new product design, hiring plans or last night's ball game without ever meeting other group members.

The networked organization differs from the conventional workplace with respect to both time and space. Computer-based communication is extremely fast in comparison with telephone or postal services, denigrated as "snail mail" by electronic mail converts. People can send a message to the other side of the globe in minutes; each message can be directed to one person or to many people. Networks can also essentially make time stand still. Electronic messages can be held indefinitely in computer memory. People can read or reread their messages at any time, copy them, change them or forward them.

Managers are often attracted to networks by the promise of faster communication and greater efficiency. In our view, the real potential of network communication has less to do with such matters than with influencing the overall work environment and the capabilities of employees. Managers can use networks to foster new kinds of task structures and reporting relationships. They can use networks to change the conventional patterns of who talks to whom and who knows what.

The capabilities that accompany networks raise significant questions for managers and for social scientists studying work organizations. Can people really work closely with one another when their only contact is through a computer? If employees interact through telecommuting, teleconferencing and electronic group discussions, what holds the organization together? Networking permits almost unlimited access to data and to other people. Where will management draw the line on freedom of access? What will the organization of the future look like?

We and various colleagues are working to understand how computer networks can affect the nature of work and relationships between managers and employees. What we are learning may help people to exploit better the opportunities that networks offer and to avoid or mitigate the potential pitfalls of networked organizations.

Our research relies on two approaches. Some questions can be studied through laboratory experiments. For instance, how do small groups respond emotionally to different forms of communication? Other questions, particularly those concerning organizational change, require field studies in actual organizations that have been routinely using computer networks. Data describing how hundreds of thousands of people currently use network communications can help predict how other people will work in the future as computer-based communications become more prevalent. Drawing on field studies and experiments, researchers gradually construct a body of evidence on how work and organizations are changing as network technology becomes more widely used. The process may sound straightforward, but in reality it is often full of exciting twists. People use technology in surprising ways, and effects often show up that contradict both theoretical predictions and managerial expectations.

One major surprise emerged as soon as the first large-scale computer network, known as the ARPANET, was begun in the late 1960s. The ARPANET was developed for the Advanced Research Projects Agency (ARPA), a part of the U.S. Department of Defense. ARPANET was intended to link computer scientists at universities and other research institutions to distant computers, thereby permitting efficient access to machines unavailable at the home institutions. A facility called electronic mail, which enabled researchers

LEE SPROULL and SARA KIESLER have spent more than a decade studying established electronic mail communities to learn about how they change patterns of communication within organizations. Sproull received a Ph.D. in social science from Stanford University in 1977. Until this year she was a professor of social sciences and sociology at Carnegie Mellon University. She is now a professor of management at Boston University's School of Management. Kiesler completed a Ph.D. in social psychology at Ohio State University in 1965. In 1979 she joined the faculty of Carnegie Mellon University, where she is a professor of social sciences and social psychology, as well as a member of the university's robotics institute.

How People Work via Electronic Mail

Global communication is possible using computer networks and electronic mail, as illustrated by the behavior of "Sue Jones," a composite based on a number of workers studied by the authors. On a typical day, Jones sends and receives from 25 to 100 pieces of electronic mail that cover both business and social topics. The maps record the links made during the course of the day, highlighting those associated with one of her working groups; the computer screens show the messages she sends to and receives from that working group. In this case, a potential crisis in the pricing of a new product is quickly resolved via electronic communication. Networks permit close, ongoing cooperation among coworkers who are physically located in very different corners of the globe.

to communicate with one another, was considered a minor additional feature of the network.

Yet electronic mail rapidly became one of the most popular features of the ARPANET. Computer scientists around the country used ARPANET to exchange ideas spontaneously and casually. Graduate students discussed problems and shared skills with professors and other students without regard to their physical location. Heads of research projects used electronic mail to coordinate activities with project members and to stay in touch with other research teams and funding agencies. A network community quickly formed, filled with friends and collaborators who rarely, if ever, met in person. Although some administrators objected to electronic mail because they did not consider it a legitimate use of computer time, demand grew sharply for more and better network connections.

Since then, many organizations have adopted internal networks that link anywhere from a few to a few thousand employees. Some of these organizational networks have also been connected to the Internet, the successor to ARPANET. Electronic mail has continued to be one of the most popular features of these computer networks.

Anyone who has a computer account on a networked system can use electronic mail software to communicate with other users on the network. Electronic mail transmits messages to a recipient's electronic "mailbox." The sender can send a message simultaneously to several mailboxes by sending the message to a group name or to a distribution list. Electronic bulletin boards and electronic conferences are common variants of group electronic mail; they too have names to identify their topic or audience. Bulletin boards post messages in chronological order as they are received. Computer conferences arrange messages by topic and display grouped messages together.

The computer communications technology in most networked organizations today is fairly similar, but there exist large differences in people's actual communication behavior that stem from policy choices made by management. In some networked organizations, electronic mail access is easy and open. Most employees have networked terminals or computers on their desks, and anyone can send mail to anyone else. Electronic mail costs are considered part of general overhead expenses and are not charged to employees or to their departments. In the open-network organizations we have studied, people typically send and receive between 25 and 100 messages a day and belong to between 10 and 50 electronic groups. These figures hold across job categories, hierarchical position, age and even amount of computer experience.

In other networked organizations, managers have chosen to limit access or charge costs directly to users, leading to much lower usage rates. Paul Schreiber, a *Newsday* columnist, describes how his own organization changed from an open-access network to a limited-access one. Management apparently believed that reporters were spending too much time sending electronic mail; management therefore had the newspaper's electronic mail software modified so that reporters could still receive mail but could no longer send it. Editors, on the other hand, could still send electronic mail to everyone. Clearly, technology by itself does not impel change. Management choices and policies are equally influential.

But even in organizations that have open access, anticipating the effect of networks on communication has proved no easy task. Some of the first researchers to study computer network communications thought the technology would improve group decision making over face-to-face discussion because computer messages were plain text. They reasoned that electronic discussions would be more purely intellectual, and so decision making would be less affected by people's social skills and personal idiosyncracies.

Research has revealed a more complicated picture. In an electronic exchange, the social and contextual cues that usually regulate and influence group dynamics are missing or attenuated. Electronic messages lack information regarding job titles, social importance, hierarchical position, race, age and appearance. The context also is poorly defined because formal and casual exchanges look essentially the same. People may have outside information about senders, receivers and situations, but few cues exist in the computer interaction itself to remind people of that knowledge.

In a series of experiments at Carnegie Mellon University, we compared how small groups make decisions using computer conferences, electronic mail and face-to-face discussion [*see illustration below*]. Using a network induced the participants to talk more frankly and more equally. Instead of one or two people doing most of the talking, as happens in many face-to-face groups, everyone had a more equal say. Furthermore, networked groups generated more proposals for action than did traditional ones.

Open, free-ranging discourse has a dark side. The increased democracy associated with electronic interactions in our experiments interfered with decision making. We observed that three-person groups took approximately four times as long to reach a decision electronically as they did face-to-face. In one case, a group never succeeded in reaching consensus, and we were ultimately forced to terminate the experiment. Making it impossible for people to interrupt one another slowed decision making and increased conflict as a few members tried to dominate control of the network. We also found that people tended to express extreme opinions and vented anger more openly in an electronic face-off than when they sat together and talked. Computer scientists using the ARPANET have called this phenomenon "flaming."

We discovered that electronic communication can influence the effects of people's status. Social or job position normally is a powerful regulator of group interaction. Group members typ-

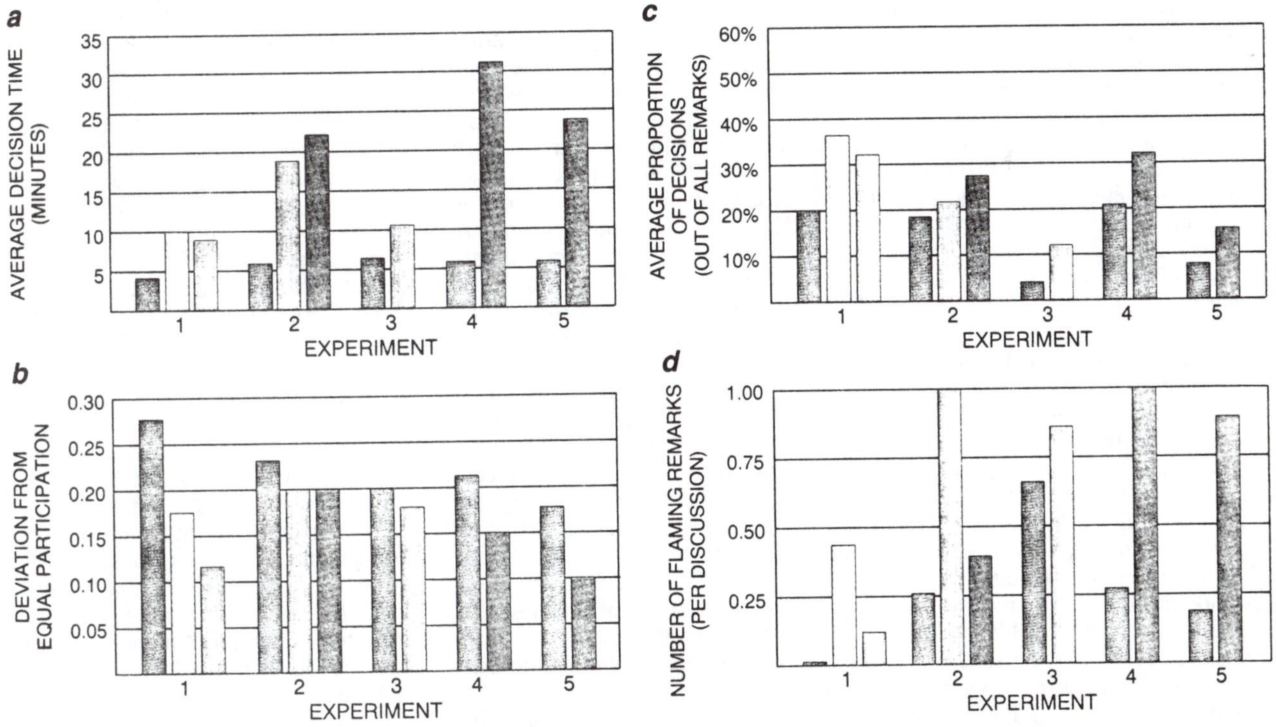

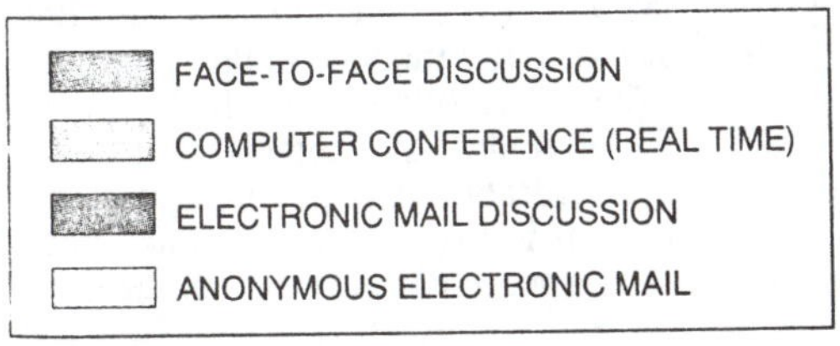

LABORATORY STUDIES reveal some ways in which networks affect how people work together. Ninety-four groups of subjects in five experiments were told to reach consensus decisions on several questions. Each group made some decisions electronically (through one or two network modes) and others face-to-face. When networked, all groups took longer to make a decision (*a*). On the other hand, they enjoyed more equal participation (*b*) and proposed more ideas (*c*). The electronic modes of discussion seemed to encourage "flaming," impassioned self-expression (*d*).

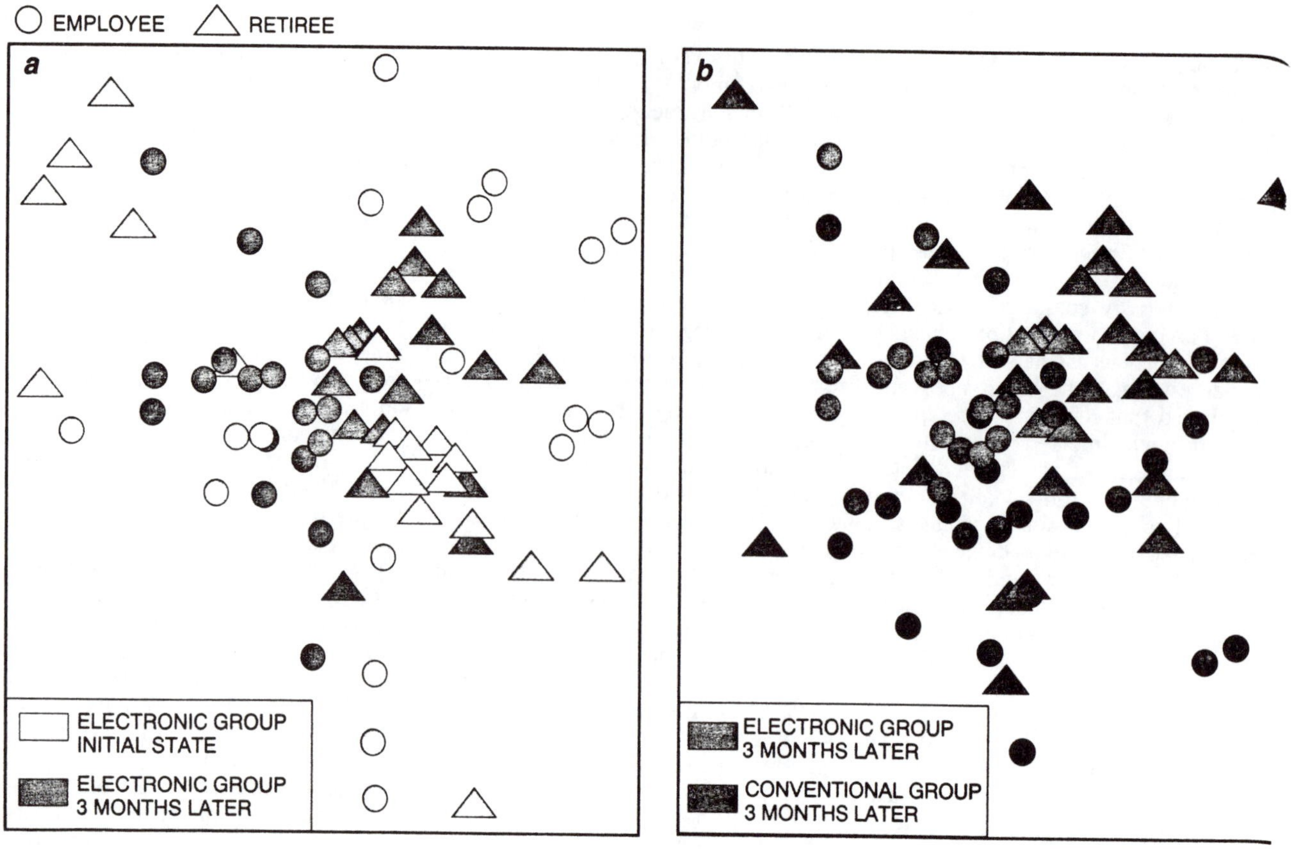

ically defer to those who have higher status and tend to follow their direction. Members' speech and demeanor become more formal in the presence of people who have high status. Higher-status people, in turn, talk more and influence group discussion more than do lower-status people.

Given that electronic conversations attenuate contextual cues, we expected that the effect of status differences within a group should also be reduced. In an experiment conducted with Vitaly Dubrovsky of Clarkson University and Beheruz Sethna of Lamar University, we asked groups containing high- and low-status members to make decisions both by electronic mail and face-to-face. The results confirmed that the proportion of talk and influence of higher-status people decreased when group members communicated by electronic mail.

Is this a good state of affairs? When higher-status members have less expertise, more democracy could improve decision making. If higher-status members truly are better qualified to make decisions, however, the results of consensus decisions may be less good.

Shoshanah Zuboff of Harvard Business School documented reduced effects of status on a computer conference system in one firm. People who regarded themselves as physically unattractive reported feeling more lively and confident when they expressed themselves over the network. Others who had soft voices or small stature reported that they no longer had to struggle to be taken seriously in a meeting.

Researchers have advanced alternative explanations for the openness and democracy of electronic talk. One hypothesis is that people who like to use computers are childish or unruly, but this hypothesis does not explain experimental results showing that the same people talk more openly on a computer than when they are face-to-face. Another hypothesis holds that text messages require strong language to get a point across; this hypothesis explains flaming but not the reduction of social and status differences. The most promising explanation of the behavior of networked individuals is that when cues about social context are absent or weak, people ignore their social situation and cease to worry about how others evaluate them. Hence, they devote less time and effort to posturing and social niceties, and they may be more honest.

Researchers have demonstrated decreased social posturing in studies that ask people to describe their own behavior. In one of our experiments, people were asked to complete a self-evaluation questionnaire either by pencil and paper or via electronic mail. Those randomly assigned to reply electronically reported significantly more undesirable social behaviors, such as illegal drug use or petty crimes. John Greist and his colleagues at the University of Wisconsin found similar decreases in posturing when taking medical histories from clinical patients. People who responded to a computerized patient history interview revealed more socially and physically undesirable behavior than did those who answered the same questions asked by a physician.

These studies show that people are willing to reveal more about undesirable symptoms and behavior to a computer, but are these reports more truthful? An investigation of alcohol consumption conducted by Jennifer J. Waterton and John C. Duffy of the University of Edinburgh suggests an affirmative answer. In traditional surveys, people report drinking only about one half as much alcohol as alcohol sales figures would suggest. Waterton and Duffy compared computer interviews with personal interviews in a survey of alcohol consumption. People who were randomly assigned to answer the computer survey reported higher alcohol consumption than those who talked to the human interviewer. The computer-derived reports of consumption extrapolated more accurately to actual alcohol sales than did the face-to-face reports.

These and other controlled studies of electronic talk suggest that such communication is relatively impersonal, yet paradoxically, it can make people feel more comfortable about talk-

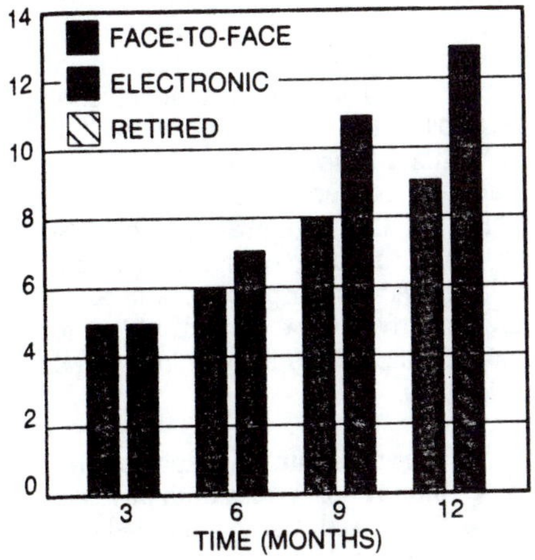

DYNAMIC GROUP STRUCTURES emerge when people converse electronically. These charts depict the behavior of two study groups, each containing a mix of employees and retired workers. One group worked in person, the other over a network. Members having the most information and social contacts appear near the center of the charts. Over time, the electronic group becomes more socially cohesive (*a*). Chart *b* compares the electronic group with the conventional group three months into the project and shows that retirees in particular become better integrated in the electronic group. Networks also encouraged more people to take on leadership roles (*c*).

ing. People are less shy and more playful in electronic discussions; they also express more opinions and ideas and vent more emotion.

Because of these behavioral effects, organizations are discovering applications for electronic group activities that nobody had anticipated. Computers can be valuable for counseling and conducting surveys about sensitive topics, situations in which many people are anxious and cover their true feelings and opinions. Networks are now being used for applications ranging from electronic Alcoholics Anonymous support groups to electronic quality circles.

Just as the dynamics of electronic communications differ from those conducted orally or by letters, so electronic groups are not just traditional groups whose members use computers. People in a networked organization are likely to belong to a number of electronic groups that span time zones and job categories. Some of these groups serve as extensions of existing work groups, providing a convenient way for members to communicate between face-to-face meetings. Other electronic groups gather together people who do not know one another personally and who may in fact have never had the opportunity to meet in person.

For example, Hewlett-Packard employs human-factors engineers who work in widely scattered locations around the world. These engineers may meet one another in person only once a year. An electronic conference creates ongoing meetings in which they can frequently and routinely discuss professional and company issues.

In some ways, electronic groups resemble nonelectronic social groups. They support sustained interactions, develop their own norms of behavior and generate peer pressure. Electronic groups often have more than 100 members, however, and involve relationships among people who do not know one another personally.

Employees whose organization is connected to the Internet or to a commercial network can belong to electronic groups whose members come from many different organizations. For example, Brian K. Reid of Digital Equipment Corporation reports that some 37,000 organizations are connected to USENET, a loosely organized network that exchanges more than 1,500 electronic discussion groups, called newsgroups. Reid estimates that 1.4 million people worldwide read at least one newsgroup.

Networked communication is only beginning to affect the structure of the workplace. The form of most current organizations has been dictated by the constraints of the nonelectronic world. Interdependent jobs must be situated in physical proximity. Formal command structures specify who reports to whom, who assigns tasks to whom and who has access to what information. These constraints reinforce the centralization of authority and shape the degree of information sharing, the number of organizational levels, the amount of interconnectivity and the structure of social relationships.

Organizations that incorporate computer networks could become more flexible and less hierarchical in structure. A field experiment conducted by Tora K. Bikson of Rand Corporation and John D. Eveland of Claremont Colleges supports the point. They formed two task forces in a large utility firm, each assigned to analyze employee retirement issues. Both groups contained 40 members, half of whom had recently retired from the company and half of whom were still employed but eligible for retirement. The only difference between the two groups was that one worked on networked computer facilities, whereas the other did not.

Both task forces created subcommittees, but the networked group created more of them and assigned people to more than one subcommittee. The networked group also organized its subcommittees in a complex, overlapping matrix structure. It added new subcommittees during the course of its work, and it decided to continue meeting even after its official one-year life span had ended. The networked task force also permitted greater input from the retirees, who were no longer located at the company. Although not every electronic group will be so flexible, eliminating the constraints of face-to-face meetings evidently facilitates trying out different forms of group organization.

Another effect of networking may be changed patterns of information sharing in organizations. Conventional organizations have formal systems of record keeping and of responsibilities for distributing information. Much of the information within an organization consists of personal experience that never appears in the formally authorized distribution system: the war stories told by service representatives (which do not appear in service manuals), the folklore about how the experimental apparatus really works (which does not appear in the journal articles) or the gossip about how workers should behave (which is not described in any personnel policy).

In the past, the spread of such personal information has been strongly determined by physical proximity and social acquaintance. As a result, distant or poorly connected employees have lacked access to local expertise; this untapped knowledge could represent an important informational resource in large organizations. Electronic groups provide a forum for sharing such expertise independent of spatial and social constraints.

One significant kind of information flow begins with the "Does anybody know...?" message that appears frequently on computer networks. A sender might broadcast an electronic request for information to an entire organization, to a particular distribution list or to a bulletin board. Anyone who sees the message can reply. We studied information inquiries on the network at Tandem Computers, Inc., in Cupertino, Calif., a computer company that employs 10,500 workers around the world. In a study we conducted with David Constant, we found an average of about six does-anybody-know messages broadcast every day to one company-wide distribution list.

Information requests typically come from field engineers or sales representatives who are soliciting personal experience or technical knowledge that they cannot find in formal documents or in their own workplace. At Tandem, about eight employees send electronic mail replies to the average question. Fewer than 15 percent of the people who answer a question are personally acquainted with the questioner or are even located in the same city.

Question askers can electronically redistribute the answers they receive by putting them in a public computer file on the network. About half of the Tandem questioners make their reply files publicly available over the company network to other employees. Tandem takes this sharing process one step further by maintaining an electronic archive of question-and-reply files that is also accessible over the company network. The firm has thereby created a repository of information and working expertise that is endlessly accessible through space and time (for example, the expertise remains available when an employee is out of the office or he or she leaves the organization). A study by Thomas Finholt in our research program found that this archive is accessed more than 1,000 times a month by employees, especially those located in field offices away from the geographic center of the company.

The discretionary information sharing we discovered at Tandem and at other networked organizations seems to run contrary to nonelectronic behavior in organizations. The askers openly admit their ignorance to perhaps hundreds or even thousands of people. The repliers respond to requests for help from people they do not know with no expectation of any direct benefit to themselves.

One might wonder why people respond so readily to information requests made by strangers. Part of the explanation is that networks make the cost of responding extremely low in time and effort expended. Also, open-access networks favor the free flow of information. Respondents seem to believe that sharing information enhances the overall electronic community and leads to a richer information environment. The result is a kind of electronic altruism quite different from the fears that networks would weaken the social fabric of organizations.

The changes in communication made possible by networks may substantially alter the relationship between an employee and his or her organization, the structure of organizations and the nature of management. Senior managers and key professionals usually have strong social and informational connections within their organizations and within their broader professional communities. Conversely, employees who reside on the organizational periphery by virtue of geographic location, job requirements or personal attributes have relatively few opportunities to make contact with other employees and colleagues.

Reducing the impediments to communication across both physical and social distance is likely to affect peripheral employees more than central ones. We, along with Charles Huff of St. Olaf College, studied this possibility for city employees in Fort Collins, Colo. Employees who used electronic mail extensively reported more commitment to their jobs and to their co-workers than did those who rarely used the network. This correlation was particularly strong for shift workers, who, because of the nature of their work, had fewer opportunities to see their colleagues than did regular day workers. As one policewoman told us,

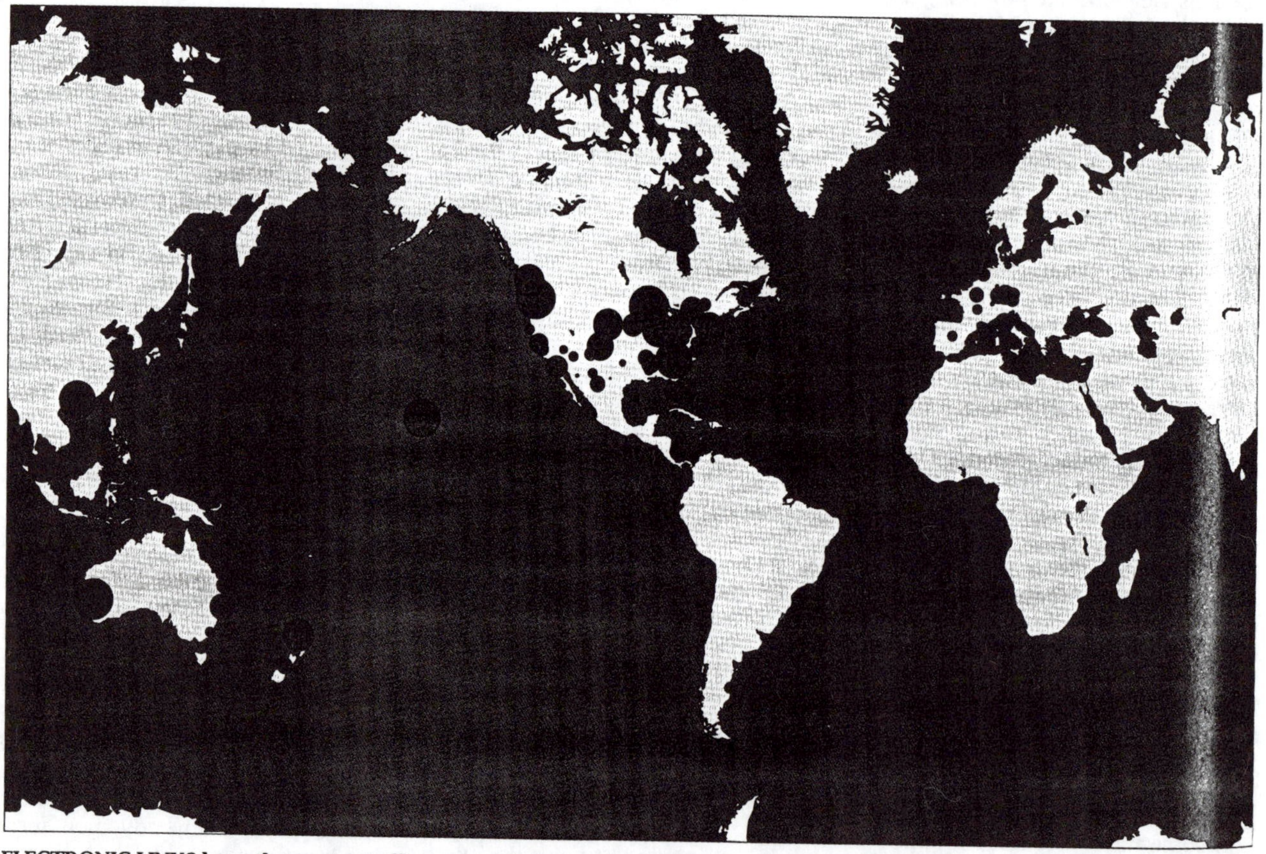

ELECTRONIC LINKS have the greatest effect on workers located at outlying sites. Workers in field offices of Tandem Computers, Inc., whose headquarters are in Cupertino, Calif., have access to data files via a network. Circles indicate how many times each office tapped into one file (consisting of employee-initiated questions and answers about company products and services) over a one-year period; the greater the usage, the larger the circle. Workers in distant or isolated offices, where local expertise is relatively limited, made the most use of the information provided through the network.

"Working the night shift, it used to be that I would hear about promotions after they happened, though I had a right to be included in the discussion. Now I have a say in the decision making."

Organizations are traditionally built around two key concepts: hierarchical decomposition of goals and tasks and the stability of employee relationships over time. In the fully networked organization that may become increasingly common in the future, task structures may be much more flexible and dynamic. Hierarchy will not vanish, but it will be augmented by distributed lattices of interconnections.

In today's organizations, executives generally know whom they manage and manage whom they know. In the future, however, managers of some electronic project groups will face the challenge of working with people they have never met. Allocating resources to projects and assigning credit and blame for performance will become more complex. People will often belong to many different groups and will be able to reach out across the network to acquire resources without management intervention or perhaps even without management knowledge.

A recent case in mathematics research hints at the nature of what may lie ahead. Mathematicians at Bell Communications Research (Bellcore) and at Digital Equipment sought to factor a large, theoretically interesting number known as the 9th Fermat number. They broadcast a message on the Internet to recruit researchers from universities, government laboratories and corporations to assist them in their project. The several hundred researchers who volunteered to help received—via electronic mail—software and a piece of the problem to solve; they also returned their solutions through electronic mail.

After results from all the volunteers were combined, the message announcing the final results of the project contained a charming admission:

> We'd like to thank everyone who contributed computing cycles to this project, but I can't: we only have records of the person at each site who installed and managed the code. If you helped us, we'd be delighted to hear from you; please send us your name as you would like it to appear in the final version of the paper. (Broadcast message from Mark S. Manasse, June 15, 1990.)

Networking in most organizations today is limited to data communications, often for economic or financial applications such as electronic data interchange, electronic funds transfer or remote transaction processing. Most organizations have not yet begun to confront the opportunities and challenges afforded by connecting their employees through networks.

Among those that have, managers have responded in a variety of ways to changes that affect their authority and control. Some managers have installed networks for efficiency reasons but ignored their potential for more profound changes. Some have restricted who can send mail or have shut down electronic discussion groups. Others have encouraged using the network for broadening participation and involving more people in the decision-making process. The last actions push responsibility down and through the organization and also produce their own managerial issues.

A democratic organization requires competent, committed, responsible employees. It requires new ways of allocating credit. It increases unpredictability, both for creative ideas and for inappropriate behavior. Managers will have to come up with new kinds of worker incentives and organizational structures to handle these changes.

The technology of networks is changing rapidly. Electronic mail that includes graphics, pictures, sound and video will eventually become widely available. These advances will make it possible to reintroduce some of the social context cues absent in current electronic communications. Even so, electronic interactions will never duplicate those conducted face-to-face.

As more people have ready access to network communications, the number and size of electronic groups will expand dramatically. It is up to management to make and shape connections. The organization of the future will depend significantly not just on how the technology of networking evolves but also on how managers seize the opportunity it presents for transforming the structure of work.

FURTHER READING

WHAT DO COMPUTERS DO? James Rule and Paul Attewell in *Social Problems*, Vol. 36, No. 3, pages 225-241; June 1989.

INTELLECTUAL TEAMWORK: THE SOCIAL AND TECHNOLOGICAL FOUNDATIONS OF COOPERATIVE WORK. Edited by Jolene Galegher, Robert E. Kraut and Carmen Egido. Lawrence Erlbaum Associates, 1990.

CONNECTIONS: NEW WAYS OF WORKING IN THE NETWORKED ORGANIZATION. Lee Sproull and Sara Kiesler. MIT Press, 1991.

SOCIAL RELATIONSHIPS IN ELECTRONIC COMMUNITIES. Charles Dunlop and Rob Kling in *Computerization and Controversy: Value Conflicts and Social Choices*. Edited by Charles Dunlop and Rob Kling. Academic Press, 1991.

GROUPWARE AND SOCIAL DYNAMICS: EIGHT CHALLENGES FOR DEVELOPERS

By JONATHAN GRUDIN Computer support has focused on organizations and individuals. Groups are different. Repeated, expensive groupware failures result from not meeting the challenges in design and evaluation that arise from these differences. • Many expensive failures in developing and marketing software that is designed to support groups are not due to technical problems. They result from not understanding the unique demands this class of software imposes on developers and users. This article briefly outlines the origins of groupware, describes eight specific problem areas, and finally examines groupware successes in search of better approaches to supporting work in group settings. • Desktop conferencing, videoconferencing, coauthoring features and applications, email and bulletin boards (b-boards), meeting support systems, voice applications, workflow systems, and group calendars are key examples of groupware. Labels vary: groupware, collaborative computing, workgroup computing, multiuser applications, computer-supported cooperative work (CSCW) applications. What is included? Not everyone agrees. Begin by asking, "Was this software designed to support groups? Is it being used to support groups?" • Email and b-boards are well known, but few other groupware prototypes and products have done as well despite considerable effort. Successes exist, but progress is slow and can lead in unanticipated directions.

Primarily Off-the-Shelf Products

The three rings of Figure 1 place groupware in the software universe somewhere between single-user applications and information systems that support organizations. Each software development area emerged independently and produced the research and development literature identified on the left.

Systems designed to support organizations achieved prominence first, because the expense of early computers required that they address major organizational goals. These include large mainframe (and, later, minicomputer) applications. "Organizational goals" are major goals typically defined by upper management. Such goals are not always fully agreed on, even among management. If they were, the course of internal systems development and acceptance would proceed more smoothly than it does. These research and development activities have variously been labeled data processing (DP), information systems (IS), management information systems (MIS), and information technology (IT).

By the early 1980s, the spread of interactive and personal computing created large markets for applications designed for individual users, such as spreadsheets and word processors. Research and development activities drew on existing human factors (HF) approaches to design and evaluation prior to the emergence in the early 1980s of conferences and journals under such banners as Computer and Human Interaction (CHI).

In the mid-1980s, the terms groupware and CSCW were coined and conference series and literature appeared. Conditions that emerged in workplaces to encourage this included (a) computation inexpensive enough to be available to all members of some groups; (b) a technological infrastructure supporting communication and coordination, notably networks and associated software; (c) a widening familiarity with computers, yielding groups willing to try the software; (d) maturing single-user application domains that pushed developers to seek new ways to enhance and differentiate products.

On the right in Figure 1 are the principal software development contexts involved in each area. Most systems addressing organizational goals are developed in-house or contracted out. Most single-user applications are commercial products, with development costs amortized over many customers. Groupware is largely a new market for product developers, along with telecommunications companies that have a focused interest in multiuser applications such as live video. Attendance at the first three CSCW conferences was primarily from software product development companies (approximately 40%) and universities (30%) with a steady telecommunications presence (5% to 10%).

To understand the problems encountered by groupware applications, it is essential to realize that most interest in groupware development is found among the developers and users of commercial off-the-shelf products who previously focused exclusively on single-user applications. The huge software markets created by standalone personal computers were once restricted to single-user applications, but as networks link the computers, groups represent large potential markets. As developers shift from supporting individual users to supporting groups, many encounter for the first time the challenges described in this article.

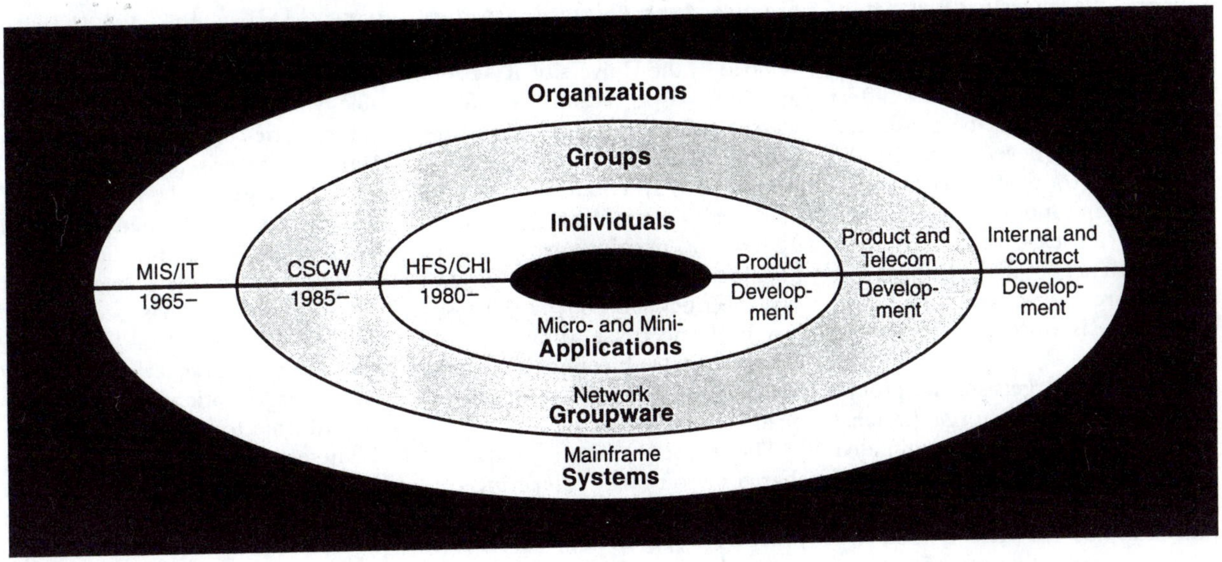

Figure 1. Development and research contexts

IS in Organizations: A Contrast to Product Development

The purchasers of a highly visible, expensive mainframe system or application anticipate a substantial benefit. They know organizational change is likely. Upper management is thus likely to commit to helping the system succeed, through (a) job redesign and creation (e.g., word processing skills are required of new secretaries and a database administrator position is created), (b) providing training in order to increase system acceptance, (c) restructuring to work around important individuals who will not use the system (e.g., a terminal-shy manager), and (d) positive leadership through inspiration or example. Even with such support, success is not assured. The system may not be salvageable or management may be divided. For example, the management of the IS group and other corporate managers may have conflicting goals.

These social and political factors that affect the introduction of large mainframe and minicomputer systems are little known to developers of single-user applications, including those moving on to groupware development. Yet similar forces affect groupware and must be considered by groupware developers. To the extent that groups share characteristics of organizations, groupware developers can learn something from the experiences of IS developers. But groups are not organizations and groupware is different from large systems.

Groupware targets smaller groups than systems serving organizational goals. Management is less committed to the less expensive groupware applications or features. An organization will not restructure itself for each new application the way it does around a major new system. In general, an organization may adapt to a large computer system, but a small application program must adapt to the organization, fitting into existing work patterns and appealing to everyone who must support it. On the other hand, groupware often benefits from user familiarity with the computer system already in place and from the relative homogeneity and shared goals of many groups.

Groupware is marketed as a product, whereas most MIS development is internal or contracted. Products are designed and evaluated to obtain a broad, competitive appeal, whereas internal IS staff have a specific set of users and must orchestrate their acceptance of a system. Each development context has its own objectives, constraints, approaches. There is little communication between product development, located in computer and software companies, and IS development, located in large companies engaged in other businesses or in companies that develop software on contract. Different research communities have grown up around each with different conferences, journals, and even languages [12, 14].

However, the MIS/IT community is interested in groupware—primarily in support for larger groups, such as workflow management systems and electronic meeting rooms. Declining technology costs bring large system software within the economic reach of groups, and thus into the product market. For example, a *group decision support system* or electronic meeting room developed by the University of Arizona and IBM was as recently as 1988 intended only for internal use by IBM. But in 1989 it was rechristened a *group support system* and in 1990 was marketed as a product, TeamFocus. The word "decision" was dropped not because of a sudden discovery that meetings serve many purposes, but rather because with declining system costs, the meeting rooms need not be used by decision makers to justify their expense.

The scope of these systems is shared by software engineering support for concurrent engineering, process programming, and other project-level activities. Thus, the middle ring could be subdivided into small-group and large-group support. CSCW research is defined to be inclusive, encompassing these and every activity at the organizational level.

Seven challenges in designing and evaluating groupware products are described. Because of the social and political factors at work in group settings, achieving groupware acceptance is much trickier than single-user product acceptance. It is difficult for "off-the-shelf" product developers to jump over the counter and help out with product acceptance, but they may have to: an eighth challenge for groupware developers.

New Problems

In addition to technical challenges, groupware poses this fundamental problem for product developers: Because individuals interact with a groupware application, it has all the interface design challenges of single-user applications, supplemented by a host of new challenges arising from its direct involvement in group processes.

Consider two relatively well-worked application areas: A review of group decision support systems concluded that after decades of effort, "their use is far below what could be expected given their need and promise," and "although some for-profit companies have built (group decision support systems), they are not yet making much money" [17]. A 1987 report stated that after 25 years of research, no company specializing in voice technology had become profitable and that projected sales of voice products were being revised sharply downward. More generally, for a panel of leading researchers titled "How can we make groupware practical?" Robert Kraut wrote "the only successful CSCW application has been email" and Lee Sproull wrote "groupware will never be practical and widely used in organizations if it follows its current trajectory." [9]

These gloomy assessments deserve an explanation, given the obvious potential in supporting something as widespread as group activity. Table 1 lists eight major problems that stem from the social dynamics of groups, drawn from developer experiences, descriptions of short-lived products and research prototypes, and experimental and modeling studies in the literature.

Overall, they call for better understanding of work environments and for corresponding adjustments by developers. Progress on the first five requires better knowledge of the intended users' workplace. The final three require changes in the development process. The final challenge in particular, addressing the sensitivity of groupware to aspects of its introduction in workplaces, demands that product developers expand their conception of the development process and product to include concerns that have been outside their sphere of activity.

As these challenges are examined in detail and illustrated with examples from various groupware areas, keep in mind that applications and use situations differ. Success and failure cannot be reliably predicted. Despite past problems and gloomy assessments, we find evidence of progress and ideas for working more effectively.

A Disparity: Work vs. Benefit

A groupware application never provides precisely the same benefit to every group member. Costs and benefits depend on preferences, prior experience, roles, and assignments. Although a groupware application is expected to provide a collective benefit, some people must adjust more than others. Ideally, each individual benefits, even if they do not benefit equally. However, this ideal is seldom realized. Most groupware requires some people to do additional work to enter or process information required or produced by the application.

Consider the automatic meeting scheduling feature that accompanies many electronic calendar systems. The underlying concept is simple: the person scheduling a meeting identifies the participants and the system checks each person's calendar, finding a time that is convenient for everyone. The direct beneficiary is the meeting convener, typically a manager or secretary, but for the feature to work efficiently, everyone in the group must maintain a personal calendar. Otherwise, the scheduling program will create conflicts by scheduling meetings in time that only seems to be open. However, studies have found that electronic calendars are typically used as communication devices by managers and are often not maintained by individual contributors [8]. Thus, successful use of automatic meeting scheduling requires additional work for those group members who would not otherwise maintain electronic calendars. Consequently, this groupware feature is rarely used.

Similarly, consider voice annotation to documents, a frequently developed feature. For speakers, digitized voice has advantages over handwritten or typed input. Speaking is faster than writing or typing, conveys emotion and nuance easily, and may be transmitted by telephone. Unfortunately, digitized voice creates problems for listeners. It is slower to take in, not easily scanned or reviewed, and more difficult to manipulate—for example, proposed edits will have to be typed in. When is it acceptable for speakers to burden listeners this way? Possibly when users speak and listen in equal measure, as in telephone conversations, or when the use of hands or a keyboard is impossible. A disparity may also be accepted when the speaker is of higher status than the listener, as with dictaphone machines, where saving one person time or effort can justify an arduous transcription. But in general, the disparity in effort and benefit works against acceptance in many situations and helps explain the failure of voice products to meet expectations.

As a third example, consider a distributed project management application that covers the scheduling and chronicling of activities, the creation and evaluation of plans and schedules, the management of product versions and changes, and the monitoring of resources and responsibilities (e.g., [27]). Its primary beneficiary is a project manager, but for it to succeed, other group members must enter information that is not typically kept on-line. This can lead to resistance. For example, a "computer-assisted management system" for a naval vessel, "its primary purpose to help the commanding officer and his department heads administer the ship," was developed over 10 years [22]. Due in part to the difficulty of getting everyone to use it, it was eventually replaced by a system that lacked management features.

Comparison: single-user applications. The problem does not arise. If a group picks one vendor for a single-user application because of the economy of purchasing a site license or in order to easily share its output, costs and benefits to group members may vary. But this is not an issue that developers can address.

Comparison: organizational IS. An expensive system is perceived to promise a substantial collective benefit. Therefore, management is more committed to take steps to ensure its success, such as hiring administrators and rewriting job descriptions. Thus, doing the additional work becomes someone's explicit job. This is much less likely for groupware. For example, it is unlikely that engineers will be required to maintain on-line calendars in order to support meeting scheduling.

Addressing the problem. Demonstrating an application's collective and indirect benefits can help. Reducing the work required of nonbeneficiaries seems to be an obvious priority, but it is very difficult to do in practice, because pleasing the principal beneficiary is critically important and the natural focus of attention. One promising approach is to design, along with the technology, processes for using it that create benefits for all group members. This has been stressed in several new meeting management applications. For example, a key element of the process in one is a specific commitment delivered by the meeting convener to act on the contributions of the participants.

Critical Mass and Prisoner's Dilemma Problems

Most groupware is only useful if a high percentage of group members use it. Different individuals may choose to use different word processors but two coauthors must agree to use the same coauthoring tool! Achieving a "critical mass" of users is essential for communication systems [8]. Even one or two defections may cause problems for meeting scheduling, decision support, or project management applications. Even in an idealized situation in which every individual will benefit once critical mass is achieved, the early adopters may well abandon it before the critical mass of users is reached.

Markus and Connolly [21] use an elegant model to demonstrate the possibility of "prisoner's dilemma" situations. In this model if *everyone* acts to further his or her personal best interest, the result is worse not only for the group but also for each individual. With some discretionary databases, as long as someone updates them, one's optimal strategy is to "freeload," but of course if everyone tries to freeload, the system is not used at all.

These analyses compound the

problem raised in the first challenge by showing that even a net benefit with equal costs and benefits for all users will not guarantee groupware success.

Comparison: single-user applications. The problem does not arise.

Comparison: organizational IS. One organizationwide voice-messaging system initially failed to obtain a critical mass of users: Those who tried to leave messages were discouraged when recipients did not use the system. This system succeeded, and even came to be appreciated by initial detractors, only after top management forced a critical mass of use by removing the alternative (message-taking receptionists). This kind of solution is available to expensive corporate systems. A less expensive groupware application or feature, such as voice annotation in word processing, is unlikely to get a forceful management shove past the critical point. Similarly, an organization can hire data entry personnel to support a large database, a solution to the prisoner's dilemma problem that most groups cannot afford.

Addressing the problem. Designers can reduce the work required of all users, build in incentives for use, and suggest a process of use that provides or emphasizes individual and collective benefits.

Table 1. Eight challenges for groupware developers

1. **Disparity in work and benefit.** Groupware applications often require additional work from individuals who do not perceive a direct benefit from the use of the application.

2. **Critical mass and Prisoner's dilemma problems.** Groupware may not enlist the "critical mass" of users required to be useful, or can fail because it is never to any one individual's advantage to use it.

3. **Disruption of social processes.** Groupware can lead to activity that violates social taboos, threatens existing political structures, or otherwise demotivates users crucial to its success.

4. **Exception handling.** Groupware may not accommodate the wide range of exception handling and improvisation that characterizes much group activity.

5. **Unobtrusive accessibility.** Features that support group processes are used relatively infrequently, requiring unobtrusive accessibility and integration with more heavily used features.

6. **Difficulty of evaluation.** The almost insurmountable obstacles to meaningful, generalizable analysis and evaluation of groupware prevent us from learning from experience.

7. **Failure of intuition.** Intuitions in product development environments are especially poor for multiuser applications, resulting in bad management decisions and an error-prone design process.

8. **The adoption process.** Groupware requires more careful implementation (introduction) in the workplace than product developers have confronted.

Social, Political and Motivational Factors

Groupware may be resisted if it interferes with the subtle and complex social dynamics that are common to groups. The computer is happiest in a world of explicit, concrete information. Central to group activity, however, are social, motivational, political and economic factors that are rarely explicit or stable. Often unconsciously, our actions are guided by social conventions and by our awareness of the personalities and priorities of people around us, knowledge not available to the computer.

Tacitly understood personal priorities are tactfully left unspoken, yet unless such information is made explicit, groupware will be insensitive to it. For example, secretaries know that managers' unscheduled time is seldom really free; unauthorized scheduling of a manager's apparently open time can lead to rejection of automatic meeting scheduling [8]. Similarly, a priority-based meeting scheduler foundered because participants were reluctant to acknowledge publicly that some of their meetings were low priority.

With one work management system, any employee who reported a "priority problem" received system-generated requests to forward progress reports to the chief executive officer—an extreme example of a design that ignores the sensitivity of certain communications. Employees stopped reporting problems. The vigilant system noted this and alerted the administrator. The employees dealt with the resulting complaint by writing a program that periodically opened files and changed dates, which satisfied the watchful, automatic monitor. Thus sabotaged, the system was of little use and was eventually removed.

As noted earlier, meeting management systems have not met expectations despite the appeal of improving the efficiency of meetings. Decision making is often complex and subtle, with participants holding partially hidden agendas, relying on knowledge of the others involved, and showing sensitivity to social customs and motivational concerns. Because such factors are not represented explicitly, the computer participates at a disadvantage. Kraemer and King [17] wrote "Most efforts have focused on the relatively narrow, rational view of the decision process . . . But as experience shows, this is limited in its utility because it specifically excludes the baffling nonrational or quasirational behaviors individuals often exhibit." In one case, a management group considered using an issue-based IS in which issues, arguments, counterarguments, and decisions are entered, creating a record of decision making that could be used to communicate, review, and explore alternatives. The plan to use the system was abandoned because the manager wanted the group to project a strong sense of consensus. The explicit record of opposing positions that the application would immortalize was politically unacceptable.

Conflicts of interest can become

major obstacles to success when group members have very different occupations or roles. Ehn [7] described such issues arising in the development of a newspaper page layout application to be used by typographers, journalists, and administrative staff.

Comparison: single-user applications. Applications that affect an individual's performance have broader effects. For example, desktop publishing software that enables anyone to produce professional quality documents can disrupt the power balance in an organization. However, these social effects are too indirect and context-specific to be addressed by single-user application developers, whose effort is more naturally directed to perceptual or cognitive interface factors that most users experience in the same way.

Comparison: organizational IS. This problem has been extensively explored in organizational settings [e.g., 6, 26]. Mainframe software developers have some advantages and some disadvantages in contrast to small-systems developers. They have well-defined target environments: Product developers must anticipate a range of sensitivities across customer sites. On the other hand, large systems inevitably affect workers whose goals conflict, whereas groupware focuses on low-conflict collaborations. A cohesive group is more likely to agree to purchase and use a piece of software. Groupware developers may risk overlooking conflict that occurs even in small groups, but organizational systems researchers may overestimate group conflict based on the higher levels of conflict found across larger organizational units.

Addressing the problem. Recognizing the magnitude of the problem and avoiding the common assumption of a "rational" work environment are first steps. Developers need sophisticated understandings of prospective users' workplaces. Working with representative users whenever possible is standard advice for developing interactive systems. It is particularly good advice for groupware developers.

Exception Handling in Workgroups

Work processes can usually be described in two ways: the way things are supposed to work and the way they do work. Software designed to support standard procedures can be too brittle. A passive strike tactic is to bring production to a halt by "working to rule" or "doing things by the book"; groupware that enforces "standard procedures" may also bring work to a halt [1]. A wide range of error handling, exception handling, and improvisation are characteristic of human activity [30]. People know when the "spirit of the law" takes precedence over the "letter of the law." Unfortunately, it is tempting to base design on available work specifications.

Ishii and Ohkubo [15] described the range of problems and consequences for designing groupware to support office procedures. "The main sources of information were an *office work handbook* made by the general affairs department and interviews with clerical workers. While collecting information, we found that the office workers made many shortcuts and modifications to the standard procedures defined in the handbook. Therefore, it was no easy task to determine the *actual standard* procedure, even when it was defined clearly in the handbook." The developers used this insight in designing the system, but it was not enough. "Unfortunately, we experienced problems in handling exceptional cases. This groupware executes predefined office procedures. However, it often happens that the standard procedure cannot be completed because of unpredicted situations." The authors concluded that AI techniques beyond the state of the art would be required to make the system useful.

A case study [26] illustrates the problem at the organizational level. Computerized stock control and sales order processing systems were introduced at a chocolate factory that is part of a large food company. Severe problems arose when the computer services division of the food company installed the systems in the chocolate factory: "[People in] computer services refer to a 'production mentality,' where [chocolate factory] staff respond to problems as and when they arise and are loathe to indulge in long-term planning and adopt specific procedures. Most important, they expect others to adjust to them, and resist the discipline the computer imposes . . . Moreover, not only did management fail to impose set procedures, but further *ad hoc* arrangements were positively encouraged by the sales department, as in the case of one customer who was assured they could amend their Friday order up to 1 P.M. on a Monday . . . No doubt they believed it was working in the best interests of the company, but its actions created considerable problems for those trying to operate the computer." In some areas the manual system continued to be used out of necessity. At one point, the general manager decided someone was sabotaging the system.

By recognizing the large amount of *ad hoc* problem solving in human activity and realizing that descriptions of "standard process" are often *post hoc* rationalizations, we can see the behavior that upset the computer services division as characteristic of efficient performance. After all, catering to the needs of specific customers is often considered a virtue, not a vice. In the case study, the general manager recommended that the system be withdrawn, but "he was overruled by group head office who were not prepared to lose face over the installation." By hiring new personnel and taking other expensive measures, the computer system was made to work. Upper management wanted this large, expensive system to succeed. A typical groupware application or feature, such as meeting scheduling, voice annotation or even meeting support, will rarely have the same degree of cost, visibility, and backing, and thus would fail under similar circumstances.

The strong interest of many organizations in supporting work flow management ensures that this complex issue will remain active. The outcome is difficult to predict: Some fear that the computer will become an enforcer of rigid procedures; others hope that greater explicitness will enable users to learn about their organization, leading to what Kari Kuutti has called "expansively mastered work."

Comparison: single-user applications. The preferences and work habits of an individual are more constant over time than those of groups, so flexibility is a greater consideration in supporting groups. Group activity is difficult to study and characterize. Even establishing the range within which group activity will vary is difficult. Single-user applications support flexible problem solving by providing a range of atomic actions and imposing few constraints on their sequencing, allowing users to construct and evolve work patterns through rapid trial and error. This approach does not work as well for group activity, because trial-and-error testing of options is slower and more public, and adjusting or evolving a group's practices requires negotiation.

Comparison: organizational IS. Groups are often more transitory and less well defined than organizations, so flexibility requirements may be greater. (Some scholars have suggested that when organizations are examined closely, groups seem to cease to exist.) The influential Cohen, March and Olsen [4] model describes an organization as "collections of choices looking for problems, issues and feelings looking for decision situations in which they might be aired, solutions looking for issues to which they might be the answer, and decision makers looking for work." A university, for example, exhibits continuity of purpose and activity at the organizational level that can persevere through dramatic shifts at the group level. An empirical study of 16 hospitals found "the predictability of the tasks confronting individual nurses was more closely associated with the characteristics of the nursing personnel on that unit than with the characteristics of the control system of the ward," according to Comstock (quoted in [24]). That is, ward-level policies did not predict behavior as well as group characteristics.

This volatility should warn groupware developers not to build software that imposes organizational controls on groups. Pfeffer [24] describes a study by Meyer and Rowan entitled "Institutionalized Organizations: Formal Structure as Myth and Ceremony": "To maintain ceremonial conformity, organizations import [views about what they should like and how they should work] and incorporate them in their structure, rules, and reporting requirements. However, since such rules and structures may have little to do with how the work can or should get performed, in fact there is little impact on task performance. . . This decoupling, Meyer and Rowan argued, is actually useful to the organization. It permits the work to get done according to the localized judgments of those doing the work, while presenting to the outside world the appearance of legitimated, rational organization of work." Myths and ceremonies can endure even as the real work processes change. In such environments, it would not be useful to impose at the group level the procedures dictated in the "myth and ceremony." (Of course, organization-level computer support can help perpetuate myths and enact ceremonies.)

Addressing the problem. To avoid the pitfall of supporting rational "myths," learn how work is actually done. Using tailorable systems is a good step to providing flexibility, but to tailor effectively is a challenge, because people are not conscious of detailed organizational functioning and how changes will affect other people. Groupware cannot count on the kind of management push that saved the large chocolate factory system. Carasik and Grantham [3] described the use of The Coordinator, a structured mail system. Users complained "this doesn't fit the way we work," but "management urging was the motivation for continued use." However, one frustrated user threw the software and documentation out of his office and after six weeks, use was discontinued.

Designing for Infrequently Used Features

If "to a hammer, everything looks like a nail," then to a groupware designer, every work situation calls out for communication or coordination support. We exaggerate the importance and frequency of the objects and events on which we focus. But many organizations are structured and responsibilities are divided in order to *minimize* the overall communication requirements and social interdependencies. As is well known, an increase in size can lead to a decrease in efficiency by increasing the communication and coordination overhead. Work has important social elements that can use support, but groupware features will be used less frequently than many features supporting individual activity. This has two important implications:

- First, groupware features will fare better if integrated with features that support individual activity. Consider coauthorship applications. Anyone who has written collaboratively can visualize the potential benefit of features to support annotation, version tracking, and effortless distribution of drafts. But most writing is done alone, whether single-authored or on a section of a jointly written document. Who would abandon their favorite word processor to use a coauthorship application? Features to support coauthorship must be integrated with those supporting authorship. Additionally, standalone groupware applications may not justify high purchase costs or may be perceived to fail if used appropriately but relatively infrequently. How often do most of us manage meetings that a group decision support system could facilitate, or embark on coauthorship projects?
- This leads to the second point: Design to be unobtrusive yet accessible. Infrequently used groupware features must not obstruct more frequently used features, yet they must be known and accessible to users. This is a difficult balancing act.

Comparison: single-user applications. Unlike groupware, the most important features are frequently used, so the problem of dealing with infrequent features is less pressing. However, avoiding clutter while ensuring awareness and access is a general and very serious challenge faced by the designers of all infrequently used features.

Comparison: organizational IS. To justify their cost, many organizational systems focus on high-frequency transaction processing,

Developers need sophisticated understandings of prospective users' workplaces. **Working with representative users whenever possible is standard advice** *for developing interactive systems.*

reducing this problem. Also, at the organizational level, more than at the group level, there are opportunities to support people who actually do spend a lot of time communicating and coordinating activity.

Addressing the problem. If possible, add groupware features to an already successful application rather than launch a new application with a fanfare that creates expectations of heavy use. Ultimately, creating awareness of and access to infrequently used features could require systems that take the initiative to educate users over time. Work in this area, mostly in AI, has proceeded slowly. Yet the need grows, as computer capability exceeds by ever greater amounts our actual use of them.

The Difficulty of Evaluation

Task analysis, design, and evaluation are much more difficult for multi-user applications than for single-user applications. An individual's success with a particular word processor is not affected by the backgrounds or personalities of other group members. Groupware is affected by such factors, and often must interface simultaneously to users with different and sometimes shifting roles, preferences, and backgrounds. Users can be tested in a laboratory on the perceptual, motor, and cognitive aspects of human-computer interaction that are central to single-user applications. But lab situations and partial prototypes cannot reliably capture complex but important social, motivational, economic, and political dynamics. Even when a full implementation is available, scheduling a test is a logistical challenge.

Evaluation takes longer. Much of a person's use of a graphics program can be observed in a single hour, for example, but group interactions unfold over days or weeks. Groupware that supports limited-duration activities such as meetings has only a modest advantage, because awareness of the preparation and consequences are critical to understanding such events. Additionally, groupware evaluation methods are less precise. Field observations are complicated by the number of people involved over time at each site, the variability in group composition, and the range of environmental factors that affect the use of the technology. The pertinent skills of social psychology and anthropology are absent in most development environments, where human factors engineers and cognitive psychologists are only slowly being accepted.

Finally, generalizing from experience is risky. Establishing success or failure is easier than identifying the factors that brought it about. A highly motivated group can find a way to use a seriously flawed product and a badly managed installation can cripple a good product, so one generally finds some successes and some failures.

Consider this example: More than 10 members of a research laboratory took part in usability tests of a coauthoring application. The data were analyzed to find interface problems. This lab produces many coauthored articles and although it required only a few minutes to bring up the application, several months later it was not being used outside the experimental setting. Why? Some people were not using the right type of computer and others did not want to give up features of their favorite word processor. They were fine-tuning the interface to an application that would not be used.

The absence of definitive studies ensures that other researchers and developers will repeat costly mistakes. More often than not, CSCW and groupware conferences include papers on automatic meeting schedulers that were developed in ignorance of the fate of a decade of commercially available products. Predictable problems were encountered: insufficiently frequent user access, an unwillingness to place true priorities on a public system, incomplete adoption of the system by group members, and so forth. Respondents to a recent Internet poll identified meeting scheduling as the most widely available and the least useful groupware application. Similarly, voice editors for nonspecialists have been marketed for a decade with little success, but they continue to appear. A typical scenario of use devised to sell an application: A sends B a voice message containing directions for driving to a party, which B edits and forwards electronically to C. Because C must transcribe the directions, probably requiring a few passes through the voice message, substantial work is required of the editor-intermediary B, of C, and of any other recipients. In a real situation, anyone in the chain could greatly reduce the overall effort by typing in the directions.

Comparison: single-user applications. As noted, most are easier to evaluate than groupware.

Comparison: organizational IS. The success or failure of a system built for one organization is generally more obvious, although proving that its benefits outweigh its costs (or vice versa) can be difficult or impossible.

Addressing the problem. Development managers must enlist the appropriate skills, provide the resources, and disseminate the results.

The Breakdown of Intuitive Decision Making

Decisions to develop unworkable applications are widespread. The problem often lies not in the detailed design but in the conception, in the nature of decision making in development environments.

Decision makers rely heavily on informed intuition. Most product development experience is based on single-user applications, for which intuition can be a more reliable guide. A manager with good intuition who quickly gets a feel for the use of a word processor or spreadsheet can fail to appreciate the intricate demands on a groupware application that requires participation by a range of users.

In particular, decision makers are drawn to applications that selectively benefit one subset of the user population: managers. Project management applications primarily benefit project managers. Meeting schedulers and meeting management systems benefit those who convene meetings. Decision support systems primarily benefit decision makers. Digitized voice products appeal to those who rely on speech (remember the dictaphone). Similarly, managers envision their own use of features such as a natural language interface and support development efforts without recognizing the drawbacks and costs.

This bias is understandable—each of us has ideas about what will help us do our job. But in the case of groupware, managers often underestimate the down side, the unwelcome extra work that an application will require of other users, resulting in neglect or resistance. For example, a group decision support or work management application can require many people to learn to enter data, it can record information that participants prefer not to have disseminated, and it can block other means to influence decision making, such as private lobbying. Intuition fails when the intricate dynamics of such situations are not appreciated. Managers can also fail to appreciate the difficulty of developing and evaluating groupware, and not recognize that users will not be required to do the work to ensure success. Finally, their interactions with customers are with customer management, who share their biases. My observation, as a product developer, was that development managers whose intuitions were generally superb could fail spectacularly with groupware. Perhaps, with more confidence in their intuition, they pushed such projects more strongly than more cautious managers would.

Good intuition for multiuser applications is unlikely to be found anywhere in a product development environment. Experience as designers, implementers, users, evaluators, or managers is heavily based on single-user applications. This has shaped the skills and outlooks that are present. For example, human factors engineers are trained to apply techniques based on perceptual, motor and cognitive psychology to study phenomena of brief duration. They are unfamiliar with the techniques needed to study group dynamics over time.

Once a project is underway, most researchers or developers rely on feedback from a few potential users, often those expected to benefit the most. For example, the greatest interface challenge for an intelligent project management application is to minimize the information entry effort required of each subordinate (or provide compensatory benefits), but attention is instead directed toward information visualization: the interface for the project manager. "Managers must know what information is needed, where to locate it, and how to interpret and use it. Equally important, they must be able to do so without great effort" [27]. This appeals to the manager sponsoring the project, but it is not wise to focus exclusively on designing for the principal beneficiary, who should already be relatively highly motivated to use the product.

The converse intuition failure also occurs: A decision maker does not recognize the value of an application that primarily benefits nonmanagers, even when it would provide a collective benefit to the group or organization. This is particularly true for applications that create additional work for managers. This point is addressed later in the context of email.

Comparison: single-user applications. Early interactive applications (e.g., line editors) were developed by and for programmers, so intuition was particularly reliable. Intuition is generally better for single-user applications than for groupware, although it is relied on too heavily.

Comparison: organizational information systems. The problem can be less severe and stronger remedies are available. An internally developed system is to support the familiar business at hand, not external customers. While personnel can be hired or retrained, customers usually cannot.

Addressing the problem. Recognition of this problem was a factor in the emphasis on user involvement in the sociotechnical and Scandinavian collective resource approaches to IS development. Product developers face obstacles in involving users that could be particularly detrimental to groupware development [13]. If development management recognizes the risks, complexities, and fallibility of intuition, we could see fewer groupware projects, but those few might have realistic design goals and the resources to meet them.

Managing Acceptance: A New Challenge

Much research in organizational information systems (IS) has addressed system acceptance (e.g., [18, 19]).[1] Product developers are usually shielded from such concerns by marketing, customer support, documentation developers, training developers, and others who stand between them and the users. Customers also accept some responsibility for their choice and may have consultants, internal developers, and other groups to tailor, supplement, or oversee the introduction of a product.

Unfortunately, groupware can be so sensitive to aspects of its introduction that these strategies fail: If sold off the shelf in the usual fashion, it can be doomed. A word processor that is immediately liked by one in five prospective customers and disliked by the rest could be a big success. A groupware application to support teams of five nurses that initially appeals to only one nurse in

[1] The word 'implementation' is generally used. Unfortunately, product developers use 'implementation' as a synonym for coding, one of many terminological differences that hinder communication.

five is a big disaster. Groupware must be introduced very carefully, leaving little to chance.

Not surprisingly, the first research articles to consider adoption from a product developer's perspective focused on groupware. Product developers have been isolated from user environments and have little awareness that factors other than utility and usability govern a product's acceptance or rejection. The following strategy for encouraging successful adoption of groupware products, drawn from the work of Ehrlich, Francik, and their colleagues [5, 8], involves cooperation between developers and marketers.

Identify a group's problems and match the computer solution to it. For example, geographic proximity of group members guides choices between voice or email, or synchronous or asynchronous decision support. Identify appropriate work processes: Our tendency to focus on structured processes can be inappropriate for communication technologies that best support important (but often unrecognized) unstructured processes. Select appropriate pilot groups and individuals: Systems can fail if placed on executive desks when secretaries are more appropriate, if restricted to secretaries when professionals should be included, and so on. Work processes can cut across an organization chart (complicating purchasing decisions). Allocate equipment properly: The positioning of peripheral equipment such as printers and scanners can be critical.

Give the adopting group a clear understanding of the mature use of the application, perhaps through a site visit, to overcome uncertainty. In particular, provide education that demonstrates a positive impact on the work day. Step-by-step training on unfamiliar features can reduce anxiety even when insufficient for complete learning. Management attitude is critical to acceptance, a common observation of special significance for applications that represent a smaller organizational investment. Finally, someone should be prepared to prevent premature rejection by anticipating and dealing quickly with early problems, and follow-through support should be in place to handle the posthoneymoon period, when the group's curiosity wanes and work returns to center stage.

These strategies, familiar to those concerned with organizational systems, have been beyond the scope of product developers. Consultation is not packaged with shrinkwrap software. But if customers walk off with a groupware product the way they do with a spreadsheet program, these steps will not be taken and the product will probably fail. Through involvement with the adoption process developers can contribute to it and learn to build support for adoption into the product itself. Recognition of this is evident in the successful marketing of the Lotus Notes groupware application: A product development company shifted to an IS approach based on direct sales of software bundled with consulting support. The same approach was used by IBM with TeamFocus. The innovative but unsuccessful developers of Wang Freestyle reached the same conclusion [5]. But most groupware has been marketed with a traditional off-the-shelf approach—and failed.

Comparison: single-user applications. Developers have not dealt with individual users. Adding consulting services to a groupware package increases the cost and shifts the transaction away from the packaged software model held by vendors of single-user applications.

Comparison: organizational IS. Groupware developers can learn from IS experience. They face a daunting challenge: They must pay more attention to system acceptance problems than product developers have in the past, yet they face more difficult acceptance problems than large systems developers have in the past, due to lower visibility and consequently less management support.

Addressing the problem. By adding groupware features to existing applications, this problem is sidestepped. Standalone groupware must first be designed to meet the real needs of group members. Developers who understand the work environment well enough to design successfully will be in a good position to help design strategies for supporting adoption as well.

Email and Other Successes

Products such as email, databases, and code management systems are used successfully in group contexts. How do they avoid the pitfalls? Are they potential models? First, consider email.

1) Who does the work and who benefits? Email provides an equitable balance for sender and recipient. The person with a message to communicate must type it, while the receiver can read it easily at a convenient time. Thus, the primary beneficiary typically does a little more work. 2) Critical mass problems: These can have an effect, although with only one other user or a path to an external b-board, email can be useful. 3) Compatibility with social practices: At times almost conversational, at times almost epistolary, email allows us to apply existing social conventions. However, differences lead to problems such as "flaming," "junk email," "smileys,"[2] and to more subtle but significant problems described later. 4) Exception-handling: The asynchronous, informal nature of most email makes it flexible. Applications that impose more structure can suffer accordingly [2, 3]. 5) Frequency of use: Email is often relatively heavily used for groupware and basic use involves few features to learn and recall. 6) Difficulty of evaluation: Organizational costs and benefits are difficult to assess, but the heavy discretionary use by individuals is a sign of success. 7) Poor intuitions for groupware: Not all email applications succeed. There has been trial and error and intuitions have improved. 8) Acceptance: An interesting anomaly is that use has spread from academic and public sources more than through product development and marketing processes, a point returned to later.

Many of the applications successful in group settings share several properties with email. As is often true of email, the primary beneficiaries of databases and code management systems are not managers or

[2]Flaming refers to the very angry messages that email seems to elicit; junk email results from the ease of adding people to distribution lists (removing individuals is often more difficult than including them); a smiley signals humorous intent or emotional context using an image of a face rotated 90 degrees, such as :-)

decision makers, but people who use computer systems more routinely. These object management applications, like email, focus on organizing and handling information without incorporating notions of role, process, and social interaction. For this reason some do not consider them groupware. Also for this reason they largely avoid being overly rigid and disrupting social processes, challenges 3 and 4.

Shifting to a Work Perspective

Email demonstrates how important it is to adopt a workplace perspective rather than a technology perspective, and how difficult it is.

As developers, we see the distinction between sender and receiver as the key role distinction in the use of email. But, as the anthropologist Constance Perin noted in [5], the key distinction in email use in many organizations is that of manager and subordinate. The technology does not recognize the supervisor-subordinate distinction, but it is critical *in the workplace*. Whatever distinctions are designed into the technology, its reception is determined by distinctions that exist in the organization.

One groupware anomaly of email is its success. Another is that its use does not selectively benefit managers or decision makers. In fact, Perin documents that the contrary can be true. The ability for anyone to disseminate information rapidly can create problems for managers whose jobs involve filtering and routing information. In a classic bureaucracy, lateral communication is minimized—information flows up and down through the hierarchy. Email, even more than a telephone on each worker's desk, supports efficient lateral communication. This may provide greater flexibility and efficiency—but also create difficulties for managers in organizations built on the hierarchical model.

Similarly, the informality of email makes it easier, less imposing, and more private to bypass hierarchical levels. People who would not think of scheduling a meeting with their manager's manager will raise an issue by email, which can provide a level of informality approaching that of a chance conversation in the hall. Being bypassed can complicate managers' jobs. Rice [25] notes a study in which 7% of the messages spanned more than one level. This number may not seem high, but many employees *never* have face-to-face skip-level meetings. A few such messages, or even the possibility of making them, could subtly shift the managerial function.

One managerial responsibility is to absorb information from higher levels and tailor its presentation to subordinates to maximize their understanding or obtain a desired response. Correspondingly, information obtained from subordinates is filtered and recast to higher management. But information received electronically is more easily forwarded without tailoring. In fact, editing such messages can be problematic: If the original electronic version is forwarded by another path, the tampering is revealed. This places managers in a no-win situation. Olson and Lucas [23] suggest that it could lead to more "rational" environments by eliminating "distortion" introduced by bad managers, but good management involves translating and adding context to messages, taking time to prepare others to receive information, and other tasks that email can make more difficult.

And, of course, the ability of anyone to send a rumor or piece of news instantly to everyone in an organization creates a volatility with which management must cope. The asynchronous quality of email, often seen as a virtue, can bother managers whose time is tightly budgeted: "Mostly, a lot of times, I won't respond. I'll print the message and stick it in their file and wait until their weekly meeting," said one manager in an interview. In support of this view, Eveland and Bikson [10] found that professionals used email steadily through the day, but managers used it primarily in the early morning or late afternoon.

Perin [in 5] analyzed field studies and suggested that "these electronic social formations represent new sources of industrial conflict . . . they are seen as subverting legitimated organizational structures." While noting the collective value of electronic communication to large organizations, she describes how it can conflict with traditional organizational practices. For example, "the very 'invisibility' of electronic social fields, which may be cultivated bureaucratically because they are believed to enhance productivity, also delegitimates them and becomes the source of managerial negativism and suspicion." A study by Fanning and Raphael, cited by Perin, concluded that email "is simply not a management tool, if by management we mean those above the level of project leader . . . a medium which allows widely separated people to aggregate their needs is, in fact, quite frightening. Some managers correctly foresee that such a system can be most upsetting to the current established order, and do not participate in it as a result."

Email can be introduced under conditions that lead to different patterns of use, perhaps at times even strengthening hierarchic control But consider the implications if the general pattern outlined earlier proves true. Some managers can discourage or terminate email use, but many organizations have introduced it. Many students and professionals are accustomed to it. Thus, the forces Perin described are likely to play themselves out over time, forcing organizations designed on outmoded notions of efficiency and control to evolve. Finding new organizational forms and minimizing the cost of shifting to them are the challenges ahead.

Can we as technology developers change our perspective or must we rely on anthropologists and others? Visionary writers have stressed the need for designers to understand the functioning and evolution of groups and organizations. But recognizing the problem is easier than escaping the technology orientation reflected in the term "groupware." And intuition-governed, technology-driven, trial-and-error approaches are proving particularly expensive and failure-prone in this area.

Through the 1970s and 1980s, the British socio-technical and Scandinavian participatory design approaches experimented with meaningful engagement of users in systems development, a slow process of mutual education. Recently these have attracted wider attention through conference presentations and published overviews [11, 28]. The June 1993 issue of *Communications* was devoted to efforts to apply these methods in Europe and the U.S.

The following methods can help overcome the behavioral and social challenges facing groupware development and use:

- Extend the use of single-user applications in group settings by adding groupware features—collaborative writing features to an existing word processor, group support features to spreadsheets, and so forth. The economic barrier to acquiring a new system to support relatively infrequent activity is bypassed and rapid adoption is replaced by incremental adoption.
- Find niches where existing groupware succeeds, either in spite of the problems described in this article or because they do not arise. Voice applications help a traveling sales force that relies on the telephone, structured email applications may succeed in autocratic organizations, and so on.
- Build on object management or shared IS that have fared better than those that incorporate elements of organizational structure and work process. Object Lens [20] and Lotus Notes combine email and databases. Electronic b-boards are used to guide research, development and marketing [e.g., 29]. Modeling group process has proved more difficult, but workflow software is reportedly successful in supporting structured activity such as processing insurance forms. The variability of much group activity is a brake to much wider application.
- Find ways to provide direct benefits for all group members. In particular, supplement the technology with a design for the process of its use. Design and evaluation are easier and intuition better if relatively homogeneous groups are involved.

Be wary of applications that will selectively benefit managers or decision makers who are typically not heavy computer users.

- Educate managers and developers about groupware, the risks involved, and the resources and approaches that are required. Successful products such as Lotus Notes were longer in development than most applications. Working with users, extensive prototyping, and iterative design can be more cost-effective, but they are expensive.
- We need a better understanding of decision-making processes in development. Too often researchers study other researchers, developers build systems because the technology exists, and managers support the development of systems that appeal to other managers. We need a more empirical approach to broaden our intuitions. Trial-and-error learning has become too slow and costly.

When you examine research prototypes and available products, keep in mind that projects have purposes other than producing something useful. Other goals include exploring an interesting technical problem or matching a competitor.

Consider adoption issues from the outset. A groupware application may lead to organizational evolution, but its introduction must be smooth. Groupware must be more "group-friendly" than mainframe systems have been. To minimize the disruption requires interfaces adapted to users' backgrounds, roles, and preferences.

Anticipate organizational change. Some technology will replace or deskill workers; groupware that handles communication and coordination—management functions—can erode authority structures. Decentralized control could in turn further dim the prospect for groupware that selectively benefits management, a description of most groupware that has been developed.

Groupware may follow the pattern of other network technologies such as the telephone and the interstate highway. They spanned existing organizational boundaries, were designed for purposes unrelated to their ultimate use, and led slowly to a wide range of indirect effects. Our tentative exploration of a new technology is a step toward organizational and societal change that is not easily predicted or hurried.

Acknowledgment
My interest in these issues arose from successes and more often failures of applications that as a developer or user I embraced enthusiastically. The analyses emerged from interactions over many years with close colleagues and others. The significance of different contexts of system development arose in discussions with colleagues at Aarhus University. Discussions with Clarence Ellis, Gerhard Fischer, Joan Greenbaum, Rob Kling, Lynne Markus, Steve Poltrock, Susan Ehrlich Rudman, and Suzanne Watzman were particularly helpful. Comments by Bob Kraut and anonymous reviewers led to improvements. ◼

References

1. Bannon, L.J. and Schmidt, K. CSCW, four characters in search of a context. In *Studies in Computer-Supported Cooperative Work,* J.M. Bowers and S.D. Benford Eds., North-Holland, Amsterdam, 1991, pp. 3–16.
2. Bullen, C.V. and Bennett, J.L. Learning from user experience with groupware. In *Proceedings of CSCW '90* (Los Angeles, Calif., Oct. 7–10, 1990).
3. Carasik, R.P. and Grantham, C.E. A case study of computer-supported cooperative work in a dispersed organization. In *Proceedings of CHI '88* (Washington D.C., May 15–19, 1988), pp. 61–66. Some specific details were given only in the verbal presentation.
4. Cohen, M.D., March, J.G., and Olsen, J.P. A garbage can model of organizational choice. *Admin. Sci. Q. 17* (1972), 1–25.
5. Commun. ACM 34, 12. Perin, C. Electronic Social Fields in Bureaucracies.
6. Curtis, B., Krasner, H. and Iscoe, N. A field study of the software design process for large systems. *Commun. ACM, 31,* 11 (1988), 1268–1287.
7. Ehn, P. *Work-Oriented Design of Computer Artifacts.* Erlbaum, Hillsdale, N.J., 1989.
8. Ehrlich, S.F. Strategies for encouraging successful adoption of office communication systems. *ACM Trans. Off. Inf. Sys. 5* (1987), 340–357.
9. Ensor, R. Moderator. How can we make groupware practical? In *Proceedings of CHI '90* (Seattle, Wash. Apr. 1–5, 1990).
10. Eveland, J.D. and Bikson, T.K. Evolving electronic communication networks: An empirical assessment. *Off. Tech People 3* (1987), 103–128.

11. Greenbaum, J. and Kyng, M. *Design at Work: Cooperative Design of Computer Systems.* Erlbaum, Hillsdale, N.J., 1991.

12. Grudin, J. Interactive systems: Bridging the gaps btween developers and users. *IEEE Comput. 24,* 4 (1991), 59–69.

13. Grudin, J. Obstacles to user involvement in software product develoment, with implications for CSCW. *Int. J. Man-Machine Studies, 34,* 3 (1991), 435–452.

14. Grudin, J. Interface: An evolving concept. *Commun. ACM 36,* 4 (1993), 110–119.

15. Ishii, H. and Ohkubo, M. Message-driven groupware design based on an office procedure model, OM-1. *J. Inf. Process. 14,* 2 (1990), 184–191. Information Processing Society of Japan.

16. Kling, R. Social analyses of computing: Theoretical perspectives in recent empirical research. *ACM Comput. Surv. 12,* 1 (1980), 61–110.

17. Kraemer, K. and King, J. Computer-based systems for cooperative work and group decision making. *ACM Comput. Surv. 20,* (1988), 115–146.

18. Lucas, H.C., Jr. *Why Information Systems Fail.* Columbia University, New York, 1975.

19. Lyytinen, K. and Lehtinen, E. Seven mortal sins of systems work. In *System Design for Human Development and Productivity: Participation and Beyond,* P. Docherty, K. Fuchs-Kittowski, P. Kolm, and L. Mathiassen Eds., North-Holland, Amsterdam, 1987.

20. Malone, T.W. and Lai, K-Y. Toward intelligent tools for information sharing and collaboration. In COMPUTER AUGMENTED TEAMWORK: A GUIDED TOUR, R.P. Bostrom, R.T. Watson and S.T. Kinney, Eds. Van Nostrand Reinhold, New York, 1992.

21. Markus, M.L. and Connolly, T. Why CSCW applications fail: Problems in the adoption of interdependent work tools. In *Proceedings of CSCW '90* (Los Angeles, Calif., Oct. 7–10, 1990).

22. McCracken, D.L. and Akscyn, R.M. Experience with the ZOG human-computer interface system. *Int. J. Man-Machine Studies 21* (1984), 293–310.

23. Olson, M.H. and Lucas, H.C., Jr. The impact of office automation on the organization: Some implications for research and practice. *Commun. ACM 25,* 11 (1982), 838–847.

24. Pfeffer, J. Organizations and organization theory. In *Handbook of Social Psychology,* G. Lindzey and E. Aronson, Eds., Random House, New York, 1985.

25. Rice, R.E. Computer-mediated communication systems network data: Theoretical concerns and empirical examples. *Int. J. Man-Machine Studies, 32* (1990), 627–647.

26. Rowe, C.J. Introducing a sales order processing system: The importance of human, organizational and ergonomic factors. *Behav. Inf. Tech. 6,* (1987), 455–465.

27. Sathi, A., Morton, T.E., and Roth, S.F. Callisto: An intelligent project management system. In *Computer-supported cooperative work: a book of readings,* I. Greif, Ed., Morgan Kaufmann, San Mateo, Calif., 269–309.

28. Schuler, D. and Namioka, A., Eds., 1993. *Participatory Design: Principles and Practices.* Erlbaum, Hillsdale, N.J., 1993.

29. Sproull, L. Using electronic mail for data collection in organizational research. *Acad. Manage. J. 29,* 1 (1986), 159–169.

30. Suchman, L. Office procedures as practical action: Models of work and system design. *ACM Trans. Off. Inf. Syst. 1* (1983), 320–328.

CR Categories and Subject Descriptors: D.2.9 [**Software Engineering**]: Management—*productivity.* H.5.3 [**Information Interfaces and Presentation**]: Group and Organization Interfaces—*theory and models*; K.4.3 [**Computers and Society**]: Organizational Impacts

General Terms: Management

Additional Key Words and Phrases: Computer-supported cooperative work groupware

About the Author:

JONATHAN GRUDIN taught in the Aarhus University Computer Science department prior to joining the faculty at Irvine. He also worked in the now defunct Human Interface Laboratory at MCC and as a developer at Wang Laboratories. His interests include human-computer interaction and the history of interactive systems development. **Author's Present Address:** Department of ICS, University of California, Irvine, CA, 92717; email: grudin@ics.uci.edu

The User-centred Iterative Design Of Collaborative Writing Software

Ronald M. Baecker, Dimitrios Nastos, Ilona R. Posner, and Kelly L. Mawby

Dynamic Graphics Project, Computer Systems Research Institute
University of Toronto
Toronto, Ontario, CANADA M5S 1A4
Phone: (416)978-6983 E-mail: baecker@dgp.utoronto.ca

ABSTRACT
This paper presents the user-centred iterative design of software that supports collaborative writing. The design grew out of a study of how people write together that included a survey of writers and a laboratory study of writing teams linked by a variety of communications media. The resulting taxonomy of collaborative writing is summarized in the paper, followed by a list of design requirements for collaborative writing software suggested by the work. The paper describes two designs of the software. The first prototype supports synchronous writing and editing from workstations linked over local area and wide area networks. The second prototype also supports brainstorming, outlining, and document review, as well as asynchronous work. Lessons learned from the user testing and actual usage of the two systems are also presented.

KEYWORDS: Computer-supported cooperative work, groupware, user-centred design, iterative design, behavioural research, collaborative writing, writing software, synchronous and asynchronous writing.

INTRODUCTION

Most authors of documents work collaboratively from time to time; many write together with others most of the time. Yet very little is understood about how people write together, and very few systems are available to support this activity. This paper summarizes the results of our research on the process of collaborative writing, lists design requirements for collaborative writing software, and presents the user-centred iterative design of such software.

Our research on process consists of interviews with writers who have worked together collaboratively and a laboratory study of writing teams linked by different communications media. The taxonomy of collaborative writing that grew out of this work is summarized in the paper.

Our software design is user-centred in that it is based on this behavioural research. It is iterative, consisting of cycles of design, implementation of prototypes, and testing and evaluation. The first prototype, SASE, supports synchronous writing and editing in both focused and peripherally aware collaborative modes from workstations linked over local area and wide are networks. The second prototype, SASSE (Synchronous Asynchronous Structured Shared Editor), also supports brainstorming, outlining, and document review, provides a rich set of views of document structure, content, and revision process, and allows asynchronous work on a document.

TAXONOMY OF COLLABORATIVE WRITING

Previous Research

Although research has been conducted on individual writing [4, 10], only recently has attention been turned to collaborative writing. Surveys have shown that the majority of all written work is performed collaboratively [1, 7]. Physical proximity of collaborators was found to be key to successful scientific writing [16]. Computer technology affects the communication between participants as well as the final product of the collaboration [9, 12, 23].

A Survey of Writers

In order to understand the process of collaborative writing, we conducted 10 interviews with individuals who had participated in a number of collaborative writing projects. The backgrounds of the individuals surveyed included medicine, computer science, psychology, journalism, and freelance writing. The 22 projects discussed included journal articles, course assignments, a TV script, and a best-selling book. These projects lasted from several days to several years. The collaborating groups were formed either voluntarily or were organized in work settings. Participants varied in status from peers to student supervisor teams. Further details on the interviews may be found in [24, 25].

We encountered a wide range of attitudes towards collaborative writing. People had different expectations about the effects of collaboration, yet most felt that having several co-writers would improve the final product.

The relative status of group members, either similar or different, can lead to problems in working groups. Equal status groups may experience struggles for leadership and the problem of confronting members who are not contributing their expected share of work. In groups of unequal status participants may feel pressured to conform not on the basis of the alternative arguments but on the basis of the status of the individual proposing the alternative.

Different individual working styles can also cause problems. Some individuals like to leave the work till the last minute, while others prefer to complete the task in advance of the deadline. Individual preferences often need to be suppressed for the benefit of group harmony.

Writing technology can also cause problems for groups. Use of different machines by collaborators introduced difficulties when the document segments had to be merged into a single format. Participants complained of problems keeping track of different versions of the document. For example, one interviewee complained, "I would get email saying change page 4 line 2, but in my version page 4 is completely different." Communication bandwidth was a problem for groups working at a distance. For these groups physical proximity was often a solution. One interviewee said, "I was tempted to just fly there, instead of trying to cope with it over a distance."

Laboratory Study

A controlled laboratory study was conducted in order to see if we would observe in that context the same collaborative writing processes that our interviewees had reported. We also wanted to observe the effects of the communication medium on the writing process.

Pairs of subjects were asked to write instructions for the assembly of two simple toys. We informed the subjects that the resulting two chapters of assembly instructions were to become part of a single book; thus there needed to be similarity in writing style, terminology, and format between the two chapters.

Groups had two computers available and were free to choose any writing approach. Subjects worked in one of five scenarios: in the same room communicating face-to-face, in different rooms communicating with a speaker-phone, in different rooms communicating with an audio-video connection, in different rooms with the audio-video connection plus an image of the partner's remote screen, and in different rooms with the audio-video connection and the SASSE shared editor. In addition, subjects had available electronic mail, facsimile, and courier services.

Results of this study are discussed in [26]. Here we'll briefly list the highlights. We ran 4 groups in each condition, 20 groups in total. Given the small number of groups we did not necessarily expect to obtain statistically significant results, but we wanted to observe trends.

Individual differences in group behaviour dominated the results. Personalities of the participants had significant effects of the writing approach chosen by the group. Autocratic individuals who actively took control of the group insisted on joint work to monitor the progress and control the final document. Groups composed of two dominant individuals often faced interpersonal conflicts. Cooperative groups often divided the work between participants each one trusting the other to complete the required task.

As in previous research [12], document quality, i.e., the useability of the instructions, did not vary significantly with medium of communication ($F[4, 15]=1.237, p<.337$).

The type of communication between participants varied with the scenario. The discussions of subjects who could see each other's work focused more on higher-level issues such as writing style, tone, and audience of their documents. Subjects that could not easily see the other document frequently discussed lower-level details such as format and wording of their chapters.

The time to complete the task did not vary significantly with the communication medium ($F[4,15]=1.774, p<.187$). The medium did affect the amount of time spent working together compared to the total working time. Face-to-face subjects spent the most time working together (76%) while the speaker-phone groups spent the least (40%). The time spent working together was negatively correlated with total writing time ($r=-.418, p<.067$), but this may be as a result of the given task, which stressed consistency between documents.

Taxonomy of Collaborative Writing

The taxonomy of collaborative writing evolved out of attempts to categorize different components of the collaborative writing process that we observed in the interviews and again in the lab study (see Table 1). Each of the four categories of the taxonomy provides a different perspective for examining the writing process. *Roles* looks at process from the individual's point of view, at the part played by each individual on the writing team. *Activities* categorizes the actions performed while working on the project. *Document control methods* describes how the writing process is managed and coordinated. Finally, *writing strategies* focuses on the text creation process.

The choice of roles can depend on several factors including organizational structure, time constraints of the participants, relative status of the group members, and skills and expertise of the contributors:

- *writer*: converts ideas into text, records the text, freely makes changes to the text
- *consultant*: actively participates in different stages of the project but does not write the text
- *editor*: corrects text written by someone else
- *reviewer*: provides comments on the document.

Activities performed on a project can be affected by time constraints, task knowledge possessed by the group members, established organizational procedures, and participants' work styles:

- *brainstorming*: generating ideas
- *researching*: gathering information from sources external to the group
- *planning*: creating an outline for the document, and often dividing the work among group members
- *writing*: transforming ideas into text
- *editing*: making changes to the written text
- *reviewing*: generating comments about the text.

Document control methods describe how the document is managed and changes to it are made and coordinated.

- *centralized*: one person maintains the document while others make suggestions to the writer
- *relay*: one person controls the document at a time, but control passes between multiple authors
- *independent*: several people support segments of the document, while each one maintains control over an individual segment

	Interview	Lab. Study
Roles		
Writer	67%	95%
Consultant	43	75
Editor	57	80
Reviewer	85	88
Activities		
Brainstorm	82	100
Research	80	0
Plan	85	95
Write	82	95
Edit	78	80
Review	93	88
Document Control Methods		
Centralized	56	10
Relay	36	45
Independent	64	85
Shared	27	20
Writing Strategies		
Single Writer	59	15
Scribe	23	15
Separate Writers	86	90
Joint Writing	41	55

Table 1: Summary of writing approaches observed in interviews and the laboratory study. [1]

- *shared*: several people jointly control the document, having equal access and write privileges.

Writing strategies describe the document creation process, demonstrating how each segment of the text is created:

- *single writer:* text of document reflects thoughts and style of one individual with minimal assistance from others
- *scribe*: most often used in group meetings when one individual records the group's discussions with minimal guidance from the group
- *separate writers*: team members take different parts of the document and write them individually; later the parts are combined to form a whole
- *joint writing*: several team members compose the text together, where each word choice and sentence structure is decided through a group effort.

DESIGN REQUIREMENTS

The taxonomy presented in the previous section provides us with a vocabulary to describe systematically the processes of group writing. This work [24, 25], insights from our other research [19, 20], and an analysis of previous research results [16, 22, 25], have enabled us to formulate in six categories a set of design requirements for collaborative writing technology (see Table 2):

General Requirements for Individual Writing

Basic word-processing. A collaborative writing system must provide basic word-processing mechanisms.

Seamlessness with other work media. Users must be able to move smoothly between new groupware technology and existing single-user software [3]. Minimally, there must be a way to exchange documents with single-user applications.

General Requirements for Collaborative Writing

Preservation of identities. Collaborative writing depends upon contributions from several individuals. A collaborative writing system should record and display the identities of the contributors.

Enhanced communication. Essential to collaboration is communication among individuals who work together. They communicate about the object of their collaboration (*substantive communication*), exchange questions, revisions, and acceptances (*annotative communication*), and discuss courses of action and process plans to achieve their goal (*procedural communication*) [28].

Enhanced collaborator awareness. We define *collaborator awareness* as the knowledge of the state or actions of one's collaborators. Two dimensions that characterize levels of awareness are the degree of engagement and the amount of planning [14]. Depending on how focused and planned shared work is, collaboration may vary from focused collaboration (where people work together closely) to general awareness (where people know roughly what others are doing). We prefer the term *peripheral awareness*.

Annotations. Contributors such as reviewers of a document often record their suggestions as annotations. Ideally, a system should support several kinds of annotations — text, voice, or hand-drawn markings.

Undo. All interactive systems such as writing and drawing tools must provide the ability to undo changes made by a user. Undoing however becomes difficult when there are interleaved changes originating from multiple sources [27].

Session control. A collaborative writing system should allow users to create, join, or leave editing sessions at arbitrary times. It must also ensure that all users access the same version of the shared document.

Requirements re Roles

Explicit roles. A shared writing environment should support the different roles individuals may play in the process of document creation.

Requirements re Activities

Variety of activities. A document is created through a number of different activities including brainstorming, planning (including both outline and process plans), writing, editing, and reviewing. Each activity requires different support and functionality from a writing system. A shared writing system should be flexible enough to allow different writers to perform different activities at the same time.

Transitions between activities. A writing system should allow seamless transitions between activities, since they do not always occur in a sequential manner.

Requirements re Document Control Methods

Several document access methods. It may be appropriate to have different types, such as read-only, write, and comment.

[1] In roles, percentages are computed out of 60 individuals participating in projects discussed in the interviews and 40 subjects in the laboratory study. In the other categories, percentages describe how many groups employed certain activities, document control methods, or writing strategies.

Requirements	Aspects	GROVE	PREP	Quilt	ShrEdit	SASE	SASSE
Individual Writing							
Basic word-processing	++	–	++	–	++	+	++
Seamlessness with other media	++	–	++	++	+	+	++
Collaborative Writing							
Preserve identities	–	++	+	++	++	++	++
Enhance communication	+	–	–	–	+	–	++
Enhance collaborator awareness							
Focused collaboration	++	++	–	–	+	++	++
Peripheral awareness	–	+	–	–	–	+	++
Annotations	–	++	++	++	–	–	+
Undo	–		+	+	–	–	–
Session control	+	++	–	++	+	–	++
Roles							
Explicit roles	–	+	++	++	–	–	–
Activities							
Variety of activities							
Brainstorming	–	++	++	+	++	+	++
Researching	–	–	–	++	–	–	–
Planning (outline)	–	++	+	+	–	–	++
Planning (process)	–	–	+	–	–	–	–
Writing	++	–	++	+	++	++	++
Editing	++	–	++	+	++	++	++
Reviewing	–	–	++	+	–	–	++
Transitions between activities	+	–	++	++	+	–	++
Document Control Methods							
Several access methods	–	++	++	++	–	–	–
Separate document segments	++	–	+	++	–	–	–
Version and change control	–	–	+	–	–	–	++
Writing Strategies							
One or several writers	++	++	++	++	++	++	++
Synchronous writing	++	++	–	–	++	++	++
Asynchronous writing	+	+	++	++	++	–	++

Notation: ++ system provides good support + system can handle – system does not support

Table 2: Design requirements and comparison of collaborative writing tools.

Separate document segments. Individuals working collaboratively often subdivide the document and work on the pieces independently. Systems should provide support for multiple document segments yet maintain connections and access into the entire document.

Version control. Knowing who wrote or changed a certain part, what changes were made, and when they were made is essential.

Requirements re Writing Strategies

One or several writers. Although designed for multiple writers, a shared writing system should also support a single writer, so that one need not use a different systems for this.

Synchronous and asynchronous writing. Participants on a project may want to access the document concurrently or sequentially. Support for synchronous writing is essential especially during the stages of brainstorming and outlining. Support for asynchronous work is particularly important in the stages of writing, editing, and reviewing.

System Comparison

These requirements are summarized in Table 2, where existing shared writing systems are also evaluated. Aspects [2] is a collaborative conferencing system that runs on networked computers and provides writing, drawing, and painting tools. GROVE [8] is an outlining tool designed for users at remote sites working on networked computers. PREP [22] is a writing tool that provides asynchronous access to documents and can be thought of as a "spreadsheet for documents," because it provides a column based interface where text is presented in columns of visually linked chunks. Quilt [17] is a multi-user hypermedia communications and coordination tool which combines computer conferencing with multi-media email. ShrEdit [5] is intended for simultaneous writing by several users working on networked computers in a conference room.

THE FIRST PROTOTYPE

Our first prototype system for collaborative writing [19] was called SASE (pronounced "sassie"). This prototype was designed to support highly interactive synchronous collaborative writing.

SASE Design Requirements

Support for focused collaboration and independent work. Groups sometimes work together in focused collaboration, yet individuals or subgroups often break off from the main group to do independent work [8, 24, 25]. We felt that SASE should support both these approaches.

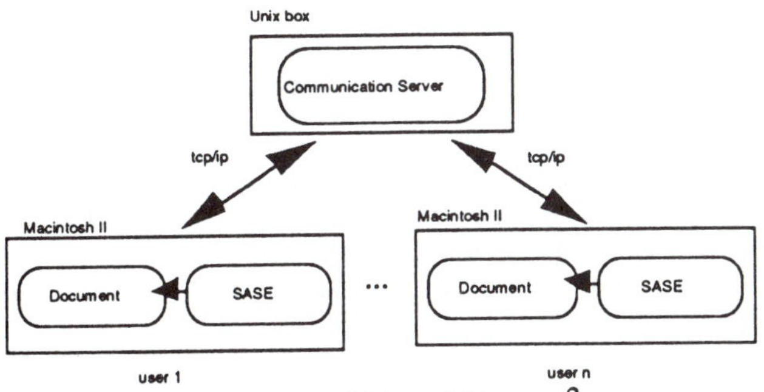

Figure 1: SASE's architecture.[2]

Support for collaborator awareness. In a synchronous writing environment, collaborators can simultaneously modify and add text to the document. Because there are multiple concurrent activities, collaborators may find it difficult to understand the changes that have been made and are currently being made to the shared document by others [6]. So SASE had to provide information to increase the individual's awareness and understanding of collaborators' actions.

Support conflict resolution. When multiple people edit the same document, it is conceivable that two or more people may attempt to modify a particular segment of text at the same time. Thus we felt SASE should provide mechanisms to help prevent users from making conflicting changes.

User Interface and Architecture

SASE allows two or more people to edit a document synchronously while working at their own Macintosh workstations. It is assumed that they will communicate via telephone or an audio/video connection.

So that collaborators can see and discuss each others' contributions as they happen, text modifications made by users immediately appear on their text windows and on the text windows of all other collaborators. Users can point to text using a hand-like pointing device called a *telepointer*. To help maintain collaborator awareness, users are provided continuous feedback of other collaborators' working locations in the document with colour coded text selections and scroll bars.

There is always one vertical scroll bar for each person currently collaborating in SASE. The rightmost scroll bar on a user's text window always belongs to that user and functions as a normal scroll bar. Additional colour-coded scroll bars indicate the current locations of collaborators, but are "read-only" and cannot be manipulated.

Users can work independently on a document in SASE, since actions such as scrolling and window sizing affect only the window of the user who initiated the action. They can also work together in a highly focused mode by locking together and synchronizing their views, thus achieving WYSIWIS (What You See Is What I See).

To avoid conflicting changes, SASE locks text at the user text selection level. This means that it is possible for collaborators to work within the same line of text. With this fine grain locking mechanism, we leave it to the collaborating group to decide how closely they will work within the shared document.

We chose a replicated architecture (Figure 1) in which a copy of the application and the shared document reside on each collaborators' workstation. This architecture is combined with a centralized communication server which resides on a Unix box. The application copies communicate via the TCP/IP communication protocol. All message traffic is routed through the central communication server which ensures that all copies of the application receive messages in the same order. This architecture supports simultaneous text editing, usually provides reasonable response, and supports conflict resolution.

User Testing

A usability study [19] was conducted with three two-person teams using SASE to perform a series of text editing tasks required to prepare collaboratively a newspaper article for publication. Subjects communicated via a CAVECAT audio/video connection [18]. All subjects were able to use SASE effectively after a brief introduction to the system.

The multiple scroll bars improved collaborator awareness. Subjects used these to match their view of the document with their partner's view, to determine how far away their partner was in the document, and to reduce the time needed to find text in the document.

When groups were asked to do a shared task such as scanning the document for typographical errors, they first negotiated how to divide the work in order to save time. When asked to collaboratively compose text, all groups used the scribe writing strategy.

Subjects liked the fact that they could work separately or together in the document. This allowed them to save time by dividing the task. They also liked that they could ask their partner for help when necessary. They suggested that the system should provide a way of seeing what changes have been made, and a way to change the text back to the original form if necessary.

THE SECOND PROTOTYPE

The second prototype, called SASSE [20], is an extension of the first, and is based on the requirements presented earlier in this paper. Our goal was to satisfy most of them, while leaving some (e.g., providing support for explicit roles) to be handled by social protocols.

Design Requirements

Support for a variety of activities. In designing the second prototype we felt that the system should support the writing activities presented previously. SASSE supports

---

[2] SASE's text editing functionality was implemented using the Word Solution Engine (WSE) [29] by DataPak Software, Inc. The WSE supports the text editing functionality of the Macintosh TextEdit Toolbox and also provides hooks into text editing procedures for purposes of customization, such as for maintaining multiple colour coded text selections .

brainstorming, outlining, and reviewing, in addition to writing and editing.

Enhanced communication and collaborator awareness. We designed views that provide information about who the collaborators are, where in the document they are working, and what they are doing.

Support for asynchronous writing. The first prototype was a synchronous shared editor. In order to support asynchronous writing, we added an annotation mechanism that allows authors to exchange notes and comments, a simple version control mechanism that shows which parts of the document were changed and by whom, as well as a centralized document storage mechanism that allows users to access shared documents easily.

SASSE User Interface and Implementation

Support for a variety of activities. SASSE's outline editor has been designed to allow writers to work with hierarchically structured shared documents. The outline editor allows users to see document structure, to display or hide parts of it, and to edit its structure as well as its contents. Baecker, et al., Colour Plate 1 shows SASSE in outlining mode. Baecker, et al., Colour Plate 2 shows the normal text display of SASSE.

During the reviewing phase writers solicit comments on versions of their document. Sometimes this results in a dialogue between the commenters and the writers, especially when the comments are unclear. SASSE's annotation mechanism allows users to write text comments that can be selectively displayed, hidden, or deleted.

Enhanced communication and collaborator awareness. SASSE's collaborator awareness mechanisms provide information about the co-authors of a document, their positions in the document, and their actions. As in SASE, colour is used to differentiate between users. Each collaborator is assigned a unique colour. This assignment is stored with the document so that the same author has the same colour each time a particular document is edited.

Collaborator awareness is further aided by views that provide information about the state or actions of collaborators. The collaborator list gives information about the authors of a document, as well as their colour assignment, and whether they are present or not present in the editing session. The shared scroll bars introduced in the first prototype were redesigned. Instead of having several scroll bars, which take up screen space, only two scroll bars are displayed: the normal scroll bar of the local user and one with multiple colour-coded indicators which correspond to the collaborators participating in an editing session. SASSE's shared scroll bars are shown in the colour plates.

Information about what user activities can range from the very abstract and global to the very concrete and local. SASSE provides two views at extremes of the spectrum. The *gestalt view* (Colour Plate 2) presents a condensed image of the entire document as well as all collaborators' positions and text selections. The *observation view* (Colour Plate 1) allows users to "look over the shoulder" of a collaborator and see exactly what they are seeing and doing. Additionally, non-speech audio cues [13] provide information about collaborators' actions such as scrolling and deleting.

Support for asynchronous writing. In order to support asynchronous writing we added an annotation mechanism. Users can selectively display or hide comments written by a specific author. The comments are colour-coded for easy identification. A simple version control mechanism (implemented but not yet installed) allows users to see which parts of the documents have been changed and what the changes are. A document server is used to store shared documents in a central storage space. Collaborators are thus able to access with ease the latest version of a document.

User Testing and Results

We conducted a usability study [20] with SASSE, again using CAVECAT to provide a voice and video link. Four two-person groups used the system to carry out a set of collaborative writing and editing tasks after a brief introduction to its functionality and user interface. The tasks were designed to test the outlining and collaborator awareness mechanisms of the system. During the first part of the study the subjects were asked to edit the outline of a travel guide. During the second part they had to do both shared and independent editing tasks on an article. Subjects were asked to use the system's awareness mechanism to obtain information about their collaborators.

Three methods were used to collect information from the usability study: observation during the study, recording it on video for later analysis with our VANNA video annotation and analysis system [15], and administration of a questionnaire and an interview with subjects after the study.

Subjects used the audio link continuously but made relatively little use of the video link. Most subjects were able to use SASSE's outlining and collaborator awareness mechanisms successfully. Yet, the character-level locking produced unacceptable delays during deletions. Some subjects could not understand why some operations were failing because they would not notice the padlock indicating that they were locked out. Finally, network delays resulting in slow system response made some subjects feel uneasy and in a few cases retry an operation.

Real Use

SASSE is becoming robust enough to be used for real work. We have done so over local area networks in our lab and over a wide area network between Toronto and California. This paper was written in part with SASSE. Observations are implied in the suggestions for future work listed below.

SUMMARY AND CONCLUSIONS

We have presented the user-centred iterative design of collaborative writing technology. The work is deeply rooted in behavioural research consisting of interviews, usability tests, and studies of the technology in actual use. This has enabled us to improve the design in successive iterations, a process which continues to this day.

Our user tests and usage suggest that a coarser locking scheme, for example, at the sentence or paragraph level, would suffice. Alternatively, locking may not be needed at all because conflicts can be negotiated through use of the voice link. This would allow us to improve performance significantly. Further work is also required to achieve true "seamlessness" with other writing technology. We are currently designing and implementing an "undo" command [27] and mechanisms for automatically collecting usage data. Finally, much more work remains to be done on the design of effective visual and auditory views to enhance collaborator awareness, and on the design of better methods for the display of document changes [21].

ACKNOWLEDGEMENTS

We gratefully acknowledge the support to our laboratory from the Natural Sciences and Engineering Research Council of Canada, the Information Technology Research Centre of Ontario, the Institute for Robotics and Intelligent Systems of Canada, Apple Computer's Human Interface Group and Advanced Technology Group, Xerox PARC and EuroPARC, Digital Equipment Corporation, and the IBM Canada Lab Centre for Advanced Studies. We are also indebted to Beverly Harrison, Marilyn Mantei, Alex Mitchell, and Abigail Sellen for assistance with this work.

REFERENCES

1. Allen, N.J., Atkinson, D., Morgan, M., Moore, T., and Snow, C., What Experienced Collaborators Say about Collaborative Writing. *Iowa State Journal of Business and Technical Communication* Sept. 1987, 70-90.
2. Aspects: The First Simultaneous Conference Software for the Macintosh, Group Technologies, Inc., 1990.
3. Baecker, R., *Readings in Groupware and Computer-supported Cooperative Work: Facilitating Human-human Collaboration,* Morgan Kaufmann, 1993.
4. Bereiter, C. and Scardamalia, M., From Conversation to Composition, in *Advances in Instructional Psychology,* R. Glaser, Editor, Erlbaum, 1982.
5. Cognitive Science and Machine Intelligence Laboratory. ShrEdit, a Multi-user Shared Text Editor: User's Manual, The University of Michigan, 1989.
6. Dourish, P. and Bellotti, V., Awareness and Coordination in Shared Workspaces, *Proceedings of CSCW'92*, 107-114.
7. Ede, L. and Lunsford, A., *Singular Texts/Plural Authors: Perspectives on Collaborative Writing.* Southern Illinois University Press, 1990.
8. Ellis, C.A., Gibbs, S.J., and Rein, G.L., Groupware: Some Issues and Experiences. *CACM* 34(1), 1991, 38-58. Reprinted in [3].
9. Eveland, J.D. and Bikson, T.K., Work Group Structures and Computer Support: A Field Experiment. *Proc of CSCW'88*, 324-343.
10. Flower, L., Schriver, K.A., Carey, L., Haas, C., and Hayes, J.R., Planning in Writing: The Cognition of a Constructive Process. Center for the Study of Writing, Carnegie Mellon University, 1989.
11. Galegher, J., Kraut, R.E., and Egido, C., Editors, *Intellectual Teamwork: Social and Technological Foundations of Cooperative Work,* Erlbaum, 1990.
12. Galegher, J., Kraut, R.E., and Egido, C.., Technology for Intellectual Teamwork: Perspectives on Research and Design, in [11], 1-20.
13. Gaver, W., Sound Support for Collaboration, *Proceedings of ECSCW '91*, 293-308. Reprinted in [3].
14. Gaver, W., Moran, T., MacLean, A., Lövstrand, L., Dourish, P., Carter, K., and Buxton, W., Realizing a Video Environment: EuroPARC's RAVE System, *Proceedings of CHI '92*, 27-35.
15. Harrison, B.L. and Baecker, R.M., Designing Video Annotation and Analysis Systems, *Proceedings of Graphics Interface '92*, 157-166.
16. Kraut, R., Egido, C., and Galegher, J., Patterns of Contact and Communication in Scientific Research Collaborations. In [11], 149-171.
17. Leland, M.D.P., Fish, R.S., and Kraut, R.E., Collaborative Document Production Using Quilt, *Proceedings of CSCW 88*, 206-215.
18. Mantei, M.M., Baecker, R.M., Sellen, A.J., Buxton, W.A.S., Milligan, T., and Wellman, B., Experiences in the Use of a Media Space, *Proceedings of CHI '91*, 203-208. Reprinted in [3].
19. Mawby, K.L., Designing Collaborative Writing Tools. 1991, Unpublished M.Sc. Thesis, Department of Computer Science, University of Toronto.
20. Nastos, D., A Structured Environment for Collaborative Writing. 1992, Unpublished M.Sc. Thesis, Department of Computer Science, University of Toronto.
21. Neuwirth, C.M., Chandhok, R., Kaufer, D.S., Erion, P., Morris, J., and Miller, D., Flexible DIFF-ing in a Collaborative Writing System, *Proceedings of CSCW'92*, 147-154.
22. Neuwirth, C.M., Kaufer, D.S., Chandhok, R., and Morris, J.H., Issues in the Design of Computer Support for Co-authoring and Commenting, *Proceedings of CSCW 90*, 183-195. Reprinted in [3].
23. Olson, J.S., Olson, G.M., Storrøsten, M., and Carter, M., How a Group-Editor Changes the Character of a Design Meeting as well as its Outcome, *Proceedings of CSCW'92*, 91-98.
24. Posner, I.R., A Study of Collaborative Writing. 1991, Unpublished M.Sc. Thesis, Department of Computer Science, University of Toronto.
25. Posner, I.R. and Baecker, R.M., How People Write Together, in *Proceedings of the Twenty-fifth Annual Hawaii International Conference on System Sciences*, 1992, 127-138. Reprinted in [3].
26. Posner, I.R. and Baecker, R.M., A Study of Collaborative Writing, journal article submittted for review, 1992.
27. Prakash, A. and Knister, M.J., Undoing Actions in Collaborative Work, *Proceedings of CSCW'92*, 273-280.
28. Suchman, L.A. and Trigg, R.H., A Framework for Studying Research Collaboration, *Proceedings of CSCW 86*, 221-228.
29. Word Solution Engine Programmer's Guide, DataPak Software, Inc., Vancouver, WA, 1990.

Baecker, et al., Colour Plate 1: SASSE is in outlining mode. The green user is working at the beginning of the document and her view appears in the upper half of the screen. An observation view of the red user appears in the lower half of the screen.

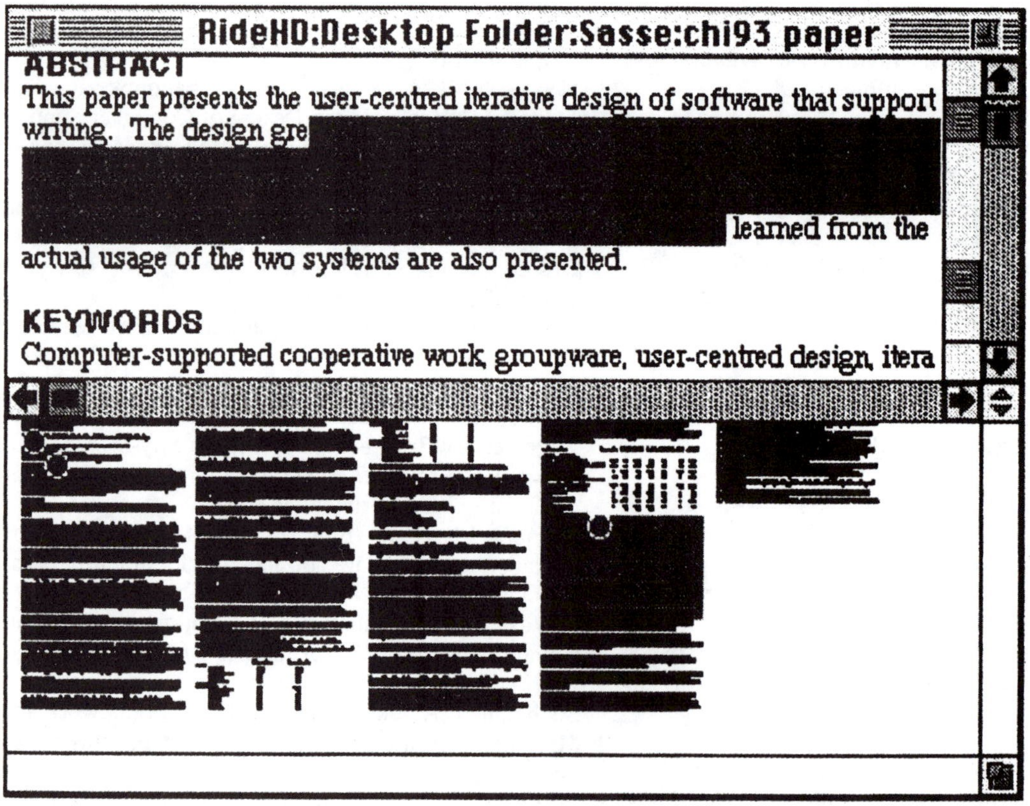

Please see the inside back cover for color image C10 which corresponds to Baecker, et al., Color Plate 2.

Baecker, et al., Colour Plate 2: SASSE's normal text display for the green user appears in the upper half of the screen. A gestalt view of the entire document appears in the lower half of the screen. There are 3 users (green, gray, and red) working concurrently on the document. The red user is working midway through the document and has selected a large region of text.

Chapter 12

From Customizable Systems to Intelligent Agents

Much of interface design is built around the premise of "the typical user." As early as Hansen's 1971 dictum "know the user" (see Chapter 2), designers' goals have included learning what typical users need, what tasks they do and how they do them, and how they react to the software that is implemented.

The problem is that there is no such thing as a typical user. Chapter 10 discussed the variations in people's abilities and needs, knowledge and training, and tasks and environments, and in the ways they engage with computers. Indeed, people's adoption of software is often less a matter of finding a perfect fit with the system than it is of conforming to organizational constraints, finding adequate functionality, and being willing to accept the challenges of learning and using a less than perfect system. Even a good match between person and system is unlikely to last. Tasks change over time, and so do we: As we gain experience we may demand more than the existing system can deliver.

There are few tasks that computers do not or could not support in some way; within each task domain a greater breadth and depth of support is continually sought. The expectations of users are on the rise. People want systems that conform to their preferences at the individual, group, and organizational levels.

In this chapter, we examine exciting new approaches to designing software that fits the needs of individuals, rather than a nonexistent "typical user." To frame this, consider Friedman's (1989) three approaches to addressing the specific needs of users.

- *Educate developers about users and their work.* A general education cannot tell us the needs of a specific group, but it helps. Friedman focuses on in-house developers who are often located close to the people they support. Contextual design, described by Holtzblatt and Jones (1993) in Chapter 3, is used by product developers to learn more about users. Gundry (1988) proposed that contractors include scenarios of workplace activity when requesting proposals.
- *Form active collaborations among users and developers when designing systems.* This is most evident in participatory or collaborative design experiments, as described by Bødker, Grønbæk, and Kyng (1992) in Chapter 3. Active collaboration works both for designing initial versions of software and for changing the software over time as the needs of users change.
- *Shift responsibility for final design decisions from the initial developers to the users or to people who are closer to the users.* This requires building flexibility and adaptability into the software and the software development process (see Boehm, 1988, in Chapter 4). The point is to make many design decisions reversible or capable of being decided at a later time by those with more information about what is needed—and often the users themselves have the most information about what is needed!

This chapter begins where the last approach leaves off. We first consider systems designed to allow "end users" to change them to conform to their needs through customization and end-user programming. We then describe systems that modify the interface during use through adaptive interfaces, programming by demonstration, and intelligent agents.

TAILORING BY EXPLICIT CUSTOMIZATION

Customizable or *tailorable* systems are applications that are designed and built to be fine-tuned or adjusted by users. The goal of providing a system so flexible that users can tailor it to their own needs is powerful and appealing. In this chapter's first reading, Henderson and Kyng (1991) argue that tailorable software can provide ongoing "design in use." Designers cannot anticipate all of a user's needs or preferences, especially since situations evolve over time. The authors define *tailoring* as an activity that is intended to have a long-term effect and that changes the tool, not the content being worked on. To embolden a document title is not tailoring; to create a "preference" setting so that all document titles default to bold is tailoring the word processor. Yet the boundary between tailoring and use is not always sharp.

Henderson and Kyng then identify types of tailoring that make different demands on users and designers:

- Users choose among alternatives. This requires designers to anticipate the range of useful alternatives.
- Users construct new behaviors from existing pieces. Here, designers must insure that the components and the language for assembling them can be applied by a user. In Unix, for example, programmers are encouraged to write programs that can be combined by allowing the output of one to be usable as the input of others.
- Users have the means to alter the system itself. Allowing users to change a program's source code is generally not realistic, but designers can supply "hooks" to a program that can be attached to user-defined actions.

Henderson and Kyng describe a good tailoring system: it is easy to use; it protects other software or users from accidental disruption by changes made during tailoring; it insures that changes are saved; it supports examination, sharing, and learning by other users; and it provides feedback on what works and doesn't work. Their conclusions are supported by a study of customization, Mackay (1990b), which found that users most often request

- the ability to browse through the useful ideas of others
- better mechanisms for sharing customizations
- methods for finding out which customizations are used and effective
- methods of identifying customizations that are ineffective

Just because a system can be tailored doesn't mean that all users will have the necessary skills or will want to do it! MacLean et al. (1990) caricature several kinds of users, each with different interests in tailoring. *Workers* are primarily interested in getting their job done. They are not expected to tailor the system, as they view the computer narrowly as a means to an end. *Tinkerers* enjoy computers to the extent that they are willing to modify the system somewhat. However, they are not computer professionals and have limited understanding of how to extend the system. *Programmers* are computer gurus who know much about the system and how to change it, but who know little about the task domain. Finally, a *handyman* is an intermediary between workers and programmers. A tailorable system must identify its audience: A system easily tailored by a programmer may be unusable by a worker.

In the following section, we catalog a variety of customization techniques—preferences and templates, customizable workspaces, and end-user programming via scripts—and close with some cautionary notes.

Preferences and Templates

Cypher (1991b, 1993) describes two common customization methods available on most computers: preferences and templates.

Preferences are sets of predefined alternatives specified in advance by the designers. Users can choose the alternative that best fits their needs. In text-based systems, such as DOS, Unix *csh*, and the emacs editor, preferences are typically indicated by modifying a script that is executed whenever the system is restarted. Most graphical interfaces supply a more easily used *control panel*, where options are displayed, selected, and adjusted graphically. Figure 12.1 shows a panel for setting the responsiveness of the Apple Macintosh mouse; the current settings and the available options are always displayed.

Templates go further by allowing an entire context to be used again and again. Examples include the setting and saving of "style sheets" in word processors and "master templates" in presentation programs. Figure 12.2 shows a slide master in Microsoft's Powerpoint presentation system. A user can specify slide attributes such as the position of the slide's title and body, the format of titles and each text level, and can even add background visuals such as logos. The master layout can be saved and reused with different sets of slides.

Preferences and templates are very useful due to their simplicity, but they are limited to the options and features that are defined in advance by the developers (Cypher, 1991b).

FIGURE 12.1

The Apple Macintosh control panel option for setting the tracking and double-click speed of the mouse.

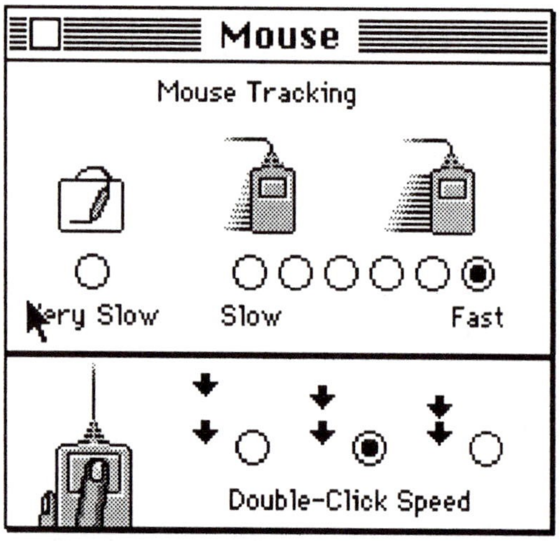

FIGURE 12.2

An example of a slide master template in Microsoft Powerpoint. Its editable layout can be applied to different collections of slides.

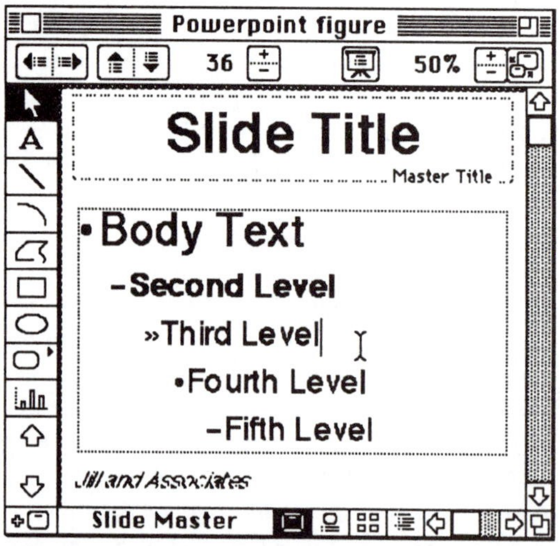

Creation of a Customizable Workspace

In the everyday world, people customize their work areas by adding their own personality and objects they like or need to use. A desk, for example, will contain documents and tools that its occupant wants to have close to hand. Although computer interfaces allow people to locate documents, few systems let people manipulate the way their common tools (or commands) are structured and presented in the workspace.

A simple (but limited) example of a customizable workspace is in Microsoft Word. Word contains around 300 commands, too many to put in its pull-down menus. Its designers created menus with a reasonable subset of the commands and allow users to customize the menus when needed. Through a simple dialog, illustrated in Figure 12.3, users can reconfigure the menus to display additional commands, add shortcut keys, or reduce clutter by removing little-used menu items.

More powerful customization happens when people can collect and pass along enhancements that they or their colleagues have defined. In the Buttons interface of MacLean et al. (1990), a person can create and place a button on the screen that executes a user-defined script. Making this simple idea usable by a community of people with different skills and motivations—workers, tinkerers, and programmers—took more thought. First, the overhead of creating buttons was minimized by *situated creation*. Anyone (including the goal-directed "worker") can easily select a text fragment—perhaps a system command that had just been typed—and attach it to a button. In addition, useful buttons can be copied and sent to other workers via e-mail. Behavior of existing buttons can also be specialized; tinkerers could view it as a set of easily recognizable and changeable attributes; programmers could see it as editable Lisp code. A handyman assigned to the Buttons project, a member of the design team who worked closely with prospective users, was seen as critical to the development of a tailoring culture.

Workbench is a graphical front end to Unix that allows people to customize their interactions with a command-line interpreter (Greenberg, 1993). Using the metaphor of a handyman's workbench, it provides a history list that predicts future commands from old ones, as well as an explicit way for users to attach buttons to commands and to further organize commands for later reuse.

Figure 12.4 is a stylized image of Workbench. The *work surface* (bottom) contains the Unix command-line interpreter, which eventually executes all commands. The *reuse area* (middle left) holds a selectable, editable, and executable history list containing the last ten unique command-lines entered. Pointing to a history entry brings up a menu that displays all other arguments the person had used with that particular command (Greenberg and Witten, 1993a, 1993b). Like Buttons, Workbench encourages situated creation and modification of temporary or permanent buttons. Users can copy items from the reuse area to the *tool panel* (middle right), where they remain available for selection, execution, and modification. Users can further customize their environment by attaching sets of commands to buttons and moving them into a "drawer" of the *tool cabinet* (top panel). Users can edit drawer contents, change a buttons label, create button-specific help messages, and alter the script attached to a button. Buttons can also be used to navigate to a drawer, and a list is kept of the drawers visited.

End-User Programming

Another approach to customization is to let the users program the system. The problem is that most (all?) computer languages are unusable by "the workers and the tinkerers"! Smith, Cypher, and Spohrer (1994) estimate that fewer than 10%, and perhaps fewer than 1%, of children who are taught to program continue to do so after a class ends. This is hardly a good omen! Be that as it may, several techniques can give users the power to program a system, albeit in limited ways.

A *scripting language* is a simplified programming language that attempts to reflect the users' language and concepts (Cypher

FIGURE 12.3

Microsoft Word's dialog for reconfiguring menus. Commands (top left) can be added or removed from menus (bottom left). Default values of particular command arguments can be established (top right). Help descriptions of commands are shown (middle right), and shortcut keys can be assigned (bottom right).

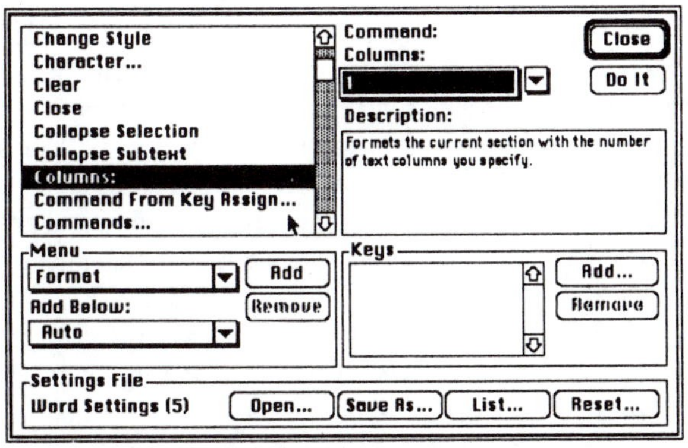

FIGURE 12.4

The Workbench system. Commands are executed in the Work Surface. The last ten unique commands entered are automatically buttonized in the Reuse Area. The user's personal cache of buttonized command-lines appears in the Tool Panel. A drawer in the Tool Cabinet contains customized buttons for carrying out task-specific actions.

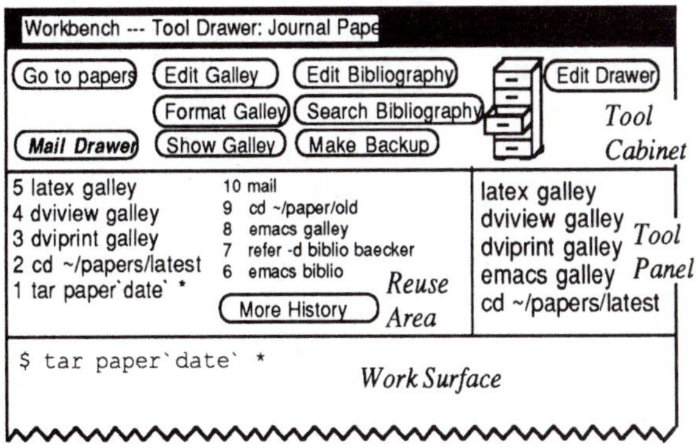

1993, 1991b). HyperTalk, the scripting language of Apple's HyperCard program, has become the development environment of choice for many people who are not professional programmers (see Chapter 13 for a discussion of its role in the creation of multimedia). But perhaps the most successful application of scripting is the spreadsheet, which provides limited programming capabilities through its formulas. Nardi and Miller (1990, 1991) examine how people use spreadsheets and conclude that one strength lies in the high degree of end-user programming and tailoring that they enable. Wilde and Lewis (1990) apply the spreadsheet model to interactive graphics. Nardi (1994) zealously promotes spreadsheet programming as a general model for empowering users.

Scripting makes it easier for nonprogrammers to learn how to program, but it still takes an effort that is beyond the desire of most users. As Cypher (1993, p. 4) succinctly states:

> *... the basic failing of scripting is that it is still programming. That is, 1) users have to learn the arcane syntax and vocabulary conventions of the language, and 2) they have to learn the standard computer science concepts of variables, loops and conditionals. For a significant number of contemporary computer users ... the hurdle of learning a scripting language is too high.*

Of course, people find ways to get over this hurdle. Nardi and Miller (1991) found that people who need programming capability often call in a coworker with some level of programming expertise (a tinkerer or handyman). The resulting spreadsheet program is a collaborative effort of people with different levels of domain and programming expertise. As Henderson and Kyng note, in the end it doesn't matter who really does the tailoring. The goal is to put this capability in the hands of those who can create the best systems for users. If not the users themselves, it is likely to be people with close involvement with the users, closer than the original developers. Perhaps it is a "designated hacker" in a user community, or a consultant hired to be a software handyman.

Cautionary Notes

One danger for interface designers is that providing tailorability can be an excuse for not doing a good initial design. Faced with design alternatives, it is tempting to say, "Instead of doing a study to see which is best, let's make it customizable and let users choose." Thus, it is ironically possible that tailorability, designed to enhance users' control, could lead to a decrease in users' involvement in the initial design of their environments.

Another danger is that designers cannot count on users to make use of a customization capability, however easy it is to use. As mentioned in Chapter 10's discussion of ergonomic furniture, people rarely understand the reasons behind the adjustable features. They often use the furniture as they receive it or adjust it improperly. The same can be true for computers.

Even experienced users may design inefficient interfaces and fail to learn from experience (Grudin and Barnard, 1985; Mackay, 1991). Mackay (1990a) found that when a new system is introduced, users typically go through a brief period of experimentation and customization, then settle on an environment that seems satisfactory. They do not optimize and may not continue to customize as they gain experience and thus have different needs. Each group she observed tended to rely on one person to take the lead in creating or distributing customizations. Most startling was the discovery that a major use of customization was to restore a new system to resemble the previous—and as a rule inferior—system, to avoid the cost of learning a new system.

Finally, customization comes at the cost of increased system complexity. As Woods (1993, p. 21) notes:

> *... the practitioner must learn about all of the available options, learn and remember how to deploy them across the variety of real operational contexts that can occur, and learn and remember the interface manipulations required to invoke different modes or features. All of this represents new burdens on the practitioner to set up and manage these capabilities and features.*

Clearly, the interface to a customization facility needs as much attention as the main system.

To summarize: Building customizable features to handle user diversity is good, but be sure that the default system design is excellent, in order to avoid crippling those who use it as they receive it.

ADAPTIVE INTERFACES

So far we have described approaches in which users appear to be in complete control. We now turn to "intelligent" interfaces in which the system is more active, where it takes the initiative by adapting its interface or its interaction model to fit the "perceived" needs of its users.

Commercial systems long ago made minor steps toward adaptive interfaces by anticipating user actions. A system that defaults to the last menu item that was selected is making a change based on anticipated behavior. It seems natural when a word processor defaults to "paste" after a user has carried out a "copy" operation. Similarly, the history systems available on many computers adapt the interface to the interaction, by making it easier for a user to recall previously submitted actions. The AI boom of the early 1980s saw numerous efforts to go much further in providing intelligent support for users, yet there were few successes (Edmonds, 1981; Innocent, 1982; Benyon, 1984). In a nice survey of intelligent interfaces, Benyon and Murray (1993) noted that earlier systems implicitly represented and anticipated user behaviors on the basis of statistical averages, while later systems constructed dynamic models of individual users and task domains.

One statistics-based adaptive interface, adaptive menus, accelerates a user's selection of items within a menu hierarchy by dynamically reconfiguring the hierarchy to bring items that are likely to be selected closer to the root (Greenberg and Witten, 1985; Greenberg et al., 1994). Its authors give the example of a large computerized telephone directory presented through a menu hierarchy. Screens contain selectable ranges of names, each representing a hierarchical progression. In the example shown in Figure 12.5, a user searching for "Otton" would select item 4 from the top-level screen, item 1 from the second-level screen, and so on, until the name "Otton" appeared as its own menu item.

Normally, the hierarchy would be constructed by splitting the name space into equal units to provide a tree with a balanced number of leaves at every point. Such menus are "frozen"; a user always navigates the same path to reach a friend's phone number, regardless of how often called. This works out to about $\log_m$ *names* screens for each access (m is the number of menu items/screen).

FIGURE 12.5

Searching through the first two levels of an adaptive menu hierarchy.

Top level screen	Second level screen
(1) Arbor – Eagan	*(1) OBrian – Rand*
(2) Farel – Kruger	*(2) Randy – Sunnel*
(3) Kwant – OBrady	*(3) Sunney – Trystan*
(4) OBrian – Zlotky	*(4) Tully – Zlotky*

However, the access frequencies of names, combined with their recency of selection, defines a probability distribution that reflects the "popularity" of the names selected. Instead of selecting regions at each stage to contain approximately equal numbers of names, the probability distribution is divided into approximately equal portions. During use, the act of selection alters the distribution and thereby increases the probability of the names selected. Thus a user is directed more quickly to entries that have already been selected, especially to those selected often and recently. The assigning of probabilities is dynamic; the hierarchy presented adapts to a user's evolving (and ever-changing) usage over time.

Adaptive menus illustrates the trade-off inherent in this style of adaptive system. The system guarantees that previous actions are almost always resubmitted in fewer keystrokes because its algorithm approaches the information-theoretic minimum of keystrokes (Witten, Cleary, and Greenberg, 1984). However, since paths change dynamically, memory cannot be used to accelerate the selection process, and users must now always search the menus for their entries. Even more serious is that the ever changing system is potentially confusing, as users may not know why the changes are occurring. In one study, this proved not to be a problem. Human factor experiments compared adaptive menus favorably with their non-adaptive counterparts (Greenberg and Witten, 1985). Selection time was reduced by 35% and, as subjects did not have to descend deep into the tree (where most selection errors occur), errors decreased by 60%. Subjects also preferred adaptive menus to the nonadaptive ones.

What if the changes made by the adaptive systems were detrimental in some cases? In a replication of the adaptive menus work, Trevellyan and Browne (1987) promote a "self-regulating" adaptive interface. The system monitors how effective its adaptations are, and if performance drops below a certain level, the system turns off the adaptive mechanism.

Intelligent tutoring and coaching systems are adaptive systems that incorporate user modeling instead of statistics. In this domain, the goal of the interaction is known to the computer (i.e., the concepts to be taught), as are the means to reach that goal (the lesson plans). The computer may contain an "expert model" that shows how an expert might learn a lesson or perform an exercise. It can then compare the student interaction with the expert model, customize the curriculum to the student's current level of knowledge, and even make suggestions as appropriate.

The ACT project (Anderson et al., 1988 video) has used theories of complex skill acquisition (see Chapter 9) to develop practical intelligent tutors to aid in learning algebra, geometry, and Lisp. The Piano Tutor (Sanchez et al., 1990 video) uses multimedia techniques to coach piano students. It observes their playing and, when errors are detected, makes corrective suggestions. It models a student's progress and modifies the lesson plan to fit the student's perceived proficiency.

A variation of intelligent tutoring, "active help" systems (see also Chapter 10) detect and flag user interaction inefficiencies. As users go about working, the system compares their interactions with inefficient or erroneous task models (buggy models), or with correct task models. When an inefficiency is detected, the system must decide when and how to interrupt the interaction. These systems can help users become proficient if their interruptions are not unduly annoying.

The promise of adaptive interfaces is tempered by a variety of pragmatic concerns, as noted by Browne (1990) (see also Edmonds, 1993):

- Adaptive systems may try to do too much with too little knowledge. System inferences are made by monitoring the user's interactions, which typically are information-poor and often contain errors.
- System and user are trying to model each other at the same time. As both are in a state of change, neither can reach a stable state (Gaines and Shaw, 1983), which Browne (1990) refers to as "hunting."
- Users can feel a lack of control when the system takes over. Adaptive interfaces that change automatically can confuse or annoy (e.g., Maskery, 1984). This also follows from Mackay's (1990a) observation that users often greet the introduction of a new and improved version by customizing it to resemble the old: we often prefer the familiar to small improvements in efficiency.
- Incorrect assumptions or modeling may cause adaptations that are worse than the default system.
- Collecting information to construct a user model may be construed as a violation of privacy, because the information could be misused by others.

Research suggests that benefits can come from adaptive interfaces, and that the problems can be mitigated. Yet adaptive interfaces are not now a substitute for careful design and customization.

Chignell and Hancock (1988) and Hancock and Chignell (1989) describe the theory and design of intelligent interfaces. Browne, Totterdell, and Norman (1990) summarize a four-year Adaptive Intelligent Dialogues project. Sullivan and Tyler (1991) collect a variety of contemporary readings on the subject. Recent papers on user modeling are found in the Kluwer journal on *User Modeling and User-Adapted Interaction*. A proceedings from a recent conference on intelligent user interfaces was published by ACM Press (Gray, Hefley, and Murray, 1993).

PROGRAMMING BY DEMONSTRATION

We now return to the idea of providing users with the ability to program the system. An alternative to direct programming is *programming by demonstration* (PBD), sometimes known as *programming by example*, where a person shows the system examples of a task and it automatically infers a program to carry out the task. The main advantage, articulated by Halbert (1984) and repeated by Smith, Cypher, and Spohrer (1994), is that a user is "programming a software system in its own user interface."

The simplest form of PBD is *macro recording*. A user performs an action sequence, and the system converts the sequence into a program that can be replayed. Simple instantiations of this idea have appeared in many systems. For example, the emacs text editor contains a macro generation facility that can be activated and invoked in a few keystrokes; a Lisp script can be optionally generated and modified by the user if desired (Stallman, 1987). Tempo (by Affinity Microsystems) and QuicKeys (by CESoftware) are popular macro recorders for capturing and replaying interactions on the Apple Macintosh. Without question, macro programs have proven useful for many repetitive tasks. However, they are not very powerful; a literal playback often fails when applied to a situation that differs even slightly from the original.

We really want programs that "generalize," that detect meaningful patterns and extend them in a wide variety of situations. Patterns could be internally coded through conventional programming concepts such as variables, branching, and loops. But automatic detection of meaningful patterns requires overlooking a user's detours and errors in the repetitive activity. It is a very challenging problem in machine learning.

One way to simplify this is to involve users. Generalization could be explicit, the user telling the system what objects are variables and where branching and looping would occur. For example, users of Halbert's early SmallStar system (1984, 1993, 1985 video) create macro recordings. Although some simple generalizations would be done by SmallStar, a user is expected to go through the program afterwards to change the way the program manages generalizations. Although the user is now "programming," Halbert's premise was that modifying code is easier than creating it afresh. Smallstar code is actually a semivisual scripting language, and many of its features could be set through options on property sheets.

Alternatively, programming by demonstration systems can infer generalizations by comparing examples: differences in data are treated as variables and program structures are examined for conditional branching and loops. Many algorithms and PBD inferencing methods are imported from the machine learning field, a branch of AI (Michalski, Carbonell, and Mitchell, 1983, 1986, 1990). Successes have been reported for some constrained domains, such as Maulsby and Witten's (1993) MetaMouse system for structured drawing. Yet, in a sense, users are still programming, in that they must carefully craft examples that capture the essence of what needs to be generalized! An open research question is how well inferencing systems scale to real-world domains, where users may create poor examples and noisy input can mislead an inference engine.

Recent PBD efforts have engaged in user-centered design to try to temper the uncertainty of inferencing systems. Maulsby, Greenberg, and Mander (1993) present a "Wizard of Oz" usability study (see Chapter 2) on Turvy, a simulated prototype of an instructable agent. They assume that teaching Turvy a program would be a cooperative task, with Turvy inferring as best it can, asking a user for assistance and explanation as needed to resolve ambiguities and correct misinterpretations. They note that users invent similar sets of commands to teach the system, and that users learn the system's "language" (i.e., terminology) by copying its speech. The study also finds that users may not identify critical features without prompting. Brennan and Ohaeri (1994) also use Wizard of Oz to study the effects of message style on people's mental models of computer agents.

The second reading in this chapter (Cypher, 1991a) describes Eager, a PBD system for the HyperCard environment that is designed to minimize intrusion (Cypher, 1991 video). Eager continuously looks for repetition (iterations) in a user's activity. When one is found, Eager displays an icon that indicates its willingness to run the program on the user's behalf. A wise user might want to check to see if the program had figured things out correctly before trusting it to take over, and Eager allows this through a method called "anticipation." It shows the user what it would do next (e.g., by highlighting the object that it expects the user to select); the person can quickly assess the correctness of Eager's predictions. This is a two-way process: Each correct anticipation confirms to Eager that its program is correct; each mistake helps Eager revise its program.

Cypher's reading is a good example of the direction that today's PBD systems are following, of the scale of programs that are being inferred, and an indication of how a PBD system works. It is also one of the few that conducts a usability study; for example, Cypher finds that subjects are uncomfortable giving total control to Eager.

Other user-centered PBD systems operate in a variety of domains. Atari (1983 video) demonstrates an early video-games-by-example system. Peridot (Myers 1988, 1988 video) lets non-programmers create GUIs. MetaMouse (Maulsby and Witten 1993; Maulsby, 1990 video), Triggers (Potter, 1993, 1993 video), and Chimera (Kurlander, 1993, 1993 video; Kurlander and Feiner, 1991 video) help users automate repetitive tasks when editing structured drawings. Tourmaline (Myers, 1991; Werth, 1993 video) and Tels (Witten and Mo, 1993) help people automate editing and formatting in word processors. Modugno and Myers (1993 video) demonstrates an easily programmable direct manipulation interface to a file system.

These and other systems are concisely summarized in Cypher et al. (1993), an excellent collection that is a source book for both novices and experts. It covers PBD history, classic papers, the diversity of approaches, interface innovations, underlying algorithms, and application domains. Myers (1992) is a survey of PBD. Other examples of recent PBD systems are included in the July 1994 *Communications of the ACM* Special Issue on Intelligent Agents. Of particular interest in that issue is KidSim, which tries to give children the power to construct and modify simulations via graphical rewrite rules and PBD (Smith, Cypher, and Spohrer, 1994).

AGENTS

When given a goal, [an intelligent agent] could carry out the details of the appropriate computer operations and could ask for and receive advice, offered in human terms, when it was stuck. (Alan Kay, 1984, p. 192).

Intelligent interface agents have been touted as a significant new direction in human-computer interface design. Videos from Apple (1990 video; Dubberly and Mitsch, 1992a, 1992b videos), Hewlett-Packard (1992, 1993 videos) and Japan's Friend21 project (Ueda, 1992 video) show futuristic interfaces in which agents play a dominant role in the dialog. Agents are shown as computerized personae such as office clerks, data base guides, and writing advisors—portrayals that were done through the wizardry of filmmaking, as the software does not exist. Fictional portrayals of self-aware computers, such as HAL in the movie 2001, bring us the extreme of what an agent could be—and what it could become! The images of agents are inspiring and sometimes frightening, but it is unlikely that the next decade will bring us software with even a trace of the capabilities envisioned. Still, modest goals in agent technology are being achieved within limited domains.

What exactly do we mean by an "intelligent interface agent"? Our reading by Maes (1994) describes an agent as "a *personal assistant* who is *collaborating with the user*" as the interaction proceeds. Unlike customizable or adaptive interfaces, where a user or a system changes the behavior of the interface directly, Maes sees the agent as an entity that sits outside, looking over the shoulder of a user, offering suggestions, being willing to handle some mundane tasks. The user remains in control and decides what advice to take and when to allow the agent to take over. Another important feature is that the agent is expected to learn about the user, and thus provide better assistance. Maes suggests that agents can learn by observing and imitating a user, by listening to user feedback, and through explicit training.

There are other eloquent descriptions of agents. Laurel (1990) defines them as "metaphors with character" that have a predisposition to behave in certain way, and whose anthropomorphism promotes a certain style of communication. Instead of the "all knowing" agent, Minsky believes that interfaces will contain many small agents specialized to handle particular tasks (Minsky and Riecken, 1994; Minsky, 1985). He coins the term *agency* to "suggest the image of an office or an organization that is composed of several interacting subagents," and he expects people to interact with an organization of agents. Bird (1993) takes a more collaborative view of agents, where a set of agents may work together on a task. As Edmonds et al. (1994) point out, this implies that agents have some shared understanding of the task.

Examples of Real Agents

Although reality is still far from the promotional visions, prototypes of intelligent agents have been implemented by researchers. Today's agents are "intelligent" in only the narrowest sense of the word. They understand only specialized or highly structured task domains. They lack flexibility in conversing with users. This is in keeping with Kay's (1984) suggestion that agents should be illusions that mirror the user's intelligence while restricting the user's agenda. Indeed, systems mentioned earlier, such as Eager and Metamouse, are state-of-the-art examples of highly specialized software agents in the domain of programming-by-demonstration systems. Dumb agents are also possible. On Wall Street, for example, computers programmed to buy or sell automatically when a stock reaches a certain price are clearly acting as agents, albeit in a very narrow task domain.

The Information Lens (Malone et al., 1989; Malone, 1987 video) demonstrates a simple example of agent technology. The system helps people manage, find, filter, sort, and prioritize electronic mail. Users compose e-mail as *semistructured messages*, hierarchical user-defined templates that specify the message type (such as Meeting Announcement) and that add extra fields to the e-mail header (such as Meeting Topic and Meeting Date). Users then import, create, or modify *active rules* that process e-mail. For example, this rule places upcoming meetings into a folder containing today's activities:

IF Message type: . . . . . .Meeting Announcement
AND Meeting Date: . . . .Today
THEN *Move to*: . . . . . . .Today's Activities

Because rules are actively monitoring and manipulating e-mail, they are semiautonomous agents. A more general system, Object Lens (Lai, Malone, and Yu, 1988), later called Oval (Malone and Lai, 1992), has a wider range of object types and capabilities.

Excellent examples of the "agent as metaphor" are the characters found in Apple's Guides system (Oren et al., 1990; Oren, Don, and Laurel, 1991 video). Given as a domain a hypertext historical document (see also Chapter 13), how do you advise readers what to read and how do you offer them different perspectives of the material? The Guides metaphor consists of several text-based and video-based characters. For example, a modern travel guide introduces the story and the other characters. Historical characters present their own point of view by walking the reader through particular paths in the document, by commenting on the material through first-person stories, and by suggesting where the reader should go next. While the agents in Guides are not intelligent (they use canned scripts), each guide certainly captures the feeling of the agent as person. The collection of guides also brings us closer to Minsky's idea of the agency.

The reading by Maes (1994) describes agents that reduce work and information overload. Maxims is an electronic mail agent that, unlike Information Lens, looks over the shoulder of a user to learn how mail is prioritized, sorted, deleted, and archived. When new situations arise, Maxims predicts what it should do with the mail, as well as its confidence in its prediction. It compares its confidence to a "do it" or "tell me" threshold that, as the name implies, causes the agent either to do the action autonomously or to ask the user about it. Maxims shows its state, confidence level, and its competence to a user through a set of emotive icons. The learning system used by Maxims is not specific to e-mail, and Maes describes how it was applied to meeting scheduling. Maes also presents a news agent for filtering news and recommending articles to read, and an entertainment agent that helps people select movies and books.

While the agents described above are far from the fictional agents hyped in the promotional press, they do show that relatively simple automations can help people in specific domains.

Towards Smarter Agents

How far are we from the goal of truly intelligent agents? The reading by Fischer and Reeves (1992) is an excerpt from a field study of successful human agents in a real-world complex environment that suggests what smart software agents will need to know. Highly experienced salespeople in a large hardware store were recorded as they responded to customer queries. Fischer and Reeves step through several of these dialogues and note a variety of difficulties inherent in complex environments. From these, they create a conceptual framework that defines how computer agents should behave. Fischer and Reeves (p. 320; see also Hutchins, 1994) see the interaction between salesperson and customer as an example of *situated cognition*, where

> *much of the problem solving is fundamentally related to the larger context in which the problem gets perceived, framed, and eventually resolved . . .*

This means that smart software agents must be very knowledgeable about world context and the nuances of situations. This is a very hard problem in AI! Agents cannot expect users to have well-defined plans for solving problems. Rather, they must work closely with the person and, within the context of the task, help them articulate the problem and possible solutions.

Will people accept agents? Researchers have always encountered problems when introducing "intelligence" or "autonomy" into interfaces. The intelligence has not been intelligent enough, and autonomy is not something we expect of our tools. The problems are numerous. As noted before, interfaces that spontaneously adapt can confuse or disrupt users. Agents that interrupt users can be annoying if they do so too frequently or at the wrong times. Another problem is that intelligence embedded in one aspect of an interface can lead users to expect intelligence throughout. This level of expectation can lead to careless assumptions, serious mistakes, and user dissatisfaction.

Gerhard Fischer has worked steadily on issues including how and when to present information to users, and how to join intelligent assistance with domain knowledge in a system (e.g., Fischer and Girgensohn, 1990; Morch, 1991 video; Fischer et al., 1993; Eisenberg and Fischer, 1994; Fischer et al., 1994). Much of this work has focused on user-invoked design critics that present advice and permit examination of the underlying reasoning.

Norman (1994) lists factors that designers should consider when creating agents:

- *Ensure that people feel in control of their computational systems;* that is, people must be comfortable, understanding what is occurring and having confidence in the result.
- *Pay attention to the nature of human-agent interaction*—how people instruct agents, how feedback is provided, and how agents and their activities are presented.
- *Employ built-in safeguards* to eliminate or minimize runaway computation and the effects of agent errors.
- *Provide a user with accurate expectations* (and eliminate false hopes), which is especially difficult when a system is presented as a human character.
- *Cater to privacy concerns* that arise when agents have access and the ability to manipulate personal records and correspondence.
- *Hide complexity* while simultaneously revealing underlying operations.

Aside from Norman's cautionary advice, designers have little to guide them on these issues. In the meantime, the best agents are probably simple ones that handle very specific tasks, with actions understandable by their users.

The literature on agents is scattered in published collections of papers on human computer interaction and artificial intelligence. Many of the papers from the July 1994 *Communications of the ACM*, which focused on intelligent agents, were discussed in this introduction. Several books relate to agents. Minsky (1985) details his ideas on agency in *The Society of Mind*. Laurel (1991) pursues the notion of "computers as theater," promoting agents as metaphors. Pollock (1989) explores the enterprise of actually "building a person" by mimicking human rationality. Videos by Schmandt (1987 video) and Davis (1989 video) illustrate simple agents working within natural language interfaces. More recent videos (Breiteneder and Gibbs, 1994 video; Takeuchi and Nagao, 1994 video) illustrate the increasing yet possibly dangerous interest (recall Norman's fourth suggestion about providing users with accurate expectations) in anthropomorphizing interfaces with facial displays.

The algorithms and methods underlying intelligent systems are available in the rich literature of artificial intelligence. For example, Engelmore and Morgan (1988) and Jagannathan, Dodhiawala, and Baum (1989) are edited collection of papers on blackboard systems. Michalski, Carbonell, and Mitchell (1983, 1986, 1990) collect influential papers in machine learning. The *Proceedings of AAAI* contain timely papers on many AI topics. Woods, Johannesen, and Potter (1991) provide a bibliography on the integration of intelligent computers and human practitioners into effective cooperative systems.

REFERENCES

Note: A ⊛ before a reference indicates a reading.

Benyon, D. (1984). Monitor: A Self-Adaptive User Interface. *Proc. Interact '84*, North-Holland, 335–341.

Benyon, D., and Murray, D. (1993). Adaptive Systems: From Intelligent Tutoring to Autonomous Agents. *Knowledge-Based Systems* 6(4), 197–219.

Bird, S. (1993). Towards a Taxonomy of Multi-Agent Systems. *International Journal of Man Machine Studies* 36, 689–704.

Bødker, S., Grønbæk, K., and Kyng, M. (1992). Cooperative Design: Techniques and Experiences from the Scandinavian Scene. In Schuler, D., and Namioka, A. (Eds.) (1993), *Participatory Design: Principles and Practices*, Lawrence Erlbaum Associates. Reprinted in Chapter 3.

Boehm, B.W. (1988). A Spiral Model of Software Development and Enhancement. *IEEE Computer* 21(2), 61–72. Reprinted in Chapter 4.

Brennan, S., and Ohaeri, J. (1994). Effects of Message Style on Users' Attributions toward Agents. *Proc. CHI '94 Conference Companion*, ACM, 281–282.

Browne, D. (1990). Chapter 7: Conclusions. In Browne, Totterdell, and Norman (1990).

Browne, D., Totterdell, P., and Norman, M. (1990). *Adaptive User Interfaces*. Academic Press.

Chignell, M., and Hancock, P. (1988). Intelligent Interface Design. In Helander, M. (Ed.) (1988), *Handbook of Human-Computer Interaction*, North-Holland, 969–995.

⊛ Cypher, A. (1991a). Eager: Programming Repetitive Tasks by Example. *Proc. CHI '91*, ACM, 33–39.

Cypher, A. (1991b). Customizing End-User Applications. *Proc. East-West HCI Conference*, ICSTI, 152–157.

Cypher, A. (1993). Introduction. In Cypher et al. (1993).

Cypher, A., Halbert, D., Kurlander, D., Lieberman, H., Maulsby, D., Myers, B., and Turransky, A. (Eds.) (1993). *Watch What I Do: Programming by Demonstration*. The MIT Press.

Edmonds, E. (1981). Adaptive Man-Computer Dialogues. In Coombs, M., and Alty, J. (Eds.) (1981), *Computing Skills and the User Interface*, Academic Press.

Edmonds, E. (1993). The Future of Intelligent Interfaces: Not Just "How?" But "What?" and "Why?" In Gray, Hefley, and Murray (1993), 13–17.

Edmonds, E., Candy, L., Jones, R., and Soufi, B. (1994). Support for Collaborative Design. *Communications of the ACM* 35(7), 41–47.

Eisenberg and Fischer (1994). Programmable Design Environments: Ingetrating End-User Programming with Domain-Oriented Assistance. *Proc. CHI '94*, ACM, 431–437.

Engelmore, R., and Morgan, T. (Eds.) (1988). *Blackboard Systems.* Addison-Wesley.

Fischer, G., and Girgensohn, A. (1990). End-User Modifiability in Design Environments. *Proc. CHI '90*, ACM, 183–191.

Fischer, G., McCall, R., Ostwald, J., Reeves, B., and Shipman, F. (1994). Seeding, Evolutionary Growth and Reseeding: Supporting the Incremental Development of Design Environments. *Proc. CHI '94*, ACM, 292–298.

Fischer, G., Nakakoji, K., Ostwald, J., Stahl, G., and Sumner, T. (1993). Embedding Computer-Based Critics in the Contexts of Design. *Proc. INTERCHI '93, ACM*, 157–164.

● Fischer, G., and Reeves, B. (1992). Beyond Intelligent Interfaces: Exploring, Analyzing, and Creating Success Models of Cooperative Problem Solving. *Journal of Applied Intelligence* 1, 311–323. (Excerpt included 311, 316–323.)

Friedman, A. (1989). *Computer Systems Development: History, Organization, and Implementation.* John Wiley & Sons.

Gaines, B., and Shaw, M. (1983). Dialog Engineering. In Sime, M., and Coombs, M. (Eds.) (1983), *Designing for Human-Computer Communication*, 23–53, Academic Press.

Gray, W., Hefley, W., and Murray, D. (Eds.) (1993). *Proc. International Workshop on Intelligent User Interfaces.* ACM.

Greenberg, S. (1993). *The Computer User As Toolsmith: The Use, Reuse, and Organization of Computer-Based Tools.* Cambridge University Press.

Greenberg, S., Darragh, J., Maulsby, D., and Witten, I. (1994). Predictive Interfaces: What Will They Think of Next? In Edwards, A. (Ed.), *Extra-Ordinary Human Computer Interaction: Interfaces for Users with Disabilities*, Cambridge University Press, 93–128.

Greenberg, S., and Witten, I. (1985). Adaptive Personalized Interfaces—A Question of Viability. *Behaviour and Information Technology* 4(1), 31–45.

Greenberg, S., and Witten, I. (1993a). Supporting Command Reuse: Empirical Foundations and Principles. *International Journal of Man-Machine Studies* 39(3), 353–390.

Greenberg, S., and Witten, I. (1993b). Supporting Command Reuse: Mechanisms For Reuse. *International Journal of Man-Machine Studies* 39(3), 391–425.

Grudin, J., and Barnard, P. (1985). When Does an Abbreviation Become a Word? and Related Questions. *Proc. CHI '85*, ACM, 121–125.

Gundry, A. (1988). Humans, Computers, and Contracts. In Jones, D., and Winder, R. (Eds.), *People and Computers IV*, Cambridge University Press.

Halbert, D. (1984). Programming by Example. Ph.D. Dissertation, Department of Electrical Engineering and Computer Science, University of California at Berkeley.

Halbert, D. (1993). SmallStar: Programming by Demonstration in the Desktop Metaphor. In Cypher et al. (1993), 103–124.

Hancock, P., and Chignell, M. (Eds.) (1989). *Intelligent Interfaces; Theory, Research and Design.* North-Holland.

Hansen, W. (1971). User Engineering Principles for Interactive Systems. *AFIPS Conference Proceedings* 39, AFIPS Press, 523–532.

● Henderson, A., and Kyng, M. (1991). There's No Place Like Home: Continuing Design in Use. In Greenbaum, J., and Kyng, M. (Eds.) (1991), *Design at Work*, Lawrence Erlbaum Associates, 219–240.

Holtzblatt, K., and Jones, S. (1993). Conducting and Analyzing a Contextual Interview. In Schuler, D., and Namioka, A. (Eds.), *Participatory Design: Principles and Practices*, Lawrence Erlbaum, 192–210. Excerpted in Chapter 3.

Hutchins, E. (1994). *Cognition in the Wild.* MIT Press.

Innocent, P. (1982). Towards Self-Adaptive Interface Systems. *International Journal of Man-Machine Studies* 16(3), 287–299.

Jagannathan, V., Dodhiawala, R., and Baum, L. S. (Eds.) (1989). *Blackboard Architectures and Applications.* Academic Press.

Kay, A. (1984). Computer Software. *Scientific American* 251(3), 191–207.

Kurlander, D. (1993). Graphical Editing by Example. Ph.D. Thesis, Department of Computer Science, Columbia University.

Lai, K.-Y., Malone, T., and Yu, K.-C. (1988). Object Lens: A "Spreadsheet" for Cooperative Work. *ACM Transactions on Office Information Systems* 6(4), 332–353.

Laurel, B. (1990). Interface Agents. In Laurel, B. (Ed.) (1990), *The Art of Human-Computer Interface Design*, Addison-Wesley, 355–365.

Laurel, B. (1991). *Computers as Theatre.* Addison-Wesley.

Mackay, W. (1990a). Patterns of Sharing Customizable Software. *Proc. CSCW '90*, ACM, 209–221.

Mackay, W. (1990b). Users and Customizable Software: A Co-Adaptive Phenomenon. Ph.D. Dissertation, Sloan School of Management, MIT.

Mackay, W. (1991). Triggers and Barriers to Customizing Software. *Proc. CHI '91*, ACM, 153–160.

MacLean, A., Carter, K., Lovstrand, L., and Moran, T. (1990). User-Tailorable Systems: Pressing the Issues with Buttons. *Proc. CHI '90*, ACM, 175–182.

● Maes, P. (1994). Agents That Reduce Work and Information Overload. *Communications of the ACM* 35(7), 31–41.

Malone, T., Grant, K., Lai, K.-Y., Rao, R., and Rosenblitt, D. (1989). The Information Lens: An Intelligent System for Information Sharing and Coordination. In Olson, M. (Ed.) (1989), *Technological Support for Work Group Collaboration*, Lawrence Erlbaum Associates.

Malone, T., and Lai, K.-Y. (1992). Experiments With Oval: A Radically Tailorable Tool for Cooperative Work. *Proc. CSCW '92*, ACM, 289–297.

Maskery, H. (1984). Adaptive Interfaces for Naive Users—An Experimental Study. *Proc. Interact '84*, North-Holland, 343–349.

Maulsby, D., Greenberg, S., and Mander, R. (1993). Prototyping an Intelligent Agent through Wizard of Oz. *Proc. INTERCHI '93*, ACM, 277–284.

Maulsby, D., and Witten, I. (1993). Metamouse: An Instructable Agent for Programming by Demonstration. In Cypher et al. (1993), 155–182.

Michalski, R., Carbonell, J., and Mitchell, T. (Eds.) (1983, 1986, 1990). *Machine Learning: An Artificial Intelligence Approach.* Vols 1–3. Morgan Kaufmann.

Minsky, M. (1985). *The Society of Mind.* Simon & Schuster.

Minsky, M., and Riecken, D. (1994). A Conversation with Marvin Minsky about Agents. *Communications of the ACM* 37(7), 22–29.

Myers, B. (1988). *Creating User Interfaces by Demonstration.* Academic Press.

Myers, B. (1991). Text Formatting by Demonstration. *Proc. CHI '91,* ACM, 251–256.

Myers, B. (1992). Demonstrational Interfaces: A Step Beyond Direct Manipulation. *IEEE Computer* 25(8), 61–73. Revision published in Cypher et al. (1993), 485–512.

Nardi, B. (1994). *A Small Matter of Programming: Perspectives on End-User Computing.* MIT Press.

Nardi, B., and Miller, J. (1990). The Spreadsheet Interface: A Basis for End-User Programming. *Proc. INTERACT '90,* North-Holland, 977–983.

Nardi, B., and Miller, J. (1991). Twinkling Lights and Nested Loops: Distributed Problem Solving and Spreadsheet Development. *International Journal of Man-Machine Studies* 34(2), 161–184. Reprinted in Greenberg, S. (Ed.) (1991), *Computer-Supported Cooperative Work and Groupware,* Academic Press.

Norman, D. (1994). How People Might Interact with Agents. *Communications of the ACM* 37(7), 69–71.

Oren, T., Salomon, G., Kreitman, K., and Don, A. (1990). Guides: Characterizing the Interface. In Laurel, B. (Ed.) (1990), *The Art of Human-Computer Interface Design,* Addison-Wesley, 367–381.

Pollock, J. L. (1989). *How to Build a Person: A Prolegomenon.* MIT.

Potter, R. (1993). Triggers: Guiding Automation with Pixels to Achieve Data Access. In Cypher et al. (1993), 361–382

Smith, D. C., Cypher, A., and Spohrer, J. (1994). KIDSIM: Programming Agents without a Programming Language. *Communications of the ACM* 37(7), 54–67.

Stallman, R. (1987). *GNU Emacs Manual.* Free Software Foundation.

Sullivan, J., and Tyler, S. (Eds.) (1991). *Intelligent User Interfaces.* ACM Press.

Trevellyan, R., and Browne, D. P. (1987). A Self-Regulating Adaptive System. *Proc. CHI+GI '87,* ACM, 103–107.

Wilde, N., and Lewis, C. (1990). Spreadsheet-based Interactive Graphics: From Prototype to Tool. *Proc. CHI '90,* ACM, 153–159.

Witten, I., Cleary, J., and Greenberg, S. (1984). On Frequency-Based Menu-Splitting Algorithms. *International Journal of Man-Machine Studies* 21(2), 135–148.

Witten, I., and Mo, D. (1993). Tels: Learning Text Editing Tasks from Examples. In Cypher et al. (1993), 183–203.

Woods, D. (1993). The Price of Flexibility. In Gray, Hefley, and Murray (1993), 19–25.

Woods, D., Johannesen, L., and Potter, S. (1991). Human Interaction with Intelligent Systems: An Overview and Bibliography. *SIGART Bulletin* 2(5), 39–50.

VIDEOS

Anderson, J., Corbett, A., Boyle, F., and Lewis, M. (1988). Intelligent Tutoring Systems: The ACT Project. *ACM SIGGRAPH Video Review (SGVR)* 59.

Apple Computer (1990). Apple 2020. Videotape of the Apple Worldwide Developer's Conference, May 9.

Atari Computer (1983). Video Games by Example. *ACM SGVR* 12.

Breiteneder, C., and Gibbs, S. (1994). Interactive Video Actors. *ACM SGVR* 97.

Cypher, A. (1991). Eager: Programming Repetitive Tasks by Example. *ACM SGVR* 64.

Davis, J. (1989). Direction Assistance. *ACM SGVR* 48.

Dubberly, H., and Mitsch, D. (1992a). Project 2000. *ACM SGVR* 78.

Dubberly, H., and Mitsch, D. (1992b). Knowledge Navigator. *ACM SGVR* 79.

Halbert, D. (1985). Programming by Example. *ACM SGVR* 18.

Hewlett Packard (1992). 1992. *ACM SGVR* 78.

Hewlett Packard (1993). Imagine. *ACM SGVR* 89.

Kurlander, D. (1993). Graphical Editing by Example. *ACM SGVR* 89.

Kurlander, D., and Feiner, S. (1991). Editable Graphical Histories. *ACM SGVR* 63.

Malone, T. (1987). The Information Lens. *ACM SGVR* 34.

Maulsby, D. (1990). Metamouse: End-User Programming by Demonstration. *ACM SGVR* 56.

Modugno, F., and Myers, B. (1993). PURSUIT: Graphically Representing Programs in a Visual Demonstrational Shell. *ACM SGVR* 97.

Morch, A. (1991). Janus: Basic Concepts and Sample Run. *ACM SGVR* 64.

Myers, B. (1988). Creating User Interfaces by Demonstration: The Peridot User Interface Management System. *ACM SGVR* 59.

Oren, T., Don, A., and Laurel, B. (1991). Guides 3.0. *ACM SGVR* 63.

Potter, R. (1993). Guiding Automation with Pixels: A Technique for Programming in the User Interface. *ACM SGVR* 89.

Sanchez, M., Joseph, A., Dannenberg, R., Capell, P., Saul, R., and Joseph, R. (1990). The Piano Tutor. *ACM SGVR* 55.

Schmandt, C. (1987). Conversational Desktop. *ACM SGVR* 27.

Takeuchi, A., and Nagao, K. (1994). Speech Dialogue with Facial Displays. *ACM SGVR* 97.

Ueda, H. (1992, tape made in 1989). Friend21. *ACM SGVR* 78.

Werth, A. (1993). Tourmaline: Macrostyles by Example. *ACM SGVR* 89.

There's No Place Like Home: Continuing Design in Use

Austin Henderson and Morten Kyng

> ... *effective design involves a co-evolution of artifacts with practice. Where artifacts can be designed by their users, this development goes on over the course of their use.*
>
> Suchman and Trigg, Chapter 4, p. 72

One of our primary goals in this book is to contribute to the creation of systems that better fit work situations, as well as the aims and intentions of the people using the systems. This implies a view of design as a process that is tightly coupled to use and that continues during the use of a system.

The preceding chapters in this part of the book have focused on the first of these aspects, showing how to incorporate use experience in the initial design process. This chapter will show what may be involved in continuing design in use, and how we, in the initial design process, may create systems are tailorable.

Case I: Tailoring?—Never Thought About It!

At Aarhus University, personnel in the payroll office were accustomed to helping people who had difficulty understanding their payslips. Because each person in the office handled only a few types of contracts, they understood the contracts thoroughly and could explain any peculiarities. However, due to the introduction of a new computer system, mandated for all state-owned Danish enterprises, the work was reorganized. As a result, each person at the payroll office handled employees according to their date of birth. This may have been the standard way of doing things at many public payroll offices, and thus an acceptable choice for the computer system, but at Aarhus University it resulted in a dramatic decline in the service provided to the employees; each person at the payroll office now handled so many different kinds of contracts that they no longer knew the details.

Although the change necessary to remedy the situation—to return to the "contract way" of working—seems conceptually simple in terms of the work being done, it was in fact infeasible. First of all, there was no support for "local variations" in the initial design of the system. Secondly, the process of maintaining the system didn't incorporate any notion of modification beyond the fixing of bugs.

Case II: Handling Modifications

As our second case, consider the Danish hospital that recently installed a new computer-based heating and ventilation control system built from a dozen standard components. The boilerman in charge of the daily operation of the system handled it quite easily. However, the personnel on duty outside normal working hours were not boilermen, and they had difficulty understanding the messages from the system and reacting appropriately. The problem was solved by having some of the "personnel on duty," together with the boilerman, redesign all messages from the system, rephrasing them in language they all understand. This second set of messages was then added to the system as the new default. As the personnel actually encounter the messages in their use of the system, those that still create problems are noted and usually modified.

In this case the system in question was prepared to accept messages in different languages, and this, in combination with a design process that deals with a number of modifications to the standard components, made the change quite feasible.

Case III: Preparing the System for Change by Its Users

As our last case we consider workers at three cooperating research facilities who are using the Xerox Common Lisp environment (XCL) for electronic paperwork, e. g. handling documents and electronic mail (cf. Sheil, 1983, for information on Lisp environments). These workers include members of the research staff, secretaries, and administrators, only some of whom can program in LISP. Although XCL is a very flexible environment for those who can program in LISP, it can be quite unfriendly to those who can't.

The researchers created Buttons to help (MacLean, Carter, Lövstrand, & Moran, 1990). A button is a screen object (actually a small window) that can be easily moved around, copied, and sent to others in documents and electronic mail. Each button contains an "action," an arbitrary piece of LISP code that is executed when the button is "pushed" by clicking on it with the mouse. Buttons are used to add to the behavior of the XCL environment.

Consider, for example, what happened when users noticed that considerable effort was being expended on remembering and typing addresses for people being sent electronic mail. A local supporter created a button, labelled with a (usually short version of) person's name, that simply typed in that person's address. Soon these "address buttons" were being copied and shared with others. Initially, users either got help in modifying buttons to capture the addresses of new people or learned how to do it themselves. The buttons were subsequently modified to make changing labels and addresses much easier. XCL was tailored by means of Buttons to meet the needs of electronic mail in ways not anticipated by its designers.

Ideal tailorable systems are those in which there are means for the users, or supporters near the users, to make them fit different work situations. The system we call Buttons is a very general tailoring mechanism which is, with varying degrees of ease, usable by workers to augment XCL behavior.

Professional system designers can match systems to users, because they have the skills to modify them. Creating systems where nonprofessional designers can do the same thing is not nearly as easy. So it is not surprising that program-literate researchers created the first address buttons. However, it should be noted that the nonprogrammers have a big advantage, in that they, as users, know the work the system is supporting, and are therefore in a much better position to determine when the system matches the work.

Why Do We Need to Continue Design in Use?

There are three main reasons why system behavior may need to change after its initial design is implemented. They are:

- As designers of technology we are usually confronted with the task of designing systems that will be used for long periods of time. And no matter how well they may have fitted the situation initially, circumstances of *the situation of use changes:* the needs change, the uses change, the users change, the organization changes. Therefore the computer systems may well have to change to match the changed circumstances. In the case of Buttons, an increase in the complexity and number of mail addresses changed the users' needs.
- The *complexity* of the world makes it difficult to anticipate all the issues that will eventually be of importance in the final situation. There are bound to be things we overlook, misunderstand, etc. The creator of the XCL electronic mail system, for example, did not provide a means for aliasing addresses (as is provided in other mail software); the address buttons were created to meet the need.
- When we are creating a product which will be purchased by many people, the need to design for many *different situations* of use is particularly clear, and in fact some of the techniques for allowing users to adjust systems in use have been motivated by market considerations; for example, producers of "plastic" software who want to satisfy as many users as possible with a single product.

Why Is It Difficult to Continue Design in Use?

Most of this book is about designing systems that fit the work of the users, and the difficulties involved in the quest of concepts and understanding that further such a task. When we want to support continued design in use, we face the same difficulties, magnified by the additional requirements that:

- the system include tools for doing this continued design;
- the continuing design be feasible for nonprofessional designers (the users);
- the "sub-system" for tailoring matches the users' work, just as required of the rest of the system.

But as with traditional systems, tailoring is more often based on concepts from the computer field than from the application domain.

First of all, the *need* for providing possibilities for tailoring has to be recognized in the development of a system. Otherwise such possibilities will be missing, or tailorable only in the implementation environment. In the development of "plastic" software this need to provide for tailoring is usually recognized. However, it seldom goes beyond the setting of software-switches (parameters), as discussed later. In custom development there is a tendency to try to provide "the right system," without regard for possible future changes. In this respect custom development may learn from plastic software design.

Recognizing the need, however, is only the beginning. Even simple capabilities such as being able to choose a default font for a word processor presuppose that there exist possibilities to choose from. To design such a space of possibilities, which is meaningful in terms of the work of the users, is no easy task; to make it possible for the users to explore this space is even more difficult.

One major problem is the lack of suitable concepts and "parts" at the levels between a full-fledged application and the programming language. With the older technologies there is usually a gradual movement from the understandable to the incomprehensible. Thus to almost any car driver, "motors" make perfect sense, most understand "spark plugs," and quite a few will even attempt to adjust the distance the spark has to travel. When trying to dig into computer applications, users are almost immediately confronted with concepts and parts that do not make sense in terms of their work. This chapter attempts to begin remedying this situation, trying to set the stage for moving from the computer bound concepts to the work of the users. But there is a long way to go, and the chapter is in some places more technical than the rest of the book.

The rest of the chapter is organized as follows: first we discuss the relationship between use and designing in use and take a brief look at the people doing the tailoring. Then in the main section of the chapter we highlight the practice of designing in use. We look first at how users change the behavior of systems, and then at how to support these activities. Following this is a section on the "down side" of tailoring, on the difficulties that may arise. The chapter concludes with a section summarizing how to support tailoring in the initial design of systems.

Tailoring and Use

Tailoring a system, continuing designing in use, is an activity different from initial design. The activity is related to specific use situations and the result is not a new system, but a modified system; that is, a system with a history which relates it to the earlier version and problems with its use.

While initial design and use thus may be treated as clearly different activities, the distinction between use and tailoring—designing in use—is somewhat blurred. For a particular system a distinction may be made, but in general it is no easy matter, because computer systems, their use and tailoring, differ as much as cars, clocks, and computers differ.

The intuition behind our presentation is coupled to the notion of change, and implicitly coupled to the related concept of stability. The distinction between tailoring and use thus rests on the understood and intended variability of artifacts and their patterns of use. Certain aspects of these artifacts we, as users, regard as stable; others we regard as more or less constantly changing. This relative stability of certain aspects is exactly what allows us to consider tailoring as an activity in itself: we tailor when we change stable aspects of an artifact.

But this stability/change dichotomy is not that crisp, as illustrated by the following examples. I may change the font of a piece of text in a text editor. Is it tailoring? Or how about modifying a spreadsheet? Or moving windows around on the screen to make working on a particular task easier?

Are these tailoring? Or are they "just" use? The text editor is designed for the creation of text in different fonts, so to take advantage of that capability seems like using the text editor, not tailoring it. Similarly, moving windows around on the screen feels more like using the window system for what it is intended than it feels like tailoring it.

We offer two more distinctions to improve understanding of the concepts of tailoring and use. The first of these rests on the view of technology as a tool for addressing certain subject matter, often conceived of as manipulating certain objects. A text editor's subject matter is text (or documents); it manipulates text. A window systems manipulates windows. The distinction then is: if the modifications that are being made are to the subject matter of the tool then we think of it as use; if the modifications are to the tool itself, then it is tailoring. So changing a font on a word in your document is use, while changing the default font—modifying the tool—is tailoring. It should be noted once again that this does not necessarily create a crisp distinction: What is it when you create a new style in your document? That act (at least in Microsoft Word) both creates a style and changes the selected paragraph; so in this distinction, creating a new style can be both use and tailoring. Note also that one person's tool is another person's subject matter, and hence, what is tailoring for one person can be use for another. For the Pascal programmer, changing the compiler is certainly tailoring, but for the team developing or maintaining the compiler, it is use.

The last distinction concerns the duration of the effect of the change. If the modification is so that an effect can be achieved later, then it is tailoring. If the modification is made so that the effect is immediate only, without any impact later, it is use. Thus, if I need a window which is buried and I move windows around on the screen so that I can access it, that is use; if I rearrange windows so that when I next want a project folder it will be easy to find, that is tailoring.

These three distinctions align fairly well in the sense that they seem to get the same answers. Usually, changing the tools is for later effect, and usually, the tools are more stable than the "material" they are used to transform. However, not all these distinctions are meaningful in all cases. The windows of the second example are the subject matter of the window system in both usages; one isn't affecting the window system (the tool) by rearranging windows. (Note that one can affect some window systems: change the layout algorithm from overlapping to tiled, or set it so that it grays out windows which have not been touched for a while.) For this reason, all three distinctions are offered as a set, complementing one another, and jointly informing the concept.

Who Are the Tailors?

After having discussed the activity of tailoring, let us briefly consider the people doing it. Who are they? The simple answer to this question is: those who design in use. In a paper by Trigg, Moran, and Halasz (1987), the discussion is restricted to activities carried out by users. However, the hospital example discussed previously illustrates what we consider to be successful tailoring of a system, but not one done by the users directly. It was done by people from the company that delivered the system in cooperation with one of the users, because the users did not have the programming skills to make such changes on their own.

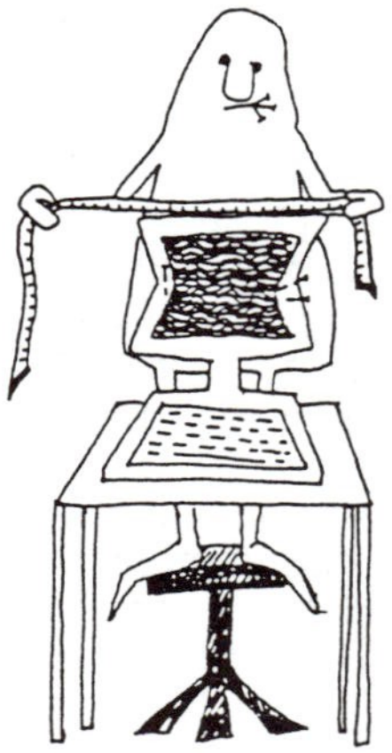

From our perspective the decisive point is not whether the users actually do it all themselves. We don't assign tailoring to one specific group. The central view is that the change is being made in response to local needs. Obviously a number of changes will be tailored by the users themselves, or not tailored at all, simply because they involve such small details that it makes no sense to involve people outside the use situation. A few examples of this kind were already illustrated. But most cases of more comprehensive tailoring involve some local expert or supporters or application specialists, because the users don't have the competence.

The Practice of Designing in Use

In this section we discuss the various activities involved in modifying computer systems. The viewpoint is that of a user turned designer who is trying to change the way in which technology behaves. It may require that a user brings in others with special skills to help achieve those changes.

We address the practice of designing in use in two parts. First, we present three kinds of activity that change the behavior of the technology. These activities are the normal focus of discussions of modifying technology. Second, we discuss the social and cognitive needs of people engaged in making such changes. These activities are often overlooked, because they do not directly change the technology.

Changing Behavior

Choosing between Alternative Anticipated Behaviors

Many systems allow the users to choose between alternative behaviors that the developers have anticipated will be needed in particular situations of use. The standard mechanism for doing this is through software switches or parameters. An electronic mail system may have multiple delivery services that it can use to deliver mail; a switch is provided to allow the user to choose the one that is appropriate for the local site. Word processors must use some font to display text when the user does not designate one; a parameter is provided which the user can set to indicate which, of all the fonts available locally, is the default font to use.

With this kind of tailoring we utilize a predetermined set of dimensions from which we choose among the different options provided in the same way as we may adjust the front seat of a car. In well-designed systems the possibilities make sense to the users and are easily identified, for example, via menus. For these reasons the users are able to adjust a system by these means. On the other hand, the possible adjustments are limited to those which have been explicitly anticipated by the designers.

In the early use of Buttons, it quickly became clear that for any particular button, the points of change were usually fixed: on the address button, people would change the label and the address (but not the font, look, size, help message, etc.). A mechanism was added to Buttons which permitted button designers to pick out these points of change; that is, parameters were added. These parameters were used to replace general editing with a simpler process of choosing as the means for altering commonly changed aspects of buttons.

Sometimes the range of choices for any particular dimension of variability can be extended by a user through simply adding new material to the environment in which the system runs. Thus, new default font choices are provided by buying and installing additional font definitions.

A limiting case of achieving different behavior from technology is to replace "the whole thing" with a different one. One word processor may provide the footnote format required by a particular journal;

when writing for that journal, a user can achieve the behavior desired by choosing that word processor. In the case of buttons which failed, or failed to meet new challenges, requests to fellow workers and supporters were a common way of getting a new button to simply replace the unsatisfactory one.

Where parameters are concerned, the major lesson for designers is that parameters themselves must be seen as elements of the resulting tailorable system. Thus parameters must be definable, and manipulable in uniform ways. Computer users must be able to find what parameters are there, what behavior they affect, what values are legitimate, etc. The supporters and designers (including, ultimately, the users) must have tools to add new parameters to the collection. This viewing of parameters as tailorable elements in their own right is the direct consequence of our requirement that the tools for tailoring be tailorable themselves.

Constructing New Behaviors from Existing Pieces

Some systems are created as configurations of smaller parts. Construction sets of all kinds exist in non-computer based technologies: office furnishings are composed of pieces of furniture; book shelves are composed of shelving and brackets; Lego and Erector sets create wonderful arrays of toys. In computer systems, file systems and folders mimic the physical world; spreadsheets are composed of linked cells; accounting structures are built of linked spreadsheets.

The behavior of such systems can be changed by changing the configuration. Sometimes the change can be simple rearrangement: in offices we push around the furniture; with desktop computers, we push around the windows. In other cases, more elaborate constructions are required to meet the changing needs of the situation.

Rooms, a Xerox system for constructing separate "screen work spaces," has one such mechanism for constructing rooms from other rooms: It was discovered in making and using rooms that many rooms would share a collection of common tools—the clock, your calendar, an application window for alerting one to the arrival of new mail, a door to get to the mailroom. To accommodate this commonality, rooms were provided with the ability to "include" other rooms, with the idea that the common tools would be put in a single "control panel" room that would be included in all relevant rooms. Subsequently, inclusion was used for other purposes too, suggesting that it is an appropriate mechanism for tailoring (cf. Henderson & Card, 1986, and Card & Henderson, 1987, for information on Rooms).

A special case of construction is that of "accelerators." A system is augmented by constructing a new operator from a sequence of operations grouped together. Ideally, the new operation may be treated in the same way as the original operations, and in particular can be used in the construction of yet larger and more powerful operators. The address buttons discussed above are accelerators. A prime factor in the success of the Unix operating system is the incorporation of such a construction philosophy for commands in the various "shell" command languages.

Another special case of construction as a way of adapting technology is "going outside the system." Here, the system is modified not by rearranging its internal parts, but by using it as a component of a larger constructed system which does what is desired. Thus, to take an example from non-computer based technology, if the range of settings for the driver's seat in our car isn't good enough, we may add a pillow to the seat.

Another argument for using a software "component" in multiple constructions is that the interface need only be learned once. For example, the task of identifying a file on the Macintosh is supported by a single dialogue which is used by most applications. However, the quality of the integration is crucial. Consider the case of spell-checking: When the first spell-checkers arrived for the Macintosh they were separate programs that could process a number of different file formats, including those used by MacWrite and Word. The spell-checkers solved the problem of spell-checking on the Mac in a uniform way, but the integration was so poor that Word users quickly abandoned them when Microsoft offered spell-checking as an integrated part of Word.

A special case of commonality is that involved in the common use of an object (with behavior) as the base for many specializations. Thus, for example, the fact that the generic button supplies a common set of interactions for moving, copying, editing, deleting, inserting in a document, etc., means that all buttons inherit these interactions and need only be learned once. Designing good specialization, in both the mechanisms and the concepts expressed using them, is hard to do well. System designers can provide good mechanisms. They can also provide good examples of how to break up concepts so that specialization is easy and productive. However, at the center of the creation of good conceptual structures is good design and good taste; teaching it may be hard.

The lesson for designers of systems that can be tailored through construction is that the elements and mechanisms which support construction must form a coherent assemblage and support a coherent tailoring activity. This lesson is present but hidden in the term "construction set," which appeals to our sense that sets are the results, not of chance, but of conscious focused design. That is, construction must be designed.

Altering the Artifact

As the most radical kind of tailoring, a last resort when other simpler means fail, we consider altering the artifact itself. (In the case of constructed systems, we consider not the reconstruction, but only the alteration of the smallest nonconstructed pieces.) If we look at the alteration of non-computer based artifacts, we may consider such examples as cutting 25 cm off the legs of the old dining table and painting it, to turn it into a coffee table for a child. Turning to computers, such alteration involves a potential alteration of all parts of a system, particularly the source code.

Changing the source code directly is in most cases infeasible. The code is usually only understandable to the designers; there is no obvious relation between the appearance and behavior of a system and the code. Consequences of specific changes are not detectable in any comprehensive way. Updating and maintenance get extremely complicated. And finally copyright concerns will in most cases make it impossible to get or provide the source code, at least at a reasonable price. Despite these difficulties, changing the source code must be retained as an option to consider.

But means of altering code other than direct change of the source are available. The most powerful of these are code architectures that make it possible to add to the behavior of code without modifying it. A number of such possibilities are found in object-oriented programming; inheritance or specialization, for example. The invocation mechanisms for functions on objects in object-oriented code make it possible to define new classes that specialize the behaviors of existing classes that one cannot examine for the reasons just mentioned. An "event hook" in LISP is another feature that allows users of a system to write LISP functions and install them on objects, to be executed whenever the corresponding event occurs for that object. For example, when the user clicks on a button, the LISP expression which is the value of the "ACTION-hook" is evaluated.

These ways of extending the behavior of code, however, require programming skills. This is the point then at which users may call on supporters for help. It should be noted that there is plenty of precedent in the non-computer world for obtaining such expert help: as the very existence of the profession of tailors makes clear, "users" of clothes do not all possess the skills needed to alter them. When dealing with computers, however, lack of knowledge about possibilities for tailoring may severely limit the users' initiative.

The preceding characterization of tailorable systems is heavily informed by the formative paper on the adapting and tailoring of the NoteCards hypertext system (Trigg et al., 1987). That paper focuses on the characteristics of technology in order to define properties of systems. Here, we focus on the activities that the tailors must do. Our understanding of the relationship between these two different perspectives is as follows. The four properties of adaptable systems are that they should be: 1. *Flexible*: a system with objects that the user can interpret in different ways. We regard such adaptability as addressing not the system but its use—a crucial capability, but not one that we are discussing here. 2. *Parameterized*: offering a range of behaviors from which to choose. We see this as focusing on a particular means of choosing. 3. *Integratable*: a system that can be used in a construction set. Using a system in a construction is only one of the activities associated with construction. 4. *Tailorable*: a system that allows the user to change the behavior of its parts through accelerators, specialization, and adding functionality. We see accelerators as construction, while adding functionality and specializing behavior are altering the artifact. In summary, these characterizations are similar and should be seen as carving up the same space according to different perspectives.

Supporting People in Changing Behavior

We now turn to supporting people engaged in the activities of designing in use. A simple view of these activities is: Some people "author" changes to the technology and make them available; others, perhaps including those authors, make use of the changes. Changes, like the technology itself, become objects to be trafficked in by users. Not only is improved behavior to be had, but membership in the "community of users" may depend on taking part in usage discussions concerning them. The interaction of people with changes becomes merely another case of involvement with design of the system; but, of course, in the case of tailoring, the design will take place locally, motivated by local needs, and often driven or implemented by the users. We can think, then, of a "life cycle" of changes, and look at the support needed to maintain its activities: creating, protecting, perpetuating, sharing, inspecting, learning, and providing feedback.

Creating

The first job is to make authoring as easy as possible. The easiest way of creating something is to copy it from someone else (see *Sharing*). This was the usual way for workers to get a button to do something they wanted. If borrowing fails, the next best move is to copy something you have that is like what you want and modify it. This was the second most common way for workers to acquire buttons. Sharing and copying require finding out what is out there, or nearby; so support for this means of creation is the support of information access: finding, negotiating, making available.

Authoring should require as little new mechanism as possible. That is, provide modification using familiar means. What particular means are already familiar to the user (turned designer/author)? Most immediately, there are the objects and mechanisms of the system being changed. If the changes can be expressed using the system itself, then mastering new mechanisms is not required. For example, a macro in Microsoft Excel is made up of commands. Commands are expressed as cell formulae. Thus, the language of commands in Microsoft Excel is an extension of the language of cell formulae that the user already knows. In contrast, the most general means for changing Buttons is the LISP expression editor, something not required in using Buttons.

Another related source of familiarity is that which a user has with the use of the system itself. This resource can be directly tapped through various means of "construction by demonstration." For example, consider creating composite commands: the user enters a demonstration mode and carries out the sequence that is to be captured; the system watches and creates a new command encapsulating the sequence. Most UNIX shells have this capability.

A third way to tap familiarity is to use the same tailoring tools in many applications. Once a user has learned how to author a change in one part of the system (e.g., in one application), authoring changes in other places will be already understood. For example, the fact that Buttons uses the LISP expression editor means that it is familiar to many LISP users because many applications appeal to this tool. And in contrast, the creation of macros in Microsoft Excel as discussed is completely idiosyncratic, working only in Excel.

Finally, familiarity with the objects of a system can be harnessed to capture regularities by letting the system extract an abstraction from a set of constructed objects, all of which are examples of the pattern (abstraction) sought (cf. Myers (Ed.), 1988).

Protecting

Ease of authoring is not an author's only need. In addition, there is the concern that in changing the system for personal use, a user may mess it up for someone else. This is not a problem if all changes affect only the local author and remain with the local author. But most authors want to share good things, which leverages the effort expended in authoring the change. Thus, for example, when making variable something that had been fixed, one can run the danger of forcing all existing users to learn about and make a new choice. To avoid this problem, an author can insure that the system default to the old behavior. Under this scheme, users need learn nothing about the new choice until they really have a need for it.

And finally, the author must make the change easy for a user to learn about, to learn, and to use. This requires documentation. Further, it is desirable that a user (who may be the author) be able to continue to evolve the change. To aid this continuing design, the history of the design can be a great help, either in conveying the thinking behind the design, or in putting a subsequent author and the original author in contact.

Perpetuating

Changes become a central part of the definition of a system, because they must be added and deleted, set and manipulated, talked about and shared, by the members of the community of users. Thus it is important that means be provided to support changes as objects (objectification of changes) that will be perpetuated while the system remains in use.

First, a change must become an object. Sometimes a change is captured as a procedure to apply to a system (e.g., adjust the timezone to your local site). These are quickly objectified by creating an object that when applied in some way to the system will carry out this change.

Changes must be objectified for the users, too. A key activity is giving them names or other short descriptions so that they may be referred to verbally and searched for in storage structures. For example, choices in programming environments are often named by the variable in which the value for the choice is held.

Means for storing and applying the changes must be provided. "Initialization files" are often used, either to encapsulate a single change, or to hold a collection of changes. An important requirement for these storage mechanisms is that they support not only individual changes, but the means of assembling them into structures.

One view of buttons is that they are objectified actions. A crucial part of their becoming a powerful mechanism for tailoring in the research communities that use them is the provision for perpetuating them. A means was provided to automatically save buttons such that when a new system was loaded, the buttons in the old one would magically (without user knowledge or action) be restored. This made it worthwhile spending effort on crafting and adjusting buttons.

Sharing

First the news must be published that a change is available. Any or all means of communication can be used. Most interesting are mechanisms that are themselves part of the system. For example, Xerox ViewPoint has a Loader mechanism that can find all enhancements and applications that have been published locally. UNIX has the MAN (manual pages) mechanism that organizes on-line documentation. Buttons were included in documents and thereby passed around as e-mail, and appeared in documentation.

Next, means must be available for acquiring the change. Here again, system-based mechanisms can organize the work, providing uniform strategies for acquiring changes. Finally, taking advantage of changes sometimes must be coordinated among collaborators. For example, if a user unilaterally acquires a new font and employs it in documents, collaborators who lack that font may have difficulty reading the documents. Such coordination requires a user to be able to know who is affected by the change being contemplated and to interact with them. When people do not want to change, it may also require more complex mechanisms for supporting out-of-sync evolution of systems, in which systems with different modifications can "inter-operate" together. For example, most document editors can upgrade a file written by an older version of the editor; fewer—but some—are prepared to read the newer (and non-understood) objects in a file created by a newer version, preserve them across editing, and write a newer version file.

The other side of this requirement is the need to help users stay current. As colleagues evolve their use of shared systems, they may find that they are operating in a way that is regarded as obsolete and outdated. Keeping completely current may be very time consuming. Knowledge of what others are doing is needed to support achieving the necessary balance between change and stability. Thus, sharing must include knowledge not only of available changes, but also of current usage patterns and understandings of acceptable practice in the local community.

A special case of coordinating with others is the establishment of the necessary assumptions upon which a change depends. Buttons created severe problems for workers on more than one occasion when e-mail containing buttons was not even readable because the receiver's environment lacked something required for the button to display itself. Eventually, button mechanisms were designed so that a failure did not disrupt the receiver's system. The lesson for the designers of tailorable systems is that the architecture of the mechanisms must be robust enough to handle errors in the practice of tailoring. Handling errors means not only minimizing failures, but also providing enough information to diagnose and report failures that do occur.

Inspecting

A user wanting to change a system will want to know what changes are already there and their history. This history includes the changes that have been made, who made them, and for what purpose, including the work practices that the users had in mind when modifying the system. All of this is needed for people to be able to continue to evolve the system coherently. For example, my Macintosh may be set up to mount certain directories automatically on the local fileservers; some directories are mounted to support working on certain projects, others are a function of people, others of social conventions of the working groups; others using my system casually may find those arrangements quite unclear.

Learning

Reading documentation and talking to people about using a system change is one thing; learning to actually use the system in its modified state is quite another. Real learning requires much additional work, both to find out how the technology actually works in detail and, more importantly, to learn how to use those capabilities in their work. This involves the mapping of task needs to system capabilities and the development of practices of work to support the use of the system. For example, making copies of large documents on certain copiers requires that there be a flat working surface to hold intermediate stacks of paper, and a large stapler, with a desk strong enough to take the pressures of using it. Buttons are easy to use (just push them), but the effect is not always so easy to predict. The central Buttons mechanism includes a means of giving a user simple help. In addition, conventions have developed encouraging the publishing of buttons in documentation, preferably in e-mail. These conventions support an important pattern (see *Feedback*) in which trouble with use can be reported by simply replying to the e-mail that brought the button to you. However, once received and put onto the desktop (put to work), buttons lose their ability to lead the user to documentation or the author.

Such learning must inevitably take place in an exploratory mode. Some attempts will fail badly. Users will therefore want an environment for supporting this learning with two important properties:

First, it must be possible to experiment in a safe way, in a way that guarantees that no damage will result from misunderstood changes to "real" information. For example, users experimenting with Excel often open a new worksheet to try out new formulae and macros, knowing that changes usually happen to the sheet in which the formula is located. Second, after exploration has settled down, "real" work may have been done in that safe but "unreal" environment which one would then like to preserve. For example, copying the newly debugged formula from a trial Excel spreadsheet to the real one is quite easy.

Providing Feedback

The final step, closing the development cycle, is to provide feedback to the creator(s) of changes, based on experience with using the modified system. This is essential for the continued tracking of user needs by the authors of changes. When a user is the author, this activity amounts to the user reflecting, on occasion, on experiences with the changes that have been created. Interestingly, the detection and reporting is often considerably easier in the case of difficulties than for success. Difficulties make themselves known by their negative results, to which the user is usually forced to attend; successes are often very much harder to see; something going right is usually the result of many things going right. And, there is the human question of motivation: "If it ain't broke, don't fix it" is the death of much feedback.

To provide feedback requires knowing what information would be useful, who to feed it back to, and how to get it there. This is the other half of sharing, and the considerations on information dissemination apply here just as they did there. Mechanisms for providing feedback can be built into the system itself. For example, the installation procedures on the Hermes message system ensured that any user with a comment could simply use the "comment" command and Hermes would get the comment to the developers (Henderson & Myers, 1977; Myers & Mooers, 1976). The user needed to know nothing at all about who the developer was. And with buttons, particularly those that came in e-mail, when they didn't work, one could reply to the e-mail (thereby getting it back to the sender without thought), including a few well-chosen words about what had gone wrong—a very easy exchange indeed. The lesson here is that tailoring should not be considered independently of the communication mechanisms that will support sharing and feedback.

More important than the mechanisms for delivering experiences of use to the authors of change is the establishment of a climate of collaboration among users and authors that fosters the learning that all use makes possible. There is a cost even to sending a comment, and more cost if the system has been very difficult to use and the user can't characterize what happened or went wrong. The investment in feedback, however, can be seen—if the larger social system is correctly constituted—as not only a duty, but as a likely source of a better tomorrow.

Some Problems with Tailoring—Why Not Tailor?

Before we conclude by summing up how to design for tailoring, we look at the down side of tailoring, at some of the major pressures against changing the behavior of a system.

Tailorability Is Hard to Provide

As discussed previously, to make tailoring possible may require implementing lots of switches, construction sets, mechanisms for adding behavior to code, and integrating into communication systems and social systems. This is not always a large job, but it always adds to the work and in some cases is a great deal of work indeed.

Second, the mechanisms for allowing design in use must be provided. An interface (or interfaces) must be designed and built. It is interesting to note that while buttons have been in use for a number of years, the mechanisms for editing them are still under development.

Third, mechanisms for saving and reestablishing the state of the system must be built. The mechanisms for appropriately saving and reestablishing can be difficult to construct. No current system does this in a principled way, the problem being to untangle the tailoring done by the possibly many authors who have provided changes to an environment, once it is in place. There is research needed on this issue; the principles have not yet been worked out. In Buttons, this difficulty manifests itself in not knowing, for a button which has passed through many hands, whom to give feedback to; or when a new version arrives in the mail, whether the new one should be used in place of one the receiver already has and is happily using.

Finally, there is the very pragmatic fact that all these additional mechanisms add to the resources necessary to use the system. Effort must be expended to create them, adding to the cost of acquisition (construction expense or price). And the system is normally larger, requiring more machine resources to run it (memory and disk space).

Learning

Turning to the user side, a system with more "stuff" in it requires more learning. A user must learn about the various design possibilities and what aspects of the system's behavior they affect. When the means for design are programming language expressions, the language, its forms and their meanings, must be learned. The interface(s) to the tailoring mechanisms must be learned too, including, where relevant, editors for creating and manipulating linguistic expressions.

Beyond learning the details of the technology of tailoring, a user will need to understand why a particular possibility has been provided by a designer. That is, what applications are better supported by the system if it behaves in one fashion or another. Consider, for example, what happened when word processors were upgraded to permit user control over the fonts in which their text appeared. People usually had no training, skills, or even taste in the arena of typographic design. In many places there was a severe outbreak of "font-itis," the inappropriate use of fonts in documents.

Finally, systems used together often must have their tailoring coordinated. Consequently, a user may well have to learn how colleagues and correspondents tailor their systems for the collaboration to work. For example, if one user employs a package of macros for the spreadsheet program Excel, those sharing these spreadsheets will have to do the same.

A variant of the learning task is the remembering task. Once committed to using certain features of a system, there can be a continuing difficulty in making use of that capability. One forgets how to use it and has to turn to manuals, examples, and colleagues to reproduce the knowledge.

Using

If one wants to or is forced to tailor, a lot of time may be required. In particular, a changed system will inevitably require changing one's practices of use. It is a very common feeling that one may never regain in time saved, the time spent learning to save it. When the mechanisms to protect against unsuccessful tailoring (breaks, wrong function) themselves are unsuccessful, this can be doubly annoying and time-consuming. Difficulties in saving and restoring buttons have on more than one occasion severely endangered their continued use in one research lab.

Tailorability produces an explosion in configurations in single systems, and when systems interact (when don't they?) the possibilities are endless. A plethora of configurations increases the likelihood of interactions that have to be dealt with by tinkering until things work. Careful factoring of effects can help manage this complexity, but trying out a new configuration may waste a great deal of time and try a lot of patience. So the users will bear the cost of possible tailoring while they are using their systems, whether they tailor them or not.

Finally, but often foremost, is the possibility that the variability provided is just not of any interest to the users. The fact that multiple fonts are available may not be of interest when writing a book which will be typeset by the editors or publishers. The provision of many features, so called "creeping feature-itis," is an ever-present source of unlooked-for and unwanted tailorability, for which users pay a price.

Babel

A common experience with tailorable systems is to sit down at a colleague's machine that runs systems that you use on your machine and discover that you can't use them because they have been tailored in ways that you are unfamiliar with. Keyboard "wirings" and macros are particularly difficult to adjust to because one's patterns of usage get "built into one's synapses"—backspace is in a certain place (the delete key, or control a, or leftarrow) and the impulse to backspace produces finger motion faster than one can easily control. In Buttons, the unavailability of buttons familiar on your own machine may make it impossible to do things you very commonly do "at home."

In some situations, it would be useful if one could install one's own personal "style," including packages, "over the top of" your colleagues' behavior. This is not usually easy to do, because the "saving technology" is not sophisticated enough to save the personal style separately from everything else. For all these reasons, people are loathe to adjust other peoples' systems to their own styles. This makes sharing machines harder when tailoring is common.

Of course, there are cases where you would not want to change to your personal style anyway. When you are trying to help figure out a problem, particularly concerning the behavior affected by personal tailoring, or when you are working collaboratively with a colleague with both of you seated at her machine, you are depending on her style being in force. However, with extensive tailoring, the unfamiliarity of styles—indeed, the languages of interaction—can greatly increase the difficulty of even talking with one another about the things that happen in the system. It becomes harder to help or debug, and collaboration can be reduced to content, not implementation. Other familiar cases are naming files or arranging directories: when collaborating using files, personal styles conflict, and compromises or decisions to live with incompatibility and inconsistency must be made.

The Missing Designers

Finally, in those cases where professional designers are absent from the "tailoring loop," tailoring may even decrease the usefulness of a system. The subtitle of this book emphasizes the cooperative nature of good design, and just as we have argued for the need to include users in the design process, the competence of designers will often be needed. Particularly in cases where the professional competence of the users does not otherwise include tailoring, it may be wise to seek assistance before modifying a system. An example of this kind is described in Grudin and Barnard (1985), in which command names tailored by naive text editing users were much less effective than those supplied by skilled designers.

Designing for Tailorability

Tailorability is no panacea, as the preceding discussion illustrates. And what is more, possibilities for tailoring will in many cases be application specific, requiring genuine design work by the creators of a system. However, the reasons for tailoring remain, and experience indicates that the resources saved in the initial development by ignoring tailorability issues will be spent several times over during the use of a system, either by the people doing the maintenance, or by the users who have to take still more elaborate action to bend the system to changing circumstances.

The lesson is design and architecture. If an artifact is created with change in mind, even if the specific change is not anticipated by the designer, the creation of change can be greatly simplified, regularized, and most importantly, supported. A simple example of this was given early in this chapter, in which new help messages were added to a system.

An important step in providing more user-accessible tailoring will be to develop new high level, or application-oriented, building blocks together with application-oriented ways of manipulating them. In terms of our characterizations in this chapter, altering of artifacts will be transformed into construction by finding decompositions of those artifacts that align with the understanding of users. The third case described in this chapter, Buttons, is a first step in this direction.

Object oriented design and implementation are a promising basis for this kind of work, since they may allow us to shorten or even bridge the gap between the structure of computer systems and their code on the one hand, and the structure of the work and concepts of the application area on the other.

Acknowledgments

Thanks to Jonathan Grudin for tailoring our language and to him and many of the authors of this book for helpful comments.

References

Brad A. M. (Ed.). (1988). *Creating user interfaces by demonstration.* San Diego, CA: Academic Press.

Card, S. K. & Henderson, A. (1987). A multiple, virtual-workspace interface to support user task switching. *Proceedings of CHI+GI '87*, (pp. 53-59). New York: ACM Press.

Grudin, J. & Barnard, P. (1985, April). When does an abbreviation become a word? and related questions. In *Proceedings CHI '85, Human factors in computing systems (San Francisco)*, (pp. 121-125). New York: ACM Press.

Henderson, A. & Card, S. K. (1986). Rooms: The use of multiple virtual workspaces to reduce space contention in a window-based graphical user interface. *ACM Transactions on Graphics, 5* (3), 211-243.

Henderson, D. A. & Myers, T. H. (1977). Issues in message technology. In *Proceedings of the Fifth ACM/IEEE Data Communications Symposium, September 27-29, 1977* (pp. 6/1-9). New York: Snowbird, UT, IEEE.

MacLean, A., Carter, K., Lövstrand, L., & Moran, T. (1990). User-tailorable systems: Pressing the issue with Buttons. In *Proceedings of CHI '90* (pp. 175-182). New York: ACM Press.

Myers, T. H. & Mooers, C. D. (1976). *HERMES user's guide.* Cambridge, MA: Bolt Beranek and Newman Inc.

Sheil, B. (1983, February). Power tools for programmers. *Datamation, 29* (2), 131-144.

Trigg, R. H., Moran, T. P., & Halasz, F. G. (1987, September). Adaptability and tailorability in NoteCards. In *Proceedings of INTERACT '87*. Stuttgart, Germany.

EAGER: PROGRAMMING REPETITIVE TASKS BY EXAMPLE

Allen Cypher

Advanced Technology Group
Apple Computer, Inc.
Cupertino, CA 95014

ABSTRACT

Eager is a Programming by Example system for the HyperCard environment. It constantly monitors the user's activities, and when it detects an iterative pattern, it writes a program to complete the iteration.

Programming by Example systems create generalized programs from examples provided by the user. They are faced with the problem of how to display these abstract procedures. Eager utilizes a new interface technique, called *anticipation*, to show how it has generalized: when it detects a repetitive activity, it highlights menus and objects on the screen to indicate what it expects the user to do next. As users continue to perform their activity, they will notice that the objects they are about to select have already been highlighted by the system. When it becomes apparent that Eager knows how to perform the task correctly, they can tell Eager to complete the task for them. The use of anticipation allows Eager to interfere minimally with the users' normal activities.

KEYWORDS: programming by example, demonstrational interfaces, user programming, intelligent interfaces, adaptive systems, agents, programmer assistants, models of user performance.

INTRODUCTION

A significant problem with today's personal computers is that users have to perform many repetitive tasks by hand. If my department decides to have a meeting every Monday, I have to go through my calendar, week by week, and paste the meeting into each Monday. If I decide to reformat a bibliography to use double-quotes instead of italics, I have to change each entry by hand. Although computers are supposed to excel at performing repetitive tasks, most users are unable to take advantage of this capability because they do not know how to program.

In Proceedings of CHI '91, New Orleans, Apr 28-May2, ACM, New York, 1991, pp. 33-39.

Programming by Example is a technique which can potentially solve this problem. Since by definition most of the steps in a repetitive task are the same as in the previous repetition, it should be possible for a computer program to automate the task by recording the steps and replaying them.

RELATED WORK

Various "macro" programs, such as *Tempo* and *QuicKeys2* on the Apple Macintosh, are effective in automating simple tasks. However, they are limited in that 1) they only record low-level events, and 2) they cannot generalize. For example, if the user clicks on a *MacWrite* icon, a macro program will only record the low-level event of clicking at that particular location on the screen. If the *MacWrite* icon is moved, the macro will no longer work correctly. The inability of macro programs to generalize is illustrated when a user selects "William" in "Dear William" and "Mrs. Julie Kincaid" in "Dear Mrs. Julie Kincaid", and the macro program is unable to select "Ms. Atkins" in "Dear Ms. Atkins", because it cannot make the generalization *all of the words following "Dear"*.

Programming by Example (PBE) systems go beyond macro programs by making generalizations about high-level events. This allows them to automate more complex tasks. The work most closely related to Eager is David Maulsby's Metamouse [6], a PBE system for a simple Draw application. Like Eager, Metamouse watches user actions and writes a program which generalizes those actions. Metamouse is more powerful than Eager in that it infers conditionals, but more restrictive in that the user must explicitly indicate the start of an example, must answer questions about how to properly generalize various steps, and must approve or reject each system action.

Eager is also related to Brad Myer's PERIDOT [7]. PERIDOT is a PBE system for building user interaction devices, such as menus and scroll bars. After the user places the first few items of a list into a menu, PERIDOT is able to infer that the entire list should comprise the menu. Like Metamouse, PERIDOT requires the user to confirm each inference it makes. PERIDOT was inspira-

Creating a Subject List

A user has a stack of message cards (a) and wants to make a list of the subjects of the messages. The user copies the subject from the first message, goes to the "**Subject List**" card, types "1. ", and pastes in the first subject (b). The user then goes to the second message, copies its subject, and adds it to the Subject List.

At this point, the Eager icon pops up (c), since Eager has detected a pattern in the user's actions. Eager highlights the right-arrow button in green (c), since it anticipates that the user will click here next. Eager continues anticipating that the user will navigate to the third message, select (d) and copy its subject, go to the Subject List, type "3. " (e) and then paste in the subject (f).

The user is now confident that Eager knows what to do, and clicks on the Eager icon. It completes the task automatically (g).

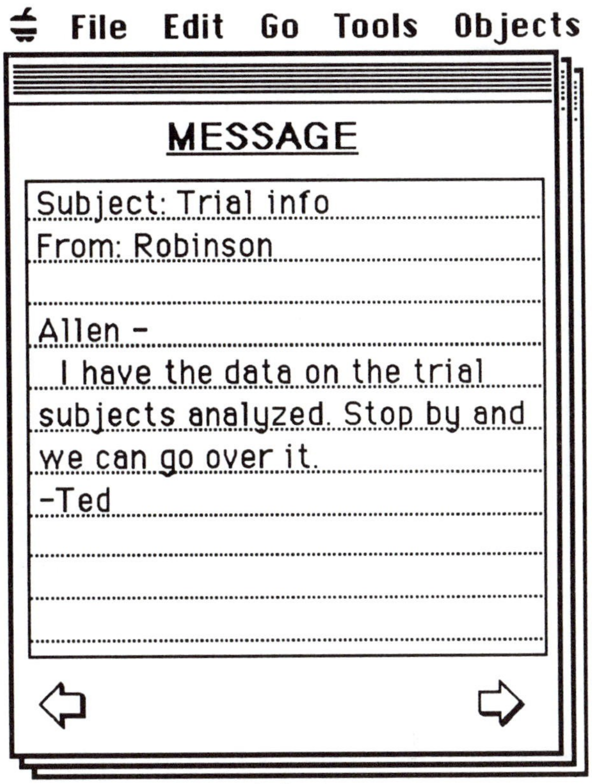

(a)

(d)

(e)

Figure 1.

File Edit Go Tools Objects
Subject List
1. Trial info

(b)

File Edit Go Tools Objects
Subject List
1. Trial info
2. Some more good ideas

(c)

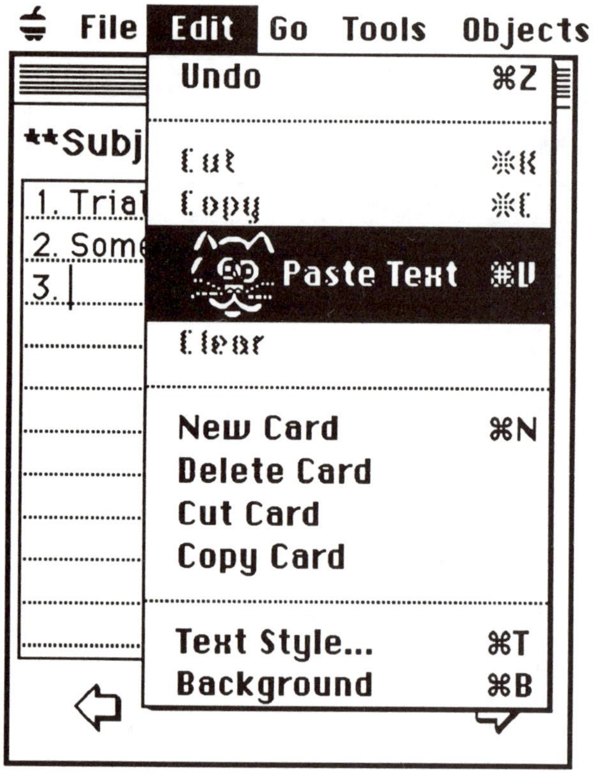
File Edit Go Tools Objects
**Subj
1. Trial
2. Some
3.
Undo ⌘Z
Paste Text ⌘V
New Card ⌘N
Delete Card
Cut Card
Copy Card
Text Style... ⌘T
Background ⌘B

(f)

File Edit Go Tools Objects
Subject List
1. Trial info
2. Some more good ideas
3. a necessary evil...
4. more on Trial info
5. Meeting this week
6. Lost data, can't fi
7. Where were you?
8. More ram
9. Lunch Weds?

(g)

tional to me in showing the potential for PBE as a practical tool for end users.

Barbara Staudt Lerner's Lantern [4] system for automated customization is similar to Eager in its concern with minimizing user interaction. Lantern adopts the radical approach of performing customizations without asking for the user's consent. It abandons a customization if it detects the user undoing its effects.

Related earlier work in PBE includes Henry Lieberman's Tinker [5], Laura Gould's Programming by Rehearsal [2], Dan Halbert's SmallStar [3], and David C. Smith's seminal PYGMALION [8].

WHAT EAGER DOES

Eager offers a solution to the *iteration* problem for Programming by Example — the problem of specifying loops by example. Eager is always on, constantly looking for repetitions in actions performed in HyperCard. When it detects an iterative pattern, the "Eager" icon pops up on the screen. As the user continues to perform the task, Eager *anticipates* each next action by turning menu items, buttons, and text selections green. When Eager is correct, the user's intended selection will appear highlighted in green before it is selected. When Eager is incorrect, the user's choice will not match the highlighted item, and Eager will use the actual choice to revise its program. Once the user is confident that Eager knows how to perform the task correctly, he or she clicks on the Eager icon and Eager writes and executes a program which completes the task automatically. Figure 1 gives an example of Eager assisting a user with a repetitive task.

USER INTERACTION

Eager differs from most other Programming by Example systems in its interaction with the user. An important design goal was to intrude minimally on the user's activities. Therefore, Eager is written so that it never asks the user for information; the only information comes from recording the user's ongoing actions. In particular, the user does not signal the start of an example, and never explicitly confirms or rejects a hypothesis — performing an action that matches the anticipation is implicitly confirming; performing any other action is implicitly rejecting.

Another important design decision was to represent actions in the same modality that the user employs for performing those actions. HyperCard has a direct-manipulation interface, so Eager represents actions by highlighting objects, menu items, and text selections rather than by displaying textual descriptions, such as *Copy the button located at 20,120.*

A significant design decision for all PBE systems concerns how generalizations will be presented to the user. Generalizations often represent abstract concepts which can be difficult to explain. In Eager, generalizations are communicated to the user through instantiations. For example, if the user *selects button 1* and then *selects button 2*, Eager makes the generalization *select button i for i = 1, 2, 3, ... ,* and instantiates this on the next iteration to *select button 3.* The hope is that users will be able to recognize through this specific instance that Eager has detected the pattern in their actions, and that this specific instance will be easier for them to understand than an abstract description such as *select button i.*

Validating programs

When I use standard macro tools to record and play back a sequence of actions, I sometimes find that the macro does not perform as expected, and I am unable to automate my task. As a result, I will sometimes not even try to create macros when I am unsure of their success. Eager minimizes such failures because the Eager icon only appears on the screen when it is able to automate the previous steps. Since it is possible that the generalization Eager has created is not what the user intended, the user may check the correctness of Eager's program by observing its anticipations. In this way, validation coincides with continuing to perform the task by hand, and no effort is wasted.

HOW EAGER WORKS

Eager is written in LISP, and runs as a background application on Macintosh computers. It receives information about high-level user events in HyperCard via interprocess communication. Whenever a new event is reported, Eager searches through previous events in the history to find one that is similar.

"Similar" means that 1) the commands are of the same type (e.g. they are both *Copy Text* commands), and 2) the objects on which the commands are performed fit into some regular pattern (e.g.*Tuesday* and *Wednesday* ; *button #6* and *button #7* ; *button #6* and *button #6* ; *the last word on line 4 of field "Address" of card 2 of stack "Rolodex"* and *the last word on line 4 of field "Address" of card 3 of stack "Rolodex"*).

For numeric data, Eager searches for constants, consecutive integers, linear sequences, and linear sequences within a given tolerance (e.g. 50, 72, 91, ... is recognized as the sequence 20*i + 30, with a tolerance ±2). Some of the numbers that HyperCard passes to Eager are: card numbers, screen coordinates for buttons, line numbers for text selections, and numbers as text and in card names.

For textual data, Eager parses the text into substrings of contiguous alphabetic characters, numbers, delimiters, and spaces. It searches for constants, alphabetic or numeric order, changes in capitalization and spacing, and known sequences such as days of the week and roman numerals. Some of the textual items that HyperCard passes to Eager are: text selections, pathnames, and the names of cards, buttons, and fields. If the user has selected some text and replaced it, Eager looks for patterns not only between the new text and the old text, but also between the new text in the current iteration and the new text in the previous iterations.

When two similar events are found, Eager assumes that the second event marks the beginning of the second iteration in the loop. All of the events before it, back to the first similar event, are presumed to constitute the first iteration in the loop. Eager now monitors each new incoming event to see if it is "similar" to the corresponding event from the first iteration. If patterns can be found for each pair of events, Eager concludes that it has detected an iterative loop, and the Eager icon pops up on the screen. Based on the generalizations formed from these two iterations, Eager instantiates the next steps in the pattern and directs HyperCard to highlight the appropriate items in green.

In the example shown in Figure 1, the first two similar events are *Copy words 2 through 3 ("Trial info") of line 1 of background field 1 of card 2 of stack "Cali:Eager Demo:Mail Messages"* and *Copy words 2 through 5 ("Some more good ideas") of line 1 of background field 1 of card 3 of stack "Cali:Eager Demo:Mail Messages".* HyperCard sends Eager a considerable amount of ancillary contextual information. For instance, the information sent with the above events includes the facts that there are 3 words on line 1 of card 2, and 5 words on line 1 of card 3, which Eager uses to recognize that the selection is from *the second through the last word of line 1.*

When the user clicks on the Eager icon, the system writes a program in HyperTalk (HyperCard's scripting language) and passes it to HyperCard for execution.

DOMAIN KNOWLEDGE

The Eager system is able to detect patterns in HyperCard because it deals with high-level events, and because it has knowledge about the structure of HyperCard. For example, instead of being given the low-level information that a mouse click occurred at location (28,142), it is given the high-level information that the click was on the button named "Phone". As an example of domain knowledge, Eager has a knowledge base about HyperCard objects which includes the relation that *Cards are PartOf Stacks*, so it can infer that a loop that copies Card 1, Card 2, ..., is an iteration over the Cards in a Stack, and that the loop should therefore terminate when the last Card in the Stack is copied. Another example of domain knowledge is that the number called "button-location-X" is of type *screen coordinate*, so Eager uses a test for similarity that recognizes linear sequences of numbers within a tolerance of 4 pixels, to allow for inexactness in where users position objects on the screen.

A forthcoming paper [1] will describe in greater detail the knowledge representation, data passing, and pattern matching algorithms used in Eager.

HIGH-LEVEL EVENTS AND USER ACTIONS

Using anticipation to communicate with the user complicates the information that must pass between Eager and HyperCard. Detecting patterns in user actions can be accomplished solely by analyzing high-level events, but anticipation must be done at the level of individual user actions, and there may well be several user actions involved in performing a single high-level event. For instance, the high-level event "Set the style of card button 5 to transparent" is performed by the user as a sequence of five actions: choosing the "button tool" from a menu, selecting button 5 by clicking on it, choosing "Button Info..." from a menu, selecting the "Transparent" style in the dialog box that appears, and clicking on the "OK" button in the dialog box. Eager handles this complication by recording and generalizing both high-level events and user actions.

Robustness

There are many equivalent ways to move to a particular card in a HyperCard stack. There are commands to move to the next, previous, first, and last cards in a stack, to jump back to the card last visited, and to select from a miniature display of the 25 most recent cards. In order to detect patterns when users do not perform an activity precisely the same way each time, Eager is written so that it only requires exact matches on major commands, such as cutting, pasting, and typing. For minor commands, such as navigating among cards, Eager will accept any command sequences which end at the same card as being equivalent.

USER STUDY

In order to understand how first-time users react to Eager, seven subjects were given three repetitive tasks to perform. The subjects were not given any information about Eager — they were simply asked to perform the three tasks.

The study showed that first-time users were generally able to understand what Eager was doing and to figure out how to use it without instruction. Three subjects clicked on the Eager icon as soon as it appeared on the screen. Three subjects noticed the icon, performed several more steps by hand, and then clicked on the icon. The verbal protocols for these subjects indicated that they were able to figure out that the anticipation highlighting indicated what they were going to do next: *"...indicates that I've been using it [the Recent command] and it's probably the next thing I'm going to do"*; *"It's almost as if it's suspecting what I want to do. Now I get it".* One subject performed all of the tasks by hand and never clicked on the icon.

When subjects were able to perform the task correctly in HyperCard (17 tasks out of 21), Eager was able to detect the patterns in their actions, even though different subjects chose different strategies for performing the tasks, and some subjects performed the task somewhat differently on each iteration. For instance, one subject originally used the "Next" button to go to the end of the stack, and on a later iteration switched to using the "Last" command. Also, some subjects made and corrected minor mistakes, such as navigating past the desired card and then backing up.

The study also pointed out significant failings in the user interface. The most striking finding was that all subjects were uncomfortable with giving up control when Eager took over. Two changes were made: Eager now saves a copy of any stacks it is going to modify so that the user can recover from an incorrect automation, and a stepping mode was added, where Eager pauses before each action for user confirmation.

There were a few cases where Eager appeared prematurely, having detected a simple but insignificant pattern. The appearance of the icon is now postponed until two complete iterations have been performed, and for extremely simple patterns, it waits for three iterations.

Some subjects did not realize that the character that popped up on the screen was related to the items being highlighted in green. To remedy this, the icon now appears in green as well.

The original icon for this program showed a man sitting in a chair. When he anticipated an iteration correctly, he would begin clapping. Some subjects expressed confusion about the character, since they could not see what the representation had to do with automating repetitive tasks. The icon was therefore changed to the less evocative image of a cat — when it takes over, the cat is shown with its paw moving the mouse.

Some subjects did not notice the icon when it first appeared, particularly if it appeared on a rich background. The cat icon now animates when it first appears.

LIMITATIONS

A limitation in using anticipation to communicate an abstract program to the user is that anticipation is unable to communicate the termination conditions for the program. A user expecting a PBE system to delete all of the documents in the current folder would be shocked to observe it blithely deleting all of the documents on the disk! At present, Eager is conservative and terminates when it reaches the end of the first structure in the PartOf hierarchy. It would be reasonable to query the user about continuing the iteration to the next level in the hierarchy.

Eager currently does not handle conditionals, nested loops, repetitions that are spread out over time (e.g. inserting the date whenever you start a new letter), or tasks that include some steps that must be left up to the user. These restrictions help to constrain the sorts of patterns that the program must detect. If Eager's search fails to detect a match between an incoming event and the corresponding event in the previous iteration, it assumes that there is no repetitive task. In fact, the correct interpretation could be that there is a conditional branch in the program, or that there is an obscure pattern that must be left up to the user (e.g. deleting the names of people who are no longer friends). Allowing for these possibilities would greatly increase the ambiguity in generalizing and the complexity of pattern-matching. Eager's success is partly due to the fact that it only tries to automate a limited, yet useful, range of tasks. Although its power is limited, it does handle almost all of the commands in HyperCard, unlike all other PBE systems which only work in limited, experimental domains.

FUTURE DIRECTIONS

Further user studies will be conducted to determine whether the changes prompted by the first user study were in fact successful in correcting the various problems.

The first user study investigated users' first experiences with Eager. To complement this data, a field study will be conducted to learn more about regular, experienced use of Eager. Most importantly, the study will investigate how often users perform tasks which Eager can automate. The study will also investigate how often Eager's automations do not coincide with the user's intentions, and how users react in such situations. The field study should also be valuable for determining whether experienced users of Eager have needs which the current user interface does not address. Finally, it seems significant that three of the subjects in the first user study clicked on the Eager icon as soon as it appeared, without following the anticipation highlighting. The field study will be able to determine whether some users remain unaware of the highlighting feature even after extensive use of Eager, and whether some users persist in invoking Eager without first validating its intended actions.

I am working on a PBE system which extends Eager's pattern recognition capabilities to include conditionals, nested loops, non-contiguous repetitions, and user steps. This extension will necessarily affect the user's interaction with the system, so the resulting program will have a redesigned interface.

It would be valuable to implement Eager-like capabilities in other application domains, such as Draw and Word Processor programs, since this would not require changing the style of user interaction.

It would be possible to apply Eager's interaction style to Intelligent Help. If Eager detected a sequence of commands for which it knew a shortcut, it could guide the user through the shorter procedure. If it detected a pattern of activity that typified a common error, it could guide the user through the correct procedure. In either case, users would see a general principle applied to their particular situation — Eager would do the instantiation, and they would not be required to puzzle over an abstract textual description or an example in an unfamiliar domain.

ACKNOWLEDGEMENTS

I would like to thank Shifteh Karimi for the user study, Ruben Kleiman for the MacFrames frame system and ipc, Donn Denman for his assembly language programming, Yin Yin for the Eager icon, and Steve Weyer, Harvey Lehtman, David Nagel, and Larry Tesler for their support of my work.

REFERENCES

1. Cypher, A. Detecting Repetitive Actions in a Direct Manipulation Environment. To be submitted to *1991 IEEE Workshop on Visual Languages*. Kobe, Japan, October, 1991.

2. Gould, L. and Finzer, W. *Programming by Rehearsal.* Xerox Palo Alto Research Center Technical Report SCL-84-1, May, 1984.
3. Halbert, D. *Programming by Example.* Xerox Office Systems Division Technical Report OSD-T8402, December, 1984.
4. Lerner, B. *Automated Customization of User Interfaces* Carnegie Mellon University School of Computer Science Technical Report CMU-CS-89-178, September, 1989.
5. Lieberman, H. An Example Based Environment for Beginning Programmers. In *Artificial Intelligence and Education.* Ablex, Norwood, N.J., 1987, pp 135-151.
6. Maulsby, D. and Witten, I. Inducing Programs in a Direct-Manipulation Environment. In *Proceedings of CHI '89* (Austin, Apr. 30 - May 4). ACM, New York, 1989, pp 57-62.
7. Myers, B. *Creating User Interfaces by Demonstration.* Academic Press, San Diego, Calif., 1988.
8. Smith, D. *Pygmalion: A Computer Program to Model and Stimulate Creative Thought.* Birkhäuser, Basel, 1977.

Agents that Reduce Work and Information Overload

Pattie Maes

Computers are becoming the vehicle for an increasing range of everyday activities. Acquisition of news and information, mail and even social interactions and entertainment have become more and more computer based. At the same time, an increasing number of untrained users are interacting with computers, and this number will continue to rise as technologies such as hand-held computers and interactive television become popular.

Unfortunately, these technological developments are not in line with a change in the way people interact with computers. The currently dominant interaction metaphor of *direct manipulation* [21] requires the user to initiate all tasks explicitly and to monitor all events. This metaphor will have to change if untrained users are to make effective use of the computer and networks of tomorrow.

Techniques from the field of AI, in particular so-called "autonomous agents," can be used to implement a complementary style of interaction, which has been referred to as *indirect management* [9]. Instead of user-initiated interaction via commands and/or direct manipulation, the user is engaged in a cooperative process in which human and computer agents both initiate communication, monitor events and perform tasks. The metaphor used is that of a *personal assistant* who is *collaborating with the user* in the same work environment. The assistant becomes gradually more effective as it learns the user's interests, habits and preferences (as well as those of his or her community). Notice that the agent is not necessarily an interface between the computer and the user. In fact, the most successful interface agents are those that do not prohibit the user from taking actions and fulfilling tasks personally (see Figure 1).

Agents assist users in a range of different ways: they hide the complexity of difficult tasks, they perform tasks on the user's behalf, they can train or teach the user, they help different users collaborate, and they monitor events and procedures.

The set of tasks or applications an agent can assist in is virtually unlimited: information filtering, information retrieval, mail management, meeting scheduling, selection of books, movies, music, and so forth.

This article focuses on a novel approach to building interface agents. It presents results from several prototype agents that have been built using this approach, including agents that provide personalized assistance with meeting scheduling, email handling, electronic news filtering and selection of entertainment.

Approaches to Building Agents

The idea of employing agents in the interface to delegate certain computer-based tasks was introduced by visionaries such as Nicholas Negroponte [19] and Alan Kay [8]. More recently, several computer manufacturers have adopted this idea to illustrate their vision of the interface of the future (cf., videos produced in 1990-1991 by Apple, Hewlett Packard, Digital and the Japanese FRIEND21 project). Even though a great amount of work has gone into the modeling and construction of agents, currently available techniques are still far from being able to produce the high-level, humanlike interactions depicted in these videos. Two main problems have to be solved when building software agents. The first problem is that of *competence:* how does an agent acquire the knowledge it needs to decide when to help the user, what to help the user with and how to help the user? The second problem is that of *trust:* how can we guarantee the user feels comfortable delegating tasks to an agent? Two previous approaches for building interface agents can be distinguished. Neither one provides a satisfactory solution to these problems.

The first approach consists in making the end-user program the interface agent. Malone and Lai's Oval (formerly Object-Lens) system [12] has "semi-autonomous agents" which consist of a collection of user-programmed rules for processing information related to a particular task. For example, the Oval user can create an email sorting agent by creating a number of rules that process incoming mail messages and sort them into different folders. Once created, these rules perform tasks for the user without having to be explicitly invoked by the user. Similarly, one can buy "agents" that can be programmed by the user to provide information filtering services (e.g., selecting any new article that mentions MIT Media Lab).

The main problem of this approach is that it does not deal with the competence criterion in a satisfactory way. The approach requires too much insight, understanding and effort from the end-user, since the user has to recognize the opportunity for employing an agent, take the initiative to create an agent, endow the agent with explicit knowledge (specifying this knowledge in an abstract language), and maintain the agent's rules over time (as work habits or interests change).

Trusting the agent is less of a problem in this approach, provided that the user trusts his or her own programming skills. However, the programs we write typically behave differently than expected, even when we trust our programming skills.

The second approach, called the "knowledge-based approach," consists in endowing an interface agent with extensive domain-specific background knowledge about the application and the user (called a domain model and user model, respectively). This approach is adopted by the majority of people working in AI on intelligent user interfaces [25]. At runtime, the interface agent uses its knowledge to recognize the user's plans and to find opportunities for contributing to them. For example, UCEgo [1] is an interface agent designed to help a user solve problems in using the Unix operating system. The UCEgo agent has a large knowledge base about how to use Unix, incorporates goals and meta-goals, and does planning (e.g., UCEgo can volunteer information or correct the user's misconceptions).

Both competence and trust constitute problems in the knowledge-based approach. The first problem related to competence is that the approach requires a huge amount of work from the knowledge engineer. A large amount of application-specific and domain-specific knowledge has to be entered into the agent's knowledge base. Little of this knowledge or the agent's control architecture can be used when building agents for other applications. The second problem is that the knowledge of the agent is fixed once and for all. It cannot be customized to individual user habits and preferences. The possibility of providing an agent with all the knowledge it needs to always comprehend the user's sometimes unpredictable actions is questionable.

In addition to the competence problem, there is also a problem with trust. It is probably not a good idea to give a user an interface agent that is very sophisticated, qualified and autonomous from the start. Schneiderman has argued convincingly that such an agent would leave the user with a feeling of loss of control and understanding [18]. Since the agent has been programmed by someone else, the user may not have a good model of the agent's limitations, the way it works, and so forth.

Training a Personal Digital Assistant

In our work, we explore an alternative approach to building interface agents that relies on machine learning techniques. A similar approach has been reported upon by Dent *et al.* [4]. The hypothesis tested is that, under certain conditions, an interface agent can "program itself" (i.e., it can acquire the knowledge it needs to assist its user). The agent is given a minimum of background knowledge, and it learns appropriate "behavior" from the user and from other agents. The particular conditions that have to be fulfilled are: (1) the use of the application has to involve a substantial amount of repetitive behavior (within the actions of one user or among users), and (2) this repetitive behavior is potentially different for different users. If the latter condition is not met (i.e., the repetitive behavior demonstrated by different users is the same), a knowledge-based approach might prove to yield results faster than a learning approach. If the former condition is not met, a learning agent will not be able to learn anything (because there are no regularities to learn in the user's actions).

The machine learning approach is inspired by the metaphor of a personal assistant. Initially, a personal assistant is not very familiar with the habits and preferences of his or her employer and may not even be very helpful. The assistant needs some time to become familiar with the particular work methods of the employer and organization at hand. However, with every experience the assistant learns, either by watching how the employer performs tasks, by receiving instructions from the employer, or by learning from other more experienced assistants within the organization. Gradually, more tasks that were initially performed directly by the employer can be taken care of by the assistant.

The goal of our research is to demonstrate that a learning interface agent can, in a similar way, become gradually more helpful and competent. In addition, we attempt to demonstrate that the learning approach also presents a satisfactory solution to the trust problem. If the agent gradually develops its abilities—as is the case in our approach—the user is also given time to gradually build up a model of how the agent makes decisions, which is one of the prerequisites for a trust relationship. Furthermore, the particular learning approach adopted allows the agent to give "explanations" for its reasoning and behavior in a language the user is familiar with, namely in terms of past examples similar to the current situation. For example, "I thought you

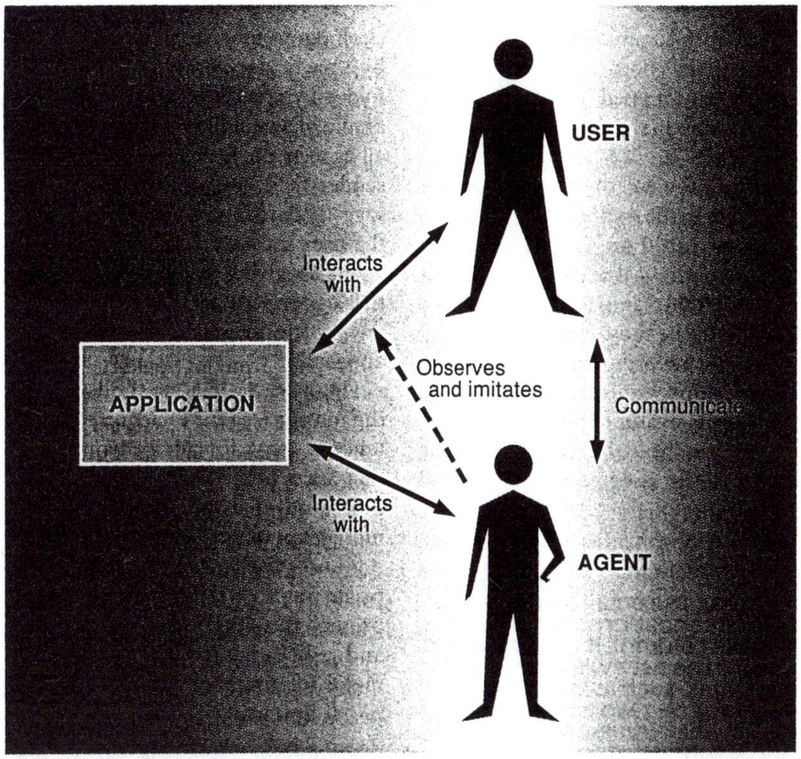

Figure 1. The interface agent does not act as interface or layer between the user and the application. It behaves as a personal assistant that cooperates with the user on the task. The user is able to bypass the agent.

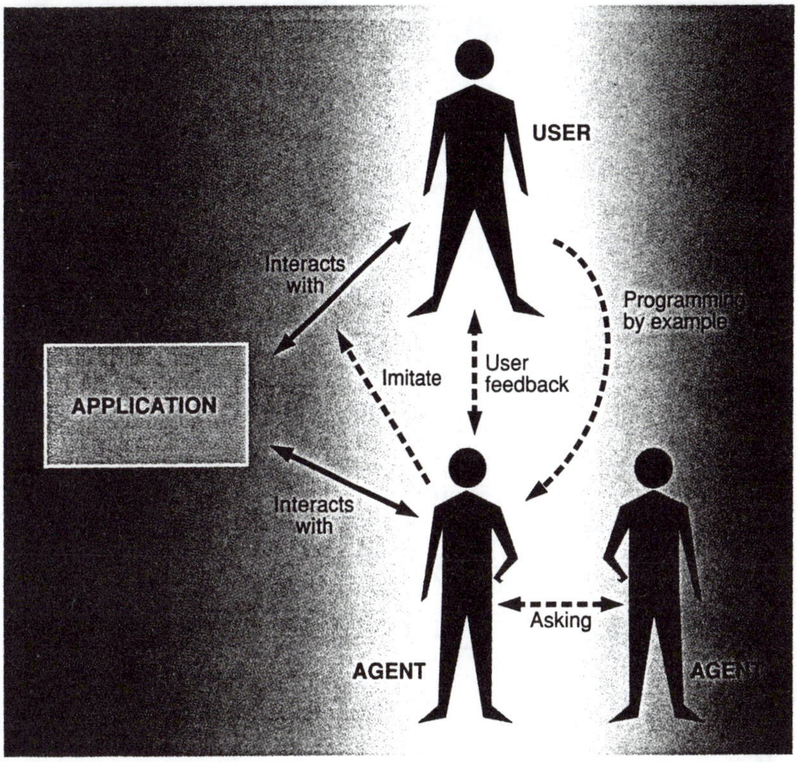

Figure 2. The interface agent learns in four different ways: (1) it observes and imitates the user's behavior, (2) it adapts based on user feedback, (3) it can be trained by the user on the basis of examples, and (4) it can ask for advice from other agents assisting other users.

might want to take this action because this situation is similar to this other situation we have experienced before, in which you also took this action" or "because assistant *Y* to person *Z* also performs tasks that way, and you and *Z* seem to share work habits."

Finally, we believe the learning approach has several advantages over the previous two approaches. First, it requires less work from the end-user and application developer. Second, the agent can more easily adapt to the user over time and become customized to individual and organizational preferences and habits. Finally, the approach helps in transferring information, habits and know-how among the different users of a community. The results described in a later section support all of these hypotheses and predictions.

A learning agent acquires its competence from four different sources (see Figure 2). First, the interface agent learns by continuously "looking over the shoulder" of the user as the user is performing actions. The interface agent can monitor the activities of the user, keep track of all of his or her actions over long periods of time (weeks or months), find regularities and recurrent patterns and offer to automate these. For example, if an email agent notices that a user almost always stores messages sent to the mailing list "intelligent-interfaces" in the folder `pattie:email:int-int.txt`, then it can offer to automate this action the next time a message sent to that mailing list is read. Similarly, if a news filtering agent detects some patterns in the articles the user reads, then it can offer similar articles to the user when it discovers them.

A second source for learning is direct and indirect user feedback. Indirect feedback happens when the user neglects the suggestion of the agent and takes a different action instead. This can be as subtle as the user changing the order in which he or she reads incoming messages, not reading some articles suggested by the agent, or reading articles not suggested by the agent. The user can also give explicit negative feedback for actions automated by the agent ("don't do this again" or "I dislike this article").

Third, the agent can learn from examples given explicitly by the user. The user can train the agent by giving it hypothetical examples of events and situations and telling the agent what to do in those cases. The interface agent records the actions, tracks relationships among objects, and changes its example base to incorporate the example that it is shown. For instance, the user can teach a mail clerk agent to save all messages sent by a particular person in a particular folder by creating a hypothetical example of an email message (which has all aspects unspecified except for the sender field) and dragging this message to the chosen folder. Similarly, the user can instruct a news filtering agent by giving it examples of (partially specified) articles (e.g., "select any article in which the word MIT appears").

Finally, a fourth method used by the interface agent to acquire competence is to ask for advice from agents that assist other users with the same task (and that may have built up more experience). If an agent does not know itself what action is appropriate in a certain situation, it can present the situation to other agents and ask "what action they recommend for that situation." For example, if an email message arrives that has been sent by Nicholas Negroponte, then the email agent can ask other agents what to do with that message. If a majority of the other agents recommends that the message has high priority and should be presented to the user for reading right away, then the agent can offer this recommendation to its user, even though the agent never previously observed the user deal with messages from Nicholas Negroponte. Rather than averaging the recommendations of all other agents in the community, a user might also inform his or her agent to accept suggestions from one or more specific agents which assist specific users. For example, if one person in the lab is an expert in the use of a particular piece of software, then other users can instruct their agents to accept advice about that software from the agent of that expert user.

Additionally, the agent can learn from experience which agents are good sources for suggestions. It can learn to trust agents that in the past

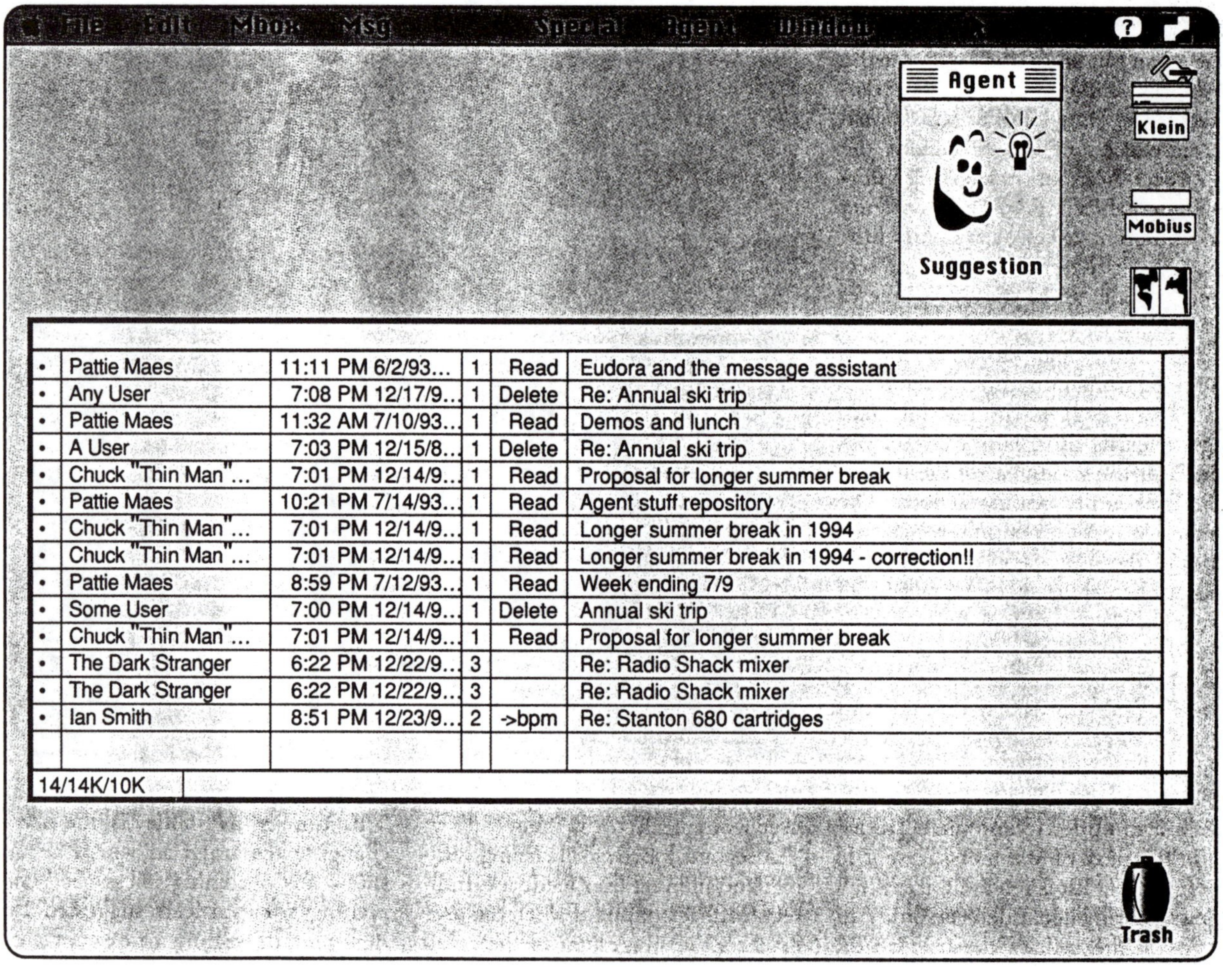

Figure 3. The email agent makes recommendations to the user (middle column). It predicts what actions the user will perform on messages, such as which messages will be read and in which order, which messages will be deleted, forwarded, archived, and so on.

have proven to recommend actions the user appreciated. The entertainment selection agent discussed next uses this technique to learn which other users have entertainment tastes similar to its user's tastes, and thus are good sources of suggestions.

Some Examples of Existing Agents

Four agents have been built using the learning approach previously discussed:

- An agent for electronic mail handling
- An agent for meeting scheduling
- An agent for electronic news filtering (Usenet Netnews).
- An agent that recommends books, music or other forms of entertainment

The choice of these domains was motivated by our dissatisfaction with the ways these tasks are currently handled. Many valuable hours are wasted dealing with junk mail, scheduling and rescheduling meetings, searching for relevant information among heaps of irrelevant information, and browsing through lists of books, music, and television programs in search of something interesting.

Electronic Mail Agent

Maxims [13] is an agent that assists the user with email. Maxims learns to prioritize, delete, forward, sort and archive mail messages on behalf of the user (Figures 3 and 4). Maxims is implemented in Macintosh Common Lisp. It communicates with the commercial email package Eudora [6] using Apple Events. The main learning technique used by Maxims is memory-based reasoning [24]. The agent continuously "looks over the shoulder" of the user as the user deals with email. As the user performs actions, the agent memorizes all of the situation-action pairs generated. For example, if the user saves a particular message after having read it, the mail agent adds a description of this situation and the action taken by the user to its memory of examples. Situations are described in terms of a set of features, which are currently handcoded. In this domain, the agent keeps track of the sender and receiver of a message, the `Cc:` list, the keywords in the `Subject:` line, whether the message has been read or not, whether it is a reply to a previous message, and so on.

When a new situation occurs that can be due to the user taking an action or due to some external event such as a message arriving, the agent will try to predict the action(s) of the user, based on the examples stored in its memory. The agent compares the

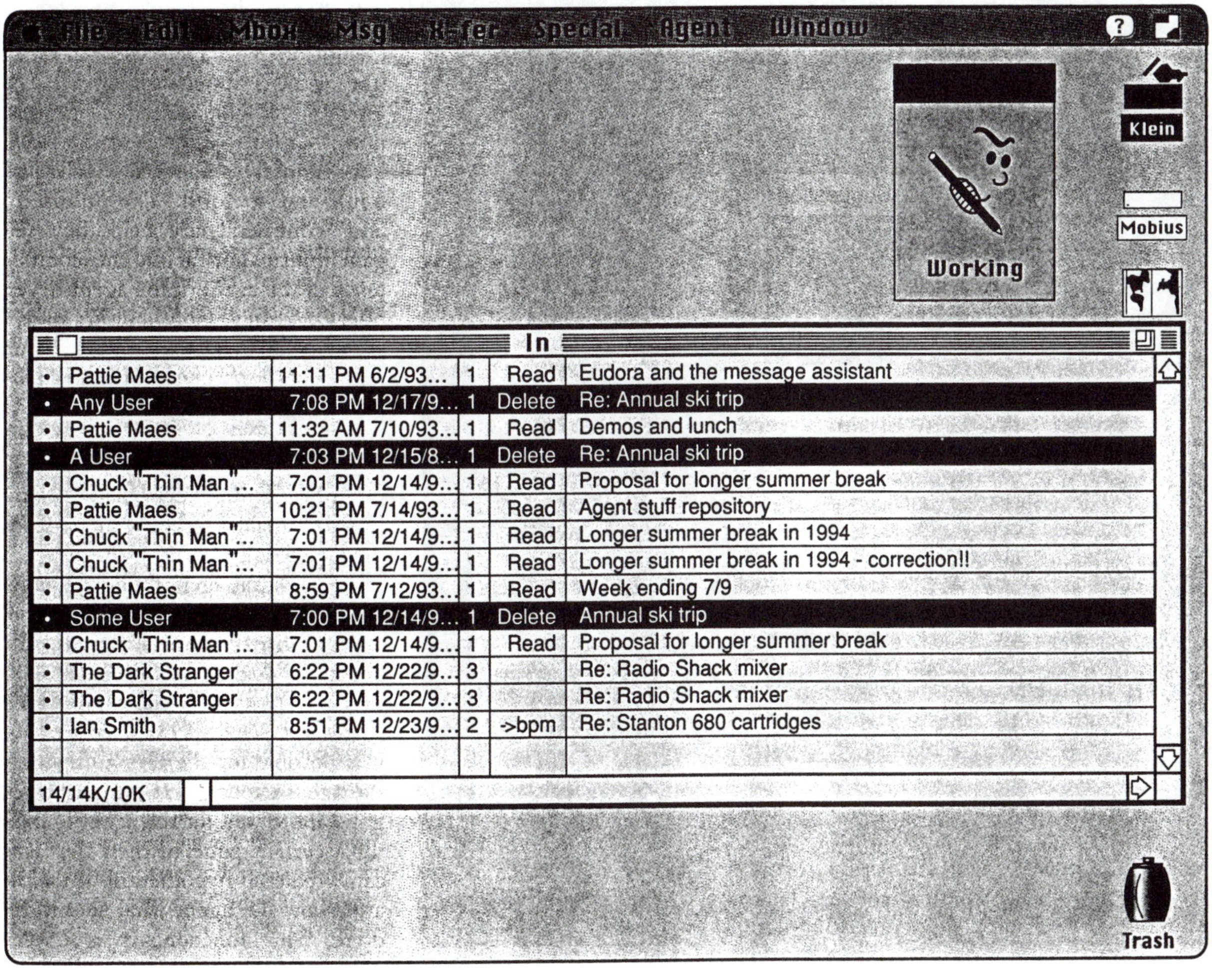

Figure 4. The user can select some of the suggestions made by the agent and ask the agent to execute them.

new situation with the memorized situations and tries to find a set of nearest neighbors (or close matches). The most similar of these memorized situations contribute to the decision of which action to take or suggest in the current situation. The distance metric used is a weighted sum of the differences for the features that make up a situation. Some features carry more weight than others. The weight of a feature is determined by the agent. Occasionally (e.g., at night), the agent analyzes its memory and determines the correlations between features and actions taken. For example, the agent may detect that the "from" field of an email message is highly correlated to whether its user reads the message, while the "date" field is not correlated. The detected correlations are employed as weights in the distance metric.

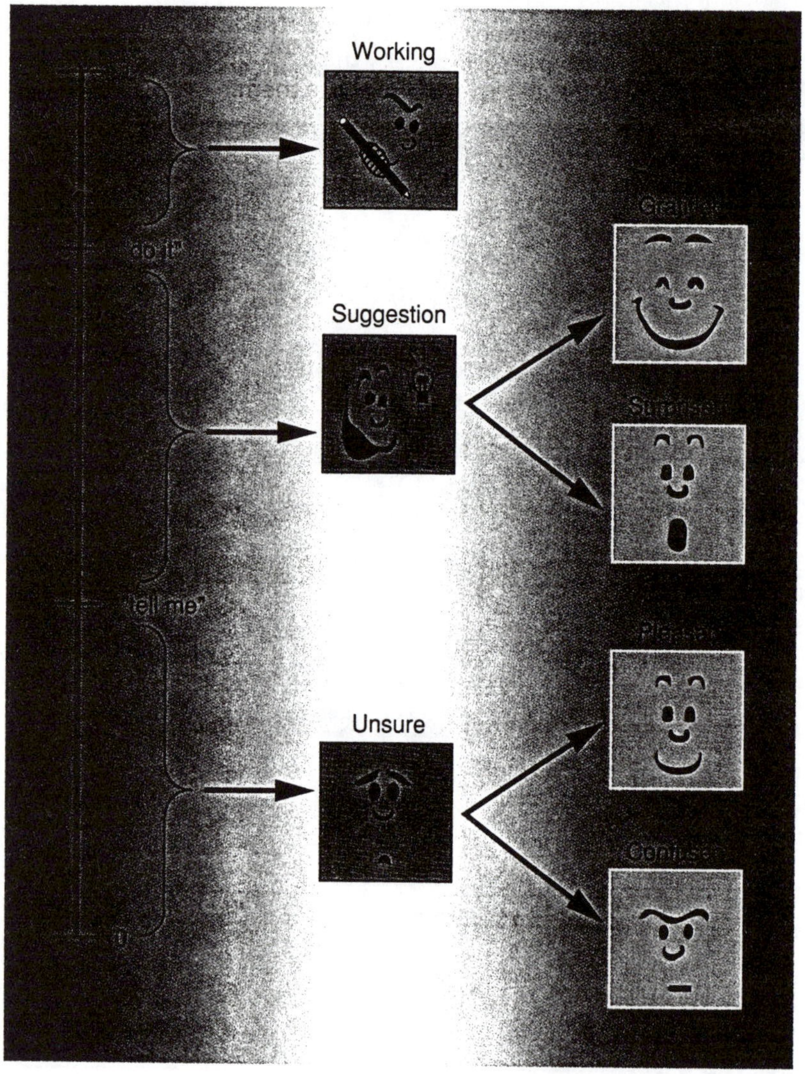

Figure 5. Simple caricatures convey the state of the agent to the user.

The agent does not only predict which action is appropriate for the current situation. It also measures its confidence in each prediction. The confidence level is determined by whether or not all the nearest neighbors recommended the same action, how close/distant the nearest neighbors are, and how many examples the agent has memorized (a measure of the accuracy of the correlation weights).

Two thresholds determine how the agent uses its prediction. When the confidence level is above the "do-it" threshold, then the agent autonomously takes the action on behalf of the user. In that case, it writes a report for the user about the action it automated. The user can ask the agent for its report of automated actions any time. If the confidence level is above the "tell-me" threshold, then the agent will offer its suggestion to the user, but will wait for the user's confirmation to automate the action. The user is responsible for setting the "tell-me" and "do-it" thresholds for actions at levels where the user feels comfortable. For example, if the user feels paranoid about the agent autonomously deleting messages, then the user can set the "do-it" threshold for that action at a maximum.

The agent communicates its internal state to the user via facial expressions (see Figure 5). These appear in a small window on the user's screen. The faces have a functional purpose: they make it possible for the user to get an update on what the agent is doing "in the blink of an eye." There are faces for "thinking" (the agent is comparing the current situation to memorized situations), "working" (the agent is automating an action), "suggestion" (the agent has a suggestion), "unsure" (the agent does not have enough confidence in its suggestion), and so forth. The "pleased" and "confused" face help the user gain information about the competence of the agent (if the agent never offers its suggestion, but it always shows a pleased face after the user takes an action, then clearly the "tell-me" threshold should be lowered. The agents have deliberately all been drawn as simple cartoon faces, in order not to encourage unwarranted attribution of human-level intelligence.

The Maxims agent gradually gains competence by observing the user and acquiring more examples. In order to deal with this slow start problem, two additional competence acquisition schemes exist. First of all, it is possible for the user to instruct the agent explicitly. If the user does not want to wait for the agent to pick up a certain pattern, then the user can create a hypothetical situation and show the agent what should be done. This functionality is imple-

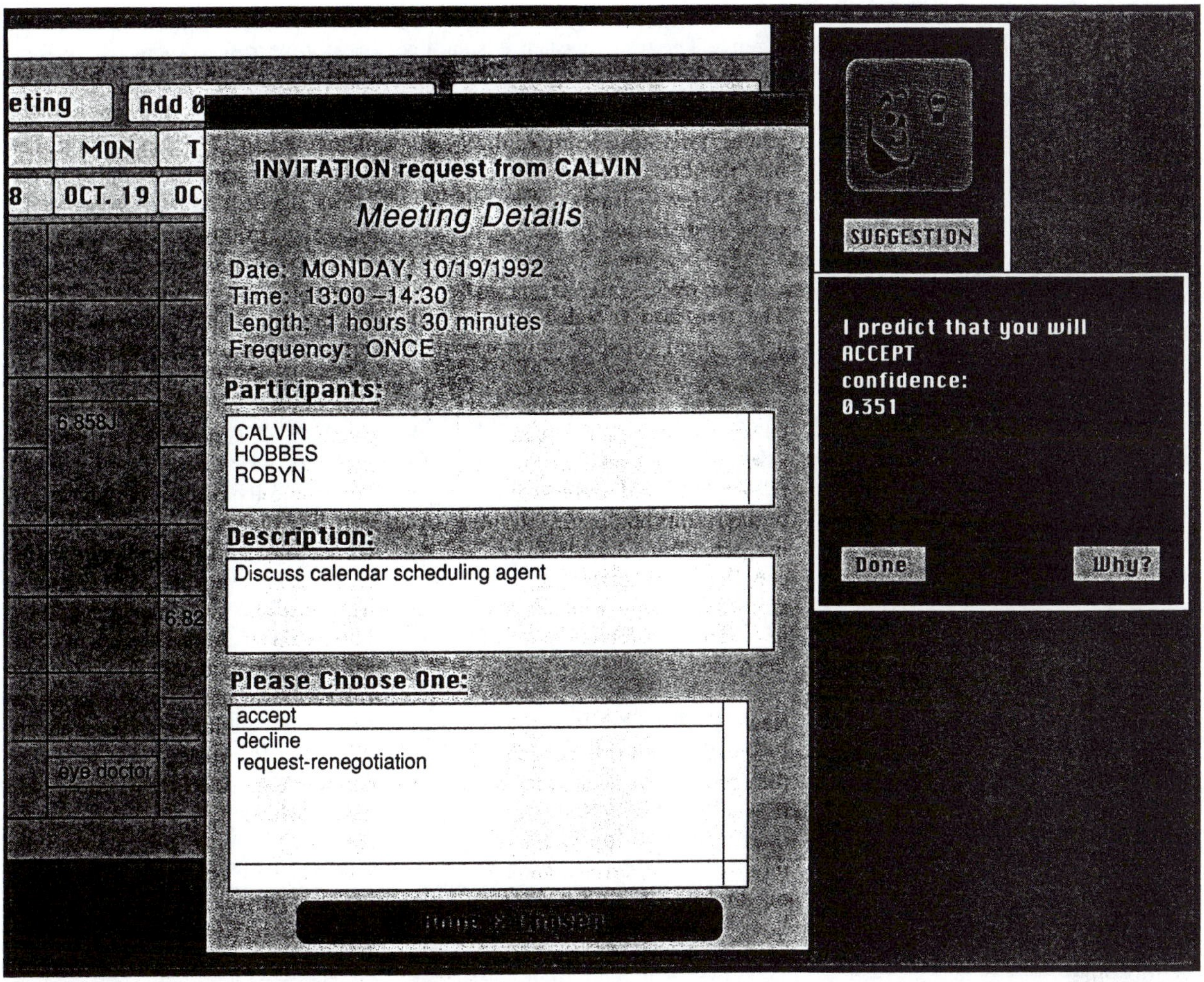

Figure 6. The calendar agent offers its suggestion to the user. The user can accept, take a different action or ask for an explanation.

mented by adding the example to the agent's memory, including "wildcards" for the features not specified in the hypothetical situation. For instance, the user can create a hypothetical message from Negroponte and show the agent that message has high priority. The new situation-action pair will match all situations in which an email message has been received from Negroponte. By varying the way in which such hypothetical examples are treated when selecting an action and when compiling statistics, both *default* and *hard-and-fast rules* can be implemented within the memory-based learning framework [11].

A second method that allows the agent to start from more than scratch is multiagent collaboration. When the agent does not have enough confidence in its prediction (confidence that is less than the "tell-me" threshold), it asks for help from other agents assisting other users with email. The agent sends part of the description of the situation to other agents via email and awaits their response. For example, if a new Media Lab user/agent pair receives a message from Negroponte, then that agent will ask other agents what it should do with that message. Some other agents will recommend that the message is important and should be immediately presented to the user for reading. The agent will make a prediction based on the different suggestions that are returned. The agent gradually learns which other agents are trustworthy sources of information for certain classes of problems. Every agent models how much it trusts other agents' advice. The trust level is increased or decreased when the action eventually taken by the user is compared with the recommendations (and confidence levels) of peer agents. The multiagent communication is an excellent method for transfer of information and competence among different users in a workgroup.

Meeting Scheduling Agent

The learning agent just described is generic. It can be attached to any application, provided the application is scriptable and recordable. The same agent was attached to a meeting scheduling software package [10, 11]. The resulting agent assists a user with the scheduling of meetings (accept/reject, schedule, reschedule, negotiate meeting times, etc.). The meetings scheduling agent is again implemented in MCL (see Figure 6). Meeting scheduling is another example of a task that fulfills the criteria for learning interface agents: the behavior of users is repetitive, but nevertheless very different for individual users. Some people prefer meetings in the morning, others in the afternoon. Some group meetings, others spread them out. Different people have different criteria for which meetings are important, which meeting initiators are important (and should be accommodated), and so on. The learning interface agent approach is ideally suited for assisting the user in a very personalized way by automating the scheduling task according to the unique habits of the user.

Both the Maxims agent and the meeting scheduling agent have been tested by real users. The results of these user tests are very encouraging. Users are eager to try out interface agents. They welcome whatever help they can get with their work overload. Users reported they felt comfortable delegating tasks to the agents. The tests revealed it is important to provide the agent with an extensive set of features to describe situations. The more features the agent has, the better the agent performs. The useless features eventually become disregarded by the agent (the weights become 0 because they do not correlate with certain actions). The tests also revealed that several areas need further improvement. First, the agents have to be made to run faster, and second, users requested they be able to instruct the agent to forget or disregard some of their behavior. Figure 7 shows some of the results obtained with the meeting scheduling agent. The agent's confidence in correct predictions increases with time, while its confidence in wrong predictions tends to decrease.

Figure 7. Typical results from a learning meeting scheduling agent. The confidence level in correct predictions increases with time, while the confidence level in wrong predictions tends to decrease.

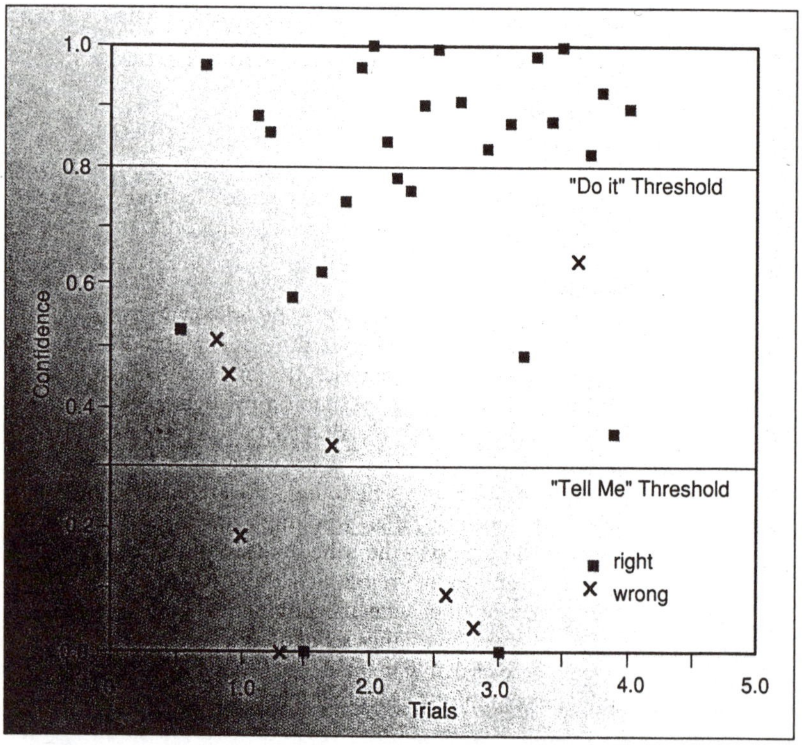

News Filtering Agent

Probably one of the more widely useful agents is an agent that helps the user select articles from a continuous stream of news [22, 23]. As more and more information becomes available on the network (see World Wide Web, on-line news feeds, etc.), users become more and more desperate for tools that will help them filter this stream of information and find articles of interest to them.

NewT is a system that helps the user filter Usenet Netnews. It is implemented in C++ on a Unix platform. A user can create one or many "news agents" and train them by means of examples of articles that should or should not be selected. For example, Figure 8 shows four agents (and icons) created by a user: one for business news, one for political news, one for computer news and one for sports news. An agent is initialized by giving it some positive and negative examples of articles to be retrieved. The agent performs a full text analysis (using the vector-space model [20] for documents) to retrieve the words in the text that may be relevant. It also remembers the structured information about the article, such as the author, source, assigned indices, and so forth. The user can also program the agent explicitly and fill out a set of templates of articles that should be selected (e.g., select all articles by Michael Schrage in the *Los Angeles Times*).

Once an agent has been bootstrapped, it will start recommending articles to the user. The user can give it positive or negative feedback for articles or portions of articles recommended. For example, the user can highlight a word or paragraph and give selective positive or negative feedback. The user can also select the author or source and give positive and negative feedback.

This will increase or decrease the probability that the agent will recommend similar articles in the future. The current implementation only performs content filtering, in the sense that the agent tries to correlate the positive and negative feedback with the contents of the article. It does not perform "social filtering," which would mean agents of different users would exchange recommendations with one another. However, a weaker form of social filtering is implemented in the NewT system: a user can train an agent for a while and then create a duplicate of that agent and give it to another user.

The NewT agents were tested by a group of 12 users. A larger group is

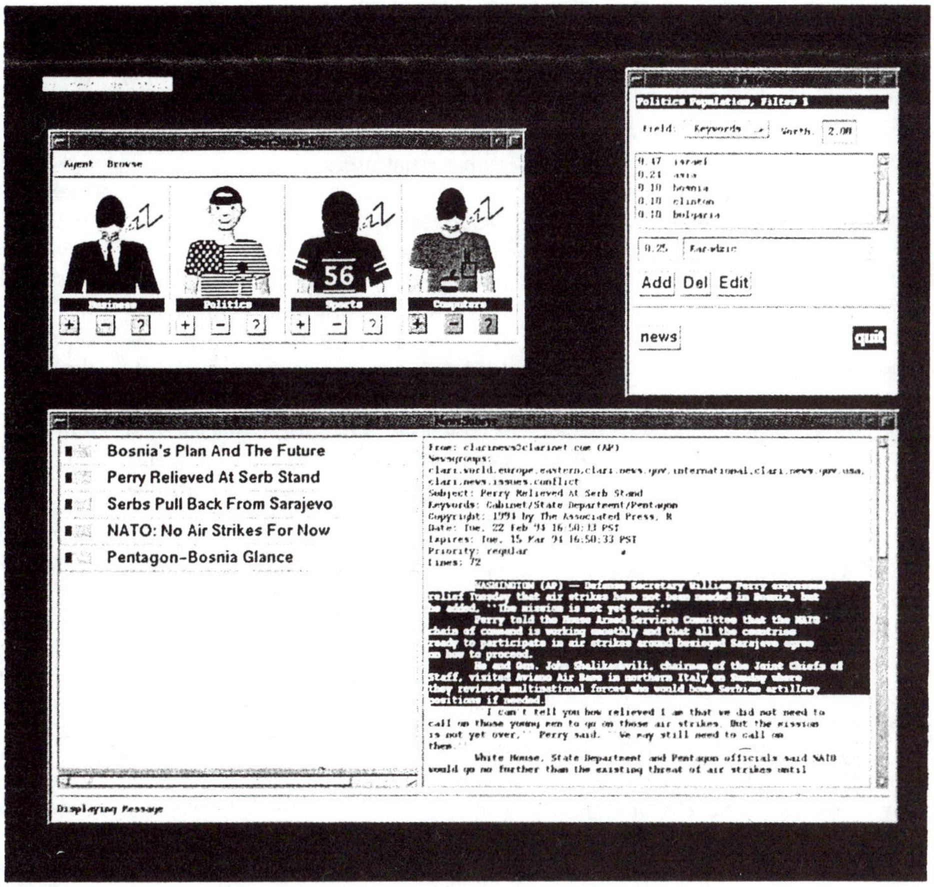

Figure 8. The NewT personalized news filtering system. A user can create a set of agents that assist the user with the filtering of an on-line news source. The agents are trained by means of positive and negative examples of articles to be selected or not selected, respectively.

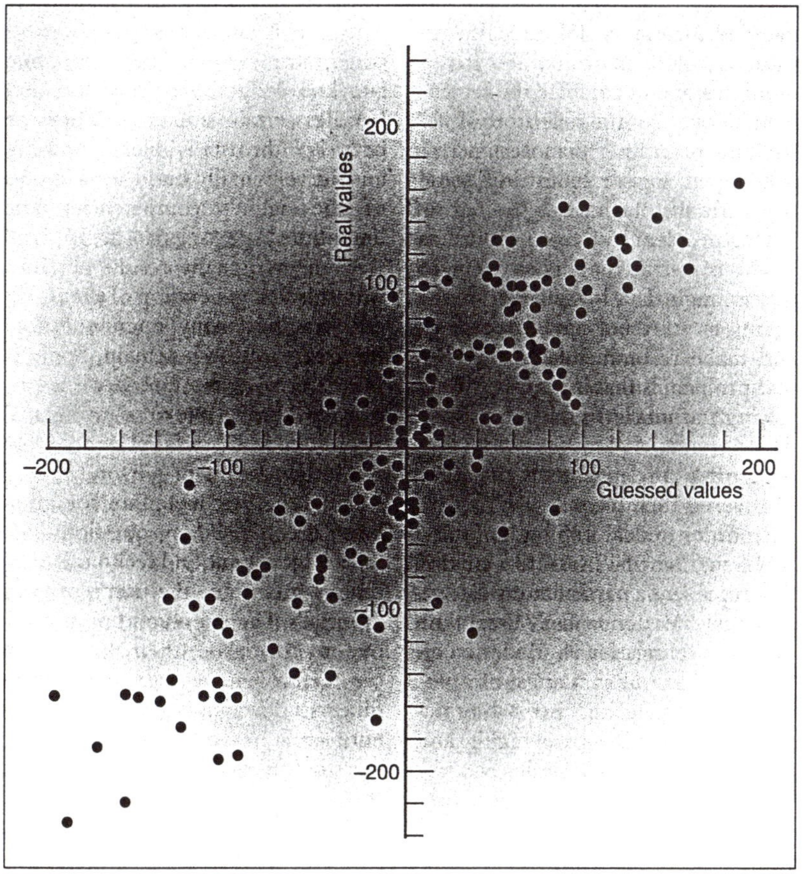

Figure 9. Results obtained with the entertainment selection agents. The Y-axis represents actual values assigned by users to items. The X-axis represents values guessed by the agents based on correlations among users.

using the system on a daily basis. As is the case with the other agent systems previously described, the NewT agents are not meant to automate all of the user's news interests. The agents are able to recommend articles to the user that concern topics (or authors or sources) in which the user has shown a continued interest. The user is still responsible for browsing the news sources to find less predictably interesting articles. Once such articles have been discovered, the user can train the agent to select those kinds of articles in the future. Again, the results obtained with the news agents were very promising. Users liked using the system and found it very useful. The main limitation of the system is its restriction to keywords only. However, if a method for deeper semantic analysis of texts becomes available (e.g., as a result of natural language understanding research), this deeper representation can be learned by using the same statistical learning techniques as are currently used for relevant keywords.

Entertainment Selection Agent

A fourth and final application area is entertainment selection. Of all four applications discussed, this one might have the best potential to become the next "killer application." Currently, critics publish reviews and recommendations which are meant for a large, general audience, but no individualized mechanisms exist to help people select movies, books, television and radio shows based on their personal tastes. However, as soon as entertainment becomes more interactive, agents can offer personalized, "readership of one" recommendations and critiques. Ringo is a personalized music recommendation system implemented on Unix platform in Perl. A similar system was built for recommending science fiction books [7]. The agents in these system use "social filtering." They do not attempt to correlate the user's interests with the contents of the items recommended. Instead, they rely solely on correlations between different users.

In these systems, every user has an agent that memorizes which books or music albums its user has evaluated, and how much the user liked them. Then, agents compare themselves with other agents. An agent finds other agents that are correlated, that is, agents that have values for similar items and whose values are positively correlated to the values of this agent. Agents accept recommendations from other correlated agents. Basically, what this means is that, if user A and user B have related musical tastes, and A has evaluated an album positively which B has not yet evaluated, then that album is recommended to user B. The actual algorithm is slightly more complex in the sense that agents combine the recommendations from a collection of related agents, rather than a single related agent. Figure 9 illustrates some of the results obtained.

One problem with this approach is how to bootstrap the whole system, so that enough data is available for the agents to start noticing correlations and make recommendations. A second problem is that users can end up relying too much on the recommendation system, and may not enter into the system any new items that they discovered themselves.

In order to deal with both of these problems, "virtual users" are created that represent a particular taste, (e.g., a virtual "Madonna fan" user, who has high ratings for all Madonna albums and no other ratings, or a virtual "cyberspace fan" user, who rates all books on cyberspace highly and has no other ratings). Similarly, a virtual user can be created for a publishing company, like the "MIT Press fan" who rates all MIT Press books highly. By entering such virtual user data into the system, the agent system can bootstrap itself, and agents for actual users can correlate themselves with virtual users.

Discussion

As computers are used for more tasks and become integrated with more services, users will need help dealing with the information and work overload. Interface agents radically change the style of human-computer interaction. The user delegates a range of tasks to personalized agents that can act on the user's behalf. We have modeled an interface agent after the metaphor of a personal assistant. The agent gradually learns how to better assist the user by:

- Observing and imitating the user
- Receiving positive and negative feedback from the user
- Receiving explicit instructions from the user
- Asking other agents for advice

These agents have been shown to tackle two of the hardest problems involved in building interface agents. The agents are *competent:* they become more helpful, as they accumulate knowledge about how the user handles certain situations. They can be *trusted:* the user is able to gradually and incrementally build up a model of the agent's competencies and limitations.

Even though the results obtained with this first generation of agents are encouraging, many open questions for future research remain. Some of these are user interface issues: Should there be one or many agents? Should agents use facial expressions and other means of personification? What is the best metaphor for interface agents? Other questions are more algorithmic and technical: How can we guarantee the user's privacy, especially if agents communicate with one another about their users? How can heterogeneous agents, built by different developers and using different techniques, collaborate? How can a system of incentives be devised, so that users are motivated to share the knowledge their experienced agents have learned? Most importantly, from a legal standpoint, should a user be held responsible for his or her agent's actions and transactions?

Acknowledgments

Beerud Sheth, Robyn Kozierok, Yezdi Lashkari, Max Metral, Carl Feynman, Upendra Shardanand, Cecile Pham and Henry Lieberman were responsible for many of the concepts and for the implementation of the four prototype agents discussed. Christie Davidson, Yezdi Lashkari and Henry Lieberman helped in the preparation of the article. C

About the Author:

PATTIE MAES is an assistant professor at the MIT Media Laboratory. Her research interests are in the areas of Artificial Intelligence, Artificial Life and Human-Computer Interaction. In particular, she is interested in modeling and building autonomous agents. **Author's Present Address:** The Media Laboratory, MIT Building E15-305B, 20 Ames St, Cambridge, MA 02139; email: pattie@media.mit.edu.

References

1. Chin, D. Intelligent interfaces as agents. In J. Sullivan and S. Tyler, eds., *Intelligent User Interfaces.* ACM Press, N.Y., 1991.
2. Crowston, K. and Malone, T. Intelligent software agents. *BYTE, 13,* 13 (Dec. 1988), 267–271.
3. Cypher, A. EAGER: Programming repetitive tasks by example. In *Proceedings of CHI'91.* ACM Press, N.Y., 1991, pp. 33–39.
4. Dent, L. Boticario, J. Mc Dermott, J. Mitchell, T. and Zabowski, D. A personal learning apprentice. In *Proceedings of the National Conference on Artificial Intelligence.* MIT Press, Cambridge, Mass., 1992.
5. Don, A. Anthropomorphism: From Eliza to Terminator 2, panel description. In *Proceedings of CHI'92.* ACM Press, N.Y., 1992, pp. 67–70.
6. Dorner, S. Eudora Reference Manual. Qualcomm Inc., 1992.
7. Feynman, C. Nearest neighbor and maximum likelihood methods for social information filtering. Internal report, MIT, Dec. 1993.
8. Kay, A. Computer software. In *Sci. Amer. 251,* 3 (Mar. 1984), 191–207.
9. Kay, A. User Interface: A personal

view. In B. Laurel, ed., *The Art of Human-Computer Interface Design*. Addison-Wesley, Reading, Mass., 1990.

10. Kozierok, R. and Maes, P. A learning interface agent for scheduling meetings. In *Proceedings of ACM SIGCHI International Workshop on Intelligent User Interfaces*. ACM Press, N.Y., 1993, pp. 81–88.

11. Kozierok, R. A learning approach to knowledge acquisition for intelligent interface agents. SM Thesis, Department of Electrical Eng. and Computer Science, MIT, May 1993.

12. Lai, K. Malone, T. and Yu, K. Object Lens: A "spreadsheet" for cooperative work. *ACM Trans. Office Inf. Syst. 6*, 4 (Apr. 1988), 332–353.

13. Lashkari, Y., Metral, M. and Maes, P. Collaborative interface agents. In *Proceedings of the National Conference on Artificial Intelligence*. MIT Press, Cambridge, Mass., 1994.

14. Laurel, B. Interface agents: Metaphors with character. In B. Laurel, ed., *The Art of Human-Computer Interface Design*. Addison-Wesley, Reading, Mass., 1990.

15. Lieberman, H. Mondrian: A teachable graphical editor. In A. Cypher, ed., *Watch what I do: Programming by Demonstration*, MIT Press, Cambridge, Mass., 1993.

16. Maes, P. and Kozierok, R. Learning interface agents. In *Proceedings of the AAAI'93 Conference*. MIT Press, Cambridge, Mass., pp. 459–465.

17. Myers, B. *Creating User Interfaces by Demonstration*. Academic Press, Boston, Mass., 1988.

18. Myers, B., ed. Demonstrational interfaces: Coming soon? In *Proceedings of CHI'91*. ACM Press, N.Y., 1991, pp. 393–396.

19. Negroponte, N. *The Architecture Machine; Towards a more Human Environment*. MIT Press, Cambridge, Mass., 1970.

20. Salton, G. and McGill, M. *Introduction to Modern Information Retrieval*. McGraw-Hill, N.Y., 1983.

21. Schneiderman, B. Direct manipulation: A step beyond programming languages. *IEEE Comput. 16*, 8 (Aug. 1988), 57–69.

22. Sheth, B. and Maes, P. Evolving agents for personalized information filtering. In *Proceedings of the Ninth Conference on Artificial Intelligence for Applications*. IEEE Computer Society Press, 1993.

23. Sheth, B. A learning approach to personalized information filtering. SM Thesis, Department of Electrical Eng. and Computer Science, MIT, Feb. 1994.

24. Stanfill, C. and Waltz, D. Toward memory-based reasoning. *Comm. ACM 29*, 12, (Dec. 1986), 1213–1228.

25. Sullivan, J.W. and Tyler, S.W., eds. *Intelligent User Interfaces*. ACM Press, N.Y., 1991.

This research is sponsored by Apple Computer, by the NSF under grant number IRI-92056688, and by the News in the Future Consortium of the MIT Media Laboratory.

Beyond Intelligent Interfaces: Exploring, Analyzing, and Creating Success Models of Cooperative Problem Solving

GERHARD FISCHER & BRENT REEVES

Department of Computer Science and Institute of Cognitive Science, University of Colorado, Campus Box 430, Boulder, CO 80309

Received March 1991, Revised August 1991

Abstract. Cooperative problem-solving systems are computer-based systems that augment a person's ability to create, reflect, design, decide, and reason. Our work focuses on supporting cooperative problem solving in the context of high-functionality computer systems. We show how the conceptual framework behind a given system determines crucial aspects of the system's behavior. Several systems are described that attempted to address specific shortcomings of prevailing assumptions, resulting in a new conceptual framework. To further test this resulting framework, we conducted an empirical study of a success model of cooperative problem solving between people in a large hardware store. The conceptual framework is instantiated in a number of new system-building efforts, which are described and discussed.

• • •

•

•

•

3. Success Models for Cooperative Problem Solving

To deepen our understanding of the problems of high-functionality systems and find ways to overcome these problems, we engaged in a search for success models of such systems. The success model idea has proven to be of great value. We have previously analyzed skiing as a success model [4] and derived architectural components for computer-based learning environments [35] from this analysis. In a similar fashion, the ideas behind spreadsheets were used as guiding principles in system-building efforts in other domains [6,36–37]. Studying success models can provide us with equally important insights as studying the role of failures [38] and their impact on the advancement of design.

In this section, we describe a study done at McGuckin Hardware, argue why it is relevant to these issues, and show how the store has successfully addressed the difficult problems mentioned previously. We then place the study in the larger context of research in situated cognition.

3.1. McGuckin: An Empirical Study

A preliminary analysis indicated the McGuckin Hardware in Boulder, Colorado, might be an ideal candidate for a success model. McGuckin carries more than 350,000 different line items in 33,000 square feet of retail space. The store's superior reputation among its customers and its continued growth and profitability make it a success model.

To get a better understanding of just how the "system" operates, we asked McGuckin Hardware for permission to observe and record interactions between customers and sales agents. Some of the dialogues were transcribed from audiotapes and carefully analyzed. Videotapes would have been a superior medium, but would have interfered too much with store operations.

The decision to observe directly as people do problem solving and design in the real world was made as a result of considering the perspective of situated cognition research. Lave [10], Schoen [7], and others have shown how problem solving in daily activity is shaped by the dynamic encounter between the culturally endowed mind and its total context. This leads to a vision of cognition as a dialectic between persons acting and the settings in which their activity is constituted. Lave [10] argued that theoretically charged, unexamined, normative models of thinking lose their descriptive and predictive power when research is moved to everyday settings and relaxes its grip on the structuring of activities.

The following dialogues illustrate the inherent difficulties in high-functionality systems mentioned above (for additional details of our study see Reeves [39]).

Users do not know about the existence of tools. In this dialogue, the customer is unsure about how to attach a sign to a metal pole. The customer does not know of self-tapping bolts and therefore cannot ask for them. Even if we assume a complete understanding of the problem, this is not enough to guarantee the knowledge of the best tool for the problem. Here the customer ends up buying a fastener that is introduced and explained by the salesperson.

Dialogue$_1$: Attaching a Sign to a Square Metal Pole[1]

1. C: *I'm looking for a small fastener maybe one-sixteenth.*
2. S: Okay. Plastic? Metal?
3. C: *Well, what I've got is to fasten a sign on to a square pole. I've got a hole in the top and it fits fine and I got to get one on the bottom.*
   `After looking at several fasteners, and asking a few more questions, the salesperson suggests a certain type of fastener.`

4. S: How about a self-tapping bolt?
   Picks one up and shows it.
5. C: *Well, what uhh, well, this would probably do it, what about, would it come back out?*
6. S: Oh sure. It'd come back out.
7. C: *But once it's in?*
8. S: As long as the hole is smaller than this thing, you can thread it in and out.

Users don't know how to access tools. The next dialogue shows that it can be difficult just to find items you "know" exist. The customer is specific about the wanted item and even seems to know the store fairly well, but still cannot find the item.

Dialogue$_2$: Finding Tool Clips

1. C: *I need clips for tools where you shove it up in them and it holds*
2. S: Yeah.
3. C: *I mean not just a single clip, a bunch of them. We tried in housewares, the cheap little ones, tools only have like funny kind of ones. Where else could they be?*
4. S: Garden center, for rakes and shovels and things like that
5. C: *Would it be there?*
6. S: Yeah.
7. C: *Okay, I know where that is, thanks.*

Users do not know when to use tools. The interaction shown in Dialogue$_3$ involves a search for scales to weigh small animals and illustrates the concept of *applicability conditions*: the conditions under which an item can be used, especially for "unintended" purposes. The salesperson is able to recognize a crucial element: namely, that there be a platform large enough to hold something of a certain approximate size and weight. He helps the customer to know *when* to use a given tool, even though that use might not have been intended by the designer of the tool. The fact that a scale is intended for food is less important than those features.

Dialogue$_3$ also illustrates the use of *differential descriptions*. The customer describes the intended item "differentially" in terms of an example, building on what the environment has to offer. The customer uses an example item (the "little tiny ones over here") to differentially describe the intended solution. The salesperson extracts the crucial information and suggests an item intended for a different domain, yet useful for accomplishing the described task.

In Dialogue$_4$ the customer wants strength, but the salesperson has to point out a crucial feature of that strength: that it comes at the expense of brittleness.

Dialogue$_3$: Scales for Small Animals

1. C: *I'm looking for some scales and I saw some little tiny ones over here, but I need something that has a large platform on it, to weigh small animals on.*
   Holds hands about 18 inches apart.
2. S: I would think something in our housewares department, for weighing food and things like that. Go on down to the last isle on the left.
3. C: *Okay.*

Dialogue$_4$: Hardened Bolts

1. C: *So if I were going to hook something would this be the best thing? What I'm going to have is I'm going to drill into the cement and have it sticking out.*
2. S: You going to have this sticking out, just the shaft of the bolt? holding a bolt and pointing to the unthreaded shaft.
3. C: *Right.*
4. S: Hmm. Interesting problem.
5. C: *A hardened bolt would give me more . . .*
6. S: Yeah, but it'll shear, they're more brittle. I don't know if you'd be any better off with a hardened.

Users can not combine or adapt tools for special uses. Although the combination in Dialogue$_5$ is simple, it does illustrate how tools can be combined in various ways. The customer doesn't know why the salesperson suggests a certain combination of tools, but ventures a guess. The salesperson allows the suggestion, but then states his reason.

Dialogue$_5$: Combining Simple Tools

1. S: After deciding that a three-sixteenth inch wire is to be looped around a half-inch bolt, which is mounted in cement
   You want a small enough loop, put it between two washers. Picks up two washers and places them on the shaft of a bolt.
2. C: *Small enough loop.*
3. S: Yeah.
4. C: *Why between two washers, so it won't rub?*
5. S: Yeah, so it won't slide off. Probably won't.

Observing interactions like these confirmed the previous analysis of the difficulties of using high-functionality systems. In addition, it raised several other issues that must be considered in building cooperative problem-solving systems.

Incremental problem specifications. Dialogue$_6$ shows that there is a close relationship between defining specifications incrementally, as seen here, and establishing shared knowledge, as will be seen in the next dialogue. The distinction is a subtle, yet useful one. Shared knowledge has more to do with establishing a common reference point with which to discuss a situation, and less to do with the specific process of identifying relevant parts of the problem domain.

Dialogue$_6$: Incrementally Refining a Query

1. C: *I need a cover for a barbecue.*
2. S: (Leading customer down an isle where several grills are lined up and accessories are displayed) Okay . . . what have we got here . . . chaise, chair barbecue grill cover. . . . Does that look kind of like what you got? (Pointing to one of the grills.) Similar? No?
3. C: *No.*
4. S: Take any measurements?
5. C: *No.*
6. S: That's a good guess there. (Pointing to a one-burner grill.)
7. C: *It's a double burner one.*
8. S: 52 inches. That's the total length it'll cover. (Measuring with the tape and holding the tape over one of the grills.)
9. C: *Yeah. I know it's not that big at all.*
10. S: You saying about 18 by 18. Well, this is 27, it'll cover up to here. (Using measuring tape again and pointing.)
11. C: *I need two.*
12. S: A couple . . . in that brand, that's all I have. Here are these Weber ones, thicker material and all that. Here are some smaller ones.
13. C: *I'll take this one.*
14. S: We'll be getting more of these pretty soon.
15. C: *You'll have them by Christmas?*
16. S: Hopefully Thursday.

Achieving shared understanding. Between the time a customer begins to interact with a sales agent and the time the customer leaves with a "satisficing" solution [23], a shared understanding must be created between the two cooperating agents. The customer must begin to appreciate relevant parts of the solution domain and the sales agent must understand the problem in enough depth to make reasonable suggestions. Dialogue$_7$ shows how establishing shared understanding is a gradual process in which each person participates, sometimes ignoring questions, sometimes volunteering information, and sometimes identifying miscommunications. Illustrated also are the problems of knowing about the existence of tools and understanding the results that they produce. The customer wants to fasten a sign to a square metal pole. The top of the sign has been fastened via a preexisting hole, but the bottom is still unattached. The customer learns about certain fasteners while the salesperson learns about the specific problem. Their shared understanding increases as each in turn asks questions and makes suggestions that are critiqued by the other.

Dialogue$_7$: Attaching a Sign to a Square Metal Pole[2]

1. C: *I'm looking for a smaller fastener. Maybe one-sixteenth.*

2. S: Okay. Plastic? Metal?
3. C: *Well, what I've got is to fasten a sign onto a square pole. I've got a hole in the top and it fits fine and I've got to get one on the bottom.*
4. S: Pole have holes in it?
5. C: *Yeah. I had a one-eighth bolt, but it's too big. Need something smaller than that.*
6. S: Round pole? Square Pole?
7. C: *Square pole.*
8. S: (Picking up a fastener and showing it) You tried these?
9. C: (Scrutinizing the fastener.) *Hmmmm.*
10. S: You've got to have a five-sixteenths hole and you fold this thing up and stick it in. Would that work?
11. C: *It's got to be five-sixteenths?*
12. S: Yes. The size of the shaft on this thing. (Pointing to the fastener.)
13. C: *It's not that big.*
14. S: No way to drill it?
15. C: *No.*
16. S: No. What did you use the first time?
17. C: *I tried a one-eighth inch.*
18. S: How thick is the metal in the pole?
19. C: *Oh, probably about one eighth inch.* (Pointing to a certain fastener.) *How about these?*
20. S: (Picking one up and showing the moving parts.) These work on hollow-core doors.
21. C: *Yeah.*
22. S: (Walking over to a different kind of fastener and picking it up) I don't know if this would be strong enough. Still need a three sixteenth hole. If the wind is blowing hard it might give way. Just putting it in with a screw-driver?
23. C: *Yeah.*
24. S: How about a self-tapping bolt? (Picks one up and shows it.) Put that in, tighten it down, (points to tip), that's a thread cutting thread there.
25. C: *Well, what, uhmm, well, this would probably do it. What about, would it come back out?*
26. S: Oh sure. It would come back out.
27. C: *But once it's in?*
28. S: As long as the hole is smaller than this thing, you can thread it in and out.

Integration between problem setting and problem solving. Dialogue$_8$ shows an interaction in which a customer wanted to buy heaters, then decided to reconceptualize the problem from one of "adding heat," to one of "retaining heat." This appears to be a trivial reframing and hardly worth notice, but we will argue that understanding exactly this kind of reframing is crucial to building cooperative problem-solving systems. The problem *itself* was redefined.

Dialogue$_8$: Generating Versus Containing Heat

1. C: *I want to get a couple of heaters for a downstairs hallway.*
2. S: What are you doing? What are you trying to heat?
3. C: *I'm trying to heat a downstairs hallway.*
4. S: How high are the ceilings?
5. C: *Normal, about eight feet.*
6. S: Okay, how about these here?
   They proceed to agree on two heaters.
7. C: *Well, the reason it gets so cold is that there's a staircase at the end of the hallway*
8. S: Where do the stairs lead?
9. C: *They go up to a landing with a cathedral ceiling.*
10. S: Ok, maybe you can just put a door across the stairs, or put a ceiling fan up to blow the hot air back down.

Summary. The findings of the McGuckin study can be summarized as follows:

Natural Language is less important than Natural Communication. People rarely spoke in complete, grammatical sentences, yet managed to communicate in a natural way. In fact, most of the dialogues shown here had to be "cleaned up" for readability. The study provided convincing evidence that the support for *natural communication* [29], allowing for breakdowns, clarifying dialogues, explanations, etc., is more important for cooperative problem solving than being able to parse syntactically complex sentences. One objective of future human-computer communication research should therefore be to understand the processes of intention communication and recognition well enough to enable a system to participate in a natural dialogue with its user [40].

Multiple Specification Techniques. Customers used a great variety of specification techniques such as bringing in a broken part, pointing to an item in a catalog or in the store, and giving general descriptions such as "I need a lock that qualifies for cheaper insurance rates."

Mixed Initiative Dialogues. People were flexible in the roles they played during a problem-solving episode. They easily switched from asking to explaining, from learning to teaching. Because $Dialogue_7$ is the longest, it probably shows this best. The structure of these dialogues was determined neither by the customer nor by the sales agent, but clearly indicated mixed initiative [28] determined by the specifics of the joint problem-solving effort.

Management of Trouble. Many breakdowns and misunderstandings occurred during the observed problem-solving episodes, but in almost all cases clarifying dialogues allowed their recovery. Problem solving among humans cannot be characterized by the absence of trouble, but by the identification and repair of breakdowns [8]. $Dialogue_6$ and $Dialogue_7$ contain examples of this.

Simultaneous Exploration of Problem and Solution Spaces. Customers and sales agents worked within both problem and solution spaces simultaneously, or at least alternatively. Typically the problem owner (customer) had a better grasp of the problem space and the problem solver (sales agent) had a better understanding of the solution space, but over time these spaces converged until there was a large enough intersection of shared knowledge within which potential solutions could be evaluated. This is seen in $Dialogue_7$ in which the customer knows what needs to be done but needs a better understanding of the possible solutions, and the salesperson knows how many different fasteners work but needs to understand the specific application.

Humans operate within the physical world. Although perhaps obvious, system designers overlook the fact that people use elements of the physical world as sources of information, as reminders, and in general as extensions of their own knowledge and reasoning systems. In most of the dialogues that deal with fasteners, both the customer and salesperson held the items and used them to guide and clarify the discussion. For example, in $Dialogue_5$, the salesperson picked up two washers and placed them on the shaft of the bolt, leaving a small gap between them to show where the cable would go, and how the loop needs to be small enough to be guided or constrained by the washers.

Humans make use of distributed intelligence. Much of people's intelligent behavior results from the interaction of mental processes with the objects and constraints of the world, and much behavior takes place through a cooperative process with others. Collaborators challenge each other's analysis of the problem and help to achieve creative solutions. One thing that surfaced in discussions with salespeople is that when they send a customer to another department, they count on the customer being able to find the items, but also expect another salesperson to be available there.

3.2. A Situated Cognition Perspective

The perspective of situated cognition researchers is important in this analysis of cooperative problem-solving success models. McGuckin Hardware provides an example of what situated cognition researchers have been claiming: much of problem solving is fundamentally related to the larger context in which the problem gets perceived, framed, and eventually resolved. Suchman [8] argued that plans are just one of the resources in the problem-solving process, not *the* guiding principles. The McGuckin study confirms this view of plans: customers do have plans, but these plans are just one resource, not the primary guide.

Lave [10] argued that the problem-solving context plays a crucial role in problem framing. The McGuckin study confirmed this finding. As customers interacted with the wide variety of hardware (e.g. two isles of fasteners), they were able to recast their perception of the problem they came in to solve.

In a critique of the approach technical rationality has encouraged professional practitioners to take toward ill-defined problems. Schoen [7] argued against abstract principles and for skills developed in domain-specific problem solving, emphasizing the role that problem setting plays. Real problems are never given, but "must be constructed from the materials of problematic situations which are puzzling, troubling, and uncertain."

The setting of a problem is as important as the problem itself. The word "setting" means two things: (1) the physical and social environment (the "context") in which a problem solver acts, and (2) the process of defining the problem. The problem context provides key resources in solving the problem, because it affects how we come to perceive the problem and the resources available to us.

Carraher, Carraher, and Schliemann [41] described how important the setting was to Brazilian school children who worked as street vendors. On the street, they were quite accurate in their calculations (98 percent correct), but when given mathematically identical problems outside the marketplace context, their accuracy dropped to a dismal 37 percent.

Attempts have been made to bring more of the environment into consideration in analyzing problem solving. Larkin et al. [42] studied several issues, such as the interaction between the person solving a problem and external memory aids such as paper and pencil, and representing situations that change over time. Situated cognition appears to push this concept of setting and problems that change over time even further into our physical environment and social relations.

When people encounter problems, these problems are embedded in an environment that provides ways in which the problem is perceived and resources with which to analyze it. Problems can be divorced neither from the social settings in which they occur, nor from the process of problem defining. The former provides structuring resources to the problem solver and the latter affects how the problem is allowed to evolve.

Problems and solutions coevolve—one cannot exist without the other. Empirical studies of people developing complex computer systems [21] have confirmed that often the problem is not to implement a given specification, but rather expressing the problem itself: deciding what problem to solve.

In the context of design problems, Rittel [43] argued that "*you cannot understand the problem without having a concept of the solution in mind; and that you cannot gather information meaningfully unless you have understood the problem but that you cannot understand the problem without information about it.*" Taken literally, this leaves no room for a beginning, but there is a way in which this view nevertheless makes sense. If one cannot begin one without the other, then the only way to proceed is with both simultaneously. In problem solving, people cannot proceed until they have a "resolution shape—a sense of an answer and a process for bringing it together with its parts" [10, p. 19].

John Dewey noted that "discovering a problem is the first step in knowing" (cited in [44]). And Wertheimer [45] observed that: "Often in great discoveries the most important thing is that a certain question is found. Envisaging, putting the productive question is often more important, often a greater achievement than the solution of a set question" (cited in VanGundy [44, p. 102]).

We are trying to understand what this means to designers of cooperative problem-solving systems. Success models of these systems provide a new perspective that informs the design of such systems built on a computing platform. Studying people at McGuckin provided an opportunity to observe "everyday cognition." These observations confirm the importance that the situated cognition perspective brings to the design of cooperative problem-solving systems.

4. Second Generation of Cooperative Problem-Solving Systems

In this section, findings from the McGuckin study are related to the framework suggested in the first section. This is followed by a description of a prototype of an integrated, domain-oriented, knowledge-based design environment.

4.1. Requirements for Cooperative Problem-Solving Systems

Beyond user interfaces. Effective human-computer communication is more than creating attractive displays on a computer screen: it requires providing the computer with a considerable body of knowledge about the world, about users, and about communication processes. This is not to say that the user interface is not of crucial importance to knowledge-based systems. Analysis of expert systems (such as the DIPMETER advisor [46]), has shown that the acceptance and real use of expert systems depends on far more than a knowledge base and an inference engine. The developers examined the relative amount of code devoted to different functions of DIPMETER and found that the *user interface portion was 42 percent* compared to 8 percent for the inference engine and 22 percent for the knowledge base. Similar data are reported for commercial knowledge-based system tools (e.g., in Intellicorp's tools, 55–60 percent of the code is interface related [47]). A good user interface is important for two groups: for the developers of knowledge-based systems and for the end-user of these systems.

The communication requirements are even more important for cooperative problem-solving systems. Because the user is actively involved in the problem-solving and decision-making process, there is an increased necessity for the interface to support the task at a level that is comprehensible by the user. In order for a knowledge-based system to support cooperative problem solving, the following components depend critically on each other:

- the structure of the knowledge and problem-solving system itself—how a system represents its problem-solving activity and retrieves the relevant portion appropriately in response to user queries
- the generation of views of this knowledge which corresponds to the needs and the knowledge of the user; for this a system must contain a model of the user
- the presentation of this knowledge on the screen; this part is mostly (explicitly or implicitly) associated with user-interface research.

Problems can be fully articulated only in the context of solving them. The McGuckin study clearly indicated that problems in realistic situations are not fixed targets. The combination of a large selection of objects and knowledgeable sales agents creates an environment in which customers can produce partial solutions and get feedback from the items in the store and from the sales agents in the form of critiques. As problem solvers tentatively explore possible solutions and evaluate how those affect their perception of the original problem, they shape the situation; in accordance with their initial appreciation of it, the situation "talks back," and they respond to the situation's back-talk [7].

The fidelity of the design situations' "back talk" must be increased. Many of the problems that are discussed at McGuckin are ill-defined. The artifacts and inventory at McGuckin are powerful to the extent that the sales agents are knowledgeable. Providing rich functionality without domain-specific expertise is not enough. In our system-building work, we originally believed that domain-oriented construction kits would be powerful enough to "talk back" by themselves, but this turned out not to be the case [31]. Construction kits support the construction of an artifact, but they do not provide any feedback on the quality of the design. Knowledgeable sales agents provide this higher level expertise and so help the situation to "talk back."

McGuckin hires experts in the various departments and considers previous experience within a field, such as plumbing, to be more important than previous sales experience in that field. The difference between working and selling experience in a field is crucial. Behind the surface or syntactic layer of the inventory, there is a semantic understanding of trade-offs, and experience in mapping specific problems to multipurpose tools.

There is a need for specialization and putting knowledge in the world. Simon [23] predicted that when a domain reaches a point where the knowledge for skillful professional practice cannot be acquired in roughly a decade, a burden on mastering all the tools and the knowledge will occur [48]. Simon predicted that the following adaptive developments will occur: (1) specialization will increase and (2) practitioners will make increasing use of books and other external reference aids in their work [49]. McGuckin addresses the tool mastery burden by (1) organizing functionality according to external task domains, and (2) incrementally making the information space relevant to the task at hand by an evolving shared understanding between customers and salespeople.

Supporting human problem-domain communication with domain-oriented architectures. The

McGuckin study illustrates the need to respond to a diverse set of tasks. There is an important need in computer science to develop domain-oriented architectures in order to avoid the pitfall of excess generality. Instead of serving all needs obscurely and insufficiently with general purpose programming languages, domain-oriented architectures serve a few needs well. The semantics of our computing environments need to be better tuned to specific domains of discourse; this involves support for different kinds of primitive entities, for specification of properties other than computational functionality, and for computational models that match the users' own models. Human-computer communication needs to be advanced to human-problem domain communication, where the computer becomes "invisible" and users have the feeling of interacting directly with a problem domain.

• • •

4. R.R. Burton, J.S. Brown, G. Fischer, "Analysis of skiing as a success model of instruction: Manipulating the learning environments to enhance skill acquisition," in *Everyday Cognition: Its Development in Social Context*, edited by B. Rogoff, J. Lave. Harvard University Press: Cambridge, MA—London, pp. 139–50, 1984.

6. G. Fischer, C. Rathke, "Knowledge-based spreadsheet systems," in *Proceedings of AAAI–88, Seventh National Conference on Artificial Intelligence (St. Paul, (MN))*, Morgan Kaufman Publishers, San Mateo, CA. 1988, pp. 802–807.

7. D.A. Schoen, *The Reflective Practitioner: How Professional Think in Action.* Basic Books: New York. 1983.

8. L.A. Suchman, *Plans and Situated Actions.* Cambridge University Press: New York, 1987.

10. J. Lave, *Cognition in Practice*, Cambridge University Press: Cambridge, UK, 1988.

21. B. Curtis, H. Krasner, N. Iscoe, "A field study of the software design process for large systems," *Communications of the ACM*, vol. 31, pp. 1268–1287, 1988.

23. H.A. Simon, *The Sciences of the Artificial*, The MIT Press, Cambridge, MA, 1981.

28. J.R. Carbonell, "Mixed-initiative man-computer instructional dialogues," Report 1971, BBN. 1970.

29. D.G. Bobrow, R.M. Kaplan, M. Kay, D.A. Norman, H. Thompson, T. Winograd, "GUS, A frame-driven dialog system," *Artificial Intelligence*, vol. 8, pp. 155–173, 1977.

31. G. Fischer, A.C. Lemke, "Construction kits and design environments: Steps toward human problem-domain communication," *Human-Computer Interaction*, vol. 3, pp. 179–222, 1988.

35. E. Wenger, *Artificial Intelligence and Tutoring Systems.* Morgan Kaufman Publishers: Los Altos, CA. 1987.

36. K.-Y. Lai, T.W. Malone, "Object lens: A 'spreadsheet' for cooperative work," in *Proceedings of the Conference on Computer-Supported Cooperative Work (CSCW '88)*, ACM, New York, 1988, pp. 115–124.

37. N. Wilde, C.H. Lewis, "Spreadsheet-based interactive graphics: From prototype to tool," in *Human Factors in Computing Systems. CHI '90 Conference Proceedings (Seattle, WA)*, ACM: New York, 1990, pp. 153–159.

38. H. Petroski, *To Engineers Is Human.* St. Martin's Press: New York, 1985.

39. B.N. Reeves, "Locating the right object in a large hardware store—An empirical study of cooperative problem solving among humans," Technical Report CU-CS-523-91, Department of Computer Science, University of Colorado, Boulder, CO, 1991.

40. T. Winograd, "A Language/Action Perspective on the Design of Cooperative Work," *Human-Computer Interaction*, vol. 3, pp. 3–30, 1988.

41. T.N. Carraher, D.W. Carraher, A.D. Schliemann, "Mathematics in the streets and in the schools," *British Journal of Development Psychology*, vol. 3., pp. 21–29, 1985.

42. J. Larkin, et al., "Expert and novice performance in solving physics problems," *Science*, vol. 208, pp. 1335–1342, 1980.

43. H.W.J. Rittel, "Second-generation design methods," in *Developments in Design Methodology*, John Wiley & Sons: New York, 1984, pp. 317–327.

44. A.B. VanGundy, *Stalking the Wild Solution: A Problem-Finding Approach to Creative Problem Solving*, Bearly Limited: Buffalo, NY, 1986.

45. M. Wertheimer, *Productive Thinking*, Harper & Row: New York, 1959.

46. R.G. Smith, "On the development of commercial expert systems," *AI Magazine*, vol. 5, pp. 61–73.

47. M. Stelzner, M.D. Williams, "The evolution of interface requirements for expert systems," in *Expert Systems: The User Interface*, Ablex Publishing Corporation: Norwood, NJ. pp. 285–306, Chapter 12, 1988.

48. F.P. Brooks, Jr., "No silver bullet, essence and accidents of software engineering," *IEEE Computer*, vol. 20, pp. 10–19, 1987.

49. D.A. Norman, *The Psychology of Everyday Things*. Basic Books: New York, 1988.

Chapter 13

Hypertext and Multimedia

In Chapter 11, we enlarged the concept of human-computer interaction to include the use of hardware and software facilitating communication, coordination, and collaboration among groups and organizations. In Chapter 12, we enlarged the concept of the human-computer interface to include computer systems that can be tailored by their users or can adapt to the behavior of their users in order to enable more productive interaction between human and machine.

In this chapter we focus on the raw material of the interaction, on the documents that often represent the tangible products of individual or collaborative use of computers. With *hypertext*, we consider how the *structure* of computerized documents can be enriched to allow more flexible browsing, searching, and retrieval of information. With *multimedia*, we consider how the *content* of documents can be enriched through the inclusion of data other than text, for example, images, sounds, and video. Hypertexts that contain multimedia are typically known as *hypermedia*.

HYPERTEXT AND HYPERMEDIA

Chapter 1 recounted the inspiration of the hypertext pioneers—Bush's visionary 1945 "MEMEX" essay, Engelbart's dramatic and influential NLS prototype, and Ted Nelson's insights into the nature and potential of hypertext. Despite this inspiration, there was relatively little progress until the mid-1980s, when workstations and development environments became powerful enough to support substantial hypertext systems.

The Xerox PARC NoteCards system (Trigg, Suchman, and Halasz; 1986; Halasz, Moran, and Trigg, 1987) was an influential research prototype, although not a successful product. Blocks of text or graphics roughly the size of an index card, called *notecards*, can be arranged and *linked* together. Different kinds of links (*typed links*) can connect objects. Notecards, electronic *fileboxes*, and links are represented iconically.

The notecards system was used as we use index cards for a research project—to formulate, structure, compare, and manage ideas. For example, if one notecard contains an hypothesis, supporting arguments can be placed on other notecards, linked to the first by links labeled "support." Opposing arguments are put on notecards with links labeled "oppose," elaborations of the hypothesis on notecards with "comment" links, and so forth. The system could be tailored to each project.

The Symbolics Document Examiner was another robust hypertext system that ran on a dying LISP machine platform in the mid-1980s (Walker, 1987, 1988, 1985 video). The Document Examiner provided instant access to the contents of well-crafted reference manuals for what was arguably the most advanced commercial programming environment of its time. It was a landmark for its well thought out interface and for being completely integrated into its environment.

In 1987, *IEEE Computer* published a special issue on hypertext. It included an overview by Jeff Conklin (1987) that is worth reading today. After arguing that the defining criterion for hypertext should be the use of machine-supported links, within or between documents, he compares and contrasts a broad range of existing systems. One category is "issue-based information systems," hypertext systems used to facilitate decision making that are based on a fixed set of node types (*issues, positions,* and *arguments*). Issue-based information systems are one approach to capturing design rationale, discussed in Chapter 2. Two examples are Conklin's gIBIS system (Conklin and Begeman, 1989) and a NoteCards successor, Aquanet (Marshall and Rogers, 1992).

Also in 1987, Apple Computer released HyperCard and bundled it with the Macintosh (i.e., it came with each new computer). HyperCard is an interface builder (see Chapter 5) and a scripting (programming) language that can also be used to implement hypertext systems and structure texts through the creation and management of navigational links.

The success of HyperCard (and that of systems such as OWL's Guide, introduced on the Mac and the PC in 1986) helped legitimize hypertext. By 1990 the community of researchers and developers was large enough and confident enough to form SIGLINK, an ACM special interest group on hypertext. By 1993 numerous significant hypertext systems and applications had become available. A major novelist and critic writing in the *New York Times* reviewed eleven "hyperfictions" from seven publishers (Coover, 1993). The Mosaic interface to World Wide Web was released, facilitating hypertext links across the Internet and triggering the explosive growth of a global hypermedia network (see Chapter 14).

These developments fully realize and surpass the initial hypertext visions. This section is devoted to understanding the technology that has been realized and the lessons that have been learned. We shall return to applications for virtual communities in Chapter 14.

Structure and Navigation within Hypertext

Hypertext consist of *nodes* connected by *links* to form *networks* or *webs*. Depending on the system, a node can be restricted to one medium (text, graphics, sound, animation, video) or can include multiple media. Links can be unidirectional or bidirectional, labeled or typed, and can store other information, such as author and creation date. *Anchors* are points or regions in a node to which a link attaches, often represented by a button or other marking that indicates a navigational possibility. When a user "navigates" to a new node, a new window may open or the existing window may expand to incorporate the new information.

A *browser* is a tool that provides a set of navigational aids. In addition to standard string searches and queries, possible navigational aids include

- *active table of contents* entries linked to their sections
- *backtracking* and *history lists*, to allow rapid retracing of steps
- *bookmarks* for quick return to points of interest
- *guided tours* of particular sequences of nodes (*paths* or *trails* also indicate preferred sequences)
- *maps* or *web viewers* of the overall network, with a "you are here" indicator
- *timestamps* indicating creation, updating, or visiting

Conklin (1987, p. 38) summarizes the perceived advantages of hypertext as follows:

- ease of tracing references: *machine support for link tracing means that all references are equally easy to follow forward to their referent, or backward to the reference;*
- ease of creating new references: *users can grow their own networks, or simply annotate someone else's document with a comment (without changing the referenced document);*
- information structuring: *both hierarchical and nonhierarchical organizations can be imposed on unstructured information; even multiple hierarchies can organize the same material;*
- global views: *browsers provide table-of-contents style views, supporting easier restructuring of large and complex documents; global and local (node or page) views can be mixed effectively;*
- customized documents: *text segments can be threaded together in many ways, allowing the same document to serve multiple functions;*
- modularity of information: *since the same text segment can be referenced from several places, ideas can be expressed with less overlap and duplication;*
- consistency of information: *references are embedded in their text, and if the text is moved, even to another document, the link information still provides direct access to the reference;*
- task stacking: *the user is supported in having several paths of inquiry active and displayed on the screen at the same time, such that any given path can be unwound to the original task;*
- collaboration: *several authors can collaborate, with the document and comments about the document being tightly interwoven . . .*

Conklin (1987) also identifies two potential disadvantages of hypertext that can affect users and developers—*disorientation*, the problem of not knowing where you are and how to get to where you would like to be (or, to put it another way, to find the information you are seeking), and *cognitive overhead*, the additional work needed to create, name, and keep track of links. Writers and readers often struggle to create and comprehend ordinary linear narrative text; hypertext can magnify these problems.

A Hypermedia Framework

Halasz (1988, 1991) assesses the state of hypermedia and frames an agenda for research and development:

- *Scope.* Hypertext systems range from small, local systems to world-spanning information systems. Particular systems will accordingly vary in their architectures and interfaces.
- *Writing space vs. information tool.* Many early proponents saw hypertext as a new form of writing, possibly collaborative, permitting a greater departure from a purely linear narrative than footnotes and reference citations. In this view, all writing might become part of one huge hypertext, with new links continually formed to provide new views or paths. Later, there was more emphasis on hypertext as an information access tool applied to new or existing texts in relatively constrained, structured ways.
- *Unlimited vs. fixed node size.* Related to the previous distinction is a choice: Should the size of textual and other objects be restricted, a central concept of the notecards metaphor, or should units of any size be permitted (e.g., entire documents or even books). Raskin (1987) refers to these two approaches as "The Card Sharks" and "The Holy Scrollers." The writing space vision suggests units of unlimited size, whereas the information tool approach is less dogmatic.
- *Literal vs. virtual links.* In many hypertext systems, such as NoteCards, typed links among text or other objects are created; navigation follows these explicit structural connections. SuperBook, the subject of our first reading in this chapter, is an example of a system in which links among objects are automatically constructed, based on a structure implicit in the text itself, such as chapter and section headings. Literal links may be powerful but often require handcrafting; virtual links may be less expensive to construct.
- *Browsing vs. authoring.* Some hypertext systems, such as on-line encyclopedias or manuals, are created for subsequent use in a browsing, "read only" fashion. Other hypertexts are created and modified continually by users, such as those that support joint project planning or document construction. Different features are emphasized in each. SuperBook is a browsing system, while NoteCards was an authoring system.
- *Structuring vs. navigation.* Another distinction is whether the focus is on the overall structure of the hypertext or on local navigation. The former approach stresses the overall coherence of the information, as seen in a browser or overview map. The latter stresses representations of information that enable users to move from node to node through an information space. These concerns are not mutually exclusive, but it is possible to attend to one and ignore the other. Aquanet and gIBIS, mentioned above,

focus on structure. Hammond and Allinson (1988) is a nice example of a strong navigation focus, an educational hypertext system based on a "tour guide" metaphor that provides several navigational alternatives.

- *Target task domain.* Different tasks have different constraints and resources, and require different approaches. An educational hypertext browser may emphasize one set of features; a hypertext system designed for document preparation may emphasize a different feature set. SuperBook is a generic system; it is relatively easily constructed and users approach all documentation through a single interface. In contrast, Perlman (1989) presents a methodology for tailoring a hypertext system to a task it supports and describes one such tailored hypertext product.

In a more recent assessment, Halasz (1991) describes technical and market issues. Technical issues include the following:

- Creating infrastructures that support hypermedia: moving beyond stand-alone hypertexts by building hypertext capabilities into open systems, allowing links across objects of different kinds
- Building support for collaborative hypermedia construction, including versioning systems
- Supporting the creation and manipulation of very large information spaces and hypertexts
- Creating hypermedia that can be extended or tailored by people with little expertise

Halasz's marketing issues begin with a familiar precept: *Focus on users.* By discovering markets for hypermedia, we can prioritize research issues. Halasz also notes that standards and copyright issues loom large in the field's future, themes that will recur in our discussion of multimedia later in this chapter.

Demonstrating the Value of Hypertext

Everyone has, at one time or another, searched tediously through text for an item that is logically related to one that is already located. The appeal of hypertext to provide such links is strong. Nevertheless, it has not proven easy to demonstrate major benefits from hypertext. One reason is that hypertext ties readers to computer displays, and until recently it was unquestionably more difficult to read from displays than from paper (Wright, 1991). However, in our first reading in this chapter, Egan et al. (1989a) describe a hypertext system and experiments that demonstrate clear advantages over text documents (see also Egan et al., 1989b; Egan et al., 1989; Egan et al., 1991).

Bellcore's SuperBook is an extraordinary HCI development project—a model of the thoughtful application of long-term research results (see the paper by Landauer, 1991, in Chapter 9), careful and inventive design, systematic iterative refinement, and well-planned laboratory experimentation (see Chapter 2). SuperBook is unusual among research prototypes in that its developers carried it forward to become a product for the regional Bell operating companies.

SuperBook is a browsing system that structures existing documents that were written in one of several standard text-formatting languages. For documents with that preexisting structure, such as an on-line version of a printed manual, SuperBook requires little handcrafting. After converting the document to hypertext, SuperBook presents a user with several browsing features available in individual windows. These include *rich indexing,* which finds relevant text using related but not necessarily identical words; *fisheye viewing,* which presents an outline that has greater detail on nearby topics and less detail on distant topics, in the way a "fisheye lens" distorts a camera image; and *word lookup,* which presents a table of contents of the document with the number of occurrences of a given word in each section, enabling a user to see where use of the word is concentrated.

In the experimental evaluation, SuperBook was contrasted with the paper documentation that it replaced. For most tasks, performance with SuperBook was equal or better than that with paper in time and in accuracy. There was also an interesting *interaction* effect—SuperBook performed better in most conditions but not in all. When people were answering a question in which the exact words in the question were not in the section headings or the text, print was slightly faster than SuperBook.

Lessons Learned

For a large, conventionally structured text, converting text to SuperBook may not be expensive. The benefits may not seem overwhelming, at first—saving a few seconds on each search. However, showing *any* advantage for on-line over printed documentation can allow the elimination of bulky, expensive paper documentation, benefiting producers and users alike.

And in some situations the potential benefits are huge. The documentation for a commercial aircraft is so extensive that it can't fit in the plane! A mechanic facing a problem in the electrical system could save a lot more than a few seconds with the right tools. Not surprisingly, Boeing is very interested in hypermedia technology (Malcolm, Poltrock, and Schuler, 1991).

Other uses of hypermedia are so new that the benefits are still speculative. Yet the creation of new hypertext-based literary forms and the World Wide Web global network (see Chapter 14) have caught the imaginations of some very creative people.

Hypertext has succeeded—but not always. An early cautionary note was Raskin's (1987) critique, "The Hype in Hypertext." A panel at CHI '88 presented mixed assessments by six leading researchers (Fischer and Weyer, 1988). As time has passed and experience with hypertext has accumulated, deeper analyses of the possibilities and pitfalls have appeared. Our second reading, by Glushko (1992), is one such analysis.

Glushko merges experience in both research and consulting in the design and development of hypertext systems. The result is "Seven Ways to Make a Hypertext Project Fail," and by implication the steps to take to succeed. His first item, "unrealistic expectations about scale and readiness," is particularly illuminating for researchers. Glushko points out that researchers (or developers working on a prototype) often lavish time on a "demonstration" portion of a planned hypertext, but will have far less time to customize other parts of the hypertext the same way. A prototype may be built quickly on a system with a nice graphical interface, whereas the final hypertext will have to run on a different system and involve a more laborious construction effort, unanticipated by the sponsors. Glushko discusses other requirements for success, including the skills needed on the development team, attention to constraints imposed by the installed user base, and provision of the necessary software tools. Some of Glushko's concerns are echoed in Malcolm, Poltrock, and Schuler's (1991) identification of requirements for an "industrial strength hypermedia."

Other researchers have provided useful descriptions based on years of experience with particular systems. Marshall and Rogers (1992) describe Aquanet, a collaborative hypertext tool that extended NoteCards. User-developed hypertexts can suffer from the lack of a coherent framework; to address this, Aquanet provides an underlying argumentation structure similar to that of gIBIS, described above. However, the system forces users to organize their knowledge domain before they have enough experience to know what they might eventually need. The authors conclude that more adaptable tools are required.

Support for this observation comes from an intriguing study of information retrieval requirements in office settings. Alison Kidd (1994) analyzes how 12 professionals organize and access information, both printed and electronic. She concludes that this large class of professionals are employed, above all else, for the perspective they contribute as a result of the information they have handled. Their work is processing information. Before completely processing it, they resist categorizing a document. After completing the processing, they very rarely ever retrieve the original. Kidd argues that many of the assumptions underlying current approaches to information retrieval should be reexamined.

After several years experience on NoteCards and Aquanet, Marshall teamed up with Frank Shipman to produce an interesting analysis of the tension between identifying structure in which software is to work while not intruding on the work process prematurely. Shipman had experience on the Virtual Notebook System (Shipman, Chaney, and Gorry, 1989) and on the Colorado high-functionality design environments discussed in Chapter 12. The successful hypermedia Virtual Notebook System, built at the Baylor College of Medicine, is based on the model of an engineering notebook. The basic unit of text and graphics is the size of a large notebook page.

Shipman and Marshall (1995) address the problem of structure in complex systems, primarily hypertext systems. Users benefit from structure, whether in text or in work processes; however, they have great difficulty in specifying such structure explicitly. Shipman and Marshall argue that this is inescapable and that to address the conflict, tools must assist users who are constructing an environment to formalize aspects of it slowly and incrementally. Information can first be captured in a relatively free form, then over time be made more formal, in a process governed by the users and guided by the system.

Standards and the Commercial Market

The first hypertext and hypermedia systems were proprietary systems that tried to provide everything: authoring support, browsing and search features, and printing capabilities. The current tools reflect the perception that the advantages to hypertext are real but more modest. Because people won't abandon other tools to obtain these benefits, systems now interface to standard desktop publishing packages or focus on converting existing documentation into hypertext.

Similarly, many users would like to build hypermedia networks linking objects or parts of objects created by different applications, perhaps on different platforms. For this to be practical, standards are necessary. The familiar controversy appears: Researchers fear that premature standardization will lock us into an inferior structure, whereas developers and users often respond to the immediate benefits of standardization.

A prominent standard in government and industry today is the Standard Generalized Markup Language (SGML), designed in the mid-1980s and rapidly attracting use (Brown, 1989). SGML consists of a set of machine-interpretable descriptors embedded in an object that identify the components of the object. Since it is difficult to "mark up" an object by hand, there are now easy-to-use SGML authoring tools and systems that generate it automatically from existing documents.

As another evolutionary step, operating systems are starting to support linking between objects created with different applications. Examples are Microsoft's Object Linking and Embedding (OLE), Apple System 7's Publish/Subscribe, and the Sun/HP Distributed Object Management Facility. These allow the embedding of a part of one object in another, but do not allow users to navigate from one to the other. Venta Technology's Microcosm is an example of a system that does support such navigation among Microsoft Windows applications.

Successful hypermedia authoring tools include HyperCard and Aldus SuperCard for the Macintosh, Asymetrix ToolBook for Windows, and MetaCard and Gain Technology's Momentum on Unix platforms. Browsing and searching tools increasingly run on multiple platforms and include Electronic Book Technologies DynaText, Frame Technology's FrameViewer, Microsoft Multimedia Viewer, and Lotus SmarText, some of which are designed to complement standard desktop publishing applications.

Information Retrieval

The fields of HCI and of information retrieval (IR) have had little overlap. Human-computer interaction draws heavily on software product developers and on the academic disciplines of computer science, cognitive psychology, and human factors. Information retrieval has drawn more heavily from library science and the developers working on library systems. Although computers are used to access information of all kinds, one natural place for IR to arise is in retrieving information *about* computers, in on-line help systems and their extensions (see Chapter 10).

The field of IR is rapidly becoming a central aspect of how humans and computers interact as a result of the explosive growth of networking and the many large data bases and other information repositories maintained and accessible worldwide. Information retrieval systems that run across the Internet, such as Mosaic and GOPHER, are major steps toward access, made possible by the increasingly reliable infrastructure of the Internet (see Chapter 14).

A psychological study led directly to a design innovation in information retrieval. Most retrieval systems require that a user formulate a query, which is then used to scan the entire information source. If the result is used to formulate a new query, it will also be run over the entire source. Williams and Hollan (1981) found that people trying to recover dim memories often use a more indirect, iterative approach. For example, someone trying to recall the names of high school classmates may first recall clubs or activities, then try to recall who was involved in each.

This study led to "query by reformulation" systems (Williams, 1984; Fischer and Nieper-Lemke, 1989). A user enters some information to guide the search, the system retrieves a single example that matches, and the user enters additional information to constrain the search, and so on, closing in on the target.

Lesk (1989) develops related approaches to help people narrow searches of a catalog that contained 800,000 book citations. One approach provides users with the book title and a hierarchical catalog structure in which the title had been placed, giving the user additional information. For example, a user might realize a search is retrieving items from an unexpected part of the catalog and reformulate the query to direct the search in the intended direction.

Korfhage (1991) extends this idea by devising systems that present the retrieved objects highlighted visually among all of the objects in the search space. This, it is argued, provides a user with additional contextual information that can be valuable in assessing the retrieved objects that are of central interest. Here we find common ground between information retrieval and information visualization (see Chapter 6).

Guide to Further Reading

In 1987, the first ACM-sponsored hypertext conference was held. The July 1988 issue of *Communications of the ACM* contains articles from that conference, including Halasz (1988), described above. Since then, ACM conferences have been held in odd-numbered years and a European hypertext conference (ECHT) held in even-numbered years. The proceedings of these conferences, published by ACM, are an excellent archival source for hypertext research.

IEEE Computer published Conklin's (1987) survey in September 1987 and in January, 1988 published an issue on electronic publishing that included work from three major hypertext projects: the Document Examiner, described earlier (see Walker, 1988); the University of Maryland's Hyperties, detailed in Shneiderman and Kearsley (1989); and Brown University's influential Intermedia, reviewed by Haan, et al. (1992).

The journal *Hypermedia* has been published since 1989. Knee and Atkinson (1990) is an annotated bibliography on hypertext with 497 entries collected through the first half of 1989.

Books include Shneiderman and Kearsley (1989), which is accompanied by software to provide a feel for the subject, and Nielsen (1990), a survey of the literature and issues. The predictions in this book were later revised for a 1993 paperback edition, since events had not gone as expected (Nielsen, personal communication). A book on on-line documentation including coverage of hypermedia is Horton (1990).

Hypertext researchers met in 1988 and 1990 to establish a common terminology and semantics. An outcome was the Dexter Hypertext Reference Model (Halasz and Schwartz, 1994), a data and process model that has guided the development of hypermedia systems. A special issue of *Communications of the ACM* on hypermedia (February 1994) publishes this model and several articles on its use and limitations.

Dumais (1988) and Salton (1989) are good introductions to information retrieval and text processing. ACM's Special Interest Group on Information Retrieval (SIGIR) has held annual conferences since the mid-1970s. *ACM Transactions on Information Systems*, the *Journal of the American Society for Information Science*, and the *Journal of Information Processing and Management* are also good sources.

MULTIMEDIA

We have spoken in Part III and especially in Chapter 8 of *multimodal* interaction, in which a system supports multiple styles of interaction using different sensory modalities, for example, voice and gesture. We noted that it was important to distinguish this concept from that of a *multimedia* computer system, which is one that transacts or interacts in more than one medium, i.e., carriers of information such as text, audio, still graphics, animation, and video (Fox, 1989a, 1989b; Frenkel, 1989; Fox, 1991a, 1991b, 1991c; Grimes and Potel, 1991; Narasimhalu and Christodoulakis, 1991; Crawford, 1993). Although multimedia systems and multimodal interaction typically occur together, we use one term or the other depending upon whether our focus is on the means by which information is conveyed or on the style of interaction.

Like hypertext, multimedia began with experiments in the 1960s and 1970s that matured into vigorous commercial activity in the 1980s and 1990s. On the technology side, the early 1970s saw the development of laser videodisks capable of storing and playing back an hour of recorded analog video (54,000 still images per side of the disk) under control of a computer. Videodisks never became a commercial reality, and for most practical purposes have been replaced by the CD-ROMs that were developed in the 1980s (Fujitani, 1984; Lambert and Ropiequet, 1986). CD-ROMs store over 600 MB of digital data, which may include text, graphics, audio, and video. The 1980s and 1990s have seen rapid progress in reducing the cost of both CD-ROM disks and disk drives, and the ease and cost of mastering, writing, and, in some cases, even erasing and rewriting the disks. The result of this and the accelerating availability of CD-ROM titles has been that more than half of the new PCs of the mid-1990s, especially those purchased for home use, have been bought with CD-ROM drives as a peripheral.

Yet hardware by itself could not make multimedia a reality. The late 1970s saw a number of prototypes of computer-based navigation, access, and control of rich image and sound libraries. Three of the most dramatic and influential of these were Dataland, the Movie Map, and the Movie Manual, all developed at the MIT Architecture Machine Project, the predecesssor of the MIT Media Laboratory (Bolt, 1984; Brand, 1987).

Dataland (Bolt, 1984) was a wall-size display of objects such as faces, maps, TVs, telephones, calculators, calendars, books, and letters. Users could wander over this data world, watch and listen to what was happening, and zoom in to see and hear more detail.

The Movie Map (Lippman, 1980) allowed a user to navigate around Aspen, a small, attractive city with streets arrayed on a rectangular grid. Every 9 feet along the streets, four photographs of the city had been taken, two parallel to the street, two perpendicular to the street. These images were then recorded onto a videodisk. Users could explore the city streets, moving forward and backwards, turning corners, and reversing directions. They could refer to maps to aid in orientation, and also enter buildings and "meet people" (see Chapter 14).

The Movie Manual (Backer, 1981; MIT, 1983 video) demonstrated the potential of electronic books by including video and sound in an electronic training manual for automobile transmission repair. Users could read text, examine still graphics, and access recorded video illustrations of specific topics. Clearly, hypertext by itself would not be sufficient to unlock the educational and research potential of electronic documents—they must and could be enlivened with multimedia. One of the first commercial realizations of this concept was Grolier's Electronic Encyclopedia in the mid-1980s (Cook, 1988).

The Encoding and Representation of Multimedia Documents

The late 1980s saw an explosion in multimedia content development (see the discussion of applications below). An enabling technology was the standardized representation and encoding of multimedia data. Standards were necessary so that multimedia documents could be transported across different hardware platforms and mass-produced inexpensively. Encoding was necessary to allow greater quantities of audio and video data to be represented and stored on a single CD-ROM, and to allow these to be transferred more quickly into a computer.

Development highlights in this area have included the following (Fox, 1989a,1989b; Fox 1991b,1991c; Luther, 1994a):

- The Phillips Compact Disk–Interactive (CD/I) standard (1986) for storing and encoding multimedia data
- The RCA Digital Video Interactive (DVI) standard (1987) for compressing, recording, and playing back over an hour of full-motion video and FM-quality audio (Ripley, 1989; Tinker, 1989; see also Dixon, 1989, for a discussion of the role graphic and video prototyping played in the development of this technology, highlighting themes presented in Chapter 2)
- An ISO standard for CD-ROM file organization (1988)
- The Quicktime standard for the digital compression, coding, and playback of motion pictures of varying quality on the Macintosh
- The JPEG standard for the digital compression and coding of continuous-tone still images (Wallace, 1991)
- The MPEG standard for the digital compression and coding of motion pictures and associated data (Le Gall, 1991), and its successor MPEG2
- The H.261 standard for the digital compression and coding of audio-visual services (e.g., videophone and videoconferencing) at data stream rates of pX64 kilobits per second (Liou, 1991)
- The HyTime (Newcomb, Kipp, and Newcomb, 1991; Erfle, 1994), MHEG (Price, 1993), and OMFI (Buford and Gopal, 1994) standards for the representation, transmission, and interchange of multimedia and hypermedia objects and documents (Buford and Brennan, 1994).

Further insight into this area is provided by Lippman and Butera (1989) and Lippman (1991), who discuss coding methods that provide the receiver with flexible control over the display of the motion picture, and Liebhold and Hoffert (1991), who stress the role of standards and the importance of developing mechanisms for the licensing and payment of royalties for the reuse of multimedia materials.

Access to and Transmission of Multimedia Data Bases

As the potential for multimedia became apparent, and as the costs of digital storage continued to plummet in the late 1980s and early 1990s, researchers began to contemplate the widespread availability of fully random access digital multimedia data bases. To realize this vision, one had to consider how to achieve the reliable transmission of these data bases over computer networks and the reassembly of them so that audio and video are properly synchronized. Approaches to this problem involve system and network architectures and protocols, such as ISDN and ATM (Sen, 1994; Vetter, 1995; Vetter and Du, 1995); representation methods for time-based media; operating systems; performance modeling; and theoretical studies of synchronization. Space precludes a detailed discussion of these issues; recent research results appear in ACM (1993), IEEE (1994), ACM (1994), and Buford (1994).

The Authoring and Use of Multimedia

Another prerequisite for the development of multimedia applications was the availability of easy-to-use tools for the authoring and use of multimedia. Whereas the influence of HyperCard on the development of significant hypertext applications was primarily symbolic, it became a real force in the development of multimedia on the Macintosh in the late 8190s. This was true for two reasons:

- Primitives for controlling videodisk and CD-ROMs were available.
- HyperCard's accessible mental model based on the metaphor of a stack of index cards (see Chapter 2), English-like syntax, and easy programmability allowed educators, graphic artists, and others who were not computer specialists to gain quickly both the confidence and the ability to produce multimedia on the Mac.

Another important authoring tool has been Macromedia Director (Canter, 1986). Here also, success has been enabled in great part by appropriate choices of metaphors, in this case a stage with a cast of characters, and a timeline for orchestrating the behavior of these characters.

Hodges, Sasnett, and Ackerman (1989) describe Athena Muse, a multimedia construction kit. Davenport, Smith, and Pincever (1991) analyze cinematic elements and how they contribute to the design of multimedia. Pea (1991) describes Multimedia Works, a system that supports the development of multimedia compositions by students. Feiner and McKeown (1991, 1991 video) describe a prototype of the automated authoring of multimedia explanations. Ueda (1993 video) demonstrates a multimedia authoring system.

Hardman, van Rossum, and Bulterman (1993) and van Rossum et al. (1994) describe an environment for structured multimedia authoring that involves the coordinated design and editing of two views, a "hierarchy" view and a "channel" view. Matthews, Gloor, and Makedon (1994) describe an extension to the Scheme programming language designed to facilitate video editing and processing. Mackay and Pagani (1994) describe an innovative application of augmented reality (see Chapter 14) that uses both computer displays and paper storyboards for movie authoring and video editing. Meira and Moura (1994) present a multimedia scripting language. Backer (1994) reviews design paradigms, user interfaces, and research issues in multimedia presentation and authoring.

Other projects have focused on the browsing, retrieval, and use of hypermedia documents, for example, Zellweger (1992, 1989 video), Davis (1993 video), and Buchanan (1993 video).

The Analysis, Annotation, and Reuse of Multimedia

As multimedia data bases stored on CD-ROM and on computer files grow exponentially, authoring is no longer the only way to create new content. Instead, one can contemplate reuse or repurposing of existing material. This leads to both legal and technical issues:

- How does one get the legal rights to reuse this material? (a topic not to be discussed here)
- How does one find, represent, and manipulate multimedia objects or sequences that appear in existing multimedia data bases?

We have already reviewed approaches to the analysis and annotation of video records of human-computer interactions in Chapter 2. Kreitman and Salomon (1988 video) demonstrate a method for specifying searches in both textual and visual data bases. Weiss, Duda, and Gifford (1994) discuss an algebraic query language for retrieving video sequences. An elegant recent approach to the more general problem of multimedia representation and reuse is the Ph.D. work of Marc Davis (Davis, 1993a, 1993b; 1994a, 1994b; 1994 video; 1995). A summary of his work appears as the last reading in this chapter (Davis, 1993a).

Davis postulates that we need deep descriptions of video in order to enable effective repurposing and reuse of archived material, and that these descriptions can only be developed by skilled human coders working with powerful tools. His system, called Media Streams, provides the coder with a hierarchical iconic language of thousands of categories to be used in indexing sequences of video. The highest level of the hierarchy includes categories that describe actions, characters, objects, locations, times, weather, recording media, cinematographic properties, and cinematic transitions. The iconic language is particularly powerful for describing video because on the order of one thousand of the icons are animated icons (recall the paper by Baecker, Small, and Mander, 1991, reprinted in Chapter 6).

Descriptions of temporal media are produced on a media timeline. An individual frame may be indexed in more than one sequence description. These descriptions provide a consistent interface for annotation, browsing, query, and editing of video and audio data, and thereby may enable the reuse and repurposing of material in video archives.

Applications of Multimedia

The most significant applications of multimedia are in

- education and training
- information resources, documentation, and research
- communications, coordination, and collaboration
- entertainment

Multimedia applications for education and training have gone far beyond the pioneering Movie Manual in scope and imagination. Applications include the study of Shakespeare (Friedlander, 1988), novels (Campbell and Hanlon, 1988), scientific investigation (Gibbon, 1988), neuroanatomy (Ackerman, 1989 video), music (Sanchez et al., 1990 video), ancient culture (Crane, 1991), and complex human-machine control systems (Yoshizawa et al., 1991 video). Mackay and Davenport (1989) and Hodges and Sasnett (1993) present an overview of multimedia applications in entertainment, learning, research, and communication at the MIT Project Athena and the MIT Media Laboratory. Woolsey (1991) presents an overview of multimedia applications for geography, history, and science developed at the Apple Multimedia Laboratory.

When the content of multimedia data bases becomes rich enough to be useful to scholars as well as students, they become applicable as information resources and for purposes of documentation and research. Hensel (1986), Lowell (1986), and Honey and White (1986) describe applications for data publishing, library catalogs, and cartographic data bases, respectively. Hoffert and Gretsch (1991) describe a prototype system for multimedia news.

In our discussion of media spaces in Chapter 11, we explored the role of video and multimedia messaging in facilitating communications, coordination, and collaboration. Crawford (1993), ACM (1993), and ACM (1994) present recent papers on this topic. Borenstein (1991) is an introduction to the prospects for multimedia electronic mail.

Finally, multimedia's biggest commercial payoff is emerging in the field of entertainment (Porter, 1994), where we have seen both the crassest of exploitations of violence and sex as well as engrossing and imaginative games of fantasy and exploration. A good example of the potential of the medium is the beauty, fantasy, mystery, and engagement of the recent CD-ROM-based game Myst (Carroll, 1994).

Multimedia and Human-Computer Interaction

Multimedia represents an important new area of application for human-computer interaction. Facilitating the creation, browsing, retrieval, and editing of rich and complex information spaces clearly requires the best in user interface design.

But, to paraphrase John F. Kennedy, ask not what human-computer interaction can do for multimedia, but also what multimedia can do for human-computer interaction. Relevant disciplines include animation, video, and nonspeech audio, all of which can enhance the communicative power of interfaces and can make them more engaging. More detailed discussions and references to the literature can be found in Chapters 6 and 8.

Guide to Further Reading

Some of the earliest compendia of writing on CD-ROM and multimedia came out of the Microsoft CD-ROM conferences (Lambert and Ropiequest, 1986; Ropiequest, Einberger, and Zoellick, 1987; Ambron and Hooper, 1988; Sherman, 1988).

Some recent useful books include Blattner and Dannenberg (1992), a collection of research papers dealing both with multimedia and with multimodal interaction; Buford (1994), a collection of survey papers dealing especially with issues of multimedia system architecture and representation; and Luther (1994b), which presents an overview of the commercial processes and technology for the authoring of multimedia.

Special issues of computer science journals devoted to multimedia are Fox (1989a), Fox (1991a), Grimes and Potel (1991), Narasimhalu and Christodoulakis (1991), and Crawford (1993). Both ACM and IEEE have recently begun annual multimedia conferences (ACM, 1993; IEEE, 1994; ACM, 1994; ACM, 1994 video). ACM Press and Springer International began a journal entitled *Multimedia Systems*, and IEEE began *Multimedia Magazine*.

REFERENCES

Note: A ● before a reference indicates a reading.

ACM (1993). *Proc. ACM Multimedia 93.*

ACM (1994). *Proc. ACM Multimedia 94.*

Ambron, S., and Hooper, K. (Eds.) (1988). *Interactive Multimedia.* Microsoft Press.

Backer, D. (1981). Personalized Visualization: Interactive Cinema for Training. *Proc. Computer Graphics '81,* London, England.

Backer, D. (1994). Multimedia Presentation and Authoring. In Buford (1994), 285–303.

Baecker, R., Small, I., and Mander, R. (1991). Bringing Icons to Life. *Proceedings of CHI '91,* ACM, 1–6. Reprinted in Chapter 6.

Blattner, M., and Dannenberg, R. (Eds.) (1992). *Multimedia Interface Design.* ACM.

Bolt, R. (1984). *The Human Interface: Where People and Computers Meet.* Lifetime Learning Publications.

Borenstein, N. (1991). Multimedia Electronic Mail: Will the Dream Become a Reality? *Communications of the ACM* 34(4), 117–119.

Brand, S. (1987). *The Media Lab: Inventing the Future at M.I.T.* Penguin Books.

Brown, H. (1989). Standards for Structured Documents. *The Computer Journal* 32(6), 505–514.

Buford, J. (Ed.) (1994). *Multimedia Systems.* ACM Press.

Buford, J., and Brennan, R. (1994). Multimedia Interchange. In Buford (1994), 323–340.

Buford, J., and Gopal, C. (1994). Standardizing a Multimedia Interchange Format: A Comparison of OMFI and MHEG. In IEEE (1994), 463–472.

Campbell, R., and Hanlon, P. (1988). Grapevine. In Ambron and Hooper (1988), 157–177.

Canter, M. (1986). The New Workstation: CD ROM Authoring Systems. In Lambert and Ropiequet (1986), 359–375.

Carroll, J. (1994). Guerrillas in the Myst. *Wired* 2(8), August 1994, 69–73.

Conklin, J. (1987). Hypertext: An Introduction and Survey. *IEEE Computer* 2(9), 17–41.

Conklin, J., and Begeman, M. (1989). gIBIS: A Tool for All Reasons. *Journal of the American Society for Information Science* 40, 200–213.

Cook, P. (1988). Multimedia Technology: An Encyclopedia Publisher's Perspective. In Ambron and Hooper (1988), 217–240.

Coover, R. (1993). Hyperfiction: Novels for the Computer. *New York Times Book Review,* August 29, 1–12.

Crane, G. (1991). Hypermedia and the Study of Ancient Culture. *IEEE Computer Graphics and Applications* 11(4), 45–51.

Crawford, D. (1993). Special Section on Multimedia in the Workplace. *Communications of the ACM* 36(1).

Davenport, G., Smith, T., and Pincever, N. (1991). Cinematic Primitives for Multimedia. *IEEE Computer Graphics and Applications* 11(4), 67–74.

● Davis, M. (1993a). Media Streams: An Iconic Visual Language for Video Representation. *Proc. 1993 Symposium on Visual Languages,* IEEE Computer Society Press, 196–202. (Revised and updated in 1995. Original title was Media Streams: An Iconic Visual Language for Video Annotation.)

Davis, M. (1993b). Media Streams: An Iconic Visual Language for Video Annotation. *Teletronikk 4.93: Cyberspace* 89(4), Norwegian Telecom Research, 59–71.

Davis, M. (1994a). Knowledge Representation for Video. *Proc. 12th National Congress on Artificial Intelligence (AAAI-94),* Seattle, Washington, 120–127.

Davis, M. (1994b). Media Streams: Representing Video for Retrieval and Repurposing. *Proc. ACM Multimedia '94,* 478–479.

Davis, M. (1995). Media Streams: Representing Video for Retrieval and Repurposing. Ph.D. Thesis, MIT.

Dixon, D. (1989). Life Before the Chips: Simulating Digital Video Interactive Technology. *Communications of the ACM* 32(7), 824–831.

Dumais, S. (1988). Textual Information Retrieval. In Helander, M. (Ed.) (1988), *Handbook of Human-Computer Interaction,* North-Holland, 673–700.

Egan, D., Lesk, M., Ketchum, R., Lochbaum, C., Remde, J., Littman, M., and Landauer, T. (1991). Hypertext for the Electronic Library? CORE Sample Results. *Proc. Hypertext '91,* ACM, 299–312.

Egan, D., Remde, J., Gomez, L., Landauer, T., Eberhardt, J., and Lochbaum, C. (1989). Formative Design-Evaluation of SuperBook. *ACM Transactions on Information Systems* 7(1), 30–57.

● Egan, D., Remde, J., Landauer, T., Lochbaum, C., and Gomez, L. (1989a). Behavioral Evaluation and Analysis of a Hypertext Browser. *Proc. CHI '89,* ACM, 205–210.

Egan, D., Remde, J., Landauer, T., Lochbaum, C., and Gomez, L. (1989b). Acquiring Information in Books and SuperBooks. *Machine-Mediated Learning* 3, 259–277.

Erfle, R. (1994). HyTime a the Multimedia Document Model of Choice. In IEEE (1994), 444–454.

Feiner, S., and McKeown, K. (1991). Automating the Generation of Coordinated Multimedia Explanations. *IEEE Computer* 24(10), 33–41.

Fischer, G., and Nieper-Lemke, H. (1989). HELGON: Extending the Retrieval by Reformulation Paradigm. *Proc. CHI '89,* ACM, 357–362.

Fischer, G., and Weyer, S. (Organizers) (1988). A Critical Assessment of Hypertext Systems. *Proc. CHI '88,* ACM, 223–227.

Fox, E. (Ed.) (1989a). Special Section on Interactive Technology. *Communications of the ACM* 32(7).

Fox, E. (1989b). The Coming Revolution in Interactive Digital Video. *Communications of the ACM* 32(7), 794–801.

Fox, E. (Ed.) (1991a). Special Section on Digital Multimedia Systems. *Communications of the ACM* 34(4).

Fox, E. (1991b). Standards and the Emergence of Digital Multimedia Systems. *Communications of the ACM* 34(4), 26–29.

Fox, E. (1991c). Advances in Interactive Digital Multimedia Systems. *IEEE Computer* 24(10), 9–21.

Frenkel, K. (1989). The Next Generation of Interactive Technologies. *Communications of the ACM* 32(7), 872–881.

Friedlander, L. (1988). The Shakespeare Project. In Ambron and Hooper (1988), 115–141.

Fujitani, L. (1984). Laser Optical Disk: The Coming Revolution in On-line Storage. *Communications of the ACM* 27(6), 546–554.

Gibbon, S., with Hooper, K. (1988). The Voyage of the MIMI. In Ambron and Hooper (1988), 181–191.

Glushko, R. (1992). Seven Ways to Make a Hypertext Project Fail. *Technical Communications* 2, 226–230.

Grimes, J., and Potel, M. (1991). Special Section on Multimedia. *IEEE Computer Graphics and Applications* 11(4).

Haan, B., Kahn, P., Riley, V., Coombs, J., and Meyrowitz, N. (1992). IRIS Hypermedia Services. *Communications of ACM* 35(1), 36–51.

Halasz, F. (1988). Reflections on Notecards: Seven Issues of the Next Generation of Hypermedia Systems. *Communications of the ACM* 31(7), 836–852.

Halasz, F. (1991). Seven Issues: Revisited. Plenary Address, Hypertext '91 Conference.

Halasz, F., Moran, T., and Trigg, R. (1987). NoteCards in a Nutshell. *Proc. CHI+GI '87,* ACM, 45–52.

Halasz, F., and Schwartz, M. (1994). The Dexter Hypertext Reference Model. *Communications of the ACM* 37(2), 30–39.

Hammond, N., and Allinson, A. (1988). Travels Around a Learning Support Environment: Rambling, Orienteering, or Touring? *Proc. CHI '88,* ACM, 269–273.

Hardman, L., van Rossum, G., and Bulterman, R. (1993). Structured Multimedia Authoring. *Proc. ACM Multimedia 93,* 283–289.

Hensel, M. (1986). Data Publishing on Optical Disks. In Lambert and Ropiequet (1986), 487—493.

Hodges, M., and Sasnett, R. (1993). *Multimedia Computing: Case Studies from MIT Project Athena.* Addison-Wesley.

Hodges, M., Sasnett, R., and Ackerman, M. (1989). A Construction Set for Multimedia Applications. *IEEE Software,* January 1989, 37–43.

Hoffert, E., and Gretsch, G. (1991). The Digital News System at EDUCOM: A Convergence of Interactive Computing, Newspapers, Television, and High-Speed Networks. *Communications of the ACM* 34(4), 113–116.

Honey, S., and White, M. (1986). Cartographic Data bases. In Lambert and Ropiequet (1986), 563—572.

Horton, W. (1990). *Designing and Writing Online Documentation.* John Wiley & Sons.

IEEE (1994). *Proc. International Conference on Multimedia Computing and Systems.* IEEE Computer Society Press.

Kidd, A. (1994). The Marks Are on the Knowledge Worker. *Proc. CHI '94,* ACM, 186–191.

Knee, M., and Atkinson, S. (1990). *Hypertext/Hypermedia: An Annotated Bibliography.* Greenwood Press.

Korfhage, R. (1991). To See, or Not to See: Is That the Query? *Proc. SIGIR '91,* ACM, 131–141.

Lambert, S., and Ropiequet, S. (Eds.) (1986). *CD-ROM: The New Papyrus.* Microsoft Press.

Landauer, T. (1991). Let's Get Real: A Position Paper on the Role of Cognitive Psychology in the Design of Humanly Useful and Usable Systems. In Carroll, J. (Ed.), *Designing Interaction,* Cambridge University Press, 60–73. Reprinted in Chapter 9.

Le Gall, D. (1991). MPEG: A Video Compression Standard for Multimedia Applications. *Communications of the ACM* 34(4), 46–58.

Lesk, M. (1989). What to Do When There's Too Much Information. *Proc. Hypertext '89,* ACM, 305–318.

Liebhold, M., and Hoffert, E. (1991). Toward an Open Environment for Digital Video. *Communications of the ACM* 34(4), 103–112.

Liou, M. (1991). Overview of the pX64 kbits/s Video Coding Standard. *Communications of the ACM* 34(4), 59–63.

Lippman, A. (1980). Movie-Maps: An Application of the Optical Video Disk to Computer Graphics. *Computer Graphics* 14(3), 32–42.

Lippman, A. (1991). Feature Sets for Interactive Images. *Communications of the ACM* 34(4), 92–102.

Lippman, A., and Butera, W. (1989). Coding Image Sequences for Interactive Retrieval. *Communications of the ACM* 32(7), 852–860.

Lowell, G. (1986). The Library of Congress on CD ROM. In Lambert and Ropiequet (1986), 517–525.

Luther, A. (1994a). Digital Video and Image Compression. In Buford (1994), 143–174.

Luther, A. (1994b). *Authoring Interactive Multimedia.* Academic Press.

Mackay, W., and Davenport, G. (1989). Virtual Video Editing in Interactive Multimedia Applications. *Communications of the ACM* 32(7), 802–810.

Mackay, W., and Pagani, D. (1994). Video Mosaic: Laying Out Time in a Physical Space. *Proc. ACM Multimedia 94,* 165–172.

Malcolm, K., Poltrock, S., and Schuler, D. (1991). Industrial Strength Hypertext: Requirements for a Large Engineering Enterprise. *Proc. Hypertext '91,* ACM, 13–24.

Marshall, C., and Rogers, R. (1992). Two Years Before the Mist: Experiences with Aquanet. *Proc. European Conference on Hypertext (ECHT '92),* 53–62.

Matthews, J., Gloor, P., and Makedon, F. (1993). VideoScheme: A Programmable Video Editing System for Automation and Media Recognition. *Proc. ACM Multimedia 93,* 419–426.

Meira, S., and Moura, A. (1994). A Scripting Language for Multimedia Presentations. In IEEE (1994), 484–489.

Narasimhalu, D., and Christodoulakis, S. (1991). Special Section on Multimedia Information Systems. *IEEE Computer* 24(10).

Newcomb, S., Kipp, N., and Newcomb, V. (1991). The "HyTime" Hypermedia/Time-based Document Structuring Language. *Communications of the ACM* 34(11), 67–83.

Nielsen, J. (1990). *Hypertext and Hypermedia.* Academic Press. (Paperback edition, 1993.)

Pea, R. (1991). Learning through Multimedia. *IEEE Computer Graphics and Applications* 11(4), 58–66.

Perlman, G. (1989). Asynchronous Design/Evaluation Methods for Hypertext Technology Development. *Proc. Hypertext '89,* ACM, 61–81.

Porter, J. (1994). The Convergence of Computers, Communications, and Entertainment Products. In Buford (1994), 27–44.

Price, R. (1993). MHEG: An Introduction to the Future International Standard for Hypermedia Object Interchange. *Proc. ACM Multimedia 93,* 121–128.

Raskin, J. (1987). The Hype in Hypertext: A Critique. *Proc. Hypertext '87,* ACM, 325–330.

Ripley, D. (1989). DVI—A Digital Multimedia Technology. *Communications of the ACM* 32(7), 811–822.

Ropiequest, S., Einberger, J., and Zoellick, B. (Eds.) 1987. *CD-ROM Volume 2: Optical Publishing.* Microsoft Press.

Salton, G. (1989). *Automatic Text Processing: The Transformation, Analysis, and Retrieval of Information by Computer.* Addison-Wesley.

Sen, P. (1994). Multimedia Services over the Public Network: Requirements, Architectures, and Protocols. In Buford (1994), 305–322.

Sherman, C. (1988). *The CD-ROM Handbook.* McGraw-Hill.

Shipman, F., Chaney, R., and Gorry, G. (1989). Distributed Hypertext for Collaborative Research: The Virtual Notebook System. *Proc. Hypertext '89,* ACM, 129–135.

Shipman, F., and Marshall, C. (1995). Formality and Interaction: Experiences, Emerging Themes, and Directions. Manuscript submitted to *Human-Computer Interaction.*

Shneiderman, B., and Kearsley, G. (1989). *Hypertext Hands-On!* Addison-Wesley.

Tinker, M. (1989). DVI Parallel Image Compression. *Communications of the ACM* 32(7), 844–851.

Trigg, R., Suchman, L., and Halasz, F. (1986). Supporting Collaboration in NoteCards. *Proc. CSCW '86,* MCC, 147–153.

Vetter, R. (1995). ATM Concepts, Architectures, and Protocols. *Communications of the ACM* 38(2), 30–38, 109.

Vetter, R., and Du, D. (1995). Introduction to the Special Issue on Issues and Challenges in ATM Networks. *Communications of the ACM* 38(2), 28–29.

van Rossum, G., Jansen, J., Mullender, S., and Bulterman, R. (1993). CMIFed: A Presentation Environment for Portable Hypermedia Documents. *Proc. ACM Multimedia 93,* 183–188.

Walker, J. (1987). Document Examiner: Delivery Interface for Hypertext Documents. *Proc. Hypertext '87.* ACM, 307–323.

Walker, J. (1988). Supporting Document Development with Concordia. *IEEE Computer* 21(1), 48–59.

Wallace, G. (1991). The JPEG Still Picture Compression Standard. *Communications of the ACM* 34(4), 30–44.

Weiss, R., Duda, A.. and Gifford, D. (1994). Content-Based Access to Algebraic Video. In IEEE (1994), 140–151.

Williams, M. (1984). What Makes RABBIT Run? *International Journal of Man-Machine Studies* 21, 333–352.

Williams, M., and Hollan, J. (1981). The Process of Retrieval from Very Long-Term Memory. *Cognitive Science* 5, 87–119.

Woolsey, K. (1991). Multimedia Scouting. *IEEE Computer Graphics and Applications* 11(4), 26–38.

Wright, P. (1991). Designing and Evaluating Documentation for I.T. Users. In Shackel, B., and Richardson, S. (Eds.), *Human Factors for Informatics Usability,* Cambridge University Press, 343–358.

Zellweger, P. (1992). Toward a Model for Active Multimedia Documents. In Blattner and Dannenberg (1992), 39–52.

VIDEOS

Ackerman, M. (1989). The Illustrated Neuroanatomy Glossary. *ACM SIGGRAPH Video Review (SGVR)* 48.

ACM (1994). *Video Proc. ACM Multimedia '94.*

Buchanan, C. (1993). Multimedia Documents as User Interfaces. *ACM SGVR* 88.

Davis, H. (1993). Microcosm: An Open Hypermedia System. *ACM SGVR* 88.

Davis, M. (1994). Media Streams: Representing Video for Retrieval and Repurposing. *Video Proc. ACM Multimedia '94.*

Feiner, S., and McKeown, K. (1991). COMET: Generating Coordinated Multimedia Explanations. *ACM SGVR* 64.

Kreitman, K., and Salomon, G. (1988). Interfaces for Accessing Textual and Visual Information in Large Data bases. *ACM SGVR* 59.

MIT (1983). Movie Manual Project. *ACM SGVR* 13.

Sanchez, M., Joseph, A., Dannenberg, R., Capell, P., Saul, R., and Joseph, R. (1990). The Piano Tutor. *ACM SGVR* 55.

Ueda, H. (1993). IMPACT: Interactive Motion Picture Authoring System for Creative Talent. *ACM SGVR* 88.

Walker, J. (1985). Document Examiner. *ACM SGVR* 19.

Yoshizawa, J., Muto, S., Ueda, T., and Nishida, S. (1991). A Hypersimulation-based Learning Environment. *ACM SGVR* 65.

Zellweger, P. (1989). Scripted Documents. *ACM SGVR* 48.

Behavioral Evaluation and Analysis of a Hypertext Browser

Dennis E. Egan, Joel R. Remde, Thomas K. Landauer, Carol C. Lochbaum, and Louis M. Gomez

Bellcore
445 South Street, Box 1910
Morristown, NJ 07960-1910

ABSTRACT

Students performed a variety of tasks using a statistics text presented either in conventional printed form or via the text browser "SuperBook" (Remde, Gomez and Landauer [18]). Students using SuperBook answered more search questions correctly, wrote higher quality "open-book" essays, and recalled certain incidental information better than students using the conventional text. Subjective ratings overwhelmingly favored SuperBook. The advantage of SuperBook appears to be particularly strong for questions that are not anticipated by the author's organization of a text.

KEYWORDS: Hypertext, Text Retrieval, Learning, Documentation, Browser

INTRODUCTION

People have long hoped that computer-based systems might facilitate the use of information from voluminous written materials (e.g. Bush [3]). Nelson [16] speculated about the possibility of finding information by taking nonlinear paths through computer-based texts (hence "hypertexts"). Engelbart and English [7] demonstrated an early system that allowed users to traverse texts in a variety of ways.

The past five years have witnessed an immense surge in the development of hypertext systems. Conklin [4] reviewed 18 hypertext systems, comparing them on a dozen different features. A reasonable guess is that 50 to 100 systems exist presently, with overlapping sets of features implemented in many different ways. Hypertext systems have been the subject of panel discussions, conferences, and special journal issues [1, 20].

Unfortunately, few hypertext systems have been evaluated to see whether and how they actually improve human performance compared to conventional printed materials. Previous comparisons of paper versus online texts generally have not been favorable to the online versions, which typically reduce reading rates and impose interface problems [19]. Perhaps the only direct comparison of hypertext and paper materials to date has been done with the Hyperties system [13]. Those studies showed that Hyperties typically resulted in longer task completion times with no gain in accuracy compared to paper materials. Users did, however, prefer the Hyperties system to paper.

The present study is a behavioral evaluation that not only demonstrates superior utility and desirability of a hypertext-like system, but also suggests which properties of the system were important under various conditions.

SUPERBOOK

Design Concepts

SuperBook fits Conklin's [4] description of a "structured browsing system." SuperBook takes as input one or more existing documents in a standard text formatting language and presents the text in a multiwindow display with search and navigation enhancements. Other browsing systems similar to SuperBook include "SAM" [17] and the "Document Examiner" [21].

Two computer-based enhancements developed and studied in our laboratory have been incorporated in SuperBook. One is *rich indexing*. Research has shown that people experience difficulty in finding information in large text databases [10, 12]. The root problem is that users try to find information using words different from those selected to index the information. Using rich indexing, each piece of information (e.g. a topic or section of a document) can be reached by many more words. Rich indexing and a related technique, *adaptive aliasing*, have been tested with favorable results in laboratory studies and prototype systems [8, 12].

The second SuperBook enhancement is a type of *fisheye viewer* [9]. Large amounts of text present severe navigation and disorientation problems for users [14, 15]. The fisheye viewer counters such problems by displaying hierarchically structured information according to a "degree of interest function." The fisheye viewer permits a user to examine detailed, low-level information in the focus of a display while it maintains successively more global, higher-level information on the display periphery.

A User's Perspective

SuperBook consists of a document preprocessor and a program to manage display and interaction. The preprocessing phase is a one-time, fully automated operation. Computer-readable source text in a standard text markup language such as *Troff*, *Scribe*, or *Interleaf* is analyzed. Rich indexing is initially implemented by full text indexing of the documents. A fisheye view "Table of Contents" is generated automatically from the format of the document's headings.

Once the preprocessing is complete, users can browse documents interactively. SuperBook functions are selected by mouse, and search words are entered at a keyboard or selected from text displays. Text in the windows can be searched, scrolled, and paged in various ways.

The SuperBook configuration for the study reported here consisted of four windows on a SUN workstation. A fifth window was used to present questions to the users (see Figure 1).

Functions

The *Word Lookup* function is used to find all occurrences of any word, word stem, or combination of words entered by the user. The *Table of Contents* window presents a dynamic, fisheye view of the hierarchy of topic headings in the document. The *Table of Contents* can be expanded or collapsed to varying levels of detail of chapters and sections. Used in conjunction with *Word Lookup*, the *Table of Contents* shows the distribution of search words in each chapter and section of the document. Search words that occur as topic headings are highlighted in the *Table of Contents* display. The *Page of Text* window displays parts of the text selected by the user. The user

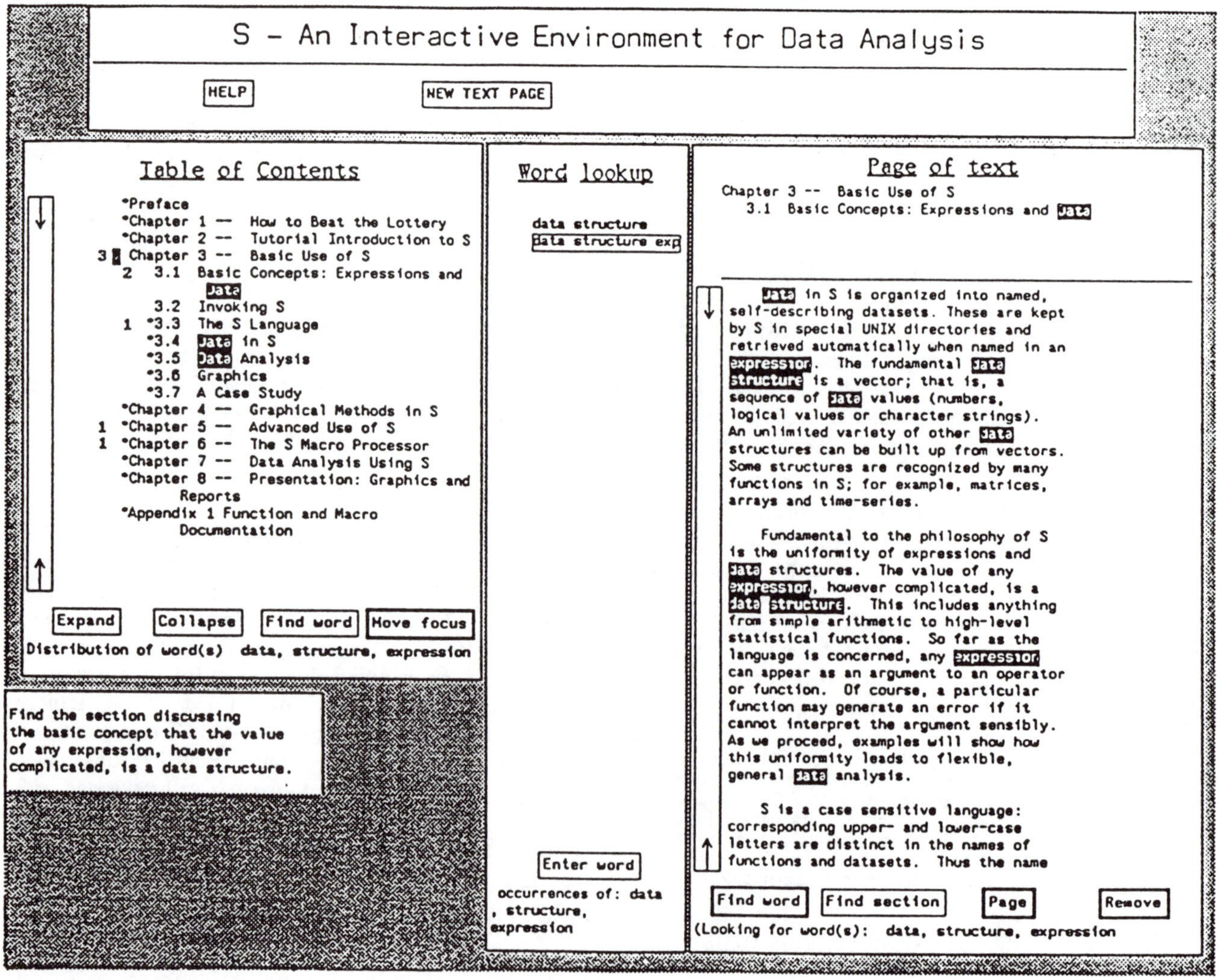

Figure 1. SuperBook display showing results of expanding the Table of Contents, looking up several terms, and displaying text containing search terms.

can select a chapter or section from the *Table of Contents*, or ask to see the context surrounding the next or previous occurrence of a search word. Active search words are highlighted automatically when the text is displayed.

Several additional functions have been implemented in SuperBook, but were not evaluated in the study to be described. These functions include an adaptive index, a "latent semantic index" [5, 6], an annotation facility, and a graphics display facility.

Implementation

The version of SuperBook used in this study evolved from the original prototype [18]. On the basis of an earlier evaluation, changes were implemented to improve the speed and accuracy of searching for information. The original Franz Lisp version was reprogrammed in C, greatly reducing system response time. The method of highlighting was changed, and effective user strategies identified in the evaluation study were made easier to use.

BEHAVIORAL EVALUATION AND ANALYSIS OF SUPERBOOK

The study examined a variety of tasks and evaluative measures. *Structured search* tasks represent the common problem of a user having to find an answer to a specific question by using a reference text with which the user is not completely familiar. The user starts with a question that may or may not correspond to the way the author has organized the material. The user may or may not know or remember some of the words the author has used in writing about the target material. The *open-book essays* represent another common but less constrained way of using reference documents. Students and professionals often look up material in different places in a document for the purpose of comparing and writing about information such as historical events, legal cases, technical specifications, and market data. *Incidental learning* tasks assess how much useful additional information about a reference document (e.g. its topic structure and common examples) users acquire while performing typical tasks without explicit directions to attend to the additional information. *Subjective ratings* assessed users' reaction to the form as well as the content of the documentation.

The *structured search* tasks explored the effect of the two factors mentioned that commonly influence the difficulty of finding information in documents. One factor is whether the user's question corresponds to the author's organization of the material. In the evaluation, half the search questions contained words cuing users to the topic heading containing the target information, and half did not. The other factor is whether the user knows some of the exact words the author used in writing about the target information. In the evaluation, half the questions included words taken from the text in the neighborhood of the target, and half did not.

We hypothesized that search performance with a conventional document would depend on topic heading cues, but searching with SuperBook would not. Several features of conventional documents simplify search if users know the appropriate topic heading: (a) the table of contents lists the author's topic headings; (b) the author's topic headings are often emphasized in the text by use of white space, bold print, and page headers; (c) words in the author's topic headings are much more likely to appear in an index than other words randomly selected from the text. These common features have the effect of emphasizing the organizational structure that an author has given to a text.

Table 1

Types of Search Questions

Words in Question Taken from:	Example Search Question
Text + Heading	"Find the section discussing the *basic concept* that the **value** of any *expression* however **complicated, is a data structure**."
Text	"**The dataset 'murder'** contains **murder rates** per 100,000 **population.** Find the section that says which **states** are included in this **dataset.**"
Heading	"Find the section that describes *pie charts* and states whether or not they are a good means for analyzing data."
Neither	"Find the section that describes the first thing you have to do to get S to print pictorial output."

Words in boldface are taken from the text, while those in italics are taken from the headings. Note that no highlighting was used in the presentation of questions to the users.

Table 2

Proportion of Correct Responses

Form of Documentation	Words in Question Taken from: Text + Heading	Text	Heading	Neither	Mean for All Types
SuperBook	**.94**	**.88**	.90	.30	**.75**
Print	**.81**	**.48**	.80	.40	**.62**

Adjacent boldface pairs in the same column differ reliably across forms of documentation.

SuperBook users do not need to work through an author's organizational scheme in order to access information. In particular, the *Word Lookup* function will work for any words in the document, whether or not the words refer to a topic heading. A descriptive phrase, an example, or any words used in the neighborhood of the target information might be good search words.

For users of conventional documents and for SuperBook users, we expected that the difficulty of searching for information would depend on knowing the exact terms the author used in presenting the information. Any means of searching conventional documents or SuperBook documents should be easier if users do not have to reformulate their questions or think of synonyms in order to match the words used by the author.

We expected that the *open-book essays* would reflect the relative ease of searching for information using conventional documents or SuperBook. If SuperBook really facilitates finding useful information, then SuperBook users might include more information in their essays compared to conventional document users.

Method

Source Text. A statistics text, *S An Interactive Environment For Data Analysis and Graphics* [2], was used in the study. The "S-manual" was selected because its size (562 pages), table of contents, and index are similar to many textbooks and documents. Subjects with a background in statistics also could be recruited easily, and the source text was available in *Troff* form.

Search questions. Four sets of search questions were written representing the crossing of the heading-word and the text-word factors described earlier. One question of each of the four types was generated from target information in each of the eight chapters of the S-manual (see Table 1).

Training tutorial. Each user was given a tutorial introduction to SuperBook using a portion of the *Texas Family Legal Code* as the text. The tutorial required users to try out each of the functions of SuperBook and concluded with four practice problems. A typical user completed training in approximately one hour.

Subjects. Users were 20 university students who had completed one or more courses in statistics.

Procedure. The experiment consisted of one training session followed by five evaluation sessions. All users initially worked through the SuperBook training tutorial, then were assigned randomly to work with the S-manual documentation in conventional print or SuperBook form. Eight search problems, two of each of the four types, were given in each of the first four evaluation sessions. Users worked on a question until they typed in the number of the section that they thought contained the target information. They were allowed to type in "Don't Know" and go on to the next question if they were unable to find the target information after 15 minutes of search.

The first part of the final session was devoted to two "open-book essay" questions. Since many users had difficulty interpreting the second essay question, only the first essay was scored. It asked users to compare three related functions of the S system.

Following the essays, users were asked to rate the documentation, the S system itself, and the likelihood that they might take additional courses in statistics. The final tasks assessed several aspects of incidental learning. Users were asked to recall as many chapter headings, commands, and datasets as they could remember, and to describe the operation of eight randomly selected S-system commands.

Results and Discussion

Search performance. SuperBook produced an overall advantage in search accuracy compared to conventional documentation (75% vs. 62%, $F(1,18)=18.50$, $p<.001$). The three-way interaction of document type, heading-word cues, and text-word cues also was reliable ($F(1,18)=22.18$, $p<.001$). As expected, performance with the printed document depended on topic heading cues, but SuperBook performance did not. SuperBook produced more accurate searches for three of the four types of questions. The advantage for SuperBook was reliably ($p<.05$) greater for both types of questions that included words taken from the text in the neighborhood of the target information. Conventional documentation tended to produce higher search accuracy than SuperBook for questions containing neither heading- nor text-words ($.10>p>.05$).

SuperBook users gave fewer erroneous responses ($p<.001$) overall. Although the three-way interaction was reliable ($p<.05$) in this analysis, conventional documentation did not have a reliable advantage in error rate for any type of question. Users of conventional documentation gave up after 15 minutes of search on 8% of all questions; SuperBook users gave up on 5% of the questions.

Table 3

Mean Search Completion Times in Minutes

Form of Documentation	Words in Question Taken from: Text + Heading	Text	Heading	Neither	Mean for All Types
SuperBook	3.7	**4.3**	4.4	**9.3**	5.4
Print	3.5	**7.5**	3.5	**8.0**	5.6

Adjacent boldface pairs in the same column differ reliably across forms of documentation.

SuperBook search times averaged 5.4 minutes compared to 5.6 minutes for conventional documentation ($F(1,18)<1.0$). The three-way interaction (see Table 3) again was reliable ($F(1,18)=10.14$, $p<.005$). SuperBook resulted in reliably ($p<.001$) faster searches for questions that included only text-word cues. Conventional documentation resulted in faster ($p<.05$) searches for questions that included neither text- nor heading-word cues.

Open-book essays. The essays were given to a statistician who is also an expert on the S system. The statistician developed her own method of scoring and rated copies of the essays that had been stripped of all identifying information. Essays written by SuperBook users were judged superior to those written by users of conventional documentation (average score 5.8 vs. 3.6 out of 7 maximum; $t(18)=3.14$, $p<.01$) For a second scoring method, a fact checklist was developed, and a point was given for each fact included in an essay. The essays then were scored "blind" by a reader working with the checklist. Scores were reliably higher for SuperBook users (average score of 8.8 facts vs. 6.0 out of 15 maximum, $t(18)=2.43$, $p<.05$). Other aspects of the writing including essay length and time spent answering the question did not differ reliably.

Subjective ratings. SuperBook users rated the documentation much easier to use than the printed manual users did (average score of 5.8 vs 3.1 on a 7-point rating scale, $t(18)=4.80$, $p<.01$). SuperBook users also gave reliably higher ratings for the S system itself ($p<.01$) and for their affect for statistics following the experiment ($p<.05$).

Incidental learning. SuperBook users recalled significantly more chapter headings than the users of the printed manual did ($t(18)=3.18$, $p<.01$). This result probably is due to the fact that the *Table of Contents* window continually displayed the chapter headings to SuperBook users. None of the other differences in incidental learning approached statistical significance ($p>.10$).

SUMMARY AND FUTURE DIRECTIONS

For most kinds of search questions, SuperBook produced advantages over conventional documentation that are statistically reliable and practically significant. When users were given questions that included words taken either from the appropriate topic heading or from the text in the vicinity of the answer, SuperBook users had between a 10% and 40% advantage in finding the target information. When given open-book essay questions that required gathering information from more than a single page of text, students using SuperBook wrote essays whose scores averaged 61% higher than those written by students using the conventional documentation. The ease of use and overall superior performance of SuperBook probably led to users' enthusiastic subjective ratings.

SuperBook's advantage over conventional documentation appears to be greatest for dealing with questions that are not anticipated by an author's organization of a document. When search questions did not cue the appropriate location in the author's topic structure, but did include words taken from the text, SuperBook had a large advantage in search accuracy and search time compared to conventional documentation. Similarly, the essay questions required users to search the documentation in a way that did not correspond to the author's organization of the material; again, SuperBook proved advantageous. Further studies including essay questions are being conducted to pinpoint the reason for this SuperBook advantage. One possibility is that SuperBook users find more relevant information in different places; another is that dynamic highlighting tailored to a user's question causes more relevant information to be included in the essays.

SuperBook allows users to access information without knowing the author's organizational scheme, but it still requires users to know the author's *words.* For questions constructed by eliminating or replacing with synonyms any words in the neighborhood of the target information, SuperBook produced poorer search performance than the conventional text did. While SuperBook users did not make reliably more errors on these questions, they took longer and tended to give up searching without finding the target information more often than users of the conventional documentation. SuperBook users approach these questions as they would any other type, using *Word Lookup* to find the occurrences of words in the question. While some of these words do occur in the S-manual, the words have been selected so that they do not occur near the target information. In such cases, SuperBook users spend much time and effort tracking down false leads.

In response to these findings, future work on SuperBook will attempt to deal with user questions phrased in terms that a document's author did not use in referring to the target information. We estimate that this situation occurs in approximately 20% of the questions users have when trying to get information from a document or database [12]. One approach would involve programming an "advisor" to detect when a strategy employed by a user is not likely to be productive. Perhaps a more interesting approach is to employ Latent Semantic Indexing (LSI), another computer-based enhancement being explored in our laboratory [5, 6]. Using LSI, it may be possible to give users a "sense" score for various parts of a document, even if the user is searching with words different from those the author has written.

REFERENCES

1. Allison, D.R. Electronic publishing technologies [Special Issue]. *IEEE Computer, 21*, 1 (Jan. 1988).
2. Becker, R.A. and Chambers, J.M. *S An Interactive Environment for Data Analysis and Graphics.* Wadsworth, Belmont, Calif., 1984.
3. Bush, V. As we may think. *Atlantic Monthly, 76*, 1 (Jan. 1945), 101-108.
4. Conklin, J. Hypertext: An introduction and survey. *IEEE Computer, 20*, 9 (Sept. 1987), 17-41.
5. Deerwester, S., Dumais, S.T., Furnas, G.W., Landauer, T.K., and Harshman, R.A. Indexing by latent semantic analysis. *JASIS*, in press.
6. Dumais, S.T., Furnas, G.W., Landauer, T.K., Deerwester, S. and Harshman, R. Using latent semantic analysis to improve access to textual information. In *Proceedings of CHI'88* (Washington, D.C., May 15-19). ACM, New York, 1988, pp. 281-285.
7. Engelbart, D.C., and English, W.K. A research center for augmenting human intellect. In *Proceedings of the 1968 Fall Joint Computer Conference* AFIPS Press, Montvale, N.J., 1968, pp. 395-410.
8. Furnas, G.W. Experience with an adaptive indexing scheme. *Proceedings of CHI'85* (San Francisco, Apr. 14-18). ACM, New York, 1985, pp. 131-135.
9. Furnas, G.W. Generalized fisheye views. In *Proceedings of CHI'86* (Boston, Apr. 13-17). ACM, New York, 1986, pp. 16-23.
10. Furnas, G.W., Landauer, T.K., Gomez, L.M., and Dumais, S.T. Statistical semantics: Analysis of the potential performance of key-word information systems. *Bell System Technical Journal, 62*, 6, 1983, pp. 1753-1806.
11. Gomez, L.M. and Lochbaum, C.C. People can retrieve more objects with enriched key-word vocabularies. But is there a human performance cost? In B. Shackel (Ed.), *Human-Computer Interaction - Interact '84.* North Holland, Amsterdam, 1984, pp. 257-261.
12. Gomez, L.M., Lochbaum, C.C. and Landauer, T.K. All the right words: A study of human performance and key-word information retrieval. *JASIS*, in press.
13. Marchionini, G. and Shneiderman, B. Finding facts vs. browsing knowledge in hypertext systems. *IEEE Computer, 21*, 1 (Jan. 1988), 70-80.
14. Mantei, M.M. *A study of disorientation behavior in ZOG.* Doctoral dissertation. University of Southern California, Los Angeles, 1982.
15. McCracken, D.L. and Akscyn, R.M. Experience with the ZOG human-computer interface system. *Int. J. Man-Mach. St., 21*, 1984, 293-310.
16. Nelson, T.H. Getting it out of our system. In G. Schechter (Ed.), *Information Retrieval: A Critical Review.* Thompson Books, Washington, D.C., 1967, pp. 191-210.
17. Perlman, G. An overview of SAM: A hypertext interface to Smith & Mosier's. Technical Report TR-87-09. Wang Institute, Tyngsboro, Mass., 1987.
18. Remde, J.R., Gomez, L.M., and Landauer, T.K. SuperBook: An Automatic Tool for Information Exploration--Hypertext? In *Proceedings of Hypertext '87.* University of North Carolina, Chapel Hill, 1987, pp. 175-188.
19. Shneiderman, B. *Designing the user interface: strategies for effective human-computer interaction.* Addison-Wesley, Reading, Mass., 1987.
20. Smith, J.B. and Weiss, S.F. Hypertext [Special issue]. *CACM, 31*, 7 (July, 1988).
21. Walker, J.H. Document Examiner: Delivery interface for hypertext documents. In *Proceedings of Hypertext '87.* University of North Carolina, Chapel Hill, 1987, pp. 307-323.

Analysis

SEVEN WAYS TO MAKE A HYPERTEXT PROJECT FAIL

Robert J. Glushko
Hypertext Engineering

SUMMARY

Hypertext is an exciting concept, but designing and developing hypertext applications of practical scale is hard. "Hypertext engineers" must overcome seven problems to make a project feasible and successful:

1. **Developing realistic expectations in the face of hypertext hype**
2. **Assembling a multidisciplinary project team**
3. **Establishing and following design guidelines**
4. **Dealing with installed base constraints**
5. **Obtaining usable source files**
6. **Finding appropriate software technology and methods**
7. **Overcoming legal uncertainties about intellectual property concerns.**

The excitement in the technical community and the popular press is rapidly inspiring others to pursue the vision of hypertext as a means to combine text, graphics, voice, and other media to make information more accessible, usable, and entertaining. Nevertheless, the novelty and the immaturity of "hypertext engineering" as a discipline cause many projects to fall short of these goals. Elsewhere *[1]* I have emphasized some of the challenging design issues that must be overcome "to make the hypertext vision happen." In this paper I take a broader view to include management and nontechnical factors and expand the list to seven ways in which hypertext projects fail. Not all of these problems are specific to hypertext projects, but together, these seven issues combine to make hypertext applications hard to design, develop, and deploy successfully.

This article has been peer reviewed.

A COMPOSITE CASE STUDY

Attracted by the excitement about hypertext, Company C decides that links and navigation features will bring enhanced usability to a problem that has traditionally been handled in a database or document archive. Since it is the first hypertext project in Company C, all of the most talented and ambitious researchers and developers find their way onto the project. No one keeps track of how much time and effort go into it, but after a few months a carefully hand-crafted demonstration system or prototype emerges using "Hyper-X." Hyper-X is a highly touted program that everyone is talking and reading about as a revolutionary software advance.

The prototype system is flashy and compelling on the 19-inch workstation screen. It contains only a tiny amount of the information contained in the application it is intended to replace, but even a casual observer is impressed by how usable and appealing it looks. The colors, the graphics scanned from documents and books, the animation, and the sound effects come together seamlessly to create a multimedia proof-of-concept.

The vice president of Company C compares the prototype with the original text-based system and declares the Hyper-X version a smashing success. All that remains is to "scale it up" by converting the remainder of the information to hypertext.

SEVEN WAYS TO FAIL

How you interpret this case study so far might depend on where you are in your project, or whether you are part of the prototype team or a member of the team that must scale it up. But the stage is now set for disaster. In the sections that follow I analyze the seven ways in which the project can fail.

Unrealistic Expectations About Scale and Readiness

When the full-scale development project begins, the organization required to carry it out usually has unrealistic expectations about how hard it is and about the capabilities and resources needed to do it. Demonstration projects often bring together the best people, who have ample resources and whose efforts benefit from ad hoc interorganizational cooperation because of the novelty of hypertext. Many demonstration projects "succeed" by using methods and tools that are impossible to scale up *[2]*.

Often the demonstration project uses an off-the-shelf software package that provides neither the capacity nor the performance to deliver the bulk of information now managed by the traditional database or file system. Worse, the information examples and links in the demonstration project may have been carefully hand-crafted, an unworkable approach for a system several orders of magnitude larger. An obsessive focus on "how it looks" often drives out serious consideration of "how it has to work."

If a demonstration project takes three months to convert five articles from an encyclopedia into an interactive hypermedia form, how long will it take to convert a thousand articles using the same techniques? Automatic, semiautomatic, or template-based techniques are the only realistic option for large conversion projects, but these are almost never applied during the initial prototyping effort, which usually focuses on user interface concerns.

Over time, organizations will acquire an experience base that allows them to make realistic estimates for large-scale projects that involve text and hypertext. But in the meantime it is better to be conservative.

Missing Skills on Design and Development Team

Organizations considering a hypertext project usually have available plenty of software design and development skills. However, hypertext projects may require (or at least benefit from) a broader mix of skills. Appropriate skills in a hypertext project team include—

- Software designers
- User-interface designers
- Usability testers and potential users
- Technical writers and editors
- Indexers
- Database designers.

Hypermedia projects can require still other talents, including graphic artists and people who understand how to integrate multiple media, sometimes called "art directors." For conversion projects, the participation of the author or editor of the original information can be invaluable in explaining the presentation conventions of the existing format. If neither is available, the project should allow additional time to develop an understanding of the design and the design rationale of the existing information. Likewise, the people who run the plant, repair the airplanes, or otherwise are expert in the application area must be involved, or the project runs the risk of building a carefully designed user interface to the wrong information.

Few organizations or individuals have expertise in more than a few of these areas. Even if the needed mix of skills for a project organization can be assembled by matrix management or by bringing in appropriate consultants, making such an interdisciplinary team work effectively together is no small challenge.

Few Published Case Studies or Design Guidelines

Because hypertext is a relatively new design field, there are few detailed published case studies or design guidelines that designers can readily use. Published reports about hypertext are not representative, being typically biased toward small-scale demonstration or research projects. While hypertext applications of practical scale have been successfully designed and implemented, such projects are generally not documented in the literature because of resource constraints in development organizations, because of proprietary considerations, or because they are classified for security reasons.

While there is a growing body of empirical research evaluating particular hypertext systems or specific design options, this work does not usually generalize well. In addition, formal experiments have been able to establish that most of the design choices, when considered in isolation, have only small impacts on system usability *[3]*. To complicate matters, sometimes small changes in the user's task or the structure of the hypertext can lead to conflicting answers about the relative merit of design features *[4]*. Individual differences in users, especially motivational differences, and the effects of different tasks seem to have major effects on system usability. Yet the hypertext system designer usually cannot control who the users are and the tasks they want to carry out.

However, designers of hypertext systems can take steps to ensure that their systems are acceptable and effective for their users. While empirically validated design guidelines remain some way off, design methodologies for hypertext are being proposed; the most comprehensive of these is that of Perlman *[5]*. Designers should be conservative in adding features and should adopt an iterative design and evaluation strategy that can identify key usability challenges when it is still early enough to do something about them.

Installed Base Constraints

Hypertext demonstration projects are often done in research organizations that have advanced technology, including workstations and high-resolution 19-inch monitors. HyperCard on the Macintosh computer is also a very popular environment for demonstration projects.

In contrast, the users for whom full-scale versions of these demonstration systems must be targeted often work with an older or different installed base of computing equipment. This installed base may consist predominantly of IBM AT-compatible processors with small display screens having limited graphics resolution.

This situation often poses a dilemma for hypertext projects. Advanced technology may be needed to demonstrate the benefits of hypertext capabilities, but the presentation of these capabilities in the demonstration projects exceeds what the installed base will support. It is essential that the funding or marketing organization promoting the project know the costs and tradeoffs implied by various technology alternatives. Which is more successful, a project that uses less-advanced technology to create lower expectations that can be met, or a project that uses state-of-the-art technology that is not readily available for the average user? There is no right answer, but to ask the question is essential when project goals are being established.

In any case, the installed base slowly changes, so hypertext designs should be prepared to take advantage of new technology capabilities as they become available. A key consideration is separating the information storage from the user interface of the hypertext system so that the user interface can be enhanced as the installed base permits it. Temporary constraints in processing power for installed-base computers can be overcome by exploiting space vs. time tradeoffs in hypertext designs. For example, navigation maps can be precomputed and stored on a CD-ROM instead of computed in real time.

Poor Quality or Availability of Source Files

Many hypertext conversion projects are plagued by the poor quality or availability of source files. Many documents have no digital form, and even when one exists, it may not be readily usable unless a hypertext version was planned or contracted for when the documents were created.

One common limitation derives from the language with which the digital version of the document was composed or marked-up. The ideal situation is when the markup language is Standard Generalized Markup Language (SGML) or some other language that specifies the logical structure of the document rather than its presentation.

Optical character recognition (OCR) technology is rapidly improving, and new OCR devices that output text in SGML form are especially promising *[6]*. Nevertheless, error rates are not negligible, so proofreading is always required, and the nature of the residual errors in OCR documents makes manual text entry preferable unless correct recognition rates exceed 98 percent *[7]*.

Taken together, potential problems with source files make it essential that hypertext projects carefully investigate source quality and availability before committing to a project schedule. A single document sample may not be representative; often a large document or document collection (such as the complete set of manuals for a large system) is assembled from parts created by different vendors or subcontractors. Each supplier may have provided documents in a different source form. If documents are obtained in various source formats, it is generally more cost-effective to have a third-party text-conversion service transform all of them to a common format than to use project software resources to carry out the conversion.

Fortunately, as the "neutral data" specifications being developed as part of CALS *[8]* and IMIS *[9]* take hold, building hypertext applications on existing information will become significantly easier.

Hypertext is an attractive vision, but practical hypertext applications are hard to build. Disciplined approaches to analyzing information, identifying constraints in its structure and in the task environment, and using the appropriate implementation technology are required.

Hypertext projects whose application involves periodic publication of text created elsewhere should define formatting standards and quality control procedures for the organization that produces the information. These measures can lead to substantial improvement in the productivity of hypertext conversion by enabling the development of automatic conversion software.

Lack of Appropriate Software Tools

Most off-the-shelf hypertext software is oriented toward creating new hypertexts and is not well suited for converting existing documents *[1-2; 10]*. Demonstration projects often use this software to create expectations about the look and feel of a full-scale implementation, and developers often get a harsh shock when they discover fundamental limitations in the software that jeopardize the viability of a project.

It may be worth waiting for the next generation of hypertext software that directly supports conversion. The CALS initiative has prompted many vendors to enter this market, and the tools are expected to improve rapidly *[11]*. Alternatively, some database programs or expert-system shells may better support hypertext features than programs that call themselves hypertext.

If off-the-shelf software must be used for a hypertext project, it is imperative that any demonstration or proof-of-concept phase carefully address the pragmatic issues of scaling up. These include both capacity concerns—can the program manage significantly larger amounts of information with acceptable performance?—and resource concerns—does the program imply or impose design methods for defining units, links, or other features that cannot be applied on a large scale *[1; 10]*?

Legal Uncertainties

In recent years there has been a rash of "look and feel" copyright infringement lawsuits and similar claims for software patents. These legal controversies have arisen because software has been defined both as a kind of "literary work," which makes it copyrightable, and as a kind of machine or method of operting one, which makes it patentable. While these legal analogies may be wrong and may someday be corrected by a new intellectual property law that recognizes the special character of software *[12]*, software designers and developers today are faced with chaos, uncertainty, and legal action.

As unclear as the situation is for software in general, the novel character of hypertext and hypermedia software raises still more complexities for intellectual property law. For example, if copyright law has different rules for "literary works," "audiovisual works," "sound recordings," and "pictorial works," into what legal category does an interactive hypermedia encyclopedia or a talking book fall? Are new links or nodes in a hypertext system considered "derivative works" under copyright law? These and other issues are not just legal curiosities; they will have considerable impact on the legal protection available and hence the economic viability of hypermedia systems.

One aspect of copyright infringement that confronts hypermedia designers and developers is clear and well-known, but new technology has made it easier to break the law. OCR, scanners, digital samplers, and video "frame grabbers" make it possible to copy almost anything and incorporate it into a hypermedia system. But having the technology does not imply the right, and a sure way to invite a lawsuit is to assume that it does. It is not a coincidence that many hypertext applications have used government documents like standards and regulations that are free of copyright restrictions.

The best defense against a copyright infringement claim is to be able to prove independent development, so keeping careful documentation of design decisions is essential. In addition, designs based on experiments or evaluations give the design a "functional" character that narrows the scope of copyright infringement claims. It is best to follow the golden rule when designing a system: Borrow from others no more than you would have them borrow from you. An alternative formulation of this principle can be found in a well-reasoned paper that presents both sides of the look-and-feel debate: Let he who has never borrowed cast the first lawsuit *[13]*.

SUMMARY

Hypertext is an attractive vision, but practical hypertext applications are hard to build. Disciplined approaches to analyzing information, identifying constraints in its structure and in the task environment, and using the appropriate implementation technology are required. Successful hypertext projects are those that take a cautious approach to problems of scale and that make the right tradeoffs along the way. Ω

REFERENCES

1. R.J. Glushko, "Visions of Grandeur?" *Unix Review* 8, no. 2 (1990): 70–80.
2. L. Alschuler, "Hand-Crafted Hypertext: Lessons from the ACM Experiment," in E. Barrett, ed., *The Society of Text: Hypertext, Hypermedia, and the Social Construction of Information* (Cambridge, MA: MIT Press, 1989), 343–361.
3. J. Nielsen, "The Matters That Really Matter for Hypertext Usability," *Hypertext '89 Proceedings* (New York: Association for Computing Machinery, 1989), 239–248.
4. P. Wright, and A. Lickorish, "An Empirical Comparison of Two Navigation Systems for Two Hypertexts," in C. Green and R. McAleese, eds., *Hypertext: Theory into Practice II* (Oxford: Intellect Press, 1990), 84–93.
5. G. Perlman, "Asynchronous Design/Evaluation Methods for Hypertext Technology Development," *Hypertext '89 Proceedings* (New York: Association for Computing Machinery, 1989), 61–81.
6. G. Grygo, "High-Volume Scanners Aid Conversion to CALS Standard," *Digital Review* 6, no. 27 (July 10, 1989): 29.
7. W. Cushman, P. Ojha, and C. Daniels, "Usable OCR: What Are the Minimum Performance Requirements? in *Proceedings of the CHI '90 Conference on Human Factors in Computing Systems* (New York: Association for Computing Machinery, 1990), 145–151.
8. Department of Defense, *Computer-Aided Acquisition and Logistic Support* (Washington, DC: Office of the Secretary of Defense CALS Office, 1985).
9. D. Thomas, and J. Clay, *Computer-Based Maintenance Aids for Technicians: Project Final Report.* Air Force Human Resources Laboratory Technical Report AFHRL-TR-87-44, Wright-Patterson Air Force Base, OH, 1988.
10. R.J. Glushko, "Using Off-the-Shelf Software to Create a Hypertext Electronic Encyclopedia," *Technical Communication* 37, no. 1 (February 1990): 28–33.
11. R. Smithmidford, "Vendors Focus on CALS Conversions for Existing Paper Documents," *Federal Computer Week* 3, no. 3 (September 4, 1989): 38.
12. P. Samuelson, "Why the Look and Feel of Software User Interfaces Should Not Be Protected by Copyright Law," *Communications of the ACM* 32, no. 5 (1989): 563–572.
13. P. Samuelson, "Protecting User Interfaces Through Copyright: The Debate," in *Proceedings of the ACM Conference on Computer-Human Interaction - CHI '89* (New York: Association for Computing Machinery, 1989), 97–103.

Media Streams: An Iconic Visual Language for Video Representation

Marc Davis
Interval Research Coporation
1801-C Page Mill Road
Palo Alto, CA 94304
davis@interval.com

Abstract

In order to enable the search and retrieval of video from large archives, we need a representation language for video content. Although some aspects of video can be automatically parsed, a sufficient representation requires that video be annotated. We discuss the design of a video representation language with special attention to the issue of creating a global, reusable video archive. Our prototype system, Media Streams, enables users to create multi-layered, iconic annotations of streams of video data. Within Media Streams, the organization and categories of the Icon Space allow users to browse and compound over 3500 iconic primitives by means of a cascading hierarchical structure that supports compounding icons across branches of the hierarchy. A Media Time Line enables users to visualize, browse, annotate, and retrieve video content. The challenges of creating a representation of human action in video are discussed in detail, with focus on the effect of the syntax of video sequences on the semantics of video shots.

1 Introduction: The Need for Video Representation

Without content representation, the development of large-scale systems for manipulating video will not happen. Currently, content providers possess massive archives of film and video for which they lack sufficient tools for search and retrieval. For the types of applications that will be developed in the near future (interactive television, personalized news, video on demand, etc.) these archives will remain a largely untapped resource, unless we are able to access their contents. Without a way of accessing video information in terms of its content, a hundred hours of video is less useful than one. With one hour of video, its content can be stored in human memory, but as we move up in orders of magnitude, we need to find ways of creating machine-readable and human-usable representations of video content. It is not simply a matter of cataloging reels or tapes, but of representing the content of video so as to facilitate the retrieval and repurposing of video according to these representations.

Given the current state of the art in machine vision and signal processing, we cannot now (and probably will not be able to for a long time) have machines parse and understand the content of digital video archives for us. Unlike text, for which we have developed sophisticated parsing technologies, and which is accessible to processing in various structured forms (ASCII, RTF, PostScript, SGML, HTML), video is still largely opaque. Some headway has been made in this area. Algorithms for the automatic annotation of shot breaks are becoming more robust and enhanced to handle special cases such as fades (Nagasaka and Tanaka 1992; Zhang and others 1993). Work on camera motion detection is close to enabling reliable automatic classification of pans and zooms (Teodosio 1992; Tonomura and others 1993; Ueda and others 1993) Problems which are still quite difficult but which are being actively worked on include: object recognition (Nagasaka and Tanaka 1992), object tracking (Ueda and others 1991), and motion segmentation (Otsuji and others 1991; Zabih and others 1993) Research is also being conducted in automatic segmentation and tagging of audio data by means of parsing the audio track for pauses and voice intensities (Arons 1993), other audio cues including sounds made by the recording devices themselves (Pincever 1990), as well as specialized audio parsers for music, laughter, and other highly distinct acoustic phenomena (Hawley 1993). Advances in signal separation and speech recognition will also contribute to automating the parsing of the content of the audio track.

Yet this information alone does not enable the creation of a sufficient representation of video content to support content-based retrieval and manipulation. Signal-based parsing and segmentation technologies must be combined with representations of the higher level semantic and syntactic structure of video data in order to support annotation, browsing, retrieval, and resequencing of video according to its content. In the near term, it is computer-supported human annotation that will enable video to become a rich, structured data type.

1.1 Video Representation Today

In developing a structured representation of video content for use in the annotation, retrieval, and repurposing of video from large archives, it is important to understand the current state of video annotation in order to create specifications for how future annotation systems should be able to perform. To begin with, we can posit a hierarchy of the efficacy of annotations:

> *At least,* Pat should be able to use Pat's annotations.
>
> *Slightly better*, Chris should be able to use Pat's annotations.

Even better, Chris's computer should be able to use Pat's annotations.

At best, Chris's computer and Chris should be able to use Pat's and Pat's computer's annotations.

Today, annotations used by video editors will typically only satisfy the first desideratum (Pat should be able to use Pat's annotations) and only for a limited length of time. Annotations used by video archivists aspire to meet the second desideratum (Chris should be able to use Pat's annotations), yet these annotations often fail to do so if the context of annotation is too distant (in either time or space) from the context of use. Current computer-supported video annotation and retrieval systems use keyword-based representations of video and ostensibly meet the third desideratum (Chris's computer should be able to use Pat's annotations), but practically do not because of the inability of keyword representations to maintain a consistent and scalable representation of the salient features of video content.

1.2 Why Keywords Are Not Enough

In the main, video has been archived and retrieved as if it were a non-temporal data type that could be adequately represented by "keywords." A good example of this approach can be seen in Apple Computer's *Visual Almanac* that describes and accesses the contents of its archive by use of "keywords" and "image keys" (Apple Multimedia Lab 1989).

This technique is successful in retrieving matches in a fairly underspecified search but lacks the level of granularity and descriptive richness necessary for computer-assisted and automatic video retrieval and repurposing. The keyword approach is inadequate for representing video content for the following reasons:

- Keywords do not describe the complex *temporal* structure of video and audio information.
- Keywords are not a *semantic* representation. They do not support inheritance, similarity, or inference between descriptors. Looking for shots of "dogs" will not retrieve shots indexed as "German shepherds" and vice versa.
- Keywords do not describe *relations* between descriptors. A search using the keywords "man," "dog," and "bite" may retrieve "dog bites man" videos as well as "man bites dog" videos—the relations between the descriptors highly determine their salience and are not represented by keyword descriptors alone.
- Keywords do not *converge*. Since they are laden with linguistic associations and not a structured, designed language, keywords, as a representation mechanism for video content, suffer from the "vocabulary problem" (Furnas and others 1987). Different users use sufficiently different keywords to describe the same materials such that keyword annotation becomes idiosyncratic rather than consensual.
- Keywords do not *scale*. As the number of keywords grows, the possibility of matching a query to the annotation diminishes. As the size of the keyword vocabulary increases, the precision and recall of searches decrease.

Because of the deficiencies of keyword-based annotation and retrieval systems, current video archives cannot rely on computers to overcome the inherent barriers to sharability and durability in human memory. In fact, even with today's "computerized" systems video archives rely on human memory as the crucial repository of the knowledge not contained in computational representations.

1.3 Towards a Global Media Archive

A video annotation language needs to create representations that are durable and sharable. The knowledge encoded in the annotation language needs to extend in time longer than one person's memory or even a collective memory, and needs to extend in space across continents and cultures. Today, and increasingly, content providers have global reach. German news teams may shoot footage in Brazil for South Korean television that is then accessed by American documentary filmmakers, perhaps ten years later. We need a global media archiving system that can be added to and accessed by people who do not share a common language, and the knowledge of whose contents is not only housed in the memories of a few people working in the basements of news archives and film libraries.

The visual language we have designed may provide an annotation language with which we can create a truly global media resource. Unlike other visual languages that are used internationally (e.g., for traffic signage, operating instructions on machines, etc.), a visual language for video annotation can take advantage of the affordances of the computer medium. We have developed an iconic visual language for video annotation that is computationally writable and readable, and makes use of a structured, semantic, searchable, generative vocabulary of iconic primitives. It also uses color, shading, anti-aliasing, and animation in order to support the creation of durable and sharable representations of video content.

2 Representing Video

Current paradigms of video representation are drawn from practices which arose primarily out of "single-use" video applications. In single-use applications, footage is shot, annotated, and edited for a given movie, story, or film. Annotations are created for one given use of the video data. There do exist certain cases today, like network news archives, film archives, and stock footage houses, in which video is used multiple times, but the level of granularity, semantics, and non-uniformity with which these organizations annotate their archives limits the repurposability of their representations and their video content. The challenge is to create representations which support "multi-use" applications of video. These are applications in which video may be dynamically resegmented, retrieved, and resequenced on the fly by a wide range of users *other than those who originally created the data.* In order to create representations for reusable video, we need to understand the structure and function of what is being represented.

2.1 Streams vs. Clips

Video is a temporal medium that represents continuities and discontinuities of space, time, and action. The first task of a representation of video content is to provide a set of units into which the temporal streams of audio and video data can be parsed. In film theory, this task of parsing the streams of video and audio data into units is called *segmentation* (Bordwell and Thompson 1990). The task of representing the basic structures of video data is the task of creating useful segmentations of that data.

One might think that for the purposes of retrieval and repurposing a segmentation of video into frames, shots, sequences, and scenes would be sufficient. However necessary these traditional segmentations are for video representation they are insufficient for representing video content. First of all, each of these segmentations has certain inherent limitations as a content representation. Frames by themselves are too fine a segmentation and remove the temporal aspects of video content from a representation. Scenes are often too large of a segmentation to be useful for repurposing; by virtue of their completeness they render their parts less easily repurposable. Shots and sequences are a useful level of granularity, but in and of themselves these segmentations do not represent their contents. Finally, and most importantly, there are many aspects of video content which *continue across shot and scene boundaries* (e.g., music, dialogue, character, etc.) or *exist within shot boundaries* (e.g., action, camera motion, etc.).

Today, most systems for representing and manipulating video create a segmentation of video into *clips*. As will be explained below, representing video by segmenting it into clips is a representational strategy that does not support multiple reuse of the representations or of the data represented. The core task of representing video for repurposing is to create *a segmentation of the data out of which multiple segmentations can be generated.* As will be explained below, a *stream-based* representation of video content enables multiple segmentations of video to be generated (Davenport and others 1991).

In most representations of video content, a stream of video frames is segmented into units called *clips* whose boundaries often, but do not necessarily, coincide with shot, sequence, or scene boundaries. Current tools for annotating video content used in film production, television production, and multimedia, add descriptors (often keywords) to clips. There is a significant problem with this approach. By taking an incoming video stream, segmenting it into various clips, and then representing the content of those clips, a clip-based representation imposes a *fixed segmentation* on the content of the video stream.

To illustrate this point, imagine a camera recording a sequence of 100 frames. Traditionally, one or more parts of the stream of frames would be segmented into clips which would then be annotated by attaching descriptors. The clip is a fixed segmentation of the video stream that separates the video from its context of origin and encodes a particular chunking of the original data.

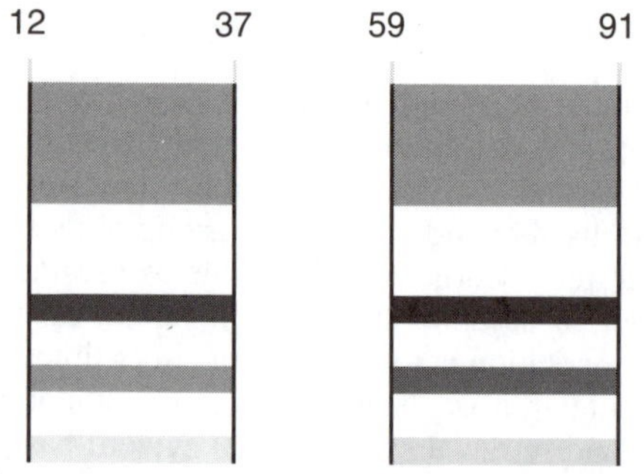

Figure 1. Two "clips" with Three Descriptors Each

In a stream-based representation, the stream of frames is left intact and is annotated by multi-layered annotations with precise time indexes (beginning and ending points in the video stream). Annotations could be made within any of the various categories for video representation discussed below (e.g., characters, character actions, objects, spatial location, camera motions, dialogue, etc.) or contain any data the user may wish.

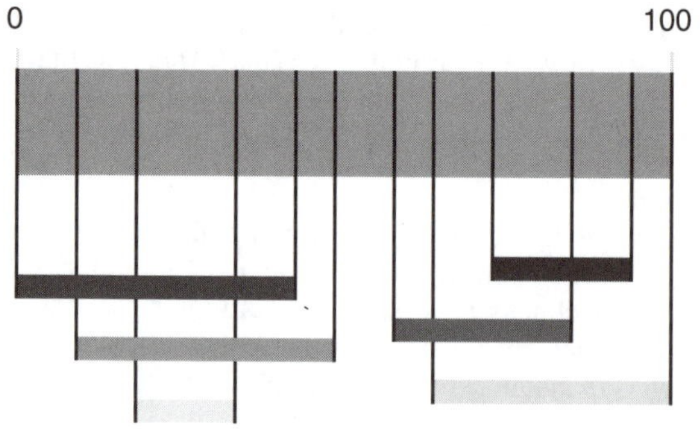

Figure 2. Stream of 100 Frames of Video with 6 Annotations Resulting in *66* Possible Segmentations of the Stream

Stream-based representation makes annotation pay off—the richer the annotation, the more numerous the possible segmentations of the video stream. Stream-based annotations generate new segmentations by virtue of their unions, intersections, overlaps, etc. Clips change from being fixed segmentations of the video stream, to being the results of retrieval queries into the network of stream-based annotations of the video stream. In short, in addressing the challenges of representing video for large archives *what we need are representations which make clips, not representations of clips.*

2.2 Video Syntax and Semantics

In attempting to create a representation of video content, an understanding of the semantics and syntax of video information is a primary concern. Video has a radically different semantic and syntactic structure than text, and attempts to represent video and index it in ways similar to text will suffer serious problems. For video, it is essential to clearly distinguish between its sequence-dependent and sequence-independent semantics. Syntax, the sequencing of individual video shots, creates new semantics which may not be present in any of the individual shots and which may supersede or contravene their existing semantics. This is evidenced by a basic property of the medium that enables not only the repurposing of video data (the resequencing of video shots taken from their original contexts and used to different ends in new contexts), but motion pictures' basic semantic and syntactic functionality: the creation of meaningful sequences through the *montage* of visual and auditory representations of discontinuous times and discontiguous spaces. Eisenstein described this property as *montage* (Eisenstein 1947).

The early experimental evidence for the effects of the syntax of shot combination on the semantics of individual shots was established by the Soviet cinematographer Lev Kuleshov early in this century (Isenhour 1975; Kuleshov 1973; Kuleshov 1974). The classic example of the "Kuleshov Effect" was evidenced by the following experiment (Pudovkin 1949). The following sequence was shown to an audience:

a long take in close-up of the Russian actor Mozhukin's expressionlessly neutral face — cut — a bowl of steaming soup

the same face of the actor — cut — a woman lying dead in a coffin

the same face of the actor — cut — a child playing with a toy bear

When audience members were asked what they saw, they said, "Oh, he was hungry, then he was sad, then he was happy." The same exact image of the actor's face was used in each of the three short sequences. What the Kuleshov Effect reveals is that the semantics of video information is highly determined by what comes before and what comes after any given shot. It is the Kuleshov Effect that makes the construction of cinematic sequences possible at all and that enables us to reuse existing footage to make new sequences.

Kuleshov's experiments began the work of cataloging the effects and principles which underlie all montage and are especially important for a representation of video that seeks to repurpose content and retrieve sequences by composing segments from various videos. Because of the impact of the syntax of video sequences on the semantics of video shots, any indexing or representational scheme for video content needs to explain how the semantics of video changes through resegmentation and resequencing. The challenge for video representation is to provide a framework for determining, representing, and relating those aspects of video content whose semantics are invariant and sequence-independent and those aspects whose semantics are variable and sequence-dependent.

What film theory teaches us is that a representation of video content cannot rely on existing representational strategies for other media or for the physical world. Video is itself a representational system with its own ontological properties and its own constraints on the construction and maintenance of representations of spaces, objects, characters, and actions through the montage of shots. In a word, video has not only its own semantics and syntax, but its own "common sense" which previous approaches to common sense knowledge, temporal, and action representation have yet to address.

2.3 Categories for Video Representation

A central question in our research is the development of a minimal set of categories for representing video content. One of the principal features that makes video unique is that it is a temporal medium. Any language for annotating the content of video must have a way of talking about temporal events—the actions of humans and objects in space over time. Therefore, we also need a way of talking about the characters and objects involved in actions as well as their mise-en-scene, that is, the spatial location, temporal location, and weather/lighting conditions in which these actions take place. The objects and characters involved in actions in particular settings also have significant positions in space relative to one another (beneath, above, inside, outside, etc.).

These categories—*actions*, *characters*, *objects*, *relative positions*, *locations*, *times*, and *weather*—would be nearly sufficient for talking about actions in the world, but video is a *recording* of actions in the world by a camera, and any representation of video content must address further specific properties. First, we need ways of talking about *cinematographic properties*, the movement and framing of the camera recording events in the world. We also need to describe the properties of the *recording medium* itself (film or video, color or black & white, graininess, etc.) Furthermore, in video, viewers see events depicted on screens, and therefore, in addition to relative positions in space, screen objects have a *screen position* in the two-dimensional grid of the frame and in the various layered vertical planes of the screen depth. Finally, video recordings of events can be manipulated as objects and rearranged. We create transitions in video in ways not possible in the physical world. Therefore, *cinematic transitions* must also be represented in an annotation language for video content. In working with video archivists from Monitor Television, we found that in their daily practice (in addition to the above mentioned intersubjective categories) video producers would ask for footage according to highly subjective *thoughts* about the video content which relate to the quality of the frame composition, color, and level of activity.

These categories need not be *sufficient* for media annotation (the range of potential things one can say is unbounded), but we believe they are *necessary* categories for media annotation in order to support retrieval and reuse of particular segments of video data from an annotated stream.

These minimal annotation categories attempt to represent information about media content that can function as a substrate:

- on top of which other annotations may be layered
- out of which new annotations may be inferred
- within which the differences between consensual and idiosyncratic annotations may be articulated

In a minimal representation of video content, the primary level of representation is of the semantically invariant, sequence-independent aspects of video. The semantically variable, sequence-dependent aspects of video content are represented in terms of this primary level of representation. Therefore, the representational system is optimized to represent that which one sees and hears in a video shot, rather than what one infers from the syntactic context of a video shot (Bordwell 1985). The process of representation is highly decontextualizing in order that these representations can support retrieval and repurposing of video content.

3 Media Streams: An Overview

Over the past four years, a small group of researchers in the MIT Media Laboratory's Machine Understanding Group (myself with the assistance of Brian Williams and Golan Levin under the direction of Prof. Kenneth Haase) has built *Media Streams,* a prototype for the representation, retrieval, and repurposing of video and audio data (Davis 1993a; Davis 1993b; Davis 1994a; Davis 1994b; Davis and others 1994; Sack and Davis 1994; Davis 1995).

Media Streams is written in two languages: the outstanding rapid prototyping environment of Macintosh Common Lisp (Apple Computer 1993a) with its CLOS (Common Lisp Object System) interface to the Macintosh ToolBox, and FRAMER (Haase 1994; Haase and Sack 1993), a persistent framework for media annotation and description that supports cross-platform knowledge representation and database functionality. Media Streams has its own Lisp interface to Apple's QuickTime digital video system software (Apple Computer 1993b). Media Streams has been developed on an Apple Macintosh Quadra 940 with two high resolution color displays.

Media Streams enables users to preprocess, annotate, browse, retrieve, and repurpose digital video and audio content with an iconic visual language designed for video representation. Its main functions are outlined in the following subsections.

3.1 Media Streams Functionality

3.1.1. Preprocessing

Media Streams makes use of existing and reliable signal-processing techniques for automatically creating meaningful segmentations and visualizations of digital video and audio data. When a QuickTime movie is first loaded into the system Media Streams creates shot-breaks for the video and pause-breaks for the audio. The system also automatically creates multiple representations of the video and audio data's structure at different temporal and spatial resolutions which are used in visualizing and navigating the data (for video: thumbnails and a videogram; for audio: waveforms and pause-break bars).

3.1.2. Annotation

In Media Streams, annotators use an iconic visual language to create stream-based annotations of video content. Media Streams utilizes a hierarchically structured semantic space of iconic primitives which are combined to form compound descriptors which are then used to create multi-layered, temporally indexed annotations of video content. These iconic primitives are grouped into the descriptive categories designed for video representation and are structured to deal with the special semantic and syntactic properties of video data discussed above. These categories include: space, time, weather, characters, objects, character actions, object actions, relative position, screen position, recording medium, cinematography, shot transitions, and subjective thoughts about the material.

In Media Streams, the annotation language is designed to support the annotation of the consensual aspects of video content—what one sees and hears, rather than what one infers from context—in order to facilitate the convergence of iconic annotations and the repurposability of the content described by these annotations. Media Streams does not aim to support all types of annotations, but only those physically-based descriptions whose semantics supports repurposing. Other types of annotations may be layered on top of and use those created in Media Streams, but the goal here is for finding the most minimalist way of saying the most salient things about the content so as to support content-based retrieval for repurposing.

Media Streams' annotations do not describe video clips, but are themselves temporal extents describing content within a video stream. As *stream-based* annotations they support multiple layers of overlapping descriptions which, unlike clip-based annotations, enable video to be dynamically resegmented at query time.

The system also supports the reuse of other people's descriptive effort through the ability to retrieve and group related iconic descriptors into palettes.

3.1.3. Browsing

Browsing in Media Streams makes use of the representations of video content which are automatically generated as well as annotations created by human users. For example, users can use a jump button (identical to the "track advance" button on consumer CD players) in order to jump by content to the next logical change in the video stream be it the next shot break or the next new character in a shot.

3.1.4. Retrieval

Media Streams supports the retrieval of annotated video segments and sequences in two ways: *by description* or *by example.* Query by description is the use of the annotation language as a query language in order to describe footage that one wants to find. Query by example is using already annotated footage itself as a query. Unlike most conventional video retrieval systems, Media Streams supports query of annotated video according to its *temporal* and *semantic* structure.

3.1.5. Repurposing

Media Streams is designed to support the repurposing of video content in all of its functions and components. The functionality that most clearly shows this is the way in which Media Streams redefines retrieval in terms of composition.

A query for a video sequence will not only search the annotated video streams for a matching sequence but will *compose* a sequence out of parts from various videos in order to satisfy the query. We refer to this retrieval strategy as *retrieval-by-composition*. In answering user queries, Media Streams can repurpose the content in its own archive in order to *make* video sequences as a way of satisfying requests to *find* them.

3.2 Media Streams System Components

Media Streams attempts to address two fundamental interface issues in video annotation and retrieval: creating and searching the space of descriptors to be used in annotation and retrieval; and visualizing, annotating, browsing, and retrieving video shots and sequences. Consequently, the system has two main interface components: the Icon Space (Figure 3) and the Media Time Line (Figure 5).

3.2.1. Icon Space

The **Icon Space** is the interface for the selection and compounding of the iconic descriptors in Media Streams (Figure 3). To date Media Streams has over 3500 iconic primitives. In the **Icon Workshop** portion of the Icon Space (the upper half) these iconic primitives can be compounded to form compound icons. Through compounding, the base set of primitives can produce millions of unique expressions.

In the **Icon Palette** portion of the Icon Space (the lower half of Figure 3), users can create palettes of iconic descriptors for use in annotation and search. By querying the space of descriptors, users can dynamically group related iconic descriptors on-the-fly. In Figure 3, the query for the union of female character icons and full body character actions has retrieved compound icons of various females doing various actions. Importantly, the Icon Palette enables users to reuse the descriptive effort of others. When annotating video, users can make use of related icons that other users have already created and used to annotate a similar piece of video.

3.2.1.1. Icon Workshop Organization

What enables the user to navigate and make use of our large number of primitives is the way the Icon Workshop organizes icons into cascading hierarchies. We refer to the iconic primitives in the Icon Workshop as *cascading icons*. The Icon Workshop has two significant forms of organization for managing navigational and descriptive complexity:

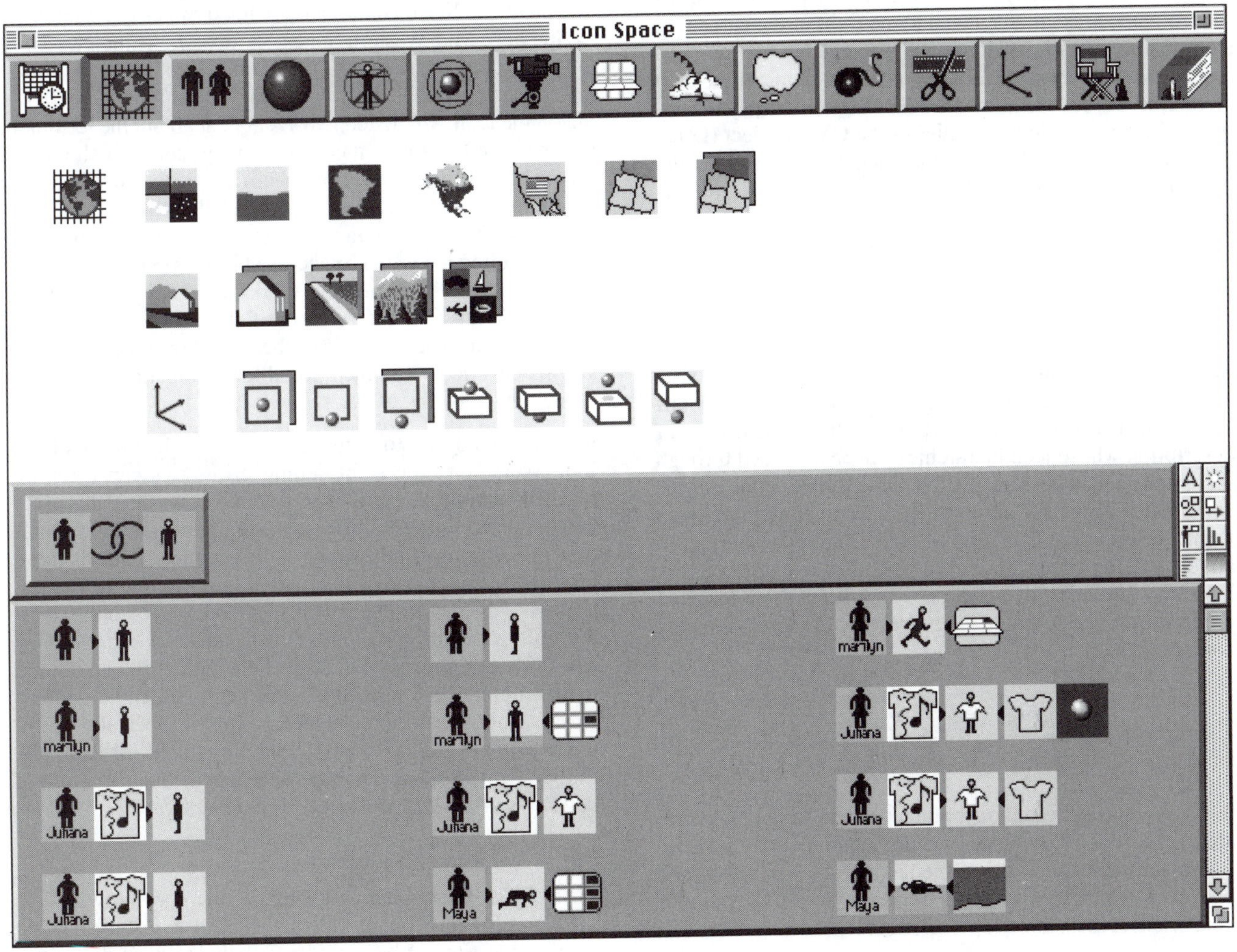

Figure 3: The Icon Space

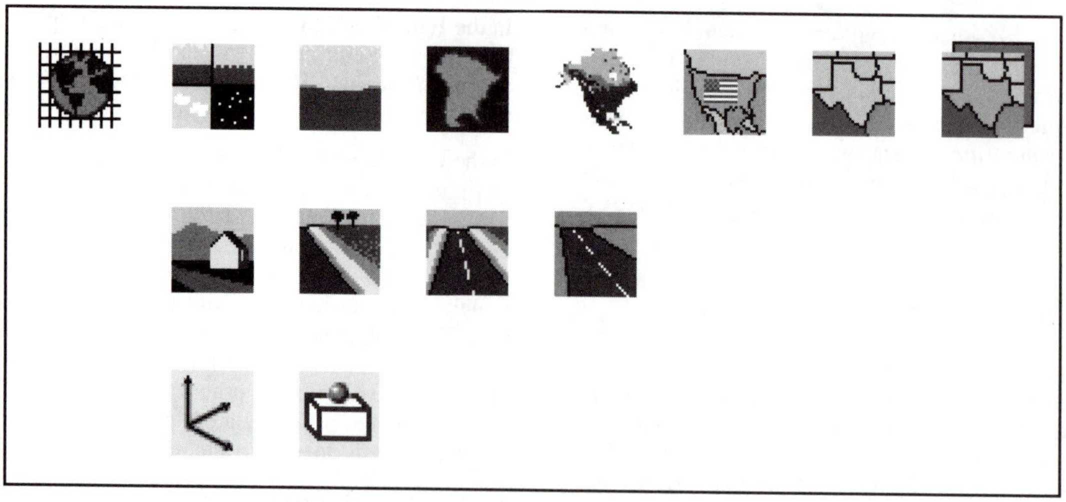

Figure 4. An Icon Path to *On Top of a Street in Texas*

- *Cascading Hierarchy with Increasing Specificity of Primitives on Subordinate Levels*

Cascading icons are organized in hierarchies from levels of generality to increasing levels of specificity. Similarly to cascading menus on the Macintosh, when a user cascades down an icon hierarchy by clicking on a cascading icon, its subordinate icons are displayed to the right of the cascading icon. These subordinate icons are arranged *horizontally* and represent an increased level of specificity. Some of the icon hierarchies cascade to as many as 7 or 8 levels deep, yet, similarly to the semantic hierarchies of the CYC Project (Lenat and Guha 1990), the design of the categories themselves and their first two or three levels is the hardest and most important representational task.

- *Compounding of Hierarchically Organized Primitives Across Multiple Axes of Description*

In many icon hierarchies in the Icon Workshop, there exists an additional form of organization. When subordinate icons are arranged *vertically,* they represent independent axes of description whose icon hierarchies can be cascaded through separately and whose respective subordinate icons can be compounded together across these axes to form compound iconic descriptors. This form of organization enables a relatively small set of primitives to be compounded into a very large and rich set of descriptors. To illustrate these forms of organization in our iconic language we can look at how the compound icon:

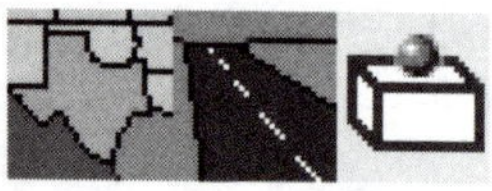

for "the scene is located on top of a street in Texas" was created. Figure 4 shows the cascading icon hierarchy for *spatial location* extended out to the icons for *Texas, street,* and *on top of,* which the user compounded to create the icon for "the scene is located on top of a street in Texas."

The user clicked on the *spatial location* icon, which cascaded to show its *vertically* arranged subordinate icons *geographical space*, *functional space*, and *topological space*. Each of these cascading icons has further *horizontally* arranged subordinate icons each of which may go several levels deep. For example, the icons in the path from *geographical space* to *Texas* each represents a distinct level of progressive specification (geographical space --> land --> continent --> North America --> United States of America --> Southern Mid-Western States --> Texas). As indicated by the gray square behind the *Texas* icon, it too has further levels of specificity below it which can be displayed by clicking on the icon. In the Icon Workshop, at all but the terminal levels in the hierarchy, there exist many icons which themselves have further levels of specification. At any level in the hierarchy, icons can be compounded across the vertical organization to create compound icons. In addition to clicking, cascading icons can be accessed by dropping an existing compound icon onto the Icon Workshop that opens the icon hierarchies up to the terminals of the components of the dropped icon. The structure of the Icon Workshop enables a vast space of icons and their possible combinations to be easily navigated by the user.

It is also important to note that in the icon hierarchy of the Icon Workshop, the same iconic primitives can often be reached by multiple paths. The system knows the paths users take to get to these primitives; this enriches the representation of the compounds which are constructed out of these primitives. Having multiple paths allows different categorization schemes to coexist in the Icon Workshop. These multiple paths are also important in retrieval because they can guide generalization and specialization of search criteria by functioning as a semantic net of hierarchically organized classes, subclasses, and instances. This is especially useful in the organization of object icons, in which, for example, the icon for *blow-dryer* may be reached under *hand-held device, heat-producing device*, or *personal device*.

3.2.2. Media Time Line

The **Media Time Line** (Figure 5) is the core browser and viewer of Media Streams. It enables users to visualize video at multiple timescales simultaneously, to read and write multi-layered iconic annotations, and provides one consistent interface for annotating, browsing, and retrieving video

Figure 5: The Media Time Line

Please see the inside back cover for color image C11 which corresponds to Figure 5.

and audio data. The Media Time Line separates annotation into various streams. These annotation streams reproduce and refine the icon categories of the Icon Space. They enable the icons used in annotation to be *viewed in context*. This design principle, like the hierarchical organization and compounding of the Icon Space, enables the large number of Media Streams' compound icons to maintain their intelligibility.

3.2.2.1. Visualizing Video Structure

Since video is a temporal medium, the first challenge for representing and annotating its content is to visualize its content and structure. In the Media Time Line we represent video at multiple timescales simultaneously by trading off temporal and spatial resolution in order to visualize both the content and the dynamics of the video data. We create a sequence of thumbnails of the video stream by subsampling the video stream at one frame per second. For longer movies, we sample at one frame per minute as well. The spatial resolution of each thumbnail enables the user to visually inspect its contents. However, the temporal resolution is not as informative because the sequence is being subsampled at one frame per second.

In order to overcome the lack of temporal resolution, we extend a technique pioneered by Ron MacNeil of the Visible Language Workshop at the MIT Media Laboratory (MacNeil 1991) and used in the work of Mills and his colleagues at Apple Computer's Advanced Technology Group (Mills and others 1992). We create a videogram. A videogram is made by grabbing a center strip from every video frame and concatenating them together. Underneath the subsampled thumbnail frames of video in the Media Time Line, the videogram represents the fine temporal resolution of the dynamics of the video with a reduced spatial resolution. However, because camera operators often strive to leave significant information within the center of the frame, a salient trace of spatial resolution is preserved.

In a videogram, a still image has an unusual salience: if a camera pans across a scene and then a center strip is taken from each video frame, a still will be recreated which is coherently deformed by the pace and direction of the camera motion and/or the pace and direction of any moving objects within the frame. Our contribution is that by presenting two different, but coordinated views of video data—the thumbnails, with good spatial resolution and poor temporal resolution, and the videogram, with poor spatial resolution but good temporal resolution—the system enables the viewer to use both representations in tandem in order to visualize the structure of the video information. In the Media Time Line, the videogram is sampled at a rate of one 4 pixel-wide strip every 1/30 second while the corresponding thumbnails appear above (outlined in a bounding box) sampled at a rate of one 32 pixel-wide thumbnail every second. This idea of playing *spatial* and *temporal* resolutions off one another is also utilized in Laura Teodosio's work on "salient stills" (Teodosio 1992) and holds promise as a general guideline for creating new visualizations of video data. An example of this spatial/temporal tradeoff can be seen in Figure 6 in

Figure 6: Media Time Line Detail — Video Thumbnails and Videogram

which the movement of Arnold through the frame is differently visible in the first thumbnails within the bounding box and in the left hand side of the videogram. In the videogram, the two swaths of extended face with the space between them correspond to Arnold's moving in the video from left to right through the center of the frame, his pausing, and then moving again.

With little practice, users can learn to quickly scan the dynamics and structure of video content from this dual temporal/spatial representation. Shot breaks are clearly visible as are camera pans, zooms, tracking, and the difference between handheld and tripod recorded video footage. Finally, the deformation of the still image in the videogram provides a coded signature of camera and/or object motion as in the example above.

3.3 Annotating Video in Media Streams

The process of annotating video in Media Streams using these components involves a few simple steps. In the Icon Space, the user can retrieve related iconic descriptors to form a customized icon palette or create iconic descriptors by cascading down hierarchies of icons in order to select or compound iconic descriptors. By dragging iconic descriptors from the Icon Space and dropping them onto a Media Time Line, the user annotates the temporal media represented in the Media Time Line. Once dropped onto a Media Time Line, an iconic description extends from its insertion point in the video stream to either a shot break or the end of the video stream. A vertical select bar specifies the current position in a movie and displays the icons that are valid at that point in time. The user can specify the end point of an annotation by dragging its icon off teh select bar and can adjust the starting and ending points of an annotation by dragging the annotation's edges. A description is built up by dropping down icons for the various categories of video representation. The granularity and specificity of the annotation are user determined. By annotating various aspects of the video and audio streams (time, space, characters, characters' actions, camera motions, etc.), the user constructs a multi-layered, temporally indexed representation of video content.

In addition to dropping individual icons onto the Media Time Line, the user can construct compound icon sentences on the Media Time Line, which, when completed, are then available for use in the Icon Space and may themselves be used as descriptors. For example, the user initially builds up the compound icon sentence for "Jane waves" by successively dropping the icons:

and

onto the Media Time Line. The user then has the follwoing "glommed" icon in the Icon Space to use in later annotation.

In addition to annotating video content, users can transcribe dialogue, and use the categories for video representation to describe events in the audio stream. In annotating the presence or absence of audio events, our representation makes use of the fact that in listening to audio, one thinks about the source that produced the audio. This concept correlates to Christian Metz's notion of "aural objects" (Metz 1980). Icons for different objects and characters are compounded with the icon for the action of producing the heard sound in order to annotate audio events.

In Media Streams, the interface for annotation is the same as the interface for retrieval: annotation is the process of describing footage one has; storyboarding is the process of describing footage one wants to make; query formulation is the process of describing footage one wants to find. In Media Streams, one interface is used for annotation and retrieval-by-composition.

4 Why Icons?

The most obvious and unique feature of Media Streams' user interface is its iconic visual language for video annotation and retrieval (Davis 1995; Davis 1993a; Davis 1993b). The representation and retrieval structures in Media Streams could be manipulated by many types of human-computer interface; however, the choice of an iconic visual language for this task is not an arbitrary or unimportant one. It represents a solution for the design of practical video annotation systems today as well as a statement about the future of systems for media manipulation. By decreasing the tedium and increasing the reusability of annotation effort, Media Streams' iconic visual language may solve many of the current problems of the stock footage industry whose antiquated technology and practices are inadequate to the task of on-time and accurate retrieval of video data (Greenway and Mouchawar 1994). A uniform and widespread iconic visual language for video annotation and retrieval will enable the creation of a global media archive in which video can be stored and reused.

Media Streams' iconic visual language also points toward the development of new forms of visual literacy which will become predominant in the coming age of computational media. We are currently in a crucial phase of a second "Gutenberg shift" (McLuhan 1962) in which video is becoming a ubiquitous data type not only for viewing (i.e., reading) but for daily communication and composition (i.e., writing). This shift will only be possible when we can construct representations of video which enable us to parse, index, browse, search, retrieve, manipulate, and resequence video according to representations of its content. These representations of visual media will themselves be visual. An iconic visual language for video annotation and retrieval will support new forms of video writing (repurposing of video content) within a widespread practice of asynchronous many-to-many daily video communication.

There have been prior, pre-computational efforts to create iconic languages to facilitate global communication (Bliss 1978; Neurath 1981) and provide international standard symbols for specific domains (Dreyfuss 1972). We developed Media Streams' iconic visual language in response to trying to meet the needs of annotating video content in large archives. It seeks to enable:

- Accurate and readable time-indexed representation of actions, expressions, and spatial relations
- Gestalt visualization of the dense, multi-layered structure of video content
- Quick recognition and browsing of content annotations
- Designed visual similarities between instances or subclasses of a class (visual resonances in the iconic language)
- Articulation of the boundaries between consensual and idiosyncratic annotations (icons can have attached textual annotations and can thus function as the explicit consensual tokens of various idiosyncratic textual descriptions)
- Global international use of annotations
- Usable by illiterate and preliterate people

Media Streams' iconic language encompasses icons which denote both things and actions and thus embodies a distinction analogous to Chang's (Chang 1986) distinction between object icons and process icons. The difference here is that the objects and processes denoted by the Media Streams' icons are not computational ones, but aspects of the video content which they represent.

The iconic language gains expressive power and range from the compounding of primitives and has set grammars of combination for various categories of icons. In Korfhage's sense Media Streams is an iconic language as opposed to being merely an iconography (Korfhage and Korfhage 1986). Similar to other syntaxes for iconic sentences (Chang and others 1992; Tanimoto and Runyan 1986), icon sentences for actions have the form of subject-action-object or subject-action-direction, while those for relative positions have the form of subject-relative position-object. Icon sentences for cinematographic properties are of the form camera-movement-object (as in "the camera-is tracking-Steve" or "the camera-zooms in on-Sally").

4.1 Extensibility of the Icon Language

Currently, we have two ways of extending the iconic visual language of Media Streams beyond the composition of iconic primitives. Icons and the components of compound icons can be titled. This enables the user to attain a level of specificity of representation while still making use of the generality and abstraction of icons. For example, if I were to annotate the video of an automobile with the descriptor "XJ7," this description may be very opaque. If, however, I title a car icon XJ7, in addition to the computer learning that XJ7 is a type of car, a human reading this annotation can simply and quickly see the visual similarity between an "XJ7" car icon and icons for other types of automobiles.

Users can also create new icons for character and object actions by means of an animated icon editor. This editor allows users to define new icons as subsets or mixtures of existing animated icons. This is very useful because a wide range of possible human motions can be described as subsets or mixtures of existing animated icons.

Applying the results of work on automatic icon incorporation would also be a fruitful path of exploration (Fuji and Korfhage 1991). Already in our icon language, there are many iconic descriptors which we designed using the principle of incorporation (by which individual iconic elements are combined to form new icons). Creating tools to allow users to automatically extend the language in this way is a logical extension of our work in this area.

5 Representation Example: A Language for Human Action

The central problem of a descriptive language for temporal media is the representation of dynamic events. For video in particular, the challenge is to come up with techniques for representing and visualizing the complex structure of the actions of characters, objects, and cameras. There exists significant work in the formalization of temporal events in order to support inferencing about their interrelationships (Allen 1985) and to facilitate the compression and retrieval of image sequences by indexing temporal and spatial changes (Arndt and Chang 1989; Del Bimbo and others 1992). Our work creates a representation of cinematic action that these and other techniques could be usefully applied to. For even if we had robust machine vision, temporal and spatial logics would still require a *representation* of the video content because such a representation would determine the units these formalizations would operate on for indexing, compression, retrieval, and inferencing.

A representation of cinematic action for video retrieval and repurposing needs to focus on the granularity, reusability, and semantics of its units. In representing the action of bodies in space, the representation needs to support the hierarchical decomposition of its units both spatially and temporally. Spatial decomposition is supported by a representation that hierarchically orders the bodies and their parts which participate in an action. For example, in a complex action like driving an automobile, the arms, head, eyes, and legs all function independently. Temporal decomposition is enabled by a hierarchical organization of units such that longer sequences of action can be broken down into their temporal subabstractions all the way down to their atomic units. Lenat and Guha (Lenat and Guha 1990) point out the need for more than a purely temporal representation of events that would include semantically relevant atomic units organized into various temporal patterns (repeated cycles, scripts, etc.). For example, the atomic unit of "walking" would be "taking a step" which repeats cyclically. An atomic unit of "opening a jar" would be "turning the lid" (which itself could theoretically be broken down into smaller units—but much of the challenge of representing action is knowing what levels of granularity are useful).

Our approach tries to address these issues in multiple ways with special attention paid to the problems of representing human action as it appears in video. It is important to note in this regard—and this holds true for all aspects of representing the content of video—that unlike the project of traditional knowledge representation that seeks to represent the world, our project is *to represent a representation of the world*. This distinction has significant consequences for the representation of human action in video. As described above, in video, actions and their units do not have a fixed semantics because their meaning can shift as the video is recut and inserted into new sequences. For example, a shot of two people shaking hands, if positioned at the beginning of a sequence depicting a business meeting, could represent "greeting," if positioned at the end, the same shot could represent "agreeing." Video brings to our attention the effects of context and order on the meaning of represented action. In addition, the prospect of annotating video for a global media archive brings forward an issue which traditional knowledge representation has largely ignored: cultural variance. The shot of two people shaking hands may signify greeting or agreeing in some cultures, but in others it does not. How are we to annotate shots of people bowing, shaking hands, waving hello and good-bye? The list goes on.

In order to address the representational challenges of action in video we do not explicitly annotate actions according to their particular semantics in a given video stream (a shot of two people shaking hands is not annotated as "greeting" or alternately as "agreeing"), but rather according to the motion of objects and people in space. We annotate using physically-based description in order to support the reuse of annotated video in different contexts—be they cinematic or cultural ones. In our representation, we index examples of sequence-dependent semantic differences in order to represent contextual synonymy or lack thereof.

In Media Streams' user interface for action representation, our icons for action are *animated* and thus take advantage of the affordances of iconography in the computer medium as opposed to those of traditional graphic arts (Baecker and others 1991). Furthermore, we represent actions for characters and objects separately because of the unique actions afforded by the human form. We *horizontally* subdivide character actions into full body actions, head actions, arm actions, and leg actions. Under each of these categories of human action (and their own subdivisions) action is represented in two ways: *abstract* physical motions and *conventionalized* physical motions.

Media Streams' *abstract* action representation provides a hierarchical decomposition of the possible motions of the human body according to articulations and rotations of joints. Since Media Streams enables multi-layered annotation, any pattern of human motion can be described with precision by layering temporally indexed descriptions of the motion of various human body parts.

There are, however, many commonly occurring, complex patterns of human motion which seem to have cross-cultural importance (e.g., walking, sitting, eating, talking, etc.). *Conventionalized* body motions compactly represent motions which may involve multiple abstract body motions.

One may ask "where is the representation of emotion in all of this?" If we remember the insights of the Kuleshov Effect, the answer becomes clear. Imagine a shot of a man *smiling*. Is it a "happy" shot? One might think so. But what if I edit this shot in a sequence so as to reveal that a gun is pointed at the head of the *smiling* man? Is he still "happy"? Perhaps the emotion is now better described as "fearful" or "pleading"? In both cases though the man is still *smiling*. Emotion is not a property of a shot that necessarily survives resequencing. Therefore Media Streams represents the underlying physiognomy of emotion by offering a typology of facial gestures, rather than emotions themselves which are the result of the semantics of video sequences, not of the semantics of video shots.

6 Conclusions and Future Work

In studying the semantic and syntactic properties of video we have developed both a representation and an interface which enable content-based annotation, retrieval, and repurposing. In the summer of 1994, Media Streams was subjected to an 8 person, 3-day user test that yielded promising resukts: we found that the system is learnable; that users reuse each other's annotation effort; and that, unlike keyword-based systems, different users' descriptions of the same footage are semantically convergent (Davis 1995). It is our hope that this technology will contribute to the creation of a stream-based, reusable, global archive of digital video. We believe that designing video representations for reusable content articulates an important challenge and opportunity for visual languages in the 1990's (Glinert and others 1991) and is the key to the development of large-scale multimedia applications in the coming decades (Davis and others 1994). Our next step is to use our system to create a large archive of annotated digital video in order to explore mechanisms for computational video storytelling. It was this goal that originally inspired the creation of Media Streams out of the necessity of having a representation of video content.

Acknowledgments

The research discussed above was conducted at the MIT Media Laboratory and during my internship at Interval Research Corporation. The support of Interval Research Corporation, the Media Laboratory and its sponsors is gratefully acknowledged. I want to thank Brian Williams and Golan Levin for their continually creative and Herculean efforts and my advisor, Prof. Kenneth Haase, for his insight, inspiration, and support. Thanks also to Wendy Buffett for enduring my dissertation.

References

Allen, James F. "Maintaining Knowledge about Temporal Intervals." In: Readings In Knowledge Representation, ed. Ronald J. Brachman and Hector J. Levesque. 510-521. San Mateo, California: Morgan Kaufmann Publishers, Inc., 1985.

Apple Computer. Macintosh Common Lisp Reference. Cupertino, California: Apple Computer, 1993a.

Apple Computer. QuickTime Developer's Guide. Cupertino, California: Apple Computer, 1993b.

Apple Multimedia Lab. The Visual Almanac. San Francisco: Apple Computer, 1989.

Arndt, Timothy and Shi-Kuo Chang. "Image Sequence Compression by Iconic Indexing." In: Proceedings of 1989 IEEE Workshop on Visual Languages in Rome, Italy, IEEE Computer Society Press, 177-182, 1989.

Arons, Barry. "Interactively Skimming Recorded Speech." Ph.D. Thesis, Massachusetts Institute of Technology, 1993.

Baecker, Ronald, Ian Small, and Richard Mander. "Bringing Icons to Life." In: Proceedings of ACM CHI'91 Conference on Human Factors in Computing Systems,1-6, 1991.

Bliss, Charles Kasiel. Semantography-Blissymbolics. 3rd ed., Sydney, N.S.W., Australia: Semantography-Blissymbolics Publications, 1978.

Bordwell, David. Narration in the Fiction Film. Madison: University of Wisconsin Press, 1985.

Bordwell, David and Kristin Thompson. Film Art: An Introduction. 3rd ed., New York: McGraw-Hill Publishing Company, 1990.

Chang, Shi-Kuo. "Visual Languages and Iconic Languages." In: Visual Languages, ed. Shi-Kuo Chang, Tadao Ichikawa, and Panos A. Ligomenides. 1-7. New York: Plenum Press, 1986.

Chang, Shi-Kuo, G. Costagliola, S. Orefice, G. Polese, and B. R. Baker. "A Methodology for Iconic Language Design with Application to Augmentative Commmunication." In: Proceedings of 1992 IEEE Workshop on Visual Languages in Seattle, Washington, IEEE Computer Society Press, 110-116, 1992.

Davenport, Glorianna, Thomas G. Aguierre-Smith, and Natalio Pincever. "Cinematic Primitives for Multimedia." IEEE Computer Graphics and Applications 11.4 (July 1991): 67-75.

Davis, Marc. "Media Streams: An Iconic Visual Language for Video Annotation." Telektronikk 4.93 (1993a): 59-71. (Also available at: http://www.nta.no/telektronikk/4.93.dir/Davis_M.html)

Davis, Marc. "Media Streams: An Iconic Visual Language for Video Annotation." In: Proceedings of 1993 IEEE Symposium on Visual Languages in Bergen, Norway, IEEE Computer Society Press, 196-202, 1993b.

Davis, Marc. "Knowledge Representation for Video." In: Proceedings of Twelfth National Conference on Artificial Intelligence (AAAI-94) in Seattle, Washington, AAAI Press, 120-127, 1994a.

Davis, Marc. "Media Streams: Representing Video for Retrieval and Repurposing." Ph.D. Thesis, Massachusetts Institute of Technology, 1995.

Davis, Marc, Catherine Baudin, Smadar Kedar, and Daniel M. Russell. "No Multimedia Without Representation." In: Proceedings of Second ACM International Conference on Multimedia in San Francisco, ACM Press, 181-182, 1994.

Del Bimbo, Alberto, Enrico Vicario, and Daniele Zingoni. "A Spatio-Temporal Logic for Image Sequence Coding and Retrieval." In: Proceedings of 1992 IEEE Workshop on Visual Languages in Seattle, Washington, IEEE Computer Society Press, 228-230, 1992.

Dreyfuss, Henry. Symbol Sourcebook: An Authoritative Guide to International Graphic Symbols. New York: McGraw-Hill, 1972.

Eisenstein, Sergei M. The Film Sense. Translated by Jay Leyda. San Diego: Harcourt Brace Jovanovich, Publishers, 1947.

Fuji, Hideo and Robert R. Korfhage. "Features and a Model for Icon Morphological Transformation." In: Proceedings of 1991 IEEE Workshop on Visual Languages in Kobe, Japan, IEEE Computer Society Press, 240-245, 1991.

Furnas, G.W., T.K. Landauer, L.M. Gomez, and S.T. Dumais. "The Vocabulary Problem in Human-System Communication." Communications of the ACM 30 (11 1987): 964-971.

Glinert, Ephraim, Meera M. Blattner, and Chrisyopher J. Frerking. "Visual Tool and Languages: Directions for the 90's." In: Proceedings of 1991 IEEE Workshop on Visual Languages in Kobe, Japan, IEEE Computer Society Press, 89-95, 1991.

Greenway, Tom and Ronaldo Mouchawar. "A Visual Language for the Management of Digital Film and Video (Motion Imagery) Archives." In: Proceedings of 136th Technical Conference and World Media Expo of the Society of Motion Picture and Television Engineers (SMPTE) in Los Angeles, California, Society of Motion

Picture and Television Engineers, Inc., 1-15, 1994.

Haase, Ken. "FRAMER: A Persistent Portable Representation Library." In: Proceedings of European Conference on Artificial Intelligence in Amsterdam, The Netherlands, 1994.

Haase, Ken and Warren Sack. "FRAMER Manual." Internal Document. Cambridge, Massachusetts: MIT Media Laboratory, 1993.

Hawley, Michael. "Structure out of Sound." Ph.D. Thesis, Massachusetts Insitute of Technology, 1993.

Isenhour, John Preston. "The Effects of Context and Order in Film Editing." AV Communications Review 23 (1 1975): 69-80.

Korfhage, Robert R. and Margaret A. Korfhage. "Criteria for Iconic Languages." In: Visual Languages, ed. Shi-Kuo Chang, Tadao Ichikawa, and Panos A. Ligomenides. 207-231. New York: Plenum Press, 1986.

Kuleshov, Lev. "The Origins of Montage." In: Cinema in Revolution, ed. Luda Schnitzer, Jean Schnitzer, and Marcel Martin. 67-76. New York: Da Capo Press, 1973.

Kuleshov, Lev. Kuleshov on Film: Writings by Lev Kuleshov. Translated by Ronald Levaco. Berkeley: University of California Press, 1974.

Lenat, Douglas B. and Ramanathan V. Guha. Building Large Knowledge-Based Systems: Representation and Inference in the Cyc Project. Reading, Massachusetts: Addison-Wesley Publishing Company, Inc., 1990.

MacNeil, Ron. "Generating Multimedia Presentations Automatically Using TYRO: the Constraint, Case-Based Designer's Apprentice." In: Proceedings of 1991 IEEE Workshop on Visual Languages in Kobe, Japan, IEEE Computer Society Press, 74-79, 1991.

McLuhan, Marshall. The Gutenberg Galaxy: The Making of Typographic Man. Toronto: University of Toronto Press, 1962.

Metz, Christian. "Aural Objects." Yale French Studies 60 (1980): 24-32.

Mills, Michael, Jonathan Cohen, and Yin Yin Wong. "A Magnifier Tool for Video Data." In: Proceedings of CHI'92 in Monterey, California, 93-98, 1992.

Nagasaka, Akio and Yuzuru Tanaka. "Automatic Video Indexing and Full-Video Search for Object Appearances." In: IFIP Transactions, Visual Database Systems II, ed. E. Knuth and L. M. Wegner. Elsevier Publishers, 1992.

Neurath, Otto. International Picture Language. New York: State Mutual Book and Periodical Service, 1981.

Otsuji, Kiyotaka, Yoshinobu Tonomura, and Yuji Ohba. "Video Browsing Using Brightness Data." SPIE Visual Communications and Image Processing '91: Image Processing SPIE 1606 (1991): 980-989.

Pincever, Natalio C. "If You Could See What I Hear: Editing Assistance Through Cinematic Parsing." M.S. Thesis, Massachusetts Institute of Technology, 1990.

Pudovkin, Vsevolod Illarionovitch. Film Technique and Film Acting. Translated by Ivor Montagu. New York: Bonanza Books, 1949.

Sack, Warren and Marc Davis. "IDIC: Assembling Video Sequences from Story Plans and Content Annotations." In: Proceedings of IEEE International Conference on Multimedia Computing and Systems in Boston, Massachusetts, IEEE Computer Society Press, 30-36, 1994.

Tanimoto, Steven L. and Marcia S. Runyan. "PLAY: An Iconic Programming System for Children." In: Visual Languages, ed. Shi Kuo Chang, Tadao Ichikawa, and Panos A. Ligomenides. 191-205. New York: Plenum Press, 1986.

Teodosio, Laura. "Salient Stills." M.S. Thesis, Massachusetts Institute of Technology Media Laboratory, 1992.

Tonomura, Yoshinobu, Akihito Akutsu, Kiyotaka Otsuji, and Toru Sadakata. "VideoMAP and VideoSpaceIcon: Tools for Anatomizing Content." In: Proceedings of INTERCHI'93 Conference on Human Factors in Computing Systems in Amsterdam, The Netherlands, ACM Press, 131-136, 1993.

Ueda, Hirotada, Takafumi Miyatake, Shigeo Sumino, and Akio Nagasaka. "Automatic Structure Visualization for Video Editing." In: Proceedings of INTERCHI'93 Conference on Human Factors in Computing Systems in Amsterdam, The Netherlands, ACM Press, 137-141, 1993.

Ueda, Hirotada, Takafumi Miyatake, and Satoshi Yoshizawa. "IMPACT: An Interactive Natural-Motion-Picture Dedicated Multimedia Authoring System." In: Proceedings of CHI '91 in New Orleans, Louisiana, ACM Press, 343-350, 1991.

Zabih, Ramin, John Woodfill, and Meg Withgott. "A Real-Time System for Automatically Annotating Unstructured Image Sequences." In: Proceedings of IEEE International Conference on Systems, Man, and Cybernetics in Le Touquet, France, IEEE Press, 345-350, 1993.

Zhang, HongJiang, Atreyi Kankanhalli, and Stephen William Smoliar. "Automatic Partitioning of Full-Motion Video." Multimedia Systems 1 (1993): 10-28.

Case C

A Multimedia Communication System

Case C is the story of the Wang Freestyle multimedia communication system (Francik, 1995), as recounted by its developers. We present it because it is a case study of product development at the frontier, and because it brings together many of the ideas presented in this book. It illustrates various aspects of advanced product development:

- The creativity, excitement, and promise of technology-driven innovation
- The application of advanced interface technologies such as pen-based and gestural input, multimedia, and computer-supported cooperative work
- The use of advanced human factors methods including awareness of work contexts, iterative design, evaluation, and anthropological field studies
- Attention to documentation and training
- A technically brilliant but realistically constrained design
- Uncertainty about the marketing strategy for a radically new kind of product

It is also a case study that tracks the successes and failures of developing a state-of-the-art system design into a marketable product.

Freestyle's ultimate failure and the uncertainty about the reasons behind the failure also typify product development at the edge. Many theories were proposed, and many factors may have contributed. Freestyle was initially constrained to run on a limited range of platforms. Pricing and marketing strategy took uncertain turns. The most promising system configurations were not immediately apparent. Unrelated company problems precluded the long-term investment that the product required.

Freestyle was launched with fanfare at Fall Comdex '88 in Las Vegas, followed by a major advertising campaign. Reaction was enthusiastic. "Freestyle: Back to the Future," wrote industry analyst Patricia Seybold, praising it as "easy to use instantly" (Millikin, 1988). "Industry Lauds Wang's New PC Networking Tack" headlined *Communications Week* (Watson, 1989). *Computerworld* described a firm that bought 200 installations and forecast a $1.2 million saving in 1989 alone (Johnson, 1989). *PC Magazine* said Freestyle "makes other graphical user interfaces seem outdated and simplistic" (Petzold, 1989). A year after its release, *PC Computing* declared it "ground-breaking," one of 16 "most valuable products of the year" (Bonner, 1990). The research and development communities also reacted favorably. Papers were published about it, and it was demonstrated at numerous trade shows and several conferences, including CHI '89.

Freestyle was novel and technically impressive. Its concept could be explained easily. The capabilities it provided will very likely be commonplace—someday. Two releases and three years later, Freestyle had disappeared. You may not have heard of it. Was it ahead of its time, as its developers suggest? Very likely, but what does that mean, and can other innovative products avoid that rueful fate?

In the first reading, Levine and Ehrlich (1991)—the principal architect and project manager, and the human factors manager, respectively—describe Freestyle's design, its rationale, and some of the trade-offs involved. In essence, Freestyle is a pen-based PC communication system that uses electronic mail to deliver annotated multimedia documents. Documents can include scanned-in paper or fax images, as well as screen snapshots from any other PC application—the user can at any time "freeze" all or part of their screen and capture the bit-mapped image. A document can then be annotated using stylus and voice. Before mailing the bit-map image to another person on the system, a person can draw on the image with the pen-shaped stylus and talk as they do so. The recipient of the message sees the image and can "replay" or reenact the sender's actions. The effect is as if a ghost were drawing and speaking simultaneously. An excellent video is available that visually demonstrates Freestyle and its expected use (Wang Laboratories, 1989 video).

Here is an example scenario (more are shown in the Wang video): An office worker freezes a page of text from a document, puts Freestyle into record mode, then uses the stylus to circle one paragraph while saying, "This may give the wrong impression, maybe we should drop it," and then mails this off electronically. The entire transaction requires no typing, is quick, and the voice message conveys hints as to how strongly the speaker feels about the matter.

Levine and Ehrlich note a problem common to the design of innovative technology—the trade-off between adopting an interface metaphor (see Chapter 2) that mimics familiar real world artifacts (in this case paper and pencil), and providing more efficient but nonintuitive approaches that exploit digital technology. Historically, new products may start by emphasizing real-world correspondences and gradually move toward greater efficiency, as early word processors mimicked the behavior of typewriters.

In the section titled "Anticipating the Relationship to Other Communication Media," Levine and Ehrlich consider where this technology could fit in a world that already has meetings, telephones, paper documents, fax, electronic and voice mail, and even videoconferencing. They note that the developers or users of a new communication technology must consider how it will fit into work processes and organizational structure, and how it will complement existing means of communication. Design decisions can be guided by issues such as the relative formality expected in a communication channel and the bandwidth it provides.

In the second reading, Perkins et al. (1989) describe the development of an on-line tutorial for Freestyle. Interestingly, the tutorial was created using a prototype and was integrated with the product from the outset. This part of the project ties together elements from several chapters in this book. Developing a training process and training materials is one element in designing to fit human capabilities, as described in Chapter 10. The authors developed in concert two aspects of usability, the training and the software interface, as recommended by Gould in Chapter 2. This tight coupling of training and interface development happens rarely—training is typically addressed too late to influence software design. It paid off when the testing of the tutorial led to changes in the software as well as in the tutorial. The study also illustrates iterative design and quantitative comparisons that demonstrated substantial benefits.

When should a user's error lead to a change in the interface and when is it acceptable to deal with it in a tutorial? One could argue that a need for training to overcome problems indicates a design flaw, requiring interface redesign. Yet we have seen in Chapter 10 that users will always make "errors" and that the purpose of a tutorial is to deal with problems that the software interface does not catch. The solution is a trade-off. Perkins et al. suggest that when a problem is solved through "one-trial learning"—when users will remember it after seeing it once—then tutorial instruction is appropriate. When users repeatedly make the same error, the interface should be changed.

So far everything appears fine. We have an innovative idea, a thoughtful consideration of the issues, followed by iterative design and evaluation of a product. What happened? Why was Freestyle not a success?

In the final reading, Francik et al. (1991) describe what they discovered from studying the introduction of Freestyle into organizations. They list problems that may seem obvious in hindsight, including the need to identify appropriate business uses involving the informal communication of annotated documents, the need to place systems and peripheral equipment in appropriate locations, and the pricing and marketing barriers that can impede widespread adoption in a particular organization. The authors outline strategies for addressing the problems:

- Provide low-cost, reduced-functionality systems to reach a "critical mass" of users.
- Provide consulting to assist customers in identifying appropriate work processes to support and appropriate sites for installation.
- Educate customers in the capabilities of the technology.

Another problem is that Freestyle-as-groupware falls between single-user software applications and large multiuser systems. As noted in Chapter 4, product developers are familiar with usability problems in the former domain and in-house developers are familiar with usability problems in the latter domain. Groupware is different from either one and seems to have most of the disadvantages of both.

This extends the theme of behavioral and social challenges to groupware development introduced in the article by Grudin in Chapter 11. The vendors of word processors, graphics packages, and spreadsheets do not have to identify their customers' work processes or help them place equipment strategically in the organization. Packaged software does not come with consulting, which is expensive. On the other hand, large systems often do come with consulting support, but they involve large expenditures for hardware and are intended to address major organizational concerns.

Another source of difficulty is that a work process that can benefit from communication support often involves individuals located in different places on the organization chart. The technology should be made available to these individuals, but equipment purchase decisions are made by organizational units. Managers are not in the habit of buying systems to sit on the desks of individuals in other areas!

Yet another issue is the vulnerability of groupware systems to social factors in groups and organizations. If a new word processor were loved by one user in five and hated by the other four, and thus captured 20% of the market, it would be considered a smashing success. But if a groupware product is developed to support groups of five office workers and is loved by one and hated by four, very few groups would adopt it and it would fail. Thus, the burden of preparing, educating, and assisting prospective users is much greater for groupware than for single-user applications.

Francik et al. (1991) conclude their article by identifying several different players who can contribute to overcoming these hurdles: vendors who have focused on minicomputer-based office systems, PC application developers, telecommunications companies, and systems integrators. One visible trend is for the developers of successful single-user applications to add support for collaboration and communication. Vendors of novel products, such as Lotus Notes (discussed in Chapters 3 and 11), have tried to find a balance between the "large system" approach of bundling consulting with their product, and the personal computer approach of off-the-shelf "shrink-wrap" sales through preexisting distribution channels. Few would deny that computer support for groups is coming, but the paths by which it will arrive are not clear.

The history of interface design at the frontier is peppered by brilliant innovations that failed to be successful products (Rudisill et al., in press). Engelbart struggled for years to commercialize his well-received NLS system (discussed in Chapter 1) as the Augment product. The Xerox Star and Apple Lisa paved the way for the Macintosh. Seven years after the introduction of Freestyle, applications resembling it are starting to appear, and some will likely succeed. Although there is no magic recipe for successful innovation in the marketplace, the insights offered by the Freestyle designers can help us avoid some of the same pitfalls.

REFERENCES

Note: A ● before a reference indicates a reading.

Bonner, P. (1990). Freestyle. *PC Computing* 3, 1.

Francik, E. (1995). Rapid, Integrated Design of a Multimedia Communication System. In Rudisill, Lewis, Polson, and McKay (1995).

● Francik, E., Rudman, S., Cooper, D., and Levine, S. (1991). Fostering the Adoption of a Multimedia Communication System. *Communications of the ACM* 34(12), 53–63.

Johnson, M. (1989). Miami Law Firm Shows Its Freestyle. *Computerworld* 23, 51.

● Levine, S., and Ehrlich, S. (1991). The Freestyle System: A Design Perspective. In Klinger, A. (Ed.), *Human-Machine Interactive Systems*, Plenum, 3–21.

Millikin, M. (1988). Freestyle: Back to the Future. *Patricia Seybold's Office Computing Report* 11, 12.

● Perkins, R., Blatt, L., Workman, D., and Ehrlich, S. (1989). Iterative Tutorial Design in the Product Development Cycle. *Proc. 33rd Annual Human Factors Society Meeting*, 268–272.

Petzold, C. (1989). Beyond the GUI: Wang Freestyle. *PC Magazine* 8, 15.

Rudisill, M., Lewis, C., Polson, P., and McKay, T. (Eds.) (in press). *Human-Computer Interface Design: Success Cases, Emerging Methods, and Real-World Context.* Morgan Kaufmann.

Watson, N. (1989). Industry Lauds Wang's New PC Networking Tack. *Communications Week* 244, April 17.

VIDEOS

Wang Laboratories (1989). Freestyle. *ACM SIGGRAPH Video Review* 45.

THE FREESTYLE SYSTEM
A DESIGN PERSPECTIVE

STEPHEN R. LEVINE AND SUSAN F. EHRLICH

1. *Introduction*

The increase in speed, memory, and display characteristics of personal computers creates a new opportunity to support a larger set of fundamental types of human communication. In order to communicate with groups of people in the past, we have used standard alphabets that are efficiently reproduced using typing, printing, word processing, and copiers. People have shared these typed messages across distance using sophisticated means of transporting both paper and electronic mail. While we have grown to accept our dependence on the written word to reach large numbers of people quickly, we have also sought ways to use technology to capture more fundamental types of human communication.

The telephone has allowed us to speak across distance, while the television has allowed us to capture most dimensions of communication—including speech, pointing, and gesture—in one-to-many communication. We have continued to look for two-way and multiway communication media that can capture these multidimensional fundamentals. Video conferencing and videophones have been tried with some limited success.[1, 2]

People can now *point* to things on computer screens with free-roaming cursors, capture *voice* in compressed computer files, as well as capture *hand-drawn input* into drawing packages, typically with a mouse. In face-to-face meetings, people rarely use these types of communication separately. There is a need, then, to simultaneously capture them as they are *used in concert* and share them via electronic mail.

The Freestyle system was designed to capture synchronized pointing, speaking, drawing, and writing with electronic versions of familiar tools: paper, pencil, and voice handset/speaker-phone (Fig. 1). People simultaneously use combinations of real world versions of these tools to

FIGURE 1. Components of the Freestyle system including pencil, tablet, and voice handset. © Wang Laboratories Inc., 1989.

communicate with each other in the initial stages of almost all work. As a project solidifies, a formal record is often kept in a typed form that can easily be reproduced and distributed. But up to this point, the computer has not supported the capture and distribution of synchronized verbal and handwritten communication. Nor has it supported such synchronized discussions *about* formal documents.

This new type of electronic mail is made possible partially because of the increasing ability of high-speed graphic interfaces to provide rich, immediate, multidimensional *feedback* that is similar to that in the real world. (See discussion of the data glove[3] and the alternate reality kit[4] below.) Even as display capabilities of personal computers have been improving, so has the ability to interconnect them. With the general introduction of networking into the work force, there has been an upsurge in the use of computer-based mail systems. The Freestyle project was in the position to take advantage of existing networks.

The design of this system was based on a combination of original ideas and discovery of needs through laboratory and field research. It was partially driven by a theory of users' communication needs and by a particular approach to graphics design based on real-world mimicry. This chapter will outline how various contributions to the design were interwoven as it evolved over time from an initial prototype through multiple versions that were tested in business environments. (See also Francik and Akagi,[5] Perkins *et al*,[6] and Hsiao and Levine[7] for details of the design process.)

STEPHEN R. LEVINE and SUSAN F. EHRLICH • *User Interface Department*, Wang Laboratories, Inc., Lowell, Massachusetts 01851.

2. *User Interface Design*

Freestyle was designed to be a voice and handwriting based communication system that sits on top of the current world of personal computing. It leaves intact the DOS operating system and PC software used for calculation, typing, or record keeping (e.g., spreadsheets, word processing, database, etc.)

2.1. *Image Annotation*

The starting point was to enable the user to capture any visible screen shown on a standard PC (including a completely blank screen, or an image that was previously scanned into the PC) and convert it into an "electronic piece of paper." Once the screen was frozen, it could then be pointed at and written on using a tablet with a pencil-shaped stylus (Francik and Akagi[5]).

The system also provided the ability to record speech via a handset/speaker-phone even as the user is writing or pointing with the stylus (Hsiao and Levine[7]), thus supporting four fundamental means for synchronized communication from the real world: pointing, speaking, drawing, and writing. The ability to type anywhere on the screen image was also provided. The combined inputs produce a dynamic multimedia message that can be mailed to others via a minicomputer network and played back. (See Fig. 2.)

The stylus and voice handset are familiar communication tools. The system capitalized on this familiarity. In order for the user to write on the screen, he or she only needs to touch the pencil to the tablet and begin writing. (No mode switch or menu navigation is required.) This mimics direct writing on a familiar piece of paper. The stylus was designed to have a pink eraser that works like a regular eraser. This direct mimicry of components of familiar tools was intended to lead people to use them without any training.

2.2. *Graphic Desktop*

The system also provides a familiar desklike environment for keeping track of the various pieces of electronic paper that are created by the user (Fig. 3). This environment was intended to be independent from the user

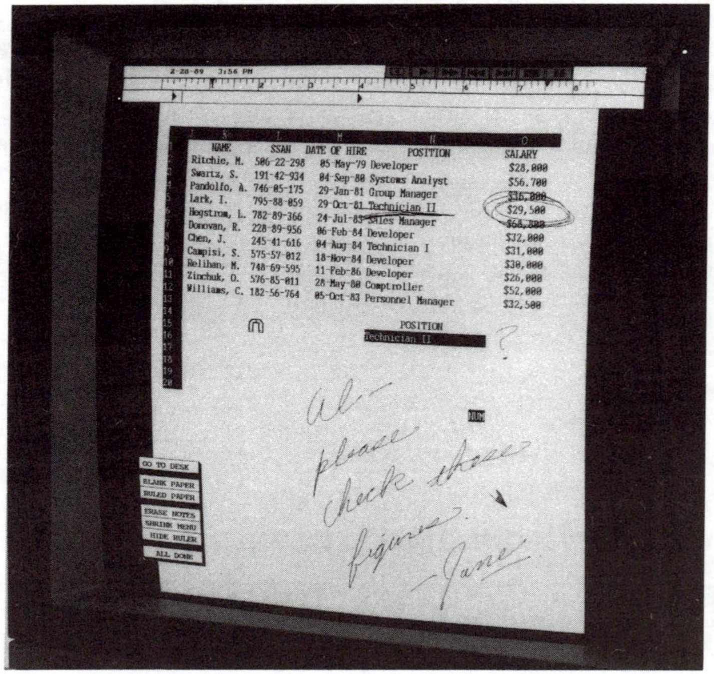

FIGURE 2. The Freestyle annotation environment. © Wang Laboratories Inc., 1989.

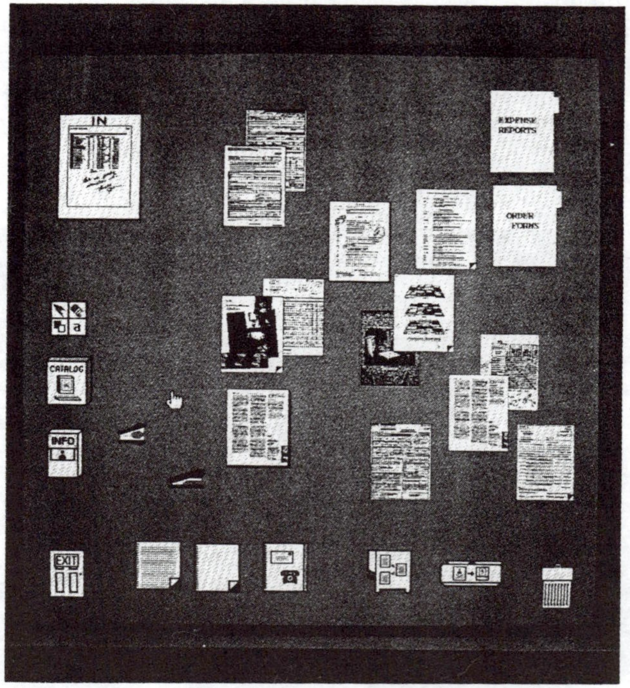

FIGURE 3. The Freestyle desktop. © Wang Laboratories Inc., 1989.

interface of the file structure of the computer (i.e., the DOS operating system).

The annotated "electronic paper" images are stored by the user in miniature form on the desk (which is accessed via a pop-up menu during annotation). The miniatures (or "stamps") first appear in a graphical "inbox." Then they can be moved around the desk with the stylus using a drag motion. A down–up motion of the pen opens selected items to full size—ready for additional annotation.

The Freestyle desktop is an environment for storing and manipulating images used primarily as electronic mail. This contrasts with desktop systems like the Apple MacIntosh that support management of editable character-based files and programs.

Recent research has shown the power of providing immediate graphic responses to fine motor input. For example, the data glove[3] allows finely articulated three-dimensional control of graphic objects on a screen via electrical feedback from the relative positions of the fingers in the glove. Another example is the alternate reality kit,[4] where graphic elements respond to mouse movements according to physical laws of nature (e.g., gravity). Commercially available desktop computers have also begun to allow users to manipulate objects with natural motion feedback (e.g., movement of icons on computer "desktops"). This allows users to predict and instantly confirm system behavior.

Real-world desks are covered with paper and folders. People maintain mental models of the spatial locations of papers and categories of papers on their desks and in their offices.[8] People overlap paper, they create piles, they put things in folders, and they put things of critical importance in places of prominence. Our goal was to provide ways to directly and flexibly mimic these activities.

For example, the miniature pieces of paper can be overlapped and laid on top of each other on haphazard or neat piles as the user wants. The movement of the elements is exactly as fast or slow as the movement of the stylus. The graphic detail of the image is stable during movement and follows rules of object constancy[9, 10] (e.g., hidden objects can be found again "behind" occluding objects). This creates an impression of delicate control over concrete objects. It was important that the stamps maintain as much of the detail of the larger images as possible to allow direct recognition without requiring labeling.

The desk also provides the icons used for organizing the stamps (e.g., stapler, staple remover, folders, trash can), and the icons used for managing communication (e.g., printer, scanner, phone book, individual "mail slots"). Individual pieces of paper can be "stapled together" by moving a stapler icon to a pile. This allows the user to move a pile of pages as a unit. A staple remover icon allows the users to separate the pages. The images can also be inserted into labeled folders.

2.3. *Controlling Communication*

The annotated images are sent around within an electronic mail network. Complete analogies to real-world experience could not be efficiently used for functions like mailing and printing, so we resorted to the use of icons on the desktop for these and related functions. Rather than taking an electronic piece of paper and putting it in an envelope and hand-writing an address, the user drags the piece of paper to a phone book icon, which results in the display of an alphabetized listing from which names can be selected with the stylus. In additon, users can set up individual mail slot icons for specific people or groups that they communicate with frequently. They can also convert an image into a voiceless FAX image to be sent out over a telephone line. Because only a few operations are required to mail or FAX items in this environment, it is more efficient than the real world of interoffice paper mail.

2.4. *Metaphor and Efficiency: A Delicate Balance*

One of the challenges was maintaining the balance between real-worl mimicry and the need for time saving though less familiar functions. The design team's goal was to minimize learning time for the screen capture and annotation functions and provide responsive feedback, but without sacrificing efficiency. For example, the eraser could be used on small areas, but there is also a much more efficient menu pick for erasing all annotations made in that session (Fig. 4). descriptive verbal labels were needed for such menu functions.

FIGURE 4. The annotation menu. © Wang Laboratories Inc., 1989.

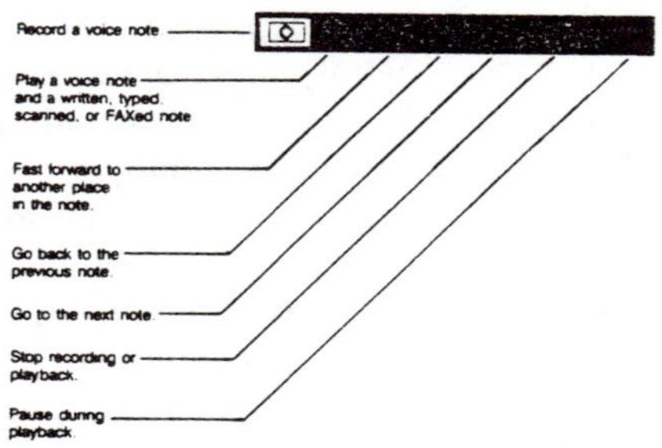

FIGURE 5. Voice playback controls. © Wang Laboratories Inc., 1989.

Also, during live conversation there are very complex social rules for stopping people speaking that were clearly beyond the powers of the Freestyle user interface (e.g., polite interruptions, a raised eyebrow). The system needed a "second best" analogy for controlling the playback of speech. The analogy that was selected was the playback controls on a tape deck or a compact disk machine (Fig. 5). These controls are not as familiar as pen, paper, and handsets.

Users are given the sensation of having successfully changed control states by several means. For example, scanned images in the system are larger than either the half page or full page monitor image and therefore need to be scrolled to be viewed in their entirety. To guide moving the image to reveal the bottom part, it was not possible to directly mimic grabbing the edge of the paper. A substitute mechanism was needed with feedback that was as natural as possible. In this case, the user moves the stylus to the edge of the screen (tablet) until a hand appears on the edge that looks like it is grabbing the image. The user thus knows that she or he is in position to touch the tablet and drag the image up and down within the screen.

A related problem was supporting the user in transitions between multiple environments. Because the Freestyle system captured any type of screen (anything from a local Lotus spreadsheet to a remote application run on a mainframe) the Freestyle system had to coexist with a multitude of "computer cultures" including the DOS file listing and Wang's regular electronic mail system. Freestyle did not attempt to provide a consistent application environment, but rather coexisted with the preexisting environments. A clean, universal mechanism was needed for switching between these environments, making it obvious when the user was in frozen annotation mode versus live application mode.

The most salient feature for distinguishing frozen annotation mode from live application mode was reversing light-on-dark screens to dark-on-light. This added to the sense of familiarity because dark writing typically appears on light paper. The context switch was also made obvious by providing a single pop-up menu and graphic pen activated controls for voice, typing, and navigation that always appear during annotation sessions.

A menu pick in the annotation environment and an icon in the desktop environment return the user to the application he or she was previously using (in the state it was left in upon touching the tablet). The number of operations was kept small within both environments. This helped minimize the conflicts in culture with "live" applications. All functions in the annotator are controllable with the pen and the handset/speaker-phone, thus requiring no memorization of keyboard commands that might conflict with other environments. In both the annotation and desk environments *only two pen motions* are available for controlling function access:

- Touch and lift on a graphic (icon, menu, stamp, button) to select a function or perform an action
- Touch and drag to relocate graphics and scroll

A cursor in the shape of a pencil point is displayed on the screen when the pen is moved around just above the tablet. Writing occurs, of course, when the user touches down on the tablet.

Extensive testing of the system with novice users provided input into iterative versions of the design of the system and showed that the concepts of pointing with the pen, writing, function selection with the pen, speaking while writing, and movement of graphic elements with the pen required minimal training. (See Perkins *et al.*[6])

3. *System Use*

While aspects of the system attempted to mimic real-world behavior, the overriding design goal of the product was to enhance communication in business environments.[11] This goal was supported by iterative evaluation of prototypes used for real business communication. The evaluation team started with interviews with potential users in a variety of business environments. As prototype versions of the product emerged and were placed into internal test applications, the users were interviewed about the match between the system features and their communication needs. Finally, the researchers followed the product out to its first customer test sites.

The field research was focused on understanding and molding two unique aspects of the system design: the ability to capture screens as the backgrounds of the messages, and dynamic multimedia annotation. As the interviews progressed, we also focused on the design of the graphical desk for supporting filing and retrieval as we shall describe below.

3.1. *Captured Screens as Background*

The background images in Freestyle can be created from familiar images in the office environment via program screen capture, scanning, or original hand drawing. The first internal business group to use Freestyle scanned in paper travel authorization forms for signature processing. Also, during design, the designers used the prototype system to send rough hand-drawn sketches of icons back and forth to each other with voice explanations of the tradeoffs between the variants in the icons.

We carried out preparatory field interviews that showed that in engineering and graphics departments, graphic materials guide the progress of work, suggesting that capture of such graphics could be an important use of Freestyle. These graphics can be complex and go through repeated revision cycles. Rough sketches are used during preliminary stages of coordination. Other materials can include CAD drawings, hand drawings, photographs, and page layouts. Revisions are required during the various review cycles or if there are any last minute changes in the product designs. These preliminary interviews anticipated the role that screen capture would play in the system.

The evaluation team later observed real use of various types of message backgrounds in the customer test sites. They included scanned images of forms, invoices, FAX's, handwritten messages, and newspaper clippings. They also included application screens such as database query results (with superimposed handwritten comments), spreadsheet screens, *and* electronic mail screens with handwritten comments.

3.2. *Dynamic Multimedia Annotations*

In Freestyle, simultaneous written and voice annotations are played back together while the receiver watches the sender point to parts of the image, write, and speak, almost as if the user is watching a video tape at her or his terminal. The business need for annotation was assessed by interviewing people in the field about their current annotation and commenting activities.

The preliminary field research showed that engineering groups use a variety of hand markings during their daily work. Some provide *focus of attention*. The prototype engineer has to locate the particular corner of a design drawing, mark it, and clearly state the problem: "Does this require a bend of a fold?" "When this grille is formed on the lathe, the lip tends to elongate—we suggest the design be changed along these dimensions." A number of the problems must be described at *multiple levels*. Pointing directs the listener's attention to particular parts within the drawing, while verbal comments explain the consequences of the desired action.

As users described how they negotiate design changes, *sequential pointing* within a diagram provides critical order information for problem resolution. This predicted a need for Freestyle's live playback capabilities.

The first internal prototype pilot was set up to support signature cycles for scanned-in forms. Signatures and handwritten/voice annotations were also used at the customer test sites. People used handwriting and voice to ask each other questions and give each other answers about the status of invoices, or the reasons for changes in database or spreadsheet information. The users also communicated with each other about problems in spatial layout. After considerable time using the system, users began to produce

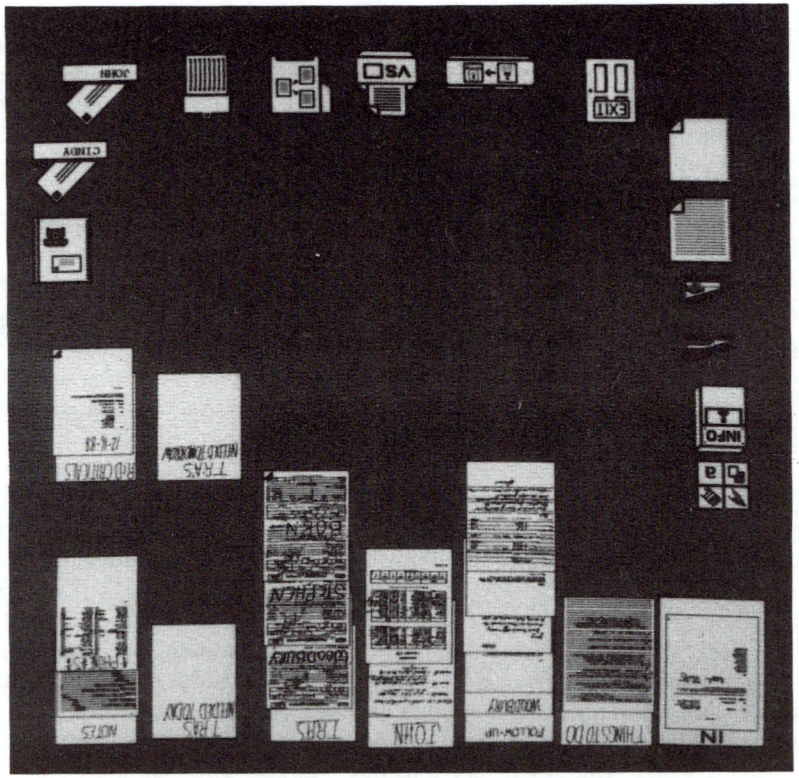

FIGURE 6. Secretary's desktop. © Wang Laboratories Inc., 1989.

"multimedia" greeting cards to, for example, congratulate a new parent on the arrival of a child with combined drawn and spoken imagery (e.g., a baby crying).

3.3. *The Graphical Desk*

The fluidity of the desktop allows it to be used as a specialized kind of indexing system supporting specific types of filing and retrieval. The basic functions that are available are (1) free, instantaneous motion of any object on the desktop; (2) the ability to overlap "stamps"; (3) the ability to create "piles"; (4) the ability to create hierarchically stapled piles; and (5) the ability to place things in folders.

These basic capabilities created indexing and organizing opportunities as illustrated in Figs. 6 and 7 below. These photographs were taken from the actual working desk of an executive user of a prototype version of the system

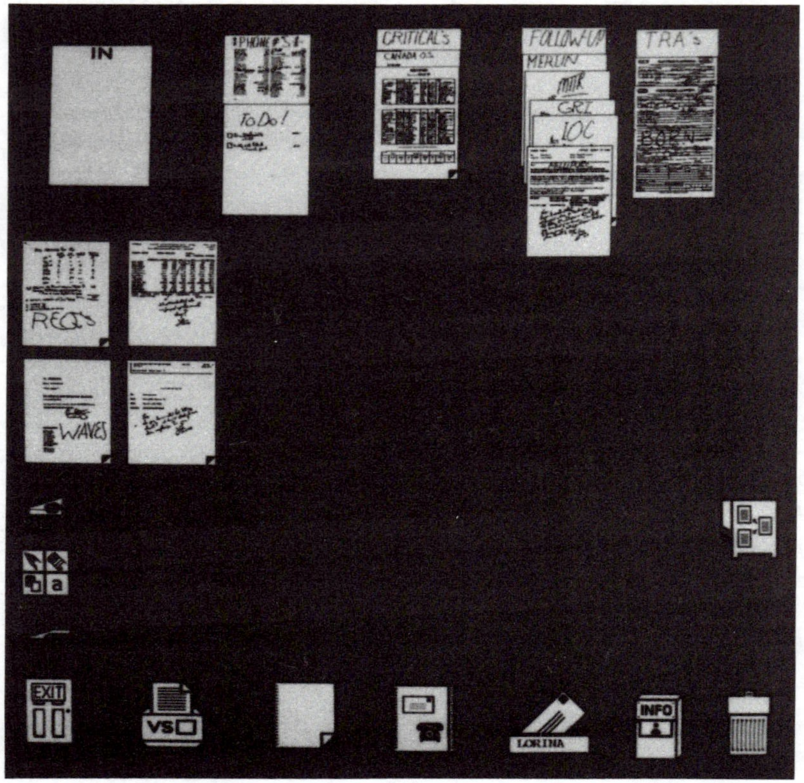

FIGURE 7. Executive's desktop. © Wang Laboratories Inc., 1989.

and his secretary after several months of experience using the system for ongoing communication (folders were not yet available). The structure of the desk evolved substantially over time, with the users themselves creating new uses of the basic desk elements. A key use was approving travel request forms for a large customer service organization (see below for description of application terms used on the desktop).

Labeling Files. Perhaps the most salient organizing tools on these users desks are the labels. Labels are created for piles by writing large leters on blank electronic pieces of paper (obtained by selecting an icon) and then overlapping image stamps on top of those blank pages. Labels are also applied to the images themselves (e.g., **PHONE**) to support easy recognition.

Grouping Files. The images can be grouped into categories that are related to specific aspects of business as shown here. The nature of the categories is flexible in that it is possible to have superordinate categories (e.g., TRA: Travel Request Approval forms) and *at the same time* view separate but related subordinate piles (TRAs today versus TRAs tomorrow). Space is reserved for time-critical communications down at the side of the executive's desk. The creation of these nonstandard hierarchies is achieved directly through labeling, physical movement, and sorting.

The visual images themselves are manipulated during sorting, not file names as in traditional hierarchical filing systems. Notice that the ability to overlap stamps is used to create a view of the approximate number of images within a pile (equal to the approximate amount of pending work) while still conserving space. A subtle clue of the size of a pile of stacked stamps is given by the variable size of a "shadow."

Regrouping Files. Regrouping of files requires no keyboard commands or file renaming but rather is done directly through motion of the miniature images. This allows a relatively high rate of change of file groupings. For example, travel request forms are moved from one pile to another on a daily basis. This provides the user with an easy way of maintaining a dynamic record of the progress of work as it goes through different stages.

Regrouping of piles is, of course, very similar to regrouping of paper piles in the real world. The miniaturization of the stamps provides a "birds's eye view" of the organization of the piles that has similar advantages to miniature models used in other environments (e.g., tactical models of military operations). The Freestyle desk is superior to spreading real paper on a conference table or the floor both because it does not compete for real space and because much smaller physical movements are required to reorganize the pages.

Locating Images. Users locate particular miniature images with a combination of visual cues in the miniatures themselves and the image's relative position on the desk (e.g., in a pile). Just as in the familiar paper world of the desktop, the images can be distinguished and selected on the basis of distinctive overall pattern or gestalt (see distinguishing characteristics of spreadsheets, electronic mail, and memos with distribution lists in Fig. 7 above). Retrieval of a particular image is very fast if the whole image or part of the image is visible on the screen. The desk does suffer from similar problems found on real desks as the volume of images increases. Things do get lost under other things, but they are found again by visual sorting.

Storage versus Throughput. The lack of file names (that can be listed in an index and searched) puts restrictions on the use of the desk for long-term filing and retrieval. Named filing was provided via a special "file cabinet" icon to help serve the need of long-term storage. But it is important to emphasize the need for "informal" visual pile structure for handling communication flow of *messages that often last only for short duration* and do not merit the investment of additional typed data entry. The Freestyle desk actively presents temporary but short shelf-life information for easy use.

Sharing Organizational Structure. One unexpected group effect was observed in the organization of desktop structure by co-workers who were cooperating on the same procedures. Even though there is no desktop organizational software shared between the users, desktop organization was shared. This included shared categories ("TRAs," "Criticals"), shared spatial organization of categories (TRAs on right side of desk), and shared images used on a repeated basis (a list of phone numbers). Slight *differences* in organization between users revealed differences in functional roles of the collaborators. For example, the secretary needed to maintain finer-level distinctions of TRAs to guide the detailed flow of communication.

The desks of other users started to reveal organizational structure. Piles are created representing *projects* as well as *people* responsible for certain activities, independent of whether the named people are accessible on the Freestyle network. We believe desktop organization may be able to support and help reveal the hidden communication structures of organizations that are sometimes obscured by official organizational charts.

3.4. Anticipating the Relationship to Other Communication Media

The design of this system had certain characteristics that position it with respect to other communication media. The role that this system will play in business communication will be influenced by the media that will be used in concert with it (meetings, telephones, paper and pencil, electronic mail, voice mail, and fascimile).[8] This section contrasts Freestyle's features with those of other media.

Meetings. Like meetings, the Freestyle multimode annotation allows sharing of paper (in electronic form), writing, voice comments, and pointing by people within the same minicomputer network. But meetings have major advantages over Freestyle, particulary in the area of turn-taking.[12] Body language, silent gesture, and spoken interruptions guide who talks next and therefore the course of the discussion. They also provide immediate interpretations of what is being said (e.g., confirmations versus rejection). With asynchronous mail turn-taking is only carried out in an extended time frame. Yet, the ability to quickly mail the multimedia annotated images around the network to people who are *geographically distributed* provides some of the advantagese of face-to-face meetings.

The fact that original Freestyle messages are played back at a different time by the receiver means that the individuals who are communicating with each other do not have to schedule some meetings in the first place. Users also can avoid traveling long distances in order to communicate informally. Our preliminary field work in a variety of departments inside Wang revealed that meeting management and scheduling were the primary causes of communication breakdowns, particulary in the graphics-dependent applications, (See also Ref. 13.)

Telephone. While telephone communication is usually very fast, there are often serious delays in completing calls because of the lack of availability of the called party—telephone tag.[14] If the topic of conversation is visual in nature (see earlier description of interpretation of an engineering drawing), then there can be serious communication breakdowns as two- and three-dimensional visual information has to be translated into a one-dimensional string of words. There is no way to point to part of a drawing in context unless both parties hold separate copies, and even there it is difficult to establish long distance frames of reference (see Bly[15]).

While there are no live conversations with Freestyle, voice comments can be sent as quickly as electronic mail messages and the juxtaposition of the voice with the image means a major increase in the amount and quality of information that can be communicated. The advantage of any type of asynchronous messaging is that all parties do not have to be at their workstations at a particular time. Telephones, of course, have the major advantage of being ubiquitous.

Paper and Pencil. The Freestyle system is both a consumer and creater of paper via scanning and printing and is therefore not really an alternative. It does provide a fast channel for moving the images on paper that does not require human sorting and physical portage. The captured computer screens that are later printed can be used in other contexts (e.g., live meetings) and can be distributed to those without Freestyle systems. The miniature images on the desktop have some characteristics in common with paper (ability to make piles, put things in folders). Though the Freestyle pencil is very similar to a regular pencil, the user must adapt to writing on a tablet rather than directly on the screen. This requires some initial adjustment.

Electronic Mail. Character-based electronic mail systems are the most common computer-based communication systems. They have been shown to have a very large impact, unifying the collaborative efforts of geographically dispersed workers. (See, for example, Eveland and Bikson[16].) But such systems have the same restrictions that telephone conversations have in that they cannot support communication that is dependent on visual information in the form of diagrams, drawings, photographs, and pictures.

Electronic mail systems have the major advantage of maintaining a machine-readable message content (as opposed to a frozen background image with machine-uninterpretable voice and hand-drawn annotations). Character-based electronic mail systems can themselves analyze the content of messages to determine actions that should be taken (e.g., Malone *et al.*[17]).

Voice Mail. Voice mail allows voice capture like Freestyle and has the same powerful forwarding and distribution capabilities, but it does not allow juxtaposition of voice with image and writing. Voice mail has found an important communication niche for people who are on the move (e.g., sales personnel) and need to communicate critical update information quickly (e.g. inventory levels) and as an immediately available message-taker that does perfect "transcription" when people are away from their phones.[11, 14] Voice mail has the same advantage as the telephone: access from any telephone in the international network.

Video Conferencing. Video conferencing captures a broader range of fundamental types of communication than Freestyle (e.g., body language, facial expressions, hand gestures). Yet attempts to support visual communication with video conferencing have not been as successfull as had been anticipated.[1, 2] Video conferencing often requires that all of the communicators assemble at the same time for meetings. Such conferencing has not therefore provided the time-independent communication that people have come to depend on with electronic mail. Communication with Freestyle also contrasts with common videoconferencing implementations that focus attention on the speakers' faces and bodies. The images of Freestyle direct the user's attention to the objects of work as opposed to the participants in the meeting. Because messages are both created and played back privately, they avoid feelings of being intruded upon.

A recent study by Bly[15] demonstrated that videoconferencing (in which the cameras *did* focus on the visual objects of work) was superior to telephone conversations about the same visual work. On the other hand, video conferencing was less satisfactory than face-to-face meetings in that study. In face-to-face meetings, participants were able to point to the visual materials being *used by the other person.* Freestyle messages do capture pointing but in asynchronously delivered messages.

Facsimile. Facsimile, like Freestyle, allows fast transmission of "electronic paper" but without the attached synchronized voice. The Freestyle system itself allows images to be FAXed directly from the workstation, avoiding the steps of printing out and scanning the image into a FAX machine. Voice comments are lost in these images, however.

It seems clear that each of the listed means of communication will be chosen on the basis of the specific communication needs of particular situations. Meetings will continue to be favored because of their high "bandwidth." With increasing geographic distance, users will make choices between character-based mail (to allow computer evaluation of content as well as such things as joint editing and programming), voice mail (to allow access from any telephone and as a "message-taker"), and Freestyle.

It is too early to tell all the possible uses of multimedia messaging, but as more systems become available, this type of system may be chosen for complex multichannel communication with commenting and review cycles and for *informal* communication of any type (e.g., planning, early design, etc.). The familiarity of the modes of communication (e.g., voice, writing) also make this type of system immediately attractive to non-computer-users/nontypists (e.g., some executives), creating a long-awaited sense of both trust of the system and opportunity for self expression.

4. *Emerging Applications*

We are still in the earliest stages of identifying where the greatest pay-off will be for this and future systems of its type. The system provides a bridge between traditional paper-based work and the use of computer programs. Both sets of human activities will continue to guide the development of new features as well as the integration requirements of the two worlds. Our field interviews helped reveal some of the new opportunities that such systems will have for supporting cooperative work.

4.1. *Preservation of Context*

Currently we take for granted the fact that long-distance communication, under time pressure, is only so effective. We have learned to live with the relatively small bandwidth of telephone communication. With the emergence of personal facsimile systems, businesses have recognized the efficiency of sending full images that do not require verbal translation. While image-based mail greatly increases the number of bits that must flow through our communication channels, it actually decreases the noise in the system by providing the context people need for *accurate interpretation* of information—"a picture is worth a thousand words." The addition of voice and handwritten annotation further reduces the noise by focusing attention on the relevant information.

One of the users interviewed told the story of a one-year negotiation between two companies on different sides of the world concerning the design of a commodity product. Miscommunications kept occurring until finally all parties decided they needed to have a conference call. But the engineering problem was essentially visual and involved the interpretation of a diagram (specific orientation of parts of the product). Fast transmission of engineering drawings with appropriate interpretation via annotation would have allowed the negotiation to be completed much more quickly.

Similar problems in interpretation were reported by a carpenter who had to build according to specification from both architects and general contractors. Miscommunications about the interpretations of the drawings often cost him weeks of effort and delays. Again, fast transmission of complex drawings with superimposed interpretation promises to have a major impact for such applications.

4.2. Planning and Iteration

Intimately related to the need for context information is the need to support rapid informal and often ad hoc communications that is the mainstay of any kind of project initiation. Design of products, organizational structures, page layouts, and buildings evolve very rapidly in the early stages, often requiring input from multiple contributors with unique expertise. The quality of collaboration is directly dependent on the ease of communication. Often the less formal, the better. Stylus and voice annotation can play roles that are similar to the white board used in a conference room. The shelf-life of an idea may be relatively short but with such informal communication mechanisms within easy reach of geographically distributed contributors, good ideas can be recognized as such more quickly by the right set of people.

4.3. An Emerging Challenge for Computer Science

There has been hope throughout the industry that users could control increasingly complex and powerful computer systems with minimal training. Much energy has been put into creating artificially intelligent machines that can understand natural language and spoken voice, can produce voice, and can make complex decisions. The Freestyle project sidestepped the need to copy the logic of users in code or to teach the computer to think. Freestyle does not attempt to understand. Instead the system captures greater and greater levels of detail to be presented to others for human interpretation.

There emerges then, a kind of debate for the future: Will our investment in computer systems development have the fastest and strongest impact by *copying* human intelligence in code, or will the larger impact come from providing more and more sophisticated high bandwidth *capture* of human intelligence for use by others and providing increasing responsiveness to human movement? The anwer to this question may depend on the extent to which both types of computer support can be interwoven to support both predictable aspects of human problem solving and the creative, ad hoc insights that help to drive innovation.

ACKNOWLEDGMENTS

We would like to thank Ellen Francik, Ron Perkins, and Victoria Moseley-Dials for valuable comments. We would also like to acknowledge the contributions of the many members of the design and evaluation teams to the ideas described here. We especially want to acknowledge the contributions provided by members of the development team, Alex Harui, Mike Schirpke, Charles Paress, Ken Knowlton, Bruce Brown, Karen Donoghue, Chuck Hsiao, Donna Ajgaonkar, Dave Wilson, Mary Ystueta, Mary Jane Boyd, Steven Teng, Steve Boylan, Pat Martin, Michael Kudla, and Betty Lorenson; the internal evaluation team, Ellen Francik, Ron Perkins, Louis Blatt, Barbara Kelly, and Kenichi Akagi; and finally those who carried out the field-based research, Ellen Francik, Donna Cooper, Constance Perin, Sharon Dodson, and Amy Bucklin.

References

1. C. Egido, Videoconferencing as a technology to support group work: A review of its failure, Proceedings of the Conference on Computer-Supported Cooperative Work, pp. 13–24, Portland, September 26–28, 1988.
2. R. Johansen and C. Bullen, Thinking ahead: What to expect from teleconferencing, in I. Greif, Ed., *Computer-Supported Cooperative Work: A Book of Readings*, pp. 185–198, Morgan Kaufman Press, San Mateo, 1988.
3. T.G. Zimmerman, J. Lanier, C. Blanchard, C. Bryson, and Y. Harvill, A hand gesture interface device, Proceedings of the CHI '87 Human Factors in Computing Systems and Graphics Interface, pp. 189–192, Toronto, April 5–9, 1987.
4. R.B. Smith, The alternate Reality Kit: An animated environment for creating interactive simulations, Proceeding of 1986 IEEE Computer Society Workshop on Visual Languages, pp. 99–106, June, 1986.
5. E. Francik and K. Akagi, Designing a computer pencil and tablet for handwriting, Proceedings of the Human Factors Society 33rd Annual Meeting, Denver, October 16–20, 1989.

6. R.D. Perkins, L.A. Blatt, D. Workman, and S.F. Ehrlich, Iterative tutorial design in the product development cycle, Proceedings of the Human Factors Society 33rd Annual Meeting, Denver, October 16–20, 1989.
7. C. Hsiao and S.F. Levine, Voice annotations on Wang Freestyle System, Official Proceedings of Speech Tech '89, pp. 365–367, New York City, May 2–4, 1989.
8. T. Malone, How do people organize their desks? Implications for the design of office information systems, *ACM Trans. Office Inf. Syst.* **1**, 99–112, 1983.
9. J. Piaget, *The Origins of Intelligence in Children*, International University Press, New York, 1952.
10. J. Piaget, *The Construction of Reality in the Child*, Basic Books, New York, 1954.
11. S.F. Ehrlich, Strategies for encouraging successful adoption of office communication systems, *ACM Trans. Office Inf. Syst.* **5**, 340–349, 1987.
12. J.C. Tang and L.J. Leifer, A framework for understanding the work space activity of design teams, Proceedings of the Conference on Computer-Supported Cooperative Work, pp. 244–249, Portland, September 26–29, 1988.
13. G. Mintzberg, *The Nature of Managerial Work*, Harper and Row, New York, 1973.
14. S.F. Ehrlich and E.A. Akiba, Successful implementation of voice store and forward technology: A case study, *ACM SIGOA Bull.*, 19–26, 1985.
15. S.A. Bly, A use of drawing surfaces in different collaborative settings, Proceedings of the Conference on Computer-Supported Cooperative Work, pp. 250–256, Portland, September 26–28, 1988.
16. J.D. Eveland and T.K. Bikson, Work group structures and computer support: A field experiment, Proceedings of the Conference on Computer-supported Cooperative Work, pp. 324–343, Portland, September 26–28, 1988.
17. T. Malone, K.R. Grant, and F.A. Turbak, The information Lens: An intelligent system for information sharing in organizations, Proceedings of the CHI '86 Human Factors in Computing Systems, pp. 1–8, Boston, April 13–17, 1986.

ITERATIVE TUTORIAL DESIGN IN THE PRODUCT DEVELOPMENT CYCLE

Ronald Perkins
Louis A. Blatt
Daniel Workman
Susan F. Ehrlich

Wang Laboratories, Inc.
Lowell, MA 01851

Abstract

Early development of a tutorial fostered a joint effort between human factors professionals, software developers and training consultants that resulted in early resolution of many problems during the development of Wang Freestyle™, a new multimedia communication system. It was decided that new users of Freestyle should be able to use the basic annotation features without referring to any hardcopy documentation. To ensure this, iterative tests of evolving prototypes of (1) the software and (2) an on-line tutorial that was designed to teach any features of the system that were not immediately intuitive were carried out. Changes were made in the software and the tutorial, resulting in improvements to both. The methods used and some of the lessons learned from this initial experience with iterative tutorial development are discussed.

Introduction

Iterative testing of user interfaces, including cycles of design, testing, evaluation and redesign, is now a well established technique for ensuring that human factors concerns are addressed early and continuously in the software development cycle (Brown, 1988; Gould and Lewis, 1985; Schneiderman, 1987; Williges and Hartson, 1986). In the Freestyle project, the iterative development process was enhanced by the concurrent development and testing of an online tutorial with prototype software. The goal of this effort was to minimize the learning time for Freestyle without hardcopy documentation.

Freestyle is a voice and handwriting based communication system. Freestyle uses a pencil-like stylus and a voice handset for synchronized annotations (Ehrlich and Levine, 1989; Francik and Akagi, 1989; Hsiao and Levine, 1989,). Freestyle captures and freezes computer screen images that can be annotated and then managed (e.g., mailed, copied, stapled, filed, etc.) on a separate "desktop" where miniature versions of the screen images are stored (see Figure 1.).

Reprinted, with permission, from *Proceedings of the Human Factors Society 33rd Annual Meeting*, 1989.

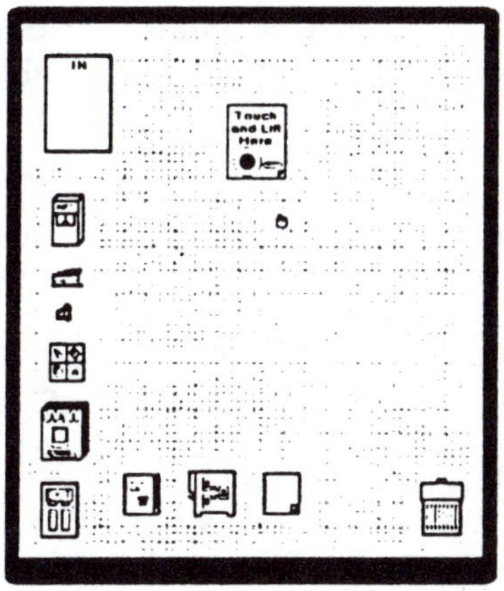

Figure 1: *The Freestyle Desktop*

For handwritten and voice annotation, the Freestyle pencil and handset are used in a familiar manner; users simply write with the pencil and speak into the handset. However, the pencil is also used as an input and manipulation device for performing all basic Freestyle functions. This presents unique interface design challenges since the pencil is used in a well learned manner for annotation but also for performing functions that are not normally performed with a pencil. Some of these functions include:

- Selecting items from pop-up menus
- Pressing "soft buttons"
- Moving objects on the Freestyle desktop
- Scrolling Freestyle images

The goal of the user interface development effort was to identify the aspects of Freestyle that were intuitive/not intuitive, then to solve the problems either through software changes or online tutorial training. Iterative testing and tutorial revision revealed which aspects of the user interface needed modification during development. This meant that even as training was being developed to deal with user interface problems, the user interface itself was changing. The methodology used effectively co-ordinated the development effort by identifying user interface problems early and correcting them either through software redesign or training via the tutorial.

Development and Testing

Four evolving prototypes of the software user interface were tested. An exploratory study was run on the initial prototype (P1) software to determine which aspects of Freestyle were intuitive and which features needed to be explicitly taught in the tutorial.

Based on the results of the exploratory study, changes were made to the P1 software to address some problems users had encountered. This new version of the software, P2, also contained additional features (for example, icon graphics and additional voice controls).

A tutorial was developed for P2, called T2 to match the software version. T2 provided two kinds of training: instruction on non-intuitive features that had not changed in the P2 software, and instruction on new features that appeared for the first time in P2. We tested the T2 tutorial with the P2 software.

These test results led us to revise both the tutorial and the software, giving rise to T3 and P3. Another round of testing led to T4 and P4. The P4 software was also tested without the tutorial as a control, to determine the usability of this final version of the software.

Tutorial

The tutorial was built utilizing existing Freestyle capabilities; it was not a separate software product. It was made up of a series of drawings that were scanned into the Freestyle annotator. Users were first presented with the tutorial in miniature form on the desktop and touched it with the pen to open it up to a full screen size (see Figure 2.). Instructions were positioned on the paper drawings so they would point to and explain the various annotation controls that were superimposed on the images by the system. Synchronized handwritten and voice annotations were added to these scanned images to provide animated illustrations of the annotation features. Particular emphasis was given to features that previous testing indicated were not intuitive. The final tutorial used illustrations to show: (1) annotation on a spreadsheet, (2) signatures on a form, (3) voice comments on an architectural drawing, and (4) synchronized voice and written directions on a map. The tutorial therefore provided both instruction on basic user interface functions and concrete examples of how to use the system.

Figure 2: *The Screen Based Tutorial*

Method

Subjects

Twenty-five subjects were tested under five conditions. Five subjects were tested in the Exploratory study. Five more subjects were tested on each of the software prototypes P2-P4 paired with tutorial versions T2-T4. Five additional subjects were tested on P4 without any tutorial as a control. All subjects were Wang employees with no experience with the Freestyle system. They included secretaries, professionals, managers and software engineers who were working on unrelated projects.

Procedure

In P2, P3, and P4 testing, subjects began by going through the current version of the Freestyle tutorial without any background information on the system. Following the completion of the tutorial, subjects were required to perform a criterion task (described below). Ss in the Exploratory and Control conditions performed the criterion task without the tutorial or any instructions. All Ss were asked to think aloud as they worked (Lewis, 1982). All Ss completed the task;

coaching was provided where needed. Participants were encouraged to try to solve problems before coaching was given.

Defining a Criterion Task

As a first step, the basic feature set of Freestyle was defined and a task was created that exercised the features listed above. A task was designed to expose the most probable user errors with the selected features. This task was used throughout the testing as the criterion task. First, each subject was instructed to: (1) open a Freestyle page which was a miniaturized spreadsheet. A spreadsheet, listing separate columns of numbers, appeared on the screen. Two subtotals were visible at the bottom of each column. Further instructions were to (2) write the total of the two numbers at the bottom of the page marked "Total". Getting to the bottom of the page required the use of the scrolling feature. The next instruction was given to (3) create a title page (this required the subject to leave the current screen), (4) add a voice message, and (5) attach the pages. The last instructions were to (6) mail a copy of the document and (7) throw the document away. Lastly, the subject was instructed to (8) exit the system.

Data Capture

Each session was videotaped with a two camera configuration which showed the contents of the screen and the subject's hand while using the graphics tablet. This allowed an examination of the position of the stylus controlled pointer on the screen as well as the position and angle of the the stylus on the tablet. Subjects were trained and prompted to use a thinking aloud protocol to describe their expectations and problem solving strategies. The video tapes were then scored by an independent researcher who identified error categories in the protocol and scored them using a PC based scoring system that was synchronized to the video recorder. The scoring system also allowed the time between events to be recorded. Thus the time it took for the criterion task, completion of the tutorial, participants comments, and the frequency of errors made were collected.

Results

The Exploratory Study revealed that the following features were intuitive (i.e., Ss made no errors in using these features):

- Pencil is used for writing
- End of the pencil is an eraser
- Screens can be annotated
- Pencil/tablet corresponds with the pointer/screen
- Handset is used for voice annotations
- Stapler is used to attach pages
- The function of desktop objects was obvious, when they were identified with labels

Each test revision resulted in the identification of new user problems which motivated changes in the software and tutorial for the next revision and test.

In order to illustrate the results of the iterative design/testing process, a subset of the non-intuitive features are tracked through the remaining iterations. These features are Voice Controls, Icon Targeting, Scrolling, and Obtaining help. The remaining results describe only these findings, and changes to the software and tutorial that pertain to these features.

Voice Controls

Subjects had both identification and feedback problems with voice controls. In the exploratory study, users did not know when to push the red button on the prototype handset (i.e., they had problems identifying the button as the voice activation feature). In P2 software, a voice On/Off switch was added to the top of the screen that helped the users identify the controls without training.

The next major change came with P4 software where a full set of voice controls was added that consisted of international symbols generally used on tape recorders. This increased the button identification problems significantly, which is shown in a comparison of error frequencies between P4 and the Control group, where no tutorial was provided from 0.5 to 2.2, ($t\,[4] = 2.23$, $p < .05$). The data verified that subjects made less errors on Voice controls when they went through the tutorial first. In the tutorial, the voice controls were represented with arrows showing the labels of each to aid identification.

Icon Targeting

The P2 software included movable icons which replaced the square boxes representing desktop objects in the P1 software. Part of the criterion task involved moving a document icon over a mail icon to activate the mail function. In the P2 software, the user was required to put a specific part of the pointer (invisible to the user) into the appropriate icon to activate its function. This resulted in many user errors in activating icons. To alleviate this problem the P3 software was changed so that only overlapping the icons was required to activate the function. The mean number of targeting errors with the P3 software was reduced from 7.8 to 1.6 ($t\,[4] = 1.9$, $p < .10$). The same method of icon activation was used in P4, resulting in an average of 0.2 targeting errors per subject.

Icon targeting was an example of a problem that could not have been detected without empirical testing. The software fix initiated by the test results provided a solution that met user expectations. However in a parallel effort, the technical writers already had illustrations carefully outlining the pointer that were discarded after the study results showed no further problems.

Scrolling

To scroll, the user moves the pen to the edge of the tablet. This causes a hand to appear on the edge of the image (as shown in Figure 3.). A touch down on the tablet and a sliding motion then causes the image to scroll, which is similar to moving paper on a desk.

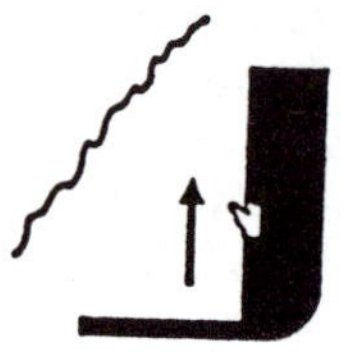

Figure 3: *Scrolling by moving the page on the screen.*

The problems subjects had learning to scroll the page emerged in the Exploratory study. Error data for scrolling indicated that without the tutorial, scrolling was nearly impossible to discover because there was no visible feedback that the mechanism existed. A description of scrolling was added to the tutorial for P2 testing. Scrolling did not change across software versions. However, the description in the tutorial was revised until scrolling errors disappeared in P4. The subjects in the Control group did not learn scrolling without coaching. The difference between P4 and the Control group show that errors significantly decreased with the tutorial from 7.8 to 1.6, ($\underline{t}$ [4] = 2.45, $p < .05$).

Help

The icon for information labeled "Info" in the Exploratory study was designed to give information on the miniaturized documents on the desktop. Most subjects erroneously picked Info to get Help on the system. In P2 software the Info icon was movable but still provided document information. The observational data showed that subjects were seeking help on the desktop icons to find how they functioned. In P3 the tutorial provided information for using the desktop icons. A t-test shows a significant decrease in errors in the group with the tutorial from 1.4 to 0.4, ($\underline{t}$ [4] = 2.49, $p < .05$). The recommendation was made to expand the function of Info to provide help whenever the Info icon was moved to another icon on the desk. This improvement resulted in an immediate reduction of errors in the P4 group.

Tutorial Effects

On the average, the tutorial decreased the time required to complete the criterion task. The tutorial users took 10.0 minutes and the non-tutorial users of the same software took 28.9 minutes. In addition, over the course of testing the tutorial itself also became more efficient. Compared to the T2 tutorial, the T4 version was shorter, yet contained training on more system features.

Discussion

We developed a tutorial for Freestyle using the first prototype version of the system and found that simultaneously developing and testing a tutorial during development highlights user problems early and fosters unique collaboration within the development team.

The software changed through four prototype versions with features changing due to human factors recommendations as well as planned upgrades. By the last software prototype, P4, the tutorial had served it's purpose; the criterion task time was reduced and the time to complete the tutorial had decreased, while the number of features covered in the tutorial had increased. As tradeoffs were made between training and prototype changes, software had also undergone changes as a result of the tutorial testing.

Tradeoffs Between Software Changes and Training

The tradeoff between reducing user errors through software design or training can be carefully examined through testing. For repeated errors that will recur due to their mismatch with user expectations, the software should be changed because training will be complicated and documentation will go unread. The icon targeting problem where the active point was invisible is the type of problem identified early and solved with software changes. This problem would have been difficult to document and the solution, which matched user expectations, needed no documentation.

If user errors can be reduced or eliminated through training with one-trial learning and the efficiency of the user interface is preserved, it is a good argument for <u>not</u> revising the software. For example, it was shown that a tutorial could eliminate the problems with the scroll feature, at least for the presently used scrolling metaphor. Scrolling became a tradeoff between design efficiency and ease of learning. The data showed that no subjects who went through the tutorial had problems scrolling whereas no subjects could learn scrolling without the tutorial. In this case the one-trial learning with training preserves screen real estate to display the full width of a page in contrast to alternative scrolling mechanisms.

Lessons Learned

After a number of iterations with a fast-paced development effort, we are now aware of the need for more controls in some aspects of this methodology. Coaching subjects for the purpose of forced completion allows the scoring of errors but introduces variance into any time data. Presently we have employed a forced completion technique with fixed time limitations for each task step. This method preserves the time data to complete each step in the criterion task and allows coaching only after a set time had transpired. By careful separation of user time and coaching it is possible to identify specific contributions to either the user interface or training materials.

Design cycles can outrun testing in that many user interface problems are identified too late for changes to the version of software tested. One solution to this problem is to test software and user documentation while the system is under development.

This testing/development method was shown to be useful because of the direct feedback loop created between human factors, software developers, and training developers. By empirically testing the product and identifying the exact places where users made errors, recommendations were made to modify either the software or the training materials to reduce user problems. Just as importantly, the early solution of user problems also prevents unnecessary documentation of the intuitive aspects of the product. Granted, with Freestyle, the task was easier because of the nature of the product and the simplicity of it's functions. But this method could be used on any product for which criterion tasks can be identified.

References

Brown, C. M. (1988). *Human Computer Interface Design*. New Jersey: Ablex.

Carroll, J. M. and Thomas, J. C. (1982). Metaphor and the Cognitive Representation of Computing Systems. *IEEE Transactions on Systems, Man and Cybernetics, 12*, 107-116.

Francik, E., and Akagi, K. (1989). Designing a Computer Pencil and Tablet for Handwriting, *Proceedings of the Human Factors Society*, this volume.

Gould, J. D. and Lewis, C. (1985). Designing for Usability: Key Principles and What Designers Think. *Communications of the ACM, 28*, 300-311.

Hsiao, C.and Levine, S. (1989). Voice Annotation on the Wang Freestyle System, *Official Proceedings of Speech Tech,* Media Dimensions, NY, N.Y.

Levine, S. R.and Ehrlich, S. F. (1989). Freestyle, A Design Perspective. In Press, *Human Machine Interactive Systems*.

Lewis, C. H. (1982). Using the "Thinking Aloud" Method in Cognitive Interface Design. *IBM Research Report, RC-9265*.

Schneiderman, B. (1987). *Designing the User Interface: Strategies for Effective Human-Computer Interaction*. MA: Addison-Wesley.

Williges, R. C. and Harston, H. R. (1986). Human-Computer Dialog Design and Research Issues. In Ehrich, R.W. and Williges, R. C. (Eds.) *Human Computer Dialog Design ,2* Amsterdam: Elsevier 367- 376.

Acknowledgments

The authors would like to thank Patty Russo for scoring the video tapes and analyzing the data, and Dick Ainsworth and Pat McCorkle for creative consulting on the design of the tutorial.

PUTTING INNOVATION TO WORK: ADOPTION STRATEGIES FOR MULTIMEDIA COMMUNICATION SYSTEMS

Multimedia communication systems promise better support for widely distributed workgroups. Their benefits for complex communication—problem-solving, negotiating, planning, and design—seem obvious. Introducing appealing new technologies into the marketplace, however, can require years of investment [13, 22]. In particular, finding productive uses for new systems takes time. Adoption strategies are needed to guide and accelerate the process.

In 1988 Wang Laboratories bundled together the familiar technologies of image capture, voice recording, and electronic mail and added pen annotation and high-resolution graphics. The result was the Freestyle system, providing multimedia communication for networked personal computers. It allowed people to capture computer screens or scanned-in paper as images, apply synchronized handwritten and voice annotations, and mail these messages to other PCs. As the voice recording played back, the accompanying pointing and writing were recreated.

This image-based annotation tool could support distributed workgroups which otherwise required more expensive, bandwidth-intensive computer or video conferencing systems. For example, design and manufacturing groups in different cities could use the system to communicate changes to design drawings more clearly, eliminating the need to travel for face-to-face meetings.

Yet despite the system's simple design, its adoption was not immediate. New technology intended to support cooperative work often risks initial rejection [3, 9, 10]. Users have difficulty envisioning how to use the technology to meet real organizational needs until they have worked with it in their own environment. Moreover, new technologies often create work pattern changes that are further resisted by the organization and it takes time for system planners to work through the resistance.

Wang had encountered these issues when introducing the Digital Voice Exchange voice mail

Ellen Francik

Susan Ehrlich Rudman

Donna Cooper

Stephen Levine

system [3] in the early 1980s. During the early years of the product's availability, voice mail systems were often given to inappropriate workgroups, such as those who sat on the same floor and could easily communicate by just walking down the hall. Customers also had difficulty identifying tasks that took advantage of voice mail's strengths. Voice mail could reduce telephone tag by allowing people to leave content-rich messages, but early users who left only name-and-number messages missed this benefit. Finally, some voice mail configurations led to unwelcome work pattern changes. When executive receptionists were replaced by voice mail systems, influential customers had problems reaching the executives and objected to the system's interference.

Over time, more workgroups found productive uses for voice mail and today, nearly 10 years later, it is a standard communication tool for many businesses. Similar adoption curves have been chronicled for previous communication advances, including the telephone itself [1, 20]. Fax technology is just now showing rapid adoption after years of slow growth: "Life Begins at 50," *FORBES* magazine wryly noted [5, 17, 21].

Introducing the Freestyle system meant developing strategies to overcome this inertia. Development, marketing, sales, and customer groups collaborated to identify potential uses of the system and to provide support for new sites. For two years Wang's human factors department worked with these groups in 15 evolving Freestyle sites, from the first rough internal implementations to full-scale deployment. We identified organizational factors that inhibited system adoption and in response developed product and consulting strategies that decreased the time needed for workgroup analysis and system introduction.

The case study presented in this article provides a pragmatic glimpse into the future of computer and video conferencing. Freestyle's combined technologies supported rich communication, yet could be rapidly deployed in diverse work sites without new investments in broadband networks, video equipment, or engineering workstations. Our experience with these sites foreshadows the challenge of putting other innovative systems to work outside of the R&D laboratory.

System Overview

Freestyle's multimedia messages are based on images, including screen snapshots and hand-drawn sketches, which users annotate with synchronized pointing, drawing, writing, and speaking. A graphical desktop displays miniature versions of the images. From the desktop, users select images to be enlarged, grouped, mailed, printed, and copied. Scanners, printers, and fax cards provide additional ways to capture and distribute images. (See Levine and Ehrlich [14] on the design and its rationale, Perkins et al. [19] for a description of iterative usability testing, and the CHI'89 video tape [24].) Descriptions of each of these component technologies and how they support group work follows:

Multimedia Annotation

To annotate a PC screen, the user captures it as a bitmap image by touching the "pencil" stylus to the tablet [7]. Users can then write and add synchronized voice annotations with a voice handset [11]. The user can also overlay typing by using the PC keyboard.

Graphic buttons above the image are used to play back the synchronized voice, hand-drawn, and typed messages. In addition, the stylus cursor's movement is also played back, allowing the user to point while talking. For instance, someone reviewing a spreadsheet can point and say, "*This* number seems out of line compared to last month's figures."

Since annotation is immediately available for any application by touching the tablet, users can capture the details of what they are working on, add comments or questions, and send the message without greatly interrupting the flow of work. In the more established test sites, people captured screens from disparate software environments—databases for tracking engineering problems, budget spreadsheets, and word processing memos—then combined them into one message.

Comments can be added as the multimedia messages pass from one person to the next. Each message holds the accumulated signatures and notes of several people on a single design drawing or report requiring action. For example, at one of the test sites invoices were commented on by buyers, passed on to management for approval, and finally sent to accounting for payment.

Although people are accustomed to annotating paper documents, combined written and spoken annotation is common only in face-to-face meetings. Users needed to discover how to combine writing and speaking for distributed, asynchronous work. A Freestyle message shows not only the end product—an image with annotations—but, equally important, the process by which it was created. Each user's annotations can be a conversational turn, with the conversation unfolding over time as the message is passed back and forth for continued annotations. So, although the Freestyle system uses asynchronous mail, it can facilitate some of the activities envisioned for experimental synchronous drawing environments [2, 23] and conferencing systems (Ishii and Miyake, this issue [12]; also see [4] for review).

Flexible Image Desktop

Newly annotated images are first displayed as miniatures in a graphical inbox on the desktop. All image mail is also received through that inbox. Items are then moved with the stylus and reorganized into overlapping piles or labelled folders. The images are distributed to other people through a mail icon, which provides access to electronic mail addresses, fax numbers, and distribution lists.

Since everything on the desktop is movable, the desktop organization of experienced users evolves to reflect the work patterns both of individuals and of workgroups [14; also see 15]. Users did learn to create and cluster desktop mail icons for frequently used addresses in their workgroup. Task-related piles or folders emerged, and these categories tended to be shared.

For example, the secretary-manager team shown in Figure 3, from one of the early internal pilot sites, agreed on common categories for piles of scanned travel request authorization forms (TRA's). The secretary then created more specific variants ("TRA's today," "TRA's tomorrow"), since her role in the workgroup was to expedite work in progress, including travel.

Scanners, Printers, Fax, and Shared Image Storage

Scanners provide gateways for printed information to enter the electronic workgroup, thereby connecting existing paper workflows to new electronic ones. One popular use of scanners in this system was to scan in paper forms (e.g., travel authorization forms and invoices) and speed their circulation, while collecting signatures and comments as the forms moved through the group. Scanners were also used to capture newspaper articles and printed documents.

Workgroups also learned to take advantage of fax option boards and printers to stretch the annotation environment to users in remote locations such as branch offices. Users viewed newly received faxes on the screen, annotated them, and

FIGURE 1

Image desktop; handwriting and voice annotation tools

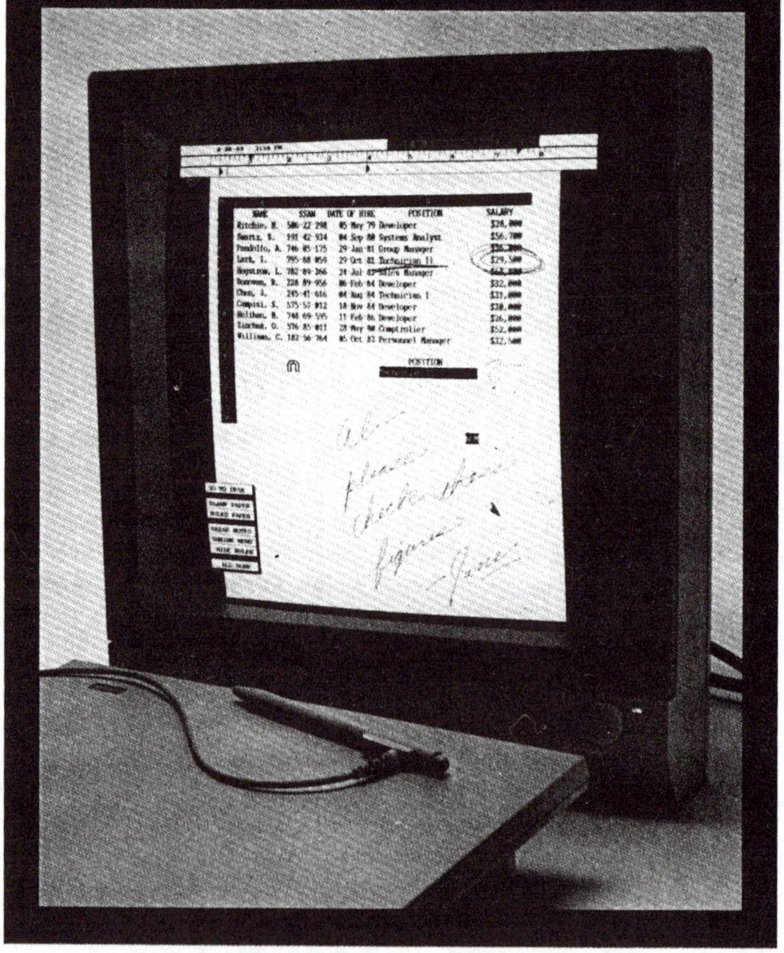

FIGURE 2

Annotation environment

routed them in Freestyle. In return, annotated images—without voice—could be faxed out or printed and mailed. With these tools, people who did not have systems were connected to the electronic workflow.

Images are also shared by moving them to a file cabinet icon on the desktop, which provides access to an indexed relational database residing on a shared server. People could thus move their work between two environments: one distributed and freeform, the other centralized, highly structured, and used for cross-organizational coordination and tracking.

Adoption Issues

The human factors department was asked by the development manager to assist in the initial design of Freestyle hardware and software [7, 19]. When the first prototypes became available, we observed system use in order to recommend design changes. Since these multimedia messages could be sent via the existing electronic mail network, however, prototypes were placed in existing organizations. This provided an unusual opportunity to observe the system's adoption even while its design was evolving. As the design solidified, we observed the introduction of systems to internal groups with targeted applications and finally to groups at customer sites. They represented many different sectors: law, finance, insurance, health, travel and entertainment, commerce, engineering, utilities, and public institutions.

People were interviewed about their work and communication patterns before systems were installed. In subsequent visits, we observed system use, collected comments on features, and documented how communication patterns were changing as new users were added to the network. This not only led to design recommendations but also suggested strategies to encourage adoption.

The system's potential was also evaluated by conducting interviews in other organizations including building construction, graphic arts, and manufacturing. These groups did not receive equipment, but they did represent markets that might have a great need for annotation during complex design tasks.

Repeatedly—in internal pilots, beta test sites, and customer sites—roadblocks that slowed system adoption appeared. Although the system had great potential benefits for individuals and groups, system planners found it hard to identify group tasks that took advantage of Freestyle's strengths, to select appropriate workgroups, and to assign equipment to individuals within workgroups. These were all similar to problems encountered with voice mail in the early 1980s.

Identifying Uses for the System

Customers had to identify specific business uses for the system in order to justify buying equipment for entire workgroups. It was not enough that multimedia mail with dynamic annotation was expected to provide generically richer, clearer communication. Department heads and system planners needed to show specific productivity increases or expense reductions. Planners, however, had difficulty envisioning the use of novel, image-based annotation in familiar work processes. Moreover, the need to select business-critical applications was not always immediately recognized.

The tendency to focus on individuals' use of the system. Customers were strongly drawn to the power and ease of use of the annotation tools per se, particularly the synchronized playback of their handwriting and voice. As a result, they initially paid less attention to group communication: that is, how the annotated documents would enter and leave their PCs. Forms would have to be scanned in by one person in order for another to receive and sign them. Documents quickly marked up by a reviewer would need to be mailed to the writer making the changes. As with other CSCW tools, the costs and benefits of Freestyle for the entire workgroup would have to be assessed. The system's appeal for individuals could not justify the volume purchases needed for critical mass.

The apparent appeal of the system for speeding forms-based paper flow. System planners who did recognize the need for cost justification searched for appropriate applications. Processes that used paper forms, especially those requiring signatures, were often suggested. In part, this was because the workflow was specified and seemed to require little additional analysis. Users did greatly benefit when processes formerly supported by paper mail were put onto the system, but the impact was more the speed of transmitting the forms than the new power provided by multidimensional annotation. For example, while the internal pilot group quickly appreciated the benefits of routing travel request forms electronically rather than handcarrying them between buildings, it was several weeks before they began using multidimensional annotation on spreadsheets to discuss new budgets.

In contrast, interviews with departments responsible for complex *design drawings* indicated those groups would be particularly sensitive to the advantages of multidimensional annotation. In construction and graphics arts departments, and in product teams where engineering passed designs on to manufacturing, between engineering and manufacturing, distributed workgroups negotiated changes on blueprints, page layouts and engineering drawings. They were already heavy users of pen annotation, hand drawing, and "yellow stickies." They also used the phone to speed up communication, but had difficulty solving spatial problems without the annotated drawings. The resulting inaccuracies during revision cycles were known to have very high costs—in some manufacturing cases, millions of dollars in design delays or retooling costs.

The tendency to use the system for structured processes. Recognizing applications that are based on spontaneous communication is difficult. Perin (this issue, [18]) discusses organizational biases that lead bureaucracies to view their work processes in structured, centralized, controlled ways. These biases may dissuade companies from implementing new communication systems, or may cause the systems to be withdrawn when they are used in unexpected ways.

In addition, the analysts who supported the test sites were not accustomed to looking for unstructured communication. Computer systems have historically been most effective for highly structured information processing, and analysts have been well trained in tracing these structured flows. In contrast, matching this system to a customer's organization meant understanding how people go through iterations, discuss options, and spontaneously include related material to buttress their arguments. It meant looking for phone calls, face-to-face conversations, yellow stickies, and scribbled notes on documents. Even experienced analysts who had supported the same customer for many years were not used to tracking this kind of data.

Selecting Workgroups

Successful system adoption required identifying members of a workgroup with a joint need for communication. Several competing factors, however, influenced group selection.

Focusing on nontyping managers. Handwritten annotation strongly appealed to managers who were not typists. When the product was first presented to existing custom-

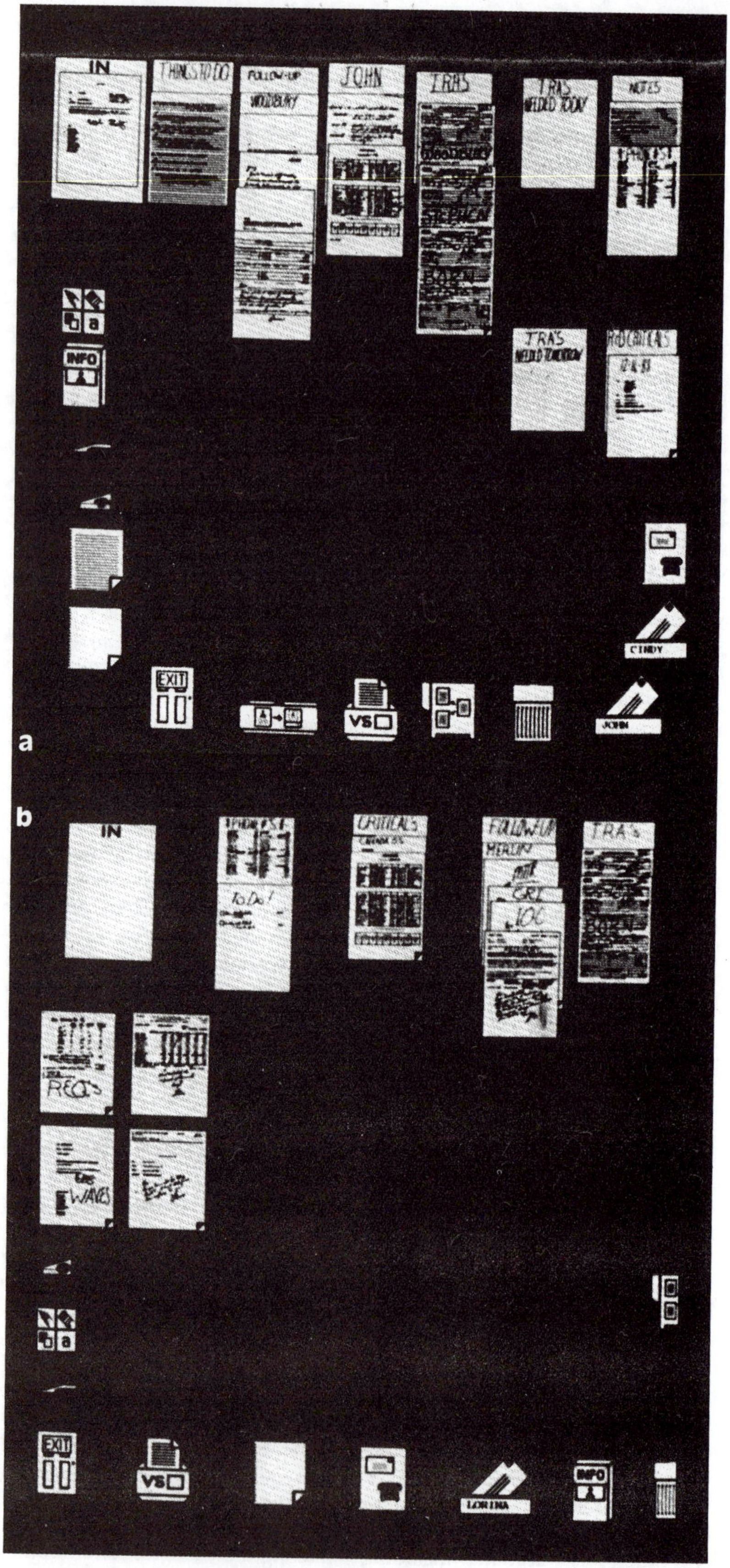

FIGURE 3

a & b Secretary's and manager's desktops

ers, both sales people and customers wanted to install systems in executive offices. In fact, the system was so appealing that some executives rolled it into their own public relations efforts, demonstrating this novel system to visiting clients. Although management support of a new system is an essential step in its adoption, we had to ensure that the system solved a business problem, serving the communication needs of a functioning workgroup. Often this meant adding users who were not executives, or even moving systems out of the executive suite.

Limiting the number of systems. Customers' system planners tended to keep test sites small, not only for technology tests but also for workgroups. This minimized their capital outlay, their risk, and their support requirements. As a result, these sites typically involved only 5 to 15 systems.

With only a few systems for each site, it was crucial to give them to the right people. Moreover, it was easy to underestimate the number of people involved in a work process, especially for existing processes supported by ubiquitous paper, mail, and telephones. In one company a four-person pilot group was proposed. This group discussed, reviewed and authorized large budgets for capital equipment. The process, however, really involved at least 13 people in several administrative sites (not to mention the dozens of people across the country who originated the budget request forms). Installing only four systems would have speeded up some steps but created new bottlenecks, requiring additional effort to scan in and print out the paper work.

Restricting geographic distribution. System managers tended to place pilots in single locations. These sites were easier to budget for, since they typically fell within one cost center. They were also easier to support; one person could handle software upgrades and hardware troubleshooting without leaving the building. The visible impact of the systems, however, was much less powerful for pilot workgroups working on the same floor than for groups stretching across buildings. One test site provided systems to users who were responsible for complex international communication that often involved design specifications. Breakdowns in communication with the Far East were known to be costly. Nevertheless, all the systems were assigned to people on the same floor who had access to other competing communication methods (including face-to-face meetings).

Following organization chart boundaries. Some methods for group selection left out key communicators. Several site proposals followed the structure of the organization chart, even though the work itself crossed organizational boundaries. Some processes, such as signature approval, were stereotyped as *vertical.* Decision makers in approval chains were scheduled to receive systems, but the need for horizontal support was underestimated. Secretaries, technical advisors, and troubleshooters in other departments also needed systems. Without them information would be frequently printed out (to include these people) and scanned back in (to resume the Freestyle workflow). The resulting extra work would be attributed to the system—not to the selection of users—and could cause the process to revert entirely to paper.

Other processes were stereotyped as *horizontal.* When system planners were actually looking for collaborative groups, they might plan to give systems to a department of 8 to 10 people. There were two problems with this plan. First, our interviews showed that the members of a department did not always collaborate closely; instead, they were matrixed into other project teams. Second, department members who did work together were often physically close enough to make face-to-face communication more convenient than electronic.

In both of these cases, systems assigned according to the organizational structure would not have supported the users' communication needs. This failure might then be mistakenly ascribed to the system.

Assigning Equipment

The system hardware and software were modular, permitting many different configurations. Voice annotation boards were optional as were scanners, printers, fax boards and high-resolution monitors. In order to reduce costs, some customers were tempted to assign options to users on the basis of rank or job title. This was a particular problem with voice boards because all users needed access to voice, if anyone in the site had it. Otherwise, messages with voice annotation could be sent to people who did not have the equipment to play them back.

Often, equipment assignment glossed over the differences in various users' tasks. This was partially because system planners lacked detailed knowledge about users' actual work practices. Even small errors created bottlenecks in the workflow, which in turn could have led to system rejection.

For example, a low-ranking public relations staff member was responsible for scanning late-breaking news articles for senior management. He needed a high-resolution monitor to confirm the legibility of small print before mailing the articles. Because of his lower status, however, he initially received a standard-resolution monitor, while senior managers received monitors that clearly displayed the small newsprint.

In the same organization, scanners were at first given only to clerical staff because scanning was considered a secretarial task like photocopying. Yet managers also needed scanners to rapidly exchange information and comments with their peers. They could not delegate this scanning to clerical staff after normal work hours or on weekends, nor did they always want to.

Short-Term Strategies for System Adoption

The human factors team advocated design changes to encourage adoption, while at the same time provided organizational consulting. Finally, the consulting was rolled into educational materials in order to reach many more customers and sales analysts. These strategies are now described.

Product Strategies for Critical Mass

The development team took several steps to reduce per-user hardware cost. These steps would allow customers to purchase additional systems necessary to include all members of a workgroup.

One step was to develop software that could be used with commonly available monitors so that purchase of a full-page, high-resolution image monitor was an option rather than a requirement. A second crucial step was the development of software that allowed mouse control of annotation, eliminating the expense of the tablet and pen. As a result, an off-the-shelf 286 PC could serve as the base workstation. Networks of users were extended by developing a version of the software that worked on local area networks (LANs), as well as on centralized hosts. It was also during this phase that the fax software and hardware were developed.

These cost-reduction strategies allowed customers to take advantage of existing fax and LANs to reach other organizations cost-effectively, thus making it easier to increase the number of systems and achieve critical mass.

Consulting

Consulting assumed greater importance as the project progressed. Usability testing and early site experience had confirmed that Freestyle was easy for individuals to use. Now, the system's costs and benefits for entire workgroups needed to be assessed, and productive uses of the system uncovered in each site.

At each customer site, human factors staff met with the sales branch and with the customer's system planner to understand their business needs and their goals for Freestyle. Then we conducted one to two days of in-depth interviews with all prospective users. At the end of the visit recommendations for changing or expanding the workgroup were discussed and techniques for encouraging system use provided. Follow-up visits were made after installation to observe system use and provide additional consulting. Some techniques for addressing the specific adoption issues we encountered will now be outlined.

Selecting uses of the system. To overcome customers' *tendency to focus on individuals' use of the system,* we reviewed the site proposal with each customer. Then, if the goal was limited to setting up a technology demonstration, we outlined potential applications, urging customers to match working pilots to their stated business needs. If a workgroup had been proposed, detailed user interviews were conducted.

Freestyle's *appeal for speeding up forms flow* meant its rich annotation capabilities might be missed. When customers proposed forms-based processes, we explored other applications, especially in engineering and design. Even within otherwise routine processes we looked for faxes, graphics, and sketches—any place where images and handwritten annotations had an advantage over text-based systems.

Using Freestyle systems for forms processing is an example of the *tendency to choose structured processes.* Although the system was best suited for problem solving, planning, and design, workgroups initially used it for signature processes and electronic distribution of scanned-in paper documents. Instead of fighting this tendency head-on, we used structured processes to provide an entry point for unstructured, spontaneous uses.

Our ideal structured process included a good deal of unstructured communication—for instance, negotiation during capital budget approval or design discussions culminating in the sign-off of an engineering change. By using the new system for these discussions, users experienced the full benefits of multimedia CSCW tools and suggested other workgroups that would also benefit. Structured-plus-unstructured processes provide opportunities for novel use of the system and foster the building of critical mass.

Selecting workgroups. A simple diagram, called a *communication constellation* (a form of link analysis), was the main interview tool. Constructed during the interview, it summarized the individual's communication patterns—not just for the target work process, but also for the rest of the job. The constellation was most useful in helping interviewees reflect on their informal, and often overlooked, communication needs.

Information collected during the interview included: names of individuals or groups, in order of importance (frequency and/or urgency); reasons for communicating; media used; location of the other person or group; whether the communication was one-way or two-way; and whether the person/group was inside or outside of the company. The interviews suggested ways in which proposed workgroups needed to be changed and expanded.

Several proposed installations had a *focus on nontyping managers* and their annotation needs. To define the workgroup, we asked about how annotated material was communicated: who it came from, and who it was sent to. We also tried to assure that the benefits were not one-sided. In one company the president and all of those who directly reported to him received systems. Though the president communicated frequently with all his reporting managers, the managers rarely communicated with one another; they dealt more frequently with their own line organizations. We helped this company identify a group of managers, professionals, and clerks who needed to communicate with each other.

To overcome *limitations on the number of systems,* we assisted customers in identifying users who only needed a subset of the options, particularly those who could use standard monitors or the mouse-annotation software. The development of the LAN and fax software further extended the potential user group.

Customers who planned to *restrict the geographic distribution* of systems needed compelling reasons to do otherwise. During workgroup interviews we asked specifically about delays and costs in communicating with other organizations, buildings, or companies. Delays ranged from hours to months (for complex design problems), and costs included time spent handcarrying, courier fees, overnight mail charges, and even use of company fleet cars to travel between buildings. In sites that already had electronic mail links between buildings, adding remote users of the new system required only an upgrade to the mail software. The fax option was especially useful for reaching field offices where no electronic mail connection existed. For example, in insurance companies, a centralized workgroup could use fax to collect information from independent insurance agents across the country.

To make sure workgroups did not automatically *follow organization chart boundaries,* we used communication constellations to verify actual communication paths. In a purchasing department, systems were proposed for buyers who worked closely with their assistants and consulted with their manager. The buyers received purchase orders, found a supplier, arranged for delivery, and invoiced the customer. Yet the buyers worked more closely with other departments than with each other. The invoicing process alone involved two other groups: Transportation, which oversaw the shipping, and Finance, which billed the customer. Any Freestyle-supported work process needed to include people in each of these groups. And for negotiations with outside firms, the fax option could be used to bring information into the electronic workgroup.

FIGURE 4

Communication constellation. Not all detail is shown

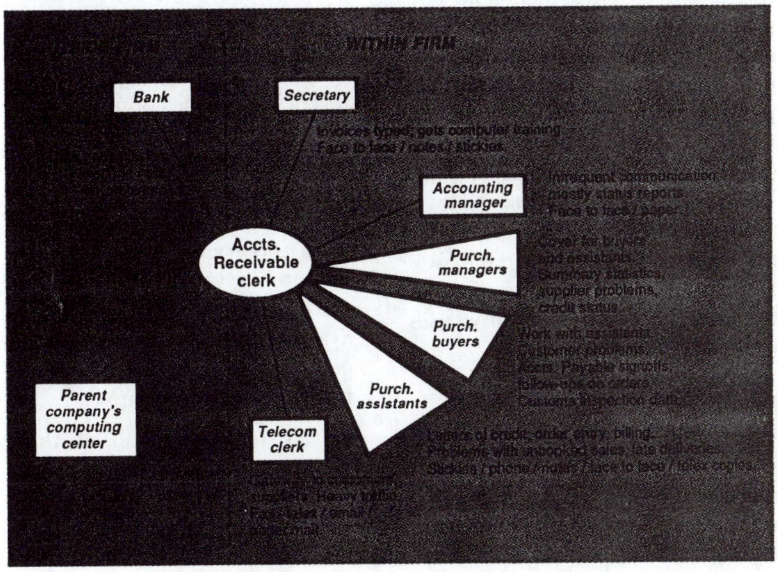

FIGURE 5

Organization chart vs. actual communication patterns

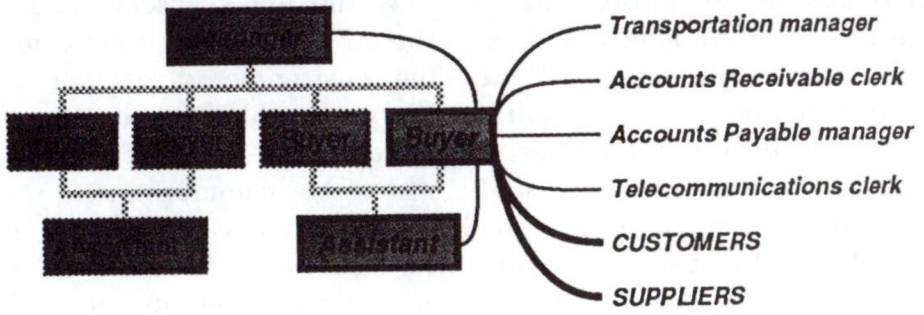

Assigning equipment. Details from the interviews, plus concrete examples from other sites, helped convince customers to place equipment where it supported the flow of work, rather than assigning it purely according to status or cost. Printers were placed to be shared, voice boards were purchased for all (to be ubiquitous), and fax and scanners were given to key individuals with a vested interest in moving information into or out of the group. For instance, in an early site, paper forms moved up the approval chain through Finance, then via the system to a senior vice president. One financial director, formerly responsible for signing up to 20 forms a day, now had the frustrating task of scanning all of them into the system before signing and mailing them. The originators of the forms were later included in the network to solve this problem.

Education

This face-to-face analysis and consulting was packaged for wider distribution. We created a videotape that walked sales staff and potential customers through the preparatory steps needed to successfully introduce a new Freestyle configuration [25]. The video focused on business problem identification, work process and communication analysis, user selection, and equipment configuration for each user. Interwoven with these approaches were concrete examples of successful installations and warnings about problems encountered in the existing sites.

Accelerating Adoption

Freestyle was a novel system for many of these workgroups. Few users had any prior experience with multimedia messaging. Some of them were working with PCs for the first time. It seemed difficult to envision, create, and sustain new work processes. Specialized hardware, not commonly available, was needed; potential uses of the system were still being discovered; and workflow issues could jeopardize each site's success.

Emerging CSCW applications face similar challenges. Consider the Freestyle system as a low-cost, asynchronous counterpart to the desktop conferencing systems that are springing up in research laboratories [12, 26]. Desktop conferencing promises rapid, flexible, multimodal communication for distributed workgroups—once the systems are widely available. But when these systems first reach the market, system planners will have to justify the workstation cost, equip them with video hardware, and place them in workgroups. Moreover, these systems require fast, wide-bandwidth networking that is not yet ubiquitous (beyond local area networks).

Therefore, desktop conferencing vendors will need adoption strategies for newly introduced products. They must identify pressing business problems the product will solve, help customers envision the many uses of multimedia tools in their workplaces, select and configure workgroups, and provide cost-effective ways to stretch the pilot workgroup and create critical mass (see also [16]).

Several of the strategies used in this project are directly applicable to other conferencing systems. For instance, desktop conferencing systems' advantage for graphic and spatial tasks needs to be shown [12], but the cost must also be justified. Videoconferencing systems are often used for structured, regularly scheduled meetings. Further examples of their use for spontaneous communication [6] are needed. And system designers who provide an array of hardware options [26] also need to demonstrate how those options are appropriately assigned—especially in lower-cost configurations—to support the flow of work.

These strategies assume critical mass is built from a modest number of systems. Visionaries can shortcut this process by making systems widely available. A well-publicized example is Price Waterhouse's planned installation of 10,000 copies of Lotus Notes to enable employees all over the world to share critical business tactics. Yet even with a large number of users, group processes need nurturing. At a CSCW 90 panel on "Commercial CSCW" [8], George John of Price Waterhouse remarked that Notes is often used by individuals to retrieve information from public databases. In his role as "evangelist," John encourages more collaborative uses of Notes.

Demands on Customers

Early adoption means customers and vendors must work together to define the customers' requirements in substantial detail. Vendors need to find customers who are keenly aware of their own communication needs and are therefore able to help recognize the match between their business problems and the vendor's solutions. This requires leadership from the customer organization, as well as a dedicated staff to nurture the early introduction through careful user education, training, and technical and organizational troubleshooting. Early adopters provide examples to other companies that have not been able to uncover technology requirements on their own but can recognize a concrete solution to familiar business problems.

Demands on Vendors

Customers, in turn, need to find CSCW vendors who have well-rounded architectural and organizational expertise. The vendors converging upon the groupware market have different strengths:

- Office automation firms, who specialize in centralized applications for *structured* group work such as word processing, databases, and financial packages. They usually offer electronic mail.
- PC application developers, whose innovative single-user applications support *unstructured* group work via local area networks and "sneakernet" (exchange of files on disks between people who are not networked). Some companies offer electronic mail systems; screen-sharing systems and conferencing applications (notably Group Technologies' Aspects) are also beginning to appear.
- Telecommunications companies, who established ubiquitous *networks* and are now offering information services using those networks.
- Systems integrators, who tie together *multiple platforms* and implicitly multiple groups.

CSCW tools need all of these qualities. Such tools should support both structured and unstructured work, to facilitate adoption in the pilot site. Systems need to be well networked to support geographically distributed users. The tool should have links to other computing environments, so that work flows smoothly between the pilot site users and the other people with whom they communicate.

Few vendors have all of these strengths, however, although some are branching out and others borrow strength through strategic alliances. Moreover, each CSCW product develops its own architectural strengths and weaknesses as designers make trade-offs. These design decisions have organizational effects.

The following provides one example: Some systems, such as MarkUp (Mainstay's document review program for the Macintosh), provide bitmap images of documents rather than live files. This increases critical mass by enabling people to share information with others who do not have the same applications: word processors, spreadsheets, databases. It also means the person receiving the comments must separately access the editable file in order to make changes. Care must be taken to minimize that burden—perhaps by providing a large monitor to display the annotated copy and the editable file side by side, or by changing the work process to spread the burden. Conversely, systems that support the sharing of live files may impose platform constraints and thereby limit critical mass, but frequently provide more sophisticated group tools for manipulating files.

At a minimum, customers need vendors who understand the work process implications of their particular designs, vendors who can help them discover how the system can be used in their own work context. Therefore, the entire vendor organization—from the development team to marketing and sales forces—must be able to describe the product in terms of the work processes it supports. Marketing and sales groups must also understand that organizational analysis is needed for successful adoption.

Development teams may need to strongly advocate this organizational analysis, especially for products that seem to have obvious benefits. Early prototypes, often under the control of development managers, provide the first opportunity for discovering adoption issues essential to the product's success. These adoption issues can influence priorities for design changes while the product is still malleable.

Finding people to do the organizational analysis is important. Most human factors departments will not be chartered or staffed for this kind of work. On the other hand, sales support staff are expected to work with customers, but work process analysis can require novel skills even for seasoned analysts. Organizational expertise can be found in consulting teams. Some vendors have these teams in-house, while other companies use contractors. Each vendor must determine how to provide this consulting. Who should be responsible? What training is needed? How should the costs be recovered?

This seems like too much effort, but only with persistent experimentation can innovative technology be matched to customers' needs. As one R&D veteran wrote, "market pull . . . is usually no more than a barely perceptible tug which you strain with all your wits to sense and interpret" [22]. Finding that pull—putting innovation to work—is doubly important for CSCW systems, which depend on critical mass. Unlike single-user applications, CSCW systems must meet the needs not just of many separate individuals but of entire groups.

Since examples of successful system use are so powerful, providing extensive consulting to early adopters can pay off. Success stories accelerate adoption, not just for a particular customer site or product line, but for an entire class of CSCW systems. If vendors become aware of adoption issues and develop specific strategies to deal with them, we shorten the delay before organizations feel the benefits of the technology.

Acknowledgments
We would like to acknowledge the contributions of Constance Perin, who was a member of the adoption team and collaborated with us on interview techniques for workflow analysis. She also increased our understanding of the system's possible uses and worked on marketing collateral to explain those uses to customers. For comments on the manuscript, we thank Tom Erickson, Jonathan Grudin, Pat Hennigan, Hiroshi Ishii, Morten Kyng, and Naomi Miyake. ■

References

1. Aronson, S.H. Bell's electrical toy: What's the use? The sociology of early telephone usage. In *The Social Impact of the Telephone,* I. de S. Pool, Ed., The MIT Press, Cambridge, Mass., 1967, 15–39.
2. Bly, S. A use of drawing surfaces in different collaborative settings. In *Proceedings of CSCW 88, Conference on Computer-Supported Cooperative Work* (Portland, Ore., Sept. 26–28). ACM, N.Y., 1988, pp. 250–256.
3. Ehrlich, S.F. Strategies for encouraging successful adoption of office communication systems. *ACM Trans. Off. Inf. Syst. 5,* 4 (Oct. 1987), 340–357.
4. Ellis, C.A., Gibbs, S.J., and Rein, G.L. Groupware: Some issues and experiences. *Commun. ACM 34,* 1 (Jan. 1991), 38–58.
5. Ellis-Simons, P. Just the fax, please. *Marketing and Media Decisions 23,* 7 (July 1988), 44–45.
6. Fish, R.S., Kraut, R.E., and Chalfonte, B.L. The VideoWindow system in informal communications. In *Proceedings of CSCW 90, Conference on Computer-Supported Cooperative Work* (Los Angeles, Oct. 7–10). ACM, N.Y., 1990, 1–11.
7. Francik, E., and Akagi, K. Designing a computer pencil and tablet for handwriting. In *Proceedings of the 33rd Human Factors Society Annual Meeting* (Denver, Oct. 16–22). Santa Monica, Calif., Human Factors Society, 1989, 445–449.
8. Greif, I., Moderator. Commercial CSCW or how to get group software out of the labs and into real use. Panel at *CSCW 90, Conference on Computer-Supported Cooperative Work* (Los Angeles, Oct. 7–10).
9. Grudin, J. Why CSCW applications fail: Problems in the design and evaluation of organizational interfaces. In *Proceedings of CSCW 88, Conference on Computer-Supported Cooperative Work* (Portland, Ore., Sept. 26–28). ACM, N.Y., 1988, 85–93.
10. Grudin, J. Seven plus one chal-

lenges for groupware developers. In Two analyses of CSCW and groupware. Tech. Rep. DAIMI PB-323. Aarhus University, Computer Science Department, Aarhus, Denmark, 1990.

11. Hsiao, C., and Levine, S.R. Voice annotation in Wang Freestyle system. In *Official Proceedings of Speech Tech '89*, 1989, pp. 365–367.
12. Ishii, H., and Miyake, N. Team-WorkStation: Toward an open shared workspace. *Commun. ACM 34* (this issue).
13. Leonard-Barton, D., and Kraus, W.A. Implementing new technology. *Harvard Bus. Rev. 63*, 6 (Nov.–Dec. 1985), 102–110.
14. Levine, S.R., and Ehrlich, S.F. The Freestyle system: A design perspective. In *Human-Machine Interactive Systems*, A. Klinger, Ed. Plenum Press, N.Y. To be published.
15. Malone, T. How do people organize their desks? Implications for the design of office information systems. *ACM Trans. Off. Inf. Syst. 1* (1983), 99–112.
16. Markus, M.L. Toward a "critical mass" theory of interactive media: Universal access, interdependence and diffusion. *Commun. Res. 14*, 5 (1987), 491–511.
17. O'Brien, L. Will the fax boom go bust? *Telephony 217*, 14 (Sept. 25, 1989), 38–46.
18. Perin, C. Electronic social fields in bureaucracies. *Commun. ACM 34* (this issue).
19. Perkins, R., Blatt, L.A., Workman, D., and Ehrlich, S.F. Iterative tutorial design in the product development cycle. In *Proceedings of the 33rd Human Factors Society Annual Meeting* (Denver, Oct. 16–21). Santa Monica, Calif., Human Factors Society, 1989, 268–272.
20. Pool, I. de S. *Forecasting the Telephone: A Retrospective Technology Assessment of the Telephone.* Ablex, Norwood, N.J., 1983.
21. Schreiber, J. Life begins at 50. *FORBES 132*, 5 (Aug. 29, 1983), 130–132.
22. Steele, L. Managers' misconceptions about technology. *Harvard Bus. Rev. 61*, 6 (Nov.–Dec. 1983), 133–140.
23. Tang, J.C., and Minneman, S.L. VideoDraw: A video interface for collaborative drawing. In *Proceedings of the CHI'90 Conference on Human Factors in Computing Systems* (Seattle, Apr. 1–5). ACM, N.Y., 1990, pp. 313–320.
24. Wang Laboratories, Inc. Freestyle. *ACM SIGGRAPH Video Review Supplement to Computer Graphics, 45*, 4. ACM, N.Y., 1989.
25. Wang Laboratories, Inc. Putting Freestyle to work. Videotape 741-7372. Wang Media Services, Lowell, Mass., 1990.
26. Watabe, K., Sakata, S., Maeno, K., Fukuoka, H., and Ohmori, T. Distributed multiparty desktop conferencing system: MERMAID. In *Proceedings of CSCW 90, Conference on Computer-Supported Cooperative Work* (Los Angeles, Oct. 7–10). ACM, N.Y., 1990, pp. 27–38.

CR Categories and Subject Descriptors: H.4.3 [**Information Systems Applications**]: Communication Applications—*electronic mail;* H.5.1. [**Information Interfaces and Presentation**]: Multimedia Information Systems—*audio input / output;* H.5.2 [**Information Interfaces and Presentation**]: User Interfaces—*input devices and strategies, interaction styles;* H.5.3 [**Information Interfaces and Presentation**]: Group and Organization Interfaces—*asynchronous interaction, evaluation / methodology;* K.4.3 [**Computers and Society**]: Organizational Impacts; K.6.2 [**Management of Computing and Information Systems**]: Installation Management

General Terms: Human Factors, Management

Additional Key Words and Phrases: Adoption, computer-supported cooperative work, CSCW, Freestyle, implementation

About the Authors:

ELLEN FRANCIK is currently in the Human Factors Engineering Laboratory at Pacific Bell, where she works on phone- and screen-based user interfaces, including those for communication systems. Her interests include the design and introduction of systems for group work, "discount" methods for usability assessment and workflow consulting, and multimedia systems. **Author's present address:** Pacific Bell, 2600 Camino Ramon, Rm. 1S 950, San Ramon, CA, USA 94583; email: epfrancik@pacbell.com

SUSAN EHRLICH RUDMAN is now a member of the technical staff at U S WEST, where she designs and evaluates communication system user interfaces. She was formerly the manager of the Human Factors Laboratory at Wang Laboratories, which was responsible for design consulting, laboratory evaluations, and field assessments of office automation technologies. **Author's present address:** U S WEST Advanced Technologies, 4001 Discovery Drive, Suite 340, Boulder, CO, USA 80303; email: crudman@uswest.com.

DONNA COOPER is in the Human Factors Laboratory at Wang Laboratories. She has a business background and has worked to implement office technologies such as voice messaging, electronic mail, and pen-based computing. Her interests include social implications of computer design and installation, justification criteria for new technologies, and user adoption. **Author's present address:** Wang Laboratories, Inc., M/S 019-490, One Industrial Avenue, Lowell, MA, USA 01851; email: donna. j..cooper@office.wang.com.

STEPHEN LEVINE was the development manager for the Freestyle system and is now an independent consultant. **Author's present address:** 95 Summer Street, North Andover, MA, USA 01845.

Chapter 14

Cyberspace

In the summer of 1993, you probably saw one or more of the movies *Jurassic Park, Sleepless in Seattle, The Fugitive,* and *The Firm,* which together grossed over a billion U.S. dollars. In each film, a computer used in a realistic fashion played a key role: Hungry velociraptors were kept at bay, a boy flew to New York to find a new mother, a one-armed killer was located, and a double-billing scheme was exposed.

The computer users who saved the day were two young girls, a doctor, and an Ivy League lawyer, respectively. The message is clear: *Computers are everywhere. They are keys to success. They are useful tools for professionals today. They will be indispensable for everyone tomorrow!*

The increasing number of Hollywood films in which computers play a significant role is due in part to an unparalleled awareness of and interest in computers among the general public. Our fascination and fear stem from the rate of change and rate of introduction of computer technologies throughout society.

Although we've been on exponential growth curves for decades, such as in the number of transistors packed on a chip, such growth is tricky: We rarely encounter it, do not reason well about it, and are astonished when it suddenly sneaks up on us and overwhelms us.

When memory went from 1K to 2K to 4K bits per chip, it still took many chips to get a job done. When we go from 16 megabits to 64 megabits to 256 megabits per chip, entire industries will change. Photography and film may change as dramatically as music recording and typesetting already have.

When the number of Internet users went from 2,000 to 4,000 to 8,000, it was an academic curiosity. When it goes from 20 million to 40 million to 80 million, a social transformation is in the making.

We shall examine in this chapter three areas of passionate current interest that stem in part from three dimensions of growth of the industry—increases in availability and connectivity of computers, increases in computational power and the ability of computers to simulate reality, and decreases in the size and manufacturing cost of computers, which allow us to have large numbers of tiny computers "everywhere."

More specifically, we shall consider three interwoven research frontiers:

- *Global networking* is computation that supports interactions among people. Whether coordinating, communicating, or collaborating, we are social beings and will never interact only *with* computers. Thus, we have devised ways to interact with other people *through* computers, via virtual encounters, virtual relationships, and virtual communities.
- *Virtual reality* is a term describing artificial environments in which computers project much or all that users see, hear, feel, and perhaps even smell. The computer becomes the environment, usually totally replacing direct contact with the world beyond.
- *Ubiquitous computing* (*ubicomp*) is computational power embedded in everything around us, often not directly noticeable. We see and interact with real but computer-enhanced objects in the world.

Although each vision provides a novel environment in which humans and computers interact, they are not the same. Our reading describes ubiquitous computing as "embedded virtuality," the *opposite* of virtual reality. Yet because all three involve novel configurations and interactions of machines and people and provide experiences dramatically different from typical human-computer interactions, we expect to find increasing links among the three approaches in the future.

They are already linked in the public mind. The word coined for this brave new world merging global networking, virtual reality, and ubiquitous computing is *cyberspace,* a term coined by Vancouver science fiction writer William Gibson around 1984. The September 1991 issue of *Scientific American,* in which our ubicomp reading appeared, is titled "How to Work, Play, and Thrive in Cyberspace." Cyberspace is "the entire Datasphere, the informational universe, the place you go when you're on the phone, the place where your money is," according to enthusiast John Perry Barlow (1993, p. 20). "Cyberspace is such a familiar environment to modern people that it is invisible to most . . . as, say, water is to a fish."

Michael Benedikt (1991a, p. 1) is more expansive:

> ***Cyberspace:*** *A new universe, a parallel universe created and sustained by the world's computers and communication lines. A world in which the global traffic of knowledge, secrets, measurements, indicators, entertainments, and alter-human agency takes on form: sights, sounds, presences never seen on the surface of the earth blossoming in a vast electronic night.*
>
> ***Cyberspace:*** *Accessed through any computer linked into the system; a place, one place, limitless; entered equally from a basement in Vancouver, a boat in Port-au-Prince, a cab in*

New York, a garage in Texas City, an apartment in Rome, an office in Hong Kong, a bar in Kyoto, a cafe in Kinshasa, a laboratory on the Moon.

Cyberspace: *The tablet becomes a page becomes a screen becomes a world, a virtual world. Everywhere and nowhere, a place where nothing is forgotten and yet everything changes.*

Cyberspace: *A common mental geography, built, in turn, by consensus and revolution, canon and experiment; a territory swarming with data and lies, with mind stuff and memories of nature, with a million voices and two million eyes in a silent, invisible concert of enquiry, deal-making, dream sharing, and simple beholding . . .*

Complex interactions of people, technology, and space were envisioned long ago. Some artists and technologists built environments that actively respond to us, virtual realities without helmets or gloves. Pioneer Myron Krueger (1991) has for decades explored ways in which people can interact with a large projected display, their movements and gestures sensed and interpreted by a computer, which adjusts the display accordingly. Virtual butterflies can be caught in your hand, or in a silhouette of your hand. Laurel (1991) explores the concept of "computers as theatre," embracing an animated, spatial, culturally deep metaphor.

Will a computer become our environment or our environment become computerized? Will our environment consist of thousands, millions, or billions of machines? The answers will depend on who we are and where we are and what we are doing. In any case, progress will require new hardware, software, and understanding of the perceptual, cognitive, and social aspects of human beings, and hardware is the easy part. The result will alter the way we work, learn, and play, and how we relate to one another.

GLOBAL NETWORKING, INFORMATION HIGHWAYS, AND VIRTUAL COMMUNITIES

Electronic mail has enjoyed exponential growth for two decades, with the number of users doubling roughly every two years. Chapter 11 discussed electronic mail and computer-mediated communications technology and usage in detail. In this chapter we review recent developments that result from the explosion of users with increasingly powerful computers linked by higher-bandwidth networks. Their numbers are great enough that massive publishing, commerce, and political activities are now beginning on the Internet, attracting media attention, which in turn fuels further growth.

Virtual Communities and the Internet

The Internet, as its name implies, is a network linking thousands of regional networks. As of 1995, thousands of e-mail-carrying networks still remain outside the Internet, mostly linking employees of specific organizations. Estimates of the number of people with Internet access at this time range from 20 million to 40 million, with at least an equal number on networks that lack a gateway to the Internet.

There are also many community-based networks or bulletin boards. Membership in these may be open or via an application process. Many are run by a single individual with a system that handles traffic via modem. Some community bulletin boards are based on specific topics. They may be moderated, or have more free-wheeling discussions. The growth of the Internet has not eliminated these boards, since they allow people to interact with a smaller, more familiar, more uniform group in ways less possible on the vast and largely anonymous Internet.

One private bulletin board, and its powerful effects on its users, was originally described in an electronic journal (Grudin, 1994):

The Beginning Teachers Computer Network

"The network is one of the most wonderful things a school can give to its students."

The students, in this case, were not really students, they were former students: graduates of the Harvard School of Education. I spent an hour on the phone with a seventh grade teacher in Augusta, Georgia, the result of a chance conversation with her mother.

50% to 60% of new teachers leave their profession within 5 years, she told me. To find out why and to see what could be done about it, several years ago Harvard set up the BTCN or Teachers Network. For $25, a graduate can rent a computer and modem for a year. The system comes set up, with an 800 dial-in line and hotline help. The documentation is primarily education on "e-mail etiquette"—actions and feelings to expect on a network.

The graduates have been through an intense twelve months of teacher training. She explained, "We get very close in the program and are then hurled off into the cruel world. The first year of teaching is awful, it's very very hard. It was the worst year I've ever had, the hardest thing I've ever done. It's brutal. It's hard. You never sleep, you're grading all the time, you're planning all the time, you're crying all the time."

About 60 in her graduating class took the offer and joined the network. Some of the on-line "forums" are devoted to specific disciplines: Humanities, Math & Science, Foreign Languages. Others are topics: Classroom Management, Evaluation. In the "Introduction" forum, new participants are guided as they try out the technology together. "Soapbox" is a general forum. Some Harvard faculty participate in the lightly facilitated forums, which are also studied for research purposes (a consent form is part of the rental agreement). "Private forums" (person-to-person e-mail) are unmonitored. (Recently they upgraded the system and added a "Chat Line" for synchronous communication. She is unsure the new features warrant the increased complexity, though.)

"It was really lifesaving for me, it kept me grounded when I needed it, helped me see what things are mountains, what are molehills. It's a time when you are feeling panicky about the world, worried about the future of society and children. Classmates really understand things so well. We could help each other in a wonderful way, not naive yet still excited."

The questions were often specific. "I'd like to stress writing, but the class is 35 kids, it seems too big . . .' 'Should I teach Julius Caesar or Macbeth?'" Other times "It was like reading an education journal, where theory and practice meet up."

After a year she bought a computer to stay on, but now finds herself participating less in the forums, which remain focused on first-year problems and populated by a new class. She mostly uses private forums (e-mail) with a few friends who also stayed on. This year for the first time current stu-

dents at Harvard can monitor and (rarely) participate. Some of her classmates who had not found teaching jobs initially got on the network but eventually stopped participating. To her surprise, arrogant classmates she "couldn't stand" in school were likable and helpful on the network, all struggling with similar problems.

"It allowed me to see the longer range. With intense, miserable experiences every day there is a tendency to say 'forget it.'" Students encourage each other or just "vent." Discussing differences in the methods that they encountered in different schools enabled her to see that some of the problems she faced in her all-white private school were not universal. After a year she transferred to an inner-city magnet school, where she says she is much happier. ("I wouldn't say Augusta has an inner city, but that's what they call it.")

It seemed a very special set of circumstances so I asked her uncertainly whether she sees any other uses for networks of this sort. She was ready. "Parents! Of kids in the same age group. I'm thinking of starting a newsletter for them. Parents of middle school kids see their kids turn into monsters and don't know what to do. It's a monstrous age, difficult to live through. The seventh grade is the height of monsterness." She laughed. 'Parents need to be told "you were a monster when you were 13 and your children's children will be monsters when they're 13.'

She sees many opportunities. "Networks for parents of infants. For people starting new businesses . . ."

Recall our discussion of synchronous and asynchronous groupware in Chapter 11. The activity on bulletin boards or newsgroups is asynchronous. Individuals read what others have left on the system, then reply, an electronic form of correspondence.

MUDs represent an electronic form of meeting, in which people interact in real time over a network or the Internet (Curtis, 1992). Interactions include discussion, and often also adding new objects that will be encountered by other participants and defining behaviors for the objects. MUD originally stood for "Multi-User Dungeons," because early use was for "dungeons and dragons" role-playing games. Others have proposed more general definitions, such as "Multi-User Dimensions" or Multi-User Discussions."

This form of interaction has been used in many ways. Kids get together to explore and build a simulated city, researchers discuss their work, and bridge players create an ongoing on-line bridge club, with games always in progress, and new players replacing those who leave or starting new games or just watching.

Despite the fact that all of the interaction in MUDs, as in e-mail and bulletin boards, takes place as text displayed on computer screens, participants become intensely involved, justifying the description of MUDs as "text-based virtual environments" or communities. With a high degree of anonymity, cultures clash and certain interpersonal restraints may break down. Many of these forums have wrestled with questions of etiquette and governance (Bruckman et al., 1994).

Two articles first published in the popular press and reprinted in Kling (1995)—Van Gelder (1985) and Dibbell (1993)—present particularly interesting and disturbing illustrations. Van Gelder describes a case in which a male psychiatrist adopted an on-line role persona as a woman paralyzed and rendered mute by an accident. In this role he managed to get numerous women to confide in him electronically, some of whom were devastated when the deception was exposed. Dibbell describes, in a colorful but subtly analytic essay, an incident in which a MUD participant outraged other members by forcing their on-line characters through a sequence of diverse sexual activities. Although this may seem like a meaningless (albeit obnoxious) thing to do, Dibbell succeeds in conveying how real these violations seemed to the victims, and he describes the agonizing process by which MUD participants attempted to deal with this unknown antisocial individual.

These extreme cases emphasize that we are inventing new forms of social interaction, and that social conventions, rules of discourse, norms, and taboos must be developed by the first homesteaders in these electronic communities. A wonderfully subtle analysis based on extensive research into MUDs is found in Turkle (1995). Turkle describes various effects on different people of living in these communities, some positive, some negative. For example, some people discover personal competencies on-line that they then translate into "real life"; others hold onto a social status on the Internet that they are losing in real life. Turkle also speculates that MUD may promote or bring out the fractionating of our sense of self into multiple personalities and identities.

The World-Wide Web

Our first reading in this chapter, Berners-Lee et al. (1994), is a description of the astoundingly successful World-Wide Web (WWW), the vast and growing hypermedia system that spans the Internet.

Mosaic, the first popular interface to the Web, was an overnight sensation when it became publicly available in 1993 from the influential National Center for Supercomputer Applications (NCSA) at the University of Illinois Urbana-Champaign (UIUC), which had previously produced Telnet, software for accessing computers over the Internet, and Eudora, a popular, elegant e-mail application. Yet their success was modest compared to that of Mosaic and the WWW, for which the world seems to have been waiting.

Why did this occur in 1993?

- A robust, reliable international network infrastructure was in place.
- Widespread deployment of computers capable of presenting multimedia objects had taken place.
- Earlier, less elegant tools for searching remote directories and retrieving text files had built up a community of practice ready to appreciate elegant new solutions.

To be useful, Mosaic requires that one can generally access a file on any computer on the Internet, ***immediately***. A few years earlier, this would have been inconceivable: breakdowns frequently isolated parts of the Internet for days at a time, and many users were connected only via intermittent transmission from Usenet, BITNET, and FIDOnet. Mosaic also handles objects that contain more than text (recall our discussion of multimedia in Chapter 13).

Let's briefly review Internet history. Originally called the ARPANET, it was designed late in the 1960s to allow the sharing of scarce resources and the transmission of files from one site to another. File transfer was implemented through "ftp," or the file transfer protocol, a somewhat cumbersome method that requires logging on to a willing remote site using the Internet address of the computer holding a file, and the location in the file system where it resides.

As often happens, people adapted the network to an unintended use—e-mail. The late J.C.R. Licklider used to recount how the amount of teletype paper sprawling over his office floor every morning grew steadily as researchers he was supporting with DARPA funds began to realize how regular e-mail reports could enhance his awareness of their work.

For two decades, the principal change was a steadily growing access to the network. By the early 1990s, better interfaces were in place for transferring files, as were tools for browsing to discover what objects were available. Archie, Veronica, WAIS, and the widely used GOPHER are examples of advanced browsing and retrieval systems. Snapshots of the rapidly evolving Internet resource discovery field are Obraczka, Danzig, and Li (1993) and Schwartz (1993).

The World-Wide Web was developed in 1991 to link physicists and engineers at different sites. The key concept was this: If everyone who contributes resources will put them into a single standard format, then different developers can build tools for accessing and displaying the materials on different platforms. WWW consists of an addressing scheme that provides an identifier for any object accessible on the Internet, together with a standard method for formatting objects. The method is extensible—people can include new object types that they have created, which can be displayed by anyone who has appropriate software and will be ignored by those who do not. Thus, any object can be reached and interpreted properly. The formatting language is html (Hypertext Markup Language), a simple application of SGML (the Standard Generalized Markup Language).

The use of WWW took off in mid-1993 with the public release of Mosaic, a browsing and retrieval interface to WWW with versions for PC, Macintosh, and XWindows (Unix) computers. The success of Mosaic is an outstanding example of the difference an interface can make. Mosaic did not provide capabilities for creating html files, nor did it provide search capabilities. However, browsing became extremely easy, motivating people to build multimedia materials for people to browse. As more materials were constructed, more browsing was encouraged, a positive feedback loop that appears unstoppable. Tools to aid searching, development, and conversion of existing objects into html soon began to appear.

Although Mosaic deserves much credit, other software contributed to its success. Lynx, a text-only browser from the University of Kansas, provided access for people with more limited computers, further motivating the development of Web sites. Infrastructure builders—server authors, maintenance and administration tools, and protocol developers—were important. The huge growth in Web sites was also driven by NCSA's server that installs current versions free, at the touch of a button. NetScape, a commercial extension of Mosaic, also contributes to the Web's growth.

Capabilities were soon added for interacting with the materials you access—for leaving comments, orders, or other specified objects, features which remind one of the Lotus Notes system described in Chapter 11. What had previously been one-way information retrieval now became interactive, possibly enabling the realization of the vision of a world-spanning, collectively constructed hypermedia.

The research issues that growth presents for Internet resource discovery is discussed in Bowman et al. (1994). They examine scalability in terms of the increasing number of on-line sources, the burgeoning user population, and the even more rapidly growing volume of data being accessed as we shift from straight text to multimedia. How should we map data that exists in different forms on the many different networks (linked by "gateways") that the Internet comprises? How can we support both browsing and searching? Intelligent approaches to replicating and caching material could significantly reduce or more evenly distribute network traffic.

Commerce on the Internet

Commercialization had long been avoided by the developers and operaters of the Internet, but prohibitions melted away in the 1990s. Vendors and customers added to the rush of people and organizations to on-line services. Specialty stores devoted to selling Internet access appeared in some shopping malls. In 1994, the "Internet Mall" was inaugurated. Modeled after a shopping mall, it was divided into six floors—media, personal items, computer hardware and software, services, clothes, and a food court. By August 1994 there were 220 shops in the Mall, with dozens being added each month.

An obstacle to commerce on the Internet was monetary exchange. The year 1994 also saw several well-financed efforts to create secure systems to support financial exchange over the Internet.

In summary, by 1995 there were physical stores selling Internet access in physical malls, and virtual stores selling physical goods in virtual malls!

The MBONE

Images, sound, and animation are among the media shipped over the Internet, as is video, the ultimate consumer of bandwidth. The prospect of transferring video is much ballyhooed, for example, movies on demand and interactive television. A more modest technology in active use by 1993 is the Multicast Backbone, or MBONE, that enables real-time multimedia interaction over the Internet (Eriksson, 1994; Macedonia and Brutzman, 1994). A camera, microphone, and computer on the Internet that can handle audio and video are all you need to broadcast an event to anyone who "tunes in" from their computer. Public domain software to handle these sessions includes capabilities such as sending "slides" as postscript files prior to a talk, thereby allowing synchronized high-resolution viewing at all sites under the control of either speaker or viewer. The video can be two-way or link multiple sites simultaneously.

This technology has been used to broadcast ("multicast") meetings, conferences, and special events (including a segment of a Rolling Stones concert). It works somewhat, but the Internet infrastructure limits video quality, which resembles a series of still pictures, one every several seconds, more than continuous motion. The priority is to preserve audio quality, which MBONE does capably. MBONE is a primitive but exciting technology, expecially since work underway on a very high speed backbone to the Internet promises substantial improvements in quality.

A New Interface Metaphor

Even when we work with standard displays, we look at our computers differently as we step into the world of the WWW, Lotus Notes, the MBONE, and other applications. Instead of the metaphor of a computer as a "container" we have the computer as a "window," in this case a window onto the limitless resources of the global network. The users of early, slow file transfer protocols linked to a distant site and then moved files from one computer to the other. The file remained in local storage until printed out or used, or perhaps indefinitely. The work and time to access it meant that one obtained a copy if it might be needed again.

The ease of access using Mosaic and other browsers means that users no longer retain copies of most of the information they see. There is little reason to create a local copy—it can be accessed with a few button presses again anytime. The impression is that one has a window looking onto the world being navigated. Of course, the material is actually residing in the local computer, but often only temporarily. Early versions of the Mosaic interface violated the metaphor by reporting the number of "bytes downloaded," even when no record of the session was being kept.

This shift in perception leads to a shift in behavior that has ramifications. I no longer keep copies of information because I believe I can return to view it again. What if the actual owner does remove it? I will complain, as will others, and slowly those who make information available will start recognizing an imperative to keep it on-line.

Let's Go Net-Surfing?

How quickly will innovations such as the World-Wide Web and the MBONE be adopted, given that they require fairly powerful systems?

The answer was clear by 1994 in the case of the World-Wide Web. Enterprising prospective students began exploring a university's WWW "home page" (probably built by university students!), and other universities had to develop pages to compete. An electronic journal publishing in html took each reference to a previously published paper and converted the authors' names to links to their home pages, if they had one—which created a large incentive for authors to create home pages. The first florist on the Internet did very well, attracted publicity, which prompted other businesses to get on. Publishers quickly anticipated that the technology was one they could not afford to ignore. About a year after Mosaic was publicly released, we began receiving requests from editors for our URL (the address for a World-Wide Web location) to include in on-line directories. Within two years, by early 1995, all of the major on-line service providers announced plans to provide WWW access.

The MBONE, a less mature technology with greater system requirements, has spread less quickly. Video communication technologies, starting with the videophone, have often come up against strong and sometimes unexpected resistance. In this case, the technology is not mature, powerful, and available enough to support significant uses, the Rolling Stones concert notwithstanding.

Information Highways

Yet universal access to interactive video may also arise from another source, the much-hyped promise of the "information highway." This term applies to a set of visions, development projects, and field trials typically run by consortia of companies from the communications, computer, and entertainment industries to provide homes with capabilities such as video on demand, home shopping and banking, communications, and information services. Although there has been little technical literature published on these developments prior to 1995, there are enormous numbers of popular articles in the media. For example, The Globe and Mail, Canada's national newspaper, ran on the order of 500 stories in 1994 that referenced information highways in some way. Thoughtful magazine articles from this period are Stix (1993), Brody (1993), Winner (1993), Steinberg (1994), and Technology Review (1994).

VIRTUAL REALITY

Aided by the media, virtual reality (VR) rivals the information highway in its hold on the public imagination. "I like reading about computers," a cab driver said. "What really interests me is virtual reality. Did you see Lawnmower Man? But when you really think about it, virtual reality gets kind of hinky."

Virtual reality comes in different flavors. Mallen (1993) argues that there are two basic approaches: simulation of reality (SOR) and simulation of complexity (SOC).

Simulation of reality focuses on reproducing aspects of reality as accurately as possible to create an illusion that conceals the larger purpose of transcending real experience. Mallen links this to a long tradition of creating myths or fictions populated with largely realistic objects and characters endowed with magical properties. Entertainment uses of virtual reality are pure examples of SOR.

Simulation of complexity focuses on creating representations that enable us to understand complex data sets better, and thus fall into the similarly long tradition of rational thought. Examples are the use of virtual reality to represent complex financial or biomedical data, enabling such data to be seen, understood, or manipulated (e.g., Robinson, 1994). Thus, VR is linked to information visualization (see Chapter 6).

Some uses of virtual reality, such as flight simulators, blend SOC and SOR, says Mallen. Erickson (1993) describes an experiment in which a shift is made from display-based information visualization to immersive virtual reality, and goes on to outline challenges and possibilities in this area.

Another distinction is the degree to which a user is "immersed" in virtual reality. At one end of the spectrum is total immersion, where everything one experiences is under computer control. A head-mounted 3D visual and auditory display, data gloves, and suitably powerful software could create such an experience (see, for example, Fisher, 1990 video). Work has also begun on force displays as another component of total immersion (Minsky et al., 1990).

As noted earlier, a less cumbersome method is to project the computer's output into the environment (Krueger, 1991; Baudel and Beaudouin-Lafon, 1993). A large monitor is less engrossing but can still hold one's entire attention. Even less immersive are "heads up" displays that overlay virtual information on visible reality, using a transparent display surface or by projecting to only one eye. Feiner, MacIntyre, and Seligmann (1993) describe the application of AI technology to such wearable displays, sometimes referred to as *augmented reality.* Drascic et al. (1993) and Milgram (1993 video) describe a system that displays synthetic computer graphic overlays on stereoscopic video.

Also of interest is the nature of the objects in the virtual environment. Often they are static, relying on users to create movement and change of focus. Some researchers are working on "virtual actors," computer-generated three-dimensional animations, possibly depicting virtual people (e.g., Zeltzer and Johnson, 1994; Thalmann, 1994). Todd and Latham (1994) describe very imaginative experiments with virtual semi abstract objects that appear to go through life stages including conception, birth, maturation, marriage, and death.

The virtual environment can also include representations of multiple human actors (e.g., Koved, 1992 video). This staple of VR arcade games is also the focus of interesting research. A set of collaborators, primarily at the Swedish Institute of Computer Science and at the University of Nottingham, are exploring ways to allow more flexible and natural ways for awareness and interaction to take place when large groups inhabit a single virtual space (Fahlén et al., 1993; Benford and Fahlén, 1993; Benford et al., 1995).

The recent prominence of virtual reality obscures its long history. Observers such as Mallen and Crampton Smith (1994) have noted a continuity in art from cave paintings to the present, and the role of technology in this evolution. For centuries artists focused on increasing realism, while embedding symbolism and considering issues of representation and framing. Photography contributed to altering the goal; painters shifted to "breaking the rules" to create effects in the viewer in other ways.

Others note that an invention more recent than art, the book, can be thought of as virtual reality. It is useful to see the continuities, without losing sight of the unique potential of computation.

In our next reading in this chapter, Ellis (1991) picks up the historical thread in this century, observing that the concept of virtual reality is found in science fiction ranging from Aldous Huxley's *Brave New World* to William Gibson's *Neuromancer* and the "cyberpunk" fiction it inspired. (Clifford D. Simak's novel *City,* published in 1952, was another visionary anticipation of VR.) Imaginations are unleashed by startling effects achieved in theme park rides, spectacular graphics on television and film, and the awesome experience of a "filmed flight around Mars" derived from digital photographic satellite data (McGreevy, 1993).

Ellis's detailed account, of which we include major excerpts, lists achievements in nonentertainment fields—simulators for training pilots and flight crews, and medical imaging technology used for diagnosis, training, and operating room assistance. The cost of these systems has fallen rapidly over time, suggesting that they will become far more widespread. For example, in 1983, a 1024 x 1024 pixel frame store occupied 3 cubic feet and cost about $100,000; ten years later it was the size of a postcard and cost $2,000 (MacDonald and Vince, 1994).

High costs have meant that much early research was conducted for military and space applications. Sterling (1993) describes the recreation of actual battlefields into virtual battlefields in which history can be relived, but details changed to see how they affect the outcome. A planned use of VR in the space program is to provide less monotonous scenery for astronauts confined to a small craft for long voyages.

Years of experience developing virtual reality technologies, much of it confined to a few laboratories equipped with expensive systems, revealed where more work is needed (see van Dam, 1993, for a discussion of software issues in the development of VR). Threaded through Ellis's excellent account of the hardware and software demands of these systems are reminders that the most critical requirement is more detailed knowledge of human psychology. How will people react to different visual, aural, tactile, and kinesthetic stimulation? Developers must know this in order to create and maintain illusions—and to avoid making dizzy a person who stands still in a dynamic virtual world!

What does the future hold? Hollan and Stornetta (1992) observe that a common tendency is to use a new technology first to replace an old technology in a more efficient way, yet over time the power arises from the completely new capabilities it enables. The future of virtual reality lies not in recreating existing realities, but in transcending them. To engage our imagination we cannot disengage from reality, but instead must develop a deep understanding of technical realities and the workplace and recreational activities that may benefit.

We also cannot predict the effects of prolonged immersion in virtual worlds. Concerns found in other domains apply here: What will be the effect on children? Should adults be allowed free reign to engage in behavior that might appear self-destructive? Could this be used to the detriment of those powerless to prevent it? Whalley (1993) explores this last point in an essay considering the use of virtual reality to treat physical and mental disorders.

UBIQUITOUS COMPUTING

The concept that computation will disappear into the woodwork, both figuratively and literally, has also captured our imaginations. This vision is rarely communicated as effectively as in our final reading, by Mark Weiser (1991). The progression from personal computer to portable to laptop to notebook to subnotebook to palmtop, and so on, is part of the picture, but Weiser paints a vivid picture of a world that is qualitatively different. When hundreds of objects in our environment have computational capabilities and are invisibly networked, and behave in ways that sensibly support our work, we will cease thinking in terms of "the computer" or of computers at all.

We all experience the first stages of this change now, in small ways. I have both analog and digital watches, but when I look at my wrist I just see the time—I don't notice whether or not a computer delivers it. Computers embedded in automobiles and household appliances help us without our knowledge.

Weiser describes many possibilities for adding computational support to our environment and asks us to imagine a world in which they are omnipresent. You may find some elements in his scenarios plausible, others less plausible, but many will find the overall picture compelling. And you may envision possibilities that he did not.

Some aspects of ubiquitous computing are reaching commercial markets. Notebook and palmtop computers are at the periphery of Weiser's vision because they are still primarily computers, yet they raise issues with which he is concerned: How do we operate these devices without a keyboard? How can we transfer information among devices with maximal ease and efficiency?

Several interesting articles appeared in the July 1993 special issue of *Communications of the ACM,* titled "Computer Augmented Environments: Back to the Real World." In one, Weiser (1993) updates his technical vision, describing hardware prototypes of electronic "tabs" and "pads," progress in wireless communication and infrared pens, and network and application issues.

The "digital desk" (Wellner, 1993, 1992 video) describes a Xerox EuroPARC effort to create in some sense a desktop conference between a user and a computer. Cameras record activity on the desktop, and computer vision software enables the computer to respond to human movements or sketching. A projector displays computer images onto the physical desktop. For example, a projector can create the image of a form; the camera and recognition system can identify the regions of the form being filled and the kinds of marks being made.

Active badges, devices that track a person's position, are part of the ubiquitous computing vision and the focus of considerable research and some commercial product development (Newman, Eldridge, and Lamming, 1991; Want et al., 1992; Hopper, 1992, 1993 videos).

Active badges can be used to keep records of who is present at meetings, alert one to who is in a room at the other end of a conference call, direct a phone call to the nearest phone, or transfer one's workstation defaults to the nearest machine. Researchers stress the positive uses of the technology, but others warn of possibilities of abuse of the monitoring capabilities. Harper (1992) examined the reactions to the technology in two different research laboratories, showing that the reactions of users can vary. Clearly these technologies give rise to complex issues of privacy and control while increasing our range of effective action.

Active badges are now used within buildings wired with sensors, but miniaturization of global positioning hardware may enable worldwide deployment of this technology. Palm-sized communication devices will merge with badge technology, bridging ubiquitous computing and the global network and enabling several of the capabilities that Weiser described. Fitzmaurice (1993) describes a prototype palm-sized device used for browsing location-dependent electronic information; for example, while in a library the device might relay information about nearby book selections.

Although portability implies physical movement, there is a sense in which, when computing is everywhere, we will always be in one place.

HOPES AND FEARS

New technologies provide benefits not imagined by their inventors—and also create unanticipated problems. Our readings in this chapter are positive in outlook. Weiser is particularly utopian. We have not commented at length in this book on the social impacts of computing. Nevertheless, a lesson of the 20th century is that technology developers must consider the consequences and work toward humane outcomes. This clearly applies to the technologies of cyberspace.

Utopianism is one side of a coin; antiutopianism is the flip side. The basic optimism of Star Trek is countered by the pessimism of Frankenstein, an early story of technology gone awry. The film *2001* captures both, as beneficial technology spins into a nightmare.

The real-life bestseller *The Cuckoo's Egg* (Stoll, 1989) describes youths who accessed government computers via telephone, with data ending up in the hands of a foreign intelligence agent. Computer programmers have rigged lotteries, defrauded banks, altered salary levels, and accessed credit records, not to mention creating mayhem with computer viruses. Law enforcement officials react to real, though often exaggerated, transgressions by employing technology in detection. Hafner and Markoff (1991), Sterling (1992), and Slatalla and Quittner (1995) provide interesting glimpses into the culture of hackers and the industry and government officials who pursue them.

Issues of privacy and information access follow as we shift from the world of cops, robbers, and thrill-seeking kids to business and pleasure in the home and office. As described above, individuals can use technology to disguise and distance themselves in ways not before possible. Monitoring technology presents new opportunities for oppressive levels of surveillance and workplace control. To address such issues, ACM sponsors an annual conference on "Computers, Freedom, and Privacy." The moderated "comp.risks" netnews group is a lively and knowledgeable forum, excerpted in Peter G. Neumann's "Inside Risks" column in *Communications of the ACM*. *Computerization and Controversy*, a set of readings edited by Rob Kling (1995), is a thought-provoking survey of contrasting positions. An excellent but more introductory text is Forester and Morrison (1994).

Physical health issues will persist. Ubiquitous technology may partly free us from keyboards, but perhaps not from displays or power sources. Chapter 10 noted possible risks from a single display—what are the effects of radiation from displays that surround us entirely, or from hundreds of computing objects that communicate with infrared light?

Psychological health is another issue. Will people who grow up shifting among virtual realities maintain a firm grip on actual reality? Weiser's scenario has both appealing and unsettling aspects. Direct human contact was relatively infrequent. Traces of the activity of children and neighbors were observed remotely. Just as ATMs eliminate interactions with tellers, we can envision stopping for coffee, shopping, having a car checkup and repair (even a medical checkup!), all transacted without direct human contact. What will be the effects on social *Homo sapiens*, which evolved through millions of years of group interaction?

The issues are not clear-cut. For example, releasing convicted criminals who agree to wear location transmitters removes them from the unhealthy prison environment and allows them to work. This sounds positive, yet early experience with the technology is mixed—since full monitoring is now prohibitively expensive, some parolees have been able to commit serious crimes. If perfected, the technology could also be abused by authorities in times of civil disobedience or in countries with few constitutional controls.

Designers and developers can ill afford, commercially or morally, to ignore the potential problems or abuses. Problems can lead to disuse as easily as abuse. Opponents of a technology must also consider the positive aspects, which are likely to generate pressure for adoption and to influence the technology's evolution.

Anticipating Consequences

The confusion that engulfs us is illustrated by the very different approaches taken to the tension between privacy and open information by two communication technologies. Consider Caller ID, a telephone feature that enables a person phoned to see the phone number of the person dialing. Those favoring this feature note, among other things, that abuses of anonymity, such as harassing phone calls, are more difficult with Caller ID. Opponents point to the potential for abuse, such as marketers recording phone numbers of people responding to an advertisement. In some places, privacy has triumphed over openness through legislation that prohibits Caller ID. (See Hillier, 1995, for a detailed history of Caller ID.)

In contrast, consider e-mail, in which a sender can virtually always be traced. A system administrator was severely criticized for creating an "anonymity server" that enabled anyone to post messages completely disguised. With e-mail, openness has generally triumphed over privacy. The degree of anonymity we eventually adopt will affect the nature, pervasiveness, and impact of electronic communications.

Our final example considers a technology with wonderful direct effects: *telemedicine,* the use of remote viewing to provide skilled medical diagnosis and intervention to people living in remote or impoverished regions. A surgeon in a major city can view X-rays or injuries by video and watch over the shoulder as a general practitioner carries out an emergency operation. Bravo! But what will be the *indirect* effects? Remote medical assistance could reduce the pressure to station doctors in remote communities, despite the fact that a doctor who lives in a community contributes in many ways, such as observing and addressing unsanitary or dangerous practices, and serving as a role model to children. Introducing the technology could cut off these indirect benefits. If not introduced thoughtfully, a wonderful technology may, in the long run, be counterproductive.

GUIDE TO FURTHER READING

Rheingold (1993) is a literate account of the recent history of computer-mediated communications. Other useful general books are cited in Chapter 11.

Perhaps the only thing growing as quickly as the Internet is the literature on the Internet. Every six months our bookstores seem to add a new shelf to the Internet section. The variety is impressive. One can find a style guide for e-mail writers (Angell and Heslop, 1994), including sections on flame control, the proper use of smileys, avoiding junk e-mail, and writing for international audiences. Even more specialized books help those unsure how to cite electronic information (Li and Crane, 1993) and provide e-mail addresses of the rich and famous (Godin, 1994)! An unusual offering is Malamud (1993), a "technical travelogue" written by a journalist who circled the globe three times seeking out interesting stories of Internet use in various parts of the world.

Most of the general guides, some of which are huge, focus on helping the inexperienced; some focus on developers; and others attempt both. Examples of the latter are *The Internet Unleashed* (Sams Publishing, 1994) and *The World-Wide Web Unleashed* (December and Randall, 1994), both in excess of 1,000 pages. Given the pace of change, these general guides may have a very short shelf life.

Selected papers from the First International Conference on the World-Wide Web are published in *Computer Networks and ISDN Systems,* Volume 27, Number 2, November 1994. The September 1993 issue of *IEEE Computer* and the August 1993 and August 1994 issues of *Communications of the ACM* are devoted to Internet technology, use, and resource discovery. A technically curious reader interested in the three major protocols specifications can consult Berners-Lee (1994), Berners-Lee, Fielding, and Frystyk Nielsen (1994), and Berners-Lee and Connolly (1994).

Ellis's 168 references provide considerable further reading for the curious. Additional history can be found in the excellent monograph by Rheingold (1991). The virtual reality research literature grows every year, spearheaded by conferences and workshops. Papers from the 1990 First Conference on Cyberspace are collected in Benedikt (1991c), published by MIT Press, which has also initiated the VR journal *Presence.*

Five collections of research papers on virtual reality originating in symposia are Middleton (1991), Helsel (1991), Bryson and Feiner (1993), Earnshaw, Gigante, and Jones (1993), and MacDonald and Vince (1994). Wexelblat (1993) has collected original articles that speculate about the new capabilities and future realities. As might be expected, these collections touch on visualization issues also covered in Chapter 6 and multimedia issues covered in Chapter 13. For example, Fairchild (1993) describes experiments in dynamic information visualization, and Chalmers (1994) describes EuroPARC multimedia systems as well as the digital desk.

Benedikt (1991b) is a long essay exploring the nature of cyberspace and some of its applications. Morningstar and Randall Farmer (1991) describe lessons learned from a large-scale, commercial, many-user, graphical virtual environment. Latta (1991) explores the commercial realities of VR. Dodsworth (1994) and Fricke (1994) are collections of articles focusing on virtual reality in interactive entertainment and art, respectively.

Ubiquitous computing literature is less extensive, although it too is growing. The July 1993 issue of *Communications of the ACM,* titled "Computer-Augmented Environments," contains articles by Myron Krueger, Mark Weiser, and other pioneers in this field.

CONCLUSION

Each time we completed a draft of this final chapter, a look toward the new millennium, our view of the future had changed. The pace of development is accelerating. Interaction paradigms introduced in this chapter are just starting to take shape in the final years of the century. Forecasting the future of computing is a difficult business, as seen in future scenario videotapes developed over the years. Listed in a special section of the references, these video forecasts have typically shown misplaced confidence that technologies such as speech recognition and software agents would soon be effective and in widespread use.

The technologies described in our readings are exciting. Challenges lie ahead, but we choose to be optimistic. Some problems may be transitory, melting with experience. For example, we should soon become less easily deceived by computer-mediated correspondents. Other problems will require continued commitment and vigilance. Computer technologies and computer-based communication media can assist us in studying and analyzing the impacts of introducing new technologies and aid us in communicating what we learn. By taking advantage of these opportunities, we can hopefully build a better world.

REFERENCES

Note: A ◉ before a reference indicates a reading.

Angell, D., and Heslop, B. (1994). *Elements of E-mail Style: Communicate Effectively Via Electronic Mail.* Addison-Wesley.

Barlow, J. (1993). Cyberspace, The Final Frontier: Response. *Communications of the ACM* 36(1), 19–20.

Baudel, T., and Beaudouin-Lafon, M. (1993). CHARADE: Remote Control of Objects Using Free-Hand Gestures. *Communications of the ACM* 36(7), 28–35.

Benedikt, M. (1991a). Introduction. In Benedikt (1991c), 1–25.

Benedikt, M. (1991b). Cyberspace: Some Proposals. In Benedikt (1991c), 119–224.

Benedikt, M. (Ed.) (1991c). *Cyberspace: First Steps.* The MIT Press.

Benford, S., Bowers, J., Fahlén, L., Greehalgh, C., and Snowdon, D. (1995). User Embodiment in Collaborative Virtual Environments. *Proc. CHI '95,* ACM, forthcoming.

Benford, S., and Fahlén, L. (1993). A Spatial Model of Interaction in Large Virtual Environments. *Proc. ECSCW '93,* Kluwer, 109–124.

Berners-Lee, T. (1994). Universal Resource Identifiers in WWW: A Unifying Syntax for the Expression of Names and Addresses of Objects on the Network as Used in the World-Wide Web, RFC 1630, CERN, June 1994. <URL:ftp://ds.internic.net/rfc/rfc1630.txt>

◉ Berners-Lee, T., Cailliau, R., Luotonen, A., Nielsen, H., and Secret, A. (1994). The World-Wide Web. *Communications of the ACM* 37(8), 76–82.

Berners-Lee, T., and Connolly, D. (1994). HyperText Markup Language Specification—2.0, Work in Progress, MIT, HaL Computer Systems, November 1994. <URL:http://www.ics.uci.edu/pub/ietf/html/>

Berners-Lee, T., Fielding, R., and Frystyk Nielsen, H. (1994). Hypertext Transfer Protocol—HTTP/1.0, Work in Progress, MIT, UC Irvine, CERN, December 1994. <URL:http://www.ics.uci.edu/pub/ietf/http/>

Bowman, C., Danzig, P., Manber, U., and Schwartz, M. (1994). Scalable Internet Resource Discovery: Research Problems and Approaches. *Communications of the ACM* 37(8), 98–107, 114.

Brody, H. (1993). Information Highway: The Home Front. *Technology Review,* Aug./Sept., 30–40

Bruckman, A., Curtis, P., Figallo, C., and Laurel, B. (1994). Approaches to Managing Deviant Social Behavior in Virtual Communities. Panel Position Statements. *CHI '94 Conference Companion,* ACM, 183–184.

Bryson, S., and Feiner, S. (1993). *Proc. Symposium on Research Frontiers in Virtual Reality.* IEEE Computer Society Press.

Chalmers, M. (1994). Information Environments. In MacDonald and Vince (1994), 187–204.

Crampton Smith, G. (1994). The Art of Interaction. In MacDonald and Vince (1994), 79–94.

Curtis, P. (1992). Mudding: Social Phenomena in Text-Based Virtual Realities. *Proc. Directions in Advanced Computing (DIAC '92),* Computer Professionals for Social Responsibility, 48–68.

December, J., and Randall, N. (1994). *The World-Wide Web Unleashed.* Sams Publishing.

Dibbell, J. (1993). A Rape in Cyberspace, or How an Evil Clown, a Haitian Trickster Spirit, Two Wizards, and a Cast of Dozens Turned a Database into a Society. *The Village Voice,* December 21, 1993, 36–42. Reprinted in Kling (1985).

Dodsworth, C. (Ed.) (1994). Special Issue on Interactive Entertainment: Design, Implementation, and Adrenaline. *Computer Graphics* 28(2), May 1994.

Drascic, D., Grodski, J., Milgram, P., Ruffo, K., Wong, P., and Zhai, S. (1993). ARGOS: A Display System for Augmenting Reality. *Proc. INTERCHI '93,* ACM, 521.

Earnshaw, R., Gigante, M., and Jones, H. (Eds.) (1993). *Virtual Reality Systems.* Academic Press.

◉ Ellis, S. (1991). Nature and Origins of Virtual Environments: A Bibliographical Essay. *Computing Systems in Engineering* 2(4), 321–347. (Excerpt included 321, 324–341, 343–47.)

Erickson, T. (1993). Artificial Realities as Data Visualization Environments: Problems and Prospects. In Wexelblat (1993), 3–22.

Eriksson, H. (1994). MBone: The Multicast Backbone. *Communications of the ACM* 37(8), 54–60.

Fahlén, L., Ståhl, O., Grant Brown, C., and Carlsson, C. (1993). A Space Based Model for User Interaction in Shared Synthetic Environments. *Proc. INTERCHI '93,* ACM, 43–48.

Fairchild, K. (1993). Information Management Using Virtual Reality-Based Visualizations. In Wexelblat (1993), 45–74.

Feiner, S., MacIntyre, B., and Seligmann, D. (1993). Knowledge-Based Augmented Reality. *Communications of the ACM* 36(7), 53–62.

Fitzmaurice, G. (1993). Situated Information Spaces and Spatially Aware Palmtop Computers. *Communications of the ACM* 36(7), 38–49.

Forester, T., and Morrison, P. (1994). *Computer Ethics: Cautionary Tales and Ethical Dilemmas in Computing,* Second Edition. MIT Press.

Fricke, K. (Ed.) (1994). Special Section on Virtual Reality: Venus Return or Vanishing Point. *Leonardo* 27(4), MIT Press.

Godin, S. (1994). *E-Mail Addresses of the Rich & Famous.* Addison-Wesley.

Grudin, J. (1994). The Beginning Teachers Computer Network. *The Network Observer* 1(3), March 1994.

Hafner, K., and Markoff, J. (1991). *Cyberpunk: Outlaws and Hackers on the Computer Frontier.* Simon and Schuster.

Harper, R. (1992). Looking at Ourselves: An Examination of the Social Organisation of Two Research Laboratories. *Proc. CSCW '92,* ACM, 330–337.

Helsel, S. (Ed.) (1991). *Beyond the Vision: The Technology, Research, and Business of Virtual Reality.* Meckler.

Hillier, W. (1995). Avoiding the Technical Fix: How Engineering Can Benefit from the Historical Study of Technology. Science and Technology Studies Global Issues Guidebook. Student Pugwash USA.

Hollan, J., and Stornetta, S. (1992). Beyond Being There. *Proc. CHI '92,* ACM, 119–125.

Kling, R. (Ed.) (in press). *Computerization and Controversy: Value Conflicts and Social Choices,* Second Edition. Academic Press.

Krueger, M. (1991). *Artificial Reality II.* Addison-Wesley.

Latta, J. (1991). When Will Reality Meet the Marketplace. In Helsel (1991), 109–141.

Laurel, B. (1991). *Computers as Theatre.* Addison-Wesley.

Li, X., and Crane, N. (1993). *Electronic Style: A Guide to Citing Electronic Information.* Meckler.

MacDonald, L., and Vince, J. (Ed.) (1994). *Interacting with Virtual Environments.* John Wiley & Sons.

Macedonia, M., and Brutzman, D. (1994). MBone Provides Audio and Video Across the Internet. *IEEE Computer* 27(4), 30–36.

Malamud, C. (1993). *Exploring the Internet: A Technical Travelogue.* Prentice Hall.

Mallen, G. (1993). Back to the Cave: Cultural Perspectives on VR. In Earnshaw, Gigante, and Jones (1993), 265–272.

McGreevy, M. (1993). Virtual Reality and Planetary Exploration. In Wexelblat (1993), 163–197.

Middleton, T. (Ed.) (1991). *Virtual Worlds: Real Challenges.* Meckler.

Minsky, M., Ouh-Young, M., Steele, O., Brooks, F., and Behensky, M. (1990). Feeling and Seeing: Issues in Force Display. *ACM Computer Graphics* 24(2), 235–243.

Morningstar, C., and Randall Farmer, F. (1991). The Lessons of Lucasfilm's Habitat. In Benedikt (1991c), 273–301.

Newman, W., Eldridge, M., and Lamming, M. (1991). PEPYS: Generating Autobiographies by Automatic Tracking. *Proc. ECSCW '91,* Kluwer, 175–188.

Obraczka, K., Danzig, P., and Li, S.-H. (1993). Internet Resource Discovery Services. *IEEE Computer* 26(9), 8–24.

Rheingold, H. (1991). *Virtual Reality.* Simon and Schuster.

Rheingold, H. (1993). *The Virtual Community: Homesteading on the Electronic Frontier.* Addison-Wesley.

Robinson, N. (1994). Biomedical Virtual Environments. In MacDonald and Vince (1994), 119–132.

Sams Publishing (50 authors contributed) (1994). *The Internet Unleashed.* Sams Publishing.

Schwartz, M. (1993). Internet Resource Discovery at the University of Colorado. *IEEE Computer* 26(9), 25–36.

Slatalla, M., and Quittner, J. (in press). *Masters of Deception: The Gang That Ruled Cyberspace.* Harper-Collins.

Steinberg, S. (1994). Travels on the Net. *Technology Review,* July, 20–31.

Sterling, B. (1992). *The Hacker Crackdown: Law and Disorder on the Electronic Frontier.* Bantam.

Sterling, B. (1993). War Is Virtual Hell. *WIRED* 1(1), 46–51, 94–99.

Stix, G. (1993). Domesticating Cyberspace. *Scientific American,* August, 101–107, 110.

Stoll, C. (1989). *The Cuckoo's Egg: Tracking a Spy Through the Maze of Computer Espionage.* Doubleday.

Technology Review (1994). Seven Thinkers in Search of an Information Highway. *Technology Review,* Aug./Sept., 42–52.

Thalmann, D. (1994). Automated Control and Behaviour of Virtual Actors. In MacDonald and Vince (1994), 217–228.

Todd, S., and Latham, W. (1994). Interacting with Artificial Life. In MacDonald and Vince (1994), 271–286.

Turkle, S. (forthcoming). *Life on the Screen: Identity in the Age of the Internet.* Simon and Schuster.

van Dam, A. (1993). VR as a Forcing Function: Software Implications of a New Paradigm. In Bryson and Feiner (1993), 5–8.

Van Gelder, L. (1985). The Strange Case of the Electronic Lover: A Real-Life Story of Deception, Seduction, and Technology. *Ms. Magazine* (October). Reprinted in Kling (1995).

Want, R., Hopper, A., Falcao, V., and Gibbons, J. (1992). The Active Badge Location System. *ACM Transactions on Information Systems* 10(1), 91–102.

● Weiser, M. (1991). The Computer for the 21st Century. *Scientific American,* September, 94–104.

Weiser, M. (1993). Some Computer Science Issues in Ubiquitous Computing. *Communications of the ACM* 36(7), 74–84.

Wellner, P. (1993). Interacting with Paper on the Digital Desk. *Communications of the ACM* 36(7), 87–96.

Wexelblat, A. (Ed.) (1993). *Virtual Reality—Applications and Explorations.* Academic Press.

Whalley, L. (1993). Ethical Issues in the Application of Virtual Reality to the Treatment of the Mental Disorders. In Earnshaw, Gigante, and Jones (1993), 273–287.

Winner, L. (1993). Beyond Inter-Passive Media. *Technology Review,* Aug./Sept., 69.

Zeltzer, D., and Johnson, M. (1994.) Virtual Actors and Virtual Environments. In MacDonald and Vince (1994), 229–255.

VIDEOS

Fisher, S. (1990). VIEW: The Ames Virtual Environment Workstation. *ACM SIGGRAPH Video Review (SGVR)* 55.

Hopper, A. (1992). The Pandora Multimedia System. *ACM SGVR* 87.

Hopper, A. (1993). The Active Badge System. *ACM SGVR* 88.

Koved, L. (1992). Rubber Rocks. *ACM SGVR* 87.

Milgram, P. (1993). ARGOS: A Display System for Augmenting Reality. *ACM SGVR* 88.

Wellner, P. (1992). Tactile Manipulation on a Digital Desk. *ACM SGVR* 79.

FUTURE SCENARIOS

(Year is publication date, not original release date.)

Apple (1992a). HyperCard 1992. *ACM SGVR* 78.

Apple (1992b). Knowledge Navigator. *ACM SGVR* 78.

Apple (1992c). Project 2000. *ACM SGVR* 78.

AT&T (1992). Residential Information Services in a Broadband Public Switched Network. *ACM SGVR* 78.

Hewlett Packard (1992). 1992. *ACM SGVR* 78.

Hewlett Packard (1993). Imagine. *ACM SGVR* 89.

Institute for Personalized Information Environment (1992). Friend21. *ACM SGVR* 78.

NTT Human Interface Laboratories (1994). Seamless Media Design. *ACM SGVR* 106.

San Francisco Art Institute (1992). Virtuality, Inc. *ACM SGVR* 78.

Telepresense Research (1992). Be There Here. *ACM SGVR* 78.

Tim Berners-Lee, Robert Cailliau, Ari Luotonen, Henrik Frystyk Nielsen, and Arthur Secret

The World-Wide Web

The World-Wide Web (W3) was developed to be a pool of human knowledge, which would allow collaborators in remote sites to share their ideas and all aspects of a common project. Physicists and engineers at CERN, the European Particle Physics Laboratory in Geneva, Switzerland, collaborate with many other institutes to build the software and hardware for high-energy physics research. The idea of the Web was prompted by positive experience of a small "home-brew" personal hypertext system used for keeping track of personal information on a distributed project. The Web was designed so that if it was used independently for two projects, and later relationships were found between the projects, then no major or centralized changes would have to be made, but the information could smoothly reshape to represent the new state of knowledge. This property of scaling has allowed the Web to expand rapidly from its origins at CERN across the Internet irrespective of boundaries of nations or disciplines.

If you haven't yet experienced the Web, the best way to find out about it is to try it. An Appendix to this article gives some recipes for getting hold of W3 clients. Given one of these, you will quickly find out all you need to know, and much more. For hard copy to read on the plane, or if you don't have Internet access from your desktop machine, refer to our paper in *Electronic Networking* (see "Glossary and Further Reading") for an overview of the project, material which we will not repeat but will summarize here.

A W3 "client" program runs on your computer. When it starts, it displays an object, normally a document with text and possibly images. Some of the phrases and images are highlighted: in blue, or boxed, or perhaps numbered, depending on what sort of a display you have and how your preferences have been set. Clicking the mouse on the highlighted area ("anchor") causes the client program to retrieve another object from some other computer, a "server." The retrieved object is normally also in a hypertext format, so the process of navigation continues (see Figure 1).

When viewing some documents, the reader can request a search, by typing in plain text (or complex commands) to send to the server, rather than following a link. In either case, the client sends a request off to the server, often a completely different machine in some other part of the world, and within (typically) a second, the related information, in either hypertext, plain text or multimedia format, is presented. This is done repeatedly, and by a sequence of selections and searches one can find anything that is "out there." Some important things to note are:

- Whatever type of server, the user interface is the same, so users do not need to understand the differences between the many protocols in common use. Before W3, access to networked information typically involved knowledge of many different access "recipes" for different systems, and a different command language for each. The model of hypertext with text input has proved sufficiently powerful to express all the user interfaces, while being sufficiently simple to require no training for a computer user.
- Links can point to anything that can be displayed, including search result lists. (When a query is applied to an object, the resulting object has an address, defined to be the address of the queried object concatenated with the text of the query. As the result object has an address, one can make links to it. Following the link later leads to a reevaluation of the query.)
- While menus and directories are available, the extra option of hypertext provides a more powerful communications tool. In simple cases, the server program can generate a hypertext view representing (for example) the directory structure of an existing file store. This allows existing data to be put "on the Web" without further human effort.
- There is a very extendable system for introducing new formats for multimedia data.
- There are many W3 client programs. As hypertext information is transmitted on the network in logical (mark-up) form, each client can interpret this in a way natural for the given platform, making optimal use of fonts, colors, and other human interface resources available on that platform.

What Does W3 Define?

W3 has come to stand for a number of things, which should be distinguished. These include

- The idea of a boundless information world in which all items have a reference by which they can be retrieved;
- The address system (URI) which the project implemented to make this world possible, despite many different protocols;
- A network protocol (HTTP) used by native W3 servers giving performance and features not otherwise available;
- A markup language (HTML) which every W3 client is required to understand, and is used for the transmission of basic things such as text, menus and simple on-line help information across the net;
- The body of data available on the Internet using all or some of the preceding listed items.

The client-server architecture of the Web is illustrated in Figure 2.

Universal Resource Identifiers

Universal Resource Identifiers[1] (URIs) are the strings used as ad-

[1]The Internet Engineering Task Force (IETF) is currently defining a similar and derived syntax known as a Uniform Resource Locator (URL). As this work is not complete, and there is no guarantee that URLs will have the same syntax or properties as URIs, we use the term URI here to avoid confusion.

dresses of objects (e.g., menus, documents, images) on the Web. For example, the URI of the main page for the WWW project happens to be

```
http://info.cern.ch/hypertext/
WWW/TheProject.html
```

URIs are "Universal" in that they encode members of the universal set of network addresses. For a new network protocol that has some concept of object, one can form an address for any object as the set of protocol parameters necessary to access the object. If these parameters are encoded into a concise string, with a prefix to identify the protocol and encoding, one has a new URI scheme. There are URIs for Internet news articles and newsgroups (the NNTP protocol), and for FTP archives, for telnet destinations, email addresses, and so on. The same can be done for names of objects in a given name space.

The prefix "http" in the preceding example indicates the address space, and defines the interpretation of the rest of the string. The HTTP protocol is to be used, so the string contains the address of the server to be contacted, and a substring to be passed to the server. Different protocols use different syntaxes, but there is a small amount of common syntax. For example, the common URI syntax reserves the "/" as a way of representing a hierarchical space, and "?" as a separator between the address of an object and a query operation applied to it. As these forms recur in several information systems, to allow expression of them in the common syntax allows the features to be retained in the common model, where appropriate. Hierarchical forms are useful for hypertext, where one "work" may be split up into many interlinked documents. Relative names exploit the hierarchical structure and allow links to be made within the work independent of the higher parts of the URI such as the server name.

URI syntax allows objects to be addressed not only using HTTP, but also using the other common networked information protocols in use today (FTP, NNTP, Gopher, and WAIS), and will allow extension when new protocols are developed.

URIs are central to the W3 architecture. The fact that it is easy to address an object anywhere on the Internet is essential for the system to scale, and for the information space to be independent of the network and server topology.

Hypertext Transfer Protocol

Perhaps misnamed, rather than being a protocol for transferring hypertext, HTTP is a protocol for transferring information with the efficiency necessary for making hypertext jumps. The data transferred may be plain text, hypertext, images, or anything else.

When a user browses the Web, objects are retrieved in rapid succession from often widely dispersed servers. For small documents, the limitations to the response time stem mainly from the number of round trip delays across the network necessary before the rendition of the object can be started. HTTP is therefore a simple request/response protocol.

HTTP does not only transfer HTML documents. Although HTML comprehension is required of W3 clients, HTTP is used for retrieving documents in an unbounded and extensible set of formats. To achieve this, the client sends a (weighted) list of the formats it can handle, and the server replies with data in any of those formats that it can produce. This allows proprietary formats to be used between consenting programs in private, without the need for standardization of those formats. This is important both for high-end users who share data in sophisticated forms, and also as a hook for formats that have yet to be invented. The same negotiation system is used for natural language (English, French, for example) where available, as well as for compression forms.

HTTP is an Internet protocol. It is similar in its readable, text-based style to the File Transfer (FTP) and Network News (NNTP) Protocols that have been used to transfer files and news on the Internet for many years. Unlike these protocols, however, HTTP, is stateless. (That is, it runs over a TCP connection that is held only for the duration of one operation.) The stateless model is efficient when a link from one object may lead equally well to an object stored on the same server, or to another distant server. The purpose of a reference such as a URI is that it should always refer to the "same" (in some sense) object. This also makes a stateless protocol appropriate, as it returns results based on the URI but irrelevant of any previous operations performed by the client.

The HTTP request from the client starts with an operation code (known as the method, in conformance with object-oriented terminology) and the URI of the object. The "GET" method used by all browsers is defined to be idempotent in that it should preserve the state of the Web (apart from billing for the information transfer, and statistics). A "PUT" method is defined for front-end update, and a "POST" method for the attachment of a new document to the Web, or submission of a filled-in form or other object to some processor. Use of PUT and POST is currently limited, partly due to scarcity of hypertext editors. The extension to other methods is a subject of study.

When objects are transferred over the network, information about them ("metainformation") is transferred in HTTP headers. The set of headers is an extension of the Multipurpose Internet Mail Extensions (MIME) set. This design decision was taken to open the door to integration of hypermedia mail, news, and information access. Unlike in email, transfer in binary, and transfer in nonstandard but mutually agreed document formats is possible. This allows, for example, servers to indicate links from, and titles of, documents (such as bit-map images) whose data format does not otherwise include such information.

The convention that unrecognized HTTP headers and parameters are ignored has made it easy to try new ideas on working production servers. This has allowed the protocol definition to evolve in a controlled way by the incorporation of tested ideas.

Hypertext Markup Language (HTML)

Despite the ability of HTTP to negotiate formats, W3 needed a common basic language of interchange for hypertext. HTML is that language, and much of the fabric of the Web is constructed out of it. It was designed

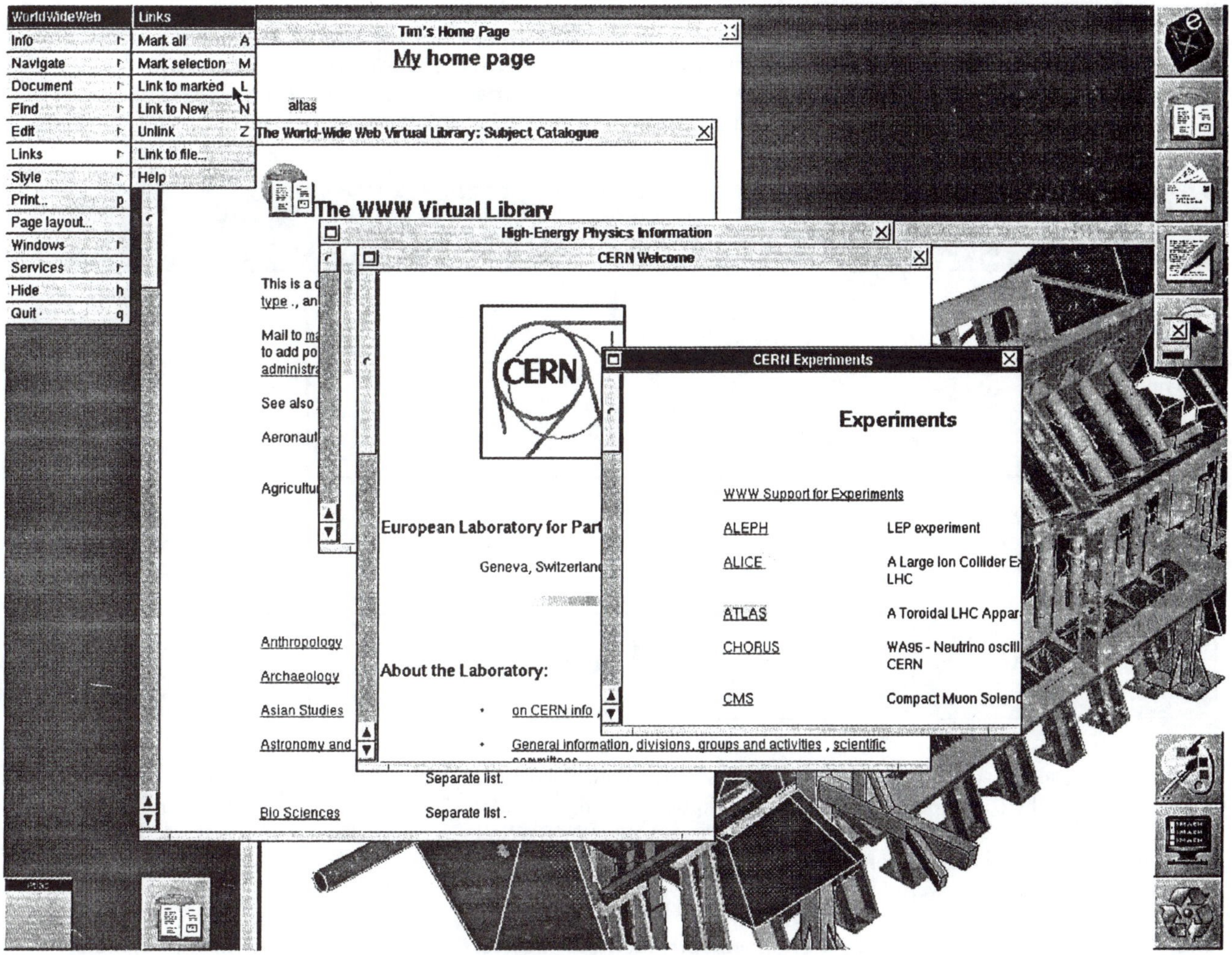

Figure 1. Using the World-Wide Web. Shown here is the authors' prototype World-Wide Web application for NextStep machines. The application initially displays the user's "home" page (top) of personal notes and links (top). Clicking on underlined text takes the reader to new documents. In this case, the user visited the Virtual Library, and, in the high energy physics department, found a link to CERN. Linked to CERN was the "Atlas" collaboration's web including an engineering drawing (background). To save having to follow the same path again, the link menu (shown) allows a new link to be made, for example from text typed into the home page, directly to the Atlas information.

to be sufficiently simple so as to be easily produced by both people and programs, but also to adhere to the SGML standard in that a valid HTML document, if attached to SGML declarations including the HTML "DTD," may be parsed by an SGML parser. HTML is a markup language that does not have to be used with HTTP. It can be used in hypertext email (it is proposed as a format for MIME), news, and anywhere basic hypertext is needed. It includes simple structure elements, such as several levels of headings, bulleted lists, menus and compact lists, all of which are useful when presenting choices, and in on-line documents.

Under development is a much enriched version of HTML known has HTML+. This includes features for more sophisticated on-line documentation, form templates for the entry of data by users, tables and mathematical formulae. Currently many browsers support a subset of the HTML+ features in addition to the core HTML set.

HTML is defined to be a language of communication, which actually flows over the network. There is no requirement that files are stored in HTML. Servers may store files in other formats, or in variations on HTML that include extra information of local interest only, and then generate HTML on the fly with each request.

W3 and Other Systems

Two other systems, WAIS (from Thinking Machines Corporation and now WAIS, Inc.) and Gopher (from the University of Minnesota), share W3's client-server architecture and a certain amount of its functionality. Table 1 indicates some of the differences.

The WAIS protocol is influenced largely by the z39.50 protocol designed for networking library catalogs. It allows a text-based search,

Table 1. A comparison of three popular network information projects.
Registered server figures taken April 27, 1993 and April 15, 1994. WAIS: from Thinking Machines Corporation directory, number of distinct hosts. Gopher: from "All the Gophers in the world" register at the University of Minnesota. W3: from Geographical registry at CERN. In all cases many more servers exist which are not directly registered, so these are a very rough guide with no indication of quantity or quality of information at each host.

	WAIS	Gopher	World-Wide Web
Original target application	Text-based information retrieval	Campus-wide information (CWIS)	Collaborative work
Typical objects			
Text	YES	YES	YES
Menus, Graphics	NO	YES	YES
Hypertext	NO	NO	YES
Search functions			
Text search	YES	YES	YES
Relevance feedback	YES	NO	NO
Reference to other servers	NO	YES	YES
Registered servers			
April 1993	113	455	62
April 1994	137	1410	829

and retrieval following a search. Indexes to be searched are found by searching in a master index. This two-stage search has been demonstrated to be sufficiently powerful to cover the current world of WAIS data. There are no navigational tools to allow the reader to be shown the available resources, however, or guided through the data: the reader is "parachuted in" to a hopefully relevant spot in the information world, but left without context.

Gopher provides a free text search mechanism, but principally uses menus. A menu is a list of titles, from which the user may pick one. While gopher space is in fact a web containing many loops, the menu system gives the user the impression of a tree. The Veronica server provides a master index for gopher space.

The W3 data model is similar to the gopher model, except that menus are generalized to hypertext documents. In both cases, simple file servers generate the menus or hypertext directly from the file structure of a server. The W3 hypertext model gives the program more power to communicate the options available to the reader, as it can include headings and various forms of list structure, for example, within the hypertext.

All three systems allow for the provision of graphics, sound and video, although because the WAIS system only has access by text search, text has to be associated with graphics files to allow them to be found.

W3 clients provide access to servers of all types, as a single simple interface to the whole Web is considered very important. Unknown to the user, several protocols are in use behind the scenes. A common code library "libwww" put into the public domain by CERN has promoted this uniformity. Whereas one would not wish to see greater proliferation of protocols, the existence of more than one protocol probably allows for the most rapid progress during this phase in the development of the field. It also allows a certain limited confidence that, if an architecture can encompass older systems and allow transition to current systems, it will, by induction, be able to provide a transition to newer and better ideas as they are invented.

Recent W3 Developments

This article, like others in this issue, was derived from material written in April 1993 for the INET'93 conference. Growth of the Web since that time has been so great that this section has been completely rewritten. There are now 829 (May: 1,248) rather than 62 registered HTTP servers, and many more client programs available as then.

The initial prototype W3 client was a "wysiwyg" hypertext browser/editor using NeXTStep. We developed a line mode browser, and were encouraging the developments of a good browser for X workstations. One year ago, NCSA's Mosaic W3 browser was in wide use on X workstations. Its easy installation and use was a major reason for the spread of the Web. Today there are many browsers available for workstations, Macintosh and IBM/PC compatible machines, and for users with character-based terminals. Of the latter category, "Lynx" from the University of Kansas provides full-screen access to the Web for users with character terminals or emulators running on personal computers. Since new software is appearing frequently, readers are advised to check the lists on the Web for those most suited to their needs.

The availability of browsers and the availability of quality information have provoked each other. One available indicator of growth has been Merit Inc.'s count of the traffic of various different protocols across the

NSF T3 backbone in the U.S. (see Figure 3).

An indicator of the uptake rate of clients is the load on the *info.cern.ch.* W3 server at CERN, which provides information about the Web itself, which more than doubled every 4 months over the three years between April 1991 and April 1994.

Information providers have also blossomed. Some of these provide simple overviews of what is available at particular institutes or in particular fields. Others use the power of the W3 model to provide a virtual world of great richness. Examples of servers that use hypertext in interesting ways are the RAL-Durham Particle Database, and the Legal Information Institute's hypertexts of several great tomes of American law. Franz Hoesel's hypertext version of the Vatican's Renaissance Culture exhibit at the Library of Congress set an example that was followed by many collections of art, history and other fields. The Palo Alto town hall runs a server with everything from building regulations to restaurants. As an example of the increasing use of the Web for commerce, a user-friendly virtual clothing store prompts for one's size, and points to a virtual store containing only those clothes that are the right size and also in stock.

The Future

The W3 initiative occupies the meeting point of many fields of technology. Users put pressure and effort into bringing about the adoption of W3 in new areas. Apart from being a place of communication and learning, and a new market place, the Web is a show ground for new developments in information technology. Some of the developments that we look forward to in the next few years include

- The implementation of a name service that will allow documents to be referenced by name, independent of their location;
- Hypertext editors allowing nonexpert users to make hypertext links to organize published information. This will bring the goal of computer-supported collaboration closer, with front-end update, and annotation;
- More sophisticated document type definitions providing for the needs of

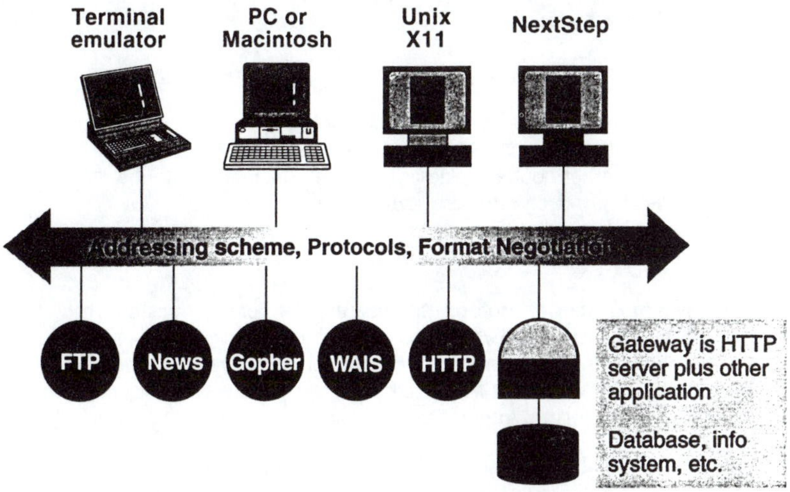

Figure 2. The World-Wide Web client-server architecture. For published information to be universally available, W3 relies on a common addressing syntax, a set of common protocols, and negotiation of data formats.

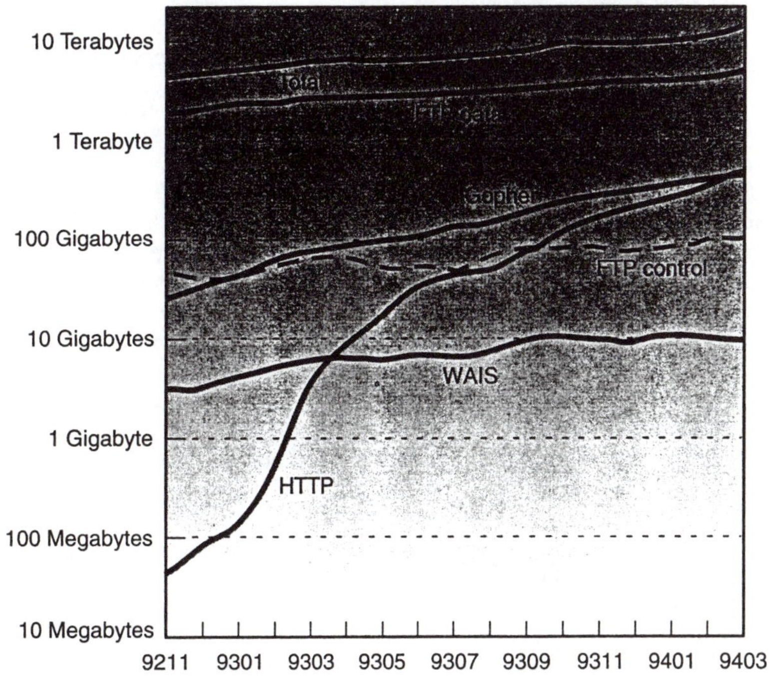

Figure 3. Traffic in bytes per month across the NSF T3 backbone in the U.S. File Transfer Protocol (FTP) was traditionally used to access archives of software. FTP uses separate connections for control and data flow. WAIS arose as an interface to text retrieval systems, Gopher protocol with menu-style interfaces, and W3's HTTP with hypertext and multimedia. W3 clients handle many protocols to access all these worlds of data as a seamless continuum, but new W3 servers use HTTP by preference. Each vertical division represents a tenfold increase in traffic. The horizontal divisions are months. Data: Merit < ftp://ftp.merit.edu/statistics/nsfnet >

Glossary and Further Reading

FTP: File Transfer Protocol. Postel, J. and Reynolds, J. File Transfer Protocol. Internet RFC 959, October 1985. <ftp://ds.internic.net/rfc/rfc959.txt>

Gopher: The Internet Gopher. Anklesaria, F. et. al. The Internet Gopher Protocol. Internet RFC 1436, March 1993. <ftp://ds.internic.net/rfc/rfc1436.txt>

HTML: Hypertext Markup Language. Berners-Lee, T., and Connolly, D. Hypertext Markup Language Protocol. <ftp://info.cern.ch/pub/www/doc/html-spec.ps, .txt>

HTTP: Hypertext Transfer Protocol. Berners-Lee, T. Hypertext Transfer Protocol. <ftp://info.cern.ch/pub/www/doc/http-spec.ps, .txt>

MIME: Multipurpose Internet Mail Extensions. Borenstein, N., and Freed, N. MIME (Multipurpose Internet Mail Extensions): Mechanisms for Specifying and Describing the Format of Internet Message Bodies. Internet RFC 1341, June 1992.

NNTP: Network News Transfer Protocol. Kantor, B. and Lapsley, P. A proposed standard for the transmission of news. Internet RFC 977, 1986.

URI: Universal Resource Identifier. Berners-Lee, T. Universal Resource Identifiers for the World-Wide Web. Submitted as an Internet RFC as yet unnumbered. See <http://info.cern.ch/hypertext/WWW/Addressing/Addressing.html> for pointers to information on this area.

WAIS: Wide Area Information Servers. See Addyman, T. WAIS: Strengths, Weaknesses and Opportunities. In *Proceedings of Information Networking 93* (London, May 1993), Meckler, London.

W3: Berners-Lee, T.J., Cailliau, R., Groff, J-F, Pollermann, B. World-Wide Web: The Information universe. *Electronic Networking: Research, Applications and Policy*, (Spring 1992), 52–58. See also documents in <ftp://info.cern.ch/pub/www/doc> and information referenced by <http://info.cern.ch/hypertext/WWW/TheProject.html>

commercial publishers of on-line material;

- The development of a common format for hypertext links from two- and three-dimensional images giving more exciting interface possibilities;
- Integration with concurrent editors and other real-time features such as teleconferencing and virtual reality;
- Easy-to-use servers for low-end machines to ease publication of information by small groups and individuals;
- Evolution of objects from being principally human-readable documents to contain more machine-oriented semantic information, allowing more sophisticated processing;
- Conventions on the Internet for charging and commercial use to allow direct access to for-profit services.

Conclusion

It is intended that after reading this article you will have an idea of what W3 is, where it fits in with other systems in the field, and where it is going. There is much more to be said, especially about providing information, but this is described on the Web itself. Also in the "Web about the Web" are lists of contributed research and development work and ideas, and pointers to work in progress, so that those interested can work together.

The Web does not yet meet its design goal as being a pool of knowledge that is as easy to update as to read. That level of immediacy of knowledge sharing waits for easy-to-use hypertext editors to be generally available on most platforms. Most information has in fact passed through publishers or system managers of one sort or another. However, the incredible diversity of information available gives great credit to the creativity and ingenuity of information providers, and points to a very exciting future. C

Appendix. Getting Started

If you have a vt100 terminal, you can try out a full-screen interface by telnet to ukanaix.cc.ukans.edu and logging in as www. With any terminal, you can telnet to info.cern.ch for the simplest interface. These browsers are also available in source and in some cases binary form. Details of status and coordinates of about 20 different browsers are available on the Web—just follow a link to World-Wide Web, and select "software available."

The kernel W3 code (a common code library, and basic server and clients) from CERN is in the public domain. (All protocols and specifications are public domain.) It is available by anonymous FTP from info.cern.ch

NCSA's "Mosaic" browser for W3 is available for X, Mac or PC/Windows by anonymous FTP from ftp.ncsa.uiuc.edu, currently without charge for academic users.

About the Authors:

TIM BERNERS-LEE originated the World-Wide Web in 1990 to enable the sharing of knowledge by complex distributed teams. At CERN he coordinates W3 development by collaborating with institutes around the world. Current research interests include text processing, graphics, communications software, and system design. email: timbl@info.cern.ch

ROBERT CAILLIAU coordinates the use of W3 by CERN experiments and other physics institutes. He is a long-time user of HyperCard, and has been working on W3 since 1991, contributing many ideas, and some software for the Macintosh. email: cailliau@www.cern.ch

ARI LUOTONEN is a member of CERN's technical student program in conjunction with his studies at Tampere University of Technology, Finland. Current research interests include developing CERN's "httpd" HTTP server for Unix and VMS systems. email: luotonen@www.cern.ch

HENRIK FRYSTYK NIELSEN, of Aalborg University, Denmark, is also a CERN technical student. He is working on the kernel code, with research interests in enhanced networking protocols. email: frystyk@info.cern.ch

ARTHUR SECRET wrote the first gateway giving W3 access to a relational database in 1992, while studying Computer Science at Ecole Internationale des Sciences du Traitement de l'Information in Paris, France, as a CERN technical student. Among other tasks in the CERN W3 team, he currently organizes the cataloging of new W3 material in the "virtual library." email: secret@info.cern.ch

Authors' Present Address: CERN, 1211 Geneva 23, Switzerland.

Computing Systems in Engineering Vol. 2, No. 4, pp. 321–347, 1991
Printed in Great Britain.

0956-0521/91 $3.00 + 0.00
Pergamon Press plc

NATURE AND ORIGINS OF VIRTUAL ENVIRONMENTS: A BIBLIOGRAPHICAL ESSAY

S. R. Ellis

NASA Ames Research Center, Moffett Field, CA 94035, U.S.A. and University of California, Berkeley, CA 94270, U.S.A.

(*Received* 30 *May* 1991)

Abstract—Virtual environments presented via head-mounted, computer-driven displays provide a new media for communication. They may be analyzed by considering: (1) what may be meant by an environment; (2) what is meant by the process of virtualization; and (3) some aspects of human performance that constrain environmental design. Their origins are traced from previous work in vehicle simulation and multimedia research. Pointers are provided to key technical references, in the dispersed, archival literature, that are relevant to the development and evaluation of virtual-environment interface systems.

Due to space limitations, this paper has been abridged, including the omission of Figures 1–3, 10–11, 14, 17, 21, and 24–26.

1. COMMUNICATION AND ENVIRONMENTS

1.1. *Virtual environments are media*

Virtual environments created through computer graphics are communications media.[1] Like other media, they have both physical and abstract components. Paper, for example, is a medium for communication. The paper is itself one possible physical embodiment of the abstraction of a two-dimensional surface onto which marks may be made.† The corresponding abstraction for head-coupled, virtual image, stereoscopic displays that synthesize a coordinated sensory experience is an environment. These so called "virtual reality" media have only recently caught the international public's imagination,[3–6] but they arise from continuous development in several technical and nontechnical areas during the past 25 years.

• • •

2. VIRTUALIZATION

2.1. *Definition of virtualization*

Virtualization may be defined as *the process by which a human viewer interprets a patterned sensory impression to be an extended object in an environment other than that in which it physically exists.*

• • •

2.2. *Levels of virtualization*

Three levels of virtualization may be distinguished: virtual space, virtual image, and virtual environments.

• • •

† As described by James Hollan at the Panel on Virtual Reality, Western Communications Forum Panel 1991, Phoenix, Arizona, some new computer interfaces may resemble handwriting-recognizing magic slates on which users write commands with a stylus. See Ref. 2.

3. ORIGINS OF VIRTUAL ENVIRONMENTS

3.1. *Early visionaries*

The intuitive appeal that virtual environment technology obviously has is probably rooted in the human fascination with vicarious experiences in imagined environments. In this respect, virtual environments may be thought of as originating with the earliest human cave art,[54] though Lewis Carroll's *Through the Looking-Glass* certainly is a more modern example of this fascination.

Fascination with alternative, synthetic realities has been continued in more contemporary literature. Aldous Huxley's "feelies" in *Brave New World* were certainly a kind of virtual environment, a cinema with sensory experience extended beyond sight and sound. A similar fascination must account for the popularity of microcomputer role playing adventure games such as *Wizzardry*. Motion pictures, and especially stereoscopic movies, of course, also provide examples of noninteractive spaces.[55]

The contemporary interest in imagined environments has been particularly stimulated by the advent of sophisticated, relatively inexpensive, interactive techniques allowing the inhabitants of these environments to move about and manually interact with computer graphics objects in three-dimensional space. This kind of environment was envisioned in the science fiction plots of the movie *TRON* and William Gibson's 1985 *Neuromancer*, yet the first actual synthesis of such a system using a head-mounted stereo display was made possible much earlier in the middle 1960s by Ivan Sutherland who developed special-purpose fast graphics hardware.[56,57]

Another early synthesis of a synthetic, interactive environment was implemented by Myron Krueger[58–60] in the 1970s. Unlike the device developed for Sutherland, Krueger's environment was projected onto a wall-sized screen. In Krueger's VIDEOPLACE, the user's image appears in a two-dimensional graphic video world created by a computer. The VIDEOPLACE computer analyzed video images to deter-

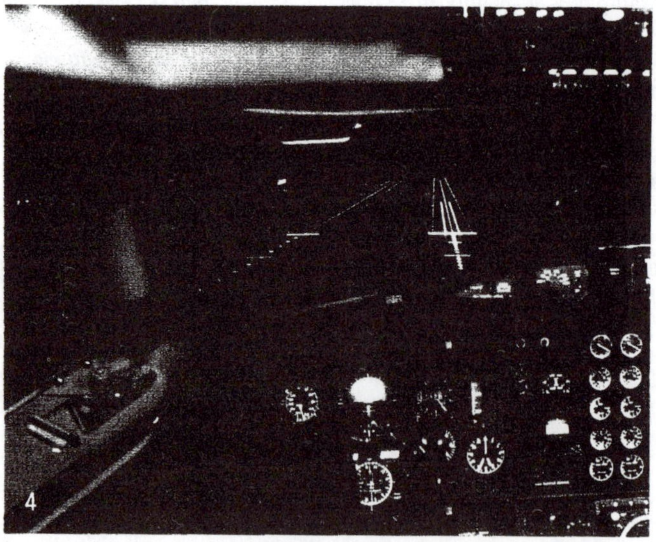

Fig. 4. View through the cockpit of a 727 simulator at the Ames Research Center which is used for human factors research. A simulated night flying environment is visible out the forward cockpit window. (Photograph courtesy of NASA.)

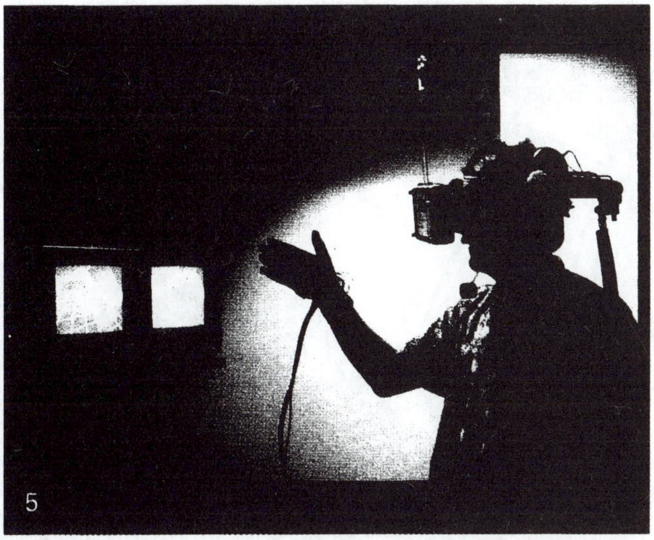

Fig. 5. This head-mounted, stereo, virtual environment display system at the Ames Research Center Advanced Display and Spatial Perception Laboratory is being used to control a remote PUMA robot in the Ames Robotics Laboratory. The simulation update rate varies from 12 to 30 Hz, depending on the complexity of the graphics. A local kinematic simulation of the remote work site aids the operator in planning complex movements and visualizing kinematic and operational constraints on the motion of the end effector. (Photography courtesy of NASA.)

mine when an object was touched by an inhabitant, and it could then generate a graphic or auditory response. One advantage of this kind of environment is that the remote video-based position measurement does not encumber the user with position sensors.

3.2. *Vehicle simulation and three-dimensional cartography*

Probably the most important source of virtual environment technology comes from previous work in fields associated with the development of realistic vehicle simulators, primarily for aircraft (see Refs 61 and 62; and Fig. 4), but also automobiles[63] and ships.[64,65] The inherent difficulties in controlling the actual vehicles often require that operators be highly trained. Since acquiring this training on the vehicles themselves could be dangerous or expensive, simulation systems synthesize the content, geometry, and

Fig. 6. As in all current relatively inexpensive, head-mounted virtual environment viewing systems, the view that the operator actually sees through the wide field (lower inset shows a part of the user's actual field of view) view finder is significantly lower resolution than that typically seen on the graphics monitors (background matched in magnification). The horizontal pixel resolution through view finder is about 22 arcmin/pixel, vertical resolution is 24 arcmin/line. Approximately 2 arcmin/pixel are required to present resolution at the center of the visual field comparable to that seen on a standard Macintosh monochrome display viewed at 57 cm. (Photograph courtesy of NASA.)

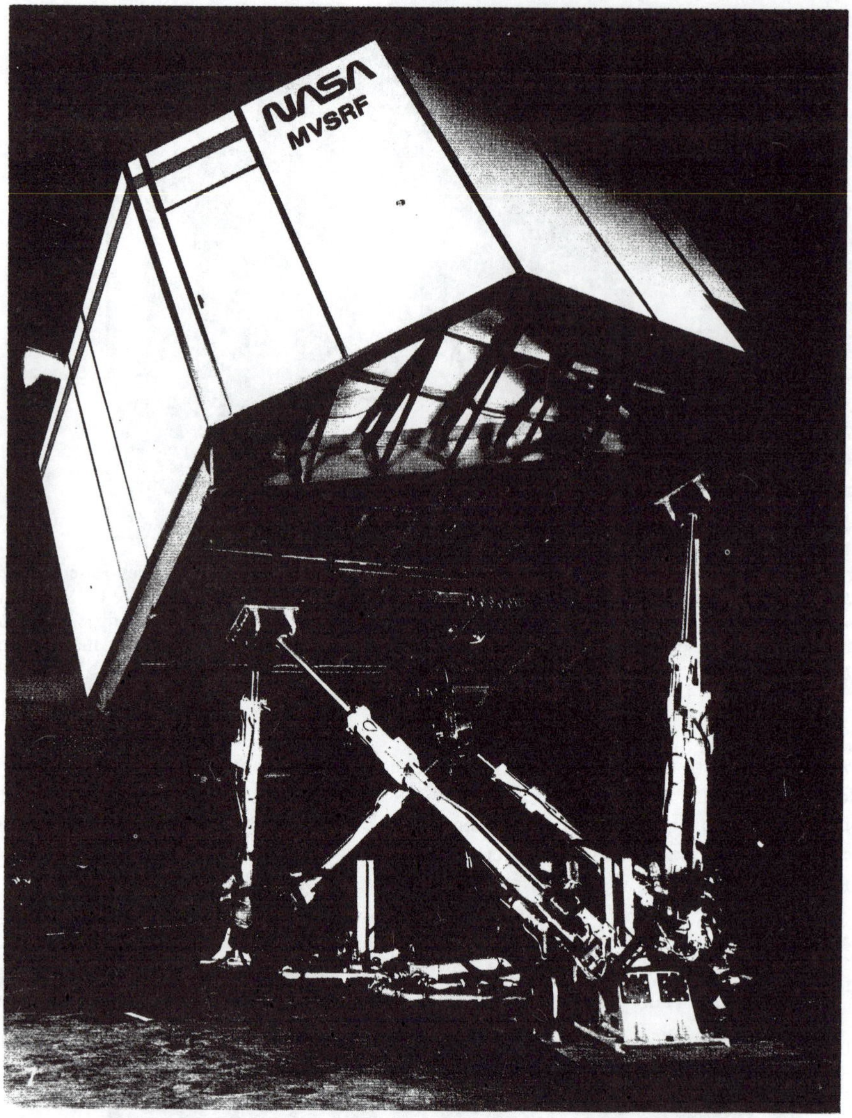

Fig. 7. Moving base simulator of the Aerospace Human Factors Division of Ames Research Center pitched so as to simulate an acceleration. (Photograph courtesy of NASA.)

dynamics of the control environment for training and for testing of new technology and procedures.

These systems have usually cost millions of dollars and have recently involved helmet-mounted displays to recreate part of the environment.[66–69] Declining costs have now brought the cost of a virtual environment display down to that of an expensive workstation and made possible "personal simulators" for everyday use (see Refs 70 and 71; and Figs 5 and 6).

The simulator's interactive visual displays are made by computer graphics hardware and algorithms. Development of special-purpose hardware, such as matrix multiplication devices, was an essential step that enabled generation of real-time, that is, greater than 20 Hz, interactive three-dimensional graphics.[56,57,72] A recent example is the "geometry engine" in Silicon Graphics IRIS workstations.[73,74] It enhances processing of the viewing transformation. These "graphics engines" can project hundreds of thousands of Gouraud shaded polygons per second.[75] Though this number may seem large, rendering of naturalistic objects and surfaces can require from 10,000 to 500,000 polygons. Software techniques are also important for improved three-dimensional graphics performance. "Oct-tree" data structures, for example, have been shown to dramatically improve processing speed for inherently volumetric structures.[76,77]

Since vehicle simulation may involve moving-base simulators, programming the appropriate correlation between visual and vestibular simulation is crucial for a complete simulation of an environment (Fig. 7). Moreover, failure to match these two stimuli correctly can lead to motion sickness.[78] Paradoxically, however, since the effective travel of most moving base simulators is limited, designers must learn how to use subthreshold visual-vestibular mismatches to produce illusions of greater freedom of movement. These allowable mismatches are built into so-called "washout" models[16,79] and are key elements for creating illusions of extended movement. For example, a slowly implemented pitch-up of a simulator can be used to help create an illusion of forward acceleration. Understanding the tolerable dynamic limits of visual-vestibular miscorrelation will be an important design consideration for wide field-of-view head-mounted displays.

The use of informative distortion is also well established in cartography[80] and is used to help create a convincing three-dimensional environment for simulated vehicles. Cartographic distortion is also obvious in global maps which must warp a spherical surface into a plane[81,82] and three-dimensional maps, which often use significant vertical scale exaggeration (6–20 ×) to clearly present topographic features. Explicit informative geometric distortion is sometimes incorporated into maps and cartograms presenting geographically indexed statistical data,[83-87] but the extent to which such informative distortion may be incorporated into simulated environments is constrained by the user's movement-related physiological reflexes. If the viewer is constrained to actually be *in* the environment, deviations from a natural environmental space can cause disorientation and motion sickness.[51,88] For this reason, virtual space or virtual image formats are more suitable when successful communication of the spatial information may be achieved through spatial distortions (Fig. 8). However, even in these formats the content of the environment may have to be enhanced by aids such as graticules to help the user discount unwanted aspects of the geometric distortion.[89-91]

In some environmental simulations the environment itself is the object of interest. Truly remarkable animations have been synthesized from image sequences taken by NASA spacecraft which mapped various planetary surfaces. When electronically combined with surface altitude data, the surface photography can be used to synthesize flights over the surface through positions never reached by the space-

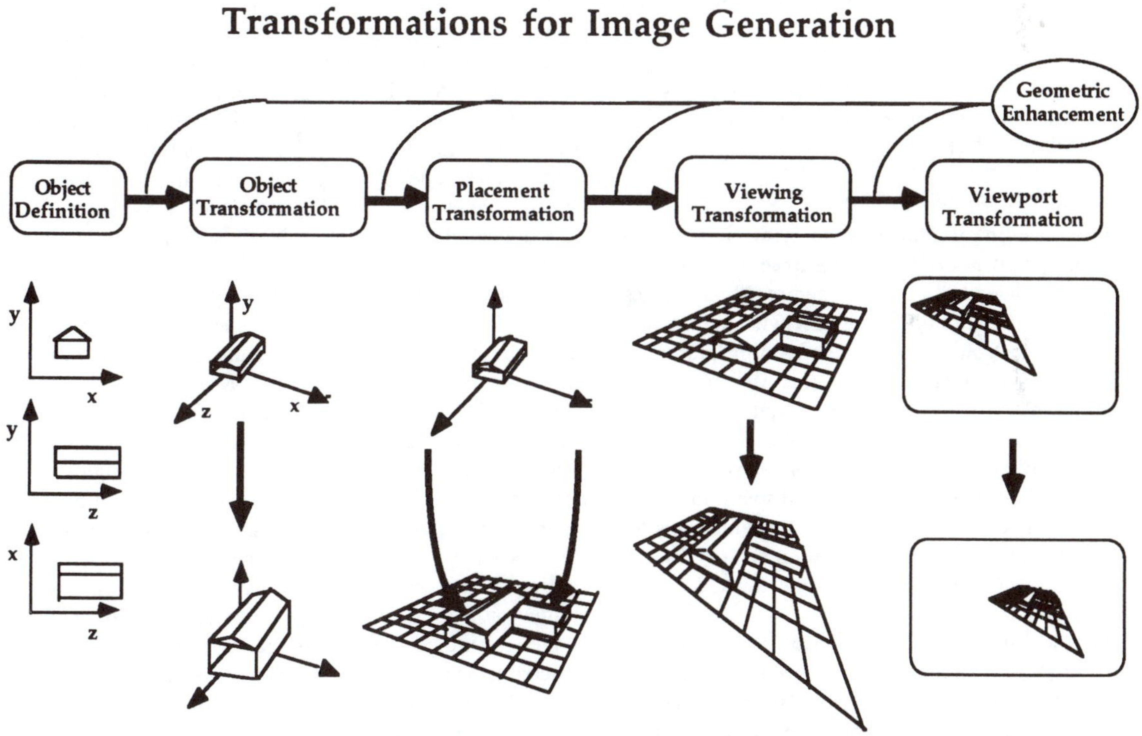

Fig. 8. Process of representing a graphic object in virtual space allows a number of different opportunities to introduce informative geometric distortions or enhancements. These may either be a modification of the transforming matrix during the process of object definition or they may be modifications of an element of a model. These modifications may take place (1) in an object relative coordinate system used to define the object's shape, or (2) in an affine or even curvilinear object shape transformation, or (3) during the placement transformation that positions the transformed object in world coordinates, or (4) in the viewing transformation or (5) in the final viewport transformation. The perceptual consequences of informative distortions are different depending on where they are introduced. For example, object transformations will not impair perceived positional stability of objects displayed in a head-mounted format, whereas changes of the viewing transformation such as magnification will.

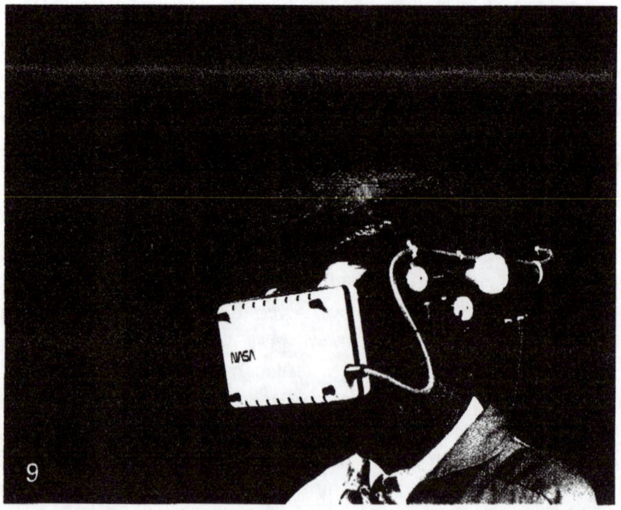

Fig. 9. When high-performance computer display technology can be matched to equally high resolution helmet display technology, planetary scientists will be able to use these systems to visualize remote environments such as the surface of Mars to plan exploration and to analyze planetary surface data. (Photograph courtesy of NASA.)

craft's camera.[92] Recent developments have made possible the use of these synthetic visualizations of planetary and Earth surfaces for interactive exploration and they promise to provide planetary scientists with the new capability of "virtual planetary exploration".[93,94] (Fig. 9).

3.3. *Physical and logical simulation*

Visualization of planetary surfaces suggests the possibility that not only the substance of the surface may be modeled but also its dynamic characteristics. Dynamic simulations for virtual environments may be developed from ordinary high-level programming languages like Pascal or C, but this usually requires considerable time for development. Interesting alternatives for this kind of simulation have been provided by simulation and modeling languages such as SLAM II, with a graphical display interface, TESS.[95] These very high languages provide tools for defining and implementing continuous or discrete dynamic models. They can facilitate construction of precise systems models.[96]

Another alternative made possible by graphical interfaces to computers is a simulation development environment in which the simulation is created through manipulation of icons representing its separate elements, such as integrators, delays, or filters, so as to connect them into a functioning *virtual machine*. A microcomputer program called "Pinball Construction Set" published in 1982 by Bill Budge is a widely distributed early example of this kind of simulation system. It allowed the user to create custom simulated pinball machines on the computer screen simply by moving icons from a tool kit into an "active region" of the display where they would become animated. A more educational, and detailed example of this kind of simulator was written as educational software by Warren Robinett. This program, called "Rocky's Boots",[97] allows users to connect icons representing logic circuits that are animated at a slow rate so the user may watch their detailed functioning. More detailed versions of this type of simulation have now been incorporated into graphical interfaces to simulation and modeling languages and are available through widely distributed systems such as the interface builder distributed with NeXt® computers.

The dynamical properties of virtual spaces and environments may also be linked to physical simulations. Prominent, noninteractive examples of this technique are James Blinn's physical animations in the video physics courses, "The Mechanical Universe" and "Beyond the Mechanical Universe."[98,99] These physically correct animations are particularly useful in providing students with subjective insights into dynamic three-dimensional phenomena such as magnetic fields. Similar educational animated visualizations have been used for courses on visual perception[100] and computer-aided design.[101] Physical simulation is more instructive, however, if it is interactive and interactive virtual spaces have been constructed which allow users to interact with nontrivial physical simulations by manipulating synthetic objects whose behavior is governed by realistic dynamics (see Refs 102 and 103; also see Figs 10 and 11).

Some unusual natural environments are difficult to work in because their inherent dynamics are unfamiliar and may be nonlinear. The immediate environment around an orbiting spacecraft is an example. When expressed in a spacecraft-relative frame of reference known as local-vertical-local-horizontal, the consequences of maneuvering thrusts becomes markedly counter-intuitive and nonlinear.[106] Consequently, a visualization tool designed to allow manual planning of maneuvers in this environment has taken account of these difficulties.[107–109] This display system most directly assists planning by providing visual feedback of the consequences of the proposed plans. Its significant features enabling interactive optimization of orbital maneuvers include an "inverse dynamics" algorithm that removes control nonlinearities. Through a "geometric spread-sheet", the display creates a synthetic environment that provides the user control of thruster burns which allows *independent* solutions to otherwise coupled problems of orbital maneuvering (Figs 12 and 13.)

3.4. *Scientific and medical visualization*

Visualizing physical phenomena may be accomplished not only by constructing simulations of the phenomena but also by animating graphs and plots of the physical parameters themselves.[98,99] For example, multiple time functions of force and torque and the joints of a manipulator or limb while it is being used for a test movement (see, for example, Ref. 110).

One application for which a virtual space display has already been demonstrated in a commercial product has been in visualization of volumetric medical data.[77] These images are typically constructed from a series of two-dimensional slices of CAT, PET, or MRI images in order to allow doctors to visualize normal or abnormal anatomical structures in three dimensions. Because the different tissue types may be identified digitally, the doctors may perform an "electronic dissection" and selectively remove particular tissues. In this way truly remarkable skeletal images may be created which currently aid orthopedic and cranio-facial surgeons to plan operations (Figs 14 and 15). These volumetric data bases are also useful for shaping custom-machined prosthetic bone implants and for directing precision robotic boring devices for precise fit between implants and surrounding bone.[111] Though these static data bases have not yet been presented to doctors as full virtual environments, existing technology is adequate to develop improved virtual space techniques for interacting with them and may be able to enhance the usability of the existing displays. Related scene-generation technology can already render detailed images of this sort based on architectural drawings and can allow prospective clients to visualize walk-throughs of buildings that have not yet been constructed.[112,113]

3.5. *Teleoperation and telerobotics and manipulative simulation*

The second major technical influence on the development of virtual environment technology is research on teleoperation and telerobotic simulation.[19,114,115] Indeed, virtual environments have existed before the name itself as telerobotic and teleoperations simulations. The display technology, however, in these cases was usually panel-mounted rather than head-mounted (but see Ref. 116). A key difficulty was lack of a convenient and cheap head tracker. The current popular, electromagnetic, six-degree-of-freedom position tracker developed by Polhemus Navigation,[117] and also see Ref. 118 and 119, consequently, was a key technological advance. In other techniques for tracking the head position, accelerometers or optical tracking hardware may be used.[61,120]

A second key component of a teleoperation work station, or of a virtual environment, is a sensor for coupling hand position of the end-effector at a remote work site. The earlier mechanical linkages used for this coupling have been replaced by joysticks or by more complex sensors that can determine hand shape, as well as position. Modern joysticks are capable of measuring simultaneously all three rotational and three translational components of motion. Some of the joysticks are isotonic[121] and allow significant travel or rotation along the sensed axes, whereas others are isometric and sense the applied forces and torques without displacement.[122] Though the isometric sticks with no moving parts benefit from simpler construction, the user's kinematic coupling in his hand make it difficult for him to use them to apply signals in one axis without cross-couples signals in other axes. Consequently, these joysticks use switches for shutting down unwanted axes during use. Careful design of the breakout forces and detentes for different axes on the isotonic sticks allow a user to minimize cross coupling in control signals while separately controlling the different axes.[61,62]

Although the mechanical bandwidth might have been only of the order of 2–5 Hz, the early mechanical linkages used for telemanipulation provided force-feedback conveniently and passively. In modern electronically coupled systems force-feed-back or "feel" must be actively provided, usually by electric motors. Although systems providing six degrees of freedom with force-feedback on all axes are mechanically complicated, they have been constructed and used for a variety of manipulative tasks.[123,124] Interestingly, force-feedback has been particularly helpful in the molecular docking work at the University of North Carolina (see Fig. 16) in which chemists manipulate molecular models of drugs in a computer graphics physical simulation in order to find optimal orientations for binding sites on other molecules.[125]

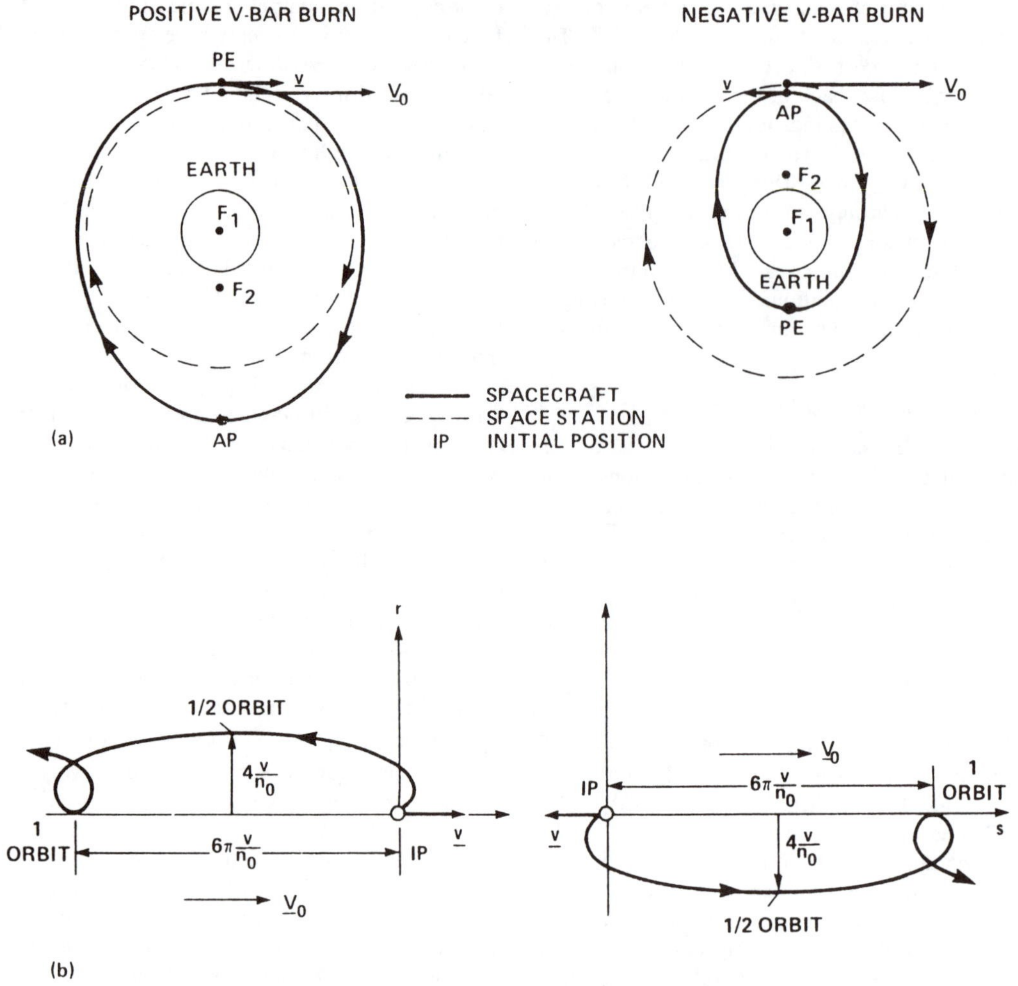

Fig. 12. Unusual environments sometimes have unusual dynamics. The orbital motion of a satellite in a low earth orbit (a) changes when thrust r is made either in the direction of orbital motion, V_0, (left) or opposed to orbital motion (right) and indicated by the change of the original orbit (dashed lines) to the new orbit (solid line). When the new trajectory is viewed in a frame of reference relative to the initial thrust point on the original orbit (Earth is down, orbital velocity is to the right; see lower panels), the consequences of the burn appear unusual. Forward thrusts (left) cause non-uniform, backward, trochoidal movement. Backward thrusts (right) cause the reverse.

High-fidelity force-feedback requires electromechanical bandwidths over 30 Hz. Most manipulators do not have this high a mechanical response. A force-reflecting joy-stick with these characteristics, however, has been designed and built (Fig. 17). Because of the required dynamic characteristics for high fidelity, it is not compact and is carefully designed to protect its operators from the strong, high-frequency forces it is capable of producing (see Refs 126–128 for some descriptions of typical manual interface specifications; and also see Ref. 129).

Manipulative interfaces may provide varying degrees of manual dexterity. Relatively crude interfaces for rate-controlled manipulators may allow experienced operators to accomplish fine manipulation tasks. Access to this level of proficiency, however, can be aided by use of position control, by more intuitive control of the interface, and by more anthropomorphic linkages on the manipulator.

An early example of a dextrous, anthropomorphic robotic end effector is the hand by Tomovic and Boni.[130] A more recent example is the Utah/MIT hand.[131] Such hand-like end effectors with large numbers of degrees of freedom may be manually controlled directly by hand-shape sensors; for example, the Exos, exoskeletal hand (see Ref. 132 and Fig. 19).

Significantly, the users of the Exos hand often turn off a number of the joints raising the possibility that there may be a limit to the number of degrees of freedom usefully incorporated into a dextrous master controller.[133] Less bulky hand shape measurement devices have also been developed using fiber optic or other sensors (Fig. 20);[134,135] however, use of these

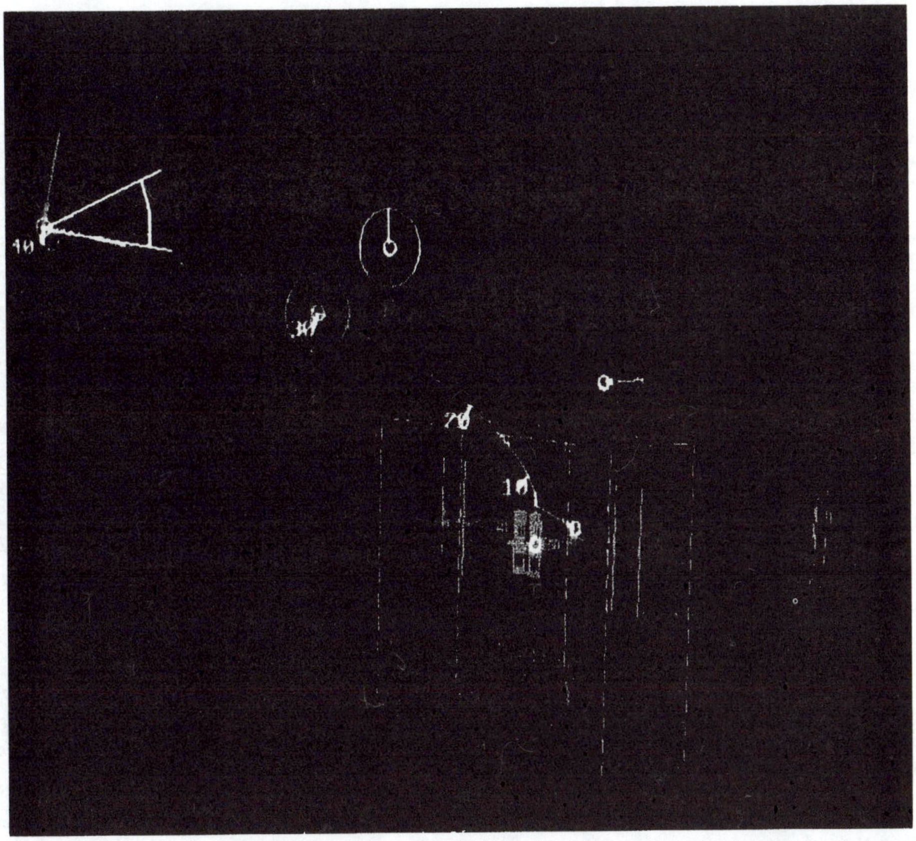

Fig. 13. Proximity operations planning display presents a virtual space that enables operators to plan orbital maneuvers despite counter-intuitive, nonlinear dynamics and operational constraints, such as plume impingement restrictions. The operator may use the display to visualize his proposed trajectories. Violations of the constraints appear as graphics objects, i.e. circles and arcs, which inform him of the nature and extent of each violation. This display provides a working example of how informed design of a planning environment's symbols, geometry, and dynamics can extend human planning capacity into new realms. (Photograph courtesy of NASA.)

alternatives involves significant trade-offs of resolution, accuracy, force-reflection and calibration stability as compared with the more bulky sensors (Figs 21–23).

3.6. *Photography, cinematography and video technology*

Since photography, cinema and television are formats for imagery that create synthetic environments, it is not surprising that technology associated with special effects for these media have been applied to virtual environments. The LEEP optics, which are commonly used in many "virtual reality" stereo-viewers, were originally developed for a stereoscopic camera system using matched camera and viewing optics to cancel the aberrations of the wide angle lens. The LEEP system field of view is approximately 110° × 55°, but it depends on how the measurement is taken.[137] Though this viewer does not allow inter-pupilary adjustment, its large entrance pupil (30 mm radius) removes the need for such an adjustment. The image pairs used, interestingly, are only 62 mm apart, closer together than the average inter-pupilary distance. This choice helpfully reduces the likelihood that users need to diverge their eyes to achieve binocular fusion.

An early development of a more complete environmental illusion through cinematic virtual space was Morton Heilig's "Sensorama". It provided a stereo, wide field-of-view, egocentric display with coordinated binaural sound, wind, and odor effects.[138] A more recent, interactive virtual space display was implemented by the MIT Architecture Machine Group in the form of a video-disk-based, interactive, map of Aspen, Colorado.[139] The interactive map provided a video display of what the user would have seen were he actually there moving through the town. Similar interactive uses of video-disk technology have been explored at the MIT Media Lab.[140] One feature that probably distinguishes the multimedia work mentioned here from the more scientific and engineering studies reported previously, is that the media artists, as users of the enabling technologies, have more interest in synthesizing highly integrated environments including sight, sound, touch and smell. A significant part of their goal is the integrated experience of a "synthetic place". On the other hand, the simulator designer is only interested in capturing the total experience insofar as this experience helps specific training and testing.

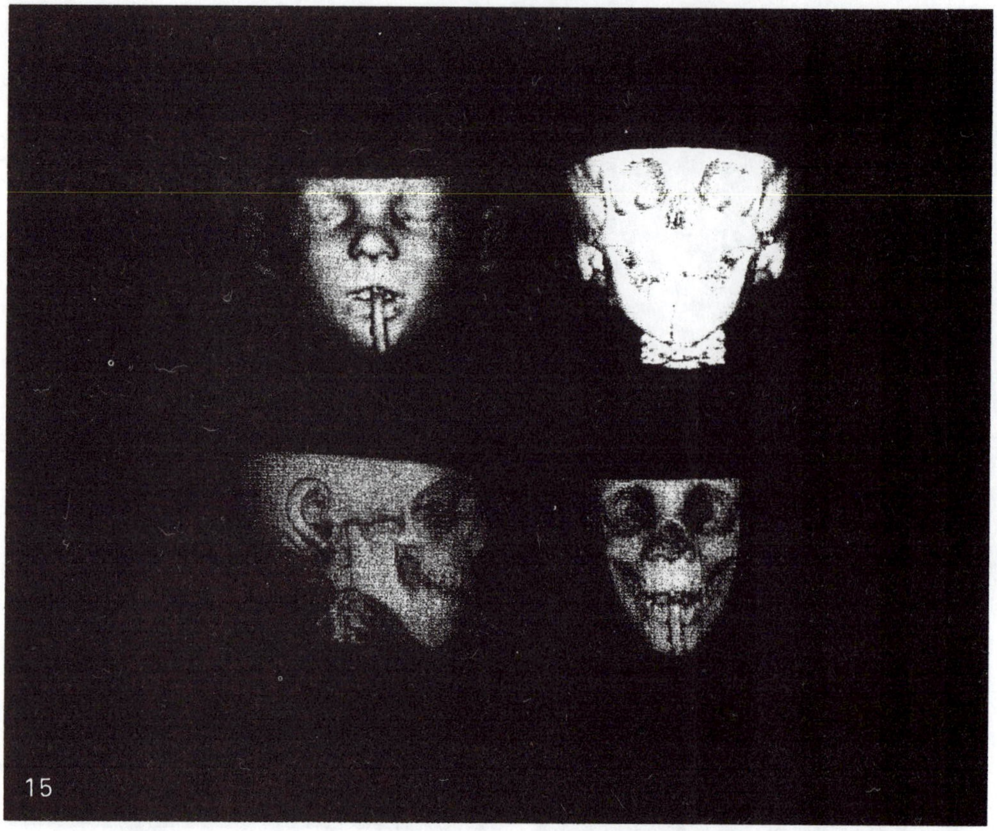

Fig. 15. Different tissues in volumetric data sets from CAT scan X-ray slices may be given arbitrary visual properties by digital processing in order to aid visualization. Here tissue surrounding the bone is made partially transparent so as to make the skin surface as well as the underlying bone of the skull clearly visible. This processing is an example of enhancement of the content of a synthetic environment. (Photograph courtesy of Octree Corporation, Cupertine California.)

3.7. *Role of engineering models*

Since the integration of the equipment necessary to synthesize a virtual environment represents such a technical challenge in itself, there is a tendency for groups working in this area to focus their attention on collecting the individual technologies. Accomplishment of specific tasks, however, places distinct performance requirements on the simulation. These requirements may be determined empirically for each task, but a more general approach is to use human performance models to help specify them. There are good general collections that can provide this background design data (e.g. Refs 141–143) and there are specific examples of how scientific engineering knowledge and computer-graphics-based visualization can be used to help designers conform to human performance constraints.[144–146] Useful sources on human sensory and motor capacities relevant to virtual environments are also available (see Refs 129, 147–151; and also Fig. 24).

Because widely available current technology limits the graphics and simulation update rate in virtual environments to less than 20 Hz, understanding the control characteristics of human movement, visual tracking, and vestibular responses is important for determining the practical limits to useful work in these environments. Theories of grasp, manual tracking,[27] spatial hearing,[148] vestibular response, and visual-vestibular correlation[88,152] all can help to determine performance guidelines.

Predictive knowledge of system performance is not only useful for matching interfaces to human capabilities, but it is also useful in developing effective displays for situations in which human operators must cope with significant time lags, for example those >250 msec, or other control difficulties. In these circumstances, accurate dynamic or kinematic models of the controlled element allow the designer to give the user control over a predictor which he may move to a desired location and which will be followed by the actual element (see Refs 15 and 18; and also Fig. 25).

Another source of guidelines is the performance and design of existing high fidelity systems themselves (see Refs 151–154; and also Figs 26 and 27). Of the virtual environment display systems, probably the one with the best visual display is the CAE Fiber Optic Helmet Mounted Display, FOHMD,[66,67] which is used in military simulators. It presents two 83.5° monocular fields of view with adjustable binocular overlap, typically about 38°, giving a full horizontal field-of-view up to 162°. The Wright–Patterson Air Force Base Visually Coupled Airborne Systems Simulator or VCASS display, which also presents a very wide field of view, has been used to study the consequences of field-of-view restriction on several visual tasks.[155] Their results support other reports that indicate that visual performance is influenced by increased field of view, but that this influence can become negligible at fields of view greater than 60°.[156]

A significant feature of the FOHMD is that the 60 Hz sampling of optical head position had to be augmented by signals from helmet-mounted accelerometers to perceptually stabilize the graphics imagery during head movement. Without the accelerometer signals, perceptual stability of the enveloping environment requires head-position sampling over 100 Hz, as illustrated by well calibrated teleoperations viewing systems developed in Japan.[157,158] In general, it is difficult to calibrate the head-mounted, virtual image displays used in these integrated systems. One solution is to use a see-through system, as illustrated by Hirose, and to compare the positions of real objects and superimposed computer-generated objects.[39]

Two integrated virtual environments systems for which performance and calibration data are not yet fully published are the NASA Ames Research Center's virtual interface[159] and the teleoperations interface at The National Advanced Robotics Research Centre, Salford, UK.[160] Technical descriptions and performance data for these and other virtual environment or visualization systems are likely to appear in journals cited in this paper, in this journal and in two new journals: *Presence: the Journal of Teleoperations and Virtual Environments*, MIT Press, Cambridge, Massacheucetts and *Pixel, the Magazine of Scientific Visualization*, Pixel Communications Inc., Watsonville, California.

4. VIRTUAL ENVIRONMENTS: PERFORMANCE AND TRADE-OFFS

4.1. *Performance advances*

With the state of off-shelf technology, it is unlikely that a fully implemented virtual environment display will today uniquely enable useful work at a price accessible to the average researcher. Those systems that have solved some of the major technological problems, that is, adequate head-tracking bandwidth, viewing resolution comparable to existing CRT technology, do so through special purpose hardware that is very expensive. The inherent cost of some enabling technologies, however, is not high and development continues, promising improved performance and flexibility (e.g. optical head tracking[120] and high quality detailed volumetric display hardware for medium cost workstations stations, see Ref. 161). However, no matter how sophisticated or cheap the display technology becomes, there will always be some costs associated with its use. With respect to practical applications, the key question is to identify those tasks that are so enabled by use of a virtual environment display, that users will choose this display format over alternatives.

4.2. *Stereoscopic visual strain*

Designers of helmet-mounted displays for military applications have known that field use of stereoscopic displays is difficult because precise alignment is required to avoid problems with visual fatigue.[162,163] Accordingly, stereo eye strain is a likely difficulty for long-term use of stereo virtual environments. However, new devices for measuring acuity, accommodation, and eye position[164] may help improve designs. Development of a self-compensating display that adjusts to the refractive state and position of the user's eyes is one possibility. As with eye strain, the neck strain caused by the helmet's mass is likely to be relieved by technical advances such as miniaturization. But there will always be a cost associated with required use of head gear.

4.3. *Resolution/field-of-view trade-off*

Another cost associated with head-mounted displays, is that though they may generally have larger fields of view than the panel-mounted alternative, they will typically have correspondingly lower spatial resolution. Eye movement recording technology has been used to avoid this trade-off by tracking the viewer's current area of fixation so that a high-resolution graphics insert can be displayed there. This technique can relieve the graphics processor of the need to display high-resolution images in the regions of the peripheral visual field that cannot resolve it.[165] Reliable and robust eye tracking technology is still, however, costly, but fortunately may be unnecessary if a high resolution insert of approximately 30° diameter may be inserted. Since in the course of daily

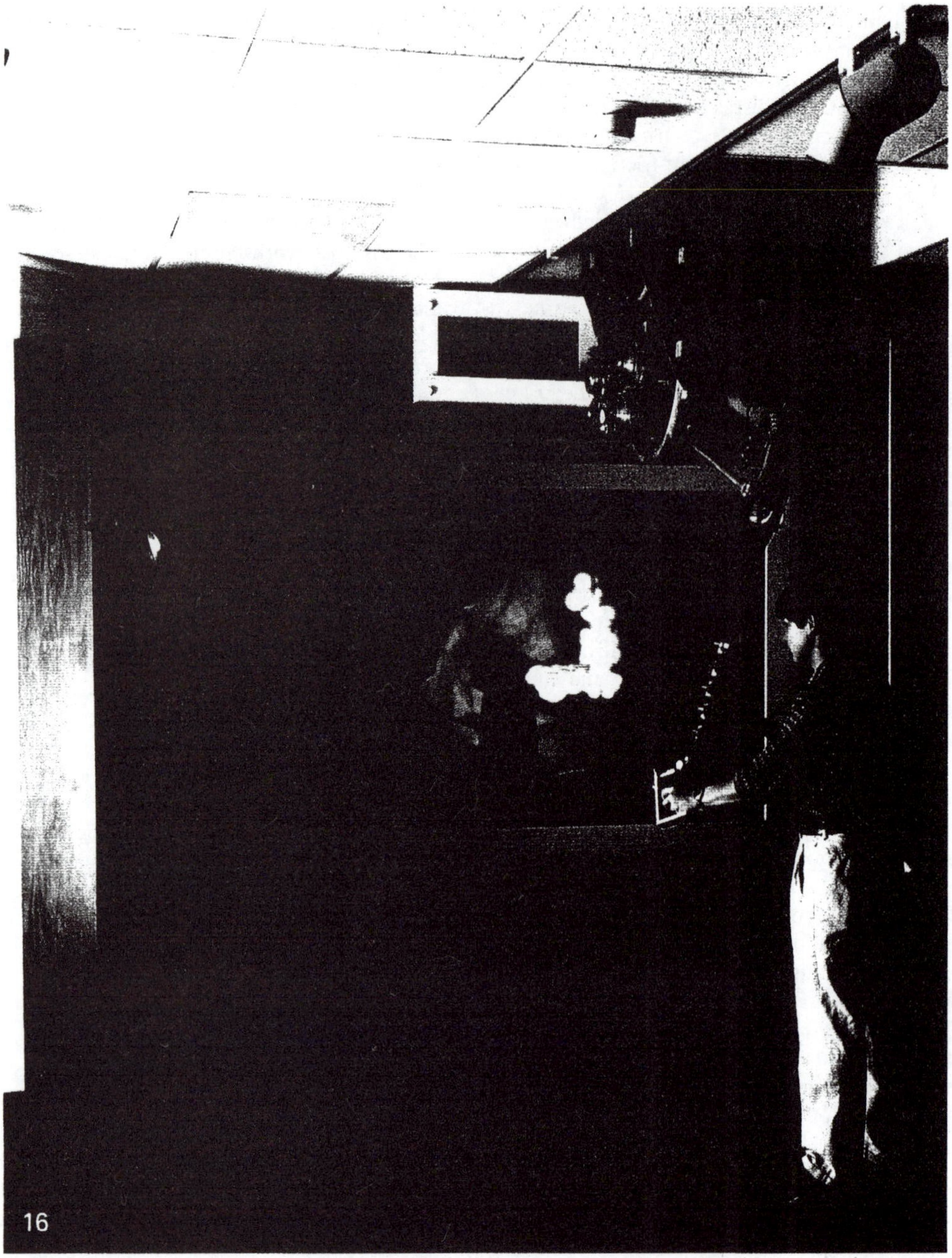

Fig. 16. Researcher at the University of North Carolina uses a multidegree-of-freedom manipulator to maneuver a computer graphics model of a drug molecule to find binding sites on a larger molecule. A dynamic simulation of the binding forces is computed in real time so the user can feel these forces through the force-reflecting manipulator and use this feel to identify the position and orientation of a binding site. (Photograph courtesy of University of North Carolina, Department of Computer Science.)

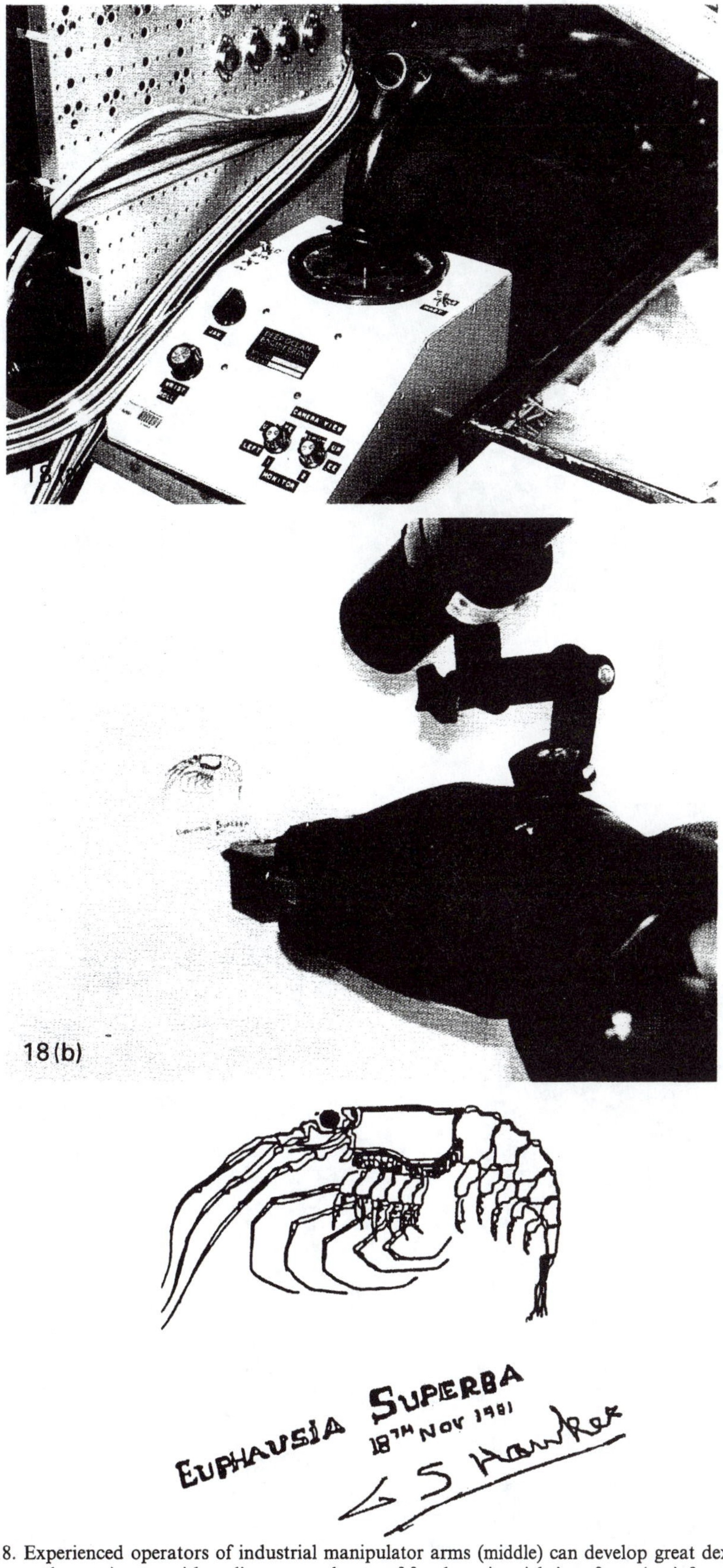

Fig. 18. Experienced operators of industrial manipulator arms (middle) can develop great dexterity (see drawing at bottom) even with ordinary two-degree-of-freedom, joystick interfaces (top) for the control of robot arms. Switches on the control box shift control to the various joints on the arm. (Photographs courtesy of Deep Ocean Engineering, San Leandro, California.)

Fig. 19. An exoskeletal hand-shape measurement system in a dextrous hand master which can drive a dextrous end-effector. (Photograph courtesy of Exos Inc., Burlington, Massachausetts.)

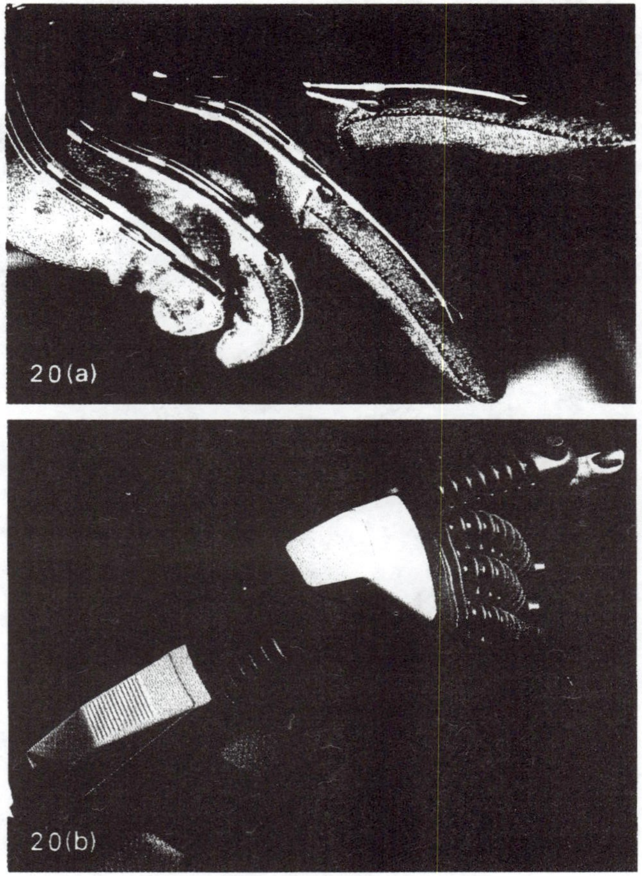

Fig. 20. Less bulky hand shape measuring instruments using flexible sensors (top panel: courtesy of VPL, Redwood City, California; bottom panel: courtesy of W. Industries, Leicester, U.K.).

Fig. 22. Fiber-optic flexion sensors used by VPL in the DataGlove have been incorporated in a body-hugging suit. Measurements of body shape can be used to dynamically control a computer-graphics image of the body which may be seen through the head-mounted viewing device.[136] (Photograph courtesy of VPL, Redwood City, California.)

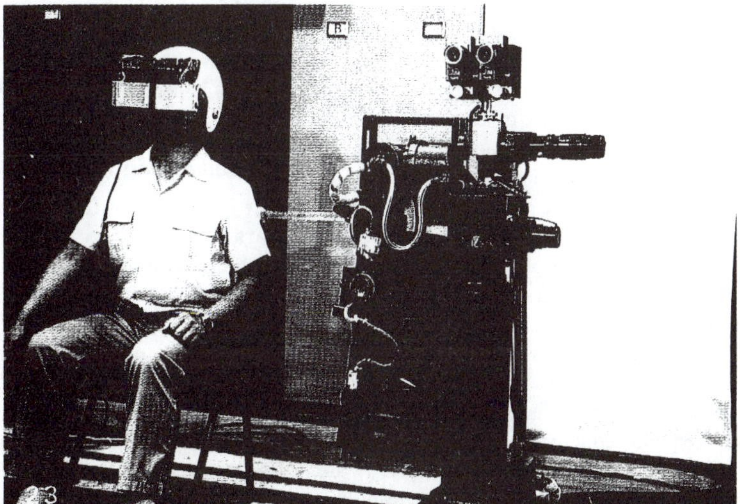

Fig. 23. Head and hand position sensors allow the user to control the head and arm position of a teleoperations robot which provides a stereo video signal that may be seen in the viewing helmet. (Photograph courtesy of Susumu Tachi.)

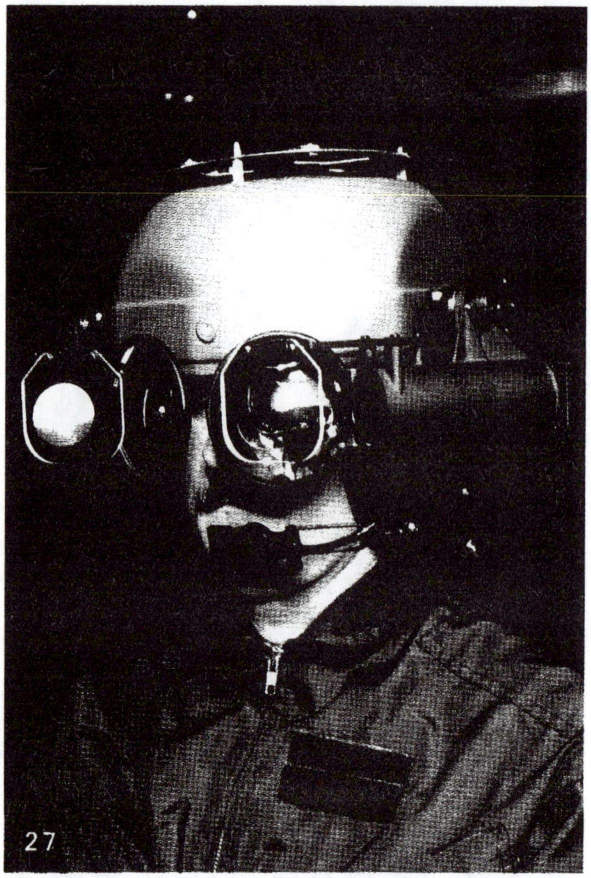

Fig. 27. Though very expensive, the CAE Fiber Optic Helmet Mounted display, FOHUD, is probably the best head-mounted, virtual environment system. It can present an overall visual field 162° × 83.5° with 5 arcmin resolution with a high resolution inset of 24° × 18° of 1.5 arcmin resolution. It has a bright display, 30 foot-Lambert, and a fast, optical head-tracker, 60 Hz sampling, with accelerometer augmentation. (Photograph courtesy of CAE Electronics, Montreal, Canada.)

life most eye movements may be less than 15°,[166] a head-mounted display system need not employ eye tracking if the performance environment does not typically require large amplitude eye movements.

4.4. *Unique capabilities*

In view of these and certainly other costs of virtual environment displays, what unique capabilities do they enable? Since these systems amount to a communications medium, they are intrinsically applicable to practically anything—education, procedure training, teleoperation, high-level programming, exploratory data analysis, and scientific visualization.[153] One unique feature of the medium, however, is that it enables multiple, simultaneous real-time foci of control in an environment. Tasks that involve manipulation of objects in complex visual environments and also require frequent, concurrent changes in viewing position, for example, laparoscopic surgery,[167] are tasks that are naturally suited for virtual environment displays. Other tasks that may be mapped into this format are also uniquely suitable. In selecting a task for which environment displays may provide useful interfaces it is important to remember that effective communication is the goal, and that consequently one need not aspire to creating a fully implemented virtual environment; a virtual space or a virtual image might even be superior. For non-entertainment applications, the illusion of an alternative reality is not necessarily the goal of the interface design.

4.5. *Future mass markets*

It is difficult to foretell the future practical mass-market applications for virtual environments. Like three-dimensional movies, the technology could only be a transient infatuation of visionary technophiles, but the situation is more likely analogous to the introduction of the first personal computer, the Altair. At its introduction, the practical uses for which small computers like it have become essential, word processing, data bases and spreadsheets, seemed well beyond its reach. In fact, spreadsheet programs like VISICALC had not even been conceived! Accordingly, some of the ultimate mass-market applications of virtual environments are likely to be unknown today. Possibly, once the world is densely criss-crossed with high bandwidth, public access, fiber-optic "information highways", mass demand will materialize for convenient, virtual environment displays of high resolution imagery.[168]

REFERENCES

1. J. C. R. Licklider, R. Taylor and E. Herbert, "The computer as a communication device," *International Science and Technology*, April 1978, 21–31 (1978).
2. J. Hollan, E. Rich, W. Hill, D. Wroblewski, K. Wittenburgh and J. Grudin, "An introduction to HITS: Human Interface Tool Suite," in *Intelligent User Interfaces* (edited by J. Sullivan and S. Yler), 1991.
3. A. Pollack, "What is artificial reality? Wear a computer and see," *New York Times*, p. A1L, April 10, 1989.
4. J. D'Arcy, "Re-creating reality," *MacCleans* **103**(6), 36–41 (1990).
5. D. Stewart, "Through the looking glass into an artificial world-via computer," *Smithsonian Magazine*, January 1991, 36–45 (1991).
6. D. Brehde "CeBIT: Cyberspace- Vorstoss in eine andere Welt (breakthrough into another world)", *Stern* **12,** 130–142 (1991) (in German).
7. G. K. Zipf, *Human Behavior and the Principle of Least Effort*, Addison-Wesley, Cambridge, Mass., 1949.
8. B. Mandelbrot, *The Fractal Geometry of Nature*, Freeman, San Francisco, California, 1982.
9. S. R. Ellis and R. J. Hitchcock, "Emergence of Zipf's Law: spontaneous encoding optimization by users of a command language," *IEEE Transactions on Systems Man and Cybernetics*, **SMC-16,** 423–427, (1986).
10. J. Grudin and D. Norman, "Language evolution and human-computer interaction," manuscript submitted for publication, (1991).
11. D. C. Smith, C. Irby, R. Kimball and E. Harslem, "The Star User Interface: an overview," in *Office Systems Technology*, pp. 1–14, Xerox Corp, El Segundo, California, 1982.
12. A. Inselberg, "The plane with parallel coordinates," *The Visual Computer* **1,** 69–91 (1985).
13. S. Feiner and C. Beshers, "Worlds within worlds: metaphors for exploring n-dimensional virtual worlds," Proceedings of 3rd Annual Symposium on User Interface Technology, Snowbird, Utah, October 3–5, 1990, ACM 429902, New York.
14. M. Levine, "The placement and misplacement of you-are-here maps," *Environment and Behavior* **16,** 139–157 (1984).
15. T. Hashimoto, T. B. Sheridan and M. V. Noyes, "Effects of predictive information in teleoperation with time delay," *Japanese Journal of Ergonomics* **22,** 2 (1986).
16. S. R. Bussolari, L. R. Young and A. T. Lee, "The use of vestibular models for design and evaluation of flight simulation motion," AGARD Conference Proceedings N. 433: Motion cues in flight simulation and simulator induced sickness, AGARD CP 433, 1988.
17. W. S. Kim, M. Takeda and L. Stark, "On-the-screen visual enhancements for a telerobotic vision system," Proceedings of the 1988 International Conference on Systems, Man, and Cybernetics, Beijing, August 8–12, pp. 126–130, 1988.
18. A. K. Bejczy, W. S. Kim and S. C. Venema, "The phantom robot: predictive displays for teleoperation with time delay," Proceedings of the IEEE International Conference on Robotics and Automation, May 13–18, 1990.
19. T. B. Sheridan, *Telerobotics and Human Supervisory Control*, MIT Press, Cambridge, Mass., 1991.
20. S. R. Ellis, "Prologue", in *Pictorial Communication in Virtual and Real Environments*, (edited by S. R. Ellis, M. K. Kaiser and A. J. Grunwald), pp. 3–11, Taylor and Francis, London, 1991.
21. R. L. Gregory "Perceptual Illusions and Brain Models," *Proceedings of the Royal Society, B* **171,** 278–296 (1968).
22. R. L. Gregory, "Perceptions as hypotheses," *Philosophical Transactions of the Royal Society, B* **290,** 181–197 (1980).
23. R. L. Gregory, *Mind in Science*, Weidenfeld and Nicolson, London, 1981.
24. R. E. Kalman, "Contributions to the theory of optimal control," *Bolatin de la Sociedad Matematico Mexicana* **5,** 102–119 (1960).
25. D. L. Kleinman, S. Baron and W. H. Levison, "An optimal control model of human response, Part I: Theory and Validation; Part II: prediction of human performance in a complex task," *Automatica* **6,** 357–369 (1970).
26. D. T. McRuer and D. H. Weir, "Theory of manual vehicular control," *Ergonomics* **12**(4), 599–633 (1969).
27. H. R. Jex, J. D. McDonnell and A. V. Phatak, "A critical tracking task for man-machine research related to the operators effective delay time," NASA CR 616, NASA, Washington D.C., 1966.
28. R. A. Hess, "Feedback control models," in *Handbook of Human Factors*, (edited by G. Salvendy), Wiley, New York.
29. R. B. Welch, *Perceptual Modification: Adapting to Altered Sensory Environments*, Academic Press, New York, 1978.
30. R. Held, A. Efstathiou and M. Greene, "Adaptation to displaced and delayed visual feedback from the hand," *Journal of Experimental Psychology* **72,** 887–891 (1966).
31. R. Held and N. Durlach, "Telepresence, time delay, and adaptation," in *Pictorial Communication in Virtual and Real Environments*, (edited by S. R. Ellis, M. K. Kaiser and A. J. Grunwald), Taylor and Francis, London, 1991.
32. G. Melvill Jones, A. Berthoz and B. Segal, "Adaptive modification of the vestibulo-ocular reflex by mental effort in darkness," *Brain Research* **56,** 149–153 (1984).
33. W. H. Zangemeister and H. C. Hansen, "Fixation suppression of the vestibular ocular reflex and head movement correlated EEG potentials," in *Eye Movements: from Physiology to Cognition*, (edited by J. K. O'Reagan and A. Levy-Schoen), pp. 247–256, Elsevier, Amsterdam, New York. 1985.
34. W. H. Zangemeister, "Voluntary presetting of the vestibular ocular reflex permits gaze stabilization despite perturbation of fast head movement," in *Pictorial Communication in Virtual and Real Environments*, (edited by S. R. Ellis, M. K. Kaiser and A. J. Grunwald), pp. 404–416, Taylor and Francis, London, 1991.
35. J. J. Gibson, *The Perception of the Visual World*, Houghton Mifflin, Boston, 1950.
36. D. J. Heeger, "Visual perception of three-dimensional motion," *Neural Computation* **2,** 127–135 (1989).
37. J. J. Koenderink and A. J. van Doorn "How an ambulant observer can construct a model of the environment from the geometrical structure of the visual inflow," in *Kybernetik*, (edited by G. Hauske and E. Butenandt), Oldenberg, Munich, 1977.
38. D. Regan and K. I. Beverley, "Visually guided locomotion: psychophysical evidence for a neural mechanism sensitive to flow patterns," *Science* **205,** 311–3 (1979).
39. M. Hirose, R. Kijima, Y. Sato and T. Ishii, "A study for modification of actual environment by see-through

HMD," Proceedings of the Human Interface Symposium, Tokyo, October, 1990 (mainly in Japanese).
40. R. A. Moses and W. M. Hart, *Adler's Physiology of the Eye*, 8th Edn (especially chapters 5, 11, 12 and 24), Mosby, Washington D.C., 1987.
41. J. M. Foley, "Binocular distance perception," *Psychological Review* **87**, 411–434 (1980).
42. J. M. Foley, "Binocular distance perception: egocentric distance tasks," *Journal Experimental Psychology: Human Perception and Performance* **11**, 133–149 (1985).
43. H. Collewijn and C. J. Erkelens, "Binocular eye movements and the perception of depth," in *Eye Movements and their Role in Visual and Cognitive Processes*, (edited by E. Kowler), pp. 213–288, Elsevier Science Publishers, North Holland, The Netherlands, 1990.
44. C. J. Erkelens and H. Collewijn, "Motion perception during dichoptic viewing of moving random dot stereograms," *Vision Research* **25**, 583–588 (1985).
45. C. J. Erkelens and H. Collewijn, "Eye movements and stereopsis during dichoptic viewing of moving random dot stereograms," *Vision Research* **25**, 1689–1700 (1985).
46. E. M. Wenzel, F. L. Wightman and S. H. Foster, "A virtual display system for conveying three-dimensional acoustic information," Proceedings of the Human Factors Society, pp. 86–90, October 22–24, 1988.
47. E. M. Wenzel, F. L. Wightman, D. J. Kistler and S. H. Foster, "Acoustic origins of individual differences in sound localization behavior," *J. Acoustical Society of America* **84**, 579 (1988).
48. F. L. Wightman and D. J. Kistler, "Headphone simulation of free-field listening I: stimulus synthesis," *Journal Acoustical Society of America* **85**, 858-867 (1989).
49. F. L. Wightman and D. J. Kistler, "Headphone simulation of free-field listening II: psycho-physical validation," *Journal of Acoustical Society of America* **85**, 868-878 (1989).
50. A. K. Bejczy, "Sensor, controls, and man-machine interface for teleoperation," *Science* **208**, 1327–1335 (1980).
51. G. H. Crampton (ed.), *Motion and Space Sickness*, CRC Press, Boca Raton, FL, 1990.
52. E. C. Poulton, *Tracking Skill and Manual Control*, Academic Press, New York, 1974.
53. C. D. Wickens, "The effects of control dynamics on performance," in *Handbook of Perception and Human Performance*, (edited by K. R. Boff, L. Kaufman and J. P. Thomas), Wiley, New York, 1986.
54. B. M. Fagan, *The Adventures of Archaeology*, p. 245, National Geographic Society, Washington D.C., 1985.
55. L. Lipton, *Foundations Of Stereoscopic Cinema*, Van Nostrand, New York, 1982.
56. I. E. Sutherland, "The ultimate display," *International Federation of Information Processing* **2**, 506 (1965).
57. I. E. Sutherland, "Computer displays," *Scientific American* **222**(6), 56–81 (1970).
58. M. W. Krueger, "Responsive environments," NCC Proceedings, pp. 375–385, 1977.
59. M. W. Krueger, *Artificial Reality*, Addison-Wesley, Reading, Massacheusetts, 1983.
60. M. W. Krueger, "VIDEOPLACE—An Artificial Reality," SIGCHI 85 Proceedings, pp. 35–40, April 1985.
61. CAE Electronics, "Product literature," St. Laurent, Quebec, Canada H4L 4X4, 1991.
62. G. M. McKinnon and R. Kruk, "Multiaxis control of telemanipulators," in *Pictorial Communication in Virtual and Real Environments*, (edited by S. R. Ellis, M. K. Kaiser and A. J. Grunwald), pp. 247–264, Taylor and Francis, London, 1991.
63. J. Stritzke, "Automobile Simulator," Daimler-Benz AG, Abt FGF/FS, Daimlerstr. 123, 1000, Berlin 48, Germany, 1991.
64. W. Veldhuyzen and H. G. Stassen, "The internal model concept: an application to modeling human control of large ships," *Human Factors* **19**, 367–380 (1977).
65. H. Schuffel, "Simulation: an interface between theory and practice elucidated with a ship's controllability study," in *Spektrum der Anthropotechnik*, (edited by R. Bernotat, K.-P. Gärtner and H. Widdel), Forschungsinstitut für Anthropotechnik, Wachtberg-Werthoven, Germany, 1987.
66. P. A. Lypaczewski, A. D. Jones and J. W. M. Vorhees, "Simulation of an advanced scout attack helicopter for crew station studies," Proceedings of the 8th Interservice/Industry Training Systems Conference, pp. 18-23, Salt Lake City, Utah 1, 1986.
67. R. Barrette, R. Dunkley, R. Kruk, D. Kurtz, S. Marshall, T. Williams, P. Weissman and S. Antos, "Flight simulation advanced wide FOV helmet mounted infinity display," AFHRL-TR-89-36, Air Force Human Resources Laboratory, Williams AFB, Arizona, 1990.
68. T. A. Furness, "The supercockpit and its human factors challenges," Proceedings of the 30th Annual Meeting of the Human Factors Society, pp. 48–52, Dayton, Ohio, 1986.
69. T. A. Furness, "Designing in virtual space," in *System Design*, (edited by W. B. Rouse and K. R. Boff), North-Holland, Amsterdam, New York, 1987.
70. J. D. Foley, "Interfaces for advanced computing," *Scientific American* **257**(4), 126–135 (1987).
71. M. W. McGreevy, Invited Address: personal simulators and planetary exploration, CHI' 89, Austin, Texas, 1989.
72. T. H. Myers and I. E. Sutherland, "On the design of display processors," *Communications of the ACM* **11**(6), 410–414 (1968).
73. J. H. Clark, "The geometry engine: a VLSI geometry system for graphics," *Computer Graphics* **16**(3), 127–133 (1982).
74. J. H. Clark, "A VLSI geometry processor for graphics," *IEEE Computer* **12**, 7 (1980).
75. Silicon Graphics, product literature, Silicon Graphics Inc. Corp., Mountain View, California, 1991.
76. C. L. Jenkins and S. I. Tanimoto, "Oct-trees and their use in representing three-dimensional objects," *Computer Graphics and Image Processing* **14**(3), 249–270 (1980).
77. D. Meagher, "A new mathematics for solids processing," *Computer Graphics World*, November 1984, 75–88 (1984).
78. AGARD, Conference Proceedings N. 433: Motion cues in flight simulation and simulator induced sickness, AGARD CP 433, 1988.
79. R. E. Curry, W. C. Hoffman and L. R. Young, "Pilot modeling for manned simulation," AFFDL-TR-76-124, Air Force Flight Dynamics Laboratory Publication, 1, December 1976.
80. M. Monmonier, *How to Lie with Maps*, University of Chicago Press, Chicago, 1991.
81. C. H. Cotter, *The Astronomical and Mathematical Foundations of Geography*, Elsevier, New York, 1966.
82. A. H. Robinson, R. D. Sale, J. L. Morrison and P. C. Muehrcke, *Elements of Cartography*, 5th edn, Wiley, New York, 1984.
83. W. R. Tobler, "Geographic area and map projections", *The Geographical Review* **53**, 59–78 (1963).
84. W. R. Tobler, "The geometry of mental maps," in *Spatial Choice and Spatial Behavior*, (edited by R. G. Golledge and G. Rushton), The Ohio State University Press, Columbus Ohio, 1976.
85. E. R. Tufte, *The Visual Display of Quantitative Information*, Graphics Press, Cheshire, CO, 1983.

86. E. R. Tufte, *Envisioning Information*, Graphics Press, Cheshire, CO, 1990.
87. J. Bertin, *Semiology of Graphics: Diagrams, Networks, Maps* (translated by W. J. Berg), University of Wisconsin Press, Madison, Wisconsin 1967/1983.
88. C. M. Oman, "Sensory conflict in motion sickness: an observer theory approach," in *Pictorial Communication in Virtual and Real Environments* (edited by S. R. Ellis, M. K. Kaiser and A. J. Grunwald), pp. 362–376, Taylor and Francis, London, 1991.
89. M. W. McGreevy and S. R. Ellis, "The effect of perspective geometry on judged direction in spatial information instruments," *Human Factors* **28**, 439–456 (1986).
90. S. Ellis, M. W. McGreevy and R. Hitchcock, "Perspective traffic display format and airline pilot traffic avoidance," *Human Factors* **29**, 371–382 (1987).
91. S. R. Ellis and S. S. Hacisalihzade, "Symbolic enhancement of perspective displays," Proceedings of the 34th Annual Meeting of the Human Factors Society, pp. 1465–1469, Human Factors Society, Santa Monica, CA, 1990.
92. K. J. Hussey (Producer/director), *Mars, the Movie*, (on video), Visualization and Earth Science Applications group, Observational system division, JPL Audiovisual Services, Pasadena California, 1990.
93. NASA, "Computerized reality comes of age," *NASA Tech. Briefs* **14**(8), 10–12 (1990).
94. M. W. McGreevy, "Virtual reality and planetary exploration," 29th AAS Goddard Memorial Symposium, March 1991, Washington D.C., 1991.
95. A. A. B. Pritsker, *Introduction to Simulation and SLAM II*, 3rd edn, Wiley, New York, 1986.
96. F. Cellier, *Modeling Continuous Systems*, Springer-Verlag, New York, 1991.
97. W. Robinett, "Rocky's boots" (Educational software product), The Learning Company, Fremont, California, 1982.
98. J. F. Blinn, "The making of the mechanical universe," in *Pictorial Communications in Virtual and Real Environments*, (edited by S. R. Ellis, M. K. Kaiser and A. J. Grunwald), Taylor and Francis, London, 1991.
99. J. F. Blinn, "The mechanical universe: an integrated view of a large animation project," (Course Notes: Course # 6), Proceedings of 14th Annual Conference on Computer Graphics and Interactive Techniques, ACM SIGGRAPH and IEEE Technical Committee on Computer Graphics, Anaheim, California, 1987.
100. M. K. Kaiser, E. MacFee and D. R. Proffitt, "Seeing beyond the obvious: understanding perception in everyday and novel environments," NASA Ames Research Center, Moffett Field, California, 1990.
101. Open University and BBC, "Components of reality," Video # 5.2 for Course T363: Computer Aided Design, Walton Hall, Milton Keynes, Buckinghamshire, England MK7 6AA, 1991.
102. A. Witkin, K. Fleisher and A. Barr, "Energy constraints on parameterised models," *Computer Graphics* **21**(4) 225–232 (1987).
103. A. Witkin, M. Gleicher and W. Welch, "Interactive dynamics," *Computer Graphics* **24**(2), 11–22 (1990).
104. I. E. McDowall, M. Bolas, S. Pieper, S. S. Fisher and J. Humphries, "Implementation and integration of a counterbalanced CRT-base stereoscopic display for interactive viewpoint control in virtual environment applications," *Stereoscopic Displays and Applications*, (edited by J. Merrit and S. Fisher), SPIE 1256, 1990.
105. C. Levit and S. Bryson (1991) "A virtual environment for the exploration of three-dimensional steady flows," in *Stereoscopic Displays and Applications II*, (edited by S. Fisher), SPIE Conference Proceedings, vol. 1457, San Jose, CA, February 1991.
106. NASA, Rendezvous/Proximity Operations Workbook, RNDZ 2102, Lyndon B. Johnson Space Center, Mission Operations Directorate Training Division, Houston, Tex., 1985.
107. A. J. Grunwald and S. R. Ellis, Interactive orbital proximity operations planning system, NASA TP 2839, NASA Ames Research Center, 1988.
108. A. J. Grunwald and S. R. Ellis, "Design and evaluation of a visual display aid for orbital maneuvering," in *Pictorial Communication in Virtual and Real Environments*, (edited by S. R. Ellis, M. K. Kaiser and A. J. Grunwald), Taylor and Francis, London, 1991.
109. S. R. Ellis and A. J. Grunwald, "The dynamics of orbital maneuvering: design and evaluation of a visual display aid for human controllers," Proceedings of the AGARD FMP Symposium on Space Vehicle Flight Mechanics, 13-16 November 1989, Luxembourg, pp. 29-1 29-13, 1989.
110. A. Pedotti, V. V. Krishnan and L. Stark, "Optimization of muscle force sequencing in human locomotion," *Mathematical Bioscience* **38**, 57–76 (1978).
111. R. H. Taylor, H. A. Paul, B. D. Mittelstadt, W. Hanson, P. Kazanzides, J. Zuhars, E. Glassman, B. L. Mustic, B. Williamson and W. L. Bargar, "An image-directed robotic system for hip replacement surgery," *Japanese R.S.J.* **8**(5) 111-116 (1990).
112. D. P. Greenberg, "Computers and architecture," *Scientific American* **264**(2), 104–109 (1991).
113. J. M. Airey, J. H. Rohlf and F. P. Brooks Jr., "Towards image realism with interactive update rates in complex virtual building environments," *Computer Graphics* **24**(2), 41–50 (1990).
114. R. C. Goertz, "Manipulator system development at ANL (Argonne National Laboratory)", Proceedings of the 12th RSTD Conference, 1964, pp. 117–136.
115. J. Vertut and P. Coiffet, *Robot Technology, Teleoperations and Robotics: Evolution and Development* (Vol. 3A), and *Applications and Technology* (Vol. 3B, English translation), Prentice-Hall, Englewood Cliffs, New Jersey, 1986.
116. R. C. Goertz, C. Potts, S. Mingesz and J. Lindberg, "An experimental head-controlled television to provide viewing for a manipulator operator", Proceedings of the 13th Remote Systems Technology Conference, pp. 57–60, 1965.
117. F. H. Raab, E. B. Blood, T. O. Steiner and H. R. Jones, "Magnetic position and orientation tracking system," IEEE Transactions on Aerospace and Electronic Systems, AES-15, No.5, 709–718, 1979.
118. Ascension Technology Corp, Product description, Burlington Vermont 05402, 1990.
119. Polhemus Navigation Systems, "Product Description," Colchester, Vermont, 05446, 1990.
120. J.-F. Wang, V. Chi and H. Fuchs, "A real-time optical 3D tracker for head-mounted display systems", *Computer Graphics* **24**, 205–215 (1990).
121. BASYS, "Product Description," Basys Gesellschaft für Anwender und Systemsoftware mbH, product description, Nürnberg, Germany, 1990.
122. Spatial Systems, "Spaceball product description," Spatial Systems Inc., Concord Massacheusetts, 01742, 1990.
123. A. K. Bejczy and K. S. Salisbury Jr., "Kinesthetic coupling between operator and remote manipulator," Advances in Computer Technology, 1, Proceedings ASME International Computer Technology Conference, San Francisco, California, 1980, pp. 197–211.
124. B. Hannaford, "A design framework for teleoperators with kinesthetic feedback," *IEEE Transactions on Robotics and Automation* **5**, 4 (1989).
125. M. Ouh-young, D. Beard and F. Brooks Jr., "Force display performs better than visual display in a simple 6D docking task," Proceedings of the IEEE Robotics and Automation Conference, May 1989, pp. 1462–1466, 1989.
126. B. D. Adelstein and M. J. Rosen, "A two degree

of freedom loading manipulandum for the study of human arm dynamics," 1987 Advances in Bioengineering. BED Vol. 3. DE Vol. 12. Proceedings of Winter Annual Meeting of the Americal Society of Mechanical Engineers, pp. 111–112, 1987.

127. B. D. Adelstein and M. J. Rosen, "A high performance two degree of freedom kinesthetic interface," in Human machine interfaces for teleoperators and virtual environments (compiled by N. I. Durlach, T. B. Sheridan and S. R. Ellis), NASA CP91035, NASA Ames Research Center, Moffett Field, California, 1991.
128. P. Fisher, R. Daniel and K. V. Siva, "Specification of input devices for teleoperation," Proceedings of the 1990 IEEE International Conference on Robotics and Automation, Cincinnati, Ohio, pp. 540–545, 1990.
129. T. L. Brooks and A. K. Bejczy, "Hand controllers for teleoperation," NASA CR 175890, JPL Publication 85-11, JPL, Pasadena, California, 1986.
130. R. Tomovic and G. Boni, "An Adaptive Artificial Hand," IRE Transactions on Automatic Control, AC-7, April 3–10, 1962.
131. S. C. Jacobson, D. F. Knutti, K. B. Biggers, E. K. Iversen and J. E. Woods, "The Utah/MIT dextrous hand: Work in progress," *International Journal of Robotics Research* 3(4), 21–50 (1984).
132. Exos, "Product literative," 8 Blanchard Rd, Burlington, MA 01803, 1990.
133. O. B. Marcus, Burlington, Massacheusetts 01803, personal communication, 1991.
134. T. Zimmerman, J. Lanier, C. Blanchard, S. Bryson and Y. Harvil, "A hand gesture interface device," Proceedings of the CHI and GI, Toronto, Canada April 5–7 1987, pp. 189–192, 1987.
135. W Industries Ltd., "Product literature," ITEC House 26–28 Chancery St., Leicester LE1 5WD, U.K., 1991.
136. A. Lasko-Harvill, C. Blanchard, W. Smithers, Y. Harvill and A. Coffman, "From DataGlove to DataSuit," Proceedings of IEEE CompConn88, February 29–March 4 1988, San Francisco, California, pp. 536–538, 1988.
137. Pop-optix, "Product literature," Waltham, MA 02154, 1991
138. M. L. Heilig, "El cine del futuro (The cinema of the future)," Espacios No. 23–24, Jan April 1955, Apartado Postal Num 20449, Espacios S. A., Mexico. (Spanish and English) (1955).
139. A. Lippman, "Movie maps: an application of optical video disks to computer graphics," *Computer Graphics*, 14(3) 32–42 (1980).
140. S. Brand, *The Media Lab: Inventing the Future at MIT*, Viking, New York, 1987.
141. J. Borah, L. R. Young and R. E. Curry, "Sensory Mechanism Modelling," USAF ASD Report AFHRL TR 78-83, Air Force Human Resources Laboratory, Williams Arizona, 1978.
142. K. R. Boff, L. Kaufman and J. P. Thomas (eds), *Handbook of Perception and Human Performance*, Wiley, New York, 1986.
143. J. I. Elkind, S. K. Card, J. Hochberg and B. M. Huey, (eds), "*Human Performance Models for Computer-aided Engineering*", National Academy Press, Washington D. C., 1989.
144. G. Monheit and N. I. Badler, "A Kinematic Model of the Human Spine and Torso," August 29, 1990, Technical Report MS-CIS-90-77, University of Pennsylvania, Philadelphia, 1990.
145. C. Phillips, J. Zhao and N. I. Badler, "Interactive real-time articulated figure manipulation using multiple kinematic constraints," *Computer Graphics* 24(2), 245–250 (1990).
146. J. Larimer, M. Prevost, A. Arditi, S. Azueta, J. Bergen and J. Lubin, "Human visual performance model for crew-station design," Proceedings of the 1991 SPIE, pp. 196–210, February, 1991 San Jose, CA, 1991.
147. I. Howard, *Human Visual Orientation*, Wiley, New York, 1982.
148. J. Blauert, *Spatial Hearing*, The MIT Press, Cambridge, MA, 1983.
149. M. A. Goodale (ed.), *Vision and Action: the Control of Grasping*, Ablex Publishing Corp., Norwood, NJ, 1990.
150. N. I. Durlach, T. B. Sheridan and Stephen R. Ellis, "Human machine interfaces for teleoperators and virtual environments, NASA CP91035, NASA Ames Research Center, Moffett Field, California, 1991.
151. S. R. Ellis, M. K. Kaiser and A. J. Grunwald (eds), *Pictorial Communication in Virtual and Real Environments*, Taylor and Francis, London, 1991.
152. C. M. Oman, B. K. Lichtenbert, K. E. Money and R. K. McCoy, "MIT/Canada Vestibular Experiment of the Spacelab 1-Mission: 4 Space motion sickness: systems, stimuli, and predictability," *Experimental Brain Research* 64, 316–334 (1986).
153. F. Brooks Jr., "Grasping reality through illusion—interactive graphics serving science," Proceedings Chi '88, Washington D. C., pp. 1–12, May 15–19, 1988.
154. S. R. Ellis, "Pictorial Communication," *Leonardo* 23, 81–86 (1990).
155. M. J. Wells and M. Venturino, "Performance and head movements using a helmet mounted display with different sized fields-of-view," *Optical Engineering* 29, 810–877 (1990).
156. T. Hatada, H. Sakata and H. Kusaka, "Psychophysical Analysis of the Sensation of Reality Induced by a Visual Wide-Field Display," *SMPTE Journal* 89, 560–569 (1980).
157. S. Tachi, A. Hirohiko and Taro Maeda, "Development of anthropomorphic tele-existence slave robot," Proceedings of the International Conference on Advanced Mechatronics, Tokyo, May 21–24, pp. 385–390, 1989.
158. S. Tachi, K. Tanie, K. Komoriya and M. Kaneko, "Tele-existence (I) design and evaluation of a visual display with sensation of presence," Proceedings of the 5th International Symposium on Theory and Practice of Robots and Manipulators, Udine, Italy June 26–29, (CISM-IFToMM-Ro Man Sy, '84), pp. 245–253, 1984.
159. S. S. Fisher, M. McGreevy, J. Humphries and W. Robinett, "Virtual environment display system," ACM 1986 Workshop on 3D Interactive Graphics, Chapel Hill, North Carolina, October 23–24, 1986.
160. R. J. Stone, The National Advanced Robotics Research Centre, Salford, United Kingdom, (personal communication), 1991.
161. OCTREE Corporation, "Company literature 4404 Adragna Court, San Jose, California 95136, 1991.
162. O. J. Edwards, Chief Technical Office: Electro-optics, S-TRON 303 Ravenswood Drive, Mt View CA 94043, personal communication, 1991.
163. J. Melzer, Senior Technical Staff Specialist, Optical Systems Engineering, Kaiser Electronics, San Jose, CA 95134, personal communication, 1991.
164. T. Takeda, Y. Fukui and T. Lida, "Three dimensional optometer, *Applied Optics* 27(12), 2595–2602 (1986).
165. D. A. Cowdry, "Advanced visuals in mission simulators," in Flight Simulation, AGARD-CP-408, AGARD, Paris, pp. 3.1–3.10, 1986.
166. A. T. Bahill, D. Adler and L. Stark, "Most naturally occuring human saccades have magnitudes of 15 degrees or less," *Investigative Opthalmology* 14, 468–469 (1975).
167. SAGES (1991) "Panel of Future Trends in Clinical Surgery," *American Surgeon*, March 1991, SAGES Scientific Session, Monterey April 18–20 1991.
168. A. Gore, "Networking the future," Editorial in *Washington Post*, July 15, 1990.

The Computer for the 21st Century

Specialized elements of hardware and software, connected by wires, radio waves and infrared, will be so ubiquitous that no one will notice their presence

by Mark Weiser

The most profound technologies are those that disappear. They weave themselves into the fabric of everyday life until they are indistinguishable from it.

Consider writing, perhaps the first information technology. The ability to represent spoken language symbolically for long-term storage freed information from the limits of individual memory. Today this technology is ubiquitous in industrialized countries. Not only do books, magazines and newspapers convey written information, but so do street signs, billboards, shop signs and even graffiti. Candy wrappers are covered in writing. The constant background presence of these products of "literacy technology" does not require active attention, but the information to be transmitted is ready for use at a glance. It is difficult to imagine modern life otherwise.

Silicon-based information technology, in contrast, is far from having become part of the environment. More than 50 million personal computers have been sold, and the computer nonetheless remains largely in a world of its own. It is approachable only through complex jargon that has nothing to do with the tasks for which people use computers. The state of the art is perhaps analogous to the period when scribes had to know as much about making ink or baking clay as they did about writing.

The arcane aura that surrounds personal computers is not just a "user interface" problem. My colleagues and I at the Xerox Palo Alto Research Center think that the idea of a "personal" computer itself is misplaced and that the vision of laptop machines, dynabooks and "knowledge navigators" is only a transitional step toward achieving the real potential of information technology. Such machines cannot truly make computing an integral, invisible part of people's lives. We are therefore trying to conceive a new way of thinking about computers, one that takes into account the human world and allows the computers themselves to vanish into the background.

Such a disappearance is a fundamental consequence not of technology but of human psychology. Whenever people learn something sufficiently well, they cease to be aware of it. When you look at a street sign, for example, you absorb its information without consciously performing the act of reading. Computer scientist, economist and Nobelist Herbert A. Simon calls this phenomenon "compiling"; philosopher Michael Polanyi calls it the "tacit dimension"; psychologist J. J. Gibson calls it "visual invariants"; philosophers Hans Georg Gadamer and Martin Heidegger call it the "horizon" and the "ready-to-hand"; John Seely Brown of PARC calls it the "periphery." All say, in essence, that only when things disappear in this way are we freed to use them without thinking and so to focus beyond them on new goals.

The idea of integrating computers seamlessly into the world at large runs counter to a number of present-day trends. "Ubiquitous computing" in this context does not mean just computers that can be carried to the beach, jungle or airport. Even the most powerful notebook computer, with access to a worldwide information network, still focuses attention on a single box. By analogy with writing, carrying a superlaptop is like owning just one very important book. Customizing this book, even writing millions of other books, does not begin to capture the real power of literacy.

Furthermore, although ubiquitous computers may use sound and video in addition to text and graphics, that does not make them "multimedia computers." Today's multimedia machine makes the computer screen into a demanding focus of attention rather than allowing it to fade into the background.

Perhaps most diametrically opposed to our vision is the notion of virtual reality, which attempts to make a world inside the computer. Users don special goggles that project an artificial scene onto their eyes; they wear gloves or even bodysuits that sense their motions and gestures so that they can move about and manipulate virtual objects. Although it may have its purpose in allowing people to explore realms otherwise inaccessible—the insides of cells, the surfaces of distant planets, the information web of data bases—virtual reality is only a map, not a territory. It excludes desks, offices, other people not wearing goggles and bodysuits, weather, trees, walks, chance encounters and, in general, the infinite richness of the universe. Virtual reality focuses an enormous apparatus on simulating the world rather than on invisibly enhancing the world that already exists.

Indeed, the opposition between the

MARK WEISER is head of the Computer Science Laboratory at the Xerox Palo Alto Research Center. He is working on the next revolution of computing after workstations, variously known as ubiquitous computing or embodied virtuality. Before working at PARC, he was a professor of computer science at the University of Maryland; he received his Ph.D. from the University of Michigan in 1979. Weiser also helped found an electronic publishing company and a video arts company and claims to enjoy computer programming "for the fun of it." His most recent technical work involved the implementation of new theories of automatic computer memory reclamation, known in the field as garbage collection.

SCIENTIFIC AMERICAN *September 1991*

UBIQUITOUS COMPUTING begins to emerge in the form of live boards that replace chalkboards as well as in other devices at the Xerox Palo Alto Research Center. Computer scientists gather around a live board for discussion. Building boards and integrating them with other tools has helped researchers understand better the eventual shape of ubiquitous computing. In conjunction with active badges, live boards can customize the information they display.

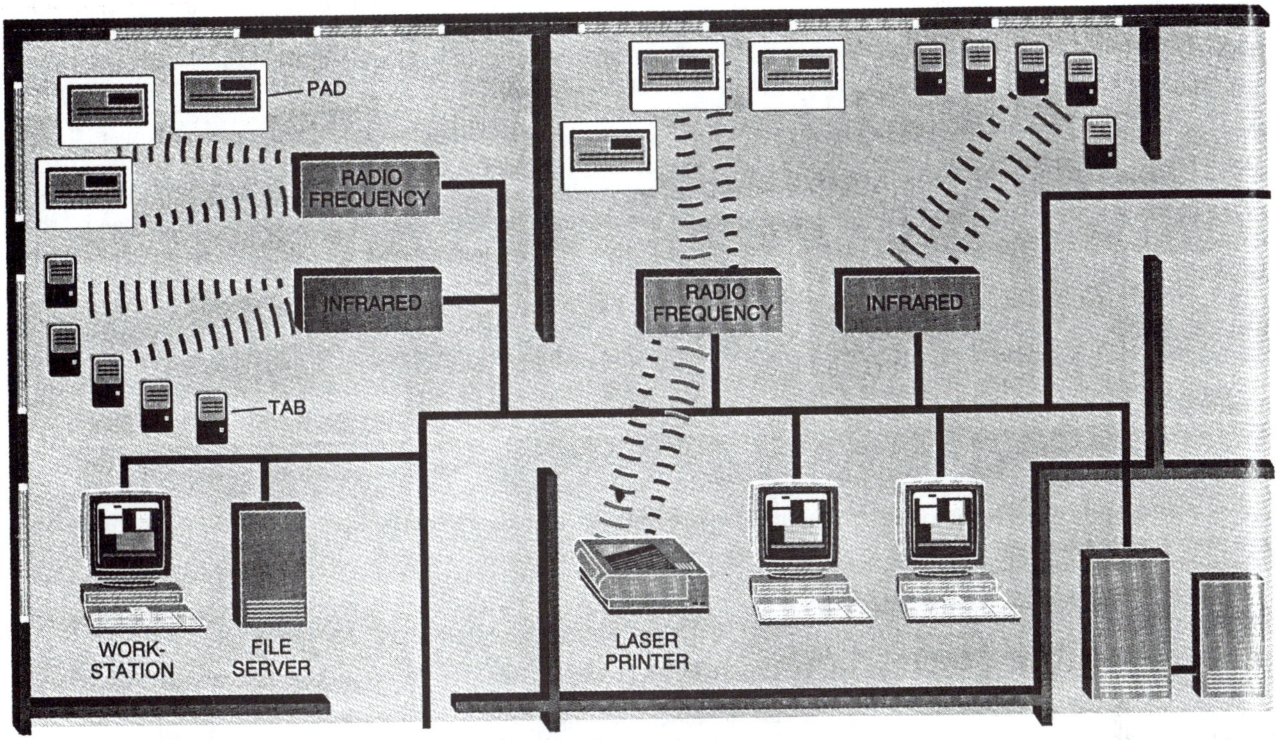

WIRED AND WIRELESS NETWORKS link computers and allow their users to share programs and data. The computers pictured here include conventional terminals and file servers, pocket-size machines known as tabs and page-size ones known as pads. Future networks must be capable of supporting hundreds of devices in a single room and must also cope with devices—ranging from tabs to laser printers or large-screen displays—that move from one place to another.

notion of virtual reality and ubiquitous, invisible computing is so strong that some of us use the term "embodied virtuality" to refer to the process of drawing computers out of their electronic shells. The "virtuality" of computer-readable data—all the different ways in which they can be altered, processed and analyzed—is brought into the physical world.

How do technologies disappear into the background? The vanishing of electric motors may serve as an instructive example. At the turn of the century, a typical workshop or factory contained a single engine that drove dozens or hundreds of different machines through a system of shafts and pulleys. Cheap, small, efficient electric motors made it possible first to give each tool its own source of motive force, then to put many motors into a single machine.

A glance through the shop manual of a typical automobile, for example, reveals 22 motors and 25 solenoids. They start the engine, clean the windshield, lock and unlock the doors, and so on. By paying careful attention, the driver might be able to discern whenever he or she activated a motor, but there would be no point to it.

Most computers that participate in embodied virtuality will be invisible in fact as well as in metaphor. Already computers in light switches, thermostats, stereos and ovens help to activate the world. These machines and more will be interconnected in a ubiquitous network. As computer scientists, however, my colleagues and I have focused on devices that transmit and display information more directly. We have found two issues of crucial importance: location and scale. Little is more basic to human perception than physical juxtaposition, and so ubiquitous computers must know where they are. (Today's computers, in contrast, have no idea of their location and surroundings.) If a computer knows merely what room it is in, it can adapt its behavior in significant ways without requiring even a hint of artificial intelligence.

Ubiquitous computers will also come in different sizes, each suited to a particular task. My colleagues and I have built what we call tabs, pads and boards: inch-scale machines that approximate active Post-it notes, foot-scale ones that behave something like a sheet of paper (or a book or a magazine) and yard-scale displays that are the equivalent of a blackboard or bulletin board.

How many tabs, pads and board-size writing and display surfaces are there in a typical room? Look around you: at the inch scale, include wall notes, titles on book spines, labels on controls, thermostats and clocks, as well as small pieces of paper. Depending on the room, you may see more than 100 tabs, 10 or 20 pads and one or two boards. This leads to our goal for initially deploying the hardware of embodied virtuality: hundreds of computers per room.

Hundreds of computers in a room could seem intimidating at first, just as hundreds of volts coursing through wires in the walls once did. But like the wires in the walls, these hundreds of computers will come to be invisible to common awareness. People will simply use them unconsciously to accomplish everyday tasks.

Tabs are the smallest components of embodied virtuality. Because they are interconnected, tabs will expand on the usefulness of existing inch-scale computers, such as the pocket calculator and the pocket organizer. Tabs will also take on functions that no computer performs today. For example, computer scientists at PARC and other research laboratories around the world have begun working with active badges—clip-on computers roughly the size of an employee I.D. card, first developed by the Olivetti Cambridge research laboratory. These badges can identify themselves to receivers placed throughout a building, thus making it possible to keep track of the people or objects to which they are attached.

In our experimental embodied virtuality, doors open only to the right badge wearer, rooms greet people by name, telephone calls can be automatically forwarded to wherever the recipient may be, receptionists actually know where people are, computer terminals retrieve the preferences of whoever is sitting at them, and appointment diaries write themselves. The automatic diary shows how such a simple task as knowing where people are can yield complex dividends: meetings, for example, consist of several people spending time in the same room, and the subject of a meeting is most probably the files called up on that room's display screen while the people are there. No revolution in artificial intelligence is needed, merely computers embedded in the everyday world.

My colleague Roy Want has designed a tab incorporating a small display that can serve simultaneously as an active badge, calendar and diary. It will also act as an extension to computer screens: instead of shrinking a program window down to a small icon on the screen, for example, a user will be able to shrink the window onto a tab display. This will leave the screen free for information and also let people arrange their computer-based projects in the area around their terminals, much as they now arrange paper-based projects in piles on desks and tables. Carrying a project to a different office for discussion is as simple as gathering up its tabs; the associated programs and files can be called up on any terminal.

The next step up in size is the pad, something of a cross between a sheet of paper and current laptop and palmtop computers. Robert Krivacic of PARC has built a prototype pad that uses two microprocessors, a workstation-size display, a multibutton stylus and a radio network with enough communications bandwidth to support hundreds of devices per person per room.

Pads differ from conventional portable computers in one crucial way. Whereas portable computers go everywhere with their owners, the pad that must be carried from place to place is a failure. Pads are intended to be "scrap computers" (analogous to scrap paper) that can be grabbed and used anywhere; they have no individualized identity or importance.

One way to think of pads is as an antidote to windows. Windows were invented at PARC and popularized by Apple in the Macintosh as a way of fitting several different activities onto the small space of a computer screen at the same time. In 20 years computer screens have not grown much larger. Computer window systems are often said to be based on the desktop metaphor—but who would ever use a desk only nine inches high by 11 inches wide?

Pads, in contrast, use a real desk. Spread many electronic pads around on the desk, just as you spread out papers. Have many tasks in front of you, and use the pads as reminders. Go beyond the desk to drawers, shelves, coffee tables. Spread the many parts of the many tasks of the day out in front of you to fit both the task and the reach of your arms and eyes rather than to fit the limitations of glassblowing. Someday pads may even be as small and light as actual paper, but meanwhile they can fulfill many more of paper's functions than can computer screens.

Yard-size displays (boards) serve a number of purposes: in the home, video screens and bulletin boards; in the office, bulletin boards, white boards or flip charts. A board might also serve as an electronic bookcase from which one might download texts to a pad or tab. For the time being, however, the ability to pull out a book and place it comfortably on one's lap remains one of the many attractions of paper. Similar objections apply to using a board as a desktop; people will have to become accustomed to having pads and tabs on a desk as an adjunct to computer screens before taking embodied virtuality any further.

Prototype boards, built by Richard Bruce and Scott Elrod of PARC, are in use at several Xerox research laboratories. They measure about 40 by 60 inches and display 1,024 × 768 black-and-white pixels. To manipulate the

The Active Badge

This harbinger of inch-scale computers contains a small microprocessor and an infrared transmitter. The badge broadcasts the identity of its wearer and so can trigger automatic doors, automatic telephone forwarding and computer displays customized to each person reading them. The active badge and other networked tiny computers are called tabs.

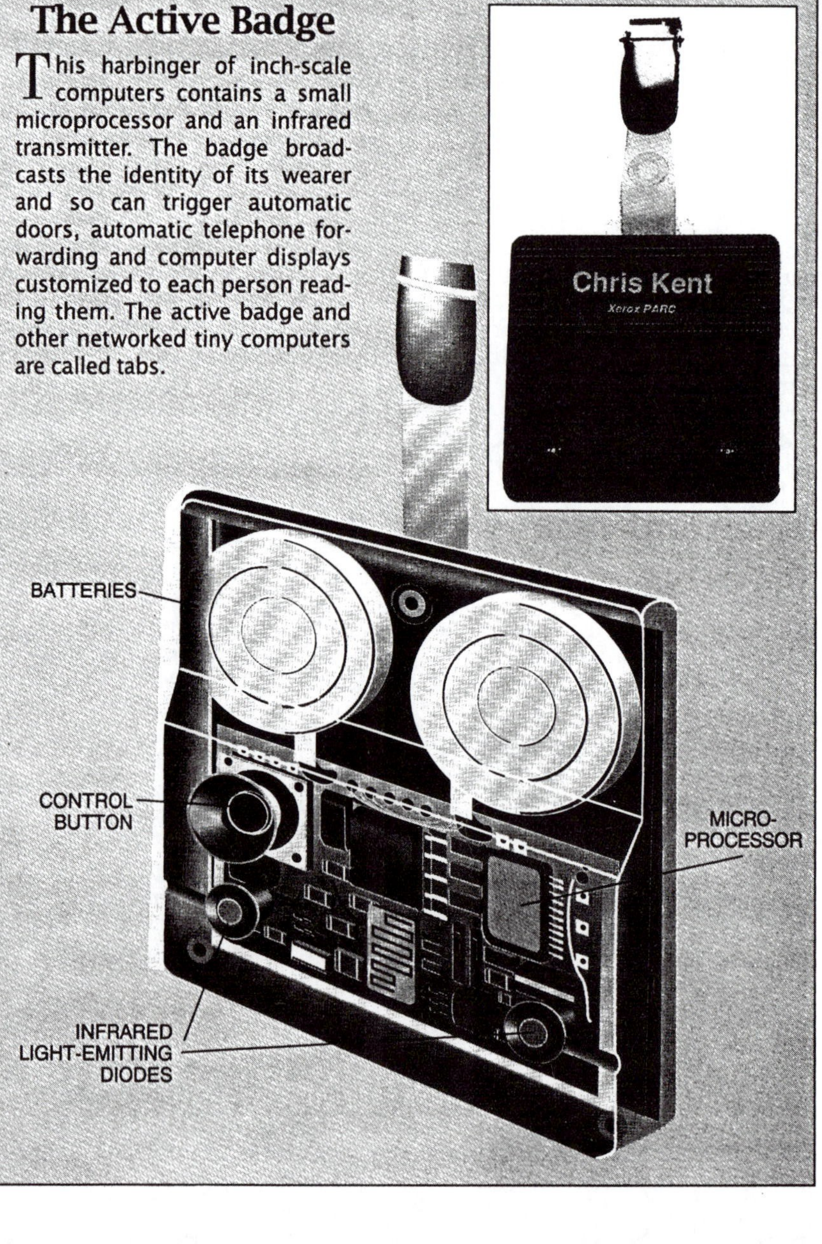

display, users pick up a piece of wireless electronic "chalk" that can work either in contact with the surface or from a distance. Some researchers, using themselves and their colleagues as guinea pigs, can hold electronically mediated meetings or engage in other forms of collaboration around a live board. Others use the boards as testbeds for improved display hardware, new "chalk" and interactive software.

For both obvious and subtle reasons, the software that animates a large shared display and its electronic chalk is not the same as that for a workstation. Switching back and forth between chalk and keyboard may involve walking several steps, and so the act is qualitatively different from using a keyboard and mouse. In addition, body size is an issue. Not everyone can reach the top of the board, so a Macintosh-style menu bar might have to run across the bottom of the screen instead.

We have built enough live boards to permit casual use: they have been placed in ordinary conference rooms and open areas, and no one need sign up or give advance notice before using them. By building and using these boards, researchers start to experience and so understand a world in which computer interaction informally enhances every room. Live boards can usefully be shared across rooms as well as within them. In experiments instigated by Paul Dourish of EuroPARC and Sara Bly and Frank Halasz of PARC, groups at widely separated sites gathered around boards—each displaying the same image—and jointly composed pictures and drawings. They have even shared two boards across the Atlantic.

Live boards can also be used as bulletin boards. There is already too much text for people to read and comprehend all of it, and so Marvin Theimer and David Nichols of PARC have built a prototype system that attunes its public information to the people reading it. Their "scoreboard" requires little or no interaction from the user other than to look and to wear an active badge.

Prototype tabs, pads and boards are just the beginning of ubiquitous computing. The real power of the concept comes not from any one of these devices—it emerges from the interaction of all of them. The hundreds of processors and displays are not a "user interface" like a mouse and windows, just a pleasant and effective "place" to get things done.

What will be most pleasant and effective is that tabs can animate objects previously inert. They can beep to help locate mislaid papers, books or other items. File drawers can open and show the desired folder—no searching. Tabs in library catalogues can make active maps to any book and guide searchers to it, even if it is off the shelf, left on a table by the last reader.

In presentations, the size of text on overhead slides, the volume of the amplified voice, even the amount of ambient light, can be determined not by guesswork but by the desires of the listeners in the room at that moment. Software tools for tallying votes instantly and consensus checking are already available in electronic meeting rooms of some large corporations; tabs can make them widespread.

The technology required for ubiquitous computing comes in three parts: cheap, low-power computers that include equally convenient displays, software for ubiquitous applications and a network that ties them all together. Current trends suggest that

COMPUTER SCRATCHPADS augment the conventional screen in this office at the Xerox Palo Alto Research Center. Prototype pads are wired to conventional computers; thus far only a handful of wireless models have been built.

the first of these requirements will easily be met. Flat-panel displays containing 640 × 480 black-and-white pixels are now common. This is the standard size for PCs and is also about right for television. As long as laptop, palmtop and notebook computers continue to grow in popularity, display prices will fall, and resolution and quality will rise. By the end of the decade, a 1,000 × 800-pixel high-contrast display will be a fraction of a centimeter thick and weigh perhaps 100 grams. A small battery will provide several days of continuous use.

Larger displays are a somewhat different issue. If an interactive computer screen is to match a white board in usefulness, it must be viewable from arm's length as well as from across a room. For close viewing, the density of picture elements should be no worse than on a standard computer screen, about 80 per inch. Maintaining a density of 80 pixels per inch over an area several feet on a side implies displaying tens of millions of pixels. The biggest computer screen made today has only about one fourth that capacity. Such large displays will probably be expensive, but they should certainly be available.

The large display will require advanced microprocessors to feed it. Central-processing-unit speeds reached a million instructions per second in 1986 and continue to double each year. Some industry observers believe that this exponential growth in raw chip speed may begin to level off about 1994 but that other measures of performance, including power consumption and auxiliary functions, will still improve. The 100-gram flat-panel display, then, might be driven by a microprocessor that executes a billion operations per second and contains 16 megabytes of on-board memory along with sound, video and network interfaces. Such a processor would draw, on average, a few percent of the power required by the display.

Auxiliary storage devices will augment main memory capacity: conservative extrapolation of current technology suggests that removable hard disks (or nonvolatile memory chips) the size of a matchbook will store about 60 megabytes each. Larger disks containing several gigabytes of information will be standard, and terabyte storage—roughly the data content of the Library of Congress—will be common. Such enormous stores will not necessarily be filled to capacity with usable information. Abundant space will, however, allow radically different strategies of information management. A terabyte of disk storage will make deleting old files virtually unnecessary, for example.

Although processors and displays should be capable of offering ubiquitous computing by the end of the decade, trends in software and network technology are more problematic. Current implementations of "distributed computing" simply make networked file servers, printers or other devices appear as if they were connected directly to each user's computer. This approach, however, does nothing to exploit the unique capabilities of physically dispersed computers and the information embodied in knowing where a particular device is located.

Computer operating systems and window-based display software will have to change substantially. The design of current operating systems, such as DOS and Unix, is based on the assumption that a computer's hardware and software configuration will not change substantially while it is running. This assumption is reasonable for conventional mainframes and personal computers, but it makes no sense in terms of ubiquitous computing. Pads, tabs and even boards may come and go at any time in any room, and it will certainly be impossible to shut down all the computers in a room to install new software in any one of them. (Indeed, it may be impossible to find all the computers in a room.)

One solution may be "micro-kernel" operating systems such as those developed by Rick Rashid of Carnegie Mellon University and A. S. Tanenbaum of Vrije University in Amsterdam. These experimental systems contain only the barest scaffolding of fixed computer code; software modules to perform specific functions can be readily added or removed. Future operating systems based on this principle could shrink and grow automatically to fit the changing needs of ubiquitous computation.

Current window display systems also are not ready to cope with ubiquitous computing. They typically assume that a particular computer will display all the information for a single application. Although the X Window System and Windows 3.0, for example, can cope with multiple screens, they do not do well with applications that start out on one screen and move to another, much less those that peregrinate from computer to computer or room to room.

Solutions to this problem are in their infancy. Certainly no existing display system can perform well while working with the full diversity of input and output forms required by embodied virtuality. Making pads, tabs and boards work together seamlessly will require changes in the kinds of protocols by which applications programs and their displayed windows communicate.

RADIO TRANSCEIVER links pads and other movable computer devices to the wired network. This unit, intended to be mounted on the ceiling, contains antennas in its crossed arms and two light-emitting diodes to signal its status.

The network that will connect ubiquitous hardware and software poses further challenges. Data transmission rates for both wired and wireless networks are increasing rapidly. Access to gigabit-per-second wired nets is already possible, although expensive, and will become progressively cheaper. (Gigabit networks will seldom devote all of their bandwidth to a single data stream; instead they will allow enormous numbers of lower-speed transmissions to proceed simultaneously.) Small wireless networks, based on digital cellular telephone principles, currently offer data rates between two and 10 megabits per second over a range of a few hundred meters. Low-power wireless networks capable of transmitting 250,000 bits per second to each station will eventually be available commercially.

Yet the problem of transparently linking wired and wireless networks resists solution. Although some stopgap methods have been developed, engineers must develop new communications protocols that explicitly recognize the concept of machines that move in physical space. Furthermore, the number of channels envisioned in most wireless network schemes is still

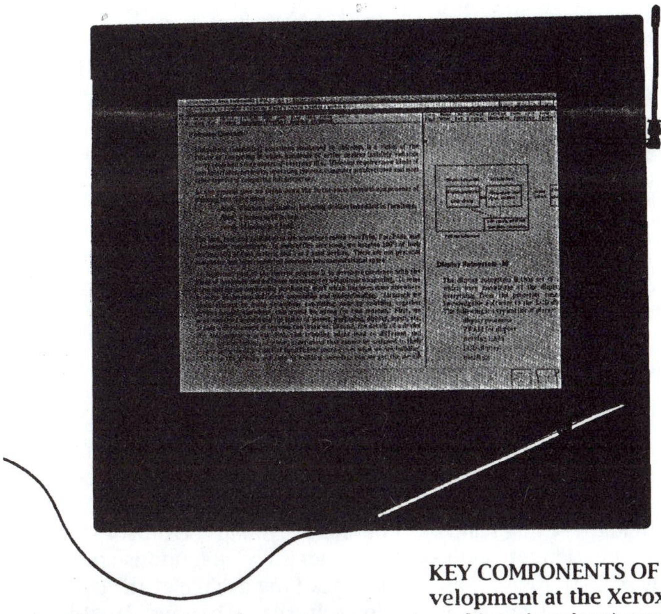

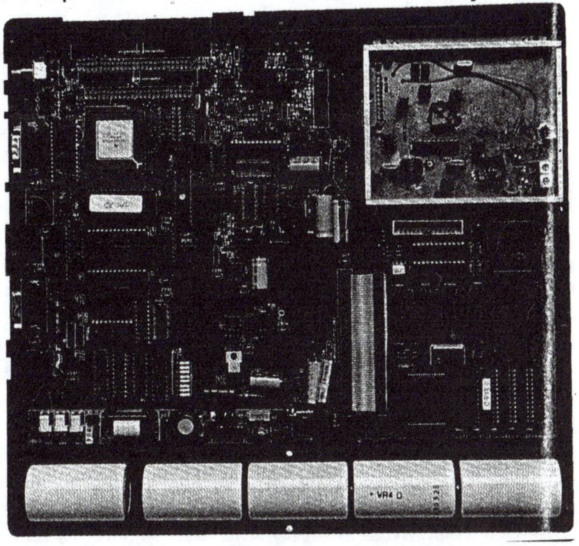

KEY COMPONENTS OF UBIQUITOUS COMPUTING are the pads and tabs under development at the Xerox Palo Alto Research Center. The page-size pad (*top, exterior and interior views*) contains two microprocessors, four million bytes of random-access memory, a high-speed radio link, a high-resolution pen interface and a black-and-white display that is 1,024 by 768 pixels. Because it uses standard window system software, the pad can communicate with most workstations. The much smaller tab (*at left*), $2\frac{3}{4}$ by $3\frac{1}{4}$ inches, has three control buttons, a pen interface, audio and an infrared link for communicating throughout a room. The author believes future homes and offices will contain hundreds of these tiny computers.

very small, and the range large (50 to 100 meters), so that the total number of mobile devices is severely limited. The ability of such a system to support hundreds of machines in every room is out of the question. Single-room networks based on infrared or newer electromagnetic technologies have enough channel capacity for ubiquitous computers, but they can work only indoors.

Present technologies would require a mobile device to have three different network connections: tiny-range wireless, long-range wireless and very high speed wired. A single kind of network connection that can somehow serve all three functions has yet to be invented.

Neither an explication of the principles of ubiquitous computing nor a list of the technologies involved really gives a sense of what it would be like to live in a world full of invisible widgets. Extrapolating from today's rudimentary fragments of embodied virtuality is like trying to predict the publication of *Finnegans Wake* shortly after having inscribed the first clay tablets. Nevertheless, the effort is probably worthwhile:

Sal awakens; she smells coffee. A few minutes ago her alarm clock, alerted by her restless rolling before waking, had quietly asked, "Coffee?" and she had mumbled, "Yes." "Yes" and "no" are the only words it knows.

Sal looks out her windows at her neighborhood. Sunlight and a fence are visible through one, and through others she sees electronic trails that have been kept for her of neighbors coming and going during the early morning. Privacy conventions and practical data rates prevent displaying video footage, but time markers and electronic tracks on the neighborhood map let Sal feel cozy in her street.

Glancing at the windows to her kids' rooms, she can see that they got up 15 and 20 minutes ago and are already in the kitchen. Noticing that she is up, they start making more noise.

At breakfast Sal reads the news. She still prefers the paper form, as do most people. She spots an interesting quote from a columnist in the business section. She wipes her pen over the newspaper's name, date, section and page number and then circles the quote. The pen sends a message to the paper, which transmits the quote to her office.

Electronic mail arrives from the company that made her garage door opener. She had lost the instruction manual and asked them for help. They have sent her a new manual and also something unexpected—a way to find the old one. According to the note, she can press a code into the opener and the missing manual will find itself. In the garage, she tracks a beeping noise to where the oil-stained manual had fallen behind some boxes. Sure enough, there is the tiny tab the manufacturer had affixed in the cover to try to avoid E-mail requests like her own.

On the way to work Sal glances in the foreview mirror to check the traffic. She spots a slowdown ahead and also notices on a side street the telltale green in the foreview of a food shop, and a new one at that. She decides to take the next exit and get a cup of coffee while avoiding the jam.

Once Sal arrives at work, the foreview helps her find a parking spot quickly. As she walks into the building, the machines in her office prepare to log her in but do not complete the sequence until she actually enters her office. On her way, she stops by the offices of four or five colleagues to exchange greetings and news.

Sal glances out her windows: a gray day in Silicon Valley, 75 percent humidity and 40 percent chance of afternoon showers; meanwhile it has been a quiet morning at the East Coast office. Usually the activity indicator shows at least one spontaneous, urgent meeting by now. She chooses not to shift the window on the home office back three hours—too much chance of being caught by surprise. But she knows others who do, usually people who never get a call from the East but just want to feel involved.

The telltale by the door that Sal programmed her first day on the job is blinking: fresh coffee. She heads for the coffee machine.

Coming back to her office, Sal picks up a tab and "waves" it to her friend Joe in the design group, with whom she has a joint assignment. They are sharing a virtual office for a few weeks. The sharing can take many forms—in this case, the two have given each other access to their location detectors and to each other's screen contents and location. Sal chooses to keep miniature versions of all Joe's tabs and pads in view and three-dimensionally correct in a little suite of tabs in the back corner of her desk. She can't see what anything says, but she feels more in touch with his work when noticing the displays change out of the corner of her eye, and she can easily enlarge anything if necessary.

A blank tab on Sal's desk beeps and displays the word "Joe" on it. She picks it up and gestures with it toward her live board. Joe wants to discuss a document with her, and now it shows up on the wall as she hears Joe's voice:

"I've been wrestling with this third paragraph all morning, and it still has the wrong tone. Would you mind reading it?"

Sitting back and reading the paragraph, Sal wants to point to a word. She gestures again with the "Joe" tab onto a nearby pad and then uses the stylus to circle the word she wants:

"I think it's this term 'ubiquitous.' It's just not in common enough use and makes the whole passage sound a little formal. Can we rephrase the sentence to get rid of it?"

"I'll try that. Say, by the way, Sal, did you ever hear from Mary Hausdorf?"

"No. Who's that?"

"You remember. She was at the meeting last week. She told me she was going to get in touch with you."

Sal doesn't remember Mary, but she does vaguely remember the meeting. She quickly starts a search for meetings held during the past two weeks with more than six people not previously in meetings with her and finds the one. The attendees' names pop up, and she sees Mary.

As is common in meetings, Mary made some biographical information about herself available to the other attendees, and Sal sees some common background. She'll just send Mary a note and see what's up. Sal is glad Mary did not make the biography available only during the time of the meeting, as many people do....

In addition to showing some of the ways that computers can enter invisibly into people's lives, this scenario points up some of the social issues that embodied virtuality will engender. Perhaps key among them is privacy: hundreds of computers in every room, all capable of sensing people near them and linked by high-speed networks, have the potential to make totalitarianism up to now seem like sheerest anarchy. Just as a workstation on a local-area network can be programmed to intercept messages meant for others, a single rogue tab in a room could potentially record everything that happened there.

Even today the active badges and self-writing appointment diaries that offer all kinds of convenience could be a source of real harm in the wrong hands. Not only corporate superiors or underlings but also overzealous government officials and even marketing firms could make unpleasant use of the same information that makes invisible computers so convenient.

Fortunately, cryptographic techniques already exist to secure messages from one ubiquitous computer to another and to safeguard private information stored in networked systems. If designed into systems from the outset, these techniques can ensure that private data do not become public. A well-implemented version of ubiquitous computing could even afford better privacy protection than exists today.

By pushing computers into the background, embodied virtuality will make individuals more aware of the people on the other ends of their computer links. This development may reverse the unhealthy centripetal forces that conventional personal computers have introduced into life and the workplace.

Even today, people holed up in windowless offices before glowing computer screens may not see their fellows for the better part of each day. And in virtual reality, the outside world and all its inhabitants effectively cease to exist. Ubiquitous computers, in contrast, reside in the human world and pose no barrier to personal interactions. If anything, the transparent connections that they offer between different locations and times may tend to bring communities closer together.

My colleagues and I at PARC believe that what we call ubiquitous computing will gradually emerge as the dominant mode of computer access over the next 20 years. Like the personal computer, ubiquitous computing will produce nothing fundamentally new, but by making everything faster and easier to do, with less strain and fewer mental gymnastics, it will transform what is apparently possible. Desktop publishing, for example, is essentially no different from computer typesetting, which dates back to the mid-1960s. But ease of use makes an enormous difference.

When almost every object either contains a computer or can have a tab attached to it, obtaining information will be trivial: "Who made that dress? Are there any more in the store? What was the name of the designer of that suit I liked last week?" The computing environment knows the suit you looked at for a long time last week because it knows both of your locations, and it can retroactively find the designer's name even though that information did not interest you at the time.

Sociologically, ubiquitous computing may mean the decline of the computer addict. In the 1910s and 1920s many people "hacked" on crystal sets to take advantage of the new high-tech world of radio. Now crystal-and-cat's-whisker receivers are rare because high-quality radios are ubiquitous. In addition, embodied virtuality will bring computers to the presidents of industries and countries for nearly the first time. Computer access will penetrate all groups in society.

Most important, ubiquitous computers will help overcome the problem of information overload. There is more information available at our fingertips during a walk in the woods than in any computer system, yet people find a walk among trees relaxing and computers frustrating. Machines that fit the human environment instead of forcing humans to enter theirs will make using a computer as refreshing as taking a walk in the woods.

FURTHER READING

THE TACIT DIMENSION. Michael Polanyi. Doubleday & Company, 1966.

TOWARD PORTABLE IDEAS. Mark Stefik and John Seely Brown in *Technological Support for Work Group Collaboration.* Edited by Margrethe H. Olson. Lawrence Erlbaum Associates, 1989.

RECENT DEVELOPMENTS IN OPERATING SYSTEMS. Special issue of *Computer (IEEE Computer Society)*, Vol. 23, No. 5; May 1990.

ACTIVITY-BASED INFORMATION RETRIEVAL: TECHNOLOGY IN SUPPORT OF HUMAN MEMORY. Mik Lamming and William Newman. Available as Rank Xerox EuroPARC Technical Report 91-03; February 1991.

LCDS AND BEYOND. Nick Baran in *Byte*, Vol. 16, No. 2, pages 229–236; February 1991.

A TALK WITH INTEL. Kenneth M. Sheldon in *Byte*, Vol. 16, No. 4, pages 131–140; April 1991.

Index

Author Index